THE HARCOURT BRACE ANTHOLOGY OF DRAMA

THE HARCOURT BRACE ANTHOLOGY OF DRAMA

SECOND EDITION

W. B. WORTHEN

Northwestern University

HARCOURT BRACE COLLEGE PUBLISHERS

Fort Worth   Philadelphia   San Diego   New York   Orlando   Austin   San Antonio
Toronto   Montreal   London   Sydney   Tokyo

Publisher	Ted Buchholz
Editor-in-chief	Christopher P. Klein
Acquisitions editor	Stephen T. Jordan / John P. Meyers
Developmental editor	Karl Yambert
Project editor	steve Norder
Production manager	Jane Tyndall Ponceti
Art director	Pat Bracken
Woodcut illustrations	David Frampton
Photo researcher	Lili Weiner
Compositor	Publications Development Company of Texas

Literary and illustration credits begin on p. 1327 and constitute a continuation of the copyright page.

Library of Congress Catalog Card Number: 95–79460

Address for Editorial Correspondence: Harcourt Brace College Publishers, 301 Commerce Street, Suite 3700, Fort Worth, TX 76102.

Address for Orders: Harcourt Brace & Company, 6277 Sea Harbor Drive, Orlando, FL 32887-6777. 1-800-782-4479, or 1-800-423-0001 (in Florida).

ISBN: 0-15-502087-0

Printed in the United States of America

8 9 0 1 2 3 4 069 10 9 8 7 6 5

PREFACE

Studying drama is more than reading plays; it requires us to study the theaters where plays were produced, the cultures that framed those theaters, and the critical and interpretive history that has framed the meanings of drama over time. *The Harcourt Brace Anthology of Drama* presents drama in these two important contexts: in the play's original theater and the society that sustained it, and in *our* culture, where the play continues to live both as literature and as theatrical performance.

The Harcourt Brace Anthology of Drama offers a comprehensive collection of classic plays from the European, American, and Asian repertory, as well as a challenging body of recent writing for the stage. Designed to be used in a variety of drama and theater courses, in general surveys of drama and theater, in courses on tragedy and/or comedy, or in classes on the modern theater, *The Harcourt Brace Anthology of Drama* offers an unusually comprehensive collection of classic theater and a rich selection of contemporary drama drawn from around the world.

This Second Edition of *The Harcourt Brace Anthology of Drama* builds on the strengths (and on the unimagined success) of the First Edition. It is divided into seven units, each focused on a significant moment in the history of drama and theater: Athens in the fifth century BC (four plays); feudal Japan (three plays); England in the late Middle Ages and Renaissance (six plays); France, Spain, and England in the seventeenth and eighteenth centuries (five plays); industrial Europe from 1850 to 1950 (eight plays); twentieth-century America (eleven plays); and the contemporary world stage (nine plays). As in the First Edition, each unit of the Second Edition begins with an extensive introduction, placing drama in the context of a specific historical era and using illustrations of theater design to develop a precise sense of stage practice. Each play is accompanied by a brief biography of the playwright and a short introduction to the play. Each unit introduction concludes with a collection of photographs, and following the plays is a selection of classic and contemporary critical readings.

However, the Second Edition of *The Harcourt Brace Anthology of Drama* has also been extensively revised and is now a more comprehensive volume for students of dramatic literature and of theater history. The Second Edition retains plays by Aeschylus, Sophocles, Aristophanes, Marlowe, Shakespeare, Molière, Racine, Behn, Ibsen, Strindberg, Chekhov, Shaw, Pirandello, Brecht, Glaspell, Williams, Baraka/Jones, Valdez, Fornes, Shange, Shepard, Hwang, Beckett, Pinter, Soyinka, and Friel. At the same time, it changes the play selection for several major authors, and now includes Euripides' *Medea*, Shakespeare's *Hamlet*, O'Neill's *Ah, Wilderness!*, Fornes's *Fefu and Her Friends*, Beckett's *Endgame*, and Churchill's *Cloud Nine*. As a whole, however, the Second Edition also is larger by eight plays, and has several distinctive new features:

- A greater number of plays by women (seven).
- More comedies (ten).
- A unit on classical Japanese theater, including a Noh play (Kan'ami Kiyotsugu's *Matsukaze*), a play from the doll theater (Chikamatsu Monzaemon's *Love Suicides at Sonezaki*), a Kabuki play (*Love Letter from the Licensed Quarter*, from the school of Chikamatsu), and four essays on classical Japanese theater and its modern performance.
- An English mystery play, The York *Crucifixion*.
- A Jacobean comedy, Ben Jonson's *Volpone*.
- Inclusion of Spanish Golden Age theater, represented by Pedro Calderón de la Barca's *Life is a Dream*.

- Plays representing the eighteenth-century and nineteenth-century theater (George Lillo's *London Merchant* and Georg Büchner's *Woyzeck*).
- Important plays in the modern tradition—Oscar Wilde's *The Importance of Being Earnest*, August Wilson's *Fences*—and significant recent drama from around the world: Marguerite Duras's *India Song*, Tom Stoppard's *Travesties*, the Split Britches-Bloolips collaboration *Belle Reprieve*, Tomson Highway's *Dry Lips Oughta Move to Kapuskasing*, Tony Kushner's *Angels in America, Part I: Millennium Approaches*.
- "Aside" sections in each unit-opening essay, devoted to topics of special importance or interest: Roman drama and theater, Sanskrit drama and theater, the masque, *commedia dell' arte*, melodrama, the Federal Theater Project, and performance art.
- A photo essay, "Restaging the Classics," helping students to see how the imagination of a production's director and designers can work to realize a play onstage in new and surprising ways.

The Second Edition retains many of the critical essays found in the First Edition, such as selections by Aristotle, Friedrich Nietzsche, Sue-Ellen Case, Sir Philip Sidney, Mikhail Bakhtin, Lynda E. Boose, Northrop Frye, Katharine Maus, Émile Zola, Bertolt Brecht, Roland Barthes, Michael Goldman, Arthur Miller, George Steiner, Raymond Williams, Amiri Baraka/LeRoi Jones, Antonin Artaud, Martin Esslin, and Fredric Jameson. However, the Second Edition adds important classic essays by Zeami Motokiyo, Chikamatsu Monzaemon, and John Dryden, and recent essays by Yamazaki Masakazu, Peter Stallybrass, Henry Louis Gates Jr., and Elin Diamond. Finally, *The Harcourt Brace Anthology of Drama* continues its effort to enable students and teachers to explore the issues of representation in the theater and the ways that culture shapes issues of identity, of gender and sexuality, of power, and of race.

The Harcourt Brace Anthology of Drama is designed for both beginning and advanced students. An introduction to writing about drama and theater furnishes beginning students with an outline of the formal and rhetorical practices used in writing about plays. The book includes a useful glossary of dramatic, theatrical, and literary terms. It also contains an extensive bibliography of drama and theater history and theory, and of works about plays and playwrights included in the volume. The book concludes with a selected list of video, film, and sound recordings. For the instructor, a thorough Instructor's Manual by Sharon Mazer of the University of Canterbury (New Zealand) offers an overview and reading suggestions for each unit, as well as a summary and commentary, and study, discussion, and writing questions for each play. *The Harcourt Brace Anthology of Drama* provides a wide-ranging survey of drama and theater, one that presents both traditional issues and the materials to interrogate those traditions.

—W.B.W.
1995

ACKNOWLEDGMENTS

My thanks again to Stephen T. Jordan of Harcourt Brace for originally proposing this project and for his help in developing this Second Edition of *The Harcourt Brace Anthology of Drama,* and to Karl Yambert for his many ideas and suggestions about how the volume could be improved for teachers and students of drama and theater. Thanks, too, to Steve Norder, and to Linda Sparkman, for their valuable and careful editing of the manuscript; my special thanks to Eleanor Garner for her heroic effort to obtain permissions; to Pat Bracken for designing the book's visual layout and overall look; to Jane Ponceti for overseeing the production; and to Lili Weiner for assembling the photographs.

I would like to thank the many instructors and scholars who commented on the First Edition, suggesting ways that we might improve the Second Edition: George R. Adams (University of Wisconsin-Whitewater), Bonnie M. Anderson (San Diego State University), Karen Buckley (University of Wisconsin-Whitewater), Kathleen Colligan Cleary (Clark State Community College), Mary Ann Emery (University of Wisconsin-Whitewater), Lawrence E. Fink (Ohio State University), Melissa Gibson (University of Pittsburgh), Kiki Gounaridou (University of Pittsburgh), Anne-Charlotte Harvey (San Diego State University), Dennis Kennedy (University of Pittsburgh), Chris Mullen (University of North Carolina-Chapel Hill), Lurana O'Malley (University of Hawaii), Gwen Orel (University of Pittsburgh), Angela Peckenpaugh (University of Wisconsin-Whitewater), and Ruth Schauer (University of Wisconsin-Whitewater). In addition, I am grateful to the following reviewers of the manuscript of the Second Edition for their valuable revision suggestions: Anne Brannen (Duquesne University), Bradley Boney (University of Texas-Austin), Susan Carlson (Iowa State University), S. Alan Chesler (Northern Illinois University), Jill Dolan (City University of New York), Anthony J. Fichera (University of North Carolina-Chapel Hill), L. W. Harrison (Santa Rosa Junior College), Margaret Knapp (Arizona State University), Josephine Lee (University of Minnesota), Michael Longrie (University of Wisconsin-Whitewater), Michael Peterson (University of Wisconsin-Madison), Eula Thompson (Jefferson State Community College), and Jon Tuttle (Francis Marion University).

I am again indebted to Sharon Mazer for writing and revising the Instructor's Manual, and for her many helpful suggestions about the contents and orientation of the anthology. I remain grateful to Oscar G. Brockett of the University of Texas at Austin, to Janelle Reinelt of the University of California at Davis, and to Bonnie Busick of the California State University–Sacramento for allowing me to think out loud about what a book such as this one might accomplish. Finally, to the many students and colleagues who have called, have dropped me a note to correct my oversights and omissions, or have graciously spoken to me about the book at professional meetings and conferences, my sincere thanks for your attention and kindness.

—W.B.W.

CONTENTS

INTRODUCTION: DRAMA, THEATER, AND CULTURE   1

UNIT I: CLASSICAL ATHENS   11

UNIT II: CLASSICAL JAPAN   115

UNIT III: MEDIEVAL AND RENAISSANCE ENGLAND   183

UNIT IV: EARLY MODERN EUROPE   389

PHOTO ESSAY: RESTAGING THE CLASSICS   557

UNIT V: MODERN EUROPE   559

UNIT VI: THE UNITED STATES 793

UNIT VII: THE WORLD STAGE   1045

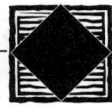

INTRODUCTION: DRAMA, THEATER, AND CULTURE

F THE MANY KINDS OF LITERATURE, DRAMA IS PERHAPS THE MOST IMMEDI-
ately involved in the life of its community. Drama shares with such other liter-
ary modes as lyric poetry, the novel, the epic, and romance the ability to
represent and challenge social, political, philosophical, and esthetic attitudes.
But unlike most literature, drama has generally been composed for performance, confronting the audience in the public, sociable confines of a theater.

To understand DRAMA, we need to understand THEATER, because the theater forges
the active interplay between drama and its community.[1] On a practical level, for instance,
the community must determine where drama will take place, and it is in the theater that a
space is carved out for dramatic performance. Not surprisingly, the place of the theater in a
city's social and physical geography often symbolizes drama's place in the culture at large.
In classical Athens, the theater adjoined a sacred precinct, and plays were part of an extensive religious and civic festival. Greek drama accordingly engages questions of moral, political, and religious authority. In seventeenth-century Paris, the close affiliation between the
theater and the court of Louis XIV is embodied in drama's concern with power, authority,
and the regulation of rebellious passions. In the United States today, most live theater takes
place either in the privileged setting of colleges and universities, or in the "theater districts"
of major cities, competing for an audience alongside movie theaters, nightclubs, and other
entertainments. Drama also seems to be struggling to define itself as part of an established
cultural tradition reaching back to Aeschylus and as part of the lively diversity of contemporary popular culture. Social attitudes are reflected in the theater in other ways, too; during
performance, the theater constructs its own "society" of performers and spectators. Staging
a play puts it immediately into a dynamic social exchange: the interaction between dramatic characters, between characters and the actors who play them, between the performers and the audience, between the drama onstage and the drama of life outside the theater.

The Greek word for "theater"—*theatron*—means "seeing place," and plays performed in
the theater engage their audiences largely through visual means. Less than a century ago,
live plays could be seen only on the stage; today, most of us see drama in a variety of
media: on film and television as well as in the theater. Yet for the past five hundred years
or so we have also had access to plays in another, nontheatrical venue: by reading them in
books. To see a play performed and to read it in a book are two very different activities, but
these distinct experiences of drama can be made to enrich one another in a number of
ways.

In the theater, a dramatic text is fashioned into an event, something existing in space
and time. The space of the stage, with whatever setting is devised, becomes the place of
the drama. The characters are embodied by specific individuals. How a given actor interprets a role tends to shape the audience's sense of that dramatic character; for the duration
of the play, it is difficult to imagine another kind of performance—a different Oedipus,
Lear, or Miss Julie than the one standing before us in the flesh. The drama onstage is also
bound by the temporal exigencies of performance. The process of performance is irre-
versible; for the duration of the performance, each moment becomes significant and yet
unrecoverable—we can't flip back a few pages to an earlier scene, or rewind the video-
tape. When a company puts a play into stage production, it inevitably confronts these

**READING
DRAMA AND
SEEING
THEATER**

---

[1] Terms are defined in the **Glossary.**

material facts of the theater: a specific cast of actors, a given theatrical space, a certain amount of money to spend, and the necessity of transforming the rich possibilities offered by the play into a clear and meaningful performance. To make the drama active and concrete, theatrical production puts a specific interpretation of the play on the stage. Whether or not to play Caliban in Shakespeare's *The Tempest* as a native of the West Indies; whether to play Torvald Helmer in Ibsen's *A Doll House* as a patriarchal autocrat or as someone bewildered by a changing world; whether to set *Phaedra* in a classical, neo-classical, or a modern setting; whether to use cross-gender or intercultural casting in *The Homecoming*—these are some of the kinds of questions that a production must face, and how the production decides such issues inevitably leads the audience toward a particular sense of the play. Everything that happens onstage becomes meaningful for an audience, something to interpret. Even apparently irrelevant facts—a short actor cast to play Hamlet in Shakespeare's play, or a beautiful actress playing Brecht's Mother Courage—become part of the audience's experience of the play, particularizing the play, lending it a definite flavor and meaning.

Reading a play presents us with a different experience of the drama. Reading plays is, first of all, a relatively recent phenomenon. In early theaters, like those of classical Athens and Rome, medieval Europe, and even Renaissance Europe of the sixteenth century, drama was almost entirely a theatrical mode, rather than a mode of literature. Although the texts of plays were written down, by and large, audiences came into contact with drama primarily through theatrical performance. By the late sixteenth century, though, the status of drama began to change. The recovery and prestige of Greek and Latin literature led to pervasive familiarity with classical texts, including plays. Throughout Europe, schooling was conducted mainly in Latin, and the plays of Roman playwrights like Plautus, Terence, and Seneca were frequently used to teach Latin grammar and rhetoric; these plays were widely imitated by playwrights writing drama in vernacular languages for emerging secular, commercial theaters. Printing made it possible to disseminate texts more widely, and plays slowly came to be regarded as worthy of publication and preservation in book form. By the late nineteenth century, widespread literacy created a large reading public and a great demand for books; continued improvements in printing technology provided the means to meet the demand. Playwrights often published their plays as books before they could be produced onstage, with some profound effects. The detailed narrative stage directions in plays by Bernard Shaw, Eugene O'Neill, or Henrik Ibsen, for instance, are useful to a stage director and set designer, but they principally fill in a kind of novelistic background for the reading audience who will experience the play only on the page.

Theater audiences are bound to the temporality and specificity of the stage, but readers have the freedom to compose the play in much more varied ways. A reader can pause over a line, teasing out possible meanings, in effect stopping the progress of the play. Readers are not bound by the linear progress of the play's action, in that they can flip back and forth in the play, looking for clues, confirmations, or connections. Nor are readers bound by the stringent physical economy of the stage, the need to embody the characters with individual actors, to specify the dramatic locale as a three-dimensional space. While actors and directors must decide on a specific interpretation of each moment and every character in the play, readers can keep several competing interpretations alive in the imagination at the same time.

Both ways of thinking about drama are demanding, and students of drama should try to develop a sensitivity to both approaches. Treating the play like a novel or poem, decomposing and recomposing it critically, leads to a much fuller sense of the play's potential meanings, its gaps and inconsistencies; it allows us to question the text without the need to come to definite conclusions. Treating the play as a design for the stage forces us to make commitments, to articulate and defend a particular version of the play, and to find ways of making those meanings active onstage, visible in performance. As readers, one way to develop a sense of the reciprocity between stage and page is to think of the play as constructed mainly of actions, not of words. Think of seeing a play in an unknown language: the *action* of the play would still emerge in its larger outlines, carried by the deeds of the characters. Not knowing the words would not prevent the audience from understanding what a character is doing onstage—threatening, lying, persuading, boasting.

When reading a play, it is easy to be seduced by the text, to think of the play's language as mainly narrative, describing the attitudes of the character. For performers onstage, however, speech—language in action—is always a way of doing something. One way for readers to attune themselves to this active quality of dramatic writing is to ask questions of the text from the point-of-view of performers or characters. What do I—Lysistrata, Everyman, Miranda—want in this speech? How can I use this speech to help me get it? What am I trying to do by speaking in this way? Although questions like these are still removed from the actual practice of performance, they can help readers unfamiliar with drama begin to read plays in theatrical terms.

Another way to enrich the reading experience of drama is to imagine staging the play: How could the design of the set, the movements of the actors, the pacing of the scenes affect the play's meaning, make the play mean something in particular? Questions of this kind can help to make the play seem more concrete, but they have one important limitation. When asking questions like these, it is tempting to imagine the play being performed in today's theaters, according to our conventions of acting and stagecraft, and within the social and cultural context that frames the theater now. To imagine the play on our stage is, of course, to produce it in our contemporary idiom, informed by our notions both of theater and of the world our theater represents. However, while envisioning performance, we should also imagine the play in the circumstances of its original theater, a theater located in a different culture and possibly sharing few practices of stagecraft with the modern theater. How would Hamlet's advice to the players have appeared on the Globe theater's empty platform stage in 1601? Are there ways in which the text capitalizes on this likeness between Shakespeare's company of actors and those Hamlet addresses fictively in the play? In a theater where a complete, "realistic" illusion was not possible (and, possibly, not even desirable), how does Shakespeare's play turn the conditions of theatrical performance to dramatic advantage? Both reading drama and staging drama involve a complex double-consciousness, inviting us to see the plays with contemporary questions in mind, while at the same time imagining them on their original stages. In this doubleness lies an important dramatic principle: Plays can speak to us in our theater but perhaps always retain something of their original accents.

DRAMA AND THEATER IN HISTORY

Throughout its development, dramatic art has changed as the theater's place in the surrounding society has changed. The categories that we apply to drama and theater today—art *vs.* entertainment, popular *vs.* classic, literary *vs.* theatrical—are categories of relatively recent vintage. They imply ways of thinking about drama and theater that are foreign to the function of theater in many other cultures. Much as drama and theater today emerge in relation to other media of dramatic performance like film and television, so in earlier eras the theater defined itself in relation to other artistic, social, and religious institutions. Placed in a different sphere of culture, drama and theater gained a different kind of significance than they have in the United States today.

Drama and theater often arise in relation to religious observance. In ancient Egypt, for instance, religious rituals involved the imitation of events in a god's or goddess's life. In Greece, drama may have had similar origins; by the sixth century BC, the performance of plays had become part of a massive religious festival celebrating the god Dionysus. The plays performed in this theater—including those of Aeschylus, Sophocles, Euripides, and Aristophanes gathered here—were highly wrought and intellectually, morally, and esthetically complex and demanding works. Aristotle classes drama among other forms of poetry, but in classical Athens these plays occupied a very different position in the spectrum of culture than do drama or "art" today, precisely because of their central role in the City Dionysia. The Roman theater set drama in the context of a much greater variety of performance—chariot racing, juggling, gladiatorial shows—and while plays were performed on religious holidays, drama was more clearly related to secular entertainments than it had been in Athens. Theater waned in Europe with the decline of the Roman Empire and the systematic efforts of the Catholic church to prevent theatrical performance. Yet, when theater was revived in the late Middle Ages, it emerged with the support of the church itself. By the year 1000, brief dramatizations illustrated the liturgy of the Catholic Mass; by the fourteenth century, a full range of dramatic forms—plays dramatizing the lives of saints, morality plays, narrative plays on Christian history—was used to illustrate Christian doctrine and to celebrate important days in the Christian year. Like plays in classical Athens, these plays were produced through community effort rather than by specialized "theaters" in the modern sense. Although we now regard medieval drama as extraordinarily rich and complex "literature," in its own era it was part of a different strand of culture, sharing space with other forms of pageantry and religious celebration, rather than being read with the poetry of Chaucer or Dante.

Similarly, in feudal Japan, the Buddhists developed a form of theater to illustrate the central concepts of their faith. Throughout the twelfth and thirteenth centuries, an increasing number of professional players came to imitate these dramatic performances on secular occasions, and for secular audiences. By the fourteenth century, it became conventional for the great samurai lords—or SHOGUNS—to patronize a theatrical company, giving rise to the classical era of the Noh theater.

Secular performance did, of course, also take place in classical and medieval Europe, including improvised farces on contemporary life, fairground shows, puppetry, mimes, and other quasi-dramatic events. Many plays were performed only on religious occasions, though, and their performers were usually itinerant, lacking the social and institutional support that would provide them with lasting and continuous existence. Only in the Renaissance of the fifteenth and sixteenth centuries did the Western theater begin to assume the function it has today: a fully secular, profit-making, commercial enterprise. Although Renaissance theaters continually vied with religious and state officials for the freedom to practice their trade, by the sixteenth century, the European theater was part of a secular entertainment market, competing with bear-baiting, animal shows, athletic contests, public executions, royal and civic pageants, public preaching, and many other attractions to draw a paying public. The theater emerged in this period as a distinct institution, supported by its own income; the theater became a trade, a profession, a business, rather than a necessary function of the state or of religious worship. Indeed, if drama in classical Athens was conceived more as religious ritual than as "art" in a modern sense, drama in Renaissance London was classed mainly as popular "entertainment." The theater only gradually became recognized as an arena for "literary" accomplishment, for literary status in this period was reserved mainly for skill demonstrated in forms like the sonnet, the prose romance, or the epic—forms that could win the author a measure of aristocratic prestige and patronage. As part of the motley, vulgar world of the public theater, plays were not considered serious, permanent literature.

However, the desire to transform drama from ephemeral theatrical "entertainment" into permanent literary "art" begins to be registered in the Renaissance. The poet and playwright Ben Jonson included plays in the 1616 edition of his *Works*, insisting on the literary importance of the volume by publishing it in the large, FOLIO format generally reserved for classical authors. In 1623, seven years after his death, William Shakespeare's friends and colleagues published a similar, folio-sized collection of his plays, a book that was reprinted several times throughout the seventeenth century. By the 1660s and 1670s, writers at the court of Louis XIV in Paris could achieve both literary and social distinction as dramatists; Jean Racine's reputation as a playwright, in part at least, helped to win his appointment as Louis's royal historiographer. Yet, despite many notable exceptions, the theatrical origins of drama prevented contemporary plays from being regarded as "literature"—although plays from earlier eras were increasingly republished and gradually seen to have "literary" merit. Indeed, by the nineteenth century, contemporary plays often achieved "literary" recognition by avoiding the theater altogether. English poets like Lord Byron and Percy Bysshe Shelley, for instance, wrote plays that were in many ways unstageable, and so preserved them from degrading contact with the tawdry stage. The English critic Charles Lamb remarked in a famous essay that he preferred reading Shakespeare's plays to seeing them in the theater; for Lamb, the practical mechanics of acting and the stage intruded on the experience of the drama's poetic dimension. In fact, the great playwrights of the late nineteenth century—Henrik Ibsen, Anton Chekhov, August Strindberg, and even the young Bernard Shaw—carved a space for themselves as dramatists by writing plays *in opposition* to the values of their contemporary audiences and to the practice of their contemporary theater—a strategy that would have seemed unimaginable to Aeschylus, Shakespeare, or even Molière. To bring their plays successfully to the stage, new theaters and new theater practices had to be devised, and a new audience had to be found, or made.

This split between the "literary drama" and the "popular theater" has become the condition of twentieth-century drama and theater: plays of the artistic AVANT-GARDE are more readily absorbed into the CANON of literature, while more conventional entertainments—television screenplays, for instance—remain outside it. The major modern playwrights from Ibsen to Luigi Pirandello to Samuel Beckett first wrote for small theaters and were produced by experimental companies playing to coterie audiences on the fringes of the theatrical "mainstream." This sense of modernist "art" as opposed to the values of bourgeois culture was not confined to drama and theater. Modernist fiction and poetry, cubist and abstract painting and sculpture, modern dance, and modern music all developed a new formal complexity, thematic abstraction, and critical self-consciousness in opposition to the sentimental superficiality they found in conventional art forms. This modernist tendency has itself produced a kind of reaction, a desire to bring the devices of popular culture and mass culture into drama, as a way of altering the place of the theater in society and changing the relationship between the spectators and the stage. Bertolt Brecht's ALIENATION EFFECT, Samuel Beckett's importation of circus and film clowns to absurdist theater, or Wole Soyinka's interweaving of African ritual and fourth-wall realism in *Death and the King's Horseman* are all examples of this reaction. For the theater has been challenged by film and television to define its space in contemporary culture, and, given the pervasive availability of other media, theater has increasingly seemed to occupy a place akin to that of opera, among the privileged, elite forms of "high culture." As a result, innovation in today's theater often takes place on the margins or fringes of mainstream theater and mainstream culture: in smaller companies experimenting with new performance forms, in subversive theaters confronting political oppression in many parts of the world, and in theaters working to form a new audience and a new sense of theater by conceiving new forms of drama.

Perhaps because its meaning must emerge rapidly and clearly in performance, drama tends to be compressed and condensed; its characters tend toward types, and its action tends toward certain general patterns as well. It is conventional to speak of these kinds of

DRAMATIC GENRES

drama as GENRES, each with its own identifying formal structure and typical themes. Following Aristotle's *Poetics*, for example, TRAGEDY is usually considered to concern the fate of an individual hero, singled out from the community through circumstances and through his or her own actions. In the course of the drama, the hero's course of action entwines with events and circumstances beyond his or her control. As a result, the hero's final downfall—usually, but not always, involving death—seems at once both chosen and inevitable. COMEDY, on the other hand, focuses on the fortunes of the community itself. While the hero of tragedy is usually unique, the heroes of comedy often come in pairs— the lovers who triumph over their parents in romantic comedies, the dupe and the trickster at the center of more ironic or satirical comic modes. While tragedy points toward the hero's downfall or death, comedy generally points toward some kind of broader reform or remaking of society, usually signalled by a wedding or other celebration at the end of the play.

To speak of genre in this way, though, is to suggest that these ideal critical abstractions actually exist in some form, exemplified more or less adequately by particular plays. Yet, as the rather different genres of Japanese theater suggest, terms like *tragedy* and *comedy*, or MELODRAMA, TRAGICOMEDY, FARCE, and others, arise from our efforts to find continuities between extraordinarily different kinds of drama: between plays written in different theaters, for different purposes, to please different audiences, under different historical pressures. When we impose these terms in a prescriptive way, we usually find that the drama eludes them or even calls them into question. Aristotle's brilliant sense of Greek tragedy in the *Poetics*, for instance, hardly "applies" with equal force to Greek plays as different as *Agamemnon*, *Oedipus Rex*, and *Medea*, or Chikamatsu's elegant doll drama, *Love Suicides at Sonezaki*, let alone later plays like *Hamlet* or *Miss Julie*. In his essay, "Tragedy and the Common Man," Arthur Miller tries to preserve "tragedy" for modern drama by redefining Aristotle's description of the hero of tragedy. Instead of Aristotle's hero—a man (not a woman) of an elevated social station—Miller argues that the modern hero should be an average, "common" man (not a woman), precisely because the "best families" do not seem normative to us or representative of our basic values. Our exemplary characters are taken from the middle classes. Yet to redefine the hero in this way calls Aristotle's other qualifications—the notion of the hero's character and actions, the meaning of the tragic "fall"—into question as well, forcing us to redefine Aristotelian tragedy in ways that make it something entirely new, something evocative in modern terms.

In approaching the question of genre, then, it is often useful to avoid asking how a play exemplifies the universal and unchanging features of tragedy or comedy. Instead, one could ask how a play or a theater *invents* tragedy or comedy for its contemporary audience. What terms does the drama present, what formal features does it use, to represent human experience? How do historically "local" genres—Renaissance REVENGE TRAGEDY, French NEOCLASSICAL DRAMA, modern THEATER OF THE ABSURD—challenge, preserve, or redefine broader notions of genre?

DRAMATIC FORM

In about 335 BC, Aristotle's *Poetics* set down the formal elements of drama, and the influence of Aristotle's description has been massive: Today we still speak of dramatic form in terms of its PLOT, CHARACTERS, LANGUAGE, THEME, and its performative elements, what Aristotle called MUSIC and SPECTACLE. Any student of drama can profit by thinking about how these formal elements function in a given play. How are the incidents of the play—its plot—arranged? What effects are achieved by *this* ordering, rather than by another? How does the plot relate to the play's narrative story, which includes events dating from before the play begins? How does the plot, the structure of the events—for instance, Nora Helmer's first act in *A Doll House* is to enter the house, and her last act is to leave it—develop the play's themes? We might then ask how the play defines its characters. What elements of human experience—family history, psychological motivation, public action—seem to be most prominent in a play's conception of "character"? How do the formal conventions of characterization—blank verse in Shakespeare's plays; the densely poetic language of Noh theater—affect our reading of the characters and our understanding of them as representations of human beings?

Although Aristotle presents these elements of drama as distinct, in practice they are mutually defining, making it very difficult to speak of them separately. A play's language, for example, can be analyzed purely for its verbal and rhetorical features, but it is more interesting to ask how the language affects our understanding of the characters or invests the play with certain thematic possibilities. Similarly, while we may regard a play's themes as inside the play, they actually arise only in our interpretation of the play. The themes are something we create by asking certain questions about the play's plotting, its characterization, its use of language. The artificiality of separating these features becomes especially clear when we turn to a play's performative or theatrical dimension. Although Aristotle suggests that a play's literary dimension and its theatrical dimensions are independent, to get a real sense of drama we must see the play both as literature and as theater. We must assess how an audience's sense of the play's plot, characters, and themes are shaped by the kinds of spectacle demanded by the play and provided by the theater. The "meaning" of Greek drama cannot be separated from its conditions of performance: the religious festival, the huge amphitheater, the masked actors, the singing, dancing chorus. The barren "sterile promontory" of *Hamlet,* Phaedra's claustral chamber, cross-dressed performance in Churchill's *Cloud Nine:* These elements of the theatrical spectacle are not outside the meaning of the drama; they are its means, the vehicle for achieving that meaning on the stage.

In a book like this one—indeed, in any book—it is difficult to convey a real sense of the power of theater. It is possible, though, to imagine this experience and to discuss it through the materials collected here: dramatic texts, descriptions of stage practice, illustrations of theaters, photographs, essays. However, an obstacle to understanding arises from a split between the disciplines we use to understand drama and theater. At many colleges and universities, this split is represented in the geography of the campus itself, where the English or Literature departments, which teach dramatic literature, are housed in one building, and the Theater or Drama department, which teaches acting, directing, design, and which actually stages the plays, is housed in another. "Literary" approaches to drama focus our attention initially, sometimes exclusively, on the text of a play and train the complex strategies of poetics and poetic interpretation on it. Such interpretation regards the dramatic text as incomplete and specifies the text's range of possible meanings by placing it in various textual and cultural contexts; in a sense, the negotiation between the text and these contexts determines what we can say the play *means.*

"Theatrical" approaches to drama tend to see a play in terms of stage practice, both in the terms of the play's original production and in the light of performance practice today. This approach interrogates the play's staging: how it can be set, what obstacles it presents to acting and casting, what the dramatic effects of costume and design will be. "Theatrical" interpretation regards the dramatic text as an incomplete design for performance and trains the complex machinery of stage representation—directing, acting, design, costuming—on the task of fleshing the script out as performed action. The meaning of the play in this regard emerges from what we can make the play *do.*

The literary and theatrical approaches to drama and theater share the assumption that plays are not fully meaningful in themselves; they share the sense that the meaning of drama emerges from the kinds of questions we ask of it, the contexts—literary, historical,

**THE STAGE
IN CRITICAL
PRACTICE**

theoretical, theatrical—in which we can make it perform, and make it mean something in particular. Although each approach can seem needlessly mysterious, involving its own specialized language and critical practice, its own set of "right" questions and "right" answers, this book has been assembled with the conviction that the literary and the theatrical approaches are necessary complements to each other. Thinking about drama requires us to think about how plays perform as literature, in culture and history, and on the stage.

CLASSICAL ATHENS

REAT DRAMA ARISES WHERE THE THEATER OCCUPIES AN IMPORTANT PLACE in the life of the community. In many respects, Western understanding of drama originated in fifth century (500–400) BC classical Athens, where the theater played a central role in politics, religion, and society. The Athenian stage invented forms of tragedy and comedy that persist to the present day. In tragedy, the Greeks dramatized climactic events in the lives of legendary heroes from prehistory and myth, bringing ethical problems of motive and action to the stage. In comedy, the theater staged satiric portraits of the life of the *POLIS* (the city-state), vividly depicting the energetic conflicts of contemporary Athens in matters of politics, war, education—even the arts of drama. Playwrights through the long history of the theater have continued to find in Greek drama both a model and a point of resistance against which to practice their own craft—see, for example, Jean Racine's *Phaedra* or Bernard Shaw's *Major Barbara* in this volume. And we need only recall Sigmund Freud's understanding of the "Oedipus complex" to sense the influence of models of action derived from the Greek theater on later Western culture.

Athens and Sparta were dominant rival powers in fifth-century Greece, which comprised many small independent city-states, each with its own political and cultural institutions, form of government, and alliances. Dramatic performances took place under a variety of circumstances in all Greek cities, but drama as we know it developed in Athens. Dramatic performance in Athens was part of citywide religious festivals honoring the god Dionysus, the most important being the CITY DIONYSIA. Plays were produced for contests, in which playwrights, actors, and choruses competed for prizes and for distinction among their fellow citizens. These contests, held in an outdoor amphitheater adjoining the sacred temple of the god, followed several days of religious parades and sacrifices. This connection between early drama and religion suggests that the essential nature of Greek drama lies in its supposed "origins" in religious ritual. But the City Dionysia was also a massive civic spectacle that went far beyond religious worship, emphasizing the theater's implication in other areas of public life. Dramatic performance contributed to this celebration of Athens' economic power, cultural accomplishment, and military might. The City Dionysia united religion and politics, enabling Athenians to celebrate both Dionysus and the achievements of their *polis*.

THE CITY DIONYSIA

The City Dionysia, the most prominent of the four religious festivals honoring Dionysus, was held between December and April in Athens and in the surrounding province of Attica. Although its purpose was primarily a religious one, the City Dionysia was structured around a series of contests between individual citizens and between major Athenian social groups—the ten (later twelve to fifteen) "tribes" that formed the city's basic political and military units. Dramatic performance was introduced to the City Dionysia during the sixth century BC and became the centerpiece of the elaborate festival. Each year a city magistrate, or *ARCHON*, honored selected wealthy citizens by choosing them to finance one of the three principal tragic dramatists competing for a prize at the festival. Each sponsor, called a *CHOREGOS*, was responsible for hiring the *CHORUS* of young men who sang and danced in the plays. He also hired musicians and provided costumes and other support for the playwright to whom he was assigned. Later in the period, the state also assigned the leading actor to the *choregos* as well, and this actor also competed for a prize. The playwright was responsible for training the chorus and the actors, and for some of the acting himself, and he shared his prize with the *choregos*.

Taking place over several days in late March or early April, the City Dionysia opened with a lavish parade of religious officials and dramatic performers through the city, followed by religious observances and sacrifices held in the theater. Athens also received its annual tribute of goods, money, and slaves from subject and allied states at this time, and war orphans raised at state expense also were displayed to the audience. After this display of religious worship and civic pride, two days were then devoted to contests of DITHYRAMBS, hymns sung and danced by a large chorus. Each of Athens' tribes sponsored two choruses: one consisting of fifty men, another consisting of fifty boys. The city's politics revolved around the tribes, and their contribution to the festival was prominent in this contest, too. The dithyrambic contest involved a thousand Athenian citizens directly in the performance. Following the dithyrambs, the main dramatic contest began. The competing playwrights each produced a TRILOGY of tragedies, staged over three days. A trilogy could take a single theme or series of events as its subject (like the three plays of Aeschylus' *Oresteia*, 458 BC), or present three distinct, unrelated dramas. A rugged farce called a SATYR PLAY followed the performance of each complete trilogy; these plays parodied a god's activities using actors dressed as satyrs—half-man, half-goat. After 486 BC, comedies were also awarded prizes, but it is unclear whether the comedies were performed on a single day or spread over several days. Prominent citizens representing each of the tribes served as judges and awarded prizes to the playwrights, their *choregoi*, and the actors.

THE THEATER OF DIONYSUS

The Greek theater was a public spectacle, a kind of cross between Inauguration Day, the Super Bowl, the Academy Awards, Memorial Day, and a major religious holiday. Plays were first produced in the AGORA (marketplace), which often served as a performance place for festivals in Athens and elsewhere. The size and importance of the City Dionysia, however, required a separate site, and a theater was built on the slope of the Acropolis, near the precinct of Dionysus. The original theater, a ring of wooden seats facing a circular floor, was later refined, enlarged, and constructed of stone. By the time of Aeschylus, Euripides, Sophocles, and Aristophanes, the Athenian theater had achieved its basic design: a circular floor for dancing and acting, ringed by a hillside AMPHITHEATER and backed by a low, rectangular building.

The focus of the classical amphitheater—which seated about 14,000 people—was the round ORCHESTRA ("dancing place"), containing the central altar of Dionysus, at which the festival sacrifices were performed. The dithyrambic choruses performed their ecstatic dances in the *orchestra*, and the bulk of the action of the plays took place there as well. Facing the *orchestra*, the hillside was divided into wedge-shaped seating areas. The citizens sat on wooden benches with their tribes: leaders and priests in the front of the sections, women perhaps toward the rear or possibly in a separate section. *Metics* (resident aliens) and visitors were probably seated in a separate area. Special front and center seats were reserved for the judges and the priests of Dionysus.

Behind the *orchestra*, a low building called the SKENE faced the audience. Although the *skene* became a permanent stone structure in the fourth century BC, in the fifth century it was a temporary wooden building, used for changing masks and possibly also for changing costumes. Playwrights quickly found the theatrical potential latent in the *skene's* facade and set of doors—through these doors the audience heard Agamemnon being murdered in his bath, or saw eyeless Oedipus return to confront the Chorus and his future in exile. In Aeschylus' *Agamemnon*, the Watchman awaits the signal fires on the palace roof, and in performance he may have waited on the roof of the *skene*. The theater also used some machinery for scenic effects: a rolling platform used to bring objects or bodies from the *skene* into the *orchestra*; a crane (MACHINA) to raise or lower characters—the gods, for instance—from the *orchestra* over the roof of the *skene*; and possibly painted panels to indicate the play's setting or location.

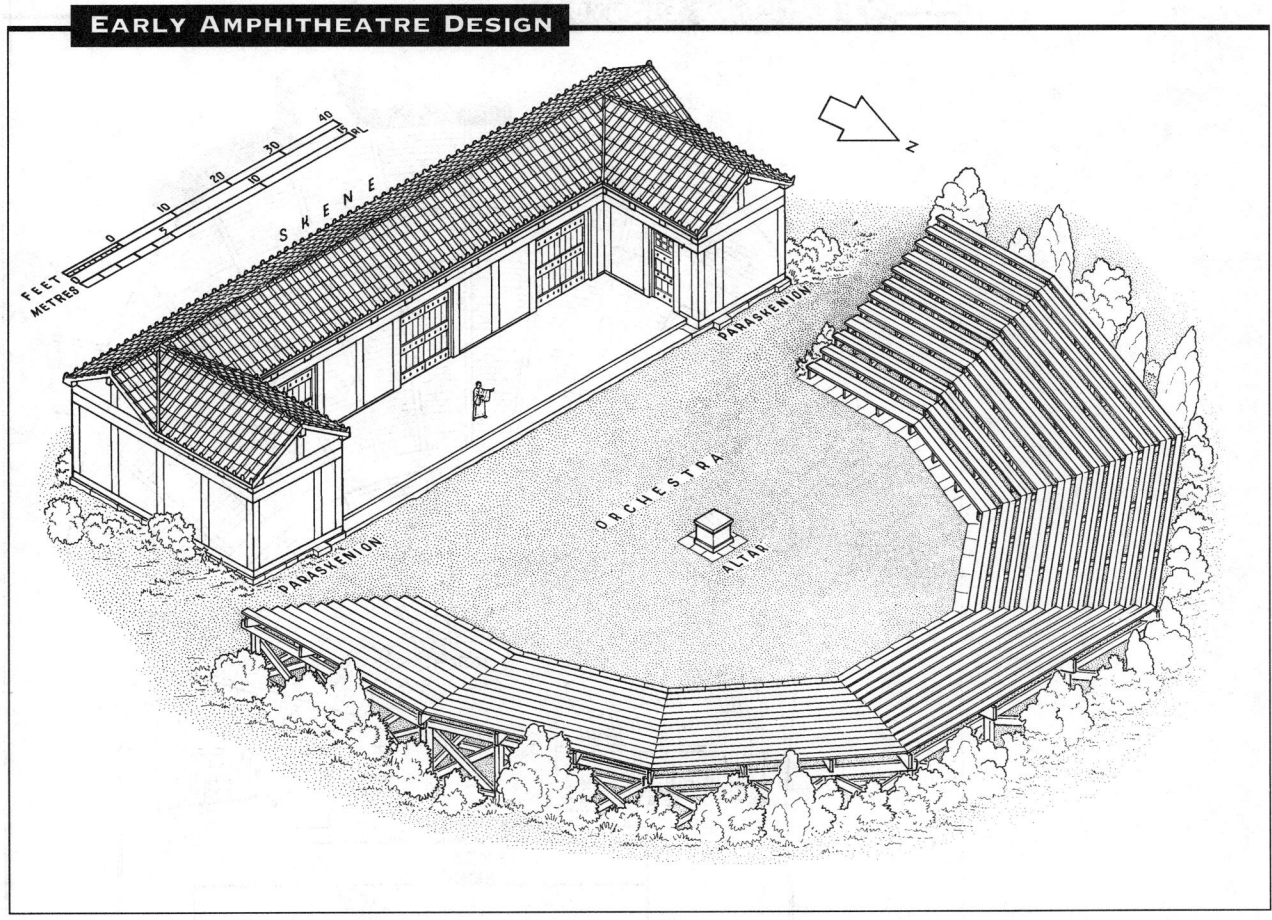

EARLY AMPHITHEATRE DESIGN

This is an artist's reconstruction of an early theater in Eretria, Greece. Notice that the seating is constructed of wooden benches and the skene *is a temporary structure.*

THEATER AND SOCIAL LIFE

The experience of theater in classical Athens was in some ways akin to participation in other institutions of civic life. Athens was a participatory democracy for its citizens, though citizenship was restricted to adult male Athenians: women, foreigners, slaves, freed slaves, and children were not citizens. Citizens sat in the assembly to discuss and vote on matters of state policy, and they were eligible to serve in all public and military offices as well. Attendance at the City Dionysia was, then, like other aspects of Athenian public life, a privilege and an obligation mainly reserved for citizens. Citizens received tickets to the festival from neighborhood officials; tickets may have been awarded on the basis of participation in other civic obligations—serving in the courts, the assembly, the army. At the theater, citizens sat together with members of their tribe. In a sense, the theater offered a visual map of the organization of Athenian society, for the tribes formed the basis of political participation outside the theater: The Athenian Assembly and the army were similarly arranged by tribe. Organized by tribes, with precedence given to religious officials and with inferior status or nonparticipation accorded to noncitizens such as women, slaves, and foreigners, the theater of Dionysus mirrored the structure of Athenian society.

The fifth century BC was the era of Athens' greatest political power and cultural vitality and an era of intense reciprocity between Athenian theater and society. Yet the tension

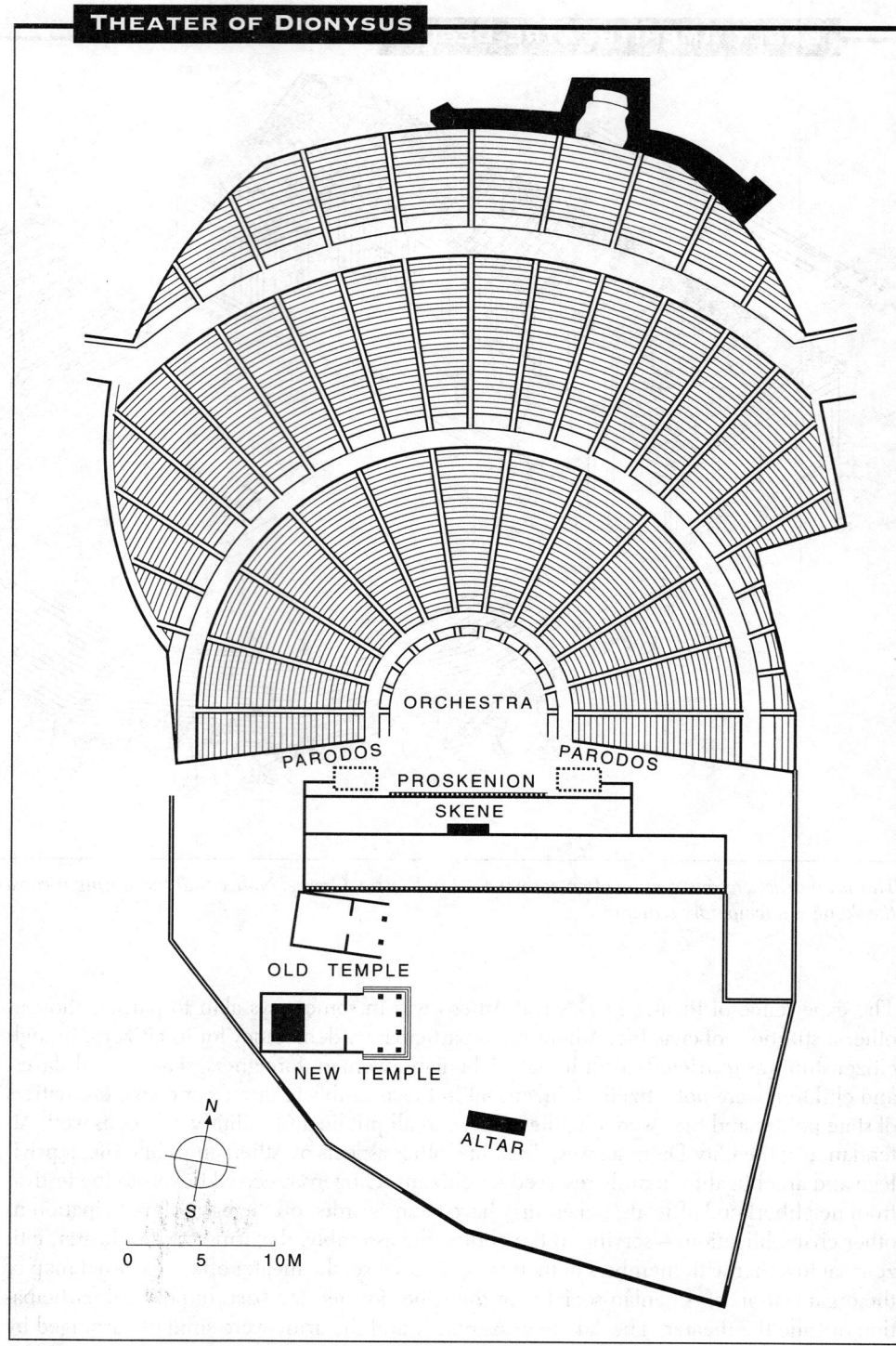

THEATER OF DIONYSUS

ORCHESTRA

PARODOS   PARODOS

PROSKENION

SKENE

OLD TEMPLE

NEW TEMPLE

ALTAR

N

S

0   5   10M

This ground plan is of the sacred precinct of Dionysus in Athens, fourth century BC. Notice that the theater is much larger than the earlier theater at provincial Eretria. The large and permanent skene was constructed after the fifth century BC.

manifest in Greek drama perhaps points to the precarious stability of the Athenian *polis*. The Athenian maritime empire, forged after the defeat of massive Persian forces in 479, was resisted by the smaller Greek states and opposed by Athens' chief rival, the military state of Sparta. Following a long period of hostility and skirmishing, Athens and Sparta declared war against each other in 431 BC, resulting in Athens' utter defeat in 404. Athenian democracy was replaced by an oppressive oligarchy, the Thirty Tyrants. Although the tyrants were rapidly overthrown and democracy restored, Athens never regained the dynamic cultural life and political power it enjoyed during the fifth century. And although dramatic performance continued after the restoration of democracy, the theater's central role in the *polis* seems to have declined after the Spartan victory. Yet, the theater became one of Greece's most widely disseminated cultural products. When Alexander the Great conquered Greece, the Near East, and northern Africa, he took Greek culture—including theater and drama—with him throughout his empire. And when the Roman Empire later absorbed Alexander's former dominions, it appropriated Greek dramatic traditions, the design of Greek theaters, and the arts and religion of Greece, as well.

In his *Poetics*, Aristotle suggests that drama originated in the singing of the dithyrambic choruses; a masked actor was first used to respond to the chorus as an individualized "character" in the mid-sixth century BC, an innovation attributed to the playwright Thespis, about whom little else is known. Aeschylus was the first to use two actors, probably taking one of the parts himself; in the 460s, Sophocles introduced a third actor and was successfully imitated by Aeschylus in his *Oresteia* in 458 BC. In general, classical tragedy can be performed with three actors, and comedy with four, though each actor may play several parts. All of the performers in the Greek theater—the dramatists, actors, musicians, and chorus members—were male citizens of Athens, as was the bulk of the audience. The dramatic choruses were perhaps composed of young men between the age of seventeen, when military training began, and twenty-one, when Athenian men entered into adulthood.

The chorus of tragedy both sang and danced, and it was expected to perform with grace and precision. Actors and choruses wore full-head masks made of painted linen or lightweight wood. The main characters' masks were individualized, but the members of the chorus all wore identical masks, giving a special force to the conflict between the unique claims of the protagonist and the more diffuse claims of his society. Costuming in comedy was somewhat more complex. Aristophanes' plays suggest that the chorus at times wore animal masks. The comic protagonists' masks, though, were again individualized; since Aristophanes often put his contemporaries in his plays—Socrates in *Clouds*, for instance, or Euripides in *Frogs*—the masks probably resembled these citizens quite closely. Comic actors often sported a leather PHALLUS, clearly visible in statues depicting comic actors and of much dramatic use in plays like *Lysistrata*.

In Athenian tragedy and comedy, female characters were played by men. Not only did men sponsor and write the plays, but the "women" onstage were literally men in disguise. Yet, many plays throw the theatrical convention of men playing women into relief. In Euripides' play *The Bacchae*, Pentheus is possessed by Dionysus when he dresses up as a woman and admires his good looks; in *Lysistrata*, the Spartan woman Lampito is closely and physically examined by Lysistrata and the other women in ways that focus the audience's attention precisely on the fact that the woman is being played by a man. Drama, then, participated fully in Athens' denial of equality to women. Athena says as much in Aeschylus' *The Eumenides* when she judges Orestes' murder of his mother as a lesser crime

DRAMA AND PERFORMANCE

WOMEN IN THE ATHENIAN THEATER

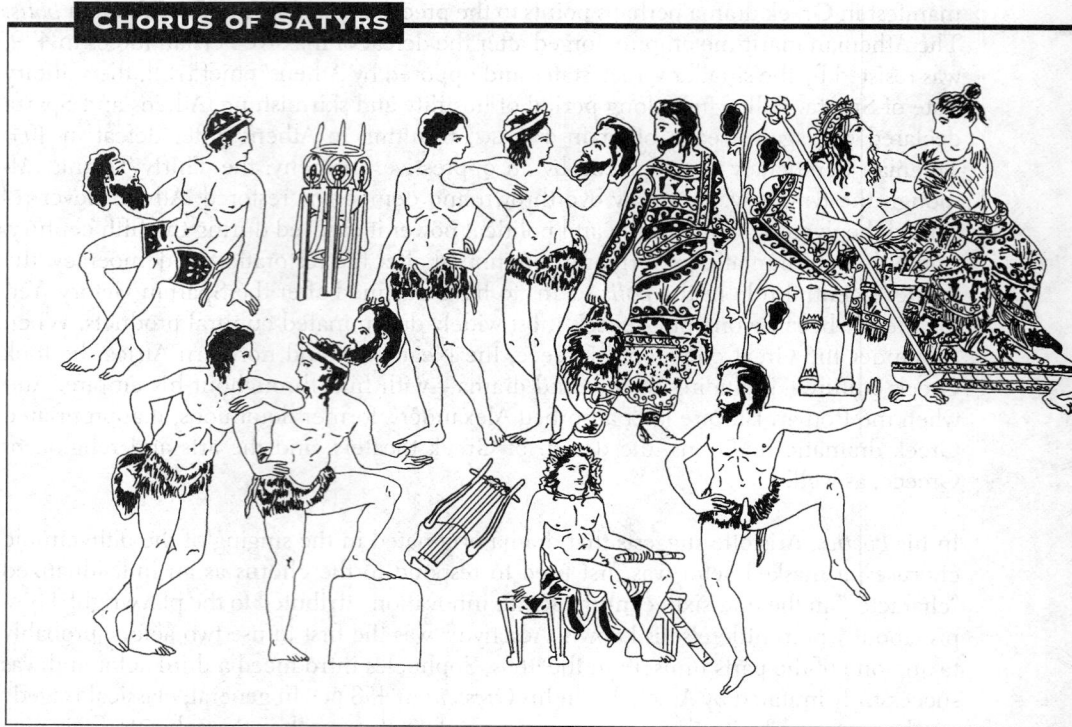

CHORUS OF SATYRS

These actors, apparently in a satyr play, appear on a vase painting. Notice that the central seated figure of Dionysus (holding the polelike thyrsus) *is surrounded by actors holding their masks. The older, bearded actor to the right of Dionysus, wearing the lion skin over his shoulder, is apparently*

than Clytaemnestra's murder of her husband. Looking closely at both the drama and its performance can help us to see how justice, power, and gender came to be arranged in Athenian society.

Yet although the theater—like Athenian society—was a male-dominated institution, Greek drama repeatedly inquires into the nature of gendered behavior and uses female characters to focus some of its most challenging questions. Given the absence of women from the stage and their marginal status in the theater and in the state, it is fascinating to note how many plays turn on the action of female characters. Women were not themselves citizens of Athens, and their prerogatives in the *polis* were defined only through marriage. Yet many of the plays raise critical moral, ethical, and political problems through the actions of women—Clytaemnestra and Cassandra in Aeschylus' *Agamemnon*, Medea in Euripides' *Medea*, and the women of Aristophanes' *Lysistrata* and *Assembly of Women*. Although Aristotle probably voices his contemporaries' views when he remarks in *The Poetics* that "a woman can be good, or a slave, although one of these classes [women] is inferior and the other, as a class, worthless," the theater stages women in ways that implicitly challenge the authority of this "natural" connection between the good, the legitimate, and the masculine.

FORMS OF GREEK DRAMA

Formally, Greek tragedy is organized somewhat differently than modern plays are, for Greek drama is based on the singing and dancing of the chorus, for whom many of the plays were named. Most plays begin with a PROLOGUE, like the Watchman's speech at the opening of *Agamemnon*, followed by the PARODOS (entrance) of the singing and

playing Hercules, the protagonist of the play. The other, younger and beardless figures may compose the chorus. While Hercules holds an individualized mask, the chorus members all hold masks similar to each other, and they wear costumes suggestive of satyrs.

dancing chorus. Several EPISODES follow, in which the central characters engage one another and the chorus; the chorus itself often sings (and dances) several ODES, which are used to enunciate and enlarge on the play's pivotal issues, and the Chorus often becomes a decisive character in the play, as it does in Aeschylus' *The Eumenides* or Euripides' *The Bacchae.* The choral odes are written in lyric meters different from the meters used for the characters' speeches. The play's CATASTROPHE, or downturn, marks some change in the hero's status and is followed by the departure of the characters from the stage and the EXODOS, or final song, dance, and departure of the chorus. Comedy—at least for Aristophanes, whose plays are the only surviving comedies from the period—is structured similarly, though Aristophanes' plays usually include a long PARABASIS, a choral ode delivered to the audience discussing political issues, and a final KOMOS, a scene of choral dancing and revelry.

This formal description, however, hardly accounts for the real and continued power of Greek drama, which arises from an intense and economical relationship between (1) a situation, usually at the point of climax as the play opens, (2) a complex of characters, each with distinctive goals and motives, (3) a chorus used both as a character and as a commentator on the action, and (4) a series of incidents that precipitates a crisis and brings the meaning of the PROTAGONIST's actions into focus. Aristotle termed this crisis the *PERIPETEIA,* or "reversal," in the external situation or fortunes of the main character, and he argued that it should be accompanied by an act of *ANAGNORISIS,* or "recognition," in which the character responds to this change. Indeed, Aristotle argued that when the pressure of the tragic action produces a close relationship between reversal and

ALTHOUGH MANY OF THEIR TRADITIONS were absorbed from Greece, the Romans developed a distinctive theater, quite different from the Athenian stage. From its beginnings, Roman theater was more varied than the Greek stage, including acrobatics, juggling, athletic events, gladiatorial combats, and skits. In the sixth and seventh centuries BC, Rome was a relatively unimportant town, ruled by the Etruscan kingdoms of northern Italy. In 509, the Romans drove out the Etruscans and founded a republic; the republic expanded its influence throughout the fourth century BC and eventually came to control many territories once governed by the Greeks and by Alexander. Much as the Romans absorbed other Greek cultural institutions, they also absorbed Greek theater and drama, which were first performed in Rome in the mid-third century, in 240 BC. As Rome's political influence expanded, particularly under the Roman Empire (27 BC–AD 476), the Romans disseminated their characteristic cultural institutions—including theater and drama—throughout Europe, North Africa, and the Middle East.

Like the Greeks, the Romans associated the drama with festivals, but the Romans not only produced plays on festival occasions throughout the year, they also developed a much wider variety of theatrical entertainments, of which drama was only a small part. Some of the Roman entertainments descended from the sixth-century, BC, *ludi Romani*, which included chariot racing, boxing, and other athletic contests, and Greek drama was first performed in Rome at these games. Moreover, Greek drama not only competed with other nondramatic entertainment, it also was rivalled by an indigenous dramatic form, known as ATELLAN FARCE. Associated with the town of Atella (near present-day Naples), these farces were probably improvised comic skits, involving stock characters and played by masked actors.

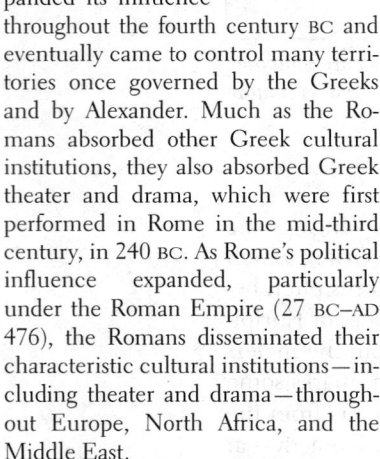

(ASIDE)

ROMAN DRAMA AND THEATER

After the introduction of tragedy and comedy to the *ludi Romani* in 240 BC, dramatic performances were introduced to several other festivals, and by 179 BC, drama was being performed at major religious festivals throughout the year: at the *ludi Romani* honoring Jupiter in September, at a second festival consecrated to Jupiter in November, at festivals honoring Flora and the Great Mother in April, and at a festival honoring Apollo in July. Dramatic performances, though still associated with festivals, were much more common in Rome than in fifth-century Athens, not only because special celebrations sometimes included theatrical performance, but also because any disruption in the rituals connected with the festivals required that the entire festival be repeated, including the dramatic performances.

Given the variety of entertainments offered in Rome—including the chariot races and gladiatorial combats that became increasingly popular in the later Empire, especially after AD 300—it is not surprising that the Romans built several different kinds of entertainment buildings, stadiums and racecourses as well as theaters. Yet until 55 BC, theaters in Rome were temporary, built and taken down for each festival. In the first century BC, the Romans began to build permanent theaters with some regularity. Like their Greek predecessors, the Roman theaters were outdoor amphitheaters, but the Romans built their theaters on level ground, and their superior engineering—particularly the Romans' use of arches in construction—enabled them to build much more massive buildings. Roman theaters were generally three stories in height. A rectangular stage house, or SCAENA stood—like the Greek *skene*—behind the semicircular orchestra and faced a steeply tiered semicircular auditorium. The facade of the *scaena* was elaborately ornamented with columns and porticos. The Romans built theaters of stone and built them throughout the Empire; many of the

recognition, it instills in the audience intense feelings of fear and pity and then effects CATHARSIS, a purgation of these emotions.

Since the plays were written for a contest, it is not surprising that their language and construction provide opportunity for powerful acting—particularly since the plays were judged only in performance. And yet the stage action of Greek drama is hardly spectacular in the modern sense. Although the visual dimension of Agamemnon's descent from the

Greek theaters that remain today were refurbished and redesigned by the Romans.

Although the Romans continued to perform plays from the Greek theater, they also developed a native strain of drama represented in the plays of Plautus, Terence, and Seneca. Titus Maccius Plautus (c. 254–c. 184 BC) is probably the most influential Roman comic playwright. His earliest surviving plays date from 205 BC, or about 35 years after Greek drama was first introduced to Rome; Plautus is thought to have based many of his comedies on Greek New Comedy, but none of these prototypes survive. Plautus is thought to have written more than one hundred comedies, many of which—*Amphitryon, The Braggart Warrior, The Rope,* and *The Menaechmus Twins,* for example—established the formal conventions of later comedy. Publius Terentius Afer (c. 195–159 BC)—usually called Terence—was probably born in Carthage and brought to Rome as a slave. Unlike the prolific Plautus, Terence wrote only six comedies, all of which survive, and strove throughout his career to adapt Greek originals to the Roman stage: *The Woman of Andros, Mother-in-Law, Self-Tormentor, Eunuch, Phormio,* and *The Brothers.* The plays of Plautus and Terence have been particularly influential on the form and structure of later European comedy; not only did they establish many of the forms and character types developed by later playwrights, but in the late Middle Ages and Renaissance, their plays were often used to teach Latin in the schools, giving rise to

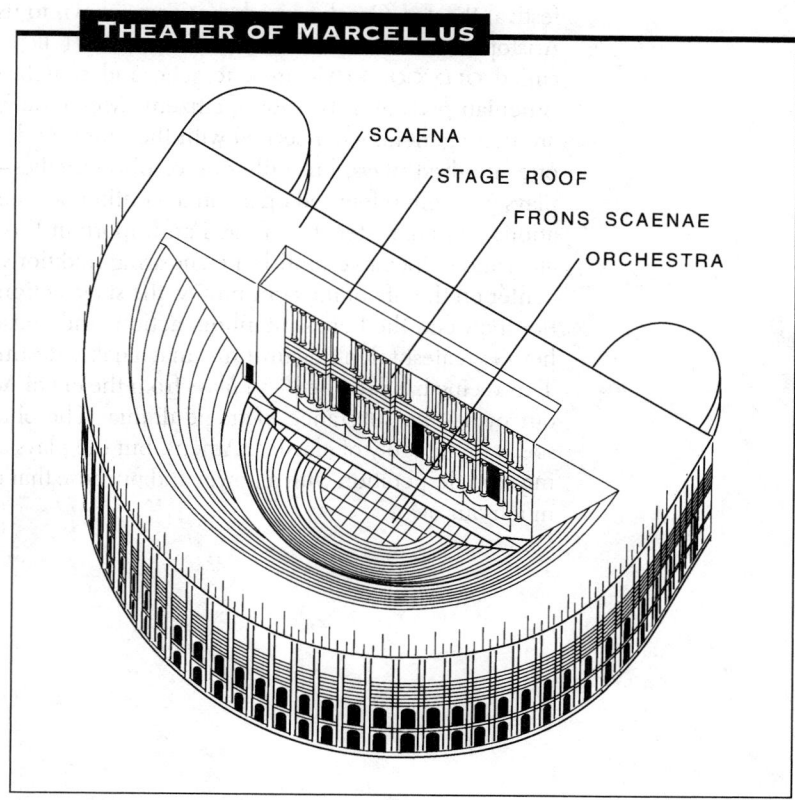

THEATER OF MARCELLUS

SCAENA
STAGE ROOF
FRONS SCAENAE
ORCHESTRA

The Theater of Marcellus was built in Rome from 13–11 BC.

generations of playwrights—including William Shakespeare, Christopher Marlowe, and Molière—who found in Roman drama a form for their own contemporary plays.

The only surviving Roman tragedies were written by Lucius Annaeus Seneca (5 BC–AD 65). Seneca's tragedies were adapted from Greek plays but tend to be more sensational and violent; indeed, it is doubtful if they were

performed in the theater. Although only nine of Seneca's plays survive—*The Trojan Women, Medea, Oedipus, Phaedra, Thyestes, Hercules on Oeta, Hercules Mad, The Phoenecian Women, Agamemnon*—Senecan tragedy also exerted an important influence on later drama, especially in the English Renaissance, where Senecan tragedy provided a prototype for the nascent English drama of the sixteenth century.

chariot onto the blood-red tapestry, or Medea's appearance in the dragon-drawn chariot, or even the aching gait of the men in *Lysistrata* is critical to any understanding of these plays, scenes of murder, suicide, or battle usually take place offstage, to be vividly reported by messengers—as in the reports of Iokaste's death and Oedipus's blinding, or of the death of Jason's young bride in *Medea.* Cassandra's graphic prophecy of Agamemnon's murder likewise provides a brutal counterpoint to the slaughter taking place offstage.

The scenic simplicity of the Greek theater enabled playwrights to achieve a special kind of concentration, one that capitalized on the special circumstances of the open-air, festival theater. Greek comedy has come down to us in the work of only two playwrights, Aristophanes and Menander (c. 342–c. 291 BC). While Aristophanes' plays—usually called OLD COMEDY—are energetic and sometimes ribald comedies lampooning the Athenian *polis* and its leading citizens, Menander's comedies—called NEW COMEDY—are more generally concerned with the mores and manners. Menander wrote more than one hundred plays, but only one of his comedies—*The Grouch*—survives. Menander's plays were often focused on a comic conflict between parents and children, devising situations and characters that forged an important link between the Greek and Roman theaters and helped to establish the enduring traditions of stage comedy. While the comedies center on the life of the community, the stage action of Greek tragedy focuses on the relation between the hero's intention, action, and consequence in ways that typically pit the hero's greatest talents against his unavoidable destiny, his society, his family, and himself. This recipe has provided—in plays from the era of Aeschylus, Sophocles, and Euripides to our own—the substance of tragic drama. The characteristic concerns of Greek drama speak undeniably of classical Athens, but the plays also represent trials of decision, suffering, and desperation with a power and purpose that continue to speak to us in accents very much our own.

This recent production of Sophocles' Oedipus Rex *uses an architectural set piece to imitate the function of the* skene *of the classical Athenian theater; similarly, although the chorus here is composed of both men and women, its performance—chanting and dancing—is also modeled on the paradigm of Greek theater.*

Framed in a doorway and lit in profile, Diana Rigg embodies the isolation and abandonment of Euripides' Medea.

■ AESCHYLUS ■

Aeschylus (c. 523–456 BC), whose life spanned the first half of the fifth century, witnessed Athens' chief political and military conflicts and became its preeminent dramatist. His epitaph suggests that he fought at the battle of Marathon against the Persians, and the detailed description of the naval battle at Salamis in his play *The Persians* implies that he may have fought there as well. Aeschylus added the second actor to dramatic performance, only one of his many achievements in the theater. He won his first victory as a playwright at the City Dionysia in 484 BC, and in 472 BC he produced *The Persians*, for which Pericles served as his sponsoring *choregos*. In 468 BC he was defeated by Sophocles but was again victorious with his trilogy *The Oresteia* and the accompanying satyr play *Proteus* (now lost) in 458. Aeschylus died in Sicily in 456 BC. Of about seventy plays that Aeschylus is said to have written, seven survive: *The Suppliants, The Persians, The Seven Against Thebes, Prometheus Bound, Agamemnon, The Libation Bearers,* and *The Eumenides.*

AGAMEMNON

Agamemnon is the first of three plays—including *The Libation Bearers* and *The Eumenides*—collectively called *The Oresteia* (458 BC). Working from the model of Homer's *Odyssey*, Aeschylus fashioned a complex and original narrative of injustice and retribution, relying on events and characters well-known to his Athenian audience. Indeed, *The Oresteia* depends on the audience's understanding of events that took place a generation before the opening of *Agamemnon*. In the previous generation, the two sons of Pelops—Atreus and Thyestes—began a bitter feud for control of Argos. Thyestes disputed his brother's claim to the throne and seduced his wife; for this he was exiled, but he later returned to Argos with his children to ask Atreus' forgiveness. Atreus received his brother but had the children secretly murdered and baked into a dish that he served to Thyestes. When the truth was revealed to him, Thyestes fled with his one remaining child, Aegisthus, leaving a terrible curse on Atreus, his family, and his descendants.

This curse gives rise to the action of *The Oresteia*, for Aeschylus shows how murder and revenge are played out across the next two generations of the house of Atreus—involving Thyestes' son, Aegisthus; Atreus' two sons, Menelaus and Agamemnon; and Agamemnon's wife, Clytaemnestra, and their children, Iphigeneia, Orestes, and Electra.

The force of much of Aeschylus' drama lies in a powerful economy of action and character, everywhere visible in *Agamemnon*. *Agamemnon* opens with a watchman awaiting the signal fire that will announce the end of the war on Troy and the return of Agamemnon. This nighttime scene immediately invests the play with a dark sense of foreboding. The opening lyrics of the chorus provide the context for Agamemnon's arrival by recounting the events of ten years before, when Agamemnon, to secure favorable winds for sailing against Troy, sacrificed his own daughter Iphigeneia. Clytaemnestra, eager to punish Agamemnon for his brutal murder of their daughter, is recognized at once as a deceptive and powerful queen, feared by the Argive elders of the chorus. Cassandra's curse—that her prophecies will never be believed—is appallingly enacted before us at the moment of Agamemnon's murder, and Aegisthus appears as a kind of thug, dehumanized by his cruel and vengeful mission. For a modern audience, the most problematic character is Agamemnon himself, seen onstage in only one scene. Yet this brief scene testifies to the intricate knotting of history and temperament in the design of Aeschylus' tragedy. We see Agamemnon's lordly ambition for success and glory, his malleability, and his insensitivity to his own wrongdoing. Treading on the crimson tapestries, Agamemnon follows a trail of blood leading him into the house of Atreus, to his accounting for the murder of Iphigeneia, to Aegisthus' fulfillment of Thyestes' curse, and to his own death.

The cycle of retribution continues in the remaining plays of the trilogy. In *The Libation Bearers*, Agamemnon's son, Orestes, returns to Argos from exile, where he had been sent by Aegisthus and Clytaemnestra, in order to avenge the murder of his father. He arrives in secret and surprises his sister, Electra (and the chorus of slave women bearing libations), at Agamemnon's grave. Brother and sister vow to avenge Agamemnon's death. Returning to the palace, they murder Aegisthus, and then Orestes executes justice on his mother, Clytaemnestra, as well. But this act summons the Furies (or Eumenides), horrible demons who haunt and torment Orestes for his crime. The final play,

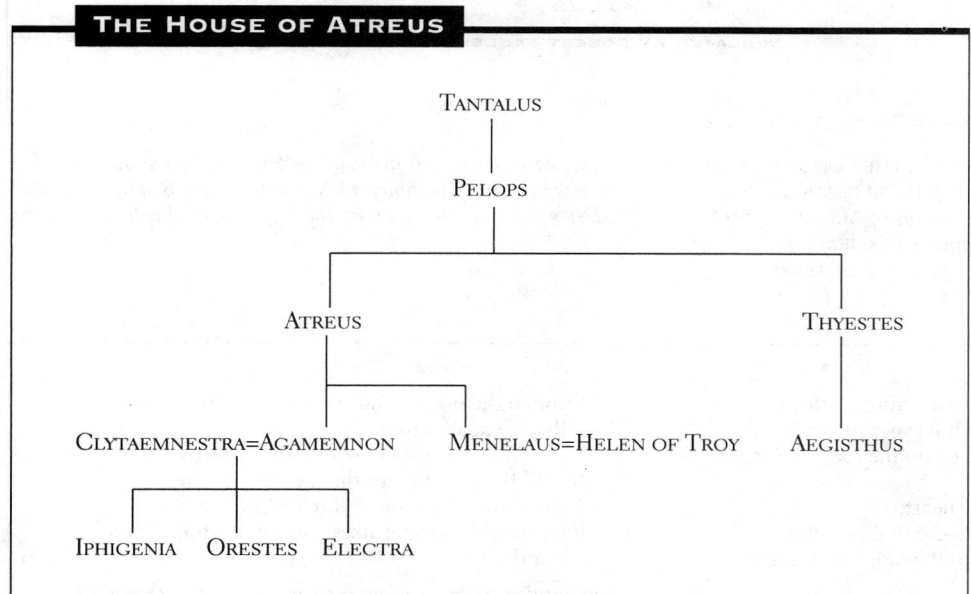

THE HOUSE OF ATREUS

TANTALUS

PELOPS

ATREUS   THYESTES

CLYTAEMNESTRA=AGAMEMNON   MENELAUS=HELEN OF TROY   AEGISTHUS

IPHIGENIA   ORESTES   ELECTRA

The family of Atreus, King of Mycenae and father of Agamemnon and Menelaus, is the focus of powerfully tragic myths and dramas.

The Eumenides, follows Orestes' search for purification. He first appeals to Apollo to release him and then to Athena. Athena calls the Furies and Orestes to a trial before a jury of mortal Athenian judges. Casting her tie-breaking vote for Orestes, Athena releases him from the Furies; to placate them, she invites them to serve as the honorary deities of Athens itself. The terrible curse of the house of Atreus is finally healed by redefining the process of justice. Revenge is replaced by the code of law.

AGAMEMNON

AESCHYLUS

TRANSLATED BY ROBERT FAGLES

— CHARACTERS —

WATCHMAN
CLYTAEMNESTRA
HERALD
AGAMEMNON
CASSANDRA
AEGISTHUS

CHORUS, THE OLD MEN OF ARGOS
    AND THEIR LEADER
Attendants of CLYTAEMNESTRA
    and of AGAMEMNON,
Bodyguard of AEGISTHUS

TIME AND SCENE: *A night in the tenth and final autumn of the Trojan war. The house of Atreus in Argos. Before it, an altar stands unlit; a watchman on the high roofs fights to stay awake.*

WATCHMAN: Dear gods, set me free from all the pain,
   the long watch I keep, one whole year awake . . .
   propped on my arms, crouched on the roofs of Atreus
   like a dog.
             I know the stars by heart,
5   the armies of the night, and there in the lead
   the ones that bring us snow or the crops of summer,
   bring us all we have —
   our great blazing kings of the sky,
   I know them, when they rise and when they fall . . .
10 and now I watch for the light, the signal-fire
   breaking out of Troy, shouting Troy is taken.
   So she commands, full of her high hopes.
   That woman — she manoeuvres like a man.

   And when I keep to my bed, soaked in dew,
15 and the thoughts go groping through the night
   and the good dreams that used to guard my sleep . . .
   not here, it's the old comrade, terror, at my neck.
   I mustn't sleep, no —

(Shaking himself awake.)

                         Look alive, sentry.
   And I try to pick out tunes, I hum a little,
20 a good cure for sleep, and the tears start,
   I cry for the hard times come to the house,
   no longer run like the great place of old.

   Oh for a blessed end to all our pain,
   some godsend burning through the dark —

(Light appears slowly in the east; he struggles to his feet and scans it.)

                              I salute you!
25 You dawn of the darkness, you turn night to day —
   I see the light at last.
   They'll be dancing in the streets of Argos
   thanks to you, thanks to this new stroke of —
                              Aieeeeee!
   There's your signal clear and true, my queen!
30 Rise up from bed — hurry, lift a cry of triumph

through the house, praise the gods for the beacon,
   if they've taken Troy . . .
                         But there it burns,
   fire all the way. I'm for the morning dances.
   Master's luck is mine. A throw of the torch
   has brought us triple-sixes — we have won!   35
   My move now —

(Beginning to dance, then breaking off, lost in thought.)

                    Just bring him home. My king,
   I'll take your loving hand in mine and then . . .
   the rest is silence. The ox is on my tongue.
   Aye, but the house and these old stones,
   give them a voice and what a tale they'd tell.   40
   And so would I, gladly . . .
   I speak to those who know; to those who don't
   my mind's a blank. I never say a word.

(He climbs down from the roof and disappears into the palace through a side entrance. A CHORUS, *the old men of Argos who have not learned the news of victory, enters and marches round the altar.)*

CHORUS: Ten years gone, ten to the day
   our great avenger went for Priam —   45
      Menelaus and lord Agamemnon,
   two kings with the power of Zeus,
   the twin throne, twin sceptre,
   Atreus' sturdy yoke of sons
   launched Greece in a thousand ships,   50
   armadas cutting loose from the land,
   armies massed for the cause, the rescue —

(From within the palace CLYTAEMNESTRA *raises a cry of triumph.)*

   the heart within them screamed for all-out war!
   Like vultures robbed of their young,
      the agony sends them frenzied,   55
   soaring high from the nest, round and
   round they wheel, they row their wings,
   stroke upon churning thrashing stroke,
   but all the labour, the bed of pain,
      the young are lost forever.   60
   Yet someone hears on high — Apollo,

---

8 **our great blazing kings** major constellations that demarcate the seasons

35 **triple-sixes** a winning throw of dice

Pan or Zeus—the piercing wail
these guests of heaven raise,
and drives at the outlaws, late
65 but true to revenge, a stabbing Fury!

(CLYTAEMNESTRA *appears at the doors and pauses with her
entourage.*)

So towering Zeus the god of guests
drives Atreus' sons at Paris,
all for a woman manned by many
the generations wrestle, knees
70 grinding the dust, the manhood drains,
the spear snaps in the first blood rites
    that marry Greece and Troy.
And now it goes as it goes
and where it ends is Fate.
75 And neither by singeing flesh
nor tipping cups of wine
nor shedding burning tears can you
enchant away the rigid Fury.

(CLYTAEMNESTRA *lights the altar-fires.*)

We are the old, dishonoured ones,
80 the broken husks of men.
Even then they cast us off,
the rescue mission left us here
to prop a child's strength upon a stick.
What if the new sap rises in his chest?
85 He has no soldiery in him,
    no more than we,
and we are aged past ageing,
gloss of the leaf shrivelled,
three legs at a time we falter on.
90 Old men are children once again,
    a dream that sways and wavers
into the hard light of day.
                    But you,
daughter of Leda, queen Clytaemnestra,
what now, what news, what message
95 drives you through the citadel
    burning victims? Look,
the city gods, the gods of Olympus,
gods of the earth and public markets—
all the altars blazing with your gifts!
100   Argos blazes! Torches
race the sunrise up her skies—
drugged by the lulling holy oils,
    unadulterated,
run from the dark vaults of kings.
105   Tell us the news!
What you can, what is right—
Heal us, soothe our fears!
Now the darkness comes to the fore,
now the hope glows through your victims,
110 beating back this raw, relentless anguish
    gnawing at the heart.

(CLYTAEMNESTRA *ignores them and pursues her rituals; they assemble for the opening chorus.*)

O but I still have power to sound the god's command at the
    roads
that launched the kings. The gods breathe power through
    my song,
    my fighting strength, Persuasion grows with the years—
I sing how the flight of fury hurled the twin command,   115
    one will that hurled young Greece
and winged the spear of vengeance straight for Troy!
The kings of birds to kings of the beaking prows, one black,
    one with a blaze of silver
        skimmed the palace spearhand right   120
        and swooping lower, all could see,
            plunged their claws in a hare, a mother
        bursting with unborn young—the babies spilling,
quick spurts of blood—cut off the race just dashing
    into life!
    Cry, cry for death, but good win out in glory in the end.   125
But the loyal seer of the armies studied Atreus' sons,
two sons with warring hearts—he saw two eagle-kings
    devour the hare and spoke the things to come,
'Years pass, and the long hunt nets the city of Priam,
        the flocks beyond the walls,   130
a kingdom's life and soul—Fate stamps them out.
Just let no curse of the gods lour on us first,
    shatter our giant armour
    forged to strangle Troy. I see
        pure Artemis bristle in pity—   135
        yes, the flying hounds of the Father
    slaughter for armies . . . their own victim . . . a
        woman
trembling young, all born to die—She loathes the eagles'
    feast!'
Cry, cry for death, but good win out in glory in the end.

'Artemis, lovely Artemis, so kind   140
to the ravening lion's tender, helpless cubs,
the suckling young of beasts that stalk the wilds—
    bring this sign for all its fortune,
        all its brutal torment home to birth!
I beg you, Healing Apollo, soothe her before   145
her crosswinds hold us down and moor the ships too long,
pressing us on to another victim . . .
    nothing sacred, no,
        no feast to be eaten
            the architect of vengeance   150

(*Turning to the palace.*)

        growing strong in the house
        with no fear of the husband
here she waits
the terror raging back and back in the future
    the stealth, the law of the hearth, the mother—   155
        Memory womb of Fury child-avenging
            Fury!'
So as the eagles wheeled at the crossroads,

---

89 **three legs** a reference to the use of a walking stick as a third leg in
old age

126 **the loyal seer** Calchas, who foretold much hardship at the outset
of the Trojan War

Calchas clashed out the great good blessings mixed with
    doom
    for the halls of kings, and singing with our fate
160 we cry, cry for death, but good win out in glory in the end.

        Zeus, great nameless all in all,
        if that name will gain his favour,
        I will call him Zeus.
    I have no words to do him justice,
165   weighing all in the balance,
        all I have is Zeus, Zeus—
    lift this weight, this torment from my spirit,
        cast it once for all.

        He who was so mighty once,
170   storming for the wars of heaven,
        he has had his day.
    And then his son who came to power
        met his match in the third fall
        and he is gone. Zeus, Zeus—
175 raise your cries and sing him Zeus the Victor!
    You will reach the truth:

        Zeus has led us on to know,
        the Helmsman lays it down as law
        that we must suffer, suffer into truth.
180 We cannot sleep, and drop by drop at the heart
    the pain of pain remembered comes again,
    and we resist, but ripeness comes as well.
From the gods enthroned on the awesome rowing-bench
        there comes a violent love.

185   So it was that day the king,
        the steersman at the helm of Greece,
    would never blame a word the prophet said—
    swept away by the wrenching winds of fortune
    he conspired! Weatherbound we could not sail,
190 our stores exhausted, fighting strength hard-pressed,
    and the squadrons rode in the shallows off Chalkis
        where the riptide crashes, drags,

  and winds from the north pinned down our hulls at Aulis,
port of anguish . . . head winds starving,
195   sheets and the cables snapped
    and the men's minds strayed,
      the pride, the bloom of Greece
    was raked as time ground on,
ground down, and then the cure for the storm
200   and it was harsher—Calchas cried,
'My captains, Artemis must have blood!'—
  so harsh the sons of Atreus
    dashed their sceptres on the rocks,
    could not hold back the tears,

205 and I still can hear the older warlord saying,
'Obey, obey, or a heavy doom will crush me!—
Oh but doom *will* crush me
    once I rend my child,
      the glory of my house—
210   a father's hands are stained,
blood of a young girl streaks the altar.
Pain both ways and what is worse?
Desert the fleets, fail the alliance?
    No, but stop the winds with a virgin's blood,
215   feed their lust, their fury?—feed their fury!—

Law is law!—
      Let all go well.'

And once he slipped his neck in the strap of Fate,
his spirit veering black, impure, unholy,
once he turned he stopped at nothing,
    seized with the frenzy   220
        blinding driving to outrage—
wretched frenzy, cause of all our grief!
Yes, he had the heart
    to sacrifice his daughter,
    to bless the war that avenged a woman's loss,   225
    a bridal rite that sped the men-of-war.
'My father, father!'—she might pray to the winds;
no innocence moves her judges mad for war.
Her father called his henchmen on,
    on with a prayer,   230
      'Hoist her over the altar
like a yearling, give it all your strength!
She's fainting—lift her,
    sweep her robes around her,
    but slip this strap in her gentle curving lips . . .   235
      here, gag her hard, a sound will curse the house'—

and the bridle chokes her voice . . . her saffron robes
pouring over the sand
          her glance like arrows showering
wounding every murderer through with pity
    clear as a picture, live,   240
she strains to call their names . . .
I remember often the days with father's guests
when over the feast her voice unbroken,
    pure as the hymn her loving father
bearing third libations, sang to Saving Zeus—   245
transfixed with joy, Atreus' offspring
    throbbing out their love.

What comes next? I cannot see it, cannot say.
The strong techniques of Calchas do their work.
But Justice turns the balance scales,   250
    sees that we suffer
and we suffer and we learn.
And we will know the future when it comes.
Greet it too early, weep too soon.
    It all comes clear in the light of day.   255
Let all go well today, well as she could want,

(Turning to CLYTAEMNESTRA.*)*

    our midnight watch, our lone defender,
      single-minded queen.
LEADER: We've come,
Clytaemnestra. We respect your power.
Right it is to honour the warlord's woman   260
once he leaves the throne.
          But why these fires?
Good news, or more good hopes? We're loyal,
we want to hear, but never blame your silence.

---

245 **third libations** offered to Zeus, following libations to the gods of
Olympus and the spirits of the dead

CLYTAEMNESTRA: Let the new day shine—as the proverb
265   says—
      glorious from the womb of Mother Night.

(Lost in prayer, then turning to the CHORUS.*)*

      You will hear a joy beyond your hopes.
      Priam's citadel—the Greeks have taken Troy!
LEADER: No, what do you mean? I can't believe it.
CLYTAEMNESTRA: Troy is ours. Is that clear enough?
LEADER: The joy of it,
270   stealing over me, calling up my tears—
CLYTAEMNESTRA: Yes, your eyes expose your loyal hearts.
LEADER: And you have proof?
CLYTAEMNESTRA: I do,
      I must. Unless the god is lying.
LEADER: That,
      or a phantom spirit sends you into raptures.
275 CLYTAEMNESTRA: No one takes me in with visions—senseless
         dreams.
LEADER: Or giddy rumour, you haven't indulged yourself—
CLYTAEMNESTRA: You treat me like a child, you mock me?
LEADER: Then when did they storm the city?
CLYTAEMNESTRA: Last night, I say, the mother of this
         morning.
280 LEADER: And who on earth could run the news so fast?
CLYTAEMNESTRA: The god of fire—rushing fire from Ida!
      And beacon to beacon rushed it on to me,
      my couriers riding home the torch.
                              From Troy
      to the bare rock of Lemnos, Hermes' Spur,
285   and the Escort winged the great light west
      to the Saving Father's face, Mount Athos hurled it
      third in the chain and leaping Ocean's back
      the blaze went dancing on to ecstasy—pitch-pine
      streaming gold like a new-born sun—and brought
290   the word in flame to Mount Makistos' brow.
      No time to waste, straining, fighting sleep,
      that lookout heaved a torch glowing over
      the murderous straits of Euripos to reach
      Messapion's watchmen craning for the signal.
295   Fire for word of fire! tense with the heather
      withered gray, they stack it, set it ablaze—
      the hot force of the beacon never flags,
      it springs the Plain of Asôpos, rears
      like a harvest moon to hit Kithairon's crest
300   and drives new men to drive the fire on.
      That relay pants for the far-flung torch,
      they swell its strength outstripping my commands
      and the light inflames the marsh, the Gorgon's Eye,
      it strikes the peak where the wild goats range—
305   my laws, my fire whips that camp!
      They spare nothing, eager to build its heat,
      and a huge beard of flame overcomes the headland
      beetling down the Saronic Gulf, and flaring south
      it brings the dawn to the Black Widow's face—
310   the watch that looms above your heads—and now

---

281 **Ida** mountain near Troy   286 **Saving Father's face** Mount Athos,
a seat of Zeus the Savior in northern Greece   309 **Black Widow's
face** "Spider Mountain," perhaps the citadel of Mycenae

the true son of the burning flanks of Ida
crashes on the roofs of Atreus' sons!
And I ordained it all.
Torch to torch, running for their lives,
one long succession racing home my fire.   315
                         One,
first in the laps and last, wins out in triumph.
There you have my proof, my burning sign, I tell you—
the power my lord passed on from Troy to me!
LEADER: We'll thank the gods, my lady—first this story,
   let me lose myself in the wonder of it all!   320
   Tell it start to finish, tell us all.
CLYTAEMNESTRA: The city's ours—in our hands this very day!
   I can hear the cries in crossfire rock the walls.
   Pour oil and wine in the same bowl,
   what have you, friendship? A struggle to the end.   325
   So with the victors and the victims—the outcries,
   you can hear them clashing like their fates.

   They are kneeling by the bodies of the dead,
   embracing men and brothers, infants over
   the aged loins that gave them life, and sobbing,   330
   as the yoke constricts their last free breath,
   for every dear one lost.
                     And the others,
   there, plunging breakneck through the night—
   the labour of battle sets them down, ravenous,
   to breakfast on the last remains of Troy.   335
   Not by rank but chance, by the lots they draw,
   they lodge in the houses captured by the spear,
   settling in so soon, released from the open sky,
   the frost and dew. Lucky men, off guard at last,
   they sleep away their first good night in years.   340
   If only they are revering the city's gods,
   the shrines of the gods who love the conquered land,
   no plunderer will be plundered in return.
   Just let no lust, no mad desire seize the armies
   to ravish what they must not touch—   345
   overwhelmed by all they've won!
                            The run for home
   and safety waits, the swerve at the post,
   the final lap of the gruelling two-lap race.
   And even if the men come back with no offence
   to the gods, the avenging dead may never rest—   350
   Oh let no new disaster strike! And here
   you have it, what a woman has to say.
   Let the best win out, clear to see.
   A small desire but all that I could want.
LEADER: Spoken like a man, my lady, loyal,   355
   full of self-command. I've heard your sign
   and now your vision.

(Reaching towards her as she turns and re-enters the palace.)

                     Now to praise the gods.
   The joy is worth the labour.
CHORUS: O Zeus my king and Night, dear Night,
   queen of the house who covers us with glories,   360
   you slung your net on the towers of Troy,
   neither young nor strong could leap
   the giant dredge net of slavery,
      all-embracing ruin.
   I adore you, iron Zeus of the guests   365

and your revenge—you drew your longbow
year by year to a taut full draw
till one bolt, not falling short
or arching over the stars,
370   could split the mark of Paris!
The sky stroke of god!—it is all Troy's to tell,
but even I can trace it to its cause:
god does as god decrees.
        And still some say
375 that heaven would never stoop to punish men
who trample the lovely grace of things
untouchable. How wrong they are!
        A curse burns bright on crime—
        full-blown, the father's crimes will blossom,
380   burst into the son's.
Let there be less suffering . . .
give us the sense to live on what we need.

                Bastions of wealth
                are no defence for the man
385   who treads the grand altar of Justice
                down and out of sight.

Persuasion, maddening child of Ruin
overpowers him—Ruin plans it all.
And the wound will smoulder on,
390   there is no cure,
a terrible brilliance kindles on the night.
He is bad bronze scraped on a touchstone:
put to the test, the man goes black.
        Like the boy who chases
395   a bird on the wing, brands his city,
            brings it down and prays,
but the gods are deaf
to the one who turns to crime, they tear him down.

                So Paris learned:
400   he came to Atreus' house
                and shamed the tables spread for guests,
                    he stole away the queen.

And she left her land *chaos*, clanging shields,
companions tramping, bronze prows, men in bronze,
405   and she came to Troy with a dowry, death,
strode through the gates
            defiant in every stride,
as prophets of the house looked on and wept,
'Oh the halls and the lords of war,
410   the bed and the fresh prints of love.
I *see* him, unavenging, unavenged,
the stun of his desolation is so clear—
    he longs for the one who lies across the sea
until her phantom seems to sway the house.

415   Her curving images,
            her beauty hurts her lord,
            the eyes starve and the touch
                of love is gone,

'and radiant dreams are passing in the night,
420 the memories throb with sorrow, joy with pain . . .
    it is pain to dream and see desires
slip through the arms,
        a vision lost for ever

winging down the moving drifts of sleep.'
So he grieves at the royal hearth   425
    yet others' grief is worse, far worse.
All through Greece for those who flocked to war
they are holding back the anguish now,
    you can feel it rising now in every house;
I tell you there is much to tear the heart.   430

            They knew the men they sent,
            but now in place of men
            ashes and urns come back
                to every hearth.

War, War, the great gold-broker of corpses   435
holds the balance of the battle on his spear!
Home from the pyres he sends them,
    home from Troy to the loved ones,
heavy with tears, the urns brimmed full,
    the heroes return in gold-dust,   440
dear, light ash for men; and they weep,
they praise them, 'He had skill in the swordplay,'
    'He went down so tall in the onslaught,'
'All for another's woman.' So they mutter
in secret and the rancour steals   445
towards our staunch defenders, Atreus' sons.

            And there they ring the walls, the young,
            the lithe, the handsome hold the graves
            they won in Troy; the enemy earth
                rides over those who conquered.   450

The people's voice is heavy with hatred,
now the curses of the people must be paid,
and now I wait, I listen . . .
    there—there is something breathing
under the night's shroud. God takes aim   455
    at the ones who murder many;
the swarthy Furies stalk the man
gone rich beyond all rights—with a twist
    of fortune grind him down, dissolve him
into the blurring dead—there is no help.   460
The reach for power can recoil,
the bolt of god can strike you at a glance.

            Make me rich with no man's envy,
            neither a raider of cities, no,
            nor slave come face to face with life   465
                overpowered by another.

(Speaking singly.)

—Fire comes and the news is good,
    it races through the streets
but is it true? Who knows?
Or just another lie from heaven?   470

—Show us the man so childish, wonderstruck,
    he's fired up with the first torch,
then when the message shifts
he's sick at heart.
                        —Just like a woman
to fill with thanks before the truth is clear.   475

—So gullible. Their stories spread like wildfire,
    they fly fast and die faster;
rumours voiced by women coming to nothing.

LEADER: Soon we'll know her fires for what they are,
480   her relay race of torches hand-to-hand—
  know if they're real or just a dream,
  the hope of a morning here to take our senses.
  I see a herald running from the beach
  and a victor's spray of olive shades his eyes
485   and the dust he kicks, twin to the mud of Troy,
  shows he has a voice—no kindling timber
  on the cliffs, no signal-fires for him.
  He can shout the news and give us joy,
  or else . . . please, not that.
                    Bring it on,
490   good fuel to build the first good fires.
  And if anyone calls down the worst on Argos
  let him reap the rotten harvest of his mind.

(*The* HERALD *rushes in and kneels on the ground.*)

HERALD: Good Greek earth, the soil of my fathers!
  Ten years out, and a morning brings me back.
495   All hopes snapped but one—I'm home at last.
  Never dreamed I'd die in Greece, assigned
  the narrow plot I love the best.
                     And now
  I salute the land, the light of the sun,
  our high lord Zeus and the king of Pytho—
500   no more arrows, master, raining on our heads!
  At Scamander's banks we took our share,
  your longbow brought us down like plague.
  Now come, deliver us, heal us—lord Apollo!
  Gods of the market, here, take my salute.
505   And you, my Hermes, Escort,
  loving Herald, the herald's shield and prayer!—
  And the shining dead of the land who launched the armies,
  warm us home . . . we're all the spear has left.
  You halls of the kings, you roofs I cherish,
510   sacred seats—you gods that catch the sun,
  if your glances ever shone on him in the old days,
  greet him well—so many years are lost.
  He comes, he brings us light in the darkness,
  free for every comrade, Agamemnon lord of men.

515   Give him the royal welcome he deserves!
  He hoisted the pickaxe of Zeus who brings revenge,
  he dug Troy down, he worked her soil down,
  the shrines of her gods and the high altars, gone!—
  and the seed of her wide earth he ground to bits.
520   That's the yoke he claps on Troy. The king,
  the son of Atreus comes. The man is blest,
  the one man alive to merit such rewards.

  Neither Paris nor Troy, partners to the end,
  can say their work outweighs their wages now.
525   Convicted of rapine, stripped of all his spoils,
  and his father's house and the land that gave it life—
  he's scythed them to the roots. The sons of Priam
  pay the price twice over.

499–502 **the king of Pytho . . . plague** at Troy, when Agamemnon refused to release a daughter of Apollo's priest, Apollo ("king of Pytho") visited a plague upon the Greeks by shooting his arrows among them 528 **pay the price twice over** in ancient Greek law, double damages were the penalty for theft

LEADER: Welcome home
  from the wars, herald, long live your joy.
HERALD: *Our* joy—
  now I could die gladly. Say the word, dear gods.   530
LEADER: Longing for your country left you raw?
HERALD: The tears fill my eyes, for joy.
LEADER: You too,
  down the sweet disease that kills a man
  with kindness . . .
HERALD: Go on, I don't see what you—
LEADER: Love
  for the ones who love you—that's what took you.   535
HERALD: You mean
  the land and the armies hungered for each other?
LEADER: There were times I thought I'd faint with longing.
HERALD: So anxious for the armies, why?
LEADER: For years now,
  only my silence kept me free from harm.
HERALD: What,
  with the kings gone did someone threaten you?   540
LEADER: So much . . .
  now as you say, it would be good to die.
HERALD: True, we *have* done well.
  Think back in the years and what have you?
  A few runs of luck, a lot that's bad.
  Who but a god can go through life unmarked?   545
  A long, hard pull we had, if I would tell it all.
  The iron rations, penned in the gangways
  hock by jowl like sheep. Whatever miseries
  break a man, our quota, every sun-starved day.

  Then on the beaches it was worse. Dug in   550
  under the enemy ramparts—deadly going.
  Out of the sky, out of the marshy flats
  the dews soaked us, turned the ruts we fought from
  into gullies, made our gear, our scalps
  crawl with lice.   555
                And talk of the cold,
  the sleet to freeze the gulls, and the big snows
  come avalanching down from Ida. Oh but the heat,
  the sea and the windless noons, the swells asleep,
  dropped to a dead calm . . .

  But why weep now?   560
  It's over for us, over for them.
  The dead can rest and never rise again;
  no need to call their muster. We're alive,
  do we have to go on raking up old wounds?
  Good-bye to all that. Glad I am to say it.   565

  For us, the remains of the Greek contingents,
  the good wins out, no pain can tip the scales,
  not now. So shout this boast to the bright sun—
  fitting it is—wing it over the seas and rolling earth:

  'Once when an Argive expedition captured Troy   570
  they hauled these spoils back to the gods of Greece,
  they bolted them high across the temple doors,
  the glory of the past!'
               And hearing that,
  men will applaud our city and our chiefs,
  and Zeus will have the hero's share of fame—   575
  he did the work.

          That's all I have to say.
LEADER: I'm convinced, glad that I was wrong.
    Never too old to learn; it keeps me young.

(CLYTAEMNESTRA enters with her women.)

    First the house and the queen, it's their affair,
580 but I can taste the riches.
CLYTAEMNESTRA: I cried out long ago!—
    for joy, when the first herald came burning
    through the night and told the city's fall.
    And there were some who smiled and said,
    'A few fires persuade you Troy's in ashes.
585 Women, women, elated over nothing.'

    You made me seem deranged.
    For all that I sacrificed—a woman's way,
    you'll say—station to station on the walls
    we lifted cries of triumph that resounded
590 in the temples of the gods. We lulled and blessed
    the fires with myrrh and they consumed our victims.

(Turning to the HERALD.)

    But enough. Why prolong the story?
    From the king himself I'll gather all I need.
    Now for the best way to welcome home
595 my lord, my good lord . . .
                No time to lose!
    What dawn can feast a woman's eyes like this?
    I can see the light, the husband plucked from war
    by the Saving God and open wide the gates.

    Tell him that, and have him come with speed,
600 the people's darling—how they long for him.
    And for his wife,
    may he return and find her true at hall,
    just as the day he left her, faithful to the last.
    A watchdog gentle to him alone,

(Glancing towards the palace.)

               savage
605 to those who cross his path. I have not changed.
    The strains of time can never break our seal.
    In love with a new lord, in ill repute I am
    as practised as I am in dyeing bronze.

    That is my boast, teeming with the truth.
610 I am proud, a woman of my nobility—
    I'd hurl it from the roofs!

(She turns sharply, enters the palace.)

LEADER: She speaks well, but it takes no seer to know
    she only says what's right.

(The HERALD attempts to leave; the leader takes him by the arm.)

          Wait, one thing.
    Menelaus, is he home too, safe with the men?
615 The power of the land—dear king.
HERALD: I doubt that lies will help my friends,
    in the lean months to come.

---

580 **I can taste the riches** according to custom, the bearer of good news was rewarded

LEADER: Help us somehow, tell the truth as well.
    But when the two conflict it's hard to hide—
    out with it.   620
HERALD: He's lost, gone from the fleets!
    He and his ship, it's true.
LEADER: After you watched him
    pull away from Troy? Or did some storm
    attack you all and tear him off the line?
HERALD: There,
    like a marksman, the whole disaster cut to a word.
LEADER: How do the escorts give him out—dead or alive? 625
HERALD: No clear report. No one knows . . .
    only the wheeling sun that heats the earth to life.
LEADER: But then the storm—how did it reach the ships?
    How did it end? Were the angry gods on hand?
HERALD: This blessed day, ruin it with *them*? 630
    Better to keep their trophies far apart.

    When a runner comes, his face in tears,
    saddled with what his city dreaded most,
    the armies routed, two wounds in one,
    one to the city, one to hearth and home . . . 635
    our best men, droves of them, victims
    herded from every house by the two-barb whip
    that Ares likes to crack,
               that charioteer
    who packs destruction shaft by shaft,
    careering on with his brace of bloody mares— 640
    When he comes in, I tell you, dragging that much pain,
    wail your battle-hymn to the Furies, and high time!
    But when he brings salvation home to a city
    singing out her heart—
    how can I mix the good with so much bad 645
    and blurt out this?—
            'Storms swept the Greeks,
    and not without the anger of the gods!'

    Those enemies for ages, fire and water,
    sealed a pact and showed it to the world—
    they crushed our wretched squadrons. 650
           Night looming,
    breakers lunging in for the kill
    and the black gales come brawling out of the north—
    ships ramming, prow into hooking prow, gored
    by the rush-and-buck of hurricane pounding rain
    by the cloudburst— 655
           ships stampeding into the darkness,
    lashed and spun by the savage shepherd's hand!

    But when the sun comes up to light the skies
    I see the Aegean heaving into a great bloom
    of corpses . . . Greeks, the pick of a generation
    scattered through the wrecks and broken spars. 660

    But not us, not our ship, our hull untouched.
    Someone stole us away or begged us off.
    No mortal—a god, death grip on the tiller,
    or lady luck herself, perched on the helm,
    she pulled us through, she saved us. Aye, 665
    we'll never battle the heavy surf at anchor,
    never shipwreck up some rocky coast.

---

648 **fire and water** lightning and the sea

But once we cleared that sea-hell, not even
trusting luck in the cold light of day,
670 we battened on our troubles, they were fresh—
the armada punished, bludgeoned into nothing.
And now if one of them still has the breath
he's saying *we* are lost. Why not?
We say the same of him. Well,
675 here's to the best.
                    And Menelaus?
Look to it, he's come back, and yet . . .
if a shaft of the sun can track him down,
alive, and his eyes full of the old fire—
thanks to the strategies of Zeus, Zeus
680 would never tear the house out by the roots—
then there's hope our man will make it home.

You've heard it all. Now you have the truth.

(Rushing out.)

CHORUS: Who—what power named the name that drove your
        fate?—
what hidden brain could divine your future,
685 steer that word to the mark,
to the bride of spears,
        the whirlpool churning armies,
                Oh for all the world a Helen!
Hell at the prows, hell at the gates
690 hell on the men-of-war,
from her lair's sheer veils she drifted
        launched by the giant western wind,
            and the long tall waves of men in armour,
huntsmen trailing the oar-blades' dying spoor
695 slipped into her moorings,
        Simois' mouth that chokes with foliage,
                bayed for bloody strife,
for Troy's Blood Wedding Day—she drives her word,
her burning will to the birth, the Fury
700 late but true to the cause,
to the tables shamed
        and Zeus who guards the hearth—
                the Fury makes the Trojans pay!
Shouting their hymns, hymns for the bride
705 hymns for the kinsmen doomed
to the wedding march of Fate.
        Troy changed her tune in her late age,
            and I think I hear the dirges mourning
'Paris, born and groomed for the bed of Fate!'
710 They mourn with their life breath,
        they sing their last, the sons of Priam
                born for bloody slaughter.

    So a man once reared
a lion cub at hall, snatched
715 from the breast, still craving milk
    in the first flush of life.
A captivating pet for the young,
and the old men adored it, pampered it
    in their arms, day in, day out,
720 like an infant just born.
Its eyes on fire, little beggar,
fawning for its belly, slave to food.

But it came of age
and the parent strain broke out
and it paid its breeders back.   725
    Grateful it was, it went
through the flock to prepare a feast,
an illicit orgy—the house swam with blood,
    none could resist that agony—
            massacre vast and raw!   730
From god there came a priest of ruin,
adopted by the house to lend it warmth.
And the first sensation Helen brought to Troy . . .
call it a spirit
    shimmer of winds dying   735
        glory light as gold
        shaft of the eyes dissolving, open bloom
        that wounds the heart with love.
But veering wild in mid-flight
she whirled her wedding on to a stabbing end,   740
slashed at the sons of Priam—hearthmate, friend to the
    death,
        sped by Zeus who speeds the guest,
a bride of tears, a Fury.

There's an ancient saying, old as man himself:
men's prosperity   745
    never will die childless,
        once full-grown it breeds.
    Sprung from the great good fortune in the race
comes bloom on bloom of pain—
insatiable wealth! But not I,   750
I alone say this. Only the reckless act
can breed impiety, multiplying crime on crime,
    while the house kept straight and just
is blessed with radiant children.

        But ancient Violence longs to breed,   755
            new Violence comes
    when its fatal hour comes, the demon comes
    to take her toll—no war, no force, no prayer
        can hinder the midnight Fury stamped
    with parent Fury moving through the house.   760

        But Justice shines in sooty hovels,
            loves the decent life.
    From proud halls crusted with gilt by filthy hands
        she turns her eyes to find the pure in spirit—
    spurning the wealth stamped counterfeit with praise, 765
        she steers all things towards their destined end.

(AGAMEMNON *enters in his chariot, his plunder borne before
him by his entourage; behind him, half hidden, stands* CASSAN-
DRA. *The old men press towards him.*)

Come, my king, the scourge of Troy,
    the true son of Atreus—
How to salute you, how to praise you
neither too high nor low, but hit   770
the note of praise that suits the hour?
So many prize some brave display,

---

725 **it paid its breeders back** on reaching maturity, children customarily made thank offerings to their parents

they prefer some flaunt of honour
    once they break the bounds.
775 When a man fails they share his grief,
but the pain can never cut them to the quick.
When a man succeeds they share his glory,
torturing their faces into smiles.
But the good shepherd knows his flock.
780 When the eyes seem to brim with love
    and it is only unction, fawning,
he will know, better than we can know.
That day you marshalled the armies
all for Helen—no hiding it now—
785 I drew you in my mind in black;
you seemed a menace at the helm,
    sending men to the grave
to bring her home, that hell on earth.
But now from the depths of trust and love
790 I say Well fought, well won—
    the end is worth the labour!
Search, my king, and learn at last
who stayed at home and kept their faith
    and who betrayed the city.

AGAMEMNON: First,
795 with justice I salute my Argos and my gods,
my accomplices who brought me home and won
my rights from Priam's Troy—the just gods.
No need to hear our pleas. Once for all
they consigned their lots to the urn of blood,
800 they pitched on death for men, annihilation
for the city. Hope's hand, hovering
over the urn of mercy, left it empty.
Look for the smoke—it is the city's seamark,
building even now.
              The storms of ruin live!
805 Her last dying breath, rising up from the ashes
sends us gales of incense rich in gold.

For that we must thank the gods with a sacrifice
our sons will long remember. For their mad outrage
of a queen we raped their city—we were right.
810 The beast of Argos, foals of the wild mare,
thousands massed in armour rose on the night
the Pleiades went down, and crashing through
their walls our bloody lion lapped its fill,
gorging on the blood of kings.
              Our thanks to the gods,
815 long drawn out, but it is just the prelude.

(CLYTAEMNESTRA *approaches with her women; they are carrying dark red tapestries.* AGAMEMNON *turns to the leader.*)

And your concern, old man, is on my mind.
I hear you and agree, I will support you.
How rare, men with the character to praise
a friend's success without a trace of envy,
820 poison to the heart—it deals a double blow.
Your own losses weigh you down but then,

look at your neighbour's fortune and you weep.
Well I know. I understand society,
the flattering mirror of the proud.
             My comrades . . .
they're shadows, I tell you, ghosts of men   825
who swore they'd die for me. Only Odysseus:
I dragged that man to the wars but once in harness
he was a trace-horse, he gave his all for me.
Dead or alive, no matter, I can praise him.

And now this cause involving men and gods.   830
We must summon the city for a trial,
found a national tribunal. Whatever's healthy,
shore it up with law and help it flourish.
Wherever something calls for drastic cures
we make our noblest effort: amputate or wield   835
the healing iron, burn the cancer at the roots.

Now I go to my father's house—
I give the gods my right hand, my first salute.
The ones who sent me forth have brought me home.

(*He starts down from the chariot, looks at* CLYTAEMNESTRA, *stops, and offers up a prayer.*)

Victory, you have sped my way before,   840
now speed me to the last.

(CLYTAEMNESTRA *turns from the king to the* CHORUS.)

CLYTAEMNESTRA: Old nobility of Argos
gathered here, I am not ashamed to tell you
how I love the man. I am older,
and the fear dies away . . . I am human.
Nothing I say was learned from others.   845
This is my life, my ordeal, long as the siege
he laid at Troy and more demanding.
             First,
when a woman sits at home and the man is gone,
the loneliness is terrible,
unconscionable . . .   850
and the rumours spread and fester,
a runner comes with something dreadful,
close on his heels the next and his news worse,
and they shout it out and the whole house can hear;
and wounds—if he took one wound for each report   855
to penetrate these walls, he's gashed like a dragnet,
more, if he had only died . . .
for each death that swelled his record, he could boast
like a triple-bodied Geryon risen from the grave,
'Three shrouds I dug from the earth, one for every body   860
that went down!'
             The rumours broke like fever,
broke and then rose higher. There were times
they cut me down and eased my throat from the noose.
I wavered between the living and the dead.

(*Turning to* AGAMEMNON.)

             And so
our child is gone, not standing by our side,   865

799–802 **they consigned . . . empty** Athenian citizens voted in law cases by placing one hand over each of two urns and dropping a voting-pebble into either the urn for acquittal or the urn for condemnation
810 **the wild mare** the Trojan Horse

826–828 **Only Odysseus . . . trace-horse** to try to evade conscription for the Trojan War, Odysseus feigned madness, but performed loyally once at war   859 **Geryon** a three-bodied giant killed by Heracles

the bond of our dearest pledges, mine and yours;
by all rights our child should be here . . .
Orestes. You seem startled.
You needn't be. Our loyal brother-in-arms
870 will take good care of him, Strophios the Phocian.
He warned from the start we court two griefs in one.
You risk all on the wars—and what if the people
rise up howling for the king, and anarchy
should dash our plans?
                    Men, it is their nature,
875 trampling on the fighter once he's down.
Our child is gone. That is my self-defence
and it is true.
              For me, the tears that welled
like springs are dry. I have no tears to spare.
I'd watch till late at night, my eyes still burn,
880 I sobbed by the torch I lit for you alone.

(Glancing towards the palace.)

I never let it die . . . but in my dreams
the high thin wail of a gnat would rouse me,
piercing like a trumpet—I could see you
suffer more than all
885 the hours that slept with me could ever bear.

I endured it all. And now, free of grief,
I would salute that man the watchdog of the fold,
the mainroyal, saving stay of the vessel,
rooted oak that thrusts the roof sky-high,
890 the father's one true heir.
Land at dawn to the shipwrecked past all hope,
light of the morning burning off the night of storm,
the cold clear spring to the parched horseman—
O the ecstasy, to flee the yoke of Fate!
895 It is right to use the titles he deserves.
Let envy keep her distance. We have suffered
long enough.

(Reaching towards AGAMEMNON.)

        Come to me now, my dearest,
down from the car of war, but never set the foot
that stamped out Troy on earth again, my great one.

900 Women, why delay? You have your orders.
Pave his way with tapestries.

(They begin to spread the crimson tapestries between the king and the palace doors.)

                Quickly.
Let the red stream flow and bear him home
to the home he never hoped to see—Justice,
lead him in!
            Leave all the rest to me.
905 The spirit within me never yields to sleep.
We will set things right, with the god's help.
We will do whatever Fate requires.
AGAMEMNON: There
is Leda's daughter, the keeper of my house.

---

908 **Leda** visited by Zeus in the form of a swan, Leda conceived both Clytaemnestra and Helen

And the speech to suit my absence, much too long.
But the praise that does us justice, 910
let it come from others, then we prize it.
                                This—
you treat me like a woman. Grovelling, gaping up at me—
what am I, some barbarian peacocking out of Asia?
Never cross my path with robes and draw the lightning.
Never—only the gods deserve the pomps of honour 915
and the stiff brocades of fame. To walk on them . . .
I am human, and it makes my pulses stir
with dread.
          Give me the tributes of a man
and not a god, a little earth to walk on,
not this gorgeous work. 920
There is no need to sound my reputation.
I have a sense of right and wrong, what's more—
heaven's proudest gift. Call no man blest
until he ends his life in peace, fulfilled.
If I can live by what I say, I have no fear. 925
CLYTAEMNESTRA: One thing more. Be true to your ideals and
   tell me—
AGAMEMNON: True to my ideals? Once I violate them I am
   lost.
CLYTAEMNESTRA: Would you have sworn this act to god in a
   time of terror?
AGAMEMNON: Yes, if a prophet called for a last, drastic rite.
CLYTAEMNESTRA: But Priam—can you see him if he had your- 930
   success?
AGAMEMNON: Striding on the tapestries of god, I see him
   now.
CLYTAEMNESTRA: And *you* fear the reproach of common
   men?
AGAMEMNON: The voice of the people—aye, they have
   enormous power.
CLYTAEMNESTRA: Perhaps, but where's the glory without a
   little gall?
AGAMEMNON: And where's the woman in all this lust for 935
   glory?
CLYTAEMNESTRA: But the great victor—it becomes him to
   give way.
AGAMEMNON: Victory in this . . . war of ours, it means so
   much to you?
CLYTAEMNESTRA: O give way! The power is yours if you
   surrender,
all of your own free will, to me!
AGAMEMNON: Enough. 940
If you are so determined—

(Turning to the women, pointing to his boots.)

Let someone help me off with these at least.
Old slaves, they've stood me well.
                            Hurry,
and while I tread his splendours dyed red in the sea,
may no god watch and strike me down with envy
from on high. I feel such shame— 945
to tread the life of the house, a kingdom's worth
of silver in the weaving.

(He steps down from the chariot to the tapestries and reveals CASSANDRA, dressed in the sacred regalia, the fillets, robes, and sceptre of Apollo.)

Done is done.
Escort this stranger in, be gentle.
Conquer with compassion. Then the gods
950 shine down upon you, gently. No one chooses
the yoke of slavery, not of one's free will—
and she least of all. The gift of the armies,
flower and pride of all the wealth we won,
she follows me from Troy.
                         And now,
955 since you have brought me down with your insistence,
just this once I enter my father's house,
trampling royal crimson as I go.

(He takes his first steps and pauses.)

CLYTAEMNESTRA: There is the sea
and who will drain it dry? Precious as silver,
inexhaustible, ever-new, it breeds the more we reap it—
960 tides on tides of crimson dye our robes blood-red.
Our lives are based on wealth, my king,
the gods have seen to that.
Destitution, our house has never heard the word.
I would have sworn to tread on legacies of robes,
965 at one command from an oracle, deplete the house—
suffer the worst to bring that dear life back!

(Encouraged, AGAMEMNON *strides to the entrance.)*

When the root lives on, the new leaves come back,
spreading a dense shroud of shade across the house
to thwart the Dog Star's fury. So you return
970 to the father's hearth, you bring us warmth in winter
like the sun—
              And you are Zeus when Zeus
tramples the bitter virgin grape for new wine
and the welcome chill steals through the halls, at last
the master moves among the shadows of his house,
    fulfilled.

*(*AGAMEMNON *goes over the threshold; the women gather up the tapestries while* CLYTAEMNESTRA *prays.)*

975 Zeus, Zeus, master of all fulfilment, now fulfil our
        prayers—
speed our rites to their fulfilment once for all!

(She enters the palace, the doors close, the old men huddle in terror.)

CHORUS: Why, why does it rock me, never stops,
this terror beating down my heart,
            this seer that sees it all—
980 it beats its wings, uncalled unpaid
thrust on the lungs
the mercenary song beats on and on
singing a prophet's strain—
            and I can't throw it off
985 like dreams that make no sense,
and the strength drains
that filled the mind with trust,
and the years drift by and the driven sand
            has buried the mooring lines

that churned when the armoured squadrons cut for Troy . . . 990
and now I believe it, I can prove he's home,
        my own clear eyes for witness—
                    Agamemnon!
Still it's chanting, beating deep so deep in the heart
this dirge of the Furies, oh dear god,
not fit for the lyre, its own master   995
    it kills our spirit
kills our hopes
and it's real, true, no fantasy—
        stark terror whirls the brain
            and the end is coming   1000
        Justice comes to birth—
I pray my fears prove false and fall
and die and never come to birth!
Even exultant health, well we know,
    exceeds its limits, comes so near disease   1005
it can breach the wall between them.

Even a man's fate, held true on course,
    in a blinding flash rams some hidden reef;
but if caution only casts the pick of the cargo—
one well-balanced cast—   1010
the house will not go down, not outright;
labouring under its wealth of grief
the ship of state rides on.

Yes, and the great green bounty of god,
sown in the furrows year by year and reaped each fall   1015
can end the plague of famine.

But a man's life-blood
    is dark and mortal.
Once it wets the earth
what song can sing it back?   1020
Not even the master-healer
    who brought the dead to life—
Zeus stopped the man before he did more harm.

Oh, if only the gods had never forged
the chain that curbs our excess,   1025
    one man's fate curbing the next man's fate,
my heart would outrace my song, I'd pour out all I feel—
        but no, I choke with anguish,
            mutter through the nights.
Never to ravel out a hope in time   1030
and the brain is swarming, burning—

*(*CLYTAEMNESTRA *emerges from the palace and goes to* CASSANDRA, *impassive in the chariot.)*

CLYTAEMNESTRA: Won't you come inside? I mean you,
    Cassandra.
Zeus in all his mercy wants you to share
some victory libations with the house.
The slaves are flocking. Come, lead them   1035
up to the altar of the god who guards
our dearest treasures.

---

969 **Dog Star** Sirius, whose rising commonly marks the hot "dog days" of summer

995 **not fit for the lyre** the lyre-god, Apollo, required songs of joy, not mourning   1021 **the master-healer** the physician Asclepius, who restored a dead man to life and was struck dead in consequence by Zeus

Down from the chariot,
this is no time for pride. Why even Heracles,
they say, was sold into bondage long ago,
1040 he had to endure the bitter bread of slaves.
But if the yoke descends on you, be grateful
for a master born and reared in ancient wealth.
Those who reap a harvest past their hopes
are merciless to their slaves.
                                        From us
1045 you will receive what custom says is right.

(CASSANDRA *remains impassive.*)

LEADER: It's *you* she is speaking to, it's all too clear.
You're caught in the nets of doom—obey
if you can obey, unless you cannot bear to.
CLYTAEMNESTRA: Unless she's like a swallow, possessed
1050 of her own barbaric song, strange, dark.
I speak directly as I can—she must obey.
LEADER: Go with her. Make the best of it, she's right.
Step down from the seat, obey her.
CLYTAEMNESTRA: Do it *now*—
I have no time to spend outside. Already
1055 the victims crowd the hearth, the Navelstone,
to bless this day of joy I never hoped to see!—
our victims waiting for the fire and the knife,
and you,
if you want to taste our mystic rites, come now.
1060 If my words can't reach you—

(*Turning to the* LEADER.)

                                        Give her a sign,
one of her exotic handsigns.
LEADER: I think
the stranger needs an interpreter, someone clear.
She's like a wild creature, fresh caught.
CLYTAEMNESTRA: She's mad,
her evil genius murmuring in her ears.
1065 She comes from a *city* fresh caught.
She must learn to take the cutting bridle
before she foams her spirit off in blood—
and that's the last I waste on her contempt!

(*Wheeling, re-entering the palace. The* LEADER *turns to* CAS-
SANDRA, *who remains transfixed.*)

LEADER: Not I, I pity her. I will be gentle.
1070 Come, poor thing. Leave the empty chariot—
Of your own free will try on the yoke of Fate.
CASSANDRA: Aieeeeee! Earth—Mother—
                                        Curse of the Earth—Apollo Apollo!
LEADER: Why cry to Apollo?
He's not the god to call with sounds of mourning.
1075 CASSANDRA: Aieeeeee! Earth—Mother—
                                        Rape of the Earth—Apollo Apollo!
LEADER: Again, it's a bad omen.
She cries for the god who wants no part of grief.

(CASSANDRA *steps from the chariot, looks slowly towards the
rooftops of the palace.*)

1038–1040 **Why even Heracles . . . slaves** as punishment, Heracles
was sold in bondage by Hermes to Omphale, queen of Lydia   1055
the Navelstone an allusion to Apollo's "World Navel," a stone erected
at Delphi

CASSANDRA: God of the long road,
                Apollo *Apollo* my destroyer—
you destroy me once, destroy me twice—   1080
LEADER: She's about to sense her own ordeal, I think.
Slave that she is, the god lives on inside her.
CASSANDRA: God of the iron marches,
                Apollo *Apollo* my destroyer—
where, where have you led me now? what house— 1085
LEADER: The house of Atreus and his sons. Really—
don't you know? It's true, see for yourself.
CASSANDRA: No . . . the house that hates god,
an echoing womb of guilt, kinsmen
        torturing kinsmen, severed heads,   1090
slaughterhouse of heroes, soil streaming blood—
LEADER: A keen hound, this stranger.
Trailing murder, and murder she will find.
CASSANDRA: See, my witnesses—
I trust to them, to the babies   1095
        wailing, skewered on the sword,
their flesh charred, the father gorging on their parts—
LEADER: We'd heard your fame as a seer,
but no one looks for seers in Argos.
CASSANDRA: Oh no, what horror, what new plot,   1100
new agony this?—
it's growing, massing, deep in the house,
        a plot, a monstrous—*thing*
                to crush the loved ones, no,
        there is no cure, and rescue's far away and— 1105
LEADER: I can't read these signs; I knew the first,
the city rings with them.
CASSANDRA: You, you godforsaken—you'd do *this*?
The lord of your bed,
you bathe him . . . his body glistens, then—   1110
        how to tell the climax?—
                comes so quickly, see,
hand over hand shoots out, hauling ropes—
                                        then lunge!
LEADER: Still lost. Her riddles, her dark words of god—
I'm groping, helpless.   1115
CASSANDRA: No no, look *there*!—
what's that? some net flung out of hell—
        No, *she* is the snare,
the bedmate, deathmate, murder's strong right arm!
        Let the insatiate discord in the race
rear up and shriek 'Avenge the victim—stone them dead!' 1120
LEADER: What Fury is this? Why rouse it, lift its wailing
through the house? I hear you and lose hope.
CHORUS: Drop by drop at the heart, the gold of life ebbs out.
We are the old soldiers . . . wounds will come
with the crushing sunset of our lives.   1125
Death is close, and quick.
CASSANDRA: Look out! *look out!*—
Ai, drag the great bull from the mate!—
a thrash of robes, she traps him—
writhing—
        black horn glints, twists—
                                she gores him through!
        And now he buckles, look, the bath swirls red— 1130
There's stealth and murder in the cauldron, do you hear?
LEADER: I'm no judge, I've little skill with the oracles,
but even I know danger when I hear it.

CHORUS: What good are the oracles to men? Words, more
words,
1135 and the hurt comes on us, endless words
and a seer's techniques have brought us
terror and the truth.
CASSANDRA: The agony—O I am breaking!—Fate's so hard,
and the pain that floods my voice is mine alone.
1140 Why have you brought me here, tormented as I am?
Why, unless to die with him, why else?
LEADER AND CHORUS: Mad with the rapture—god speeds
you on
to the song, the deathsong,
like the nightingale that broods on sorrow,
1145 mourns her son, her son,
her life inspired with grief for him,
she lilts and shrills, dark bird that lives for night.
CASSANDRA: The nightingale—O for a song, a fate like hers!
The gods gave her a life of ease, swathed her in wings,
1150 no tears, no wailing. The knife waits for me.
They'll splay me on the iron's double edge.
LEADER AND CHORUS: Why?—what god hurls you on, stroke
on stroke
to the long dying fall?
Why the horror clashing through your music,
1155 terror struck to song?—
why the anguish, the wild dance?
Where do your words of god and grief begin?
CASSANDRA: Ai, the wedding, wedding of Paris,
death to the loved ones. Oh Scamander,
1160 you nursed my father . . . once at your banks
I nursed and grew, and now at the banks
of Acheron, the stream that carries sorrow,
it seems I'll chant my prophecies too soon.
LEADER AND CHORUS: What are you saying? Wait, it's clear,
1165 a child could see the truth, it wounds within,
like a bloody fang it tears—
I hear your destiny—breaking sobs,
cries that stab the ears.
CASSANDRA: Oh the grief, the grief of the city
1170 ripped to oblivion. Oh the victims,
the flocks my father burned at the wall,
rich herds in flames . . . no cure for the doom
that took the city after all, and I,
her last ember, I go down with her.
1175 LEADER AND CHORUS: You cannot stop, your song goes on—
some spirit drops from the heights and treads you down
and the brutal strain grows—
your death-throes come and come and
I cannot see the end!
1180 CASSANDRA: Then off with the veils that hid the fresh
young bride—
we will see the truth.
Flare up once more, my oracle! Clear and sharp
as the wind that blows towards the rising sun,
I can feel a deeper swell now, gathering head
1185 to break at last and bring the dawn of grief.

1145 **her son** Itys, son of Philomela, the mother was transformed into a
nightingale after she inadvertently tricked her husband, Tereus, into
eating their son's flesh

No more riddles. I will teach you.
Come, bear witness, run and hunt with me.
We trail the old barbaric works of slaughter.

These roofs—look up—there is a dancing troupe
that never leaves. And they have their harmony 1190
but it is harsh, their words are harsh, they drink
beyond the limit. Flushed on the blood of men
their spirit grows and none can turn away
their revel breeding in the veins—the Furies!
They cling to the house for life. They sing, 1195
sing of the frenzy that began it all,
strain rising on strain, showering curses
on the man who tramples on his brother's bed.

There. Have I hit the mark or not? Am I a fraud,
a fortune-teller babbling lies from door to door? 1200
Swear how well I know the ancient crimes
that live within this house.
LEADER: And if I did?
Would an oath bind the wounds and heal us?
But you amaze me. Bred across the sea,
your language strange, and still you sense the truth 1205
as if you had been here.
CASSANDRA: Apollo the Prophet
introduced me to his gift.
LEADER: A *god*—and moved with love?
CASSANDRA: I was ashamed to tell this once,
but now . . . 1210
LEADER: We spoil ourselves with scruples,
long as things go well.
CASSANDRA: He came like a wrestler,
magnificent, took me down and breathed his fire
through me and—
LEADER: You bore him a child?
CASSANDRA: I yielded,
then at the climax I recoiled—I deceived Apollo!
LEADER: But the god's skills—they seized you even then? 1215
CASSANDRA: Even then I told my people all the grief to come.
LEADER: And Apollo's anger never touched you?—is it
possible?
CASSANDRA: Once I betrayed him I could never be believed.
LEADER: We believe you. Your visions seem so true.
CASSANDRA: Aieeeee!—
the pain, the terror! the birth-pang of the seer 1220
who tells the truth—
it whirls me, oh,
the storm comes again, the crashing chords!
Look, you see them nestling at the threshold?
Young, young in the darkness like a dream,
like children really, yes, and their loved ones 1225
brought them down . . .
their hands, they fill their hands
with their own flesh, they are serving it like food,
holding out their entrails . . . now it's clear,
I can see the armfuls of compassion, see the father
reach to taste and— 1230
For so much suffering,
I tell you, someone plots revenge.
A lion who lacks a lion's heart,
he sprawled at home in the royal lair

and set a trap for the lord on his return.
1235   My lord . . . I must wear his yoke, I am his slave.
The lord of the men-of-war, he obliterated Troy—
he is so blind, so lost to that detestable hellhound
who pricks her ears and fawns and her tongue draws out
her glittering words of welcome—
                      No, he cannot see
1240   the stroke that Fury's hiding, stealth, and murder.
What outrage—the woman kills the man!
                          What to call
that . . . monster of Greece, and bring my quarry down?
Viper coiling back and forth?
                      Some sea-witch?—
Scylla crouched in her rocky nest—nightmare of sailors?
1245   Raging mother of death, storming deathless war against
the ones she loves!
             And how she howled in triumph,
boundless outrage. Just as the tide of battle
broke her way, she seems to rejoice that he
is safe at home from war, saved for her.
1250   Believe me if you will. What will it matter
if you won't? It comes when it comes,
and soon you'll see it face to face
and say the seer was all too true.
You will be moved with pity.
  LEADER: Thyestes' feast,
1255   the children's flesh—that I know,
and the fear shudders through me. It's true,
real, no dark signs about it. I hear the rest
but it throws me off the scent.
  CASSANDRA: Agamemnon.
You will see him dead.
  LEADER: Peace, poor girl!
1260   Put those words to sleep.
  CASSANDRA: No use,
the Healer has no hand in this affair.
  LEADER: Not if it's true—but god forbid it is!
  CASSANDRA: You pray, and they close in to kill!
  LEADER: What man prepares this, this dreadful—
  CASSANDRA: Man?
1265   You *are* lost, to every word I've said.
  LEADER: Yes—
I don't see who can bring the evil off.
  CASSANDRA: And yet I know my Greek, too well.
  LEADER: So does the Delphic oracle,
but he's hard to understand.
  CASSANDRA: His *fire!*—
1270   sears me, sweeps me again—the torture!
Apollo Lord of the Light, you burn,
you blind me—
             Agony!
                 She is the lioness,
she rears on her hind legs, she beds with the wolf
when her lion king goes ranging—
                     she will kill me—
1275   Ai, the torture!
           She is mixing her drugs,
adding a measure more of hate for me.

_____

1244 **Scylla** a many-headed monster who terrorized sailors

She gloats as she whets the sword for him.
He brought me home and we will pay in carnage.

  Why mock yourself with these—trappings, the rod,
the god's wreath, his yoke around my throat?   1280
Before I die I'll tread you—

(Ripping off her regalia, stamping it into the ground.)

                    Down, out,
die die die!
Now you're down. I've paid you back.
Look for another victim—I am free at last—
make her rich in all your curse and doom.   1285

(Staggering backwards as if wrestling with a spirit tearing at her robes.)

                        See,
Apollo himself, his fiery hands—I feel him again,
he's stripping off my robes, the Seer's robes!
And after he looked down and saw me mocked,
even in these, his glories, mortified by friends   1290
I loved, and they hated me, they were so blind
to their own demise—
                I went from door to door,
I was wild with the god, I heard them call me
'Beggar! Wretch! Starve for bread in hell!'

  And I endured it all, and now he will
extort me as his due. A seer for the Seer.   1295
He brings me here to die like this,
not to serve at my father's altar. No,
the block is waiting. The cleaver steams
with my life blood, the first blood drawn
for the king's last rites.   1300

(Regaining her composure and moving to the altar.)

                  We will die,
but not without some honour from the gods.
There will come another to avenge us,
born to kill his mother, born
his father's champion. A wanderer, a fugitive
driven off his native land, he will come home   1305
to cope the stones of hate that menace all he loves.
The gods have sworn a monumental oath: as his father lies
upon the ground he draws him home with power like a
    prayer.

  Then why so pitiful, why so many tears?
I have seen my city faring as she fared,   1310
and those who took her, judged by the gods,
faring as they fare. I must be brave.
It is my turn to die.

(Approaching the doors.)

  I address you as the Gates of Death.
I pray it comes with one clear stroke,   1315
no convulsions, the pulses ebbing out
in gentle death. I'll close my eyes and sleep.
  LEADER: So much pain, poor girl, and so much truth,
you've told so much. But if you *see* it coming,
clearly—how can you go to your own death,   1320
like a beast to the altar driven on by god,
and hold your head so high?

CASSANDRA: No escape, my friends,
       not now.
LEADER: But the last hour should be savoured.
CASSANDRA: My time has come. Little to gain from flight.
1325 LEADER: You're brave, believe me, full of gallant heart.
CASSANDRA: Only the wretched go with praise like that.
LEADER: But to go nobly lends a man some grace.
CASSANDRA: My noble father—you and your noble children.

(She nears the threshold and recoils, groaning in revulsion.)

LEADER: What now? what terror flings you back?
1330   Why? Unless some horror in the brain—
CASSANDRA: Murder.
       The house breathes with murder—bloody shambles!
LEADER: No, no, only the victims at the hearth.
CASSANDRA: I know that odour. I smell the open grave.
LEADER: But the Syrian myrrh, it fills the halls with
          splendour,
1335   can't you sense it?
CASSANDRA: Well, I must go in now,
       mourning Agamemnon's death and mine.
       Enough of life!

(Approaching the doors again and crying out.)

              Friends—I cried out,
       not from fear like a bird fresh caught,
       but that you will testify to *how* I died.
1340   When the queen, woman for woman, dies for me,
       and a man falls for the man who married grief.
       That's all I ask, my friends. A stranger's gift
       for one about to die.
LEADER: Poor creature, you
       and the end you see so clearly. I pity you.
1345 CASSANDRA: I'd like a few words more, a kind of dirge,
       it is my own. I pray to the sun,
       the last light I'll see,
       that when the avengers cut the assassins down
       they will avenge me too, a slave who died,
1350   an easy conquest.
              Oh men, your destiny.
       When all is well a shadow can overturn it.
       When trouble comes a stroke of the wet sponge,
       and the picture's blotted out. And that,
       I think that breaks the heart.

(She goes through the doors.)

1355 CHORUS: But the lust for power never dies—
          men cannot have enough.
       No one will lift a hand to send it
       from his door, to give it warning,
       'Power, never come again!'
1360   Take this man: the gods in glory
       gave him Priam's city to plunder,
       brought him home in splendour like a god.
       But now if he must pay for the blood
          his fathers shed, and die for the deaths
1365   he brought to pass, and bring more death
       to avenge his dying, show us one
          who boasts himself born free
       of the raging angel, once he hears—

(Cries break out within the palace.)

AGAMEMNON: Aagh!
       Struck deep—the death-blow, deep—
LEADER: Quiet. Cries,
       but who? Someone's stabbed—   1370
AGAMEMNON: Aaagh, again . . .
       second blow—struck home.
LEADER: The work is done,
       you can feel it. The king, and the great cries—
       Close ranks now, find the right way out.

(But the old men scatter, each speaks singly.)

CHORUS: —I say send out heralds, muster the guard,
       they'll save the house.   1375
              —And I say rush in now,
       catch them red-handed—butchery running on their
          blades.
—Right with you, do something—now or never!
—Look at them, beating the drum for insurrection.
                              —Yes,
       we're wasting time. They rape the name of caution,
       their hands will never sleep.   1380
              —Not a plan in sight.
       Let men of action do the planning, too.
—I'm helpless. Who can raise the dead with words?
—What, drag out our lives? bow down to the tyrants,
       the ruin of the house?
              —Never, better to die
       on your feet than live on your knees.   1385
              —Wait,
       do we take the cries for signs, prophesy like seers
       and give him up for dead?
              —No more suspicions,
       not another word till we have proof.
              —Confusion
       on all sides—one thing to do. See how it stands
       with Agamemnon, once and for all we'll see—   1390

*(He rushes at the doors. They open and reveal a silver cauldron
that holds the body of AGAMEMNON shrouded in bloody robes,
with the body of CASSANDRA to his left and CLYTAEMNESTRA
standing to his right, sword in hand. She strides towards the
chorus.)*

CLYTAEMNESTRA: Words, endless words I've said to serve the
          moment—
       now it makes me proud to tell the truth.
       How else to prepare a death for deadly men
       who seem to love you? How to rig the nets
       of pain so high no man can overleap them?   1395
       I brooded on this trial, this ancient blood feud
       year by year. At last my hour came.
       Here I stand and here I struck
       and here my work is done.
       I did it all. I don't deny it, no.   1400
       He had no way to flee or fight his destiny—

*(Unwinding the robes from AGAMEMNON's body, spreading
them before the altar where the old men cluster around them,
unified as a chorus once again.)*

our never-ending, all embracing net, I cast it
wide for the royal haul, I coil him round and round
in the wealth, the robes of doom, and then I strike him
1405 once, twice, and at each stroke he cries in agony—
he buckles at the knees and crashes here!
And when he's down I add the third, last blow,
to the Zeus who saves the dead beneath the ground
I send that third blow home in homage like a prayer.

1410 So he goes down, and the life is bursting out of him—
great sprays of blood, and the murderous shower
wounds me, dyes me black and I, I revel
like the Earth when the spring rains come down,
the blessed gifts of god, and the new green spear
1415 splits the sheath and rips to birth in glory!

So it stands, elders of Argos gathered here.
Rejoice if you can rejoice—I glory.
And if I'd pour upon his body the libation
it deserves, what wine could match my words?
1420 It is right and more than right. He flooded
the vessel of our proud house with misery,
with the vintage of the curse and now
he drains the dregs. My lord is home at last.

LEADER: You appal me, you, your brazen words—
1425 exulting over your fallen king.

CLYTAEMNESTRA: And you,
you try me like some desperate woman.
My heart is steel, well you know. Praise me,
blame me as you choose. It's all one.
Here is Agamemnon, my husband made a corpse
1430 by this right hand—a masterpiece of Justice.
Done is done.

CHORUS: Woman!—what poison cropped from the soil
or strained from the heaving sea, what nursed you,
drove you insane? You brave the curse of Greece.
You have cut away and flung away and now
1435 the people cast you off to exile,
broken with our hate.

CLYTAEMNESTRA: And now you sentence me?—
you banish *me* from the city, curses breathing
down my neck? But *he*—
name one charge you brought against him then.
1440 He thought no more of it than killing a beast,
and his flocks were rich, teeming in their fleece,
but he sacrificed his own child, our daughter,
the agony I laboured into love
to charm away the savage winds of Thrace.
1445 Didn't the law demand you banish him?—
hunt him from the land for all his guilt?
But now you witness what I've done
and you are ruthless judges.

Threaten away!
I'll meet you blow for blow. And if I fall
1450 the throne is yours. If god decrees the reverse,
late as it is, old men, you'll learn your place.

CHORUS: Mad with ambition,
shrilling pride!—some Fury
crazed with the carnage rages through your brain—
1455 I can see the flecks of blood inflame your eyes!
But vengeance comes—you'll lose your loved ones,
stroke for painful stroke.

CLYTAEMNESTRA: Then learn this, too, the power of my oaths.
By the child's Rights I brought to birth,
by Ruin, by Fury—the three gods to whom 1460
I sacrificed this man—I swear my hopes
will never walk the halls of fear so long
as Aegisthus lights the fire on my hearth.
Loyal to me as always, no small shield
to buttress my defiance. 1465
Here he lies.
He brutalized me. The darling of all
the golden girls who spread the gates of Troy.
And here his spear-prize . . . what wonders she beheld!—
the seer of Apollo shared my husband's bed,
his faithful mate who knelt at the rowing-benches, 1470
worked by every hand.
They have their rewards.
He as you know. And she, the swan of the gods
who lived to sing her latest, dying song—
his lover lies beside him.
She brings a fresh, voluptuous relish to my bed! 1475

CHORUS: Oh quickly, let me die—
no bed of labour, no, no wasting illness . . .
bear me off in the sleep that never ends,
now that he has fallen,
now that our dearest shield lies battered— 1480
Woman made him suffer,
woman struck him down.

Helen the wild, maddening Helen,
one for the many, the thousand lives
you murdered under Troy. Now you are crowned 1485
with this consummate wreath, the blood
that lives in memory, glistens age to age.
Once in the halls she walked and she was war,
angel of war, angel of agony, lighting men to death.

CLYTAEMNESTRA: Pray no more for death, broken 1490
as you are. And never turn
your wrath on her, call her
the scourge of men, the one alone
who destroyed a myriad Greek lives—
Helen the grief that never heals. 1495

CHORUS: The *spirit!*—you who tread
the house and the twinborn sons of Tantalus—
you empower the sisters, Fury's twins
whose power tears the heart!
Perched on the corpse your carrion raven 1500
glories in her hymn,
her screaming hymn of pride.

CLYTAEMNESTRA: Now you set your judgement straight,
you summon *him!* Three generations
feed the spirit in the race. 1505
Deep in the veins he feeds our bloodlust—
aye, before the old wound dies
it ripens in another flow of blood.

CHORUS: The great curse of the house, the spirit,
dead weight wrath—and you can praise it! 1510

1472 **the swan** the bird of Apollo, reputed to sing only when about to die 1497 **the twinborn sons of Tantalus** here, Agamemnon and Menelaus

Praise the insatiate doom that feeds
relentless on our future and our sons.
Oh all through the will of Zeus,
the cause of all, the one who works it all.
1515   What comes to birth that is not Zeus?
Our lives are pain, what part not come from god?

        Oh my king, my captain,
        how to salute you, how to mourn you?
        What can I say with all my warmth and love?
1520   Here in the black widow's web you lie,
        gasping out your life
        in a sacrilegious death, dear god,
        reduced to a slave's bed,
        my king of men, yoked by stealth and Fate,
1525   by the wife's hand that thrust the two-edged sword.
CLYTAEMNESTRA: You claim the work is mine, call me
        Agamemnon's wife—you are so wrong.
        Fleshed in the wife of this dead man,
            the spirit lives within me,
1530   our savage ancient spirit of revenge.
        In return for Atreus' brutal feast
        he kills his perfect son—for every
        murdered child, a crowning sacrifice.
CHORUS: And *you*, innocent of his murder?
1535   And who could swear to that? and how? . . .
        and still an avenger could arise,
        bred by the fathers' crimes, and lend a hand.
        He wades in the blood of brothers,
        stream on mounting stream—black war erupts
1540   and where he strides revenge will stride,
        clots will mass for the young who were devoured.

        Oh my king, my captain,
        how to salute you, how to mourn you?
        What can I say with all my warmth and love?
1545   Here in the black widow's web you lie,
        gasping out your life
        in a sacrilegious death, dear god,
        reduced to a slave's bed,
        my king of men, yoked by stealth and Fate,
1550   by the wife's hand that thrust the two-edged sword.
CLYTAEMNESTRA: No slave's death, I think—
        no stealthier than the death he dealt
        our house and the offspring of our loins,
            Iphigeneia, girl of tears!
1555   Act for act, wound for wound!
        Never exult in Hades, swordsman,
        here you are repaid. By the sword
        you did your work and by the sword you die.
CHORUS: The mind reels—where to turn?
1560   All plans dashed, all hope! I cannot think . . .
        the roofs are toppling, I dread the drumbeat thunder
            the heavy rains of blood will crush the house
                the first light rains are over—
            Justice brings new acts of agony, yes,
1565   on new grindstones Fate is grinding sharp the sword of
            Justice.
        Earth, dear Earth,
        if only you'd drawn me under
        long before I saw him huddled
        in the beaten silver bath.
1570   Who will bury him, lift his dirge?

(*Turning to* CLYTAEMNESTRA.)
    You, can you dare *this*?
    To kill your lord with your own hand
    then mourn his soul with tributes, terrible tributes—
    do his enormous works a great dishonour.
    This god-like man, this hero. Who at the grave   1575
    will sing his praises, pour the wine of tears?
    Who will labour there with truth of heart?
CLYTAEMNESTRA: This is no concern of yours.
    The hand that bore and cut him down
    will hand him down to Mother Earth.   1580
    This house will never mourn for him.
        Only our daughter Iphigeneia,
    by all rights, will rush to meet him
    first at the churning straits,
    the ferry over tears—   1585
    she'll fling her arms around her father,
    pierce him with her love.
CHORUS: Each charge meets counter-charge.
        None can judge between them. Justice.
    The plunderer plundered, the killer pays the price. 1590
    The truth still holds while Zeus still holds the throne:
            the one who acts must suffer—
        that is law. Who can tear from the veins
    the bad seed, the curse? The race is welded to its ruin.
CLYTAEMNESTRA: At last you see the future and the truth! 1595
    But I will swear a pact with the spirit
    born within us. I embrace his works,
    cruel as they are but done at last,
        if he will leave our house
    in the future, bleed another line   1600
    with kinsmen murdering kinsmen.
    Whatever he may ask. A few things
    are all I need, once I have purged
    our fury to destroy each other—
        purged it from our halls.   1605

(AEGISTHUS *has emerged from the palace with his bodyguard
and stands triumphant over the body of* AGAMEMNON.)

AEGISTHUS: O what a brilliant day
    it is for vengeance! Now I can say once more
    there are gods in heaven avenging men,
    blazing down on all the crimes of earth.
    Now at last I see this man brought down
    in the Furies' tangling robes. It feasts my eyes—   1610
    he pays for the plot his father's hand contrived.

    Atreus, this man's father, was king of Argos.
    My father, Thyestes—let me make this clear—
    Atreus' brother challenged him for the crown,
    and Atreus drove him out of house and home   1615
    then lured him back, and home Thyestes came,
    poor man, a suppliant to his own hearth,
    to pray that Fate might save him.
                        So it did.
    There was no dying, no staining our native ground
    with *his* blood. Thyestes was the guest,   1620
    and this man's godless father—

1585 **the ferry** Charon's ferry across the River Styx into the underworld

(Pointing to AGAMEMNON.*)*

the zeal of the host outstripping a brother's love,
made my father a feast that seemed a feast for gods,
a love feast of his children's flesh.
                                    He cuts
1625 the extremities, feet and delicate hands
into small pieces, scatters them over the dish
and serves it to Thyestes throned on high.
He picks at the flesh he cannot recognize,
the soul of innocence eating the food of ruin—
1630 look,

(Pointing to the bodies at his feet.)

            that feeds upon the house! And then,
when he sees the monstrous thing he's done, he shrieks,
he reels back head first and vomits up that butchery,
tramples the feast—brings down the curse of Justice:
'Crash to ruin, all the race of Pleisthenes, crash down!'

1635 So you see him, down. And I, the weaver of Justice,
plotted out the kill. Atreus drove us into exile,
my struggling father and I, a babe-in-arms,
his last son, but I became a man
and Justice brought me home. I was abroad
1640 but I reached out and seized my man,
link by link I clamped the fatal scheme
together. Now I could die gladly, even I—
now I see this monster in the nets of Justice.
LEADER: Aegisthus, you revel in pain—you sicken me.
1645 You say you killed the king in cold blood,
single-handed planned his pitiful death?
I say there's no escape. In the hour of judgement,
trust to this, your head will meet the people's
rocks and curses.
AEGISTHUS: You say! you slaves at the oars—
1650 while the master on the benches cracks the whip?
You'll learn, in your late age, how much it hurts
to teach old bones their place. We have techniques—
chains and the pangs of hunger,
two effective teachers, excellent healers.
1655 They can even cure old men of pride and gall.
Look—can't you see? The more you kick
against the pricks, the more you suffer.
LEADER: You, pathetic—
the king had just returned from battle.
1660 You waited out the war and fouled his lair,
you planned my great commander's fall.
AEGISTHUS: Talk on—
you'll scream for every word, my little Orpheus.
We'll see if the world comes dancing to your song,
your absurd barking—snarl your breath away!
1665 I'll make you dance, I'll bring you all to heel!
LEADER: *You* rule Argos? You who schemed his death
but cringed to cut him down with your own hand?
AEGISTHUS: The treachery was the woman's work, clearly.
I was a marked man, his enemy for ages.
1670 But I will use his riches, stop at nothing

to civilize his people. All but the rebel:
him I'll yoke and break—
no cornfed colt, running free in the traces.
Hunger, ruthless mate of the dark torture-chamber,
trains her eyes upon him till he drops!   1675
LEADER: Coward, why not kill the man yourself?
Why did the woman, the corruption of Greece
and the gods of Greece, have to bring him down?
Orestes—
            If he still sees the light of day,
bring him home, good Fates, home to kill   1680
this pair at last. Our champion in slaughter!
AEGISTHUS: Bent on insolence? Well, you'll learn, quickly.
At them, men—you have your work at hand!

(His men draw swords; the old men take up their sticks.)

LEADER: At them, first at the hilt, to the last man—
AEGISTHUS: First at the hilt, I'm not afraid to die.   1685
LEADER: It's death you want and death you'll have—
we'll make that word your last.

*(*CLYTAEMNESTRA *moves between them, restraining* AEGISTHUS.*)*

CLYTAEMNESTRA: No more, my dearest,
no more grief. We have too much to reap
right here, our mighty harvest of despair.
Our lives are based on pain. No bloodshed now.   1690

Fathers of Argos, turn for home before you act
and suffer for it. What we did was destiny.
If we could end the suffering, how we would rejoice.
The spirit's brutal hoof has struck our heart.
And that is what a woman has to say.   1695
Can you accept the truth?

*(*CLYTAEMNESTRA *turns to leave.)*

AEGISTHUS: But these . . . mouths
that bloom in filth—spitting insults in my teeth.
You tempt your fates, you insubordinate dogs—
to hurl abuse at me, your master!
LEADER: No Greek
worth his salt would grovel at your feet.   1700
AEGISTHUS: I—I'll stalk you all your days!
LEADER: Not if the spirit brings Orestes home.
AEGISTHUS: Exiles feed on hope—well I know.
LEADER: More,
gorge yourself to bursting—soil justice, while you can.
AEGISTHUS: I promise you, you'll pay, old fools—in good   1705
time, too!
LEADER: Strut on your own dunghill, you cock beside your
mate.
CLYTAEMNESTRA: Let them howl—they're impotent. You and
I have power now.
We will set the house in order once for all.

(They enter the palace; the great doors close behind them; the old men disband and wander off.)

1634 **Pleisthenes** an unidentified ancestral figure, perhaps Atreus or Pelops   1662 **Orpheus** a musician who enchanted even rocks and trees with his lyre

■ SOPHOCLES ■

Like Aeschylus, Sophocles (c. 496–406 BC) had an important career in the civic life of Athens as well as in the theater. He was treasurer for the Athenian imperial league, and served as one of ten generals who led a campaign against Samos, an island threatening to secede from the Athenian alliance. In 411 BC, he was appointed to a committee called to examine Athens' disastrous military campaign in Sicily. Sophocles' greatest achievements, though, were in the theater. Sophocles is responsible for introducing a third actor into dramatic performance, an innovation rapidly imitated by other playwrights, including Aeschylus and Euripides. He also enlarged the size of the chorus from twelve to fifteen men. Sophocles won his first victory, against Aeschylus, in 468 BC; he was victorious twenty-four times in his career and never finished lower than second in the dramatic competition. Of the one hundred twenty plays attributed to Sophocles, only seven survive: *Ajax, Trachiniae, Antigone, Oedipus Rex, Electra, Philoctetes,* and *Oedipus at Colonus.* Fragments of a satyr play, *The Trackers,* also remain. The three "Theban" plays—*Antigone, Oedipus Rex,* and *Oedipus at Colonus*—are thematically related, but, unlike *The Oresteia* of Aeschylus, were not composed as a single trilogy. *Antigone,* a play about Oedipus' daughters after his banishment from Thebes, was composed around the year 441 BC; *Oedipus Rex* was first produced sometime shortly after the declaration of war with Sparta in 431 BC; and *Oedipus at Colonus* was first produced after Sophocles' death and Athens' defeat.

OEDIPUS REX

Oedipus Rex is framed by two acts of identification, recognition, and acknowledgment. The action of the play is about the deepening and horrible understanding of what it means for the hero to recognize who he is, what it means to *be* Oedipus.

In his *Poetics,* written nearly a century later (about 335 BC), Aristotle frequently refers to *Oedipus Rex* as a definitive example of the form and purpose of tragedy. Modern audiences, though, sometimes find the play baffling, in part because the prophecy delivered to Oedipus' parents, Laïos and Iokaste—that their son will murder his father and marry his mother—seems to rob Oedipus of the ability to act, to decide his fate through his own deeds. The tension between destiny and discovery is central to the play, and to understand it, we should pay attention to the function of the oracle at Delphi both in the Greek world and in *Oedipus Rex.* The Greeks consulted the oracle at Delphi on a variety of matters, ranging from personal decisions to problems of state. In the play, Laïos and Iokaste, for example, have consulted the oracle to learn the future of their child, and Oedipus turns to Delphi to find out whether Polybos is actually his father; at the same time, the oracle also speaks on important public issues—about the cause of the plague afflicting Thebes and about what should be done with Oedipus after his blinding. Sophocles lived in an era of increasing skepticism, when political conflict and the rise of rhetorical training raised questions about the nature and significance of truth—even the truth of oracular revelation. It is not surprising that characters in *Oedipus Rex* frequently question such prophecy or have difficulty learning how to accept and interpret it—as when Oedipus flees Corinth to avoid murdering his father.

Critical as the prophecy is to Oedipus' life, Oedipus' deeds are really at issue in *Oedipus Rex.* Sophocles chose to begin and end his drama on the day of Oedipus' discovery of his own identity. The play focuses less on the prophecy than on the course and meaning of Oedipus' actions, on *how* he comes to recognize himself as the criminal he seeks. Oedipus arrives at this recognition only through an extraordinary effort of action and decision: Oedipus calls for the exile of Laïos' murderer; he insults Teiresias when the prophet tries to evade his questions; he accuses Kreon; he threatens the old shepherd with torture in order to learn the truth of his birth. The oracle says that Oedipus will commit his terrible crimes of murder and incest, but Oedipus *chooses* the relentless, brutal pursuit of the truth himself, even to the point of his own incrimination and destruction. The tragedy of *Oedipus Rex* lies in the fearsome turn of events caused by Oedipus' inflexible compulsion to discover the truth.

Aristotle considers the hero of tragedy at some length, in terms that are at once compelling and confusing, particularly in the case of Oedipus. Aristotle suggests in his *Poetics* that the hero of tragedy should be "a man who is neither a paragon of virtue and justice nor undergoes the change to misfortune through any real badness or wickedness but because of some mistake," a description that leads some to look for the cause of this error within Oedipus' character, in a so-called "tragic flaw." But, in fact, when he says that the character's "mistake"—or *HAMARTIA*—is not the result of "any real badness or wickedness," Aristotle seems to deny that the hero's downfall is the effect of any moral "flaw" at all. It might help us to remember that to his audience, Oedipus may have seemed to share some typically "Athenian" characteristics. Oedipus' passion for inquiry, his abrupt decisiveness, and his impulsive desire to act were seen as the stereotypical traits of Athenian citizens and of Athens as a city. Far from being "flaws," these are just the qualities that made Oedipus (and Athens) successful. What is "tragic" about Oedipus' fate in *Oedipus Rex* is the way that his own surest strengths, the aggressive, pragmatic qualities that enabled him to outwit the Sphinx, lead, on this one occasion, to his destruction. Oedipus' "mistake" is neither a moral failing nor a deed that he might have avoided; it is simply that he is Oedipus and acts like Oedipus—intelligent, masterful, assertive, impatient, impulsive. The tragedy lies in the way that acting like Oedipus leads him, as it has always led him in the past, to the discovery of the truth he seeks, this time with ruinous consequences.

OEDIPUS REX

SOPHOCLES

TRANSLATED BY DUDLEY FITTS AND ROBERT FITZGERALD

— CHARACTERS —

OEDIPUS	MESSENGER
A PRIEST	SHEPHERD OF LAÏOS
KREON	SECOND MESSENGER
TEIRESIAS	CHORUS OF THEBAN ELDERS
IOKASTE	CHORAGOS

SCENE: *Before the palace of Oedipus, King of Thebes. A central door and two lateral doors open onto a platform which runs the length of the façade. On the platform, right and left, are altars; and three steps lead down into the "orchestra," or chorus-ground. At the beginning of the action these steps are crowded by suppliants who have brought branches and chaplets of olive leaves and who lie in various attitudes of despair.* OEDIPUS *enters.*

— PROLOGUE —

OEDIPUS: My children, generations of the living
  In the line of Kadmos, nursed at his ancient
    hearth:
  Why have you strewn yourselves before these altars
  In supplication, with your boughs and garlands?
5 The breath of incense rises from the city
  With a sound of prayer and lamentation.
  Children,
  I would not have you speak through messengers,
  And therefore I have come myself to hear you—
10 I, Oedipus, who bear the famous name.

(*To a* PRIEST.)

  You, there, since you are eldest in the company,
  Speak for them all, tell me what preys upon you,
  Whether you come in dread, or crave some
    blessing:
  Tell me, and never doubt that I will help you
15 In every way I can; I should be heartless
  Were I not moved to find you suppliant here.
PRIEST: Great Oedipus, O powerful King of Thebes!
  You see how all the ages of our people
  Cling to your altar steps: here are boys
20 Who can barely stand alone, and here are priests
  By weight of age, as I am a priest of God,
  And young men chosen from those yet unmarried;
  As for the others, all that multitude,
  They wait with olive chaplets in the squares,
25 At the two shrines of Pallas, and where Apollo
  Speaks in the glowing embers.
  Your own eyes
  Must tell you: Thebes is tossed on a murdering sea
  And can not lift her head from the death surge.
30 A rust consumes the buds and fruits of the earth;
  The herds are sick; children die unborn,
  And labor is vain. The god of plague and pyre
  Raids like detestable lightning through the city,
  And all the house of Kadmos is laid waste,
35 All emptied, and all darkened: Death alone
  Battens upon the misery of Thebes.

  You are not one of the immortal gods, we know;
  Yet we have come to you to make our prayer
  As to the man surest in mortal ways
  And wisest in the ways of God. You saved us 40
  From the Sphinx, that flinty singer, and the tribute
  We paid to her so long; yet you were never
  Better informed than we, nor could we teach you;
  A god's touch, it seems, enabled you to help us.

  Therefore, O mighty power, we turn to you: 45
  Find us our safety, find us a remedy,
  Whether by counsel of the gods or of men.
  A king of wisdom tested in the past
  Can act in a time of troubles, and act well.
  Noblest of men, restore 50
  Life to your city! Think how all men call you
  Liberator for your boldness long ago;
  Ah, when your years of kingship are remembered,
  Let them not say *We rose, but later fell*—
  Keep the State from going down in the storm! 55
  Once, years ago, with happy augury,
  You brought us fortune; be the same again!
  No man questions your power to rule the land:
  But rule over men, not a dead city!
  Ships are only hulls, high walls are nothing, 60
  When no life moves in the empty passageways.
OEDIPUS: Poor children! You may be sure I know
  All that you longed for in your coming here.
  I know that you are deathly sick; and yet,
  Sick as you are, not one is as sick as I. 65
  Each of you suffers in himself alone
  His anguish, not another's; but my spirit
  Groans for the city, for myself, for you.

  I was not sleeping, you are not waking me.
  No, I have been in tears for a long while 70
  And in my restless thought walked many ways.
  In all my search I found one remedy,
  And I have adopted it: I have sent Kreon,
  Son of Menoikeus, brother of the Queen,
  To Delphi, Apollo's place of revelation, 75
  To learn there, if he can,
  What act or pledge of mine may save the city.
  I have counted the days, and now, this very day,
  I am troubled, for he has overstayed his time.
  What is he doing? He has been gone too long. 80
  Yet whenever he comes back, I should do ill
  Not to take any action the god orders.

PRIEST: It is a timely promise. At this instant
    They tell me Kreon is here.
85 OEDIPUS: O Lord Apollo!
    May his news be fair as his face is radiant!
PRIEST: Good news, I gather: he is crowned with bay,
    The chaplet is thick with berries.
OEDIPUS: We shall soon know;
90   He is near enough to hear us now.

(Enter KREON.*)*

    O Prince:
    Brother: son of Menoikeus
    What answer do you bring us from the God?
KREON: A strong one. I can tell you, great afflictions
95   Will turn out well, if they are taken well.
OEDIPUS: What was the oracle? These vague words
    Leave me still hanging between hope and fear.
KREON: Is it your pleasure to hear me with all these
    Gathered around us? I am prepared to speak,
100   But should we not go in?
OEDIPUS: Speak to them all.
    It is for them I suffer, more than for myself.
KREON: Then I will tell you what I heard at Delphi.
    In plain words
105   The god commands us to expel from the land of Thebes
    An old defilement we are sheltering.
    It is a deathly thing, beyond cure;
    We must not let it feed upon us longer.
OEDIPUS: What defilement? How shall we rid ourselves of it?
110 KREON: By exile or death, blood for blood. It was
    Murder that brought the plague-wind on the city.
OEDIPUS: Murder of whom? Surely the god has named him?
KREON: My lord: Laïos once ruled this land,
    Before you came to govern us.
115 OEDIPUS: I know;
    I learned of him from others; I never saw him.
KREON: He was murdered; and Apollo commands us now
    To take revenge upon whoever killed him.
OEDIPUS: Upon whom? Where are they? Where shall we find
    a clue
120   To solve that crime, after so many years?
KREON: Here in this land, he said. Search reveals
    Things that escape an inattentive man.
OEDIPUS: Tell me: Was Laïos murdered in his house,
    Or in the fields, or in some foreign country?
125 KREON: He said he planned to make a pilgrimage.
    He did not come home again.
OEDIPUS: And was there no one,
    No witness, no companion, to tell what happened?
KREON: They were all killed but one, and he got away
130   So frightened that he could remember one thing only.
OEDIPUS: What was that one thing? One may be the key
    To everything, if we resolve to use it.
KREON: He said that a band of highwaymen attacked them,
    Outnumbered them, and overwhelmed the King.
135 OEDIPUS: Strange, that a highwayman should be so daring—
    Unless some faction here bribed him to do it.
KREON: We thought of that. But after Laïos' death
    New troubles arose and we had no avenger.
OEDIPUS: What troubles could prevent your hunting down the
    killers?

KREON: The riddling Sphinx's song   140
    Made us deaf to all mysteries but her own.
OEDIPUS: Then once more I must bring what is dark to light.
    It is most fitting that Apollo shows,
    As you do, this compunction for the dead.
    You shall see how I stand by you, as I should,   145
    Avenging this country and the god as well,
    And not as though it were for some distant friend,
    But for my own sake, to be rid of evil.
    Whoever killed King Laïos might—who knows?—
    Lay violent hands even on me—and soon.   150
    I act for the murdered king in my own interest.

    Come, then, my children: leave the altar steps,
    Lift up your olive boughs!
    One of you go
    And summon the people of Kadmos to gather here.   155
    I will do all that I can; you may tell them that.

(Exit a PAGE.*)*

    So, with the help of God.
    We shall be saved—or else indeed we are lost.
PRIEST: Let us rise, children. It was for this we came,
    And now the King has promised it.   160
    Phoibos has sent us an oracle; may he descend
    Himself to save us and drive out the plague.

(Exeunt OEDIPUS *and* KREON *into the palace by the central
door. The* PRIEST *and the* SUPPLIANTS *disperse right and left.
After a short pause the* CHORUS *enters the* ORCHESTRA.*)*

PARODOS

Strophe 1

CHORUS: What is God singing in his profound
    Delphi of gold and shadow?
    What oracle for Thebes, the sunwhipped city?   165

    Fear unjoints me, the roots of my heart tremble.

    Now I remember, O Healer, your power and wonder:
    Will you send doom like a sudden cloud, or weave it
    Like nightfall of the past?

    Speak to me, tell me, O   170
    Child of golden Hope, immortal Voice.

Antistrophe 1

    Let me pray to Athene, the immortal daughter of Zeus,
    And to Artemis her sister
    Who keeps her famous throne in the market ring,

    And to Apollo, archer from distant heaven—   175

    O gods, descend! Like three streams leap against
    The fires of our grief, the fires of darkness;
    Be swift to bring us rest!

    As in the old time from the brilliant house
    Of air you stepped to save us, come again!   180

Strophe 2

    Now our afflictions have no end,
    Now all our stricken host lies down
    And no man fights off death with his mind;

    The noble plowland bears no grain,
    And groaning mothers can not bear—   185

See, how our lives like birds take wing,
Like sparks that fly when a fire soars,
To the shore of the god of evening.

Antistrophe 2

190   The plague burns on, it is pitiless,
Though pallid children laden with death
Lie unwept in the stony ways,

And old gray women by every path
Flock to the strand about the altars

There to strike their breasts and cry
195   Worship of Phoibos in wailing prayers:
Be kind, God's golden child!

Strophe 3

There are no swords in this attack by fire,
No shields, but we are ringed with cries.

Send the besieger plunging from our homes
200   Into the vast sea-room of the Atlantic
Or into the waves that foam eastward of Thrace—

For the day ravages what the night spares—

Destroy our enemy, lord of the thunder!
Let him be riven by lightning from heaven!

Antistrophe 3

205   Phoibos Apollo, stretch the sun's bowstring,
That golden cord, until it sing for us,
Flashing arrows in heaven!
Artemis, Huntress,
Race with flaring lights upon our mountains!

210   O scarlet god, O golden-banded brow,
O Theban Bacchos in a storm of Maenads,

(*Enter* OEDIPUS, *center.*)

Whirl upon Death, that all the Undying hate!
Come with blinding torches, come in joy!

SCENE I

OEDIPUS: Is this your prayer? It may be answered. Come,
Listen to me, act as the crisis demands,
And you shall have relief from all these evils.

Until now I was a stranger to this tale.
5   As I had been a stranger to the crime.
Could I track down the murderer without a clue?
But now, friends,
As one who became a citizen after the murder,
I make this proclamation to all Thebans:

10   If any man knows by whose hand Laïos, son of Labdakos,
Met his death, I direct that man to tell me everything,
No matter what he fears for having so long withheld it.
Let it stand as promised that no further trouble
Will come to him, but he may leave the land in safety.

15   Moreover: If anyone knows the murderer to be foreign,
Let him not keep silent: he shall have his reward from me.
However, if he does conceal it; if any man
Fearing for his friend or for himself disobeys this edict,
Hear what I propose to do:

I solemnly forbid the people of this country,   20
Where power and throne are mine, ever to receive that
    man
Or speak to him, no matter who he is, or let him
Join in sacrifice, lustration, or in prayer.
I decree that he be driven from every house,
Being, as he is, corruption itself to us: the Delphic   25
Voice of Apollo has pronounced this revelation.
Thus I associate myself with the oracle
And take the side of the murdered king.

As for the criminal, I pray to God—
Whether it be a lurking thief, or one of a number—   30
I pray that that man's life be consumed in evil and
    wretchedness.
And as for me, this curse applies no less
If it should turn out that the culprit is my guest here,
Sharing my hearth.
You have heard the penalty.   35

I lay it on you now to attend to this
For my sake, for Apollo's, for the sick
Sterile city that heaven has abandoned.
Suppose the oracle had given you no command:
Should this defilement go uncleansed for ever?   40
You should have found the murderer: your king,
A noble king, had been destroyed!
Now I,
Having the power that he held before me,
Having his bed, begetting children there   45
Upon his wife, as he would have, had he lived—
Their son would have been my children's brother,
If Laïos had had luck in fatherhood!
(And now his bad fortune has struck him down)—
I say I take the son's part, just as though   50
I were his son, to press the fight for him
And see it won! I'll find the hand that brought
Death to Labdakos' and Polydoros' child,
Heir of Kadmos' and Agenor's line.
And as for those who fail me,   55
May the gods deny them the fruit of the earth,
Fruit of the womb, and may they rot utterly!
Let them be wretched as we are wretched, and worse!

For you, my loyal Thebans, and for all
Who find my actions right, I pray the favor   60
Of justice, and of all the immortal gods.
CHORAGOS: Since I am under oath, my lord, I swear
I did not do the murder, I can not name
The murderer. Phoibos ordained the search;
Why did he not say who the culprit was?   65
OEDIPUS: An honest question. But no man in the world
Can make the gods do more than the gods will.
CHORAGOS: There is an alternative, I think—
OEDIPUS: Tell me.
Any or all, you must not fail to tell me.   70
CHORAGOS: A lord clairvoyant to the lord Apollo,
As we all know, is the skilled Teiresias.
One might learn much about this from him, Oedipus.
OEDIPUS: I am not wasting time:
Kreon spoke of this, and I have sent for him—   75
Twice, in fact; it is strange that he is not here.

CHORAGOS: The other matter—that old report—seems
   useless.
OEDIPUS: What was that? I am interested in all reports.
CHORAGOS: The King was said to have been killed by
   highwaymen.
80 OEDIPUS: I know. But we have no witnesses to that.
CHORAGOS: If the killer can feel a particle of dread,
   Your curse will bring him out of hiding!
OEDIPUS: No.
   The man who dared that act will fear no curse.

(Enter the blind seer TEIRESIAS, *led by a* PAGE.)

85 CHORAGOS: But there is one man who may detect the
      criminal.
   This is Teiresias, this is the holy prophet
   In whom, alone of all men, truth was born.
OEDIPUS: Teiresias: seer: student of mysteries,
   Of all that's taught and all that no man tells,
90 Secrets of Heaven and secrets of the earth:
   Blind though you are, you know the city lies
   Sick with plague; and from this plague, my lord,
   We find that you alone can guard or save us.

   Possibly you did not hear the messengers?
95 Apollo, when we sent to him,
   Sent us back word that this great pestilence
   Would lift, but only if we established clearly
   The identity of those who murdered Laïos.
   They must be killed or exiled.
100 Can you use
   Birdflight or any art of divination
   To purify yourself, and Thebes, and me
   From this contagion? We are in your hands.
   There is no fairer duty
105 Than that of helping others in distress.
TEIRESIAS: How dreadful knowledge of the truth can be
   When there's no help in truth! I knew this well,
   But did not act on it: else I should not have come.
OEDIPUS: What is troubling you? Why are your eyes so cold?
110 TEIRESIAS: Let me go home. Bear your own fate, and I'll
   Bear mine. It is better so: trust what I say.
OEDIPUS: What you say is ungracious and unhelpful
   To your native country. Do not refuse to speak.
TEIRESIAS: When it comes to speech, your own is neither
      temperate
115 Nor opportune. I wish to be more prudent.
OEDIPUS: In God's name, we all beg you—
TEIRESIAS: You are all ignorant.
   No; I will never tell you what I know.
   Now it is my misery; then it would be yours.
120 OEDIPUS: What! You do know something, and will not tell us?
   You would betray us all and wreck the State?
TEIRESIAS: I do not intend to torture myself, or you.
   Why persist in asking? You will not persuade me.
OEDIPUS: What a wicked old man you are! You'd try a stone's
125 Patience! Out with it. Have you no feeling at all?
TEIRESIAS: You call me unfeeling. If you could only see
   The nature of your own feelings . . .
OEDIPUS: Why,
   Who would not feel as I do? Who could endure
130 Your arrogance toward the city?

TEIRESIAS: What does it matter?
   Whether I speak or not, it is bound to come.
OEDIPUS: Then, if 'it' is bound to come, you are bound to
   tell me.
TEIRESIAS: No, I will not go on. Rage as you please.
OEDIPUS: Rage? Why not!   135
   And I'll tell you what I think:
   You planned it, you had it done, you all but
   Killed him with your own hands: if you had eyes,
   I'd say the crime was yours, and yours alone.
TEIRESIAS: So? I charge you, then,   140
   Abide by the proclamation you have made:
   From this day forth
   Never speak again to these men or to me;
   You yourself are the pollution of this country.
OEDIPUS: You dare say that! Can you possibly think you have 145
   Some way of going free, after such insolence?
TEIRESIAS: I have gone free. It is the truth sustains me.
OEDIPUS: Who taught you shamelessness? It was not your
      craft.
TEIRESIAS: You did. You made me speak. I did not want to.
OEDIPUS: Speak what? Let me hear it again more clearly.   150
TEIRESIAS: Was it not clear before? Are you tempting me?
OEDIPUS: I did not understand it. Say it again.
TEIRESIAS: I say that you are the murderer whom you seek.
OEDIPUS: Now twice you have spat out infamy. You'll pay
   for it!
TEIRESIAS: Would you care for more? Do you wish to be   155
   really angry?
OEDIPUS: Say what you will. Whatever you say is worthless.
TEIRESIAS: I say you live in hideous shame with those
   Most dear to you. You can not see the evil.
OEDIPUS: Can you go on babbling like this for ever?
TEIRESIAS: I can, if there is power in truth.   160
OEDIPUS: There is:
   But not for you, not for you,
   You sightless, witless, senseless, mad old man!
TEIRESIAS: You are the madman. There is no one here
   Who will not curse you soon, as you curse me.   165
OEDIPUS: You child of total night! I would not touch you;
   Neither would any man who sees the sun.
TEIRESIAS: True: it is not from you my fate will come.
   That lies within Apollo's competence,
   As it is his concern.   170
OEDIPUS: Tell me, who made
   These fine discoveries? Kreon? Or someone else?
TEIRESIAS: Kreon is no threat. You weave your own doom.
OEDIPUS: Wealth, power, craft of statesmanship!
   Kingly position, everywhere admired!   175
   What savage envy is stored up against these,
   If Kreon, whom I trusted, Kreon my friend,
   For this great office which the city once
   Put in my hands unsought—if for this power
   Kreon desires in secret to destroy me!   180

   He has brought this decrepit fortune-teller, this
   Collector of dirty pennies, this prophet fraud—
   Why, he is no more clairvoyant than I am!
   Tell us:
   Has your mystic mummery ever approached the truth?   185
   When that hellcat the Sphinx was performing here,

What help were you to these people?
Her magic was not for the first man who came along:
It demanded a real exorcist. Your birds—
190 What good were they? or the gods, for the matter of that?
But I came by,
Oedipus, the simple man, who knows nothing—
I thought it out for myself, no birds helped me!
And this is the man you think you can destroy,
195 That you may be close to Kreon when he's king!
Well, you and your friend Kreon, it seems to me,
Will suffer most. If you were not an old man,
You would have paid already for your plot.

CHORAGOS: We can not see that his words or yours
200 Have been spoken except in anger, Oedipus,
And of anger we have no need. How to accomplish
The god's will best: that is what most concerns us.

TEIRESIAS: You are a king. But where argument's concerned
I am your man, as much a king as you.
205 I am not your servant, but Apollo's.
I have no need of Kreon's name.

Listen to me. You mock my blindness, do you?
But I say that you, with both your eyes, are blind:
You can not see the wretchedness of your life,
210 Nor in whose house you live, no, nor with whom.
Who are your father and mother? Can you tell me?
You do not even know the blind wrongs
That you have done them, on earth and in the world
    below.
But the double lash of your parents' curse will whip you
215 Out of this land some day, with only night
Upon your precious eyes.
Your cries then—where will they not be heard?
What fastness of Kithairon will not echo them?
And that bridal-descant of yours—you'll know it then,
220 The song they sang when you came here to Thebes
And found your misguided berthing.
All this, and more, that you can not guess at now,
Will bring you to yourself among your children.

Be angry, then. Curse Kreon. Curse my words.
225 I tell you, no man that walks upon the earth
Shall be rooted out more horribly than you.

OEDIPUS: Am I to bear this from him?—Damnation
Take you! Out of this place! Out of my sight!

TEIRESIAS: I would not have come at all if you had not
    asked me.
230 OEDIPUS: Could I have told that you'd talk nonsense, that
You'd come here to make a fool of yourself, and of me?

TEIRESIAS: A fool? Your parents thought me sane enough.

OEDIPUS: My parents again!—Wait: who were my parents?

TEIRESIAS: This day will give you a father, and break your
    heart.

235 OEDIPUS: Your infantile riddles! Your damned abracadabra!

TEIRESIAS: You were a great man once at solving
    riddles.

OEDIPUS: Mock me with that if you like; you will find it true.

TEIRESIAS: It was true enough. It brought about your ruin.

OEDIPUS: But if it saved this town?

240 TEIRESIAS (*To the* PAGE.): Boy, give me your hand.

OEDIPUS: Yes, boy; lead him away.
    —While you are here

We can do nothing. Go; leave us in peace.

TEIRESIAS: I will go when I have said what I have to say.
How can you hurt me? And I tell you again: 245
The man you have been looking for all this time,
The damned man, the murderer of Laïos,
That man is in Thebes. To your mind he is foreign-born,
But it will soon be shown that he is a Theban,
A revelation that will fail to please. 250
A blind man,
Who has his eyes now; a penniless man, who is rich now;
And he will go tapping the strange earth with his staff.
To the children with whom he lives now he will be
Brother and father—the very same; to her 255
Who bore him, son and husband—the very same
Who came to his father's bed, wet with his father's blood.

Enough. Go think that over.
If later you find error in what I have said,
You may say that I have no skill in prophecy. 260

(*Exit* TEIRESIAS, *led by his* PAGE. OEDIPUS *goes into the palace.*)

ODE I

Strophe 1

CHORUS: The Delphic stone of prophecies
Remembers ancient regicide
And a still bloody hand.
That killer's hour of flight has come.
He must be stronger than riderless 265
Coursers of untiring wind,
For the son of Zeus armed with his father's thunder
Leaps in lightning after him;
And the Furies hold his track, the sad Furies.

Antistrophe 1

Holy Parnassos' peak of snow 270
Flashes and blinds that secret man,
That all shall hunt him down:
Though he may roam the forest shade
Like a bull gone wild from pasture
To rage through glooms of stone. 275
Doom comes down on him; flight will not avail him;
For the world's heart calls him desolate,
And the immortal voices follow, for ever follow.

Strophe 2

But now a wilder thing is heard
From the old man skilled at hearing Fate in the wingbeat of 280
    a bird.
Bewildered as a blown bird, my soul hovers and can not
    find
Foothold in this debate, or any reason or rest of mind.
But no man ever brought—none can bring
Proof of strife between Thebes' royal house,
Labdakos' line, and the son of Polybos; 285
And never until now has any man brought word
Of Laïos' dark death staining Oedipus the King.

Antistrophe 2

Divine Zeus and Apollo hold
Perfect intelligence alone of all tales ever told;
And well though this diviner works, he works in his own 290
    night;

No man can judge that rough unknown or trust in second
   sight,
For wisdom changes hands among the wise.
Shall I believe my great lord criminal
At a raging word that a blind old man let fall?
295 I saw him, when the carrion woman faced him of old,
Prove his heroic mind. These evil words are lies.

SCENE II

KREON: Men of Thebes:
  I am told that heavy accusations
  Have been brought against me by King Oedipus.

  I am not the kind of man to bear this tamely.

5 If in these present difficulties
  He holds me accountable for any harm to him
  Through anything I have said or done—why, then,
  I do not value life in this dishonor.

  It is not as though this rumor touched upon
10 Some private indiscretion. The matter is grave.
  The fact is that I am being called disloyal
  To the State, to my fellow citizens, to my friends.
CHORAGOS: He may have spoken in anger, not from his
    mind.
KREON: But did you not hear him say I was the one
15 Who seduced the old prophet into lying?
CHORAGOS: The thing was said: I do not know how seriously.
KREON: But you were watching him! Were his eyes steady?
  Did he look like a man in his right mind?
CHORAGOS: I do not know.
20 I can not judge the behavior of great men.
  But here is the King himself.

(Enter OEDIPUS.*)*

OEDIPUS: So you dared come back.
  Why? How brazen of you to come to my house,
  You murderer!
25 Do you think I do not know
  That you plotted to kill me, plotted to steal my throne?
  Tell me, in God's name: am I coward, a fool,
  That you should dream you could accomplish this?
  A fool who could not see your slippery game?
30 A coward, not to fight back when I saw it?
  You are the fool, Kreon, are you not? hoping
  Without support or friends to get a throne?
  Thrones may be won or bought: you could do neither.
KREON: Now listen to me. You have talked; let me talk, too.
35 You can not judge unless you know the facts.
OEDIPUS: You speak well: there is one fact; but I find it hard
  To learn from the deadliest enemy I have.
KREON: That above all I must dispute with you.
OEDIPUS: That above all I will not hear you deny.
40 KREON: If you think there is anything good in being stubborn
  Against all reason, then I say you are wrong.
OEDIPUS: If you think a man can sin against his own kind
  And not be punished for it, I say you are mad.
KREON: I agree. But tell me: what have I done to you?
45 OEDIPUS: You advised me to send for that wizard, did you
    not?
KREON: I did. I should do it again.

OEDIPUS: Very well. Now tell me:
  How long has it been since Laïos—
KREON: What of Laïos?
OEDIPUS: Since he vanished in that onset by the road?   50
KREON: It was long ago, a long time.
OEDIPUS: And this prophet,
  Was he practicing here then?
KREON: He was; and with honor, as now.
OEDIPUS: Did he speak of me at that time?   55
KREON: He never did;
  At least, not when I was present.
OEDIPUS: But . . . the enquiry?
  I suppose you held one?
KREON: We did, but we learned nothing.   60
OEDIPUS: Why did the prophet not speak against me then?
KREON: I do not know; and I am the kind of man
  Who holds his tongue when he has no facts to go on.
OEDIPUS: There's one fact that you know, and you could
    tell it.
KREON: What fact is that? If I know it, you shall have it.   65
OEDIPUS: If he were not involved with you, he could not say
  That it was I who murdered Laïos.
KREON: If he says that, you are the one that knows it!—
  But now it is my turn to question you.
OEDIPUS: Put your questions. I am no murderer.   70
KREON: First, then: You married my sister?
OEDIPUS: I married your sister.
KREON: And you rule the kingdom equally with her?
OEDIPUS: Everything that she wants she has from me.
KREON: And I am the third, equal to both of you?   75
OEDIPUS: That is why I call you a bad friend.
KREON: No. Reason it out, as I have done.
  Think of this first: Would any sane man prefer
  Power, with all a king's anxieties,
  To that same power and the grace of sleep?   80
  Certainly not I.
  I have never longed for the king's power—only his rights.
  Would any wise man differ from me in this?
  As matters stand, I have my way in everything
  With your consent, and no responsibilities.   85
  If I were king, I should be a slave to policy.
  How could I desire a sceptre more
  Than what is now mine—untroubled influence?
  No, I have not gone mad; I need no honors,
  Except those with the perquisites I have now.   90
  I am welcome everywhere; every man salutes me,
  And those who want your favor seek my ear,
  Since I know how to manage what they ask.
  Should I exchange this ease for that anxiety?
  Besides, no sober mind is treasonable.   95
  I hate anarchy
  And never would deal with any man who likes it.
  Test what I have said. Go to the priestess
  At Delphi, ask if I quoted her correctly.
  And as for this other thing: If I am found   100
  Guilty of treason with Teiresias,
  Then sentence me to death. You have my word
  It is a sentence I should cast my vote for—
  But not without evidence!
  You do wrong   105
  When you take good men for bad, bad men for good.

A true friend thrown aside—why, life itself
Is not more precious!
In time you will know this well:
110   For time, and time alone, will show the just man,
Though scoundrels are discovered in a day.
CHORAGOS: This is well said, and a prudent man would
    ponder it.
Judgments too quickly formed are dangerous.
OEDIPUS: But is he not quick in his duplicity?
115   And shall I not be quick to parry him?
Would you have me stand still, hold my peace, and let
This man win everything, through my inaction?
KREON: And you want—what is it, then? To banish me?
OEDIPUS: No, not exile. It is your death I want,
120   So that all the world may see what treason means.
KREON: You will persist then? You will not believe me?
OEDIPUS: How can I believe you?
KREON: Then you are a fool.
OEDIPUS: To save myself?
125   KREON: In justice, think of me.
OEDIPUS: You are evil incarnate.
KREON: But suppose that you are wrong?
OEDIPUS: Still I must rule.
KREON: But not if you rule badly.
130   OEDIPUS: O city, city!
KREON: It is my city, too!
CHORAGOS: Now, my lords, be still. I see the Queen,
    Iokastê, coming from her palace chambers;
And it is time she came, for the sake of you both,
135   This dreadful quarrel can be resolved through her.

(Enter IOKASTE.*)*

IOKASTE: Poor foolish men, what wicked din is this?
    With Thebes sick to death, is it not shameful
That you should rake some private quarrel up?

(To OEDIPUS.*)*

    Come into the house.
140   And you, Kreon, go now:
Let us have no more of this tumult over nothing.
KREON: Nothing? No, sister: what your husband plans for me
    Is one of two great evils: exile or death.
OEDIPUS: He is right.
145   Why, woman I have caught him squarely
Plotting against my life.
KREON: No! Let me die
    Accurst if ever I have wished you harm!
IOKASTE: Ah, believe it, Oedipus!
150   In the name of the gods, respect this oath of his
For my sake, for the sake of these people here!

Strophe 1

CHORAGOS: Open your mind to her, my lord. Be ruled by
    her, I beg you!
OEDIPUS: What would you have me do?
CHORAGOS: Respect Kreon's word. He has never spoken like
    a fool,
155   And now he has sworn an oath.
OEDIPUS: You know what you ask?
CHORAGOS: I do.

OEDIPUS: Speak on, then.
CHORAGOS: A friend so sworn should not be baited so,
    In blind malice, and without final proof.   160
OEDIPUS: You are aware, I hope, that what you say
    Means death for me, or exile at the least.

Strophe 2

CHORAGOS: No, I swear by Helios, first in Heaven!
    May I die friendless and accurst,
The worst of deaths, if ever I meant that!   165
    It is the withering fields
That hurt my sick heart:
Must we bear all these ills,
    And now your bad blood as well?
OEDIPUS: Then let him go. And let me die, if I must,   170
    Or be driven by him in shame from the land of Thebes.
It is your unhappiness, and not his talk,
That touches me.
As for him—
    Wherever he goes, hatred will follow him.   175
KREON: Ugly in yielding, as you were ugly in rage!
    Natures like yours chiefly torment themselves.
OEDIPUS: Can you not go? Can you not leave me?
KREON: I can.
    You do not know me; but the city knows me,   180
And in its eyes I am just, if not in yours.

(Exit KREON.*)*

Antistrophe 1

CHORAGOS: Lady Iokastê, did you not ask the King to go to
    his chambers?
IOKASTE: First tell me what has happened.
CHORAGOS: There was suspicion without evidence; yet
    it rankled
As even false charges will.   185
IOKASTE: On both sides?
CHORAGOS: On both.
IOKASTE: But what was said?
CHORAGOS: Oh let it rest, let it be done with!
    Have we not suffered enough?   190
OEDIPUS: You see to what your decency has brought you:
    You have made difficulties where my heart saw none.

Antistrophe 2

CHORAGOS: Oedipus, it is not once only I have told you—
    You must know I should count myself unwise
To the point of madness, should I now forsake you—   195
    You, under whose hand,
        In the storm of another time,
    Our dear land sailed out free.
        But now stand fast at the helm!

IOKASTE: In God's name, Oedipus, inform your wife as well: 200
    Why are you so set in this hard anger?
OEDIPUS: I will tell you, for none of these men deserves
    My confidence as you do. It is Kreon's work,
His treachery, his plotting against me.
IOKASTE: Go on, if you can make this clear to me.   205
OEDIPUS: He charges me with the murder of Laïos.
IOKASTE: Has he some knowledge? Or does he speak from
    hearsay?

OEDIPUS: He would not commit himself to such a charge,
But he has brought in that damnable soothsayer
210 To tell his story.
IOKASTE: Set your mind at rest.
If it is a question of soothsayers, I tell you
That you will find no man whose craft gives knowledge
Of the unknowable.

215 Here is my proof:
An oracle was reported to Laïos once
(I will not say from Phoibos himself, but from
His appointed ministers, at any rate)
That his doom would be death at the hands of his own
son—
220 His son, born of his flesh and of mine!

Now, you remember the story: Laïos was killed
By marauding strangers where three highways meet;
But his child had not been three days in this world
Before the King had pierced the baby's ankles
225 And left him to die on a lonely mountainside.
Thus, Apollo never caused that child
To kill his father, and it was not Laïos' fate
To die at the hands of his son, as he had feared.
This is what prophets and prophecies are worth!
230 Have no dread of them.
It is God himself
Who can show us what he wills, in his own way.
OEDIPUS: How strange a shadowy memory crossed my mind,
Just now while you were speaking; it chilled my heart.
235 IOKASTE: What do you mean? What memory do you speak
of?
OEDIPUS: If I understand you, Laïos was killed
At a place where thee roads meet.
IOKASTE: So it was said;
We have no later story.
240 OEDIPUS: Where did it happen?
IOKASTE: Phokis, it is called: at a place where the Theban
Way
Divides into the roads toward Delphi and Daulia.
OEDIPUS: When?
IOKASTE: We had the news not long before you came
245 And proved the right to your succession here.
OEDIPUS: Ah, what net has God been weaving for me?
IOKASTE: Oedipus! Why does this trouble you?
OEDIPUS: Do not ask me yet.
First, tell me how Laïos looked, and tell me
250 How old he was.
IOKASTE: He was tall, his hair just touched
With white; his form was not unlike your own.
OEDIPUS: I think that I myself may be accurst
By my own ignorant edict.
255 IOKASTE: You speak strangely.
It makes me tremble to look at you, my King.
OEDIPUS: I am not sure that the blind man can not see.
But I should know better if you were to tell me—
IOKASTE: Anything—though I dread to hear you ask it.
260 OEDIPUS: Was the King lightly escorted, or did he ride
With a large company, as a ruler should?
IOKASTE: There were five men with him in all: one was
a herald;

And a single chariot, which he was driving.
OEDIPUS: Alas, that makes it plain enough!
But who—   265
Who told you how it happened?
IOKASTE: A household servant,
The only one to escape.
OEDIPUS: And is he still
A servant of ours?   270
IOKASTE: No; for when he came back at last
And found you enthroned in the place of the dead king,
He came to me, touched my hand with his, and begged
That I would send him away to the frontier district
Where only the shepherds go—   275
As far away from the city as I could send him.
I granted his prayer; for although the man was a slave,
He had earned more than this favor at my hands.
OEDIPUS: Can he be called back quickly?
IOKASTE: Easily.   280
But why?
OEDIPUS: I have taken too much upon myself
Without enquiry; therefore I wish to consult him.
IOKASTE: Then he shall come.
But am I not one also   285
To whom you might confide these fears of yours?
OEDIPUS: That is your right; it will not be denied you,
Now least of all; for I have reached a pitch
Of wild foreboding. Is there anyone
To whom I should sooner speak?   290
Polybos of Corinth is my father.
My mother is a Dorian: Meropê.
I grew up chief among the men of Corinth
Until a strange thing happened—
Not worth my passion, it may be, but strange.   295

At a feast, a drunken man maundering in his cups
Cries out that I am not my father's son!
I contained myself that night, though I felt anger
And a sinking heart. The next day I visited
My father and mother, and questioned them. They   300
stormed,
Calling it all the slanderous rant of a fool;
And this relieved me. Yet the suspicion
Remained always aching in my mind;
I knew there was talk; I could not rest;
And finally, saying nothing to my parents,   305
I went to the shrine at Delphi.

The god dismissed my question without reply;
He spoke of other things.
Some were clear,
Full of wretchedness, dreadful, unbearable: 310
As, that I should lie with my own mother, breed
Children from whom all men would turn their eyes;
And that I should be my father's murderer.

I heard all this, and fled. And from that day
Corinth to me was only in the stars   315
Descending in that quarter of the sky,
As I wandered farther and farther on my way
To a land where I should never see the evil
Sung by the oracle. And I came to this country
Where, so you say, King Laïos was killed.   320

I will tell you all that happened there, my lady.

There were three highways
Coming together at a place I passed;
And there a herald came towards me, and a chariot
325 Drawn by horses, with a man such as you describe
Seated in it. The groom leading the horses
Forced me off the road at his lord's command;
But as this charioteer lurched over towards me
I struck him in my rage. The old man saw me
330 And brought his double goad down upon my head
As I came abreast.
He was paid back, and more!
Swinging my club in this right hand I knocked him
Out of his car, and he rolled on the ground.
335 I killed him.
I killed them all.
Now if that stranger and Laïos were—kin,
Where is a man more miserable than I?
More hated by the gods? Citizen and alien alike
340 Must never shelter me or speak to me—
I must be shunned by all.
And I myself
Pronounced this malediction upon myself!

Think of it: I have touched you with these hands,
345 These hands that killed your husband. What defilement!

Am I all evil, then? It must be so,
Since I must flee from Thebes, yet never again
See my own countrymen, my own country,
For fear of joining my mother in marriage
350 And killing Polybos, my father.
Ah,
If I was created so, born to this fate,
Who could deny the savagery of God?

O holy majesty of heavenly powers!
355 May I never see that day! Never!
Rather let me vanish from the race of men
Than know the abomination destined me!
CHORAGOS: We too, my lord, have felt dismay at this.
But there is hope: you have yet to hear the shepherd.
360 OEDIPUS: Indeed, I fear no other hope is left me.
IOKASTE: What do you hope from him when he comes?
OEDIPUS: This much:
If his account of the murder tallies with yours,
Then I am cleared.
365 IOKASTE: What was it that I said
Of such importance?
OEDIPUS: Why, 'marauders', you said,
Killed the King, according to this man's story.
If he maintains that still, if there were several,
370 Clearly the guilt is not mine: I was alone.
But if he says one man, singlehanded, did it,
Then the evidence all points to me.
IOKASTE: You may be sure that he said there were several;
And can he call back that story now? He can not.
375 The whole city heard it as plainly as I.
But suppose he alters some detail of it:
He can not ever show that Laïos' death
Fulfilled the oracle: for Apollo said

My child was doomed to kill him; and my child—
Poor baby!—it was my child that died first. 380

No. From now on, where oracles are concerned,
I would not waste a second thought on any.
OEDIPUS: You may be right.
But come: let someone go
For the shepherd at once. This matter must be settled. 385
IOKASTE: I will send for him.
I would not wish to cross you in anything,
And surely not in this.—Let us go in.

(*Exeunt into the palace.*)

ODE II
Strophe 1
CHORUS: Let me be reverent in the ways of right,
Lowly the paths I journey on; 390
Let all my words and actions keep
The laws of the pure universe
From highest Heaven handed down.
For Heaven is their bright nurse,
Those generations of the realms of light; 395
Ah, never of mortal kind were they begot,
Nor are they slaves of memory, lost in sleep:
Their Father is greater than Time, and ages not.

Antistrophe 1
The tyrant is a child of Pride
Who drinks from his great sickening cup 400
Recklessness and vanity,
Until from his high crest headlong
He plummets to the dust of hope.
That strong man is not strong.
But let no fair ambition be denied; 405
May God protect the wrestler for the State
In government, in comely policy,
Who will fear God, and on His ordinance wait.

Strophe 2
Haughtiness and the high hand of disdain
Tempt and outrage God's holy law; 410
And any mortal who dares hold
No immortal Power in awe
Will be caught up in a net of pain:
The price for which his levity is sold.
Let each man take due earnings, then, 415
And keep his hands from holy things,
And from blasphemy stand apart—
Else the crackling blast of heaven
Blows on his head, and on his desperate heart.
Though fools will honor impious men, 420
In their cities no tragic poet sings.

Antistrophe 2
Shall we lose faith in Delphi's obscurities,
We who have heard the world's core
Discredited, and the sacred wood
Of Zeus at Elis praised no more? 425
The deeds and the strange prophecies
Must make a pattern yet to be understood.

Zeus, if indeed you are lord of all,
Throned in light over night and day,
430   Mirror this in your endless mind:
Our masters call the oracle
Words on the wind, and the Delphic vision blind!
Their hearts no longer know Apollo,
And reverence for the gods has died away.

SCENE III

(Enter IOKASTE.*)*

IOKASTE: Princes of Thebes, it has occurred to me
To visit the altars of the gods, bearing
These branches as a suppliant, and this incense.
Our King is not himself: his noble soul
5   Is overwrought with fantasies of dread,
Else he would consider
The new prophecies in the light of the old.
He will listen to any voice that speaks disaster,
And my advice goes for nothing.

(She approaches the altar, right.)

10   To you, then, Apollo,
Lycéan lord, since you are nearest, I turn in prayer.

Receive these offerings, and grant us deliverance
From defilement. Our hearts are heavy with fear
When we see our leader distracted, as helpless sailors
15   Are terrified by the confusion of their helmsman.

(Enter MESSENGER.*)*

MESSENGER: Friends, no doubt you can direct me:
Where shall I find the house of Oedipus,
Or, better still, where is the King himself?
CHORAGOS: It is this very place, stranger; he is inside.
20   This is his wife and mother of his children.
MESSENGER: I wish her happiness in a happy house,
Blest in all the fulfillment of her marriage.
IOKASTE: I wish as much for you: your courtesy
Deserves a like good fortune. But now, tell me:
25   Why have you come? What have you to say to us?
MESSENGER: Good news, my lady, for your house and your
husband.
IOKASTE: What news? Who sent you here?
MESSENGER: I am from Corinth.
The news I bring ought to mean joy for you,
30   Though it may be you will find some grief in it.
IOKASTE: What is it? How can it touch us in both ways?
MESSENGER: The word is that the people of the Isthmus
Intend to call Oedipus to be their king.
IOKASTE: But old King Polybos—is he not reigning still?
35   MESSENGER: No. Death holds him in his sepulchre.
IOKASTE: What are you saying? Polybos is dead?
MESSENGER: If I am not telling the truth, may I die myself.
IOKASTE *(To a* MAIDSERVANT.*):* Go in, go quickly; tell this to
your master.

O riddlers of God's will, where are you now!
40   This was the man whom Oedipus, long ago,
Feared so, fled so, in dread of destroying him—
But it was another fate by which he died.

(Enter OEDIPUS, *center.)*

OEDIPUS: Dearest Iokastê, why have you sent for me?
IOKASTE: Listen to what this man says, and then tell me
What has become of the solemn prophecies.   45
OEDIPUS: Who is this man? What is his news for me?
IOKASTE: He has come from Corinth to announce your
father's death!
OEDIPUS: Is it true, stranger? Tell me in your own words.
MESSENGER: I can not say it more clearly: the King is dead.
OEDIPUS: Was it by treason? Or by an attack of illness?   50
MESSENGER: A little thing brings old men to their rest.
OEDIPUS: It was sickness, then?
MESSENGER: Yes, and his many years.
OEDIPUS: Ah!
Why should a man respect the Pythian hearth, or   55
Give heed to the birds that jangle above his head?
They prophesied that I should kill Polybos,
Kill my own father; but he is dead and buried,
And I am here—I never touched him, never,
Unless he died of grief for my departure,   60
And thus, in a sense, through me. No. Polybos
Has packed the oracles off with him underground.
They are empty words.
IOKASTE: Had I not told you so?
OEDIPUS: You had; it was my faint heart that betrayed me. 65
IOKASTE: From now on never think of those things again.
OEDIPUS: And yet—must I not fear my mother's bed?
IOKASTE: Why should anyone in this world be afraid,
Since Fate rules us and nothing can be foreseen?
A man should live only for the present day.   70

Have no more fear of sleeping with your mother:
How many men, in dreams, have lain with their mothers!
No reasonable man is troubled by such things.
OEDIPUS: That is true; only—
If only my mother were not still alive!   75
But she is alive. I can not help my dread.
IOKASTE: Yet this news of your father's death is wonderful.
OEDIPUS: Wonderful. But I fear the living woman.
MESSENGER: Tell me, who is this woman that you fear?
OEDIPUS: It is Meropê, man; the wife of King Polybos.   80
MESSENGER: Meropê? Why should you be afraid of her?
OEDIPUS: An oracle of the gods, a dreadful saying.
MESSENGER: Can you tell me about it or are you sworn
to silence?
OEDIPUS: I can tell you, and I will.
Apollo said through his prophet that I was the man   85
Who should marry his own mother, shed his father's blood
With his own hands. And so, for all these years
I have kept clear of Corinth, and no harm has come—
Though it would have been sweet to see my parents again.
MESSENGER: And is this the fear that drove you out of   90
Corinth?
OEDIPUS: Would you have me kill my father?
MESSENGER: As for that
You must be reassured by the news I gave you.
OEDIPUS: If you could reassure me, I would reward you.
MESSENGER: I had that in mind, I will confess: I thought   95
I could count on you when you returned to Corinth.
OEDIPUS: No: I will never go near my parents again.

MESSENGER: Ah, son, you still do not know what you are
doing—
OEDIPUS: What do you mean? In the name of God tell me!
100 MESSENGER: —If these are your reasons for not going home.
OEDIPUS: I tell you, I fear the oracle may come true.
MESSENGER: And guilt may come upon you through your
parents?
OEDIPUS: That is the dread that is always in my heart.
MESSENGER: Can you not see that all your fears are
groundless?
105 OEDIPUS: Groundless? Am I not my parents' son?
MESSENGER: Polybos was not your father.
OEDIPUS: Not my father?
MESSENGER: No more your father than the man speaking to
you.
OEDIPUS: But you are nothing to me!
110 MESSENGER: Neither was he.
OEDIPUS: Then why did he call me son?
MESSENGER: I will tell you:
Long ago he had you from my hands, as a gift.
OEDIPUS: Then how could he love me so, if I was not his?
115 MESSENGER: He had no children, and his heart turned to
you.
OEDIPUS: What of you? Did you buy me? Did you find me by
chance?
MESSENGER: I came upon you in the woody vales of
Kithairon.
OEDIPUS: And what were you doing there?
MESSENGER: Tending my flocks.
120 OEDIPUS: A wandering shepherd?
MESSENGER: But your savior, son, that day.
OEDIPUS: From what did you save me?
MESSENGER: Your ankles should tell you that.
OEDIPUS: Ah, stranger, why do you speak of that childhood
pain?
125 MESSENGER: I pulled the skewer that pinned your feet
together.
OEDIPUS: I have had the mark as long as I can remember.
MESSENGER: That was why you were given the name you
bear.
OEDIPUS: God! Was it my father or my mother who did it?
Tell me!
130 MESSENGER: I do not know. The man who gave you to me
Can tell you better than I.
OEDIPUS: It was not you that found me, but another?
MESSENGER: It was another shepherd gave you to me.
OEDIPUS: Who was he? Can you tell me who he was?
135 MESSENGER: I think he was said to be one of Laïos' people.
OEDIPUS: You mean the Laïos who was king here years ago?
MESSENGER: Yes; King Laïos; and the man was one of his
herdsmen.
OEDIPUS: Is he still alive? Can I see him?
MESSENGER: These men here
140 Know best about such things.
OEDIPUS: Does anyone here
Know this shepherd that he is talking about?
Have you seen him in the fields, or in the town?
If you have, tell me. It is time things were made plain.
145 CHORAGOS: I think the man he means is that same shepherd
You have already asked to see. Iokastê perhaps
Could tell you something.

OEDIPUS: Do you know anything
About him, Lady? Is he the man we have summoned?
Is that the man this shepherd means? 150
IOKASTE: Why think of him?
Forget this herdsman. Forget it all.
This talk is a waste of time.
OEDIPUS: How can you say that,
When the clues to my true birth are in my hands? 155
IOKASTE: For God's love, let us have no more questioning!
Is your life nothing to you?
My own is pain enough for me to bear.
MESSENGER: You need not worry. Suppose my mother a
slave,
And born of slaves: no baseness can touch you. 160
IOKASTE: Listen to me, I beg of you: do not do this thing!
OEDIPUS: I will not listen; the truth must be made known.
IOKASTE: Everything that I say is for your own good!
OEDIPUS: My own good
Snaps my patience, then; I want none of it. 165
IOKASTE: You are fatally wrong! May you never learn who you
are!
OEDIPUS: Go, one of you, and bring the shepherd here.
Let us leave this woman to brag of her royal name.
IOKASTE: Ah, miserable!
That is the only word I have for you now. 170
That is the only word I can ever have.

(Exit into the palace.)

CHORAGOS: Why has she left us, Oedipus? Why has she gone
In such a passion of sorrow? I fear this silence:
Something dreadful may come of it.
OEDIPUS: Let it come! 175
However base my birth, I must know about it.
The Queen, like a woman, is perhaps ashamed
To think of my low origin. But I
Am a child of Luck; I can not be dishonored.
Luck is my mother; the passing months, my brothers, 180
Have seen me rich and poor.
If this is so,
How could I wish that I were someone else?
How could I not be glad to know my birth?

ODE III

Strophe

CHORUS: If ever the coming time were known 185
To my heart's pondering,
Kithairon, now by Heaven I see the torches
At the festival of the next full moon,
And see the dance, and hear the choir sing
A grace to your gentle shade: 190
Mountain where Oedipus was found,
O mountain guard of a noble race!
May the god who heals us lend his aid,
And let that glory come to pass
For our King's cradling-ground. 195

Antistrophe

Of the nymphs that flower beyond the years,
Who bore you, royal child,
To Pan of the hills or the timberline Apollo,
Cold in delight where the upland clears,

200 Or Hermês for whom Kyllenês heights are piled?
    Or flushed as evening cloud,
    Great Dionysos, roamer of mountains,
    He—was it he who found you there,
    And caught you up in his own proud
205 Arms from the sweet god-ravisher
    Who laughed by the Muses' fountains?

SCENE IV

OEDIPUS: Sirs: though I do not know the man,
    I think I see him coming, this shepherd we want:
    He is old, like our friend here, and the men
    Bringing him seem to be servants of my house.
5   But you can tell, if you have ever seen him.

(Enter SHEPHERD *escorted by servants.)*

CHORAGOS: I know him, he was Laïos' man. You can trust
    him.
OEDIPUS: Tell me first, you from Corinth: is this the shepherd
    We were discussing?
MESSENGER: This is the very man.
10 OEDIPUS (*To* SHEPHERD.): Come here. No, look at me. You
    must answer
    Everything I ask.—You belonged to Laïos?
SHEPHERD: Yes: born his slave, brought up in his house.
OEDIPUS: Tell me: what kind of work did you do for him?
SHEPHERD: I was a shepherd of his, most of my life.
15 OEDIPUS: Where mainly did you go for pasturage?
SHEPHERD: Sometimes Kithairon, sometimes the hills
    near-by.
OEDIPUS: Do you remember ever seeing this man out there?
SHEPHERD: What would he be doing there? This man?
OEDIPUS: This man standing here. Have you ever seen him
    before?
20 SHEPHERD: No. At least, not to my recollection.
MESSENGER: And that is not strange, my lord. But I'll refresh
    His memory: he must remember when we two
    Spent three whole seasons together, March to September,
    On Kithairon or thereabouts. He had two flocks;
25 I had one. Each autumn I'd drive mine home
    And he would go back with his to Laïos' sheepfold.—
    Is this not true, just as I have described it?
SHEPHERD: True, yes; but it was all so long ago.
MESSENGER: Well, then: do you remember, back in those
    days,
30 That you gave me a baby boy to bring up as my own?
SHEPHERD: What if I did? What are you trying to say?
MESSENGER: King Oedipus was once that little child.
SHEPHERD: Damn you, hold your tongue!
OEDIPUS: No more of that!
35 It is your tongue needs watching, not this man's.
SHEPHERD: My King, my Master, what is it I have done
    wrong?
OEDIPUS: You have not answered his question about the boy.
SHEPHERD: He does not know . . . He is only making
    trouble . . .
OEDIPUS: Come, speak plainly, or it will go hard with you.
40 SHEPHERD: In God's name, do not torture an old man!
OEDIPUS: Come here, one of you; bind his arms behind him.
SHEPHERD: Unhappy king! What more do you wish to learn?

OEDIPUS: Did you give this man the child he speaks of?
SHEPHERD: I did.
    And I would to God I had died that very day.   45
OEDIPUS: You will die now unless you speak the truth.
SHEPHERD: Yet if I speak the truth, I am worse than dead.
OEDIPUS (*To* attendant.): He intends to draw it out,
    apparently—
SHEPHERD: No! I have told you already that I gave him the
    boy.
OEDIPUS: Where did you get him? From your house?   50
    From somewhere else?
SHEPHERD: Not from mine, no. A man gave him to me.
OEDIPUS: Is that man here? Whose house did he belong to?
SHEPHERD: For God's love, my King, do not ask me any
    more!
OEDIPUS: You are a dead man if I have to ask you again.
SHEPHERD: Then . . . Then the child was from the palace of   55
    Laïos.
OEDIPUS: A slave child? or a child of his own line?
SHEPHERD: Ah, I am on the brink of dreadful speech!
OEDIPUS: And I of dreadful hearing. Yet I must hear.
SHEPHERD: If you must be told, then . . .
    They said it was Laïos' child;   60
    But it is your wife who can tell you about that.
OEDIPUS: My wife!—Did she give it to you?
SHEPHERD: My lord, she did.
OEDIPUS: Do you know why?
SHEPHERD: I was told to get rid of it.   65
OEDIPUS: Oh heartless mother!
SHEPHERD: But in dread of prophecies . . .
OEDIPUS: Tell me.
SHEPHERD: It was said that the boy would kill his own father.
OEDIPUS: Then why did you give him over to this old man?   70
SHEPHERD: I pitied the baby, my King,
    And I thought that this man would take him far away
    To his own country.
    He saved him—but for what a fate!
    For if you are what this man says you are,   75
    No man living is more wretched than Oedipus.
OEDIPUS: Ah God!
    It was true!
    All the prophecies!
    —Now,   80
    O Light, may I look on you for the last time!
    I, Oedipus,
    Oedipus, damned in his birth, in his marriage damned,
    Damned in the blood he shed with his own hand!

(He rushes into the palace.)

ODE IV

Strophe 1

CHORUS: Alas for the seed of men.   85

    What measure shall I give these generations
    That breathe on the void and are void
    And exist and do not exist?

    Who bears more weight of joy
    Than mass of sunlight shifting in images,   90
    Or who shall make his thought stay on
    That down time drifts away?

Your splendor is all fallen.

O naked brow of wrath and tears,
95   O change of Oedipus!
I who saw your days call no man blest—
Your great days like ghosts gone.

Antistrophe 1

That mind was a strong bow.

Deep, how deep you drew it then, hard archer,
100   At a dim fearful range,

And brought dear glory down!

You overcame the stranger—
The virgin with her hooking lion claws—
And though death sang, stood like a tower
105   To make pale Thebes take heart.

Fortress against our sorrow!

True king, giver of laws,
Majestic Oedipus!
No prince in Thebes had ever such renown,
110   No prince won such grace of power.

Strophe 2

And now of all men ever known
Most pitiful is this man's story:
His fortunes are most changed, his state
Fallen to a low slave's
115   Ground under bitter fate.

O Oedipus, most royal one!
The great door that expelled you to the light
Gave at night—ah, gave night to your glory:
As to the father, to the fathering son.

120   All understood too late.

How could that queen whom Laïos won,
The garden that he harrowed at his height,
Be silent when that act was done?

Antistrophe 2

But all eyes fail before time's eye,
125   All actions come to justice there.
Your bed, your dread sirings,
Are brought to book at last.

Child by Laïos doomed to die,
Then doomed to lose that fortunate little death,
130   Would God you never took breath in this air
That with my wailing lips I take to cry:

For I weep the world's outcast.

I was blind, and now I can tell why:
Asleep, for you had given ease of breath
135   To Thebes, while the false years went by.

— EXODOS —

(*Enter, from the palace,* SECOND MESSENGER.)

SECOND MESSENGER: Elders of Thebes, most honored in
   this land,
What horrors are yours to see and hear, what weight

Of sorrow to be endured, if, true to your birth,
You venerate the line of Labdakos!
I think neither Istros nor Phasis, those great rivers,   5
Could purify this place of all the evil
It shelters now, or soon must bring to light—
Evil not done unconsciously, but willed.

The greatest griefs are those we cause ourselves.
CHORAGOS: Surely, friend, we have grief enough already;   10
   What new sorrow do you mean?
SECOND MESSENGER: The Queen is dead.
CHORAGOS: O miserable Queen! But at whose hand?
SECOND MESSENGER: Her own.
The full horror of what happened you can not know,   15
For you did not see it; but I, who did, will tell you
As clearly as I can how she met her death.

When she had left us,
In passionate silence, passing through the court,
She ran to her apartment in the house,   20
Her hair clutched by the fingers of both hands.
She closed the doors behind her; then, by that bed
Where long ago the fatal son was conceived—
That son who should bring about his father's death—
We heard her call upon Laïos, dead so many years,   25
And heard her wail for the double fruit of her marriage,
A husband by her husband, children by her child.

Exactly how she died I do not know:
For Oedipus burst in moaning and would not let us
Keep vigil to the end: it was by him   30
As he stormed about the room that our eyes were caught.
From one to another of us he went, begging a sword,
Hunting the wife who was not his wife, the mother
Whose womb had carried his own children and himself.
I do not know: it was none of us aided him,   35
But surely one of the gods was in control!
For with a dreadful cry
He hurled his weight, as though wrenched out of himself,
At the twin doors: the bolts gave, and he rushed in.
And there we saw her hanging, her body swaying   40
From the cruel cord she had noosed about her neck.
A great sob broke from him, heartbreaking to hear,
As he loosed the rope and lowered her to the ground.

I would blot out from my mind what happened next!
For the King ripped from her gown the golden brooches   45
That were her ornament, and raised them, and plunged
   them down
Straight into his own eyeballs, crying, 'No more,
No more shall you look on the misery about me,
The horrors of my own doing! Too long you have known
The faces of those whom I should never have seen,   50
Too long been blind to those for whom I was searching!
From this hour, go in darkness!' And as he spoke,
He struck at his eyes—not once, but many times;
And the blood spattered his beard,
Bursting from his ruined sockets like red hail.   55

So from the unhappiness of two this evil has sprung,
A curse on the man and woman alike. The old
Happiness of the house of Labdakos
Was happiness enough: where is it today?
It is all wailing and ruin, disgrace, death—all   60

The misery of mankind that has a name—
And it is wholly and for ever theirs.
CHORAGOS: Is he in agony still? Is there no rest for him?
SECOND MESSENGER: He is calling for someone to open the
doors wide
65 So that all the children of Kadmos may look upon
His father's murderer, his mother's—no,
I can not say it!
And then he will leave Thebes,
Self-exiled, in order that the curse
70 Which he himself pronounced may depart from the house.
He is weak, and there is none to lead him,
So terrible is his suffering.
But you will see:
Look, the doors are opening; in a moment
75 You will see a thing that would crush a heart of stone.

(*The central door is opened;* OEDIPUS, *blinded, is led in.*)

CHORAGOS: Dreadful indeed for men to see.
Never have my own eyes
Looked on a sight so full of fear.

Oedipus!
80 What madness came upon you, what daemon
Leaped on your life with heavier
Punishment than a mortal man can bear?
No: I can not even
Look at you, poor ruined one.
85 And I would speak, question, ponder,
If I were able. No.
You make me shudder.
OEDIPUS: God.   God.
Is there a sorrow greater?
90 Where shall I find harbor in this world?
My voice is hurled far on a dark wind.
What has God done to me?
CHORAGOS: Too terrible to think of, or to see.

Strophe 1

OEDIPUS: O cloud of night,
95 Never to be turned away: night coming on,
I can not tell how: night like a shroud!

My fair winds brought me here.
O God. Again
The pain of the spikes where I had sight,
100 The flooding pain
Of memory, never to be gouged out.
CHORAGOS: This is not strange.
You suffer it all twice over, remorse in pain,
Pain in remorse.

Antistrophe 1

105 OEDIPUS: Ah dear friend
Are you faithful even yet, you alone?
Are you still standing near me, will you stay here,
Patient, to care for the blind?
The blind man!
110 Yet even blind I know who it is attends me,
By the voice's tone—
Though my new darkness hide the comforter.
CHORAGOS: Oh fearful act!

What god was it drove you to rake black
Night across your eyes?   115

Strophe 2

OEDIPUS: Apollo. Apollo. Dear
Children, the god was Apollo.
He brought my sick, sick fate upon me.
But the blinding hand was my own!
How could I bear to see   120
When all my sight was horror everywhere?
CHORAGOS: Everywhere; that is true.
OEDIPUS: And now what is left?
Images? Love? A greeting even,
Sweet to the senses? Is there anything?   125
Ah, no, friends: lead me away.
Lead me away from Thebes.
Lead the great wreck
And hell of Oedipus, whom the gods hate.
CHORAGOS: Your misery, you are not blind to that.   130
Would God you had never found it out!

Antistrophe 2

OEDIPUS: Death take the man who unbound
My feet on the hillside
And delivered me from death to life! What life?
If only I had died,   135
This weight of monstrous doom
Could not have dragged me and my darlings down.
CHORAGOS: I would have wished the same.
OEDIPUS: Oh never to have come here
With my father's blood upon me! Never   140
To have been the man they call his mother's husband!
Oh accurst! Oh child of evil,
To have entered that wretched bed—
The selfsame one!
More primal than sin itself, this fell to me.   145
CHORAGOS: I do not know what words to offer you.
You were better dead than alive and blind.
OEDIPUS: Do not counsel me any more. This punishment
That I have laid upon myself is just.
If I had eyes,   150
I do not know how I could bear the sight
Of my father, when I came to the house of Death,
Or my mother: for I have sinned against them both
So vilely that I could not make my peace
By strangling my own life.   155
Or do you think my children,
Born as they were born, would be sweet to my eyes?
Ah never, never! Nor this town with its high walls,
Nor the holy images of the gods.
For I,   160
Thrice miserable!—Oedipus, noblest of all the line
Of Kadmos, have condemned myself to enjoy
These things no more, by my own malediction
Expelling that man whom the gods declared
To be a defilement in the house of Laïos.   165
After exposing the rankness of my own guilt,
How could I look men frankly in the eyes?
No, I swear it,
If I could have stifled my hearing at its source,
I would have done it, and made all this body   170

A tight cell of misery, blank to light and sound:
So I should have been safe in my dark mind
Beyond external evil.
Ah Kithairon!
175 Why did you shelter me? When I was cast upon you,
Why did I not die? Then I should never
Have shown the world my execrable birth.

Ah, Polybos! Corinth, city that I believed
The ancient seat of my ancestors: how fair
180 I seemed, your child! And all the while this evil
Was cancerous within me!
For I am sick
In my own being, sick in my origin,

O three roads, dark ravine, woodland and way
185 Where three roads met: you, drinking my father's blood,
My own blood, spilled by my own hand: can you remember
The unspeakable things I did there, and the things
I went on from there to do?
O marriage, marriage!
190 The act that engendered me, and again the act
Performed by the son in the same bed—
Ah, the net
Of incest, mingling fathers, brothers, sons,
With brides, wives, mothers: the last evil
195 That can be known by men: no tongue can say
How evil!
No. For the love of God, conceal me
Somewhere far from Thebes; or kill me; or hurl me
Into the sea, away from men's eyes for ever.
200 Come, lead me. You need not fear to touch me.
Of all men, I alone can bear this guilt.

(Enter KREON.*)*

CHORAGOS: Kreon is here now. As to what you ask,
He may decide the course to take. He only
Is left to protect the city in your place.
205 OEDIPUS: Alas, how can I speak to him? What right have I
To beg his courtesy whom I have deeply wronged?
KREON: I have not come to mock you, Oedipus,
Or to reproach you, either.

(To Attendants.)

—You, standing there:
210 If you have lost all respect for man's dignity,
At least respect the flame of Lord Helios:
Do not allow this pollution to show itself
Openly here, an affront to the earth
And Heaven's rain and the light of day. No, take him
215 Into the house as quickly as you can.
For it is proper
That only the close kindred see his grief.
OEDIPUS: I pray you in God's name, since your courtesy
Ignores my dark expectation, visiting
220 With mercy this man of all men most execrable:
Give me what I ask—for your good, not for mine.
KREON: And what is it that you turn to me begging for?
OEDIPUS: Drive me out of this country as quickly as may be
To a place where no human voice can ever greet me.
225 KREON: I should have done that before now—only,
God's will had not been wholly revealed to me.

OEDIPUS: But his command is plain: the parricide
Must be destroyed. I am that evil man.
KREON: That is the sense of it, yes; but as things are,
We had best discover clearly what is to be done.   230
OEDIPUS: You would learn more about a man like me?
KREON: You are ready now to listen to the god.
OEDIPUS: I will listen. But it is to you
That I must turn for help. I beg you, hear me.

The woman in there—   235
Give her whatever funeral you think proper:
She is your sister.
—But let me go, Kreon!
Let me purge my father's Thebes of the pollution
Of my living here, and go out to the wild hills,   240
To Kithairon, that has won such fame with me,
The tomb my mother and father appointed for me,
And let me die there, as they willed I should.
And yet I know
Death will not ever come to me through sickness   245
Or in any natural way: I have been preserved
For some unthinkable fate. But let that be.

As for my sons, you need not care for them.
They are men, they will find some way to live.
But my poor daughters, who have shared my table,   250
Who never before have been parted from their father—
Take care of them, Kreon; do this for me.
And will you let me touch them with my hands
A last time, and let us weep together?
Be kind, my lord,   255
Great prince, be kind!
Could I but touch them.
They would be mine again, as when I had my eyes.

(Enter ANTIGONE *and* ISMENE, *attended.)*

Ah, God!
Is it my dearest children I hear weeping?   260
Has Kreon pitied me and sent my daughters?
KREON: Yes, Oedipus: I knew that they were dear to you
In the old days, and you must love them still.
OEDIPUS: May God bless you for this—and be a friendlier
Guardian to you than he has been to me!   265

Children, where are you?
Come quickly to my hands: they are your brother's—
Hands that have brought your father's once clear eyes
To this way of seeing—
Ah dearest ones,   270
I had neither sight nor knowledge then, your father
By the woman who was the source of his own life!
And I weep for you—having no strength to see you—,
I weep for you when I think of the bitterness
That men will visit upon you all your lives.   275
What homes, what festivals can you attend
Without being forced to depart again in tears?
And when you come to marriageable age,
Where is the man, my daughters, who would dare
Risk the bane that lies on all my children?   280
Is there any evil wanting? Your father killed
His father; sowed the womb of her who bore him;
Engendered you at the fount of his own existence!

That is what they will say of you.

285   Then, whom
Can you ever marry? There are no bridegrooms for you,
And your lives must wither away in sterile dreaming.

O Kreon, son of Menoikeus!
You are the only father my daughters have,
290   Since we, their parents, are both of us gone for ever.
They are your own blood: you will not let them
Fall into beggary and loneliness;
You will keep them from the miseries that are mine!
Take pity on them; see, they are only children,
295   Friendless except for you. Promise me this,
Great Prince, and give me your hand in token of it.

(KREON clasps his right hand.)

Children:
I could say much, if you could understand me,
But as it is, I have only this prayer for you:
300   Live where you can, be as happy as you can—
Happier, please God, than God has made your father.

KREON: Enough. You have wept enough. Now go within.
OEDIPUS: I must; but it is hard.
KREON: Time eases all things.
305 OEDIPUS: You know my mind, then?
KREON: Say what you desire.

OEDIPUS: Send me from Thebes!
KREON: God grant that I may!
OEDIPUS: But since God hates me . . .
KREON: No, he will grant your wish.   310
OEDIPUS: You promise?
KREON: I can not speak beyond my knowledge.
OEDIPUS: Then lead me in.
KREON: Come now, and leave your children.
OEDIPUS: No! Do not take them from me!   315
KREON: Think no longer
That you are in command here, but rather think
How, when you were, you served your own destruction.

(Exeunt into the house all but the CHORUS; *the* CHORAGOS *chants directly to the audience.)*

CHORAGOS: Men of Thebes: look upon Oedipus.

This is the king who solved the famous riddle   320
And towered up, most powerful of men.
No mortal eyes but looked on him with envy,
Yet in the end ruin swept over him.

Let every man in mankind's frailty
Consider his last day; and let none   325
Presume on his good fortune until he find
Life, at his death, a memory without pain.

■ EURIPIDES ■

Euripides (c. 484–406 BC) was the youngest of the three tragic playwrights whose plays remain today. Although he first competed in the City Dionysia in 455 BC, and won his first victory in 441 BC, he won only four victories in his lifetime and left Athens about the year 408 BC for the court of King Archileus of Macedon, where he died. We do not know why Euripides won so infrequently, but his tragedies are much more bitter and ironic than those of Aeschylus or Sophocles, brilliantly unfolding the selfish capriciousness of gods and heroes alike. Of the roughly ninety plays Euripides is thought to have written, eighteen survive, and most of these were written and produced during the war with Sparta: *Alcestis, Medea, Heracleidae, Hippolytus, Cyclops* (a satyr play), *Heracles, Iphigeneia in Tauris, Helen, Hecuba, Andromache, The Trojan Women, Ion, The Suppliant Women, Orestes, Electra, The Phoenician Women.* Three additional plays—*Iphigeneia at Aulis, The Bacchae,* and *Alcmaeon at Corinth* (now lost)—were written in Macedon and brought to Athens by the playwright's son Euripides the Younger. This trilogy, produced after Euripides' death, won him his final prize at the City Dionysia.

MEDEA

Although many Greek tragedies center on female characters—think of Clytaemnestra in Aeschylus' *Agamemnon*, for example, or Sophocles' *Antigone*—Euripides was famous in Athens for centering his tragedies so frequently on women. Euripides was hardly a feminist in any modern sense, yet more than his contemporaries, Euripides used his tragic heroines to explore the relationship between gender and the other conceptual, political, social, and esthetic categories organizing Athenian life.

Like all roles in the Athenian theater, the role of Medea was played by a male actor; nonetheless, in many ways *Medea* illustrates Euripides' skeptical and ironic regard for conventional attitudes, and his tendency toward a more sensational form of tragic action. Like Shakespeare's *Hamlet*, *Medea* is a tragedy of revenge, in which Medea poisons her husband Jason's newly married wife and her father Creon, and in the play's climactic moment executes her own children from her marriage with Jason. What sometimes seems most monstrous to modern readers and audiences is that Medea herself—in one of Euripides' most striking uses of the *machina*—flees Corinth alive at the end of the play, rising above the *skene* in a dragon-drawn chariot, draped in the bodies of her dead children, taunting and reviling the impotent Jason. That is, modern audiences sometimes feel that Medea herself should die at the play's close if *Medea* is to be a truly tragic drama, as though by dying Medea would be "punished" for her revenge in some appalling vision of tragic "justice." But Euripides seems uninterested in such a moralized version of tragedy. Indeed, as Aristotle implies in *The Poetics*, tragedy is a deeply dialectical, contradictory way of representing human experience: tragedy arises from the unresolvable tension between pity and fear, from the relationship between the hero's actions (remembering that the tragic hero is neither a "paragon of virtue" nor inherently wicked) and their terrible, somehow fitting consequences. And while Aristotle praises Sophocles' *Oedipus Rex* as the best-constructed tragedy, he also remarks that Euripides "is felt by the audience to be the most tragic, at least, of the poets." To grasp Euripides' sense of tragedy means placing Medea's execution of the children within the context of the action as a whole, an act that brings her history to bear in one exacting deed, an act like Agamemnon's treading on the carpet or Oedipus' blistering interrogation of the ancient shepherd.

At the play's opening, Medea is an outcast, a foreign exile in Corinth, and the play repeatedly stresses Medea's otherness—she is an Eastern exotic, she has little respect for Greek culture and its institutions, and she is a sorceress as well. Medea is consistently shown to be a figure of willful passion, brought into exile through her love for Jason. Falling in love with Jason when he went to Colchis in search of the Golden Fleece, Medea used her sorcery to help Jason gain the Fleece, betraying her father and killing her brother in the bargain. When the play opens, Jason has returned to Greece with Medea and their children; in Corinth, however, Jason decides to marry the daughter of King Creon. Creon, no doubt recognizing that Medea and her children will pose a constant threat to his own line of succession, has ruled that Medea and her children must again be sent into exile.

Yet as Medea suggests to the Chorus, the indignity that Jason has thrust upon her—being doubly exiled, from her country and from her marriage—is in an important sense merely an extension of the state of all women in Greek culture. For once women "buy a husband and take for our bodies / A master," they are exiled from their own homes, and from the mastery of their own lives. Inasmuch as women are represented as creatures of passion, they are "exiled" as well from the organizing principles of the Greek state: reason, the law, and legitimate society are identified in the play as the preserve of men. Euripides makes Jason the spokesman for these values. When Jason first confronts Medea, he takes pride in his talents as a speaker, listing his arguments in support of taking a new wife almost as though he were arguing in the courtroom or conducting a philosophical demonstration. But while Oedipus, for instance, uses the strategies of philosophic inquiry to discover the truth, Jason's arguments seem to conceal the truth—he is betraying Medea and their children, after all—behind a smoke-screen of sophistic rhetoric. Having brought Medea into exile, Jason argues that she is fortunate merely to "inhabit a Greek land and understand our ways / How to live by law instead of the sweet will of force." Yet the law that Jason praises seems designed to enable him to act out his own "sweet will"—taking a second wife—while it prevents Medea from acting on hers. And the more Jason insists that he is acting reasonably, the more unreasonable his arguments become; he becomes increasingly irritable, and finally insulting: "you women have got into such a state of mind / That, if your life at night is good, you think you have / Everything." Euripides' treatment of Jason is typical of his tendency to present an ironic view of the heroes of Greek mythology. Here, in making Jason the representative of Greek values—reason, law, justice—Euripides suggests the limits of those values. For the Chorus clearly sees Jason's "reason" as a self-indulgent pretense: "though you have made this speech of yours look well, / . . . / You have betrayed your wife and are acting badly."

As Medea comes to recognize, both Jason and the masculine laws of Corinth are willing to betray her, to call her fidelity and love merely irrational, to force her again into exile. Having poisoned Creon and his daughter, Medea first claims to kill the children in order that they not be slain "by another hand less kindly to them." But it is also clear that in killing the children, Medea revenges herself on Jason in the only way open to her; he has little regard for her love for him, but the children are his property, an extension of himself, of his identity. More importantly, the children are his successors, representing his continued presence in the world. For, as Jason laments, Medea has contrived a punishment for him that no Greek woman would have dared: in leaving him childless, Medea transforms Jason into an exile like herself, prophesying that he will die "without distinction."

Medea's acts epitomize the ethical ambiguity that drives Greek tragedy. Agamemnon strides on the blood-red carpet, magisterially desecrating the honor of his family as he had once done in sacrificing Iphigeneia; Oedipus sentences the hidden criminal to exile, only to discover that he is the criminal he seeks. To force Jason into a childless exile, Medea commits the kind of crime that Jason has repeatedly drawn her to enact: she murders what she loves in order to insist on the priority and power of her love for him. As in other classical tragedies, the hero chooses to act in a way that is not only consistent with her past, but a self-conscious reenactment of it. The *peripeteia*, the reversal that defines the tragic action, seems in many ways to be a kind of restoration as well, revealing destructive consequences that have been latent in the action from the beginning.

It should be clear that while Euripides interrogates the relationship between reason and passion, culture and nature, the rational and the irrational, science and magic, *Medea* does not finally disrupt or overturn this relationship. Nor does the play finally question the way that Greek culture gendered these categories as masculine and feminine, expressing the conceptual and political hierarchies of its own making as the "natural" outgrowth of some essential gender difference. Euripides exposes the destructive tension lurking in Greek conceptions of gender, power, and identity, but the language of tragedy is not the language of revolution. For although tragedy frequently exposes the values of its world as contradictory and destructive, it also accepts those values as somehow inevitable, unavoidable. Medea flees Corinth and the abusive Jason, but only by destroying herself in the same way she destroys Jason; Medea triumphs over Jason, but only by destroying her family and becoming an exile yet again. The only alternative that *Medea* offers to the way that Medea—and, she argues, all women—is positioned as an outsider, an "exile" to the governing categories of Greek life, is a deeper, more permanent isolation.

MEDEA

Euripides

TRANSLATED BY REX WARNER

— CHARACTERS —

MEDEA, PRINCESS OF COLCHIS AND WIFE OF
JASON, SON OF AESON, KING OF IOLCUS
TWO CHILDREN OF MEDEA AND JASON
CREON, KING OF CORINTH
AEGEUS, KING OF ATHENS
NURSE TO MEDEA

TUTOR TO MEDEA'S CHILDREN
MESSENGER
CHORUS OF CORINTHIAN WOMEN

SCENE: *In front of* MEDEA's *house in Corinth.*

Enter from the house MEDEA'S NURSE.

NURSE: How I wish the Argo never had reached the land
    Of Colchis, skimming through the blue Symplegades,
    Nor ever had fallen in the glades of Pelion
    The smitten fir-tree to furnish oars for the hands
5   Of heroes who in Pelias' name attempted
    The Golden Fleece! For then my mistress Medea
    Would not have sailed for the towers of the land of Iolcus,
    Her heart on fire with passionate love for Jason;
    Nor would she have persuaded the daughters of Pelias
10   To kill their father, and now be living here
    In Corinth with her husband and children. She gave
    Pleasure to the people of her land of exile,
    And she herself helped Jason in every way.
    This is indeed the greatest salvation of all—
15   For the wife not to stand apart from the husband.
    But now there's hatred everywhere, Love is diseased.
    For, deserting his own children and my mistress,
    Jason has taken a royal wife to his bed,
    The daughter of the ruler of this land, Creon.
20   And poor Medea is slighted, and cries aloud on the
    Vows they made to each other, the right hands clasped
    In eternal promise. She calls upon the gods to witness
    What sort of return Jason has made to her love.
    She lies without food and gives herself up to suffering,
25   Wasting away every moment of the day in tears.
    So it has gone since she knew herself slighted by him.
    Not stirring an eye, not moving her face from the ground,
    No more than either a rock or surging sea water
    She listens when she is given friendly advice.
30   Except that sometimes she twists back her white neck and
    Moans to herself, calling out on her father's name,
    And her land, and her home betrayed when she came away
    with
    A man who now is determined to dishonor her.
    Poor creature, she has discovered by her sufferings
35   What it means to one not to have lost one's own country.

---

1 **Argo** Jason's ship on the expedition of the Argonauts, sent by Pelias, king of Iolcus in Thessaly (Jason's uncle, who had usurped the throne), to Colchis on the Black Sea. The Symplegades were clashing rocks, one of the obstacles along the way. Pelion is a mountain in Thessaly. Medea was a princess of Colchis who fell in love with Jason and followed him back to Greece

She has turned from the children and does not like to see
    them.
    I am afraid she may think of some dreadful thing,
    For her heart is violent. She will never put up with
    The treatment she is getting. I know and fear her
    Lest she may sharpen a sword and thrust to the heart,   40
    Stealing into the palace where the bed is made,
    Or even kill the king and the new-wedded groom,
    And thus bring a greater misfortune on herself.
    She's a strange woman. I know it won't be easy
    To make an enemy of her and come off best.   45
    But here the children come. They have finished playing.
    They have no thought at all of their mother's trouble.
    Indeed it is not usual for the young to grieve.

(Enter from the right the slave who is the TUTOR *to Medea's two small* CHILDREN. *The* CHILDREN *follow him.)*

TUTOR: You old retainer of my mistress' household,
    Why are you standing here all alone in front of the   50
    Gates and moaning to yourself over your misfortune?
    Medea could not wish you to leave her alone.
NURSE: Old man, and guardian of the children of Jason,
    If one is a good servant, it's a terrible thing
    When one's master's luck is out; it goes to one's heart.   55
    So I myself have got into such a state of grief
    That a longing stole over me to come outside here
    And tell the earth and air of my mistress' sorrows.
TUTOR: Has the poor lady not yet given up her crying?
NURSE: Given up? She's at the start, not halfway through her   60
    tears.
TUTOR: Poor fool—if I may call my mistress such a name—
    How ignorant she is of trouble more to come.
NURSE: What do you mean, old man? You needn't fear to
    speak.
TUTOR: Nothing. I take back the words which I used just now.
NURSE: Don't, by your beard, hide this from me, your   65
    fellow-servant.
    If need be, I'll keep quiet about what you tell me.
TUTOR: I heard a person saying, while I myself seemed
    Not to be paying attention, when I was at the place
    Where the old draught-players sit, by the holy fountain,
    That Creon, ruler of the land, intends to drive   70
    These children and their mother in exile from Corinth.
    But whether what he said is really true or not
    I do not know. I pray that it may not be true.

NURSE: And will Jason put up with it that his children
75   Should suffer so, though he's no friend to their mother?
TUTOR: Old ties give place to new ones. As for Jason, he
  No longer has a feeling for this house of ours.
NURSE: It's black indeed for us, when we add new to old
  Sorrows before even the present sky has cleared.
80 TUTOR: But you be silent, and keep all this to yourself.
  It is not the right time to tell our mistress of it.
NURSE: Do you hear, children, what a father he is to you?
  I wish he were dead—but no, he is still my master.
  Yet certainly he has proved unkind to his dear ones.
85 TUTOR: What's strange in that? Have you only just discovered
  That everyone loves himself more than his neighbor?
  Some have good reason, others get something out of it.
  So Jason neglects his children for the new bride.
NURSE: Go indoors, children. That will be the best thing.
90   And you, keep them to themselves as much as possible.
  Don't bring them near their mother in her angry mood.
  For I've seen her already blazing her eyes at them
  As though she meant some mischief and I am sure that
  She'll not stop raging until she has struck at someone.
95   May it be an enemy and not a friend she hurts!

(MEDEA is heard inside the house.)

MEDEA: Ah, wretch! Ah, lost in my sufferings,
  I wish, I wish I might die.
NURSE: What did I say, dear children? Your mother
  Frets her heart and frets it to anger.
100   Run away quickly into the house,
  And keep well out of her sight.
  Don't go anywhere near, but be careful
  Of the wildness and bitter nature
  Of that proud mind.
105   Go now! Run quickly indoors.
  It is clear that she soon will put lightning
  In that cloud of her cries that is rising
  With a passion increasing. O, what will she do,
  Proud-hearted and not to be checked on her course,
110   A soul bitten into with wrong?

(The TUTOR takes the children into the house.)

MEDEA: Ah, I have suffered
  What should be wept for bitterly. I hate you,
  Children of a hateful mother. I curse you
  And your father. Let the whole house crash.
115 NURSE: Ah, I pity you, you poor creature.
  How can your children share in their father's
  Wickedness? Why do you hate them? Oh children,
  How much I fear that something may happen!
  Great people's tempers are terrible, always
120   Having their own way, seldom checked,
  Dangerous they shift from mood to mood.
  How much better to have been accustomed
  To live on equal terms with one's neighbors.
  I would like to be safe and grow old in a
125   Humble way. What is moderate sounds best,
  Also in practice is best for everyone.
  Greatness brings no profit to people.
  God indeed, when in anger, brings
  Greater ruin to great men's houses.

(Enter, on the right, a CHORUS of Corinthian women. They have
come to inquire about MEDEA and to attempt to console her.)

CHORUS: I heard the voice, I heard the cry 130
  Of Colchis' wretched daughter.
  Tell me, mother, is she not yet
  At rest? Within the double gates
  Of the court I heard her cry. I am sorry
  For the sorrow of this home. O, say, what has happened? 135
NURSE: There is no home. It's over and done with.
  Her husband holds fast to his royal wedding,
  While she, my mistress, cries out her eyes
  There in her room, and takes no warmth from
  Any word of any friend. 140
MEDEA: O, I wish
  That lightning from heaven would split my head open.
  Oh, what use have I now for life?
  I would find my release in death
  And leave hateful existence behind me. 145
CHORUS: O God and Earth and Heaven!
  Did you hear what a cry was that
  Which the sad wife sings?
  Poor foolish one, why should you long.
  For that appalling rest? 150
  The final end of death comes fast.
  No need to pray for that.
  Suppose your man gives honor
  To another woman's bed.
  It often happens. Don't be hurt. 155
  God will be your friend in this.
  You must not waste away
  Grieving too much for him who shared your bed.
MEDEA: Great Themis, lady Artemis, behold
  The things I suffer, though I made him promise, 160
  My hateful husband. I pray that I may see him,
  Him and his bride and all their palace shattered
  For the wrong they dare to do me without cause.
  Oh, my father! Oh, my country! In what dishonor
  I left you, killing my own brother for it. 165
NURSE: Do you hear what she says, and how she cries
  On Themis, the goddess of Promises, and on Zeus,
  Whom we believe to be the Keeper of Oaths?
  Of this I am sure, that no small thing
  Will appease my mistress' anger. 170
CHORUS: Will she come into our presence?
  Will she listen when we are speaking
  To the words we say?
  I wish she might relax her rage
  And temper of her heart. 175
  My willingness to help will never
  Be wanting to my friends.
  But go inside and bring her
  Out of the house to us,
  And speak kindly to her: hurry, 180
  Before she wrongs her own.
  This passion of hers moves to something great.

---

159 **Themis, Artemis** goddesses: Themis was the goddess of justice, the virgin Artemis would be sensitive to the plight of women   165 **brother** during the escape from Colchis, to delay her father's pursuit

NURSE: I will, but I doubt if I'll manage
  To win my mistress over.
185 But still I'll attempt it to please you.
  Such a look she will flash on her servants
  If any comes near with a message,
  Like a lioness guarding her cubs.
  It is right, I think, to consider
190 Both stupid and lacking in foresight
  Those poets of old who wrote songs
  For revels and dinners and banquets,
  Pleasant sounds for men living at ease;
  But none of them all has discovered
195 How to put to an end with their singing
  Or musical instruments grief,
  Bitter grief, from which death and disaster
  Cheat the hopes of a house. Yet how good
  If music could cure men of this! But why raise
200 To no purpose the voice at a banquet? For *there* is
  Already abundance of pleasure for men
  With a joy of its own.

(*The* NURSE *goes into the house.*)

CHORUS: I heard a shriek that is laden with sorrow.
  Shrilling out her hard grief she cries out
205 Upon him who betrayed both her bed and her marriage.
  Wronged, she calls on the gods,
  On the justice of Zeus, the oath sworn,
  Which brought her away
  To the opposite shore of the Greeks
210 Through the gloomy salt straits to the gateway
  Of the salty unlimited sea.

(MEDEA, *attended by servants, comes out of the house.*)

MEDEA: Women of Corinth, I have come outside to you
  Lest you should be indignant with me; for I know
  That many people are overproud, some when alone,
215 And others when in company. And those who live
  Quietly, as I do, get a bad reputation.
  For a just judgment is not evident in the eyes
  When a man at first sight hates another, before
  Learning his character, being in no way injured;
220 And a foreigner especially must adapt himself.
  I'd not approve of even a fellow-countryman
  Who by pride and want of manners offends his neighbors.
  But on me this thing has fallen so unexpectedly,
  It has broken my heart. I am finished. I let go
225 All my life's joy. My friends, I only want to die.
  It was everything to me to think well of one man,
  And he, my own husband, has turned out wholly vile.
  Of all things which are living and can form a judgment
  We women are the most unfortunate creatures.
230 Firstly, with an excess of wealth it is required
  For us to buy a husband and take for our bodies
  A master; for not to take one is even worse.
  And now the question is serious whether we take
  A good or bad one; for there is no easy escape
235 For a woman, nor can she say no to her marriage.
  She arrives among new modes of behavior and manners,
  And needs prophetic power, unless she has learned at
    home,
  How best to manage him who shares the bed with her.

And if we work out all this well and carefully,
And the husband lives with us and lightly bears his yoke, 240
Then life is enviable. If not, I'd rather die.
A man, when he's tired of the company in his home,
Goes out of the house and puts an end to his boredom
And turns to a friend or companion of his own age.
But we are forced to keep our eyes on one alone. 245
What they say of us is that we have a peaceful time
Living at home, while they do the fighting in war.
How wrong they are! I would very much rather stand
Three times in the front of battle than bear one child.
Yet what applies to me does not apply to you. 250
You have a country. Your family home is here.
You enjoy life and the company of your friends.
But I am deserted, a refugee, thought nothing of
By my husband—something he won in a foreign land.
I have no mother or brother, nor any relation 255
With whom I can take refuge in this sea of woe.
This much then is the service I would beg from you:
If I can find the means or devise any scheme
To pay my husband back for what he has done to me—
Him and his father-in-law and the girl who married him— 260
Just to keep silent. For in other ways a woman
Is full of fear, defenseless, dreads the sight of cold
Steel; but, when once she is wronged in the matter of love,
No other soul can hold so many thoughts of blood.

CHORUS: This I will promise. You are in the right, Medea, 265
  In paying your husband back. I am not surprised at you
  For being sad.
            But look! I see our King Creon
  Approaching. He will tell us of some new plan.

(*Enter, from the right,* CREON, *with attendants.*)

CREON: You, with that angry look, so set against your husband,
  Medea, I order you to leave my territories 270
  An exile, and take along with you your two children,
  And not to waste time doing it. It is my decree,
  And I will see it done. I will not return home
  Until you are cast from the boundaries of my land.

MEDEA: Oh, this is the end for me. I am utterly lost. 275
  Now I am in the full force of the storm of hate
  And have no harbor from ruin to reach easily.
  Yet still, in spite of it all, I'll ask the question:
  What is your reason, Creon, for banishing me?

CREON: I am afraid of you—why should I dissemble it?— 280
  Afraid that you may injure my daughter mortally.
  Many things accumulate to support my feeling.
  You are a clever woman, versed in evil arts,
  And are angry at having lost your husband's love.
  I hear that you are threatening, so they tell me, 285
  To do something against my daughter and Jason
  And me, too. I shall take my precautions first.
  I tell you, I prefer to earn your hatred now
  Than to be soft-hearted and afterward regret it.

MEDEA: This is not the first time, Creon. Often previously 290
  Through being considered clever I have suffered much.
  A person of sense ought never to have his children
  Brought up to be more clever than the average.
  For, apart from cleverness bringing them no profit,
  It will make them objects of envy and ill-will. 295
  If you put new ideas before the eyes of fools

They'll think you foolish and worthless into the bargain;
And if you are thought superior to those who have
Some reputation for learning, you will become hated.
300 I have some knowledge myself of how this happens;
For being clever, I find that some will envy me,
Others object to me. Yet all my cleverness
Is not so much.
                    Well, then, are you frightened, Creon,
That I should harm you? There is no need. It is not
305 My way to transgress the authority of a king.
How have you injured me? You gave your daughter away
To the man you wanted. Oh, certainly I hate
My husband, but you, I think, have acted wisely;
Nor do I grudge it you that your affairs go well.
310 May the marriage be a lucky one! Only let me
Live in this land. For even though I have been wronged,
I will not raise my voice, but submit to my betters.
CREON: What you say sounds gentle enough. Still in my heart
I greatly dread that you are plotting some evil,
315 And therefore I trust you even less than before.
A sharp-tempered woman, or, for that matter, a man,
Is easier to deal with than the clever type
Who holds her tongue. No. You must go. No need for more
Speeches. The thing is fixed. By no manner of means
320 Shall you, an enemy of mine, stay in my country.
MEDEA: I beg you. By your knees, by your new-wedded girl.
CREON: Your words are wasted. You will never persuade me.
MEDEA: Will you drive me out, and give no heed to my
        prayers?
CREON: I will, for I love my family more than you.
325 MEDEA: O my country! How bitterly now I remember you!
CREON: I love my country too—next after my children.
MEDEA: O what an evil to men is passionate love!
CREON: That would depend on the luck that goes along with it.
MEDEA: O God, do not forget who is the cause of this!
330 CREON: Go. It is no use. Spare me the pain of forcing you.
MEDEA: I'm spared no pain. I lack no pain to be spared me.
CREON: Then you'll be removed by force by one of my men.
MEDEA: No, Creon, not that! But do listen, I beg you.
CREON: Woman, you seem to want to create a disturbance.
335 MEDEA: I *will* go into exile. *This* is not what I beg for.
CREON: Why then this violence and clinging to my hand?
MEDEA: Allow me to remain here just for this one day,
    So I may consider where to live in my exile,
    And look for support for my children, since their father
340 Chooses to make no kind of provision for them.
    Have pity on them! You have children of your own.
    It is natural for you to look kindly on them.
    For myself I do not mind if I go into exile.
    It is the children being in trouble that I mind.
345 CREON: There is nothing tyrannical about my nature,
    And by showing mercy I have often been the loser.
    Even now I know that I am making a mistake.
    All the same you shall have your will. But this I tell you,
    That if the light of heaven tomorrow shall see you,
350 You and your children in the confines of my land,
    You die. This word I have spoken is firmly fixed.
    But now, if you must stay, stay for this day alone.
    For in it you can do none of the things I fear.

(Exit CREON *with his attendants.*)

CHORUS: Oh, unfortunate one! Oh, cruel!
    Where will you turn? Who will help you?   355
    What house or what land to preserve you
    From ill can you find?
    Medea, a god has thrown suffering
    Upon you in waves of despair.
MEDEA: Things have gone badly every way. No doubt of that 360
    But not these things this far, and don't imagine so.
    There are still trials to come for the new-wedded pair,
    And for their relations pain that will mean something.
    Do you think that I would ever have fawned on that man
    Unless I had some end to gain or profit in it?   365
    I would not even have spoken or touched him with my hands.
    But he has got to such a pitch of foolishness
    That, though he could have made nothing of all my plans
    By exiling me, he has given me this one day
    To stay here, and in this I will make dead bodies   370
    Of three of my enemies—father, the girl, and my husband.
    I have many ways of death which I might suit to them,
    And do not know, friends, which one to take in hand;
    Whether to set fire underneath their bridal mansion,
    Or sharpen a sword and thrust it to the heart,   375
    Stealing into the palace where the bed is made.
    There is just one obstacle to this. If I am caught
    Breaking into the house and scheming against it,
    I shall die, and give my enemies cause for laughter.
    It is best to go by the straight road, the one in which 380
    I am most skilled, and make away with them by poison.
    So be it then.
    And now suppose them dead. What town will receive me?
    What friend will offer me a refuge in his land,
    Or the guaranty of his house and save my own life?   385
    There is none. So I must wait a little time yet,
    And if some sure defense should then appear for me,
    In craft and silence I will set about this murder.
    But if my fate should drive me on without help,
    Even though death is certain, I will take the sword   390
    Myself and kill, and steadfastly advance to crime.
    It shall not be—I swear it by her, my mistress,
    Whom most I honor and have chosen as partner,
    Hecate, who dwells in the recesses of my hearth—
    That any man shall be glad to have injured me.   395
    Bitter I will make their marriage for them and mournful,
    Bitter the alliance and the driving me out of the land.
    Ah, come, Medea, in your plotting and scheming
    Leave nothing untried of all those things which you know.
    Go forward to the dreadful act. The test has come   400
    For resolution. You see how you are treated. Never
    Shall you be mocked by Jason's Corinthian wedding,
    Whose father was noble, whose grandfather Helius.
    You have the skill. What is more, you were born a woman,
    And women, though most helpless in doing good deeds,   405
    Are of every evil the cleverest of contrivers.
CHORUS: Flow backward to your sources, sacred rivers,
    And let the world's great order be reversed.
    It is the thoughts of *men* that are deceitful,
    Their pledges that are loose.   410

394 **Hecate** a goddess of the night   403 **Helius** sun god

Story shall now turn my condition to a fair one,
Women are paid their due.
No more shall evil-sounding fame be theirs.

Cease now, you muses of the ancient singers,
415   To tell the tale of my unfaithfulness;
For not on us did Phoebus, lord of music,
Bestow the lyre's divine
Power, for otherwise I should have sung an answer
To the other sex. Long time
420   Has much to tell of us, and much of them.

You sailed away from your father's home,
With a heart on fire you passed
The double rocks of the sea.
And now in a foreign country
425   You have lost your rest in a widowed bed,
And are driven forth, a refugee
In dishonor from the land.

Good faith has gone, and no more remains
In great Greece a sense of shame.
430   It has flown away to the sky.
No father's house for a haven
Is at hand for you now, and another queen
Of your bed has dispossessed you and
Is mistress of your home.

(Enter JASON, *with attendants.)*

435   JASON: This is not the first occasion that I have noticed
How hopeless it is to deal with a stubborn temper.
For, with reasonable submission to our ruler's will,
You might have lived in this land and kept your home.
As it is you are going to be exiled for your loose speaking.
440   Not that I mind myself. You are free to continue
Telling everyone that Jason is a worthless man.
But as to your talk about the king, consider
Yourself most lucky that exile is your punishment.
I, for my part, have always tried to calm down
445   The anger of the king, and wished you to remain.
But you will not give up your folly, continually
Speaking ill of him, and so you are going to be banished.
All the same, and in spite of your conduct, I'll not desert
My friends, but have come to make some provision for you,
450   So that you and the children may not be penniless
Or in need of anything in exile. Certainly
Exile brings many troubles with it. And even
If you hate me, I cannot think badly of you.

MEDEA: O coward in every way—that is what I call you,
455   With bitterest reproach for your lack of manliness,
You have come, you, my worst enemy, have come to me!
It is not an example of overconfidence
Or of boldness thus to look your friends in the face,
Friends you have injured—no, it is the worst of all
460   Human diseases, shamelessness. But you did well
To come, for I can speak ill of you and lighten
My heart, and you will suffer while you are listening.
And first I will begin from what happened first.
I saved your life, and every Greek knows I saved it,
465   Who was a shipmate of yours aboard the Argo,

When you were sent to control the bulls that breathed fire
And yoke them, and when you would sow that deadly field.
Also that snake, who encircled with his many folds
The Golden Fleece and guarded it and never slept,
I killed, and so gave you the safety of the light.   470
And I myself betrayed my father and my home,
And came with you to Pelias' land of Iolcus.
And then, showing more willingness to help than wisdom,
I killed him, Pelias, with a most dreadful death
At his own daughters' hands, and took away your fear.   475
This is how I behaved to you, you wretched man,
And you forsook me, took another bride to bed,
Though you had children; for, if that had not been,
You would have had an excuse for another wedding.
Faith in your word has gone. Indeed, I cannot tell   480
Whether you think the gods whose names you swore by then
Have ceased to rule and that new standards are set up,
Since you must know you have broken your word to me.
O my right hand, and the knees which you often clasped
In supplication, how senselessly I am treated   485
By this bad man, and how my hopes have missed their mark!
Come, I will share my thoughts as though you were a
   friend—
You! Can I think that you would ever treat me well?
But I will do it, and these questions will make you
Appear the baser. Where am I to go? To my father's?   490
Him I betrayed and his land when I came with you.
To Pelias' wretched daughters? What a fine welcome
They would prepare for me who murdered their father!
For this is my position—hated by my friends
At home, I have, in kindness to you, made enemies   495
Of others whom there was no need to have injured.
And how happy among Greek women you have made me
On your side for all this! A distinguished husband
I have—for breaking promises. When in misery
I am cast out of the land and go into exile,   500
Quite without friends and all alone with my children,
That will be a fine shame for the new-wedded groom,
For his children to wander as beggars and she who saved
   him.
O God, you have given to mortals a sure method
Of telling the gold that is pure from the counterfeit;   505
Why is there no mark engraved upon men's bodies,
By which we could know the true ones from the false ones?

CHORUS: It is a strange form of anger, difficult to cure,
When two friends turn upon each other in hatred.

JASON: As for me, it seems I must be no bad speaker.   510
But, like a man who has a good grip of the tiller,
Reef up his sail, and so run away from under
This mouthing tempest, woman, of your bitter tongue.
Since you insist on building up your kindness to me,
My view is that Cypris was alone responsible   515
Of men and gods for the preserving of my life.
You are clever enough—but really I need not enter
Into the story of how it was love's inescapable
Power that compelled you to keep my person safe.
On this I will not go into too much detail.   520

---

416 **Phoebus** Apollo

515 **Cypris** Aphrodite, goddess of love

In so far as you helped me, you did well enough.
But on this question of saving me, I can prove
You have certainly got from me more than you gave.
Firstly, instead of living among barbarians,
525 You inhabit a Greek land and understand our ways,
How to live by law instead of the sweet will of force.
And all the Greeks considered you a clever woman.
You were honored for it; while, if you were living at
The ends of the earth, nobody would have heard of you.
530 For my part, rather than stores of gold in my house
Or power to sing even sweeter songs than Orpheus,
I'd choose the fate that made me a distinguished man.
There is my reply to your story of my labors.
Remember it was you who started the argument.
535 Next for your attack on my wedding with the princess:
Here I will prove that, first, it was a clever move,
Secondly, a wise one, and, finally, that I made it
In your best interests and the children's. Please keep calm.
When I arrived here from the land of Iolcus,
540 Involved, as I was, in every kind of difficulty,
What luckier chance could I have come across than this,
An exile to marry the daughter of the king?
It was not—the point that seems to upset you—that I
Grew tired of your bed and felt the need of a new bride;
545 Nor with any wish to outdo your number of children.
We have enough already. I am quite content.
But—this was the main reason—that we might live well,
And not be short of anything. I know that all
A man's friends leave him stone-cold if he becomes poor.
550 Also that I might bring my children up worthily
Of my position, and, by producing more of them
To be brothers of yours, we would draw the families
Together and all be happy. You need no children.
And it pays me to do good to those I have now
555 By having others. Do you think this a bad plan?
You wouldn't if the love question hadn't upset you.
But you women have got into such a state of mind
That, if your life at night is good, you think you have
Everything; but, if in that quarter things go wrong,
560 You will consider your best and truest interests
Most hateful. It would have been better far for men
To have got their children in some other way, and women
Not to have existed. Then life would have been good.
CHORUS: Jason, though you have made this speech of yours
    look well,
565 Still I think, even though others do not agree,
You have betrayed your wife and are acting badly.
MEDEA: Surely in many ways I hold different views
From others, for I think that the plausible speaker
Who is a villain deserves the greatest punishment.
570 Confident in his tongue's power to adorn evil,
He stops at nothing. Yet he is not really wise.
As in your case. There is no need to put on the airs
Of a clever speaker, for one word will lay you flat.
If you were not a coward, you would not have married
575 Behind my back, but discussed it with me first.
JASON: And you, no doubt, would have furthered the proposal,
If I had told you of it, you who even now
Are incapable of controlling your bitter temper.
MEDEA: It was not that. No, you thought it was not
    respectable
580 As you got on in years to have a foreign wife.

JASON: Make sure of this: it was not because of a woman
I made the royal alliance in which I now live,
But, as I said before, I wished to preserve you
And breed a royal progeny to be brothers
To the children I have now, a sure defense to us. 585
MEDEA: Let me have no happy fortune that brings pain with it,
Or prosperity which is upsetting to the mind!
JASON: Change your ideas of what you want, and show more
    sense.
Do not consider painful what is good for you,
Nor, when you are lucky, think yourself unfortunate. 590
MEDEA: You can insult me. You have somewhere to turn to.
But I shall go from this land into exile, friendless.
JASON: It was what you chose yourself. Don't blame others
    for it.
MEDEA: And how did I choose it? Did I betray my husband?
JASON: You called down wicked curses on the king's family. 595
MEDEA: A curse, that is what I am become to your house too.
JASON: I do not propose to go into all the rest of it;
But, if you wish for the children or for yourself
In exile to have some of my money to help you,
Say so, for I am prepared to give with open hand, 600
Or to provide you with introductions to my friends
Who will treat you well. You are a fool if you do not
Accept this. Cease your anger and you will profit.
MEDEA: I shall never accept the favors of friends of yours,
Nor take a thing from you, so you need not offer it. 605
There is no benefit in the gifts of a bad man.
JASON: Then, in any case, I call the gods to witness that
I wish to help you and the children in every way,
But you refuse what is good for you. Obstinately
You push away your friends. You are sure to suffer for it. 610
MEDEA: Go! No doubt you hanker for your virginal bride,
And are guilty of lingering too long out of her house.
Enjoy your wedding. But perhaps—with the help of God—
You will make the kind of marriage that you will regret.

(JASON *goes out with his attendants.*)

CHORUS: When love is in excess 615
    It brings a man no honor
    Nor any worthiness.
    But if in moderation Cypris comes,
    There is no other power at all so gracious.
    O goddess, never on me let loose the unerring 620
    Shaft of your bow in the poison of desire.

    Let my heart be wise.
    It is the gods' best gift.
    On me let mighty Cypris
    Inflict no wordy wars or restless anger 625
    To urge my passion to a different love.
    But with discernment may she guide women's weddings,
    Honoring most what is peaceful in the bed.

    O country and home,
    Never, never may I be without you, 630
    Living the hopeless life,
    Hard to pass through and painful,
    Most pitiable of all.
    Let death first lay me low and death
    Free me from this daylight. 635
    There is no sorrow above
    The loss of a native land.

I have seen it myself,
Do not tell of a secondhand story.
640 Neither city nor friend
Pitied you when you suffered
The worst of sufferings.
O let him die ungraced whose heart
Will not reward his friends,
645 Who cannot open an honest mind
No friend will he be of mine.

(*Enter* AEGEUS, *king of Athens, an old friend of* MEDEA.)

AEGEUS: Medea, greeting! This is the best introduction
Of which men know for conversation between friends.
MEDEA: Greeting to you too, Aegeus, son of King Pandion.
650 Where have you come from to visit this country's soil?
AEGEUS: I have just left the ancient oracle of Phoebus.
MEDEA: And why did you go to earth's prophetic center?
AEGEUS: I went to inquire how children might be born to me.
MEDEA: Is it so? Your life still up to this point is childless?
655 AEGEUS: Yes. By the fate of some power we have no children.
MEDEA: Have you a wife, or is there none to share your bed?
AEGEUS: There is. Yes, I am joined to my wife in marriage.
MEDEA: And what did Phoebus say to you about children?
AEGEUS: Words too wise for a mere man to guess their
meaning.
660 MEDEA: It is proper for me to be told the god's reply?
AEGEUS: It is. For sure what is needed is cleverness.
MEDEA: Then what was his message? Tell me, if I may hear.
AEGEUS: I am not to loosen the hanging foot of the wine-
skin . . .
MEDEA: Until you have done something, or reached some
country?
665 AEGEUS: Until I return again to my hearth and house.
MEDEA: And for what purpose have you journeyed to this
land?
AEGEUS: There is a man called Pittheus, king of Troezen.
MEDEA: A son of Pelops, they say, a most righteous man.
AEGEUS: With him I wish to discuss the reply of the god.
670 MEDEA: Yes. He is wise and experienced in such matters.
AEGEUS: And to me also the dearest of all my spear-friends.
MEDEA: Well, I hope you have good luck, and achieve your
will.
AEGEUS: But why this downcast eye of yours, and this pale
cheek?
MEDEA: O Aegeus, my husband has been the worst of all
to me.
675 AEGEUS: What do you mean? Say clearly what has caused this
grief.
MEDEA: Jason wrongs me, though I have never injured him.
AEGEUS: What has he done? Tell me about it in clearer words.
MEDEA: He has taken a wife to his house, supplanting me.
AEGEUS: Surely he would not dare to do a thing like that.
680 MEDEA: Be sure he has. Once dear, I now am slighted by him.
AEGEUS: Did he fall in love? Or is he tired of your love?
MEDEA: He was greatly in love, this traitor to his friends.
AEGEUS: Then let him go, if, as you say, he is so bad.
MEDEA: A passionate love—for an alliance with the king.
685 AEGEUS: And who gave him his wife? Tell me the rest of it.
MEDEA: It was Creon, he who rules this land of Corinth.
AEGEUS: Indeed, Medea, your grief was understandable.
MEDEA: I am ruined. And there is more to come: I am
banished.

AEGEUS: Banished? By whom? Here you tell me of a new
wrong.
690 MEDEA: Creon drives me an exile from the land of Corinth.
AEGEUS: Does Jason consent? I cannot approve of this.
MEDEA: He pretends not to, but he will put up with it.
Ah, Aegeus, I beg and beseech you, by your beard
And by your knees I am making myself your suppliant,
695 Have pity on me, have pity on your poor friend,
And do not let me go into exile desolate,
But receive me in your land and at your very hearth.
So may your love, with God's help, lead to the bearing
Of children, and so may you yourself die happy.
700 You do not know what a chance you have come on here.
I will end your childlessness, and I will make you able
To beget children. The drugs I know can do this.
AEGEUS: For many reasons, woman, I am anxious to do
This favor for you. First, for the sake of the gods,
705 And then for the birth of children which you promise,
For in that respect I am entirely at my wits' end.
But this is my position: if you reach my land,
I, being in my rights, will try to befriend you.
But this much I must warn you of beforehand:
710 I shall not agree to take you out of this country;
But if you by yourself can reach my house, then you
Shall stay there safely. To none will I give you up
But from this land you must make your escape yourself,
For I do not wish to incur blame from my friends.
715 MEDEA: It shall be so. But, if I might have a pledge from you
For this, then I would have from you all I desire.
AEGEUS: Do you not trust me? What is it rankles with you?
MEDEA: I trust you, yes. But the house of Pelias hates me,
And so does Creon. If you are bound by this oath,
720 When they try to drag me from your land, you will not
Abandon me; but if our pact is only words,
With no oath to the gods, you will be lightly armed,
Unable to resist their summons. I am weak,
While they have wealth to help them and a royal house.
725 AEGEUS: You show much foresight for such negotiations.
Well, if you will have it so, I will not refuse.
For, both on my side this will be the safest way
To have some excuse to put forward to your enemies,
And for you it is more certain. You may name the gods.
730 MEDEA: Swear by the plain of Earth, and Helius, father
Of my father, and name together all the gods. . .
AEGEUS: That I will act or not act in what way? Speak.
MEDEA: That you yourself will never cast me from your land,
Nor, if any of my enemies should demand me,
735 Will you, in your life, willingly hand me over.
AEGEUS: I swear by the Earth, by the holy light of Helius,
By all the gods, I will abide by this you say.
MEDEA: Enough. And, if you fail, what shall happen to you?
AEGEUS: What comes to those who have no regard for
heaven.
740 MEDEA: Go on your way. Farewell. For I am satisfied.
And I will reach your city as soon as I can,
Having done the deed I have to do and gained my end.

(AEGEUS *goes out*.)

CHORUS: May Hermes, god of travelers,
Escort you, Aegeus, to your home!
And may you have the things you wish
745 So eagerly; for you

Appear to me to be a generous man.
MEDEA: God, and God's daughter, justice, and light of
   Helius!
Now, friends, has come the time of my triumph over
750 My enemies, and now my foot is on the road.
Now I am confident they will pay the penalty.
For this man, Aegeus, has been like a harbor to me
In all my plans just where I was most distressed.
To him I can fasten the cable of my safety
755 When I have reached the town and fortress of Pallas.
And now I shall tell to you the whole of my plan.
Listen to these words that are not spoken idly.
I shall send one of my servants to find Jason
And request him to come once more into my sight.
760 And when he comes, the words I'll say will be soft ones.
I'll say that I agree with him, that I approve
The royal wedding he has made, betraying me.
I'll say it was profitable, an excellent idea.
But I shall beg that my children may remain here:
765 Not that I would leave in a country that hates me
Children of mine to feel their enemies' insults,
But that by a trick I may kill the king's daughter.
For I will send the children with gifts in their hands
To carry to the bride, so as not to be banished—
770 A finely woven dress and a golden diadem.
And if she takes them and wears them upon her skin
She and all who touch the girl will die in agony;
Such poison will I lay upon the gifts I send.
But there, however, I must leave that account paid.
775 I weep to think of what a deed I have to do
Next after that; for I shall kill my own children.
My children, there is none who can give them safety.
And when I have ruined the whole of Jason's house,
I shall leave the land and flee from the murder of my
780 Dear children, and I shall have done a dreadful deed.
For it is not bearable to be mocked by enemies.
So it must happen. What profit have I in life?
I have no land, no home, no refuge from my pain.
My mistake was made the time I left behind me
785 My father's house, and trusted the words of a Greek,
Who, with heaven's help, will pay me the price for that.
For those children he had from me he will never
See alive again, nor will he on his new bride
Beget another child, for she is to be forced
790 To die a most terrible death by these my poisons.
Let no one think me a weak one, feeble-spirited,
A stay-at-home, but rather just the opposite,
One who can hurt my enemies and help my friends;
For the lives of such persons are most remembered.
795 CHORUS: Since you have shared the knowledge of your plan
   with us,
I both wish to help you and support the normal
Ways of mankind, and tell you not to do this thing.
MEDEA: I can do no other thing. It is understandable
For you to speak thus. You have not suffered as I have.
800 CHORUS: But can you have the heart to kill your flesh and
   blood?
MEDEA: Yes, for this is the best way to wound my husband.

CHORUS: And you, too. Of women you will be most unhappy.
MEDEA: So it must be. No compromise is possible.

(*She turns to the* NURSE.)

Go, you, at once, and tell Jason to come to me.
You I employ on all affairs of greatest trust.   805
Say nothing of these decisions which I have made,
If you love your mistress, if you were born a woman.
CHORUS: From of old the children of Erechtheus are
Splendid, the sons of blessed gods. They dwell
In Athens' holy and unconquered land,   810
Where famous Wisdom feeds them and they pass gaily
Always through that most brilliant air where once, they say,
That golden Harmony gave birth to the nine
Pure Muses of Pieria.

And beside the sweet flow of Cephisus' stream,   815
Where Cypris sailed, they say, to draw the water,
And mild soft breezes breathed along her path,
And on her hair were flung the sweet-smelling garlands
Of flowers of roses by the Lovers, the companions
Of Wisdom, her escort, the helpers of men   820
In every kind of excellence.

How then can these holy rivers
Or this holy land love you,
Or the city find you a home,
You, who will kill your children,   825
You, not pure with the rest?
O think of the blow at your children
And think of the blood that you shed.
O, over and over I beg you,
By your knees I beg you do not   830
Be the murderess of your babes!

O where will you find the courage
Or the skill of hand and heart,
When you set yourself to attempt
A deed so dreadful to do?   835
How, when you look upon them,
Can you tearlessly hold the decision
For murder? You will not be able,
When your children fall down and implore you,
You will not be able to dip   840
Steadfast your hand in their blood.

(*Enter* JASON *with attendants.*)

JASON: I have come at your request. Indeed, although you are
Bitter against me, this you shall have: I will listen
To what new thing you want, woman, to get from me.
MEDEA: Jason, I beg you to be forgiving toward me   845
For what I said. It is natural for you to bear with
My temper, since we have had much love together.
I have talked with myself about this and I have
Reproached myself. "Fool" I said, "why am I so mad?
Why am I set against those who have planned wisely?   850
Why make myself an enemy of the authorities
And of my husband, who does the best thing for me
By marrying royalty and having children who
Will be as brothers to my own? What is wrong with me?

---

755 **fortress of Pallas** Athens, the town of Athena

808 **children of Erechtheus** the Athenians   815 **beside . . . stream** at
Athens

855 Let me give up anger, for the gods are kind to me.
Have I not children, and do I not know that we
In exile from our country must be short of friends?"
When I considered this I saw that I had shown
Great lack of sense, and that my anger was foolish.
860 Now I agree with you. I think that you are wise
In having this other wife as well as me, and I
Was mad. I should have helped you in these plans of yours,
Have joined in the wedding, stood by the marriage bed,
Have taken pleasure in attendance on your bride.
865 But we women are what we are—perhaps a little
Worthless; and you men must not be like us in this,
Nor be foolish in return when we are foolish.
Now, I give in, and admit that then I was wrong.
I have come to a better understanding now.

(She turns toward the house.)

870 Children, come here, my children, come outdoors to us!
Welcome your father with me, and say goodbye to him,
And with your mother, who just now was his enemy,
Join again in making friends with him who loves us.

(Enter the CHILDREN, attended by the TUTOR.)

We have made peace, and all our anger is over.
875 Take hold of his right hand—O God, I am thinking
Of something which may happen in the secret future.
O children, will you just so, after a long life,
Hold out your loving arms at the grave? O children,
How ready to cry I am, how full of foreboding!
880 I am ending at last this quarrel with your father,
And, look my soft eyes have suddenly filled with tears.
CHORUS: And the pale tears have started also in my eyes.
O may the trouble not grow worse than now it is!
JASON: I approve of what you say. And I cannot blame you
885 Even for what you said before. It is natural
For a woman to be wild with her husband when he
Goes in for secret love. But now your mind has turned
To better reasoning. In the end you have come to
The right decision, like the clever woman you are.
890 And of you, children, your father is taking care.
He has made, with God's help, ample provision for you.
For I think that a time will come when you will be
The leading people in Corinth with your brothers.
You must grow up. As to the future, your father
895 And those of the gods who love him will deal with that.
I want to see you, when you have become young men,
Healthy and strong, better men than my enemies.
Medea, why are your eyes all wet with pale tears?
Why is your cheek so white and turned away from me?
900 Are not these words of mine pleasing for you to hear?
MEDEA: It is nothing. I was thinking about these children.
JASON: You must be cheerful. I shall look after them well.
MEDEA: I will be. It is not that I distrust your words,
But a woman is a frail thing, prone to crying.
905 JASON: But why then should you grieve so much for these
children?
MEDEA: I am their mother. When you prayed that they might
live
I felt unhappy to think that these things will be.
But come, I have said something of the things I meant
To say to you, and now I will tell you the rest.

910 Since it is the king's will to banish me from here—
And for me, too, I know that this is the best thing,
Not to be in your way by living here or in
The king's way, since they think me ill-disposed to them—
I then am going into exile from this land;
915 But do you, so that you may have the care of them,
Beg Creon that the children may not be banished.
JASON: I doubt if I'll succeed, but still I'll attempt it.
MEDEA: Then you must tell your wife to beg from her father
That the children may be reprieved from banishment.
920 JASON: I will, and with her I shall certainly succeed.
MEDEA: If she is like the rest of us women, you will.
And I, too, will take a hand with you in this business,
For I will send her some gifts which are far fairer,
I am sure of it, than those which now are in fashion,
925 A finely woven dress and a golden diadem,
And the children shall present them. Quick, let one of you
Servants bring here to me that beautiful dress.

(One of her attendants goes into the house.)

She will be happy not in one way, but in a hundred,
Having so fine a man as you to share her bed,
930 And with this beautiful dress which Helius of old,
My father's father, bestowed on his descendants.

(Enter attendant carrying the poisoned dress and diadem.)

There, children, take these wedding presents in your hands.
Take them to the royal princess, the happy bride,
And give them to her. She will not think little of them.
935 JASON: No, don't be foolish, and empty your hands of these.
Do you think the palace is short of dresses to wear?
Do you think there is no gold there? Keep them, don't give
them
Away. If my wife considers me of any value,
She will think more of me than money, I am sure of it.
940 MEDEA: No, let me have my way. They say the gods themselves
Are moved by gifts, and gold does more with men than
words.
Hers is the luck, her fortune that which god blesses;
She is young and a princess; but for my children's reprieve
I would give my very life, and not gold only.
945 Go children, go together to that rich palace,
Be suppliants to the new wife of your father,
My lady, beg her not to let you be banished.
And give her the dress—for this is of great importance,
That she should take the gift into her hand from yours.
950 Go, quick as you can. And bring your mother good news
By your success of those things which she longs to gain.

*(JASON goes out with his attendants, followed by the TUTOR and
the CHILDREN carrying the poisoned gifts.)*

CHORUS: Now there is no hope left for the children's lives.
Now there is none. They are walking already to murder.
The bride, poor bride, will accept the curse of the gold,
Will accept the bright diadem.
955 Around her yellow hair she will set that dress
Of death with her own hands.

The grace and the perfume and glow of the golden robe
Will charm her to put them upon her and wear the wreath,
And now her wedding will be with the dead below,
960 Into such a trap she will fall,

Poor thing, into such a fate of death and never
Escape from under that curse.

You, too, O wretched bridegroom, making your match with
kings,
965 You do not see that you bring
Destruction on your children and on her,
Your wife, a fearful death.
Poor soul, what a fall is yours!

In your grief, too, I weep, mother of little children,
970 You who will murder your own,
In vengeance for the loss of married love
Which Jason has betrayed
As he lives with another wife.

(Enter the TUTOR with the CHILDREN.)

TUTOR: Mistress, I tell you that these children are reprieved,
975 And the royal bride has been pleased to take in her hands
Your gifts. In that quarter the children are secure.
But come,
Why do you stand confused when you are fortunate?
Why have you turned round with your cheek away from me?
980 Are not these words of mine pleasing for you to hear?
MEDEA: Oh! I am lost!
TUTOR: That word is not in harmony with my tidings.
MEDEA: I am lost, I am lost!
TUTOR: Am I in ignorance telling you
Of some disaster, and not the good news I thought?
985 MEDEA: You have told what you have told. I do not blame
you.
TUTOR: Why then this downcast eye, and this weeping of
tears?
MEDEA: Oh, I am forced to weep, old man. The gods and I,
I in a kind of madness, have contrived all this.
TUTOR: Courage! You, too, will be brought home by your
children.
990 MEDEA: Ah, before that happens I shall bring others home.
TUTOR: Others before you have been parted from their
children.
Mortals must bear in resignation their ill luck.
MEDEA: That is what I shall do. But go inside the house,
And do for the children your usual daily work.

(The TUTOR goes into the house. MEDEA turns to her CHILDREN.)

995 O children, O my children, you have a city,
You have a home, and you can leave me behind you,
And without your mother you may live there forever.
But I am going in exile to another land
Before I have seen you happy and taken pleasure in you,
1000 Before I have dressed your brides and made your marriage
beds
And held up the torch at the ceremony of wedding.
Oh, what a wretch I am in this my self-willed thought!
What was the purpose, children, for which I reared you?
For all my travail and wearing myself away?
1005 They were sterile, those pains I had in the bearing of you.
Oh surely once the hopes in you I had, poor me,
Were high ones: you would look after me in old age,
And when I died would deck me well with your own hands;
A thing which all would have done. Oh but now it is gone,
1010 That lovely thought. For, once I am left without you,

Sad will be the life I'll lead and sorrowful for me.
And you will never see your mother again with
Your dear eyes, gone to another mode of living.
Why, children, do you look upon me with your eyes?
Why do you smile so sweetly that last smile of all? 1015
Oh, Oh, what can I do? My spirit has gone from me,
Friends, when I saw that bright look in the children's eyes.
I cannot bear to do it. I renounce my plans
I had before. I'll take my children away from
This land. Why should I hurt their father with the pain 1020
They feel, and suffer twice as much of pain myself?
No, no, I will not do it. I renounce my plans.
Ah, what is wrong with me? Do I want to let go
My enemies unhurt and be laughed at for it?
I must face this thing. Oh, but what a weak woman 1025
Even to admit to my mind these soft arguments.
Children, go into the house. And he whom law forbids
To stand in attendance at my sacrifices,
Let him see to it. I shall not mar my handiwork.
Oh! Oh! 1030
Do not, O my heart, you must not do these things!
Poor heart, let them go, have pity upon the children.
If they live with you in Athens they will cheer you.
No! By Hell's avenging furies it shall not be—
This shall never be, that I should suffer my children 1035
To be the prey of my enemies' insolence.
Every way is it fixed. The bride will not escape.
No, the diadem is now upon her head, and she,
The royal princess, is dying in the dress, I know it.
But—for it is the most dreadful of roads for me 1040
To tread, and them I shall send on a more dreadful still—
I wish to speak to the children.

(She calls the CHILDREN to her.)

Come, children, give
Me your hands, give your mother your hands to kiss them.
Oh the dear hands, and O how dear are these lips to me,
And the generous eyes and the bearing of my children! 1045
I wish you happiness, but not here in this world.
What is here your father took. Oh how good to hold you!
How delicate the skin, how sweet the breath of children!
Go, go! I am no longer able, no longer
To look upon you. I am overcome by sorrow. 1050

(The CHILDREN go into the house.)

I know indeed what evil I intend to do,
But stronger than all my afterthoughts is my fury,
Fury that brings upon mortals the greatest evils.

(She goes out to the right, toward the royal palace.)

CHORUS: Often before
I have gone through more subtle reasons, 1055
And have come upon questionings greater
Than a woman should strive to search out.
But we too have a goddess to help us
And accompany us into wisdom.
Not all of us. Still you will find 1060
Among many women a few,
And our sex is not without learning.
This I say, that those who have never
Had children, who know nothing of it,

1065   In happiness have the advantage
       Over those who are parents.
       The childless, who never discover
       Whether children turn out as a good thing
       Or as something to cause pain, are spared
1070   Many troubles in lacking this knowledge.
       And those who have in their homes
       The sweet presence of children, I see that their lives
       Are all wasted away by their worries.
       First they must think how to bring them up well and
1075   How to leave them something to live on.
       And then after this whether all their toil
       Is for those who will turn out good or bad,
       Is still an unanswered question.
       And of one more trouble, the last of all,
1080   That is common to mortals I tell.
       For suppose you have found them enough for their living,
       Suppose that the children have grown into youth
       And have turned out good, still, if God so wills it,
       Death will away with your children's bodies,
1085   And carry them off into Hades.
       What is our profit, then, that for the sake of
       Children the gods should pile upon mortals
       After all else
       This most terrible grief of all?

(Enter MEDEA, *from the spectators' right.)*

1090   MEDEA: Friends, I can tell you that for long I have waited
       For the event. I stare toward the place from where
       The news will come. And now, see one of Jason's servants
       Is on his way here, and that labored breath of his
       Shows he has tidings for us, and evil tidings.

(Enter, also from the right, the MESSENGER.*)*

1095   MESSENGER: Medea, you who have done such a dreadful
          thing,
       So outrageous, run for your life, take what you can,
       A ship to bear you hence or chariot on land.
       MEDEA: And what is the reason deserves such flight as this?
       MESSENGER: She is dead, only just now, the royal princess,
1100   And Creon dead, too, her father, by your poisons.
       MEDEA: The finest words you have spoken. Now and hereafter
       I shall count you among my benefactors and friends.
       MESSENGER: What! Are you right in the mind? Are you not
          mad,
       Woman? The house of the king is outraged by you.
1105   Do you enjoy it? Not afraid of such doings?
       MEDEA: To what you say I on my side have something too
       To say in answer. Do not be in a hurry, friend,
       But speak. How did they die? You will delight me twice
       As much again if you say they died in agony.
1110   MESSENGER: When those two children, born of you, had
          entered in,
       Their father with them, and passed into the bride's house,
       We were pleased, we slaves who were distressed by your
          wrongs.
       All through the house we were talking of but one thing,
       How you and your husband had made up your quarrel.
1115   Some kissed the children's hands and some their yellow hair,
       And I myself was so full of my joy that I
       Followed the children into the women's quarters.

Our mistress, whom we honor now instead of you,
Before she noticed that your two children were there,
Was keeping her eye fixed eagerly on Jason.   1120
Afterwards, however, she covered up her eyes,
Her cheek paled, and she turned herself away from him,
So disgusted was she at the children's coming there.
But your husband tried to end the girl's bad temper,
And said "You must not look unkindly on your friends.   1125
Cease to be angry. Turn your head to me again.
Have as your friends the same ones as your husband has.
And take these gifts, and beg your father to reprieve
These children from their exile. Do it for my sake."
She, when she saw the dress, could not restrain herself.   1130
She agreed with all her husband said, and before
He and the children had gone far from the palace,
She took the gorgeous robe and dressed herself in it,
And put the golden crown around her curly locks,
And arranged the set of the hair in a shining mirror,   1135
And smiled at the lifeless image of herself in it.
Then she rose from her chair and walked about the room,
With her gleaming feet stepping most soft and delicate,
All overjoyed with the present. Often and often
She would stretch her foot out straight and look along it.   1140
But after that it was a fearful thing to see.
The color of her face changed, and she staggered back,
She ran, and her legs trembled, and she only just
Managed to reach a chair without falling flat down.
An aged woman servant who, I take it, thought   1145
This was some seizure of Pan or another god,
Cried out "God bless us," but that was before she saw
The white foam breaking through her lips and her rolling
The pupils of her eyes and her face all bloodless.
Then she raised a different cry from that "God bless us,"   1150
A huge shriek, and the women ran, one to the king,
One to the newly wedded husband to tell him
What had happened to his bride; and with frequent sound
The whole of the palace rang as they went running.
One walking quickly round the course of a race-track   1155
Would now have turned the bend and be close to the goal,
When she, poor girl, opened her shut and speechless eye,
And with a terrible groan she came to herself.
For a twofold pain was moving up against her.
The wreath of gold that was resting around her head   1160
Let forth a fearful stream of all-devouring fire,
And the finely woven dress your children gave to her,
Was fastening on the unhappy girl's fine flesh.
She leapt up from the chair, and all on fire she ran,
Shaking her hair now this way and now that, trying   1165
To hurl the diadem away; but fixedly
The gold preserved its grip, and, when she shook her hair,
Then more and twice as fiercely the fire blazed out.
Till, beaten by her fate, she fell down to the ground,
Hard to be recognized except by a parent.   1170
Neither the setting of her eyes was plain to see,
Nor the shapeliness of her face. From the top of
Her head there oozed out blood and fire mixed together.
Like the drops on pine-bark, so the flesh from her bones
Dropped away, torn by the hidden fang of the poison.   1175
It was a fearful sight; and terror held us all
From touching the corpse. We had learned from what had
   happened.
But her wretched father, knowing nothing of the event,

1180 Came suddenly to the house, and fell upon the corpse,
And at once cried out and folded his arms about her,
And kissed her and spoke to her, saying, "O my poor child,
What heavenly power has so shamefully destroyed you?
And who has set me here like an ancient sepulcher,
Deprived of you? O let me die with you, my child!"
1185 And when he had made an end of his wailing and crying,
Then the old man wished to raise himself to his feet;
But, as the ivy clings to the twigs of the laurel,
So he stuck to the fine dress, and he struggled fearfully.
For he was trying to lift himself to his knee,
1190 And she was pulling him down, and when he tugged hard
He would be ripping his aged flesh from his bones.
At last his life was quenched, and the unhappy man
Gave up the ghost, no longer could hold up his head.
There they lie close, the daughter and the old father,
1195 Dead bodies, an event he prayed for in his tears.
As for your interests, I will say nothing of them,
For you will find your own escape from punishment.
Our human life I think and have thought a shadow,
And I do not fear to say that those who are held
1200 Wise among men and who search the reasons of things
Are those who bring the most sorrow on themselves.
For of mortals there is no one who is happy.
If wealth flows in upon one, one may be perhaps
Luckier than one's neighbor, but still not happy.

(Exit.)

1205 CHORUS: Heaven, it seems, on this day has fastened many
Evils on Jason, and Jason has deserved them.
Poor girl, the daughter of Creon, how I pity you
And your misfortunes, you who have gone quite away
To the house of Hades because of marrying Jason.
1210 MEDEA: Women, my task is fixed: as quickly as I may
To kill my children, and start away from this land,
And not, by wasting time, to suffer my children
To be slain by another hand less kindly to them.
Force every way will have it they must die, and since
1215 This must be so, then I, their mother, shall kill them.
Oh, arm yourself in steel, my heart! Do not hang back
From doing this fearful and necessary wrong.
Oh, come, my hand, poor wretched hand, and take the
sword,
Take it, step forward to this bitter starting point,
1220 And do not be a coward, do not think of them,
How sweet they are, and how you are their mother. Just for
This one short day be forgetful of your children,
Afterward weep; for even though you will kill them,
They were very dear—Oh, I am an unhappy woman!

(With a cry she rushes into the house.)

1225 CHORUS: O Earth, and the far shining
Ray of the Sun, look down, look down upon
This poor lost woman, look, before she raises
The hand of murder against her flesh and blood.
Yours was the golden birth from which
1230 She sprang, and now I fear divine
Blood may be shed by men.
O heavenly light, hold back her hand,
Check her, and drive from out the house
The bloody Fury raised by fiends of Hell.

Vain waste, your care of children; 1235
Was it in vain you bore the babes you loved,
After you passed the inhospitable strait
Between the dark blue rocks, Symplegades?
O wretched one, how has it come,
This heavy anger on your heart, 1240
This cruel bloody mind?
For God from mortals asks a stern
Price for the stain of kindred blood
In like disaster falling on their homes.

(A cry from ONE OF THE CHILDREN *is heard.)*

CHORUS: Do you hear the cry, do you hear the children's cry? 1245
O you hard heart, O woman fated for evil!
ONE OF THE CHILDREN: *(From within.)* What can I do and
how escape my mother's hands?
ANOTHER CHILD: *(From within.)* O my dear brother, I cannot
tell. We are lost.
CHORUS: Shall I enter the house? Oh, surely I should
Defend the children from murder. 1250
A CHILD: *(From within.)* O help us, in God's name, for now
we need your help.
Now, now we are close to it. We are trapped by the sword.
CHORUS: O your heart must have been made of rock or steel,
You who can kill
With your own hand the fruit of your own womb. 1255
Of one alone I have heard, one woman alone
Of those of old who laid her hands on her children,
Ino, sent mad by heaven when the wife of Zeus
Drove her out from her home and made her wander;
And because of the wicked shedding of blood 1260
Of her own children she threw
Herself, poor wretch, into the sea and stepped away
Over the sea-cliff to die with her two children.
What horror more can be? O women's love,
So full of trouble, 1265
How many evils have you caused already!

(Enter JASON, *with attendants.)*

JASON: You women, standing close in front of this dwelling,
Is she, Medea, she who did this dreadful deed,
Still in the house, or has she run away in flight?
For she will have to hide herself beneath the earth, 1270
Or raise herself on wings into the height of air,
If she wishes to escape the royal vengeance.
Does she imagine that, having killed our rulers,
She will herself escape uninjured from this house?
But I am thinking not so much of her as for 1275
The children—her the king's friends will make to suffer
For what she did. So I have come to save the lives
Of my boys, in case the royal house should harm them
While taking vengeance for their mother's wicked deed.
CHORUS: O Jason, if you but knew how deeply you are 1280
Involved in sorrow, you would not have spoken so.
JASON: What is it? That she is planning to kill me also?
CHORUS: Your children are dead, and by their own mother's
hand.
JASON: What! That is it? O woman, you have destroyed me!
CHORUS: You must make up your mind your children are no 1285
more.
JASON: Where did she kill them? Was it here or in the house?
CHORUS: Open the gates and there you will see them murdered.

JASON: Quick as you can unlock the doors, men, and undo
  The fastenings and let me see this double evil,
1290 My children dead and her—Oh her I will repay.

(His attendants rush to the door. MEDEA *appears above the house in a chariot drawn by dragons. She has the dead bodies of the* CHILDREN *with her.)*

MEDEA: Why do you batter these gates and try to unbar them,
  Seeking the corpses and for me who did the deed?
  You may cease your trouble, and, if you have need of me,
  Speak, if you wish. You will never touch me with your hand,
1295 Such a chariot has Helius, my father's father,
  Given me to defend me from my enemies.

JASON: You hateful thing, you woman most utterly loathed
  By the gods and me and by all the race of mankind,
  You who have had the heart to raise a sword against
1300 Your children, you, their mother, and left me childless—
  You have done this, and do you still look at the sun
  And at the earth, after these most fearful doings?
  I wish you dead. Now I see it plain, though at that time
  I did not, when I took you from your foreign home
1305 And brought you to a Greek house, you, an evil thing,
  A traitress to your father and your native land.
  The gods hurled the avenging curse of yours on me.
  For your own brother you slew at your own hearthside,
  And then came aboard that beautiful ship, the Argo.
1310 And that was your beginning. When you were married
  To me, your husband, and had borne children to me,
  For the sake of pleasure in the bed you killed them.
  There is no Greek woman who would have dared such
    deeds,
  Out of all those whom I passed over and chose you
1315 To marry instead, a bitter destructive match,
  A monster, not a woman, having a nature
  Wilder than that of Scylla in the Tuscan sea.
  Ah! no, not if I had ten thousand words of shame
  Could I sting you. You are naturally so brazen.
1320 Go, worker in evil, stained with your children's blood.
  For me remains to cry aloud upon my fate,
  Who will get no pleasure from my newly wedded love,
  And the boys whom I begot and brought up, never
  Shall I speak to them alive. Oh, my life is over!
1325 MEDEA: Long would be the answer which I might have
    made to
  These words of yours, if Zeus the father did not know
  How I have treated you and what you did to me.
  No, it was not to be that you should scorn my love,
  And pleasantly live your life through, laughing at me;
1330 Nor would the princess, nor he who offered the match,
  Creon, drive me away without paying for it.
  So now you may call me a monster, if you wish,
  A Scylla housed in the caves of the Tuscan sea.
  I too, as I had to, have taken hold of your heart.
1335 JASON: You feel the pain yourself. You share in my sorrow.
MEDEA: Yes, and my grief is gain when you cannot mock it.
JASON: O children, what a wicked mother she was to you!
MEDEA: They died from a disease they caught from their
    father.

1317 **Scylla** a monster in the *Odyssey*

JASON: I tell you it was not my hand that destroyed them.
MEDEA: But it was your insolence, and your virgin wedding. 1340
JASON: And just for the sake of that you chose to kill them.
MEDEA: Is love so small a pain, do you think, for a woman?
JASON: For a wise one, certainly. But you are wholly evil.
MEDEA: The children are dead. I say this to make you suffer.
JASON: The children, I think, will bring down curses on you. 1345
MEDEA: The gods know who was the author of this sorrow.
JASON: Yes, the gods know indeed, they know your loathsome
    heart.
MEDEA: Hate me. But I tire of your barking bitterness.
JASON: And I of yours. It is easier to leave you.
MEDEA: How then? What shall I do? I long to leave you too. 1350
JASON: Give me the bodies to bury and to mourn them.
MEDEA: No, that I will not. I will bury them myself,
  Bearing them to Hera's temple on the promontory;
  So that no enemy may evilly treat them
  By tearing up their grave. In this land of Corinth 1355
  I shall establish a holy feast and sacrifice
  Each year for ever to atone for the blood guilt.
  And I myself go to the land of Erechtheus
  To dwell in Aegeus' house, the son of Pandion.
  While you, as is right, will die without distinction, 1360
  Struck on the head by a piece of the Argo's timber,
  And you will have seen the bitter end of my love.
JASON: May a Fury for the children's sake destroy you,
  And justice, Requitor of blood.
MEDEA: What heavenly power lends an ear 1365
  To a breaker of oaths, a deceiver?
JASON: Oh, I hate you, murderess of children.
MEDEA: Go to your palace. Bury your bride.
JASON: I go, with two children to mourn for.
MEDEA: Not yet do you feel it. Wait for the future. 1370
JASON: Oh, children I loved!
MEDEA: I loved them, you did not.
JASON: You loved them, and killed them.
MEDEA: To make you feel pain.
JASON: Oh, wretch that I am, how I long
  To kiss the dear lips of my children!
MEDEA: Now you would speak to them, now you would kiss 1375
    them.
  Then you rejected them.
JASON: Let me, I beg you,
  Touch my boys' delicate flesh.
MEDEA: I will not. Your words are all wasted.
JASON: O God, do you hear it, this persecution,
  These my sufferings from this hateful 1380
  Woman, this monster, murderess of children?
  Still what I can do that I will do:
  I will lament and cry upon heaven,
  Calling the gods to bear me witness
  How you have killed my boys and prevent me from 1385
  Touching their bodies or giving them burial.
  I wish I had never begot them to see them
  Afterward slaughtered by you.
CHORUS: Zeus in Olympus is the overseer
  Of many doings. Many things the gods 1390
  Achieve beyond our judgment. What we thought
  Is not confirmed and what we thought not god
  Contrives. And so it happens in this story.

■ ARISTOPHANES ■

Aristophanes (c. 450–c. 388 BC) pursued his career as a playwright throughout the Peloponnesian War. As he observed the decline and defeat of Athens, his comedies relentlessly attacked the war and the individuals and attitudes that supported it. Aristophanes first entered the City Dionysia in 427 BC and first won in 426 BC with a now-lost play that satirized the policies and character of the military leader Cleon. Many of Aristophanes' plays—*Birds*, *Lysistrata*, *Assembly of Women*—use a utopian premise to criticize the war, but in other plays, Aristophanes lampoons other aspects of city life. In *Frogs*, for instance, a pompous Aeschylus and an embittered Euripides come from Hades to vie with one another once again; in *Clouds*, Aristophanes ridicules the sophists—professional teachers of rhetoric—for their ability to argue any side of an issue, and he particularly singles out Socrates for blame. The impact of Aristophanes' comedy on Athens should not be underestimated. In Plato's *Apology*, Socrates cites Aristophanes' portrayal of him in *Clouds* as one of the factors that turned Athenian sentiment against him, resulting in his trial and sentence of execution. Aristophanes' plays include *Acharnians*, *Knights*, *Clouds*, *Wasps*, *Peace*, *Birds*, *Lysistrata*, *Women Celebrating the Thesmophoria*, *Frogs*, *Assembly of Women*, and *Plutus*.

LYSISTRATA

Lysistrata is one of several plays critical of Athens' war with Sparta. Produced in 411 BC, it follows shortly on a disastrous phase of the war for Athens. Two years earlier, the Athenian raid on Sicily had failed, and the navy was decimated, leaving Athens vulnerable to attack by Sparta. Although the navy was rebuilt before Sparta mounted its final assault, Athens fell to Sparta in 404 BC.

Lysistrata explores the premise that the women of Greece—drawn from all the major city-states and regions—could unite to oppose the war. Led by the Athenian Lysistrata (her name means "disband the army"), the women barricade themselves on the Acropolis, withholding sex from the men until peace can be declared. Aristophanes provides each of his women with the physical attributes and accent typical of her region. The large and powerful Spartan woman Lampito, for example, is both an expert in the Spartan rump-kicking dance and speaks in what was—to an Athenian audience—an outlandish accent (to make this clear for English-speaking readers, this translation gives Lampito a Scots accent).

Lysistrata addresses the politics of its era in a variety of ways. It is, of course, a passionate plea for peace, concluding with a scene of comic feasting and dancing enjoyed by all the characters in the play, Athenians and Spartans, men and women. For modern audiences, though, the play's connection between gender and politics may seem more immediate. On one hand, the play implies an equality between men and women. The women claim that the morality of their domestic sphere is superior to the military morality pursued by the men, and to get the women back, the men are forced to compromise with them. On the other hand, although *Lysistrata* seems to provide women with political power, their power resides wholly in their sexuality; they can interrupt, but not change, the fact that they are the property of men. The Theater of Dionysus could not, of course, put women on the stage, and Lysistrata, Lampito, Calonice, and the rest—even the naked girl Reconciliation—were all played by men in padded costumes. We might also take this stage convention as an indication of the place of gender in the politics of Athens and its theater: women's concerns are only represented or impersonated by men. In the play and in the *polis*, women were defined principally through their relation to men. The limited influence women could exert was subordinate to the civil power that Aristophanes and his audience took to be the "natural" preserve of the male audience. Despite the play's earthy humor and apparent feminism, *Lysistrata* documents the actual status of women in classical Athens; their power is restricted to the sphere of the *oikos*, or home, and can be practiced only through their subservience to men, who—as citizens—finally can command women's bodies, the home, and the state as well.

LYSISTRATA

ARISTOPHANES
TRANSLATED BY ALAN H. SOMMERSTEIN

— CHARACTERS —

LYSISTRATA
CALONICE } *Athenian women*
MYRRHINE
LAMPITO, *a Spartan woman*
CHORUS OF OLD MEN
CHORUS OF OLD WOMEN
STRATYLLIS, *leader of the Women's Chorus*
A MAGISTRATE, *member of the Committee of Ten for the Safety of the State*
FIVE YOUNG WOMEN
CINESIAS, *husband to Myrrhine*
BABY, *son to Cinesias and Myrrhine*
A SPARTAN HERALD

A SPARTAN AMBASSADOR
AN ATHENIAN NEGOTIATOR
TWO LAYABOUTS
DOORKEEPER, *of the Acropolis*
TWO DINERS
ISMENIA, *a Boeotian woman*
A CORINTHIAN WOMAN
RECONCILIATION, *maidservant to Lysistrata*
FOUR SCYTHIAN POLICEMEN
A SCYTHIAN POLICEWOMAN
ATHENIAN CITIZENS, SPARTAN AMBASSADORS,
  ATHENIAN AND SPARTAN WOMEN, SLAVES, *etc.*

— ACT ONE —

SCENE: *In front of the entrance to the Athenian Acropolis. At the back of the stage stands the Great Gateway (the Propylaea); to the right, a stretch of the Acropolis wall with a little shrine to Athena Niké (Victory) built into it; to the left, a statue of the tyrannicides Harmodius and Aristogeiton. It is early morning.*

(LYSISTRATA *is standing in front of the Propylaea looking, with increasing impatience, to see if anyone is coming.*)

LYSISTRATA: (*Stamping her foot and bursting into impatient speech.*) Just think if it had been a Bacchic celebration they'd been asked to attend—or something in honour of Pan or Aphrodite—particularly Aphrodite! You wouldn't have been
5 able to move for all the drums. And now look—not a woman here!

(*Enter* CALONICE.)

Ah! here's one at last. One of my neighbours, I—Why, hello, Calonice.

CALONICE: Hello, Lysistrata. What's bothering you, dear?
10 Don't screw up your face like that. It really doesn't suit you, you know, knitting your eyebrows up like a bow or something.

LYSISTRATA: Sorry, Calonice, but I'm furious. I'm disappointed in womankind. All our husbands think we're such
15 clever villains—

CALONICE: Well, aren't we?

LYSISTRATA: And here I've called a meeting to discuss a very important matter, and they're all still fast asleep!

CALONICE: Don't worry, dear, they'll come. It's not so easy for
20 a wife to get out of the house, you know. They'll all be rushing to and fro for their husbands, waking up the servants, putting the baby to bed or washing and feeding it—

LYSISTRATA: Damn it, there are more important things than that!

25 CALONICE: Tell me, Lysistrata dear, what is it you've summoned this meeting of the women for? Is it something big?

LYSISTRATA: Very.

CALONICE: (*Thinking she detects a significant intonation in that word.*) Not thick as well?

LYSISTRATA: As a matter of fact, yes. 30

CALONICE: Then why on earth aren't they here?

LYSISTRATA: (*Realizing she has been misleading.*) No, not that kind of thing—well, not exactly. If it had been, I can assure you, they'd have been here as quick as you can bat an eyelid. No, I've had an idea, which for many sleepless nights I've 35 been tossing to and fro—

CALONICE: Must be a pretty flimsy one, in that case.

LYSISTRATA: Flimsy? Calonice, we women have the salvation of Greece in our hands.

CALONICE: In our hands? We might as well give up hope, 40 then.

LYSISTRATA: The whole future of the City is up to us. Either the Peloponnesians are all going to be wiped out—

CALONICE: Good idea, by Zeus!

LYSISTRATA: —and the Boeotians be destroyed too— 45

CALONICE: Not all of them, please! Do spare the eels.

LYSISTRATA: —and Athens—well, I won't say it, but you know what might happen. But if all the women join together—not just us, but the Peloponnesians and Boeotians as well—then we can save Greece. 50

CALONICE: The women!—what could they ever do that was any use? Sitting at home putting flowers in their hair, putting on cosmetics and saffron gowns and Cimberian see-through shifts, with slippers on our feet?

LYSISTRATA: But don't you see, that's exactly what I mean to 55 use to save Greece. Those saffron gowns and slippers and see-through dresses, yes, and our scent and rouge as well.

CALONICE: How are you going to do that?

LYSISTRATA: I am going to bring it about that the men will no longer lift up their spears against one another— 60

CALONICE: I'm going to get some new dye on my yellow gown!

---

46 **eels** Boeotia was well known for its seafood

78

LYSISTRATA: —nor take up their shields—

CALONICE: I'll put on a see-through right away!

LYSISTRATA: —or their swords.

65 CALONICE: Slippers, here I come!

LYSISTRATA: *Now* do you think the women ought to be here by now?

CALONICE: By Zeus, yes—they ought to have taken wing and flown here.

70 LYSISTRATA: No such luck, old girl; what do you expect?—they're Athenian, and everything they do too late. But really—for nobody to have come at all! None from the Paralia, none of the Salaminians—

CALONICE: Oh, they'll have been on the go since the small

75 hours. *(Aside.)* They probably will too.

LYSISTRATA: And the ones I was most counting on being here first—the Acharnians—they haven't come either.

CALONICE: Well, as to that, I did see Theagenes' wife consulting the shrine of Hecate in front of her door, so I imagine

80 she's going to come.

(Enter, from various directions MYRRHINE *and other women.)*

Ah, here are some coming—and here are some more. Ugh! *(Puckering up her nose.)* where do this lot come from?

LYSISTRATA: Ponchidae.

CALONICE: I can well believe it!

85 MYRRHINE: *(A little out of breath.)* We're not late, are we, Lysistrata?

*(*LYSISTRATA *frowns and says nothing.)*

Well? Why aren't you saying anything?

LYSISTRATA: Myrrhine, I don't think much of people who come this late when such an important matter is to be discussed.

90 MYRRHINE: *(Lamely.)* Well, I had some difficulty finding my girdle in the dark. If it is so important, don't let's wait for the rest; tell us about it now.

LYSISTRATA: Let's just wait a moment. The Boeotian and Peloponnesian women should be here any time now.

95 MYRRHINE: Good idea. Ah, here comes Lampito!

(Enter LAMPITO, *with several other Spartan women, their dresses fringed at the bottom with sheepskin, and with representatives from Corinth and Boeotia.)*

LYSISTRATA: Welcome, Lampito, my dear. How are things in Sparta? Darling, you look simply beautiful. Such colour, such resilience! Why, I bet you could throttle a bull.

LAMPITO: Sae cuid you, my dear, if ye were in training. Dinna

100 ken, I practise rump-jumps every day.

LYSISTRATA: *(Prodding her.)* And such marvellous tits, too.

LAMPITO: *(Indignantly.)* I'd thank ye not tae treat me as though ye were just aboot tae sacrifice me.

LYSISTRATA: Where's this other girl come from?

105 LAMPITO: *(Presenting* ISMENIA.) By the Twa Gudes, this is the Boeotian Ambassadress that's come tae ye.

LYSISTRATA: *(Inspecting* ISMENIA.) I should have known—look what a fertile vale she's got there!

CALONICE: Yes, and with all the grass so beautifully cropped,

110 too!

LYSISTRATA: And this one?

LAMPITO: Och, she's a braw bonny lass—a Corinthian.

CALONICE: Yes, I can see why you call her that! *(Indicating a prominent part of the Corinthian's person.)*

LAMPITO: Who's the convener of this female assembly?   115

LYSISTRATA: I am.

LAMPITO: Then tell us the noo what ye have tae say.

MYRRHINE: Yes, dear, tell us what this important business is.

LYSISTRATA: I will tell you. But before I do, I want to ask you just one little question.   120

MYRRHINE: By all means.

LYSISTRATA: The fathers of your children—don't you miss them when they're away at the war? I know not one of you has a husband at home.

CALONICE: I know, my dear. My husband has been away for   125
five months, five months, my dear, in Thrace I think, keeping an eye on our general there.

MYRRHINE: And mine has been in Pylos for the last seven months.

LAMPITO: And as for my mon, if he ever turns up at home, it's   130
anely to pit a new strap on his shield and fly off again.

LYSISTRATA: That's what it's like. There isn't anyone even to have an affair with—not a sausage! Talking of which, now the Milesians have rebelled, we can't even get our six-inch Ladies' Comforters which we used to keep as leather rations 135
for when all else failed. Well then, if I found a way to do it, would you be prepared to join with me in stopping the war?

MYRRHINE: By the Holy Twain, I would! Even if I had to take off my cloak this very day and—drink!

CALONICE: And so would I—even if I had to cut myself in two, 140
like a flatfish, and give half of myself for the cause.

LAMPITO: And I too, if I had tae climb tae the top o' Taygetus, so I cuid see the licht o' peace whenas I got there.

LYSISTRATA: Then I will tell you my plan: there is no need to keep it back. Ladies, if we want to force our husbands to   145
make peace, we must give up—*(She hesitates.)*

CALONICE: What must we give up? Go on.

LYSISTRATA: Then you'll do it?

CALONICE: If need be, we'll lay down our lives for it.

LYSISTRATA: Very well then. We must give up—sex.   150

(Strong murmurs of disapproval, shaking of heads, etc. Several of the company begin to walk off.)

Why are you turning away from me? Where are you going? What's all this pursing of lips and shaking of heads mean? You're all going pale—I can see tears! Will you do it or won't you? Answer!

MYRRHINE: I won't do it. Better to let the war go on.   155

CALONICE: I won't do it either. Let the war go on.

LYSISTRATA: Weren't you the flatfish who was ready to cut herself in half a moment ago?

CALONICE: I still am! I'll do that, or walk through the fire, or anything—but give up sex, never! Lysistrata, darling, there's 160
just nothing like it.

LYSISTRATA: *(To* MYRRHINE.) How about you?

MYRRHINE: I'd rather walk through the fire too!

LYSISTRATA: I didn't know we women were so beyond redemption. The tragic poets are right about us after all: all we're 165

---

105 **Twa Gudes** to a Spartan, this means Castor and Polydeuces (Pollux)

138 **Holy Twain** to an Athenian, Demeter and her daughter, Persephone

interested in is having our fun and then getting rid of the baby. My Spartan friend, will you join me? Even if it's just the two of us, we might yet succeed.

170 LAMPITO: Well—it's a sair thing, the dear knows, for a woman tae sleep alone wi'oot a prick—but we maun do it, for the sake of peace.

LYSISTRATA: *(Enthusiastically embracing her.)* Lampito, darling, you're the only real woman among the lot of them.

175 CALONICE: But look, suppose we did give up—what you said—which may heaven forbid—but if we did, how would that help to end the war?

LYSISTRATA: How? Well, just imagine: we're at home, beautifully made up, wearing our sheerest lawn negligées and nothing underneath, and with our—our triangles carefully
180 plucked; and the men are all like ramrods and can't wait to leap into bed, and then we absolutely refuse—that'll make them make peace soon enough, you'll see.

LAMPITO: Din ye mind how Menelaus threw away his sword when he saw but a glimpse of Helen's breasties?

185 CALONICE: But look, what if they divorce us?

LYSISTRATA: Well, that wouldn't help them much, would it? Like Pherecrates says, it would be no more use than skinning the same dog twice.

CALONICE: *(Misunderstanding her.)* You know what you can
190 do with those imitation dogskin things. Anyway, what if they take hold of us and drag us into the bedroom by force?

LYSISTRATA: Cling to the door.

CALONICE: And if they hit us and force us to let go?

LYSISTRATA: Why, in that case you've got to be as damned un-
195 responsive as possible. There's no pleasure in it if they have to use force and give pain. They'll give up trying soon enough. And no man is ever happy if he can't please his woman.

CALONICE: Well—if you really think it's a good idea—we
200 agree.

LAMPITO: And we'll do the same thing and see if we can persuade oor men tae mak peace and mean it. But I dinna see how ye're ever going to get the Athenian riff-raff tae see sense.

205 LYSISTRATA: We will, you'll see.

LAMPITO: Not sae lang as their warships have sails and they have that bottomless fund o' money in Athena's temple.

LYSISTRATA: Oh, don't think we haven't seen to that! We're going to occupy the Acropolis. While we take care of the
210 sexual side of things, so to speak, all the older women have been instructed to seize the Acropolis under pretence of going to make sacrifices.

LAMPITO: A guid notion; it sounds as if it will wark.

LYSISTRATA: Well then, Lampito, why don't we confirm the
215 whole thing now by taking an oath?

LAMPITO: Tell us the aith and we'll sweir.

LYSISTRATA: Well spoken. Officeress!

(Enter a SCYTHIAN POLICEWOMAN, with bow and arrows and a shield. She stares open-eyed about her.)

Stop gawping like an idiot! Put your shield face down in front of you—so. Now someone give me the limbs of the
220 sacrificial victim.

183–184 **Din ye . . . breasties** when he was about to kill her at Troy for her infidelity   187 **Pherecrates** a contemporary comic writer

---

(The severed limbs of a ram are handed to her.)

CALONICE: *(Interrupting.)* Lysistrata, what sort of oath is this you're giving us?

LYSISTRATA: Why, the one that Aeschylus talks about somewhere, 'filling a shield with blood of fleecy sheep.'

225 CALONICE: But Lysistrata, this oath is about peace! We can't possibly take it over a shield.

LYSISTRATA: What do you suggest, then?

CALONICE: Well, if we could slaughter a full-grown cock . . .

LYSISTRATA: You've got a one-track mind.

230 CALONICE: Well, how are you going to take the oath, then?

MYRRHINE: I've got an idea, if you like. Put a large black cup on the ground, and pour some Thasian vine's blood into it, and then we can swear over the cup that we won't—put any water in.

235 LAMPITO: Whew, that's the kind of aith I like!

LYSISTRATA: A cup and a wine-jar, somebody!

(These are brought. Both are of enormous size.)

CALONICE: My dears, isn't it a whopper? It cheers you up even to touch it!

LYSISTRATA: Put the cup down, and take up the sacrificial jar.

(The attendant elevates the jar, and LYSISTRATA stretches out her hands towards it and prays.)

240 O holy Goddess of Persuasion, and thou, O Lady of the Loving Cup, receive with favour this sacrifice from your servants the women of Greece. Amen.

(The attendant begins to pour the wine into the cup.)

CALONICE: What lovely red blood! And how well it flows!

LAMPITO: And how sweet it smells forby, by Castor!

245 MYRRHINE: *(Pushing to the front.)* Let me take the oath first!

CALONICE: Not unless you draw the first lot, you don't!

LYSISTRATA: Lampito and all of you, take hold of the cup. One of you repeat the oath after me, and everybody else signify assent.

(All put their hands on the cup. CALONICE comes forward; and as she repeats each line of the following oath, all the others bow their heads.)

250 LYSISTRATA: I will not allow either boyfriend or husband—

CALONICE: I will not allow either boyfriend or husband—

LYSISTRATA: —to approach me in an erect condition. Go on!

CALONICE: —to approach me in an—erect—condition— help, Lysistrata, my knees are giving way! *(She nearly faints,
255 but recovers herself.)*

LYSISTRATA: And I will live at home without any sexual activity—

CALONICE: And I will live at home without any sexual activity—

LYSISTRATA: —wearing my best make-up and my most seduc-
260 tive dresses—

CALONICE: —wearing my best make-up and my most seductive dresses—

LYSISTRATA: —to inflame my husband's ardour.

CALONICE: —to inflame my husband's ardour.

265 LYSISTRATA: But I will never willingly yield to his desires.

CALONICE: But I will never willingly yield to his desires.

---

223 **Aeschylus** in his *Seven Against Thebes*

LYSISTRATA: And should he force me against my will—
CALONICE: And should he force me against my will—
LYSISTRATA: I will be wholly passive and unresponsive.
270 CALONICE: I will be wholly passive and unresponsive.
LYSISTRATA: I will not raise my legs towards the ceiling.
CALONICE: I will not raise my legs towards the ceiling.
LYSISTRATA: I will not take up the lion-on-a-cheese-grater position.
275 CALONICE: I will not take up the lion-on-a-cheese-grater position.
LYSISTRATA: As I drink from this cup, so will I abide by this oath.
CALONICE: As I drink from this cup, so will I abide by this
280 oath.
LYSISTRATA: And if I do not abide by it, may the cup prove to be filled with water.
CALONICE: And if I do not abide by it, may the cup prove to be filled with water.
285 LYSISTRATA: (*To the others.*) Do you all join in this oath?
ALL: We do.

(CALONICE *drinks from the cup.*)

LYSISTRATA: (*Taking the cup.*) I'll dispose of the sacred remains.
MYRRHINE: Not all of them, my friend—let's share them, as friends should.

(LYSISTRATA *drinks part of the remaining wine and, with some reluctance, hands the rest to* MYRRHINE. *As she is drinking it off a shout of triumph is heard backstage.*)

290 LAMPITO: What was that?
LYSISTRATA: What I said we were going to do. The Citadel of Athena is now in our hands. Well then, Lampito, you'll be wanting to go and see to your side of the business at home; but you'd better leave your friends here (*Indicating the other
295 Peloponnesian women.*) as hostages with us. We'll go up on to the Acropolis now and join the others—the first thing we must do is bar the doors. (*Exit* LAMPITO.)
CALONICE: Won't the men be coming soon to try to get us out?
LYSISTRATA: They can if they like—it won't bother me. Doesn't
300 matter what they threaten to do—even if they try to set fire to the place—they won't make us open the gates except on our own terms.
CALONICE: No, by Aphrodite, they won't. We must show that it's not for nothing that women are called impossible.

(*All the women retire into the Acropolis, and the gates are closed and barred. Enter the* CHORUS OF MEN, *twelve in number, advanced in years, carrying heavy logs and pitchers—the latter containing, as we shall see, lighted embers.*)

305 LEADER: (*Recitative.*) Keep moving, Draces, even if the weight
      Of olive wood is hurting your poor shoulder.
CHORUS: Incredible! Impossible!
      Our women, if you please!
    We've kept and fed within our doors
310   A pestilent disease!
    They've seized our own Acropolis,
      With bars they've shut the gate!
    They hold the statue of the Maid,
      Protectress of our state!

---

313 **the Maid** Athena, also called "the Protectress" and "Pallas"

Come on and let us hurry there   315
    And put these logs around,
  Smoke out the whole conspiracy
    From Pallas' sacred ground!

With one accord we vote that all
    Have forfeited their life,   320
  And first in the indictment-roll
    (Who else?) stands Lycon's wife.
LEADER: And shall these females hold the sacred spot
    That mighty King Cleomenes could not?
CHORUS: The grand old Spartan king,   325
    He had six hundred men,
  He marched them into the Acropolis
    And he marched them out again.
  And he entered breathing fire,
    But when he left the place   330
  He hadn't washed for six whole years
    And had hair all over his face.

  We slept before the gates;
    We wore our shields asleep;
  We all of us laid siege to him   335
    In units twenty deep.
  And the King came out half starved,
    And wore a ragged cloak,
  And 'I surrender—let me go!'
    Were all the words he spoke.   340

  Now the enemies of the gods
    And of Euripides
  Have seized the Acropolis and think
    They can beat us to our knees.
  Well, we swear that they will not,   345
    And we will take them on,
  Or else we never fought and beat
    The Medes at Marathon.
LEADER: I doubt if I have any hope
    Of hauling these logs up the slope.   350
    My legs they are wonky,
    I haven't a donkey,
  But somehow I'll just have to cope.

  And I'd better make sure that I've got
    Some fire still left in my pot;   355
    For it would be so sad
    If I thought that I had
  And I found in the end that I'd not.

(*He blows on the embers in the pitcher. A pungent smoke arises, which hurts his eyes.*)

    Yow!
  This smoke is so stinging and hot.   360
  I think a mad dog in disguise
  Has jumped up and bitten my eyes!
    With precision more fine
    One might call it a swine,
  'Cos just look what it's done to my styes.   365

---

322 **Lycon's wife** a lady noted for her immorality   324 **Cleomenes** a Spartan king who occupied the Acropolis nearly a century before the events of *Lysistrata*

But come, let us go to the aid
Of Pallas the Warrior-Maid;
  For now is the time,
  As to glory we climb,
370 And we must not, must not be afraid.

(Blows on the embers again.)

  Yow!
This smoke fairly has me dismayed.
Ah, that's woken the old flame up all right, the gods be
praised! Now, suppose we put the logs down here, and put
375 tapers into the pots, lighting them first of all of course, and
then go for the door like a battering ram? We'll call on them
to let the bars down, and if they refuse, then we'll set fire to
all the doors and smoke them out. Let's put this stuff down
first.

(They lay down the logs. The LEADER *has some difficulty in sorting out his logs and his pitcher.)*

380 Ugh! Can the generals in Samos hear us? Will some of them
come and help? Well, at least these things aren't crushing my
backbone any longer. *(He puts a taper into his pitcher.)* It's
up to you now, pot; let's have the coal burning, and let me be
the fist to have my taper alight. *(Turning towards the shrine
385 of Victory.)* Our Lady of Victory, be with us now, and may we
set up a trophy to thee when we have conquered the audacious attempt of the women to occupy thy holy Acropolis.

(The CHORUS OF MEN *continue to make preparations. Just now,
however, the voices of the* CHORUS OF OLD WOMEN, *also twelve
in number, are heard in the distance.)*

STRATYLLIS: *(Off.)* I think I see the smoke and vapour rising.
The fire has started, ladies; we must hasten.
390 CHORUS OF WOMEN: *(Off, approaching.)* Come, come and
    help
  Before our friends are fried.
    Some evil men
  Have lit a fire outside.

    Are we too late?
395 It's early in the day,
    But at the spring
  We suffered great delay.

    The jostling slaves,
  The crash as pitchers fall,
400   The crush, the noise—
  It's no damn fun at all.

  But now I come with water to the aid
  Of thy beleaguered servants, holy Maid!

(Hereabouts the WOMEN *begin to enter, carrying pitchers full of
water.)*

    Some frail old men
405 Approach with limping gait,
    And carry logs
  Of an enormous weight.

Dire threats they make,
Our friends they hope to see
  Roasted alive.   410
O Maid, this must not be!

  No, may they save
All Greece from war insane,
  For that is why
They occupy thy fane.   415

If seeds of fire around thy hill are laid,
Bear water with thy servants, holy Maid!

*(*STRATYLLIS, *at the* WOMEN'S *head, almost collides with the*
MEN, *who were just about to begin their rush at the doors.)*

STRATYLLIS: Hold it! What do you think you're up to, you
scoundrels?

(The LEADER *tries to protest.)*

If you were honest, or had any respect for the gods, you   420
wouldn't be doing what you're doing now.
LEADER: This is the end! A swarm of women come as
reinforcements!
STRATYLLIS: What are you so frightened for? We don't out
number you, after all. Still, remember you haven't seen the   425
millionth part of us yet!
LEADER: *(To his neighbour.)* Are we going to let them go on
blethering like this? Shouldn't we be bringing down our logs
on their backs rather? *(All the* MEN *put down their pitchers.)*
STRATYLLIS: *(To her followers.)* Put down your jars too. We   430
don't want any encumbrances in case it comes to a fight.
LEADER: *(Raising his fist.)* Someone ought to give them a Bupalus or two on the jaw—that might shut them up for a bit.
STRATYLLIS: *(Presenting her cheek to him.)* All right; there you
are; hit me; I won't shy away. Only, if you do, no dog will   435
ever grab your balls again!
LEADER: If you don't shut up, you old crone, I'll knock the
stuffing out of you!
STRATYLLIS: If you so much as touch me with the tip of your
finger—   440
LEADER: All right, suppose I do; what then?
STRATYLLIS: I'll bite your chest and tear out your inside!
LEADER: *(With calculated insolence.)* Euripides was right!
'There is no beast so shameless as a woman'!
STRATYLLIS: *(With cold determination.)* Rhodippe! Everybody! 445
Take up—jars! *(They do so.)*
LEADER: Damn you, what have you brought water for?
STRATYLLIS: Well, how about *you*, you warmed-up corpse?
What's that fire for? Your funeral?
LEADER: No—those pals of yours, for their funeral.   450
STRATYLLIS: And we've got the water here to put your fire out!
LEADER: Put our fire out?
STRATYLLIS: You'll see!

*(She prepares to throw the contents of her pitcher on the wood,
but the* LEADER *keeps her off with his lighted taper.)*

LEADER: I'm just making up my mind whether to give *you* a
roasting.   455

---

380 **Samos** an island in the Aegean that was the headquarters of the
Athenian navy

432 **Bupalus** a sculptor ridiculed by the satirist Hipponax as the recipient of blows to the jaw

STRATYLLIS: You wouldn't happen to have any soap, would
you? How would you like a bath?
LEADER: A bath, you toothless wonder?
STRATYLLIS: A bridal bath, if you like.
460 LEADER: Of all the barefaced—
STRATYLLIS: I'm not a slave, you know.
LEADER: I'll shut your big mouth.
STRATYLLIS: If you try, you'll never sit on a jury again.
LEADER: Come on, let's set fire to her hair!
465 STRATYLLIS: Over to you, water!

(The WOMEN *all empty their pitchers over the* MEN, *who are
thus thoroughly drenched.)*

MEN: Help, I'm soaking!
WOMEN: *(With affected concern.)* Was it hot?
MEN: No, it certainly was not!
What're you doing? Let me go!
470 WOMEN: *(Continuing to wet them.)* We're watering you to
make you grow.
MEN: Stop it! Stop! I'm numb with cold!
WOMEN: Well, if I may make so bold,

(Pointing to the MEN's *fires.)*

Warm yourselves before the grate.
475 MEN: Stop it! Help! Help! Magistrate!

(As if in answer to their call, an elderly MAGISTRATE *of severe appearance enters, attended by four* SCYTHIAN POLICEMEN. *The*
WOMEN *put down their empty pitchers and await developments.
The* MAGISTRATE *has not, in fact, come in answer to the* MEN's
*appeal, and he at first takes no notice of their bedraggled ap-
pearance. Of the* WOMEN *he takes no notice at all.)*

MAGISTRATE: I hear it's the same old thing again—the unbri-
dled nature of the female sex coming out. All their banging
of drums in honour of that Sabazius god, and singing to
Adonis on the roofs of houses, and all that nonsense. I re
480 member once in the Assembly—Demostratus, may he come
to no good end, was saying we ought to send the expedition
to Sicily, and this woman, who was dancing on the roof, she
cried, 'O woe for Adonis!', and then he went on and said we
should include some heavy infantry from Zacynthus, and
485 the woman on the roof—she'd had a bit to drink, I fancy—
she shouted, 'Mourn for Adonis, all ye people!' But the
damnable scoundrel from Angeriae just blustered on and
on. Anyway *(Rather lamely.)* that's the sort of outrage that
women get up to.
490 LEADER: Wait till you hear what this lot have done. We have
been brutally assaulted, and what is more, we have been
given an unsolicited cold bath out of these pots *(Kicking one
of them and breaking it.),* and all our clothes are wringing
wet. Anybody would think we were incontinent!
495 MAGISTRATE: Disgraceful. Disgraceful. But by Poseidon the
Shipbuilder, I'm not surprised. Look at the way we pander to
the women's vices—we positively teach them to be wicked.
That's why we get this kind of conspiracy. Think of when we
go to the shops, for example. We might go to the goldsmith's

and say, 'Goldsmith, the necklace you made for my wife— 500
she was dancing last night and the clasp came unstuck. Now
I've got to go off to Salamis; so if you've got time, could you
go down to my place tonight and put the pin back in the hole
for her?' Or perhaps we go in to a shoemaker's, a great strap-
ping well-hung young fellow, and we say, 'Shoemaker, the 505
toe-strap on my wife's sandal is hurting her little toe—it's
rather tender, you know. Could you go down around
lunchtime perhaps and ease the strap off for her, enlarge the
opening a little?' And now look what's happened! I, a member of the Committee of Ten, having found a source of sup- 510
ply for timber to make oars, and now requiring money to buy
it, come to the Acropolis and find the women have shut the
doors in my face! No good standing around. Fetch the crowbars, somebody, and we'll soon put a stop to this nonsense.
(To two of the POLICEMEN.) What are you gawping at, you 515
fool? And you? Dreaming about pubs, eh?

(Crowbars are brought in.)

Let's get these bars under the doors and lever them up. I'll
help.

(They begin to move the crowbars into position, when LYSIS-
TRATA, CALONICE *and* MYRRHINE *open the gates and come out.)*

LYSISTRATA: No need to use force. I'm coming out of my own
free will. What's the use of crowbars? It's intelligence and 520
common sense that we need, not violence.
MAGISTRATE: You disgusting creature! Officer!—take her and
tie her hands behind her back.
LYSISTRATA: By Artemis, if he so much as touches me, I'll
teach him to know his place! 525

(The POLICEMAN *hesitates.)*

MAGISTRATE: Frightened, eh? Go on, the two of you, up-end
her and tie her up!
CALONICE: *(Interposing herself between* SECOND POLICEMAN
and LYSISTRATA.) If you so much as lay a finger on her, by
Pandrosus, I'll hit you so hard you'll shit all over the place. 530
MAGISTRATE: Obscene language! Officer! *(To* THIRD POLICE-
MAN.) Tie this one up first, and stop her mouth.
MYRRHINE: *(Interposing herself between* THIRD POLICEMAN
and CALONICE.) By the Giver of Light, if you touch her,
you'll soon be crying out for a cupping-glass! 535
MAGISTRATE: What's all this? Officer! *(To* FOURTH POLICE-
MAN.) Get hold of her. I'm going to stop this relay some time.
STRATYLLIS: *(Intervening in her turn.)* By the Bull Goddess, if
you go near her, I'll make you scream! *(Giving an exemplary
tug to* FOURTH POLICEMAN's *hair.)* 540
MAGISTRATE: Heaven help me, I've no more archers! Well, we
mustn't let ourselves be worsted by women. Come on, officers, we'll charge them, all together.
LYSISTRATA: If you do, by the Holy Twain, you'll find out that
we've got four whole companies of fighting women in there, 545
fully armed.
MAGISTRATE: *(Calling her bluff.)* Twist their arms behind
them, officers.

(The POLICEMEN *approach the four women with intent to do
this.)*

---

478 **Sabazius** an Asiatic god, often identified with Dionysus and worshipped mainly by women   479 **Adonis** a youth beloved by Aphrodite
who died young and was honored yearly in a women's festival

530 **Pandrosus** Artemis, who is also the Giver of Light and the Bull
Goddess

LYSISTRATA: *(To the women inside.)* Come out, the reserve!
550   Lettuce-seed-pancake-vendors of the Market Square! Inn-keepers, bakers and garlic-makers! Come to our help! *(Four bands of women emerge from the Acropolis.)* Drag them along! Hit them! Shout rude words in their faces!

(The POLICEMEN *are quickly brought to the ground, and punched and kicked as they lie there.)*

    All right—withdraw—no plunder will be taken.

(The women retire into the Acropolis.)

555 MAGISTRATE: *(His hand to his head.)* My bowmen have been utterly defeated!
LYSISTRATA: Well, what did you expect? Did you think we were slaves?—or that women couldn't have any stomach for a fight?
560 MAGISTRATE: I must admit I thought they only had one for booze.
LEADER: Our noble magistrate, why waste your words
    On these sub-human creatures? Know you not
    How we were given a bath when fully clothed,
565   And that without the benefit of soap?
STRATYLLIS: Well, he who uses force without good reason
    Should not complain on getting a black eye.
    We only want to stay at home content
    And hurting no-one; but if you provoke us,
570   You'll find you're stirring up a hornets' nest!
CHORUS OF MEN: Monsters, enough!—our patience now is gone.
    It's time for you to tell
    Why you are barricaded here upon
575   Our hallowed citadel.
LEADER: *(To* MAGISTRATE.*)* Now question her, and test her out, and never own she's right:
    It's shameful to surrender to a girl without a fight.
MAGISTRATE: *(To* LYSISTRATA.*)* Well, the first thing I want to
580   know is—what in Zeus' name do you mean by shutting and barring the gates of our own Acropolis against us?
LYSISTRATA: We want to keep the money safe and stop you from waging war.
MAGISTRATE: The war has nothing to do with money—
585 LYSISTRATA: Hasn't it? Why are Peisander and the other office-seekers always stirring things up? Isn't it so they can take a few more dips in the public purse? Well, as far as we're concerned they can do what they like; only they're not going to lay their hands on the money in there.
590 MAGISTRATE: Why, what are you going to do?
LYSISTRATA: Do? Why, we'll be in charge of it.
MAGISTRATE: *You* in charge of *our* finances?
LYSISTRATA: Well, what's so strange about that? We've been in charge of all your housekeeping finances for years.
595 MAGISTRATE: But that's not the same thing.
LYSISTRATA: Why not?
MAGISTRATE: Because the money here is needed for the war!
LYSISTRATA: Ah, but the war itself isn't necessary.
MAGISTRATE: Not necessary! How is the City going to be saved
600   then?
LYSISTRATA: We'll save it for you.
MAGISTRATE: You!!!

LYSISTRATA: Us.
MAGISTRATE: This is intolerable!
LYSISTRATA: It may be, but it's what's going to happen.
605 MAGISTRATE: But Demeter!—I mean, it's against nature!
LYSISTRATA: *(Very sweetly.)* We've got to save you, after all, Sir.
MAGISTRATE: Even against my will?
LYSISTRATA: That only makes it all the more essential.
MAGISTRATE: Anyway, what business are war and peace of
610   yours?
LYSISTRATA: I'll tell you.
MAGISTRATE: *(Restraining himself with difficulty.)* You'd better or else.
LYSISTRATA: I will if you'll listen and keep those hands of yours
615   under control.
MAGISTRATE: I can't—I'm too livid.
STRATYLLIS: *(Interrupting.)* It'll be you that regrets it.
MAGISTRATE: I hope it's you, you superannuated crow! *(To*
620   LYSISTRATA.*)* Say what you have to say.
LYSISTRATA: In the last war we were too modest to object to anything you men did—and in any case you wouldn't let us say a word. But don't think we approved! We knew every-
625   thing that was going on. Many times we'd hear at home about some major blunder of yours, and then when you came home we'd be burning inside but we'd have to put on a smile and ask what it was you'd decided to inscribe on the pillar underneath the Peace Treaty.—And what did my hus-
630   band always say?—'Shut up and mind your own business!' And I did.
STRATYLLIS: *I* wouldn't have done!
MAGISTRATE: *(Ignoring her—to* LYSISTRATA.*)* He'd have given you one if you hadn't!
635 LYSISTRATA: Exactly—so I kept quiet. But sure enough, next thing we knew you'd take an even sillier decision. And if I so much as said, 'Darling, why are you carrying on with this silly policy?' he would glare at me and say, 'Back to your weaving, woman, or you'll have a headache for a month.
640   "Go and attend to your work; let war be the care of the men-folk."'
MAGISTRATE: Quite right too, by Zeus.
LYSISTRATA: Right? That we should not be allowed to make the least little suggestion to you, no matter how much you mismanage the City's affairs? And now, look, every time two
645   people meet in the street, what do they say? 'Isn't there a man in the country?' and the answer comes, 'Not one.' That's why we women got together and decided we were going to save Greece. What was the point of waiting any longer, we asked ourselves. Well now, we'll make a deal. You
650   listen to us—and we'll talk sense, not like you used to—listen to us and keep quiet, as we've had to do up to now, and we'll clear up the mess you've made.
MAGISTRATE: Insufferable effrontery! I will not stand for it!
LYSISTRATA: *(Magisterially.)* Silence!
655 MAGISTRATE: You, confound you, a woman with your face veiled, dare to order me to be silent! Gods, let me die!
LYSISTRATA: Well, if that's what's bothering you—

(During the ensuing trio the women put a veil on the MAGIS-TRATE's *head, and give him a sewing-basket and some uncarded wool.)*

---

585 **Peisander** leader of a short-lived oligarchic revolt in Athens

639–640 "**Go . . . menfolk**" from the *Iliad*, Hector's parting—and final—words to his wife at Troy

With veiling bedeck
Your head and your neck,
660   And then, it may be, you'll be quiet.
    MYRRHINE:
       This basket fill full—
    CALONICE:
       By carding this wool—
    LYSISTRATA: Munching beans—they're an excellent diet.
       So hitch up your gown
665   And really get down
       To the job—you could do with some
          slimmin'.
       And keep this refrain
       Fixed firm in your brain—
670   ALL: That war is the care of the *women!*

(During the song and dance of the women the MAGISTRATE *has
been sitting, a ludicrous figure, with not the least idea what to do
with the wool. During the following chorus, fuming, he tears off
the veil, flings away wool and basket, and stands up.)*

    STRATYLLIS: Come forward, ladies: time to lend a hand
       Of succour to our heroine's brave stand!
    CHORUS OF WOMEN: I'll dance for ever, never will I tire,
       To aid our champions here.
675   For theirs is courage, wisdom, beauty, fire;
       And Athens hold they dear.
    STRATYLLIS: *(To* LYSISTRATA.*)* Now, child of valiant ancestors
       of stinging-nettle stock,
       To battle!—do not weaken, for the foe is seized with shock.
680   LYSISTRATA: If Aphrodite of Cyprus and her sweet son Eros
       still breathe hot desire into our bosoms and our thighs, and if
       they still, as of old, afflict our men with that distressing ail-
       ment, club-prick—then I prophecy that before long we
       women will be known as the Peacemakers of Greece.
685   MAGISTRATE: Why, what will you do?
    LYSISTRATA: Well, for one thing, there'll be no more people
       clomping round the Market Square in full armour, like
       lunatics.
    CALONICE: By Aphrodite, never a truer word!
690   LYSISTRATA: You see them every day—going round the veg-
       etable and pottery stalls armed to the teeth. You'd think they
       were Corybants!
    MAGISTRATE: Of course: that's what every true Athenian ought
       to do.
695   LYSISTRATA: But a man carrying a shield with a ferocious Gor-
       gon on it—and buying minnows at the fishmonger's! Isn't it
       ridiculous?
    CALONICE: Like that cavalry captain I saw, riding round the
       market with his lovely long hair, buying a pancake from an
700   old stallholder and stowing it in his helmet! And there was a
       Thracian too—coming in brandishing his light-infantry
       equipment for all the world as if he were a king or some-
       thing. The fruiteress fainted away with fright, and he an-
       nexed everything on her stall!
705   MAGISTRATE: But the international situation at present is in a
       hopeless muddle. How do you propose to unravel it?
    LYSISTRATA: Oh, it's dead easy.
    MAGISTRATE: Would you explain?
    LYSISTRATA: Well, take a tangled skein of wool for example.

---

692 **Corybants** priests of Cybele, who wore full armor during their
ceremonies

We take it so, put it to the spindle, unwind it this way, now   710
that way. *(Miming with her fingers.)* That's how we'll unravel
this war, if you'll let us. Send ambassadors first to Sparta, this
way, then to Thebes, that way—
    MAGISTRATE: Are you such idiots as to think that you can solve
       serious problems with spindles and bits of wool?   715
    LYSISTRATA: As a matter of fact, it might not be so idiotic as you
       think to run the whole City entirely on the model of the way
       we deal with wool.
    MAGISTRATE: How d'you work that out?
    LYSISTRATA: The first thing you do with wool is wash the   720
       grease out of it; you can do the same with the City. Then you
       stretch out the citizen body on a bench and pick out the
       burrs—that is, the parasites. After that you prise apart the
       club-members who form themselves into knots and clots to
       get into power, and when you've separated them, pick them   725
       out one by one. Then you're ready for the carding: they can
       all go into the basket of Civic Goodwill—including the resi-
       dent aliens and any foreigners who are your friends—yes,
       and even those who are in debt to the Treasury! Not only
       that. Athens has many colonies. At the moment these are   730
       lying around all over the place, like stray bits and pieces of
       the fleece. You should pick them up and bring them here,
       put them all together, and then out of all this make an enor-
       mous great ball of wool—and from that you can make the
       People a coat.   735
    MAGISTRATE: Burrs—balls of wool—nonsense! What right
       have you to talk about these things? What have you done for
       the war effort?
    LYSISTRATA: Done, you puffed-up old idiot! We've contributed
       to it twice over and more. For one thing, we've given you   740
       sons, and then had to send them off to fight.
    MAGISTRATE: Enough, don't let's rub the wound.
    LYSISTRATA: For another, we're in the prime of our lives, and
       how can we enjoy it? Even if we've got husbands, we're war
       widows just the same. And never mind us—think of the un-   745
       married ones, getting on in years and with never a hope—
       that's what really pains me.
    MAGISTRATE: But for heaven's sake, it's not only women that
       get older.
    LYSISTRATA: Yes, I know, but it's not the same thing, is it? A   750
       man comes home—he may be old and grey—but he can get
       himself a young wife in no time. But a woman's not in
       bloom for long, and if she doesn't succeed quickly, there's no
       one will marry her, and before long she's going round to the
       fortune-tellers to ask them if she's any chance.   755
    MAGISTRATE: That's right—any man who's still got a service-
       able—

*(Whatever he was going to say, it is drowned by music. During
the following trio the women supply him with two half-obols, a
filleted head-dress and a wreath, and dress him up as a corpse.)*

    LYSISTRATA: Shut up! It's high time that you died.
       You'll find a fine coffin outside.
          Myself I will bake
          Your Cerberus-cake,   760
       And here is the fare for the ride.

---

761 **Cerberus-cake** a cake placed with the dead with which to distract
Cerberus, the hound guarding the gates of Hades   762 **fare for the
ride** a coin with which to pay Charon, who ferried the dead across the
River Styx to Hades

CALONICE: Look, here are your fillets all red—
LYSISTRATA: So why do you wait?
765 You'll make Charon late!
Push off! Don't you realize? You're dead!
MAGISTRATE: (*Spluttering with rage.*) This is outrageous! I
shall go at once and show my colleagues what these women
have done to me.
770 LYSISTRATA: What's your complaint? You haven't been properly laid out? Don't worry; we'll be with you early the day
after tomorrow to complete the funeral!

(*The* MAGISTRATE *goes out.* LYSISTRATA, CALONICE *and*
MYRRHINE *go back into the Acropolis.*)

LEADER: No time to laze; our freedom's now at risk;
Take off your coats, and let the dance be brisk!
775 CHORUS OF MEN: There's more in this than meets the eye,
Or so it seems to me.
The scum will surface by and by:
It stinks of Tyranny!

Those Spartan rogues are at their games
780 (Their agent's Cleisthenes)—
It's them that's stirring up these dames
To seize our jury fees!
LEADER: Disgraceful!—women venturing to prate
In public so about affairs of State!
785 They even (men could not be so naive)
The blandishments of Sparta's wolves believe!
The truth the veriest child could surely see:
This is a Monarchist Conspiracy.
I'll fight autocracy until the end:
790 My freedom I'll unswervingly defend.
As once our Liberators did, so now
'I'll bear my sword within a myrtle bough,'
And stand beside them, thus.

(*He places himself beside the statue of Harmodius and Aristogeiton, imitating the attitude of the latter.*)

And from this place
795 I'll give this female one upon the face!

(*He slaps* STRATYLLIS *hard on the cheek.*)

STRATYLLIS: (*Giving him a blow in return that sends him reel-
ing.*) Don't trifle with us, rascals, or we'll show you
Such fisticuffs, your mothers will not know you!
CHORUS OF WOMEN: My debt of love today
800 To the City I will pay,
And I'll pay it in the form of good advice;
For the City gave me honour
(Pallas' blessing be upon her!),
And the things I've had from her deserve their price.

805 For at seven years or less
I became a girl priestess
In the Erechthean temple of the Maid;
And at ten upon this hill
I made flour in the mill
810 For the cakes which to our Lady are displayed.

Then I went to Brauron town
And put on a yellow gown
To walk in the procession as the Bear;
To complete my perfect score
I the sacred basket bore   815
At Athena's feast when I was young and fair.
STRATYLLIS: See why I think I have a debt to pay?
'But women can't talk politics,' you say.
Why not? What is it you insinuate?
That we contribute nothing to the State?   820
Why, we give more than you! See if I lie:
We cause men to be born, you make them die.
What's more, you've squandered all the gains of old,
The Persians' legacy, the allies' gold;
And now, the taxes you yourselves assess   825
You do not pay. *Who's* got us in this mess?
Do you complain? Another grunt from you,
And you will feel the impact of this shoe!

(*She takes off her shoe and hits the* MEN'S LEADER *with it.*)

MEN: Assault! Assault! This impudence
Gets yet more aggravated.   830
Why don't we act in self-defence?
Or are we all castrated?
LEADER: Let's not be all wrapped up, let's show we're men,
Not sandwiches! Take off your cloaks again!
CHORUS OF MEN: Come, party-sandalled men of war,   835
The tyrants' foes in days of yore,
Those days when we were men;
The time has come to grow new wings
And think once more of martial things;
We must be young again.   840
LEADER: If once we let these women get the semblance of
start,
Before we know, they'll be adept at every manly art.
They'll build a navy, quickly master strategy marine,
And fight against the City's fleet, just like that Carian
queen.
And if to form a cavalry contingent they decide,   845
They'd soon be teaching *our* equestrian gentry how to ride!
For riding on cock-horses suits a woman best of all;
Her seat is sure, and when it bolts she doesn't often fall.
Just look at Micon's painting, and you'll see the sort of
thing:
The Amazonian cavalry engaging Athens' king.   850
I think that we should seize them now, that's what we ought
to do,
And shove them in the stocks—and I will start by seizing
you!

(*He grabs* STRATYLLIS *by the scruff of the neck but is forced to let
her go by a well-aimed bite.*)

---

780 **Cleisthenes** Athenian statesman and well-known homosexual
782 **jury fees** a main source of income for older men, and stored in the
Citadel on the Acropolis   791 **Liberators** Harmodius and Aristogeiton, who tried to assassinate the last Tyrant of Athens in 514 BC

811–813 **Brauron town . . . the Bear** a reference to a festival for
Artemis, who evidently supplanted a local bear-goddess   815 **sacred
basket** containing objects sacred to Athena and a great honor for an
Athenian girl to carry in a festival   844 **Carian queen** Artemisia, who
distinguished herself against the Athenian navy at Salamis in 480 BC
849 **Micon's painting** a fresco depicting the battle between Theseus
and the Amazons

WOMEN: Our anger now is all afire,
  And, by the Holy Twain,
855 We'll give you such a dose of ire
  You'll scream and scream again.
STRATYLLIS: Take off your coats and feel the heart beneath:
  We're women, and our wrath is in our teeth!
CHORUS OF WOMEN: The man who lays a hand on me
860 Will never more eat celery
  Or beans—he won't be able.
  I burn with anger: I will strike
  And smash his bloody eggs, just like
  The beetle in the fable.
865 STRATYLLIS: Friend Lampito from Sparta and Ismenia from
    the north
  Are still alive, and so I scorn the threats you vomit forth.
  You cannot hurt us, though you pass your motions six
    times o'er:

(Pointing at a well-known politician in the audience.)

  You're hated by the People here and by the folks next door.
  The other day I asked a friend to share a sacred meal
870 To Hecate; my friend (she is a rich Boeotian eel)
  Sent word to say, 'I cannot come, my dear; forgive me,
    please;
  I can't get through to Athens 'cause of You Know Who's
    decrees.'
  These damn decrees will never stop, until we make a
    frontal
  Assault on you and grab your legs and make you horizontal!

(Each of the women grabs a man by the leg and brings him to the ground. The MEN, *defeated, retire down stage; the* WOMEN *move closer to the Acropolis gates.)*

— ACT TWO —

SCENE I

The same. It is five days later.

*(*LYSISTRATA *comes out of the Acropolis, in great agitation.)*

STRATYLLIS: *(In tragic tones.)* Lady who did this daring plot
    invent,
  Why from thy fortress com'st thou grim-look'd out?
LYSISTRATA: It is the thoughts of evil women's minds
  That makes me wander restless to and fro.
5 WOMEN: What sayest thou?
LYSISTRATA: 'Tis true, 'tis true.
STRATYLLIS: But what hath caused it? Speak; we are thy
    friends.
LYSISTRATA: Silence is hard, but it were shame to speak.
STRATYLLIS: Hide not the ill that we are suffering from.
10 LYSISTRATA: I will but one word speak: 'tis sex-starvation.
WOMEN: Alas, great Zeus!
LYSISTRATA: Why cry to Zeus? for 'tis natural. *(In her ordinary voice.)* I just can't keep them to their vow of abstinence any longer. They're deserting. One I caught clearing out the
15 stopped-up hole in the wall near Pan's Grotto—another

letting herself down by a rope—another leaving her post as sentry—and there was even one yesterday who was trying to fly down on sparrow-back—aiming straight for the nearest pimpshop! I was able to grab her by the hair and pull her back. And they invent every kind of excuse just to be allowed 20 to go home. Here's one now. *(To* FIRST WOMAN, *who is trying to leave the Acropolis swiftly and stealthily.)* Hey, you, where do you think you're going?
FIRST WOMAN: I want to go home. I've got some fleeces there from Miletus, and the moths will be eating them up. 25
LYSISTRATA: No nonsense about moths! Go back inside.
FIRST WOMAN: But I promise you, I swear, I'll come right back. I'll only spread it out on the bed.
LYSISTRATA: No you won't; you're not going anywhere.
FIRST WOMAN: Am I to leave my fleeces to be destroyed, then? 30
LYSISTRATA: *(Unyielding.)* If necessary, yes.
SECOND WOMAN: *(Rushing out of the Acropolis.)* Help! My flax, my Amorgian flax! I left it at home without taking the bark off!
LYSISTRATA: Here's another—flax this time. *(To* SECOND 35 WOMAN.*)* Come back.
SECOND WOMAN: But by Artemis I will, as soon as I've stripped it off!
LYSISTRATA: No. Once I let you strip anything off, they'll all be wanting to. 40
THIRD WOMAN: *(Coming out as if heavily pregnant.)* Not yet, holy Eilithuia, not yet! Wait till I've got somewhere where it's lawful to give birth!
LYSISTRATA: What's all this nonsense?
THIRD WOMAN: Can't you see? I'm in labour! 45
LYSISTRATA: But you weren't even pregnant yesterday!
THIRD WOMAN: Well, I am today! Lysistrata, let me go home right away. The midwife's waiting.
LYSISTRATA: What do you think you're talking about? *(Pokes her stomach.)* Rather hard, isn't it? What have you got there? 50
THIRD WOMAN: Hard?—yes, of course—it's—it's a baby, a boy.
LYSISTRATA: *(Tapping it.)* Nonsense! It's made of bronze— and hollow—Let's have a look at it.

(Dives under THIRD WOMAN's *dress and emerges with an enormous bronze helmet.)*

  Athena's sacred helmet! What were you trying to kid me, 55 saying you were pregnant?
THIRD WOMAN: But I am, I swear.
LYSISTRATA: What's this, then?
THIRD WOMAN: Well, I thought—if I found it coming upon me before I got out of the Acropolis—I could nest in the hel- 60 met like the pigeons do, and give birth there.
LYSISTRATA: No good trying to get out of it. You're caught. You can stay here until the day your baby *(Pointing to the helmet.)* is named.

(Two more women rush out of the Acropolis.)

FOURTH WOMAN: I can't sleep in there any longer! I've seen 65 the Guardian Serpent!

863–864 **smash . . . fable** in Aesop's fable, an eagle steals the beetle's young, and the beetle retaliates by destroying the eagle's eggs

42 **Eilithuia** goddess of childbirth   42–43 **somewhere . . . birth** that is, not on the Acropolis, which was sacred ground   66 **Guardian Serpent** symbolic of Athena's protection and supposed to dwell on the Acropolis

FIFTH WOMAN: I can't either! Those owls are keeping me awake with their infernal hooting!

LYSISTRATA: (*Stopping them firmly.*) Tall tales will get you n
70 nowhere, ladies. I know you miss your husbands; but don't you realize they miss you as well? Think of the sort of nights they'll be spending! Be strong, sisters; you won't have to endure much longer. There is an oracle (*Unrolls a scroll.*) that we will triumph if only we don't fall out among ourselves. I
75 have it here.

(*The women all gather round.*)

FIFTH WOMAN: What does it say?

LYSISTRATA: Listen. (*Reads.*) 'When that the swallows escape from the hoopoes and gather together,
Keeping away from the cock-birds, then trouble and sorrow will perish,
80 Zeus will make high into low—'

THIRD WOMAN: What, will we be on top when we do it?

LYSISTRATA: 'But if the swallows rebel and fly from the sacred enclosure,
Then will it manifest be that there is no creature more sex-mad.'

FIFTH WOMAN: Pretty blunt, isn't it? So help us the gods, we
85 won't give up the fight now. Let's go inside. It would be disgraceful, my dears, wouldn't it, to flag or fail now we've heard what the oracle says.

(*They all go into the Acropolis. The two* CHORUSES *move to the centre of the stage, facing each other.*)

MEN: I feel a rather pressing need
To exercise my tongue:
90 I'll tell a little fairy tale
I heard when I was young.

Well, once upon a time there was
A wise young man who fled
From women and from marriage, and
95 He roamed the hills instead.

He hunted hares with nets, and had
A faithful little hound,
And hated girls so much he ne'er
Came back to his native ground.

100 Yes, he was truly wise, this lad,
Loathed women through and through,
And following his example we
Detest the creatures too.

LEADER: (*To* STRATYLLIS.) Give us a kiss.
105 STRATYLLIS: (*Slapping him.*) You can take this!
LEADER: (*Raising his tunic and kicking her.*) That's got you there.
STRATYLLIS: (*Giggling.*) Look at that hair!
MEN: A sign of valour is such hair
Upon the crotch, you know;
110 Myronides had lots of it,
And so had Phormio.

77–78 **When that . . . together** a reference to the story of Tereus' lustful pursuit of Procne, even after he was transformed into a hoopoe and she into a swallow 110 **Myronides** victorious Athenian general 111 **Phormio** victorious Athenian admiral

WOMEN: I'll tell a little tale myself
(I like this little game)
About a man who had no home,
And Timon was his name. 115

He lived among the thorns and briars,
And never served on juries;
Some said his mother really was
A sister of the Furies.

This Timon went away and lived 120
So far from mortal ken
Not out of hate for women but
Because of hate for men.

He loathed them for their wickedness,
Their company abhorred, 125
And cursed them loud and long and deep—
But *women* he adored.

STRATYLLIS: (*To leader.*) One on the cheek! (*Slaps him.*)
LEADER: (*In mockery.*) Oh, how I shriek!
STRATYLLIS: Let's have a go! (*Prepares to kick him.*) 130
LEADER: Think what you'll show!

(STRATYLLIS *hastily lets her skirt fall again.*)

WOMEN: At least, despite our age, it's not
With hirsute mantle fringed:
With utmost care and frequently
Our triangles are singed. 135

(LYSISTRATA *appears on the battlements. She looks away to the right, and cries out.*)

LYSISTRATA: Women! Women! Come here, quickly!

(*Several women join her, among them* CALONICE *and* MYRRHINE.)

CALONICE: What is it dear? What are you shouting for?

LYSISTRATA: A man! There's a man coming—and by the look of him he's equipped for the Mysteries of Aphrodite!

CALONICE: Aphrodite, Lady of Cyprus, Paphos and Cytherá, 140 as thou hast gone with us till now, so aid us still!—Where is he, whoever he is?

LYSISTRATA: There, down by the shrine of Chloe.

CALONICE: So he is; but who on earth is he?

LYSISTRATA: Have a look, all of you. Does anyone know him? 145

MYRRHINE: Yes, by Zeus! It's Cinesias, my husband!

LYSISTRATA: Well, dear, you know what you have to do: keep him on toast. Tantalize him. Lead him on. Say no, say yes. You can do anything—except what you swore over the cup not to do. 150

MYRRHINE: Don't worry, I'll do as you say.

LYSISTRATA: I'll stay here and start the process of toasting. Off you go.

(*All go within except* LYSISTRATA.)

(*Enter, right,* CINESIAS *and a* SLAVE, *the latter carrying a* BABY.)

CINESIAS: Gods help me, I'm so bloody stretched out I might just as well be on the rack! 155

LYSISTRATA: Who goes there?

CINESIAS: Me.

LYSISTRATA: A man?

---

115 **Timon** famous misanthrope

160 CINESIAS: I certainly am!

LYSISTRATA: Well, off with you.

CINESIAS: Who do you think you are, sending me away?

LYSISTRATA: I'm on guard duty.

CINESIAS: Well—for the god's sake—ask Myrrhine to come out to me.

165 LYSISTRATA: You want me to get you Myrrhine? Who might you be?

CINESIAS: Her husband—Cinesias from Paeonidae.

LYSISTRATA: Cinesias! That name we know well. It's for ever in your wife's mouth. She can't eat an egg or an apple but she 170 says, 'Here's to my love Cinesias.'

CINESIAS: (*Breathing more rapidly.*) Gods!

LYSISTRATA: It's true, I swear by Aphrodite. And if we happen to get talking about our husbands, she always says, 'The rest are nothing to my Cinesias!'

175 CINESIAS: Bring her to me! Bring her to me!

LYSISTRATA: Well, aren't you going to give me anything?

CINESIAS: If you want. Look, this is all I've got; catch.

(*Throws up a purse of silver.*)

LYSISTRATA: Thanks. I'll go and get her. (*She disappears.*)

CINESIAS: Quickly, please! I've no joy in life any longer since 180 she left home. It pains me to enter the place, it all seems so empty—and my food doesn't agree with me. I'm permanently rigid!

MYRRHINE: (*Appearing on the battlements, pretending to talk to somebody within.*) I love him, I love him! But he won't 185 love me. Don't ask me to go out to him.

CINESIAS: Myrrie darling, why on earth not? Come down here.

MYRRHINE: No, I won't.

CINESIAS: Aren't you going to come down when I call you, 190 Myrrhine?

MYRRHINE: You don't really want me.

CINESIAS: What! I'm dying for love of you.

MYRRHINE: I'm going. (*Turns to go back inside.*)

CINESIAS: No—don't—listen to your child!

(*The* SLAVE *caresses the* BABY *without result.*)

195 Come on, damn you—say 'mama'! (*Strikes the* BABY.)

BABY: Mama, mama, mama!

CINESIAS: What's wrong with you? Surely you can't harden your heart against your baby! It's five days now since he had a bath or a feed.

200 MYRRHINE: I pity him all right. His father hasn't looked after him very well.

CINESIAS: For heaven's sake, won't you come down to your own child?

MYRRHINE: How powerful motherhood is! My feelings compel 205 me. I will come down. (*She leaves the battlements.*)

CINESIAS: I think she looks much younger and more beautiful than she was! And all this spurning and coquetting—why, it just inflames my desire even more!

MYRRHINE: (*Coming out and taking the* BABY *in her arms.*) 210 Come on there, darling, you've got a bad daddy, haven't you? Come on, do you want a little drink, then? (*She feeds him.*)

CINESIAS: Tell me, darling, why do you behave like this and shut yourself up in there with the other women? Why do you give me pain—and yourself too? (*Attempts to caress her* 215 *breast.*)

MYRRHINE: Keep your hands off me!

CINESIAS: And our things at home—they belong to you as well as me—they're going to ruin!

MYRRHINE: (*Playing with the* BABY.) I don't care!

CINESIAS: What, you don't care if the chickens are pulling all 220 your wool to pieces?

MYRRHINE: No, I don't.

CINESIAS: And what about the rites of Aphrodite? How long is it since you performed them? (*Puts his arm around her.*) Come along home. 225

MYRRHINE: (*Wriggling free.*) No, I won't. Not until you stop the war and make peace.

CINESIAS: Then, if you want, we'll do that.

MYRRHINE: *Then*, if you want, I'll go home. Till then, I've sworn not to. 230

CINESIAS: But won't you let me make love to you? It's been such a long time!

MYRRHINE: No. Mind you, I'm not saying I don't love you . . .

CINESIAS: You do, Myrrie love? Why won't you let me, then?

MYRRHINE: What, you idiot, in front of the baby? 235

CINESIAS: No—er—Manes, take it home.

(*The* SLAVE *departs with the* BABY.)

All right, darling, it's out of the way. Let's get on with it.

MYRRHINE: Don't be silly, there's nowhere we can do it here.

CINESIAS: What's wrong with Pan's Grotto?

MYRRHINE: And how am I supposed to purify myself before 240 going back into the Acropolis? It's sacred ground, you know.

CINESIAS: Why, there's a perfectly good spring next to it.

MYRRHINE: You're not asking me to break my oath!

CINESIAS: On my own head be it. Don't worry about that, darling. 245

MYRRHINE: All right, I'll go and get a camp bed.

CINESIAS: Why not on the ground?

MYRRHINE: By Apollo—I love you very much—but not on the ground! (*She goes into the Acropolis.*)

CINESIAS: Well, at least she does love me, that I can be sure of. 250

MYRRHINE: (*Returning with a bare camp bed.*) Here you are. You just lie down, while I take off my—Blast it! We need a— what do you call it?—a mattress.

CINESIAS: Mattress? I certainly don't!

MYRRHINE: In the name of Artemis, you're not proposing we 255 should do it on the cords!

CINESIAS: At least give us a kiss first.

MYRRHINE: (*Doing so.*) There. (*She goes.*)

CINESIAS: Mmmm! Come back quickly!

MYRRHINE: (*Returning with a mattress.*) There. Now just lie 260 down, and I'll—But look, you haven't got a pillow!

CINESIAS: I don't want one. (*He lies down on the mattress.*)

MYRRHINE: But I do! (*She goes in.*)

CINESIAS: This is a Heracles' supper and no mistake!

MYRRHINE: (*Returning with a pillow.*) Lift up your head. So. 265

CINESIAS: That's everything.

MYRRHINE: Everything?

CINESIAS: Yes. Come to me now, precious.

MYRRHINE: (*Her back to him.*) I'm just undoing my bra. Remember, don't let me down on what you said about making 270 peace.

---

264 **Heracles' supper** a stock bit in comedies in which the ravenous Heracles is cheated of his dinner

CINESIAS: May Zeus strike me dead if I do!

MYRRHINE: But look now, you haven't got a blanket!

CINESIAS: But I don't want one! All I want is you, darling!

275 MYRRHINE: In a moment, love. I'll just pop in for the blanket.

(Goes into the Acropolis.)

CINESIAS: These bedclothes will be the end of me!

MYRRHINE: *(Returning with a blanket and a box of ointment.)* Lift yourself up.

CINESIAS: You can see very well I did that long ago.

280 MYRRHINE: Do you want me to anoint you?

CINESIAS: No, dammit, I don't!

MYRRHINE: Too bad, then, because I'm going to anyway.

CINESIAS: *(Aside.)* Zeus, make her spill the stuff!

MYRRHINE: Hold out your hand and you can rub it on.

285 CINESIAS: *(Smelling the ointment.)* I don't care for it. I only like sexy ones, and besides, this positively reeks of prevarication!

MYRRHINE: *(Pretending to sniff it in her turn.)* Why, silly me, I brought the wrong one!

290 CINESIAS: Well, never mind, darling, let it be.

MYRRHINE: Don't talk such nonsense. *(She goes in with the box.)*

CINESIAS: Curse whoever invented these ointments!

MYRRHINE: *(Returning with another unguent in a bottle.)* Here

295 you are, take this bottle.

CINESIAS: I've got one already and it's fit to burst! *(Indicating what he is referring to.)* Come here and lie down, damn you, and stop this stupid game.

MYRRHINE: I will, I swear it by Artemis. I've got both my shoes

300 off now. But darling, don't forget about making peace.

CINESIAS: I'll—

(MYRRHINE runs off into the Acropolis and the gates slam behind her.)

She's gone! She's been having me on! Just when I was all ripe for her, she ran away! *(Bursts into sorrowful song.)*

Oh what, tell me what, can this woeful laddie do?

305 And who, tell me who, can this woeful laddie screw?

Philostratus, I need you, do come and help me quick:

Could I please hire a nurse for my poor young orphan prick?

CHORUS OF MEN: It's clear, my poor lad, that you're in a baddish way.

And I pity you—O alack and well-a-day!

310 What heart, what soul, what bollocks could long endure this plight,

Having no one to screw in the middle of the night?

CINESIAS: O Zeus! Hear me, Zeus! I am suffering tortures dire.

MEN: It's that female's fault; she inflamed you with false fire. I think she is a villain and deserves to suffer death!

315 WOMEN: She's a heroine, and I will praise her while I've breath.

MEN: A heroine you call her?—to that I'll ne'er agree.

I'll tell you just what I would really like to see:

To see a whirlwind catch her, just like a heap of hay,

And to waft her aloft, take her up, up and away.

Then let the whirlwind drop, after tossing her around   320

Till giddy and dizzy she falls back to the ground,

Where suddenly she finds that there still is more in store:

We'd be queuing and screwing a dozen times or more.

SCENE II

The same.

(Enter severally a HERALD *from Sparta and the Athenian* MAGISTRATE *we met before. Both appear to be suffering from acute priapism but the* HERALD *is ineffectually endeavouring to conceal the fact.)*

HERALD: Where are the lairds o' the Athenian council, or the Executive Committee? I wuid hae words wi' them.

MAGISTRATE: *(Guffawing.)* Ha! ha! ha! What are you—a man or a phallic symbol?

HERALD: My dear lad, I'm a herald, and I'm come frae Sparta   5 tae talk aboot peace.

MAGISTRATE: *(Pointing.)* Which is why you've got a spear under your clothes, I suppose?

HERALD: *(Turning his back on him.)* No, I hanna.

MAGISTRATE: What have you turned round for, then? Why are   10 you holding your cloak in that funny way? Did you get a rupture on the way here?

HERALD: *(To himself.)* By Castor, the man's senile!

MAGISTRATE: Why, you rascal, you've got prickitis!

HERALD: No, I hanna. Dinna be stupid.   15

MAGISTRATE: Well, what's that, then?

HERALD: It's a standard Spartan cipher rod.

MAGISTRATE: *(Indicating his counter-part.)* Yes, and so is this. You needn't think I'm a fool; you can tell me the truth. What is the present situation in Sparta?   20

HERALD: Tae be colloquial, things ha' reached a total cock-up. All our allies ha' risen, and we canna get hold o' Pellene.

(Looks longingly at the WOMEN'S CHORUS.)

MAGISTRATE: What's the cause of it all? Do you think Pan was responsible?

HERALD: Pan? Och, no, it was Lampito, and then a' the ither   25 women—almost as though there were some kind of plot in it—they a' pit up a Keep Oot notice over their whatnots.

MAGISTRATE: So how are you getting on?

HERALD: Verra badly, verra badly. We a' bend double as we walk roond the toon, as though we were carrying lamps.   30 D'ye ken, the women won't even let us sae much as touch their knobs, till we a' consent tae mak a general peace for the whole of Greece.

MAGISTRATE: Ah, now I see the plot! They're all in it—all the women everywhere. Tell your people at once to send dele-   35 gates here with full powers to negotiate for peace. I'll go and tell the Council to choose delegates to represent Athens. When they see my—my cipher rod I don't think they'll hesitate a moment.

HERALD: That's a' fine by me. I'll fly.   40

---

306 **Philostratus** a pimp

---

17 **Spartan cipher rod** Spartans wrote coded messages on strips wound around a rod; these were then decoded by the recipient by winding them around an identical rod   22 **Pellene** both a city considering an alliance with Sparta against Athens and an infamous woman of pleasure

(Exeunt severally.)

(The two CHORUSES *advance.)*

LEADER: There is no beast more stubborn than a woman,
  And neither fire nor leopard is more shameless.
STRATYLLIS: If you know that, why do you hate us so?
  We would be faithful friends, if you would let us.
45 LEADER: Women I loathe, both now and evermore.
STRATYLLIS: Well, as you please. But really, you look stupid
  Without your coat. Come on now, put it on.
  Or no, I know, I'll put your coat on for you.
LEADER: *(When she has done so.)* That was a good turn that
  you did to me,
50 And I was wrong to yield to wrath and doff it.
STRATYLLIS: There, you look better now, and not so comic.
  And now, if you'll keep still, I'll take that gnat
  Out of your eye.
LEADER: A gnat! that's what it was
  Was biting me! Come, dig it out and show me.
55 I've had these bites for hours and hours and hours.
STRATYLLIS: All right. *(She explores his eye carefully; he
  winces.)*
            You *are* a difficult old man.
  Great Zeus, it's monstrous! Look, just look at it!
  It must be from the Marsh of Marathon!
LEADER: Thank you so much. The gnat was digging deep,
60 And now the tears are streaming from my eyes.
STRATYLLIS: Don't worry, I've a handkerchief to wipe them—
  You *are* a bad old man, you know—and now
  I'll kiss you.
LEADER: No, you don't.
ALL THE WOMEN: Oh, yes, we do!

(And each of them kisses one of the MEN.*)*

LEADER: Damn you, you wheedlers! Still the saying's true—
65 We can't live with you, we can't live without you!
  Let us make peace, that's what we ought to do;
  You won't hit us, we promise not to flout you;
    Let us all form a single happy ring
    And in that union our next number sing.

(The two CHORUSES *join hands and are from now on united in
a single chorus. They sing the following two songs together.)*

70   No citizen need fear that we
        Will dent his reputation;
      We rather think you've had enough
        Of toil and tribulation.

      So what we'll do is not to jest
75   Or try to be buffoons;
      Instead we'd like to publicize
        Some unexpected boons.

      If anyone is short of drachs,
        Two hundred (say) and twenty,
80   Just call on us, because we've got
        Good money-bags in plenty.

      It's true they have no cash inside;
        Still, I should not complain:
      That means that you will never need
85   To pay it back again!

I'm entertaining some friends from Carystus tonight,
  tonight,
The table's prepared and you'll find the menu just right,
  just right.
There's plenty of soup and I've sacrificed a sow, a sow,
And—I think I can smell it—the pork should be roasting
  now, 'sting now.
You'd best be quick; it's a well-attended affair, affair,   90
So bath the kids and then get along right there, right there.
Walk in—no questions—pretend that you're in your own
  place, own place;
There's just one thing: the door will be shut in your face,
  your face.

(Enter a group of SPARTAN AMBASSADORS, *again looking very
distended.)*

LEADER: Here come our bearded Spartan friends. Why,
  anyone would swear
  That each of them was carrying a pig-pen under there!   95
  Welcome, gentlemen. How are you?
AMBASSADOR: I dinna need tae answer that in words; ye can
  see for yersel's how we are.
LEADER: Whew! You're certainly under severe tension—I
  should say things were quite inflammatory.   100
AMBASSADOR: And that's no lie. We dinna mind where, we
  dinna mind how, but we maun hae peace!

(Enter several ATHENIAN NEGOTIATORS.*)*

LEADER: Ah, here are our true-born Athenian representatives.
  Look as if they'd dropped from a great height and broken
  their backs, the way they're bending over. Yes, definitely a   105
  case of dropsy, I'd say. And look how they're holding their
  clothes miles away from their bodies!
NEGOTIATOR: Will somebody tell us where Lysistrata is? We're
  at the *point* of collapse.
LEADER: You've both got the same thing, I think. When does it   110
  get worst? In the small hours?
NEGOTIATOR: Not just then—all the time—and it's killing us.
  If we don't make peace right away, we shall all end up screwing Cleisthenes.

(The SPARTAN AMBASSADORS *take off their coats.)*

LEADER: I shouldn't do that if I were you. You wouldn't want   115
  your sacred emblems mutilated, would you?
NEGOTIATOR: *(To* AMBASSADOR.*)* They're right, you know.
AMBASSADOR: I'm thinking so too. Here, let's pit them on
  again.
NEGOTIATOR: Well now, old chap, this is a pretty pass we've all   120
  come to!
AMBASSADOR: Not sae bad as it wuid be, my dear fellow, if one
  of those amateur sculptors saw us like this.
NEGOTIATOR: Anyway, to business. What are you here for?
AMBASSADOR: Tae mak peace.   125
NEGOTIATOR: That's good to hear. So are we. Why don't we
  ask Lysistrata to come out? She's the only one who can rec-
  oncile us properly.

---

116 **sacred emblems mutilated** a reference to the recent mutilation by
vandals of the heads and phalluses of all the statues of Hermes in
Athenian streets

AMBASSADOR: Ay, by the Twa Gudes, Lysistratus, Lysistrata,
130   Lysistratum, masculine, feminine or neuter, I couldna care
less, sae we can bring this war to an end!

(*Music. The Propylaea opens wide, and* LYSISTRATA *appears,
magnificently arrayed.*)

NEGOTIATOR: No need to summon her, it seems; here she is!
CHORUS: Mighty lady with a mission—
Paragon of common sense—
135   Running fount of erudition—
Miracle of eloquence!
Greece is torn, and would be healed;
War is rife—let peace be sealed;
Thou hast conquered by thy charm;
140   Make the cities all disarm.
Mighty lady with a mission—
Paragon of common sense—
Running fount of erudition—
Miracle of eloquence!

145   LYSISTRATA: It's not hard, if you catch them when they're
aroused but not satisfied. We'll soon see. Reconciliation!

(*An extremely beautiful and totally unclothed girl enters from
the Acropolis.*)

Bring the Spartans to me first of all. Don't be rough or
brusque; handle them very gently, not in the brutal way men
lay hold on us, but the way a lady should—very civilized.

(RECONCILIATION *goes up to one of the* SPARTAN AMBASSADORS
and offers him her hand. He refuses.)

150   Well, if he won't give you his hand, try that leather thing.
That's right. Now the Athenians. You can take hold of anything they offer you. Now you, Spartans, stand on this side of
me, and you, Athenians, on the other side, and listen to what
I have to say.

(*The* AMBASSADORS *and* NEGOTIATORS, *guided by* RECONCILI-
ATION, *take their places on either side of* LYSISTRATA.)

155   I am a woman, but I am not brainless:
I have my share of native wit, and more,
Both from my father and from other elders
Instruction I've received. Now listen, both:
Hard will my words be, but not undeserved.
160   You worship the same gods at the same shrines,
Use the same lustral water, just as if
You were a single family—which you are—
Delphi, Olympia, Thermopylae—
How many other Panhellenic shrines
165   Could I make mention of, if it were needed!
And yet, although the Mede is at our gates,
You ruin Greece with mad intestine wars.
This is my first reproach to both of you.
NEGOTIATOR: (*Who has been eyeing* RECONCILIATION *all
170   through this speech.*) I hope she doesn't take much longer. I
doubt if this giant carrot will stand it.
LYSISTRATA: The next is for the Spartans. Know you not
How Pericleidas came to Athens once,
And sat a suppliant at our holy altar,
175   In scarlet uniform and death-white face,
Beseeching us to send a force to help you?
For then two perils threatened you at once:

The Helots, and Poseidon with his earthquake.
So Cimon took four thousand infantry
And saved the Spartan people from destruction.   180
This, Spartans, the Athenians did for you:
Is it then just to ravage Athens' land?
NEGOTIATOR: Yes, Lysistrata, they're in the wrong.
AMBASSADOR: We are. But by the Twa Gudes, she's a fine
bottom.   185
LYSISTRATA: Think not, Athenians, you are guiltless either.
Remember once you had to dress like slaves,
Until the Spartans came in force, and slew
The foreign mercenaries of Hippias
And many of his allies and confederates.   190
They fought for you alone upon that day
And set you free, removed your servile cloak
And clothed you with Democracy again.
AMBASSADOR: (*Still intent on* RECONCILIATION.) I havena
seen a bonnier lass.   195
NEGOTIATOR: Nor I a shapelier cunt.
LYSISTRATA: So why on fighting are your hearts so set?
For each of you is in the other's debt.
Why don't you make peace? What's the problem?
AMBASSADOR: (*Who has got hold of* RECONCILIATION; *both he   200
and his opposite number map out their demands on her per-
son.*) We will, if ye'll give us back this little promontory.
NEGOTIATOR: Which one, sir?
AMBASSADOR: Pylos. We've set oor hearts on it and been prod-
prodding at it for years.   205
NEGOTIATOR: By Poseidon, you shan't have it!
LYSISTRATA: Give it them.
NEGOTIATOR: Who will we have left to stimulate, then? To re-
volt, I mean.
LYSISTRATA: Well, you ask for somewhere else in exchange.   210
NEGOTIATOR: Very well . . . give us (*Mapping the areas out.*)
first of all the Echinian Triangle here, then the Malian
Gulf—I mean the one round behind, of course—and lastly—
er—the Long Legs—I mean the Long Walls of Megara.
AMBASSADOR: Are ye crazy? There's naething left!   215
LYSISTRATA: Come now, don't quarrel over a pair of legs—I
mean walls.
NEGOTIATOR: I'm ready to go back to my husbandry now.
AMBASSADOR: And I'm wanting tae do some manuring.
LYSISTRATA: Time enough for that when you've made peace. If   220
that's what you want to do, go and have a conference with
your allies and agree it with them.
NEGOTIATOR: Allies, ma'am?—look at the state we're in! We
know what the allies will say—the same as we do: 'Peace!
Peace! Bed! Bed!'   225
AMBASSADOR: And oors the same.
NEGOTIATOR: And we certainly needn't ask the Carystians.
LYSISTRATA: Fine then. Now we had better ratify the treaty in
the usual way. The women will entertain you in the Acropolis; they have plenty of good food in their picnic baskets. And   230
over that you can clasp hands and take the oaths. And then,
let everyone take his wife and live happily ever after!

---

178 **Helots** Spartan serfs, who rebelled following an earthquake in 464
BC   189 **Hippias** an Athenian ruler dethroned by a coalition of Athenian nobles and Spartans   227 **Carystians** a notoriously lustful folk

NEGOTIATOR: Let's go right away.
AMBASSADOR: Lead the way, my dear.
235 NEGOTIATOR: Yes, and quickly.

(All except the CHORUS go inside.)

CHORUS: Embroidered upholstery—magnificent cloaks—
    Fine ornaments fashioned of gold:
If your daughter is chosen the Basket to bear,
    Don't ask where these items are sold.

240 For all that I've got for the taking is yours;
    The seals on the boxes are weak;
Remove them, and then from whatever's inside
    Take just what it is that you seek.

There's one little thing I should warn you of first,
245   For if not, I'd be being unfair:
That unless you have got sharper eyesight than me,
    You'll find there ain't anything there!

If anyone who's short of bread
Has slaves and kids that must be fed,
250 I've got some loaves of finest milling,
Quadruple size, and very filling.

Let any who provisions lack
Come round to me with bag or sack;
My servant is enjoined by me
255 To give them all these loaves for free.

One thing I should have said before—
They'd better not come near the door;
I have a dog who at the sight
Of strangers will not bark but bite.

(Some LAYABOUTS come in, and begin pounding on the Acropolis gates.)

260 FIRST LAYABOUT: Open up! Open up!
DOORKEEPER: (Coming to the door.) Get away from here!
FIRST LAYABOUT: (To his companions.) What are you waiting
    for? (To the DOORKEEPER and others inside.) Do you want
    me to burn you up with my torch? No, on second thoughts,
265   that's an absolute comic cliché and I won't do it.

(Protests from the audience.)

Oh—very well—to please you, I'll go through with it.
SECOND LAYABOUT: And we'll be with you.
DOORKEEPER: (Coming out.) Get off with you! I'll pull your
    long hair out! Shoo! Get out of the way of the Spartans—the
270   banquet's nearly over, and they'll soon be coming out!

(He drives them away and goes back inside. Presently the door
opens, and two well-fed ATHENIAN DINERS emerge.)

FIRST DINER: Never known a party like it. The Spartans were
    the life and soul of it, weren't they? And we were pretty
    clever, considering how sozzled we were.
SECOND DINER: Not surprising really. We couldn't be as stu-
275   pid as we are when we're sober. If the Athenians took my ad-
    vice they'd always get drunk when going on diplomatic mis-
    sions. As it is, you see, we go to Sparta sober, and so we're al-
    ways looking for catches. We don't hear what they do say,
    and we hunt for implications in what they don't say—and we
280   bring back quite incompatible reports of what went on. And
    yet we only have to have a few, and everything's all right.

Even if one of them starts singing 'Telamon' when he should
be singing 'Cleitagora,' all we do is slap him on the back and
swear that 'Telamon' was just what was wanted!

(They go out. The LAYABOUTS return.)

DOORKEEPER: Here come these no-goods again. Bugger off, 285
all of you!
FIRST LAYABOUT: We'd better. They're coming out. (They run
off.)

(Enter ATHENIANS and SPARTANS, one of whom carries bagpipes.)

SPARTAN: Here, my dear fellow, tak the pipes, and I'll dance a
    reel and sing a song in honour of the Athenians and of 290
    oursel's forby.
ATHENIAN: Yes, do. There's nothing I enjoy so much as a good
    old Spartan dance.

(The PIPER takes the pipes and strikes up. The SPARTAN dances a
solo as he sings.)

Raise the song o' Sparta's fame,
And tae valiant Athens' name 295
Kindle an undying flame,
    Holy Memory.

How they focht in days of yore
Off the Artemisium shore—
They were few, the Medes were more— 300
    Theirs the victory!

While we Spartans quit oor hame—
Boarlike from oor mouths ran faem—
Brave our King, and high our aim—
    'Hellas shall be free!' 305

Nocht cuid frighten us that day,
Nocht cuid mak us run away,
And we won renown for aye
    At Thermopylae.

Artemis the Virgin Queen, 310
Huntress in the wuids sae green,
Come and bless this happy scene,
    Come, we call on thee!

Pour thy grace upon oor peace;
Make the artful foxes cease; 315
Let guidwill and love increase
    And prosperity!

(The Propylaea opens wide, and LYSISTRATA appears, flanked by
all the Athenian and Spartan women.)

LYSISTRATA: Well, gentlemen, it's all happily settled. Spartans,
    here are your wives back. And here are yours. Now form up
    everyone, two by two, and let us have a dance of thanksgiving. 320
    And may the gods vouchsafe to give us sense
    Ne'er to repeat our former dire offence!
CHORUS: Come, let us on the Graces call,
    Apollo next who healeth all,
    On Artemis and Hera too, 325

282–284 **Even if . . . wanted** a reference to an after-dinner singing
game   298 **How . . . yore** the following lines allude to the Spartan attempt to block the Persian (Mede) advance at Thermopylae and to the
Athenian naval victory at Artemisium in 480 BC

On Bacchus and his Maenad crew,
And most on Zeus above:

Let all the gods come witness now
The making of our solemn vow
330   To stay our hands from mutual war
And keep the peace for evermore
Made by the power of Love.
O great Apollo, hail!
O let it be that we
335   May win the victory!
O great Apollo, hail!
O great Apollo, hail!
Evoi! Evoi! Evoi!

(The CHORUS *dance joyfully out. The* ATHENIANS *and* SPARTANS
and their wives remain.)

LYSISTRATA: *(Recitative.)* To hail the peace for which we've
pined so long,
340   There's time, I fancy, for another song!

*(As a spectacular dance is performed by a soloist and everyone else
dances in the background.)*

SPARTAN: Muse, now be Sparta praisin',
Muse, Phoebus' name be raisin',
And in her temple brazen
Let Pallas hear:
345   Come, sons of Tyndareus's,
Castor and Polydeuces,
Favourites of a' the Muses,
Famed far and near.

Dance, dance tae Sparta's might!
350   Swing, swing yer sheepskins light!

Let's praise oor noble city,
Home o' songs and dances pretty—
Home of the sacred chorus,
Home of our sires before us,
Stout shield and mantle o'er us,   355
Sparta the brave!

Girls, shake your pretty tresses,
Whirl roond yer Doric dresses,
See your display expresses
Joy and relief: 360
Joy at the end o' slaughter—
See, Leda's beauteous daughter,
Purer than mountain water,
Helen's the chief.

Dance, dance for Helen fair!   365
Smooth, smooth yer flowing hair!
Tak off wi' both yer feet and
Stamp on every ither beat and
Pray that Athena never
Her link tae Sparta sever,   370
May she protect for ever
Sparta the brave!

(All kneel facing the shrine of Victory.)

ALL: Athena, hail, thou Zeus-born Maid!
Who war and death in Greece hast stayed:
Hail, fount from whom all blessings fall;   375
All hail, all hail, Protectress of us all!

(General dance.)

CRITICAL CONTEXTS

Born near Macedonia, Aristotle entered the Academy in Athens at the age of seventeen to study with Plato. After Plato's death, Aristotle conducted research in natural history—mainly botany and zoology—throughout the Aegean region and served as the tutor of the young Alexander the Great in Macedon, before returning to Athens to found the Lyceum in 355 BC.

Aristotle wrote extensively on topics ranging from ethics, rhetoric, and metaphysics to physics and natural history. In The Poetics, *he analyzes the field of poetry into different "species" or genres (epic, tragedy, comedy, dithyramb) and attempts to discover the basic features of each. The Poetics demonstrates Aristotle's extensive knowledge of drama, which he uses to refine a keen sense of the form and purpose of tragedy. We should remember that* The Poetics *was written sometime after 335 BC, roughly a century after the height of the Athenian theater. And although* The Poetics *is the cornerstone of Western dramatic criticism, the meaning of several of Aristotle's key terms—*MIMESIS *(imitation), catharsis (purgation),* HAMARTIA *(error)—remain controversial.*

ARISTOTLE
(384–322 BC)

FROM *THE POETICS*
(C. 335 BC)

TRANSLATED BY
GERALD F. ELSE

The art of poetic composition in general and its various species, the function and effect of each of them; how the plots should be constructed if the composition is to be an artistic success; how many other component elements are involved in the process, and of what kind; and similarly all the other questions that fall under this same branch of inquiry—these are the problems we shall discuss; let us begin in the right and natural way, with basic principles.

Epic composition, then; the writing of tragedy, and of comedy also; the composing of dithyrambs; and the greater part of the making of music with flute and lyre: these are all in point of fact, taken collectively, imitative processes. They differ from each other, however, in three ways, namely by virtue of having (1) different means, (2) different objects, and (3) different methods of imitation.

First, in the same way that certain people imitate a variety of things by means of shapes and colors, making visible replicas of them (some doing this on the basis of art, others out of habit), while another group produces its mimicry with the voice, so in the case of the arts we just mentioned: they all carry on their imitation through the media of rhythm, speech, and melody, but with the latter two used separately or together. Thus the arts of flute and lyre music, and any others of similar nature and effect such as the art of the panpipe, produce their imitation using melody and rhythm alone, while there is another which does so using speeches or verses alone, bare of music, and either mixing the verses with one another or employing just one certain kind—an art which is, as it happens, nameless up to the present time. In fact we could not even assign a common name to the mimes of Sophron and Xenarchus and the Socratic discourses; nor again if somebody should compose his imitation in trimeters or elegiac couplets or certain other verses of that kind; (Except people do link up poetic composition with verse and speak of "elegiac poets," "epic poets," not treating them as poets by virtue of their imitation, but employing the term as a common appellation going along with the use of verse. And in fact the name is also applied to anyone who treats a medical or scientific topic in verses, yet Homer and Empedocles actually have nothing in common except their verse; hence the proper term for the one is "poet," for the other, "science-writer" rather than "poet.") and likewise if someone should mix all the kinds of verse together in composing his imitation, as Chaeremon composed a *Centaur* using all the verses.

Such is the disjunction we feel is called for in these cases. There are on the other hand certain arts which use all the aforesaid media, I mean such as rhythm, song, and verse. The composition of dithyrambs and of nomes does so, and both tragedy and comedy. But there is a difference in that some of these arts use all the media at once while others use them in different parts of the work.

These then are the differentiations of the poetic arts with respect to the media in which the poets carry on their imitation.

BASIC CONSIDERATIONS

THE DIFFERENTIATION ACCORDING TO MEDIUM

THE OBJECTS OF IMITATION

Since those who imitate men in action, and these must necessarily be either worthwhile or worthless people (for definite characters tend pretty much to develop in men of action), it follows that they imitate men either better or worse than the average, as the painters do—for Polygnotus used to portray superior and Pauson inferior men; and it is evident that each of the forms of imitation aforementioned will include these differentiations, that is, will differ by virtue of imitating objects which are different in this sense. Indeed it is possible for these dissimilarities to turn up in flute and lyre playing, and also in prose dialogues and bare verses: thus Homer imitated superior men and Hegemon of Thasos, the inventor of parody, and Nicochares, the author of the *Deiliad*, inferior ones; likewise in connection with dithyrambs and nomes, for one can make the imitation the way Timotheus and Philoxenus did their Cyclopes. Finally, the difference between tragedy and comedy coincides exactly with the master-difference: namely the one tends to imitate people better, the other one people worse, than the average.

THE MODES OF IMITATION

The third way of differentiating these arts is by the mode of imitation. For it is possible to imitate the same objects, and in the same media, (1) by narrating part of the time and dramatizing the rest of the time, which is the way Homer composes (mixed mode), or (2) with the same person continuing without change (straight narrative), or (3) with all the persons who are performing the imitation acting, that is, carrying on for themselves (straight dramatic mode).

JOTTINGS, CHIEFLY ON COMEDY

Poetic imitation, then, shows these three *differentiae*, as we said at the beginning: in the media, objects, and modes of imitation. So in one way Sophocles would be the same (kind of) imitator as Homer, since they both imitate worthwhile people, and in another way the same as Aristophanes, for they both imitate people engaged in action, doing things. In fact some authorities maintain that that is why plays are called dramas, because the imitation is of men acting (*drôntas*, from *drân*, 'do, act'). It is also the reason why both tragedy and comedy are claimed by the Dorians: comedy by the Megarians, both those from hereabouts, who say that it came into being during the period of their democracy, and those in Sicily, and tragedy by some of those in the Peloponnese. They use the names "comedy" and "drama" as evidence; for they say that *they* call their outlying villages *kômai* while the Athenians call theirs "demes" (*dêmoi*)—the assumption being that the participants in comedy were called *kômôidoi* not from their being revelers but because they wandered from one village to another, being degraded and excluded from the city—and that they call "doing" or "acting" *drân* while the Athenians designate it by *prattein*.

THE ORIGIN AND DEVELOPMENT OF POETRY

So much, then, for the *differentiae* of imitation, their number and identity. As to the origin of the poetic art as a whole, it stands to reason that two operative causes brought it into being, both of them rooted in human nature. Namely (1) the habit of imitating is congenital to human beings from childhood (actually man differs from the other animals in that he is the most imitative and learns his first lessons through imitation), and so is (2) the pleasure that all men take in works of imitation. A proof of this is what happens in our experience. There are things which we see with pain so far as they themselves are concerned but whose images, even when executed in very great detail, we view with pleasure. Such is the case for example with renderings of the least favored animals, or of cadavers. The cause of this also is that learning is eminently pleasurable not only to philosophers but to the rest of mankind in the same way, although their share in the pleasure is restricted. For the reason they take pleasure in seeing the images is that in the process of viewing they find themselves learning, that is, reckoning what kind a given thing belongs to: "This individual is a So-and-so." Because if the viewer happens not to have seen such a thing before, the reproduction will not produce the pleasure *qua* reproduction but through its workmanship or color or something else of that sort.

Since, then, imitation comes naturally to us, and melody and rhythm too (it is obvious that verses are segments of the respective rhythms), in the beginning it was those who were most gifted in these respects who, developing them little by little, brought the making of poetry into being out of improvisations. And the poetic enterprise split into two branches, in accordance with the two kinds of character. Namely, the soberer spirits were imitating noble actions and the actions of noble persons, while the cheaper ones were imitating those of the worthless, producing lampoons and invectives at first just as the other sort were producing hymns and encomia. (. . .) In them (i.e., the invectives), in accordance with what is suitable and fitting, iambic verse also put in its appearance; indeed that is why it is called "iambic" now, because it is the verse in which they used to "iambize," that is, lampoon, each other. And so some of the early poets became composers of epic, the others of iambic, verses.

Now it happens that we cannot name anyone before Homer as the author of that kind of poem (i.e., an iambic poem), though it stands to reason that there were many who were; but from Homer on we can do so: thus his *Margites* and other poems of that sort. However, just as on the serious side Homer was most truly a poet, since he was the only one who not only composed well but constructed dramatic imitations, so too he was the first to adumbrate the forms of comedy by producing a (1) dramatic presentation, and not of invective but of (2) the ludicrous. For as the *Iliad* stands in relation to our tragedies, so the *Margites* stands in relation to our comedies.

Once tragedy and comedy had been partially brought to light, those who were out in pursuit of the two kinds of poetic activity, in accordance with their own respective natures, became in the one case comic poets instead of iambic poets, in the other case producers of tragedies instead of epics, because these genres were higher and more esteemed than the others. Now to review the question whether even tragedy is adequate to the basic forms or not—a question which is (can be) judged both by itself, in the abstract, and in relationship to our theater audiences—that is another story. However that may be, it did spring from an improvisational beginning (both it and comedy: the one from those who led off the dithyramb, the other from those who did so for the phallic performances [?] which still remain on the program in many of our cities); it did expand gradually, each feature being further developed as it appeared; and after it had gone through a number of phases it stopped upon attaining its full natural growth. Thus Aeschylus was the first to expand the troupe of assisting actors from one to two, shorten the choral parts, and see to it that the dialogue takes first place; (. . .) at the same time the verse became iambic trimeter instead of trochaic tetrameter. For in the beginning they used the tetrameter because the form of composition was "satyr-like," that is, more given over to dancing, but when speech came along the very nature of the case turned up the appropriate verse. For iambic is the most speech-like of verses. An indication of this is that we speak more iambics than any other kind of verse in our conversation with each other, whereas we utter hexameters rarely, and when we do we abandon the characteristic tone-pattern of ordinary speech.

Further, as to plurality of episodes and the other additions which are recorded as having been made to tragedy, let our account stop here; for no doubt it would be burdensome to record them in detail.

COMEDY

Comedy is as we said it was, an imitation of persons who are inferior; not, however, going all the way to full villainy, but imitating the ugly, of which the ludicrous is one part. The ludicrous, that is, is a failing or a piece of ugliness which causes no pain or destruction; thus, to go no farther, the comic mask is something ugly and distorted but painless.

Now the stages of development of tragedy, and the men who were responsible for them, have not escaped notice, but comedy did escape notice in the beginning because it was not taken seriously. (In fact it was late in its history that the presiding magistrate officially "granted a chorus" to the comic poets; until then they were volunteers.) Thus comedy already possessed certain defining characteristics when the first "comic poets," so-called, appear in the record. Who gave it masks, or prologues, or troupes of actors and all that sort of thing, is not known. The composing of plots came originally from Sicily; of the Athenian poets, Crates was the first to abandon the lampooning mode and compose arguments, that is, plots, of a general nature.

EPIC AND TRAGEDY

Well then, epic poetry followed in the wake of tragedy up to the point of being a (1) good-sized (2) imitation (3) in verse (4) of people who are to be taken seriously; but in its having its verse unmixed with any other and being narrative in character, there they differ. Further, so far as its length is concerned tragedy tries as hard as it can to exist during a single daylight period, or to vary but little, while the epic is not limited in its time and so differs in that respect. Yet originally they used to do this in tragedies just as much as they did in epic poems.

The constituent elements are partly identical and partly limited to tragedy. Hence anybody who knows about good and bad tragedy knows about epic also; for the elements that the epic possesses appertain to tragedy as well, but those of tragedy are not all found in the epic.

TRAGEDY AND ITS SIX CONSTITUENT ELEMENTS

Our discussions of imitative poetry in hexameters, and of comedy, will come later; at present let us deal with tragedy, recovering from what has been said so far the definition of its essential nature, as it was in development. Tragedy, then, is a process of imitating an action which has serious implications, is complete, and possesses magnitude; by means of language which has been made sensuously attractive, with each of its varieties found separately in the parts; enacted by the persons themselves and not presented through narrative; through a course of pity and fear completing the purification of tragic acts which have those emotional characteristics. By "language made sensuously attractive" I mean language that has rhythm and melody, and by "its varieties found separately" I mean the fact that certain parts of the play are carried on through spoken verses alone and others the other way round, through song.

Now first of all, since they perform the imitation through action (by acting it), the adornment of their visual appearance will perforce constitute some part of the making of tragedy; and song-composition and verbal expression also, for those are the media in which they perform the imitation. By "verbal expression" I mean the actual composition of the verses, and by "song-composition" something whose meaning is entirely clear.

Next, since it is an imitation of an action and is enacted by certain people who are performing the action, and since those people must necessarily have certain traits both of character and thought (for it is thanks to these two factors that we speak of people's actions also as having a defined character, and it is in accordance with their actions that all either succeed or fail); and since the imitation of the action is the plot, for by "plot" I mean here the structuring of the events, and by the "characters" that in accordance with which we say that the persons who are acting have a defined moral character, and by "thought" all the passages in which they attempt to prove some thesis or set forth an opinion—it follows of necessity, then, that tragedy as a whole has just six constituent elements, in relation to the essence that makes it a distinct species; and they are plot, characters, verbal expression, thought, visual adornment, and song-composition. For the elements by which they imitate are two (i.e., verbal expression and song-composition), the manner in which they imitate is one (visual adornment), the things they imitate are three (plot, characters, thought), and there is nothing more beyond these. These then are the constituent forms they use.

THE RELATIVE IMPORTANCE OF THE SIX ELEMENTS

The greatest of these elements is the structuring of the incidents. For tragedy is an imitation not of men but of a life, an action, and they have moral quality in accordance with their characters but are happy or unhappy in accordance with their actions; hence they are not active in order to imitate their characters, but they include the characters along with the actions for the sake of the latter. Thus the structure of events, the plot, is the goal of tragedy, and the goal is the greatest thing of all.

Again: a tragedy cannot exist without a plot, but it can without characters: thus the tragedies of most of our modern poets are devoid of character, and in general many poets are like that; so also with the relationship between Zeuxis and Polygnotus, among the painters: Polygnotus is a good portrayer of character, while Zeuxis' painting has no dimension of character at all.

Again: if one strings end to end speeches that are expressive of character and carefully worked in thought and expression, he still will not achieve the result which we said was the aim of tragedy; the job will be done much better by a tragedy that is more deficient in these other respects but has a plot, a structure of events. It is much the same case as with painting: the most beautiful pigments smeared on at random will not give as much pleasure as a black-and-white outline picture. Besides, the most powerful means tragedy has for swaying our feelings, namely the peripeties and recognitions, are elements of the plot.

Again: an indicative sign is that those who are beginning a poetic career manage to hit the mark in verbal expression and character portrayal sooner than they do in plot construction; and the same is true of practically all the earliest poets.

So plot is the basic principle, the heart and soul, as it were, of tragedy, and the characters come second: (. . .) it is the imitation of an action and imitates the persons primarily for the sake of their action.

Third in rank is thought. This is the ability to state the issues and appropriate points pertaining to a given topic, an ability which springs from the arts of politics and rhetoric; in fact the earlier poets made their characters talk "politically," the present-day poets rhetorically. But "character" is that kind of utterance which clearly reveals the bent of a man's moral choice (hence there is no character in that class of utterances in which there is nothing at all that the speaker is choosing or rejecting), while "thought" is the passages in which they try to prove that something is so or not so, or state some general principle.

Fourth is the verbal expression of the speeches. I mean by this the same thing that was said earlier, that the "verbal expression" is the conveyance of thought through language: a statement which has the same meaning whether one says "verses" or "speeches."

The song-composition of the remaining parts is the greatest of the sensuous attractions, and the visual adornment of the dramatic persons can have a strong emotional effect but is the least artistic element, the least connected with the poetic art; in fact the force of tragedy can be felt even without benefit of public performance and actors, while for the production of the visual effect the property man's art is even more decisive than that of the poets.

With these distinctions out of the way, let us next discuss what the structuring of the events should be like, since this is both the basic and the most important element in the tragic art. We have established, then, that tragedy is an imitation of an action which is complete and whole and has some magnitude (for there is also such a thing as a whole that has no magnitude). "Whole" is that which has beginning, middle, and end. "Beginning" is that which does not necessarily follow on something else, but after it something else naturally is or happens; "end," the other way round, is that which naturally follows on something else, either necessarily or for the most part, but nothing else after it; and "middle" that which naturally follows on something else and something else on it. So, then, well-constructed plots should neither begin nor end at any chance point but follow the guidelines just laid down.

Furthermore, since the beautiful, whether a living creature or anything that is composed of parts, should not only have these in a fixed order to one another but also possess a definite size which does not depend on chance—for beauty depends on size and order; hence neither can a very tiny creature turn out to be beautiful (since our perception of it grows blurred as it approaches the period of imperceptibility) nor an excessively huge one (for then it cannot all be perceived at once and so its unity and wholeness are lost), if for example there were a creature a thousand miles long—so, just as in the case of living creatures they must have some size, but one that can be taken in in a single view, so with plots: they should have length, but such that they are easy to remember. As to a limit of the length, the one is determined by the tragic competitions and the ordinary span of attention. (If they had to compete with a hundred tragedies they would compete by the water clock, as they say used to be done [?].) But the limit fixed by the very nature of the case is: the longer the plot, up to the point of still being perspicuous as a whole, the finer it is so far as size is concerned; or to put it in general terms, the length in which, with things happening in unbroken sequence, a shift takes place either probably or necessarily from bad to good fortune or from good to bad—that is an acceptable norm of length.

But a plot is not unified, as some people think, simply because it has to do with a single person. A large, indeed an indefinite number of things can happen to a given individual, some of which go to constitute no unified event; and in the same way there can be many acts of a given individual from which no single action emerges. Hence it seems clear that those poets are wrong who have composed *Heracleïds*, *Theseïds*, and the like. They think that since Heracles was a single person it follows that the plot will be single too. But Homer, superior as he is in all other respects, appears to have grasped this point well also, thanks either to art or nature, for in composing an *Odyssey* he did not incorporate into it everything that happened to the hero, for example how he was wounded on Mt. Parnassus or how he feigned madness at the muster, neither of which events, by happening, made it at all necessary or probable that the other should happen. Instead, he composed the *Odyssey*—and the *Iliad* similarly—around a unified action of the kind we have been talking about.

A poetic imitation, then, ought to be unified in the same way as a single imitation in any other mimetic field, by having a single object: since the plot is an imitation of an action, the latter ought to be both unified and complete, and the component events ought to be so firmly compacted that if any one of them is shifted to another place, or removed, the whole is loosened up and dislocated; for an element whose addition or subtraction makes no perceptible extra difference is not really a part of the whole.

GENERAL PRINCIPLES OF THE TRAGIC PLOT

From what has been said it is also clear that the poet's job is not to report what has happened but what is likely to happen: that is, what is capable of happening according to the rule of probability or necessity. Thus the difference between the historian and the poet is not in their utterances being in verse or prose (it would be quite possible for Herodotus' work to be translated into verse, and it would not be any the less a history with verse than it is without it); the difference lies in the fact that the historian speaks of what has happened, the poet of the kind of thing that *can* happen. Hence also poetry is a more philosophical and serious business than history; for poetry speaks more of universals, history of particulars. "Universal" in this case is what kind of person is likely to do or say certain kinds of things, according to probability or necessity; that is what poetry aims at, although it gives its persons particular names afterward; while the "particular" is what Alcibiades did or what happened to him.

In the field of comedy this point has been grasped: our comic poets construct their plots on the basis of general probabilities and then assign names to the persons quite arbitrarily, instead of dealing with individuals as the old iambic poets did. But in tragedy they still cling to the historically given names. The reason is that what is possible is persuasive; so what has not happened we are not yet ready to believe is possible, while what has happened is, we feel, obviously possible: for it would not have happened if it were impossible. Nevertheless, it is a fact that even in our tragedies, in some cases only one or two of the names are traditional, the rest being invented, and in some others none at all. It is so, for example, in Agathon's *Antheus*—the names in it are as fictional as the events—and it gives no less pleasure because of that. Hence the poets ought not to cling at all costs to the traditional plots, around which our tragedies are constructed. And in fact it is absurd to go searching for this kind of authentication, since even the familiar names are familiar to only a few in the audience and yet give the same kind of pleasure to all.

So from these considerations it is evident that the poet should be a maker of his plots more than of his verses, insofar as he is a poet by virtue of his imitations and what he imitates is actions. Hence even if it happens that he puts something that has actually taken place into poetry, he is none the less a poet; for there is nothing to prevent some of the things that have happened from being the kind of things that can happen, and that is the sense in which he is their maker.

SIMPLE AND COMPLEX PLOTS

Among simple plots and actions the episodic are the worst. By "episodic" plot I mean one in which there is no probability or necessity for the order in which the episodes follow one another. Such structures are composed by the bad poets because they are bad poets, but by the good poets because of the actors: in composing contest pieces for them, and stretching out the plot beyond its capacity, they are forced frequently to dislocate the sequence.

Furthermore, since the tragic imitation is not only of a complete action but also of events that are fearful and pathetic, and these come about best when they come about contrary to one's expectation yet logically, one following from the other; that way they will be more productive of wonder than if they happen merely at random, by chance—because even among chance occurrences the ones people consider most marvelous are those that seem to have come about as if on purpose: for example the way the statue of Mitys at Argos killed the man who had been the cause of Mitys' death, by falling on him while he was attending the festival; it stands to reason, people think, that such things don't happen by chance—so plots of that sort cannot fail to be artistically superior.

Some plots are simple, others are complex; indeed the actions of which the plots are imitations already fall into these two categories. By "simple" action I mean one the development of which being continuous and unified in the manner stated above, the reversal comes without peripety or recognition, and by "complex" action one in which the reversal is continuous but with recognition or peripety or both. And these developments must grow out of the very structure of the plot itself, in such a way that on the basis of what has happened previously this particular outcome follows either by necessity or in accordance with probability; for there is a great difference in whether these events happen because of those or merely after them.

"Peripety" is a shift of what is being undertaken to the opposite in the way previously stated, and that in accordance with probability or necessity as we have just been saying; as for example in the *Oedipus* the man who has come, thinking that he will reassure Oedipus, that is, relieve him of his fear with respect to his mother, by revealing who he once was, brings about the opposite; and in the *Lynceus*, as he (Lynceus) is being led away with every prospect of being executed, and Danaus pursuing him with every prospect of doing the executing, it comes about as a result of the other things that have happened in the play that *he* is executed and Lynceus is saved. And "recognition" is, as indeed the name indicates, a shift from ignorance to awareness, pointing in the direction either of close blood ties or of hostility, of people who have previously been in a clearly marked state of happiness or unhappiness.

The finest recognition is one that happens at the same time as a peripety, as is the case with the one in the *Oedipus*. Naturally, there are also other kinds of recognition: it is possible for one to take place in the prescribed manner in relation to inanimate objects and chance occurrences, and it is possible to recognize whether a person has acted or not acted. But the form that is most integrally a part of the plot, the action, is the one aforesaid; for that kind of recognition combined with peripety will excite either pity or fear (and these are the kinds of action of which tragedy is an imitation according to our definition), because both good and bad fortune will also be most likely to follow that kind of event. Since, further, the recognition is a recognition of persons, some are of one person by the other one only (when it is already known who the "other one" is), but sometimes it is necessary for both persons to go through a recognition, as for example Iphigenia is recognized by her brother through the sending of the letter, but of him by Iphigenia another recognition is required.

These then are two elements of plot: peripety and recognition; third is the *pathos*. Of these, peripety and recognition have been discussed; a *pathos* is a destructive or painful act, such as deaths on stage, paroxysms of pain, woundings, and all that sort of thing.

The "parts" of tragedy which should be used as constituent elements were mentioned earlier; (. . .) but what one should aim at and what one should avoid in composing one's plots, and whence the effect of tragedy is to come, remains to be discussed now, following immediately upon what has just been said.

Since, then, the construction of the finest tragedy should be not simple but complex, and at the same time imitative of fearful and pitiable happenings (that being the special character of this kind of poetry), it is clear first of all that (1) neither should virtuous men appear undergoing a change from good to bad fortune, for that is not fearful, nor pitiable either, but morally repugnant; nor (2) the wicked from bad fortune to good—that is the most untragic form of all, it has none of the qualities that one wants: it is productive neither of ordinary sympathy nor of pity nor of fear—nor again (3) the really wicked man changing from good fortune to bad, for that kind of structure will excite sympathy but neither pity nor fear, since the one (pity) is directed towards the man who does not deserve his misfortune and the other (fear) towards the one who is like the rest of mankind—what is left is the man who falls between these extremes. Such is a man who is neither a paragon of virtue and justice nor undergoes the change to misfortune through any real badness or wickedness but because of some mistake; one of those who stand in great repute and prosperity, like Oedipus and Thyestes: conspicuous men from families of that kind.

So, then, the artistically made plot must necessarily be single rather than double, as some maintain, and involve a change not from bad fortune to good fortune but the other way round, from good fortune to bad, and not thanks to wickedness but because of some mistake of great weight and consequence, by a man such as we have described or else on the good rather than the bad side. An indication comes from what has been happening in tragedy: at the beginning the poets used to "tick off" whatever plots came their way, but nowadays the finest tragedies are composed about a few houses: they deal with Alcmeon, Oedipus, Orestes, Meleager, Thyestes, Telephus, and whichever others have had the misfortune to do or undergo fearful things.

Thus the technically finest tragedy is based on this structure. Hence those who bring charges against Euripides for doing this in his tragedies are making the same mistake. His practice is correct in the way that has been shown. There is a very significant indication: on our stages and in the competitions, plays of this structure are accepted as the most tragic, *if* they are handled successfully, and Euripides, though he may not make his other arrangements effectively, still is felt by the audience to be the most tragic, at least, of the poets.

Second comes the kind which is rated first by certain people, having its structure double like the *Odyssey* and with opposite endings for the good and bad. Its being put first is due to the weakness of the audiences; for the poets follow along, catering to their wishes. But this particular pleasure is not the one that springs from tragedy but is more characteristic of comedy.

THE TRAGIC SIDE OF TRAGEDY: PITY AND FEAR AND THE PATTERNS OF THE COMPLEX PLOT

PITY AND FEAR AND THE TRAGIC ACT

Now it is possible for the fearful or pathetic effect to come from the actors' appearance, but it is also possible for it to arise from the very structure of the events, and this is closer to the mark and characteristic of a better poet. Namely, the plot must be so structured, even without benefit of any visual effect, that the one who is hearing the events unroll shudders with fear and feels pity at what happens: which is what one would experience on hearing the plot of the *Oedipus.* To set out to achieve this by means of the masks and costumes is less artistic, and requires technical support in the staging. As for those who do not set out to achieve the fearful through the masks and costumes, but only the monstrous, they have nothing to do with tragedy at all; for one should not seek any and every pleasure from tragedy, but the one that is appropriate to it.

Since it is the pleasure derived from pity and fear by means of imitation that the poet should seek to produce, it is clear that these qualities must be built into the constituent events. Let us determine, then, which kinds of happening are felt by the spectator to be fearful, and which pitiable. Now such acts are necessarily the work of persons who are near and dear (close blood kin) to one another, or enemies, or neither. But when an enemy attacks an enemy there is nothing pathetic about either the intention or the deed, except in the actual pain suffered by the victim; nor when the act is done by "neutrals"; but when the tragic acts come within the limits of close blood relationship, as when brother kills or intends to kill brother or do something else of that kind to him, or son to father or mother to son or son to mother—those are the situations one should look for.

Now although it is not admissible to break up the transmitted stories—I mean for instance that Clytemestra was killed by Orestes, or Eriphyle by Alcmeon—one should be artistic both in inventing stories and in managing the ones that have been handed down. But what we mean by "artistic" requires some explanation.

It is possible, then, (1) for the act to be performed as the older poets presented it, knowingly and wittingly; Euripides did it that way also, in Medea's murder of her children. It is possible (2) to refrain from performing the deed, with knowledge. Or it is possible (3) to perform the fearful act, but unwittingly, then recognize the blood relationship later, as Sophocles' Oedipus does; in that case the act is outside the play, but it can be in the tragedy itself, as with Astydamas' Alcmeon, or Telegonus in the *Wounding of Odysseus.* A further mode, in addition to these, is (4) while intending because of ignorance to perform some black crime, to discover the relationship before one does it. And there is no other mode besides these; for one must necessarily either do the deed or not, and with or without knowledge of what it is.

Of these modes, to know what one is doing but hold off and not perform the act (no. 2) is worst: it has the morally repulsive character and at the same time is not tragic; for there is no tragic act. Hence nobody composes that way, or only rarely, as, for example, Haemon threatens Creon in the *Antigone.* Performing the act (with knowledge) (no. 1) is second (poorest). Better is to perform it in ignorance and recognize what one has done afterward (no. 3); for the repulsive quality does not attach to the act, and the recognition has a shattering emotional effect. But the best is the last (no. 4): I mean a case like the one in the *Cresphontes* where Merope is about to kill her son but does not do so because she recognizes him first; or in *Iphigenia in Tauris* the same happens with sister and brother; or in the *Helle* the son recognizes his mother just as he is about to hand her over to the enemy.

The reason for what was mentioned a while ago, namely that our tragedies have to do with only a few families, is this: It was because the poets, when they discovered how to produce this kind of effect in their plots, were conducting their search on the basis of chance, not art; hence they have been forced to focus upon those families which happen to have suffered tragic happenings of this kind.

THE TRAGIC CHARACTERS

Enough, then, concerning the structure of events and what traits the tragic plots should have. As for the characters, there are four things to be aimed at. First and foremost, that they be good. The persons will have character if in the way previously stated their speech or their action reveals the moral quality of some choice, and good character if a good choice. Good character exists, moreover, in each category of persons; a woman can be good, or a slave, although one of these classes (*sc.* women) is inferior and the other, as a class, worthless. Second, that they be appropriate; for it is possible for a character to be brave, but inappropriately to a woman. Third is likeness to human nature in general; for this is different from making the character good and appropriate according to the criteria previously mentioned. And fourth is consistency. For even if the person being imitated is inconsistent, and that kind of character has been taken as the theme, he should be inconsistent in a consistent fashion.

An example of moral depravity that accomplishes no necessary purpose is the Menelaus in Euripides' *Orestes*; of an unsuitable and inappropriate character, the lamentation of Odysseus in the *Scylla* and the speech of Melanippe; and of the inconsistent, Iphigenia at Aulis; for the girl who pleads for her life is in no way like the later one.

In character portrayal also, as in plot construction, one should always strive for either the necessary or the probable, so that it is either necessary or probable for that kind of person to do or say that kind of thing, just as it is for one event to follow the other. It is evident, then, that the dénouements of plots also should come out of the character itself, and not from the "machine" as in the *Medea* or with the sailing of the fleet in the *Aulis*. Rather the machine should be used for things that lie outside the drama proper, either previous events that a human being cannot know, or subsequent events which require advance prophecy and exposition; for we grant the gods the ability to foresee everything. But let there be no illogicality in the web of events, or if there is, let it be outside the play like the one in Sophocles' *Oedipus*.

Since tragedy is an imitation of persons who are better than average, one should imitate the good portrait painters, for in fact, while rendering likenesses of their sitters by reproducing their individual appearance, they also make them better-looking; so the poet, in imitating men who are irascible or easygoing or have other traits of that kind, should make them, while still plausibly drawn, morally good, as Homer portrayed Achilles as good yet like other men.

TECHNIQUES OF RECOGNITION

What recognition is generically, was stated earlier; now as to its varieties: First comes the one that is least artistic and is most used, merely out of lack of imagination, that by means of tokens. Of these some are inherited, like "the lance that all the Earth-born wear," or "stars" such as Carcinus employs in his *Thyestes*; some are acquired, and of those some are on the body, such as scars, others are external, like the well-known amulets or the recognition in the *Tyro* by means of the little ark. There are better and poorer ways of using these; for example, Odysseus was recognized in different ways by means of his scar, once by the nurse and again by the swineherds. Those that are deliberately cited for the sake of establishing an identity, and all that kind, are less artistic, while those that develop naturally but unexpectedly, like the one in the foot-washing scene, are better.

Second poorest are those that are contrived by the poet and hence are inartistic; for example the way, in the *Iphigenia*, she recognizes that it is Orestes: *she* was recognized by means of the letter, but *he* goes out of his way to say what the poet, rather than the plot, wants him to say. Thus this mode is close kin to the error mentioned above: he might as well have actually worn some tokens. Similarly, in Sophocles' *Tereus*, the "voice of the shuttle."

Third poorest is that through recollection, by means of a certain awareness that follows on seeing or hearing something, like the one in the *Cypriotes* of Dicaeogenes where the hero bursts into tears on seeing the picture, and the one in Book 8 of the *Odyssey*: Odysseus weeps when he hears the lyre-player and is reminded of the War; in both cases the recognition follows.

Fourth in ascending order is the recognition based on reasoning; for example in the *Libation-Bearers*: "Somebody like me has come; nobody is like me but Orestes; therefore he has come." And the one suggested by the sophist Polyidus in speaking of the *Iphigenia*: it would have been natural, he said, for Orestes to draw the conclusion (aloud): "My sister was executed as a sacrifice, and now it is my turn." Also in the *Tydeus* of Theodectes: "I came expecting to find my son, and instead I am being destroyed myself." Or the one in the *Daughters of Phineus*: when they see the spot they reflect that it was indeed their fate to die here; for they had been exposed here as babies also. There is also one based on mistaken inference on the part of the audience, as in *Odysseus the False Messenger*. In that play, that he and no once else can string the bow is an assumption, a premise invented by the poet, and also his saying that he would recognize the bow when in fact he had not seen it; whereas the notion that he (the poet) has made his invention for the sake of the other person who would make the recognition, that is a mistaken inference.

The best recognition of all is the one that arises from the events themselves; the emotional shock of surprise is then based on probabilities, as in Sophocles' *Oedipus* and in the *Iphigenia*; for it was only natural that she should wish to send a letter. Such recognitions are the only ones that dispense with artificial inventions and visible tokens. And second-best are those based on reasoning. . . .

**FRIEDRICH
NIETZSCHE**
(1844–1900)

FROM *THE BIRTH
OF TRAGEDY*
(1872)

TRANSLATED BY
WALTER KAUFMANN

SECTION 1

Throughout his career, the German philosopher and poet Friedrich Nietzsche criticized the limitations of modern conceptual and moral categories. This revolutionary subversion of the premises of philosophy forms the core of his most famous works— The Gay Science *(1882),* Also Spoke Zarathustra *(1883–1892), and* Beyond Good and Evil *(1886). In* The Birth of Tragedy *(1872), Nietzsche argues that Greek tragedy arose from the collision between Athenian rationalism—symbolized by Apollo, Socrates, and Euripides—and an earlier, irrational mysticism, symbolized by Dionysus. Although Nietzsche's reading of Greek history has been generally discredited, the essay offers a powerful and influential reading of the tension between the rational and irrational informing Greek drama. Nietzsche was admired by several modern playwrights represented in this volume, including Bernard Shaw, August Strindberg, and Eugene O'Neill.*

We shall have gained much for the science of aesthetics, once we perceive not merely by logical inference, but with the immediate certainty of vision, that the continuous development of art is bound up with the *Apollinian* and *Dionysian* duality—just as procreation depends on the duality of the sexes, involving perpetual strife with only periodically intervening reconciliations. The terms Dionysian and Apollinian we borrow from the Greeks, who disclose to the discerning mind the profound mysteries of their view of art, not, to be sure, in concepts, but in the intensely clear figures of their gods. Through Apollo and Dionysus, the two art deities of the Greeks, we come to recognize that in the Greek world there existed a tremendous opposition, in origin and aims, between the Apollinian art of sculpture, and the nonimagistic, Dionysian art of music. These two different tendencies run parallel to each other, for the most part openly at variance; and they continually incite each other to new and more powerful births, which perpetuate an antagonism, only superficially reconciled by the common term "art"; till eventually, by a metaphysical miracle of the Hellenic "will," they appear coupled with each other, and through this coupling ultimately generate an equally Dionysian and Apollinian form of art—Attic tragedy.

In order to grasp these two tendencies, let us first conceive of them as the separate art worlds of *dreams* and *intoxication*. These physiological phenomena present a contrast analogous to that existing between the Apollinian and the Dionysian. It was in dreams, says Lucretius, that the glorious divine figures first appeared to the souls of men; in dreams the great shaper beheld the splendid bodies of superhuman beings; and the Hellenic poet, if questioned about the mysteries of poetic inspiration, would likewise have suggested dreams and he might have given an explanation like that of Hans Sachs in the *Meistersinger:*

> The poet's task is this, my friend,
> to read his dreams and comprehend.
> The truest human fancy seems
> to be revealed to us in dreams:
> all poems and versification
> are but true dreams' interpretation.

The beautiful illusion of the dream worlds, in the creation of which every man is truly an artist, is the prerequisite of all plastic art, and, as we shall see, of an important part of poetry also. In our dreams we delight in the immediate understanding of figures; all forms speak to us; there is nothing unimportant or superfluous. But even when this dream reality is most intense, we still have, glimmering through it, the sensation that it is *mere appearance*: at least this is my experience, and for its frequency—indeed, normality—I could adduce many proofs, including the sayings of the poets.

Philosophical men even have a presentiment that the reality in which we live and have our being is also mere appearance, and that another, quite different reality lies beneath it. Schopenhauer actually indicates as the criterion of philosophical ability the occasional ability to view men and things as mere phantoms or dream images. Thus the aesthetically sensitive man stands in the same relation to the reality of dreams as the philosopher does to the reality of existence; he is a close and willing observer, for these images afford him an interpretation of life, and by reflecting on these processes he trains himself for life.

It is not only the agreeable and friendly images that he experiences as something universally intelligible: the serious, the troubled, the sad, the gloomy, the sudden restraints, the tricks of accident, anxious expectations, in short, the whole divine comedy of life, including the inferno, also pass before him, not like mere shadows on a wall—for he lives and suffers with these scenes—and yet not without that fleeting sensation of illusion. And perhaps many will, like myself, recall how amid the dangers and terrors of dreams they have occasionally said to themselves in self-encouragement, and not without success: "It is a dream! I will dream on!" I have likewise heard of people who were able to continue one and the same dream for three and even more successive nights—facts which indicate clearly how our innermost being, our common ground, experiences dreams with profound delight and a joyous necessity.

This joyous necessity of the dream experience has been embodied by the Greeks in their Apollo: Apollo, the god of all plastic energies, is at the same time the soothsaying god. He, who (as the etymology of the name indicates) is the "shining one," the deity of light, is also ruler over the beautiful illusion of the inner world of fantasy. The higher truth, the perfection of these states in contrast to the incompletely intelligible everyday world, this deep consciousness of nature, healing and helping in sleep and dreams, is at the same time the symbolical analogue of the soothsaying faculty and of the arts generally, which make life possible and worth living. But we must also include in our image of Apollo that delicate boundary which the dream image must not overstep lest it have a pathological effect (in which case mere appearance would deceive us as if it were crude reality). We must keep in mind that measured restraint, that freedom from the wilder emotions, that calm of the sculptor god. His eye must be "sunlike," as befits his origin; even when it is angry and distempered it is still hallowed by beautiful illusion. And so, in one sense, we might apply to Apollo the words of Schopenhauer when he speaks of the man wrapped in the veil of *māyā* [illusion]: "Just as in a stormy sea that, unbounded in all directions, raises and drops mountainous waves, howling, a sailor sits in a boat and trusts in his frail bark: so in the midst of a world of torments the individual human being sits quietly, supported by and trusting in the *principium individuationis*." In fact, we might say of Apollo that in him the unshaken faith in this *principium* and the calm repose of the man wrapped up in it receive their most sublime expression; and we might call Apollo himself the glorious divine image of the *principium individuationis*, through whose gestures and eyes all the joy and wisdom of "illusion," together with its beauty, speak to us.

In the same work Schopenhauer has depicted for us the tremendous *terror* which seizes man when he is suddenly dumbfounded by the cognitive form of phenomena because the principle of sufficient reason, in some one of its manifestations, seems to suffer an exception. If we add to this terror the blissful ecstasy that wells from the innermost depths of man, indeed of nature, at this collapse of the *principium individuationis*, we steal a glimpse into the nature of the *Dionysian*, which is brought home to us most intimately by the analogy of intoxication.

Either under the influence of the narcotic draught, of which the songs of all primitive men and peoples speak, or with the potent coming of spring that penetrates all nature with joy, these Dionysian emotions awake, and as they grow in intensity everything subjective vanishes into complete self-forgetfulness. In the German Middle Ages, too, singing and dancing crowds, ever increasing in number, whirled themselves from place to place under this same Dionysian impulse. In these dancers of St. John and St. Vitus, we rediscover the Bacchic choruses of the Greeks, with their prehistory in Asia Minor, as far back as Babylon and the orgiastic Sacaea. There are some who, from obtuseness or lack of experience, turn away from such phenomena as from "folk-diseases," with contempt or pity born of the consciousness of their own "healthy-mindedness." But of course such poor wretches have no idea how corpselike and ghostly their so-called "healthy-mindedness" looks when the glowing life of the Dionysian revelers roars past them.

Under the charm of the Dionysian not only is the union between man and man reaffirmed, but nature which has become alienated, hostile, or subjugated, celebrates once more her reconciliation with her lost son, man. Freely, earth proffers her gifts, and peacefully the beasts of prey of the rocks and desert approach. The chariot of Dionysus is covered with flowers and garlands; panthers and tigers walk under its yoke. Transform Beethoven's "Hymn to Joy" into a painting; let your imagination conceive the multitudes bowing to the dust, awestruck—then you will approach the Dionysian. Now the slave is a free man; now all the rigid, hostile barriers that necessity, caprice, or "impudent convention" have fixed between man and man are broken. Now, the gospel of universal harmony, each one feels himself not only united, reconciled, and fused with his neighbor, but as one with him, as if the veil of māyā had been torn aside and were now merely fluttering in tatters before the mysterious primordial unity.

In song and in dance man expresses himself as a member of a higher community; he has forgotten how to walk and speak and is on the way toward flying into the air, dancing. His very gestures express enchantment. Just as the animals now talk, and the earth yields milk and honey, supernatural sounds emanate from him, too: he feels himself a god, he himself now walks about enchanted, in ecstasy, like the gods he saw walking in his dreams. He is no longer an artist, he has become a work of art: in these paroxysms of intoxication the artistic power of all nature reveals itself to the highest gratification of the primordial unity. The noblest clay, the most costly marble, man, is here kneaded and cut, and to the sound of the chisel stokes of the Dionysian world-artist rings out the cry of the Eleusinian mysteries: "Do you prostrate yourselves, millions? Do you sense your Maker, world?" . . .

SECTION 10   The tradition is undisputed that Greek tragedy in its earliest form had for its sole theme the sufferings of Dionysus and that for a long time the only stage hero was Dionysus himself. But it may be claimed with equal confidence that until Euripides, Dionysus never ceased to be the tragic hero; that all the celebrated figures of the Greek stage—Prometheus, Oedipus, etc.—are mere masks of this original hero, Dionysus. That behind all these masks there is a deity, that is one essential reason for the typical "ideality" of these famous figures which has caused so much astonishment. Somebody, I do not know who, has claimed that all individuals, taken as individuals, are comic and hence untragic—from which it would follow that the Greeks simply *could* not suffer individuals on the tragic stage. In fact, this is what they seem to have felt; and the Platonic distinction and evaluation of the "idea" and the "idol," the mere image, is very deeply rooted in the Hellenic character.

Using Plato's terms we should have to speak of the tragic figures of the Hellenic stage somewhat as follows: the one truly real Dionysus appears in a variety of forms, in the mask of a fighting hero, and entangled, as it were, in the net of the individual will. The god who appears talks and acts so as to resemble an erring, striving, suffering individual. That he *appears* at all with such epic precision and clarity is the work of the dream-interpreter, Apollo, who through this symbolic appearance interprets to the chorus its Dionysian state. In truth, however, the hero is the suffering Dionysus of the Mysteries, the god experiencing in himself the agonies of individuation, of whom wonderful myths tell that as a boy he was torn to pieces by the Titans and now is worshiped in this state as Zagreus. Thus it is intimated that this dismemberment, the properly Dionysian *suffering,* is like a transformation into air, water, earth, and fire, that we are therefore to regard the state of individuation as the origin and primal cause of all suffering, as something objectionable in itself. From the smile of this Dionysus sprang the Olympian gods, from his tears sprang man. In this existence as a dismembered god, Dionysus possesses the dual nature of a cruel, barbarized demon and a mild, gentle ruler. But the hope of the epopts [initiates] looked toward a rebirth of Dionysus, which we must now dimly conceive as the end of individuation. It was for this coming third Dionysus that the epopts' roaring hymns of joy resounded. And it is this hope alone that casts a gleam of joy upon the features of a world torn asunder and shattered into individuals; this is symbolized in the myth of Demeter, sunk in eternal sorrow, who *rejoices* again for the first time when told that she may *once more* give birth to Dionysus. This view of things already provides us with all the elements of a profound and pessimistic view of the world, together with the *mystery doctrine of tragedy:* the fundamental knowledge of the oneness of everything existent, the conception of individuation as the primal cause of evil, and of art as the joyous hope that the spell of individuation may be broken in augury of a restored oneness.

We have already suggested that the Homeric epos is the poem of Olympian culture, in which this culture has sung its own song of victory over the terrors of the war of the Titans. Under the predominating influence of tragic poetry, these Homeric myths are now born anew; and this metempsychosis reveals that in the meantime the Olympian culture also has been conquered by a still more profound view of the world. The defiant Titan Prometheus has announced to his Olympian tormentor that some day the greatest danger will menace his rule, unless Zeus should enter into an alliance with him in time. In Aeschylus we recognize how the terrified Zeus, fearful of his end, allies himself with the Titan. Thus the former age of the Titans is once more recovered from Tartarus and brought to the light.

The philosophy of wild and naked nature beholds with the frank, undissembling gaze of truth the myths of the Homeric world as they dance past: they turn pale, they tremble under the piercing glance of this goddess—till the powerful fist of the Dionysian artist forces them into the service of the new deity. Dionysian truth takes over the entire domain of myth as the symbolism of *its* knowledge which it makes known partly in the public cult of tragedy and partly in the secret celebrations of dramatic mysteries, but always in the old mythical garb.

What power was it that freed Prometheus from his vultures and transformed the myth into a vehicle of Dionysian wisdom? It is the Heraclean power of music: having reached its highest manifestation in tragedy, it can invest myths with a new and most profound significance. This we have already characterized as the most powerful function of music. For it is the fate of every myth to creep by degrees into the narrow limits of some alleged historical reality, and to be treated by some later generation as a unique fact with historical claims: and the Greeks were already fairly on the way toward restamping the whole of their mythical juvenile dream sagaciously and arbitrarily into a historico-pragmatical *juvenile history*. For this is the way in which religions are wont to die out: under the stern, intelligent eyes of an orthodox dogmatism, the mythical premises of a religion are systematized as a sum total of historical events; one begins apprehensively to defend the credibility of the myths, while at the same time one opposes any continuation of their natural vitality and growth; the feeling for myth perishes, and its place is taken by the claim of religion to historical foundations. This dying myth was now seized by the new-born genius of Dionysian music; and in these hands it flourished once more with colors such as it had never yet displayed, with a fragrance that awakened a longing anticipation of a metaphysical world. After this final effulgence it collapses, its leaves wither, and soon the mocking Lucians of antiquity catch at the discolored and faded flowers carried away by the four winds. Through tragedy the myth attains its most profound content, its most expressive form; it rises once more like a wounded hero, and its whole excess of strength, together with the philosophic calm of the dying, burns in its eyes with a last powerful gleam.

What did you want, sacrilegious Euripides, when you sought to compel this dying myth to serve you once more? It died under your violent hands—and then you needed a copied, masked myth that, like the ape of Heracles, merely knew how to deck itself out in the ancient pomp. And just as the myth died on you, the genius of music died on you, too. Though with greedy hands you plundered all the gardens of music, you still managed only copied, masked music. And because you had abandoned Dionysus, Apollo abandoned you: rouse all the passions from their resting places and conjure them into your circle, sharpen and whet a sophistical dialectic for the speeches of your heroes—your heroes, too, have only copied, masked passions and speak only copied, masked speeches. . . .

A prominent scholar and theoretician of feminism and theater, Sue-Ellen Case examines the complicity of traditional theatrical practices—cross-dressing in the Greek theater, for example—in the patriarchal structure of Western culture. Professor Case has written many influential studies of gender, sexuality, and theater and is the author of Feminism and Theatre *(1988).*

SUE-ELLEN CASE

FROM "CLASSIC DRAG: THE GREEK CREATION OF FEMALE PARTS" (1985)

From a feminist perspective, the initial observations about the history of theatre noted the absences of women within the tradition. Since traditional scholarship has focused on evidence related to written texts, the absence of women playwrights became central to early feminist investigations. The fact that there was no significant number of extant texts written by women for the stage until the seventeenth century produced a rather astounding sense of absence in the classical traditions of the theatre. The silence of women's voices in these traditions led feminist historians who were interested in women playwrights to concentrate on periods in which they did emerge: primarily the seventeenth century in England, the nineteenth century in America, and the twentieth century in Europe and America. These studies produced a number of new anthologies of plays by women and biographies of women playwrights that began to appear in the early seventies.

Work on the classical periods became possible by studying the image of women within plays written by men. Many scholars attribute the beginning to this type of textual discovery to the popular book by Kate Millett entitled *Sexual Politics* (1970). Millett's book illustrated a way to recognize and interpret the images of women in male literature as misogynistic. *Sexual Politics* offered a way to read against texts by becoming aware of their gendered bias and, as the title suggests, to foreground the notion that art is not distinct from politics. While Millett's book concentrated on describing the images of women, other early works such as Judith Fetterly's *The Resisting Reader* articulated a posture for resisting reading texts by men as they were conventionally read. Fetterly outlined ways to read against texts to discover the feminist subtext latent in such subversions. Works on images of women still predominate in the feminist criticism of historical texts. Numerous re-visions of Aeschylus and Shakespeare are currently being produced. The images are commonly identified as being one of two basic types: positive roles, which depict women as independent, intelligent, and even heroic and a surplus of misogynistic roles commonly identified as the Bitch, the Witch, the Vamp, or the Virgin/Goddess. These roles reflect the perspective of the playwright or of the theatrical tradition on women. Originally, feminist historians used these theatrical images of women as evidence of the kind of lives actual women might have lived in the period. For example, what the characters and situations of Medea or Phaedra might tell us about the lives of powerful women in Greece. This approach was useful because traditional socio-economic histories tend to exhibit the same absence of women as does the literature. In the seventies, groundbreaking work on women in history was done in both realms: the socio-historical evidence identified in theatrical texts, and the publication of newly-collated documents on laws, social practices, and economic restrictions on women in history. This work enabled feminist critics and historians to produce a new kind of cultural analysis, which is based on the interplay of cultural phenomena, such as plays, theatre practice, and socio-economic evidence, to discover the nature of women's lives in the classical periods.

Yet, the discovery of the complicity of art with political projects, as well as the complicity of traditional history with the patriarchy led to new discoveries which reverse the original interpretations of these documents. The feminist critic may no longer believe that the portrayal of women in classical plays by men relates to the lives of actual women. Instead, the feminist critic may assume that the images of women in these plays represent a fiction of women constructed by the patriarchy. This assumption originates in a central practice within classical cultures: the division between private and public life. The public life becomes privileged in the classical plays and histories, while the private life remains relatively invisible. The new feminist analyses prove that this division is gender-specific, i.e., the public life is the property of men and women are relegated to the invisible private sphere. The result of the suppression of actual women in the classical world created the invention of a representation of the gender "Woman" within the culture. This "Woman" appeared on the stage, in the myths, and in the plastic arts, representing the patriarchal values attached to the gender of "Woman" while suppressing the experiences, stories, feelings, and fantasies of actual women.[1] The new feminist approach to these cultural fictions divides this "Woman" as a male-produced fiction from historical women, insisting that there is little connection between the two categories. Within theatre practice, the clearest illustration of this division is in the tradition of the all-male stage. "Woman" was played by male actors in drag, while actual women were banned from the stage. The classical acting practice reveals the construction of the fictional gender created by the patriarchy. The classical plays and theatrical conventions can now be regarded as allies in the project of suppressing actual women and replacing them with the masks of patriarchal production.

The beginning of the activity and literature known as theatre is traditionally assigned to the plays and practices of the Athenian festivals of Dionysos in sixth and fifth century BC. Our notions of plays, acting, physical theatre space, costume, mask, and relation of play to audience begin with these Athenian festivals. In the sixth century, both women and men participated in these ceremonies, but by the fifth century, when the ceremonies were becoming what is known as theatre, women disappeared from the practice. Scholars do not record any evidence for specific laws or codes forbidding women to appear in the songs and dances, nor is there any evidence for the specific date or occasion of the beginning of their omission. Margarete Bieber, a recognized authority on this history, merely notes that it was part of "Attic morality" which "banished women from public life."[2] This implies, then, that the

---

[1] See Teresa de Lauretis, *Alice Doesn't: Feminism, Semiotics, Cinema* (Bloomington: Indiana University Press, 1984), for a thorough development of the concept of "Woman."

[2] Margarete Bieber, *The History of the Greek and Roman Theatre* (Princeton: Princeton University Press, 1939), p. 9.

reason for this practice must be sought in the emerging cultural codes of Athens, rather than in specific political or theatrical practices. Three elements of Athenian culture help to understand the emerging theatrical practice: the new economic practices, the new cultural project and the new genealogy of the gods. The intersection of all of these elements will be theatrically legitimatized in the text of *The Oresteia*.

Among the new economic practices, the rise of the family unit radically altered the role of women in Greek public life. Ironically, the important role women began to assume within the family unit was the cause of their removal from public life. The family unit became the new site for the creation and transmission of personal wealth. With the rise of the *polis*, the large network inherent in aristocracies gave way to single families. The rise of metals as commodities and the small-scale cultivation of land made it possible for individuals to control their own wealth. Yet while ownership became more individual and located within the family unit, it was limited to the male gender. Women were restricted to limited conditions of ownership and exchange. For example, women could only enter into inheritance transactions in the absence of a male and women were not allowed to barter for property over one medimnos (bushel). Within this new economy, women became a medium of exchange and marriage became an institution of ownership.[3] In fact, the word for marriage, *ekdosis*, meant loan—women were loaned to their husbands by their fathers, and in the case of a divorce, they were returned to their fathers.

With this change in the organization of wealth came a concomitant change in the organization of political units. The *oikos*, or household, became the basic unit for citizenship.[4] Citizenship was dependent upon family lines—a son was granted citizenship only if his parents were citizens, but without a son the parents could not retain their citizenship. This new condition for citizenship led to the strict definition and regulation of the sex life of the woman. The mother/wife assumed a new moral/legal dimension for the legitimacy and security of heirs and, by extension, political membership in the *polis*. Clear lines of reproduction were vital to the *polis*, making adultery a crime against society, rather than a sign of personal transgression. At the same time that the household became controlled by needs of the state, its activities became totally separate from those which were considered the business of the state, the mark of the citizen, or the activities of public life. Nancy Hartsock, in her book *Money, Sex, and Power*, describes it this way: the Greeks defined the household as a private, apolitical space from the public, political space of the *polis*. "The result was a theorization of politics and political power as activities that occurred in a masculine arena characterized by freedom from necessary labor, dominance of intellect or soul," while the domestic space was defined by necessary labor and as a place where bodily needs were dominant.[5] Since Athenian women were confined to the house (explicitly in the laws of Solon), they were removed from the public life of the intellect and the soul and confined to the world of domestic labor, childbearing, and concomitant sexual activities. Actual women disappeared from the public life of the *polis*, lost their economic and legal powers and became objects of exchange. Within the socio-economic life of the *polis*, it is not surprising that their participation in the Dionysian festivals was restricted to private practices, resulting in their eventual exclusion from the stage.

Alongside these new legal and economic practices came new cultural institutions. Athens created new architecture, new religions, new myths, and the practice of theatre. These cultural institutions became allied with the suppression of women by creating the new gender role of "Woman" that would privilege the masculine gender and oppress the feminine one. At base, the new cultural categories of gender were constructed as categories of difference and polarity.[6] "Woman" appeared as the opposite of man. This move can best be seen in the new myths and architectural depictions of the amazons. The image of amazons is central to the female gender conflated with the outsider

---

[3] See Gayle Rubin, "The Traffic in Women: Notes on the 'Political Economy' of Sex," in *Toward an Anthropology of Women*, ed. Rayna R. Reiter (New York: Monthly Review Press, 1975), for a discussion of women as a medium of exchange through the institution of marriage and kinship laws.

[4] Marilyn Arthur, "'Liberated' Women: The Classical Era," in *Becoming Visible: Women in European History*, eds. Renate Bridenthal and Claudia Koonz (Boston: Houghton Mifflin, 1977), pp. 67–68.

[5] Nancy Hartsock, *Money, Sex and Power: Toward a Feminist Historical Materialism* (New York: Longman, 1983), p. 187.

[6] Page duBois, *Centaurs and Amazons* (Ann Arbor: University of Michigan Press, 1982), p. 2.

and with polar differences from the Greek male citizen. The amazons, dangerous but defeated, reverse the "natural" gender roles. They are warriors who force men to do "women's" work, such as child rearing, while the women go off to war.[7] The amazons also embody other myths of gender reversal—they keep female babies and dispose of the male ones, while the custom was to dispose of female babies.[8] Moreover, the word "amazon" (no breast) ties such practices to a biological, secondary sex characteristic specific to the female. The new architecture of the Acropolis, the civic center of Athens, displays the downfall of the amazons and the rise of Athena. Central to the new political order, then, is the demise of these women who would defy correct gender associations and the rise of a woman who would enforce the new image of "Woman" in the *polis*. This demise of the old images of women and the rise of Athena are central themes in *The Oresteia*.

The genealogy of the gods provides the mytho-historical context for this creation of the new "Woman." The history of the gods explains why genders are opposite, locked in conflict, and why the male gender must defeat the former female one. The myth of the first earth-mother-goddess, Gaia, is a story of the dangers of her womb—the story of her children is one of murders and castrations. It concludes with the final conquest by Zeus, who swallows his wife Metis in order to gain her power of reproduction and then gives birth to Athena. Athena represents the end of the dangers of the womb, for she has no mother (breaking with matriarchal and female-identification), has no sexuality (she remains a virgin), defeats the amazons, allies herself with the reign of Zeus and Apollo, and thereby brings order to Athens. About this same time, Dionysos, a new god, appears in Athens and usurps the role of fertility and sexuality which the earlier female goddesses had retained. This male usurpation of female fertility will later be idealized by Plato in his famous midwife metaphor, while the assimilation of female sexuality will be usurped by boys in the social practice of male homosexuality (also later idealized by Plato). The genealogy of the gods thus divides female sexuality from power, assimilating female sexuality in the figure of Dionysos and isolating power in the image of the motherless virgin, Athena.

The rise of drama, within the Athenian state festivals dedicated to the celebration of Dionysos, places theatre securely within this new patriarchal institution of gender wars. Theatre must be gender-specific to the male and enact the suppression of actual women as well as the representation of the new "Woman." The maenads (the female celebrants of the Dionysian festivals) must dance into oblivion, while the satyrs (the male celebrants) must become the first choruses of the drama. "The singer Arion is said to have given to the singers of the dithyramb . . . the costume of the satyrs. The practice of representing someone other than oneself grew out of this ecstasy and led to the mimic art of the actors."[9] In other words, the power of representation was given only to the male celebrants. The invention of acting was gender-specific—the actor was the satyr. The gender-specific quality of the actor in the satyr play was even underscored by his wearing of the leather phallus. Yet in order to dramatize the battle of the genders, the female must somehow be represented: the male actor would need to perform the female role. Though scholars and theatre historians never mention this strange phenomenon in more than passing remarks, Bieber does note one specific problem for male actors in their representations of women: on the vases, the maenads seem to be in a state of ecstasy—to play maenads, the male actors needed the comprehension of the religious emotion felt by these women.[10] Yet a more central problem emerges: how does one depict a woman? How does the male actor signal to the audience that he is a woman? Along with the female costume of the shorter tunic and the female mask with longer hair, he might have indicated through gesture, movement, and vocal intonation that the character was female. In considering this portrayal, it is important to remember that the notion of the female derived from the male point of view, which remained alien to female experience and reflected the perspective of her gendered opposite. This vocabulary of gestures initiated the image of "Woman" as she is seen on the stage—institutionalized through patriarchal culture and represented by male-originated signs of her appropriate gender behavior. Moreover, the practice of male actors playing women probably encouraged the creation of female

---

[7] William Blake Tyrell, *Amazons: A Study in Athenian Mythmaking* (Baltimore: The Johns Hopkins University Press, 1984), p. 47.

[8] Tyrell, p. 55.

[9] Bieber, p. 1.

[10] Bieber, p. 9.

roles which lent themselves to generalization and stereotype. The depiction and development of female characters in the written texts must have accommodated the practice of their representation onstage. Though all characters were formalized and masked, the cross-gender casting for female characters distinguished them in kind from the male characters. A subtextual message was delivered about the nature of the female gender, its behavior, appearance, and formal distance from the representation of the male.

The Athenian theatre practice created a political and aesthetic arena for ritualized and codified gender behavior, linking it to civic privileges and restrictions. The elevation of this gender principle to the term "classic" canonizes it as a paradigmatic element of the history of theatre, connoting the expulsion of women from the canon and the ideal. The etymology of "classic," connoting class, indicates that this expulsion is also related to the economic and legal privileges of the "first class"—a class to which women were denied admittance. The consonance of aesthetic criteria with economic ones becomes clear in the term itself. In each of the cultures which has produced "classics" for the stage (not only the Athenian, but the Roman and the Elizabethan) women were denied access to the stage and to legal and economic enfranchisement. These same production values are embedded in the texts of these periods. Female characters are derived from the absence of actual women on the stage and from the reasons for their absence. Each culture which valorizes the reproduction of those "classic" texts actively participates in the same patriarchal subtext which created those female characters as "Woman." Though we cannot examine a production of the Greek classics, we can examine one of the "classic" texts produced for the Dionysian festivals and reproduced in the history of theatrical productions, history, and criticism within our own contemporary culture. The trilogy of *The Oresteia* exhibits all of the themes and practices discussed above. Moreover, its elevated position in the canon illustrates its lasting value. A feminist reading of *The Oresteia* illustrates the defeat of the old matriarchal genealogy, the nature of "Woman" as portrayed on the stage, the rise of Athena, and the legacy of the suppression of actual women.

THE ORESTEIA

Many feminist critics and historians have analyzed *The Oresteia* as a text central to the formalization of misogyny. Simone de Beauvoir and Kate Millett describe it as the mythical rendering of a patriarchal takeover. Nancy Hartsock argues that it associates the female gender with sexuality and nature, those forces that must be tamed in outside activities and within the inner person for the survival of the *polis*.[11] Hartsock describes *The Oresteia* within the dramatic festivals that are themselves associated with male gender activities. The drama, like the four-horse chariot race, is a contest. It formalizes *agons* (contests) and the notion of winners and losers. The festivals associate the heroic ideal of valor in battle with the peacetime ideal of rhetorical and dramatic competition.[12] The subject of the drama is the subject of war—the male warrior hero. When this *agon* is inscribed with the conflicts of gender, the dramatic dice are loaded for the same gender-specific hero to win. *The Oresteia* enacts the "battle of the sexes," using Athenian cultural and political codes to prescribe that women must lose the battle.

Early in the first play of the trilogy, *Agamemnon*, the chorus of old men explicates the dramatic situation within the perspective of male-female problems. The old men describe a promiscuous woman (Helen) as the cause of the Trojan war in which Agamemnon is presently engaged and they tell of the war fleet launched by Agamemnon's sacrifice of his virgin-daughter Iphigenia. The Trojan war and the relationship of Agamemnon and Clytemnestra are already fraught with conflicts embedded in gender roles. Then the chorus prepares the audience for the entrance of Clytemnestra by linking gender with certain attributes of character. They suggest that steady resolve and intensity of purpose are gender-specific when they refer to the male (inner) strength of Clytemnestra (line 10).[13] Within this context Clytemnestra enters, played by a man. After s/he speaks, the chorus congratulates her for thinking like a man and dismisses her announcement of the end of the war as just "like a woman to take rapture before fact" (line 483). These lines presume certain gender roles regarding the judgment of evidence and decision-making. Within the theatre practice, they also

---

[11] Hartsock, p. 192.

[12] Hartsock, p. 198.

[13] All citations of *The Oresteia* are from Aeschylus, *The Oresteia in Complete Greek Tragedies, Aeschylus*, eds. David Greene, Richmond Lattimore (Chicago: Chicago University Press, 1960).

play with a certain level of irony since a man in drag plays a woman who "thinks like a man." Clearly, the primary referent is the male. The notion of female, like the notion of the amazon, disrupts the male order. Clytemnestra is introduced as a figure of that disruption. The absence of the male king has provided her with "unnatural" political power. In his absence, she has taken a male lover. By this act, she disrupts the gender code of female sexuality, for the tradition was that women were to remain monogamous even during ten year wars. The chorus treats Clytemnestra's liaison as dangerous. Yet when Agamemnon enters with his sexual war booty, Cassandra, the implication of social disruption is not in the text. In fact, the dramatic pathos of the drama favors Agamemnon, despite his treatment of women as evidenced by his rape of Cassandra or his murder of Iphigenia.

Cassandra provides the Athenian image of the woman in the public arena (even though she is played by a man). She has certain privileges of belonging (she is the priestess of Apollo which assures her of sexual liaisons with citizens of rank such as Agamemnon), but she does not have the privilege of effective public speech because of her prior refusal to be violated by Apollo. Cassandra's entrance, as an outsider, as Agamemnon's booty, mute to Clytemnestra and expelled from effective dialogue, even portrayed by a male actor, projects the strength of the misogyny embedded in the Athenian patriarchal order. What remains in the play is only Clytemnestra's murder of Agamemnon and her complete vilification. At the end, the chorus mourns Agamemnon as one who had to fight a war for a woman and then be killed by one (lines 1453–1454).

The third play, *The Eumenides*, decides the winner of the battle of the sexes within the play, within Athens, and within the genealogy of the gods. From a feminist perspective, it is ironic that this play dramatizes the so-called beginnings of democracy. Moreover, within theatre history, *The Eumenides* is often marked as the play of the new order of civilization which created our western tradition of reason and fair play. This may be an accurate description, for it does make the deciding gender judgments of Athenian culture and condemns women to their subservient role in Western civilization. The play rests upon a new genealogy of the gods. It opens with the old order, the vile goddesses, the Eumenides. They create an ugly, frightening characterization of the earlier Cthonic female religions. The masks created for them were famous for their disgusting appearance. An extant remark about them states that "Aeschylus' Eumenides horrified women into miscarriages"[14]— an interesting anecdote for its gender and sexual connotations. The Eumenides have arrived in Athens, while pursuing Orestes to revenge his murder of his mother. They describe their role as the punishment of matricide (line 210). Orestes appeals to Apollo for help and Athena appears to solve the problem. She institutes a trial, exhibiting Athenian methods of justice, to try Orestes for his murder. The decision is to set Orestes free. This conclusion is damning evidence for the public rationalization of misogyny, for it rests upon establishing the parental line as male. The mother is not the parent, but the nurse of the child. The parent is defined as he who mounts (lines 658–661). Athena is the supreme proof of this fact because she had no mother and was begat by the male god Zeus (lines 734–738). The Eumenides are confined to a cave and their function is no longer to revenge matricide, but to preside over marriages. Thus, the trilogy which began with the end of the Trojan war and proceeded through the house of Agamemnon ends with the institution of democracy deciding the role of gender and the definition of procreation. This ending can be seen as paradigmatic of future plot structures in the Western playwriting tradition. A majority of plays will conclude various kinds of civic, historical, and psychological problems with the institution of marriage. The proper gender role for women is inscribed in this conclusion.

The feminist reader of *The Oresteia* discovers that she must read against the text, resisting not only its internal sense of pathos and conclusion, but also the historical and cultural codes which surround it, including its treatment within theatre history. The pathos the feminist reader feels may be for Iphigenia and Clytemnestra rather than for Agamemnon. She may perceive Athena as a male-identified woman in alliance with the male network of power rather than as a hero of Athens. She definitely feels excluded from the conventions of the stage, bewildered by the convention of cross-gender casting which is only practiced in terms of female characters. Mimesis is not possible for her. Perhaps the feminist reader will decide that the female roles have nothing to do with women, that these roles should be played by men, as fantasies of "Woman" as "Other" than men, disruptions of a

---

[14] Sir Arthur Pickard-Cambridge, *The Dramatic Festivals of Athens* (Oxford: Clarendon Press, 1968), p. 265.

patriarchal society which illustrates its fear and loathing of the female parts. In fact, the feminist reader might become persuaded that the Athenian roles of Medea, Clytemnestra, Cassandra or Phaedra are properly played as drag roles. The feminist reader might conclude that women need not relate to these roles or even attempt to identify with them. Moreover, the feminist historian might conclude that these roles contain no information about the experience of real women in the classical world. Nevertheless, the feminist scholars must recognize that theatre originated in this kind of cultural climate and that the Athenian experience will continue to provide a certain paradigm of theatrical practice for the rest of Western theatrical/cultural history. By linking practice, text, and cultural practice in this new way, she may enhance her understanding of how the hegemonic structure of patriarchal practice was instituted in Athens. . . .

CLASSICAL JAPAN

THE DRAMA AND THEATER OF THE ASIAN WORLD HAS A HISTORY AS COMPLEX and multifaceted as the histories of the many civilizations, peoples, and nations that have been said—by the West—to comprise the "Asian world." India, for example, has a literature—in SANSKRIT—over three thousand years old; although the "golden age" of Sanskrit theater took place in the fourth and fifth centuries, theater of various kinds—folk, classical, and modern—thrives in India today. The conventions of Indian theater have pervasively influenced the theater of southeast Asia; the Sanskrit epic poems *Mahabharata* and *Ramayana* provide the characters and settings, for example, for the beautiful shadow-puppet theater of Java in Indonesia—the WAYANG KULIT—and related forms of performance using dolls or live actors.

The masked dance drama of Korea—called KAMYONGUK—is related both to Chinese and Japanese theater, and Korea, like other Asian countries, has developed an important modern theater as well.

European knowledge of China's theater probably dates from Marco Polo's visits (1254–1324); we know of more than 550 playwrights who wrote after the Mongol invasion during China's Yüan dynasty (1279–1368), part of a theatrical tradition that is recorded as early as 1000 BC, and that developed throughout the Han (206 BC–AD 221), Hui (589–614), T'ang (618–904), and Sung (960–1279) periods. Several plays from the Yüan theater have been adapted by European playwrights; Voltaire's *The Orphan of China* (1755), an adaptation of Chi Chünhsiang's *The House of Chao*, was the first Chinese play to become widely known in Europe, and Li Hsing's *The Story of the Chalk Circle* has been adapted several times, notably by Bertolt Brecht in *The Caucasian Chalk Circle* (1944). After the Mongols were expelled during the Ming dynasty (1368–1644), the center of theatrical activity shifted from northern China toward southern cities such as Hangchow. It was only during the eighteenth and nineteenth centuries—under the Ch'ing dynasty (1644–1912)—that the most characteristic form of modern Chinese theater, the PEKING OPERA, began to take the shape that it has today, sharing the stage with both Western and Western-style plays, and with a vigorous experimental theater working in a more distinctly Chinese dramatic idiom.

Although no one theater can be said to "represent" these rich and diverse theatrical traditions, the classical theater of Japan shares many features common to other Asian theaters: it blends aristocratic and popular affiliations; it is ritualized, descending from social and religious ritual traditions; it coordinates acting, dance, music, and spectacle; many of its plots and characters are derived from familiar literary and historical narratives and legends; its performance conventions are elaborately stylized and refined; and its performers are often trained with a level of formality not found in Western theater. This is hardly surprising, in that the introduction of Buddhism into Japan during the sixth century coincided with an important period of Japanese cultural and political expansion; for the next two centuries, Japan was actively in contact with the vital cultures of India, China, and Korea. And while the period of "classical" Japanese theater—roughly the twelfth through the eighteenth centuries—coincides with an extended period of cultural isolation, the expansion of Japan's military, political, and economic power in the nineteenth and twentieth centuries has again brought Japanese culture into dialogue with Asia and the West. Indeed, while Japan's imperial ambitions—the invasion of China and much of the Pacific Rim before and during World War II—were extinguished with the atomic bombing of Hiroshima and Nagasaki, Japanese theater and drama has continued to develop both in response to Western culture, and through the experimental innovation of its own traditions.

The classical Japanese theater is a product of a distinctive period in the history of Japan, extending from 1192, when the emperor gave all civil and secular power to a *SHOGUN,* a hereditary military leader, to 1868, when the emperor regained state as well as religious authority. For better than 750 years the Japanese emperors lived in Kyoto engaged in largely ceremonial duties, while the *shoguns,* based in Edo, exercised all political and judicial authority. The Genroku period (1680–1730) saw an extraordinary flowering of Japanese art and culture supported by the shogunate: this is the period of Basho, the famous *haiku* poet; of Ihara Saikaku, the novelist; and of Chikamatsu Monzaemon, Japan's greatest playwright. Although the Noh theater was in decline by the Genroku period, the three principal modes of Japanese classical theater—NOH, DOLL THEATER, and KABUKI—are in different ways the product of the elaborately hierarchical culture of feudal Japan, and of the increasing tension between the class of warriors who ruled Japan and a class of artisans and merchants—sometimes called simply *CHONIN,* or townsmen— whose economic power was centered in Japan's cities. With the rise of the shogunate, Japanese society assumed a feudal character that represented the interests and values of its ruling class of *SAMURAI* warriors. Owing their allegiance to the *shogun,* the ranks of the *samurai* were comprised of various warrior lords, or *DAIMYO,* and their attendant warriors. As in other feudal societies, in Japan it was both a right and an obligation to display the signs and behavior of one's caste; the *samurai,* for example, were expected to obey a stringent honor code, one that required their absolute loyalty to the *shogun,* to the *samurai* caste, and to its military ethos. If a *samurai* betrayed his lord, he and his followers risked becoming outcasts, called *RONIN* or "men adrift." The most famous Kabuki drama, *Chushingura* (1748), takes the fortunes of such a *samurai* lord and his forty-seven followers as its subject, and *ronin* are common figures in the Japanese theater.

Under the Ashikaga shogunate, which began in 1338 and ended in a civil war in the late sixteenth century, not only were the values of the *samurai* dominant, but the privileges of the *samurai* relative to other castes—such as the many ranks of merchants, artisans, farmers, and peasants—were rigidly observed. The principal forms of theatrical entertainment, especially Noh (or Nō) theater, were both sponsored by and largely reserved for the elite *samurai* castes, and represented the literary and cultural values of their patrons. Under the Tokugawa shogunate (1603–1867), however, Japan entered a period of extended peace and increasing cultural isolation. In the seventeenth century, the *shoguns* began to expel all foreigners from Japan, reserving specific enclaves in port cities like Nagasaki as protected zones where foreign trade might be undertaken. More important, as cities like Osaka, Tokyo, and Kyoto became significant urban centers, the merchant classes became wealthier and more powerful. While their status was lower than that of the *samurai,* many of the merchants amassed huge fortunes that far exceeded the wealth of many *samurai.* The *samurai* still exerted political authority—in 1705 the *samurai* confiscated the fortune of a merchant to whom many of them were indebted—but the merchant classes came to dominate the cultural sphere, as they became the principal audience for poetry, fiction, and theater. Although all three forms of classical Japanese theater are preserved and performed today, they first became popular in different eras of Japan's history: the Noh as it is now known was developed largely between the fourteenth and early seventeenth centuries; the doll theater's greatest popularity was in the late seventeenth century; Kabuki, which is said to have originated when Okuni, a dancer and prostitute from the Izumo Shrine in Kyoto, began to perform satirical skits in Kyoto in 1603, developed largely between the late seventeenth and mid-eighteenth centuries.

THE NOH THEATER

Although Noh theater achieved its highly literary and ceremonial form in the fourteenth century, it is usually said to have developed from performance modes popular throughout the tenth and eleventh centuries, the *SARUGAKU-NO,* and a related form, *DENGAKU-NO.*

"Noh" means "accomplishment" or "performance," and both forms of entertainment contributed elements to the development of Noh theater and drama. *Dengaku-no* may have had more explicit ritual elements, and was initially associated with the native Japanese religion of Shinto, but both forms involved acrobatics, comic role-playing, and dance. *Sarugaku* means "monkey music," which may give some idea of the exuberance of these performances. In the twelfth century, however, *sarugaku-no* was adapted by Buddhist priests to illustrate tenets of Buddhist thought and belief, and performances were given to large audiences at major temples, acted by lower-ranking priests. In time, professional players both imitated these performances outside the temples and were hired to replace the priests in temple performances; by the mid-twelfth century, guilds of performers were attached to major temples. In return for free performances during religious ceremonies and festivals, the professional guilds were given a monopoly on performing in the region of the temple.

Although the *sarugaku-no* and *dengaku-no* seem to have been energetic and spirited forms of entertainment, it was the association with the contemplative and literary elements of Buddhism that were to have the greatest effect on the formation of Noh theater. In 1374, Kan'ami Kiyotsugu (1333–1384)—a leader of one of the four main *sarugaku-no* troupes—performed before the *shogun* Yoshimitsu Ashikaga (1358–1408). Kan'ami was one of the great innovators of his era and is thought to have contributed to giving the Noh its current form: he emphasized the rhythmic nature of the musical accompaniment, developed a greater use of mime in acting, and correlated dance and musical elements more closely with a dramatic plot. These innovations might well have been lost, however, had the *shogun* not been so impressed that he took Kan'ami and his son Zeami Motokiyo (1363–1444) under his patronage; Kan'ami's troupe became the most influential in Japan, and after his death Zeami assumed control of the company, until he was exiled from the court in 1434 by one of Yoshimitsu's sons. Together, Kan'ami and Zeami gave the Noh drama its now-traditional ethos and shape. Kan'ami's innovations were explored and formalized by Zeami, who wrote or revised more than 100 of the 241 plays that make up the Noh repertoire, and described the philosophical, esthetic, and practical goals of Noh performance in several theoretical essays. In time, the *daimyo*, emulating the *shogun*, came to sponsor their own Noh performers. Because the performers and performances were so closely bound to the status of the *samurai* caste, however, Noh never became a popular or even very public form of theater. While *samurai* occasionally sponsored "subscription" performances of Noh for the "townsmen," these highly refined, intensely literary dramas were definitively the entertainment of the elite.

The esthetics of Noh derive from the Buddhist emphasis on ZEN, or contemplation, an attitude of repose and withdrawal from worldly desire and distraction. Noh performance aims to induce a similar kind of attentive repose in its audience, to evoke what is called YUGEN (often translated as "grace," though for Western readers this may have irrelevant Christian connotations), a mood or state of mind responsive to the mysterious, graceful, and impermanent beauty of the performance. For this reason, perhaps, Noh drama is not really driven by the cause-and-effect narrative logic of Western drama. Noh plays are typically centered on scenes of revelation that climax in the main actor's principal dance. Rather than imitating life, a Noh play should evoke the "flower," as Zeami termed the fusion of esthetic, spiritual, and moral beauty arising from the performance.

A "typical" Noh play might begin with the WAKI, or secondary actor, meeting the SHITE, or principal actor, at a site of historical, legendary, or mythological importance. The *waki* enters first, and in his opening song—sometimes called the TRAVELING SONG, because he sings it while making his entrance—announces who he is (often a priest), and where he is going. The *shite* then enters, taking the role of an ordinary person. They discuss the significance of the place, perhaps where a legendary warrior was killed in battle.

The characters speak a densely literary language, for part of the Noh dramatist's skill is shown in his cunning ability to borrow allusions and quotations from Japanese literature; the actors repeat and emphasize a network of phrases and images that convey the play's central theme. The chorus—kneeling stage left—also contributes to this "literary" texture, narrating some of the action and singing or reciting some of the dialogue. The *shite* then leaves the stage, and in some Noh productions a KYŌGEN (a brief farce also descended from *sarugaku*) is performed. When the *shite* returns, however, he reveals who he really is, usually a god, hero, or demon connected with the place whose destiny is troubled; he might, for example, be the ghost of the legendary warrior. In a manner of speaking, the character continues to haunt this place because he or she is unable to let go of the world, of the "character" and its investment in the world that are the essence of his or her being. The ghost is haunted by the tortuous attitude or emotion that keeps him or her connected to the world. Unlike a Greek or Shakespearean tragedy, a Noh play does not conclude with a speech of recognition or response; instead, Noh drama concludes with an intricate dance, a beautiful interplay of dialogue, dance, narration, and music for the audience's contemplation.

Since the active repertoire of Noh drama has remained more or less the same for over 400 years, it is perhaps not surprising that other elements of Noh theater and performance have become highly systematic and conventionalized. There are five types of Noh drama—plays praising the gods, plays about warriors, plays about women, plays about madness or spirits, and plays about demons—and in classical Japan, a program of Noh performance included one play from each of these categories, performed in this order, with a *kyōgen* between each Noh play. In modern Japan, it has become more common to perform only two or three plays followed by a *kyōgen*, in part because the pace of performance is much slower today. Although women at one time performed in Noh theater, in 1629 women were banned from the Japanese stage; while women do perform in the modern Japanese theater, Noh companies are now traditionally all male. Plays are performed by the *shite*, who is masked, an unmasked *waki*, and actors who play the *shite's* companions (TSURE). A chorus of six to ten men both sings and narrates from a position to the side of the stage, and musicians—a flute and two or three drums—are positioned at the rear of the stage. The drums beat rhythmically, punctuating and accentuating the actors' delivery, while the flute plays in a kind of counterpoint to their speech. The *shite's* mask is drawn from one of five categories—old person, male, female, gods, monsters—and the clothing of the performers is similarly stylized: the actors sometimes wear elaborate headdresses, and sumptuous silk clothing, arranged and layered in particular ways for certain roles. The chorus wears the traditional dress of the *samurai*. Attendants clothed in black are present onstage throughout the performance, helping the actors with costumes and masks, and placing and removing properties when needed; they are always senior actors of the company, since they may also need to step in to finish a performance if an actor is unable to continue. The stage is bare of sets, and hand properties are few and conventional; a bundle of firewood might be represented by a few sticks bound with flowers. Similarly, many of the properties are purely symbolic: a twig carried by a grieving woman is the sign of her madness. Throughout the performance, the actors move slowly and ceremonially; indeed, many of their actions must take place at a prescribed area of the stage.

Although the Noh stage was shaped somewhat differently in Kan'ami and Zeami's era, by 1615 it had assumed the shape it retains to this day. A stage (BUTAI), roughly eighteen feet square, extends into the audience area; the stage is roofed like the early shrines from which it derives, and the audience is seated in front and on the stage-left side. A painted backdrop behind the stage always pictures the Yogo Pine at the Kasuga Shrine in Nara. The stage is always of highly-polished wood with sounding jars concealed beneath it to resonate with the emphatic stamping that is part of the actors' performance. The

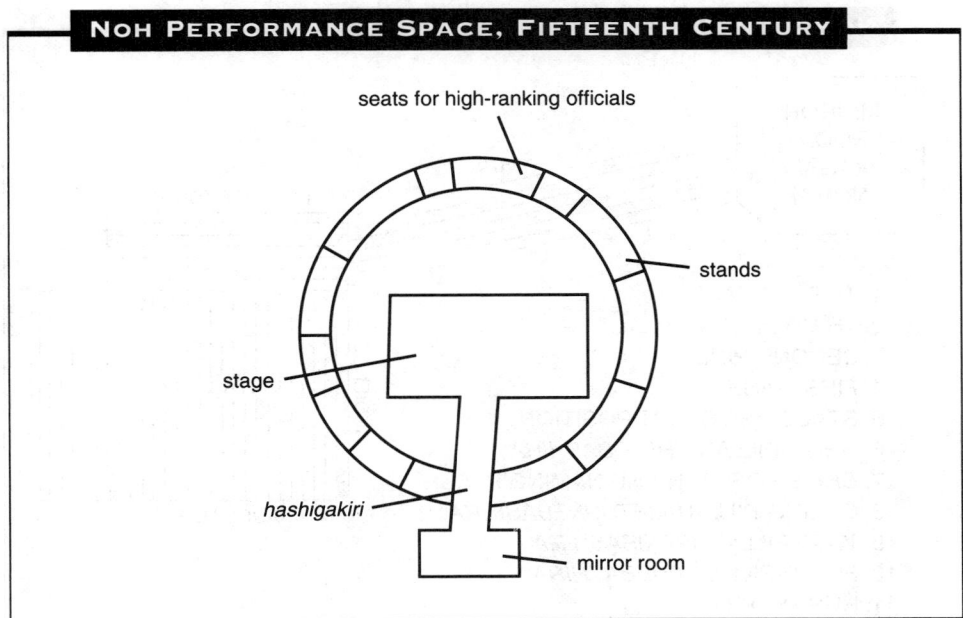

NOH PERFORMANCE SPACE, FIFTEENTH CENTURY

seats for high-ranking officials

stands

stage

hashigakiri

mirror room

This is the ground plan of the performance space in the time of Zeami.

musicians are seated directly behind the main stage area on a second, narrow stage (**ATOZA**); they are in full view of the audience and are able to see the actors and adjust their playing to the actors' performance throughout the play. A small entrance, called the "**HURRY DOOR**," leads off the stage-left side of the *atoza,* which is used by the stage assistants, the chorus, and for the exit of dead characters. A second narrow stage runs along the stage-left side of the stage, the **WAKI-ZA,** where the chorus is seated, again in view of the audience and able to adjust their narration and singing to the pace of the actors. Finally, a long bridge, the **HASHIGAKARI,** leads from the upstage right corner of the stage out to the **MIRROR ROOM,** where the costumed actors have been studying themselves in order to get into the character. The *hashigakari* is six feet wide by 33 to 52 feet long; it is bordered by a narrow strip of white pebbles, on which stand three pine trees, representing heaven, earth, and man.

The four pillars that support the roof over the stage also have specific functions in the performance, and provide a sense of the ceremonial formality of Noh theater. The upstage right pillar closest to the *hashigakari* is called the **SHITEBASHIRA,** or *shite's* pillar. When the *shite* enters the *hashigakari,* he slides his feet (which are bound in cotton cloth) slowly along the floor; reaching the *shitebashira* he pauses to announce who he is, where he is coming from, and where he is going (sometimes the *waki* will make this announcement when the *shite* reaches the *shitebashira*). The pillar down stage right is called the **MET-SUKEBASHIRA,** the gazing or eye-fixing pillar. It is the place where the *shite* looks while delivering his speech, and which he watches through the slits in his mask to help orient his performance; given the tiny eye-openings in Noh masks, the *metsukebashira* is nearly all the *shite* can see. Down stage left, diagonally across from the *shitebashira,* is the **WAKIBASHIRA,** where the *waki* is often stationed when the *shite* enters. Upstage left is the **FUEBASHIRA,** the flute-player's pillar, where the flute-player is positioned.

As Zeami suggests in "Teachings on Style and the Flower" (see Critical Contexts), the training of a Noh actor in the fourteenth century was presumed to be life-long, more

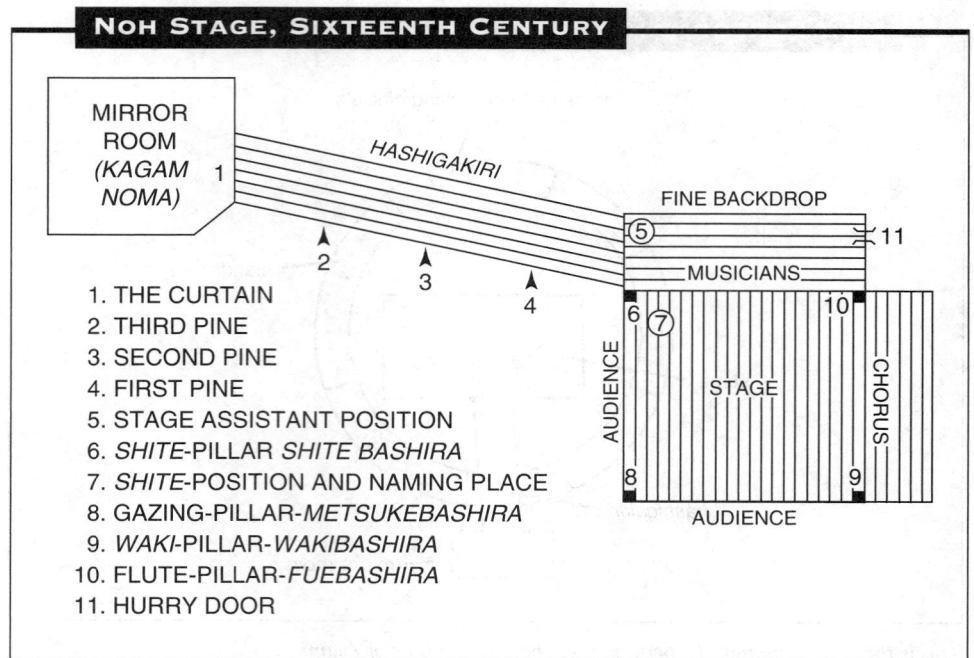

NOH STAGE, SIXTEENTH CENTURY

MIRROR ROOM (KAGAM NOMA)   1

HASHIGAKIRI

FINE BACKDROP

2   3   4

5   11

MUSICIANS

6   10
7

AUDIENCE   STAGE   CHORUS

8   9

AUDIENCE

1. THE CURTAIN
2. THIRD PINE
3. SECOND PINE
4. FIRST PINE
5. STAGE ASSISTANT POSITION
6. *SHITE*-PILLAR *SHITE BASHIRA*
7. *SHITE*-POSITION AND NAMING PLACE
8. GAZING-PILLAR-*METSUKEBASHIRA*
9. *WAKI*-PILLAR-*WAKIBASHIRA*
10. FLUTE-PILLAR-*FUEBASHIRA*
11. HURRY DOOR

This ground plan shows the stage with the mirror room, the hashigakiri, *the* shitebashira, *the* wakibashira, *the* metsukebashira, *and the* fuebashira, *as well as the locations for the musicians and the chorus.*

a vocation than an occupation. Under the shogunate, Noh performers were given the privileges of the *samurai* caste, and five schools for training Noh actors were founded. These schools were run by hereditary masters, and certain families of Noh performers have influenced the theater over several generations; indeed, we owe the preservation of many documents (including Zeami's treatises), properties, and masks to the unusually closed and traditional ways in which Noh training has been passed from generation to generation. Four of the five current Noh companies were founded in Zeami's lifetime. Although Japan is no longer a caste society, acting in a Noh company today still requires years of dedication and intense training, something between the priesthood and the military. Moreover, because the relatively small number of classical Noh plays was stabilized in the early seventeenth century, Noh actors have generally mastered all the roles of the repertoire and perform without rehearsal. Their intensive training in movement, song, and dance prepares the actors, chorus, musicians, and stage assistants to be closely responsive to the many subtleties of their collective performance. And given the stability of the repertoire, of training, and of performance conventions, Noh theater has been performed in an unbroken tradition from Zeami's era to the present day.

DOLL THEATER

Like the Noh theater, the doll theater owes something to the desire of Buddhist priests to educate a wider Japanese audience in their teachings; unlike the Noh, however, the doll theater was not supported or protected directly by the shogunate, and it came to enjoy a more popular audience. The doll theater arose from the confluence of two kinds of performance: puppet shows and storytelling to music. Much like the itinerant performers of *sarugaku-no,* wandering puppeteers became associated with shrines and temples in the twelfth century. At the same time, a form of live storytelling also became popular, the singing and recitation of legends and stories to the accompaniment of the BIWA, a four-stringed, plucked instrument. One of the most popular of these narratives was *The Tale of Jōruri*, a love story about a wealthy girl named Jōruri; although the story dates from the fifteenth century, it became popular when it was performed to a musical instrument imported from the Ryukyu Islands between 1558 and 1569, the SAMISEN. The *samisen*, a three-stringed instrument that is both plucked and struck, has a much wider tonal and dynamic range than the *biwa*. *Samisen*-accompanied dialogue and narrative became so popular that this kind of performance was termed simply *JŌRURI*. In effect, the doll theater is a form of *jōruri* in which the song and spoken narrative is accompanied by puppet performance.

Although puppets had been used in Japan for several centuries, puppets were first used in conjunction with *jōruri* performances in the sixteenth century; puppet-*jōruri* performances have been recorded in Kyoto as early as 1596, and by the late seventeenth century there were important doll theaters in both Tokyo and Osaka. As in the Noh, the plays performed in the doll theaters used narrative, dialogue, music, and acting to convey the dramatic action, and in the seventeenth century playwrights writing for the doll theaters adapted plots and characters directly from Noh models. In part, however, because of their derivation from the romantic *jōruri* narratives, in part because their audiences were well-to-do merchants and citizens rather than the aristocratic *samurai*, and in part because they were competing with the more salacious Kabuki theaters for that audience, the doll theaters came to dramatize events more closely approaching contemporary life. Although the earliest doll theater plays were on historical and legendary subjects (like the Noh plays), by the late seventeenth and early eighteenth century, doll drama concerned stagings of current events, and romanticized portrayals of contemporary life, called "domestic plays" or SEWAMONO. Although the shogunate forbade the staging of current events in 1703, the shoguns were more concerned about the satirical portrayals of *samurai* common in Kabuki; playwrights continued to write about contemporary events.

The doll theater played a major role in the development of Japanese theater generally. When Gidayu Takemoto (1651–1714), a famous performer of *jōruri*, opened the Takemoto Theater in Osaka in 1684, he began a collaboration with Chikamatsu Monzaemon (1653–1725), now generally recognized as Japan's greatest dramatist. Chikamatsu wrote an important body of plays for the doll theater, on historical subjects as well as on contemporary life. His play *Love Suicides at Sonezaki* (1703) concerns the double suicide of a young merchant and a prostitute in 1703, and was renowned for the beauty of its language and the power of its performance. The genre became so popular that in 1722 the shogunate banned plays about double suicide, which were common in both the doll theater and the Kabuki theater, perhaps fearing that Chikamatsu's play would be imitated by romantic young Japanese. Not only did Chikamatsu and other playwrights—notably Chikamatsu Hanji (1725–1783) and Uemura Bunrakuken (1737–1810), for whom the current puppet theater of Japan, BUNRAKU, is named—produce an extraordinarily rich body of plays, but these plays were immediately mined by the Kabuki theaters, providing a source of material for living actors as well as the doll theater's elaborate puppets.

The stage of the doll theater is 36 feet wide by 26 feet deep and is divided into three sections, each separated by a low screen. The three puppeteers who operate each puppet are visible throughout the performance. They are costumed in elegant traditional clothes and are seated behind the screens. The puppeteers and their dolls share the stage with several other performers: the stage assistants, dressed in black as in the Noh theater; the announcer; the narrator; and the *samisen* player. The announcer begins the performance by announcing the title of the play and introducing the narrator and the *samisen* player. The narrator is responsible for the verbal art of the play in a direct development of his role in the *jōruri*: he narrates the story of the play, speaks the dialogue of the characters and expresses their emotions as well, smiling, laughing, weeping, and so on. Later in the eighteenth century, several narrators were used, one for each of the major characters in the drama. The *samisen* is played to augment, clarify, and deepen the narrator's performance, lending it a special plangency.

As in the Noh theater, performance in the doll theater is extremely ceremonial and precise, and performers undergo years of training to achieve their craft. Although marionettes were used in the seventeenth century, hand-operated puppets became increasingly popular and by 1736 had supplanted earlier forms. The typical doll is three or four feet tall and is operated by three puppeteers. The most senior operator, dressed in a formal nineteenth-century costume, stands behind the doll and holds it up; he works a system of strings and pulleys within the head that control the doll's head, eyebrows, and eyelids, and he also operates the doll's right arm and right hand by means of hidden strings. His two assistants are clothed in black like the stage assistants, and their faces are covered; one assistant operates the left arm and hand, and the other assistant operates the legs and feet. Much as training in the Noh theater resembles that of a traditional art, so learning to operate the puppets of the doll theater entails a lifetime of commitment. Puppeteers take an apprenticeship of ten years to learn to operate the legs and feet of the dolls with sufficient grace; they then take another ten years to learn the correct operation of the left arm and hand before spending the final ten years on mastering the subtleties of the right arm, right hand, and head.

Doll theater contributed extensively to the dramatic repertoire of the Kabuki theater, and the fixed poses of the puppets are sometimes thought to contribute to the exaggerated expressive stance of the Kabuki actors, the MIE. But the doll theater contributed other innovations to Japanese theater, and to world theater generally. Much as the dolls increased in complexity throughout the late seventeenth century and early eighteenth century—gaining eye movement in 1730, finger joints and movements in 1733, and so on—so the stage itself became increasingly mechanized. By 1715 the doll theaters were using movable settings, and by 1727 elevator traps were used to raise and lower scenery visibly through the floor of the stage. This machinery not only was put to use in the more spectacular Kabuki theater, but also was adapted and imitated by theaters around the world. Although the doll theater was surpassed in popularity by the Kabuki in the nineteenth century, it continues to be sponsored by the Japanese government and performed regularly in Osaka and Tokyo.

KABUKI THEATER

Kabuki is in many ways the most energetic and spectacular mode of classical Japanese theater, using live actors to stage intense and passionate dramas whose effect is heightened by an elaborately mechanized stage. Like the doll theater, Kabuki arose as a popular form of entertainment, supported by audiences outside the aristocratic sphere of Noh performance. And while Kabuki drama, like the drama of the doll theaters, was initially derived from the plays of the Noh theater, Kabuki theater rapidly developed its own dramatic style and performance esthetics.

Unlike Noh and doll theater, Kabuki did not originate in medieval performance forms like the *sarugaku-no* and the *biwa*-accompanied narratives that became *jōruri*. Instead, Kabuki began in 1603, when Okuni—who claimed to be a priestess from the Izumo Grand Shrine—set up an impromptu stage in the Kyoto riverbed, where she performed dances and satirical skits. Okuni's company was largely composed of women, and they performed licentious dances during the day and worked as prostitutes in the evening. Kabuki rapidly became a popular kind of performance in Japan's cities, and several troupes quickly followed Okuni's lead. Although comic roles—called SARUWAKA—were always performed by men, the earliest troupes were composed mainly of women, called either ONNA KABUKI (women's Kabuki) or YUJO KABUKI (prostitutes' Kabuki). At the same time, however, other Kabuki companies composed mainly of adolescent boys, also prostitutes, became popular.

Although the Tokugawa shogunate licensed both Kabuki theaters and prostitution, the increasing popularity of Kabuki—which mingled the two activities—made it difficult to maintain strict governmental supervision. When a riot between *samurai* broke out during a Noh performance by the prostitute Yoshino in 1629, the *shogun* prohibited women from appearing onstage. Although the boys' Kabuki—*WAKASHU KABUKI*—continued to be performed, its days were numbered; it was banned by the *shogun* in 1652. Thereafter, the only Kabuki companies that were licensed to perform were the *YARO KABUKI*, or adult male Kabuki companies, which are now traditional.

The repertoire of Kabuki theater contains two kinds of plays, one based on historical or legendary incidents, and *sewamono* or "domestic plays" based on contemporary events. Okuni had once acted the role of a young *samurai* soliciting a prostitute, and plays based on the visit of a wealthy and powerful young man to the "licensed quarter" became a popular Kabuki genre, particularly in Kyoto and Osaka. Many of these plays, including *Love Letter from the Licensed Quarter* (1780), concern the fortunes of Yūgiri, a well-known courtesan of the Osaka Shinmachi quarter who died in 1678. Chikamatsu—whose *Love Suicides at Sonezaki* (1703) adapted the conventions of the Kabuki prostitute play to the doll stage—played a central role in this regard as well, for he worked as the house playwright for over twenty years to a famous Kabuki company. Although plays that dramatize love suicides and plays staging the scandals of the *samurai* caste were banned after 1722,

KABUKI STAGE, NINETEENTH CENTURY

Notice the screens to the side of the stage, the hanamichi *(which attaches to the front of the stage in the lower left-center of the picture), and a revolving platform in the center of the stage.*

The cultures, languages, and theater of the Indian subcontinent have been transformed by three massive invasions: by the Aryans sometime between 3000 and 2000 BC; by the Moslems, who brought both Persian and the Koran, in the tenth and eleventh centuries; and by the British, beginning in the seventeenth century. The Aryan language—Sanskrit literally, "the perfected tongue")—became the foundation of ancient Indian culture. Sanskrit was a spoken language until early in the first millennium, when Prakit became the vernacular. Something like Latin in medieval Europe, Sanskrit was reserved for ritual, religious, and academic uses, and for India's rich literature and theater. Sanskrit is the language of the *Rgveda*, a collection of prayers and hymns composed between 1500 and 1000 BC that is the oldest work in any Indo-European language. The two major epics of Indian culture—the *Mahabharata* and the *Ramayana*—date from around 1000 BC, but took their current form during India's "golden age," which lasted from the second century AD into the ninth century. Although it had long been thought in the West that Sanskrit theater gradually disappeared after the Moslem invasions of the tenth and eleventh centuries, Sanskrit plays were still performed in Kerala—a state in the southwest of India—by performers who were part of a hereditary caste connected to religious temples.

Hindu belief and the caste structure of ancient Indian society inform the esthetics of Sanskrit theater and drama. Ancient India was a rigidly stratified society composed of four hereditary castes, each of which was subdivided: the *Brahmins* (priests and intellectuals), *Kshatriyas* (aristocrats, warriors), *Vaisyas* (craftsmen, farmers), and *Sudras* (unskilled workers, peasants). Although these castes were devised and perpetuated along racial and economic lines, they also translated Hindu religious beliefs into the organizing structure of society. Hindu is based on a belief in Brahman, or "world-soul." Although different aspects of Brahman are often represented as distinct gods—Brahma the creator, Siva the destroyer, Vishnu the preserver, for example—these gods are really aspects of Brahman, the only whole, perfect, and unchanging being. The created universe is arrayed hierarchically, according to the degree that each being is able to contemplate or participate in this sense of wholeness or perfection.

In performance, Sanskrit drama emblematizes this dichotomy between the distracting diversity of lived experience and the contemplation of wholeness and perfection; Sanskrit theater offers its audience a richly varied performance while inducing the audience to adopt a unifying and impersonal, even contemplative mood. Most of our understanding of Sanskrit drama derives from the second-century *Natyasastra*, or *Art of the Theater*, usually attributed to the playwright Bharata, from several other treatises, and from the twenty-five plays that remain. Much as ancient Greek plays were based on myth and legend mainly drawn from the *Iliad* and the *Odyssey*, Sanskrit plays were generally based on heroic stories taken from the *Mahabharata* and the *Ramayana*, and were divided into two groups, RUPAKA (major drama) and UPA-RUPAKA (minor drama). *Rupaka* are of various lengths, and include the plays of Bharata, Bhasa's second-century plays *The Vision of Vasavadatta* and *Carudatta*, King Sudraka's *The Clay Cart* (written sometime between the fourth and eighth centuries), Kalidasa's fifth-century *Sakuntala*, and the plays of King Harsa and Bhavabhuti (seventh century). As in the Japanese Noh, the narrative of the play is less critical than the attitude it produces, the impersonal and contemplative mood of wholeness called RASA. According to the *Natyasastra*, there are eight basic *rasas* or moods that a play should strive to produce—erotic, comic, pathetic, furious, heroic, terrible, odious, marvelous—and while a given play may include several *rasas*, it should be designed so that one mood dominates. Moreover, these *rasas* are related to the BHAVA, the emotions or feelings displayed in the play by the characters. The eight *bhavas* (desire, comic or sympathetic laughter, sadness, anger, vigor or power, fear, loathing, and wonder) are the organizing, "stable"

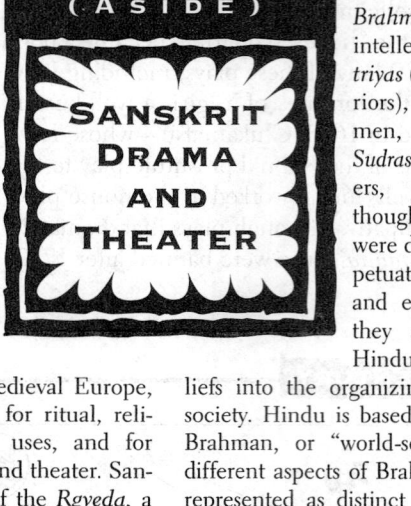

(A S I D E)

SANSKRIT DRAMA AND THEATER

---

playwrights continued to write about contemporary life under the guise of the other major genre of Kabuki theater, the history play. It quickly became apparent that by changing names and setting the drama in the past, playwrights were able to write domestic plays thinly veiled as history. For example, in 1703 the forty-seven retainers of Lord Asano took revenge on their master's disgrace at the hands of a shogunate official by killing the official

emotions staged in the play, and are complicated by thirty-three "unstable" emotions. The subtle balance and interplay of the *bhavas* should evoke a sense of harmony and perfection, the dominant *rasa* of the play.

As in Hindu philosophy, Sanskrit drama aims to produce a sense of oneness from the diversity of experience; *rasa* arises from each play's cunning interplay of the range of *bhavas*, of dialogue written in both verse and prose, of Sanskrit and Prakit, and of character types ranging from gods, kings, and heroes to servants, peasants, and children. Yet despite this diversity, Sanskrit plays have several common characteristics. Each play not only produces its main mood or *rasa*; it also illustrates the workings of *karma* or cosmic justice. For this reason, Sanskrit drama falls outside the Western understanding of tragedy, and Sanskrit playwrights are urged by the *Natyasastra* not to represent death onstage. Sanskrit is spoken by all the male Brahmin and Kshatriya characters in the play, while women, peasants, and children speak Prakit, as does the jester character who appears in most plays, often as the hero's sidekick. Although plays vary in length from one act to ten acts, each act generally takes place within a single day; the action usually takes place in several earthly and heavenly locations.

Plays were performed on a variety of occasions in ancient India—at festivals, weddings, coronations, and at other public events—and the play's *rasa* was appropriate to the occasion. The *Natyasastra* describes three kinds

CLASSICAL SANSKRIT PERFORMANCE

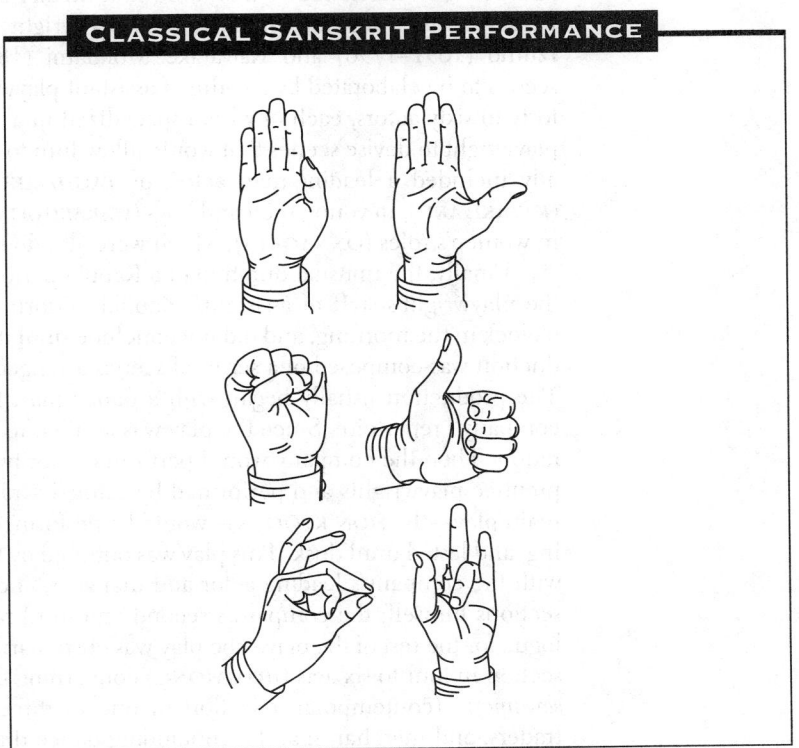

These six hand positions are used in a classical Sanskrit performance.

of theater structure—square, rectangular, and triangular—each in three different sizes. The rectangular theaters were divided into two equal areas. The audience area was supported by four pillars, representing both the four compass points and the four principal castes; the stage area was divided into two parts—a relatively shallow performing space divided from a backstage area by a wall.

Performances were accompanied by a variety of musical instruments, and were elaborately ceremonial in

character: actors used an elaborate system of movement, gesture, and speech. Since the performers were to represent codified *bhavas*, the *Natyasastra* described the gestures appropriate to them: it describes, for instance, thirty-two different eye-movements, thirty-two positions for the feet, twenty-four gestures for one hand. Both the Sanskrit drama and texts like the *Natyasastra* document the extraordinary theatrical vitality of the "golden age" of classical Indian culture.

and then committing *seppuku*, or ritual disembowelment. Within two weeks, a Kabuki play alluding to the incident was staged, and then rapidly closed by the government. When Chikamatsu turned to these events in 1706, he set the play in the fourteenth century in order to sidestep the ban, and one of the most famous Kabuki plays—*Chushingura* (1748)—concerns these events as well.

Kabuki is very much a performance genre, and its plays were organized around the abilities of its actors rather than around a literary script. For this reason, even the plays written by the most influential Kabuki playwrights—Chikamatsu Monzaemon, Takedo Izumo (1691–1756) and Kawatake Mokuami (1816–1893)—began as an outline of scenes to be elaborated by a cadre of assistant playwrights. A Kabuki company contained forty to sixty actors, each of whom specialized in a certain kind of role and expected the playwright to devise scenes that would allow him to display his talents. Companies generally included a leading-man actor, or *TACHIYAKU*, and specialists in villainous men (*KATAKIYAKU*), in young men and boys (*WAKASHUGATA*), in comic roles (*DOKEKATA*), and in women's roles (*ONNAGATA*), which were also divided according to age and type.

Finally, the unusual duration of a Kabuki performance also demanded the talents of the playwright's staff of assistants. Kabuki performances originally began around three o'clock in the morning, and did not conclude until dusk; the fourteen- to fifteen-hour production was composed of a series of scenes arranged around a common theme or mood. The production usually began with a dance play, followed by a familiar play from the company's repertoire. Since the play was familiar to the company, it required little preparation. Then the company would perform one or two short practice plays, written by apprentice playwrights and performed by actors-in-training as part of their education. The main play—the *HON KYŌGEN*—would be performed at about seven o'clock in the morning, and lasted until dusk. This play was outlined by the house playwright in collaboration with the company's leading actor and manager, and he would write the most important sections himself; the company's second and third rank playwrights would elaborate dialogue for the rest of the play. The play was customarily divided into four sections: a history section in four to six acts (*JIDAIMONO*) concerning the exploits of the *samurai*; a dance; a *sewamono* (contemporary) section in one to three acts, set in the milieu of artisans, traders, and merchants; and a concluding dance drama. Kabuki performances today are generally given in two programs, lasting from eleven to four o'clock and from four-thirty until nine-thirty in the evening. Although it is rare to see a full-length Kabuki play performed today, the four-part sequence is still followed.

Kabuki is very much an actor's theater. The actors undergo a long period of training, and as in Noh theater, certain families of actors have dominated the history of Kabuki. Indeed, Kabuki actors often wear their family crest in performance, and audiences frequently compare an actor's performance in a given role with his father's or his uncle's. Originating as a form of dance, Kabuki places a premium on choreography, which accompanies gesture and speech as a means of realizing the character's essential tone or feeling in a precise and elegant image. Yet the actors play directly to the audience, and the most striking moments in the performance—the *mie*, a posed performance of passion— are underscored *as* performance when the stage assistants clap two pieces of wood loudly and rhythmically together. The actors play conventional roles, and each role in the Kabuki repertoire has a conventional costume associated with it. The costumes are extremely cumbersome, so the actors are often helped by stage assistants clothed in black who position properties and move pieces of the set. The actors are not masked, but wear an elaborate and conventionalized makeup, usually of red and black lines and patterns ranged over a white base; *onnagata* actors generally add only eyebrow lines and rouged cheeks and lips to an otherwise white face. Given its close relationship to *jōruri* and doll theater, it is not surprising that Kabuki usually requires a narrator onstage as well, who not only sets the scene, but comments on the action throughout; he also occasionally speaks dialogue as well. Kabuki actors never sing, and so their songs are sung by the narrator and by an onstage chorus as well. Moreover, each play is accompanied by traditional music, played by musicians wearing the traditional *samurai* costume; the orchestra for Kabuki is considerably larger than that for Noh and makes use of flutes, bells, drums, cymbals, and gongs, as well as the *samisen*.

Although the first Kabuki companies played on impromptu stages, they soon were allowed to use Noh theaters; given their raffish character, however, Kabuki companies were not allowed to have roofed theaters until 1724. Like the doll theater, Kabuki theater quickly made use of scenic technology; the elevator stage was in use by 1736, and by the late eighteenth century it was common for Kabuki theaters to have a revolving stage, sometimes two independent turntables with one turning inside the other. Kabuki makes extensive use of scenery, though much of it is of a symbolic or ornamental nature. Like properties in this theater, which tend to be suggestive of the objects they represent, the scenery of a Kabuki performance is openly theatrical in character: the scenery is changed in view of the audience by visible assistants (who help the actors as well) and aims to suggest the locale of the scene rather than put it on the stage in a realistic way. It is a measure, though, of the relationship between the extroverted Kabuki performance and its audience that its most distinguishing feature involves the audience more directly in the production. In the early eighteenth century, Kabuki theaters added a *HANAMICHI,* or elevated bridge, extending from the rear of the auditorium to the stage. Actors made their exits and entrances here, and scenes could be played on the *hanamichi* as well. By the 1770s, a second *hanamichi* was added, and the area between the two *hanamichi* was divided into floor boxes, while other rows of seating ran along the sides of the auditorium. Although the second *hanamichi* is still required for some plays, it is generally no longer in use.

The restoration of the emperor in 1868 not only brought about the collapse of the shogunate, but also ended Japan's isolation. It also dramatized the economic weakness of the *samurai* relative to the merchant class. In many respects, Japan's theater was vulnerable to extinction, especially the Noh and doll theaters, which had no truly popular audience; Kabuki was the only theater which continued to attract new plays, playwrights, and audiences in the nineteenth and twentieth centuries. But the Japanese worked to preserve their classical theater and it is still possible today to see plays from the Noh, doll theater, and Kabuki repertoire in excellent, traditional productions.

This performance of Chikamatsu's Love Suicides at Sonezaki *is enacted in the style of Kabuki theater, rather than with dolls. Here the* onnagata Ohatsu—*played by a man—confronts her lover Tokubei in the brothel.*

In this scene from the Kabuki play Love Letter from the Licensed Quarter, *Izaemon returns to the brothel to spy on his lover Yūgiri.*

■ KAN'AMI KIYOTSUGU ■

Kan'ami Kiyotsugu (1333–1384) was one of the principal performers of *sarugaku-no*, and the leader of a prominent company. When he appeared before the *shogun* Yoshimitsu Ashikiga in 1374, the *shogun* was so impressed with the company that he retained them as his players. Kan'ami is generally credited with refining and systematizing the Noh for his aristocratic audience, and with writing many of the plays that became part of the standard Noh repertoire. Kan'ami's son, Zeami Motokiyo (1363–1444), succeeded his father as the leader of the company, and had a massive influence on the development of the Noh. Zeami both reworked older plays and wrote many new plays of his own; of the 241 plays in the Noh repertoire, more than 100 are connected to Zeami. Zeami influenced the development of Noh in other respects as well, mainly in writing sixteen essays on Noh esthetics. These essays cover a range of topics, including the training of actors, the proper style of dramatic writing, and the goals of performance. Although Zeami enjoyed the favor of Yoshimitsu until the *shogun's* death in 1408, he fared less well under the rule of Yoshimitsu's son, Yoshimochi (1386–1428), and was banished to the remote island of Sado in 1434 when Yoshimochi's younger brother Yoshinori (1394–1441) became *shogun*. The reasons for Yoshinori's hostility to Zeami are not clear, but may involve Yoshinori's preference for another playwright, On'ami. Zeami did succeed in passing his essays on to his son-in-law Komparu Zenchiku (1405–1468), who became an important Noh playwright and theoretician. Not much is known about the end of Zeami's life; legend has it that he was able to return to the mainland after Yoshinori was assassinated in 1441.

MATSUKAZE

Matsukaze was originally written by Kan'ami and extensively reworked by Zeami; it has remained in the Noh repertoire since the fifteenth century, and is performed by all Noh companies.

This elegant drama, like most Noh plays, takes place in a setting familiar from the classic literature of Japan, the Bay of Suma. Suma is principally associated with the famous poet, courtier, and scholar Ariwaka no Yukihira (818–893), whose exile at Suma was recounted in his own poetry and formed the basis for many stories and legends. It also inspired the narrative of Genji's exile at Suma in the Japanese epic *Tale of Genji*. The narrative of the play, though, seems to have been invented by Kan'ami. The play opens when the *waki*—playing a priest—enters the stage, singing a traveling song about his arrival at Suma. He asks the *kyōgen* (playing a villager) about the significance of the pine tree, and he is informed that it memorializes two fisher girls, Murasame and Matsukaze, who have long since died. Shortly thereafter Murasame—played by the *tsure*—enters, followed by the *shite*, Matsukaze. The two girls elaborately mime dipping brine into their cart with their fans, and in speeches that quote from Yukihira and from other poets, they describe their desolation. Their language here is rich with imagery, particularly of the changing sea, the hard lives of the fishermen, and of the moon, a Buddhist symbol of enlightenment. As is typical of the Noh, many of their lines are spoken by the Chorus.

Although the *shite* and his *tsure* do not leave the stage, they retire to the *shitebashira*, where they mime sitting in their small hut. The *waki*—who has observed them throughout the first scene, approaches the hut and asks for shelter, quoting one of Yukihira's poems in passing. The girls then reveal that they are the ghosts of Matsukaze and Murasame, still "steeped in longing" for the exiled poet, even in death. They had fallen in love with Yukihira during his exile at Suma, and he had given them their names, "Wind in the Pines" (*matsukaze*), and "Autumn Rain" (*murasame*), names redolent of the imagery of classical Japanese poetry. The girls were not able to follow Yukihira when he returned to court after his exile; all they have in his memory is his hunting cloak and court hat. Driven nearly to madness with her eternal grief, Matsukaze puts on Yukihira's cloak and hat for her final dance.

Matsukaze is an evocative example of the way Noh theater attempts to capture a particular mood through the collaborative interplay between each of its highly wrought arts. The beauty of the language, the delicacy of characterization, the succinct action, the music of the flute and drums, the chanting of the chorus, and the refinement of the acting combine to capture the subtle intensity of feeling for which Noh theater is famous.

MATSUKAZE

KAN'AMI KIYOTSUGU

TRANSLATED BY ROYALL TYLER

— CHARACTERS —

AN ITINERANT PRIEST (*waki*)   MATSUKAZE (*shite*)   PLACE: *Suma Bay in Settsu Province*
A VILLAGER (*kyōgen*)   MURASAME (*tsure*)   TIME: *Autumn, the Ninth Month*

(The stage assistant places a stand with a pine sapling set into it at the front of the stage. The PRIEST *enters and stands at the naming-place. He carries a rosary.)*

PRIEST: I am a priest who travels from province to province. Lately I have been in the Capital. I visited the famous sites and ancient ruins, not missing a one. Now I intend to make a pilgrimage to the western provinces. *(He faces forward.)* I

5   have hurried, and here I am already at the Bay of Suma in Settsu Province. *(His attention is caught by pine tree.)* How strange! That pine on the beach has a curious look. There must be a story connected with it. I'll ask someone in the neighborhood. *(He faces the bridgeway.)* Do you live in

10   Suma?

(The VILLAGER *comes down the bridgeway to the first pine. He wears a short sword.)*

VILLAGER: Perhaps I am from Suma; but first tell me what you want.

PRIEST: I am a priest and I travel through the provinces. Here on the beach I see a solitary pine tree with a wooden tablet

15   fixed to it, and a poem slip hanging from the tablet. Is there a story connected with the tree? Please tell me what you know.

VILLAGER: The pine is linked with the memory of two fisher girls, Matsukaze and Murasame. Please say a prayer for them

20   as you pass.

PRIEST: Thank you. I know nothing about them, but I will stop at the tree and say a prayer for them before I move on.

VILLAGER: If I can be of further service, don't hesitate to ask.

PRIEST: Thank you for your kindness.

25 VILLAGER: At your command, sir.

(The VILLAGER *exits. The* PRIEST *goes to stage center and turns toward the pine tree.)*

PRIEST: So, this pine tree is linked with the memory of two fisher girls, Matsukaze and Murasame. It is sad! Though their bodies are buried in the ground, their names linger on. This lonely pine tree lingers on also, ever green and un-

30   touched by autumn, their only memorial. Ah! While I have been chanting sutras and invoking Amida Buddha for their repose, the sun, as always on autumn days, has quickly set. That village at the foot of the mountain is a long way. Perhaps I can spend the night in this fisherman's salt shed.

(He kneels at the waki-*position. The stage assistant brings out the prop, a cart for carrying pails of brine, and sets it by the gazing-pillar. He places a pail on the cart.)*

MURASAME *enters and comes down the bridgeway as far as the first pine. She wears the* tsure *mask.* MATSUKAZE *follows her and stops at the third pine. She wears the* wakaonna *mask. Each carries a water pail. They face each other.)*

MATSUKAZE AND MURASAME: A brine cart wheeled along the 35
beach
Provides a meager livelihood:
The sad world rolls
Life by quickly and in misery!

MURASAME: Here at Suma Bay
The waves shatter at our feet, 40
And even the moonlight wets our sleeves
With its tears of loneliness.

*(*MURASAME *goes to stage center while* MATSUKAZE *moves to the* shite-*position.)*

MATSUKAZE: The autumn winds are sad.
When the Middle Counselor Yukihira
Lived here back a little from the sea, 45
They inspired his poem,
"Salt winds blowing from the mountain pass. . . ."
On the beach, night after night,
Waves thunder at our door;
And on our long walks to the village 50
We've no companion but the moon.
Our toil, like all of life, is dreary,
But none could be more bleak than ours.
A skiff cannot cross the sea,
Nor we this dream world. 55
Do we exist, even?
Like foam on the salt sea,
We draw a cart, friendless and alone,
Poor fisher girls whose sleeves are wet
With endless spray, and tears 60
From our hearts' unanswered longing.

CHORUS: Our life is so hard to bear
That we envy the pure moon

---

47 From the poem by Yukihira, no. 876 in the *Shinkokinshū:* "The sleeves of the traveler have turned cold; the wind from Suma Bay blows through the pass." 51 A modified quotation from the poem by Hōkyō Chūmei, no. 187 in the *Kin'yōshū:* "Pillow of grass—as I sleep on my journey I realize I have no companion but the moon." 57–58 The words "salt sea," which can also be translated "brine," lead to mention of the brine cart even though the cart does not logically belong in the context. 63 From the poem by Fujiwara Takamitsu, no. 435 in the *Shūishū:* "In this world which seems difficult to pass through, how I envy the pure moon!"

132

Now rising with the tide.
65 But come, let us dip brine,
Dip brine from the rising tide!
Our reflections seem to shame us!

(*They look down as if catching a glimpse of their reflections in the water. The movement of their heads "clouds" the expression on their masks, making it seem sad.*)

Yes, they shame us!
Here, where we shrink from men's eyes,
70 Drawing our timorous cart;
The withdrawing tide
Leaves stranded pools behind.
How long do they remain?
If we were the dew on grassy fields,
75 We would vanish with the sun.
But we are sea tangle,
Washed up on the shore,
Raked into heaps by the fishermen,
Fated to be discarded, useless,
80 Withered and rotting,
Like our trailing sleeves,
Like our trailing sleeves.

(*They look down again.*)

Endlessly familiar, still how lovely
The twilight at Suma!
85 The fishermen call out in muffled voices;
At sea, the small boats loom dimly.
Across the faintly glowing face of the moon
Flights of wild geese streak,
And plovers flock below along the shore.
90 Fall gales and stiff sea winds:
These are things, in such a place,
That truly belong to autumn.
But oh, the terrible, lonely nights!

(*They hide their faces.*)

MATSUKAZE: Come, dip the brine
95 MURASAME: Where the seas flood and fall.
Let us tie our sleeves back to our shoulders
MATSUKAZE: Think only, "Dip the brine."
MURUSAME: We ready ourselves for the task,
MATSUKAZE: But for women, this cart is too hard.
100 CHORUS: While the rough breakers surge and fall,

(MURASAME *moves upstage to stand beside* MATSUKAZE.)

While the rough breakers surge and fall,
And cranes among the reeds
Fly up with sharp cries.
The four winds add their wailing.
105 How shall we pass the cold night?

(*They look up.*)

The late moon is so brilliant—
What we dip is its reflection!
Smoke from the salt fires
May cloud the moon—take care!

Are we always to spend only 110
The sad autumns of fishermen?
At Ojima in Matsushima

(MATSUKAZE *half-kneels by the brine cart and mimes dipping with her fan.*)

The fisherfolk, like us,
Delight less in the moon
Than in the dipping of its reflection; 115
There they take delight in dipping
Reflections of the moon.

(MATSUKAZE *returns to the* shite-*position.*)

We haul our brine from afar,
As in far-famed Michinoku
And at the salt kilns of Chika— 120
Chika, whose name means "close by."
MATSUKAZE: Humble folk hauled wood for salt fires
At the ebb tide on Akogi Shore;
CHORUS: On Ise Bay there's Twice-See Beach—
Oh, could I live my life again! 125

(MATSUKAZE *looks off into the distance.*)

MATSUKAZE: On days when pine groves stand hazy,
And the sea lanes draw back
From the coast at Narumi—
CHORUS: You speak of Narumi; this is Naruo,
Where pines cut off the moonlight 130
From the reed-thatched roofs of Ashinoya.
MATSUKAZE: Who is to tell of our unhappiness
Dipping brine at Nada?
With boxwood combs set in our hair,
From rushing seas we draw the brine, 135
Oh look! I have the moon in my pail!

(MURASAME *kneels before the brine cart and places her pail on it.* MATSUKAZE, *still standing, looks into her pail.*)

MATSUKAZE: In my pail too I hold the moon!
CHORUS: How lovely! A moon here too!

---

84 The following description is generally inspired by the "Exile at Suma" chapter of *The Tale of Genji*.

112 Ojima is one of the islands at Matsushima, a place renowned for its scenic beauty. Both names are conventionally associated in poetry with *ama*, fisherwomen. 119 The following passage is a *tsukushi*, or "exhaustive enumeration," of place-names associated with the sea, including allusions and plays on words. This passage was apparently borrowed from an older work, a play called *Tōei* that was set by Ashinoya Bay. Michinoku is a general name for the northern end of the island of Honshu. Chika was another name for Shiogama ("Salt Kiln"), and sounds like the word meaning "near." 123 Akogi is the name of a stretch of shore on Ise Bay. The pulling in of the nets and the hauling of the wood for the salt kilns at Akogi were frequently mentioned in poetry. 124 Futami-ga-ura (Twice-See Beach) is a word evocative of Ise and often used in poetry for the meaning of its name. 128 Narumi was often mentioned in poetry because of its dry flats that appeared at low tide. 131 Ashinoya (modern Ashiya) and Naruo are two places near Suma. Ashinoya means literally "reed house." 133 Derived from the poem in the 87th episode of the *Ise Monogatari*: "At Nada by Ashinoya, I have no respite from boiling brine for salt; I have come without even putting a boxwood comb in my hair." 134 The line recalls the poem quoted in previous note, but it is used because of the pivot-word *tsuge no*, "of boxwood," and *tsuge*, "to inform." Similarly, *kushi sashi*, "Setting a comb (in the hair)," leads into *sashi-kuru nami*, "in-rushing waves."

(MURASAME *picks up the rope tied to the cart and gives it to* MATSUKAZE, *then moves to the* shite-*position.* MATSUKAZE *looks up.*)

MATSUKAZE: The moon above is one;
140   Below it has two, no, three reflections

(*She looks into both pails.*)

Which shine in the flood tide tonight,

(*She pulls the cart to a spot before the musicians.*)

And on our cart we load the moon!
No, life is not all misery
Here by the sea lanes.

(*She drops the rope. The stage assistant removes the cart.* MAT-SUKAZE *sits on a low stool and* MURASAME *kneels beside her, a sign that the two women are resting inside their hut. The* PRIEST *rises.*)

145   PRIEST: The owner of the salt shed has returned. I shall ask for a night's lodging. (*To* MATSUKAZE *and* MURASAME.) I beg your pardon. Might I come inside?
MURASAME: (*Standing and coming forward a little.*) Who might you be?
150   PRIEST: A traveler, overtaken by night on my journey. I should like to ask lodging for the night.
MURASAME: Wait here. I must ask the owner. (*She kneels before* MATSUKAZE.) A traveler outside asks to come in and spend the night.
155   MATSUKAZE: That is little enough, but our hut is so wretched we cannot ask him in. Please tell him so.
MURASAME: (*Standing, to the* PRIEST.) I have spoken to the owner. She says the house is too wretched to put anyone up.
PRIEST: I understand those feelings
160   perfectly, but poverty makes
no difference at all to me.
I am only a priest. Please
say I beg her to let
me spend the night.
165   MURASAME: No, we really cannot put you up.
MATSUKAZE: (*To* MURASAME.) Wait!
I see in the moonlight
One who has renounced the world.
He will not mind a fisherman's hut,
170   With its rough pine pillars and bamboo fence;
I believe it is very cold tonight,
So let him come in and warm himself
At our sad fire of rushes.
You may tell him that.
175   MURASAME: Please come in.
PRIEST: Thank you very much. Forgive me for intruding.

(*He takes a few steps forward and kneels.* MURASAME *goes back beside* MATSUKAZE.)

MATSUKAZE: I wished from the beginning to invite you in, but this place is so poor I felt I must refuse.
PRIEST: You are very kind. I am a priest and a traveler, and
180   never stay anywhere very long. Why prefer one lodging to another? In any case, what sensitive person would not prefer to live here at Suma, in the quiet solitude. Yukihira wrote, "If ever anyone
Chances to ask for me,

Say I live alone,   185
Soaked by the dripping seaweed
On the shore of Suma Bay."
(*He looks at the pine tree.*) A while ago I asked someone the meaning of that solitary pine on the beach. I was told it grows there in memory of two fisher girls, Matsukaze and   190
Murasame. There is no connection between them and me, but I went to the pine anyway and said a prayer for them. (MATSUKAZE *and* MURASAME *weep. The* PRIEST *stares at them.*) This is strange! They seem distressed at the mention of Matsukaze and Murasame. Why?   195
MATSUKAZE AND MURASAME: Truly, when a grief is hidden,
Still, signs of it will show.
His poem, "If ever anyone
Chances to ask for me,"
Filled us with memories which are far too fond.   200
Tears of attachment to the world
Wet our sleeves once again.
PRIEST: Tears of attachment to the world? You speak as though you are no longer of the world. Yukihira's poem overcame you with memories. More and more bewildering! Please,   205
both of you, tell me who you are.
MATSUKAZE AND MURASAME: We would tell you our names,
But we are too ashamed!
No one, ever,
Has chanced to ask for us,   210
Long dead as we are,
And so steeped in longing
For the world by Suma Bay
That pain has taught us nothing.
Ah, the sting of regret!   215
But having said this,
Why should we hide our names any longer?
At twilight you said a prayer
By a mossy grave under the pine
For two fisher girls,   220
Matsukaze and Murasame.
We are their ghosts, come to you.
When Yukihira was here he whiled away
Three years of weary exile
Aboard his pleasure boat,   225
His heart refreshed
By the moon of Suma Bay.
There were, among the fisher girls
Who hauled brine each evening,
Two sisters whom he chose for his favors.   230
"Names to fit the season!"
He said, calling us
Pine Wind and Autumn Rain.
We had been Suma fisher girls,
Accustomed to the moon,   235
But he changed our salt makers' clothing
To damask robes,
Burnt with the scent of faint perfumes.
MATSUKAZE: Then, three years later, Yukihira
Returned to the Capital.   240

---

187 Poem no. 962 in the *Kokinshū*.   238 Derived from a poem by Fu-jiwara Tameuji, no. 361 in the *Shingo-senshū*: "The fishermen of Suma are accustomed to the moon, spending the autumn in clothes wet with waves blown by the salt wind."

MURASAME: Soon, we heard he had died, oh so young!
MATSUKAZE: How we both loved him!
　　Now the message we pined for
　　Would never, never come.
245 CHORUS: Pine Wind and Autumn Rain
　　Both drenched their sleeves with the tears
　　Of hopeless love beyond their station,
　　Fisher girls of Suma.
250　　Our sin is deep, o priest.
　　Pray for us, we beg of you!

(They press their palms together in supplication.)

　　Our love grew rank as wild grasses;
　　Tears and love ran wild.
　　It was madness that touched us.
　　Despite spring purification,
255　　Performed in our old robes,
　　Despite prayers inscribed on paper streamers,
　　The gods refused us their help.
　　We were left to melt away
　　Like foam on the waves,
260　　And, in misery, we died.

(MATSUKAZE looks down, shading her mask.)

　　Alas! How the past evokes our longing!
　　Yukihira, the Middle Counselor,

(The stage assistant puts a man's cloak and court hat in MAT-SUKAZE's left hand.)

　　Lived three years here by Suma Bay.
　　Before he returned to the Capital,
265　　He left us these keepsakes of his stay:
　　A court hat and a hunting cloak.
　　Each time we see them,

(She looks at the cloak.)

　　Our love grows again,
　　And gathers like dew
270　　On the tip of a leaf
　　So that there's no forgetting,
　　Not for an instant.
　　Oh endless misery!

(She places the cloak in her lap.)

　　"This keepsake
275　　Is my enemy now;
　　For without it

(She lifts the cloak.)

　　I might forget."

(She stares at the cloak.)

　　The poem says that
　　And it's true:
280　　My anguish only deepens.

(She weeps.)

MATSUKAZE: "Each night before I go to sleep,
　　I take off the hunting cloak
CHORUS: And hang it up . . ."

(The keepsakes in her hand, she stands and, as in a trance, takes a few steps toward the gazing-pillar.)

　　I hung all my hopes
　　On living in the same world with him,　　285
　　But being here makes no sense at all
　　And these keepsakes are nothing.

(She starts to drop the cloak, only to cradle it in her arms and press it to her.)

　　I drop it, but I cannot let it lie;
　　So I take it up again
　　To see his face before me yet once more.　　290

(She turns to her right and goes toward the naming-place, then stares down the bridgeway as though something were coming after her.)

　　"Awake or asleep,
　　From my pillow, from the foot of my bed,
　　Love rushes in upon me."
　　Helplessly I sink down,
　　Weeping in agony.　　295

(She sits at the shite-position, weeping. The stage assistant helps her take off her outer robe and replace it with the cloak. He also helps tie on the court hat.)

MATSUKAZE: The River of Three Fords
　　Has gloomy shallows
　　Of never-ending tears;
　　I found, even there,
　　An abyss of wildest love.　　300
　　Oh joy! Look! Over there!
　　Yukihira has returned!

(She rises, staring at the pine tree.)

　　He calls me by my name, Pine Wind!
　　I am coming!

(She goes to the tree. MURASAME hurriedly rises and follows. She catches MATSUKAZE's sleeve.)

MURASAME: For shame! For such thoughts as these　　305
　　You are lost in the sin of passion.
　　All the delusions that held you in life—
　　None forgotten!

(Both step back from the tree.)

　　That is a pine tree.
　　And Yukihira is not here.　　310
MATSUKAZE: You are talking nonsense!

(She looks at the pine tree.)

---

256 Literally, "purification on the day of the serpent." The ceremony was performed on the first day of the serpent in the third month. Genji had the ceremony performed while he was at Suma. The streamers were conventional Shinto offerings.　277 A slightly modified quotation of the anonymous poem, no. 746 in the *Kokinshū*. It is also quoted in *Lady Han.*

283 The first part of a poem by Ki no Tomomori, no. 593 in the *Kokinshū.* The last two lines run: "When I wear it there is no instant when I do not long for him."　293 The first part of an anonymous poem, no. 1023 in the *Kokinshū.* The last part runs: "Helpless, I stay in the middle of the bed."　296 The river of the afterworld.

This pine *is* Yukihira!
"Though we may part for a time,
If I hear you are pining for me,
315   I'll hurry back."
Have you forgotten those words he wrote?
MURASAME: Yes, I had forgotten!
  He said, "Though we may part for a time,
  If you pine, I will return to you."
320 MATSUKAZE: I have not forgotten.
  And I wait for the pine wind
  To whisper word of his coming.
MURASAME: If that word should ever come,
  My sleeves for a while
325   Would be wet with autumn rain.
MATSUKAZE: So we await him. He will come,
  Constant ever, green as a pine.
MURASAME: Yes, we can trust
MATSUKAZE: his poem:
330 CHORUS: "I have gone away

(MURASAME, *weeping, kneels before the flute player.* MAT-
SUKAZE *goes to the first pine on the bridgeway, then returns to
the stage and dances.*)

MATSUKAZE: Into the mountains of Inaba,
  Covered with pines,
  But if I hear you pine,
  I shall come back at once."
335   Those are the mountain pines
  Of distant Inaba,

---

315 A paraphrase of the poem by Yukihira, no. 365 in the *Kokinshū*. Another paraphrase is given in the following speech by Murasame, and the poem is given in its correct form below. In Japanese *matsu* means both "pine tree" and "to wait."   334 The poem by Yukihira mentioned in the previous note.

(*She looks up the bridgeway.*)

  And these are the pines
  On the curving Suma shore.
  Here our dear prince once lived.
  If Yukihira comes again,
  I shall go stand under the tree   340

(*She approaches the tree.*)

  Bent by the sea-wind,
  And, tenderly, tell him

(*She stands next to the tree.*)

  I love him still!

(*She steps back a little and weeps. Then she circles the tree, her dancing suggesting madness.*)

CHORUS: Madly the gale howls through the pines,   345
  And breakers crash in Suma Bay;
  Through the frenzied night
  We have come to you
  In a dream of deluded passion.
  Pray for us! Pray for our rest!   350

(*At stage center,* MATSUKAZE *presses her palms together in supplication.*)

  Now we take our leave. The retreating waves
  Hiss far away, and a wind sweeps down
  From the mountain to Suma Bay.
  The cocks are crowing on the barrier road.
  Your dream is over. Day has come.   355
  Last night you heard the autumn rain;
  This morning all that is left
  Is the wind in the pines,
  The wind in the pines.

■ CHIKAMATSU MONZAEMON ■

Chikamatsu Monzaemon (1653–1725) is probably the first professional playwright in Japanese history; he is certainly the most famous. Chikamatsu, born Sugimori Nobumori, was the second son of the Sugimori *samurai* family. Though born in provincial Echizen, Chikamatsu and his family moved to Kyoto when he was in his teens, where he served as a page in an aristocratic household. He seems to have taken the stage name Chikamatsu sometime around the age of thirty, perhaps in association with the Chikamatsu Temple in Omi. In any event, by 1683 he had written his first successful play, *The Soga Successors*, which opened Gidayu Takemoto's (1651–1714) new doll theater in Osaka in 1684. Chikamatsu had a long and profitable association with Gidayu, and his second play, *Kagekiyo Victorious*, helped to establish the new *jōruri* theater.

Chikamatsu also collaborated with Tojuro Sakata (1647–1709), the most famous Kabuki actor of his era. From 1684 through 1695, Chikamatsu wrote a number of Kabuki plays while continuing to write plays for the doll theater. He wrote mainly for the Kabuki theater between 1695 and 1705, when he then returned his attention primarily to puppet plays. The enormous success of *The Love Suicides at Sonezaki* (1703) may have been partly responsible for Chikamatsu's renewed interest in puppet theater; perhaps he was also influenced by the impending retirement of Tojuro. Chikamatsu moved from Kyoto to Osaka—where Gidayu's theater, and doll theater in general, were thriving—in 1706. Working in the doll theater, Chikamatsu not only explored the possibilities of *sewamono*, the "domestic play," but also developed his talents in *jidaimono*, the "history play," writing one of the most famous, *The Battles of Coxinga*, in 1715. Like many of the history plays, *The Battles of Coxinga* requires the elaborate special effects of the doll theater: huge battles, dream sequences, ghostly figures who suddenly disappear, and a rainbow bridge spanning a large gorge that suddenly vanishes. In the generations following Chikamatsu's death, playwrights would increasingly exploit the spectacular potential of the doll theater, and the *jōruri* narrators would develop a more hyperbolic performance style. But although Chikamatsu's plays eventually fell out of favor (the music that originally accompanied them has been lost), generations of playwrights in both the doll theater and the Kabuki theater paid him the homage of adapting his classic plays to the changing tastes of their audiences.

THE LOVE SUICIDES AT SONEZAKI

The Love Suicides at Sonezaki is the earliest of Chikamatsu's efforts in the *sewamono*, or "domestic play" genre; like other plays in this genre, it concerns the lives of contemporary "townsmen." The suicides it dramatizes took place on May 22, 1703, and it is a measure both of Chikamatsu's skill and of his audience's appetite for the staging of such current events that the play was produced less than one month later, on June 20. *The Love Suicides at Sonezaki* spurred a vogue for the "love suicide" play, and Chikamatsu and other playwrights wrote many plays in this genre. They became so popular that they were banned by the shogunate in 1722. Chikamatsu revised the play in 1715, but the text printed here is a translation of his original 1703 version.

Not long before he died, Chikamatsu remarked, "I was born into a hereditary family of *samurai* but left the martial profession. I served in personal attendance on the nobility but never obtained the least court rank. I drifted in the market place but learned nothing of trade." Although Chikamatsu may have regretted his failings in other professions, growing up in a relatively impoverished *samurai* household and having to turn his hand to trade seems to have given Chikamatsu a keen appreciation of the pressured lives of Japan's merchant classes, the *chonin* or "townsmen" who flocked to see his plays in the doll theaters and on the Kabuki stages. *The Love Suicides at Sonezaki* dramatizes the straitened lives of the merchants, bound like the *samurai* to a code of family honor while at the same time striving, sometimes unscrupulously, to succeed in the competitive world of trade.

The play begins with the return of Tokubei, the nephew of a prominent soy sauce merchant, to Osaka, where he hopes to be reunited with his lover, the courtesan Ohatsu. As in other courtesan plays, Tokubei's return coincides with the arrival of a new customer for Ohatsu; Tokubei had mysteriously disappeared, apparently deserting her. But although Ohatsu is distraught, Tokubei begins to calm her by telling her why he has been gone. Tokubei's uncle, the soy sauce merchant, had been so impressed by his nephew's diligence and honesty that he made Tokubei an offer: he would marry Tokubei to his wife's niece, provide a large dowry of two *kamme* (about two thousand dollars, a lot of money in eighteenth-century Japan), and set him up in business. But although Tokubei was cool to the deal, the uncle gave the dowry to Tokubei's stepmother as an incentive. When Tokubei finally refused to be married, his uncle fired him from his job, demanded the dowry back, and promised to chase him from Osaka. Tokubei's stepmother, however, refused to return the money, so he fled Osaka for Kyoto, where he hoped to borrow the money from one of his business connections. Although this strategy failed, Tokubei was finally able to shame his stepmother into returning him the money. Yet just as he was going to return the dowry to his uncle, Tokubei made a fateful mistake: he loaned the money to Kuheiji the oil merchant, who promised to return the money in time for Tokubei to make the repayment. But just as Tokubei is telling Ohatsu about the loan, Kuheiji arrives and manages to cheat Tokubei out of his money by persuading the other merchants that Tokubei is trying to cheat him out of the two *kamme*.

Tokubei is beaten, but worse awaits him. When he returns in secret and is hidden by Ohatsu in the Temma House, he hears Kuheiji describe how he has destroyed Tokubei's honor and reputation as a merchant, and will force him to leave Osaka forever. For Tokubei, a life without honor and a life without Ohatsu are insupportable, and he decides to commit suicide. In an elaborate scene, Ohatsu signals to Tokubei her willingness to accompany him in death, and in the play's beautiful finale, Ohatsu and Tokubei journey to the Sonezaki shrine and commit suicide.

This outline of the plot of *The Love Suicides at Sonezaki*, however, hardly does justice to Chikamatsu's art as a *jōruri* playwright. Not only is the play's language exquisite, but the play provides terrific opportunities for both narrators and puppeteers to demonstrate their mastery of puppet performance. From the outset, the narrator is required both to describe and to express the intense passion that draws the lovers together, and as is common in *jōruri* theater, he is given many scenes of weeping. He also describes the characters' movements in detail, and gives us some sense of the puppeteers' extraordinary skill. In the second scene of the play, for example, Ohatsu conceals Tokubei beneath the porch while she negotiates with Kuheiji, and the narrator describes the actions of the puppets: "She taps with her foot, and Tokubei, weeping, takes it in his hands and reverently touches it to his forehead. He embraces her knees and sheds tears of love. She too can hardly conceal her emotions. Though no word is spoken, answering each other heart to heart, they silently weep." Although the doll theater hardly aims to achieve verisimilitude in the modern sense—the puppeteers, their assistants, the narrator, and the musicians are all fully in view—scenes like this one suggest the special power of the doll theater: the way it concentrates its dramatic power through the refined artifice of the performance.

THE LOVE SUICIDES AT SONEZAKI

CHIKAMATSU MONZAEMON

TRANSLATED BY DONALD KEENE

— CHARACTERS —

TOKUBEI, *aged 25, employee of a dealer in soy sauce*
KUHEIJI, *an oil merchant*
HOST *of Temma House*
CHŌZŌ, *an apprentice*
CUSTOMER *of Ohatsu*

TOWNSMEN
OHATSU, *aged 19, a courtesan*
HOSTESS
COURTESANS
SERVANTS

SCENE 1

The grounds of the Ikudama Shrine in Osaka.

TIME

May 21, 1703.

NARRATOR: This graceful young man has served many springs
 With the firm of Hirano in Uchihon Street;
 He hides the passion that burns in his breast
 Lest word escape and the scandal spread.
5 He drinks peach wine, a cup at a time,
 And combs with care his elegant locks.
 "Toku" he is called, and famed for his taste,
 But now, his talents buried underground,
 He works as a clerk, his sleeves stained with oil,
10 A slave to his sweet remembrances of love.
 Today he makes the rounds of his clients
 With a lad who carries a cask of soy:
 They have reached the shrine of Ikudama.
 A woman's voice calls from a bench inside a refreshment
15 stand.

OHATSU: Tokubei—that's you, isn't it?

NARRATOR: She claps her hands, and Tokubei nods in recognition.

TOKUBEI: Chōzō, I'll be following later. Make the rounds of
20 the temples in Tera Street and the uptown mansions, and
 then return to the shop. Tell them that I'll be back soon.
 Don't forget to call on the dyer's in Azuchi Street and collect
 the money he owes us. And stay away from Dōtombori.

NARRATOR: He watches as long as the boy remains in sight,
25 then lifts the bamboo blinds.

TOKUBEI: Ohatsu—what's the matter?

NARRATOR: He starts to remove his bamboo hat.

OHATSU: Please keep your hat on just now. I have a customer
 from the country today who's making a pilgrimage to all
30 thirty-three temples of Kwannon. He's been boasting that he
 intends to spend the whole day drinking. At the moment he's

gone off to hear the impersonators' show, but if he returns
and finds us together, there might be trouble. All the chair-
bearers know you. It's best you keep your face covered.

 But to come back to us. Lately you haven't written me a 35
word. I've been terribly worried but, not knowing what the
situation might be in your shop, I couldn't very well write
you. I must have called a hundred times at the Tamba
House, but they hadn't any news of you either. Somebody—
yes, it was Taichi, the blind musician—asked his friends, and 40
they said you'd gone back to the country. I couldn't believe it
was true. You've really been too cruel. Didn't you even want
to ask about me? Perhaps you hoped things would end that
way, but I've been sick with worry. If you think I'm lying, feel
this swelling! 45

NARRATOR: She takes his hand and presses it to her breast,
weeping reproachful and entreating tears, exactly as if they
were husband and wife. Man though he is, he also weeps.

TOKUBEI: You're right, entirely right, but what good would it
have done to tell you and make you suffer? I've been going 50
through such misery that I couldn't be more distracted if
Bon, New Year, the Ten Nights, and every other feast in the
calendar came all at once. My mind's been in a turmoil, and
my finances in chaos. To tell the truth, I went up to Kyoto to
raise some money, among other things. It's a miracle I'm still 55
alive. If they make my story into a three-act play, I'm sure the
audiences will weep.

NARRATOR: Words fail and he can only sigh.

OHATSU: And is this the comic relief of your tragedy? Why
couldn't you have trusted me with your worries when you 60
tell me even trivial little things? You must've had some reason for hiding. Why don't you take me into your confidence?

NARRATOR: She leans over his knee. Bitter tears soak her handkerchief.

TOKUBEI: Please don't cry or be angry with me. I wasn't hiding 65
anything, but it wouldn't have helped to involve you. At any
rate, my troubles have largely been settled, and I can tell you
the whole story now.

 My master has always treated me with particular kindness because I'm his nephew. For my part, I've served 70
him with absolute honesty. There's never been a penny's

16 **that's you** his face is covered by a deep wicker hat, commonly worn
by visitors to the quarters of prostitution   17 **Tokubei** the pronunciation of the name given in the text is Tokubyoe, but I have followed the
more normal modern pronunciation   23 **Dōtombori** a street in Osaka
famed for its theaters and houses of pleasure

32 **impersonators' show** within the precincts of the Ikudama Shrine
were booths where various types of entertainment were presented. The
impersonators mimicked the speech and posture of popular actors

discrepancy in the accounts. It's true that recently I used his name when I bought on credit a bolt of Kaga silk to make into a summer kimono, but that's the one and only time, and if I
75 have to raise the money on the spot, I can always sell back the kimono without taking a loss. My master has been so impressed by my honesty that he proposed I marry his wife's niece with a dowry of two *kamme*, and promised to set me up in business. That happened last year, but how could I shift
80 my affections when I have you? I didn't give his suggestion a second thought, but in the meantime my mother—she's really my stepmother—conferred with my master, keeping it a secret from me. She went back to the country with the two *kamme* in her clutches. Fool that I am, I never dreamt what
85 had happened.

The trouble began last month when they tried to force me to marry. I got angry and said, "Master, you surprise me. You know how unwilling I am to get married, and yet you've inveigled my old mother into giving her consent. You've
90 gone too far, master. I can't understand the mistress's attitude either. If I took as my wife this young lady whom I've always treated with the utmost deference and accepted her dowry in the bargain, I'd spend my whole life dancing attendance on my wife. How could I ever assert myself? I've re-
95 fused once, and even if my father were to return from his grave, the answer would still be no."

The master was furious that I should have answered so bluntly. His voice shook with rage. "I know your real reasons. You're involved with Ohatsu, or whatever her name is, from
100 the Temma House in Dōjima. That's why you seem so averse to my wife's niece. Very well—after what's been said, I'm no longer willing to give you the girl, and since there's to be no wedding, return the money. Settle without fail by the twenty-second of the month and clear your business accounts. I'll
105 chase you from Osaka and never let you set foot here again!"

I too have my pride as a man. "Right you are!" I answered, and rushed off to my village. But my so-called mother wouldn't let the money from her grip, not if this world turned into the next. I went to Kyoto, hoping to bor-
110 row the money from the wholesale soy sauce dealers in the Fifth Ward. I've always been on good terms with them. But, as ill luck would have it, they had no money to spare. I retraced my steps to the country, and this time, with the intercession of the whole village, I managed to extract the money
115 from my mother. I intended to return the dowry immediately and settle things for once and for all. But if I can't remain in Osaka, how shall I be able to meet you?

My bones may be crushed to powder, my flesh be torn away, and I may sink, an empty shell, in the slime of Shijimi
120 River. Let that happen if it must, but if I am parted from you, what shall I do?

NARRATOR: He weeps, suffocated by his grief. Ohatsu, holding back the welling tears of sympathy, strengthens and comforts him.

125 OHATSU: How you've suffered! And when I think that it's been because of me, I feel happy, sad, and most grateful all at once. But please, show more courage. Pull yourself together. Your uncle may have forbidden you to set foot in Osaka

again, but you haven't committed robbery or arson. I'll think of some way to keep you here. And if a time should come 130 when we can no longer meet, did our promises of love hold only for this world? Others before us have chosen reunion through death. To die is simple enough—none will hinder and none be hindered on the journey to the Mountain of Death and the River of Three Ways. 135

NARRATOR: Ohatsu falters among these words of encouragement, choked by tears. She resumes.

OHATSU: The twenty-second is tomorrow. Return the money early, since you must return it anyway. Try to get in your master's good graces again. 140

TOKUBEI: I want to, and I'm impatient to return the money, but on the thirteenth of the month Kuheiji the oil merchant—I think you know him—begged me desperately for the money. He said he needed it only for one day, and promised to return it by the morning of the eighteenth. I de- 145 cided to lend him the money since I didn't need it until the twenty-second, and it was for a friend close as a brother. He didn't get in touch with me on the eighteenth or nineteenth. Yesterday he was out and I couldn't see him. I intended to call on him this morning, but I've spent it making the 150 rounds of my customers in order to wind up my business by tomorrow. I'll go to him this evening and settle everything. He's a man of honor and he knows my predicament. I'm sure nothing will go wrong. Don't worry. Oh—look there, Ohatsu! 155

NARRATOR: "Hatsuse is far away,
　　Far too is Naniwa-dera:
　　So many temples are renowned
　　For the sound of their bells,
　　Voices of the Eternal Law. 160
　　If, on an evening in spring,
　　You visit a mountain temple
　　You will see . . ."
At the head of a band of revelers

TOKUBEI: Kuheiji! That's a poor performance! You've no busi- 165 ness running off on excursions when you haven't cleared up your debt with me. Today we'll settle our account.

NARRATOR: He grasps Kuheiji's arm and restrains him. Kuheiji's expression is dubious.

KUHEIJI: What are you talking about, Tokubei? These people 170 with me are all residents of the ward. We've had a meeting in Ueshio Street to raise funds for a pilgrimage to Ise. We've drunk a little saké, but we're on our way home now. What do you mean by grabbing my arm? Don't be rowdy!

NARRATOR: He removes his wicker hat and glares at Tokubei. 175

TOKUBEI: I'm not being rowdy. All I ask is that you return the two *kamme* of silver I lent you on the thirteenth, which you were supposed to repay on the eighteenth.

NARRATOR: Before he can finish speaking, Kuheiji bursts out laughing. 180

---

78 *kamme* a measure of silver, worth about one thousand dollars

134–135 **Mountain . . . Ways** places in the Japanese afterworld
156–163 **Hatsuse . . . see** a passage from the Nō play *Miidera*, here quoted mainly because the first word, "Hatsuse," echoes the name Ohatsu in the preceding line. The last words similarly point to the arrival of Kuheiji. Most of this passage would be sung not by a single chanter but by a chorus, as in a Nō play   165 **performance** Tokubei, relieved to see Kuheiji, at first teases him about his singing of the Nō passage, but his words have an undertone of criticism of Kuheiji's past behavior

KUHEIJI: Are you out of your mind, Tokubei? I can't remember having borrowed a penny from you in all the years I've known you. Don't make any accusations which you'll regret.

NARRATOR: He shakes himself free. His companions also re-185 move their hats. Tokubei pales with astonishment.

TOKUBEI: Don't say that, Kuheiji! You came to me in tears, saying that you couldn't survive your monthly bills, and I thought that this was the kind of emergency for which we'd 190 been friends all these years. I lent you the money as an act of generosity, though I needed it desperately myself. I told you that I didn't even require a receipt, but you insisted on putting your seal to one, for form's sake. You made me write out a promissory note and you sealed it. Don't try to deny it, Kuheiji!

195 NARRATOR: Tokubei rebukes him heatedly.

KUHEIJI: What's that? I'd like to see the seal.

TOKUBEI: Do you think I'm afraid to show you?

NARRATOR: He produces the paper from his wallet.

TOKUBEI: If these gentlemen are from the ward, I am sure that 200 they will recognize your seal. Will you still dispute it?

NARRATOR: When he unfolds the paper and displays it, Kuheiji claps his hands in recollection.

KUHEIJI: Yes, it's my seal all right. Oh, Tokubei, I never thought you'd do such a thing, not even if you were starving 205 and forced to eat dirt. On the tenth of the month I lost a wallet containing the seal. I advertised for it everywhere, but without success, so as of the sixteenth of this month, as I've informed these gentlemen, I've changed my seal. Could I have affixed the seal I lost on the tenth to a document on the 210 thirteenth? No—what happened was that you found my wallet, wrote the promissory note, and affixed my seal. Now you're trying to extort money from me—that makes you a worse criminal than a forger. You'd do better, Tokubei, to commit out-and-out robbery. You deserve to have your head 215 cut off, but for old times' sake, I'll forgive you. Let's see if you can make any money out of this!

NARRATOR: He throws the note in Tokubei's face and glares at him fiercely in an extraordinary display of feigned innocence. Tokubei, furious, cries aloud.

220 TOKUBEI: You've been damned clever. You've put one over on me. I'm dishonored. What am I to do? Must I let you take my money brazenly from me? You've planned everything so cleverly that even if I go to court, I'm sure to lose. I'll take back my money with my fists! See here! I'm Tokubei of the 225 Hirano-ya, a man of honor. Do you follow me? I'm not a man to trick a friend out of his money the way you have. Come on!

NARRATOR: He falls on Kuheiji.

KUHEIJI: You impudent little apprentice! I'll knock the inso-230 lence out of you!

NARRATOR: He seizes the front of Tokubei's kimono and they grapple, trading blows and shoves. Ohatsu rushes barefoot to them.

---

185 **remove their hats** readying themselves to come to Kuheiji's defense   187 **bills** I have converted all dates to the Western calendar, but the dates in the lunar calendar correspond to the end of the third moon. Kuheiji needs the money to pay end-of-the-month bills 232 **barefoot** in her agitation she fails to slip on her *geta*. We suppose that her country customer has returned during the dialogue between Tokubei and Kuheiji

OHATSU: (*To townsmen.*) Please everybody, stop the fight! He's a friend of mine. Where are the chair-bearers? Why don't 235 they do something? Tokubei's being beaten!

NARRATOR: She writhes in anguish, but is helpless. Her customer, country bumpkin that he is, bundles her forcibly into a palanquin.

CUSTOMER: It won't do for you to get hurt. 240

OHATSU: Please wait just a moment! Oh, I'm so unhappy!

NARRATOR: The palanquin is rushed off, leaving only the echoes of her weeping voice.

Tokubei is alone; Kuheiji has five companions. Men rush out from the nearby booths and drive them all with sticks to 245 the lotus pond. Who tramples Tokubei? Who beats him? There is no way to tell. His hair is disheveled, his sash undone. He stumbles and falls to this side and that.

TOKUBEI: Kuheiji, you swine! Do you think I'll let you escape alive? 250

NARRATOR: He staggers about searching for Kuheiji, but he has fled and vanished. Tokubei falls heavily in his tracks and, weeping bitterly, he cries aloud.

TOKUBEI: (*To bystanders.*) I feel humiliated and ashamed that you've seen me this way. There was not a false word in my 255 accusation. I've always treated Kuheiji like a brother, and when he begged me for the money, saying he'd never forget it as long as he lived, I lent it to him, sure that he'd do the same for me, though the money was precious as life, and I knew that without it tomorrow, the twenty-second, I'd have 260 to kill myself. He made me write the note in my own hand, then put his seal to it. But it was a seal which he had already reported as lost, and now he's turned the accusations against me! It's mortifying, infuriating—to be kicked and beaten this way, dishonored and forced to my knees. It would've 265 been better if I had died while smashing and biting him!

NARRATOR: He strikes the ground and gnashes his teeth, clenches his fists and moans, a sight to stir compassion.

TOKUBEI: There's no point in my talking this way. Before three days have passed I, Tokubei, will make amends by showing 270 all Osaka the purity at the bottom of my heart.

NARRATOR: The meaning of these words is later known.

TOKUBEI: I'm sorry to have bothered you all. Please forgive me.

NARRATOR: He speaks his apologies, picks up his battered hat 275 and puts it on. His face, downcast in the sinking rays of the sun, is clouded by tears that engulf him. Dejectedly he leaves, a sight too pitiful to behold.

SCENE 2

Inside the Temma House.

TIME

Evening of the same day.

NARRATOR: The breezes of love are all-pervasive
By Shijimi River, where love-drowned guests
Like empty shells, bereft of their senses,

---

246 **lotus pond** this pond still may be seen today at the Ikudama Shrine

2 **Shijimi River** the word *shijimi* means the corbicula, a kind of small shellfish, and the name of the river thus occasions mention of shells

5   Wander the dark ways of love
     Lit each night by burning lanterns,
     Fireflies that glow in the four seasons,
     Stars that shine on rainy nights.
     By Plum Bridge, blossoms show even in summer.
     Rustics on a visit, city connoisseurs,
10   All journey the varied roads of love,
     Where adepts wander and novices play:
     What a lively place this New Quarter is!

But alas for Ohatsu of the Temma House—even after she returns the day's events still weigh on her. She cannot swal-
15 low her saké, she feels on edge. As she sits weeping, some courtesans from the neighboring houses and other friends come for a little chat.

FIRST COURTESAN: Have you heard, Ohatsu? They say that Toku was given a thrashing for something bad he did. Is it
20 true?

SECOND COURTESAN: No, my customer told me that Toku was trampled to death.

NARRATOR: They say he was fettered for fraud or trussed for counterfeiting a seal. Not one decent thing have they to re-
25 port: every expression of sympathy makes their visit the more painful.

OHATSU: No, please, not another word. The more I hear, the worse my breast pains me. I'm sure I'll be the first to die. I wish I were dead already.

30 NARRATOR: She can only weep. But amidst her tears she hap-pens to look outside and catches a glimpse of Tokubei, a pathetic figure wearing a wicker hat, even at night. Her heart leaps, and she wants to run to him, but in the sitting room are the master and his wife, and by the entrance stands the cook,
35 while in the kitchen a maid is hovering: with so many sharp eyes watching, she cannot do as she pleases.

OHATSU: I feel terribly depressed. I think I'll step outside for a moment.

NARRATOR: She slips out softly.

40 OHATSU: What happened? I've heard rumors of every sort about you. They've driven me out of my mind with worry.

NARRATOR: She thrusts her face under the brim of his wicker hat and weeps in secret, soundless, painful tears. He too is lost in tears.

45 TOKUBEI: I've been made the victim of a clever plot, as no doubt you've heard, and the more I struggle, the worse off I am. Everything has turned against me now. I can't survive this night. I've made up my mind to it.

NARRATOR: As he whispers, voices are heard from within.

50 VOICES: Come inside, Ohatsu. There's enough gossip about you as it is.

OHATSU: There—did you hear? We can't go on talking. Do as I show you.

NARRATOR: She hides him under the train of her mantle. He
55 crawls behind her to the garden door, where he slips beneath the porch at the step. Ohatsu sits by the entrance and, pulling the tobacco tray to her, lights her pipe. She assumes an air of unconcern.

At this moment Kuheiji and a couple of his loudmouthed
60 friends burst in, accompanied by a blind musician.

KUHEIJI: Hello, girls. You're looking lonesome. Would you like me for a customer? Hello there, host. I haven't seen you in ages.

NARRATOR: He strides arrogantly into the room.

65 HOST: Bring a tobacco tray and some saké cups.

NARRATOR: He makes the customary fuss over the guests.

KUHEIJI: No, don't bother about saké. We were drinking before we came. I have something to tell you. Tokubei, the number one customer of your Ohatsu, found a seal I'd lost and tried
70 to cheat me out of two *kamme* in silver with a forged note. The facts were too much for him, and he finally met with some unpleasantness from which he was lucky to escape alive. His reputation has been ruined. Be on your guard if he comes here again. Everybody will tell you that I speak the
75 truth, so even if Tokubei tells you the exact opposite, don't believe him for a moment. You'd do best not to let him in at all. Sooner or later he's bound to end up on the gallows.

NARRATOR: He pours out his words convincingly. Tokubei, un-derneath the porch, gnashes his teeth and trembles with
80 rage. Ohatsu, afraid that he may reveal himself, calms him with her foot, calms him gently. The host is loath to answer yes or no, for Tokubei's a customer of long standing.

HOST: Well, then, how about some soup?

NARRATOR: Covering his confusion, he leaves the room.
85 Ohatsu, weeping bitterly, exclaims.

OHATSU: You needn't try your clever words on me. Tokubei and I have been intimate for years. We've told each other our inmost secrets. He hasn't a particle of deceit in him, the poor boy. His generosity has been his undoing. He's been tricked,
90 but he hasn't the evidence to prove it. After what has hap-pened Tokubei has no choice but to kill himself. I wish I knew whether or not he was resolved to die.

NARRATOR: She pretends to be talking to herself, but with her foot she questions him. He nods, and taking her ankle,
95 passes it across his throat, to let her know that he is bent on suicide.

OHATSU: I knew it. I knew it. No matter how long one lives, it comes to the same thing. Only death can wipe out the disgrace.

100 NARRATOR: Kuheiji is startled by her words.

KUHEIJI: What is Ohatsu talking about? Why should Tokubei kill himself? Well, if he kills himself, I'll take good care of you after he's gone! I think you've fallen for me too!

OHATSU: That's most generous of you, I'm sure. But would
105 you object if, by way of thanks for your kindness, I killed you? Could I go on living even a moment if separated from Toku? Kuheiji, you dirty thief! Anyone hearing your silly lies can only suspect you. I'm sure that Toku intends to die with me, as I with him.

---

8 **Plum Bridge** Umeda Bridge, the name of which means literally "plum field"   12 **New Quarter** the Dojima New Quarter of Osaka was opened about 1700   32 **wicker hat** the hat was worn for concealment, but at night this precaution was normally unnecessary   50 **gossip** standing in the street outside a teahouse was likely to occasion gossip about secret lovers

---

77 **gallows** literally, "he's bound to end up at Noe or Tobita." Noe and Tobita were execution grounds on the outskirts of Osaka

110 NARRATOR: She taps with her foot, and Tokubei, weeping, takes it in his hands and reverently touches it to his forehead. He embraces her knees and sheds tears of love. She too can hardly conceal her emotions. Though no word is spoken, answering each other heart to heart, they silently weep. That
115 no one knows makes it sadder still.
    Kuheiji feels uncomfortable.

KUHEIJI: The wind's against us today. Let's get out of here. The whores in this place are certainly peculiar—they seem to have an aversion for customers like ourselves with plenty of
120 money to spend. Let's stop at the Asa House and have a drink there. We'll rattle around a couple of gold pieces, then go home to bed. Oh—my wallet is so heavy I can hardly walk.

NARRATOR: Spewing forth all manner of abuse, they noisily depart. The host and his wife call to the servants.

125 HOST: It's time to put out the lights for the night. Lay out beds for the guests who are staying on. Ohatsu, you sleep upstairs. Get to bed early.

OHATSU: (*To herself.*) Master, mistress, I shall probably never see you again. Farewell. Farewell to all the servants too.

130 NARRATOR: Thus inwardly taking leave, she goes to her bedchamber. Later they will learn that this was a parting for life; how pitiful the foolish hearts of men who do not realize the truth in time!

HOST: See that the fire is out under the kettle. Don't let the
135 mice get at the relishes.

NARRATOR: They shut the place and bar the gate. Hardly have their heads touched their pillows than all are snoring merrily. So short is the night that before they've had a chance to dream, two o'clock in the morning has come. Ohatsu is
140 dressed for death, a black cloak dark as the ways of love thrown over her kimono of spotless white. She tiptoes to the staircase and looks down. Tokubei shows his face from under the porch. He beckons, nods, points, communicating his intent without a word. Below the stairs a servant girl is sleep-
145 ing. A hanging lantern brightly shines. Ohatsu in desperation attaches her fan to a palm-leaf broom, and from the second step of the staircase attempts in vain to extinguish the flame. At last, by stretching every inch, she puts it out, only to tumble suddenly down the stairs. The lamp is out,
150 and in the darkness the servant girl turns in her sleep. Trembling, the lovers grope for each other—a fearful moment. The host awakens in his room to the back.

HOST: What was that noise just now? Servants! The night lamp has gone out. Get up and light it!

155 NARRATOR: The servant girl, aroused, sleepily rubs her eyes and gets up from the bed stark naked.

SERVANT: I can't find the flint box.

NARRATOR: She wanders about the room searching, and Ohatsu, faint with terror, dodges this way and that to avoid
160 her. At last she catches Tokubei's hand, and softly they creep to the entranceway. They unfasten the latch, but the hinges creak, and frightened by the noise, they hesitate. Just then the maid begins to strike the flints; they time their actions to the rasping sound, and with each rasp open the door farther
165 until, huddled together and their sleeves twisted round them, they pass through the door one after the other, feeling as though they tread on a tiger's tail. They exchange glances and cry out for joy, happy that they are to die—a painful, heart-rending sight. The life left them now is as brief as
170 sparks that fly from blocks of flint.

SCENE 3

The journey from Dōjima to the Sonezaki Shrine.

NARRATOR: Farewell to this world, and to the night farewell. We who walk the road to death, to what should we be likened?
  To the frost by the road that leads to the graveyard,
  Vanishing with each step we take ahead:
  How sad is this dream of a dream!   5

TOKUBEI: Ah, did you count the bell? Of the seven strokes
  That mark the dawn, six have sounded.
  The remaining one will be the last echo
  We shall hear in this life.

OHATSU: It will echo the bliss of nirvana.   10

NARRATOR: Farewell, and not to the bell alone—
  They look a last time on the grass, the trees, the sky.
  The clouds, the river go by unmindful of them;
  The Dipper's bright reflection shines in the water.

TOKUBEI: Let's pretend that Umeda Bridge   15
  Is the bridge the magpies built
  Across the Milky Way, and make a vow
  To be husband and wife stars for eternity.

OHATSU: I promise. I'll be your wife forever.

NARRATOR: They cling together—the river waters   20
  Will surely swell with the tears they shed.
  Across the river, in a teahouse upstairs,
  Some revelers, still not gone to bed,
  Are loudly talking under blazing lamps—
  No doubt gossiping about the good or bad   25
  Of this year's crop of lovers' suicides;
  Their hearts sink to hear these voices.

TOKUBEI: How strange! but yesterday, even today,
  We spoke as if such things did not concern us.
  Tomorrow we shall figure in their gossip.   30
  If the world will sing about us, let it sing.

NARRATOR: This is the song that now they hear.
    "I'm sure you'll never have me for your wife,
    I know my love means nothing to you . . ."
  Yes, for all our love, for all our grieving,   35
  Our lives, our lots, have not been as we wished.
  Never, until this very day, have we known
  A single night of heart's relaxation—
  Instead, the tortures of an ill-starred love.
    "What is this bond between us?   40
    I cannot forget you.
    But you would shake me off and go—
    I'll never let you!
    Kill me with your hands, then go.
    I'll never release you!"   45
  So she said in tears.

OHATSU: Of all the many songs, that one, tonight!

TOKUBEI: Who is it singing? We who listen

BOTH: Suffer the ordeal of those before us.

NARRATOR: They cling to each other, weeping bitterly.   50
  Any other night would not matter

---

15 **bridge** allusion to the Chinese legend, familiar also in Japan, which tells of two stars (known as the Herd Boy and the Weaver Girl) that meet once a year, crossing over a bridge in the sky built by magpies 40–45 **What is . . . you** the song overheard by Ohatsu and Tokubei is derived from a popular ballad of the time that describes a love suicide

If tonight were only a little longer,
But the heartless summer night, as is its wont,
Breaks as cockcrows hasten their last hour.

55 TOKUBEI: It will be worse if we wait for dawn.
Let us die in the wood of Tenjin.
NARRATOR: He leads her by the hand.
At Umeda Embankment, the night ravens.
TOKUBEI: Tomorrow our bodies may be their meal.

60 OHATSU: It's strange, this is your unlucky year
Of twenty-five, and mine of nineteen.
It's surely proof how deep are our ties
That we who love each other are cursed alike.
All the prayers I have made for this world

65 To the gods and to the Buddha, I here and now
Direct to the future: in the world to come
May we be reborn on the same lotus!
NARRATOR: One hundred eight the beads her fingers tell
On her rosary; tears increase the sum.

70 No end to her grief, but the road has an end:
Their minds are numbed, the sky is dark, the wind still,
They have reached the thick wood of Sonezaki.
    Shall it be here, shall it be there? When they brush the
grass, the falling dew vanishes even quicker than their lives,

75 in this uncertain world a lightning flash—or was it something else?
OHATSU: I'm afraid. What was that now?
TOKUBEI: That was a human spirit. I thought we alone would
die tonight, but someone else has preceded us. Whoever it

80 may be, we'll have a companion on the journey to the
Mountain of Death. *Namu Amida Butsu. Namu Amida
Butsu.*
NARRATOR: She weeps helplessly.
OHATSU: To think that others are dying tonight too! How

85 heartbreaking!
NARRATOR: Man though he is, his tears fall freely.
TOKUBEI: Those two spirits flying together—do you suppose
they belong to anyone else? They must be yours and mine!

90 OHATSU: Those two spirits? Then, are we dead already?
TOKUBEI: Normally, if we saw a spirit, we'd knot our clothes
and murmur prayers to keep our souls with us, but now we
hurry towards our end, hoping instead our two souls will
find the same dwelling. Do not mistake the way, do not lose

95 me!
NARRATOR: They embrace, flesh to flesh, then fall to the
ground and weep—how pitiful they are! Their strings of
tears unite like entwining branches, or the pine and palm
that grow from a single trunk, a symbol of eternal love. Here

100 the dew of their unhappy lives will at last settle.
TOKUBEI: Let this be the spot.

---

56 **Tenjin** the shrine of Sonezaki, sacred to Tenjin (*Sugawara no Michizane*)   60 **unlucky year** according to yin-yang divination, a man's twenty-fifth, forty-second, and sixtieth years   69 **rosary** the Buddhist rosary of 108 beads, one for each of the sufferings occasioned by the passions   78 **human spirit** *Hitodama*, a kind of will-o'-the-wisp believed to be a human soul   81 *Namu Amida Butsu* the invocation to Amida Buddha used in Pure Land Buddhism   91–92 **knot . . . prayers** exorcism practiced to prevent the soul from leaving the body   98 **pine and palm** such a tree actually existed, as contemporary accounts of the Sonezaki Shrine show

NARRATOR: He unfastens the sash of his cloak. Ohatsu removes her tear-stained outer robe, and throws it on the palm
tree; the fronds might now serve as a broom to sweep away
the sad world's dust. Ohatsu takes a razor from her sleeve. 105
OHATSU: I had this razor prepared in case we were overtaken
on the way and separated. I was determined not to forfeit our
name as lovers. How happy I am that we are to die together
as we hoped!
TOKUBEI: How wonderful of you to have thought of that! I am 110
so confident in our love that I have no fears even about
death. And yet it would be unfortunate if because of the pain
we are to suffer people said that we looked ugly in death. Let
us secure our bodies to this twin-trunked tree and die im-
maculately! We will become an unparalleled example of a 115
lovers' suicide.
OHATSU: Yes, let us do that.
NARRATOR: Alas! She little thought she thus would use her
light blue undersash! She draws it taut, and with her razor
slashes it through.
OHATSU: The sash is cut, but you and I will never be torn 120
apart.
NARRATOR: She sits, and he binds her twice, thrice to the tree,
firmly so that she will not stir.
TOKUBEI: Is it tight?
OHATSU: Very tight. 125
NARRATOR: She looks at her husband, and he at her—they
burst into tears.
BOTH: This is the end of our unhappy lives!
TOKUBEI: No I mustn't give way to grief.
NARRATOR: He lifts his head and joins his hands in prayer. 130
TOKUBEI: My parents died when I was a boy, and I grew up
thanks to the efforts of my uncle, who was my master. It dis-
graces me to die without repaying his kindness. Instead I
shall cause him trouble which will last even after my death.
Please forgive my sins. 135
    Soon I shall see my parents in the other world. Father,
Mother, welcome me there!
NARRATOR: He weeps. Ohatsu also joins her hands.
OHATSU: I envy you. You say you will meet your parents in the
world of the dead. My father and mother are in this world 140
and in good health. I wonder when I shall see them again. I
heard from them this spring, but I haven't seen them since
the beginning of last autumn. Tomorrow, when word reaches
the village of our suicides, how unhappy they will be! Now I
must bid farewell for this life to my parents, my brothers and 145
sisters. If at least my thoughts can reach you, please appear
before me, if only in dreams. Dear Mother, beloved Father!
NARRATOR: She sobs and wails aloud. Her husband also cries
out and sheds incessant tears in all too understandable
emotion. 150
OHATSU: We could talk forever, but it serves no purpose. Kill
me, kill me quickly!
NARRATOR: She hastens the moment of death.
TOKUBEI: I'm ready.
NARRATOR: He swiftly draws his dagger. 155
TOKUBEI: The moment has come. *Namu Amida. Namu
Amida.*
NARRATOR: But when he tries to bring the blade against the
skin of the woman he's loved, and held and slept with so
many months and years, his eyes cloud over, his hand 160
shakes. He tries to steady his weakening resolve, but still he

trembles, and when he thrusts, the point misses. Twice or thrice the flashing blade deflects this way and that until a cry tells it has struck her throat.

165   TOKUBEI: *Namu Amida. Namu Amida. Namu Amida Butsu.*

NARRATOR: He twists the blade deeper and deeper, but the strength has left his arm. When he sees her weaken, he stretches forth his hands. The last agonies of death are indescribable.

170   TOKUBEI: Must I lag behind you? Let's draw our last breaths together.

NARRATOR: He thrusts and twists the razor in his throat, until it seems the handle or the blade must snap. His eyes grow dim, and his last painful breath is drawn away at its appointed hour. No one is there to tell the tale, but the wind that blows through Sonezaki Wood transmits it, and high and low alike gather to pray for these lovers who beyond a doubt will in the future attain Buddhahood. They have become models of true love.

175

---

174 **appointed hour** it was believed by practitioners of yin-yang divination that a person's hour of death was determined at his birth and could be foretold by an examination of the celestial stems governing his birth. Death normally occurred with the receding of the tide

■ LOVE LETTER FROM THE ■ LICENSED QUARTER

As with many Kabuki plays, *Love Letter from the Licensed Quarter* was devised by a Kabuki playwright with help of his assistant playwrights and the company's actors. The play is one of many dramatizing the life of Yūgiri, a famous prostitute. Chikamatsu Monzaemon, for example, wrote a Kabuki play on Yūgiri, *Seventh Anniversary of Yūgiri's Death* in 1678, and a *jōruri* play, *Yūgiri and the Straits of Naruto* in 1712. This version of *Love Letter from the Licensed Quarter* is based on the first act of Chikamatsu's *jōruri*, and takes about half its lines from it as well; it was first performed in 1780.

In many respects, *Love Letter from the Licensed Quarter* relies on its audience's familiarity with the story of Yūgiri and Izaemon; how Izaemon, disgraced and outcast from his wealthy merchant family, returns to the Yoshida House only to spy his lover, the prostitute Yūgiri, apparently entertaining a new client, the *samurai* Hiraoka. Kabuki audiences would know, however, that "Hiraoka" is actually the *samurai's* wife, who has come to the brothel disguised as her husband in order to care for Izaemon and Yūgiri's seven-year-old child. After a long scene in which Izaemon bemoans his poverty—he is wearing a "paper kimono," made of Yūgiri's love letters—and challenges Yūgiri's love for him, the couple are reconciled. In the play's brilliant finale, eighteen clerks from Izaemon's family march down the *hanamichi*, bearing strongboxes which they pile in a huge pyramid. They tell Izaemon that he has been accepted back into his family and that the boxes each contain a thousand *ryo*, enough money to settle all of Izaemon's debts and to buy Yūgiri out of her contract with the brothel-keeper Kizaemon.

In part because the play was adapted from Chikamatsu's original, and in part due to the historical relationship between doll theater and Kabuki, *Love Letter from the Licensed Quarter* shares some features with plays like *The Love Suicides at Sonezaki*, particularly the use of narration and songs to develop aspects of characterization. But in most respects, the play is clearly in the Kabuki mode. It has the mixed tonality of the prostitute-buying Kabuki genre, ranging from the crude "pounding the mochi" jokes in the first scene, to the comic scenes between the brothel-keeper Kizaemon and his wife, to the more serious and passionate confrontation between Izaemon and Yūgiri. More important, it provides many opportunities for Kabuki actors to display their talents in these familiar and highly-conventional roles, calling on them not only to engage the changing verse and prose forms of the text, but also to perform many scenes—like the final scene between Yūgiri and Izaemon—in dance as well.

LOVE LETTER FROM THE LICENSED QUARTER

Anonymous

TRANSLATED BY JAMES R. BRANDON

— CHARACTERS —

HIRAOKA	LEAD SINGER
IZAEMON	SOLO SINGER
KIZAEMON	TAKEMOTO SINGERS
UME	TOKIWAZU SINGERS
YŪGIRI	MAIDS, COURTESANS, SERVANTS, PLAYERS

SCENE 1

Outside the Yoshida brothel

Stick drum and flute play lively Tōri Kagura, *"Shrine Dance Procession," and* shamisen *play* Shikoru, *"Harden," behind the striped kabuki curtain. Two ki clacks. Ki clacks accelerate as the curtain is run open. The main entrance of Yoshida House, in New Town licensed quarter, Osaka, opening onto the street. Lattice strips cover the front of the house. A festive display of a Shintō sacred straw rope hanging under the eaves and great tubs of cut bamboo, plum, and pine branches flanking the entry in the center of the stage indicate that it is the New Year season. Music tapers off. Silence. The stage is empty. A single ki clack: music resumes. Shouts are heard from inside the house. A group of male* SERVANTS *bursts through the curtain in the entry. They wear short* happi *coats over plain cotton kimonos. They carry a large tree stump as a mortar and a long-handled maul for pounding the traditional New Year's rice-cake dough. One* SERVANT *puts a huge ball of rice dough in the hollow of the stump. As the others clap their hands and sing, the* SERVANT *with the maul strikes rhythmically, moving around the stump in a circle.*

SERVANTS: (*Sing* Kome Tsuki, *"Rice Pounding," to the accompaniment of* shamisen *and small drums.*)

Pounding rice five men are right, pound together in rhythm;
  When a great lord is passing, even he must stop to watch.

(*They repeat the song several times, until the* SERVANT *who is pounding drops the* maul *to the ground and plops down cross-legged.*)

5   FIRST SERVANT: (*Wiping his forehead.*) Whew! I could use a drink.

(*The others laugh and hoot.*)

SECOND SERVANT: (*Playfully slapping his shoulder.*) He'd rather pound the mochi with debutante whores or old women . . .

10   THIRD SERVANT: . . . but he can't today. The Awa millionaire's bought them all.

FOURTH SERVANT: So our pounding goes into rice cake!

(*They laugh good-naturedly.*)

FIFTH SERVANT: Each year it's the custom to make felicitous rice cakes . . .

SIXTH SERVANT: . . . to celebrate the New Year . . .   15

SEVENTH SERVANT: . . . the first business of the year . . .

EIGHTH SERVANT: . . . is drinking, treated by the master of Yoshida House.

NINTH SERVANT: If there's trouble abroad, why the only trouble . . .   20

TENTH SERVANT: . . . is drinking our fill!

FIRST SERVANT: Remember last year, when the great courtesan Oyama took a shine . . .

SECOND SERVANT: . . . to the best . . .

THIRD SERVANT: . . . singer and dancer at the feast?   25

FOURTH SERVANT: (*Puffing up.*) I'll do my best this year . . .

FIFTH SERVANT: . . . in the hope she'll fall for me!

(*They all laugh, and some jokingly push the* FOURTH SERVANT.)

SIXTH SERVANT: Forget it. Let's stuff ourselves . . .

SEVENTH SERVANT: . . . and hope the Awa patron treats us . . .

EIGHTH SERVANT: . . . to his Awa-cakes . . .   30

NINTH SERVANT: . . . and maybe some of his girls!

TENTH SERVANT: Oh, how great . . .

ALL: . . . that would be!

(*Shamisen* resume Shikoru *and stick drum and flute* Tōri Kagura. HIRAOKA, *a wealthy* samurai *from Awa, appears on the* hanamichi. *He is dressed in sober but expensive dark kimono and cloak. He is escorted by four adult* MAIDS, *two teahouse* GIRLS, *and two* CHILD MAIDS, *whose brilliant colored kimonos catch the eye.* HIRAOKA *stops at seven-three and faces the audience. Music stops.*)

HIRAOKA: "Even travelers can't help being late sleepers, when the year end comes," someone has written. I have come from   35 faroff Awa, at New Year, to see the whores of Osaka and drink love's liquor from the pink blossoms of wintertime. I proclaim it publicly: I want to meet the famous courtesan Yūgiri. Sweet girls, skilled in love's affairs, intercede for me. Five days straight I have waited at Yoshida House for her.   40 Please arrange it, please.

FIRST MAID: (*Sweetly flattering.*) A lord so enamored that he lets his heart stray to the port of Osaka, far from home, is surely a millionaire who knows the ways of love . . .

SS **Yoshida House** an *ageya* or house of assignation. In 1678, the time of the play, a customer did not visit the house where a courtesan lived. Instead he met her at an *ageya* where they were entertained and where they spent the night   8 **mochi** a small rice cake, a traditional New Year's delicacy. The dough is prepared by pounding steamed rice in a pestle, so "to pound mochi" meant in popular parlance sexual intercourse

30 **Awa-cakes** since *Awa* can mean either an area of the island of Shikoku or millet, the line can mean either "millet cakes" or "(the man from) Awa's cakes"   SD **Awa** on Shikoku Island facing Osaka across the Inland Sea   35 **year end** travelers who had long distances to cover on foot were notoriously early risers in Japan. But even they slack off and share in the festivities, which mark the end of the year

45   SECOND MAID: . . . for among all the courtesans of New Town Quarter, the famous one you visit unceasingly is Evening Mist of Fan House.

THIRD MAID: We deeply understand your passion, and wish your quest to meet her meets success, yet . . .

50   FOURTH COURTESAN: *(Sadly.)* . . . since mid-autumn she has been ill . . .

FIRST SERVANT: *(Confidentially.)* . . . master and mistress both worry about forcing things too much . . .

SECOND SERVANT: . . . but she has pride and with luck her

55   heart might melt . . .

ALL: . . . tonight.

HIRAOKA: *(Fervently.)* And so please intercede, please.

FIRST MAID: *(Bowing.)* In any case, great millionaire . . .

ALL: . . . do come this way.

(Shamisen and stick drum play Migi no Uta, *"Song of the Right," as the procession crosses onstage. A black-robed stage assistant places a folding stool center.* HIRAOKA *sits and fans himself importantly. The others flutter around him. Music stops.)*

60   FIRST SERVANT: *(Bowing obsequiously.)* Welcome, welcome . . .

SERVANTS: *(In unison.)* . . . great millionaire from Awa.

HIRAOKA: *(Jovially.)* Well, well. I see you are all lined up before me. Tell me, is the mochi pounding over?

FIRST SERVANT: *(Ingratiatingly.)* We finished it off a moment

65   ago. A generous patron came to Yoshida House this New Year . . .

SECOND SERVANT: . . . passing out tips to us every day, so we really put our hearts in it.

THIRD SERVANT: Why, you made us feel so good . . .

70   FOURTH SERVANT: . . . we beat the rice in rhythm . . .

FIFTH SERVANT: . . . as a welcome . . .

ALL: *(Bowing.)* . . . Master.

HIRAOKA: *(Frowning.)* I wish I had seen it. But I have come daily to see Yūgiri.

(A FIFTH MAID *hurries from the entrance and bows to* HIRAOKA.*)*

75   FIFTH MAID: Ah, have you just returned, sir? Wonderful news. It must have been the auspicious mochi pounding. When our master personally went to Yūgiri and implored her, as you might expect of a high-ranking courtesan, she consented, for the honor of Yoshida House, to appear today!

80   HIRAOKA: You say Yūgiri will come out?

FIRST SERVANT: *(Rubbing his hands gleefully.)* If Yūgiri is coming out, let's go quickly in . . .

SECOND SERVANT: . . . to the banquet hall and feast and drink . . .

85   THIRD SERVANT: . . . as we usually do . . .

ALL: . . . at our great lord's pleasure!

HIRAOKA: Here, here, now. You don't have to say it. As if I didn't know!

(Laughing, he throws a handful of coins onto the ground. The SERVANTS *eagerly scramble for them.)*

ALL: Thank you! Thank you, sir!

90   FIRST SERVANT: *(Slyly.)* They say a millionaire has sticky fingers!

SECOND SERVANT: When you're alone with Yūgiri . . .

THIRD SERVANT: . . . side by side in Yoshida's private cottage . . .

FOURTH SERVANT: . . . you'll be today's mochi-pounding pestle . . .

FIFTH SERVANT: . . . she a mortar dripping with love . . .   95

SIXTH SERVANT: . . . never ceasing through eternity!

SEVENTH SERVANT: Congratulations . . .

ALL: . . . on getting in her bed!

(There is nothing salacious in their attitudes. They laugh good-naturedly. HIRAOKA *waggles his fan at them.)*

HIRAOKA: Flatterers! Flatterers!

FIRST SERVANT: *(Expansively.)* Then, great millionaire, enter   100

the banquet hall . . .

HIRAOKA: . . . come with me, all of you . . .

ALL: . . . with pleasure, sir!

(Shamisen play fast Sugagaki brothel music. HIRAOKA *rises and leads the way through the curtain into Yoshida House. The others follow ad-libbing "This will be a great feast," "I'll drink all day," "We'll never have a feast like this one."* SERVANTS *carry off the mortar and pestle. Music fades. The stage is empty. Two ki clacks: paper doors slide open stage left revealing a raised platform on which are seated three* TAKEMOTO SINGERS *and three shamisen* PLAYERS. *After a short* shamisen *introductory section, the* LEAD SINGER *sings a capella.)*

LEAD SINGER: Winter's woven hat of straw covered with grime;

Letter-paper kimono frayed at sleeves and knees.   105

SINGERS: *(In unison, to shamisen accompaniment.)*

A heath fern blown by the wind, enduring during;

Hiding concealed though he is, in past times it was not so.

A windblown flower, chin tucked into his collar . . .

(Shamisen continues to play as the lights come up on the hana-michi and IZAEMON *enters. He wears a "paper kimono," supposedly made of Yūgiri's love letters, that shows his poverty. The characters of her "letters" are embroidered in silver thread on the purple and black silk patches that make up the kimono. A sedge hat hides his face. A short sword is tucked in a plain black sash. He wears straw sandals. Hunched over against the bitter winter cold, he has tucked his arms inside his kimono sleeves. He walks slowly, wearily. At seven-three he stops and looks toward Yoshida House. He turns back and faces the audience. Takemoto singing resumes to shamisen accompaniment.)*

SINGERS: Teeth clamped tight still chattering in the evening cold.

(He shivers and hugs himself. He steps back, stumbles, and recovers his balance. He blows gently on his hands to warm them. His head shakes as if crying.)

Protruding sword hilt and guard are worn smooth with age;   110

End of the scabbard cut short by the approaching year's end.

*(*IZAEMON *brushes dust from his kimono sleeve, then pulls out the thin red inner kimono of his right sleeve and places it protectively over the sword hilt. He holds the scabbard tip gently in his*

---

90 **sticky fingers** *nurete de awa*, part of a proverb meaning to handle "millet with wet fingers" (that is, to get rich without effort) leads into *awa no odaijinsama,* "Awa's millionaire." *Awa* is a kakekotoba. *Nurete* also suggests his fingers are wet with love

---

106–107 **heath . . . not so** this complicated passage contains many puns. Part of the line goes *kaza fukishinogu* (to bear the blowing wind) *shinobugusa* (fern), *shinobu to suredo* (though he hides)   111 **year's end** traditionally all debts had to be paid at the end of the year. A person down on his luck might have to settle for wearing a short sword that has been cut down from a broken long one

left hand, sighing. He looks toward the house and slaps his thigh determinedly. He tucks his hands once more into his sleeves and walks onstage, arrogant and pathetic, a fancy, funny, and thoroughly miserable young man.)

LEAD SINGER: *(Chanting rapidly, without* shamisen *accompaniment.)* Like a hunted fugitive he peeps furtively into the brothel.

(He parts the split curtain in the entry and calls inside. His voice is delicate and wan.)

IZAEMON: Are you there, Kizaemon? *(Pouting.)* Kiza. Kiza.

115　LEAD SINGER: *(Singing to* shamisen *accompaniment.)* Haughtily, fan held before his nose . . . young men pour from the house!

(IZAEMON poses facing front with his left hand tucked arrogantly in his breast. He flicks his fan half open and holds it before his face. Offstage stick drum and shamisen *play* Odoriji, *"Dance Music." A dozen* SERVANTS *rush out brandishing brooms. Music softens.)*

ALL: *(Ad-libbing.)* Yes, Master Kizaemon is in. He's here. Who wants him?

120　FIRST SERVANT: *(Contemptuously, looking* IZAEMON *up and down.)* Ehh? What kind of windblown ghost are you?

SECOND SERVANT: Damned scarecrow, what do you mean impudently calling . . .

THIRD SERVANT: . . . "Kiza, Kiza," to a gentleman?

125　FOURTH SERVANT: You talk as bold as a spender spewing out a thousand gold pieces!

FIFTH SERVANT: Idiot. What shack did they throw you out of?

SIXTH SERVANT: Don't stand before Master Kizaemon's gate . . .

SEVENTH SERVANT: . . . with your face covered, blabbing like

130　you owned the world!

EIGHTH SERVANT: Impudent beggar . . .

NINTH SERVANT: . . . know your place . . .

TENTH SERVANT: . . . or you'll see what it means to joke with us!

(They turn their backs on him. IZAEMON *lowers the fan and poses.)*

135　IZAEMON: *(Blithely.)* Who cares about a thousand gold pieces? His name is Kizaemon. I'll call him Kiza if I like. Now, I want to meet him.

(He flicks open the fan and poses, pouting. The SERVANTS *are incensed. They push their sleeves up, tie towels around their heads, and raise their brooms to beat him. Stick drum and* shamisen *play* Odoriji.)*

ALL: Meet him? What nerve! Meet this!

LEAD SINGER: *(Chanting rapidly.)* Brooms whirl! Kizaemon

140　rushes out!

(KIZEAMON, the owner of Yoshida House, flicks open the entry curtain and enters, frowning. He is middle-aged and wears a formal black cloak and tan divided trousers over a townsman's gray kimono. He restrains his employees with a gesture.)

KIZAEMON: *(Dignified.)* Come, come. There should be no disturbance on the day for auspicious New Year's rice-pounding. Think of what would happen if you injured someone with your brooms.

(Though IZAEMON *looks thoroughly disreputable,* KIZAEMON *bows politely.)*

I am Kizaemon. But who are you? Why do you want to meet　145
me?

(IZAEMON does not move or speak. KIZAEMON *edges in and tries to peer under the hat.)*

LEAD SINGER: *(Sings to* shamisen *accompaniment.)* Peering under the sedge hat . . .

IZAEMON: *(Delicately, pouting.)* It's me, Kiza.

(IZAEMON lifts the hat slightly to show his face. KIZAEMON *falls back astonished.)*

KIZAEMON: Ehh? Master Izaemon?　　　　　　　　　　　　150

IZAEMON: *(Feigning the reason he has come.)* I've wanted to meet you. So I've come.

(IZAEMON tucks his hands in his sleeves, tosses his head, and poses.)

KIZAEMON: Welcome, young Master, welcome!

(He bows very low and wipes away a tear. He turns to the SERVANTS *severely.)*

See what you've done. Who did you think this was? It is our honored Master Izaemon. Put up your brooms. Drop your　155
sleeves. Apologize and hope the Master will be good enough to forgive you. *(Bows to* IZAEMON.) Please, please forgive us.

(The SERVANTS *look sheepishly at one another, adjust their clothes, and kneel abjectly before* IZAEMON.)*

FIRST SERVANT: We were rude without thinking.

SECOND SERVANT: We were inexcusably careless . . .

THIRD SERVANT: . . . not to know a valued customer.　　160

FOURTH SERVANT: Please, excuse the dreadful thing . . .

ALL: . . . we have done.

IZAEMON: Then you will not beat me?

ALL: *(Bowing.)* Oh, no.

IZAEMON: And you won't scold me any more?　　　　　165

ALL: *(Bowing.)* Oh no, Master.

IZAEMON: *(Still piqued.)* You've made a mistake, have you?

FIRST SERVANT: We blundered, we blundered. In years we haven't made . . .

ALL: *(Prostrating themselves.)* . . . such a blunder!　　170

IZAEMON: *(Pleased with himself.)* Hmph. I should say you haven't.

KIZAEMON: Be quick now. Fix a room for our young master.

(Bowing and ad-libbing apologies, the SERVANTS *tumble over each other in their hurry to escape inside.)*

They're a troublesome bunch of boys. Ha, ha, ha! But, my how strange to see you like this. *(He shakes his head sadly　175
and blinks back tears.)* When I heard you had been disowned, two, three times I searched as far as Nara and Fushimi. How good to see you again! Come, we will go to your favorite small room. We have two years of tales to exchange. Please come this way.　　　　　　　　　　180

(Deeply moved, KIZAEMON *takes the trailing sleeve of* IZAEMON's *kimono to guide him.)*

LEAD SINGER: *(Sings to* shamisen *accompaniment.)* As he tugs upon the sleeve . . .

IZAEMON: *(Pathetically trying to maintain his dignity.)* Here. Here. Kiza. My kimono is paper, your touch is rough . . . rough.　　　　　　　　　　　　　　　　　　185

LEAD SINGER: *(Slowly, singing to* shamisen *accompaniment.)*

Pull on it and it will tear, hold it and a crease remains;
   Wandering through December.

(IZAEMON *brushes loose his sleeve, pats it gently, and poses holding it protectively to his chest.*)

In olden times the servants rushed forth to greet him;
190   Now they come out to meet him with poles raised high.

(KIZAEMON *backs off politely.* IZAEMON *gestures warningly to* KIZAEMON *with his fan, then tucks it back into his sash. He slips both arms nonchalantly inside the breast of his kimono and poses, sulking.*)

Removing his straw sandals and deep woven hat;
   Grandly he swaggers into the small banquet room.

(*He stamps and kicks off his right sandal. Instantly a black-robed stage assistant takes it away.* KIZAEMON *removes his wooden clogs and places them before his honored guest.* IZAEMON *steps into them and stands proudly in his newfound height. He unties the cord under his chin and removes the hat. His face has delicate features and is powdered white. Courtesans, forced to entertain the coarsest men, find the handsome gentleness of a man like* IZAEMON *extremely attractive. The audience applauds and shouts, "We've waited for this."* IZAEMON, *striving to maintain his dignity, flicks open his fan and turns to go.* KIZAEMON *respectfully holds his hat and gestures that it would be wiser not to enter.* IZAEMON, *determined to meet* YŪGIRI, *pulls his hat free and stamps loudly on the floor with his clog. He pouts.* KIZAEMON *bows low to his customer.* IZAEMON *smiles and passes the hat to a stage assistant. Overcome with shame at his pathetic state,* IZAEMON *holds the fan before his face. Then he flicks the other arm inside his sleeve, lifts his nose in the air, and swaggers into Yoshida House as if he owned it. Stick drum and shamisen play Odoriji.* KIZAEMON *admires* IZAEMON's *sensuous gait. He does a comic imitation: he picks up* IZAEMON's *sandals, hikes up his trousers, and walks mincingly inside.*)

SCENE 2

A guest room in the Yoshida brothel

A single ki clack signals the change of scene: lights partially dim, the front of Yoshida House is flown and the pots of pine and bamboo disappear right and left. A second ki clack signals lights to come up full. A guest room in the brothel. Snow scenes are painted on large sliding doors at the rear to the right. Left are sliding doors covered with translucent paper. New Year offerings and hanging decorations brighten the room. The TAKEMOTO SINGERS *and shamisen* PLAYERS *remain in view. Offstage Odoriji music swells. Two young* MAIDS *enter and place lighted lamps at the rear of the stage. A stage assistant in formal dress places a charcoal brazier under a frame which is covered by a gaily colored quilt to make a heater. This is put center stage.* KIZAEMON *enters from the right carrying small lacquered trays of sweets and of cakes. He puts them beside the heater. The* MAIDS *kneel by the door and bow.* IZAEMON *breezes in, his mood completely changed. He is at ease and smiles happily. After two years of penniless wandering he relishes being pampered again.* KIZAEMON *places a cushion by the heater and gestures for* IZAEMON *to accept it. He takes it as if it were his right. The* MAIDS *slip away, closing the door behind them.* KIZAEMON *kneels a respectful distance away and bows very low to welcome* IZAEMON. *He speaks with marked deference, merchant to important customer.*)

KIZAEMON: I can't say how good it is to see you well. Ah, it's so cold outside again today, please warm yourself.
IZAEMON: (*Grandly.*) I shall. Ahh. It's warm. It's warm.

(*He tries to pretend nothing is wrong, but he is chilled to the bone from the January cold and he cannot help shivering. Sliding his legs under the quilt, he rubs his hands pathetically.*)

KIZAEMON: The chill in the air is terrible. Young Master, you must be cold. Ah, my cloak!   5

(*The stage assistant places a tray holding a black cloak beside* KIZAEMON. *He crosses to* IZAEMON *and gently places the cloak over his trembling shoulders.*)

LEAD SINGER: (*Singing sadly to* shamisen *accompaniment.*) He lightly drapes the cloak . . .
IZAEMON: (*Noticing the cloak, half melancholy, half proud.*) A generous gift is presented to frozen Izaemon. Out of understanding for your feeling, he accepts it.   10

(*As if he were dressed in the height of fashion, he precisely arranges the folds of the cloak and ties the breast cord in a perfectly shaped knot. He inspects the look of the cloak and is satisfied.*)

LEAD SINGER: (*Occasional* shamisen *chords punctuate chanted phrases.*) Kizaemon carefully, gazes at the form, newly dressed in borrowed cloak.

(*Offstage* shamisen *and stick drum play* Odoriji *quietly in the background.* KIZAEMON *blinks back tears of sympathy.*)

KIZAEMON: It is clear why people say man's fate is unknowable. Who would have thought Izaemon, honored young   15
master of Fuji House, would ever wear Kizaemon's cloak, though it be made of Chinese silk or antique gold brocade. When I think how pained you must feel, hot tears boil forth.

(*His voice breaks. He places open palms to his eyes.* IZAEMON *saunters airily left.*)

IZAEMON: Ah, Kiza, no. I'm not the least bit in fashion, but I don't care. Do I complain, do I complain? No. No one really   20
knows this Izaemon. Though I've come to look like this, I don't feel vexed. And do you know why? (*He preens.*) There's a saying, "no one thinks it strange to see a horse or cow bearing heavy loads of logs, but people cheer to see a cat or a mouse do it." I suppose I shouldn't say it, but I stand un-   25
daunted though I've nothing but a paper kimono to my name. On and on, I carry on, carrying a crushing debt of half-a-million dollars. For I am Fujiya Izaemon, Japan's greatest man!

(*He smirks and poses with both hands tucked inside his kimono breast.*)

15–17 **Who . . . brocade** paraphrased from the *Wakan Sansai Zue*, a 105-volume encyclopedia, whose first volumes were published the year before the play was written   28 **half-a-million dollars** eleven thousand gold *ryō*, worth between $330,000 and $500,000. Even allowing for the fact that Izaemon is deliberately exaggerating the figure to gain sympathy, great sums were required to cut a fine figure in the licensed quarter. It was because Izaemon had squandered much of the family fortune that he had been disinherited two years before. The play does not make clear what type of business Fuji House is in, but it is a merchant family

30   My fortune is my person, my person is my gold, and so . . .
      ohhh, I'm cold. I'm cold.

*(The audience laughs as he drops his pose and scurries to the
heater to warm his hands.)*

KIZAEMON: *(Gravely.)* How fortunate for you, you are your for-
      tune. And how auspicious for us that you bring your body of
35   gold to Yoshida House in time to celebrate the New Year. Be
      fore long your disinheritance will be revoked and then you
      will return as before. That will be a happy day. *(Calls off
      right.)* Ume, where are the New Year's offerings? Bring an of-
      fering for eternal youth, quickly, in the spirit of the New
40   Year.

UME: *(Off.)* I'm coming.

LEAD SINGER: *(Singing to* shamisen *accompaniment.)* Saying
      "I shall," his wife Ume places on the shelf;
      An offering of new leaves, pomegranates, dried chestnuts,
      Tangerines, and oranges, variously arranged.

*(KIZAEMON's wife UME, carries on a small wooden tray heaped
with fruits and nuts. She places it as an offering in the alcove up
left, then kneels beside her husband. She wears a matron's dark
blue and gray kimono. Two MAIDS place a lacquered wine
pitcher and cups beside IZAEMON, bow and exit right, closing
the sliding door after them.)*

45   IZAEMON: *(Coyly.)* Yes, Ume, it's me you see.

UME: *(Bowing repeatedly.)* Ah, welcome, Master Izaemon!
      Welcome! Since you've gone we've worried about you end-
      lessly. And now to see you . . . *(She breaks off, nearly in tears.)*
      Ah, it is good to see you!

50   IZAEMON: You have not changed at all, Ume. *(Savoring his
      misery.)* Congratulations.

UME: *(Bowing.)* Thank you.

IZAEMON: And now, having congratulated you, it is time to ask
      some questions.

*(He thinks of YŪGIRI and rises on his knees, yearning for her.
Then he catches himself and looks ahead proudly.)*

55   Why is it since I've been here you haven't uttered one word
      about Yūgiri? Are the rumors I have heard true—that pining
      for me, she has fallen ill? *(Emotionally.)* Does Evening Mist,
      unsubstantial, fade and die? Well, Kizaemon, tell me. What
      has happened? Are you silent because you think I'll snivel?
60   Why should I cry? I . . . will not . . . cry. I want to hear her
      story, so I can laugh.

*(His eyes fill with tears at the thought of YŪGIRI. His lips trem-
ble. To control himself, he grasps the charcoal tongs and poses.
The tongs slip and he falls over. He laughs sheepishly and adjusts his kimono.)*

LEAD SINGER: *(Sings to* shamisen *accompaniment.)* The voice
      which says "I will not, I will not cry"
      Is clouded over by tears of anxious concern.

*(Delicately he pulls out the red inner kimono sleeve and daubs
his eyes.)*

---

57 **Evening Mist** a play on the name Yūgiri, Evening Mist, which combined with *kieru* (fade away) can mean "evening mist vanishes" or
"Yūgiri dies"

KIZAEMON: *(Quickly, bowing low.)* Surely we were impolite   65
      not to speak of Yūgiri before. Your feeling is natural. *(To
      UME.)* Ume, tell Master Izaemon the news.

*(He gestures for her to move forward. She sits quietly with hands
folded in her lap.)*

UME: In every way it would be better for you to talk with the
      young master.

KIZAEMON: *(Annoyed.)* A woman's better at something like this.   70

UME: *(Stubbornly.)* It's men's work and you should do it.

KIZAEMON: Is there no difference between a man and a
      woman? A woman is responsible in the house. You should
      tell him.

UME: No, you should tell him.   75

KIZAEMON: *(Firmly.)* You shall be the one to speak!

UME: If it's hard to do, it's always my work. Ho, ho, ho!

(The men smile. She moves closer to IZAEMON.)

      In the middle of autumn, Yūgiri fell sick with worry, but hap-
      pily, Master Izaemon, her spirits have revived. She stayed se-
      cluded in her room and I worried that she would only get   80
      worse, but fortunately a wealthy samurai from Awa has re-
      quested her.

IZAEMON: *(Shocked.)* What?

UME: For days he has insisted she must come out for New Year.
      At last she has consented. She meets him in the inner room   85
      today.

*(IZAEMON rushes desperately to her. Like a little boy pleading for
a favor from his mother, he falls to his knees, placing both hands
on her waist.)*

IZAEMON: Really, is it true? Are you fibbing to me?

UME: If you want to know whether it's true or not, look
      through the doors yourself.

LEAD SINGER: *(Sings rapidly to strong* shamisen *accompani-*   90
      ment.) Izaemon's face is stricken!

(In time to rhythmic chords of Takemoto shamisen *music, IZAE-
MON rises and turns toward the sliding paper doors left. He
scarcely knows what he is doing. The cloak falls unnoticed to the
floor. Like a drunken man, he reels and staggers to the doors. His
hands tremble so violently he can hardly grasp them, then he
flings them open revealing an empty room with another set of
sliding doors at the rear. Music gradually accelerates. Dancing
in time to the music, he throws these doors open and stands
transfixed at the sight of the shadows of YŪGIRI and HIRAOKA
cast on the thin paper of yet another set of inner sliding doors.
They are drinking and gesticulating animatedly. Their heads
blend together. He falls back helplessly. Silently he appeals to
UME.)*

LEAD SINGER: For a moment there are no words he can utter!

*(UME approaches with the cloak. He turns wildly, as if to burst
through the doors into the adjoining room. Then his resolution
ebbs and he turns to UME. She drapes the cloak over his shoulders, kneels, and restrains him by placing both hands on his
sash. They pose. The cloak slips to the floor and a stage assistant
whisks it out of sight. Takemoto* shamisen *play quietly in the
background.)*

IZAEMON: *(Wretchedly.)* Oh! She seems in miraculously good
      spirits all right. In my good-natured way, I couldn't conceive
      of such a thing happening. It's true, from the time the world   95

began, who has ever heard of a sincere whore or a bespectacled blind man? You think I came here today wanting to see Yūgiri's face. How mortifying. I didn't at all. *(Nose in the air.)* There's not a smidgen of love left in my heart for that . . . har
100 lot, but as you know the wretch bore me a son. He's just seven this year.

(Sinks to his knees with a self-pitying sigh.)

One of your old crones said he's been put out for adoption, but I don't believe he's been adopted. I suppose you've had him strangled . . . and his body thrown away. Ohhhh!

(He rises and stamps in pique. UME *and* KIZAEMON *exchange shocked looks.* IZAEMON *is oblivious to everything except his own problems.)*

105 There's no mistake about it: I thought I was a rake buying a whore, but what I raked up was trash.
UME: *(Protesting.)* But why do you say that?
IZAEMON: *(Petulant.)* Can you ask why? I've spent a fortune and all I've got from her are love letters—eleven thousand
110 ryō of waste paper! *(He gestures with his fan.)* Why, if I piled them up, I'll bet I could build Mt. Fuji in papier-mâché! Oh, look. *(He sinks slowly to his knees.)* I've soaked my precious paper kimono crying out useless tears. How absurd.

(He realizes he has been daubing his eyes with the trailing sleeve of his kimono. Gently he wipes the dampened right sleeve. This finished, he flips both arms inside his kimono, stands erect, and strikes a martyred pose.)

And now, before the seams of my kimono sleeves disinte
115 grate, I think I shall go.

(With his nose in the air and a self-pitying look on his face, he sashays toward the door, hoping of course to be stopped. UME *kneels before him, blocking his way.)*

UME: Master Izaemon, let the fact that the guest in the inner room is no ordinary person be food for thought.
IZAEMON: *(Brightly.)* Hah! He could be a fancy dish or pot luck for all I care. I've had my fill, thank you!
120 UME: You musn't fly off the handle so, young Master.
IZAEMON: If I do, I'll hit her with it. Hmph! "Evening Mist." I haven't missed her evenings!
LEAD SINGER: *(Singing.)* Hiding her smile . . .

(UME can't help smiling. Proud of his witticisms, IZAEMON *nods grandly to them and starts to go. She detains him by holding his sleeve.)*

IZAEMON: No, I'm thinking of going away. You shouldn't try to
125 prevent me.

(He pulls gently on his sleeve; she continues to hold it.)

96–97 **who . . . blind man** "No one has seen a sincere prostitute nor a picture of a *karyōbinga* rooster" (a mythical bird mentioned in Buddhist sutras) in Chikamatsu's text is usually changed to this easier form. Few in the Japanese audience would understand the original 106 **trash** a pun on *keiseigai* (buying a prostitute) and *kamikuzukai* (trash man) 116 **guest** Hiraoka's wife, who is caring for the child of Izaemon and Yūgiri. She has come disguised as her husband. This is not important in the versions of the play performed now, for none of the preceding nor following acts are done. These lines and following contain a number of puns on food and dishes

I'm going to go.

(He pulls again but she does not release her hold. He claps his hands delightedly.)

I know what I'll do. I'll walk around the room.

(UME covers a smile and releases his sleeve. He adjusts his kimono and fixes his hair, as if getting ready for a public promenade. Takemoto shamisen play occasional chords as accompaniment. He flicks his arms inside the kimono sleeves and casually circles the room. He passes the doors to the inner room, then stops, drawn back irresistibly toward them. He is enraged to see the shadows on the paper doors. He clenches his fists. He is about to throw the doors open, but then realizes he is powerless to interfere. Furious at his impotence, he stamps toward the door.)

Ahh! I'm going!

(UME restrains him. He pretends to struggle.)

UME: Do not go. I'll warm some sake.
IZAEMON: No, no. I'm leaving. *(Hesitates.)* Or should I stay? 130 Or should I go? *(Blithely.)* I'll just take a nap.

(In an instant he is curled up under the quilt of the heater, head resting on his arm and for all the world asleep.)

KIZAEMON: *(In a whisper.)* You didn't have to say so much about Yūgiri.
UME: Eh? "Tell, tell him," you said. I told him, that's all.
KIZAEMON: You didn't have to jabber on and on. Well, get him 135 a pillow. Quickly, now.
UME: Yes, yes.

(A stage assistant passes her a headrest which she gently places under IZAEMON's *head.* IZAEMON *pretends to be asleep.* KIZAEMON *and* UME *tiptoe to the door. Fondly, they look back at* IZAEMON.)*

KIZAEMON: It's so like the young master, he hasn't changed a bit. In the past, I honored him like the God of Fortune and now he's destitute. Yet he doesn't grudge us our good life. 140 Ah, he's the son of a great family for certain. In the end, he'll apologize or the family will relent. He'll be taken back, I'm sure. Stay here ten thousand days, young Master.
LEAD SINGER: *(Singing to shamisen accompaniment.)* There is fondness in their hearts as they leave the room. Looking after 145 them, Izaemon . . .

(They slip silently through the doors up right and close them.)

IZAEMON: *(Sighs and sits up.)* That kind couple still cares for me, even as I am. I can never forget it. Comparing them with Yūgiri . . . agh!

(His heart is torn by the thought of YŪGIRI *with another man. Yet there is nothing he can do. Fuming, he flounces over to the wine tray and plops down on his knees. A half-dozen graduated wine cups stand in a pile. He carelessly tosses the small ones over his shoulder. When he reaches the last, large, saucerlike cup, he fills it and lifts it to his lips. He stops, gazing forlornly ahead.)*

How changed is my appearance. What hasn't changed is the 150 gaiety of the quarter.

(He doesn't really like sake, but he tosses the drink down and then chokes. Offstage Nagauta singing begins from the geza.)

SOLO SINGER: (*Lyric singing to* shamisen *accompaniment expressing* YŪGIRI's *feelings.*) Looking back through time; Even one's bitter grief is remembered fondly.

(*Noticing a drop of wine on his precious kimono sleeve, he wipes it away.*)

155   More painful still than meeting an endearing man; At Osaka's barrier gate are the world's lessons.

(*He puts away the wine cup, slaps his thigh determinedly, and begins to mime playing a shamisen.*)

IZAEMON: (*Wistfully.*) Play away, play away. Hearing that song reminds me of autumn a year ago, when we viewed the moon, enraptured, from our private room. We were so happy.

(*He realizes he should be angry. He folds his arms across his chest.*)

160   Of all people, to think that you would deceive me . . .

(*He clenches his teeth and makes a fist, looking about for someone on whom to vent his anger. Then, realizing how foolish he looks, his shoulders slump.*)

SOLO SINGER: (*Continuing offstage.*) The flow of their affections blocked unexpectedly; Turns into stagnant marshland, a brackish pool.

(*Seeing no way out, he drops down by the wine tray, pours and drinks recklessly. He seizes the headrest and rushes to the sliding doors as if to hurl it into the inner room. He feels the seams of his paper kimono straining. Quickly he drops the headrest to the floor. Again his mood changes: like a pampered prince, he delicately arranges the kimono's folds and poses.*)

IZAEMON: (*Lightly, ruefully.*) It's true, every person in the world feels love and sorrow. But an outcast like me isn't even considered. When I rage or pout in the corner, no one pays any attention. Very well then, I'm going home. Hmph. Sincere harlot. I'm going home.

(*To occasional chords of offstage* Sugagaki shamisen *music, he arranges his dress, and walks elegantly to seven-three on the* hanamichi. *He tries to pose grandly, arms tucked inside his kimono sleeves, but the effect is marred by a hangdog look in his eyes. He faces the audience, speaking with deep melancholy.*)

170   I have been shown kindness by some. Forgive me, for leaving without saying goodbye . . . Kizaemon.

SOLO SINGER: (*Continues offstage.*) The heart's innermost feelings go misunderstood; Until the moonlight makes clear our affection.

(*He turns back for what he intends to be a final look, but he cannot take his eyes from the doors separating him from* YŪGIRI. *Without realizing what he is doing, he runs back pell-mell, clambering over the heater in his haste. He stops, knowing he can't do anything, and sits inelegantly on the heater. A single* ki *clack: doors upstage right open showing a* TOKIWAZU *ensemble of four* SINGERS *and four* shamisen PLAYERS *seated on a dais. They wear formal black kimonos and outer garments of deep green.*)

TOKIWAZU SINGERS: (*In a high, lyric style to* shamisen *accompaniment.*) How pitiful she, this Yūgiri; Times of long ago flow past, fond remembrance.

(*A* CHILD MAID, *dressed in a brilliant red kimono with trailing sleeves, demurely brings on* YŪGIRI's *tobacco tray. She places it beside* IZAEMON *and exits. He pretends indifference until the* MAID *is gone, then he almost falls from the heater in his excitement. He straightens his kimono and slicks down his hair with moistened palms. He cannot decide how to receive* YŪGIRI. *First he plans to treat her formally: he kneels at the far edge of the room, placing his hands deliberately on his knees and looking coldly ahead.*)

Within the inner chamber he heart leaps with joy; Ties of their affection still happily undestroyed.

(*A second* CHILD MAID, *dressed like the first, places a small tray of sweets beside the tobacco tray and exits. It is torture for* IZAEMON *to keep from peeking to see if* YŪGIRI *is coming. Finally he cranes his neck to look. She isn't there. He gets an idea: he claps his hands and tiptoes to the door, tripping and almost falling on the way. He tries to peek in. Then he hides at the side of the door, ready to shout "Surprise!" when she enters. Again he changes his mind. He sits cross-legged, fingers laced over his knees.*)

Breast from breast and heart from heart a mountain divides; And just as much divided by the sliding doors.   180

(IZAEMON *gives up his pose on the heater and jumps to his feet. Now frantic over her impending arrival, he tries out various attitudes—aloof, stern, friendly, casual—but in the end abandons them all to slide under the quilt. With one motion he scoops in the headrest and feigns sleep. Tempo of Tokiwazu music quickens. The sliding doors center open and* YŪGIRI *enters, followed by the two* CHILD MAIDS. *Her blushing pink kimono is almost completely hidden by a long outer robe of black silk embroidered with cranes and pine branches symbolic of the New Year. A thick wad of folded paper held before her downcast eyes hides her face. She enters slowly, moving sensuously.*)

Yearning to glimpse his dear face from morning till night, She joyfully approaches, rushing to his side.

(*She drops the paper from her eyes and looks up. Her white face is delicately formed and extremely beautiful. Fans shout the actor's name. She pivots gracefully to face upstage, then slowly turns her head to gaze over her shoulder at* IZAEMON. YŪGIRI *embodies all the attractive features of the Genroku courtesan; she is physically alluring, accomplished, sophisticated, and, in spite of her profession, can lose her heart to an attractive man. She is deeply in love with* IZAEMON.)

I bring my body next to yours, within the same robe; Let it cover both of us, quickly let us sleep; Enfolding holding him fast Yūgiri weeps.   185

(YŪGIRI *dismisses the* MAIDS *with a gesture. They exit up center. Looking at* IZAEMON, *she has to stifle tears. Quickly she crosses beside him and drops to her knees. With a deliberate gesture, she sweeps the trailing robe protectively over him.*)

---

156 **Osaka's barrier** one of the great barriers that had to be passed in traveling between Kyoto and Edo, and in poetry its mention suggests melancholy parting

185 **Yūgiri weeps** the Tokiwazu lyrics are particularly rich with puns, internal rhymes, and engo

YŪGIRI: (*Speaking with exquisite sadness, each word greatly pro-longed.*) Izaemon. Izaemon. Do open your eyes. I . . . am ill.

TOKIWAZU SINGERS: (*Continuing.*) Although death long ago would have come surely;

190   Until today the thread of life is unbroken,
Held firm by compassionate Gods and the Buddha.

(*She falls back as if in sudden pain. She immediately pretends nothing has happened, posing sadly, gazing at his closed eyes.*)

"Have you no feeling of yearning for me?
Don't you wish to see my face?" she asks tenderly.
Hoping to rouse him she lifts and cradles his head.

(*She places her hand gently on his shoulder and rocks him back and forth. She leans closer, half-cradling his head in her arms. He does not react. Hurt, she pokes his shoulder.*)

195   TAKEMOTO SINGER: (*To shamisen accompaniment.*) She sharply pushes him . . .

(IZAEMON *sits up and pushes her away. He adopts a lordly atti-tude, not even looking in her direction.*)

IZAEMON: (*Rudely.*) Here, here. What are you doing, Miss Whatever-they-call-you. Miss Evening Mist—or is it Miss Evening Meal?—I'm not like you, indolently carousing
200   around at the year's end. This Izaemon labors night and day to earn a living for he carries a debt of eleven thousand ryō. He has to sleep whenever he can, so he thanks you not to dis-turb him. (*Coldly, over his shoulder.*) Miss Street Slut.

(*He slaps the floor for emphasis, pulls in the headrest, and snug-gles down under the quilt.*)

TAKEMOTO SINGER: (*Singing to shamisen accompaniment.*)
205   Rolling over on his side, he pretends to snore . . .

YŪGIRI: Izaemon! You have no reason to speak that way. Why are you angry? Tell me or you will not sleep. I shall not allow it.

(*She shakes his shoulders, first gently, then more firmly when he does not move. Suddenly he sits up, shaking her off.*)

IZAEMON: (*Coldly, furious.*) Stop it! Don't come close to me! I
210   may have been disinherited, but no courtesan who's been kicked and tumbled in the next room gets near Fujiya Izae-mon! See here, Miss Streetwalker, come back in spring when the weather suits your trade. Now get out. Get out!

(*He flicks open his fan and waves her away as if she were some kind of loathsome beggar. He stamps away left to be rid of her.*)

TAKEMOTO SINGERS: (*In unison.*) Though he says, "get out,
215   get out . . ."

(*She gasps and covers her mouth to hide her anguish. Suddenly afraid he has gone too far,* IZAEMON *peeps at her from behind his open fan.*)

YŪGIRI: (*Faintly.*) What? You call Yūgiri a streetwalker?

IZAEMON: Can you say you don't know why? When you let a *samurai* kick his way into your affections, that's what you are, a streetwalker, I say!

TAKEMOTO SINGERS: (*Singing in unison to* shamisen *accom-   220
paniment.*) "Felicitous morn," some write this New Year.

(*He points to his foot and mimes kicking her. He thrusts his leg forward again, this time with erotic suggestiveness.*)

IZAEMON: Furthermore, he probably did it wearing clogs! Hah!

(IZAEMON *stamps and derisively scuffs his foot in her direction.*)

TAKEMOTO SINGERS: (*Continuing in unison.*) Highly stilted passages honor the year end;   225
"Felicitous morn," some write this New Year.

(*Takemoto* shamisen *and small offstage drums play strong, rhythmic accompaniment as* IZAEMON, *in a fit of pique, drops to his knees by the food trays and pelts* YŪGIRI *with soft rice cakes. He is about to throw the cake stand as well, until he notices it is similar in shape to the small* nō *shoulder drum. Instantly forget-ting his anger, he dances and mimes playing the drum.* YŪGIRI *slowly lowers her head, weeping.*)

IZAEMON: (*Cruelly.*) In any case, it's all part of a day's work, isn't it. There's no harm done if a customer kicks you. Be-cause if there's no lust in him you can't make a living! Agh!

(IZAEMON *drops the stand. He coldly turns from* YŪGIRI *and poses with his arms tucked in the breast of his kimono.*)

TAKEMOTO SINGERS: (*Continuing in unison.*) Youths lustfully   230
greet their revered streetwalkers;
Highly stilted passages honor the year end;
"Felicitous morn," some write this New Year.

(IZAEMON *flicks open his fan and turns on* YŪGIRI *spitefully.*)

IZAEMON: If a *samurai* can kick Yūgiri, so can a merchant. If a merchant can kick you, so can Izaemon. Kick, kick, kick!   235

(*He was worked himself into such a rage he can scarcely speak. He stamps repeatedly on the floor, then plops down by the trays.*)

Ah, Kiza! Who cares if it's mochi or stale rice for a street slut!

(*He knocks the tray to the floor. Suddenly facing her, he pulls back his kimono sleeve and raises his fist.*)

TAKEMOTO SINGER: (*Sings rapidly to* shamisen *accompani-ment.*) His long pent-up grievances burst out in tearful words;
Pulling tobacco tray close he lights the long pipe.   240

190–191 **thread . . . Buddha** in popular belief Shintō gods or the Bud-dha could hold a person back from death with an unseen rope (*hikaezuna*)   198 **Miss Evening Meal** this is a direct translation of a rather cruel pun on the name Yūgiri-*dono* (Miss Evening Mist) and the made-up word *yūmeshi-dono* (Miss Evening Meal)

220 **singing . . . accompaniment** Chikamatsu here paraphrases the lyrics of a New Year's song of low-class street entertainers (*manzai*) to whom Izaemon has just compared Yūgiri, calling her a *manzai geisei*, "street prostitute"   221 **some write** Chikamatsu intends *sorai* (is) to suggest *samurai*, as in translation "some write" could be heard in performance as "felicitous morn, *samurai*, this New Year"   232 **highly stilted passages** Chikamatsu's *kakekotoba* in this line is *ashida* (high clog), which also suggests *ashita* (morning). Courtesans wore tall clogs, often fourteen inches high, when they paraded through the quar-ter. "Stilted passages" becomes the *kakekotoba* in translation. The line can be taken to mean "streetwalkers' highly stilted passages" (parade of clogs) or "stilted (poetic) passages honor the New Year"

(He tries to smoke, but is so furious he can't get the tobacco into the small bowl and can't hold the pipe still enough over the coals to get a light. This enrages him even more. He knocks the tobacco out and half turning to her, raises the pipe as if to strike her. She recoils. With an expression of helpless disgust, he whirls front and slams the pipe onto the floor. He sighs.)

He adopts an attitude of cool unconcern.

(He turns his back on her and sits with fingers laced casually around his knees. He poses sadly. A stage assistant takes off trays and cakes.)

TOKIWAZU SINGERS: *(Sing slowly to lyric shamisen accompaniment.)* Though they may say the bitter grief Yūgiri feels;
Teardrops brimming in her eyes to be so reviled;
245   Is natural in a quarrel between two lovers.

(To stifle her tears YŪGIRI clenches the wad of tissue between her teeth. Rising on her knees, she poses, gazing at IZAEMON. She puts most of the paper back in the front of her kimono. The rest she rolls into a ball, which she almost throws angrily at his back. It hurts her that he seems so unconcerned, and she tucks the paper away in her sleeve pathetically.)

From the day our flirtation, thin as watery blue,
    Became deep-eyed with loving one another;

(IZAEMON tucks both hands in the breast of his kimono. He rises grandly and turns to go. Quickly she blocks his way. Gently placing her hands against his chest, she forces him back one, two, three steps. Pretending unconcern, he drops to one knee. She kneels beside him and arranges his hair with a pin that she takes from her elaborate hairdo. Although this is a sign of deep affection, he shakes her off, sulking.)

Have such ties of love been known, even in Cathay?

(He rises to leave again, but she drapes her arms over his shoulders to restrain him. With an elegant movement he pivots, holding the lapel of her robe so it falls from one of her shoulders and onto his in one motion. She kneels. They pose holding the robe between them. Then he breaks away, wearing the robe himself. With a disdainful shrug, he poses.)

Flaunting our great affair, I lived joyously;

(He shivers and huddles under the robe, then, like a sulking boy, pulls the robe over his head. A hand snakes out from the robe hunting for a pipe. She hurries to his side, picks up a pipe, wipes it with her sleeve, and offers it to him.)

250   Though people spoke slanderously of my obligations.

(Peeping out from the robe and seeing her grief-stricken face, he is almost moved, but his hand gets tangled in the bulky sleeve as he reaches for the pipe and he ends up angry once more. Together, they lean over the coals of the tobacco tray to light their pipes. She purposely brings her pipe near his, only to have him knock it out of the way so he can go first. He raises the pipe as if to strike her. When she recoils, he slaps the pipe down loudly on the floor and poses with his back to her.)

246–247 **thin . . . deep-dyed** there is a double engo in these lines (*mizuasagi omoisometa*): water engo (*mizu* means water and *someta* dyed in liquid); and color engo (*mizuasagi* means watery blue and *someta*, dyed, implies color)

TAKEMOTO SINGER: *(Sings to slow shamisen accompaniment.)*
    Though seen sharing the same bed, sleeping back-to-back;
    They stretch the fragile ties of love unthinkingly.

(They rise and stand back-to-back. She blinks back tears; he sighs with self-pity. Thinking of their unhappy situation, he slowly drops to his knees. She kneels beside him and when she reaches out to touch his shoulder, he coldly brushes the hand away.)

Their lovers' quarrel ended, morning bells sounding;
    Hatefully it seems to them, the birds sing at dawn.   255

(He rises and crosses elegantly to the heater where he sits in a swaggering pose, hands tucked into the back of his sash. She kneels at his feet. She takes one of the sleeves of the black robe and wraps it around her arm, tying them together. She looks up imploringly. They pose.)

Love cannot be as you wish, it goes its own way;
    Yet the only happiness in this broad world;
    True love to true love.

(She leans against his thigh seductively. Still not mollified, IZAEMON pushes her away and throws off the robe, which a stage assistant quickly takes off. She pulls his sleeve to show him a letter scroll that she takes up from a small tray stage left. He snatches it from her, extends it like a telescope, and peers at the audience. He lifts it as if to strike her. She gently retrieves the scroll, then throws it across stage with a flourish. It unrolls some ten or twelve feet, stopping in front of IZAEMON. They hold opposite ends of the love letter. They recall the past, posing sadly. Then he remembers he is angry with her: he yanks on the letter, ripping it in half. She sinks to the floor, her half of the crumpled letter clutched to her breast. Again they pose.)

TAKEMOTO SINGER: *(Chants in regular rhythm to strong shamisen accompaniment.)* "Can you still think of Yūgiri as a   260
    prostitute?"

(Reading the letter and recalling the past, she is near tears. He lets it slip idly from his fingers, circles the stage nonchalantly, and slides under the quilt to go to sleep.)

"Am I not really your wife? I had just turned fifteen the year end we met. Now our child is seven."

(With the love letter dangling a few inches from his face, IZAEMON can't resist the impulse to see what YŪGIRI has written. He comes across a complimentary passage. Flattered, he beams and nods approvingly. He catches himself and rolls over as if asleep.)

"When writing your family, isn't it true that I sign 'Izaemon's   265
wife' without any blame?"

(She rises on her knees and points to the letter. He shrugs and thrusts his hands deeper into the quilt.)

"If you feel bitterly toward me, I too have reason to feel bitterness toward you."

(Passing the letter to a stage assistant, she reaches under the quilt from the opposite side of the heater, searching for his hands. With a childish smirk, he lifts the heater, quilt and all, and crosses past the startled YŪGIRI to sit stage left.)

"A full year and more has passed without a word of news."

(She kneels beside him, lovingly putting her arms around his shoulders. He shrugs free and escapes, with the heater, to the other side of the stage.)

"Worrying about you constantly, I became ill."

(*Very agitated,* YŪGIRI *rises, not knowing what to do. She feels a sharp pain and, uttering a tiny cry, collapses to the floor.*)

270 Can it be you have not noticed her wasted form, her life but barely extended by ointments and potions, massages and acupuncture?

(*He rushes to her and begins to massage her back. This has no effect, so he crosses to the door, calling for help in mime. In the end he stands helplessly watching her.*)

"I had thought to greet you with, 'I have waited for our meeting so long,' but instead I am met with abuse."

(*He pours a cup of wine for her, but her accusing face shames him so he turns away and passes the wine over his shoulder. She places her hands on his sash and looks up into his eyes. He is deeply moved. They pose.*)

275 "If you think I no longer love you, why don't you just kick me, why don't you just beat me?"

(*He proudly circles the stage and drops under the quilt again. She poses, holding a lavender and red silk scarf which a stage assistant has passed to her. She holds it up for him to see: on it are the intertwined crests of the actors playing* YŪGIRI *and* IZAEMON, *showing the linking of their lives.*)

"Yūgiri is dying. My only prayer: that I may see your smiling face."

(*She crosses behind him and gently forces him to his knees. She poses with the cloth clenched between her teeth to stop the pain. Then she falls to the floor, quietly weeping.*)

280 Raising her tearful voice, "How can you remain so heartless, hating me this way," she gropes across the floor. Thinking neither of past nor of future, their hearts are turbulent.

(*They grope toward each other. Center, their hands touch. He places his hands on her thighs. She looks up coquettishly. They embrace, reconciled. They hear someone approaching. He scurries to the door. She rises on her knees and places her palms together in prayer. He kneels beside her and gently separates her hands with his own clasped palms, indicating it is for him to pray, not her. They sit silently, heads bowed. Then they both begin to weep quietly. Suddenly loud bata-bata tsuke beats are heard. Stick drum and shamisen play lively* Odoriji. IZAEMON *moves protectively behind* YŪGIRI. KIZAEMON, UME, *and the* MAIDS *file on from inside and kneel. They are beaming and chattering animatedly. Music changes to rhythmic, rapid Hayawatari, "Rapid*

Crossing." *The curtain at the end of the* hanamichi *flies open and a procession of eighteen* CLERKS *and* SERVANTS *from the House of Fuji march on. They wear conservative brown and blue kimonos. Each carries a heavy, locked strongbox, filled with gold pieces. They chant in unison as they walk, "Essa! Essa! Essa!" Music fades away.*)

UME: (*Bowing.*) Wonderful news, young Master! Your family has relented. They wish you back and all the people of your house are here to welcome you.

IZAEMON: (*With a delighted expression.*) Really? They aren't 285 angry any more?

KIZAEMON: Nothing could be greater cause for rejoicing! Enter! Enter!

(*He waves the procession onstage. Hayawatari resumes. The men stack the boxes in an impressive pyramid in the center of the stage. Each box contains a thousand ryō, together enough to retire* IZAEMON's *debts and release* YŪGIRI *from her contract.*)

MEN: (*Bowing.*) We rejoice for you, young Master!

IZAEMON: (*Almost dancing for joy.*) How marvelous! What 290 great good fortune! Come everyone! Clap with me!

(*All join him in the ritual ten hand claps—three, three, three, one—that celebrate an auspicious event.*)

ALL: (*Bowing to* IZAEMON.) We offer our congratulations!

(IZAEMON *preens delightedly.* YŪGIRI *and* UME *exchange knowing glances and smile.* IZAEMON *struts back to get* YŪGIRI's *black robe from a stage assistant. She rises and they exchange positions. He drapes the robe over her shoulders.*)

TOKIWAZU SINGERS: (*Sing slowly, lyrically to* shamisen *accompaniment.*) Izaemon's eyes twinkle in carefree happiness;
The name of Yūgiri shall bloom, like a spring flower; 295
Before admiring eyes, through all the ages.

(YŪGIRI *drops to her knees and faces front.* IZAEMON *sits possessively on the money boxes, grins, and flicks open his fan. He glances happily at* YŪGIRI. *A single ki clack. The cast poses in a group, or hippari, mie as Odoriji swells and the curtain is run quickly closed to a crescendo of ki clacks. Two ki clacks signal large drum to play Uchidashi, which concludes the performance.*)

SD **each box** the amount—eighteen thousand *ryō,* or between $540,000 and $800,000—presumably in the chests, is not to be taken literally. The point is that a certain number of chests must be brought in to make an appropriately big pyramid on stage

CRITICAL CONTEXTS

Although Zeami's treatises describe the practical and esthetic foundations of the Noh theater, they were not well known until the twentieth century. Since the Noh was organized around prominent families of actors, Zeami's texts were passed on in private and shown only to those who had been properly initiated. The first definitive edition of the treatises was published in 1940.

In "Teachings on Style and the Flower," Zeami discusses the training of Noh performers, emphasizing the interplay between physical training, spiritual development, and acting style in the production of the "flower"—beauty—in Noh performance. In this translation, the central term yugen *has been translated as "Grace."*

In searching for the origins of *sarugaku* and *ennen*, some say they came from India, and some say they have been handed down since the age of the gods. Yet as time moves on and those ages grow remote, any proper skill is lacking to learn the ancient ways precisely. The origin of the *nō*, which all enjoy today, goes back to the reign of the Empress Suiko, when Prince Shōtoku commanded Hata no Kōkatsu (some say for the sake of peace in the country, some say to entertain the people) to create sixty-six public entertainments, which were named *sarugaku*. From that time onward, men in every age must have used images of the beauties of nature as a means to render this entertainment more elegant. Later, the descendants of Kōkatsu inherited this art and served as the Kasuga and Hie shrines.[1] This is why, even now, those performers from Yamato and Ōmi perform rites at both temples, which are still flourishing. Therefore, while studying the old and admiring the new, the great traditions of elegance must never be slighted. A truly skillful player is one whose speech lacks no refinement and whose appearance creates a feeling of Grace. One who wishes to follow the path of the *nō* must engage himself in no other art. There is one exception: the art of poetry deserves study, for it is a means to open the actor to the profound beauties of nature and enrich his life. I will note here in general various things I have seen and heard since my youth concerning the practice of the *nō*.

—Sensual pleasures, gambling, heavy drinking represent the Three Prohibitions. Such was the precept of my late father.

—Rehearse with the greatest effort; do not be overbearing with others.

AGE SEVEN   It may be said of our art that one may begin at seven.[2] When a boy practices at this age, he will naturally of his own accord show some elements of beauty in what he does. If, by chance, he should show some special skill in dancing, movement, chanting, or in the kind of powerful gestures required for demon roles, he should be left free to perform them in his own manner, according to his own desires. He should certainly not be instructed as to what he did well and what he did poorly. If rehearsals are too strict, and if the child is admonished too much, he will lose his enthusiasm. If the *nō* becomes unpleasant for him, then his progress will cease. He should only be taught dancing, movement, and the chant. In particular, he should not be instructed in the fine points of Role Playing, even though he may show aptitude for it. He must not be permitted to perform in a *waki sarugaku*, especially on an open stage. Let him perform at a time that seems appropriate, in the third or fourth play in the day's program, when he can be given a part he can perform with skill.

AGE OF ELEVEN OR TWELVE   From this age onward, the voice begins to achieve its proper pitch, and the actor can begin to comprehend the *nō*. Therefore, various aspects of the art can now

**FROM
"TEACHINGS ON
STYLE AND THE
FLOWER"
(1402)**

TRANSLATED BY
J. THOMAS RIMER AND
YAMAZAKI MASAKAZU

**ITEMS
CONCERNING
THE PRACTICE
OF THE NŌ IN
RELATION TO
THE AGE OF
THE ACTOR**

---

[1]The Yamato *sarugaku* troupe had an official affiliation with the Kasuga Shrine in Nara. A series of *nō* performances was included in the important Wakamiya festival held there. The Ōmi troupe had official ties with the Hie Shrine on Mount Hiei, to the north of Kyoto, the site of the great Buddhist temple complex of Enryakuji.

[2]Traditionally, ages were calculated so that a person was considered one year old at birth and two at the beginning of the next calendar year. Thus the ages given here are higher than would have been assigned to a Western actor at the same stage of development. Thus Zeami's actor at the age of seventeen or eighteen would probably be, by Western reckoning, between fourteen and sixteen.

be explained. In the first place, a boy's appearance, no matter in what aspect, will produce the sensation of Grace. And his voice at this age will always sound charming as well. Because of those two strong points, any defects can be hidden and the good points will be made all the more evident. On the whole, it is better not to teach any fine points concerning Role Playing for a child's performance, for such knowledge would make his performances at this stage seem inappropriate and, in fact, hinder further progress in his art. Later, as he becomes more skillful, he should be allowed to practice every element of the art. With the appearance and voice of a child, a boy actor, if he shows skill in his performance, can hardly give a bad impression. Still, this Flower is not the true Flower. It is only a temporary bloom. For that reason, practice at this time is easily managed. This does not mean that, because of this one flowering, he will always appear to be so skillful. As rehearsal at this age will always allow the young actor to create the impression of the Flower through his good points, the development of his basic skills is crucial. His movements must be authentic, the words of his chanting distinct, and his positions for dancing must be well fixed. These skills must be carefully and thoroughly rehearsed.

FROM THE AGE OF SEVENTEEN OR EIGHTEEN This is a particularly crucial period, and not too many kinds of training can be arranged. First of all, since the actor's voice is changing, he loses his first Flower. His physical figure changes as well, and his movements become awkward. Before, his voice was full and beautiful, and it was easy for him to perform; now, realizing that the rules have changed, the actor's will falters. What is more, since the audience may look scornfully at his performance, he now feels embarrassed and discouraged. As concerns training, then, at this age, the actor, even though there are those who may point to him and laugh, must take no note, but retire to his own house, and, in a pitch comfortable to him, practice his chanting, using appropriate techniques for morning and evening.[3] Most important of all, he must vow to himself that, although he is now in a crucial period, he will truly stake his life on the *nō* and never abandon it. Should any actor give up his training at this point, his skill can never increase. In general, although the pitch of the individual voice at this age may vary, it usually lies between the *ōshiki* and the *banshiki*.[4] If the actor tries to regulate the pitch too strictly [by forcing], he risks getting into bad habits with his posture. Then too, this may be the cause of damage to the actor's voice in later life.

FROM TWENTY-FOUR OR TWENTY-FIVE It is in this period that the level of artistry of the performer begins to become established. The limits of the actor will be fixed by his training and his self-discipline. His voice will by now have settled, and his body will have matured. These are the strong points required in our art: voice and physical appearance. Both of these become fixed at this period. This is the time in an actor's life when the art is born that will lead to the skills of his later years. In the eyes of others, it may well appear that a new and highly skilled performer has appeared. Therefore, even though he is being judged against a performer who is already highly regarded, it may seem on the occasion of his performance that his Flower is a new and fresh one, and, should he win a competition, others may praise him beyond his due, so that the actor himself comes to believe that he is already highly skilled. I cannot stress often enough that such an attitude serves as an enemy to the actor. For such is not the true Flower. A truly novel Flower comes about because of the actor's age and experience, when his spectators can truly be surprised. Spectators of real discernment are able to make this distinction. It would indeed be a shame if this early Flower, which actually represents only the actor's first level of accomplishment, should somehow be fixed in the actor's thoughts, so that he sees this phase as the culmination of his art, and therefore indulges himself in what is a deviation from the true path. Actually, even if an actor is praised by his audience and manages to win a competition over a famous performer, he must take cognizance of the fact that his Flower is merely a temporary one; therefore, he will begin at once to study Role Playing with the utmost seriousness and will ask every detail of those who have already achieved a real reputation for their performances, so that he may rehearse all the more diligently. One who believes

---

[3] Zeami's remark suggests that a certain caution must be used when exercising the voice in the morning, whereas in the evening the voice is freer and can thus be exercised more vigorously.

[4] *Ōshiki* and *banshiki* are two of the twelve pitches in the traditional Japanese musical scales. *Ōshiki* is considered to correspond roughly to the pitch A in the Western musical scale, *banshiki* to B.

that this temporary Flower is the real Flower is one who has separated himself from the true way. And indeed, any performer can be taken in by this temporary Flower and so fail to realize that he is losing the real one. Such is the situation of a young actor.

Here is one point that must be considered carefully. If one has a true ability to understand his own level of perfection in his art, then he can never lose that level of the Flower. If an actor thinks he has attained a higher level of skill than he has reached, however, he will lose even the level that he has achieved. This matter must be thought over carefully.

THIRTY-FOUR OR THIRTY-FIVE YEARS This age represents the peak of perfection in our art. If an actor grasps the various items set down here, and masters them, he will truly be acknowledged by the public and will achieve a reputation as a great actor. If such public recognition does not come, however, and he does not obtain such a reputation, then no matter how skillful the actor may be, he must recognize the fact that he is not one who has yet found the true Flower. And if he has not obtained such a Flower by this time, his art will begin to decline when he is forty. The proof of this fact will become clear as the actor grows older. An actor is on the rise until he is thirty-four or thirty-five, and he begins to decline after forty. This fact cannot be repeated too often—those who do not achieve a reputation at this stage of their career have not actually mastered the art of the *nō*. Therefore it is in this period that the actor must perfect his self-discipline. At this time in his career, he can recall all that he has learned; it is also the moment when he is able to plan for the means to accomplish what he wishes to in the future. If such things are not mastered at this age, then, let me repeat again, it will be difficult for an actor to find success with audiences later in his career.

FORTY-FOUR, FORTY-FIVE YEARS From this point on, the actor must find new means of showing his skills. Even if he has achieved a fine reputation and has mastered the art of the *nō*, he must be able in turn to have in his troupe young actors who will follow him. Although his real art may not decline, yet, as his years advance, his physical presence and the beauty others find in him will be diminished. Leaving aside the exceptionally handsome performer, even a fairly good-looking actor, as he grows older, should no longer be seen playing roles that do not require a mask. Thus this former aspect of his art will now be lacking. From this point onward, it is best not to perform elaborate parts. On the whole, an actor should choose roles that are congenial to him and that can be played in a relaxed manner without physical strain. He should allow the younger actors to show off their own abilities, and he should play with them in a modest fashion, as an associate. Even if he has no young successor of a suitable caliber, an actor should not himself perform any highly complicated and strenuous roles. In any case, the audience will find no Flower in this sort of performance. If, on the other hand, an actor has not lost his Flower by this age, then it will remain truly his possession. If an actor still possesses his Flower as he approaches fifty, then he must have achieved a real reputation before the age of forty. Even an actor who has gained such a reputation however, if he is truly a master, must most of all know himself, and, therefore, work to give the young actors proper training; he will exert himself to the utmost, without performing roles that may betray his own weaknesses. One who truly knows how to see and reflect upon himself—it is he who has really grasped the nature of our art.

FIFTY YEARS OLD AND LATER From this point onward, for the most part, there is little more that can be done. There is a saying that "even *ch'i lin*, when old, is worse than a worn out packhorse."[5] Nevertheless, an actor who has truly mastered his art, even though he has lost his ability to perform many of his roles, and although he may manifest less and less of his art in performance, will still have something of his Flower left about him.

My late father died at the age of fifty-two on the nineteenth day of the fifth month [of 1384], and on the fourth day of that same month, he performed the *nō* in connection with religious services at the Sengen shrine in the province of Suruga.[6] The performances that day were particularly

---

[5] *Ch'i-lin,* (*kirin* in Japanese) famous in ancient Chinese historical chronicles was, rather like the Greek Pegasus, a horse with the miraculous ability to travel enormous distances very quickly.

[6] Generally identified as the Sengen Shrine in the present city of Shizuoka, a little over a hundred miles south of Tokyo.

colorful, and all the spectators, high-ranking and commoner alike, praised his performances. At that time the various plays were given over to the younger actors, and he performed a few easy roles in a modest way. Yet the beauty of his Flower was all the more striking. For when an artist has achieved a real Flower, then the art of the *nō*, even if the foliage is slight and the tree grows old, still retains its blooms. This is the very proof that, even in an ancient frame, the Flower remains.

What has been written above constitutes the appropriate stages of *nō* training at various ages.

VARIOUS ITEMS CONCERNING ROLE PLAYING

It would be impossible to describe in writing all the various aspects of Role Playing. Yet as this skill forms the fundamental basis of our art, various roles must be studied with the greatest care. In general, Role Playing involves an imitation, in every particular, with nothing left out. Still, depending on the circumstances, one must know how to vary the degree of imitation involved. For example, when it comes to playing the part of a ruler or a high official, it is extremely difficult to perform with the necessary detail, since the actor cannot know the real way of life of the court nobility, or the bearing appropriate to a great lord. Still, he can study carefully their way of speaking, observe their circumstances, and ask the opinion of those noblemen who watch the performances. Next, he must imitate down to the smallest detail the various things done by persons of high profession, especially those elements related to high artistic pursuits. On the other hand, when it comes to imitating laborers and rustics, their commonplace actions should not be copied too realistically. In the case of woodcutters, grass cutters, charcoal burners, and salt workers, however, they should be imitated in detail insofar as they have traditionally been found congenial as poetic subjects. In general, men of lowly occupation should not be imitated in any meticulous fashion, nor shown to men of refined taste. Should they see such things, they will merely find them vulgar, and the performance will hold no attraction for them. The need for prudence in this matter can be fully understood. Thus the degree of imitation must vary, depending on the kind of role being performed.

WOMEN'S ROLES   In general, a young *shite* is the most suitable actor to play the part of a woman. Nevertheless, playing such a part represents a considerable undertaking. If the actor's style of dress is unseemly, there will be nothing worth watching in the performance. When it comes to impersonating high-ranking women of the court, such as ladies-in-waiting, for example, since the actor cannot easily view their actual deportment, he must make serious, detailed inquiries concerning such matters. As for items of clothing such as the *kinu* and the *hakama*, these too cannot merely be chosen on the basis of the actor's personal preference. The actor must make a proper investigation concerning what is correct. When it comes to impersonating an ordinary woman, however, the actor will be familiar with the appropriate details, and so the task will not be difficult. If the actor dresses in an appropriate *kinu* or *kosode*, that will doubtless suffice. When performing *kusemai*, *shirabyōshi*, or mad women's roles, the actor should hold a fan or a sprig of flowers, for example, loosely in his hand in order to represent female gentleness. The *kinu* and the *hakama*, as well, should be long enough to conceal his steps, his hips and knees should be straight, and his bodily posture pliable. As for his head posture, if he bends backward, his face will appear coarse. If the actor looks down, on the other hand, his appearance from the back will be unseemly. Then too, if he holds his neck too stiffly, he will not look feminine. He should certainly wear a robe with long sleeves, and he should avoid showing the tips of his hands. His *obi* should be loosely tied. The fact that an actor takes great care with his costume means that he is truly anxious to perform his role as well as possible. No matter what the role, bad costuming will never be effective, and, in the case of a woman's role, proper dressing is essential.

OLD MEN   Playing the role of an old man represents the very pinnacle of our art. These roles are crucial, since the spectators who watch can gauge immediately the real skills of the actor. There are many *shite* who have mastered the art of *nō* quite well, but who cannot achieve the appearance of an old man. When an actor plays a woodcutter, salt scooper, or a similar part that contains conspicuous gestures, it is easy enough for the spectators to be deceived and to make a false judgment too quickly concerning the performer's talents. But to play the part of an old man of high rank whose gestures involve no characteristic movement is truly difficult and requires the skills of a master actor. Unless an actor rehearses over the years until his art is at its peak, he cannot properly present this kind of role. Without a proper Flower, such a restrained performance can have nothing of interest about it.

In terms of stage deportment, most actors, thinking to appear old, bend their loins and hips, shrink their bodies, lose their Flower, and give a withered, uninteresting performance. Thus there is little that is attractive in what such actors do. It is particularly important that the actor refrain from performing in a limp or weak manner, but bear himself with grace and dignity. Most crucial of all is the dancing posture chosen for the role of an old man. One must study assiduously the precept: portray an old man while still possessing the Flower. The results should resemble an old tree that puts forth flowers.

PERFORMING WITHOUT A MASK   This too represents an important aspect of our art. As such roles are those representing ordinary persons, they may seem to be easy to perform, but, surprisingly, unless the highest level of skill in the *nō* is used, such a performance will not be worth watching. The actor must of necessity study the object of each role individually [since the face is visible]. Although it is not possible to imitate any particular individual countenance in performance, actors sometimes alter their own ordinary facial expressions in an attempt to create some particular effect. The results are always without interest. The performance should rather be constructed from the movements and general feeling of the person being portrayed. The actor must always use his own natural facial expressions and never try to alter them.

ROLES OF MAD PERSONS   This skill represents the most fascinating aspect of our art. In this category there are many types of roles, and an actor who has truly taken up this specialty can play successfully all types of roles. I must repeat again and again that an actor must fully commit himself to rehearse and practice continuously, as I have admonished. In general, there are various types of possessed beings; for example, those inhabited by the curse of a god, a Buddha, the spirit of a living person, or of a dead person. Therefore, if the actor studies the nature of the spirit who possesses the character, he should be able to manage the part well. On the other hand, the really difficult parts involve those characters whose thoughts have become confused because their minds have become crazed—a parent searching for a lost child, for example, a wife thrown over by her husband, or a husband who lives on after his wife. Even a relatively skillful *shite* may fail to make the distinction between them, and he will create his mad gestures in the same manner, so that no emotional response is engendered in those who watch him. In the case of characters of this sort, the actor must have as his intention the manifestation of the precise feelings that can indicate the character's emotional disturbance, and make them the core of his Flower; then, if he feigns madness with all the skill he has at his command, there will certainly be many arresting elements in his performance. If an actor possesses this kind of skill, and if he can make his spectators weep, his art will represent the highest attainment possible. Reflect as fully as possible on what I have written above.

It goes without saying that a costume appropriate for the role of a mad person is essential. Still, as the character is a mad person, the costume might, depending on the occasion, be more gaudy than usual. The actor can carry in his hand a sprig of flowers appropriate to the season.

Then again, while I have spoken in terms of acting that imitates surface realities, there is another point that must be seriously considered. Although I said that the madness of the character must be performed in terms of the being who possesses that character, when it comes to playing a madwoman possessed by a warrior or a demon, for example, the circumstances are made quite difficult for the actor. Thinking to act out the true nature of the being who possesses such a character, the actor will show masculine wrath while playing a woman, and his performance will seem quite inappropriate. On the other hand, if the actor concentrates on the womanly traits of his character, there will be no logic to the possession. Similarly, when a male character is possessed by a woman, the same difficulty arises. In sum, to avoid plays with such characters represents an important secret of our art. Those who compose such texts simply do not understand the nature of our art. A writer who truly understands the art of *nō* would never compose a text that showed such a lack of harmony. To possess this truth is another secret of our art.

When it comes to playing the role of a mad person without a mask, the performance will not be complete unless the actor has truly mastered his art. For, if the expressions on the actor's face are not properly descriptive, there will be no sense of madness conveyed. If the actor changes his face without a profound understanding of his art, on the other hand, the results will be merely ugly. The deepest arts of Role Playing are required for these paradoxical circumstances.

Thus, in important performances, inexperienced actors must participate with the greatest caution. Playing without a mask is very difficult. Acting a mad role is also very difficult. To combine these two elements into one: how difficult indeed to elevate such a role to the level of the Flower. Rehearsal and study are the only methods possible.

ROLES OF BUDDHIST PRIESTS   Although such roles exist, they are few in number and do not require so much practice. In general, when playing a gorgeously robed cleric or a priest of high rank, the actor must use the majesty and dignity of the character as the basis for his performance. When it comes to lesser-ranking priests, such as those who have abandoned the world and practice austerities, their religious pilgrimage is of paramount importance to them, and so it is crucial for the actor to create the impression that such characters are absorbed in their religious devotions. In the end, when it comes to the materials on which to build a performance, more pains may be required than might be expected.

SHURA   Here is still another type of role. Such dead warrior roles, even when well performed, are seldom arresting. Thus they should not be performed too often. Nevertheless, when it comes to events dealing with the famous Genji or Heike warriors,[7] if the various elements are knit together with suitable elegance, so that the text is a good one, such a performance can be more moving than one of any other variety. In such plays, some spectacular moment is particularly important. The wildness of the *shura* style may well lead to the kind of behavior appropriate to a demon role. Then again, such a role risks turning entirely into a dance performance. If there is a section in the play that resembles *kusemai*, it is allowable to include some appropriate dancelike gestures. As it is customary for the actor to carry with him a bow and quiver and to wear some variety of sword, the performer should undertake a careful study of how to carry and use such objects, making efforts to exhibit the essence of this type of role. The actor must take special care to avoid both those movements appropriate to a demon role on the one hand, and the use of purely dancelike motions on the other.

ROLES OF GODS   In general, this kind of Role Playing is related to that appropriate for the demon roles. As the appearance of such a figure is always fierce, no particular difficulties are created by playing the part in the manner of a demon, depending, of course, on the role of the god involved. However, there is one essential difference between the two types of characters. Dancelike gestures are the most appropriate for the role of a god, but they are not suitable for a demon role. Particularly in the case of a god role, the only means available to the actor to represent such a being lies in his being properly dressed, and therefore he must give particular attention to the creation of a properly noble appearance. The actor must decorate his costume correctly and adjust his clothing in an appropriate manner.

DEMON ROLES   These roles are a particular specialty of the Yamato school. They are extremely difficult to perform successfully. True, it is simple to play effectively the demon roles of vengeful ghosts or possessed beings, as they offer visible elements of interest that can make them arresting. The performer, directing himself toward his acting partner, should use small foot and hand motions and make his movements in accordance with the effect created by his headgear. In the case of a real demon from hell, however, even if the actor studies well, his performance is likely to be merely frightening. There are no real means to make such roles truly enjoyable for the spectators. In fact, these are such difficult roles to play that there are few actors who can perform them in an effective way, it seems.

The essence of such roles lies in forcefulness and frightfulness. Yet such qualities do not stimulate feelings of enjoyment. For this reason, the role of a demon is particularly difficult to play. Logically, the harder the actor tries to perform them, the less interesting they become. The essence of such a role is frightfulness, yet the qualities of frightfulness and enjoyment are as different as black

---

[7] The Genji and Heike clans were the chief rivals in the disastrous civil wars of 1185 that brought an end to the political domination by the Kyoto court. Many important *nō* texts by Zeami dealt with characters and incidents from those battles.

and white. Thus, it might be said that an actor who can perform such a role in an enjoyable way would indeed be a performer of the highest talent. Indeed, an actor who strives for nothing but to play demon roles well can never really attain the Flower. Therefore, a performance by a young actor, even if it seems well done, will not really be effective. Is it not then true that an actor who only strives to play demon roles well can never actually perform them well? This paradox must be carefully studied. For the interest the spectator finds in the performance of a demon role is like a flower blooming among the rocks.

CHINESE ROLES   As these are special kinds of characters, there is no fixed form of practice for the actor. The element of appearance is essential. In choosing a mask—even though the character is of course a human being just like anyone else—it is best for the actor to wear something with an unusual appearance so as to maintain the effect of something somehow out of the ordinary.

Such parts are effectively played by older artists with talent and experience. Still, other than costuming, there are no special techniques required. In any case, since any attempt to imitate the Chinese style directly, either in chant or in movement, will not in itself be effective, it is better to add just one representative element to an ordinary performance. The selection of just such an element, slight in itself, can serve as a means to animate the whole. Although usually such changes are not considered appropriate, there is no way truly to copy the style, and so such a slight change in gesture will add something of the Chinese flavor and can give the spectators an appropriate sensation. Such methods have been practiced for a long time.

In general, such are the various elements of Role Playing. It is difficult to express any finer details in writing. Nevertheless, an actor who has fully grasped the points enumerated above will be able by himself to grasp them.

An actor must not only rehearse thoroughly with his teachers but he must learn through practice to imitate their peerless performances. Indeed, it is precisely because the art of these great performers has been brought to the highest levels of training that they can present in their acting an appearance of total mastery and ease, thus fascinating their audiences. If a beginner wishes merely to imitate this level of accomplishment, he may seem to achieve its semblance, yet there will be nothing moving in his performance. A truly great artist has for many years succeeded in training both his body and his spirit; he can hold back much of his potential in reserve and perform in an easy fashion, so that only seven-tenths of his art is visible. If a beginner tries to perform in this fashion, without the proper practice, he will only imitate what he can observe, and so his spirit and his performance cannot reach beyond that seven-tenths he can grasp. What is more, his own progress will be blocked.

Therefore, when a student is learning his craft, the teacher should show not his own high level of ability [in which there is a reserve of artistry], but, as he did when he too was a beginner, indicate to his pupils how to use fully both their minds and bodies. After such lessons have been absorbed, the students will gradually reach a level of mastery and attain a level of ease in their own performances, understand how to hold in reserve a certain amount of their own physical energy, and grasp of themselves the principle that "what is felt by the heart is ten, what appears in movement seven."

In general, a performance of Perfect Fluency cannot be imitated. And if an actor makes an attempt to imitate it, the very effort involved in the attempt will produce a tension that cannot be a part of Perfect Fluency. Only something that is meant to appear difficult can actually be imitated. "The truth and what looks like it are two different things,"[1] it is said. Thus, could there be any way to imitate the truth of the master actor's easy performance? Indeed, ease and difficulty are two aspects of the same thing. There is a separate teaching on this matter. The means by which a student learns from a teacher are well known, and so no special comment is needed here. However, the teacher's official certification of the student must be based on a thorough examination of his capacities and devotion; otherwise, certification should not be given. If the student's basic abilities are

ZEAMI MOTOKIYO
(1363–1444)

FROM "A MIRROR HELD TO THE FLOWER" (1424)

TRANSLATED BY
J. THOMAS AND
YAMAZAKI MASAKAZU

UNDERSTANDING THE PROPER MEANING OF LEARNING OUR ART

---

[1] A popular saying found in many texts circulated in this period.

insufficient, no certification is possible. Should certification be given when talent is lacking, a level of accomplishment is suggested that cannot actually be matched. The certification will be fraudulent and the results meaningless; therefore, it should not be given. In the *Book of Changes* it is written that "if suitable teachings are given to those who are not suitable, the hatred of Heaven will be aroused."[2] In order that such a suitable person can be created, three conditions must be present. First, he must possess himself the requisite talent. Secondly, he must adore his art and show a total dedication to the path of *nō*. Thirdly, he must have a teacher capable of showing him the proper way. If these three conditions cannot be met, the candidate will not be suitable. A suitable person is one who has the capacity to achieve the highest reaches of his art, to be recognized himself as a teacher.

When I observe the artistic abilities of young performers now, it appears that "skipping"[3] has become commonplace. This situation comes about because they imitate without study. An actor must begin by studying the Two Basic Arts and the Three Role Types, continue to practice all that is appropriate for his age, and carry on his studies in the proper sequence, so that he will reach a stage of mastery in all the arts of the *nō* that can permit him to perform in any artistic style. To learn only by imitation and so only manage a temporary resolution seems indeed to represent a kind of "skipping." For example, when studying the Two Basic Arts, one must not study the Three Role Types. When the time comes to study the Three Role Types, one must put off for a certain time the study of military roles [as they demand intense physical effort]. When an actor does come to study the military roles, then the demon roles in both the Delicacy within Strength and Rough styles of movement should be put off for a certain time, since there is an appropriate moment to learn them as well. To attempt to learn all these roles at once—what a terribly difficult thing it would be. And the degree of difficulty would be unexpectedly high. Therefore, even if by "skipping" a young performer manages to fool the public into thinking that he is a master, he will achieve a momentary Flower. And as such an artist grows older, his art will decline. And even should his art not decline, it would be impossible for him to achieve true renown. This point must be firmly kept in mind.

Concerning "skipping," there is another matter to consider. If an actor is inordinately fond of new plays, and should he come step by step to abandon the older repertory he performed in the past, he can never master the art of *nō* and will only be "skipping." Rather, the actor must fix a repertory of standard plays at which he excels and then mix new plays in with them. If he plays only fresh pieces and neglects the plays to which he is accustomed, the results, in terms of the art of the *nō*, will be a disgraceful "skipping" indeed. Besides, if only unusual pieces are performed, then that procedure of itself loses its novelty. If a mixture of old and new is achieved, then both the old and the new alike will seem novel. Such becomes the undying flower. As Confucius said, "He who by reanimating the Old can gain knowledge of the New is fit to be a teacher."[4]

HAVING A REAL UNDERSTANDING OF SKILL

If an actor has become fully proficient at music and dance, he may be called skillful. If he has not become fully accomplished, there will be no denying his shortcomings. On the other hand, there is a kind of real skill based on still different considerations. For example, there are actors whose abilities in dance and chant show no shortcomings, yet who have not achieved a high reputation. Then again, there are actors whose voices are not attractive and whose mastery of dancing and singing show defects, yet who are widely thought of as accomplished performers. The reason for this is that both dancing and gesture are external skills. The essentials of our art lie in the spirit. They represent a true enlightenment established through art. Thus, if an actor knows how to create interest and can perform from an understanding of this spirit, he will gain a reputation as a fine actor even if he has not mastered every aspect of his craft. Such being the case, if an actor really wants to become a master, he cannot simply depend on his skill in dance and gesture. Rather, mastery seems to depend on the actor's own state of self-understanding and the sense of style with which he has been blessed. Real discernment of the nature of the differences between external skill and interior understanding forms the basis of true mastery. Thus it is that an actor who has merely perfected his technique will

[2] The quotation as recorded here does not appear in the *Book of Changes* (*I ching*).
[3] "Skipping" (*tendoku*) was a term originally used to mean "turning the *sutras*," chanting the first few lines and then skipping the rest to save time, as a kind of devotional exercise. Zeami of course uses the term ironically.
[4] See Arthur Waley, *The Analects of Confucius*, Book II, no. 11, p. 90.

have little of interest to show. Other actors, from the beginning of their careers, can fascinate their audiences. So it is that an actor, from the time he is young until he masters seven-tenths, eight-tenths, even all of his technique and reaches the level of a master, will continue to interest others for quite separate considerations.

Still higher than the level of interest, there is a level of skill that will simply make the audience gasp, without reflection, in surprise and pleasure. This level will be termed one of a pure Feeling that Transcends Cognition. The response to such a performance is such that there is no occasion for reflection, no time for a spectator to realize how well the performance is contrived. Such a state might be referred to as "purity unmixed."[5] In the *Book of Changes*, when the Chinese character for "feeling" (*kan* 感) is written, the element that stands for "mind" (*kokoro* 心) is eliminated [and the character is written as 咸] in order to illustrate the fact that when true feeling is involved, there is no room in the concept for reflection as a function of the mind.[6]

Thus it is that the actor comes to possess various levels of artistic skill. If a beginning actor continues on through all the various stages of his training, he will be called a good actor, but not necessarily anything more. Yet there is still a higher level where real mastery is possible. If the spectators are truly fascinated with an actor's performance, he can be said to have reached the level of a master. If, in addition, he possesses the ability to create for his audience an intensity of pure feeling that goes beyond the workings of the mind, he will have achieved the level of greatest reputation. Thus an actor should pursue his study of *nō* through these various levels, develop his skills, and through his own spiritual understanding, bring his art to the highest possible level of fulfillment.

SHALLOW AND DEEP

Concerning *nō* performance, there is one matter that must be given particularly serious consideration. If a performance is given without sufficient attention to detail, it will be without interest. On the other hand, if too much attention is given by the performer to details, the whole performance risks to shrink in scale. Then again, if the actor thinks to play his part as liberally as possible, the opportunities for the audience to witness his skill will be fewer, and there will be a tendency for his performance to become slow and monotonous. An understanding of this distinction is of the greatest importance. An actor might, on first reflection, think that the parts of the play requiring intricate skills should be played in as complex a fashion as possible, while those moments requiring a more general approach should be played as broadly as possible. Yet in fact this kind of distinction cannot be made unless an actor knows the art of *nō* very well indeed. A student must question his teacher closely on such matters, so that these distinctions become clear. There is, however, one general principle that can be kept in mind. For the chant, the dance, and the various sorts of gestures that will be employed, the actor's spirit should be as delicately attuned as possible, but, at the same time, his physical stance should be as relaxed and broad as possible. An actor must comprehend these principles and stick to them.

In general, it can be said that, in the case of the *nō*, an art that is based on general and flexible principles can be made subtle and detailed. But a *nō* that is merely meticulous in conception cannot easily develop on a large and relaxed scale. After all, the small can be contained in the large, but not the large in the small. A great deal of skill needs to be given over to this matter. A *nō* that possesses both these qualities will truly be full and rich. Indeed, when ice formed during the deep cold melts, the ice formed during a brief chilly spell will melt as well.

ENTERING THE REALM OF GRACE

The aesthetic quality of Grace is considered the highest ideal of perfection in many arts. Particularly in the *nō*, Grace can be regarded as the highest principle. However, although the quality of Grace is manifested in performance and audiences give it high appreciation, there are very few actors who in fact possess that quality. This is because they have never had a taste of the real Grace themselves. So it is that few actors have entered this world.

What kind of realm is represented by what is termed Grace? For example, if we take the general appearance of the world and observe the various sorts of people who live there, it might be said

---

[5] A term sometimes used to indicate the high level of excellence in *waka* poetry. The term is probably of Zen origin.

[6] For a translation into English of this section of the *I ching*, see Richard Wilhelm, tr., *The I Ching or Book of Changes*, pp. 122–125. The interpretation of the passage is evidently Zeami's.

that Grace is best represented in the character of the nobility, whose deportment is of such a high quality and who receive the affection and respect not given to others in society. If such is the case, then their dignified and mild appearance represents the essence of Grace. Therefore, the stage appearance of Grace is best indicated by their refined and elegant carriage. If an actor examines closely the nobility's beautiful way of speaking and studies the words and habitual means of expression that such elevated persons use, even to observing their tasteful choice of language when saying the smallest things, such can be taken to represent the Grace of speech. In the case of the chant, when the melody flows smoothly and naturally on the ear and sounds suitably mild and calm, this quality can be said to represent the Grace of music. In the case of the dance, if the actor studies until he is truly fluent, so that his appearance on stage will be sympathetic and his carriage both unostentatious and moving to those who observe him, he will surely manifest the Grace of the dance. When he is acting a part, if he makes his appearance beautiful in the Three Role Types, he will have achieved Grace in his performance. Again, when presenting a role of fearsome appearance, a demon's role for example, even should the actor use a rough manner to a certain extent, he must not forget to preserve a graceful appearance, and he must remember the principles of "what is felt in the heart is ten," and "violent body movements, gentle foot movements," so that his stage appearance will remain elegant. Thus he may manifest the Grace of a demon's role.

An actor must come to grasp those various types of Grace and absorb them within himself; for no matter what kind of role he may assume, he must never separate himself from the virtue of Grace. No matter what the role—whether the character be of high or low rank, a man, a woman, a priest or lay person, a farmer or country person, even a beggar or an outcast—it should seem as though each were holding a branch of flowers in his hand. In this one respect they exhibit the same appeal, despite whatever differences they may show in their social positions. This Flower represents the beauty of their stance in the *nō*; and the ability to reveal this kind of stance in performance represents, of course, its spirit. In order to study the Grace of words, the actor must study the art of composing poetry; and to study the Grace of physical appearance, he must study the aesthetic qualities of elegant costume, so that, in every aspect of his art, no matter how the role may change that the actor is playing, he will always maintain one aspect in his performance that shows Grace. Such it is to know the seed of Grace.

However, it may well happen that an actor will put such an importance on his impersonation of the particulars of his role, regarding this aspect of his performance as the highest of his art, that he will neglect to maintain the beauty of the stance he has properly assumed. Thus he will fail to enter the world of Grace. And if he does not enter into the world of Grace, he cannot approach the level of Highest Fruition. And unless he reaches this highest level of accomplishment, he will never be recognized as a great actor. There are indeed few masters who have attained those heights. Thus an actor must rehearse with the utmost diligence on this critical point of the representation of Grace.

This Highest Fruition of an actor represents precisely the appearance of this deeply beautiful posture. I cannot repeat too often that an actor must rehearse with the need for the proper preparation of his body always in mind. Thus it is of crucial importance that, beginning with the Two Basic Arts down to the specifics of any role that may be played, the stance of the actor be attractive so as to represent this Highest Fruition in every circumstance. If the actor's posture is unattractive, his art will invariably appear vulgar. In any case, whatever gestures may be seen or music may be heard, however great the variety, the fact that the actor's stance is beautifully assumed represents the true attainment of Grace. An actor may be said to have entered the world of Grace when he has of his own accord studied these principles and made himself master of them. If an actor does not work to fulfill them and thinks that, without mastering every aspect of his art, he can still try to attain this Grace, he will, in fact, never know it during his entire lifetime.

PAYING HEED TO THE ACCUMULATION OF SKILLS

Studying the art of the *nō*, having the reputation of a superior actor, and rising in merit as the years pass by depends on a proper accumulation of skills. Yet the nature of such an accumulation will differ depending on where the actor lives and performs. Even if he earns a reputation as a fine actor, if the praise he earns is not from those who live in the capital, it can have little significance for him. Even an actor who has earned genuine praise in the capital, should he return to his native place and continue to perform in the countryside, will merely expend his energies in attempting not to forget those means of expression that he learned in the capital, and because of his false sense that he still remembers how to perform properly, he will little by little slacken in his persistence in maintaining his beauty of performance. The result will be an accumulation of bad experiences. Such a stagnation of experience must be shunned.

In the capital, on the other hand, the actor will be performing before discerning spectators so that, should he become careless concerning any element in his art and so fail to progress, he will soon notice a response from his audience; then too, as criticism and comment come to him, he will eventually disregard the unsatisfactory elements in his art, accumulate only positive artistic experiences, and discover that his art has become polished. Of its own accord his skill will become as burnished as a jewel. There is a saying that "sagebrush, which has the ability to bend, even should it grow up among flax plants, will come out straight, without correction, while white sand, when mixed with earth, will become black like the rest."[7] Thus by living in the capital, an actor is in the proper environment, and the insufficiencies in his art will naturally disappear. This gradual lessening of error is in itself the accumulation of good experience. There is no way that an artist can simply set out to pile up these experiences of his own accord. Rather, let me repeat again and again a warning that, if an actor does not take cognizance of his good experiences, they will stagnate and turn into an accumulation of bad experiences.

So it is that even a skilled performer as he grows older will come to depend on his increasingly old-fashioned art, which has become so through an accumulation caused by his own stagnation. Although audiences may dislike his performances, he thinks only that he has been recognized as an artist of great merit for a long time. Thus he does not recognize the real feelings of his audiences. He therefore loses the chance to make his final appearances on the stage successful — such an important opportunity in an actor's career.

All of this is the result of piling up of such bad experiences. The greatest caution must be taken against this.

It is often commented on by audiences that "many times a performance is effective when the actor does nothing." Such an accomplishment results from the actor's greatest, most secret skill. From the techniques involved in the Two Basic Arts down to all the gestures and the various kinds of Role Playing, all such skills are based on the abilities found in the actor's body. Thus to speak of an actor "doing nothing" actually signifies that interval which exists between two physical actions. When one examines why this interval "when nothing happens" may seem so fascinating, it is surely because of the fact that, at the bottom, the artist never relaxes his inner tension. At the moment when the dance has stopped, or the chant has ceased, or indeed at any of those intervals that can occur during the performance of a role, or, indeed, during any pause or interval, the actor must never abandon his concentration but must keep his consciousness of that inner tension. It is this sense of inner concentration that manifests itself to the audience and makes the moment enjoyable.

However, it is wrong to allow an audience to observe the actor's inner state of control directly. If the spectators manage to witness this, such concentration will merely become another ordinary skill or action, and the feeling in the audience that "nothing is happening" will disappear.

The actor must rise to a selfless level of art, imbued with a concentration that transcends his own consciousness, so that he can bind together the moments before and after that instant when "nothing happens." Such a process constitutes that inner force that can be termed "connecting all the arts through one intensity of mind."

"Indeed, when we come to face death, our life might be likened to a puppet on a cart (decorated for a great festival). As soon as one string is cut, the creature crumbles and fades."[8] Such is the image given of the existence of man, caught in the perpetual flow of life and death. This constructed puppet, on a cart, shows various aspects of himself but cannot come to life of itself. It represents a deed performed by moving strings. At the moment when the strings are cut, the figure falls and crumbles. *Sarugaku* too is an art that makes use of just such artifice. What supports these illusions and gives them life is the intensity of mind of the actor. Yet the existence of this intensity must not be shown directly to the audience. Should they see it, it would be as though they could see the

CONNECTING ALL THE ARTS THROUGH ONE INTENSITY OF MIND

---

[7] An expression widely circulated during the medieval period in various forms, probably originating in the writings of Tseng Ts'an, one of the most important disciples of Confucius.

[8] A saying attributed to a priest of the Rinzai sect of Zen Buddhism in Japan, Gettan Sōkō (1316?–1389).

strings of a puppet. Let me repeat again: the actor must make his spirit the strings, and without letting his audience become aware of them, he will draw together the forces of his art. In that way, true life will reside in his *nō*.

In general, such attitudes need not be limited to the moments involved in actual performance. Morning and night alike, and in all the activities of daily life, an actor must never abandon his concentration, and he must retain his resolve. Thus, if without ever slackening, he manages to increase his skills, his art of the *nō* will grow ever greater. This particular point represents one of the most secret of all the teachings concerning our art. However, in actual rehearsal, there must be within this concentration some variations of tension and relaxation.

THE MOMENT OF PEERLESS CHARM

The character *myō* in the term *myōsho* [Peerless Charm] means "exquisite" or "delicate." But it also has the meaning of an appearance that transcends any specific form. Such a transcendence of form represents an expression of this Peerless Charm.

When one speaks of such moments in terms of the *nō*, this Charm should exist in every aspect of our art, from the Two Basic Arts to gesture. Yet precisely where can it be located? It seems to be found nowhere. If an actor can possess this arresting power, he must be a performer of surpassing skill. However, if an actor is truly blessed with great talent, he will show from his beginnings some shadow of this Charm. The actor will not himself be conscious of it, but spectators of discernment will always find this quality within him. Ordinary spectators, on the other hand, will merely find that his performances are enjoyable in some mysterious fashion. And indeed even in the case of an actor of the highest skill, he will at best have come only to the realization that he somehow does possess this skill. Still, he will have no consciousness that he is practicing it at any given moment. An actor will possess this quality precisely because he does not recognize it; if such a moment could in any way be put into words, this Charm could no longer exist.

When one ponders carefully the substance of this Peerless Charm, can it not be said that an artist may approach it when he has truly learned his craft and attained Perfect Fluency, when he has transcended all stages of his art to the point where he performs everything with ease and exhibits every skill without care, thus achieving a selfless art that rises above any artifice? When an actor manages to ascend to the aesthetic level of Grace, will he indeed not be somewhat closer to this power of beauty? These matters must be pondered deeply.

JUDGING THE NŌ

When it comes to making crucial judgments concerning the *nō*, people invariably have different ideas. It is difficult indeed for any particular *nō* to match the tastes of everyone. Thus the basis of judgment should be made on the strength of the performances of accomplished actors who enjoy a wide reputation.

First of all, one should look and listen with great care during actual performances so as to understand why some plays succeed and why others do not. Plays that succeed possess three qualities: Sight, Sound, and Heart.

As for the *nō* that succeeds through Sight, the stage atmosphere will be colorful from the beginning, the dancing and music will have an attractive air, the spectators, noblemen and commoners alike, will be spontaneous in their praise, the atmosphere brilliant. Such is the *nō* that is effective to the eye. It goes without saying that such a performance will please the discriminating; even those who know nothing of the *nō* will find such a performance enjoyable. However, concerning such performances, there is one point that an actor must keep in mind. If the performance passes by altogether too well and with too much appeal, and if every aspect seems enjoyable, then the feelings of the audience will tend to become over-stimulated, and their sensibilities in appreciating the details of the acting will be coarsened. For his part, an actor may be impetuous and, since he wants to exhaust every aspect of his art, will make no allowance for a slackening of pace, either for himself or for the audience. In an attempt to make every aspect of the performance successful, a surface brilliance is achieved, but the end results may be unsatisfactory. This kind of abuse arises when the play goes too well. On such an occasion, the play should be performed in a more restrained manner, all the artistic appearances made more moderate, and the eyes and ears of the spectators given some surcease, so that they can have an occasion to rest and breathe easily and the audience can be given the quiet necessary to observe the really skillful elements in the performance. Then, if the results are successful, the plays that follow will seem stronger, so that, whatever the number of plays that may be staged, their fascination for the audience will never be exhausted. So it is that an effective *nō* performance can be said to succeed through the art of Sight.

Nō that can be said to succeed through Sound shows from the very beginning a serious atmosphere. The music and text are chosen in accord with the season [and the time of day], thus creating a gentle, relaxed, and enjoyable effect. Above all, it is the chant that should create the main impression. Only a peerless artist of highest experience can achieve this effect during a performance. However, the kind of sober flavor engendered by such a performance cannot be understood by country audiences and the like.

This kind of *nō*, when performed by a peerless actor, can give rise through his spiritual resources to various aesthetic qualities that make the play become more and more enjoyable as it goes along. In the case of an artist of the second rank, however, whose art has not fully matured, he will cause the day's performance to lag if he decides to follow such a presentation by a famous actor with one of his own in a *nō* that is also of this particular variety. When such a player follows the kind of performance that has successfully created a cool and quiet atmosphere, as he continues on he will only create a gloomy mood in the succeeding plays. An actor must be aware of this difficulty and put his energies into his performance in order to begin to increase the number of stimulating moments in the play, so as to bring an element of surprise to his audience. Of course, as a truly peerless player has naturally a wide repertory and is highly trained in body and mind, his art will be effectively manifested in his dance and chant, so that his performance will naturally progress in an enjoyable manner. A player of the second rank, however, must take great care so that, as the performance continues, the atmosphere does not go dead. Concerning this point, when thinking to keep up the atmosphere of his performance, the actor must not reveal his methods to the audience. The spectators must merely feel that the performance is enjoyable. Such is the actor's secret, based on long-mastered precedents as to how to perform successfully. All I have written above can explain how a *nō* can succeed through Sound.

When it comes to the *nō* that succeeds through the Heart, a truly gifted actor of *sarugaku*, after he has mastered the whole repertory, will have the ability even when performing a play of no particular distinction in terms of chant, dance, gesture, or plot, to create even in the midst of a certain dullness a particular poetic quality that can move the hearts of his audience. This level of attainment is not usually grasped even by connoisseurs; how much more beyond any imaginings of a country audience must be such an art. Indeed, such a quality must seem to represent the propitious manifestation of an actor of the highest abilities. Such a performance can be termed a *nō* that succeeds through the Heart, a *nō* that surpasses technique, a *nō* that transcends outward manifestation.

An actor must learn to discriminate between the kinds of artistic qualities that display those various differences. There are spectators of discernment who do not really understand the art of the *nō*. On the other hand, there are those spectators who possess a true grasp of the essential nature of the *nō* but who cannot observe subtle differences. Those who have both a practical and a theoretical understanding of *nō* represent the highest level of spectator. For example, there are occasions when a fine performance does not meet with success, and times when an unskilled performance pleases, but no one must use these exceptions as a basis for one's general judgments. For example, truly gifted players customarily have success with outdoor and other large-scale performances, while lesser actors perform profitably at smaller playing areas at country fairs or on other such occasions.

An actor who understands how to make his performance attractive to his audience brings good fortune to the *nō*. Then too, a spectator who understands the heart of the actor as he watches a performance is a gifted spectator. The following might be said concerning making judgments: forget the specifics of a performance and examine the whole. Then forget the performance and examine the actor. Then forget the actor and examine his inner spirit. Then, forget that spirit, and you will grasp the nature of the *nō*.

THE MATTER OF MASTERING THE CHANT

There are two aspects to the study of the chant. The person who composes the text should know the principles of music and how to make the words flow together in a euphonious fashion. For his part, the performer who sings must know how to fit the melody to the words and to chant the syllables and words in a clear and correct manner. Since the beauty of the chant derives from the syllables and the words performed, the melodies must be composed in such a way that the pronunciation is always correctly represented, and the linking between the phrases smooth and flexible. When the chant is performed, if the singer has mastered these principles and really knows them well, both the composition and the performance will reinforce each other and produce an enjoyable effect. As this is true, a standard should be established by which the melody is attached to the chant. The flow of the phrases must be attractive, and the sound characteristics of the text must be in harmony with the melody, so that the results will of themselves be musical. That is, the melody provides the basic frame for the musical composition, and the artistic effect derives from the spirit of the performer, who shades the melody in terms of the flow of the phrases. Thus an actor has various elements of music that he must master—the physical problems of using the breath, the development of his own emotional concentration in order to direct it properly, and the understanding of the melody, as well as the music that lies behind the melody. In terms of practicing the musical aspects of *nō*, the following should be taken to heart: forget the voice and understand the shading of the melody. Forget the melody and understand the pitch. Forget the pitch and understand the rhythm.

In learning the art of musical performance, there is a proper order to be followed: first, the words of the text must be learned thoroughly; then the melody must be mastered; then the actor must learn how to color the melody; finally, he must learn how to apply the proper pitch accent. After all these steps are taken, the actor must concentrate on how to bring his performances to flower. At every stage, an emphasis must be placed on the rhythm. When practicing the voice, miss no occasion to obtain this kind of training, so beneficial to personal development.

Then there is the matter of accent in musical performance. In the case of auxiliary words or particles, the problem is not a serious one. However, mistaken accents on such substantive words as nouns, verbs, and adjectives[9] are harmful. Understanding the importance of this distinction is crucial. Serious study must be given to this point. When speaking of mistaken accents on these substantive words, I refer to pronunciations with improper pitch accent, which affect the meaning of the words. In the case of particles and auxiliary words, the problem has to do with the voicing of such sounds as *te, ni, ha*, and the like. Concerning correct pronunciation for these sounds, when the flow of words in the course of the singing moves effectively, even if the pronunciation becomes altered to some extent, so long as the rhythm is correct, the problem is not a serious one. It is said that words that make a heavy or a light effect, that are clear or complex in sound, depend on the forward flow of the text. In addition, there are various customs and rules concerning sound changes when words are juxtaposed together. Study the transmitted teachings carefully on this matter. As concerns particles that come at the end of phrases, such as *ha, ni, no, o, ka, te, mo, shi*, and so forth, even if there should be some deviation in their pronunciation, there will be nothing disagreeable in the sound as long as the melody is tasteful. In other words, the movement of the melody should be supported by these various particles. In the chanting, every syllable must not simply be pronounced in a flat manner, with an equal length and emphasis given to all of them. Those sounds which represent substantive words should be pronounced briskly, so that their meaning remains clear, while the sound of the auxiliary syllables can be rather freely regulated—slow or fast—in order to make the melody more colorful.

[Remember that] the principle of using four basic tones is used [in Chinese].[10]

In *The History of the Former Han* by Pan Ku,[11] it is written [concerning the legendary origin of the melody] that "as for the origins of the twelve-pitch gamut, a man [named Ling Lun] climbed Mount Kun-lun and, hearing the voice of the male and female phoenix, created the six *ryo* pitches and six *ritsu* pitches of the twelve-pitch gamut." *Ritsu*, since it is derived from the voice of the male phoenix, represents the principle of *yang*. *Ryo*, which imitates the voice of the female phoenix, represents *yin*. *Ritsu* represents the kind of sound that goes from high to low, and the breath is inhaled. *Ryo* represents a sound that goes from low to high, and the breath is exhaled. Breathing appropriate to *ritsu* is produced through a state of tension; *ryo* is produced in a state of ease. Then too, *ritsu* can

---

[9] That is, independent, uninflected words usually written with Chinese characters.

[10] Zeami doubtless wished to stress the importance of proper pitch accent for substantive words in Japanese, usually written in Chinese characters, by this reference to the Chinese language. For a concise description of the function of tones in classical Chinese, see James J. Y. Liu, *The Art of Chinese Poetry*, pp. 21–22.

[11] Pan Ku's history was the first of the so-called dynastic histories of China. For a general description of the text and its subject matter, see Burton Watson, *Early Chinese Literature*, pp. 103–109. Zeami's quotation contains minor errors. For an explanation of the significance of the passage in the history of Chinese music, see Kenneth J. DeWoskin, *A Song for One or Two*, pp. 59–61.

be considered as appropriate to Non-Being, *ryo* appropriate to Being. Thus, a thin, high voice [a "vertical" voice] is appropriate for *ritsu*, while a thick, low voice [a "horizontal" voice] is appropriate for *ryo*.

In the *Analects*,[12] it is written that "the hides of the bear, the tiger, and the panther are used as targets [for the hunter's] arrow. The tiger is the prince's target, the panther the nobleman's target, and the bear the target of the officers of state." If this sequence is followed, it would doubtless be correct to write "tiger, panther, bear." But for the sake of euphony, the order is changed to "bear, tiger, and panther."

The contents of this work have now all been set forth. There is nothing to learn in addition to what has been set down here. Indeed, there is nothing else involved but to "understand the *nō*" with one's very being. If this fundamental principle is not observed, the various matters discussed here will serve no purpose. If an actor really wishes to master the *nō*, he must set aside all other pursuits and truly give his whole soul to our art; then, as his learning increases and his experience grows, he will gradually of himself reach a level of awareness and so come to understand the *nō*.

First of all, an actor must deeply believe what his teacher tells him and take those instructions to heart. The numerous teachings involved are contained in the various points discussed in this book, but the actor must truly master them and engrave them on his heart, so that, when he is actually in a performance, he can try out in practice the various things that he has learned. Then, as a result, he will value those principles, and, as he comes to revere the art of *nō*, he will as time passes come to understand the real secret of success in our art. In whatever artistic pursuit, one studies and then understands, studies and then understands, so that he will know how to carry out his art in actual practice. In *sarugaku* as well, one must study and learn, so that these various principles can be put into practice.

All these secret teachings can be summed up by saying that an actor must continually earn mastery through constant practice, from his apprenticeship through his old age. When I speak of studying through old age, I refer to the fact that from the time of an actor's apprenticeship until the peak of his maturity there are various arts that must be mastered. It is only from the time that an actor passes forty that he can slowly begin to make use of restraint in his physical performance. In other words, he must learn the means of artistic expression appropriate for an actor of his age. When the actor passes fifty, then he can begin to use the technique of "doing nothing." This represents a crucial stage in an actor's career. The first thing to learn at this point is the necessity to limit the kinds of plays in the actor's repertory. His musical performance now becomes the center of his style of performance, his acting style becomes simpler, and his dancing and gestures grow more restrained. He should only give a hint of his former colorful appearance. In fact, the art of music remains the one area in which an actor at this age can excel. This is true because an older voice will have exhausted its natural and untrained qualities, and the voice that remains will be highly polished, in whatever style of vocal production the actor may wish to use; thus whatever music is chanted, the results will always be enjoyable. This is a sure means to achieve a successful performance. Thus an older actor should learn carefully to make his age serve his own artistic purposes and work all the harder to train himself appropriately.

Concerning roles that can be played by older actors, old men and women are doubtless the most appropriate. However, depending on the strong points of a particular actor, he may not necessarily be limited to these two. Still, an actor who wishes to create an atmosphere of serenity in his performance will find the roles of older characters best suited to him. If his special strength lies in roles demanding energetic movement, however, those will not be suitable for the aesthetic qualities appropriate to the art of older actors. In any case, within these limits, he should perform his dances and gestures while limiting himself to six-tenths or seven-tenths of "what is felt by the heart is ten," so as to perform in a manner appropriate to his age. Such is the means to master the art suitable for the older actor.

THE ULTIMATE KEYS OF OUR ART

---

[12] No such passage appears in the *Analects*, but a somewhat similar one does appear in the *Chou li* or *Rites of Chou*. Both this passage and the preceding section on *The History of the Former Han* were added to Zeami's text in the form of notes, and may not be by his hand.

In our Kanze school, there is one phrase that is of infinite value concerning the fundamentals of any artistic accomplishment: an actor must never forget the experiences he has undergone as a beginning artist. In the transmitted teaching, there are three explanations provided for this. Accordingly:

—he must never forget the fresh experiences he first went through as a young performer.

—at each level of accomplishment, there are new levels of fresh experience that the actor must encounter for the first time, as though he were a beginner, and then never forget.

—after the actor becomes older, there are still new stages of fresh experience that must never be forgotten.

Here are the teachings contained in these maxims in more detail.

Concerning the maxim that "he must never forget the fresh experiences he first went through as a young performer," it can be said that, if the actor retains the feelings he had at that time, he will profit from them in many ways as he grows older. As the expression has it, "an understanding of errors in the past will turn them into advantages in the future." Or, "seeing the cart in front turn over serves as a warning to the cart that follows." Forgetting the arts one has learned as a beginner amounts in fact to forgetting the skills an actor may possess at a later point in his career. The fact that his art has been perfected and his reputation has been made can only be the result of the development of his own skill. But if he does not take cognizance of how his skills have improved, he will unknowingly revert to the level he possessed as a beginner. Such a reversal means that his art is actually degenerating. His ability to maintain a sense of his present level of accomplishment shows that he has not forgotten the skills learned as a young performer. I cannot stress this principle too strongly: if an actor loses his memory of his unmatured skills, he will be forced to revert to them. On the other hand, if he does not forget them, his later accomplishments will be genuine. And, if they are genuine, his abilities, as they increase, will insure that his art can never retrogress. Thus, this truth can serve as a distinction between truth and error.

Young actors must therefore take cognizance of the current level of their accomplishment, realize that they are still only beginners, and understand that they must not lose sight of their own skills that still remain to be developed. In this way, they can truly work to lift the level of their art. To lose consciousness of the level of one's ability is to forget how to advance in the art; under such circumstances, an artist's skill will not increase. Therefore, young artists must never lose their perceptions of their actual level of ability.

Secondly, there is the principle that "at each level of accomplishment, there are new levels of fresh experience that the actor must encounter for the first time, as though he were a beginner, and then never forget." This means that, for the actor, from his beginnings through the height of his career and into his old age, there are always various suitable means of expression he must practice and learn. On all these occasions he can be seen as a beginner. Therefore, if at each stage he abandons and forgets what has come before, he will only possess the artistic ability that matches what he is doing at that particular moment in his career. If, on the other hand, he has managed to maintain in himself all the skills that he has previously mastered, so that he can still make use of them, then he can perform in an ever-increasing variety of styles. These "new skills" refer to those he has learned for the first time at every successive stage in his career. Maintaining them all and combining them together at one time means that he has forgotten none of them. It is just through such efforts that a *shite* becomes an artist of wide-ranging abilities. Thus one must never forget what he has learned at each stage of his career.

Finally, "after the actor becomes older, there are still new stages of fresh experience that must never be forgotten." Truly, although there are limits on a human life, the *nō* never comes to an end. If an actor has mastered every technique appropriate to each stage in his career, then when it comes time to learn what is correct for an older actor, he will still be able to enjoy a new experience even at this late stage in his career. If an actor still possesses this attitude when he reaches this high level, his art will still contain everything about the *nō* that he has managed to learn before. When he passes the age of fifty, as I have said, an actor need have no other plan than to "do nothing special." To face the challenge of having no other technique than to "do nothing special"—is the art of an older actor really so different than that of a beginner?

So it is that if an actor manages to live his whole life without forgetting how and what he has learned at any one time in his career, the level of his art will steadily increase during his last years, and his abilities will never degenerate. To live one's life without ever exhausting the depths of the *nō* represents the most profound principle of our school, a principle that must be passed on from child to grandchild, generation to generation as a secret teaching of our house. Passing on the importance of these attitudes I have described above will serve as a means to develop the artistry of all generations to come. On the other hand, if an actor forgets this "experience of a beginner," he will surely not be able to pass the conception along to others in later generations. An artist must not forget this "experience of a beginner," but must convey it to those who follow, for countless generations.

In addition to what I have written here, another who studies the *nō* may, depending on his own abilities and discernment, be able to discover still other truths.

All of the *Teachings on Style and the Flower*, beginning with the chapter called "The Practice of the *Nō* in Relation to the Age of the Actor" down to the "Separate Secret Teaching," is a secret document that makes clear the *nō* by using the metaphor of the flower. That text represents an account of various elements in the art of my father Kan'ami, set down twenty years after his death, and serves as a record of what I learned from him. The present treatise, on the other hand, represents discoveries that have occurred to me from time to time concerning the *nō* over a period of forty years, down to the time of my own advanced age. Summing them up, I have written out my observations in six sections and twenty parts,[13] which I leave behind as a memento of my art.

> Ōe 31 [1424], 1st day of the 6th month
> Zeami

This teaching was passed on by Zeami himself for the succeeding generations of his house and should not be shown to actors from other troupes. Luckily, thanks to the Will of Heaven, which knows that my heart reveres the art of the *nō*, this manuscript has come into my hands. This secret teaching forms the very core of the art of our school, and it has been written down to guide the art of our family. It is a text of fearsome power. Thus it must not be shown carelessly to others.

> Eikyō 9 [1437], 8th month, 8th day
> Komparu Zenchiku[14]

---

[13] The indication of twenty parts suggests that the manuscript was originally arranged in some different fashion.
[14] Komparu's signature is an attribution; the identity of the writer is not altogether certain.

CHIKAMATSU MONZAEMON (1653–1725)

"CHIKAMATSU ON THE ART OF THE PUPPET STAGE" (1738)

TRANSLATED BY DONALD KEENE

Chikamatsu's remarks on the art of the doll theater were written down by his friend Hozumi Ikan in 1738. In a few brief comments, Chikamatsu appears to outline many of the most admired features of his own work as a playwright: the way emotional restraint can lead to a more powerful sense of feeling, the ways that artifice can be employed to develop a stronger sense of "reality," and the interplay between literary and performative elements in the play.

This is what Chikamatsu told me when I visited him many years ago:

Jōruri differs from other forms of fiction in that, since it is primarily concerned with puppets, the words must all be living and full of action. Because *jōruri* is performed in theatres that operate in close competition with those of the *kabuki*, which is the art of living actors, the author must impart to lifeless wooden puppets a variety of emotions, and attempt in this way to capture the interest of the audience. It is thus generally very difficult to write a work of great distinction.

Once when I was young and reading a story about the court,[1] I came across a passage which told how, on the occasion of a festival, the snow had fallen heavily and piled up. An order was given to a guard to clear away the snow from an orange tree. When this happened, the pine next to it, apparently resentful that its boughs were still bent with snow, recoiled its branches. This was a stroke of the pen which gave life to the inanimate tree. It did so because the spectacle of the pine, resentful that the snow had been cleared from the orange tree, recoiling its branches and shaking off the snow that bends it down, is one which creates the feeling of a living, moving thing. Is that not so?

---

[1] "The Tale of Genji." The particular reference is to a passage in the chapter translated by Waley as "The Village of Falling Flowers."

From this model I learned how to put life into my *jōruri*. Thus, even descriptive passages like the *michiyuki*,[2] to say nothing of the narrative phrases and dialogue, must be charged with feeling or they will be greeted with scant applause. This is the same thing as what is called evocative power in poetry. For example, if a poet should fail to bring emotion to his praise of even the superb scenery of Matsushima or Miyajima in his poem, it would be like looking at the carelessly drawn portrait of a beautiful woman. For this reason, it should be borne in mind that feeling is the basis of writing.

When a composition is filled with particles, its literary quality is somehow lowered. Authors of no merit inevitably try to cast their writings exactly in the form of *waka* or linked-verse, stringing together alternating lines of five and seven syllables. This naturally results in the use of many unnecessary particles. For example, when one should say *"Toshi mo yukanu musume wo,"* they say such things as *"Toshiha mo yukanu, musume wo ba."* This comes from concerning one's self with the syllable count, and naturally causes the language to sound vulgar. Thus, while verse is generally written by arranging long and short lines in order, the *jōruri* is basically a musical form, and the length of the lines recited is therefore determined by the melody. If an author adheres implicitly to the rules of metrics, his lines may prove awkward to recite. For this reason I am not concerned with metrics in my writings and I use few particles.

The old *jōruri* was just like our modern street storytelling,[3] and was without either flower or fruit. From the time I first began to write *jōruri*, I have used care in my works, which was not true of the old *jōruri*. As a result, the medium was raised considerably. For example, inasmuch as the nobility, the samurai, and the lower classes all have different social stations, it is essential that they be distinguished in their representation from their appearance down to their speech. Similarly, even within the same samurai class, there are both daimyō and retainers, as well as others of lower rank, each rank possessed of its distinct qualities; such differences must be established. This is because it is essential that they be well pictured in the emotions of the reader.

In writing *jōruri*, one attempts first to describe facts as they really are, but in so doing one writes things which are not true, in the interest of art. In recent plays many things have been said by female characters which real women could not utter. Such things fall under the heading of art; it is because they say what could not come from a real woman's lips that their true emotions are disclosed. If in such cases the author were to model his character on the ways of a real woman and conceal her feelings, such realism, far from being admired, would permit no pleasure in the work. Thus, if one examines a play without paying attention to the question of art, one will certainly criticize it for containing many unpleasant words which are not suitable for women. But such things should be considered art. In addition, there are numerous instances in the portrayal of a villain as excessively cowardly, or of a clown as funny, which are outside the truth and which must be regarded as art. The spectator must bear this consideration in mind.

There are some who, thinking that pathos is essential to a *jōruri*, make frequent use of such expressions as "It was touching" in their writing, or who when chanting do so in voices thick with tears. This is foreign to my style. I take pathos to be entirely a matter of restraint. It is moving when the whole of a play is controlled by the dramatic situation, and the stronger and firmer the melody and words, the sadder will be the impression created. For this reason, when one says of something which is sad that it is sad, one loses the implications, and in the end, even the impression of sadness is slight. It is essential that one not say of a thing that "it is sad," but that it be sad of itself. For example, when one praises a place renowned for its scenery such as Matsushima by saying, "Ah, what a fine view!" one has said in one phrase all that one can about the sight, but without effect. If one wishes to praise the view, and one says numerous things indirectly about its appearance, the quality of the view may be known of itself, without one's having to say, "It is a fine view." This is true of everything of its kind.

Someone said, "People nowadays will not accept plays unless they are realistic and well reasoned out. There are many things in the old stories which people will not now tolerate. It is thus that such people as *kabuki* actors are considered skillful to the degree that their acting resembles reality. The first consideration is to have the retainer in the play resemble a real retainer, and to have the daimyō look like a real daimyō. People will not stand for childish nonsense as they did in the past." I

---

[2] The journey, such as that of the lovers in "The Love Suicides at Sonezaki."
[3] These were popular recitations of ballads, gossip, etc., which flourished particularly about this time.

answered, "Your view seems plausible, but it is a theory which does not take into account the real methods of art. Art is something which lies in the slender margin between the real and the unreal. Of course it seems desirable, in view of the current taste for realism, to have the retainer in the play copy the gestures and speech of a real retainer, but in that case should a real retainer put rouge and powder on his face like an actor? Or, would it prove entertaining if an actor, on the grounds that real retainers do not make up their faces, were to appear on the stage and perform with his beard growing wild and his head shaven? This is what I mean by the slender margin between the real and the unreal. It is unreal, and yet it is not unreal; it is real, and yet it is not real. Entertainment lies between the two."

In this connection, there is the story of a certain court lady who had a lover. The two loved each other very passionately, but the lady lived far deep in the women's palace, and the man could not visit her quarters. She could see him therefore only very rarely, from between the cracks of her screen of state at the court. She longed for him so desperately that she had a wooden image carved of the man. Its appearance was not like that of an ordinary doll, but did not differ in any particle from the man. It goes without saying that the color of his complexion was perfectly rendered; even the pores of his skin were delineated. The openings in his ears and nostrils were fashioned, and there was no discrepancy even in the number of teeth in the mouth. Since it was made with the man posing beside it, the only difference between the man and this doll was the presence in one, and the absence in the other, of a soul. However, when the lady drew the doll close to her and looked at it, the exactness of the reproduction of the living man chilled her, and she felt unpleasant and rather frightened. Court lady that she was, her love was also chilled, and as she found it distressing to have the doll by her side, she soon threw it away.

In view of this we can see that if one makes an exact copy of a living being, even if it happened to be Yang Kuei-fei, one will become disgusted with it. If when one paints an image or carves it of wood there are, in the name of artistic license, some stylized parts in a work otherwise resembling the real form; this is, after all, what people love in art. The same is true of literary composition. While bearing resemblance to the original, it should have stylization; this makes it art, and is what delights men's minds. Theatrical dialogue written with this in mind is apt to be worth while.

Yamazaki Masakazu teaches at Osaka University in Japan; he is both a scholar of Japanese theater and a well-known playwright whose plays have been translated into a variety of languages. In this essay, he outlines the major themes of Zeami's essays.

YAMAZAKI MASAKAZU

"THE AESTHETICS OF AMBIGUITY: THE ARTISTIC THEORIES OF ZEAMI" (1984)

When compared with the other views of the theater in the world, particularly with various dramatic theories of the West, Zeami's artistic theory clearly demonstrates three major characteristics. First, Zeami attached great importance to the audience that witnessed a performance; second, he laid a particular emphasis on the actor's mental and physical acting among the diverse elements that constitute the theater; third, he gave a high place to stylization in acting.

When speaking of classical dramatic theories of the West, one would cite Aristotle's *Poetics* as the first comprehensive attempt; but in an almost symbolic fashion, this first dramatic theory in the world almost completely lacks reference to the three elements mentioned above. This work by Aristotle is, first of all, a theory of the creation of the drama (as its title in Greek, ΠΕΡΙ ΠΟΙΗΤΙΚΗΣ, shows) and analyzes its structure. Although the author describes precisely and thoroughly how a play should be written, he does not go at all into how the play will be acted or seen by the audience. Aristotle compares literary works, including the drama, with historical narratives, or analyzes art in relation to reality, but he never looks into the relationship between creation and appreciation, or between the work and the audience. One can even say that the very fact the audience does affect the production of art in various subtle ways, and does participate actively in making the theater what it is, was not present in his mind.

Needless to say, according to Aristotle, the essence of the theater is the imitation of action in the form of action, and here the definition "in the form of action," is merely set against the idea of "in the form of narration." In other words, the philosopher is saying that when writing a play the dramatist should not portray his characters from the outside in the fashion of an epic poet, but should enter into them and look at the world from their viewpoints. Within this framework, Aristotle does not completely ignore the importance of acting. In Chapter 17, he even demands of the dramatist a kind of empathic acting.[1] Aristotle insisted that a man who is himself feeling real sorrow and real rage can express such emotions convincingly and make his audience believe in them effectively. However, this view concerned only the internal acting by the dramatist; Aristotle's demand did not extend to the imitation of action by a real actor making use of his voice and body. If the actor's body movements or voice production is considered in Aristotle's theory of the drama at all, it is only in connection with the aural or visual effects of the performance, and even as such, it is subsidiary to references to the plot, characterization, thought, or diction, and is clearly given a peripheral position.[2]

One may say that in the *Poetics* the performance of a play itself is a secondary subject; and if that is so, it is natural that questions of stylization in acting or directing are not seriously considered.

Aristotle was apparently a realist of a sort in his view of internal acting by the dramatist, and seems to have thought that the only function of acting is to communicate unadulterated emotions precisely. From their characteristics known today, we may deduce that classical Greek tragedies required highly stylized acting, but the fact that such acting was not of aesthetic interest to Aristotle was decisive for the history of dramatic theories of the West.

Later in the Renaissance period, the West saw signs of Aristotelian poetics reviving along with the resurgence of the theater itself, and on that foundation many literary scholars developed their own dramatic theories. The central argument was again on the writing of the drama—its subject matter, construction, or style. Very little attention was given to the techniques of performance.

The only exception was an Italian humanist, Leone de Somi (1527–1592), who turned his eyes to the art of acting in the latter half of the sixteenth century and wrote a discourse called "A Dialogue on Acting." The eighteenth century finally saw some growth in the interest in the theory of acting: Luigi Riccoboni's *On the Art of Declamation*, his son François Riccoboni's *L'Art du théâtre*, and Pierre Rémond de Sainte-Albine's *Le comédien* were published. This led to the writing of the famous *Paradoxe sur le comédien* by Denis de Diderot.[3]

All these, however, were but fragmentary technical discussions on acting that lacked any firm aesthetic foundation. They were interested in some limited aspect of acting. Their only major argument revolved around opposing ideas as to whether acting should be based on real emotions or on intellectual observation that excluded emotion. In one sense it represented a dispute between the Aristotelian theory of acting and the theory that opposed it.

This conflict was continued into the nineteenth century, when William Archer discussed the choice between two alternatives, masks or faces. Even then, one may conclude that the mainstream of opinion descended from Aristotle's theory of empathy. For example, Stanislavsky's "method" of realistic acting later came to dominate the modern theater worldwide; it, in short, valued the truth of emotion and denied all stylized acting.

This tradition of the denial of stylization goes back many centuries. In existing records of the Roman era, one can see traces of the fact that actors at that time aimed principally to be realistic. According to Aulus Gellius, the actor named Polus was praised for keeping to himself the sorrow he felt at the death of his son and so making a clever use of it in acting the role of Orestes.[4]

The famous lines in Scene 2 of Act III of *Hamlet* are often cited as an indication of Shakespeare's theory of acting, and the idea that actors should hold a mirror up to nature must also be read as a manifesto on realism in a wider sense of the word. It is widely known that French classicists

---

[1] "Again, the poet should work out his play, to the best of his power, with appropriate gestures; for those who feel emotion are most convincing through natural sympathy with the characters they represent; and one who is agitated storms, one who is angry rages, with the most life-like reality." S. M. Butcher, trans., *Aristotle's Theory of Poetry and Fine Art* (New York: Dover, 1951), pp. 61–62.

[2] "The spectacle has, indeed, an emotional attraction of its own, but, of all the parts, it is the least artistic, and connected least with the art of poetry. For the power of tragedy, we may be sure, is felt even apart from representation and actors." Butcher, *Aristotle*, p. 29. "Again, tragedy like epic poetry produces its effect even without action; it reveals its power by mere reading." Butcher, *Aristotle*, p. 109.

[3] Details concerning these various treatises and translations of important sections from them can be found in various entries in Toby Cole and Helen K. Chinoy, eds., *Actors on Acting* (New York: Crown, 1972). A discussion and evaluation of certain aspects of these treatises from the point of view of a pioneer of the modern theater can be found in chapter 2 of William Archer's *Masks or Faces? A Study in the Psychology of Acting* (London and New York: Longmans, Green & Co., 1888).

[4] See *Actors on Acting*, pp. 14–15.

always asked for the pursuit of "naturalness" at the same time as they demanded a recapitulation of the classics in their concept of the theater. On the Shakespearean stage and in the acting of French classics, various types of stylization were actually required, and lines were written in magnificent verse; yet no theoretical attempt was made to affirm that fact in any positive fashion.

Moreover, even in the modern age, when Stanislavsky and his successors took the center stage, the audience was always treated as a subordinate factor in a performance and was never regarded as an essential part of dramatic creation. Ironically, modern dramatic theories were devised rather as an inquiry into the necessary means to allow the actor to forget the audience and make him independent of it. When the proscenium arch came to be an integral part of theaters and succeeded in physically separating the auditorium from the stage, then and only then did modern realistic acting in the strict sense of the word come into being. Stanislavsky's actors tried to guard the truth of the emotions to be expressed by imagining an invisible "fourth wall" on the auditorium side of the stage and by deliberately disregarding the audience on the other side of that wall.

It is no exaggeration to say that the idea of demanding that the audience participate actively in the performance and the recognition of their worth in dramatic creation as a whole appeared in the West for the first time in the latter half of the twentieth century.

In contrast to these Western views of drama, it is obvious how great an importance Zeami placed on the audience. At the very beginning of his *Teachings on Style and the Flower* (Fūshikaden), he insisted that the ideal of the performing arts is to gain the love and respect of the people. To perform in front of an audience consisting of people of diverse tastes and to capture the heart of all of them was the basic task of an actor. Zeami went so far as to place an extremely difficult responsibility on the actor, which was to perform the *nō* so that it would be enjoyable even to those who have no eye for it. On the one hand, Zeami was an artist who pursued purity in the theater and gave birth to a highly sophisticated theatrical taste, but on the other hand he set for himself the almost contradictory task of pleasing the popular audience at all times.[5] One must not overlook the fact that this emphasis on the audience penetrates deep into his essential idea of the theater and further into his fundamental thoughts on beauty.

Zeami uses the word Flower (*hana*) to describe the beauty of the performing arts or the aesthetic effect of the theater. According to his definition, this Flower is none other than Fascination, and Fascination none other than Novelty. Novelty means something the audience has not seen before, something that always remains fresh in its creative power. In Zeami's mind, Novelty did not mean something odd or something that was singular in kind. It was a quality that emerged out of the technique of making the old look new by various devices used in theatrical presentation. Spectators become bored when shown the same thing repeatedly; on the other hand, it is impossible for an artist to go on producing different qualities infinitely. Zeami managed to repeat the familiar and, by skillfully alternating it with different or unfamiliar elements, to revitalize the image in the spectator's mind. Therein lay the secret of his art.

In that sense, the reason why he compared the beauty of the performing arts to a flower was not simply because a flower is perceived as beautiful in a sensuous fashion. To this great artist, a flower was beautiful because it would shed its petals. In the sense that a flower undergoes constant changes in front of the viewer, it can be compared to an artistic ideal.

His well-known saying, "If hidden, acting shows the Flower; if unhidden, it cannot," for example, comes out of his consideration for his audience and his profound analysis of their psychology. If the audience can see beforehand the performer's calculations in his acting or becomes conscious of his inventions, the dramatic effect that is produced as a result can be neither novel nor fresh. As a consequence, Zeami demands that while showing the results of his acting to the audience, the actor should at all costs hide his self-awareness or the psychological processes that lead to such results from the spectators' eyes. Later this demand was taken even one level higher. The actor was asked to

---

[5] Zeami was active at the period when Kyoto, the aristocratic capital, was becoming swollen with new arrivals of different classes—warriors, farmers, merchants—all resulting from the establishment of a new military regime, the Ashikaga bakufu, which took over the middle of the city. Intellectuals of the time, such as Yoshida Kenkō, were keenly aware of the discrepancy in aesthetic tastes between the serene and individualistic "men of breeding," and the crazed "rustic boors who take all their pleasures grossly." See Yoshida Kenkō, *Essays in Idleness*, translated by Donald Keene (New York: Columbia University Press, 1967), p. 118.

"hide his own mind from himself" or to hide from himself what the awareness of his own efforts does to him. That is the state the actor reaches when he has completely digested his artistic skills through repeated and thorough training and rehearsals, thus integrating his mind and body so that dramatic effects appear almost automatically or spontaneously. In other words, the actor keeps back from the audience the impression that he is controlling their emotions and takes care not to give the impression of the expansion of his self to the audience.

This emphasis on the audience is characteristic not only of Japanese dramatic theories but of its artistic theories in general. Donald Keene in his *Japanese Literature: An Introduction for Western Readers* quotes Ki no Tsurayuki's preface to the early anthology of court poetry, the *Kokinshū*, and points out that an idea completely opposed to Western aesthetics is recognizable in Tsurayuki's thought. The Japanese poet held that poetry grows out of the human heart, touches it and goes beyond human beings to move even nature and supernatural beings. According to Mr. Keene, Western poetics believe that poetry is born out of the supernatural and moves human beings in the guise of human language.[6] The traditional view of art in the West held that art came into being out of the relations between the artist as an individual and what was called a god or an ideal—in other words, between man and the supernatural. In this context, a work of art was created by a lonely genius outside the common or mundane world; therefore another man's appreciation had only a secondary significance.

From the point of view of this idealistic aestheticism, the value that art must pursue, whether it be beauty or truth, must always be seen as at the end of a one-directional road. Since all realities are but copies of their ideas, the correct appearance of reality is produced by approaching as close as possible to that idea. In classicism, the ideal of beauty was given as an objective canon, whereas romanticism sought to achieve more direct and subjective unity with ideas. In either case, the artist was required to pursue a pure and one-dimensional objective at all times.

Needless to say, even in the West attempts were made apart from idealism to see man as an ambiguous being, and to understand reality as a paradoxical world. It is widely known that Socrates was a genius of paradoxes. Shakespeare's plays are studded with lines that portray the ambiguity of man's existence, such as "Fair is foul, foul is fair" at the beginning of *Macbeth*. Nevertheless, the fundamental aesthetics of the West ultimately aim to capture an ideal in its purest form, and have tried to eliminate all that is inconclusive or ambiguous; in other words, an attempt has been made to exclude compromises between the artist and the rest of humanity.

Even in the modern age, when people began to believe that art must portray reality, the basic idealism did not change. Realism allowed no compromise on the part of the actor, and demanded that he portray social injustices and human uglinesses relentlessly. In addition, the Western tradition required that the artist be aloof to his secular surroundings. He was expected to make his art outside the framework of actual human relations.

In the Japanese tradition, by contrast, art almost always stemmed from actual human relations. Take lyric poetry, for instance. *Waka* poems were customarily made at various parties and later specifically at poetry parties, which were a unique form of social gathering. At such a party, a poem was considered completed when it was appreciated and evaluated by those present as soon as it was made. Afterwards this custom developed further and produced the form of *renga* in which a number of persons contributed to create one unified work. In the case of the fine arts, as well, a painting was deemed completed only when it was seen by people at a salon and their impression was inscribed on the picture in the form of a poem. Furthermore, Japan produced a unique form of art, the tea ceremony. The fact that social formalities were heightened into art is enough to suggest how the Japanese traditional view of art functioned.

Reflecting such a tradition, Japanese aesthetic thought did not and does not encourage pursuit of any aesthetic ideal in one direction of purification. Rather, to the contrary, all aesthetic effects are believed to become what they are while containing contradictory elements within themselves.

According to Yoshida Kenkō (1283–1350), a noted essayist of the medieval period, a man of good taste should not look directly at anything beautiful, whether it be the moon or a flower. The

---

[6] See Donald Keene, *Japanese Literature, An Introduction for Western Readers* (New York: Grove Press, 1955), p. 22.

CRITICAL CONTEXTS **179**

correct attitude is *yosonagara ni miru,* or to long for it indirectly from some distance.[7] This idea was later succeeded by the aesthetics of *wabi,* according to which anything gorgeous becomes truly beautiful when joined with something subdued, so as to become half concealed by it. One of the originators of the tea ceremony, Murata Shukō (1422–1502), said, "I do not like the moon without clouds." The point of the aesthetics of *wabi* was summed up in the words of Rikyū (1521–1591), the greatest of the tea masters, as "a fine steed tethered in a thatched shack."

In Japanese literature from the Heian to the Edo period, the technique of allusion (*honkadori*) in poetry and of parody (*mojiri*) in fiction were particularly liked, reflecting a taste that valued the duality of imagery—creating, in other words, an aesthetics of paradox.

Whereas a transcendental being essentially represents a single value and never varies its demand, man's existence cannot be separated from his physical senses, and so he cannot endure the pureness of any singular and homogeneous value. However much a man may like brightness, he cannot keep his eyes open in the direct rays of the sun. A man may have a sweet tooth, but if he were forced to keep on taking pure sugar forever, he would find it painful. Man's senses easily become fatigued and bored with any unadulterated object; the only way to keep them satisfied is to change continuously the nature of the stimulation. Moreover, just as sweetness is enhanced by a small amount of salt or bitterness mixed in with it, it is well known that man's sensitivity is heightened by the addition of an opposing element.

Such observations help us to see that since Japanese art is created not before a transcendental being but by one human being for another, it is natural for its aesthetic ideal to show an essentially paradoxical and ambiguous character. It is also easily understandable how in the thinking of Zeami, who worked face to face with his audiences as an artist in the theater, such an aesthetics of paradox came to rule his thought. For example, he set the concept of Grace (*yūgen*) as the supreme goal of his art, but this idea of beauty, of which sophistication and grace constituted the essence, could not be achieved by pursuing it directly.

Zeami's family, who came originally from the farming district in Iga and who represented the artistic taste of the powerful local clan, was particularly good at acting out stories with many dramatic ups and downs and at presenting various characters in a realistic manner. One can imagine that their original style lay in portraying diverse characters with clearly marked personalities. On the technical side they laid emphasis on descriptive gestures and stage speech. Starting from this base of unsophisticated realism, Zeami achieved an urban refinement of expression. In more specific terms, he developed a style that emphasized song and dance. He called this new form of beauty "grace."

In this sense, from the beginning his idea of Grace presupposed its opposite as the condition for its existence, and it came into being through the unification of reality and idealization, of individuality and refinement, of popular traits and aristocratic taste. When an actor is to play the part of a fierce warrior, for instance, Zeami demands that a trace of Grace be added to the realistic representation of the character. According to his own words, the effect must be "like a flower blooming on a rock." In the portrayal of an old man, while demanding an expression of the decline of strength and of the anguish that accompanies human life, Zeami required a shade of splendor and charm; he described the effect as "a flower blooming on a dead tree." Needless to say, what he demanded in these instances was not mere compromise or eclecticism, but a dramatic conflict between two contradictory elements, the rock and the flower, or the dead tree and the flower.

In passing, one should note that Zeami showed a special liking for the figure of a beautiful woman who had lost her sanity. In this case, contrary to the examples above, a realistic element of madness is mixed into the portrayal of elegance, with an aim of unifying the charm of static beauty and that of mobility.

In his *Teachings on Style and the Flower,* Zeami cites the basic components of the *nō,* which he calls the Two Basic Arts of song and dance (*nikyoku*) and the Three Role Types (*santai*). From one point of view, the essential opposition also exists between the Two Basic Arts and the Three Role Types. For a man to sing and dance is to leave the reality of his life, but to play a role is to face reality directly and to reconfirm it. Clearly the former represents the lyrical aspects of acting and

---

[7] See *Essays in Idleness,* pp. 115–118.

the latter the epic. Whereas the former aims for fluidity of movement, the latter attempts at articulation. Zeami regarded the unification of this essential opposition as the central task of acting, and in his mind, acting was itself a paradoxical action. Hegel saw dramatic literature as unifying the lyrical and the epic, and explained it as the dialectic between the subjective spirit and the objective spirit; but Zeami saw the unification occurring in physical acting itself.

Going one step further and looking into Zeami's analysis of actual acting, one notices that he counterposes two basic methods, imitation and becoming. "Imitation" means to copy gestures and facial expressions realistically. It means to observe a human action, analyze it, and reproduce it consciously in detail. On the other hand, "becoming" means that the actor assimilates himself into the emotions of the character. It means that he sees human action as a stream of consciousness that never slackens, throws himself into the stream, and is carried along by it.

When the actor tries to imitate something, he manipulates his body as an object, or paints, as it were, using his body as the canvas; but he transcends the break between his body and mind when he attempts to "become" the character. When he has completely assimilated himself into the character, he fills his heart and mind with the emotions of that character alone, and tries to allow those emotions to move his body with their own force. At such times, he has become completely united with his own body, and he can forget about each specific gesture and facial expression, while keeping hold on the continuous flow of consciousness.

According to Zeami, ideal acting is founded on the unity of these two methods. He describes it, for instance, as "connecting all the arts through one intensity of mind." All arts here denote the various technical skills of acting that enable the actor to represent the character's actions objectively and analytically. Zeami likens their working to the movements of the limbs of a lifeless puppet. What gives life to this mechanical contraption and incorporates it in flowing movement is Zeami's "one mind," the act of keeping a certain level of heightened tension in the mind. In other words, the former is the actor turning the eye of consciousness toward the outside, and the latter toward the inside. It is by no means easy to unite the two in a balanced state. In reality, man tends to control and manipulate his own body as an object, and the actor inclines more toward "imitation" and forgets the maintenance of "one mind."

Well aware of this, Zeami demands that the actor hold the function of "all arts" deliberately in check, and communicate his internal tension directly to the audience. To help achieve that purpose, he quotes a phrase used in criticizing the *nō*, "the less done the better." Through these words, he is teaching the fact that even when the actor has stopped all exterior movement of his body, the well-disciplined dynamism of the body itself can move the audience.[8]

In regard to the style of dance in the *nō*, Zeami first defines the two opposing basic forms of Self-Conscious Movement (*shuchi*) and Movement beyond Consciousness (*buchi*), and places above them Mutuality in Balance (*sōkyokuchi*), which comes into being as the unification of the two. Self-Conscious Movement is the style based on the articulated movement of various parts of the body, including the limbs, and Movement beyond Consciousness is born out of the actor's committing his body to the continuous flow of movement itself. In explaining the dance in terms of Movement beyond Consciousness, Zeami likens it to a bird spreading its wings and floating in the air. This static state, which is full of tension, must correspond to the ideal of "the less done the better." For Zeami, this internal tension was always the foundation of acting, and any external and articulated movement was to be added on top of it. Needless to say, the ideal was a perfect balance between the two. Indeed, in regard to the dance, he defined that state specifically as the original style called Mutuality in Balance.

What Zeami stresses in his teachings to actors, however, is none other than "becoming" and the possession of "one mind." He calls the actor who has acquired that ability one who can show Internalization (*yūshufū*). Internalization requires that an actor become the complete master of his

---

[8] In performances of *nō* as presently staged, it may seem to some members of the audience that the aspect of "becoming" is overemphasized, and that the technique of "the less done the better" is excessively abused by the actors. It is certainly true that throughout the Tokugawa period (1600–1867), efforts were made, under the strong pressure of the Shōguns, to remove the *nō* from the life of the ordinary people and to reduce realistic and expressive acting in order to make the form as aristocratic as possible. Zeami's assertions must be understood in the context of his own historical period.

own movements, and according to Zeami it denotes a state in which the flow of movement has become so well assimilated that the actor loses even the consciousness of controlling it.

In this regard, one can say that this great artist's theory of acting went beyond the argument prevalent in the West since the eighteenth century concerning the opposition between masks and faces. Diderot's stand was that acting which moves the audience rises out of the actor's conscious manipulation of his body. Archer's idea was that, on the contrary, such acting came spontaneously from the actor's own feelings. These two views clearly correspond to the contrast between Zeami's "imitation" and "becoming." However, Zeami did not see the mask and the face as requiring a choice among alternatives; rather he wanted the actor to unify the two while retaining a positive consciousness of their opposition. In connection with the expression of a strong emotion, in particular, Zeami strictly demanded this ambiguous attitude. He carefully warned the actor against indulging in his own emotions as well as using his technique to manipulate them. This concept is clearly shown in his teaching, "What is felt by the heart is ten; what appears in movement is seven," and "Violent body movement, gentle foot movement." He wanted the actor to place his body under a certain amount of control. This idea led Zeami to form a particular attitude about the role of a demon, for example. He insisted that even while playing the part of a ferocious demon, the actor's physical expressions must, to some extent, be elegant and delicate.

What Zeami taught specifically to the actors in order to make them tackle this contradictory task of acting was, first, to understand a role in terms of an attitude and, second, to see action as a rhythmical structure. Either of these can become a direct aim for an actor's efforts, and they may be described as the focus for his consciousness, giving him a target for his attention and saving him from confusion and disruption.

Zeami divides nō characters into three basic types, the old man, the woman, and the warrior, and it is obvious that these three represent the basic attitudes of man toward his world. The old man represents the attitude of retiring from life, and the calm contemplation of it. The warrior shows an aggressive and vigorous attitude. The woman stands between the two, symbolizing an attitude of harmony with the world.

This artist, however, did not see attitudes of man on the spiritual plane alone but also regarded them as very concrete attitudes of the body. For example, the old man's attitude is described in the following single sentence: "Relaxed Heart Looking Afar." In this brief summation, the contradictory characteristics of an old man's behavior are united; that is to say, he has given up on this life but still possesses a final concern over the future, which is physically expressed in his calm look directed afar. Zeami warns the actor who plays the old man's part against merely imitating the decline in physical appearance, and encourages him rather to express the man's desire to remain young. In this feat, also, "imitating" and "becoming" need to be united, and as a specific psychological technique, Zeami teaches his actors to assume one particular mental and bodily attitude.

He also pointed out that there is a modulating structure of *jo*, *ha*, and *kyū* in human actions. He believed that it was a duty of acting to unify actions into one complete image by bringing out this rhythmic structure. All actions form one unit when they begin in an easy manner (*jo*), develop dramatically (*ha*), and finish rapidly (*kyū*); and then they can give the viewer the impression of an organic unity.

In real life, this rhythmical structure meets many obstructions posed by various conditions. Part of the process is broken down or its order disturbed. The structure is manifested in its complete form only when such obstacles are eliminated, and when man can move while consciously giving his attention to it. This kind of special action represents acting, which includes singing and dancing. Or rather, according to Zeami, acting makes a positive use of external conditions in order to give the impression of this rhythm, and the actor can take even the atmosphere of the theater and the general feeling of the audience into the structure of *jo*, *ha*, and *kyū*. By acting well, he gives order to his environment, or, to use a different expression, he reflects the rhythm of reality in his body.

This bodily and mental attitude and the rhythm of action complement each other in acting; the former is the spatial support of acting, and the latter its chronological axis. But, needless to say, each of them takes its reciprocal place in the character of acting in its entirety, which achieves a happy balance between those two aspects. One attitude consists of the internal workings of a man as manifested directly on his outward appearance, and also represents a point of contact between the conscious and the unconscious in movement. When a man takes this attitude, he keeps his consciousness in a completely awakened state, but the details of his action emanate almost automatically from that attitude. Therefore, a man takes an attitude through an active use of his will, but once that attitude is established, he is passively carried along by it. Exactly the same is true of rhythm. A man may consciously create a rhythm, and at the same time be moved by it as if intoxicated. A rhythm is founded on the unity between contradictory elements—drive and restraint, flow and articulation. A man can therefore view it from the outside and also make it three-dimensional by immersing himself in it. As far as his actions are concerned, as long as he makes them sufficiently rhythmical, he is, so to speak, automatically uniting the fact of being outside his actions and inside them.

Attitude and rhythm are found, of course, in all of man's actions. It is obvious that in daily life they are distorted in almost all cases, and often destroyed; man tries to control his actions too consciously or, on the contrary, often leaves them to completely habitual and unconscious progression.

In real life, man tends to be concerned only with the aim and results of his action and, as a consequence, is engrossed only in efficiency and economy of labor for achieving them. When it is difficult to attain his aims, man manipulates his body as a tool and makes haste, leaning forward in the effort. When the goal is easy to attain, man throws away the tension necessary to assume any one attitude and so becomes one with his body, simply carried along by its movement. It goes without saying that in either case his attitude loses its essential balance, and the ambiguous character of the rhythm is destroyed. Acting, as a consequence, will become either imprecise, with the aspect of its fluidity accentuated, or will be reduced to a mechanical and clumsy level, with the aspect of its articulatedness more apparent. In all probability, so long as human civilization swings undecided between utilitarianism and laziness, man's action will always be threatened by both of them, and so will fail to attain a sound and beautiful appearance.

Having discussed this much, it is not necessary any longer to explain why Zeami showed no interest in realism of acting but endeavored to establish a stylized form for it. To this artist, it was song and dance, or the Two Basic Arts, and three basic characters, or Three Role Types, that stylized acting. The reason for this was that they gave action both a stable rhythm and an attitude. To Zeami, a beautiful style meant nothing other than the beautiful attitude for action and the ideal rhythm that all actions should possess. In other words, a style of acting is not a fiction for the stage but a form that all actions should possess in order to attain perfection as action. It is, however, a framework that actions tend to miss in reality. In this sense, if one is to state on Zeami's behalf his tacit and basic understanding, probably one should say that there is no perfect action that one must imitate in this world of reality, and a real action is restored to its ideal state only in stylized acting.

MEDIEVAL AND RENAISSANCE ENGLAND

T HE FIFTEENTH, SIXTEENTH, AND SEVENTEENTH CENTURIES SAW EUROPE transformed by the extraordinary cultural revolution we now call the European Renaissance. Fueled by new technology, like printing, and by new scientific, political, and religious ideas, explosive change transformed European culture. The known world expanded beyond the sea to embrace the New World; the recovery of Greek and Latin literature spurred a sweeping intellectual revolution; strong centralized monarchies in Spain, Portugal, France, and England created new empires abroad and fought to control an increasingly restive populace at home; the Protestant Reformation undermined the religious and political authority of the Catholic Church, beginning a period of violent religious conflict; the "new philosophy"—modern science—of Copernicus, Bacon, and Galileo seemed to put even the physical world of heaven and earth in doubt. "'Tis all in pieces, all coherence gone," the poet John Donne wrote in 1611, voicing the profound anxiety and exhilaration of many of his contemporaries: "Prince, subject, father, son are things forgot./For every man alone thinks that he hath got/To be a Phoenix." The changing tides of thought swept away the crumbling edifice of the medieval world—the feudal state, the universal Church, scholastic philosophy, an ordered heaven, and revealed truth—and opened the way for the modern world.

This revolution also infused the theater; the Renaissance—especially in Italy, France, Spain, and England—is one of the great ages of theatrical and dramatic achievement. In England, the professional theater as we know it originated at this time: the history of the secular, profit-making, commercial theater is conventionally dated from the opening of the first theater building, The Theatre, in London in 1576. Licensed and protected as an aristocratic entertainment, the theater was also a popular institution in which commoners such as William Shakespeare, Richard Burbage, Edward Alleyn, Inigo Jones, and others, could indeed rise like the phoenix. However, to understand the revolutionary impact of theater and drama in Shakespeare's era, we need to understand their conservative inheritance, their deep indebtedness to the medieval stage that preceded them.

Dramatic performance in medieval Europe was thoroughly conditioned by the Catholic Church's central role in the life of the community. Having closed the Roman theaters in the sixth century, the Church maintained a vigilant opposition to the secular theater and the vices associated with it. Yet the revival of theater in Europe, beginning in the tenth century, was inspired and sponsored by the Church itself. The four major dramatic forms in the late Middle Ages were connected with the Church, its rituals, and its calendar of religious observances: LITURGICAL DRAMA, enacted as part of the liturgy of the Catholic Mass; CYCLE PLAYS, illustrating scriptural history and performed by craft guilds on the feast of Corpus Christi; MORALITY DRAMA, enacting the symbolic structure of Christian life; and plays written and performed in schools and universities, sometimes imitating classical plays. In England, cycle and morality plays particularly influenced the later, secular drama of the sixteenth century.

The earliest dramatic records, dating from the ninth century, are musical TROPES, brief elaborations of the authorized liturgy, written to amplify the scriptural text and enhance its impact and appeal. These compositions were set to music and sung in ANTIPHONAL PERFORMANCE (back and forth, in dialogue) between monks or boy choristers to accompany the liturgy of the Mass. In England, Ethelwold, Bishop of Winchester, wrote a series of lessons concerning the conduct of the Mass, the *Regularis Concordia* (965–975), including instructions for such performances. These are his instructions to the priests for representing

DRAMA AND THEATER IN MEDIEVAL ENGLAND

the visit of the three Marys to the tomb of Christ after the Crucifixion (translated from Latin):

> While the third lesson is being chanted, let four brethren vest themselves; of whom, let one, vested in an alb, enter as if to take part in the service, and let him without being observed approach the place of the sepulchre [i.e., near the altar], and there, holding a palm in his hand, let him sit down quietly. While the third responsory is being sung, let the remaining three follow, all of them vested in copes, and carrying in their hands censers filled with incense; and slowly, in the manner of seeking something, let them come before the place of the sepulchre. These things are done in imitation of the angel seated in the monument, and of the women coming with spices to anoint the body of Jesus. When therefore that one seated shall see the three, as if straying about and seeking something, approach him, let him begin in a dulcet voice of medium pitch to sing:

> *Whom seek ye in the sepulchre, O followers of Christ?*

When he has sung this to the end, let the three respond in unison:

> *Jesus of Nazareth, which was crucified, O celestial one.*

To whom that one:

> *He is not here; he is risen; just as he foretold.*
> *Go, announce that he is risen from the dead.*

At the word of this command let those three turn themselves to the choir, saying:

> *Alleluia! The Lord is risen to-day.*
> *The strong lion, the Christ, the Son of God. Give thanks to God.*

This said, let the former, again seating himself, as if recalling them, sing the anthem:

> *Come, and see the place where the Lord was laid. Alleluia! Alleluia!*

And saying this, let him rise and let him lift the veil and show them the place bare of the cross, but only the cloths laid there with which the cross was wrapped. Seeing which, let them set down the censers which they carried into the same sepulchre, and let them take up the cloth and spread it out before the eyes of the clergy; and as if making known that the Lord had risen and was not now therein wrapped, let them sing this anthem:

> *The Lord is risen from the sepulchre.*
> *Who for us hung upon the cross.*

And let them place the cloth upon the altar. The anthem being ended, let the Prior, rejoicing with them at the triumph of our King, in that, having conquered death, he arose, begin the hymn:

> *We praise thee, O God.*

This begun, all the bells chime out together.[1]

---

[1] *Regularis Concordia,* in *Chief Pre-Shakespearean Dramas,* ed. Joseph Quincy Adams (Boston: Houghton Mifflin, 1924), 9–10.

Despite its brevity, and the limitations imposed by the liturgy itself, this trope has the elements of drama: a progressive plot, the involvement of specific characters, conflict and resolution. Ethelwold's "stage directions" convey a subtle sense of how character can be created by performance and a fine sense of visual spectacle as well, all within the narrow scope allowed by the Mass.

Throughout the Middle Ages and beyond, liturgical plays of this kind became increasingly common and complex. Enacted in different locations—called MANSIONS— within the church, liturgical drama provided a model for the forms of religious drama that came to be performed outside the church and outside the framework of the liturgy. In the tenth and eleventh centuries, the church sponsored dramatized scenes from the life of Christ or the lives of the saints, staged on important Christian holidays. A town, for example, might commemorate the entrance of Christ into Jerusalem on Palm Sunday with a procession to the cathedral in which townspeople enacted various roles. In addition, the church oversaw the production of cycles of plays, which became a principal mode of theatrical and dramatic innovation. These cycles were performed sixty days after Easter as part of the Feast of Corpus Christi, a holiday inaugurated in the fourteenth century to celebrate the doctrine of the Eucharist. The Corpus Christi festival frequently featured the performance of a series of plays dramatizing scriptural history—the Creation, Old Testament events (Noah and the Flood, Abraham and Isaac), scenes from the New Testament (the Annunciation, Herod and the Slaughter of the Innocents), and prophetic plays concerning the Harrowing of Hell and the Last Judgment. The production of these plays could last several days or weeks and called on the services of the entire town. Each craft guild (or *mystery*, as the guilds were called; the cycles are sometimes called MYSTERY CYCLES) financed and produced a different play, often on a subject appropriate to the guild. The shipwrights' guild might undertake the Noah play, the Three Kings play might be assigned to the goldsmiths, and so on. The plays were the property of the guilds and passed through generations of guild members. In major towns with many craft guilds, the cycles often included a large number of plays. Of the English cycles, the York cycle is the longest, containing forty-eight plays, the Wakefield cycle has thirty-two, and the Chester cycle has twenty-four.

Although they were produced for a popular, largely illiterate audience, the cycle dramas are extremely sophisticated and involved the talents of trained performers. One of the cycles' most powerful and typical features is their use of ANACHRONISM—the blending of the historical past with contemporary events and characters. Many of the characters who appear in the plays are medieval English peasants, who often display an ironic, even theatrical sense of their involvement in the scriptural events of the past. One of the most telling uses of this technique occurs in the York *Crucifixion*, for one of the ways that the York playwright conveys the Roman soldiers' hardness to the message of Christ is by making them jest with him about the cruxifixion they are performing:

> 1 SOLDIER: (to Christ) Say, Sir, how likes you now
>   This work that we have wrought?
> 2 SOLDIER: We pray you say us how
>   Ye feel, or faint ye aught.
> JESUS: . . . My Father, that all bales [evils] may beet [abate].
>   Forgive these men that do me pine [pain].
>   What they work wot [know] they nought;
>   Therefore, my Father, I crave,
>   Let never their sins be sought,
>   But see their souls to save.
> 1 SOLDIER: We! Hark! he jangles like a jay.

By characterizing the jesting Roman soldiers as, in effect, contemporaries of the medieval audience, the play implies that biblical events are part of the audience's contemporary

One actor is playing in the street in front of the wagon.

history. Seeing their neighbors enacting the biblical scenes, and seeing contemporary characters share the stage with biblical figures, must have emphasized the immediacy of the ongoing Christian story.

Like the cycle plays, morality plays dramatized elements of Christian life. Instead of staging events from scriptural history, morality drama stages a symbolic **ALLEGORY** of the Christian's spiritual journey through life. Increasingly popular throughout the fourteenth and fifteenth centuries, plays like *The Castle of Perseverance* (c. 1425), *Mankind* (c. 1470), and *Everyman* (c. 1500) emphasized the individual's struggle with sin, while the cycle plays emphasized the larger patterns of Christian history. Later playwrights, including

Shakespeare, found both models useful. The cycles provided a pattern for staging the epic sweep of secular English history, and morality drama provided a supple device for representing psychological and moral conflict. Morality plays often provided the structure for the secular plays written at schools and universities, as well, and for the INTERLUDES performed at court as a break from holiday feasting. They also provided a staple technique for characterization in the later secular drama. Christopher Marlowe's *Doctor Faustus* (1590) uses the Good and Evil Angels to externalize Faustus's moral conflict, and other playwrights frequently used the devices of morality drama to dramatize the difficulties of political choice. In John Skelton's interlude, *Magnificence* (1516)—written for Henry VIII—or Thomas Sackville and Thomas Norton's *Gorboduc* (1561), the monarch is shown to make his decisions framed by a host of allegorized counsellors, good and bad advisers who approximate the role played in morality drama by angels and demons.

Medieval plays were often acted on or near PAGEANT WAGONS. In some towns, it appears that the audience remained stationary at various locations, while the wagons and their plays proceeded past them; at others, the wagons were drawn in a procession of TABLEAUX VIVANTS (posed scenes) through the town and then arranged in an open area for the performance, allowing the audience to move from play to play. The plays combined historical and contemporary elements; in performance, the staging produced a close and powerful relationship between the dramatic characters and the audience. In the Coventry play of the Magi, for example, Herod raves when he discovers that the three kings have escaped him:

> I Stamp! I Stare! I look all about!
> Might I them take, I should them burn at a glede [fire]!
> I rant! I run! and now run I wode [mad]
> A! That these villain traitors hath marred this my mood!
> They shall be hanged, if I may come them to!
> *Here Herod rages in the pagond* [pageant wagon] *and in the street also.*[2]

Herod's rage was certainly one of the highlights of the medieval cycles. Shakespeare, at least, seems to refer to it in *Hamlet* (1600), when he has Hamlet remind his actors that they should be restrained and natural in their performance, for overacting "out-Herods Herod." The stage direction also suggests that Herod's frenzy carried him from the wagon and into the street, into a closer and more effective relationship to his audience. This interaction between actor and audience is characteristic of popular theater and is a feature of medieval performance carried into Renaissance acting. It also suggests that the "place" of medieval drama, the fictitious locale of the play, was not firmly localized onstage; the actors/ characters could move easily back and forth between Herod's Jerusalem and the medieval audience, and even onstage places could be rapidly and easily transformed. This flexibility also allowed medieval playwrights to treat stage space symbolically. The ground plot for *The Castle of Perseverance*, for instance—with its scaffolds for various evils, its moat, and its central castle—clearly offers us a symbolic locale rather than an actual geography. The various demons on their scaffolds stand at a symbolic distance, not an actual distance, from the central castle.

This complex of dramatic conventions, staging practices, and audience attitudes is a legacy of the medieval theater passed on to later theater. Although the medieval stage was only one of many influences on it, the drama of the sixteenth and seventeenth centuries is reminiscent of medieval drama in many ways. Renaissance drama frequently treats secular history according to a providential design similar to that of the cycles; it often treats its

STAGING MEDIEVAL DRAMA

---

[2] The Coventry *Magi, Herod, and the Slaughter of the Innocents*, in *Chief Pre-Shakespearean Dramas*, ed. Joseph Quincy Adams (Boston: Houghton Mifflin, 1924), 163.

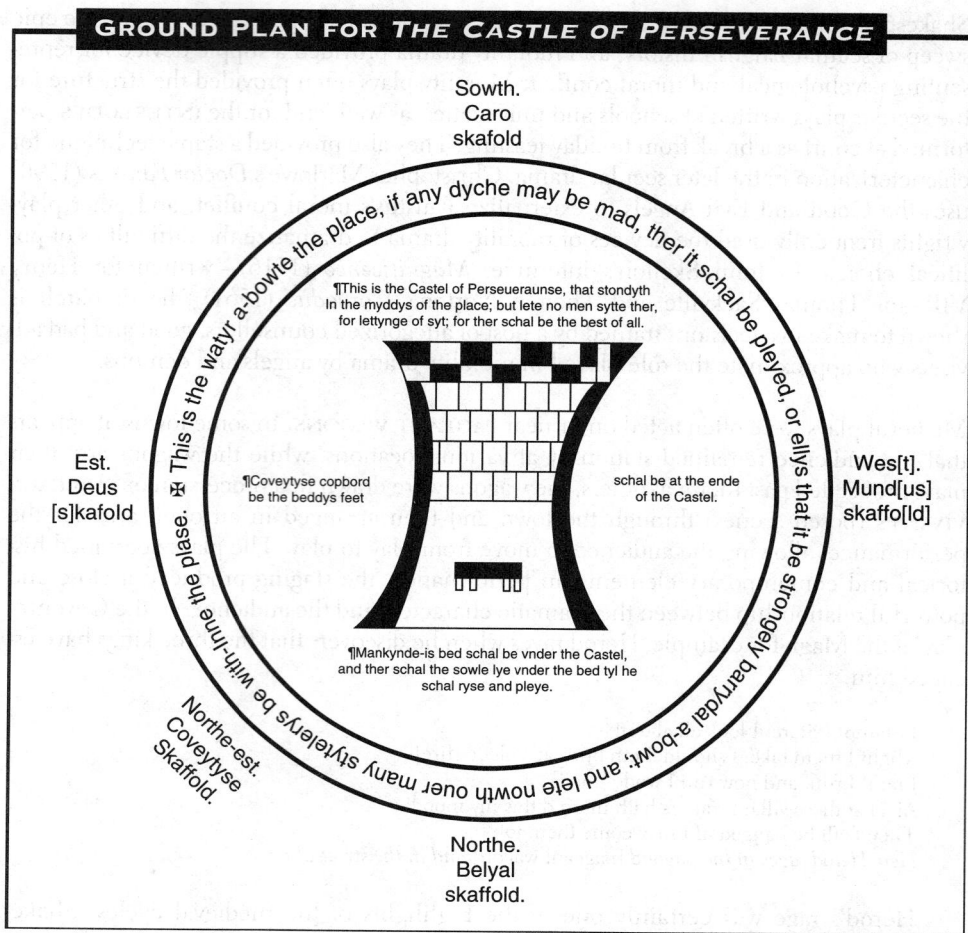

GROUND PLAN FOR *THE CASTLE OF PERSEVERANCE*

Sowth.
Caro
skafold

¶This is the watyr a-bowte the place, if any dyche may be mad, ther it schal be pleyed, or ellys that it be strongly barryd al a-bowt; and lete nowth ouer many stytelerys be with-inne the plase.

¶This is the Castel of Perseuerraunse, that stondyth
In the myddys of the place; but lete no men sytte ther,
for lettynge of syt; for ther schal be the best of all.

Est.
Deus
[s]kafold

¶Coveytyse copbord
be the beddys feet

schal be at the ende
of the Castel.

Wes[t].
Mund[us]
skaffo[ld]

¶Mankynde-is bed schal be vnder the Castel,
and ther schal the sowle lye vnder the bed tyl he
schal ryse and pleye.

Northe-est.
Coveytyse
Skaffold.

Northe.
Belyal
skaffold.

The ground-plot for the medieval morality play shows five scaffolds (North, Northeast, South, East, and West) arranged around a playing area, with a castle in the center. A ditch enclosed the castle to keep spectators at a distance. In the manuscript, a note beneath the drawing describes the costumes and special effects: "He that shall play Belial [a devil], look that he have gunpowder burning in pipes in his hands and in his ears, and in his arse, when he goes to battle. The four daughters should be clad in mantles; Mercy in white, Ruthwiseness in red, all together, Truth in sad green, and Peace all in black; and they shall play in the place all together until they bring up the soul."

characters in the symbolic terms of the medieval moralities; and it uses both acting and stage space to create an immediacy between the fictive play and its audience. These habits take on very different meanings in Renaissance London, in a city and in a state in which the Anglican Protestant church is the state religion and where signs of Catholicism—or, in fact, of any religious subject matter—in the theater could be read as an act of sedition. The medieval theater provided the forms of drama and the practices of theater that were refashioned by the political, social, and theatrical pressures of the new era.

DRAMA AND THEATER IN RENAISSANCE LONDON

The explosion of theatrical and dramatic activity in London can be marked by two dates: 1567, when John Brayne built the Red Lion, London's first purpose-built theater (his brother-in-law, James Burbage, built The Theatre in 1576); and 1642, when plays were suspended and theaters were closed at the outbreak of the Civil War. The theater underwent profound changes from the reign of Elizabeth I (ruled 1558–1603) to the reigns of her successors James I (1603–1625) and Charles I (1625–1642, executed 1649), and yet at the same time it endured the intense social and cultural upheavals of the period with remarkable consistency. As an institution, the new professional theater witnessed the emergence of England as a modern state; the rise of England as an important mercantile and naval power, aided by the defeat of the Spanish Armada in 1588; the expansion of English interests in the New World; the growth of the city of London to roughly 250,000 inhabitants; and the ascendance of the Puritan faction that closed the theaters and deposed and executed the king.

The professional theater—a new institution in England, though already established on the continent—necessarily reflected the political and social strains of the time. These strains are most readily visible in the many laws regulating theatrical performance. The location of theater buildings, the structure and organization of theater companies, and the entire scene of theatrical activity in Renaissance London epitomized the fundamental tensions of English society as it moved from the medieval to the modern world.

The sixteenth century witnessed intense religious and civil controversy, dating in part from Henry VIII's divorce from Catherine of Aragon in 1532 and his consequent excommunication from the Catholic church in 1533. Once Henry established the Protestant Church of England as the religion of the realm in 1535, English politics were often dictated by England's vulnerability to the massive, hostile powers of the Catholic church in Rome and Catholic states such as France and Spain. Within England, a variety of Protestant sects competed with each other, with the government, and with the Church of England for power. This was also a period of profound changes in the ordering of society, a period of growing mercantile power, of aristocratic discontent with the power of the Crown, and of the rise of new merchants and other social groups into prominence and power. As a result, the Crown was eternally on guard to suppress civil unrest or religious nonconformity.

Given this volatile political climate, it is not surprising that the Crown sought to limit and control public assembly, including theatrical performances. Laws were frequently directed against the theater, particularly against productions identified with England's Catholic past. In 1548, for example, the English church cancelled the Feast of Corpus Christi, and the production of the cycle plays was systematically suppressed. In 1569, the York cycle was performed for the last time, and in 1575, the Mayor of Chester was arrested for allowing cycle plays to be performed. Morality plays may have seemed less sectarian in the kind of instruction they offered; features of morality drama were more readily absorbed by the secular theater.

Yet while the Crown limited and censored the stage, it also maintained its traditional patronage of the theater as well. The famous "Act for the punishment of Vagabonds" of 1572 is a case in point. The law prohibited itinerant players and entertainers from wandering throughout the realm, but its ultimate effect was to establish permanent theatrical companies under the protection of noble patrons. The law ordered that "all Fencers, Bearwards, Common Players in Interludes, and Minstrels, not belonging to any Baron of this Realm, or towards any other honorable Personage of greater Degree . . . [who] wander abroad and have not License of two Justices of the Peace at the least . . . shall be taken adjudged and deemed Rogues Vagabonds and Sturdy Beggars." Unless they belonged to the retinue of a nobleman, players were classed with common vagrants and could be arrested and fined. Protected as servants, a company of players could receive a license to perform in public.

The statute points to the strong bond between the theater and the aristocracy, and patents granted by Elizabeth entitled noblemen to retain companies of actors as servants. These patents—granted for the Lord Chamberlain's Men (Shakespeare's company), the

THE PROFESSIONAL THEATER AND ITS SOCIETY

Lord Admiral's Men (who produced Marlowe's plays), and others—shaped the professional theater of Renaissance London. Elizabeth authorized such companies to perform "Comedies, Tragedies, Interludes, and stage plays" in public, both in London and elsewhere. Yet, in granting these privileges, the Crown made significant qualifications. Elizabeth required the companies to submit their plays to her Master of Revels for approval. She also stipulated that plays "be not published or shown in the time of common prayer, or in the time of great and common plague in our said City of London." Religious and civic officials exerted considerable authority over when and where plays could actually be performed and where theaters could legally be built, and they often closed theaters for months at a time due to plague or civil strife.

The City of London, like many towns, had its own ordinances prohibiting plays within the city limits, and for this reason James Burbage—a member of the Earl of Leicester's company—built The Theatre to the north of the city. Within a decade theaters had been built both to the north of the city and to the south, across the Thames River.

Although they were technically "servants," the major acting companies—the most famous being the Lord Chamberlain's Men, patented in 1593 and then given royal sponsorship as the King's Men when King James I succeeded Elizabeth in 1603—were organized as stockholding, profit-making corporations, that is, as business enterprises in the modern sense. Their economic survival depended on their public performances, for their patron might command and finance only a few productions per year. Several investors, or **SHARERS,** put up the capital to finance the company and took a percentage of its profits. The sharers were not just investors, they were involved in all aspects of the theater. The sharers of the King's Men, for example, included Shakespeare (playwright and actor), Richard Burbage (James Burbage's son and the company's principal actor, who was the first to play Shakespeare's King Lear, Hamlet, and Macbeth), the actors John Heminges and Henry Condell (who later published Shakespeare's plays), and several others. The sharers were responsible for building or leasing a theater, for purchasing plays, for taking on boy actors as apprentices, and for hiring other actors for each production. They also were liable when legal proceedings were brought against the company.

Although several companies flourished during the theater's heyday, life for actors and playwrights was hard. Any company could be forced (by theatrical fashion, plague, or fear of unrest) to leave the relative profit and security of London to take up the dangerous life of an itinerant troupe. Playwrights, who were paid a flat fee by the company for the script of a play, hustled to scrape together a living, and even a famous dramatist like Ben Jonson could die in penury. On the other hand, the theater also provided an opportunity for advancement as well. Several actors, including Richard Burbage and Edward Alleyn, were able to amass considerable fortunes. Shakespeare used the money he received as sharer to invest in property both in London and in his home, Stratford-upon-Avon, where he purchased a large house and land. Such careers were the exception rather than the rule, however, in an era when the theater was widely regarded as illicit and was frequently declared illegal.

THE THEATERS

English companies performed on three kinds of stage—large, open, outdoor buildings called **PUBLIC THEATERS** that held as many as 3,000 people; smaller, indoor, more elite **PRIVATE THEATERS** holding perhaps 700; and private performances at court or at the home of the patron. Public theaters, inspired both by the innyard booths where itinerant companies performed and by the circular arenas used for animal baiting, were outdoor buildings accommodating a large and diverse audience for afternoon performances. Although one theater, the Fortune, was rectangular, most public theaters were eight- to twelve-sided structures. The roughly circular, three-story gallery surrounded an open pit for standing audiences, into which a stage extended at about the height of five feet. The

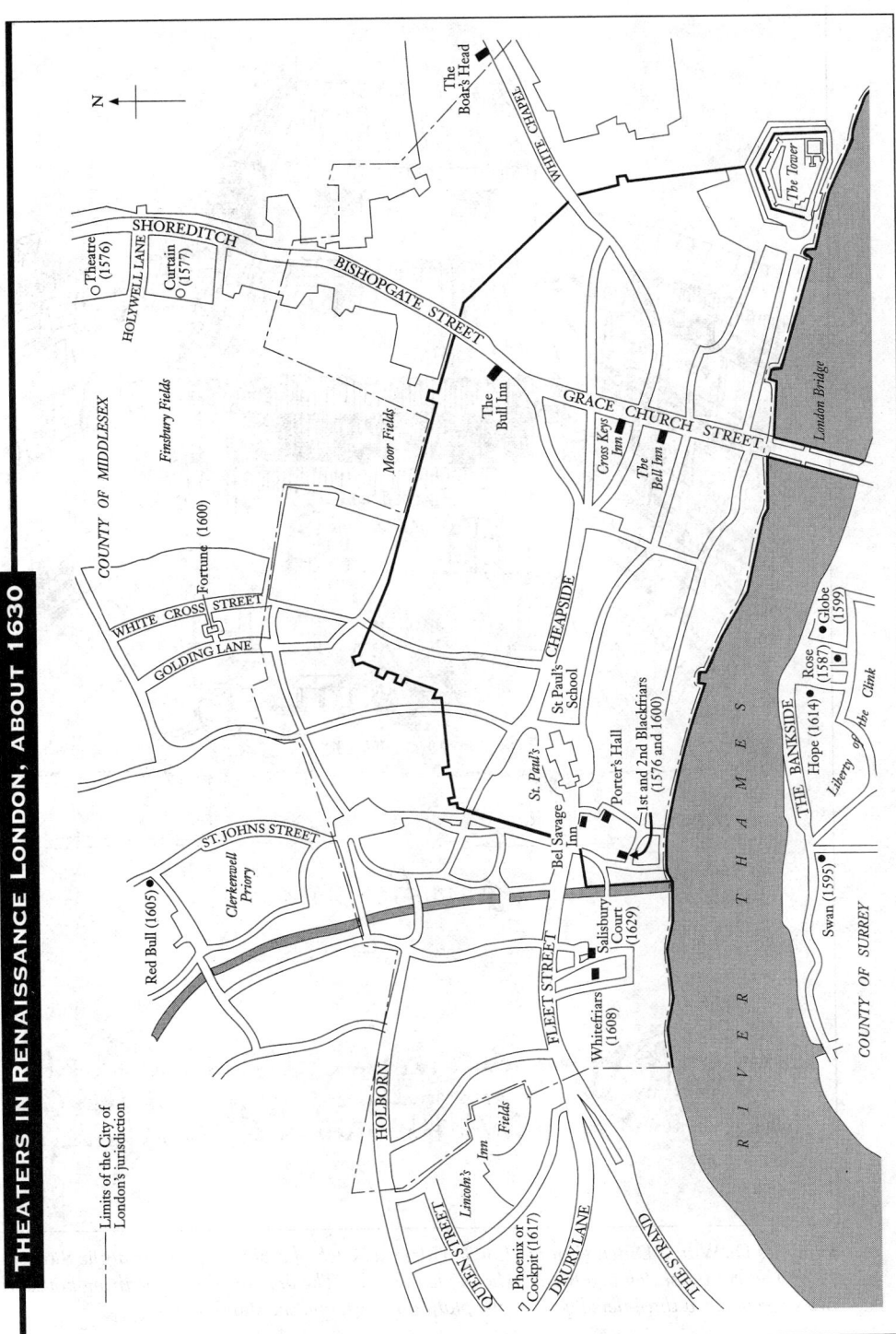

THEATERS IN RENAISSANCE LONDON, ABOUT 1630

—————— Limits of the City of
London's jurisdiction

A number of theaters were constructed in London after 1574. The dark line extending from The Tower (lower right) to Blackfriars in the west is the old city wall. Note that, with the exception of the first and second Blackfriars theaters, the theaters are either north of the city (the Fortune, The Theatre, the Curtain, the Red Bull) or south of the Thames River (the Swan, the Hope, the Rose, the Globe).

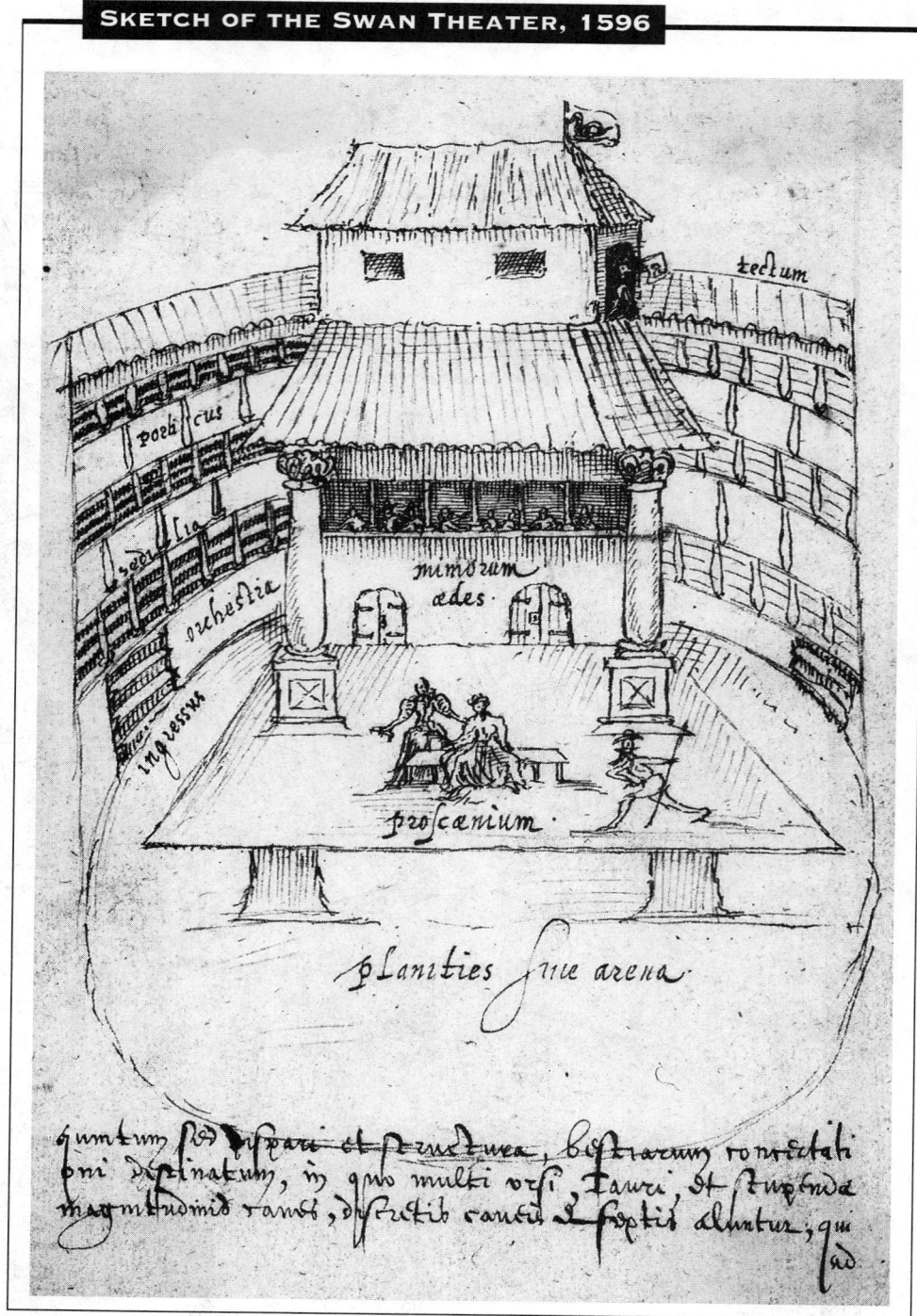

SKETCH OF THE SWAN THEATER, 1596

Johannes De Witt, a Dutch visitor to London, drew a sketch of a play in progress at the Swan in 1596. He sent the sketch to a friend, who made this copy. The drawing shows the tiring house with its two stage doors, a three-tiered gallery, the platform stage, and the standing pit.

MODERN RECONSTRUCTION OF THE SWAN THEATER

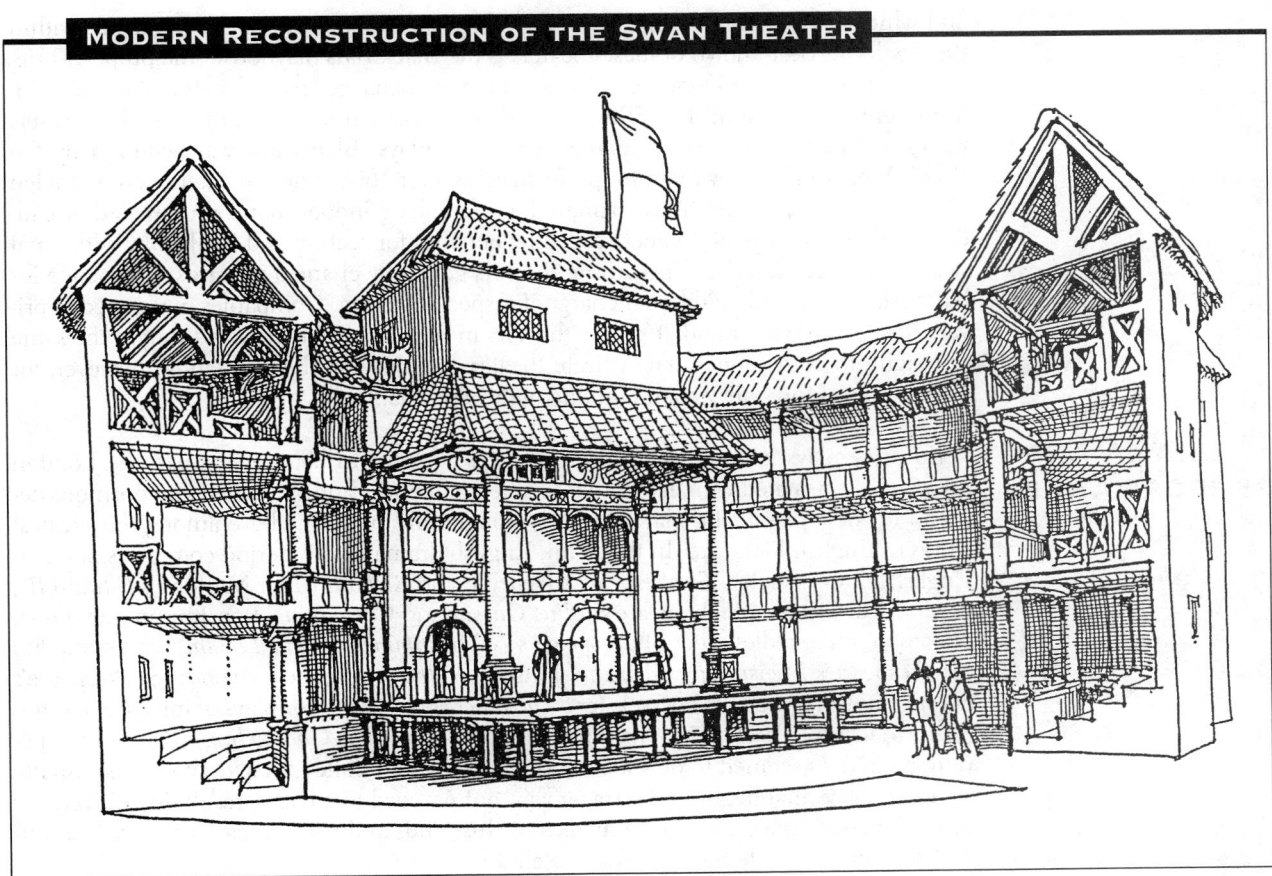

C. Walter Hodges based this reconstruction on the De Witt sketch.

stage was partly roofed, and two doors used for entrances were set into the rear wall, or **TIRING HOUSE.** On the gallery level above the stage, small rooms were used for aristocratic seating, for music, and for scenes requiring action above the stage—as in the balcony scene in *Romeo and Juliet,* or when Prospero appears "aloft" in *The Tempest.* The stage had a central trapdoor (or **GRAVE TRAP**), and its roofed area held a pulley for raising or lowering actors or properties. The public theaters catered to a paying audience, charging one penny to enter the pit and an additional penny to enter each of the galleries, where seating was provided on benches. Estimates on the size of the theaters vary, but the largest—like the Globe or the Fortune—were about 99 feet in external diameter, with a standing pit about 70 feet across, and a stage 45 feet wide and 27 feet deep; they could hold audiences of 2,000 to 3,000 people. Some theaters were considerably smaller. The Rose theater (whose foundation was discovered in 1988) was a twelve-sided building about 70 feet across, with a pit 50 feet in diameter and a stage roughly 25 by 15 feet. Most of the plays we associate with the Renaissance theater—those of Marlowe, Shakespeare, Jonson, John Webster, John Fletcher, and others—were produced in public theaters like the Globe, the Rose, the Hope, the Swan, or the Fortune.

Although a number of theaters were built in this period, the prestige of the public theaters seems to have declined in the 1620s and 1630s as companies shifted much of their attention to the more lucrative private theaters. These theaters stood within the City of London, on lands called "liberties"—property which had once belonged to monasteries and which had remained outside the city's legal jurisdiction, even though it was within the city limit. Best-known of these theaters is the Blackfriars playhouse (the property originally belonged to the Dominican friars, who wore black gowns). Blackfriars was used intermittently throughout the 1590s by boys' companies, troupes of boy chapel choristers who on occasion formed companies for acting plays. Blackfriars was acquired by the King's Men and used by them for performances after 1608. These theaters were modeled along the lines of a great-house banqueting room: long indoor rooms illuminated by candles, with a low stage at one end, faced by benches for seating and flanked by additional seats along side galleries. The private theaters generally charged upwards of sixpence for basic admission, with additional charges for special seating. Companies performed at private theaters in winter and at public theaters in summer and generally brought the same repertoire to both venues. The private theaters did develop the reputation, however, for originating a more satirical and erudite body of drama.

DRAMA AND PERFORMANCE

Performing plays in **REPERTORY** over perhaps as many as 200 days a year, the London companies competed with each other for their audiences and generated an enormous demand for new plays. The plays that they bought and performed are among the greatest works of English literature. In the main, English drama in this period comprises plays on English history (such as Shakespeare's *Henry V* and *Richard III*, or Marlowe's *Edward II*); on classical history (Shakespeare's *Julius Caesar* and *Coriolanus*, Ben Jonson's *Sejanus*); of romantic comedies (like Shakespeare's *A Midsummer Night's Dream*); city comedies (Shakespeare's *Measure for Measure*, Jonson's *Volpone*); heroic tragedies (Shakespeare's *Hamlet* and *King Lear*, John Webster's *The Duchess of Malfi*); or plays of intrigue or satire (John Marston's *The Malcontent*, Thomas Middleton's *The Changeling*). Later in the period, audiences seemed to develop a taste for plays they called **TRAGICOMEDIES,** usually romantic plays that begin in the tragic vein but proceed to a happy resolution. Several of John Fletcher's plays are tragicomedies of this kind, and Shakespeare's *Cymbeline* and *The Tempest* resemble tragicomedy as well.

This list of genres suggests both the fertile range of innovation in the Renaissance theater and the drama's dependence on models drawn from the classical and medieval theaters. Roman drama—the comedies of Plautus and Terence, and the tragedies of Seneca—was widely used in schools and universities as part of the teaching of Latin, and university students often staged these plays in Latin. It is not surprising, then, that some features of classical drama made their way into the Renaissance theater. The model of Shakespearean romantic comedy—mistaken identities, separated lovers, an irascible old man or father, a wily servant—derives directly from Plautus' plays; indeed, Shakespeare's *Comedy of Errors* directly adapts Plautus' *Menaechmi*. In a similar fashion, the violence of Seneca's tragedies makes its way directly into the action of Elizabethan drama. Formally and thematically, however, Renaissance drama also differs sharply from its classical ancestors. Renaissance plays tend to be more diffuse, involving a greater variety of characters and multiple plots; in tragedy, the action is often not quite as closely focused on the fortunes of a single hero as it is in classical tragedy. In these and other ways—in the Christian providence that seems to stand behind the action of many plays, in its variety of contemporary characters, in its use of symbolic anachronism, and in the complex relationship between the dramatic world and the world of the audience—Renaissance drama bears the signs of its medieval inheritance.

Playwrights generally wrote in **BLANK VERSE,** an unrhymed **IAMBIC PENTAMETER** line (ten syllables with alternating stress), and occasionally used other verse forms as well. They often used prose, sometimes for emphasis, sometimes to develop the qualities of a particular character. Although modern editors divided the plays into five acts, in most cases Renaissance playwrights probably did not compose their plays in this form. Performance on the public theater stage was rapid and continuous. The theaters used an open stage, few large properties, and had little or no scenery onstage, so that scenes could follow one another without interruption.

Despite the absence of elaborate stage sets, performance in the Renaissance theater was nonetheless spectacular. Actors used costumes, properties, and language to transform the midafternoon stage into a dramatic locale—Prospero's desert island, Lear's heath, Faustus's study. Some larger properties could be wheeled out from the rear doors, or perhaps raised from the trap: a throne, for instance, or a bed for Desdemona in *Othello,* or the hell-mouth used at the end of *Doctor Faustus.* A cannon fired during a production of Shakespeare's *Henry VIII* in 1613 unfortunately set fire to the Globe and burned it to the ground.

The unlocalized stage of medieval drama can be seen as the forerunner of the Renaissance theater's fluid use of stage space. The open stage made for a kind of cinematic flexibility in performance, as the play could range rapidly from scene to scene, place to place. Costuming was eclectic and anachronistic: the actors wore mainly Elizabethan clothing, adding armor, royal finery, motley, or some "classical" style of gowns when needed. The actors—Burbage, Alleyn, Will Kemp, among many others—were widely praised for their power and effectiveness. Their acting style was oratorical in tragedy and extemporaneous in comedy, but there is no doubt that many were consummate performers, in command of dozens of roles that could be put into play at short notice.

WOMEN IN DRAMA AND PERFORMANCE

Boy actors played a significant part in the experience of English theater, for boy actors played the parts of women and girls onstage, including major roles like Lady Macbeth, Ophelia, and Cleopatra. Much as they did in classical Athens, "women" emerged onstage in Renaissance London only as a side-effect of masculine attitudes and performances. In the English theater, this CROSS-DRESSING came into special prominence, though, because the romantic, sexual, and political intrigue so popular in Renaissance plays was often focused on female characters and therefore on the performance of the boy actors. Indeed, the drama frequently uses cross-dressing as a way of interrogating the power and perquisites of gender, in ways that sometimes confirm and sometimes question the role of gender in English society. English society was an overtly hierarchical one, and despite the power of the "Virgin Queen," women had little access to education, most could not hold property, and they were generally subject to discrimination of many kinds. In this social economy—and in a theater in which Puritan opposition to the stage frequently criticized the theater's "effeminacy"—the absence of women from the stage became a powerful sign of their absence from other scenes of power. Much as sumptuary laws prevented individuals from wearing jewels and clothing above their social station, so, too, was cross-dressing a legal offense in sixteenth-century England, punishable by whipping and a prison sentence. The license of the theater, the freedom to create magical new worlds on the stage, was, like other forms of power in the period, the prerogative of men, and the images that men created for the stage are in important ways imprinted with the signs of a specifically masculine imagination. As with all stage conventions, cross-dressing was deeply implicated in the values of the culture outside the theater, so much so that when women did perform onstage in England—a French company used actresses at Blackfriars in 1629— they met with hostility, ridicule, and rejection.

The theater had an extraordinary hold on the English imagination. In their many progresses, pageants, and allegorical entertainments, the English monarchs revealed a keen sense of the power of fictive images to represent reality, or a version of it, and so to shape their subjects' understanding of royal power. Playwrights and audiences also found in the theater a magical image of human possibility. Think of Prospero summoning the storm, Ariel, and other spirits with his stagey magic; or of the playwright John Webster's

One of the principal obligations of the professional companies was to perform at court or for their patron. Performances at court often took place during holidays and were commanded with increasing frequency by James I and Charles I. The companies performed many of their staple plays at court, but they also performed special entertainments called MASQUES, plays written in verse, usually on mythological subjects, that involved dancing, fanciful costumes, music, and special scenic machinery and effects. While the actors spoke the lines in these plays, they shared the stage with members of the court, who performed in the elaborate dances that began, ended, and punctuated the masques. The little play that Prospero puts on for Ferdinand and Miranda in Shakespeare's *The Tempest* resembles court masques in many ways, with its cast of goddesses, its formal singing and dancing, and the ceremonial quality of the occasion it celebrates.

Masques were an elaborate and expensive entertainment; some were performed on special state occasions—Jonson's *Hymenaei* (1605) celebrated the marriage of Lady Essex, and *The Masque of Oberon* (1610) was written to celebrate Prince Henry's investiture as Prince of Wales—and all had important implications for the mythology of the Stuart dynasty. Since members of the royal and aristocratic families performed in the masques, the poet was challenged to devise a setting and dramatic narrative that were elevated enough for the courtly audience. More important, each masque included several "grand masquing dances," which were performed by members of the court, often costumed as "characters" in the masque. Jonson was by far the most renowned writer of masques, though the playwrights James Shirley, William

(ASIDE)

THE JACOBEAN COURT MASQUE

Davenant (who became a critically important theater manager after the restoration of the monarchy in 1660), and others also wrote masques. Jonson however, wrote more than a dozen masques, and in the course of his long career innovated the genre in several ways. While the earlier Stuart masques tend to have a relatively simple narrative, later masques—beginning with *The Masque of Queens* (1609)—adopted a more complicated structure. *The Masque of Queens* begins with an ANTI-MASQUE, a scene involving witches, goblins, or demons who are magically transformed into goddesses or allegorical virtues in the course of the action.

His majesty, then, being set, and the whole company in full expectation, the part of the scene which first presented itself was an ugly hell, which flaming beneath, smoked unto the top of the roof. And in respect all evils are, morally said to come from hell, . . . these witches, with a kind of hollow and infernal music, came forth from thence. First one, then two, and three, and more, till their number increased to eleven, all differently attired: some with rats on their head, some on their shoulders; others with ointment pots at their girdles; all with spindles, timbrels, rattles or other venefical [having to do with witchcraft] instruments, making a confused noise, with strange gestures.

The witches dance and pronounce a series of charms until, suddenly, "with a strange and sudden music,"

they fell into a magical dance full of preposterous change and gesticulation . . . . In the heat of their dance on the sudden was heard a sound of loud music, as if many instruments had made one blast; with which not only the hags themselves but the hell into which they ran quite

vanished, and the whole face of the scene altered, scarce suffering the memory of such a thing. But in the place of it appeared a glorious and magnificent building figuring the House of Fame, in the top of which were discovered the twelve masquers sitting upon a throne triumphal erected in form of a pyramid and circled with all store of light. From whom a person, by this time descended, in the furniture of Perseus, and expressing heroic and masculine virtue began to speak.[1]

The antimasque establishes a world of demonic disorder, which suddenly vanishes when the members of the court appear in the House of Fame, among classical heroes and virtues. We can get a sense of the delicacy of Jonson's situation when we recognize that the performers of the masque included the queen herself, as well as the countesses of Arundel, Derby, Huntington, Bedford, Essex, and Montgomery, Viscountess Cranborne, and several ladies in waiting. The court was both performer and audience of this self-enclosed spectacle, which almost of necessity reflected back on its audience an idealized vision of courtly perfection.

As an ambitious writer, it is understandable that Jonson thought the masques were essentially a vehicle for his splendid poetry. But as even this brief description suggests, the masques were highly dependent on the development of new scenic technology, and on the skills of the architect and designer Inigo Jones (1573–1652). The masques were unusually expensive—one of King James's masques cost more than £4,000, and one of King Charles's cost £21,000. Much of this money was spent on the elaborate changeable scenery that accompanied the masques, the first changeable scenery in the English theater. Inigo Jones designed the theater space where masques were performed, the banqueting hall of

---

[1] From *Ben Jonson: Selected Masques*, ed. Stephen Orgel (New Haven, CT: Yale University Press, 1970).

Whitehall Palace. Jones had visited Italy in 1600; he may have visited again during 1607–1608, and he is known to have been in Italy from 1613–1615. In Italy, he came into contact with the theater designs of Andrea Palladio (1518–1580), who adapted the design of classical Roman theaters for indoor stages: Palladio's Teatro Olimpico had a curved amphitheater-like auditorium and a proscenium stage. As court architect and designer, Jones had the opportunity both to import Palladio's understanding of theatrical design, and to develop his own interest in elaborate spectacle. The stage at Whitehall was about 40 feet wide by 28 feet deep, and gently raked; although Jones's theater at Whitehall changed during his long tenure at court, it eventually consisted of staggered wings and a backdrop to convey a sense of perspective. Unlike both the public and private theaters of Renaissance London, Jones's theater was the first to use changeable scenery, and when the theaters reopened in 1660, the English companies brought this aristocratic inheritance with them: Jones's **WINGS-AND-BACKDROP** designs became the basic model for changeable scenery throughout the eighteenth century.

Jones's interest in spectacle was far-reaching, and he devised the instruments to execute many of Jonson's most elaborate poetic images: flying machines, a globe which opened to reveal several aristocratic dancers, and brilliant costumes to dress the masques' allegorical characters. But it was Jones's development of a perspective in the theater that was most deeply implicated in the rhetoric of court life. For at Whitehall performances, the King sat on a raised, central dais directly in front of the stage; since none of the other courtiers could be seated with their backs to the King, those closer to the stage were seated along the side walls of the room, while others were seated behind the royal spectator. It has been argued that the King was positioned in a complex relation to the stage and to the rest of the audience: not only was he the only spectator for whom the illusion of perspective

FIERY SPIRIT

Inigo Jones created this costume for a fiery spirit in 1635.

was complete (the other spectators could probably see between the wings, for example), but the rest of the audience could *see* that only the king had a perfect vision of the world onstage. The closer one sat to the royal seat, the more one's view of the illusion onstage approximated the king's ideal vantage. Spectators and performers, in other words, engaged in a richly hierarchical sense of illusion, in which the King's centrality—and, in a sense, his omniscience—was constantly displayed, and each spectator's distance from that sense of illusion was constantly experienced. Like Jonson, whose texts frequently betray his intense awareness of his royal audience and aristocratic performers, Jones's perspective theater reflects the increasingly absolutist ideology of the Stuart monarchy.

The banqueting hall at Whitehall played one more ironic role in the history of performance. Charles I became increasingly hostile to Parliament—he refused to call Parliament from 1629–1640—and when civil war broke out in 1642, Charles fled London. The Royalist forces were concentrated in Oxford, and in 1647 Charles was defeated and captured by the Parliamentary army. In 1649, he was sentenced to death by Parliament, and he visited the Whitehall banquet hall on his way to his execution. The executioner's block was set on a large public stage outside a window of the banquet hall; Charles was led through the room where the masques' brilliant fantasies had been staged for him to his own last performance, the public stage where he was beheaded.

Dating from about 1595, this drawing appears to show a scene from Titus Andronicus, *by William Shakespeare. Two of the actors wear pseudoclassical Roman costumes; the others are dressed in Elizabethan clothing.*

description of "an excellent actor": "All men have been of his occupation, and indeed what he doth feignedly, that do others essentially: this day one plays a Monarch, the next a private person. Here one acts a Tyrant, on the morrow an Exile; a Parasite [tricky servant] this man tonight, tomorrow a Precisian [Puritan], and so of divers others." Acting and the theater provided a liberating image of human—or, at least, masculine—power: the power to transform oneself and the world. However, the rich, strange, transforming freedom of the theater could also seem empty and terrifying, even demonic. Rather than an image of human potential, the theater could seem to offer an image of the poverty of human action, the sterile and deceptive emptiness of the world we make and inhabit. As King Lear preaches to blinded Gloucester: "When we are born, we cry that we are come/ To this great stage of fools." Puritan critics of the theater insistently reminded audiences that the stage's methods—to seduce with the vain and showy image of a false reality— were also Satan's, and that the theater subversively invited audiences to "unman, unChristian, uncreate themselves." Yet it is precisely this transforming power that lies at the heart of the Renaissance theater's fascination for its audience. For while the theater sometimes seemed to depict a world threatened with constant change and loss, it also presented the power of illusion to recreate the real.

In this scene from an American Shakespeare Theater production of The Tempest, *Ariel describes how he has performed Prospero's commands.*

As the "cavalier" costumes suggest, John Gielgud's acclaimed 1934 production of Hamlet *was set in the later seventeenth century, rather than in the Elizabethan era; here, Hamlet and Laertes duel in the play's final scene.*

■ THE YORK *CRUCIFIXION* ■

The cycle of Corpus Christi pageants produced in the city of York is the oldest and best-recorded of any of the English Corpus Christi cycles. The cycle was devised as part of the celebration of the Feast of Corpus Christi and was first produced during the late fourteenth century. In the late Middle Ages, York was a flourishing and important city, with the wealth necessary to stage a great cycle of forty-seven plays; the York cycle continued to be performed as late as the 1560s. As in other towns, craft guilds—sometimes called "mysteries"—were given the responsibility for staging individual pageants, and the pageants were occasionally assigned to "appropriate" guilds. In the York cycle, for example, the shipwrights produced the "Building of the Ark" pageant, the fishers and mariners produced "The Flood," the masons and the goldsmiths guilds produced "Herod" and "The Magi," and the bakers produced "The Last Supper." The pinners—or pin-makers—guild produced the play on the Crucifixion. Each guild elected an officer called a **PAGEANT MASTER,** who was responsible for gathering money from the guild's members to finance the pageant and for hiring an individual to supervise the play's production—hiring, rehearsing, and paying the actors.

In York, each play in the Corpus Christi cycle was performed on a separate pageant wagon; the wagons were arranged in the order of the plays—from the first play, "The Fall of the Angels," to the last, "The Last Judgment"—and proceeded through the city, stopping at each of twelve stations. Audiences could choose one station and watch while each of the forty-seven pageants was performed in order. The procession began at 4:30 in the morning, and the last play was probably performed at the twelfth station sometime after midnight. Although little is known about the pageant wagons themselves, records suggest that the wagons were elaborately decorated and often included impressive scenery and special effects. The York mercers guild, which produced "The Last Judgment," had a wagon that held a complicated set, including a "heaven," a winch to raise and lower God, and a "hell-mouth." Some device operated the nine mechanical angels who sat with God, among the brightly-colored clouds (made of cloth) in the "heaven." Because the pageant wagons were expensive to build and decorate and were owned by the guild, they were stored between annual performances of the cycle; when a pageant wagon became dilapidated or the guild became wealthier, a new wagon would be devised for the pageant.

Each guild was responsible for maintaining the text of its pageant; the city of York, however, began keeping an official record of the Corpus Christi plays sometime between 1463 and 1477. This volume, called the "Register," is the sole manuscript of the York cycle of plays. Comparison with other surviving documents from the period reveals that the cycle underwent several changes during two centuries of performance. Some pageants were reassigned to different guilds and several were revised. The most notable of these revisions took place in the fifteenth century and are attributed to an unknown playwright now called the "York Realist"; *The Crucifixion* is a particularly fine example of this work. As in other cycle plays, the York Realist uses recognizably contemporary characters as part of the setting of Biblical events. Like the author of the Wakefield *Second Shepherds' Play*, who makes the Bethlehem shepherds appear to be much like fifteenth-century peasants, the York Realist makes the four Roman soldiers seem like familiar members of the medieval community: they are medieval laborers, and share many of the audience's attitudes and prejudices, notably its deep antisemitism. But the York playwright's skill goes well beyond an eye for realistic characterization. With a sure sense of drama, he gives Christ only two speeches in the play, one as the soldiers bring him to the cross, and another after the cross has been raised and jarringly dropped into its mortise. Christ's silence stands out against the soldiers' cruel joking as they nail him to the cross, and the playwright clearly contrasts Christ's effort to redeem mankind with the selfish and earthbound imagination of the soldiers, who ridicule his final words and fall to gambling for his cloak. Like many cycle plays, the York *Crucifixion* asked its audience to contemplate the relationship between the eternal and the temporal by staging the Christian narrative in the everyday terms of medieval life.

THE YORK *CRUCIFIXION*

ANONYMOUS

EDITED BY A. C. CAWLEY

— CHARACTERS —

JESUS
FOUR SOLDIERS

SCENE: *Calvary.*

---

1 SOLDIER: Sir knights, take heed hither in hie:
 This deed undree we may not draw;
 Ye wot yourselves as well as I
 How lords and leaders of our law
5 Have given doom that this dote shall die.
2 SOLDIER: Sir, all their counsel well we know.
 Since we are come to Calvary,
 Let ilk man help now as him owe.
3 SOLDIER: We are all ready, lo,
10 That forward to fulfil.
4 SOLDIER: Let hear how we shall do,
 And go we tite theretill.

1 SOLDIER: It may not help here for to hone,
 If we shall any worship win.
15 2 SOLDIER: He must be dead needlings by noon.
3 SOLDIER: Then it is good time that we begin.
4 SOLDIER: Let ding him down! Then is he done.
 He shall not dere us with his din.
1 SOLDIER: He shall be set and learned soon,
20 With care to him and all his kin.
2 SOLDIER: The foulest death of all
 Shall he die for his deeds.
3 SOLDIER: That means cross him we shall.
4 SOLDIER: Behold, so right he redes.

25 1 SOLDIER: Then to this work as must take heed,
 So that our working be not wrong.
2 SOLDIER: None other note to neven is need,
 But let us haste him for to hang.
3 SOLDIER: And I have gone for gear, good speed,
30 Both hammers and nails large and long.
4 SOLDIER: Then may we boldly do this deed;
 Come on, let kill this traitor strong.
1 SOLDIER: Fair might ye fall in fere,
 That have wrought on this wise.
35 2 SOLDIER: Us needs not for to lere
 Such faitours to chastise.

3 SOLDIER: Since ilka thing is right arrayed,
 The wiselier now work may we.
4 SOLDIER: The cross on ground is goodly graid,
 And bored even as it ought to be. 40
1 SOLDIER: Look that the lad on length be laid,
 And made be ta'en unto this tree.
2 SOLDIER: For all his fare he shall be flayed:
 That on essay soon shall ye see.
3 SOLDIER: Come forth, thou cursed knave, 45
 Thy comfort soon shall keel.
4 SOLDIER: Thine hire here shalt thou have.
1 SOLDIER: Walk on! Now work we well.

JESUS: Almighty God, my Father free,
 Let these matters be marked in mind: 50
 Thou bade that I should buxom be,
 For Adam's plight to be pined.
 Here to death I oblige me,
 From that sin for to save mankind,
 And sovereignly beseech I thee 55
 That they for me may favour find;
 And from the fiend them fend,
 So that their souls be safe
 In wealth withouten end;
 I keep not else to crave. 60

1 SOLDIER: We! hark, sir knights, for Mahound's blood!
 Of Adam's kind is all his thought.
2 SOLDIER: The warlock waxes worse than wood;
 This doleful death ne dreadeth he nought.
3 SOLDIER: Thou shouldst have mind, with main and mood, 65
 Of wicked works that thou has wrought.

---

4 SOLDIER: I hope that he had been as good
    Have ceased of saws that he up sought.

1 SOLDIER: Those saws shall rue him sore,
70   For all his sauntering, soon.

2 SOLDIER: Ill speed them that him spare
    Till he to death be done!

3 SOLDIER: Have done belive, boy, and make thee boun,
    And bend thy back unto this tree.

(JESUS *lies down.*)

75 4 SOLDIER: Behold, himself has laid him down,
    In length and breadth as he should be.

1 SOLDIER: This traitor here tainted of treason,
    Go fast and fetter him then, ye three;
    And since he claimeth kingdom with crown,
80   Even as a king here hang shall he.

2 SOLDIER: Now, certes, I shall not fine
    Ere his right hand be fast.

3 SOLDIER: The left hand then is mine;
    Let see who bears him best.

85 4 SOLDIER: His limbs on length then shall I lead,
    And even unto the bore them bring.

1 SOLDIER: Unto his head I shall take heed,
    And with my hand help him to hang.

2 SOLDIER: Now since we four shall do this deed,
90   And meddle with this unthrifty thing,
    Let no man spare for special speed,
    Till that we have made ending.

2 SOLDIER: This forward may not fail;
    Now we are right arrayed.

95 4 SOLDIER: This boy here in our bail
    Shall bide full bitter braid.

1 SOLDIER: Sir knights, say now, work we ought?

2 SOLDIER: Yes, certes, I hope I hold this hand.

3 SOLDIER: And to the bore I have it brought
100   Full buxomly withouten band.

1 SOLDIER: Strike on then hard, for him thee bought.

2 SOLDIER: Yes, here is a stub will stiffly stand;
    Through bones and sinews it should be sought.
    This work is well, I will warrant.

105 1 SOLDIER: Say, sir, how do we there?

    This bargain may not blin.

3 SOLDIER: It fails a foot and more;
    The sinews are so gone in.

4 SOLDIER: I hope that mark amiss be bored.

2 SOLDIER: Then must he bide in bitter bale.   110

3 SOLDIER: In faith, it was over-scantily scored;
    That makes it foully for to fail.

1 SOLDIER: Why carp ye so? Fast on a cord,
    And tug him to, by top and tail.

3 SOLDIER: Yea, thou commandest lightly as a lord;   115
    Come help to hale him, will ill hail!

1 SOLDIER: Now certes that shall I do—
    Full snelly as a snail.

3 SOLDIER: And I shall tache him to,
    Full nimbly with a nail.   120

    This work will hold, that dare I heet,
    For now are fest fast both his hend.

4 SOLDIER: Go we all four then to his feet,
    So shall our space be speedily spent.

2 SOLDIER: Let see what bourd his bale might beet;   125
    Thereto my back now would I bend.

4 SOLDIER: Oh! this work is all unmeet:
    This boring must all be amend.

1 SOLDIER: Ah, peace, man, for Mahoun!
    Let no man wot that wonder;   130
    A rope shall rug him down,
    If all his sinews go asunder.

2 SOLDIER: That cord full kindly can I knit,
    The comfort of this carl to keel.

1 SOLDIER: Fest on then fast that all be fit;   135
    It is no force how fell he feel.

2 SOLDIER: Lug on, ye both, a little yet.

3 SOLDIER: I shall not cease, as I have sele.

4 SOLDIER: And I shall fond him for to hit.

2 SOLDIER: Oh, hale!   140

4 SOLDIER: Ho now! I hold it well.

1 SOLDIER: Have done, drive in that nail,
    So that no fault be found.

4 SOLDIER: This working would not fail,
    If four bulls here were bound.

67–70 **I hope . . . soon** I think he would have done well to stop telling those tales he made up. . . . Soon he shall bitterly regret all his babbling 71 **Ill speed** bad luck to 73 **Have done . . . boun** Be quick, knave, and get ready 77 **tainted** convicted 81 **certes** certainly; **fine** stop 84 **Let see . . . best** Let's see who acquits himself best 85 **His limbs . . . lead** Then I shall draw his limbs to their full length 86 **bore** hole 90 **unthrifty** unprofitable 91 **Let no . . . speed** Let no one use less than his best possible speed 93 **This forward . . . fail** i.e., we must not fail to carry out our agreement 94 **right arrayed** properly prepared 95 **boy** knave; **bail** charge 96 **Shall bide . . . braid** Shall suffer a most bitter onslaught 97 **Sir knights . . . ought** Are we doing anything? (The First Soldier is evidently in charge) 98 **hope** think 100 **Full buxomly . . . band** Quite obediently without [having to use a] rope 101 **for him . . . bought** by Him who redeemed you 102–103 **here . . . be sought** Here is a nail that will stand fast; [in order to find it] we shall have to look for it through bones and sinews

---

106–108 **This bargain . . . in** This business may not cease (i.e., must go on). . . . It [the hole] is out by a foot or more; his sinews are so shrunken 109 **I hope . . . bored** I think that mark is bored wrongly (i.e., the hole has not been bored in the place marked for it) 110 **bittle bale** grievous torment 111–112 **It was . . . fail** i.e., the mark was put in the wrong place; that is why the hole is badly out 113 **carp** prate; **Fast** fasten 114 **And tug . . . tail** And tug him to [the holes] by his head and feet 115 **lightly** readily 116 **Come help . . . hail** Come and help pull him, confound you! 118 **snelly** quickly (A sarcastic aside by the First Soldier, who considers himself a foreman, not a workman) 119 **tache him to** fasten him to [the cross] 121 **heet** promise 122 **For now . . . hend** For now both his hands are firmly fastened 124–125 **So shall . . . beet** So shall our time be well spent. . . . Let's see what jest can lighten his misery 127 **unmeet** unfit 128 **amend** improved 130 **Let no . . . wonder** Let no one know about this extraordinary thing. (The First Soldier seems to believe that their work has been undone by magic) 131 **rug** pull 133 **kindly** thoroughly 134 **carl** churl 135–136 **Fest on . . . feel** Get hold of it firmly then so that all shall be ready; it doesn't matter how cruelly he feels it 138 **I shall . . . sele** As I hope for happiness 139 **fond** try 140 **hale** pull

145 1 SOLDIER: These cords have evil increased his pains,
Ere he were till the borings brought.
2 SOLDIER: Yea, asunder are both sinews and veins
On ilka side, so have we sought.
3 SOLDIER: Now all his gauds nothing him gains;
150 His sauntering shall with bale be bought.
4 SOLDIER: I will go say to our sovereigns
Of all these works how we have wrought.
1 SOLDIER: Nay, sirs, another thing
Falls first to you and me:
155 They bade we should him hang
On high that men might see.
2 SOLDIER: We wot well so their words were;
But, sir, that deed will do us dere.
1 SOLDIER: It may not mend for to moot more;
160 This harlot must be hanged here.
2 SOLDIER: The mortice is made fit therefor.
3 SOLDIER: Fest on your fingers then, in fere.
4 SOLDIER: I ween it will never come there;
We four raise it not right to-year.
165 1 SOLDIER: Say, man, why carp'st thou so?
Thy lifting was but light.
2 SOLDIER: He means there must be mo
To heave him up on height.
3 SOLDIER: Now certes, I hope it shall not need
170 To call to us more company.
Methink we four should do this deed,
And bear him to yon hill on high.
1 SOLDIER: It must be done, without dread.
No more, but look ye be ready,
175 And this part shall I lift and lead;
On length he shall no longer lie.
Therefore now make ye boun:
Let bear him to yon hill.
4 SOLDIER: Then will I bear here down,
180 And tent his toes until.
2 SOLDIER: We two shall see till either side,
For else this work will wry all wrong.
3 SOLDIER: We are ready, good sirs. Abide,
And let me first his feet up fong.
185 2 SOLDIER: Why tent ye so to tales this tide?
1 SOLDIER: Lift up!

(They lift the cross.)

4 SOLDIER: Let see!
2 SOLDIER: Oh, lift along!
3 SOLDIER: From all this harm he should him hide,
And he were God.
4 SOLDIER: The devil him hang!
1 SOLDIER: For-great harm have I hent:
My shoulder is asunder. **190**
2 SOLDIER: And certes I am near shent,
So long have I borne under.
3 SOLDIER: This cross and I in two must twin,
Else breaks my back asunder soon.
4 SOLDIER: Lay down again and leave your din; **195**
This deed for us will never be done.

(They lay it down.)

1 SOLDIER: Essay, sirs, let see if any gin
May help him up withouten hone;
For here should wight men worship win,
And not with gauds all day to gone. **200**
2 SOLDIER: More wighter men than we
Full few I hope ye find.
3 SOLDIER: This bargain will not be,
For certes me wants wind.
4 SOLDIER: So will of work never we were; **205**
I hope this carl some cautels cast.
2 SOLDIER: My burden sat me wondrous sore;
Unto the hill I might not last.
1 SOLDIER: Lift up, and soon he shall be there;
Therefore fest on your fingers fast. **210**
3 SOLDIER: Oh, lift!

(They lift up the cross again.)

1 SOLDIER: We lo!
4 SOLDIER: A little more.
2 SOLDIER: Hold then!
1 SOLDIER: How now!
2 SOLDIER: The worst is past.
3 SOLDIER: He weighs a wicked weight.
2 SOLDIER: So may we all four say,
Ere he was heaved on height, **215**
And raised in this array.
4 SOLDIER: He made us stand as any stones,
So boistous was he for to bear.
1 SOLDIER: Now raise him nimbly for the nonce,
And set him by this mortice here; **220**
And let him fall in all at once,
For certes that pain shall have no peer.
3 SOLDIER: Heave up!

---

145 **evil** severely 146 **borings** boreholes 148 **On ilka . . . sought** Everywhere, so fare as we have looked 149 **gauds** tricks 150 **His saintering . . . bought** His babbling shall be paid for with suffering 152 **Of all . . . wrought** How well we have done our work 157 **We wot . . . were** We know well that their words were so (i.e., that they said so) 158 **dere** harm 159 **It may . . . more** It won't help to argue any more 160 **harlot** rascal 161 **fit therefor** ready for it 162 **Fest on . . . fere** Fasten your fingers on to it then, all together 163 **ween** think 164 **We four . . . to-year** We four won't lift it upright this year 166 **light** feeble 167 **mo** more 168 **height** high 173 **dread** doubt 174 **No more** No more [talking] 175 **this part** i.e., the head of the cross; **lead** carry 176 **length** prone 179–180 **Then will . . . until** Then I will carry him down here (i.e., at the foot of the cross), and attend to his toes 181 **We two . . . side** i.e., to each arm of the cross 182 **wry** go 184 **fong** take 185 **Why tent . . . tide** Why do you now listen to such talk [when there's work to be done]?

---

186 **along** lengthwise 187 **hide** protect 188 **And if** 189 **For-great** very great; **hent** suffered 191 **shent** exhausted 192 **borne under** held it up 193 **twin** part 197 **gin** contrivance 198 **hone** delay 199 **wight** valiant 200 **And not . . . gone** And not spend all day playing pranks 203–204 **This bargain . . . wind** This business won't get finished, for certainly I am short of breath 205–206 **So will . . . cast** We were never at such a loss in our work; I think this fellow has played some tricks [magic] 207 **sore** grieved 211 **We lo!** Ah well! 216 **array** fashion 217–218 **He made . . . bear** He brought us to a standstill; he was so bulky to carry 219 **for the nonce** [a metrical tag]

4 SOLDIER: Let down, so all his bones
Are asunder now on sides sere.

(They drop the cross into its mortice.)

225 1 SOLDIER: This falling was more fell
Than all the harms he had;
Now may a man well tell
The least lith of this lad.

3 SOLDIER: Methinketh this cross will not abide,
230 Ne stand still in this mortice yet.
4 SOLDIER: At the first time was it made over-wide:
That makes it wave, thou mayst well wit.
1 SOLDIER: It shall be set on ilka side,
So that it shall not further flit;
235 Good wedges shall we take this tide,
And fest the foot, then all is fit.
2 SOLDIER: Here are wedges arrayed
For that, both great and small.
3 SOLDIER: Where are our hammers laid,
240 That we should work withal?

4 SOLDIER: We have them here even at our hand.
2 SOLDIER: Give me this wedge; I shall it in drive.
4 SOLDIER: Here is another yet ordand.
3 SOLDIER: Do take it me hither belive.
245 1 SOLDIER: Lay on then fast.
3 SOLDIER: Yes, I warrant
I thring them sam, so mote I thrive.
Now will this cross full stably stand;
All if he rave, they will not rive.
1 SOLDIER: *(To Christ.)* Say, sir, how likes you now
250 This work that we have wrought?
4 SOLDIER: We pray you say us how
Ye feel, or faint ye aught.

JESUS: All men that walk by way or street,
Take tent ye shall no travail tine;
255 Behold my head, my hands, my feet,
And fully feel now, ere ye fine,
If any mourning may be meet,
Or mischief measured unto mine.
My Father, that all bales may beet,
260 Forgive these men that do me pine.
What they work wot they nought;

Therefore, my Father, I crave,
Let never their sins be sought,
But see their souls to save.

1 SOLDIER: We! hark! he jangles like a jay. 265
2 SOLDIER: Methink he patters like a pie.
3 SOLDIER: He has been doing so all day,
And made great moving of mercy.
4 SOLDIER: Is this the same that gan us say
That he was God's Son almighty? 270
1 SOLDIER: Therefore he feels full fell affray,
And deemed this day for to die.
2 SOLDIER: *Vah! qui destruis templum. . .*
3 SOLDIER: His saws were so, certain.
4 SOLDIER: And, sirs, he said to some 275
He might raise it again.

1 SOLDIER: To muster that he had no might,
For all the cautels that he could cast;
All if he were in word so wight,
For all his force now he is fast. 280
As Pilate deemed, is done and dight;
Therefore I rede that we go rest.
2 SOLDIER: This race mun be rehearsed right,
Through the world both east and west.
3 SOLDIER: Yea, let him hang there still, 285
And make mows on the moon.
4 SOLDIER: Then may we wend at will.
1 SOLDIER: Nay, good sirs, not so soon.

For certes us needs another note:
This kirtle would I of you crave. 290
2 SOLDIER: Nay, nay, sir, we will look by lot
Which of us four falls it to have.
3 SOLDIER: I rede we draw cut for this coat—
Lo, see how soon—all sides to save.
4 SOLDIER: The short cut shall win, that well ye wot, 295
Whether it fall to knight or knave.
1 SOLDIER: Fellows, ye thar not flite,
For this mantle is mine.
2 SOLDIER: Go we then hence tite;
This travail here we tine. 300

223–224 **so all . . . sere** so that all his bones break asunder everywhere 225 **fell** painful 227 **tell** count 228 **lith** limb; **lad** fellow 229 **not abide** not stand firm 230 **Ne** nor 231 **it** i.e., the mortice 232 **it** i.e., the cross; **wave** move; **wit** know 233 **set on . . . side** fixed on each side 234 **flit** move 237 **arrayed** prepared 240 **withal** with 243–244 **Here is. . . believe** Here is yet another made ready. . . . Bright it here to me quickly 246 **I thring . . . thrive** I shall press them (i.e., wedge and cross) together, as I hope to prosper 247 **stably** firmly 248 **All if . . . rive** All if he rave, they will not rive 249 **how likes you** do you like 252 **or faint . . . aught** or whether you are faint at all 254 **Take tent . . . tine** Take care that you waste none of my suffering 256 **fine** stop 257 **meet** fitting 258 **mischief** misfortune 259 **that all . . . beet** who may remedy all ills 260–261 **do me . . . nought** that inflict suffering on me. They know not what they do

263 **sought** examined 264 **But see . . . save** But see that their souls are saved 265 **jangles** clatters 266 **pie** magpie 268 **made great. . . mercy** made a great show of moving God to mercy 269 **gan** did 271 **Therefore he . . . affray** That is why he suffers this deadly assault 272 **deemed** was judged 273 **Vah! . . . templum** Ah, thou that destroyest the temple (Mark xiv.58; John ii.19) 274 **saws** words 277 **muster** show 278 **cautels** tricks; **cast** play 279 **All if. . . wight** Even if he was so valiant in work 281 **As Pilate . . . dight** It is done and performed as Pilate decreed 283 **This race . . . right** This action must be rightly reported 286 **mows on** grimaces at 287 **wend** go 289 **For certes . . . note** For, to be sure, there's another thing we need to do 291–292 **we will . . . have** we shall draw lots to see which of us four is to have it 293 **rede** advise; **cut** lots 294 **all sides . . . save** to protect all our interests 297 **thar** need; **flite** wrangle 299 **tite** quickly 300 **This travail . . . tine** We are wasting our efforts here

■ EVERYMAN ■

Everyman was written late in the fifteenth century and strongly resembles a Flemish play, *Elckerlijc* ("Everyman"), which was printed in 1495. It seems likely that one of the two plays is a translation of the other, but scholars are uncertain about which is the original. Given the play's subtle treatment of the Catholic doctrine of salvation, it has sometimes been argued that *Everyman* was written by a monk or cleric. Yet *Everyman* is hardly a theological treatise; it brims with a vitality that brings the reality of impending death vividly to the stage.

In the play, God orders Death to seek out Everyman and prepare him to die. Like most people, though, Everyman is not ready to meet his end. He first tries to bribe Death and then pleads unsuccessfully for mercy. When Death does not relent, Everyman begins a kind of spiritual journey, confronting several allegorical figures and asking them to accompany him to the grave. Medieval allegory often involved the personification of moral or psychological abstractions, much like the characters that Everyman meets: Fellowship, Kindred, Goods, Good Deeds, Knowledge, and so on. In performance, however, these abstractions become vividly fleshed-out, for the playwright gives these characters traits and behaviors that make them powerfully "real" and recognizable as individuals on the stage rather than as abstract moral emblems. As Everyman proceeds toward death, he is deserted by most of his worldly attributes, but Good Deeds remains faithful to him, especially once he has repented. Although the playwright concludes *Everyman* with a moralizing sermon by the Doctor, we may well feel that the theatrical lesson of the play has at least as much to do with the humanizing of Everyman and his poignant confrontation with our common mortality.

EVERYMAN

Anonymous

EDITED BY A. C. CAWLEY

— CHARACTERS —

GOD	COUSIN	STRENGTH
MESSENGER	GOODS	DISCRETION
DEATH	GOOD DEEDS	FIVE WITS
EVERYMAN	KNOWLEDGE	ANGEL
FELLOWSHIP	CONFESSION	DOCTOR
KINDRED	BEAUTY	

Here beginneth a treatise how the High Father of Heaven sendeth death to summon every creature to come and give account of their lives in this world, and is in manner of a moral play.

MESSENGER: I pray you all give your audience,
  And hear this matter with reverence,
  By figure a moral play:
  The *Summoning of Everyman* called it is,
5 That of our lives and ending shows
  How transitory we be all day.
  This matter is wondrous precious,
  But the intent of it is more gracious,
  And sweet to bear away.
10 The story saith: Man, in the beginning
  Look well, and take good heed to the ending,
  Be you never so gay!
  Ye think sin in the beginning full sweet,
  Which in the end causeth the soul to weep,
15 When the body lieth in clay.
  Here shall you see how Fellowship and Jollity,
  Both Strength, Pleasure, and Beauty,
  Will fade from thee as flower in May;
  For ye shall hear how our Heaven King
20 Calleth Everyman to a general reckoning:
  Give audience, and hear what he doth say.   *(Exit.)*

*(*GOD *speaketh:)*

GOD: I perceive, here in my majesty,
  How that all creatures be to me unkind,
  Living without dread in worldly prosperity:
25 Of ghostly sight the people be so blind,
  Drowned in sin, they know me not for their God;
  In worldly riches is all their mind,
  They fear not my righteousness, the sharp rod.
  My law that I showed, when I for them died,
30 They forget clean, and shedding of my blood red;
  I hanged between two, it cannot be denied;
  To get them life I suffered to be dead;
  I healed their feet, with thorns hurt was my head.
  I could do no more than I did, truly;
35 And now I see the people do clean forsake me:

They use the seven deadly sins damnable,
As pride, covetise, wrath, and lechery
Now in the world be made commendable;
And thus they leave of angels the heavenly company.
Every man liveth so after his own pleasure,   40
And yet of their life they be nothing sure:
I see the more that I them forbear
The worse they be from year to year.
All that liveth appaireth fast;
Therefore I will, in all the haste,   45
Have a reckoning of every man's person;
For, and I leave the people thus alone
In their life and wicked tempests,
Verily they will become much worse than beasts;
For now one would by envy another up eat;   50
Charity they do all clean forget.
I hoped well that every man
In my glory should make his mansion,
And thereto I had them all elect;
But now I see, like traitors deject,   55
They thank me not for the pleasure that I to them meant,
Nor yet for their being that I them have lent,
I proffered the people great multitude of mercy,
And few there be that asketh it heartily.
They be so cumbered with worldly riches   60
That needs on them I must do justice,
On every man living without fear.
Where art thou, Death, thou mighty messenger?

(Enter DEATH.*)*

DEATH: Almighty God, I am here at your will,
  Your commandment to fulfill.   65
GOD: Go thou to Everyman,
  And show him, in my name,
  A pilgrimage he must on him take,
  Which he in no wise may escape;

---

3 **By figure** in form 6 **all day** always 8 **But . . . gracious** but the purpose of it is more devout 23 **unkind** ungrateful 25 **Of ghostly sight** in spiritual vision 32 **I . . . dead** I consented to die

37 **covetise** covetousness 41 **and . . . sure** and yet their lives are by no means obscure 44 **appaireth** degenerates 47 **and** if 48 **tempests** tumults 55 **deject** abject 59 **heartily** earnestly

70   And that he bring with him a sure reckoning
       Without delay or any tarrying.   (GOD *withdraws.*)
      DEATH: Lord, I will in the world go run overall,
        And cruelly outsearch both great and small;
        Every man will I beset that liveth beastly
75   Out of God's laws, and dreadeth not folly.
        He that loveth riches I will strike with my dart,
        His sight to blind, and from heaven to depart—
        Except that alms be his good friend—
        In hell for to dwell, world without end.
80   Lo, yonder I see Everyman walking.
        Full little he thinketh on my coming;
        His mind is on fleshly lusts and his treasure,
        And great pain it shall cause him to endure
        Before the Lord, Heaven King.

      (*Enter* EVERYMAN.)

85   Everyman, stand still! Whither art thou going
        Thus gaily? Hast thou thy Maker forget?
      EVERYMAN: Why askest thou?
        Wouldest thou wit?
      DEATH: Yea, sir; I will show you:
90   In great haste I am sent to thee
        From God out of his majesty.
      EVERYMAN: What, sent to me?
      DEATH: Yea, certainly.
        Though thou have forget him here,
95   He thinketh on thee in the heavenly sphere,
        As, ere we depart, thou shalt know.
      EVERYMAN: What desireth God of me?
      DEATH: That shall I show thee:
        A reckoning he will needs have
100   Without any longer respite.
      EVERYMAN: To give a reckoning longer leisure I crave;
        This blind matter troubleth my wit.
      DEATH: On thee thou must take a long journey;
        Therefore thy book of count with thee thou bring,
105   For turn again thou cannot by no way.
        And look thou be sure of thy reckoning,
        For before God thou shalt answer, and show
        Thy many bad deeds, and good but a few;
        How thou hast spent thy life, and in what wise,
110   Before the chief Lord of paradise.
        Have ado that we were in that way,
        For, wit thou well, thou shalt make none
          attorney.
      EVERYMAN: Full unready I am such reckoning to give.
        I know thee not. What messenger art thou?
115   DEATH: I am Death, that no man dreadeth,
        For every man I rest, and no man spareth;
        For it is God's commandment
        That all to me should be obedient.
      EVERYMAN: O Death, thou comest when I had thee
          least in mind!
120   In thy power it lieth me to save;

        Yet of my good will I give thee, if thou will be kind:
        Yea, a thousand pound shalt thou have,
        And defer this matter till another day.
      DEATH: Everyman, it may not be, by no way.
        I set not by gold, silver, nor riches,   125
        Ne by pope, emperor, king, duke, ne princes;
        For, and I would receive gifts great,
        All the world I might get;
        But my custom is clean contrary.
        I give thee no respite. Come hence, and not tarry.   130
      EVERYMAN: Alas, shall I have no longer respite?
        I may say Death giveth no warning!
        To think on thee, it maketh my heart sick,
        For all unready is my book of reckoning.
        But twelve year and I might have abiding,   135
        My counting-book I would make so clear
        That my reckoning I should not need to fear.
        Wherefore, Death, I pray thee, for God's mercy,
        Spare me till I be provided of remedy.
      DEATH: Thee availeth not to cry, weep, and pray;   140
        But haste thee lightly that thou were gone that journey,
        And prove thy friends if thou can;
        For, wit thou well, the tide abideth no man,
        And in the world each living creature
        For Adam's sin must die of nature.   145
      EVERYMAN: Death, if I should this pilgrimage take,
        And my reckoning surely make,
        Show me, for saint charity,
        Should I not come again shortly?
      DEATH: No, Everyman; and thou be once there,   150
        Thou mayst never more come here,
        Trust me verily.
      EVERYMAN: O gracious God in the high seat celestial,
        Have mercy on me in this most need!
        Shall I have no company from this vale terrestrial   155
        Of mine acquaintance, that way me to lead?
      DEATH: Yea, if any be so hardy
        That would go with thee and bear thee company.
        Hie thee that thou were gone to God's magnificence,
        Thy reckoning to give before his presence.   160
        What, weenest thou thy life is given thee,
        And thy worldly goods also?
      EVERYMAN: I had wend so, verily.
      DEATH: Nay, nay; it was but lent thee;
        For as soon as thou art go,   165
        Another a while shall have it, and then go therefro,
        Even as thou hast done.
        Everyman, thou art mad! Thou hast thy wits five,
        And here on earth will not amend thy life;
        For suddenly I do come.   170
      EVERYMAN: O wretched caitiff, whither shall I flee,
        That I might scape this endless sorrow?
        Now, gentle Death, spare me till to-morrow,
        That I may amend me
        With good advisement.   175
      DEATH: Nay, thereto I will not consent,

---

72 **overall** everywhere   77 **depart** separate   88 **wit** know   102 **blind** obscure   104 **count** account   105 **turn again** return   111 **Have . . . way** i.e., let's see about making that journey   112 **none attorney** no one [your] advocate   115 **that . . . dreadeth** who fears no man   116 **rest** arrest

121 **good** goods   123 **And defer** if you defer   125 **set not by** care not for   143 **tide** time   161 **weenest** suppose   163 **wend** supposed   165 **go** gone   166 **therefro** from it   175 **advisement** reflection

Nor no man will I respite;
But to the heart suddenly I shall smite
Without any advisement.
180 And now out of thy sight I will me hie;
See thou make thee ready shortly,
For thou mayst say this is the day
That no man living may scape away. (*Exit* DEATH.)
EVERYMAN: Alas, I may well weep with sighs deep!
185 Now have I no manner of company
To help me in my journey, and me to keep;
And also my writing is full unready.
How shall I do now for to excuse me?
I would to God I had never be get!
190 To my soul a full great profit it had be;
For now I fear pains huge and great.
The time passeth. Lord, help, that all wrought!
For though I mourn it availeth nought.
The day passeth, and is almost ago;
195 I wot not well what for to do.
To whom were I best my complaint to make?
What and I to Fellowship thereof spake,
And showed him of this sudden chance?
For in him is all mine affiance;
200 We have in the world so many a day
Be good friends in sport and play.
I see him yonder, certainly.
I trust that he will bear me company;
Therefore to him will I speak to ease my sorrow.
205 Well met, good Fellowship, and good morrow!

(FELLOWSHIP *speaketh:*)

FELLOWSHIP: Everyman, good morrow, by this day!
Sir, why lookest thou so piteously?
If any thing be amiss, I pray thee me say,
That I may help to remedy.
210 EVERYMAN: Yea, good Fellowship, yea;
I am in great jeopardy.
FELLOWSHIP: My true friend, show to me your mind;
I will not forsake thee to my life's end,
In the way of good company.
215 EVERYMAN: That was well spoken, and lovingly.
FELLOWSHIP: Sir, I must needs know your heaviness;
I have pity to see you in any distress.
If any have you wronged, ye shall revenged be,
Though I on the ground be slain for thee—
220 Though that I know before that I should die.
EVERYMAN: Verily, Fellowship, gramercy.
FELLOWSHIP: Tush! by thy thanks I set not a straw.
Show me your grief, and say no more.
EVERYMAN: If I my heart should to you break,
225 And then you to turn your mind from me,
And would not me comfort when ye hear me speak,
Then should I ten times sorrier be.
FELLOWSHIP: Sir, I say as I will do indeed.

EVERYMAN: Then be you a good friend at need:
I have found you true herebefore.
230 FELLOWSHIP: And so ye shall evermore;
For, in faith, and thou go to hell,
I will not forsake thee by the way.
EVERYMAN: Ye speak like a good friend; I believe you well.
I shall deserve it, and I may. 235
FELLOWSHIP: I speak of no deserving, by this day!
For he that will say, and nothing do,
Is not worthy with good company to go;
Therefore show me the grief of your mind,
As to your friend most loving and kind. 240
EVERYMAN: I shall show you how it is:
Commanded I am to go a journey,
A long way, hard and dangerous,
And give a strait count, without delay,
Before the high Judge, Adonai. 245
Wherefore, I pray you, bear me company,
As ye have promised, in this journey.
FELLOWSHIP: That is matter indeed. Promise is duty;
But, and I should take such a voyage on me,
I know it well, it should be to my pain; 250
Also it maketh me afeard, certain.
But let us take counsel here as well as we can,
For your words would fear a strong man.
EVERYMAN: Why, ye said if I had need
Ye would me never forsake, quick ne dead, 255
Though it were to hell, truly.
FELLOWSHIP: So I said, certainly,
But such pleasures be set aside, the sooth to say;
And also, if we took such a journey,
When should we come again? 260
EVERYMAN: Nay, never again, till the day of doom.
FELLOWSHIP: In faith, then will not I come there!
Who hath you these tidings brought?
EVERYMAN: Indeed, Death was with me here.
FELLOWSHIP: Now, by God that all hath bought, 265
If Death were the messenger,
For no man that is living to-day
I will not go that loath journey—
Not for the father that begat me!
EVERYMAN: Ye promised, otherwise, pardie. 270
FELLOWSHIP: I wot well I said so, truly;
And yet if thou wilt eat, and drink, and make good cheer,
Or haunt to women the lusty company,
I would not forsake you while the day is clear,
Trust me verily. 275
EVERYMAN: Yea, thereto ye would be ready!
To go to mirth, solace, and play,
Your mind will sooner apply,
Than to bear me company in my long journey.
FELLOWSHIP: Now, in good faith, I will not that way. 280
But and thou will murder, or any man kill,
In that I will help thee with a good will.

---

186 **keep** guard   187 **writing** the writing of Everyman's accounts   189 **be get** been born   194 **ago** gone   197 **and if**   199 **affiance** trust   206 **by this day** an asseveration   216 **heaviness** sorrow   224 **break** open

235 **deserve** repay   244 **strait count** strict account   245 **Adonai** a Hebrew name for God   248 **That . . . indeed** that is a good reason indeed [for asking me]   253 **fear** frighten   265 **bought** redeemed   268 **loath** loathsome   270 **pardie** by God   273 **Or . . . company** or frequent the pleasant company of women   274 **while . . . clear** until daybreak   278 **apply** attend

EVERYMAN: O, that is a simple advice indeed.
  Gentle fellow, help me in my necessity!
285   We have loved long, and now I need;
  And now, gentle Fellowship, remember me.
FELLOWSHIP: Whether ye have loved me or no,
  By Saint John, I will not with thee go.
EVERYMAN: Yet, I pray thee, take the labour, and do so much
  for me
290   To bring me forward, for saint charity,
  And comfort me till I come without the town.
FELLOWSHIP: Nay, and thou would give me a new gown,
  I will not a foot with thee go;
  But, and thou had tarried, I would not have left thee so.
295   And as now God speed thee in thy journey,
  For from thee I will depart as fast as I may.
EVERYMAN: Whither away, Fellowship? Will thou forsake me?
FELLOWSHIP: Yea, by my fay! To God I betake thee.
EVERYMAN: Farewell, good Fellowship; for thee my heart is
  sore.
300   Adieu for ever! I shall see thee no more.
FELLOWSHIP: In faith, Everyman, farewell now at the ending;
  For you I will remember that parting is mourning.

(*Exit* FELLOWSHIP.)

EVERYMAN: Alack! shall we thus depart indeed—
  Ah, Lady, help!—without any more comfort?
305   Lo, Fellowship forsaketh me in my most need.
  For help in this world whither shall I resort?
  Fellowship herebefore with me would merry make,
  And now little sorrow for me doth he take.
  It is said, 'In prosperity men friends may find,
310   Which in adversity be full unkind.'
  Now whither for succour shall I flee,
  Sith that Fellowship hath forsaken me?
  To my kinsmen I will, truly,
  Praying them to help me in my necessity;
315   I believe that they will do so,
  For kind will creep where it may not go.
  I will go say, for yonder I see them.
  Where be ye now, my friends and kinsmen?

(*Enter* KINDRED *and* COUSIN.)

KINDRED: Here be we now at your commandment.
320   Cousin, I pray you show us your intent
  In any wise, and do not spare.
COUSIN: Yea, Everyman, and to us declare
  If ye be disposed to go anywhither;
  For, wit you well, we will live and die together.
325 KINDRED: In wealth and woe we will with you hold,
  For over his kin a man may be bold.
EVERYMAN: Gramercy, my friends and kinsmen kind.
  Now shall I show you the grief of my mind:
  I was commanded by a messenger,

  That is a high king's chief officer;   330
  He bade me go a pilgrimage, to my pain,
  And I know well I shall never come again;
  Also I must give a reckoning strait,
  For I have a great enemy that hath me in wait,
  Which intendeth me for to hinder.   335
KINDRED: What account is that which ye must render?
  That would I know.
EVERYMAN: Of all my works I must show
  How I have lived and my days spent;
  Also of ill deeds that I have used   340
  In my time, sith life was me lent;
  And of all virtues that I have refused.
  Therefore, I pray you, go thither with me
  To help to make mine account, for saint charity.
COUSIN: What, to go thither? Is that the matter?   345
  Nay, Everyman, I had liefer fast bread and water
  All this five year and more.
EVERYMAN: Alas, that ever I was bore!
  For now shall I never be merry,
  If that you forsake me.   350
KINDRED: Ah, sir, what ye be a merry man!
  Take good heart to you, and make no moan.
  But one thing I warn you, by Saint Anne—
  As for me, ye shall go alone.
EVERYMAN: My Cousin, will you not with me go?   355
COUSIN: No, by our Lady! I have the cramp in my toe.
  Trust not to me, for, so God me speed,
  I will deceive you in your most need.
KINDRED: It availeth not us to tice.
  Ye shall have my maid with all my heart;   360
  She loveth to go to feasts, there to be nice,
  And to dance, and abroad to start:
  I will give her leave to help you in that journey,
  If that you and she may agree.
EVERYMAN: Now show me the very effect of your mind: 365
  Will you go with me, or abide behind?
KINDRED: Abide behind? Yea, that will I, and I may!
  Therefore farewell till another day.   (*Exit* KINDRED.)
EVERYMAN: How should I be merry or glad?
  For fair promises men to me make,   370
  But when I have most need they me forsake.
  I am deceived; that maketh me sad.
COUSIN: Cousin Everyman, farewell now,
  For verily I will not go with you.
  Also of mine own an unready reckoning   375
  I have to account; therefore I make tarrying.
  Now God keep thee, for now I go.   (*Exit* COUSIN.)
EVERYMAN: Ah, Jesus, is all come hereto?
  Lo, fair words maketh fools fain;
  They promise, and nothing will do, certain.   380
  My kinsmen promised me faithfully
  For to abide with me steadfastly,
  And now fast away do they flee:

---

290 **bring me forward** escort me 298 **fay** faith; **betake** commend 303 **depart** part 312 **Sith** since 316 **For . . . go** For kinship will creep where it cannot walk, that is, blood is thicker than water 317 **go say** essay, try 321 **In . . . spare** without fail, and do not hold back 323 **anywhither** anywhere 325 **hold** side 326 **For . . . bold** for a man may be sure of his kinsfolk

---

334 **For . . . wait** a great enemy (the devil) who has me under observation 340 **used** practised 346 **I . . . water** I had rather fast on bread and water 348 **bore** born 351 **what . . . man** what a merry man you are 359 **It . . . tice** it is no use trying to entice us 361 **nice** wanton 362 **abroad to start** go out and about 365 **effect** tenor

Even so Fellowship promised me.
385 What friend were best me of to provide?
I lose my time here longer to abide.
Yet in my mind a thing there is:
All my life I have loved riches;
If that my Good now help me might,
390 He would make my heart full light.
I will speak to him in this distress—
Where art thou, my Goods and riches?

(GOODS *speaks from a corner.*)

GOODS: Who calleth me? Everyman? What! hast thou haste?
I lie here in corners, trussed and piled so high,
395 And in chests I am locked so fast,
Also sacked in bags. Thou mayst see with thine eye
I cannot stir; in packs low I lie.
What would ye have? Lightly me say.
EVERYMAN: Come hither, Goods, in all the haste thou may,
400 For of counsel I must desire thee.
GOODS: Sir, and ye in the world have sorrow or adversity,
That can I help you to remedy shortly.
EVERYMAN: It is another disease that grieveth me;
In this world it is not, I tell thee so.
405 I am sent for, another way to go,
To give a strait count general
Before the highest Jupiter of all;
And all my life I have had joy and pleasure in thee,
Therefore, I pray thee, go with me;
410 For, peradventure, thou mayst before God Almighty
My reckoning help to clean and purify;
For it is said ever among
That money maketh all right that is wrong.
GOODS: Nay, Everyman, I sing another song.
415 I follow no man in such voyages;
For, and I went with thee,
Thou shouldst fare much the worse for me;
For because on me thou did set thy mind,
Thy reckoning I have made blotted and blind,
420 That thine account thou cannot make truly;
And that hast thou for the love of me.
EVERYMAN: That would grieve me full sore,
When I should come to that fearful answer.
Up, let us go thither together.
425 GOODS: Nay, not so! I am too brittle, I may not endure;
I will follow no man one foot, be ye sure.
EVERYMAN: Alas, I have thee loved, and had great pleasure
All my life-days on good and treasure.
GOODS: That is to thy damnation, without leasing,
430 For my love is contrary to the love everlasting;
But if thou had me loved moderately during,
As to the poor to give part of me,
Then shouldst thou not in this dolour be,
Nor in this great sorrow and care.

EVERYMAN: Lo, now was I deceived ere I was ware, 435
And all I may wite misspending of time.
GOODS: What, weenest thou that I am thine?
EVERYMAN: I had wend so.
GOODS: Nay, Everyman, I say no.
As for a while I was lent thee; 440
A season thou hast had me in prosperity.
My condition is man's soul to kill;
If I save one, a thousand I do spill.
Weenest thou that I will follow thee?
Nay, not from this world, verily. 445
EVERYMAN: I had wend otherwise.
GOODS: Therefore to thy soul Goods is a thief;
For when thou art dead, this is my guise—
Another to deceive in this same wise
As I have done thee, and all to his soul's reprief. 450
EVERYMAN: O false Goods, cursed may thou be,
Thou traitor to God, that hast deceived me
And caught me in thy snare!
GOODS: Marry, thou brought thyself in care,
Whereof I am glad; 455
I must needs laugh, I cannot be sad.
EVERYMAN: Ah, Goods, thou hast had long my heartly love;
I gave thee that which should be the Lord's above.
But wilt thou not go with me indeed?
I pray thee truth to say. 460
GOODS: No, so God me speed!
Therefore farewell, and have good day.

(*Exit* GOODS.)

EVERYMAN: O, to whom shall I make my moan
For to go with me in that heavy journey?
First Fellowship said he would with me gone; 465
His words were very pleasant and gay,
But afterward he left me alone.
Then spake I to my kinsmen, all in despair,
And also they gave me words fair;
They lacked no fair speaking, 470
But all forsook me in the ending.
Then went I to my Goods, that I loved best,
In hope to have comfort, but there had I least;
For my Goods sharply did me tell
That he bringeth many into hell. 475
Then of myself I was ashamed,
And so I am worthy to be blamed;
Thus may I well myself hate.
Of whom shall I now counsel take?
I think that I shall never speed 480
Till that I go to my Good Deed.
But, alas, she is so weak
That she can neither go nor speak;
Yet will I venture on her now.
My Good Deeds, where be you? 485

(GOOD DEEDS *speaks from the ground.*)

---

385 **me . . . provide** to provide myself with   389 **Good** Goods   398
Lightly quickly   400 **For . . . thee** for I must entreat your advice   403
disease trouble   412 **For . . . among** for it is sometimes said   419
blind obscure   429 **without leasing** without a lie, that is, truly
431–432 **But . . . me** but if you had loved me moderately during your
lifetime, so as to give part of me to the poor   433 **dolour** distress

---

435 **ware** aware   436 **And . . . time** and I may blame it all on the bad
use I have made of time   438 **wend** supposed   442 **condition** nature
443 **spill** ruin   448 **guise** practice   450 **reprief** shame   457 **heartly**
heartfelt   483 **go** walk   484 **venture** gamble

GOOD DEEDS: Here I lie, cold in the ground;
　Thy sins hath me sore bound,
　That I cannot stir.
EVERYMAN: O Good Deeds, I stand in fear!
490　I must you pray of counsel,
　For help now should come right well.
GOOD DEEDS: Everyman, I have understanding
　That ye be summoned account to make
　Before Messias, of Jerusalem King;
495　And you do by me, that journey with you will I take.
EVERYMAN: Therefore I come to you, my moan to make;
　I pray you that ye will go with me.
GOOD DEEDS: I would full fain, but I cannot stand, verily.
EVERYMAN: Why, is there anything on you fall?
500　GOOD DEEDS: Yea, sir, I may thank you of all;
　If ye had perfectly cheered me,
　Your book of count full ready had be.
　Look, the books of your works and deeds eke!
　Behold how they lie under the feet,
505　To your soul's heaviness.
EVERYMAN: Our Lord Jesus help me!
　For one letter here I cannot see.
GOOD DEEDS: There is a blind reckoning in time of distress.
EVERYMAN: Good Deeds, I pray you help me in this need,
510　Or else I am for ever damned indeed;
　Therefore help me to make reckoning
　Before the Redeemer of all thing,
　That King is, and was, and ever shall.
GOOD DEEDS: Everyman, I am sorry of your fall,
515　And fain would I help you, and I were able.
EVERYMAN: Good Deeds, your counsel I pray you give me.
GOOD DEEDS: That shall I do verily;
　Though that on my feet I may not go,
　I have a sister that shall with you also,
520　Called Knowledge, which shall with you abide,
　To help you to make that dreadful reckoning.

(*Enter* KNOWLEDGE.)

KNOWLEDGE: Everyman, I will go with thee, and be thy
　　guide,
　In thy most need to go by thy side.
EVERYMAN: In good condition I am now in every thing,
525　And am wholly content with this good thing,
　Thanked be God my creator.
GOOD DEEDS: And when she hath brought you there
　Where thou shalt heal thee of thy smart,
　Then go you with your reckoning and your Good Deeds
　　together,
530　For to make you joyful at heart
　Before the blessed Trinity.
EVERYMAN: My Good Deeds, gramercy!
　I am well content, certainly,
　With your words sweet.

KNOWLEDGE: Now go we together lovingly   535
　To Confession, that cleansing river.
EVERYMAN: For joy I weep; I would we were there!
　But, I pray you, give me cognition
　Where dwelleth that holy man, Confession.
KNOWLEDGE: In the house of salvation: 540
　We shall find him in that place,
　That shall us comfort, by God's grace.

(KNOWLEDGE *takes* EVERYMAN *to* CONFESSION.)

　Lo, this is Confession. Kneel down and ask mercy,
　For he is in good conceit with God Almighty.
EVERYMAN: O glorious fountain, that all uncleanness doth   545
　　clarify,
　Wash from me the spots of vice unclean,
　That on me no sin may be seen.
　I come with Knowledge for my redemption,
　Redempt with heart and full contrition;
　For I am commanded a pilgrimage to take,   550
　And great accounts before God to make.
　Now I pray you, Shrift, mother of salvation,
　Help my Good Deeds for my piteous exclamation.
CONFESSION: I know your sorrow well, Everyman.
　Because with Knowledge ye come to me,   555
　I will you comfort as well as I can,
　And a precious jewel I will give thee,
　Called penance, voider of adversity;
　Therewith shall your body chastised be,
　With abstinence and perseverance in God's service.   560
　Here shall you receive that scourge of me,
　Which is penance strong that ye must endure,
　To remember thy Saviour was scourged for thee
　With sharp scourges, and suffered it patiently;
　So must thou, ere thou scape that painful pilgrimage.   565
　Knowledge, keep him in this voyage,
　And by that time Good Deeds will be with thee.
　But in any wise be siker of mercy,
　For your time draweth fast; and ye will saved be,
　Ask God mercy, and he will grant truly.   570
　When with the scourge of penance man doth him bind,
　The oil of forgiveness then shall he find.
EVERYMAN: Thanked be God for his gracious work!
　For now I will my penance begin;
　This hath rejoiced and lighted my heart,   575
　Though the knots be painful and hard within.
KNOWLEDGE: Everyman, look your penance that ye fulfil,
　What pain that ever it to you be;
　And Knowledge shall give you counsel at will
　How your account ye shall make clearly.   580
EVERYMAN: O eternal God, O heavenly figure,
　O way of righteousness, O goodly vision,
　Which descended down in a virgin pure
　Because he would every man redeem,

---

491 **For . . . well** For help would now be very welcome   495 **And . . . me** if you do as I advise   499 **fall** befallen   500 **of** for   501 **If . . . me** If you had encouraged me fully   503 **eke** also   508 **There . . . distress** a sinful person in this hour of need finds that the account of his good deeds is dimly written and difficult to read   520 **Knowledge** the meaning of Knowledge here is acknowledgment or recognition of sins   528 **smart** pain

---

538 **cognition** knowledge   540 **In . . . salvation** in the church   544 **conceit** esteem   549 **Redempt . . . contrition** redeemed by heartfelt and full contrition   552 **Shrift** confession   553 **for . . . exclamation** in answer to my piteous cry   558 **voider** expeller   568 **siker** sure   569 **draweth fast** draws quickly to an end; **and** if   571 **him** himself   575 **lighted** lightened   576 **Though . . . within** though the knots [of the scourge] be painful and hard to my body

585   Which Adam forfeited by his disobedience:
O blessed Godhead, elect and high divine,
Forgive my grievous offence;
Here I cry thee mercy in this presence.
O ghostly treasure, O ransomer and redeemer,
590   Of all the world hope and conductor,
Mirror of joy, and founder of mercy,
Which enlumineth heaven and earth thereby,
Hear my clamorous complaint, though it late be;
Receive my prayers, of thy benignity;
595   Though I be a sinner most abominable,
Yet let my name be written in Moses' table.
O Mary, pray to the Maker of all thing,
Me for to help at my ending;
And save me from the power of my enemy,
600   For Death assaileth me strongly.
And, Lady, that I may by mean of thy prayer
Of your Son's glory to be partner,
By the means of his passion, I it crave;
I beseech you help my soul to save.
605   Knowledge, give me the scourge of penance;
My flesh therewith shall give acquittance:
I will now begin, if God give me grace.
KNOWLEDGE: Everyman, God give you time and space!
Thus I bequeath you in the hands of our Saviour;
610   Now may you make your reckoning sure.
EVERYMAN: In the name of the Holy Trinity,
My body sore punished shall be:
Take this, body, for the sin of the flesh!

(Scourges himself.)

Also thou delightest to go gay and fresh,
615   And in the way of damnation thou did me bring,
Therefore suffer now strokes and punishing.
Now of penance I will wade the water clear,
To save me from purgatory, that sharp fire.

(GOOD DEEDS rises from the ground.)

GOOD DEEDS: I thank God, now I can walk and go,
620   And am delivered of my sickness and woe.
Therefore with Everyman I will go, and not spare;
His good works I will help him to declare.
KNOWLEDGE: Now, Everyman, be merry and glad!
Your Good Deeds cometh now; ye may not be sad.
625   Now is your Good Deeds whole and sound,
Going upright upon the ground.
EVERYMAN: My heart is light, and shall be evermore;
Now will I smite faster than I did before.
GOOD DEEDS: Everyman, pilgrim, my special friend,
630   Blessed be thou without end;
For thee is preparate the eternal glory.

Ye have me made whole and sound,
Therefore I will bide by thee in every stound.
EVERYMAN: Welcome, my Good Deeds; now I hear thy voice,
I weep for very sweetness of love.   635
KNOWLEDGE: Be no more sad, but ever rejoice;
God seeth thy living in his throne above.
Put on this garment to thy behoof,
Which is wet with your tears,
Or else before God you may it miss,   640
When ye to your journey's end come shall.
EVERYMAN: Gentle Knowledge, what do ye it call?
KNOWLEDGE: It is a garment of sorrow:
From pain it will you borrow;
Contrition it is,   645
That geteth forgiveness;
It pleaseth God passing well.
GOOD DEEDS: Everyman, will you wear it for your heal?
EVERYMAN: Now blessed be Jesu, Mary's Son,
For now have I on true contrition.   650
And let us go now without tarrying;
Good Deeds, have we clear our reckoning?
GOOD DEEDS: Yea, indeed, I have it here.
EVERYMAN: Then I trust we need not fear;
Now, friends, let us not part in twain.   655
KNOWLEDGE: Nay, Everyman, that will we not, certain.
GOOD DEEDS: Yet must thou lead with thee
Three persons of great might.
EVERYMAN: Who should they be?
GOOD DEEDS: Discretion and Strength they hight,   660
And thy Beauty may not abide behind.
KNOWLEDGE: Also ye must call to mind
Your Five Wits as for your counsellors.
GOOD DEEDS: You must have them ready at all hours.
EVERYMAN: How shall I get them hither?   665
KNOWLEDGE: You must call them all together,
And they will hear you incontinent.
EVERYMAN: My friends, come hither and be present,
Discretion, Strength, my Five Wits, and Beauty.

(Enter BEAUTY, STRENGTH, DISCRETION, and FIVE WITS.)

BEAUTY: Here at your will we be all ready.   670
What will ye that we should do?
GOOD DEEDS: That ye would with Everyman go,
And help him in his pilgrimage.
Advise you, will ye with him or not in that voyage?
STRENGTH: We will bring him all thither,   675
To his help and comfort, ye may believe me.
DISCRETION: So will we go with him all together.
EVERYMAN: Almighty God, lofed may thou be!
I give thee laud that I have hither brought
Strength, Discretion, Beauty, and Five Wits. Lack   680
   I nought.
And my Good Deeds, with Knowledge clear,
All be in my company at my will here;
I desire no more to my business.

---

586 **divine** divinity   588 **in this presence** in the presence of this company   592 **thereby** besides   596 **Yet . . . table** medieval theologians regarded the two tables given on Sinai as symbols of baptism and penance, respectively. Thus Everyman is asking to be numbered among those who have escaped damnation by doing penance for their sins.   599 **my enemy** the devil   601–603 **And . . . crave** and, Lady, I beg that through the mediation of thy prayer I may share in your Son's glory, in consequence of His passion   606 **acquittance** satisfaction (as a part of the sacrament of penance)   608 **space** opportunity   631 **preparate** prepared

---

633 **stound** trial   638 **behoof** advantage   644 **borrow** release   647 **passing** exceedingly   648 **heal** salvation   660 **hight** are called   663 **wits** senses   667 **incontinent** immediately   674 **Advise** consider   678 **lofed** praised   683 **to** for

STRENGTH: And I, Strength, will by you stand in distress,
685 Though thou would be in battle fight on the ground.
FIVE WITS: And though it were through the world round,
We will not depart for sweet ne sour.
BEAUTY: No more will I unto death's hour
Whatsoever thereof befall.
690 DISCRETION: Everyman, advise you first of all;
Go with a good advisement and deliberation.
We all give you virtuous monition
That all shall be well.
EVERYMAN: My friends, harken what I will tell:
695 I pray God reward you in his heavenly sphere.
Now harken, all that be here,
For I will make my testament
Here before you all present:
In alms half my good I will give with my hands twain
700 In the way of charity, with good intent,
And the other half still shall remain
In queth, to be returned there it ought to be.
This I do in despite of the fiend of hell,
To go quit out of his peril
705 Ever after and this day.
KNOWLEDGE: Everyman, harken what I say:
Go to priesthood, I you advise,
And receive of him in any wise
The holy sacrament and ointment together.
710 Then shortly see ye turn again hither;
We will all abide you here.
FIVE WITS: Yea, Everyman, hie you that ye ready were.
There is no emperor, king, duke, ne baron,
That of God hath commission
715 As hath the least priest in the world being;
For of the blessed sacraments pure and benign
He beareth the keys, and thereof hath the cure
For man's redemption—it is ever sure—
Which God for our soul's medicine
720 Gave us out of his heart with great pine.
Here in this transitory life, for thee and me,
The blessed sacraments seven there be:
Baptism, confirmation, with priesthood good,
And the sacrament of God's precious flesh and blood,
725 Marriage, the holy extreme unction, and penance;
These seven be good to have in remembrance,
Gracious sacraments of high divinity.
EVERYMAN: Fain would I receive that holy body,
And meekly to my ghostly father I will go.
730 FIVE WITS: Everyman, that is the best that ye can do.
God will you to salvation bring,
For priesthood exceedeth all other thing:
To us Holy Scripture they do teach,
And converteth man from sin heaven to reach;
735 God hath to them more power given

Than to any angel that is in heaven.
With five words he may consecrate,
God's body in flesh and blood to make,
And handleth his Maker between his hands.
740 The priest bindeth and unbindeth all bands,
Both in earth and in heaven.
Thou ministers all the sacraments seven;
Though we kissed thy feet, thou were worthy;
Thou art surgeon that cureth sin deadly:
745 No remedy we find under God
But all only priesthood.
Everyman, God gave priests that dignity,
And setteth them in his stead among us to be;
Thus be they above angels in degree.

(EVERYMAN *goes to the priest to receive the last sacraments.*)

KNOWLEDGE: If priests be good, it is so, surely.
750 But when Jesus hanged on the cross with great smart,
There he gave out of his blessed heart
The same sacrament in great torment:
He sold them not to us, that Lord omnipotent.
755 Therefore Saint Peter the apostle doth say
That Jesu's curse hath all they
Which God their Saviour do buy or sell,
Or they for any money do take or tell.
Sinful priests giveth the sinners example bad;
760 Their children sitteth by other men's fires, I have heard;
And some haunteth women's company
With unclean life, as lusts of lechery:
These be with sin made blind.
FIVE WITS: I trust to God no such may we find;
765 Therefore let us priesthood honour,
And follow their doctrine for our souls' succour.
We be their sheep, and they shepherds be
By whom we all be kept in surety.
Peace, for yonder I see Everyman come,
770 Which hath made true satisfaction.
GOOD DEEDS: Methink it is he indeed.

(*Re-enter* EVERYMAN.)

EVERYMAN: Now Jesu be your alder speed!
I have received the sacrament for my redemption,
And then mine extreme unction:
775 Blessed be all they that counselled me to take it!
And now, friends, let us go without longer respite;
I thank God that ye have tarried so long.
Now set each of you on this rood your hand,
And shortly follow me:
780 I go before there I would be; God be our guide!
STRENGTH: Everyman, we will not from you go
Till ye have done this voyage long.
DISCRETION: I, Discretion, will bide by you also.

---

687 **for . . . sour** that is, in happiness or adversity   688 **unto** until   691 **advisement** reflection   692 **monition** forewarning   701–702 **And . . . be** the meaning seems to be that Everyman's immovable property (his body) will lie at rest in the earth   704–705 **To . . . day** to go free out of his power today and ever after   708 **in any wise** without fail   712 **hie . . . were** hurry and prepare yourself   714 **commission** authority   715 **being** living   720 **pine** suffering   728 **that holy body** the sacrament   729 **ghostly** spiritual

737 **five words** *Hoc est enim corpus meum* ("This is my body")   742 **ministers** administer   746 **But . . . priesthood** except only from the priesthood   750 **it is so** that they are above the angels   755–757 **Therefore . . . sell** the reference here is to the sin of simony (Acts viii.18 ff.)   760 **Their . . . fires** their children are illegitimate   772 **be . . . speed** be the helper of you all   778 **rood** cross

KNOWLEDGE: And though this pilgrimage be never so strong,
785   I will never part you fro.
STRENGTH: Everyman, I will be as sure by thee
    As ever I did by Judas Maccabee.

(EVERYMAN comes to his grave.)

EVERYMAN: Alas, I am so faint I may not stand;
    My limbs under me doth fold.
790   Friends, let us not turn again to this land,
    Not for all the world's gold;
    For into this cave must I creep
    And turn to earth, and there to sleep.
BEAUTY: What, into this grave? Alas!
795 EVERYMAN: Yea, there shall ye consume, more and less.
BEAUTY: And what, should I smother here?
EVERYMAN: Yea, by my faith, and never more appear.
    In this world live no more we shall,
    But in heaven before the highest Lord of all.
800 BEAUTY: I cross out all this; adieu, by Saint John!
    I take my cap in my lap, and am gone.
EVERYMAN: What, Beauty, whither will ye?
BEAUTY: Peace, I am deaf; I look not behind me,
    Not and thou wouldest give me all the gold in thy chest.

(Exit BEAUTY.)

805 EVERYMAN: Alas, whereto may I trust?
    Beauty goeth fast away from me;
    She promised with me to live and die.
STRENGTH: Everyman, I will thee also forsake and deny;
    Thy game liketh me not at all.
810 EVERYMAN: Why, then, ye will forsake me all?
    Sweet Strength, tarry a little space.
STRENGTH: Nay, sir, by the rood of grace!
    I will hie me from thee fast,
    Though thou weep till thy heart to-brast.
815 EVERYMAN: Ye would ever bide by me, ye said.
STRENGTH: Yea, I have you far enough conveyed.
    Ye be old enough, I understand,
    Your pilgrimage to take on hand;
    I repent me that I hither came.
820 EVERYMAN: Strength, you to displease I am to blame;
    Yet promise is debt, this ye well wot.
STRENGTH: In faith, I care not.
    Thou art but a fool to complain;
    You spend your speech and waste your brain.
825   Go thrust thee into the ground!

(Exit STRENGTH.)

EVERYMAN: I had wend surer I should you have found.
    He that trusteth in his Strength
    She him deceiveth at the length.
    Both Strength and Beauty forsaketh me;
830   Yet they promised me fair and lovingly.

DISCRETION: Everyman, I will after Strength be gone;
    As for me, I will leave you alone.
EVERYMAN: Why, Discretion, will you forsake me?
DISCRETION: Yea, in faith, I will go from thee,
    For when Strength goeth before   835
    I follow after evermore.
EVERYMAN: Yet, I pray thee, for the love of the Trinity,
    Look in my grave once piteously.
DISCRETION: Nay, so nigh will I not come;
    Farewell, every one!   840

(Exit DISCRETION.)

EVERYMAN: O, all thing faileth, save God alone—
    Beauty, Strength, and Discretion;
    For when Death bloweth his blast,
    They all run from me full fast.
FIVE WITS: Everyman, my leave now of thee I take;   845
    I will follow the other, for here I thee forsake.
EVERYMAN: Alas, then may I wail and weep,
    For I took you for my best friend.
FIVE WITS: I will no longer thee keep;
    Now farewell, and there an end.   850

(Exit FIVE WITS.)

EVERYMAN: O Jesu, help! All hath forsaken me.
GOOD DEEDS: Nay, Everyman; I will bide with thee.
    I will not forsake thee indeed;
    Thou shalt find me a good friend at need.
EVERYMAN: Gramercy, Good Deeds! Now may I true friends   855
    see.
    They have forsaken me, every one;
    I loved them better than my Good Deeds alone.
    Knowledge, will ye forsake me also?
KNOWLEDGE: Yea, Everyman, when ye to Death shall go;
    But not yet, for no manner of danger.   860
EVERYMAN: Gramercy, Knowledge, with all my heart.
KNOWLEDGE: Nay, yet I will not from hence depart
    Till I see where ye shall become.
EVERYMAN: Methink, alas, that I must be gone
    To make my reckoning and my debts pay,   865
    For I see my time is nigh spent away.
    Take example, all ye that this do hear or see,
    How they that I loved best do forsake me,
    Except my Good Deeds that bideth truly.
GOOD DEEDS: All earthly things is but vanity: 870
    Beauty, Strength, and Discretion do man forsake,
    Foolish friends, and kinsmen, that fair spake—
    All fleeth save Good Deeds, and that am I.
EVERYMAN: Have mercy on me, God most mighty;
    And stand by me, thou mother and maid, holy Mary.   875
GOOD DEEDS: Fear not; I will speak for thee.
EVERYMAN: Here I cry God mercy.
GOOD DEEDS: Short our end, and minish our pain;
    Let us go and never come again.
EVERYMAN: Into thy hands, Lord, my soul I commend;   880
    Receive it, Lord, that it be not lost,
    As thou me boughtest, so me defend,

---

784 **strong** grievous   785 **you fro** from you   786–787 **Everyman . . .
Maccabee** I will stand by you as steadfastly as ever I did by Judas Mac-
cabaeus (I Macc. iii)   795 **consume . . . less** decay, all of you   800 **I
. . . this** I cancel all this, that is, my promise to stay with you   801 **I . . .
lap** I doff my cap (so low that it comes) into my lap   809 **liketh** pleases
811 **space** while   814 **to-brast** break   820 **you . . . blame** I am to
blame for displeasing you

---

863 **where . . . become** what shall become of you   878 **Short . . . pain**
shorten our end, and diminish our pain

And save me from the fiend's boast,
That I may appear with that blessed host
885 That shall be saved at the day of doom.
In manus tuas, of mights most
For ever, *commendo spiritum meum.*

(He sinks into his grave.)

KNOWLEDGE: Now hath he suffered that we all shall endure;
The Good Deeds shall make all sure.
890 Now hath he made ending;
Methinketh that I hear angels sing,
And make great joy and melody
Where Everyman's soul received shall be.

ANGEL: Come, excellent elect spouse, to Jesu!
895 Hereabove thou shalt go
Because of thy singular virtue.
Now the soul is taken the body fro,
Thy reckoning is crystal-clear.
Now shalt thou into the heavenly sphere,
900 Unto the which all ye shall come
That liveth well before the day of doom.

(Enter DOCTOR.)

DOCTOR: This moral men may have in mind.
Ye hearers, take it of worth, old and young,
And forsake Pride, for he deceiveth you in the end;
And remember Beauty, Five Wits, Strength, and   905
   Discretion,
They all at the last do every man forsake,
Save his Good Deeds there doth he take.
But beware, for and they be small
Before God, he hath no help at all;
None excuse may be there for every man.   910
Alas, how shall he do then?
For after death amends may no man make,
For then mercy and pity doth him forsake.
If his reckoning be not clear when he doth come,
God will say: '*Ite, maledicti, in ignem eternum.*'   915
And he that hath his account whole and sound,
High in heaven he shall be crowned;
Unto which place God bring us all thither,
That we may live body and soul together.
Thereto help the Trinity!   920
Amen, say ye, for saint charity.

886–887 *In . . . meum* Into thy hands, most mighty One for ever, I commend my spirit   894 **spouse** bride of Jesus [a common medieval metaphor to express the idea of the soul's union with God]

---

903 **take . . . worth** value it   907 **Save** unless   915 *Ite . . . eternum* depart, ye cursed, into everlasting fire (Matt. xxv.41)

◆ THUS ENDETH THIS MORAL PLAY OF EVERYMAN ◆

■ CHRISTOPHER MARLOWE ■

Born in the same year as Shakespeare, Christopher Marlowe (1564–1593) pursued a very different kind of life than his famous contemporary. Unlike Shakespeare, Marlowe had a university education; schooled at the King's School in Canterbury, Marlowe then attended Corpus Christi college, Cambridge. Marlowe left Cambridge in 1587, and his first play—*Tamburlaine*, in two full-length parts—was produced later that year. He wrote several important plays in the course of the next six years: *Doctor Faustus* (c. 1589), *The Jew of Malta* (c. 1590), *Edward II* (c. 1591). Marlowe also wrote *Dido, Queen of Carthage,* possibly while still at Cambridge, and a play about the St. Bartholomew massacre of Huguenots in Paris, *The Massacre at Paris* (1593). Marlowe was an accomplished poet and wrote the narrative poem *Hero and Leander* (published in 1598), among many others. He was known at court and to influential advisers to Queen Elizabeth, such as Sir Walter Raleigh and Sir Francis Walsingham. It is not surprising that Marlowe's life has been much-romanticized, especially given his reputation for iconoclasm, his association with occultists, and his service as one of Elizabeth's spies in Europe. Marlowe was arrested on several occasions for fighting and died from injuries he received in a tavern fight in 1593; there is some speculation that he may have been assassinated. He was 29 years old.

Despite the brevity of his career, Marlowe is deservedly ranked among the greatest of English playwrights. The rhetorical flourish of what Ben Jonson called his "mighty line" and the brilliance of his language are unsurpassed in their majesty and power. His plays were popular in part no doubt because they starred Edward Alleyn, the major actor of the 1580s and early 1590s. Alleyn was the son-in-law of Philip Henslowe, a theatrical entrepreneur who built several theaters in London; their efforts, and Marlowe's plays, made them rich men. Indeed, Marlowe's plays remain alive today through the depth and force of their principal roles. In Faustus and Tamburlaine, Marlowe created roles of a rich and involved subjectivity, characters of the psychological complexity that would become one of the hallmarks of English drama.

DOCTOR FAUSTUS

Marlowe based his play on a popular German narrative, the *History of Doctor Johann Faust,* published in 1587. Audiences might also have seen in Faustus some resemblance to John Dee, Queen Elizabeth's royal astrologer. *Doctor Faustus* was celebrated in its day and would certainly have made a spectacular impression on audiences in the public theater. We know from Henslowe's accounts that his theater had a "hell mouth for Doctor Faustus"—some kind of grotesque opening from which the devils could leap to snare Faustus and haul him off to damnation. The devils themselves were covered with flames, fireworks, and firecrackers; tradition has it that Alleyn—clearly a real showman—wore a cross prominently displayed around his neck, as a way of "defending" himself should real devils be summoned by his performance of Faustus.

The magic of the play, however, arises from the attraction exerted by Faustus himself. Like many of Marlowe's heroes, Faustus is an "overreacher," a man who magnificently and self-destructively tries to go beyond his own limitations, perhaps even beyond the limits of human nature itself. We can see this magnificent energy at the play's opening, when Faustus turns away from Aristotle and philosophy, from medicine, from the law, and from theology to the seductive arts of magic, striking the bargain with the devil that gives him the power to gratify his insatiable curiosity in exchange for his mortal soul.

Modern readers are sometimes confused by *Doctor Faustus*'s morality-play elements, the pageant of the Seven Deadly Sins, and the Good and Bad angels who frame Faustus's temptation. Marlowe brings a medieval vision of the tragic "fall of those who stood in high degree" into collision with the more psychologically oriented vision of tragedy that is characteristic of the modern secular world. Certainly the Good and Bad angels point to what is right and wrong about Faustus's temptation. What is fascinating about the play is the way that Faustus's desire to be ravished by new experiences not only overcomes *his* scruples, but *ours* in the audience as well. Marlowe's play relies on the fact that despite the angels' warnings, we will want to see where Faustus's overreaching will take him.

Faustus—like Prospero in Shakespeare's *The Tempest*—could be taken as a figure for the Renaissance sense of human potential, here realized in its negative or self-destructive dimension. Faustus also seems to provide a figure for the morality of the theater itself, for the power that Faustus exercises in the play increasingly seems to be illusory, merely theatrical. The spectacles that Faustus conjures are finally *only* shows—Mephostophilis and Helen are just devils in disguise— and the power he wields has increasingly trivial results: tricking the Pope degenerates into hoodwinking the horse-courser and setting antlers on Benvolio's head. Faustus is damned for bargaining away his soul, but what finally seems to turn the play toward tragedy is what he sells his soul for: not for the world, but for the illusion of a world, a kind of endless and impoverished theater. We might well recall that the illusions that damn Faustus are, in many ways, the same illusions we have come to the theater to see. The theater makes Faustus's temptation real to its audience by tempting it with many of the same arts.

DOCTOR FAUSTUS

CHRISTOPHER MARLOWE
EDITED BY SYLVAN BARNET

— CHARACTERS —

CHORUS
DOCTOR FAUSTUS
WAGNER, *his student and servant*
GOOD ANGEL
BAD ANGEL
VALDES ⎱ *magicians*
CORNELIUS ⎰
THREE SCHOLARS
LUCIFER, *prince of devils*
MEPHOSTOPHILIS, *a devil*
ROBIN, *a clown*
BELZEBUB, *a devil*
PRIDE
COVETOUSNESS
ENVY
WRATH ⎰ *the Seven Deadly Sins*
GLUTTONY
SLOTH
LECHERY
DICK, *a clown*
POPE ADRIAN
RAYMOND, *King of Hungary*

BRUNO, *rival Pope appointed by the Emperor*
TWO CARDINALS
ARCHBISHOP OF RHEIMS
FRIARS
VINTNER
MARTINO ⎱
FREDERICK ⎰ *gentlemen at the Emperor's court*
BENVOLIO
THE GERMAN EMPEROR, CHARLES THE FIFTH
DUKE OF SAXONY
TWO SOLDIERS
HORSE-COURSER, *a clown*
CARTER, *a clown*
HOSTESS OF A TAVERN
DUKE OF VANHOLT
DUCHESS OF VANHOLT
SERVANT
OLD MAN
DARIUS OF PERSIA, ALEXANDER THE GREAT, ALEXANDER'S PARAMOUR, HELEN OF TROY, DEVILS, PIPER, CARDINALS, MONKS, FRIARS, ATTENDANTS, SOLDIERS, SERVANTS, TWO CUPIDS

— PROLOGUE —

(Enter CHORUS.*)*

Not marching in the fields of Trasimene
Where Mars did mate the warlike Carthagens,
Nor sporting in the dalliance of love
In courts of kings where state is overturned,
5 Nor in the pomp of proud audacious deeds
Intends our muse to vaunt his heavenly verse.
Only this, gentles—We must now perform
The form of Faustus' fortunes, good or bad:
And now to patient judgments we appeal
10 And speak for Faustus in his infancy.
Now is he born of parents base of stock
In Germany within a town called Rhode;
At riper years to Wittenberg he went
Whereas his kinsmen chiefly brought him up.

So much he profits in divinity   15
That shortly he was graced with doctor's name,
Excelling all, and sweetly can dispute
In th' heavenly matters of theology;
Till swoll'n with cunning, of a self-conceit,
His waxen wings did mount above his reach   20
And melting, heavens conspired his overthrow!
For falling to a devilish exercise
And glutted now with learning's golden gifts
He surfeits upon cursèd necromancy:
Nothing so sweet as magic is to him   25
Which he prefers before his chiefest bliss—
And this the man that in his study sits.

(Exit.)

Prologue s.d. **Chorus** a single actor (here, perhaps, Wagner, Faustus' servant-student)   1 **Trasimene** Lake Trasimene, site of one of Hannibal's victories over the Romans, 217 B.C. (Marlowe is not known to have written on this subject, though lines 3–4 may refer to his *Edward II*, and line 5 to his *Tamburlaine*)   2 **Mars did mate** i.e., the Roman army encountered   4 **state** government   6 **muse** poet; **vaunt** proudly display   12 **Rhode** Roda   14 **Whereas** where

16 **graced** (alluding to the official "grace" permitting the student to take his degree)   19 **cunning, of a self-conceit** ingenuity, born of arrogance   20 **waxen wings** (alluding to Icarus, who flew by means of wings made of feathers waxed to a framework; despite the warning of his father, Icarus soared too near the sun, the wax melted, and he plunged to his death)   24 **necromancy** (literally divination by means of the spirits of the dead, but here probably equivalent to black magic)   26 **prefers before his chiefest bliss** sets above his hope of salvation

— ACT ONE —

SCENE I

FAUSTUS *in his study.*

FAUSTUS: Settle thy studies Faustus, and begin
    To sound the depth of that thou wilt profess.
    Having commenced, be a divine in show—
    Yet level at the end of every art
5   And live and die in Aristotle's works.
    Sweet *Analytics,* 'tis thou hast ravished me.
    Bene disserere est finis logices.
    Is to dispute well logic's chiefest end?
    Affords this art no greater miracle?
10 Then read no more, thou has attained that end.
    A greater subject fitteth Faustus' wit:
    Bid *on kai me on* farewell, and Galen come:
    Be a physician Faustus, heap up gold,
    And be eternized for some wondrous cure.
15 *Summum bonum medicinae sanitas,*
    The end of physic is our body's health.
    Why Faustus hast thou not attained that end?
    Are not thy bills hung up as monuments
    Whereby whole cities have escaped the plague
20 And thousand desperate maladies been cured?
    Yet art thou still but Faustus and a man.
    Could'st thou make men to live eternally
    Or being dead raise them to life again,
    Then this profession were to be esteemed.
25 Physic farewell! Where is Justinian?
    Si una eademque res legatur duobus, alter rem, alter
        valorem rei, et cetera.
    A petty case of paltry legacies.
    Exhereditare filium non potest pater, nisi—
30 Such is the subject of the *Institute*
    And universal body of the law!
    This study fits a mercenary drudge
    Who aims at nothing but external trash,
    Too servile and illiberal for me.
35 When all is done, divinity is best.
    Jerome's Bible, Faustus, view it well.
    Stipendium peccati mors est. Ha! *Stipendium et cetera.* The

reward of sin is death? That's hard: *Si peccasse negamus, fal-*
limur, et nulla est in nobis veritas. If we say that we have no
sin, we deceive ourselves, and there is no truth in us. Why,   40
then belike, we must sin, and so consequently die.
Ay, we must die an everlasting death.
What doctrine call you this? *Che serà, serà:*
What will be, shall be! Divinity, adieu!
These metaphysics of magicians   45
And negromantic books are heavenly;
Lines, circles, letters, characters—
Ay, these are those that Faustus most desires.
O, what a world of profit and delight,
Of power, of honor, and omnipotence   50
Is promised to the studious artisan!
All things that move between the quiet poles
Shall be at my command: emperors and kings
Are but obeyed in their several provinces
But his dominion that exceeds in this   55
Stretcheth as far as doth the mind of man:
A sound magician is a demi-god!
Here tire my brains to get a deity!

(*Enter* WAGNER.)

Wagner, commend me to my dearest friends.
The German Valdes and Cornelius.   60
Request them earnestly to visit me.

WAGNER: I will, sir.   (*Exit.*)

FAUSTUS: Their conference will be a greater help to me
    Than all my labors, plod I ne'er so fast.

(*Enter the* [GOOD] ANGEL *and* [*the* EVIL] SPIRIT.)

GOOD ANGEL: O Faustus, lay that damnèd book aside   65
    And gaze not on it lest it tempt thy soul
    And heap God's heavy wrath upon thy head!
    Read, read the Scriptures—that is blasphemy!

BAD ANGEL: Go forward Faustus, in that famous art
    Wherein all nature's treasure is contained.   70
    Be thou on earth as Jove is in the sky,
    Lord and commander of these elements!

(*Exeunt* ANGELS.)

FAUSTUS: How am I glutted with conceit of this!
    Shall I make spirits fetch me what I please?
    Resolve me of all ambiguities?   75
    Perform what desperate enterprise I will?
    I'll have them fly to India for gold,
    Ransack the ocean for orient pearl,

I.i. s.d. **Faustus in his study** (probably at his last line the Chorus drew back a curtain at the rear of the stage, disclosing Faustus)   2 **profess** study and teach   3 **commenced** taken a degree   4 **level** aim   6 **Analytics** title of two treatises by Aristotle on logic   7 **Bene . . . logices** the end (i.e., purpose) of logic is to argue well (Latin)   11 **wit** intelligence   12 **on kai me on** being and not being (Greek); **Galen** Greek authority on medicine, 2nd century AD   15 **Summum . . . sanitas** health is the greatest good of medicine (Latin, translated from Aristotle's *Nichomachean Ethics*)   16 **physic** medicine   18 **bills** prescriptions   25 **Justinian** Roman emperor and authority on law (483–565) who ordered the compilation of the *Institutes*   26–27 **Si . . . et cetera** if one thing is willed to two persons, one of them shall have the thing itself, the other the value of the thing, and so forth (Latin)   29 **Exhereditare . . . nisi** a father cannot disinherit his son unless (Latin)   36 **Jerome's Bible** the Latin translation made by St. Jerome (c.340–420)   37 **Stipendium . . . est** the wages of sin is death (Romans 6:23; if Faustus had gone on to read the rest of the verse, he would have found that "the gift of God is eternal life through Jesus Christ our Lord")

38–39 **Si . . . veritas** from I John 1:8, translated in the next two lines; Faustus neglects the following verse: "If we confess our sins, He is faithful and just to forgive us our sins, and to cleanse us from all unrighteousness"   43 **Che serà, serà** (Italian, translated in the first half of the next line)   45 **metaphysics** subjects lying beyond (or studied after) physics   46 **negromantic** black magical (though probably here also associated with "necromantic," i.e., concerned with raising the spirits of the dead)   51 **artisan** i.e., expert   52 **quiet** motionless   55 **this** i.e., magic   58 **get** beget   63 **conference** conversation.   s.d. **Spirit** Bad Angel, devil (the two angels probably enter the stage from separate doors)   68 **that** i.e., the book of magic   73 **conceit of this** i.e., the conception of being a magician   75 **Resolve me of** explain to me   77 **India** either the West Indies (America) or the East Indies   78 **orient** lustrous and precious

And search all corners of the new-found world
80   For pleasant fruits and princely delicates;
        I'll have them read me strange philosophy
        And tell the secrets of all foreign kings;
        I'll have them wall all Germany with brass
        And make swift Rhine circle fair Wittenberg;
85   I'll have them fill the public schools with silk
        Wherewith the students shall be bravely clad.
        I'll levy soldiers with the coin they bring
        And chase the Prince of Parma from our land
        And reign sole king of all the provinces!
90   Yea, stranger engines for the brunt of war
        Than was the fiery keel at Antwerp bridge
        I'll make my servile spirits to invent.

        (Enter VALDES *and* CORNELIUS.)

        Come German Valdes and Cornelius
        And make me blest with your sage conference.
95   Valdes, sweet Valdes, and Cornelius,
        Know that your words have won me at the last
        To practice magic and concealèd arts.
        Philosophy is odious and obscure,
        Both law and physic are for petty wits,
100   Divinity is basest of the three—
        Unpleasant, harsh, contemptible, and vile.
        'Tis magic, magic, that hath ravished me!
        Then, gentle friends, aid me in this attempt
        And I, that have with subtle syllogisms
105   Graveled the pastors of the German church
        And made the flow'ring pride of Wittenberg
        Swarm to my problems as th' infernal spirits
        On sweet Musaeus when he came to hell,
        Will be as cunning as Agrippa was,
110   Whose shadows made all Europe honor him.
        VALDES: Faustus, these books, thy wit, and our experience
        Shall make all nations to canonize us.
        As Indian Moors obey their Spanish lords,
        So shall the spirits of every element
115   Be always serviceable to us three:
        Like lions shall they guard us when we please,
        Like Almain rutters with their horsemen's staves
        Or Lapland giants trotting by our sides;
        Sometimes like women or unwedded maids
120   Shadowing more beauty in their airy brows
        Than has the white breasts of the queen of love;
        From Venice shall they drag huge argosies
        And from America the golden fleece
        That yearly stuffs old Philip's treasury,
125   If learnèd Faustus will be resolute.

FAUSTUS: Valdes, as resolute am I in this
        As thou to live; therefore object it not.
CORNELIUS: The miracles that magic will perform
        Will make thee vow to study nothing else.
        He that is grounded in astrology,   130
        Enriched with tongues, well seen in minerals,
        Hath all the principles magic doth require.
        Then doubt not Faustus but to be renowned
        And more frequented for this mystery
        Than heretofore the Delphian oracle.   135
        The spirits tell me they can dry the sea
        And fetch the treasure of all foreign wracks,
        Yea, all the wealth that our forefathers hid
        Within the massy entrails of the earth.
        Then tell me Faustus, what shall we three want?   140
FAUSTUS: Nothing, Cornelius. O, this cheers my soul!
        Come, show me some demonstrations magical
        That I may conjure in some bushy grove
        And have these joys in full possession.
VALDES: Then haste thee to some solitary grove,   145
        And bear wise Bacon's and Albanus' works,
        The Hebrew Psalter, and New Testament;
        And whatsoever else is requisite
        We will inform thee ere our conference cease.
CORNELIUS: Valdes, first let him know the words of art,   150
        And then, all other ceremonies learned,
        Faustus may try his cunning by himself.
VALDES: First I'll instruct thee in the rudiments,
        And then wilt thou be perfecter than I.
FAUSTUS: Then come and dine with me, and after meat   155
        We'll canvass every quiddity thereof,
        For ere I sleep I'll try what I can do:
        This night I'll conjure though I die therefor!

        (Exeunt omnes.)

SCENE II

Enter two SCHOLARS.

1 SCHOLAR: I wonder what's become of Faustus that was wont
        to make our schools ring with *sic probo.*

(Enter WAGNER.)

2 SCHOLAR: That shall we presently know. Here comes his
        boy.
1 SCHOLAR: How now sirrah, where's thy master?   5
WAGNER: God in heaven knows.
1 SCHOLAR: Why, dost not thou know then?
WAGNER: Yes, I know, but that follows not.
1 SCHOLAR: Go to sirrah, leave your jesting and tell us where
        he is.   10

---

85 **public schools** universities   86 **bravely** splendidly   88 **Prince of Parma** Spanish governor-general of the Low Countries during 1579–1592   90 **brunt** assault   91 **fiery keel** burning ship sent by the Netherlanders in 1585 against a bridge erected by Parma to blockade Antwerp (Antwerp here is adjectival, not genitive)   105 **Graveled** confounded   107 **problems** questions proposed for disputation   108 **Musaeus** legendary Greek poet   109 **Agrippa** Cornelius Agrippa of Nettesheim (1486–1535), German author of *De occulta philosophia,* a survey of Renaissance magic; Agrippa was believed to have raised spirits ("shadows") from the dead   113 **Indian Moors** American Indians   117 **Almain rutters** German cavalrymen   120 **Shadowing** sheltering   124 **Philip** King Philip II of Spain (1527–1598)

---

131 **well seen** skilled   134 **frequented for this mystery** resorted to for this art   135 **Delphian oracle** oracle of Apollo at Delphi   139 **massy** massive   140 **want** lack   143 **conjure** raise spirits   146 **Bacon** Roger Bacon, medieval friar and scientist; **Albanus** perhaps Pietro d'Abano, medieval writer on medicine and philosophy   156 **canvass every quiddity** discuss every essential detail.   s.d. **omnes** all (Latin)

I.ii.2 **sic probo** thus I prove it (Latin)   3 **presently** at once   4 **boy** servant (an impoverished student)   5 **sirrah** (term of address used to an inferior)   9 **Go to** (exclamation of impatience)

WAGNER: That follows not by force of argument, which you, being licentiates, should stand upon; therefore, acknowledge your error and be attentive.

2 SCHOLAR: Then you will not tell us?

15 WAGNER: You are deceived, for I will tell you. Yet if you were not dunces, you would never ask me such a question. For is he not corpus naturale? And is not that mobile? Then wherefore should you ask me such a question? But that I am by na-

20 ture phlegmatic, slow to wrath, and prone to lechery—to love, I would say—it were not for you to come within forty foot of the place of execution—although I do not doubt but to see you both hanged the next sessions. Thus, having triumphed over you, I will set my countenance like a pre-

25 cisian and begin to speak thus: Truly, my dear brethren, my master is within at dinner, with Valdes and Cornelius, as this wine, if it could speak, would inform your worships; and so, the Lord bless you, preserve you, and keep you, my dear brethren.

(Exit.)

1 SCHOLAR: O Faustus, then I fear that which I have long suspected,

30 That thou art fall'n into that damnèd art
For which they two are infamous through the world.

2 SCHOLAR: Were he a stranger, not allied to me,
The danger of his soul would make me mourn.
But come, let us go and inform the rector.

35 It may be his grave counsel may reclaim him.

1 SCHOLAR: I fear me nothing will reclaim him now.

2 SCHOLAR: Yet let us see what we can do.

(Exeunt.)

SCENE III

Thunder. Enter LUCIFER *and four* DEVILS. FAUSTUS *to them with this speech.*

FAUSTUS: Now that the gloomy shadow of the night,
Longing to view Orion's drizzling look,
Leaps from th' antarctic world unto the sky
And dims the welkin with her pitchy breath,

5 Faustus, begin thine incantations
And try if devils will obey thy hest,
Seeing thou hast prayed and sacrificed to them.
Within this circle is Jehovah's name
Forward and backward anagrammatized,

10 Th' abbreviated names of holy saints,

Figures of every adjunct to the heavens,
And characters of signs and erring stars,
By which the spirits are enforced to rise:
Then fear not, Faustus, to be resolute
And try the utmost magic can perform.   15

(Thunder.)

Sint mihi dei Acherontis propitii! Valeat numen triplex Iehovae! Ignei, aerii, aquatici, spiritus, salvete! Orientis princeps, Belzebub inferni ardentis monarcha, et Demogorgon, propitiamus vos ut appareat et surgat Mephostophilis! Quid tu moraris? Per Iehovam, Gehennam, et consecratam aquam 20 *quam nunc spargo, signumque crucis quod nunc facio, et per vota nostra, ipse nunc surgat nobis dicatus Mephostophilis!*

(Enter a DEVIL.*)*

I charge thee to return and change thy shape,
Thou art too ugly to attend on me.
Go, and return an old Franciscan friar: 25
That holy shape becomes a devil best.

(Exit DEVIL.*)*

I see there's virtue in my heavenly words.
Who would not be proficient in this art?
How pliant is this Mephostophilis,
Full of obedience and humility,   30
Such is the force of magic and my spells.

(Enter MEPHOSTOPHILIS.*)*

MEPHOSTOPHILIS: Now Faustus, what wouldst thou have me do?

FAUSTUS: I charge thee wait upon me whilst I live
To do whatever Faustus shall command,
Be it to make the moon drop from her sphere   35
Or the ocean to overwhelm the world.

MEPHOSTOPHILIS: I am a servant to great Lucifer
And may not follow thee without his leave.
No more than he commands must we perform.

FAUSTUS: Did not he charge thee to appear to me?   40

MEPHOSTOPHILIS: No, I came now hither of mine own accord.

FAUSTUS: Did not my conjuring raise thee? Speak.

MEPHOSTOPHILIS: That was the cause, but yet *per accidens:*
For when we hear one rack the name of God,
Abjure the Scriptures and his savior Christ,   45
We fly in hope to get his glorious soul.

---

12 **licentiates** possessors of a degree preceding the master's degree; **stand upon** make much of   16 **dunces** (1) fools (2) hairsplitters   17 **corpus naturale . . . mobile** natural matter . . . movable (Latin, scholastic definition of the subject-matter of physics)   19 **phlegmatic** sluggish   21 **the place of execution** the place of action, i.e., the dining room (with quibble on gallows)   22 **sessions** sittings of a court   23 **precisian** Puritan (Wagner goes on to parody the style of the Puritans)   34 **rector** head of the university

I.iii. s.d. **Enter . . . Devils** (they are invisible to Faustus; perhaps they enter through a trapdoor and climb to the upper playing area, as implied in V.ii. s.d.)   2 **Orion** constellation appearing at the beginning of winter, associated with rain   4 **welkin** sky   8 **circle** circle the conjuror draws around him on the ground, to call the spirits and to protect himself from them

---

11 **adjunct to** heavenly body fixed to   12 **signs and erring stars** signs of the Zodiac and planets   16–22 **Sint . . . Mephostophilis** may the gods of the lower region be favorable to me. Away with the trinity of Jehovah. Hail, spirits of fire, air, water. Prince of the east, Belzebub monarch of burning hell, and Demogorgon, we pray to you that Mephostophilis may appear and rise. Why do you delay? By Jehovah, Gehenna, and the holy water which now I sprinkle, and the sign of the cross which now I make, and by our vows, may Mephostophilis himself now rise to serve us (Latin).   s.d. **Devil** (the word "dragon" oddly appears, after "surgat Mephostophilis," in the preceding conjuration. It makes no sense in the sentence, and it has therefore been omitted from the present text, but perhaps it indicates that a dragon briefly appears at that point, or perhaps the devil referred to in the present stage direction is disguised as a dragon)   43 **per accidens** the immediate (but not ultimate) cause (Latin)   44 **rack** torture   46 **glorious** (1) splendid (2) presumptuous

Nor will we come unless he use such means
Whereby he is in danger to be damned.
Therefore the shortest cut for conjuring
50 Is stoutly to abjure the Trinity
And pray devoutly to the prince of hell.
FAUSTUS: So Faustus hath already done, and holds this
    principle,
There is no chief but only Belzebub:
To whom Faustus doth dedicate himself.
55 This word "damnation" terrifies not me
For I confound hell in Elysium:
My ghost be with the old philosophers!
But leaving these vain trifles of men's souls,
Tell me, what is that Lucifer thy Lord?
60 MEPHOSTOPHILIS: Arch-regent and commander of all spirits.
FAUSTUS: Was not that Lucifer an angel once?
MEPHOSTOPHILIS: Yes Faustus, and most dearly loved of God.
FAUSTUS: How comes it then that he is prince of devils?
MEPHOSTOPHILIS: O, by aspiring pride and insolence,
65 For which God threw him from the face of heaven.
FAUSTUS: And what are you that live with Lucifer?
MEPHOSTOPHILIS: Unhappy spirits that fell with Lucifer,
Conspired against our God with Lucifer,
And are forever damned with Lucifer.
70 FAUSTUS: Where are you damned?
MEPHOSTOPHILIS: In hell.
FAUSTUS: How comes it then that thou art out of hell?
MEPHOSTOPHILIS: Why this is hell, nor am I out of it.
Think'st thou that I who saw the face of God
75 And tasted the eternal joys of heaven
Am not tormented with ten thousand hells
In being deprived of everlasting bliss?
O Faustus, leave these frivolous demands
Which strikes a terror to my fainting soul!
80 FAUSTUS: What, is great Mephostophilis so passionate
For being deprivèd of the joys of heaven?
Learn thou of Faustus manly fortitude
And scorn those joys thou never shalt possess.
Go bear these tidings to great Lucifer:
85 Seeing Faustus hath incurred eternal death
By desperate thoughts against Jove's deity,
Say he surrenders up to him his soul
So he will spare him four and twenty years,
Letting him live in all voluptuousness,
90 Having thee ever to attend on me,
To give me whatsoever I shall ask,
To tell me whatsoever I demand,
To slay mine enemies and to aid my friends
And always be obedient to my will.
95 Go and return to mighty Lucifer
And meet me in my study at midnight,
And then resolve me of my master's mind.
MEPHOSTOPHILIS: I will, Faustus.
FAUSTUS: Had I as many souls as there be stars
100 I'd give them all for Mephostophilis.

By him I'll be great emperor of the world,
And make a bridge through the moving air
To pass the ocean with a band of men;
I'll join the hills that bind the Afric shore
105 And make that country continent to Spain,
And both contributary to my crown;
The Emperor shall not live but by my leave,
Nor any potentate of Germany.
Now that I have obtained what I desired
110 I'll live in speculation of this art
Till Mephostophilis return again.

(Exit.)

(Exeunt LUCIFER *and* DEVILS.*)*

SCENE IV

Enter WAGNER *and* [ROBIN] *the clown.*

WAGNER: Come hither, sirrah boy.
ROBIN: Boy! O, disgrace to my person! Zounds, boy in your
    face! You have seen many boys with such pickadevants, I am
    sure.
WAGNER: Sirrah, hast thou no comings in?   5
ROBIN: Yes, and goings out too, you may see sir.
WAGNER: Alas, poor slave! See how poverty jests in his naked-
    ness. I know the villain's out of service, and so hungry that I
    know he would give his soul to the devil for a shoulder of
    mutton, though it were blood-raw.   10
ROBIN: Not so, neither! I had need to have it well roasted, and
    good sauce to it, if I pay so dear, I can tell you.
WAGNER: Sirrah, wilt thou be my man and wait on me? And I
    will make thee go like *Qui mihi discipulus.*
ROBIN: What, in verse?   15
WAGNER: No, slave, in beaten silk and stavesacre.
ROBIN: Stavesacre? That's good to kill vermin! Then, belike, if
    I serve you I shall be lousy.
WAGNER: Why, so thou shalt be, whether thou dost it or no; for
    sirrah, if thou dost not presently bind thyself to me for seven   20
    years, I'll turn all the lice about thee into familiars and make
    them tear thee in pieces.
ROBIN: Nay sir, you may save yourself a labor, for they are as
    familiar with me as if they paid for their meat and drink, I
    can tell you.   25
WAGNER: Well sirrah, leave your jesting and take these guilders.
ROBIN: Yes marry sir, and I thank you too.
WAGNER: So, now thou art to be at an hour's warning whenso-
    ever and wheresoever the devil shall fetch thee.
ROBIN: Here, take your guilders, I'll none of 'em!   30

---

56 **confound hell in Elysium** do not distinguish between hell and Elysium   57 **ghost** spirit; **old** i.e., pre-Christian   60 **spirits** devils   79
strikes (it is not unusual to have a plural subject—especially when it
has a collective force—take a verb ending in -s)   80 **passionate** emotional   97 **resolve** inform

102 **through** (pronounced "thorough")   105 **continent to** continuous
with   110 **speculation** contemplation

I.iv. s.d. **Clown** buffoon   2 **Zounds** by God's wounds   3 **pickade-
vants** pointed beards   5 **comings in** income (the Clown then quibbles
on "goings out," i.e., expenses and also holes in his clothes through
which his body pokes   14 **Qui mihi discipulus** one who is my disciple, i.e., like the servant of a learned man (the Latin is the beginning of
a poem, familiar to Renaissance schoolboys on proper behavior)   16
beaten embroidered (leading to the quibble on the sense "hit");
stavesacre preparation from seeds of delphinium, used to kill vermin
21 **familiars** attendant demons   26 **guilders** Dutch coins   27 **marry**
indeed (a mild oath, from "by the Virgin Mary")

WAGNER: Not I, thou art pressed. Prepare thyself, for I will
     presently raise up two devils to carry thee away. Banio!
     Belcher!
ROBIN: Belcher! And Belcher come here I'll belch him. I am
35   not afraid of a devil!

(Enter two DEVILS.)

WAGNER: How now sir, will you serve me now?
ROBIN: Ay, good Wagner, take away the devil then.
WAGNER: Spirits, away! *(Exeunt* DEVILS.) Now sirrah, follow
     me.
40 ROBIN: I will sir! But hark you master, will you teach me this
     conjuring occupation?
WAGNER: Ay sirrah, I'll teach thee to turn thyself to a dog or a
     cat or a mouse or a rat or anything.
ROBIN: A dog or a cat or a mouse or a rat? O brave Wagner!
45 WAGNER: Villain, call me Master Wagner. And see that you
     walk attentively, and let your right eye be always diametrally
     fixed upon my left heel, that thou mayst *quasi vestigiis nostris*
     insistere.
ROBIN: Well sir, I warrant you.

(Exeunt.)

— ACT TWO —

SCENE I

Enter FAUSTUS *in his study.*

FAUSTUS: Now, Faustus, must thou needs be damned;
     Canst thou not be saved!
     What boots it then to think on God or heaven?
     Away with such vain fancies, and despair—
5   Despair in God and trust in Belzebub!
     Now go not backward, Faustus, be resolute!
     Why waver'st thou? O something soundeth in mine ear,
     "Abjure this magic, turn to God again."
     Ay, and Faustus will turn to God again.
10   To God? He loves thee not;
     The god thou serv'st is thine own appetite
     Wherein is fixed the love of Belzebub!
     To him I'll build an altar and a church
     And offer lukewarm blood of newborn babies!

(Enter the two ANGELS.)

15 BAD ANGEL: Go forward, Faustus, in that famous art.
GOOD ANGEL: Sweet Faustus, leave that execrable art.
FAUSTUS: Contrition, prayer, repentance, what of these?
GOOD ANGEL: O, they are means to bring thee unto heaven.
BAD ANGEL: Rather illusions, fruits of lunacy,
20   That make men foolish that do use them most.
GOOD ANGEL: Sweet Faustus, think of heaven and heavenly
     things.
BAD ANGEL: No Faustus, think of honor and of wealth.

(Exeunt ANGELS.)

FAUSTUS: Wealth!
     Why, the signory of Emden shall be mine!
     When Mephostophilis shall stand by me   25
     What power can hurt me? Faustus, thou art safe.
     Cast no more doubts! Mephostophilis, come,
     And bring glad tidings from great Lucifer.
     Is't not midnight? Come Mephostophilis,
     Veni, veni, Mephostophile!   30

(Enter MEPHOSTOPHILIS.)

     Now tell me, what saith Lucifer thy Lord?
MEPHOSTOPHILIS: That I shall wait on Faustus whilst he lives,
     So he will buy my service with his soul.
FAUSTUS: Already Faustus hath hazarded that for thee.
MEPHOSTOPHILIS: But now thou must bequeath it solemnly   35
     And write a deed of gift with thine own blood,
     For that security craves Lucifer.
     If thou deny it I must back to hell.
FAUSTUS: Stay Mephostophilis and tell me
     What good will my soul do thy lord?   40
MEPHOSTOPHILIS: Enlarge his kingdom.
FAUSTUS: Is that the reason why he tempts us thus?
MEPHOSTOPHILIS: *Solamen miseris socios habuisse doloris.*
FAUSTUS: Why, have you any pain that torture other?
MEPHOSTOPHILIS: As great as have the human souls of men.   45
     But tell me, Faustus, shall I have thy soul—
     And I will be thy slave and wait on thee
     And give thee more than thou hast wit to ask?
FAUSTUS: Ay Mephostophilis, I'll give it him.
MEPHOSTOPHILIS: Then, Faustus, stab thy arm courageously   50
     And bind thy soul that at some certain day
     Great Lucifer may claim it as his own.
     And then be thou as great as Lucifer!
FAUSTUS: Lo, Mephostophilis, for love of thee
     Faustus hath cut his arm and with his proper blood   55
     Assures his soul to be great Lucifer's,
     Chief lord and regent of perpetual night.
     View here this blood that trickles from mine arm
     And let it be propitious for my wish.
MEPHOSTOPHILIS: But Faustus,   60
     Write it in manner of a deed of gift.
FAUSTUS: Ay so I do—But Mephostophilis,
     My blood congeals and I can write no more.
MEPHOSTOPHILIS: I'll fetch thee fire to dissolve it straight.

(Exit.)

FAUSTUS: What might the staying of my blood portend?   65
     Is it unwilling I should write this bill?
     Why streams it not that I may write afresh:
     "Faustus gives to thee his soul"? O there it stayed.
     Why shouldst thou not? Is not thy soul thine own?
     Then write again: "Faustus gives to thee his soul."   70

(Enter MEPHOSTOPHILIS *with the chafer of fire.)*

---

31 **pressed** enlisted into service   34 **And** if   44 **brave** splendid   46 **diametrally** directly   47 **quasi vestigiis nostris insistere** as if to step in our footsteps
II.i.3 **boots** avails

24 **signory of Emden** lordship of the rich German port at the mouth of the Ems   30 **Veni, veni, Mephostophile** come, come, Mephostophilis (Latin)   43 **Solamen . . . doloris** misery loves company (Latin)   44 **other** others   49 **him** i.e., to Lucifer   55 **proper** own   56 **Assures** conveys by contract   66 **bill** contract   s.d. **chafer** portable grate

MEPHOSTOPHILIS: See Faustus, here is fire. Set it on.
FAUSTUS: So, now the blood begins to clear again.
   Now will I make an end immediately.
MEPHOSTOPHILIS: *(Aside.)* What will not I do to obtain his
   soul!
75 FAUSTUS: *Consummatum est!* This bill is ended:
   And Faustus hath bequeathed his soul to Lucifer.
   —But what is this inscription on mine arm?
   Homo fuge! Whither should I fly?
   If unto God, He'll throw me down to hell.
80   My senses are deceived, here's nothing writ.
   O yes, I see it plain! Even here is writ.
   Homo fuge! Yet shall not Faustus fly!
MEPHOSTOPHILIS: *(Aside.)* I'll fetch him somewhat to delight
   his mind.

(Exit.)

(Enter DEVILS *giving crowns and rich apparel to* FAUSTUS. *They
dance and then depart.)*

(Enter MEPHOSTOPHILIS.*)*

FAUSTUS: What means this show? Speak, Mephostophilis.
85 MEPHOSTOPHILIS: Nothing Faustus, but to delight thy mind
   And let thee see what magic can perform.
FAUSTUS: But may I raise such spirits when I please?
MEPHOSTOPHILIS: Ay Faustus, and do greater things than
   these.
FAUSTUS: Then, Mephostophilis, receive this scroll,
90   A deed of gift of body and of soul:
   But yet conditionally that thou perform
   All covenants and articles between us both.
MEPHOSTOPHILIS: Faustus, I swear by hell and Lucifer
   To effect all promises between us both.
95 FAUSTUS: Then hear me read it, Mephostophilis:
   "On these conditions following:
   First, that Faustus may be a spirit in form and substance.
   Secondly, that Mephostophilis shall be his servant and be by
   him commanded.
100   Thirdly, that Mephostophilis shall do for him and bring him
   whatsoever.
   Fourthly, that he shall be in his chamber or house invisible.
   Lastly, that he shall appear to the said John Faustus at all
   times in what form or shape soever he please:
105   I, John Faustus of Wittenberg, Doctor, by these presents, do
   give both body and soul to Lucifer, prince of the east, and
   his minister Mephostophilis, and furthermore grant unto
   them that, four and twenty years being expired, and these
   articles above written being inviolate, full power to fetch or
110   carry the said John Faustus, body and soul, flesh, blood, or
   goods, into their habitation wheresoever.
                                  By me John Faustus."
MEPHOSTOPHILIS: Speak Faustus, do you deliver this as your
   deed?

FAUSTUS: Ay, take it, and the devil give thee good of it!
MEPHOSTOPHILIS: So now Faustus, ask me what thou wilt.   115
FAUSTUS: First will I question with thee about hell.
   Tell me, where is the place that men call hell?
MEPHOSTOPHILIS: Under the heavens.
FAUSTUS: Ay, so are all things else, but whereabouts?
MEPHOSTOPHILIS: Within the bowels of these elements   120
   Where we are tortured and remain forever.
   Hell hath no limits nor is circumscribed
   In one self place, but where we are is hell,
   And where hell is there must we ever be.
   And to be short, when all the world dissolves   125
   And every creature shall be purified
   All places shall be hell that is not heaven!
FAUSTUS: I think hell's a fable.
MEPHOSTOPHILIS: Ay, think so still—till experience change
   thy mind!
FAUSTUS: Why, dost thou think that Faustus shall be damned? 130
MEPHOSTOPHILIS: Ay, of necessity, for here's the scroll
   In which thou hast given thy soul to Lucifer.
FAUSTUS: Ay, and body too; but what of that?
   Think'st thou that Faustus is so fond to imagine
   That after this life there is any pain?   135
   No, these are trifles and mere old wives' tales.
MEPHOSTOPHILIS: But I am an instance to prove the contrary,
   For I tell thee I am damned and now in hell!
FAUSTUS: Nay, and this be hell, I'll willingly be damned—
   What, sleeping, eating, walking, and disputing?   140
   But leaving this, let me have a wife, the fairest maid in
     Germany, for I am wanton and lascivious and cannot
     live without a wife.
MEPHOSTOPHILIS: Well Faustus, thou shalt have a wife.

(He fetches in a woman DEVIL *[with fireworks].)*

FAUSTUS: What sight is this?   145
MEPHOSTOPHILIS: Now Faustus, wilt thou have a wife?
FAUSTUS: Here's a hot whore indeed! No, I'll no wife.
MEPHOSTOPHILIS: Marriage is but a ceremonial toy,

(Exit SHE-DEVIL.*)*

   And if thou lovest me, think no more of it.
   I'll cull thee out the fairest courtesans   150
   And bring them every morning to thy bed.
   She whom thine eye shall like thy heart shall have,
   Were she as chaste as was Penelope,
   As wise as Saba, or as beautiful
   As was bright Lucifer before his fall.   155
   Here, take this book and peruse it well.
   The iterating of these lines brings gold;
   The framing of this circle on the ground
   Brings thunder, whirlwinds, storm, and lightning;
   Pronounce this thrice devoutly to thyself,   160
   And men in harness shall appear to thee,
   Ready to execute what thou command'st.

---

71 **it** i.e., the receptacle containing the congealed blood   75 **Consummatum est** it is finished (Latin; a blasphemous repetition of Christ's words on the cross; see John 19:30)   78 **Homo fuge** fly, man (Latin)   97 **spirit** evil spirit, devil (but to see Faustus as transformed now into a devil deprived of freedom to repent is to deprive the remainder of the play of much of its meaning)   109 **inviolate** unviolated

---

134 **fond** foolish   148 **toy** trifle   150 **cull thee out** select for you   153 **Penelope** wife of Ulysses, famed for her fidelity   154 **Saba** the Queen of Sheba   157 **iterating** repetition   158 **framing** drawing   161 **harness** armor

FAUSTUS: Thanks Mephostophilis for this sweet book.
  This will I keep as chary as my life.   *(Exeunt.)*

SCENE II

Enter FAUSTUS *in his study and* MEPHOSTOPHILIS.

FAUSTUS: When I behold the heavens, then I repent
  And curse thee, wicked Mephostophilis,
  Because thou has deprived me of those joys.
MEPHOSTOPHILIS: 'Twas thine own seeking Faustus, thank
  thyself.
5 But think'st thou heaven is such a glorious thing?
  I tell thee, Faustus, it is not half so fair
  As thou or any man that breathe on earth.
FAUSTUS: How prov'st thou that?
MEPHOSTOPHILIS: 'Twas made for man; then he's more
  excellent.
10 FAUSTUS: If heaven was made for man, 'twas made for me!
  I will renounce this magic and repent.

(Enter the two ANGELS.)

GOOD ANGEL: Faustus, repent: yet God will pity thee!
BAD ANGEL: Thou art a spirit: God cannot pity thee!
FAUSTUS: Who buzzeth in mine ears I am a spirit?
15 Be I a devil, yet God may pity me—
  Yea, God will pity me if I repent.
BAD ANGEL: Ay, but Faustus never shall repent.

(Exit ANGELS.)

FAUSTUS: My heart is hardened, I cannot repent.
  Scarce can I name salvation, faith, or heaven,
20 Swords, poison, halters, and envenomed steel
  Are laid before me to dispatch myself.
  And long ere this I should have done the deed
  Had not sweet pleasure conquered deep despair.
  Have not I made blind Homer sing to me
25 Of Alexander's love and Oenon's death?
  And hath not he that built the walls of Thebes
  With ravishing sound of his melodious harp
  Made music with my Mephostophilis?
  Why should I die then or basely despair?
30 I am resolved, Faustus shall not repent!
  Come Mephostophilis, let us dispute again
  And reason of divine astrology.
  Speak, are there many spheres above the moon?
  Are all celestial bodies but one globe
35 As is the substance of this centric earth?
MEPHOSTOPHILIS: As are the elements, such are the heavens,

Even from the moon unto the empyreal orb
Mutually folded in each others' spheres,
And jointly move upon one axle-tree,
Whose terminè is termed the world's wide pole.   40
Nor are the names of Saturn, Mars, or Jupiter
Feigned but are erring stars.
FAUSTUS: But have they all one motion,
  Both *situ et tempore?*
MEPHOSTOPHILIS: All move from east to west in four and   45
  twenty hours upon the poles of the world but differ in their
  motions upon the poles of the zodiac.
FAUSTUS: These slender questions Wagner can decide.
  Hath Mephostophilis no greater skill?
  Who knows not the double motion of the planets?   50
  That the first is finished in a natural day.
  The second thus: Saturn in thirty years;
  Jupiter in twelve; Mars in four; the sun, Venus, and Mercury
  in a year; the moon in twenty-eight days. These are fresh-
  men's suppositions. But tell me, hath every sphere a domin-   55
  ion or *intelligentia?*
MEPHOSTOPHILIS: Ay.
FAUSTUS: How many heavens or spheres are there?
MEPHOSTOPHILIS: Nine: the seven planets, the firmament,
  and the empyreal heaven.   60
FAUSTUS: But is there not *coelum igneum et crystallinum?*
MEPHOSTOPHILIS: No Faustus, they be but fables.
FAUSTUS: Resolve me then in this one question. Why are not
  conjunctions, oppositions, aspects, eclipses all at one time,
  but in some years we have more, in some less?   65
MEPHOSTOPHILIS: *Per inaqualem motum respectu totius.*
FAUSTUS: Well, I am answered. Now tell me, who made the
  world?
MEPHOSTOPHILIS: I will not.
FAUSTUS: Sweet Mephostophilis, tell me.   70
MEPHOSTOPHILIS: Move me not, Faustus!
FAUSTUS: Villain, have not I bound thee to tell me anything?
MEPHOSTOPHILIS: Ay, that is not against our kingdom. This is.
  Thou art damned. Think thou of hell!
FAUSTUS: Think, Faustus, upon God, that made the world.   75
MEPHOSTOPHILIS: Remember this!

(Exit.)

FAUSTUS: Ay, go accursèd spirit to ugly hell!
  'Tis thou hast damned distressèd Faustus' soul—
  Is't not too late?

(Enter the two ANGELS.)

BAD ANGEL: Too late.   80
GOOD ANGEL: Never too late, if Faustus will repent.
BAD ANGEL: If thou repent, devils will tear thee in pieces.
GOOD ANGEL: Repent, and they shall never raze thy skin.

(Exeunt ANGELS.)

---

164 s.d. **Exeunt** (a scene following this stage direction has probably
been lost. Earlier Wagner hired the Clown; later the Clown is an
ostler possessed of one of Faustus' conjuring books. Possibly, then, the
lost scene was a comic one, showing the Clown stealing a book and
departing)
II.ii.12 **yet** still, even now   25 **Alexander . . . Oenone** Paris, also
called Alexander, was Oenone's lover, but he later deserted her for
Helen of Troy, causing the Trojan War, the subject of Homer's *Iliad*
26 **he** Amphion, whose music charmed stones to form the walls of
Thebes   35 **centric** central   36 **such** i.e., separate but combined; the
idea is that the heavenly bodies are separate but their spheres are con-
centric ("folded"), and all—from the nearest (the moon) to the farthest
("the empyreal orb" or empyrean)—move on one axletree

40 **terminè** end, extremity   42 **erring stars** planets   44 **situ et tempore** in place and in time   51 **natural day** twenty-four hours   55 **suppositions** premises; **dominion or intelligentia** governing angel or
intelligence (believed to impart motion to the sphere)   61 **coelum
igneum et crystallinum** a heaven of fire and a crystaline sphere (Latin)
64 **at one time** i.e., at regular intervals   66 **Per . . . totius** because of
unequal speed within the system (Latin)   71 **Move** anger   83 **raze**
scratch

FAUSTUS: O Christ, my savior, my savior!
85   Help to save distressèd Faustus' soul.

(*Enter* LUCIFER, BELZEBUB, *and* MEPHOSTOPHILIS.)

LUCIFER: Christ cannot save thy soul, for He is just.
    There's none but I have interest in the same.
FAUSTUS: O, what art thou that look'st so terribly?
LUCIFER: I am Lucifer
90   And this is my companion prince in hell.
FAUSTUS: O Faustus, they are come to fetch thy soul!
BELZEBUB: We are come to tell thee thou dost injure us.
LUCIFER: Thou call'st on Christ contrary to thy promise.
BELZEBUB: Thou should'st not think on God.
LUCIFER: Think on the Devil.
95 BELZEBUB: And his dam too.
FAUSTUS: Nor will Faustus henceforth. Pardon him for this,
    And Faustus vows never to look to heaven!
    Never to name God or to pray to Him,
    To burn His Scriptures, slay His ministers,
100   And make my spirits pull His churches down.
LUCIFER: So shalt thou show thyself an obedient servant,
    And we will highly gratify thee for it.
BELZEBUB: Faustus, we are come from hell in person to show
    thee some pastime. Sit down and thou shalt behold the
105   Seven Deadly Sins appear to thee in their own proper shapes
    and likeness.
FAUSTUS: That sight will be as pleasant to me as Paradise was
    to Adam the first day of his creation.
LUCIFER: Talk not of Paradise or creation but mark the show.
110   Go Mephostophilis, fetch them in.

(*Enter the* SEVEN DEADLY SINS [*led by a* PIPER].)

BELZEBUB: Now Faustus, question them of their names and
    dispositions.
FAUSTUS: That shall I soon. What art thou, the first?
PRIDE: I am Pride. I disdain to have any parents. I am like to
115   Ovid's flea, I can creep into every corner of a wench: some-
    times, like a periwig I sit upon her brow; next, like a neck-
    lace I hang about her neck; then, like a fan of feathers I kiss
    her; and then, turning myself to a wrought smock, do what I
    list—But fie, what a smell is here! I'll not speak a word more
120   for a king's ransom unless the ground be perfumed and cov-
    ered with cloth of arras.
FAUSTUS: Thou art a proud knave indeed. What art thou, the
    second?
COVETOUSNESS: I am Covetousness, begotten of an old churl
125   in a leather bag; and might I now obtain my wish, this house,
    you and all, should turn to gold that I might lock you safe
    into my chest. O my sweet gold!
FAUSTUS: And what art thou, the third?
ENVY: I am Envy, begotten of a chimney-sweeper and an
130   oysterwife. I cannot read and therefore wish all books
    burned. I am lean with seeing others eat. O, that there would

come a famine over all the world that all might die and I live
alone! Then thou shouldst see how fat I'd be. But must thou
sit and I stand? Come down, with a vengeance!
FAUSTUS: Out, envious wretch! But what art thou, the fourth?   135
WRATH: I am Wrath. I had neither father nor mother. I leapt
    out of a lion's mouth when I was scarce an hour old and ever
    since have run up and down the world with these case of
    rapiers, wounding myself when I could get none to fight
    withal. I was born in hell! And look to it, for some of you   140
    shall be my father.
FAUSTUS: And what art thou, the fifth?
GLUTTONY: I am Gluttony. My parents are all dead, and the
    devil a penny they have left me, but a small pension: and
    that buys me thirty meals a day and ten bevers, a small trifle   145
    to suffice nature. I come of a royal pedigree. My father was a
    gammon of bacon, and my mother was a hogshead of claret
    wine. My godfathers were these: Peter Pickled-herring and
    Martin Martlemas-beef. But my godmother, O, she was an
    ancient gentlewoman: her name was Margery March-beer.   150
    Now Faustus, thou hast heard all my progeny, wilt thou bid
    me to supper?
FAUSTUS: Not I.
GLUTTONY: Then the devil choke thee!
FAUSTUS: Choke thyself, glutton! What art thou, the sixth?   155
SLOTH: Heigh-ho! I am Sloth. I was begotten on a sunny bank.
    Heigh-ho, I'll not speak a word more for a king's ransom.
FAUSTUS: And what are you, Mistress Minx, the seventh and
    last?
LECHERY: Who, I, I sir? I am one that loves an inch of raw   160
    mutton better than an ell of fried stockfish, and the first let-
    ter of my name begins with Lechery.
LUCIFER: Away to hell, away! On, piper!

(*Exeunt the* SEVEN SINS.)

FAUSTUS: O, how this sight doth delight my soul!
LUCIFER: But Faustus, in hell is all manner of delight.   165
FAUSTUS: O, might I see hell and return again safe, how happy
    were I then!
LUCIFER: Faustus, thou shalt. At midnight I will send for
    thee.
    Meanwhile peruse this book and view it thoroughly,
    And thou shalt turn thyself into what shape thou wilt.   170
FAUSTUS: Thanks mighty Lucifer.
    This will I keep as chary as my life.
LUCIFER: Now Faustus, farewell.
FAUSTUS: Farewell great Lucifer. Come Mephostophilis.

(*Exeunt omnes several ways.*)

---

87 **interest in** legal claim on 95 **dam** mother 105 **Seven Deadly
Sins** (so called because they cause spiritual death; they are Pride, Covetousness, Envy, Wrath, Gluttony, Sloth, Lechery) 115 **Ovid's flea**
flea in *Carmen de pulce,* a lewd poem mistakenly attributed to Ovid
118 **wrought smock** decorated petticoat 121 **cloth of arras** Flemish
cloth used for tapestries 125 **leather bag** moneybag (?) 129–130
chimney-sweeper . . . oysterwife i.e., dirty and smelly

138 **these case** this pair 145 **bevers** snacks (literally drinks) 147
gammon haunch 149 **Martlemas-beef** cattle slaughtered at Martin-
mas (11 November) and salted for winter consumption 150 **March-
beer** strong beer brewed in March 151 **progeny** ancestry 156
Heigh-ho (a yawn or tired greeting) 160–161 **inch of raw mutton**
i.e., penis ("mutton" in a bawdy sense commonly alludes to a prostitute, but since here the speaker is a woman, the allusion must be to a
male) 161 **an ell of . . . stockfish** forty-five inches of dried cod 172
chary carefully s.d. **several** various

SCENE III

Enter [ROBIN] *the clown.*

ROBIN: What, Dick, look to the horses there till I come again!
I have gotten one of Doctor Faustus' conjuring books, and
now we'll have such knavery as't passes.

(Enter DICK.*)*

DICK: What, Robin, you must come away and walk the horses.

5 ROBIN: I walk the horses? I scorn't, faith. I have other matters
in hand. Let the horses walk themselves an they will. *(Reading.)* A *per se*—a; t, h, e—the; o *per se*—o; deny orgon—gorgon. Keep further from me, O thou illiterate and unlearned
hostler!

10 DICK: 'Snails, what hast thou got there, a book? Why, thou
canst not tell ne'er a word on't.

ROBIN: That thou shalt see presently. Keep out of the circle, I
say, lest I send you into the hostry with a vengeance.

DICK: That's like, 'faith! You had best leave your foolery, for an
15 my master come, he'll conjure you, 'faith.

ROBIN: My master conjure me? I'll tell thee what. An my master come here, I'll clap as fair a pair of horns on's head as e'er
thou sawest in thy life.

DICK: Thou need'st not do that, for my mistress hath done it.

20 ROBIN: Ay, there be of us here that have waded as deep into
matters as other men—if they were disposed to talk.

DICK: A plague take you! I thought you did not sneak up and
down after her for nothing. But I prithee tell me in good sadness Robin, is that a conjuring book?

25 ROBIN: Do but speak what thou't have me to do, and I'll do't. If
thou't dance naked, put off thy clothes, and I'll conjure thee
about presently. Or if thou't go but to the tavern with me, I'll
give thee white wine, red wine, claret wine, sack, muscadine,
malmsey, and whippincrust—hold-belly-hold. And we'll not
30 pay one penny for it.

DICK: O brave! Prithee let's to it presently, for I am as dry as a
dog.

ROBIN: Come then, let's away.

(Exeunt.)

— ACT THREE —

Enter the CHORUS.

Learnèd Faustus,
To find the secrets of astronomy
Graven in the book of Jove's high firmament,
Did mount him up to scale Olympus' top:
5 Where, sitting in a chariot burning bright
Drawn by the strength of yokèd dragons' necks,
He views the clouds, the planets, and the stars,
The tropics, zones, and quarters of the sky,

From the bright circle of the hornèd moon
Even to the height of *primum mobile*:   10
And whirling round with this circumference
Within the concave compass of the pole,
From east to west his dragons swiftly glide
And in eight days did bring him home again.
Not long he stayed within his quiet house   15
To rest his bones after his weary toil
But new exploits do hale him out again.
And mounted then upon a dragon's back,
That with his wings did part the subtle air,
He now is gone to prove cosmography,   20
That measures coasts and kingdoms of the earth,
And as I guess will first arrive at Rome
To see the Pope and manner of his court
And take some part of holy Peter's feast,
The which this day is highly solemnized.   25

(Exit.)

SCENE I

Enter FAUSTUS *and* MEPHOSTOPHILIS.

FAUSTUS: Having now, my good Mephostophilis,
Passed with delight the stately town of Trier,
Environed round with airy mountain tops,
With walls of flint, and deep-entrenchèd lakes,
Not to be won by any conquering prince: 5
From Paris next, coasting the realm of France,
We saw the river Main fall into Rhine,
Whose banks are set with groves of fruitful vines:
Then up to Naples, rich Campania,
Whose buildings fair and gorgeous to the eye,   10
The streets straight forth and paved with finest brick,
Quarters the town in four equivalents.
There saw we learnèd Maro's golden tomb,
The way he cut an English mile in length
Through a rock of stone in one night's space.   15
From thence to Venice, Padua, and the rest,
In one of which a sumptuous temple stands
That threats the stars with her aspiring top,
Whose frame is paved with sundry colored stones
And roofed aloft with curious work in gold.   20
Thus hitherto hath Faustus spent his time.
But tell me now, what resting-palace is this?
Hast thou, as erst I did command,
Conducted me within the walls of Rome?

MEPHOSTOPHILIS: I have, my Faustus, and for proof thereof   25
This is the goodly palace of the Pope,
And cause we are no common guests
I choose his privy chamber for our use.

FAUSTUS: I hope his Holiness will bid us welcome.

MEPHOSTOPHILIS: All's one, for we'll be bold with his venison. 30
But now my Faustus, that thou may'st perceive

II.iii.6 **an** if   7 **per se** by itself (Latin; the idea is, "A by itself spells A");
deny orgon—gorgon (Robin is trying to read the name "Demogorgon")   10 **'Snails** by God's nails   13 **hostry** hostelry inn   17 **horns**
(as the next speech indicates, horns were said to adorn the head of a
man whose wife was unfaithful)   23 **in good sadness** seriously   28
sack sherry   29 **whippincrust** illiterate pronunciation of "hippocras,"
a spiced wine

III **Chorus** 8 **zones** segments of the sky

---

9 **circle** orbit   10 **primun mobile** the outermost sphere, the empyrean
20 **prove cosmography** test maps, i.e., explore the universe
III.i.2 **Trier** German city on the Moselle, also known as Trèves   4
deep-entrenchèd lakes moats   13 **Maro** Vergil (Publius Vergilius
Maro, 70–19 BC)   15 **Through** (pronounced "thorough")

What Rome contains for to delight thine eyes,
Know that this city stands upon seven hills
That underprop the groundwork of the same:
35 Just through the midst runs flowing Tiber's stream
With winding banks that cut it in two parts,
Over the which four stately bridges lean
That make safe passage to each part of Rome.
Upon the bridge called Ponte Angelo
40 Erected is a castle passing strong
Where thou shalt see such store of ordinance
As that the double cannons forged of brass
Do match the number of the days contained
Within the compass of one complete year,
45 Beside the gates and high pryamides
That Julius Caesar brought from Africa.
FAUSTUS: Now, by the kingdoms of infernal rule,
Of Styx, of Acheron, and the fiery lake
Of ever-burning Phlegethon, I swear
50 That I do long to see the monuments
And situation of bright-splendent Rome.
Come therefore, let's away.
MEPHOSTOPHILIS: Nay stay my Faustus. I know you'd see the
Pope
And take some part of holy Peter's feast,
55 The which this day with high solemnity,
This day, is held through Rome and Italy
In honor of the Pope's triumphant victory.
FAUSTUS: Sweet Mephostophilis, thou pleasest me.
Whilst I am here on earth let me be cloyed
60 With all things that delight the heart of man.
My four and twenty years of liberty
I'll spend in pleasure and in dalliance,
That Faustus' name, whilst this bright frame doth stand,
May be admirèd through the furthest land.
65 MEPHOSTOPHILIS: Tis well said, Faustus, come then, stand
by me
And thou shalt see them come immediately.
FAUSTUS: Nay stay, my gentle Mephostophilis,
And grant me my request, and then I go.
Thou know'st, within the compass of eight days
70 We viewed the face of heaven, of earth, and hell.
So high our dragons soared into the air
That looking down the earth appeared to me
No bigger than my hand in quantity—
There did we view the kingdoms of the world,
75 And what might please mine eye I there beheld.
Then in this show let me an actor be
That this proud Pope may Faustus' cunning see!
MEPHOSTOPHILIS: Let it be so, my Faustus, but first stay
And view their triumphs as they pass this way.
80 And then devise what best contents thy mind
By cunning in thine art to cross the Pope
Or dash the pride of this solemnity—
To make his monks and abbots stand like apes
And point like antics at his triple crown,
85 To beat the beads about the friars' pates,

Or clap huge horns upon the cardinals' heads,
Or any villainy thou canst devise—
And I'll perform it, Faustus. Hark, they come!
This day shall make thee be admired in Rome!

(*Enter the* CARDINALS *and* BISHOPS, *some bearing crosiers, some
the pillars;* MONKS *and* FRIARS *singing their procession; then the*
POPE *and* RAYMOND *King of Hungary, with* BRUNO *led in
chains.*)

POPE: Cast down our footstool.   90
RAYMOND: Saxon Bruno, stoop,
Whilst on thy back his Holiness ascends
Saint Peter's chair and state pontifical.
BRUNO: Proud Lucifer, that state belongs to me—
But thus I fall to Peter, not to thee.
POPE: To me and Peter shalt thou grov'lling lie   95
And crouch before the papal dignity!
Sound triumpets then, for thus Saint Peter's heir
From Bruno's back ascends Saint Peter's chair!

(*A flourish while he ascends.*)

Thus as the gods creep on with feet of wool
Long ere with iron hands they punish men,   100
So shall our sleeping vengeance now arise
And smite with death thy hated enterprise.
Lord Cardinals of France and Padua,
Go forthwith to our holy consistory
And read amongst the statutes decretal   105
What by the holy council held at Trent
The sacred synod hath decreed for him
That doth assume the papal government
Without election and a true consent.
Away, and bring us word with speed!   110
1 CARDINAL: We go my lord.

(*Exeunt [two]* CARDINALS.)

POPE: Lord Raymond—

(*Talks to him apart.*)

FAUSTUS: Go haste thee, gentle Mephostophilis,
Follow the cardinals to the consistory
And as they turn their superstitious books   115
Strike them with sloth and drowsy idleness
And make them sleep so sound that in their shapes
Thyself and I may parley with this Pope,
This proud confronter of the Emperor!
—And in despite of all his holiness   120
Restore this Bruno to his liberty
And bear him to the states of Germany!
MEPHOSTOPHILIS: Faustus, I go.
FAUSTUS: Dispatch it soon.
The Pope shall curse that Faustus came to Rome.   125

(*Exit* FAUSTUS *and* MEPHOSTOPHILIS.)

---

37 **lean** bend   45 **pyramides** obelisk (pronounced py-ràm-i-des)
48–49 **Styx, Acheron, Phlegethon** rivers of the underworld   79 **triumphs** spectacular displays   84 **antics** grotesque figures, buffoons

89 **admired** wondered at   s.d. **Raymond King of Hungary . . . Bruno**
(unhistorical figures; Bruno is the emperor's nominee for the papal
throne)   92 **state** throne   s.d. **flourish** trumpet fanfare   104 **consistory** i.e., meeting-place of the papal consistory or senate   105 **statutes
decretal** i.e., ecclesiastical laws   106 **council held at Trent** (intermittently from 1545 to 1563)   107 **synod** council

BRUNO: Pope Adrian, let me have some right of law:
    I was elected by the Emperor.
POPE: We will depose the Emperor for that deed
    And curse the people that submit to him.
130   Both he and thou shalt stand excommunicate
    And interdict from church's privilege
    And all society of holy men.
    He grows too proud in his authority,
    Lifting his lofty head above the clouds,
135   And like a steeple overpeers the church.
    But we'll pull down his haughty insolence.
    And as Pope Alexander, our progenitor,
    Trod on the neck of German Frederick,
    Adding this golden sentence to our praise:
140   "That Peter's heirs should tread on emperors
    And walk upon the dreadful adder's back,
    Treading the lion and the dragon down,
    And fearless spurn the killing basilisk"—
    So will we quell that haughty schismatic
145   And by authority apostolical
    Depose him from his regal government.
BRUNO: Pope Julius swore to princely Sigismond,
    For him and the succeeding Popes of Rome,
    To hold the emperors their lawful lords.
150 POPE: Pope Julius did abuse the church's rites
    And therefore none of his decrees can stand.
    Is not all power on earth bestowed on us?
    And therefore though we would, we cannot err.
    Behold this silver belt whereto is fixed
155   Seven golden keys fast sealed with seven seals
    In token of our sevenfold power from heaven
    To bind or loose, lock fast, condemn, or judge,
    Resign or seal, or whatso pleaseth us.
    Then he and thou and all the world shall stoop—
160   Or be assurèd of our dreadful curse
    To light as heavy as the pains of hell.

(Enter FAUSTUS *and* MEPHOSTOPHILIS *like the* CARDINALS.)

MEPHOSTOPHILIS: *(Aside.)* Now tell me Faustus, are we not
    fitted well?
FAUSTUS: *(Aside.)* Yes Mephostophilis, and two such cardinals
    Ne'er served a holy Pope as we shall do.
165   But whilst they sleep within the consistory
    Let us salute his reverend Fatherhood.
RAYMOND: Behold my lord, the cardinals are returned.
POPE: Welcome grave fathers, answer presently,
    What have our holy council there decreed
170   Concerning Bruno and the Emperor
    In quittance of their late conspiracy
    Against our state and papal dignity?
FAUSTUS: Most sacred patron of the church of Rome,
    By full consent of all the synod
175   Of priests and prelates it is thus decreed:
    That Bruno and the German Emperor

Be held as lollards and bold schismatics
And proud disturbers of the church's peace.
And if that Bruno by his own assent,
Without enforcement of the German peers,   180
Did seek to wear the triple diadem
And by your death to climb Saint Peter's chair,
The statutes decretal have thus decreed:
He shall be straight condemned of heresy
And on a pile of fagots burnt to death.   185
POPE: It is enough. Here, take him to your charge
    And bear him straight to Ponte Angelo
    And in the strongest tower enclose him fast.
    Tomorrow, sitting in our consistory
    With all our college of grave cardinals   190
    We will determine of his life or death.
    Here, take his triple crown along with you
    And leave it in the church's treasury.
    Make haste again, my good lord cardinals,
    And take our blessing apostolical.   195
MEPHOSTOPHILIS: *(Aside.)* So, so! Was never devil thus blessed
    before.
FAUSTUS: *(Aside.)* Away sweet Mephostophilis, be gone!
    The cardinals will be plagued for this anon.

(Exeunt FAUSTUS *and* MEPHOSTOPHILIS *[with* BRUNO*].)*

POPE: Go presently and bring a banquet forth,
    That we may solemnize Saint Peter's feast   200
    And with Lord Raymond, King of Hungary,
    Drink to our late and happy victory.

(Exeunt.)

SCENE II

A sennet *while the banquet is brought in, and then enter*
FAUSTUS *and* MEPHOSTOPHILIS *in their own shapes.*

MEPHOSTOPHILIS: Now Faustus, come prepare thyself for
    mirth.
    The sleepy cardinals are hard at hand
    To censure Bruno, that is posted hence,
    And on a proud-paced steed as swift as thought
    Flies o'er the Alps to fruitful Germany,   5
    There to salute the woeful Emperor.
FAUSTUS: The Pope will curse them for their sloth today
    That slept both Bruno and his crown away.
    But now, that Faustus may delight his mind
    And by their folly make some merriment,   10
    Sweet Mephostophilis, so charm me here
    That I may walk invisible to all
    And do whate'er I please unseen of any.
MEPHOSTOPHILIS: Faustus, thou shalt. Then kneel down
    presently,
    Whilst on thy head I lay my hand   15
    And charm thee with this magic wand.
    First wear this girdle, then appear
    Invisible to all are here:
    The planets seven, the gloomy air,

---

137 **Pope Alexander** Pope Alexander III (d. 1181) compelled the Emperor Frederick Barbarossa to kneel before him; **progenitor** predecessor   143 **basilisk** fabulous monster said to kill with a glance   158 **Resign** unseal   168 **presently** immediately   171 **quittance of** requital for

177 **lollards** heretics   194 **again** i.e., to return

III.ii. s.d. **sennet** set of notes played on a trumpet signaling an approach or a departure

20 Hell, and the Furies' forkèd hair,
    Pluto's blue fire, and Hecat's tree
    With magic spells so compass thee
    That no eye may thy body see.
    So Faustus, now for all their holiness,
25 Do what thou wilt, thou shalt not be discerned.
FAUSTUS: Thanks Mephostophilis. Now friars, take heed
    Lest Faustus make your shaven crowns to bleed.
MEPHOSTOPHILIS: Faustus, no more. See where the cardinals
    come.

(Enter POPE *[and* FRIARS*] and all the* LORDS *[with* KING RAY-
MOND *and the* ARCHBISHOP OF RHEIMS*]. Enter the [two]* CAR-
DINALS *with a book.)*

POPE: Welcome lord cardinals. Come, sit down.
30 Lord Raymond, take your seat. Friars, attend,
    And see that all things be in readiness
    As best beseems this solemn festival.
1 CARDINAL: First may it please your sacred Holiness
    To view the sentence of the reverend synod
35 Concerning Bruno and the Emperor.
POPE: What needs this question? Did I not tell you
    Tomorrow we would sit i' th' consistory
    And there determine of his punishment?
    You brought us word, even now, it was decreed
40 That Bruno and the cursèd Emperor
    Were by the holy council both condemned
    For loathèd lollards and base schismatics.
    Then wherefore would you have me view that book?
1 CARDINAL: Your Grace mistakes. You gave us no such
    charge.
45 RAYMOND: Deny it not; we all are witnesses
    That Bruno here was late delivered you
    With his rich triple crown to be reserved
    And put into the church's treasury.
BOTH CARDINALS: By holy Paul we saw them not.
50 POPE: By Peter you shall die
    Unless you bring them forth immediately.
    Hale them to prison, lade their limbs with gyves.
    False prelates, for this hateful treachery
    Cursèd be your souls to hellish misery.

(Exeunt ATTENDANTS *with two* CARDINALS*.)*

55 FAUSTUS: So, they are safe. Now Faustus, to the feast.
    The Pope had never such a frolic guest.
POPE: Lord Archbishop of Rheims, sit down with us.
ARCHBISHOP: I thank your Holiness.
FAUSTUS: Fall to, the devil choke you an you spare!
60 POPE: Who's that spoke? Friars, look about.
    Lord Raymond, pray fall to. I am beholding
    To the Bishop of Milan for this so rare a present.
FAUSTUS: *(Aside.)* I thank you, sir!

(Snatches the dish.)

POPE: How now! Who snatched the meat from me?
    Villains, why speak you not?   65
    My good Lord Archbishop, here's a most dainty dish
    Was sent me from a cardinal in France.
FAUSTUS: *(Aside.)* I'll have that too!

(Snatches the dish.)

POPE: What lollards do attend our Holiness
    That we receive such great indignity!   70
    Fetch me some wine.
FAUSTUS: *(Aside.)* Ay, pray do, for Faustus is adry.
POPE: Lord Raymond, I drink unto your Grace.
FAUSTUS: *(Aside.)* I pledge your Grace.

(Snatches the goblet.)

POPE: My wine gone too? Ye lubbers, look about   75
    And find the man that doth this villainy,
    Or by our sanctitude you all shall die.
    I pray, my lords, have patience at this troublesome
    banquet.
ARCHBISHOP: Please it your Holiness, I think it be some ghost
    crept out of purgatory, and now is come unto your Holiness 80
    for his pardon.
POPE: It may be so:
    Go then, command our priests to sing a dirge
    To lay the fury of this same troublesome ghost.

(Exit ATTENDANT*.)*

(The POPE *crosses himself before eating.)*

FAUSTUS: How now! Must every bit be spicèd with a cross? 85
    Nay then, take that!

(Strikes the POPE*.)*

POPE: O, I am slain! Help me my lords!
    O come and help to bear my body hence.
    Damned be this soul forever for this deed.

(Exeunt the POPE *and his train.)*

MEPHOSTOPHILIS: Now Faustus, what will you do now?   90
    For I can tell you, you'll be cursed with bell, book, and
    candle.
FAUSTUS: Bell, book, and candle. Candle, book, and bell.
    Forward and backward, to curse Faustus to hell!

(Enter the FRIARS, *with bell, book, and candle for the dirge.)*

1 FRIAR: Come brethren, let's about our business with good 95
    devotion.
    Cursèd be he that stole his Holiness' meat from the table.
      Maledicat Dominus!
    Cursèd be he that struck his Holiness a blow on the face.
      Maledicat Dominus!

*(*FAUSTUS *strikes a* FRIAR*.)*

    Cursèd be he that took Friar Sandelo a blow on the pate. 100
      Maledicat Dominus!
    Cursèd be he that disturbeth our holy dirge.
      Maledicat Dominus!

---

20 **Furies' forkèd hair** (the hair of the Furies consisted of snakes, whose forked tongues may be implied here) 21 **Hecat** Hecate, goddess of magic (possibly her "tree" is the gallows-tree, but possibly "tree" is a slip for "three," Hecate being the triple goddess of heaven, earth, and hell) 52 **gyves** fetters 59 **Fall to** set to work (here, as commonly, "start eating")

91–92 **bell, book, and candle** implements used in excommunicating (the bell was tolled, the book closed, the candle extinguished) 98 **Maledicat Dominus** may the Lord curse him (Latin)

Cursèd be he that took away his Holiness' wine.
105   *Maledicat Dominus!*

([FAUSTUS and MEPHOSTOPHILIS] beat the FRIARS, fling fire-works among them and exeunt.)

SCENE III

Enter [ROBIN] the clown and DICK with a cup.

DICK: Sirrah Robin, we were best look that your devil can answer the stealing of this same cup, for the vintner's boy follows us at the hard heels.

ROBIN: 'Tis no matter, let him come! An he follow us I'll so
5   conjure him as he was never conjured in his life, I warrant him. Let me see the cup.

(Enter VINTNER.)

DICK: Here 'tis. Yonder he comes. Now Robin, now or never show thy cunning.

VINTNER: O, are you here? I am glad I have found you. You are
10   a couple of fine companions! Pray, where's the cup you stole from the tavern?

ROBIN: How, how! We steal a cup? Take heed what you say. We look not like cup-stealers, I can tell you.

VINTNER: Never deny't, for I know you have it, and I'll search
15   you.

ROBIN: Search me? Ay, and spare not! *(Aside.)* Hold the cup, Dick.—Come, come. Search me, search me.

(VINTNER searches him.)

VINTNER: Come on sirrah, let me search you now.

DICK: Ay ay, do do. *(Aside.)* Hold the cup, Robin.—I fear not
20   your searching. We scorn to steal your cups, I can tell you.

(VINTNER searches him.)

VINTNER: Never outface me for the matter, for sure the cup is between you two.

ROBIN: Nay, there you lie! 'Tis beyond us both.

VINTNER: A plague take you. I thought 'twas your knavery to
25   take it away. Come, give it me again.

ROBIN: Ay, much! When, can you tell? *(Aside.)* Dick, make me a circle and stand close at my back and stir not for thy life. Vintner, you shall have your cup anon. *(Aside.)* Say nothing, Dick! O *per se,* o; Demogorgon, Belcher, and
30   Mephostophilis!

(Enter MEPHOSTOPHILIS. Exit VINTNER.)

MEPHOSTOPHILIS: You princely legions of infernal rule, How am I vexèd by these villains' charms! From Constantinople have they brought me now Only for pleasure of these damnèd slaves.

35   ROBIN: By lady sir, you have had a shrewd journey of it. Will it please you to take a shoulder of mutton to supper and a tester in your purse and go back again?

DICK: Ay, I pray you heartily, sir. For we called you but in jest, I promise you.

MEPHOSTOPHILIS: To purge the rashness of this cursèd deed,   40 First be thou turnèd to this ugly shape, For apish deeds transformèd to an ape.

ROBIN: O brave! An ape! I pray sir, let me have the carrying of him about to show some tricks.

MEPHOSTOPHILIS: And so thou shalt. Be thou transformed to   45 a dog and carry him upon thy back. Away, be gone!

ROBIN: A dog! That's excellent. Let the maids look well to their porridge-pots, for I'll into the kitchen presently. Come Dick, come.

(Exeunt the two CLOWNS.)

MEPHOSTOPHILIS: Now with the flames of ever-burning fire   50 I'll wing myself and forthwith fly amain Unto my Faustus, to the Great Turk's court.

(Exit.)

— ACT FOUR —

Enter CHORUS.

When Faustus had with pleasure ta'en the view Of rarest things and royal courts of kings, He stayed his course and so returnèd home, Where such as bare his absence but with grief, I mean his friends and nearest companions,   5 Did gratulate his safety with kind words. And in their conference of what befell Touching his journey through the world and air They put forth questions of astrology Which Faustus answered with such learnèd skill   10 As they admired and wondered at his wit Now is his fame spread forth in every land. Amongst the rest the Emperor is one, Carolus the Fifth, at whose palace now Faustus is feasted 'mongst his noblemen.   15 What there he did in trial of his art I leave untold, your eyes shall see performed.

(Exit.)

SCENE I

Enter MARTINO and FREDERICK at several doors.

MARTINO: What ho, officers, gentlemen! Hie to the presence to attend the Emperor. Good Frederick, see the rooms be voided straight, His Majesty is coming to the hall. Go back and see the state in readiness.   5

FREDERICK: But where is Bruno, our elected Pope, That on a fury's back came post from Rome? Will not his Grace consort the Emperor?

MARTINO: O yes, and with him comes the German conjurer, The learnèd Faustus, fame of Wittenberg,   10

III.iii.3 **at the hard heels** hard at heel, closely   10 **companions** fellows (contemptuous)   23 **beyond us both** (apparently Robin has managed to place the cup at some distance from where he now stands) 26 **When, can you tell** (a scornful reply)   35 **shrewd** bad   36 **tester** sixpence

42 **apish** (1) foolish (2) imitative

IV Chorus 6 **gratulate** express joy in   7 **conference** discussion   14 **Carolus the Fifth** Charles V (1500–1558), Holy Roman Emperor

IV.i. s.d. **several** separate   2 **presence** presence-chamber   3 **voided straight** emptied immediately   5 **state** chair of state, throne   8 **consort** attend

The wonder of the world for magic art:
And he intends to show great Carolus
The race of all his stout progenitors
And bring in presence of his Majesty
15 The royal shapes and warlike semblances
Of Alexander and his beauteous paramour.

FREDERICK: Where is Benvolio?

MARTINO: Fast asleep, I warrant you.
He took his rouse with stoups of Rhenish wine
So kindly yesternight to Bruno's health
20 That all this day the sluggard keeps his bed.

FREDERICK: See, see, his window's ope. We'll call to him.

MARTINO: What ho, Benvolio!

(Enter BENVOLIO *above at a window, in his nightcap, buttoning.)*

BENVOLIO: What a devil ail you two?

MARTINO: Speak softly sir, lest the devil hear you,
25 For Faustus at the court is late arrived
At his heels a thousand furies wait
To accomplish whatsoever the doctor please.

BENVOLIO: What of this?

MARTINO: Come, leave thy chamber first, and thou shalt see
30 This conjurer perform such rare exploits
Before the Pope and royal Emperor
As never yet was seen in Germany.

BENVOLIO: Has not the Pope enough of conjuring yet?
He was upon the devil's back late enough!
35 And if he be so far in love with him
I would he would post with him to Rome again.

FREDERICK: Speak, wilt thou come and see this sport?

BENVOLIO: Not I.

MARTINO: Wilt thou stand in thy window and see it then?

BENVOLIO: Ay, and I fall not asleep i' th' meantime.

40 MARTINO: The Emperor is at hand, who comes to see
What wonders by black spells may compassed be.

BENVOLIO: Well, go you attend the Emperor. I am content for
this once to thrust my head out at a window, for they say if a
man be drunk overnight the devil cannot hurt him in the
45 morning. If that be true, I have a charm in my head shall
control him as well as the conjurer, I warrant you.

*(Exit [*MARTINO *with* FREDERICK. BENVOLIO *remains at
window].)*

SCENE II

A *sennet.* CHARLES *the German Emperor,* BRUNO, [DUKE *of*]
SAXONY, FAUSTUS, MEPHOSTOPHILIS, FREDERICK, MARTINO,
and ATTENDANTS.

EMPEROR: Wonder of men, renowned magician,
Thrice-learnèd Faustus, welcome to our court,

This deed of thine in setting Bruno free
From his and our professèd enemy,
Shall add more excellence unto thine art   5
Than if by powerful necromantic spells
Thou could'st command the world's obedience.
For ever be beloved of Carolus!
And if this Bruno thou hast late redeemed
In peace possess the triple diadem   10
And sit in Peter's chair despite of chance,
Thou shalt be famous through all Italy
And honored of the German Emperor.

FAUSTUS: These gracious words, most royal Carolus
Shall make poor Faustus to his utmost power   15
Both love and serve the German Emperor
And lay his life at holy Bruno's feet.
For proof whereof, if so your Grace be pleased,
The doctor stands prepared by power of art
To cast his magic charms that shall pierce through   20
The ebon gates of ever-burning hell,
And hale the stubborn furies from their caves
To compass whatsoe'er your Grace commands.

BENVOLIO: Blood! He speaks terribly. But for all that I do not
greatly believe him. He looks as like a conjurer as the Pope   25
to a costermonger.

EMPEROR: Then Faustus, as thou late didst promise us,
We would behold that famous conqueror
Great Alexander and his paramour
In their true shapes and state majestical,   30
That we may wonder at their excellence.

FAUSTUS: Your Majesty shall see them presently. —
Mephostophilis away,
And with a solemn noise of trumpets' sound
Present before this royal Emperor   35
Great Alexander and his beauteous paramour.

MEPHOSTOPHILIS: Faustus, I will.

(Exit.)

BENVOLIO: Well master doctor, an your devils come not away
quickly, you shall have me asleep presently. Zounds, I could
eat myself for anger to think I have been such an ass all this   40
while to stand gaping after the devils' governor and can see
nothing.

FAUSTUS: I'll make you feel something anon if my art fail me
not!
My lord, I must forewarn your Majesty
That when my spirits present the royal shapes   45
Of Alexander and his paramour,
Your Grace demand no questions of the King
But in dumb silence let them come and go.

EMPEROR: Be it as Faustus please; we are content.

BENVOLIO: Ay ay, and I am content too. And thou bring   50
Alexander and his paramour before the Emperor, I'll be
Actaeon and turn myself to a stag.

FAUSTUS: *(Aside.)* And I'll play Diana and send you the horns
presently.

---

16 **Alexander and his beauteous paramour** Alexander the Great and
his mistress Thaïs   18 **took his rouse with stoups** had drinking bouts
with full goblets   31 **the Pope** i.e., Bruno   s.d. **Benvolio remains at
window** (because Benvolio does not leave the stage, this scene cannot
properly be said to be ended. But the present edition, following its predecessors for convenience of reference, begins a new scene)

IV.ii. s.d. **sennet** trumpet fanfare (the absence of a verb in the rest of
the stage direction perhaps indicates that the Emperor and his party do
not enter but rather are "discovered," as Faustus may have been discovered at the beginning of I.i, if the Chorus drew back a curtain)

---

9 **redeemed** freed   26 **costermonger** fruit-seller   39 **Zounds** by
God's wounds   52 **Actaeon** legendary hunter who saw the naked goddess Diana bathing. She transformed him into a stag, and he was torn
to pieces by his own hounds

(Sennet. Enter at one [door] the EMPEROR ALEXANDER, *at the other* DARIUS. *They meet.* DARIUS *is thrown down.* ALEXANDER *kills him, takes off his crown, and offering to go out, his* PARA-MOUR *meets him. He embraceth her and sets* DARIUS' *crown upon her head, and coming back both salute the* EMPEROR; *who leaving his state offers to embrace them, which* FAUSTUS *seeing suddenly stays him. Then trumpets cease and music sounds.)*

55   My gracious lord, you do forget yourself.
        These are but shadows, not substantial.
     EMPEROR: O pardon me, my thoughts are so ravished
        With sight of this renownèd Emperor,
        That in mine arms I would have compassed him.
60   But Faustus, since I may not speak to them,
        To satisfy my longing thoughts at full,
        Let me this tell thee: I have heard it said
        That this fair lady whilst she lived on earth,
        Had on her neck a little wart or mole.
65   How may I prove that saying to be true?
     FAUSTUS: Your Majesty may boldly go and see.
     EMPEROR: Faustus, I see it plain!
        And in this sight thou better pleasest me
        Than if I gained another monarchy.
70   FAUSTUS: Away, be gone!

     (Exit show.)

        See, see my gracious lord, what strange beast is yon that
        thrusts his head out at the window!
     EMPEROR: O wondrous sight! See, Duke of Saxony,
        Two spreading horns most strangely fastened
75   Upon the head of young Benvolio.
     SAXONY: What, is he asleep or dead?
     FAUSTUS: He sleeps my lord, but dreams not of his horns.
     EMPEROR: This sport is excellent. We'll call and wake him.
        What ho, Benvolio!
80   BENVOLIO: A plague upon you! Let me sleep awhile.
     EMPEROR: I blame thee not to sleep much, having such a head
        of thine own.
     SAXONY: Look up Benvolio! 'Tis the Emperor calls.
     BENVOLIO: The Emperor! Where? O zounds, my head!
85   EMPEROR: Nay, and thy horns hold, 'tis no matter for thy head,
        for that's armed sufficiently.
     FAUSTUS: Why, how now Sir Knight? What, hanged by the
        horns? This is most horrible! Fie fie, pull in your head for
        shame! Let not all the world wonder at you.
90   BENVOLIO: Zounds doctor, is this your villainy?
     FAUSTUS: Oh, say not so sir: The doctor has no skill,
        No art, no cunning to present these lords
        Or bring before this royal Emperor
        The mighty monarch, warlike Alexander.
95   If Faustus do it, you are straight resolved
        In bold Actaeon's shape to turn a stag.
        And therefore my lord, so please your Majesty,
        I'll raise a kennel of hounds shall hunt him so
        As all his footmanship shall scarce prevail
100   To keep his carcass from their bloody fangs.
        Ho, Belimote, Argiron, Asterote!

     BENVOLIO: Hold, hold! Zounds, he'll raise up a kennel of
        devils I think, anon. Good my lord, entreat for me. 'Sblood,
        I am never able to endure these torments.
     EMPEROR: Then good master doctor,   105
        Let me entreat you to remove his horns.
        He has done penance now sufficiently.
     FAUSTUS: My gracious lord, not so much for injury done to
        me, as to delight your Majesty with some mirth, hath Faustus
        justly requited this injurious knight; which being all I desire, 110
        I am content to remove his horns. Mephostophilis, trans-
        form him. And hereafter sir, look you speak well of scholars.
     BENVOLIO: *(Aside.)* Speak well of ye! 'Sblood, and scholars be
        such cuckold-makers to clap horns of honest men's heads o'
        this order, I'll ne'er trust smooth faces and small ruffs more. 115
        But an I be not revenged for this, would I might be turned to
        a gaping oyster and drink nothing but salt water.

     (Exit.)

     EMPEROR: Come Faustus, while the Emperor lives,
        In recompense of this thy high desert,
        Thou shalt command the state of Germany   120
        And live beloved of mighty Carolus.

     (Exeunt omnes.)

SCENE III

Enter BENVOLIO, MARTINO, FREDERICK, *and* SOLDIERS.

     MARTINO: Nay, sweet Benvolio, let us sway thy thoughts
        From this attempt against the conjurer.
     BENVOLIO: Away! You love me not to urge me thus.
        Shall I let slip so great an injury
        When every servile groom jests at my wrongs   5
        And in their rustic gambols proudly say,
        "Benvolio's head was graced with horns today"?
        O, may these eyelids never close again
        Till with my sword I have that conjurer slain!
        If you will aid me in this enterprise,   10
        Then draw your weapons and be resolute;
        If not, depart. Here will Benvolio die
        But Faustus' death shall quit my infamy.
     FREDERICK: Nay, we will stay with thee, betide what may,
        And kill that doctor if he come this way.   15
     BENVOLIO: Then, gentle Frederick, hie thee to the grove
        And place our servants and our followers
        Close in an ambush there behind the trees.
        By this, I know, the conjurer is near.
        I saw him kneel and kiss the Emperor's hand   20
        And take his leave laden with rich rewards.
        Then soldiers, boldly fight. If Faustus die,
        Take you the wealth, leave us the victory.
     FREDERICK: Come soldiers, follow me unto the grove.
        Who kills him shall have gold and endless love.   25

     (Exit FREDERICK *with the* SOLDIERS.)

     BENVOLIO: My head is lighter than it was by th' horns—
        But yet my heart more ponderous than my head,
        And pants until I see that conjurer dead.

---

s.d. **Darius** King of Persia, defeated by Alexander in 334 BC   59 **com-passed** encompassed, embraced   87–88 **hanged by the horns** (the spreading horns prevent Benvolio from pulling his head inside of the window)

103 **'Sblood** by God's blood   110 **injurious** insulting   115 **small ruffs** (worn by scholars, in contrast to the large ruffs worn by courtiers)   IV.iii.4 **let slip** ignore   13 **But** unless; **quit** avenge

MARTINO: Where shall we place ourselves, Benvolio?

30 BENVOLIO: Here will we stay to bide the first assault.
O, were that damnèd hell-hound but in place
Thou soon should'st see me quit my foul disgrace.

(*Enter* FREDERICK.)

FREDERICK: Close, close! The conjurer is at hand
And all alone comes walking in his gown.
35 Be ready then and strike the peasant down!

BENVOLIO: Mine be that honor then! Now sword, strike
home!
For horns he gave I'll have his head anon.

(*Enter* FAUSTUS *with the false head.*)

MARTINO: See see, he comes.

BENVOLIO: No words. This blow ends all!

(*Strikes* FAUSTUS.)

FAUSTUS: O!

40 FREDERICK: Groan you, master doctor?

BENVOLIO: Break may his heart with groans! Dear Frederick,
see,
Thus will I end his griefs immediately.

(*Cuts off* FAUSTUS' *false head.*)

MARTINO: Strike with a willing hand! His head is off.

BENVOLIO: The devil's dead, the furies now may laugh.

45 FREDERICK: Was this that stern aspect, that awful frown,
Made the grim monarch of infernal spirits
Tremble and quake at his commanding charms?

MARTINO: Was this that damnèd head whose heart conspired
Benvolio's shame before the Emperor?

50 BENVOLIO: Ay, that's the head, and here the body lies
Justly rewarded for his villainies.

FREDERICK: Come let's devise how we may add more shame
To the black scandal of his hated name.

BENVOLIO: First, on his head in quittance of my wrongs
55 I'll nail huge forkèd horns and let them hang
Within the window where he yoked me first
That all the world may see my just revenge.

MARTINO: What use shall we put his beard to?

BENVOLIO: We'll sell it to a chimney-sweeper. It will wear out
60 ten birchen brooms, I warrant you.

FREDERICK: What shall eyes do?

BENVOLIO: We'll put out his eyes, and they shall serve for buttons to his lips to keep his tongue from catching cold.

MARTINO: An excellent policy! And now sirs, having divided
65 him, what shall the body do?

(FAUSTUS *rises.*)

BENVOLIO: Zounds, the devil's alive again!

FREDERICK: Give him his head for God's sake!

FAUSTUS: Nay keep it. Faustus will have heads and hands,
Ay, all your hearts, to recompense this deed.
70 Knew you not, traitors, I was limited
For four and twenty years to breathe on earth?
And had you cut my body with your swords
Or hewed this flesh and bones as small as sand,
Yet in a minute had my spirit returned

And I had breathed a man made free from harm. 75
But wherefore do I dally my revenge?
Asteroth, Belimoth, Mephostophilis!

(*Enter* MEPHOSTOPHILIS *and other* DEVILS.)

Go horse these traitors on your fiery backs
And mount aloft with them as high as heaven,
Thence pitch them headlong to the lowest hell. 80
Yet stay, the world shall see their misery,
And hell shall after plague their treachery.
Go Belimoth, and take this caitiff hence
And hurl him in some lake of mud and dirt:
Take thou this other, drag him through the woods 85
Amongst the pricking thorns and sharpest briars:
Whilst with my gentle Mephostophilis
This traitor flies unto some steepy rock
That rolling down may break the villain's bones
As he intended to dismember me. 90
Fly hence, dispatch my charge immediately!

FREDERICK: Pity us, gentle Faustus, save our lives!

FAUSTUS: Away!

FREDERICK: He must needs go that the devil drives.

(*Exeunt* SPIRITS *with the* KNIGHTS.)

(*Enter the ambushed* SOLDIERS.)

1 SOLDIER: Come sirs, prepare yourselves in readiness.
Make haste to help these noble gentlemen. 95
I heard them parley with the conjurer.

2 SOLDIER: See where he comes, dispatch, and kill the slave!

FAUSTUS: What's here, an ambush to betray my life?
Then Faustus, try thy skill. Base peasants, stand!
For lo, these trees remove at my command 100
And stand as bulwarks 'twixt yourselves and me
To shield me from your hated treachery!
Yet to encounter this your weak attempt
Behold an army comes incontient.

(FAUSTUS *strikes the door, and enter a* DEVIL *playing on a drum,
after him another bearing an ensign, and divers with weapons:*
MEPHOSTOPHILIS *with fireworks: they set upon the* SOLDIERS
and drive them out. [Exeunt all.])

SCENE IV

Enter at several doors BENVOLIO, FREDERICK, *and* MARTINO,
*their heads and faces bloody and besmeared with mud and dirt,
all having horns on their heads.*

MARTINO: What ho, Benvolio!

BENVOLIO: Here! What, Frederick, ho!

FREDERICK: O, help me gentle friend. Where is Martino?

MARTINO: Dear Frederick, here,
Half smothered in a lake of mud and dirt,
Through which the furies dragged me by the heels. 5

FREDERICK: Martino, see, Benvolio's horns again.

MARTINO: O misery! How now Benvolio?

BENVOLIO: Defend me, heaven! Shall I be haunted still?

---

35 **peasant** low fellow

83 **caitiff** wretch   100 **remove** move   104 **incontinent** immediately
IV.iv.8 **haunted** (the following line suggests that there is a quibble on
"hunted," Benvolio now resembling a stag)

MARTINO: Nay fear not man, we have no power to kill.

10 BENVOLIO: My friends transformèd thus! O hellish spite,
　　Your heads are all set with horns.
FREDERICK:　　　　　　　　　You hit it right:
　　It is your own you mean. Feel on your head.
BENVOLIO: Zounds, horns again!
MARTINO:　　　　　　　　Nay chafe not man, we all are sped.
BENVOLIO: What devil attends this damned magician,
15　　That spite of spite our wrongs are doubled?
FREDERICK: What may we do that we may hide our shames?
BENVOLIO: If we should follow him to work revenge
　　He'd join long asses' ears to these huge horns
　　And make us laughing-stocks to all the world.
20 MARTINO: What shall we then do, dear Benvolio?
BENVOLIO: I have a castle joining near these woods,
　　And thither we'll repair and live obscure
　　Till time shall alter this our brutish shapes.
　　Sith black disgrace hath thus eclipsed our fame,
25　　We'll rather die with grief than live with shame.

(Exeunt omnes.)

SCENE V

Enter FAUSTUS *and the* HORSE-COURSER.

HORSE-COURSER: I beseech your worship, accept of these forty
　　dollars.
FAUSTUS: Friend, thou canst not buy so good a horse for so
　　small a price. I have no great need to sell him, but if thou lik-
5　　est him for ten dollars more, take him, because I see thou
　　hast a good mind to him.
HORSE-COURSER: I beseech you sir, accept of this. I am a very
　　poor man and have lost very much of late by horse-flesh, and
　　this bargain will set me up again.
10 FAUSTUS: Well, I will not stand with thee. Give me the money.
　　Now sirrah, I must tell you that you may ride him o'er hedge
　　and ditch and spare him not. But, do you hear, in any case
　　ride him not into the water.
HORSE-COURSER: How sir, not into the water! Why, will he
15　　not drink of all waters?
FAUSTUS: Yes, he will drink of all waters, but ride him not into
　　the water: o'er hedge and ditch or where thou wilt, but not
　　into the water. Go bid the hostler deliver him unto you, and
　　remember what I say.
20 HORSE-COURSER: I warrant you sir. O joyful day! Now am I a
　　made man forever.

(Exit.)

FAUSTUS: What art thou, Faustus, but a man condemned to
　　die?
　　Thy fatal time draws to a final end;
　　Despair doth drive distrust into my thoughts.
25　　Confound these passions with a quiet sleep.

　　Tush, Christ did call the thief upon the cross!
　　Then rest thee Faustus, quiet in conceit.

(He sits to sleep.)

(Enter the HORSE-COURSER *wet.)*

HORSE-COURSER: O what a cozening doctor was this! I riding
　　my horse into the water, thinking some hidden mystery had
　　been in the horse, I had nothing under me but a little straw　30
　　and had much ado to escape drowning. Well, I'll go rouse
　　him and make him give me my forty dollars again. Ho, sirrah
　　doctor, you cozening scab! Master doctor, awake and rise,
　　and give me my money again, for your horse is turned to a
　　bottle of hay. Master doctor!　　　　　　　　　　　　　35

(He pulls off his leg.)

　　Alas, I am undone! What shall I do? I have pulled off his leg.
FAUSTUS: O help, help! The villain hath murdered me!
HORSE-COURSER: Murder or not murder, now he has but one
　　leg I'll outrun him, and cast this leg into some ditch or other.
FAUSTUS: Stop him, stop him, stop him!—Ha, ha, ha! Faustus　40
　　hath his leg again, and the horse-courser a bundle of hay for
　　his forty dollars.

(Enter WAGNER.)

　　How now, Wagner? What news with thee?
WAGNER: If it please you, the Duke of Vanholt doth earnestly
　　entreat your company, and hath sent some of his men to at-　45
　　tend you with provision fit for your journey.
FAUSTUS: The Duke of Vanholt's an honorable gentleman,
　　and one to whom I must be no niggard of my cunning.
　　Come, away!

(Exeunt.)

SCENE VI

Enter [ROBIN] *the clown,* DICK, HORSE-COURSER, *and a* CARTER.

CARTER: Come my masters, I'll bring you to the best beer in
　　Europe. What ho, hostess! Where be these whores?

(Enter HOSTESS.)

HOSTESS: How now? What lack you? What, my old guests,
　　welcome.
ROBIN: *(Aside.)* Sirrah Dick, dost thou know why I stand so　5
　　mute?
DICK: *(Aside.)* No Robin, why is't?
ROBIN: *(Aside.)* I am eighteen pence on the score. But say
　　nothing. See if she have forgotten me.
HOSTESS: Who's this that stands so solemnly by himself?　10
　　What, my old guest!
ROBIN: O, hostess, how do you? I hope my score stands still.
HOSTESS: Ay, there's no doubt of that, for methinks you make
　　no haste to wipe it out.
DICK: Why hostess, I say, fetch us some beer!　　　　　　15
HOSTESS: You shall, presently.—Look up into th' hall there,
　　ho!

(Exit.)

---

13 **chafe** fret; **sped** done for, ruined (because of the horns)　24 **Sith** since

IV.v. s.d. **Horse-courser** horse trader　2 **dollars** German coins　8 **horse-flesh** (the possibility of a quibble on "whores' flesh" is increased by "set me up" and "stand" in the ensuing dialogue)　10 **stand** haggle　16 **drink of all waters** i.e., go anywhere　23 **fatal time** life span

26 **Christ . . . cross** (in Luke 23:39–43 Christ promised one of the thieves that he would be with Christ in paradise)　27 **quiet in conceit** with a quiet mind　28 **cozening** deceiving　35 **bottle** bundle

IV.vi.8 **on the score** in debt

DICK: Come sirs, what shall we do now till mine hostess comes?

20 CARTER: Marry sir, I'll tell you the bravest tale how a conjurer served me. You know Doctor Faustus?

HORSE-COURSER: Ay, a plague take him! Here's some on's have cause to know him. Did he conjure thee too?

CARTER: I'll tell you how he served me. As I was going to Wit-
25 tenberg t'other day with a load of hay, he met me and asked me what he should give me for as much hay as he could eat. Now sir, I thinking that a little would serve his turn, bad him take as much as he would for three farthings. So he presently gave me my money and fell to eating; and as I am a cursen
30 man, he never left eating till he had eat up all my load of hay.

ALL: O monstrous, eat a whole load of hay!

ROBIN: Yes yes, that may be, for I have heard of one that has eat a load of logs.

35 HORSE-COURSER: Now sirs, you shall hear how villainously he served me. I went to him yesterday to buy a horse of him, and he would by no means sell him under forty dollars. So sir, because I knew him to be such a horse as would run over hedge and ditch and never tire, I gave him his money. So,
40 when I had my horse, Doctor Faustus bade me ride him night and day and spare him no time. "But," quoth he, "in any case ride him not into the water." Now sir, I thinking the horse had had some quality that he would not have me know of, what did I but rid him into a great river—and when I
45 came just in the midst, my horse vanished away and I sate straddling upon a bottle of hay.

ALL: O brave doctor!

HORSE-COURSER: But you shall hear how bravely I served him for it. I went me home to his house, and there I found him
50 asleep. I kept ahallowing and whooping in his ears, but all could not wake him. I seeing that, took him by the leg and never rested pulling till I had pulled me his leg quite off, and now 'tis at home in mine hostry.

DICK: And has the doctor but one leg then? That's excellent,
55 for one of his devils turned me into the likeness of an ape's face.

CARTER: Some more drink, hostess!

ROBIN: Hark you, we'll into another room and drink awhile, and then we'll go seek out the doctor.

(Exeunt omnes.)

SCENE VII

Enter the DUKE OF VANHOLT, *his* [SERVANTS,] DUCHESS, FAUS-
TUS, *and* MEPHOSTOPHILIS.

DUKE: Thanks master doctor, for these pleasant sights. Nor know I how sufficiently to recompense your great deserts in erecting that enchanted castle in the air, the sight whereof so delighted me,
5 As nothing in the world could please me more.

FAUSTUS: I do think myself, my good lord, highly recom-
pensed in that it pleaseth your Grace to think but well of that which Faustus hath performed.—But gracious lady, it may

be that you have taken no pleasure in those sights. Therefore I pray you tell me what is the thing you most desire to have: 10 be it in the world it shall be yours. I have heard that great-bellied women do long for things are rare and dainty.

DUCHESS: True master doctor, and since I find you so kind, I will make known unto you what my heart desires to have: and were it now summer, as it is January, a dead time of the 15 winter, I would request no better meat than a dish of ripe grapes.

FAUSTUS: This is but a small matter. Go Mephostophilis, away!

(Exit MEPHOSTOPHILIS.*)*

Madam, I will do more than this for your content.

(Enter MEPHOSTOPHILIS *again with the grapes.)*

Here, now taste ye these. They should be good, 20
For they come from a far country, I can tell you.

DUKE: This makes me wonder more than all the rest, that at this time of the year when every tree is barren of his fruit, from whence you had these ripe grapes.

FAUSTUS: Please it your Grace, the year is divided into two cir- 25 cles over the whole world, so that when it is winter with us, in the contrary circle it is likewise summer with them, as in India, Saba, and such countries that lie far east, where they have fruit twice a year. From whence, by means of a swift spirit that I have, I had these grapes brought as you see. 30

DUCHESS: And trust me, they are the sweetest grapes that e'er I tasted.

(The CLOWNS *[*ROBIN, DICK, CARTER, *and* HORSE-COURSER*] bounce at the gate within.)*

DUKE: What rude disturbers have we at the gate?
Go pacify their fury, set it ope,
And then demand of them what they would have. 35

(They knock again and call out to talk with FAUSTUS.*)*

A SERVANT: Why, how now masters, what a coil is there! What is the reason you disturb the Duke?

DICK: We have no reason for it, therefore a fig for him!

SERVANT: Why saucy varlets, dare you be so bold!

HORSE-COURSER: I hope sir, we have wit enough to be more 40 bold than welcome.

SERVANT: It appears so. Pray be bold elsewhere
And trouble not the Duke.

DUKE: What would they have?

SERVANT: They all cry out to speak with Doctor Faustus. 45

CARTER: Ay, and we will speak with him.

DUKE: Will you sir? Commit the rascals.

DICK: Commit with us! He were as good commit with his father as commit with us!

FAUSTUS: I do beseech your Grace, let them come in. 50
They are good subject for a merriment.

---

29 **cursen** i.e., Christian (dialect form)   33–34 **eat a load of logs** been drunk   53 **hostry** inn

---

IV.vii.11 **great-bellied** i.e., pregnant   16 **meat** food   25 **two circles** i.e., the northern and the southern hemispheres (though later in the speech he talks of east and west rather than of north and south)   s.d. **bounce** knock   36 **coil** turmoil   37 **reason** (pronounced like "raisin," leading to the quibble on "fig"; a "fig" here is an obscene contemptuous gesture in which the hand is clenched and the thumb is thrust between the first and second fingers, making the thumb resemble the stem of a fig, or a penis)   47 **Commit** imprison (Dick proceeds to quibble on the idea of committing adultery)

DUKE: Do as thou wilt, Faustus, I give thee leave.

FAUSTUS: I thank your Grace.

(*Enter* [ROBIN] *the clown,* DICK, CARTER, *and* HORSE-COURSER.)

       Why, how now my good friends?
  'Faith, you are too outrageous; but come near,
55 I have procured your pardons. Welcome all.

ROBIN: Nay sir, we will be welcome for our money, and we will pay for what we take. What ho, give's half a dozen of beer here, and be hanged!

FAUSTUS: Nay, hark you, can you tell me where you are?

60 CARTER: Ay, marry can I, we are under heaven.

SERVANT: Ay, but Sir Sauce-box, know you in what place?

HORSE-COURSER: Ay ay, the house is good enough to drink in. Zounds, fill us some beer, or we'll break all the barrels in the house and dash out all your brains with your bottles.

65 FAUSTUS: Be not so furious. Come, you shall have beer.
  My lord, beseech you give me leave awhile;
  I'll gage my credit 'twill content your Grace.

DUKE: With all my heart, kind doctor, please thyself.
  Our servants and our court's at thy command.

70 FAUSTUS: I humbly thank your Grace.—Then fetch some beer.

HORSE-COURSER: Ay marry, there spake a doctor indeed! And 'faith, I'll drink a health to thy wooden leg for that word.

FAUSTUS: My wooden leg? What dost thou mean by that?

75 CARTER: Ha, ha, ha, dost hear him Dick? He has forgot his leg.

HORSE-COURSER: Ay ay, he does not stand much upon that.

FAUSTUS: No, 'faith, not much upon a wooden leg.

CARTER: Good lord, that flesh and blood should be so frail with your worship! Do not you remember a horse-courser
80 you sold a horse to?

FAUSTUS: Yes, I remember I sold one a horse.

CARTER: And do you remember you bid he should not ride into the water?

FAUSTUS: Yes, I do very well remember that.

85 CARTER: And do you remember nothing of your leg?

FAUSTUS: No, in good sooth.

CARTER: Then I pray remember your curtsy.

FAUSTUS: I thank you sir.

CARTER: 'Tis not so much worth. I pray you tell me one thing.

90 FAUSTUS: What's that?

CARTER: Be both your legs bedfellows every night together?

FAUSTUS: Would'st thou make a colossus of me that thou askest me such questions?

CARTER: No, truly sir, I would make nothing of you, but I
95 would fain know that.

(*Enter* HOSTESS *with drink.*)

FAUSTUS: Then I assure thee certainly they are.

CARTER: I thank you, I am fully satisfied.

FAUSTUS: But wherefore dost thou ask?

CARTER: For nothing, sir, but methinks you should have a
100 wooden bedfellow of one of 'em.

HORSE-COURSER: Why, do you hear sir, did not I pull off one of your legs when you were asleep?

FAUSTUS: But I have it again now I am awake. Look you here sir.

ALL: O horrible! Had the doctor three legs?

CARTER: Do you remember sir, how you cozened me and eat 105
up my load of—

(FAUSTUS *charms him dumb.*)

DICK: Do you remember how you made me wear an ape's—

(FAUSTUS *charms him.*)

HORSE-COURSER: You whoreson conjuring scab! Do you remember how you cozened me with a ho—

(FAUSTUS *charms him.*)

ROBIN: Ha' you forgotten me? You think to carry it away with 110
your "hey-pass" and "re-pass"? Do you remember the dog's fa—

([FAUSTUS *charms him.] Exeunt* CLOWNS.)

HOSTESS: Who pays for the ale? Hear you master doctor, now you have sent away my guests, I pray who shall pay me for
my a—   115

([FAUSTUS *charms her.] Exit* HOSTESS.)

DUCHESS: My Lord,
  We are much beholding to this learnèd man.

DUKE: So are we madam, which we will recompense
  With all the love and kindness that we may:
  His artful sport drives all sad thoughts away. 120

(*Exeunt.*)

— ACT FIVE —

SCENE I

Thunder and lightning. Enter DEVILS *with covered dishes:* MEPHOSTOPHILIS *leads them into* FAUSTUS' *study. Then enter* WAGNER.

WAGNER: I think my master means to die shortly. He has made his will and given me his wealth: his house, his goods, and store of golden plate—besides two thousand ducats ready coined. I wonder what he means. If death were nigh, he would not frolic thus. He's now at supper with the scholars, 5
where there's such belly-cheer as Wagner in his life ne'er saw the like! And see where they come. Belike the feast is done.

(*Exit.*)

(*Enter* FAUSTUS, MEPHOSTOPHILIS, *and two or three* SCHOLARS.)

1 SCHOLAR: Master Doctor Faustus, since our conference about fair ladies, which was the beautifulest in all the world, we have determined with ourselves that Helen of Greece 10

---

67 **gage** pledge 76 **stand much upon** (quibble on "attach much importance to") 87 **curtsy** (also called "a leg," hence there is a quibble on the Carter's previous speech) 92 **colossus** huge statue in the harbor at Rhodes, between whose legs ships were said to have sailed

---

111 **hey-pass, re-pass** conjuring expressions

V.i.7 Belike most likely 1–7 **I think . . . done** (though printed as prose in the quarto, as here, perhaps this speech should be verse, the lines ending *shortly, wealth, plate, coined, nigh, supper, belly-cheer, like, done*)

was the admirablest lady that ever lived. Therefore master
doctor, if you will do us so much favor as to let us see that
peerless dame of Greece, whom all the world admires for
majesty, we should think ourselves much beholding unto
15   you.

FAUSTUS: Gentlemen,
For that I know your friendship is unfeigned,
It is not Faustus' custom to deny
The just request of those that wish him well:
20   You shall behold that peerless dame of Greece
No otherwise for pomp or majesty
Than when Sir Paris crossed the seas with her
And brought the spoils to rich Dardania.
Be silent then, for danger is in words.

(Music sounds. MEPHOSTOPHILIS *brings in* HELEN: *she passeth
over the stage.)*

25   2 SCHOLAR: Was this fair Helen, whose admired worth
Made Greece with ten years' wars afflict poor Troy?
3 SCHOLAR: Too simple is my wit to tell her worth,
Whom all the world admires for majesty.
1 SCHOLAR: Now we have seen the pride of nature's work,
30   We'll take our leaves, and for this blessèd sight
Happy and blest be Faustus evermore.
FAUSTUS: Gentlemen, farewell, the same wish I to you.

(Exeunt scholars.)

(Enter an OLD MAN.*)*

OLD MAN: O gentle Faustus, leave this damnèd art,
This magic that will charm thy soul to hell
35   And quite bereave thee of salvation.
Though thou hast now offended like man,
Do not persever in it like a devil.
Yet, yet, thou hast an amiable soul
If sin by custom grow not into nature.
40   Then, Faustus, will repentance come too late!
Then, thou are banished from the sight of heaven!
No mortal can express the pains of hell!
It may be this my exhortation
Seems harsh and all unpleasant. Let it not.
45   For gentle son, I speak it not in wrath
Or envy of thee but in tender love
And pity of thy future misery:
And so have hope that this my kind rebuke,
Checking thy body, may amend thy soul.
50   FAUSTUS: Where art thou, Faustus? Wretch, what hast thou
done!

*(*MEPHOSTOPHILIS *gives him a dagger.)*

Hell claims his right and with a roaring voice
Says "Faustus, come, thine hour is almost come!"
And Faustus now will come to do thee right!
OLD MAN: O stay, good Faustus, stay thy desperate steps!
55   I see an angel hover o'er thy head,
And with a vial full of precious grace
Offers to pour the same into thy soul:
Then call for mercy and avoid despair.

FAUSTUS: O friend,
I feel thy words to comfort my distressèd soul: 60
Leave me awhile to ponder on my sins.
OLD MAN: Faustus, I leave thee, but with grief of heart,
Fearing the enemy of thy hapless soul.

(Exit.)

FAUSTUS: Accursèd Faustus! Wretch, what hast thou done!
I do repent, and yet I do despair: 65
Hell strives with grace for conquest in my breast!
What shall I do to shun the snares of death?
MEPHOSTOPHILIS: Thou traitor Faustus, I arrest thy soul
For disobedience to my sovereign lord.
Revolt, or I'll in piecemeal tear thy flesh.   70
FAUSTUS: I do repent I e'er offended him.
Sweet Mephostophilis, entreat thy lord
To pardon my unjust presumption,
And with my blood again I will confirm
The former vow I made to Lucifer.   75
MEPHOSTOPHILIS: Do it then, Faustus, with unfeignèd heart
Lest greater dangers do attend thy drift.
FAUSTUS: Torment, sweet friend, that base and agèd man
That durst dissuade me from thy Lucifer,
With greatest torment that our hell affords.   80
MEPHOSTOPHILIS: His faith is great. I cannot touch his soul.
But what I may afflict his body with
I will attempt, which is but little worth.
FAUSTUS: One thing, good servant, let me crave of thee
To glut the longing of my heart's desire: 85
That I may have unto my paramour
That heavenly Helen which I saw of late,
Whose sweet embraces may extinguish clear
Those thoughts that do dissuade me from my vow,
And keep mine oath I made to Lucifer.   90
MEPHOSTOPHILIS: This or what else my Faustus shall desire
Shall be performed in twinkling of an eye.

(Enter HELEN *again, passing over between two* CUPIDS.*)*

FAUSTUS: Was this the face that launched a thousand ships
And burnt the topless towers of Ilium?
Sweet Helen, make me immortal with a kiss.   95
Her lips suck forth my soul. See where it flies!
Come Helen, come, give me my soul again.
Here will I dwell, for heaven is in these lips
And all is dross that is not Helena.
I will be Paris, and for love of thee   100
Instead of Troy shall Wittenberg be sacked;
And I will combat with weak Menelaus
And wear thy colors on my plumèd crest.
Yea, I will wound Achilles in the heel
And then return to Helen for a kiss.   105
O, thou art fairer than the evening's air
Clad in the beauty of a thousand stars,
Brighter art thou than flaming Jupiter
When he appeared to hapless Semele,
More lovely than the monarch of the sky   110

---

23 **spoils** booty (including Helen); **Dardania** Troy   35 **bereave** deprive   37 **persever** (accent on second syllable)   38 **an amiable soul** a
soul worthy of love   49 **Checking** rebuking

70 **Revolt** return (to your allegiance)   94 **topless** i.e., so tall their tops
are beyond sight; **Ilium** Troy   102 **Menelaus** Greek king, deserted by
Helen for Paris   104 **Achilles** greatest of the Greek warriors   109
Semele beloved by Jupiter, who promised to do whatever she wished;
she asked to see him in his full splendor, and the sight incinerated her

In wanton Arethusa's azure arms,
And none but thou shalt be my paramour.   *(Exeunt.)*

SCENE II

Thunder. Enter LUCIFER, BELZEBUB, *and* MEPHOSTOPHILIS.

LUCIFER: Thus from infernal Dis do we ascend
    To view the subjects of our monarchy,
    Those souls which sin seals the black sons of hell.
    'Mong which as chief, Faustus, we come to thee,
5   Bringing with us lasting damnation
    To wait upon thy soul. The time is come
    Which makes it forfeit.
MEPHOSTOPHILIS: And this gloomy night
    Here in this room will wretched Faustus be.
BELZEBUB: And here we'll stay
10   To mark him how he doth demean himself.
MEPHOSTOPHILIS: How should he but in desperate lunacy?
    Fond worldling, now his heart blood dries with grief.
    His conscience kills it, and his laboring brain
    Begets a world of idle fantasies
15   To overreach the devil; but all in vain:
    His store of pleasures must be sauced with pain!
    He and his servant Wagner are at hand.
    Both come from drawing Faustus' lastest will.
    See where they come.

(Enter FAUSTUS *and* WAGNER.)

20 FAUSTUS: Say Wagner, thou hast perused my will;
    How dost thou like it?
WAGNER: Sir, so wondrous well
    As in all humble duty I do yield
    My life and lasting service for your love.

(Enter the SCHOLARS.)

FAUSTUS: Gramercies, Wagner—Welcome gentlemen.

(Exit WAGNER.)

25 1 SCHOLAR: Now worthy Faustus, methinks your looks are
      changed.
FAUSTUS: O gentlemen!
2 SCHOLAR: What ails Faustus?
FAUSTUS: Ah my sweet chamber-fellow, had I lived with thee,
    then had I lived still!—But now must die eternally. Look sirs,
30   comes he not, comes he not?
1 SCHOLAR: O my dear Faustus, what imports this fear?
2 SCHOLAR: Is all our pleasure turned to melancholy?
3 SCHOLAR: He is not well with being over-solitary.
2 SCHOLAR: If it be so, we'll have physicians and Faustus shall
35   be cured.
3 SCHOLAR: 'Tis but a surfeit sir, fear nothing.
FAUSTUS: A surfeit of deadly sin that hath damned both body
    and soul!
2 SCHOLAR: Yet Faustus, look up to heaven and remember
40   mercy is infinite.

---

111 **Arethusa** a nymph, here apparently loved by Jupiter, "the monarch
of the sky"
V.ii. s.d. **Enter Lucifer, Belzebub, and Mephostophilis** (probably
they rise out of a trapdoor and ascend to the upper stage,
Mephostophilis descending to the main stage at line 86) 1 **infernal
Dis** the underworld (named for its ruler) 12 **Fond** foolish 24
Gramercies thank you 36 **a surfeit** indigestion

FAUSTUS: But Faustus' offense can ne'er be pardoned. The serpent that tempted Eve may be saved, but not Faustus! O gentlemen, hear with patience and tremble not at my speeches.
Though my heart pant and quiver to remember that I have
been a student here these thirty years, O, would I had never   45
seen Wittenberg, never read book.—And what wonders I
have done all Germany can witness, yea all the world, for
which Faustus hath lost both Germany and the world, yea
heaven itself—heaven, the seat of God, the throne of the
blessèd, the kingdom of joy—and must remain in hell for   50
ever! hell, O hell forever! Sweet friends, what shall become
of Faustus being in hell forever?
2 SCHOLAR: Yet Faustus, call on God.
FAUSTUS: On God, whom Faustus hath abjured? On God,
whom Faustus hath blasphemed? O my God, I would weep,   55
but the devil draws in my tears! Gush forth blood instead of
tears, yea life and soul! O, he stays my tongue! I would lift up
my hands, but see, they hold 'em, they hold 'em!
ALL: Who, Faustus?
FAUSTUS: Why, Lucifer and Mephostophilis. O gentlemen, I   60
gave them my soul for my cunning.
ALL: O, God forbid!
FAUSTUS: God forbade it indeed, but Faustus hath done it. For
the vain pleasure of four and twenty years hath Faustus lost
eternal joy and felicity. I writ them a bill with mine own   65
blood. The date is expired. This is the time. And he will
fetch me.
1 SCHOLAR: Why did not Faustus tell us of this before, that di-
vines might have prayed for thee?
FAUSTUS: Oft have I thought to have done so, but the devil   70
threatened to tear me in pieces if I named God—to fetch me
body and soul if I once gave ear to divinity; and now 'tis too
late! Gentlemen, away, lest you perish with me.
2 SCHOLAR: O, what may we do to save Faustus?
FAUSTUS: Talk not of me but save yourselves and depart.   75
3 SCHOLAR: God will strengthen me. I will stay with Faustus.
1 SCHOLAR: Tempt not God, sweet friend, but let us into the
next room and pray for him.
FAUSTUS: Ay, pray for me, pray for me. And what noise soever
you hear, come not unto me, for nothing can rescue me.   80
2 SCHOLAR: Pray thou, and we will pray that God may have
mercy upon thee.
FAUSTUS: Gentlemen, farewell! If I live till morning, I'll visit
you. If not, Faustus is gone to hell.
ALL: Faustus, farewell.   85

(Exeunt SCHOLARS.)

MEPHOSTOPHILIS: Ay, Faustus, now thou hast no hope of
    heaven.
    Therefore, despair! Think only upon hell,
    For that must be thy mansion, there to dwell.
FAUSTUS: O thou bewitching fiend, 'twas thy temptation
    Hath robbed me of eternal happiness.   90
MEPHOSTOPHILIS: I do confess it Faustus, and rejoice.
    'Twas I, that when thou wert i'the way to heaven
    Damned up thy passage. When thou took'st the book
    To view the Scriptures, then I turned the leaves
    And led thine eye.   95
    What, weep'st thou! 'Tis too late, despair, farewell!
    Fools that will laugh on earth, most weep in hell.

(Exit.)

(Enter the GOOD ANGEL *and the* BAD ANGEL *at several doors.)*

GOOD ANGEL: O Faustus, if thou hadst given ear to me
    Innumerable joys had followèd thee.
100   But thou did'st love the world.
BAD ANGEL: Gave ear to me,
    And now must taste hell's pains perpetually.
GOOD ANGEL: O, what will all thy riches, pleasures, pomps
    Avail thee now?
BAD ANGEL: Nothing but vex thee more,
    To want in hell, that had on earth such store.

(Music while the throne descends.)

105 GOOD ANGEL: O, thou hast lost celestial happiness,
    Pleasures unspeakable, bliss without end.
    Had'st thou affected sweet divinity,
    Hell or the devil had had no power on thee.
    Had'st thou kept on that way, Faustus behold
110   In what resplendent glory thou had'st sat
    In yonder throne, like those bright shining saints,
    And triumphed over hell! That hast thou lost.

(Throne ascends.)

    And now, poor soul, must thy good angel leave thee,
    The jaws of hell are open to receive thee.

(Exit.)

(Hell is discovered.)

115 BAD ANGEL: Now Faustus, let thine eyes with horror stare
    Into that vast perpetual torture-house.
    There are the furies, tossing damnèd souls
    On burning forks. Their bodies boil in lead.
    There are live quarters broiling on the coals,
120   That ne'er can die: this ever-burning chair
    Is for o'er-tortured souls to rest them in.
    These that are fed with sops of flaming fire
    Were gluttons and loved only delicates
    And laughed to see the poor starve at their gates.
125   But yet all these are nothing. Thou shalt see
    Ten thousand tortures that more horrid be.
FAUSTUS: O, I have seen enough to torture me.
BAD ANGEL: Nay, thou must feel them, taste the smart of all:
    He that loves pleasure must for pleasure fall.
130   And so I leave thee Faustus, till anon:
    Then wilt thou tumble in confusion.   *(Exit.)*

(The clock strikes eleven.)

FAUSTUS: O Faustus!
    Now hast thou but one bare hour to live
    And then thou must be damned perpetually.
135   Stand still, you ever-moving spheres of Heaven
    That time may cease and midnight never come:
    Fair nature's eye, rise, rise again and make
    Perpetual day, or let this hour be but a year,
    A month, a week, a natural day—
140   That Faustus may repent and save his soul.

O lente lente currite noctis equi!
    The stars move still, time runs, the clock will strike:
    The devil will come, and Faustus must be damned!
    O, I'll leap up to my God! Who pulls me down?
    See, see where Christ's blood streams in the firmament!   145
    One drop of blood will save me. O my Christ!—
    Rend not my heart for naming of my Christ!
    Yet will I call on Him! O spare me, Lucifer!—
    Where is it now? 'Tis gone: and see where God
    Stretcheth out His arm and bends His ireful brows!   150
    Mountains and hills, come, come and fall on me
    And hide me from the heavy wrath of God!
    No?
    Then will I headlong run into the earth.
    Gape earth! O no, it will not harbor me.   155
    You stars that reigned at my nativity,
    Whose influence hath allotted death and hell,
    Now draw up Faustus like a foggy mist
    Into the entrails of yon laboring cloud
    That when you vomit forth into the air,   160
    My limbs may issue from your smoky mouths—
    But let my soul mount and ascend to heaven!

(The watch strikes.)

    O half the hour is passed! 'Twill all be passed anon!
    O God,
    If thou wilt not have mercy on my soul   165
    Yet for Christ's sake, whose blood hath ransomed me,
    Impose some end to my incessant pain!
    Let Faustus live in hell a thousand years,
    A hundred thousand, and at last be saved!
    No end is limited to damnèd souls!   170
    Why wert thou not a creature wanting soul?
    Or why is this immortal that thou hast?
    O, Pythagoras' metempsychosis, were that true
    This soul should fly from me and I be changed
    Into some brutish beast.   175
    All beasts are happy, for when they die
    Their souls are soon dissolved in elements.
    But mine must live still to be plagued in hell!
    Cursed be the parents that engendered me!
    No Faustus, curse thyself, curse Lucifer   180
    That hath deprived thee of the joys of heaven.

(The clock strikes twelve.)

    It strikes, it strikes! Now body, turn to air,
    Or Lucifer will bear thee quick to hell!:
    O soul, be changed into small water-drops
    And fall into the ocean, ne'er be found.   185

(Thunder, and enter the DEVILS.*)*

    My God, my God! Look not so fierce on me!
    Adders and serpents, let me breathe awhile!

---

141 **O . . . equi** slowly, slowly run, O horses of the night (Latin, adapted from Ovid's *Amores,* I.xiii.40, where a lover regretfully thinks of the coming of the dawn) 170 **limited** to set for 173 **metempsychosis** transmigration of souls (a doctrine held by Pythagoras, philosopher of the sixth century BC) 178 **still** always 183 **quick** alive

---

s.d. **throne** (symbolic of heaven) 107 **affected** preferred 119 **quarters** bodies 131 **confusion** destruction

Ugly Hell, gape not! Come not Lucifer!
I'll burn my books!—O Mephostophilis!

*(Exeunt [*DEVILS *with* FAUSTUS*].)*

SCENE III

(Enter the SCHOLARS.*)*

1 SCHOLAR: Come gentlemen, let us go visit Faustus,
For such a dreadful night was never seen
Since first the world's creation did begin!
Such fearful shrieks and cries were never heard!
5   Pray heaven, the doctor have escaped the danger.
2 SCHOLAR: O, help us heaven, see, here are Faustus' limbs
All torn asunder by the hand of death!
3 SCHOLAR: The devils whom Faustus served have torn him
      thus:
For 'twixt the hours of twelve and one, methought
10 I heard him shriek and call aloud for help,
At which self time the house seemed all on fire
With dreadful horror of these damnèd fiends.
2 SCHOLAR: Well gentlemen, though Faustus' end be such
As every Christian heart laments to think on,

Yet for he was a scholar once admired   15
For wondrous knowledge in our German schools,
We'll give his mangled limbs due burial;
And all the students, clothed in mourning black,
Shall wait upon his heavy funeral.

(Exeunt.)

(Enter CHORUS.*)*

Cut is the branch that might have grown full straight   20
And burnèd is Apollo's laurel bough
That sometime grew within this learnèd man.
Faustus is gone: regard his hellish fall,
Whose fiendful fortune may exhort the wise
Only to wonder at unlawful things,   25
Whose deepness doth entice such forward wits
To practice more than heavenly power permits.

(Exit.)

(Terminat hora diem; terminat Author opus.)

---

s.d. **Exeunt [Devils with Faustus]** (possibly the devils drag Faustus into the "hell" that was "discovered" at V.ii.114, and then toss his limbs onto the stage, or possibly the limbs are revealed in V.iii.6 by withdrawing a curtain at the rear of the stage)
V.iii.11 self same

---

19 **wait upon** attend; **heavy** sad **Chorus** 21 **laurel bough** symbol of wisdom, here associated with Apollo, god of divination   25 **Only to wonder at** i.e., merely to observe at a distance, with awe   s.d. **Terminat . . . opus** the hour ends the day; the author ends his work (this Latin tag probably is not Marlowe's but the printer's, though it is engaging to believe Marlowe wrote it, ending his play at midnight, the hour of Faustus' death)

■ WILLIAM SHAKESPEARE ■

Given the fact that William Shakespeare (1564–1616) was a commoner and that he worked in the ephemeral trades of the theater, what we know about his life is extraordinarily rich and revealing, especially in comparison to the lives of other playwrights of the period like Christopher Marlowe or John Webster. William Shakespeare was born in Stratford-on-Avon, a town to the northwest of London in Warwickshire. He was baptized on April 26, 1564, and was probably born a few days earlier — his birth date is conventionally given as April 23, the feast day of St. George, the patron saint of England, and the day on which Shakespeare died fifty-two years later in 1616, again at his home in Stratford. One of eight children, Shakespeare was the son of a glover — a tradesman who worked with a variety of leather goods. It is not known whether Shakespeare attended the local school, the King's New School, but like other schools of the period it would have provided him with an extensive grounding in Latin grammar, rhetoric, and literature. Later in his career, Shakespeare often drew on works he could have read at such a school: plays by Terence and Plautus, the poetry of Virgil and Ovid, the writings of Caesar.

He married Anne Hathaway in November of 1582; she was twenty-six and he was eighteen. In May of 1583 they had their first daughter, Susannah, followed by twins, Hamnet and Judith, born in 1585. Although his wife and children remained in Stratford throughout his career, Shakespeare went to London sometime in the late 1580s, possibly joining one of the theater companies that passed through Stratford.

By the 1590s, Shakespeare was established in London as an up-and-coming playwright; he was associated with the Lord Chamberlain's Men; he had written several plays on English history; and he was at work on several comedies and tragedies. When plague closed the theaters in London from the summer of 1592 through the spring of 1594, Shakespeare wrote two narrative poems, *Venus and Adonis* and *The Rape of Lucrece*, which he dedicated to Henry Wriothesley, the third Earl of Southampton, in a bid for patronage. He later wrote *The Phoenix and the Turtle* and circulated a brilliant and ambitious sequence of sonnets in manuscript before publishing it in 1609. As a shareholder of the Lord Chamberlain's Men, Shakespeare would have had many duties; no doubt he acted many parts, and we know he appeared in two plays by his contemporary Ben Jonson — *Every Man In His Humour* and *Sejanus.* In 1598, the Lord Chamberlain's men tore down The Theatre, brought the timbers south of the city and used them to build a new theater, the Globe. The Globe would remain the principal public-theater venue for the rest of Shakespeare's career, complemented by court and private-theater performances.

Shakespeare became the most popular playwright in London. He profited handsomely from his efforts at the Globe and from the patronage of the court, particularly after James I came to the throne in 1603 and took on the Lord Chamberlain's company as his own King's Men. Shakespeare used his income to buy a large house — called New Place — in Stratford, and throughout his career added to his property there; he retired and returned to Stratford in 1613. He drew up a will shortly before he died in 1616, leaving property to his family and mentioning gifts for several of his friends, including members of the King's Men: Richard Burbage, John Heminges, and Henry Condell. Heminges and Condell proved true to Shakespeare, for in 1623 they took Shakespeare's plays and published them in a single large volume. In an era when plays were not regarded as "literature," this was an important event. Although many of Shakespeare's plays had been published individually during his lifetime, roughly half of Shakespeare's plays (*Macbeth, Antony and Cleopatra,* and *The Tempest,* for instance) existed only in manuscript form at Shakespeare's death and certainly would not have survived without the efforts of Heminges and Condell. This complete volume is now usually called the "First Folio" because it is printed in a large, FOLIO-sized format (about twice the dimensions of this book). The First Folio contains 36 of Shakespeare's plays; two more plays published in his lifetime (*Pericles* and *The Two Noble Kinsmen*) were left out of the Folio, and it is generally thought that Shakespeare contributed to a thirty-ninth play, *Sir Thomas More.* Finally, although many people have advanced the thesis that someone else actually wrote the "Shakespeare" plays — Sir Francis Bacon, Francis Walsingham, the Earl of Oxford, among others — these claims belong to the realm of myth, not to the realm of history.

The range of Shakespeare's accomplishment as a playwright is astonishing. Early in his career, Shakespeare wrote two cycles of plays on English history — *Henry VI (Parts 1, 2,* and *3),* and *Richard*

III; and *Richard II, Henry IV* (*Parts 1* and *2*), and *Henry V*—that not only established a vogue for history plays but gave the English audience an epic version of the struggles that founded the Tudor and Stuart dynasties. Shakespeare's early comedies—*The Comedy of Errors, Two Gentlemen of Verona*—are very much in the vein of Plautus. Later comedies—*A Midsummer Night's Dream, As You Like It, Twelfth Night, The Merchant of Venice*—explore a variety of complex relations between love, sexuality, adulthood, ethnic discrimination, power, politics, and money. To many audiences today, Shakespeare is most remembered for *Hamlet* and the magisterial series of tragedies that followed, including *Othello, King Lear,* and *Macbeth*. Shakespeare's achievements often began with experimentation. The major tragedies benefitted from his earlier efforts in the mode of the Roman playwright Seneca in *Titus Andronicus*, in morality drama in *Richard III*, in romantic tragedy in *Romeo and Juliet*, and political intrigue-drama in *Julius Caesar*. In his final years as a playwright, Shakespeare seems to have collaborated with John Fletcher on a few occasions and to have turned his hand to plays in the vein of "tragicomedy," now generally called ROMANCE: *Pericles, Cymbeline, The Winter's Tale,* and *The Tempest*.

HAMLET

In his landmark study, *The Idea of a Theater*, the actor and scholar Francis Fergusson characterized *Hamlet* as one of the "sphinxes of literature," a play that has repeatedly drawn actors, audiences, and scholars into its labyrinthine mystery. Yet while *Hamlet*, like the brooding young prince of Denmark, may now seem like a difficult and philosophical problem, to its original audiences the play was a version of a popular genre on the Elizabethan stage, the revenge tragedy. As in many of his other plays, Shakespeare adapted his tragedy from a variety of known materials. The story of Amlethus, a disinherited Danish prince who uses feigned madness and cunning to avenge his father's murder and regain the throne from his villainous uncle, dates from the twelfth-century *Historia Danica* of the Danish historian Saxo Grammaticus; it was later adapted as a tragic narrative by François de Belleforest and included in his *Histoires tragiques* in 1576. While Shakespeare may have known these versions, it is more certain that he knew a now-lost play on the subject of Hamlet's revenge that was staged in the 1580s. This play—usually called the *Ur-Hamlet* by scholars—was possibly written by Thomas Kyd, the author of another popular revenge tragedy, *The Spanish Tragedy*. While little is known about this play, we do know that it had at least one element of Shakespeare's play; in 1596, the playwright and novelist Thomas Lodge remarked on a play in which a pale ghost "cried so miserably at the Theater, like an oyster-wife, '*Hamlet, revenge!*'"

A ghost, a sinister and deceptive family, a court full of busybodies and spies, a broken romance, an elaborate play-within-the-play, a command—sometimes from beyond the grave—to take revenge, an elaborate finale in which the stage is littered with corpses: these devices were common in revenge tragedies preceeding Shakespeare's play, such as *The Spanish Tragedy*, and common also in those that capitalized on *Hamlet's* success in 1601, plays like John Marston's *The Malcontent* and Cyril Tourneur's *The Revenger's Tragedy* (which opens with a man speaking to a skull) and John Webster's *The White Devil*. While *Hamlet* avails itself of all these devices, it also reflects and refracts them; the play seems to question what it means to take action, simply to *act* let alone take revenge, in a world of such complete duplicity that any behavior might seem the treacherous "actions that a man might play." In his famous essay, "The World of *Hamlet*," Maynard Mack suggests that the play is in the "interrogative mood": not only does Hamlet repeatedly ask questions of himself and others ("To be or not to be . . . ," "Is it not monstrous . . . ," and so on), but much of the action of the play involves, as Polonius suggests, using theatrical "indirections" to "find directions out": Polonius sends Reynaldo to spread dishonorable rumors about Laertes, to see whether Laertes is being virtuous in Paris; Claudius and Polonius "stage" Ophelia for Hamlet, hoping to discover whether he's mad for revenge or madly in love; Hamlet hopes that the players' *Murder of Gonzago* will reveal Claudius' guilt; Polonius hides fatally behind the arras while Hamlet interrogates Gertrude; Claudius stages a "duel" between Hamlet and Laertes that is really a design for murder.

The world of *Hamlet* is a world in which appearances sometimes deceive and sometimes speak the truth: not being able to read the signs—as Ophelia, Rosencrantz and Guildenstern, and Polonius all discover—can be fatal. Indeed, the play's obsession with seeming ("Seems, madam? Nay, it is. I know not 'seems,'" Hamlet declares in his first scene in the play) perhaps explains its obsession with the arts of seeming, with acting, performance, theater. In *Hamlet*, Shakespeare undertakes an extended meditation on the purpose and limits of theater. Hamlet, of course, is quite familiar with the theater, and Shakespeare clearly characterizes the troupe of players as his audience's contemporaries: not only is the company all male, but they seem to have left England—as many professional companies did in the late 1590s—as a result of the "war of the theaters," the contemporary vogue for companies of boy-actors performing satirical plays. Moreover, Hamlet's famous advice to the players (3.2) suggests that he has a keen eye for performance. He chastens the actors not to "mouth it, as many of our players do," not to "saw the air too much with your hand," but to "Suit the action to the word, the word to the action." Yet in *Hamlet*, words and actions are more often than not suited to deception, to the extent that to Hamlet "this goodly frame, the earth, seems . . . a sterile promontory." Hamlet's blatant reference to the Globe itself—an actor, surrounded by the circular frame of the Globe, standing on the bare platform of the stage—suggests a skeptical regard for the theater's creation. While plays like *A Midsummer Night's Dream* or perhaps *The Tempest* suggest the theater's ability to present healing fictions, the theater in *Hamlet* is presented from a more ironic, even disaffected perspective: to be trapped in a theatrical world, a world where performance outruns truth, is to be trapped in a world of empty and sterile pretending.

Shakespeare was clearly captivated by the character of Hamlet, which is often described as the richest acting role in the theatrical repertoire. But the theatricality that besets Hamlet in the shady world of Elsinore also poses problems for Hamlet's many interpreters, not only for Polonius and Claudius—who spend much of the play trying to "read" Hamlet, figure him out—but for the generations of actors, audiences, and scholars who have attempted to "pluck out the heart of [his] mystery." The difficulties of sounding Hamlet, however, are also part of the play's elaborate design. From his opening scene in the play, in which Hamlet both wears the conventional black of mourning and chides his mother for presuming that he is seeming to be in mourning, Hamlet's performance challenges his audiences (both onstage and off) to "read" him, to interpret his character through the signs and signals of his behavior. That is, Hamlet presents the audience with the same challenges that any actor does, inviting us to interpret "that within" from the various behaviors that pass "show." And, contrary to Laurence Olivier—whose brilliant film of the play opens with a voice intoning that *Hamlet* is the story "of a man who could not make up his mind"—Hamlet seems to act decisively throughout the play; what's difficult about reading Hamlet is that it's hard to tell when he's *acting* and when he's "acting in earnest." Hamlet feigns madness in some scenes, but seems madly out of control in others, such as the "nunnery" scene with Ophelia or the scene in Gertrude's closet. He asks the player to act the part of vengeful Pyrrhus, then seems to adopt the murderous swagger of the stage revenger, and then to question his performance ("Why, what an ass am I"). He directs the players to insert a scene into *The Murder of Gonzago* in order to trick Claudius into revealing his guilt, and then can't seem to keep himself off the stage, interrupting and interpreting the play as they play it. He's so offended when Laertes stagily leaps into Ophelia's grave that he outperforms Laertes' overacting: "Nay, an thou'lt mouth, / I'll rant as well as thou." Even Hamlet's soliloquies are problematic in this regard. For although we might think that we hear the "true" Hamlet when he speaks alone onstage, how can we know that Hamlet isn't trying on another role, either for his own benefit or ours—as he seems to do when he plays the revenger in the "O what a rogue and peasant slave am I" speech? And as the play proceeds, Hamlet's soliloquies become less frequent, and less revealing: when he returns from England in Act 5—having sent his friends Rosencrantz and Guildenstern to their deaths—the play provides him with no more solo speeches; like the court, we have only Hamlet's abrupt and irritable actions to go on.

Hamlet was evidently a success when it was first performed in 1600 or 1601; a pirated version of the play (the so-called bad quarto, Q1) was published in 1603, presumably because the play's popularity suggested that a published text could make some money. A version of the play authorized by the King's Men was published in 1604 (the second quarto, Q2), and the play was later included in the 1623 Folio (F); while Q1 is the most corrupt version of the play, Q2 and F are by no means identical, and most modern texts collate elements of both versions. From its inception, *Hamlet* has been a popular play with actors and audiences, and from Richard Burbage's creation of the role, Hamlet has been a mark of distinction in the history of English acting: the Restoration actor Thomas Betterton and the great eighteenth-century actor David Garrick were both admired in the part (Henry

Fielding's novel *Tom Jones* contains a memorable parody of Garrick's performance). In the late nineteenth century Sir Henry Irving, the first actor to be knighted in England, gave a celebrated performance in which Hamlet never left the stage but several other characters (Rosencrantz and Guildenstern, for instance) were cut entirely. In the twentieth century, the play has, if anything, confirmed its reputation as an obligatory test for great actors, who have given a host of brilliant performances: Sir John Gielgud and Sir Laurence Olivier both produced fine stage versions of the play, and Olivier later won a Best Film Oscar for his film version. Since World War II, Richard Burton, Jonathan Pryce, Derek Jacobi, and Michael Pennington are among the many actors to have given distinguished performances of this demanding play. The complexity of the play is something that faces actors even more immediately than readers of the play, for they will have to find a way to suit their acting to Hamlet's wild and whirling character. As Michael Pennington remarked in an essay on playing Hamlet, "to pull it off will take the actor further down into his psyche, memory and imagination, and further outwards to the limits of his technical knowledge and equipment, than he has probably been before."[1]

---

[1] Philip Brockbank, ed., *Players of Shakespeare: Essays in Shakespearean performance by twelve players with the Royal Shakespeare Company.* Cambridge: Cambridge University Press, 1985, p. 117.

HAMLET

WILLIAM SHAKESPEARE

EDITED BY CYRUS HOY

— CHARACTERS —

CLAUDIUS, *King of Denmark*
HAMLET, *son to the late, and nephew to the present king*
POLONIUS, *Lord Chamberlain*
HORATIO, *friend to Hamlet*
LAERTES, *son to Polonius*
VOLTEMAND
CORNELIUS
ROSENCRANTZ
GUILDENSTERN   } *courtiers*
OSRIC
A GENTLEMAN
A PRIEST
MARCELLUS   } *officers*
BERNARDO

FRANCISCO, *a soldier*
REYNALDO, *servant to Polonius*
PLAYERS
TWO CLOWNS, *grave-diggers*
FORTINBRAS, *Prince of Norway*
A NORWEGIAN CAPTAIN
ENGLISH AMBASSADORS
GERTRUDE, *Queen of Denmark, and mother of Hamlet*
OPHELIA, *daughter to Polonius*
GHOST OF HAMLET'S FATHER
LORDS, LADIES, OFFICERS, SOLDIERS, SAILORS, MESSENGERS,
    and ATTENDANTS

SCENE: *Denmark.*

— ACT ONE —

SCENE I

Enter BERNARDO *and* FRANCISCO, *two sentinels.*

BERNARDO: Who's there?
FRANCISCO: Nay, answer me. Stand, and unfold yourself.
BERNARDO: Long live the king!
FRANCISCO: Bernardo?
5 BERNARDO: He.
FRANCISCO: You come most carefully upon your hour.
BERNARDO: 'Tis now struck twelve. Get thee to bed, Francisco.
FRANCISCO: For this relief much thanks. 'Tis bitter cold,
    And I am sick at heart.
10 BERNARDO: Have you had quiet guard?
FRANCISCO: Not a mouse stirring.
BERNARDO: Well, good night.
    If you do meet Horatio and Marcellus,
    The rivals of my watch, bid them make haste.

(Enter HORATIO *and* MARCELLUS.*)*

FRANCISCO: I think I hear them. Stand, ho! Who is there?
15 HORATIO: Friends to this ground.
MARCELLUS: And liegemen to the Dane.
FRANCISCO: Give you good night.
MARCELLUS: O, farewell, honest soldier!
    Who hath relieved you?
FRANCISCO: Bernardo hath my place.
    Give you good night.

(Exit FRANCISCO.*)*

MARCELLUS: Holla, Bernardo!
BERNARDO: Say—
    What, is Horatio there?

HORATIO: A piece of him.
BERNARDO: Welcome, Horatio. Welcome, good Marcellus.   20
HORATIO: What, has this thing appeared again to-night?
BERNARDO: I have seen nothing.
MARCELLUS: Horatio says 'tis but our fantasy,
    And will not let belief take hold of him
    Touching this dreaded sight twice seen of us.   25
    Therefore I have entreated him along
    With us to watch the minutes of this night,
    That if again this apparition come,
    He may approve our eyes and speak to it.
HORATIO: Tush, tush, 'twill not appear.   30
BERNARDO: Sit down awhile,
    And let us once again assail your ears,
    That are so fortified against our story,
    What we have two nights seen.
HORATIO: Well, sit we down,
    And let us hear Bernardo speak of this.
BERNARDO: Last night of all,   35
    When yond same star that's westward from the pole
    Had made his course t' illume that part of heaven
    Where now it burns, Marcellus and myself,
    The bell then beating one—

(Enter GHOST.*)*

MARCELLUS: Peace, break thee off. Look where it comes again.   40
BERNARDO: In the same figure like the king that's dead.
MARCELLUS: Thou art a scholar; speak to it, Horatio.
BERNARDO: Looks 'a not like the king? Mark it, Horatio.
HORATIO: Most like. It harrows me with fear and wonder.
BERNARDO: It would be spoke to.   45
MARCELLUS: Question it, Horatio.
HORATIO: What art thou that usurp'st this time of night

I.i.13 **rivals** partners   15 **Dane** King of Denmark

29 **approve** confirm   36 **pole** polestar   44 **harrows** afflicts, distresses

Together with that fair and warlike form
In which the majesty of buried Denmark
Did sometimes march? By heaven I charge thee, speak.
50 MARCELLUS: It is offended.
BERNARDO: See, it stalks away.
HORATIO: Stay. Speak, speak. I charge thee, speak.

(*Exit* GHOST.)

MARCELLUS: 'Tis gone and will not answer.
BERNARDO: How now, Horatio! You tremble and look pale.
   Is not this something more than fantasy?
55 What think you on't?
HORATIO: Before my God, I might not this believe
   Without the sensible and true avouch
   Of mine own eyes.
MARCELLUS: Is it not like the king?
HORATIO: As thou art to thyself.
60 Such was the very armour he had on
   When he the ambitious Norway combated.
   So frowned he once when, in an angry parle,
   He smote the sledded Polacks on the ice.
   'Tis strange.
65 MARCELLUS: Thus twice before, and jump at this dead hour,
   With martial stalk hath he gone by our watch.
HORATIO: In what particular thought to work I know not,
   But in the gross and scope of mine opinion,
   This bodes some strange eruption to our state.
70 MARCELLUS: Good now, sit down, and tell me he that knows,
   Why this same strict and most observant watch
   So nightly toils the subject of the land,
   And why such daily cast of brazen cannon
   And foreign mart for implements of war;
75 Why such impress of shipwrights, whose sore task
   Does not divide the Sunday from the week.
   What might be toward that this sweaty haste
   Doth make the night joint-laborer with the day?
   Who is't that can inform me?
HORATIO: That can I.
80 At least, the whisper goes so. Our last king,
   Whose image even but now appeared to us,
   Was as you know by Fortinbras of Norway,
   Thereto pricked on by a most emulate pride,
   Dared to the combat; in which our valiant Hamlet
85 (For so this side of our known world esteemed him)
   Did slay this Fortinbras; who by a sealed compact
   Well ratified by law and heraldry,
   Did forfeit, with his life, all those his lands
   Which he stood seized of, to the conqueror;
90 Against the which a moiety competent
   Was gagéd by our king; which had returned
   To the inheritance of Fortinbras,

Had he been vanquisher; as, by the same comart
And carriage of the article designed,
His fell to Hamlet. Now, sir, young Fortinbras,   95
Of unimprovéd mettle hot and full,
Hath in the skirts of Norway here and there
Sharked up a list of lawless resolutes
For food and diet to some enterprise
That hath a stomach in't; which is no other,   100
As it doth well appear unto our state,
But to recover of us by strong hand
And terms compulsatory, those foresaid lands
So by his father lost; and this, I take it,
Is the main motive of our preparations,   105
The source of this our watch, and the chief head
Of this post-haste and romage in the land.
BERNARDO: I think it be no other but e'en so.
   Well may it sort that this portentous figure
   Comes arméd through our watch; so like the king   110
   That was and is the question of these wars.
HORATIO: A mote it is to trouble the mind's eye.
   In the most high and palmy state of Rome,
   A little ere the mightiest Julius fell,
   The graves stood tenantless and the sheeted dead   115
   Did squeak and gibber in the Roman streets;
   As stars with trains of fire, and dews of blood,
   Disasters in the sun; and the moist star,
   Upon whose influence Neptune's empire stands,
   Was sick almost to doomsday with eclipse.   120
   And even the like precurse of feared events,
   As harbingers preceding still the fates
   And prologue to the omen coming on,
   Have heaven and earth together demonstrated
   Unto our climatures and countrymen.   125

(*Enter* GHOST.)

   But soft, behold, lo where it comes again!
   I'll cross it though it blast me.—Stay, illusion.

([GHOST] *spreads his arms.*)

   If thou hast any sound or use of voice,
   Speak to me.
   If there be any good thing to be done,   130
   That may to thee do ease, and grace to me,
   Speak to me.
   If thou art privy to thy country's fate,
   Which happily foreknowing may avoid,
   O, speak!   135
   Or if thou hast uphoarded in thy life
   Extorted treasure in the womb of earth,
   For which, they say, you spirits oft walk in death,

(*The cock crows.*)

---

48 **buried Denmark** the buried King of Denmark   49 **sometimes** formerly   57 **sensible** confirmed by one of the senses   61 **Norway** King of Norway   62 **parle** parley   63 **sledded Polacks** the Poles mounted on sleds or sledges   65 **jump** just, exactly   68 **gross and scope** general drift   72 **toils** causes to toil; **subject** people   74 **mart** traffic, bargaining   75 **impress** conscription   77 **toward** imminent, impending   83 **emulate** ambitious   87 **heraldry** the law of arms, regulating tournaments and state combats   89 **seized** possessed   90 **moiety competent** sufficient portion   91 **gagéd** pledged

93 **comart** joint bargain   94 **carriage** import   96 **unimprovéd** unrestrained   98 **Sharked up** picked up indiscriminately   100 **stomach** spice of adventure   106 **head** fountainhead   107 **romage** turmoil   109 **sort** suit, be in accordance   112 **mote** particle of dust   113 **palmy** flourishing   115 **sheeted** in shrouds   118 **Disasters** ominous signs; **moist star** the moon   121 **precurse** heralding, foreshadowing   122 **harbingers** forerunners; **still** ever   123 **omen** ominous event   125 **climatures** regions   127 **cross it** cross its path   134 **happily** haply, perchance

Speak of it. Stay, and speak. Stop it, Marcellus.
140 MARCELLUS: Shall I strike at it with my partisan?
HORATIO: Do, if it will not stand.
BERNARDO: 'Tis here.
HORATIO: 'Tis here!

(Exit GHOST.*)*

MARCELLUS: 'Tis gone!
    We do it wrong, being so majestical,
    To offer it the show of violence;
145 For it is as the air, invulnerable,
    And our vain blows malicious mockery.
BERNARDO: It was about to speak when the cock crew.
HORATIO: And then it started like a guilty thing
    Upon a fearful summons. I have heard
150 The cock, that is the trumpet to the morn,
    Doth with his lofty and shrill-sounding throat
    Awake the god of day and at his warning,
    Whether in sea or fire, in earth or air,
    Th' extravagant and erring spirit hies
155 To his confine; and of the truth herein
    This present object made probation.
MARCELLUS: It faded on the crowing of the cock.
    Some say that ever 'gainst that season comes
    Wherein our Saviour's birth is celebrated,
160 The bird of dawning singeth all night long,
    And then, they say, no spirit dare stir abroad.
    The nights are wholesome, then no planets strike,
    No fairy takes, nor witch hath power to charm,
    So hallowed and so gracious is that time.
165 HORATIO: So have I heard and do in part believe it.
    But look, the morn in russet mantle clad
    Walks o'er the dew of yon high eastward hill.
    Break we our watch up, and by my advice
    Let us impart what we have seen to-night
170 Unto young Hamlet, for, upon my life
    This spirit, dumb to us, will speak to him.
    Do you consent we shall acquaint him with it,
    As needful in our loves, fitting our duty?
MARCELLUS: Let's do't, I pray, and I this morning know
175 Where we shall find him most convenient.

(Exeunt.)

SCENE II

Flourish. Enter CLAUDIUS, KING OF DENMARK, GERTRUDE
THE QUEEN, COUNCILLORS, *[including]* POLONIUS *and his
son* LAERTES, HAMLET, *cum aliis [including* VOLTEMAND *and*
CORNELIUS.*]*

KING: Though yet of Hamlet our dear brother's death
    The memory be green, and that it us befitted
    To bear our hearts in grief, and our whole kingdom
    To be contracted in one brow of woe,
5   Yet so far hath discretion fought with nature
    That we with wisest sorrow think on him,
    Together with remembrance of ourselves.
    Therefore our sometime sister, now our queen,
    Th' imperial jointress to this warlike state,
    Have we, as 'twere with a defeated joy,   10
    With an auspicious and a dropping eye,
    With mirth in funeral and with dirge in marriage,
    In equal scale weighing delight and dole,
    Taken to wife; nor have we herein barred
    Your better wisdoms, which have freely gone   15
    With this affair along. For all, our thanks.
    Now follows that you know young Fortinbras,
    Holding a weak supposal of our worth,
    Or thinking by our late dear brother's death
    Our state to be disjoint and out of frame,   20
    Colleaguéd with this dream of his advantage,
    He hath not failed to pester us with message
    Importing the surrender of those lands
    Lost by his father, with all bands of law,
    To our most valiant brother. So much for him.   25
    Now for ourself, and for this time of meeting,
    Thus much the business is: we have here writ
    To Norway, uncle of young Fortinbras—
    Who, impotent and bedrid, scarcely hears
    Of this his nephew's purpose—to suppress   30
    His further gait herein, in that the levies,
    The lists, and full proportions are all made
    Out of his subject; and we here dispatch
    You, good Cornelius, and you, Voltemand,
    For bearers of this greeting to old Norway,   35
    Giving to you no further personal power
    To business with the king, more than the scope
    Of these delated articles allow.
    Farewell, and let your haste commend your duty.
CORNELIUS: ⎫ In that and all things will we show our duty. 40
VOLTEMAND: ⎭
KING: We doubt it nothing, heartily farewell.

(Exeunt VOLTEMAND *and* CORNELIUS.*)*

    And now, Laertes, what's the news with you?
    You told us of some suit. What is't, Laertes?
    You cannot speak of reason to the Dane
    And lose your voice. What wouldst thou beg, Laertes, 45
    That shall not be my offer, not thy asking?
    The head is not more native to the heart,
    The hand more instrumental to the mouth,
    Than is the throne of Denmark to thy father.
    What wouldst thou have, Laertes?   50
LAERTES: My dread lord,
    Your leave and favour to return to France,
    From whence, though willingly, I came to Denmark
    To show my duty in your coronation,
    Yet now I must confess, that duty done,
    My thoughts and wishes bend again toward France,   55
    And bow them to your gracious leave and pardon.

---

140 **partisan** pike 154 **extravagant** straying, vagrant; **erring** wandering 156 **probation** proof 158 **'gainst** just before 162 **strike** blast, destroy by malign influence 163 **takes** bewitches
I.ii. s.d. **cum aliis** with others

9 **jointress** a widow who holds a jointure or life interest in an estate
14 **barred** excluded 21 **Colleaguéd** united 31 **gait** proceeding
32 **proportions** forces or supplies for war 38 **delated** expressly stated
44 **Dane** King of Denmark 45 **lose your voice** speak in vain 47 **native** joined by nature 48 **instrumental** serviceable 56 **pardon** indulgence

KING: Have you your father's leave? What says Polonius?

POLONIUS: He hath, my lord, wrung from me my slow leave
  By laborsome petition, and at last
60   Upon his will I sealed my hard consent.
  I do beseech you give him leave to go.

KING: Take thy fair hour, Laertes. Time be thine,
  And thy best graces spend it at thy will.
  But now, my cousin Hamlet, and my son—

65 HAMLET: (*Aside.*) A little more than kin, and less than kind.

KING: How is it that the clouds still hang on you?

HAMLET: Not so, my lord. I am too much in the sun.

QUEEN: Good Hamlet, cast thy nighted color off,
  And let thine eye look like a friend on Denmark.
70   Do not for ever with thy vailéd lids
  Seek for thy noble father in the dust.
  Thou know'st 'tis common—all that lives must die,
  Passing through nature to eternity.

HAMLET: Ay, madam, it is common.

QUEEN: If it be,
75   Why seems it so particular with thee?

HAMLET: Seems, madam? Nay, it is. I know not 'seems.'
  'Tis not alone my inky cloak, good mother,
  Nor customary suits of solemn black,
  Nor windy suspiration of forced breath,
80   No, nor the fruitful river in the eye,
  Nor the dejected haviour of the visage,
  Together with all forms, moods, shapes of grief,
  That can denote me truly. These indeed seem,
  For they are actions that a man might play,
85   But I have that within which passeth show—
  These but the trappings and the suits of woe.

KING: 'Tis sweet and commendable in your nature, Hamlet,
  To give these mourning duties to your father,
  But you must know your father lost a father,
90   That father lost, lost his, and the survivor bound
  In filial obligation for some term
  To do obsequious sorrow. But to persever
  In obstinate condolement is a course
  Of impious stubbornness. 'Tis unmanly grief.
95   It shows a will most incorrect to heaven,
  A heart unfortified, a mind impatient,
  An understanding simple and unschooled.
  For what we know must be, and is as common
  As any the most vulgar thing to sense,
100   Why should we in our peevish opposition
  Take it to heart? Fie, 'tis a fault to heaven,
  A fault against the dead, a fault to nature,
  To reason most absurd, whose common theme
  Is death of fathers, and who still hath cried,
105   From the first corse till he that died to-day,
  'This must be so.' We pray you throw to earth
  This unprevailing woe, and think of us
  As of a father, for let the world take note

  You are the most immediate to our throne,
  And with no less nobility of love   110
  Than that which dearest father bears his son
  Do I impart toward you. For your intent
  In going back to school in Wittenberg,
  It is most retrograde to our desire,
  And we beseech you, bend you to remain   115
  Here in the cheer and comfort of our eye,
  Our chiefest courtier, cousin, and our son.

QUEEN: Let not thy mother lose her prayers, Hamlet.
  I pray thee stay with us, go not to Wittenberg.

HAMLET: I shall in all my best obey you, madam.   120

KING: Why, 'tis a loving and a fair reply.
  Be as ourself in Denmark. Madam, come.
  This gentle and unforced accord of Hamlet
  Sits smiling to my heart, in grace whereof,
  No jocund health that Denmark drinks to-day   125
  But the great cannon to the clouds shall tell,
  And the king's rouse the heaven shall bruit again,
  Respeaking earthly thunder. Come away.

(*Flourish. Exeunt all but* HAMLET.)

HAMLET: O, that this too too sallied flesh would melt,
  Thaw and resolve itself into a dew,   130
  Or that the Everlasting had not fixed
  His canon 'gainst self-slaughter. O God, God,
  How weary, stale, flat, and unprofitable
  Seem to me all the uses of this world!
  Fie on't, ah, fie, 'tis an unweeded garden   135
  That grows to seed. Things rank and gross in nature
  Possess it merely. That it should come to this,
  But two months dead, nay, not so much, not two.
  So excellent a king, that was to this
  Hyperion to a satyr, so loving to my mother,   140
  That he might not beteem the winds of heaven
  Visit her face too roughly. Heaven and earth,
  Must I remember? Why, she would hang on him
  As if increase of appetite had grown
  By what it fed on, and yet, within a month—   145
  Let me not think on't. Frailty, thy name is woman—
  A little month, or ere those shoes were old
  With which she followed my poor father's body
  Like Niobe, all tears, why she—
  O God, a beast that wants discourse of reason   150
  Would have mourned longer—married with my uncle,

---

114 **retrograde** contrary   127 **rouse** full draught of liquor; **bruit** echo 129 **sallied** sullied. "Sallied" is the reading of *Quarto 2 (Q2,* also *Q1). Folio (F)* reads "solid." Since Hamlet's primary concern is with the fact of the flesh's impurity, not with its corporeality, the choice as between Q and F clearly lies with Q. "Sally" is a legitimate sixteenth-century form of "sully"; it occurs in Dekker's *Patient Grissil* (I.i.12), printed in 1603, as F. T. Bowers has pointed out (in "Hamlet's 'Sullied' or 'Solid' Flesh. A Bibliographical Case-History," *Shakespeare Survey* 9 [1956]: p. 44); and it occurs as a noun at II.i.39 of *Hamlet*   132 **canon** law 137 **merely** entirely   140 **Hyperion** the sun god   141 **beteem** allowed   149 **Niobe** wife of Amphion, King of Thebes, she boasted of having more children than Leto and was punished when her seven sons and seven daughters were slain by Apollo and Artemis, children of Leto; in her grief she was changed by Zeus into a stone, which continually dropped tears   150 **wants** lacks; **discourse of reason** the reasoning faculty

---

60 **hard** reluctant   64 **cousin** kinsman of any kind except parent, child, brother, or sister   65 **kin** related as nephew; **kind** (1) affectionate (2) natural, lawful   70 **vailéd** lowered   75 **particular** personal, individual   92 **obsequious** dutiful in performing funeral obsequies or manifesting regard for the dead; **persever** persevere   105 **corse** corpse

My father's brother, but no more like my father
Than I to Hercules. Within a month,
Ere yet the salt of most unrighteous tears
155 Had left the flushing in her gallèd eyes,
She married. O, most wicked speed, to post
With such dexterity to incestuous sheets!
It is not, nor it cannot come to good.
But break my heart, for I must hold my tongue.

(Enter HORATIO, MARCELLUS, *and* BERNARDO.*)*

160 HORATIO: Hail to your lordship!
HAMLET: I am glad to see you well.
     Horatio—or I do forget myself.
HORATIO: The same, my lord, and your poor servant ever.
HAMLET: Sir, my good friend, I'll change that name with you.
     And what make you from Wittenberg, Horatio?
165 Marcellus?
MARCELLUS: My good lord!
HAMLET: I am very glad to see you. *(To* BERNARDO.*)* Good
     even, sir.—
     But what, in faith, make you from Wittenberg?
HORATIO: A truant disposition, good my lord.
170 HAMLET: I would not hear your enemy say so,
     Nor shall you do my ear that violence
     To make it truster of your own report
     Against yourself. I know you are no truant.
     But what is your affair in Elsinore?
175 We'll teach you to drink deep ere you depart.
HORATIO: My lord, I came to see your father's funeral.
HAMLET: I prithee, do not mock me, fellow-student,
     I think it was to see my mother's wedding.
HORATIO: Indeed, my lord, it followed hard upon.
180 HAMLET: Thrift, thrift, Horatio. The funeral baked meats
     Did coldly furnish forth the marriage tables.
     Would I had met my dearest foe in heaven
     Or ever I had seen that day, Horatio!
     My father—methinks I see my father.
185 HORATIO: Where, my lord?
HAMLET: In my mind's eye, Horatio.
HORATIO: I saw him once, 'a was a goodly king.
HAMLET: 'A was a man, take him for all in all,
     I shall not look upon his like again.
HORATIO: My lord, I think I saw him yesternight.
190 HAMLET: Saw who?
HORATIO: My lord, the king your father.
HAMLET: The king my father?
HORATIO: Season your admiration for a while
     With an attent ear, till I may deliver
     Upon the witness of these gentlemen
195 This marvel to you.
HAMLET: For God's love, let me hear!
HORATIO: Two nights together had these gentlemen,
     Marcellus and Bernardo, on their watch
     In the dead waste and middle of the night
     Been thus encountered. A figure like your father,
200 Armed at point exactly, cap-a-pe,

Appears before them, and with solemn march
Goes slow and stately by them. Thrice he walked
By their oppressed and fear-surprisèd eyes
Within his truncheon's length, whilst they, distilled
Almost to jelly with the act of fear,   205
Stand dumb and speak not to him. This to me
In dreadful secrecy impart they did,
And I with them the third night kept the watch,
Where, as they had delivered, both in time,
Form of the thing, each word made true and good,   210
The apparition comes. I knew your father.
These hands are not more like.
HAMLET: But where was this?
MARCELLUS: My lord, upon the platform where we watch.
HAMLET: Did you not speak to it?
HORATIO: My lord, I did,
     But answer made it none. Yet once methought   215
     It lifted up it head and did address
     Itself to motion, like as it would speak;
     But even then the morning cock crew loud,
     And at the sound it shrunk in haste away
     And vanished from our sight.   220
HAMLET: 'Tis very strange.
HORATIO: As I do live, my honoured lord, 'tis true,
     And we did think it writ down in our duty
     To let you know of it.
HAMLET: Indeed, sirs, but
     This troubles me. Hold you the watch to-night?
ALL: We do, my lord.   225
HAMLET: Armed, say you?
ALL: Armed, my lord.
HAMLET: From top to toe?
ALL: My lord, from head to foot.
HAMLET: Then saw you not his face.
HORATIO: O yes, my lord, he wore his beaver up.
HAMLET: What, looked he frowningly?
HORATIO: A countenance more in sorrow than in anger.   230
HAMLET: Pale or red?
HORATIO: Nay, very pale.
HAMLET: And fixed his eyes upon you?
HORATIO: Most constantly.
HAMLET: I would I had been there.
HORATIO: It would have much amazed you.
HAMLET: Very like.
     Stayed it long?   235
HORATIO: While one with moderate haste might tell a
     hundred.
BOTH: Longer, longer.
HORATIO: Not when I saw't.
HAMLET: His beard was grizzled, no?
HORATIO: It was as I have seen it in his life,
     A sable silvered.
HAMLET: I will watch to-night.
     Perchance 'twill walk again.   240
HORATIO: I warr'nt it will.
HAMLET: If it assume my noble father's person,

---

155 **gallèd** sore from rubbing or chafing   163 **change** exchange
164 **make** do   182 **dearest** direst   192 **Season** temper, moderate; **admiration** wonder, astonishment   200 **at point exactly** in every particular; **cap-a-pe** from head to foot

---

204 **truncheon** military leader's baton   216 **it** its   228 **beaver** the part
of the helmet that was drawn down to cover the face   235 **tell** count
237 **grizzled** grayish   239 **sable silvered** black mixed with white

I'll speak to it though hell itself should gape
And bid me hold my peace. I pray you all,
If you have hitherto concealed this sight,
245 Let it be tenable in your silence still,
And whatsomever else shall hap to-night,
Give it an understanding but no tongue.
I will requite your loves. So fare you well.
Upon the platform 'twixt eleven and twelve
250 I'll visit you.
ALL: Our duty to your honor.
HAMLET: Your loves, as mine to you. Farewell.

(Exeunt [all but HAMLET.*])*

My father's spirit in arms? All is not well.
I doubt some foul play. Would the night were come!
Till then sit still, my soul. Foul deeds will rise,
255 Though all the earth o'erwhelm them, to men's eyes.

(Exit.)

SCENE III

Enter LAERTES *and* OPHELIA *his sister.*

LAERTES: My necessaries are embarked. Farewell.
And, sister, as the winds give benefit
And convoy is assistant, do not sleep,
But let me hear from you.
OPHELIA: Do you doubt that?
5 LAERTES: For Hamlet, and the trifling of his favor,
Hold it a fashion and a toy in blood,
A violet in the youth of primy nature,
Forward, not permanent, sweet, not lasting,
The perfume and suppliance of a minute,
10 No more.
OPHELIA: No more but so?
LAERTES: Think it no more.
For nature crescent does not grow alone
In thews and bulk, but as this temple waxes
The inward service of the mind and soul
Grows wide withal. Perhaps he loves you now,
15 And now no soil nor cautel doth besmirch
The virtue of his will, but you must fear,
His greatness weighed, his will is not his own,
For he himself is subject to his birth.
He may not, as unvalued persons do,
20 Carve for himself, for on his choice depends
The safety and health of this whole state,
And therefore must his choice be circumscribed
Unto the voice and yielding of that body
Whereof he is the head. Then if he says he loves you,
25 It fits your wisdom so far to believe it
As he in his particular act and place
May give his saying deed, which is no further
Than the main voice of Denmark goes withal.

Then weigh what loss your honor may sustain
If with too credent ear you list his songs, 30
Or lose your heart, or your chaste treasure open
To his unmastered importunity.
Fear it, Ophelia, fear it, my dear sister,
And keep you in the rear of your affection,
Out of the shot and danger of desire. 35
The chariest maid is prodigal enough
If she unmask her beauty to the moon.
Virtue itself scapes not calumnious strokes.
The canker galls the infants of the spring
Too oft before their buttons be disclosed, 40
And in the morn and liquid dew of youth
Contagious blastments are most imminent.
Be wary then; best safety lies in fear.
Youth to itself rebels, though none else near.
OPHELIA: I shall the effect of this good lesson keep 45
As watchman to my heart. But, good my brother,
Do not as some ungracious pastors do,
Show me the steep and thorny way to heaven,
Whiles like a puffed and reckless libertine
Himself the primrose path of dalliance treads 50
And recks not his own rede.
LAERTES: O, fear me not.

(Enter POLONIUS.*)*

I stay too long. But here my father comes.
A double blessing is a double grace;
Occasion smiles upon a second leave.
POLONIUS: Yet here, Laertes? Aboard, aboard, for shame! 55
The wind sits in the shoulder of your sail,
And you are stayed for. There, my blessing with thee,
And these few precepts in thy memory
Look thou character. Give thy thoughts no tongue,
Nor any unproportioned thought his act. 60
Be thou familiar, but by no means vulgar.
Those friends thou hast, and their adoption tried,
Grapple them to thy soul with hoops of steel,
But do not dull thy palm with entertainment
Of each new-hatched, unfledged courage. Beware 65
Of entrance to a quarrel, but being in,
Bear't that th' opposed may beware of thee.
Give every man thy ear, but few thy voice;
Take each man's censure, but reserve thy judgement.
Costly thy habit as thy purse can buy, 70
But not expressed in fancy; rich not gaudy,
For the apparel oft proclaims the man,
And they in France of the best rank and station
Are of a most select and generous chief in that.
Neither a borrower nor a lender be, 75
For loan oft loses both itself and friend,
And borrowing dulls th' edge of husbandry.
This above all, to thine own self be true,
And it must follow as the night the day

---

245 **tenable** retained 246 **whatsomever** whatsoever 253 **doubt** suspect

I.iii.6 **fashion** the creation of a season only; **toy in blood** passing fancy 7 **primy** of the springtime 11 **crescent** growing 12 **thews** sinews, strength; **this temple** the body 15 **cautel** deceit 16 **will** desire 17 **greatness weighed** high position considered 19 **unvalued persons** persons of no social importance 20 **Carve for himself** act according to his own inclination 23 **yielding** assent

30 **credent** trusting 34 **affection** feeling 39 **canker** canker-worm (which feeds on roses); **galls** injures 40 **buttons** buds 42 **blastments** blights 51 **recks** regards; **rede** counsel 59 **character** engrave 60 **unproportioned** inordinate 61 **vulgar** common 65 **courage** young blood, man of spirit 74 **chief** eminence 77 **husbandry** thriftiness

80   Thou canst not then be false to any man.
         Farewell. My blessing season this in thee!
LAERTES: Most humbly do I take my leave, my lord.
POLONIUS: The time invites you. Go, your servants tend.
LAERTES: Farewell, Ophelia, and remember well
85   What I have said to you.
OPHELIA: 'Tis in my memory locked,
         And you yourself shall keep the key of it.
LAERTES: Farewell.

(Exit LAERTES.)

POLONIUS: What is 't, Ophelia, he hath said to you?
OPHELIA: So please you, something touching the Lord Hamlet.
90 POLONIUS: Marry, well bethought.
         'Tis told me he hath very oft of late
         Given private time to you, and you yourself
         Have of your audience been most free and bounteous.
         If it be so—as so 'tis put on me,
95   And that in way of caution—I must tell you,
         You do not understand yourself so clearly
         As it behooves my daughter and your honor.
         What is between you? Give me up the truth.
OPHELIA: He hath, my lord, of late made many tenders
100   Of his affection to me.
POLONIUS: Affection? Pooh! You speak like a green girl,
         Unsifted in such perilous circumstance.
         Do you believe his tenders, as you call them?
OPHELIA: I do not know, my lord, what I should think.
105 POLONIUS: Marry, I will teach you. Think yourself a baby
         That you have ta'en these tenders for true pay
         Which are not sterling. Tender yourself more dearly,
         Or (not to crack the wind of the poor phrase,
         Running it thus) you'll tender me a fool.
110 OPHELIA: My lord, he hath importuned me with love
         In honorable fashion.
POLONIUS: Ay, fashion you may call it. Go to, go to.
OPHELIA: And hath given countenance to his speech, my lord,
         With almost all the holy vows of heaven.
115 POLONIUS: Ay, springes to catch woodcocks. I do know,
         When the blood burns, how prodigal the soul
         Lends the tongue vows. These blazes, daughter,
         Giving more light than heat, extinct in both
         Even in their promise, as it is a-making,
120   You must not take for fire. From this time
         Be something scanter of your maiden presence.
         Set your entreatments at a higher rate
         Than a command to parle. For Lord Hamlet,
         Believe so much in him that he is young,
125   And with a larger tether may he walk
         Than may be given you. In few, Ophelia,
         Do not believe his vows, for they are brokers,
         Not of that dye which their investments show,
         But mere implorators of unholy suits,
130   Breathing like sanctified and pious bawds,
         The better to beguile. This is for all:

         I would not, in plain terms, from this time forth
         Have you so slander any moment leisure
         As to give words or talk with the Lord Hamlet.
         Look to 't, I charge you. Come your ways.   135
OPHELIA: I shall obey, my lord.

(Exeunt.)

SCENE IV

Enter HAMLET, HORATIO, *and* MARCELLUS.

HAMLET: The air bites shrewdly; it is very cold.
HORATIO: It is a nipping and an eager air.
HAMLET: What hour now?
HORATIO: I think it lacks of twelve.
MARCELLUS: No, it is struck.
HORATIO: Indeed? I heard it not. It then draws near the season   5
         Wherein the spirit held his wont to walk.

(A flourish of trumpets, and two pieces go off.)

         What does this mean, my lord?
HAMLET: The king doth wake to-night and takes his rouse,
         Keeps wassail, and the swagg'ring up-spring reels,
         And as he drains his draughts of Rhenish down,   10
         The kettledrum and trumpet thus bray out
         The triumph of his pledge.
HORATIO: Is it a custom?
HAMLET: Ay, marry, is 't,
         But to my mind, though I am native here
         And to the manner born, it is a custom   15
         More honored in the breach than the observance.
         This heavy-headed revel east and west
         Makes us traduced and taxed of other nations.
         They clepe us drunkards, and with swinish phrase
         Soil our addition, and indeed it takes   20
         From our achievements, though performed at height,
         The pith and marrow of our attribute.
         So oft it chances in particular men,
         That for some vicious mole of nature in them,
         As, in their birth, wherein they are not guilty   25
         (Since nature cannot choose his origin),
         By the o'ergrowth of some complexion,
         Oft breaking down the pales and forts of reason,
         Or by some habit that too much o'er-leavens
         The form of plausive manners—that these men,   30
         Carrying, I say, the stamp of one defect,
         Being nature's livery or fortune's star,
         His virtues else, be they as pure as grace,
         As infinite as man may undergo,
         Shall in the general censure take corruption   35
         From that particular fault. The dram of evil
         Doth all the noble substance often doubt
         To his own scandal.

---

81 **season** ripen 83 **tend** attend, wait 90 **Marry** by Mary 99 **tenders** offers 102 **Unsifted** untried 115 **springes** snares 122 **entreatments** military negotiations for surrender 127 **brokers** go-betweens 128 **investments** clothes 129 **implorators** solicitors

---

I.iv.2 **eager** sharp 9 **wassail** carousal; **up-spring** a German dance 18 **taxed of** censured by 19 **clepe** call 20 **addition** title added to a man's name to denote his rank 22 **attribute** reputation 26 **his** its 27 **complexion** one of the four temperaments (sanguine, melancholy, choleric, and phlegmatic) 29 **o'er-leavens** works change throughout 30 **plausive** pleasing 32 **livery** badge; **star** a person's fortune, rank, or destiny, viewed as determined by the stars 37 **doubt** put out, obliterate 38 **his** its

(Enter GHOST.*)*

HORATIO: Look, my lord, it comes.
HAMLET: Angels and ministers of grace defend us!
40   Be thou a spirit of health or goblin damned,
      Bring with thee airs from heaven or blasts from hell,
      Be thy intents wicked or charitable,
      Thou com'st in such a questionable shape
      That I will speak to thee. I'll call thee Hamlet,
45   King, father, royal Dane. O, answer me!
      Let me not burst in ignorance, but tell
      Why thy canonized bones, hearséd in death,
      Have burst their cerements; why the sepulchre
      Wherein we saw thee quietly interred,
50   Hath oped his ponderous and marble jaws
      To cast thee up again. What may this mean
      That thou, dead corse, again in complete steel
      Revisits thus the glimpses of the moon,
      Making night hideous, and we fools of nature
55   So horridly to shake our disposition
      With thoughts beyond the reaches of our souls?
      Say, why is this? wherefore? What should we do?

([GHOST] *beckons.)*

HORATIO: It beckons you to go away with it,
      As if it some impartment did desire
60   To you alone.
MARCELLUS: Look, with what courteous action
      It waves you to a more removéd ground.
      But do not go with it.
HORATIO: No, by no means.
HAMLET: It will not speak; then I will follow it.
HORATIO: Do not, my lord.
HAMLET: Why, what should be the fear?
65   I do not set my life at a pin's fee,
      And for my soul, what can it do to that,
      Being a thing immortal as itself?
      It waves me forth again. I'll follow it.
HORATIO: What if it tempt you toward the flood, my lord,
70   Or to the dreadful summit of the cliff
      That beetles o'er his base into the sea,
      And there assume some other horrible form,
      Which might deprive your sovereignty of reason
      And draw you into madness? Think of it.
75   The very place puts toys of desperation,
      Without more motive, into every brain
      That looks so many fathoms to the sea
      And hears it roar beneath.
HAMLET: It waves me still.
      Go on. I'll follow thee.
80 MARCELLUS: You shall not go, my lord.
HAMLET: Hold off your hands.
HORATIO: Be ruled; You shall not go.
HAMLET: My fate cries out,
      And makes each petty artere in this body
      As hardy as the Nemean lion's nerve.

      Still am I called. Unhand me, gentlemen.
      By heaven, I'll make a ghost of him that lets me.   85
      I say, away!—Go on. I'll follow thee.

([Exeunt] GHOST *and* HAMLET.*)*

HORATIO: He waxes desperate with imagination.
MARCELLUS: Let's follow. 'Tis not fit thus to obey him.
HORATIO: Have after. To what issue will this come?
MARCELLUS: Something is rotten in the state of Denmark.   90
HORATIO: Heaven will direct it.
MARCELLUS: Nay, let's follow him.

(Exeunt.)

SCENE V

Enter GHOST *and* HAMLET.

HAMLET: Whither wilt thou lead me? Speak. I'll go no further.
GHOST: Mark me.
HAMLET: I will.
GHOST: My hour is almost come
      When I to sulph'rous and tormenting flames
      Must render up myself.
HAMLET: Alas, poor ghost!
GHOST: Pity me not, but lend thy serious hearing   5
      To what I shall unfold.
HAMLET: Speak. I am bound to hear.
GHOST: So art thou to revenge, when thou shalt hear.
HAMLET: What?
GHOST: I am thy father's spirit,
      Doomed for a certain term to walk the night,   10
      And for the day confined to fast in fires,
      Till the foul crimes done in my days of nature
      Are burnt and purged away. But that I am forbid
      To tell the secrets of my prison house,
      I could a tale unfold whose lightest word   15
      Would harrow up thy soul, freeze thy young blood,
      Make thy two eyes like stars start from their spheres,
      Thy knotted and combinéd locks to part,
      And each particular hair to stand an end,
      Like quills upon the fretful porpentine.   20
      But this eternal blazon must not be
      To ears of flesh and blood. List, list, O, list!
      If thou didst ever thy dear father love—
HAMLET: O God!
GHOST: Revenge his foul and most unnatural murder.   25
HAMLET: Murder!
GHOST: Murder most foul, as in the best it is,
      But this most foul, strange, and unnatural.
HAMLET: Haste me to know't, that I, with wings as swift
      As meditation or the thoughts of love,   30
      May sweep to my revenge.
GHOST: I find thee apt,
      And duller shouldst thou be than the fat weed
      That roots itself in ease on Lethe wharf,
      Wouldst thou not stir in this. Now, Hamlet, hear.
      'Tis given out that, sleeping in my orchard,   35

---

47 **canonized** buried according to the church's rule; **hearséd** coffined, buried   59 **impartment** communication   71 **beetles** juts out   73 **sovereignty of reason** state of being ruled by reason   75 **toys** fancies, impules   82 **artere** artery   83 **Nemean lion** slain by Hercules in the performance of one of his twelve labors

---

85 **lets** hinders

I.v.19 **an** on   20 **porpentine** porcupine   21 **eternal blazon** proclamation of the secrets of eternity   33 **Lethe** the river in Hades that brings forgetfulness

A serpent stung me. So the whole ear of Denmark
Is by a forgéd process of my death
Rankly abused. But know, thou noble youth,
The serpent that did sting thy father's life
40 Now wears his crown.
HAMLET: O my prophetic soul!
My uncle!
GHOST: Ay, that incestuous, that adulterate beast,
With witchcraft of his wits, with traitorous gifts—
O wicked wit and gifts that have the power
45 So to seduce!—won to his shameful lust
The will of my most seeming virtuous queen.
O Hamlet, what a falling off was there,
From me, whose love was of that dignity
That it went hand in hand even with the vow
50 I made to her in marriage, and to decline
Upon a wretch whose natural gifts were poor
To those of mine!
But virtue, as it never will be moved,
Though lewdness court it in a shape of heaven,
55 So lust, though to a radiant angel linked,
Will sate itself in a celestial bed
And prey on garbage.
But soft, methinks I scent the morning air.
Brief let me be. Sleeping within my orchard,
60 My custom always of the afternoon,
Upon my secure hour thy uncle stole,
With juice of cursed hebona in a vial,
And in the porches of my ears did pour
The leperous distilment, whose effect
65 Holds such an enmity with blood of man
That swift as quicksilver it courses through
The natural gates and alleys of the body,
And with a sudden vigor it doth posset
And curd, like eager droppings into milk,
70 The thin and wholesome blood. So did it mine,
And a most instant tetter barked about
Most lazar-like with vile and loathsome crust
All my smooth body.
Thus was I sleeping by a brother's hand
75 Of life, of crown, of queen, at once dispatched,
Cut off even in the blossoms of my sin,
Unhouseled, disappointed, unaneled,
No reck'ning made, but sent to my account
With all my imperfections on my head.
80 O, horrible! O, horrible! most horrible!
If thou hast nature in thee, bear it not,
Let not the royal bed of Denmark be
A couch for luxury and damnéd incest.
But howsomever thou pursues this act,
85 Taint not thy mind, nor let thy soul contrive
Against thy mother aught. Leave her to heaven,
And to those thorns that in her bosom lodge
To prick and sting her. Fare thee well at once.

The glowworm shows the matin to be near,
And gins to pale his uneffectual fire.   90
Adieu, adieu, adieu. Remember me.
(Exit.)
HAMLET: O all you host of heaven! O earth! What else?
And shall I couple hell? O, fie! Hold, hold, my heart,
And you, my sinews, grow not instant old,
But bear me stiffly up. Remember thee?   95
Ay, thou poor ghost, whiles memory holds a seat
In this distracted globe. Remember thee?
Yea, from the table of my memory
I'll wipe away all trivial fond records,
All saws of books, all forms, all pressures past   100
That youth and observation copied there,
And thy commandment all alone shall live
Within the book and volume of my brain,
Unmixed with baser matter. Yes, by heaven!
O most pernicious woman!   105
O villain, villain, smiling, damnéd villain!
My tables—meet it is I set it down
That one may smile, and smile, and be a villain
At least I am sure it may be so in Denmark.   *(Writing.)*
So, uncle, there you are. Now to my word: 110
It is 'Adieu, adieu! Remember me,'
I have sworn't.

(Enter HORATIO *and* MARCELLUS.*)*

HORATIO: My lord, my lord!
MARCELLUS: Lord Hamlet!
HORATIO: Heavens secure him!
HAMLET: So be it!
MARCELLUS: Illo, ho, ho, my lord!   115
HAMLET: Hillo, ho, ho, boy! Come, bird, come.
MARCELLUS: How is't, my noble lord?
HORATIO: What news, my lord?
HAMLET: O, wonderful!
HORATIO: Good my lord, tell it.
HAMLET: No, you will reveal it.
HORATIO: Not I, my lord, by heaven.   120
MARCELLUS: Nor I, my lord.
HAMLET: How say you then, would heart of man once think it?
But you'll be secret?
BOTH: Ay, by heaven, my lord.
HAMLET: There's never a villain dwelling in all Denmark
But he's an arrant knave.
HORATIO: There needs no ghost, my lord, come from the grave   125
To tell us this.
HAMLET: Why, right, you are in the right,
And so without more circumstance at all
I hold it fit that we shake hands and part,
You, as your business and desire shall point you,
For every man has business and desire   130
Such as it is, and for my own poor part,
I will go pray.

---

37 **process** account   61 **secure** free from suspicion   62 **hebona** an
imaginary poison, associated with henbane   68 **posset** curdle
69 **eager** acid   71 **tetter** a skin eruption; **barked** covered as with bark
77 **Unhouseled** without having received the sacrament; **disappointed**
unprepared; **unaneled** without extreme unction   83 **luxury** lust

89 **matin** morning   97 **globe** head   98 **table** writing tablet, memo-
randum book (as at line 107, below; here metaphorically of the mind)
99 **fond** foolish   100 **saws** sayings; **forms** concepts; **pressures** impressions   115 **Illo, ho, ho** cry of the falconer to summon his hawk

HORATIO: These are but wild and whirling words, my lord.
HAMLET: I am sorry they offend you, heartily;
135   Yes, faith, heartily.
HORATIO: There's no offence, my lord.
HAMLET: Yes, by Saint Patrick, but there is, Horatio,
      And much offence too. Touching this vision here,
      It is an honest ghost, that let me tell you
      For your desire to know what is between us,
140   O'ermaster't as you may. And now, good friends,
      As you are friends, scholars, and soldiers,
      Give me one poor request.
HORATIO: What is't, my lord? We will.
HAMLET: Never make known what you have seen to-night.
145 BOTH: My lord, we will not.
HAMLET: Nay, but swear't.
HORATIO: In faith,
      My lord, not I.
MARCELLUS: Nor I, my lord, in faith.
HAMLET: Upon my sword.
MARCELLUS: We have sworn, my lord, already.
HAMLET: Indeed, upon my sword, indeed.

(Ghost cries under the stage.)

GHOST: Swear.
HAMLET: Ha, ha, boy, say'st thou so? Art thou there, truepenny?
150   Come on. You hear this fellow in the cellarage.
      Consent to swear.
HORATIO: Propose the oath, my lord.
HAMLET: Never to speak of this that you have seen,
      Swear by my sword.
GHOST: (*Beneath.*) Swear.
155 HAMLET: Hic et ubique? Then we'll shift our ground.
      Come hither, gentlemen,
      And lay your hands again upon my sword.
      Swear by my sword
      Never to speak of this that you have heard.
160 GHOST: (*Beneath.*) Swear by his sword.
HAMLET: Well said, old mole! Canst work i' th' earth so fast?
      A worthy pioneer! Once more remove, good friends.
HORATIO: O day and night, but this is wondrous strange!
HAMLET: And therefore as a stranger give it welcome.
165   There are more things in heaven and earth, Horatio,
      Than are dreamt of in your philosophy.
      But come.
      Here as before, never, so help you mercy,
      How strange or odd some'er I bear myself
170   (As I perchance hereafter shall think meet
      To put an antic disposition on),
      That you, at such times, seeing me, never shall,
      With arms encumbered thus, or this head-shake,
      Or by pronouncing of some doubtful phrase,
175   As 'Well, well, we know,' or 'We could, and if we would'
      Or 'If we list to speak,' or 'There be, and if they might'
      Or such ambiguous giving out, to note

      That you know aught of me—this do swear,
      So grace and mercy at your most need help you.
GHOST: (*Beneath.*) Swear.   180
HAMLET: Rest, rest, perturbèd spirit! So, gentlemen,
      With all my love I do commend me to you,
      And what so poor a man as Hamlet is
      May do t' express his love and friending to you,
      God willing, shall not lack. Let us go in together,   185
      And still your fingers on your lips, I pray.
      The time is out of joint. O cursèd spite
      That ever I was born to set it right!
      Nay, come, let's go together.

(Exeunt.)

— **ACT TWO** —

SCENE I

Enter old POLONIUS *with his man [*REYNALDO*].*

POLONIUS: Give him this money and these notes, Reynaldo.
REYNALDO: I will, my lord.
POLONIUS: You shall do marvellous wisely, good Reynaldo,
      Before you visit him, to make inquire
      Of his behavior.   5
REYNALDO: My lord, I did intend it.
POLONIUS: Marry, well said, very well said. Look you, sir,
      Enquire me first what Danskers are in Paris,
      And how, and who, what means, and where they keep,
      What company, at what expense; and finding
      By this encompassment and drift of question   10
      That they do know my son, come you more nearer
      Than your particular demands will touch it.
      Take you as 'twere some distant knowledge of him,
      As thus, 'I know his father and his friends,
      And in part him.' do you mark this, Reynaldo?   15
REYNALDO: Ay, very well, my lord.
POLONIUS: 'And in part him, but,' you may say, 'not well,
      But if't be he I mean, he's very wild,
      Addicted so and so.' And there put on him
      What forgeries you please; marry, none so rank   20
      As may dishonour him. Take heed of that.
      But, sir, such wanton, wild, and usual slips
      As are companions noted and most known
      To youth and liberty.
REYNALDO: As gaming, my lord?
POLONIUS: Ay, or drinking, fencing, swearing, quarrelling,   25
      Drabbing—you may go so far.
REYNALDO: My lord, that would dishonour him.
POLONIUS: Faith, no, as you may season it in the charge.
      You must not put another scandal on him,
      That he is open to incontinency.   30
      That's not my meaning. But breathe his faults so quaintly
      That they may seem the taints of liberty,
      The flash and outbreak of a fiery mind,

---

136 Saint Patrick associated, in the late middle ages, with purgatory, whence the ghost has presumably come   **149 truepenny** honest fellow   **155 Hic et ubique** here and everywhere   **162 pioneer** miner   **171 antic** mad   **173 encumbered** folded

II.i.7 Danskers Danes   **8 means** wealth   **10 encompassment** talking round the matter   **20 forgeries** invented wrongdoings   **24 liberty** license   **26 Drabbing** whoring   **28 season** moderate   **31 quaintly** delicately

A savageness in unreclaiméd blood,
35   Of general assault.
REYNALDO: But, my good lord—
POLONIUS: Wherefore should you do this?
REYNALDO: Ay, my lord,
  I would know that.
POLONIUS: Marry, sir, here's my drift,
  And I believe it is a fetch of warrant.
  You laying these slight sullies on my son,
40   As 'twere a thing a little soiled i' th' working,
  Mark you,
  Your party in converse, him you would sound,
  Having ever seen in the prenominate crimes
  The youth you breathe of guilty, be assured
45   He closes with you in this consequence,
  'Good sir', or so, or 'friend', or 'gentleman',
  According to the phrase or the addition
  Of man and country.
REYNALDO: Very good, my lord.
POLONIUS: And then, sir, does 'a this—'a does—What was I
  about to say?
50   By the mass, I was about to say something.
  Where did I leave?
REYNALDO: At 'closes in the consequence.'
POLONIUS: At 'closes in the consequence'—ay, marry,
  He closes thus: 'I know the gentleman.
55   I saw him yesterday, or th' other day,
  Or then, or then, with such, or such, and as you say,
  There was 'a gaming, there o'ertook in 's rouse;
  There falling out at tennis', or perchance
  'I saw him enter such a house of sale',
60   Videlicet, a brothel, or so forth.
  See you, now—
  Your bait of falsehood takes this carp of truth,
  And thus do we of wisdom and of reach,
  With windlasses and with assays of bias,
65   By indirections find directions out;
  So by my former lecture and advice
  Shall you my son. You have me, have you not?
REYNALDO: My lord, I have.
POLONIUS: God bye ye; fare ye well.
REYNALDO: Good my lord.
70 POLONIUS: Observe his inclination in yourself.
REYNALDO: I shall, my lord.
POLONIUS: And let him ply his music.
REYNALDO: Well, my lord.
POLONIUS: Farewell.

(*Exit* REYNALDO.)

(*Enter* OPHELIA.)

        How now, Ophelia! what's the matter?
OPHELIA: O my lord, my lord, I have been so affrighted!
75 POLONIUS: With what, i' th' name of God?
OPHELIA: My lord, as I was sewing in my closet,

Lord Hamlet, with his doublet all unbraced,
No hat upon his head, his stockings fouled,
Ungartered, and down-gyvéd to his ankle,
Pale as his shirt, his knees knocking each other,   80
And with a look so piteous in purport
As if he had been looséd out of hell
To speak of horrors—he comes before me.
POLONIUS: Mad for thy love?
OPHELIA: My lord, I do not know,
  But truly I do fear it.
POLONIUS: What said he?   85
OPHELIA: He took me by the wrist, and held me hard,
  Then goes he to the length of all his arm,
  And with his other hand thus o'er his brow,
  He falls to such perusal of my face
  As 'a would draw it. Long stayed he so.   90
  At last, a little shaking of mine arm
  And thrice his head thus waving up and down,
  He raised a sigh so piteous and profound
  As it did seem to shatter all his bulk
  And end his being. That done, he lets me go,   95
  And with his head over his shoulder turned,
  He seemed to find his way without his eyes,
  For out adoors he went without their helps,
  And to the last bended their light on me.
POLONIUS: Come, go with me. I will go seek the king.   100
  This is the very ecstasy of love,
  Whose violent property fordoes itself,
  And leads the will to desperate undertakings
  As oft as any passion under heaven
  That does afflict our natures. I am sorry.   105
  What, have you given him any hard words of late?
OPHELIA: No, my good lord, but as you did command
  I did repel his letters, and denied
  His access to me.
POLONIUS: That hath made him mad.
  I am sorry that with better heed and judgement   110
  I had not quoted him. I feared he did but trifle,
  And meant to wrack thee; but beshrew my jealousy.
  By heaven, it is as proper to our age
  To cast beyond ourselves in our opinions
  As it is common for the younger sort   115
  To lack discretion. Come, go we to the king.
  This must be known, which being kept close, might move
  More grief to hide than hate to utter love.
  Come.

(*Exeunt.*)

SCENE II

Flourish. Enter KING *and* QUEEN, ROSENCRANTZ, *and* GUILDEN-STERN [*and* ATTENDANTS].

KING: Welcome, dear Rosencrantz and Guildenstern.
  Moreover that we much did long to see you,
  The need we have to use you did provoke
  Our hasty sending. Something have you heard

---

34 **unreclaiméd** untamed   35 **Of general assault** assailing all
38 **fetch of warrant** allowable device   43 **prenominate** before-named
45 **closes** agrees; **in this consequence** as follows   47 **addition** title
60 **Videlicet** namely   63 **reach** ability   64 **windlasses** roundabout approaches; **assays of bias** indirect attempts   68 **God buy ye** God be
with you   76 **closet** private room

---

77 **unbraced** unlaced   79 **down-gyvéd** hanging down, like gyves or
fetters on a prisoner's ankles   101 **ecstasy** madness   102 **fordoes** destroys   111 **quoted** observed   112 **wrack** ruin   113 **proper to** characteristic of   117 **close** secret; **move** cause

5 Of Hamlet's transformation—so call it,
Sith nor th' exterior nor the inward man
Resembles that it was. What it should be,
More than his father's death, that thus hath put him
So much from th' understanding of himself,
10 I cannot dream of. I entreat you both
That, being of so young days brought up with him,
And sith so neighboured to his youth and havior,
That you vouchsafe your rest here in our court
Some little time, so by your companies
15 To draw him on to pleasures, and to gather
So much as from occasion you may glean,
Whether aught to us unknown afflicts him thus,
That opened, lies within our remedy.
QUEEN: Good gentlemen, he hath much talked of you,
20 And sure I am two men there is not living
To whom he more adheres. If it will please you
To show us so much gentry and good will
As to expend your time with us awhile
For the supply and profit of our hope,
25 Your visitation shall receive such thanks
As fits a king's remembrance.
ROSENCRANTZ: Both your majesties
Might, by the sovereign power you have of us,
Put your dread pleasures more into command
Than to entreaty.
GUILDENSTERN: But we both obey,
30 And here give up ourselves in the full bent
To lay our service freely at your feet,
To be commanded.
KING: Thanks, Rosencrantz and gentle Guildenstern.
QUEEN: Thanks, Guildenstern and gentle Rosencrantz.
35 And I beseech you instantly to visit
My too much changed son. Go, some of you,
And bring these gentlemen where Hamlet is.
GUILDENSTERN: Heavens make our presence and our
    practices
Pleasant and helpful to him!
QUEEN: Ay, amen!

(*Exeunt* ROSENCRANTZ *and* GUILDENSTERN [*with some*
ATTENDANTS].)

(*Enter* POLONIUS.)

40 POLONIUS: Th' ambassadors from Norway, my good lord,
    Are joyfully returned.
KING: Thou still hast been the father of good news.
POLONIUS: Have I, my lord? I assure my good liege,
    I hold my duty as I hold my soul,
45 Both to my God and to my gracious king;
    And I do think—or else this brain of mine
    Hunts not the trail of policy so sure
    As it hath used to do—that I have found
    The very cause of Hamlet's lunacy.
50 KING: O, speak of that, that do I long to hear.
POLONIUS: Give first admittance to th' ambassadors.
    My news shall be the fruit to that great feast.
KING: Thyself do grace to them, and bring them in.

(*Exit* POLONIUS.)

He tells me, my dear Gertrude, he hath found
The head and source of all your son's distemper.   55
QUEEN: I doubt it is no other but the main,
    His father's death and our o'erhasty marriage.
KING: Well, we shall sift him.

(*Enter Ambassadors [(*VOLTEMAND *and* CORNELIUS), *with*
POLONIUS].)

                      Welcome, my good friends,
    Say, Voltemand, what from our brother Norway?
VOLTEMAND: Most fair return of greetings and desires.   60
    Upon our first, he sent out to suppress
    His nephew's levies, which to him appeared
    To be a preparation 'gainst the Polack,
    But better looked into, he truly found
    It was against your highness, whereat grieved,   65
    That so his sickness, age, and impotence
    Was falsely borne in hand, sends out arrests
    On Fortinbras, which he in brief obeys,
    Receives rebuke from Norway, and in fine,
    Makes vow before his uncle never more   70
    To give th' assay of arms against your majesty.
    Whereon old Norway, overcome with joy,
    Gives him three score thousand crowns in annual fee,
    And his commission to employ those soldiers,
    So levied as before, against the Polack,   75
    With an entreaty, herein further shown,   (*Gives a paper.*)
    That it might please you to give quiet pass
    Through your dominions for this enterprise,
    On such regards of safety and allowance
    As therein are set down.   80
KING: It likes us well,
    And at our more considered time we'll read,
    Answer, and think upon this business.
    Meantime we thank you for your well-took labor.
    Go to your rest; at night we'll feast together.
    Most welcome home!   85

(*Exeunt* AMBASSADORS.)

POLONIUS: This business is well ended.
    My liege and madam, to expostulate
    What majesty should be, what duty is,
    Why day is day, night night, and time is time,
    Were nothing but to waste night, day and time.
    Therefore, since brevity is the soul of wit,   90
    And tediousness the limbs and outward flourishes,
    I will be brief. Your noble son is mad.
    Mad call I it, for to define true madness,
    What is 't but to be nothing else but mad?
    But let that go.   95
QUEEN: More matter with less art.
POLONIUS: Madam, I swear I use no art at all.
    That he is mad, 'tis true: 'tis true 'tis pity.
    And pity 'tis 'tis true. A foolish figure,
    But farewell it, for I will use no art.
    Mad let us grant him, then, and now remains   100
    That we find out the cause of this effect,

II.ii.6 **Sith** since   18 **opened** disclosed   22 **gentry** courtesy   42 **still**
ever

56 **doubt** suspect   63 **the Polack** the Polish nation   67 **borne in**
hand deceived   69 **in fine** in the end   71 **assay** trial   79 **regards**
considerations   90 **wit** understanding   95 **matter** meaning, sense

Or rather say the cause of this defect,
For this effect defective comes by cause.
Thus it remains, and the remainder thus.
105 Perpend.
I have a daughter—have while she is mine—
Who in her duty and obedience, mark,
Hath given me this. Now gather, and surmise. *(Reads.)*
'To the celestial, and my soul's idol, the most beautified
110 Ophelia,'—That's an ill phrase, a vile phrase, 'beautified' is
a vile phrase. But you shall hear. Thus: *(Reads.)*
'In her excellent white bosom, these, etc.'
QUEEN: Came this from Hamlet to her?
POLONIUS: Good madam, stay awhile. I will be faithful.
(Reads Letter.)
115   'Doubt thou the stars are fire,
                 Doubt that the sun doth move;
                 Doubt truth to be a liar;
                 But never doubt I love.

           'O dear Ophelia, I am ill at these numbers. I have not
120 art to reckon my groans, but that I love thee best, O most
best, believe it. Adieu.
                 'Thine evermore, most dear lady, whilst
                      this machine is to him, HAMLET.'
This in obedience hath my daughter shown me,
125 And more above, hath his solicitings,
As they fell out by time, by means and place,
All given to mine ear.
KING: But how hath she
Received his love?
POLONIUS: What do you think of me?
KING: As of a man faithful and honourable.
130 POLONIUS: I would fain prove so. But what might you think,
When I had seen this hot love on the wing,
(As I perceived it, I must tell you that,
Before my daughter told me), what might you,
Or my dear majesty your queen here, think,
135 If I had played the desk or table-book,
Or given my heart a winking, mute and dumb,
Or looked upon this love with idle sight,
What might you think? No, I went round to work,
And my young mistress thus I did bespeak:
140 'Lord Hamlet is a prince out of thy star.
This must not be'. and then I prescripts gave her,
That she should lock herself from his resort,
Admit no messengers, receive no tokens,
Which done, she took the fruits of my advice;
145 And he repelled, a short tale to make,
Fell into a sadness, then into a fast,
Thence to a watch, thence into a weakness,
Thence to a lightness, and, by this declension,
Into the madness wherein now he raves,
150 And all we mourn for.
KING: Do you think 'tis this?
QUEEN: It may be, very like.

POLONIUS: Hath there been such a time—I would fain know
    that—
That I have positively said "Tis so,'
When it proved otherwise?
KING: Not that I know.
POLONIUS: *(Pointing to his head and shoulder.)* Take this from   155
    this, if this be otherwise:
If circumstances lead me, I will find
Where truth is hid, though it were hid indeed
Within the centre.
KING: How may we try it further?
POLONIUS: You know, sometimes he walks four hours together
Here in the lobby.
QUEEN: So he does, indeed.   160
POLONIUS: At such a time I'll loose my daughter to him.
Be you and I behind an arras then.
Mark the encounter. If he love her not,
And be not from his reason fall'n thereon,
Let me be no assistant for a state,   165
But keep a farm and carters.
KING: We will try it.
(Enter HAMLET *[reading on a book].)*
QUEEN: But look where sadly the poor wretch comes reading.
POLONIUS: Away, I do beseech you both away,
I'll board him presently.

([Exeunt] KING *and* QUEEN *[with* ATTENDANTS.*])*
                 O, give me leave.
How does my good Lord Hamlet?   170
HAMLET: Well, God-a-mercy.
POLONIUS: Do you know me, my lord?
HAMLET: Excellent well, you are a fishmonger.
POLONIUS: Not I, my lord.
HAMLET: Then I would you were so honest a man.   175
POLONIUS: Honest, my lord?
HAMLET: Ay, sir, to be honest as this world goes, is to be one
    man picked out of ten thousand.
POLONIUS: That's very true, my lord.
HAMLET: For if the sun breed maggots in a dead dog, being a   180
    good kissing carrion—Have you a daughter?
POLONIUS: I have, my lord.
HAMLET: Let her not walk i' th' sun. Conception is a blessing,
    but as your daughter may conceive—friend, look to 't.
POLONIUS: *(Aside.)* How say you by that? Still harping on my   185
    daughter. Yet he knew me not at first. 'A said I was a fish-
    monger. 'A is far gone. And truly in my youth I suffered
    much extremity for love, very near this. I'll speak to him
    again.—What do you read, my lord?
HAMLET: Words, words, words.   190
POLONIUS: What is the matter, my lord?
HAMLET: Between who?
POLONIUS: I mean the matter that you read, my lord.
HAMLET: Slanders, sir; for the satirical rogue says here that old
    men have grey beards, that their faces are wrinkled, their   195
    eyes purging thick amber and plum-tree gum, and that they
    have a plentiful lack of wit, together with most weak
    hams—all which, sir, though I most powerfully and po-
    tently believe, yet I hold it not honesty to have it thus set

---

105 **Perpend** consider   119 **numbers** verses   123 **machine** body
135 **played . . . table-book** acted as silent go-between   138 **round** directly   147 **watch** sleeplessness   148 **lightness** lightheadedness

---

158 **centre** centre of the earth and of the Ptlolemaic universe
169 **board** accost; **presently** immediately

200   down, for yourself, sir, shall grow old as I am, if like a crab
      you could go backward.

      POLONIUS: (*Aside.*) Though this be madness, yet there is
      method in 't.—Will you walk out of the air, my lord?

      HAMLET: Into my grave?

205   POLONIUS: (*Aside.*) Indeed, that's out of the air. How pregnant
      sometimes his replies are! a happiness that often madness
      hits on, which reason and sanity could not so prosperously
      be delivered of. I will leave him, and suddenly contrive the
      means of meeting between him and my daughter.—My

210   lord, I will take my leave of you.

      HAMLET: You cannot take from me anything that I will not
      more willingly part withal—except my life, except my life,
      except my life.

      (*Enter* GUILDENSTERN *and* ROSENCRANTZ.)

      POLONIUS: Fare you well, my lord.

215   HAMLET: These tedious old fools!

      POLONIUS: You go to seek the Lord Hamlet. There he is.

      ROSENCRANTZ: (*To* POLONIUS.) God save you, sir!

      (*Exit* POLONIUS.)

      GUILDENSTERN: My honored lord!

      ROSENCRANTZ: My most dear lord!

220   HAMLET: My excellent good friends! How dost thou,
      Guildenstern?
      Ah, Rosencrantz! Good lads, how do ye both?

      ROSENCRANTZ: As the indifferent children of the earth.

      GUILDENSTERN: Happy in that we are not over-happy;

225   On Fortune's cap we are not the very button.

      HAMLET: Nor the soles of her shoe?

      ROSENCRANTZ: Neither, my lord.

      HAMLET: Then you live about her waist, or in the middle of
      her favors?

230   GUILDENSTERN: Faith, her privates we.

      HAMLET: In the secret parts of Fortune? O, most true, she is a
      strumpet. What news?

      ROSENCRANTZ: None, my lord, but that the world's grown
      honest.

235   HAMLET: Then is doomsday near. But your news is not true.
      Let me question more in particular. What have you, my
      good friends, deserved at the hands of Fortune, that she
      sends you to prison hither?

      GUILDENSTERN: Prison, my lord!

240   HAMLET: Denmark's a prison.

      ROSENCRANTZ: Then is the world one.

      HAMLET: A goodly one, in which there are many confines,
      wards, and dungeons, Denmark being one o' th' worst.

      ROSENCRANTZ: We think not so, my lord.

245   HAMLET: Why then 'tis none to you; for there is nothing either
      good or bad, but thinking makes it so. To me it is a prison.

      ROSENCRANTZ: Why then your ambition makes it one. 'Tis
      too narrow for your mind.

      HAMLET: O God, I could be bounded in a nutshell and count

250   myself a king of infinite space, were it not that I have bad
      dreams.

      GUILDENSTERN: Which dreams indeed are ambition; for the
      very substance of the ambitious is merely the shadow of a
      dream.

      HAMLET: A dream itself is but a shadow.   255

      ROSENCRANTZ: Truly, and I hold ambition of so airy and light
      a quality that it is but a shadow's shadow.

      HAMLET: Then are our beggars bodies, and, our monarchs and
      outstretched heroes the beggars' shadows. Shall we to th'
      court? for, by my fay, I cannot reason.   260

      BOTH: We'll wait upon you.

      HAMLET: No such matter. I will not sort you with the rest of my
      servants; for to speak to you like an honest man, I am most
      dreadfully attended. But in the beaten way of friendship,
      what make you at Elsinore?   265

      ROSENCRANTZ: To visit you, my lord; no other occasion.

      HAMLET: Beggar that I am, I am ever poor in thanks, but I
      thank you; and sure, dear friends, my thanks are too dear a
      halfpenny. Were you not sent for? Is it your own inclining? Is
      it a free visitation? Come, come, deal justly with me. Come,   270
      come, nay speak.

      GUILDENSTERN: What should we say, my lord?

      HAMLET: Anything but to the purpose. You were sent for, and
      there is a kind of confession in your looks, which your mod-
      esties have not craft enough to color. I know the good king   275
      and queen have sent for you.

      ROSENCRANTZ: To what end, my lord?

      HAMLET: That you must teach me. But let me conjure you by
      the rights of our fellowship, by the consonancy of our youth,
      by the obligation of our ever-preserved love, and by what   280
      more dear a better proposer can charge you withal be even
      and direct with me whether you were sent for or no.

      ROSENCRANTZ: (*Aside to* GUILDENSTERN.) What say you?

      HAMLET: (*Aside.*) Nay, then, I have an eye of you.—If you love
      me, hold not off.   285

      GUILDENSTERN: My lord, we were sent for.

      HAMLET: I will tell you why; so shall my anticipation prevent
      your discovery, and your secrecy to the king and queen
      moult no feather. I have of late—but wherefore I know not—
      lost all my mirth, forgone all custom of exercises; and indeed   290
      it goes so heavily with my disposition, that this goodly frame
      the earth seems to me a sterile promontory, this most excel-
      lent canopy the air, look you, this brave o'er-hanging firma-
      ment, this majestical roof fretted with golden fire, why it
      appeareth nothing to me but a foul and pestilent congrega-   295
      tion of vapors. What a piece of work is a man, how noble in
      reason, how infinite in faculties, in form and moving, how
      express and admirable in action, how like an angel in appre-
      hension, how like a god: the beauty of the world, the paragon
      of animals. And yet to me, what is this quintessence   300
      of dust? Man delights not me, nor woman neither, though by
      your smiling you seem to say so.

      ROSENCRANTZ: My lord, there was no such stuff in my
      thoughts.

      HAMLET: Why did ye laugh, then, when I said 'Man delights   305
      not me'?

---

206 **pregnant** full of meaning   206 **happiness** aptness   223 **indifferent** average   225 **button** knob on the top of the cap

260 **fay** faith   262 **sort you with** put you in the same class with
287 **prevent** forestall   288 **discovery** disclosure   294 **fretted** decorated with fretwork

ROSENCRANTZ: To think, my lord, if you delight not in man, what lenten entertainment the players shall receive from you. We coted them on the way, and hither are they coming
310 to offer you service.

HAMLET: He that plays the king shall be welcome—his majesty shall have tribute on me; the adventurous knight shall use his foil and target; the lover shall not sigh gratis; the humorous man shall end his part in peace; the clown shall
315 make those laugh whose lungs are tickle o' th' sere; and the lady shall say her mind freely, or the blank verse shall halt for 't. What players are they?

ROSENCRANTZ: Even those you were wont to take such delight in, the tragedians of the city.

320 HAMLET: How chances it they travel? Their residence, both in reputation and profit, was better both ways.

ROSENCRANTZ: I think their inhibition comes by the means of the late innovation.

HAMLET: Do they hold the same estimation they did when I
325 was in the city? Are they so followed?

ROSENCRANTZ: No, indeed, are they not.

HAMLET: How comes it? Do they grow rusty?

ROSENCRANTZ: Nay, their endeavour keeps in the wonted pace; but there is, sir, an eyrie of children, little eyases, that
330 cry out on the top of question, and are most tyrannically clapped for't. These are now the fashion, and so berattle the common stages (so they call them) that many wearing rapiers are afraid of goose quills and dare scarce come thither.

HAMLET: What, are they children? Who maintains 'em? How
335 are they escoted? Will they pursue the quality no longer than they can sing? Will they not say afterwards, if they should grow themselves to common players (as it is most like, if their means are no better), their writers do them wrong to make them exclaim against their own succession?

340 ROSENCRANTZ: 'Faith, there has been much to do on both sides; and the nation holds it no sin to tarre them to controversy. There was for a while no money bid for argument, unless the poet and the player went to cuffs in the question.

HAMLET: Is't possible?

345 GUILDENSTERN: O, there has been much throwing about of brains.

HAMLET: Do the boys carry it away?

ROSENCRANTZ: Ay, that they do, my lord, Hercules and his load too.

HAMLET: It is not very strange, for my uncle is King of Den-
350 mark, and those that would make mouths at him while my father lived give twenty, forty, fifty, a hundred ducats apiece for his picture in little. 'Sblood, there is something in this more than natural, if philosophy could find it out.

(A flourish.)

GUILDENSTERN: There are the players.

355 HAMLET: Gentlemen, you are welcome to Elsinore. Your hands. Come then th' appurtenance of welcome is fashion and ceremony. Let me comply with you in this garb, lest my extent to the players, which I tell you must show fairly outwards, should more appear like entertainment than yours.
360 You are welcome. But my uncle-father and aunt-mother are deceived.

GUILDENSTERN: In what, my dear lord?

HAMLET: I am but mad north-north-west; when the wind is southerly I know a hawk from a handsaw.

365

(Enter POLONIUS.)

POLONIUS: Well be with you, gentlemen.

HAMLET: Hark you, Guildenstern—and you too—at each ear a hearer. That great baby you see there is not yet out of his swaddling clouts.

ROSENCRANTZ: Happily he is the second time come to them,
370 for they say an old man is twice a child.

HAMLET: I will prophesy he comes to tell me of the players. Mark it.—You say right, sir, a Monday morning, 'twas then indeed.

POLONIUS: My lord, I have news to tell you.

375 HAMLET: My lord, I have news to tell you. When Roscius was an actor in Rome—

POLONIUS: The actors are come hither, my lord.

HAMLET: Buzz, buzz.

POLONIUS: Upon my honor—

380 HAMLET: Then came each actor on his ass—

POLONIUS: The best actors in the world, either for tragedy, comedy, history, pastoral, pastoral-comical, historical-pastoral, tragical-historical, tragical-comical-historical-pastoral, scene individable, or poem unlimited. Seneca cannot be too heavy
385 nor Plautus too light. For the law of writ and the liberty, these are the only men.

HAMLET: O Jephthah, judge of Israel, what a treasure hadst thou!

---

308 **lenten** scanty   309 **coted** passed   313 **foil and target** spear and shield   314 **humorous man** the actor who plays the eccentric character dominated by one of the four humors   315 **tickle o' th' sere** easily set off (**sere** is that part of a gunlock which keeps the hammar at full or half cock)   316 **halt** limp   322 **inhibition** prohibition of plays by authority (possibly with reference to decree of the Privy Council of 22 June 1600, limiting the number of London theater companies to two, and stipulating that the two were to perform only twice a week)   323 **innovation** meaning uncertain (sometimes taken to refer to the reintroduction, ca. 1600, on the London theatrical scene of companies of boy actors performing in private theaters; sometimes interpreted as "political upheaval," with special reference to Essex's rebellion, February, 1601)   329 **eyrie** nest; **eyases** nestling hawks (here, the boys in the children's companies training as actors)   330 **on the top of question** louder than all others on matter of dispute   332 **common stages** public theaters of the **common players** (below, line 337), organized in companies composed mainly of adult actors   333 **goose quills** pens (of the satiric dramatists writing for the private theaters)   335 **escoted** maintained; **pursue the quality** continue in the profession of acting   336 **sing** i.e., until their voices change   341 **tarre** incite   342 **argument** plot of a play

---

349 **load** i.e., the world (the sign of the Globe Theatre represented Hercules bearing the world on his shoulders)   351 **mouths** grimaces   353 **in little** in miniature   357 **appurtenance** adjuncts   359 **extent** welcome   365 **hawk** mattock or pickaxe (also called "hack," here used with a play on *hawk* as a bird); **handsaw** a saw managed with one hand (here used with a play on some corrupt form of *hernshaw*, "heron")   370 **Happily** perhaps   376 **Roscius** the greatest of Roman actors, though regarded by the Elizabethans as a tragic one   384 **scene individable** i.e., a play that observes the unities of time and place   385 **poem unlimited** a play that does not observe the unities; **Seneca** Roman writer of tragedies   386 **Plautus** Roman comic dramatist; **law of writ and the liberty** i.e., plays according to strict classical rules, and those that ignored the unities of time and place   388 **Jephthah** was compelled to sacrifice a beloved daughter (Judges II). Hamlet quotes from a contemporary ballad titled *Jephthah, Judge of Israel* at lines 392-393, 401, and 403

390 POLONIUS: What a treasure had he, my lord?
HAMLET: Why—

> 'One fair daughter, and no more,
> The which he loved passing well.'

POLONIUS: (*Aside*.) Still on my daughter.
395 HAMLET: Am I not i' th' right, old Jephthah?
POLONIUS: If you call me Jephthah, my lord, I have a daughter that I love passing well.
HAMLET: Nay, that follows not.
POLONIUS: What follows then, my lord?
400 HAMLET: Why—

> 'As by lot, God wot,'

and then, you know,

> 'It came to pass, as most like it was.'

The first row of the pious chanson will show you more, for
405 look where my abridgement comes.

(*Enter the* PLAYERS.)

You are welcome, masters; welcome, all.—I am glad to see thee well.—Welcome, good friends. O, old friend! Why thy face is valanced since I saw thee last. Come'st thou to beard me in Denmark?—What, my young lady and mistress? By'r
410 lady, your ladyship is nearer to heaven than when I saw you last by the altitude of a chopine. Pray God, your voice, like a piece of uncurrent gold, be not cracked within the ring.—Masters, you are all welcome. We'll e'en to't like French falconers, fly at any thing we see. We'll have a
415 speech straight. Come give us a taste of your quality, come a passionate speech.
1 PLAYER: What speech, my good lord?
HAMLET: I heard thee speak me a speech once, but it was never acted, or if it was, not above once, for the play, I re
420 member, pleased not the million; 'twas caviary to the general. But it was—as I received it, and others whose judgements in such matters cried in the top of mine—an excellent play, well digested in the scenes, set down with as much modesty as cunning. I remember one said there were
425 no sallets in the lines to make the matter savory, nor no matter in the phrase that might indict the author of affectation, but called it an honest method, as wholesome as sweet, and by very much more handsome than fine. One speech in't I chiefly loved. 'Twas Æneas' tale to Dido and thereabout of it
430 especially when he speaks of Priam's slaughter. If it live in your memory, begin at this line—let me see, let me see:

> 'The rugged Pyrrhus, like th' Hyrcanian beast'—

'tis not so;—it begins with Pyrrhus—

> 'The rugged Pyrrhus, he whose sable arms,
435 Black as his purpose, did the night resemble

> When he lay couchéd in the ominous horse,
> Hath now this dread and black complexion smeared
> With heraldry more dismal; head to foot
> Now is he total gules, horridly tricked
> With blood of fathers, mothers, daughters, sons,   440
> Baked and impasted with the parching streets,
> That lend a tyrannous and a damnéd light
> To their lord's murder. Roasted in wrath and fire,
> And thus o'er-sizéd with coagulate gore,
> With eyes like carbuncles, the hellish Pyrrhus   445
> Old grandsire Priam seeks.'

So, proceed you.
POLONIUS: Fore God, my lord, well spoken, with good accent and good discretion.
1 PLAYER: 'Anon he finds him   450
> Striking too short at Greeks. His antique sword,
> Rebellious to his arm, lies where it falls,
> Repugnant to command. Unequal matched,
> Pyrrhus at Priam drives, in rage strikes wide.
> But with the whiff and wind of his fell sword   455
> Th' unnervéd father falls. Then senseless Ilium,
> Seeming to feel this blow, with flaming top
> Stoops to his base, and with a hideous crash
> Takes prisoner Pyrrhus' ear. For, lo! his sword,
> Which was declining on the milky head   460
> Of reverend Priam, seemed i' th' air to stick.
> So as a painted tyrant Pyrrhus stood,
> And like a neutral to his will and matter,
> Did nothing.
> But as we often see, against some storm,   465
> A silence in the heavens, the rack stand still,
> The bold winds speechless, and the orb below
> As hush as death, anon the dreadful thunder
> Doth rend the region; so, after Pyrrhus' pause,
> A rouséd vengeance sets him new awork,   470
> And never did the Cyclops' hammers fall
> On Mars's armor, forged for proof eterne
> With less remorse than Pyrrhus' bleeding sword
> Now falls on Priam.
> Out, out, thou strumpet, Fortune! All you gods,   475
> In general synod take away her power,
> Break all the spokes and fellies from her wheel,
> And bowl the round nave down the hill of heaven
> As low as to the fiends.'
POLONIUS: This is too long.   480
HAMLET: It shall to the barber's with your beard.—Prithee, say on. He's for a jig, or a tale of bawdry, or he sleeps. Say on, come to Hecuba.
1 PLAYER: 'But who, ah woe! had seen the mobled queen—'
HAMLET: 'The mobled queen'?   485
POLONIUS: That's good.

---

404 **row** stanza   408 **valanced** bearded   409 **young lady** i.e., the boy who plays female roles   411 **chopine** a shoe with high cork heel and sole   412 **cracked within the ring** a coin cracked within the circle surrounding the head of the sovereign was no longer legal tender and so *uncurrent*   415 **straight** immediately   420 **caviary** caviare; **general** multitude   423 **digested** arranged   425 **sallets** salads, highly seasoned passages   428 **more handsome than fine** admirable rather than appealing by mere cleverness   432 **Hyrcanian beast** tiger

436 **horse** i.e., the Trojan horse   439 **gules** heraldic term for red; **tricked** delineated   444 **o'er-sizéd** covered as with size; **coagulate** clotted   453 **Repugnant** refractory   455 **fell** fierce, cruel   465 **against** just before   466 **rack** mass of cloud   469 **region** air   471 **Cyclops** giant workmen who made armor in the smithy of Vulcan   472 **proof eterne** to be forever impenetrable   477 **fellies** the curved pieces forming the rim of a wheel   478 **nave** hub of a wheel   484 **mobled** muffled

1 PLAYER: 'Run barefoot up and down, threat'ning the flames
    With bisson rheum; a clout upon that head
    Where late the diadem stood, and for a robe,
490   About her lank and all o'er-teemed loins,
    A blanket, in the alarm of fear caught up—
    Who this had seen, with tongue in venom steeped,
    'Gainst Fortune's state would treason have pronounced.
    But if the gods themselves did see her then,
495   When she saw Pyrrhus make malicious sport
    In mincing with his sword her husband's limbs,
    The instant burst of clamor that she made,
    Unless things mortal move them not at all,
    Would have made milch the burning eyes of heaven,
500   And passion in the gods.'
POLONIUS: Look whe'r he has not turned his color, and has
    tears in's eyes. Prithee no more.
HAMLET: 'Tis well. I'll have thee speak out the rest of this
    soon.—Good my lord, will you see the players well be-
505   stowed? Do you hear, let them be well used, for they are the
    abstract and brief chronicles of the time; after your death you
    were better have a bad epitaph than their ill report while
    you live.
POLONIUS: My lord, I will use them according to their desert.
510 HAMLET: God's bodkin, man, much better. Use every man
    after his desert, and who shall 'scape whipping? Use them
    after your own honor and dignity. The less they deserve, the
    more merit is in your bounty. Take them in.
POLONIUS: Come, sirs.
515 HAMLET: Follow him, friends. We'll hear a play tomorrow.
    (*Aside to First Player.*) Dost thou hear me, old friend, can
    you play the 'Murder of Gonzago'?
1 PLAYER: Ay, my lord.
HAMLET: We'll ha't tomorrow night. You could for a need
520   study a speech of some dozen or sixteen lines which I would
    set down and insert in't, could you not?
1 PLAYER: Ay, my lord.
HAMLET: Very well. Follow that lord. and look you mock him
    not.

(*Exeunt* POLONIUS *and* PLAYERS.)

525   My good friends, I'll leave you till night. You are welcome to
    Elsinore.
ROSENCRANTZ: Good my lord!

(*Exeunt [*ROSENCRANTZ *and* GUILDENSTERN*].*)

HAMLET: Ay, so God buy to you. Now I am alone.
    O, what a rogue and peasant slave am I!
530   Is it not monstrous that this player here,
    But in a fiction, in a dream of passion,
    Could force his soul so to his own conceit
    That from her working all his visage wanned;
    Tears in his eyes, distraction in his aspect,
535   A broken voice, and his whole function suiting
    With forms to his conceit? And all for nothing,
    For Hecuba!
    What's Hecuba to him or he to Hecuba,

    That he should weep for her? What would he do
    Had he the motive and the cue for passion   540
    That I have? He would drown the stage with tears,
    And cleave the general ear with horrid speech,
    Make mad the guilty, and appal the free,
    Confound the ignorant, and amaze indeed
    The very faculties of eyes and ears.   545
    Yet I,
    A dull and muddy-mettled rascal, peak
    Like John-a-dreams, unpregnant of my cause,
    And can say nothing; no, not for a king
    Upon whose property and most dear life   550
    A damned defeat was made. Am I a coward?
    Who calls me villain, breaks my pate across,
    Plucks off my beard and blows it in my face,
    Tweaks me by the nose, gives me the lie i' th' throat
    As deep as to the lungs? Who does me this?   555
    Ha, 'swounds, I should take it; for it cannot be
    But I am pigeon-livered and lack gall
    To make oppression bitter, or ere this
    I should 'a fatted all the region kites
    With this slave's offal. Bloody, bawdy villain!   560
    Remorseless, treacherous, lecherous, kindless villain!
    Why, what an ass am I! This is most brave,
    That I, the son of a dear father murdered,
    Prompted to my revenge by heaven and hell,
    Must like a whore unpack my heart with words,   565
    And fall a-cursing like a very drab,
    A scullion! Fie upon 't! foh!
    About, my brains! Hum—I have heard
    That guilty creatures sitting at a play,
    Have by the very cunning of the scene   570
    Been struck so to the soul that presently
    They have proclaimed their malefactions;
    For murder, though it have no tongue, will speak
    With most miraculous organ. I'll have these players
    Play something like the murder of my father   575
    Before mine uncle. I'll observe his looks.
    I'll tent him to the quick. If 'a do blench,
    I know my course. The spirit that I have seen
    May be the devil, and the devil hath power
    T' assume a pleasing shape, yea, and perhaps   580
    Out of my weakness and my melancholy,
    As he is very potent with such spirits,
    Abuses me to damn me. I'll have grounds
    More relative than this. The play's the thing
    Wherein I'll catch the conscience of the king   585

(*Exit.*)

---

542 **general** public   547 **muddy-mettled** dull-spirited; **peak** mope
548 **unpregnant** not quickened to action   559 **region kites** kites of the
air   561 **kindless** unnatural. Following this line, *F* adds the words "Oh
Vengeance!" Their inappropriateness to the occasion is noted by Professor Harold Jenkins (in his "Playhouse Interpolations in the Folio
Text of Hamlet," *Studies in Bibliography* 13 [1960]: 37). Professor Jenkins remarks that the folio text, by introducing Hamlet's "call for
vengeance while he is still absorbed in self-reproaches, both anticipates
and misconstrues" the crisis of his passion and of the speech, which
comes in fact at line 568 ("**About, my brains**"), when "he abandons
his self-reproaches and plans action"   567 **scullion** kitchen wench
571 **presently** immediately   577 **tent** probe; **blench** flinch
583 **Abuses** deludes   584 **relative** relevant

---

488 **bisson rheum** blinding tears   490 **o'er-teemed** exhausted by
many births   493 **state** government   499 **milch** moist, tearful (lit.,
milk-giving)   506 **abstract** summary account   510 **God's bodkin** by
God's dear body   532 **conceit** imagination

— ACT THREE —

SCENE I

Enter KING, QUEEN, POLONIUS, OPHELIA, ROSENCRANTZ, GUILDENSTERN, LORDS.

KING: And can you by no drift of conference
  Get from him why he puts on this confusion,
  Grating so harshly all his days of quiet
  With turbulent and dangerous lunacy?
5 ROSENCRANTZ: He does confess he feels himself distracted,
  But from what cause 'a will by no means speak.
GUILDENSTERN: Nor do we find him forward to be sounded,
  But with a crafty madness keeps aloof
  When we would bring him on to some confession
10   Of his true state.
QUEEN: Did he receive you well?
ROSENCRANTZ: Most like a gentleman.
GUILDENSTERN: But with much forcing of his disposition.
ROSENCRANTZ: Niggard of question, but of our demands
  Most free in his reply.
QUEEN: Did you assay him
15 To any pastime?
ROSENCRANTZ: Madam, it so fell out that certain players
  We o'er-raught on the way. Of these we told him,
  And there did seem in him a kind of joy
  To hear of it. They are here about the court,
20   And as I think, they have already order
  This night to play before him.
POLONIUS: 'Tis most true,
  And he beseeched me to entreat your majesties
  To hear and see the matter.
KING: With all my heart, and it doth much content me
25   To hear him so inclined.
  Good gentlemen, give him a further edge,
  And drive his purpose into these delights.
ROSENCRANTZ: We shall, my lord.

(Exeunt ROSENCRANTZ *and* GUILDENSTERN.*)*

KING: Sweet Gertrude, leave us too;
  For we have closely sent for Hamlet hither,
30   That he, as 'twere by accident, may here
  Affront Ophelia.
  Her father and myself (lawful espials)
  We'll so bestow ourselves that, seeing unseen,
  We may of their encounter frankly judge,
35   And gather by him, as he is behaved,
  If 't be th' affliction of his love or no
  That thus he suffers for.
QUEEN: I shall obey you. —
  And for your part, Ophelia, I do wish
  That your good beauties be the happy cause
40   Of Hamlet's wildness. So shall I hope your virtues
  Will bring him to his wonted way again,
  To both your honors.
OPHELIA: Madam, I wish it may.

(Exit QUEEN *with* LORDS.*)*

POLONIUS: Ophelia, walk you here. —Gracious, so please you,
  We will bestow ourselves. —*(To* OPHELIA.*)* Read on this book,
  That show of such an exercise may color   45
  Your loneliness. —We are oft to blame in this,
  'Tis too much proved, that with devotion's visage
  And pious action we do sugar o'er
  The devil himself.
KING: *(Aside.)*   O, 'tis too true.
  How smart a lash that speech doth give my conscience! 50
  The harlot's cheek, beautied with plast'ring art,
  Is not more ugly to the thing that helps it
  Then is my deed to my most painted word.
  O heavy burden!
POLONIUS: I hear him coming. Let's withdraw, my lord. 55

(Exeunt KING *and* POLONIUS.*)*

(Enter HAMLET.*)*

HAMLET: To be, or not to be, that is the question:
  Whether 'tis nobler in the mind to suffer
  The slings and arrows of outrageous fortune,
  Or to take arms against a sea of troubles,
  And by opposing end them. To die, to sleep— 60
  No more; and by a sleep to say we end
  The heartache, and the thousand natural shocks
  That flesh is heir to: 'tis a consummation
  Devoutly to be wished. To die, to sleep—
  To sleep, perchance to dream, ay there's the rub; 65
  For in that sleep of death what dreams may come
  When we have shuffled off this mortal coil
  Must give us pause. There's the respect
  That makes calamity of so long life:
  For who would bear the whips and scorns of time, 70
  Th' oppressor's wrong, the proud man's contumely,
  The pangs of despised love, the law's delay,
  The insolence of office, and the spurns
  That patient merit of th' unworthy takes,
  When he himself might his quietus make 75
  With a bare bodkin? Who would fardels bear,
  To grunt and sweat under a weary life,
  But that the dread of something after death,
  The undiscovered country, from whose bourn
  No traveller returns, puzzles the will, 80
  And makes us rather bear those ills we have
  Than fly to others that we know not of?
  Thus conscience does make cowards of us all,
  And thus the native hue of resolution
  Is sicklied o'er with the pale cast of thought, 85
  And enterprises of great pitch and moment
  With this regard their currents turn awry
  And lose the name of action. Soft you now,
  The fair Ophelia. —Nymph, in thy orisons
  Be all my sins remembered. 90
OPHELIA: Good my lord,
  How does your honor for this many a day?

III.i.7 forward willing **14 assay** try to win **17 o'er-raught** overtook **26 give him a further edge** sharpen his inclination **29 closely** privately **31 Affront** meet face to face **32 espials** spies

45 exercise act of devotion; **color** give an appearance of naturalness to **52 to** compared to **65 rub** obstacle (lit., obstruction encountered by bowler's ball) **67 coil** bustle, turmoil **75 quietus** settlement **76 bodkin** dagger; **fardels** burdens **79 bourn** realm **86 pitch** height **87 regard** consideration **89 orisons** prayers

HAMLET: I humbly thank you, well.

OPHELIA: My lord, I have remembrances of yours
   That I have longed long to re-deliver.
95   I pray you now receive them.

HAMLET: No, not I,
   I never gave you aught.

OPHELIA: My honored lord, you know right well you did,
   And with them words of so sweet breath composed
   As made the things more rich. Their perfume lost,
100   Take these again, for to the noble mind
   Rich gifts wax poor when givers prove unkind.
   There, my lord.

HAMLET: Ha, ha! are you honest?

OPHELIA: My lord?

105   HAMLET: Are you fair?

OPHELIA: What means your lordship?

HAMLET: That if you be honest and fair, your honesty should
   admit no discourse to your beauty.

OPHELIA: Could beauty, my lord, have better commerce than
110   with honesty?

HAMLET: Ay, truly, for the power of beauty will sooner transform honesty from what it is to a bawd than the force of honesty can translate beauty into his likeness. This was sometime
   a paradox, but now the time gives it proof. I did love you
115   once.

OPHELIA: Indeed, my lord, you made me believe so.

HAMLET: You should not have believed me, for virtue cannot
   so inoculate our old stock but we shall relish of it. I loved
   you not.

120   OPHELIA: I was the more deceived.

HAMLET: Get thee to a nunnery. Why wouldst thou be a
   breeder of sinners? I am myself indifferent honest, but yet
   I could accuse me of such things that it were better my
   mother had not borne me: I am very proud, revengeful, am-
125   bitious, with more offences at my beck than I have thoughts
   to put them in, imagination to give them shape, or time to
   act them in. What should such fellows as I do crawling between earth and heaven? We are arrant knaves all; believe
   none of us. Go thy ways to a nunnery. Where's your father?

130   OPHELIA: At home, my lord.

HAMLET: Let the doors be shut upon him, that he may play the
   fool nowhere but in's own house. Farewell.

OPHELIA: O, help him, you sweet heavens!

HAMLET: If thou dost marry, I'll give thee this plague for thy
135   dowry: be thou as chaste as ice, as pure as snow, thou shalt
   not escape calumny. Get thee to a nunnery, farewell. Or if
   thou wilt needs marry, marry a fool, for wise men know well
   enough what monsters you make of them. To a nunnery, go,
   and quickly too. Farewell.

140   OPHELIA: Heavenly powers, restore him!

HAMLET: I have heard of your paintings well enough. God
   hath given you one face, and you make yourselves another.
   You jig and amble, and you lisp; you nickname God's creatures, and make your wantonness your ignorance. Go to, I'll
145   no more on't, it hath made me mad. I say we will have no

moe marriage. Those that are married already, all but one,
shall live. The rest shall keep as they are. To a nunnery, go.

(Exit.)

OPHELIA: O, what a noble mind is here o'erthrown!
   The courtier's, soldier's, scholar's, eye, tongue, sword,
   Th' expectancy and rose of the fair state,   150
   The glass of fashion and the mould of form,
   Th' observed of all observers, quite quite down!
   And I of ladies most deject and wretched,
   That sucked the honey of his musiced vows,
   Now see that noble and most sovereign reason   155
   Like sweet bells jangled, out of time and harsh;
   That unmatched form and feature of blown youth
   Blasted with ecstasy. O, woe is me
   T' have seen what I have seen, see what I see!

(Enter KING *and* POLONIUS.*)*

KING: Love? His affections do not that way tend,   160
   Nor what he spake, though it lacked form a little,
   Was not like madness. There's something in his soul,
   O'er which his melancholy sits on brood,
   And I do doubt the hatch and the disclose
   Will be some danger; which for to prevent,   165
   I have in quick determination
   Thus set it down: he shall with speed to England
   For the demand of our neglected tribute.
   Haply the seas and countries different,
   With variable objects, shall expel   170
   This something-settled matter in his heart
   Whereon his brains still beating puts him thus
   From fashion of himself. What think you on't?

POLONIUS: It shall do well. But yet do I believe
   The origin and commencement of his grief   175
   Sprung from neglected love.—How now, Ophelia?
   You need not tell us what Lord Hamlet said;
   We heard it all.—My lord, do as you please,
   But if you hold it fit, after the play
   Let his queen-mother all alone entreat him   180
   To show his grief. Let her be round with him,
   And I'll be placed, so please you, in the ear
   Of all their conference. If she find him not,
   To England send him; or confine him where
   Your wisdom best shall think.   185

KING: It shall be so.
   Madness in great ones must not unwatched go.

(Exeunt.)

SCENE II

Enter HAMLET *and three of the* PLAYERS.

HAMLET: Speak the speech, I pray you, as I pronounced it to
   you, trippingly on the tongue; but if you mouth it as many of
   our players do, I had as lief the town-crier spoke my lines.
   Nor do not saw the air too much with your hand thus, but
   use all gently, for in the very torrent, tempest, and as I may   5

---

103 **honest** chaste   118 **inoculate** graft   122 **indifferent honest**
moderately respectable   144 **make your wantonness your ignorance**
excuse your wanton behavior with the plea that you don't know any
better

---

146 **moe** more   150 **expectancy** hope   151 **glass** mirror   157 **blown**
blooming   158 **ecstasy** madness   160 **affections** emotions
164 **doubt** fear   181 **round** plain-spoken

say, whirlwind of your passion, you must acquire and beget a
temperance that may give it smoothness. O, it offends me
to the soul to hear a robustious periwig-pated fellow tear a
passion to tatters, to very rags, to split the ears of the
groundlings, who for the most part are capable of nothing
10   but inexplicable dumb shows and noise. I would have such
a fellow whipped for o'erdoing Termagant. It out-Herods
Herod. Pray you avoid it.

1 PLAYER: I warrant your honour.

15   HAMLET: Be not too tame neither, but let your own discretion
be your tutor. Suit the action to the word, the word to the action, with this special observance, that you o'erstep not the
modesty of nature; for any thing so o'erdone is from the purpose of playing, whose end both at the first, and now, was
20   and is, to hold as 'twere the mirror up to nature, to show
virtue her own feature, scorn her own image, and the very
age and body of the time his form and pressure. Now this
overdone, or come tardy off, though it make the unskilful
laugh, cannot but make the judicious grieve, the censure of
25   the which one must in your allowance o'erweigh a whole
theatre of others. O, there be players that I have seen play—
and heard others praise, and that highly—not to speak it profanely, that neither having th' accent of Christians, nor the
gait of Christian, pagan, nor man, have so strutted and bel-
30   lowed that I have thought some of nature's journeymen had
made men, and not made them well, they imitated humanity so abominably.

1 PLAYER: I hope we have reformed that indifferently with us.

HAMLET: O, reform it altogether. And let those that play your
35   clowns speak no more than is set down for them, for there be
of them that will themselves laugh, to set on some quantity of
barren spectators to laugh too, though in the meantime
some necessary question of the play be then to be considered. That's villanous, and shows a most pitiful ambition in
40   the fool that uses it. Go, make you ready.

(*Exeunt* PLAYERS.)

(*Enter* POLONIUS, GUILDENSTERN, *and* ROSENCRANTZ.)

How now, my lord? Will the king hear this piece of work?

POLONIUS: And the queen too, and that presently.

HAMLET: Bid the players make haste.

(*Exit* POLONIUS.)

Will you two help to hasten them?

45   ROSENCRANTZ: Ay, my lord.

(*Exeunt they two.*)

HAMLET: What, ho! Horatio!

(*Enter* HORATIO.)

HORATIO: Here, sweet lord, at your service.

HAMLET: Horatio, thou art e'en as just a man
As e'er my conversation coped withal.

50   HORATIO: O my dear lord!

HAMLET: Nay, do not think I flatter,
For what advancement may I hope from thee,
That no revenue hast but thy good spirits
To feed and clothe thee? Why should the poor be flattered?
No, let the candied tongue lick absurd pomp,
And crook the pregnant hinges of the knee   55
Where thrift may follow fawning. Dost thou hear?
Since my dear soul was mistress of her choice
And could of men distinguish her election,
S'hath sealed thee for herself, for thou hast been
As one in suff'ring all that suffers nothing,   60
A man that Fortune's buffets and rewards
Hast ta'en with equal thanks; and blest are those
Whose blood and judgment are so well commeddled
That they are not a pipe for Fortune's finger
To sound what stop she please. Give me that man   65
That is not passion's slave, and I will wear him
In my heart's core, ay, in my heart of heart,
As I do thee. Something too much of this.
There is a play to-night before the king.
One scene of it comes near the circumstance   70
Which I have told thee of my father's death.
I prithee, when thou seest that act afoot,
Even with the very comment of thy soul
Observe my uncle. If his occulted guilt
Do not itself unkennel in one speech,   75
It is a damnéd ghost that we have seen,
And my imaginations are as foul
As Vulcan's stithy. Give him heedful note,
For I mine eyes will rivet to his face,
And after we will both our judgements join   80
In censure of his seeming.

HORATIO: Well, my lord.
If 'a steal aught the whilst this play is playing,
And 'scape detecting, I will pay the theft.

(*Enter Trumpets and Kettledrums,* KING, QUEEN, POLONIUS,
OPHELIA, [ROSENCRANTZ, GUILDENSTERN, *and other* LORDS
attendant].)

HAMLET: They are coming to the play. I must be idle.
Get you a place.   85

KING: How fares our cousin Hamlet?

HAMLET: Excellent, i' faith, of the chameleon's dish. I eat the
air, promise-crammed. You cannot feed capons so.

KING: I have nothing with this answer, Hamlet. These words
are not mine.   90

HAMLET: No, nor mine now. (*To* POLONIUS.) My lord, you
played once i' th' university, you say?

POLONIUS: That did I, my lord; and was accounted a good
actor.

HAMLET: What did you enact?   95

POLONIUS: I did enact Julius Caesar. I was killed i' th' Capitol;
Brutus killed me.

III.ii.10 groundlings spectators who paid least and stood on the
ground   **12 Termagant** thought to be a Mohammedan deity, and represented in medieval mystery plays as a violent and ranting personage;
Herod represented in the mystery plays as a blustering tyrant   **24 censure** judgment, opinion   **33 indifferently** fairly well   **49 coped** encountered

55 pregnant ready   **56 thrift** profit   **58 election** choice   **63 comed-
dled** mingled   **73 the very comment of thy soul** with a keenness of
observation that penetrates to the very being   **74 occulted** hidden
75 unkennel reveal   **78 stithy** forge   **81 censure** opinion   **84 idle**
crazy   **87 chameleon's dish** the air, on which the chameleon was supposed to feed

HAMLET: It was a brute part of him to kill so capital a calf there. Be the players ready?

100 ROSENCRANTZ: Ay, my lord, they stay upon your patience.

QUEEN: Come hither, my dear Hamlet, sit by me.

HAMLET: No, good mother, here's metal more attractive.

POLONIUS: (*To the* KING.) O, ho! do you mark that?

HAMLET: Lady, shall I lie in your lap?

(*Lying down at* OPHELIA'S *feet.*)

105 OPHELIA: No, my lord.

HAMLET: I mean, my head upon your lap?

OPHELIA: Ay, my lord.

HAMLET: Do you think I meant country matters?

OPHELIA: I think nothing, my lord.

110 HAMLET: That's a fair thought to lie between maids' legs.

OPHELIA: What is, my lord?

HAMLET: Nothing.

OPHELIA: You are merry, my lord.

HAMLET: Who, I?

115 OPHELIA: Ay, my lord.

HAMLET: O God, your only jig-maker! What should a man do but be merry? For look you how cheerfully my mother looks, and my father died within's two hours.

OPHELIA: Nay, 'tis twice two months, my lord.

120 HAMLET: So long? Nay then, let the devil wear black, for I'll have a suit of sables. O heavens! die two months ago, and not forgotten yet? Then there's hope a great man's memory may outlive his life half a year, but, by'r lady 'a must build churches then, or else shall 'a suffer not thinking on, with

125 the hobby-horse, whose epitaph is 'For O, for O, the hobby-horse is forgot!'

(*The trumpets sound. Dumb Show follows.*)

(*Enter a* KING *and a* QUEEN [*very lovingly*]; *the* QUEEN *embracing him and he her.* [*She kneels, and makes show of protestation unto him.*] *He takes her up, and declines his head upon her neck. He lies him down upon a bank of flowers; she, seeing him asleep, leaves him. Anon comes in another man, takes off his crown, kisses it, pours poison in the sleeper's ears, and leaves him. The* QUEEN *returns, finds the* KING *dead, makes passionate action. The* POISONER *with some three or four come in again, seem to condole with her. The dead body is carried away. The* POISONER *woos the* QUEEN *with gifts; she seems harsh awhile, but in the end accepts love.*)

(*Exeunt.*)

OPHELIA: What means this, my lord?

HAMLET: Marry, this is miching mallecho; it means mischief.

OPHELIA: Belike this show imports the argument of the play.

(*Enter* PROLOGUE.)

130 HAMLET: We shall know by this fellow. The players cannot keep counsel; they'll tell all.

OPHELIA: Will 'a tell us what this show meant?

HAMLET: Ay, or any show that you will show him. Be not you ashamed to show, he'll not shame to tell you what it means.

135 OPHELIA: You are naught, you are naught. I'll mark the play.

PROLOGUE:

> For us, and for our tragedy,
> Here stooping to your clemency,
> We beg your hearing patiently.

(*Exit.*)

HAMLET: Is this a prologue, or the posy of a ring?

OPHELIA: 'Tis brief, my lord.   140

HAMLET: As woman's love.

(*Enter [the* PLAYER] KING *and* QUEEN.)

PLAYER KING: Full thirty times hath Phoebus' cart gone round
Neptune's salt wash and Tellus' orbéd ground,
And thirty dozen moons with borrowed sheen
About the world have times twelve thirties been,   145
Since love our hearts and Hymen did our hands
Unite comutual in most sacred bands.

PLAYER QUEEN: So many journeys may the sun and moon
Make us again count o'er ere love be done!
But woe is me, you are so sick of late,   150
So far from cheer and from your former state,
That I distrust you. Yet though I distrust,
Discomfort you, my lord, it nothing must.
For women's fear and love hold quantity,
In neither aught, or in extremity.   155
Now what my love is proof hath made you know,
And as my love is sized, my fear is so.
Where love is great, the littlest doubts are fear;
Where little fears grow great, great love grows there.

PLAYER KING: Faith, I must leave thee, love, and shortly too;   160
My operant powers their functions leave to do.
And thou shalt live in this fair world behind,
Honored, beloved; and haply one as kind
For husband shalt thou—

PLAYER QUEEN: O, confound the rest!
Such love must needs be treason in my breast.   165
In second husband let me be accurst!
None wed the second but who killed the first.

HAMLET: That's wormwood.

PLAYER QUEEN: The instances that second marriage move
Are base respects of thrift, but none of love.   170
A second time I kill my husband dead,
When second husband kisses me in bed.

PLAYER KING: I do believe you think what now you speak,
But what we do determine oft we break.
Purpose is but the slave to memory,   175
Of violent birth, but poor validity;
Which now, like fruit unripe, sticks on the tree,
But fall unshaken when they mellow be.
Most necessary 'tis that we forget
To pay ourselves what to ourselves is debt.   180
What to ourselves in passion we propose,

---

125 **hobby-horse** the figure of a horse fastened round the waist of a morris dancer. Puritan efforts to suppress the country sports in which the hobby-horse figured led to a popular ballad lamenting the fact that "the hobby-horse is forgot"   128 **miching mallecho** skulking or crafty crime

---

135 **naught** naughty, lewd   139 **posy** brief motto engraved on a finger-ring   142 **Phœbus' cart** the sun's chariot   143 **Tellus' orbed ground** the earth (Tellus was the Roman goddess of the earth)   146 **Hymen** god of marriage   152 **distrust** fear for   154 **hold quantity** are proportional, weigh alike   157 **as my love is sized** according to the greatness of my love   161 **operant** vital   169 **instances** motives   176 **validity** endurance

The passion ending, doth the purpose lose.
The violence of either grief or joy
Their own enactures with themselves destroy.
185   Where joy most revels, grief doth most lament;
Grief joys, joy grieves, on slender accident.
This world is not for aye, nor 'tis not strange
That even our loves should with our fortunes change;
For 'tis a question left us yet to prove,
190   Whether love lead fortune, or else fortune love.
The great man down, you mark his favorite flies;
The poor advanced makes friends of enemies;
And hitherto doth love on fortune tend,
For who not needs shall never lack a friend,
195   And who in want a hollow friend doth try,
Directly seasons him his enemy.
But orderly to end where I begun,
Our wills and fates do so contrary run
That our devices still are overthrown;
200   Our thoughts are ours, their ends none of our own.
So think thou wilt no second husband wed,
But die thy thoughts when thy first lord is dead.
PLAYER QUEEN: Nor earth to me give food, nor heaven light,
Sport and repose lock from me day and night.
205   To desperation turn my trust and hope,
An anchor's cheer in prison be my scope,
Each opposite that blanks the face of joy
Meet what I would have well, and it destroy,
Both here and hence pursue me lasting strife,
210   If once a widow, ever I be wife!
HAMLET: If she should break it now!
PLAYER KING: 'Tis deeply sworn. Sweet, leave me here awhile.
My spirits grow dull, and fain I would beguile
The tedious day with sleep.

(Sleeps.)

PLAYER QUEEN: Sleep rock thy brain.
215   And never come mischance between us twain!

(Exit.)

HAMLET: Madam, how like you this play?
QUEEN: The lady doth protest too much, methinks.
HAMLET: O, but she'll keep her word.
KING: Have you heard the argument? Is there no offence in't?
220   HAMLET: No, no, they do but jest, poison in jest; no offence i'
th' world.
KING: What do you call the play?
HAMLET: 'The Mouse-trap.' Marry, how? Tropically. This play
is the image of a murder done in Vienna. Gonzago is
225   the duke's name; his wife, Baptista. You shall see anon. 'Tis a
knavish piece of work, but what of that? Your majesty, and
we that have free souls, it touches us not. Let the galled jade
winch, our withers are unwrung.

(Enter LUCIANUS.)

This is one Lucianus, nephew to the king.
230   OPHELIA: You are as good as a chorus, my lord.
HAMLET: I could interpret between you and your love, if I
could see the puppets dallying.

OPHELIA: You are keen, my lord, you are keen.
HAMLET: It would cost you a groaning to take off mine edge.
OPHELIA: Still better, and worse.   235
HAMLET: So you mis-take your husbands.—Begin, murderer.
Leave thy damnable faces and begin. Come, the croaking
raven doth bellow for revenge.
LUCIANUS: Thoughts black, hands apt, drugs fit, and time
agreeing,
Confederate season, else no creature seeing.   240
Thou mixture rank, of midnight weeds collected,
With Hecate's ban thrice blasted, thrice infected,
Thy natural magic and dire property
On wholesome life usurp immediately.

(Pours the poison in his ears.)

HAMLET: 'A poisons him i' th' garden for his estate. His name's   245
Gonzago. The story is extant, and written in very choice Ital-
ian. You shall see anon how the murderer gets the love of
Gonzago's wife.
OPHELIA: The king rises.
HAMLET: What, frighted with false fire?   250
QUEEN: How fares my lord?
POLONIUS: Give o'er the play.
KING: Give me some light. Away!
POLONIUS: Lights, lights, lights!

(Exeunt all but HAMLET and HORATIO.)

HAMLET: Why, let the strucken deer go weep,   255
                    The hart ungallèd play.
            For some must watch, while some must sleep;
                    Thus runs the world away.

Would not this, sir, and a forest of feathers—if the rest of my
fortunes turn Turk with me—with two Provincial roses on   260
my razed shoes, get me a fellowship in a cry of players?
HORATIO: Half a share.
HAMLET: A whole one, I.

            For thou dost know, O Damon dear,
                    This realm dismantled was   265
            Of Jove himself, and now reigns here
                    A very, very—pajock.

HORATIO: You might have rhymed.
HAMLET: O good Horatio, I'll take the ghost's word for a thou-
sand pound. Didst perceive?   270
HORATIO: Very well, my lord.
HAMLET: Upon the talk of the poisoning.
HORATIO: I did very well note him.
HAMLET: Ah, ha! Come, some music. Come, the recorders.

            For if the king like not the comedy,   275
                    Why then, belike, he likes it not, perdy.

Come, some music.

---

242 **Hecate** goddess of witchcraft; **blasted** fallen under a blight
259 **feathers** plumes for actors' costumes   260 **Provincial roses** i.e.,
Provençal roses. Ribbon rosettes resembling these French roses were
used to decorate shoes   261 **razed** with ornamental slashing; **cry** company   267 **pajock** presumably a variant form of "patch-cock," a despicable person. Cf. III.iv. 104   275 **For if . . . comedy** a seeming parody
of *The Spanish Tragedy,* IV.i. 197–198 ("And if the world like not this
tragedy,/Hard is the hap of old Hieronimo"), where another revenger's
dramatic entertainment is referred to

---

184 **enactures** enactments   187 **aye** ever   196 **seasons him** ripens
him into   206 **anchor's** anchorite's   227 **gallad jade** sorebacked
horse

(Enter ROSENCRANTZ *and* GUILDENSTERN.)

GUILDENSTERN: Good my lord, vouchsafe me a word with you.

HAMLET: Sir, a whole history.

280 GUILDENSTERN: The king, sir—

HAMLET: Ay, sir, what of him?

GUILDENSTERN: Is in his retirement marvellous distempered.

HAMLET: With drink, sir?

GUILDENSTERN: No, my lord, with choler.

285 HAMLET: Your wisdom should show itself more richer to signify this to the doctor, for for me to put him to his purgation would perhaps plunge him into more choler.

GUILDENSTERN: Good my lord, put your discourse into some frame, and start not so wildly from my affair.

290 HAMLET: I am tame, sir. Pronounce.

GUILDENSTERN: The queen, your mother, in most great affliction of spirit, hath sent me to you.

HAMLET: You are welcome.

GUILDENSTERN: Nay, good my lord, this courtesy is not of the right breed. If it shall please you to make me a wholesome answer, I will do your mother's commandment. If not, your pardon and my return shall be the end of my business.

HAMLET: Sir, I cannot.

GUILDENSTERN: What, my lord?

300 HAMLET: Make you a wholesome answer; my wit's diseased. But, sir, such answer as I can make, you shall command, or rather, as you say, my mother. Therefore no more, but to the matter. My mother, you say—

ROSENCRANTZ: Then thus she says: your behaviour hath struck her into amazement and admiration.

HAMLET: O wonderful son, that can so stonish a mother! But is there no sequel at the heels of this mother's admiration? Impart.

ROSENCRANTZ: She desires to speak with you in her closet ere you go to bed.

HAMLET: We shall obey, were she ten times our mother. Have you any further trade with us?

ROSENCRANTZ: My lord, you once did love me.

HAMLET: And do still, by these pickers and stealers.

315 ROSENCRANTZ: Good my lord, what is your cause of distemper? You do surely bar the door upon your own liberty, if you deny your griefs to your friend.

HAMLET: Sir, I lack advancement.

320 ROSENCRANTZ: How can that be, when you have the voice of the king himself for your succession in Denmark?

HAMLET: Ay, sir, but 'While the grass grows'—the proverb is something musty.

(Enter the PLAYERS *with recorders.)*

O, the recorders! Let me see one. To withdraw with you—why do you go about to recover the wind of me, as if you would drive me into a toil?

GUILDENSTERN: O, my lord, if my duty be too bold, my love is too unmannerly.

HAMLET: I do not well understand that. Will you play upon this pipe?

330 GUILDENSTERN: My lord, I cannot.

HAMLET: I pray you.

GUILDENSTERN: Believe me, I cannot.

HAMLET: I beseech you.

GUILDENSTERN: I know no touch of it, my lord.

335 HAMLET: It is as easy as lying. Govern these ventages with your fingers and thumb, give it breath with your mouth, and it will discourse most eloquent music. Look you, these are the stops.

GUILDENSTERN: But these cannot I command to any utt'rance of harmony. I have not the skill.

340 HAMLET: Why look you now, how unworthy a thing you make of me! You would play upon me, you would seem to know my stops, you would pluck out the heart of my mystery, you would sound me from my lowest note to the top of my compass; and there is much music, excellent voice, in this little organ, yet cannot you make it speak. 'Sblood, do you think I am easier to be played on than a pipe? Call me what instrument you will, though you can fret me, you cannot play upon me.

(Enter POLONIUS.)

God bless you, sir!

350 POLONIUS: My lord, the queen would speak with you, and presently.

HAMLET: Do you see yonder cloud that's almost in shape of a camel?

355 POLONIUS: By th' mass and 'tis, like a camel indeed.

HAMLET: Methinks it is like a weasel.

POLONIUS: It is backed like a weasel.

HAMLET: Or like a whale.

POLONIUS: Very like a whale.

360 HAMLET: Then I will come to my mother by and by. *(Aside.)* They fool me to the top of my bent.—I will come by and by.

POLONIUS: I will say so.

(Exit POLONIUS.)

HAMLET: 'By and by' is easily said. Leave me, friends.

(Exeunt all but HAMLET.)

'Tis now the very witching time of night,
When churchyards yawn and hell itself breathes out
Contagion to this world. Now could I drink hot blood,
And do such bitter business as the day
Would quake to look on. Soft, now to my mother.
O heart, lose not thy nature; let not ever
The soul of Nero enter this firm bosom.
Let me be cruel, not unnatural;
I will speak daggers to her, but use none.
My tongue and soul in this be hypocrites:
How in my words somever she be shent,
To give them seals never my soul consent!

(Exit.)

---

287 **choler** one of the four bodily humors, an excess of which gave rise to anger   295 **wholesome** reasonable   307 **admiration** wonder   314 **pickers and stealers** hands   321 **"while the grass grows"** a proverb ending "the horse starves"   323 **withdraw** step aside for private conversation   325 **toil** net, snare

335 **ventages** holes or stops in the recorder   348 **fret** (1) a stop on the fingerboard of a guitar (2) annoy   370 **Nero** Roman emperor who murdered his mother   374 **somever** soever; **shent** reproved, abused

SCENE III

Enter KING, ROSENCRANTZ, *and* GUILDENSTERN.

KING: I like him not, nor stands it safe with us
    To let his madness range. Therefore prepare you.
    I your commission will forthwith dispatch,
    And he to England shall along with you.
5   The terms of our estate may not endure
    Hazard so near's as doth hourly grow
    Out of his brows.
GUILDENSTERN: We will ourselves provide,
    Most holy and religious fear it is
    To keep those many many bodies safe
10   That live and feed upon your majesty.
ROSENCRANTZ: The single and peculiar life is bound
    With all the strength and armor of the mind
    To keep itself from noyance, but much more
    That spirit upon whose weal depends and rests
15   The lives of many. The cess of majesty
    Dies not alone, but like a gulf doth draw
    What's near it with it. It is a massy wheel
    Fixed on the summit of the highest mount,
    To whose huge spokes ten thousand lesser things
20   Are mortised and adjoined, which when it falls,
    Each small annexment, petty consequence,
    Attends the boist'rous ruin. Never alone
    Did the king sigh, but with a general groan.
KING: Arm you, I pray you, to this speedy voyage,
25   For we will fetters put about this fear,
    Which now goes too free-footed.
ROSENCRANTZ: We will haste us.

*(Exeunt Gentlemen [*ROSENCRANTZ *and* GUILDENSTERN*].)*

(Enter POLONIUS.*)*

POLONIUS: My lord, he's going to his mother's closet.
    Behind the arras I'll convey myself
    To hear the process. I'll warrant she'll tax him home,
30   And as you said, and wisely was it said,
    'Tis meet that some more audience than a mother,
    Since nature makes them partial, should o'erhear
    The speech of vantage. Fare you well, my liege.
    I'll call upon you ere you go to bed,
35   And tell you what I know.
KING: Thanks, dear my lord.

(Exit POLONIUS.*)*

    O, my offence is rank, it smells to heaven;
    It hath the primal eldest curse upon't,
    A brother's murder. Pray can I not,
    Though inclination be as sharp as will.
40   My stronger guilt defeats my strong intent,
    And like a man to double business bound,
    I stand in pause where I shall first begin,
    And both neglect. What if this cursèd hand

Were thicker than itself with brother's blood,
Is there not rain enough in the sweet heavens   45
To wash it white as snow? Whereto serves mercy
But to confront the visage of offence?
And what's in prayer but this twofold force,
To be forestallèd ere we come to fall,
Or pardoned being down? Then I'll look up.   50
My fault is past. But, O, what form of prayer
Can serve my turn? 'Forgive me my foul murder'?
That cannot be, since I am still possessed
Of those effects for which I did the murder—
My crown, mine own ambition, and my queen.   55
May one be pardoned and retain th' offence?
In the corrupted currents of this world
Offence's gilded hand may shove by justice,
And oft 'tis seen the wicked prize itself
Buys out the law. But 'tis not so above   60
There is no shuffling; there the action lies
In his true nature, and we ourselves compelled,
Even to the teeth and forehead of our faults,
To give in evidence. What then? What rests?
Try what repentance can. What can it not?   65
Yet what can it when one can not repent?
O wretched state! O bosom black as death!
O limèd soul, that struggling to be free
Art more engaged! Help, angels! Make assay.
Bow, stubborn knees, and heart with strings of steel,   70
Be soft as sinews of the new-born babe.
All may be well.

(He kneels.)

(Enter HAMLET.*)*

HAMLET: Now might I do it pat, now 'a is a-praying,
    And now I'll do't—and so 'a goes to heaven,
    And so am I revenged. That would be scanned.   75
    A villain kills my father, and for that,
    I, his sole son, do this same villain send
    To heaven.
    Why, this is hire and salary, not revenge.
    'A took my father grossly, full of bread,   80
    With all his crimes broad blown, as flush as May;
    And how his audit stands who knows save heaven?
    But in our circumstance and course of thought
    'Tis heavy with him; and am I then revenged
    To take him in the purging of his soul,   85
    When he is fit and seasoned for his passage?
    No.
    Up, sword, and know thou a more horrid hent.
    When he is drunk asleep, or in his rage,
    Or in th' incestuous pleasure of his bed,   90
    At game a-swearing, or about some act
    That has no relish of salvation in't—
    Then trip him, that his heels may kick at heaven,
    And that his soul may be as damned and black

III.iii.5 **terms of our estate** conditions required for our rule as king
7 **brows** threatening looks that suggest the dangerous plots Hamlet's
brain is hatching 11 **peculiar** private 13 **noyance** harm 15 **cess**
cessation, extinction 20 **mortised** jointed (as with mortise and tenon)
33 **of vantage** (1) in addition; (2) from a convenient place for listening
39 **will** carnal desire

---

61 **shuffling** doubledealing; **action** legal action 68 **limèd soul**
caught by sin as the bird by lime 69 **assay** an effort 80 **grossly** unprepared spiritually 81 **as flush as May** in full flower 83 **in our circumstance** considering all evidence; **course** beaten way, habit
88 **hent** occasion, opportunity

95　As hell, whereto it goes. My mother stays.
　　This physic but prolongs thy sickly days.

(Exit.)

KING: *(Rising.)* My words fly up, my thoughts remain below.
　　Words without thoughts never to heaven go.

(Exit.)

SCENE IV

*Enter [*QUEEN*]* GERTRUDE *and* POLONIUS.

POLONIUS: 'A will come straight. Look you lay home to him.
　　Tell him his pranks have been too broad to bear with,
　　And that your grace hath screened and stood between
　　Much heat and him. I'll silence me even here.
5　Pray you be round.
　　QUEEN:　　　　　I'll warrant you. Fear me not.
　　Withdraw, I hear him coming.

*(*POLONIUS *goes behind the arras.)*

(Enter HAMLET.*)*

HAMLET: Now, mother, what's the matter?
QUEEN: Hamlet, thou hast thy father much offended.
HAMLET: Mother, you have my father much offended.
10　QUEEN: Come, come, you answer with an idle tongue.
HAMLET: Go, go, you question with a wicked tongue.
QUEEN: Why, how now, Hamlet?
HAMLET:　　　　　　　　What's the matter now?
QUEEN: Have you forgot me?
HAMLET:　　　　　　　No, by the rood, not so:
　　You are the queen, your husband's brother's wife,
15　And would it were not so, you are my mother.
QUEEN: Nay, then I'll set those to you that can speak.
HAMLET: Come, come, and sit you down. You shall not
　　　budge.
　　You go not till I set you up a glass
　　Where you may see the inmost part of you.
20　QUEEN: What wilt thou do? Thou wilt not murder me?
　　Help, ho!
POLONIUS: *(Behind.)* What, ho! help!
HAMLET: *(Draws.)* How now! a rat?
　　Dead for a ducat, dead!

(Thrusts his sword through the arras and kills POLONIUS*)*

25　POLONIUS: *(Behind.)* O, I am slain!
QUEEN: O me, what hast thou done?
HAMLET:　　　　　　　　　　Nay, I know not.
　　Is it the king?
QUEEN: O, what a rash and bloody deed is this!
HAMLET: A bloody deed? Almost as bad, good mother,
30　As kill a king and marry with his brother.
QUEEN: As kill a king?
HAMLET:　　　　　Ay, lady, it was my word.

(Lifts up the arras and sees the body of POLONIUS.*)*

　　Thou wretched, rash, intruding fool, farewell!
　　I took thee for thy better. Take thy fortune.

III.iv.5 Following Polonius's "Pray you be round" (which in *F* reads "Pray you be round with him"), *F* adds the line: "*Hamlet within.* Mother, mother, mother" 13 **rood** cross

---

Thou find'st to be too busy is some danger.—
Leave wringing of your hands. Peace, sit you down 35
And let me wring your heart, for so I shall
If it be made of penetrable stuff,
If damnéd custom have not brazed it so
That it be proof and bulwark against sense.
QUEEN: What have I done that thou dar'st wag thy tongue 40
　　In noise so rude against me?
HAMLET:　　　　　　　　Such an act
　　That blurs the grace and blush of modesty,
　　Calls virtue hypocrite, takes off the rose
　　From the fair forehead of an innocent love,
　　And sets a blister there, makes marriage-vows 45
　　As false as dicers' oaths. O, such a deed
　　As from the body of contraction plucks
　　The very soul, and sweet religion makes
　　A rhapsody of words. Heaven's face does glow
　　O'er this solidity and compound mass 50
　　With heated visage, as against the doom—
　　Is thought-sick at the act.
QUEEN:　　　　　　　Ay me, what act,
　　That roars so loud, and thunders in the index?
HAMLET: Look here, upon this picture and on this.
　　The counterfeit presentment of two brothers. 55
　　See what a grace was seated on this brow:
　　Hyperion's curls, the front of Jove himself,
　　An eye like Mars, to threaten and command,
　　A station like the herald Mercury
　　New lighted on a heaven-kissing hill— 60
　　A combination and a form indeed
　　Where every god did seem to set his seal
　　To give the world assurance of a man.
　　This was your husband. Look you now what follows.
　　Here is your husband, like a mildewed ear 65
　　Blasting his wholesome brother. Have you eyes?
　　Could you on this fair mountain leave to feed,
　　And batten on this moor? Ha! have you eyes?
　　You cannot call it love, for at your age
　　The heyday in the blood is tame, it's humble, 70
　　And waits upon the judgement, and what judgement
　　Would step from this to this? Sense sure you have,
　　Else could you not have motion, but sure that sense
　　Is apoplexed, for madness would not err
　　Nor sense to ecstasy was ne'er so thralled 75
　　But it reserved some quantity of choice
　　To serve in such a difference. What devil was't
　　That thus hath cozened you at hoodman-blind?
　　Eyes without feeling, feeling without sight,
　　Ears without hands or eyes, smelling sans all, 80

---

38 **brazed** plated it as with brass 39 **proof** impenetrable, as of armor 47 **contraction** the contract of marriage 50 **this solidity and compound mass** the earth, as compounded of the four elements 51 **doom** Judgment Day 53 **index** table of contents; thus, indication of what is to follow 55 **counterfeit presentment** portrait 57 **front** forehead 59 **station** bearing, figure 68 **batten** feed like an animal 70 **heyday** ardor 72 **Sense** the senses collectively, which according to Aristotelian tradition are found in all creatures that have the power of locomotion 75 **ecstasy** madness 78 **hoodman-blind** blindman's bluff 80 **sans** without

Or but a sickly part of one true sense
Could not so mope. O shame! where is thy blush?
Rebellious hell,
If thou canst mutine in a matron's bones,
85 To flaming youth let virtue be as wax
And melt in her own fire. Proclaim no shame
When the compulsive ardor gives the charge,
Since frost itself as actively doth burn,
And reason pandars will.
QUEEN: O Hamlet, speak no more!
90 Thou turn'st mine eyes into my very soul,
And there I see such black and grainéd spots
As will not leave their tinct.
HAMLET: Nay, but to live
In the rank sweat of an enseaméd bed,
Stewed in corruption, honeying and making love
95 Over the nasty sty—
QUEEN: O, speak to me no more!
These words like daggers enter in mine ears.
No more, sweet Hamlet.
HAMLET: A murderer and a villain,
A slave that is not twentieth part the tithe
Of your precedent lord, a vice of kings,
100 A cutpurse of the empire and the rule,
That from a shelf the precious diadem stole
And put it in his pocket—
QUEEN: No more.

(Enter GHOST.*)*

HAMLET: A king of shreds and patches—
105 Save me and hover o'er me with your wings,
You heavenly guards! What would your gracious figure?
QUEEN: Alas, he's mad.
HAMLET: Do you not come your tardy son to chide,
That lapsed in time and passion lets go by
110 Th' important acting of your dread command?
O, say!
GHOST: Do not forget. This visitation
Is but to whet thy almost blunted purpose.
But look, amazement on thy mother sits.
115 O, step between her and her fighting soul!
Conceit in weakest bodies strongest works.
Speak to her, Hamlet.
HAMLET: How is it with you, lady?
QUEEN: Alas, how is't with you,
That you do bend your eye on vacancy,
120 And with th' incorporal air do hold discourse?
Forth at your eyes your spirits wildly peep,
And as the sleeping soldiers in th' alarm,
Your bedded hair like life in excrements
Start up and stand an end. O gentle son,
125 Upon the heat and flame of thy distemper
Sprinkle cool patience. Whereon do you look?

HAMLET: On him, on him! Look you how pale he glares.
His form and cause conjoined, preaching to stones,
Would make them capable.—Do not look upon me,
Lest with this piteous action you convert   130
My stern effects. Then what I have to do
Will want true color—tears perchance for blood.
QUEEN: To whom do you speak this?
HAMLET: Do you see nothing there?
QUEEN: Nothing at all, yet all that is I see.   135
HAMLET: Nor did you nothing hear?
QUEEN: No, nothing but ourselves.
HAMLET: Why, look you there. Look, how it steals away.
My father, in his habit as he lived!
Look where he goes even now out at the portal.   140

(Exit GHOST.*)*

QUEEN: This is the very coinage of your brain.
This bodiless creation ecstasy
Is very cunning in.
HAMLET: My pulse as yours doth temperately keep time,
And makes us healthful music. It is not madness   145
That I have uttered. Bring me to the test,
And I the matter will re-word, which madness
Would gambol from. Mother, for love of grace,
Lay not that flattering unction to your soul,
That not your trespass but my madness speaks.   150
It will but skin and film the ulcerous place
Whiles rank corruption, mining all within,
Infects unseen. Confess yourself to heaven,
Repent what's past, avoid what is to come,
And do not spread the compost on the weeds,   155
To make them ranker. Forgive me this my virtue,
For in the fatness of these pursy times
Virtue itself of vice must pardon beg,
Yea, curb and woo for leave to do him good.
QUEEN: O Hamlet, thou hast cleft my heart in twain.   160
HAMLET: O, throw away the worser part of it,
And live the purer with the other half.
Good night—but go not to my uncle's bed.
Assume a virtue, if you have it not.
That monster custom, who all sense doth eat,   165
Of habits devil, is angel yet in this,
That to the use of actions fair and good
He likewise gives a frock or livery
That aptly is put on. Refrain to-night,
And that shall lend a kind of easiness   170
To the next abstinence; the next more easy;
For use almost can change the stamp of nature,
And either curb the devil, or throw him out
With wondrous potency. Once more, good night,

---

129 **capable** able to respond   132 **want** lack   148 **gambol** leap or start, as a shying horse   149 **unction** ointment; hence, soothing notion   152 **mining** undermining   157 **fatness** grossness, slackness; **pursy** corpulent   165 **who all sense doth eat** who consumes all human sense, both bodily and spiritual   166 **Of habits devil** being a devil in, or in respect of, habits (with a play on "habits," as meaning both settled practices and garments, whereby devilish practices contrast with "actions fair and good," line 167, and devilish garments contrast with the "frock or livery" of line 168, which custom in its angelic aspect provides)

---

82 **mope** act without full use of one's wits   89 **will** desire   91 **grainéd spots** indelible stains   92 **tinct** color   93 **enseaméd** greasy   99 **vice** a character in the morality plays, presented often as a buffoon (here, a caricature)   116 **Conceit** imagination   123 **excrements** nails, hair (whatever grows out of the body)   124 **an** on

175 And when you are desirous to be blest,
I'll blessing beg of you. For this same lord,
I do repent; but heaven hath pleased it so,
To punish me with this, and this with me,
That I must be their scourge and minister.
180 I will bestow him and will answer well
The death I gave him. So, again, good night.
I must be cruel only to be kind.
This bad begins and worse remains behind.
One word more, good lady.
QUEEN: What shall I do?
185 HAMLET: Not this, by no means, that I bid you do:
Let the bloat king tempt you again to bed,
Pinch wanton on your cheek, call you his mouse,
And let him, for a pair of reechy kisses,
Or paddling in your neck with his damned fingers,
190 Make you to ravel all this matter out,
That I essentially am not in madness,
But mad in craft. 'Twere good you let him know,
For who that's but a queen, fair, sober, wise,
Would from a paddock, from a bat, a gib,
195 Such dear concernings hide? Who would so do?
No, in despite of sense and secrecy,
Unpeg the basket on the house's top,
Let the birds fly, and like the famous ape,
To try conclusions, in the basket creep
200 And break your own neck down.
QUEEN: Be thou assured, if words be made of breath
And breath of life, I have no life to breathe
What thou hast said to me.
HAMLET: I must to England; you know that?
QUEEN: Alack,
205 I had forgot. 'Tis so concluded on.
HAMLET: There's letters sealed, and my two school-fellows,
Whom I will trust as I will adders fanged,
They bear the mandate; they must sweep my way
And marshal me to knavery. Let it work,
210 For 'tis the sport to have the engineer
Hoist with his own petar; and 't shall go hard
But I will delve one yard below their mines
And blow them at the moon. O, 'tis most sweet
When in one line two crafts directly meet.
215 This man shall set me packing.
I'll lug the guts into the neighbour room.
Mother, good night indeed. This counsellor
Is now most still, most secret and most grave,
Who was in life a foolish prating knave.
220 Come sir, to draw toward an end with you.
Good night, mother.

*(Exit [*HAMLET *tugging in* POLONIUS*].)*

---

183 **This** i.e., the death of Polonius (cf. line 178); **remains behind** is yet to come   188 **reechy** dirty   191 **essentially** in fact   194 **paddock** toad; **gib** tom-cat   197–200 **Unpeg the basket . . . neck down** the story is lost (in it, apparently, the ape carries a cage of birds to the top of a house, releases them by accident, and, surprised at their flight, imagines he can imitate it by first creeping into the basket and then leaping out. The moral of the story, for the queen, is not to expose herself to destruction by making public what good sense decrees should be kept secret.)   211 **petar** a bomb or charge for blowing in gates   217 **indeed** in earnest (cf. lines 163, 174, 181)

— ACT FOUR —

SCENE I

Enter KING [*to the*] QUEEN, *with* ROSENCRANTZ *and* GUILDEN-
STERN.

KING: There's matter in these sighs, these profound heaves,
You must translate, 'tis fit we understand them.
Where is your son?
QUEEN: Bestow this place on us a little while.

(Exeunt ROSENCRANTZ *and* GUILDENSTERN.*)*

Ah, mine own lord, what have I seen to-night!   5
KING: What, Gertrude, how does Hamlet?
QUEEN: Mad as the sea and wind when both contend
Which is the mightier. In his lawless fit,
Behind the arras hearing something stir,
Whips out his rapier, cries 'A rat, a rat!'   10
And in this brainish apprehension kills
The unseen good old man.
KING: O heavy deed!
It had been so with us had we been there.
His liberty is full of threats to all—
To you yourself, to us, to every one.   15
Alas, how shall this bloody deed be answered?
It will be laid to us, whose providence
Should have kept short, restrained, and out of haunt,
This mad young man. But so much was our love,
We would not understand what was most fit,   20
But like the owner of a foul disease,
To keep it from divulging, let it feed
Even on the pith of life. Where is he gone?
QUEEN: To draw apart the body he hath killed,
O'er whom his very madness, like some ore   25
Among a mineral of metals base,
Shows itself pure: 'a weeps for what is done.
KING: O Gertrude, come away!
The sun no sooner shall the mountains touch
But we will ship him hence, and this vile deed   30
We must with all our majesty and skill,
Both countenance and excuse. Ho, Guildenstern!

(Enter ROSENCRANTZ *and* GUILDENSTERN.*)*

Friends both, go join you with some further aid.
Hamlet in madness hath Polonius slain,
And from his mother's closet hath he dragged him.   35
Go seek him out; speak fair, and bring the body
Into the chapel. I pray you haste in this.

(Exeunt ROSENCRANTZ *and* GUILDENSTERN.*)*

Come, Gertrude, we'll call up our wisest friends
And let them know both what we mean to do
And what's untimely done; so haply slander—   40
Whose whisper o'er the world's diameter,
As level as the cannon to his blank,

IV.i. The action is continuous with that of the preceding scene. The Queen does not leave the stage.   2 **translate** explain   11 **brainish apprehension** frenzied delusion   18 **out of haunt** away from society   26 **mineral** mine   42 **As level** as sure of aim; **blank** target

Transports his poisoned shot—may miss our name,
And hit the woundless air. O, come away!
45   My soul is full of discord and dismay.

(*Exeunt.*)

SCENE II

Enter HAMLET.

HAMLET: Safely stowed.—But soft, what noise? who calls on
Hamlet? O, here they come.

(*[Enter]* ROSENCRANTZ, *[*GUILDENSTERN,*] and* OTHERS.)

ROSENCRANTZ: What have you done, my lord, with the dead
body?
5   HAMLET: Compounded it with dust, whereto 'tis kin.
ROSENCRANTZ: Tell us where 'tis, that we may take it thence
And bear it to the chapel.
HAMLET: Do not believe it.
ROSENCRANTZ: Believe what?
10   HAMLET: That I can keep your counsel and not mine own. Besides, to be demanded of a sponge—what replication should
be made by the son of a king?
ROSENCRANTZ: Take you me for a sponge, my lord?
HAMLET: Ay, sir, that soaks up the king's countenance, his re-
15   wards, his authorities. But such officers do the king best service in the end. He keeps them, like an apple in the corner
of his jaw, first mouthed to be last swallowed. When he
needs what you have gleaned, it is but squeezing you and,
sponge, you shall be dry again.
20   ROSENCRANTZ: I understand you not, my lord.
HAMLET: I am glad of it. A knavish speech sleeps in a foolish
ear.
ROSENCRANTZ: My lord, you must tell us where the body is,
and go with us to the king.
25   HAMLET: The body is with the king, but the king is not with
the body.
     The king is a thing—
GUILDENSTERN: A thing, my lord!
HAMLET: Of nothing. Bring me to him. Hide fox, and all after.

(*Exeunt.*)

SCENE III

Enter KING, *and two or three.*

KING: I have sent to seek him, and to find the body.
How dangerous is it that this man goes loose!
Yet must not we put the strong law on him.
He's loved of the distracted multitude,
5   Who like not in their judgement but their eyes,
And where 'tis so, th' offender's scourge is weighed,
But never the offence. To bear all smooth and even,
This sudden sending him away must seem

Deliberate pause. Diseases desperate grown
By desperate appliance are relieved,   10
Or not at all.

(*Enter* ROSENCRANTZ, *[*GUILDENSTERN,*] and all the rest.*)

     How now! what hath befall'n?
ROSENCRANTZ: Where the dead body is bestowed, my lord,
We cannot get from him.
KING: But where is he?
ROSENCRANTZ: Without, my lord; guarded, to know your
pleasure.
KING: Bring him before us.   15
ROSENCRANTZ: Ho! bring in the lord.

(*They enter [with* HAMLET*].*)

KING: Now, Hamlet, where's Polonius?
HAMLET: At supper.
KING: At supper? Where?
HAMLET: Not where he eats, but where 'a is eaten. A certain
convocation of politic worms are e'en at him. Your worm is   20
your only emperor for diet. We fat all creatures else to fat us,
and we fat ourselves for maggots. Your fat king and your lean
beggar is but variable service—two dishes, but to one table.
That's the end.
KING: Alas, alas!   25
HAMLET: A man may fish with the worm that hath eat of a
king, and eat of the fish that hath fed of that worm.
KING: What dost thou mean by this?
HAMLET: Nothing but to show you how a king may go a prog-
ress through the guts of a beggar.   30
KING: Where is Polonius?
HAMLET: In heaven. Send thither to see. If your messenger
find him not there, seek him i' th' other place yourself. But
if, indeed, you find him not within this month, you shall
nose him as you go up the stairs into the lobby.   35
KING: (*To* ATTENDANTS.) Go seek him there.
HAMLET: 'A will stay till you come.

(*Exeunt* ATTENDANTS.)

KING: Hamlet, this deed, for thine especial safety—
Which we do tender, as we dearly grieve
For that which thou hast done—must send thee hence   40
With fiery quickness. Therefore prepare thyself.
The bark is ready, and the wind at help,
Th' associates tend, and everything is bent
For England.
HAMLET: For England?
KING: Ay, Hamlet.
HAMLET: Good.
KING: So is it, if thou knew'st our purposes.   45
HAMLET: I see a cherub that sees them. But come, for
England!
Farewell, dear mother.
KING: Thy loving father, Hamlet.

IV.ii.1 After the words "Safely stowed," *F* adds the line: "*Gentlemen within. Hamlet, Lord Hamlet.*" Here, as at III.iv.5 "when a character speaks of hearing someone coming, *F* provides, though *Q* does not, for the audience to hear it too" (Jenkins, *SB*, 13.35)   11 **replication** reply 29 **Hide fox, and all after** presumably a cry in some game such as hide-and-seek. The words, which do not occur in *Q2*, may be an actor's addition

IV.iii.9 **Deliberate pause** carefully considered   29 **progress** the state journey of a ruler   39 **tender** value   46 **cherub** one of the cherubim, the watchmen or sentinels of heaven, and thus endowed with the keen-est vision

HAMLET: My mother. Father and mother is man and wife, man
50   and wife is one flesh. So, my mother. Come, for England.

(Exit.)

KING: Follow him at foot; tempt him with speed aboard.
  Delay it not; I'll have him hence to-night.
  Away! for every thing is sealed and done
  That else leans on th' affair. Pray you make haste.

(Exeunt all but the KING.*)*

55   And, England, if my love thou hold'st at aught—
  As my great power thereof may give thee sense,
  Since yet thy cicatrice looks raw and red
  After the Danish sword, and thy free awe
  Pays homage to us—thou mayst not coldly set
60   Our sovereign process, which imports at full
  By letters congruing to that effect
  The present death of Hamlet. Do it, England.
  For like the hectic in my blood he rages,
  And thou must cure me. Till I know 'tis done,
65   Howe'er my haps, my joys were ne'er begun.

(Exit.)

SCENE IV

Enter FORTINBRAS *with his* ARMY *over the stage.*

FORTINBRAS: Go, captain, from me greet the Danish king.
  Tell him that by his license Fortinbras
  Craves the conveyance of a promised march
  Over his kingdom. You know the rendezvous.
5   If that his majesty would aught with us,
  We shall express our duty in his eye,
  And let him know so.
CAPTAIN: I will do't, my lord.
FORTINBRAS: Go softly on.

(Exeunt all but the CAPTAIN.*)*

(Enter HAMLET, ROSENCRANTZ, [GUILDENSTERN,] *and* OTHERS.*)*

HAMLET: Good sir, whose powers are these?
10 CAPTAIN: They are of Norway, sir.
HAMLET: How purposed, sir, I pray you?
CAPTAIN: Against some part of Poland.
HAMLET: Who commands them, sir?
CAPTAIN: The nephew to old Norway, Fortinbras.
15 HAMLET: Goes it against the main of Poland, sir,
  Or for some frontier?
CAPTAIN: Truly to speak, and with no addition,
  We go to gain a little patch of ground
  That hath in it no profit but the name.
20   To pay five ducats, five, I would not farm it;
  Nor will it yield to Norway or the Pole
  A ranker rate should it be sold in fee.

HAMLET: Why, then the Polack never will defend it.
CAPTAIN: Yes, it is already garrisoned.
HAMLET: Two thousand souls and twenty thousand ducats   25
  Will not debate the question of this straw.
  This is th' imposthume of much wealth and peace,
  That inward breaks, and shows no cause without
  Why the man dies. I humbly thank you, sir.
CAPTAIN: God buy you, sir.   30

(Exit.)

ROSENCRANTZ: Will 't please you go, my lord?
HAMLET: I'll be with you straight. Go a little before.

(Exeunt all but HAMLET.*)*

  How all occasions do inform against me,
  And spur my dull revenge! What is a man,
  If his chief good and market of his time
  Be but to sleep and feed? A beast, no more.   35
  Sure he that made us with such large discourse,
  Looking before and after, gave us not
  That capability and godlike reason
  To fust in us unused. Now, whether it be
  Bestial oblivion, or some craven scruple   40
  Of thinking too precisely on th' event—
  A thought which, quartered, hath but one part wisdom
  And ever three parts coward—I do not know
  Why yet I live to say 'This thing's to do',
  Sith I have cause, and will, and strength, and means,   45
  To do 't. Examples gross as earth exhort me:
  Witness this army of such mass and charge,
  Led by a delicate and tender prince,
  Whose spirit, with divine ambition puffed,
  Makes mouths at the invisible event,   50
  Exposing what is mortal and unsure
  To all that fortune, death, and danger dare,
  Even for an eggshell. Rightly to be great
  Is not to stir without great argument,
  But greatly to find quarrel in a straw   55
  When honor's at the stake. How stand I then,
  That have a father killed, a mother stained,
  Excitements of my reason and my blood,
  And let all sleep, while to my shame I see
  The imminent death of twenty thousand men   60
  That for a fantasy and trick of fame
  Go to their graves like beds, fight for a plot
  Whereon the numbers cannot try the cause,
  Which is not tomb enough and continent
  To hide the slain? O, from this time forth,   65
  My thoughts be bloody, or be nothing worth!

(Exit.)

---

57 **cicatrice** scar, used here of memory of a defeat   59 **coldly set** regard with indifference   60 **process** mandate   61 **congruing to** in accordance with   63 **hectic** consumptive fever   65 **haps** fortunes
IV.iv.3 conveyance conduct   6 **eye** presence   15 **main** chief part   17 **addition** exaggeration   20 **To pay** i.e., for a yearly rental   22 **a ranker rate** a greater price; **sold in fee** sold with absolute and perpetual possession

27 **imposthume** abscess   32 **inform** take shape   34 **market** profit   36 **discourse** power of reasoning   39 **fust** grow musty   50 **Makes mouths at** makes scornful faces at, derides   53–56 **Rightly to be great . . . honor's at the stake** i.e., to be rightly great is *not* to refuse to act ("stir") in a dispute ("argument") because the grounds are insufficient, but to be moved to action even in trivial circumstances where a question of honor is involved   63 **try the cause** settle by combat   64 **continent** receptacle

SCENE V

Enter HORATIO, [QUEEN] GERTRUDE, *and a* GENTLEMAN.

QUEEN: I will not speak with her.

GENTLEMAN: She is importunate, indeed distract.
Her mood will needs be pitied.

QUEEN: What would she have?

GENTLEMAN: She speaks much of her father, says she hears

5   There's tricks i' th' world, and hems, and beats her heart,
Spurns enviously at straws, speaks things in doubt
That carry but half sense. Her speech is nothing,
Yet the unshaped use of it doth move
The hearers to collection; they aim at it,

10   And botch the words up fit to their own thoughts,
Which, as her winks and nods and gestures yield them,
Indeed would make one think there might be thought,
Though nothing sure, yet much unhappily.

HORATIO: 'Twere good she were spoken with, for she may
        strew

15   Dangerous conjectures in ill-breeding minds.

QUEEN: Let her come in.

(Exit GENTLEMAN.*)*

(*Aside.*) To my sick soul, as sin's true nature is,
Each toy seems prologue to some great amiss.
So full of artless jealousy is guilt,

20   It spills itself in fearing to be spilt.

(Enter OPHELIA *[distracted].)*

OPHELIA: Where is the beauteous majesty of Denmark?

QUEEN: How now, Ophelia!

OPHELIA: (*She sings.*)

            How should I your true love know
                From another one?

25   By his cockle hat and staff,
                And his sandal shoon.

QUEEN: Alas, sweet lady, what imports this song?

OPHELIA: Say you? Nay, pray you mark.   (*Song.*)

            He is dead and gone, lady,

30   He is dead and gone;
            At his head a grass-green turf,
                At his heels a stone.

    O, ho!

QUEEN: Nay, but Ophelia—

OPHELIA: Pray you mark.

(*Sings.*)

35   White his shroud as the mountain snow—

(Enter KING.*)*

QUEEN: Alas, look here, my lord.

OPHELIA:

            Larded all with sweet flowers;   (*Song.*)
            Which bewept to the grave did not go
                With true-love showers.

KING: How do you, pretty lady?   40

OPHELIA: Well, good dild you! They say the owl was a baker's
    daughter. Lord, we know what we are, but know not what we
    may be. God be at your table!

KING: Conceit upon her father.

OPHELIA: Pray let's have no words of this, but when they ask 45
    you what it means, say you this:

(*Song.*)

            To-morrow is Saint Valentine's day,
                All in the morning betime,
            And I a maid at your window,
                To be your Valentine.   50
            Then up he rose, and donned his clo'es,
                And dupped the chamber-door,
            Let in the maid, that out a maid
                Never departed more.

KING: Pretty Ophelia—   55

OPHELIA: Indeed, without an oath, I'll make an end on't:

(*Sings.*)

            By Gis and by Saint Charity,
                Alack, and fie for shame!
            Young men will do't, if they come to't;
                By cock, they are to blame.   60
            Quoth she 'Before you tumbled me,
                You promised me to wed.'

    He answers:

            'So would I a' done, by yonder sun,
                An thou hadst not come to my bed.'   65

KING: How long hath she been thus?

OPHELIA: I hope all will be well. We must be patient, but I
    cannot choose but weep, to think they would lay him i' th'
    cold ground. My brother shall know of it, and so I thank you
    for your good counsel. Come, my coach! Good night, ladies, 70
    good night. Sweet ladies, good night, good night.

(Exit.)

KING: Follow her close; give her good watch, I pray you.

(Exeunt HORATIO *and* GENTLEMEN.*)*

    O, this is the poison of deep grief; it springs
    All from her father's death, and now behold!
    O Gertrude, Gertrude,   75
    When sorrows come, they come not single spies,
    But in battalions: first, her father slain;
    Next, your son gone, and he most violent author

IV.v.6 **Spurns enviously at straws** takes exception, spitefully, to trifles
7 **nothing** nonsense 8 **unshaped use** disordered manner 9 **collection** attempts at shaping meaning; **aim** guess 13 **sure** certain 18 **toy** trifle 19 **artless jealousy** ill-concealed suspicion 20 **spills** destroys 25 **cockle hat** hat bearing a cockle shell, worn by a pilgrim who had been to the shrine of St. James of Compostella, in Spain 26 **shoon** shoes

37 **Larded** garnished, strewn 41 **good dild you** God yield (require) you; **They say the owl was a baker's daughter** allusion to a folktale in which a baker's daughter was transformed into an owl because of her ungenerous behavior (giving short measure) when Christ asked for bread in the baker's shop 44 **Conceit upon her father** i.e., obsessed with her father's death 48 **betime** early 52 **dupped** opened 57 **Gis** Jesus 60 **Cock** corruption of God

Of his own just remove; the people muddied,
80 Thick and unwholesome in their thoughts and whispers
For good Polonius' death; and we have done but greenly
In hugger-mugger to inter him; poor Ophelia
Divided from herself and her fair judgement,
Without the which we are pictures, or mere beasts;
85 Last, and as much containing as all these,
Her brother is in secret come from France,
Feeds on his wonder, keeps himself in clouds,
And wants not buzzers to infect his ear
With pestilent speeches of his father's death.
90 Wherein necessity, of matter beggared,
Will nothing stick our person to arraign
In ear and ear. O my dear Gertrude, this,
Like to a murd'ring piece, in many places
Gives me superfluous death. Attend,   (*A noise within.*)

(*Enter a* MESSENGER.)

95 Where are my Switzers? Let them guard the door.
What is the matter?
MESSENGER: Save yourself, my lord.
The ocean, overpeering of his list,
Eats not the flats with more impiteous haste
Then young Laertes, in a riotous head,
100 O'erbears your officers. The rabble call him lord,
And as the world were now but to begin,
Antiquity forgot, custom not known,
The ratifiers and props of every word,
They cry 'Choose we, Laertes shall be king'.
105 Caps, hands, and tongues, applaud it to the clouds,
'Laertes shall be king, Laertes king!'
QUEEN: How cheerfully on the false trail they cry!

(*A noise within.*)

O, this is counter, you false Danish dogs!
KING: The doors are broke.

(*Enter* LAERTES *with* OTHERS.)

110 LAERTES: Where is this king?—Sirs, stand you all without.
ALL: No, let's come in.
LAERTES: I pray you give me leave.
ALL: We will, we will.

(*Exeunt his followers.*)

LAERTES: I thank you. Keep the door.—O thou vile king,
Give me my father!
QUEEN: Calmly, good Laertes.
115 LAERTES: That drop of blood that's calm proclaims me bastard,
Cries cuckold to my father, brands the harlot
Even here between the chaste unsmirchéd brow
Of my true mother.

79 **remove** banishment, departure; **muddied** stirred up and confused
81 **greenly** without judgment   82 **hugger-mugger** secrecy and disorder   87 **in clouds** i.e., of suspicion and rumor   88 **wants** lacks   90 **of matter beggared** lacking facts   91 **nothing stick** in no way hesitate   93 **murd'ring piece** cannon loaded with shot meant to scatter   94 F omits the King's "Attend," but substitutes, by way of drawing attention to the "noise within"   95 **Switzers** Swiss bodyguard   97 **list** boundary   99 **riotous head** turbulent mob   108 **counter** hunting backward on the trail

KING: What is the cause, Laertes,
That thy rebellion looks so giant-like?
Let him go, Gertrude. Do not fear our person.   120
There's such divinity doth hedge a king
That treason can but peep to what it would,
Acts little of his will. Tell me, Laertes.
Why thou art thus incensed. Let him go, Gertrude.
Speak, man.   125
LAERTES: Where is my father?
KING: Dead.
QUEEN: But not by him.
KING: Let him demand his fill.
LAERTES: How came he dead? I'll not be juggled with.
To hell allegiance, vows to the blackest devil,
Conscience and grace to the profoundest pit!   130
I dare damnation. To this point I stand,
That both the worlds I give to negligence,
Let come what comes, only I'll be revenged
Most thoroughly for my father.
KING: Who shall stay you?   135
LAERTES: My will, not all the world's.
And for my means, I'll husband them so well
They shall go far with little.
KING: Good Laertes,
If you desire to know the certainty
Of your dear father, is't writ in your revenge
That, swoopstake, you will draw both friend and foe,   140
Winner and loser?
LAERTES: None but his enemies.
KING: Will you know them, then?
LAERTES: To his good friends thus wide I'll ope my arms,
And like the kind life-rend'ring pelican,
Repast them with my blood.   145
KING: Why, now you speak
Like a good child and a true gentleman.
That I am guiltless of your father's death,
And am most sensibly in grief for it,
It shall as level to your judgement 'pear
As day does to your eye.   150

(*A noise within: 'Let her come in.'*)

LAERTES: How now! what noise is that?

(*Enter* OPHELIA.)

O heat, dry up my brains! tears seven times salt
Burn out the sense and virtue of mine eye!
By heaven, thy madness shall be paid with weight
Till our scale turn the beam. O rose of May,   155
Dear maid, kind sister, sweet Ophelia!
O heavens! is 't possible a young maid's wits
Should be as mortal as an old man's life?
Nature is fine in love, and where 'tis fine
It sends some precious instance of itself   160
After the thing it loves.

120 **fear** fear for   134 **throughly** thoroughly   140 **swoopstake** sweepstake, taking all the stakes on the gambling table   144 **pelican** supposed to feed her young with her own blood   149 **level** plain   153 **virtue** power   159 **fine** refined to purity

OPHELIA: *(Song.)*

　　　They bore him barefac'd on the bier;
　　　Hey non nonny, nonny, hey nonny;
　　　And in his grave rain'd many a tear—

165　Fare you well, my dove!

LAERTES: Hadst thou thy wits, and didst persuade revenge,
　　It could not move thus.

OPHELIA: You must sing 'A-down, a-down,' and you 'Call him
　　a-down-a.' O, how the wheel becomes it! It is the false stew
170　ard, that stole his master's daughter.

LAERTES: This nothing's more than matter.

OPHELIA: There's rosemary, that's for remembrance. Pray you,
　　love, remember. And there is pansies, that's for thoughts.

LAERTES: A document in madness, thoughts and remembrance
175　fitted.

OPHELIA: There's fennel for you, and columbines. There's rue
　　for you, and here's some for me. We may call it herb of grace
　　a Sundays. O, you must wear your rue with a difference.
　　There's a daisy. I would give you some violets, but they with
180　ered all when my father died. They say 'a made a good end,

(Sings.)　　For bonny sweet Robin is all my joy.

LAERTES: Thought and affliction, passion, hell itself,
　　She turns to favor and to prettiness.

OPHELIA: *(Song.)*

　　　And will 'a not come again?
185　　　And will 'a not come again?
　　　　No, no, he is dead:
　　　　Go to thy death-bed:
　　　　He never will come again.

　　　His beard was as white as snow,
190　　　All flaxen was his poll;
　　　　He is gone, he is gone,
　　　　And we cast away moan:
　　　　God ha' mercy on his soul!

And of all Christian souls, I pray God. God buy you. *(Exit.)*

195　LAERTES: Do you see this, O God?

KING: Laertes, I must commune with your grief,
　　Or you deny me right. Go but apart,
　　Make choice of whom your wisest friends you will,
　　And they shall hear and judge 'twixt you and me.
200　If by direct or by collateral hand
　　They find us touched, we will our kingdom give,

Our crown, our life, and all that we call ours,
To you in satisfaction; but if not,
Be you content to lend your patience to us,
And we shall jointly labour with your soul　　　　205
To give it due content.

LAERTES:　　　　　　Let this be so.
His means of death, his obscure funeral—
No trophy, sword, nor hatchment, o'er his bones,
No noble rite nor formal ostentation—
Cry to be heard, as 'twere from heaven to earth,　　210
That I must call't in question.

KING:　　　　　　　　So you shall;
And where th' offence is let the great axe fall.
I pray you go with me.

(Exeunt.)

SCENE VI

Enter HORATIO *and* OTHERS.

HORATIO: What are they that would speak with me?

GENTLEMAN: Sea-faring men, sir. They say they have letters
　　for you.

HORATIO: Let them come in.

(Exit GENTLEMAN.*)*

　　I do not know from what part of the world
　　I should be greeted, if not from Lord Hamlet.　　5

(Enter SAILORS.*)*

SAILOR: God bless you, sir.

HORATIO: Let him bless thee too.

SAILOR: 'A shall sir, an't please him. There's a letter for you,
　　sir—it comes from th' ambassador that was bound for
　　England—if your name be Horatio, as I am let to know it is.　　10

HORATIO: *(Reads.)* 'Horatio, when thou shalt have overlooked
　　this, give these fellows some means to the king. They have
　　letters for him. Ere we were two days old at sea, a pirate of
　　very warlike appointment gave us chase. Finding ourselves
　　too slow of sail, we put on a compelled valor, and in the grap　　15
　　ple I boarded them. On the instant they got clear of our ship,
　　so I alone became their prisoner. They have dealt with me
　　like thieves of mercy, but they knew what they did; I am to
　　do a good turn for them. Let the king have the letters I have
　　sent, and repair thou to me with as much speed as thou　　20
　　wouldest fly death. I have words to speak in thine ear will
　　make thee dumb; yet are they much too light for the bore of
　　the matter. These good fellows will bring thee where I am.
　　Rosencrantz and Guildenstern hold their course for En
　　gland. Of them I have much to tell thee. Farewell.　　25
　　　　　　'He that thou knowest thine, HAMLET.'

Come, I will give you way for these your letters,
And do't the speedier that you may direct me
To him from whom you brought them.

(Exeunt.)

---

169 **wheel** burden, refrain　172–180 Harold Jenkins in his Arden edition of *Hamlet* (London and New York, 1982) 536–42, suggests that
Ophelia gives rosemary (emblematic of remembrance) and pansies (of
thoughts) to Laertes; that she gives fennel and columbines (both signifying marital infidelity) to the Queen; she gives rue (for repentance) to
the King (keeping some for herself as a sign of her sorrow, but noting
that the King is to wear his rue with **a difference,** an heraldic term designating a mark for distinguishing one branch of a family from another
in a coat-of-arms). The daisy, an emblem of love's victims, is given to
the King as substitute for the absent Hamlet, whose absence he has
caused. The King would also be given the violets (emblems of faithfulness, associated both with Ophelia's love for Hamlet, and Polonius's
service to the state, both now lost) were these still available. Each gift of
flowers represents a symbolic reproach to the recipient　190 **poll** head

---

208 **hatchment** coat of arms

IV.vi.22 **bore** literally, caliber of a gun; hence, size, importance

SCENE VII

Enter KING *and* LAERTES.

KING: Now must your conscience my acquittance seal,
    And you must put me in your heart for friend,
    Sith you have heard, and with a knowing ear,
    That he which hath your noble father slain
5   Pursued my life.
LAERTES: It well appears. But tell me
    Why you proceeded not against these feats,
    So criminal and so capital in nature,
    As by your safety, wisdom, all things else,
    You mainly were stirred up.
KING: O, for two special reasons,
10 Which may to you, perhaps, seem much unsinewed,
    But yet to me th' are strong. The queen his mother
    Lives almost by his looks, and for myself—
    My virtue or my plague, be it either which—
    She's so conjunctive to my life and soul
15 That, as the star moves not but in his sphere,
    I could not but by her. The other motive,
    Why to a public count I might not go,
    Is the great love the general gender bear him,
    Who, dipping all his faults in their affection,
20 Work, like the spring that turneth wood to stone,
    Convert his gyves to graces; so that my arrows,
    Too slightly timbered for so loud a wind,
    Would have reverted to my bow again,
    And not where I had aimed them.
25 LAERTES: And so have I a noble father lost,
    A sister driven into desp'rate terms,
    Whose worth, if praises may go back again,
    Stood challenger on mount of all the age
    For her perfections. But my revenge will come.
30 KING: Break not your sleeps for that. You must not think
    That we are made of stuff so flat and dull
    That we can let our beard be shook with danger,
    And think it pastime. You shortly shall hear more.
    I loved your father, and we love our self,
35 And that, I hope, will teach you to imagine—

(Enter a MESSENGER *with letters.)*

MESSENGER: These to your majesty; this to the queen.
KING: From Hamlet! Who brought them?
MESSENGER: Sailors, my lord, they say. I saw them not.
    They were given me by Claudio; he received them
40 Of him that brought them.

KING: Laertes, you shall hear them.—
    Leave us.

(Exit MESSENGER.*)*

(Reads.) 'High and mighty, you shall know I am set naked on
    your kingdom. To-morrow shall I beg leave to see your
    kingly eyes, when I shall, first asking your pardon, thereunto
    recount the occasion of my sudden and more strange return. 45
                                                        HAMLET.'
    What should this mean? Are all the rest come back?
    Or is it some abuse, and no such thing?
LAERTES: Know you the hand?
KING: 'Tis Hamlet's character. 'Naked!' 50
    And in a postscript here, he says 'alone'.
    Can you devise me?
LAERTES: I am lost in it, my lord. But let him come.
    It warms the very sickness in my heart
    That I shall live and tell him to his teeth 55
    'Thus didst thou.'
KING: If it be so, Laertes—
    As how should it be so, how otherwise?—
    Will you be ruled by me?
LAERTES: Ay, my lord,
    So you will not o'errule me to a peace.
KING: To thine own peace. If he be now returned, 60
    As checking at his voyage, and that he means
    No more to undertake it, I will work him
    To an exploit now ripe in my device,
    Under the which he shall not choose but fall;
    And for his death no wind of blame shall breathe 65
    But even his mother shall uncharge the practice
    And call it accident.
LAERTES: My lord, I will be ruled;
    The rather if you could devise it so
    That I might be the organ.
KING: It falls right.
    You have been talked of since your travel much, 70
    And that in Hamlet's hearing, for a quality
    Wherein they say you shine. Your sum of parts
    Did not together pluck such envy from him
    As did that one, and that, in my regard,
    Of the unworthiest siege. 75
LAERTES: What part is that, my lord?
KING: A very riband in the cap of youth,
    Yet needful too, for youth no less becomes
    The light and careless livery that it wears
    Than settled age his sables and his weeds,
    Importing health and graveness. Two months since 80
    Here was a gentleman of Normandy.
    I have seen myself, and served against, the French,
    And they can well on horseback, but this gallant
    Had witchcraft in't. He grew unto his seat,
    And to such wondrous doing brought his horse, 85
    As had he been incorpsed and demi-natured

IV.vii.7 **capital** punishable by death   10 **unsinewed** weak   14 **conjunctive** closely joined   17 **count** reckoning   18 **general gender** common people   21 **gyves** fetters   35 Following the entrance of the Messenger, the King says in *F* "How now? What Newes?" and the Messenger replies, "Letters my Lord from *Hamlet*." Jenkins comments (*SB* 13.36): "In Q the King is not told the letters come from Hamlet; he is left to find this out as he reads, and his cry 'From *Hamlet*' betokens his astonishment on doing so. I think Hamlet would not have approved of the *F* messenger who robs his bomb of the full force of its explosion. Shakespeare's messenger did not even know he carried such a bomb, for the letters had reached him via sailors who were ignorant of their sender. They took him for 'th' Embassador that was bound for *England*' (IV.vi.9). *F*, with its too knowledgeable messenger, by seeking to enhance the effect, destroys it"

---

52 **devise** explain to   61 **checking at** turning aside from (like a falcon turning from its quarry for other prey)   66 **uncharge the practice** regard the deed as free from villainy   69 **organ** instrument   75 **siege** rank   79 **weeds** garments   86 **incorpsed** made one body; **demi-natured** like a centaur, half man half horse

With the brave beast. So far he topped my thought
That I, in forgery of shapes and tricks,
Come short of what he did.
LAERTES: A Norman was't?
90 KING: A Norman.
LAERTES: Upon my life, Lamord.
KING: The very same.
LAERTES: I know him well. He is the brooch indeed
And gem of all the nation.
95 KING: He made confession of you,
And gave you such a masterly report
For art and exercise in your defence,
And for your rapier most especial,
That he cried out 'twould be a sight indeed
If one could match you. The scrimers of their nation,
100 He swore had neither motion, guard, nor eye,
If you opposed them. Sir, this report of his
Did Hamlet so envenom with his envy
That he could nothing do but wish and beg
Your sudden coming o'er, to play with you.
105 Now out of this—
LAERTES: What out of this, my lord?
KING: Laertes, was your father dear to you?
Or are you like the painting of a sorrow,
A face without a heart?
LAERTES: Why ask you this?
KING: Not that I think you did not love your father,
110 But that I know love is begun by time,
And that I see, in passages of proof,
Time qualifies the spark and fire of it.
There lives within the very flame of love
A kind of wick or snuff that will abate it,
115 And nothing is at a like goodness still,
For goodness, growing to a plurisy,
Dies in his own too much. That we would do,
We should do when we would; for this 'would' changes,
And hath abatements and delays as many
120 As there are tongues, are hands, are accidents,
And then this 'should' is like a spendthrift's sigh,
That hurts by easing. But to the quick of th' ulcer—
Hamlet comes back; what would you undertake
To show yourself in deed your father's son
125 More than in words?
LAERTES: To cut his throat i' th' church.
KING: No place, indeed, should murder sanctuarize;
Revenge should have no bounds. But good Laertes,
Will you do this, keep close within your chamber;
Hamlet returned shall know you are come home;
130 We'll put on those shall praise your excellence,
And set a double varnish on the fame
The Frenchman gave you, bring you in fine together,
And wager on your heads. He, being remiss,
Most generous, and free from all contriving,
135 Will not peruse the foils, so that with ease,
Or with a little shuffling, you may choose

A sword unbated, and in a pass of practice
Requite him for your father.
LAERTES: I will do't,
And for that purpose I'll anoint my sword.
I bought an unction of a mountebank   140
So mortal that but dip a knife in it,
Where it draws blood no cataplasm so rare,
Collected from all simples that have virtue
Under the moon, can save the thing from death
That is but scratched withal. I'll touch my point   145
With this contagion, that if I gall him slightly,
It may be death.
KING: Let's further think of this,
Weigh what convenience both of time and means
May fit us to our shape. If this should fail,
And that our drift look through our bad performance,   150
'Twere better not assayed. Therefore this project
Should have a back or second that might hold
If this should blast in proof. Soft! let me see.
We'll make a solemn wager on your cunnings—
I ha't.   155
When in your motion you are hot and dry—
As make your bouts more violent to that end—
And that he calls for drink, I'll have preferred him
A chalice for the nonce, whereon but sipping,
If he by chance escape your venomed stuck,   160
Our purpose may hold there.—But stay, what noise?

(Enter QUEEN.)

QUEEN: One woe doth tread upon another's heel,
So fast they follow. Your sister's drowned, Laertes.
LAERTES: Drowned! O, where?
QUEEN: There is a willow grows askant the brook   165
That shows his hoar leaves in the glassy stream.
Therewith fantastic garlands did she make
Of crowflowers, nettles, daisies, and long purples
That liberal shepherds give a grosser name,
But our cold maids do dead men's fingers call them.   170
There on the pendent boughs her crownet weeds
Clamb'ring to hang, an envious sliver broke,
When down her weedy trophies and herself
Fell in the weeping brook. Her clothes spread wide,
And mermaid-like awhile they bore her up,   175
Which time she chanted snatches of old lauds,
As one incapable of her own distress,
Or like a creature native and indued
Unto that element. But long it could not be
Till that her garments, heavy with their drink,   180
Pulled the poor wretch from her melodious lay
To muddy death.
LAERTES: Alas, then, she is drowned?

---

87 **topped** excelled 88 **forgery** invention 99 **scrimers** fencers (French *escrimeurs*) 111 **passages of proof** incidents of experience 112 **qualifies** weakens 116 **plurisy** excess 122 **quick** sensitive flesh 126 **sanctuarize** give sanctuary to 133 **remiss** careless 135 **peruse** inspect

137 **unbated** not blunted; **pass of practice** treacherous thrust 142 **cataplasm** poultice 143 **simples** medicinal herbs 149 **shape** plan 150 **drift** scheme 152 **back or second** something in support 153 **blast in proof** burst during trial (like a faulty cannon) 156 **motion** exertion 158 **preferred** offered to 159 **nonce** occasion 160 **stuck** thrust 165 **askant** alongside 166 **hoar** gray 169 **liberal** free-spoken, licentious 170 **cold** chaste 171 **crownet** coronet 172 **envious** malicious 176 **lauds** hymns 177 **incapable of** insensible to 178 **indued** endowed

QUEEN: Drowned, drowned.

LAERTES: Too much of water hast thou, poor Ophelia,
185   And therefore I forbid my tears; but yet
    It is our trick; nature her custom holds,
    Let shame say what it will. When these are gone,
    The woman will be out. Adieu, my lord.
    I have a speech o' fire that fain would blaze
190   But that this folly drowns it.

(Exit.)

KING: Let's follow, Gertrude.
    How much I had to do to calm his rage!
    Now fear I this will give it start again;
    Therefore let's follow.

(Exeunt.)

— ACT FIVE —

SCENE I

Enter two CLOWNS.

CLOWN: Is she to be buried in Christian burial when she wil-
    fully seeks her own salvation?

OTHER: I tell thee she is, therefore make her grave straight.
    The crowner hath sat on her, and finds it Christian burial.

5   CLOWN: How can that be, unless she drowned herself in her
    own defence?

OTHER: Why, 'tis found so.

CLOWN: It must be 'se offendendo', it cannot be else. For here
    lies the point: if I drown myself wittingly, it argues an act,
10   and an act hath three branches—it is to act, to do, and to
    perform; argal, she drowned herself wittingly.

OTHER: Nay, but hear you, Goodman Delver.

CLOWN: Give me leave. Here lies the water; good. Here stands
    the man; good. If the man go to this water and drown him-
15   self, it is, will he, nill he, he goes—mark you that. But if the
    water come to him and drown him, he drowns not himself.
    Argal, he that is not guilty of his own death shortens not his
    own life.

OTHER: But is this law?

20   CLOWN: Ay, marry, is't; crowner's quest law.

OTHER: Will you ha' the truth on 't? If this had not been a gen-
    tlewoman, she should have been buried out o' Christian
    burial.

CLOWN: Why, there thou say'st. And the more pity that great
25   folk should have count'nance in this world to drown or hang
    themselves more than their even-Christen. Come, my spade.
    There is no ancient gentlemen but gard'ners, ditchers, and
    grave-makers. They hold up Adam's profession.

OTHER: Was he a gentleman?

30   CLOWN: 'A was the first that ever bore arms.

OTHER: Why, he had none.

CLOWN: What, art a heathen? How dost thou understand the
    Scripture? The Scripture says Adam digged. Could he dig

without arms? I'll put another question to thee. If thou an-
swerest me not to the purpose, confess thyself—   35

OTHER: Go to.

CLOWN: What is he that builds stronger than either the mason,
    the shipwright, or the carpenter?

OTHER: The gallows-maker for that frame outlives a thousand
    tenants.   40

CLOWN: I like thy wit well, in good faith. The gallows does
    well. But how does it well? It does well to those that do ill.
    Now thou dost ill to say the gallows is built stronger than the
    church. Argal, the gallows may do well to thee. To't again,
    come.   45

OTHER: 'Who builds stronger than a mason, a shipwright, or a
    carpenter?'

CLOWN: Ay tell me that, and unyoke.

OTHER: Marry, now I can tell.

CLOWN: To't.   50

OTHER: Mass, I cannot tell.

(Enter HAMLET *and* HORATIO *afar off.)*

CLOWN: Cudgel thy brains no more about it, for your dull ass
    will not mend his pace with beating. And when you are
    asked this question next, say 'a grave-maker.' The houses he
    makes lasts till doomsday. Go, get thee in, and fetch me a   55
    stoup of liquor.

(Exit OTHER CLOWN.*)*

*(*HAMLET *and* HORATIO *come forward as* CLOWN *digs and
sings.)*

(Song.)

        In youth, when I did love, did love,
            Methought it was very sweet,
        To contract–O–the time, for–a–my behove,
            O, methought, there–a–was nothing–a–meet.   60

HAMLET: Has this fellow no feeling of his business, that 'a sings
    at gravemaking?

HORATIO: Custom hath made it in him a property of easiness.

HAMLET: 'Tis e'en so. The hand of little employment hath the
    daintier sense.   65

CLOWN: *(Song.)*

        But age, with his stealing steps,
            Hath clawed me in his clutch,
        And hath shipped me into the land,
            As if I had never been such.

(Throws up a skull.)

HAMLET: That skull had a tongue in it, and could sing once.   70
    How the knave jowls it to the ground, as if 'twere Cain's jaw-
    bone, that did the first murder! This might be the pate of a
    politician, which this ass now o'erreaches; one that would
    circumvent God, might it not?

HORATIO: It might, my lord.   75

---

188 **woman** unmanly part of nature

V.i. s.d. **CLOWNS** rustics   4 **crowner** coroner   8 **se offendendo** the
Clown's blunder for **se defendendo** ("in self-defense")   11 **argal**
therefore (corrupt form of *ergo*)   20 **quest** inquest   26 **even-Christen**
fellow Christian

---

48 **tell me that, and unyoke** answer the question and then you can
relax   56 **stoup** tankard   59 **behove** benefit   59–60 The repeated *a*
and *o* may represent the Clown's vocal embellishments, but more
probably they represent his grunting as he takes breath in the course of
his digging   63 **a property of easiness** a habit that comes easily to him
71 **jowls** hurls   74 **circumvent** cheat

HAMLET: Or of a courtier, which could say 'Good morrow, sweet lord! How dost thou, sweet lord?' This might be my Lord Such-a-one, that praised my Lord Such-a-one's horse, when 'a went to beg it, might it not?

80 HORATIO: Ay, my lord.

HAMLET: Why, e'en so, and now my Lady Worm's, chopless, and knock'd about the mazzard with a sexton's spade. Here's fine revolution, an we had the trick to see't. Did these bones cost no more the breeding but to play at loggats with them?

85 Mine ache to think on't.

CLOWN: *(Song.)*

A pick-axe and a spade, a spade,
For and a shrouding sheet:
O, a pit of clay for to be made
For such a guest is meet.

(Throws up another skull.)

90 HAMLET: There's another. Why may not that be the skull of a lawyer? Where be his quiddities now, his quillets, his cases, his tenures, and his tricks? Why does he suffer this mad knave now to knock him about the sconce with a dirty shovel, and will not tell him of his action of battery? Hum!

95 This fellow might be in's time a great buyer of land, with his statutes, his recognizances, his fines, his double vouchers, his recoveries. Is this the fine of his fines, and the recovery of his recoveries, to have his fine pate full of fine dirt? Will his vouchers vouch him no more of his purchases, and double

100 ones too, than the length and breadth of a pair of indentures? The very conveyances of his lands will scarcely lie in this box, and must th' inheritor himself have no more, ha?

HORATIO: Not a jot more, my lord.

HAMLET: Is not parchment made of sheepskins?

105 HORATIO: Ay, my lord, and of calves' skins too.

HAMLET: They are sheep and calves which seek out assurance in that. I will speak to this fellow. Whose grave's this, sirrah?

CLOWN: Mine, sir. *(Sings.)*

O, a pit of clay for to be made—

110 HAMLET: I think it be thine indeed, for thou liest in't.

CLOWN: You lie out on't, sir, and therefore 'tis not yours. For my part, I do not lie in't, yet it is mine.

HAMLET: Thou dost lie in't, to be in't and say it is thine. 'Tis for the dead, not for the quick; therefore thou liest.

115 CLOWN: 'Tis a quick lie, sir; 'twill away again from me to you.

HAMLET: What man dost thou dig it for?

CLOWN: For no man, sir.

HAMLET: What woman, then?

CLOWN: For none neither.

120 HAMLET: Who is to be buried in't?

CLOWN: One that was a woman, sir; but, rest her soul, she's dead.

HAMLET: How absolute the knave is! We must speak by the card, or equivocation will undo us. By the Lord, Horatio, this three years I have took note of it, the age is grown so 125 picked that the toe of the peasant comes so near the heel of the courtier, he galls his kibe. How long hast thou been a grave-maker?

CLOWN: Of all the day i' th' year, I came to't that day that our last King Hamlet overcame Fortinbras. 130

HAMLET: How long is that since?

CLOWN: Cannot you tell that? Every fool can tell that. It was that very day that young Hamlet was born—he that is mad, and sent into England.

HAMLET: Ay, marry, why was he sent into England? 135

CLOWN: Why, because 'a was mad. 'A shall recover his wits there; or, if 'a do not, 'tis no great matter there.

HAMLET: Why?

CLOWN: 'Twill not be seen in him there. There the men are as mad as he. 140

HAMLET: How came he mad?

CLOWN: Very strangely, they say.

HAMLET: How strangely?

CLOWN: Faith, e'en with losing his wits.

HAMLET: Upon what ground? 145

CLOWN: Why, here in Denmark. I have been sexton here, man and boy, thirty years.

HAMLET: How long will a man lie i' th' earth ere he rot?

CLOWN: Faith, if 'a be not rotten before 'a die—as we have many pocky corses now-a-days that will scarce hold the lay 150 ing in—'a will last you some eight year or nine year. A tanner will last you nine year.

HAMLET: Why he more than another?

CLOWN: Why, sir, his hide is so tanned with his trade that 'a will keep out water a great while and your water is a sore de- 155 cayer of your whoreson dead body. Here's a skull now hath lain you i' th' earth three and twenty years.

HAMLET: Whose was it?

CLOWN: A whoreson mad fellow's it was. Whose do you think it was? 160

HAMLET: Nay, I know not.

CLOWN: A pestilence on him for a mad rogue! 'a poured a flagon of Rhenish on my head once. This same skull, sir, was, sir, Yorick's skull, the king's jester.

HAMLET: *(Takes the skull.)* This? 165

CLOWN: E'en that.

HAMLET: Alas, poor Yorick! I knew him, Horatio—a fellow of infinite jest, of most excellent fancy. He hath bore me on his back a thousand times, and now how abhorred in my imagination it is! My gorge rises at it. Here hung those lips that I 170 have kissed I know not how oft. Where be your gibes now, your gambols, your songs, your flashes of merriment that were wont to set the table on a roar? Not one now to mock your own grinning? Quite chop-fall'n? Now get you to my lady's chamber, and tell her, let her paint an inch thick, to 175 this favour she must come. Make her laugh at that. Prithee, Horatio, tell me one thing.

HORATIO: What's that, my lord?

---

81 **chopless** with lower jaw missing 82 **mazzard** head 84 **loggats** small logs of wood for throwing at a mark 91 **quiddities** subtle distinctions; **quillets** quibbles 96 **recognizances** legal bonds, defining debts; **vouchers** persons vouched or called on to warrant a title 97 **recoveries** legal processes to break an entail 100 **pair of indentures** deed or legal agreement in duplicate 101 **conveyances** deeds by which property is transferred

123 **absolute** positive 124 **card** card on which the points of the mariner's compass are marked (i.e., absolutely to the point) 126 **picked** fastidious 127 **kibe** chilblain 150 **pocky** infected with pox (syphilis) 163 **Rhenish** Rhine wine

HAMLET: Dost thou think Alexander looked o' this fashion i'
180 th' earth?

HORATIO: E'en so.

HAMLET: And smelt so? Pah!

(Throws down the skull.)

HORATIO: E'en so, my lord.

HAMLET: To what base uses we may return, Horatio! Why may
185 not imagination trace the noble dust of Alexander till 'a find
it stopping a bung-hole?

HORATIO: 'Twere to consider too curiously to consider so.

HAMLET: No, faith, not a jot, but to follow him thither with
modesty enough, and likelihood to lead it. Alexander died,
190 Alexander was buried, Alexander returneth to dust; the dust
is earth; of earth we make loam; and why of that loam
whereto he was converted might they not stop a beer-barrel?

Imperious Caesar, dead and turned to clay,
Might stop a hole to keep the wind away.
195 O, that that earth which kept the world in awe
Should patch a wall t'expel the winter's flaw!

But soft, but soft awhile! Here comes the king,
The queen, the courtiers.

(Enter KING, QUEEN, LAERTES, *and the Corse [with a Doctor of
Divinity as* PRIEST *and* LORDS *attendant]*.)

                          Who is this they follow?
And with such maiméd rites? This doth betoken
200 The corse they follow did with desperate hand
Fordo it own life. 'Twas of some estate.
Couch we awhile and mark.

(Retires with HORATIO.)

LAERTES: What ceremony else?

HAMLET: That is Laertes, a very noble youth. Mark.
205 LAERTES: What ceremony else?

DOCTOR: Her obsequies have been as far enlarged
As we have warranty. Her death was doubtful,
And but that great command o'ersways the order,
She should in ground unsanctified been lodged
210 Till the last trumpet. For charitable prayers,
Shards, flints and pebbles should be thrown on her.
Yet here she is allowed her virgin crants,
Her maiden strewments and the bringing home
Of bell and burial.

215 LAERTES: Must there no more be done?

DOCTOR: No more be done.
We should profane the service of the dead
To sing a requiem and such rest to her
As to peace-parted souls.

LAERTES: Lay her i' th' earth,
And from her fair and unpolluted flesh
220 May violets spring! I tell thee, churlish priest,
A minist'ring angel shall my sister be
When thou liest howling.

HAMLET: What, the fair Ophelia!

QUEEN: Sweets to the sweet. Farewell!

(Scatters flowers.)

I hoped thou shouldst have been my Hamlet's wife.
I thought thy bride-bed to have decked, sweet maid,   225
And not have strewed thy grave.

LAERTES: O, treble woe
Fall ten times treble on that curséd head,
Whose wicked deed thy most ingenious sense
Deprived thee of! Hold off the earth awhile,
Till I have caught her once more in mine arms.   230

(Leaps into the grave.)

Now pile your dust upon the quick and dead,
Till of this flat a mountain you have made
T' o'er-top old Pelion or the skyish head
Of blue Olympus.

HAMLET: *(Coming forward.)* What is he whose grief
Bears such an emphasis, whose phrase of sorrow   235
Conjures the wand'ring stars, and makes them stand
Like wonder-wounded hearers? This is I,
Hamlet the Dane.

*(*LAERTES *climbs out of the grave.)*

LAERTES: The devil take thy soul!

(Grappling with him.)

HAMLET: Thou pray'st not well.
I prithee take thy fingers from my throat,   240
For though I am not splenitive and rash,
Yet have I in me something dangerous,
Which let thy wisdom fear. Hold off thy hand.

KING: Pluck them asunder.

QUEEN: Hamlet! Hamlet!   245

ALL: Gentlemen!

HORATIO: Good my lord, be quiet.

(The ATTENDANTS *part them.)*

HAMLET: Why, I will fight with him upon this theme
Until my eyelids will no longer wag.

QUEEN: O my son, what theme?   250

HAMLET: I loved Ophelia. Forty thousand brothers
Could not with all their quantity of love
Make up my sum. What wilt thou do for her?

KING: O, he is mad, Laertes.

QUEEN: For love of God, forbear him.   255

HAMLET: 'Swounds, show me what thou't do.
Woo't weep, woo't fight, woo't fast, woo't tear thyself,
Woo't drink up eisel, eat a crocodile?
I'll do't. Dost come here to whine?
To outface me with leaping in her grave?   260
Be buried quick with her, and so will I,
And if thou prate of mountains, let them throw
Millions of acres on us, till our ground,
Singeing his pate against the burning zone,
Make Ossa like a wart! Nay, an thou'lt mouth,   265
I'll rant as well as thou.

---

228 **most ingenious** of quickest apprehension   233 **Pelion** a mountain in Thessaly, like Olympus, line 234, and Ossa, line 265 (the allusion is to the war in which the Titans fought the gods and, in their
attempt to scale heaven, heaped Ossa and Olympus on Pelion, or Pelion and Ossa on Olympus)   235 **such an emphasis** so vehement an
expression or display   241 **splenitive** fiery-tempered (from the spleen,
seat of anger)   257 **Woo't** wilt (thou)   258 **eisel** vinegar

---

187 **too curiously** over ingeniously   196 **flaw** gust   201 **Fordo** destroy; **it** its   211 **Shards** bits of broken pottery   212 **crants** garland

QUEEN: This is mere madness;
    And thus awhile the fit will work on him.
    Anon, as patient as the female dove
    When that her golden couplets are disclosed,
270 His silence will sit drooping.
HAMLET: Hear you, sir.
    What is the reason that you use me thus?
    I loved you ever. But it is no matter.
    Let Hercules himself do what he may,
    The cat will mew, and dog will have his day.
275 KING: I pray thee, good Horatio, wait upon him.

    (*Exit* HAMLET *and* HORATIO.)

    (*To* LAERTES.) Strengthen your patience in our last night's
        speech.
    We'll put the matter to the present push.—
    Good Gertrude, set some watch over your son.—
    This grave shall have a living monument.
280 An hour of quiet shortly shall we see;
    Till then in patience our proceeding be.

    (*Exeunt.*)

SCENE II

Enter HAMLET *and* HORATIO.

HAMLET: So much for this, sir; now shall you see the other.
    You do remember all the circumstance?
HORATIO: Remember it, my lord!
HAMLET: Sir, in my heart there was a kind of fighting
5   That would not let me sleep. Methought I lay
    Worse than the mutines in the bilboes. Rashly,
    And praised be rashness for it—let us know,
    Our indiscretion sometime serves us well,
    When our deep plots do pall; and that should learn us
10   There's a divinity that shapes our ends,
    Rough-hew them how we will—
HORATIO: That is most certain.
HAMLET: Up from my cabin,
    My sea-gown scarfed about me, in the dark
    Groped I to find out them, had my desire,
15   Fingered their packet, and in fine withdrew
    To mine own room again, making so bold,
    My fears forgetting manners, to unseal
    Their grand commission; where I found, Horatio—
    Ah, royal knavery!—an exact command,
20   Larded with many several sorts of reasons
    Importing Denmark's health and England's too,
    With, ho! such bugs and goblins in my life,
    That on the supervise, no leisure bated,
    No, not to stay the grinding of the axe,
25   My head should be struck off.
HORATIO: Is't possible?
HAMLET: Here's the commission; read it at more leisure.
    But wilt thou hear me how I did proceed?

---

269 **couplets** newly-hatched pair
V.ii.6 **mutines** mutineers; **bilboes** fetters   9 **pall** fail   15 **Fingered** filched   20 **Larded** garnished   22 **bugs and goblins** imaginary horrors (here, horrendous crimes attributed to Hamlet, and represented as dangers should he be allowed to live)   23 **supervise** perusal; **bated** deducted, allowed   24 **stay** await

HORATIO: I beseech you.
HAMLET: Being thus benetted round with villianies,
    Or I could make a prologue to my brains,   30
    They had begun the play. I sat me down,
    Devised a new commission, wrote it fair.
    I once did hold it, as our statists do,
    A baseness to write fair, and laboured much
    How to forget that learning; but sir, now   35
    It did me yeoman's service. Wilt thou know
    Th' effect of what I wrote?
HORATIO: Ay, good my lord.
HAMLET: An earnest conjuration from the king,
    As England was his faithful tributary,
    As love between them like the palm might flourish,   40
    As peace should still her wheaten garland wear
    And stand a comma 'tween their amities,
    And many such like as's of great charge,
    That on the view and knowing of these contents,
    Without debatement further more or less,   45
    He should the bearers put to sudden death,
    Not shriving-time allowed.
HORATIO: How was this sealed?
HAMLET: Why, even in that was heaven ordinant,
    I had my father's signet in my purse,
    Which was the model of that Danish seal,   50
    Folded the writ up in the form of th' other,
    Subscribed it, gave't th' impression, placed it safely,
    The changeling never known. Now the next day
    Was our sea-fight, and what to this was sequent
    Thou knewest already.   55
HORATIO: So Guildenstern and Rosencrantz go to't.
HAMLET: Why, man, they did make love to this employment.
    They are not near my conscience; their defeat
    Does by their own insinuation grow.
    'Tis dangerous when the baser nature comes   60
    Between the pass and fell incensèd points
    Of mighty opposites.
HORATIO: Why, what a king is this!
HAMLET: Does it not, think thee, stand me now upon—
    He that hath killed my king and whored my mother,
    Popped in between th' election and my hopes,   65
    Thrown out his angle for my proper life,
    And with such coz'nage—is't not perfect conscience,
    To quit him with this arm? And is't not to be damned
    To let this canker of our nature come
    In further evil?   70
HORATIO: It must be shortly known to him from England
    What is the issue of the business there.
HAMLET: It will be short; the interim is mine.
    And a man's life's no more than to say 'one.'
    But I am very sorry, good Horatio,   75

---

30 **Or** ere   33 **statists** statesmen   42 **comma** a connective that also acknowledges separateness   43 **charge** (1) importance (2) burden (the double meaning fits the play that makes "as's" into "asses")   48 **ordinant** guiding   52 **Subscribed** signed   59 **insinuation** intrusion   61 **pass** thrust; **fell** fierce   63 **Does it not . . . stand me now upon** is it not incumbent upon me   65 **election** i.e., to the kingship, Denmark being an elective monarchy   66 **angle** fishing line; **proper** own   68 **quit** repay

That to Laertes I forgot myself;
For by the image of my cause I see
The portraiture of his. I'll court his favours.
But sure the bravery of his grief did put me
80 Into a tow'ring passion.
HORATIO: Peace; who comes here?

*(Enter [*OSRIC*] a courtier.)*

OSRIC: Your lordship is right welcome back to Denmark.
HAMLET: I humbly thank you, sir. *(Aside to* HORATIO.*)* Dost
  know this water-fly?
HORATIO: *(Aside to* HAMLET.*)* No, my good lord.
85 HAMLET: *(Aside to* HORATIO.*)* Thy state is the more gracious,
  for 'tis a vice to know him. He hath much land, and fertile.
  Let a beast be lord of beasts, and his crib shall stand at the
  king's mess. 'Tis a chough, but as I say, spacious in the possession of dirt.
90 OSRIC: Sweet lord, if your lordship were at leisure, I should
  impart a thing to you from his majesty.
HAMLET: I will receive it, sir, with all diligence of spirit. Put
  your bonnet to his right use. 'Tis for the head.
OSRIC: I thank you lordship, it is very hot.
95 HAMLET: No, believe me, 'tis very cold; the wind is northerly.
OSRIC: It is indifferent cold, my lord, indeed.
HAMLET: But yet methinks it is very sultry and hot for my
  complexion.
OSRIC: Exceedingly, my lord; it is very sultry, as 'twere—I can
100 not tell how. My lord, his majesty bade me signify to you that
  'a has laid a great wager on your head. Sir, this is the matter—
HAMLET: I beseech you, remember.

*(*HAMLET *moves him to put on his hat.)*

OSRIC: Nay, good my lord; for my ease, in good faith. Sir, here
  is newly come to court Laertes; believe me, an absolute gen-
105 tleman, full of most excellent differences, of very soft society
  and great showing. Indeed, to speak feelingly of him, he is
  the card or calendar of gentry, for you shall find in him the
  continent of what part a gentleman would see.
HAMLET: Sir, his definement suffers, no perdition in you,
110 though I know to divide him inventorially would dozy th'
  arithmetic of memory, and yet but yaw neither in respect of
  his quick sail. But in the verity of extolment, I take him to be
  a soul of great article, and his infusion of such dearth and
  rareness as, to make true diction of him, his semblable is his
115 mirror, and who else would trace him, his umbrage, nothing
  more.
OSRIC: Your lordship speaks most infallibly of him.
HAMLET: The concernancy, sir? Why do we wrap the gentleman in our more rawer breath?
120 OSRIC: Sir?

HORATIO: Is't not possible to understand in another tongue?
  You will to't, sir, really.
HAMLET: What imports the nomination of this gentleman?
OSRIC: Of Laertes?
HORATIO: *(Aside.)* His purse is empty already. All's golden 125
  words are spent.
HAMLET: Of him, sir.
OSRIC: I know you are not ignorant—
HAMLET: I would you did, sir; yet, in faith, if you did, it would
  not much approve me. Well, sir. 130
OSRIC: You are not ignorant of what excellence Laertes is—
HAMLET: I dare not confess that, lest I should compare with
  him in excellence; but to know a man well were to know
  himself.
OSRIC: I mean, sir, for his weapon; but in the imputation laid 135
  on him by them in his meed, he's unfellowed.
HAMLET: What's his weapon?
OSRIC: Rapier and dagger.
HAMLET: That's two of his weapons—but well.
OSRIC: The king, sir, hath wagered with him six Barbary 140
  horses, against the which he has impawned, as I take it, six
  French rapiers and poniards, with their assigns, as girdle,
  hangers, and so. Three of the carriages, in faith, are very dear
  to fancy, very responsive to the hilts, most delicate carriages,
  and of very liberal conceit. 145
HAMLET: What call you the carriages?
HORATIO: *(Aside to* HAMLET.*)* I knew you must be edified by
  the margent ere you had done.
OSRIC: The carriages, sir, are the hangers.
HAMLET: The phrase would be more germane to the matter if 150
  we could carry cannon by our sides. I would it might be
  hangers till then. But on! Six Barbary horses against six
  French swords, their assigns, and three liberal conceited carriages; that's the French bet against the Danish. Why is this
  all impawned, as you call it? 155
OSRIC: The king, sir, hath laid, sir, that in a dozen passes between yourself and him he shall not exceed you three hits;
  he hath laid on twelve for nine, and it would come to immediate trial if your lordship would vouchsafe the answer.
HAMLET: How if I answer no? 160
OSRIC: I mean, my lord, the opposition of your person in trial.
HAMLET: Sir, I will walk here in the hall. If it please his
  majesty, it is the breathing time of day with me. Let the foils
  be brought, the gentleman willing, and the king hold his
  purpose; I will win for him an I can. If not, I will gain noth- 165
  ing but my shame and the odd hits.
OSRIC: Shall I deliver you so?

---

79 **bravery** ostentatious display   88 **mess** table; **chough** jackdaw; thus,
a chatterer   96 **indifferent** somewhat   98 **complexion** temperament
105 **differences** distinguishing qualities   106 **great showing** distinguished appearance   107 **card** map   108 **continent** all-containing
embodiment   109 **definement** definition   110 **divide him inventorially** classify him in detail; **dozy** dizzy   111 **yaw** hold to a course unsteadily like a ship that steers wild   113 **article** scope, importance;
infusion essence; **dearth** scarcity   114 **semblable** likeness   115 **trace**
(1) draw (2) follow; **umbrage** shadow   118 **concernancy** import, rel-
evance

---

122 **to't** i.e., to get an understanding   123 **nomination** mention
130 **approve** commend   132 **compare** compete   136 **meed** pay; **unfellowed** unequaled   141 **impawned** staked   142 **assigns** appendages
143 **carriages** an affected word for **hangers**, i.e., straps from which the
weapon was hung   145 **liberal conceit** elaborate design   148 **margent** margin (where explanatory notes were printed)   156–157 **in a
dozen passes . . . he shall not exceed you three hits** the odds the King
proposes seem to be that in a match of twelve bouts, Hamlet will win at
least five. Laertes would need to win by at least eight to four   158 **he
hath laid on twelve for nine** "he" apparently is Laertes, who has seemingly raised the odds against himself by wagering that out of twelve
bouts he will win nine   163 **breathing time** time for taking exercise
165 **an** if

HAMLET: To this effect, sir, after what flourish your nature will.

170 OSRIC: I commend my duty to your lordship.

HAMLET: Yours. (*Exit* OSRIC.) He does well to commend it himself; there are no tongues else for's turn.

HORATIO: This lapwing runs away with the shell on his head.

HAMLET: 'A did comply, sir, with his dug, before 'a sucked it.

175 Thus has he, and many more of the same bevy that I know the drossy age dotes on, only got the tune of the time; and out of an habit of encounter, a kind of yesty collection which carries them through and through the most fanned and win-nowed opinions; and do but blow them to their trial, the

180 bubbles are out.

(*Enter a* LORD.)

LORD: My lord, his majesty commended him to you by young Osric, who brings back to him that you attend him in the hall. He sends to know if your pleasure hold to play with Laertes, or that you will take longer time.

185 HAMLET: I am constant to my purposes; they follow the king's pleasure. If his fitness speaks, mine is ready; now or whenso-ever, provided I be so able as now.

LORD: The king and queen and all are coming down.

HAMLET: In happy time.

190 LORD: The queen desires you to use some gentle entertain-ment to Laertes before you fall to play.

HAMLET: She well instructs me.

(*Exit* LORD.)

HORATIO: You will lose, my lord.

HAMLET: I do not think so. Since he went into France, I have

195 been in continual practice. I shall win at the odds. But thou wouldst not think how ill all's here about my heart. But it is no matter.

HORATIO: Nay, good my lord—

HAMLET: It is but foolery, but it is such a kind of gaingiving as

200 would perhaps trouble a woman.

HORATIO: If your mind dislike any thing, obey it. I will forestall their repair hither, and say you are not fit.

HAMLET: Not a whit, we defy augury. There is a special provi-dence in the fall of a sparrow. If it be now, 'tis not to come; if

205 it be not to come, it will be now; if it be not now, yet it will come. The readiness is all. Since no man of aught he leaves knows, what is't to leave betimes? Let be.

(*A table prepared.* [Enter] *trumpets, drums, and* OFFICERS *with cushions;* KING, QUEEN, [OSRIC,] *and all the* STATE, [with] *foils, daggers, and* LAERTES.)

KING: Come, Hamlet, come, and take this hand from me.

(*The* KING *puts* LAERTES' *hand into* HAMLET's.)

HAMLET: Give me your pardon, sir. I have done you wrong,

210 But pardon 't as you are a gentleman.

This presence knows, and you must needs have heard,
how I am punished with a sore distraction.
What I have done
That might your nature, honour, and exception,
Roughly awake, I here proclaim was madness.   215
Was 't Hamlet wronged Laertes? Never Hamlet.
If Hamlet from himself be ta'en away,
And when he's not himself does wrong Laertes,
Then Hamlet does it not, Hamlet denies it.
Who does it then? His madness. If 't be so,   220
Hamlet is of the faction that is wronged;
His madness is poor Hamlet's enemy.
Sir, in this audience,
Let my disclaiming from a purposed evil
Free me so far in your most generous thoughts   225
That I have shot mine arrow o'er the house,
And hurt my brother.

LAERTES: I am satisfied in nature,
Whose motive in this case should stir me most
To my revenge. But in my terms of honor
I stand aloof, and will no reconcilement   230
Till by some elder masters of known honor,
I have a voice and precedent of peace
To keep my name ungored. But till that time
I do receive your offered love like love,
And will not wrong it.   235

HAMLET: I embrace it freely,
And will this brother's wager frankly play.
Give us the foils.

LAERTES: Come, one for me.

HAMLET: I'll be your foil, Laertes. In mine ignorance
Your skill shall, like a star i' th' darkest night,
Stick fiery off indeed.   240

LAERTES: You mock me, sir.

HAMLET: No, by this hand.

KING: Give them the foils, young Osric. Cousin Hamlet,
You know the wager?

HAMLET: Very well, my lord;
Your Grace has laid the odds o' th' weaker side.

KING: I do not fear it, I have seen you both;   245
But since he is bettered, we have therefore odds.

LAERTES: This is too heavy; let me see another.

HAMLET: This likes me well. These foils have all a length?

(*They prepare to play.*)

OSRIC: Ay, my good lord.

KING: Set me the stoups of wine upon that table.   250
If Hamlet give the first or second hit,
Or quit in answer of the third exchange,
Let all the battlements their ordnance fire.
The king shall drink to Hamlet's better breath,
And in the cup an union shall he throw,   255
Richer than that which four successive kings
In Denmark's crown have worn. Give me the cups,
And let the kettle to the trumpet speak,

---

173 **lapwing** a bird reputedly so precocious as to run as soon as hatched 174 **comply** observe the formalities of courtesy; **dug** mother's nipple 175 **bevy** a covey of quails or lapwings 176 **drossy** frivolous 177 **en-counter** manner of address or accosting; **yesty collection** a frothy and superficial patchwork of terms from the conversation of others 178 **winnowed** tested, freed from inferior elements 186 **fitness** con-venience, inclination 199 **gaingiving** misgiving

232 **voice and precedent** authoritative statement justified by prece-dent 238 **foil** (1) setting for gem (2) weapon 246 **bettered** perfected through training 248 **have all a length** are all of the same length 252 **quit in answer** literally, give as good as he gets (i.e., if the third bout is a draw) 255 **union** pearl

The trumpet to the cannoneer without,
260 The cannons to the heavens, the heaven to earth,
'Now the king drinks to Hamlet.' Come begin—

(Trumpets the while.)

And you, the judges, bear a wary eye.
HAMLET: Come on, sir.
LAERTES: Come, my lord.

(They play.)

HAMLET: One.
LAERTES: No.
HAMLET: Judgment.
OSRIC: A hit, a very palpable hit.

(Drums, trumpets, and shot. Flourish; a piece goes off.)

265 LAERTES: Well, again.
KING: Stay, give me drink. Hamlet, this pearl is thine.
    Here's to thy health. Give him the cup.
HAMLET: I'll play this bout first; set it by awhile.
    Come.

(They play.)

270 Another hit; what say you?
LAERTES: I do confess't.
KING: Our son shall win.
QUEEN: He's fat, and scant of breath.
    Here, Hamlet, take my napkin, rub thy brows.
    The queen carouses to thy fortune, Hamlet.
275 HAMLET: Good madam!
KING: Gertrude, do not drink.
QUEEN: I will, my lord; I pray you pardon me.
KING: *(Aside.)* It is the poisoned cup; it is too late.
HAMLET: I dare not drink yet, madam; by and by.
280 QUEEN: Come, let me wipe thy face.
LAERTES: My lord, I'll hit him now.
KING: I do not think't.
LAERTES: *(Aside.)* And yet it is almost against my conscience.
HAMLET: Come, for the third, Laertes. You but dally.
    I pray you pass with your best violence;
285 I am afeard you make a wanton of me.
LAERTES: Say you so? come on.

(They play.)

OSRIC: Nothing, neither way.
LAERTES: Have at you now!

(LAERTES wounds HAMLET; then, in scuffling, they change rapiers.)

KING: Part them. They are incensed.
290 HAMLET: Nay, come again.

(HAMLET wounds LAERTES. The QUEEN falls.)

OSRIC: Look to the queen there, ho!
HORATIO: They bleed on both sides. How is it, my lord?
OSRIC: How is't, Laertes?
LAERTES: Why, as a woodcock to mine own springe, Osric.
295 I am justly killed with mine own treachery.

HAMLET: How does the queen?
KING: She swoons to see them bleed.
QUEEN: No, no, the drink, the drink! O my dear Hamlet!
    The drink, the drink! I am poisoned.

(Dies.)

HAMLET: O villany! Ho! let the door be locked.
    Treachery! Seek it out.   300

(LAERTES falls. Exit OSRIC.)

LAERTES: It is here, Hamlet. Hamlet, thou art slain;
    No med'cine in the world can do thee good.
    In thee there is not half an hours' life.
    The treacherous instrument is in thy hand,
    Unbated and envenomed. The foul practice   305
    Hath turned itself on me. Lo, here I lie,
    Never to rise again. Thy mother's poisoned.
    I can no more. The king, the king's to blame.
HAMLET: The point envenomed too!
    Then, venom, to thy work.   310

(Wounds the KING.)

ALL: Treason! treason!
KING: O, yet defend me, friends. I am but hurt.
HAMLET: Here, thou incestuous, murd'rous, damnéd Dane,
    Drink off this potion. Is thy union here?
    Follow my mother.   315

(KING dies.)

LAERTES: He is justly served.
    It is a poison tempered by himself.
    Exchange forgiveness with me, noble Hamlet.
    Mine and my father's death come not upon thee,
    Nor thine on me!

(Dies.)

HAMLET: Heaven make thee free of it! I follow thee.   320
    I am dead, Horatio. Wretched queen, adieu!
    You that look pale and tremble at this chance,
    That are but mutes or audience to this act,
    Had I but time, as this fell sergeant Death
    Is strict in his arrest, O, I could tell you—   325
    But let it be. Horatio, I am dead:
    Thou livest; report me and my cause aright
    To the unsatisfied.
HORATIO: Never believe it:
    I am more an antique Roman than a Dane.
    Here 's yet some liquor left.   330
HAMLET: As th'art a man,
    Give me the cup. Let go. By heaven, I'll ha't.
    O God, Horatio, what a wounded name,
    Things standing thus unknown, shall live behind me!
    If thou didst ever hold me in thy heart,
    Absent thee from felicity awhile,   335
    And in this harsh world draw thy breath in pain,
    To tell my story.

---

272 **fat** out of training   285 **make a wanton of me** trifle with me
294 **springe** trap

305 **Unbated** unblunted; **practice** plot   324 **fell** cruel; **sergeant** an officer whose duty is to summon persons to appear before a court

(A march afar off.)

        What warlike noise is this?

(Enter OSRIC.*)*

OSRIC: Young Fortinbras, with conquest come from Poland,
    To th' ambassadors of England gives
340   This warlike volley.
  HAMLET: O, I die, Horatio!
    The potent poison quite o'er-crows my spirit.
    I cannot live to hear the news from England,
    But I do prophesy th' election lights
    On Fortinbras. He has my dying voice.
345   So tell him, with th' occurrents, more and less,
    Which have solicited—the rest is silence.

(Dies.)

HORATIO: Now cracks a noble heart. Good night, sweet prince,
    And flights of angels sing thee to thy rest!

(March within.)

    Why does the drum come hither?

(Enter FORTINBRAS, *with the* AMBASSADORS *[and with drum,
colors, and* ATTENDANTS*].)*

350 FORTINBRAS: Where is this sight?
  HORATIO: What is it you would see?
    If aught of woe or wonder, cease your search.
  FORTINBRAS: This quarry cries on havoc. O proud Death,
    What feast is toward in thine eternal cell
    That thou so many princes at a shot
355   So bloodily hast struck?
  AMBASSADORS: The sight is dismal;
    And our affairs from England come too late.
    The ears are senseless that should give us hearing
    To tell him his commandment is fulfilled,
    That Rosencrantz and Guildenstern are dead.
360   Where should we have our thanks?

HORATIO: Not from his mouth,
    Had it th' ability of life to thank you.
    He never gave commandment for their death.
    But since, so jump upon this bloody question,
    You from the Polack wars, and you from England,
    Are here arrived, give order that these bodies   365
    High on a stage be placéd to the view,
    And let me speak to th' yet unknowing world
    How these things came about. So shall you hear
    Of carnal, bloody, and unnatural acts;
    Of accidental judgements, casual slaughters;   370
    Of deaths put on by cunning and forced cause;
    And, in this upshot, purposes mistook
    Fall'n on th' inventors' heads. All this can I
    Truly deliver.
  FORTINBRAS: Let us haste to hear it,
    And call the noblest to the audience.   375
    For me, with sorrow I embrace my fortune.
    I have some rights of memory in this kingdom,
    Which now to claim my vantage doth invite me.
  HORATIO: Of that I shall have also cause to speak,
    And from his mouth whose voice will draw on more.   380
    But let this same be presently performed,
    Even while men's minds are wild, lest more mischance
    On plots and errors happen.
  FORTINBRAS: Let four captains
    Bear Hamlet like a soldier to the stage,
    For he was likely, had he been put on,   385
    To have proved most royal; and for his passage
    The soldier's music and the rite of war
    Speak loudly for him.
    Take up the bodies. Such a sight as this
    Becomes the field, but here shows much amiss.   390
    Go, bid the soldiers shoot.

(Exeunt [marching. A peal of ordnance shot off].)

---

341 **o'er-crows** triumphs over   344 **voice** vote   345 **more and less**
great and small   346 **solicited** incited, prompted   352 **quarry** pile of
dead   353 **toward** impending

363 **jump** exactly   371 **put on** instigated; **forced cause** by reason of
compulsion   385 **put on** set to perform in office   386 **passage** death

■ WILLIAM SHAKESPEARE ■

The Tempest

The Tempest was staged at court in 1611. It is probably the last play that Shakespeare wrote without a collaborator, and generations of readers and audiences have taken Prospero as an image of Shakespeare himself: when Prospero puts aside his powerful, theatrical magic, Shakespeare may in a sense be making his farewell to the stage.

Renaissance audiences might have taken *The Tempest* as an example of a new kind of play becoming increasingly popular in the early seventeenth century: *tragicomedy*. Renaissance tragicomedy generally opens in the severe, disturbing mood of tragedy and builds to a moment of crisis; it then resolves into a comic finale of festivity, marriage, and harmony. That is, this version of "tragicomedy" concerns the play's plot structure, rather than its tone or mood. Shakespeare's company, the King's Men, had staged several plays by John Fletcher, one of the premier writers of tragicomedy, and it is inviting to see Shakespeare trying out his hand at the new genre late in his career in plays such as *Pericles, Cymbeline, The Winter's Tale*, and *The Tempest. The Tempest* begins as something like a revenge tragedy: Prospero plots to revenge himself on his usurping brother Antonio, and Sebastian's plot to murder Alonso also smacks of tragic intrigue. However, *The Tempest*, while raising the problems of tragedy, resolves them in the mode of comedy. Instead of murdering his brother, Prospero marries his daughter, Miranda, to Alonso's son, Ferdinand. The spirit Ariel prompts Prospero to discover that "The rarer action is/In virtue than in vengeance."

In other respects, *The Tempest* shares the forms and moods of Shakespearean comedy. In a plot reminiscent of many of Shakespeare's earlier comedies, Prospero's daughter Miranda falls instantly in love with Alonso's son Ferdinand, for in *The Tempest*, virtue "naturally" recognizes virtue in others. The marriage also promises to heal the political rifts between Milan and Naples, and Prospero devises an elegant entertainment to lend the engagement an aura of sanctity. In its mythological characters, verse, song, and dance, Prospero's play resembles the masques frequently performed at court on such occasions. The romantic comedy of Ferdinand and Miranda is balanced by the play's more ironic treatment of Caliban, Stephano, and Trinculo. If the magical meeting of the lovers urges us to believe that the virtuous are drawn naturally together, the fact that Caliban takes the boozy Stephano and Trinculo for gods, and that the three of them try to overthrow Prospero from his second kingdom, suggests a parallel recognition—that bad nature also seeks itself out in others.

Although Prospero and Doctor Faustus may practice different kinds of magic, both are figures of the common desire to transcend nature through art. But much as Faustus is finally damned for his bargain with Mephostophilis, so Prospero learns that his own nature, and human nature generally, cannot be overcome. Prospero must learn to forgive in order to return to the world from his magic island-prison. Indeed, if the power of Prospero's artful magic is symbolized by the capable spirit Ariel, its limitations are suggested by Caliban. In some ways, Caliban represents a European imagination of human nature in its elemental form, an image of human nature that in the sixteenth and seventeenth centuries was often reinforced by European contacts with the indigenous peoples of the Americas and Africa. For although Prospero's island is located in the Mediterranean, many of its features—and the shipwreck motif—seem to be drawn from pamphlets describing the exploration of the New World. In 1609, a fleet of English ships bound for Virginia was wrecked by a storm in the Bermudas; and while many of the ships eventually reached Jamestown, one, the *Sea Adventure*, remained lost for nearly a year. When the ship finally reached Virginia in May of 1610, the Englishmen's story of survival and their encounters with the natives of the "still-vexed Bermoothes" was widely published in pamphlets that Shakespeare seems to have read while writing the play.

The play's setting and sources have led critics to see *The Tempest* as a play not only about the state of human nature, but also about the conquest and subjection of the native peoples represented by Caliban. Caliban is clearly seen from the point of view of the European settlers: Prospero calls him a devil and a slave and uses him as a beast of burden; his language is simple; and instead of using the arts of romance on Miranda, as Ferdinand does, he tries to rape Miranda in an effort to people the island with Calibans. Caliban was the master of the island's nature, its "fresh springs, brine pits, barren place and fertile," but in attempting to civilize Caliban, Prospero has succeeded only in deforming him. Caliban is now neither "natural" nor civilized, but a parody of European "humanity": "You taught me language, and my profit on't/Is, I know how to curse."

Prospero's stagey magic, his ability to conjure storms and spectacles, is a glorious image of Renaissance "overreaching." As in *A Midsummer Night's Dream* or *Hamlet,* Shakespeare uses *The Tempest* to frame his final, most subtle imaging of the extraordinary powers of art—the arts of magic, of civilization, of the theater. At the same time, *The Tempest* also expresses the limitations of that art: neither Sebastian nor Antonio seems fundamentally changed by Prospero's magic. And much as Caliban has been changed, the play finally can find no voice, no language for Caliban to speak.

THE TEMPEST

WILLIAM SHAKESPEARE

EDITED BY DAVID BEVINGTON

— CHARACTERS —

ALONSO, *King of Naples*
SEBASTIAN, *his brother*
PROSPERO, *the right Duke of Milan*
ANTONIO, *his brother, the usurping Duke of Milan*
FERDINAND, *son to the King of Naples*
GONZALO, *an honest old Counselor*
ADRIAN *and*
FRANCISCO, } *Lords*
CALIBAN, *a savage and deformed Slave*
TRINCULO, *a Jester*
STEPHANO, *a drunken Butler*

MASTER *of a Ship*
BOATSWAIN
MARINERS
MIRANDA, *daughter to Prospero*
ARIEL, *an airy Spirit*
IRIS,
CERES,
JUNO, } *[presented by]* SPIRITS
NYMPHS,
REAPERS,
[Other SPIRITS *attending on Prospero.]*

— ACT ONE —

SCENE I

An uninhabited island.

(A tempestuous noise of thunder and lightning heard. Enter a SHIP-MASTER *and a* BOATSWAIN.)

MASTER: Boatswain!

BOATSWAIN: Here, master. What cheer?

MASTER: Good speak to th' mariners. Fall to 't, yarely, or we run ourselves aground. Bestir, bestir.

(Exit.)

(Enter MARINERS.)

5 BOATSWAIN: Heigh, my hearts! Cheerly, cheerly, my hearts! Yare, yare! Take in the topsail. Tend to th' master's whistle.— Blow till thou burst thy wind, if room enough!

(Enter ALONSO, SEBASTIAN, ANTONIO, FERDINAND, GONZALO, *and others.)*

ALONSO: Good boatswain, have care. Where's the master? Play the men.

10 BOATSWAIN: I pray now, keep below.

ANTONIO: Where is the master, bos'n?

BOATSWAIN: Do you not hear him? You mar our labor. Keep your cabins; you do assist the storm.

GONZALO: Nay, good, be patient.

15 BOATSWAIN: When the sea is. Hence! What cares these roarers for the name of king? To cabin! Silence! Trouble us not.

GONZALO: Good, yet remember whom thou hast aboard.

BOATSWAIN: None that I more love than myself. You are a counselor; if you can command these elements to silence, and work the peace of the present, we will not hand a rope

20

more. Use your authority. If you cannot, give thanks you have liv'd so long, and make yourself ready in your cabin for the mischance of the hour, if it so hap.—Cheerly, good hearts!—Out of our way, I say.

(Exit.)

GONZALO: I have great comfort from this fellow. Methinks he 25 hath no drowning mark upon him; his complexion is perfect gallows. Stand fast, good Fate, to his hanging! Make the rope of his destiny our cable, for our own doth little advantage. If he be not born to be hang'd, our case is miserable.

(Exeunt.)

(Enter BOATSWAIN.)

BOATSWAIN: Down with the topmast! Yare! Lower, lower! 30 Bring her to try with main-course. *(A cry within.)* A plague upon this howling! They are louder than the weather or our office.

(Enter SEBASTIAN, ANTONIO, *and* GONZALO.)

Yet again? What do you here? Shall we give o'er and drown? Have you a mind to sink? 35

SEBASTIAN: A pox o' your throat, you bawling, blasphemous, incharitable dog!

BOATSWAIN: Work you then.

ANTONIO: Hang, cur! Hang, you whoreson, insolent noise-maker! We are less afraid to be drown'd than thou art. 40

GONZALO: I'll warrant him for drowning, though the ship were no stronger than a nutshell and as leaky as an unstanch'd wench.

I.i. Location: On a ship at sea. **3 Good** i.e., it's good you've come; or, my good fellow; **yarely** nimbly **6 Tend** attend **7 Blow** (Addressed to the wind); **if room enough** as long as we have sea-room enough **8–9 Play the men** act like men (?) ply, urge the men to exert themselves (?) **15 roarers** waves or winds, or both; spoken to as though they were "bullies" or "blusterers" **20 hand** handle

26–27 **complexion . . . gallows** appearance shows he was born to be hanged (and therefore, according to the proverb, in no danger of drowning) 28 **our . . . advantage** i.e., our own cable is of little benefit 31 **Bring . . . course** sail her close to the wind by means of the mainsail 32 **our office** i.e., the noise we make at our work 41 **warrant him for drowning** guarantee that he will never be drowned 42 **unstanch'd** insatiable, loose, unrestrained

BOATSWAIN: Lay her a-hold, a-hold! Set her two courses off to
45 sea again! Lay her off!

(Enter MARINERS *wet.)*

MARINERS: All lost! To prayers, to prayers! All lost!

(Exeunt.)

BOATSWAIN: What, must our mouths be cold?
GONZALO: The King and Prince at prayers! Let's assist them,
For our case is as theirs.
SEBASTIAN: I am out of patience.
50 ANTONIO: We are merely cheated of our lives by drunkards.
This wide-chopp'd rascal! Would thou mightst lie drowning
The washing of ten tides!
GONZALO: He'll be hang'd yet,
Though every drop of water swear against it
And gape at wid'st to glut him.

(A confused noise within:)

                              "Mercy on us!"—
55 "We split, we split!"—"Farewell my wife and children!"–
"Farewell, brother!"—"We split, we split, we split!"

(Exit BOATSWAIN.*)*

ANTONIO: Let's all sink wi' th' King.
SEBASTIAN: Let's take leave of him.

(Exit [with ANTONIO*].)*

GONZALO: Now would I give a thousand furlongs of sea for an
60 acre of barren ground, long heath, brown furze, anything.
The wills above be done! But I would fain die a dry death.

(Exit.)

SCENE II

Enter PROSPERO *[in his magic robes] and* MIRANDA.

MIRANDA: If by your art, my dearest father, you have
Put the wild waters in this roar, allay them.
The sky, it seems, would pour down stinking pitch,
But that the sea, mounting to th' welkin's cheek,
5 Dashes the fire out. O, I have suffered
With those that I saw suffer! A brave vessel,
Who had, no doubt, some noble creature in her,
Dash'd all to pieces. O, the cry did knock
Against my very heart! Poor souls, they perish'd.
10 Had I been any god of power, I would
Have sunk the sea within the earth or ere
It should the good ship so have swallow'd and
The fraughting souls within her.
PROSPERO: Be collected.

No more amazement. Tell your piteous heart
There's no harm done.   15
MIRANDA: O, woe the day!
PROSPERO: No harm.
I have done nothing but in care of thee,
Of thee, my dear one, thee, my daughter, who
Art ignorant of what thou art, nought knowing
Of whence I am, nor that I am more better
Than Prospero, master of a full poor cell,   20
And thy no greater father.
MIRANDA: More to know
Did never meddle with my thoughts.
PROSPERO: 'Tis time
I should inform thee farther. Lend thy hand,
And pluck my magic garment from me. So,

(Lays down his magic robe and staff.)

Lie there, my art. Wipe thou thine eyes; have comfort. 25
The direful spectacle of the wrack, which touch'd
The very virtue of compassion in thee,
I have with such provision in mine art
So safely ordered that there is no soul—
No, not so much perdition as an hair   30
Betid to any creature in the vessel
Which thou heard'st cry, which thou saw'st sink. Sit down;
For thou must now know farther.
MIRANDA: You have often
Begun to tell me what I am, but stopp'd
And left me to a bootless inquisition,   35
Concluding, "Stay, not yet."
PROSPERO: The hour's now come;
The very minute bids thee ope thine ear.
Obey and be attentive. Canst thou remember
A time before we came unto this cell?
I do not think thou canst, for then thou wast not   40
Out three years old.
MIRANDA: Certainly, sir, I can.
PROSPERO: By what? By any other house or person?
Of anything the image, tell me, that
Hath kept with thy remembrance.
MIRANDA: 'Tis far off,
And rather like a dream than an assurance   45
That my remembrance warrants. Had I not
Four or five women once that tended me?
PROSPERO: Thou hadst, and more, Miranda. But how is it
That this lives in thy mind? What seest thou else
In the dark backward and abysm of time?   50
If thou remem'brest aught ere thou cam'st here,
How thou cam'st here thou mayst.
MIRANDA: But that I do not.
PROSPERO: Twelve year since, Miranda, twelve year since,
Thy father was the Duke of Milan and
A prince of power.   55
MIRANDA: Sir, are not you my father?
PROSPERO: Thy mother was a piece of virtue, and

---

44 **a-hold** a-hull, close to the wind; **courses** sails, i.e., foresail as well as mainsail, set in an attempt to get the ship back out into open water   47 **must . . . cold** i.e., let us heat up our mouths with liquor   50 **merely** quite   51 **wide-chopp'd** with mouth wide open   51–52 **lie . . . tides** (Pirates were hanged on the shore and left until three tides had come in.)   54 **glut** swallow   60 **heath** uncultivated ground; heather; **furze** a weed growing on waste land
I.ii. Location: The island. Before Prospero's cell.   4 **welkin's cheek** sky's face   6 **brave** gallant, splendid   11 **or ere** before   13 **fraughting** forming the cargo; **collected** calm, composed

14 **amazement** consternation   20 **full** very   30 **perdition** loss   31 **Betid** happened   35 **bootless inquisition** profitless inquiry   41 **Out** fully   45–46 **assurance . . . warrants** certainty that my memory guarantees   56 **piece** masterpiece, exemplar

She said thou wast my daughter; and thy father
Was Duke of Milan; and thou his only heir
And princess no worse issued.
MIRANDA: O the heavens!
60 What foul play had we, that we came from thence?
Or blessed was 't we did?
PROSPERO: Both, both, my girl.
By foul play, as thou say'st, were we heav'd thence,
But blessedly holp hither.
MIRANDA: O, my heart bleeds
To think o' th' teen that I have turn'd you to,
65 Which is from my remembrance! Please you, farther.
PROSPERO: My brother and thy uncle, call'd Antonio—
I pray thee mark me—that a brother should
Be so perfidious!—he whom next thyself
Of all the world I lov'd, and to him put
70 The manage of my state, as at that time
Through all the signories it was the first
And Prospero the prime duke, being so reputed
In dignity, and for the liberal arts
Without a parallel; those being all my study,
75 The government I cast upon my brother
And to my state grew stranger, being transported
And rapt in secret studies. Thy false uncle—
Dost thou attend me?
MIRANDA: Sir, most heedfully.
PROSPERO: Being once perfected how to grant suits,
80 How to deny them, who t' advance and who
To trash for overtopping, new created
The creatures that were mine, I say, or chang'd 'em,
Or else new form'd 'em; having both the key
Of officer and office, set all hearts i' th' state
85 To what tune pleas'd his ear, that now he was
The ivy which had hid my princely trunk,
And suck'd my verdure out on 't. Thou attend'st not.
MIRANDA: O, good sir, I do.
PROSPERO: I pray thee mark me.
I, thus neglecting worldly ends, all dedicated
90 To closeness and the bettering of my mind
With that which, but by being so retir'd,
O'er-priz'd all popular rate, in my false brother
Awak'd an evil nature; and my trust,
Like a good parent, did beget of him
95 A falsehood in its contrary as great
As my trust was, which had indeed no limit,
A confidence sans bound. He being thus lorded,
Not only with what my revenue yielded,
But what my power might else exact—like one

Who having into truth, by telling of it,   100
Made such a sinner of his memory
To credit his own lie—he did believe
He was indeed the Duke, out o' th' substitution,
And executing th' outward face of royalty,
With all prerogative. Hence his ambition growing—   105
Dost thou hear?
MIRANDA: Your tale, sir, would cure deafness.
PROSPERO: To have no screen between this part he play'd
And him he play'd it for, he needs will be
Absolute Milan. Me, poor man, my library
Was dukedom large enough. Of temporal royalties   110
He thinks me now incapable; confederates—
So dry he was for sway—wi' th' King of Naples
To give him annual tribute, do him homage,
Subject his coronet to his crown, and bend
The dukedom yet unbow'd—alas, poor Milan!—   115
To most ignoble stooping.
MIRANDA: O the heavens!
PROSPERO: Mark his condition and th' event, then tell me
If this might be a brother.
MIRANDA: I should sin
To think but nobly of my grandmother.
Good wombs have borne bad sons   120
PROSPERO: Now the condition.
This King of Naples, being an enemy
To me inveterate, hearkens my brother's suit,
Which was that he, in lieu o' th' premises
Of homage and I know not how much tribute,
Should presently extirpate me and mine   125
Out of the dukedom and confer fair Milan
With all the honors on my brother. Whereon,
A treacherous army levied, one midnight
Fated to th' purpose, did Antonio open
The gates of Milan, and, i' th' dead of darkness,   130
The ministers for th' purpose hurried thence
Me and thy crying self.
MIRANDA: Alack, for pity!
I, not rememb'ring how I cried out then,
Will cry it o'er again. It is a hint
That wrings mine eyes to 't.   135
PROSPERO: Hear a little further,
And then I'll bring thee to the present business
Which now's upon 's, without the which this story
Were most impertinent.
MIRANDA: Wherefore did they not
That hour destroy us?
PROSPERO: Well demanded, wench.
My tale provokes that question. Dear, they durst not,   140

---

59 **issued** born, descended   63 **holp** helped   64 **teen . . . to** trouble I've caused you to remember, or put you to   65 **from** out of   71 **signories** i.e., city-states of northern Italy   79 **perfected** grown skillful   81 **trash** check a hound by tying a weight to its neck; **overtopping** running too far ahead of the pack; or, growing too tall   82 **creatures** dependents; **or** either   83 **key** (1) key for unlocking (2) tool for tuning stringed instruments   90 **closeness** retirement, seclusion   91–92 **but . . . rate** except that it was done in retirement, (would have) surpassed in value all popular estimate   94 **good parent** (Alludes to the proverb that good parents often bear bad children; see also l. 120.)   97 **sans** without; **lorded** raised to lordship, with power and wealth

100–102 **Who . . . lie** i.e., who, by repeatedly telling the lie (that he was indeed Duke of Milan), made his memory such a confirmed sinner against truth that he began to believe his own lie   103 **out o'** as a result of   104 **And . . . royalty** and (as a result) his carrying out all the ceremonial functions of royalty   108 **him** i.e., himself   109 **Absolute Milan** unconditional Duke of Milan   110 **temporal royalties** practical prerogatives and responsibilities of a sovereign   111 **confederates** conspires, allies himself   112 **dry** thirsty   113 **him** i.e., the King of Naples   114 **his . . . his** Antonio's . . . the King of Naples'   117 **condition** pact; **event** outcome   123 **in . . . premises** in return for the stipulation   125 **presently extirpate** at once remove   134 **hint** occasion   138 **impertinent** irrelevant

So dear the love my people bore me, nor set
A mark so bloody on the business, but
With colors fairer painted their foul ends.
In few, they hurried us aboard a bark,
145 Bore us some leagues to sea, where they prepar'd
A rotten carcass of a butt, not rigg'd,
Nor tackle, sail, nor mast; the very rats
Instinctively have quit it. There they hoist us,
To cry to th' sea that roar'd to us, to sigh
150 To th' winds whose pity, sighing back again,
Did us but loving wrong.
MIRANDA: Alack, what trouble
Was I then to you!
PROSPERO: O, a cherubin
Thou wast that did preserve me. Thou didst smile,
Infused with a fortitude from heaven,
155 When I have deck'd the sea with drops full salt,
Under my burden groan'd, which rais'd in me
An undergoing stomach, to bear up
Against what should ensue.
MIRANDA: How came we ashore?
PROSPERO: By Providence divine.
160 Some food we had, and some fresh water, that
A noble Neapolitan, Gonzalo,
Out of his charity, who being then appointed
Master of this design, did give us, with
Rich garments, linens, stuffs, and necessaries,
165 Which since have steaded much. So, of his gentleness,
Knowing I lov'd my books, he furnish'd me
From mine own library with volumes that
I prize above my dukedom.
MIRANDA: Would I might
But ever see that man!
PROSPERO: Now I arise.

(Resumes his magic robes.)

170 Sit still, and hear the last of our sea-sorrow.
Here in this island we arriv'd; and here
Have I, thy schoolmaster, made thee more profit
Than other princess' can that have more time
For vainer hours and tutors not so careful.
175 MIRANDA: Heavens thank you for 't! And now, I pray you, sir,
For still 'tis beating in my mind, your reason
For raising this sea-storm?
PROSPERO: Know thus far forth.
By accident most strange, bountiful Fortune,
Now my dear lady, hath mine enemies
180 Brought to this shore; and by my prescience
I find my zenith doth depend upon
A most auspicious star, whose influence
If now I court not but omit, my fortunes
Will ever after droop. Here cease more questions.

Thou art inclin'd to sleep; 'tis a good dullness,   185
And give it way. I know thou canst not choose.

(MIRANDA sleeps.)

Come away, servant, come! I am ready now.
Approach, my Ariel, come.

(Enter ARIEL.)

ARIEL: All hail, great master! Grave sir, hail! I come
To answer thy best pleasure; be 't to fly,   190
To swim, to dive into the fire, to ride
On the curl'd clouds. To thy strong bidding, task
Ariel and all his quality.
PROSPERO: Hast thou, spirit,
Perform'd to point the tempest that I bade thee?
ARIEL: To every article.   195
I boarded the King's ship; now on the beak,
Now in the waist, the deck, in every cabin,
I flam'd amazement. Sometime I'd divide,
And burn in many places; on the topmast,
The yards, and boresprit, would I flame distinctly,   200
Then meet and join. Jove's lightnings, the precursors
O' th' dreadful thunder-claps, more momentary
And sight-outrunning were not; the fire and cracks
Of sulphurous roaring the most mighty Neptune
Seem to besiege and make his bold waves tremble,   205
Yea, his dread trident shake.
PROSPERO: My brave spirit!
Who was so firm, so constant, that this coil
Would not infect his reason?
ARIEL: Not a soul
But felt a fever of the mad and play'd
Some tricks of desperation. All but mariners   210
Plung'd in the foaming brine and quit the vessel;
Then all afire with me, the King's son, Ferdinand,
With hair up-staring—then like reeds, not hair—
Was the first man that leapt; cried, "Hell is empty,
And all the devils are here."   215
PROSPERO: Why, that's my spirit!
But was not this nigh shore?
ARIEL: Close by, my master.
PROSPERO: But are they, Ariel, safe?
ARIEL: Not a hair perish'd.
On their sustaining garments not a blemish,
But fresher than before; and, as thou bad'st me,
In troops I have dispers'd them 'bout the isle.   220
The King's son have I landed by himself,
Whom I left cooling of the air with sighs
In an odd angle of the isle and sitting,
His arms in this sad knot.

(Folds his arms.)

---

144 **few** few words   146 **butt** cask, tub   151 **loving wrong** (i.e., the winds pitied Prospero and Miranda though of necessity they blew them from shore.)   155 **deck'd** covered (with salt tears); adorned   156 **which** i.e., the smile   157 **undergoing stomach** courage to go on   165 **steaded much** been of much use   172 **more profit** profit more   173 **princess'** princesses   181 **zenith** height of fortune (Astrological term.)   182 **influence** astrological power

---

187 **Come away** come   192 **task** make demands upon   193 **quality** (1) fellow-spirits (2) abilities   194 **to point** to the smallest detail   196 **beak** prow   197 **waist** midships; **deck** poopdeck at the stern   198 **flam'd amazement** struck terror in the guise of fire, i.e., St. Elmo's fire   200 **boresprit** bowsprit; **distinctly** in different places   207 **coil** tumult   209 **of the mad** i.e., such as madmen feel   213 **up-staring** standing on end   218 **sustaining garments** garments that buoyed them up in the sea   223 **angle** corner   224 **sad knot** (Folded arms are indicative of melancholy.)

PROSPERO: Of the King's ship,
225   The mariners, say how thou hast dispos'd,
        And all the rest o' th' fleet.
        ARIEL: Safely in harbor
        Is the King's ship; in the deep nook, where once
        Thou call'dst me up at midnight to fetch dew
        From the still-vex'd Bermoothes, there she's hid;
230   The mariners all under hatches stow'd,
        Who, with a charm join'd to their suff'red labor,
        I have left asleep; and for the rest o' th' fleet,
        Which I dispers'd, they all have met again
        And are upon the Mediterranean flote
235   Bound sadly home for Naples,
        Supposing that they saw the King's ship wrack'd
        And his great person perish.
        PROSPERO: Ariel, thy charge
        Exactly is perform'd. But there's more work.
        What is the time o' th' day?
        ARIEL: Past the mid season.
240   PROSPERO: At least two glasses. The time 'twixt six and now
        Must by us both be spent most preciously.
        ARIEL: Is there more toil? Since thou dost give me pains,
        Let me remember thee what thou hast promis'd,
        Which is not yet perform'd me.
        PROSPERO: How now? Moody?
245   What is 't thou canst demand?
        ARIEL: My liberty.
        PROSPERO: Before the time be out? No more!
        ARIEL: I prithee,
        Remember I have done thee worthy service,
        Told thee no lies, made thee no mistakings, serv'd
        Without or grudge or grumblings. Thou didst promise
250   To bate me a full year.
        PROSPERO: Dost thou forget
        From what a torment I did free thee?
        ARIEL: No.
        PROSPERO: Thou dost, and think'st it much to tread the ooze
        Of the salt deep,
        To run upon the sharp wind of the north,
255   To do me business in the veins o' th' earth
        When it is bak'd with frost.
        ARIEL: I do not, sir.
        PROSPERO: Thou liest, malignant thing! Hast thou forgot
        The foul witch Sycorax, who with age and envy
        Was grown into a hoop? Hast thou forgot her?
260   ARIEL: No, sir.
        PROSPERO: Thou hast. Where was she born? Speak. Tell me.
        ARIEL: Sir, in Argier.
        PROSPERO: O, was she so? I must
        Once in a month recount what thou hast been,
        Which thou forget'st. This damn'd witch Sycorax,
265   For mischiefs manifold and sorceries terrible
        To enter human hearing, from Argier,

Thou know'st, was banish'd; for one thing she did
They would not take her life. Is not this true?
ARIEL: Ay, sir.
PROSPERO: This blue-ey'd hag was hither brought with child   270
        And here was left by th' sailors. Thou, my slave,
        As thou report'st thyself, was then her servant;
        And, for thou wast a spirit too delicate
        To act her earthy and abhorr'd commands,
        Refusing her grand hests, she did confine thee,   275
        By help of her more potent ministers,
        And in her most unmitigable rage,
        Into a cloven pine, within which rift
        Imprison'd thou didst painfully remain
        A dozen years; within which space she died   280
        And left thee there, where thou did'st vent thy groans
        As fast as mill-wheels strike. Then was this island—
        Save for the son that she did litter here,
        A freckled whelp hag-born—not honor'd with
        A human shape.   285
        ARIEL: Yes, Caliban her son.
PROSPERO: Dull thing, I say so; he, that Caliban
        Whom now I keep in service. Thou best know'st
        What torment I did find thee in; thy groans
        Did make wolves howl and penetrate the breasts
        Of ever angry bears. It was a torment   290
        To lay upon the damn'd, which Sycorax
        Could not again undo. It was mine art,
        When I arriv'd and heard thee, that made gape
        The pine and let thee out.
        ARIEL: I thank thee, master.
PROSPERO: If thou more murmur'st, I will rend an oak   295
        And peg thee in his knotty entrails till
        Thou hast howl'd away twelve winters.
        ARIEL: Pardon, master;
        I will be correspondent to command
        And do my spriting gently.
        PROSPERO: Do so, and after two days   300
        I will discharge thee.
        ARIEL: That's my noble master!
        What shall I do? Say what? What shall I do?
PROSPERO: Go make thyself like a nymph o' th' sea.
        Be subject
        To no sight but thine and mine, invisible
        To every eyeball else. Go take this shape   305
        And hither come in 't. Go, hence with diligence!

(Exit [ARIEL].*)*

        Awake, dear heart, awake! Thou hast slept well;
        Awake!
MIRANDA: The strangeness of your story put
        Heaviness in me.   310
PROSPERO: Shake it off. Come on;
        We'll visit Caliban my slave, who never
        Yields us kind answer.
MIRANDA: 'Tis a villain, sir,
        I do not love to look on.

---

227 **nook** bay   229 **still-vex'd Bermoothes** ever stormy Bermudas
(Perhaps refers to the then-recent Bermuda shipwreck; see Play Introduction.)   231 **with . . . labor** by means of a spell added to all the
labor they have undergone   234 **flote** sea   239 **mid season** noon
240 **glasses** i.e., hourglasses   243 **remember** remind   250 **bate** remit,
deduct   258 **envy** malice   262 **Argier** Algiers

---

267 **one . . . did** (Perhaps a reference to her pregnancy, for which her
life would be spared.)   270 **blue-ey'd** with dark circles under the eyes
273 **for** because   275 **hests** commands   296 **his** its   298 **correspon-
dent** responsive, submissive

PROSPERO: But, as 'tis,
We cannot miss him. He does make our fire,
315 Fetch in our wood, and serves in offices
That profit us. What, ho! Slave! Caliban!
Thou earth, thou! Speak.
CALIBAN: *(Within.)*   There's wood enough within.
PROSPERO: Come forth, I say! There's other business for thee.
Come, thou tortoise! When?

(Enter ARIEL *like a water-nymph.)*

320 Fine apparition! My quaint Ariel,
Hark in thine ear.

(Whispers.)

ARIEL: My lord, it shall be done.

(Exit.)

PROSPERO: Thou poisonous slave, got by the devil himself
Upon thy wicked dam, come forth!

(Enter CALIBAN.*)*

CALIBAN: As wicked dew as e'er my mother brush'd
325 With raven's feather from unwholesome fen
Drop on you both! A south-west blow on ye
And blister you all o'er!
PROSPERO: For this, be sure, tonight thou shalt have cramps,
Side-stitches that shall pen thy breath up; urchins
330 Shall, for that vast of night that they may work,
All exercise on thee. Thou shalt be pinch'd
As thick as honeycomb, each pinch more stinging
Than bees that made 'em.
CALIBAN: I must eat my dinner.
This island's mine, by Sycorax my mother,
335 Which thou tak'st from me. When thou cam'st first,
Thou strok'st me and made much of me, wouldst
give me
Water with berries in 't, and teach me how
To name the bigger light, and how the less,
That burn by day and night; and then I lov'd thee
340 And show'd thee all the qualities o' th' isle,
The fresh springs, brine-pits, barren place and fertile.
Curs'd be I that did so! All the charms
Of Sycorax, toads, beetles, bats, light on you!
For I am all the subjects that you have,
345 Which first was mine own king; and here you sty me
In this hard rock, whiles you do keep from me
The rest o' th' island.
PROSPERO: Thou most lying slave,
Whom stripes may move, not kindness! I have us'd
thee,
Filth as thou art, with humane care, and lodg'd
thee
350 In mine own cell, till thou didst seek violate
The honor of my child.

CALIBAN: O ho, O ho! Would 't had been done!
Thou didst prevent me; I had peopled else
This isle with Calibans.
MIRANDA: Abhorred slave,
Which any print of goodness wilt not take,   355
Being capable of all ill! I pitied thee,
Took pains to make thee speak, taught thee each
hour
One thing or other. When thou didst not, savage,
Know thine own meaning, but wouldst gabble like
A thing most brutish, I endow'd thy purposes   360
With words that made them known. But thy vile
race,
Though thou didst learn, had that in 't which
good natures
Could not abide to be with; therefore wast thou
Deservedly confin'd into this rock,
Who hadst deserv'd more than a prison.   365
CALIBAN: You taught me language, and my profit on 't
Is, I know how to curse. The red plague rid you
For learning me your language!
PROSPERO: Hag-seed, hence!
Fetch us in fuel; and be quick, thou 'rt best,
To answer other business. Shrug'st thou, malice?   370
If thou neglect'st or dost unwillingly
What I command, I'll rack thee with old cramps,
Fill all thy bones with aches, make thee roar
That beasts shall tremble at thy din.
CALIBAN: No, pray thee.
(Aside.) I must obey. His art is of such pow'r,   375
It would control my dam's god, Setebos,
And make a vassal of him.
PROSPERO: So, slave, hence!

(Exit CALIBAN.*)*

(Enter FERDINAND; *and* ARIEL, *invisible, playing and singing.*
*[*FERDINAND *does not see* PROSPERO *and* MIRANDA.*])*

(ARIEL'*s song.)*

Come unto these yellow sands,
And then take hands.
Curtsied when you have and kiss'd,   380
The wild waves whist,
Foot it featly here and there;
And, sweet sprites, the burden bear.
Hark, hark!

(Burden, dispersedly [within].)

Bow-wow.   385
The watch-dogs bark.

(Burden, dispersedly [within].)

---

314 **miss** do without   320 **quaint** ingenious   323 **wicked** mischievous, harmful   326 **south-west** i.e., wind thought to bring disease
329 **urchins** hedgehogs; here, suggesting goblins in the guise of hedgehogs   330 **vast** lengthy, desolate time; **that . . . work** (Malignant spirits were thought to be restricted to the hours of darkness.)   348 **stripes** lashes

354–365 **Abhorred . . . prison** (Sometimes assigned by editors to Prospero.)   360 **purposes** meanings, desires   361 **race** natural disposition; species, nature   367 **red plague** bubonic plague; **rid** destroy   368 **learning** teaching; **Hag-seed** offspring of a female demon   369 **thou'rt best** you'd be well advised   372 **old** such as old people suffer; or, plenty of   373 **aches** (Pronounced "aitches.")   381 **whist** being hushed   382 **featly** nimbly   383 **burden** refrain, undersong   s.d. **dispersedly** i.e., from all directions

Bow-wow.
Hark, hark! I hear
The strain of strutting chanticleer
390   Cry, Cock-a-diddle-dow.

FERDINAND: Where should this music be? I' th' air or
   th' earth?
   It sounds no more; and, sure, it waits upon
   Some god o' th' island. Sitting on a bank,
395   Weeping again the King my father's wrack,
   This music crept by me upon the waters,
   Allaying both their fury and my passion
   With its sweet air. Thence I have follow'd it,
   Or it hath drawn me rather. But 'tis gone.
   No, it begins again.

            (ARIEL's *song*.)

400   Full fathom five thy father lies;
         Of his bones are coral made;
         Those are pearls that were his eyes.
         Nothing of him that doth fade
         But doth suffer a sea-change
405   Into something rich and strange.
         Sea-nymphs hourly ring his knell:

(Burden [within].)

         Ding-dong.
         Hark, now I hear them—Ding-dong,
            bell.

FERDINAND: The ditty does remember my drown'd father.
410   This is no mortal business, nor no sound
   That the earth owes. I hear it now above me.
PROSPERO: The fringed curtains of thine eye advance
   And say what thou seest yond.
MIRANDA: What is 't! A spirit!
   Lord, how it looks about! Believe me, sir,
415   It carries a brave form. But 'tis a spirit.
PROSPERO: No, wench, it eats and sleeps and hath such senses
   As we have, such. This gallant which thou seest
   Was in the wrack; and, but he's something stain'd
   With grief, that's beauty's canker, thou mightst call him
420   A goodly person. He hath lost his fellows
   And strays about to find 'em.
MIRANDA: I might call him
   A thing divine, for nothing natural
   I ever saw so noble.
PROSPERO: (*Aside.*) It goes on, I see,
   As my soul prompts it. Spirit, fine spirit, I'll free thee
425   Within two days for this.
FERDINAND: (*Seeing* MIRANDA.) Most sure, the goddess
   On whom these airs attend!—Vouchsafe my pray'r
   May know if you remain upon this island,
   And that you will some good instruction give
   How I may bear me here. My prime request,

Which I do last pronounce, is, O you wonder!   430
If you be maid or no?
MIRANDA: No wonder, sir,
   But certainly a maid.
FERDINAND: My language? Heavens!
   I am the best of them that speak this speech,
   Were I but where 'tis spoken.
PROSPERO: (*Coming forward.*) How? The best?
   What wert thou, if the King of Naples heard thee?   435
FERDINAND: A single thing, as I am now, that wonders
   To hear thee speak of Naples. He does hear me;
   And that he does I weep. Myself am Naples,
   Who with mine eyes, never since at ebb, beheld
   The King my father wrack'd.   440
MIRANDA: Alack, for mercy!
FERDINAND: Yes, faith, and all his lords, the Duke of Milan
   And his brave son being twain.
PROSPERO: (*Aside.*)   The Duke of Milan
   And his more braver daughter could control thee,
   If now 'twere fit to do 't. At the first sight
   They have chang'd eyes. Delicate Ariel,   445
   I'll set thee free for this. (*To* FERDINAND.) A word, good sir.
   I fear you have done yourself some wrong. A word!
MIRANDA: (*Aside.*) Why speaks my father so ungently? This
   Is the third man that e'er I saw, the first
   That e'er I sigh'd for. Pity move my father   450
   To be inclin'd my way!
FERDINAND: O, if a virgin,
   And your affection not gone forth, I'll make you
   The Queen of Naples.
PROSPERO: Soft, sir! One word more.
   (*Aside.*) They are both in either's pow'rs; but this swift
      business
   I must uneasy make, lest too light winning   455
   Make the prize light. (*To* FERDINAND.) One word more: I
      charge thee
   That thou attend me. Thou dost here usurp
   The name thou ow'st not, and hast put thyself
   Upon this island as a spy, to win it
   From me, the lord on 't.   460
FERDINAND: No, as I am a man.
MIRANDA: There's nothing ill can dwell in such a temple.
   If the ill spirit have so fair a house,
   Good things will strive to dwell with 't.
PROSPERO: Follow me.—
   Speak not you for him; he's a traitor.—Come,
   I'll manacle thy neck and feet together.   465
   Sea-water shalt thou drink; thy food shall be
   The fresh-brook mussels, wither'd roots, and husks
   Wherein the acorn cradled. Follow.
FERDINAND: No.

---

409 **remember** commemorate 411 **owes** owns 412 **advance** raise 415 **brave** excellent 418 **but** except that; **something stain'd** somewhat disfigured 419 **canker** cankerworm (feeding on buds and leaves) 423 **It goes on** i.e., my plan works 427 **remain** dwell 429 **bear me** conduct myself; **prime** chief

433 **best** i.e., in birth 436 **single** (1) solitary (2) feeble 437–438 **He . . . weep** i.e., this man to whom I speak (Prospero) hears me as I hear him, proving to me I am indeed alive, not dreaming, and am in the sad plight I imagined (?) 438 **Naples** the King of Naples (also in l. 437) 442 **son** (The only reference in the play to a son of Antonio.) 443 **control** confute 445 **chang'd eyes** exchanged amorous glances 447 **done . . . wrong** i.e., spoken falsely 455 **uneasy** difficult 455–456 **light . . . light** easy . . . cheap 458 **ow'st** ownest

470 I will resist such entertainment till
Mine enemy has more pow'r.

(He draws, and is charmed from moving.)

MIRANDA: O dear father,
Make not too rash a trial of him, for
He's gentle, and not fearful.

PROSPERO: What, I say,
My foot my tutor?—Put thy sword up, traitor,
Who mak'st a show but dar'st not strike, thy conscience
475 Is so possess'd with guilt. Come, from thy ward,
For I can here disarm thee with this stick
And make thy weapon drop.

(Brandishes his staff.)

MIRANDA: *(Trying to hinder him.)*   Beseech you, father.
PROSPERO: Hence! Hang not on my garments.
MIRANDA: Sir, have pity!
I'll be his surety.

PROSPERO: Silence! One word more
480 Shall make me chide thee, if not hate thee. What,
An advocate for an imposter? Hush!
Thou think'st there is no more such shapes as he,
Having seen but him and Caliban. Foolish wench,
To th' most of men this is a Caliban
485 And they to him are angels.

MIRANDA: My affections
Are then most humble; I have no ambition
To see a goodlier man.

PROSPERO: *(To FERDINAND.)* Come on, obey.
Thy nerves are in their infancy again
And have no vigor in them.

FERDINAND: So they are.
490 My spirits, as in a dream, are all bound up.
My father's loss, the weakness which I feel,
The wrack of all my friends, nor this man's threats
To whom I am subdu'd, are but light to me,
Might I put through my prison once a day
495 Behold this maid. All corners else o' th' earth
Let libery make use of; space enough
Have I in such a prison.

PROSPERO: *(Aside.)* It works. *(To FERDINAND.)* Come on.—
Thou hast done well, fine Ariel! *(To FERDINAND.)* Follow
me.
(To ARIEL.) Hark what thou else shalt do me.

MIRANDA: *(To FERDINAND.)*   Be of comfort.
500 My father's of a better nature, sir,
Than he appears by speech. This is unwonted
Which now came from him.

PROSPERO: *(To ARIEL.)*   Thou shalt be as free
As mountain winds, but then exactly do
All points of my command.

ARIEL: To th' syllable.
505 PROSPERO: *(To FERDINAND.)* Come, follow. *(To MIRANDA.)*
Speak not for him.

(Exeunt.)

---

469 **entertainment** treatment 472 **gentle** wellborn; **fearful** cowardly
473 **foot** subordinate (Miranda, the foot, presumes to instruct Prospero, the head.) 475 **ward** defensive posture (in fencing) 484 **To**
compared to 488 **nerves** sinews 499 **me** for me

— ACT TWO —

SCENE I

Enter ALONSO, SEBASTIAN, ANTONIO, GONZALO, ADRIAN,
FRANCISCO, *and others.*

GONZALO: Beseech you, sir, be merry. You have cause,
So have we all, of joy, for our escape
Is much beyond our loss. Our hint of woe
Is common; every day some sailor's wife,
The masters of some merchant, and the merchant,   5
Have just our theme of woe; but for the miracle,
I mean our preservation, few in millions
Can speak like us. Then wisely, good sir, weigh
Our sorrow with our comfort.

ALONSO: Prithee, peace.

SEBASTIAN: *(To ANTONIO.)* He receives comfort like cold   10
porridge.

ANTONIO: *(To SEBASTIAN.)* The visitor will not give him o'er
so.

SEBASTIAN: Look, he's winding up the watch of his wit; by and
by it will strike.   15

GONZALO: Sir—

SEBASTIAN: *(To ANTONIO.)* One. Tell.

GONZALO: When every grief is entertain'd that's offer'd,
Comes to th' entertainer—

SEBASTIAN: A dollar.   20

GONZALO: Dolor comes to him, indeed. You have spoken truer
than you purpos'd.

SEBASTIAN: You have taken it wiselier than I meant you should.

GONZALO: Therefore, my lord—

ANTONIO: Fie, what a spendthrift is he of his tongue!   25

ALONSO: I prithee, spare.

GONZALO: Well, I have done. But yet—

SEBASTIAN: He will be talking.

ANTONIO: Which, of he or Adrian, for a good wager, first begins
to crow?   30

SEBASTIAN: The old cock.

ANTONIO: The cock'rel.

SEBASTIAN: Done. The wager?

ANTONIO: A laughter.

SEBASTIAN: A match!   35

ADRIAN: Though this island seem to be desert—

SEBASTIAN: Ha, ha, ha!

ANTONIO: So, you're paid.

II.i. Location: Another part of the island. 3 **hint of** occasion for 5
masters . . . the merchant officers of some merchant vessel and the
merchant himself, the owner 11 **porridge** (with a pun on *peace* and
pease, a usual ingredient of porridge) 12 **visitor** one taking nourishment and comfort to the sick, i.e., Gonzalo; **give him o'er** abandon
him 17 **Tell** keep count 18–19 **When . . . entertainer** when every
sorrow that presents itself is accepted without resistance, there comes
to the recipient 20 **dollar** widely-circulated coin, the German *Thaler*
and the Spanish *piece of eight.* (Sebastian puns on *entertainer* in the
sense of *innkeeper*; to Gonzalo, *dollar* suggests *dolor*, grief.) 29–30
Which . . . crow which of the two, Gonzalo or Adrian, do you bet will
speak (crow) first 31 **old cock** i.e., Gonzalo 32 **cock'rel** i.e., Adrian
34 **laughter** (1) burst of laughter (2) sitting of eggs. (When Adrian, the
cock'rel, begins to speak two lines later, Sebastian loses the bet. Some
editors alter the speech prefixes in ll. 37–38 so that Antonio enjoys his
laugh as the prize for winning, but possibly Sebastian pays for losing
with a laugh.) 35 **A match** a bargain; agreed

ADRIAN: Uninhabitable and almost inaccessible—

40 SEBASTIAN: Yet—

ADRIAN: Yet—

ANTONIO: He could not miss 't.

ADRIAN: It must needs be of subtle, tender, and delicate
temperance.

45 ANTONIO: Temperance was a delicate wench.

SEBASTIAN: Ay, and a subtle, as he most learnedly deliver'd.

ADRIAN: The air breathes upon us here most sweetly.

SEBASTIAN: As if it had lungs, and rotten ones.

ANTONIO: Or as 'twere perfum'd by a fen.

50 GONZALO: Here is everything advantageous to life.

ANTONIO: True, save means to live.

SEBASTIAN: Of that there's none, or little.

GONZALO: How lush and lusty the grass looks! How green!

ANTONIO: The ground indeed is tawny.

55 SEBASTIAN: With an eye of green in 't.

ANTONIO: He misses not much.

SEBASTIAN: No; he doth but mistake the truth totally.

GONZALO: But the rarity of it is—which is indeed almost beyond credit—

60 SEBASTIAN: As many vouch'd rarities are.

GONZALO: That our garments, being, as they were, drench'd
in the sea, hold notwithstanding their freshness and glosses,
being rather new-dyed than stain'd with salt water.

ANTONIO: If but one of his pockets could speak, would it not
65 say he lies?

SEBASTIAN: Ay, or very falsely pocket up his report.

GONZALO: Methinks our garments are now as fresh as when
we put them on first in Afric, at the marriage of the King's
fair daughter Claribel to the King of Tunis.

70 SEBASTIAN: 'Twas a sweet marriage, and we prosper well in our
return.

ADRIAN: Tunis was never grac'd before with such a paragon to
their queen.

GONZALO: Not since widow Dido's time.

75 ANTONIO: Widow! A pox o' that! How came that widow in?
Widow Dido!

SEBASTIAN: What if he had said "widower Aeneas" too? Good
Lord, how you take it!

ADRIAN: "Widow Dido" said you? You make me study of that.
80 She was of Carthage, not of Tunis.

GONZALO: This Tunis, sir, was Carthage.

ADRIAN: Carthage?

GONZALO: A assure you, Carthage.

ANTONIO: His word is more than the miraculous harp.

SEBASTIAN: He hath rais'd the wall and houses too. 85

ANTONIO: What impossible matter will he make easy next?

SEBASTIAN: I think he will carry this island home in his pocket
and give it his son for an apple.

ANTONIO: And, sowing the kernels of it in the sea, bring forth
more islands. 90

GONZALO: Ay.

ANTONIO: Why, in good time.

GONZALO: (*To* ALONSO.) Sir, we were talking that our garments seem now as fresh as when we were at Tunis at the
marriage of your daughter, who is now queen. 95

ANTONIO: And the rarest that e'er came there.

SEBASTIAN: Bate, I beseech you, widow Dido.

ANTONIO: O, widow Dido? Ay, widow Dido.

GONZALO: Is not, sir, my doublet as fresh as the first day I wore
it? I mean, in a sort. 100

ANTONIO: That "sort" was well fish'd for.

GONZALO: When I wore it at your daughter's marriage?

ALONSO: You cram these words into mine ears against
The stomach of my sense. Would I had never
Married my daughter there! For, coming thence, 105
My son is lost and, in my rate, she too,
Who is so far from Italy removed
I ne'er again shall see her. O thou mine heir
Of Naples and of Milan, what strange fish
Hath made his meal on thee? 110

FRANCISCO: Sir, he may live.
I saw him beat the surges under him,
And ride upon their backs. He trod the water,
Whose enmity he flung aside, and breasted
The surge most swoll'n that met him. His bold head
'Bove the contentious waves he kept, and oared 115
Himself with his good arms in lusty stroke
To th' shore, that o'er his wave-worn basis bowed,
As stooping to relieve him. I not doubt
He came alive to land.

ALONSO: No, no, he's gone.

SEBASTIAN: Sir, you may thank yourself for this great loss, 120
That would not bless our Europe with your daughter,
But rather loose her to an African,
Where she at least is banish'd from your eye,
Who hath cause to wet the grief on 't.

ALONSO: Prithee, peace.

SEBASTIAN: You were kneel'd to and importun'd otherwise 125

---

42 **miss 't** (1) avoid saying "Yet" (2) miss the island   44 **temperance**
climate   45 **Temperance** a girl's name; **delicate** (Here it means *given
to pleasure, voluptuous*; in l. 43, *pleasant*. Antonio is evidently suggesting that "tender, and delicate temperance" sounds like a Puritan
phrase, which Antonio then mocks by applying the words to a woman
rather than an island. He began this bawdy comparison with a double
entendre on *inaccessible*, l. 39.)   46 **subtle** (Here it means *tricky*; in l.
43, *delicate*.); **deliver'd** uttered. (Sebastian joins in the Puritan baiting
of Antonio with his use of the pious cant phrase "learnedly deliver'd.")
53 **lusty** healthy   54 **tawny** dull brown, yellowish   55 **eye** tinge, or
spot (perhaps with reference to Gonzalo's eye or judgment)   60
vouch'd certified   64 **pockets** i.e., because they are muddy   66
pocket up receive unprotestingly, fail to respond to a challenge   72 **to**
for   74 **widow Dido** Queen of Carthage, deserted by Aeneas. (She
was in fact a widow when Aeneas, a widower, met her, but Antonio may
be amused at the term "widow" to describe a woman deserted by her
lover.)

---

84 **miraculous harp** (Alludes to Amphion's harp with which he raised
the walls of Thebes; Gonzalo has exceeded that deed by creating a
modern Carthage—walls *and* houses—mistakenly on the site of
Tunis.)   91 **Ay** (Gonzalo may be reasserting his point about Carthage,
or he may be responding ironically to Antonio who in turn answers sarcastically.)   92 **in good time** (An expression of ironical acquiescence
or amazement; i.e., *sure, right away.*)   96 **rarest** most remarkable,
beautiful   97 **Bate** abate, except, leave out. (i.e., don't forget Dido; or,
let's have no more talk of Dido.)   100 **in a sort** in a way   104 **stomach** appetite   105 **Married** given in marriage   106 **rate** estimation,
consideration   116 **lusty** vigorous   117 **that . . . bowed** that hung out
over its wave-worn foot   118 **As** as if   124 **Who** which, i.e., the eye

By all of us, and the fair soul herself
Weigh'd between loathness and obedience, at
Which end o' th' beam should bow. We have lost your son,
I fear, for ever. Milan and Naples have
130 Moe widows in them of their business' making
Than we bring men to comfort them.
The fault's your own.

ALONSO: So is the dear'st o' th' loss.

GONZALO: My lord Sebastian,
The truth you speak doth lack some gentleness,
135 And time to speak it in. You rub the sore,
When you should bring the plaster.

SEBASTIAN: Very well.

ANTONIO: And most chirurgeonly.

GONZALO: It is foul weather in us all, good sir,
When you are cloudy.

SEBASTIAN: (*To* ANTONIO.) Foul weather?

ANTONIO: (*To* SEBASTIAN.)   Very foul.

140 GONZALO: Had I plantation of this isle, my lord—

ANTONIO: He'd sow 't with nettle-seed.

SEBASTIAN: Or docks, or mallows.

GONZALO: And were the king on 't, what would I do?

SEBASTIAN: Scape being drunk for want of wine.

GONZALO: I' th' commonwealth I would by contraries
145 Execute all things; for no kind of traffic
Would I admit; no name of magistrate;
Letters should not be known; riches, poverty,
And use of service, none; contract, succession,
Bourn, bound of land, tilth, vineyard, none;
150 No use of metal, corn, or wine, or oil;
No occupation; all men idle, all,
And women too, but innocent and pure;
No sovereignty—

SEBASTIAN: Yet he would be king on 't.

ANTONIO: The latter end of his commonwealth forgets the
      beginning.
155 GONZALO: All things in common nature should produce
Without sweat or endeavor. Treason, felony,
Sword, pike, knife, gun, or need of any engine,
Would I not have; but nature should bring forth,
Of it own kind, all foison, all abundance,
160 To feed my innocent people.

SEBASTIAN: No marrying 'mong his subjects?

ANTONIO: None, man; all idle—whores and knaves.

GONZALO: I would with such perfection govern, sir,
T' excel the golden age.

SEBASTIAN: Save his Majesty!

165 ANTONIO: Long live Gonzalo!

GONZALO: And—do you mark me, sir?

ALONSO: Prithee, no more. Thou dost talk nothing to me.

GONZALO: I do well believe your Highness, and did it to minister occasion to these gentlemen, who are of such sensible
and nimble lungs that they always use to laugh at nothing.

ANTONIO: 'Twas you we laugh'd at.   170

GONZALO: Who in this kind of merry fooling am nothing to
you; so you may continue and laugh at nothing still.

ANTONIO: What a blow was there given!

SEBASTIAN: An it had not fall'n flat-long.

GONZALO: You are gentlemen of brave mettle; you would lift 175
the moon out of her sphere, if she would continue in it five
weeks without changing.

(*Enter* ARIEL *[invisible] playing solemn music.*)

SEBASTIAN: We would so, and then go a-batfowling.

ANTONIO: Nay, good my lord, be not angry.

GONZALO: No, I warrant, you, I will not adventure my discre- 180
tion so weakly. Will you laugh me asleep? For I am very
heavy.

ANTONIO: Go sleep, and hear us.

(*All sleep except* ALONSO, SEBASTIAN, *and* ANTONIO.)

ALONSO: What, all so soon asleep? I wish mine eyes
Would, with themselves, shut up my thoughts. I find   185
They are inclin'd to do so.

SEBASTIAN: Please you, sir,
Do not omit the heavy offer of it.
It seldom visits sorrow; when it doth,
It is a comforter.

ANTONIO: We two, my lord,
Will guard your person while you take your rest,   190
And watch your safety.

ALONSO: Thank you. Wondrous heavy.

(ALONSO *sleeps. Exit* ARIEL.)

SEBASTIAN: What a strange drowsiness possesses them!

ANTONIO: It is the quality o' th' climate.

SEBASTIAN: Why
Doth it not then our eyelids sink? I find not
Myself dispos'd to sleep.   195

ANTONIO: Nor I; my spirits are nimble.
They fell together all, as by consent;
They dropp'd, as by a thunder-stroke. What might,
Worthy Sebastian? O, what might—? No more—
And yet methinks I see it in thy face,
What thou shouldst be. Th' occasion speaks thee, and   200
My strong imagination sees a crown
Dropping upon thy head.

SEBASTIAN: What, art thou waking?

126–128 **the fair . . . bow** i.e., Claribel herself was poised uncertain
between unwillingness to marry and obedience to her father as to
which end of the scale sink, which should prevail   130 **Moe**
more   133 **dear'st** heaviest, most costly   135 **time** appropriate time
137 **chirurgeonly** like a skilled surgeon. (Antonio mocks Gonzalo's
medical analogy of a *plaster* applied curatively to a wound.)   140
plantation colonization (with subsequent wordplay on the literal
meaning)   141 **docks, mallows** (Various weeds.)   144 **by contraries**
by what is directly opposite to usual custom   145 **traffic** trade   147
Letters learning   148 **use of service** custom of employing servants;
succession holding of property by right of inheritance   149 **Bourn**
boundaries; **bound of land** landmarks; **tilth** tillage of soil   150 **corn**
grain   157 **engine** instrument of warfare   159 **it** its; **foison** plenty
164 **Save** God save

167–168 **minister occasion** furnish opportunity   168 **sensible** sensitive   174 **An** if; **flat-long** with the flat of the sword, i.e., ineffectually.
(Cf. *fallen flat.*)   178 **a-batfowling** hunting birds at night with lantern
and stick; also, gulling a simpleton. (Gonzalo is the simpleton, or fowl,
and Sebastian will use the moon as his lantern.)   180–181 **adventure
. . . weakly** risk my reputation for discretion for so trivial a cause (by
getting angry at these sarcastic fellows)   182 **heavy** sleep   183 **Go . . .
us** let our laughing send you to sleep, or, go to sleep and hear us laugh
at you   187 **omit** neglect; **heavy** drowsy   200 **speaks** calls upon; or,
pronounces, proclaims (Sebastian as usurper of Alonso's crown)

ANTONIO: Do you not hear me speak?

SEBASTIAN: I do; and surely
It is a sleepy language and thou speak'st
205 Out of thy sleep. What is it thou didst say?
This is a strange repose, to be asleep
With eyes wide open—standing, speaking, moving—
And yet so fast asleep.

ANTONIO: Noble Sebastian,
Thou let'st thy fortune sleep—die, rather; wink'st
210 Whiles thou art waking.

SEBASTIAN: Thou dost snore distinctly;
There's meaning in thy snores.

ANTONIO: I am more serious than my custom. You
Must be so too, if heed me; which to do
Trebles thee o'er.

SEBASTIAN: Well, I am standing water.

215 ANTONIO: I'll teach you how to flow.

SEBASTIAN: Do so. To ebb
Hereditary sloth instructs me.

ANTONIO: O,
If you but knew how you the purpose cherish
Whiles thus you mock it! How, in stripping it,
You more invest it! Ebbing men, indeed,
220 Most often do so near the bottom run
By their own fear or sloth.

SEBASTIAN: Prithee say on.
The setting of thine eye and cheek proclaim
A matter from thee, and a birth indeed
Which throes thee much to yield.

ANTONIO: Thus, sir:
225 Although this lord of weak remembrance, this,
Who shall be of as little memory
When he is earth'd, hath here almost persuaded—
For he's a spirit of persuasion, only
Professes to persuade—the King his son's alive,
230 'Tis as impossible that he's undrown'd
As he that sleeps here swims.

SEBASTIAN: I have no hope
That he's undrown'd.

ANTONIO: O, out of that "no hope"
What great hope have you! No hope that way is
Another way so high a hope that even
235 Ambition cannot pierce a wink beyond,
But doubt discovery there. Will you grant with me
That Ferdinand is drown'd?

SEBASTIAN: He's gone.

ANTONIO: Then, tell me,
Who's the next heir of Naples?

SEBASTIAN: Claribel.

ANTONIO: She that is Queen of Tunis; she that dwells
Ten leagues beyond man's life; she that from Naples   240
Can have no note, unless the sun were post—
The man i' th' moon's too slow—till new-born chins
Be rough and razorable; she that from whom
We all were sea-swallow'd, though some cast again,
And by that destiny to perform an act   245
Whereof what's past is prologue, what to come
In yours and my discharge.

SEBASTIAN: What stuff is this? How say you?
'Tis true, my brother's daughter's Queen of Tunis;
So is she heir of Naples; 'twixt which regions   250
There is some space.

ANTONIO: A space whose ev'ry cubit
Seems to cry out, "How shall that Claribel
Measure us back to Naples? Keep in Tunis,
And let Sebastian wake." Say this were death
That now hath seiz'd them; why, they were no worse   255
Than now they are. There be that can rule Naples
As well as he that sleeps; lords that can prate
As amply and unnecessarily
As this Gonzalo; I myself could make
A chough of as deep chat. O, that you bore   260
The mind that I do! What a sleep were this
For your advancement! Do you understand me?

SEBASTIAN: Methinks I do.

ANTONIO: And how does your content
Tender your own good fortune?

SEBASTIAN: I remember
You did supplant your brother Prospero.   265

ANTONIO: True.
And look how well my garments sit upon me,
Much feater than before. My brother's servants
Were then my fellows; now they are my men.

SEBASTIAN: But, for your conscience?

ANTONIO: Ay, sir; where lies that? If 'twere a kibe,   270
'Twould put me to my slipper; but I feel not
This deity in my bosom. Twenty consciences,
That stand 'twixt me and Milan, candied be they
And melt ere they molest! Here lies your brother,
No better than the earth he lies upon,   275
If he were that which now he's like—that's dead,
Whom I, with this obedient steel, three inches of it,
Can lay to bed forever; whiles you, doing thus,
To the perpetual wink for aye might put

---

209 **wink'st** shut your eyes   214 **Trebles thee o'er** makes you three times as great and rich; **standing water** water which neither ebbs nor flows, at a standstill, indecisive   216 **Hereditary sloth** natural laziness   217 **purpose** i.e., of being king; **cherish** i.e., make dear, enrich   219 **invest** clothe. (Antonio's paradox is that by sceptically stripping away illusions Sebastian can see the essence of a situation and the opportunity it presents, or that by disclaiming and deriding his purpose Sebastian shows how he values it.)   220 **the bottom** i.e., on which unadventurous men may go aground and miss the tide of fortune   222 **setting** set expression (of earnestness)   223 **matter** matter of importance   224 **throes** causes pain, as in giving birth   225 **this lord** i.e., Gonzalo; **remembrance** (1) power of remembering (2) being remembered after his death   227 **earth'd** buried   228–229 **only . . . persuade** i.e., whose whole function (as a privy councilor) is to persuade   233 **that way** i.e., in regard to Ferdinand's being saved   235–236 **Ambition . . . there** ambition itself cannot see any further than that hope (of the crown), but is unsure of itself in seeing even so far, is dazzled by daring to think so high

---

240 **Ten . . . life** i.e., it would take more than a lifetime to get there   241 **note** news, intimation; **post** messenger   243 **from** on our voyage from   244 **cast** were disgorged (with a pun on *casting* of parts for a play)   247 **discharge** performance   253 **Measure us** i.e., traverse the cubits, find her way   254 **wake** i.e., to his good fortune   259–260 **I . . . chat** I could teach a jackdaw to talk as wisely, or, be such a garrulous talker myself   263 **content** desire, inclination   264 **Tender** regard, look after   267 **feater** more becomingly, fittingly   270 **kibe** chilblain, sore on the heel   271 **put me to** oblige me to wear   273 **Milan** the dukedom of Milan; **candied** frozen, congealed in crystalline form   279 **wink** sleep, closing of eyes

280 This ancient morsel, this Sir Prudence, who
Should not upbraid our course. For all the rest,
They'll take suggestion as a cat laps milk;
They'll tell the clock to any business that
We say befits the hour.
SEBASTIAN: Thy case, dear friend,
285 Shall be my precedent. As thou got'st Milan,
I'll come by Naples. Draw thy sword. One stroke
Shall free thee from the tribute which thou payest,
And I the king shall love thee.
ANTONIO: Draw together;
And when I rear my hand, do you the like,
290 To fall it on Gonzalo.

(They draw.)

SEBASTIAN: O, but one word.

(They talk apart.)

(Enter ARIEL [invisible], with music and song.)

ARIEL: My master through his art foresees the danger
That you, his friend, are in, and sends me forth—
For else his project dies—to keep them living.

(Sings in GONZALO's ear.)

                While you here do snoring lie,
295   Open-ey'd conspiracy
                His time doth take.
                If of life you keep a care,
                Shake off slumber, and beware.
                Awake, awake!

300 ANTONIO: Then let us both be sudden.
GONZALO: *(Waking.)* Now, good angels preserve the King!

(The others wake.)

ALONSO: Why, how now, ho, awake? Why are you drawn?
Wherefore this ghastly looking?
GONZALO: What's the matter?
SEBASTIAN: Whiles we stood here securing your repose,
305 Even now, we heard a hollow burst of bellowing
Like bulls, or rather lions. Did 't not wake you?
It struck mine ear most terribly.
ALONSO: I heard nothing.
ANTONIO: O, 'twas a din to fright a monster's ear,
To make an earthquake! Sure it was the roar
310 Of a whole herd of lions.
ALONSO: Heard you this, Gonzalo?
GONZALO: Upon mine honor, sir, I heard a humming,
And that a strange one too, which did awake me.
I shak'd you, sir, and cried. As mine eyes open'd,
315 I saw their weapons drawn. There was a noise,
That's verily. 'Tis best we stand upon our guard,
Or that we quit this place. Let's draw our weapons.
ALONSO: Lead off this ground, and let's make further search
For my poor son.
GONZALO: Heavens keep him from these beasts!
320 For he is, sure, i' th' island.

ALONSO: Lead away.
ARIEL: *(Aside.)* Prospero my lord shall know what I have done.
So, King, go safely on to seek thy son.

(Exeunt [severally].)

SCENE II

Enter CALIBAN with a burden of wood. A noise of thunder heard.

CALIBAN: All the infections that the sun sucks up
From bogs, fens, flats, on Prosper fall and make him
By inch-meal a disease! His spirits hear me,
And yet I needs must curse. But they'll nor pinch,
Fright me with urchin-shows, pitch me i' th' mire,   5
Nor lead me, like a firebrand, in the dark
Out of my way, unless he bid 'em; but
For every trifle are they set upon me;
Sometime like apes that mow and chatter at me
And after bite me, then like hedgehogs which   10
Lie tumbling in my barefoot way and mount
Their pricks at my footfall; sometime am I
All wound with adders who with cloven tongues
Do hiss me into madness.

(Enter TRINCULO.)

                Lo, now, lo!
Here comes a spirit of his, and to torment me   15
For bringing wood in slowly. I'll fall flat;
Perchance he will not mind me.

(Lies down.)

TRINCULO: Here's neither bush nor shrub, to bear off any
weather at all, and another storm brewing; I hear it sing i' th'
wind. Yond same black cloud, yond huge one, looks like a   20
foul bombard that would shed his liquor. If it should thunder
as it did before, I know not where to hide my head. Yond
same cloud cannot choose but fall by pailfuls. *(Sees CAL-
IBAN.)* What have we here? A man or a fish? Dead or alive? A
fish, he smells like a fish; a very ancient and fish-like smell; a 25
kind of not of the newest Poor-John. A strange fish! Were I in
England now, as once I was, and had but this fish painted,
not a holiday fool there but would give a piece of silver.
There would this monster make a man; any strange beast
there makes a man. When they will not give a doit to relieve 30
a lame beggar, they will lay out ten to see a dead Indian. Leg-
g'd like a man! And his fins like arms! Warm, o' my troth! I
do now let loose my opinion, hold it no longer: this is no
fish, but an islander, that hath lately suffer'd by a thunderbolt. *(Thunder.)* Alas, the storm is come again! My best way 35
is to creep under his gaberdine; there is no other shelter
hereabout. Misery acquaints a man with strange bedfellows.
I will here shroud till the dregs of the storm be past.

II.ii. Location: Another part of the island.   3 By inch-meal inch by
inch   **4 nor** neither   **5 urchin-shows** apparitions shaped like hedgehogs   **6 like a firebrand** in the guise of a will-o'-the-wisp   **9 mow**
make faces   **17 mind** notice   **18 bear off** keep off   **21 foul bombard**
dirty leathern bottle; **his** its   **26 Poor-John** salted hake, type of poor
fare   **27 painted** i.e., painted on a sign set up outside a booth or tent at
a fair   **29 make a man** make one's fortune   **30 doit** small coin   **36
gaberdine** cloak, loose upper garment   **38 shroud** take shelter; **dregs**
i.e., last remains

---

283 **tell the clock** i.e., answer appropriately, chime   287 **tribute** (See
I.ii. 113–124)   296 **time** opportunity   304 **securing** standing guard
over

(Creeps under CALIBAN's *garment.)*

(Enter STEPHANO, *singing, [a bottle in his hand].)*

STEPHANO: "I shall no more to sea, to sea,
40   Here shall I die ashore—"

This is a very scurvy tune to sing at a man's funeral.
Well, here's my comfort.

(Drinks.)

(Sings.)

    "The master, the swabber, the boatswain and I,
         The gunner and his mate
45   Lov'd Mall, Meg, and Marian, and Margery,
         But none of us car'd for Kate;
         For she had a tongue with a tang,
         Would cry to a sailor, 'Go hang!'
     She lov'd not the savor of tar nor of pitch,
50   Yet a tailor might scratch her where'er she did
            itch.
         Then to sea, boys, and let her go hang!"

This is a scurvy tune too; but here's my comfort.

(Drinks.)

CALIBAN: Do not torment me! Oh!

STEPHANO: What's the matter? Have we devils here? Do you
55   put tricks upon 's with savages and men of Ind, ha? I have
not scap'd drowning to be afeard now of your four legs; for it
hath been said, "As proper a man as ever went on four legs
cannot make him give ground"; and it shall be said so again
while Stephano breathes at' nostrils.

60 CALIBAN: This spirit torments me! Oh!

STEPHANO: This is some monster of the isle with four legs,
who hath got, as I take it, an ague. Where the devil should
he learn our language? I will give him some relief, if it be but
for that. If I can recover him and keep him tame and get to
65   Naples with him, he's a present for any emperor that ever
trod on neat's-leather.

CALIBAN: Do not torment me, prithee. I'll bring my wood
home faster.

STEPHANO: He's in his fit now and does not talk after the wis-
70   est. He shall taste of my bottle; if he have never drunk wine
afore, it will go near to remove his fit. If I can recover him
and keep him tame, I will not take too much for him; he
shall pay for him that hath him, and that soundly.

CALIBAN: Thou dost me yet but little hurt;
75   Thou wilt anon, I know it by thy trembling.
Now Prosper works upon thee.

STEPHANO: Come on your ways; open your mouth; here is that
which will give language to you, cat. Open your mouth; this
will shake your shaking, I can tell you, and that soundly.
80   *(Gives* CALIBAN *drink.)* You cannot tell who's your friend.
Open your chaps again.

TRINCULO: I should know that voice. It should be—but he is
drown'd; and these are devils. O defend me!

STEPHANO: Four legs and two voices; a most delicate monster!
His forward voice now is to speak well of his friend; his back- 85
ward voice is to utter foul speeches and to detract. If all the
wine in my bottle will recover him, I will help his ague.
Come. *(Gives drink.)* Amen! I will pour some in thy other
mouth.

TRINCULO: Stephano! 90

STEPHANO: Doth thy other mouth call me? Mercy, mercy!
This is a devil, and no monster. I will leave him; I have no
long spoon.

TRINCULO: Stephano! If thou beest Stephano, touch me and
speak to me; for I am Trinculo—be not afeard—thy good 95
friend Trinculo.

STEPHANO: If thou beest Trinculo, come forth. I'll pull thee by
the lesser legs. If any be Trinculo's legs, these are they. *(Pulls
him out.)* Thou art very Trinculo indeed! How cam'st thou
to be the siege of this moon-calf? Can he vent Trinculos? 100

TRINCULO: I took him to be kill'd with a thunder-stroke. But
art thou not drown'd, Stephano? I hope now thou art not
drown'd. Is the storm overblown? I hid me under the dead
moon-calf's gaberdine for fear of the storm. And art thou living, Stephano? O Stephano, two Neapolitans scap'd! 105

STEPHANO: Prithee, do not turn me about; my stomach is not
constant.

CALIBAN: These be fine things, an if they be not sprites.
That's a brave god and bears celestial liquor.
I will kneel to him. 110

STEPHANO: How didst thou scape? How cam'st thou hither?
Swear by this bottle how thou cam'st hither. I escap'd upon a
butt of sack which the sailors heav'd o'erboard—by this bottle, which I made of the bark of a tree with mine own hands
since I was cast ashore. 115

CALIBAN: *(Kneeling.)* I'll swear upon that bottle to be thy true
subject, for the liquor is not earthly.

STEPHANO: Here; swear then how thou escap'dst.

TRINCULO: Swum ashore, man, like a duck. I can swim like a
duck, I'll be sworn. 120

STEPHANO: Here, kiss the book. Though thou canst swim like
a duck, thou art made like a goose.

(Gives drink.)

TRINCULO: O Stephano, hast any more of this?

STEPHANO: The whole butt, man. My cellar is in a rock by the
sea-side where my wine is hid. How now, moon-calf? How 125
does thine ague?

CALIBAN: Hast thou not dropp'd from heaven?

STEPHANO: Out o' th' moon, I do assure thee. I was the man i'
th' moon when time was.

CALIBAN: I have seen thee in her and I do adore thee. 130
My mistress show'd me thee and thy dog and thy bush.

STEPHANO: Come, swear to that; kiss the book. I will furnish it
anon with new contents. Swear.

(Gives drink.)

---

55 **Ind** India 57 **proper** handsome; **four legs** (The conventional
phrase would supply *two legs.*) 59 **at'** at the 64 **for that** i.e., for
knowing our language; **recover** restore 66 **neat's-leather** cowhide
72 **I will . . . much** i.e., no sum can be too much 73 **hath** possesses,
receives 78 **cat . . . mouth** (Allusion to the proverb, "Good liquor
will make a cat speak.") 81 **chaps** jaws

93 **long spoon** (Allusion to the proverb, "He that sups with the devil
has need of a long spoon.") 100 **siege** excrement; **moon-calf** monster, abortion. (Supposed to be caused by the influence of the moon.);
vent emit 106–107 **not constant** unsteady 108 **an if** if 109 **brave**
fine, magnificent 113 **butt of sack** barrel of Canary wine 121 **book**
i.e., bottle 129 **when time was** once upon a time 131 **dog . . . bush**
(The man in the moon was popularly imagined to have with him a dog
and a bush of thorn.)

TRINCULO: By this good light, this is a very shallow monster! I
135   afeard of him? A very weak monster! The man i' th' moon? A
       most poor credulous monster! Well drawn, monster, in good
       sooth!
CALIBAN: I'll show thee every fertile inch o' th' island;
       And I will kiss thy foot. I prithee, by my god.
140 TRINCULO: By this light, a most perfidious and drunken mon-
       ster! When's god's asleep, he'll rob his bottle.
CALIBAN: I'll kiss thy foot. I'll swear myself thy subject.
STEPHANO: Come on then; down, and swear.

(CALIBAN swears.)

TRINCULO: I shall laugh myself to death at this puppy-headed
145   monster. A most scurvy monster! I could find in my heart to
       beat him—
STEPHANO: Come, kiss.
TRINCULO: But that the poor monster's in drink. An abom-
       inable monster!
150 CALIBAN: I'll show thee the best springs; I'll pluck thee berries;
       I'll fish for thee and get thee wood enough.
       A plague upon the tyrant that I serve!
       I'll bear him no more sticks, but follow thee,
       Thou wondrous man.
155 TRINCULO: A most ridiculous monster, to make a wonder of a
       poor drunkard!
CALIBAN: I prithee, let me bring thee where crabs grow;
       And I with my long nails will dig thee pig-nuts,
       Show thee a jay's nest, and instruct thee how
160   To snare the nimble marmoset. I'll bring thee
       To clust'ring filberts, and sometimes I'll get thee
       Young scamels from the rock. Wilt thou go with me?
STEPHANO: I prithee now, lead the way without any more talk-
       ing. Trinculo, the King and all our company else being
165   drown'd, we will inherit here. Here! Bear my bottle. Fellow
       Trinculo, we'll fill him by and by again.
CALIBAN: *(Sings drunkenly.)*

            Farewell, master; farewell, farewell!

TRINCULO: A howling monster; a drunken monster!
CALIBAN:

       No more dams I'll make for fish,
170   Nor fetch in firing
          At requiring,
       Nor scrape trenchering, nor wash dish.
          'Ban, 'Ban, Ca-Caliban
          Has a new master, get a new man.
175   Freedom, high-day! High-day, freedom! Freedom,
       high-day, freedom!

STEPHANO: O brave monster! Lead the way.

(Exeunt.)

---

134 **By . . . light** by God's light, by this good light from heaven   136
Well drawn well pulled (on the bottle)   157 **crabs** crab apples   158
pig-nuts peanuts   160 **marmoset** small monkey   162 **scamels** (Possibly "seamews," mentioned in Strachey's letter, or shellfish; or perhaps
from *squamelle*, furnished with little scales. Contemporary French and
Italian travel accounts report that the natives of Patagonia in South
America ate small fish described as *fort scameux* and *squame*.)   165 **inherit** take possession   172 **trenchering** trenchers, wooden plates
175 **high-day** holiday (?)

— ACT THREE —

SCENE I

Enter FERDINAND, *bearing a log.*

FERDINAND: There be some sports are painful, and their labor
       Delight in them sets off; some kinds of baseness
       Are nobly undergone; and most poor matters
       Point to rich ends. This my mean task
       Would be as heavy to me as odious, but   5
       The mistress which I serve quickens what's dead
       And makes my labors pleasures. O, she is
       Ten times more gentle than her father's crabbed,
       And he's compos'd of harshness. I must remove
       Some thousands of these logs and pile them up,   10
       Upon a sore injunction. My sweet mistress
       Weeps when she sees me work, and says such baseness
       Had never like executor. I forget;
       But these sweet thoughts do even refresh my labors,
       Most busy lest, when I do it.   15

(Enter MIRANDA; *and* PROSPERO *[at a distance, unseen].)*

MIRANDA: Alas, now, pray you,
       Work not so hard. I would the lightning had
       Burnt up those logs that you are enjoin'd to pile!
       Pray, set it down and rest you. When this burns,
       'Twill weep for having wearied you. My father
       Is hard at study; pray now, rest yourself.   20
       He's safe for these three hours.
FERDINAND: O most dear mistress,
       The sun will set before I shall discharge
       What I must strive to do.
MIRANDA: If you'll sit down,
       I'll bear your logs the while. Pray give me that.
       I'll carry it to the pile.   25
FERDINAND: No, precious creature,
       I had rather crack my sinews, break my back,
       Than you should such dishonor undergo
       While I sit lazy by.
MIRANDA: It would become me
       As well as it does you; and I should do it
       With much more ease, for my good will is to it,   30
       And yours it is against.
PROSPERO: *(Aside.)*   Poor worm, thou art infected!
       This visitation shows it.
MIRANDA: You look wearily.
FERDINAND: No, noble mistress, 'tis fresh morning with me
       When you are by at night. I do beseech you—
       Chiefly that I might set it in my prayers—   35
       What is your name?
MIRANDA: Miranda.—O my father,
       I have broke your hest to say so.
FERDINAND: Admir'd Miranda!
       Indeed the top of admiration! Worth
       What's dearest to the world! Full many a lady

III.i. Location: Before Prospero's cell.   **2 sets off** makes seem
greater by contrast   **6 quickens** gives life to   **11 sore injunction** severe command   **15 Most . . . it** i.e., least troubled by my labor when
I think of her (?) (The line may be in need of emendation.)   **32 visitation** (1) visit (2) visitation of the plague, i.e., infection of love   **37
hest** command

40 I have ey'd with best regard, and many a time
Th' harmony of their tongues hath into bondage
Brought my too diligent ear. For several virtues
Have I lik'd several women, never any
With so full soul but some defect in her
45 Did quarrel with the noblest grace she ow'd
And put it to the foil. But you, O you,
So perfect and so peerless, are created
Of every creature's best!

MIRANDA: I do not know
One of my sex; no woman's face remember,
50 Save, from my glass, mine own. Nor have I seen
More that I may call men than you, good friend,
And my dear father. How features are abroad,
I am skilless of; but, by my modesty,
The jewel in my dower, I would not wish
55 Any companion in the world but you,
Nor can imagination form a shape,
Besides yourself, to like of. But I prattle
Something too wildly, and my father's precepts
I therein do forget.

FERDINAND: I am in my condition
60 A prince, Miranda; I do think, a king—
I would, not so!—and would no more endure
This wooden slavery than to suffer
The flesh-fly blow my mouth. Hear my soul speak:
The very instant that I saw you, did
65 My heart fly to your service; there resides,
To make me slave to it; and for your sake
Am I this patient log-man.

MIRANDA: Do you love me?
FERDINAND: O heaven, O earth, bear witness to this sound,
And crown what I profess with kind event
70 If I speak true! If hollowly, invert
What best is boded me to mischief! I
Beyond all limit of what else i' th' world
Do love, prize, honor you.

MIRANDA: *(Weeping.)*   I am a fool
To weep at what I am glad of.

PROSPERO: *(Aside.)*   Fair encounter
75 Of two most rare affections! Heavens rain grace
On that which breeds between 'em!

FERDINAND: Wherefore weep you?
MIRANDA: At mine unworthiness, that dare offer
What I desire to give, and much less take
What I shall die to want. But this is trifling,
80 And all the more it seeks to hide itself
The bigger bulk it shows. Hence, bashful cunning,
And prompt me, plain and holy innocence!
I am your wife, if you will marry me;
If not, I'll die your maid. To be your fellow
85 You may deny me, but I'll be your servant,
Whether you will or no.

FERDINAND: My mistress, dearest,
And I thus humble ever.

MIRANDA: My husband, then?
FERDINAND: Ay, with a heart as willing
As bondage e'er of freedom. Here's my hand.
MIRANDA: And mine, with my heart in 't. And now farewell   90
Till half an hour hence.
FERDINAND: A thousand thousand!

*(Exeunt [*FERDINAND *and* MIRANDA *severally].)*

PROSPERO: So glad of this as they I cannot be,
Who are surpris'd with all; but my rejoicing
At nothing can be more. I'll to my book,
For yet ere supper-time must I perform   95
Much business appertaining.

SCENE II

Enter CALIBAN, STEPHANO, *and* TRINCULO.

STEPHANO: Tell not me. When the butt is out, we will drink
water, not a drop before. Therefore bear up, and board 'em.
Servant-monster, drink to me.
TRINCULO: Servant-monster? The folly of this island! They say
there's but five upon this isle; we are three of them. If th'   5
other two be brain'd like us, the state totters.
STEPHANO: Drink, servant-monster, when I bid thee. Thy eyes
are almost set in thy head.

(Gives drink.)

TRINCULO: Where should they be set else? He were a brave
monster indeed if they were set in his tail.   10
STEPHANO: My man-monster hath drown'd his tongue in sack.
For my part, the sea cannot drown me; I swam, ere I could
recover the shore, five and thirty leagues off and on. By this
light, thou shalt be my lieutenant, monster, or my standard.
TRINCULO: Your lieutenant, if you list; he's no standard.   15
STEPHANO: We'll not run, Monsieur Monster.
TRINCULO: Nor go neither, but you'll lie like dogs and yet say
nothing neither.
STEPHANO: Moon-calf, speak once in thy life, if thou beest a
good moon-calf.   20
CALIBAN: How does thy honor? Let me lick thy shoe.
I'll not serve him; he is not valiant.
TRINCULO: Thou liest, most ignorant monster, I am in case to
justle a constable. Why, thou debosh'd fish thou, was there
ever man a coward that hath drunk so much sack as I today?   25
Wilt thou tell a monstrous lie, being but half a fish and half
a monster?
CALIBAN: Lo, how he mocks me! Wilt thou let him, my lord?
TRINCULO: "Lord," quoth he? That a monster should be such
a natural!   30

---

45 **ow'd** owned   46 **put . . . foil** (1) overthrew it (as in wrestling) (2)
served as a "foil" or contrast to set it off   53 **skilless** ignorant   63 **blow**
befoul with fly-eggs   69 **kind event** favorable outcome   70 **hollowly**
insincerely, falsely   71 **boded** destined for   79 **want** lack   84 **fellow**
mate, equal

III.ii. Location: Another part of the island.   1 **out** empty   2 **bear
. . . 'em** (Stephano uses the terminology of maneuvering at sea and
boarding a vessel under attack as a way of urging an assault on the
liquor supply.)   8 **set** fixed in a drunken stare; or sunk, like the sun   9
brave fine, splendid   13 **recover** arrive at   14 **standard** standard-
bearer, ancient, i.e., ensign (as distinguished from *lieutenant*, l. 15)
15 **list** prefer; **no standard** i.e., not able to stand up   16 **run** (1) retreat
(2) urinate (taking Trinculo's *standard* l. 15, in the old sense of *conduit*)   17 **go** walk; **lie** (1) tell lies (2) lie prostrate (3) excret   23–24
case . . . constable i.e., in fit condition, made valiant by drink, to taunt
or challenge the police; **debosh'd** i.e., debauched   30 **natural** (1) idiot
(2) natural as opposed to unnatural, monster-like

CALIBAN: Lo, lo, again! Bite him to death, I prithee.

STEPHANO: Trinculo, keep a good tongue in your head. If you prove a mutineer—the next tree! The poor monster's my subject and he shall not suffer indignity.

35 CALIBAN: I thank my noble lord. Wilt thou be pleas'd
To hearken once again to the suit I made to thee?

STEPHANO: Marry, will I. Kneel and repeat it; I will stand, and so shall Trinculo.

(CALIBAN kneels.)

(Enter ARIEL, invisible.)

CALIBAN: As I told thee before, I am subject to a tyrant,
40 A sorcerer, that by his cunning hath
Cheated me of the island.

ARIEL: Thou liest.

CALIBAN: Thou liest, thou jesting monkey, thou!
I would my valiant master would destroy thee.
I do not lie.

45 STEPHANO: Trinculo, if you trouble him any more in 's tale, by this hand, I will supplant some of your teeth.

TRINCULO: Why, I said nothing.

STEPHANO: Mum, then, and no more.—Proceed.

CALIBAN: I say, by sorcery he got this isle;
50 From me he got it. If thy greatness will
Revenge it on him—for I know thou dar'st,
But this thing dare not—

STEPHANO: That's most certain.

CALIBAN: Thou shalt be lord of it, and I'll serve thee.

55 STEPHANO: How now shall this be compass'd? Canst thou being me to the party?

CALIBAN: Yea, yea, my lord. I'll yield him thee asleep,
Where thou mayst knock a nail into his head.

ARIEL: Thou liest; thou canst not.

60 CALIBAN: What a pied ninny's this! Thou scurvy patch!
I do beseech thy greatness, give him blows
And take his bottle from him. When that's gone
He shall drink nought but brine, for I'll now show him
Where the quick freshes are.

65 STEPHANO: Trinculo, run into no further danger. Interrupt the monster one word further, and, by this hand, I'll turn my mercy out o' doors and make a stock-fish of thee.

TRINCULO: Why, what did? I did nothing. I'll go farther off.

STEPHANO: Didst thou not say he lied?

70 ARIEL: Thou liest.

STEPHANO: Do I so? Take thou that. *(Beats TRINCULO.)* As you like this, give me the lie another time.

TRINCULO: I did not give the lie. Out o' your wits and hearing too? A pox o' your bottle! This can sack and drinking do. A
75 murrain on your monster, and the devil take your fingers!

CALIBAN: Ha, ha, ha!

STEPHANO: Now, forward with your tale.

(To TRINCULO.)

Prithee, stand further off.

CALIBAN: Beat him enough. After a little time
I'll beat him too.   80

STEPHANO: Stand farther.—Come, proceed.

CALIBAN: Why, as I told thee, 'tis a custom with him
I' th' afternoon to sleep. There thou mayst brain him,
Having first seiz'd his books, or with a log
Batter his skull, or paunch him with a stake,   85
Or cut his wezand with thy knife. Remember
First to possess his books; for without them
He's but a sot, as I am, nor hath not
One spirit to command. They all do hate him
As rootedly as I. Burn but his books.   90
He has brave utensils—for so he calls them—
Which, when he has a house, he'll deck withal.
And that most deeply to consider is
The beauty of his daughter. He himself
Calls her a nonpareil. I never saw a woman,   95
But only Sycorax my dam and she;
But she as far surpasseth Sycorax
As great'st does least.

STEPHANO: Is it so brave a lass?

CALIBAN: Ay, lord; she will become thy bed, I warrant,   100
And bring thee forth brave brood.

STEPHANO: Monster, I will kill this man. His daughter and I will be king and queen—save our Graces!—and Trinculo and thyself shall be viceroys. Dost thou like the plot, Trinculo?

TRINCULO: Excellent.   105

STEPHANO: Give me thy hand. I am sorry I beat thee; but, while thou liv'st, keep a good tongue in thy head.

CALIBAN: Within this half hour will he be asleep.
Wilt thou destroy him then?

STEPHANO: Ay, on mine honor.   110

ARIEL: *(Aside.)* This will I tell my master.

CALIBAN: Thou mak'st me merry; I am full of pleasure.
Let us be jocund. Will you troll the catch
You taught me but while-ere?

STEPHANO: At thy request, monster, I will do reason, any rea-   115
son. Come on, Trinculo, let us sing.

(Sings.)

"Flout 'em and scout 'em
And scout 'em and flout 'em!
Thought is free."

CALIBAN: That's not the tune.   120

(ARIEL plays the tune on a tabor and pipe.)

STEPHANO: What is this same?

TRINCULO: This is the tune of our catch, play'd by the picture of Nobody.

STEPHANO: If thou beest a man, show thyself in thy likeness. If thou beest a devil, take 't as thou list.   125

TRINCULO: O, forgive me my sins!

---

33 **the next tree** i.e., you'll hang   37 **Marry** i.e., indeed (Originally an oath by the Virgin Mary.)   52 **this thing** i.e., Trinculo   60 **pied ninny** fool in motley; **patch** fool   64 **quick freshes** running springs   67 **stock-fish** dried cod beaten before cooking   72 **give me the lie** call me a liar to my face   75 **murrain** plague (Literally, a cattle disease.)

85 **paunch** stab in the belly   86 **wezand** windpipe   88 **sot** fool   91 **brave utensils** fine furnishings   113 **troll the catch** sing the round   114 **while-ere** a short time ago   118 **scout** deride   s.d. **tabor** small drum   122–123 **picture of Nobody** (Refers to a familiar figure with head, arms, and legs, but no trunk.)   125 **take 't . . . list** i.e., take my defiance as you please, as best you can

STEPHANO: He that dies pays all debts. I defy thee. Mercy
   upon us!
CALIBAN: Art thou afeard?
130 STEPHANO: No, monster, not I.
CALIBAN: Be not afeard. This isle is full of noises,
   Sounds and sweet airs, that give delight and hurt not.
   Sometimes a thousand twangling instruments
   Will hum about mine ears, and sometimes voices
135 That, if I then had wak'd after long sleep,
   Will make me sleep again; and then, in dreaming,
   The clouds methought would open and show riches
   Ready to drop upon me, that, when I wak'd,
   I cried to dream again.
140 STEPHANO: This will prove a brave kingdom to me, where I
   shall have my music for nothing.
CALIBAN: When Prospero is destroy'd.
STEPHANO: That shall be by and by. I remember the story.
TRINCULO: The sound is going away. Let's follow it, and after
145 do our work.
STEPHANO: Lead, monster; we'll follow. I would I could see
   this taborer; he lays it on.
TRINCULO: Wilt come? I'll follow, Stephano.

(Exeunt [following ARIEL'S *music].)*

SCENE III

Enter ALONSO, SEBASTIAN, ANTONIO, GONZALO, ADRIAN,
FRANCISCO, *etc.*

GONZALO: By 'r lakin, I can go no further, sir;
   My old bones aches. Here's a maze trod indeed
   Through forth-rights and meanders! By your patience,
   I needs must rest me.
ALONSO: Old lord, I cannot blame thee,
5 Who am myself attach'd with weariness,
   To th' dulling of my spirits. Sit down, and rest.
   Even here I will put off my hope and keep it
   No longer for my flatterer. He is drown'd
   Whom thus we stray to find, and the sea mocks
10 Our frustrate search on land. Well, let him go.

*(*ALONSO *and* GONZALO *sit.)*

ANTONIO: *(Aside to* SEBASTIAN.*)* I am right glad that he's so
   out of hope.
   Do not, for one repulse, forego the purpose
   That you resolv'd t' effect.
SEBASTIAN: *(To* ANTONIO.*)* The next advantage
   Will we take throughly.
ANTONIO: *(To* SEBASTIAN.*)* Let it be tonight,
15 For, now they are oppress'd with travail, they
   Will not, nor cannot, use such vigilance
   As when they are fresh.
SEBASTIAN: *(To* ANTONIO.*)* I say tonight. No more.

(Solemn and strange music; and PROSPERO *on the top,
invisible.)*

ALONSO: What harmony is this? My good friends, hark!
GONZALO: Marvelous sweet music!

*(Enter several strange shapes, bringing in a banquet, and dance
about it with gentle actions of salutations; and, inviting the
KING, etc., to eat, they depart.)*

ALONSO: Give us kind keepers, heavens! What were these?   20
SEBASTIAN: A living drollery. Now I will believe
   That there are unicorns, that in Arabia
   There is one tree, the phoenix' throne, one phoenix
   At this hour reigning there.
ANTONIO: I'll believe both;
   And what does else want credit, come to me,   25
   And I'll be sworn 'tis true. Travelers ne'er did lie,
   Though fools at home condemn 'em.
GONZALO: If in Naples
   I should report this now, would they believe me
   If I should say I saw such islanders?
   For, certes, these are people of the island,   30
   Who, though they are of monstrous shape, yet, note,
   Their manners are more gentle, kind, than of
   Our human generation you shall find
   Many, nay, almost any.
PROSPERO: *(Aside.)*   Honest lord,
   Thou hast said well; for some of you there present   35
   Are worse than devils.
ALONSO: I cannot too much muse
   Such shapes, such gesture, and such sound, expressing,
   Although they want the use of tongue, a kind
   Of excellent dumb discourse.
PROSPERO: *(Aside.)*   Praise in departing.
FRANCISCO: They vanish'd strangely.   40
SEBASTIAN: No matter, since
   They have left their viands behind; for we have stomachs.
   Will 't please you taste of what is here?
ALONSO: Not I.
GONZALO: Faith, sir, you need not fear. When we were boys,
   Who would believe that there were mountaineers
   Dew-lapp'd like bulls, whose throats had hanging at 'em   45
   Wallets of flesh? Or that there were such men
   Whose heads stood in their breasts? Which now we find
   Each putter-out of five for one will bring us
   Good warrant of.
ALONSO: I will stand to and feed,
   Although my last—no matter, since I feel   50
   The best is past. Brother, my lord the Duke,
   Stand to and do as we.

(They approach the table.)

III.iii. Location: Another part of the island.   **1 By'r lakin** by our La-
dykin, by our Lady   **3 forth-rights and meanders** paths straight and
crooked   **5 attach'd** seized   **12 for** because of   **14 throughly** thoroughly   s.d. **on the top** at some high point of the tiring-house or the
theatre

20 **kind keepers** guardian angels   21 **drollery** puppet show   25 **want
credit** lack credence   30 **certes** certainly   36 **muse** wonder at   39
Praise in departing i.e., save your praise until the end of the performance   45 **Dew-lapp'd** having a dewlap, or fold of skin hanging from
the neck, like cattle   47 **in their breasts** (i.e., like the Anthropophagi
described in *Othello*)   48 **putter-out . . . one** one who invests money,
or gambles on the risks of travel on the condition that, if he returns
safely, he is to receive five times the amount deposited; hence, any traveler   49 **stand to** fall to; take the risk

(Thunder and lightning. Enter ARIEL, *like a harpy; claps his wings upon the table; and, with a quaint device, the banquet vanishes.)*

ARIEL: You are three men of sin, whom Destiny,
That hath to instrument this lower world
55 And what is in 't, the never-surfeited sea
Hath caus'd to belch up you, and on this island
Where man doth not inhabit—you 'mongst men
Being most unfit to live. I have made you mad;
And even with such-like valor men hang and drown
60 Their proper selves.

*(*ALONSO, SEBASTIAN, *and* ANTONIO *draw their swords.)*

                    You fools! I and my fellows
Are ministers of Fate. The elements,
Of whom your swords are temper'd, may as well
Wound the loud winds, or with bemock'd-at stabs
Kill the still-closing waters, as diminish
65 One dowle that's in my plume. My fellow-ministers
Are like invulnerable. If you could hurt,
Your swords are now too massy for your strengths
And will not be uplifted. But remember—
For that's my business to you—that you three
70 From Milan did supplant good Prospero;
Expos'd unto the sea, which hath requit it,
Him and his innocent child; for which foul deed
The pow'rs, delaying, not forgetting, have
Incens'd the seas and shores, yea, all the creatures,
75 Against your peace. Thee of thy son, Alonso,
They have bereft; and do pronounce by me
Ling'ring perdition, worse than any death
Can be at once, shall step by step attend
You and your ways; whose wraths to guard you from—
80 Which here, in this most desolate isle, else falls
Upon your heads—is nothing but heart's sorrow
And a clear life ensuring.

(He vanishes in thunder; then, to soft music, enter the shapes again, and dance, with mocks and mows, and carrying out the table.)

PROSPERO: Bravely the figure of this harpy hast thou
Perform'd, my Ariel; a grace it had devouring.
85 Of my instruction hast thou nothing bated
In what thou hadst to say. So, with good life
And observation strange, my meaner ministers

---

s.d. **harpy** a fabulous monster with a woman's face and vulture's body, supposed to be a minister of divine vengeance; **quaint device** ingenious stage contrivance; **banquet vanishes** i.e., the food vanishes; the table remains until l.82   54 **to** i.e., as its   59 **such-like valor** i.e., the reckless valor derived from madness   60 **proper** own   62 **whom** which   64 **still-closing** always closing again when parted   65 **dowle** soft, fine feather   66 **like** likewise, similarly; **If** even if   71 **requit** requited, avenged   79 **whose** (Refers to the heavenly powers.)   s.d. **mocks and mows** mocking gestures and grimaces   83 **Bravely** finely, dashing   84 **a grace . . . devouring** i.e., you gracefully caused the banquet to disappear as if you had consumed the meal (with puns on *grace* meaning "gracefulness" and "a blessing on the meal," and on *devouring* meaning "a literal eating" and "an all-consuming or ravishing grace")   85 **bated** abated, diminished   86 **good life** faithful reproduction   87 **observation strange** exceptional attention to detail; **meaner** i.e., subordinate to Ariel

---

Their several kinds have done. My high charms work,
And these mine enemies are all knit up
In their distractions. They now are in my pow'r;   90
And in these fits I leave them, while I visit
Young Ferdinand, whom they suppose is drown'd,
And his and mine lov'd darling.

(Exit above.)

GONZALO: I' th' name of something holy, sir, why stand you
In this strange stare?   95
ALONSO: O, it is monstrous, monstrous!
Methought the billows spoke and told me of it;
The winds did sing it to me, and the thunder,
That deep and dreadful organ-pipe, pronounc'd
The name of Prosper; it did bass my trespass.
Therefore my son i' th' ooze is bedded, and   100
I'll seek him deeper than e'er plummet sounded
And with him there lie mudded.

(Exit.)

SEBASTIAN: But one fiend at a time,
I'll fight their legions o'er.
ANTONIO: I'll be thy second.

*(Exeunt [*SEBASTIAN *and* ANTONIO*].)*

GONZALO: All three of them are desperate. Their great guilt,   105
Like poison given to work a great time after,
Now 'gins to bite the spirits. I do beseech you,
That are of suppler joints, follow them swiftly
And hinder them from what this ecstasy
May now provoke them to.   110
ADRIAN: Follow, I pray you.

(Exeunt omnes.)

— **ACT FOUR** —

SCENE 1

Enter PROSPERO, FERDINAND, *and* MIRANDA.

PROSPERO: If I have too austerely punish'd you,
Your compensation makes amends, for I
Have given you here a third of mine own life,
Or that for which I live; who once again
I tender to thy hand. All thy vexations   5
Were but my trials of thy love, and thou
Hast strangely stood the test. Here, afore Heaven,
I ratify this my rich gift. O Ferdinand,
Do not smile at me that I boast her off,
For thou shalt find she will outstrip all praise   10
And make it halt behind her.

---

88 **several kinds** individual parts   94 **why** (Gonzalo was not addressed in Ariel's speech to the "three men of sin," l.53, and is not as they are in a maddened state; see ll. 105–107.)   95 **it** i.e., my sin   99 **bass my trespass** proclaim my trespass like a bass note in music   104 **o'er** one after another

IV.i. Location: Before Prospero's cell.   3 **a third** i.e., Miranda, into whose education Prospero has put a third of his life (?) or who represents a large part of what he cares about, along with his dukedom and his learned study (?)   7 **strangely** extraordinarily   9 **boast her off** i.e., praise her so   11 **halt** limp

FERDINAND: I do believe it
  Against an oracle.
PROSPERO: Then, as my gift and thine own acquisition
  Worthily purchas'd, take my daughter. But
15   If thou dost break her virgin-knot before
  All sanctimonious ceremonies may
  With full and holy rite be minist'red,
  No sweet aspersion shall the heavens let fall
  To make this contract grow; but barren hate,
20   Sour-ey'd disdain, and discord shall bestrew
  The union of your bed with weeds so loathly
  That you shall hate it both. Therefore take heed,
  As Hymen's lamps shall light you.
FERDINAND: As I hope
  For quiet days, fair issue, and long life,
25   With such love as 'tis now, the murkiest den,
  The most opportune place, the strong'st suggestion
  Our worser genius can, shall never melt
  Mine honor into lust, to take away
  The edge of that day's celebration
30   When I shall think or Phoebus' steeds are founder'd
  Or Night kept chain'd below.
PROSPERO: Fairly spoke.
  Sit then and talk with her; she is thine own.

(FERDINAND and MIRANDA sit.)

  What, Ariel! My industrious servant, Ariel!

(Enter ARIEL.)

ARIEL: What would my potent master? Here I am.
35 PROSPERO: Thou and thy meaner fellows your last service
  Did worthily perform; and I must use you
  In such another trick. Go bring the rabble,
  O'er whom I give thee pow'r, here to this place.
  Incite them to quick motion, for I must
40   Bestow upon the eyes of this young couple
  Some vanity of mine art. It is my promise,
  And they expect it from me.
ARIEL: Presently?
PROSPERO: Ay, with a twink.
ARIEL: Before you can say "come" and "go,"
45   And breathe twice and cry "so, so,"
  Each one, tripping on his toe,
  Will be here with mop and mow.
  Do you love me, master? No?
PROSPERO: Dearly, my delicate Ariel. Do not approach
50   Till thou dost hear me call.
ARIEL: Well, I conceive.

(Exit.)

PROSPERO: Look thou be true; do not give dalliance
  Too much the rein. The strongest oaths are straw

To th' fire i' th' blood. Be more abstemious,
  Or else good night your vow!
FERDINAND: I warrant you, sir;
  The white cold virgin snow upon my heart   55
  Abates the ardor of my liver.
PROSPERO: Well.
  Now come, my Ariel! Bring a corollary,
  Rather than want a spirit. Appear, and pertly!
  No tongue! All eyes! Be silent.

(Soft music.)

(Enter IRIS.)

IRIS: Ceres, most bounteous lady, thy rich leas   60
  Of wheat, rye, barley, vetches, oats, and pease;
  Thy turfy mountains, where live nibbling sheep,
  And flat meads thatch'd with stover, them to keep;
  Thy banks with pioned and twilled brims,
  Which spongy April at thy hest betrims,   65
  To make cold nymphs chaste crowns; and thy
    broom-groves,
  Whose shadow the dismissed bachelor loves,
  Being lass-lorn; thy pole-clipt vineyard;
  And thy sea-marge, sterile and rocky-hard,
  Where thou thyself dost air—the queen o' th' sky,   70
  Whose wat'ry arch and messenger am I,
  Bids thee leave these, and with her sovereign grace.

(JUNO descends [slowly in her car].)

  Here on this grass-plot, in this very place,
  To come and sport. Her peacocks fly amain.
  Approach, rich Ceres, her to entertain.   75

(Enter CERES.)

CERES: Hail, many-color'd messenger, that ne'er
  Dost disobey the wife of Jupiter,
  Who with thy saffron wings upon my flow'rs
  Diffusest honey-drops, refreshing show'rs,
  And with each end of thy blue bow dost crown   80
  My bosky acres and my unshrubb'd down,
  Rich scarf to my proud earth; why hath thy Queen
  Summon'd me hither, to this short-grass'd green?
IRIS: A contract of true love to celebrate,
  And some donation freely to estate   85
  On the bless'd lovers.
CERES: Tell me, heavenly bow,
  If Venus or her son, as thou dost know,
  Do now attend the Queen? Since they did plot

---

12 **Against an oracle** i.e., even if an oracle should declare otherwise
16 **sanctimonious** sacred   18 **aspersion** dew, shower   23 **Hymen's**
(Hymen was the Greek and Roman god of marriage.)   27 **worser genius** evil genius, or evil attendant spirit   30 **or** either; **founder'd** broken down, made lame (i.e., Ferdinand will wait impatiently for the
bridal night.)   37 **rabble** band, i.e., the *meaner fellows* of l. 35   41
vanity illusion   47 **mop and mow** gestures and grimaces   50 **conceive** understand

---

56 **liver** (as the presumed seat of the passions)   57 **corollary** surplus,
extra supply   58 **want** lack; **pertly** briskly   s.d. **Iris** goddess of the
rainbow, and Juno's messenger   60 **Ceres** goddess of the generative
power of nature; **leas** meadows   61 **vetches** plants for forage, fodder
63 **stover** winter fodder for cattle   64 **pioned and twilled** undercut by
the swift current and protected by roots and branches woven into a mat
(?)   66 **broom-groves** clumps of broom, gorse, yellow-flowered shrub
67 **dismissed bachelor** rejected male lover   68 **pole-clipt** hedged in
with poles; or pruned   70 **queen o' th' sky** i.e., Juno   71 **wat'ry arch**
rainbow   s.d. **Juno descends** i.e., starts her descent from the "heavens" above the stage (?)   74 **peacocks** birds sacred to Juno, and used to
pull her chariot; **amain** with full speed   75 **entertain** receive   81
bosky wooded;   **down** upland   85 **estate** bestow   87 **son** i.e., Cupid

90 The means that dusky Dis my daughter got,
Her and her blind boy's scandal'd company
I have forsworn.
IRIS: Of her society
Be not afraid. I met her deity
Cutting the clouds towards Paphos, and her son
Dove-drawn with her. Here thought they to have done
95 Some wanton charm upon this man and maid,
Whose vows are, that no bed-right shall be paid
Till Hymen's torch be lighted; but in vain;
Mars's hot minion is return'd again;
Her waspish-headed son has broke his arrows,
100 Swears he will shoot no more, but play with sparrows
And be a boy right out.

(JUNO alights.)

CERES: Highest Queen of state,
Great Juno, comes; I know her by her gait.
JUNO: How does my bounteous sister? Go with me
To bless this twain, that they may prosperous be
105 And honor'd in their issue.

(They sing.)

JUNO:

Honor, riches, marriage-blessing,
Long continuance, and increasing,
Hourly joys be still upon you!
Juno sings her blessings on you.

CERES:

110 Earth's increase, foison plenty,
Barns and garners never empty,
Vines with clust'ring bunches growing,
Plants with goodly burden bowing;
Spring come to you at the farthest
115 In the very end of harvest!
Scarcity and want shall shun you;
Ceres' blessing so is on you.

FERDINAND: This is a most majestic vision, and
Harmonious charmingly. May I be bold
120 To think these spirits?
PROSPERO: Spirits, which by mine art
I have from their confines call'd to enact
My present fancies.
FERDINAND: Let me live here ever;
So rare a wond'red father and a wife
Makes this place Paradise.

(JUNO and CERES whisper, and send IRIS on employment.)

PROSPERO: Sweet now, silence!
125 Juno and Ceres whisper seriously;

There's something else to do. Hush and be mute,
Or else our spell is marr'd.
IRIS: You nymphs, call'd Naiads, of the windring brooks,
With your sedg'd crowns and ever-harmless looks,
Leave your crisp channels, and on this green land   130
Answer your summons; Juno does command.
Come, temperate nymphs, and help to celebrate
A contract of true love; be not too late.

(Enter certain NYMPHS.)

You sunburnt sicklemen, of August weary,
Come hither from the furrow and be merry.   135
Make holiday; your rye-straw hats put on
And these fresh nymphs encounter every one
In country footing.

(Enter certain REAPERS, properly habited. They join with the NYMPHS in a graceful dance, towards the end whereof PROSPERO starts suddenly, and speaks; after which, to a strange, hollow, and confused noise, they heavily vanish.)

PROSPERO: *(Aside.)* I had forgot that foul conspiracy
Of the beast Caliban and his confederates   140
Against my life. The minute of their plot
Is almost come. *(To the SPIRITS.)* Well done! Avoid;
no more!
FERDINAND: This is strange. Your father's is some passion
That works him strongly.
MIRANDA: Never till this day
Saw I him touch'd with anger so distemper'd.   145
PROSPERO: You do look, my son, in a mov'd sort,
As if you were dismay'd. Be cheerful, sir.
Our revels now are ended. These our actors,
As I foretold you, were all spirits and
Are melted into air, into thin air;   150
And, like the baseless fabric of this vision,
The cloud-capp'd tow'rs, the gorgeous palaces,
The solemn temples, the great globe itself,
Yea, all which it inherit, shall dissolve
And, like this insubstantial pageant faded,   155
Leave not a rack behind. We are such stuff
As dreams are made on, and our little life
Is rounded with a sleep. Sir, I am vex'd.
Bear with my weakness; my old brain is troubled.
Be not disturb'd with my infirmity.   160
If you be pleas'd, retire into my cell
And there repose. A turn or two I'll walk
To still my beating mind.
FERDINAND, MIRANDA: We wish your peace.

(Exeunt.)

PROSPERO: Come with a thought! I thank thee, Ariel. Come.

(Enter ARIEL.)

---

89 **Dis . . . got** (Pluto, or *Dis*, god of the infernal regions, carried off Persephone, daughter of Ceres, to be his bride in Hades.)   90 **Her** i.e., Venus; **scandal'd** scandalous   92 **her deity** i.e., her highness   93 **Paphos** place on the island of Cyprus, sacred to Venus   98 **Mars' hot minion** i.e., Venus, the beloved of Mars   99 **waspish-headed** fiery, hotheaded, peevish   100 **sparrows** (Supposed lustful, and sacred to Venus.)   101 **right out** outright   110 **foison plenty** plentiful harvest   111 **garners** granaries   123 **wond'red** wonder-performing, wondrous; **wife** (Sometimes emended to *wise.*)

---

128 **windring** wandering, winding (?)   130 **crisp** curled, rippled   132 **temperate** chaste   138 **country footing** country dancing   s.d. **heavily** slowly, dejectedly   142 **Avoid** depart, withdraw   146 **mov'd sort** troubled state, condition   148 **revels** entertainments, pageants   151 **baseless** without substance   154 **which it inherit** who occupy it   156 **rack** wisp of cloud   157 **on** of   164 **with a thought** i.e., on the instant, or summoned by my thought, no sooner thought on than here

165 ARIEL: Thy thoughts I cleave to. What's thy pleasure?
PROSPERO: Spirit,
     We must prepare to meet with Caliban.
     ARIEL: Ay, my commander. When I presented Ceres,
        I thought to have told thee of it, but I fear'd
        Lest I might anger thee.
170 PROSPERO: Say again, where didst thou leave these varlets?
     ARIEL: I told you, sir, they were red-hot with drinking,
        So full of valor that they smote the air
        For breathing in their faces; beat the ground
        For kissing of their feet; yet always bending
175   Towards their project. Then I beat my tabor,
        At which, like unback'd colts, they prick'd their ears,
        Advanc'd their eyelids, lifted up their noses
        As they smelt music. So I charm'd their ears
        That calf-like they my lowing follow'd through
180   Tooth'd briers, sharp furzes, pricking goss, and thorns,
        Which ent'red their frail shins. At last I left them
        I' th' filthy-mantled pool beyond your cell,
        There dancing up to th' chins, that the foul lake
        O'erstunk their feet.
     PROSPERO: This was well done, my bird.
185   Thy shape invisible retain thou still.
        The trumpery in my house, go bring it hither,
        For stale to catch these thieves.
     ARIEL: I go, I go.

(Exit.)

PROSPERO: A devil, a born devil, on whose nature
        Nurture can never stick; on whom my pains,
190   Humanely taken, all, all lost, quite lost!
        And as with age his body uglier grows,
        So his mind cankers. I will plague them all,
        Even to roaring.

(Enter ARIEL, *loaden with glistering apparel, etc.)*

        Come, hang them on this line.

*([*ARIEL *hangs up the showy finery;* PROSPERO *and* ARIEL *remain, invisible.] Enter* CALIBAN, STEPHANO, *and* TRINCULO, *all wet.)*

CALIBAN: Pray you, tread softly, that the blind mole may not
195   Hear a foot fall. We now are near his cell.
STEPHANO: Monster, your fairy, which you say is a harmless
     fairy, has done little better than play'd the Jack with us.
TRINCULO: Monster, I do smell all horse-piss, at which my
     nose is in great indignation.
200 STEPHANO: So is mine. Do you hear, monster? If I should take
     a displeasure against you, look you—
TRINCULO: Thou wert but a lost monster.
CALIBAN: Good my lord, give me thy favor still.

        Be patient, for the prize I'll bring thee to
        Shall hoodwink this mischance. Therefore speak softly.   205
        All's hush'd as midnight yet.
TRINCULO: Ay, but to lose our bottles in the pool—
STEPHANO: There is not only disgrace and dishonor in that,
     monster, but an infinite loss.
TRINCULO: That's more to me than my wetting. Yet this is your   210
     harmless fairy, monster!
STEPHANO: I will fetch off my bottle, though I be o'er ears for
     my labor.
CALIBAN: Prithee, my King, be quiet. See'st thou here,
     This is the mouth o' th' cell. No noise, and enter.   215
     Do that good mischief which may make this island
     Thine own for ever, and I, thy Caliban,
     For aye thy foot-licker.
STEPHANO: Give me thy hand. I do begin to have bloody
     thoughts.   220
TRINCULO: *(Seeing the finery.)* O King Stephano! O peer! O
     worthy Stephano! Look what a wardrobe here is for thee!
CALIBAN: Let it alone, thou fool! It is but trash.
TRINCULO: O, ho, monster! We know what belongs to a frip-
     pery. O King Stephano!   *(Takes a gown.)*   225
STEPHANO: Put off that gown, Trinculo. By this hand, I'll have
     that gown.
TRINCULO: Thy Grace shall have it.
CALIBAN: The dropsy drown this fool! What do you mean
     To dote thus on such luggage? Let's alone   230
     And do the murder first. If he awake,
     From toe to crown he'll fill our skins with pinches,
     Make us strange stuff.
STEPHANO: Be you quiet, monster. Mistress line, is not this my
     jerkin? *(Takes it down.)* Now is the jerkin under the line.   235
     Now, jerkin, you are like to lose your hair and prove a bald
     jerkin.
TRINCULO: Do, do! We steal by line and level, an 't like your
     Grace.
STEPHANO: I thank thee for that jest. Here's a garment for 't.   240
     (Gives a garment.) Wit shall not go unrewarded while I am
     king of this country. "Steal by line and level" is an excellent
     pass of pate. There's another garment for 't.
TRINCULO: Monster, come, put some lime upon your fingers,
     and away with the rest.   245
CALIBAN: I have none on 't. We shall lose our time,
     And all be turn'd to barnacles, or to apes
     With foreheads villainous low.

---

205 **hoodwink** cover up, make you not see (A hawking term.)   221 **King . . . peer** (Alludes to the old ballad beginning, "King Stephen was a worthy peer.")   224 **frippery** place where cast-off clothes are sold   230 **luggage** cumbersome trash   235 **jerkin** jacket make of leather; **under the line** under the lime tree (with punning sense of being south of the equinoctial line or equator; sailors were popularly supposed to lose their hair from scurvy or other diseases. Stephano also quibbles bawdily on losing hair through syphilis, and in *Mistress* and *jerkin*.)   238 **by line and level** i.e., by means of plumb-line and carpenter's level, methodically (with pun on *line*, "lime tree," l. 235, and *steal* pronounced *stale*, i.e., prostitute, continuing Stephano's bawdy quibble); **an 't like** if it please   243 **pass of pate** sally of wit   244 **lime** birdlime, sticky substance (to give Caliban sticky fingers)   247 **barnacles** barnacle geese, formerly supposed to be hatched from seashells attached to trees and to fall thence into the water; here evidently used, like *apes*, as types of simpletons   248 **villainous** miserably

---

167 **presented** acted the part of, or introduced   176 **unback'd** unbroken, unridden   177 **Advanc'd** lifted up   180 **goss** gorse, a prickly shrub   182 **filthy-mantled** covered with a slimy coating   186 **trumpery** cheap goods, the *glistering apparel* mentioned in the following stage direction   187 **stale** (1) decoy (2) out of fashion garments (with possible further suggestions of *fit for a stale* or prostitute, *stale* meaning "horse-piss," l. 198, and *steal*, pronounced like *stale*)   192 **cankers** festers, grows malignant   193 **line** lime tree or linden   197 **Jack** (1) Knave (2) will-o-the wisp

250 STEPHANO: Monster, lay to your fingers. Help to bear this away
where my hogshead of wine is, or I'll turn you out of my
kingdom. Go to, carry this.

TRINCULO: And this.

STEPHANO: Ay, and this.

(They collect more and more garments.)

(A noise of hunters heard. Enter divers SPIRITS, *in shape of dogs
and hounds, hunting them about,* PROSPERO *and* ARIEL *setting
them on.)*

PROSPERO: Hey, Mountain, hey!

255 ARIEL: Silver! There it goes, Silver!

PROSPERO: Fury, Fury! There, Tyrant, there! Hark! Hark!

*(*CALIBAN, STEPHANO, *and* TRINCULO *are driven out.)*

Go charge my goblins that they grind their joints
With dry convulsions, shorten up their sinews
With aged cramps, and more pitch-spotted make them
260 Than pard or cat o' mountain.

ARIEL: Hark, they roar!

PROSPERO: Let them be hunted soundly. At this hour
Lies at my mercy all mine enemies.
Shortly shall all my labors end, and thou
Shalt have the air at freedom. For a little
265 Follow, and do me service.

(Exeunt.)

— ACT FIVE —

SCENE I

Enter PROSPERO *in his magic robes, [with his staff,] and* ARIEL.

PROSPERO: Now does my project gather to a head.
My charms crack not, my spirits obey, and Time
Goes upright with his carriage. How's the day?

ARIEL: On the sixth hour; at which time, my lord,
5 You said our work should cease.

PROSPERO: I did say so,
When first I rais'd the tempest. Say, my spirit,
How fares the King and 's followers?

ARIEL: Confin'd together
In the same fashion as you gave in charge,
Just as you left them; all prisoners, sir,
10 In the line-grove which weather-fends your cell.
They cannot budge till your release. The King,
His brother, and yours, abide all three distracted,
And the remainder mourning over them,
Brimful of sorrow and dismay; but chiefly
15 Him that you term'd, sir, "The good old lord, Gonzalo."
His tears runs down his beard like winter's drops
From eaves of reeds. Your charm so strongly works 'em
That if you now beheld them, your affections
Would become tender.

PROSPERO: Dost thou think so, spirit?

ARIEL: Mine would, sir, were I human.   20

PROSPERO: And mine shall.
Hast thou, which art but air, a touch, a feeling
Of their afflictions, and shall not myself,
One of their kind, that relish all as sharply,
Passion as they, be kindlier mov'd than thou art?
25 Though with their high wrongs I am struck to th' quick,
Yet with my nobler reason 'gainst my fury
Do I take part. The rarer action is
In virtue than in vengeance. They being penitent,
The sole drift of my purpose doth extend
30 Not a frown further. Go release them, Ariel.
My charms I'll break, their senses I'll restore,
And they shall be themselves.

ARIEL: I'll fetch them, sir.

(Exit.)

*(*PROSPERO *traces a charmed circle with his staff.)*

PROSPERO: Ye elves of hills, brooks, standing lakes, and groves,
And ye that on the sands with printless foot
35 Do chase the ebbing Neptune, and do fly him
When he comes back; you demi-puppets that
By moonshine do the green sour ringlets make,
Whereof the ewe not bites; and you whose pastime
Is to make midnight mushrooms, that rejoice
40 To hear the solemn curfew; by whose aid,
Weak masters though ye be, I have bedimm'd
The noontide sun, call'd forth the mutinous winds,
And 'twixt the green sea and the azur'd vault
Set roaring war; to the dread rattling thunder
45 Have I given fire, and rifted Jove's stout oak
With his own bolt; the strong-bas'd promontory
Have I made shake, and by the spurs pluck'd up
The pine and cedar; graves at my command
Have wak'd their sleepers, op'd, and let 'em forth
50 By my so potent art. But this rough magic
I here abjure, and, when I have requir'd
Some heavenly music, which even now I do,
To work mine end upon their senses that
This airy charm is for, I'll break my staff,
55 Bury it certain fathoms in the earth,
And deeper than did ever plummet sound
I'll drown my book.

(Solemn music.)

(Here enters ARIEL *before; then* ALONSO, *with a frantic gesture,
attended by* GONZALO; SEBASTIAN *and* ANTONIO *in like manner, attended by* ADRIAN *and* FRANCISCO. *They all enter the circle which* PROSPERO *had made, and there stand charm'd; which*
PROSPERO *observing, speaks:)*

---

258 **dry** associated with age, arthritic (?); **convulsions** cramps 259
aged characteristic of old age 260 **pard** panther or leopard; **cat o'
mountain** wildcat

V.i. Location: Before Prospero's cell. 3 **his carriage** its burden (i.e.,
Time is unstopped, runs smoothly.) 10 **line-grove** grove of lime trees;
weather-fends protects from the weather 11 **your release** you release
them 17 **eaves of reeds** thatched roofs

---

23 **relish all** experience quite 24 **Passion** experience deep feeling
27 **rarer** nobler 33–50 **Ye . . . art** (This famous passage is an embell-
ished paraphrase of Golding's translation of Ovid's *Metamorphoses*, vii.
197–219.) 36 **demi-puppets** puppets of half-size, i.e., elves and
fairies 37 **green sour ringlets** fairy rings, circles in grass (actually produced by mushrooms) 44–45 **to . . . fire** I have discharged the dread
rattling thunderbolt 45 **rifted** riven, split 47 **spurs** roots 51 **requir'd** requested

A solemn air, and the best comforter
To an unsettled fancy, cure thy brains,

60 Now useless, boil'd within thy skull! There stand,
For you are spell-stopp'd.
Holy Gonzalo, honorable man,
Mine eyes, ev'n sociable to the show of thine,
Fall fellowly drops. The charm dissolves apace,

65 And as the morning steals upon the night,
Melting the darkness, so their rising senses
Begin to chase the ignorant fumes that mantle
Their clearer reason. O good Gonzalo,
My true preserver, and a loyal sir

70 To him thou follow'st! I will pay thy graces
Home both in word and deed. Most cruelly
Didst thou, Alonso, use me and my daughter.
Thy brother was a furtherer in the act.
Thou art pinch'd for 't now, Sebastian. Flesh and blood,

75 You, brother mine, that entertain'd ambition,
Expell'd remorse and nature, who, with Sebastian,
Whose inward pinches therefore are most strong,
Would here have kill'd your king, I do forgive thee,
Unnatural though thou art.—Their understanding

80 Begins to swell, and the approaching tide
Will shortly fill the reasonable shore
That now lies foul and muddy. Not one of them
That yet looks on me, or would know me. Ariel,
Fetch me the hat and rapier in my cell.

(ARIEL goes to the cell and returns immediately.)

85 I will discase me, and myself present
As I was sometime Milan. Quickly, spirit;
Thou shalt ere long be free.

(ARIEL sings and helps to attire him.)

ARIEL: Where the bee sucks, there suck I;
In a cowslip's bell I lie;

90   There I couch when owls do cry.
On the bat's back I do fly
After summer merrily.
Merrily, merrily shall I live now
Under the blossom that hangs on the bough.

95 PROSPERO: Why, that's my dainty Ariel! I shall miss thee;
But yet thou shalt have freedom. So, so, so.
To the King's ship, invisible as thou art!
There shalt thou find the mariners asleep
Under the hatches. The master and the boatswain

100   Being awake, enforce them to this place,
And presently, I prithee.
ARIEL: I drink the air before me, and return
Or ere your pulse twice beat.   *(Exit.)*
GONZALO: All torment, trouble, wonder, and amazement

105   Inhabits here. Some heavenly power guide us
Out of this fearful country!
PROSPERO: Behold, sir King,
The wronged Duke of Milan, Prospero.

For more assurance that a living prince
Does now speak to thee, I embrace thy body;
And to thee and thy company I bid   110
A hearty welcome.

(Embraces him.)

ALONSO: Whe'er thou be'st he or no,
Or some enchanted trifle to abuse me,
As late I have been, I not know. Thy pulse
Beats as of flesh and blood; and, since I saw thee,
Th' affliction of my mind amends, with which,   115
I fear, a madness held me. This must crave,
An if this be at all, a most strange story.
Thy dukedom I resign, and do entreat
Thou pardon me my wrongs. But how should Prospero
Be living and be here?   120
PROSPERO: *(To* GONZALO.)   First, noble friend,
Let me embrace thine age, whose honor cannot
Be measur'd or confin'd.

(Embraces him.)

GONZALO: Whether this be
Or be not, I'll not swear.
PROSPERO: Yet do yet taste
Some subtleties o' th' isle, that will not let you
Believe things certain. Welcome, my friends all!   125
(Aside to SEBASTIAN *and* ANTONIO.) But you, my brace of
    lords, were I so minded,
I here could pluck his Highness' frown upon you
And justify you traitors. At this time
I will tell no tales.
SEBASTIAN: The devil speaks in him.
PROSPERO: No.
For you, most wicked sir, whom to call brother   130
Would even infect my mouth, I do forgive
Thy rankest fault—all of them; and require
My dukedom of thee, which perforce I know
Thou must restore.
ALONSO: If thou be'st Prospero,
Give us particulars of thy preservation,   135
How thou hast met us here, who three hours since
Were wrack'd upon this shore; where I have lost—
How sharp the point of this remembrance is!—
My dear son Ferdinand.
PROSPERO: I am woe for 't, sir.
ALONSO: Irreparable is the loss, and Patience   140
Says it is past her cure.
PROSPERO: I rather think
You have not sought her help, of whose soft grace
For the like loss I have her sovereign aid
And rest myself content.
ALONSO: You the like loss?
PROSPERO: As great to me as late; and, supportable   145
To make the dear loss, have I means much weaker

---

58 **and** i.e., which is   63 **sociable** sympathetic; **show** appearance   64 **Fall** let fall   70 **pay thy graces** reward your favors   71 **Home** fully   76 **remorse** pity; **nature** natural feeling   85 **discase** disrobe   86 **As . . . Milan** in my former appearance as Duke of Milan   96 **So, so, so** (Expresses approval of Ariel's help as valet.)

112 **trifle** trick of magic; **abuse** deceive   116 **crave** require   117 **An . . . all** if this is actually happening   118 **Thy . . . resign** (Alonso made arrangement with Antonio at the time of Prospero's banishment for Milan to pay tribute to Naples; see I.ii. 113–127.)   124 **subtleties** illusions, magical powers   128 **justify you** prove you to be   139 **woe** sorry   145 **late** recent

Than you may call to comfort you, for I
Have lost my daughter.

ALONSO: A daughter?

150   O heavens, that they were living both in Naples,
The king and queen there! That they were, I wish
Myself were mudded in that oozy bed
Where my son lies. When did you lose your daughter?

PROSPERO: In this last tempest. I perceive these lords

155   At this encounter do so much admire
That they devour their reason and scarce think
Their eyes do offices of truth, their words
Are natural breath. But, howsoev'r you have
Been justled from your senses, know for certain

160   That I am Prospero and that very duke
Which was thrust forth of Milan, who most strangely
Upon this shore, where you were wrack'd, was landed,
To be the lord on 't. No more yet of this,
For 'tis a chronicle of day by day,

165   Not a relation for a breakfast nor
Befitting this first meeting. Welcome, sir;
This cell's my court. Here have I few attendants
And subjects none abroad. Pray you look in.
My dukedom since you have given me again,

170   I will requite you with as good a thing,
At least bring forth a wonder, to content ye
As much as me my dukedom.

(Here PROSPERO *discovers* FERDINAND *and* MIRANDA, *playing at chess.)*

MIRANDA: Sweet lord, you play me false.

FERDINAND: No, my dearest love,

175   I would not for the world.

MIRANDA: Yes, for a score of kingdoms you should wrangle,
And I would call it fair play.

ALONSO: If this prove
A vision of the island, one dear son
Shall I twice lose.

SEBASTIAN: A most high miracle!

180 FERDINAND: Though the seas threaten, they are merciful;
I have curs'd them without cause. *(Kneels.)*

ALONSO: Now all the blessings
Of a glad father compass thee about!
Arise, and say how thou cam'st here.

MIRANDA: O, wonder!
How many goodly creatures are there here!

185   How beauteous mankind is! O brave new world,
That has such people in 't!

PROSPERO: 'Tis new to thee.

ALONSO: What is this maid with whom thou wast at play?
Your eld'st acquaintance cannot be three hours.

---

155 admire wonder   **156–158 scarce . . . breath** scarcely believe that their eyes inform them accurately what they see or that their words are naturally spoken   s.d. **discovers** i.e., by opening a curtain, presumably rear-stage   **176–177 Yes . . . play** i.e., yes, even if we were playing for twenty kingdoms, something less than the whole world, you would still contend mightily against me and play me false, and I would let you do it as though it were fair play; or, if you were to play not just for stakes but literally for kingdoms, my accusation of false play would be out of order in that your "wrangling" would be proper   **185 brave** splendid, gorgeously appareled, handsome   **188 eld'st** longest

---

Is she the goddess that hath sever'd us,
And brought us thus together?   190

FERDINAND: Sir, she is mortal;
But by immortal Providence she's mine.
I chose her when I could not ask my father
For his advice, nor thought I had one. She
Is daughter to this famous Duke of Milan,
Of whom so often I have heard renown,   195
But never saw before; of whom I have
Receiv'd a second life; and second father
This lady makes him to me.

ALONSO: I am hers.
But, O, how oddly will it sound that I
Must ask my child forgiveness!   200

PROSPERO: There, sir, stop.
Let us not burden our remembrances with
A heaviness that's gone.

GONZALO: I have inly wept
Or should have spoke ere this. Look down, you gods,
And on this couple drop a blessed crown!
For it is you that have chalk'd forth the way   205
Which brought us hither.

ALONSO: I say Amen, Gonzalo!

GONZALO: Was Milan thrust from Milan, that his issue
Should become kings of Naples? O, rejoice
Beyond a common joy, and set it down
With gold on lasting pillars: In one voyage   210
Did Claribel her husband find at Tunis,
And Ferdinand, her brother, found a wife
Where he himself was lost; Prospero his dukedom
In a poor isle; and all of us ourselves
When no man was his own.   215

ALONSO: *(To* FERDINAND *and* MIRANDA.*)* Give me your hands.
Let grief and sorrow still embrace his heart
That doth not wish you joy!

GONZALO: Be it so! Amen!

(Enter ARIEL, *with the* MASTER *and* BOATSWAIN *amazedly following.)*

O, look, sir, look, sir! Here is more of us.
I prophesied, if a gallows were on land,
This fellow could not drown. Now, blasphemy,   220
That swear'st grace o'erboard, not an oath on shore?
Hast thou no mouth by land? What is the news?

BOATSWAIN: The best news is that we have safely found
Our King and company; the next, our ship—
Which, but three glasses since, we gave out split—   225
Is tight and yare and bravely rigg'd as when
We first put out to sea.

ARIEL: *(Aside to* PROSPERO.*)* Sir, all this service
Have I done since I went.

PROSPERO: *(Aside to* ARIEL.*)* My tricksy spirit!

ALONSO: These are not natural events; they strengthen
From strange to stranger. Say, how came you hither?   230

BOATSWAIN: If I did think, sir, I were well awake,
I'd strive to tell you. We were dead of sleep,

---

207 Was Milan was the Duke of Milan   **216 still** always; **his** that man's   **217 That** who   **225 glasses** i.e., hours; **gave out** reported   **226 yare** ready

And—how we know not—all clapp'd under hatches;
Where but even now with strange and several noises
235 Of roaring, shrieking, howling, jingling chains,
And moe diversity of sounds, all horrible,
We were awak'd; straightway, at liberty;
Where we, in all her trim, freshly beheld
Our royal, good, and gallant ship, our master
240 Cap'ring to eye her. On a trice, so please you,
Even in a dream, were we divided from them
And were brought moping hither.
ARIEL: *(Aside to* PROSPERO.)   Was 't well done?
PROSPERO: *(Aside to* ARIEL.) Bravely, my diligence. Thou shalt
     be free.
ALONSO: This is as strange a maze as e'er men trod,
245 And there is in this business more than nature
Was ever conduct of. Some oracle
Must rectify our knowledge.
PROSPERO: Sir, my liege,
Do not infest your mind with beating on
The strangeness of this business. At pick'd leisure,
250 Which shall be shortly, single I'll resolve you,
Which to you shall seem probable, of every
These happen'd accidents; till when, be cheerful
And think of each thing well. *(Aside to* ARIEL.) Come
     hither, spirit.
Set Caliban and his companions free;
255 Untie the spell. *(Exit* ARIEL.) How fares my gracious sir?
There are yet missing of your company
Some few odd lads that you remember not.

(Enter ARIEL, *driving in* CALIBAN, STEPHANO, *and* TRINCULO,
in their stol'n apparel.)

STEPHANO: Every man shift for all the rest, and let no man
     take care of himself; for all is but fortune. Coragio, bully-
260   monster, coragio!
TRINCULO: If these be true spies which I wear in my head,
     here's a goodly sight.
CALIBAN: O Setebos, these be brave spirits indeed!
How fine my master is! I am afraid
265 He will chastise me.
SEBASTIAN: Ha, ha!
What things are these, my lord, Antonio?
Will money buy 'em?
ANTONIO: Very like. One of them
Is a plain fish, and no doubt marketable.
270 PROSPERO: Mark but the badges of these men, my lords,
Then say if they be true. This misshapen knave,
His mother was a witch, and one so strong
That could control the moon, make flows and ebbs,
And deal in her command without her power.
275 These three have robb'd me; and this demi-devil—

For he's a bastard one—had plotted with them
To take my life. Two of these fellows you
Must know and own; this thing of darkness I
Acknowledge mine.
CALIBAN: I shall be pinch'd to death.
ALONSO: Is not this Stephano, my drunken butler?   280
SEBASTIAN: He is drunk now. Where had he wine?
ALONSO: And Trinculo is reeling ripe. Where should they
Find this grand liquor that hath gilded 'em?
How cam'st thou in this pickle?
TRINCULO: I have been in such a pickle since I saw you last   285
     that, I fear me, will never out of my bones. I shall not fear fly-
     blowing.
SEBASTIAN: Why, how now, Stephano?
STEPHANO: O, touch me not! I am not Stephano, but a
     cramp.   290
PROSPERO: You'd be king o' the isle, sirrah?
STEPHANO: I should have been a sore one then.
ALONSO: *(Pointing to* CALIBAN.) This is a strange thing as e'er
     I look'd on.
PROSPERO: He is as disproportion'd in his manners
As in his shape. Go, sirrah, to my cell;   295
Take with you your companions. As you look
To have my pardon, trim it handsomely.
CALIBAN: Ay, that I will; and I'll be wise hereafter
And seek for grace. What a thrice-double ass
Was I to take this drunkard for a god   300
And worship this dull fool!
PROSPERO: Go to; away!
ALONSO: Hence, and bestow your luggage where you found it.
SEBASTIAN: Or stole it, rather.

(Exeunt CALIBAN, STEPHANO, *and* TRINCULO.)*

PROSPERO: Sir, I invite your Highness and your train
To my poor cell, where you shall take your rest   305
For this one night; which, part of it, I'll waste
With such discourse as, I not doubt, shall make it
Go quick away—the story of my life,
And the particular accidents gone by
Since I came to this isle. And in the morn   310
I'll bring you to your ship, and so to Naples,
Where I have hope to see the nuptial
Of these our dear-belov'd solemnized;
And thence retire me to my Milan, where
Every third thought shall be my grave.   315
ALONSO: I long
To hear the story of your life, which must
Take the ear strangely.
PROSPERO: I'll deliver all;
And promise you calm seas, auspicious gales,
And sail so expeditious that shall catch

---

240 **Cap'ring to eye** dancing for joy to see   242 **moping** in a daze
246 **conduct** guide, leader   248 **infest** harass, disturb   249 **pick'd**
chosen, convenient   250 **single** i.e., by my own human powers   252
accidents occurrences   259 **Coragio** courage; **bully-monster** gallant
monster (Ironical.)   264 **fine** splendidly attired   270 **badges** emblems of cloth or silver worn on the arms of retainers (Prospero refers
here to the stolen clothes as emblems of their villainy.)   271 **true** honest   274 **deal . . . power** wield the moon's power, either without her
authority or beyond her influence

---

278 **own** recognize, admit as belonging to you   283 **gilded** (1)
flushed, made drunk (2) covered with gilt (suggesting the horse-urine)
284 **pickle** (1) fix, predicament (2) pickling brine (in this case, horse
urine)   286–287 **fly-blowing** i.e., being fouled by fly-eggs (from
which he is saved by being pickled)   291 **sirrah** (Standard form of address to an inferior.)   292 **sore** (1) tyrannical (2) wracked by pain
306 **waste** spend   309 **accidents** occurrences   317 **Take** take effect
upon, enchant; **deliver** declare, relate

320 Your royal fleet far off. (*Aside to* ARIEL.) My Ariel, chick,
     That is thy charge. Then to the elements
     Be free, and fare thou well!—Please you, draw near.

(*Exeunt omnes.*)

— EPILOGUE —

Spoken by PROSPERO.

     Now my charms are all o'erthrown,
     And what strength I have 's mine own,
     Which is most faint. Now, 'tis true,
     I must be here confin'd by you,
  5 Or sent to Naples. Let me not,
     Since I have my dukedom got
     And pardon'd the deceiver, dwell
     In this bare island by your spell,
     But release me from my bands
     With the help of your good hands.   10
     Gentle breath of yours my sails
     Must fill, or else my project fails,
     Which was to please. Now I want
     Spirits to enforce, art to enchant,
     And my ending is despair,   15
     Unless I be reliev'd by prayer,
     Which pierces so that it assaults
     Mercy itself and frees all faults.
     As you from crimes would pardon'd be,
     Let your indulgence set me free.   20

(*Exit.*)

---

322 **draw near** i.e., enter my cell

Epilogue. 9 **bands** bonds   10 **hands** i.e., applause (the noise of which would break the spell of silence)   13 **want** lack   16 **prayer** i.e., Prospero's petition to the audience   17 **assaults** rightfully gains the attention of   18 **frees** obtains forgiveness of   19 **crimes** sins

■ BEN JONSON ■

The playwright Ben Jonson (1572–1637) was Shakespeare's colleague in the theater in the late sixteenth century and early seventeenth century, the period in which both were working as professional playwrights. Shakespeare acted in several of Jonson's plays, and while Jonson alludes ironically to several of Shakespeare's plays in his own works, he also contributed a warm memorial poem to the volume of Shakespeare's plays published in 1623. But in many respects Jonson's life stands in marked contrast to Shakespeare's: where Shakespeare seems to have led a life of increasing "respectability," steadily accumulating wealth and real estate in provincial Stratford, Jonson's career seems to have followed a more mercurial course. Jonson was born in or near London, probably in 1572. His father had been imprisoned and had lost his estate during the reign of Queen Mary; he became a minister but died a month before Jonson was born. Jonson's mother married a bricklayer within a year or two of Jonson's birth, and his stepfather seems to have intended Jonson to follow in his footsteps. A patron, however, paid for Jonson to be enrolled at the Westminster school, where he gained command of Greek and Latin authors and developed a lifelong friendship with the famous scholar and antiquary William Camden. Though a student of Jonson's abilities graduating from Westminster would have been destined for Cambridge University, Jonson seems to have been denied this route and was apprenticed to his stepfather.

In the early 1590s, Jonson left bricklaying (though he was inducted as a "freeman" into the Company of Tylers and Bricklayers in 1598). He was married, served as a soldier in the Low Countries, and appeared as a strolling player in London. Although little is known about this period of his life, by 1597 he was in the employ of the theatrical impresario Philip Henslowe. Jonson may have played the leading role of Hieronymo in Thomas Kyd's hugely popular play, *The Spanish Tragedy*; in 1601, Henslowe commissioned Jonson to compose several additions to the play. The course of Jonson's career in the theater, however, was never a smooth one. In 1597, he collaborated with the playwright Thomas Nashe on a (now lost) play called *The Isle of Dogs*; Jonson was called before the Privy Council for the play's "lewd," "seditious and slanderous matter." In 1598, Jonson killed an actor—Gabriel Spencer—in a duel, and was imprisoned and sentenced to the gallows. He was released on a reduced sentence: all his property was confiscated and his thumb was branded. In 1598, however, Jonson also scored his first success in the theater: his play, *Every Man In His Humour* (1598), was performed by the Lord Chamberlain's Men at the Curtain theater, and Shakespeare was a member of the cast. The play capitalized on the vogue of "humour" comedies of the late sixteenth century, comedies in which each character is governed by a single ruling passion, his or her "humour." Jonson followed this play with a second comedy, *Every Man Out of His Humour* (1599), also performed by the Lord Chamberlain's men; he also spent part of 1599 in prison for debt. At the turn of the century, Jonson became embroiled in conflict with the poet and playwright John Marston. Marston and Jonson seized on the vogue of children's companies—the "little eyases" that have driven the players from London in *Hamlet*—to conduct a bitter rivalry. Jonson contributed two plays to this "war of the theaters" between 1599 and 1601, *Cynthia's Revels* and *Poetaster*; the actor Nathaniel Field, who was to become a friend of Jonson's, had a leading part in *Poetaster*.

In 1603 Jonson's son died (the subject of one of his most moving poems), and Jonson wrote his first classical tragedy, *Sejanus*. Though Jonson made *Sejanus* a model of his classical erudition, this tragedy of the Roman empire under Tiberius was not popular with audiences. One of his enemies at court also managed to have him summoned before the Privy Council again, this time for treason. Jonson landed in more difficult circumstances, however, when he collaborated with John Marston and John Chapman on a satire, *Eastward Ho!*. The play's satiric portrayal of Scotland and the Scots seemed seditious—King James V of Scotland had assumed the English throne as James I in 1603— and resulted in the arrest of the playwrights. Although he was threatened with the usual punishment (having his ears and nose cut off), Jonson was again released from prison. He was soon summoned again by the Privy Council on a more serious matter. In October, Jonson dined with a group of Catholics who were eventually involved in the failed Gunpowder Plot—a plan to undermine Parliament with explosives and blow it up on November 5. It is sometimes thought that Jonson met with the conspirators as a spy for the government, for by November 7 he was working to assist the Privy Council in their arrest.

Nonetheless, the first decades of the seventeenth century were the period of Jonson's greatest success as a writer. He was lionized as a poet and met with a group of younger poets—the "Tribe of Ben," including Robert Herrick—who both admired and imitated his classically inflected style. By 1605 he was regularly writing the Christmas masque for James's court and would continue to write holiday entertainments, as well as masques for state occasions, for the next decade. Jonson's career in the theater reached its peak at this time as well, with a stunning series of comedies: *Volpone* (1606), *Epicoene; or, The Silent Woman* (1609), *The Alchemist* (1610), *Bartholomew Fair* (1614); only *The Devil Is an Ass* (1616) and Jonson's second tragedy, *Catiline* (1611), failed to be popular in the theater. He also published a collection of *Epigrams* and a prose work, *The Forest*, in 1612. By 1616, Jonson was at the height of his career: he oversaw the publication of a lavish volume, *The Works of Benjamin Jonson*, and was granted a royal pension, becoming in effect England's poet laureate. Jonson's *Works* are a signal event in the history of publishing, in part because Jonson supervised the publication with such care, and in part because the *Works* were published in the large-format folio size usually reserved for classical authors. Jonson also collected nine of his plays and several of the masques in the volume, granting dramatic texts a status as "literature" that was unique in the period and marking the way for Heminges and Condell to publish Shakespeare's plays in folio in 1623.

In 1618, Jonson walked from London to Scotland, where he was publicly honored by the city council of Edinburgh. He was entertained at the home of William Drummond of Hawthornden, who later published a volume of his conversations with the famous poet. Drummond's portrait of Jonson captures Jonson's energy and ambition:

> a great lover and praiser of himself; a condemer and scorner of others; given rather to lose a friend than a jest, jealous of every word and action of those about him, especially after drink (which is one of the elements in which he lives). . . . He is passionately kind and angry; careless either to gain or keep; vindictive, but if he be well answered, at himself.

Although Jonson received an honorary Master of Arts from Oxford University in 1619 in recognition of his learning and skill as a poet, his later career was marked by failure and disappointment. His library—known for its extensive holdings of classical and modern languages—was destroyed in a fire in 1623. With the succession of James's son Charles I to the throne in 1625, Jonson's fortunes at court took a turn for the worse as well. Jonson had long feuded with Inigo Jones, the brilliant designer who oversaw the elaborate productions of the court masques; while Jonson saw the masque as a vehicle for his poetry, Jones saw the poetry as the vehicle for his splendid scenic displays. Under Charles, Jonson's popularity at court waned. Jonson wrote only two masques and returned to writing for the public theater. His first new play, *The Staple of News* (1626), was performed by the King's Men without much success; it was followed by *The New Inn* (1629), *The Magnetic Lady* (1631), and *The Tale of a Tub* (1633). These plays were not popular and brought Jonson little additional income. Jonson was paralyzed in 1628 and confined to his home. His annual pension was increased to £100 per year (six or seven times the annual wage of a craftsman or artisan) in 1629, and he continued to write professionally: Jonson was appointed London historian in 1628 and was writing a play—*The Sad Shepherd*—when he died.

In its outlines, Jonson's career was much different from Shakespeare's. Shakespeare is, in a sense, one of the success stories of an emerging English "middle class": joining the theater as actor and playwright, Shakespeare became an investor (or sharer) in the era's most prestigious company and reaped a steady profit. In the late 1590s, while Jonson was laboring to foresake the life of a strolling player, to keep out of jail, and to write for the stage, Shakespeare had already bought his home in Stratford, New Place. When Shakespeare died in 1616, he left a sizable estate in rural Stratford but was not memorialized in London; he was buried in Stratford, and his principal "monument" was the publication of his plays in 1623. Jonson actively pursued a career as a court writer but was never attached as a "sharer" to a theatrical company, and he sustained himself through patronage, preferment, and the publication of his *Works*. When he died on August 6, 1637, his belongings were valued at about £8. Nonetheless, he was given an elaborate public funeral and buried in Westminster Abbey. Typically, though, the monument that was to be placed on his tomb never materialized; a stone was later cut to mark his grave, bearing the simple, eloquent epitaph: "O rare Ben Jonson."

Volpone

Volpone is Jonson's best-known play today, and in many ways it is exemplary of Jonson's talents as a playwright. The play is set in Venice—the wealthiest city in Europe and the emblem of mercantile riches and excess to the English audience—and concerns Volpone's various schemes to trick his neighbors. The characters in the play are named for animals—Volpone (the fox), Mosca (the fly), Voltore (the vulture), Corbaccio (the raven), Corvino (the crow)—and in some ways the play resembles the moralized beast-fables common in medieval and Renaissance literature, in which the fox tricks his enemies, the vulture, raven, and crow. In the famous medieval epic *Reynard the Fox,* for example, Reynard the Fox feigns death to seduce the Crow's wife, is taken to court for raping a she-wolf, and becomes a kind of false preacher, something like Volpone's performance as the mountebank in Jonson's play. But while beast-fables anatomize human failings in vignettes in which animals behave like human beings, Jonson's satire uses the opposite strategy: in *Volpone,* Jonson castigates human beings for showing the rapacious instincts of animals.

Volpone opens with Volpone on his "deathbed" and the play revolves around his central scheme: to trick the wealthy citizens of Venice into believing that he is soon to die, so that they will bribe him in order to be included in his will. Volpone's energetic opening speech—"Good morning to the day; and next, my gold! / Open the shrine, that I may see my saint"—shows us that the fox is hardly near death; he has more than enough energy to outwit his greedy opponents. Indeed, Volpone's energy is constantly on display to the audience as he continually plays different roles, leaping from the deathbed performances of Act 1 to play the mountebank in Act 2, returning home to seduce Celia in Act 3, and giving a brilliant reprise of his deathbed performance to the Venetian Senate in Act 4. Volpone's talents are harnessed to his massive greed, an insatiable appetite that leads him not only to revel in his own wealth and power, but also to conspire against virtuous characters like Bonario and Celia as well as against scavengers like Voltore, Corbaccio, and Corvino. Jonson's brilliant talents as a poet are fully visible here, however, for he uses the richness of language to create a sense of the enormous power of Volpone's rich desire. When he attempts to seduce Celia with a vision of earthly pleasure, for example, his language works to ravish the audience as well:

> If thou hast wisdom, hear me, Celia.
> Thy baths shall be the juice of July-flowers,
> Spirit of roses, and of violets,
> The milk of unicorns, and panthers' breath
> Gathered in bags and mixed with Cretan wines.
> Our drink shall be prepared gold and amber,
> Which we will take until my roof whirl round
> With the vertigo; and my dwarf shall dance,
> My eunuch sing, my fool make up the antic.
> Whilst we, in changed shapes, act Ovid's tales,
> Thou like Europa now, and I like Jove,
> Then I like Mars, and thou like Erycine;
> So of the rest till we have quite run through
> And wearied all the fables of the gods.

In the play, Volpone's power is in many ways the power of rhetoric, the power to seduce his audience by giving range and voice to their own deepest fantasies. But fantasy—like rhetoric, like acting—is a dangerous thing, threatening to undermine the moral values that Jonson wants to locate at the heart of a civil society. It's one thing for Volpone to trick cunning fortune hunters like Voltore, Corbaccio, and Corvino: his devices work, after all, by playing on their own evil natures. But Volpone's performance is in other ways deeply antisocial, and Jonson's satire takes a moral turn when the fox uses his performance to pervert the public identity and reputation of the "good" characters. Volpone's brilliant performance to the Senate in Act 4—persuading them that Bonario is a potential murderer and that Celia is a well-known prostitute—succeeds brilliantly in convincing the Senate, but also traps Volpone in his role, the exhausting performance of his own illness and death. When Volpone feigns his own death in Act 5, he seems finally to misjudge both his victims and the limits of his ability to deceive. Mosca—the parasite who has absorbed Volpone's talents for transformation—inherits Volpone's fortune, but turns the tables on the fox: once Volpone has "died" and Mosca has inherited, there is no reason for Mosca to obey his still-living master.

Jonson is often remembered for remarking on Shakespeare's "little Latin, and less Greek" in the memorial poem he contributed to the 1623 folio of Shakespeare's plays, and *Volpone* is indebted in many ways to Jonson's extensive learning: Lady Pol is modeled on one of Juvenal's satires, the famous song to Celia in Act 3 adapts Catullus, and Jonson's language and imagery alludes frequently to Ovid, Petronius, and other Latin poets. But *Volpone* is indebted to the moral tradition of classical satire more deeply in its fundamental moral structure. For while Jonson satirizes Volpone's greed—and that of Mosca, Voltore, Corbaccio, Corvino, and the rest—he also brings his villains to sure punishment: Mosca is sentenced to the slave galleys, and Volpone is stripped of his wealth and left to die. Taking to his deathbed to corrupt the values of Venice, Volpone becomes a symbol of the enervating sterility that drives the city, where the lust for gold deforms nearly all social relationships and threatens to undermine justice as well. Fittingly, when the fox is finally exposed, he is "imprisoned" in the part he has used to corrupt the city: this time, Volpone will play the part of a sick and dying old man for real.

VOLPONE

BEN JONSON
EDITED BY M. L. WINE

— CHARACTERS —

VOLPONE, *a Magnifico*[1]
MOSCA, *his Parasite*
VOLTORE, *an Advocate*
CORBACCIO, *an old Gentleman*
CORVINO, *a Merchant*
AVOCATORI, *four Magistrates*
NOTARIO, *the Register*
NANO, *a Dwarf*
CASTRONE, *an Eunuch*
GREGE[2]
[SIR] POLITIC WOULD-BE, *a Knight*

PEREGRINE, *a Gent[leman]-traveler*
BONARIO, *a young Gentleman*
FINE MADAME WOULD-BE, *the Knight's wife*
CELIA, *the Merchant's wife*
COMMENDATORI, *Officers*
MERCATORI, *three Merchants*
ANDROGYNO, *a Hermaphrodite*
SERVITORE, *a Servant*
WOMEN

THE SCENE: *Venice.*

— THE ARGUMENT —

V olpone, childless, rich, feigns sick, despairs,
O ffers his state to hopes of several heirs,
L ies languishing; his Parasite receives
P resents of all, assures, deludes, then weaves
O ther cross plots, which ope' themselves, are told.
N ew tricks for safety are sought; they thrive; when, bold,
E ach tempts th'other again, and all are sold.

— PROLOGUE —

Now, luck yet send us, and a little wit
   Will serve to make our play hit;
According to the palates of the season,
   Here is rhyme, not empty of reason.
5 This we were bid to credit from our poet,
   Whose true scope, if you would know it,
In all his poems still hath been this measure:
   To mix profit with your pleasure;
And not as some (whose throats their envy failing)
10   Cry hoarsely, "All he writes is railing,"
And, when his plays come forth, think they can flout them,
   With saying, "He was a year about them."
To these there needs no lie but this his creature,
   Which was, two months since, no feature;
15 And, though he dares give them five lives to mend it,
   'Tis known, five weeks fully penned it,
From his own hand, without a coadjutor,
   Novice, journeyman, or tutor.
Yet thus much can I give you as a token
20   Of his play's worth: no eggs are broken,
Nor quaking custards with fierce teeth affrighted,
   Wherewith your rout are so delighted;

Nor hales he in a gull, old ends reciting,
   To stop gaps in his loose writing,
With such a deal of monstrous and forced action, 25
   As might make Bedlam a faction;
Nor made he his play for jests stol'n from each table,
   But makes jests to fit his fable.
And so presents quick comedy refined,
   As best critics have designed; 30
The laws of time, place, persons be observeth,
   From no needful rule he swerveth.
All gall and copp'ras from his ink he draineth,
   Only a little salt remaineth,
Wherewith he'll rub your cheeks till, red with laughter, 35
   They shall look fresh a week after.

— ACT ONE —

SCENE I

VOLPONE, MOSCA.

VOLPONE: Good morning to the day; and, next, my gold!
   Open the shrine that I may see my saint.

(MOSCA *opens a curtain, revealing great treasure.*)

   Hail the world's soul, and mine! More glad than is
The teeming earth to see the longed-for sun
Peep through the horns of the celestial Ram 5
Am I, to view thy splendor darkening his,
That, lying here amongst my other hoards,
Show'st like a flame by night, or like the day
Struck out of chaos, when all darkness fled
Unto the center. O thou son of Sol, 10
But brighter than thy father, let me kiss,
With adoration, thee and every relic
Of sacred treasure in this blessed room.

---

[1] **Magnifico** Venetian nobleman   [2] **Grege** the mob
7 **still** constantly, always

26 **Bedlam** Bethlehem Hospital, an asylum for the insane   29 **quick**
lively   33 **copp'ras** vitriol
10 **center** the earth's center; **Sol** the sun

Well did wise poets, by thy glorious name,
15   Title that age which they would have the best,
Thou being the best of things and far transcending
All style of joy in children, parents, friends,
Or any other waking dream on earth.
Thy looks when they to Venus did ascribe,
20   They should have giv'n her twenty thousand Cupids;
Such are thy beauties and our loves! Dear saint,
Riches, the dumb god that giv'st all men tongues,
That canst do naught, and yet mak'st men do all things;
The price of souls! Even hell, with thee to boot,
25   Is made worth heaven! Thou art virtue, fame,
Honor, and all things else! Who can get thee,
He shall be noble, valiant, honest, wise—
MOSCA: And what he will, sir. Riches are in fortune
A greater good than wisdom is in nature.
30 VOLPONE: True, my belovèd Mosca. Yet, I glory
More in the cunning purchase of my wealth
Than in the glad possession since I gain
No common way: I use no trade, no venture;
I wound no earth with ploughshares; fat no beasts
35   To feed the shambles; have no mills for iron,
Oil, corn, or men, to grind 'hem into poulder;
I blow no subtle glass; expose no ships
To threat'nings of the furrow-facèd sea;
I turn no monies in the public bank,
40   Nor usure private—
MOSCA: No, sir, nor devour
Soft prodigals. You shall ha' some will swallow
A melting heir as glibly as your Dutch
Will pills of butter, and ne'er purge for't;
Tear forth the fathers of poor families
45   Out of their beds and coffin them, alive,
In some kind, clasping prison, where their bones
May be forthcoming when the flesh is rotten.
But your sweet nature doth abhor these courses;
You loathe the widow's or the orphan's tears
50   Should wash your pavements, or their piteous cries
Ring in your roofs, and beat the air for vengeance—
VOLPONE: Right, Mosca, I do loathe it.
MOSCA: And, besides, sir,
You are not like the thresher that doth stand
With a huge flail, watching a heap of corn,
55   And, hungry, dares not taste the smallest grain
But feeds on mallows and such bitter herbs;
Nor like the merchant, who hath filled his vaults
With Romagnìa and rich Candian wines,
Yet drinks the lees of Lombard's vinegar.
60   You will not lie in straw whilst moths and worms
Feed on your sumptuous hangings and soft beds.
You know the use of riches and dare give, now,
From that bright heap, to me, your poor observer,
Or to your dwarf, or your hermaphrodite,
65   Your eunuch, or what other household trifle
Your pleasure allows maint'nance—
VOLPONE: Hold thee, Mosca,
Take of my hand; thou strik'st on truth in all,
And they are envious term thee parasite.

---

36 **poulder** powder   63 **observer** obsequious servant

Call forth my dwarf, my eunuch, and my fool,
And let 'hem make me sport.   70

(*Exit* MOSCA.)

                     What should I do
But cocker up my genius and live free
To all delights my fortune calls me to?
I have no wife, no parent, child, ally
To give my substance to; but whom I make
Must be my heir: and this makes men observe me.   75
This draws me clients, daily, to my house,
Women and men of every sex and age,
That bring me presents, send me plate, coin, jewels,
With hope that when I die (which they expect
Each greedy minute) it shall then return   80
Tenfold upon them; whilst some, covetous
Above the rest, seek to engross me, whole,
And counterwork the one unto the other,
Contend in gifts, as they would seem in love:
All which I suffer, playing with their hopes,   85
And am content to coin 'hem into profit,
And look upon their kindness, and take more,
And look on that; still bearing them in hand,
Letting the cherry knock against their lips,
And draw it by their mouths, and back again.—   90
How now!

SCENE II

NANO, ANDROGYNO, CASTRONE, VOLPONE, MOSCA.

NANO: Now, room for fresh gamesters, who do will you to know
   They do bring you neither play nor university show;
And therefore do entreat you that whatsoever they rehearse
May not fare a whit the worse for the false pace of the verse.
If you wonder at this, you will wonder more, ere we pass,   5
For know, here

(*He points to* ANDROGYNO.)

              is enclosed the soul of Pythagoras,
That juggler divine, as hereafter shall follow;
Which soul, fast and loose, sir, came first from Apollo,
And was breathed into Æthalides, Mercurius his son,
Where it had the gift to remember all that ever was done.   10
From thence it fled forth and made quick transmigration
To goldy-locked Euphorbus, who was killed, in good fashion,
At the siege of old Troy, by the cuckold of Sparta.
Hermotimus was next (I find it in my charta)
To whom it did pass, where no sooner it was missing   15
But with one Pyrrhus of Delos it learned to go afishing;
And thence did it enter into the sophist of Greece.
From Pythagore, she went into a beautiful piece,
Hight Aspasia, the meretrix; and the next toss of her

---

71 **cocker up** indulge, pamper   75 **observe** notice, pander to
88 **bearing them in hand** deceiving them
4 **false pace** uneven or doggerel rhythm   19 **hight** called, named;
meretrix whore, harlot

20 Was, again, of a whore she became a philosopher,
Crates the Cynic (as itself doth relate it).
Since, kings, knights, and beggars, knaves, lords, and fools
    gat it,
Besides ox, and ass, camel, mule, goat, and brock,
In all which it hath spoke, as in the cobbler's cock.
25 But I come not here to discourse of that matter,
Or his one, two, or three, or his great oath, "By quater!"
His musics, his trigon, his golden thigh,
Or his telling how elements shift; but I
Would ask, how of late thou hast suffered translation,
30 And shifted thy coat in these days of reformation?
ANDROGYNO: Like one of the reformèd, a fool, as you can see,
    Counting all old doctrine heresy.
NANO: But not on thine own forbid meats hast thou ventured?
ANDROGYNO: On fish, when first a Carthusian I entered.
35 NANO: Why, then thy dogmatical silence hath left thee?
ANDROGYNO: Of that an obstreperous lawyer bereft me.
NANO: O wonderful change! When Sir Lawyer forsook thee,
    For Pythagore's sake, what body then took thee?
ANDROGYNO: A good, dull moil.
NANO: And how! By that means
40 Thou wert brought to allow of the eating of beans?
ANDROGYNO: Yes.
NANO: But from the moil into whom didst thou pass?
ANDROGYNO: Into a very strange beast, by some writers called
    an ass;
By others, a precise, pure, illuminate brother,
Of those devour flesh, and sometimes one another,
45 And will drop you forth a libel or a sanctified lie
Betwixt every spoonful of a Nativity pie.
NANO: Now quit thee, for heaven, of that profane nation,
    And gently report they next transmigration.
ANDROGYNO: To the same that I am.
NANO: A creature of delight?
50 And, what is more than a fool, an hermaphrodite?
Now, pray thee, sweet soul, in all thy variation,
Which body wouldst thou choose to take up thy station?
ANDROGYNO: Troth, this I am in, even here would I tarry.
NANO: 'Cause here the delight of each sex thou canst vary?
55 ANDROGYNO: Alas, those pleasures be stale and forsaken;
No, 'tis your fool wherewith I am so taken,
The only one creature that I can call blessèd;
For all other forms I have proved most distressèd.
NANO: Spoke true, as thou wert in Pythagoras still.
60 This learned opinion we celebrate will,
Fellow eunuch, as behooves us, with all our wit and art,
To dignify that whereof ourselves are so great and special
    a part.
VOLPONE: Now, very, very pretty!—Mosca, this
    Was thy invention?
MOSCA: If it please my patron,
65 Not else.

---

23 **brock** badger   24 **cobbler's cock** Lucian's dialogue *The Cock* is the source of this passage   26 **by quater** by the tetractys, a geometrical figure representing the number 10 as the triangle of 4   27 **trigon** triangular lyre   29–30 **how . . . reformation** what other transmigrations of the soul have you experienced since the Protestant Reformation?   35 **silence** referring to Pythagoras' injunction to his followers of a five-year period of silence   39 **moil** mule   43 **precise** puritanical

VOLPONE: It doth, good Mosca.
MOSCA: Then it was, sir.

            (Song)
Fools, they are the only nation
Worth men's envy or admiration;
Free from care or sorrow-taking,
Selves and others merry making:
All they speak or do is sterling. 70
Your fool, he is your great man's dearling,
And your ladies' sport and pleasure;
Tongue and bable are his treasure.
E'en his face begetteth laughter,
And he speaks truth free from slaughter; 75
He's the grace of every feast
And, sometimes, the chiefest guest;
Hath his trencher and his stool,
When wit waits upon the fool.
    O, who would not be 80
    He, he, he?

(One knocks without.)

VOLPONE: Who's that? Away! Look, Mosca.
MOSCA: Fool, begone!

(Exeunt NANO, CASTRONE, *and* ANDROGYNO.)
    'Tis Signor Voltore, the advocate;
    I know him by his knock.
VOLPONE: Fetch me my gown,
My furs, and night-caps; say my couch is changing, 85
And let him entertain himself awhile
Without i'th'gallery.

(Exit MOSCA.)
           Now, now, my clients
Begin their visitation! Vulture, kite,
Raven, and gorcrow, all my birds of prey,
That think me turning carcass, now they come. 90
I am not for 'hem yet.

(Enter MOSCA.)
           How now? the news?
MOSCA: A piece of plate, sir.
VOLPONE: Of what bigness?
MOSCA: Huge,
Massy, and antique, with your name inscribed,
And arms engraven.
VOLPONE: Good! and not a fox
Stretched on the earth, with fine delusive sleights 95
Mocking a gaping crow? Ha, Mosca?
MOSCA: Sharp, sir.
VOLPONE: Give me my furs. Why dost thou laugh so, man?
MOSCA: I cannot choose, sir, when I apprehend
What thoughts he has, without, now, as he walks:
That this might be the last gift he should give; 100
That this would fetch you; if you died today,
And gave him all, what he should be tomorrow;

---

71 **dearling** darling   73 **bable** babble; bauble; the male organ
89 **gorcrow** carrion crow

What large return would come of all his ventures;
How he should worshipped be and reverenced;
105 Ride with his furs and foot-cloths; waited on
By herds of fools and clients; have clear way
Made for his moil, as lettered as himself;
Be called the great and learned advocate:
And then concludes, there's naught impossible.
110 VOLPONE: Yes, to be learned, Mosca.
MOSCA: O, no: rich
Implies it. Hood an ass with reverend purple,
So you can hide his two ambitious ears,
And he shall pass for a cathedral doctor.
VOLPONE: My caps, my caps, good Mosca. Fetch him in.
115 MOSCA: Stay, sir; your ointment for your eyes.
VOLPONE: That's true;
Dispatch, dispatch! I long to have possession
Of my new present.
MOSCA: That, and thousands more,
I hope to see you lord of.
VOLPONE: Thanks, kind Mosca.
MOSCA: And that, when I am lost in blended dust,
120 And hundred such as I am, in succession—
VOLPONE: Nay, that were too much, Mosca.
MOSCA: You shall live
Still to delude these harpies.
VOLPONE: Loving Mosca,
'Tis well! My pillow now, and let him enter.

(*Exit* MOSCA.)

Now, my feigned cough, my phthisic, and my gout,
125 My apoplexy, palsy, and catarrhs,
Help, with your forcèd functions, this my posture,
Wherein, this three year, I have milked their hopes.
He comes, I hear him—uh! uh! uh! uh! O—

SCENE III

MOSCA, VOLTORE, VOLPONE.

MOSCA: You still are what you were, sir. Only you,
Of all the rest, are he commands his love;
And you do wisely to preserve it thus,
With early visitation and kind notes
5 Of your good meaning to him, which, I know,
Cannot but come most grateful.—Patron, sir!
Here's Signor Voltore is come—
VOLPONE: What say you?
MOSCA: Sir, Signor Voltore is come this morning
To visit you.
VOLPONE: I thank him.
MOSCA: And hath brought
10 A piece of antique plate, bought of Saint Mark,
With which he here presents you.
VOLPONE: He is welcome.
Pray him to come more often.
MOSCA: Yes.
VOLTORE: What says he?

---

112 **ambitious** prominent; flapping   113 **cathedral doctor** university professor
10 **Saint Mark** at a goldsmith's shop in Saint Mark's Place

MOSCA: He thanks you and desires you see him often.
VOLTORE: Mosca!
MOSCA: My patron?
VOLPONE: Bring him near; where is he?
I long to feel his hand.   15
MOSCA: The plate is here, sir.
VOLTORE: How fare you, sir?
VOLPONE: I thank you, Signor Voltore.
Where is the plate? Mine eyes are bad.
VOLTORE: (*Putting the plate into his hands.*) I'm sorry
To see you still thus weak.
MOSCA: (*Aside.*)   That he is not weaker.
VOLPONE: You are too munificent.
VOLTORE: No, sir; would to heaven
I could as well give health to you as that plate!   20
VOLPONE: You give, sir, what you can. I thank you. Your love
Hath taste in this and shall not be unanswered.
I pray you see me often.
VOLTORE: Yes, I shall, sir.
VOLTORE: Be not far from me.
MOSCA: (*To* VOLTORE.)   Do you observe that, sir?
VOLPONE: Harken unto me still; it will concern you.   25
MOSCA: You are a happy man, sir; know your good.
VOLPONE: I cannot now last long—
MOSCA: (*Aside to* VOLTORE.)   You are his heir, sir.
VOLTORE: (*Aside.*) Am I?
VOLPONE: I feel me going—uh! uh! uh! uh!
I am sailing to my port—uh! uh! uh! uh!
And I am glad I am so near my haven.   30
MOSCA: Alas, kind gentleman; well, we must all go—
VOLTORE: But, Mosca—
MOSCA: Age will conquer.
VOLTORE: Pray thee, hear me.
Am I inscribed his heir for certain?
MOSCA: Are you?
I do beseech you, sir, you will vouchsafe
To write me i' your family. All my hopes   35
Depend upon your worship. I am lost
Except the rising sun do shine on me.
VOLTORE: It shall both shine and warm thee, Mosca.
MOSCA: Sir,
I am a man that have not done your love
All the worst offices: Here I wear your keys,   40
See all your coffers and your caskets locked,
Keep the poor inventory of your jewels,
Your plate, and monies; am your steward, sir,
Husband your goods here.
VOLTORE: But am I sole heir?
MOSCA: Without a partner, sir, confirmed this morning;   45
The wax is warm yet, and the ink scarce dry
Upon the parchment.
VOLTORE: Happy, happy me!
By what good chance, sweet Mosca?
MOSCA: Your desert, sir;
I know no second cause.
VOLTORE: Thy modesty
Is loath to know it; well, we shall requite it.   50
MOSCA: He ever liked your course, sir; that first took him.
I oft have heard him say how he admired
Men of your large profession, that could speak
To every cause, and things mere contraries,

55 Till they were hoarse again, yet all be law;
That, with most quick agility, could turn,
And re-turn; make knots, and undo them;
Give forkèd counsel; take provoking gold
On either hand, and put it up. These men,
60 He knew, would thrive with their humility.
And, for his part, he thought he should be blessed
To have his heir of such a suffering spirit,
So wise, so grave, of so perplexed a tongue,
And loud withal, that would not wag, nor scarce
65 Lie still, without a fee; when every word
Your worship but lets fall is chequin!

(Another knocks.)

Who's that? One knocks. I would not have you seen, sir.
And yet—pretend you came and went in haste;
I'll fashion an excuse. And, gentle sir,
70 When you do come to swim in golden lard,
Up to the arms in honey, that your chin
Is borne up stiff with fatness of the flood,
Think on your vassal; but remember me:
I ha' not been your worst of clients.

VOLTORE: Mosca—
75 MOSCA: When will you have your inventory brought, sir?
Or see a copy of the will?—Anon!—
I'll bring 'em to you, sir. Away, be gone;
Put business i' your face.

(Exit VOLTORE.*)*

VOLPONE: Excellent, Mosca!
Come hither, let me kiss thee.
MOSCA: Keep you still, sir.
80 Here is Corbaccio.
VOLPONE: Set the plate away;
The vulture's gone, and the old raven's come.

SCENE IV

MOSCA, CORBACCIO, VOLPONE.

MOSCA: Betake you to your silence and your sleep.—
Stand there, and multiply.

(He sets the plate among the treasures.)

                          —Now shall we see
A wretch who is, indeed, more impotent
Than this can feign to be, yet hopes to hop
5 Over his grave.

(Enter CORBACCIO.*)*

                  Signor Corbaccio!
You're very welcome, sir.
CORBACCIO: How does your patron?
MOSCA: Troth, as he did, sir; no amends.
CORBACCIO: What? Mends he?
MOSCA: No, sir; he is rather worse.
CORBACCIO: That's well. Where is he?
MOSCA: Upon his couch, sir, newly fall'n asleep.
10 CORBACCIO: Does he sleep well?

MOSCA: No wink, sir, all this night,
Nor yesterday, but slumbers.
CORBACCIO: Good! He should take
Some counsel of physicians. I have brought him
An opiate here from mine own doctor—
MOSCA: He will not hear of drugs.
CORBACCIO: Why? I myself
Stood by while't was made; saw all th'ingredients,   15
And know it cannot but most gently work.
My life for his, 'tis but to make him sleep.
VOLPONE: *(Aside.)* Ay, his last sleep if he would take it.
MOSCA: Sir,
He has no faith in physic.
CORBACCIO: Say you? Say you?
MOSCA: He has no faith in physic: he does think   20
Most of your doctors are the greater danger,
And worse disease, t'escape. I often have
Heard him protest that your physician
Should never be his heir.
CORBACCIO: Not I his heir?
MOSCA: Not your physician, sir.   25
CORBACCIO: O, no, no, no,
I do not mean it.
MOSCA: No, sir, nor their fees
He cannot brook; he says they flay a man
Before they kill him.
CORBACCIO: Right, I do conceive you.
MOSCA: And then they do it by experiment,
For which the law not only doth absolve 'hem   30
But gives them great reward; and he is loath
To hire his death so.
CORBACCIO: It is true, they kill
With as much license as a judge.
MOSCA: Nay, more;
For he but kills, sir, where the law condemns,
And these can kill him too.   35
CORBACCIO: Ay, or me,
Or any man. How does his apoplex?
Is that strong on him still?
MOSCA: Most violent.
His speech is broken, and his eyes are set,
His face drawn longer than't was wont—
CORBACCIO: How? how?
Stronger that he was wont?   40
MOSCA: No, sir; his face
Drawn longer than't was wont.
CORBACCIO: O, good!
MOSCA: His mouth
Is ever gaping, and his eyelids hang.
CORBACCIO: Good.
MOSCA: A freezing numbness stiffens all his joints
And makes the color of his flesh like lead.
CORBACCIO: 'Tis good.
MOSCA: His pulse beats slow and dull.   45
CORBACCIO: Good symptoms still.
MOSCA: And from his brain—
CORBACCIO: Ha! How? Not from his brain?
MOSCA: Yes, sir; and from his brain—

---

66 **chequin** Venetian gold coin

19 **physic** medicine   28 **conceive** understand

CORBACCIO: I conceive you; good.
MOSCA: Flows a cold sweat, with a continual rheum,
   Forth the resolvèd corners of his eyes.
50 CORBACCIO: Is't possible? Yet I am better, ha!
   How does he with the swimming of his head?
MOSCA: O, sir, 'tis past the scotomy; he now
   Hath lost his feeling and hath left to snort;
   You can hardly perceive him that he breathes.
55 CORBACCIO: Excellent, excellent! Sure I shall outlast him!
   This makes me young again, a score of years.
MOSCA: I was a-coming for you, sir.
CORBACCIO: Has he made his will?
   What has he given me?
MOSCA: No, sir.
CORBACCIO: Nothing? Ha?
MOSCA: He has not made his will, sir.
CORBACCIO: O, O, O!
60 What then did Voltore, the lawyer, here?
MOSCA: He smelt a carcass, sir, when he but heard
   My master was about his testament;
   As I did urge him to it for your good—
CORBACCIO: He came unto him, did he? I thought so.
65 MOSCA: Yes, and presented him this piece of plate.
CORBACCIO: To be his heir?
MOSCA: I do not know, sir.
CORBACCIO: True, I know it too.
MOSCA: (Aside.) By your own scale, sir.
CORBACCIO: Well,
   I shall prevent him yet. See, Mosca, look;
   Here I have brought a bag of bright chequins
70 Will quite weigh down his plate.
MOSCA: Yea, marry, sir!
   This is true physic, this your sacred medicine;
   No talk of opiates to this great elixir!
CORBACCIO: 'Tis *aurum palpabile*, if not *potabile*.
MOSCA: It shall be ministered to him in his bowl?
75 CORBACCIO: Ay, do, do, do.
MOSCA: Most blessed cordial!
   This will recover him.
CORBACCIO: Yes, do, do, do.
MOSCA: I think it were not best, sir.
CORBACCIO: What?
MOSCA: To recover him.
CORBACCIO: O, no, no, no; by no means!
MOSCA: Why, sir, this
   Will work some strange effect if he but feel it.
80 CORBACCIO: 'Tis true; therefore forbear. I'll take my venture;
   Give me't again.
MOSCA: At no hand, pardon me;
   You shall not do yourself that wrong, sir. I
   Will so advise you, you shall have it all.
CORBACCIO: How?
MOSCA: All, sir; 'tis your right, your own; no man
85 Can claim a part: 'tis yours without a rival,
   Decreed by destiny.

CORBACCIO: How? How, good Mosca?
MOSCA: I'll tell you, sir. This fit he shall recover—
CORBACCIO: I do conceive you.
MOSCA: And, on first advantage
   Of his gained sense, will I re-importune him
   Unto the making of his testament   90
   And show him this.

(He points to CORBACCIO's *gift.)*

CORBACCIO: Good, Good.
MOSCA: 'Tis better yet
   If you will hear, sir.
CORBACCIO: Yes, with all my heart.
MOSCA: Now would I counsel you, make home with speed;
   There, frame a will whereto you shall inscribe
   My master your sole heir.   95
CORBACCIO: And disinherit
   My son?
MOSCA: O, sir, the better: for that color
   Shall make it much more taking.
CORBACCIO: O, but color?
MOSCA: This will, sir, you shall send it unto me.
   Now, when I come to enforce (as I will do)
   Your cares, your watchings, and your many prayers,   100
   Your more than many gifts, your this day's present,
   And, last, produce your will, where, without thought
   Or least regard unto your proper issue,
   A son so brave and highly meriting,
   The stream of your diverted love hath thrown you   105
   Upon my master, and made him your heir:
   He cannot be so stupid, or stone dead,
   But out of conscience and mere gratitude—
CORBACCIO: He must pronounce me his?
MOSCA: 'Tis true.
CORBACCIO: This plot
   Did I think on before.   110
MOSCA: I do believe it.
CORBACCIO: Do you not believe it?
MOSCA: Yes, sir.
CORBACCIO: Mine own project.
MOSCA: Which, when he hath done, sir—
CORBACCIO: Published me his heir?
MOSCA: And you so certain to survive him—
CORBACCIO: Ay.
MOSCA: Being so lusty a man—
CORBACCIO: 'Tis true.
MOSCA: Yes, sir—
CORBACCIO: I thought on that too. See, how he should be   115
   The very organ to express my thoughts!
MOSCA: You have not only done yourself a good—
CORBACCIO: But multiplied it on my son?
MOSCA: 'Tis right, sir.
CORBACCIO: Still my invention.
MOSCA: 'Las, sir, heaven knows
   It hath been all my study, all my care   120
   (I e'en grow gray withal), how to work things—
CORBACCIO: I do conceive, sweet Mosca.

---

49 **resolvèd** dissolved   52 **scotomy** dizziness   68 **prevent** anticipate;
go before   73 *aurum palpabile* palpable gold (can be felt); *potabile*
drinkable (also refers to the gold), supposedly an efficacious medicinal
remedy; the philosopher's stone

---

96 **color** pretense, pretext   103 **proper** own

MOSCA: You are he
  For whom I labor here.
CORBACCIO: Ay, do, do, do.
  I'll straight about it.
MOSCA: *(Aside.)*   Rook go with you, raven!
125 CORBACCIO: I know thee honest.
MOSCA: *(Aside.)*   You do lie, sir.
CORBACCIO: And—
MOSCA: *(Aside.)* Your knowledge is no better than your
      ears, sir.
CORBACCIO: I do not doubt to be a father to thee.
MOSCA: *(Aside.)* Nor I to gull my brother of his blessing.
CORBACCIO: I may ha' my youth restored to me; why not?
130 MOSCA: *(Aside.)* Your worship is a precious ass—
CORBACCIO: What sayst thou?
MOSCA: I do desire your worship to make haste, sir.
CORBACCIO: 'Tis done, 'tis done; I go.

(Exit.)

VOLPONE: *(Leaping up from his bed.)* O, I shall burst!
  Let out my sides, let out my sides—
MOSCA: Contain
  Your flux of laughter, sir; you know this hope
135 Is such a bait it covers any hook.
VOLPONE: O, but thy working, and thy placing it!
  I cannot hold; good rascal, let me kiss thee.
  I never knew thee in so rare a humor.
MOSCA: Alas, sir, I but do as I am taught;
140 Follow your grave instructions; give 'hem words;
  Pour oil into their ears, and send them hence.
VOLPONE: 'Tis true, 'tis true. What a rare punishment
  Is avarice to itself!
MOSCA: Ay, with our help, sir.
VOLPONE: So many cares, so many maladies,
145 So many fears attending on old age;
  Yea, death so often called on as no wish
  Can be more frequent with 'hem; their limbs faint,
  Their senses dull, their seeing, hearing, going,
  All dead before them; yea, their very teeth,
150 Their instruments of eating, failing them.
  Yet this is reckoned life! Nay, here was one
  Is now gone home, that wishes to live longer!
  Feels not his gout, nor palsy; feigns himself
  Younger by scores of years, flatters his age
155 With confident belying it; hopes he may
  With charms, like Aeson, have his youth restored;
  And with these thoughts so battens as if fate
  Would be as easily cheated on as he,
  And all turns air!

(Another knocks.)

                Who's that, there, now? A third?
160 MOSCA: Close to your couch again; I hear his voice.
  It is Corvino, our spruce merchant.
VOLPONE: *(Lying down again.)* Dead!
MOSCA: Another bout, sir, with your eyes.—Who's there?

---

124 **rook . . . you** may you be rooked or cheated (pun on "rook" ["gull"], "crow") 148 **going** faculty of walking 156 **Aeson** rejuvenated by the magic of Medea, his son Jason's wife 162 **bout** application of eye ointment used as a disguise

SCENE V

MOSCA, CORVINO, VOLPONE.

MOSCA: Signor Corvino! Come most wished for! O,
  How happy were you, if you knew it, now!
CORVINO: Why? What? Wherein?
MOSCA: The tardy hour is come, sir.
CORVINO: He is not dead?
MOSCA: Not dead, sir, but as good;
  He knows no man.   5
CORVINO: How shall I do then?
MOSCA: Why, sir?
CORVINO: I have brought him here a pearl.
MOSCA: Perhaps he has
  So much remembrance left as to know you, sir;
  He still calls on you; nothing but your name
  Is in his mouth. Is your pearl orient, sir?
CORVINO: Venice was never owner of the like.   10
VOLPONE: Signor Corvino!
MOSCA: Hark!
VOLPONE: Signor Corvino!
MOSCA: He calls you; step and give it him. He's here, sir,
  And he has brought you a rich pearl.
CORVINO: How do you, sir?
  Tell him it doubles the twelfth caract.
MOSCA: Sir,
  He cannot understand; his hearing's gone,   15
  And yet it comforts him to see you—
CORVINO: Say
  I have a diamond for him, too.
MOSCA: Best show't, sir;
  Put it into his hand; 'tis only there
  He apprehends—he has his feeling yet.
  See how he grasps it!   20
CORVINO: 'Las, good gentleman.
  How pitiful the sight is!
MOSCA: Tut, forget, sir.
  The weeping of an heir should still be laughter
  Under a visor.
CORVINO: Why, am I his heir?
MOSCA: Sir, I am sworn, I may not show the will
  Till he be dead. But here has been Corbaccio,   25
  Here has been Voltore, here were others too,
  I cannot number 'hem, they were so many,
  All gaping here for legacies; but I,
  Taking the vantage of his naming you
  ("Signor Corvino, Signor Corvino!"), took   30
  Paper, and pen, and ink, and there I asked him
  Whom he would have his heir? "Corvino." Who
  Should be executor? "Corvino." And
  To any question he was silent to,
  I still interpreted the nods he made,   35
  Through weakness, for consent; and sent home th'others,
  Nothing bequeathed them but to cry and curse.
CORVINO: O, my dear Mosca!

(They embrace.)

                Does he not perceive us?
MOSCA: No more than a blind harper. He knows no man,

---

8 **still** continually 9 **orient** lustrous

40   No face of friend, nor name of any servant,
     Who't was that fed him last, or gave him drink;
     Not those he hath begotten, or brought up,
     Can he remember.
     CORVINO: Has he children?
     MOSCA: Bastards,
45   Some dozen, or more, that he begot on beggars,
     Gypsies, and Jews, and blackmoors when he was drunk,
     Knew you not that, sir? 'Tis the common fable.
     The dwarf, the fool, the eunuch are all his;
     He's the true father of his family,
     In all save me, but he has given 'hem nothing.
50   CORVINO: That's well, that's well! Art sure he does not hear us?
     MOSCA: Sure, sir? Why, look you, credit your own sense.

     (He shouts in VOLPONE's *ear.)*

     The pox approach and add to your diseases
     If it would send you hence the sooner, sir;
     For your incontinence, it hath deserved it
55   Throughly and throughly, and the plague to boot! —
     You may come near, sir. — Would you would once close
     Those filthy eyes of yours that flow with slime
     Like two frog-pits, and those same hanging cheeks,
     Covered with hide instead of skin — Nay, help, sir! —
60   That look like frozen dish-clouts set on end!
     CORVINO: Or like an old smoked wall, on which the rain
     Ran down in streaks!
     MOSCA: Excellent, sir, speak out;
     You may be louder yet: a culverin
     Dischargèd in his ear would hardly bore it.
65   CORVINO: His nose is like a common sewer, still running.
     MOSCA: 'Tis good! And what his mouth?
     CORVINO: A very draught.
     MOSCA: O, stop it up —
     CORVINO: By no means.
     MOSCA: Pray you, let me.
     Faith, I could stifle him rarely with a pillow,
     As well as any woman that should keep him.
70   CORVINO: Do as you will, but I'll be gone.
     MOSCA: Be so;
     It is your presence makes him last so long.
     CORVINO: I pray you, use no violence.
     MOSCA: No, sir? Why?
     Why should you be thus scrupulous, pray you, sir?
     CORVINO: Nay, at your discretion.
     MOSCA: Well, good sir, be gone.
75   CORVINO: I will not trouble him now to take my pearl?
     MOSCA: Puh! nor your diamond. What a needless care
     Is this afflicts you! Is not all here yours?
     Am not I here whom you have made? Your creature?
     That owe my being to you?
     CORVINO: Grateful Mosca!
80   Thou are my friend, my fellow, my companion,
     My partner, and shalt share in all my fortunes.
     MOSCA: Excepting one.
     CORVINO: What's that?
     MOSCA: Your gallant wife, sir.

     (Exit CORVINO.*)*

     Now is he gone; we had no other means
     To shoot him hence but this.
     VOLPONE: My divine Mosca!
     Thou hast today outgone thyself.   85

     (Another knocks.)

                                —Who's there?
     I will be troubled with no more. Prepare
     Me music, dances, banquets, all delights;
     The Turk is not more sensual in his pleasures
     Than will Volpone.

     (Exit MOSCA.*)*

                         Let me see — a pearl!
     A diamond! plate! chequins! Good morning's purchase.   90
     Why, this is better than rob churches, yet,
     Or fat, by eating once a month a man. —

     (Enter MOSCA.*)*

     Who is't?
     MOSCA: The beauteous Lady Would-be, sir,
     Wife to the English knight, Sir Politic Would-be —
     This is the style, sir, is directed me —   95
     Hath sent to know how you have slept tonight
     And if you would be visited.
     VOLPONE: Not now.
     Some three hours hence —
     MOSCA: I told the squire so much.
     VOLPONE: When I am high with mirth and wine, then, then.
     'Fore heaven, I wonder at the desperate valor   100
     Of the bold English, that they dare let loose
     Their wives to all encounters!
     MOSCA: Sir, this knight
     Had not his name for nothing: he is politic,
     And knows, howe'er his wife affect strange airs,
     She hath not yet the face to be dishonest.   105
     But had she Signor Corvino's wife's face —
     VOLPONE: Has she so rare a face?
     MOSCA: O, sir, the wonder,
     The blazing star of Italy, a wench
     O' the first year! A beauty ripe as harvest!
     Whose skin is whiter than a swan, all over!   110
     Than silver, snow, or lilies! A soft lip,
     Would tempt you to eternity of kissing!
     And flesh that melteth in the touch to blood!
     Bright as your gold! And lovely as your gold!
     VOLPONE: Why had not I known this before?   115
     MOSCA: Alas, sir,
     Myself but yesterday discovered it.
     VOLPONE: How might I see her?
     MOSCA: O, not possible;
     She's kept as warily as is your gold;
     Never does come abroad, never takes air
     But at a windore. All her looks are sweet   120
     As the first grapes or cherries and are watched
     As near as they are.
     VOLPONE: I must see her —

---

55 **throughly** thoroughly   63 **culverin** small cannon   98 **squire** messenger   105 **dishonest** unchaste   120 **windore** window

MOSCA: Sir,
    There is a guard, of ten spies thick, upon her;
    All his whole household; each of which is set
125   Upon his fellow, and have all their charge,
    When he goes out, when he comes in, examined.
VOLPONE: I will go see her, though but at her windore.
MOSCA: In some disguise then.
VOLPONE: That is true. I must
    Maintain mine own shape still the same: we'll think.

(Exeunt.)

— ACT TWO —

SCENE I

[SIR] POLITIC WOULD-BE, PEREGRINE.

SIR POLITIC: Sir, to a wise man, all the world's his soil.
    It is not Italy, nor France, nor Europe
    That must bound me if my fates call me forth.
    Yet, I protest, it is no salt desire
5   Of seeing countries, shifting a religion,
    Nor any disaffection to the state
    Where I was bred (and unto which I owe
    My dearest plots) hath brought me out; much less
    That idle, antique, stale, gray-headed project
10   Of knowing men's minds and manners, with Ulysses,
    But a peculiar humor of my wife's,
    Laid for this height of Venice, to observe,
    To quote, to learn the language, and so forth.
    I hope you travel, sir, with license?
PEREGRINE: Yes.
15 SIR POLITIC: I dare the safelier converse. How long, sir,
    Since you left England?
PEREGRINE: Seven weeks.
SIR POLITIC: So lately!
    You ha' not been with my lord ambassador?
PEREGRINE: Not yet, sir.
SIR POLITIC: Pray you, what news, sir, vents our climate?
    I heard, last night, a most strange thing reported
20   By some of my lord's followers, and I long
    To hear how 'twill be seconded.
PEREGRINE: What was't, sir?
SIR POLITIC: Marry, sir, of a raven, that should build
    In a ship royal of the king's.
PEREGRINE: *(Aside.)*   This fellow,
    Does he gull me, trow? or is gulled?—Your name, sir?
25 SIR POLITIC: My name is Politic Would-be.
PEREGRINE: *(Aside.)*   O, that speaks him.—
    A knight, sir?
SIR POLITIC: A poor knight, sir.
PEREGRINE: Your lady
    Lies here, in Venice, for intelligence
    Of tires and fashions and behavior
    Among the courtesans? The fine Lady Would-be?
30 SIR POLITIC: Yes, sir, the spider and the bee ofttimes
    Suck from one flower.

PEREGRINE: Good Sir Politic!
    I cry you mercy; I have heard much of you.
    'Tis true, sir, of your raven.
SIR POLITIC: On your knowledge?
PEREGRINE: Yes, and your lion's whelping in the Tower.
SIR POLITIC: Another whelp!   35
PEREGRINE: Another, sir.
SIR POLITIC: Now, heaven!
    What prodigies be these? The fires at Berwick!
    And the new star! These things concurring, strange!
    And full of omen! Saw you those meteors?
PEREGRINE: I did, sir.
SIR POLITIC: Fearful! Pray you, sir, confirm me,
    Were there three porpoises seen above the bridge,   40
    As they give out?
PEREGRINE: Six, and a sturgeon, sir.
SIR POLITIC: I am astonished!
PEREGRINE: Nay, sir, be not so;
    I'll tell you a greater prodigy than these—
SIR POLITIC: What should these things portend?
PEREGRINE: The very day
    (Let me be sure) that I put forth from London,   45
    There was a whale discovered in the river,
    As high as Woolwich, that had waited there—
    Few know how many months—for the subversion
    Of the Stode fleet.
SIR POLITIC: Is't possible? Believe it,
    'Twas either sent from Spain or the Archduke's!   50
    Spinola's whale, upon my life, my credit!
    Will they not leave these projects? Worthy sir,
    Some other news.
PEREGRINE: Faith, Stone the fool is dead;
    And they do lack a tavern fool extremely.
SIR POLITIC: Is Mas' Stone dead?   55
PEREGRINE: He's dead, sir; why, I hope
    You thought him not immortal?—*(Aside.)* Oh, this knight,
    Were he well known, would be a precious thing
    To fit our English stage: He that should write
    But such a fellow should be thought to feign
    Extremely, if not maliciously.—   60
SIR POLITIC: Stone dead!
PEREGRINE: Dead. Lord, how deeply, sir, you apprehend it!
    He was no kinsman to you?
SIR POLITIC: That I know of.
    Well, that same fellow was an unknown fool.
PEREGRINE: And yet you knew him, it seems?
SIR POLITIC: I did so. Sir,
    I knew him one of the most dangerous heads   65
    Living within the state, and so I held him.
PEREGRINE: Indeed, sir?
SIR POLITIC: While he lived, in action.
    He has received weekly intelligence,
    Upon my knowledge, out of the Low Countries,
    For all parts of the world, in cabbages;   70
    And those dispensed, again, t'ambassadors,
    In oranges, musk-melons, apricots,

---

4 **salt** inordinate   12 **height** latitude   13 **quote** note down; observe
14 **license** passport   24 **trow** do you suppose?   28 **tires** attires, dress

---

34 **Tower** of London   36 **fires at Berwick** town on the Scottish border
where ghostly armies were reported fighting in 1604   37 **new star** discovered by Kepler in 1604   51 **Spinola** Spanish general in the Netherlands   68 **intelligence** information from spies; communication

Lemons, pome-citrons, and suchlike; sometimes
In Colchester oysters, and your Selsey cockles.
75 PEREGRINE: You make me wonder.
SIR POLITIC: Sir, upon my knowledge.
Nay, I have observed him at your public ordinary
Take his advertisement from a traveler
(A concealed statesman) in a trencher of meat;
And, instantly, before the meal was done,
80 Convey an answer in a toothpick.
PEREGRINE: Strange!
How could this be, sir?
SIR POLITIC: Why, the meat was cut
So like his character, and so laid as he
Must easily read the cipher.
PEREGRINE: I have heard
He could not read, sir.
SIR POLITIC: So 'twas given out,
85 In polity, by those that did employ him;
But he could read and had your languages,
And, to't, as sound a noddle—
PEREGRINE: I have heard, sir,
That your baboons were spies and that they were
A kind of subtle nation near to China.
90 SIR POLITIC: Ay, ay, your Mamuluchi. Faith, they had
Their hand in a French plot, or two; but they
Were extremely given to women as
They made discovery of all; yet I
Had my advices here, on Wednesday last,
95 From one of their own coat, they were returned,
Made their relations (as the fashion is)
And now stand fair for fresh employment.
PEREGRINE: *(Aside.)*   Heart!
This Sir Pol will be ignorant of nothing.—
It seems, sir, you know all.
SIR POLITIC: Not all, sir. But
100 I have some general notions; I do love
To note and to observe: though I live out,
Free from the active torrent, yet I'd mark
The currents and the passages of things
For mine own private use and know the ebbs
105 And flows of state.
PEREGRINE: Believe it, sir, I hold
Myself in no small tie unto my fortunes
For casting me thus luckily upon you,
Whose knowledge, if your bounty equal it,
May do me great assistance in instruction
110 For my behavior and my bearing, which
Is yet so rude and raw—
SIR POLITIC: Why? Came you forth
Empty of rules for travel?
PEREGRINE: Faith, I had
Some common ones, from out that vulgar grammar,
Which he that cried Italian taught me.
115 SIR POLITIC: Why, this it is that spoils all our brave bloods,
Trusting our hopeful gentry unto pedants,

Fellows of outside and mere bark. You seem
To be a gentleman, of ingenuous race—
I not profess it, but my fate hath been
To be where I have been consulted with,   120
In this high kind, touching some great men's sons,
Persons of blood and honor—
PEREGRINE: Who be these, sir?

SCENE II

MOSCA, [SIR] POLITIC, PEREGRINE, NANO, GREGE.

(MOSCA and NANO start to erect a platform.)

MOSCA: Under that windore, there't must be. The same.
SIR POLITIC: Fellows to mount a bank! Did your instructor
In the dear tongues never discourse to you
Of the Italian mountebanks?
PEREGRINE: Yes, sir.
SIR POLITIC: Why,
Here shall you see one.   5
PEREGRINE: They are quacksalvers,
Fellows that live by venting oils and drugs.
SIR POLITIC: Was that the character he gave you of them?
PEREGRINE: As I remember.
SIR POLITIC: Pity his ignorance.
They are the only knowing men of Europe!
Great general scholars, excellent physicians,   10
Most admired statesmen, professed favorites
And cabinet counselors to the greatest princes!
The only languaged men of all the world!
PEREGRINE: And I have heard they are the most lewd impostors,
Made all of terms and shreds; no less beliers   15
Of great men's favors than their own vile med'cines;
Which they will utter upon monstrous oaths,
Selling that drug for twopence, ere they part,
Which they have valued at twelve crowns before.
SIR POLITIC: Sir, calumnies are answered best with silence. 20
Yourself shall judge.—Who is it mounts, my friends?
MOSCA: Scoto of Mantua, sir.
SIR POLITIC: Is't he? Nay, then,
I'll proudly promise, sir, you shall behold
Another man than has been phant'sied to you.
I wonder, yet, that he should mount his bank   25
Here, in this nook, that has been wont t'appear
In face of the Piazza!—Here he comes.

(Enter VOLPONE, disguised as a mountebank doctor.)

VOLPONE: Mount, zany.
GREGE: Follow, follow, follow, follow, follow!
SIR POLITIC: See how the people follow him! He's a man   30
May write ten thousand crowns in bank here. Note,

(VOLPONE mounts the platform.)

Mark but his gesture. I do use to observe
The stage he keeps in getting up!
PEREGRINE: 'Tis worth it, sir.

VOLPONE: Most noble gentlemen and my worthy patrons! It
may seem strange that I, your Scoto Mantuano, who was
ever wont to fix my bank in face of the public Piazza, near
the shelter of the Portico to the Procuratia, should now, after
eight months' absence from this illustrious city of Venice,
humbly retire myself into an obscure nook of the Piazza.

SIR POLITIC: Did not I now object the same?

PEREGRINE: Peace, sir.

VOLPONE: Let me tell you: I am not, as your Lombard proverb
saith, cold on my feet or content to part with my commodities at a cheaper rate than I accustomed: look not for it. Nor
that the calumnious reports of that impudent detractor, and
shame to our profession (Alessandro Buttone, I mean), who
gave out, in public, I was condemned *a sforzato* to the galleys for poisoning the Cardinal Bembo's——cook, hath at all
attached, much less dejected me. No, no, worthy gentlemen; to tell you true, I cannot endure to see the rabble of
these ground *ciarlitani* that spread their cloaks on the pavement as if they meant to do feats of activity, and then come
in lamely, with their moldy tales out of Boccacio, like stale
Tabarine, the fabulist: some of them discoursing their travels, and of their tedious captivity in the Turks' galleys, when,
indeed, were the truth known, they were the Christians' galleys, where very temperately they eat bread and drunk water
as a wholesome penance, enjoined them by their confessors,
for base pilferies.

SIR POLITIC: Note but his bearing and contempt of these.

VOLPONE: These turdy-facy-nasty-paty-lousy-fartical rogues,
with one poor groatsworth of unprepared antimony, finely
wrapt up in several *scartoccios*, are able, very well, to kill
their twenty a week, and play; yet these meager, starved spirits, who have half stopped the organs of their minds with
earthy oppilations, want not their favorers among your shriveled salad-eating artisans, who are overjoyed that they may
have their half-pe'rth of physic; though it purge 'hem into
another world, 't makes no matter.

SIR POLITIC: Excellent! Ha' you heard better language, sir?

VOLPONE: Well, let 'hem go. And, gentlemen, honorable gentlemen, know, that for this time, our bank, being thus removed from the clamors of the *canaglia*, shall be the scene
of pleasure and delight; for I have nothing to sell, little or
nothing to sell.

SIR POLITIC: I told you, sir, his end.

PEREGRINE: You did so, sir.

VOLPONE: I protest, I and my six servants are not able to make
of this precious liquor so fast as it is fetched away from my
lodging by gentlemen of your city, strangers of the Terrafirma, worshipful of merchants, ay, and senators too, who,
ever since my arrival, have detained me to their uses by their
splendidous liberalities. And worthily; for what avails your
rich man to have his magazines stuffed with *moscadelli*, or of
the purest grape, when his physicians prescribe him, on pain
of death, to drink nothing but water cocted with aniseeds? O
health! health! the blessing of the rich! the riches of the
poor! Who can buy thee at too dear a rate since there is no

enjoying this world without thee? Be not then so sparing of
your purses, honorable gentlemen, as to abridge the natural
course of life—

PEREGRINE: You see his end.

SIR POLITIC: Ay, is't not good?

VOLPONE: For, when a humid flux or catarrh, by the mutability of air, falls from your head into an arm or shoulder, or any
other part, take you a ducat, or your chequin of gold, and
apply to the place affected: see what good effect it can work.
No, no, 'tis this blessed *unguento*, this rare extraction, that
hath only power to disperse all malignant humors that proceed either of hot, cold, moist, or windy causes—

PEREGRINE: I would he had put in dry too.

SIR POLITIC: Pray you observe.

VOLPONE: To fortify the most indigest and crude stomach, ay,
were it of one that, through extreme weakness, vomited
blood, applying only a warm napkin to the place, after the
unction and fricace; for the *vertigine* in the head, putting but
a drop into your nostrils, likewise behind the ears; a most
sovereign and approved remedy: the *mal-caduco*, cramps,
convulsions, paralyses, epilepsies, *tremorcordia*, retired
nerves, ill vapors of the spleen, stoppings of the liver, the
stone, the strangury, *hernia ventosa, iliaca passio*; stops a
dysenteria immediately; easeth the torsion of the small guts;
and cures *melancholia hypocondriaca*, being taken and applied according to my printed receipt. (*Pointing to his bill
and his glass.*) For this is the physician, this the medicine;
this counsels, this cures; this gives the direction, this works
the effect; and, in sum, both together may be termed an abstract of the theoric and practic in the Æsculapian art. 'Twill
cost you eight crowns. And, Zan Fritada, pray thee sing a
verse, extempore, in honor of it.

SIR POLITIC: How do you like him, sir?

PEREGRINE: Most strangely, I!

SIR POLITIC: Is not his language rare?

PEREGRINE: But alchemy
I never heard the like, or Broughton's books.

(*NANO sings.*)

(Song)

Had old Hippocrates or Galen,
That to their books put med'cines all in,
But known this secret, they had never
(Of which they will be guilty ever)
Been murderers of so much paper,
Or wasted many a hurtless taper:
No Indian drug had e'er been famèd,
Tobacco, sassafras not namèd;
Ne yet of guacum one small stick, sir,
Nor Raymund Lully's great elixir.
Ne had been known the Danish Gonswart,
Or Paracelsus, with his long sword.

---

46 *a sforzato* to hard labor   48 **attached** in a legal suit   50 *ciarlitani* petty impostors or charlatans   62 *scartoccios* waste folds of paper   65 **oppilations** obstructions   67 **half-pe'rth** half-pennyworth   72 *canaglia* rabble, mob   78 **terrafirma** mainland   82 *moscadelli* muscatel wines   84 **cocted** boiled

95 *unguento* ointment   102 **fricace** salve that is rubbed on; *vertigine* vertigo, dizziness   104 *mal-caduco* epilepsy   105 *tremorcordia* palpitation of the heart   107 *iliaca passio* colic   119 **Broughton's books** Old Testament commentaries by the Puritan minister, Hugh Broughton   128 **ne** nor   131 **Paracelsus ... sword** in the hilt of which this German physician-alchemist was supposed to have kept his "essences"

PEREGRINE: All this, yet, will not do; eight crowns is high.
VOLPONE: No more.—Gentlemen, if I had but time to discourse to you the miraculous effects of this my oil, surnamed
135 *Oglio del Scoto*, with the countless catalogue of those I have cured of th'aforesaid and many more diseases; the patents and privileges of all the princes and commonwealths of Christendom; or but the depositions of those that appeared on my part before the signory of the *Sanita* and most learned
140 College of Physicians, where I was authorized, upon notice taken of the admirable virtues of my medicaments, and mine own excellency in matter of rare and unknown secrets, not only to disperse them publicly in this famous city but in all the territories that happily joy under the government of the
145 most pious and magnificent states of Italy. But may same other gallant fellow say, "O, there be divers that make profession to have as good and as experimented receipts as yours." Indeed, very many have assayed, like apes, in imitation of that, which is really and essentially in me, to make of this oil;
150 bestowed great cost in furnaces, stills, alembics, continual fires, and preparation of the ingredients (as indeed there goes to it six hundred several simples, besides some quantity of human fat, for the conglutination, which we buy of the anatomists), but, when these practitioners come to the last
155 decoction, blow, blow, puff, puff, and all flies *in fumo*. Ha, ha, ha! Poor wretches! I rather pity their folly and indiscretion than their loss of time and money; for those may be recovered by industry, but to be a fool born is a disease incurable. For myself, I always from my youth have endeav-
160 ored to get the rarest secrets, and book them, either in exchange or for money; I spared nor cost nor labor where anything was worthy to be learned. And, gentlemen, honorable gentlemen, I will undertake, by virtue of chemical art, out of the honorable hat that covers your head, to extract the
165 four elements; that is to say, the fire, air, water, and earth, and return you your felt without burn or stain. For, whilst others have been at the balloo, I have been at my book, and am now past the craggy paths of study and come to the flowery plains of honor and reputation.
170 SIR POLITIC: I do assure you, sir, that is his aim.
VOLPONE: But to your price—
PEREGRINE: And that withal, Sir Pol.
VOLPONE: You all know, honorable gentlemen, I never valued this *ampulla*, or vial, at less than eight crown; but for this time I am content to be deprived of it for six: six crowns is
175 the price, and less in courtesy I know you cannot offer me; take it or leave it, howsoever, both it and I am at your service. I ask you not as the value of the thing, for then I should demand of you a thousand crowns; so the Cardinals Montalto, Fernese, the great Duke of Tuscany, my gossip, with divers
180 other princes have given me; but I despise money. Only to show my affection to you, honorable gentlemen, and your illustrious state here, I have neglected the messages of these princes, mine own offices, framed my journey hither, only to present you with the fruits of my travels.—Tune your voices
185 once more to the touch of your instruments, and give the honorable assembly some delightful recreation.
PEREGRINE: What monstrous and most painful circumstance

---

139 *Sanita* medical board of Venice   155 *in fumo* in fumes   167 **balloo** Venetian ball game   179 **gossip** intimate friend

Is here, to get some three or four *gazets!*
Some threepence i'th' whole, for that 'twill come to.
(NANO *sings.*)

(Song)
You that would last long, list to my song;   190
Make no more coil, but buy of this oil.
Would you be ever fair? and young?
Stout of teeth? and strong of tongue?
Tart of palate? quick of ear?
Sharp of sight? of nostril clear?   195
Moist of hand? and light of foot?
Or, I will come nearer to't,
Would you live free from all diseases?
Do the act your mistress pleases,
Yet fright all achès from your bones?   200
Here's a med'cine for the nones.

VOLPONE: Well, I am in a humor, at this time, to make a present of the small quantity my coffer contains: to the rich in courtesy, and to the poor for God's sake. Wherefore, now mark: I asked you six crowns; and six crowns, at other times, 205 you have paid me; you shall not give me six crowns, nor five, not four, nor three, nor two, nor one; nor half a ducat; no, nor a *moccenigo*. Sixpence it will cost you, or six hundred pound—expect no lower price, for, by the banner of my front, I will not bate a bagatine; that I will have, only, a 210 pledge of your loves, to carry something from amongst you to show I am not contemned by you. Therefore, now, toss your handkerchiefs cheerfully, cheerfully; and be advertised that the first heroic spirit that deigns to grace me with a handkerchief, I will give it a little remembrance of something beside, 215 shall please it better than if I had presented it with a double pistolet.
PEREGRINE: Will you be that heroic spark, Sir Pol?
(CELIA *at a windo[w] throws down her handkerchief.*)
O, see! the windore has prevented you.
VOLPONE: Lady, I kiss your bounty; and for this timely grace 220 you have done your poor Scoto of Mantua, I will return you, over and above my oil, a secret of that high and inestimable nature shall make you forever enamored on that minute wherein your eye first descended on so mean, yet not altogether to be despised, an object. Here is a poulder concealed 225 in this paper, of which, if I should speak to the worth, nine thousand volume were but as one page, that page as a line, that line as a word: so short is this pilgrimage of man (which some call life) to the expressing of it. Would I reflect on the price? Why, the whole world is but as an empire, that empire 230 as a province, that province as a bank, that bank as a private purse to the purchase of it. I will only tell you: it is the poulder that made Venus a goddess (given her by Apollo), that kept her perpetually young, cleared her wrinkles, firmed her gums, filled her skin, colored her hair; from her derived to 235

---

188 **gazets** Venetian coins of little worth   191 **coil** disturbance   201 **nones** occasion   208 *moccenigo* small coin   210 **bagatine** small Italian coin   217 **pistolet** Spanish gold coin   219 **prevented** anticipated   225 **poulder** powder

Helen, and at the sack of Troy unfortunately lost; till now, in this our age, it was as happily recovered, by a studious anti-quary, out of some ruins of Asia, who sent a moiety of it to the court of France (but much sophisticated) wherewith the 240 ladies there now color their hair. The rest, at this present, re-mains with me; extracted to a quintessence, so that, wher-ever it but touches, in youth it perpetually preserves, in age restores the complexion; seats your teeth, did they dance like virginal jacks, firm as a wall; makes them white as ivory, that 245 were black as—

SCENE III

CORVINO, [SIR] POLITIC, PEREGRINE.

CORVINO: *(To* CELIA.*)* Spite o' the devil, and my shame!
    —*(To* VOLPONE.*)* Come down here;
    Come down! No house but mine to make your scene?
    Signor Flaminio, will you down, sir? Down?
    What, is my wife your Franciscina, sir?
5 No windores on the whole Piazza here
    To make your properties but mine? but mine?

(He beats away the mountebank, etc.)

    Heart! ere tomorrow I shall be new christened
    And called the Pantalone di Besogniosi
    About the town.
PEREGRINE: What should this mean, Sir Pol?
10 SIR POLITIC: Some trick of state, believe it. I will home.
PEREGRINE: It may be some design on you.
SIR POLITIC: I know not.
    I'll stand upon my guard.
PEREGRINE: It is your best, sir.
SIR POLITIC: This three weeks, all my advices, all my letters,
    They have been intercepted.
PEREGRINE: Indeed, sir?
15 Best have a care.
SIR POLITIC: Nay, so I will.
PEREGRINE: *(Aside.)*   This knight,
    I may not lose him for my mirth, till night.

(Exeunt.)

SCENE IV

VOLPONE, MOSCA.

VOLPONE: O, I am wounded!
MOSCA: Where, sir?
VOLPONE: Not without;
    Those blows were nothing: I could bear them ever.
    But angry Cupid, bolting from her eyes,
    Hath shot himself into me like a flame,
5 Where, now, he flings about his burning heat,
    As in a furnace an ambitious fire
    Whose vent is stopped. The fight is all within me.
    I cannot live except thou help me, Mosca.

    My liver melts; and I, without the hope
    Of some soft air from her refreshing breath,
    Am but a heap of cinders.   10
MOSCA: 'Las, good sir!
    Would you had never seen her!
VOLPONE: Nay, would thou
    Hadst never told me of her!
MOSCA: Sir, 'tis true;
    I do confess I was unfortunate,
    And you unhappy; but I'm bound in conscience,   15
    No less than duty, to effect my best
    To your release of torment, and I will, sir.
VOLPONE: Dear Mosca, shall I hope?
MOSCA: Sir, more than dear,
    I will not bid you despair of aught
    Within a human compass.   20
VOLPONE: O, there spoke
    My better angel. Mosca, take my keys,
    Gold, plate, and jewels—all's at thy devotion;
    Employ them how thou wilt; nay, coin me too,
    So thou in this but crown my longings. Mosca?
MOSCA: Use but your patience.   25
VOLPONE: So I have.
MOSCA: I doubt not
    To bring success to your desires.
VOLPONE: Nay, then,
    I not repent me of my late disguise.
MOSCA: If you can horn him, sir, you need not.
VOLPONE: True;
    Besides, I never meant him for my heir.
    Is not the color o' my beard and eyebrows   30
    To make me known?
MOSCA: No jot.
VOLPONE: I did it well.
MOSCA: So well, would I could follow you in mine
    With half the happiness; and, yet, I would
    Escape your epilogue.
VOLPONE: But were they gulled
    With a belief that I was Scoto?   35
MOSCA: Sir,
    Scoto himself could hardly have distinguished!
    I have not time to flatter you now; we'll part,
    And, as I prosper, so applaud my art.

(Exeunt.)

SCENE V

CORVINO, CELIA, SERVITORE *[later]*.

CORVINO: Death of mine honor, with the city's fool?
    A juggling, tooth-drawing, prating mountebank?
    And at a public windore? where, whilst he,
    With his strained action, and his dole of faces,
    To his drug-lecture draws your itching ears,   5
    A crew of old, unmarried, noted lechers
    Stood leering up like satyrs: and you smile

---

239 **sophisticated** adulterated

8 **Pantalone di Besogniosi** literally, "fool of beggars"—a stock charac-ter (the old, cuckolded merchant), along with Flaminio (head of a noted company of actors) and Franciscina (the light-of-love serving maid), of the *Commedia dell' arte*

6 **ambitious** swelling

---

9 **liver** regarded as the seat of love   22 **devotion** service, disposal
28 **horn** give (him) the horns of a cuckold   34 **epilogue** beating
4 **dole of faces** distribution of grimaces

Most graciously, and fan your favors forth,
To give your hot spectators satisfaction!
10   What, was your mountebank their call? Their whistle?
Or were y'enamored on his copper rings?
His saffron jewel, with the toad-stone in't?
Or his embroidèred suit, with the cope-stitch,
Made of a hearse cloth? Or his old tilt-feather?
15   Or his starched beard? Well, you shall have him, yes.
He shall come home and minister unto you
The fricace for the mother. Or, let me see,
I think you had rather mount? Would you not mount?
Why, if you'll mount, you may; yes, truly, you may,
20   And so you may be seen, down to th' foot.
Get you a cittern, Lady Vanity,
And be a dealer with the virtuous man;
Make one: I'll but protest myself a cuckold,
And save your dowry. I am a Dutchman, I!
25   For, if you thought me an Italian,
You would be damned ere you did this, you whore!
Thou'ldst tremble to imagine that the murder
Of father, mother, brother, all thy race,
Should follow as the subject of my justice.
30   CELIA: Good sir, have patience!
CORVINO: What couldst thou propose
Less to thyself than in this heat of wrath,
And stung with my dishonor, I should strike
This steel unto thee, with as many stabs
As thou wert gazed upon with goatish eyes?
35   CELIA: Alas, sir, be appeased! I could not think
My being at the windore should more now
Move your impatience than at other times.
CORVINO: No? Not to seek and entertain a parley
With a known knave? Before a multitude?
40   You were an actor with your handkerchief,
Which he, most sweetly, kissed in the receipt
And might, no doubt, return it with a letter
And point the place where you might meet: your sister's,
Your mother's, or your aunt's might serve these excuses?
45   CELIA: Why, dear sir, when do I make these excuses?
Or ever stir abroad but to the church?
And that so seldom—
CORVINO: Well, it shall be less;
And thy restraint before was liberty
To what I now decree; and, therefore, mark me.
50   First, I will have this bawdy light dammed up;
And, till't be done, some two or three yards off
I'll chalk a line, o'er which, if thou but chance
To set thy desp'rate foot, more hell, more horror,
More wild, remorseless rage shall seize on thee
55   Than on a conjuror that had heedless left
His circle's safety ere his devil was laid.
Then, here's a lock which I will hang upon thee;
And, now I think on't, I will keep thee backwards;
Thy lodging shall be backwards, thy walks backwards,
60   Thy prospect—all be backwards, and no pleasure
That thou shalt know but backwards. Nay, since you force
My honest nature, know it is your own

Being too open makes me use you thus.
Since you will not contain your subtle nostrils
In a sweet room, but they must snuff the air   65
Of rank and sweaty passengers—

(Knock within.)

                                        One knocks.
Away, and be not seen, pain of thy life;
Not look toward the windore; if thou dost—
Nay, stay, hear this—let me not prosper, whore,
But I will make thee an anatomy,   70
Dissect thee mine own self, and read a lecture
Upon thee to the city, and in public.
Away!

(Exit CELIA.*)*

(Enter SERVITORE.*)*

        Who's there?
SERVITORE: 'Tis Signor Mosca, sir.

SCENE VI

CORVINO, MOSCA.

CORVINO: Let him come in; his master's dead: there's yet
Some good to help the bad.—My Mosca, welcome!
I guess your news.
MOSCA: I fear you cannot, sir.
CORVINO: Is't not his death?
MOSCA: Rather the contrary.
CORVINO: Not his recovery?   5
MOSCA: Yes, sir.
CORVINO: I am cursed,
I am bewitched; my crosses meet to vex me.
How? how? how? how?
MOSCA: Why, sir, with Scoto's oil!
Corbaccio and Voltore brought of it
Whilst I was busy in an inner room—
CORVINO: Death! That damned mountebank! But for the law   10
Now, I could kill the rascal; 't cannot be
His oil should have that virtue. Ha' not I
Known him a common rogue, come fiddling in
To th' *osteria*, with a tumbling whore,
And, when he has done all his forced tricks, been glad   15
Of a poor spoonful of dead wine, with flies in't?
It cannot be. All his ingredients
Are a sheep's gall, a roasted bitch's marrow,
Some few sod earwigs, pounded caterpillars,
A little capon's grease, and fasting spittle—   20
I know 'hem to a dram.
MOSCA: I know not, sir;
But some on't, there, they poured into his ears,
Some in his nostrils, and recovered him,
Applying but the fricace.
CORVINO: Pox o' that fricace!
MOSCA: And since, to seem the more officious   25
And flatt'ring of his health, there they have had
(At extreme fees) the College of Physicians

---

17 **mother** hysteria   21 **cittern** guitar-like instrument; zither; **Lady Vanity** character in the morality plays   30 **propose** expect   56 **laid** exorcised   58 **backwards** in the back of the house

70 **anatomy** skeleton; cadaver
14 *osteria* inn, hostelry   19 **sod** sodden, boiled

Consulting on him how they might restore him;
Where one would have a cataplasm of spices,
30 Another a flayed ape clapped to his breast,
A third would ha' it a dog, a fourth an oil
With wild cats' skins. At last, they all resolved
That, to preserve him, was no other means
But some young woman must be straight sought out,
35 Lusty, and full of juice, to sleep by him;
And to this service, most unhappily
And most unwillingly, am I now employed,
Which here I thought to pre-acquaint you with,
For your advice, since it concerns you most,
40 Because I would not do that thing might cross
Your ends, on whom I have my whole dependence, sir.
Yet, if I do it not, they may delate
My slackness to my patron, work me out
Of his opinion; and there all your hopes,
45 Ventures, or whatsoever, are all frustrate.
I do but tell you, sir. Besides, they are all
Now striving who shall first present him. Therefore,
I could entreat you briefly, conclude somewhat;
Prevent 'hem if you can.
CORVINO: Death to my hopes!
50 This is my villanous fortune! Best to hire
Some common courtesan?
MOSCA: Ay, I thought on that, sir.
But they are all so subtle, full of art,
And age again doting and flexible,
So as—I cannot tell—we may perchance
55 Light on a quean may cheat us all.
CORVINO: 'Tis true.
MOSCA: No, no: it must be one that has no tricks, sir,
Some simple thing, a creature made unto it;
Some wench you may command. Ha' you no kinswoman?
God's so—Think, think, think, think, think, think, think, sir.
60 One o' the doctors offered there his daughter.
CORVINO: How!
MOSCA: Yes, Signor Lupo, the physician.
CORVINO: His daughter!
MOSCA: And a virgin, sir. Why? Alas,
He knows the state of's body, what it is;
That naught can warm his blood, sir, but a fever,
65 Nor any incantation raise his spirit;
A long forgetfulness hath seized that part.
Besides, sir, who shall know it? Some one or two—
CORVINO: I pray thee give me leave.

(He walks aside.)

                          If any man
But I had had this luck—The thing in'tself,
70 I know, is nothing—Wherefore should not I
As well command my blood and my affections
As this dull doctor? In the point of honor,
The cases are all one of wife and daughter.
MOSCA: *(Aside.)* I hear him coming.
CORVINO: She shall do't: 'tis done.
75 'Slight, if this doctor, who is not engaged,
Unless't be for his counsel, which is nothing,
Offer his daughter, what should I that am

So deeply in? I will prevent him. Wretch!
Covetous wretch!—Mosca, I have determined.
MOSCA: How, sir?   80
CORVINO: We'll make all sure. The party you wot of
Shall be mine own wife, Mosca.
MOSCA: Sir, the thing,
But that I would not seem to counsel you,
I should have motioned to you at the first;
And, make your count, you have cut all their throats.
Why, 'tis directly taking a possession!   85
And, in his next fit, we may let him go.
'Tis but to pull the pillow from his head,
And he is thr[o]ttled; 't had been done before
But for your scrupulous doubts.
CORVINO: Ay, a plague on't,
My conscience fools my wit! Well, I'll be brief,   90
And so be thou, lest they should be before us.
Go home, prepare him, tell him with what zeal
And willingness I do it; swear it was
On the first hearing (as thou mayst do, truly)
Mine own free motion.   95
MOSCA: Sir, I warrant you,
I'll so possess him with it that the rest
Of his starved clients shall be banished all,
And only you received. But come not, sir,
Until I send, for I have something else
To ripen for your good—you must not know't.   100
CORVINO: But do not you forget to send now.
MOSCA: Fear not.

(Exit.)

SCENE VII

CORVINO, CELIA.

CORVINO: Where are you, wife? My Celia? Wife?

(Enter CELIA, *weeping.)*

                          What, blubbering?
Come, dry those tears. I think thou thought'st me in
     earnest?
Ha? By this light, I talked so but to try thee.
Methinks the lightness of the occasion
Should ha' confirmed thee. Come, I am not jealous.   5
CELIA: No?
CORVINO: Faith, I am not, I, nor never was:
It is a poor, unprofitable humor.
Do not I know if women have a will
They'll do 'gainst all the watches o' the world?
And that the fiercest spies are tamed with gold?   10
Tut, I am confident in thee, thou shalt see't;
And see I'll give thee cause, too, to believe it.
Come, kiss me. Go, and make thee ready straight,
In all thy best attire, thy choicest jewels;
Put 'hem all on, and, with 'hem, thy best looks.   15
We are invited to a solemn feast
At old Volpone's, where it shall appear
How far I am free from jealousy or fear.

(Exeunt.)

---

29 **cataplasm** poultice   42 **delate** denounce; accuse, blame
55 **quean** harlot, prostitute   75 **'slight** contraction of "by God's light!"

80 **wot** know   83 **motioned** proposed

— ACT THREE —

SCENE I

MOSCA.

MOSCA: I fear I shall begin to grow in love
With my dear self and my most prosp'rous parts,
They do so spring and burgeon; I can feel
A whimsy i' my blood. I know not how,
5   Success hath made me wanton. I could skip
Out of my skin now, like a subtle snake,
I am so limber. O! your parasite
Is a most precious thing, dropped from above,
Not bred 'mongst clods and clo[d]polls here on earth.
10 I muse the mystery was not made a science,
It is so liberally professed! Almost
All the wise world is little else in nature
But parasites or sub-parasites. And yet
I mean not those that have your bare town-art,
15 To know who's fit to feed 'hem; have no house,
No family, no care, and therefore mold
Tales for men's ears, to bait that sense; or get
Kitchen-invention and some stale receipts
To please the belly and the groin; nor those,
20 With their court-dog-tricks, that can fawn and fleer,
Make their revènue out of legs and faces,
Echo my lord, and lick away a moth:
But your fine, elegant rascal, that can rise
And stoop, almost together, like an arrow;
25 Shoot through the air as nimbly as a star;
Turn short as doth a swallow; and be here,
And there, and here, and yonder, all at once;
Present to any humor, all occasion;
And change a visor swifter than a thought!
30 This is the creature had the art born with him;
Toils not to learn it, both doth practice it
Out of most excellent nature: and such sparks
Are the true parasites, others but their zanies.

SCENE II

MOSCA, BONARIO.

MOSCA: (Aside.) Who's this? Bonario? Old Corbaccio's son?
The person I was bound to seek.—Fair sir,
You are happ'ly met.
BONARIO: That cannot be by thee.
MOSCA: Why, sir?
BONARIO: Nay, pray thee know thy way and leave me:
5   I would be loath to interchange discourse
With such a mate as thou art.
MOSCA: Courteous sir,
Scorn not my poverty.
BONARIO: Not I, by heaven;
But thou shalt give me leave to hate thy baseness.
MOSCA: Baseness?
BONARIO: Ay, answer me, is not thy sloth
10 Sufficient argument? Thy flattery?
Thy means of feeding?

MOSCA: Heaven be good to me!
These imputations are too common, sir,
And eas'ly stuck on virtue when she's poor.
You are unequal to me, and howe'er
Your sentence may be righteous, yet you are not,   15
That, ere you know me, thus proceed in censure.
Saint Mark bear witness 'gainst you, 'tis inhuman!

(He weeps.)

BONARIO: (Aside.) What? Does he weep? The sign is soft and
good.
I do repent me that I was so harsh.
MOSCA: 'Tis true that, swayed by strong necessity,   20
I am enforced to eat my careful bread
With too much obsequy; 'tis true, beside,
That I am fain to spin mine one poor raiment
Out of my mere observance, being not born
To a free fortune; but that I have done   25
Base offices, in rending friends asunder,
Dividing families, betraying counsels,
Whispering false lies, or mining men with praises,
Trained their credulity with perjuries,
Corrupted chastity, or am in love   30
With mine own tender ease, but would not rather
Prove the most rugged and laborious course
That might redeem my present estimation,
Let me here perish, in all hope of goodness.
BONARIO: (Aside.) This cannot be a personated passion!—   35
I was to blame, so to mistake thy nature;
Pray thee forgive me, and speak out thy business.
MOSCA: Sir, it concerns you; and, though I may seem,
At first, to make a main offense in manners,
And in my gratitude unto my master,   40
Yet, for the pure love which I bear all right,
And hatred of the wrong, I must reveal it.
This very hour your father is in purpose
To disinherit you—
BONARIO: How!
MOSCA: And thrust you forth
As a mere stranger to his blood; 'tis true, sir.   45
The work in no way engageth me, but as
I claim an interest in the general state
Of goodness and true virtue, which I hear
T'abound in you, and for which mere respect,
Without a second aim, sir, I have done it.   50
BONARIO: This tale hath lost thee much of the late trust
Thou hadst with me; it is impossible:
I know not how to lend it any thought
My father should be so unnatural.
MOSCA: It is a confidence that well becomes   55
Your piety; and formed, no doubt, it is
From your own simple innocence, which makes
Your wrong more monstrous and abhorred. But, sir,
I now will tell you more. This very minute
It is, or will be doing; and, if you   60
Shall be but pleased to go with me, I'll bring you

---

10 **mystery** profession   18 **kitchen-invention** elaborate or ingenious
recipes (*receipts*)
6 **mate** low fellow

---

14 **unequal** unjust, unfair   21 **careful** acquired with care or difficulty
24 **observance** service   29 **trained** tricked, lured   39 **main** great
45 **mere** complete   49 **for . . . respect** for this reason only   56 **piety**
filial love

(I dare not say where you shall see, but) where
Your ear shall be a witness of the deed,
Hear yourself written bastard and professed
65   The common issue of the earth.
BONARIO: I'm 'mazed!
MOSCA: Sir, if I do it not, draw your just sword
  And score your vengeance on my front and face;
  Mark me your villain. You have too much wrong,
  And I do suffer for you, sir. My heart
70   Weeps blood in anguish—
BONARIO: Lead; I follow thee.

(Exeunt.)

SCENE III

VOLPONE, NANO, ANDROGYNO, CASTRONE.

VOLPONE: Mosca stays long, methinks. Bring forth your sports
  And help to make the wretched time more sweet.
NANO: Dwarf, fool, and eunuch, well met here we be.
  A question it were now, whether of us three,
5   Being all the known delicates of a rich man,
  In pleasing him, claim the precedency can?
CASTRONE: I claim for myself.
ANDROGYNO: And so doth the fool.
NANO: 'Tis foolish indeed; let me set you both to school.
  First, for your dwarf, he's little and witty,
10   And everything, as it is little, is pretty;
  Else, why do men say to a creature of my shape,
  So soon as they see him, "It's a pretty little ape"?
  And why a pretty ape but for pleasing imitation
  Of greater men's action in a ridiculous fashion.
15   Beside, this feat body of mine doth not crave
  Half the meat, drink, and cloth one of your bulks will have.
  Admit your fool's face be the mother of laughter,
  Yet, for his brain, it must always come after;
  And, though that do feed him, it's a pitiful case
20   His body is beholding to such a bad face.

(One knocks.)

VOLPONE: Who's there? My couch! Away! Look, Nano, see!

(Exeunt ANDROGYNO and CASTRONE.)

Give me my caps first—go, inquire.

(Exit NANO.)

                                    Now Cupid
  Send it be Mosca, and with fair return.
NANO: *(Within.)* It is the beauteous Madam—
VOLPONE: Would-be—is it?
25   NANO: The same.
VOLPONE: Now, torment on me! Squire her in,
  For she will enter or dwell here forever.
  Nay, quickly, that my fit were past.

(He lies down on his couch.)

                                    I fear
  A second hell too, that my loathing this
  Will quite expel my appetite to the other.
30   Would she were taking, now, her tedious leave.
  Lord, how it threats me what I am to suffer!

SCENE IV

LADY [WOULD-BE], VOLPONE, NANO, WOMEN 2 *[later].*

LADY WOULD-BE: *(To NANO.)* I thank you, good sir. Pray you
    signify
  Unto your patron I am here.—This band
  Shows not my neck enough.—I trouble you, sir;
  Let me request you bid one of my women
  Come hither to me. In good faith, I am dressed   5
  Most favorably today! It is no matter;
  'Tis well enough.

(Enter 1 WAITING-WOMAN.)

                    Look, see these petulant things!
  How they have done this!
VOLPONE: *(Aside.)*   I do feel the fever
  Ent'ring in at mine ears. O, for a charm
  To fright it hence!   10
LADY WOULD-BE: Come nearer. Is this curl
  In his right place? Or this? Why is this higher
  Than all the rest? You ha' not washed your eyes yet?
  Or do they not stand even i' your head?
  Where's your fellow? Call her.

(Exit 1 WOMAN.)

NANO: *(Aside.)*   Now, Saint Mark
  Deliver us! Anon she'll beat her women   15
  Because her nose is red.

(Enter 1 and 2 WOMEN.)

LADY WOULD-BE: I pray you, view
  This tire, forsooth; are all things apt, or no?
[1] WOMAN: One hair a little, here, sticks out, forsooth.
LADY WOULD-BE: Dost so, forsooth? And where was your dear
    sight
  When it did so, forsooth? What now! Bird-eyed?   20
  And you, too? Pray you both approach and mend it.
  Now, by that light, I muse you're not ashamed!
  I, that have preached these things, so oft, unto you,
  Read you the principles, argued all the grounds,
  Disputed every fitness, every grace,   25
  Called you to counsel of so frequent dressings—
NANO: *(Aside.)* More carefully than of your fame or honor.
LADY WOULD-BE: Made you acquainted what an ample dowry
  The knowledge of these things would be unto you,
  Able, alone, to get you noble husbands   30
  At your return; and you, thus, to neglect it!
  Besides, you seeing what a curious nation
  Th'Italians are, what will they say of me?
  "The English lady cannot dress herself."
  Here's a fine imputation to our country!   35
  Well, go your ways, and stay i' the next room.
  This fucus was too coarse, too; it's no matter.—
  Good sir, you'll give 'hem entertainment?

(Exeunt NANO and WAITING-WOMEN.)

VOLPONE: *(Aside.)* The storm comes toward me.
LADY WOULD-BE: How does my Volp?
VOLPONE: Troubled with noise, I cannot sleep; I dreamt   40
  That a strange fury entered now my house,

---

4 **whether** which   15 **feat** neatly formed, delicate

17 **tire** headdress   32 **curious** fastidious   37 **fucus** cosmetic; rouge

And, with the dreadful tempest of her breath,
Did cleave my roof asunder.
LADY WOULD-BE: Believe me, and I
Had the most fearful dream, could I remember't—
45 VOLPONE: *(Aside.)* Out on my fate! I ha' giv'n her the occasion
How to torment me: she will tell me hers.
LADY WOULD-BE: Methought the golden mediocrity,
Polite and delicate—
VOLPONE: O, if you do love me,
No more; I sweat, and suffer, at the mention
50 Of any dream; feel how I tremble yet.
LADY WOULD-BE: Alas, good soul! The passion of the heart!
Seed-pearl were good now, boiled with syrup of apples,
Tincture of gold, and coral, citron-pills,
Your elecampane root, myrobalanes—
55 VOLPONE: Ay me, I have ta'en a grasshopper by the wing!
LADY WOULD-BE: Burnt silk and amber. You have muscadel
Good i' the house—
VOLPONE: You will not drink and part?
LADY WOULD-BE: No, fear not that. I doubt we shall not get
Some English saffron (half a dram would serve),
60 Your sixteen cloves, a little musk, dried mints,
Burgloss, and barley-meal—
VOLPONE: *(Aside.)*   She's in again!
Before I feigned diseases; now I have one.
LADY WOULD-BE: And these applied with a right scarlet cloth.
VOLPONE: *(Aside.)* Another flood of words! A very torrent!
65 LADY WOULD-BE: Shall I, sir, make you a poultice?
VOLPONE: No, no, no;
I'm very well; you need prescribe no more.
LADY WOULD-BE: I have, a little, studied physic; but now
I'm all for music, save i' the forenoons
An hour or two for painting. I would have
70 A lady, indeed, t'have all—letters and arts,
Be able to discourse, to write, to paint,
But principal, as Plato holds, your music
(And so does wise Pythagoras, I take it)
Is your true rapture when there is concent
75 In face, in voice, and clothes, and is, indeed,
Our sex's chiefest ornament.
VOLPONE: The poet
As old in time as Plato, and as knowing,
Says that your highest female grace is silence.
LADY WOULD-BE: Which o' your poets? Petrarch? or Tasso? or
Dante?
80 Guarini? Ariosto? Aretine?
Cieco di Hadria? I have read them all.
VOLPONE: *(Aside.)* Is everything a cause to my destruction?
LADY WOULD-BE: I think I ha' two or three of 'hem about me.
VOLPONE: *(Aside.)* The sun, the sea, will sooner both stand
still
85 Than her eternal tongue! Nothing can 'scape it.
LADY WOULD-BE: Here's *Pastor Fido*—
VOLPONE: *(Aside.)*   Profess obstinate silence;
That's now my safest.
LADY WOULD-BE: All our English writers,
I mean such as are happy in th'Italian,

Will deign to steal out of this author, mainly,
Almost as much as from Montagniè;   90
He has so modern and facile a vein,
Fitting the time, and catching the court-ear.
Your Petrarch is more passionate, yet he,
In days of sonneting, trusted 'hem with much.
Dante is hard, and few can understand him.   95
But, for a desperate wit, there's Aretine!
Only his pictures are a little obscene—
You mark me not?
VOLPONE: Alas, my mind's perturbed.
LADY WOULD-BE: Why, in such cases, we must cure ourselves,
Make use of our philosophy—   100
VOLPONE: O'y me!
LADY WOULD-BE: And, as we find our passions do rebel,
Encounter 'hem with reason or divert 'hem
By giving scope unto some other humor
Of lesser danger: as, in politic bodies,
There's nothing more doth overwhelm the judgment,   105
And clouds the understanding, than too much
Settling and fixing and, as 'twere, subsiding
Upon one object. For the incorporating
Of these same outward things into that part
Which we call mental leaves some certain feces   110
That stop the organs and, as Plato says,
Assassinates our knowledge.
VOLPONE: *(Aside.)*   Now, the spirit
Of patience help me!
LADY WOULD-BE: Come, in faith, I must
Visit you more now adays and make you well;
Laugh and be lusty.   115
VOLPONE: *(Aside.)* My good angel save me!
LADY WOULD-BE: There was but one sole man in all the world
With whom I e'er could sympathize; and he
Would lie you often, three, four hours together
To hear me speak, and be sometime so rapt
As he would answer me quite from the purpose,   120
Like you; and you are like him, just. I'll discourse
(And't be but only, sir, to bring you asleep)
How we did spend our time and loves together,
For some six years.
VOLPONE: O, O, O, O, O, O!
LADY WOULD-BE: For we were *coætanei*, and brought up—   125
VOLPONE: *(Aside.)* Some power, some fate, some fortune
rescue me!

SCENE V

MOSCA, LADY [WOULD-BE], VOLPONE.

MOSCA: God save you, madam!
LADY WOULD-BE: Good sir.
VOLPONE: Mosca?
Welcome!
Welcome to my redemption.
MOSCA: Why, sir?
VOLPONE: *(Aside.)*   O,
Rid me of this my torture quickly, there,
My madam with the everlasting voice;

---

51 **passion of the heart** heartburn   58 **doubt** fear   74 **concent** harmony   76 **poet** Sophocles (*Ajax*, 293)   86 *Pastor Fido* Guarini's pastoral play *The Faithful Shepherd*

---

90 **Montagniè** the French essayist Montaigne, pronounced as four syllables   118 **lie you** lie   125 *coætanei* of the same age

5   The bells in time of pestilence ne'er made
     Like noise or were in that perpetual motion!
     The cock-pit comes not near it. All my house,
     But now, steamed like a bath with her thick breath.
     A lawyer could not have been heard; nor scarce
10   Another woman, such a hail of words
     She has let fall. For hell's sake, rid her hence.
  MOSCA: *(Aside.)* Has she presented?
  VOLPONE: *(Aside.)*   O, I do not care;
     I'll take her absence upon any price,
     With any loss.
  MOSCA: Madam—
  LADY WOULD-BE: I ha' brought your patron
15   A toy, a cap here, of mine own work—
  MOSCA: 'Tis well.
     I had forgot to tell you I saw your knight
     Where you'd little think it—
  LADY WOULD-BE: Where?
  MOSCA: Marry,
     Where yet, if you make haste, you may apprehend him,
     Rowing upon the water in a gondole,
20   With the most cunning courtesan of Venice.
  LADY WOULD-BE: Is't true?
  MOSCA: Pursue 'hem, and believe your
     eyes.
     Leave me to make your gift.

(Exit LADY WOULD-BE.*)*

           —I knew 'twould take.
     For, lightly, they that use themselves most license
     Are still most jealous.
  VOLPONE: Mosca, hearty thanks
25   For thy quick fiction and delivery of me.
     Now to my hopes, what sayest thou?

(Re-enter LADY WOULD-BE.*)*

  LADY WOULD-BE: But do you hear, sir?
  VOLPONE: *(Aside.)* Again! I fear a paroxysm.
  LADY WOULD-BE: Which way
     Rowed they together?
  MOSCA: Toward the Rialto.
  LADY WOULD-BE: I pray you lend me your dwarf.
  MOSCA: I pray you
     take him.

(Exit LADY WOULD-BE.*)*

30   Your hopes, sir, are like happy blossoms, fair,
     And promise timely fruit, spell will stay
     But the maturing; keep you at your couch.
     Corbaccio will arrive straight with the will;
     When he is gone, I'll tell you more.

(Exit.)

  VOLPONE: My blood,
35   My spirits are returned; I am alive;
     And, like your wanton gamester at primero,
     Whose thought had whispered to him, not go less,
     Methinks I lie and draw—for an encounter.

(He draws the curtains across the bed.)

---

23 **lightly** generally

SCENE VI

MOSCA, BONARIO.

MOSCA: Sir, here concealed you may hear all. But pray you
     Have patience, sir.

(One knocks.)

             The same's your father knocks.
     I am compelled to leave you.
BONARIO: Do so. Yet
     Cannot my thought imagine this a truth.

(He hides himself.)

SCENE VII

MOSCA, CORVINO, CELIA, BONARIO, VOLPONE.

MOSCA: Death on me! You are come too soon; what meant
     you?
     Did not I say I would send?
CORVINO: Yes, but I feared
     You might forget it, and then they prevent us.
MOSCA: Prevent!—*(Aside.)* Did e'er man haste so for his horns?
     A courtier would not play it so for a place.—   5
     Well, now there's no helping it, stay here;
     I'll presently return.

(Exit.)

CORVINO: Where are you, Celia?
     You know not wherefore I have brought you hither?
CELIA: Not well, except you told me.
CORVINO: Now I will.
     Hark hither.   10

(They walk apart.)

(Re-enter MOSCA.*)*

MOSCA: *(To* BONARIO.*)* Sir, your father hath sent word,
     It will be half an hour ere he come;
     And, therefore, if you please to walk the while
     Into that gallery—at the upper end
     There are some books to entertain the time;
     And I'll take care no man shall come unto you, sir.   15
BONARIO: Yes, I will stay there.—*(Aside.)* I do doubt this fellow.

(Exit.)

MOSCA: There, he is far enough; he can hear nothing;
     And, for his father, I can keep him off.

(He draws open the curtains of VOLPONE's *bed.)*

CORVINO: Nay, now, there is no starting back, and therefore
     Resolve upon it; I have so decreed.   20
     It must be done. Nor would I move't afore.
     Because I would avoid all shifts and tricks
     That might deny me.
CELIA: Sir, let me beseech you,
     Affect not these strange trials; if you doubt
     My chastity, why, lock me up forever;   25
     Make me the heir of darkness. Let me live
     Where I may please your fears, if not your trust.

---

7 **presently** immediately

CORVINO: Believe it, I have no such humor, I.
  All that I speak I mean; yet I am not mad:
30 Not horn-mad, see you? Go to, show yourself
  Obedient and a wife.
CELIA: O heaven!
CORVINO: I say it,
  Do so.
CELIA: Was this the train?
CORVINO: I've told you reasons:
  What the physicians have set down; how much
  It may concern me; what my engagements are;
35 My means, and the necessity of those means
  For my recovery; wherefore, if you be
  Loyal and mine, be won, respect my venture.
CELIA: Before your honor?
CORVINO: Honor! Tut, a breath;
  There's no such thing in nature; a mere term
40 Invented to awe fools. What, is my gold
  The worse for touching? Clothes for being looked on?
  Why, this's no more. An old, decrepit wretch,
  That has no sense, no sinew; takes his meat
  With others' fingers; only knows to gape
45 When you do scald his gums; a voice, a shadow;
  And what can this man hurt you?
CELIA: Lord! What spirit
  Is this hath entered him?
CORVINO: And for your fame,
  That's such a jig; as if I would go tell it,
  Cry it, on the Piazza! Who shall know it
50 But he that cannot speak it, and this fellow,
  Whose lips are i' my pocket, save yourself—
  If you'll proclaim't, you may—I know no other
  Should come to know it.
CELIA: Are heaven and saints then nothing?
  Will they be blind or stupid?
CORVINO: How?
CELIA: Good sir,
55 Be jealous still, emulate them, and think
  What hate they burn with toward every sin.
CORVINO: I grant you: if I thought it were a sin,
  I would not urge you. Should I offer this
  To some young Frenchman, or hot Tuscan blood
60 That had read Aretine, conned all his prints,
  Knew every quirk within lust's labyrinth,
  And were professed critic in lechery,
  And I would look upon him, and applaud him,
  This were a sin; but here, 'tis contrary,
65 A pious work, mere charity, for physic
  And honest polity to assure mine own.
CELIA: O heaven! canst thou suffer such a change?
VOLPONE: (*Aside.*) Thou art mine honor, Mosca, and my
    pride,
  My joy, my tickling, my delight! Go, bring 'hem.
70 MOSCA: Please you draw near, sir.
CORVINO: Come on, what—
  You will not be rebellious? By that light—

MOSCA: Sir, Signor Corvino, here, is come to see you.
VOLPONE: O!
MOSCA: And hearing of the consultation had,
  So lately, for your health, is come to offer,
  Or rather, sir, to prostitute—   75
CORVINO: Thanks, sweet Mosca.
MOSCA: Freely, unasked, or unentreated—
CORVINO: Well.
MOSCA: As the true, fervent instance of his love,
  His own most fair and proper wife, the beauty
  Only of price in Venice—
CORVINO: 'Tis well urged.
MOSCA: To be your comfortress, and to preserve you.   80
VOLPONE: Alas, I am past already! Pray you, thank him
  For his good care and promptness; but for that,
  'Tis a vain labor e'en to fight 'gainst heaven,
  Applying fire to a stone—uh, uh, uh, uh!—
  Making a dead leaf grow again. I take   85
  His wishes gently, though; and you may tell him
  What I have done for him. Marry, my state is hopeless!
  Will him to pray for me, and t'use his fortune
  With reverence when he comes to't.
MOSCA: Do you hear, sir?
  Go to him with your wife.   90
CORVINO: Heart of my father!
  Wilt thou persist thus? Come, I pray thee, come.
  Thou seest 'tis nothing, Celia. By this hand
  I shall grow violent. Come; do't, I say.
CELIA: Sir, kill me rather. I will take down poison,
  Eat burning coals, do anything—   95
CORVINO: Be damned!
  Heart! I will drag thee hence home by the hair;
  Cry thee a strumpet through the streets; rip up
  Thy mouth unto thine ears; and slit thy nose,
  Like a raw rotchet!—Do not tempt me, come.
  Yield, I am loath—Death! I will buy some slave,   100
  Whom I will kill, and bind thee to him, alive;
  And at my windore hang you forth, devising
  Some monstrous crime, which I, in capital letters,
  Will eat into thy flesh with *aquafortis*
  And burning cor'sives on this stubborn breast.   105
  Now, by the blood thou hast incensed, I'll do't!
CELIA: Sir, what you please, you may; I am your martyr.
CORVINO: Be not thus obstinate; I ha' not deserved it.
  Think who it is entreats you. Pray thee, sweet;
  Good faith, thou shalt have jewels, gowns, attires, 110
  What thou wilt, think and ask. Do but go kiss him.
  Or touch him but. For my sake. At my suit.
  This once. No? Not? I shall remember this.
  Will you disgrace me thus? D'you thirst my undoing?
MOSCA: Nay, gentle lady, be advised.   115
CORVINO: No, no.
  She has watched her time. God's precious, this is scurvy;
  'Tis very scurvy; and you are—
MOSCA: Nay, good sir.

---

30 **horn-mad** raving mad or jealous (pun on cuckoldry) **32 train**
stratagem, trick, plot 48 **jig** farce

99 **rotchet** red fish 104 ***aquafortis*** sulphuric acid 105 **cor'sives** cor-
rosives

CORVINO: An errant locust, by heaven, a locust! Whore,
  Crocodile, that hast thy tears prepared.
120 Expecting how thou'lt bid 'hem flow.
MOSCA: Nay, pray you, sir!
  She will consider.
CELIA: Would my life would serve
  To satisfy.
CORVINO: 'Sdeath! If she would but speak to him,
  And save my reputation, 'twere somewhat;
  But, spitefully, to effect my utter ruin!
125 MOSCA: Ay, now you have put your fortune in her hands.
  Why, i' faith, it is her modesty, I must quit her.
  If you were absent, she would be more coming;
  I know it, and dare undertake for her.
  What woman can before her husband? Pray you,
130 Let us depart and leave her here.
CORVINO: Sweet Celia,
  Thou mayst redeem all yet; I'll say no more.
  If not, esteem yourself as lost. Nay, stay there.

(Exeunt CORVINO and MOSCA.)

CELIA: O God and his good angels! Whither, whither
  Is shame fled human breasts? that with such ease
135 Men dare put off your honors, and their own?
  Is that, which ever was a cause of life,
  Now placed beneath the basest circumstance,
  And modesty an exile made for money?
VOLPONE: *(He leaps off from his couch.)* Ay, in Corvino, and
  such earth-fed minds,
140 That never tasted the true heaven of love.
  Assure thee, Celia, he that would sell thee,
  Only for hope of gain, and that uncertain,
  He would have sold his part of Paradise
  For ready money had he met a cope-man.
145 Why art thou 'mazed to see me thus revived?
  Rather applaud thy beauty's miracle;
  'Tis thy great work that hath, not now alone,
  But sundry times, raised me in several shapes,
  And, but this morning, like a mountebank,
150 To see thee at thy windore. Ay, before
  I would have left my practice for thy love,
  In varying figures I would have contended
  With the blue Proteus or the hornèd flood.
  Now art thou welcome.
CELIA: Sir!
VOLPONE: Nay, fly me not.
155 Nor let thy false imagination
  That I was bed-rid make thee think I am so:
  Thou shalt not find it. I am, now, as fresh,
  As hot, as high, and in as jovial plight
  As when (in that so celebrated scene
160 At recitation of our comedy,
  For entertainment of the great Valois)
  I acted young Antinous and attracted
  The eyes and ears of all the ladies present,
  T'admire each graceful gesture, note, and footing.

(Song)

Come, my Celia, let us prove,   165
While we can, the sports of love;
Time will not be ours forever;
He, at length, our good will sever;
Spend not then his gifts in vain.
Suns that set may rise again;   170
But, if once we lose this light,
'Tis with us perpetual night.
Why should we defer our joys?
Fame and rumor are but toys.
Cannot we delude the eyes   175
Of a few poor household spies?
Or his easier ears beguile,
Thus removèd by our wile?
'Tis no sin love's fruits to steal
But the sweet thefts to reveal: 180
To be taken, to be seen,
These have crimes accounted been.
CELIA: Some serene blast me, or dire lightning strike
  This my offending face!
VOLPONE: Why droops my Celia?
  Thou hast in place of a base husband found   185
  A worthy lover: use thy fortune well,
  With secrecy and pleasure. See, behold,
  What thou art queen of; not in expectation,
  As I feed others, but possessed and crowned.
  See, here, a rope of pearl, and each more orient   190
  Than that the brave Egyptian queen caroused;
  Dissolve and drink 'hem. See, a carbuncle
  May put out both the eyes of our Saint Mark;
  A diamond would have bought Lollia Paulina
  When she came in like star-light, hid with jewels   195
  That were the spoils of provinces; take these,
  And wear, and lose 'hem; yet remains an earring
  To purchase them again and this whole state.
  A gem but worth a private patrimony
  Is nothing; we will eat such at a meal.   200
  The heads of parrots, tongues of nightingales,
  The brains of peacocks and of estriches
  Shall be our food; and, could we get the phoenix,
  Though nature lost her kind, she were our dish.
CELIA: Good sir, these things might move a mind affected   205
  With such delights; but I, whose innocence
  Is all I can think wealthy, or worth th'enjoying,
  And which, once lost, I have naught to lose beyond it,
  Cannot be taken with these sensual baits.
  If you have conscience—   210
VOLPONE: 'Tis the beggar's virtue;
  If thou hast wisdom, hear me, Celia.
  Thy baths shall be the juice of July-flowers,
  Spirit of roses, and of violets,
  The milk of unicorns, and panthers' breath
  Gathered in bags and mixed with Cretan wines.   215

---

126 **quit** acquit, excuse 144 **cope-man** chapman; merchant 151 **practice** deceit, craft

165 **prove** test, try 183 **serene** harmful damp evening air 190 **orient** precious; pure 191 **queen** Cleopatra 194 **Lollia Paulina** wife of a Roman provincial governor who adorned herself with the jewels plundered by her husband 202 **estriches** ostriches 212 **July-flowers** gillyflowers

Our drink shall be preparèd gold and amber,
Which we will take until my roof whirl round
With the vertigo; and my dwarf shall dance,
My eunuch sing, my fool make up the antic.
220   Whilst we, in changèd shapes, act Ovid's tales,
Thou like Europa now, and I like Jove,
Then I like Mars, and thou like Erycine;
So of the rest till we have quite run through
And wearied all the fables of the gods.
225   Then will I have thee in more modern forms,
Attirèd like some sprightly dame of France,
Brave Tuscan lady, or proud Spanish beauty;
Sometimes unto the Persian Sophy's wife,
Or the Grand Signor's mistress; and, for change,
230   To one of our most artful courtesans,
Or some quick Negro, or cold Russian;
And I will meet thee in as many shapes:
Where we may so transfuse our wand'ring souls
Out at our lips and score up sums of pleasures,
235   That the curious shall not know
                    How to tell them as they flow;
               And the envious, when they find
                    What their number is, be pined.
CELIA: If you have ears that will be pierced, or eyes
240   That can be opened, a heart may be touched,
Or any part that yet sounds man about you;
If you have touch of holy saints, or heaven,
Do me the grace to let me 'scape. If not,
Be bountiful and kill me. You do know
245   I am a creature hither ill betrayed
By one whose shame I would forget it were.
If you will deign me neither of these graces,
Yet feed your wrath, sir, rather than your lust
(It is a vice comes nearer manliness),
250   And punish that unhappy crime of nature,
Which you miscall my beauty: flay my face,
Or poison it with ointments for seducing
Your blood to this rebellion. Rub these hands
With what may cause an eating leprosy,
255   E'en to my bones and marrow; anything
That may disfavor me, save in my honor,
And I will kneel to you, pray for you, pay down
A thousand hourly vows, sir, for your health,
Report and think you virtuous—
VOLPONE: Think me cold,
260   Frozen, and impotent, and so report me?
That I had Nestor's hernia thou wouldst think.
I do degenerate and abuse my nation
To play with opportunity thus long;
I should have done the act and then have parleyed.
265   Yield, or I'll force thee.

(He seizes her.)

CELIA: O! just God!
VOLPONE: In vain—
BONARIO: *(He leaps out from where* MOSCA *had placed him.)*
Forbear, foul ravisher! Libidinous swine!

---

219 **antic** grotesque performance   222 **Erycine** Venus   229 **Grand Signor** Sultan of Turkey   231 **quick** lively   236 **tell** count   238 **be pined** be made to pine away   261 **Nestor's hernia** the impotence of an old man like Homer's Nestor

Free the forced lady, or thou diest, impostor!
But that I am loath to snatch thy punishment
Out of the hand of justice, thou shouldst yet
Be made the timely sacrifice of vengeance   270
Before this altar and this dross, thy idol.—
Lady, let's quit the place; it is the den
Of villainy. Fear naught; you have a guard:
And he, ere long, shall meet his just reward.

(Exeunt BONARIO *and* CELIA.)

VOLPONE: Fall on me, roof, and bury me in ruin!   275
Become my grave, that wert my shelter! O!
I am unmasked, unspirited, undone,
Betrayed to beggary, to infamy—

SCENE VIII

MOSCA, VOLPONE.

MOSCA: Where shall I run, most wretched shame of men,
To beat out my unlucky brains?
VOLPONE: Here, here.
What! Dost thou bleed?
MOSCA: O, that his well-driven sword
Had been so courteous to have cleft me down
Unto the navel, ere I lived to see   5
My life, my hopes, my spirits, my patron, all
Thus desperately engagèd by my error!
VOLPONE: Woe on thy fortune!
MOSCA: And my follies, sir.
VOLPONE: Th'hast made me miserable.
MOSCA: And myself, sir.
Who would have thought he would have hearkened so?   10
VOLPONE: What shall we do?
MOSCA: I know not; if my heart
Could expiate the mischance, I'd pluck it out.
Will you be pleased to hang me? Or cut my throat?
And I'll requite you, sir. Let's die like Romans
Since we have lived like Grecians.   15

(They knock without.)

VOLPONE: Hark! Who's there?
I hear some footing; officers, the *Saffi*,
Come to apprehend us! I do feel the brand
Hissing already at my forehead; now,
Mine ears are boring.
MOSCA: To your couch, sir; you
Make that place good, however. Guilty men   20
Suspect what they deserve still.—Signor Corbaccio!

SCENE IX

CORBACCIO, MOSCA, VOLTORE, VOLPONE.

CORBACCIO: Why, how now, Mosca?
MOSCA: O, undone, amazed, sir.
Your son, I know not by what accident,
Acquainted with your purpose to my patron,
Touching your will, and making him your heir,
Entered our house with violence, his sword drawn,   5

---

7 **engagèd** trapped   16 *saffi* bailiffs; Venetian police

Sought for you, called you wretch, unnatural,
Vowed he would kill you.

CORBACCIO: Me?

MOSCA: Yes, and my patron.

CORBACCIO: This act shall disinherit him indeed;
Here is the will.

MOSCA: 'Tis well, sir.

CORBACCIO: Right and well.

10   Be you as careful now for me.

(Enter VOLTORE *behind.)*

MOSCA: My life, sir,
Is not more tendered; I am only yours.

CORBACCIO: How does he? Will he die shortly, think'st thou?

MOSCA: I fear
He'll outlast May.

CORBACCIO: Today?

MOSCA: No, last out May, sir.

CORBACCIO: Couldst thou not gi'him a dram?

MOSCA: O, by no means, sir.

15 CORBACCIO: Nay, I'll not bid you.

VOLTORE: *(Coming forward.)*   This is a knave, I see.

MOSCA: *(Aside.)* How! Signor Voltore! Did he hear me?

VOLTORE: Parasite!

MOSCA: Who's that?—O, sir, most timely welcome.

VOLTORE: Scarce
To the discovery of your tricks, I fear.
You are his only? And mine, also, are you not?

20 MOSCA: Who? I, sir?

VOLTORE: You, sir. What device is this
About a will?

MOSCA: A plot for you, sir.

VOLTORE: Come,
Put not your foists upon me; I shall scent 'hem.

MOSCA: Did you not hear it?

VOLTORE: Yes, I hear Corbaccio
Hath made your patron, there, his heir.

MOSCA: 'Tis true,
25 By my device, drawn to it by my plot,
With hope—

VOLTORE: Your patron should reciprocate?
And you have promised?

MOSCA: For your good I did, sir.
Nay, more, I told his son, brought, hid him here,
Where he might hear his father pass the deed;
30 Being persuaded to it by this thought, sir:
That the unnaturalness, first, of the act,
And then his father's oft disclaiming in him
(Which I did mean t'help on) would sure enrage him
To do some violence upon his parent.
35 On which the law should take sufficient hold,
And you be stated in a double hope.
Truth be my comfort, and my conscience,
My only aim was to dig you a fortune
Out of these two old, rotten sepulchres—

40 VOLTORE: I cry thee mercy, Mosca.

MOSCA: Worth your patience,
And your great merit, sir. And see the change!

VOLTORE: Why? What success?

MOSCA: Most hapless! You must help, sir.
Whilst we expected th'old raven, in comes
Corvino's wife, sent hither by her husband—

VOLTORE: What, with a present?   45

MOSCA: No, sir, on visitation
(I'll tell you how anon), and, staying long,
The youth he grows impatient, rushes forth,
Seizeth the lady, wounds me, makes her swear
(Or he would murder her, that was his vow)
T'affirm my patron to have done her rape,   50
Which how unlike it is, you see! And hence,
With that pretext, he's gone t'accuse his father,
Defame my patron, defeat you—

VOLTORE: Where's her husband?
Let him be sent for straight.

MOSCA: Sir, I'll go fetch him.

VOLTORE: Bring him to the *Scrutineo*.   55

MOSCA: Sir, I will.

VOLTORE: This must be stopped.

MOSCA: O, you do nobly, sir.
Alas, 'twas labored all, sir, for your good;
Nor was there want of counsel in the plot:
But Fortune can, at any time, o'erthrow
The projects of a hundred learned clerks, sir. 60

CORBACCIO: *(Straining to hear.)* What's that?

VOLTORE: Will't please
you, sir, to go along?

(Exit with CORBACCIO.*)*

MOSCA: Patron, go in and pray for our success.

VOLPONE: Need makes devotion: heaven your labor bless!

— ACT FOUR —

SCENE I

[SIR] POLITIC, PEREGRINE.

SIR POLITIC: I told you, sir, it was a plot: you see
What observation is! You mentioned me
For some instructions; I will tell you, sir
(Since we are met here in this height of Venice),
Some few particulars I have set down   5
Only for this meridian, fit to be known
Of your crude traveler; and they are these.
I will not touch, sir, at your phrase or clothes,
For they are old.

PEREGRINE: Sir, I have better.

SIR POLITIC: Pardon;
I meant as they are themes.   10

PEREGRINE: O, sir, proceed;
I'll slander you no more of wit, good sir.

SIR POLITIC: First, for your garb, it must be grave and serious,
Very reserved and locked; not tell a secret
On any terms, not to your father; scarce
A fable but with caution; make sure choice   15

---

10 **careful** concerned   11 **tendered** watched over, attended to
22 **foists** tricks, deceits   32 **disclaiming** denying (kinship)

55 *Scrutineo* Senate house   60 **clerks** scholars
1 **it** the mountebank scene above   12 **garb** demeanor

Both of your company and discourse; beware
You never speak a truth—
PEREGRINE: How!
SIR POLITIC: Not to strangers,
  For those be they you must converse with most;
  Others I would not know, sir, but at distance,
20 So as I still might be a saver in 'hem.
  You shall have tricks else passed upon you hourly.
  And then, for your religion, profess none,
  But wonder at the diversity of all;
  And, for your part, protest, were there no other
25 But simply the laws o'th'land, you could content you.
  Nick Machiavel and Monsieur Bodin both
  Were of this mind. Then must you learn the use
  And handling of your silver fork at meals,
  The metal of your glass (these are main matters
30 With your Italian), and to know the hour
  When you must eat your melons and your figs.
PEREGRINE: Is that a point of state too?
SIR POLITIC: Here it is.
  For your Venetian, if he see a man
  Preposterous in the least, he has him straight;
35 He has, he strips him. I'll acquaint you, sir.
  I now have lived here 'tis some fourteen months;
  Within the first week of my landing here,
  All took me for a citizen of Venice,
  I know the forms so well—
PEREGRINE: (*Aside.*)   And nothing else.
40 SIR POLITIC: I had read Contarine, took me a house,
  Dealt with my Jews to furnish it with movables—
  Well, if I could but find one man, one man
  To mine own heart, whom I durst trust, I would—
PEREGRINE: What, what, sir?
SIR POLITIC: Make him rich, make him a fortune:
45 He should not think again. I would command it.
PEREGRINE: As how?
SIR POLITIC: With certain projects that I have,
  Which I may not discover.
PEREGRINE: (*Aside.*)   If I had
  But one to wager with, I would lay odds now
  He tells me instantly.
SIR POLITIC: One is (and that
50 I care not greatly who knows) to serve the state
  Of Venice with red herrings for three years,
  And at a certain rate, from Rotterdam,
  Where I have correspondence. There's a letter
  Sent me from one o'th'States, and to that purpose;
55 He cannot write his name, but that's his mark.
PEREGRINE: He is a chandler?
SIR POLITIC: No, a cheesemonger.
  There are some other, too, with whom I treat
  About the same negotiation;
  And I will undertake it: for 'tis thus
60 I'll do't with ease; I've cast it all. Your hoy

Carries but three men in her and a boy,
And she shall make me three returns a year;
So, if there come but one of three, I save;
If two, I can defalk. But this is now
If my main project fail.   65
PEREGRINE: Then you have others?
SIR POLITIC: I should be loath to draw the subtle air
  Of such a place without my thousand aims.
  I'll not dissemble, sir; where'er I come
  I love to be considerative; and, 'tis true,
  I have at my free hours thought upon   70
  Some certain goods unto the state of Venice,
  Which I do call my cautions, and, sir, which
  I mean, in hope of pension, to propound
  To the Great Council, then unto the Forty,
  So to the Ten. My means are made already—   75
PEREGRINE: By whom?
SIR POLITIC: Sir, one that though his place
      b'obscure,
  Yet he can sway, and they will hear him. He's
  A *commendatore*.
PEREGRINE: What, a common sergeant?
SIR POLITIC: Sir, such as they are put it in their mouths
  What they should say, sometimes, as well as greater.   80
  I think I have my notes to show you—
PEREGRINE: Good sir—
SIR POLITIC: But you shall swear unto me, on your gentry,
  Not to anticipate—
PEREGRINE: I, sir?
SIR POLITIC: Nor reveal
  A circumstance—My paper is not with me.
PEREGRINE: O, but you can remember, sir.   85
SIR POLITIC: My first is
  Concerning tinderboxes. You must know
  No family is here without its box.
  Now, sir, it being so portable a thing,
  Put case that you or I were ill affected
  Unto the state; sir, with it in our pockets,   90
  Might not I go into the Arsenal?
  Or you? Come out again? And none the wiser?
PEREGRINE: Except yourself, sir.
SIR POLITIC: Go to, then. I, therefore,
  Advertise to the state how fit it were
  That none but such as were known patriots,   95
  Sound lovers of their country, should be suffered
  T'enjoy them in their houses; and even those
  Sealed at some office and at such a bigness
  As might not lurk in pockets.
PEREGRINE: Admirable!
SIR POLITIC: My next is, how t'inquire, and be resolved   100
  By present demonstration, whether a ship
  Newly arrivèd from S[y]ria, or from
  Any suspected part of all the Levant,
  Be guilty of the plague. And where they use
  To lie out forty, fifty days sometimes,   105
  About the *Lazaretto* for their trial,

---

26 **Machiavel . . . Bodin** the famous Florentine and French political writers   34 **preposterous** incorrect according to convention   40 **Contarine** Cardinal Contarini, famed for a work on Venice that was translated into English in 1599   60 **cast** calculated, reckoned; **hoy** small vessel

---

64 **defalk** make retrenchments   72 **cautions** precautions   101 **present** immediate   106 **Lazaretto** island used for quarantine

I'll save that charge and loss unto the merchant
And in an hour clear the doubt.
PEREGRINE: Indeed, sir?
SIR POLITIC: Or—I will lose my labor.
PEREGRINE: My faith, that's much.
110 SIR POLITIC: Nay, sir, conceive me. 'Twill cost me, in onions,
    Some thirty livres—
PEREGRINE: Which is one pound sterling.
SIR POLITIC: Beside my waterworks; for this I do, sir:
    First, I bring in your ship 'twixt two brick walls
    (But those the state shall venture); on the one
115 I strain me a fair tarpaulin, and in that
    I stick my onions, cut in halves; the other
    Is full of loopholes, out at which I thrust
    The noses of my bellows; and those bellows
    I keep, with waterworks, in perpetual motion,
120 Which is the easi'st matter of a hundred.
    Now, sir, your onion, which doth naturally
    Attract th'infection, and your bellows blowing
    The air upon him, will show instantly
    By his changed color if there be contagion,
125 Or else remain as fair as the first.
    Now 'tis known, 'tis nothing.
PEREGRINE: You are right, sir.
SIR POLITIC: I would I had my note.
PEREGRINE: Faith, so would I;
    But you 'ha done well for once, sir.
SIR POLITIC: Were I false,
    Or would be made so, I could show you reasons
130 How I could sell this state now to the Turk,
    Spite of their galleys or their—

(He searches for his notes.)

PEREGRINE: Pray you, Sir Pol.
SIR POLITIC: I have 'hem not about me.
PEREGRINE: That I feared.
    They're there, sir?
SIR POLITIC: No, this is my diary,
    Wherein I note my actions of the day.
135 PEREGRINE: Pray you let's see, sir. What is here?

(He reads.)

                              "*Notandum,*
    A rat had gnawn my spur leathers; notwithstanding,
    I put on new and did go forth; but, first,
    I threw three beans over the threshold. *Item,*
    I went and bought two toothpicks, whereof one
140 I burst, immediately, in a discourse
    With a Dutch merchant, 'bout *ragion del stato.*
    From him I went and paid a *moccenigo*
    For piecing my silk stockings; by the way,
    I cheapened sprats, and at Saint Mark's I urined."—
145 Faith, these are politic notes!
SIR POLITIC: Sir, I do slip
    No action of my life, thus but I quote it.
PEREGRINE: Believe me, it is wise!
SIR POLITIC: Nay, sir, read forth.

SCENE II

LADY [WOULD-BE], NANO, WOMEN, [SIR] POLITIC, PEREGRINE.

LADY WOULD-BE: Where should this loose knight be, trow?
    Sure, he's housed.
NANO: Why, then he's fast.
LADY WOULD-BE: Ay, he plays both with me.
    I pray you stay. This heat will do more harm
    To my complexion than his heart is worth.
    I do not care to hinder, but to take him.   5

(She rubs her cheeks.)

    How it comes off!
1 WOMAN: My master's yonder.
LADY WOULD-BE: Where?
2 WOMAN: With a young gentleman.
LADY WOULD-BE: That's the same party!
    In man's apparel! Pray you, sir, jog my knight.
    I will be tender to his reputation,
    However he demerit.   10
SIR POLITIC: *(Seeing his wife.)* My lady!
PEREGRINE: Where?
SIR POLITIC: 'Tis she indeed, sir; you shall know her. She is,
    Were she not mine, a lady of that merit
    For fashion and behavior; and for beauty
    I durst compare—
PEREGRINE: It seems you are not jealous,
    That dare commend her.   15
SIR POLITIC: Nay, and for discourse—
PEREGRINE: Being your wife, she cannot miss that.
SIR POLITIC: Madam,
    Here is a gentleman; pray you, use him fairly;
    He seems a youth, but he is—
LADY WOULD-BE: None?
SIR POLITIC: Yes, one
    Has put his face as soon into the world—
LADY WOULD-BE: You mean, as early? But today?   20
SIR POLITIC: How's this?
LADY WOULD-BE: Why, in this habit, sir; you apprehend me!
    Well, Master Would-be, this doth not become you;
    I had thought the odor, sir, of your good name
    Had been more precious to you, that you would not
    Have done this dire massàcre on your honor.   25
    One of your gravity and rank besides!
    But knights, I see, care little for the oath
    They make to ladies, chiefly their own ladies.
SIR POLITIC: Now, by my spurs, the symbol of my
    knighthood—
PEREGRINE: *(Aside.)* Lord, how his brain is humbled for an 30
    oath!
SIR POLITIC: I reach you not.
LADY WOULD-BE: Right sir, your polity
    May bear it through thus.—*(To* PEREGRINE.*)* Sir, a word
    with you.
    I would be loath to contest publicly
    With any gentlewoman, or to seem
    Froward or violent (as *The Courtier* says);   35

---

110 **conceive** understand   111 **livres** French coins   135 *notandum*
let it be noted   141 *ragion del stato* affairs of the state; politics
144 **cheapened** bargained for

1 **housed** in a house of prostitution   2 **plays both** fast and
loose   10 **demerit** is at fault   31 **reach** understand   35 *The Courtier* the Renaissance handbook of conduct by Castiglione

It comes too near rusticity in a lady,
Which I would shun by all means. And, however
I may deserve from Master Would-be, yet
T'have one fair gentlewoman thus be made
40 Th'unkind instrument to wrong another,
And one she knows not, ay, and to persèver,
In my poor judgment, is not warranted
From being a solecism in our sex,
If not in manners.
PEREGRINE: How is this!
SIR POLITIC: Sweet madam,
45 Come nearer to your aim.
LADY WOULD-BE: Marry, and will, sir.
Since you provoke me with your impudence
And laughter of your light land-siren here,
Your Sporus, your hermaphrodite—
PEREGRINE: What's here?
Poetic fury and historic storms!
50 SIR POLITIC: The gentleman, believe it, is of worth
And of our nation.
LADY WOULD-BE: Ay, your Whitefriars nation!
Come, I blush for you, Master Would-be, ay;
And am ashamed you should ha' no more forehead
Than thus to be the patron, or Saint George,
55 To a lewd harlot, a base fricatrice,
A female devil in a male outside.
SIR POLITIC: Nay,
And you be such a one, I must bid adieu
To your delights! The case appears too liquid.

(Exit.)

LADY WOULD-BE: Ay, you may carry't clear with your
state-face!
60 But for your carnival concupiscence,
Who where is fled for liberty of conscience,
From furious persecution of the marshal,
Her will I disc'ple.
PEREGRINE: This is fine, i'faith!
And do you use this often? Is this part
65 Of your wit's exercise, 'gainst you have occasion?
Madam—
LADY WOULD-BE: Go to, sir.
PEREGRINE: Do you hear me, lady?
Why, if your knight have set you to beg shirts,
Or to invite me home, you might have done it
A nearer way by far.
LADY WOULD-BE: This cannot work you
70 Out of my snare.
PEREGRINE: Why, am I in it, then?
Indeed, your husband told me you were fair,
And so you are; only your nose inclines
(That side that's next the sun) to the queen-apple.
LADY WOULD-BE: This cannot be endured by any patience.

---

48 **Sporus** Emperor Nero's favorite   49 **historic** histrionic, dramatic
51 **Whitefriars** notorious part of London where evildoers were immune from the law and from arrest   53 **forehead** shame   55 **fricatrice** prostitute   58 **liquid** clear   59 **state-face** public or official
manner   60 **carnival** with pun on carnal   63 **disc'ple** discipline
65 **'gainst** when   73 **queen-apple** particularly red

SCENE III

MOSCA, LADY [WOULD-BE], PEREGRINE [,NANO, WOMEN].

MOSCA: What's the matter, madam?
LADY WOULD-BE: If the Senate
Right not my quest in this, I will protest 'hem
To all the world no aristocracy.
MOSCA: What is the injury, lady?
LADY WOULD-BE: Why, the callet
You told me of, here I have ta'en disguised.   5
MOSCA: Who? This! What means your ladyship? The creature
I mentioned to you is apprehended now
Before the Senate. You shall see her—
LADY WOULD-BE: Where?
MOSCA: I'll bring you to her. This young gentleman,
I saw him land this morning at the port.   10
LADY WOULD-BE: Is't possible? How has my judgment
wandered!
Sir, I must, blushing, say to you, I have erred,
And plead your pardon.
PEREGRINE: What! more changes yet?
LADY WOULD-BE: I hope yo' ha' not the malice to remember
A gentlewoman's passion. If you stay   15
In Venice here, please you to use me, sir—
MOSCA: Will you go, madam?
LADY WOULD-BE: Pray you, sir, use me.
In faith,
The more you see me, the more I shall conceive
You have forgot our quarrel.

(Exeunt all but PEREGRINE.)

PEREGRINE: This is rare!
Sir Politic Would-be? No, Sir Politic Bawd,   20
To bring me thus acquainted with his wife!
Well, wise Sir Pol, since you have practiced thus
Upon my freshmanship, I'll try your salt-head,
What proof it is against a counterplot.

(Exit.)

SCENE IV

VOLTORE, CORBACCIO, CORVINO, MOSCA.

VOLTORE: Well, now you know the carriage of the business,
Your constancy is all that is required
Unto the safety of it.
MOSCA: Is the lie
Safely conveyed amongst us? Is that sure?
Knows every man his burden?   5
CORVINO: Yes.
MOSCA: Then shrink not.
CORVINO: *(Aside to* MOSCA.*)* But knows the advocate the
truth?
MOSCA: O, sir,
By no means. I devised a formal tale
That salved your reputation. But be valiant, sir.
CORVINO: I fear no one but him, that this his pleading
Should make him stand for a co-heir—   10

---

4 **callet** wanton, wench, strumpet   23 **salt-head** lechery

MOSCA: Co-halter!
Hang him! we will but use his tongue, his noise,
As we do Croaker's here.

(He points to CORBACCIO.*)*

CORVINO: Ay, what shall he do?
MOSCA: When we ha' done, you mean?
CORVINO: Yes.
MOSCA: Why, we'll think.
Sell him for mummia, he's half dust already.—
15 *(To* VOLTORE.*)* Do not you smile to see this buffalo,
How he doth sport it with his head?—*(Aside.)* I should
If all were well and past.—*(To* CORBACCIO.*)* Sir, only you
Are he that shall enjoy the crop of all,
And these not know for whom they toil.
CORBACCIO: Ay, peace.
20 MOSCA: *(To* CORVINO.*)* But you shall eat it.—*(Aside.)* Much!

(Then to VOLTORE *again.)*

—Worshipful sir,
Mercury sit upon your thund'ring tongue,
Or the French Hercules, and make your language
As conquering as his club, to beat along,
As with a tempest, flat, our adversaries;
25 But much more yours, sir.
VOLTORE: Here they come; ha' done.
MOSCA: I have another witness, if you need, sir,
I can produce.
VOLTORE: Who is it?
MOSCA: Sir, I have her.

SCENE V

AVOCATORI 4, BONARIO, CELIA, VOLTORE, CORBACCIO,
CORVINO, MOSCA, NOTARIO, COMMENDATORI.

AVOCATORE 1: The like of this the Senate never heard of.
AVOCATORE 2: 'Twill come most strange to them when we
report it.
AVOCATORE 4: The gentlewoman has been ever held
Of unreprovèd name.
AVOCATORE 3: So the young man.
5 AVOCATORE 4: The more unnatural part, that of his father.
AVOCATORE 2: More of the husband.
AVOCATORE 1: I not know to give
His act a name, it is so monstrous!
AVOCATORE 4: But the impostor, he is a thing created
T'exceed example!
AVOCATORE [1]: And all after times!
10 AVOCATORE 2: I never heard a true voluptuary
Described but him.
AVOCATORE 3: Appear yet those were cited?
NOTARIO: All but the old magnifico, Volpone.
AVOCATORE 1: Why is not he here?
MOSCA: Please your fatherhoods,
Here is his advocate. Himself's so weak,
15 So feeble—

AVOCATORE 4: What are you?
BONARIO: His parasite,
His knave, his pander! I beseech the court
He may be forced to come, that your grave eyes
May bear strong witness of his strange impostures.
VOLTORE: Upon my faith and credit with your virtues,
He is not able to endure the air. 20
AVOCATORE 2: Bring him, however.
AVOCATORE 3: We will see him.
AVOCATORE 4: Fetch him.
VOLTORE: Your fatherhoods' fit pleasures be obeyed.

(Exeunt COMMENDATORI.*)*

But sure the sight will rather move your pities
Than indignation. May it please the court,
In the meantime, he may be heard in me: 25
I know this place most void of prejudice,
And therefore crave it, since we have no reason
To fear our truth should hurt our cause.
AVOCATORE 3: Speak free.
VOLTORE: Then know, most honored fathers, I must now
Discover to your strangely abusèd ears 30
The most prodigious and most frontless piece
Of solid impudence and treachery
That ever vicious nature yet brought forth
To shame the state of Venice. This lewd woman,
That wants not artificial looks or tears 35
To help the visor she has now put on,
Hath long been known a close adulteress
To that lascivious youth there; not suspected,
I say, but known, and taken in the act
With him, and by this man, the easy husband, 40
Pardoned; whose timeless bounty makes him now
Stand here, the most unhappy, innocent person
That ever man's own goodness made accused.
For these, not knowing how to owe a gift
Of that dear grace but with their shame, being placed 45
So above all powers of their gratitude,
Began to hate the benefit and in place
Of thanks devise t'extirp the memory
Of such an act. Wherein, I pray your fatherhoods,
To observe the malice, yea, the rage of creatures 50
Discovered in their evils, and what heart
Such take even from their crimes. But that anon
Will more appear. This gentleman, the father,
Hearing of this foul fact, with many others,
Which daily struck at his too tender ears, 55
And grieved in nothing more than that he could not
Preserve himself a parent (his son's ills
Growing to that strange flood) at last decreed
To disinherit him.
AVOCATORE 1: These be strange turns!
AVOCATORE 2: The young man's fame was ever fair and 60
honest.
VOLTORE: So much more full of danger is his vice
That can beguile so under shade of virtue.
But, as I said, my honored sires, his father

---

14 **mummia** medicine supposedly made from mummies   15 **buffalo**
jest referring to Corvino's horns   22 **French Hercules** Ognius, symbol, like Mercury, of eloquence

7 **monstrous** pronounced as "monsterous"

---

31 **frontless** shameless   37 **close** secret   41 **timeless** untimely
44 **owe** own   54 **fact** deed; crime

65 Having this settled purpose (by what means
To him betrayed, we know not), and this day
Appointed for the deed, that parricide
(I cannot style him better), by confederacy
Preparing this his paramour to be there,
70 Entered Volpone's house (who was the man,
Your fatherhoods must understand, designed
For the inheritance), there sought his father:
But with what purpose sought he him, my lords?
I tremble to pronounce it, that a son
Unto a father, and to such a father,
75 Should have so foul, felonious intent!
It was to murder him! When, being prevented
By his more happy absence, what then did he?
Not check his wicked thoughts? No, now new deeds
(Mischief doth ever end where it begins),
80 An act of horror, fathers! He dragged forth
The agèd gentleman, that had there [lain] bed-rid
Three years and more, out off his innocent couch,
Naked, upon the floor, there left him; wounded
His servant in the face; and, with this strumpet,
85 The stale to his forged practice, who was glad
To be so active (I shall here desire
Your fatherhoods to note but my collections
As most remarkable), thought at once to stop
His father's ends, discredit his free choice
90 In the old gentleman, redeem themselves
By laying infamy upon this man,
To whom, with blushing, they should owe their lives.
AVOCATORE 1: What proofs have you of this?
BONARIO: Most honored fathers,
I humbly crave there be no credit given
95 To this man's mercenary tongue.
AVOCATORE 2:   Forbear.
BONARIO: His soul moves in his fee.
AVOCATORE 3:   O, sir!
BONARIO: This fellow
For six sols more would plead against his Maker.
AVOCATORE 1: You do forget yourself.
VOLTORE: Nay, nay, grave fathers,
Let him have scope. Can any man imagine
100 That he will spare's accuser, that would not
Have spared his parent?
AVOCATORE 1:   Well, produce your proofs.
CELIA: I would I could forget I were a creature!
VOLTORE: Signor Corbaccio!
AVOCATORE 4:   What is he?
VOLTORE: The father.
AVOCATORE 2: Has he had an oath?
NOTARIO: Yes.
CORBACCIO: What must I do now?
105 NOTARIO: Your testimony's craved.
CORBACCIO: Speak to the knave?
I'll ha' my mouth first stopped with earth; my heart
Abhors his knowledge. I disclaim in him.
AVOCATORE 1: But for what cause?

CORBACCIO: The mere portent of nature.
He is an utter stranger to my loins.
BONARIO: Have they made you to this?   110
CORBACCIO: I will not hear thee,
Monster of men, swine, goat, wolf, parricide!
Speak not, thou viper!
BONARIO: Sir, I will sit down
And rather wish my innocence should suffer
Than I resist the authority of a father.
VOLTORE: Signor Corvino!   115
AVOCATORE 2:   This is strange.
AVOCATORE 1:   Who's that?
NOTARIO: The husband.
AVOCATORE 4:   Is he sworn?
NOTARIO: He is.
AVOCATORE 3:   Speak, then.
CORVINO: This woman, please your fatherhoods, is a whore
Of most hot exercise, more than a partridge,
Upon record—
AVOCATORE 1: No more.
CORVINO: Neighs like a jennet.
NOTARIO: Preserve the honor of the court!   120
CORVINO: I shall,
And modesty of your most reverend ears.
And yet I hope that I may say these eyes
Have seen her glued unto that piece of cedar,
That fine, well-timbered gallant; and that here

(He points to his forehead.)

The letters may be read, thorough the horn,   125
That make the story perfect.
MOSCA: Excellent, sir!
CORVINO: *(Aside to* MOSCA.*)* There is no shame in this now,
is there?
MOSCA: *(Aside.)* None.
CORVINO: Or if I said I hoped that she were onward
To her damnation, if there be a hell
Greater than whore and woman, a good Catholic   130
May make the doubt.
AVOCATORE 3:   His grief hath made him frantic.
AVOCATORE 1: Remove him hence.

(She swoons.)

AVOCATORE 2:   Look to the woman!
CORVINO: Rare!
Prettily feigned! Again!
AVOCATORE 4:   Stand from about her!
AVOCATORE 1: Give her the air.
AVOCATORE 3: *(To* MOSCA.*)*   What can you say?
MOSCA: My wound,
May't please your wisdoms, speaks for me, received   135
In aid of my good patron, when he missed
His sought-for father, when that well-taught dame
Had her cue given her to cry out a rape.
BONARIO: O most laid impudence! Fathers—
AVOCATORE 3:   Sir, be silent;
You had your hearing free, so must they theirs.   140

---

85 **stale** decoy; mask   87 **collections** conclusions, evidences   97 **sols** small coins

108 **mere portent** an absolute monster   125 **horn** hornbook (used as a pun on horns of a cuckold)   126 **perfect** complete   139 **laid** well-contrived

AVOCATORE 2: I do begin to doubt th'imposture here.
AVOCATORE 4: This woman has too many moods.
VOLTORE: Grave fathers,
  She is a creature of a most professed
  And prostituted lewdness.
CORVINO: Most impetuous,
145 Unsatisfied, grave fathers!
VOLTORE: May her feignings
  Not take your wisdoms; but, this day, she baited
  A stranger, a grave knight, with her loose eyes
  And more lascivious kisses. This man saw 'hem
  Together on the water in a gondola.
150 MOSCA: Here is the lady herself that saw 'hem too,
  Without, who then had in the open streets
  Pursued them but for saving her knight's honor.
AVOCATORE 1: Produce that lady.
AVOCATORE 2:   Let her come.

(Exit MOSCA.*)*

AVOCATORE 4:   These things,
  They strike with wonder!
AVOCATORE 3:   I am turned a stone!

SCENE VI

MOSCA, LADY [WOULD-BE], AVOCATORI, *etc.*

MOSCA: Be resolute, madam.
LADY WOULD-BE: Ay, this same is she.
  Out, thou chameleon harlot! Now thine eyes
  Vie tears with the hyena. Dar'st thou look
  Upon my wrongèd face?—I cry your pardons.
5 I fear I have forgettingly transgressed
  Against the dignity of the court—
AVOCATORE 2:   No, madam.
LADY WOULD-BE: And been exorbitant—
AVOCATORE [2]:   You have not, lady.
AVOCATORE 4: These proofs are strong.
LADY WOULD-BE: Surely, I had no purpose
  To scandalize your honors or my sex's.
10 AVOCATORE 3: We do believe it.
LADY WOULD-BE: Surely, you may believe it.
AVOCATORE 2: Madam, we do.
LADY WOULD-BE: Indeed, you may; my breeding
  Is not so coarse—
AVOCATORE 4:   We know it.
LADY WOULD-BE: To offend
  With pertinacy—
AVOCATORE 3:   Lady—
LADY WOULD-BE: Such a presence.
  No, surely.
AVOCATORE 1: We well think it.
LADY WOULD-BE: You may think it.
15 AVOCATORE 1: Let her o'ercome.—What witnesses have you
  To make good your report?
BONARIO: Our consciences.
CELIA: And heaven, that never fails the innocent.
AVOCATORE 4: These are no testimonies.
BONARIO: Not in your courts,
  Where multitude and clamor overcomes.
20 AVOCATORE 1: Nay, then you do wax insolent.

*(*VOLPONE *is brought in, as impotent.)*

*(*LADY WOULD-BE *kisses him.)*

VOLTORE: Here, here,
  The testimony comes that will convince
  And put to utter dumbness their bold tongues.
  See here, grave fathers, here's the ravisher,
  The rider on men's wives, the great impostor,
  The grand voluptuary! Do you not think   25
  These limbs should affect venery? Or these eyes
  Covet a concubine? Pray you, mark these hands.
  Are they not fit to stroke a lady's breasts?
  Perhaps he doth dissemble!
BONARIO: So he does.
VOLTORE: Would you ha' him tortured?   30
BONARIO: I would have him
  proved.
VOLTORE: Best try him, then, with goads or burning irons;
  Put him to the strappado; I have heard
  The rack hath cured the gout. Faith, give it him,
  And help him of a malady; be courteous.
  I'll undertake, before these honored fathers,   35
  He shall have yet as many left diseases
  As she has known adulterers, or thou strumpets.
  O, my most equal hearers, if these deeds,
  Acts of this bold and most exorbitant strain,
  May pass with sufferance, what one citizen   40
  But owes the forfeit of his life, yea, fame,
  To him that dares traduce him? Which of you
  Are safe, my honored fathers? I would ask,
  With leave of your grave fatherhoods, if their plot
  Have any face or color like to truth?   45
  Or if, unto the dullest nostril here,
  It smell not rank and most abhorrèd slander?
  I crave your care of this good gentleman,
  Whose life is much endangered by their fable;
  And, as for them, I will conclude with this,   50
  That vicious persons, when they are hot and fleshed
  In impious acts, their constancy abounds:
  Damned deeds are done with greatest confidence.
AVOCATORE 1: Take 'hem to custody, and sever them.
AVOCATORE 2: 'Tis pity two such prodigies should live. 55
AVOCATORE 1: Let the old gentleman be returned with care;

(Exeunt COMMENDATORI *with* VOLPONE.*)*

  I'm sorry our credulity wronged him.
AVOCATORE 4: These are two creatures!
AVOCATORE 3:   I have an earthquake
  in me!
AVOCATORE 2: Their shame, even in their cradles, fled their
  faces.
AVOCATORE 4: *(To* VOLTORE.*)* You've done a worthy service 60
  to the state, sir.
  In their discovery.
AVOCATORE 1:   You shall hear, ere night,
  What punishment the court decrees upon 'hem.
VOLTORE: We thank your fatherhoods.

---

7 **exorbitant** disorderly   13 **pertinacy** pertinacity

30 **proved** tested   38 **equal** impartial   51 **fleshed** confirmed
55 **prodigies** portents; monsters

(*Exeunt* AVOCATORI, NOTARIO, *and* COMMENDATORI *with* BONARIO *and* CELIA.)

                                        How like you it?

MOSCA: Rare!

   I'ld ha' your tongue, sir, tipped with gold for this;

65   I'ld ha' you be the heir to the whole city;

   The earth I'ld have want men, ere you want living.

   They're bound to erect your statue in Saint Mark's. —

   Signor Corvino, I would have you go

   And show yourself, that you have conquered.

CORVINO: Yes.

70 MOSCA: It was much better that you should profess

   Yourself a cuckold, thus, than that the other

   Should have been proved.

CORVINO: Nay, I considered that;

   Now, it is her fault.

MOSCA: Then, it had been yours.

CORVINO: True, I do doubt this advocate still.

MOSCA: I'faith,

75   You need not; I dare ease you of that care.

CORVINO: I trust thee, Mosca.

MOSCA: As your own soul, sir.

(*Exit* CORVINO.)

CORBACCIO: Mosca!

MOSCA: Now for your business, sir.

CORBACCIO: How! Ha' you business?

MOSCA: Yes, yours, sir.

CORBACCIO: O, none else?

MOSCA: None else, not I.

CORBACCIO: Be careful then.

MOSCA: Rest you with both your eyes, sir.

80 CORBACCIO: Dispatch it.

MOSCA: Instantly.

CORBACCIO: And look that all

   Whatever be put in: jewels, plate, moneys,

   Household stuff, bedding, curtains.

MOSCA: Curtain-rings, sir;

   Only the advocate's fee must be deducted.

CORBACCIO: I'll pay him now; you'll be too prodigal.

85 MOSCA: Sir, I must tender it.

CORBACCIO: Two chequins is well?

MOSCA: No, six, sir.

CORBACCIO: 'Tis too much.

MOSCA: He talked a great while —

   You must consider that, sir.

CORBACCIO: Well, there's three —

MOSCA: I'll give it him.

CORBACCIO: Do so, and there's for thee.

(*Exit.*)

MOSCA: Bountiful bones! What horrid, strange offense

90   Did he commit 'gainst nature in his youth

   Worthy this age? —(*To* VOLTORE.) You see, sir, how I work

   Unto your ends; take you no notice.

VOLTORE: No,

   I'll leave you.

(*Exit.*)

MOSCA: All is yours — the devil and all,

   Good advocate! —madam, I'll bring you home.

95 LADY WOULD-BE: No, I'll go see your patron.

MOSCA: That you shall not;

   I'll tell you why: my purpose is to urge

   My patron to reform his will; and for

   The zeal you've shown today, whereas before

   You were but third or fourth, you shall be now

   Put in the first, which would appear as begged   100

   If you were present. Therefore—

LADY WOULD-BE: You shall sway me.

(*Exeunt.*)

— ACT FIVE —

SCENE I

VOLPONE.

VOLPONE: Well, I am here, and all this brunt is past.

   I ne'er was in dislike with my disguise

   Till this fled moment; here 'twas good, in private;

   But in your public—*cavè*, whilst I breathe.

   'Fore God, my left leg 'gan to have the cramp,   5

   And I apprehended straight some power had struck me

   With a dead palsy. Well, I must be merry

   And shake it off. A many of these fears

   Would put me into some villainous disease

   Should they come thick upon me. I'll prevent 'hem.   10

   Give me a bowl of lusty wine to fright

   This humor from my heart.

(*He drinks.*)

                     Hum, hum, hum!

   'Tis almost gone already; I shall conquer.

   Any device now of rare, ingenious knavery

   That would possess me with a violent laughter   15

   Would make me up again.

(*Drinks again.*)

                 So, so, so, so!

   This heat is life; 'tis blood by this time! —Mosca!

SCENE II

MOSCA, VOLPONE, [NANO, CASTRONE *later*].

MOSCA: How now, sir? Does the day look clear again?

   Are we recovered? And wrought out of error

   Into our way to see our path before us?

   Is our trade free once more?

VOLPONE: Exquisite Mosca!

MOSCA: Was it not carried learnedly?   5

VOLPONE: And stoutly.

   Good wits are greatest in extremities.

MOSCA: It were a folly beyond thought to trust

   Any grand act unto a cowardly spirit.

   You are not taken with it enough, methinks?

VOLPONE: O, more than if I had enjoyed the wench: 10

   The pleasure of all womankind's not like it.

MOSCA: Why, now you speak, sir! We must here be fixed;

   Here we must rest. This is our masterpiece:

   We cannot think to go beyond this.

---

4 **cavè** beware

VOLPONE: True,
15   Th'ast played thy prize, my precious Mosca.
     MOSCA: Nay, sir,
     To gull the court—
     VOLPONE: And quite divert the torrent
     Upon the innocent.
     MOSCA: Yes, and to make
     So rare a music out of discords—
     VOLPONE: Right.
     That yet to me's the strangest—how th'ast borne it!—
20   That these, being so divided 'mongst themselves,
     Should not scent somewhat, or in me or thee,
     Or doubt their own side.
     MOSCA: True, they will not see't.
     Too much light blinds 'hem, I think. Each of 'hem
     Is so possessed and stuffed with his own hopes
25   That anything unto the contrary,
     Never so true or never so apparent,
     Never so palpable, they will resist it—
     VOLPONE: Like a temptation of the devil.
     MOSCA: Right, sir.
     Merchants may talk of trade, and your great signors
30   Of land that yields well; but, if Italy
     Have any glebe more fruitful than these fellows,
     I am deceived. Did not your advocate rare?
     VOLPONE: O—"My most honored fathers, my grave fa-
          thers,
     Under correction of your fatherhoods,
35   What face of truth is here? If these strange deeds
     May pass, most honored fathers"—I had much ado
     To forbear laughing.
     MOSCA: 'T seemed to me you sweat, sir.
     VOLPONE: In troth, I did a little.
     MOSCA: But confess, sir,
     Were you not daunted?
     VOLPONE: In good faith, I was
40   A little in a mist, but not dejected:
     Never but still myself.
     MOSCA: I think it, sir.
     Now, so truth help me, I must needs say this, sir,
     And out of conscience for your advocate:
     He's taken pains, in faith, sir, and deserved
45   (In my poor judgment, I speak it under favor,
     Not to contrary you, sir) very richly—
     Well—to be cozened.
     VOLPONE: Troth, and I think so too,
     By that I heard him in the latter end.
     MOSCA: O, but before, sir, had you heard him first
50   Draw it to certain heads, then aggravate,
     Then use his vehement figures—I looked still
     When he would shift a shirt; and doing this
     Out of pure love, no hope of gain—
     VOLPONE: 'Tis right.
     I cannot answer him, Mosca, as I would,
55   Not yet; but for thy sake, at thy entreaty,
     I will begin e'en now to vex 'hem all,
     This very instant.

MOSCA: Good, sir.
VOLPONE: Call the dwarf
     And eunuch forth.
     MOSCA: Castrone! Nano!
(Enter CASTRONE *and* NANO.)
NANO: Here.
VOLPONE: Shall we have a jig now?
MOSCA: What you please, sir.
VOLPONE: Go,
     Straight give out about the streets, you two,   60
     That I am dead; do it with constancy,
     Sadly, do you hear? Impute it to the grief
     Of this late slander.
(Exeunt CASTRONE *and* NANO.)
MOSCA: What do you mean, sir?
VOLPONE: O,
     I shall have, instantly, my vulture, crow,
     Raven, come flying hither on the news   65
     To peck for carrion, my she-wolf and all,
     Greedy and full of expectation—
MOSCA: And then to have it ravished from their mouths?
VOLPONE: 'Tis true. I will ha' thee put on a gown,
     And take upon thee as thou wert mine heir;   70
     Show 'hem a will. Open that chest, and reach
     Forth one of those that has the blanks. I'll straight
     Put in thy name.
MOSCA: It will be rare, sir.
(He gives him a paper.)
                              Ay,
     When they e'en gape and find themselves deluded—
MOSCA: Yes.   75
VOLPONE: And thou use them scurvily! Dispatch;
     Get on thy gown.
MOSCA: But what, sir, if they ask
     After the body?
VOLPONE: Say it was corrupted.
MOSCA: I'll say it stunk, sir, and was fain t'have it
     Coffined up instantly and sent away.
VOLPONE: Anything, what thou wilt. Hold, here's my will.   80
     Get thee a cap, a count-book, pen and ink,
     Papers afore thee; sit as thou wert taking
     An inventory of parcels. I'll get up
     Behind the curtain, on a stool, and hearken;
     Sometime peep over, see how they do look,   85
     With what degrees their blood doth leave their faces.
     O, 'twill afford me a rare meal of laughter!
MOSCA: Your advocate will turn stark dull upon it.
VOLPONE: It will take off his oratory's edge.
MOSCA: But your *clarissimo,* old round-back, he   90
     Will crump you like a hog-louse with the touch.
VOLPONE: And what Corvino?
MOSCA: O, sir, look for him
     Tomorrow morning with a rope and a dagger
     To visit all the streets; he must run mad.

---

21 **or** either   31 **glebe** cultivated land   47 **cozened** cheated   52 **shift a shirt** by the violence of his gestures   54 **answer** repay

61 **constancy** boldness   62 **sadly** seriously, gravely   90 *clarissimo* a Venetian grandee (here, Corbaccio)

95   My lady, too, that came into the court
     To bear false witness for your worship—
VOLPONE: Yes,
     And kissed me 'fore the fathers, when my face
     Flowed all with oils—
MOSCA: And sweat, sir. Why, your gold
     Is such another med'cine, it dries up
100 All those offensive savors! It transforms
     The most deformèd and restores 'hem lovely
     As 'twere the strange poetical girdle. Jove
     Could not invent t'himself a shroud more subtle
     To pass Acrisius' guards. It is the thing
105 Makes all the world her grace, her youth, her beauty.
VOLPONE: I think she loves me.
MOSCA: Who? The lady, sir?
     She's jealous of you.
VOLPONE: Dost thou say so?
MOSCA: Hark,
     There's some already.
VOLPONE: Look!
MOSCA: It is the vulture;
     He has the quickest scent.
VOLPONE: I'll to my place,
110 Thou to thy posture.
MOSCA: I am set.
VOLPONE: But, Mosca,
     Play the artificer now; torture 'hem rarely.

SCENE III

VOLTORE, MOSCA, [CORBACCIO, CORVINO, LADY WOULD-BE,
later], VOLPONE.

VOLTORE: How now, my Mosca?
MOSCA: *(Writing.)*   Turkey carpets, nine—
VOLTORE: Taking an inventory? That is well.
MOSCA: Two suits of bedding, tissue—
VOLTORE: Where's the will?
     Let me read that the while.

(Enter SERVANTS *carrying* CORBACCIO *in a chair.)*

CORBACCIO: So, set me down,
5   And get you home.

(Exeunt SERVANTS.*)*

VOLTORE: Is he come now to trouble us?
MOSCA: Of cloth of gold, two more—
CORBACCIO: Is it done, Mosca?
MOSCA: Of several vellets, eight—
VOLTORE: I like his care.
CORBACCIO: Dost thou not hear?

(Enter CORVINO.*)*

CORVINO: Ha! Is the hour come, Mosca?

*(*VOLPONE *peeps from behind a traverse.)*

VOLPONE: *(Aside.)* Ay, now they muster.
CORVINO: What does the advocate here?
     Or this Corbaccio?   10
CORBACCIO: What do these here?

(Enter LADY WOULD-BE.*)*

LADY WOULD-BE: Mosca!
     Is his thread spun?
MOSCA: Eight chests of linen—
VOLPONE: *(Aside.)*   O,
     My fine Dame Would-be, too!
CORVINO: Mosca, the will,
     That I may show it these and rid 'hem hence.
MOSCA: Six chests of diaper, four of damask—There!

(He hands them the will and continues to write.)

CORBACCIO: Is that the will?   15
MOSCA: Down-beds and bolsters—
VOLPONE: *(Aside.)*   Rare!
     Be busy still. Now they begin to flutter;
     They never think of me. Look, see, see, see!
     How their swift eyes run over the long deed
     Unto the name and to the legacies
     What is bequeathed them there.   20
MOSCA: Ten suits of hangings—
VOLPONE: *(Aside.)* Ay, i'their garters, Mosca! Now their hopes
     Are at the gasp.
VOLTORE: Mosca the heir!
CORBACCIO: What's that?
VOLPONE: *(Aside.)* My advocate is dumb. Look to my
     merchant;
     He has heard of some strange storm, a ship is lost,
     He faints. My lady will swoon. Old glazen-eyes,   25
     He hath not reached his despair yet.
CORBACCIO: All these
     Are out of hope; I'm sure the man.
CORVINO: But, Mosca—
MOSCA: Two cabinets—
CORVINO: Is this in earnest?
MOSCA: One
     Of ebony—
CORVINO: Or do you but delude me?
MOSCA: The other, mother of pearl—I am very busy.   30
     Good faith, it is a fortune thrown upon me—
     Item, one salt of agate—not my seeking.
LADY WOULD-BE: Do you hear, sir?
MOSCA: A perfumed box—
     Pray you forbear;
     You see I am troubled—made of an onyx—
LADY WOULD-BE: How?
MOSCA: Tomorrow, or next day, I shall be at leisure   35
     To talk with you all.
CORVINO: Is this my large hope's issue?
LADY WOULD-BE: Sir, I must have a fairer answer.
MOSCA: Madam!
     Marry, and shall: pray you, fairly quit my house.
     Nay, raise no tempest with your looks; but, hark you,
     Remember what your ladyship offered me   40

---

102 **strange poetical girdle** Jonson's marginal note at this point reads *"cestus"*—the girdle of Venus, into which were woven all her seductive powers   104 **Acrisius' guards** referring to Jove's seduction of Danaë, daughter of Acrisius, in a shower of gold
7 **vellets** velvets

14 **diaper** fine patterned linen   32 **salt** saltcellar

To put you in an heir; go to, think on't.
And what you said e'en your best madams did
For maintenance, and why not you? Enough.
Go home and use the poor Sir Pol, your knight, well,
45   For fear I tell some riddles. Go, be melancholic.

(Exit LADY WOULD-BE.*)*

VOLPONE: *(Aside.)* O, my fine devil!
CORVINO: Mosca, pray you a word.
MOSCA: Lord! Will not you take your dispatch hence yet?
    Methinks of all you should have been th'example.
    Why should you stay here? With what thought? What
        promise?
50   Hear you, do not you know I know you an ass?
    And that you would most fain have been a wittol
    If fortune would have let you? That you are
    A declared cuckold, on good terms? This pearl,
    You'll say, was yours? Right. This diamond?
55   I'll not deny't, but thank you. Much here else?
    It may be so. Why, think that these good works
    May help to hide you[r] bad. I'll not betray you,
    Although you be but extraordinary,
    And have it only in title, it sufficeth.
60   Go home, be melancholic too, or mad.

(Exit CORVINO.*)*

VOLPONE: *(Aside.)* Rare, Mosca! How his villainy becomes
    him!
VOLTORE: Certain he doth delude all these for me.
CORBACCIO: Mosca the heir?
VOLPONE: *(Aside.)*   O, his four eyes have found it!
CORBACCIO: I'm cozened, cheated, by a parasite slave!
65   Harlot, th'ast gulled me!
MOSCA: Yes, sir. Stop your mouth,
    Or I shall draw the only tooth is left.
    Are not you he, that filthy, covetous wretch,
    With the three legs, that here, in hope of pray,
    Have, any time this three year, snuffed about
70   With your most grov'ling nose and would have hired
    Me to the pois'ning of my patron, sir?
    Are not you he that have today in court
    Professed the disinheriting of your son?
    Perjured yourself? Go home, and die, and stink.
75   If you but croak a syllable, all comes out.
    Away, and call your porters! Go, go, stink!

(Exit CORBACCIO.*)*

VOLPONE: *(Aside.)* Excellent varlet!
VOLTORE: Now, my faithful Mosca,
    I find thy constancy—
MOSCA: Sir?
VOLTORE: Sincere.
MOSCA: *(Writing.)*   A table
    Of porphyry—I mar'l you'll be thus troublesome.
80 VOLTORE: Nay, leave off now; they are gone.
MOSCA: Why, who are you?
    What? Who did send for you? O, cry you mercy,
    Reverend sir! Good faith, I am grieved for you,

That any chance of mine should thus defeat
Your (I must needs say) most deserving travails;
But I protest, sir, it was cast upon me,   85
And I could almost wish to be without it,
But that the will o'th'dead must be observed.
Marry, my joy is that you need it not;
You have a gift, sir (thank your education),
Will never let you want while there are men   90
And malice to breed causes. Would I had
But half the like, for all my fortune, sir.
If I have any suits (as I do hope,
Things being so easy and direct, I shall not),
I will make bold with your obstreperous aid,   95
Conceive me, for your fee, sir. In meantime,
You that have so much law I know ha' the conscience
Not to be covetous of what is mine.
Good sir, I thank you for my plate; 'twill help
To set up a young man. Good faith, you look   100
As you were costive; best go home and purge, sir.

(Exit VOLTORE.*)*

VOLPONE: *(Coming out from hiding.)* Bid him eat lettuce
    well! My witty mischief,
    Let me embrace thee. O, that I could now
    Transform thee to a Venus—Mosca, go,
    Straight take my habit of *clarissimo*   105
    And walk the streets. Be seen, torment 'hem more:
    We must pursue as well as plot. Who would
    Have lost this feast?
MOSCA: I doubt it will lose them.
VOLPONE: O, my recovery shall recover all.
    That I could now but think on some disguise   110
    To meet 'hem in and ask 'hem questions.
    How I would vex 'hem still at every turn!
MOSCA: Sir, I can fit you.
VOLPONE: Canst thou?
MOSCA: Yes, I know
    One o' the *commendatori*, sir, like you;
    Him will I straight make drunk and bring you his habit.   115
VOLPONE: A rare disguise, and answering thy brain!
    O, I will be a sharp disease unto 'hem.
MOSCA: Sir, you must look for curses—
VOLPONE: Till they burst;
    The fox fares ever best when he is cursed.

(Exeunt.)

SCENE IV

PEREGRINE, MERCATORI 3, WOMAN *[later]*, [SIR] POLITIC.

PEREGRINE: Am I enough disguised?
MERCATORE 1:   I warrant you.
PEREGRINE: All my ambition is to fright him only.
MERCATORE 2: If you could ship him away, 'twere excellent.
MERCATORE 3: To Zant or to Aleppo?
PEREGRINE: Yes, and ha' his
    Adventures put i'th'*Book of Voyages*,   5
    And his gulled story registered for truth?

---

51 **wittol** a willing and contented cuckold   65 **harlot** knave   68 **three
legs** that is, with a cane   79 **mar'l** marvel

---

91 **causes** lawsuits   101 **costive** constipated   102 **lettuce** a laxative
5 *Book of Voyages* such as Hakluyt's

Well, gentlemen, when I am in a while,
And that you think us warm in our discourse,
Know your approaches.
MERCATORE 1:   Trust it to our care.

(*Exeunt* MERCATORI.)

(*Enter* WOMAN.)

10 PEREGRINE: Save you, fair lady! Is Sir Pol within?
WOMAN: I do not know, sir.
PEREGRINE: Pray you say unto him,
Here is a merchant, upon earnest business,
Desires to speak with him.
WOMAN: I will see, sir.
PEREGRINE: Pray you.

(*Exit* WOMAN.)

I see the family is all female here.

(*Re-enter* WOMAN.)

15 WOMAN: He says, sir, he has weighty affairs of state
That now require him whole; some other time
You may possess him.
PEREGRINE: Pray you say again,
If those require him whole, these will exact him,
Whereof I bring him tidings.

(*Exit* WOMAN.)

                        —What might be
20 His grave affair of state now? How to make
Bolognian sausages here in Venice, sparing
One o'th'ingredients?

(*Re-enter* WOMAN.)

WOMAN: Sir, he says he knows
By your word "tidings" that you are no statesman,
And therefore wills you stay.
PEREGRINE: Sweet, pray you return him:
25 I have not read so many proclamations,
And studied them for words, as he has done,
But—Here he deigns to come.

(*Exit* WOMAN.)

(*Enter* SIR POLITIC.)

SIR POLITIC: Sir, I must crave
Your courteous pardon. There hath chanced today
Unkind disaster 'twixt my lady and me,
30 And I was penning my apology
To give her satisfaction as you came now.
PEREGRINE: Sir, I am grieved I bring you worse disaster:
The gentleman you met at th'port today,
That told you he was newly arrived—
SIR POLITIC: Ay, was
35 A fugitive punk?
PEREGRINE: No, sir, a spy set on you,
And he has made relation to the Senate
That you professed to him to have a plot
To sell the state of Venice to the Turk.

SIR POLITIC: O me!
PEREGRINE: For which warrants are signed by this time
To apprehend you and to search your study   40
For papers—
SIR POLITIC: Alas, sir, I have none but notes
Drawn out of play-books—
PEREGRINE: All the better, sir.
SIR POLITIC: And some essays. What shall I do?
PEREGRINE: Sir, best
Convey yourself into a sugar-chest,
Or, if you could lie round, a frail were rare,   45
And I could send you aboard.
SIR POLITIC: Sir, I but talked so
For discourse' sake merely.

(*They knock without.*)

PEREGRINE: Hark, they are there!
SIR POLITIC: I am a wretch, a wretch!
PEREGRINE: What will you do, sir?
Ha' you ne'er a curran[t]-butt to leap into?
They'll put you to the rack; you must be sudden.   50
SIR POLITIC: Sir, I have an engine—
MERCATORE 3: (*Within.*)   Sir Politic Would-be?
MERCATORE 2: (*Within.*) Where is he?
SIR POLITIC: That I have thought
upon beforetime.
PEREGRINE: What is it?
SIR POLITIC: (*Aside.*)   I shall ne'er endure the torture!—
Marry, it is, sir, of a tortoise shell,
Fitted for these extremities. Pray you, sir, help me.   55

(PEREGRINE *helps him into a large tortoise shell.*)

Here I've a place, sir, to put back my legs;
Please you to lay it on, sir. With this cap
And my black gloves, I'll lie, sir, like a tortoise,
Till they are gone.
PEREGRINE: And call you this an engine?
SIR POLITIC: Mine own device.—Good sir, bid my wife's   60
women
To burn my papers.

(*Exit* PEREGRINE.)

(*They rush in.*)

MERCATORE 1:   Where's he hid?
MERCATORE 3:   We must,
And will, sure, find him.
MERCATORE 2:   Which is his study?

(*Re-enter* PEREGRINE.)

MERCATORE 1:   What
Are you, sir?
PEREGRINE: I'm a merchant that came here
To look upon this tortoise.
MERCATORE 3:   How?
MERCATORE 1:   Saint Mark!
What beast is this?   65
PEREGRINE: It is a fish.

---

18 **exact** finish off (completely); force   23 **tidings** instead of the statesman's "intelligence"   35 **punk** prostitute

45 **frail** rush basket   49 **curran[t]-butt** wine cask   51 **engine** mechanical contrivance

MERCATORE 2: *(Striking the shell.)* Come out here!

PEREGRINE: Nay, you may strike him, sir, and tread upon him;
   He'll bear a cart.

MERCATORE 1:   What, to run over him?

PEREGRINE: Yes.

MERCATORE 3: Let's jump upon him.

MERCATORE 2:   Can he not go?

PEREGRINE: He creeps, sir.

MERCATORE 1: Let's see him creep.

PEREGRINE: No, good sir, you will hurt him.

70 MERCATORE 2: Heart! I'll see him creep, or prick his guts.

MERCATORE 3: Come out here!

PEREGRINE: Pray you, sir.—(Creep a little!)

MERCATORE 1:   Forth!

MERCATORE 2: Yet further.

PEREGRINE: Good sir!—(Creep!)

MERCATORE 2:   We'll see his legs.

(They pull off the shell and discover him.)

MERCATORE 3: Godso, he has garters!

MERCATORE 1:   Ay, and gloves!

MERCATORE 2:   Is this
   Your fearful tortoise?

PEREGRINE: *(Discovering himself.)*
        Now, Sir Pol, we are even;

75 For your next project I shall be prepared.
  I am sorry for the funeral of your notes, sir.

MERCATORE 1: 'Twere a rare motion to be seen in Fleet Street!

MERCATORE 2: Ay, i'the term.

MERCATORE 1:   Or Smithfield, in the fair.

MERCATORE 3: Methinks 'tis but a melancholic sight.

80 PEREGRINE: Farewell, most politic tortoise!

(Exeunt PEREGRINE and MERCHANTS.)

(Re-enter WOMAN.)

SIR POLITIC: Where's my lady?
  Knows she of this?

WOMAN: I know not, sir.

SIR POLITIC: Inquire.—

(Exit WOMAN.)

  O, I shall be the fable of all feasts,
  The freight of the *gazetti*, ship-boys' tale,
  And, which is worst, even talk for ordinaries.

(Re-enter WOMAN.)

85 WOMAN: My lady's come most melancholic home
  And says, sir, she will straight to sea for physic.

SIR POLITIC: And I, to shun this place and clime forever,
  Creeping with house on back, and think it well
  To shrink my poor head in my politic shell.

(Exeunt.)

---

68 **go** walk   77 **motion** spectacle   78 **term** sitting of the sessions of court; **Smithfield** Bartholomew Fair, with its sideshows   83 **freight . . . gazetti** theme of the newspapers

SCENE V

VOLPONE, MOSCA; *the first in the habit of a commendatore; the other, of a clarissimo.*

VOLPONE: Am I then like him?

MOSCA: O, sir, you are he;
  No man can sever you.

VOLPONE: Good.

MOSCA: But what am I?

VOLPONE: 'Fore heaven, a brave *clarissimo*; thou becom'st it!
  Pity thou wert not born one.

MOSCA: *(Aside.)*   If I hold
  My made one, 'twill be well.   5

VOLPONE: I'll go and see
  What news first at the court.

(Exit.)

MOSCA: Do so.—My fox
  Is out on his hole; and, ere he shall re-enter,
  I'll make him languish in his borrowed case,
  Except he come to composition with me.—
  Androgyno, Castrone, Nano!   10

(Enter ANDROGYNO, CASTRONE, and NANO.)

ALL: Here!

MOSCA: Go, recreate yourselves abroad; go, sport.

(Exeunt the others.)

  So, now I have the keys and am possessed.
  Since he will needs be dead afore his time,
  I'll bury him or gain by him. I'm his heir,
  And so will keep me till he share at least.   15
  To cozen him of all were but a cheat
  Well placed; no man would construe it a sin.
  Let his sport pay for't: this is called the fox-trap.

(Exit.)

SCENE VI

CORBACCIO, CORVINO, VOLPONE *[later]*.

CORBACCIO: They say the court is set.

CORVINO: We must maintain
  Our first tale good, for both our reputations.

CORBACCIO: Why, mine's no tale! My son would there have killed me.

CORVINO: That's true; I had forgot. Mine is, I am sure.
  But for your will, sir—   5

CORBACCIO: Ay, I'll come upon him
  For that hereafter, now his patron's dead.

(Enter VOLPONE.)

VOLPONE: Signor Corvino! And Corbaccio! Sir,
  Much joy unto you.

CORVINO: Of what?

VOLPONE: The sudden good
  Dropped down upon you—

CORBACCIO: Where?

---

8 **case** disguise   9 **composition** terms, agreement

VOLPONE: *(Aside.)*   And none knows how.—
10 From old Volpone, sir.
CORBACCIO: Out, arrant knave!
VOLPONE: Let not your too much wealth, sir, make you
      furious.
CORBACCIO: Away, thou varlet!
VOLPONE: Why, sir?
CORBACCIO: Dost thou mock me?
VOLPONE: You mock the world, sir; did not you change wills?
CORBACCIO: Out, harlot!
VOLPONE: O! Be like you are the man,
15   Signor Corvino? Faith, you carry it well;
      You grow not mad withal: I love your spirit.
      You are not over-leavened with your fortune.
      You should ha' some would swell now like a wine-fat
      With such an autumn.—Did he gi' you all, sir?
20 CORVINO: Avoid, you rascal!
VOLPONE: Troth, your wife has shown
      Herself a very woman! But you are well;
      You need not care. You have a good estate
      To bear it out, sir, better by this chance—
      Except Corbaccio have a share?
CORBACCIO: Hence, varlet!
25 VOLPONE: You will not be a'known, sir? Why, 'tis wise.
      Thus do all gamesters, at all games, dissemble.
      No man will seem to win.

(Exeunt CORVINO *and* CORBACCIO.*)*
                          —Here comes my vulture,
      Heaving his beak up i'the air, and snuffing.

SCENE VII

VOLTORE, VOLPONE.

VOLTORE: Outstripped thus, by a parasite! A slave,
      Would run on errands, and make legs for crumbs!
      Well, what I'll do—
VOLPONE: The court stays for you[r] worship.
      I e'en rejoice, sir, at your worship's happiness
5   And that it fell into so learned hands,
      That understand the fingering.
VOLTORE: What do you mean?
VOLPONE: I mean to be a suitor to your worship
      For the small tenement, out of reparations,
      That at the end of your long row of houses,
10   By the *Pescheria*—it was, in Volpone's time,
      Your predecessor, ere he grew diseased,
      A handsome, pretty, customed bawdy-house
      As any in Venice (none dispraised)
      But fell with him. His body and that house
15   Decayed together.
VOLTORE: Come, sir, leave your prating.
VOLPONE: Why, if your worship give me but your hand
      That I may ha' the refusal, I have done.
      'Tis a mere toy to you, sir, candle-rents.
      As your learned worship knows—

VOLTORE: What do I know?
VOLPONE: Marry, no end of your wealth, sir; God decrease it!   20
VOLTORE: Mistaking knave! What, mock'st thou my
      misfortune?
VOLPONE: His blessing on your heart, sir; would 'twere more!

(Exit VOLTORE.*)*
                —Now, to my first again, at the next corner.

SCENE VIII

CORBACCIO, CORVINO, *(*MOSCA, *passant)*, VOLPONE.

CORBACCIO: See, in our habit! See the impudent varlet!
CORVINO: That I could shoot mine eyes at him, like gunstones!
VOLPONE: But is this true, sir, of the parasite?
CORBACCIO: Again t'afflict us? Monster!
VOLPONE: In good faith, sir,
      I'm heartily grieved a beard of your grave length   5
      Should be so over-reached. I never brooked
      That parasite's hair; methought his nose should cozen.
      There still was somewhat in his look did promise
      The bane of a *clarissimo*.
CORBACCIO: Knave—
VOLPONE: Methinks
      Yet you, that are so traded i'the world,   10
      A witty merchant, the fine bird Corvino,
      That should have such moral emblems on your name,
      Should not have sung your shame and dropped your cheese
      To let the fox laugh at your emptiness.
CORVINO: Sirrah, you think the privilege of the place   15
      And your red, saucy cap, that seems to me
      Nailed to your jolt-head with those two chequins
      Can warrant your abuses. Come you hither:
      You shall perceive, sir, I dare beat you. Approach!
VOLPONE: No haste, sir. I do know your valor well   20
      Since you durst publish what you are, sir.
CORVINO: Tarry;
      I'ld speak with you.
VOLPONE: Sir, sir, another time—
CORVINO: Nay, now.
VOLPONE: O God, sir! I were a wise man
      Would stand the fury of a distracted cuckold.

*(*MOSCA *walks by 'hem.)*

CORBACCIO: What! Come again?   25
VOLPONE: *(Aside.)*   Upon 'hem, Mosca; save me.
CORBACCIO: The air's infected where he breathes.
CORVINO: Let's fly him.

(Exeunt CORVINO *and* CORBACCIO.*)*

VOLPONE: Excellent basilisk! Turn upon the vulture.

SCENE IX

VOLTORE, MOSCA, VOLPONE.

VOLTORE: Well, flesh-fly, it is summer with you now;
      Your winter will come on.

---

12 **varlet** base person; but here, also court sergeant   18 **wine-fat** wine
vat   25 **a'known** acknowledged, recognized

2 **make legs** bows   8 **reparations** repairs   10 *Pescheria* fish market
12 **customed** well-frequented   18 **candle-rents** rents from deteriorat-
ing properties

---

s.d. *passant* passing (over the stage)   17 **chequins** here, gilt buttons
27 **basilisk** a fabled serpent whose glance was fatal

1 **flesh-fly** definition of Mosca's name

MOSCA: Good advocate,
Pray thee not rail nor threaten out of place thus;
Thou'lt make a solecism, as Madam says.
5   Get you a biggen more; your brain breaks loose.

(Exit.)

VOLTORE: Well, sir.
VOLPONE: Would you ha' me beat the insolent slave?
Throw dirt upon his first good clothes?
VOLTORE: This same
Is doubtless some familiar!
VOLPONE: Sir, the court,
In troth, stays for you. I am mad, a mule
10 That never read Justinian should get up
And ride an advocate! Had you no quirk
To avoid gullage, sir, by such a creature?
I hope you do but jest; he has not done't;
This's but confederacy to blind the rest.
15 You are the heir?
VOLTORE: A strange, officious,
Troublesome knave! Thou dost torment me.
VOLPONE: *(Aside.)* I know.—
It cannot be, sir, that you should be cozened;
'Tis not within the wit of man to do it:
You are so wise, so prudent, and 'tis fit
20 That wealth and wisdom still should go together.

(Exeunt.)

SCENE X

AVOCATORI 4, NOTARIO, COMMENDATORI, BONARIO, CELIA,
CORBACCIO, CORVINO, VOLTORE, VOLPONE *[the last two later].*

AVOCATORE 1: Are all the parties here?
NOTARIO: All but the advocate.
AVOCATORE 2: And here he comes.

(Enter VOLTORE *and* VOLPONE.*)*

AVOCATORE [1]: Then bring 'hem forth to
sentence.
VOLTORE: O, my most honored fathers, let your mercy
Once win upon your justice to forgive—
5   I am distracted—
VOLPONE: *(Aside.)* What will he do now?
VOLTORE: O,
I know not what t'address myself to first,
Whether your fatherhoods or these innocents—
CORVINO: *(Aside.)* Will he betray himself?
VOLTORE: Whom equally
I have abused, out of most covetous ends—
10 CORVINO: *(Aside.)* The man is mad!
CORBACCIO: *(Aside.)* What's that?
CORVINO: *(Aside.)* He is possessed.
VOLTORE: For which, now struck in conscience, here I
prostrate
Myself at your offended feet, for pardon.

---

5 **biggen** lawyer's cap   8 **familiar** attendant spirit   10 **Justinian** the
6th-century Byzantine emperor who ordered the compilation of
Roman law   11 **quirk** trick
10 **possessed** i.e., by the devil

AVOCATORE 1, 2: Arise.
CELIA: O heaven, how just thou art!
VOLPONE: *(Aside.)* I'm caught
I'mine own noose—
CORVINO: *(To* CORBACCIO.*)* Be constant, sir; naught now
Can help but impudence.   15
AVOCATORE 1: Speak forward.
COMMENDATORE: Silence!
VOLTORE: It is not passion in me, reverend fathers,
But only conscience, conscience, my good sires,
That makes me now tell truth. That parasite,
That knave, hath been the instrument of all.
AVOCATORE [1]: Where is that knave? Fetch him.   20
VOLPONE: I go.

(Exit.)

CORVINO: Grave fathers,
This man's distracted; he confessed it now;
For, hoping to be old Volpone's heir,
Who now is dead—
AVOCATORE 3: How!
AVOCATORE 2: Is Volpone dead?
CORVINO: Dead since, grave fathers—
BONARIO: O sure vengeance!
AVOCATORE 1: Stay;   25
Then he was no deceiver?
VOLTORE: O, no, none;
The parasite, grave fathers.
CORVINO: He does speak
Out of mere envy 'cause the servant's made
The thing he gaped for. Please your fatherhoods,
This is the truth, though I'll not justify
The other, but he may be somedeal faulty.   30
VOLTORE: Ay, to your hopes, as well as mine, Corvino;
But I'll use modesty. Pleaseth your wisdoms
To view these certain notes and but confer them;
As I hope favor, they shall speak clear truth.
CORVINO: The devil has entered him!   35
BONARIO: Or bides in you.
AVOCATORE 4: We have done ill, by a public officer
To send for him, if he be heir.
AVOCATORE 2: By whom?
AVOCATORE 4: Him that they call the parasite.
AVOCATORE 3: 'Tis true;
He is a man of great estate now left.
AVOCATORE 4: Go you, and learn his name; and say the court 40
Entreats his presence here but to the clearing
Of some few doubts.

(Exit NOTARIO.*)*

AVOCATORE 2: This same's a labyrinth!
AVOCATORE 1: Stand you unto your first report?
CORVINO: My state,
My life, my fame—
BONARIO: Where is't?
CORVINO: Are at the stake.
AVOCATORE 1: Is yours so, too?   45

---

30 **somedeal** somewhat   32 **modesty** moderation   33 **confer** compare

CORBACCIO: The advocate's a knave,
And has a forkèd tongue—
AVOCATORE 2:   Speak to the point.
CORBACCIO: So is the parasite, too.
AVOCATORE 1:   This is confusion.
VOLTORE: I do beseech your fatherhoods, read but those—

(He gives them papers.)

CORVINO: And credit nothing the false spirit hath writ;
50   It cannot be but he is possessed, grave fathers.

(Exeunt.)

SCENE XI

VOLPONE, NANO, ANDROGYNO, CASTRONE, *[the last three later]*.

VOLPONE: To make a snare for mine own neck! And run
My head into it wilfully, with laughter!
When I had newly 'scaped, was free and clear!
Out of mere wantonness! O, the dull devil
5   Was in this brain of mine when I devised it,
And Mosca gave it second; he must now
Help to sear up this vein, or we bleed dead.—

(Enter NANO, ANDROGYNO, and CASTRONE.)

How now! Who let you loose? Whither go you now?
What, to buy gingerbread or to drown kitlings?
10   NANO: Sir, Master Mosca called us out of doors,
And bid us all go play, and took the keys.
ANDROGYNO: Yes.
VOLPONE: Did Master Mosca take the keys? Why, so!
I am farther in. These are my fine conceits!
I must be merry, with a mischief to me!
15   What a vile wretch was I, that could not bear
My fortune soberly. I must ha' my crotchets
And my conundrums! Well, go you and seek him:
His meaning may be truer than my fear.
Bid him, he straight come to me to the court;
20   Thither will I and, if 't be possible,
Unscrew my advocate upon new hopes.
When I provoked him, then I lost myself.

(Exeunt.)

SCENE XII

AVOCATORI, *etc.*

AVOCATORE 1: These things can ne'er be reconciled. He, here,

(He points to VOLTORE's papers.)

Professeth that the gentleman was wronged
And that the gentlewoman was brought thither,
Forced by her husband, and there left.
VOLTORE: Most true.
5   CELIA: How ready is heaven to those that pray!
AVOCATORE 1:   But that
Volpone would have ravished her, he holds
Utterly false, knowing his impotence.
CORVINO: Grave fathers, he is possessed; again, I say,

Possessed. Nay, if there be possession
And obsession, he has both.   10
AVOCATORE 3:   Here comes our officer.

(Enter VOLPONE, still disguised.)

VOLPONE: The parasite will straight be here, grave fathers.
AVOCATORE 4: You might invent some other name, sir varlet.
AVOCATORE 3: Did not the notary meet him?
VOLPONE: Not that I know.
AVOCATORE 4: His coming will clear all.
AVOCATORE 2:   Yes, it is misty.
VOLTORE: May 't please your fatherhoods—   15

(VOLPONE whispers to the Advocate.)

VOLPONE: Sir, the parasite
Willed me to tell you that his master lives;
That you are still the man; your hopes the same;
And this was only a jest—
VOLTORE: How?
VOLPONE: Sir, to try
If you were firm and how you stood affected.
VOLTORE: Art sure he lives?   20
VOLPONE: Do I live, sir?
VOLTORE: O me!
I was to[o] violent.
VOLPONE: Sir, you may redeem it:
They said you were possessed; fall down, and seem so.
I'll help to make it good.

(VOLTORE falls.)

                              —God bless the man!—
(Stop your wind hard, and swell.)—See, see, see, see!
He vomits crooked pins! His eyes are set   25
Like a dead hare's hung in a poulter's shop!
His mouth's running away! Do you see, signor?
Now, 'tis his belly.
CORVINO: *(Aside.)* Ay, the devil!
VOLPONE: Now in his throat.
CORVINO: *(Aside.)*   Ay, I perceive it plain.
VOLPONE: 'Twill out, 'twill out! Stand clear. See where it   30
flies!
In shape of a blue toad, with a bat's wings!—
Do not you see it, sir?
CORBACCIO: What? I think I do.
CORVINO: 'Tis too manifest.
VOLPONE: Look! He comes t'himself.
VOLTORE: Where am I?
VOLPONE: Take good heart; the worst is past, sir.
You are dispossessed.   35
AVOCATORE 1:   What accident is this?
AVOCATORE [2]: Sudden, and full of wonder!
AVOCATORE 3:   If he were
Possessed, as it appears, all this is nothing.
CORVINO: He has been often subject to these fits.
AVOCATORE 1: Show him that writing.—Do you know it, sir?
VOLPONE: *(Whispering to VOLTORE.)* Deny it, sir; forswear it;   40
know it not.

---

9 **kitlings** kittens

9–10 **possession and obsession** possessed by the devil, from within the body and from without

VOLTORE: Yes, I do know it well; it is my hand:
   But all that it contains is false.
BONARIO: O, practice!
AVOCATORE 2: What maze is this!
AVOCATORE 1:   Is he not guilty then,
   Whom you, there, name the parasite?
VOLTORE: Grave fathers,
45   No more than his good patron, old Volpone.
AVOCATORE 4: Why, he is dead.
VOLTORE: O, no, my honored fathers.
   He lives—
AVOCATORE 1: How! Lives?
VOLTORE: Lives.
AVOCATORE 2:   This is subtler yet!
AVOCATORE 3: You said he was dead.
VOLTORE: Never.
AVOCATORE 3:   You said so!
CORVINO: I heard so.
AVOCATORE 4: Here comes the gentleman; make him way.

(Enter MOSCA.)

AVOCATORE 3:   A stool!
50 AVOCATORE 4: *(Aside.)* A proper man and, were Volpone
    dead,
   A fit match for my daughter.
AVOCATORE 3:   Give him way.
VOLPONE: *(Aside to* MOSCA.) Mosca, I was a'most lost; the
    advocate
   Had betrayed all; but now it is recovered.
   All's o'the hinge again.—Say I am living.
55 MOSCA: What busy knave is this?—Most reverend fathers,
   I sooner had attended your grave pleasures,
   But that my order for the funeral
   Of my dear patron did require me—
VOLPONE: *(Aside.)*   Mosca!
MOSCA: Whom I intend to bury like a gentleman.
60 VOLPONE: *(Aside.)* Ay, quick, and cozen me of all.
AVOCATORE 2:   Still stranger!
   More intricate!
AVOCATORE 1:   And come about again!
AVOCATORE 4: *(Aside.)* It is a match: my daughter is bestowed.
MOSCA: *(Aside to* VOLPONE.) Will you gi' me half?
VOLPONE: *(Aside.)*   First I'll be hanged.
MOSCA: *(Aside.)*   I know
   Your voice is good; cry not so loud.
AVOCATORE 1:   Demand
65 The advocate.—Sir, did not you affirm
   Volpone was alive.
VOLPONE: Yes, and he is;
   This gent'man told me so.

(Aside to MOSCA.)

           Thou shalt have half.
MOSCA: Whose drunkard is this same? Speak, some that know
   him.
   I never saw his face.—*(Aside to* VOLPONE.) I cannot now
70 Afford it to you so cheap.

VOLPONE: *(Aside.)*   No?
AVOCATORE 1:   What say you?
VOLTORE: The officer told me.
VOLPONE: I did, grave fathers,
   And will maintain he lives with mine own life,
   And that this creature told me.—

(He points to MOSCA.)

                (Aside.) I was born
   With all good stars my enemies!
MOSCA: Most grave fathers,
   If such insolence as this must pass   75
   Upon me, I am silent; 'twas not this
   For which you sent, I hope.
AVOCATORE 2:   Take him away.
VOLPONE: *(Aside.)* Mosca!
AVOCATORE 3:   Let him be whipped.
VOLPONE: *(Aside.)*   Wilt thou betray me?
   Cozen me?
AVOCATORE 3: And taught to bear himself
   Toward a person of his rank.   80
AVOCATORE 4:   Away!

(The COMMENDATORE *seizes* VOLPONE.)

MOSCA: I humbly thank your fatherhoods.
VOLPONE: *(Aside.)*   Soft, soft! Whipped?
   And [lose] all that I have? If I confess,
   It cannot be much more.
AVOCATORE 4: *(To* MOSCA.) Sir, are you married?
VOLPONE: *(Aside.)* They'll be allied anon; I must be resolute:
   The fox shall here uncase.   85

(He puts off his disguise.)

MOSCA: Patron!
VOLPONE: Nay, now
   My ruins shall not come alone; your match
   I'll hinder sure. My substance shall not glue you,
   Nor screw you, into a family.
MOSCA: Why, patron!
VOLPONE: I am Volpone, and this is my knave;

(He points to MOSCA.)

   This *(To* VOLTORE.), his own knave; this *(To* CORBACCIO.), 90
    avarice's fool;
   This *(To* CORVINO.), a chimera of wittol, fool, and knave.
   And, reverend fathers, since we all can hope
   Naught but a sentence, let's not now despair it.
   You hear me brief.
CORVINO: May it please your fatherhoods—
COMMENDATORE: Silence!
AVOCATORE 1: The knot is now undone by miracle!   95
AVOCATORE 2: Nothing can be more clear.
AVOCATORE 3:   Or can more prove
   These innocent.
AVOCATORE 1:   Give 'hem their liberty.
BONARIO: Heaven could not long let such gross crimes be hid.
AVOCATORE 2: If this be held the highway to get riches,
   May I be poor!   100
AVOCATORE 3:   This's not the gain, but torment.

---

42 **practice** deceit 50 **proper** handsome 60 **quick** alive 64 **de-mand** question

91 **chimera** monster

AVOCATORE 1: These possess wealth as sick men possess
   fevers,
  Which trulier may be said to possess them.
AVOCATORE 2: Disrobe that parasite.
CORVINO: ⎫   Most honored
MOSCA: ⎬ fathers—
AVOCATORE 1: Can you plead aught to stay the course of
   justice?
105   If you can, speak.
CORVINO: ⎫
          ⎬ We beg favor.
VOLTORE: ⎭
CELIA: And mercy.
AVOCATORE 1: You hurt your innocence, suing for the guilty.
  Stand forth; and, first, the parasite. You appear
  T'have been the chiefest minister, if not plotter,
  In all these lewd impostures; and now, lastly,
110   Have, with your impudence, abused the court
  And habit of a gentleman of Venice,
  Being a fellow of no birth or blood:
  For which our sentence is, first thou be whipped,
  Then live perpetual prisoner in our galleys.
115 VOLPONE: I thank you for him.
MOSCA: Bane to thy wolfish nature!
AVOCATORE 1: Deliver him to the *Saffi*.—

(MOSCA *is led out*.)

                      Thou, Volpone,
  By blood and rank a gentleman, canst not fall
  Under like censure; but our judgment on thee
  Is that thy substance all be straight confiscate
120   To the hospital of the *Incurabili*,
  And, since the most was gotten by imposture,
  By feigning lame, gout, palsy, and such diseases,
  Thou art to lie in prison, cramped with irons,
  Till thou be'st sick and lame indeed. Remove him!
125 VOLPONE: This is called mortifying of a fox.
AVOCATORE 1: Thou, Voltore, to take away the scandal
  Thou hast giv'n all worthy men of thy profession,
  Art banished from their fellowship and our state.—
  Corbaccio, bring him near! We here possess

Thy son of all thy state and confine thee   130
To the monastery of San Spirito,
Where, since thou knew'st not how to live well here,
Thou shalt be learned to die well.
CORBACCIO: Ha! What said he?
COMMENDATORE: You shall know anon, sir.
AVOCATORE [1]:   Thou, Corvino,
  shalt
  Be straight embarked from thine own house and rowed   135
  Round about Venice, through the Grand Canal,
  Wearing a cap with fair long ass's ears
  Instead of horns; and so to mount—a paper
  Pinned on thy breast—to the *Berlin[a]*—
CORVINO: Yes,
  And have mine eyes beat out with stinking fish,   140
  Bruised fruit, and rotten eggs—'Tis well; I'm glad
  I shall not see my shame yet.
AVOCATORE 1:   And to expiate
  Thy wrongs done to thy wife, thou art to send her
  Home to her father, with her dowry trebled:
  And these are all your judgments—   145
ALL: Honored fathers!
AVOCATORE 1: Which may not be revoked. Now you begin,
  When crimes are done and past, and to be punished,
  To think what your crimes are. Away with them!
  Let all that see these vices thus rewarded
  Take heart and love to study 'hem. Mischiefs feed   150
  Like beasts till they be fat, and then they bleed.

(*Exeunt*.)

(VOLPONE [*comes forward*].)

VOLPONE: The seasoning of a play is the applause.
  Now, though the fox be punished by the laws,
  He yet doth hope there is no suff'ring due
  For any fact which he hath done 'gainst you.   155
  If there be, censure him: here he doubtful stands.
  If not, fare jovially, and clap your hands.

---

130 **state** estate   139 **berlina** pillory   155 **fact** crime

CRITICAL CONTEXTS

**SIR PHILIP
SIDNEY**
(1554–1586)

**FROM *APOLOGY
FOR POETRY*
(1598)**
EDITED BY
FORREST G. ROBINSON

Philip Sidney was one of the preeminent courtiers of his day. He was a familiar figure at the court of Queen Elizabeth I, led an ill-fated military expedition to the Netherlands (where he was fatally wounded), wrote an important sonnet sequence, Astrophil and Stella, *and a prose romance,* Arcadia. *His* Apology for Poetry *develops a defense of poets and poetry based on their ability to offer a fictive "golden world," an idealized image of reality that can edify, entertain, and instruct.*

. . . There is no art delivered to mankind that hath not the works of nature for his principal object, without which they could not consist, and on which they so depend, as they become actors and players, as it were, of what nature will have set forth. So doth the astronomer look upon the stars, and by that he seeth, setteth down what order nature hath taken therein. So do the geometrician and arithmetician in their diverse sorts of quantities. So doth the musician in times tell you which by nature agree, which not. The natural philosopher thereon hath his name, and the moral philosopher standeth upon the natural virtues, vices, and passions of man; and follow nature (saith he) therein, and thou shalt not err. The lawyer saith what men have determined; the historian what men have done. The grammarian speaketh only of the rules of speech, and the rhetorician and logician, considering what in nature will soonest prove and persuade, thereon give artificial[1] rules, which still are compassed within the circle of a question, according to the proposed matter. The physician weigheth the nature of a man's body, and the nature of things helpful or hurtful unto it. And the metaphysic, though it be in the second and abstract notions, and therefore be counted supernatural, yet doth he indeed build upon the depth of nature. Only the poet, disdaining to be tied to any such subjection, lifted up with the vigor of his own invention, doth grow in effect another nature, in making things either better than nature bringeth forth, or quite anew, forms such as never were in nature, as the Heroes, Demigods, Cyclops, Chimeras, Furies, and such like; so as he goeth hand in hand with nature, not enclosed within the narrow warrant of her gifts, but freely ranging only within the zodiac of his own wit.

Nature never set forth the earth in so rich tapestry as divers poets have done, neither with pleasant rivers, fruitful trees, sweet smelling flowers, nor whatsoever else may make the too much loved earth more lovely. Her world is brazen, the poets only deliver a golden. . . .

Our tragedies and comedies (not without cause cried out against), observing rules neither of honest civility nor of skillful poetry, excepting *Gorboduc*[2] (again I say, of those that I have seen), which notwithstanding, as it is full of stately speeches and well sounding phrases, climbing to the height of Seneca his[3] style, and as full of notable morality, which it doth most delightfully teach, and so obtain the very end of poesy; yet in troth it is very defectious in the circumstances, which grieveth me, because it might not remain as an exact model of all tragedies. For it is faulty both in place and time, the two necessary companions of all corporal actions. For where the stage should always represent but one place, and the uttermost time presupposed in it should be, both by Aristotle's precept and common reason, but one day, there is both many days and many places inartificially[4] imagined.

But if it be so in *Gorboduc*, how much more in all the rest? where you shall have Asia of the one side, and Afric of the other, and so many other under-kingdoms, that the player, when he cometh in, must ever begin with telling where he is, or else the tale will not be conceived. Now ye shall have three ladies walk to gather flowers, and then we must believe the stage to be a garden. By and by we hear news of shipwreck in the same place, and then we are to blame if we accept it not for a rock. Upon the back of that comes out a hideous monster with fire and smoke, and then the miserable beholders are bound to take it for a cave. While in the meantime two armies fly in, represented with four swords and bucklers, and then what hard heart will not receive it for a pitched field?

[1] **artificial** humanly contrived, rather than natural
[2] *Gorboduc* an early English play (first performed in 1562), modelled on the tragedies of Seneca
[3] **Seneca his** Seneca's
[4] **inartificially** artlessly

Now of time they are much more liberal, for ordinary it is that two young princes fall in love. After many traverses, she is got with child, delivered of a fair boy, he is lost, groweth a man, falls in love, and is ready to get another child, and all this in two hours' space: which, how absurd it is in sense, even sense may imagine, and art hath taught, and all ancient examples justified, and at this day, the ordinary players in Italy will not err in. Yet will some bring in an example of *Eunuchus* in Terence, that containeth matter of two days, yet far short of twenty years. True it is, and so was it to be played in two days, and so fitted to the time it set forth. And though Plautus hath in one place done amiss, let us hit with him, and not miss with him. But they will say, how then shall we set forth a story which containeth both many places and many times? And do they not know that a tragedy is tied to the laws of poesy, and not of history, not bound to follow the story, but having liberty, either to feign a quite new matter, or to frame the history to the most tragical conveniency? Again, many things may be told which cannot be showed, if they know the difference betwixt reporting and representing. . . .

Mikhail Bakhtin, a major Russian philosopher, linguist, and literary theorist, spent much of his career attempting to subvert the Stalinist oppression of intellectuals in the Soviet Union of the 1930s. His book on Rabelais, written in the 1930s, was published only in 1965. This selection, on the "grotesque body," develops an influential reading of how the body can be used to represent the social order, its dominant classes and its points of resistance. Although Bakhtin developed this reading of the body in connection with Rabelais's novels, it is applicable to the grotesque bodies appearing on the English stage as well—insatiable Volpone, or Caliban.

MIKHAIL BAKHTIN
(1895–1975)

FROM *RABELAIS AND HIS WORLD* (1965)

TRANSLATED BY
HÉLÈNE ISWOLSKY

. . . We find at the basis of grotesque imagery a special concept of the body as a whole and of the limits of this whole. The confines between the body and the world and between separate bodies are drawn in the grotesque genre quite differently than in the classic and naturalist images. We have already seen this difference in a number of Rabelaisian images. In the present chapter we must broaden our observations, systematize them, and disclose the sources of Rabelais' grotesque concept of the body.

But let us first have a look at another example cited by Schneegans: the caricature of Napoleon and the exaggeration of the size of his nose. According to Schneegans, the grotesque starts when the exaggeration reaches fantastic dimensions, the human nose being transformed into a snout or beak. We shall not discuss the nature of these caricatures per se; it is but superficial satire, deprived of true grotesque character. We are interested in the theme of the nose itself, which occurs throughout world literature in nearly every language, as well as in abusive and degrading gesticulations. Schneegans correctly points out the grotesque character of the transformation of the human element into an animal one; the combination of human and animal traits is, as we know, one of the most ancient grotesque forms. But the author does not grasp the meaning of the grotesque image of the nose: that it always symbolizes the phallus. Laurent Joubert, the famous sixteenth-century physician and a contemporary of Rabelais, whose theory of laughter we have already mentioned, wrote a book on popular superstitions in medicine.[1] In Part 5, Chapter 6 of this book he speaks of the popular belief that the size and potency of the genital organs can be inferred from the dimensions and form of the nose. Friar John also expresses this belief in his monastic jargon. Such is the usual interpretation of this image in the literature of the Middle Ages and the Renaissance, linked with the popular-festive system. The most widely known example of this symbolism is the famous carnival "Dance of the Noses" of Hans Sachs *(Nasentanz).*

Of all the features of the human face, the nose and mouth play the most important part in the grotesque image of the body; the head, ears, and nose also acquire a grotesque character when they adopt the animal form or that of inanimate objects. The eyes have no part in these comic images; they express an individual, so to speak, self-sufficient human life, which is not essential to the

---

[1] Laurent Joubert, *Erreurs populaires et propos vulgaires touchant la médecine et le régime de santé.* Bordeaux, 1579.

grotesque. The grotesque is interested only in protruding eyes, like the eyes of the stutterer in the scene described earlier. It is looking for that which protrudes from the body, all that seeks to go out beyond the body's confines. Special attention is given to the shoots and branches, to all that prolongs the body and links it to other bodies or to the world outside. Moreover, the bulging eyes manifest a purely bodily tension. But the most important of all human features for the grotesque is the mouth. It dominates all else. The grotesque face is actually reduced to the gaping mouth; the other features are only a frame encasing this wide-open bodily abyss.

The grotesque body, as we have often stressed, is a body in the act of becoming. It is never finished, never completed; it is continually built, created, and builds and creates another body. Moreover, the body swallows the world and is itself swallowed by the world (let us recall the grotesque image in the episode of Gargantua's birth on the feast of cattle-slaughtering). This is why the essential role belongs to those parts of the grotesque body in which it outgrows its own self, transgressing its own body, in which it conceives a new, second body: the bowels and the phallus. These two areas play the leading role in the grotesque image, and it is precisely for this reason that they are predominantly subject to positive exaggeration, to hyperbolization; they can even detach themselves from the body and lead an independent life, for they hide the rest of the body, as something secondary (The nose can also in a way detach itself from the body.) Next to the bowels and the genital organs is the mouth, through which enters the world to be swallowed up. And next is the anus. All these convexities and orifices have a common characteristic; it is within them that the confines between bodies and between the body and the world are overcome: there is an interchange and an interorientation. This is why the main events in the life of the grotesque body, the acts of the bodily drama, take place in this sphere. Eating, drinking, defecation and other elimination (sweating, blowing of the nose, sneezing), as well as copulation, pregnancy, dismemberment, swallowing up by another body—all these acts are performed on the confines of the body and the outer world, or on the confines of the old and new body. In all these events the beginning and end of life are closely linked and interwoven.

Thus the artistic logic of the grotesque image ignores the closed, smooth, and impenetrable surface of the body and retains only its excrescences (sprouts, buds) and orifices, only that which leads beyond the body's limited space or into the body's depths.[2] Mountains and abysses, such is the relief of the grotesque body; or speaking in architectural terms, towers and subterranean passages.

Grotesque images may, of course, present other members, organs and parts of the body (especially dismembered parts), but they play a minor role in the drama. They are never stressed unless they replace a leading image.

Actually, if we consider the grotesque image in its extreme aspect, it never presents an individual body; the image consists of orifices and convexities that present another, newly conceived body. It is a point of transition in a life eternally renewed, the inexhaustible vessel of death and conception.

As we have said, the grotesque ignores the impenetrable surface that closes and limits the body as a separate and completed phenomenon. The grotesque image displays not only the outward but also the inner features of the body: blood, bowels, heart and other organs. The outward and inward features are often merged into one.

We have already sufficiently stressed the fact that grotesque imagery constructs what we might call a double body. In the endless chain of bodily life it retains the parts in which one link joins the other, in which the life of one body is born from the death of the preceding, older one.

Finally, let us point out that the grotesque body is cosmic and universal. It stresses elements common to the entire cosmos: earth, water, fire, air; it is directly related to the sun, to the stars. It contains the signs of the zodiac. It reflects the cosmic hierarchy. This body can merge with various natural phenomena, with mountains, rivers, seas, islands, and continents. It can fill the entire universe.

The grotesque mode of representing the body and bodily life prevailed in art and creative forms of speech over thousands of years. From the point of view of extensive use, this mode of representation still exists today; grotesque forms of the body not only predominate in the art of European peoples but

---

[2] This grotesque logic is also extended to images of nature and of objects in which depths (holes) and convexities are emphasized.

also in their folklore, especially in the comic genre. Moreover, these images predominate in the extra-official life of the people. For example, the theme of mockery and abuse is almost entirely bodily and grotesque. The body that figures in all the expressions of the unofficial speech of the people is the body that fecundates and is fecundated, that gives birth and is born, devours and is devoured, drinks, defecates, is sick and dying. In all languages there is a great number of expressions related to the genital organs, the anus and buttocks, the belly, the mouth and nose. But there are few expressions for the other parts of the body: arms and legs, face, and eyes. Even these comparatively few forms of speech have, in most cases, a narrow, practical character; they are related to the nearby area, determine distance, dimensions, or number. They have no broader, symbolic meaning, nor are they especially expressive. They do not participate in abuse and mockery.

Wherever men laugh and curse, particularly in a familiar environment, their speech is filled with bodily images. The body copulates, defecates, overeats, and men's speech is flooded with genitals, bellies, defecations, urine, disease, noses, mouths, and dismembered parts. Even when the flood is contained by norms of speech, there is still an eruption of these images into literature, especially if the literature is gay or abusive in character. The common human fund of familiar and abusive gesticulations is also based on these sharply defined images.

This boundless ocean of grotesque bodily imagery within time and space extends to all languages, all literatures, and the entire system of gesticulation; in the midst of it the bodily canon of art, belles lettres, and polite conversation of modern times is a tiny island. This limited canon never prevailed in antique literature. In the official literature of European peoples it has existed only for the last four hundred years.

We shall give a brief characterization of the new canon, concerning ourselves less with the pictorial arts than with literature. We shall build this characterization by comparing it to the grotesque conception and bringing out the differences.

The new bodily canon, in all its historic variations and different genres, presents an entirely finished, completed, strictly limited body, which is shown from the outside as something individual. That which protrudes, bulges, sprouts, or branches off (when a body transgresses its limits and a new one begins) is eliminated, hidden, or moderated. All orifices of the body are closed. The basis of the image is the individual, strictly limited mass, the impenetrable façade. The opaque surface and the body's "valleys" acquire an essential meaning as the border of a closed individuality that does not merge with other bodies and with the world. All attributes of the unfinished world are carefully removed, as well as all the signs of its inner life. The verbal norms of official and literary language, determined by the canon, prohibit all that is linked with fecundation, pregnancy, childbirth. There is a sharp line of division between familiar speech and "correct" language. . . .

In the new canon, such parts of the body as the genital organs, the buttocks, belly, nose and mouth cease to play the leading role. Moreover, instead of their original meaning they acquire an exclusiveness; in other words, they convey a merely individual meaning of the life of one single, limited body. The belly, nose, and mouth, are of course retained in the image and cannot be hidden, but in an individual, completed body they either fulfill purely expressive functions (this is true of the mouth only) or the functions of characterization and individualization. There is no symbolic, broad meaning whatever in the organs of this body. If they are not interpreted as a characterization and an expressive feature, they are referred to on the merely practical level in brief explanatory comments. Generally speaking, all that does not contain an element of characterization in the literary image is reduced to a simple bodily remark added to speech or action.

In the modern image of the individual body, sexual life, eating, drinking, and defecation have radically changed their meaning: they have been transferred to the private and psychological level where their connotation becomes narrow and specific, torn away from the direct relation to the life of society and to the cosmic whole. In this new connotation they can no longer carry on their former philosophical functions.

In the new bodily canon the leading role is attributed to the individually characteristic and expressive parts of the body: the head, face, eyes, lips, to the muscular system, and to the place of the body in the external world. The exact position and movements of this finished body in the finished outside world are brought out, so that the limits between them are not weakened.

The body of the new canon is merely one body; no signs of duality have been left. It is self-sufficient and speaks in its name alone. All that happens within it concerns it alone, that is, only the individual, closed sphere. Therefore, all the events taking place within it acquire one single meaning: death is only death, it never coincides with birth; old age is torn away from youth; blows merely hurt, without assisting an act of birth. All actions and events are interpreted on the level of a single, individual life. They are enclosed within the limits of the same body, limits that are the absolute beginning and end and can never meet.

In the grotesque body, on the contrary, death brings nothing to an end, for it does not concern the ancestral body, which is renewed in the next generation. The events of the grotesque sphere are always developed on the boundary dividing one body from the other and, as it were, at their points of intersection. One body offers its death, the other its birth, but they are merged in a two-bodied image.

In the new canon the duality of the body is preserved only in one theme, a pale reflection of its former dual nature. This is the theme of nursing a child.[3] But the image of the mother and the child is strictly individualized and closed, the line of demarcation cannot be removed. This is a completely new phase of the artistic conception of bodily interaction.

Finally, the new canon is completely alien to hyperbolization. The individualized image has no place for it. All that is permitted is a certain accentuation of expressive and characterized features. The severance of the organs from the body or their independent existence is no longer permitted.

We have roughly sketched the basic outlines of the modern canon, as they generally appear in the norms of literature and speech.[4] . . .

---

[3] Let us recall Goethe's remarks as reported by Eckermann in "Conversations with Goethe" concerning Correggio's painting "The Weaning of a Child." Goethe is attracted by the duality of the image, preserved in an attenuated form.

[4] Similar classical concepts of the body form the basis of the new canon of behavior. Good education demands: not to place the elbows on the table, to walk without protruding the shoulder blades or swinging the hips, to hold in the abdomen, to eat without loud chewing, not to snort and pant, to keep the mouth shut, etc.; in other words, to close up and limit the body's confines and to smooth the bulges. It is interesting to trace the struggle of the grotesque and classical concept in the history of dress and fashion. Even more interesting is this struggle in the history of dance.

LYNDA E. BOOSE

FROM *"THE FATHER AND THE BRIDE IN SHAKESPEARE"* (1982)

In this article, the feminist scholar Lynda Boose examines the relationship between gender and power in the Elizabethan family and the rituals that govern the transfer of women in Shakespeare's plays. Drawing on the methods of social anthropology, Boose provides a way of describing how masculine power is enacted in society through the disposition of women as a kind of property.

The aristocratic family of Shakespeare's England was, according to social historian Lawrence Stone, "patrilinear, primogenitural, and patriarchal." Parent-child relations were in general remote and formal, singularly lacking in affective bonds and governed solely by a paternal authoritarianism through which the "husband and father lorded it over his wife and children with the quasi-authority of a despot" (*Crisis* 271). Stone characterizes the society of the sixteenth and early seventeenth centuries as one in which "a majority of individuals . . . found it very difficult to establish close emotional ties to any other person" (*Family* 99)[1] and views the nuclear family as a burdensome social unit, valued only for its ability to provide the means of patrilineal descent. Second and third sons counted for little and daughters for even less. A younger son could, it is true, be kept around as a "walking sperm bank in case the elder son died childless," but daughters "were often unwanted and might be regarded as no more than a tiresome drain on the economic resources of the family" (Stone, *Family* 88, 112).[2]

Various Elizabethan documents, official and unofficial, that comment on family relations support Stone's hypothesis of the absence of affect.[3] Yet were we to turn from Stone's conclusions to those we might draw from Shakespeare's plays, the disparity of implication—especially if we assume that the plays to some extent mirror the life around them—must strike us as significant. Shakespeare's dramas consistently explore affective family dynamics with an intensity that justifies the

growing inference among Shakespearean scholars that the plays may be primarily "about" family relations and only secondarily about the macrocosm of the body politic.[4] Not the absence of affect but
the possessive overabundance of it is the force that both defines and threatens the family in Shakespeare. When we measure Stone's assertions against the Shakespeare canon, the plays must seem
startlingly ahistorical in focusing on what would seem to have been the least valued relationship of
all: that between father and daughter.

While father and son appear slightly more often in the canon, figuring in twenty-three plays,
father and daughter appear in twenty-one dramas and in one narrative poem. As different as these
father-daughter plays are, they have one thing in common: almost without exception the relationships they depict depend on significant underlying substructures of ritual. Shakespeare apparently
created his dramatic mirrors not solely from the economic and social realities that historians infer as
having dictated family behavior but from archetypal models, psychological in import and ritual in
expression. And the particular ritual model on which Shakespeare most frequently drew for the
father-daughter relationship was the marriage ceremony.[5]

In an influential study of the sequential order or "relative positions within ceremonial wholes,"
Arnold van Gennep isolated three phases in ritual enactment that always recur in the same underlying arrangement and that form, in concert, "the pattern of the rites of passage": separation, transition, and reincorporation.[6] The church marriage service—as familiar to a modern audience as it
was to Shakespeare's—contains all three phases. When considered by itself, it is basically a separation rite preceding the transitional phase of consummation and culminating in the incorporation of
a new family unit. In Hegelian terms, the ceremonial activities associated with marriage move from
thesis through antithesis to synthesis; the anarchic release to fertility is positioned between two
phases of relative stasis. The ritual enables society to allow for a limited transgression of its otherwise
universal taboo against human eroticism. Its middle movement is the dangerous phase of transition
and transgression; its conclusion, the controlled reincorporation into the stability of family. But before the licensed transgression can take place—the transgression that generates the stability and
continuity of society itself—the ritual must separate the sanctified celebrants from the sterile forces
of social interdiction. The marriage ritual is thus a pattern of and for the community that surrounds
it, as well as a rite of passage of and for the individuals who enact it. It serves as an especially effective substructure for the father-daughter relation because within its pattern lies the paradigm of all
the conflicts that define this bond at its liminal moment of severance. The ceremony ritualizes two
particularly significant events: a daughter and a son are being incorporated into a new family unit, an
act that explicitly breaks down the boundaries of two previously existing families; yet, at the same
time, the bonds being dissolved, particularly those between father and daughter, are being memorialized and thus, paradoxically, reasserted. In early comedies like *The Taming of the Shrew*, Shakespeare followed the Roman design of using the father of the young male lover as the *senex iratus*, a
blocking figure to be circumvented. The mature comedies, tragedies, and romances reconstruct the
problems of family bonds, filial obedience, and paternal possessiveness around the father and daughter, the relation put into focus by the marriage ceremony. When marriage activities are viewed from
the perspective of their ritual implications, the bride and groom are not joined until the transitional
phase of the wedding-night consummation; before that, a marriage may be annulled. What the
church service is actually all about is the separation of the daughter from the interdicting father.

The wedding ceremony of Western tradition has always recognized the preeminence of the
father-daughter bond. Until the thirteenth century, when the church at last managed to gain control of marriage law, marriage was considered primarily a private contract between two families
concerning property exchange. The validity and legality of matrimony rested on the *consensus
nuptialis* and the property contract, a situation that set up a potential for conflict by posing the mutual consent of the two children, who owed absolute obedience to their parents, against the desires
of their families, who must agree beforehand to the contract governing property exchange. However true it was that the couple's willing consent was necessary for valid matrimony and however
vociferously the official conduct books urged parents to consider the compatibility of the match, fathers like Cymbeline, Egeus, and Baptista feel perfectly free to disregard these requirements. Although lack of parental consent did not affect the validity of a marriage and, after 1604, affected
the legality only when a minor was involved,[7] the family control over the dowry was a powerful psychological as well as economic weapon. Fathers like Capulet, Lear, and Brabantio depend on

threats of disinheritance to coerce their children. When their daughters nonetheless wed without the paternal blessing, the marriages are adversely affected not because any legal statutes have been breached but because the ritual base of marriage has been circumvented and the psychological separation of daughter from father thus rendered incomplete. For in Shakespeare's time—as in our own—the ceremony acknowledged the special bond between father and daughter and the need for the power of ritual to release the daughter from its hold.

As specified in the 1559 *Book of Common Prayer*, the marriage ritual enjoins that the father (or, in his absence, the legal guardian)[8] deliver his daughter to the altar, stand by her in mute testimony that there are no impediments to her marriage, and then witness her pledge henceforth to forsake all others and "obey and serve, love honor and keep" the man who stands at her other side. To the priest's question, "Who giveth this woman to be married unto this man?"—a question that dates in English tradition back to the York manual (*Book of Common Prayer* 290–99; 408, n.)—the father must silently respond by physically relinquishing his daughter, only to watch the priest place her right hand into the possession of another man. Following this expressly physical symbolic transfer, the father's role in his daughter's life is ended; custom dictates that he now leave the stage, resign his active part in the rite, and become a mere observer. After he has withdrawn, the couple plight their troths, and the groom receives the ring, again from the priest. Taking the bride's hand into his, the groom places the ring on her finger with the words, "With this ring I thee wed, with my body I thee worship, and with all my worldly goods I thee endow," thus solemnizing the transfer in its legal, physical and material aspects.[9]

Before us we have a tableau paradigmatic of the problematic father-daughter relation: decked in the symbols of virginity, the bride stands at the altar between her father and husband, pulled as it were between the two important male figures in her life. To resolve the implied dilemma, the force of the priest and the community presides over and compels the transfer of an untouched daughter into the physical possession of a male whom the ceremony authorizes both as the invested successor to the father's authority and as the sanctified transgressor of prohibitions that the father has been compelled to observe.[10] By making the father transfer his intact daughter to the priest in testimony that he knows of no impediments to her lawful union, the service not only reaffirms the taboo against incest but implicitly levels the full weight of that taboo on the relationship between father and daughter. The groom's family does not enter into the archetypal dynamics going on at this altar except through the priest's reference to marriage as the cause why a man "shall leave father and mother and shall be joined unto his wife." The mother of the bride is a wholly excluded figure—as indeed she is throughout almost the entire Shakespeare canon. Only the father must act out, must dramatize his loss before the audience of the community. Within the ritual circumscription, the father is compelled to give his daughter to a rival male; and as Georges Bataille comments:

> The gift itself is a renunciation. . . . Marriage is a matter less for the partners than for the man who gives the woman away, the man whether father or brother who might have freely enjoyed the woman, daughter or sister, yet who bestows her on someone else. This gift is perhaps a substitute for the sexual act; for the exuberance of giving has a significance akin to that of the act itself; it is also a spending of resources.[11]

By playing out his role in the wedding ceremony, the father implicitly gives the blessing that licenses the daughter's deliverance from family bonds that might otherwise become a kind of bondage. Hence in *A Midsummer Night's Dream*, a play centered on marriage, the intransigent father Egeus, supported by the king-father figure Theseus, poses a threat that must be converted to a blessing to ensure the comic solution. In *Love's Labor's Lost*, the sudden death of the Princess' father, who is likewise the king-father figure for all the French ladies, prevents the necessary blessing, thus cutting sharply across the movement toward comic resolution and postponing the happy ending. In plots constructed around a daughter without a father, the absent father frequently assumes special dramatic prominence. This absence felt almost as a presence may well contribute to the general unease and unresolved tensions emanating from the three "problem plays," for Helena, Isabella, and Cressida are all daughters severed from their fathers. . . .

In tragedies like *Lear*, *Othello*, and *Romeo and Juliet*, the father's failure to act out his required role has a special significance, one that we can best apprehend by looking not at the logic of causal narrative progression but at the threat implied by the violation of ritual. . . .

Through the use of ceremonial substructures, Shakespeare invokes a sacramentality, a context of sacredness, for a certain moment and space within the play. Such structures temporally and spatially set the ritualized moments away from the undifferentiated profane events of the drama. But once a ritual has been invoked, has in effect drawn a circle of archetypal reference around the moment and space, any events from the nonsacramental surrounding world that interrupt or counter its prescribed direction take on special, portentous significance.[12] By interrupting or converting the invoked ritual to parody, such profane invasions rupture its sacramental context. . . .

The opening scene of *King Lear*, however, is infused with the additional tension of colliding, incompatible ritual structures: the attempt of the man who is both king and father to substitute the illegitimate transfer of his kingdom for the legitimate one of his daughter.

In *King Lear*, the father's grudging recognition of the need to confer his *daughter* on younger strengths while he unburdened crawls toward death should be understood as the basal structure underlying his divestiture of his kingdom. Lear has called his court together in the opening scene because he must at last face the postponed reckoning with Cordelia's two princely suitors, who "Long in our court have made their amorous sojourn,/And here are to be answer'd" (1.1.47–48). But instead of justly relinquishing his daughter, Lear tries to effect a substitution of paternal divestitures: he portions out his kingdom as his "daughters' several dowers," attaching to Cordelia's share a stipulation designed to thwart her separation. In substituting his public paternity for his private one, the inherently indivisible entity for the one that biologically must divide and recombine, Lear violates both his kingly role in the hierarchical universe and his domestic one in the family. Nor is it accident—as it was in *Hamlet* 5.1—that brings these two incompatible rituals into collision in *Lear* 1.1. It is the willful action of the king and father, the lawgiver and protector of both domain and family, that is fully responsible for this explosion of chaos.

Yet of course Lear's bequest of his realm is in no way an unconditional transfer of the kingdom from one rulership to another. Instead, Lear wants to retain the dominion he theoretically casts off and to "manage those authorities/That he hath given away" (1.3.17–18). Likewise, the bequest of his daughter is actually an attempt to keep her, a motive betrayed by the very words he uses. When he *dis*claims "all my paternal care" and orders Cordelia "as a stranger to my heart and me/Hold thee from this for ever" (113, 115–16), his verb holds to his heart rather than expels from it the daughter he says is "adopted to our hate" (203), another verbal usage that betrays his retentive motives. His disastrous attempts to keep the two dominions he sheds are structurally linked through the parodic divestiture of his kingdom as dowry. In recognition of the family's economic interest in marriage, the terms of sixteenth-century dowries were required to be fully fixed before the wedding, thus making the property settlement a precondition for the wedding.[13] But Lear the father will not freely give his daughter her endowment unless she purchases it with pledges that would nullify those required by the wedding ceremony. If she will not love him all, she will mar her fortunes, lose her dowry, and thus forfeit the symbolic separation. And yet, as she asserts, she cannot marry if she loves her father all. The circularity of Lear's proposition frustrates the ritual phase of separation: by disinheriting Cordelia, Lear casts her away not to let her go but to prevent her from going. In Lévi-Strauss' terms, Lear has to give up Cordelia because the father must obey the basic social rule of reciprocity, which has a necessarily communal effect, functioning as a "distribution to undo excess." Lear's refusal is likewise communal in its effect, and it helps create the universe that he has "ta'en too little care of."

Insofar as Burgundy's suit is concerned, Lear's quantitatively constructed presumption works. Playing the mime priest and intentionally desecrating the sacramental ritual question he imitates, Lear asks the first bridegroom-candidate:

> Will you, with those infirmities she owes,
> Unfriended, new adopted to our hate,
> Dow'r'd with our curse, and stranger'd with our oath,
> Take her, or leave her? (1.1.202–05)

Burgundy's hedged response is what Lear anticipates—this suitor will gladly "take Cordelia by the hand" only if Lear will give "but that portion which yourself propos'd" (243, 242). Shrewdly intuiting

---

EDITOR'S NOTE: Boose's citations are to a different edition of Shakespeare plays than is used in this anthology; act, scene, and line references will differ from those here.

that France cannot be dissuaded by so quantitative a reason as "her price is fallen," Lear then adopts a strategy based on qualitative assumptions in his attempt to discourage the rival he most greatly fears. Insisting to France that

> For you, great King
> I would not from your love make such a stray
> To match you where I hate; therefore beseech you
> T'avert your liking a more worthier way   (208–11)

Lear tries to avoid even making the required ritual offer. By calling his own daughter "a wretch whom Nature is asham'd/Almost t'acknowledge hers" (212–13), Lear implies by innuendo the existence of some unnatural impediment in Cordelia that would make her unfit to marry and would thus prevent her separation. Effectively, the scene presents an altar tableau much like that in *Much Ado*, with a bride being publicly pronounced unfit for marriage. In *Lear*, however, it is the father rather than the groom who defames the character of the bride, and his motives are to retain her rather than to reject her. In this violated ceremony, the slandered daughter—instead of fainting—staunchly denies the alleged impediments by demanding that her accuser "make known/It is no vicious blot . . . No unchaste action, or dishonored step,/That hath deprived me of your grace and favor" (226–29). And here the groom himself takes up the role implicit in his vows, defending Cordelia's suborned virtue by his statement that to believe Lear's slanders would require "a faith that reason without miracle/Should never plant in me" (222–23). The physical separation of the daughter from the father is finally achieved only by France's perception that "this unpriz'd precious maid . . . is herself a dowry" (259, 241); France recognizes the qualitative meaning of the dowry that Burgundy could only understand quantitatively.

In Cordelia's almost archetypal definition of a daughter's proper loyalties (1.1.95–104), Shakespeare uses a pun to link the fundamental predicament of the daughter—held under the aegis of the father—to its only possible resolution in the marriage troth: "That lord whose hand must take my plight shall carry/Half my love with him" (101–02), says Cordelia. When France later addresses his bride as "Fairest Cordelia, that art most rich being poor,/Most choice forsaken, and most lov'd despis'd" (250–51), he echoes the husband's traditional pledge to love "for richer, for poorer" the daughter who has "forsaken all others." And France himself then endows Lear's "dow'rless daughter" with all his worldly goods by making her "queen of us, of ours, and our fair France" (256–57). His statement "Be it lawful I take up what's cast away" (253) even suggests a buried stage direction through its implied allusion to the traditional conclusion of the *consensus nuptialis* as explained in the Sarum and York manuals: the moment when the bride, in token of receiving a dowry of land from her husband, prostrates herself at her husband's feet and he responds by lifting her up again (*Rathen* 36, Legg 190, Howard 306–07).

The visual and verbal texts of this important opening scene allude to the separation phase of the marriage ritual; the ritual features are emphasized because here, unlike the similar scene in *Othello*, the daughter's right to choose a husband she loves is not at issue. Because the ritual is sacred, Cordelia dispassionately refuses to follow her sisters in prostituting it. Lear, in contrast, passionately destroys his kingdom in order to thwart the fixed movement of the ritual pattern and to convert the pattern's linear progression away from the father into a circular return to him.[14] The discord his violation engenders continues to be projected through accumulating ritual substructures: in a parody of giving his daughter's hand, Lear instead gives her "father's heart from her" (126); in a parody of the ring rite, Lear takes the golden round uniting king and country and parts it, an act that both dramatizes the consequences of dividing his realm and demonstrates the anguish he feels at losing his daughter to a husband.

Once Lear has shattered the invoked sacred space by collapsing two incompatible rituals into it, he shatters also all claims to paternal authority. From this scene onward, the question of Lear's paternal relation to his daughters and his kingdom pervades the drama through the King's ceremonial invocations of sterility against the daughters he has generated and the land he has ruled. In the prototype of a harmonious wedding that concludes *As You Like It*, Hymen—who "peoples every town"—defines Duke Senior's correct paternal role as that of the exogamous giver of the daughter created in heaven:

Hymen from heaven brought her,
    Yea, brought her hither,
That thou mightst join her hand with his
Whose heart within his bosom is.   (5.4.112–15)[15]

Hymen characterizes the generating of children as a gift from heaven, an essential spending of the self designed to increase the world. By contrast, Lear's image of the father is the "barbarous Scythian,/Or he that makes his generation messes/To gorge his appetite" (1.1.116–18). The definition is opposite to the very character of ritual. It precludes the possibility of transformation, for the father devours the flesh he begets. Here, generation becomes primarily an autogamous act, a retention and recycling of the procreative energies, which become mere extensions of private appetite feeding on its own production. The unnatural appetite of the father devouring his paternity is implicit even in the motive Lear reveals behind his plan to set his rest on Cordelia's "kind nursery" (124), an image in which the father pictures himself as an infant nursing from his daughter. The implied relationship is unnatural because it allows the father to deflect his original incestuous passions into Oedipal ones, thus effecting a newly incestuous proximity to the daughter, from whom the marriage ritual is designed to detach him. And when this form of appetite is thwarted by France's intervention, Lear effects yet another substitution of state for daughter: having ordered Cornwall and Albany to "digest the third" part of his kingdom, he and his gluttonous knights proceed to feed off it and through their "Epicurism and lust/Make . . . it more like a tavern or a brothel/Than a grac'd palace" (1.4.244–46). Compelled by nature to give up his daughter, he unnaturally gives up his kingdom; when his appetites cannot feed on her, they instead devour the paternity of his land.

The father devouring his own flesh is the monstrous extension of the circular terms of Lear's dowry proposal. The image belongs not only to the play's pervasive cluster of monsters from the deep but also to its dominant spatial pattern of circularity. Within both the narrative movement and the repeated spatial structure inside the drama, the father's retentive passions deny the child's rite of passage. When Cordelia departs from the father's realm for a new life in her husband's, ostensibly fulfilling the ritual separation, the journey is condemned to futility at its outset, for Cordelia departs dowered with Lear's curse: "Without our grace, our love, our benison" (1.1.265). Although the bride and groom have exchanged vows, the denial of the father's blessing renders the separation incomplete and the daughter's future blighted. Cordelia, like Rosalind, must therefore return to be reincorporated with her father before she can undergo the ritual severance that will enable her to progress. She thus chooses father over husband, returning to Lear to ask his blessing: "look upon me, sir,/And hold your hand in benediction o'er me" (4.7.56–57). In lines that indicate how futile the attempt at incorporation has been when the precedent rites of passage have been perverted, Cordelia asserts, "O dear father,/It is thy business that I go about" (4.4.23–24), and characterizes her life with France as having been one of constant mourning for the father to whom she is still bound.

Shakespeare rewrote the source play *Leir* to make Cordelia remain in England alone (rather than with France at her side) to fight, lose, and die with her father, a revision that vividly illustrates the tragic failure of the family unit to divide, recombine, and regenerate. The only respite from pain the tragedy offers is the beauty of Lear's reunion with Cordelia, but that reunion takes place at the cost of both the daughter's life and the future life of the family. And for all the poignancy of this reunion, the father's intransigence—which in this play both initiates and conditions the tragedy—remains unchanged: it is still writ large in his fantasy that he and his daughter will be forever imprisoned together like birds in a cage.[16] At the end of the play, excluding any thought of Cordelia's new life with France, Lear focuses solely on the father-daughter merger, which he joyfully envisions enclosed in a perpetuity where no interlopers—short of a divine messenger—can threaten it: "He that parts us shall bring a brand from heaven,/And fire us hence like foxes" (5.3.22–23). The rejoining is the precise opposite of that in *As You Like It*. To Rosalind's question, "if I bring in your Rosalind,/You will bestow her on Orlando here?" Duke Senior responds, "That would I, had I kingdoms to give with her" (*AYL* 5.4.6–7, 8). In the Duke's characterization of Orlando's newly received endowment as "a potent Dukedom" (5.4.169), the implied fertility of both kingdom and family is ensured through the father's submission to the necessary movement of ritual. In *King Lear,* the father who imagined that he "gave his daughters all" extracts from his daughter at the end of the play the same price he demanded in the opening scene—that she love her father all. The play's tragic circles find their counterpart in its ritual movements. Cordelia returns to her father, and the final scene stages the most sterile of altar tableaux: a dead father with his three dead daughters, the wheel having come full circle back to the opening scene of the play. Initially barren of mothers, the play concludes with the death of all the fathers and all the daughters; the only figures who survive to emphasize the sterility of the final tableau are Albany, a widower, and Edgar, an unmarried son. . . .

. . . [F]requently throughout the canon, Shakespeare draws on ritual substructures for the conclusions of his plays. Within these patterns, tragedy ends with an emphasis on broken or inverted ritual designs; comedy ends with the scattered elements of ritual regrouped and correctly enacted. And in the four late romances—plays in which oracular prophecies and the sudden descent of divine beings constantly reshape the linear narrative—the shattered human world, through obsessive reenactments of broken rituals, strives to recapture what has been lost and thus to reconnect itself with the sacred world of its origins. The design closely approximates Mircea Eliade's description of the ritual process as humanity's attempt to effect the "myth of the eternal return." Within these late plays, the declining world of inflexible paternal authority rediscovers a redemptive teleology through the ritualized reclamation of that particular bond which could only be viewed as a liability to the family's prospects for economic and patrilineal prosperity. In *The Winter's Tale,* the murderous wrath Leontes directs against his innocent wife and daughter is punished by the immediately conjunctive death of the son he imagines will carry his lineal posterity. Only when he comes to value "that which has been lost"—the daughter Perdita, who is a matrilineal rather than a patrilineal extension—is Leontes allowed the partial restitution implicit in his adoption of Florizel. And even this compensation is made possible only through the return and affirmation of the hitherto unvalued daughter. . . .

The father-daughter relation in *The Tempest,* the last of the romances, is somewhat similar, in that Miranda, like Perdita [in *The Winter's Tale*] and Marina [in *Pericles*], is the force that preserves her father. Here, however, there is no mother for Prospero to rediscover when he at last gives up his daughter and abandons his island. Instead of the miraculous reunion with a lost daughter as the force that suddenly resuscitates life, *The Tempest* shows us a father who has never lost his child and whose concern for her welfare has always given him his will to live. And of all the Shakespearean fathers of daughters, Prospero is undoubtedly the most successful in enacting his proper role. His purpose, much like that defined by Hymen in *As You Like It,* has always been to educate, discipline, and nurture Miranda so that he can set her free, as he does Ariel. Prospero understands the need to play the father's mock role as the barrier to young love, the need to make Ferdinand realize the value of his daughter through laboring to earn her lest "too light winning/Make the prize light" (1.2.452–53). He also understands the need for the daughter to choose her husband over her father, a choice that Desdemona and Cordelia could not make their fathers accept. When he commands Miranda not to talk with his prisoner or reveal her name, he is purposely acting to fulfill both roles. While Lear casts Cordelia away so that he can keep her, Prospero ties Miranda to him so that she will disobey his commands and initiate the required transition of loyalties from father to husband. Yet, for all his awareness, Prospero turns aside from watching Miranda and Ferdinand play out the parts he himself has written for them and makes the pained commend "So glad of this as they I cannot be" (3.1.92).

Shakespeare shows us that it is no easier for Prospero to give up Miranda, even to a husband he himself has chosen, than it was for poor Brabantio to relinquish Desdemona. Throughout the play Prospero remains disproportionately preoccupied with tormenting thoughts of his daughter sexually possessed by another male, an obsession that has its analogue in Brabantio's dream. Hence the father lectures Ferdinand—the future son-in-law whom old Prospero never manages to like very much—that

> If thou dost break her virgin-knot before
> All sanctimonious ceremonies may . . . be minist'red,
> . . . barren hate . . . and discord shall bestrew
> The union of your bed with weeds so loathly
> That you shall hate it both.   (4.1.15–22)

And hence he sets Ferdinand to work hauling logs, doing the labor that Caliban refused to do, thereby domesticating Ferdinand's energies in a way that could never reform the uneducable lust of Caliban. In his betrothal gift to Miranda and Ferdinand, the dowry masque he evokes out of the powers of his mind, Prospero includes the rainbow goddess Iris, the emblematic fertility of Ceres, and the archetypal wife-consort Juno. Significantly, from this vision the father banishes Venus and her son, turning them back on their way to the celebration, where he fears they would have done "some wanton charm upon this man and maid/Whose vows are, that no bedright shall be paid / Till Hymen's torch be lighted" (4.1.95–97).

The forces of erotic chaos that Prospero hoped to banish from his daughter's prothalamion are, however, not so easily vanquished. For before the masque has ended, Prospero realizes that Caliban and his confederates are on their way, and the very thought of the would-be rapist abruptly dissolves the insubstantial pageant into thin air.

In *The Tempest*, Prospero essentially overcomes his incestuous desire to retain his daughter imprisoned on his island. He recognizes his own repressed but monstrous wishes in confessing that Caliban, who would people the island with Calibans, is a "thing of darkness I / [must] Acknowledge mine" (5.1.275–76). Caliban, the monster of *The Tempest*, whose name suggests an anagram for "cannibal," refigures the incestuous, self-consumptive desires imaged in Lear's "barbarous Scythian" and in the "monstrous lust" between Antiochus and his daughter in *Pericles*. He is also a force on whose nature nurture will not stick. And so while daughter and father are simultaneously released from the enchantment of living together forever isolated on an island controlled by the father's shaping fancies, Caliban must remain enslaved on it. Their release and their ability to return to the natural order of civilization are made possible only by the arrival of Ferdinand, who comes—like the prince of the fairy tale—to take the bride away from her father's fortress and lead her out into generative space and time.

The end of *The Tempest* leaves us with a father who has learned what nature requires of him: the father must take part with his nobler reason against his fury and let his admired Mirando go. Yet doing so leaves Prospero with the lonely emptiness apparent in his confession to Alonzo: "I / Have lost my daughter . . . In this last tempest" (5.1.147–48, 153). As in *Pericles* and *The Winter's Tale*, the ritual dissolution of the father-daughter bond is dramatically realized; but in this final play the relationship gains added depth through the exploration of the central paradox always inherent in its resolution. Here, we are not left entirely with the "brave new world" imagined by Miranda and in some respects promised to the reclaimed families of the two earlier romances. For Shakespeare goes beyond the happy ending to show us the pain and loss bequeathed to the isolated father who has acted out the required rite of separation. For while at first glance the church ceremony might seem only to dramatize the transfer of a passive female object from one male to another, in reality it ritualizes the community's coercion, not of the bride, but of her father. Ultimately, it is he who must pay the true "bride price" at the altar and, by doing so, become the displaced and dispossessed actor. As the celebratory reunification that concludes Shakespeare's comedy begins in the final scene, it is therefore left up to Prospero to complete the demands dictated by his role and—like every father of every bride—retire from the scene to seek out his seat in the congregation. Thus Prospero concludes the ritual and the play with his only remaining expectation:

> to see the nuptial
> Of these our dear-belov'd solemnized,
> And thence retire me to my Milan, where
> Every third thought shall be my grave.   (5.1.309–12)

NOTES

[1] Stone accounts for the drama and poetry of the sixteenth and early seventeenth centuries by modifying his "rather pessimistic view of a society with little love and generally low affect" to allow for "romantic love and sexual intrigue . . . in one very restricted social group . . . that is the households of princes and great nobles" (*Family* 103–04). This qualification does not extend to his view of parent-child relationships.

[2] Stone also points out that the high infant-mortality rate, "which made it folly to invest too much emotional capital in such ephemeral beings," was as much responsible for this lack of affective family ties as were any economic motives (*Family* 105). For Stone, paternal authority—not affection—was the almost exclusive source of the family's coherence. Furthermore, the domestic patriarchy of the sixteenth century was not

merely a replica of family structures inherited from the past but a social pattern consciously exploited and reinforced by the state to emphasize the injunctions of obedience and authority; nor was it replaced until absolute monarchy was overthrown (see *Family* 151–218). Meanwhile, because of the prevalent child-rearing practices, the maternal impact was relatively insignificant, hence not nearly so important to the psychological process of maturation; in Stone's estimate, our familiar "maternal, child-oriented, affectionate and permissive mode" of child rearing did not emerge till about 1800 (*Family* 405). During the Elizabethan era, the upper-class practice of transferring a newborn infant immediately to a village wet nurse, who nurtured the child for two years, substantially muted any maternal influence on child development and no doubt created an inestimable psychological distance between mother and child. Stone cites the strained and formal relationship between Juliet and Lady Capulet as vivid testimony of the absence of affective mother-child bonds that results from such an arrangement (106); in the Capulet household, it is even left up to the nurse, not the mother, to remember Juliet's birthday. Yet Stone does not measure the relationship between Juliet and her father against his hypothesis of the absence of affect. Old Capulet is indeed the authoritarian dictator of Stone's model, but he is also a "careful father" who deeply loves his child. Instead of being eager to have her off his hands, Capulet is notably reluctant to give up the daughter he calls "the hopeful lady of my earth" (1.2.15; all Shakespeare quotations are from the Evans ed.); his bull-headed determination to marry her to Paris following Tybalt's death is born, paradoxically enough, from the deeply rooted affection that Stone's hypothesis excludes.

[3] As Christopher Hill suggests in his review of Stone's *Family*, much of the evidence used could well imply its opposite: "The vigour of the preachers' propaganda on behalf . . . of breaking children's wills, suggests that such attitudes were by no means so universally accepted as they would have wished" (461). Hill and others have criticized Stone for asserting that love and affection were negligible social phenomena before 1700 and for presuming throughout "that values percolate downwards from the upper to the lower classes" (Hill 462). Because of the scope and importance of Stone's subject, his book has been widely reviewed. As David Berkowitz comments, "the possibility of endless symposia on Stone's vision and performance looms as a fashionable activity for the next half-dozen years" (396). Hill's review and the reviews by Keith Thomas and John Demos seem particularly well balanced.

[4] One could chart the new emphasis on the family by reviewing the Shakespeare topics at recent MLA conventions. The 1979 convention featured Marriage and the Family in Shakespeare, Shirley Nelson Garner chairing, as its Shakespeare Division topic and also included a related special session, The Love between Shakespeare's Fathers and Daughters, Paul A. Jorgensen chairing. Before becoming the division topic, the subject had been examined in special sessions for three consecutive years: 1976, Marianne Novy chairing; 1977, John Bean and Coppélia Kahn chairing; and 1978, Carol Thomas Neely chairing. Special sessions continued in 1980 and 1981, with Shirley Nelson Garner and Madelon S. Gohlke as chairs. A parallel phenomenon has meanwhile been taking place in sixteenth-, seventeenth-, and eighteenth-century historical scholarship, which Hill explains by saying that ". . . the family as an institution rather suddenly became fashionable,

perhaps as a by-product of the women's liberation movement" (450).

Most of the work on fathers and daughters in Shakespeare has been done, as might be expected, on the romances. See the essays by Cyrus Hoy, D. W. Harding, and Charles Frey. Of particular interest is the Schwartz and Kahn collection, which was published after I had written this paper but which includes several essays that express views related to my own. See esp. David Sundelson's "So Rare a Wonder'd Father: Prospero's *Tempest*," C. L. Barber's "The Family in Shakespeare's Development: Tragedy and Sacredness," and Coppélia Kahn's "The Providential *Tempest* and the Shakespearean Family."

[5] Margaret Loftus Ranald has done substantial work on the legal background of marriage in Shakespeare plays. I have found no marriages (or funerals) staged literally in the plays of Shakespeare or of his contemporaries. Although, for instance, the marriage of Kate and Petruchio would seem to offer a rich opportunity for an indecorously comic scene appropriate for *The Taming of the Shrew*, the action occurs offstage and we only hear of it secondhand. Nor do we witness the Olivia-Sebastian marriage in *Twelfth Night*. Even the fragment of the botched ceremony in *Much Ado* does not follow the liturgy with any precision but presents a dramatized version of it. This omission—apparently consistent in Elizabethan and Jacobean drama—may have resulted from the 1559 Act of Uniformity of Common Prayer and Divine Service in the Church, which stipulates sanctions against "any persone or persones whatsoever . . . [who] shall in anye Entreludes Playes Songes, Rymes or by other open Woordes, declare or speake anye thing in the derogation depraving or despising of the same Booke, or of any thing therein conteyned" (1 Elizabeth i, c. 2, in *Statutes* 4:355–58). Given the rising tempo of the Puritan attack on the theaters at this time, we may reasonably infer that the omission of liturgy reflects the dramatists' conscientious wish to avoid conflict. Richmond Noble's study corroborates this assumption (82). Of the services to which Shakespeare does refer, Noble notes that the allusions to "distinctive features, words, and phrases of Holy Matrimony are extremely numerous" (83).

[6] Van Gennep built his study on the work of Hartland, Frazer, Ciszewski, Hertz, Crowley, and others who had noted resemblances among the components of various disparate rites. His tripartite diachronic structure provides the basis for Victor W. Turner's discussions in the essay "Liminality and Communitas" (*Ritual Process* 94–203).

[7] The church canons of 1604 seem to have confused the situation further by continuing to recognize the validity of the nuptial pledge but forbidding persons under twenty-one to marry without parental consent; this ruling would make the marriage of minors illegal but nonetheless binding for life and hence valid (Stone, *Family* 32). Until the passage of Lord Hardwicke's Marriage Act in 1753, confusion was rife over what constituted a legal marriage and what a valid one. In addition to bringing coherence to the marriage laws, this act was designed to protect increasingly threatened parental interests by denying the validity as well as the legality of a religious ceremony performed without certain conditions, including parental consent for parties under twenty-one (Stone, *Family* 35–36).

The concern for parental approval has always focused on, and in fact ritualized, the consent of the bride's father. In 1858, the Reverend Charles Wheatly, a noted authority on church law, attributed the father's giving away his daughter as signifying the care that must be taken of the female sex, "who are always supposed to be under the tuition of a father or guardian, whose consent is necessary to make their acts valid" (496). For supportive authority Wheatly looks back to Richard Hooker, whose phrasing is substantially harsher. Hooker felt that the retention of the custom "hath still this vse that it putteth we men in mind of a dutie whereunto the verie imbecillitie of their [women's] nature and sex doth binde them, namely to be alwaies directed, guided and ordered by others . . . (215).

Even though the validity of a marriage was not vested in parental consent, "the Protestants, including the Anglicans, considered the consent of the parents to be as essential to the marriage as the consent of the bride and bridegroom" (Flandrin 131). Paradoxically, "both Church and State claimed to be supporting, at one and the same time, freedom of marriage and the authority of parents" (Flandrin 132). The ambiguity arose because the child was obliged, under pain of mortal sin, to obey the parent. Technically, the child was free to choose a marriage partner, but since the church never took steps against the prerogatives of the father, the notion of choice was problematic.

[8] Given the high parent mortality rate, a number of brides necessarily went to the altar on the arms of their legal guardians. Peter Laslett notes that in Manchester between 1553–1657 over half of the girls marrying for the first time were fatherless (103), but some historians have criticized his reliance on parish registers as the principal demographic barometer.

[9] The groom's pledge suggests the wedding ring's dual sexual and material symbolism. Historically, the ring symbolizes the dowry payment that the woman will receive from her husband by the entitlement of marriage; it apparently superseded the custom of placing tokens of espousal on the prayer book (see *Book of Common Prayer* 408). It also signifies the physical consummation, a point frequently exploited in Renaissance drama and also implied by the rubrics in the older Roman Catholic manuals, which direct the placing of the ring. The Martène manual specifies that the bride is to wear it on the left hand to signify "a difference between the estate and the episcopal order, by whom the ring is publicly worn on the right hand as a symbol of full and entire chastity" (Legg 207). *The Rathen Manual*, which follows the Use of Sarum, contains a rather charming piece of folklore widely believed through the eighteenth century. It, too, allusively suggests the sexual significance of the ring: "For in the fourth finger there is a certain vein proceeding to the heart and by the chime of silver there is represented the internal affection which ought always to be fresh between them" (35–36; see also Wheatly 503). Even after the priest took over the ceremonial role of transferring the bride's hand from her father's to her husband's, he did not also become the intermediary in transferring the ring from the groom's keeping to the bride's finger. Such an incorporation of duties might seem logical were it not that this part of the ritual simultaneously imitates and licenses the sexual act.

The English reformers retained both the symbol of the ring and the groom's accompanying pledge to "worship" his wife's body, a retention that generated considerable attack from the more radical reformers. The controversy over this wording occupies the major portion of Hooker's defense of the Anglican marriage rite (see also Stone, *Family* 522, on the attempts in 1641 and 1661 to alter the wording of the vow from "worship" to "honor"). Hooker justifies the husband's "worship" as a

means of transferring to the wife the "dignitie" incipient in her husband's legitimizing of the children he now allows her to bear. She furthermore receives, by this annexation of his worship, a right to participate in his material possessions. The movement of the vow, from sexual to material pledge, thus sequences a formal rite of passage, a pattern alluded to in Hooker's phrase, "the former branch hauing granted the principall, the latter graunteth that which is annexed thereunto" (216).

[10] The ceremonial transfer of the father's authority to the husband is acknowledged by the Reverend John Shepherd in his historical commentary accompanying the 1853 Family Prayer Book: ". . . the ceremony shows the father's consent; and that the authority, which he before possessed, he now resigns to the husband" (Brownell 465). By implication, however, the ceremony resolves the incestuous attraction between father and daughter by ritualizing his "gift" of her hand, a signification unlikely to be discussed in the commentary of church historians. When first the congregation and next the couple are asked to name any impediments to the marriage, there are, Wheatly says, three specific impediments the church is charging all knowledgeable parties to declare: a preceding marriage or contract, consanguinity or affinity, and want of consent (483). The final act of Ben Jonson's *Epicoene* enumerates all the possible legal impediments that might be subsumed under these three.

The bride's father, by virtue of his special prominence in the ritual, functions as a select witness whose presence attests to the validity of the contract. The Friar in *Much Ado* asks Hero and Claudio whether they "know any inward impediment why you should not be cojoin'd" (4.1.12–13). Leonato dares to respond for Claudio, "I dare make his answer, none," because, as father of the bride, he presumes to have full knowledge that no impediment exists. When he learns of Hero's supposed taint, the rage he vents over the loss of his own honor is the more comprehensible when we understand his special position in the ceremony as a sworn witness to the transfer of an intact daughter.

[11] The sections on the celebration of "Festiuall daies" and times of fast that precede Hooker's defense of the English "Celebration of Matrimonie" are especially helpful in understanding Elizabethan ritual, for in these sections Hooker expands his defense of the Anglican rites into an explanation of, and rationale for, the whole notion of ritual. Having first isolated three sequential elements necessary for festival—praise, bounty, and rest—he goes on to justify "bountie" in terms remarkably compatible with the theories of both Bataille and Lévi-Strauss on the essential "spending-gift" nature of marriage. To Hooker, the "bountie" essential to celebration represents the expression of a "charitable largenesse of somewhat more then common bountie. . . . Plentifull and liberall expense is required in them that abounde, partly as a signe of their owne joy in the goodnesse of God toward them" (292, 293). Bounty is important to all festival rites, but within the marriage rite this "spending" quality incorporates the specific idea of sexual orgasm as the ultimate and precious expenditure given the bride by her husband, a notion alluded to in Bataille and one that functioned as a standard Elizabethan metaphor apparent in phrases like "Th' expense of spirit" (sonnet 129) or Othello's comment to Desdemona, "The purchase made, the fruits are to ensue;/ That profit's yet to come 'tween me and you" (2.3.9–10). The

wedding ceremony ritualizes this notion of bounty as the gift of life by having the father give the groom the family treasure, which the father cannot "use" but can only bequeath or hoard. The groom, who ritually places coins or a gold ring on the prayer book as a token "bride price," then fully "purchases" the father's treasure through his own physical expenditure, an act that guarantees the father's "interest" through future generations. This money-sex image complex is pervasive and important in many of Shakespeare's plays. The pattern and its relation to festival are especially evident in Juliet's ecstatic and impatient speech urging night to come and bring her husband:

> O, I have bought the mansion of a love,
> But not possess'd it, and though I am sold,
> Not yet enjoy'd. So tedious is this day
> As is the night before some festival.   (3.2.26–29)

In another context, this pattern enables us fully to understand Shylock's miserly refusal to give or spend and the implications of his simultaneous loss of daughter and hoarded fortune. His confusion of daughter and ducats is foreshadowed when he recounts the story of Jacob and equates the increase of the flock through the "work of generation" to the increase of money through retentive "use." To Antonio's question, "Or is your gold and silver ewes and rams?" Shylock responds, "I cannot tell, I make it breed as fast" (MV 1.3.95–96).

[12] Hooker also makes the point that the sacramentality invoked by ritual is profaned when festival celebration overflows the measure or when the form of ceremony becomes parodic. Hooker asserts that the festivals of the "Israelites and heathens," though they contained the necessary elements, "failed in the ende it self, so neither could they discerne rightly what forme and measure Religion therein should obserue. . . . they are in every degree noted to haue done amisse, their Hymnes or songs of praise were idolatrie, their bountie excesse, and their rest wantonnesse" (294). On the use of ritual as the human means to recover the sacred dimension of existence, see Eliade: "Driven from religious life in the strict sense, the *celestial sacred* remains active through symbolism. A religious symbol conveys its message even if it is no longer consciously understood in every part. For a symbol speaks to the whole human being and not only to the intelligence. . . . Hence the supreme function

of the myth is to "fix" the paradigmatic models for all rites and all significant human activities. . . . By the continuous reactualization of paradigmatic divine gestures, the world is sanctified." (129, 98–99). Unquestionably, the late C. L. Barber's study is the best book to date on the relation of Shakespeare's plays to underlying patterns of ritual.

[13] *Measure for Measure* provides the most dramatic testimony to the importance of fixing the dowry provisions before the wedding. Although Juliet is nearly nine months pregnant and although she and Claudio believe themselves spiritually married, they have not legalized the wedding in church because of still unresolved dowry provisions.

[14] Alan Dundes points out the psychological dimensions of various folktale types underlying a number of Shakespeare's plays; significantly, the central figure in the folktale is usually the daughter-heroine. The theme of incest, which Freud himself recognized as a powerful undercurrent in *King Lear*, is manifest in the folktale father who demands that his daughter marry him; Shakespeare transforms the overt demand into a love test requiring that she love her father all (358). In Dundes' interpretation, the more obvious father-daughter incest wish is actually an Electral daughter-father desire that has been transformed through projection. Dundes also lists other discussions of the father-daughter incest theme in *King Lear* (359).

[15] Hymen's verses emphasize the religious sense of the marriage ritual. In this context the genetic father is only a surrogate parent, appointed by the heavenly parent to act out the specific role of bequeathing the daughter to a new union; Hymen himself functions as the mythic priest, the agent authorized by heaven to oversee the transfer. Wheatly's notes reflect this same sense of the religious meaning of the roles played by father and priest: ". . . the woman is to be given not to the man, but to the Minister; for the rubric orders, that the minister shall receive her *at her father's or friend's hands*; which signifies, to be sure, that the father resigns her up to God, and that it is God, who, by His Priest, now gives her in marriage . . ." (497).

[16] See Barber's essay in Schwartz and Kahn, esp. pp. 198–221. Barber additionally provides a striking iconographic association, noting the image of Lear with Cordelia in his arms as being effectively "a *pietá* with the roles reversed, not Holy Mother with her Dead Son, but father with his dead daughter" (200).

WORKS CITED

Barber, C. L. *Shakespeare's Festive Comedy*. Princeton: Princeton Univ. Press, 1959.

Bataille, Georges. *Death and Sensuality: A Study of Eroticism and the Taboo*. 1962; rpt. New York: Arno, 1977.

Berkowitz, David. *Renaissance Quarterly* 32 (1979): 396–403.

The Book of Common Prayer, 1559 Ed. John E. Booty. Charlottesville: Univ. of Virginia Press, 1967.

Brownell, Thomas Church, ed. *The Family Prayer Book; or, The Book of Common Prayer according to the Use of the Protestant Episcopal Church*. New York: Stanford and Swords, 1853.

Demos, John. *New York Times Book Review*, 25 Dec. 1977, 1.

Dundes, Alan. "'To Love My Father All': A Psychoanalytic Study of the Folktale Source of *King Lear*." *Southern Folklore Quarterly* 40 (1976): 353–66.

Eliade, Mircea. *The Sacred and the Profane*. Trans. Willard R. Trask. New York: Harcourt, 1959.

Evans, G. Blakemore, ed. *The Riverside Shakespeare*. Boston: Houghton, 1974.

Flandrin, Jean-Louis. *Families in Former Times: Kinship, Household and Sexuality*. Trans. Richard Southern. Cambridge: Cambridge Univ. Press, 1979.

Frey, Charles. "'O sacred, shadowy, cold, and constant queen': Shakespeare's Imperiled and Chastening Daughters of Romance." *South Atlantic Bulletin* 43 (1978):125–40.

Harding, D. W. "Father and Daughter in Shakespeare's Last Plays." *TLS*, 30 Nov. 1979, 59–61.

Hill, Christopher. "Sex, Marriage and the Family in England." *Economic History Review*, 2nd ser., 31 (1978):450–63.

Hooker, Richard. *Of the Lawes of Ecclesiasticall Politie*. 1594; facsim. rpt. Amsterdam: Theatrum Orbis Terrarum, 1971.

Hoy, Cyrus. "Fathers and Daughters in Shakespeare's Romances." In *Shakespeare's Romances Reconsidered*. Ed. Carol McGinnis Kay and Henry E. Jacobs. Lincoln: Univ. of Nebraska Press, 1978, 77–90.

Laslett, Peter. *The World We Have Lost*. 2nd ed. 1965; rpt. London: Methuen, 1971.

Legg, J. Wickham. *Ecclesiological Essays*. London: De La More Press, 1905.

Lévi-Strauss, Claude. *The Elementary Structures of Kinship*. Trans. James Harle Bell. Ed. John Richard von Sturmer and Rodney Needham. Paris, 1949; rpt. Boston: Beacon, 1969.

Noble, Richmond. *Shakespeare's Use of the Bible and* The Book of Common Prayer. London: Society for the Promotion of Biblical Knowledge, 1935.

Ranald, Margaret Loftus. "'As Marriage Binds, and Blood Breaks': English Marriage and Shakespeare." *Shakespeare Quarterly* 30 (1979):68–81.

Schwartz, Murray M., and Coppélia Kahn, eds. *Representing Shakespeare: New Psychoanalytic Essays*. Baltimore: Johns Hopkins Univ. Press, 1980.

The Statutes of the Realm. London: Record Commissions, 1820–28; facsim. ed. 1968.

Stone, Lawrence. *The Crisis of the Aristrocracy: 1558–1660*. Abridged ed. London: Oxford Univ. Press, 1971.

_____. *The Family, Sex and Marriage in England: 1500–1800*. New York: Harper, 1977.

Thomas, Keith. *TLS*, 21 Oct. 1977, 1226.

Turner, Victor W. *The Ritual Process: Structure and Anti-Structure*. Chicago: Aldine, 1969.

Van Gennep, Arnold. *The Rites of Passage*. Trans. Monika B. Vizedom and Gabrielle L. Caffee. 1908; rpt. London: Routledge and Kegan Paul, 1960.

Wheatly, Charles. *A Rational Illustration of* The Book of Common Prayer *According to the Use of the Church of England*. Cambridge: Cambridge Univ. Press, 1858.

Peter Stallybrass is a well-known scholar of Renaissance literature and culture; in addition to many articles, he is the author, with Allon White, of The Politics and Poetics of Transgression *(1986). In this article, he considers the ways that a Renaissance audience might have* seen *and interpreted the body of the boy actor performing women's roles in the theater. Rather than arguing (as earlier critics have often done) that the audience ignored or overlooked the sex-and-gender dissonance between the actor and role, Stallybrass is interested in the ways that the display of the boy/woman's body staged a complex of attitudes, relating anxieties about the ordering of sexuality and gender in the state to the morality of theatrical performance.*

PETER STALLYBRASS

FROM "TRANSVESTISM AND THE 'BODY BENEATH': SPECULATING ON THE BOY ACTOR"[1] **(1992)**

My paper starts from a puzzle: what did a Renaissance audience *see* when boy actors undressed on stage? The puzzle could, of course, be resolved by a simple (and, for my argument, damaging) move. The boy actor doesn't undress, or, at least, doesn't undress to the point of disturbing the illusion; the audience *sees* nothing. Against such a move, I want on the one hand to think quite bluntly about the prosthetic devices through which gender is rendered visible upon the stage. In that sense, the visible is an empirical question (although a question to which we seem to have surprisingly few answers). But, on the other hand, I want to suggest the degree to which the Renaissance spectator is required to *speculate* upon a boy actor who undresses, and thus to speculate upon the relation between the boy actor and the woman he plays. This speculation depends upon a cultural fantasy of sight, but a fantasy, I shall argue, that plays back and forth between sexual difference as a site of indeterminacy (the undoing of any stable or given difference) and sexual difference (and sexuality itself) as the production of contradictory fixations (fixations articulated through a fetishistic attention to particular items of clothing, particular parts of the body of an imagined woman, particular parts of an actual boy actor). I want to suggest that on the Renaissance stage the demand that the spectator *sees* is at its most intense in the undressing of the boy actor, at the very moment when *what* is seen is most vexed, being the point of intersection between spectatorship, the specular, and the speculative.

THE PROSTHETIC BODY

Perhaps the most substantial theatrical property of many Renaissance companies was a bed. It is a property which is called for in play after play, mainly in tragedy, but also in history and comedy. *Volpone* revolves around the bed in which Volpone simulates death, the bed from which he rises in his attempted rape of Celia; *Cymbeline* hinges upon Iachimo spying upon Imogen while she lies asleep in bed; in *The Maid's Tragedy*, Evadne ties the king to the bed in which they have made love before she kills him; in *Othello*, the bed bears the bodies of Desdemona, Emilia and Othello in the final scene. One becomes accustomed to stage directions like: 'King a bed' (Beaumont and Fletcher 1610: 5.1.12); 'Enter Othello, and Desdemona in her bed' (Shakespeare 1623b: 5.12); 'Enter Imogen in her Bed, and a Lady' (Shakespeare 1623d: 2.2). The bed becomes a focal point of scenes of sleep, of sex, of death. But bed scenes also focus upon facts so obvious that they resist interpretation as we hasten on to find out what these scenes are *about*: they draw attention to undressing or being undressed, to the process of shedding those garments through which class and gender were made visible and staged. They stage clothes as signs which can be put on and off, outward signs which can be assumed or shed.

At the same time, bed scenes foreground the body: the body which is either literally or symbolically about to be exposed. And here we come to a peculiar problem. The consensus of recent scholars on Renaissance transvestism has been that it is self-consciously staged mainly, or only, in comedy. Lisa Jardine, in her important work on the boy actor to which I am deeply indebted, states what has now become a commonplace:[2]

> the eroticism of the boy player is invoked in the drama whenever it is openly alluded to: on the whole this means in comedy, where role-playing and disguise is part of the genre. In tragedy, the willing suspension of disbelief does customarily extend, I think, to the taking of the female parts of boy players; taken for granted, it is not alluded to.   (Jardine 1983: 23)

But in bed scene after bed scene in Renaissance tragedy, we begin to witness an undressing or we are asked to see or to imagine an undressed (or partially undressed) body within the bed. What is it we are being asked to see?

If we take *Othello* as our starting point, we may reach some puzzling conclusions. As Lynda Boose has finely argued, the 'ocular proof' that Othello demands is reworked in the play as the audience's voyeuristic desire to *see*, to grossly gape (Boose 1987). But what are we to gape *at*? From the beginning of the eighteenth century, as Michael Neill has shown, illustrators of *Othello* were obsessively concerned with the depiction of the final bed scene. Even as Desdemona's 'Will to come to bed, my Lord?' (5.2.24) was cut from theatrical productions, illustrators focused upon the dead Desdemona lying in bed (Neill 1989: 35 fn.). And what the illustrators above all reveal (requiring that the spectator grossly gape) are the bedclothes and clothing pulled back to show a single exposed breast (see the illustrations by Boitard (1709), Loutherbourg (1785), Metz (1789), and Leney (1799), in Neill 1989: 386–9). The bed scene, then, is taken by the illustrators as an opportunity for the display of the female body, and in particular of a woman's breast.

Although we cannot take such illustrations as reflecting eighteenth-century stage productions, we do, in fact, find the exposure of the female breast recurrently called for by stage directions after the introduction of women actors to the stage in the previous century. On the Renaissance stage, actual boys played seeming 'boys' who were 'revealed' to be women—Ganymede as Rosalind, Cesario as Viola.[3] But on the Restoration stage, women played boys who were revealed to be women. And they were often revealed as women by the exposure of their breasts.

In fact, the commonest technique for the revelation of the 'woman beneath' after the Restoration was the removal of a wig, whereupon the female actor's 'true' hair would be seen. In Boyle's *Guzman* (1669), for instance, a woman disguised as a priest is exposed when 'Francisco pulls off her Peruque, and her Woman's Hair falls about her ears' (quoted in Wilson 1958: 84). Now this, of course, can depend upon the interplay of prostheses, an interplay which would have been perfectly possible on the Renaissance stage. The audience would have no means of knowing (any more than we do today) whether the hair beneath the wig was the hair of the actor or another wig. The play of difference (male wig/female hair) had no necessary relation to the anatomical specificities of the actor's body. If, then, the distinction of the sexes is staged as a distinction of hair (and above all of hair length), it will be constantly transformed by changes in hair styles. Sexual difference may, in this case, seem essentially prosthetic: the addition (or subtraction) of detachable (or growable/cuttable) parts.

It is precisely such a prosthetic view which William Prynne had denounced in *The Unlovelinesse of Lovelockes* (1628). There, he elaborates at length on St Paul: 'Doth not even nature itself teach you, that, if a man have long hair, it is a shame unto him? But if a woman have long hair it is a glory to her' (*I Corinthians* 11.14–15). From Prynne's perspective, the problem is precisely that 'nature' doesn't seem to have taught its lesson thoroughly enough. Cavalier men flaunt their long hair (and, from 1641, were to ridicule their opponents as 'Roundheads', in reference to their close-cropped hair). Prynne asserts that gender is defined by 'the outward Culture of [our] Heads, and Bodies' (Prynne 1628: A3v), and that the long hair of men and the short hair of women erase sexual difference. We live, he claims, in 'Unnaturall, and Unmanly times: wherein . . . sundry of our

Mannish, Impudent, and inconstant Female sexe, are Hermaphrodited, and transformed into men'
because they 'unnaturally clip, and cut their Haire' (ibid.: A3, G2). Asserting hair as a sign of *natural*
difference, Prynne is particularly fierce in his denunciation of wigs: 'the wearing of counterfeite,
false, and suppositious Haire, is *utterly unlawfull*' (ibid.: C4v, original emphasis). In using the
putting on and the taking off of wigs as the mark of gender difference, the Restoration stage turned
Prynne on his head. 'Natural' signs became the artifices of malleable gender.

But, as I noted above, the Restoration theatre used a second, overlapping method of revealing
the 'woman beneath': the exposure of the female actor's breasts. The methods are overlapping because they could be used together: in Wycherley's *The Plain Dealer* (1676), when Fidelia, in disguise, confesses that she is a woman, Vernish 'Pulls off her peruke and feels her breasts'; and in
Hopkins' *Friendship Improv'd* (1699), Locris, refusing to fight with her lover, says: 'Here's my bare
Breast, now if thou dar'st, strike here. (*She loosens her robe a little, her Helmet drops off, and her
Hair appears*)' (Wilson 1958: 84–5). Here, the stage directions are ambiguous: if Vernish feels Fidelia's breast and Locris 'loosens her robe', we cannot be sure what it was that an audience was sup-
posed actually to *see*.

The revelation of the female actor's breasts, though, is central to the staging of Aphra Behn's
The Younger Brother; Or, the Amorous Jilt (1696). In that play, there is an elaborate bed scene in
which Mirtilla, in love with the cross-dressed Olivia, says 'Come to my Bed' (stage direction: '*She
leading him [sic] to her Bed*'), while the Prince, who is in love with Mirtilla, breaks in upon the
scene. The prince grabs hold of the cross-dressed Olivia, and the stage direction reads: '*The* Prince
holding Olivia *by the Bosom of her Coat, her Breast appears to* Mirtilla.' Mirtilla: 'Ha! what do I
see?—Two Female rising Breasts. / By heav'n, a Woman.' The Prince, however, has not seen these
signs of Olivia's gender, and so the revelation is repeated by Mirtilla who, as a later stage direction
reads, '*Opens* Olivia's *Bosom, shows her Breasts*' (Behn 1696: 5.2.390). It is worth remarking that
Aphra Behn uses the revelation convention to play with the relation between woman and woman (it
is Mirtilla who first sees Olivia's breasts, it is she who opens Olivia's bosom).[4]

But there can be little doubt that such stagings of the female actor's breasts were usually constituted for arousal of the heterosexual male spectator. (A more extended discussion of this point
would look at the significant position of the Restoration theatre in the *construction* of the 'heterosexual male spectator'.) According to Colley Cibber, the very presence of female actors upon the
stage helped to constitute a new audience (or rather new spectators): 'The additional Objects then
of real, beautiful Women, could not but draw a portion of new Admirers to the Theatre' (Cibber
1968: 55). In the Epilogue to Nathaniel Lee's *The Rival Queens* (1677), the actors protest that if
their male spectators continue to lure female actors away from the stage, they will return to using
boy actors:

> For we have vow'd to find a sort of Toys
> Known to black Fryars, a Tribe of choopping Boys.
> If once they come, they'l quickly spoil your sport;
> There's not one Lady will receive your Court:
> But for the Youth in Petticoats run wild,
> With oh the archest Wagg, the sweetest Child.
> The panting Breasts, white Hands and little Feet
> No more shall your pall'd thoughts with pleasure meet.
> The Woman in Boys Cloaths, all Boy shall be,
> And never raise your thoughts above the Knee.   (Lee 1677: 282)

There are several interesting features about this epilogue: first, the threat to replace women with boy
actors is not imagined as a *general* loss but as a loss to the male spectator alone. The female spectator, on the contrary, is imagined as running wild after the 'Youth in Petticoats'. The boy actor is thus
depicted as particularly alluring to women, a possibility that has been addressed by Stephen Orgel
(1989b: 8).

But the grammar of the Epilogue is strangely playful about the crucial question: the difference
between a boy actor and a female actor. 'The panting Breasts, white Hands and little Feet' seem at
first to follow directly on from, and thus to be the attributes of, the archest wags, the sweetest children, but this possibility is retracted in the next line: 'No more' shall such breasts, hands and feet be
seen when boy actors return. Yet the *feet* of the boy actor would seem to be adequate enough for his

female role, if we are to take literally that he will 'never raise your thoughts above the Knee'. The crucial point of that latter line, of course, is what the boy actor does *not* have: implicitly a vagina; explicitly breasts.

It is that explicit absence upon which I want to dwell here. For recent criticism has been particularly concerned with the 'part' that the boy actor has which is not in his part. (I would want to suggest, incidentally, that that part has been peculiarly distorted [and enlarged] by being thought of as a 'phallus', as if a boy's small parts weren't peculiarly—and interestingly—at variance with the symbolic weight of THE phallus.) Criticism has thus been concerned with what Shakespeare calls the 'addition' which the boy actor brings to a female role. But in bed scene after bed scene, what is staged is a tableau in which we are about to witness the female body (and most particularly the female breast), even as it is a boy who is undressing. Indeed, there seems to be something so odd about this fact that it has simply been overlooked (an important exception, to which I am deeply indebted, is Shapiro 1990; for an earlier attempt to touch on this subject, see Rosenberg 1971: 17, 19).

So let me declare first of all what the puzzles are to which I have no solution. Did boy actors wear false breasts? There seem to be no records of such a practice, but the female fury at the beginning of *Salmacida Spolia* was presumably played by a professional actor and his/her *'breasts hung bagging down to her waist'* (quoted in Gossett 1988: 112). Or did boys use tight lacing to gather up their flesh so as to create a cleavage, or were they simply flat-chested, or . . . ? While John Rainolds denounces Achilles' transvestism, which William Gager had used in defense of the academic stage, he notes that Achilles had learned from Deidamia 'howe *he must hold his naked brest*' (Rainolds 1599: 17). A further question: in undressing scenes, how far did the boy actor go in actually removing his clothes or, if he was in bed, how much of his flesh was revealed? These are the questions I shall *not* be attempting to resolve.

Indeed, I want less to suggest a resolution than to express the dimensions of the problem. Lisa Jardine, whom I quoted above, assumes that the significance of the boy actor is virtually erased in tragedy (although her argument as a whole finely attends to the crucial importance of the cross-dressed boy). And Kathleen McLuskie (in what I take to be an implicit critique of Jardine) pushes for a *generally* conventional view of the boy actor (McLuskie 1987). To support her argument, she draws upon R. A. Foakes' *Illustrations of the English Stage*, which reproduces title pages and illustrations to play quartos in which women are represented with their breasts fully or partially exposed. McLuskie appears to conclude that this is how we are meant to think of the boy actors: within the convention, we can imagine them fully as women. But Foakes' *Illustrations* are themselves puzzling when we try to relate them to the practices of the English Renaissance stage and to the boy actor. (Only one of the illustrations to which I will refer can, in my view, be thought of as in any way an illustration *of* the stage; the others are illustrations (some presumably re-uses of woodcuts made for other purposes) *for* a *reader* of play quartos, a very different matter.)

How do these illustrations depict the female body, and, in particular, women's breasts? There is no one answer to this. To start with the three different title pages to *If You Know Not Me, You Know Nobody* in 1605, 1623, and 1639. All depict Elizabeth I, conventionally enough, in an elaborate gown with a low cut bodice (Foakes 1985: 91–3). But there is no suggestion of a cleavage, and only in the 1605 woodcut do two loops of pearls suggest the shape of her breasts. If a boy actor should want to imitate such an appearance, he would have no difficulty in doing so with the help of costume alone. And the same is true for the women represented on the title pages of *The Fair Maid of the West* (1631) and of *Englishmen for my Money* (1616) in which the attributes of gender depend upon hair and costume, and the bodices in these cases extend up to the neck (Foakes 1985: 130, 166). But the title page of William Alabaster's *Roxana* (1632) is more complicated. It is famous for the fact that in one of its panels it shows actors upon a stage (Foakes 1985: 73). The woman on the stage is clearly depicted as having swelling breasts. Another panel of the title page shows a couple in classical clothes, the man touching the woman's breasts, which are clearly depicted, as is her right nipple. At the furthest extreme, there are the title pages of Beaumont and Fletcher's *Philaster* (1620) and Sir William Lower's *The Enchanted Lovers* (1658), both of which depict women with fully exposed breasts (Foakes 1985: 118, 146). (On 30 May 1668, Pepys went to see *Philaster*, 'where it is pretty to see how I could remember almost all along, ever since I was a boy, Arethusa, the part which I was to have acted at Sir Robert Cookes's; and it was very pleasant to me, but more to think what a ridiculous thing it would have been for me to have acted a beautiful woman' [Pepys 1916:

94–5].) Some play quartos, then, draw attention to the specifications of women's bodies in ways which would be extremely difficult (if not impossible) to represent upon the stage.

Now this whole discussion would be irrelevant if we assumed that the convention of the boy actor meant that the physical body of the boy was subsumed by the conventions of femininity signified by costume and gesture. That such subsumptions are, indeed, one feature of Renaissance theatrical and non-theatrical texts is a point to which I shall return. But what I want to emphasize here is the extent to which such subsumptions were also played with to the point of their undoing. That they *could* be played with has something to do with systematic dislocations between visual and linguistic systems of representation in the Renaissance. I noted above the extent to which visual representations of women in play quartos move between representations which depend upon costume/hair/gesture and those which also depend upon a display of the naked body, and in particular of the naked breast. The displayed breast is a metonymy for woman. Since for us, both 'breast' and 'bosom' are always already gendered, this comes as little surprise. But in the Renaissance, both 'breast' and 'bosom' are used interchangeably for men and women. ('Pap', on the other hand, was usually applied only to women.) 'Bosom', indeed, seems to be more frequently gendered as *masculine*. For instance, after the 1611 translation of the Bible which introduced the Hebraic 'wife of thy bosome' and 'husband of her bosome', it was only the *former* expression which became current, thus re-emphasizing the bosom as male (see *OED*). In Ford's *'Tis Pity She's a Whore*, Giovanni offers his dagger to his sister, Annabella, and says: 'And here's my breast; strike home! / Rip up my bosom' (1633a, 1.3) The language of breasts and bosoms tended to be either ungendered or absorbed into the power of the patriarch. To 'toy' with breasts verbally, then, had no obvious implications for the relation of the boy actor to his female role.

But this indeterminacy of gender at the verbal level (an indeterminacy which, I would argue, was determined by a motivated absorption of the female body) was opposed by the visual codes in which the breast was insistently gendered as female. What remains extraordinary is the extent to which this female-gendered breast is staged by the boy actor. In Jonson's *The Devil is an Ass*, for instance, as Wittipol approaches '[t]hese sister-swelling brests' of Frances Fitz-Dottrell, the stage direction reads: *'he growes more familiar in his Courtship, plays with her paps, kisseth her hands, &'* (1631: 2.6.71). (Michael Shapiro gives other striking examples [1990: 1–2].) But the boy actor's 'female body' is most commonly the object of attention in tragedy and tragi-comedy. There, we are asked not to *imagine* the boy actor as he is dressed *up*, but literally to *gaze* at him whilst he *un*dresses.

This staging of the undressing boy is particularly striking in death scenes and bed scenes which draw attention to the boy actor's 'breast'. In Ford's *Love's Sacrifice*, the Duke says to Bianca 'Prepare to die', and she responds:

> I do; and to the point
> Of thy sharp sword with open breast I'll run
> Half way thus naked.   (1633b, 5.1)

But even more striking is the way in which Shakespeare in both *Antony and Cleopatra* and *Cymbeline* changes his sources so as to stage the boy's breast. In Plutarch, Cleopatra attaches an asp to her *arm*. Shakespeare retains this, but only after she has already placed an asp upon her *breast*. And Cleopatra/the boy actor, who has already imagined seeing '[s]ome squeaking *Cleopatra* Boy my greatnesse', focuses upon the contradictory vision of Cleopatra's nursing breast/the boy actor's breast: 'Dost thou not see my Baby at my breast, / That suckes the Nurse asleepe' (1623c, 5.2.218, 308–9).[5] An audience seems to be required to observe the splitting apart of what later critics assumed to be a stable 'convention'. More than that, critics have appealed to the presence of the boy actor to 'explain' that certain stagings would have been 'impossible'. Enobarbus's description of Cleopatra is thus taken as a technique of avoidance, by which the audience is spared the embarrassment of gazing at a transvestite boy. But what becomes of such explanations when, again and again, we find Renaissance dramatists going beyond their sources to demand that we witness the boy actor at the very point which a later audience has ruled unimaginable?

In *Cymbeline*, for instance, as Iachimo observes Imogen asleep in bed, he fetishizes both the chamber, the bracelet which will represent her lost honour, and a 'mole Cinque-spotted' upon 'her left brest' (1623d, 2.2.37–8). This last detail, like the asp on Cleopatra's breast, is truly remarkable.

It has been argued that Shakespeare used *Frederyke of Jennen* as a source for *Cymbeline*, and in that pamphlet John of Florence notes *not* a mole on the *breast*, but a wart on the *arm* of Ambrose's wife: 'it fortuned that her lefte arme lay on the bed; and on that arme she had a blacke warte' (Anon. 1560: 197). But Shakespeare replaces the wart with a mole (thus following Boccaccio's version of the story), a mole which is given a *precise* but *imaginary* location upon the body of the boy actor. To make the left breast the object of this voyeuristic scene is to focus our attention on one of the sites of the cultural differentiation of gender. But that site produces antithetical readings: Imogen's swelling breast; the breast of a boy actor. It is as if within the dramatic fiction, the fetishistic signs of presence are forced to confront the absences which mark the actor's body. Or perhaps we might rather say that two contradictory realities are forced to peer into each other's faces. In *Cymbeline*, at the very moment where a later audience would expect a discrete effacement of the theatrical means by which gender is produced, those means are verbally and visually staged.

The specifically erotic charge of such bed scenes is suggested by Aphra Behn, even as she attempts to defend herself against the supposed indecency of her plays. Accused of staging lewd revelations of the actor's body ('they cry, *That Mr.* Leigh *opens his Night Gown, when he comes into the Bride chamber*'), she responds that the best plays are full of such things:

> *Valentinian* all loose and ruffld a Moment after the Rape . . . , the *Moor of Venice* in many places. The *Maids Tragedy*—see the Scene of undressing the Bride, and between the *King* and *Amintor*, and after between the *King* and *Evadne* . . .   (Behn 1967: 186)

It is striking that Behn, in thinking of the erotics of the theatre, thinks of Rochester's *Valentinian*, a Restoration play which explicitly stages homoeroticism,[6] and Renaissance plays in which the undressing of the bride was performed by a boy. Behn, of course, would have seen the plays performed with female actors, but she nevertheless emphasizes the extent to which these plays reveal the body.

To be aware of the fetishistic staging of the boy actor, of the insistence that we see what is not there to see, is to conceptualize the erotics of Renaissance drama in totally unfamiliar ways. Think, for instance, of the end of *Othello* (1623b: 4.3). 'Prithee, tonight / Lay on my bed our wedding-sheets', Desdemona says to Emilia. But interpolated between the command and the on-stage arrival of the bed itself, we are asked to witness the boy actor prepare for bed. In one sense, the scene suggests that this preparation is itself a kind of transvestism—a crossing from day to night, from the clothes of a Venetian noble to a shift. And it is curious to note how such 'closet' scenes are frequently—and strangely—marked by an explicit movement from formal to informal dress. Even ghosts obey this convention, if we are to believe the first quarto of *Hamlet*, where Hamlet Senior, appearing to his son in Gertrude's closet, has put off his armour and put on his nightgown. Both in *Othello* and *Hamlet*, the body seems to be simultaneously sexualized and made vulnerable. But in *Othello*, the movement from one set of clothes to another is curiously truncated. Desdemona's command to Emilia, 'Give me my nightly wearing', is followed some twenty lines later by Emilia's enquiry, 'Shall I go fetch your nightgown?' to which Desdemona answers 'No'. In fact, the absence of the nightgown makes all the more insistent the fact that we are witnessing Desdemona/a boy actor undress. The undressing is the more *present* as a strip-tease for the *absence* of any substitute clothing. 'Prithee unpin me', Desdemona says, and later, rejecting the nightgown, 'No, unpin me here.'[7]

Before I return to this moment of voyeuristic suspense where the staged body prepares to split into the unpinned clothes and the 'body beneath', I want to note how the scene as a whole stages a series of splittings or—to put it another way—a series of radical crossings of perspective. First, there is the presentation to the audience of Emilia's impressively relativistic view of sexual morality, a view which threatens to re-present the whole play as grotesque farce, the absurd magnification of 'a *small* vice'. Curiously, and to the disturbance of many critics, the 'sport' which Emilia commends seems to migrate into the language of Desdemona:

> DESDEMONA: unpin me here;
>   This Lodovico is a proper man.
> EMILIA: A very handsome man.
> DESDEMONA: He speaks well.
> EMILIA: I know a lady in Venice would have walk'd
>   barefoot to Palestine for a touch of his nether lip.

As Desdemona is unpinned, Othello is displaced by that 'proper man', Lodovico. At the same time, Desdemona herself takes on the voice of a maidservant called Barbary. (I am here indebted to Raima Evans's work on this scene.) The willow song is the song of that maid, whose name is itself a curious transposing of Iago's slur against Othello as he goads Brabantio: 'you'll have your daughter cover'd with a Barbary horse; you'll have your nephews neigh to you'. Barbary: the name for bestial male sexuality; the name for a maid betrayed in love—'poor Barbary'. A single signifier slides between male and female, animal and human, betrayer and betrayed, and at the same time between opposed notions of the 'barbarian' as oppressor and as victim. And it is the song of a poor maid which the Venetian noble will reiterate.

I want to draw attention to these slippages within the signifier because they provide one possible model through which we could read the undressing of Desdemona. On such a reading, the closure of the play would be unsettled by a startling moment of indeterminancy when we are held in suspension between cultural antitheses and, at the same time, between the fiction of Desdemona and the staging of the boy actor. But I do not believe that 'indeterminacy' is an adequate way of thinking about these moments. Rather, we are forced into contradictory attitudes about both sexuality and gender: on the one hand, gender as a set of prosthetic devices (in which case, the *object* of sexual attention is absorbed into the play of those devices); on the other, gender as the 'given' marks of the body (the breast, the vagina, the penis) which (however analogous in Galenic medicine) are read as the signs of an absolute difference (in which case, sexuality, whether between man and woman, woman and woman, or man and man, tends to be organized through a fixation upon the supposedly 'essential' features of gender). But on the Renaissance stage, even those 'essential' features are located—whether prosthetically or at the level of the imaginary—upon *another body*.

In comedy, the relation between the boy's body, the female role and erotic play is at times explicitly articulated. In *The Taming of a Shrew*, the Lord says to the boy in the first scene:

And dresse yourselfe like some lovelie ladie,
And when I call see that you come to me.
For I will say to him thou art his wife,
Dallie with him and hug him in thine armes,
And if he desire to goe to bed with thee,
Then faine some scuse and say thou wilt anon.   (Anon. 1594: 71)

And Sly puts 'The boy in Woman's attire' on his knee and says that 'she and I will go to bed anon' (72). In Shakespeare's *The Taming of the Shrew*, the Lord requires of the boy that he greet Sly not only with 'kinde embracements' but with 'tempting kisses' (Shakespeare 1623a: Ind. 1.116), and there is an expanded invocation of the pleasures of the bed:

Wee'l have thee to a Couch,
Softer and sweeter then the lustfull bed
On purpose trim'd up for Semiramis.   (Ind. 2.38–40)

Sly's invitation to bed is also amplified: 'Madam undresse you, and come now to bed' (Ind. 2.118). In both plays, any undressing or bed scene is explicitly circumvented, and this draws attention to the fact that in bed scenes (such as the ones I have looked at above) female clothes and boy actor are separated out.

But even here, I think, we can note a radical oscillation between a sense of the absolute difference of the boy from his role and the total absorption of the boy into the role. In other words, if Renaissance theatre constructs an eroticism that depends upon a play of differences (the boy's breast / the woman's breast), it also equally conjures up an eroticism which depends upon the total absorption of male into female, female into male. In the printed text of Shakespeare's *The Shrew* in 1623, the boy is named as 'Bartholomew my Page' (Ind. I. 103) and yet, in changing into the clothes of a woman, he is entirely subsumed into her role. When in *A Shrew*, a stage direction reads '*Enter the boy in Woman's attire*', in *The Shrew* it reads: '*Enter Lady with Attendants*' (Ind. 2. 99). Moreover, the speech prefixes are all for '*Lady*' or '*La*'. The text thus accomplishes what John Rainolds warns against in *Th' Overthrow of Stage-Playes*: 'beware the beautifull boyes *transformed into women* by putting on their raiment, their feature, lookes and facions' (1599: 34, my emphasis). This transformation is carefully erased by a modern editor like Brian Morris, who emends the stage direction to read '*Enter* [PAGE *as a*] *lady*' and changes the speech prefixes to read '*Page*' (Morris 1981: 168). In the Folio *The Shrew*, we are thus presented with a wild oscillation between contradictory positions: the plot of the induction demands that we remain aware of Bartholomew *as* Bartholomew, while the language of the text simply cuts Bartholomew, replacing him with 'Lady'.

Such wild oscillations are peculiarly resonant upon the stage, precisely because of the boy actor. But comparable shifts are also characteristic of non-dramatic texts. In *Frederyke of Jennen*, as soon as 'Ambroses wyfe' takes on the name of 'Frederyke' she becomes 'he'. Where a modern text would want to register the 'body beneath' (that is, 'she dressed as he'), *Frederyke* inscribes the transformation of female into male through name and clothes. But, on the other hand, the transformation of Frederick back into Ambrose's wife *does* depend upon the revelation of the body beneath:

> in the meane whyle went the lorde Frederyke secretly away, and came into the chamber, where she did unclothe her al naked saving a clothe before her membres, and than came into the hall before the kyng and al his lordes . . . (Anon. 1560: 202)

Yet this 'revelation' itself suggests no simple hierarchical relation of 'reality' between what would later be read as 'disguise' and the 'true' body: clothed, he is 'lorde Frederyke'; naked, she is 'the woman' and then 'his [Ambrose's] wyfe'.

This oscillation of gender within a single sentence is even more striking in Barnabe Rich's tale 'Of Apolonius and Silla': Silla dresses in men's clothes and assumes the name of her brother, Silvio. When accused by Julina of impregnating her, Silvio/Silla reveals 'his' body:

> here with all loosing his garmentes doune to his stomacke, and shewed *Iulina* his breastes and pretie teates, surmountyng farre the whitenesse of Snowe it self, saiying: . . . see I am a woman the daughter of a noble Duke . . . (Rich 1581: 177)

Silvio shows '*his*' breasts which show that he is a woman (but also, curiously, that he is a nobleman's daughter). The phrase 'his breastes and pretie teates' thus enacts the very cross-gendering at the grammatical level which the sentence is undoing at the level of narrative. The garments which are 'his'—the social inscriptions of masculinity—retain, however briefly, their power to name a body which is equally powerfully asserted as *hers* ('I am a woman'). And the body which is 'hers' is in turn reinscribed as 'his' through the name of father and husband ('the daughter of a noble Duke', 'Ambroses wyfe').

The power of clothes, like language, to *do* things to the body is suggested in both these romances, and it is this power of clothes which is so insistently asserted by anti-theatricalists. Calvin, in his sermons on Deuteronomy, if he sometimes thinks of clothes as *manifesting* sexual difference, equally thinks of them as *creating* difference: 'God intended to shew us that every bodies attyring of themselves ought to be such, *as there may be difference betweene men and women*' (1583: 773, my emphasis). Similarly, Prynne thinks of women who 'mimic' masculinity as 'hermaphrodited and transformed into men' (1628: A3) and of male actors 'metamorphosed into women on the Stage' (1633: 171). And he follows Calvin in arguing that 'a mans attyring himselfe in womans array . . . perverts one principall use of garments, *to difference men from women*' (1633: 207, original emphasis).

The anti-theatricalists thus feared the power of clothes to *produce* new subjects, to metamorphose boy into woman, commoner into aristocrat. John Rainolds' powerful attack upon the academic stage (and, by extension, upon all theatrical activity) was provoked in the first instance by the almost magical properties of transvestism (Boas 1914: 231–4; Young 1916: 593–604; Binns 1974: 95–101; Jardine 1983: 14–17). Rainolds, one of the greatest scholars of his day, had himself cross-dressed in his youth (Boas 1914: 105–6) and in *Th' Overthrow of Stage-Playes* he admits that 'he did play a womans part upon the same stage, the part of Hippolyta' (Rainolds 1599: 45). But what exactly *is* the danger of transvestism? Here, Rainolds' citations are frequently opaque, as, for instance, the following from Dionysius Carthusianus:

> the apparell of wemen (*saith he*) is a great provocation of men to lust and leacherie: because a womans garment being put on a man doeth vehemently touch and move him with the remembrance and imagination of a woman: and the imagination of a thing desirable doth stir up the desire. (Rainolds 1599: 96)

What does Rainolds' translation imply? That the woman's body is imprinted upon or within the clothes? That women's clothes, when they touch and move the male wearer, will awaken the desire *for* women (whom he will remember and imagine) or the desire *to be* a woman? Will the desire be homo- or heteroerotic and will it be directed towards another or towards the self?

The Renaissance theatre was thus the site for the prosthetic production of the sexualized body through the clothing of the body and the mimed gestures of love. But it was also the site where the prosthetic production was dramatically staged and speculated upon, as the boy actor undressed, as the fixations of spectators were drawn back and forth between the clothes which embodied and determined a particular sexual identity and contradictory fantasies of the 'body beneath'—the body of a woman, the body of a boy; a body with and without breasts.

THE TRANSVESTITE BODY[8]

The interplay between clothing and undressing on the Renaissance stage organized gender around a process of fetishizing, which is conceived *both* as a process of fixation *and* as indeterminable. If the Renaissance stage demands that we '*see*' particular body parts (the breast, the penis, the naked body), it also reveals that such fixations are inevitably unstable. The actor is both boy and woman, and he/she embodies the fact that sexual fixations are not the product of any categorical fixity of gender. Indeed, all attempts to fix gender are necessarily *prosthetic*: that is, they suggest the attempt to supply an imagined deficiency by the exchange of male clothes for female clothes or of female clothes for male clothes; by displacement from male to female space or from female to male space; by the replacement of male with female tasks or of female with male tasks. But all elaborations of the prosthesis which will supply the 'deficiency' can secure no essence. On the contrary, they suggest that gender itself is a fetish, the production of an identity through the fixation upon specific 'parts'. The imagined 'truth' of gender which a post-Renaissance culture would later construct is dependent upon the disavowal of the fetishism of gender, the disavowal of gender as fetish. In its place, it would put a fantasized biology of the 'real'.

But it is this notion of the 'real' which seems to be dramatically undone in undressing scenes, as in *Othello* when Desdemona/the boy actor is unpinned. Lynda Boose has demonstrated how the play itself demands both concealment (of the sexual scene, of the bed and its burden which 'poisons sight') and exposure (the stimulated desire that we should *see*, should 'grossly gape'). But, as I have argued, *what* we should see is radically uncertain. It is not so much a moment of indeterminacy as of contradictory fixations. On the one hand, the clothes themselves—the marks of Desdemona's gender and status—are held up to our attention; on the other, we teeter on the brink of seeing the boy's breastless but 'pinned' body revealed. It is as if, at the moments of greatest dramatic tension, the Renaissance theatre stages its own transvestism.

Contradictory fixations, though, are precisely what mobilize *Othello*. Think, for instance, of how Iago constructs the narrative of Desdemona's betrayal so that Othello can approach the 'grossly gaping' of her being 'topp'd'. He does it by casting *himself* in the role of Desdemona:

> I lay with *Cassio* lately . . .
> In sleepe I heard him say, sweet *Desdemona*,
> Let us be wary, let us hide our Loves,
> And then (Sir) would he gripe, and wring my hand:
> Cry, oh sweet Creature: then kisse me hard,
> As if he pluckt up kisses by the rootes,
> That grew upon my lippes, laid his Leg ore my Thigh,
> And sigh, and kisse . . .   (1623b: 3.3.419–31)

It is these contradictory fixations (Desdemona and/as the boy actor, Desdemona and/as Iago) which a later theatre would attempt to erase, precisely because the *site* of the audience's sexual fixation is so uncertain.

This uncertainty is, paradoxically, most powerfully felt by anti-theatrical writers. They oscillate between seeing the boy actor as woman, as neither woman nor man, as alluring boy, as male prostitute (or 'dogge', to use Rainolds' term). Prynne, for instance, incorporates Cyprian's account of how the theatre taught 'how a man might be effeminated into a female, how their sex might be changed by Art' (1633: 169). But he can also think of actors as those who, 'by unchaste infections of their members, effeminate their manly nature, being both effeminate men and women, yea, being neither men nor women' (ibid.). Yet the uncertainty of *what* anti-theatricalists saw in no way inhibited the fascinated fixity of their (imaginary) gaze. What they gazed at was a theatre imagined *as a bedroom*, a bedroom which spills off the stage and into the lives of players and audience alike:

> O . . . that thou couldest in that sublime watch-tower insinuate thine eyes into these Players secrets; or set open the closed dores of their bed-chambers, and bring all their innermost hidden Cels unto the conscience of thine eyes. . . . [M]en rush on men with outragious lusts. (Prynne 1633: 135)

So writes Prynne, translating Cyprian. And Phillip Stubbes sees the actors as contaminating the spectators so that, 'these goodly pageants being done, every mate sorts to his mate . . . and in their secret conclaves (covertly) they play *the Sodomits*, or worse' (Stubbes 1583: 144–5). But *what* anti-theatricalists saw in the 'secret conclaves' of the theatrical bedroom constantly shifted, thus mimicking the shifting perspectives of the Renaissance stage itself.

For the bed scenes and undressing scenes with which I have been concerned produce moments of dizzying indeterminacy. It was such moments that Freud attempted to describe in his essay on 'Fetishism', where the fetish stands in for and mediates between the marks of sexual difference.[9] Freud writes:

> In very subtle instances both the disavowal and the affirmation of the castration (of woman) have found their way into the construction of the fetish itself. This was so in the case of a man whose fetish was an athletic support-belt which could also be worn as bathing drawers. This piece of clothing covered up the genitals entirely and concealed the distinction between them. Analysis showed that it signified that women were castrated *and* that they were not castrated; and it also allowed of the hypothesis that men were castrated, for all these possibilities could equally well be concealed under the belt. . . .

The athletic support-belt, through its concealments, supports contradictory hypotheses. But for Freud, all those hypotheses must be grounded in the fantasy of castration. Why? Because Freud needs to find a fixed point (and a *male* point) outside the play of fetishism, a point to which all other fetishes will teleologically point. The fetishist is, Freud suggests, someone whose interest '*comes to a halt half-way, as it were*' (my emphasis). 'Thus the foot or shoe owes its preference as a fetish—or a part of it—to the circumstance that the inquisitive boy peered at the woman's genitals from below, from her legs up.' The fetish is, for Freud, but part of the larger category of perversions. 'Perversions', he writes in the 'Three essays on the theory of sexuality':

> are sexual activities which either a) *extend*, in an anatomical sense, beyond the regions of the body that are designed for sexual union, or b) *linger*, over the intermediate relations to the sexual object which should normally be traversed rapidly on the path towards the sexual aim. (Freud 1905: 62)

The very notion of the perverse, like that of the fetish, can only emerge in relation to a) the parts of the body which are 'naturally' sexual and b) a teleological path towards the genitals. The transvestite theatre of the Renaissance, though, does not allow for any such distinction between the 'perverse' and the normal teleological path.

From a Freudian perspective, it 'comes to a halt half-way, as it were'. It does so because it resists the sexual and narrative teleologies which would be developed in the eighteenth and nineteenth centuries. But that resistance is, I believe, less a matter of indeterminacy than of the production of contradictory fixations: the imagined body of a woman, the staged body of a boy actor, the material presence of clothes. Freud's brilliant insight was to see that the 'real person' was itself a displacement of fetishism:

> The progressive concealment of the body which goes along with civilization keeps sexual curiosity awake. This curiosity seeks to complete the sexual object by revealing its hidden parts. It can, however, be diverted ('sublimated') in the direction of art, if its interest can be shifted away from the genitals on to the shape of the body as a whole.   (Freud 1905: 69)

'The body as a whole', then, is itself a fantasy, a sublimation. But for Freud, the real tends to reappear *behind* or *beneath* that fantasy, a real which always tends towards the formation of sexual difference. In the 'mingle-mangle', the 'hodge-podge', the 'gallimaufry' of Renaissance tragedy, though, contradictory fetishisms (body parts, costumes, handkerchiefs, sheets) are staged not in the play of pure difference but in the play between indeterminacy and fixation.

NOTES

[1] I am deeply indebted for ideas, references and challenges to Lynda Boose, Greg Bredbeck, Linda Charnes, Lisa Jardine, David Kastan, Michael Shapiro, and Valerie Traub; and I couldn't even have begun without the stimulus of Jonathan Dollimore, Marjorie Garber, Ann Rosalind Jones, Stephen Orgel, Phyllis Rackin and Susan Zimmerman.

[2] For important revisions to Lisa Jardine's earlier work, see her 'Twins and travesties' in this volume.

[3] On the occasional presence of women on English stages prior to the Restoration, see for instance Stokes (1985–6: 335–6); Bentley (1941: 25); and Gossett (1988).

[4] Interestingly, it seems that it was for the revelation of the *male* body that Behn was most virulently criticized: taxing her with indecency, her critics, she writes, claim 'That Mr. Leigh *opens his Night Gown, when he comes into the Bride-Chamber;* if he do, which is a Jest of his own making, and which I never saw, I hope he has his Cloaths on underneath. And if so, where is the Indecency?' Behn goes on to imply that the charge of indecency is specifically levelled against her as a woman writer: 'had the Plays I have writ come forth under any Mans Name, and never known to have been mine; I appeal to all unbyast Judges of Sense, if they had not said that Person had made as many good Comedies, as any one Man that has writ in our Age; but a Devil on't the Woman damns the Poet' (Behn 1687: 186, 184).

[5] For other accounts of Cleopatra and the boy actor, see Rackin (1972), Shapiro (1982), and Gruber (1985).

[6] *Valentinian* 5.5 opens with 'Valentinian *and the* Eunuch *discovered on a Couch'.* Valentinian says:

> Oh let me press these balmy Lips all day,
> And bath my Love scorch'd Soul in thy moist Kisses.
> Now by my Joys thou art all sweet And soft,
> And thou shalt be the Altar of my love;
> Upon thy Beauties hourly will I offer,
> And pour out Pleasure and blest Sacrifice,
> To the dear Memory of my Lucina . . .
>
> (Rochester 1696: 215)

[7] John Russell Brown has pointed out to me that, in the dominant theatrical tradition, the 'unpinning' refers to Desdemona's *hair.* That there is no Renaissance warrant for this is suggested by the *OED*, which actually quotes Desdemona's lines as referring to the unpinning of *clothes*, and also gives further examples.

[8] My account of transvestism, and of the boy actor in general, is deeply indebted to Jonathan Dollimore's brilliant essay on 'Subjectivity, sexuality and transgression' (1986).

[9] My account of fetishism is deeply indebted to Marjorie Garber (1989). See also her fine, wide-ranging study, *Vested Interests.*

WORKS CITED

Agnew, J. -C. (1986) *Worlds Apart: The Market and the Theater in Anglo-American Thought, 1550–1750*, Cambridge: Cambridge University Press.

Anon. (1560) *Frederyke of Jennen*, in J. M. Nosworthy (ed.) *Cymbeline*, the Arden Shakespeare, London and New York: Methuen, 1955, 191–204.

Anon. (1594) *The Taming of a Shrew*, in G. Bullough (ed.) *Narrative and Dramatic Sources of Shakespeare*, vol. 1, London: Routledge & Kegan Paul, 1957.

Appadurai, A. (1986) 'Introduction: Commodities and the politics of value', in A. Appadurai (ed.) *The Social Life of Things: Commodities in Cultural Perspective*, Cambridge: Cambridge University Press, 3–63.

Beaumont, F. and Fletcher, J. (1610) *The Maid's Tragedy*, ed. A. Gurr, Berkeley: University of California Press, 1969.

Behn, A. (1687) *The Lucky Chance; Or, An Alderman's Bargain*, in M. Summers (ed.) *The Works of Aphra Behn*, vol. 3, New York: Phaeton, 1967 (1915).

_____ (1696) *The Younger Brother; Or, the Amorous Jilt*, in M. Summers (ed.) *The Works of Aphra Behn*, vol. 4, New York: Phaeton, 1967 (1915), 311–99.

Bentley, G. E. (1941) *The Jacobean and Caroline Stage*, vol. 1, Oxford: Clarendon Press.

_____ (1984) *The Profession of Player in Shakespeare's Time*, Princeton: Princeton University Press.

Binns, J. W. (1974) 'Women or transvestites on the Elizabethan stage?: an Oxford controversy', *Sixteenth Century Journal*, 5, 2: 95–120.

Boas, F. S. (1914) *University Drama in the Tudor Age*, Oxford: Oxford University Press.

Boose, L. (1987) '"Let it be Hid": Iago, Renaissance pornography, and *Othello's* "grossly gaping" audience', unpublished ms.

Calvin, J. (1583) *The Sermons of M. John Calvin Upon . . . Deuteronomie*, trans. A. Golding, London.

Chambers, E. K. (1923) *The Elizabethan Stage*, vol. 4, Oxford: Clarendon Press.

Cibber, C. (1968) *An Apology for the Life of Colley Cibber*, ed. B. R. S. Fone, Ann Arbor: University of Michigan Press.

Dollimore, J. (1986) 'Subjectivity, sexuality and transgression: the Jacobean connection', *Renaissance Drama*, n.s. 17: 53–81.

_____ (1990) 'The cultural politics of perversion: Augustine, Shakespeare, Freud, Foucault', *Genders*, 8: 1–16.

Foakes, R. A. (1985) *Illustrations of the English Stage 1580–1642*, London: Scolar Press.

Ford, J. (1633a) *'Tis Pity She's a Whore*, in H. Ellis (ed.) *John Ford*, New York: Hill & Wang (1957), 5–163.

_____ (1633b) *Love's Sacrifice*, in H. Ellis (ed.) *John Ford*, New York: Hill & Wang (1957), 257–340.

Freeburg, V. O. (1915) *Disguise Plots in Elizabethan Drama: A Study in Stage Tradition*, New York: Columbia University Press.

Freud, S. (1905) 'Three essays on the theory of sexuality', in James Strachey and Angela Richards (eds) *On Sexuality*, trans. James Strachey, Harmondsworth: Penguin, 1977, 33–204.

Garber, M. (1989) 'Fetish envy', paper given at the Modern Languages Association, New Orleans.

_____ (1991a) 'The logic of the transvestite: *The Roaring Girl*', in D. S. Kastan and P. Stallybrass (eds) *Staging the Renaissance: Reinterpretations of Elizabethan and Jacobean Drama*, London and New York: Routledge, 221–34.

_____ (1991b) *Vested Interests: Cross-Dressing and Cultural Anxiety*, New York and London: Routledge.

Gossett, S. (1988) '"Man-maid, begone!": Women in masques', *English Literary Renaissance* 18: 96–113.

Gruber, W. (1985) 'The actor in the script: affective strategies in Shakespeare's *Antony and Cleopatra*', *Comparative Drama* 19, 1:30–48.

Hillebrand, H. N. (1926) *The Child Actors: A Chapter in Elizabethan Stage History*, New York: Russell & Russell, 1964.

Howard, J. (1988) 'Crossdressing, the theatre, and gender struggle in early modern England', *Shakespeare Quarterly* 39, 4:418–40.

Jamieson, M. (1968) 'Shakespeare's celibate stage', in G. E. Bentley (ed.) *The Seventeenth-Century Stage: A Collection of Critical Essays*, Chicago: University of Chicago Press, 70–93.

Jardine, L. (1983) *Still Harping on Daughters: Women and Drama in the Age of Shakespeare*, Brighton: Harvester.

Jonson, B. (1607) *Volpone, or the Foxe*, in C. H. H. Percy and E. Simpson (eds) *Ben Jonson*, vol. 5, Oxford: Clarendon Press, 1938.

_____ (1631) *The Devil is an Ass*, in C. H. H. Percy and E. Simpson (eds) *Ben Jonson*, vol. 6, Oxford: Clarendon Press, 1938.

Lee, N. (1677) *The Rival Queens*, in T. B. Stroup and A. L. Cooke (eds) *The Works of Nathaniel Lee*, New Brunswick: Scarecrow, 1954, 211–13.

McLuskie, K. (1987) 'The act, the role, and the actor: Boy actresses on the Elizabethan stage', *New Theatre Quarterly* 3, 10: 120–30.

Marston, J. (1906) *John Marston's The Wonder of Women or The Tragedy of Sophonisba*, ed. W. Kemp, New York and London: Garland, 1979.

Maus, K. E. (1979) '"Playhouse flesh and blood": Sexual ideology and the Restoration actress', *ELH* 46, 4: 595–617.

Morris, B. (ed.) (1981) *The Taming of the Shrew*, the Arden Shakespeare, London and New York: Methuen.

Neill, M. (1989) 'Unproper beds: Race, adultery, and the hideous in *Othello*', *Shakespeare Quarterly* 40, 4: 383–412.

Orgel, S. (1985) 'Making greatness familiar', in D. M. Bergeron (ed.) *Pageantry in the Shakespearean Theatre*, Athens: University of Georgia Press, 19–25.

_____ (1989a) 'Nobody's perfect: or why did the English stage take boys for women?' *South Atlantic Quarterly* 88, 1: 7–29.

_____ (1989b) 'The boys in the back room: Shakespeare's apprentices and the economics of theatre', a paper given at the Modern Languages Association, New Orleans.

Pepys, S. (1916) *Pepys on the Restoration Stage*, ed. H. McAfee, New Haven: Yale University Press.

Prynne, W. (1628) *The Unlovelinesse of Lovelockes*, London.

_____ (1633) *Histrio-Mastix*, London.

Rackin, P. (1972) 'Shakespeare's boy Cleopatra, the decorum of nature, and the golden world of poetry', *PMLA* 87: 201–12.

_____ (1987) 'Androgyny, mimesis, and the marriage of the boy heroine on the English Renaissance stage', *PMLA* 102: 29–41.

Rainolds, J. (1599) *Th' Overthrow of Stage-Playes*, London.

Rich, B. (1581) 'Of Apolonius and Silla' in J. M. Lothian and T. W. Craik (eds) *Twelfth Night*, the Arden Shakespeare, London and New York: Metheun, 1975, 157–79.

Rochester, J., Earl of (1696) *Poems On Several Occasions with Valentinian*, London.

Rosenburg, M. (1971) *The Masks of Othello*, Berkeley: University of California Press.

_____ (1978) *The Masks of Macbeth*, Berkeley: University of California Press.

Shakespeare, W. (1623a) *The Taming of the Shrew*, in C. Hinman (ed.) *The First Folio of Shakespeare: The Norton Facsimile*, New York: Norton, 1968.

_____ (1623b) *Othello*, in C. Hinman (ed.) *The First Folio of Shakespeare: The Norton Facsimile*, New York: Norton, 1968.

_____ (1623c) *Antony and Cleopatra*, in C. Hinman (ed.) *The First Folio of Shakespeare: The Norton Facsimile*, New York: Norton, 1968.

_____ (1623d) *Cymbeline*, in C. Hinman (ed.) *The First Folio of Shakespeare: The Norton Facsimile*, New York: Norton, 1968.

Shapiro, M. (1977) *Children of the Revels: The Boy Companies of Shakespeare's Time and Their Plays*, New York: Columbia University Press.

_____ (1982) 'Boying her greatness: Shakespeare's use of coterie drama in *Antony and Cleopatra*', *Modern Language Review* 77, 1: 1–15.

_____ (1990) 'Crossgender casting, crossgender disguise, and anxieties of intimacy in *Twelfth Night* and other plays', paper given at the Shakespeare Association of America, Philadelphia.

Stokes, J. (1985–6) 'The Wells Cordwainers show: New evidence concerning guild entertainments in Somerset', *Comparative Drama* 19, 4: 332–46.

Stubbes, P. (1583) *The Anatomie of Abuses*, F. J. Furnivall (ed.), New Shakespeare Society, London: Trübner, 1877–9.

Styan, J. L. (1986) *Restoration Comedy in Performance*, Cambridge: Cambridge University Press.

Traub, V. (1991) 'Getting hot: Female erotic pleasure and the early modern theatre', paper given at the Shakespeare Association of America, Vancouver.

Wilson, J. H. (1958) *All the King's Ladies: Actresses of the Restoration*, Chicago: University of Chicago Press.

Young, K. (1916) 'William Gager's defence of the academic stage', *Transactions of the Wisconsin Academy of Sciences, Arts, and Letters* 18: 593–638.

EARLY MODERN EUROPE

I N LONDON, PARIS, AND MADRID, THEATER AND DRAMA EXPERIENCED A second "renaissance," in the later seventeenth century. In these cities, the theater came under the influence and protection of the king and his court, and the theaters of both London and Paris adapted Italian staging practices, as did the theaters of the Spanish court. As scenic technology became increasingly complex and spectacular, theater buildings achieved the form they would hold well into the nineteenth century, and the work of new playwrights and new dramatic designs invigorated the dramatic repertoire.

Yet for all their similarities, the theaters of Restoration England, of Louis XIV's France, and of the Spanish "Golden Age" were sustained by very different social and political climates. In France, Louis XIV declared *"L'état, c'est moi"*—"I am the state"—in 1660, confidently drawing all state authority into the person of the king and his magnificent court. The later seventeenth century in France was a period of royal absolutism, as the throne worked to consolidate its power. In England, conditions were very different, for 1660 brought the restoration of the monarchy. The Restoration period saw an ongoing negotiation between newly installed Charles II and Parliament for power, in which Parliament gradually gained control of many royal prerogatives. In both countries, the theater became associated with the throne and reflected the tensions animating social and political life.

In France, a character in Molière's play *Tartuffe* drew the official portrait of the absolute monarch: "A Prince who sees into our inmost hearts, / And can't be fooled by any trickster's arts." Yet the authoritarian policies of the French government, the internecine competition among members of the court, and even the fortunes of the theater suggest that the king's claim of absolute power was challenged in a variety of ways. Under Louis XIII (reigned 1610–1643) and Louis XIV (reigned 1643–1715), the Crown strove to centralize its power by crushing the claims of the landed nobility and by expanding French rule in a series of costly wars. Since Louis XIII came to the throne at the age of nine, when his father—Henry IV—was assassinated, much of this expansion was carried on by his chief minister, Cardinal Richelieu (1585–1642), and Richelieu's successor, Cardinal Mazarin (1602–1661). The suppression of the traditional nobility was achieved largely through Richelieu's formation of a new bureaucracy loyal to the Crown, partly composed of politically active clergy and partly of commoners promoted over the heads of the nobility to critical positions in the government. Allowing these "new men" to buy aristocratic titles, the Crown raised money and further diluted the power of the nobility. The Crown's ravenous appetite for cash to pay for the lavish life of the court and for expensive building projects, such as the palace of Versailles (built by Louis XIV in 1673), further weakened the nobility and alienated the peasantry. Using tax-farmers, who paid a fixed sum to the government in exchange for the authority to collect taxes and pocket the excess as profit, the Crown squeezed the nobles' wealth directly into the royal coffers, impoverishing their lands and making the peasantry increasingly rebellious.

A poor and disaffected peasantry, a jealous aristocracy, an upstart bourgeoisie, and an increasingly authoritarian and isolated monarchy: this became the recipe for revolution. Although the French Revolution did not erupt until 1789, France suffered civil convulsions throughout the seventeenth century that dramatize the tension between Louis's absolutist rhetoric and the political realities of his reign. The nobles led a series of rebellions called the Fronde throughout the 1640s and 1650s, in an effort to unseat Louis and his powerful ministers. Louis defeated these uprisings and finally sealed the fate of his enemies when he required the nobility to attend him at Versailles, so he could keep his eye on their activities. However, the Fronde was part of a more pervasive unrest. Relentless taxation, economic stagnation, and repeated famines throughout the seventeenth century made the peasants angry, as well, and peasant riots and rebellions took place in nearly every province of France in nearly every decade of the century. Finally, Louis XIV also had difficulty with the most volatile issue of seventeenth-century Europe—religious dissent. The close ties between the Crown and the church often resulted in the suppression of Protestant sects, particularly the Calvinist French Huguenots. Protestant rebellion had forced the enactment of the Edict of Nantes in 1598, granting the Huguenots considerable religious freedom. Louis XIV revoked the Edict in 1685, giving the government wider latitude to suppress increasingly energetic religious protest. Louis XIV carefully crafted the image of the "Le Roi Soleil"—the Sun King—whose absolute authority seemed almost a force of nature, not a fact of politics. Throughout his reign, though, Louis had to contend with recalcitrant factions who refused to accept completely his characterization of the king's power.

In England, resistance to royal authority had been much more successful. Between 1603 and 1642, the Stuart kings James I (reigned 1603–1625) and his son, Charles I (reigned 1625–1649), worked to limit the power of Parliament and to enforce increasingly strict religious laws that suppressed the Protestant Puritan sects and demanded conformity with the Church of England. In 1642, Parliament passed legislation limiting the powers of the throne, and Civil War between Parliamentary and Royalist forces erupted. Charles I was executed in 1649, while his wife and children (including the future king, Charles II) escaped to France. From 1653 to 1658, Oliver Cromwell served as Lord Protector of the realm, but Royalist sentiments eventually prevailed and established Charles II (reigned 1660–1685) on the throne.

Although the monarchy was restored—the term *Restoration* refers generally to the period of Charles II's reign and the remainder of the seventeenth century—Charles II was in no position to command the nation, and English politics in the later seventeenth century mainly concerned the negotiation of power between the Crown and Parliament. Charles's death in 1685 spurred a crisis in that his son James II (reigned 1685–1688) was Catholic and threatened to compromise English religious and civil autonomy from the Catholic church and the Catholic states of Europe. In 1689, Parliament effectively deposed James, inviting his Protestant daughter Mary (reigned as Mary II, 1689–1694) and her husband, William of Orange (reigned as William III, 1689–1702), to return to England and assume the throne. While Louis XIV increasingly insisted on the autonomous power of the throne in France, the Parliament in England finally achieved a lasting compromise with the Crown in the form of a constitutional monarchy. In bringing William and Mary into power, Parliament gained the authority of consent over royal succession, a power it confirmed in 1702 in naming James II's daughter Anne as successor (reigned as Queen Anne, 1702–1714).

While in an important sense the gulf separating French and English culture has always been narrow and deep, like the English Channel, Spanish culture in the Renaissance arises from a very different history. Spain was occupied by the Moors in 711 and is still marked by its five centuries of Islamic culture. In 1479, Ferdinand of Aragon and Isabella of Castile were married, forming the alliance that gave rise to modern Spain; in 1480 they joined forces with the Catholic Inquisition, expelling Jews from the country. At the Conquest of Granada in 1492, the Moors were finally driven out of Spain.

Having formed a single state, the Spanish monarchy successfully expanded its reach into a global empire during the sixteenth century. Under Charles V, Spain's territory included its many New World colonies as well as the Netherlands and the Holy Roman Empire of central Europe, and the culture of the Spanish court was unrivaled in Europe: this is the era of Velasquéz and El Greco. But during the reign of Philip II (1556–1598), Spain's domination of Europe began to wane. Spain became involved in a brutal and expensive effort to keep control of the Netherlands, a hotbed of Protestant resistance. English soldiers—Sir Philip Sidney and Ben Jonson, among others—fought the Spanish in the Netherlands, and Philip tried in several ways to outmaneuver the English. He proposed marriage to Queen Elizabeth, but as she did with other suitors, she strung him along for political purposes and finally refused him. He also mounted a massive naval invasion of England, the Spanish Armada of 1588, which was surprisingly defeated. Spain continued to wane in the seventeenth century, eventually losing the Netherlands, and losing Portugal in 1657. By 1665, Spain was ruled by the last of the Hapsburg kings, the deformed imbecile Charles II (1665–1700).

Louis XIV's familiar sobriquet, "Le Roi Soleil," derives from a role he played in a court ballet devised for him in 1653. A fine dancer, Louis sponsored and took part in a wide variety of entertainments. Moreover, the centralization of power in the king and the court paralleled the increasing institutionalization of the arts under Louis XIV, as a means of advancing his own prestige and of keeping control over potentially seditious activities. The most famous of these institutions—the ACADÉMIE FRANÇAISE—was chartered in 1637, and used by Cardinal Richelieu to evaluate a critical controversy surrounding Pierre Corneille's play *The Cid*. Corneille's detractors had sharply attacked the play, and Richelieu urged the Académie to resolve whether *The Cid* could legitimately be described as effective tragedy in neoclassical terms (on *neoclassicism*, see page 401). In return, Richelieu promoted the Académie and its aims, the purification of French language and literature, and the advancement of official French culture. Louis XIV assumed the role of official protector of the Académie Française in 1672 and sponsored other institutions as ornaments to his reign: the Académie Royale de Musique (1672), the Académie Royale de Peinture et de Sculpture (1648), the Académie des Inscriptions (1663), the Académie des Sciences (1666), and the Académie de l'Architecture (1671). The institution of the stage was no exception. Theatrical companies had always needed the king's license to play in Paris, and Louis licensed several companies and named Molière's company as the *Troupe du roi*. After Molière's death in 1673, the leading tragic actress in Paris, Mademoiselle Champmeslé, joined with Molière's troupe and gained the king's patronage. The new company—the COMÉDIE FRANÇAISE—opened in August of 1680. It held a MONOPOLY on the production of all spoken drama in French, and although this monopoly has long since vanished, the Comédie Française remains the principal company performing the French classical repertoire.

    In Louis XIV's Paris, the institutions of art—including the theater—were identified with the prerogatives of the king and his court, though the structure of the theater had its roots in practices dating back to the Middle Ages. Throughout the later Middle Ages and into the sixteenth century, stage production in Paris was controlled by the Confrérie de la Passion, a guild-like corporation initially formed to stage religious drama. In 1545 the Confrérie purchased land in Paris from the Duke of Burgundy and erected the Hôtel de Bourgogne, at the time probably the only permanent theater building in Europe (*hôtel* in this case means "hall" or "large building"). Extensively remodelled in 1647, the Hôtel de Bourgogne served as the model for other theaters built in the seventeenth century: the Théâtre du Marais (built in a tennis court in 1629, rebuilt in 1644); the Palais-Cardinal (built by Richelieu in 1640; later renamed the Palais-Royal); the Salle des Machines (1642), and the Comédie Française (1689).

    The shape of these theaters owes something to the Hôtel de Bourgogne, and something to tennis courts as well, for tennis courts were often used as theaters. (In the sixteenth and seventeenth centuries, tennis courts were long indoor rooms with side galleries.)

THEATER IN FRANCE, 1660–1700

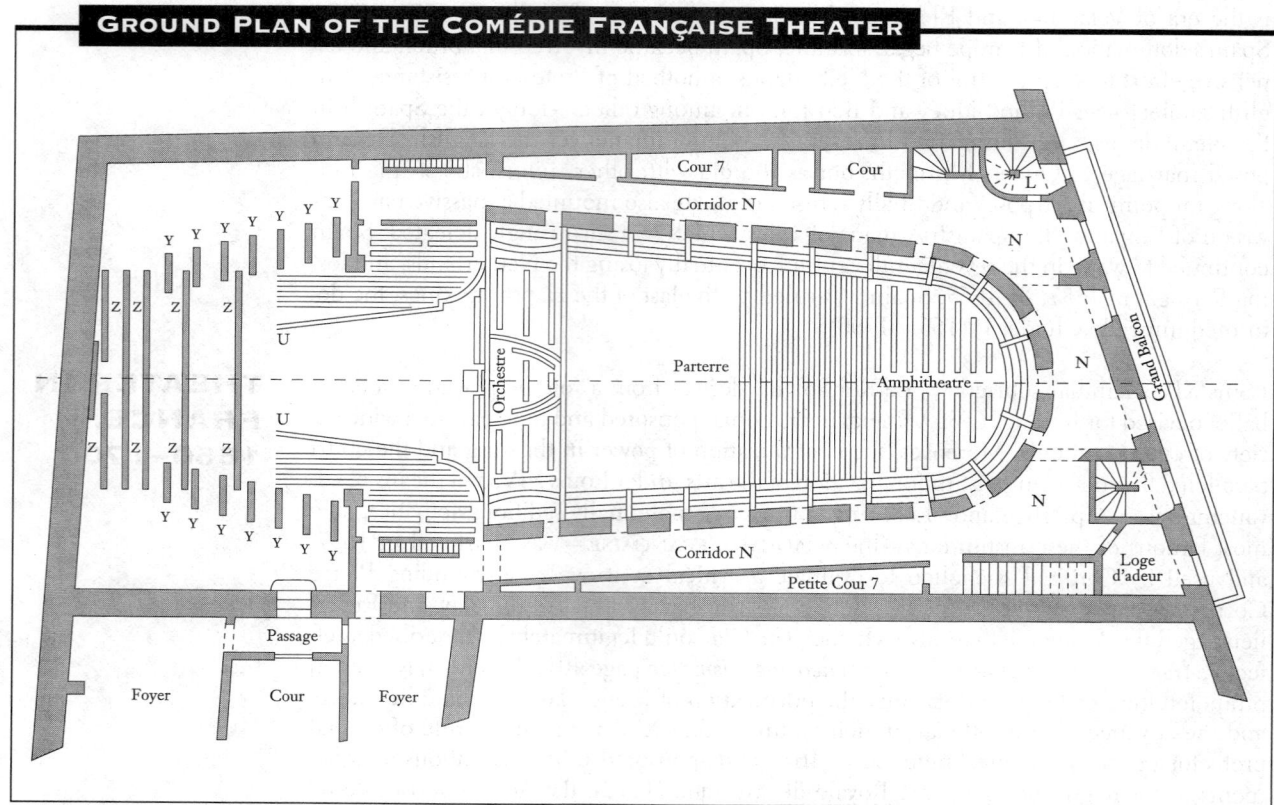

GROUND PLAN OF THE COMÉDIE FRANÇAISE THEATER

The Comédie Française *had this basic design from 1689 to 1770. Note the open* parterre, *the wings (marked Y), and the backdrops (Z). The benches on the stage were added during the eighteenth century.*

These theaters generally had deep, **RAKED STAGES** (40 feet deep, 45 feet wide at the Hôtel de Bourgogne) that faced an open **PIT** called the **PARTERRE** (literally, "on the ground") which was used for standing spectators. The auditorium had **BOXES** on three sides; **GALLERY** seating rose above the boxes opposite the stage; some patrons were also seated on the stage itself. The theaters were large—the Hôtel de Bourgogne initially held 1,600 spectators, the Comédie Française held 2,000—and many theaters made extensive use of stage scenery, sometimes concocting extraordinary spectacles. In a fantasy celebrating Louis XIV's wedding in 1662, the entire royal family and its entourage were "flown" by machines in the Salle des Machines; in a production in 1671, 300 deities were lifted aloft. The dramatic theaters—the Hôtel de Bourgogne, the Palais-Royal, the Comédie Française— tended to avoid such effects, using instead a single setting for each play, depending on the genre of the play. The theaters generally used a series of staggered **WINGS AND BACKDROP** to create the effect of perspective, adapting both scenic practices and scene-changing technology from Italian theaters.

Acting companies in Paris were organized as investment corporations requiring the patronage of the Crown and had long included women in their ranks. Louis XIV's reign saw a series of great actresses take the stage, Mademoiselle DuParc and Mademoiselle Champmeslé among them. Companies were comprised of twelve members (eight men, four women), who shared the company's profits. The company hired additional actors when necessary. The Comédie Française standardized this practice: its twelve main ac- tors—called **SOCIÉTAIRES**—ran the company for twenty years, and new *sociétaires* could be recruited only after the retirement of current members. Actors in the Comédie Française received an annual subsidy from the Crown and a retirement pension if they completed their twenty years with the company. The company purchased plays, which were cast by the author. Throughout the 1650s and 1660s the major companies kept about 70 plays in repertoire and generally played three or four times per week. After the 1680s, the Comédie Française began daily performances, beginning at 5 P.M.

We should recall that life at court was itself a kind of performance, and that attending the theater provided ample opportunity for aristocrats, courtiers, and aspiring courtiers to display and preen themselves. In a milieu so dependent on the king's preference, we can easily imagine how stage seating and side boxes emphasized that the evening's entertainment included the audience's performances as well as the actors'. This sense of the reciprocity between court and stage is signalled more concretely by the fortunes of the Parisian theaters after Louis XIV moved the court to Versailles. Although five companies flourished in Paris while Louis kept court in the city, by 1700 only two remained.

At the outbreak of the English Civil War in 1642, Parliament closed the London theaters, putting a stop to dramatic performance. Some companies managed to mount secret productions between 1642 and 1660, but Parliament and city officials moved quickly to suppress them, sometimes by destroying the theater buildings. In the 1650s, however, William Davenant (1606–1668), a Royalist supporter of Charles I and successor to Ben Jonson as writer of court masques, attempted to mount operas. In 1656 he succeeded in staging a production of *The Siege of Rhodes* at Rutland House, performing it again in 1658 and 1659 at the Cockpit theater and elsewhere in London.

The restoration of Charles II to the throne in 1660 inaugurated a period of renewed theatrical vitality. As in France—where Charles developed a taste for theater during his exile—the theater was closely associated with royal prerogatives. Upon his return, Charles rewarded PATENTS to William Davenant and Thomas Killegrew (1612–1683) to open theaters under royal authority. These PATENT THEATERS (also called "theaters royal")—Davenant's Duke's company, and Killigrew's King's company—thus held a royal monopoly on the production of spoken English drama. Although they underwent huge modifications, the patent theaters dominated the legitimate theater until the mid-nineteenth century, when legislation was passed that finally broke their monopoly. Yet monopoly could not guarantee support. The two companies, unable to turn a profit, were united into a single company from 1682 to 1695.

When the theaters reopened in 1660, theatrical taste had changed significantly. Although a few of the older, pre-1642 theater buildings were still standing, they could not handle the new theater technology. For, as in the French theater, the English theater rapidly encouraged the development of scenic practices already well-known in Italy—a PROSCENIUM stage and moveable painted wings and backdrop used to create a visual setting for the play. Onstage, theaters used stock sets—one for classical tragedy, one for romantic comedy, and so on—that conformed to the dramatic genre of the play. In 1661, Davenant converted Lisle's Tennis Court to the Lincoln's Inn Fields Theater, which measured 30 by 70 feet; he replaced this theater with the Dorset Garden Theater in 1671. Killegrew erected his Theatre Royal in Bridges Street in 1663. When it burned in 1672, he built a new Theatre Royal in Drury Lane, which opened in 1674; a theater has occupied this site down to the present time.

The new English theaters were much smaller than the French theaters. The Drury Lane theater, for example, held 650-700 people, though it was expanded throughout the late seventeenth and eighteenth centuries and eventually held more than 2,000. Nonetheless, like the French theaters, the English houses also introduced new design and staging practices: a proscenium stage flanked by a large APRON, footlights to illuminate

THEATER IN ENGLAND, 1660–1700

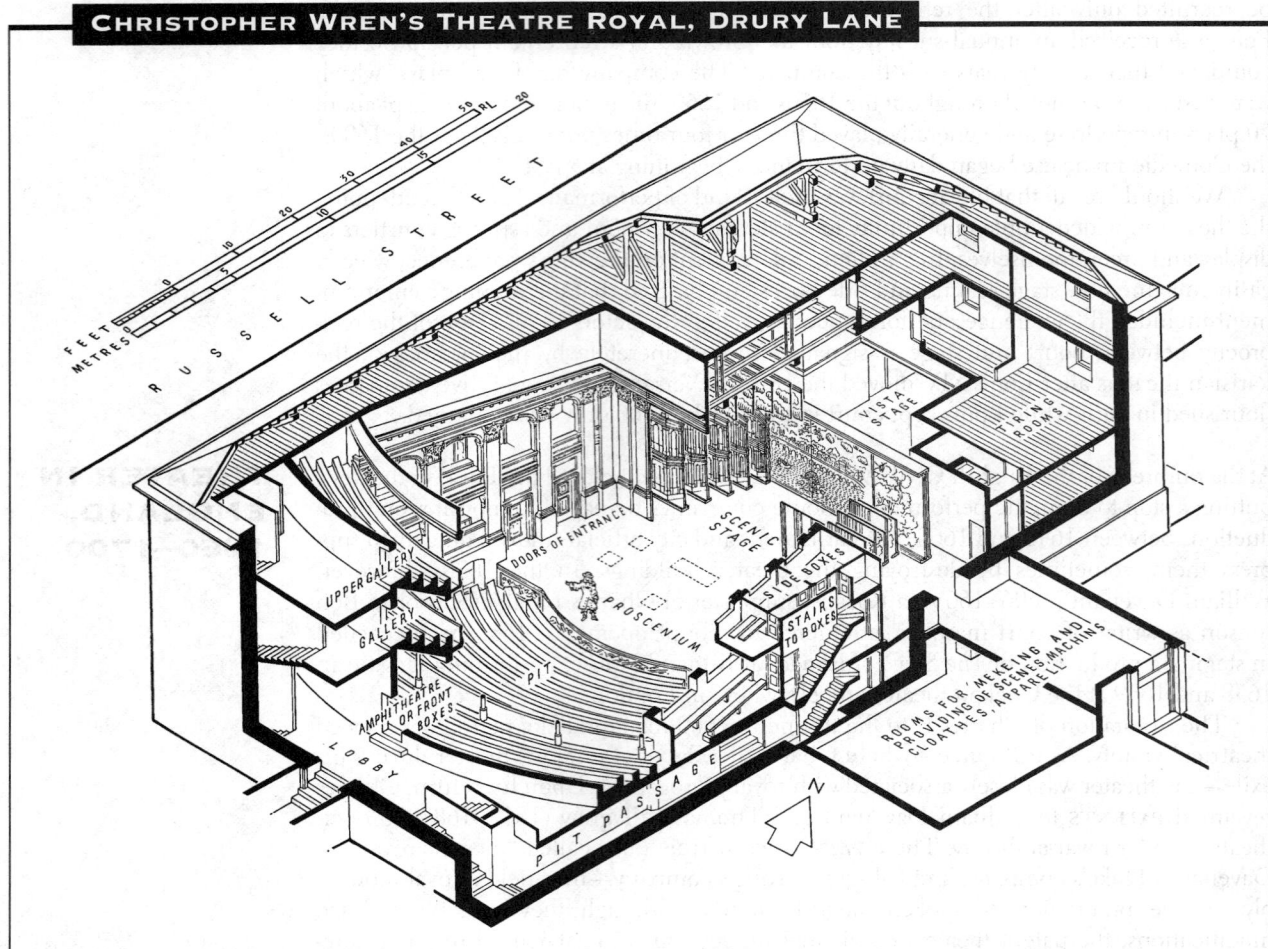

In 1674, Christopher Wren designed a new Theatre Royal, Drury Lane. Note that the acting area extends to the apron, in front of the wing and backdrop stage scenery. Pit seating, side boxes, and two galleries also are visible.

the stage, a raked pit with benches (the French *parterre* was flat and had no seats), side and rear box seats, and a rear gallery. This division of the house accorded with social and class distinctions in the audience, which was in any event a narrow selection of the English public, in part because the theater was recognized as the ornament of the privileged, and—not incidentally—because plays were produced in the afternoon, when working people could not easily attend. The entire auditorium was lighted by chandeliers, making the audience itself very much a part of the show: in an important sense the performance did not stop at the edge of the stage. Although the theaters were not at the court itself, they were frequently patronized by courtiers and the nobility, who preened and displayed themselves to the audience—sometimes from seats onstage. Charles II—who numbered the well-known actress Nell Gwynne (1650–1687) among his many mistresses—was also frequently in the audience.

Companies were generally managed by one of the actors, and they avoided the need for lengthy casting and rehearsal by developing LINES OF BUSINESS, in which each actor would specialize in a particular type of character: heroic lead, comic lead, male heavy, female heavy, utility player, and so on. Acting style was relatively formal, and actors often played downstage on the apron directly to the audience; a famous speech—one of Hamlet's soliloquies, for example—would be delivered directly to the audience, something like an operatic aria today, a practice called **POINTING**. As the theater developed in the later seventeenth century, sharing companies were replaced by companies financed by outside investors, who paid the actors salaries and took a percentage of the profits. Companies were large and salaries low; actors were compensated by **BENEFIT** performances, in which the actor (on his or her benefit night) received the entire profit from a given evening's performance, minus the operating expenses of the house. The practice of supplementing salaries with benefit performances continued well into the nineteenth century, and although most benefit nights—after the house expenses were deducted—left the actors with little additional pay, benefits provided an excuse to keep actors' salaries low.

By far the greatest innovation in the English theater, though, was the introduction of actresses onstage. English comedies in this period were often frankly concerned with sexual intrigue, and the actresses who played in them—and in the new heroic tragedies, and in the plays by Shakespeare, Jonson, Fletcher, and other Renaissance playwrights who continued to hold the stage—also had a reputation for sexual licentiousness. Yet, while several actresses, like Nell Gwynne, were mistresses of the famous and powerful, the phenomenon of regarding actresses as sexual objects, of classing them with prostitutes, has more to do with the status and vulnerability of working women in a highly stratified and patriarchal society than it does with the immorality of the stage or its performers. Indeed, actresses' ongoing struggle to assert themselves as legitimate performers was born at this time as well, epitomized in the careers of Elizabeth Barry (1658–1713), Anne Bracegirdle (1663–1748), and many others.

As in medieval England and France, medieval Spanish theater was strongly influenced by the church, which saw in the drama a source of instruction and inspiration. Although there is some evidence for liturgical drama as early as the twelfth century, the principal form of medieval theater was the *AUTO SACRAMENTALE,* a form of allegorical religious drama initially devised to celebrate the feast of Corpus Christi. But while the mystery cycles were suppressed in Protestant England, the Spanish *autos* continued to be performed alongside the secular theater until they were banned in 1765. Like the English cycles, the *autos* were in civic hands, and by the late sixteenth century major cities would perform *autos* as many as three times per year, usually in the central city plaza before a gathering of citizens and civic officials. Professional actors were hired for the *autos* and were drawn through the city on wagons (**CARROS**); the *carros* were heavily decorated, and a prize was given for the most spectacular *carro.* Despite their abstract themes, the *autos* remained extremely popular and drew on the talents of the best playwrights of the era—between 1647 and 1681, for instance, all the *autos* performed in Madrid were written by Pedro Calderón de la Barca.

Philip II, Philip III, and Philip IV were all interested in theater and commissioned playwrights to devise entertainments; during the reign of Philip III, Spain developed an impressive court theater. Early in the seventeenth century, this court theater merely occupied a hall at the Alcázar palace, as Ben Jonson and Inigo Jones had done at Whitehall palace in England, and it produced a similar kind of entertainment: mythological dramas that required spectacular scenery, effects, and costumes. But by the 1630s, the center of court theater shifted to the new palace of Buen Retiro. Here, in 1640 Cosme Lotti (d. 1643) was retained to build a permanent theater that could perform the scenic effects of the Italian theater. This theater was roofed, but in its basic design resembled the most influential of Spanish theaters in the Golden Age, the public theater or *CORRAL.*

Although the Spanish public theater resembled the public theaters of Elizabethan London, it stood in a much different relationship to city life. While the English theaters

THEATER IN SPAIN'S GOLDEN AGE, 1580–1680

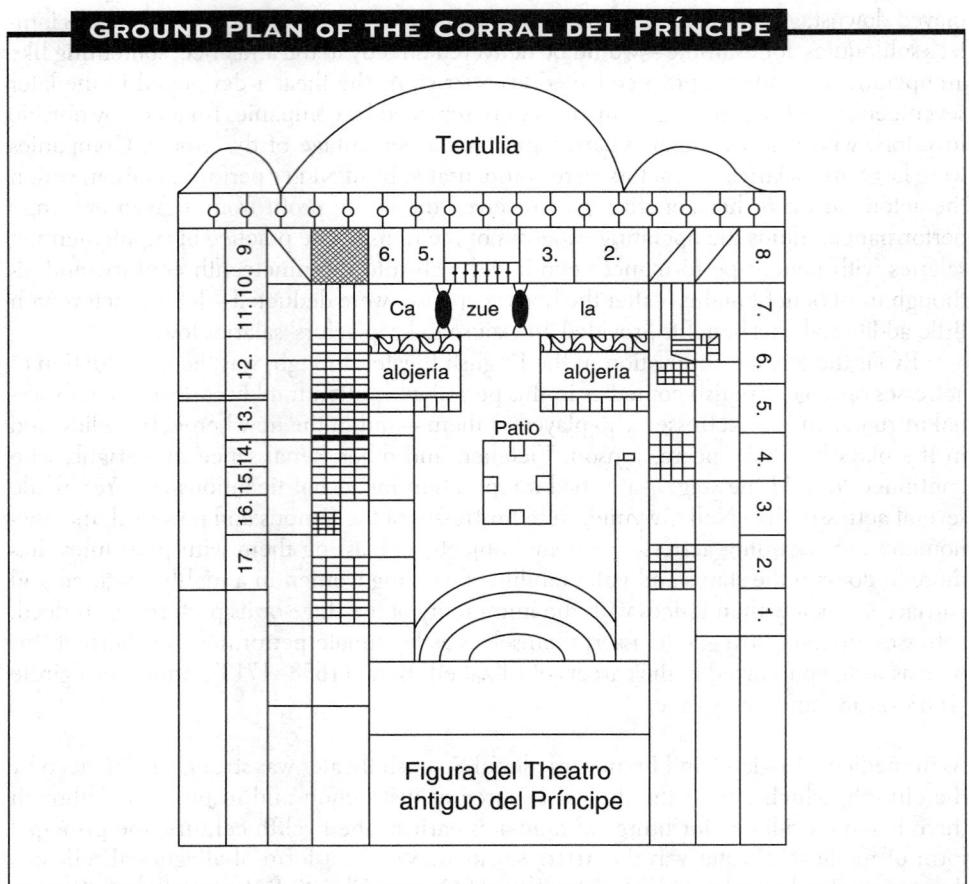

GROUND PLAN OF THE CORRAL DEL PRÍNCIPE

Tertulia

9. 6. 5. 3. 2. 8.

11. 10.

Ca zue la 7.

12. alojería alojería 6.

13. 5.

16. 15. 14. Patio 4.

3.

17. 2.

1.

Figura del Theatro
antiguo del Príncipe

Made in 1730, this drawing of the Corral del Príncipe shows the important features of the theater: the patio, *the* alojería, *the* gradas, *and the* cazuela.

were banned from the city proper and were erected across the Thames in Southwark, the Spanish theaters were public institutions. Since the medieval church held the rights to theatrical production, the public theaters were licensed by religious confraternities in the sixteenth century, which used the funds for various charitable purposes, including maintaining the general hospital of Madrid. By the early seventeenth century, these funds were paid directly to the city, and theaters continued to subsidize charities well into the nineteenth century. Companies of actors were licensed to play in the city, and took a lease on a *corral* for a stated period of time. In general, Spanish companies toured major cities and towns, and only Seville and Madrid allowed two companies to perform at the same time. While playwrights were initially associated with individual companies, by the seventeenth century playwrights would sell their plays to the company: they were paid very well for an *auto,* and adequately for a regular play—about 500 reales, or about 10 times the daily wage of a laborer. Although companies were composed of men and boys until 1587, when women were allowed to appear onstage, the church issued a decree banning women from performing onstage in 1596. By 1599, however, a royal council ruled that actresses could be permitted, providing they were married to a member of the company; it also ruled against cross-dressing, so that when Rosaura appeared dressed as a man in Calderón's *Life is a Dream,* the actress wore a man's costume only down to the waist with a skirt below.

VIEW OF THE CORRAL DEL PRÍNCIPE

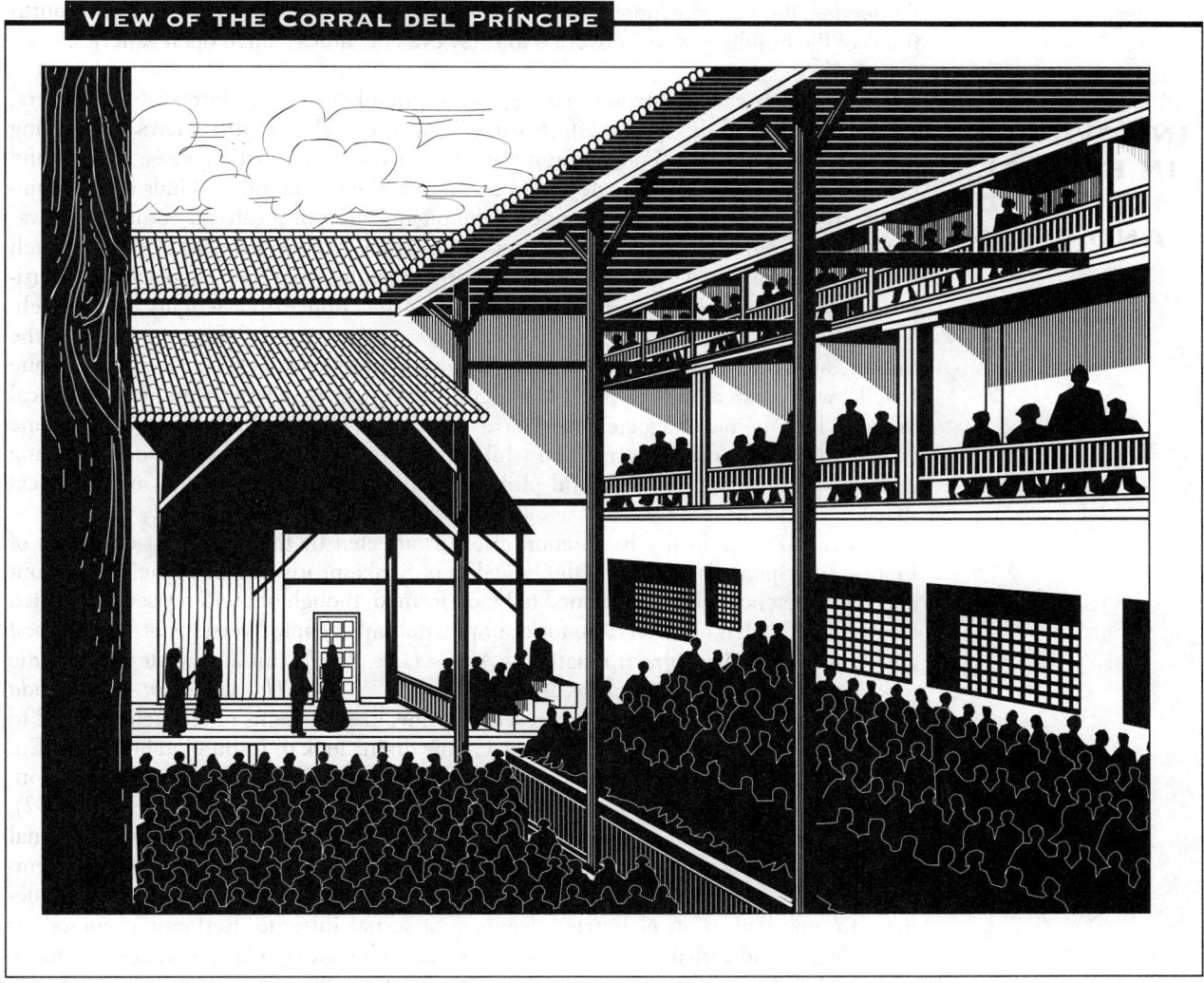

This illustration provides a view of the Corral del Príncipe from the rear of the patio, *perhaps from the* cazuela.

The reciprocity between the city and the theater is also revealed in the design of public theaters of the golden age, particularly the two principal theaters of Madrid, the Corral de la Cruz, opened in 1579 as Spain's first theater, and the Corral del Príncipe, opened in 1583. The theaters were originally merely stages placed in a courtyard enclosed on three or four sides by four story buildings; over time the theaters gradually acquired possession of these structures, but in the meantime the buildings' galleries and windows could be sold to spectators separately. The central courtyard or *PATIO* was unroofed, and like the pit of English theaters was occupied by standing spectators. In the seventeenth century, a few rows of benches (called *TABURETES*) were erected near the stage, on a raised and fenced dais. Along the sides of the *patio* rose the *GRADAS,* steeply raked rows of seats that rose to the second floor. The *ALOJERÍA,* a tavern, served refreshments, and was located at the rear of the *patio*; above the *alojería,* were several stories of galleries: the *CAZUELA,* or women's gallery, on the second floor; above it galleries for the City of Madrid and Council of Castile officials; and a gallery for intellectual and church officials, the *TERTULIA.* Above the *gradas*, the grated windows of the houses served as box seats. The third and fourth floors of the buildings were converted to *DESVANES* or "attics," small open galleries.

DRAMATIC INNOVATION IN FRANCE, ENGLAND, AND SPAIN

Although theatrical production extended into a number of other forms—ballet, opera, royal pageants, and the special-effects extravaganzas called MACHINE PLAYS—prevailing attitudes, particularly in France, prohibited the mixing of dramatic genres: tragedy and comedy were firmly discriminated from one another and from others kinds of entertainment. In France, comedy—and, indeed, the organization of theatrical companies—was particularly influenced by the techniques of the Italian *COMMEDIA DELL' ARTE.* French tragic drama inherited a taste for classical subject matter from the schools and universities, which had led Europe in translating Greek and Roman playwrights into French. Throughout the sixteenth century, the court sponsored a variety of efforts to classicize the theater, supporting several important playwrights, including Robert Garnier and Étienne Jodelle, who created highly wrought and refined tragedies based on the model of classical drama. The heroic tragedies of Pierre Corneille (1606–1684) and Jean Racine (1639–1699) epitomize this tradition while also turning it in a new direction, refracting contemporary moral, political, and philosophical issues through the lens of a classical style.

English drama in the Restoration also was affected by the HEROIC TRAGEDIES of France and Spain, as well as by the tragedies of Shakespeare, and of Francis Beaumont and John Fletcher, which continued to be performed, though often in revised or adapted form. John Dryden (1631–1700), for example, not only adapted versions of *The Tempest* and *Antony and Cleopatra* (the latter as *All for Love,* 1677), but also wrote plays in the mode of heroic tragedy, such as *Aureng-Zebe* (1675) and *The Conquest of Granada* (1669). Heroic tragedy generally represents the idealized passions of characters forced to choose between love and personal honor. Comic drama took its inspiration both from European models—Molière's plays, for example—and from the earlier plays of Ben Jonson, but in the plays of William Wycherley (1640–1716), Sir George Etherege (1635–1692), and William Congreve (1670–1729), English comedy rapidly developed its own original style. Restoration comedies are most often in the vein of COMEDY OF MANNERS, contemporary dramas in which witty aristocrats, city dupes and dandies, and dull country gentlemen are engaged in an elaborate adventure of sexual intrigue. Restoration comedy is often elegant and verbally polished, and obsessed with issues of class, privilege, manners, and sex. In addition, much as the Restoration theater witnessed the rise of actresses onstage, it also saw the first women to achieve success as playwrights: Aphra Behn (1640–1689), Catharine Trotter (1679–1749), and Susanna Centlivre (1670–1723).

After the turn of the century, the risqué character of many plays spurred one of the perennial movements to restrain the theater as an immoral institution. Partly as a result of Jeremy Collier's diatribe *A Short View of the Immorality and Profaneness of the English Stage* (1698), and partly as a result of changing attitudes and social mores, English comedy after 1700—the plays of Sir Richard Steele (1672–1729), Colley Cibber (1671–1757), George Farquhar (1678–1707), Oliver Goldsmith (1728–1774), and Richard Brinsley Sheridan (1751–1816), for instance—became more romantic and sentimental. Moreover, political satire in English theater was also sharply limited with the passing of the Stage Licensing Act of 1737. After 1737, all plays produced for public entertainment had to be submitted for censorship prior to production. The censor could require changes, delete words, passages, or scenes, or refuse to grant permission entirely. Confronting the Act by producing a nonlicensed play was to risk the fining and imprisonment of everyone involved in the production. While theaters found a variety of ways to subvert or sidestep the law, the censorship remained in effect—with some modifications—until 1968, inhibiting the possibility of dramatic innovation.

In the early sixteenth century, a Spanish theatrical manager may well have written his own plays and acted in them himself. Lope de Rueda (1510–1565), for example, was a touring performer and the author of both *autos* and secular plays. But by the late sixteenth century, companies would pay a playwright for the play, and the theaters had made several genres popular: the CAPA Y ESPADA or heroic/romantic "cape and sword" play was very popular, as was the *RUIDO* or "noise" play. But the forms of Golden Age drama were in many ways determined by the extraordinary and prolific career of Lope Félix de Vega Carpio (1562–1635). Lope de Vega is frequently said to have written more than 1,500 plays—which points to the immense popularity of the theater and its constant need for new material—and more than 450 of his plays have survived. He is particularly associated with *COMEDIA NUEVA*, a genre mixing the tragic and the comic, high and low characters (including the *GRACIOSO*, a comic fool), and usually having a romantic plot. In the intervals between the acts of his plays, short interludes *(ENTREMESES)* were performed, which were coherent plays in themselves. Like other playwrights in this period, Lope de Vega also wrote *autos*, but his best-known work is *Fuente Ovejuna* (1614), a play about a vicious tyrant that critics have seen as an allegory on Portuguese independence.

Lope shared the stage with several equally brilliant playwrights, principally with Pedro Calderón de la Barca (1600–1681), who succeeded Lope de Vega as Spain's most influential dramatist. Miguel de Cervantes (1547–1616), the author of *Don Quixote*, wrote about thirty plays, of which sixteen remain. Tirso de Molina (1584–1648) was a friar who had written more than 400 plays—eighty survive—before he was reprimanded by the Council of Castile; his most well-known play, *El Burlador de Seville (The Barber of Seville)* is the earliest play on the subject of Don Juan. The playwright Guillén de Castro (1569–1631) was a friend of Lope de Vega; his influence on the French theater is perhaps as marked as it was in Spain. Guillén de Castro wrote *Las Mocedades del Cid (The Youthful Adventures of the Cid)*, which was adapted by Corneille as *Le Cid* and ignited a furious controversy about neoclassical esthetics.

In both France and England, the arts in general and drama in particular were closely regulated by the state, a state of affairs sustained by the rise of NEOCLASSICISM. Neoclassicism is, in the simplest sense, the revival of what was taken to be a "classical" ordering of the arts. The literature of classical Greece and Rome began to be recovered in the fourteenth and fifteenth centuries, first through the dissemination of texts preserved in monasteries and later through expanded contact with the Islamic world in the sixteenth and seventeenth centuries. Translating, imitating, and adapting classical texts, European writers in the later seventeenth century appeared to "revive" the principles of classical art. In practice, however, neoclassicism offered an *interpretation* of the classics, emphasizing order, control, decorum, reason, and harmony.

In many respects, neoclassicism relied on the authority of Aristotle's *Poetics*, published first in Latin translation in 1498 and then in Italian in 1549, and on the series of critical commentaries written on Aristotle throughout the sixteenth century. Aristotle's *Poetics* is something of a naturalist's description of the several species of poetry and their characteristics, but readers in the sixteenth and seventeenth centuries fell under the influence of Aristotle's enormous authority (see *Doctor Faustus*, Act 1) and quickly transformed the *Poetics* into a prescription, a series of rules, for producing the most perfect and effective tragedies. Two central precepts of the *Poetics* regard the tragic hero's actions: those acts must seem both necessary and probable, and they should not entirely violate moral expectations. Neoclassical critics and playwrights schematized Aristotle's descriptions as necessary features of dramatic composition, arguing that a tragedy should be rigorously and causally plotted and should reveal the workings of providential justice through the actions of universalized or typical characters. These goals were transformed

NEOCLASSICISM, DRAMA, AND THEATER

The term *commedia dell' arte* means the "comedy of the professional players," and *commedia* became popular throughout Europe in the sixteenth century. *Commedia* companies were itinerant (though one was established in Paris for part of Louis XIV's reign), organized around ten or twelve actors, men and women, each of whom played a stock character who could be easily recognized by typical and routine behavior. Although the characters were fixed, the plots that *commedia* companies played were generally improvised; the actor relied on the traits of his or her

(ASIDE)

COMMEDIA DELL' ARTE

character and a core of stage business from which to invent action and dialogue. The cast usually included one or two pairs of young lovers (the **INNAMORATO** and **INNAMORATA**), good-looking, aristocratic, or fashionable characters played without masks. The rest of the cast was masked and played more stereotypical roles: the **CAPITANO**, a military braggart and coward, played with sword and cape; the **PANTALONE**, an elderly dupe, often in love, played in stockings, breeches and slippers; the **DOTTORE**, sometimes actually a doctor, but otherwise a

pedantic friend of the Pantalone's; and a variety of comic parts called **ZANNI**, usually sly servants. The most familiar of these parts is *Arlecchino*, or **HARLEQUIN**, a cunning character who is usually an acrobat, wearing a patched costume (later refined to diamond-shaped pattern), a black cap, and carrying his slapstick—the origin of our term "slapstick," which gives some idea of what *commedia* humor was like. *Commedia* was also popular in England, but it had fewer long-term effects on the comic drama than on the rise of English **PANTOMIME**. In England, plays were often followed by a short **AFTERPIECE**, which frequently led Harlequin into adventures with mythological characters. John Rich (1692–1761), taking the name Lun, was the most famous Harlequin of the early eighteenth-century English stage.

PANTALONE AND HARLEQUIN

Note the mask and breeches of the Pantalone (left), and the mask, slapstick, and diamond-shaped patches of the Harlequin (right).

into the famous "unities" of neoclassicism: a play should take place within a single day (unity of time), in one location (unity of place), and consist of a single line of action, a single plot (unity of action). The action of neoclassical tragedy, therefore, is concentrated, maintaining a uniformity of tone and style called DECORUM. Plays in this mode maintain a single, narrow range of language and behavior; the action is either idealized (rather than realistic) in tragedy, or commonplace in comedy: tragic characters are classic and heroic, while comic characters are contemporary, even bourgeois; tragedy undertakes the conflict between the ideal passions of love and honor, while comedy takes its cue from more earthly desires—lust, greed, hypocrisy, and so on. Following the recovery of Vitruvius' *De Architectura* (15 BC) in 1414, this neoclassical sensibility urged the modern stage to imitate Vitruvius's distinction between the proper stage settings of tragedy and comedy: classical architecture for tragedy, urban architecture for comedy. Especially in seventeenth-century Paris, theaters adjusted their stagecraft to these ideals of regularity and decorum, assigning a generalized palace setting to the elevated world of tragedy, and the *chambre à quatre portes*—the room with four doors—to the lower, contemporary world of comedy.

Writing later in the eighteenth century, the Englishman Thomas Davies characterized the differences between French and English audiences and suggests that neoclassical ideals did not take root as deeply in the English theater as they did in France:

> The Frenchman, when he goes to a play, seems to make his entertainment a matter of importance. The long speeches in the plays of Corneille, Racine, Crebillon, and Voltaire, which would disgust an English ear, are extremely pleasing to our light neighbours: they sit in silence, and enjoy the beauty of sentiment, and energy of language; and are taught habitually to cry at scenes of distress. The Englishman looks upon the theatre as a place of amusement; he does not expect to be alarmed with terror, or wrought upon by scenes of commiseration; but he is surprised into the feeling of those passions, and sheds tears because he cannot avoid it. The theatre, to most Englishmen, becomes a place of instruction by chance.

Davies, of course, betrays a common chauvinism of the English toward the French: while the French are pedantic and calculating, the English are spontaneous. But this distinction between English and French theaters—one for "art," one for "entertainment"; one tragic, one comic—conceals the fundamental likenesses between the two institutions and the plays they put on the stage. As the plays of Corneille, Racine, and Dryden suggest, neoclassical tragedy imposes severe and artificial forms on the irrepressible forces of the passions, which inevitably break through the formal speech and decorous behavior of the characters to destroy them and sometimes the state as well. Comedy of the period in England and in France reveals a cognate tension, as the formal acting styles and stereotyped characters common in Restoration comedy seem barely able to contain the bottomless appetites of the plays' heroes. To this extent, neoclassical decorum embodies a barely contained anxiety about the power of forms—forms of conduct, forms of art, forms of state—to prevent a revolution of unreason and disorder.

In the opening scene of Pedro Calderón de la Barca's Life is a Dream, *Rosaura defends herself against Segismund, who is clothed in animal hides.*

In one of the most famous scenes of Molière's Tartuffe, *Orgon hides under the table to listen to the hypocrite Tartuffe attempt to seduce his wife Elmire.*

■ PEDRO CALDERÓN DE LA BARCA ■

Like many of his contemporaries, Pedro Calderón de la Barca (1600–1681) was a prolific playwright; he is thought to have written more than 200 plays, of which about 100 survive. Calderón was born in Madrid on January 17, 1600, the son of a minor court official. He was educated at a Jesuit "college," or preparatory school, before attending the University of Alcalá de Henares and the University of Salamanca. In 1620 he entered and won a poetry competition in honor of St. Isidore, which brought his writing to the attention of Lope de Vega, one of the judges of the contest. His first play, *Love, Honor, and Power,* was performed at court in 1623, but Calderón—who served intermittently in the military in the early 1620s—did not become established as a playwright until some time after 1626, when his plays were popular both at court and in the public theaters. With the death of Lope in 1635, Calderón became the most important playwright in Spain; he was knighted by Philip IV and became the principal court playwright in 1636.

Many of Calderón's plays in this period are either *capa y espada* plays, like *The Phantom Lady* (1629), or "love and honor" plays. *El alcalde de Zalamea (The Mayor of Zalamea,* 1642) is typical of the "love and honor" genre. In the play, a peasant's daughter is raped by a soldier; through a series of coincidents, the peasant becomes the mayor just as the soldier is apprehended, and he is torn between his desire for revenge, his obligation to enforce the process of law, and Christian charity. Calderón's most important play, *La vida es sueño (Life is a Dream)* was produced in 1636. Throughout his career, Calderón also wrote *autos sacramentales,* but these became more significant later in his life. Calderón's mistress died in 1648, and Calderón entered the priesthood in 1651, possibly in grief over her loss; he also adopted and raised her child, who may have been his natural son. He was appointed priest of a Toledo parish, but the bishop objected to his playwriting, and Calderón devoted himself to *autos* thereafter; his *autos* were so popular that between 1647 and 1681 the only *autos* performed in Madrid were by Calderón. Calderón was made chaplain to the king in 1663 and died in retirement in 1681.

LIFE IS A DREAM

Life is a Dream typifies the concerns of Calderón's mature drama: it is a play that tests the relationship between love and honor and conducts a searching meditation on human nature itself. The play is set in a mythological Poland, ruled by King Basil. Several years before the current action, it was predicted that if Basil's son, Segismund, were to succeed to the throne, he "would be the most outrageous / Of all men, the most cruel of all princes, / And impious of all monarchs, by whose acts / The kingdom would be torn up and divided." Basil, not willing to murder his son to save his country, has had Segismund removed from court and imprisoned in a cave, where he is attended only by the old courtier Clotaldo. This is where Rosaura—a well-born woman, also forsaken by her father—finds Segismund at the opening of the play.

Calderón begins his interrogation of human nature in the characterization of Segismund. Raised like a beast, Segismund is impulsive and untamed; though he opens the play complaining about his life of constant punishment, when he sees Rosaura (disguised as a man) watching him, he seizes and threatens to kill her. And yet when Rosaura kneels to him and begs for mercy, Segismund feels a strange sensation:

> Your voice has softened me, your presence halted me,
> And now, confusingly, I feel respect
> For you.

Living in captivity and isolation, Segismund is a "human monster": his behavior is ruled neither by reason nor by the conventions of polite society. Yet Segismund responds to Rosaura's plea for mercy as though some element of human sympathy were native to him. At the outset of the play, Calderón presents two contrasting views of human nature. In one perspective, human beings—like other animals—are ruled by their passions, which can only be governed by the civilizing force of law and reason; since Segismund has been raised without benefit of culture, he represents humanity in this unadorned state. Yet at the same time, Segismund's innate response to Rosaura suggests a second view of human nature, one in which sympathy, kindness, and morality are not imposed on human nature by education and society, but are somehow innate to humanity itself.

Just as Segismund relents toward Rosaura, Clotaldo suddenly bursts in and arrests her; Basil has decreed that even the existence of his son must remain a secret. But in arresting Rosaura, Clotaldo takes her sword, which he immediately recognizes as the sword he had left "fair Violante" years before: Rosaura—who has traveled to Poland disguised as a man for protection—must be Clotaldo's "son." Clotaldo is now caught in the classic "love-and-honor" bind. His duty to his king requires him to arrest and eventually execute anyone who spies Basil's secret son; yet to honor his bond to the king, he must betray the natural love he should show to his own child.

As the play proceeds, Clotaldo's effort to reclaim his son is paralleled by Basil's guilty desire to restore his own son to society. Basil hits on an experiment: he will put Segismund to sleep and awaken him at court; when he awakens, Segismund will be told that he is now the king. If his behavior is civilized and restrained, then Basil will know that the prophecy was wrong and will acknowledge Segismund as his heir; if his behavior is threatening, he will be sent back to prison. But Basil's plan has one flaw: having been raised in solitude, Segismund has no understanding of the elaborate conventions of courtly behavior. When he awakens as "king," he is rude to Prince Astolfo, offensively forward to Stella, and murderously impulsive to the servants who try to restrain and control his behavior. His behavior is so outrageous that he is again knocked unconscious and sent back to his prison.

Returned to captivity, Segismund can only understand his sojourn at court as a beautiful dream, a dream that becomes an image for the fleeting and illusory joys of life itself. But this recognition reforms Segismund, enables him to recognize that he can only assume his full humanity by governing his passions. In the play's final moments, Segismund is released from prison by a rebellious mob, who have come to release Segismund in order to overthrow Basil. When Segismund and his army confront Basil, the old king not only assumes that he has lost his kingdom, but that Segismund will kill him, in part to repay Basil for stealing the better part of his life. But Segismund now understands that although Basil's treatment has made him "savage" in his passions—an "inhuman monster"—the only way to regain his humanity is to govern his desire for revenge. So Segismund submits himself to Basil, who recognizes that his son has been reformed and gives him the kingdom: in conquering himself, Segismund wins the throne as well.

Calderón's drama is a deeply philosophical play, and the characters meditate extensively on the nature and meaning of their behavior. But *Life is a Dream* is in some sense also a political play; its rich examination of "human nature" is conducted from a deeply aristocratic perspective. The only way that Segismund can demonstrate his humanity, after all, is to recognize and accept the conventions of courtly behavior as "natural." It is a sign of Segismund's acceptance of those values that his first act as king is to sentence the soldier who liberated him from prison to a life imprisonment of his own.

LIFE IS A DREAM

Pedro Calderón de la Barca

TRANSLATED BY ROY CAMPBELL

— CHARACTERS —

BASIL, *King of Poland*
SEGISMUND, *Prince*
ASTOLFO, *Duke of Muscovy*
CLOTALDO, *old man*
CLARION, *a comical servant*
ROSAURA, *a lady*

STELLA, *a princess*
Soldiers, guards, musicians, servants, retinues, women

*The scene is laid in the court of Poland, a nearby fortress, and
the open country.*

— ACT ONE —

*On one side a craggy mountain: on the other a rude tower whose
base serves as a prison for* SEGISMUND. *The door facing the
spectators is open. The action begins at nightfall.*

(ROSAURA, *dressed as a man, appears on the rocks climbing
down to the plain: behind her comes* CLARION.)

ROSAURA: You headlong hippogriff who match the gale
    In rushing to and fro, you lightning-flicker
    Who give no light, you scaleless fish, you bird
    Who have no coloured plumes, you animal
5   Who have no natural instinct, tell me whither
    You lead me stumbling through this labyrinth
    Of naked crags! Stay here upon this peak
    And be a Phaëthon to the brute-creation!
    For I, pathless save only for the track
10   The laws of destiny dictate for me,
    Shall, blind and desperate, descend this height
    Whose furrowed brows are frowning at the sun.
    How rudely, Poland, you receive a stranger
    (Hardly arrived, but to be treated hardly)
15   And write her entry down in blood with thorns.
    My plight attests this well, but after all,
    Where did the wretchèd ever pity find?

CLARION: Say *two* so wretchèd. Don't you leave me out
    When you complain! If we two sallied out
20   From our own country, questing high adventure,
    And after so much madness and misfortune
    Are still two here, and were two when we fell
    Down those rough crags—shall I not be offended
    To share the trouble yet forego the credit?

25 ROSAURA: I did not give you shares in my complaint
    So as not to rob you of the right to sorrow
    Upon your own account. There's such relief
    In venting grief that a philosopher
    Once said that sorrows should not be bemoaned
30   But sought for pleasure.

CLARION: Philosopher?
    I call him a long-bearded, drunken sot
    And would they'd cudgelled him a thousand blows
    To give him something worth his while lamenting!
    But, madam, what should we do, by ourselves,
35   On foot and lost at this late hour of day,
    Here on this desert mountain far away—

The sun departing after fresh horizons?

ROSAURA: Clarion, how can I answer, being both
    The partner of your plight and your dilemma?

CLARION: Would anyone believe such strange events?   40

ROSAURA: If there my sight is not deceived by fancy,
    In the last timid light that yet remains
    I seem to see a building.

CLARION: Either my hopes
    Are lying or I see the signs myself.

ROSAURA: Between the towering crags, there stands so small   45
    A royal palace that the lynx-eyed sun
    Could scarce perceive it at midday, so rude
    In architecture that it seems but one
    Rock more down-toppled from the sun-kissed crags
    That form the jaggèd crest.   50

CLARION: Let's go closer,
    For we have stared enough: it would be better
    To let the inmates makes us welcome.

ROSAURA: See:
    The door, or, rather, that funereal gap,
    Is yawning wide—whence night itself seems born,
    Flowing out from its black, rugged centre.   55

(A sound of chains is heard.)

CLARION: Heavens! What's that I hear?

ROSAURA: I have become
    A block immovable of ice and fire.

CLARION: Was that a little chain? Why, I'll be hanged
    If that is not the clanking ghost of some
    Past galley-slave—my terror proves it is!   60

SEGISMUND: Oh, miserable me! Unhappy me!

ROSAURA: How sad a cry that is! I fear new trials
    And torments.

CLARION: It's a fearful sound.

ROSAURA: Oh, come,
    My Clarion, let us fly from suffering!

CLARION: I'm in such sorry trim, I've not the spirit   65
    Even to run away.

ROSAURA: And if you had,
    You'd not have seen that door, not known of it.
    When one's in doubt, the common saying goes
    One walks between two lights.

CLARION: I'm the reverse.
    It's not that way with me.   70

ROSAURA: What then disturbs you?

CLARION: I walk in doubt between two darknesses.

ROSAURA: Is not that feeble exhalation there

A light? That pallid star whose fainting tremors,

Pulsing a doubtful warmth of glimmering rays,

75 Make even darker with its spectral glow

That gloomy habitation? Yes! because

By its reflection (though so far away)

I recognise a prison, grim and sombre,

The sepulchre of some poor living carcase.

80 And, more to wonder at, a man lies there

Clothed in the hides of savage beasts, with limbs

Loaded with fetters, and a single lamp

For company. So, since we cannot flee,

Let us stay here and listen to his plaint

85 And what his sorrows are.

SEGISMUND: Unhappy me!

Oh, miserable me! You heavens above,

I try to think what crime I've done against you

By being born. Although to have been born,

I know, is an offence, and with just cause

90 I bear the rigours of your punishment:

Since to be born is man's worst crime. But yet

I long to know (to clarify my doubts)

What greater crime, apart from being born,

Can thus have earned my greater chastisement.

95 Aren't others born like me? And yet they seem

To boast a freedom that I've never known.

The bird is born, and in the hues of beauty

Clothed with its plumes, yet scarce has it become

A feathered posy—or a flower with wings—

100 When through ethereal halls it cuts its way,

Refusing the kind shelter of its nest.

And I, who have more soul than any bird,

Must have less liberty?

The beast is born, and with its hide bright-painted,

105 In lovely tints, has scarce become a spangled

And starry constellation (thanks to the skilful

Brush of the Painter) than its earthly needs

Teach it the cruelty to prowl and kill,

The monster of its labyrinth of flowers.

110 Yet I, with better instincts than a beast,

Must have less liberty?

The fish is born, the birth of spawn and slime,

That does not even live by breathing air.

No sooner does it feel itself a skiff

115 Of silver scales upon the wave than swiftly

It roves about in all directions taking

The measure of immensity as far

As its cold blood's capacity allows.

Yet I, with greater freedom of the will,

120 Must have less liberty?

The brook is born, and like a snake unwinds

Among the flowers. No sooner, silver serpent,

Does it break through the blooms than it regales

And thanks them with its music for their kindness,

125 Which opens to its course the majesty

Of the wide plain. Yet I, with far more life,

Must have less liberty?

This fills me with such passion, I become

Like the volcano Etna, and could tear

130 Pieces of my own heart out of my breast!

What law, justice, or reason can decree

That man alone should never know the joys

And be alone excepted from the rights

God grants a fish, a bird, a beast, a brook?

ROSAURA: His words have filled me full of fear and pity. 135

SEGISMUND: Who is it overheard my speech? Clotaldo?

CLARION: Say "yes!"

ROSAURA: It's only a poor wretch, alas,

Who in these cold ravines has overheard

Your sorrows.

SEGISMUND: Then I'll kill you

(Seizes her.)

So as to leave no witness of my frailty. 140

I'll tear you into bits with these strong arms!

CLARION: I'm deaf. I wasn't able to hear that.

ROSAURA: If you were human born, it is enough

That I should kneel to you for you to spare me.

SEGISMUND: Your voice has softened me, your presence 145

halted me,

And now, confusingly, I feel respect

For you. Who are you? Though here I have learned

So little of the world, since this grim tower

Has been my cradle and my sepulchre;

And though since I was born (if you can say 150

I really have been born) I've only seen

This rustic desert where in misery

I dwell alone, a living skeleton,

An animated corpse; and though till now,

I never spoke, save to one man who hears 155

My griefs and through whose converse I have heard

News of the earth and of the sky; and though,

To astound you more, and make you call me

A human monster, I dwell here, and am

A man of the wild animals, a beast 160

Among the race of men; and though in such

Misfortune, I have studied human laws,

Instructed by the birds, and learned to measure

The circles of the gentle stars, you only

Have curbed my furious rage, amazed my vision, 165

And filled with wonderment my sense of hearing.

Each time I look at you, I feel new wonder!

The more I see of you, the more I long

To go on seeing more of you. I think

My eyes are dropsical, to go on drinking 170

What it is death for them to drink, because

They go on drinking that which I am dying

To see and that which, seen, will deal me death.

Yet let me gaze on you and die, since I

Am so bewitched I can no longer think 175

What not seeing you would do to me—the sight

Itself being fatal! that would be more hard

Than dying, madness, rage, and fiercest grief:

It would be life—worst fate of all because

The gift of life to such a wretchèd man 180

Would be the gift of death to happiness!

ROSAURA: Astonished as I look, amazed to hear,

I know not what to say nor what to ask.

All I can say is that heaven guided me

Here to be comforted, if it is comfort 185

To see another sadder than oneself.

They say a sage philosopher of old,

Being so poor and miserable that he

Lived on the few plain herbs he could collect,
190 One day exclaimed: "Could any man be poorer
Or sadder than myself?"—when, turning round,
He saw the very answer to his words.
For there another sage philosopher
Was picking up the scraps he'd thrown away.
195 I lived cursing my fortune in this world
And asked within me: "Is there any other
Suffers so hard a fate?" Now out of pity
You've given me the answer. For within me
I find upon reflection that my griefs
200 Would be as joys to you and you'd receive them
To give you pleasure. So if they perchance
In any measure may afford relief,
Listen attentively to my misfortune
And take what is left over for yourself.
205 I am . . .

CLOTALDO: *(Within.)* Guards of the tower! You sluggards
Or cowards, you have let two people pass
Into the prison bounds . . .
ROSAURA: Here's more confusion!
SEGISMUND: That is Clotaldo, keeper of my prison.
Are my misfortunes still not at an end?
210 CLOTALDO: Come. Be alert, and either seize or slay them
Before they can resist!
VOICES: *(Within.)*   Treason! Betrayal!
CLARION: Guards of the tower who let us pass unhindered,
Since there's a choice, to seize us would be simpler.

(Enter CLOTALDO *with soldiers. He holds a pistol and they all
wear masks.)*

CLOTALDO: *(Aside to the soldiers.)* Cover your faces, all! It's a
precaution
215 Imperative that nobody should know us
While we are here.
CLARION: What's this? A masquerade?
CLOTALDO: O you, who ignorantly passed the bounds
And limits of this region, banned to all—
Against the king's decree which has forbidden
220 That any should find out the prodigy
Hidden in these ravines—yield up your weapons
Or else this pistol, like a snake of metal,
Will spit the piercing venom of two shots
With scandalous assault upon the air.
225 SEGISMUND: Tyrannic master, ere you harm these people
Let my life be the spoil of these sad bonds
In which (I swear it by Almighty God)
I'll sooner rend myself with hands and teeth
Amid these rocks than see them harmed and mourn
230 Their suffering.
CLOTALDO: Since you know, Segismund,
That your misfortunes are so huge that, even
Before your birth, you died by heaven's decree,
And since you know these walls and binding chains
Are but the brakes and curbs to your proud frenzies,
235 What use is it to bluster?

(To the guards.)

Shut the door
Of this close prison! Hide him in its depths!
SEGISMUND: Ah, heavens, how justly you denied me freedom!
For like a Titan I would rise against you,

Pile jasper mountains high on stone foundations
And climb to burst the windows of the sun!   240
CLOTALDO: Perhaps you suffer so much pain today
Just to forestall that feat.
ROSAURA: Now that I see
How angry pride offends you, I'd be foolish
Not to plead humbly at your feet for life.
Be moved by me to pity. It would be   245
Notoriously harsh that neither pride
Nor humbleness found favour in your eyes!
CLARION: And if neither Humility nor Pride
Impress you (characters of note who act
And motivate a thousand mystery plays)   250
Let me, here, who am neither proud nor humble,
But merely something halfway in between,
Plead to you both for shelter and for aid.
CLOTALDO: Ho, there!
SOLDIER: Sir?
CLOTALDO: Take their weapons. Bind their eyes
So that they cannot see the way they're led.   255
ROSAURA: This is my sword. To nobody but you
I yield it, since you're, after all, the chief.
I cannot yield to one of meaner rank.
CLARION: My sword is such that I will freely give it
To the most mean and wretched.   260

(To one soldier.)

                              Take it, you!

ROSAURA: And if I have to die, I'll leave it to you
In witness of your mercy. It's a pledge
Of great worth and may justly be esteemed
For someone's sake who wore it long ago.
CLOTALDO: *(Apart.)* Each moment seems to bring me new   265
misfortune!
ROSAURA: Because of that, I ask you to preserve
This sword with care. Since if inconstant Fate
Consents to the remission of my sentence,
It has to win me honour. Though I know not
The secret that it carries, I do know   270
It has got one—unless I trick myself—
And prize it just as the sole legacy
My father left me.
CLOTALDO: Who then was your father?
ROSAURA: I never knew.
CLOTALDO: And why have you come here?
ROSAURA: I came to Poland to avenge a wrong.   275
CLOTALDO: *(Apart.)* Sacred heavens!

(On taking the sword he becomes very perturbed.)

                    What's this? Still worse and worse.
I am perplexed and troubled with more fears.

(Aloud.)

Tell me: who gave that sword to you?
ROSAURA: A woman.
CLOTALDO: Her name?
ROSAURA: A secret I am forced to keep.
CLOTALDO: What makes you think this sword contains a   280
secret?
ROSAURA: That she who gave it to me said: "Depart
To Poland. There with subtlety and art
Display it so that all the leading people

And noblemen can see you wearing it,
285 And I know well that there's a lord among them
Who will both shelter you and grant you favour."
But, lest he should be dead, she did not name him.
CLOTALDO: *(Aside.)* Protect me, heavens! What is this I hear?
I cannot say if real or imagined
290 But here's the sword I gave fair Violante
In token that, whoever in the future
Should come from her to me wearing this sword,
Would find in me a tender father's love.
Alas, what can I do in such a pass,
295 When he who brings the sword to win my favour
Brings it to find his own red death instead
Arriving at my feet condemned already?
What strange perplexity! How hard a fate!
What an inconstant fortune to be plagued with!
300 This is my son not only by all signs
But also by the promptings of my heart,
Since, seeing him, my heart seems to cry out
To him, and beat its wings, and, though unable
To break the locks, behaves as one shut in,
305 Who, hearing noises in the street outside,
Cranes from the window-ledge. Just so, not knowing
What's really happening, but hearing sounds,
My heart runs to my eyes which are its windows
And out of them flows into bitter tears.
310 Protect me, heaven! What am I to do?
To take him to the king is certain death.
To hide him is to break my sacred oath
And the strong law of homage. From one side
Love of one's own, and from the other loyalty—
315 Call me to yield. Loyalty to my king
(Why do I doubt?) comes before life and honour.
Then live my loyalty, and let him die!
When I remember, furthermore, he came
To avenge an injury—a man insulted
320 And unavenged is in disgrace. My son
Therefore he is not, nor of noble blood.
But if some danger has mischanced, from which
No one escapes, since honour is so fragile
That any act can smash it, and it takes
325 A stain from any breath of air, what more
Could any nobleman have done than he,
Who, at the cost of so much risk and danger,
Comes to avenge his honour? Since he's so brave
He is my son, and my blood's in his veins.
330 And so betwixt the one doubt and the other,
The most important mean between extremes
Is to go to the king and tell the truth—
That he's my son, to kill, if so he wishes.
Perhaps my loyalty thus will move his mercy
335 And if I thus can merit a live son
I'll help him to avenge his injury.
But if the king prove constant in his rigour
And deal him death, he'll die in ignorance
That I'm his father.

(Aloud to ROSAURA *and* CLARION.*)*

          Come then, strangers, come!
340 And do not fear that you have no companions
In your misfortunes, since, in equal doubt,

Tossed between life and death, I cannot guess
Which is the greater evil or the less.

A hall at the royal palace, in court.

(Enter ASTOLFO *and soldiers at one side: from the other side*
PRINCESS STELLA *and ladies. Military music and salvos.)*

ASTOLFO: To greet your excellent bright beams
As brilliant as a comet's rays,   345
The drums and brasses mix their praise
With those of fountains, birds, and streams.
With sounds alike, in like amaze,
Your heavenly face each voice salutes,
Which puts them in such lively fettle,   350
The trumpets sound like birds of metal,
The songbirds play like feathered flutes.
And thus they greet you, fair señora—
The salvos, as their queen, the brasses,
As to Minerva when she passes,   355
The songbirds to the bright Aurora,
And all the flowers and leaves and grasses
As doing homage unto Flora,
Because you come to cheat the day
Which now the night has covered o'er—   360
Aurora in your spruce array,
Flora in peace, Pallas in war,
But in my heart the queen of May.
STELLA: If human voice could match with acts
You would have been unwise to say   365
Hyperboles that a few facts
May well refute some other day
Confounding all this martial fuss
With which I struggle daringly,
Since flatteries you proffer thus   370
Do not accord with what I see.
Take heed that it's an evil thing
And worthy of a brute accursed,
Loud praises with your mouth to sing
When in your heart you wish the worst.   375
ASTOLFO: Stella, you have been badly misinformed
If you doubt my good faith. Here let me beg you
To listen to my plea and hear me out.
The third Eugtorgius died, the King of Poland.
Basil, his heir, had two fair sisters who   380
Bore you, my cousin, and myself. I would not
Tire you with all that happened here. You know
Clorilene was your mother who enjoys,
Under a better reign, her starry throne.
She was the elder. Lovely Recisunda   385
(Whom may God cherish for a thousand years!)
The younger one, my mother and your aunt,
Was wed in Muscovy. Now to return:
Basil has yielded to the feebleness
Of age, loves learnèd study more than women,   390
Has lost his wife, is childless, will not marry.
And so it comes that you and I both claim
The heirdom of the realm. You claim that you
Were daughter to the elder daughter. I
Say that my being born a man, although   395
Son of the younger daughter, gives me title

To be preferred. We've told the king, our uncle,
Of both of our intentions. And he answered
That he would judge between our rival claims,
400 For which the time and place appointed was
Today and here. For the same reason I
Have left my native Muscovy. With that
Intent I come—not seeking to wage war
But so that you might thus wage war on me!
405 May Love, wise god, make true what people say
(Your "people" is a wise astrologer)
By settling this through your being chosen queen—
Queen and my consort, sovereign of my will;
My uncle crowning you, for greater honour;
410 Your courage conquering, as it deserves;
My love applauding you, its emperor!
STELLA: To such chivalrous gallantry, my breast
Cannot hold out. The imperial monarchy
I wish were mine only to make it yours—
415 Although my love is not quite satisfied
That you are to be trusted since your speech
Is somewhat contradicted by that portrait
You carry in the locket round your neck.
ASTOLFO: I'll give you satisfaction as to that.

(Drums.)

420 But these loud instruments will not permit it
That sound the arrival of the king and council.

(Enter KING BASIL *with his following.)*

STELLA: Wise Thales . . .
ASTOLFO: Learned Euclid . . .
STELLA: Among the signs . . .
ASTOLFO: Among the stars . . .
STELLA: Where you preside in power . . .
ASTOLFO: Where you reside . . .
425 STELLA: And plot their paths . . .
ASTOLFO: And trace their fiery trails . . .
STELLA: Describing . . .
ASTOLFO: . . . Measuring and judging them . . .
STELLA: Please read my stars that I, in humble bonds . . .
ASTOLFO: Please read them, so that I in soft embraces . . .
STELLA: May twine as ivy to this tree!
ASTOLFO: May find
430 Myself upon my knees before these feet!
BASIL: Come and embrace me, niece and nephew. Trust me,
Since you're both loyal to my loving precepts,
And come here so affectionately both—
In nothing shall I leave you cause to cavil,
435 And both of you as equals will be treated.
The gravity of what I have to tell
Oppresses me, and all I ask of you
Is silence: the event itself will claim
Your wonderment. So be attentive now,
440 Belovèd niece and nephew, illustrious courtiers,
Relatives, friends, and subjects! You all know
That for my learning I have merited
The surname of The Learnèd, since the brush
Of great Timanthes, and Lisippus' marbles—
445 Stemming oblivion (consequence of time)—
Proclaimed me to mankind Basil the Great.
You know the science that I most affect

And most esteem is subtle mathematics
(By which I forestall time, cheat fame itself)
Whose office is to show things gradually.   450
For when I look my tables up and see,
Present before me, all the news and actions
Of centuries to come, I gain on Time—
Since Time recounts whatever I have said
After I say it. Those snowflaking haloes,   455
Those canopies of crystal spread on high,
Lit by the sun, cut by the circling moon,
Those diamond orbs, those globes of radiant crystal
Which the bright stars adorn, on which the signs
Parade in blazing excellence, have been   460
My chiefest study all through my long years.
They are the volumes on whose adamantine
Pages, bound up in sapphire, heaven writes,
In lines of burnished gold and vivid letters,
All that is due to happen, whether adverse   465
Or else benign. I read them in a flash,
So quickly that my spirit tracks their movements—
Whatever road they take, whatever goal
They aim at. Would to heaven that before
My genius had been the commentary   470
Writ in their margins, or the index to
Their pages, that my life had been the rubble,
The ruin, and destruction of their wrath,
And that my tragedy in them had ended,
Because, to the unlucky, even their merit   475
Is like a hostile knife, and he whom knowledge
Injures is but a murderer to himself.
And this I say myself, though my misfortunes
Say it far better, which, to marvel at,
I beg once more for silence from you all.   480
With my late wife, the queen, I had a son,
Unhappy son, to greet whose birth the heavens
Wore themselves out in prodigies and portents.
Ere the sun's light brought him live burial
Out of the womb (for birth resembles death)   485
His mother many times, in the delirium
And fancies of her sleep, saw a fierce monster
Bursting her entrails in a human form,
Born spattered with her lifeblood, dealing death,
The human viper of this century!   490
The day came for his birth, and every presage
Was then fulfilled, for tardily or never
Do the more cruel ones prove false. At birth
His horoscope was such that the bright sun,
Stained in its blood, entered ferociously   495
Into a duel with the moon above.
The whole earth seemed a rampart for the strife
Of heaven's two lights, who—though not hand-to-hand—
Fought light-to-light to gain the mastery!
The worst eclipse the sun has ever suffered   500
Since Christ's own death horrified earth and sky.
The whole earth overflowed with conflagrations
So that it seemed the final paroxysm
Of existence. The skies grew dark. Buildings shook.
The clouds rained stones. The rivers ran with blood. 505
In this delirious frenzy of the sun,
Thus, Segismund was born into the world,
Giving a foretaste of his character

By killing his own mother, seeming to speak thus
510 By his ferocity: "I am a man,
Because I have begun now to repay
All kindnesses with evil." To my studies
I went forthwith, and saw in all I studied
That Segismund would be the most outrageous
515 Of all men, the most cruel of all princes,
And impious of all monarchs, by whose acts
The kingdom would be torn up and divided
So as to be a school of treachery
And an academy of vices. He,
520 Risen in fury, amidst crimes and horrors,
Was born to trample me (with shame I say it)
And make of my grey hairs his very carpet.
Who is there but believes an evil Fate?
And more if he discovers it himself,
525 For self-love lends its credit to our studies.
So I, believing in the Fates, and in
The havoc that their prophecies predestined,
Determined to cage up this newborn tiger
To see if on the stars we sages have
530 Some power. I gave out that the prince had died
Stillborn, and, well-forewarned, I built a tower
Amidst the cliffs and boulders of yon mountains
Over whose tops the light scarce finds its way,
So stubbornly their obelisks and crags
535 Defend the entry to them. The strict laws
And edicts that I published then (declaring
That nobody might enter the forbidden
Part of the range) were passed on that account.
There Segismund lives to this day, a captive,
540 Poor and in misery, where, save Clotaldo,
His guardian, none have seen or talked to him.
The latter has instructed him in all
Branches of knowledge and in the Catholic faith,
Alone the witness of his misery.
545 There are three things to be considered now:
Firstly, Poland, that I love you greatly,
So much that I would free you from the oppression
And servitude of such a tyrant king.
He would not be a kindly ruler who
550 Would put his realm and homeland in such danger.
The second fact that I must bear in mind
Is this: that to deny my flesh and blood
The rights which law, both human and divine,
Concedes, would not accord with Christian charity,
555 For no law says that, to prevent another
Being a tyrant, I may be one myself,
And if my son's a tyrant, to prevent him
From doing outrage, I myself should do it.
Now here's the third and last point I would speak of,
560 Namely, how great an error it has been
To give too much belief to things predicted,
Because, even if his inclination should
Dictate some headlong, rash precipitancies,
They may perhaps not conquer him entirely,
565 For the most accursèd destiny, the most
Violent inclination, the most impious
Planet—all can but influence, not force,
The free will which man holds direct from God.
And so, between one motive and another
570 Vacillating discursively, I hit

On a solution that will stun you all.
I shall tomorrow, but without his knowing
He is my son—your king—place Segismund
(For that's the name with which he was baptised)
Here on my throne, beneath my canopy,   575
Yes, in my very place, that he may govern you
And take command. And you must all be here
To swear him fealty as his loyal subjects.
Three things may follow from this test, and these
I'll set against the three which I proposed.   580
The first is that should the prince prove prudent,
Stable, and benign—thus giving the lie
To all that prophecy reports of him—
Then you'll enjoy in him your rightful ruler
Who was so long a courtier of the mountains   585
And neighbour to the beasts. Here is the second:
If he prove proud, rash, cruel, and outrageous,
And with a loosened rein gallop unheeding
Across the plains of vice, I shall have done
My duty, and fulfilled my obligation   590
Of mercy. If I then re-imprison him,
That's incontestably a kingly deed—
Not cruelty but merited chastisement.
The third thing's this: that if the prince should be
As I've described him, then—by the love I feel   595
For you, my vassals—I shall give you worthier
Rulers to wear the sceptre and the crown;
Because your king and queen will be my nephew
And niece, each with an equal right to rule,
Each gaining the inheritance he merits,   600
And joined in faith of holy matrimony.
This I command you as a king, I ask you
As a kind father, as a sage I pray you,
As an experienced old man I tell you,
And (if it's true, as Spanish Seneca   605
Says, that the king is slave unto his nation)
This, as a humble slave, I beg of you.
ASTOLFO: If it behoves me to reply (being
The person most involved in this affair)
Then, in the name of all, let Segismund   610
Appear! It is enough that he's your son!
ALL: Give us our prince: we want him for our king!
BASIL: Subjects, I thank you for your kindly favour.
Accompany these, my two Atlases,
Back to their rooms. Tomorrow you shall see him.   615
ALL: Long live the great King Basil! Long live Basil!

(*Exeunt all, accompanying* STELLA *and* ASTOLFO. *The* KING *remains.*

Enter CLOTALDO *with* ROSAURA *and* CLARION.)

CLOTALDO: May I have leave to speak, sire?
BASIL: Oh, Clotaldo!
You're very welcome.
CLOTALDO: Thus to kneel before you
Is always welcome, sire—yet not today
When sad and evil Fate destroys the joy   620
Your presence normally concedes.
BASIL: What's wrong?
CLOTALDO: A great misfortune, sire, has come upon me
Just when I should have met it with rejoicing.
BASIL: Continue.

CLOTALDO: Sire, this beautiful young man
625   Who inadvertently and daringly
      Came to the tower, wherein he saw the prince,
      Is my . . .
      BASIL: Do not afflict yourself, Clotaldo.
      Had it not been just now, I should have minded,
      I must confess. But I've revealed the secret,
630   And now it does not matter if he knows it.
      Attend me afterwards. I've many things
      To tell you. You in turn have many things
      To do for me. You'll be my minister,
      I warn you, in the most momentous action
635   The world has ever seen. These prisoners, lest you
      Should think I blame your oversight, I'll pardon.

      (Exit.)

      CLOTALDO: Long may you live, great sire! A thousand years!

      (Aside.)

      Heaven improves our fates. I shall not tell him
      Now that he is my son, since it's not needed
640   Till he's avenged.

      (Aloud.)

      Strangers, you may go free.
      ROSAURA: Humbly I kiss your feet.
      CLARION: Whilst I'll just *miss* them—
      Old friends will hardly quibble at one letter.
      ROSAURA: You've granted me my life, sir. I remain
645   Your servant and eternally your debtor.
      CLOTALDO: No! It was not your life I gave you. No!
      Since any wellborn man who, unavenged,
      Nurses an insult does not live at all.
      And seeing you have told me that you came
650   For that sole reason, it was not life I spared—
      Life in disgrace is not a life at all.

      (Aside.)

      I see this spurs him.
      ROSAURA: Freely I confess it—
      Although you spared my life, it was no life.
      But I will wipe my honour's stain so spotless
655   That after I have vanquished all my dangers
      Life well may seem a shining gift from you.
      CLOTALDO: Take here your burnished steel: 'twill be enough,
      Bathed in your enemies' red blood, to right you.
      For steel that once was mine (I mean of course
660   Just for the time I've had it in my keeping)
      Should know how to avenge you.
      ROSAURA: Now, in your name I gird it on once more
      And on it I will swear to take revenge
      Although my foe were even mightier.
665   CLOTALDO: Is he so powerful?
      ROSAURA: So much so that . . .
      Although I have no doubt in your discretion . . .
      I say no more because I'd not estrange
      Your clemency.
      CLOTALDO: You would have won me had you told me, since
670   That would prevent me helping him.

      (Aside.)

      If only I could discover who he is!

      ROSAURA: So that you'll not think that I value lightly
      Such confidence, know that my adversary
      Is no less than Astolfo, Duke of Muscovy.
      CLOTALDO: (Aside.) (I hardly can withstand the grief it   675
        gives me
      For it is worse than aught I could imagine!
      Let us inquire of him some further facts.)

      (Aloud.)

      If you were born a Muscovite, your ruler
      Could never have affronted you. Go back
      Home to your country. Leave this headstrong valour.   680
      It will destroy you.
      ROSAURA: Though he's been my prince,
      I know that he has done me an affront.
      CLOTALDO: Even though he slapped your face, that's no
        affront.

      (Aside.)

      O heavens!
      ROSAURA: My insult was far deeper!
      CLOTALDO: Tell it:
      Since nothing I imagine could be deeper.   685
      ROSAURA: Yes. I will tell it, yet, I know not why,
      With such respect I look upon your face,
      I venerate you with such true affection,
      With such high estimation do I weigh you,
      That I scarce dare to tell you—these men's clothes   690
      Are an enigma, not what they appear.
      So now you know. Judge if it's no affront
      That here Astolfo comes to wed with Stella
      Although betrothed to me. I've said enough.

      (Exeunt ROSAURA *and* CLARION.)

      CLOTALDO: Here! Listen! Wait! What mazed confusion!   695
      It is a labyrinth wherein the reason
      Can find no clue. My family honour's injured.
      The enemy's all powerful. I'm a vassal
      And she's a woman. Heavens! Show a path
      Although I don't believe there is a way!   700
      There's nought but evil bodings in the sky.
      The whole world is a prodigy, say I.

      — ACT TWO —

      A hall in the royal palace.

      (Enter BASIL *and* CLOTALDO.)

      CLOTALDO: All has been done according to your orders.
      BASIL: Tell me, Clotaldo, how it went?
      CLOTALDO: Why, thus:
      I took to Segismund a calming drug
      Wherein are mixed herbs of especial virtue,
      Tyrannous in their overpowering strength,   5
      Which seize and steal and alienate man's gift
      Of reasoning, thus making a live corpse
      Of him. His violence evaporated
      With all his faculties and senses too.
      There is no need to prove it's possible   10
      Because experience teaches us that medicine
      Is full of natural secrets, that there is no

Animal, plant, or stone that has not got
Appointed properties. If human malice
15 Explores a thousand poisons which deal death,
Who then can doubt, that being so, that other
Poisons, less violent, cause only sleep?
But (leaving that doubt aside, as proven false
By every evidence) hear then the sequel:
20 I went down into Segismund's close prison
Bearing the drink wherein, with opium,
Henbane and poppies had been mixed. With him
I talked a little while of the humanities,
In which dumb Nature has instructed him,
25 The mountains and the heavens and the stars,
In whose divine academies he learned
Rhetoric from the birds and the wild creatures.
To lift his spirit to the enterprise
Which you require of him, I chose for subject
30 The swiftness of a stalwart eagle, who,
Deriding the base region of the wind,
Rises into the sphere reserved for fire,
A feathered lightning, an untethered comet.
Then I extolled such lofty flight and said:
35 "After all, he's the king of birds, and so
Takes precedence, by right, over the rest."
No more was needful for, in taking up
Majesty for his subject, he discoursed
With pride and high ambition, as his blood
40 Naturally moves, incites, and spurs him on
To grand and lofty things, and so he said
That in the restless kingdom of the birds
There should be those who swear obedience, too!
"In this, my miseries console me greatly,
45 Because if I'm a vassal here, it's only
By force, and not by choice. Of my own will
I would not yield in rank to any man."
Seeing that he grew furious—since this touched
The theme of his own griefs—I gave the potion
50 And scarcely had it passed from cup to breast
Before he yielded all his strength to slumber.
A chill sweat ran through all his limbs and veins.
Had I not known that this was mere feigned death
I would have thought him dead. Then came the men
55 To whom you've trusted this experiment,
Who placed him in a coach and brought him here
To your own rooms, where all things were prepared
In royalty and grandeur as befitting
His person. In your own bed they have laid him
60 Where, when the torpor wanes, they'll do him service
As if he were Your Majesty himself.
All has been done as you have ordered it,
And if I have obeyed you well, my lord,
I'd beg a favour (pardon me this freedom)—
65 To know what your intention is in thus
Transporting Segismund here to the palace.
BASIL: Your curiosity is just, Clotaldo,
And yours alone I'll satisfy. The star
Which governs Segismund, my son, in life,
70 Threatens a thousand tragedies and woes.
And now I wish to see whether the stars
(Which never lie—and having shown to us
So many cruel signs seem yet more certain)
May yet be brought to moderate their sentence,

Whether by prudence charmed or valour won,   75
For man does have the power to rule his stars.
I would examine this, bringing him here
Where he may know he is my son, and make
Trial of his talent. If magnanimously
He conquers and controls himself, he'll reign,   80
But if he proves a tyrant and is cruel,
Back to his chains he'll go. Now, you will ask,
Why did we bring him sleeping in this manner
For the experiment? I'll satisfy you,
Down to the smallest detail, with my answer.   85
If he knows that he is my son today,
And if tomorrow he should find himself
Once more reduced to prison, to misery,
He would despair entirely, knowing truly
Who, and whose son, he is. What consolation   90
Could he derive, then, from his lot? So I
Contrive to leave an exit for such grief,
By making him believe it was a dream.
By these means we may learn two things at once:
First, his character—for he will really be   95
Awake in all he thinks and all his actions;
Second, his consolation—which would be
(If he should wake in prison on the morrow,
Although he saw himself obeyed today)
That he might understand he had been dreaming,   100
And he will not be wrong, for in this world,
Clotaldo, all who live are only dreaming.
CLOTALDO: I've proofs enough to doubt of your success,
But now it is too late to remedy it.
From what I can make out, I think he's awakened   105
And that he's coming this way, by the sound.
BASIL: I shall withdraw. You, as his tutor, go
And guide him through his new bewilderments
By answering his queries with the truth.
CLOTALDO: You give me leave to tell the truth of it?   110
BASIL: Yes, because knowing all things, he may find
Known perils are the easiest to conquer.

(*Exit* BASIL. *Enter* CLARION.)

CLARION: It cost me four whacks to get here so quickly.
I caught them from a red-haired halberdier
Sprouting a ginger beard over his livery,   115
And I've come to see what's going on.
No windows give a better view than those
A man brings with him in his head, not asking
For tickets of admission or paid seats,
Since at all functions, festivals, or feasts   120
He looks out with the same nice self-composure.
CLOTALDO: (*Aside.*) Here's Clarion who's the servant of that
person—
That trader in woes, importer from Poland
Of my disgrace.

(*Aloud.*)

Come, Clarion, what news?
CLARION: Item the first: encouraged by the fact   125
Your clemency's disposed to venge her insult,
Rosaura has resumed her proper clothing.
CLOTALDO: That's right: it's less indecorous and bold.
CLARION: Item: she's changed her name, and given out
That she's your niece. And now they've made so much   130

Of her that she's been raised to maid of honour
To the unique and only princess, Stella.
CLOTALDO: That's right: her honour stands to my account.
CLARION: Indeed she merely bides the time till you
135   Will settle all accounts about her honour.
CLOTALDO: Biding the time is wise, for in the end
It's Time that's going to settle all accounts!
CLARION: Item: that she's attended like a queen,
Because they take her for your niece. Item:
140   That I, who trudged along with her, am dying
Of hunger. Nobody remembers me,
Nor yet remembers that I'm like my name
And (should I sound my Clarion) could tell
All to the king and Stella and Astolfo.
145   For I am both a Clarion and a servant—
Two things which ill-accord with secrecy.
If silence should, by chance, let slip my hand,
Then there's a chorus which would fit me well:
"Dawn-breaking Clarion plays no better tune!"
150 CLOTALDO: You've reason for complaint. I'll satisfy it
If you'll but serve me . . .
CLARION: Hush, here's Segismund!

(Enter musicians, singing, and servants arraying SEGISMUND,
who seems amazed.)

SEGISMUND: Heavens above! What's this that I am seeing?
I wonder at it all, with naught of fear!
But with a mighty doubt, I disbelieve it!
155   I?—in a sumptuous palace? I—encircled
With rich brocades and silks? I—overwhelmed
With servants in such brilliant liveries?
I—to awake in such a gorgeous bed?
I—in the middle of so many footmen
160   Who clothe me in rich garments? I'm awake:
It would be false to take this for a dream.
Am I not Segismund? Heavens! disabuse me
If I'm mistaken. Say, what could have happened
In my imagination while I slept—
165   That I should find myself in such a place?
But why should I worry, whatever it was?
I'll let myself be served and entertained—
Befall what may.
FIRST SERVANT: *(Aside to* SECOND SERVANT *and* CLARION.*)*
He's very melancholy!
SECOND SERVANT: Who would not be, considering all that's
happened
170   To him?
CLARION: I would not be!
SECOND SERVANT: You, speak to him.
FIRST SERVANT: Shall they begin to sing again?
SEGISMUND: Why, no,
I would not have them sing.
SECOND SERVANT: You're so distraught,
I wish you entertained.
SEGISMUND: My griefs are such
That no mere voices can amuse me now—
175   Only the martial music pleased my mind.
CLOTALDO: Your Highness, mighty prince, give me your hand
To kiss. I'm glad to be the first to offer
Obedience at your feet.

SEGISMUND: *(Aside.)*   This is Clotaldo.
How is it he, that tyrannised my thralldom,
Should now be treating me with such respect?   180

(Aloud.)

Tell me what's happening all round me here.
CLOTALDO: With the perplexities of your new state,
Your reason will encounter many doubts,
But I shall try to free you from them all
(If that may be) because you now must know   185
You are hereditary Prince of Poland.
If you have been withdrawn from public sight
Under restraint, it was in strict obedience
To Fate's inclemency, which will permit
A thousand woes to fall upon this empire   190
The moment that you wear the sovereign's crown.
But trusting that you'll prudently defeat
Your own malignant stars (since they can be
Controlled by magnanimity) you've been
Brought to this palace from the tower you knew   195
Even while your soul was yielded up to sleep.
My lord the king, your father, will be coming
To see you, and from him you'll learn the rest.
SEGISMUND: Then, vile, infamous traitor, what have I
To know more than this fact of who I am,   200
To show my pride and power from this day onward?
How have you played your country such a treason
As to deny me, against law and right,
The rank which is my own?
CLOTALDO: Unhappy me!
SEGISMUND: You were a traitor to the law, a flattering liar   205
To your own king, and cruel to myself.
And so the king, the law, and I condemn you,
After such fierce misfortunes as I've borne,
To die here by my hands.
SECOND SERVANT: My lord!
SEGISMUND: Let none
Get in the way. It is in vain. By God!   210
If you intrude, I'll throw you through the window.
SECOND SERVANT: Clotaldo, fly!
CLOTALDO: Alas, poor Segismund!
That you should show such pride, all unaware
That you are dreaming this.

(Exit.)

SECOND SERVANT: Take care! Take care!
SEGISMUND: Get out!   215
SECOND SERVANT: He was obeying the king's orders.
SEGISMUND: In an injustice, no one should obey
The king, and I'm his prince.
SECOND SERVANT: He had no right
To look into the rights and wrongs of it.
SEGISMUND: You must be mad to answer back at me.
CLARION: The prince is right. It's you who're in the wrong!   220
SECOND SERVANT: Who gave you right to speak?
CLARION: I simply took it.
SEGISMUND: And who are you?
CLARION: I am the go-between,
And in this art I think I am a master—
Since I'm the greatest jackanapes alive.
SEGISMUND: *(To* CLARION.*)* In all this new world, you're the   225
only one

Of the whole crowd who pleases me.
CLARION: Why, my lord,
    I am the best pleaser of Segismunds
    That ever was: ask anybody here!

(Enter ASTOLFO.*)*

ASTOLFO: Blessèd the day, a thousand times, my prince,
230   On which you landed here on Polish soil
    To fill with so much splendour and delight
    Our wide horizons, like the break of day!
    For you arise as does the rising sun
    Out of the rugged mountains, far away.
235   Shine forth then! And although so tardily
    You bind the glittering laurels on your brows,
    The longer may they last you still unwithered.
SEGISMUND: God save you.
ASTOLFO: That you do not know me, sir,
    Is some excuse for greeting me without
240   The honour due to me. I am Astolfo
    The Duke of Muscovy. You are my cousin.
    We are of equal rank.
SEGISMUND: Then if I say,
    "God save you," do I not display good feeling?
    But since you take such note of who you are,
245   The next time that I see you, I shall say
    "God save you *not*," if you would like that better.
SECOND SERVANT: *(To* ASTOLFO.*)* Your Highness, make
        allowance for his breeding
    Amongst the mountains. So he deals with all.

(To SEGISMUND.*)*

    Astolfo does take precedence, Your Highness—
250   SEGISMUND: I have no patience with the way he came
    To make his solemn speech, then put his hat on!
SECOND SERVANT: He's a grandee!
SEGISMUND: I'm grander than grandees!
SECOND SERVANT: For all that, there should be respect
        between you,
    More than among the rest.
SEGISMUND: And who told you
255   To mix in my affairs?

(Enter STELLA.*)*

STELLA: Many times welcome to Your Royal Highness,
    Now come to grace the dais that receives him
    With gratitude and love. Long may you live
    August and eminent, despite all snares,
260   And count your life by centuries, not years!
SEGISMUND: *(Aside to* CLARION.*)* Now tell me, who's this sov-
        ereign deity
    At whose divinest feet Heaven lays down
    The fleece of its aurora in the east?
CLARION: Sir, it's your cousin Stella.
SEGISMUND: She were better
265   Named "sun" than "star"!

(To STELLA.*)*

                              Though your speech was fair,
    Just to have seen you and been conquered by you
    Suffices for a welcome in itself.
    To find myself so blessed beyond my merit
    What can I do but thank you, lovely Stella,
270   For you could add more brilliance and delight

To the most blazing star? When you get up
    What work is left the sun to do? O give me
    Your hand to kiss, from out whose cup of snow
    The solar horses drink the fires of day!
STELLA: Be a more gentle courtier.   275
ASTOLFO: I am lost.
SECOND SERVANT: I know Astolfo's hurt. I must divert him.

(To SEGISMUND.*)*

    Sir, you should know that thus to woo so boldly
    Is most improper. And, besides, Astolfo . . .
SEGISMUND: Did I not tell you not to meddle with me?
SECOND SERVANT: I only say what's just.   280
SEGISMUND: All this annoys me.
    Nothing seems just to me but what I want.
SECOND SERVANT: Why, sir, I heard you say that no obedience
    Or service should be lent to what's unjust.
SEGISMUND: You also heard me say that I would throw
    Anyone who annoys me from that balcony.   285
SECOND SERVANT: With men like me you cannot do such
        things.
SEGISMUND: No? Well, by God, I'll have to prove it then!

*(He takes him in his arms and rushes out, followed by many, to
return soon after.)*

ASTOLFO: What on earth have I seen? Can it be true?
STELLA: Go, all, and stop him!
SEGISMUND: *(Returning.)*   From the balcony
    He's fallen in the sea. How strange it seems!   290
ASTOLFO: Measure your acts of violence, my lord:
    From crags to palaces, the distance is
    As great as that between man and the beasts.
SEGISMUND: Well, since you are for speaking out so boldly,
    Perhaps one day you'll find that on your shoulders   295
    You have no head to place your hat upon.

(Exit ASTOLFO. *Enter* BASIL.*)*

BASIL: What's happened here?
SEGISMUND: Nothing at all. A man
    Wearied me, so I threw him in the sea.
CLARION: *(To* SEGISMUND.*)* Be warned. That is the king.
BASIL: On the first day,
    So soon, your coming here has cost a life?   300
SEGISMUND: He said I couldn't: so I won the bet.
BASIL: It grieves me, Prince, that, when I hoped to see you
    Forewarned, and overriding Fate, in triumph
    Over your stars, the first thing I should see
    Should be such rigour—that your first deed here   305
    Should be a grievous homicide. Alas!
    With what love, now, can I offer my arms,
    Knowing your own have learned to kill already?
    Who sees a dirk, red from a mortal wound,
    But does not fear it? Who can see the place   310
    Soaking in blood, where late a man was murdered,
    But even the strongest must respond to nature?
    So in your arms seeing the instrument
    Of death, and looking on a blood-soaked place,
    I must withdraw myself from your embrace,   315
    And though I thought in loving bonds to bind
    Your neck, yet fear withholds me from your arms.
SEGISMUND: Without your loving arms I can sustain
    Myself as usual. That such a loving father

320   Could treat me with such cruelty, could thrust me
From his side ungratefully, could rear me
As a wild beast, could hold me for a monster,
And pray that I were dead, that such a father
Withholds his arms from winding round my neck,
325   Seems unimportant, seeing that he deprives
Me of my very being as a man.
BASIL: Would to heaven I had never granted it,
For then I never would have heard your voice,
Nor seen your outrages.
SEGISMUND: Had you denied
330   Me being, then I would not have complained,
But that you took it from me when you gave it—
That is my quarrel with you. Though to give
Is the most singular and noble action,
It is the basest action if one gives
335   Only to take away.
BASIL: How well you thank me
For being raised from pauper to a prince!
SEGISMUND: In this what is there I should thank you for?
You tyrant of my will! If you are old
And feeble, and you die, what can you give me
340   More than what is my own by right of birth?
You are my father and my king, therefore
This grandeur comes to me by natural law.
Therefore, despite my present state, I'm not
Indebted to you, rather can I claim
345   Account of all those years in which you robbed me
Of life and being, liberty, and honour.
You ought to thank me that I press no claim
Since you're my debtor, even to bankruptcy.
BASIL: Barbarous and outrageous brute! The heavens
350   Have now fulfilled their prophecy: I call
Them to bear witness to your pride. Although
You know now, disillusioned, who you are,
And see yourself where you take precedence,
Take heed of this I say: be kind and humble
355   Since it may be that you are only dreaming,
Although it seems to you you're wide-awake.

(Exit BASIL.)

SEGISMUND: Can I perhaps be dreaming, though I seem
So wide-awake? No: I am not asleep,
Since I can touch, and realise what I
360   Have been before, and what I am today.
And if you even now relented, Father,
There'd be no cure since I know who I am
And you cannot, for all your signs and groans,
Cheat me of my hereditary crown.
365   And if I was submissive in my chains
Before, then I was ignorant of what I am,
Which I now know (and likewise know that I
Am partly man but partly beast as well).

(Enter ROSAURA in woman's clothing.)

ROSAURA: *(Aside.)* I came in Stella's train. I am afraid
370   Of meeting with Astolfo, since Clotaldo
Says he must not know who I am, not see me,
Because (he says) it touches on my honour.
And well I trust Clotaldo since I owe him
The safety of my life and honour both.

CLARION: What pleases you, and what do you admire   375
Most, of the things you've seen here in the world?
SEGISMUND: Why, nothing that I could not have foreseen—
Except the loveliness of women! Once,
I read among the books I had out there
That who owes God most grateful contemplation   380
Is Man: who is himself a tiny world.
But I think who owes God more grateful study
Is Woman—since she is a tiny heaven,
Having as much more beauty than a man
As heaven than earth. And even more, I say,   385
If she's the one that I am looking at.
ROSAURA: *(Aside.)* That is the prince. I'll go.
SEGISMUND: Stop! Woman! Wait!
Don't join the sunset with the breaking day
By fading out so fast. If east and west
Should clash like that, the day would surely suffer   390
A syncope. But what is this I see?
ROSAURA: What I am looking at I doubt, and yet
Believe.
SEGISMUND: *(Aside.)* This beauty I have seen before.
ROSAURA: *(Aside.)* This pomp and grandeur I have seen before
Cooped in a narrow dungeon.   395
SEGISMUND: *(Aside.)*   I have found
My life at last.

(Aloud.)

         Woman (for that sole word
Outsoars all wooing flattery of speech
From one that is a man), woman, who are you?
If even long before I ever saw you
You owed me adoration as your prince,   400
How much the more should you be conquered by me
Now I recall I've seen you once before!
Who are you, beauteous woman?
ROSAURA: *(Aside.)*   I'll pretend.

(Aloud.)

In Stella's train, I am a luckless lady.
SEGISMUND: Say no such thing. You are the sun from which   405
The minor star that's Stella draws its life,
Since she receives the splendour of your rays.
I've seen how in the kingdom of sweet odours,
Commander of the squadrons of the flowers,
The rose's deity presides, and is   410
Their empress by divine right of her beauty.
Among the precious stones which can be listed
In the academy of mines, I've seen
The diamond much preferred above the rest,
And crowned their emperor, for shining brightest.   415
In the revolving empire of the stars
The morning star takes pride among the others.
In their perfected spheres, when the sun calls
The planets to his council, he presides
And is the very oracle of day.   420
Then if among stars, gems, planet, and flowers
The fairest are exalted, why do you
Wait on a lessor beauty than yourself
Who are, in greater excellence and beauty,
The sun, the morning star, the diamond, and the rose!   425

(Enter CLOTALDO, who remains by the stage-curtain.)

CLOTALDO: *(Aside.)*
 I wish to curb him, since I brought him up.
 But, what is this?
ROSAURA: I reverence your favour,
 And yet reply, rhetorical, with silence,
 For when one's mind is clumsy and untaught,
430 He answers best who does not speak at all.
SEGISMUND: Stay! Do not go! How can you wish to go
 And leave me darkened by my doubts?
ROSAURA: Your Highness,
 I beg your leave to go.
SEGISMUND: To go so rudely
 Is not to beg my leave but just to take it.
435 ROSAURA: But if you will not grant it, I must take it.
SEGISMUND: That were to change my courtesy to rudeness.
 Resistance is like venom to my patience.
ROSAURA: But even if this deadly, raging venom
 Should overcome your patience, yet you dare not
440 And could not treat me with dishonour, sir.
SEGISMUND: Why, just to see then if I can, and dare to—
 You'll make me lose the fear I bear your beauty,
 Since the impossible is always tempting
 To me. Why, only now I threw a man
445 Over this balcony who said I couldn't:
 And so to find out if I can or not
 I'll throw your honour through the window too.
CLOTALDO: *(Aside.)*
 He seems determined in this course. Oh, heavens!
 What's to be done that for a second time
450 My honour's threatened by a mad desire?
ROSAURA: Then with good reason it was prophesied
 Your tyranny would wreak this kingdom
 Outrageous scandals, treasons, crimes, and deaths.
 But what can such a creature do as you
455 Who are not even a man, save in the name—
 Inhuman, barbarous, cruel, and unbending
 As the wild beasts amongst whom you were nursed?
SEGISMUND: That you should not insult me in this way
 I spoke to you most courteously, and thought
460 I'd thereby get my way; but if you curse me thus
 Even when I am speaking gently, why,
 By the living God, I'll really give you cause.
 Ho there! Clear out, the lot of you, at once!
 Leave her to me! Close all the doors upon us.
465 Let no one enter!

(Exeunt CLARION *and other attendants.)*

ROSAURA: I am lost . . . I warn you . . .
SEGISMUND: I am a tyrant and you plead in vain.
CLOTALDO: *(Aside.)*
 Oh, what a monstrous thing! I must restrain him
 Even if I die for it.

(Aloud.)

             Sir! Wait! Look here!
SEGISMUND: A second time you have provoked my anger,
470 You feeble, mad old man! Do you prize lightly
 My wrath and rigour that you've gone so far?
CLOTALDO: Brought by the accents of her voice, I came
 To tell you you must be more peaceful
 If still you hope to reign, and warn you that

You should not be so cruel, though you rule—   475
 Since this, perhaps, is nothing but a dream.
SEGISMUND: When you refer to disillusionment
 You rouse me near to madness. Now you'll see,
 Here as I kill you, if it's truth or dreaming!

(As he tries to pull out his dagger, CLOTALDO *restrains him and throws himself on his knees before him.)*

CLOTALDO: It's thus I'd save my life: and hope to do so—   480
SEGISMUND: Take your presumptuous hand from off this steel.
CLOTALDO: Till people come to hold your rage and fury
 I shall not let you go.
ROSAURA: O heavens!
SEGISMUND: Loose it,

(They struggle.)

 I say, or else—you interfering fool—
 I'll crush you to your death in my strong arms!   485
ROSAURA: Come quickly! Here's Clotaldo being killed!

(Exit.
ASTOLFO *appears as* CLOTALDO *falls on the floor, and the former stands between* SEGISMUND *and* CLOTALDO.)*

ASTOLFO: Why, what is this, most valiant prince? What?
 Staining
 Your doughty steel in such old, frozen blood?
 For shame! For shame! Sheathe your illustrious weapon!
SEGISMUND: When it is stained in his infamous blood!   490
ASTOLFO: At my feet here he has found sanctuary
 And there he's safe, for it will serve him well.
SEGISMUND: Then serve me well by dying, for like this
 I will avenge myself for your behaviour
 In trying to annoy me first of all.   495
ASTOLFO: To draw in self-defence offends no king,
 Though in his palace.

*(ASTOLFO *draws his sword and they fight.)*

CLOTALDO: *(To* ASTOLFO.*)* Do not anger him!

(Enter BASIL, STELLA, *and attendants.)*

BASIL: Hold! Hold! What's this? Fighting with naked swords?
STELLA: *(Aside.)* It is Astolfo! How my heart misgives me!
BASIL: Why, what has happened here?   500
ASTOLFO: Nothing, my Lord,
 Since you've arrived.

(Both sheathe their swords.)

SEGISMUND: Much, though you *have* arrived.
 I tried to kill the old man.
BASIL: Had you no
 Respect for those white hairs?
CLOTALDO: Sire, since they're only
 Mine, as you well can see, it does not matter!
SEGISMUND: It is in vain you'd have me hold white hairs   505
 In such respect, since one day you may find
 Your own white locks prostrated at my feet
 For still I have not taken vengeance on you
 For the foul way in which you had me reared.

(Exit.)

BASIL: Before that happens you will sleep once more   510
 Where you were reared, and where what's happened may

Seem just a dream (being mere earthly glory).

(All save ASTOLFO *and* STELLA *leave.)*

ASTOLFO: How seldom does prediction fail, when evil!
　　　How oft, foretelling good! Exact in harm,
515　　Doubtful in benefit! Oh, what a great
　　　Astrologer would be one who foretold
　　　Nothing but harms, since there's no doubt at all
　　　That they are always due! In Segismund
　　　And me the case is illustrated clearly.
520　　In him, crimes, cruelties, deaths, and disasters
　　　Were well predicted, since they all came true.
　　　But in my own case, to predict for me
　　　(As I foresaw beholding rays which cast
　　　The sun into the shade and outface heaven)
525　　Triumphs and trophies, happiness and praise,
　　　Was false—and yet was true: it's only just
　　　That when predictions start with promised favours
　　　They should end in disdain.

STELLA:　　　　　　　　I do not doubt
　　　Your protestations are most heartfelt; only
530　　They're not for me, but for another lady
　　　Whose portrait you were wearing round your neck
　　　Slung in a locket when you first arrived.
　　　Since it is so, she only can deserve
　　　These wooing flatteries. Let her repay you
535　　For in affairs of love, flatteries and vows
　　　Made for another are mere forged credentials.

*(*ROSAURA *enters but waits by the curtain.)*

ROSAURA: *(Aside.)* Thanks be to God, my troubles are near
　　　　ended!
　　　To judge from what I see, I've naught to fear.

ASTOLFO: I will expel that portrait from my breast
540　　To make room for the image of your beauty
　　　And keep it there. For there where Stella is
　　　Can be no room for shade, and where the sun is
　　　No place for any star. I'll fetch the portrait.

(Aside.)

　　　Forgive me, beautiful Rosaura, that,
545　　When absent, men and women seldom keep
　　　More faith than this.

(Exit.

ROSAURA *comes forward.)*

ROSAURA: *(Aside.)* I could not hear a word. I was afraid
　　　That they would see me.

STELLA:　　　　　　　Oh, Astrea!

ROSAURA:　　　　　　　　　My lady!

STELLA: I am delighted that you came. Because
　　　To you alone would I confide a secret.

550　ROSAURA: Thereby you greatly honour me, your servant.

STELLA: Astrea, in the brief time I have known you
　　　I've given you the latchkey of my will.
　　　For that, and being who you are, I'll tell you
　　　A secret which I've very often hidden
555　　Even from myself.

ROSAURA:　　　　　I am your slave.

STELLA:　　　　　　　　　Then, briefly:
　　　Astolfo, who's my cousin (the word cousin
　　　Suffices, since some things are plainly said

Even by thinking them), is to wed me
If Fortune thus can wipe so many cares
Away with one great joy. But I am troubled   560
In that, the day he first came here, he carried
A portrait of a lady round his neck.
I spoke to him about it courteously.
He was most amiable, he loves me well,
And now he's gone for it. I am embarrassed   565
That he should give it me himself. Wait here,
And tell him to deliver it to you.
Do not say more. Since you're discreet and fair:
You'll surely know just what love is.

(Exit.)

ROSAURA:　　　　　　　　　Great heavens!
How I wish that I did not! For who could be   570
So prudent or so skilful as would know
What to advise herself in such a case?
Lives there a person on this earth today
Who's more beset by the inclement stars,
Who has more cares besieging him, or fights   575
So many dire calamities at once?
What can I do in such bewilderment
Wherein it seems impossible to find
Relief or comfort? Since my first misfortune
No other thing has chanced or happened to me   580
But was a new misfortune. In succession
Inheritors and heirs of their own selves
(Just like the Phoenix, his own son and father)
Misfortunes reproduce themselves, are born,
And live by dying. In their sepulchre   585
The ashes they consume are hot forever.
A sage once said misfortunes must be cowards
Because they never dare to walk alone
But come in crowds. I say they are most valiant
Because they always charge so bravely on   590
And never turn their backs. Who charges with them
May dare all things because there is no fear
That they'll ever desert him; and I say it
Because in all my life I never once
Knew them to leave me, nor will they grow tired   595
Of me till, wounded and shot through and through
By Fate, I fall into the arms of death.
Alas, what can I do in this dilemma?
If I reveal myself, then old Clotaldo,
To whom I owe my life, may take offence,   600
Because he told me to await the cure
And mending of my honour in concealment.
If I don't tell Astolfo who I am
And he detects me, how can I dissimulate?
Since even if I say I am not I,   605
The voice, the language, and the eyes will falter,
Because the soul will tell them that they lie.
What shall I do? It is in vain to study
What I should do, when I know very well
That, whatsoever way I choose to act,   610
When the time comes I'll do as sorrow bids,
For no one has control over his sorrows.
Then since my soul dares not decide its actions
Let sorrow fill my cup and let my grief
Reach its extremity and, out of doubts   615

And vain appearances, once and for all
Come out into the light—and Heaven shield me!

(*Enter* ASTOLFO.)

ASTOLFO: Here, lady, is the portrait . . . but . . . great God!
ROSAURA: Why does Your Highness halt, and stare astonished?
620 ASTOLFO: Rosaura! Why, to see you here!
ROSAURA: Rosaura?
    Sir, you mistake me for some other lady.
    I am Astrea, and my humble station
    Deserves no perturbation such as yours.
ASTOLFO: Enough of this pretence, Rosaura, since
625 The soul can never lie. Though as Astrea
    I see you now, I love you as Rosaura.
ROSAURA: Not having understood Your Highness' meaning
    I can make no reply except to say
    That Stella (who might be the star of Venus)
630 Told me to wait here and to tell you from her
    To give to me the portrait you were fetching
    (Which seems a very logical request)
    And I myself will take it to my lady.
    Thus Stella bids: even the slightest things
635 Which do me harm are governed by some star.
ASTOLFO: Even if you could make a greater effort
    How poorly you dissimulate, Rosaura!
    Tell your poor eyes they do not harmonise
    With your own voice, because they needs must jangle
640 When the whole instrument is out of time.
    You cannot match the falsehood of your words
    With the sincerity of what you're feeling.
ROSAURA: All I can say is—that I want the portrait.
ASTOLFO: As you require a fiction, with a fiction
645 I shall reply. Go and tell Stella this:
    That I esteem her so, it seems unworthy
    Only to send the counterfeit to her
    And that I'm sending her the original.
    And you, take the original along with you,
650 Taking yourself to her.
ROSAURA: When a man starts
    Forth on a definite task, resolved and valiant,
    Though he be offered a far greater prize
    Than what he seeks, yet he returns with failure
    If he returns without his task performed.
655 I came to get that portrait. Though I bear
    The original with me, of greater value,
    I would return in failure and contempt
    Without the copy. Give it me, Your Highness,
    Since I cannot return without it.
ASTOLFO: But
660 If I don't give it you, how can you do so?
ROSAURA: Like this, ungrateful man! I'll take it from you.

(*She tries to wrest it from him.*)

ASTOLFO: It is in vain.
ROSAURA: By God, it shall not come
    Into another woman's hands!
ASTOLFO: You're terrifying!
ROSAURA: And you're perfidious!
ASTOLFO: Enough, my dear
665 Rosaura!
ROSAURA: I, your dear? You lie, you villain!

(*They are both clutching the portrait.*
Enter STELLA.)

STELLA: Astrea and Astolfo, what does this mean?
ASTOLFO: (*Aside.*) Here's Stella.
ROSAURA: (*Aside.*)   Love, grant me the strength to win
    My portrait.

(*To* STELLA.)

            If you want to know, my lady,
    What this is all about, I will explain.
ASTOLFO: (*To* ROSAURA, *aside.*) What do you mean?   670
ROSAURA: You told me to await
    Astolfo here and ask him for a portrait
    On your behalf. I waited here alone
    And as one thought suggests another thought,
    Thinking of portraits, I recalled my own
    Was here inside my sleeve. When one's alone,   675
    One is diverted by a foolish trifle
    And so I took it out to look at it.
    It slipped and fell, just as Astolfo here,
    Bringing the portrait of the other lady,
    Came to deliver it to you as promised.   680
    He picked my portrait up, and so unwilling
    Is he to give away the one you asked for,
    Instead of doing so, he seized upon
    The other portrait which is mine alone
    And will not give it back though I entreated   685
    And begged him to return it. I was angry
    And tried to snatch it back. That's it he's holding,
    And you can see yourself if it's not mine.
STELLA: Let go the portrait.

(*She snatches it from him.*)

ASTOLFO: Madam!
STELLA: The draughtsman
    Was not unkind to truth.   690
ROSAURA: Is it not mine?
STELLA: Why, who could doubt it?
ROSAURA: Ask him for the other.
STELLA: Here, take your own, Astrea. You may leave us.
ROSAURA: (*Aside.*) Now I have got my portrait, come what will.

(*Exit.*)

STELLA: Now give me up the portrait that I asked for
    Although I'll see and speak to you no more.   695
    I do not wish to leave it in your power
    Having been once so foolish as to beg it.
ASTOLFO: (*Aside.*) Now how can I get out of this foul trap?

(*To* STELLA.)

    Beautiful Stella, though I would obey you,
    And serve you in all ways, I cannot give you   700
    The portrait, since . . .
STELLA: You are a crude, coarse villain
    And ruffian of a wooer. For the portrait—
    I do not want it now, since, if I had it,
    It would remind me I had asked you for it.

(*Exit.*)

ASTOLFO: Listen! Look! Wait! Let me explain!   705

(*Aside.*)

Oh, damn
Rosaura! How the devil did she get
To Poland for my ruin and her own?

The prison of SEGISMUND *in the tower.*

(SEGISMUND *lying on the ground loaded with fetters and
clothed in skins as before.* CLOTALDO, *two attendants, and*
CLARION.)

CLOTALDO: Here you must leave him—since his reckless pride
 Ends here today where it began.
ATTENDANT: His chain
710 I'll rivet as it used to be before.
CLARION: O Prince, you'd better not awake too soon
 To find how lost you are, how changed your fate,
 And that your fancied glory of an hour
 Was but a shade of life, a flame of death!
715 CLOTALDO: For one who knows so well to wield his tongue
 It's fit a worthy place should be provided
 With lots of room and lots of time to argue.
 This is the fellow that you have to seize

(*To the attendants.*)

 And that's the room in which you are to lock him.

(*Points to the nearest cell.*)

720 CLARION: Why me?
CLOTALDO: Because a Clarion who knows
 Too many secrets must be kept in gaol—
 A place where even clarions are silent.
CLARION: Have I, by chance, wanted to kill my father
 Or thrown an Icarus from a balcony?
725 Am I asleep or dreaming? To what end
 Do you imprison me?
CLOTALDO: You're Clarion.
CLARION: Well, say I swear to be a cornet now,
 A silent one, a wretched instrument . . . ?

(*They hustle him off.* CLOTALDO *remains.
Enter* BASIL, *wearing a mask.*)

BASIL: Clotaldo.
CLOTALDO: Sire . . . and is it thus alone
730 Your Majesty has come?
BASIL: Vain curiosity
 To see what happens here to Segismund.
CLOTALDO: See where he lies, reduced to misery!
BASIL: Unhappy prince! Born at a fatal moment!
 Come waken him, now he has lost his strength
735 With all the opium he's drunk.
CLOTALDO: He's stirring
 And talking to himself.
BASIL: What is he dreaming?
 Let's listen now.
SEGISMUND: He who chastises tyrants
 Is a most pious prince . . . Now let Clotaldo
 Die by my hand . . . my father kiss my feet . . .
740 CLOTALDO: He threatens me with death!
BASIL: And me with insult
 And cruelty.
CLOTALDO: He'd take my life away.
BASIL: And he'd humiliate me at his feet.

SEGISMUND: (*Still in a dream.*) Throughout the expanse of
 this world's theatre
 I'll show my peerless valour, let my vengeance
 Be wreaked, and the Prince Segismund be seen   745
 To triumph—over his father . . . but, alas!

(*Awakening.*)

 Where am I?
BASIL: (*To* CLOTALDO.) Since he must not see me here,
 I'll listen further off. You know your cue.

(*Retires to one side.*)

SEGISMUND: Can this be I? Am I the same who, chained 750
 And long imprisoned, rose to such a state?
 Are you not still my sepulchre and grave,
 You dismal tower? God! What things I have dreamed!
CLOTALDO: (*Aside.*) Now I must go to him to disenchant him.

(*Aloud.*)

 Awake already?   755
SEGISMUND: Yes: it was high time.
CLOTALDO: What? Do you have to spend all day asleep?
 Since I was following the eagle's flight
 With tardy discourse, have you still lain here
 Without awaking?
SEGISMUND: No. Nor even now
 Am I awake. It seems I've always slept,   760
 Since, if I've dreamed what I've just seen and heard
 Palpably and for certain, then I am dreaming
 What I see now—nor is it strange I'm tired,
 Since what I, sleeping, see, tells me that I
 Was dreaming when I thought I was awake.   765
CLOTALDO: Tell me your dream.
SEGISMUND: That's if it *was* a dream!
 No, I'll not tell you what I dreamed; but what
 I lived and saw, Clotaldo, I *will* tell you.
 I woke up in a bed that might have been
 The cradle of the flowers, woven by Spring.   770
 A thousand nobles, bowing, called me Prince,
 Attiring me in jewels, pomp, and splendour.
 My equanimity you turned to rapture
 Telling me that I was the Prince of Poland.
CLOTALDO: I must have got a fine reward!   775
SEGISMUND: Not so:
 For as a traitor, twice, with rage and fury,
 I tried to kill you.
CLOTALDO: Such cruelty to me?
SEGISMUND: I was the lord of all, on all I took revenge,
 Except I loved one woman . . . I believe
 That *that* was true, though all the rest has faded. 780

(*Exit* BASIL.)

CLOTALDO: (*Aside.*) I see the king was moved, to hear him
 speak.

(*Aloud.*)

 Talking of eagles made you dream of empires,
 But even in your dreams it's good to honour
 Those who have cared for you and brought you up.
 For Segismund, even in dreams, I warn you   785
 Nothing is lost by trying to do good.

(*Exit.*)

SEGISMUND: That's true, and therefore let us subjugate
   The bestial side, this fury and ambition,
   Against the time when we may dream once more,
790   As certainly we shall, for this strange world
   Is such that but to live here is to dream.
   And now experience shows me that each man
   Dreams what he is until he is awakened.
   The king dreams he's a king and in this fiction
795   Lives, rules, administers with royal pomp.
   Yet all the borrowed praises that he earns
   Are written in the wind, and he is changed
   (How sad a fate!) by death to dust and ashes.
   What man is there alive who'd seek to reign
800   Since he must wake into the dream that's death.
   The rich man dreams his wealth which is his care
   And woe. The poor man dreams his sufferings.
   He dreams who thrives and prospers in this life.
   He dreams who toils and strives. He dreams who injures,
805   Offends, and insults. So that in this world
   Everyone dreams the thing he is, though no one
   Can understand it. I dream I am here,
   Chained in these fetters. Yet I dreamed just now
   I was in a more flattering, lofty station.
810   What is this life? A frenzy, an illusion,
   A shadow, a delirium, a fiction.
   The greatest good's but little, and this life
   Is but a dream, and dreams are only dreams.

— ACT THREE —

The tower.

(Enter CLARION.)

CLARION: I'm held in an enchanted tower, because
   Of all I know. What would they do to me
   For all I don't know, since—for all I know—
   They're killing me by starving me to death.
5   O that a man so hungry as myself
   Should live to die of hunger while alive!
   I am so sorry for myself that others
   May well say "I can well believe it," since
   This silence ill accords with my name "Clarion",
10   And I just can't shut up. My fellows here?
   Spiders and rats—fine feathered songsters those!
   My head's still ringing with a dream of fifes
   And trumpets and a lot of noisy humbug
   And long processions as of penitents
15   With crosses, winding up and down, while some
   Faint at the sight of blood besmirching others.
   But now to tell the truth, I am in prison.
   For knowing secrets, I am kept shut in,
   Strictly observed as if I were a Sunday,
20   And feeling sadder than a Tuesday, where
   I neither eat nor drink. They say a secret
   Is sacred and should be as strictly kept
   As any saint's day on the calendar.
   Saint Secret's Day for me's a working day
25   Because I'm never idle then. The penance
   I suffer here is merited, I say:
   Because being a lackey, I was silent,
   Which, in a servant, is a sacrilege.

(A noise of drums and trumpets.)

FIRST SOLDIER: *(Within.)* Here is the tower in which he is
      imprisoned.
   Smash in the door and enter, everybody!   30
CLARION: Great God! They've come to seek me. That is certain
   Because they say I'm here. What can they want?

(Enter several soldiers.)

FIRST SOLDIER: Go in.
SECOND SOLDIER: He's here!
CLARION: No, he's not here!
ALL THE SOLDIERS: Our lord!
CLARION: What, are they drunk?
FIRST SOLDIER: You are our rightful prince.
   We do not want and never shall allow   35
   A stranger to supplant our trueborn prince.
   Give us your feet to kiss!
ALL THE SOLDIERS: Long live the prince!
CLARION: Bless me, if it's not real! In this strange kingdom
   It seems the custom, everyday, to take
   Some fellow and to make him prince and then   40
   Shut him back in this tower. That *must* be it!
   So I must play my role.
ALL THE SOLDIERS: Give us your feet.
CLARION: I can't. They're necessary. After all
   What sort of use would be a footless prince?
SECOND SOLDIER: All of us told your father, as one man,   45
   We want no prince of Muscovy but you!
CLARION: You weren't respectful to my father? Shame!
FIRST SOLDIER: It was our loyalty that made us tell him.
CLARION: If it was loyalty, you have my pardon.
SECOND SOLDIER: Restore your empire. Long live Segismund!   50
CLARION: *(Aside.)* That is the name they seem to give to all
   These counterfeited princes.

(Enter SEGISMUND.)

SEGISMUND: Who called Segismund?
CLARION: *(Aside.)* I seem to be a hollow sort of prince.
FIRST SOLDIER: Which of you's Segismund?
SEGISMUND: I am.
SECOND SOLDIER: *(To CLARION.)*   Then why,
   Rash fool, did you impersonate the prince   55
   Segismund?
CLARION: What? I, Segismund? Yourselves
   Be-Segismunded me without request.
   All yours was both the rashness and the folly.
FIRST SOLDIER: Prince Segismund, whom we acclaim our
      lord,
   Your father, great King Basil, in his fear   60
   That heaven would fulfil a prophecy
   That one day he would kneel before your feet
   Wishes now to deprive you of the throne
   And give it to the Duke of Muscovy.
   For this he called a council, but the people   65
   Discovered his design and knowing, now,
   They have a native king, will have no stranger.
   So scorning the fierce threats of destiny,
   We've come to seek you in your very prison,
   That aided by the arms of the whole people,   70
   We may restore you to the crown and sceptre,
   Taking them from the tyrant's grasp. Come, then:
   Assembling here, in this wide desert region,

Hosts of plebeians, bandits, and freebooters,
75 Acclaim you king. Your liberty awaits you!
Hark to its voice!

(Shouts within.)

Long life to Segismund!
SEGISMUND: Once more, you heavens will that I should dream
Of grandeur, once again, 'twixt doubts and shades,
Behold the majesty of pomp and power
80 Vanish into the wind, once more you wish
That I should taste the disillusion and
The risk by which all human power is humbled,
Of which all human power should live aware.
It must not be. I'll not be once again
85 Put through my paces by my fortune's stars.
And since I know this life is all a dream,
Depart, vain shades, who feign, to my dead senses,
That you have voice and body, having neither!
I want no more feigned majesty, fantastic
90 Display, nor void illusions, that one gust
Can scatter like the almond tree in flower,
Whose rosy buds, without advice or warning,
Dawn in the air too soon and then, as one,
Are all extinguished, fade, and fall, and wither
95 In the first gust of wind that comes along!
I know you well. I know you well by now.
I know that all that happens in yourselves
Happens as in a sleeping man. For me
There are no more delusions and deceptions
100 Since I well know this life is all a dream.
SECOND SOLDIER: If you think we are cheating, just sweep
Your gaze along these towering peaks, and see
The hosts that wait to welcome and obey you.
SEGISMUND: Already once before I've seen such crowds
105 Distinctly, quite as vividly as these:
And yet it was a dream.
SECOND SOLDIER: No great event
Can come without forerunners to announce it
And this is the real meaning of your dream.
SEGISMUND: Yes, you say well. It was the fore-announcement
110 And just in case it was correct, my soul,
(Since life's so short) let's dream the dream anew!
But it must be attentively, aware
That we'll awake from pleasure in the end.
Forewarned of that, the shock's not so abrupt,
115 The disillusion's less. Evils anticipated
Lose half their sting. And armed with this precaution—
That power, even when we're sure of it, is borrowed
And must be given back to its true owner—
We can risk anything and dare the worst.
120 Subjects, I thank you for your loyalty.
In me you have a leader who will free you,
Bravely and skilfully, from foreign rule.
Sound now to arms, you'll soon behold my valour.
Against my father I must march and bring
125 Truth from the stars. Yes: he must kneel to me.

(Aside.)

But yet, since I may wake before he kneels,
Perhaps I'd better not proclaim what may not happen.
ALL: Long live Segismund!

(Enter CLOTALDO.)

CLOTALDO: Gracious heavens! What is
This riot here?
SEGISMUND: Clotaldo!
CLOTALDO: Sir!

(Aside.)

He'll prove
His cruelty on me.   130
CLARION: I bet he throws him
Over the mountain.
CLOTALDO: At your royal feet
I kneel, knowing my penalty is death.
SEGISMUND: Rise, rise, my foster father, from the ground,
For you must be the compass and the guide
In which I trust. You brought me up, and I   135
Know what I owe your loyalty. Embrace me!
CLOTALDO: What's that you say?
SEGISMUND: I know I'm in a dream,
But I would like to act well, since good actions,
Even in a dream, are not entirely lost.
CLOTALDO: Since doing good is now to be your glory,   140
You will not be offended that I too
Should do what's right. You march against your father!
I cannot give you help against my king.
Here at your feet, my lord, I plead for death.
SEGISMUND: *(Aloud.)* Villain!   145

(Aside.)

But let us suffer this annoyance.
Though my rage would slay him, yet he's loyal.
A man does not deserve to die for that.
How many angry passions does this leash
Restrain in me, this curb of knowing well
That I must wake and find myself alone!   150
SECOND SOLDIER: All this fine talk, Clotaldo, is a cruel
Spurn of the public welfare. We are loyal
Who wish our own prince to reign over us.
CLOTALDO: Such loyalty, after the king were dead,
Would honour you. But while the king is living   155
He is our absolute, unquestioned lord.
There's no excuse for subjects who oppose
His sovereignty in arms.
FIRST SOLDIER: We'll soon see well
Enough, Clotaldo, what this loyalty
Is worth.   160
CLOTALDO: You would be better if you had some.
It is the greatest prize.
SEGISMUND: Peace, peace, I pray you.
CLOTALDO: My lord!
SEGISMUND: Clotaldo, if your feelings
Are truly thus, go you, and serve the king;
That's prudence, loyalty, and common sense.
But do not argue here with anyone   165
Whether it's right or wrong, for every man
Has his own honour.
CLOTALDO: Humbly I take my leave.

(Exit.)

SEGISMUND: Now sound the drums and march in rank and
order
Straight to the palace.
ALL: Long live Segismund!

170 SEGISMUND: Fortune, we go to reign! Do not awake me
      If I am dreaming! Do not let me fall
      Asleep if it is true! To act with virtue
      Is what matters, since if this proves true,
      That truth's sufficient reason in itself;
175   If not, we win us friends against the time
      When we at last awake.

A room in the royal palace.

(Enter BASIL *and* ASTOLFO.*)*

      BASIL: Whose prudence can rein in a bolting horse?
      Who can restrain a river's pride, in spate?
      Whose valour can withstand a crag dislodged
180   And hurtling downwards from a mountain peak?
      All these are easier by far than to hold back
      A crowd's proud fury, once it has been roused.
      It has two voices, both proclaiming war,
      And you can hear them echoing through the mountains,
185   Some shouting "Segismund," others "Astolfo."
      The scene I set for swearing of allegiance
      Lends but an added horror to this strife:
      It has become the back cloth to a stage
      Where Fortune plays out tragedies in blood.
190   ASTOLFO: My lord, forget the happiness and wealth
      You promised me from your most blessèd hand.
      If Poland, which I hope to rule, refuses
      Obedience to my right, grudging me honour,
      It is because I've got to earn it first.
195   Give me a horse, that I with angry pride
      May match the thunder in my voice and ride
      To strike, like lightning, terror far and wide.

(Exit ASTOLFO.*)*

      BASIL: No remedy for what's infallible!
      What is foreseen is perilous indeed!
200   If something has to be, there's no way out;
      In trying to evade it, you but court it.
      This law is pitiless and horrible.
      Thinking one can evade the risk, one meets it:
      My own precautions have been my undoing,
205   And I myself have quite destroyed my kingdom.

(Enter STELLA.*)*

      STELLA: If you, my lord, in person do not try
      To curb the vast commotion that has started
      In all the streets between the rival factions,
      You'll see your kingdom, swamped in waves of crimson,
210   Swimming in its own blood, with nothing left
      But havoc, dire calamity, and woe.
      So frightful is the damage to your empire
      That, seen, it strikes amazement; heard, despair.
      The sun's obscured, the very winds are hindered.
215   Each stone is a memorial to the dead.
      Each flower springs from a grave while every building
      Appears a mausoleum, and each soldier
      A premature and walking skeleton.

(Enter CLOTALDO.*)*

      CLOTALDO: Praise be to God, I reach your feet alive!
220   BASIL: Clotaldo! What's the news of Segismund?

CLOTALDO: The crowd, a headstrong monster blind with rage,
      Entered his dungeon tower and set him free.
      He, now exalted for the second time,
      Conducts himself with valour, boasting how
      He will bring down the truth out of the stars.   225
BASIL: Give me a horse, that I myself, in person,
      May vanquish such a base, ungrateful son!
      For I, in the defence of my own crown,
      Shall do by steel what science failed to do.

(Exit.)

STELLA: I'll be Bellona to your Sun, and try   230
      To write my name next yours in history.
      I'll ride as though I flew on outstretched wings
      That I may vie with Pallas.

(Exit.
Enter ROSAURA, *holding back* CLOTALDO.*)*

ROSAURA: I know that all is war, Clotaldo, yet
      Although your valour calls you to the front,   235
      First hear me out. You know quite well that I
      Arrived in Poland poor and miserable,
      Where, shielded by your valour, I found mercy.
      You told me to conceal myself, and stay
      Here in the palace, hiding from Astolfo.   240
      He saw me in the end, and so insulted
      My honour that (although he saw me clearly)
      He nightly speaks with Stella in the garden.
      I have the key to it and I will show you
      How you can enter there and end my cares.   245
      Thus bold, resolved, and strong, you can recover
      My honour, since you're ready to avenge me
      By killing him.
CLOTALDO: It's true that I intended,
      Since first I saw you (having heard your tale)
      With my own life to rectify your wrongs.   250
      The first step that I took was bid you dress
      According to your sex, for fear Astolfo
      Might see you as you were, and deem you wanton.
      I was devising how we could recover
      Your honour (so much did it weigh on me)   255
      Even though we had to kill him. (A wild plan—
      Though since he's not my king, I would not flinch
      From killing him.) But then, when suddenly
      Segismund tried to kill me, it was he
      Who saved my life with his surpassing valour.   260
      Consider: how can I requite Astolfo
      With death for giving me my life so bravely,
      And when my soul is full of gratitude?
      So torn between the two of you I stand—
      Rosaura, whose life I saved, and Astolfo,   265
      Who saved my life. What's to be done? Which side
      To take, and whom to help, I cannot judge.
      What I owe you in that I gave you life
      I owe to him in that he gave me life.
      And so there is no course that I can take   270
      To satisfy my love. I am a person
      Who has to act, yet suffer either way.
ROSAURA: I should not have to tell so brave a man
      That if it is nobility to give,
      It's baseness to receive. That being so   275
      You owe no gratitude to him, admitting

That it was he who gave you life, and you
Who gave me life, since he forced you to take
A meaner role, and through me you assumed
280   A generous role. So you should side with me:
My cause is so far worthier than his own
As giving is than taking.
CLOTALDO: Though nobility
Is with the giver, it is gratitude
That dwells with the receiver. As a giver
285   I have the name of being generous:
Then grant me that of being grateful too
And let me earn the title and be grateful,
As I am liberal, giving or receiving.
ROSAURA: You granted me my life, at the same time
290   Telling me it was worthless, since dishonoured,
And therefore was no life. Therefore from you
I have received no life at all. And since
You should be liberal first and grateful after
(Since so you said yourself) I now entreat you
295   Give me the life, the life you never gave me!
As giving magnifies the most, give first
And then be grateful after, if you will!
CLOTALDO: Won by your argument, I will be liberal.
Rosaura, I shall give you my estate
300   And you shall seek a convent, there to live.
This measure is a happy thought, for, see,
Fleeing a crime, you find a sanctuary.
For when the empire's threatened with disasters
And is divided thus, I, born a noble,
305   Am not the man who would augment its woes.
So with this remedy which I have chosen
I remain loyal to the kingdom, generous
To you, and also grateful to Astolfo.
And thus I choose the course that suits you best.
310   Were I your father, what could I do more?
ROSAURA: Were you my father, then I would accept
The insult. Since you are not, I refuse.
CLOTALDO: What do you hope to do then?
ROSAURA: Kill the duke!
CLOTALDO: A girl who never even knew her father
315   Armed with such courage?
ROSAURA: Yes.
CLOTALDO: What spurs you on?
ROSAURA: My good name.
CLOTALDO: In Astolfo you will find . . .
ROSAURA: My honour rides on him and strikes him down!
CLOTALDO: Your king, too, Stella's husband!
ROSAURA: Never, never
Shall that be, by almighty God, I swear!
320   CLOTALDO: Why, this is madness!
ROSAURA: Yes it is!
CLOTALDO: Restrain it.
ROSAURA: That I cannot.
CLOTALDO: Then you are lost forever!
ROSAURA: I know it!
CLOTALDO: Life and honour both together!
ROSAURA: I well believe it!
CLOTALDO: What do you intend?
ROSAURA: My death.
CLOTALDO: This is despair and desperation.
325   ROSAURA: It's honour.
CLOTALDO: It is nonsense.

ROSAURA: It is valour.
CLOTALDO: It's frenzy.
ROSAURA: Yes, it's anger! Yes, it's fury!
CLOTALDO: In short you cannot moderate your passion?
ROSAURA: No.
CLOTALDO: Who is there to help you?
ROSAURA: I, myself.
CLOTALDO: There is no cure?
ROSAURA: There is no cure!
CLOTALDO: Think well
If there's not some way out . . .   330
ROSAURA: Some other way
To do away with me . . .

(Exit.)

CLOTALDO: If you are lost,
My daughter, let us both be lost together!

In the country.

(Enter SEGISMUND *clothed in skins. Soldiers marching.* CLAR-
ION. *Drums beating.)*

SEGISMUND: If Rome, today, could see me here, renewing
Her olden triumphs, she might laugh to see
A wild beast in command of mighty armies,   335
A wild beast, to whose fiery aspirations
The firmament were all too slight a conquest!
But stoop your flight, my spirit. Do not thus
Be puffed to pride by these uncertain plaudits
Which, when I wake, will turn to bitterness   340
In that I won them only to be lost.
The less I value them, the less I'll miss them.

(A trumpet sounds.)

CLARION: Upon a rapid courser (pray excuse me,
Since if it comes to mind I must describe it)
In which it seems an atlas was designed   345
Since if its body is earth, its soul is fire
Within its breast, its foam appears the sea,
The wind its breath, and chaos its condition,
Since in its soul, its foam, its breath and flesh,
It seems a monster of fire, earth, sea, and wind,   350
Upon the horse, all of a patchwork colour,
Dappled, and rushing forward at the will
Of one who plies the spur, so that it flies
Rather than runs—see how a woman rides
Boldly into your presence.   355
SEGISMUND: Her light blinds me.
CLARION: Good God! Why, here's Rosaura!
SEGISMUND: It is heaven
That has restored her to my sight once more.

(Enter ROSAURA *with sword and dagger in riding costume.)*

ROSAURA: Generous Segismund, whose majesty
Heroically rises in the lustre
Of his great deeds out of his night of shadows,   360
And as the greatest planet, in the arms

343–355 **Upon a . . . presence** Clarion's speech is a parody of exaggerated style including Calderón's. [R.C.]

Of his aurora, lustrously returns
To plants and roses, over hills and seas,
When, crowned with gold, he looks abroad, dispersing
365 Radiance, flashing his rays, bathing the summits,
And broidering the fringes of the foam,
So may you dawn upon the world, bright sun
Of Poland, that a poor unhappy woman
May fall before your feet and beg protection
370 Both as a woman and unfortunate—
Two things that must oblige you, sire, as one
Who prizes yourself as valiant, each of them
More than suffices for your chivalry.
Three times you have beheld me now, three times
375 Been ignorant of who I am, because
Three times you saw me in a different clothing.
The first time you mistook me for a man,
Within that rigorous prison, where your hardships
Made mine seem pleasure. Next time, as a woman,
380 You saw me, when your pomp and majesty
Were as a dream, a phantasm, a shade.
The third time is today when, as a monster
Of both the sexes, in a woman's costume
I bear a soldier's arms. But to dispose you
385 The better to compassion, hear my story.
My mother was a noble in the court
Of Moscow, who, since most unfortunate,
Must have been beautiful. Then came a traitor
And cast his eyes on her (I do not name him,
390 Not knowing who he is). Yet I deduce
That he was valiant too from my own valour,
Since he gave form to me—and I could wish
I had been born in pagan times, that I might
Persuade myself he was some god of those
395 Who rain in showers of gold, turn into swans
Or bulls, for Danaës, Ledas, or Europas.
That's strange: I thought I was just rambling on
By telling old perfidious myths, yet find
I've told you how my mother was cajoled.
400 Oh, she was beautiful as no one else
Has been, but was unfortunate like all.
He swore to wed her (that's an old excuse)
And this trick reached so nearly to her heart
That thought must weep, recalling it today.
405 The tyrant left her only with his sword
As Aeneas left Troy. I sheathed its blade here
Upon my thigh, and I will bare it too
Before the ending of this history.
Out of this union, this poor link which neither
410 Could bind the marriage nor handcuff the crime,
Myself was born, her image and her portrait,
Not in her beauty, but in her misfortune,
For mine's the same. That's all I need to say.
The most that I can tell you of myself
415 Is that the man who robbed me of the spoils
And trophies of my honour is Astolfo.
Alas! to name him my heart rages so
(As hearts will do when men name enemies).
Astolfo was my faithless and ungrateful
420 Lord, who (quite forgetful of our happiness,
Since of a past love even the memory fades)
Came here to claim the throne and marry Stella

For she's the star who rises as I set.
It's hard to credit that a star should sunder
Lovers the stars had made conformable! 425
So hurt was I, so villainously cheated,
That I became mad, brokenhearted, sick,
Half wild with grief, and like to die, with all
Hell's own confusion ciphered on my mind
Like Babel's incoherence. Mutely I told 430
My griefs (since woes and griefs declare themselves
Better than can the mouth, by their effects),
When, with my mother (we were by ourselves),
She broke the prison of my pent-up sorrows
And from my breast they all rushed forth in troops. 435
I felt no shyness, for in knowing surely
That one to whom one's errors are recounted
Has also been an ally in her own,
One finds relief and rest, since bad example
Can sometimes serve for a good purpose too. 440
She heard my plaint with pity, and she tried
To palliate my sorrows with her own.
How easily do judges pardon error
When they've offended too! An example,
A warning, in herself, she did not trust 445
To idleness, or the slow cure of time,
Nor try to find a remedy for her honour
In my misfortunes, but, with better counsel,
She bade me follow him to Poland here
And with prodigious gallantry persuade him 450
To pay the debt to honour that he owes me.
So that it would be easier to travel,
She bade me don male clothing, and took down
This ancient sword which I am wearing now.
Now it is time that I unsheathe the blade 455
As I was bid, for, trusting in its sign,
She said: "Depart to Poland, show this sword
That all the nobles may behold it well,
And it may be that one of them will take
Pity on you, and counsel you, and shield you." 460
I came to Poland and, you will remember,
Entered your cave. You looked at me in wonder.
Clotaldo passionately took my part
To plead for mercy to the king, who spared me,
Then, when he heard my story, bade me change 465
Into my own clothes and attend on Stella,
There to disturb Astolfo's love and stop
Their marriage. Again you saw me in woman's dress
And were confused by the discrepancy.
But let's pass to what's new: Clotaldo, now 470
Persuaded that Astolfo must, with Stella,
Come to the throne, dissuades me from my purpose,
Against the interests of my name and honour.
But seeing you, O valiant Segismund,
Are claiming your revenge, now that the heavens 475
Have burst the prison of your rustic tower,
(Wherein you were the tiger of your sorrows,
The rock of sufferings and direful pains)
And sent you forth against your sire and country,
I come to aid you, mingling Dian's silks 480
With the hard steel of Pallas. Now, strong Captain,
It well behoves us both to stop this marriage—
Me, lest my promised husband should be wed,

485 You, lest, when their estates are joined, they weigh
More powerfully against your victory.
I come, as a mere woman, to persuade you
To right my shame; but, as a man, I come
To help you battle for your crown. As woman,
490 To melt your heart, here at your feet I fall;
But, as a man, I come to serve you bravely
Both with my person and my steel, and thus,
If you today should woo me as a woman,
Then I should have to kill you as a man would
495 In honourable service of my honour;
Since I must be three things today at once—
Passionate, to persuade you: womanly,
To ply you with my woes: manly, to gain
Honour in battle.
SEGISMUND: Heavens! If it is true I'm dreaming,
Suspend my memory, for in a dream
500 So many things could not occur. Great heavens!
If I could only come free of them all!
Or never think of any! Who ever felt
Such grievous doubts? If I but dreamed that triumph
In which I found myself, how can this woman
505 Refer me to such sure and certain facts?
Then all of it was true and not a dream.
But if it be the truth, why does my past life
Call it a dream? This breeds the same confusion.
Are dreams and glories so alike, that fictions
510 Are held for truths, realities for lies?
Is there so little difference in them both
That one should question whether what one sees
And tastes is true or false? What? Is the copy
So near to the original that doubt
515 Exists between them? Then if that is so,
And grandeur, power, majesty, and pomp,
Must all evaporate like shades at morning,
Let's profit by it, this time, to enjoy
That which we only can enjoy in dreams.
520 Rosaura's in my power: my soul adores her beauty.
Let's take the chance. Let love break every law
On which she has relied in coming here
And kneeling, trustful, prostrate at my feet.
This is a dream. If so, dream pleasures now
525 Since they must turn to sorrows in the end!
But with my own opinions, I begin
Once again to convince myself. Let's think.
If it is but vainglory and a dream,
Who for mere human vainglory would lose
530 True glory? What past blessing is not merely
A dream? Who has known heroic glories,
That deep within himself, as he recalls them
Has never doubted that they might be dreams?
But if this all should end in disenchantment,
535 Seeing that pleasure is a lovely flame
That's soon converted into dust and ashes
By any wind that blows, then let us seek
That which endures in thrifty, lasting fame
In which no pleasures sleep, nor grandeurs dream.
540 Rosaura's without honour. In a prince
It's worthier to restore it than to steal it.
I shall restore it, by the living God,
Before I win my throne! Let's shun the danger

And fly from the temptation which is strong!
Then sound to arms!   545

(To a soldier.)

Today I must give battle before darkness
Buries the rays of gold in green-black waves!
ROSAURA: My lord! Alas, you stand apart, and offer
No word of pity for my plight. How is it
You neither hear nor see me nor even yet   550
Have turned your face on me?
SEGISMUND: Rosaura, for your honour's sake
I must be cruel to you, to be kind.
My voice must not reply to you because
My honour must reply to you. I am silent
Because my deeds must speak to you alone.   555
I do not look at you since, in such straits,
Having to see your honour is requited,
I must not see your beauty.

(Exit with soldiers.)

ROSAURA: What strange enigma's this? After such trouble
Still to be treated with more doubtful riddles!   560

(Enter CLARION.*)*

CLARION: Madam, may you be visited just now?
ROSAURA: Why, Clarion, where have you been all this time?
CLARION: Shut in the tower, consulting cards
About my death: "to be or not to be."
And it was a near thing.   565
ROSAURA: Why?
CLARION: Because I know
The secret who you are: in fact, Clotaldo . . .

(Drums.)

But hush what noise is that?
ROSAURA: What can it be?
CLARION: From the beleaguered palace a whole squadron
Is charging forth to harry and defeat
That of fierce Segismund.   570
ROSAURA: Why, what a coward
Am I, not to be at his side, the terror
And scandal of the world, while such fierce strife
Presses all round in lawless anarchy.

(Exit.)

VOICES OF SOME: Long live our king!
VOICES OF OTHERS: Long live our liberty!
CLARION: Long live both king and liberty. Yes, live! 575
And welcome to them both! I do not worry.
In all this pother, I behave like Nero
Who never grieved at what was going on.
If I had anything to grieve about
It would be me, myself. Well hidden here   580
Now, I can watch the sport that's going on.
This place is safe and hidden between crags,
And since death cannot find me here, two figs for death!

*(He hides. Drums and the clash of arms are heard.
Enter* BASIL, CLOTALDO, *and* ASTOLFO, *fleeing.)*

BASIL: Was ever king so hapless as myself
Or father more ill used?   585

CLOTALDO: Your beaten army
Rush down, in all directions, in disorder.
ASTOLFO: The traitors win!
BASIL: In battles such as these
Those on the winning side are ever "loyal,"
And traitors the defeated. Come, Clotaldo,
590   Let's flee from the inhuman cruelty
Of my fierce son!

(Shots are fired within. CLARION *falls wounded.)*

CLARION: Heavens, save me!
ASTOLFO: Who is this
Unhappy soldier bleeding at our feet?
CLARION: I am a most unlucky man who, wishing
To guard myself from death, have sought it out
595   By fleeing from it. Shunning it, I found it,
Because, to death, no hiding-place is secret.
So you can argue that whoever shuns it
Most carefully runs into it the quickest.
Turn, then, once more into the thick of battle:
600   There is more safety there amidst the fire
And clash of arms than here on this secluded
Mountain, because no hidden path is safe
From the inclemency of Fate; and so,
Although you flee from death, yet you may find it
605   Quicker than you expect, if God so wills.

(He falls dead.)

BASIL: "If God so wills" . . . With what strange eloquence
This corpse persuades our ignorance and error
To better knowledge, speaking from the mouth
Of its fell wound, where the red liquid flowing
610   Seems like a bloody tongue which teaches us
That the activities of man are vain
When they are pitted against higher powers.
For I, who wished to liberate my country
From murder and sedition, gave it up
615   To the same ills from which I would have saved it.
CLOTALDO: Though Fate, my lord, knows every path, and finds
Him whom it seeks even in the midst of crags
And thickets, it is not a Christian judgment
To say there is no refuge from its fury.
620   A prudent man can conquer Fate itself.
Though you are not exempted from misfortune,
Take action to escape it while you can!
ASTOLFO: Clotaldo speaks as one mature in prudence,
And I as one in valour's youthful prime.
625   Among the thickets of this mount is hidden
A horse, the very birth of the swift wind.
Flee on him, and I'll guard you in the rear.
BASIL: If it is God's will I should die, or if
Death waits here for my coming, I will seek
630   Him out today, and meet him face to face.

(Enter SEGISMUND, STELLA, ROSAURA, *soldiers, and their train.)*

A SOLDIER: Amongst the thickets of this mountain
The king is hiding.
SEGISMUND: Seek him out at once!
Leave no foot of the summit unexplored
But search from stem to stem and branch to branch!

CLOTALDO: Fly, sir!   635
BASIL: What for?
ASTOLFO: What do you mean to do?
BASIL: Astolfo, stand aside!
CLOTALDO: What is your wish?
BASIL: To take a cure I've needed for sometime.

(To SEGISMUND.*)*

If you have come to seek me, here I am.

(Kneeling.)

Your father, prince, kneels humbly at your feet.
The white snow of my hair is now your carpet.   640
Tread on my neck and trample on my crown!
Lay low and drag my dignity in dust!
Take vengeance on my honour! Make a slave
Of me and, after all I've done to thwart them,
Let Fate fulfil its edict and claim homage   645
And Heaven fulfil its oracles at last!
SEGISMUND: Illustrious court of Poland, who have been
The witnesses of such unwonted wonders,
Attend to me, and hear your prince speak out.
What Heaven decrees and God writes with his finger 650
(Whose prints and ciphers are the azure leaves
Adorned with golden lettering of the stars)
Never deceives nor lies. They only lie
Who seek to penetrate the mystery
And, having reached it, use it to ill purpose.   655
My father, who is here to evade the fury
Of my proud nature, made me a wild beast:
So, when I, by my birth of gallant stock,
My generous blood, and inbred grace and valour,
Might well have proved both gentle and forbearing, 660
The very mode of life to which he forced me,
The sort of bringing up I had to bear
Sufficed to make me savage in my passions.
What a strange method of restraining them!
If one were to tell any man: "One day   665
You will be killed by an inhuman monster,"
Would it be the best method he could choose
To wake that monster when it was asleep?
Or if they told him: "That sword which you're wearing
Will be your death," what sort of cure were it   670
To draw it forth and aim it at his breast?
Or if they told him: "Deep blue gulfs of water
Will one day be your sepulchre and grave
Beneath a silver monument of foam,"
He would be mad to hurl himself in headlong   675
When the sea highest heaved its showy mountains
And crystalline sierras plumed with spray.
The same has happened to the king as to him
Who wakes a beast which threatens death, to him
Who draws a naked sword because he fears it,   680
To him who dives into the stormy breakers.
Though my ferocious nature (hear me now)
Was like a sleeping beast, my inborn rage
A sheathèd sword, my wrath a quiet ripple,
Fate should not be coerced by man's injustice—   685
This rouses more resentment. So it is
That he who seeks to tame his fortune must

Resort to moderation and to measure.
He who foresees an evil cannot conquer it
690 Thus in advance, for though humility
Can overcome it, this it can do only
When the occasion's there, for there's no way
To dodge one's fate and thus evade the issue.
Let this strange spectacle serve as example—
695 This prodigy, this horror, and this wonder,
Because it is no less than one, to see,
After such measures and precautions taken
To thwart it, that a father thus should kneel
At his son's feet, a kingdom thus be shattered.
700 This was the sentence of the heavens above,
Which he could not evade, much though he tried.
Can I, younger in age, less brave, and less
In science than the king, conquer that fate?

(To the KING.*)*

Sire, rise, give me your hand, now that the heavens
705 Have shown you that you erred as to the method
To vanquish them. Humbly I kneel before you
And offer you my neck to tread upon.
BASIL: Son, such a great and noble act restores you
Straight to my heart. Oh, true and worthy prince!
710 You have won both the laurel and the palm.
Crown yourself with your deeds! For you *have* conquered!
ALL: Long live Segismund! Long live Segismund!
SEGISMUND: Since I have other victories to win,
The greatest of them all awaits me now:
715 To conquer my own self. Astolfo, give
Your hand here to Rosaura, for you know
It is a debt of honour and must be paid.
ASTOLFO: Although, it's true, I owe some obligations—
She does not know her name or who she is,
720 It would be base to wed a woman who . . .
CLOTALDO: Hold! Wait! Rosaura's of as noble stock
As yours, Astolfo. In the open field
I'll prove it with my sword. She is my daughter
And that should be enough.

ASTOLFO: What do you say?
CLOTALDO: Until I saw her married, righted, honoured,   725
I did not wish for it to be discovered.
It's a long story but she is my daughter.
ASTOLFO: That being so, I'm glad to keep my word.
SEGISMUND: And now, so that the princess Stella here
Will not remain disconsolate to lose   730
A prince of so much valour, here I offer
My hand to her, no less in birth and rank.
Give me your hand.
STELLA: I gain by meriting
So great a happiness.
SEGISMUND: And now, Clotaldo,
So long so loyal to my father, come   735
To my arms. Ask me anything you wish.
FIRST SOLDIER: If thus you treat a man who never served you,
What about me who led the revolution
And brought you from your dungeon in the tower?
What will you give me?   740
SEGISMUND: That same tower and dungeon
From which you never shall emerge till death.
No traitor is of use after his treason.
BASIL: All wonder at your wisdom!
ASTOLFO: What a change
Of character!
ROSAURA: How wise and prudent!
SEGISMUND: Why
Do you wonder? Why do you marvel, since   745
It was a dream that taught me and I still
Fear to wake up once more in my close dungeon?
Though that may never happen, it's enough
To dream it might, for thus I came to learn
That all our human happiness must pass   750
Away like any dream, and I would here
Enjoy it fully ere it glide away,
Asking (for noble hearts are prone to pardon)
Pardon for faults in the actors or the play.

■ MOLIÈRE ■

Jean-Baptiste Poquelin (1622–1673) was born into a prosperous mercantile family with connections at court; his father, Jean Poquelin, secured the honor of *tapissier ordinaire du roi*, the upholsterer to the court, which carried an annual pension. Jean Poquelin also educated his son in the traditional disciplines of the humanities, philosophy, and the classics and must have intended a life at court for him. In 1643, Jean-Baptiste joined with the Illustre Théâtre, a theatrical company run by the Béjart family, took the stage name Molière, and after a brief period performing in Parisian tennis courts, left with the company to play in the provinces. In 1658, after several hard and impoverished years of touring, when Molière is thought to have mastered the techniques of *commedia dell' arte*, the company was invited to perform in Paris.

Molière's career was closely tied to the court. When his brother died in 1660, he received the position of court upholsterer and the income it provided. More important, Molière became an important playwright and both wrote and acted in a splendid series of plays that satirized the manners and morals of elegant society: *Les Précieuses Ridicules* (1659), *Sganarelle* (1660), *School for Husbands* (1661), *School for Wives* (1662), *Don Juan* (1665), *The Misanthrope* (1666), *The Doctor in Spite of Himself* (1666), *The Miser* (1668), *The Learned Ladies* (1672), and *The Imaginary Invalid* (1673). Molière also prepared other entertainments at court, including many royal pageants, ballets, and machine plays devised by and for Louis XIV. In addition to being a great dramatist, Molière was a fine comic actor as well and performed in his own plays; he died shortly after playing the title role in the fourth performance of *The Imaginary Invalid*.

The fortunes of *Tartuffe* suggest Molière's importance at court. When Molière initially produced the first three acts of the play in 1664, the clergy protested and banned the play from production in Paris. Many of Molière's plays had excited controversy, and in this case Molière appealed to the king and proceeded to revise the play. Louis's attitude is perhaps revealed by the fact that he made Molière's company the *Troupe du roi* ("King's Company") in 1665, but even the throne could not prevent the clergy from censoring Molière's second version of the play in 1667, newly titled *The Impostor*. Molière finally produced the play to acclaim in 1669, and the record of his efforts is preserved in the series of letters and prefaces included here.

Molière's theatrical company was the most influential of its day. After his death, his young wife Amanda Béjart and the actress Mademoiselle Champmeslé—newly defected from the rival company at the Hôtel de Bourgogne—established a new company, the Comédie Française. Yet although Molière achieved extraordinary status at court, because he was an actor he remained stigmatized in ways that playwrights like Racine and Corneille were not. Following its standard practice, and perhaps because of *Tartuffe*'s notoriety, the church refused to bury Molière in sacred ground. Louis XIV intervened, but was only able to persuade the Archbishop of Paris to bury Molière in a parish cemetery. The burial was conducted at night, by two priests, with no funeral ceremony.

TARTUFFE

The Catholic church criticized *Tartuffe* for its portrait of hypocritical piety, but the fact that Molière played the part of Orgon may suggest that the play is as much about Tartuffe's effect on that benighted householder as it is about the title character. For if Tartuffe is hypocritical, Orgon is obsessed, less with piety than with his own desire to achieve a kind of total power and authority in his household, a kind of domestic absolutism; he is, in a sense, a comic, bourgeois Louis XIV in miniature. Moreover, Tartuffe dupes Orgon not by tricking him, but by inviting Orgon to fulfill his own fantasy of autonomy and authority. As he brags to the sensible Cléante, under Tartuffe's teaching, "my soul's been freed/From earthly loves, and every human tie:/My mother, children, brother, and wife could die,/And I'd not feel a single moment's pain." Helping Orgon to realize this fantasy, Tartuffe transforms him into a kind of monster: Orgon comes near to selling his daughter, disinheriting his son, allowing his wife to be raped, and losing his family's property and fortune.

Tartuffe is very much a play of the world, a satiric comedy. Set in an urban landscape, the play insistently translates the idealized passions of tragedy and romantic comedy—love, honor, loyalty—

into their ironic counterparts—lust, hypocrisy, betrayal. Molière peoples the play with individual-ized versions of the unchanging types of *commedia dell' arte* and the Roman comedy that inspired it: the reasonable and attractive heroes; an old, pedantic, self-absorbed dupe; a wily and conniving villain; a clever and witty servant. Yet Molière reinvents this range of stock characters, brilliantly turning his play toward an exploration of the folly of self-deception. For while we might take the neoclassical conflict between reason and the passions to be the hallmark of tragedy, it surges through this play as well. Orgon's passionate solipsism is, for all its ridiculousness, no less profound, troubling, or destructive than the obsessed affections of Racine's Phaedra and Hippolytus. Also, Orgon's redemption, by fiat of the king, seems no less arbitrary than the vengeful caprice of Venus or Neptune in Racine's tragedy.

Since the characters cannot change in Molière's comedy, then change must happen to them. Molière's most brilliant device here arises in the person of the king's officer, who appears to appre-hend Tartuffe and to restore Orgon and his family to their property: property is what establishes the position, the place, the social and individual identity of these characters. Although Molière's DEUS EX MACHINA might be regarded as an elegant (though somewhat clumsy) compliment to the king—and, perhaps, as a sly jab at the clerical critics who attacked *Tartuffe*—this device plays a subtle role in dramatizing the nature of royal authority. For in *Tartuffe*, the king has the power to assign every person to his or her proper place, to see into our inmost hearts, to structure the moral and social order of the world as the reflection of his own will and judgment: "*L'état, c'est moi.*" In this sense, even though *Tartuffe* unleashes the uncontrollable power of self-delusion, and the power and de-structive fantasies of absolute authority, it concludes by asserting the legitimacy of that absolute power. Molière's *deus ex machina* testifies both to the power and to the arbitrariness of the king's authority.

PREFACE[1]

TRANSLATED BY RICHARD WILBUR

Here is a comedy that has excited a good deal of discussion and that has been under attack for a long time; and the persons who are mocked by it have made it plain that they are more powerful in France than all whom my plays have satirized up to this time. Noblemen, ladies of fashion, cuck-olds, and doctors all kindly consented to their presentation, which they themselves seemed to enjoy along with everyone else; but hypocrites do not understand banter: they became angry at once, and found it strange that I was bold enough to represent their actions and to care to describe a profession shared by so many good men. This is a crime for which they cannot forgive me, and they have taken up arms against my comedy in a terrible rage. They were careful not to attack it at the point that had wounded them: they are too crafty for that and too clever to reveal their true character. In keeping with their lofty custom, they have used the cause of God to mask their private interests; and *Tartuffe*, they say, is a play that offends piety: it is filled with abominations from beginning to end, and nowhere is there a line that does not deserve to be burned. Every syllable is wicked, the very ges-tures are criminal, and the slightest glance, turn of the head, or step from right to left conceals mys-teries that they are able to explain to my disadvantage. In vain did I submit the play to the criticism of my friends and the scrutiny of the public: all the corrections I could make, the judgment of the king and queen who saw the play,[2] the approval of great princes and ministers of state who honored it with their presence, the opinion of good men who found it worthwhile; all this did not help. They will not let go of their prey, and every day of the week they have pious zealots abusing me in public and damning me out of charity.

I would care very little about all they might say except that their devices make enemies of men whom I respect and gain the support of genuinely good men, whose faith they know and who, be-cause of the warmth of their piety, readily accept the impressions that others present to them. And it is this which forces me to defend myself. Especially to the truly devout do I wish to vindicate my

---

[1] Molière added his three petitions to Louis XIV; they follow the preface.
[2] Louis XIV was married to Marie Thérèse of Austria.

play, and I beg of them with all my heart not to condemn it before seeing it, to rid themselves of pre-conceptions, and not aid the cause of men dishonored by their actions.

If one takes the trouble to examine my comedy in good faith, he will surely see that my intentions are innocent throughout, and tend in no way to make fun of what men revere; that I have presented the subject with all the precautions that its delicacy imposes; and that I have used all the art and skill that I could to distinguish clearly the character of the hypocrite from that of the truly devout man. For that purpose I used two whole acts to prepare the appearance of my scoundrel. Never is there a moment's doubt about his character; he is known at once from the qualities I have given him; and from one end of the play to the other, he does not say a word, he does not perform an action which does not depict to the audience the character of a wicked man, and which does not bring out in sharp relief the character of the truly good man which I oppose to it.

I know full well that by way of reply, these gentlemen try to insinuate that it is not the role of the theater to speak of these matters; but with their permission, I ask them on what do they base this fine doctrine. It is a proposition they advance as no more than a supposition, for which they offer not a shred of proof; and surely it would not be difficult to show them that comedy, for the ancients, had its origin in religion and constituted a part of its ceremonies; that our neighbors, the Spaniards, have hardly a single holiday celebration in which a comedy is not a part; and that even here in France, it owes its birth to the efforts of a religious brotherhood who still own the Hôtel de Bourgogne, where the most important mystery plays of our faith were presented;[3] that you can still find comedies printed in gothic letters under the name of a learned doctor of the Sorbonne;[4] and without going so far, in our own day the religious dramas of Pierre Corneille[5] have been performed to the admiration of all France.

If the function of comedy is to correct men's vices, I do not see why any should be exempt. Such a condition in our society would be much more dangerous than the thing itself; and we have seen that the theater is admirably suited to provide correction. The most forceful lines of a serious moral statement are usually less powerful than those of satire; and nothing will reform most men better than the depiction of their faults. It is a vigorous blow to vices to expose them to public laughter. Criticism is taken lightly, but men will not tolerate satire. They are quite willing to be mean, but they never like to be ridiculed.

I have been attacked for having placed words of piety in the mouth of my impostor. Could I avoid doing so in order to represent properly the character of a hypocrite? It seemed to me sufficient to reveal the criminal motives which make him speak as he does, and I have eliminated all ceremonial phrases, which nonetheless he would not have been found using incorrectly. Yet some say that in the fourth act he sets forth a vicious morality; but is not this a morality which everyone has heard again and again? Does my comedy say anything new here? And is there any fear that ideas so thoroughly detested by everyone can make an impression on men's minds; that I make them dangerous by presenting them in the theater; that they acquire authority from the lips of a scoundrel? There is not the slightest suggestion of any of this; and one must either approve the comedy of *Tartuffe* or condemn all comedies in general.

This has indeed been done in a furious way for some time now, and never was the theater so much abused.[6] I cannot deny that there were Church Fathers who condemned comedy; but neither will it be denied me that there were some who looked on it somewhat more favorably. Thus authority, on which censure is supposed to depend, is destroyed by this disagreement; and the only conclusion that can be drawn from this difference of opinion among men enlightened by the same wisdom is that they viewed comedy in different ways, and that some considered it in its purity, while others regarded it in its corruption and confused it with all those wretched performances which have been rightly called performances of filth.

---

[3] A reference to the *Confrérie de la Passion et Résurrection de Notre-Seigneur* (the Fraternity of the Passion and Resurrection of Our Saviour), founded in 1402. The Hôtel de Bourgogne was a rival theater of Molière.

[4] Probably Maitre Jehán Michel, a medical doctor who wrote mystery plays.

[5] Pierre Corneille (1606–1684) and Racine were France's two greatest writers of classic tragedy. The two dramas Molière doubtlessly had in mind were *Polyeucte* (1643) and *Théodore, vierge et martyre* (1645).

[6] Molière had in mind Nicole's two attacks on the theater: *Visionnaries* (1666) and *Traité de Comédie*, the Prince de Conti's *Traité de Comédie* (1666).

And in fact, since we should talk about things rather than words, and since most misunderstanding comes from including contrary notions in the same word, we need only to remove the veil of ambiguity and look at comedy in itself to see if it warrants condemnation. It will surely be recognized that as it is nothing more than a clever poem which corrects men's faults by means of agreeable lessons, it cannot be condemned without injustice. And if we listened to the voice of ancient times on this matter, it would tell us that its most famous philosophers have praised comedy—they who professed so austere a wisdom and who ceaselessly denounced the vices of their times. It would tell us that Aristotle spent his evenings at the theater[7] and took the trouble to reduce the art of making comedies to rules. It would tell us that some of its greatest and most honored men took pride in writing comedies themselves,[8] and that others did not disdain to recite them in public; that Greece expressed its admiration for this art by means of handsome prizes and magnificent theaters to honor it; and finally, that in Rome this same art also received extraordinary honors; I do not speak of Rome run riot under the license of the emperors, but of disciplined Rome, governed by the wisdom of the consuls, and in the age of the full vigor of Roman dignity.

I admit that there have been times when comedy became corrupt. And what do men not corrupt every day? There is nothing so innocent that men cannot turn it to crime; nothing so beneficial that its values cannot be reversed; nothing so good in itself that it cannot be put to bad uses. Medical knowledge benefits mankind and is revered as one of our most wonderful possessions; and yet there was a time when it fell into discredit, and was often used to poison men. Philosophy is a gift of Heaven; it has been given to us to bring us to the knowledge of a God by contemplating the wonders of nature; and yet we know that often it has been turned away from its function and has been used openly in support of impiety. Even the holiest of things are not immune from human corruption, and every day we see scoundrels who use and abuse piety, and wickedly make it serve the greatest of crimes. But this does not prevent one from making the necessary distinctions. We do not confuse in the same false inference the goodness of things that are corrupted with the wickedness of the corrupt. The function of an art is always distinguished from its misuse; and as medicine is not forbidden because it was banned in Rome,[9] nor philosophy because it was publicly condemned in Athens,[10] we should not suppress comedy simply because it has been condemned at certain times. This censure was justified then for reasons which no longer apply today; it was limited to what was then seen; and we should not seize on these limits, apply them more rigidly than is necessary, and include in our condemnation the innocent along with the guilty. The comedy that this censure attacked is in no way the comedy that we want to defend. We must be careful not to confuse the one with the other. There may be two persons whose morals may be completely different. They may have no resemblance to one another except in their names, and it would be a terrible injustice to want to condemn Olympia, who is a good woman, because there is also an Olympia who is lewd. Such procedures would make for great confusion everywhere. Everything under the sun would be condemned; now since this rigor is not applied to the countless instances of abuse we see every day, the same should hold for comedy, and those plays should be approved in which instruction and virtue reign supreme.

I know there are some so delicate that they cannot tolerate a comedy, who say that the most decent are the most dangerous, that the passions they present are all the more moving because they are virtuous, and that men's feelings are stirred by these presentations. I do not see what great crime it is to be affected by the sight of a generous passion; and this utter insensitivity to which they would lead us is indeed a high degree of virtue! I wonder if so great a perfection resides within the strength of human nature, and I wonder if it is not better to try to correct and moderate men's passions than to try to suppress them altogether. I grant that there are places better to visit than the theater; and if we want to condemn every single thing that does not bear directly on God and our salvation, it is right that comedy be included, and I should willingly grant that it be condemned

---

[7] A reference to Aristotle's *Poetics* (composed between 335 and 322 BC, the year of his death).

[8] The Roman consul and general responsible for the final destruction of Carthage in 146 BC, Scipio Africanus Minor (*ca.* 185–129 BC), collaborated with the writer of comedies, Terence (Publius Terentius Afer, *ca.* 195 or 185 –*ca.* 159 BC).

[9] Pliny the Elder says that the Romans expelled their doctors at the same time that the Greeks did theirs.

[10] An allusion to Socrates' condemnation to death.

along with everything else. But if we admit, as is in fact true, that the exercise of piety will permit interruptions, and that men need amusement, I maintain that there is none more innocent than comedy. I have dwelled too long on this matter. Let me finish with the words of a great prince on the comedy, *Tartuffe*.[11]

Eight days after it had been banned, a play called *Scaramouche the Hermit*[12] was performed before the court; and the king, on his way out, said to this great prince: "I should really like to know why the persons who make so much noise about Molière's comedy do not say a word about *Scaramouche*." To which the prince replied, "It is because the comedy of *Scaramouche* makes fun of Heaven and religion, which these gentlemen do not care about at all, but that of Molière makes fun of *them*, and that is what they cannot bear."

Molière

FIRST PETITION[13]
(Presented to the King on the Comedy of Tartuffe)

Sire,

As the duty of comedy is to correct men by amusing them, I believed that in my occupation I could do nothing better than attack the vices of my age by making them ridiculous; and as hypocrisy is undoubtedly one of the most common, most improper, and most dangerous, I thought, Sire, that I would perform a service for all good men of your kingdom if I wrote a comedy which denounced hypocrites and placed in proper view all of the contrived poses of these incredibly virtuous men, all of the concealed villainies of these counterfeit believers who would trap others with a fraudulent piety and a pretended virtue.

I have written this comedy, Sire, with all the care and caution that the delicacy of the subject demands; and so as to maintain all the more properly the admiration and respect due to truly devout men, I have delineated my character as sharply as I could; I have left no room for doubt; I have removed all that might confuse good with evil, and have used for this painting only the specific colors and essential lines that make one instantly recognize a true and brazen hypocrite.

Nevertheless, all my precautions have been to no avail. Others have taken advantage of the delicacy of your feelings on religious matters, and they have been able to deceive you on the only side of your character which lies open to deception: your respect for holy things. By underhanded means, the Tartuffes have skillfully gained Your Majesty's favor, and the models have succeeded in eliminating the copy, no matter how innocent it may have been and no matter what resemblance was found between them.

Although the suppression of this work was a serious blow for me, my misfortune was nonetheless softened by the way in which Your Majesty explained his attitude on the matter; and I believed, Sire, that Your Majesty removed any cause I had for complaint, as you were kind enough to declare that you found nothing in this comedy that you would forbid me to present in public.

Yet, despite this glorious declaration of the greatest and most enlightened king in the world, despite the approval of the Papal Legate[14] and of most of our churchmen, all of whom, at private readings of my work, agreed with the views of Your Majesty, despite all this, a book has appeared by a certain priest[15] which boldly contradicts all of these noble judgments. Your Majesty expressed himself in vain, and the Papal Legate and churchmen gave their opinion to no avail: sight unseen, my

---

[11] One of Molière's benefactors who liked the play was the Prince de Condé; de Condé had *Tartuffe* read to him and also privately performed for him.

[12] A troupe of Italian comedians had just performed the licentious farce, where a hermit dressed as a monk makes love to a married woman, announcing that *questo e per mortificar la carne* ("this is to mortify the flesh").

[13] The first of the three *petitions* or *placets* to Louis XIV concerning the play. On May 12, 1664, *Tartuffe*—or at least the first three acts roughly as they now stand—was performed at Versailles. A cabal unfavorable to Molière, including the Archbishop of Paris, Hardouin de Péréfixe, Queen-Mother Anne of Austria, certain influential courtiers, and the Brotherhood or Company of the Holy Sacrament (formed in 1627 to enforce morality), arranged that the play be banned and Molière censured.

[14] Cardinal Legate Chigi, nephew to Pope Alexander VII, heard a reading of *Tartuffe* at Fontainebleau on August 4, 1664.

[15] Pierre Roullé, the curate of St. Barthélémy, who wrote a scathing attack on the play and sent his book to the king.

comedy is diabolical, and so is my brain; I am a devil garbed in flesh and disguised as a man,[16] a libertine, a disbeliever who deserves a punishment that will set an example. It is not enough that fire expiate my crime in public, for that would be letting me off too easily: the generous piety of this good man will not stop there; he will not allow me to find any mercy in the sight of God; he demands that I be damned, and that will settle the matter.

This book, Sire, was presented to Your Majesty; and I am sure that you see for yourself how unpleasant it is for me to be exposed daily to the insults of these gentlemen, what harm these abuses will do my reputation if they must be tolerated, and finally, how important it is for me to clear myself of these false charges and let the public know that my comedy is nothing more than what they want it to be. I will not ask, Sire, for what I need for the sake of my reputation and the innocence of my work: enlightened kings such as you do not need to be told what is wished of them; like God, they see what we need and know better than we what they should give us. It is enough for me to place my interests in Your Majesty's hands, and I respectfully await whatever you may care to command.

(August, 1664)

SECOND PETITION[17]
(PRESENTED TO THE KING IN HIS CAMP BEFORE THE CITY OF LILLE, IN FLANDERS)

Sire,

It is bold indeed for me to ask a favor of a great monarch in the midst of his glorious victories; but in my present situation, Sire, where will I find protection anywhere but where I seek it, and to whom can I appeal against the authority of the power that crushes me,[18] if not to the source of power and authority, the just dispenser of absolute law, the sovereign judge and master of all?

My comedy, Sire, has not enjoyed the kindnesses of Your Majesty. All to no avail, I produced it under the title of *The Hypocrite* and disguised the principal character as a man of the world; in vain I gave him a little hat, long hair, a wide collar, a sword, and lace clothing,[19] softened the action and carefully eliminated all that I thought might provide even the shadow of grounds for discontent on the part of the famous models of the portrait I wished to present; nothing did any good. The conspiracy of opposition revived even at mere conjecture of what the play would be like. They found a way of persuading those who in all other matters plainly insist that they are not to be deceived. No sooner did my comedy appear than it was struck down by the very power which should impose respect; and all that I could do to save myself from the fury of this tempest was to say that Your Majesty had given me permission to present the play and I did not think it was necessary to ask this permission of others, since only Your Majesty could have refused it.

I have no doubt, Sire, that the men whom I depict in my comedy will employ every means possible to influence Your Majesty, and will use, as they have used already, those truly good men who are all the more easily deceived because they judge of others by themselves.[20] They know how to display all of their aims in the most favorable light; yet, no matter how pious they may seem, it is surely not the interests of God which stir them; they have proven this often enough in the comedies they have allowed to be performed hundreds of times without making the least objection. Those plays attacked only piety and religion, for which they care very little; but this play attacks and makes fun of them, and that is what they cannot bear. They will never forgive me for unmasking their hypocrisy in the eyes of everyone. And I am sure that they will not neglect to tell Your Majesty that people are

---

[16] Molière took some of these phrases from Roullé.

[17] On August 5, 1667, *Tartuffe* was performed at the Palais-Royal. The opposition—headed by the First President of Parliament—brought in the police, and the play was stopped. Since Louis was campaigning in Flanders, friends of Molière brought the second *placet* to Lille. Louis had always been favorable toward the playwright; in August 1665, Molière's company, the *Troupe de Monsieur* (nominally sponsored by Louis's brother Philippe, Duc d'Orléans) had become the *Troupe du Roi*.

[18] President de Lanvignon, in charge of the Paris police.

[19] There is evidence that in 1664 Tartuffe played his role dressed in a cassock, thus allying him more directly to the clergy.

[20] Molière apparently did not know that de Lanvignon had been affiliated with the Company of the Holy Sacrament for the previous ten years.

shocked by my comedy. But the simple truth, Sire, is that all Paris is shocked only by its ban, that the most scrupulous persons have found its presentation worthwhile, and men are astounded that individuals of such known integrity should show so great a deference to people whom everyone should abominate and who are so clearly opposed to the true piety which they profess.

I respectfully await the judgment that Your Majesty will deign to pronounce: but it's certain, Sire, that I need not think of writing comedies if the Tartuffes are triumphant, if they thereby seize the right to persecute me more than ever, and find fault with even the most innocent lines that flow from my pen.

Let your goodness, Sire, give me protection against their envenomed rage, and allow me, at your return from so glorious a campaign, to relieve Your Majesty from the fatigue of his conquests, give him innocent pleasures after such noble accomplishments, and make the monarch laugh who makes all Europe tremble!

(August, 1667)

THIRD PETITION
(PRESENTED TO THE KING)

Sire,

A very honest doctor[21] whose patient I have the honor to be, promises and will legally contract to make me live another thirty years if I can obtain a favor for him from Your Majesty. I told him of his promise that I do not deserve so much, and that I should be glad to help him if he will merely agree not to kill me. This favor, Sire, is a post of canon at your royal chapel of Vincennes, made vacant by death.

May I dare to ask for this favor from Your Majesty on the very day of the glorious resurrection of *Tartuffe*, brought back to life by your goodness? By this first favor I have been reconciled with the devout, and the second will reconcile me with the doctors.[22] Undoubtedly this would be too much grace for me at one time, but perhaps it would not be too much for Your Majesty, and I await your answer to my petition with respectful hope.

(February, 1669)

---

[21] A physician friend, M. de Mauvillain, who helped Molière with some of the medical details of *Le Malada imaginaire*.

[22] Doctors are ridiculed to varying degrees in earlier plays of Molière: *Dom Juan, L'Amour médecin,* and *Le Médecin malgré lui.*

TARTUFFE

Molière

TRANSLATED BY RICHARD WILBUR

— CHARACTERS —

MADAME PERNELLE, *Orgon's mother*
ORGON, *Elmire's husband*
ELMIRE, *Orgon's wife*
DAMIS, *Orgon's son, Elmire's stepson*
MARIANE, *Orgon's daughter, Elmire's stepdaughter, in love with Valère*
VALÈRE, *in love with Mariane*
CLÉANTE, *Orgon's brother-in-law*

TARTUFFE, *a hypocrite*
DORINE, *Mariane's lady's-maid*
M. LOYAL, *a bailiff*
A POLICE OFFICER
FLIPOTE, *Mme Pernelle's maid*

The scene throughout: Orgon's house in Paris

— ACT ONE —

SCENE I

MADAME PERNELLE *and* FLIPOTE, *her maid,* ELMIRE, MARIANE, DORINE, DAMIS, CLÉANTE

MADAME PERNELLE: Come, come, Flipote; it's time I left this
    place.
ELMIRE: I can't keep up, you walk at such a pace.
MADAME PERNELLE: Don't trouble, child; no need to show
    me out.
    It's not your manners I'm concerned about.
5 ELMIRE: We merely pay you the respect we owe.
    But, Mother, why this hurry? Must you go?
MADAME PERNELLE: I must. This house appals me. No one
    in it
    Will pay attention for a single minute.
    Children, I take my leave much vexed in spirit.
10   I offer good advice, but you won't hear it.
    You all break in and chatter on and on.
    It's like a madhouse with the keeper gone.
DORINE: If . . .
MADAME PERNELLE: Girl, you talk too much, and I'm afraid
    You're far too saucy for a lady's-maid.
15   You push in everywhere and have your say.
DAMIS: But . . .
MADAME PERNELLE: You, boy, grow more foolish every day.
    To think my grandson should be such a dunce!
    I've said a hundred times, if I've said it once,
    That if you keep the course on which you've started,
20   You'll leave your worthy father broken-hearted.
MARIANE: I think . . .
MADAME PERNELLE: And you, his sister, seem so pure,
    So shy, so innocent, and so demure.
    But you know what they say about still waters.
    I pity parents with secretive daughters.
25 ELMIRE: Now, Mother . . .
MADAME PERNELLE: And as for you, child, let me add
    That your behavior is extremely bad,
    And a poor example for these children, too.
    Their dear, dead mother did far better than you.
    You're much too free with money, and I'm distressed
30   To see you so elaborately dressed.

When it's one's husband that one aims to please,
    One has no need of costly fripperies.
CLÉANTE: Oh, Madam, really . . .
MADAME PERNELLE: You are her brother, Sir,
    And I respect and love you; yet if I were
    My son, this lady's good and pious spouse,   35
    I wouldn't make you welcome in my house.
    You're full of worldly counsels which, I fear,
    Aren't suitable for decent folk to hear.
    I've spoken bluntly, Sir; but it behooves us
    Not to mince words when righteous fervor moves us.   40
DAMIS: Your man Tartuffe is full of holy speeches . . .
MADAME PERNELLE: And practises precisely what he preaches.
    He's a fine man, and should be listened to.
    I will not hear him mocked by fools like you.
DAMIS: Good God! Do you expect me to submit   45
    To the tyranny of that carping hypocrite?
    Must we forgo all joys and satisfactions
    Because that bigot censures all our actions?
DORINE: To hear him talk—and he talks all the time—
    There's nothing one can do that's not a crime.   50
    He rails at everything, your dear Tartuffe.
MADAME PERNELLE: Whatever he reproves deserves reproof.
    He's out to save your souls, and all of you
    Must love him, as my son would have you do.
DAMIS: Ah no, Grandmother, I could never take   55
    To such a rascal, even for my father's sake.
    That's how I feel, and I shall not dissemble.
    His every action makes me seethe and tremble
    With helpless anger, and I have no doubt
    That he and I will shortly have it out.   60
DORINE: Surely it is a shame and a disgrace
    To see this man usurp the master's place—
    To see this beggar who, when first he came,
    Had not a shoe or shoestring to his name
    So far forget himself that he behaves   65
    As if the house were his, and we his slaves.
MADAME PERNELLE: Well, mark my words, your souls would
    fare far better
    If you obeyed his precepts to the letter.
DORINE: You see him as a saint. I'm far less awed;
    In fact, I see right through him. He's a fraud.   70
MADAME PERNELLE: Nonsense!

DORINE: His man Laurent's the same, or worse;
　　I'd not trust either with a penny purse.
MADAME PERNELLE: I can't say what his servant's morals may
　　be;
　　His own great goodness I can guarantee.
75　　You all regard him with distaste and fear
　　Because he tells you what you're loath to hear,
　　Condemns your sins, points out your moral flaws,
　　And humbly strives to further Heaven's cause.
DORINE: If sin is all that bothers him, why is it
80　　He's so upset when folk drop in to visit?
　　Is Heaven so outraged by a social call
　　That he must prophesy against us all?
　　I'll tell you what I think: if you ask me,
　　He's jealous of my mistress' company.
85　MADAME PERNELLE: Rubbish! (*To* ELMIRE.) He's not alone,
　　child, in complaining
　　Of all of your promiscuous entertaining.
　　Why, the whole neighborhood's upset, I know,
　　By all these carriages that come and go,
　　With crowds of guests parading in and out
90　　And noisy servants loitering about.
　　In all of this, I'm sure there's nothing vicious;
　　But why give people cause to be suspicious?
CLÉANTE: They need no cause; they'll talk in any case.
　　Madam, this world would be a joyless place
95　　If, fearing what malicious tongues might say,
　　We locked our doors and turned our friends away.
　　And even if one did so dreary a thing,
　　D'you think those tongues would cease their chattering?
　　One can't fight slander; it's a losing battle;
100　　Let us instead ignore their tittle-tattle.
　　Let's strive to live by conscience' clear decrees,
　　And let the gossips gossip as they please.
DORINE: If there is talk against us, I know the source:
　　It's Daphne and her little husband, of course.
105　　Those who have greatest cause for guilt and shame
　　Are quickest to besmirch a neighbor's name.
　　When there's a chance for libel, they never miss it;
　　When something can be made to seem illicit
　　They're off at once to spread the joyous news,
110　　Adding to fact what fantasies they choose.
　　By talking up their neighbor's indiscretions
　　They seek to camouflage their own transgressions,
　　Hoping that others' innocent affairs
　　Will lend a hue of innocence to theirs,
115　　Or that their own black guilt will come to seem
　　Part of a general shady color-scheme.
MADAME PERNELLE: All that is quite irrelevant. I doubt
　　That anyone's more virtuous and devout
　　Than dear Orante; and I'm informed that she
120　　Condemns your mode of life most vehemently.
DORINE: Oh, yes, she's strict, devout, and has no taint
　　Of worldliness; in short, she seems a saint.
　　But it was time which taught her that disguise;
　　She's thus because she can't be otherwise.
125　　So long as her attractions could enthrall,
　　She flounced and flirted and enjoyed it all,
　　But now that they're no longer what they were
　　She quits a world which fast is quitting her,
　　And wears a veil of virtue to conceal

Her bankrupt beauty and her lost appeal.　　　　130
That's what becomes of old coquettes today:
Distressed when all their lovers fall away,
They see no recourse but to play the prude,
And so confer a style on solitude.
Thereafter, they're severe with everyone,　　　　135
Condemning all our actions, pardoning none,
And claiming to be pure, austere, and zealous
When, if the truth were known, they're merely jealous,
And cannot bear to see another know
The pleasures time has forced them to forgo.　　　140
MADAME PERNELLE: (*Initially to* ELMIRE.) That sort of talk is
　　what you like to hear;
　　Therefore you'd have us all keep still, my dear,
　　While Madam rattles on the livelong day.
　　Nevertheless, I mean to have my say.
　　I tell you that you're blest to have Tartuffe　　　145
　　Dwelling, as my son's guest, beneath this roof;
　　That Heaven has sent him to forestall its wrath
　　By leading you, once more, to the true path;
　　That all he reprehends is reprehensible,
　　And that you'd better heed him, and be sensible.　　150
　　These visits, balls, and parties in which you revel
　　Are nothing but inventions of the Devil.
　　One never hears a word that's edifying:
　　Nothing but chaff and foolishness and lying,
　　As well as vicious gossip in which one's neighbor　　155
　　Is cut to bits with epee, foil, and saber.
　　People of sense are driven half-insane
　　At such affairs, where noise and folly reign
　　And reputations perish thick and fast.
　　As a wise preacher said on Sunday last,　　　　160
　　Parties are Towers of Babylon, because
　　The guests all babble on with never a pause;
　　And then he told a story which, I think . . .

(*To* CLÉANTE.)

　　I heard that laugh, Sir, and I saw that wink!
　　Go find your silly friends and laugh some more!　　165
　　Enough; I'm going; don't show me to the door.
　　I leave this household much dismayed and vexed;
　　I cannot say when I shall see you next.

(*Slapping* FLIPOTE.)

　　Wake up, don't stand there gaping into space!
　　I'll slap some sense into that stupid face.　　　170
　　Move, move, you slut.

SCENE II

CLÉANTE, DORINE

CLÉANTE: I think I'll stay behind;
　　I want no further pieces of her mind.
　　How that old lady . . .
DORINE: Oh, what wouldn't she say
　　If she could hear you speak of her that way!
　　She'd thank you for the *lady*, but I'm sure　　　5
　　She'd find the *old* a little premature.
CLÉANTE: My, what a scene she made, and what a din!
　　And how this man Tartuffe has taken her in!
DORINE: Yes, but her son is even worse deceived;

10 His folly must be seen to be believed.
In the late troubles, he played an able part
And served his king with wise and loyal heart,
But he's quite lost his senses since he fell
Beneath Tartuffe's infatuating spell.
15 He calls him brother, and loves him as his life,
Preferring him to mother, child, or wife.
In him and him alone will he confide;
He's made him his confessor and his guide;
He pets and pampers him with love more tender
20 Than any pretty mistress could engender,
Gives him the place of honor when they dine,
Delights to see him gorging like a swine,
Stuffs him with dainties till his guts distend,
And when he belches, cries "God bless you, friend!"
25 In short, he's mad; he worships him; he dotes;
His deeds he marvels at, his words he quotes,
Thinking each act a miracle, each word
Oracular as those that Moses heard.
Tartuffe, much pleased to find so easy a victim,
30 Has in a hundred ways beguiled and tricked him,
Milked him of money, and with his permission
Established here a sort of Inquisition.
Even Laurent, his lackey, dares to give
Us arrogant advice on how to live;
35 He sermonizes us in thundering tones
And confiscates our ribbons and colognes.
Last week he tore a kerchief into pieces
Because he found it pressed in a *Life of Jesus*:
He said it was a sin to juxtapose
40 Unholy vanities and holy prose.

SCENE III

ELMIRE, MARIANE, DAMIS, CLÉANTE, DORINE

ELMIRE: *(To* CLÉANTE.*)* You did well not to follow; she stood
     in the door
And said *verbatim* all she'd said before.
I saw my husband coming. I think I'd best
Go upstairs now, and take a little rest.
5 CLÉANTE: I'll wait and greet him here; then I must go.
I've really only time to say hello.
DAMIS: Sound him about my sister's wedding, please.
I think Tartuffe's against it, and that he's
Been urging Father to withdraw his blessing.
10 As you well know, I'd find that most distressing.
Unless my sister and Valère can marry,
My hopes to wed *his* sister will miscarry,
And I'm determined . . .
DORINE: He's coming.

SCENE IV

ORGON, CLÉANTE, DORINE

ORGON: Ah, Brother, good-day.
CLÉANTE: Well, welcome back. I'm sorry I can't stay.
How was the country? Blooming, I trust, and green?
ORGON: Excuse me, Brother; just one moment.

(To DORINE.*)*

                          Dorine . . .

(To CLÉANTE.*)*

To put my mind at rest, I always learn   5
The household news the moment I return.

(To DORINE.*)*

Has all been well, these two days I've been gone?
How are the family? What's been going on?
DORINE: Your wife, two days ago, had a bad fever,
And a fierce headache which refused to leave her.   10
ORGON: Ah. And Tartuffe?
DORINE: Tartuffe? Why, he's round and red,
Bursting with health, and excellently fed.
ORGON: Poor fellow!
DORINE: That night, the mistress was unable
To take a single bite at the dinner-table.
Her headache-pains, she said, were simply hellish. 15
ORGON: Ah. And Tartuffe?
DORINE: He ate his meal with relish,
And zealously devoured in her presence
A leg of mutton and a brace of pheasants.
ORGON: Poor fellow!
DORINE: Well, the pains continued strong,
And so she tossed and tossed the whole night long, 20
Now icy-cold, now burning like a flame.
We sat beside her bed till morning came.
ORGON: Ah. And Tartuffe?
DORINE: Why, having eaten, he rose
And sought his room, already in a doze,
Got into his warm bed, and snored away   25
In perfect peace until the break of day.
ORGON: Poor fellow!
DORINE: After much ado, we talked her
Into dispatching someone for the doctor.
He bled her, and the fever quickly fell.
ORGON: Ah. And Tartuffe?   30
DORINE: He bore it very well.
To keep his cheerfulness at any cost,
And make up for the blood *Madame* had lost,
He drank, at lunch, four beakers full of port.
ORGON: Poor fellow!
DORINE: Both are doing well, in short.
I'll go and tell *Madame* that you've expressed   35
Keen sympathy and anxious interest.

SCENE V

ORGON, CLÉANTE

CLÉANTE: That girl was laughing in your face, and though
I've no wish to offend you, even so
I'm bound to say that she had some excuse.
How can you possibly be such a goose?
Are you so dazed by this man's hocus-pocus   5
That all the world, save him, is out of focus?
You've given him clothing, shelter, food, and care;
Why must you also . . .
ORGON: Brother, stop right there.
You do not know the man of whom you speak.
CLÉANTE: I grant you that. But my judgment's not so weak 10
That I can't tell, by his effect on others . . .
ORGON: Ah, when you meet him, you two will be like brothers!
There's been no loftier soul since time began.

He is a man who . . . a man who . . . an excellent man.

15 To keep his precepts is to be reborn,
And view this dunghill of a world with scorn.
Yes, thanks to him I'm a changed man indeed.
Under his tutelage my soul's been freed
From earthly loves, and every human tie:
20 My mother, children, brother, and wife could die,
And I'd not feel a single moment's pain.

CLÉANTE: That's a fine sentiment, Brother; most humane.

ORGON: Oh, had you seen Tartuffe as I first knew him,
Your heart, like mine, would have surrendered to him.
25 He used to come into our church each day
And humbly kneel nearby, and start to pray.
He'd draw the eyes of everybody there
By the deep fervor of his heartfelt prayer;
He'd sigh and weep, and sometimes with a sound
30 Of rapture he would bend and kiss the ground;
And when I rose to go, he'd run before
To offer me holy-water at the door.
His serving-man, no less devout than he,
Informed me of his master's poverty;
35 I gave him gifts, but in his humbleness
He'd beg me every time to give him less.
"Oh, that's too much," he'd cry, "too much by twice!
I don't deserve it. The half, Sir, would suffice."
And when I wouldn't take it back, he'd share
40 Half of it with the poor, right then and there.
At length, Heaven prompted me to take him in
To dwell with us, and free our souls from sin.
He guides our lives, and to protect my honor
Stays by my wife, and keeps an eye upon her;
45 He tells me whom she sees, and all she does,
And seems more jealous than I ever was!
And how austere he is! Why, he can detect
A mortal sin where you would least suspect;
In smallest trifles, he's extremely strict.
50 Last week, his conscience was severely pricked
Because, while praying, he had caught a flea
And killed it, so he felt, too wrathfuly.

CLÉANTE: Good God, man! Have you lost your common sense—
Or is this all some joke at my expense?
55 How can you stand there and in all sobriety . . .

ORGON: Brother, your language savors of impiety.
Too much free-thinking's made your faith unsteady,
And as I've warned you many times already,
'Twill get you into trouble before you're through.

60 CLÉANTE: So I've been told before by dupes like you:
Being blind, you'd have all others blind as well;
The clear-eyed man you call an infidel,
And he who sees through humbug and pretense
Is charged, by you, with want of reverence.
65 Spare me your warnings, Brother; I have no fear
Of speaking out, for you and Heaven to hear,
Against affected zeal and pious knavery.
There's true and false in piety, as in bravery,
And just as those whose courage shines the most
70 In battle, are the least inclined to boast,
So those whose hearts are truly pure and lowly
Don't make a flashy show of being holy.
There's a vast difference, so it seems to me,
Between true piety and hypocrisy:

How do you fail to see it, may I ask? 75
Is not a face quite different from a mask?
Cannot sincerity and cunning art,
Reality and semblance, be told apart?
Are scarecrows just like men, and do you hold
That a false coin is just as good as gold? 80
Ah, Brother, man's a strangely fashioned creature
Who seldom is content to follow Nature,
But recklessly pursues his inclination
Beyond the narrow bounds of moderation,
And often, by transgressing Reason's laws, 85
Perverts a lofty aim or noble cause.
A passing observation, but it applies.

ORGON: I see, dear Brother, that you're profoundly wise;
You harbor all the insight of the age.
You are our one clear mind, our only sage, 90
The era's oracle, its Cato too,
And all mankind are fools compared to you.

CLÉANTE: Brother, I don't pretend to be a sage,
Nor have I all the wisdom of the age.
There's just one insight I would dare to claim: 95
I know that true and false are not the same;
And just as there is nothing I more revere
Than a soul whose faith is steadfast and sincere,
Nothing that I more cherish and admire
Than honest zeal and true religious fire, 100
So there is nothing that I find more base
Than specious piety's dishonest face—
Than these bold mountebanks, these histrios
Whose impious mummeries and hollow shows
Exploit our love of Heaven, and make a jest 105
Of all that men think holiest and best;
These calculating souls who offer prayers
Not to their Maker, but as public wares,
And seek to buy respect and reputation
With lifted eyes and sighs of exaltation; 110
These charlatans, I say, whose pilgrim souls
Proceed, by way of Heaven, toward earthly goals,
Who weep and pray and swindle and extort,
Who preach the monkish life, but haunt the court,
Who make their zeal the partner of their vice— 115
Such men are vengeful, sly, and cold as ice,
And when there is an enemy to defame
They cloak their spite in fair religion's name,
Their private spleen and malice being made
To seem a high and virtuous crusade, 120
Until, to mankind's reverent applause,
They crucify their foe in Heaven's cause.
Such knaves are all too common; yet, for the wise,
True piety isn't hard to recognize,
And, happily, these present times provide us 125
With bright examples to instruct and guide us.
Consider Ariston and Périandre;
Look at Oronte, Alcidamas, Clitandre;
Their virtue is acknowledged; who could doubt it?
But you won't hear them beat the drum about it. 130
They're never ostentatious, never vain,
And their religion's moderate and humane;
It's not their way to criticize and chide:
They think censoriousness a mark of pride,
And therefore, letting others preach and rave, 135
They show, by deeds, how Christians should behave.

They think no evil of their fellow man,
But judge of him as kindly as they can.
They don't intrigue and wangle and conspire;
140 To lead a good life is their one desire;
The sinner wakes no rancorous hate in them;
It is the sin alone which they condemn;
Nor do they try to show a fiercer zeal
For Heaven's cause than Heaven itself could feel.
145 These men I honor, these men I advocate
As models for us all to emulate.
Your man is not their sort at all, I fear:
And, while your praise of him is quite sincere,
I think that you've been dreadfully deluded.
150 ORGON: Now then, dear Brother, is your speech concluded?
CLÉANTE: Why, yes.
ORGON: Your servant, Sir.

(He turns to go.)

CLÉANTE: No, Brother; wait.
There's one more matter. You agreed of late
That young Valère might have your daughter's hand.
ORGON: I did.
CLÉANTE: And set the date, I understand.
155 ORGON: Quite so.
CLÉANTE: You've now postponed it; is that true?
ORGON: No doubt.
CLÉANTE: The match no longer pleases you?
ORGON: Who knows?
CLÉANTE: D'you mean to go back on your word?
ORGON: I won't say that.
CLÉANTE: Has anything occurred
Which might entitle you to break your pledge?
160 ORGON: Perhaps.
CLÉANTE: Why must you hem, and haw, and hedge?
The boy asked me to sound you in this affair . . .
ORGON: It's been a pleasure.
CLÉANTE: But what shall I tell Valère?
ORGON: Whatever you like.
CLÉANTE: But what have you decided?
What are your plans?
ORGON: I plan, Sir, to be guided
165 By Heaven's will.
CLÉANTE: Come, Brother, don't talk rot.
You've given Valère your word; will you keep it, or not?
ORGON: Good day.
CLÉANTE: This looks like poor Valère's undoing;
I'll go and warn him that there's trouble brewing.

— **ACT TWO** —

SCENE I

ORGON, MARIANE

ORGON: Mariane.
MARIANE: Yes, Father?
ORGON: A word with you; come here.
MARIANE: What are you looking for?
ORGON:

(Peering into a small closet.)

                              Eavesdroppers, dear.
I'm making sure we shan't be overheard.

Someone in there could catch our every word.
Ah, good, we're safe. Now, Mariane, my child,   5
You're a sweet girl who's tractable and mild,
Whom I hold dear, and think most highly of.
MARIANE: I'm deeply grateful, Father, for your love.
ORGON: That's well said, Daughter; and you can repay me
If, in all things, you'll cheerfully obey me.   10
MARIANE: To please you, Sir, is what delights me best.
ORGON: Good, good. Now, what d'you think of Tartuffe, our
   guest?
MARIANE: I, Sir?
ORGON: Yes. Weigh your answer; think it through.
MARIANE: Oh, dear. I'll say whatever you wish me to.
ORGON: That's wisely said, my Daughter. Say of him, then,   15
That he's the very worthiest of men,
And that you're fond of him, and would rejoice
In being his wife, if that should be my choice.
Well?
MARIANE: What?
ORGON: What's that?
MARIANE: I . . .
ORGON: Well?
MARIANE: Forgive me, pray.
ORGON: Did you not hear me?   20
MARIANE: Of *whom*, Sir, must I say
That I am fond of him, and would rejoice
In being his wife, if that should be your choice?
ORGON: Why, of Tartuffe.
MARIANE: But, Father, that's false, you know.
Why would you have me say what isn't so?
ORGON: Because I am resolved it shall be true.   25
That it's my wish should be enough for you.
MARIANE: You can't mean, Father . . .
ORGON: Yes, Tartuffe shall be
Allied by marriage to this family,
And he's to be your husband, is that clear?
It's a father's privilege . . .   30

SCENE II

DORINE, ORGON, MARIANE

ORGON: *(To DORINE.)*   What are you doing in here?
Is curiosity so fierce a passion
With you, that you must eavesdrop in this fashion?
DORINE: There's lately been a rumor going about—
Based on some hunch or chance remark, no doubt—   5
That you mean Mariane to wed Tartuffe.
I've laughed it off, of course, as just a spoof.
ORGON: You find it so incredible?
DORINE: Yes, I do.
I won't accept that story, even from you.
ORGON: Well, you'll believe it when the thing is done.   10
DORINE: Yes, yes, of course. Go on and have your fun.
ORGON: I've never been more serious in my life.
DORINE: Ha!
ORGON: Daughter, I mean it; you're to be his wife.
DORINE: No, don't believe your father; it's all a hoax.
ORGON: See here, young woman . . .   15
DORINE: Come, Sir, no more
   jokes;
You can't fool us.
ORGON: How dare you talk that way?

DORINE: All right, then: we believe you, sad to say.
But how a man like you, who looks so wise
And wears a moustache of such splendid size,
20 Can be so foolish as to . . .
ORGON: Silence, please!
My girl, you take too many liberties.
I'm master here, as you must not forget.
DORINE: Do let's discuss this calmly; don't be upset.
You can't be serious, Sir, about this plan.
25 What should that bigot want with Mariane?
Praying and fasting ought to keep him busy.
And then, in terms of wealth and rank, what is he?
Why should a man of property like you
Pick out a beggar son-in-law?
ORGON: That will do.
30 Speak of his poverty with reverence.
His is a pure and saintly indigence
Which far transcends all worldly pride and pelf.
He lost his fortune, as he says himself,
Because he cared for Heaven alone, and so
35 Was careless of his interests here below.
I mean to get him out of his present straits
And help him to recover his estates—
Which, in his part of the world, have no small fame.
Poor though he is, he's a gentleman just the same.
40 DORINE: Yes, so he tells us; and, Sir, it seems to me
Such pride goes very ill with piety.
A man whose spirit spurns this dungy earth
Ought not to brag of lands and noble birth;
Such worldly arrogance will hardly square
45 With meek devotion and the life of prayer.
. . . But this approach, I see, has drawn a blank;
Let's speak, then, of his person, not his rank.
Doesn't it seem to you a trifle grim
To give a girl like her to a man like him?
50 When two are so ill-suited, can't you see
What the sad consequences is bound to be?
A young girl's virtue is imperilled, Sir,
When such a marriage is imposed on her;
For if one's bridegroom isn't to one's taste,
55 It's hardly an inducement to be chaste,
And many a man with horns upon his brow
Has made his wife the thing that she is now.
It's hard to be a faithful wife, in short,
To certain husbands of a certain sort,
60 And he who gives his daughter to a man she hates
Must answer for her sins at Heaven's gates.
Think, Sir, before you play so risky a role.
ORGON: This servant-girl presumes to save my soul!
DORINE: You would do well to ponder what I've said.
65 ORGON: Daughter, we'll disregard this dunderhead.
Just trust your father's judgment. Oh, I'm aware
That I once promised you to young Valère;
But now I hear he gambles, which greatly shocks me;
What's more, I've doubts about his orthodoxy.
70 His visits to church, I note, are very few.
DORINE: Would you have him go at the same hours as you,
And kneel nearby, to be sure of being seen?
ORGON: I can dispense with such remarks, Dorine.

(To MARIANE.*)*

Tartuffe, however, is sure of Heaven's blessing,
And that's the only treasure worth possessing.   75
This match will bring you joys beyond all measure;
Your cup will overflow with every pleasure;
You two will interchange your faithful loves
Like two sweet cherubs, or two turtle-doves.
No harsh word shall be heard, no frown be seen,   80
And he shall make you happy as a queen.
DORINE: And she'll make him a cuckold, just wait and see.
ORGON: What language!
DORINE: Oh, he's a man of destiny;
He's *made* for horns, and what the stars demand
Your daughter's virtue surely can't withstand.   85
ORGON: Don't interrupt me further. Why can't you learn
That certain things are none of your concern?
DORINE: It's for your own sake that I interfere.

(She repeatedly interrupts ORGON *just as he is turning to speak to his daughter.)*

ORGON: Most kind of you. Now, hold your tongue, d'you hear?
DORINE: If I didn't love you . . .   90
ORGON: Spare me your affection.
DORINE: I'll love you, Sir, in spite of your objection.
ORGON: Blast!
DORINE: I can't bear, Sir, for your honor's sake,
To let you make this ludicrous mistake.
ORGON: You mean to go on talking?
DORINE: If I didn't protest
This sinful marriage, my conscience couldn't rest.   95
ORGON: If you don't hold your tongue, you little shrew . . .
DORINE: What, lost your temper? A pious man like you?
ORGON: Yes! Yes! You talk and talk. I'm maddened by it.
Once and for all, I tell you to be quiet.
DORINE: Well, I'll be quiet. But I'll be thinking hard.   100
ORGON: Think all you like, but you had better guard
That saucy tongue of yours, or I'll . . .

(Turning back to MARIANE.*)*

               Now, child,
I've weighed this matter fully.
DORINE:

(Aside.)

              It drives me wild
That I can't speak.

*(*ORGON *turns his head, and she is silent.)*

ORGON: Tartuffe is no young dandy,
But, still, his person . . .   105
DORINE:

(Aside.)

              Is as sweet as candy.
ORGON: Is such that, even if you shouldn't care
For his other merits . . .

(He turns and stands facing DORINE, *arms crossed.)*

DORINE:

(Aside.)

              They'll make a lovely pair.
If I were she, no man would marry me

Against my inclination, and go scot-free.
110 He'd learn, before the wedding-day was over,
How readily a wife can find a lover.
ORGON:

(*To* DORINE.)

It seems you treat my orders as a joke.
DORINE: Why, what's the matter? 'Twas not to you I spoke.
ORGON: What *were* you doing?
DORINE: Talking to myself, that's all.
115 ORGON: Ah! (*Aside.*) One more bit of impudence and gall,
And I shall give her a good slap in the face.

(*He puts himself in position to slap her;* DORINE, *whenever he glances at her, stands immobile and silent.*)

Daughter, you shall accept, and with good grace,
The husband I've selected . . . Your wedding-day . . .

(*To* DORINE.)

Why don't you talk to yourself?
DORINE: I've nothing to say.
120 ORGON: Come, just one word.
DORINE: No thank you, Sir. I pass.
ORGON: Come, speak; I'm waiting.
DORINE: I'd not be such an ass.
ORGON:

(*Turning to* MARIANE.)

In short, dear Daughter, I mean to be obeyed,
And you must bow to the sound choice I've made.
DORINE:

(*Moving away.*)

I'd not wed such a monster, even in jest.

(ORGON *attempts to slap her, but misses.*)

125 ORGON: Daughter, that maid of yours is a thorough pest;
She makes me sinfully annoyed and nettled.
I can't speak further; my nerves are too unsettled.
She's so upset me by her insolent talk,
I'll calm myself by going for a walk.

SCENE III

DORINE, MARIANE

DORINE:

(*Returning.*)

Well, have you lost your tongue, girl? Must I play
Your part, and say the lines you ought to say?
Faced with a fate so hideous and absurd,
Can you not utter one dissenting word?
5 MARIANE: What good would it do? A father's power is great.
DORINE: Resist him now, or it will be too late.
MARIANE: But . . .
DORINE: Tell him one cannot love at a father's
whim;
That you shall marry for yourself, not him;
That since it's you who are to be the bride,
10 It's you, not he, who must be satisfied;
And that if his Tartuffe is so sublime,
He's free to marry him at any time.

MARIANE: I've bowed so long to Father's strict control,
I couldn't oppose him now, to save my soul.
DORINE: Come, come, Mariane. Do listen to reason, won't   15
you?
Valère has asked your hand. Do you love him, or don't
you?
MARIANE: Oh, how unjust of you! What can you mean
By asking such a question, dear Dorine?
You know the depth of my affection for him;
I've told you a hundred times how I adore him.   20
DORINE: I don't believe in everything I hear;
Who knows if your professions were sincere?
MARIANE: They were, Dorine, and you do me wrong to doubt
it;
Heaven knows that I've been all too frank about it.
DORINE: You love him, then?   25
MARIANE: Oh, more than I can express.
DORINE: And he, I take it, cares for you no less?
MARIANE: I think so.
DORINE: And you both, with equal fire,
Burn to be married?
MARIANE: That is our one desire.
DORINE: What of Tartuffe, then? What of your father's plan?
MARIANE: I'll kill myself, if I'm forced to wed that man.   30
DORINE: I hadn't thought of that recourse. How splendid!
Just die, and all your troubles will be ended!
A fine solution. Oh, it maddens me
To hear you talk in that self-pitying key.
MARIANE: Dorine, how harsh you are! It's most unfair.   35
You have no sympathy for my despair.
DORINE: I've none at all for people who talk drivel
And, faced with difficulties, whine and snivel.
MARIANE: No doubt I'm timid, but it would be wrong . . .
DORINE: True love requires a heart that's firm and strong.   40
MARIANE: I'm strong in my affection for Valère,
But coping with my father is his affair.
DORINE: But if your father's brain has grown so cracked
Over his dear Tartuffe that he can retract
His blessing, though your wedding-day was named,   45
It's surely not Valère who's to be blamed.
MARIANE: If I defied my father, as you suggest,
Would it not seem unmaidenly, at best?
Shall I defend my love at the expense
Of brazenness and disobedience?   50
Shall I parade my heart's desires, and flaunt . . .
DORINE: No, I ask nothing of you. Clearly you want
To be Madame Tartuffe, and I feel bound
Not to oppose a wish so very sound.
What right have I to criticize the match?   55
Indeed, my dear, the man's a brilliant catch.
Monsieur Tartuffe! Now, there's a man of weight!
Yes, yes, Monsieur Tartuffe, I'm bound to state,
Is quite a person; that's not to be denied;
'Twill be no little thing to be his bride.   60
The world already rings with his renown;
He's a great noble—in his native town;
His ears are red, he has a pink complexion,
And all in all, he'll suit you to perfection.
MARIANE: Dear God!   65
DORINE: Oh, how triumphant you will feel
At having caught a husband so ideal!

MARIANE: Oh, do stop teasing, and use your cleverness
      To get me out of this appalling mess.
      Advise me, and I'll do whatever you say.
70 DORINE: Ah no, a dutiful daughter must obey
      Her father, even if he weds her to an ape.
      You've a bright future; why struggle to escape?
      Tartuffe will take you back where his family lives,
      To a small town aswarm with relatives—
75   Uncles and cousins whom you'll be charmed to meet.
      You'll be received at once by the elite,
      Calling upon the bailiff's wife, no less—
      Even, perhaps, upon the mayoress,
      Who'll sit you down in the *best* kitchen chair.
80 Then, once a year, you'll dance at the village fair
      To the drone of bagpipes—two of them, in fact—
      And see a puppet-show, or an animal act.
      Your husband . . .
MARIANE: Oh, you turn my blood to ice!
      Stop torturing me, and give me your advice.
DORINE:

(Threatening to go.)

85   Your servant, Madam.
MARIANE: Dorine, I beg of you . . .
DORINE: No, you deserve it; this marriage must go through.
MARIANE: Dorine!
DORINE: No.
MARIANE: Not Tartuffe! You know I think him . . .
DORINE: Tartuffe's your cup of tea, and you shall drink him.
MARIANE: I've always told you everything, and relied . . .
90 DORINE: No. You deserve to be tartuffified.
MARIANE: Well, since you mock me and refuse to care,
      I'll henceforth seek my solace in despair:
      Despair shall be my counsellor and friend,
      And help me bring my sorrows to an end.

(She starts to leave.)

95 DORINE: There now, come back; my anger has subsided.
      You do deserve some pity, I've decided.
MARIANE: Dorine, if Father makes me undergo
      This dreadful martyrdom, I'll die, I know.
DORINE: Don't fret; it won't be difficult to discover
100   Some plan of action . . . But here's Valère, your lover.

SCENE IV

VALÈRE, MARIANE, DORINE

VALÈRE: Madam, I've just received some wondrous news
      Regarding which I'd like to hear your views.
MARIANE: What news?
VALÈRE: You're marrying Tartuffe.
MARIANE: I find
      That Father does have such a match in mind.
5 VALÈRE: Your father, Madam . . .
MARIANE: . . . has just this minute said
      That it's Tartuffe he wishes me to wed.
VALÈRE: Can he be serious?
MARIANE: Oh, indeed he can;
      He's clearly set his heart upon the plan.
VALÈRE: And what position do you propose to take,
10   Madam?

MARIANE: Why—I don't know.
VALÈRE: For heaven's sake—
      You don't know?
MARIANE: No.
VALÈRE: Well, well!
MARIANE: Advise me, do.
VALÈRE: Marry the man. That's my advice to you.
MARIANE: That's your advice?
VALÈRE: Yes.
MARIANE: Truly?
VALÈRE: Oh, absolutely.
      You couldn't choose more wisely, more astutely.
MARIANE: Thanks for this counsel; I'll follow it, of course.   15
VALÈRE: Do, do; I'm sure 'twill cost you no remorse.
MARIANE: To give it didn't cause your heart to break.
VALÈRE: I gave it, Madam, only for your sake.
MARIANE: And it's for your sake that I take it, Sir.
DORINE:

(Withdrawing to the rear of the stage.)

      Let's see which fool will prove the stubborner.   20
VALÈRE: So! I am nothing to you, and it was flat
      Deception when you . . .
MARIANE: Please, enough of that.
      You've told me plainly that I should agree
      To wed the man my father's chosen for me,
      And since you've deigned to counsel me so wisely,   25
      I promise, Sir, to do as you advise me.
VALÈRE: Ah, no, 'twas not by me that you were swayed.
      No, your decision was already made;
      Though now, to save appearances, you protest
      That you're betraying me at my behest.   30
MARIANE: Just as you say.
VALÈRE: Quite so. And I now see
      That you were never truly in love with me.
MARIANE: Alas, you're free to think so if you choose.
VALÈRE: I choose to think so, and here's a bit of news:
      You've spurned my hand, but I know where to turn   35
      For kinder treatment, as you shall quickly learn.
MARIANE: I'm sure you do. Your noble qualities
      Inspire affection . . .
VALÈRE: Forget my qualities, please.
      They don't inspire you overmuch, I find.
      But there's another lady I have in mind   40
      Whose sweet and generous nature will not scorn
      To compensate me for the loss I've borne.
MARIANE: I'm no great loss, and I'm sure that you'll transfer
      Your heart quite painlessly from me to her.
VALÈRE: I'll do my best to take it in my stride.   45
      The pain I feel at being cast aside
      Time and forgetfulness may put an end to.
      Or if I can't forget, I shall pretend to.
      No self-respecting person is expected
      To go on loving once he's been rejected.   50
MARIANE: Now, that's a fine, high-minded sentiment.
VALÈRE: One to which any sane man would assent.
      Would you prefer it if I pined away
      In hopeless passion till my dying day?
      Am I to yield you to a rival's arms   55
      And not console myself with other charms?
MARIANE: Go then: console yourself; don't hesitate.

I wish you to; indeed, I cannot wait.
VALÈRE: You wish me to?
MARIANE: Yes.
VALÈRE: That's the final straw.
60   Madam, farewell. Your wish shall be my law.

(He starts to leave, and then returns: this repeatedly.)

MARIANE: Splendid.
VALÈRE:

(Coming back again.)

                    This breach, remember, is of your making;
    It's you who've driven me to the step I'm taking.
MARIANE: Of course.
VALÈRE:

(Coming back again.)

                    Remember, too, that I am merely
    Following your example.
MARIANE: I see that clearly.
65 VALÈRE: Enough. I'll go and do your bidding, then.
MARIANE: Good.
VALÈRE:

(Coming back again.)

                    You shall never see my face again.
MARIANE: Excellent.
VALÈRE:

(Walking to the door, then turning about.)

                    Yes?
MARIANE: What?
VALÈRE: What's that? What did you
    say?
MARIANE: Nothing. You're dreaming.
VALÈRE: Ah. Well, I'm on my
    way.
    Farewell, *Madame.*

(He moves slowly away.)

MARIANE: Farewell.
DORINE:

(To MARIANE.)

                                    If you ask me,
70   Both of you are as mad as mad can be.
    Do stop this nonsense, now. I've only let you
    Squabble so long to see where it would get you.
    Whoa there, Monsieure Valère!

(She goes and seizes VALÈRE by the arm; he makes a great show of resistance.)

VALÈRE: What's this, Dorine?
DORINE: Come here.
VALÈRE: No, no, my heart's too full of spleen.
75   Don't hold me back; her wish must be obeyed.
DORINE: Stop!
VALÈRE: It's too late now; my decision's made.
DORINE: Oh, pooh!
MARIANE:

(Aside.)

    He hates the sight of me, that's plain.
    I'll go, and so deliver him from pain.
DORINE:

(Leaving VALÈRE, running after MARIANE.)

    And now *you* run away! Come back.
MARIANE: No, no.
    Nothing you say will keep me here. Let go!   80
VALÈRE:

(Aside.)

    She cannot bear my presence, I perceive.
    To spare her further torment, I shall leave.
DORINE:

(Leaving MARIANE, running after VALÈRE.)

    Again! You'll not escape, Sir; don't you try it.
    Come here, you two. Stop fussing, and be quiet.

(She takes VALÈRE by the hand, then MARIANE, and draws them together.)

VALÈRE:

(To DORINE.)

    What do you want of me?   85
MARIANE:

(To DORINE.)

                                    What is the point of this?
DORINE: We're going to a have little armistice.

(To VALÈRE.)

    Now, weren't you silly to get so overheated?
VALÈRE: Didn't you see how badly I was treated?
DORINE:

(To MARIANE.)

    Aren't you a simpleton, to have lost your head?
MARIANE: Didn't you hear the hateful things he said?   90
DORINE:

(To VALÈRE.)

    You're both great fools. Her sole desire, Valère,
    Is to be yours in marriage. To that I'll swear.

(To MARIANE.)

    He loves you only, and he wants no wife
    But you, Mariane. On that I'll stake my life.
MARIANE:

(To VALÈRE.)

    Then why you advised me so, I cannot see.   95
VALÈRE:

(To MARIANE.)

    On such a question, why ask advice of *me?*
DORINE: Oh, you're impossible. Give me your hands, you
    two.

(To VALÈRE.)

    Yours first.
VALÈRE:

(Giving DORINE his hand.)

But why?

DORINE:

(To MARIANE.*)*

And now a hand from you.

MARIANE:

(Also giving DORINE *her hand.)*

What are you doing?

DORINE: There: a perfect fit.
100   You suit each other better than you'll admit.

*(*VALÈRE *and* MARIANE *hold hands for some time without look-ing at each other.)*

VALÈRE:

(Turning toward MARIANE.*)*

Ah, come, don't be so haughty. Give a man
A look of kindness, won't you, Mariane?

*(*MARIANE *turns toward* VALÈRE *and smiles.)*

DORINE: I tell you, lovers are completely mad!

VALÈRE:

(To MARIANE.*)*

Now come, confess that you were very bad
105   To hurt my feelings as you did just now.
I have a just complaint, you must allow.

MARIANE: *You* must allow that you were most unpleasant . . .

DORINE: Let's table that discussion for the present;
Your father has a plan which must be stopped.

110   MARIANE: Advise us, then; what means must we adopt?

DORINE: We'll use all manner of means, and all at once.

(To MARIANE.*)*

Your father's addled; he's acting like a dunce.
Therefore you'd better humor the old fossil.
Pretend to yield to him, be sweet and docile,
115   And then postpone, as often as necessary,
The day on which you have agreed to marry.
You'll thus gain time, and time will turn the trick.
Sometimes, for instance, you'll be taken sick,
And that will seem good reason for delay;
120   Or some bad omen will make you change the day—
You'll dream of muddy water, or you'll pass
A dead man's hearse, or break a looking-glass.
If all else fails, no man can marry you
Unless you take his ring and say "I do."
125   But now, let's separate. If they should find
Us talking here, our plot might be divined.

(To VALÈRE.*)*

Go to your friends, and tell them what's occurred,
And have them urge her father to keep his word.
Meanwhile, we'll stir her brother into action,
130   And get Elmire, as well, to join our faction.
Good-bye.

VALÈRE:

(To MARIANE.*)*

Though each of us will do his best,
It's your true heart on which my hopes shall rest.

MARIANE:

(To VALÈRE.*)*

Regardless of what Father may decide,
None but Valère shall claim me as his bride.

VALÈRE: Oh, how those words content me! Come what will . . .   135

DORINE: Oh, lover, lovers! Their tongues are never still.
Be off, now.

VALÈRE:

(Turning to go, then turning back.)

One last word . . .

DORINE: No time to chat:
You leave by this door; and *you* leave by that.

*(*DORINE *pushes them, by the shoulders, toward opposing doors.)*

— ACT THREE —

SCENE I

DAMIS, DORINE

DAMIS: May lightning strike me even as I speak,
May all men call me cowardly and weak,
If any fear or scruple holds me back
From settling things, at once, with that great quack!

DORINE: Now, don't give way to violent emotion.   5
Your father's merely talked about this notion,
And words and deeds are far from being one.
Much that is talked about is left undone.

DAMIS: No, I must stop that scoundrel's machinations;
I'll go and tell him off; I'm out of patience.   10

DORINE: Do calm down and be practical. I had rather
My mistress dealt with him—and with your father.
She has some influence with Tartuffe, I've noted.
He hangs upon her words, seems most devoted,
And may, indeed, be smitten by her charm.   15
Pray Heaven it's true! 'Twould do our cause no harm.
She sent for him, just now, to sound him out
On this affair you're so incensed about;
She'll find out where he stands, and tell him, too,
What dreadful strife and trouble will ensue   20
If he lends countenance to your father's plan.
I couldn't get in to see him, but his man
Says that he's almost finished with his prayers.
Go, now. I'll catch him when he comes downstairs.

DAMIS: I want to hear this conference, and I will.   25

DORINE: No, they must be alone.

DAMIS: Oh, I'll keep still.

DORINE: Not you. I know your temper. You'd start a brawl,
And shout and stamp your foot and spoil it all.
Go on.

DAMIS: I won't; I have a perfect right . . .

DORINE: Lord, you're a nuisance! He's coming; get out of sight.   30

*(*DAMIS *conceals himself in a closet at the rear of the stage.)*

SCENE II

TARTUFFE, DORINE

TARTUFFE:

(Observing DORINE, *and calling to his manservant offstage.)*

Hang up my hair-shirt, put my scourge in place,
And pray, Laurent, for Heaven's perpetual grace.
I'm going to the prison now, to share

My last few coins with the poor wretches there.
DORINE:

(Aside.)

5   Dear God, what affectation! What a fake!
TARTUFFE: You wished to see me?
DORINE: Yes . . .
TARTUFFE:

(Taking a handkerchief from his pocket.)

                                        For mercy's sake,
    Please take this handkerchief, before you speak.
DORINE: What?
TARTUFFE: Cover that bosom, girl. The flesh is weak,
    And unclean thoughts are difficult to control.
10   Such sights as that can undermine the soul.
DORINE: Your soul, it seems, has very poor defenses,
    And flesh makes quite an impact on your senses.
    It's strange that you're so easily excited;
    My own desires are not so soon ignited,
15   And if I saw you naked as a beast,
    Not all your hide would tempt me in the least.
TARTUFFE: Girl, speak more modestly; unless you do,
    I shall be forced to take my leave of you.
DORINE: Oh, no, it's I who must be on my way;
20   I've just one little message to convey.
    Madame is coming down, and begs you, Sir,
    To wait and have a word or two with her.
TARTUFFE: Gladly.
DORINE:

(Aside.)

                        That had a softening effect!
    I think my guess about him was correct.
25   TARTUFFE: Will she be long?
DORINE: No: that's her step I hear.
    Ah, here she is, and I shall disappear.

SCENE III

ELMIRE, TARTUFFE

TARTUFFE: May Heaven, whose infinite goodness we adore,
    Preserve your body and soul forevermore,
    And bless your days, and answer thus the plea
    Of one who is its humblest votary.
5   ELMIRE: I thank you for that pious wish. But please,
    Do take a chair and let's be more at ease.

(They sit down.)

TARTUFFE: I trust that you are once more well and strong?
ELMIRE: Oh, yes: the fever didn't last for long.
TARTUFFE: My prayers are too unworthy, I am sure,
10   To have gained from Heaven this most gracious
            cure;
    But lately, Madam, my every supplication
    Has had for object your recuperation.
ELMIRE: You shouldn't have troubled so. I don't deserve it.
TARTUFFE: Your health is priceless, Madam, and to preserve it
15   I'd gladly give my own, in all sincerity.
ELMIRE: Sir, you outdo us all in Christian charity.
    You've been most kind. I count myself your debtor.
TARTUFFE: 'Twas nothing, Madam. I long to serve you better.
ELMIRE: There's a private matter I'm anxious to discuss.

I'm glad there's no one here to hinder us.   20
TARTUFFE: I too am glad; it floods my heart with bliss
    To find myself alone with you like this.
    For just this chance I've prayed with all my power—
    But prayed in vain, until this happy hour.
ELMIRE: This won't take long, Sir, and I hope you'll be   25
    Entirely frank and unconstrained with me.
TARTUFFE: Indeed, there's nothing I had rather do
    Than bare my inmost heart and soul to you.
    First, let me say that what remarks I've made
    About the constant visits you are paid   30
    Were prompted not by any mean emotion,
    But rather by a pure and deep devotion,
    A fervent zeal . . .
ELMIRE: No need for explanation.
    Your sole concern, I'm sure, was my salvation.
TARTUFFE:

(Taking ELMIRE's hand and pressing her fingertips.)

    Quite so; and such great fervor do I feel . . .   35
ELMIRE: Ooh! Please! You're pinching!
TARTUFFE: 'Twas from excess of
        zeal.
    I never meant to cause you pain, I swear.
    I'd rather . . .

(He places his hand on ELMIRE's knee.)

ELMIRE: What can your hand be doing there?
TARTUFFE: Feeling your gown; what soft, fine-woven stuff!
ELMIRE: Please, I'm extremely ticklish. That's enough.   40

(She draws her chair away; TARTUFFE pulls his after her.)

TARTUFFE:

(Fondling the lace collar of her gown.)

    My, my, what lovely lacework on your dress!
    The workmanship's miraculous, no less.
    I've not seen anything to equal it.
ELMIRE: Yes, quite. But let's talk business for a bit.
    They say my husband means to break his word   45
    And give his daughter to you, Sir. Had you heard?
TARTUFFE: He did once mention it. But I confess
    I dream of quite a different happiness.
    It's elsewhere, Madam, that my eyes discern
    The promise of that bliss for which I yearn.   50
ELMIRE: I see: you care for nothing here below.
TARTUFFE: Ah, well—my heart's not made of stone, you
        know.
ELMIRE: All your desires mount heavenward, I'm sure,
    In scorn of all that's earthly and impure.
TARTUFFE: A love of heavenly beauty does not preclude   55
    A proper love for earthly pulchritude;
    Our senses are quite rightly captivated
    By perfect works our Maker has created.
    Some glory clings to all that Heaven has made;
    In you, all Heaven's marvels are displayed.   60
    On that fair face, such beauties have been lavished,
    The eyes are dazzled and the heart is ravished;
    How could I look on you, O flawless creature,
    And not adore the Author of all Nature,
    Feeling a love both passionate and pure   65
    For you, his triumph of self-portraiture?
    At first, I trembled lest that love should be

A subtle snare that Hell had laid for me;
I vowed to flee the sight of you, eschewing
70 A rapture that might prove my soul's undoing;
But soon, fair being, I became aware
That my deep passion could be made to square
With rectitude, and with my bounden duty.
I thereupon surrendered to your beauty.
75 It is, I know, presumptuous on my part
To bring you this poor offering of my heart,
And it is not my merit, Heaven knows,
But your compassion on which my hopes repose.
You are my peace, my solace, my salvation;
80 On you depends my bliss—or desolation;
I bide your judgment and, as you think best,
I shall be either miserable or blest.

ELMIRE: Your declaration is most gallant, Sir,
But don't you think it's out of character?
85 You'd have done better to restrain your passion
And think before you spoke in such a fashion.
It ill becomes a pious man like you . . .

TARTUFFE: I may be pious, but I'm human too:
With your celestial charms before his eyes,
90 A man has not the power to be wise.
I know such words sound strangely, coming from me,
But I'm no angel, nor was meant to be,
And if you blame my passion, you must needs
Reproach as well the charms on which it feeds.
95 Your loveliness I had no sooner seen
Than you became my soul's unrivalled queen;
Before your seraph glance, divinely sweet,
My heart's defenses crumbled in defeat,
And nothing fasting, prayer, or tears might do
100 Could stay my spirit from adoring you.
My eyes, my sighs have told you in the past
What now my lips make bold to say at last,
And if, in your great goodness, you will deign
To look upon your slave, and ease his pain,—
105 If, in compassion for my soul's distress,
You'll stoop to comfort my unworthiness,
I'll raise to you, in thanks for that sweet manna,
An endless hymn, an infinite hosanna.
With me, of course, there need be no anxiety.
110 No fear of scandal or of notoriety.
These young court gallants, whom all the ladies fancy,
Are vain in speech, in action rash and chancy;
When they succeed in love, the world soon knows it;
No favor's granted them but they disclose it
115 And by the looseness of their tongues profane
The very altar where their hearts have lain.
Men of my sort, however, love discreetly,
And one may trust our reticence completely.
My keen concern for my good name insures
120 The absolute security of yours;
In short, I offer you, my dear Elmire,
Love without scandal, pleasure without fear.

ELMIRE: I've heard your well-turned speeches to the end,
And what you urge I clearly apprehend.
125 Aren't you afraid that I may take a notion
To tell my husband of your warm devotion,
And that, supposing he were duly told,
His feelings toward you might grow rather cold?

TARTUFFE: I know, dear lady, that your exceeding charity

Will lead your heart to pardon my temerity;   130
That you'll excuse my violent affection
As human weakness, human imperfection;
And that—O fairest!—you will bear in mind
That I'm but flesh and blood, and am not blind.

ELMIRE: Some women might do otherwise, perhaps,   135
But I shall be discreet about your lapse;
I'll tell my husband nothing of what's occurred
If, in return, you'll give your solemn word
To advocate as forcefully as you can
The marriage of Valère and Mariane,   140
Renouncing all desire to dispossess
Another of his rightful happiness,
And . .

SCENE IV

DAMIS, ELMIRE, TARTUFFE

DAMIS:

(Emerging from the closet where he has been hiding.)

        No! We'll not hush up this vile affair;
I heard it all inside that closet there,
Where Heaven, in order to confound the pride
Of this great rascal, prompted me to hide.
Ah, now I have my long-awaited chance   5
To punish his deceit and arrogance,
And give my father clear and shocking proof
Of the black character of his dear Tartuffe.

ELMIRE: Ah no, Damis; I'll be content if he
Will study to deserve my leniency.   10
I've promised silence—don't make me break my word;
To make a scandal would be too absurd.
Good wives laugh off such trifles, and forget them;
Why should they tell their husbands, and upset them?

DAMIS: You have your reasons for taking such a course, 15
And I have reasons, too, of equal force.
To spare him now would be insanely wrong.
I've swallowed my just wrath for far too long
And watched this insolent bigot bringing strife
And bitterness into our family life.   20
Too long he's meddled in my father's affairs,
Thwarting my marriage-hopes, and poor Valère's.
It's high time that my father was undeceived,
And now I've proof that can't be disbelieved—
Proof that was furnished me by Heaven above.   25
It's too good not to take advantage of.
This is my chance, and I deserve to lose it
If, for one moment, I hesitate to use it.

ELMIRE: Damis . . .

DAMIS: No, I must do what I think right.
Madam, my heart is bursting with delight,   30
And, say whatever you will, I'll not consent
To lose the sweet revenge on which I'm bent.
I'll settle matters without more ado;
And here, most opportunely, is my cue.

SCENE V

ORGON, DAMIS, TARTUFFE, ELMIRE

DAMIS: Father, I'm glad you've joined us. Let us advise you
Of some fresh news which doubtless will surprise you.
You've just now been repaid with interest

For all your loving-kindness to our guest.
5 He's proved his warm and grateful feelings toward you;
It's with a pair of horns he would reward you.
Yes, I surprised him with your wife, and heard
His whole adulterous offer, every word.
She, with her all too gentle disposition,
10 Would not have told you of his proposition;
But I shall not make terms with brazen lechery,
And feel that not to tell you would be treachery.
ELMIRE: And I hold that one's husband's peace of mind
Should not be spoilt by tattle of this kind.
15 One's honor doesn't require it: to be proficient
In keeping men at bay is quite sufficient.
These are my sentiments, and I wish, Damis,
That you had heeded me and held your peace.

SCENE VI

ORGON, DAMIS, TARTUFFE

ORGON: Can it be true, this dreadful thing I hear?
TARTUFFE: Yes, Brother, I'm a wicked man, I fear:
A wretched sinner, all depraved and twisted,
The greatest villain that has ever existed.
5 My life's one heap of crimes, which grows each minute;
There's naught but foulness and corruption in it;
And I perceive that Heaven, outraged by me,
Has chosen this occasion to mortify me.
Charge me with any deed you wish to name;
10 I'll not defend myself, but take the blame.
Believe what you are told, and drive Tartuffe
Like some base criminal from beneath your roof;
Yes, drive me hence, and with a parting curse:
I shan't protest, for I deserve far worse.
ORGON:

(To DAMIS.)

15 Ah, you deceitful boy, how dare you try
To stain his purity with so foul a lie?
DAMIS: What! Are you taken in by such a bluff?
Did you not hear . . . ?
ORGON: Enough, you rogue, enough!
TARTUFFE: Ah, Brother, let him speak: you're being unjust.
20 Believe his story; the boy deserves your trust.
Why, after all, should you have faith in me?
How can you know what I might do, or be?
Is it on my good actions that you base
Your favor? Do you trust my pious face?
25 Ah, no, don't be deceived by hollow shows;
I'm far, alas, from being what men suppose;
Though the world takes me for a man of worth,
I'm truly the most worthless man on earth.

(To DAMIS.)

Yes, my dear son, speak out now: call me the chief
30 Of sinners, a wretch, a murderer, a thief;
Load me with all the names men most abhor;
I'll not complain; I've earned them all, and more;
I'll kneel here while you pour them on my head
As a just punishment for the life I've led.
ORGON:

(To TARTUFFE.)

This is too much, dear Brother.   35

(To DAMIS.)

                              Have you no heart?
DAMIS: Are you so hoodwinked by this rascal's art. . . ?
ORGON: Be still, you monster.

(To TARTUFFE.)

                              Brother, I pray you, rise.

(To DAMIS.)

Villain!
DAMIS: But . . .
ORGON: Silence!
DAMIS: Can't you realize. . . ?
ORGON: Just one word more, and I'll tear you limb from limb.
TARTUFFE: In God's name, Brother, don't be harsh with him. 40
I'd rather far be tortured at the stake
Than see him bear one scratch for my poor sake.
ORGON:

(To DAMIS.)

Ingrate!
TARTUFFE: If I must beg you, on bended knee,
To pardon him . . .
ORGON:

(Falling to his knees, addressing TARTUFFE.)

                    Such goodness cannot be!

(To DAMIS.)

Now, *there's* true charity!   45
DAMIS: What, you. . . ?
ORGON: Villain, be still!
I know your motives; I know you wish him ill:
Yes, all of you—wife, children, servants, all—
Conspire against him and desire his fall,
Employing every shameful trick you can
To alienate me from this saintly man.   50
Ah, but the more you seek to drive him away,
The more I'll do to keep him. Without delay,
I'll spite this household and confound its pride
By giving him my daughter as his bride.
DAMIS: You're going to force her to accept his hand? 55
ORGON: Yes, and this very night, d'you understand?
I shall defy you all, and make it clear
That I'm the one who gives the orders here.
Come, wretch, kneel down and clasp his blessed feet,
And ask his pardon for your black deceit.   60
DAMIS: I ask that swindler's pardon? Why, I'd rather . . .
ORGON: So! You insult him, and defy your father!
A stick! A stick! (To TARTUFFE.) No, no—release me, do.

(To DAMIS.)

Out of my house this minute! Be off with you,
And never dare set foot in it again.   65
DAMIS: Well, I shall go, but . . .
ORGON: Well, go quickly, then.
I disinherit you; an empty purse
Is all you'll get from me—except my curse!

SCENE VII

ORGON, TARTUFFE

ORGON: How he blasphemed your goodness! What a son!
TARTUFFE: Forgive him, Lord, as I've already done.

(To ORGON.*)*

You can't know how it hurts when someone tries
To blacken me in my dear Brother's eyes.
5 ORGON: Ahh!
TARTUFFE: The mere thought of such ingratitude
Plunges my soul into so dark a mood . . .
Such horror grips my heart . . . I gasp for breath,
And cannot speak, and feel myself near death.
ORGON:

(He runs, in tears, to the door through which he has just driven his son.)

You blackguard! Why did I spare you? Why did I not
10 Break you in little pieces on the spot?
Compose yourself, and don't be hurt, dear friend.
TARTUFFE: These scenes, these dreadful quarrels, have got to
end.
I've much upset your household, and I perceive
That the best thing will be for me to leave.
15 ORGON: What are you saying!
TARTUFFE: They're all against me here;
They'd have you think me false and insincere.
ORGON: Ah, what of that? Have I ceased believing in you?
TARTUFFE: Their adverse talk will certainly continue,
And charges which you now repudiate
20 You may find credible at a later date.
ORGON: No, Brother, never.
TARTUFFE: Brother, a wife can sway
Her husband's mind in many a subtle way.
ORGON: No, no.
TARTUFFE: To leave at once is the solution;
Thus only can I end their persecution.
25 ORGON: No, no, I'll not allow it; you shall remain.
TARTUFFE: Ah, well; 'twill mean much martyrdom and pain,
But if you wish it . . .
ORGON: Ah!
TARTUFFE: Enough; so be it.
But one thing must be settled, as I see it.
For your dear honor, and for our friendship's sake,
30 There's one precaution I feel bound to take.
I shall avoid your wife, and keep away . . .
ORGON: No, you shall not, whatever they may say.
It pleases me to vex them, and for spite
I'd have them see you with her day and night.
35 What's more, I'm going to drive them to despair
By making you my only son and heir;
This very day, I'll give to you alone
Clear deed and title to everything I own.
A dear, good friend and son-in-law-to-be
40 Is more than wife, or child, or kin to me.
Will you accept my offer, dearest son?
TARTUFFE: In all things, let the will of Heaven be done.
ORGON: Poor fellow! Come, we'll go draw up the deed.
Then let them burst with disappointed greed!

— ACT FOUR —

SCENE I

CLÉANTE, TARTUFFE

CLÉANTE: Yes, all the town's discussing it, and truly,
Their comments do not flatter you unduly.
I'm glad we've met, Sir, and I'll give my view
Of this sad matter in a word or two.
As for who's guilty, that I shan't discuss;   5
Let's say it was Damis who caused the fuss;
Assuming, then, that you have been ill-used
By young Damis, and groundlessly accused,
Ought not a Christian to forgive, and ought
He not to stifle every vengeful thought?   10
Should you stand by and watch a father make
His only son an exile for your sake?
Again I tell you frankly, be advised:
The whole town, high and low, is scandalized;
This quarrel must be mended, and my advice is   15
Not to push matters to a further crisis.
No, sacrifice your wrath to God above,
And help Damis regain his father's love.
TARTUFFE: Alas, for my part I should take great joy
In doing so. I've nothing against the boy.   20
I pardon all, I harbor no resentment;
To serve him would afford me much contentment.
But Heaven's interest will not have it so:
If he comes back, then I shall have to go.
After his conduct—so extreme, so vicious—   25
Our further intercourse would look suspicious.
God knows what people would think! Why, they'd describe
My goodness to him as a sort of bribe;
They'd say that out of guilt I made pretense
Of loving-kindness and benevolence—   30
That, fearing my accuser's tongue, I strove
To buy his silence with a show of love.
CLÉANTE: Your reasoning is badly warped and stretched,
And these excuses, Sir, are most far-fetched.
Why put yourself in charge of Heaven's cause?   35
Does Heaven need our help to enforce its laws?
Leave vengeance to the Lord, Sir; while we live,
Our duty's not to punish, but forgive;
And what the Lord commands, we should obey
Without regard to what the world may say.   40
What! Shall the fear of being misunderstood
Prevent our doing what is right and good?
No, no; let's simply do what Heaven ordains,
And let no other thoughts perplex our brains.
TARTUFFE: Again, Sir, let me say that I've forgiven   45
Damis, and thus obeyed the laws of Heaven;
But I am not commanded by the Bible
To live with one who smears my name with libel.
CLÉANTE: Were you commanded, Sir, to indulge the whim
Of poor Orgon, and to encourage him   50
In suddenly transferring to your name
A large estate to which you have no claim?
TARTUFFE: 'Twould never occur to those who know me best
To think I acted from self-interest.
The treasures of this world I quite despise;   55
Their specious glitter does not charm my eyes;

And if I have resigned myself to taking
The gift which my dear Brother insists on making,
I do so only, as he well understands,
60 Lest so much wealth fall into wicked hands,
Lest those to whom it might descend in time
Turn it to purposes of sin and crime,
And not, as I shall do, make use of it.
For Heaven's glory and mankind's benefit.
65 CLÉANTE: Forget these trumped-up fears. Your argument
Is one the rightful heir might well resent;
It *is* a moral burden to inherit
Such wealth, but give Damis a chance to bear it.
And would it not be worse to be accused
70 Of swindling, than to see that wealth misused?
I'm shocked that you allowed Orgon to broach
This matter, and that you feel no self-reproach;
Does true religion teach that lawful heirs
May freely be deprived of what is theirs?
75 And if the Lord has told you in your heart
That you and young Damis must dwell apart,
Would it not be the decent thing to beat
A generous and honorable retreat,
Rather than let the son of the house be sent,
80 For your convenience, into banishment?
Sir, if you wish to prove the honesty
Of your intentions . . .
TARTUFFE: Sir, it is half-past three.
I've certain pious duties to attend to,
And hope my prompt departure won't offend you.
CLÉANTE:

(*Alone.*)

Damn.

SCENE II

ELMIRE, MARIANE, CLÉANTE, DORINE

DORINE: Stay, Sir, and help Mariane, for Heaven's sake!
She's suffering so, I fear her heart will break.
Her father's plan to marry her off tonight
Has put the poor child in a desperate plight.
5 I hear him coming. Let's stand together, now,
And see if we can't change his mind, somehow,
About this match we all deplore and fear.

SCENE III

ORGON, ELMIRE, MARIANE, CLÉANTE, DORINE

ORGON: Hah! Glad to find you all assembled here.

(*To* MARIANE.)

This contract, child, contains your happiness,
And what it says I think your heart can guess.
MARIANE:

(*Falling to her knees.*)

Sir, by that Heaven which sees me here distressed,
5 And by whatever else can move your breast,
Do not employ a father's power, I pray you,
To crush my heart and force it to obey you,
Nor by your harsh commands oppress me so
That I'll begrudge the duty which I owe—

And do not so embitter and enslave me   10
That I shall hate the very life you gave me.
If my sweet hopes must perish, if you refuse
To give me to the one I've dared to choose,
Spare me at least—I beg you, I implore—
The pain of wedding one whom I abhor;   15
And do not, by a heartless use of force,
Drive me to contemplate some desperate course.
ORGON:

(*Feeling himself touched by her.*)

Be firm, my soul. No human weakness, now.
MARIANE: I don't resent your love for him. Allow
Your heart free rein, Sir; give him your property,   20
And if that's not enough, take mine from me;
He's welcome to my money; take it, do,
But don't, I pray, include my person too.
Spare me, I beg you; and let me end the tale
Of my sad days behind a convent veil.   25
ORGON: A convent! Hah! When crossed in their amours,
All lovesick girls have the same thought as yours.
Get up! The more you loathe the man, and dread
    him,
The more ennobling it will be to wed him.
Marry Tartuffe, and mortify your flesh!   30
Enough; don't start that whimpering afresh.
DORINE: But why. . . ?
ORGON: Be still, there. Speak when you're
    spoken to.
Not one more bit of impudence out of you.
CLÉANTE: If I may offer a word of counsel here . . .
ORGON: Brother, in counseling you have no peer;   35
All your advice is forceful, sound, and clever;
I don't propose to follow it, however.
ELMIRE:

(*To* ORGON.)

I am amazed, and don't know what to say;
Your blindness simply takes my breath away.
You are indeed bewitched, to take no warning   40
From our account of what occurred this morning.
ORGON: Madam, I know a few plain facts, and one
Is that you're partial to my rascal son;
Hence, when he sought to make Tartuffe the victim
Of a base lie, you dared not contradict him.   45
Ah, but you underplayed your part, my pet;
You should have looked more angry, more upset.
ELMIRE: When men make overtures, must we reply
With righteous anger and a battle-cry?
Must we turn back their amorous advances   50
With sharp reproaches and with fiery glances?
Myself, I find such offers merely amusing,
And make no scenes and fusses in refusing;
My taste is for good-natured rectitude,
And I dislike the savage sort of prude   55
Who guards her virtue with her teeth and claws,
And tears men's eyes out for the slightest cause;
The Lord preserve me from such honor as that,
Which bites and scratches like an alley-cat!
I've found that a polite and cool rebuff   60
Discourages a lover quite enough.

ORGON: I know the facts, and I shall not be shaken.
ELMIRE: I marvel at your power to be mistaken.
     Would it, I wonder, carry weight with you
65   If I could *show* you that our tale was true?
ORGON: Show me?
ELMIRE: Yes.
ORGON: Rot.
ELMIRE: Come, what if I found a way
     To make you see the facts as plain as day?
ORGON: Nonsense.
ELMIRE: Do answer me; don't be absurd.
     I'm not now asking you to trust our word.
70   Suppose that from some hiding-place in here
     You learned the whole sad truth by eye and ear—
     What would you say of your good friend, after that?
ORGON: Why, I'd say . . . nothing, by Jehoshaphat!
     It can't be true.
ELMIRE: You've been too long deceived,
75   And I'm quite tired of being disbelieved.
     Come now: let's put my statements to the test,
     And you shall see the truth made manifest.
ORGON: I'll take that challenge. Now do your uttermost.
     We'll see how you make good your empty boast.
ELMIRE:

(To DORINE.)

80   Send him to me.
DORINE: He's crafty; it may be hard
     To catch the cunning scoundrel off his guard.
ELMIRE: No, amorous men are gullible. Their conceit
     So blinds them that they're never hard to cheat.
     Have him come down *(To* CLÉANTE *and* MARIANE.) Please
          leave us, for a bit.

SCENE IV

ELMIRE, ORGON

ELMIRE: Pull up this table, and get under it.
ORGON: What?
ELMIRE: It's essential that you be well-hidden.
ORGON: Why there?
ELMIRE: Oh, Heavens! Just do as you are bidden
     I have my plans; we'll soon see how they fare.
5   Under the table, now; and once you're there,
     Take care that you are neither seen nor heard.
ORGON: Well, I'll indulge you, since I gave my word
     To see you through this infantile charade.
ELMIRE: Once it is over, you'll be glad we played.

(To her husband, who is now under the table.)

10   I'm going to act quite strangely, now, and you
     Must not be shocked at anything I do.
     Whatever I may say, you must excuse
     As part of that deceit I'm forced to use.
     I shall employ sweet speeches in the task
15   Of making that impostor drop his mask;
     I'll give encouragement to his bold desires,
     And furnish fuel to his amorous fires.
     Since it's for your sake, and for his destruction,
     That I shall seem to yield to his seduction,
20   I'll gladly stop whenever you decide

That all your doubts are fully satisfied.
I'll count on you, as soon as you have seen
What sort of man he is, to intervene,
And not expose me to his odious lust
One moment longer than you feel you must.   25
Remember: you're to save me from my plight
Whenever . . . He's coming! Hush! Keep out of sight!

SCENE V

TARTUFFE, ELMIRE, ORGON

TARTUFFE: You wish to have a word with me, I'm told.
ELMIRE: Yes. I've a little secret to unfold.
     Before I speak, however, it would be wise
     To close that door, and look about for spies.

*(*TARTUFFE *goes to the door, closes it, and returns.)*

     The very last thing that must happen now   5
     Is a repetition of this morning's row.
     I've never been so badly caught off guard.
     Oh, how I feared for you! You saw how hard
     I tried to make that troublesome Damis
     Control his dreadful temper, and hold his peace.   10
     In my confusion, I didn't have the sense
     Simply to contradict his evidence;
     But as it happened, that was for the best,
     And all has worked out in our interest.
     This storm has only bettered your position;   15
     My husband doesn't have the least suspicion,
     And now, in mockery of those who do,
     He bids me be continually with you.
     And that is why, quite fearless of reproof,
     I now can be alone with my Tartuffe,   20
     And why my heart—perhaps too quick to yield—
     Feels free to let its passion be revealed.
TARTUFFE: Madam, your words confuse me. Not long ago,
     You spoke in quite a different style, you know.
ELMIRE: Ah, Sir, if that refusal made you smart,   25
     It's little that you know of woman's heart,
     Or what that heart is trying to convey
     When it resists in such a feeble way!
     Always, at first, our modesty prevents
     The frank avowal of tender sentiments;   30
     However high the passion which inflames us,
     Still, to confess its power somehow shames us.
     Thus we reluct, at first, yet in a tone
     Which tells you that our heart is overthrown,
     That what our lips deny, our pulse confesses,   35
     And that, in time, all noes will turn to yesses.
     I fear my words are all too frank and free,
     And a poor proof of woman's modesty;
     But since I'm started, tell me, if you will—
     Would I have tried to make Damis be still,   40
     Would I have listened, calm and unoffended,
     Until your lengthy offer of love was ended,
     And been so very mild in my reaction,
     Had your sweet words not given me satisfaction?
     And when I tried to force you to undo   45
     The marriage-plans my husband has in view,
     What did my urgent pleading signify
     If not that I admired you, and that I

50   Deplored the thought that someone else might own
    Part of a heart I wished for mine alone?
  TARTUFFE: Madam, no happiness is so complete
    As when, from lips we love, come words so sweet;
    Their nectar floods my every sense, and drains
    In honeyed rivulets through all my veins.
55   To please you is my joy, my only goal;
    Your love is the restorer of my soul;
    And yet I must beg leave, now, to confess
    Some lingering doubts as to my happiness
    Might this not be a trick? Might not the catch
60   Be that you wish me to break off the match
    With Mariane, and so have feigned to love me?
    I shan't quite trust your fond opinion of me
    Until the feelings you've expressed so sweetly
    Are demonstrated somewhat more concretely,
65   And you have shown, by certain kind concessions,
    That I may put my faith in your professions.
  ELMIRE:

(She coughs, to warn her husband.)

    Why be in such a hurry? Must my heart
    Exhaust its bounty at the very start?
    To make that sweet admission cost me dear,
70   But you'll not be content, it would appear,
    Unless my store of favors is disbursed
    To the last farthing, and at the very first.
  TARTUFFE: The less we merit, the less we dare to hope,
    And with our doubts, mere words can never cope.
75   We trust no promised bliss till we receive it;
    Not till a joy is ours can we believe it.
    I, who so little merit your esteem,
    Can't credit this fulfillment of my dream,
    And shan't believe it, Madam, until I savor
80   Some palpable assurance of your favor.
  ELMIRE: My, how tyrannical your love can be,
    And how it flusters and perplexes me!
    How furiously you take one's heart in hand,
    And make your every wish a fierce command!
85   Come, must you hound and harry me to death?
    Will you not give me time to catch my breath?
    Can it be right to press me with such force,
    Give me no quarter, show me no remorse,
    And take advantage, by your stern insistence,
90   Of the fond feelings which weaken my resistance?
  TARTUFFE: Well, if you look with favor upon my love,
    Why, then, begrudge me some clear proof thereof?
  ELMIRE: But how can I consent without offense
    To Heaven, toward which you feel such reverence?
95   TARTUFFE: If Heaven is all that holds you back, don't worry.
    I can remove that hindrance in a hurry.
    Nothing of that sort need obstruct our path.
  ELMIRE: Must one not be afraid of Heaven's wrath?
  TARTUFFE: Madam, forget such fears, and be my pupil,
100   And I shall teach you how to conquer scruple.
    Some joys, it's true, are wrong in Heaven's eyes;
    Yet Heaven is not averse to compromise;
    There is a science, lately formulated,
    Whereby one's conscience may be liberated,
105   And any wrongful act you care to mention
    May be redeemed by purity of intention.

    I'll teach you, Madam, the secrets of that science;
    Meanwhile, just place on me your full reliance.
    Assuage my keen desires, and feel no dread:
    The sin, if any, shall be on my head.   110

(ELMIRE coughs, this time more loudly.)

  You've a bad cough.
  ELMIRE: Yes, yes. It's bad indeed.
  TARTUFFE:

(Producing a little paper bag.)

    A bit of licorice may be what you need.
  ELMIRE: No, I've a stubborn cold, it seems. I'm sure it
    Will take much more than licorice to cure it.
  TARTUFFE: How aggravating.   115
  ELMIRE: Oh, more than I can say.
  TARTUFFE: If you're still troubled, think of things this way:
    No one shall know our joys, save us alone,
    And there's no evil till the act is known;
    It's scandal, Madam, which makes it an offense,
    And it's no sin to sin in confidence.   120
  ELMIRE:

(Having coughed once more.)

    Well, clearly I must do as you require,
    And yield to your importunate desire.
    It is apparent, now, that nothing less
    Will satisfy you, and so I acquiesce.
    To go so far is much against my will;   125
    I'm vexed that it should come to this; but still,
    Since you are so determined on it, since you
    Will not allow mere language to convince you,
    And since you ask for concrete evidence, I
    See nothing for it, now, but to comply.   130
    If this is sinful, if I'm wrong to do it,
    So much the worse for him who drove me to it.
    The fault can surely not be charged to me.
  TARTUFFE: Madam, the fault is mine, if fault there be,
    And . . .   135
  ELMIRE: Open the door a little, and peek out;
    I wouldn't want my husband poking about.
  TARTUFFE: Why worry about the man? Each day he grows
    More gullible; one can lead him by the nose.
    To find us here would fill him with delight,
    And if he saw the worst, he'd doubt his sight.   140
  ELMIRE: Nevertheless, do step out for a minute
    Into the hall, and see that no one's in it.

SCENE VI

ORGON, ELMIRE

ORGON:

(Coming out from under the table.)

    That man's a perfect monster, I must admit!
    I'm simply stunned. I can't get over it.
  ELMIRE: What, coming out so soon? How premature!
    Get back in hiding, and wait until you're sure.
    Stay till the end, and be convinced completely;   5
    We mustn't stop till things are proved concretely.
  ORGON: Hell never harbored anything so vicious!

ELMIRE: Tut, don't be hasty. Try to be judicious.
   Wait, and be certain that there's no mistake.
10 No jumping to conclusions, for Heaven's sake!

(*She places* ORGON *behind her, as* TARTUFFE *re-enters.*)

SCENE VII

TARTUFFE, ELMIRE, ORGON

TARTUFFE:

(*Not seeing* ORGON.)

   Madam, all things have worked out to perfection;
   I've given the neighboring rooms a full inspection;
   No one's about; and now I may at last . . .

ORGON:

(*Intercepting him.*)

   Hold on, my passionate fellow, not so fast!
5 I should advise a little more restraint.
   Well, so you thought you'd fool me, my dear saint!
   How soon you wearied of the saintly life—
   Wedding my daughter, and coveting my wife!
   I've long suspected you, and had a feeling
10 That soon I'd catch you at your double-dealing.
   Just now, you've given me evidence galore;
   It's quite enough; I have no wish for more.

ELMIRE:

(*To* TARTUFFE.)

   I'm sorry to have treated you so slyly.
   But circimstances forced me to be wily.
15 TARTUFFE: Brother, you can't think . . .
   ORGON: No more talk from
      you;
   Just leave this household, without more ado.
   TARTUFFE: What I intended . . .
   ORGON: That seems fairly clear.
   Spare me your falsehoods and get out of here.
   TARTUFFE: No, I'm the master, and you're the one to go!
20 This house belongs to me, I'll have you know,
   And I shall show you that you can't hurt *me*
   By this contemptible conspiracy,
   That those who cross me know not what they do,
   And that I've means to expose and punish you,
25 Avenge offended Heaven, and make you grieve
   That ever you dared order me to leave.

SCENE VIII

ELMIRE, ORGON

ELMIRE: What was the point of all that angry chatter?
ORGON: Dear God, I'm worried. This is no laughing matter.
ELMIRE: How so?
ORGON: I fear I understood his drift.
   I'm much disturbed about that deed of gift.
5 ELMIRE: You gave him. . . ?
   ORGON: Yes, it's all been drawn and
      signed.
   But one thing more is weighing on my mind.
ELMIRE: What's that?
ORGON: I'll tell you; but first let's see if there's
   A certain strong-box in his room upstairs.

— ACT FIVE —

SCENE I

ORGON, CLÉANTE

CLÉANTE: Where are you going so fast?
ORGON: God knows!
CLÉANTE: Then wait;
   Let's have a conference, and deliberate
   On how this situation's to be met.
ORGON: That strong-box has me utterly upset;
   This is the worst of many, many shocks.   5
CLÉANTE: Is there some fearful mystery in that box?
ORGON: My poor friend Argas brought that box to me
   With his own hands, in utmost secrecy;
   'Twas on the very morning of his flight.
   It's full of papers which, if they came to light,   10
   Would ruin him—or such is my impression.
CLÉANTE: Then why did you let it out of your possession?
ORGON: Those papers vexed my conscience, and it seemed
      best
   To ask the counsel of my pious guest.
   The cunning scoundrel got me to agree   15
   To leave the strong-box in his custody,
   So that, in case of an investigation,
   I could employ a slight equivocation
   And swear I didn't have it, and thereby,
   At no expense to conscience, tell a lie.   20
CLÉANTE: It looks to me as if you're out on a limb.
   Trusting him with that box, and offering him
   That deed of gift, were actions of a kind
   Which scarcely indicate a prudent mind.
   With two such weapons, he has the upper hand,   25
   And since you're vulnerable, as matters stand,
   You erred once more in bringing him to bay,
   You should have acted in some subtler way.
ORGON: Just think of it: behind that fervent face,
   A heart so wicked, and a soul so base!   30
   I took him in, a hungry beggar, and then . . .
   Enough, by God! I'm through with pious men:
   Henceforth I'll hate the whole false brotherhood.
   And persecute them worse than Satan could.
CLÉANTE: Ah, there you go—extravagant as ever.   35
   Why can you not be rational? You never
   Manage to take the middle course, it seems,
   But jump, instead, between absurd extremes
   You've recognized your recent grave mistake
   In falling victim to a pious fake;   40
   Now, to correct that error, must you embrace
   An even greater error in its place,
   And judge our worthy neighbors as a whole
   By what you've learned of one corrupted soul?
   Come, just because one rascal made you swallow   45
   A show of zeal which turned out to be hollow,
   Shall you conclude that all men are deceivers,
   And that, today, there are no true believers?
   Let atheists make that foolish inference;
   Learn to distinguish virtue from pretense,   50
   Be cautious in bestowing admiration,
   And cultivate a sober moderation.
   Don't humor fraud, but also don't asperse

True piety; the latter fault is worse,
55   And it is best to err, if err one must,
As you have done, upon the side of trust.

SCENE II

DAMIS, ORGON, CLÉANTE

DAMIS: Father, I hear that scoundrel's uttered threats
Against you; that he pridefully forgets
How, in his need, he was befriended by you,
And means to use your gifts to crucify you.
5   ORGON: It's true, my boy. I'm too distressed for tears.
DAMIS: Leave it to me, Sir; let me trim his ears.
Faced with such insolence, we must not waver.
I shall rejoice in doing you the favor
Of cutting short his life, and your distress.
10   CLÉANTE: What a display of young hotheadedness!
Do learn to moderate your fits of rage.
In this just kingdom, this enlightened age,
One does not settle things by violence.

SCENE III

MADAME PERNELLE, MARIANE, ELMIRE, DORINE, DAMIS,
ORGON, CLÉANTE

MADAME PERNELLE: I hear strange tales of very strange events.
ORGON: Yes, strange events which these two eyes beheld.
The man's ingratitude is unparalleled.
I save a wretched pauper from starvation.
5   House him, and treat him like a blood relation,
Shower him every day with my largesse,
Give him my daughter, and all that I possess;
And meanwhile the unconscionable knave
Tries to induce my wife to misbehave;
10   And not content with such extreme rascality,
Now threatens me with my own liberality,
And aims, by taking base advantage of
The gifts I gave him out of Christian love,
To drive me from my house, a ruined man,
15   And make me end a pauper, as he began.
DORINE: Poor fellow!
MADAME PERNELLE: No, my son, I'll never bring
Myself to think him guilty of such a thing.
ORGON: How's that?
MADAME PERNELLE: The righteous always were maligned.
ORGON: Speak clearly, Mother. Say what's on your mind.
20   MADAME PERNELLE: I mean that I can smell a rat, my dear.
You know how everybody hates him, here.
ORGON: That has no bearing on the case at all.
MADAME PERNELLE: I told you a hundred times, when you
were small,
That virtue in this world is hated ever;
25   Malicious men may die, but malice never.
ORGON: No doubt that's true, but how does it apply?
MADAME PERNELLE: They've turned you against him by a
clever lie.
ORGON: I've told you, I was there and saw it done.
MADAME PERNELLE: Ah, slanderers will stop at nothing, Son.
30   ORGON: Mother, I'll lose my temper . . . For the last time,
I tell you I was witness to the crime.

MADAME PERNELLE: The tongues of spite are busy night and
noon
And to their venom no man is immune.
ORGON: You're talking nonsense. Can't you realize
I saw it; saw it; saw it with my eyes?   35
Saw, do you understand me? Must I shout it
Into your ears before you'll cease to doubt it?
MADAME PERNELLE: Appearances can deceive, my son.
Dear me,
We cannot always judge by what we see.
ORGON: Drat! Drat!   40
MADAME PERNELLE: One often interprets things awry;
Good can seem evil to a suspicious eye.
ORGON: Was I to see his pawing at Elmire
As an act of charity?
MADAME PERNELLE: Till his guilt is clear,
A man deserves the benefit of the doubt.
You should have waited, to see how things turned out. 45
ORGON: Great God in Heaven, what more proof did I need?
Was I to sit there, watching, until he'd . . .
You drive me to the brink of impropriety.
MADAME PERNELLE: No, no, a man of such surpassing piety
Could not do such a thing. You cannot shake me.   50
I don't believe it, and you shall not make me.
ORGON: You vex me so that, if you weren't my mother,
I'd say to you . . . some dreadful thing or other.
DORINE: It's your turn now, Sir, not to be listened to;
You'd not trust us, and now she won't trust you.   55
CLÉANTE: My friends, we're wasting time which should be
spent
In facing up to our predicament.
I fear that scoundrel's threats weren't made in sport.
DAMIS: Do you think he'd have the nerve to go to court?
ELMIRE: I'm sure he won't: they'd find it all too crude   60
A case of swindling and ingratitude.
CLÉANTE: Don't be too sure. He won't be at a loss
To give his claims a high and righteous gloss;
And clever rogues with far less valid cause
Have trapped their victims in a web of laws.   65
I say again that to antagonize
A man so strongly armed was most unwise.
ORGON: I know it; but the man's appalling cheek
Outraged me so, I couldn't control my pique.
CLÉANTE: I wish to Heaven that we could devise   70
Some truce between you, or some compromise.
ELMIRE: If I had known what cards he held, I'd not
Have roused his anger by my little plot.
ORGON:

(To DORINE, *as* M. LOYAL *enters.*)

What is that fellow looking for? Who is he?
Go talk to him—and tell him that I'm busy.   75

SCENE IV

MONSIEUR LOYAL, MADAME PERNELLE, ORGON, DAMIS, MARI-
ANE, DORINE, ELMIRE, CLÉANTE

MONSIEUR LOYAL: Good day, dear sister. Kindly let me see
Your master.
DORINE: He's involved with company,
And cannot be disturbed just now, I fear.

MONSIEUR LOYAL: I hate to intrude; but what has brought me
here

5   Will not disturb your master, in any event.
Indeed, my news will make him most content.

DORINE: Your name?

MONSIEUR LOYAL: Just say that I bring greetings from
Monsieur Tartuffe, on whose behalf I've come.

DORINE:

(To ORGON.*)*

Sir, he's a very gracious man, and bears

10   A message from Tartuffe, which, he declares,
Will make you most content.

CLÉANTE: Upon my word,
I think this man had best be seen, and heard.

ORGON: Perhaps he has some settlement to suggest.
How shall I treat him? What manner would be best?

15 CLÉANTE: Control your anger, and if he should mention
Some fair adjustment, give him your full attention.

MONSIEUR LOYAL: Good health to you, good Sir. May
Heaven confound
Your enemies, and may your joys abound.

ORGON:

(Aside, to CLÉANTE.*)*

A gentle salutation: it confirms

20   My guess that he is here to offer terms.

MONSIEUR LOYAL: I've always held your family most dear;
I served your father, Sir, for many a year.

ORGON: Sir, I must ask your pardon; to my shame,
I cannot now recall your face or name.

25 MONSIEUR LOYAL: Loyal's my name; I come from Normandy,
And I'm a bailiff, in all modesty.
For forty years, praise God, it's been my boast
To serve with honor in that vital post,
And I am here, Sir, if you will permit

30   The liberty, to serve you with this writ . . .

ORGON: To—*what?*

MONSIEUR LOYAL: Now, please, Sir, let us have no friction:
It's nothing but an order of eviction.
You are to move your goods and family out
And make way for new occupants, without

35   Deferment or delay, and give the keys . . .

ORGON: I? Leave this house?

MONSIEUR LOYAL: Why yes, Sir, if you please.
This house, Sir, from the cellar to the roof,
Belongs now to the good Monsieur Tartuffe,
And he is lord and master of your estate

40   By virtue of a deed of present date,
Drawn in due form, with clearest legal phrasing . . .

DAMIS: Your insolence is utterly amazing!

MONSIEUR LOYAL: Young man, my business here is not with
you,
But with your wise and temperate father, who,

45   Like every worthy citizen, stands in awe
Of justice, and would never obstruct the law.

ORGON: But . . .

MONSIEUR LOYAL: Not for a million, Sir, would you rebel
Against authority; I know that well.
You'll not make trouble, Sir, or interfere

50   With the execution of my duties here.

DAMIS: Someone may execute a smart tattoo
On that black jacket of yours, before you're through.

MONSIEUR LOYAL: Sir, bid your son be silent. I'd much regret
Having to mention such a nasty threat
Of violence, in writing my report.   55

DORINE:

(Aside.)

This man Loyal's a most disloyal sort!

MONSIEUR LOYAL: I love all men of upright character,
And when I agreed to serve these papers, Sir,
It was your feelings that I had in mind.
I couldn't bear to see the case assigned   60
To someone else, who might esteem you less
And so subject you to unpleasantness.

ORGON: What's more unpleasant than telling a man to leave
His house and home?

MONSIEUR LOYAL: You'd like a short reprieve?
If you desire, Sir, I shall not press you,   65
But wait until tomorrow to dispossess you.
Splendid. I'll come and spend the night here, then,
Most quietly, with half a score of men.
For form's sake, you might bring me, just before
You go to bed, the keys to the front door.   70
My men, I promise, will be on their best
Behavior, and will not disturb your rest.
But bright and early, Sir, you must be quick
And move out all your furniture, every stick;
The men I've chosen are both young and strong,   75
And with their help it shouldn't take you long.
In short, I'll make things pleasant and convenient,
And since I'm being so extremely lenient,
Please show me, Sir, a like consideration,
And give me your entire cooperation.   80

ORGON:

(Aside.)

I may be all but bankrupt, but I vow
I'd give a hundred louis, here and now,
Just for the pleasure of landing one good clout
Right on the end of that complacent snout.

CLÉANTE: Careful; don't make things worse.   85

DAMIS: My bootsole
itches
To give that beggar a good kick in the breeches.

DORINE: Monsieur Loyal, I'd love to hear the whack
Of a stout stick across your fine broad back.

MONSIEUR LOYAL: Take care: a woman too may go to jail if
She uses threatening language to a bailiff.   90

CLÉANTE: Enough, enough, Sir. This must not go on.
Give me that paper, please, and then begone.

MONSIEUR LOYAL: Well, *au revoir.* God give you all good
cheer!

ORGON: May God confound you, and him who sent you here!

SCENE V

ORGON, CLÉANTE, MARIANE, ELMIRE, MADAME PERNELLE,
DORINE, DAMIS

ORGON: Now, Mother, was I right or not? This writ
Should change your notion of Tartuffe a bit.
Do you perceive his villainy at last?

MADAME PERNELLE: I'm thunderstruck. I'm utterly aghast.
5 DORINE: Oh, come, be fair. You mustn't take offense
At this new proof of his benevolence.
He's acting out of selfless love, I know.
Material things enslave the soul, and so
He kindly has arranged your liberation
10 From all that might endanger your salvation.
ORGON: Will you not ever hold your tongue, you dunce?
CLÉANTE: Come, you must take some action, and at once.
ELMIRE: Go tell the world of the low trick he's tried.
The deed of gift is surely nullified
15 By such behavior, and public rage will not
Permit the wretch to carry out his plot.

SCENE VI

VALÈRE, ORGON, CLÉANTE, ELMIRE, MARIANE, MADAME PER-
NELLE, DAMIS, DORINE

VALÈRE: Sir, though I hate to bring you more bad news,
Such is the danger that I cannot choose.
A friend who is extremely close to me
And knows my interest in your family
5 Has, for my sake, presumed to violate
The secrecy that's due to things of state,
And sends me word that you are in a plight
From which your one salvation lies in flight.
That scoundrel who's imposed upon you so
10 Denounced you to the King an hour ago
And, as supporting evidence, displayed
The strong-box of a certain renegade
Whose secret papers, so he testified,
You had disloyally agreed to hide.
15 I don't know just what charges may be pressed,
But there's a warrant out for your arrest;
Tartuffe has been instructed, furthermore,
To guide the arresting officer to your door.
CLÉANTE: He's clearly done this to facilitate
20 His seizure of your house and your estate.
ORGON: That man, I must say, is a vicious beast!
VALÈRE: Quick, Sir; you mustn't tarry in the least.
My carriage is outside, to take you hence;
This thousand louis should cover all expense.
25 Let's lose no time, or you shall be undone;
The sole defense, in this case, is to run.
I shall go with you all the way, and place you
In a safe refuge to which they'll never trace you.
ORGON: Alas, dear boy, I wish that I could show you
30 My gratitude for everything I owe you.
But now is not the time; I pray the Lord
That I may live to give you your reward.
Farewell, my dears; be careful . . .
CLÉANTE: Brother, hurry.
We shall take care of things; you needn't worry.

SCENE VII

The OFFICER, TARTUFFE, VALÈRE, ORGON, ELMIRE, MARIANE,
MADAME PERNELLE, DORINE, CLÉANTE, DAMIS

TARTUFFE: Gently, Sir, gently; stay right where you are.
No need for haste; your lodging isn't far.
You're off to prison, by order of the Prince.

ORGON: This is the crowning blow, you wretch; and since
5 It means my total ruin and defeat,
Your villainy is now at last complete.
TARTUFFE: You needn't try to provoke me; it's no use.
Those who serve Heaven must expect abuse.
CLÉANTE: You are indeed most patient, sweet, and blameless.
DORINE: How he exploits the name of Heaven! It's shameless. 10
TARTUFFE: Your taunts and mockeries are all for naught;
To do my duty is my only thought.
MARIANE: Your love of duty is more meritorious,
And what you've done is little short of glorious.
TARTUFFE: All deeds are glorious, Madam, which obey 15
The sovereign prince who sent me here today.
ORGON: I rescued you when you were destitute,
Have you forgotten that, you thankless brute?
TARTUFFE: No, no, I well remember everything;
But my first duty is to serve my King. 20
That obligation is so paramount
That other claims, beside it, do not count;
And for it I would sacrifice my wife,
My family, my friend, or my own life.
ELMIRE: Hypocrite! 25
DORINE: All that we most revere, he uses
To cloak his plots and camouflage his ruses.
CLÉANTE: If it is true that you are animated
By pure and loyal zeal, as you have stated,
Why was this zeal not roused until you'd sought
To make Orgon a cuckold, and been caught? 30
Why weren't you moved to give your evidence
Until your outraged host had driven you hence?
I shan't say that the gift of all his treasure
Ought to have damped your zeal in any measure;
But if he is a traitor, as you declare, 35
How could you condescend to be his heir?
TARTUFFE:

(*To the* OFFICER.)

Sir, spare me all this clamor; it's growing shrill.
Please carry out your orders, if you will.
OFFICER: Yes, I've delayed too long, Sir. Thank you kindly.
You're just the proper person to remind me. 40
Come, you are off to join the other boarders
In the King's prison, according to his orders.
TARTUFFE: Who? I, Sir?
OFFICER: Yes.
TARTUFFE: To prison? This can't be true!
OFFICER: I owe an explanation, but not to you.

(*To* ORGON.)

Sir, all is well; rest easy, and be grateful. 45
We serve a Prince to whom all sham is hateful,
A Prince who sees into our inmost hearts,
And can't be fooled by any trickster's arts.
His royal soul, though generous and human,
Views all things with discernment and acumen; 50
His sovereign reason is not lightly swayed,
And all his judgments are discreetly weighed.
He honors righteous men of every kind,
And yet his zeal for virtue is not blind,
Nor does his love of piety numb his wits 55
And make him tolerant of hypocrites.

'Twas hardly likely that this man could cozen
A King who's foiled such liars by the dozen.
With one keen glance, the King perceived the whole
60 Perverseness and corruption of his soul,
And thus high Heaven's justice was displayed:
Betraying you, the rogue stood self-betrayed.
The King soon recognized Tartuffe as one
Notorious by another name, who'd done
65 So many vicious crimes that one could fill
Ten volumes with them, and be writing still.
But to be brief: our sovereign was appalled
By this man's treachery toward you, which he called
The last, worst villainy of a vile career,
70 And bade me follow the impostor here
To see how gross his impudence could be,
And force him to restore your property.
Your private papers, by the King's command,
I hereby seize and give into your hand.
75 The King, by royal order, invalidates
The deed which gave this rascal your estates,
And pardons, furthermore, your grave offense
In harboring an exile's documents.
By these decrees, our Prince rewards you for
80 Your loyal deeds in the late civil war,
And shows how heartfelt is his satisfaction
In recompensing any worthy action,

How much he prizes merit, and how he makes
More of men's virtues than of their mistakes.
DORINE: Heaven be praised!   85
MADAME PERNELLE: I breathe again, at last.
ELMIRE: We're safe.
MARIANE: I can't believe the danger's past.
ORGON:

(To TARTUFFE.*)*

Well, traitor, now you see . . .
CLÉANTE: Ah, Brother, please,
Let's not descend to such indignities.
Leave the poor wretch to his unhappy fate,
And don't say anything to aggravate   90
His present woes; but rather hope that he
Will soon embrace an honest piety,
And mend his ways, and by a true repentance
Move our just King to moderate his sentence.
Meanwhile, go kneel before your sovereign's throne   95
And thank him for the mercies he has shown.
ORGON: Well said: let's go at once and, gladly kneeling,
Express the gratitude which all are feeling.
Then, when that first great duty has been done,
We'll turn with pleasure to a second one,   100
And give Valère, whose love has proven so true,
The wedded happiness which is his due.

■ JEAN RACINE ■

Jean Racine (1639–1699) pursued a career closely connected with the dominant institutions of Parisian culture: the court, the church, and the stage. Racine's parents both died in his early childhood, and he was raised by his grandfather and enrolled at the school of the famous and controversial abbey at Port-Royal. Port-Royal was associated with an emphatically unworldly Catholic sect—the Jansenists—that was brutally suppressed in the seventeenth century. Racine's education at Port-Royal played a decisive role in his intellectual life and in the course of his career as a dramatist.

At Port-Royal, Racine perfected his study of Greek and Latin, considered a career in the church, and became ambitious for public success and for a life at court. By the early 1660s he had written several courtly poems—on Louis XIV's marriage, on his illness—that brought him to the attention of the established writers at court: Jean La Fontaine, Nicholas Boileau-Despréaux, and Molière. His first surviving play, *La Thebaïde* was performed by Molière's company in 1664. In 1665, he gave *Alexandre* to Molière's company, as well, but was dissatisfied with Molière's production. He then gave the play to the rival company at the Hôtel de Bourgogne, where it played opposite Molière's production. Molière withdrew the play, and the hostilities between the two playwrights intensified in 1667 when Mademoiselle DuParc, Molière's leading lady—and possibly Racine's mistress—defected from Molière's company to create the title role in Racine's *Andromaque*. This play initiates the stunning series of Racine's major plays, *Britannicus* (1669), *Bérénice* (1670), *Bajazet* (1672), *Mithradate* (1673), *Iphigénie* (1674), and *Phaedra* (1677). *Phaedra* is Racine's most celebrated play, and his most controversial. The play, originally entitled *Phaedra and Hippolytus*, opened in January 1677 at the Hôtel de Bourgogne, but Racine's enemies at court persuaded Jacques Pradon (1632–1698), a minor playwright, to open his own play about Phaedra at the Palais-Royal theater. The plays ran against one another, inviting comparison and criticism. After *Phaedra*, Racine married and retired from Paris to Port-Royal. He was also appointed to the coveted position of court historiographer and in 1684 wrote a history of Louis XIV's wars. Racine's two last plays, *Esther* (1688) and *Athalie* (1690), are religious dramas, written at the request of Louis's second wife, Madame de Maintenon, to be performed privately at St. Cyr, a girls' academy. Racine was buried at Port-Royal in 1699, and his remains were moved when the abbey was subsequently destroyed.

Throughout his career, Racine maintained contact with Port-Royal, responding to its criticism of his work in the theater, defending Port-Royal in ecclesiastical matters, and writing a history of the abbey. However, Port-Royal's most pervasive influence on Racine's drama has to do with the Jansenist sense of sin, of the impossibility of redeeming human action. Inspired by the writing of Cornelius Otto Jansen (1558–1638), the Jansenists held that mankind lives in a state of essential sin and corruption, and summoned their followers to retire from the world in order to contemplate the moral abyss dividing mankind from God's mercy. What made Jansenism particularly threatening to the church in the seventeenth century was its resistance to the authority of Rome, and its call for a solitary and contemplative clergy, which challenged the massive public and political role played by the church in the affairs of the French state. Racine's plays touch only metaphorically on the strictly religious issues surrounding the Jansenist debate, but they are directly concerned with the philosophical themes of Jansenist belief: the sense of unavoidable guilt, the tortuous process of introspection, the desire to escape the world of action.

PHAEDRA

If René Descartes' famous *cogito ergo sum* ("I think, therefore I am") can be taken to represent a neoclassical concern for rational order, *Phaedra* might be said to illustrate a similar principle in terms of tragedy: "I feel, therefore I suffer." The play's main characters, particularly Hippolytus and Phaedra, feel and suffer precisely because reason falls to control the massive passions welling up within them, passions that deepen the rift between the corruption they feel and the uncorrupted ideals they never can achieve.

Racine's Jansenist beliefs have an indirect but profound impact in *Phaedra*. The world of the play is a world of unavoidable sin, in which action leads inevitably to wrongdoing and catastrophe, and in which flight is impossible. The characters define themselves according to fixed and unattainable ideals that are subverted by their irresistible, even criminal passions. Hippolytus pursues an ideal of heroic innocence and self-containment, violated in his own eyes by his love for Aricia. Theseus is consumed by his passion for power, conquest, and authority, and feels betrayed when he believes that he has been usurped by his son. Phaedra's honor, and even her humanity, is shattered by her adulterous, incestuous desire for her stepson. The play's elegant compression concentrates the action exclusively on these characters; their confidants—Theramenes, Oenone—function largely as screens on which Racine projects the tempestuous passions of the main characters. Although the characters blame the gods for the desire they suffer, the destructive force of the characters' passions really rises from within. In the world of *Phaedra*, action is impossible and sin is inevitable. The characters are each destroyed by the monsters they become.

PREFACE
TRANSLATED BY R. C. KNIGHT

Here is another tragedy on a subject taken from Euripides. The action follows a somewhat different course, but I have enriched my play with everything in his that I considered most strikingly beautiful. Had I borrowed no more than the conception of Phaedra's character, I might say I owe him the most reasonable thing, perhaps, that I have given to the theatre. I am not surprised that this character was so successful in Euripides' time, and now again in our own, considering that it has every quality required by Aristotle in the tragic hero, and proper to arouse compassion and terror. For Phaedra is not altogether guilty, and not altogether innocent. She is drawn by her destiny, and the anger of the Gods, into an unlawful passion which she is the first to hold in horror. She makes every endeavour to overcome it. She chooses death rather than disclose it to anyone. And when forced to reveal it, she speaks of it with such shame and confusion as leave no doubt that her crime is rather a punishment from the Gods, than an impulse of her own will.

I have even taken pains to make her a little less odious than she is in the tragedies of antiquity, where she brings herself, unprompted, to accuse Hippolytus. I felt that a false testimony was something too base, too black, to put into the mouth of a Princess possessed otherwise of sentiments so noble and virtuous. Such baseness seemed to me more fitting to a Nurse, who might have more slave-like propensities; though even she only enters upon the lying accusation to save the life and honour of her mistress. If Phaedra acquiesces, it is because she is beside herself in the agitation of her thoughts, and the next moment she comes on with the intention of vindicating the guiltless and publishing the truth.

Hippolytus is accused, in Euripides and in Seneca, of actually raping his step-mother—*vim corpus tulit*; here, of no more than the intention. I desired to spare Theseus a sense of shame which might have made him less acceptable to my audience.

As for the figure of Hippolytus, I had read in ancient authors that Euripides was blamed for depicting him as a philosopher free of all imperfection—so that the death of the youthful Prince gave rise to far more indignation than pity. I felt I should give him a failing that might render him somewhat guilty towards his father, without detracting at all from that magnanimity which makes him spare Phaedra's honour and go to his doom without accusing her. By failing I mean his involuntary passion for Aricia, the daughter and the sister of his father's mortal enemies.

This Aricia is not a child of my invention. Virgil relates that Hippolytus married her, and she bore him a son, after Aesculapius had brought him back to life. And I have read too, in certain authors, that Hippolytus had married and brought into Italy an Athenian maiden of high birth, named Aricia, who had given her name to an Italian township.

I adduce these authorities, because I have most scrupulously endeavoured to keep close to the legend. I have even taken the history of Theseus just as it is in Plutarch.

It is this historian who mentions that the belief in Theseus' descent to the underworld to abduct Proserpine was occasioned by a journey he made into Epirus towards the source of the Acheron, where a King, whose wife Pirithous sought to carry off, held Theseus prisoner after putting Pirithous to death. Thus I have tried to retain the verisimilitude of history, and yet to lose none of the embellishments of fable, so rich in the stuff of poetry. And the rumour of Theseus' death, based on the legendary journey, gives rise to that declaration of Phaedra's love which proves one of the principal causes of her unhappy plight, and which she would never have dared utter while she believed her husband to be alive.

For the rest, I dare not yet assert this play to be in truth the best of my tragedies. I leave my readers, and time, to set its rightful price upon it. What I can assert is that I have composed none where virtue is shown to more advantage than here. The slightest faults are severely punished. The bare thought of crime is regarded with no less horror than crime itself. The failings of love are treated as real failings. The passions are offered to view only to show all the ravage they create. And vice is everywhere painted in such hues, that its hideous face may be recognised and loathed. Here is the proper aim for every man to keep in sight who works for the public. And this, above all, was the purpose of the earliest tragic poets. Their stage was a school where virtue was taught no less well than in the schools of the philosophers. Thus Aristotle consented to draw up the rules of the dramatic poem; Socrates, the sagest of the philosophers, thought it no shame to set his hand to the tragedies of Euripides. It were much to be desired that our works should be found as serious and as full of useful instruction as the pages of those poets. It might bring about a reconciliation between the tragic art and a number of persons, noted for their religion and learning, who have denounced it of late, but might well look upon it with less disfavour if authors cared as much to instruct as to entertain their audience, and carried out thereby the true purpose of tragedy.

Jean Racine
(1677)

PHAEDRA

TRANSLATED BY R. C. KNIGHT

— CHARACTERS —

THESEUS, *son of Aegeus, King of Athens*
PHAEDRA, *wife of Theseus, daughter of Minos and Pasiphaë*
HIPPOLYTUS, *son of Theseus by Antiope Queen of the Amazons*
ARICIA, *daughter of Pallas, descended from the ancient kings of Athens*
OENONE, *nurse and confidant of Phaedra*

THERAMENES, *governor of Hippolytus*
ISMENE, *confidant to Aricia*
PANOPE, *one of Phaedra's women*
GUARDS

The scene is in Trozen, a town in the Peloponnese.

— ACT ONE —

HIPPOLYTUS, THERAMENES

HIPPOLYTUS: My mind's made up: I sail, Theramenes.
  No more for me the tranquil days of Trozen,
  For in the mortal tempest of my doubts
  I am dishonoured if I linger here.
5 Six months ago my father sailed and left me
  Ignorant what befalls a head so cherished,
  Ignorant even where he may be hidden—
  THERAMENES: So where will you go to look for him, my lord?
  Already, to relieve a fear I shared,
10 I have scoured the two seas that Corinth holds asunder.
  Demanded Theseus of the tribes that live
  Where Acheron drives down headlong into Hell,
  Searched Elis, skirted Taenarum, and even
  Traversed the waves where Icarus fell and perished.
15 What hope new-risen or what happier skies
  Will light you to his footsteps? Why, perhaps,
  Who knows, perhaps the King your father wishes
  Not to unveil the mystery of his venture,
  And while his peril fills your thought and ours,
20 Serene, weaving the latest of his loves,
  The hero waits to seize the unguarded moment—
  HIPPOLYTUS: Stop, good Theramenes. You slander Theseus;
  There is a nobler cause for these delays;
  After the follies of forgotten youth
25 The wanderings of his inconstant heart
  Are fixed at length, and Phaedra fears no rival.
  So once more—I shall go where duty points
  And fly a land I cannot bear to see.
  THERAMENES: But my lord, how long have you despised the presence
30 Of these calm fields, the pleasure of your childhood
  Whose solitude was dearer to you than
  The splendid stir of Athens and the court?
  What fear has banished you, or else what heartache?
  HIPPOLYTUS: Those days are past. Pleasure and peace have vanished
35 Since first the Gods directed to our shore
  The child of Minos and Pasiphaë.
  THERAMENES: I see: there is the cause, the hated presence—
  Phaedra, who came, your father's dangerous bride,
  Looked on you once, and by your prompt exile
40 Gave the first measure of her new-won power.

But all that dogged hate and old aversion
Has passed with time, passed or at least abated;
And after all what danger lies in her,
A woman dying, crying out for death?
Stricken by ills that none can make her utter,   45
Tired of her life, tired of the day that lights her,
What can she do to you?
HIPPOLYTUS: I do not fear
  Anything her aversion could devise.
  I sail to fly another enemy,
  I do admit: I fly Aricia,   50
  The youngest and the last of all that house
  In fatal league against ours.
THERAMENES: You, my lord,
  Are turned against her too? But Pallas' daughter
  Surely had no part in her brothers' treason,
  And must you hate that unoffending grace?   55
HIPPOLYTUS: I would not fly her if I hated her.
THERAMENES: My lord, have I permission to interpret
  Your flight? Must I suppose that you are not
  The old implacable Hippolytus,
  The outlaw of Love's empire, he that vowed   60
  Never to wear the yoke his father wore?
  Can it be that a slighted and a smarting Goddess
  Will press you to the service of her shrine,
  Reduce you to the rank of common men
  And vindicate that father by your fate?   65
  Can it be love, my lord?
HIPPOLYTUS: How can you say it,
  My friend, that knew the childhood of my heart
  And all its growth in pride and fierce resolve?
  Shall I dishonour it, disown myself?
  First, as a babe, at an Amazonian breast   70
  I drank the resolution that astounds you,
  But once of age to look upon myself
  I wished to be no other than I was.
  Then, in the faithful service of your kindness
  As you rehearsed for me my father's story,   75
  Do you remember how my soul blazed up
  At each particular in the noble toils
  Of the intrepid hero, as we showed him
  Turning the world from thoughts of lost Alcides
  By monsters strangled and by brigands slain—   80
  Procrustes, Sinnis, Sciro, Cercyon
  And Epidaurus scattered with the limbs

462

Of her gigantic tyrant, and the gore
Reeking from all Crete, of the Minotaur?
85   But when you told other ignobler feats—
A faith so cheaply pledged, and ever new,
Helen torn from a mother's arms in Sparta,
In Salamis the sighs of Periboea,
So many more than he can even name,
90   Victims too credulous of a lover's tongue;
What barren rocks heard Ariadne's sorrows;
How Phaedra, last and under happier auspice,
Followed him—then I wished the tale untold;
Often I urged you hasten and be done;
95   And would my wishes had redeemed from fame
That darker half of such a fair renown!
And now, by the spite of Heaven, shall I be
Degraded to the same indignity?
—Baseness beyond excuse, for those were frailties
100 Unseen amid a multitude of honours,
While not one trophy of a monster slain
Entitles me to fail as he has failed.
Even if I lost my freedom and my pride
How could I yield them to Aricia?
105 How could my disobedient sense forget
That which divides us irremovably?
The King denies her, denies her fallen brothers,
By violent laws, continuance of their line;
Their name must die for ever in her death,
110 Their guilty branch must bear no other fruit,
And till the tomb, submissive and sequestered,
The torch of wedlock must not burn for her.
Am I to oppose my father and his wrath?
Embrace her claims? and give a precedent
115 To treason? and embark my youth—
THERAMENES: My lord,
If the marked hour draws on, our arguments
Escape the notice of the incurious Heavens.
No. Theseus wished you blind, and gave you eyes;
His hate inflames the passion he forbids you,
120 And adds enchantment to his prisoner's charms.
But come, why look askance at honest love?
Why not make trial where its sweetness lies?
Why be enchained by vain and foolish scruples?
Who fears to stray that follows Hercules?
125 Many a stubborn heart has Venus bent—
Where would you be yourself and your defiance
Had chaste Antiope been as chaste as you
And never warmed to Theseus' flame? But why
Face out a falsehood with the pride of words?
130 Confess how things have changed: not now as once,
Aloof, intractable, we see you guide
A skimming chariot along the beaches
Or, adept in the mystery Neptune taught,
Break an unmastered courser to the curb;
135 Less often our halloos awake the forests;
Your eyes droop, weighted with a secret fire . . .
The case is clear—you are in love, in flame,
In torment, and you will not show your wound.
Is it Aricia?
HIPPOLYTUS: Theramenes,
140 I sail today, and go to find my father.
THERAMENES: Without an audience of Phaedra?

HIPPOLYTUS: No.
I will see her; I cannot well do less.
You may send word.—But what is the fresh misfortune
Disturbs her favorite Oenone so?

(Enter OENONE.*)*

OENONE: Alas, my lord, what grief can equal mine?   145
The Queen is near her utmost bourne of fate;
She that I watch by night and day unsleeping
Dies in my arms, and will not tell her sickness.
Her thought is all at variance with itself;
Her sick disquiet drives her from her bed   150
To see the light of day. But by her orders
No eye of man may see her suffering.
—Here she is.
HIPPOLYTUS: Very well; then I retire
Not to offend with this unwelcome face.

(Exeunt HIPPOLYTUS *and* THERAMENES.*)*

(Enter PHAEDRA.*)*

PHAEDRA: No more, for I can move no more, Oenone.   155
Let me rest; I am faint, my strength has left me.
My darkened eyes are dazzled by the light,
My wavering knees are weak beneath my weight.
Ah me!

(Sits.)

OENONE: High Gods, relent and see our tears!
PHAEDRA: These fripperies, these veils, they hang so heavy!   160
Whose was the unkind hand that piled and bound
These clustering locks that weigh upon my brow?
So feeble and so weary, all these things
Grieve me and weary me.
OENONE: How can we please you?
Yourself, repentant of your wicked thoughts,   165
You called in haste for clothes and ornaments;
Yourself you rallied your forgotten vigour,
You wanted to be out and see the sunlight.
Now you are here, my lady, and it seems
You loathe the very light that you desired.   170
PHAEDRA: Splendid begetter of a seed afflicted,
Father from whom my mother claimed her birth,
O blushing Sun ashamed of my despair,
Now, for the last time, I salute thy face.
OENONE: What, still possessed of such a fearful purpose?   175
Shall I for ever see you, turned from life,
Enact the mournful ritual of your death?
PHAEDRA: Oh give me the shadow of the forest glades!
Or let my eye piercing the glorious dust
Follow the wheeling chariot in the course!   180
OENONE: My lady?
PHAEDRA: Oh, I am mad. What have I said?
Where am I, where are my thoughts, my wandering mind?
Lost, for the Gods have taken it away.
My face is hot, Oenone, with my shame;
I cannot hide my guilty sufferings   185
And tears descend that I cannot restrain.
OENONE: Blush if you must, but blush to keep a silence
That doubles all the misery you suffer.
Rebellious to all tending, deaf to all pleas,
Will you unpitying allow your life   190

To flow away? What madness cuts it short?
What spell, what poison stanches up its course?
Thrice has the sky been muffled up in shade
And still is sleep a stranger to your eyes;
195   Thrice has the day displaced the gloom of night
And still you fast, and still your body wastes.
What dark temptation leads you on? What right
Invests you with the power to take your life—
Wronging the Gods from whom you draw your being,
200   Failing the husband who received your promise,
Failing still more your helpless children, doomed
To bitter lives of bondage; for reflect,
The very day that takes their mother from them
Rebuilds the hope of that Barbarian's child,
205   That arrogant enemy of you and yours,
The boy the Amazonian stranger bore,
Hippolytus—
PHAEDRA: O Gods!
OENONE: That charge strikes home!
PHAEDRA: Woman, how dare you name that name to me?
OENONE: Why, now your anger is most justly roused.
210   It heartens me that you should shrink to hear
That fatal name. Then live. For love, for duty,
Live; if you would not have the Scythian's son,
Bending your children to his hated yoke,
Lord it over the fairest blood of Greece
215   And of the Gods. But do not wait, each moment
You die. Rally, betimes, your prostrate vigour
While yet your almost spent and guttering life
Still glows, and may be kindled once again.
PHAEDRA: I have outlived the right to live already.
220 OENONE: Why, is there some remorse that feeds upon you?
What have you done that drives you so distraught?
Your hands have never dipped in guiltless blood?
PHAEDRA: I thank the Gods my hands are free of evil.
Would that my heart were innocent as they!
225 OENONE: What resolution, then, have you conceived
To terrify your heart before the time?
PHAEDRA: I have said enough. Ask me no more, have pity;
For if I die it is to keep within me
This dreadful secret.
OENONE: Keep it then, and die;
230   But other hands, not mine, will close your eyes.
Yours is a weak and flickering fire, but I
Will lose my spirit first among the dead;
There are many avenues and all unbarred;
An injured heart will soon perceive the best.—
235   Ungrateful mistress, when did I betray you?
Have you forgotten that these hands received you
When you were born? My children and my home,
I have left all for you: and all for this.
PHAEDRA: What do you think to gain by this beseeching?
240   You will shrink with horror if I break my silence.
OENONE: What can you tell me then more horrible
Than thus to see you die before my face?
PHAEDRA: And when you know my destiny and my weakness
Still I shall die, and only die more guilty.
245 OENONE: My lady, by the tears I shed for you,
By these your trembling knees I hold entwined,
Deliver me from deadly fear and doubt.

PHAEDRA: You wish it. Rise.
OENONE: Speak on, and I will listen.
PHAEDRA: How shall I tell, ye Gods, or where begin?
OENONE: Your fears are insults to my loyalty.   250
PHAEDRA: O deathless hate of Venus, fatal vengeance!
O heavy doom of love upon my mother!
OENONE: Forget, my lady. Hide that memory
And keep it from the ears of later times.
PHAEDRA: Love left thee dying, sweet sister Ariadne,   255
Lying forsaken by the alien waters.
OENONE: Let by, my lady. Must your mortal grief
Be vented on the dearest of your blood?
PHAEDRA: Of this doomed blood, I, by the will of Venus,
I perish now the last and most accursed.   260
OENONE: You love!
PHAEDRA: To madness and to ecstasy.
OENONE: Who?
PHAEDRA: There's the horror that surpasses horror:
I love . . . at the fatal name I blench and tremble—
I love . . .
OENONE: But who?
PHAEDRA: You know the Amazon's son,
The young Prince who endured so much, through me . . .   265
OENONE: O Gods! Hippolytus!
PHAEDRA: You spoke the name!
OENONE: Sweet Heavens! You have chilled my very blood.
O race polluted, hopeless, lamentable!
Woe worth the day that brought us to these shores!
Why did we venture?   270
PHAEDRA: It was long ago
And far from here. When first the rite of Hymen
Bound my obedience to the son of Aegeus—
My happiness, my peace then seemed so plain—
Careless in Athens stood my conqueror.
I saw and gazed, I blushed and paled again,   275
A blind amazement rose and blurred my mind;
My eyes were dim, my lips forgot to speak,
This, I knew, was the awful flame of Venus,
The fated torment of her chosen victims.
I tried to ward it off with prayers, with vows   280
And offerings, a temple built and decked,
And in the midst of endless sacrifices
I searched the entrails for my erring wisdom.
Weak drugs for irremediable love!
Even as my hand spilt incense at the shrine,   285
Even as my lips invoked the name of Venus
I prayed Hippolytus, my eyes beheld
Hippolytus, and while the altars steamed
I offered all to him I dared not name.
I fled him everywhere. O bitterness,   290
He looked upon me in his father's features.
At last, I turned upon myself. I forced
Myself to play the torturer against
The dreaded enemy I loved too well,
Put on the bride's abhorrence of the stepson,   295
Pleaded and pressed until I banished him
Out of his father's arms, his father's heart.
Once more I breathed; and after this, Oenone,
My life, serener, flowed in blameless ways,
Pleasing my husband, covering my pain,   300

Tending the fruits of his unhappy bed:
Foolish expedients! and inexorable
Hardness of destiny!—My lord himself
Brought me to Trozen and my banished foe.
305   The ancient wound gaped deep, and bled again.
No longer is it a secret flame that flickers
About my veins: headlong in onset Venus
Hangs on her quarry! I abhorred my guilt,
Life was a curse, my love a misery;
310   I looked for death to save my name, and bury
Far from the day the darkness of these fires.
I could not face your strivings and your tears.
Now you know all; and it is well, if you
Stand but aside from my advancing death.
315   Abstain at last from undeserved reproaches,
And leave your useless effort to revive
The embers of a fast-expiring fire.

(Enter PANOPE.)

PANOPE: I wish that I could hide the news, my lady,
That I am forced to bring you. Death has taken
320   Your lord, our most indomitable King;
And you alone are ignorant of your loss.
OENONE: What is this, Panope?
                              My lady's prayers
Will never now bring Theseus back to Athens,
And mariners that landed here today
325   Have told Hippolytus that he is dead.
PHAEDRA: Gods!
PANOPE: Athens wavers in the choice of masters.
One boasts allegiance to the Prince your son;
One, reckless of the statutes of the land,
Presumes to favour the Barbarian's child,
330   My lady; and they say a rank sedition
Proclaims Aricia and the blood of Pallas.
I knew it was my duty to report
Such perils. Hippolytus is ready now
To sail, and many fear if he arrives
335   In this tempestuous season, he will sway
A fickle multitide.
OENONE: Panope, thank you:
Your news was precious, and the Queen has heard.

(Exit PANOPE.)

OENONE: My lady, I had thrown away all pleadings,
All hope to move you, and my only thought
340   Was to attend you past the gates of the tomb,
But new disaster points new purposes,
An altered fortune, and an altered duty.
   Theseus is dead, and you are his successor,
My lady, with a son that looks to you—
345   A slave alone, and if you live a king.
No other will uphold his friendless quarrel,
No other wipe away his orphan tears;
Only in Heaven will his hearers be
The Gods, your judges and his ancestors.
350   Live then, in liberty from all misgiving;
Your love is now as unremarkable
As any love, for death disjoins the bond

That made its foulness and its infamy.
Henceforth the image of Hippolytus
Is not so terrible, and you may see him   355
With perfect guiltlessness. But what if now,
Despairing of a better understanding,
He takes command of these rebellious throngs?
Open his eyes, soften that stubborn heart.
Prince of these smiling coasts, his patrimony   360
Is here in Trozen, but he knows the laws;
He knows that they deliver to your son
The queenly ramparts that Minerva reared.
Your rightful enemy is also his:
Unite your forces to defeat Aricia.   365
PHAEDRA: So be it. I commit my way to you.
I will live, if I still have strength to live
And if a mother's love can even now
Revive in my wasted flesh the seeds of life.

— ACT TWO —

ARICIA, ISMENE

ARICIA: He asked to see me here? Hippolytus
Wanted to see me and to say farewell?
Are you quite certain? Is this true, Ismene?
ISMENE: Much more than this, now that the King is dead.
Prepare yourself, my lady; all the hearts   5
He kept at bay will cluster at your feet.
All Greece will bring its tributes to Aricia,
Enfranchised now and sovereign of her fortunes.
ARICIA: So then, Ismene, it is no idle talk.
And I have no oppressor and no foe?   10
ISMENE: My lady, none. The Heavens have relented
And Theseus walks among your fathers' shades.
ARICIA: What enterprise has brought him to his death?
Do they say?
ISMENE: Rumours wild and past belief;
Some say that in a lover's last adventure   15
The seas have claimed this ever-wandering husband;
Some say, and everywhere the news is sown,
That with Pirithous he went down to Hell,
Saw the Cocytus and the coasts of darkness
And stood alive amid a world of shadows,   20
But could not scale the gloomy track again
Nor pass the bourne men never pass but once.
ARICIA: Shall mortal men, before the last leave-taking,
Fathom those sullen deeps of the Departed?
What sorcery lured him to their awful shore?   25
ISMENE: My lady, he is dead, and you alone
Doubt it. All Athens grieves for him, all Trozen
Knows, and salutes Hippolytus for Prince.
And in these walls, despairing for her son,
Phaedra takes counsel of her trembling friends.   30
ARICIA: And you suppose that, kinder than his father,
Hippolytus will make my bondage sweeter
And pity me?
ISMENE: My lady, yes, I do.
ARICIA: But do you know the hard Hippolytus?
What makes you fancy he could feel compassion   35

For me alone, who never felt for woman?
He never joins our customary paths
And hides himself wherever we are not.
ISMENE: Oh, I know all the legend of his coldness;
40   But when you met the proud Hippolytus
I own the strangeness of his reputation
Sharpened the edge of my curiosity.
I saw a face at variance with the fable;
At once your eyes disturbed that hard assurance
45   And his, avoiding you but all in vain,
Melted at once, and could not turn away.
His pride may yet refuse the name of lover
But I'll believe his looks, and not his tongue.
ARICIA: Ah, sweet Ismene, how my heart devours
50   The unhoped-for comfort of a mere perhaps!
You that have known me, did you once imagine
This heart, the plaything of unpitying Fortune,
Starved of all sustenance except despair, ·
Would learn of love and the wild woes of love?
55   Child of Earth's child, last of a royal lineage,
Sole remnant spared by battlefield and hatred,
I lost the last proud blossoms of our tree,
Six brothers, in the springtime of their year.
The steel reaped all, and Earth's unwilling furrows
60   Drank her own blood, the blood of her Erechtheus.
Since then you know what rigorous decree
Defies all Greeks to lift their eyes to mine—
For a mutinous ardour in the sister's breast
Might wake the embers in her brothers' urns—
65   And you remember how I laughed to scorn
Those calculations of the victor's fear;
I held that love itself was slavery
And even thanked the King for a constraint
So fit and favourable to my distaste—
70   Then, yes; but then I had not seen his son.
Not that subservient to the eye's seduction
I love him for that beauty, that demeanour,
Graces of partial Nature, gifts that he
Ignores, if ever he has noticed them;
75   I see richer and dearer treasures in him—
His father's parts, and not his father's failings;
For I confess I love the manly pride
That never bent under the yoke of Love.
Phaedra was flattered by the doubtful glory
80   Of Theseus' courtly sighs: but I am prouder
And will not stoop to share an easy prize
Or occupy an undefended heart.
No, but to shape a will as yet unbending,
To waken pain in a proof-armoured bosom,
85   To lead a slave that never thought to serve,
Vainly at war against the pleasing chain—
There's a reward worthy of my ambition;
Hercules was an easier adversary
Who readily disarmed and quick to yield
90   Lent no such lustre to his overthrow.
But dear Ismene, these are reckless dreams:
Resistance there will be, and all too stubborn,
And you shall hear me soon in humbler strain
Lament the coldness that I praise today.
95   He love, Hippolytus? What heights of fortune
Could ever bring him—

ISMENE: Only let him speak;
He is coming now.

(*Enter* HIPPOLYTUS.)

HIPPOLYTUS: My lady, before I sail
I owe you some account of my intentions.
My father's dead: and well enough my fears
Foretold the causes of his late homecoming—   100
Death only, and the closure of his toils
Could hold him from the world so long. The Gods
At last abandon to the fatal Spinners
Alcides' friend, his fellow, his successor.
—I know your enmity will not forbid   105
His son to assert these titles he has earned.—
One hope alleviates my deepest sorrow,
For I can end a harsh and long subjection:
I here revoke laws that have caused me grief—
The full bestowal of your life and hand   110
Is yours alone, and in my patrimony,
This Trozen, seat of Pittheus my grandfather,
Which willingly defers his crown to me
I leave you free and freer than its Prince.
ARICIA: Show me less kindness, I could bear it better.   115
So much regard for me in my abjection
Binds me, my lord, more even than you know,
To that constraint you would have put away.
HIPPOLYTUS: Doubtful who stands the next in title, Athens
Canvasses you, and me, and Phaedra's son.   120
ARICIA: Me, my lord?
HIPPOLYTUS: I have never shut my eyes
To arrogant laws that seem to bar my claim:
The Greeks reject me for my mother's race.
But if my brother were my only rival
I could appeal to certain natural laws   125
And make them good against the law's caprice.
I have a better reason to refrain:
To you I yield, say rather I restore
The seat, the sceptre, that your fathers held
Of the illustrious mortal, son of Earth.   130
It only passed to Aegeus by adoption;
And next my father, Athens' second founder,
Was hailed and crowned for all his benefits
While your unhappy brothers lay forgotten.
Now, Athens calls you home within her ramparts, 135
Too long the ancient quarrel lives in pain,
Too long your blood, that flowed along her fields,
Reeks from the furrows where it found its birth.—
Trozen I hold. As for the son of Phaedra
The Cretan acres yield him rich retirement.   140
Attica falls to you. I sail, to join
My partisans with yours, in your support.
ARICIA: At every word more troubled and bewildered,
Can I, or dare I, think I heard you rightly?
Have I my senses, is this your intent?   145
What God, my lord, what God inspired your mind?
Rightly your glory sounds in every climate
But reputation falls behind the truth.
What, will you cheat yourself on my behalf?
It was enough indeed to think that you   150
Hated me not, and held a mind untainted
By this long enmity—

HIPPOLYTUS: How could I hate you?
    Men may deride this proud unconquered heart
    But do they think a monster gave me birth?
155 What brutishness or what inveterate malice
    Could see your face and not forget its fury?
    And how should I withstand this subtle spell—
ARICIA: My lord! . . .
HIPPOLYTUS: My tongue has carried me too far;
    But wisdom fails and yields to the compulsion . . .
160 Now that my silence has been partly broken,
    My lady, I must needs go on, and speak
    The secret that my soul cannot contain.—
    Here stands a Prince of all men most unhappy,
    A monument of overthrown presumption;
165 I, long a truant from the law of love
    And long a mocker of its votaries,
    That stayed ashore watching the luckless sailor
    And never thought myself to fight the tempest,
170 By strange tides I am borne far from myself.
    My wanton liberty has learnt to yield
    And in an instant this bold heart was tamed.
    Six months or nearly, in despair and shame,
    I've borne the arrow burning in my side;
175 Vainly I pit my strength against myself
    And you. I fly you where you are, and find you
    Where you are not; deep in the forest glade
    Your picture chases me; sunlight and shade
    Alike retrace your features and alike
180 Betray the fugitive that would be free,
    And I, for all my fruitless pains, look round
    To find Hippolytus, and know him not.
    My bow, my bounds, my spear, my chariot,
    Weary me. Neptune's lessons are forgotten;
185 Only my lamentations fill the groves,
    My stabled coursers know my voice no more.
      Perhaps this tale I tell of uncouth passion
    Will make you blush to own your handiwork:
    Wild terms, indeed, to offer up a heart!
190 And chains too fair for such a slave to claim!
    And yet my tribute therefore ranks the higher;
    Consider that I speak an unknown language
    And do not spurn these faltered words of love
    That you alone could teach Hippolytus.

    (Enter THERAMENES.*)*

195 THERAMENES: Close on my heels, my lord, the Queen
     approaches
   Asking for you.
HIPPOLYTUS: For me?
THERAMENES: In what intention
    I do not know, but messengers have come
    Bidding you wait on her before you sail.
HIPPOLYTUS: The Queen? What should I say to her? Or she . . .
200 ARICIA: You cannot disappoint her wish, my lord.
    Even to such an enemy is due
    Some sign of formal pity for her grief.
HIPPOLYTUS: So you go. And I sail. And still I know not
    Whether my worship has incensed my goddess,
205 Whether this heart I leave in your two hands . . .
ARICIA: Sail, Prince. Pursue your noble purposes;

    Bring me the realm of Athens for dominion;
    Whatever gift you make shall be accepted,
    But that imperial, that unhoped-for state
    Is not the dearest of your offerings.   210

 (Exeunt ARICIA *and* ISMENE.*)*

HIPPOLYTUS: Good friend, are all things ready?—But I hear
    The Queen.—Have all things ordered for our sailing.
    Send out the signal. Haste, command, return
    And free me from the burden of this meeting.

 (Exit THERAMENES.*)*

 (Enter PHAEDRA *and* OENONE.*)*

PHAEDRA: He is here. My blood retreats toward my heart.   215
    I see him, and forget what I should speak.
OENONE: Be mindful of the son that trusts in you!
PHAEDRA: They say that you are taking ship at once,
    My lord. I came to join my grief with yours,
    And with the story of a mother's terrors—   220
    My child is fatherless, and soon the day
    Will dawn that brings him to another deathbed;
    So fiercely even now assailed and threatened,
    Your strength alone can champion his weakness.—
    But deep within me throbs the preying thought   225
    That his complaint will never reach your ear,
    That through my child your angry justice soon
    Will strike a hated memory.
HIPPOLYTUS: My lady,
    So infamous a wish was never mine.
PHAEDRA: But you have seen me unremittingly   230
    Pursue your hate, my lord; and how could you
    Explore the bottom of my soul and read
    My secret there? I threw myself upon
    Your just resentment; I would not suffer you
    Within the self-same frontiers; privily   235
    And openly I waged my war, and set
    The width of seas between your path and mine.
    I even gave explicit orders not
    To breathe your name before my presence. Yet,
    If by the wrong the penalty were measured,   240
    If only hatred could achieve your hatred,
    Never did woman more deserve your tears,
    My lord, and less your enmity.
HIPPOLYTUS: No mother
    That watches for her children's interest
    Forgives the other children of her house;   245
    I know, my lady. Untoward mistrust
    Is always near when men have married twice.
    Another in your place would have conceived
    No less suspicion, and I might have suffered
    Deeper indignities.   250
PHAEDRA: Ah but, my lord,
    The Gods—as now they stand my witnesses—
    Deigned to release me from this general law.
    How different are the thoughts that ravage me!
HIPPOLYTUS: It is too soon, my lady, for such thoughts;
    The sunshine may still light your husband's eye,   255
    And Heaven still may yield him to our prayers;
    Neptune's his friend, and that high patronage
    Will not in vain be canvassed by my father.

PHAEDRA: No man has twice explored the coasts of Death,
260 My lord. If Theseus touched the sullen shores
Vainly we look for Gods to send him home:
Harsh Acheron is grasping and holds fast
His prey. But did I say that he is dead?
He breathes again in you; I see the King,
265 See him, speak to him, thrill . . . My mind is wandering,
My lord, my madness speaks the thing it should not.
HIPPOLYTUS: This is a prodigy of loyal love:
Theseus is gone, yet lives within your mind
And fires the ardour of your loving heart.
270 PHAEDRA: Yes, Prince, for him indeed I yearn, I languish;
I love him—not the man that Hell has claimed,
The butterfly that every beauty lured,
The adulterous ravisher that would have stained
The God of Hell's own bed; but faithful, fine,
275 Sometimes aloof, and pure, gallant and gay,
Young, stealing every heart upon his road—
So do they character our Gods, and so
I see you now; those eyes, that voice, were his,
That generous red of virtue in your cheek,
280 When first he drove across the Cretan foam,
Meet meditation for the virgin dreams
Of Minos' daughters. You, where were you then
Among the flower and chivalry of Greece?
Where was Hippolytus—alas, too young—
285 The day his vessel grounded on our shore?
You would have slain the terror of the island,
The monster lapped in labyrinthine wiles;
Into your hand my sister would have thrust,
To unweave those riddling and deceitful ways,
290 The thread of life and death. But no, she would not—
Love would have found a readier wit in me,
And I, Prince, I, devoted and assured,
Could have resolved the devious Labyrinth;
What would I not have done for that sweet head?
295 How should a thread content your fearful lover?
Half-claimant in the peril that you claimed
I would have walked before you in the way,
And Phaedra, steadfast in the Labyrinth,
Would have returned again with you, or else
300 With you remained.
HIPPOLYTUS: Great Gods, what have you said?
My lady, can it be that you forget
That Theseus is my father, and your husband?
PHAEDRA: And why do you suppose I had forgotten,
Prince? Do I appear so careless of my honour?
305 HIPPOLYTUS: Forgive, my lady. I own, I blush to own
How blameless are the words that I reproved.
My shame can face it out no more before you,
So let me go . . .
PHAEDRA: Ah, leave your heartless lying.
You understand and you have heard enough.
310 Very well then, you shall learn what Phaedra is
And all her frenzy. Yes; I am in love.
But never think that even while I love you
I can absolve myself, or hide my face
From my own guiltiness. And never think
315 The wanton love that blurs my better mind
Grew with the treachery of my consent.
I, singled out for a celestial vengeance,

Unpitied victim, I abhor myself
More than you hate me. Let the Gods bear witness,
Those Gods that set the fire within my breast, 320
The fatal fire of my accursed line;
Those Gods whose majesty and might exulted
In the beguiling of a mortal's weakness.
Turn back the past yourself; how I have laboured
To seem malignant, savage, how I fostered 325
Your hatred as my ally in the fight.
Did I escape you? No, I banished you.
What fruit repaid these unavailing cares?
You loathed me more, I could not love you less;
Your suffering doubled the spell that binds me, 330
The withering ravage of my flames, my tears.
Your eyes can testify that this is true—
If for one moment they could bear my sight.
Why, this confession of my bitter secret,
My shameful secret, do you think that I 335
Have made it willingly? I came in fear
For one defenceless that I dare not fail:
I came to pray you not to hate my child.
Precarious resolution of a mind
Too full of what it loves! I came, and spoke 340
Of nothing else but you. So now, do justice.
Punish me for this execrable passion.
Approve yourself a hero's son indeed
And sweep this monster from the universe.
Dare Theseus' widow love Hippolytus? 345
Truly so vile a monster must not live.
My heart is here, and here is where you strike.
Eager to make atonement for its fault
I feel it swell and bound to meet your hand:
Strike. Or am I unworthy of your steel, 350
Or will your hate refuse to sweet a doom,
Or would ignoble blood sully your fingers?
Then hold your hand and let me have your sword.
Give it me.
OENONE: Stop, my lady. Heavenly powers!
What would you do? But somebody is coming: 355
Escape their sight, be quick, come back, or face
Inevitable shame.

(*Exeunt* PHAEDRA *and* OENONE. *Enter* THERAMENES.)

THERAMENES: Was that the Queen
Half dragged, half rushing out? What, my lord, what
Are all these marks of grief? You stand disarmed,
Dumb, pale . . .
HIPPOLYTUS: Come, let us go, Theramenes. 360
I cannot think of what I have heard and witnessed;
I cannot see myself without disgust.
Phaedra . . . No more, great Gods! Oblivion
Must shroud away the secret and the shame.
THERAMENES: If you would leave, my lord, the sail hangs 365
ready;
But Athens is beforehand with her answer:
Her chiefs have counted votes among the tribes;
Your brother has their suffrage, Phaedra wins.
HIPPOLYTUS: Phaedra!
THERAMENES: A herald of the will of Athens
Will bring the reins of state into her hands. 370
Her son is King.

HIPPOLYTUS: Ye Gods that know her heart,
  Is it her righteousness you would repay?
THERAMENES: And now dark rumours speak again of Theseus:
  Some tell that men have seen him in Epirus
375 Alive; though, I, who went to seek him there,
  I know full well, my lord . . .
HIPPOLYTUS: It may be so.
  But I would hear whatever rumour tells,
  Consult this public cry, divine its sources.
  If it be worthless to delay our journey
380 We sail; and cost the venture what it will
  I'll save the sceptre for a worthy hand.

— ACT THREE —

PHAEDRA, OENONE

PHAEDRA: Send them away, these heralds and these honours.
  Have they a balm to ease a tortured mind?
  Unkind, is Phaedra fit for public show?
  Rather conceal me, for my secret's out:
5 Intemperate desire has seen the light,
  And what these lips had never thought to utter
  He heard. Immortal Gods! and how he listened,
  How long he parried, how deviously he turned
  To baffle the approaches of my speech!
10 How visibly he yearned to leave my presence!
  How painfully his blush revived my shame!
  Why did you disappoint me of my death?
  Ah, when his weapon pointed at my breast
  Did he blench? Did he stir to snatch it back?
15 Enough for him my fingers at the hilt
  And in his heartless reckoning it was vile,
  Profaned, a blade that would defile his hand.
OENONE: And so complaining, dwelling on your sorrow,
  You feed a fire that wisdom would have quenched.
20 Should not a worthy child of Minos' blood
  Look for serenity in nobler tasks,
  Fly from a stuggle that you cannot win,
  Learn to assume the guidance of a kingdom
  And be a Queen?
PHAEDRA: Queen, I? And hold command,
25 While my own senses rage in mutiny,
  While in my soul wisdom has lost dominion,
  While shame and slavery has bowed my head,
  And death is waiting?
OENONE: Fly.
PHAEDRA: I cannot leave him.
OENONE: You drove him away, and cannot go from him?
30 PHAEDRA: I cannot now. He has seen my raging soul,
  Seen me transgress the rigid pale of virtue;
  Before those stony eyes I have poured out
  My shame, and now, unbidden, secret hope
  Has slipped into my breast. Ay, you yourself,
35 Rallying the wasted forces of my life,
  The parting spirit ready on my lips,
  Wooed me from death with false and soothing words;
  You half persuaded me that I might love.
OENONE: Ah, call me guilty, or call me innocent,
40 I would do worse if anything could save you.
  But, if resentment ever stung your mind,

Can you forget the blow of his rebuff,
  The insolence, the icy cruelty
  That eyed you all but prostrate at his feet,
  The arrogant disdain?—how odious   45
  Had Phaedra only seen him as I saw!
PHAEDRA: What if he lost this arrogance, Oenone?
  He has the harshness of his forest ways,
  And in his arduous life Hippolytus
  Has never heard of love until today.   50
  What if surprise had robbed him of his speech?
  What if we blamed him more than he deserved?
OENONE: He was conceived in a Barbarian's womb.
PHAEDRA: Barbarian, Scythian, still she learned to love.
OENONE: He hates our sex with firm and deadly hate. 55
PHAEDRA: So I shall never fear another woman.
  Enough: such counsels had their season once;
  My passion now commands you, and not my reason.
  Though hard and inaccessible to love,
  Another side lies weaker to attack—   60
  The sweets of empire tempted him, I think;
  Athens allured him more than he could hide.
  His ships already turned their prows to sea
  With canvas rigged and offered to the breeze.
  Find him, Oenone, find the ambitious boy,   65
  Show him the glitter of the Athenian crown,
  Bid him assume the diadem and the glory;
  I only ask to lay it on his brow,
  Into his hand descends authority
  I cannot grasp, and he shall teach my son   70
  The science of command—even he might
  Look as a father on him. In his power
  I now resign the orphan and the mother.
  Incline his heart by any means you know,
  Use—do not blush—the voice of supplication,   75
  I sanction all. I have no other hope;
  Go, till you come again I cannot tell
  What else I have to do.

(*Exit* OENONE.)

PHAEDRA: (*Alone.*)   O Thou, that knowest
  How deep in shame my soul is overwhelmed,
  Venus, O Venus unappeasable,   80
  This is the consummation of thy hatred.
  These must be the limits of thy cruelty.
  Thy triumph is entire, each shot has told.
  Art thou not sated yet with victory?
  Find tougher quarry then: Hippolytus   85
  Rejects thy deity, derides thy wrath,
  He never bent the knee before thy altar;
  Thy name seems hideous in his stubborn ears,
  Goddess, avenge; our grievances are one!
  Teach him to love . . . Oenone, here so soon?   90
  I am rejected then, you were not heard.

(*Enter* OENONE.)

OENONE: Stifle the memory of a hopeless passion,
  My lady; summon up your earlier virtue.
  The King's not dead, and you will see him soon.
  Theseus has landed. He is coming here.   95
  The populace are rushing to salute him,

And as I passed obedient to your mission
Unending cheers rose up on every hand—
PHAEDRA: He is not dead. Nothing else signifies,
100 Oenone. I revealed a lawless love
That wounds him in his honour. And he lives.
What needs there more?
OENONE: But yet—
PHAEDRA: I told you so;
And you would not. Foreboding and remorse
Have yielded to your tears. Only this morning
105 My death was not unworthy to be pitied:
I took your counsel, and I die disgraced.
OENONE: Die?
PHAEDRA: Righteous Gods! The things this day has seen!
And now, as I meet my husband and his son
I know this witness of adulterous passion
110 Studies my countenance before his father—
My heart heavy with sighs he would not hear,
My eyelids drenched with tears that he despised.
Do you think his tenderness for Theseus' honour
Would hide away the memory of my falsehood,
115 My treason to a father and a King?
Will he repress the loathing I inspire?
What if he did? I know my treachery,
Oenone. And if there are intrepid women
Who taste a flawless quietude in crime
120 And force their countenance to show no shame,
I am not such. My misdeeds rise before me;
And even now these over-arching walls
Seem full of tongues, impatient to accuse me
Before my husband, and proclaim his wrong.
125 Oh for a death, and surcease from this anguish!
Is life so precious and so hard to leave?
Need the tormented hesitate to die?
Only I fear the name I leave behind—
The legacy of horror for my children,
130 Whose blood, the very blood of Jupiter,
Should swell their hearts with pride: now they must lift
The burden of a mother's infamy.
My soul foretells that malice, soon or late,
Will throw my black reproach into their faces,
135 And crushed so cruelly they may never dare
To look with level eyes upon their kind.
OENONE: It is most true. They both are to be pitied,
And never sorrow was foretold more surely.
But why abandon them to the ordeal?
140 Why be the witness that betrays your cause?
For all is lost; and all the world will judge
That Phaedra knows her guilt, and dare not wait
The awful presence of an outraged husband.
Hippolytus should thank you for a deed
145 Stronger than all his words on his behalf;
And what can I respond to your accuser?
Confounded, tongue-tied, I must live to see
Him taste a hideous triumph undisturbed
And chronicle your shame to all mankind.
150 May fire from Heaven fall upon me sooner!
But tell me this, and tell without dissembling:
Do you still love him, this presumptuous Prince?
How does he now appear. . . ?

PHAEDRA: I see him now
Grim as a monster and as terrible.
OENONE: Then why concede him victory unresisted?   155
Do you fear him? Attack before he strikes
And use the imputation he prepares
For you. What can refute you? Every sign
Informs against him—first his sword that Fortune
Leaves in your hands, and then this day's distress,   160
And those disconsolate months of misery,
And long ago his father's mind prepared
When long ago you claimed his banishment.
PHAEDRA: Shall I defame and murder innocence?
OENONE: Lend me but silence and my zeal suffices.   165
Like you I shudder at my remedy
And dread it deeper than a thousand deaths.
But either this, or else I lose my mistress,
And in your loss all other values fade.
So I will speak. Theseus will rage, but still   170
He'll take no more revenge than banishment.
A father punishing is still a father
Whose love is louder than the voice of justice;
But guiltless blood is nothing in the scales
Against the imperilled honour of your name.   175
That is a jewel far too dear to hazard;
It is a law we dare not disobey;
And when our honour stands at such a cost
Virtue itself must go for sacrifice.
—Here they are. I see Theseus.   180
PHAEDRA: And I see
Hippolytus, and his unflinching eyes
Spell my dishonour. Do what you will, Oenone.
I am in your hands. In this tormented hour
To save myself is more than I can do.

(*Enter* THESEUS, HIPPOLYTUS, *and* THERAMENES.)

THESEUS: Fortune has smiled again, my dearest lady,   185
And now your sweet embrace—
PHAEDRA: No, Theseus; stop,
Do not pollute this love and this delight.
No longer I deserve this tenderness.
You have been wronged. The jealousy of Fortune
Has not respected her you left behind you;   190
And now, unworthy to approach your love,
My sole desire must be for solitude.

(*Exit* PHAEDRA.)

THESEUS: What is this cheerless welcome that I find here,
My son?
HIPPOLYTUS: A riddle Phaedra must interpret,
No one else can. But now if prayers can move   195
I ask but this, my lord, never to see
Her face again, but to live out my life
Safe, far away, forgotten by the Queen.
THESEUS: Now you, my son, forsake me!
HIPPOLYTUS: For you know
I never sought her, but you brought her here   200
At your departure; and the coasts of Trozen
Became the dwelling of Aricia
And of the Queen. I was to be their guardian.
But now what duty keeps me from my life?

205 Inglorious victories among the forests
   Weary my idle youth, my wasted skill.
   I long to waken from obscurity
   And tip my hunter's spear in a nobler red.
   Before you had spent the years that I have counted
210 What robbers, what oppressors, and what monsters
   Had known the weight of that revengeful arm,
   Victor and scourge of wanton insolence!
   While on the quiet shore of either sea
   The traveller learnt to take his road in peace;
215 Hercules heard your prowess and drew breath,
   Leaving his triumphs and his toils to you—
   And I, the unknown son of such a father,
   Have much to do to reach my mother's footsteps.
   Now let my unfledged valour learn to dare;
220 Let me, if anywhere some monster yet
   Escapes you, drag its trophy to your feet,
   Or by the record of a glorious failure
   Find life for ever in a fitting death
   And show posterity I was your son.
225 THESEUS: What is it, what invading blast of fear
   Empties my very home at my approach?
   Why, O ye Gods, to face these shrinking looks,
   This lack of love, did ye deliver me?
   I had one friend. His unregarding passion
230 Conspired to carry back from far Epirus
   The tyrant's Queen. I helped, against my will,
   But Fate was pitiless, and we were blind.
   The villain caught me all unarmed, unwatching,
   And these two eyes—that weep him yet—beheld
235 Pirithous under the fangs of beasts
   Fatted on human slaughter; and I spent
   Deep in the sightless silence of his dungeons
   Down near the horrible empire of the Dead,
   Six months. Then Heaven thought on me again.
240 I tricked the watchful eyes. I purged creation
   Of one perfidious enemy, and his blood
   Glutted his own fell monsters. Now at length
   Free, and restored to all that's left to love,
   Now that my soul aspires to nothing more
245 Than the enjoyment of their blessed sight,
   Grief and lament is all my salutation,
   None will abide to suffer my embraces;
   And, chilled by the contagion of the fears
   That breathe about my path, I'd rather be
250 A prisoner again and in Epirus.
    Speak out. Phaedra declares I've been betrayed.
   Who wronged me? Why is not the wrong avenged?
   Has Greece, so long beholden to this arm,
   Offered a refuge to the criminal?
255 —You will not answer? Is my son, my son,
   A shield and ally of my enemies?
   I will go in, for this suspense unmans me.
   I will find out the culprit and the offence.
   Phaedra must tell me what her sorrow is.

   (*Exit* THESEUS.)

260 HIPPOLYTUS: What did her words portend? They froze my
     blood:
   Would Phaedra in her ecstasy of frenzy

Denounce her guilt and give her case away?
Gods, when the King is told! Death-dealing Love,
What blighting mists thou hast wrapped around his house!
And I with my secret of disloyal passion,   265
What was I once, what will he think me now!
My mind is dark with unaccomplished shapes
Of evil: but need innocence be afraid?
I must look for better times and better ways
To move my father's heart, and then reveal   270
Love he may doom to parting and to tears
But fixed beyond his force to overthrow.

— ACT FOUR —

THESEUS, OENONE

THESEUS: Ah! What have you said? The rebel, the betrayer
  Conceived this outrage on his father's honour?
  How unrelenting is thy hand upon me,
  O Destiny! I know not where I go,
  I know not what I do. All my long kindness   5
  Wasted, paid with this hideous wanton plot!
  And with the argument and threat of steel
  To enforce his dark design! I know that sword,
  I gave it him, I strapped it to his side—
  For nobler work than this. Not all the bonds   10
  Of blood itself could hold him back; and she
  Could hesitate to punish, and her silence
  Showed mercy to the wrongdoer!
OENONE: Say rather
  Showed mercy to a father's suffering.
  Shamed by a lover's frenzy, and ashamed   15
  That her chaste eyes could kindle such a fire,
  She would have died, my lord, and dimmed for ever
  Herself the innocent lustre of those eyes.
  The arm was raised. I hastened, I preserved
  Her life for the embraces of her lord,   20
  And pitying your fears and her confusion
  Became the unwilling spokesman of her tears.
THESEUS: The perfidy! Yes, for all his craft, he paled;
  He quaked with fear, I saw it as he came;
  I marvelled then to feel his joylessness   25
  And froze against the chill of his embrace.
  —Did you not say, the love that burns in him
  Had shown itself in Athens long before?
OENONE: My lord, remember how the Queen abhorred him;
  It was unhallowed love that caused her hatred.   30
THESEUS: And now, in Trozen, it has flared again?
OENONE: I have told you all, my lord; but I have left
  My lady too long now with her deadly sorrow,
  And, by your leave, my place is at her side.

(*Exit* OENONE. *Enter* HIPPOLYTUS.)

THESEUS: So, here he comes. Great Gods, that noble carriage 35
  Would it not blind another's eye, as mine?
  Then sacrilegious and adulterous heads
  May flaunt the sacred emblem of the pure?
  Why is there no infallible badge to blazon
  The minds of our dissembling race of men?   40

HIPPOLYTUS: May I not know, my lord, why such a weight
    Of cloud darkens the majesty of your brow?
    Must this be secret from my loyalty?
    THESEUS: Dissembler! Dare you come so near to me?
45   Monster the thunderbolts reprieve too long,
    Corrupted straggler of the brigand race
    I cleansed the earth of once, how dare you still
    Parade that odious face, here where your frenzy
    Clutched at a father's bed? How dare you pace
50   These halls where all things tell of your dishonour?
    Why are you not far hence, where skies unknown
    Illumine coasts that never knew my name?
    Away, you traitor. Do not stand and tempt
    A hate, an anger hardly to be stayed.
55   Enough for me the indelible reproach
    Of fathering you, without the soil of murder
    To smother my bright deeds from memory.
    —Away. And if you would not share the sentence
    Of all the villains that this hand has felled
60   Take care that never again the sun that lights us
    Finds your rebellious feet upon this shore.
    Away, I tell you, out of my dominions
    And cleanse them for ever of your loathsome presence.
        And now hear, Neptune, hear. If once my courage
65   Scoured off a scum of bandits from thy coasts
    Remember thou hast sworn in recompense
    To grant one prayer. In long and stern confinement
    I called not thy undying power; I saved thee
    Thrifty of all the aid I hoped for, till
70   A greater need. Today I pray: avenge
    A mourning father. To thy wrath I leave
    This profligate. Still his lust in his blood.
    Let Theseus read thy kindness in thy rage.
    HIPPOLYTUS: With such a love Hippolytus is charged
75   By Phaedra! Weight of horror crushes me;
    So many assaults unlooked-for, stroke on stroke,
    Leave me no words.
    THESEUS: And so you judged that Phaedra's
    Compliant silence would have muffled up
    Your savage insolence. You might have waited
80   To gather up the sword that now, in her hands,
    Helps to convict you. Or why not, better still,
    Heap up the measure of your infamy
    With one good blow to finish breath and life?
    HIPPOLYTUS: After a calumny so infamous
85   I should let truth be heard—but for a secret
    That touches you, my lord. I beg you sanction
    Respect that silences what I might say;
    Labour no more to probe into your pain,
    Look on my life, consider what I am:
90   The greatest crimes have lesser crimes before them;
    The rest is easy when the way is known;
    Like virtue, vice is gradual. No one day
    Made any good man vile, murderous, incestuous,
    And innocence is slow to dare, and slow
95   To push beyond the boundaries of law.
    I had a mother, as chaste as she was valiant,
    Nor have I derogated from my blood;
    Pittheus, wise among men, took up my nurture
    After her hands. I would not praise myself,
100   But, if one virtue was allotted mine,

May I not claim, my lord, to loathe that act
    My enemies presume to speak of? This
    Has made Hippolytus his name in Greece—
    Unstudied honour rude in its excess,
    Rugged, intractable austerity.   105
    The daylight is no cleaner than the deeps
    Of this my heart. What, sacrilegious lust
    Could stain Hippolytus?
    THESEUS: And this condemns you:
    That was the foul source fed your vaunted coldness—
    No one but Phaedra could bewitch your eyes;   110
    No other woman's love was worth your interest
    Unless it offered pleasures more than lawful.
    HIPPOLYTUS: No, father, you shall hear the truth. This heart
    Has not refused an honourable yoke.
    Here at your feet I will confess—I love,   115
    And love in disobedience to your will.
    Aricia's beauty holds my heart enslaved
    And Pallas' daughter has subdued your son.
    I worship her, forgetful of my duty
    And have no room to feel another passion.   120
    THESEUS: You love her! No—a pitiful pretence;
    You feign that crime to clear yourself of this.
    HIPPOLYTUS: These six months I have hid from love, and
        loved,
    My lord; I came here to confess to you
    In trembling. But is it so? Will nothing move you?   125
    What fearful oath will win you to believe?
    Witness the Earth, the Heavens, and all Nature . . .
    THESEUS: What felon ever feared a perjury?
    Peace, peace. Waste no more time on idle stories
    If that fine virtue rests on aids like these.   130
    HIPPOLYTUS: You see it as a mockery, a lie:
    But Phaedra in her heart of hearts knows better.
    THESEUS: Shall I endure so much effrontery?
    HIPPOLYTUS: What place of exile, and how long a time
    Do you appoint?   135
    THESEUS: Past the Pillars of Hercules
    A traitor's presence is too close for me.
    HIPPOLYTUS: What friendship shall I find to comfort me
    When you have cast me out, dishonoured thus?
    THESEUS: Find yourself friends whose dangerous regard
    Goes to adultery and honours incest,   140
    Deceivers, ingrates, free of law and shame,
    Fit to protect a criminal like you.
    HIPPOLYTUS: And still you taunt me with adultery
    And incest. How can I reply? But Phaedra
    Came of a mother, Phaedra's is a blood,   145
    My lord, you do not need me to recall it,
    More laden with their awful taint than mine.
    THESEUS: How dare you go so far before my face?
    For the last time, villain, avoid my sight,
    Leave me; or force a father in his rage   150
    To have you flung with infamy from the place.

(*Exit* HIPPOLYTUS.)

And now you go towards your waiting doom
    Irrevocably. For by that River's name
    Terrible even to the immortal Gods,
    Neptune has sworn his oath, and will perform it.   155
    Yes, and I loved you, and in spite of all,

Before the hour is come, my bowels yearn
For pity of you. But I have too much cause—
Did ever a deeper injury wound a father?
160 Ye righteous Gods, that see me thus prostrated,
Did I give being to a son like this?

(Enter PHAEDRA.)

PHAEDRA: My lord, you see me here impelled by terror:
Just now, when that terrible voice assailed my ears,
I thought the threat might come to a fulfilment.
165 Let me beg you, if there still is time, have pity
On your own race, your own blood; do not force me,
My lord, to hear it crying from the earth.
Spare me the endless misery of laying
That fearful stain on a paternal hand.
170 THESEUS: My lady, I have kept my hand unstained
And still the unnatural boy has not escaped;
Immortal hands will undertake his doom,
Neptune's my debtor; you shall be avenged.
PHAEDRA: Your debtor, Neptune! Then your prayer of hate . . .
175 THESEUS: Are you afraid it might be heard too soon?
No, join your own entreaty with my curses,
Paint me his crimes once more in all their blackness
Inflame my faint and still-too-sluggish rage—
He has added guilt more than the guilt you knew;
180 His frenzy spends itself in railing on you,
He swears that all your words are perjuries,
He says Aricia claims his heart, his love,
His loyalty.
PHAEDRA: No, my lord!
THESEUS: That is what he told me;
Not that a flimsy lie could impose on me.
185 I hope to hear that Neptune's justice falls
Swiftly, and till that hour I'll ply his altars
And keep him mindful of his undying word.

(Exit THESEUS.)

PHAEDRA: He leaves me, with this dreadful news, alone.
Ah Gods, the fire that I dreamed was safely stifled
190 To wake no more! Dreadful, unlooked-for news!
All trepidation and remorse, all speed
Out of Oenone's clinging arms of fear
I came to save his son. And who can tell
What might have been had conscience had its way?
195 Whether I might have spoken of my guilt,
Might have let slip, had he but left me time,
The entire and awful truth?—He has felt love,
Hippolytus, who never felt for me;
Aricia claims his loyalty, his heart . . .
200 Gods! while I pleaded, while my prayer beat
On those rigid eyes, that unrelenting brow,
I thought he bore impenetrable armour
Always the same and closed to all alike.
And now another has overthrown his pride,
205 Another finds favour in the tyrant's eyes;
Perhaps his heart is easy to entreat
And condescends to any plea but mine.
And I am fool enough to be his friend!

(Enter OENONE.)

—Oenone, do you know what I have heard?
OENONE: No; I have tried to find you in alarm,   210
Wondering what sudden impulse drove you here
And how it may imperil you . . .
PHAEDRA: Oenone,
Who would have thought there was another woman?
OENONE: You say—
PHAEDRA: Hippolytus, I tell you, loves—   215
The adversary I could never shake,
Vexed by submission, impatient of complaining,
The ogre that I never could encounter
Undaunted; he is tamed and brought to heel,
Aricia has forced the access to his heart.
OENONE: Aricia!   220
PHAEDRA: Oh, I never thought of these,
These newest tortures that I live to taste:
All the old despairs, the ecstasies, the broodings,
Raging of flame, and horror of remorse,
And that slight of unendurable denial   225
Were barely foretastes of my torment here.
They, lovers! Did they bewitch these watchful eyes?
What time did they find to meet? Since when? What place?
What furtive means? You knew. Why was I left
To treasure foolish dreams? You might have told me
Of their stolen pleasure. Were they often seen   230
Speaking, or lingering? Was it the forest shades
That sheltered them? Ah, but they had liberty
To see the face they sought. The Heavens smiled
On the innocence of their embrace, no fear
Restrained their eager steps, and each fair day   235
Rose clear and candid on their love. And I
Disowned, dishonoured in the whole creation
I fled the sun, I could not face the daylight,
Death was the only godhead I could pray;
Gall on my tongue, and tears my only drink;   240
Happy, if any privacy of grief
Had left me this one pitiable solace,
To taste a last precarious luxury;
But the forced travesty of a smiling face
Deprived me even of the right to weep.   245
OENONE: They reap no harvest of their vain desires:
They'll meet no more.
PHAEDRA: They'll love for evermore.
Now as I speak—the poison of the thought!—
Mocking the fury of a rival wronged,
Forgetful of the exile that divides them,   250
They swear a thousand times never to part.
No, I will not yield to the insult of their joy,
Oenone. Help me, pity my jealousy.
Aricia must be crushed. I must stir up
My husband's wrath against that hated house—   255
No feeble sentence serves, the sister's crime
Is more than all her brothers'. I'll entreat him
In rage and jealousy.
                      What am I doing?
Where is reason in my wandering mind? I, jealous?
I, entreat Theseus? He, my husband, lives   260
And still I burn—for whom? Still yearn—for whom?
At every word each separate hair lifts up
Upon my head. My guilt has filled the measure—
I crave for incest, dream of calumny,

265 My murderous hands, avid of vengeance, burn
To bathe in the blood of innocence. Misery!
And dare I live, and dare I face the sight
Of that sacred Sun, the giver of my life,
I, grandchild of the high Father of the Gods,
270 My forebears crowding Heaven and all creation?
Where may I hide? Flee to the night of Hell?
No, no, not there; for there my father's hands
Inexorable lift the doomsday urn,
They say, and Minos stands in deathly justice
275 Over the pallid multitudes of men.
Will that great shade not start in ghastly anger
When I in shame before his awful gaze,
His daughter, plead my guilt, and deeds perhaps
Unheard in all the calendar of Hell?
280 Father, what will you say to these? I see
The tremendous urn roll thundering at your feet;
I see you ponder unknown penalties
To execute yourself upon your own . . .
Forgive. A cruel God detests your seed,
285 A heavenly vengeance breathed in me the frenzy
You see. Alas, and still of all the guilt
And all the shame that never will release me
My fearful heart has never reaped the sweets.
Pursued while yet I breathe by ceaseless evils
290 I wait to yield a bruised and broken life.
OENONE: My lady, come, dismiss a causeless terror,
Be more indulgent to a venial failing—
You love; but driven by a fatal charm.
It is not ours to challenge Destiny.
295 Was this a wonder never seen till now?
Were you the first that Love has overthrown?
Weakness was ever part of man's condition;
So, mortal, bow to a mortal's destiny.
You struggle against an immemorial yoke:
300 Even the Gods that live in high Olympus
Whose judgements hold a guilty world in dread
Have loved, and sometimes loved against the law.
PHAEDRA: Still you dare speak? And this is your advice,
And till the end you mean to drug my mind?
305 I hate you. All your help has been my downfall.
You dragged me back to the unbearable sunshine;
Your prayers were louder than the voice of right;
The man that I shunned, you made me see.
Was it your business? And now have all the lies
310 Of those false lips dared blacken such a life?
You may have killed him. His father's impious vows
And blind revenge perhaps are gratified
Already. I'll hear no more. Leave me alone,
Loathly inhuman monster; leave my sight,
315 Leave me alone to shape my bitter future.
On you I pray the justice of the Gods;
And may they make you the eternal warning
Of all cringing cunning sycophants that nourish
Their masters' dearest weakness, urge the way
320 Their cravings tend, and smooth the slope of crime;
Accursed flatterers, deadliest gift of all
That angry Heaven inflicts upon a King!

(Exit.)

OENONE: *(Alone.)* O ye Gods! To have borne so much for
her, forgone
So much!—This is my pay. And it is just.

— ACT FIVE —

HIPPOLYTUS, ARICIA, ISMENE

ARICIA: And in this extremity you will not speak
And will not undeceive a loving father?
Cruel, if you can disregard my tears
And lightly say goodbye to me for ever,
Then sail, and leave Aricia with her grief;   5
But do not go in certainty of death.
Fight the foul imputation on your honour,
Constrain your father to unsay his curses.
There is time yet. What reason, or what folly
Makes you leave all the advantage to the accuser?   10
Tell Theseus what you know.
HIPPOLYTUS: Have I not told
What may be told? Would you have me reveal
To light the shameful mystery of his bed
Or by too scrupulous report bring down
Confusion on a father's honoured head?   15
Alone you know this horror. You, and the Gods,
Alone receive the outpouring of my heart.
See if I love you: I have shown to you
What I would fain have veiled from my own thoughts.
But under what a seal, you know. Forget,   20
My lady, if you can, that I have spoken;
Let me believe this hideous affair
Will never be breathed between those blameless lips.
We set our trust upon the righteous Heavens.
My cause is theirs; and Phaedra, whether soon   25
Or in the slow procedure of their justice,
Will not escape disgrace. This deference
I ask of you; and all the rest I sweep
Before the liberty of my wrath. I bid you
No longer be a slave. I bid you dare   30
To come with me, dare to be banned with me.
Break from a poisoned house where Virtue breathes
A deathly and a desecrated air;
Turn into profit for a headlong flight
All the disorder following on my fall.   35
The means I offer: you have still no guard
But my own men. Most powerful patrons wait us—
Argos extends her arms, and Sparta welcomes;
Let common friends receive our just laments,
Otherwise Phaedra rakes our wreckage up,   40
Evicts us both from a throne our fathers left us,
And strips us both for spoils to deck her son.
The moment beckons, grasp it. But what fear
Restrains you? What suspends your doubtful mind?
Only for your sake have I dared so far.   45
When I am all on fire, why are you ice?
Are you unwilling to adventure on
An outlaw's path?
ARICIA: Oh, but how happily,
My lord, I'd taste of exile so; how eagerly
Embrace a life forgotten of all beside   50

And linked with yours! But lacking that sweet bond
Can I in honour join your wanderings?
I know the sternest laws do not forbid me
To fly your father's power: he is not mine,
55 I owe him no obedience; and to fly
From an oppressor is the right of all.
But you, my lord, love me. And anxious honour . . .
    HIPPOLYTUS: And can you think I rate that honour cheaply?
No, no. I came with worthier designs—
60 Escape your foes, and follow as my bride.
Free in adversity, since Heaven has freed us,
Our pledges need no words but ours, and Hymen
Robbed of his torchlit rites is Hymen still.
        By Trozen's gates, among those sepulchres,
65 Antique memorials of my father's pride,
A wayside temple holy and renowned
Stands grim protector of the plighted word;
There falsehood dare not raise her voice, or falls
Blasted at once, and certitude of death
70 Lays chains invincible on perjury.
May we not there with solemn mutual oath
Give and receive our hearts' enduring faith
Before the shrine, and pray the Deity
For his protection and paternal love?
75 I will invoke each mighty God to hear me—
Maiden Diana, Juno's majesty,
And every name whose present patronage
Shall seal and sanctify my true intent.
    ARICIA: The King is here. Fly, Prince, depart at once.
80 I shall remain awhile to hide my purpose.
Away—but send me back a trusty servant
To guide my footsteps safely to your side.

(Exit HIPPOLYTUS.*)*

(Enter THESEUS.*)*

THESEUS: Lighten the mists, ye Gods, and show my eyes
The truth they seek for here!
                                Now, sweet Ismene,
85 See everything is done. Be ready quickly.

(Exit ISMENE.*)*

THESEUS: You seem disturbed, your colour fails, my lady.
What was Hippolytus doing in this place?
ARICIA: Taking an everlasting leave, my lord.
THESEUS: And so your eyes have tamed that rebel heart
90 And brought him to his earliest thoughts of love.
ARICIA: I must not hide the truth from you, my lord.
He has not learnt your unjust hate from you;
He did not treat me like a criminal.
THESEUS: You mean he vowed you everlasting passion.
95 I should not build on that unsettled heart.
He swore as deep to others.
ARICIA: He, my lord?
THESEUS: I wish you could have taught him constancy.
How could you bear that loathsome competition?
ARICIA: And how can you bear loathsome calumnies
100 To blacken all the lustre of his fame?
Have you so little knowledge of his nature?
Can you not tell the guiltless from the guilty?
Only your eyes are darkened by a cloud

That lets his goodness gleam on all the world.
Oh stop, relent. He must not be the victim   105
Of false accusers. Repent your murderous curses.
Tremble, my lord, tremble, lest frowning Heaven
Hate you enough to take you at your word—
Gods may accept our offerings in anger
And punish with the presents we entreated.   110
THESEUS: No, blind as you are with ill-requited love
You will not blind me to his villainy;
For I have witnesses, beyond reproach,
Beyond suspicion—I have seen tears flow,
Tears that were true.   115
ARICIA: Look to yourself, my lord:
Your matchless weight of arm redeemed mankind
From monsters past all counting—but not all,
The breed is not destroyed, and you have saved
One . . . I must say no more; your son forbids me.
Knowing what deference his heart still holds   120
I should increase his suffering too much
Dared I continue. Let me imitate
His generous scruple, and excuse myself
While nothing forces me to break my silence.

(Exit ARICIA.*)*

THESEUS: *(Alone.)* But what is in her mind? What lurks below 125
A tale so often broached, and never told?
Is it a stratagem without a meaning?
Is it conspiracy to bind me on
A rack of doubt? And secret in my heart
Steeled to be cruel, what is the small voice   130
That pleads for mercy, and unmans my wrath,
Perplexes me and tears me?—I must see
Her woman once again; I know too little.
—Guard! Fetch Oenone, and send her in alone.

(Enter PANOPE.*)*

PANOPE: I cannot say what thoughts are in her heart, 135
But the distraction motions of the Queen
Fill me with fear, my lord. Death and despair
Are painted on her face, and the deathly tint
Sits even now upon her cheeks. Already
Pursued with scorn and chiding from her side,   140
Oenone has plunged to death among the waves.
None knows what wild will drove her, and her voice
Is covered in the murmur of the tide.
THESEUS: What have you said?
PANOPE: Her going gave no peace;
Confusion gains in the Queen's divided soul: 145
One moment, soothing her mysterious grief,
She takes her children, bathes them in her tears;
And suddenly, her motherhood dismissed,
She drives them from her with a look of loathing.
Her restless steps come and go purposeless   150
And we are strangers in her fevered eyes.
Thrice she has written, only to repent,
And thrice destroyed the message uncompleted.
My lord, be gracious: see her, comfort her.
THESEUS: Is it so? Oenone's dead, and Phaedra waits 155
For death? Call for my son, let him plead his cause,
Let him speak to me, and I will listen.

(Exit PANOPE.)

                             Neptune,
Delay thy deadly gift, be not too sudden,
Rather refuse it utterly. What if
160   I was seduced too soon by worthless words?
What if my cruel hands were raised too rashly?
What wretchedness would follow from that vow!

(Enter THERAMENES.)

THESEUS: Is it you, Theramenes? Where is my son?
    What have you done with him? His careful tending
165   Has been your charge from earliest infancy.
    But why the tears I see upon your cheeks?
    What of my son?
THERAMENES: O late, O vain regret,
    O useless love! Hippolytus is no more.
THESEUS: Oh Gods!
THERAMENES: I saw him die, the best and sweetest
170   Of human kind—and, let me say, my lord,
    The purest also.
THESEUS: Is my son dead? Now,
    Now that these arms reached out for him, the Gods
    Impatient urged his execution on?
    How did I lose him? What immortal stroke. . . ?
175 THERAMENES: Still close behind us lay the gates of Trozen.
    He drove his chariot, his grieving guard
    Matching his silence, marched on either hand.
    Sunk in his thought, the loose reins lying free,
    He brought us on the causeway to Mycenae;
180   And the noble beasts, so eager once to leap
    At the least inflexion of a master's voice,
    Now bent dull eyes to earth and drooping crests
    As if communing with his bitter mood.
    —Suddenly from the sea an awful cry
185   Shattered the silence of the air. And then
    A second voice wailed answer from the landward.
    Our blood was frozen in our inmost hearts.
    Stiffly rose up the listening horses' manes.
    And now from the level deep immense there heaves
190   A boiling mount of brine, and still it swells,
    Rears wavelike foaming down on us and breaks
    To belch a ravening monster at our feet
    Whose threatening brow is broadened with huge horns,
    Whose body, cased in golden glint of scales,
195   Thrashes a train of sinuous writhing whorls.
    Indomitable bull, malignant dragon,
    Its long-drawn bellows rumble down the shore;
    Heaven quails, earth shudders at the portent, air
    Reeks with its pestilential breath. The wave
200   Withdraws again, aghast at what it bore.
    We fly to the nearby temple; not one lingers
    Or wraps himself in unavailing valour.
    Hippolytus, honouring his hero blood,
    Hippolytus alone checks, wheels his team,
205   Snatches the spears, charges upon the creature,
    Aims, and unerring flings. A gaping slash
    Fair in the monster's flank drives it in bounds
    Of pain and fury to the horses' feet
    To roar and wallow and from flaming jaws

To spatter them with blood and cloud and fire.   210
Reckless, they plunge aside. They hear no more,
Answer no more to bridle or to voice.
The charioteer spends all his strength in vain
While they redden the bits with spume that is bright with
   blood.
Even, men say, some more than mortal shape   215
Borne on the horrible confusion plied
Their dusty flanks with goads. Where terror leads them
Stand rocks. The axle screeches, snaps. The car
Crashes in fragments; and my fearless master
Drops tangled in the reins. . .—Forgive my weakness.   220
In that tormenting image lives a source
Of quenchless tears.—I watched, my lord, I watched
Your helpless son dragging behind the steeds
His hands had fed. He tried to call to them:
Instead, his cries startle them. So they gallop   225
And make one wound of all his living flesh.
    Now as the plain is pealing with our grief
The violent fit is spent. They slacken speed,
And stop, where close at hand his father's tombs
And ancient sculptures hold the chill remains   230
And memories of Kings. I run, behind me
Run all his guard, reading the traces painted
By his gallant blood, past the empurpled crags,
Past dripping brambles hung about with spoils
Of bloody hair. I reach him, I speak; he gives me   235
A hand and greets me with a dying gaze
That quickly closes. And I hear these words:
    'My guiltless days are forfeit to the Gods.
Do you after my death be watchful over
The sad Aricia; and, sweet friend, if ever   240
My father undeceived should come to mourn
The misadventure of a slandered son,
To lay in peace my blood and wailing shade
Bid him be gentle to the captive maiden,
Render her . . .' On the word the lifeless youth   245
Fell back into my arms a ravaged corpse,
The dreadful triumph of an angry Heaven,
Where not a father's eye could undertake
To know his child.
THESEUS: O child! O dearest hope
I cast away! Gods, ye unswerving Gods,   250
Too faithfully ye served me! Now must life
Henceforward be a death of long-drawn sorrow.
THERAMENES: And now in fear and haste Aricia,
    Stealing, my lord, from your captivity
    To hear his nuptial vow before the Gods,   255
    Approached. There are the red and steaming grasses,
    And there—what welcome for a bride's regard!—
    There is Hippolytus, but motionless,
    Featureless, bloodless. First she seeks to question
    Her misery, and, seeing, still demands   260
    Hippolytus. Then, too pitifully assured,
    After one glance reproachful to the skies
    Cold, with one cry, lifeless upon the dead
    She falls. Ismene, weeping, is beside her
    And draws her back to life and life's despair;   265
    And I, still subject to the hostile daylight,
    Return to speak a hero's last desires

And so fulfil the grievous ministry
His dying heart committed to my love.
270   —But here I see the deadliest of his foes.

(*Enter* PHAEDRA, PANOPE *and* GUARDS.)

THESEUS: Well, victory is yours: my son is gone.
Much, much I could suspect; deep rankling doubt
Acquits him in my heart and troubled mind—
But he is dead: your sacrifice, my lady;
275   Take it, find satisfaction in the forfeit
Unmerited or just. It matters little
That evermore my eyes be blindfolded;
Let him be criminal if you accuse.
His loss alone is theme enough for sorrow,
280   No need to look for new and fearful knowledge
That, impotent to bring the dead again,
Could pile at most new suffering on the old.
Let me escape, leave you and leave these shores,
Flying the bloody image of a son
285   Mangled—before that harrying memory
I could long for exile from the world of men.
All things upbraid me, all increase my anguish—
My very name (for nameless, I could hide),
The very honours that the Gods bestowed,
290   Whose murderous grace I'll mourn, and not again
Importune them with fruitless prayers of mine;
Do what they might, their fatal condescension
Could not console for what they took away.
PHAEDRA: Theseus, I have repented of my silence.
295   Your son requires his innocence from my lips;
Yes, he was guiltless.
THESEUS: This to me, his father!
And on your solemn faith I sentenced him.
Can any pretext for an act so vile—
PHAEDRA: My time is measured. Listen to me, Theseus.
300   I, on your dutiful and temperate son,

Looked with profaning and incestuous eyes—
The flame of Heaven lighted in my bosom
A fatal fire. Oenone did the rest;
She feared Hippolytus, my passion known,
Would publish all the madness that he loathed;   305
Presuming on my feebleness, she came
With that base story of my victim's guilt.
Self-chosen, easy death among the waves
Punished her perfidy and foiled my anger,
And by now the knife would have cleft my destiny,   310
But goodness still cried out for vindication.
I chose the slower path. I chose to pour
Into your ears before I joined the dead
The chronicle of my remorse. I have drained
And mingled with my burning blood a draught   315
Medea left in Athens. Now already
Her poison makes it progress toward my heart
Striking that heart with cold it never knew;
Faintly already I perceive the daylight
And you I wrong by my unworthy presence;   320
And death, blurring the sunbeams from these eyes
Whose glance polluted them, restores the light
To perfect purity.
PANOPE: My lord, she is dying.
THESEUS: And would the dark remembrance too might die
Of what she has done! Come, all is now too plain.   325
I must enfold what still remains to touch
Of my dear son, and expiate in tears
The blind curse I shall evermore bewail
With dear-bought honours rendered at his tomb;
And, better to placate his injured spirit,   330
I will forget the voice of ancient vengeance
And look upon his lover as my child.

■ APHRA BEHN ■

Little is known about the early life of England's first female professional playwright, Aphra Behn (1640–1689). As a child, she moved to Surinam with her parents, where she lived until returning to England in the late 1650s. In 1658, she married a merchant named Behn and served Charles II as a spy in Antwerp in the mid-1660s. When she returned to England penniless in 1667, she was sent to debtors' prison and appealed to the government for her wages. Between 1670 and her death in 1689, Behn became one of the most popular of English playwrights. Behn wrote fifteen plays beginning with *The Forced Marriage: or, The Jealous Bridegroom*, a tragicomedy produced by Thomas Betterton at Lincoln's Inn Fields. Behn's major plays are mainly in the mode of Restoration comedy, including *The Rover* (1677), *The Feigned Courtesans* (1679), *The Second Part of The Rover* (1681), and *The City Heiress* (1682). In 1688, Behn published a novel, *Oronooko: or, The Royal Slave*, set in the West Indies. The novel was dramatized by Thomas Southerne in 1695 and was popular onstage throughout the eighteenth century. An important figure in the history of the novel, and a brilliantly successful playwright, Aphra Behn is appropriately buried in Westminster Abbey.

THE ROVER

The Rover is a comedy of intrigue, set in Naples during the Carnival. The play concerns the sexual adventures of a band of Englishmen—Belvile, Willmore (the Rover), and Blunt—and their efforts to seduce the heroine Florinda and her sister Hellena. Like many Restoration comedies, *The Rover* takes a frank attitude toward sexual and financial negotiation, which are often paired in the play. The play opens with Hellena's rejection of a life in the convent and her decision to "provide my self this Carnival, if there be e'er a handsome proper fellow." In the course of the play, Hellena flirts with Willmore; Willmore wins the services (and, unfortunately, the love) of the courtesan Angelica, who eventually tries to murder him; Willmore and Blunt nearly rape Florinda on several occasions; and Blunt is tricked by a prostitute and turned out into the street in his shirt and underwear, "before consummation."

Yet despite the licentiousness of its action, the play clearly depends on a deeply ingrained sense of propriety, much of which operates through class distinctions. While it "would anger us vilely to be trussed up for a rape upon a maid of quality," one of the gentlemen declares, it seems otherwise acceptable to "ruffle a harlot." Morality, in *The Rover*, is in many ways determined by class and wealth. These distinctions are both troubled and confirmed by the important function of disguise and masking in the play. Since the action of *The Rover* takes place during Carnival, the main characters meet only in disguise. Masking enables the characters both to flirt without dishonoring themselves and to discover the truth about one another. In fact, masking in the play empowers the women, in that the temporary masking of the Carnival allows the women to escape their enforced lives at home and to meet men in public. Florinda and Hellena, for instance, can marry only with their brother Pedro's permission. He wants to marry his sisters to the wealthiest—and oldest—suitors, who will be able to settle large fortunes on them. However, the young Englishmen who attract the two sisters are Royalist supporters of Charles II, currently exiled from Cromwell's Protectorate because they support the Crown. As a result, although they are well-born, they are currently without funds and so are a poor match for Florinda and Hellena, at least in Pedro's eyes.

Masking also enables the women to escape Pedro's control, to act on their own behalf. Indeed, although the women are more modest than the Rover, they are equally devious in their pursuit of a lover—though the women insist on marriage as the price of their virginity. In Behn's brilliant comedy, the women emerge as the agents—as well as the objects—of the play's erotic intrigue.

THE ROVER
OR THE BANISH'D CAVALIERS

APHRA BEHN
EDITED BY MONTAGUE SUMMERS

— CHARACTERS —

Don ANTONIO, *the Vice-Roy's Son*
Don PEDRO, *a Noble Spaniard, his Friend*
BELVILE, *an English Colonel in love with Florinda*
WILLMORE, *the Rover*
FREDERICK, *an English Gentleman, and Friend to Belvile and Blunt*
BLUNT, *an English Country Gentleman*
STEPHANO, *Servant to Don Pedro*
PHILIPPO, *Lucetta's Gallant*
SANCHO, *Pimp to Lucetta*
BISKEY *and* SEBASTIAN, *two Bravoes to Angelica*
DIEGO, *Page to Don Antonio*
PAGE *to Hellena*
BOY, *Page to Belvile*

Blunt's MAN
OFFICERS *and* SOLDIERS
FLORINDA, *Sister to Don Pedro*
HELLENA, *a gay young Woman design'd for a Nun, and Sister to Florinda*
VALERIA, *a Kinswoman to Florinda*
ANGELICA BIANCA, *a famous Curtezan*
MORETTA, *her Woman*
CALLIS, *Governess to Florinda and Hellena*
LUCETTA, *a jilting Wench*
SERVANTS, *other* MASQUERADERS, MEN *and* WOMEN

SCENE: *Naples, in Carnival-time.*

— PROLOGUE —
WRITTEN BY A PERSON OF QUALITY

WITS, like Physicians, never can agree,
When of a different Society;
And Rabel's Drops were never more cry'd down
By all the Learned Doctors of the Town,
5   Than a new Play, whose Author is unknown:
Nor can those Doctors with more Malice sue
(And powerful Purses) the dissenting Few,
Than those with an insulting Pride do rail
At all who are not of their own Cabal.
10   If a Young Poet hit your Humour right,
You judge him then out of Revenge and Spite;
So amongst Men there are ridiculous Elves,
Who Monkeys hate for being too like themselves:
So that the Reason of the Grand Debate,
15   Why Wit so oft is damn'd, when good Plays take,
Is, that you censure as you love or hate.
Thus, like a learned Conclave, Poets sit
Catholick Judges both of Sense and Wit,
And damn or save, as they themselves think fit.
20   Yet those who to others Faults are so severe,
Are not so perfect, but themselves may err.
Some write correct indeed, but then the whole
(Bating their own dull Stuff i'th' Play) is stole:
As Bees do suck from Flowers their Honey-dew,
25   So they rob others, striving to please you.
    Some write their Characters genteel and fine,
But then they do so toil for every Line,
That what to you does easy seem, and plain,
Is the hard issue of their labouring Brain.
30   And some th' Effects of all their Pains we see,
Is but to mimick good Extempore.
Others by long Converse about the Town,
Have Wit enough to write a leud Lampoon,

But their chief Skill lies in a Baudy Song.
In short, the only Wit that's now in Fashion   35
Is but the Gleanings of good Conversation.
As for the Author of this coming Play,
I ask'd him what he thought fit I should say,
In thanks for your good Company to day:
He call'd me Fool, and said it was well known,   40
You came not here for our sakes, but your own.
New Plays are stuff'd with Wits, and with Debauches,
That croud and sweat like Cits in *May*-day Coaches.

— ACT ONE —

SCENE I

A chamber.

(Enter FLORINDA *and* HELLENA.*)*

FLORINDA: What an impertient thing is a young Girl bred in a Nunnery! How full of Questions! Prithee no more, Hellena; I have told thee more than thou understand'st already.

HELLENA: The more's my Grief; I wou'd fain know as much as you, which makes me so inquisitive; nor is't enough to know   5
you're a Lover, unless you tell me too, who 'tis you sigh for.

FLORINDA: When you are a Lover, I'll think you fit for a Secret of that nature.

HELLENA: 'Tis true, I was never a Lover yet—but I begin to have a shreud Guess, what 'tis to be so, and fancy it very   10
pretty to sigh, and sing, and blush and wish, and dream and wish, and long and wish to see the Man; and when I do, look pale and tremble; just as you did when my Brother brought home the fine *English* Colonel to see you—what do you call him? Don *Belvile.*   15

FLORINDA: Fie, *Hellena.*

HELLENA: That Blush betrays you—I am sure 'tis so—or is it Don *Antonio* the Vice-Roy's Son?—or perhaps the rich old

20 Don *Vincentio*, whom my father designs for your Husband?—Why do you blush again?

FLORINDA: With Indignation; and how near soever my Father thinks I am to marrying that hated Object, I shall let him see I understand better what's due to my Beauty, Birth and Fortune, and more to my Soul, than to obey those unjust

25 Commands.

HELLENA: Now hang me, if I don't love thee for that dear Disobedience. I love Mischief strangely, as most of our Sex do, who are come to love nothing else—But tell me, dear *Florinda*, don't you love that fine *Anglese?*—for I vow next to

30 loving him my self, 'twill please me most that you do so, for he is so gay and so handsom.

FLORINDA: *Hellena*, a Maid design'd for a Nun ought not to be so curious in a Discourse of Love.

HELLENA: And dost thou think that ever I'll be a Nun? Or at

35 least till I'm so old, I'm fit for nothing else. Faith no, Sister; and that which makes me long to know whether you love *Belvile*, is because I hope he has some mad Companion or other, that will spoil my Devotion; nay I'm resolv'd to provide my self this Carnival, if there be e'er a handsom Fellow

40 of my Humour above Ground, tho I ask first.

FLORINDA: Prithee be not so wild.

HELLENA: Now you have provided your self with a Man, you take no Care for poor me—Prithee tell me, what dost thou see about me that is unfit for Love—have not I a world of

45 Youth? a Humour gay? a Beauty passable? a Vigour desirable? well shap'd? clean limb'd? sweet breath'd? and Sense enough to know how all these ought to be employ'd to the best Advantage: yes, I do and will. Therefore lay aside your Hopes of my Fortune, by my being a Devotee, and tell me

50 how you came acquainted with this *Belvile*; for I perceive you knew him before he came to *Naples.*

FLORINDA: Yes, I knew him at the Siege of *Pampelona,* he was then a Colonel of *French* Horse, who when the Town was ransack'd, nobly treated my Brother and my self, preserving

55 us from all Insolencies; and I must own, (besides great Obligations) I have I know not what, that pleads kindly for him about my Heart, and will suffer no other to enter—But see my Brother.

(Enter DON PEDRO, STEPHANO, *with a Masquing Habit, and* CALLIS.)

PEDRO: Good morrow, Sister. Pray, when saw you your Lover

60 Don *Vincentio?*

FLORINDA: I know not, Sir—*Callis,* when was he here? for I consider it so little, I know not when it was.

PEDRO: I have a Command from my Father here to tell you, you ought not to despise him, a Man of so vast a Fortune,

65 and such a Passion for you—*Stephano,* my things—

(Puts on his Masquing Habit.)

FLORINDA: A Passion for me! 'tis more than e'er I saw, or had a desire should be known—I hate *Vincentio,* and I would not have a Man so dear to me as my Brother follow the ill Customs of our Country, and make a Slave of his Sister—And

70 Sir, my Father's Will, I'm sure, you may divert.

PEDRO: I know not how dear I am to you, but I wish only to be rank'd in your Esteem, equal with the *English* Colonel *Belvile*—Why do you frown and blush? Is there any Guilt belongs to the Name of that Cavalier?

FLORINDA: I'll not deny I value *Belvile:* when I was expos'd to   75 such Dangers as the licens'd Lust of common Soldiers threatned, when Rage and Conquest flew thro the City— then *Belvile,* this Criminal for my sake, threw himself into all Dangers to save my Honour, and will you not allow him my Esteem?   80

PEDRO: Yes, pay him what you will in Honour—but you must consider Don *Vincentio's* Fortune, and the Jointure he'll make you.

FLORINDA: Let him consider my Youth, Beauty and Fortune; which ought not to be thrown away on his Age and Jointure.   85

PEDRO: 'Tis true, he's not so young and fine a Gentleman as that *Belvile*—but what Jewels will that Cavalier present you with? those of his Eyes and Heart?

HELLENA: And are not those better than any Don *Vincentio* has brought from the *Indies?*   90

PEDRO: Why how now! Has your Nunnery-breeding taught you to understand the Value of Hearts and Eyes?

HELLENA: Better than to believe *Vincentio* deserves Value from any woman—He may perhaps encrease her Bags, but not her Family.   95

PEDRO: This is fine—Go up to your Devotion, you are not design'd for the Conversation of Lovers.

HELLENA: *(Aside.)* Nor Saints yet a while I hope.
Is't not enough you make a Nun of me, but you must cast my Sister away too, exposing her to a worse confinement than a   100 religious Life?

PEDRO: The Girl's mad—Is it a Confinement to be carry'd into the Country, to an antient Villa belonging to the Family of the *Vincentio's* these five hundred Years, and have no other Prospect than that pleasing one of seeing all her own   105 that meets her Eyes—a fine Air, large Fields and Gardens, where she may walk and gather Flowers?

HELLENA: When? By Moon-Light? For I'm sure she dares not encounter with the heat of the Sun; that were a Task only for Don *Vincentio* and his *Indian* Breeding, who loves it in the   110 Dog-days—And if these be her daily Divertisements, what are those of the Night? to lie in a wide Moth-eaten Bed-Chamber with Furniture in Fashion in the Reign of King *Sancho* the First; the Bed that which his Forefathers liv'd and dy'd in.   115

PEDRO: Very well.

HELLENA: This Apartment (new furbisht and fitted out for the young Wife) he (out of Freedom) makes his Dressing-room; and being a frugal and a jealous Coxcomb, instead of a Valet to uncase his feeble Carcase, he desires you to do that Of-   120 fice—Signs of Favour, I'll assure you, and such as you must not hope for, unless your Woman be out of the way.

PEDRO: Have you done yet?

HELLENA: That Honour being past, the Giant stretches it self, yawns and sighs a Belch or two as loud as a Musket, throws   125

---

52 **Siege of Pampelona** Pampluna, the strongly fortified capital of Navarra and very frequently a center of military operations

114 **King Sancho the First** Sancho I, 'the Fat,' of Castile and Leon, reigned 955–67: Sancho I of Aragon 1067–94. But the phrase is here only in a vague general sense to denote some musty and immemorial antiquity without any exact reference

himself into Bed, and expects you in his foul Sheets, and e'er
you can get your self undrest, calls you with a Snore or two—
And are not these fine Blessings to a young Lady?

PEDRO: Have you done yet?

130 HELLENA: And this man you must kiss, nay, you must kiss none
but him too—and nuzle thro his Beard to find his Lips—and
this you must submit to for threescore Years, and all for a
Jointure.

PEDRO: For all your Character of Don *Vincentio*, she is as like

135 to marry him as she was before.

HELLENA: Marry Don *Vincentio*! hang me, such a Wedlock
would be worse than Adultery with another Man: I had
rather see her in the *Hostel de Dieu*, to waste her Youth there
in Vows, and be a Handmaid to Lazers and Cripples, than to

140 lose it in such a Marriage.

PEDRO: You have consider'd, Sister, that *Belvile* has no Fortune to bring you to, is banisht his Country, despis'd at
home, and pity'd abroad.

HELLENA: What then? the Vice-Roy's Son is better than that

145 Old Sir Fisty. Don *Vincentio*! Don *Indian*! he thinks he's
trading to *Gambo* still, and wou'd barter himself (that Bell
and Bawble) for your Youth and Fortune.

PEDRO: *Callis*, take her hence, and lock her up all this Carnival, and at Lent she shall begin her everlasting Penance in a

150 Monastery.

HELLENA: I care not, I had rather be a Nun, than be oblig'd to
marry as you wou'd have me, if I were design'd for't.

PEDRO: Do not fear the Blessing of that Choice—you shall be
a Nun.

155 HELLENA: Shall I so? you may chance to be mistaken in my
way of Devotion—*(Aside.)* A Nun! yes I am like to make a
fine Nun! I have an excellent Humour for a Grate: No, I'll
have a Saint of my own to pray to shortly, if I like any that
dares venture on me.

160 PEDRO: *Callis*, make it your Business to watch this wild Cat.
As for you, *Florinda*, I've only try'd you all this while, and
urg'd my Father's Will; but mine is, that you would love *Antonio*, he is brave and young, and all that can compleat the
Happiness of a gallant Maid—This Absence of my Father

165 will give us opportunity to free you from *Vincentio*, by marrying here, which you must do to morrow.

FLORINDA: To morrow!

PEDRO: To morrow, or 'twill be too late—'tis not my Friendship
to *Antonio*, which makes me urge this, but Love to thee, and

170 Hatred to *Vincentio*—therefore resolve upon't to morrow.

FLORINDA: Sir, I shall strive to do, as shall become your Sister.

PEDRO: I'll both believe and trust you—Adieu.

(Exeunt PEDRO *and* STEPHANO.*)*

HELLENA: As become his Sister!—That is, to be as resolved
your way, as he is his—

*(*HELLENA *goes to* CALLIS.*)*

175 FLORINDA: I ne'er till now perceiv'd my Ruin near,
I've no Defence against *Antonio's* Love,

For he has all the Advantages of Nature,
The moving Arguments of Youth and Fortune.

HELLENA: But hark you, *Callis*, you will not be so cruel to lock
me up indeed: will you? 180

CALLIS: I must obey the Commands I hate—besides, do you
consider what a Life you are going to lead?

HELLENA: Yes, *Callis*, that of a Nun: and till then I'll be indebted a World of Prayers to you, if you let me now see, what
I never did, the Divertisements of a Carnival. 185

CALLIS: What, go in Masquerade? 'twill be a fine farewell to
the World I take it—pray what wou'd you do there?

HELLENA: That which all the World does, as I am told, be as
mad as the rest, and take all innocent Freedom—Sister,
you'll go too, will you not? come prithee be not sad—We'll 190
out-wit twenty Brothers, if you'll be ruled by me—Come put
off this dull Humour with your Clothes, and assume one as
gay, and as fantastick as the Dress my Cousin *Valeria* and I
have provided, and let's ramble.

FLORINDA: *Callis*, will you give us leave to go? 195

CALLIS: *(Aside.)* I have a youthful Itch of going my self.
—Madam, if I thought your Brother might not know it, and
I might wait on you, for by my troth I'll not trust young Girls
alone.

FLORINDA: Thou see'st my Brother's gone already, and thou 200
shalt attend and watch us.

(Enter STEPHANO.*)*

STEPHANO: Madam, the Habits are come, and your Cousin
Valeria is drest, and stays for you.

FLORINDA: 'Tis well—I'll write a Note, and if I chance to see
Belvile, and want an opportunity to speak to him, that shall 205
let him know what I've resolv'd in favour of him.

HELLENA: Come, let's in and dress us.

(Exeunt.)

SCENE II

A Long Street.

(Enter BELVILE, *melancholy,* BLUNT *and* FREDERICK.*)*

FREDERICK: Why, what the Devil ails the Colonel, in a time
when all the World is gay, to look like mere Lent thus? Hadst
thou been long enough in *Naples* to have been in love, I
should have sworn some such Judgment had befall'n thee.

BELVILE: No, I have made no new Amours since I came to 5
Naples.

FREDERICK: You have left none behind you in Paris.

BELVILE: Neither.

FREDERICK: I can't divine the Cause then; unless the old
Cause, the want of Mony. 10

BLUNT: And another old Cause, the want of a Wench—Wou'd
not that revive you?

BELVILE: You're mistaken, *Ned*.

BLUNT: Nay, 'Sheartlikins, then thou art past Cure.

FREDERICK: I have found it out; thou hast renew'd thy Ac- 15
quaintance with the Lady that cost thee so many Sighs at
the Siege of *Pampelona*—pox on't, what d'ye call her—her
Brother's a noble *Spaniard*—Nephew to the dead General—

---

138 **Hostel de Dieu** The first Spanish hospital was erected at Granada
by St. Juan de Dios before 1550   146 **Gambo** The Gambia in West
Africa has been a British Colony since 1664, when a fort, now Fort
James, was founded at the mouth of the river

14 **'sheartlikins** by God's heart

20 *Florinda*—ay, *Florinda*—And will nothing serve thy turn but that damn'd virtuous Woman, whom on my Conscience thou lov'st in spite too, because thou seest little or no possibility of gaining her?

BELVILE: Thou art mistaken, I have Interest enough in that
25 lovely Virgin's Heart, to make me proud and vain, were it not abated by the Severity of a Brother, who perceiving my Happiness—

FREDERICK: Has civilly forbid thee the House?

BELVILE: 'Tis so, to make way for a powerful Rival, the Vice-
30 Roy's Son, who has the advantage of me, in being a Man of Fortune, a *Spaniard*, and her Brother's Friend; which gives him liberty to make his Court, whilst I have recourse only to Letters, and distant Looks from her Window, which are as soft and kind as those which Heav'n sends down on Penitents.

BLUNT: Hey day! 'Sheartlikins, Simile! by this Light the Man
35 is quite spoil'd—*Frederick*, what the Devil are we made of, that we cannot be thus concern'd for a Wench?—'Sheartlikins, our *Cupids* are like the Cooks of the Camp, they can roast or boil a Woman, but they have none of the fine Tricks to set 'em off, no Hogoes to make the Sauce pleasant, and
40 the Stomach sharp.

FREDERICK: I dare swear I have had a hundred as young, kind and handsom as this *Florinda*; and Dogs eat me, if they were not as troublesom to me i'th' Morning as they were welcome o'er night.

45 BLUNT: And yet, I warrant, he wou'd not touch another Woman, if he might have her for nothing.

BELVILE: That's thy Joy, a cheap Whore.

BLUNT: Why, 'dsheartlikins, I Love a frank Soul—When did you ever hear of an honest Woman that took a Man's Mony?
50 I warrant 'em good ones—But, Gentlemen, you may be free, you have been kept so poor with Parliaments and Protectors, that the little Stock you have is not worth preserving—but I thank my Stars, I have more Grace than to forfeit my Estate by Cavaliering.

55 BELVILE: Methinks only following the Court should be sufficient to entitle 'em to that.

BLUNT: 'Sheartlikins, they know I follow it to do it no good, unless they pick a hole in my Coat for lending you Mony now and then; which is a greater Crime to my Conscience,
60 Gentlemen, than to the Common-wealth.

(Enter WILLMORE.*)*

WILLMORE: Ha! dear *Belvile!* noble Colonel!

BELVILE: *Willmore!* welcome ashore, my dear Rover!—what happy Wind blew us this good Fortune?

WILLMORE: Let me salute you my dear *Fred*, and then com-
65 mand me—How is't honest Lad?

FREDERICK: Faith, Sir, the old Complement, infinitely the better to see my dear mad *Willmore* again—Prithee why camest thou ashore? and where's the Prince?

WILLMORE: He's well, and reigns still Lord of the watery Ele-
70 ment—I must aboard again within a Day or two, and my Business ashore was only to enjoy my self a little this Carnival.

BELVILE: Pray know our new Friend, Sir, he's but bashful, a raw Traveller, but honest, stout, and one of us.

---

39 **Hogoes** Haut-goût, a relish

(Embraces BLUNT.*)*

WILLMORE: That you esteem him, gives him an Interest here.

BLUNT: Your Servant, Sir. 75

WILLMORE: But well—Faith I'm glad to meet you again in a warm Climate, where the kind Sun has its god-like Power still over the Wine and Woman.—Love and Mirth are my Business in *Naples*; and if I mistake not the Place, here's an excellent Market for Chapmen of my Humour. 80

BELVILE: See here be those kind Merchants of Love you look for.

(Enter several MEN *in masquing Habits, some playing on Musick, others dancing after;* WOMEN *drest like Curtezans, with Papers pinn'd to their Breasts, and Baskets of Flowers in their Hands.)*

BLUNT: 'Sheartlikins, what have we here!

FREDERICK: Now the Game begins.

WILLMORE: Fine pretty Creatures! may a stranger have leave 85 to look and love?—What's here—*(Reads the Paper.) Roses for every Month!*

BLUNT: Roses for every Month! what means that?

BELVILE: They are, or wou'd have you think they're Curtezans, who here in *Naples* are to be hir'd by the Month. 90

WILLMORE: Kind and obliging to inform us—Pray where do these Roses grow? I would fain plant some of 'em in a Bed of mine.

WOMAN: Beware such Roses, Sir.

WILLMORE: A Pox of fear: I'll be bak'd with thee between a pair 95 of Sheets, and that's thy proper Still, so I might but strow such Roses over me and under me—Fair one, wou'd you wou'd give me leave to gather at your Bush this idle Month, I wou'd go near to make some Body smell of it all the Year after. 100

BELVILE: And thou hast need of such a Remedy, for thou stinkest of Tar and Rope-ends, like a Dock or Pesthouse.

(The WOMAN *puts her self into the Hands of a* MAN, *and Exit.)*

WILLMORE: Nay, nay, you shall not leave me so.

BELVILE: By all means use no Violence here.

WILLMORE: Death! just as I was going to be damnably in love, 105 to have her led off! I could pluck that Rose out of his Hand, and even kiss the Bed, the Bush it grew in.

FREDERICK: No Friend to Love like a long Voyage at Sea.

BLUNT: Except a Nunnery, *Frederick*.

WILLMORE: Death! but will they not be kind, quickly be kind? 110 Thou know'st I'm no tame Sigher, but a rampant Lion of the Forest.

(Two MEN *drest all over with Horns of several sorts, making Grimaces at one another, with Papers pinn'd on their Backs, advance from the farther end of the Scene.)*

BELVILE: Oh the fantastical Rogues, how they are dress'd! 'tis a Satir against the whole Sex.

WILLMORE: Is this a Fruit that grows in this warm Country? 115

BELVILE: Yes: 'Tis pretty to see these *Italian* start, swell, and stab at the Word *Cuckold*, and yet stumble at Horns on every Threshold.

WILLMORE: See what's on their Back—*(Reads.) Flowers for every Night.*—Ah Rogue! And more sweet than Roses of ev'ry 120 Month! This is a Gardiner of *Adam's* own breeding.

(They dance.)

BELVILE: What think you of those grave People?—is a Wake in *Essex* half so mad or extravagant?

WILLMORE: I like their sober grave way, 'tis a kind of legal au-
125 thoriz'd Fornication, where the Men are not chid for 't, nor the Women despis'd, as amongst our dull *English*; even the Monsieurs want that part of good Manners.

BELVILE: But here in *Italy* a Monsieur is the humblest best-
130 bred Gentleman—Duels are so baffled by Bravo's that an age shews not one, but between a *Frenchman* and a Hang-man, who is as much too hard for him on the Piazza, as they are for a *Dutchman* on the new Bridge—But see another Crew.

(Enter FLORINDA, HELLENA, *and* VALERIA, *drest like Gipsies;* CALLIS *and* STEPHANO, LUCETTA, PHILIPPO *and* SANCHO *in Masquerade.)*

HELLENA: Sister, there's your *Englishman*, and with him a
135 handsome proper Fellow—I'll to him, and instead of telling him his Fortune, try my own.

WILLMORE: Gipsies, on my Life—Sure these will prattle if a Man cross their Hands. *(Goes to Hellena.)*—Dear pretty (and I hope) young Devil, will you tell an amorous Stranger
140 what Luck he's like to have?

HELLENA: Have a care how you venture with me, Sir, lest I pick your Pocket, which will more vex your *English* Hu-mour, than an *Italian* Fortune will please you.

WILLMORE: How the Devil cam'st thou to know my Country
145 and Humour?

HELLENA: The first I guess by a certain forward Impudence, which does not displease me at this time; and the Loss of your Money will vex you, because I hope you have but very little to lose.

150 WILLMORE: Egad Child, thou'rt i'th' right; it is so little, I dare not offer it thee for a Kindness—But cannot you divine what other things of more value I have about me, that I would more willingly part with?

HELLENA: Indeed no, that's the Business of a Witch, and I am
155 but a Gipsy yet—Yet, without looking in your Hand, I have a parlous Guess, 'tis some foolish Heart you mean, an incon-stant *English* Heart, as little worth stealing as your Purse.

WILLMORE: Nay, then thou dost deal with the Devil, that's cer-tain—Thou hast guess'd as right as if thou hadst been one of
160 that Number it has languisht for—I find you'll be better ac-quainted with it; nor can you take it in a better time, for I am come from Sea, Child; and *Venus* not being propitious to me in her own Element, I have a world of Love in store—Wou'd you would be good-natur'd, and take some on't off my Hands.

165 HELLENA: Why—I could be inclin'd that way—but for a fool-ish Vow I am going to make—to die a Maid.

WILLMORE: Then thou art damn'd without Redemption; and as I am a good Christian, I ought to charity to divert so wicked a Design—therefore prithee, dear Creature, let me
170 know quickly when and where I shall begin to set a helping hand to so good a Work.

HELLENA: If you should prevail with my tender Heart (as I begin to fear you will, for you have horrible loving Eyes) there will be difficulty in't that you'll hardly undergo for my
175 sake.

WILLMORE: Faith, Child, I have been bred in Dangers, and wear a Sword that has been employ'd in a worse Cause, than for a handsom kind Woman—Name the Danger—let it be any thing but a long Siege, and I'll undertake it.

HELLENA: Can you storm?   180

WILLMORE: Oh, most furiously.

HELLENA: What think you of a Nunnery-wall? for he that wins me, must gain that first.

WILLMORE: A Nun! Oh how I love thee for't! there's no Sinner like a young Saint—Nay, now there's no denying me: the old 185
Law had no Curse (to a Woman) like dying a Maid; witness *Jephtha's* Daughter.

HELLENA: A very good Text this, if well handled; and I per-ceive, Father Captain, you would impose no severe Penance on her who was inclin'd to console her self before she took 190
Orders.

WILLMORE: If she be young and handsom.

HELLENA: Ay, there's it—but if she be not—

WILLMORE: By this Hand, Child, I have an implicit Faith, and dare venture on thee with all Faults—besides, 'tis more mer- 195
itorious to leave the World when thou hast tasted and prov'd the Pleasure on't; then 'twill be a Virtue in thee, which now will be pure Ignorance.

HELLENA: I perceive, good Father Captain, you design only to make me fit for Heaven—but if on the contrary you should 200
quite divert me from it, and bring me back to the World again, I should have a new Man to seek I find; and what a grief that will be—for when I begin, I fancy I shall love like any thing: I never try'd yet.

WILLMORE: Egad, and that's kind—Prithee, dear Creature, 205
give me Credit for a Heart, for faith, I'm a very honest Fel-low—Oh, I long to come first to the Banquet of Love; and such a swinging Appetite I bring—Oh, I'm impatient. Thy Lodging, Sweetheart, thy Lodging, or I'm a dead man.

HELLENA: Why must we be either guilty of Fornication or 210
Murder, if we converse with you Men?—And is there no dif-ference between leave to love me, and leave to lie with me?

WILLMORE: Faith, Child, they were made to go together.

LUCETTA: *(Pointing to* BLUNT.) Are you sure this is the Man?

SANCHO: When did I mistake your Game?   215

LUCETTA: This is a stranger, I know by his gazing; if he be brisk he'll venture to follow me; and then, if I understand my Trade, he's mine: he's *English* too, and they say that's a sort of good natur'd loving People, and have generally so kind an opinion of themselves, that a Woman with any Wit may flat- 220
ter 'em into any sort of Fool she pleases.

BLUNT: 'Tis so—she is taken—I have Beauties which my false Glass at home did not discover.

(She often passes by BLUNT *and gazes on him; he struts, and cocks, and walks, and gazes on her.)*

FLORINDA: This Woman watches me so, I shall get no Oppor-tunity to discover my self to him, and so miss the intent of my 225
coming—But as I was saying, Sir—*(Looking in his Hand.)* by this Line you should be a Lover.

BELVILE: I thought how right you guess'd, all Men are in love, or pretend to be so—Come, let me go, I'm weary of this fooling.   230

(Walks away.)

FLORINDA: I will not, till you have confess'd whether the Passion that you have vow'd *Florinda* be true or false.

(*She holds him, he strives to get from her.*)

BELVILE: *Florinda!*

(*Turns quick towards her.*)

FLORINDA: Softly.

235 BELVILE: Thou hast nam'd one will fix me here for ever.

FLORINDA: She'll be disappointed then, who expects you this Night at the Garden-gate, and if you'll fail not—as let me see the other Hand—you will go near to do—she vows to die or make you happy.

(*Looks on* CALLIS, *who observes 'em.*)

240 BELVILE: What canst thou mean?

FLORINDA: That which I say—Farewel.

(*Offers to go.*)

BELVILE: Oh charming Sybil, stay, complete that Joy, which, as it is, will turn into Distraction!—Where must I be? at the Garden-gate? I know it—at night you say—I'll sooner forfeit
245 Heaven than disobey.

(*Enter* DON PEDRO *and other Masquers, and pass over the Stage.*)

CALLIS: Madam, your Brother's here.

FLORINDA: Take this to instruct you farther.

(*Gives him a Letter, and goes off.*)

FREDERICK: Have a care, Sir, what you promise; this may be a Trap laid by her Brother to ruin you.

250 BELVILE: Do not disturb my Happiness with Doubts.

(*Opens the Letter.*)

WILLMORE: My dear pretty Creature, a Thousand Blessings on thee; still in this Habit, you say, and after Dinner at this Place.

HELLENA: Yes, if you will swear to keep your Heart, and not
255 bestow it between this time and that.

WILLMORE: By all the little Gods of Love I swear, I'll leave it with you; and if you run away with it, those Deities of Justice will revenge me.

(*Exeunt all the Women except* LUCETTA.)

FREDERICK: Do you know the Hand?

260 BELVILE: 'Tis *Florinda's.*
All Blessings fall upon the virtuous Maid.

FREDERICK: Nay, no Idolatry, a sober Sacrifice I'll allow you.

BELVILE: Oh Friends! the welcom'st News, the softest Letter!—nay, you shall see it; and could you now be serious, I
265 might be made the happiest Man the Sun shines on.

WILLMORE: The Reason of this mighty Joy.

BELVILE: See how kindly she invites me to deliver her from the threaten'd Violence of her Brother—will you not assist me?

WILLMORE: I know not what thou mean'st, but I'll make one at
270 any Mischief where a Woman's concern'd—but she'll be grateful to us for the Favour, will she not?

BELVILE: How mean you?

WILLMORE: How should I mean? Thou know'st there's but one way for a Woman to oblige me.

275 BELVILE: Don't prophane—the Maid is nicely virtuous.

WILLMORE: Who pox, then she's fit for nothing but a Husband; let her e'en go, Colonel.

FREDERICK: Peace, she's the Colonel's Mistress, Sir.

WILLMORE: Let her be the Devil; if she be thy Mistress, I'll serve her—name the way.   280

BELVILE: Read here this Postcript.

(*Gives him a Letter.*)

WILLMORE: (*Reads.*) *At Ten at night—at the Garden-Gate—of which, if I cannot get the Key, I will contrive a way over the Wall—come attended with a Friend or two.—Kind heart, if* 285 *we three cannot weave a String to let her down a Garden-Wall, 'twere pity but the Hangman wove one for us all.*

FREDERICK: Let her alone for that: your Woman's Wit, your fair kind Woman, will not out-trick a Brother or a Jew, and contrive like a Jesuit in Chains—but see, *Ned Blunt* is stoln 290 out after the Lure of a Damsel.

(*Exit* BLUNT *and* LUCETTA.)

BELVILE: So he'll scarce find his way home again, unless we get him cry'd by the Bell-man in the Market-place, and 'twou'd sound prettily—a lost *English* Boy of Thirty.

FREDERICK: I hope 'tis some common crafty Sinner, one that will fit him; it may be she'll sell him for *Peru,* the Rogue's 295 sturdy and would work well in a Mine; at least I hope she'll dress him for our Mirth; cheat him of all, then have him well-favour'dly bang'd, and turn'd out naked at Midnight.

WILLMORE: Prithee what Humour is he of, that you wish him so well?   300

BELVILE: Why, of an *English* Elder Brother's Humour, educated in a Nursery, with a Maid to tend him till Fifteen, and lies with his Grand-mother till he's of Age; one that knows no Pleasure beyond riding to the next Fair, or going up to *London* with his right Worshipful Father in Parliament-time; 305 wearing gay Clothes, or making honourable Love to his Lady Mother's Landry-Maid; gets drunk at a Hunting-Match, and ten to one then gives some Proofs of his Prowess—A pox upon him, he's our Banker, and has all our Cash about him, and if he fail we are all broke.   310

FREDERICK: Oh let him alone for that matter, he's of a damn'd stingy Quality, that will secure our Stock. I know not in what Danger it were indeed, if the Jilt should pretend she's in love with him, for 'tis a kind believing Coxcomb; otherwise if he part with more than a Piece of Eight—geld him: for which 315 offer he may chance to be beaten, if she be a Whore of the first Rank.

BELVILE: Nay the Rogue will not be easily beaten, he's stout enough; perhaps if they talk beyond his Capacity, he may chance to exercise his Courage upon some of them; else I'm 320 sure they'll find it as difficult to beat as to please him.

WILLMORE: 'Tis a lucky Devil to light upon so kind a Wench!

FREDERICK: Thou hadst a great deal of talk with thy little Gipsy, coud'st thou do no good upon her? for mine was hard-hearted.   325

WILLMORE: Hang her, she was some damn'd honest Person of Quality, I'm sure, she was so very free and witty. If her Face be but answerable to her Wit and Humour, I would be

---

315 **a Piece of Eight** A piastre, a coin of varying values in different countries

330   bound to Constancy this Month to gain her. In the mean time, have you made no kind Acquaintance since you came to Town?—You do not use to be honest so long, Gentlemen.

FREDERICK: Faith Love has kept us honest, we have been all fir'd with a Beauty newly come to Town, the famous *Padu-ana Angelica Bianca*.

335   WILLMORE: What, the Mistress of the dead *Spanish* General?

BELVILE: Yes, she's now the only ador'd Beauty of all the Youth in *Naples*, who put on all their charms to appear lovely in her sight, their Coaches, Liveries, and themselves, all gay, as

340   on a Monarch's Birth-Day, to attract the Eyes of this fair Charmer, while she has the Pleasure to behold all languish for her that see her.

FREDERICK: 'Tis pretty to see with how much Love the Men regard her, and how much Envy the Women.

WILLMORE: What Gallant has she?

345   BELVILE: None, she's exposed to Sale, and four Days in the Week she's yours—for so much a Month.

WILLMORE: The very Thought of it quenches all manner of Fire in me—yet prithee let's see her.

BELVILE: Let's first to Dinner, and after that we'll pass the Day

350   as you please—but at Night ye must all be at my Devotion.

WILLMORE: I will not fail you.

(Exeunt.)

— ACT TWO —

SCENE I

The Long Street.

(Enter BELVILE *and* FREDERICK *in Masquing-Habits, and* WILLMORE *in his own Clothes, with a Vizard in his Hand.)*

WILLMORE: But why thus disguis'd and muzzl'd?

BELVILE: Because whatever Extravagances we commit in these Faces, our own may not be oblig'd to answer 'em.

5   WILLMORE: I should have chang'd my Eternal Buff too: but no matter, my little Gipsy wou'd not have found me out then: for if she should change hers, it is impossible I should know her, unless I should hear her prattle—A Pox on't, I cannot get her out of my Head: Pray Heaven, if ever I do see her again, she prove damnable ugly, that I may fortify my self

10   against her Tongue.

BELVILE: Have a care of Love, for o' my conscience she was not of a Quality to give thee any hopes.

WILLMORE: Pox on 'em, why do they draw a Man in then? She has play'd with my Heart so, that 'twill never lie still till I

15   have met with some kind Wench, that will play the Game out with me—Oh for my Arms full of soft, white, kind—Woman! such as I fancy *Angelica*.

BELVILE: This is her House, if you were but in stock to get admittance; they have not din'd yet; I perceive the Picture is

20   not out.

(Enter BLUNT.*)*

WILLMORE: I long to see the Shadow of the fair Substance, a Man may gaze on that for nothing.

BLUNT: Colonel, thy Hand—and thine, *Frederick*. I have been an Ass, a deluded Fool, a very Coxcomb from my Birth till

25   this Hour, and heartily repent my little Faith.

BELVILE: What the Devil's the matter with thee *Ned?*

BLUNT: Oh such a Mistress, *Frederick*, such a Girl!

WILLMORE: Ha! where? *Frederick.* Ay where!

BLUNT: So fond, so amorous, so toying and fine! and all for sheer Love, ye Rogue! Oh how she lookt and kiss'd! and 30 sooth'd my Heart from my Bosom. I cannot think I was awake, and yet methinks I see and feel her Charms still—*Frederick.*—Try if she have not left the Taste of her balmy Kisses upon my Lips—

(Kisses him.)

BELVILE: Ha, ha, ha! *Willmore.* Death Man, where is she? 35

BLUNT: What a Dog was I to stay in dull *England* so long—How have I laught at the Colonel when he sigh'd for Love! but now the little Archer has reveng'd him, and by his own Dart, I can guess at all his Joys, which then I took for Fancies, mere Dreams and Fables—Well, I'm resolved to sell all 40 in *Essex*, and plant here for ever.

BELVILE: What a Blessing 'tis, thou hast a Mistress thou dar'st boast of; for I know thy Humour is rather to have a proclaim'd Clap, than a secret Amour.

WILLMORE: Dost know her Name? 45

BLUNT: Her Name? No, 'sheartlikins: what care I for Names?—She's fair, young, brisk and kind, even to ravishment: and what a Pox care I for knowing her by another Title?

WILLMORE: Didst give her anything?

BLUNT: Give her!—Ha, ha, ha! why, she's a Person of Quality—That's a good one, give her! 'sheartlikins dost think such 50 Creatures are to be bought? Or are we provided for such a Purchase? Give her, quoth ye? Why she presented me with this Bracelet, for the Toy of a Diamond I us'd to wear: No, Gentlemen, *Ned Blunt* is not every Body—She expects me 55 again to night.

WILLMORE: Egad that's well; we'll all go.

BLUNT: Not a Soul: No, Gentlemen, you are Wits; I am a dull Country Rogue, I.

FREDERICK: Well, Sir, for all your Person of Quality, I shall be 60 very glad to understand your Purse be secure; 'tis our whole Estate at present, which we are loth to hazard in one Bottom: come, Sir, unload.

BLUNT: Take the necessary Trifle, useless now to me, that am belov'd by such a Gentlewoman—'sheartlikins Money! Here 65 take mine too.

FREDERICK: No, keep that to be cozen'd, that we may laugh.

WILLMORE: Cozen'd!—Death! wou'd I cou'd meet with one, that wou'd cozen me of all the Love I cou'd spare to night.

FREDERICK: Pox 'tis some common Whore upon my Life. 70

BLUNT: A Whore! yes with such Clothes! such Jewels! such a House! such Furniture, and so attended! a Whore!

BELVILE: Why yes, Sir, they are Whores, tho they'll neither entertain you with Drinking, Swearing, or Baudy; are Whores in all those gay Clothes, and right Jewels; are Whores with 75 great Houses richly furnisht with Velvet Beds, Store of Plate, handsome Attendance, and fine Coaches, are Whores and errant ones.

WILLMORE: Pox on't, where do these fine Whores live?

BELVILE: Where no Rogue in Office yclep'd Constables dare 80 give 'em laws, nor the Wine-inspired Bullies of the Town break their Windows; yet they are Whores, tho this *Essex* Calf believe them Persons of Quality.

BLUNT: 'Sheartlikins, y'are all Fools, there are things about this *Essex* Calf, that shall take with the Ladies, beyond all your 85

Wits and Parts—This Shape and Size, Gentlemen, are not to be despis'd; my Waste tolerably long, with other inviting Signs, that shall be nameless.

WILLMORE: Egad I believe he may have met with some Person of Quality that may be kind to him.

90

BELVILE: Dost thou perceive any such tempting things about him, should make a fine Woman, and of Quality, pick him out from all Mankind, to throw away her Youth and Beauty upon, nay, and her dear Heart too?—no, no, *Angelica* has rais'd the Price too high.

95

WILLMORE: May she languish for Mankind till she die, and be damn'd for that one Sin alone.

(Enter two BRAVOES, *and hang up a great Picture of* ANGELICA'S, *against the Balcony, and two little ones at each side of the Door.)*

BELVILE: See there the fair Sign to the Inn, where a Man may lodge that's Fool enough to give her Price.

*(*WILLMORE *gazes on the Picture.)*

100

BLUNT: 'Sheartlikins, Gentlemen, what's this?

BELVILE: A famous Curtezan that's to be sold.

BLUNT: How! to be sold! nay then I have nothing to say to her—sold! what Impudence is practis'd in this Country?— With Order and Decency Whoring's established here by virtue of the Inquisition—Come let's be gone, I'm sure we're no Chapmen for this Commodity.

105

FREDERICK: Thou art none, I'm sure, unless thou could'st have her in thy Bed at the Price of a Coach in the Street.

WILLMORE: How wondrous fair she is—a Thousand Crowns a Month—by Heaven as many Kingdoms were too little. A plague of this Poverty—of which I ne'er complain, but when it hinders my Approach to Beauty, which Virtue ne'er could purchase.

110

(Turns from the Picture.)

115

BLUNT: What's this?—*(Reads.)* A Thousand Crowns a Month! —'Sheartlikins, here's a Sum! sure 'tis a mistake. —Hark you, Friend, does she take or give so much by the Month!

FREDERICK: A Thousand Crowns! Why, 'tis a Portion for the *Infanta.*

120

BLUNT: Hark ye, Friends, won't she trust?

BRAVO: This is a Trade, Sir, that cannot live by Credit.

(Enter DON PEDRO *in Masquerade, follow'd by* STEPHANO.)*

BELVILE: See, here's more Company, let's walk off a while.

*(*PEDRO *reads. Exeunt English. Enter* ANGELICA *and* MORETTA *in the Balcony, and draw a Silk Curtain.)*

PEDRO: Fetch me a Thousand Crowns, I never wish to buy this Beauty at an easier Rate.

(Passes off.)

125

ANGELICA: Prithee what said those Fellows to thee?

BRAVO: Madam, the first were Admirers of Beauty only, but no purchasers; they were merry with your Price and Picture, laught at the Sum, and so past off.

130

ANGELICA: No matter, I'm not displeas'd with their rallying; their Wonder feeds my Vanity, and he that wishes to buy, gives me more Pride, than he that gives my Price can make me Pleasure.

BRAVO: Madam, the last I knew thro all his disguises to be Don *Pedro,* Nephew to the General, and who was with him in *Pampelona.*

135

ANGELICA: Don *Pedro!* my old Gallant's Nephew! When his Uncle dy'd, he left him a vast Sum of Money; it is he who was so in love with me at *Padua,* and who us'd to make the General so jealous.

MORETTA: Is this he that us'd to prance before our Window and take such care to shew himself an amorous Ass? if I am not mistaken, he is the likeliest Man to give your Price.

140

ANGELICA: The Man is brave and generous, but of an Humour so uneasy and inconstant, that the victory over his Heart is as soon lost as won; a Slave that can add little to the Triumph of the Conqueror; but inconstancy's the Sin of all Mankind, therefore I'm resolv'd that nothing but Gold shall charm my Heart.

145

MORETTA: I'm glad on't; 'tis only interest that Women of our Profession ought to consider: tho I wonder what has kept you from that general Disease of our Sex so long, I mean that of being in love.

150

ANGELICA: A kind, but sullen Star, under which I had the Happiness to be born; yet I have had no time for Love; the bravest and noblest of Mankind have purchas'd my Favours at so dear a Rate, as if no Coin but Gold were current with our Trade—But here's Don *Pedro* again, fetch me my Lute—for 'tis for him or Don *Antonio* the Vice-Roy's Son, that I have spread my Nets.

155

(Enter at one Door Don PEDRO, *and* STEPHANO; *Don* ANTONIO *and* DIEGO *[his page], at the other Door, with people following him in Masquerade, antickly attir'd, some with Musick: they both go up to the Picture.)*

ANTONIO: A thousand Crowns! had not the Painter flatter'd her, I should not think it dear.

160

PEDRO: Flatter'd her! by Heaven he cannot. I have seen the Original, nor is there one Charm here more than adorns her Face and Eyes; all this soft and sweet, with a certain languishing Air, that no Artist can represent.

165

ANTONIO: What I heard of her Beauty before had fir'd my Soul, but this confirmation of it has blown it into a flame.

PEDRO: Ha!

PAGE: Sir, I have known you throw away a Thousand Crowns on a worse Face, and tho y' are near your Marriage, you may venture a little Love here; *Florinda*—will not miss it.

170

PEDRO: Ha! *Florinda!* Sure 'tis *Antonio.*

(Aside.)

ANTONIO: *Florinda!* name not those distant Joys, there's not one thought of her will check my Passion here.

PEDRO: Florinda scorn'd! and all my Hopes defeated of the Possession of Angelica! (A noise of a Lute above. Antonio gazes up.) Her Injuries by Heaven he shall not boast of.

175

(Song to a Lute above.)

SONG

When *Damon* first began to love,
He languisht in a soft Desire,
And knew not how the Gods to move,
To lessen or increase his Fire,
For *Caelia* in her charming Eyes
    Wore all Love's Sweet, and all his Cruelties.

180

II

185 But as beneath a Shade he lay,
Weaving of Flow'rs for *Caelia's* Hair,
She chanc'd to lead her Flock that way,
And saw the am'rous Shepherd there.
She gaz'd around upon the Place,
190 And saw the Grove (resembling Night)
To all the Joys of Love invite,
Whilst guilty Smiles and Blushes drest her Face.
At this the bashful Youth all Transport grew,
And with kind Force he taught the Virgin how
To yield what all his Sighs cou'd never do.

195 ANTONIO: By Heav'n she's charming fair!

(ANGELICA *throws open the Curtains, and bows to* ANTONIO, *who pulls off his Vizard, and bows and blows up Kisses.* PEDRO *unseen looks in his Face.*)

PEDRO: 'Tis he, the false *Antonio!*
ANTONIO: Friend, where must I pay my offering of Love?

(*To the bravo.*)

My Thousand Crowns I mean.
PEDRO: That offering I have design'd to make,
200 And yours will come too late.
ANTONIO: Prithee be gone, I shall grow angry else,
And then thou art not safe.
PEDRO: My Anger may be fatal, Sir, as yours;
And he that enters here may prove this Truth.
205 ANTONIO: I know not who thou art, but I am sure thou'rt
worth my killing, and aiming at *Angelica.*

(*They draw and fight.*)

(*Enter* WILLMORE *and* BLUNT, *who draw and part 'em.*)

BLUNT: 'Sheartlikins, here's fine doings.
WILLMORE: Tilting for the Wench I'm sure—nay gad, if that
wou'd win her, I have as good a Sword as the best of ye—Put
210 up—put up, and take another time and place, for this is design'd for Lovers only.

(*They all put up.*)

PEDRO: We are prevented; dare you meet me to morrow on the
Molo?
For I've a Title to a better quarrel,
215 That of *Florinda,* in whose credulous Heart
Thou'st made an Int'rest, and destroy'd my Hopes.
ANTONIO: Dare?
I'll meet thee there as early as the Day.
PEDRO: We will come thus disguis'd, that whosoever chance to
220 get the better, he may escape unknown.
ANTONIO: It shall be so.

(*Exit* PEDRO *and* STEPHANO.)

Who shou'd this Rival be? unless the *English* Colonel, of
whom I've often heard Don *Pedro* speak; it must be he, and
time he were removed, who lays a Claim to all my Happiness.

(WILLMORE *having gaz'd all this while on the Picture, pulls down a little one.*)

225 WILLMORE: This posture's loose and negligent,
The sight on't wou'd beget a warm desire

In Souls, whom Impotence and Age had chill'd.
—This must along with me.
BRAVO: What means this rudeness, Sir?—restore the Picture.
ANTONIO: Ha! Rudeness committed to the fair *Angelica!*— 230
Restore the Picture, Sir.
WILLMORE: Indeed I will not, Sir.
ANTONIO: By Heav'n but you shall.
WILLMORE: Nay, do not shew your Sword; if you do, by this
dear Beauty—I will shew mine too. 235
ANTONIO: What right can you pretend to't?
WILLMORE: That of Possession which I will maintain—you
perhaps have 1000 Crowns to give for the Original.
ANTONIO: No matter, Sir, you shall restore the Picture.
ANGELICA: Oh, *Moretta!* what's the matter? 240

(ANGELICA *and* MORETTA *above.*)

ANTONIO: Or leave your Life behind.
WILLMORE: Death! you lye—I will do neither.
ANGELICA: Hold, I command you, if for me you fight.

(*They fight, the Spaniards join with* ANTONIO, BLUNT *laying on like mad. They leave off and bow.*)

WILLMORE: How heavenly fair she is!—ah Plague of her Price.
ANGELICA: You Sir in Buff, you that appear a Soldier, that first 245
began this Insolence.
WILLMORE: 'Tis true, I did so, if you call it Insolence for a Man
to preserve himself; I saw your charming Picture, and was
wounded: quite thro my Soul each pointed Beauty ran; and
wanting a Thousand Crowns to procure my Remedy, I laid 250
this little Picture to my Bosom—which if you cannot allow
me, I'll resign.
ANGELICA: No, you may keep the Trifle.
ANTONIO: You shall first ask my leave, and this.

(*Fight again as before.*)

(*Enter* BELVILE *and* FREDERICK *who join with the English.*)

ANGELICA: Hold; will you ruin me?—*Biskey, Sebastian,* part 255
them.

(*The* SPANIARDS *are beaten off.*)

MORETTA: Oh Madam, we're undone, a pox upon that rude
Fellow, he's set on to ruin us: we shall never see good days,
till all these fighting poor Rogues are sent to the Gallies.

(*Enter* BELVILE, BLUNT *and* WILLMORE, *with his shirt bloody.*)

BLUNT: 'Sheartlikins, beat me at this Sport, and I'll ne'er wear 260
Sword more.
BELVILE: The Devil's in thee for a mad Fellow, thou art always
one at an unlucky Adventure.—Come, let's be gone whilst
we're safe, and remember these are *Spaniards,* a sort of People that know how to revenge an Affront. 265
FREDERICK: (*To* WILLMORE.) You bleed; I hope you are not
wounded.
WILLMORE: Not much:—a plague upon your Dons, if they
fight no better they'll ne'er recover *Flanders.*—What the
Devil was't to them that I took down the Picture? 270
BLUNT: Took it! 'Sheartlikins, we'll have the great one too; 'tis
ours by Conquest.—Prithee, help me up, and I'll pull it
down.—

ANGELICA: Stay, Sir, and e'er you affront me further, let me
275 know how you durst commit this Outrage—To you I speak,
Sir, for you appear like a Gentleman.

WILLMORE: To me, Madam?—Gentlemen, your Servant.

(BELVILE stays him.)

BELVILE: Is the Devil in thee? Do'st know the danger of en-
280 tring the house of an incens'd Curtezan?

WILLMORE: I thank you for your care—but there are other
matters in hand, there are, tho we have no great Temptation.—Death! let me go.

FREDERICK: Yes, to your Lodging, if you will, but not in
here.—Damn these gay Harlots—by this Hand I'll have as
285 sound and hansome a Whore for a Patacoone.—Death,
Man, she'll murder thee.

WILLMORE: Oh! fear me not, shall I not venture where a
Beauty calls? a lovely charming Beauty? for fear of danger!
when by Heaven there's none so great as to long for her,
290 whilst I want Money to purchase her.

FREDERICK: Therefore 'tis loss of time, unless you had the
thousand Crowns to pay.

WILLMORE: It may be she may give a Favour, at least I shall
have the pleasure of saluting her when I enter, and when I
295 depart.

BELVILE: Pox, she'll as soon lie with thee, as kiss thee, and
sooner stab than do either—you shall not go.

ANGELICA: Fear not, Sir, all I have to wound with, is my Eyes.

BLUNT: Let him go, 'Sheartlikins, I believe the Gentlewoman
300 means well.

BELVILE: Well, take thy Fortune, we'll expect you in the next
Street.—Farewell Fool,—farewell—

WILLMORE: B'ye Colonel—

(Goes in.)

FREDERICK: The Rogue's stark mad for a Wench.

(Exeunt.)

SCENE II

A Fine Chamber.

(Enter WILLMORE, ANGELICA, and MORETTA.)

ANGELICA: Insolent, Sir, how durst you pull down my Picture?

WILLMORE: Rather, how durst you set it up, to tempt poor
amorous Mortals with so much Excellence? which I find
you have but too well consulted by the unmerciful price you
5 set upon't.—Is all this Heaven of Beauty shewn to move Despair in those that cannot buy? and can you think the effects
of that Despair shou'd be less extravagant than I have shewn?

ANGELICA: I sent for you to ask my Pardon, Sir, not to aggravate your Crime.—I thought I shou'd have seen you at my
10 Feet imploring it.

WILLMORE: You are deceived, I came to rail at you, and talk
such Truths, too, as shall let you see the Vanity of that Pride,
which taught you how to set such a Price on Sin. For such it
is, whilst that which is Love's due is meanly barter'd for.

ANGELICA: Ha, ha, ha, alas, good Captain, what pity 'tis your 15
edifying Doctrine will do no good upon me—*Moretta*, fetch
the Gentleman a Glass, and let him survey himself, to see
what Charms he has,—*(Aside in a soft tone.)* and guess my
Business.

MORETTA: He knows himself of old, I believe those Breeches 20
and he have been acquainted ever since he was beaten at
Worcester.

ANGELICA: Nay, do not abuse the poor Creature.—

MORETTA: Good Weather-beaten Corporal, will you march
off? we have no need of your Doctrine, tho you have of our 25
Charity; but at present we have no Scraps, we can afford no
kindness for God's sake; in fine, Sirrah, the Price is too high
i'th' Mouth for you, therefore troop, I say.

WILLMORE: Here, good Fore-Woman of the Shop, serve me,
and I'll be gone. 30

MORETTA: Keep it to pay your Landress, your Linen stinks of
the Gun-Room; for here's no selling by Retail.

WILLMORE: Thou hast sold plenty of thy stale Ware at a cheap
Rate.

MORETTA: Ay, the more silly kind Heart I, but this is an Age 35
wherein Beauty is at higher Rates.—In fine, you know the
price of this.

WILLMORE: I grant you 'tis here set down a thousand Crowns a
Month—Baud, take your black Lead and sum it up, that I
may have a Pistole-worth of these vain gay things, and I'll 40
trouble you no more.

MORETTA: Pox on him, he'll fret me to Death:—abominable
Fellow, I tell thee, we only sell by the whole Piece.

WILLMORE: 'Tis very hard, the whole Cargo or nothing—
Faith, Madam, my Stock will not reach it, I cannot be your 45
Chapman.—Yet I have Countrymen in Town, Merchants of
Love, like me; I'll see if they'll put for a share, we cannot lose
much by it, and what we have no use for, we'll sell upon the
Friday's Mart, at—*Who gives more?* I am studying, Madam,
how to purchase you, tho at present I am unprovided of 50
Money.

ANGELICA: Sure, this from any other Man would anger me—
nor shall he know the Conquest he has made—Poor angry
Man, how I despise this railing.

WILLMORE: Yes, I am poor—but I'm a Gentleman, 55
And one that scorns this Baseness which you practise.
Poor as I am, I would not sell my self,
No, not to gain your charming high-priz'd Person.
Tho I admire you strangely for your Beauty,
Yet I contemn your Mind. 60
—And yet I wou'd at any rate enjoy you;
At your own rate—but cannot—See here
The only Sum I can command on Earth;
I know not where to eat when this is gone:
Yet such a Slave I am to Love and Beauty, 65
This last reserve I'll sacrifice to enjoy you.
—Nay, do not frown, I know you are to be bought,
And wou'd be bought by me, by me,
For a mean trifling Sum, if I could pay it down.
Which happy knowledge I will still repeat, 70
And lay it to my Heart, it has a Virtue in't,
And soon will cure those Wounds your Eyes have made.

285 **Patacoone** A Spanish coin

40 **Pistole** A gold coin

—And yet—there's something so divinely powerful there—
Nay, I will gaze—to let you see my Strength.

(Holds her, looks on her, and pauses and sighs.)

75 By Heaven, bright Creature—I would not for the World
Thy Fame were half so fair as thy Face.

(Turns her away from him.)

ANGELICA: *(Aside.)* His words go thro me to the very Soul.
—If you have nothing else to say to me.
WILLMORE: Yes, you shall hear how infamous you are—
80 For which I do not hate thee:
But that secures my Heart, and all the Flames it feels
Are but so many Lusts,
I know it by their sudden bold intrusion.
The Fire's impatient and betrays, 'tis false—
85 For had it been the purer Flame of Love,
I should have pin'd and languish'd at your Feet,
E'er found the Impudence to have discover'd it.
I now dare stand your Scorn, and your Denial.
MORETTA: Sure she's bewitcht, that you can stand thus tamely,
90 and hear his saucy railing.—Sirrah, will you be gone?
ANGELICA: How dare you take this liberty?—*(To* MORETTA.*)*
Withdraw.—Pray, tell me, Sir, are not you guilty of the same
mercenary Crime? When a Lady is proposed to you for a
Wife, you never ask, how fair, discreet, or virtuous she is; but
95 what's her Fortune—which if but small, you cry—She will
not do my business—and basely leave her, tho she languish
for you.—Say, is not this as poor?
WILLMORE: It is a barbarous Custom, which I will scorn to de-
fend in our Sex, and do despise in yours.
100 ANGELICA: Thou art a brave Fellow! put up thy Gold, and
know
That were thy Fortune large, as is thy Soul,
Thou shouldst not buy my Love,
Couldst thou forget those mean Effects of Vanity,
Which set me out to sale; and as a Lover, prize
105 My yielding Joys.
Canst thou believe they'l be entirely thine,
Without considering they were mercenary?
WILLMORE: *(Aside.)* I cannot tell, I must bethink me first—ha,
Death, I'm going to believe her.
110 ANGELICA: Prithee, confirm that Faith—or if thou canst not—
flatter me a little, 'twill please me from thy Mouth.
WILLMORE: Curse on thy charming Tongue! dost thou return
My feign'd Contempt with so much subtilty?

(Aside.)

Thou'st found the easiest way into my Heart,
115 Tho I yet know that all thou say'st is false.

(Turning from her in a Rage.)

ANGELICA: By all that's good 'tis real,
I never lov'd before, tho oft a Mistress.
—Shall my first Vows be slighted?
WILLMORE: *(Aside.)* What can she mean?
120 ANGELICA: *(In an angry tone.)* I find you cannot credit me.
WILLMORE: I know you take me for an errant Ass,
An Ass that may be sooth'd into Belief,
And then be us'd at pleasure.
—But, Madam, I have been so often cheated

By perjur'd, soft, deluding Hypocrites,   125
That I've no Faith left for the cozening Sex,
Especially for Women of your Trade.
ANGELICA: The low esteem you have of me, perhaps
May bring my Heart again:
For I have Pride that yet surmounts my Love.   130

(She turns with Pride, he holds her.)

WILLMORE: Throw off this Pride, this Enemy to Bliss,
And shew the Power of Love: 'tis with those Arms
I can be only vanquisht, made a Slave.
ANGELICA: Is all my mighty Expectation vanisht?
—No, I will not hear thee talk,—thou hast a Charm   135
In every word, that draws my Heart away.
And all the thousand Trophies I design'd,
Thou hast undone—Why are thou soft?
Thy Looks are bravely rough, and meant for War.
Could thou not storm on still?   140
I then perhaps had been as free as thou.
WILLMORE: *(Aside.)* Death! how she throws her Fire about my
Soul!
—Take heed, fair Creature, how you raise my Hopes,
Which once assum'd pretend to all Dominion.
There's not a Joy thou hast in store   145
I shall not then command:
For which I'll pay thee back my Soul, my Life.
Come, let's begin th' account this happy minute.
ANGELICA: And will you pay me then the Price I ask?
WILLMORE: Oh, why dost thou draw me from an awful   150
Worship,
By shewing thou art no Divinity?
Conceal the Fiend, and shew me all the Angel;
Keep me but ignorant, and I'll be devout,
And pay my Vows for ever at this Shrine.

(Kneels, and kisses her Hand.)

ANGELICA: The Pay I mean is but thy Love for mine.—Can   155
you give that?
WILLMORE: Intirely—come, let's withdraw: where I'll renew
my vows,—and breathe 'em with such Ardour, thou shalt not
doubt my Zeal.
ANGELICA: Thou hast a Power too strong to be resisted.   160

(Exit WILLMORE *and* ANGELICA.*)*

MORETTA: Now my Curse go with you—Is all our Project
fallen to this? to love the only Enemy to our Trade? Nay, to
love such a Shameroon, a very Beggar; nay, a Pirate-Beggar,
whose Business is to rifle and be gone, a No-Purchase, No-
Pay Tatterdemalion, an English Piccaroon; a Rogue that   165
fights for daily Drink, and takes a Pride in being loyally
lousy—Oh, I could curse now, if I durst—This is the Fate of
most Whores.

Trophies, which from believing Fops we win,
Are Spoils to those who cozen us again.   170

---

163 **shameroon** A trickster, a cozening rascal

— ACT THREE —

SCENE I

A Street.

(*Enter* FLORINDA, VALERIA, HELLENA, *in Antick different Dresses from what they were in before,* CALLIS *attending.*)

FLORINDA: I wonder what should make my Brother in so ill a Humour: I hope he has not found out our Ramble this Morning.

HELLENA: No, if he had, we should have heard on't at both Ears, and have been mew'd up this Afternoon; which I would not for the World should have happen'd—Hey ho! I'm sad as a Lover's Lute.

VALERIA: Well, methinks we have learnt this Trade of Gipsies as readily as if we had been bred upon the Road to *Loretto:* and yes I did so fumble, when I told the Stranger his Fortune, that I was afraid I should have told my own and yours by mistake—But methinks *Hellena* has been very serious ever since.

FLORINDA: I would give my Garters she were in love, to be reveng'd upon her, for abusing me—How is't, *Hellena?*

HELLENA: Ah!—would I had never seen my mad Monsieur—and yet for all your laughing I am not in love—and yet this small Acquaintance, o'my Conscience, will never out of my Head.

VALERIA: Ha, ha, ha—I laugh to think how thou art fitted with a Lover, a Fellow that, I warrant, loves every new Face he sees.

HELLENA: Hum—he has not kept his Word with me here—and may be taken up—that thought is not very pleasant to me—what the Duce should this be now that I feel?

VALERIA: What is't like?

HELLENA: Nay, the Lord knows—but if I should be hanged, I cannot chuse but be angry and afraid, when I think that mad Fellow should be in love with any Body but me—What to think of my self I know not—Would I could meet with some true damn'd Gipsy, that I might know my Fortune.

VALERIA: Know it! why there's nothing so easy; thou wilt love this wandering Inconstant till thou find'st thy self hanged about his Neck, and then be as mad to get free again.

FLORINDA: Yes, *Valeria;* we shall see her bestride his Baggage-horse, and follow him to the Campaign.

HELLENA: So, so; now you are provided for, there's no care taken of poor me—But since you have set my Heart a wishing, I am resolv'd to know for what. I will not die of the Pip, so I will not.

FLORINDA: Art thou mad to talk so? Who will like thee well enough to have thee, that hears what a mad Wench thou art?

HELLENA: Like me! I don't intend every he that likes me shall have me, but he that I like: I shou'd have staid in the Nunnery still, if I had lik'd my Lady Abbess as well as she lik'd me. No, I came thence, not (as my wise Brother imagines) to take an eternal Farewel of the World, but to love and to be belov'd; and I will be belov'd, or I'll get one of your Men, so I will.

VALERIA: Am I put into the Number of Lovers?

HELLENA: You! my Couz, I know thou art too good natur'd to leave us in any Design: Thou wou't venture a Cast, tho thou comest off a Loser, especially with such a Gamester—I observ'd your Man, and your willing ears incline that way; and if you are not a Lover, 'tis an Art soon learnt—that I find.

(*Sighs.*)

FLORINDA: I wonder how you learnt to love so easily, I had a thousand Charms to meet my Eyes and Ears, e'er I cou'd yield; and 'twas the knowledge of *Belvile's* Merit, not the surprising Person, took my Soul—Thou art too rash to give a Heart at first sight.

HELLENA: Hang your considering Lover; I ne'er thought beyond the Fancy, that 'twas a very pretty, idle, silly kind of Pleasure to pass ones time with, to write little, soft, nonsensical Billets, and with great difficulty and danger receive Answers; in which I shall have my Beauty prais'd, my Wit admir'd (tho little or none) and have the Vanity and Power to know I am desirable; then I have the more Inclination that way, because I am to be a Nun, and so shall not be suspected to have any such earthly Thoughts about me—But when I walk thus—and sigh thus—they'll think my Mind's upon my Monastery, and cry, how happy 'tis she's so resolv'd!—But not a Word of Man.

FLORINDA: What a mad Creature's this!

HELLENA: I'll warrant, if my Brother hears either of you sigh, he cries (gravely)—I fear you have the Indiscretion to be in love, but take heed of the Honour of our House, and your own unspotted Fame; and so he conjures on till he has laid the soft-wing'd God in your Hearts, or broke the Birds-nest—But see here comes your Lover: but where's my inconstant? let's stop aside, and we may learn something.

(*Go aside.*)

(*Enter* BELVILE, FREDERICK *and* BLUNT.)

BELVILE: What means this? the Picture's taken in.

BLUNT: It may be the Wench is good-natur'd, and will be kind *gratis.* Your Friend's a proper handsom Fellow.

BELVILE: I rather think she has cut his Throat and is fled: I am mad he should throw himself into Dangers—Pox on't, I shall want him to night—let's knock and ask for him.

HELLENA: My heart goes a-pit a-pat, for fear 'tis my Man they talk of.

(*Knock,* MORETTA *above.*)

MORETTA: What would you have?

BELVILE: Tell the Stranger that enter'd here about two Hours ago, that his Friends stay here for him.

MORETTA: A Curse upon him for *Moretta,* would he were at the Devil—but he's coming to you.

(*Enter* WILLMORE.)

HELLENA: I, I, 'tis he. Oh how this vexes me.

BELVILE: And how, and how, dear Lad, has Fortune smil'd? Are we to break her Windows, or raise up Altars to her! hah!

WILLMORE: Does not my Fortune sit triumphant on my Brow? dost not see the little wanton God there all gay and smiling? have I not an Air about my Face and Eyes, that distinguish me from the Croud of common Lovers? By Heav'n, *Cupid's* Quiver has not half so many Darts as her Eyes—Oh such a Bona Roba, to sleep in her Arms is lying in Fresco, all perfum'd Air about me.

HELLENA: (*Aside.*) Here's fine encouragement for me to fool on.

WILLMORE: Hark ye, where didst thou purchase that rich Canary we drank to-day? Tell me, that I may adore the Spigot, and sacrifice to the Butt: the Juice was divine, into which I

must dip my Rosary, and then bless all things that I would
have bold or fortunate.

110 BELVILE: Well, Sir, let's go take a Bottle, and hear the Story of
your Success.

FREDERICK: Would not *French* Wine do better?

WILLMORE: Damn the hungry Balderdash; cheerful Sack has
a generous Virtue in't, inspiring a successful Confidence,
115 gives Eloquence to the Tongue, and Vigour to the Soul; and
has in a few Hours compleated all my Hopes and Wishes.
There's nothing left to raise a new Desire in me—Come let's
be gay and wanton—and, Gentlemen, study, study what you
want, for here are Friends,—that will supply, Gentlemen,—
120 hark! what a charming sound they make—'tis he and she
Gold whilst here, shall beget new Pleasures every moment.

BLUNT: But hark ye, Sir, you are not married, are you?

WILLMORE: All the Honey of Matrimony, but none of the
Sting, Friend.

125 BLUNT: 'Sheartlikins, thou'rt a fortunate Rogue.

WILLMORE: I am so, Sir, let these inform you.—Ha, how
sweetly they chime! Pox of Poverty, it makes a Man a Slave,
makes Wit and Honour sneak, my Soul grew lean and rusty
for want of Credit.

130 BLUNT: 'Sheartlikins, this I like well, it looks like my lucky Bargain! Oh how I long for the Approach of my Squire, that is to
conduct me to her House again. Why! here's two provided
for.

FREDERICK: By this light y're happy Men.

135 BLUNT: Fortune is pleased to smile on us, Gentlemen,—to
smile on us.

(*Enter* SANCHO, *and pulls* BLUNT *by the Sleeve. They go aside.*)

SANCHO: Sir, my Lady expects you—she has remov'd all that
might oppose your Will and Pleasure—and is impatient till
you come.

140 BLUNT: Sir, I'll attend you—Oh the happiest Rogue! I'll take
no leave, lest they either dog me, or stay me.

(*Exit with* SANCHO.)

BELVILE: But then the little Gipsy is forgot?

WILLMORE: A Mischief on thee for putting her into my
thoughts; I had quite forgot her else, and this Night's De-
145 bauch had drunk her quite down.

HELLENA: Had it so, good Captain?

(*Claps him on the Back.*)

WILLMORE: Ha! I hope she did not hear.

HELLENA: What, afraid of such a Champion!

WILLMORE: Oh! you're a fine Lady of your word, are you not?
150 to make a Man languish a whole day—

HELLENA: In tedious search of me.

WILLMORE: Egad, Child, thou'rt in the right, hadst thou seen
what a melancholy Dog I have been ever since I was a Lover,
how I have walkt the Streets like a *Capuchin*, with my Hands
155 in my Sleeves—Faith, Sweetheart, thou wouldst pity me.

HELLENA: Now, if I should be hang'd, I can't be angry with
him, he dissembles so heartily—Alas, good Captain, what
pains you have taken—Now were I ungrateful not to reward
so true a Servant.

160 WILLMORE: Poor Soul! that's kindly said, I see thou bearest a
Conscience—come then for a beginning shew me thy dear
Face.

HELLENA: I'm afraid, my small Acquaintance, you have been
staying that swinging stomach you boasted of this morning; I
remember then my little Collation would have gone down 165
with you, without the Sauce of a handsom Face—Is your
Stomach so quesy now?

WILLMORE: Faith long fasting, Child, spoils a Man's Appetite—yet if you durst treat, I could so lay about me still.

HELLENA: And would you fall to, before a Priest says Grace? 170

WILLMORE: Oh fie, fie, what an old out-of-fashion'd thing hast
thou nam'd? Thou could'st not dash me more out of Countenance, shouldst thou shew me an ugly Face.

(*Whilst he is seemingly courting* HELLENA, *enter* ANGELICA,
MORETTA, BISKEY, *and* SEBASTIAN, *all in Masquerade:* ANGEL-
ICA *sees* WILLMORE *and starts.*)

ANGELICA: Heavens, is't he? and passionately fond to see another Woman? 175

MORETTA: What cou'd you expect less from such a Swaggerer?

ANGELICA: Expect! as much as I paid him, a Heart intire,
Which I had pride enough to think when e'er I gave
It would have rais'd the Man above the Vulgar,
Made him all Soul, and that all soft and constant. 180

HELLENA: You see, Captain, how willing I am to be Friends
with you, till Time and Ill-luck make us Lovers; and ask you
the Question first, rather than put your Modesty to the blush,
by asking me: for alas, I know you Captains are such strict
Men, severe Observers of your Vows to Chastity, that 185
'twill be hard to prevail with your tender Conscience to
marry a young willing Maid.

WILLMORE: Do not abuse me, for fear I should take thee at thy
word, and marry thee indeed, which I'm sure will be Revenge sufficient. 190

HELLENA: O' my Conscience, that will be our Destiny, because we are both of one humour; I am as inconstant as you,
for I have considered, Captain, that a handsom Woman has
a great deal to do whilst her Face is good, for then is our Har-
vest-time to gather Friends; and should I in these days of my 195
Youth, catch a fit of foolish Constancy, I were undone; 'tis
loitering by day-light in our great Journey: therefore declare,
I'll allow but one year for Love, one year for Indifference,
and one year for Hate—and then—go hang your self—for I
profess myself the gay, the kind, and the inconstant—the 200
Devil's in't if this won't please you.

WILLMORE: Oh most damnably!—I have a Heart with a hole
quite thro it too, no Prison like mine to keep a Mistress in.

ANGELICA: (*Aside.*) Purjur'd Man! how I believe thee now!

HELLENA: Well, I see our Business as well as Humours are 205
alike, yours to cozen as many Maids as will trust you, and I as
many Men as have Faith—See if I have not as desperate a
lying look, as you can have for the heart of you.

(*Pulls off her Vizard; he starts.*)

—How do you like it, Captain?

WILLMORE: Like it! by Heav'n, I never saw so much Beauty. 210
Oh the Charms of those sprightly black Eyes, that strangely
fair Face, full of Smiles and Dimples! those soft round melting cherry Lips! and small even white Teeth! not to be ex-
prest, but silently adored!—Oh one Look more, and strike
me dumb, or I shall repeat nothing else till I am mad. 215

(*He seems to court her to pull off her Vizard: she refuses.*)

ANGELICA: I can endure no more—nor is it fit to interrupt him; for if I do, my Jealousy has so destroy'd my Reason,—I shall undo him—Therefore I'll retire. And you *Sebastian (To one of her bravoes.)* follow that Woman, and learn who 'tis; while you tell the Fugitive, I would speak to him instantly.

(To the other bravo. Exit.)

(This while FLORINDA *is talking to* BELVILE, *who stands sullenly.* FREDERICK *courting* VALERIA.)

VALERIA: Prithee, dear Stranger, be not so sullen; for tho you have lost your Love, you see my Friend frankly offers you hers, to play with in the mean time.

BELVILE: Faith, Madam, I am sorry I can't play at her Game.

FREDERICK: Pray leave your Intercession, and mind your own Affair, they'll better agree apart; he's a model Sigher in Company, but alone no Woman escapes him.

FLORINDA: Sure he does but rally—yet if it should be true—I'll tempt him farther—Believe me, noble Stranger, I'm no common Mistress—and for a little proof on't—wear this Jewel—nay, take it, Sir, 'tis right, and Bills of Exchange may sometimes miscarry.

BELVILE: Madam, why am I chose out of all Mankind to be the Object of your Bounty?

VALERIA: There's another civil Question askt.

FREDERICK: Pox of's Modesty, it spoils his own Markets, and hinders mine.

FLORINDA: Sir, from my Window I have often seen you; and Women of Quality have so few opportunities for Love, that we ought to lose none.

FREDERICK: Ay, this is something! here's a Woman!—When shall I be blest with so much kindness from your fair Mouth?—*(Aside to* BELVILE.) Take the Jewel, Fool.

BELVILE: You tempt me strangely, Madam, every way.

FLORINDA: *(Aside.)* So, if I find him false, my whole Repose is gone.

BELVILE: And but for a Vow I've made to a very fine Lady, this Goodness had subdu'd me.

FREDERICK: Pox on't be kind, in pity to me be kind, for I am to thrive here but as you treat her Friend.

HELLENA: Tell me what did you in yonder House, and I'll unmasque.

WILLMORE: Yonder House—oh—I went to—a—to—why, there's a Friend of mine lives there.

HELLENA: What a she, or a he Friend?

WILLMORE: A Man upon my Honour! a Man—A she Friend! no, no, Madam, you have done my Business, I thank you.

HELLENA: And was't your Man Friend, that had more Darts in's Eyes than *Cupid* carries in a whole Budget of Arrows?

WILLMORE: So—

HELLENA: Ah such a *Bona Roba:* to be in her Arms is lying in *Fresco*, all perfumed Air about me—Was this your Man Friend too?

WILLMORE: So—

HELLENA: That gave you the He, and the She—Gold, that begets young Pleasures.

WILLMORE: Well, well, Madam, then you see there are Ladies in the World, that will not be cruel—there are, Madam, there are—

HELLENA: And there be Men too as fine, wild, inconstant Fellows as your self, there be, Captain, there be, if you go to that now—therefore I'm resolv'd—

WILLMORE: Oh!

HELLENA: To see your Face no more—

WILLMORE: Oh!

HELLENA: Till to morrow.

WILLMORE: Egad you frighted me.

HELLENA: Nor then neither, unless you'l swear never to see that Lady more.

WILLMORE: See her!—why! never to think of Womankind again?

HELLENA: Kneel, and swear.

(Kneels, she gives him her hand.)

WILLMORE: I do, never to think—to see—to love—nor lie with any but thy self.

HELLENA: Kiss the Book.

WILLMORE: Oh, most religiously.

(Kisses her Hand.)

HELLENA: Now what a wicked Creature am I, to damn a proper Fellow.

CALLIS: *(To* FLORINDA.) Madam, I'll stay no longer, 'tis e'en dark.

FLORINDA: However, Sir, I'll leave this with you—that when I'm gone, you may repent the opportunity you have lost by your modesty.

(Gives him the Jewel, which is her Picture, and Exits. He gazes after her.)

WILLMORE: 'Twill be an Age till to morrow,—and till then I will most impatiently expect you—Adieu, my dear pretty Angel.

(Exeunt all the WOMEN.)

BELVILE: Ha! *Florinda's* Picture! 'twas she her self—what a dull Dog was I? I would have given the World for one minute's discourse with her.—

FREDERICK: This comes of your Modesty,—ah pox on your Vow, 'twas ten to one but we had lost the Jewel by't.

BELVILE: *Willmore!* the blessed'st Opportunity lost!—*Florinda*, Friends, *Florinda!*

WILLMORE: Ah Rogue! such black Eyes, such a Face, such a Mouth, such Teeth,—and so much Wit!

BELVILE: All, all, and a thousand Charms besides.

WILLMORE: Why, dost thou know her?

BELVILE: Know her! ay, ay, and a Pox take me with all my Heart for being modest.

WILLMORE: But hark ye, Friend of mine, are you my Rival? and have I been only beating the Bush all this while?

BELVILE: I understand thee not—I'm mad—see here—

(Shews the Picture.)

WILLMORE: Ha! whose Picture is this?—'tis a fine Wench.

FREDERICK: The Colonel's Mistress, Sir.

WILLMORE: Oh, oh, here—I thought it had been another Prize—come, come, a Bottle will set thee right again.

(Gives the Picture back.)

BELVILE: I am content to try, and by that time 'twill be late enough for our Design.

WILLMORE: Agreed.

*Love does all day the Soul's great Empire keep,
But Wine at night lulls the soft God asleep.*

(Exeunt.)

SCENE II

LUCETTA's *House.*

(*Enter* BLUNT *and* LUCETTA *with a Light.*)

LUCETTA: Now we are safe and free, no fears of the coming home of my old jealous Husband, which made me a little thoughtful when you came in first—but now Love is all the business of my Soul.

5   BLUNT: (*Aside.*) I am transported—Pox on't, that I had but some fine things to say to her, such as Lovers use—I was a Fool not to learn of *Frederick* a little by Heart before I came—something I must say.—
'Sheartlikins, sweet Soul, I am not us'd to complement, but 10   I'm an honest Gentleman, and thy humble Servant.

LUCETTA: I have nothing to pay for so great a Favour, but such a Love as cannot but be great, since at first sight of that sweet Face and Shape it made me your absolute Captive.

BLUNT: (*Aside.*) Kind heart, how prettily she talks! Egad I'll 15   show her Husband a *Spanish* Trick; send him out of the World, and marry her: she's damnably in love with me, and will ne'er mind Settlements, and so there's that sav'd.

LUCETTA: Well, Sir, I'll go and undress me, and be with you instantly.

20   BLUNT: Make haste then, for 'dsheartlikins, dear Soul, thou canst not guess at the pain of a longing Lover, when his Joys are drawn within the compass of a few minutes.

LUCETTA: You speak my Sense, and I'll make haste to provide it.

(*Exit.*)

25   BLUNT: 'Tis a rare Girl, and this one night's enjoyment with her will be worth all the days I ever past in Essex.—Would she'd go with me into *England*, tho to say truth, there's plenty of Whores there already.—But a pox on 'em they are such mercenary prodigal Whores, that they want such a one 30   as this, that's free and generous, to give 'em good Examples:—Why, what a House she has! how rich and fine!

(*Enter* SANCHO.)

SANCHO: Sir, my Lady has sent me to conduct you to her Chamber.

BLUNT: Sir, I shall be proud to follow—Here's one of her Ser-35   vants too: 'dsheartlikins, by his Garb and Gravity he might be a Justice of Peace in *Essex,* and is but a Pimp here.

(*Exeunt.*)

(*The Scene changes to a Chamber with an Alcove-Bed in it, a Table, &c.* LUCETTA *in Bed. Enter* SANCHO *and* BLUNT, *who takes the Candle of* SANCHO *at the Door.*)

SANCHO: Sir, my Commission reaches no farther.

BLUNT: Sir, I'll excuse your Complement:—what, in Bed, my sweet Mistress?

40   LUCETTA: You see, I still out-do you in kindness.

BLUNT: And thou shalt see what haste I'll make to quit scores—oh the luckiest Rogue!

(*Undresses himself.*)

LUCETTA: Shou'd you be false or cruel now!

BLUNT: False, 'Sheartlikins, what dost thou take me for a *Jew?*
45   an insensible Heathen,—A Pox of thy old jealous Husband: and he were dead, egad, sweet Soul, it shou'd be none of my fault, if I did not marry thee.

LUCETTA: It never shou'd be mine.

BLUNT: Good Soul, I'm the fortunatest Dog!

LUCETTA: Are you not undrest yet?   50

BLUNT: As much as my Impatience will permit.

(*Goes towards the Bed in his Shirt and Drawers.*)

LUCETTA: Hold, Sir, put out the Light, it may betray us else.

BLUNT: Any thing, I need no other Light but that of thine Eyes!—(*Aside.*) 'sheartlikins, there I think I had it.

(*Puts out the Candle, the Bed descends, he gropes about to find it.*)

—Why—why—where am I got? what, not yet?—where are   55
your sweetest?—ah, the Rogue's silent now—a pretty Love-trick this—how she'll laugh at me anon!—you need not, my dear Rogue! you need not! I'm all on a fire already—come, come, now call me in for pity—Sure I'm enchanted! I have been round the Chamber, and can find neither Woman, nor   60
Bed—I lockt the Door, I'm sure she cannot go that way; or if she cou'd, the Bed cou'd not—Enough, enough, my pretty Wanton, do not carry the Jest too far—Ha, betray'd! Dogs! Rogues! Pimps! help! help!

(*Lights on a Trap, and is let down. Enter* LUCETTA, PHILIPPO, *and* SANCHO *with a Light.*)

PHILIPPO: Ha, ha, ha, he's dispatcht finely.   65

LUCETTA: Now, Sir, had I been coy, we had mist of this Booty.

PHILIPPO: Nay when I saw 'twas a substantial Fool, I was molli-fied; but when you doat upon a Serenading Coxcomb, upon a Face, fine Clothes, and a Lute, it makes me rage.

LUCETTA: You know I never was guilty of that Folly, my dear   70
Philippo, but with your self—But come let's see what we have got by this.

PHILIPPO: A rich Coat!—Sword and Hat!—these Breeches too—are well lin'd!—see here a Gold Watch!—a Purse—ha! Gold!—at least two hundred Pistoles! a bunch of Diamond   75
Rings; and one with the Family Arms!—a Gold Box!—with a Medal of his King! and his Lady Mother's Picture!—these were sacred Reliques, believe me!—see, the Wasteband of his Breeches have a Mine of Gold!—Old *Queen Bess's.* We have a Quarrel to her ever since Eighty Eight, and may   80
therefore justify the Theft, the Inquisition might have com-mitted it.

LUCETTA: See, a Bracelet of bow'd Gold, these his Sister ty'd about his Arm at parting—but well—for all this, I fear his being a Stranger may make a noise, and hinder our Trade   85
with them hereafter.

PHILIPPO: That's our security; he is not only a Stranger to us, but to the Country too—the Common-Shore into which he is descended, thou know'st, conducts him into another Street, which this Light will hinder him from ever finding   90
again—he knows neither your Name, nor the Street where your House is, nay, nor the way to his own Lodgings.

LUCETTA: And art not thou an unmerciful Rogue, not to af-ford him one Night for all this?—I should not have been such a *Jew.*   95

PHILIPPO: Blame me not, *Lucetta,* to keep as much of thee as I can to my self—come, that thought makes me wanton,—let's to Bed,—*Sancho,* lock up these.

---

83 **bow'd Gold** Bowed is still used in the North of England for bent: 'A bowed pin'

> *This is the Fleece which Fools do bear,*
> 100   *Design'd for witty Men to sheer.*

(Exeunt.)

(The Scene changes, and discovers BLUNT, *creeping out of a Common Shore, his Face, &c., all dirty.)*

BLUNT: Oh Lord!

(Climbing up.)

I am got out at last, and (which is a Miracle) without a Clue—and now to Damning and Cursing—but if that would ease me, where shall I begin? with my Fortune, my 105 self, or the Quean that cozen'd me—What a dog was I to believe in Women! Oh Coxcomb—ignorant conceited Coxcomb! to fancy she cou'd be enamour'd with my Person, at the first sight enamour'd—Oh, I'm a cursed Puppy, 'tis plain, Fool was writ upon my Forehead, she perceiv'd it,— 110 saw the *Essex* Calf there—for what Allurements could there be in this Countenance? which I can indure, because I'm acquainted with it—Oh, dull silly Dog! to be thus sooth'd into a Cozening! Had I been drunk, I might fondly have credited the young Quean! but as I was in my right Wits, to 115 be thus cheated, confirms I am a dull believing *English* Country Fop.—But my Comrades! Death and the Devil, there's the worst of all—then a Ballad will be sung to Morrow on the *Prado*, to a lousy Tune of the enchanted Squire, and the annihilated Damsel—But *Frederick* that Rogue, and 120 the Colonel, will abuse me beyond all Christian patience— had she left me my Clothes, I have a Bill of Exchange at home wou'd have sav'd my Credit—but now all hope is taken from me—Well, I'll home (if I can find the way) with this Consolation, that I am not the first kind believing Cox 125 comb; but there are, Gallants, many such good Natures amongst ye.

> *And tho you've better Arts to hide your Follies,*
> *Adsheartlikins y'are all as errant Cullies.*

SCENE III

The Garden, in the Night.

(Enter FLORINDA, *undress'd, with a Key, and a little Box.)*

FLORINDA: Well, thus far I'm in my way to Happiness; I have got my self free from *Callis*; my Brother too, I find by yonder light, is gone into his Cabinet, and thinks not of me: I have by good Fortune got the Key of the Garden Back-door,—I'll 5 open it, to prevent *Belvile's* knocking,—a little noise will now alarm my Brother. Now am I as fearful as a young Thief. *(Unlocks the Door.)*—Hark,—what noise is that?—Oh, 'twas the Wind that plaid amongst the Boughs.—*Belvile* stays long, methinks—it's time—stay—for fear of a surprize, I'll 10 hide these Jewels in yonder Jessamin.

(She goes to lay down the Box.)

(Enter WILLMORE *drunk.)*

WILLMORE: What the Devil is become of these Fellows, *Belvile* and *Frederick*? They promis'd to stay at the next corner for me, but who the Devil knows the corner of a full Moon?— Now—whereabouts am I?—hah—what have we here? a 15 Garden!—a very convenient place to sleep in—hah—what has God sent us here?—a Female—by this light, a Woman; I'm a Dog if it be not a very Wench.—

FLORINDA: He's come!—hah—who's there?

WILLMORE: Sweet Soul, let me salute thy Shoe-string.

FLORINDA: 'Tis not my *Belvile*—good Heavens, I know him 20 not.—Who are you, and from whence come you!

WILLMORE: Prithee—prithee, Child—not so many hard Questions—let it suffice I am here, Child—Come, come kiss me.

FLORINDA: Good Gods! what luck is mine? 25

WILLMORE: Only good luck, Child, parlous good luck.— Come hither,—'tis a delicate shining Wench,—by this Hand she's perfum'd, and smells like any Nosegay.—Prithee, dear Soul, let's not play the Fool, and lose time,—precious time—for as Gad shall save me, I'm as honest a Fellow as 30 breathes, tho I am a little disguis'd at present.—Come, I say,—why, thou may'st be free with me, I'll be very secret. I'll not boast who 'twas oblig'd me, not I—for hang me if I know thy Name.

FLORINDA: Heavens! what a filthy beast is this! 35

WILLMORE: I am so, and thou oughtst the sooner to lie with me for that reason,—for look you, Child, there will be no Sin in't, because 'twas neither design'd nor premeditated; 'tis pure Accident on both sides—that's a certain thing now— Indeed should I make love to you, and you vow Fidelity— 40 and swear and lye till you believ'd and yielded—Thou art therefore (as thou art a good Christian) oblig'd in Conscience to deny me nothing. Now—come, be kind, without any more idle prating.

FLORINDA: Oh, I am ruin'd—wicked Man, unhand me. 45

WILLMORE: Wicked! Egad, Child, a Judge, were he young and vigorous, and saw those Eyes of thine, would know 'twas they gave the first blow—the first provocation.—Come, prithee let's lose no time, I say—this is a fine convenient place.

FLORINDA: Sir, let me go, I conjure you, or I'll call out. 50

WILLMORE: Ay, ay, you were best to call Witness to see how finely you treat me—do.—

FLORINDA: I'll cry Murder, Rape, or any thing, if you do not instantly let me go.

WILLMORE: A Rape! Come, come, you lye, you Baggage, you 55 lye: What, I'll warrant you would fain have the World believe now that you are not so forward as I. No, not you,—why at this time of Night was your Cobweb-door set open, dear Spider—but to catch Flies?—Hah come—or I shall be damnably angry.—Why what a Coil is here.— 60

FLORINDA: Sir, can you think—

WILLMORE: That you'd do it for nothing? oh, oh, I find what you'd be at—look here, here's a Pistole for you—here's a work indeed—here—take it, I say.—

FLORINDA: For Heaven's sake, Sir, as you're a Gentleman— 65

WILLMORE: So—now—she would be wheedling me for more—what, you will not take it then—you're resolv'd you will not.—Come, come, take it, or I'll put it up again; for, look ye, I never give more.—Why, how now, Mistress, are you so high i'th' Mouth, a Pistole won't down with you?— 70 hah—why, what a work's here—in good time—come, no struggling, be gone—But an y'are good at a dumb Wrestle, I'm for ye,—look ye,—I'm for ye.—

(She struggles with him.)

(Enter BELVILE *and* FREDERICK.)*

---

31 **disguis'd** A common phrase for drunk

BELVILE: The Door is open, a Pox of this mad Fellow, I'm angry
that we've lost him, I durst have sworn he had follow'd us.
FREDERICK: But you were so hasty, Colonel, to be gone.
FLORINDA: Help, help,—Murder!—help—oh, I'm ruin'd.
BELVILE: Ha, sure that's *Florinda's* Voice.

(Comes up to them.)

—A Man! Villain, let go that Lady.

(A noise.)

(WILLMORE turns and draws, FREDERICK interposes.)

FLORINDA: *Belvile!* Heavens! my Brother too is coming, and
'twill be impossible to escape.—*Belvile*, I conjure you to walk
under my Chamber-window, from whence I'll give you some
instructions what to do—This rude Man has undone us.

(Exit.)

WILLMORE: *Belvile!*

(Enter PEDRO, STEPHANO, and other Servants with Lights.)

PEDRO: I'm betray'd; run, *Stephano*, and see if *Florinda* be safe.

(Exit STEPHANO.)

So who'er they be, all is not well, I'll to *Florinda's* Chamber.

*(They fight, and PEDRO's Party beats 'em out; going out, meets
STEPHANO.)*

STEPHANO: You need not, Sir, the poor Lady's fast asleep, and
thinks no harm: I wou'd not wake her, Sir, for fear of fright-
ning her with your danger.
PEDRO: I'm glad she's there—Rascals, how came the Garden-
Door open?
STEPHANO: That Question comes too late, Sir: some of my
Fellow-Servants Masquerading I'll warrant.
PEDRO: Masquerading! a leud Custom to debauch our
Youth—there's something more in this than I imagine.
(Exeunt.)

SCENE IV

Changes to the Street.

*(Enter BELVILE in Rage, FREDERICK holding him, and WILL-
MORE melancholy.)*

WILLMORE: Why, how the Devil shou'd I know *Florinda*?
BELVILE: Ah plague of your ignorance! if it had not been
Florinda, must you be a Beast?—a Brute, a senseless Swine?
WILLMORE: Well, Sir, you see I am endu'd with Patience—I
can bear—tho egad y're very free with me methinks,—I was
in good hopes the Quarrel wou'd have been on my side, for
so uncivilly interrupting me.
BELVILE: Peace, Brute, whilst thou'rt safe—oh, I'm distracted.
WILLMORE: Nay, nay, I'm an unlucky Dog, that's certain.
BELVILE: Ah curse upon the Star that rul'd my Birth! or what-
soever other Influence that makes me still so wretched.
WILLMORE: Thou break'st my Heart with these Complaints;
there is no Star in fault, no Influence but Sack, the cursed
Sack I drank.
FREDERICK: Why, how the Devil came you so drunk?
WILLMORE: Why, how the Devil came you so sober?
BELVILE: A curse upon his thin Skull, he was always before-
hand that way.

FREDERICK: Prithee, dear Colonel, forgive him, he's sorry for
his fault.
BELVILE: He's always so after he has done a mischief—a
plague on all such Brutes.
WILLMORE: By this Light I took her for an errant Harlot.
BELVILE: Damn your debaucht Opinion: tell me, Sot, hadst
thou so much sense and light about thee to distinguish her to
be a Woman, and could'st not see something about her Face
and Person, to strike an awful Reverence into thy Soul?
WILLMORE: Faith no, I consider'd her as mere a Woman as I
could wish.
BELVILE: 'Sdeath I have no patience—draw, or I'll kill you.
WILLMORE: Let that alone till to morrow, and if I set not all
right again, use your Pleasure.
BELVILE: To morrow, damn it.
The spiteful Light will lead me to no happiness.
To morrow is *Antonio's*, and perhaps
Guides him to my undoing;—oh that I could meet
This Rival, this powerful Fortunate.
WILLMORE: What then?
BELVILE: Let thy own Reason, or my Rage instruct thee.
WILLMORE: I shall be finely inform'd then, no doubt; hear
me, Colonel—hear me—shew me the Man and I'll do his
Business.
BELVILE: I know him no more than thou, or if I did, I should
not need thy aid.
WILLMORE: This you say is *Angelica's* House, I promis'd the
kind Baggage to lie with her to Night.

(Offers to go in.)

*(Enter ANTONIO and his Page. ANTONIO knocks on the Hilt of
his Sword.)*

ANTONIO: You paid the thousand Crowns I directed?
PAGE: To the Lady's old Woman, Sir, I did.
WILLMORE: Who the Devil have we here?
BELVILE: I'll now plant my self under *Florinda's* Window, and
if I find no comfort there, I'll die.

(Exit BELVILE and FREDERICK. Enter MORETTA.)

MORETTA: Page!
PAGE: Here's my Lord.
WILLMORE: How is this, a Piccaroon going to board my
Frigate! here's one Chase-Gun for you.

*(Drawing his Sword, justles ANTONIO who turns and draws.
They fight, ANTONIO falls.)*

MORETTA: Oh, bless us, we are all undone!

(Runs in, and shuts the Door.)

PAGE: Help, Murder!

(BELVILE returns at the noise of fighting.)

BELVILE: Ha, the mad Rogue's engag'd in some unlucky Adventure again.

(Enter two or three MASQUERADERS.)

MASQUERADER: Ha, a Man kill'd!
WILLMORE: How! a Man kill'd! then I'll go home to sleep.

(Puts up, and reels out. Exeunt MASQUERADERS another way.)

BELVILE: Who shou'd it be! pray Heaven the Rogue is safe, for
all my Quarrel to him.

(As BELVILE *is groping about, enter an* OFFICER *and six* SOLDIERS.*)*

SOLDIER: Who's there?

65 OFFICER: So, here's one dispatcht—secure the Murderer.

BELVILE: Do not mistake my Charity for Murder: I came to his Assistance.

*(*SOLDIERS *sieze on* BELVILE.*)*

OFFICER: That shall be tried, Sir.—St. *Jago,* Swords drawn in the Carnival time!

(Goes to ANTONIO.*)*

70 ANTONIO: Thy Hand prithee.

OFFICER: Ha, Don *Antonio!* look well to the Villain there.— How is't, Sir?

ANTONIO: I'm hurt.

BELVILE: Has my Humanity made me a Criminal?

75 OFFICER: Away with him.

BELVILE: What a curst Chance is this!

(Exeunt SOLDIERS *with* BELVILE.*)*

ANTONIO: *(To the* OFFICER.*)* This is the Man that has set upon me twice—carry him to my Apartment till you have further Orders from me.

(Exit. ANTONIO *led.)*

— ACT FOUR —

SCENE I

A fine Room.

(Discovers BELVILE, *as by Dark alone.)*

BELVILE: When shall I be weary of railing on Fortune, who is resolv'd never to turn with Smiles upon me?—Two such De- feats in one Night—none but the Devil and that mad Rogue could have contriv'd to have plagued me with—I am here a
5   Prisoner—but where?—Heaven knows—and if there be Murder done, I can soon decide the Fate of a Stranger in a Nation without Mercy—Yet this is nothing to the Torture my Soul bows with, when I think of losing my fair, my dear *Florinda.*—Hark—my Door opens—a Light—a Man—and
10   seems of Quality—arm'd too.—Now shall I die like a Dog without defence.

(Enter ANTONIO *in a Night-Gown, with a Light; his Arm in a Scarf, and a Sword under his Arm: He sets the Candle on the Table.)*

ANTONIO: Sir, I come to know what Injuries I have done you, that could provoke you to so mean an Action, as to attack me basely, without allowing time for my Defence.

15 BELVILE: Sir, for a Man in my Circumstances to plead Inno- cence, would look like Fear—but view me well, and you will find no marks of a Coward on me, nor any thing that betrays that Brutality you accuse me of.

ANTONIO: In vain, Sir, you impose upon my Sense,
20   You are not only he who drew on me last Night,
       But yesterday before the same House, that of *Angelica.*
       Yet there is something in your Face and Mein—

BELVILE: I own I fought to day in the defence of a Friend of mine, with whom you (if you're the same) and your

Party were first engag'd.   25
Perhaps you think this Crime enough to kill me,
But if you do, I cannot fear you'll do it basely.

ANTONIO: No, Sir, I'll make you fit for a Defence with this.

(Gives him the Sword.)

BELVILE: This Gallantry surprizes me—nor know I how to use this Present, Sir, against a Man so brave.   30

ANTONIO: You shall not need;
       For know, I come to snatch you from a Danger
       That is decreed against you;
       Perhaps your Life, or long Imprisonment:
       And 'twas with so much Courage you offended,   35
       I cannot see you punish.

BELVILE: How shall I pay this Generosity?

ANTONIO: It had been safer to have kill'd another,
       Than have attempted me:
       To shew your Danger, Sir, I'll let you know my Quality; 40
       And 'tis the Vice-Roy's Son whom you have wounded.

BELVILE: *(Aside.)* The Vice-Roy's Son!
       Death and Confusion! was this Plague reserved
       To compleat all the rest?—oblig'd by him!
       The Man of all the World I would destroy.   45

ANTONIO: You seem disorder'd, Sir.

BELVILE: Yes, trust me, Sir, I am, and 'tis with pain
       That Man receives such Bounties,
       Who wants the pow'r to pay 'em back again.

ANTONIO: To gallant Spirits 'tis indeed uneasy;   50
       —But you may quickly over-pay me, Sir.

BELVILE: Then I am well—*(Aside.)* kind Heaven! but set us even,
       That I may fight with him, and keep my Honour safe.
       —Oh, I'm impatient, Sir, to be discounting
       The mighty Debt I owe you; command me quickly— 55

ANTONIO: I have a Quarrel with a Rival, Sir,
       About the Maid we love.

BELVILE: *(Aside.)* Death, 'tis *Florinda* he means—
       That Thought destroys my Reason, and I shall kill him—

ANTONIO: My Rival, Sir,   60
       Is one has all the Virtues Man can boast of.

BELVILE: Death! who shou'd this be?

ANTONIO: He challeng'd me to meet him on the *Molo,*
       As soon as Day appear'd; but last Night's quarrel
       Has made my Arm unfit to guide a Sword.   65

BELVILE: I apprehend you, Sir, you'd have me kill the Man
       That lays a claim to the Maid you speak of.
       —I'll do't—I'll fly to do it.

ANTONIO: Sir, do you know her?

BELVILE: —No, Sir, but 'tis enough she is admired by you. 70

ANTONIO: Sir, I shall rob you of the Glory on't,
       For you must fight under my Name and Dress.

BELVILE: That Opinion must be strangely obliging that makes
       You think I can personate the brave *Antonio,*
       Whom I can but strive to imitate.   75

ANTONIO: You say too much to my Advantage.
       Come, Sir, the Day appears that calls you forth.
       Within, Sir, is the Habit.

(Exit ANTONIO.*)*

BELVILE: Fantastick Fortune, thou deceitful Light,
       That cheats the wearied Traveller by Night,   80

Tho on a Precipice each step you tread,
I am resolv'd to follow where you lead.

(Exit.)

SCENE II

The Molo.

(Enter FLORINDA *and* CALLIS *in Masques, with* STEPHANO.*)*

FLORINDA: *(Aside.)* I'm dying with my fears; *Belvile's* not
    coming,
    As I expected, underneath my Window,
    Makes me believe that all those Fears are true.
    —Canst thou not tell with whom my Brother fights?

5 STEPHANO: No, Madam, they were both in Masquerade, I was
    by when they challeng'd one another, and they had decided
    the Quarrel then, but were prevented by some Cavaliers;
    which made 'em put it off till now—but I am sure 'tis about
    you they fight.

10 FLORINDA: *(Aside.)* Nay then 'tis with *Belvile,* for what other
    Lover have I that dares fight for me, except *Antonio?* and he
    is too much in favour with my Brother—If it be he, for whom
    shall I direct my Prayers to Heaven?
    STEPHANO: Madam, I must leave you; for if my Master see me,

15 I shall be hang'd for being your Conductor.—I escap'd nar-
    rowly for the Excuse I made for you last night i'th' Garden.
    FLORINDA: And I'll reward thee for't—prithee no more.

(Exit STEPHANO.*)*

(Enter Don PEDRO *in his Masquing Habit.)*

PEDRO: *Antonio's* late to day, the place will fill, and we may be
    prevented.

(Walks about.)

20 FLORINDA: (Aside.) Antonio! sure I heard amiss.
    PEDRO: But who would not excuse a happy Lover.
    When soft fair Arms comfine the yielding Neck;
    And the kind Whisper languishingly breathes,
    Must you be gone so soon?

25 Sure I had dwelt for ever on her Bosom.
    —But stay, he's here.

(Enter BELVILE *drest in* ANTONIO's *Clothes.)*

FLORINDA: 'Tis not *Belvile,* half my Fears are vanisht.
PEDRO: *Antonio!*—
BELVILE: *(Aside.)* This must be he.

30 You're early, Sir,—I do not use to be out-done this way.
    PEDRO: The wretched, Sir, are watchful, and 'tis enough
    You have the advantage of me in *Angelica.*
    BELVILE: *(Aside.)* Angelica!
    Or I've mistook my Man! Or else *Antonio,*

35 Can he forget his Interest in *Florinda,*
    And fight for common Prize?
    PEDRO: Come, Sir, you know our terms—
    BELVILE: *(Aside.)* Be Heaven, not I.
    —No talking, I am ready, Sir.

(Offers to fight. FLORINDA *runs in.)*

40 FLORINDA: *(To* BELVILE.*)* Oh, hold! who'er you be, I do con-
    jure you hold. If you strike here—I die—
    PEDRO: *Florinda!*

BELVILE: *Florinda* imploring for my Rival!
PEDRO: Away, this Kindness is unseasonable.

(Puts her by, they fight; she runs in just as BELVILE *disarms*
PEDRO.*)*

FLORINDA: Who are you, Sir, that dare deny my Prayers?   45
BELVILE: Thy Prayers destroy him; if thou wouldst preserve
    him.
    Do that thou'rt unacquainted with, and curse him.

(She holds him.)

FLORINDA: By all you hold most dear, by her you love,
    I do conjure you, touch him not.
BELVILE: By her I love!   50
    See—I obey—and at your Feet resign
    The useless Trophy of my Victory.

(Lays his sword at her Feet.)

PEDRO: *Antonio,* you've done enough to prove you love
    Florinda.
BELVILE: Love *Florinda!*   55
    Does Heaven love Adoration, Pray'r, or Penitence?
    Love her! here Sir,—your Sword again.

(Snatches up the Sword, and gives it him.)

    Upon this Truth I'll fight my Life away.
PEDRO: No, you've redeem'd my Sister, and my Friendship.
BELVILE: Don *Pedro!*   60

(He gives him FLORINDA *and pulls off his Vizard to shew his
Face, and puts it on again.)*

PEDRO: Can you resign your Claims to other Women,
    And give your Heart intirely to *Florinda?*
BELVILE: Intire, as dying Saints Confessions are.
    I can delay my happiness no longer.
    This minute let me make *Florinda* mine: 65
PEDRO: This minute let it be—no time so proper,
    This Night my Father will arrive from *Rome,*
    And possibly may hinder what we propose.
FLORINDA: Oh Heavens! this Minute!

(Enter MASQUERADERS, *and pass over.)*

BELVILE: Oh, do not ruin me!   70
PEDRO: The place begins to fill; and that we may not be ob-
    serv'd, do you walk off to St. *Peter's* Church, where I will
    meet you, and conclude your Happiness.
BELVILE: I'll meet you there—*(Aside.)* if there be no more
    Saints Churches in *Naples.*   75
FLORINDA: Oh stay, Sir, and recall your hasty Doom:
    Alas I have not yet prepar'd my Heart
    To entertain so strange a Guest.
PEDRO: Away, this silly Modesty is assum'd too late.
BELVILE: Heaven, Madam! what do you do?   80
FLORINDA: Do! despise the Man that lays a Tyrant's Claim
    To what he ought to conquer by Submission.
BELVILE: You do not know me—move a little this way.

(Draws her aside.)

FLORINDA: Yes, you may even force me to the Altar,
    But not the holy Man that offers there   85
    Shall force me to be thine.

*(*PEDRO *talks to* CALLIS *this while.)*

BELVILE: Oh do not lose so blest an opportunity!
See—'tis your *Belvile*—not *Antonio*,
Whom your mistaken Scorn and Anger ruins.

(*Pulls off his Vizard.*)

90 FLORINDA: *Belvile!*
Where was my Soul it cou'd not meet thy Voice,
And take this knowledge in?

(*As they are talking, enter* WILLMORE *finely drest, and* FREDERICK.)

WILLMORE: No Intelligence! no News of *Belvile* yet—well I
am the most unlucky Rascal in Nature—ha!—am I de-
95 ceiv'd—or is it he—look, *Frederick*—'tis he—my dear
Belvile.

(*Runs and embraces him.* BELVILE'S *Vizard falls out on's Hand.*)

BELVILE: Hell and Confusion seize thee!
PEDRO: Ha! *Belvile!* I beg your Pardon, Sir.

(*Takes* FLORINDA *from him.*)

BELVILE: Nay, touch her not, she's mine by Conquest, Sir.
100 I won her by my Sword.
WILLMORE: Did'st thou so—and egad, Child, we'll keep her
by the Sword.

(*Draws on* PEDRO, BELVILE *goes between.*)

BELVILE: Stand off.
Thou'rt so profanely leud, so curst by Heaven,
105 All Quarrels thou espousest must be fatal.
WILLMORE: Nay, an you be so hot, my Valour's coy,
And shall be courted when you want it next.

(*Puts up his Sword.*)

BELVILE: You know I ought to claim a Victor's Right,

(*To* PEDRO.)

But you're the Brother to divine *Florinda,*
110 To whom I'm such a Slave—to purchase her,
I durst not hurt the Man she holds so dear.
PEDRO: 'Twas by *Antonio's,* not by *Belvile's* Sword,
This Question should have been decided, Sir:
I must confess much to your Bravery's due,
115 Both now, and when I met you last in Arms.
But I am nicely punctual in my word,
As Men of Honour ought, and beg your Pardon.
(*Aside to* FLORINDA *as they are going out.*)
—For this Mistake another Time shall clear.
—This was some Plot between you and *Belvile:*
120 But I'll prevent you.

(BELVILE *looks after her, and begins to walk up and down in a Rage.*)

WILLMORE: Do not be modest now, and lose the Woman: but
if we shall fetch her back, so—
BELVILE: Do not speak to me.
WILLMORE: Not speak to you!—Egad, I'll speak to you, and
125 will be answered too.
BELVILE: Will you, Sir?
WILLMORE: I know I've done some mischief, but I'm so dull a
Puppy, that I am the Son of a Whore, if I know how, or
where—prithee inform my Understanding.—

BELVILE: Leave me I say, and leave me instantly. 130
WILLMORE: I will not leave you in this humour, nor till I know
my Crime.
BELVILE: Death, I'll tell you, Sir—

(*Draws and runs at* WILLMORE; *he runs out;* BELVILE *after him,* FREDERICK *interposes.*)

(*Enter* ANGELICA, MORETTA, *and* SEBASTIAN.)

ANGELICA: Ha—*Sebastian*—Is not that *Willmore*? haste,
haste, and bring him back. 135
FREDERICK: The Colonel's mad—I never saw him thus before; I'll after 'em, lest he do some mischief, for I am sure
Willmore will not draw on him.

(*Exit.*)

ANGELICA: I am all Rage! my first desires defeated
For one, for ought he knows, that has no 140
Other Merit than her Quality,—
Her being Don *Pedro's* Sister—He loves her:
I know 'tis so—dull, dull, insensible—
He will not see me now tho oft invited;
And broke his Word last night—false perjur'd Man! 145
—He that but yesterday fought for my Favours,
And would have made his Life a Sacrifice
To've gain'd one Night with me,
Must now be hired and courted to my Arms.
MORETTA: I told you what wou'd come on't, but *Moretta's* an 150
old doating Fool—Why did you give him five hundred
Crowns, but to set himself out for other Lovers? You shou'd
have kept him poor, if you had meant to have had any good
from him.
ANGELICA: Oh, name not such mean Trifles.—Had I given 155
him all
My Youth has earn'd from Sin,
I had not lost a Thought nor Sigh upon't.
But I have given him my eternal Rest,
My whole Repose, my future Joys, my Heart;
My Virgin Heart. *Moretta!* oh' tis gone! 160
MORETTA: Curse on him, here he comes;
How fine she has made him too!

(*Enter* WILLMORE *and* SEBASTIAN. ANGELICA *turns and walks away.*)

WILLMORE: How now, turn'd Shadow?
Fly when I pursue, and follow when I fly!

(*Sings.*)

> Stay gentle Shadow of my Dove, 165
> And tell me e'er I go,
> Whether the Substance may not prove
> A fleeting Thing like you.

There's a soft kind Look remaining yet.

(*As she turns she looks on him.*)

ANGELICA: Well, Sir, you may be gay; all Happiness, all Joys 170
pursue you still, Fortune's your Slave, and gives you every
hour choice of new Hearts and Beauties, till you are cloy'd
with the repeated Bliss, which others vainly languish for—
But know, false Man, that I shall be reveng'd.

(*Turns away in a Rage.*)

175 WILLMORE: So, 'gad, there are of those faint-hearted Lovers, whom such a sharp Lesson next their Hearts would make as impotent as Fourscore—pox o' this whining—my Bus'ness is to laugh and love—a pox on't; I hate your sullen Lover, a Man shall lose as much time to put you in Humour now, as

180 would serve to gain a new Woman.

ANGELICA: I scorn to cool that Fire I cannot raise, Or do the Drudgery of your virtuous Mistress.

WILLMORE: A virtuous Mistress! Death, what a thing thou hast found out for me! why what the Devil should I do with a vir-

185 tuous Woman?—a fort of ill'natur'd Creatures, that take a Pride to torment a Lover. Virtue is but an Infirmity in Women, a Disease that renders even the handsom ungrateful; whilst the ill-favour'd, for want of Sollicitations and Address, only fancy themselves so.—I have lain with a Woman

190 of Quality, who has all the while been railing at Whores.

ANGELICA: I will not answer for your Mistress's Virtue, Tho she be young enough to know no Guilt: And I could wish you would persuade my Heart, 'Twas the two hundred thousand Crowns you courted.

195 WILLMORE: Two hundred thousand Crowns! what Story's this?—what Trick?—what Woman?—ha.

ANGELICA: How strange you make it! have you forgot the Creature you entertain'd on the Piazza last night?

WILLMORE: Ha, my Gipsy worth two hundred thousand

200 Crowns!—oh how I long to be with her—pox, I knew she was of Quality.

ANGELICA: False Man, I see my Ruin in thy Face. How many vows you breath'd upon my Bosom, Never to be unjust—have you forgot so soon?

205 WILLMORE: Faith no, I was just coming to repeat 'em—but here's a Humour indeed—would make a Man a Saint— (Aside.) Wou'd she'd be angry enough to leave me, and command me not to wait on her.

(Enter HELLENA, drest in Man's Clothes.)

HELLENA: This must be *Angelica*, I know it by her mumping

210 Matron here—Ay, ay, 'tis she: my mad Captain's with her too, for all his swearing—how this unconstant Humour makes me love him:—pray, good grave Gentlewoman, is not this *Angelica*?

MORETTA: My too young Sir, it is—I hope 'tis one from Don

215 *Antonio*.

(Goes to ANGELICA.)

HELLENA: (Aside.) Well, something I'll do to vex him for this.

ANGELICA: I will not speak with him; am I in humour to receive a Lover?

WILLMORE: Not speak with him! why I'll be gone—and wait

220 your idler minutes—Can I shew less Obedience to the thing I love so fondly?

(Offers to go.)

ANGELICA: A fine Excuse this—stay—

WILLMORE: And hinder your Advantage: should I repay your Bounties so ungratefully?

225 ANGELICA: Come, hither, Boy,—that I may let you see How much above the Advantages you name I prize one Minute's Joy with you.

WILLMORE: Oh, you destroy me with this Endearment.

(Impatient to be gone.)

—Death, how shall I get away!—Madam, 'twill not be fit I should be seen with you—besides, it will not be conve-
230 nient—and I've a Friend—that's dangerously sick.

ANGELICA: I see you're impatient—yet you shall stay.

WILLMORE: And miss my Assignation with my Gipsy.

(Aside, and walks about impatiently. MORETTA brings HELLENA, who addresses her self to ANGELICA.)

HELLENA: Madam, You'l hardly pardon my Intrusion, When you shall know my Business;
235 And I'm too young to tell my Tale with Art: But there must be a wondrous store of Goodness Where so much Beauty dwells.

ANGELICA: A pretty Advocate, whoever sent thee, —Prithee proceed—Nay, Sir, you shall not go.
240

(To WILLMORE who is stealing off.)

WILLMORE: Then shall I lose my dear Gipsy for ever. (Aside.)—Pox on't, she stays me out of spite.

HELLENA: I am related to a Lady, Madam, Young, rich, and nobly born, but has the fate To be in love with a young *English* Gentleman.
245 Strangely she loves him, at first sight she lov'd him, But did adore him when she heard him speak; For he, she said, had Charms in every word, That fail'd not to surprize, to wound, and conquer—

WILLMORE: (Aside.) Ha, Egad I hope this concerns me.
250 ANGELICA: 'Tis my false Man, he means—wou'd he were gone. This Praise will raise his Pride and ruin me—(To WILLMORE.) Well, Since you are so impatient to be gone. I will release you, Sir.

WILLMORE: (Aside.) Nay, then I'm sure 'twas me he spoke of,
255 this cannot be the Effects of Kindness in her. —No, Madam, I've consider'd better on't, And will not give you cause of Jealousy.

ANGELICA: But, Sir, I've—business, that—

WILLMORE: This shall not do, I know 'tis but to try me.
260 ANGELICA: (Aside.) Well, to your Story, Boy,—tho 'twill undo me.

HELLENA: With this Addition to his other Beauties, He won her unresisting tender Heart, He vow'd and sigh'd, and swore he lov'd her dearly; And she believ'd the cunning Flatterer,
265 And thought her self the happiest Maid alive: To day was the appointed time by both, To consummate their Bliss; The Virgin, Altar, and the Priest were drest, And whilst she languisht for the expected Bridegroom,
270 She heard, he paid his broken Vows to you.

WILLMORE: (Aside.) So, this is some dear Rogue that's in love with me, and this way lets me know it; or if it be not me, she means some one whose place I may supply.

ANGELICA: Now I perceive
275 The cause of thy Impatience to be gone, And all the business of this glorious Dress.

WILLMORE: Damn the young Prater, I know not what he means.

HELLENA: Madam, In your fair Eyes I read too much concern
280 To tell my farther Business.

ANGELICA: Prithee, sweet Youth, talk on, thou may'st perhaps
　　Raise here a Storm that may undo my Passion,
　　And then I'll grant thee any thing.

285　HELLENA: Madam, 'tis to intreat you, (oh unreasonable!)
　　You wou'd not see this Stranger;
　　For if you do, she vows you are undone,
　　Tho Nature never made a Man so excellent;
　　And sure he'ad been a God, but for Inconstancy.

290　WILLMORE: (*Aside.*) Ah, Rogue, how finely he's instructed!
　　—'Tis plain some Woman that has seen me *en passant.*
　　ANGELICA: Oh, I shall burst with Jealousy! do you know the
　　Man you speak of?—
　　HELLENA: Yes, Madam, he us'd to be in Buff and Scarlet.

295　ANGELICA: (*To* WILLMORE.) Thou, false as Hell, what canst
　　thou say to this?
　　WILLMORE: By Heaven—
　　ANGELICA: Hold, do not damn thy self—
　　HELLENA: Nor hope to be believ'd.

(*He walks about, they follow.*)

300　ANGELICA: Oh, perjur'd Man!
　　Is't thus you pay my generous Passion back?
　　HELLENA: Why wou'd you, Sir, abuse my Lady's Faith?
　　ANGELICA: And use me so unhumanly?
　　HELLENA: A Maid so young, so innocent—

305　WILLMORE: Ah, young Devil!
　　ANGELICA: Dost thou not know thy Life is in my Power?
　　HELLENA: Or think my Lady cannot be reveng'd?
　　WILLMORE: (*Aside.*) So, so, the Storm comes finely on.
　　ANGELICA: Now thou art silent, Guilt has struck thee dumb.

310　Oh, hadst thou still been so, I'd liv'd in safety.

(*She turns away and weeps.*)

WILLMORE: (*Aside to* HELLENA, *looks towards* ANGELICA *to
　　watch her turning; and as she comes towards them, he meets
　　her.*) Sweetheart, the Lady's Name and House—quickly: I'm
　　impatient to be with her.—

315　HELLENA: (*Aside.*) So now is he for another Woman.
　　WILLMORE: The impudent'st young thing in Nature!
　　I cannot persuade him out of his Error, Madam.
　　ANGELICA: I know he's in the right,—yet thou'st a Tongue
　　That wou'd persuade him to deny his Faith.

(*In Rage walks away.*)

320　WILLMORE: (*Said softly to* HELLENA.) Her Name, her Name,
　　dear Boy—
　　HELLENA: Have you forgot it, Sir?
　　WILLMORE: (*Aside.*) Oh, I perceive he's not to know I am a
　　Stranger to his Lady.

325　—Yes, yes, I do know—but—I have forgot the—

(ANGELICA *turns.*)

—By Heaven, such early confidence I never saw.
　　ANGELICA: Did I not charge you with this Mistress, Sir?
　　Which you denied, tho I beheld your Perjury.
　　This little Generosity of thine has render'd back my Heart.

(*Walks away.*)

330　WILLMORE: So, you have made sweet work here, my little
　　mischief;
　　Look your Lady be kind and good-natur'd now, or
　　I shall have but a cursed Bargain on't.

(ANGELICA *turns towards them.*)

—The Rogue's bred up to Mischief,
　　Art thou so great a Fool to credit him?
ANGELICA: Yes, I do; and you in vain impose upon me.　335
　　—Come hither, Boy—Is not this he you speak of?
HELLENA: (HELLENA *looks in his Face, he gazes on her.*) I
　　think—it is; I cannot swear, but I vow he has just such an-
　　other lying Lover's look.
WILLMORE: (*Aside.*) Hah! do not I know that Face?—　340
　　By Heaven, my little Gipsy! what a dull Dog was I?
　　Had I but lookt that way, I'd known her.
　　Are all my hopes of a new Woman banisht?
　　—Egad, if I don't fit thee for this, hang me.
　　—Madam, I have found out the Plot.　345
HELLENA: Oh Lord, what does he say? am I discover'd now?
WILLMORE: Do you see this young Spark here?
HELLENA: He'll tell her who I am.
WILLMORE: Who do you think this is?
HELLENA: Ay, ay, he does know me.—Nay, dear Captain, I'm　350
　　undone if you discover me.
WILLMORE: Nay, nay, no cogging; she shall know what a pre-
　　cious Mistress I have.
HELLENA: Will you be such a Devil?
WILLMORE: Nay, nay, I'll teach you to spoil sport you will not　355
　　make.—This small Ambassador comes not from a Person of
　　Quality, as you imagine, and he says; but from a very errant
　　Gipsy, the talkingst, pratingst, cantingst little Animal thou
　　ever saw'st.
ANGELICA: What news you tell me! that's the thing I mean.　360
HELLENA: (*Aside.*) Wou'd I were well off the place.—If ever I
　　go a Captain-hunting again.—
WILLMORE: Mean that thing? that Gipsy thing? thou may'st as
　　well be jealous of thy Monkey, or Parrot as her: a *German*
　　Motion were worth a dozen of her, and a Dream were a bet-　365
　　ter Enjoyment, a Creature of Constitution fitter for Heaven
　　than Man.
HELLENA: (*Aside.*) Tho I'm sure he lyes, yet this vexes me.
ANGELICA: You are mistaken, she's a *Spanish* Woman
　　Made up of no such dull Materials.　370
WILLMORE: Materials! Egad, and she be made of any that will
　　either dispense, or admit of Love, I'll be bound to conti-
　　nence.
HELLENA: (*Aside to him.*) Unreasonable Man, do you think so?
WILLMORE: You may Return, my little Brazen Head, and tell　375
　　your Lady, that till she be handsom enough to be belov'd, or I
　　dull enough to be religious, there will be small hopes of me.
ANGELICA: Did you not promise then to marry her?
WILLMORE: Not I, by Heaven.
ANGELICA: You cannot undeceive my fears and torments, till　380
　　you have vow'd you will not marry her.
HELLENA: If he swears that, he'll be reveng'd on me indeed for
　　all my Rogueries.
ANGELICA: I know what Arguments you'll bring against me,
　　Fortune and Honour.　385
WILLMORE: Honour! I tell you, I hate it in your Sex; and those
　　that fancy themselves possest of that Foppery, are the most
　　impertinently troublesom of all Woman-kind, and will

---

352 **cogging** To cog = to trick, wheedle or cajole

transgress nine Commandments to keep one: and to satisfy
390 your Jealousy I swear—
     HELLENA: *(Aside to him.)* Oh, no swearing, dear Captain—
     WILLMORE: If it were possible I should ever be inclin'd to
     marry, it should be some kind young Sinner, one that has
395 Generosity enough to give a favour handsomely to one that
     can ask it discreetly, one that has Wit enough to manage an
     Intrigue of Love—oh, how civil such a Wench is, to a Man
     than does her the Honour to marry her.
     ANGELICA: By Heaven, there's no Faith in any thing he says.

(Enter SEBASTIAN.*)*

     SEBASTIAN: Madam, *Don Antonio—*
400 ANGELICA: Come hither.
     HELLENA: Ha, *Antonio!* he may be coming hither, and he'll cer-
     tainly discover me, I'll therefore retire without a Ceremony.

(Exit HELLENA.*)*

     ANGELICA: I'll see him, get my Coach ready.
     SEBASTIAN: It waits you, Madam.
405 WILLMORE: This is lucky: what, Madam, now I may be gone
     and leave you to the enjoyment of my Rival?
     ANGELICA: Dull Man, that canst not see how ill, how poor
         That false dissimulation looks—Be gone,
         And never let me see thy cozening Face again,
410   Lest I relapse and kill thee.
     WILLMORE: Yes, you can spare me now,—farewell till you are
     in a better Humour—I'm glad of this release—
         Now for my Gipsy:
         For tho to worse we change, yet still we find
415   New Joys, New Charms, in a new Miss that's kind.

(Exit WILLMORE.*)*

     ANGELICA: He's gone, and in this Ague of My Soul
         The shivering Fit returns;
         Oh with what willing haste he took his leave,
         As if the long'd for Minute were arriv'd,
420   Of some blest Assignation.
         In vain I have consulted all my Charms,
         In vain this Beauty priz'd, in vain believ'd
         My eyes cou'd kindle any lasting Fires.
         I had forgot my Name, my Infamy,
425   And the Reproach that Honour lays on those
         That dare pretend a sober passion here.
         Nice Reputation, tho it leave behind
         More Virtues than inhabit where that dwells,
         Yet that once gone, those virtues shine no more.
430   —Then since I am not fit to belov'd,
         I am resolv'd to think on a Revenge
         On him that sooth'd me thus to my undoing.

(Exeunt.)

SCENE III

A Street.

(Enter FLORINDA *and* VALERIA *in Habits different from what
they have been seen in.)*

FLORINDA: We're happily escap'd, yet I tremble still.
VALERIA: A Lover and fear! why, I am but half a one, and yet I
have Courage for any Attempt. Would *Hellena* were here. I

wou'd fain have had her as deep in this Mischief as we, she'll
fare but ill else I doubt.   5
FLORINDA: She pretended a Visit to the *Augustine* Nuns, but I
believe some other design carried her out, pray Heavens we
light on her.
VALERIA: When I saw no reason wou'd go good on her, I follow'd her into the Wardrobe, and as she was looking for   10
something in a great Chest, I tumbled her in by the Heels,
snatcht the Key of the Apartment where you were confin'd,
lockt her in, and left her bauling for help.
FLORINDA: 'Tis well you resolve to follow my Fortunes, for
thou darest never appear at home again after such an Action. 15
VALERIA: That's according as the young Stranger and I shall
agree—But to our business—I deliver'd your Letter, your
Note to *Belvile,* when I got out under pretence of going to
Mass, I found him at his Lodging, and believe me it came
seasonably; for never was Man in so desperate a Condition. I 20
told him of your Resolution of making your escape to day, if
your Brother would be absent long enough to permit you;
if not, die rather than be *Antonio's.*
FLORINDA: Thou shou'dst have told him I was confin'd to my
Chamber upon my Brother's suspicion, that the Business on 25
the *Molo* was a Plot laid between him and I.
VALERIA: I said all this, and told him your Brother was now
gone to his Devotion, and he resolves to visit every Church
till he find him; and not only undeceive him in that, but caress him so as shall delay his return home.   30
FLORINDA: Oh Heavens! he's here, and *Belvile* with him too.

(They put on their Vizards.)

(Enter Don PEDRO, BELVILE, WILLMORE; BELVILE *and Don*
PEDRO *seeming in serious Discourse.)*

VALERIA: Walk boldly by them, I'll come at a distance, lest he
suspect us.

(She walks by them, and looks back on them.)

WILLMORE: Ha! A Woman! and of an excellent Mien!
PEDRO: She throws a kind look back on you.   35
WILLMORE: Death, tis a likely Wench, and that kind look shall
not be cast away—I'll follow her.
BELVILE: Prithee do not.
WILLMORE: Do not! By Heavens to the Antipodes, with such
an Invitation.   40

(She goes out, and WILLMORE *follows her.)*

BELVILE: 'Tis a mad Fellow for a Wench.

(Enter FREDERICK.*)*

FREDERICK: Oh Colonel, such News.
BELVILE: Prithee what?
FREDERICK: News that will make you laugh in spite of Fortune.
BELVILE: What, *Blunt* has had some damn'd Trick put upon   45
him, cheated, bang'd, or clapt?
FREDERICK: Cheated, Sir, rarely cheated of all but his Shirt
and Drawers; the unconscionable Whore too turn'd him
out before Consummation, so that traversing the Streets at
Midnight, the Watch found him in this *Fresco,* and con-   50
ducted him home: By Heaven 'tis such a slight, and yet I
durst as well have been hang'd as laugh at him, or pity him;
he beats all that do but ask him a Question, and is in such
an Humour—

55 PEDRO: Who is't has met with this ill usage, Sir?

BELVILE: (*Aside.*) A Friend of ours, whom you must see for Mirth's sake. I'll imploy him to give *Florinda* time for an escape.

PEDRO: Who is he?

60 BELVILE: A young Countryman of ours, one that has been educated at so plentiful a rate, he yet ne'er knew the want of Money, and 'twill be a great Jest to see how simply he'll look without it. For my part I'll lend him none, and the Rogue knows not how to put on a borrowing Face, and ask first. I'll 65 let him see how good 'tis to play our parts whilst I play his— Prithee, *Frederick* do go home and keep him in that posture till we come.

(*Exeunt.*)

(*Enter* FLORINDA *from the farther end of the Scene, looking behind her.*)

FLORINDA: I am follow'd still—hah—my Brother too advancing this way, good Heavens defend me from being seen by 70 him.

(*She goes off.*)

(*Enter* WILLMORE, *and after him* VALERIA, *at a little distance.*)

WILLMORE: Ah! There she sails, she looks back as she were willing to be boarded, I'll warrant her Prize.

(*He goes out,* VALERIA *following.*)

(*Enter* HELLENA, *just as he goes out, with a* PAGE.)

HELLENA: Hah, is not that my Captain that has a Woman in chase?—'tis not *Angelica.* Boy, follow those People at a dis-75 tance, and bring me an Account where they go in.—I'll find his Haunts, and plague him every where.—ha—my Brother!

(*Exit* PAGE. BELVILE, WILLMORE, *and* PEDRO *cross the Stage:* HELLENA *runs off.*)

(*Scene changes to another Street. Enter* FLORINDA.)

FLORINDA: What shall I do, my Brother now pursues me. Will no kind Power protect me from his Tyranny?—Hah, here's a Door open, I'll venture in, since nothing can be worse than 80 to fall into his Hands, my Life and Honour are at stake, and my Necessity has no choice.

(*She goes in. Enter* VALERIA, *and* HELLENA'S PAGE *peeping after* FLORINDA.)

PAGE: Here she went in, I shall remember this House.

(*Exit* BOY.)

VALERIA: This is *Belvile's* Lodgings; she's gone in as readily as if she knew it—hah—here's that mad Fellow again, I dare not 85 venture in—I'll watch my Opportunity.

(*Goes aside. Enter* WILLMORE, *gazing about him.*)

WILLMORE: I have lost her hereabouts—Pox on't she must not scape me so.

(*Goes out.*)

(*Scene changes to* BLUNT'S *chamber, discovers him sitting on a couch in his shirt and drawers, reading.*)

BLUNT: So, now my Mind's a little at Peace, since I have resolv'd Revenge—A Pox on this Taylor tho, for not bringing 90 home the Clothes I bespoke; and a Pox of all poor Cavaliers,

a Man can never keep a spare Suit for 'em; and I shall have these Rogues come in and find me naked; and then I'm undone; but I'm resolv'd to arm my self—the Rascals shall not insult over me too much.

(*Puts on an old rusty Sword and Buff-Belt.*)

—Now, how like a Morrice-Dancer I am equipt—a fine 95 Lady-like Whore to cheat me thus, without affording me a Kindness for my Money, a Pox light on her, I shall never be reconciled to the Sex more, she has made me as faithless as a Physician, as uncharitable as a Churchman, and as ill-natur'd as a Poet. O how I'll use all Womenkind hereafter! 100 what wou'd I give to have one of 'em within my reach now! any Mortal thing in Petticoats, kind Fortune, send me; and I'll forgive thy last Night's Malice—Here's a cursed Book too, (a Warning to all young Travellers) that can instruct me how to prevent such Mischiefs now 'tis too late. Well 'tis a 105 rare convenient thing to read a little now and then, as well as hawk and hunt.

(*Sits down again and reads.*)

(*Enter to him* FLORINDA.)

FLORINDA: This House is haunted sure, 'tis well furnisht and no living thing inhabits it—hah—a Man! Heavens how he's attir'd! sure 'tis some Rope-dancer, or Fencing-Master; I 110 tremble now for fear, and yet I must venture now to speak to him—Sir, if I may not interrupt your Meditations—

(*He starts up and gazes.*)

BLUNT: Hah—what's here? Are my wishes granted? and is not that a she Creature? Adsheartlikins 'tis! what wretched thing art thou—hah! 115

FLORINDA: Charitable Sir, you've told your self already what I am; a very wretched Maid, forc'd by a strange unlucky Accident, to seek a safety here, and must be ruin'd, if you do not grant it.

BLUNT: Ruin'd! Is there any Ruin so inevitable as that which 120 now threatens thee? Dost thou know, miserable Woman, into what Den of Mischiefs thou art fall'n? what a Bliss of Confusion?—hah—dost not see something in my looks that frights thy guilty Soul, and makes thee wish to change that Shape of Woman for any humble Animal, or Devil? for those 125 were safer for thee, and less mischievous.

FLORINDA: Alas, what mean you, Sir? I must confess your Looks have something in 'em makes me fear; but I beseech you, as you seem a Gentleman, pity a harmless Virgin, that takes your House for Sanctuary. 130

BLUNT: Talk on, talk on, and weep too, till my faith return. Do, flatter me out of my Senses again—a harmless Virgin with a Pox, as much one as t'other, adsheartlikins. Why, what the Devil can I not be safe in my House for you? not in my Chamber? nay, even being naked too cannot secure me. 135 This is an Impudence greater than has invaded me yet.— Come, no Resistance.

(*Pulls her rudely.*)

FLORINDA: Dare you be so cruel?

BLUNT: Cruel, adsheartlikins as a Gally-slave, or a *Spanish* Whore: Cruel, yes, I will kiss and beat thee all over; kiss, and 140 see thee all over; thou shalt lie with me too, not that I care for the Injoyment, but to let you see I have ta'en deliberated Malice to thee, and will be revenged on one Whore for the

145 Sins of another; I will smile and deceive thee, flatter thee, and beat thee, kiss and swear, and lye to thee, imbrace thee and rob thee, as she did me, fawn on thee, and strip thee stark naked, then hang thee out at my Window by the Heels, with a Paper of scurvey Verses fasten'd to thy Breast, in praise of damnable Women—Come, come along.

150 FLORINDA: Alas, Sir, must I be sacrific'd for the Crimes of the most infamous of my Sex? I never understood the Sins you name.

BLUNT: Do, persuade the Fool you love him, or that one of you
155 can be just or honest; tell me I was not an easy Coxcomb, or any strange impossible Tale: it will be believ'd sooner than thy false Showers or Protestations. A Generation of damn'd Hypocrites, to flatter my very Clothes from my back! dissembling Witches! are these the Returns you make an honest Gentleman that trusts, believes, and loves you?—But if I be
160 not even with you—Come along, or I shall—

(Pulls her again.)

(Enter FREDERICK.*)*

FREDERICK: Hah, what's here to do?

BLUNT: Adsheartlikins, *Frederick* I am glad thou art come, to be a Witness of my dire Revenge.

FREDERICK: What's this, a Person of Quality too, who is upon
165 the Ramble to supply the Defects of some grave impotent Husband?

BLUNT: No, this has another Pretence, some very unfortunate Accident brought her hither, to save a Life pursued by I
170 know not who, or why, and forc'd to take Sanctuary here at Fools Haven. Adsheartlikins to me of all Mankind for Protection? Is the Ass to be cajol'd again, think ye? No, young one, no Prayers or Tears shall mitigate my Rage; therefore prepare for both my Pleasure of Enjoyment and Revenge, for I am resolved to make up my Loss here on thy Body, I'll take
175 it out in kindness and in beating.

FREDERICK: Now, Mistress of mine, what do you think of this?

FLORINDA: I think he will not—dares not be so barbarous.

FREDERICK: Have a care, *Blunt*, she fetch'd a deep Sigh, she is inamour'd with thy Shirt and Drawers, she'll strip thee even
180 of that. There are of her Calling such unconscionable Baggages, and such dexterous Thieves, they'll flea a Man, and he shall ne'er miss his Skin, till he feels the Cold. There was a Country-man of ours robb'd of a Row of Teeth whilst he was sleeping, which the Jilt made him buy again when he
185 wak'd—You see, Lady, how little Reason we have to trust you.

BLUNT: 'Dsheartlikins, why, this is most abominable.

FLORINDA: Some such Devils there may be, but by all that's holy I am none such, I entered here to save a Life in danger.
190 BLUNT: For no goodness I'll warrant her.

FREDERICK: Faith, Damsel, you had e'en confess the plain Truth, for we are Fellows not to be caught twice in the same Trap: Look on that Wreck, a tight Vessel when he set out of Haven, well trim'd and laden, and see how a Female Picca-
195 roon of this Island of Rogues has shatter'd him, and canst thou hope for any Mercy?

BLUNT: No, no, Gentlewoman, come along, adsheartlikins we must be better acquainted—we'll both lie with her, and then let me alone to bang her.
200 FREDERICK: I am ready to serve you in matters of Revenge, that has a double Pleasure in't.

BLUNT: Well said. You hear, little one, how you are condemn'd by publick Vote to the Bed within, there's no resisting your Destiny, Sweetheart.

(Pulls her.)

205 FLORINDA: Stay, Sir, I have seen you with *Belvile*, an *English* Cavalier, for his sake use me kindly; you know how, Sir.

BLUNT: *Belvile!* why, yes, Sweeting, we do know *Belvile*, and wish he were with us now, he's a Cormorant at Whore and Bacon, he'd have a Limb or two of thee, my Virgin Pullet:
210 but 'tis no matter, we'll leave him the Bones to pick.

FLORINDA: Sir, if you have any Esteem for that *Belvile*, I conjure you to treat me with more Gentleness; he'll thank you for the Justice.

FREDERICK: Hark ye, *Blunt*, I doubt we are mistaken in this matter.
215

FLORINDA: Sir, If you find me not worth *Belvile's* Care, use me as you please; and that you may think I merit better treatment than you threaten—pray take this Present—

(Gives him a Ring: He looks on it.)

BLUNT: Hum—A Diamond! why, 'tis a wonderful Virtue now that lies in this Ring, a mollifying Virtue; adsheartlikins 220 there's more persuasive Rhetorick in't, than all her Sex can utter.

FREDERICK: I begin to suspect something; and 'twou'd anger us vilely to be truss'd up for a Rape upon a Maid of Quality, when we only believe we ruffle a Harlot. 225

BLUNT: Thou art a credulous Fellow, but adsheartlikins I have no Faith yet; why, my Saint prattled as parlously as this does, she gave me a Bracelet too, a Devil on her: but I sent my Man to sell it to day for Necessaries, and it prov'd as counterfeit as her Vows of Love. 230

FREDERICK: However let it reprieve her till we see *Belvile*.

BLUNT: That's hard, yet I will grant it.

(Enter a SERVANT.*)*

SERVANT: Oh, Sir, the Colonel is just come with his new Friend and a *Spaniard* of Quality, and talks of having you to Dinner with 'em. 235

BLUNT: 'Dsheartlikins, I'm undone—I would not see 'em for the World: Harkye, *Frederick* lock up the Wench in your Chamber.

FREDERICK: Fear nothing, Madam, whate'er he threatens, you're safe whilst in my Hands. 240

(Exit FREDERICK *and* FLORINDA.*)*

BLUNT: And, Sirrah—upon your Life, say—I am not at home—or that I am asleep—or—or any thing—away—I'll prevent them coming this way.

(Locks the Door and Exeunt.)

— ACT FIVE —

SCENE 1

BLUNT'S *Chamber.*

(After a great knocking as at his Chamber-door, enter BLUNT *softly, crossing the Stage in his Shirt and Drawers, as before.)*

(Call within.) Ned, Ned Blunt, Ned Blunt.

BLUNT: The Rogues are up in Arms, 'dsheartlikins, this villain-ous *Frederick* has betray'd me, they have heard of my blessed Fortune.

5 (*And knocking within.*) *Ned Blunt, Ned, Ned*—

BELVILE: Why, he's dead, sir, without dispute dead, he has not been seen to day; let's break open the Door—here—Boy—

BLUNT: Ha, break open the Door! 'dsheartlikins that mad Fel-low will be as good as his word.

10 BELVILE: Boy, bring something to force the Door.

(*A great noise within at the Door again.*)

BLUNT: So, now must I speak in my own Defence, I'll try what Rhetorick will do—hold—hold, what do you mean, Gentle-men, what do you mean?

BELVILE: Oh Rogue, art alive? prithee open the Door, and
15 convince us.

BLUNT: Yes, I am alive, Gentlemen—but at present a little busy.

BELVILE: (*Within.*) How! *Blunt* grown a man of Business! come, come, open, and let's see this Miracle.

20 BLUNT: No, no, no, no, Gentlemen, 'tis no great Business—but—I am—at—my Devotion,—'dsheartlikins, will you not allow a man time to pray?

BELVILE: (*Within.*) Turn'd religious! a greater Wonder than the first, therefore open quickly, or we shall unhinge, we
25 shall.

BLUNT: This won't do—Why, hark ye, Colonel; to tell you the plain Truth, I am about a necessary Affair of Life.—I have a Wench with me—you apprehend me? the Devil's in't if they be so uncivil as to disturb me now.

30 WILLMORE: How, a Wench! Nay, then we must enter and par-take; no Resistance,—unless it be your Lady of Quality, and then we'll keep our distance.

BLUNT: So, the Business is out.

WILLMORE: Come, come, lend more hands to the Door,—
35 now heave altogether—so, well done, my Boys—

(*Breaks open the Door. Enter* BELVILE, WILLMORE, FREDER-ICK, PEDRO *and* BELVILE'S PAGE: BLUNT *looks simply, they all laugh at him, he lays his hand on his Sword, and comes up to* WILLMORE.)

BLUNT: Hark ye, Sir, laugh out your laugh quickly, d'ye hear, and be gone, I shall spoil your sport else; 'dsheartlikins, Sir, I shall—the Jest has been carried on too long,—(*Aside.*) a Plague upon my Taylor.

40 WILLMORE: 'Sdeath, how the Whore has drest him! Faith, Sir, I'm sorry.

BLUNT: Are you so, Sir? keep't to your self then, Sir, I advise you, d'ye hear? for I can as little endure your Pity as his Mirth.

(*Lays his Hand on's Sword.*)

45 BELVILE: Indeed, *Willmore*, thou wert a little too rough with *Ned Blunt's* Mistress; call a Person of Quality Whore, and one so young, so handsome, and so eloquent!—ha, ha, ha.

BLUNT: Hark ye, Sir, you know me, and know I can be angry; have a care—for 'dsheartlikins I can fight too—I can, Sir,—
50 do you mark me—no more.

BELVILE: Why so peevish, good *Ned?* some Disappointments, I'll warrant—What! did the jealous Count her Husband re-turn just in the nick?

(*They laugh.*)

BLUNT: Or the Devil, Sir,—d'ye laugh?
Look ye, settle me a good sober Countenance, and that
55 quickly too, or you shall know *Ned Blunt* is not—

BELVILE: Not every Body, we know that.

BLUNT: Not an Ass, to be laught at, Sir.

WILLMORE: Unconscionable Sinner, to bring a Lover so near his Happiness, a vigorous passionate Lover, and then not
60 only cheat him of his Moveables, but his Desires too.

BELVILE: Ah, Sir, a Mistress is a Trifle with *Blunt*, he'll have a dozen the next time he looks abroad; his Eyes have Charms not to be resisted: There needs no more than to expose that taking Person to the view of the Fair, and he leads 'em all in
65 Triumph.

PEDRO: Sir, tho I'm a stranger to you, I'm ashamed at the rude-ness of my Nation; and could you learn who did it, would as-sist you to make an Example of 'em.

BLUNT: Why, ay, there's one speaks sense now, and hand-
70 somly; and let me tell you Gentlemen, I should not have shew'd my self like a Jack-Pudding, thus to have made you Mirth, but that I have revenge within my power; for know, I have got into my possession a Female, who had better have fallen under any Curse, than the Ruin I design her: 'dsheart-
75 likins, she assaulted me here in my own Lodgings, and had doubtless committed a Rape upon me, had not this Sword defended me.

FREDERICK: I knew not that, but o' my Conscience thou hadst ravisht her, had she not redeem'd her self with a Ring—let's
80 see't, *Blunt.*

(BLUNT *shews the Ring.*)

BELVILE: (*Goes to whisper to him.*) Hah!—the Ring I gave *Florinda* when we exchang'd our Vows!—hark ye, *Blunt*—

WILLMORE: No whispering, good Colonel, there's a Woman in the case, no whispering.
85

BELVILE: Hark ye, Fool, be advis'd, and conceal both the Ring and the Story, for your Reputation's sake; don't let People know what despis'd Cullies we *English* are: to be cheated and abus'd by one Whore, and another rather bribe thee than be kind to thee, is an Infamy to our Nation.
90

WILLMORE: Come, come, where's the Wench! we'll see her, let her be what she will, we'll see her.

PEDRO: Ay, ay, let us see her, I can soon discover whether she be of Quality, or for your Diversion.

BLUNT: She's in *Frederick's* Custody.
95

WILLMORE: Come, come, the Key.

(*To* FREDERICK *who gives him the Key, they are going.*)

BELVILE: Death! what shall I do?—stay, Gentlemen—yet if I hinder 'em, I shall discover all—hold, let's go one at once—give me the Key.

WILLMORE: Nay, hold there, Colonel, I'll go first.
100

FREDERICK: Nay, no Dispute, *Ned* and I have the property of her.

WILLMORE: Damn Property—then we'll draw Cuts.

(BELVILE *goes to whisper* WILLMORE.)

Nay, no Corruption, good Colonel: come, the longest Sword carries her.—
105

(*They all draw, forgetting Don* PEDRO, *being a Spaniard, had the longest.*)

BLUNT: I yield up my Interest to you Gentlemen, and that will be Revenge sufficient.

WILLMORE: The Wench is yours—*(To* PEDRO.*)* Pox of his *Toledo*, I had forgot that.

110 FREDERICK: Come, Sir, I'll conduct you to the Lady.

(Exit FREDERICK *and* PEDRO.*)*

BELVILE: *(Aside.)* To hinder him will certainly discover—Dost know, dull Beast, what Mischief thou hast done?

*(*WILLMORE *walking up and down out of Humour.)*

WILLMORE: Ay, ay, to trust our Fortune to Lots, a Devil on't, 'twas madness, that's the Truth on't.

115 BELVILE: Oh intolerable Sot!

(Enter FLORINDA, *running masqu'd,* PEDRO *after her,* WILLMORE *gazing round her.)*

FLORINDA: *(Aside.)* Good Heaven, defend me from discovery.

PEDRO: 'Tis but in vain to fly me, you are fallen to my Lot.

BELVILE: Sure she is undiscover'd yet, but now I fear there is no way to bring her off.

120 WILLMORE: Why, what a Pox is not this my Woman, the same I follow'd but now?

*(*PEDRO *talking to* FLORINDA, *who walks up and down.)*

PEDRO: As if I did not know ye, and your Business here.

FLORINDA: *(Aside.)* Good Heaven! I fear he does indeed—

PEDRO: Come, pray be kind, I know you meant to be so when 125 you enter'd here, for these are proper Gentlemen.

WILLMORE: But, Sir—perhaps the Lady will not be impos'd upon, she'll chuse her Man.

PEDRO: I am better bred, than not to leave her Choice free.

(Enter VALERIA, *and is surpriz'd at the Sight of Don* PEDRO.*)*

VALERIA: *(Aside.)* Don *Pedro* here! there's no avoiding him.

130 FLORINDA: *(Aside.)* *Valeria!* then I'm undone—

VALERIA: *(To* PEDRO, *running to him.)* Oh! have I found you, Sir—
—The strangest Accident—if I had breath—to tell it.

PEDRO: Speak—is *Florinda* safe? *Hellena* well?

135 VALERIA: Ay, ay, Sir—*Florinda*—is safe—from any fears of you.

PEDRO: Why, where's *Florinda?*—speak.

VALERIA: Ay, where indeed, Sir? I wish I could inform you,—But to hold you no longer in doubt—

FLORINDA: *(Aside.)* Oh, what will she say!

140 VALERIA: She's fled away in the Habit of one of her Pages, Sir—but *Callis* thinks you may retrieve her yet, if you make haste away; she'll tell you, Sir, the rest—*(Aside.)* if you can find her out.

PEDRO: Dishonourable Girl, she has undone my Aim—Sir— 145 you see my necessity of leaving you, and I hope you'll pardon it: my Sister, I know, will make her flight to you; and if she do, I shall expect she should be render'd back.

BELVILE: I shall consult my Love and Honour, Sir.

(Exit PEDRO.*)*

FLORINDA: *(To* VALERIA.*)* My dear Preserver, let me imbrace 150 thee.

WILLMORE: What the Devil's all this?

BLUNT: Mystery by this Light.

VALERIA: Come, come, make haste and get your selves married quickly, for your Brother will return again.

155 BELVILE: I am so surpriz'd with Fears and Joys, so amaz'd to find you here in safety, I can scarce persuade my Heart into a Faith of what I see—

WILLMORE: Harkye, Colonel, is this that Mistress who has cost you so many Sighs, and me so many Quarrels with you?

160 BELVILE: It is—*(To* FLORINDA.*)* Pray give him the Honour of your Hand.

WILLMORE: Thus it must be receiv'd then.

(Kneels and kisses her Hand.)

And with it give your Pardon too.

FLORINDA: The Friend to *Belvile* may command me anything.

165 WILLMORE: *(Aside.)* Death, wou'd I might, 'tis a surprizing Beauty.

BELVILE: Boy, run and fetch a Father instantly.

(Exit BOY.*)*

FREDERICK: So, now do I stand like a Dog, and have not a Syl-lable to plead my own Cause with: by this Hand, Madam, I 170 was never thorowly confounded before, nor shall I ever more dare look up with Confidence, till you are pleased to pardon me.

FLORINDA: Sir, I'll be reconcil'd to you on one Condition, that you'll follow the Example of your Friend, in marrying a 175 Maid that does not hate you, and whose Fortune (I believe) will not be unwelcome to you.

FREDERICK: Madam, had I no Inclinations that way, I shou'd obey your kind Commands.

BELVILE: Who, *Frederick* marry; he has so few Inclinations for 180 Womankind, that had he been possest of Paradise, he might have continu'd there to this Day, if no Crime but Love cou'd have disinherited him.

FREDERICK: Oh, I do not use to boast of my Intrigues.

BELVILE: Boast! why thou do'st nothing but boast; and I dare 185 swear, wer't thou as innocent from the Sin of the Grape, as thou art from the Apple, thou might'st yet claim that right in *Eden* which our first Parents lost by too much loving.

FREDERICK: I wish this Lady would think me so modest a Man.

190 VALERIA: She shou'd be sorry then, and not like you half so well, and I shou'd be loth to break my Word with you; which was, That if your Friend and mine are agreed, it shou'd be a Match between you and I.

(She gives him her Hand.)

FREDERICK: Bear witness, Colonel, 'tis a Bargain.

(Kisses her Hand.)

195 BLUNT: *(To* FLORINDA.*)* I have a Pardon to beg too; but ads-heartlikins I am so out of Countenance, that I am a Dog if I can say any thing to purpose.

FLORINDA: Sir, I heartily forgive you all.

BLUNT: That's nobly said, sweet Lady—*Belvile*, prithee present 200 her her Ring again, for I find I have not Courage to approach her my self.

(Gives him the Ring, he gives it to FLORINDA. *Enter* BOY.*)*

BOY: Sir, I have brought the Father that you sent for.

BELVILE: 'Tis well, and now my dear *Florinda*, let's fly to com-pleat that mighty Joy we have so long wish'd and sigh'd for. Come, *Frederick* you'll follow? 205

FREDERICK: Your Example, Sir, 'twas ever my Ambition in War, and must be so in Love.

WILLMORE: And must not I see this juggling Knot ty'd?

BELVILE: No, thou shalt do us better Service, and be our Guard, lest Don *Pedro's* sudden Return interrupt the Ceremony.

210 WILLMORE: Content; I'll secure this Pass.

(Exit BELVILE, FLORINDA, FREDERICK, *and* VALERIA. *Enter* BOY.*)*

BOY: *(To* WILLMORE.*)* Sir, there's a Lady without wou'd speak to you.

WILLMORE: Conduct her in, I dare not quit my Post.

215 BOY: And, Sir, your Taylor waits you in your Chamber.

BLUNT: Some comfort yet, I shall not dance naked at the Wedding.

(Exit BLUNT *and* BOY.*)*

(Enter again the BOY, *conducting in* ANGELICA *in a masquing Habit and a Vizard,* WILLMORE *runs to her.)*

WILLMORE: This can be none but my pretty Gipsy—Oh, I see you can follow as well as fly—Come, confess thy self the
220 most malicious Devil in Nature, you think you have done my Bus'ness with *Angelica*—

ANGELICA: Stand off, base Villain—

(She draws a Pistol and holds to his Breast.)

WILLMORE: Hah, 'tis not she: who art thou? and what's thy Business?

225 ANGELICA: One thou hast injur'd, and who comes to kill thee for't.

WILLMORE: What the Devil canst thou mean?

ANGELICA: By all my Hopes to kill thee—

(Holds still the Pistol to his Breast, he going back, she following still.)

WILLMORE: Prithee on what Acquaintance? for I know thee
230 not.

ANGELICA: Behold this Face!—so lost to thy Remembrance! And then call all thy Sins about thy Soul,

(Pulls off her Vizard.)

And let them die with thee.

WILLMORE: *Angelica!*

235 ANGELICA: Yes, Traitor.
Does not thy guilty Blood run shivering thro thy Veins? Hast thou no Horrour at this Sight, that tells thee, Thou hast not long to boast thy shameful Conquest?

WILLMORE: Faith, no Child, my Blood keeps its old Ebbs and
240 Flows still, and that usual Heat too, that cou'd oblige thee with a Kindness, had I but opportunity.

ANGELICA: Devil! dost wanton with my Pain—have at thy Heart.

WILLMORE: Hold, dear Virago! hold thy Hand a little,
245 I am not now at leisure to be kill'd—hold and hear me—
(Aside.) Death, I think she's in earnest.

ANGELICA: *(Aside, turning from him.)* Oh if I take not heed, My coward Heart will leave me to his Mercy.
—What have you, Sir, to say?—but should I hear thee,
250 Thoud'st talk away all that is brave about me:

(Follows him with the Pistol to his Breast.)

And I have vow'd thy Death, by all that's sacred.

WILLMORE: Why, then, there's an end of a proper handsom Fellow, that might have liv'd to have done good Service yet:—That's all I can say to't.

255 ANGELICA: *(Pausingly.)* Yet—I wou'd give thee—time for Penitence.

WILLMORE: Faith, Child, I thank God, I have ever took care to lead a good, sober, hopeful Life, and am of a Religion that teaches me to believe, I shall depart in Peace.

260 ANGELICA: So will the Devil: tell me
How many poor believing Fools thou hast undone;
How many Hearts thou hast betray'd to ruin!
—Yet, these are little Mischiefs to the Ills
Thou'st taught mine to commit: thou'st taught it Love.

265 WILLMORE: Egad, 'twas shreudly hurt the while.

ANGELICA: —Love, that has robb'd it of its Unconcern,
Of all that Pride that taught me how to value it,
And in its room a mean submissive Passion was convey'd,
That made me humbly bow, which I ne'er did
270 To any thing but Heaven.
—Thou, perjur'd Man, didst this, and with thy Oaths,
Which on thy Knees thou didst devoutly make,
Soften'd my yielding Heart—And then, I was a Slave—
Yet still had been content to've worn my Chains,
275 Worn 'em with Vanity and Joy for ever,
Hadst thou not broke those Vows that put them on.
—'Twas then I was undone.

(All this while follows him with a Pistol to his Breast.)

WILLMORE: Broke my Vows! why, where hast thou lived?
Amongst the Gods! For I never heard of mortal Man,
That has not broke a thousand Vows.
280
ANGELICA: Oh, Impudence!

WILLMORE: *Angelica!* that Beauty has been too long tempting,
Not to have made a thousand Lovers languish,
Who in the amorous Favour, no doubt have sworn
285 Like me; did they all die in that Faith? still adoring?
I do not think they did.

ANGELICA: No, faithless Man: had I repaid their Vows, as I did thine, I wou'd have kill'd the ungrateful that had abandon'd me.

290 WILLMORE: This old General has quite spoil'd thee, nothing makes a Woman so vain, as being flatter'd; your old Lover ever supplies the Defects of Age, with intolerable Dotage, vast Charge, and that which you call Constancy; and attributing all this to your own Merits, you domineer, and
295 throw your Favours in's Teeth, upbraiding him still with the Defects of Age, and cuckold him as often as he deceives your Expectations. But the gay, young, brisk Lover, that brings his equal Fires, and can give you Dart for Dart, he'll be as nice as you sometimes.

300 ANGELICA: All this thou'st made me know, for which I hate thee.
Had I remain'd in innocent Security,
I shou'd have thought all Men were born my Slaves;
And worn my Pow'r like Lightning in my Eyes,
To have destroy'd at Pleasure when offended.
305 —But when Love held the Mirror, the undeceiving Glass
Reflected all the Weakness of my Soul, and made me know,

My richest Treasure being lost, my Honour,
All the remaining Spoil cou'd not be worth
The Conqueror's Care or Value.
310 —Oh how I fell like a long worship'd Idol,
Discovering all the Cheat!
Wou'd not the Incense and rich Sacrifice,
Which blind Devotion offer'd at my Altars,
Have fall'n to thee?
315 Why woud'st thou then destroy my fancy'd Power?
WILLMORE: By Heaven thou art brave, and I admire thee
       strangely.
I wish I were that dull, that constant thing,
Which thou woud'st have, and Nature never meant me:
I must, like chearful Birds, sing in all Groves,
320 And perch on every Bough,
Billing the next kind She that flies to meet me;
Yet after all cou'd build my Nest with thee,
Thither repairing when I'd lov'd my round,
And still reserve a tributary Flame.

(Offers her a Purse of Gold.)

325 —To gain your Credit, I'll pay you back your Charity,
And be oblig'd for nothing but for Love.
ANGELICA: Oh that thou wert in earnest!
So mean a Thought of me,
Wou'd turn my Rage to Scorn, and I shou'd pity thee,
330 And give thee leave to live;
Which for the publick Safety of our Sex,
And my own private Injuries, I dare not do.
Prepare—

(Follows still, as before.)

—I will no more be tempted with Replies.
335 WILLMORE: Sure—
ANGELICA: Another Word will damn thee! I've heard thee talk
       too long.

*(She follows him with a Pistol ready to shoot: he retires still
amaz'd.)*

(Enter Don ANTONIO, *his Arm in a Scarf, and lays hold on the
Pistol.)*

ANTONIO: Hah! *Angelica!*
ANGELICA: *Antonio!* What Devil brought thee hither?
ANTONIO: Love and Curiosity, seeing your Coach at Door.
340 Let me disarm you of this unbecoming Instrument of
Death.—

(Takes away the Pistol.)

Amongst the Number of your Slaves, was there not one worthy
the Honour to have fought your Quarrel?
—Who are you, Sir, that are so very wretched
345 To merit Death from her?
WILLMORE: One, sir, that cou'd have made a better End of an
       amorous Quarrel without you, than with you.
ANTONIO: Sure 'tis some Rival—hah—the very Man took
       down her Picture yesterday—the very same that set on me
350 last night—Blest opportunity—

(Offers to shoot him.)

ANGELICA: Hold, you're mistaken, Sir.

ANTONIO: By Heaven the very same!
—Sir, what pretensions have you to this Lady?
WILLMORE: Sir, I don't use to be examin'd, and am ill at all
       Disputes but this—   355

(Draws, ANTONIO *offers to shoot.)*

ANGELICA: *(To* WILLMORE.) Oh, hold! you see he's arm'd
       with certain Death:
—And you, *Antonio,* I command you hold,
By all the Passion you've so lately vow'd me.

(Enter Don PEDRO, *sees* ANTONIO, *and stays.)*

PEDRO: *(Aside.)* Hah, *Antonio!* and *Angelica!*
ANTONIO: When I refuse Obedience to your Will,   360
May you destroy me with your mortal Hate.
By all that's Holy I adore you so,
That even my Rival, who has Charms enough
To make him fall a Victim to my Jealousy,
Shall live, nay, and have leave to love on still.   365
PEDRO: *(Aside.)* What's this I hear?
ANGELICA: *(Pointing to* WILLMORE.) Ah thus, 'twas thus he
       talk'd, and I believ'd.
—*Antonio,* yesterday,
I'd not have sold my Interest in his Heart,
For all the Sword has won and lost in Battle.   370
—But now to show my utmost of Contempt,
I give thee Life—which if thou would'st preserve,
Live where my Eyes may never see thee more,
Live to undo some one, whose Soul may prove
So bravely constant to revenge my Love.   375

(Goes out, ANTONIO *follows, but* PEDRO *pulls him back.)*

PEDRO: *Antonio*—stay.
ANTONIO: Don *Pedro*—
PEDRO: What Coward Fear was that prevented thee
From meeting me this Morning on the *Molo?*
ANTONIO: Meet thee?   380
PEDRO: Yes me; I was the Man that dar'd thee to't.
ANTONIO: Hast thou so often seen me fight in War,
To find no better Cause to excuse my Absence?
—I sent my Sword and one to do thee Right,
Finding my self uncapable to use a Sword.   385
PEDRO: But 'twas *Florinda's* Quarrel that we fought,
And you to shew how little you esteem'd her,
Sent me your Rival, giving him your Interest.
—But I have found the Cause of this Affront,
But when I meet you fit for the Dispute,   390
—I'll tell you my Resentment.
ANTONIO: I shall be ready, Sir, e'er long to do your Reason.

(Exit ANTONIO.)

PEDRO: If I cou'd find *Florinda,* now whilst my Anger's high, I
       think I shou'd be kind, and give her to *Belvile* in Revenge.
WILLMORE: Faith, Sir, I know not what you wou'd do, but I be- 395
       lieve the Priest within has been so kind.
PEDRO: How! my Sister married?
WILLMORE: I hope by this time she is, and bedded too, or he
       has not my longings about him.
PEDRO: Dares he do thus? Does he not fear my Pow'r?   400
WILLMORE: Faith not at all. If you will go in, and thank him

for the Favour he has done your Sister, so; if not, Sir, my Power's greater in this House than yours; I have a damn'd surly Crew here, that will keep you till the next Tide, and then clap you an board my Prize; my Ship lies but a League off the *Molo,* and we shall show your Donship a damn'd *Tramontana* Rover's Trick.

(Enter BELVILE.*)*

BELVILE: This Rogue's in some new Mischief—hah, *Pedro* return'd!

PEDRO: Colonel *Belvile,* I hear you have married my Sister.

BELVILE: You have heard truth then, Sir.

PEDRO: Have I so? then, Sir, I wish you Joy.

BELVILE: How!

PEDRO: By this Embrace I do, and I glad on't.

BELVILE: Are you in earnest?

PEDRO: By our long Friendship and my Obligations to thee, I am. The sudden Change I'll give you Reasons for anon. Come lead me into my Sister, that she may know I now approve her Choice.

(Exit BELVILE *with* PEDRO. WILLMORE *goes to follow them. Enter* HELLENA *as before in Boy's Clothes, and pulls him back.)*

WILLMORE: Ha! my Gipsy—Now a thousand Blessings on thee for this Kindness. Egad, Child, I was e'en in despair of ever seeing thee again; my Friends are all provided for within, each Man his kind Woman.

HELLENA: Hah! I thought they had serv'd me some such Trick.

WILLMORE: And I was e'en resolv'd to go aboard, condemn my self to my lone Cabin, and the Thoughts of thee.

HELLENA: And cou'd you have left me behind? wou'd you have been so ill-natur'd?

WILLMORE: Why, 'twou'd have broke my Heart, Child—but since we are met again, I defy foul Weather to part us.

HELLENA: And wou'd you be a faithful Friend now, if a Maid shou'd trust you?

WILLMORE: For a Friend I cannot promise, thou art of a Form so excellent, a Face and Humour too good for cold dull Friendship; I am parlously afraid of being in love, Child, and you have not forgot how severely you have us'd me.

HELLENA: That's all one, such Usage you must still look for, to find out all your Haunts, to rail at you to all that love you, till I have made you love only me in your own Defence, because no body else will love.

WILLMORE: But hast thou no better Quality to recommend thy self by?

HELLENA: Faith none, Captain—Why, 'twill be the greater Charity to take me for thy Mistress, I am a lone Child, a kind of Orphan Lover; and why I shou'd die a Maid, and in a Captain's Hands too, I do not understand.

WILLMORE: Egad, I was never claw'd away with Broad-Sides from any Female before, thou hast one Virtue I adore, good-Nature; I hate a coy demure Mistress, she's as troublesom as a Colt, I'll break none; no, give me a mad Mistress when mew'd, and in flying on[e] I dare trust upon the Wing, that whilst she's kind will come to the Lure.

HELLENA: Nay, as kind as you will, good Captain, whilst it lasts, but let's lose no time.

WILLMORE: My time's as precious to me, as thine can be; therefore, dear Creature, since we are so well agreed, let's retire to my Chamber, and if ever thou were treated with such savory Love—Come—My Bed's prepar'd for such a Guest, all clean and sweet as thy fair self; I love to steal a Dish and a Bottle with a Friend, and hate long Graces—Come, let's retire and fall to.

HELLENA: 'Tis but getting my Consent, and the Business is soon done; let but old Gaffer *Hymen* and his Priest say Amen to't, and I dare lay my Mother's Daughter by as proper a Fellow as your Father's Son, without fear or blushing.

WILLMORE: Hold, hold, no Bugg Words, Child, Priest and *Hymen:* prithee add Hangman to 'em to make up the Consort—No, no, we'll have no Vows but Love, Child, nor Witness but the Lover; the kind Diety injoins naught but love and enjoy. *Hymen* and Priest wait still upon Portion, and Joynture; Love and Beauty have their own Ceremonies. Marriage is as certain a Bane to Love, as lending Money is to Friendship: I'll neither ask nor give a Vow, tho I could be content to turn Gipsy, and become a Left-hand Bridegroom, to have the Pleasure of working that great Miracle of making a Maid a Mother, if you durst venture; 'tis upse Gipsy that, and if I miss, I'll lose my Labour.

HELLENA: And if you do not lose, what shall I get? A Cradle full of Noise and Mischief, with a Pack of Repentance at my Back? Can you teach me to weave Incle to pass my time with? 'Tis upse Gipsy that too.

WILLMORE: I can teach thee to weave a true Love's Knot better.

HELLENA: So can my Dog.

WILLMORE: Well, I see we are both upon our Guard, and I see there's no way to conquer good Nature, but by yielding—here—give me thy Hand—one Kiss and I am thine.

HELLENA: One Kiss! How like my Page he speaks; I am resolv'd you shall have none, for asking such a sneaking Sum—He that will be satisfied with one Kiss, will never die of that Longing; good Friend single-Kiss, is all your talking come to this? A Kiss, a Caudle! farewel, Captain single-Kiss.

(Going out he stays her.)

WILLMORE: Nay, if we part so, let me die like a Bird upon a Bough, at the Sheriff's Charge. By Heaven, both the *Indies* shall not buy thee from me. I adore thy Humour and will marry thee, and we are so of one Humour, it must be a Bargain—give me thy Hand—

(Kisses her hand.)

And now let the blind ones (Love and Fortune) do their worst.

HELLENA: Why, God-a-mercy, Captain!

WILLMORE: But harkye—The Bargain is now made; but is it not fit we should know each other's Names? That when we have Reason to curse one another hereafter, and People ask me who 'tis I give to the Devil, I may at least be able to tell what Family you came of.

---

406 **Tramontana** Italian and Spanish *tramontano* = from beyond the mountains

476 **upse** Op zijn = in the fashion or manner of, *Upse Gipsy* = like a gipsy   480 **Incle** Linen thread or yarn which was woven into a tape once very much in use

HELLENA: Good reason, Captain; and where I have cause, (as I doubt not but I shall have plentiful) that I may know at whom to throw my—Blessings—I beseech ye your Name.

WILLMORE: I am call'd *Robert the Constant.*

510 HELLENA: A very fine Name! pray was it your Faulkner or Butler that christen'd you? Do they not use to whistle when then call you?

WILLMORE: I hope you have a better, that a Man may name without crossing himself, you are so merry with mine.

515 HELLENA: I am call'd *Hellena the Inconstant.*

(*Enter* PEDRO, BELVILE, FLORINDA, FREDERICK, *and* VALERIA.)

PEDRO: Hah! *Hellena!*

FLORINDA: *Hellena!*

HELLENA: The very same—hah my Brother! now, Captain, shew your Love and Courage; stand to your Arms, and de

520 fend me bravely, or I am lost for ever.

PEDRO: What's this I hear? false Girl, how came you hither, and what's your Business? Speak.

(*Goes roughly to her.*)

WILLMORE: Hold off, Sir, you have leave to parly only.

(*Puts himself between.*)

HELLENA: I had e'en as good tell it, as you guess it. Faith,

525 Brother, my Business is the same with all living Creatures of my Age, to love, and be loved, and here's the Man.

PEDRO: Perfidious Maid, hast thou deceiv'd me too, deceiv'd thy self and Heaven?

HELLENA: 'Tis time enough to make my Peace with that: Be

530 you but kind, let me alone with Heaven.

PEDRO: *Belvile,* I did not expect this false Play from you; was't not enough you'd gain *Florinda* (which I pardon'd) but your leud Friends too must be inrich'd with the Spoils of a noble Family?

535 BELVILE: Faith, Sir, I am as much surpriz'd at this as you can be: Yet, Sir, my Friends are Gentlemen, and ought to be esteem'd for their Misfortunes, since they have the Glory to suffer with the best of Men and Kings; 'tis true, he's a Rover of Fortune, yet a Prince aboard his little wooden World.

540 PEDRO: What's this to the maintenance of a Woman or her Birth and Quality?

WILLMORE: Faith, Sir, I can boast of nothing but a Sword which does me Right where-e'er I come, and has defended a worse Cause than a Woman's: and since I lov'd her before I

545 either knew her Birth or Name, I must pursue my Resolution, and marry her.

PEDRO: And is all your holy Intent of becoming a Nun debauch'd into a Desire of Man?

HELLENA: Why—I have consider'd the matter, Brother, and

550 find the Three hundred thousand Crowns my Uncle left me (and you cannot keep from me) will be better laid out in Love than in Religion, and turn to as good an Account—let most Voices carry it, for Heaven or the Captain?

ALL CRY: Captain, a Captain.

555 HELLENA: Look ye, Sir, 'tis a clear Case.

PEDRO: (*Aside.*) Oh I am mad—if I refuse, my Life's in Danger—Come—There's one motive induces me—take her—I shall now be free from the fear of her Honour; guard it you now, if you can, I have been a Slave to't long enough.

(*Gives her to him.*)

WILLMORE: Faith, Sir, I am of a Nation, that are of opinion a

560 Woman's Honour is not worth guarding when she has a mind to part with it.

HELLENA: Well said, Captain.

PEDRO: (*To* VALERIA.) This was your Plot, Mistress, but I hope you have married one that will revenge my Quarrel to you—

565 VALERIA: There's no altering Destiny, Sir.

PEDRO: Sooner than a Woman's Will, therefore I forgive you all—and wish you may get my Father's Pardon as easily; which I fear.

(*Enter* BLUNT *drest in a Spanish Habit, looking very ridiculously; his* MAN *adjusting his Band.*)

MAN: 'Tis very well, Sir.

570

BLUNT: Well, Sir, 'dsheartlikins I tell you 'tis damnable ill, Sir—a Spanish Habit, good Lord! cou'd the Devil and my Taylor devise no other Punishment for me, but the Mode of a Nation I abominate?

BELVILE: What's the matter, *Ned?*

575

BLUNT: Pray view me round, and judge—

(*Turns round.*)

BEVILE: I must confess thou art a kind of an odd Figure.

BLUNT: In a Spanish Habit with a Vengeance! I had rather be in the Inquisition for Judaism, than in this Doublet and Breeches; a Pillory were an easy Collar to this, three Hand-

580 fuls high; and these Shoes too are worse than the Stocks, with the Sole an Inch shorter than my Foot: In fine, Gentlemen, methinks I look altogether like a Bag of Bays stuff'd full of Fools Flesh.

BELVILE: Methinks 'tis well, and makes the look *en Cavalier:*

585 Come, Sir, settle your Face, and salute our Friends, Lady—

BLUNT: Hah! Say'st thou so, my little Rover?

(*To* HELLENA.)

Lady—(if you be one) give me leave to kiss your Hand, and tell you, adsheartlikins, for all I look so, I am your humble Servant—A Pox of my *Spanish* Habit.

590

WILLMORE: Hark—what's this?

(*Musick is heard to Play. Enter* BOY.)

BOY: Sir, as the Custom is, the gay People in Masquerade, who make every Man's House their own, are coming up.

(*Enter several* MEN *and* WOMEN *in masquing Habits, with Musick, they put themselves in order and dance.*)

BLUNT: Adsheartlikins, wou'd 'twere lawful to pull off their false Faces, that I might see if my Doxy were not amongst

595 'em.

BELVILE: Ladies and Gentlemen, since you are come so *a propos,* you must take a small Collation with us.

(*To the* MASQUERADERS.)

WILLMORE: Whilst we'll to the Good Man within, who stays to give us a Cast of his Office.

600

(*To* HELLENA.)

—Have you no trembling at the near approach?

HELLENA: No more than you have in an Engagement or a Tempest.

WILLMORE: Egad, thou'rt a brave Girl, and I admire thy Love and Courage.

605

Lead on, no other Dangers they can dread,
Who venture in the Storms o'th' Marriage-Bed.

(Exeunt.)

— EPILOGUE —

THE banisht Cavaliers! a Roving Blade!
A popish Carnival! a Masquerade!
The Devil's in't if this will please the Nation,
In these our blessed Times of Reformation,
5   When Conventicling is so much in Fashion.
And yet—
That mutinous Tribe less Factions do beget,
Than your continual differing in Wit;
Your Judgment's (as your Passions) a Disease:
10   Nor Muse nor Miss your Appetite can please;
You're grown as nice as queasy Consciences,
Whose each Convulsion, when the Spirit moves,
Damns every thing that Maggot disapproves.
        With canting Rule you wou'd the Stage refine,
15   And to dull Method all our Sense confine.
With th' Insolence of Common-wealths you rule,
Where each gay Fop, and politick brave Fool
On Monarch Wit impose without controul.
As for the last who seldom sees a Play,
20   Unless it be the old Black-Fryers way,
Shaking his empty Noodle o'er Bamboo,

He crys—Good Faith, these Plays will never do.
—Ah, Sir, in my young days, what lofty Wit,
What high-strain'd Scenes of Fighting there were writ:
These are slight airy Toys. But tell me, pray,   25
What has the House of Commons done to day?
Then shews his Politicks, to let you see
Of State Affairs he'll judge as notably,
As he can do of Wit and Poetry.
        The younger Sparks, who hither do resort,   30
Cry—
Pox o' your gentle things, give us more Sport;
—Damn me, I'm sure 'twill never please the Court.
        Such Fops are never pleas'd, unless the Play
Be stuff'd with Fools, as brisk and dull as they: 35
Such might the Half-Crown spare, and in a Glass
At home behold a more accomplisht Ass,
Where they may set their Cravats, Wigs and Faces,
And practice all their Buffoonry Grimaces;
See how this—Huff becomes—this Dammy—flare—   40
Which they at home may act, because they dare,
But—must with prudent Caution do elsewhere.
Oh that our Nokes, or Tony Lee could show
A Fop but half so much to th' Life as you.

---

43 **Nokes, or Tony Lee** James Nokes and Antony Leigh, the two famous actors, were the leading low comedians of the day

■ GEORGE LILLO ■

George Lillo (1693–1739) was a London merchant, a goldsmith-jeweler with a shop in Moorgate Street, whose family was of Flemish descent. As his play *The London Merchant* suggests, Lillo was sensitive to the ways that an increasingly mercantile and industrial economy was changing the social landscape of eighteenth-century England. Indeed, the character of Thorowgood is reminiscent of the novelist Henry Fielding's description of Lillo's personality: "He had a perfect knowledge of human nature, though his contempt of all base means of application, which are the necessary steps to great acquaintance, restrained his conversation within very narrow bounds. . . . He was content with his little state of life, in which his excellent temper of mind gave him an happiness beyond the power of riches. . . . In short, he was one of the best of men, and those who knew him best will most regret his loss." Lillo wrote several successful plays in the 1730s—a ballad opera, *Sylvia* (1730); *The Christian Hero* (1735); *Guilt Its Own Punishment; or, Fatal Curiosity* (1736); a play based on Shakespeare's *Pericles, Marina* (1739); *Elmerick; or Justice Triumphant* (1740)—but none of these rivaled the success of *The London Merchant* (1731).

THE LONDON MERCHANT

The London Merchant was one of the most popular plays to appear on the eighteenth-century London stage. Opening at the Theatre Royal, Drury Lane, in the summer of 1731, the play was immediately successful and was acted hundreds of times in the remainder of the century; in 1796, the famous tragic actress Sarah Siddons played the evil Millwood to her brother Charles Kemble's George Barnwell. By mid-century, it had become traditional in the theater to play *The London Merchant* during the Christmas and Easter seasons, as well as on Lord Mayor's day in November, as a warning to the apprentices who were usually free to go to the theater only during the holidays.

Drawing the outline of his narrative from a familiar English ballad about George Barnwell and Sarah Millwood, Lillo worked to write a bourgeois tragedy, a tragedy centered not on the "fall of princes," but instead on "the circumstances of the generality of mankind," as he said in his dedication to Sir John Eyles. In this sense, *The London Merchant*, generally regarded as the first English middle-class tragedy, is the forerunner of modern tragedies of the "common man" such as Arthur Miller's *Death of a Salesman* or August Wilson's *Fences*. Despite using middle-class characters, who speak prose rather than verse, Lillo's play adapts many of the themes common in eighteenth-century tragedies to his mercantile subject. For in an important sense, the play uses the tragic conflict between reason and the passions as the mainspring of its cautionary tale.

The London Merchant is set during the 1580s, on the eve of the Spanish Armada, but Lillo's play is less a historical romance about an earlier era than fantasia on the virtues of the contemporary merchant class. The play advances a relatively straightforward moral structure: as Thorowgood says to his good apprentice Trueman in the opening scene of the play, "as the name of merchant never degrades the gentleman, so by no means does it exclude him; only take heed not to purchase the character of complaisant at the expense of your sincerity." The merchants in the play are not merely sincere and honest, they are sentimentally invested in the social order itself: Thorowgood treats his apprentices with compassion and dignity; Trueman and George Barnwell feel no stronger calling than to serve their master well; when George's uncle is murdered, he dies while asking God to forgive his murderer. Society is shown to be ordered along reasonable lines, and the play's virtuous characters not only accept that order, but *feel* its justness with passionate intensity.

Although we might expect Lillo's revolutionary decision to depose the princes of traditional tragedy and replace them with middle-class heroes to lead to a more skeptical attitude toward society at large, *The London Merchant* urgently reinforces the status quo. The play represents the social order not as a function of economic forces, nor as a structure of aristocratic privilege, but as the "natural" expression of the innate virtues and abilities of its citizens. For this reason, the play's principal crime is not so much theft or murder, but Millwood's scheme to manipulate George Barnwell's passions, to turn him from his natural desire to obey and serve his master. Once Barnwell is seduced, the play's benevolent society begins to collapse: he is rude to his friend Trueman, who is astonished by the change, and Trueman and Thorowgood's daughter Maria are led to replace the money Barnwell has stolen in order to protect him.

Yet the play's bourgeois society is not really threatened by Millwood's villainy, for even as Barnwell is murdering his uncle, Millwood's servants virtuously decide to turn her in. Barnwell is so divided against himself that it seems only a matter of time before his massive remorse destroys him. What prevents the play from seeming tragic to modern audiences, then, has less to do with the social class of the characters than with the clarity with which good and evil, right and wrong, justice and injustice can be distinguished and known. Although Barnwell is seduced by Millwood, his fundamentally virtuous character is unchanged throughout the play, as Lillo demonstrates when Thorowgood visits Barnwell in prison in Act 5:

> THOROWGOOD: See there the bitter fruits of passion's detested reign, and sensual appetite
>   indulged; severe reflections, penitence, and tears.
> BARNWELL: My honoured, injured master, whose goodness has covered me a thousand
>   times with shame . . .

When Phaedra is unable to control her desire for Hippolytus, she becomes a monster to herself, and engenders the complete destruction of her world: she is dead, and Hippolytus lies in pieces over the landscape. *Phaedra*, that is, challenges a neoclassical faith in the ordering power of reason. In *The London Merchant*, Barnwell's passion leads him into bad behavior, but the fundamental structure of Lillo's "reasonable" world is never questioned: women are less rational than men, masters deserve to be obeyed, and apprentices must rule themselves or be destroyed.

DEDICATION
TO

SIR JOHN EYLES, Bart., Member of Parliament for, and Alderman of, the City of *London*, and Sub-Governor of the *South-Sea* Company.

Sir,

If tragic poetry be, as Mr. Dryden has some where said, the most excellent and most useful kind of writing, the more extensively useful the moral of any tragedy is, the more excellent that piece must be of its kind.

I hope I shall not be thought to insinuate that this, to which I have presumed to prefix your name, is such; that depends on its fitness to answer the end of tragedy, the exciting of the passions in order to the correcting such of them as are criminal, either in their nature, or through their excess. Whether the following scenes do this in any tolerable degree, is, with the deference that becomes one who would not be thought vain, submitted to your candid and impartial judgment.

What I would infer is this, I think, evident truth: that tragedy is so far from losing its dignity by being accommodated to the circumstances of the generality of mankind that it is more truly august in proportion to the extent of its influence, and the numbers that are properly affected by it. As it is more truly great to be the instrument of good to many, who stand in need of our assistance, than to a very small part of that number.

If princes, &c., were alone liable to misfortunes arising from vice or weakness in themselves or others, there would be good reason for confining the characters in tragedy to those of superior rank; but, since the contrary is evident, nothing can be more reasonable than to proportion the remedy to the disease.

I am far from denying that tragedies founded on any instructive and extraordinary events in history, or a well-invented fable where the persons introduced are of the highest rank, are without their use, even to the bulk of the audience. The strong contrast between a *Tamerlane* and a *Bajazet*,[1] may have its weight with an unsteady people and contribute to the fixing of them in the interest of a prince of the character of the former, when, thro' their own levity or the arts of designing men, they are rendered factious and uneasy though they have the highest reason to be satisfied.

---

[1] Characters in Nicholas Rowe's *Tamerlane* (1702).

The sentiments and example of a *Cato*,[2] may inspire his spectators with a just sense of the value of liberty when they see that honest patriot prefer death to an obligation from a tyrant who would sacrifice the constitution of his country and the liberties of mankind to his ambition or revenge. I have attempted, indeed, to enlarge the province of the graver kind of poetry, and should be glad to see it carried on by some abler hand. Plays founded on moral tales in private life may be of admirable use by carrying conviction to the mind with such irresistible force as to engage all the faculties and powers of the soul in the cause of virtue by stifling vice in its first principles. They who imagine this to be too much to be attributed to tragedy must be strangers to the energy of that noble species of poetry. Shakespeare, who has given such amazing proofs of his genius in that as well as in comedy, in his *Hamlet*, has the following lines:

> Had he the motive and the cause for passion
> That I have, he would drown the stage with tears
> And cleave the general ear with horrid speech;
> Make mad the guilty, and appall the free,
> Confound the ignorant, and amaze indeed
> The very faculty of eyes and ears.

And farther, in the same speech,

> I've heard that guilty creatures at a play,
> Have, by the very cunning of the scene,
> Been so struck to the soul that presently
> They have proclaim'd their malefactions.

Prodigious! yet strictly just. But I shan't take up your valuable time with my remarks; only give me leave just to observe that he seems so firmly persuaded of the power of a well wrote piece to produce the effect here ascribed to it, as to make Hamlet venture his soul on the event, and rather trust that, than a messenger from the other world, though it assumed, as he expresses it, his noble father's form, and assured him that it was his spirit. I'll have, says Hamlet, grounds more relative.

> . . . The Play's the thing
> Wherein I'll catch the conscience of the king.

Such plays are the best answers to them who deny the lawfulness of the stage.

Considering the novelty of this attempt, I thought it would be expected from me to say something in its excuse; and I was unwilling to lose the opportunity of saying something of the usefulness of tragedy in general, and what may be reasonably expected from the farther improvement of this excellent kind of poetry.

Sir, I hope you will not think I have said too much of an art, a mean specimen of which I am ambitious enough to recommend to your favor and protection. A mind conscious of superior worth as much despises flattery as it is above it. Had I found in myself an inclination to so contemptible a vice, I should not have chose Sir John Eyles for my patron. And indeed the best writ panegyric, though strictly true, must place you in a light, much inferior to that in which you have long been fixed by the love and esteem of your fellow citizens, whose choice of you for one of their representatives in Parliament has sufficiently declared their sense of your merit. Nor hath the knowledge of your worth been confined to the City. The proprietors in the South-Sea Company, in which are included numbers of persons as considerable for their rank, fortune, and understanding as any in the kingdom, gave the greatest proof of their confidence in your capacity and probity when they chose you Sub-Governor of their company, at a time when their affairs were in the utmost confusion, and their properties in the greatest danger.[3] Nor is the court insensible of your importance. I shall not therefore attempt your character, nor pretend to add any thing to a reputation so well established.

---

[2] Addison's *Cato* (1713).
[3] After the collapse of the South Sea Bubble in 1720.

Whatever others may think of a dedication, wherein there is so much said of other things and so little of the person to whom it is addressed, I have reason to believe that you will the more easily pardon it on that very account.

I am, sir,
Your most obedient
humble servant,
George Lillo

THE LONDON MERCHANT
OR THE HISTORY OF GEORGE BARNWELL

GEORGE LILLO
EDITED BY JOHN HAROLD WILSON

— CHARACTERS —

THOROWGOOD
BARNWELL, *uncle to George*
GEORGE BARNWELL
TRUEMAN

BLUNT
MARIA
MILLWOOD
LUCY

Officers with their attendants, Keeper, and Footmen

SCENE: *London and an adjacent village*

— PROLOGUE —
SPOKE BY MR. CIBBER, JUN.

The tragic muse, sublime, delights to show
Princes distressed, and scenes of royal woe;
In awful pomp, majestic, to relate
The fall of nations or some hero's fate,
5   That sceptered chiefs may by example know
The strange vicissitude of things below;
What dangers on security attend;
How pride and cruelty in ruin end;
Hence Providence supreme to know, and own
10 Humanity adds glory to a throne.
    In ev'ry former age, and foreign tongue,
With native grandeur thus the goddess sung.
Upon our stage indeed with wished success
You've sometimes seen her in a humbler dress,
15 Great only in distress. When she complains
In Southerne's, Rowe's, or Otway's moving strains
The brilliant drops that fall from each bright eye,
The absent pomp with brighter gems supply.
Forgive us then, if we attempt to show
20 In artless strains a tale of private woe.
A London 'prentice ruined is our theme,
Drawn from the famed old song that bears his name.
We hope your taste is not so high to scorn
A moral tale esteemed e'er you were born,
25 Which for a century of rolling years
Has filled a thousand-thousand eyes with tears.
If thoughtless youth to warn and shame the age
From vice destructive well becomes the stage,
If this example innocence insure,
30 Prevent our guilt, or by reflection cure,
If Millwood's dreadful guilt, and sad despair,
Commend the virtue of the good and fair,
Though art be wanting, and our numbers fail,
Indulge th' attempt, in justice to the tale.

---

prologue **Spoke . . . Jun.** Prologues and epilogues were conventionally spoken by one of the play's leading actors, but not "in character." Cibber played the role of George Barnwell in the first production

---

— ACT ONE —

SCENE I

A Room in THOROWGOOD's *House.*

(Enter THOROWGOOD *and* TRUEMAN.*)*

TRUEMAN: Sir, the packet from Genoa is arrived.

(Gives letters.)

THOROWGOOD: Heaven be praised, the storm that threatened our royal mistress, pure religion, liberty, and laws is for a time diverted; the haughty and revengeful Spaniard, disappointed of the loan on which he depended from Genoa, 5 must now attend the slow return of wealth from his new world to supply his empty coffers, e'er he can execute his purposed invasion of our happy island; by which means time is gained to make such preparations on our part as may, Heaven concurring, prevent his malice or turn the meditated mischief on himself. 10

TRUEMAN: He must be insensible indeed who is not affected when the safety of his country is concerned. Sir, may I know by what means—if I am too bold—

THOROWGOOD: Your curiosity is laudable; and I gratify it with 15 the greater pleasure because from thence you may learn how honest merchants, as such, may sometimes contribute to the safety of their country as they do at all times to its happiness; that if hereafter you should be tempted to any action that has the appearance of vice or meanness in it, upon reflecting on 20 the dignity of our profession, you may with honest scorn reject whatever is unworthy of it.

TRUEMAN: Should Barnwell or I, who have the benefit of your example, by our ill conduct bring any imputation on that honorable name, we must be left without excuse. 25

THOROWGOOD: You compliment, young man. *(*TRUEMAN *bows respectfully.)* Nay, I'm not offended. As the name of merchant never degrades the gentleman, so by no means does it exclude him; only take heed not to purchase the character of complaisant at the expense of your sincerity. But to 30 answer your question—the bank of Genoa had agreed, at excessive interest and on good security, to advance the King of Spain a sum of money sufficient to equip his vast armada, of which our peerless Elizabeth (more than in name the

---

8 **purposed . . . island** The time of the play is about 1587

515

35   mother of her people), being well informed, sent Walsingham, her wise and faithful secretary, to consult the merchants of this loyal city, who all agreed to direct their several agents to influence, if possible, the Genoese to break their contract with the Spanish court. 'Tis done; the state and

40   bank of Genoa, having maturely weighed and rightly judged of their true interest, prefer the friendship of the merchants of London to that of a monarch who proudly styles himself King of both Indies.

TRUEMAN: Happy success of prudent councils. What an ex-

45   pense of blood and treasure is here saved! Excellent queen! O how unlike to former princes, who made the danger of foreign enemies a pretense to oppress their subjects by taxes great and grievous to be borne.

THOROWGOOD: Not so our gracious queen, whose richest ex-

50   chequer is her people's love, as their happiness her greatest glory.

TRUEMAN: On these terms to defend us is to make our protection a benefit worthy her who confers it, and well worth our acceptance. Sir, have you any commands for me at this

55   time?

THOROWGOOD: Only to look carefully over the files to see whether there are any tradesmen's bills unpaid; and if there are, to send and discharge 'em. We must not let artificers lose their time, so useful to the public and their families, in un-

60   necessary attendance.

(*Exit* TRUEMAN.)

(*Enter* MARIA.)

THOROWGOOD: Well, Maria, have you given orders for the entertainment? I would have it in some measure worthy the guests. Let there be plenty, and of the best, that the courtiers, though they should deny us citizens politeness, may at least

65   commend our hospitality.

MARIA: Sir, I have endeavored not to wrong your well-known generosity by an ill-timed parsimony.

THOROWGOOD: Nay, 'twas a needless caution; I have no cause to doubt your prudence.

70   MARIA: Sir, I find myself unfit for conversation at present. I should but increase the number of the company, without adding to their satisfaction.

THOROWGOOD: Nay, my child, this melancholy must not be indulged.

75   MARIA: Company will but increase it. I wish you would dispense with my absence; solitude best suits my present temper.

THOROWGOOD: You are not insensible that it is chiefly on your account these noble lords do me the honor so frequently to grace my board; should you be absent, the disap-

80   pointment may make them repent their condescension and think their labor lost.

MARIA: He that shall think his time or honor lost in visiting you, can set no real value on your daughter's company, whose only merit is that she is yours. The man of quality,

85   who chooses to converse with a gentleman and merchant of your worth and character, may confer honor by so doing, but he loses none.

---

75 **dispense with** excuse

THOROWGOOD: Come, come, Maria, I need not tell you that a young gentleman may prefer your conversation to mine, yet intend me no disrespect at all; for though he may lose no   90 honor in my company, 'tis very natural for him to expect more pleasure in yours. I remember the time when the company of the greatest and wisest man in the kingdom would have been insipid and tiresome to me, if it had deprived me of an opportunity of enjoying your mother's.   95

MARIA: Yours no doubt was as agreeable to her; for generous minds know no pleasure in society but where 'tis mutual.

THOROWGOOD: Thou know'st I have no heir, no child, but thee; the fruits of many years' successful industry must all be thine. Now it would give me pleasure great as my love, to see   100 on whom you would bestow it. I am daily solicited by men of the greatest rank and merit for leave to address you, but I have hitherto declined it, in hopes that by observation I should learn which way your inclination tends; for as I know love to be essential to happiness in the marriage state, I had   105 rather my approbation should confirm your choice than direct it.

MARIA: What can I say? How shall I answer as I ought this tenderness, so uncommon even in the best of parents; but you are without example; yet had you been less indulgent, I had   110 been most wretched. That I look on the crowd of courtiers that visit here with equal esteem but equal indifference you have observed, and I must needs confess; yet had you asserted your authority, and insisted on a parent's right to be obeyed, I had submitted, and to my duty sacrificed my   115 peace.

THOROWGOOD: From your perfect obedience in every other instance, I feared as much; and therefore would leave you without a bias in an affair wherein your happiness is so immediately concerned.   120

MARIA: Whether from a want of that just ambition that would become your daughter or from some other cause I know not; but I find high birth and titles don't recommend the man who owns them, to my affections.

THOROWGOOD: I would not that they should, unless his merit   125 recommends him more. A noble birth and fortune, though they make not a bad man good, yet they are a real advantage to a worthy one, and place his virtues in the fairest light.

MARIA: I cannot answer for my inclinations, but they shall ever be submitted to your wisdom and authority; and as you will   130 not compel me to marry where I cannot love, so love shall never make me act contrary to my duty. Sir, have I your permission to retire?

THOROWGOOD: I'll see you to your chamber.

(*Exeunt.*)

SCENE II

A Room in MILLWOOD's *House.*

(MILLWOOD [*at her toilet*]. LUCY *waiting.*)

MILLWOOD: How do I look to-day, Lucy?

LUCY: Oh, killingly, madam! A little more red, and you'll be irresistible! But why this more than ordinary care of your dress and complexion? What new conquest are you aiming at?   5

MILLWOOD: A conquest would be new indeed!

LUCY: Not to you, who make 'em every day, but to me—well! 'tis what I'm never to expect, unfortunate as I am. But your wit and beauty—

10 MILLWOOD: First made me a wretch, and still continue me so. Men, however generous or sincere to one another, are all selfish hypocrites in their affairs with us. We are no otherwise esteemed or regarded by them, but as we contribute to their satisfaction.

15 LUCY: You are certainly, madam, on the wrong side in this argument. Is not the expense all theirs? And I am sure it is our own fault if we haven't our share of the pleasure.

MILLWOOD: We are but slaves to men.

LUCY: Nay, 'tis they that are slaves most certainly; for we lay
20 them under contribution.

MILLWOOD: Slaves have no property; no, not even in themselves. All is the victor's.

LUCY: You are strangely arbitrary in your principles, madam.

MILLWOOD: I would have my conquests complete, like those
25 of the Spaniards in the New World, who first plundered the natives of all the wealth they had, and then condemned the wretches to the mines for life to work for more.

LUCY: Well, I shall never approve of your scheme of government. I should think it much more politic, as well as just, to
30 find my subjects an easier employment.

MILLWOOD: It's a general maxim among the knowing part of mankind that a woman without virtue, like a man without honor or honesty, is capable of any action, though never so vile; and yet what pains will they not take, what arts not use,
35 to seduce us from our innocence and make us contemptible and wicked even in their own opinions? Then is it not just, the villains, to their cost, should find us so? But guilt makes them suspicious, and keeps them on their guard; therefore we can take advantage only of the young and innocent part
40 of the sex, who, having never injured women, apprehend no injury from them.

LUCY: Ay, they must be young indeed.

MILLWOOD: Such a one, I think, I have found. As I've passed through the City, I have often observed him receiving and
45 paying considerable sums of money; from thence I conclude he is employed in affairs of consequence.

LUCY: Is he handsome?

MILLWOOD: Ay, ay, the stripling is well made.

LUCY: About—

50 MILLWOOD: Eighteen.

LUCY: Innocent, handsome, and about eighteen. You'll be vastly happy. Why, if you manage well, you may keep him to your self these two or three years.

MILLWOOD: If I manage well, I shall have done with him
55 much sooner. Having long had a design on him, and meeting him yesterday, I made a full stop and gazing wishfully on his face, asked him his name. He blushed, and bowing very low, answered George Barnwell. I begged his pardon for the freedom I had taken, and told him that he was the person I
60 had long wished to see, and to whom I had an affair of importance to communicate at a proper time and place. He named a tavern; I talked of honor and reputation, and invited him to my house. He swallowed the bait, promised to come, and this is the time I expect him. *(Knocking at the*
65 *door.)* Somebody knocks—d'ye hear? I am at home to nobody to-day, but him.—*(Exit* LUCY.) Less affairs must give

way to those of more consequence; and I am strangely mistaken if this does not prove of great importance to me and him, too, before I have done with him. Now, after what manner shall I receive him? Let me consider. What manner of 70 person am I to receive? He is young, innocent, and bashful; therefore I must take care not to shock him at first. But then, if I have any skill in physiognomy, he is amorous, and, with a little assistance, will soon get the better of his modesty. I'll trust to nature, who does wonders in these matters. If to 75 seem what one is not, in order to be the better liked for what one really is; if to speak one thing, and mean the direct contrary, be art in a woman, I know nothing of nature.

(Enter BARNWELL *bowing very low.* LUCY *at a distance.)*

MILLWOOD: Sir, the surprise and joy!—

BARNWELL: Madam—   80

MILLWOOD: *(Advancing.)* This is such a favor—

BARNWELL: Pardon me, madam—

MILLWOOD: So unhoped for—

(Still advances. BARNWELL *salutes her, and retires in confusion.)*

To see you here—Excuse the confusion—

BARNWELL: I fear I am too bold.   85

MILLWOOD: Alas, sir! All my apprehensions proceed from my fears of your thinking me so. Please, sir, to sit. I am as much at a loss how to receive this honor as I ought, as I am surprised at your goodness in conferring it.

BARNWELL: I thought you had expected me. I promised to   90 come.

MILLWOOD: That is the more surprising; few men are such religious observers of their word.

BARNWELL: All who are honest are.

MILLWOOD: To one another. But we silly women are seldom   95 thought of consequence enough to gain a place in your remembrance.

(Laying her hand on his, as by accident.)

BARNWELL: *(Aside.)* Her discomfort is so great, she don't perceive she has laid her hand on mine. Heaven! how she trembles! What can this mean!   100

MILLWOOD: The interest I have in all that relates to you (the reason of which you shall know hereafter) excites my curiosity; and, were I sure you would pardon my presumption, I should desire to know your real sentiments on a very particular subject.   105

BARNWELL: Madam, you may command my poor thoughts on any subject; I have none that I would conceal.

MILLWOOD: You'll think me bold.

BARNWELL: No, indeed.

MILLWOOD: What then are your thoughts of love?   110

BARNWELL: If you mean the love of women, I have not thought of it at all. My youth and circumstances make such thoughts improper in me yet. But if you mean the general love we owe to mankind, I think no one has more of it in his temper than myself. I don't know that person in the world   115 whose happiness I don't wish, and wouldn't promote, were it in my power. In an especial manner I love my uncle and my master, but above all my friend.

MILLWOOD: You have a friend then whom you love?

BARNWELL: As he does me, sincerely.   120

MILLWOOD: He is, no doubt, often blessed with your company and conversation.

BARNWELL: We live in one house together, and both serve the same worthy merchant.

125 MILLWOOD: Happy, happy youth!—Who e'er thou art, I envy thee, and so must all who see and know this youth.—What I have lost, by being formed a woman! I hate my sex, myself. Had I been a man, I might, perhaps, have been as happy in your friendship as he who now enjoys it. But as it is—oh!

130 BARNWELL: *(Aside.)* I never observed women before, or this is sure the most beautiful of her sex.—You seem disordered, madam! May I know the cause?

MILLWOOD: Do not ask me. I can never speak it, whatever is the cause. I wish for things impossible. I would be a servant,
135 bound to the same master as you are, to live in one house with you.

BARNWELL: *(Aside.)* How strange, and yet how kind, her words and actions are! And the effect they have on me is as strange. I feel desires I never knew before. I must be gone, while I
140 have power to go. Madam, I humbly take my leave.

MILLWOOD: You will not sure leave me so soon!

BARNWELL: Indeed I must.

MILLWOOD: You cannot be so cruel! I have prepared a poor supper, at which I promised myself your company.

145 BARNWELL: I am sorry I must refuse the honor that you designed me, but my duty to my master calls me hence. I never yet neglected his service. He is so gentle and so good a master that should I wrong him, though he might forgive me, I never should forgive myself.

150 MILLWOOD: Am I refused, by the first man, the second favor I ever stooped to ask? Go then, thou proud, hard-hearted youth. But know, you are the only man that could be found who would let me sue twice for greater favors.

BARNWELL: *(Aside.)* What shall I do? How shall I go or stay!

155 MILLWOOD: Yet do not, do not, leave me. I wish my sex's pride would meet your scorn; but when I look upon you, when I behold those eyes—oh! spare my tongue, and let my blushes—this flood of tears, too, that will force its way—declare what woman's modesty should hide.

160 BARNWELL: *(Aside.)* Oh, heavens! she loves me, worthless as I am; her looks, her words, her flowing tears confess it. And can I leave her then? Oh, never, never!—Madam, dry up your tears. You shall command me always; I will stay here for ever, if you'd have me.

165 LUCY: *(Aside.)* So! she has wheedled him out of his virtue of obedience already and will strip him of all the rest, one after another, till she has left him as few as her ladyship or myself.

MILLWOOD: Now you are kind, indeed; but I mean not to detain you always. I would have you shake off all slavish obedi-
170 ence to your master, but you may serve him still.

LUCY: *(Aside.)* Serve him still! Aye, or he'll have no opportunity of fingering his cash, and then he'll not serve your end, I'll be sworn.

(Enter BLUNT.*)*

BLUNT: Madam, supper's on the table.

175 MILLWOOD: Come, sir, you'll excuse all defects. My thoughts were too much employed on my guest to observe the entertainment.

(Exeunt MILLWOOD *and* BARNWELL.*)*

BLUNT: What! is all this preparation, this elegant supper, variety of wines and music, for the entertainment of that young fellow! 180

LUCY: So it seems.

BLUNT: What! is our mistress turned fool at last! She's in love with him, I suppose.

LUCY: I suppose not, but she designs to make him in love with her if she can. 185

BLUNT: What will she get by that? He seems under age, and can't be supposed to have much money.

LUCY: But his master has; and that's the same thing, as she'll manage it.

BLUNT: I don't like this fooling with a handsome young fellow; 190 while she's endeavoring to ensnare him, she may be caught herself.

LUCY: Nay, were she like me, that would certainly be the consequence; for, I confess, there is something in youth and innocence that moves me mightily. 195

BLUNT: Yes, so does the smoothness and plumpness of a partridge move a mighty desire in the hawk to be the destruction of it.

LUCY: Why, birds are their prey, as men are ours; though, as you observed, we are sometimes caught ourselves. But that, I 200 dare say, will never be the case with our mistress.

BLUNT: I wish it may prove so; for you know we all depend upon her. Should she trifle away her time with a young fellow that there's nothing to be got by, we must all starve.

LUCY: There's no danger of that, for I am sure she has no view 205 in this affair but interest.

BLUNT: Well, and what hopes are there of success in that?

LUCY: The most promising that can be. 'Tis true, the youth has his scruples; but she'll soon teach him to answer them by stifling his conscience. Oh, the lad is in a hopeful way, depend 210 upon't.

(Exeunt.)

SCENE III

Draws and discovers BARNWELL *and* MILLWOOD *at supper. An entertainment of music and singing. After which they come forward.*

BARNWELL: What can I answer! All that I know is, that you are fair and I am miserable.

MILLWOOD: We are both so, and yet the fault is in ourselves.

BARNWELL: To ease our present anguish by plunging into guilt is to buy a moment's pleasure with an age of pain. 5

MILLWOOD: I should have thought the joys of love as lasting as they are great. If ours prove otherwise, 'tis your inconstancy must make them so.

BARNWELL: The law of heaven will not be reversed, and that requires us to govern our passions. 10

MILLWOOD: To give us sense of beauty and desires, and yet forbid us to taste and be happy, is cruelty to nature. Have we passions only to torment us!

BARNWELL: To hear you talk, though in the cause of vice, to gaze upon your beauty, press your hand, and see your snow- 15 white bosom heave and fall, enflames my wishes; my pulse beats high, my senses all are in a hurry, and I am on the

rack of wild desire; yet for a moment's guilty pleasure, shall
I lose my innocence, my peace of mind, and hopes of solid
20 happiness?
MILLWOOD: Chimeras all! Come on with me and prove,
No joy's like woman-kind, nor heaven like love.
BARNWELL: I would not, yet must on.—
Reluctant thus, the merchant quits his ease
25 And trusts to rocks, and sands, and stormy seas;
In hopes some unknown golden coast to find,
Commits himself, though doubtful, to the wind,
Longs much for joys to come, yet mourns those left behind.

(Exeunt.)

— ACT TWO —

SCENE I

A Room in THOROWGOOD's *House.*

(Enter BARNWELL.)

BARNWELL: How strange are all things round me! Like some
thief, who treads forbidden ground, fearful I enter each
apartment of this well-known house. To guilty love, as if that
were too little, already have I added breach of trust. A thief!
5 Can I know myself that wretched thing, and look my honest
friend and injured master in the face? Though hypocrisy
may a while conceal my guilt, at length it will be known, and
public shame and ruin must ensue. In the meantime, what
must be my life? Ever to speak a language foreign to my
10 heart; hourly to add to the number of my crimes in order to
conceal 'em. Sure, such was the condition of the grand apostate, when first he lost his purity; like me disconsolate he
wandered, and, while yet in heaven, bore all his future hell
about him.

(Enter TRUEMAN.)

15 TRUEMAN: Barnwell! Oh, how I rejoice to see you safe! So will
our master and his gentle daughter, who during your absence often inquired after you.
BARNWELL: *(Aside.)* Would he were gone! his officious love
will pry into the secrets of my soul.
20 TRUEMAN: Unless you knew the pain the whole family has felt
on your account, you can't conceive how much you are
beloved. But why thus cold and silent? When my heart is full
of joy for your return, why do you turn away? Why thus avoid
me? What have I done? How am I altered since you saw me
25 last? Or rather what have you done, and why are you thus
changed, for I am still the same?
BARNWELL: *(Aside.)* What have I done, indeed?
TRUEMAN: Not speak nor look upon me!
BARNWELL: *(Aside.)* By my face he will discover all I would
30 conceal; methinks already I begin to hate him.
TRUEMAN: I cannot bear this usage from a friend, one whom
till now I ever found so loving, whom yet I love, though this
unkindness strikes at the root of friendship, and might destroy it in any breast but mine.
35 BARNWELL: I am not well. *(Turning to him.)* Sleep has been a
stranger to these eyes since you beheld them last.

---

11 **grand apostate** Lucifer

TRUEMAN: Heavy they look indeed, and swollen with tears;
now they o'erflow; rightly did my sympathizing heart fore-
bode last night, when thou wast absent, something fatal to
our peace.   40
BARNWELL: Your friendship engages you too far. My troubles,
whate'er they are, are mine alone; you have no interest in
them, nor ought your concern for me give you a moment's
pain.
TRUEMAN: You speak as if you knew of friendship nothing but   45
the name. Before I saw your grief I felt it. Since we parted
last I have slept no more than you, but, pensive in my chamber, sat alone and spent the tedious night in wishes for your
safety and return; e'en now, though ignorant of the cause,
your sorrow wounds me to the heart.   50
BARNWELL: 'Twill not be always thus. Friendship and all engagements cease, as circumstances and occasions vary; and,
since you once may hate me, perhaps it might be better for
us both that now you loved me less.
TRUEMAN: Sure I but dream! Without a cause would Barnwell   55
use me thus? Ungenerous and ungrateful youth, farewell.
(Going.) I shall endeavor to follow your advice. *(Aside.)* Yet
stay, perhaps I am too rash, and angry when the cause demands compassion. Some unforeseen calamity may have be-
fallen him, too great to bear.   60
BARNWELL: *(Aside.)* What part am I reduced to act! 'Tis vile
and base to move his temper thus, the best of friends and
men.
TRUEMAN: I am to blame; prithee forgive me, Barnwell. Try to
compose your ruffled mind, and let me know the cause that   65
thus transports you from yourself. My friendly counsel may
restore your peace.
BARNWELL: All that is possible for man to do for man, your
generous friendship may effect; but here even that's in vain.
TRUEMAN: Something dreadful is laboring in your breast. Oh,   70
give it vent and let me share your grief! 'Twill ease your pain
should it admit no cure and make it lighter by the part I bear.
BARNWELL: Vain supposition! My woes increase by being observed; should the cause be known, they would exceed all
bounds.   75
TRUEMAN: So well I know thy honest heart, guilt cannot har-
bor there.
BARNWELL: *(Aside.)* Oh, torture insupportable!
TRUEMAN: Then why am I excluded? Have I a thought I
would conceal from you?   80
BARNWELL: If still you urge me on this hated subject, I'll never
enter more beneath this roof, nor see your face again.
TRUEMAN: 'Tis strange. But I have done; say but you hate me
not.
BARNWELL: Hate you! I am not that monster yet.   85
TRUEMAN: Shall our friendship still continue?
BARNWELL: It's a blessing I never was worthy of, yet now must
stand on terms, and but upon conditions can confirm it.
TRUEMAN: What are they?
BARNWELL: Never hereafter, though you should wonder at my   90
conduct, desire to know more than I am willing to reveal.
TRUEMAN: 'Tis hard, but upon any conditions I must be your
friend.
BARNWELL: Then, as much as one lost to himself can be an-
other's, I am yours.   95

(Embracing.)

TRUEMAN: Be ever so, and may heaven restore your peace.

BARNWELL: Will yesterday return? We have heard the glorious sun, that till then incessant rolled, once stopped his rapid course, and once went back. The dead have risen; and parched rocks poured forth a liquid stream to quench a people's thirst. The sea divided and formed walls of water while a whole nation passed in safety through its sandy bosom. Hungry lions have refused their prey; and men unhurt have walked amidst consuming flames; but never yet did time, once past, return.

TRUEMAN: Though the continued chain of time has never once been broke, nor ever will, but uninterrupted must keep on its course till, lost in eternity, it ends there where it first begun; yet as heaven can repair whatever evils time can bring upon us, we ought never to despair. But business requires our attendance, business the youth's best preservative from ill, as idleness his worst of snares. Will you go with me?

BARNWELL: I'll take a little time to reflect on what has past, and follow you.—   *(Exit* TRUEMAN.*)*

I might have trusted Trueman and engaged him to apply to my uncle to repair the wrong I have done my master; but what of Millwood? Must I expose her too? Ungenerous and base! Then heaven requires it not. But heaven requires that I forsake her. What! Never see her more! Does heaven require that! I hope I may see her, and heaven not be offended. Presumptuous hope! Dearly already have I proved my frailty; should I once more tempt heaven, I may be left to fall never to rise again. Yet shall I leave her, forever leave her, and not let her know the cause? She who loves me with such a boundless passion? Can cruelty be duty? I judge of what she then must feel, by what I now endure. The love of life and fear of shame, opposed by inclination strong as death or shame, like wind and tide in raging conflict met, when neither can prevail, keep me in doubt. How then can I determine?

(Enter THOROWGOOD.*)*

THOROWGOOD: Without a cause assigned, or notice given, to absent yourself last night was a fault, young man, and I came to chide you for it, but hope I am prevented. That modest blush, the confusion so visible in your face, speak grief and shame. When we have offended heaven, it requires no more; and shall man, who needs himself to be forgiven, be harder to appease? If my pardon or love be of moment to your peace, look up, secure of both.

BARNWELL: *(Aside.)* This goodness has o'er-come me.—Oh, sir! you know not the nature and extent of my offence; and I should abuse your mistaken bounty to receive it. Though I had rather die than speak my shame; though racks could not have forced the guilty secret from my breast, your kindness has.

THOROWGOOD: Enough, enough! Whate'er it be, this concern shows you're convinced, and I am satisfied. *(Aside.)* How painful is the sense of guilt to an ingenuous mind!—some youthful folly, which it were prudent not to enquire into. When we consider the frail condition of humanity, it may raise our pity, not our wonder, that youth should go astray; when reason, weak at the best when opposed to inclination,

scarce formed, and wholly unassisted by experience, faintly contends, or willingly becomes the slave of sense. The state of youth is much to be deplored, and the more so because they see it not; being then to danger most exposed when they are least prepared for their defence.

BARNWELL: It will be known, and you recall your pardon and abhor me.

THOROWGOOD: I never will; so heaven confirm to me the pardon of my offences. Yet be upon your guard in this gay, thoughtless season of your life; now, when the sense of pleasure's quick, and passion high, the voluptuous appetites, raging and fierce, demand the strongest curb; take heed of a relapse. When vice becomes habitual, the very power of leaving it is lost.

BARNWELL: Hear me, on my knees confess.

THOROWGOOD: I will not hear a syllable more upon this subject; it were not mercy, but cruelty, to hear what must give you such torment to reveal.

BARNWELL: This generosity amazes and distracts me.

THOROWGOOD: This remorse makes thee dearer to me than if thou hadst never offended; whatever is your fault, of this I'm certain, 'twas harder for you to offend than me to pardon.

(Exit THOROWGOOD.*)*

BARNWELL: Villain, villain, villain! basely to wrong so excellent a man. Should I again return to folly?—detested thought!—But what of Millwood then? Why, I renounce her! I give her up; the struggle's over, and virtue has prevailed. Reason may convince, but gratitude compels. This unlooked for generosity has saved me from destruction.

(Going.)

(Enter a Footman.)

FOOTMAN: Sir, two ladies, from your uncle in the country, desire to see you.

BARNWELL: *(Aside.)* Who should they be?—Tell them I'll wait upon 'em.—

(Exit Footman.)

Methinks I dread to see 'em. Guilt, what a coward hast thou made me! Now everything alarms me.

(Exit.)

SCENE II

Another Room in THOROWGOOD's *House.*

(Enter MILLWOOD *and* LUCY, *and to them a Footman.)*

FOOTMAN: Ladies, he'll wait upon you immediately.

MILLWOOD: 'Tis very well. I thank you.

(Exit Footman.)

(Enter BARNWELL.*)*

BARNWELL: *(Aside.)* Confusion! Millwood!

MILLWOOD: That angry look tells me that here I'm an unwelcome guest; I feared as much—the unhappy are so everywhere.

BARNWELL: Will nothing but my utter ruin content you?

MILLWOOD: Unkind and cruel! Lost myself, your happiness is now my only care.

BARNWELL: How did you gain admission?

---

133 prevented anticipated

MILLWOOD: Saying we were desired by your uncle to visit and deliver a message to you, we were received by the family without suspicion, and with much respect conducted here.

BARNWELL: Why did you come at all?

15 MILLWOOD: I never shall trouble you more; I'm come to take my leave forever. Such is the malice of my fate, I go hopeless, despairing ever to return. This hour is all I have left. One short hour is all I have to bestow on love and you, for whom I thought the longest life too short.

20 BARNWELL: Then we are met to part forever?

MILLWOOD: It must be so; yet think not that time or absence shall ever put a period to my grief or make me love you less; though I must leave you, yet condemn me not.

BARNWELL: Condemn you? No, I approve your resolution, and rejoice to hear it; 'tis just, 'tis necessary. I have well weighed, and found it so.

25

LUCY: (*Aside.*) I'm afraid the young man has more sense than she thought he had.

BARNWELL: Before you came I had determined never to see you more.

35

MILLWOOD: (*Aside.*) Confusion!

LUCY: (*Aside.*) Ay! we are all out; this is a turn so unexpected that I shall make nothing of my part; they must e'en play the scene betwixt themselves.

30 MILLWOOD: 'Twas some relief to think, though absent, you would love me still; but to find, though fortune had been indulgent, that you, more cruel and inconstant, had resolved to cast me off—this, as I never could expect, I have not learnt to bear.

40 BARNWELL: I am sorry to hear you blame in me a resolution that so well becomes us both.

MILLWOOD: I have reason for what I do, but you have none.

BARNWELL: Can we want a reason for parting, who have so many to wish we never had met?

45 MILLWOOD: Look on me, Barnwell; am I deformed or old, that satiety so soon succeeds enjoyment? Nay, look again; am I not she whom yesterday you thought the fairest and the kindest of her sex, whose hand, trembling with ecstasy, you pressed and molded thus, while on my eyes you gazed with such delight, as if desire increased by being fed?

50

BARNWELL: No more! Let me repent my former follies, if possible, without remembering what they were.

MILLWOOD: Why?

BARNWELL: Such is my frailty that 'tis dangerous.

55 MILLWOOD: Where is the danger, since we are to part?

BARNWELL: The thought of that already is too painful.

MILLWOOD: If it be painful to part, then I may hope at least you do not hate me?

BARNWELL: No—no—I never said I did!—Oh, my heart!

60 MILLWOOD: Perhaps you pity me?

BARNWELL: I do, I do, indeed, I do.

MILLWOOD: You'll think upon me?

BARNWELL: Doubt it not while I can think at all.

MILLWOOD: You may judge an embrace at parting too great a favor, though it would be the last? (*He draws back.*) A look shall then suffice—farewell forever.

65

(*Exeunt* MILLWOOD *and* LUCY.)

BARNWELL: If to resolve to suffer be to conquer, I have conquered. Painful victory!

(*Re-enter* MILLWOOD *and* LUCY.)

MILLWOOD: One thing I had forgot. I never must return to my own house again. This I thought proper to let you know, lest your mind should change, and you should seek in vain to find me there. Forgive me this second intrusion; I only came to give you this caution, and that, perhaps, was needless.

70

BARNWELL: I hope it was, yet it is kind, and I must thank you for it.

75

MILLWOOD: (*To* LUCY.) My friend, your arm. Now I am gone forever. (*Going.*)

BARNWELL: One thing more. Sure, there's no danger in my knowing where you go? If you think otherwise—

MILLWOOD: (*Weeping.*) Alas!

80

LUCY: (*Aside.*) We are right I find, that's my cue.—Ah, dear sir, she's going she knows not whither, but go she must.

BARNWELL: Humanity obliges me to wish you well. Why will you thus expose yourself to needless troubles?

LUCY: Nay, there's no help for it. She must quit the town immediately, and the kingdom as soon as possible; it was no small matter, you may be sure, that could make her resolve to leave you.

85

MILLWOOD: No more, my friend; since he for whose dear sake alone I suffer, and am content to suffer, is kind and pities me. Where'er I wander through wilds and deserts, benighted and forlorn, that thought shall give me comfort.

90

BARNWELL: For my sake! Oh, tell me how; which way am I so cursed as to bring such ruin on thee?

MILLWOOD: No matter, I am contented with my lot.

95

BARNWELL: Leave me not in this incertainty.

MILLWOOD: I have said too much.

BARNWELL: How, how am I the cause of your undoing?

MILLWOOD: To know it will but increase your troubles.

BARNWELL: My troubles can't be greater than they are.

100

LUCY: Well, well, sir, if she won't satisfy you, I will.

BARNWELL: I am bound to you beyond expression.

MILLWOOD: Remember, sir, that I desired you not to hear it.

BARNWELL: Begin, and ease my racking expectation.

LUCY: Why you must know, my lady here was an only child; but her parents dying while she was young, left her and her fortune, (no inconsiderable one, I assure you) to the care of a gentleman who has a good estate of his own.

105

MILLWOOD: Ay, ay, the barbarous man is rich enough—but what are riches when compared to love?

110

LUCY: For a while he performed the office of a faithful guardian, settled her in a house, hired her servants—but you have seen in what manner she lived, so I need say no more of that.

MILLWOOD: How I shall live hereafter, heaven knows.

115

LUCY: All things went on as one could wish, till, some time ago, his wife dying, he fell violently in love with his charge, and would fain have married her. Now the man is neither old nor ugly, but a good, personable sort of man, but I don't know how it was, she could never endure him. In short, her ill usage so provoked him that he brought in an account of his executorship, wherein he makes her debtor to him.

120

MILLWOOD: A trifle in itself, but more than enough to ruin me, whom, by his unjust account, he had stripped of all before.

125

LUCY: Now she having neither money nor friend, except me, who am as unfortunate as herself, he compelled her to pass his account, and give bond for the sum he demanded; but still provided handsomely for her and continued his

130 courtship, till, being informed by his spies (truly I suspect some in her own family) that you were entertained at her house and stayed with her all night, he came this morning raving and storming like a madman, talks no more of marriage (so there's no hopes of making up matters that way)
135 but vows her ruin, unless she'll allow him the same favor that he supposes she granted you.

BARNWELL: Must she be ruined, or find her refuge in another's arms?

MILLWOOD: He gave me but an hour to resolve in, that's hap-
140 pily spent with you—and now I go.

BARNWELL: To be exposed to all the rigors of the various seasons; the summer's parching heat, and winter's cold; unhoused to wander friendless through the unhospitable world, in misery and want; attended with fear and danger,
145 and pursued by malice and revenge—wouldst thou endure all this for me, and can I do nothing, nothing to prevent it?

LUCY: 'Tis really a pity, there can be no way found out.

BARNWELL: Oh, where are all my resolutions now? Like early vapors, or the morning dew, chased by the sun's warm beams
150 they're vanished and lost, as though they had never been.

LUCY: Now I advised her, sir, to comply with the gentleman; that would not only put an end to her troubles, but make her fortune at once.

BARNWELL: Tormenting fiend, away! I had rather perish, nay,
155 see her perish, than have her saved by him; I will myself prevent her ruin, though with my own. A moment's patience, I'll return immediately.

(Exit.)

LUCY: 'Twas well you came, or, by what I can perceive, you had lost him.
160 MILLWOOD: That, I must confess, was a danger I did not foresee; I was only afraid he should have come without money. You know a house of entertainment like mine is not kept without expense.

LUCY: That's very true; but then you should be reasonable in
165 your demands; 'tis pity to discourage a young man.

(Re-enter BARNWELL, *with a bag of money.)*

BARNWELL: *(Aside.)* What am I about to do! Now you, who boast your reason all sufficient, suppose yourselves in my condition, and determine for me whether it's right to let her suffer for my faults, or, by this small addition to my guilt, pre
170 vent the ill effects of what is past.

LUCY: *(Aside.)* These young sinners think everything in the ways of wickedness so strange,—but I could tell him that this is nothing but what's very common; for one vice as naturally begets another, as a father a son. But he'll find out that him
175 self, if he lives long enough.

BARNWELL: Here, take this, and with it purchase your deliverance; return to your house, and live in peace and safety.

MILLWOOD: So I may hope to see you there again.

BARNWELL: Answer me not, but fly—lest, in the agonies of my
180 remorse, I take again what is not mine to give, and abandon thee to want and misery.

MILLWOOD: Say but you'll come!

BARNWELL: You are my fate, my heaven, or my hell. Only leave me now, dispose of me hereafter as you please.—

(Exeunt MILLWOOD *and* LUCY.)

What have I done? Were my resolutions founded on rea- 185 son, and sincerely made? why then has heaven suffered me to fall? I sought not the occasion; and, if my heart deceives me not, compassion and generosity were my motives. Is virtue inconsistent with itself, or are vice and virtue only empty names? Or do they depend on accidents beyond our 190 power to produce, or to prevent, wherein we have no part, and yet must be determined by the event? But why should I attempt to reason? All is confusion, horror, and remorse. I find I am lost, cast down from all my late erected hopes and plunged again in guilt, yet scarce know how or why— 195
    Such undistinguished horrors make my brain,
    Like hell, the seat of darkness, and of pain.

(Exit.)

— ACT THREE —

SCENE I

A Room in THOROWGOOD's *House.*

*(*THOROWGOOD *and* TRUEMAN *discovered sitting at a table.)*

THOROWGOOD: Methinks I would not have you only learn the method of merchandise and practise it hereafter merely as a means of getting wealth. 'Twill be well worth your pains to study it as a science, to see how it is founded in reason and the nature of things, how it has promoted humanity, as it has 5 opened and yet keeps up an intercourse between nations far remote from one another in situation, customs, and religion; promoting arts, industry, peace and plenty, by mutual benefits diffusing mutual love from pole to pole.

TRUEMAN: Something of this I have considered, and hope, by 10 your assistance, to extend my thoughts much farther. I have observed those countries where trade is promoted and encouraged do not make discoveries to destroy, but to improve mankind by love and friendship, to tame the fierce, and polish the most savage, to teach them the advantages of honest 15 traffic by taking from them with their own consent their useless superfluities, and giving them in return what, from their ignorance in manual arts, their situation, or some other accident, they stand in need of.

THOROWGOOD: 'Tis justly observed. The populous east, luxu- 20 riant, abounds with glittering gems, bright pearls, aromatic spices, and health-restoring drugs. The late found western world glows with unnumbered veins of gold and silver ore. On every climate, and on every country, heaven has bestowed some good peculiar to itself. It is the industrious mer- 25 chant's business to collect the various blessings of each soil and climate, and, with the product of the whole, to enrich his native country.

    Well! I have examined your accounts. They are not only just, as I have always found them, but regularly kept, and 30 fairly entered. I commend your diligence. Method in business is the surest guide. He who neglects it frequently stumbles, and always wanders perplexed, uncertain, and in danger. Are Barnwell's accounts ready for my inspection? He does not use to be the last on these occasions. 35

TRUEMAN: Upon receiving your orders he retired, I thought in some confusion. If you please, I'll go and hasten him. I hope he hasn't been guilty of any neglect.

THOROWGOOD: I'm now going to the Exchange; let him
40   know, at my return I expect to find him ready.

(Exeunt.)

(Enter MARIA *with a book; sits and reads.)*

MARIA: How forcible is truth! The weakest mind, inspired with
love of that, fixed and collected in itself, with indifference
beholds the united force of earth and hell opposing. Such
45   souls are raised above the sense of pain, or so supported that
they regard it not. The martyr cheaply purchases his heaven.
Small are his sufferings, great is his reward. Not so the
wretch who combats love with duty, when the mind, weakened and dissolved by the soft passion, feeble and hopeless,
50   opposes its own desire. What is an hour, a day, a year of pain,
to a whole life of tortures such as these?

(Enter TRUEMAN.*)*

TRUEMAN: Oh, Barnwell! Oh, my friend, how art thou fallen!
MARIA: Ha! Barnwell! What of him? Speak, say what of Barn-
well?
TRUEMAN: 'Tis not to be concealed. I've news to tell of him
55   that will afflict your generous father, yourself, and all who
knew him.
MARIA: Defend us, Heaven!
TRUEMAN: I cannot speak it. See there.

(Gives a letter, MARIA *reads.)*

MARIA:

Trueman,
60   I know my absence will surprise my honored master and
yourself; and the more, when you shall understand that the reason of my withdrawing, is my having embezzled part of the
cash with which I was entrusted. After this, 'tis needless to inform you that I intend never to return again. Though this
65   might have been known by examining my accounts; yet, to prevent that unnecessary trouble, and to cut off all fruitless expectations of my return, I have left this from the lost
                                        George Barnwell.

TRUEMAN: Lost indeed! Yet how he should be guilty of what
70   he there charges himself withal, raises my wonder equal to
my grief. Never had youth a higher sense of virtue. Justly he
thought, and as he thought he practised; never was life more
regular than his; an understanding uncommon at his years;
an open, generous, manliness of temper; his manners easy,
75   unaffected and engaging.
MARIA: This and much more you might have said with truth.
He was the delight of every eye, and joy of every heart that
knew him.
TRUEMAN: Since such he was, and was my friend, can I sup-
80   port his loss? See, the fairest and happiest maid this wealthy
city boasts, kindly condescends to weep for thy unhappy fate,
poor, ruined Barnwell!
MARIA: Trueman, do you think a soul so delicate as his, so sensible of shame, can e'er submit to live a slave to vice?
85   TRUEMAN: Never, never! So well I know him, I'm sure this act
of his, so contrary to his nature, must have been caused by
some unavoidable necessity.
MARIA: Is there no means yet to preserve him?
TRUEMAN: Oh, that there were! But few men recover reputa-
90   tion lost, a merchant never. Nor would he, I fear, though I

should find him, ever be brought to look his injured master
in the face.
MARIA: I fear as much—and therefore would never have my father know it.
TRUEMAN: That's impossible.   95
MARIA: What's the sum?
TRUEMAN: 'Tis considerable. I've marked it here, to show it,
with the letter, to your father, at his return.
MARIA: If I should supply the money, could you so dispose of
that, and the account, as to conceal this unhappy misman-   100
agement from my father?
TRUEMAN: Nothing more easy. But can you intend it? Will
you save a helpless wretch from ruin? Oh! 'twere an act
worthy such exalted virtue as Maria's. Sure, heaven in mercy
to my friend inspired the generous thought!   105
MARIA: Doubt not but I would purchase so great a happiness at
a much dearer price. But how shall he be found?
TRUEMAN: Trust to my diligence for that. In the meantime, I'll
conceal his absence from your father, or find such excuses
for it that the real cause shall never be suspected.   110
MARIA: In attempting to save from shame one whom we hope
may yet return to virtue, to heaven and you, the judges of
this action, I appeal, whether I have done anything misbe-
coming my sex and character.
TRUEMAN: Earth must approve the deed, and heaven, I doubt   115
not, will reward it.
MARIA: If heaven succeeds it, I am well rewarded. A virgin's
fame is sullied by suspicion's slightest breath; and therefore
as this must be a secret from my father and the world, for
Barnwell's sake, for mine, let it be so to him.   120

SCENE II

MILLWOOD'S *House.*

(Enter LUCY *and* BLUNT.*)*

LUCY: Well! what do you think of Millwood's conduct now?
BLUNT: I own it is surprising. I don't know which to admire
most, her feigned, or his real passion, though I have sometimes been afraid that her avarice would discover her. But
his youth and want of experience make it the easier to im-   5
pose on him.
LUCY: No, it is his love. To do him justice, notwithstanding his
youth, he don't want understanding; but you men are much
easier imposed on in these affairs than your vanity will allow
you to believe. Let me see the wisest of you all as much in   10
love with me as Barnwell is with Millwood, and I'll engage
to make as great a fool of him.
BLUNT: And all circumstances considered, to make as much
money of him, too?
LUCY: I can't answer for that. Her artifice in making him rob   15
his master at first, and the various strategems, by which she
has obliged him to continue in that course, astonish even
me, who know her so well.
BLUNT: But then you are to consider that the money was his
master's.   20
LUCY: There was the difficulty of it. Had it been his own, it
had been nothing. Were the world his, she might have it for
a smile. But those golden days are done; he's ruined, and
Millwood's hopes of farther profits there are at an end.
BLUNT: That's no more than we all expected.   25

LUCY: Being called by his master to make up his accounts, he was forced to quit his house and service, and wisely flies to Millwood for relief and entertainment.

BLUNT: I have not heard of this before! How did she receive
30   him?

LUCY: As you would expect. She wondered what he meant, was astonished at his impudence, and, with an air of modesty peculiar to herself, swore so heartily that she never saw him before that she put me out of countenance.

35   BLUNT: That's much indeed! But how did Barnwell behave?

LUCY: He grieved, and at length, enraged at this barbarous treatment, was preparing to be gone; and, making toward the door, showed a sum of money, which he had brought from his master's—the last he's ever like to have from thence.

40   BLUNT: But then Millwood?

LUCY: Aye, she, with her usual address, returned to her old arts of lying, swearing, and dissembling, hung on his neck, and wept, and swore 'twas meant in jest. The amorous youth melted into tears, threw the money into her lap, and swore
45   he had rather die than think her false.

BLUNT: Strange infatuation!

LUCY: But what followed was stranger still. As doubts and fears followed by reconcilement ever increase love where the passion is sincere, so in him it caused so wild a transport of ex-
50   cessive fondness, such joy, such grief, such pleasure, and such anguish, that nature in him seemed sinking with the weight, and the charmed soul disposed to quit his breast for hers. Just then, when every passion with lawless anarchy prevailed, and reason was in the raging tempest lost, the cruel,
55   artful Millwood prevailed upon the wretched youth to promise what I tremble but to think on.

BLUNT: I am amazed! What can it be?

LUCY: You will be more so to hear it is to attempt the life of his nearest relation, and best benefactor.

60   BLUNT: His uncle, whom we have often heard him speak of as a gentleman of a large estate and fair character in the country where he lives?

LUCY: The same. She was no sooner possessed of the last dear purchase of his ruin, but her avarice, insatiate as the grave,
65   demanded this horrid sacrifice. Barnwell's near relation and unsuspected virtue must give too easy means to seize the good man's treasure, whose blood must seal the dreadful secret, and prevent the terrors of her guilty fears.

BLUNT: Is it possible she could persuade him to do an act like
70   that! He is, by nature, honest, grateful, compassionate, and generous. And though his love and her artful persuasions have wrought him to practise what he most abhors; yet we all can witness for him with what reluctance he has still complied! So many tears he shed o'er each offence, as might, if
75   possible, sanctify theft, and make a merit of a crime.

LUCY: 'Tis true, at the naming the murder of his uncle, he started into rage; and, breaking from her arms, where she till then had held him with well dissembled love and false endearments, called her cruel, monster, devil; and told her she
80   was born for his destruction. She thought it not for her purpose to meet his rage with rage, but affected a most passionate fit of grief, railed at her fate, and cursed her wayward stars, that still her wants should force her to press him to act such deeds as she must needs abhor as well as he; but told
85   him necessity had no law and love no bounds; that therefore he never truly loved, but meant in his necessity to forsake

her. Then kneeled and swore, that since by his refusal he had given her cause to doubt his love, she never would see him more, unless, to prove it true, he robbed his uncle to supply her wants, and murdered him to keep it from discov-   90
ery.

BLUNT: I am astonished! What said he?

LUCY: Speechless he stood; but in his face you might have read that various passions tore his very soul. Oft he in anguish threw his eyes towards heaven, and then as often bent their   95
beams on her; then wept and groaned and beat his troubled breast; at length, with horror not to be expressed, he cried, "Thou cursed fair! have I not given dreadful proofs of love? What drew me from my youthful innocence to stain my then unspotted soul but love? What caused me to rob my worthy,   100
gentle master but cursed love? What makes me now a fugitive from his service, loathed by myself, and scorned by all the world, but love? What fills my eyes with tears, my soul with torture never felt on this side death before? Why love, love, love! And why, above all, do I resolve (for, tearing his   105
hair, he cried, I do resolve!) to kill my uncle?"

BLUNT: Was she not moved? It makes me weep to hear the sad relation.

LUCY: Yes, with joy that she had gained her point. She gave him no time to cool, but urged him to attempt it instantly.   110
He's now gone; if he performs it and escapes, there's more money for her; if not, he'll ne'er return, and then she's fairly rid of him.

BLUNT: 'Tis time the world was rid of such a monster.

LUCY: If we don't do our endeavors to prevent this murder, we   115
are as bad as she.

BLUNT: I'm afraid it is too late.

LUCY: Perhaps not. Her barbarity to Barnwell makes me hate her. We have run too great a length with her already. I did not think her or myself so wicked, as I find upon reflection   120
we are.

BLUNT: 'Tis true, we have all been too much so. But there is something so horrid in murder that all other crimes seem nothing when compared to that. I would not be involved in the guilt of that for all the world.   125

LUCY: Nor I, heaven knows; therefore let us clear ourselves by doing all that is in our power to prevent it. I have just thought of a way that, to me, seems probable. Will you join with me to detect this cursed design?

BLUNT: With all my heart. He who knows of a murder in-   130
tended to be committed and does not discover it, in the eye of the law and reason is a murderer.

LUCY: Let us lose no time; I'll acquaint you with the particulars as we go.

SCENE III

A Walk at Some Distance from a County Seat.

(*Enter* BARNWELL.)

BARNWELL: A dismal gloom obscures the face of day; either the sun has slipped behind a cloud, or journeys down the west of heaven with more than common speed to avoid the sight of what I'm doomed to act. Since I set forth on this accursed design, where'er I tread, methinks, the solid earth trembles   5
beneath my feet. Yonder limpid stream, whose hoary fall has made a natural cascade, as I passed by, in doleful accents seemed to murmur, "Murder." The earth, the air, the water,

seem concerned; but that's not strange, the world is pun-
10 ished, and nature feels the shock when Providence permits a
good man's fall! Just heaven! Then what should I be! for him
that was my father's only brother, and since his death has
been to me a father, who took me up an infant, and an orphan, reared me with tenderest care, and still indulged me
15 with most paternal fondness; yet here I stand avowed his destined murderer! I stiffen with horror at my own impiety; 'tis
yet unperformed. What if I quit my bloody purpose and fly
the place! (*Going, then stops.*) But whither, oh, whither,
shall I fly? My master's once friendly doors are ever shut
20 against me; and without money Millwood will never see me
more, and life is not to be endured without her! She's got
such firm possession of my heart, and governs there with
such despotic sway! Aye, there's the cause of all my sin and
sorrow. 'Tis more than love; 'tis the fever of the soul and
25 madness of desire. In vain does nature, reason, conscience,
all oppose it; the impetuous passion bears down all before it,
and drives me on to lust, to theft, and murder.—Oh conscience! feeble guide to virtue, who only shows us when we
go astray, but wants the power to stop us in our course.—Ha!
30 in yonder shady walk I see my uncle. He's alone. Now for my
disguise. (*Plucks out a visor.*) This is his hour of private meditation. Thus daily he prepares his soul for heaven, whilst I—
but what have I to do with heaven!—Ha! No struggles,
conscience.—
35 Hence! Hence remorse, and ev'ry thought that's good;
The storm that lust began must end in blood.

(*Puts on visor, draws a pistol, and exit.*)

SCENE IV

A *Close Walk in a Wood.*

(*Enter* UNCLE.)

UNCLE: If I were superstitious, I should fear some danger
lurked unseen, or death were nigh. A heavy melancholy
clouds my spirits; my imagination is filled with gashly forms
of dreary graves, and bodies changed by death, when the
5 pale lengthened visage attracts each weeping eye, and fills
the musing soul at once with grief and horror, pity and aversion. I will indulge the thought. The wise man prepares
himself for death by making it familiar to his mind. When
strong reflections hold the mirror near, and the living in the
10 dead behold their future selves, how does each inordinate
passion and desire cease or sicken at the view. The mind
scarce moves; the blood, curdling and chilled, creeps slowly
through the veins. Fixed, still, and motionless we stand, so
like the solemn object of our thoughts, we are almost at
15 present what we must be hereafter—till curiosity awakes the
soul and sets it on enquiry.

(*Enter* GEORGE BARNWELL *at a distance.*)

—O death, thou strange mysterious power, seen every day,
yet never understood but by the incommunicative dead,
what art thou? The extensive mind of man, that with a
20 thought circles the earth's vast globe, sinks to the center, or
ascends above the stars; that worlds exotic finds, or thinks
it finds, thy thick clouds attempts to pass in vain; lost and

---
3 **gashly** ghastly

bewildered in the horrid gloom, defeated she returns more
doubtful than before; of nothing certain, but of labor lost.

(*During this speech,* BARNWELL *sometimes presents the pistol,
and draws it back again; at last he drops it, at which his* UNCLE
starts, and draws his sword.)

BARNWELL: Oh, 'tis impossible!   25
UNCLE: A man so near me, armed and masked!
BARNWELL: Nay, then there's no retreat.

(*Plucks a poniard from his bosom, and stabs him.*)

UNCLE: Oh! I am slain! All-gracious heaven, regard the prayer
of thy dying servant! Bless with thy choicest blessings my
dearest nephew, forgive my murderer, and take my fleeting   30
soul to endless mercy!

(BARNWELL *throws off his mask, runs to him, and, kneeling by
him, raises and chafes him.*)

BARNWELL: Expiring saint! Oh, murdered, martyred uncle!
Lift up your dying eyes, and view your nephew in your murderer. Oh, do not look so tenderly upon me! Let indignation
lighten from your eyes, and blast me ere you die. By heaven,   35
he weeps in pity of my woes. Tears, tears, for blood! The
murdered, in the agonies of death, weeps for his murderer!
Oh, speak your pious purpose, pronounce my pardon then,
and take me with you!—He would, but cannot.—Oh, why,
with such fond affection do you press my murdering hand!   40
What! will you kiss me! (*Kisses him.*— UNCLE *groans and
dies.*) Life, that hovered on his lips but till he had sealed my
pardon, in that sigh expired. He's gone forever, and oh! I
follow.—(*Swoons away upon his* UNCLE's *dead body.*) Do I
still live to press the suffering bosom of the earth? Do I still   45
breathe, and taint with my infectious breath the wholesome
air? Let heaven, from its high throne, in justice or in mercy,
now look down on that dear murdered saint, and me the
murderer. And, if his vengeance spares, let pity strike and
end my wretched being. Murder the worst of crimes, and   50
parricide the worst of murders, and this the worst of parri-
cides! Cain, who stands on record from the birth of time,
and must to its last final period, as accursed, slew a brother
favored above him. Detested Nero, by another's hand, dispatched a mother, that he feared and hated. But I, with my   55
own hand, have murdered a brother, mother, father, and a
friend; most loving and beloved. This execrable act of mine's
without a parallel! Oh, may it ever stand alone!—the last of
murders, as it is the worst!
    The rich man thus, in torment and despair,   60
    Preferred his vain, but charitable prayer.
    The fool, his own soul lost, would fain be wise
    For others' good; but heaven his suit denies.
    By laws and means well known we stand or fall,
    And one eternal rule remains for all.   65

— ACT FOUR —

SCENE I

A *Room in* THOROWGOOD's *House.*

(*Enter* MARIA.)

MARIA: How falsely do they judge who censure or applaud, as
we're afflicted or rewarded here! I know I am unhappy, yet

cannot charge myself with any crime more than the common frailties of our kind that should provoke just heaven to mark me out for sufferings so uncommon and severe. Falsely to accuse ourselves, heaven must abhor; then it is just and right that innocence should suffer, for heaven must be just in all its ways. Perhaps by that we are kept from moral evils much worse than penal, or more improved in virtue; or may not the lesser ills that we sustain, be the means of greater good to others? Might all the joyless days and sleepless nights that I have passed, but purchase peace for thee—

> Thou dear, dear cause of all my grief and pain,
> Small were the loss, and infinite the gain;
> Though to the grave in secret love I pine,
> So life, and fame, and happiness were thine.

(Enter TRUEMAN.*)*

What news of Barnwell?

TRUEMAN: None. I have sought him with the greatest diligence, but all in vain.

MARIA: Does my father yet suspect the cause of his absenting himself?

TRUEMAN: All appeared so just and fair to him, it is not possible he ever should; but his absence will no longer be concealed. Your father's wise; and though he seems to harken to the friendly excuses I would make for Barnwell, yet I am afraid he regards 'em only as such, without suffering them to influence his judgment.

MARIA: How does the unhappy youth defeat all our designs to serve him. Yet I can never repent what we have done. Should he return, 'twill make his reconciliation with my father easier, and preserve him from future reproach from a malicious, unforgiving world.

(Enter THOROWGOOD *and* LUCY.*)*

THOROWGOOD: This woman here has given me a sad, and (bating some circumstances) too probable account of Barnwell's defection.

LUCY: I am sorry, sir, that my frank confession of my former unhappy course of life should cause you to suspect my truth on this occasion.

THOROWGOOD: It is not that; your confession has in it all the appearance of truth. *(To them.)* Among many other particulars, she informs me that Barnwell has been influenced to break his trust, and wrong me, at several times, of considerable sums of money; now, as I know this to be false, I would fain doubt the whole of her relation, too dreadful to be willingly believed.

MARIA: Sir, your pardon; I find myself on a sudden so indisposed, that I must retire. *(Aside.)* Providence opposes all attempts to save him. Poor ruined Barnwell! Wretched lost Maria!

(Exit MARIA.*)*

THOROWGOOD: How am I distressed on every side! Pity for that unhappy youth, fear for the life of a much valued friend—and then my child—the only joy and hope of my declining life. Her melancholy increases hourly and gives me painful apprehension of her loss.—Oh, Trueman! this person informs me that your friend, at the instigation of an impious woman, is gone to rob and murder his venerable uncle.

TRUEMAN: Oh, execrable deed! I am blasted with the horror of the thought.

LUCY: This delay may ruin all.

THOROWGOOD: What to do or think I know not; that he ever wronged me, I know is false; the rest may be so too—there's all my hope.

TRUEMAN: Trust not to that, rather suppose all true than lose a moment's time; even now the horrid deed may be a-doing—dreadful imagination! or it may be done, and we be vainly debating on the means to prevent what is already past.

THOROWGOOD: *(Aside.)* This earnestness convinces me that he knows more than he has yet discovered—What ho! Without there! who waits?

(Enter a Servant.)

Order the groom to saddle the swiftest horse, and prepare himself to set out with speed. An affair of life and death demands his diligence.—

(Exit Servant.)

(To LUCY.*)* For you, whose behavior on this occasion I have no time to commend as it deserves, I must engage your farther assistance. Return and observe this Millwood till I come. I have your directions, and will follow you as soon as possible.—

(Exit LUCY.*)*

Trueman, you, I am sure, would not be idle on this occasion,

(Exit THOROWGOOD.*)*

TRUEMAN: He only who is a friend can judge of my distress.

(Exit.)

SCENE II

MILLWOOD'*s House.*

(Enter MILLWOOD.*)*

MILLWOOD: I wish I knew the event of his design; the attempt without success would ruin him. Well! what have I to apprehend from that? I fear too much. The mischief being only intended, his friends, in pity of his youth, turn all their rage on me. I should have thought of that before. Suppose the deed done; then, and then only, I shall be secure. Or what if he returns without attempting it at all?

(Enter BARNWELL, *bloody.)*

But he is here, and I have done him wrong; his bloody hands show he has done the deed; but show he wants the prudence to conceal it.

BARNWELL: Where shall I hide me? Whither shall I fly to avoid the swift unerring hand of justice?

MILLWOOD: Dismiss those fears; though thousands had pursued you to the door, yet being entered here, you are safe as innocence. I have such a cavern, by art so cunningly contrived, that the piercing eyes of jealousy and revenge may search in vain, nor find the entrance to the safe retreat. There will I hide you if any danger's near.

BARNWELL: Oh, hide me from myself if it be possible, for while I bear my conscience in my bosom, though I were hid where man's eye never saw, nor light e'er dawned, 'twere all in vain. For oh! that inmate, that impartial judge, will try, convict, and sentence me for murder, and execute me with never-ending torments. Behold these hands all crimsoned o'er with my dear uncle's blood! Here's a sight to make a statue start with horror or turn a living man into a statue.

MILLWOOD: Ridiculous! Then it seems you are afraid of your own shadow; or what's less than a shadow, your conscience.

BARNWELL: Though to man unknown I did the accursed act, what can we hide from heaven's all-seeing eye?

MILLWOOD: No more of this stuff. What advantage have you made of his death, or what advantage may yet be made of it? Did you secure the keys of his treasure? Those no doubt were about him? What gold, what jewels, or what else of value have you brought me?

BARNWELL: Think you I added sacrilege to murder? Oh! had you seen him as his life flowed from him in a crimson flood, and heard him praying for me by the double name of nephew and of murderer—alas, alas! he knew not then that his nephew was his murderer—how would you have wished as I did, though you had a thousand years of life to come, to have given them all to have lengthened his one hour. But, being dead, I fled the sight of what my hands had done, nor could I, to have gained the empire of the world, have violated by theft his sacred corpse.

MILLWOOD: Whining, preposterous, canting villain! to murder your uncle, rob him of life, nature's first, last, dear prerogative, after which there's no injury—then fear to take what he no longer wanted! and bring to me your penury and guilt. Do you think I'll hazard my reputation, nay, my life, to entertain you?

BARNWELL: Oh! Millwood! This from thee? But I have done; if you hate me, if you wish me dead, then are you happy—for oh! 'tis sure my grief will quickly end me.

MILLWOOD: (Aside.) In his madness he will discover all, and involve me in his ruin; we are on a precipice from whence there's no retreat for both. Then to preserve myself— (Pauses.) There is no other way—'tis dreadful, but reflection comes too late when danger's pressing, and there's no room for choice. It must be done.

(Rings a bell.)

(Enter a Servant.)

MILLWOOD: Fetch me an officer and seize this villain; he has confessed himself a murderer. Should I let him escape, I justly might be thought as bad as he.

(Exit Servant.)

BARNWELL: Oh, Millwood! sure you do not, cannot mean it. Stop the messenger; upon my knees I beg you would call him back. 'Tis fit I die indeed, but not by you. I will this instant deliver myself into the hands of justice; indeed I will, for death is all I wish. But thy ingratitude so tears my wounded soul, 'tis worse ten thousand times than death with torture!

MILLWOOD: Call it what you will, I am willing to live; and live secure; which nothing but your death can warrant.

BARNWELL: If there be a pitch of wickedness that seats the author beyond the reach of vengeance, you must be secure. But what remains for me but a dismal dungeon, hard-galling fetters, an awful trial, and an ignominious death, justly to fall unpitied and abhorred?—after death to be suspended between heaven and earth, a dreadful spectacle, the warning

and horror of a gaping crowd. This I could bear, nay, wish not to avoid, had it but come from any hand but thine.

(Enter BLUNT, *Officer and Attendants*.)

MILLWOOD: Heaven defend me! Conceal a murderer! Here, sir, take this youth into your custody; I accuse him of murder and will appear to make good my charge.

(They seize him.)

BARNWELL: To whom, of what, or how shall I complain? I'll not accuse her; the hand of heaven is in it, and this the punishment of lust and parricide! Yet heaven, that justly cuts me off, still suffers her to live, perhaps to punish others. Tremendous mercy! So fiends are cursed with immortality to be the executioners of heaven—

> Be warned, ye youths, who see my sad despair,
> Avoid lewd women, false as they are fair,
> By reason guided, honest joys pursue.
> The fair, to honor, and to virtue true,
> Just to herself, will ne'er be false to you.
> By my example learn to shun my fate,
> (How wretched is the man who's wise too late!)
> Ere innocence, and fame, and life be lost,
> Here purchase wisdom cheaply, at my cost.

(Exeunt BARNWELL, *Officer, and Attendants*.)

MILLWOOD: Where's Lucy? Why is she absent at such a time?

BLUNT: Would I had been so too! Lucy will soon be here; and I hope to thy confusion, thou devil!

MILLWOOD: Insolent! This to me?

BLUNT: The worst that we know of the devil is that he first seduces to sin and then betrays to punishment.

(Exit BLUNT.)

MILLWOOD: They disapprove of my conduct then, and mean to take this opportunity to set up for themselves. My ruin is resolved; I see my danger, but scorn both it and them. I was not born to fall by such weak instruments.

(Going.)

(Enter THOROWGOOD.)

THOROWGOOD: Where is the scandal of her own sex, and curse of ours?

MILLWOOD: What means this insolence? Who do you seek?

THOROWGOOD: Millwood.

MILLWOOD: Well, you have found her then. I am Millwood.

THOROWGOOD: Then you are the most impious wretch that e'er the sun beheld.

MILLWOOD: From your appearance I should have expected wisdom and moderation, but your manners belie your aspect. What is your business here? I know you not.

THOROWGOOD: Hereafter you may know me better; I am Barnwell's master.

MILLWOOD: Then you are master to a villain, which, I think, is not much to your credit.

THOROWGOOD: Had he been as much above thy arts as my credit is superior to thy malice, I need not have blushed to own him.

MILLWOOD: My arts? I don't understand you, sir! If he has done amiss, what's that to me? Was he my servant, or yours? You should have taught him better.

THOROWGOOD: Why should I wonder to find such uncommon impudence in one arrived to such a height of wickedness! When innocence is banished, modesty soon follows. Know, sorceress, I'm not ignorant of any of the arts by which you first deceived the unwary youth. I know how, step by step, you've led him on, reluctant and unwilling, from crime to crime to this last horrid act, which you contrived and by your cursed wiles even forced him to commit.

MILLWOOD: (*Aside.*) Ha! Lucy has got the advantage, and accused me first; unless I can turn the accusation, and fix it upon her and Blunt, I am lost.

THOROWGOOD: Had I known your cruel design sooner, it had been prevented. To see you punished as the law directs is all that now remains. Poor satisfaction, for he, innocent as he is compared to you, must suffer too. But heaven, who knows our frame, and graciously distinguishes between frailty and presumption, will make a difference, though man cannot, who sees not the heart, but only judges by the outward action.

MILLWOOD: I find, sir, we are both unhappy in our servants. I was surprised at such ill treatment, without cause, from a gentleman of your appearance, and therefore too hastily returned it, for which I ask your pardon. I now perceive you have been so far imposed on as to think me engaged in a former correspondence with your servant, and, some way or other, accessory to his undoing.

THOROWGOOD: I charge you as the cause, the sole cause of all his guilt, and all his suffering, of all he now endures, and must endure, till a violent and shameful death shall put a dreadful period to his life and miseries together.

MILLWOOD: 'Tis very strange; but who's secure from scandal and detraction? So far from contributing to his ruin, I never spoke to him till since that fatal accident, which I lament as much as you. 'Tis true, I have a servant, on whose account he has of late frequented my house; if she has abused my good opinion of her, am I to blame? Hasn't Barnwell done the same by you?

THOROWGOOD: I hear you; pray go on.

MILLWOOD: I have been informed he had a violent passion for her, and she for him; but till now I always thought it innocent; I know her poor and given to expensive pleasures. Now who can tell but she may have influenced the amorous youth to commit this murder, to supply her extravagancies? It must be so. I now recollect a thousand circumstances that confirm it. I'll have her and a man servant that I suspect as an accomplice, secured immediately. I hope, sir, you will lay aside your ill-grounded suspicions of me, and join to punish the real contrivers of this bloody deed.

(*Offers to go.*)

THOROWGOOD: Madam, you pass not this way. I see your design, but shall protect them from your malice.

MILLWOOD: I hope you will not use your influence and the credit of your name to screen such guilty wretches. Consider, sir, the wickedness of persuading a thoughtless youth to such a crime.

THOROWGOOD: I do, and of betraying him when it was done.

MILLWOOD: That which you call betraying him, may convince you of my innocence. She who loves him, though she contrived the murder, would never have delivered him into the hands of justice, as I, struck with the horror of his crimes, have done.

THOROWGOOD: (*Aside.*) How should an unexperienced youth escape her snares? The powerful magic of her wit and form might betray the wisest to simple dotage and fire the blood that age had froze long since. Even I, that with just prejudice came prepared, had, by her artful story, been deceived, but that my strong conviction of her guilt makes even a doubt impossible.—Those whom subtly you would accuse, you know are your accusers; and—what proves unanswerably their innocence and your guilt—they accused you before the deed was done, and did all that was in their power to prevent it.

MILLWOOD: Sir, you are very hard to be convinced; but I have such a proof, which, when produced, will silence all objections.

(*Exit.*)

(*Enter* LUCY, TRUEMAN, BLUNT, *Officers, &c.*)

LUCY: Gentlemen, pray place yourselves, some on one side of that door, and some on the other; watch her entrance, and act as your prudence shall direct you.—This way—(*To* THOROWGOOD.) and note her behavior; I have observed her, she's driven to the last extremity, and is forming some desperate resolution. I guess at her design.

(*Enter* MILLWOOD *with a Pistol.* TRUEMAN *secures her.*)

TRUEMAN: Here thy power of doing mischief ends, deceitful, cruel, bloody woman!

MILLWOOD: Fool, hypocrite, villain!—man! thou can'st not call me that.

TRUEMAN: To call thee woman were to wrong the sex, thou devil!

MILLWOOD: That imaginary being is an emblem of thy cursed sex collected. A mirror, wherein each particular man may see his own likeness and that of all mankind!

TRUEMAN: Think not, by aggravating the fault of others, to extenuate thy own, of which the abuse of such uncommon perfections of mind and body is not the least.

MILLWOOD: If such I had, well may I curse your barbarous sex, who robbed me of 'em ere I knew their worth, then left me, too late, to count their value by their loss! Another and another spoiler came, and all my gain was poverty and reproach. My soul disdained, and yet disdains, dependence and contempt. Riches, no matter by what means obtained, I saw, secured the worst of men from both; I found it therefore necessary to be rich; and, to that end, I summoned all my arts. You call 'em wicked; be it so! They were such as my conversation with your sex had furnished me withal.

THOROWGOOD: Sure, none but the worst of men conversed with thee.

MILLWOOD: Men of all degrees and all professions I have known, yet found no difference but in their several capacities; all were alike wicked to the utmost of their power. In pride, contention, avarice, cruelty, and revenge, the reverend priesthood were my unerring guides. From suburb-magistrates, who live by ruined reputations, as the unhospitable natives of Cornwall do by shipwrecks, I

---

236 **surburb-magistrates** Magistrates outside the City were notoriously venal   238 **Cornwall . . . shipwrecks** The natives of Cornwall were notorious for plundering ships wrecked on their rocky coast

240 learned that to charge my innocent neighbors with my crimes was to merit their protection; for to screen the guilty is the less scandalous when many are suspected, and detraction, like darkness and death, blackens all objects and levels all distinction. Such are your venal magistrates, who favor none but such as, by their office, they are sworn to punish.

245 With them, not to be guilty is the worst of crimes; and large fees privately paid are every needful virtue.

THOROWGOOD: Your practice has sufficiently discovered your contempt of laws, both human and divine; no wonder then that you should hate the officers of both.

250 MILLWOOD: I know you, and I hate you all; I expect no mercy, and I ask for none. I followed my own inclinations, and that the best of you do every day. All actions seem alike natural and indifferent to man and beast, who devour, or are devoured, as they meet with others weaker or stronger than

255 themselves.

THOROWGOOD: What pity it is, a mind so comprehensive, daring, and inquisitive, should be a stranger to religion's sweet and powerful charms.

MILLWOOD: I am not fool enough to be an atheist, though I

260 have known enough of men's hypocrisy to make a thousand simple women so. Whatever religion is in itself, as practised by mankind it has caused the evils you say it was designed to cure. War, plague, and famine have not destroyed so many of the human race as this pretended piety has done, and with

265 such barbarous cruelty, as if the only way to honor heaven were to turn the present world into hell.

THOROWGOOD: Truth is truth, though from an enemy and spoke in malice. You bloody, blind, and superstitious bigots, how will you answer this?

270 MILLWOOD: What are your laws, of which you make your boast, but the fool's wisdom and the coward's valor—the instrument and screen of all your villainies, by which you punish in others what you act yourselves, or would have acted had you been in their circumstances? The judge who con-

275 demns the poor man for being a thief had been a thief himself had he been poor. Thus you go on deceiving and being deceived, harassing, plaguing, and destroying one another; but women are your universal prey.

Women, by whom you are, the source of joy,

280 With cruel arts you labor to destroy.
A thousand ways our ruin you pursue,
Yet blame in us those arts, first taught by you.
Oh, may, from hence, each violated maid,
By flattering, faithless, barb'rous man betrayed,

285 When robbed of innocence and virgin fame,
From your destruction raise a nobler name;
To right their sex's wrongs devote their mind,
And future Millwoods prove, to plague mankind.

— ACT FIVE —

SCENE I

A Room in a Prison.

(*Enter* THOROWGOOD, BLUNT *and* LUCY.)

THOROWGOOD: I have recommended to Barnwell a reverend divine whose judgment and integrity I am well acquainted with; nor has Millwood been neglected, but she, unhappy woman, still obstinate, refuses his assistance.

LUCY: This pious charity to the afflicted well becomes your 5 character; yet pardon me, sir, if I wonder you were not at their trial.

THOROWGOOD: I knew it was impossible to save him, and I and my family bear so great a part in his distress, that to have been present would have aggravated our sorrows without re- 10 lieving his.

BLUNT: It was mournful, indeed. Barnwell's youth and modest deportment as he passed drew tears from every eye. When placed at the bar and arraigned before the reverend judges, with many tears and interrupting sobs he confessed and ag- 15 gravated his offences, without accusing, or once reflecting on, Millwood, the shameless author of his ruin, who, dauntless and unconcerned, stood by his side, viewing with visible pride and contempt the vast assembly, who all with sympathizing sorrow wept for the wretched youth. Millwood, when 20 called upon to answer, loudly insisted upon her innocence, and made an artful and a bold defence; but finding all in vain, the impartial jury and the learned bench concurring to find her guilty, how did she curse herself, poor Barnwell, us, her judges, all mankind! But what could that avail? She was 25 condemned, and is this day to suffer with him.

THOROWGOOD: The time draws on; I am going to visit Barnwell, as you are Millwood.

LUCY: We have not wronged her, yet I dread this interview. She's proud, impatient, wrathful, and unforgiving. To be the 30 branded instruments of vengeance, to suffer in her shame, and sympathize with her in all she suffers, is the tribute we must pay for our former ill-spent lives, and long confederacy with her in wickedness.

THOROWGOOD: Happy for you it ended when it did. What you 35 have done against Millwood, I know, proceeded from a just abhorrence of her crimes, free from interest, malice, or revenge. Proselytes to virtue should be encouraged. Pursue your proposed reformation, and know me hereafter for your friend. 40

LUCY: This is a blessing as unhoped for as unmerited, but heaven, that snatched us from impending ruin, sure intends you as its instrument to secure us from apostasy.

THOROWGOOD: With gratitude to impute your deliverance to heaven is just. Many, less virtuously disposed than Barnwell 45 was, have never fallen in the manner he has done; may not such owe their safety rather to Providence than to themselves? With pity and compassion let us judge him. Great were his faults, but strong was the temptation. Let his ruin learn us diffidence, humanity and circumspection; for we, 50 who wonder at his fate—perhaps had we like him, been tried, like him, we had fallen, too.

SCENE II

A Dungeon, a Table and Lamp.

(BARNWELL *reading. Enter* THOROWGOOD.)

THOROWGOOD: See there the bitter fruits of passion's detested reign and sensual appetite indulged—severe reflections, penitence, and tears!

BARNWELL: (*Rising.*) My honored, injured master, whose goodness has covered me a thousand times with shame, for- 5 give this last unwilling disrespect. Indeed I saw you not.

THOROWGOOD: 'Tis well. I hope you were better employed in viewing of yourself; your journey's long, your time for

10 preparation almost spent. I sent a reverend divine to teach you to improve it and should be glad to hear of his success.

BARNWELL: The word of truth, which he recommended for my constant companion in this my sad retirement, has at length removed the doubts I labored under. From thence I've learned the infinite extent of heavenly mercy; that my of-
15 fences, though great, are not unpardonable; and that 'tis not my interest only, but my duty, to believe and to rejoice in that hope. So shall heaven receive the glory, and future pen-itents the profit of my example.

THOROWGOOD: Proceed!

20 BARNWELL: 'Tis wonderful that words should charm despair, speak peace and pardon to a murderer's conscience; but truth and mercy flow in every sentence, attended with force and energy divine. How shall I describe my present state of mind? I hope in doubt, and trembling I rejoice. I feel my
25 grief increase, even as my fears give way. Joy and gratitude now supply more tears than the horror and anguish of de-spair before.

THOROWGOOD: These are the genuine signs of true recep-tance, the only preparatory, the certain way to everlasting
30 peace. Oh, the joy it gives to see a soul formed and prepared for heaven! For this the faithful minister devotes himself to meditation, abstinence, and prayer, shunning the vain de-lights of sensual joys, and daily dies that others may live for-ever. For this he turns the sacred volumes o'er, and spends
35 his life in painful search of truth. The love of riches and the lust of power, he looks upon with just contempt and detesta-tion, who only counts for wealth the souls he wins, and whose highest ambition is to serve mankind. If the reward of all his pains be to preserve one soul from wandering or turn
40 one from the error of his ways, how does he then rejoice and own his little labors over-paid!

BARNWELL: What do I owe for all your generous kindness! But though I cannot, heaven can, and will, reward you.

THOROWGOOD: To see thee thus is joy too great for words.
45 Farewell! Heaven strengthen thee! Farewell!

BARNWELL: Oh, sir, there's something I could say, if my sad swelling heart would give me leave.

THOROWGOOD: Give it vent a while and try.

BARNWELL: I had a friend ('tis true I am unworthy), yet me
50 thinks your generous example might persuade—could I not see him once before I go from whence there's no return?

THOROWGOOD: He's coming, and as much thy friend as ever; but I'll not anticipate his sorrow. (*Aside.*) Too soon he'll see the sad effect of this contagious ruin. This torrent of domes-
55 tic misery bears too hard upon me; I must retire to indulge a weakness I find impossible to overcome.—Much loved and much lamented youth, farewell! Heaven strengthen thee! Eternally farewell!

BARNWELL: The best of masters and men, farewell! While I
60 live, let me not want your prayers!

THOROWGOOD: Thou shalt not. Thy peace being made with heaven, death's already vanquished; bear a little longer the pains that attend this transitory life, and cease from pain for-ever.

(*Exit.*)

65 BARNWELL: I find a power within that bears my soul above the fears of death, and, spite of conscious shame and guilt, gives me a taste of pleasure more than mortal.

(*Enter* TRUEMAN *and Keeper.*)

KEEPER: Sir, there's the prisoner.

(*Exit.*)

BARNWELL: Trueman! My friend, whom I so wished to see, yet now he's here I dare not look upon him. 70

TRUEMAN: Oh, Barnwell! Barnwell!

BARNWELL: Mercy! Mercy! gracious heaven! For death, but not for this, was I prepared!

TRUEMAN: What have I suffered since I saw you last! What pain has absence given me! But oh! to see thee thus! 75

BARNWELL: I know it is dreadful! I feel the anguish of thy gen-erous soul—but I was born to murder all who love me.

(*Both weep.*)

TRUEMAN: I came not to reproach you; I thought to bring you comfort. But I'm deceived, for I have none to give. I came to share thy sorrow, but cannot bear my own. 80

BARNWELL: My sense of guilt, indeed, you cannot know; 'tis what the good and innocent like you can ne'er conceive; but other griefs at present I have none but what I feel for you. In your sorrow I read you love me still, but yet methinks 'tis strange, when I consider what I am. 85

TRUEMAN: No more of that. I can remember nothing but thy virtues, thy honest, tender friendship, our former happy state and present misery. Oh, had you trusted me when first the fair seducer tempted you, all might have been prevented!

BARNWELL: Alas, thou know'st not what a wretch I've been! 90 Breach of friendship was my first and least offence. So far was I lost to goodness, so devoted to the author of my ruin, that had she insisted on my murdering thee, I think I should have done it.

TRUEMAN: Prithee, aggravate they faults no more. 95

BARNWELL: I think I should! Thus good and generous as you are, I should have murdered you!

TRUEMAN: We have not yet embraced, and may be inter-rupted. Come to my arms.

BARNWELL: Never, never will I taste such joys on earth; never 100 will I so soothe my just remorse. Are those honest arms and faithful bosom fit to embrace and to support a murderer? These iron fetters only shall clasp and flinty pavement bear me. (*Throwing himself on the ground.*) Even these too good for such a bloody monster! 105

TRUEMAN: Shall fortune sever those whom friendship joined! Thy miseries cannot lay thee so low, but love will find thee. (*Lies down by him.*) Upon this rugged couch then let us lie, for well it suits our most deplorable condition. Here will we offer to stern calamity, this earth the altar, and ourselves the 110 sacrifice. Our mutual groans shall echo to each other through the dreary vault. Our signs shall number the mo-ments as they pass, and mingling tears communicate such anguish as words were never made to express.

BARNWELL: Then be it so. (*Rising.*) Since you propose an in- 115 tercourse of woe, pour all your griefs into my breast, and in exchange take mine. (*Embracing.*) Where's now the anguish that you promised? You've taken mine, and make me no re-turn. Sure peace and comfort dwell within these arms, and sorrow can't approach me while I'm here! This, too, is the 120 work of heaven, who, having before spoke peace and pardon to me, now sends thee to confirm it. Oh, take, take some of the joy that overflows my breast!

125 TRUEMAN: I do, I do. Almighty Power, how have you made us capable to bear, at once, the extremes of pleasure and of pain?

(Enter Keeper.)

KEEPER: Sir.

TRUEMAN: I come.

(Exit Keeper.)

BARNWELL: Must you leave me? Death would soon have
130 parted us forever.

TRUEMAN: Oh, my Barnwell, there's yet another task behind. Again your heart must bleed for others' woes.

BARNWELL: To meet and part with you, I thought was all I had to do on earth! What is there more for me to do or suffer?

135 TRUEMAN: I dread to tell thee, yet it must be known. Maria—

BARNWELL: Our master's fair and virtuous daughter!

TRUEMAN: The same.

BARNWELL: No misfortune, I hope, has reached that lovely maid! Preserve her, heaven, from every ill, to show mankind
140 that goodness is your care.

TRUEMAN: Thy, thy misfortunes, my unhappy friend, have reached her. Whatever you and I have felt, and more, if more be possible, she feels for you.

BARNWELL: *(Aside.)* I know he doth abhor a lie, and would not
145 trifle with his dying friend. This is, indeed, the bitterness of death!

TRUEMAN: You must remember, for we all observed it, for some time past a heavy melancholy weighed her down. Disconsolate she seemed, and pined and languished from a
150 cause unknown; till hearing of your dreadful fate, the long stifled flame blazed out. She wept, she wrung her hands, and tore her hair, and in the transport of her grief discovered her own lost state, whilst she lamented yours.

BARNWELL: Will all the pain I feel restore thy case, lovely, un-
155 happy maid? *(Weeping.)* Why didn't you let me die and never know it?

TRUEMAN: It was impossible; she makes no secret of her passion for you, and is determined to see you ere you die. She waits for me to introduce her.

(Exit.)

160 BARNWELL: Vain busy thoughts be still! What avails it to think on what I might have been. I now am what I've made myself.

(Enter TRUEMAN *and* MARIA.*)*

TRUEMAN: Madam, reluctant I lead you to this dismal scene. This is the seat of misery and guilt. Here awful justice reserves her public victims. This is the entrance to shameful
165 death.

MARIA: To this sad place, then, no improper guest, the abandoned, lost Maria brings despair; and see the subject and the cause of all this world of woe! Silent and motionless he stands, as if his soul had quitted her abode, and the lifeless
170 form alone was left behind; yet that so perfect that beauty and death, ever at enmity, now seem united there.

BARNWELL: I groan, but murmur not. Just Heaven, I am your own; do with me what you please.

MARIA: Why are your streaming eyes still fixed below as
175 though thou'dst give the greedy earth thy sorrows, and rob me of my due? Were happiness within your power, you should bestow it where you pleased; but in your misery I must and will partake.

BARNWELL: Oh! say not so, but fly, abhor, and leave me to my fate. Consider what you are! How vast your fortune, and how
180 bright your fame! Have pity on your youth, your beauty, and unequalled virtue, for which so many noble peers have sighed in vain. Bless with your charms some honorable lord. Adorn with your beauty and, by your example, improve the English court, that justly claims such merit; so shall I
185 quickly be to you as though I had never been.

MARIA: When I forget you, I must be so, indeed. Reason, choice, virtue, all forbid it. Let women like Millwood, if there be more such women, smile in prosperity and in adversity forsake. Be it the pride of virtue to repair or to partake
190 the ruin such have made.

TRUEMAN: Lovely, ill-fated maid! Was there ever such generous distress before? How must this pierce his grateful heart and aggravate his woes!

BARNWELL: Ere I knew guilt or shame, when fortune smiled,
195 and when my youthful hopes were at the highest—if then to have raised my thoughts to you had been presumption in me, never to have been pardoned, think how much beneath yourself you condescend to regard me now.

MARIA: Let her blush, who, professing love, invades the free-
200 dom of your sex's choice and meanly sues in hopes of a return. Your inevitable fate hath rendered hope impossible as vain. Then why should I fear to avow a passion so just and so disinterested?

TRUEMAN: If any should take occasion from Millwood's
205 crimes to libel the best and fairest part of the creation, here let them see their error. The most distant hopes of such a tender passion from so bright a maid might add to the happiness of the most happy and make the greatest proud. Yet here
210 'tis lavished in vain. Though by the rich present the generous donor is undone, he on whom it is bestowed receives no benefit.

BARNWELL: So the aromatic spices of the East, which all the living covet and esteem, are with unavailing kindness wasted
215 on the dead.

MARIA: Yes, fruitless is my love, and unavailing all my sighs and tears. Can they save thee from approaching death, from such a death? Oh, terrible idea! What is her misery and distress, who sees the first, last object of her love, for whom
220 alone she'd live, for whom she'd die a thousand, thousand deaths if it were possible, expiring in her arms? Yet she is happy, when compared to me. Were millions of words mine, I'd gladly give them in exchange for her condition. The most consummate woe is light to mine. The last of curses to other
225 miserable maids is all I ask; and that's denied me.

TRUEMAN: Time and reflection cure all ills.

MARIA: All but this; his dreadful catastrophe virtue herself abhors. To give a holiday to suburb slaves, and, passing, entertain the savage herd who, elbowing each other for a sight,
230 pursue and press upon him like his fate. A mind with piety and resolution armed may smile on death. But public ignominy! everlasting shame! shame the death of souls! to die a thousand times and yet survive even death itself in neverdying infamy, is this to be endured? Can I, who live in him,

---

228 **passing** through the City on his way to execution

235 and must each hour of my devoted life feel all these woes renewed—can I endure this!

TRUEMAN: Grief has impaired her spirits; she pants as in the
agonies of death.

BARNWELL: Preserve her, heaven, and restore her peace, nor
240 let her death be added to my crimes! *(Bell tolls.)* I am summoned to my fate.

(Enter Keeper.)

KEEPER: The officers attend you, sir. Mrs. Millwood is already
summoned.

BARNWELL: Tell 'em I'm ready.—And now, my friend, fare-
245 well. *(Embracing.)* Support and comfort the best you can
this mourning fair. No more! Forget not to pray for me—
(Turning to MARIA.*)* Would you, bright excellence, permit
me the honor of a chaste embrace, the last happiness this
world could give were mine. *(She inclines towards him; they*
250 *embrace.)* Exalted goodness! Oh, turn your eyes from earth
and me to heaven, where virtue like yours is ever heard. Pray
for the peace of my departing soul.—Early my race of
wickedness began and soon has reached the summit. Ere nature has finished her work, and stamped me man, just at the
255 time that others begin to stray, my course is finished!
Though short my span of life, and few my days, yet count my
crimes for years, and I have lived whole ages. Justice and
mercy are in heaven the same. Its utmost severity is mercy to
the whole, thereby to cure man's folly and presumption,
260 which else would render even infinite mercy vain and ineffectual. Thus justice in compassion to mankind cuts off a
wretch like me, by one such example to secure thousands
from future ruin.

If any youth, like you, in future times,
265 Shall mourn my fate, though he abhor my crimes;
Or tender maid, like you, my tale shall hear,
And to my sorrows give a pitying tear:
To each such melting eye, and throbbing heart,
Would gracious heaven this benefit impart,
270 Never to know my guilt, nor feel my pain;
Then must you own, you ought not to complain;
Since you nor weep, nor shall I die, in vain.

(Exeunt Keeper and BARNWELL.*)*

(Enter BLUNT *and* LUCY.*)*

LUCY: Heart-breaking sight! O wretched, wretched Millwood!

TRUEMAN: You came from her then—how is she disposed to
275 meet her fate?

BLUNT: Who can describe unalterable woe?

---

264 **like you** pointing into the audience

LUCY: She goes to death encompassed with horror, loathing
life, and yet afraid to die; no tongue can tell her anguish and
despair.

TRUEMAN: Heaven be better to her than her fears; may she 280
prove a warning to others, a monument of mercy in herself.

LUCY: O sorrow insupportable! Break, break, my heart!

TRUEMAN: In vain
With bleeding hearts and weeping eyes we show
A human gen'rous sense of others' woe; 285
Unless we mark what drew their ruin on,
And by avoiding that, prevent our own.

— EPILOGUE —
WRITTEN BY COLLEY CIBBER, ESQ. AND SPOKE
BY MRS. CIBBER

Since Fate has robbed me of the hopeless youth,
For whom my heart had hoarded up its truth;
By all the laws of love and honor, now,
I'm free again to choose—and one of you.

But soft! With caution first I'll round me peep; 5
Maids, in my case, should look before they leap.
Here's choice enough, of various sorts and hue,
The cit, the wit, the rake cocked up in cue,
The fair, spruce mercer, and the tawny Jew.

Suppose I search the sober gallery. No, 10
There's none but prentices, and cuckolds all a row;
And these, I doubt, are those that make 'em so.

(Points to the boxes.)

'Tis very well, enjoy the jest. But you,
Fine powdered sparks, nay, I'm told 'tis true,
Your happy spouses—can make cuckolds too. 15
'Twixt you and them, the diff'rence this perhaps,
The cit's ashamed whene'er his duck he traps;
But you, when madam's tripping, let her fall,
Cock up your hats, and take no shame at all.

What if some favored poet I could meet, 20
Whose love would lay his laurels at my feet?
No,—painted passion real love abhors,—
His flame would prove the suit of creditors.

Not to detain you then with longer pause,
In short; my heart to this conclusion draws, 25
I yield it to the hand, that's loudest in applause.

---

epilogue **Written . . . Mrs. Cibber** Mrs. Cibber played the role of
Maria in the first production   8 **cocked up in cue** with hat tipped over
the queue of his wig   9 **tawny** yellow, referring to the yellow head
dress, which Jews had been compelled to wear   23 **His flame . . .**
creditors The poet would be seeking a means of support

CRITICAL CONTEXTS

JOHN DRYDEN
(1631–1700)

"PREFACE TO
TROILUS AND
CRESSIDA,
CONTAINING THE
GROUNDS OF
CRITICISM IN
TRAGEDY"
(1679)

EDITED BY
ARTHUR C. KIRSCH

John Dryden is the most important English critic and poet of the late seventeenth century; he was appointed poet laureate and royal historiographer in 1668 and was also the author of many plays, both comedies and heroic tragedies. In 1679, he wrote an adaptation of Shakespeare's Troilus and Cressida, *and in his "Preface" to the play Dryden argues for neoclassical principles of unity and decorum.*

The poet Æschylus was held in the same veneration by the Athenians of after ages as Shakespeare is by us; and Longinus has judged, in favor of him, that he had a noble boldness of expression, and that his imaginations were lofty and heroic; but, on the other side, Quintilian affirms that he was daring to extravagance. 'Tis certain that he affected pompous words, and that his sense too often was obscured by figures. Notwithstanding these imperfections, the value of his writings after his decease was such that his countrymen ordained an equal reward to those poets who could alter his plays to be acted on the theater, with those whose productions were wholly new, and of their own. The case is not the same in England; though the difficulties of altering are greater, and our reverence for Shakespeare much more just, than that of the Grecians for Æschylus. In the age of that poet, the Greek tongue was arrived to its full perfection; they had then amongst them an exact standard of writing and of speaking. The English language is not capable of such a certainty; and we are at present so far from it that we are wanting in the very foundation of it, a perfect grammar. Yet it must be allowed to the present age that the tongue in general is so much refined since Shakespeare's time that many of his words, and more of his phrases, are scarce intelligible. And of those which we understand, some are ungrammatical, others coarse; and his whole style is so pestered with figurative expressions, that it is as affected as it is obscure. 'Tis true, that in his later plays he had worn off somewhat of the rust; but the tragedy which I have undertaken to correct was, in all probability, one of his first endeavors on the stage.[1]

The original story was written by one Lollius, a Lombard, in Latin verse, and translated by Chaucer into English; intended, I suppose, a satire on the inconstancy of women: I find nothing of it among the Ancients; not so much as the name Cressida once mentioned. Shakespeare (as I hinted), in the apprenticeship of his writing, modeled it into that play which is now called by the name of *Troilus and Cressida*; but so lamely is it left to us, that it is not divided into acts; which fault I ascribe to the actors who printed it after Shakespeare's death; and that too so carelessly, that a more uncorrect copy I never saw. For the play itself, the author seems to have begun it with some fire; the characters of Pandarus and Thersites are promising enough; but as if he grew weary of his task, after an entrance or two, he lets 'em fall: and the later part of the tragedy is nothing but a confusion of drums and trumpets, excursions and alarms. The chief persons, who give name to the tragedy, are left alive; Cressida is false, and is not punished. Yet after all, because the play was Shakespeare's, and that there appeared in some places of it the admirable genius of the author, I undertook to remove that heap of rubbish under which many excellent thoughts lay wholly buried. Accordingly, I new modeled the plot; threw out many unnecessary persons; improved those characters which were begun and left unfinished: as Hector, Troilus, Pandarus, and Thersites; and added that of Andromache. After this I made, with no small trouble, an order and connection of all the scenes; removing them from the places where they were inartificially set; and though it was impossible to keep 'em all unbroken, because the scene must be sometimes in the city and sometimes in the camp, yet I have so ordered them that there is a coherence of 'em with one another, and a dependence on the main design: no leaping from Troy to the Grecian tents, and thence back again in the same act; but a due proportion of time allowed for every motion. I need not say that I have refined his language, which before was obsolete; but I am willing to acknowledge that as I have often drawn his English nearer to our times, so I have sometimes conformed my own to his; and consequently, the language is not altogether so pure as it is significant. The scenes of Pandarus and Cressida, of Troilus and

---

[1] Actually, *Troilus and Cressida*, which was probably written around 1602, came at the mid-point of Shakespeare's career.

Pandarus, of Andromache with Hector and the Trojans, in the second act, are wholly new; together with that of Nestor and Ulysses with Thersites, and that of Thersites with Ajax and Achilles. I will not weary my reader with the scenes which are added of Pandarus and the lovers, in the third; and those of Thersites, which are wholly altered; but I cannot omit the last scene in it, which is almost half the act, betwixt Troilus and Hector. The occasion of raising it was hinted to me by Mr. Betterton: the contrivance and working of it was my own. They who think to do me an injury by saying that it is an imitation of the scene betwixt Brutus and Cassius, do me an honor by supposing I could imitate the incomparable Shakespeare; but let me add that if Shakespeare's scene, or that faulty copy of it in *Amintor and Melantius*, had never been, yet Euripides had furnished me with an excellent example in his *Iphigenia*, between Agamemnon and Menelaus; and from thence, indeed, the last turn of it is borrowed.[2] The occasion which Shakespeare, Euripides, and Fletcher have all taken is the same; grounded upon friendship: and the quarrel of two virtuous men, raised by natural degrees to the extremity of passion, is conducted in all three to the declination of the same passion, and concludes with a warm renewing of their friendship. But the particular groundwork which Shakespeare has taken is incomparably the best; because he has not only chosen two of the greatest heroes of their age, but has likewise interested the liberty of Rome, and their own honors who were the redeemers of it, in this debate. And if he has made Brutus, who was naturally a patient man, to fly into excess at first, let it be remembered in his defense that, just before, he has received the news of Portia's death; whom the poet, on purpose neglecting a little chronology, supposes to have died before Brutus, only to give him an occasion of being more easily exasperated. Add to this that the injury he had received from Cassius had long been brooding in his mind; and that a melancholy man, upon consideration of an affront, especially from a friend, would be more eager in his passion than he who had given it, though naturally more choleric.

Euripides, whom I have followed, has raised the quarrel betwixt two brothers who were friends. The foundation of the scene was this: the Grecians were windbound at the port of Aulis, and the oracle had said that they could not sail, unless Agamemnon delivered up his daughter to be sacrificed: he refuses; his brother Menelaus urges the public safety; the father defends himself by arguments of natural affection, and hereupon they quarrel. Agamemnon is at last convinced, and promises to deliver up Iphigenia, but so passionately laments his loss that Menelaus is grieved to have been the occasion of it and, by a return of kindness, offers to intercede for him with the Grecians, that his daughter might not be sacrificed. But my friend Mr. Rymer has so largely, and with so much judgment, described this scene, in comparing it with that of Melantius and Aminton, that it is superfluous to say more of it; I only named the heads of it, that any reasonable man might judge it was from thence I modeled my scene betwixt Troilus and Hector. I will conclude my reflections on it with a passage of Longinus, concerning Plato's imitation of Homer: "We ought not to regard a good imitation as a theft, but as a beautiful idea of him who undertakes to imitate, by forming himself on the invention and the work of another man; for he enters into the lists like a new wrestler, to dispute the prize with the former champion. This sort of emulation, says Hesiod, is honorable, 'this strife is wholesome to man,'[3] when we combat for victory with a hero, and are not without glory even in our overthrow. Those great men whom we propose to ourselves as patterns of our imitation serve us as a torch, which is lifted up before us to enlighten our passage; and often elevate our thoughts as high as the conception we have of our author's genius."[4]

I have been so tedious in three acts that I shall contract myself in the two last. The beginning scenes of the fourth act are either added or changed wholly by me; the middle of it is Shakespeare altered, and mingled with my own; three or four of the last scenes are altogether new. And the whole fifth act, both the plot and the writing, are my own additions.

But having written so much for imitation of what is excellent, in that part of the preface which related only to myself, methinks it would neither be unprofitable nor unpleasant to inquire how far

---

[2] The comparison of the quarrels between Amintor and Melantius in Beaumont and Fletcher's *Maid's Tragedy* and Agamemnon and Menelaus in Euripides's *Iphigenia in Aulis* had already been made by Rymer in his *Tragedies of the Last Age* (1678), as Dryden acknowledges in the following paragraph.

[3] "ἀγαθὴ δ' ἔρις ἐστὶ βροτοῖσιν" (*Works and Days*, 1.24).

[4] *On the Sublime*, xiii. 4.

we ought to imitate our own poets, Shakespeare and Fletcher, in their tragedies: and this will occasion another inquiry, how those two writers differ between themselves. But since neither of these questions can be solved unless some measures be first taken by which we may be enabled to judge truly of their writings, I shall endeavor, as briefly as I can, to discover the grounds and reason of all criticism, applying them in this place only to tragedy. Aristotle with his interpreters, and Horace, and Longinus, are the authors to whom I owe my lights; and what part soever of my own plans, or of this, which no mending could make regular, shall fall under the condemnation of such judges, it would be impudence in me to defend. I think it no shame to retract my errors, and am well pleased to suffer in the cause, if the art may be improved at my expense: I therefore proceed to

THE GROUNDS OF CRITICISM IN TRAGEDY

Tragedy is thus defined by Aristotle (omitting what I thought unnecessary in his definition). 'Tis an imitation of one entire, great, and probable action; not told, but represented; which, by moving in us fear and pity, is conducive to the purging of those two passions in our minds. More largely thus, tragedy describes or paints an action, which action must have all the proprieties above named. First, it must be one or single, that is, it must not be a history of one man's life; suppose of Alexander the Great, or Julius Caesar, but one single action of theirs. This condemns all Shakespeare's historical plays, which are rather chronicles represented than tragedies, and all double action of plays. As to avoid a satire upon others, I will make bold with my own *Marriage a-la-Mode*, where there are manifestly two actions, not depending on one another: but in *Oedipus* there cannot properly be said to be two actions, because the love of Adrastus and Eurydice has a necessary dependence on the principal design, into which it is woven. The natural reason of rule is plain; for two different independent actions distract the attention and concernment of the audience, and consequently destroy the intention of the poet: if his business be to move terror and pity, and one of his actions be comical, the other tragical, the former will divert the people, and utterly make void his greater purpose. Therefore, as in perspective, so in tragedy, there must be a point of sight in which all the lines terminate; otherwise the eye wanders, and the work is false. This was the practice of the Grecian stage. But Terrence made an innovation in the Roman: all his plays have double actions; for it was his custom to translate two Greek comedies, and to weave them into one of his, yet so that both the actions were comical, and one was principal, the other but secondary or subservient. And this has obtained on the English stage, to give us the pleasure of variety.

As the action ought to be one, it ought, as such, to have order in it, that is, to have a natural beginning, a middle, and an end. A natural beginning, says Aristotle, is that which could not necessarily have been placed after another thing, and so of the rest. This consideration will arraign all plays after the new model of Spanish plots, where accident is heaped upon accident, and that which is first might as reasonably be last: an inconvenience not to be remedied but by making one accident naturally produce another, otherwise 'tis a farce and not a play. Of this nature is the *Slighted Maid*,[5] where there is no scene in the first act which might not by as good reason be in the fifth. And if the action ought to be one, the tragedy ought likewise to conclude with the action of it. Thus in *Mustapha*,[6] the play should naturally have ended with the death of Zanger, and not have given us the grace cup after dinner of Solyman's divorce from Roxolana.

The following properties of the action are so easy that they need not my explaining. It ought to be great, and to consist of great persons, to distinguish it from comedy, where the action is trivial, and the persons of inferior rank. The last quality of the action is that it ought to be probable, as well as admirable and great. 'Tis not necessary that there should be historical truth in it; but always necessary that there should be a likeness of truth, something that is more than barely possible, *probable* being that which succeeds or happens oftener than it misses. To invent therefore a probability, and to make it wonderful, is the most difficult undertaking in the art of poetry; for that which is not wonderful is not great; and that which is not probable will not delight a reasonable audience. This action, thus described, must be represented and not told, to distinguish dramatic poetry from epic: but I hasten to the end or scope of tragedy, which is to rectify or purge our passions, fear and pity.

To instruct delightfully is the general end of all poetry. Philosophy instructs, but it performs its work by precept: which is not delightful, or not so delightful as example. To purge the passions by

---

[5] By Sir Robert Stapylton (1663).
[6] By Roger Boyle, Earl of Orrery (first performed in 1665).

example is therefore the particular instruction which belongs to tragedy. Rapin, a judicious critic, has observed from Aristotle that pride and want of commiseration are the most predominant vices in mankind: therefore, to cure us of these two, the inventors of tragedy have chosen to work upon two other passions, which are fear and pity. We are wrought to fear by their setting before our eyes some terrible example of misfortune, which happened to persons of the highest quality; for such an action demonstrates to us that no condition is privileged from the turns of fortune; this must of necessity cause terror in us, and consequently abate our pride. But when we see that the most virtuous, as well as the greatest, are not exempt from such misfortunes, that consideration moves pity in us, and insensibly works us to be helpful to, and tender over, the distressed, which is the noblest and most god-like of moral virtues. Here 'tis observable that it is absolutely necessary to make a man virtuous, if we desire he should be pitied: we lament not, but detest, a wicked man; we are glad when we behold his crimes are punished, and that poetical justice[7] is done upon him. Euripides was censured by the critics of his time for making his chief characters too wicked: for example, Phaedra, though she loved her son-in-law with reluctancy, and that it was a curse upon her family for offending Venus, yet was thought too ill a pattern for the stage. Shall we therefore banish all characters of villainy? I confess I am not of that opinion; but it is necessary that the hero of the play be not a villain; that is, the characters which should move our pity ought to have virtuous inclinations, and degrees of moral goodness in them. As for a perfect character of virtue, it never was in nature, and therefore there can be no imitation of it; but there are allays of frailty to be allowed for the chief persons, yet so that the good which is in them shall outweigh the bad, and consequently leave room for punishment on the one side, and pity on the other.

After all, if anyone will ask me whether a tragedy cannot be made upon any other grounds than those of exciting pity and terror in us, Bossu,[8] the best of modern critics, answers thus in general: that all excellent arts, and particularly that of poetry, have been invented and brought to perfection by men of a transcendent genius; and that therefore they who practice afterwards the same arts are obliged to tread in their footsteps, and to search in their writings the foundation of them; for it is not just that new rules should destroy the authority of the old. But Rapin writes more particularly thus:[9] that no passions in a story are so proper to move our concernment as fear and pity; and that it is from our concernment we receive our pleasure, is undoubted; when the soul becomes agitated with fear for one character, or hope for another, then it is that we are pleased in tragedy by the interest which we take in their adventures.

Here, therefore, the general answer may be given to the first question, how far we ought to imitate Shakespeare and Fletcher in their plots: namely, that we ought to follow them so far only as they have copied the excellencies of those who invented and brought to perfection dramatic poetry: those things only excepted which religion, customs of countries, idioms of languages, etc., have altered in the superstructures, but not in the foundation of the design.

How defective Shakespeare and Fletcher have been in all their plots, Mr. Rymer has discovered in his criticisms: neither can we who follow them be excused from the same or greater errors; which are the more unpardonable in us, because we want their beauties to countervail our faults. The best of their designs, the most approaching to antiquity, and the most conducing to move pity, is the *King and No King*; which, if the farce of Bessus were thrown away, is of that inferior sort of tragedies which end with a prosperous event. 'Tis probably derived from the story of Oedipus, with the character of Alexander the Great, in his extravagancies, given to Arbaces. The taking of this play, amongst many others, I cannot wholly ascribe to the excellency of the action; for I find it moving when it is read: 'tis true, the faults of the plot are so evidently proved that they can no longer be denied. The beauties of it must therefore lie either in the lively touches of the passion: or we must conclude, as I think we may, that even in imperfect plots there are less degrees of nature, by which some faint emotions of pity and terror are raised in us: as a less engine will raise a less proportion of weight, though not so much as one of Archimedes' making; for nothing can move our nature, but

---

[7] A phrase first coined by Rymer in *The Tragedies of the Last Age*.
[8] Le Bossu, author of *Traité du poème épique* (1675).
[9] In *Réflexions sur la poétique d'Aristote* (1674).

by some natural reason, which works upon passions. And since we acknowledge the effect, there must be something in the cause.

The difference between Shakespeare and Fletcher in their plotting seems to be this: that Shakespeare generally moves more terror, and Fletcher more compassion. For the first had a more masculine, a bolder and more fiery genius; the second, a more soft and womanish. In the mechanic beauties of the plot, which are the observation of the three unities, time, place, and action, they are both deficient; but Shakespeare most. Ben Jonson reformed those errors in his comedies, yet one of Shakespeare's was regular before him; which is, *The Merry Wives of Windsor*. For what remains concerning the design, you are to be referred to our English critic. That method which he has prescribed to raise it from mistake, or ignorance of the crime, is certainly the best, though 'tis not the only: for amongst all the tragedies of Sophocles, there is but one, *Oedipus*, which is wholly built after that model.

After the plot, which is the foundation of the play, the next thing to which we ought to apply our judgment is the manners, for now the poet comes to work above ground: the ground-work indeed is that which is most necessary, as that upon which depends the firmness of the whole fabric; yet it strikes not the eye so much as the beauties or imperfections of the manners, the thoughts, and the expressions.

The first rule which Bossu prescribes to the writer of an heroic poem, and which holds too by the same reason in all dramatic poetry, is to make the moral of the work, that is, to lay down to yourself what that precept of morality shall be, which you would insinuate into the people; as namely, Homer's (which I have copied in my *Conquest of Granada*) was, that union preserves a commonwealth, and discord destroys it; Sophocles, in his *Oedipus*, that no man is to be accounted happy before his death. 'Tis the moral that directs the whole action of the play to one center; and that action or fable is the example built upon the moral, which confirms the truth of it to our experience: when the fable is designed, then and not before, the persons are to be introduced with their manners, characters, and passions.

The manners in a poem are understood to be those inclinations, whether natural or acquired, which move and carry us to actions, good, bad, or indifferent, in a play; or which incline the persons to such or such actions. I have anticipated part of this discourse already, in declaring that a poet ought not to make the manners perfectly good in his best persons; but neither are they to be more wicked in any of his characters than necessity requires. To produce a villain, without other reason than a natural inclination to villainy is, in poetry, to produce an effect without a cause; and to make him more a villain than he has just reason to be, is to make an effect which is stronger than the cause.

The manners arise from many causes; and are either distinguished by complexion, as choleric and phlegmatic, or by the differences of age or sex, of climates, or quality of the persons, or their present condition. They are likewise to be gathered from the several virtues, vices, or passions, and many other commonplaces which a poet must be supposed to have learned from natural philosophy, ethics, and history; of all which whosoever is ignorant, does not deserve the name of poet.

But as the manners are useful in this art, they may be all comprised under these general heads: first, they must be apparent; that is, in every character of the play, some inclinations of the person must appear: and these are shown in the actions and discourse. Secondly, the manners must be suitable, or agreeing to the persons; that is, to the age, sex, dignity, and the other general heads of manners: thus, when a poet has given the dignity of a king to one of his persons, in all his actions and speeches, that person must discover majesty, magnanimity, and jealousy of power, because these are suitable to the general manners of a king. The third property of manners is resemblance; and this is founded upon the particular characters of men, as we have them delivered to us by relation or history; that is, when a poet has the known character of this or that man before him, he is bound to represent him such, at least not contrary to that which fame has reported him to have been. Thus, it is not a poet's choice to make Ulysses choleric, or Achilles patient, because Homer has described 'em quite otherwise. Yet this is a rock on which ignorant writers daily split; and the absurdity is as monstrous as if a painter should draw a coward running from a battle, and tell us it was the picture of Alexander the Great.

The last property of manners is that they be constant and equal, that is, maintained the same through the whole design: thus, when Virgil had once given the name of *pious* to Æneas, he was bound to show him such, in all his words and actions through the whole poem. All these properties

Horace has hinted to a judicious observer: "1. you must mark the manners of each age; 2. or follow tradition; 3. or create your own convention; 4. let each character remain constant and consistent with itself."[10]

From the manners, the characters of persons are derived; for indeed the characters are no other than the inclinations, as they appear in the several persons of the poem; a character being thus defined, that which distinguishes one man from another. Not to repeat the same things over again which have been said of the manners, I will only add what is necessary here. A character, or that which distinguishes one man from all others, cannot be supposed to consist of one particular virtue, or vice, or passion only; but 'tis a composition of qualities which are not contrary to one another in the same person; thus the same man may be liberal and valiant, but not liberal and covetous; so in a comical character, or humour (which is an inclination to this or that particular folly), Falstaff is a liar, and a coward, a glutton, and a buffoon, because all these qualities may agree in the same man; yet it is still to be observed that one virtue, vice, and passion ought to be shown in every man, as predominant over all the rest; as covetousness in Crassus, love of his country in Brutus; and the same in characters which are feigned.

The chief character or hero in a tragedy, as I have already shown, ought in prudence to be such a man who has so much more in him of virtue than of vice, that he may be left amiable to the audience, which otherwise cannot have any concernment for his sufferings; and 'tis on this one character that the pity and terror must be principally, if not wholly, founded—a rule which is extremely necessary, and which none of the critics that I know have fully enough discovered to us. For terror and compassion work but weakly when they are divided into many persons. If Creon had been the chief character in *Oedipus*, there had neither been terror nor compassion moved; but only detestation of the man and joy for his punishment; if Adrastus and Eurydice had been made more appealing characters, then the pity had been divided, and lessened on the part of Oedipus: but making Oedipus the best and bravest person, and even Jocasta but an underpart to him, his virtues and the punishment of his fatal crime drew both the pity and the terror to himself.

By what had been said of the manners, it will be easy for a reasonable man to judge whether the characters be truly or falsely drawn in a tragedy; for if there be no manners appearing in the characters, no concernment for the persons can be raised; no pity or horror can be moved, but by vice or virtue; therefore, without them, no person can have any business in the play. If the inclinations be obscure, 'tis a sign the poet is in the dark, and knows not what manner of man he presents to you; and consequently you can have no idea, or very imperfect, of that man; nor can judge what resolutions he ought to take; or what words or actions are proper for him. Most comedies made up of accidents or adventures are liable to fall into this error; and tragedies with many turns are subject to it; for the manners never can be evident where the surprises of fortune take up all the business of the stage; and where the poet is more in pain to tell you what happened to such a man than what he was. 'Tis one of the excellencies of Shakespeare that the manners of his persons are generally apparent, and you see their bent and inclinations. Fletcher comes far short of him in this, as indeed he does almost in everything: there are but glimmerings of manners in most of his comedies, which run upon adventures: and in his tragedies, *Rollo, Otto,* the *King and No King, Melantius,*[11] and many others of his best, are but pictures shown you in the twilight; you know not whether they resemble vice or virtue, and they are either good, bad, or indifferent, as the present scene requires it. But of all poets, this commendation is to be given to Ben Jonson, that the manners even of the most inconsiderable persons in his plays are everywhere apparent.

By considering the second quality of manners, which is that they be suitable to the age, quality, country, dignity, etc., of the character, we may likewise judge whether a poet has followed nature. In this kind, Sophocles and Euripides have more excelled among the Greeks than Æschylus; and Terence more than Plautus among the Romans. Thus Sophocles gives to Oedipus the true qualities of a king, in both those plays which bear his name; but in the latter, which is the *Oedipus Colonœus,* he lets fall on purpose his tragic style; his hero speaks not in the arbitrary tone, but remembers, in the softness of his complaints, that he is an unfortunate blind old man, that he is banished from his

---

[10] "*1. notandi sunt tibi mores; 2. aut famam sequere; 3. aut sibi convenientia finge; 4. servetur ad imum, qualis ab incepto processerit, et sibi constet*" (*Ars poetica,* ll. 156, 119, 126–127).

[11] Otto is Rollo's brother; Melantius is a character in *The Maid's Tragedy.*

country, and persecuted by his next relations. The present French poets are generally accused that wheresoever they lay the scene, or in whatsoever age, the manners of their heroes are wholly French. Racine's Bajazet is bred at Constantinople, but his civilities are conveyed to him, by some secret passage, from Versailles into the Seraglio. But our Shakespeare, having ascribed to Henry the Fourth the character of a king and of a father, gives him the perfect manners of each relation, when either he transacts with his son or with his subjects. Fletcher, on the other side, gives neither to Arbaces, nor to his King in the *Maid's Tragedy*, the qualities which are suitable to a monarch; though he may be excused a little in the latter, for the King there is not uppermost in the character; 'tis the lover of Evadne, who is King only in a second consideration; and though he be unjust, and has other faults which shall be nameless, yet he is not the hero of the play. 'Tis true, we find him a lawful prince (though I never heard of any King that was in Rhodes), and therefore Mr. Rymer's criticism stands good; that he should not be shown in so vicious a character. Sophocles has been more judicious in his *Antigona*; for though he represents in Creon a bloody prince, yet he makes him not a lawful king, but an usurper, and Antigona herself is the heroine of the tragedy. But when Philaster wounds Arethusa and the boy; and Perigot his mistress, in the *Faithful Shepherdess*, both these are contrary to the character of manhood. Nor is Valentinian managed much better, for though Fletcher has taken his picture truly, and shown him as he was, an effeminate, voluptuous man, yet he has forgotten that he was an Emperor, and has given him none of those royal marks which ought to appear in a lawful successor of the throne. If it be inquired what Fletcher should have done on this occasion: ought he not to have represented Valentinian as he was? Bossu shall answer this question for me, by an instance of the like nature: Mauritius, the Greek Emperor, was a prince far surpassing Valentinian, for he was endued with many kingly virtues; he was religious, merciful, and valiant, but withal he was noted of extreme covetousness, a vice which is contrary to the character of a hero, or a prince: therefore, says the critic, that emperor was no fit person to be represented in a tragedy, unless his good qualities were only to be shown, and his covetousness (which sullied them all) were slurred over by the artifice of the poet.[12] To return once more to Shakespeare: no man ever drew so many characters, or generally distinguished 'em better from one another, excepting only Jonson. I will instance but in one, to show the copiousness of his invention: 'tis that of Caliban, or the Monster in the *Tempest*. He seems there to have created a person which was not in nature, a boldness which at first sight would appear intolerable; for he makes him a species of himself, begotten by an incubus on a witch; but this, as I have elsewhere proved, is not wholly beyond the bounds of credibility, at least the vulgar still believe it. We have the separated notions of a spirit, and of a witch (and spirits, according to Plato, are vested with a subtle body; according to some of his followers, have different sexes); therefore, as from the distinct apprehensions of a horse, and of a man, imagination has formed a centaur; so from those of an incubus and a sorceress, Shakespeare has produced his monster. Whether or no his generation can be defended, I leave to philosophy; but of this I am certain, that the poet has most judiciously furnished him with a person, a language, and a character, which will suit him, both by father's and mother's side: he has all the discontents and malice of a witch, and of a devil, besides a convenient proportion of the deadly sins; gluttony, sloth, and lust are manifest; the dejectedness of a slave is likewise given him, and the ignorance of one bred up in a desert island. His person is monstrous, as he is the product of unnatural lust; and his language is as hobgoblin as his person; in all things he is distinguished from other mortals. The characters of Fletcher are poor and narrow, in comparison of Shakespeare's; I remember not one which is not borrowed from him; unless you will except that strange mixture of a man in the *King and No King*; so that in this part Shakespeare is generally worth our imitation; and to imitate Fletcher is but to copy after him who was a copier.

Under this general head of manners, the passions are naturally included, as belonging to the characters. I speak not of pity and of terror, which are to be moved in the audience by the plot; but of anger, hatred, love, ambition, jealousy, revenge, etc., as they are shown in this or that person of the play. To describe these naturally, and to move them artfully, is one of the greatest commendations which can be given to a poet: to write pathetically, says Longinus, cannot proceed but from a lofty genius. A poet must be born with this quality; yet, unless he help himself by an acquired knowledge of the passions, what they are in their own nature, and by what springs they are to be moved, he

---

[12]*Traité du poème épique*, IV. vii.

will be subject either to raise them where they ought not to be raised, or not to raise them by the just degrees of nature, or to amplify them beyond the natural bounds, or not to observe the crisis and turns of them, in their cooling and decay: all which errors proceed from want of judgment in the poet, and from being unskilled in the principles of moral philosophy. Nothing is more frequent in a fanciful writer than to foil himself by not managing his strength; therefore, as in a wrestler, there is first required some measure of force, a well-knit body, and active limbs, without which all instruction would be vain; yet, these being granted, if he want the skill which is necessary to a wrestler, he shall make but small advantage of his natural robustuousness: so, in a poet, his inborn vehemence and force of spirit will only run him out of breath the sooner, if it be not supported by the help of art. The roar of passion indeed may please an audience, three parts of which are ignorant enough to think all is moving which is noise, and it may stretch the lungs of an ambitious actor, who will die upon the spot for a thundering clap; but it will move no other passion than indignation and contempt from judicious men. Longinus, whom I have hitherto followed, continues thus: *If the passions be artfully employed, the discourse becomes vehement and lofty: if otherwise, there is nothing more ridiculous than a great passion out of season:* and to this purpose he animadverts severely upon Æschylus, who writ nothing in cold blood, but was always in a rapture, and in fury with his audience:[13] the inspiration was still upon him, he was ever tearing it upon the tripos;[14] or (to run off as madly as he does, from one similitude to another) he was always at high flood of passion, even in the dead ebb and lowest water-mark of the scene. He who would raise the passion of a judicious audience, says a learned critic, must be sure to take his hearers along with him; if they be in a calm, 'tis in vain for him to be in a huff: he must move them by degrees, and kindle with 'em; otherwise he will be in danger of setting his own heap of stubble on a fire, and of burning out by himself without warming the company that stand about him. They who would justify the madness of poetry from the authority of Aristotle have mistaken the text, and consequently the interpretation: I imagine it to be false read, where he says of poetry that it is εὐφυοῦς ἢ μανικοῦ, that it had always somewhat in it either of a genius, or of a madman. 'Tis more probable that the original ran thus, that poetry was εὐφυοῦς οὐ μανικοῦ, that it belongs to a witty man, but not to a madman.[15] Thus then the passions, as they are considered simply and in themselves, suffer violence when they are perpetually maintained at the same height; for what melody can be made on that instrument, all whose strings are screwed up at first to their utmost stretch, and to the same sound? But this is not the worst: for the characters likewise bear a part in the general calamity, if you consider the passions embodied in them; for it follows of necessity that no man can be distinguished from another by his discourse, when every man is ranting, swaggering, and exclaiming with the same excess: as if it were the only business of all the characters to contend with each other for the prize at Billingsgate; or that the scene of the tragedy lay in Bet'lem.[16] Suppose the poet should intend this man to be choleric, and that man to be patient; yet when they are confounded in the writing, you cannot distinguish them from one another: for the man who was called patient and tame is only so before he speaks; but let his clack be set a-going, and he shall tongue it as impetuously, and as loudly, as the errantest hero in the play. By this means, the characters are only distinct in name; but, in reality, all the men and women in the play are the same person. No man should pretend to write who cannot temper his fancy with his judgment: nothing is more dangerous to a raw horseman than a hot-mouthed jade without a curb.

'Tis necessary therefore for a poet who would concern an audience by describing of a passion, first to prepare it, and not to rush upon it all at once. Ovid has judiciously shown the difference of these two ways, in the speeches of Ajax and Ulysses: Ajax, from the very beginning, breaks out into his exclamations, and is swearing by his Maker, "'By Jupiter,' he cried."[17] Ulysses, on the contrary,

---

[13] *On the Sublime*, iii.
[14] A reference to the tripod at Delphi on which the priestess of Apollo delivered her raving oracles.
[15] Aristotle, *Poetics*, xvii.
[16] Bedlam, a London hospital for the insane.
[17] "*agimus, proh Jupiter, inquit*" (Metamorphoses, xiii. 5).

prepares his audience with all the submissiveness he can practice, and all the calmness of a reasonable man; he found his judges in a tranquillity of spirit, and therefore set out leisurely and softly with 'em, till he had warmed 'em by degrees; and then he began to mend his pace, and to draw them along with his own impetuousness: yet so managing his breath, that it might not fail him at his need, and reserving his utmost proofs of ability even to the last. The success, you see, was answerable; for the crowd only applauded the speech of Ajax:

and the applause of the crowd followed his closing words.[18]

But the judges awarded the prize for which they contended to Ulysses:

the assembly was very moved; and the power of eloquence was revealed, and the skillful orator carried off the hero's arms.[19]

The next necessary rule is to put nothing into the discourse which may hinder your moving of the passions. Too many accidents, as I have said, encumber the poet, as much as the arms of Saul did David; for the variety of passions which they produce are ever crossing and jostling each other out of the way. He who treats of joy and grief together is in a fair way of causing neither of those effects. There is yet another obstacle to be removed, which is pointed wit, and sentences affected out of season; these are nothing of kin to the violence of passion: no man is at leisure to make sentences and similes when his soul is in an agony. I the rather name this fault that it may serve to mind me of my former errors; neither will I spare myself, but give an example of this kind from my *Indian Emperor*. Montezuma, pursued by his enemies, and seeking sanctuary, stands parleying without the fort, and describing his danger to Cydaria, in a simile of six lines:

As on the sands the frighted traveller
Sees the high seas come rolling from afar, etc.[20]

My Indian potentate was well skilled in the sea for an inland prince, and well improved since the first act, when he sent his son to discover it. The image had not been amiss from another man, at another time: "but not now, in this place";[21] he destroyed the concernment which the audience might otherwise have had for him; for they could not think the danger near when he had the leisure to invent a simile.

If Shakespeare be allowed, as I think he must, to have made his characters distinct, it will easily be inferred that he understood the nature of the passions: because it has been proved already that confused passions make undistinguishable characters. Yet I cannot deny that he has his failings; but they are not so much in the passions themselves as in his manner of expression: he often obscures his meaning by his words, and sometimes makes it unintelligible. I will not say of so great a poet that he distinguished not the blown puffy style from true sublimity; but I may venture to maintain that the fury of his fancy often transported him beyond the bounds of judgment, either in coining of new words and phrases or racking words which were in use into the violence of a catachresis.[22] 'Tis not that I would explode[23] the use of metaphors from passions, for Longinus thinks 'em necessary to raise it: but to use 'em at every word, to say nothing without a metaphor, a simile, an image, or description, is I doubt to smell a little too strongly of the buskin. I must be forced to give an example of expressing passion figuratively; but that I may do it with respect to Shakespeare, it shall not be

---

[18]   *vulgique secutum*
ultima mumur erat.
       Ibid., 123.

[19] *mota manus procerum est; et quid facundia posset*
tum patuit, fortisque viri tulit arma disertus.
       Ibid., 282–283.

[20] Act V.

[21] "*sed nunc non erat hisce locus*" (*Ars poetica*, 1. 19).

[22] A misuse of terms.

[23] Banish, reject.

taken from anything of his: 'tis an exclamation against Fortune, quoted in his *Hamlet,* but written by some other poet:

> Out, out, thou strumpet Fortune! all you gods,
> In general synod, take away her power;
> Break all the spokes and felleys from her wheel,
> And bowl the round nave down the hill of Heav'n,
> As low as to the fiends.

And immediately after, speaking of Hecuba, when Priam was killed before her eyes:

> The mobbled queen ran up and down,
> Threatening the flame with bisson rheum; a clout
>   about that head
> Where late the diadem stood; and for a robe,
> About her lank and all o'er-teemed loins,
> A blanket in th' alarm of fear caught up.
> Who this had seen, with tongue in venom steep'd
> 'Gainst Fortune's state would treason have
>   pronounced;
> But if the gods themselves did see her then,
> When she saw Pyrrhus make malicious sport
> In mincing with his sword her husband's limbs,
> The instant burst of clamour that she made
> (Unless things mortal move them not at all)
> Would have made milch the burning eyes of Heaven,
> And passion in the gods.[24]

What a pudder is here kept in raising the expression of trifling thoughts! Would not a man have thought that the poet had been bound prentice to a wheelwright, for his first rant? and had followed a ragman for the clout and blanket, in the second? Fortune is painted on a wheel, and therefore the writer, in a rage, will have poetical justice down upon every member of that engine: after this execution, he bowls the nave down hill, from Heaven to the fiends (an unreasonable long mark, a man would think); 'tis well there are no solid orbs to stop it in the way, or no element of fire to consume it: but when it came to the earth, it must be monstrous heavy, to break ground as low as to the center. His making milch the burning eyes of Heaven was a pretty tolerable flight too: and I think no man ever drew milk out of eyes before him: yet to make the wonder greater, these eyes were burning. Such a sight indeed were enough to have raised passion in the gods; but to excuse the effects of it, he tells you perhaps they did not see it. Wise men would be glad to find a little sense couched under all those pompous words; for bombast is commonly the delight of that audience which loves poetry, but understands it not: and as commonly has been the practice of those writers who, not being able to infuse a natural passion into the mind, have made it their business to ply the ears and to stun their judges by the noise. But Shakespeare does not often thus; for the passions in his scene between Brutus and Cassius are extremely natural, the thoughts are such as arise from the matter, and the expression of 'em not viciously figurative. I cannot leave this subject before I do justice to that divine poet by giving you one of his passionate descriptions: 'tis of Richard the Second when he was deposed, and led in triumph through the streets of London by Henry of Bolingbroke: the painting of it is so lively, and the words so moving, that I have scarce read anything comparable to it in any other language. Suppose you have seen already the fortunate usurper passing through the crowd, and followed by the shouts and acclamations of the people; and now behold King Richard entering upon the scene: consider the wretchedness of his condition, and his carriage in it; and refrain from pity if you can:

---

[24] *Hamlet,* II, ii, 515–519, 524, 528–541.

> As in a theater, the eyes of men,
> After a well-graced actor leaves the stage,
> Are idly bent on him that enters next,
> Thinking his prattle to be tedious:
> Even so, or with much more contempt, men's eyes
> Did scowl on Richard: no man cried, God save him:
> No joyful tongue gave him his welcome home,
> But dust was thrown upon his sacred head,
> Which with such gentle sorrow he shook off,
> His face still combating with tears and smiles
> (The badges of his grief and patience),
> That had not God (for some strong purpose) steel'd
> The hearts of men, they must perforce have melted,
> And barbarism itself have pitied him.[25]

To speak justly of this whole matter: 'tis neither height of thought that is discommended, nor pathetic vehemence, nor any nobleness of expression in its proper place; but 'tis a false measure of all these, something which is like 'em, and is not them; 'tis the Bristol-stone,[26] which appears like a diamond; 'tis an extravagant thought, instead of a sublime one; 'tis roaring madness, instead of vehemence; and a sound of words, instead of sense. If Shakespeare were stripped of all the bombast in his passions, and dressed in the most vulgar words, we should find the beauties of his thoughts remaining; if his embroideries were burnt down, there would still be silver at the bottom of the melting-pot: but I fear (at least let me fear it for myself) that we who ape his sounding words have nothing of his thought, but are all outside; there is not so much as a dwarf within our giant's clothes. Therefore, let not Shakespeare suffer for our sakes; 'tis our fault, who succeed him in an age which is more refined, if we imitate him so ill that we copy his failings only, and make a virtue of that in our writings which in his was an imperfection.

For what remains, the excellency of that poet was, as I have said, in the more manly passions; Fletcher's in the softer: Shakespeare writ better betwixt man and man; Fletcher, betwixt man and woman: consequently, the one described friendship better; the other love: yet Shakespeare taught Fletcher to write love: and Juliet, and Desdemona, are originals. 'Tis true, the scholar had the softer soul; but the master had the kinder. Friendship is both a virtue and a passion essentially; love is a passion only in its nature, and is not a virtue but by accident: good nature makes friendship, but effeminacy love. Shakespeare had an universal mind, which comprehended all characters and passions; Fletcher a more confined and limited: for though he treated love in perfection, yet honor, ambition, revenge, and generally all the stronger passions, he either touched not, or not masterly. To conclude all, he was a limb of Shakespeare.

I had intended to have proceeded to the last property of manners, which is that they must be constant, and the characters maintained the same from the beginning to the end; and from thence to have proceeded to the thoughts and expressions suitable to a tragedy: but I will first see how this will relish with the age. 'Tis, I confess, but cursorily written; yet the judgment which is given here is generally founded upon experience: but because many men are shocked at the name of rules, as if they were a kind of magisterial prescription upon poets, I will conclude with the words of Rapin, in his reflections on Aristotle's work of poetry: "If the rules be well considered, we shall find them to be made only to reduce nature into method, to trace her step by step, and not to suffer the least mark of her to escape us: 'tis only by these that probability in fiction is maintained, which is the soul of poetry. They are founded upon good sense, and sound reason, rather than on authority; for though Aristotle and Horace are produced, yet no man must argue that what they write is true because they writ it; but 'tis evident, by the ridiculous mistakes and gross absurdities which have been made by those poets who have taken their fancy only for their guide, that if this fancy be not regulated, 'tis a mere caprice, and utterly incapable to produce a reasonable and judicious poem."[27]

---

[25] *Richard II*, V, ii, 23–36.
[26] A rock crystal.
[27] *Réflexions*, xii.

**NORTHROP
FRYE**
(1912–1991)

**FROM *ANATOMY
OF CRITICISM*
(1957)**

Northrop Frye was the author of many influential works of literary and cultural criticism, and his Anatomy of Criticism *is one of the most important works of literary theory written in the twentieth century. In it, Frye attempts a systematic overview of the ordering structures and themes of Western literature. In this selection, he discusses character types commonly found in literature and suggests how they have been drawn from comic types first used in the comedies of Plautus and Terence. The specificity of a work of literature, Frye argues, arises from its adaptation of, and confrontation with, basic elements such as these.*

Dramatic comedy, from which fictional comedy is mainly descended, has been remarkably tenacious of its structural principles and character types. Bernard Shaw remarked that a comic dramatist could get a reputation for daring originality by stealing his method from Molière and his characters from Dickens: if we were to read Menander and Aristophanes for Molière and Dickens the statement would be hardly less true, at least as a general principle. The earliest extant European comedy, Aristophanes' *The Acharnians*, contains the *miles gloriosus* or military braggart who is still going strong in Chaplin's *Great Dictator*; the Joxer Daly of O'Casey's *Juno and the Paycock* has the same character and dramatic function as the parasites of twenty-five hundred years ago, and the audiences of vaudeville, comic strips, and television programs still laugh at the jokes that were declared to be outworn at the opening of *The Frogs*.

The plot structure of Greek New Comedy, as transmitted by Plautus and Terence, in itself less a form than a formula, has become the basis for most comedy, especially in its more highly conventionalized dramatic form, down to our own day. It will be most convenient to work out the theory of comic construction from drama, using illustrations from fiction only incidentally. What normally happens is that a young man wants a young woman, that his desire is resisted by some opposition, usually paternal, and that near the end of the play some twist in the plot enables the hero to have his will. In this simple pattern there are several complex elements. In the first place, the movement of comedy is usually a movement from one kind of society to another. At the beginning of the play the obstructing characters are in charge of the play's society, and the audience recognizes that they are usurpers. At the end of the play the device in the plot that brings hero and heroine together causes a new society to crystallize around the hero, and the moment when this crystallization occurs is the point of resolution in the action, the comic discovery, *anagnorisis* or *cognitio*.

The appearance of this new society is frequently signalized by some kind of party or festive ritual, which either appears at the end of the play or is assumed to take place immediately afterward. Weddings are most common, and sometimes so many of them occur, as in the quadruple wedding at the end of *As You Like It*, that they suggest also the wholesale pairing off that takes place in a dance, which is another common conclusion, and the normal one for the masque. The banquet at the end of *The Taming of the Shrew* has an ancestry that goes back to Greek Middle Comedy; in Plautus the audience is sometimes jocosely invited to an imaginary banquet afterwards; Old Comedy, like the modern Christmas pantomime, was more generous, and occasionally threw bits of food to the audience. As the final society reached by comedy is the one that the audience has recognized all along to be the proper and desirable state of affairs, an act of communion with the audience is in order. Tragic actors expect to be applauded as well as comic ones, but nevertheless the word "plaudite" at the end of a Roman comedy, the invitation to the audience to form part of the comic society, would seem rather out of place at the end of a tragedy. The resolution of comedy comes, so to speak, from the audience's side of the stage; in a tragedy it comes from some mysterious world on the opposite side. In the movie, where darkness permits a more erotically oriented audience, the plot usually moves toward an act which, like death in Greek tragedy, takes place offstage, and is symbolized by a closing embrace.

The obstacles to the hero's desire, then, form the action of the comedy, and the overcoming of them the comic resolution. The obstacles are usually parental, hence comedy often turns on a clash between a son's and a father's will. Thus the comic dramatist as a rule writes for the younger men in his audience, and the older members of almost any society are apt to feel that comedy has something subversive about it. This is certainly one element in the social persecution of drama, which is not peculiar to Puritans or even Christians, as Terence in pagan Rome met much the same kind of social opposition that Ben Jonson did. There is one scene in Plautus where a son and father are making love to the same courtesan, and the son asks his father pointedly if he really does love mother. One has to see this scene against the background of Roman family life to understand its importance as psychological release. Even in Shakespeare there are startling outbreaks of baiting older men, and in contemporary movies the triumph of youth is so relentless that the moviemakers find some difficulty in getting anyone over the age of seventeen into their audiences.

The opponent to the hero's wishes, when not the father, is generally someone who partakes of the father's closer relation to established society: that is, a rival with less youth and more money. In Plautus and Terence he is usually either the pimp who owns the girl, or a wandering soldier with a supply of ready cash. The fury with which these characters are baited and exploded from the stage shows that they are father-surrogates, and even if they were not, they would still be usurpers, and their claim to possess the girl must be shown up as somehow fraudulent. They are, in short, impostors, and the extent to which they have real power implies some criticism of the society that allows them their power. In Plautus and Terence this criticism seldom goes beyond the immorality of brothels and professional harlots, but in Renaissance dramatists, including Jonson, there is some sharp observation of the rising power of money and the sort of ruling class it is building up.

The tendency of comedy is to include as many people as possible in its final society: the blocking characters are more often reconciled or converted than simply repudiated. Comedy often includes a scapegoat ritual of expulsion which gets rid of some irreconcilable character, but exposure and disgrace make for pathos, or even tragedy. *The Merchant of Venice* seems almost an experiment in coming as close as possible to upsetting the comic balance. If the dramatic role of Shylock is ever so slightly exaggerated, as it generally is when the leading actor of the company takes the part, it is upset, and the play becomes the tragedy of the Jew of Venice with a comic epilogue. *Volpone* ends with a great bustle of sentences to penal servitude and the galleys, and one feels that the deliverance of society hardly needs so much hard labor; but then *Volpone* is exceptional in being a kind of comic imitation of a tragedy, with the point of Volpone's hybris carefully marked.

The principle of conversion becomes clearer with characters whose chief function is the amusing of the audience. The original *miles gloriosus* in Plautus is a son of Jove and Venus who has killed an elephant with his fist and seven thousand men in one day's fighting. In other words, he is trying to put on a good show: the exuberance of his boasting helps to put the play over. The convention says that the braggart must be exposed, ridiculed, swindled, and beaten. But why should a professional dramatist, of all people, want so to harry a character who is putting on a good show—*his* show at that? When we find Falstaff invited to the final feast in *The Merry Wives*, Caliban reprieved, attempts made to mollify Malvolio, and Angelo and Parolles allowed to live down their disgrace, we are seeing a fundamental principle of comedy at work. The tendency of the comic society to include rather than exclude is the reason for the traditional importance of the parasite, who has no business to be at the final festival but is nevertheless there. The word "grace," with all its Renaissance overtones from the graceful courtier of Castiglione to the gracious God of Christianity, is a most important thematic word in Shakespearean comedy.

The action of comedy in moving from one social center to another is not unlike the action of a lawsuit, in which plaintiff and defendant construct different versions of the same situation, one finally being judged as real and the other as illusory. This resemblance of the rhetoric of comedy to the rhetoric of jurisprudence has been recognized from earliest times. A little pamphlet called the *Tractatus Coislinianus*, closely related to Aristotle's *Poetics*, which sets down all the essential facts about comedy in about a page and a half, divides the *dianoia* of comedy into two parts, opinion (*pistis*) and proof (*gnosis*). These correspond roughly to the usurping and the desirable societies respectively. Proofs (i.e., the means of bringing about the happier society) are subdivided into oaths, compacts, witnesses, ordeals (or tortures), and laws—in other words the five forms of material proof in law cases listed in the *Rhetoric*. We notice how often the action of a Shakespearean comedy begins with some absurd, cruel, or irrational law: the law of killing Syracusans in the *Comedy of Errors*, the law of compulsory marriage in *A Midsummer Night's Dream*, the law that confirms Shylock's bond, the attempts of Angelo to legislate people into righteousness, and the like, which the action of the comedy then evades or breaks. Compacts are as a rule the conspiracies formed by the hero's society; witnesses, such as overhearers of conversations or people with special knowledge (like the hero's old nurse with her retentive memory for birthmarks), are the commonest devices for bringing about the comic discovery. Ordeals (*basanoi*) are usually tests or touchstones of the hero's character: the Greek word also means touchstones, and seems to be echoed in Shakespeare's Bassanio whose ordeal it is to make a judgment on the worth of metals.

There are two ways of developing the form of comedy: one is to throw the main emphasis on the blocking characters; the other is the throw it forward on the scenes of discovery and reconciliation. One is the general tendency of comic irony, satire, realism, and studies of manners; the other is the tendency of Shakespearean and other types of romantic comedy. In the comedy of manners the main ethical interest falls as a rule on the blocking characters. The technical hero and heroine are not often very interesting people: the *adulescentes* of Plautus and Terence are all alike, as hard to tell apart in the dark as Demetrius and Lysander, who may be parodies of them. Generally the hero's character has the neutrality that enables him to represent a wish-fulfilment. It is very different with the miserly or ferocious parent, the boastful or foppish rival, or the other characters who stand in the way of the action. In Molière we have a simple but fully tested formula in which the ethical interest is focussed on a single blocking character, a heavy father, a miser, a misanthrope, a hypocrite, or a hypochondriac. These are the figures that we remember, and the plays are usually named after them, but we can seldom remember all the Valentins and Angeliques who wriggle out of their clutches. In *The Merry Wives* the technical hero, a man named Fenton, has only a bit part, and this play has picked up a hint or two from Plautus's *Casina*, where the hero and heroine are not even brought on the stage at all. Fictional comedy, especially Dickens, often follows the same practice of grouping its interesting characters around a somewhat dullish pair of technical leads. Even Tom Jones, though far more fully realized, is still deliberately associated, as his commonplace name indicates, with the conventional and typical.

Comedy usually moves toward a happy ending, and the normal response of the audience to a happy ending is "this should be," which sounds like a moral judgment. So it is, except that it is not moral in the restricted sense, but social. Its opposite is not the villainous but the absurd, and comedy finds the virtues of Malvolio as absurd as the vices of Angelo. Molière's misanthrope, being committed to sincerity, which is a virtue, is morally in a strong position, but the audience soon realizes that his friend Philinte, who is ready to lie quite cheerfully in order to enable other people to preserve their self-respect, is the more genuinely sincere of the two. It is of course quite possible to have a moral comedy, but the result is often the kind of melodrama that we have described as comedy without humor, and which achieves its happy ending with a self-righteous tone that most comedy avoids. It is hardly possible to imagine a drama without conflict, and it is hardly possible to imagine a conflict without some kind of enmity. But just as love, including sexual love, is a very different thing from lust, so enmity is a very different thing from hatred. In tragedy, of course, enmity almost always includes hatred; comedy is different, and one feels that the social judgement against the absurd is closer to the comic norm than the moral judgement against the wicked.

The question then arises of what makes the blocking character absurd. Ben Jonson explained this by his theory of the "humor," the character dominated by what Pope calls a ruling passion. The humor's dramatic function is to express a state of what might be called ritual bondage. He is obsessed by his humor, and his function in the play is primarily to repeat his obsession. A sick man is not a humor, but a hypochondriac is, because, *qua* hypochondriac, he can never admit to good health, and can never do anything inconsistent with the role that he has prescribed for himself. A miser can do and say nothing that is not connected with the hiding of gold or saving of money. In *The Silent Woman*, Jonson's nearest approach to Molière's type of construction, the whole action recedes from the humor of Morose, whose determination to eliminate noise from his life produces so loquacious a comic action.

The principle of the humor is the principle that unincremental repetition, the literary imitation of ritual bondage, is funny. In a tragedy—*Oedipus Tyrannus* is the stock example—repetition leads logically to catastrophe. Repetition overdone or not going anywhere belongs to comedy, for laughter is partly a reflex, and like other reflexes it can be conditioned by a simple repeated pattern. In Synge's *Riders to the Sea* a mother, after losing her husband and five sons at sea, finally loses her last son, and the result is a very beautiful and moving play. But if it had been a full-length tragedy plodding glumly through the seven drownings one after another, the audience would have been helpless with unsympathetic laughter long before it was over. The principle of repetition as the basis of humor both in Jonson's sense and in ours is well known to the creators of comic strips, in which a character is established as a parasite, a glutton (often confined to one dish), or a shrew, and who begins to be funny after the point has been made every day for several months. Continuous comic radio programs, too, are much more amusing to habitués than to neophytes. The girth of Falstaff and the hallucinations of Quixote are based on much the same comic laws. Mr. E. M. Forster speaks with disdain of Dickens's Mrs. Micawber, who never says anything except that she will never desert Mr. Micawber: a strong contrast is marked here between the refined writer too finicky for popular formulas, and the major one who exploits them ruthlessly.

The humor in comedy is usually someone with a good deal of social prestige and power, who is able to force much of the play's society into line with his obsession. Thus the humor is intimately connected with the theme of the absurd or irrational law that the action of comedy moves toward breaking. It is significant that the central character of our earliest humor comedy, *The Wasps*, is obsessed by law cases: Shylock, too, unites a craving for the law with the humor of revenge. Often the absurd law appears as a whim of a bemused tyrant whose will is law, like Leontes or the humorous Duke Frederick in Shakespeare, who makes some arbitrary decision or rash promise: here law is replaced by "oath," also mentioned in the *Tractatus*. Or it may take the form of a sham Utopia, a society of ritual bondage constructed by an act of humorous or pedantic will, like the academic retreat in *Love's Labor's Lost*. This theme is also as old as Aristophanes, whose parodies of Platonic social schemes in *The Birds* and *Ecclesiazusae* deal with it.

The society emerging at the conclusion of comedy represents, by contrast, a kind of moral norm, or pragmatically free society. Its ideals are seldom defined or formulated: definition and formulation belong to the humors, who want predictable activity. We are simply given to understand that the newly-married couple will live happily ever after, or that at any rate they will get along in a relatively unhumorous and clear-sighted manner. That is one reason why the character of the successful hero is so often left undeveloped: his real life begins at the end of the play, and we have to believe him to be potentially a more interesting character than he appears to be. In Terence's *Adelphoi*, Demea, a harsh father, is contrasted with his brother Micio, who is indulgent. Micio being more liberal, he leads the way to the comic resolution, and converts Demea, but then Demea points out the indolence inspiring a good deal of Micio's liberality, and releases him from a complementary humorous bondage.

Thus the movement from *pistis* to *gnosis*, from a society controlled by habit, ritual bondage, arbitrary law and the older characters to a society controlled by youth and pragmatic freedom is fundamentally, as the Greek words suggest, a movement from illusion to reality. Illusion is whatever is fixed or definable, and reality is best understood as its negation: whatever reality is, it's not *that*. Hence the importance of the theme of creating and dispelling illusion in comedy: the illusions caused by disguise, obsession, hypocrisy, or unknown parentage.

The comic ending is generally manipulated by a twist in the plot. In Roman comedy the heroine, who is usually a slave or courtesan, turns out to be the daughter of somebody respectable, so that the hero can marry her without loss of face. The *cognitio* in comedy, in which the characters find out who their relatives are, and who is left of the opposite sex not a relative, and hence available for marriage, is one of the features of comedy that have never changed much: *The Confidential Clerk* indicates that it still holds the attention of dramatists. There is a brilliant parody of a *cognitio* at the end of *Major Barbara* (the fact that the hero of this play is a professor of Greek perhaps indicates an unusual affinity to the conventions of Euripides and Menander), where Undershaft is enabled to break the rule that he cannot appoint his son-in-law as successor by the fact that the son-in-law's own father married his deceased wife's sister in Australia, so that the son-in-law is his own first cousin as well as himself. It sounds complicated, but the plots of comedy often are complicated because there is something inherently absurd about complications. As the main character interest in comedy is so often focussed on the defeated characters, comedy regularly illustrates a victory of arbitrary plot over consistency of character. Thus, in striking contrast to tragedy, there can hardly be such a thing as inevitable comedy, as far as the action of the individual play is concerned. That is, we may know that the convention of comedy will make some kind of happy ending inevitable, but still for each play the dramatist must produce a distinctive "gimmick" or "weenie," to use two disrespectful Hollywood synonyms for *anagnorisis*. Happy endings do not impress us as true, but as desirable, and they are brought about by manipulation. The watcher of death and tragedy has nothing to do but sit and wait for the inevitable end; but something gets born at the end of comedy, and the watcher of birth is a member of a busy society.

The manipulation of plot does not always involve metamorphosis of character, but there is no violation of comic decorum when it does. Unlikely conversions, miraculous transformations, and providential assistance are inseparable from comedy. Further, whatever emerges is supposed to be there for good: if the curmudgeon becomes lovable, we understand that he will not immediately relapse again into his ritual habit. Civilizations which stress the desirable rather than the real, and the religious as opposed to the scientific perspective, think of drama almost entirely in terms of comedy. In the classical drama of India, we are told, the tragic ending was regarded as bad taste, much as the manipulated endings of comedy are regarded as bad taste by novelists interested in ironic realism.

The total *mythos* of comedy, only a small part of which is ordinarily presented, has regularly what in music is called a ternary form: the hero's society rebels against the society of the *senex* and triumphs, but the hero's society is a Saturnalia, a reversal of social standards which recalls a golden age in the past before the main action of the play begins. Thus we have a stable and harmonious order disrupted by folly, obsession, forgetfulness, "pride and prejudice," or events not understood by the characters themselves, and then restored. Often there is a benevolent grandfather, so to speak, who overrules the action set up by the blocking humor and so links the first and third parts. An example is Mr. Burchell, the disguised uncle of the wicked squire, in *The Vicar of Wakefield*. A very long play, such as the Indian *Sakuntala*, may present all three phases; a very intricate one, such as many of Menander's evidently were, may indicate their outlines. But of course very often the first phase is not given at all: the audience simply understands an ideal state of affairs which it knows to be better than what is revealed in the play, and which it recognizes as like that to which the action leads. This ternary action is, ritually, like a contest of summer and winter in which winter occupies the middle action; psychologically, it is like the removal of a neurosis or blocking point and the restoring of an unbroken current of energy and memory. The Jonsonian masque, with the antimasque in the middle, gives a highly conventionalized or "abstract" version of it.

We pass now to the typical characters of comedy. In drama, characterization depends on function; what a character is follows from what he has to do in the play. Dramatic function in its turn depends on the structure of the play; the character has certain things to do because the play has such and such a shape. The structure of the play in its turn depends on the category of the play; if it is a comedy, its structure will require a comic resolution and a prevailing comic mood. Hence when we speak of typical characters, we are not trying to reduce lifelike characters to stock types, though we certainly are suggesting that the sentimental notion of an antithesis between the lifelike character and the stock type is a vulgar error. All lifelike characters, whether in drama or fiction, owe their consistency to the appropriateness of the stock type which belongs to their dramatic function. That stock type is not the character but it is as necessary to the character as a skeleton is to the actor who plays it.

With regard to the characterization of comedy, the *Tractatus* lists three types of comic characters: the *alazons* or impostors, the *eirons* or self-deprecators, and the buffoons (*bomolochoi*). This list is closely related to a passage in the *Ethics* which contrasts the first two, and then goes on to contrast the buffoon with a character whom Aristotle calls *agroikos* or churlish, literally rustic. We may reasonably accept the churl as a fourth character type, and so we have two opposed pairs. The contest of *eiron* and *alazon* forms the basis of the comic action, and the buffoon and the churl polarize the comic mood.

We have previously dealt with the terms *eiron* and *alazon*. The humorous blocking characters of comedy are nearly always impostors, though it is more frequently a lack of self-knowledge than simple hypocrisy that characterizes them. The multitudes of comic scenes in which one character complacently soliloquizes while another makes sarcastic asides to the audience show the contest of *eiron* and *alazon* in its purest form, and show too that the audience is sympathetic to the *eiron* side. Central to the *alazon* group is the *senex iratus* or heavy father, who with his rages and threats, his obsessions and his gullibility, seems closely related to some of the demonic characters of romance, such as Polyphemus. Occasionally a character may have the dramatic function of such a figure without his characteristics: an example is Squire Allworthy in *Tom Jones*, who as far as the plot is concerned behaves almost as stupidly as Squire Western. Of heavy-father surrogates, the *miles gloriosus* has been mentioned: his popularity is largely due to the fact that he is a man of words rather than deeds, and is consequently far more useful to a practising dramatist than any tight-lipped hero could ever be. The pedant, in Renaissance comedy often a student of the occult sciences, the fop or coxcomb, and similar humors, require no comment. The female *alazon* is rare: Katharina the shrew represents to some extent a female *miles gloriosus*, and the *précieuse ridicule* a female pedant, but the "menace" or siren who gets in the way of the true heroine is more often found as a sinister figure of melodrama or romance than as a ridiculous figure in comedy.

The *eiron* figures need a little more attention. Central to this group is the hero, who is an *eiron* figure because, as explained, the dramatist tends to play him down and make him rather neutral and unformed in character. Next in importance is the heroine, also often played down: in Old Comedy, when a girl accompanies a male hero in his triumph, she is generally a stage prop, a *muta persona* not previously introduced. A more difficult form of *cognitio* is achieved when the heroine disguises herself or through some other device brings about the comic resolution, so that the person whom the hero is seeking turns out to be the person who has sought him. The fondness of Shakespeare for this "she stoops to conquer" theme needs only to be mentioned here, as it belongs more naturally to the *mythos* of romance.

Another central *eiron* figure is the type entrusted with hatching the schemes which bring about the hero's victory. This character in Roman comedy is almost always a tricky slave *(dolosus servus)*, and in Renaissance comedy he becomes the scheming valet who is so frequent in Continental plays, and in Spanish drama is called the *gracioso*. Modern audiences are most familiar with him in Figaro and in the Leporello of *Don Giovanni*. Through such intermediate nineteenth-century figures as Micawber and the Touchwood of Scott's *St. Ronan's Well*, who, like the gracioso, have buffoon affiliations, he evolves into the amateur detective of modern fiction. The Jeeves of P. G. Wodehouse is a more direct descendant. Female confidantes of the same general family are often brought in to oil the machinery of the well-made play. Elizabethan comedy had another type of trickster, represented by the Matthew Merrygreek of *Ralph Roister Doister*, who is generally said to be developed from the vice or iniquity of the morality plays: as usual, the analogy is sound enough, whatever historians decide about origins. The vice, to give him that name, is very useful to a comic dramatist because he acts from pure love of mischief, and can set a comic action going with the minimum of motivation. The vice may be as light-hearted as Puck or as malignant as Don John in *Much Ado*, but as a rule the vice's activity is, in spite of his name, benevolent. One of the tricky slaves in Plautus, in a soliloquy, boasts that he is the *architectus* of the comic action: such a character carries out the will of the author to reach a happy ending. He is in fact the spirit of comedy, and the two clearest examples of the type in Shakespeare, Puck and Ariel, are both spiritual beings. The tricky slave often has his own freedom in mind as the reward of his exertions: Ariel's longing for release is in the same tradition.

The role of the vice includes a great deal of disguising, and the type may often be recognized by disguise. A good example is the Brainworm of Jonson's *Every Man in His Humour*, who calls the action of the play the day of his metamorphoses. Similarly Ariel has to surmount the difficult stage direction of "Enter invisible." The vice is combined with the hero whenever the latter is a cheeky, improvident young man who hatches his own schemes and cheats his rich father or uncle into giving him his patrimony along with the girl.

Another *eiron* type has not been much noticed. This is a character, generally an older man, who begins the action of the play by withdrawing from it, and ends the play by returning. He is often a father with the motive of seeing what his son will do. The action of *Every Man in His Humour* is set going in this way by Knowell Senior. The disappearance and return of Lovewit, the owner of the house which is the scene of *The Alchemist*, has the same dramatic function, though the characterization is different. The clearest Shakespearean example is the Duke in *Measure for Measure*, but Shakespeare is more addicted to the type than might appear at first glance. In Shakespeare the vice is rarely the real *architectus*: Puck and Ariel both act under orders from an older man, if one may call Oberon a man for the moment. In *The Tempest* Shakespeare returns to a comic action established by Aristophanes, in which an older man, instead of retiring from the action, builds it up on the stage. When the heroine takes the vice role in Shakespeare, she is often significantly related to her father, even when the father is not in the play at all, like the father of Helena, who gives her his medical knowledge, or the father of Portia, who arranges the scheme of the caskets. A more conventionally treated example of the same benevolent Prospero figure turned up recently in the psychiatrist of *The Cocktail Party*, and one may compare the mysterious alchemist who is the father of the heroine of *The Lady's Not for Burning*. The formula is not confined to comedy: Polonius, who shows so many of the disadvantages of a literary education, attempts the role of a retreating paternal *eiron* three times, once too often. *Hamlet* and *King Lear* contain subplots which are ironic versions of stock comic themes, Gloucester's story being the regular comedy theme of the gullible *senex* swindled by a clever and unprincipled son.

We pass now to the buffoon types, those whose function it is to increase the mood of festivity rather than to contribute to the plot. Renaissance comedy, unlike Roman comedy, had a great variety of such characters, professional fools, clowns, pages, singers, and incidental characters with established comic habits like malapropism or foreign accents. The oldest buffoon of this incidental nature is the parasite, who may be given something to do, as Jonson gives Mosca the role of a vice in *Volpone*, but who, *qua* parasite, does nothing but entertain the audience by talking about his appetite. He derives chiefly from Greek Middle Comedy, which appears to have been very full of food, and where he was, not unnaturally, closely associated with another established buffoon type, the cook, a conventional figure who breaks into comedies to bustle and order about and make long speeches about the mysteries of cooking. In the role of cook the buffoon or entertainer appears, not simply as a gratuitous addition like the parasite, but as something more like a master of ceremonies, a center for the comic mood. There is no cook in Shakespeare, though there is a superb description of one in the *Comedy of Errors*, but a similar role is often attached to a jovial and loquacious host, like the "mad host" of *The Merry Wives* or the Simon Eyre of *The Shoemakers Holiday*. In Middleton's *A Trick to Catch the Old One* the mad host type is combined with the vice. In Falstaff and Sir Toby Belch we can see the affinities of the buffoon or entertainer type both with the parasite and with the master of revels. If we study this entertainer or host role carefully we shall soon realize that it is a development of what in Aristophanic comedy is represented by the chorus, and which in its turn goes back to the *komos* or revel from which comedy is said to be descended.

Finally, there is a fourth group to which we have assigned the word *agroikos*, and which usually means either churlish or rustic, depending on the context. This type may also be extended to cover the Elizabethan gull and what in vaudeville used to be called the straight man, the solemn or inarticulate character who allows the humor to bounce off him, so to speak. We find churls in the miserly, snobbish, or priggish characters whose role is that of the refuser of festivity, the killjoy who tries to stop the fun, or, like Malvolio, locks up the food and drink instead of dispensing it. The melancholy Jaques of *As You Like It*, who walks out on the final festivities, is closely related. In the sulky and self-centered Bertram of *All's Well* there is a most unusual and ingenious combination of this type with the hero. More often, however, the churl belongs to the *alazon* group, all miserly old men in comedies, including Shylock, being churls. In *The Tempest* Caliban has much the same relation to the churlish type that Ariel has to the vice or tricky slave. But often, where the mood is more light-hearted, we may translate *agroikos* simply by rustic, as with the innumerable country squires and similar characters who provide amusement in the urban setting of drama. Such types do not refuse the mood of festivity, but they mark the extent of its range. In a pastoral comedy the idealized virtues of rural life may be represented by a simple man who speaks for the pastoral ideal, like Corin in *As You Like It*. Corin has the same *agroikos* role as the "rube" or "hayseed" of more citified comedies, but the moral attitude to the role is reversed. Again we notice the principle that dramatic structure is a permanent and moral attitude a variable factor in literature.

In a very ironic comedy a different type of character may play the role of the refuser of festivity. The more ironic the comedy, the more absurd the society, and an absurd society may be condemned by, or at least contrasted with, a character that we may call the plain dealer, an outspoken advocate of a kind of moral norm who has the sympathy of the audience. Wycherley's Manly, though he provides the name for the type, is not a particularly good example of it: a much better one is the Cléante of *Tartuffe*. Such a character is appropriate when the tone is ironic enough to get the audience confused about its sense of the social norm: he corresponds roughly to the chorus in a tragedy, which is there for a similar reason. When the tone deepens from the ironic to the bitter, the plain dealer may become a malcontent or railer, who may be morally superior to his society, as he is to some extent in Marston's play of that name, but who may also be too motivated by envy to be much more than another aspect of his society's evil, like Thersites, or to some extent Apemantus. . . .

Katharine Eisaman Maus has written widely about seventeenth-century literature, including a book on the playwright Ben Jonson. In this essay, Maus explores the relationship between Restoration actresses, their reputation for sexual promiscuity, and the politics of gender in the Restoration theater and society.

Sometime in the fall of 1660—no one is quite sure when or at which theater—the first professional English actress made her debut on the public stage. Her appearance was not entirely without precedents. In the first half of the seventeenth century, Queen Henrietta Maria and her ladies performed extensively in the English court theater. During the interregnum, when the theaters were officially closed, William D'Avenant used at least one woman—a Mrs. Edward Coleman—in his opera *The Siege of Rhodes*. On the Continent, women had been employed on the stage since the sixteenth century, and many royalists became familiar with the French custom when they followed Prince Charles into exile. However, women had never been used on the English stage in any regular or systematic way.

Before the war, adolescent boys had performed the women's parts in the public theater. In November, 1629, when a French company with actresses came to London, Thomas Brand informed Archbishop Laud that "those women . . . giving just offense to all virtuous and well disposed persons in this town . . . were hissed, hooted, and pippin-pelted from the stage."[1] By the Restoration, though, attitudes toward women on the stage seem to have changed radically. The new actresses were accepted almost immediately into the life of the theater, and there was surprisingly little controversy over their suitability for the stage.

What caused this striking reversal of audience attitudes? Was it merely a case of English theatergoers belatedly relinquishing a set of absurd scruples? Discussions of seventeenth-century actresses have assumed that they succeeded on the stage because they could provide a more plausible portrayal of women characters than transvestite actors could.[2] There are two objections to this kind of explanation. For one thing, there is no evidence which implies that the female impersonators were incompetent. Female parts written by Shakespeare, Webster, Ford, Middleton, and others suggests no mean estimate by the playwrights of the boys' abilities; Elizabethan and Jacobean audiences applauded male Juliets, Rosalinds, and Cleopatras. The usual explanation of the actresses' success further assumes that naturalism is an obvious and desirable goal in theatrical representation—an assumption which is questionable to say the least. E. H. Gombrich has shown that standards of naturalism—what will seem "true to life" in a drawing or painting—vary from generation to generation depending upon the conventions which inform and have informed artistic production. What seems natural or conventional is not universal across time and space, but is historically and culturally conditioned.[3] There is no reason to suppose that naturalism in the theater is any less problematic than naturalism in the visual arts. Why should male impersonation of women seem more intolerable than other kinds of artificiality—extravagantly exotic sets, or a highly rhetorical acting style? The Restoration audience expected, and enjoyed, stage conventions which grievously ignore the demands of realism as understood by, say, Ibsen or Chekhov.

The orthodox explanation of the actresses' new acceptability is, if not entirely wrong, at least seriously insufficient. What is required is an examination of the issues in terms of the attitudes prevailing in Restoration culture. This examination logically begins with the contemporary accounts of the actresses, and inevitably widens to include analysis of Restoration attitudes toward women and the theater in general.

Unfortunately, there is very little comment upon the actresses in the years when they are first introduced, when the quality of contemporary response might best help illuminate the reasons for their professional success. Since no one seriously questioned women's fitness for the stage, the few attempts to account for the innovation involve no very elaborate process of justification. In 1660, the players and owners of theatrical companies were complaining that the hiatus in the theatrical tradition had created a dearth of well-trained female inpersonators. The available actors were all too masculine-looking, they claimed, to excel in women's parts. As Thomas Jordan lamented in his preface to a revival of *Othello*:

KATHARINE EISAMAN MAUS

FROM "*PLAYHOUSE FLESH AND BLOOD*': SEXUAL IDEOLOGY AND THE RESTORATION ACTRESS" (1979)

> Our women are defective, and so siz'd
> You'ld think they were some of the guard disguis'd
> For to speak truth, men act that are between
> Forty and fifty, wenches of fifteen
> With bone so large and nerve so incompliant
> When you call Desdemona, enter Geant.[4]

According to this line of argument, the peculiar circumstances of the Restoration theater necessitated the employment of women. The closing of the theaters during the interregnum had interrupted the old system of apprenticeship, which had supplied the Elizabethan and Jacobean companies with adequately-trained female impersonators.

This explanation, even if true, would only reveal by what chance women arrived on the stage, and not how and why they were successful once they got there. Furthermore, the plight of the producers was not nearly so severe as Jordan represents it. According to John Downes in *Roscius Anglicanus*, the King's Company at its inception included four actors "Bred up from Boys, under the Master ACTORS."[5] The Duke's Company included six actors, who "commonly Acted Women's Parts"—notably Edward Kynaston, who "being young made a complete Femal Stage Beauty, performing his part so well . . . that it hath since been disputable among the Judicious, whether any Woman that succeeded him so sensibly touched the audience as he."[6] Pepys and Cibber, as well as Downes, comment upon the excellence of Kynaston's impersonations, as well as upon the more than passable abilities of the lesser actors.[7] Surely if the Restoration audience had greeted the women players with the hisses and orange pips of an earlier generation, the companies would have made do for a while with ungainly performances by untrained adolescent boys. The perceived unsuitability of male actors for female roles is really more a symptom than an explanation of changing attitudes.

As the theaters reopened, actors and producers urged yet another argument for the introduction of actresses, which seems at least in retrospect equally unsatisfactory as a real explanation. Initially some people hoped that the presence of women on the stage would eliminate the obscene and corrupt aspects of English drama, and encourage the adoption of purer standards for theatrical spectacle. The patents issued to William D'Avenant and Thomas Killigrew in 1660, and reissued in 1662, contain the following clause:

> forasmuch as many plays formerly acted, do conteine severall prophane, obscene, and scurrilous passages, and the women's parts therein have been acted by men in the habit of women, at which some have taken offense; for the preventing of these abuses for the future, we doe straitly charge, command, and enjoyn that henceforth no . . . play shall be acted by either of the said companies conteining any passages offensive to piety or good manners . . . And we doe likewise permit and give leave that all the women's parts to be acted in either of the said two companies may be performed by women so long as these recreations, which by reason of the abuses aforesaid were scandalous and offensive, may by such reformation be esteemed not only harmlesse delight but useful instruction.[8]

By this account the actresses were introduced in order to help the dramatic arts exert a beneficial effect upon the community. Whether or not this apparently pious hope was initially a sincere one, it remained unrealized on the Restoration stage. Restoration drama, especially comedy, tends to be sexually more explicit and morally more subversive than the drama of earlier decades—and the sexual explicitness, at least, largely depends upon the physical presence of genuine women on the stage. "We can only conclude," writes a twentieth century critic, "that [the actresses'] chief effect on dramatic literature was to push it steadily in the direction of sex and sensuality."[9] The threat implied in the language of the patents—that the women's continued employment depended upon their moral efficacy—was of course never carried out. If women were now considered appropriate on the public stage, it was not for their purifying influence, any more than it was due to a shortage of teenage boys.

Since the overt attempts at contemporary justification seem inadequate, it is reasonable to suspect that the new acceptability of actresses is associated with ideological changes more fundamental or far-reaching than a mere modification of theatrical custom might indicate. The first such change which needs to be examined is the transformation in audience attitudes toward players in the latter part of the seventeenth century—a change which makes the success of the Restoration actress even more striking. Before the war, even the most appreciative playgoers seem not have been particularly interested in the offstage lives of Burbage, Kempe, or Alleyn. In the more intimate Restoration theater, though, the personalities of both male and female players intrigued the comparatively small and loyal audience. Actresses as well as actors were praised not for their ability to depict any character with equal skill, but for their ability to inform their dramatic portrayals with the force of their personal talent and idiosyncratic vision. In James Wright's *Historia Histrionica* (London, 1699), Truewit assumes that even in reading an old play one is curious about the personalities of the original actors:

> I wish they had printed in the last age (so I call the times before the rebellion) the actors names over against the parts they acted, as they have done since the restoration: and thus one might have guess'd at the action of the men, by the parts which we now read in the old plays.   (p. 3)

Restoration theater did not really challenge the actor to submit himself to the demands of a fictional role; rather it provided, at least for the leading players, manifold opportunities for self-expression. In the case of women like Nell Gwynn, Elizabeth Barry, or Ann Bracegirdle, this kind of attention constituted a virtually unprecedented celebration of female personality—at least of middle- and lower-class female personality.

As Restoration playwrights worked very closely with the theatrical companies, they inevitably wrote with particular performers in mind. They were thus able to play upon the spectator's sense of the relationship between an actor's personality and the roles he was required to enact. Nell Gwynn and Charles Hart, lovers behind the scenes, played witty, amoral "mad couples" together—Florimel and Celadon in Dryden's *Secret Love*, Miridia and Philidor in Howard's *All Mistaken*, Jacintha and Wildblood in Dryden's *Evening's Love*, Olivia and Wildish in Sedley's *Mulberry Garden*. Ann Bracegirdle, who resisted the advances of enamored aristocrats throughout her career, and who was the object of a melodramatic rape attempt, became famous for her portrayal of chaste women in distress. She was applauded when, as Cordelia in the revised *Lear*, she described herself as "Arm'd in my Virgin Innocence"—although the promiscuous Mrs. Barry, "in the same part, more fam'd for her Stage Performance than the other, at the words, *Virgin Innocence*, has created a Horse-laugh . . . and the scene of generous Pity and Compassion at the close turn'd to Ridicule."[10]

Prologues and epilogues, with their ambiguous position between the fictional and the real, provided ideal opportunities to exploit the relation between the player and the part. The most extreme, and probably the funniest, example occurs at the end of Dryden's *Tyrannic Love*. Nell Gwynn, playing a doomed princess despite her generally recognized ineptitude in tragic roles, finally expires. Servants load her corpse onto a litter and are carrying it out when she suddenly sits bolt upright and exclaims, "Hold, are you mad? You damn'd confounded Dog! I am to rise, and speak the Epilogue!" She leaps off the bier and begins the final speech:

> I come, kind Gentlemen, strange news to tell ye
> I am the ghost of poor departed Nelly . . .
> To tell you truth, I walk because I die
> Out of my calling, in a Tragedy.
> O Poet, dam'd dull Poet, who could prove
> So senseless to make Nelly die for love! . . .
> As for my epitaph when I am gone,
> I'll trust no poet, but will write my own:
> "Here Nelly lies, who, though she liv'd a Slattern
> Yet dy'd a princess, acting in Saint Cathar'n."[11]

In *An Essay of Dramatic Poetry*, and *The Grounds of Criticism in Tragedy*, Dryden's qualified admiration for the French tradition testifies to his interest in and sensitivity to the requirements of theatrical decorum. But the demands of the tragic situation, even for Dryden, are overridden by the demands of Nell's personality.

It is tempting to think of the new acceptance of female assertiveness on the stage as part of a general revaluation of women's status—a reassessment that would eventually allow them to participate more fully in all aspects of public life. Certainly all the evidence suggests that although the actresses were never as numerous or as well-paid as their male colleagues, they participated extensively in the life of the companies to which they belonged. They were granted the same special privileges as the actors—most significantly a relative immunity from prosecution for debt. And with the formation of the Lincoln's Inn Fields Company in 1695, two actresses—Ann Bracegirdle and Mary Saunderson Betterton—became shareholders, with a right to a certain percentage of the company's profits.

The employment of actresses does not, however, coincide with a more general broadening of female participation in public life. In fact, during the second half of the seventeenth century women seem to have been losing rather than acquiring opportunities for gainful employment. Men were encroaching upon such traditionally female occupations as brewing, textile manufacture, dressmaking, and midwifery. Women were less and less likely to run businesses or enter trades independently of their husbands, to help their husbands in a family venture, or to continue such a venture when they were widowed. By the beginning of the eighteenth century, there were few alternatives for undowered, unmarried women—or married women whose husbands could not support them—other than domestic service or prostitution.[12] The success of the actress has to be explained in ways which take into account the drastically different experience of women in other professions.

Actresses, in other words, seem to be anomalous rather than typical; the task is to isolate the factors that make their case so special. It is reasonable to look more closely to the audience's actual response to the women on the stage, in order to establish revealing patterns of assumptions. One such pattern is so obvious as to be unavoidable. Everyone from Dryden on has remarked upon the audience's extraordinarily lively, even obsessive, concern with the actresses' sexuality. John Downes, in *Roscius Angelicanus*, regales the reader with sly anecdotes:

> And all the Women's Parts admirably Acted: chiefly *Celia* [Moll Davis], a Shepherdess being Mad for Love; especially in Singing several Wild and Mad Songs. *My Lodging is on the Cold Ground*, etc. She perform'd that so Charmingly, that not long after, it Rais'd her from her Bed on the Cold Ground, to a Bed Royal.

> Note, Mrs. Johnson in this Comedy, Dancing a Jigg so Charming Well, Love's power in a little time after Coerc'd her to Dance more Charming else where.[13]

Others were less delicate. The anonymous author of "Satyr on Players" (London, ca. 1685), declares that actresses are "so lewd in every kind/You'd swear that Rogue and Whore had both combin'd," and goes on to support his claim in explicit detail:

> Sue Percival so long has known the Stage
> She grows in Lewdness faster, than in Age:
> From Eight or Nine she there has swiving been;
> So calls that Nature, which is truly Sin. (page 2)

Despite the difference in tone, Downes and the author of the "Satyr" both assume that the sexual exploits of the actress are an extension of her histrionic function rather than an irrelevant side-issue. Moll Davis's change of beds is described as the direct result of her fine performance; Mrs. Johnson gets invited to dance elsewhere because she has danced so well on the stage; Sue Percival's theatrical and sexual exploits coincide. Modern critics like John Harold Wilson and Allardyce Nicoll conclude that the presence of the actresses debased the theater, by lending it the atmosphere of a brothel.[14] . . .

No doubt the fuss is partly due to the fact that the actresses' sex lives really were fairly unorthodox. As Allardyce Nicoll primly declares, "very few of these women led chaste lives."[15] Elizabeth Barry was the mistress of John, Earl of Rochester; Elizabeth Hall the mistress of Sir Philip Howard; the Mrs. Johnson of Downe's anecdote the mistress of Henry, Earl of Peterborough. Margaret Hughes was the mistress of Prince Rupert, Susannah Hall the mistress of Sir Robert Howard, Ann

Reeves the mistress of Dryden, Elizabeth Barry (again) of Otway, and Ann Bracegirdle (perhaps) of Congreve. Hester Davenport was irregularly married to the Earl of Oxford—when she refused to become his mistress he dressed up one of his servants as a parson, and had an invalid marriage ceremony performed. Nell Gwynn and Moll Davis went all the way to the top, and became mistresses of Charles II. Others, like Elizabeth Boutell and Rebecca Marshall, played the field.

Nonetheless, there were alternative models, like Mary Saunderson Betterton, who was the leading tragic actress before Mrs. Barry, and who seems to have led a faithful married life throughout her long career. An actress like Nell Gwynn, however, whose stage career lasted only five years, and whose histrionic talents were probably much smaller, seemed a much more exemplary specimen. When Ann Bracegirdle proved unexpectedly chaste, the audience did not divert its attention from her sexuality, but focused upon it all the more sharply.

> RAMBLE: And Mrs. Bracegirdle . . .
> CRITIC: Is a haughty conceited Woman, that has got more Money by dissembling her
>   Lewdness, than others by professing it.
> SULLEN: But does that Romantick Virgin still keep up her great reputation?
> CRITIC: D'ye mean her Reputation for Acting?
> SULLEN: I mean her Reputation for not acting; you understand me.—[16]

By contrast, audience interest in the male players tended not to involve such an avid concern with their sex lives. Actors like Charles Hart, Edward Kynaston, and Cardell Goodman were "kept" by aristocratic ladies—in Goodman's case his connection with Lady Castlemaine obtained him a pardon after he had been convicted of highway robbery, a capital crime. But contemporary comment on their situation is muted; their sexuality is not considered part and parcel with their histrionic vocation. . . .

If hierarchical assumptions dominate conceptions of gender difference, boys and women occupy a similar position—they are inferior versions of mature men, *hommes manqués*. From one point of view, as *As You Like It*'s Rosalind-Ganymede knows, boys and women are cattle of the same color. The convention of the boy-actresses has a certain logic; at any rate it does not pose a profound or necessary challenge to the audience's ideological convictions. If sexual difference is understood in terms of opposition, however, transvestite role-playing involves a much greater rupture of decorum—a rupture which may be ludicrous, implausible, or titillating depending upon the context. Boys no longer seem appropriate in women's tragic roles; a Cleopatra who shaves is the occasion for a jest.[17] The Restoration audience was more eager to see women in male disguise, but arguably this eagerness is rooted in the same attitudes which make the boy impersonators seem obsolete. John Harold Wilson has remarked upon the surprisingly "indelicate" methods by which women players in male disguise were unmasked in Restoration comedy.[18] Surely all the loosened hair, all the naked breasts in the fifth act are meant to heighten an incongruity of which the audience was already aware; the unmasking reinforces a histrionic appeal which depends upon the seductive appeal of female difference.

From this perspective one can see why the actresses appeared on the pubic stage for the first time at the Restoration; why their success could coincide with a more general withdrawal of women from public life; and also why their achievement took the specific forms that it did. It is not merely new attitudes toward women and the theater, but the persistence of old ones, which make possible the novel phenomenon of the Restoration actress, and which condition the highly selective enthusiasm of her audience.

NOTES

[1]John Payne Collier, *History of Dramatic Poetry to the Time of Shakespeare: And Annals of the Stage to the Restoration* (London: John Murray, 1831), II, pp. 23–24.

[2]e.g., Colley Cibber, *An Apology of the Life of Colley Cibber* (London, 1740), p. 55: "The characters of Women, on former Theatres, were perform'd by Boys, or young Men of the most effeminate Aspect. And what Grace, or Master-Stroke of Action, can we conceive such ungain Hoydens to have been capable of?"

Allardyce Nicoll, *The History of Restoration Drama 1660–1700* (Cambridge: Cambridge Univ. Press, 1928), p. 71: "the actresses certainly made possible a more charming presentation of Shakespearean tragedy and comedy, shedding a fresh light on the Desdemonas and Ophelias of the past."

Rosamund Gilder, *Enter the Actresses* (London: George C. Harrup, 1931), pp. 134–35: "In England the curtain of legal prohibition drops in 1642 on a stage peopled by squeaking Cleopatras, and rises eighteen years later on a rout of beautiful, witty, and accomplished actresses."

John Harold Wilson, *All the King's Ladies: Actresses of the Restoration* (Chicago: Univ. of Chicago Press, 1958), p. 90: "As creators of character there can be little doubt that the new actresses were superior to their juvenile predecessors . . . the stage life of the female impersonator was usually short, and his interpretation of a character could never be more than superficially correct."

[3] E. H. Gombrich, *Art and Illusion* (New York: Pantheon, 1960), esp. pp. 181–287.

[4] Thomas Jordan, "A Prologue, to introduce the first Woman that came to act on the Stage, in the tragedy called The Moor of Venice," in *A Royal Arbour of Loyal Poesie* (London, 1664), p. 22.

[5] John Downes, *Roscius Anglicanus, or An Historical View of the Stage* (London, 1708), p. 2.

[6] *Ibid.*, p. 19.

[7] Samuel Pepys, *The Diary of Samuel Pepys*, ed. R. Latham and W. Matthews (London: G. Bell, 1970), I, 224 (August 18, 1660) and II, 7 (January 7, 1660–61). Cibber, p. 71.

[8] Nicoll, pp. 285–86n.

[9] Wilson, p. 107.

[10] William Chetwood, *A General History of the Stage* (London, 1749), p. 28.

[11] John Dryden, *The Dramatic Works*, ed. Montague Summers (London: Nonesuch, 1931), II, p. 395.

[12] The standard work on the subject is still Alice Clark's *Working Life of Women in the Seventeenth Century* (London: Routledge and Sons, 1919). Her conclusion—that women were progressively excluded from the job market during the seventeenth century—though not her Marxist analysis, has recently been supported by Roger Thompson, *Women In Stuart England and America* (London: Routledge and Kegan Paul, 1974), pp. 74–75.

[13] Downes, pp. 23–24, p. 33.

[14] Wilson, *passim.*; Nicoll, p. 72.

[15] Nicoll, p. 72.

[16] Anon. (sometimes ascribed to Charles Gildon), *A Comparison Between The Two Stages* (London, 1702), p. 17.

[17] Cibber, p. 71.

[18] Wilson, p. 85.

RESTAGING THE CLASSICS

Throughout the twentieth century, stage directors have used the *mise-en-scène* both to comment on classic drama and to invite audiences to understand classic plays in terms of modern analogies of action and behavior.

This recent production of Aeschylus' Agamemnon at the American Repertory Theatre recalls Fredric Jameson's discussion of postmodern pastiche, in that it appears to combine elements from several historical eras: Agamemnon, costumed as a modern general, arrives on a military transport vehicle to confront Clytaemnestra in an evening dress. While the backdrop of the set resembles a Greek skene, the people of Argos (lower right) resemble modern townspeople.

This production of Christopher Marlowe's Doctor Faustus uses an open stage and relatively minimal costuming and properties to emphasize both the power of Faustus's imagination and the fact that Mephostophilis has only illusion to offer Faustus. Here, while Faustus "sees" his "bride," the audience sees a demon disguised as a woman.

JoAnne Akalaitis's 1994 production of Aphra Behn's The Rover set the play in a modern carnival setting, as a way to make the sexual license associated with the carnival more evident to modern audiences. Much as Behn's cavaliers comment on the fashionable ornateness of the Spaniards' clothing, here the men's costumes in particular seem to allude to modern Italian fashions.

For this production of Anton Chekhov's The Cherry Orchard *at the American Repertory Theatre, designer George Tsypin deconstructed the "box set" of naturalistic staging (typified by the Moscow Art Theater's production; see picture on p. 572). Instead, he set the play on an open stage, littered with the remains of that homogeneous social world—an armoire, a table and chair, a rocking horse—and illuminated by harsh phosphorescent lights. As the actors' isolated and statuesque positioning suggests, this production used the play's visual design to literalize the isolation of the characters.*

This New York Shakespeare Festival production of Bertolt Brecht's Mother Courage and Her Children *used multiracial casting and set the play in the period of American westward expansion. Brecht frequently adapted classic plays to new historical settings; his* Threepenny Opera *was based on John Gay's eighteenth-century* Beggar's Opera, *and he updated the story of Joan of Arc to gangster-land Chicago in* Saint Joan of the Stockyards. *Brecht might well have been impressed by the idea of relocating* Mother Courage's *critique of war and business from seventeenth-century Europe to nineteenth-century America.*

Occasionally, a director's restaging of a classic may restore elements of the playwright's design that have been lost or suppressed in the history of the play's theatrical production. This 1994 New York production of Tennessee Williams's The Glass Menagerie, *for example, used the projections—including "The Sky Falls"—that Williams had included in his original script but that were dropped from later stage versions of the play.*

MODERN EUROPE

I N MANY WAYS THE WORLD WE LIVE IN TODAY WAS FORGED BETWEEN 1850 and 1950. Since the mid-nineteenth century, enormous political changes have redrawn the map of the planet: two world wars; the rise of the United States and the rise and fall of the Union of Soviet Socialist Republics as world superpowers; revolutions in Russia and China; worldwide liberation from European colonial rule in Mexico, the Philippines, Latin America, Africa, India, and Southeast Asia. Political change was spurred by a series of industrial and technological revolutions. This is the century of the telephone, radio, film, and television; of the automobile and the highway; of the airplane and the rocket; of penicillin, anesthetics, vaccinations, and artificial organs; of the assembly line and mass production; of multinational corporations extending their markets and influence around the globe. The acceleration of technological change altered the fabric of daily life, creating new forms of living, working, and relating to one another, and new ways of measuring our lives: suburbs and housing developments, trade unions and public corporations, the time clock and the wristwatch, public education and compulsory retirement. It witnessed huge changes in the landscape of life: the growth of the modern cityscape, of modern slums, skyscrapers, subways, and even city streets; of massive public projects like the Panama and Suez canals, the Empire State Building, the Eiffel Tower, and their grim cousins—the gas chambers of Auschwitz and the nuclear bombing of Hiroshima and Nagasaki.

Political and social changes were rivaled by the intellectual and cultural revolutions that gave—or attempted to give—meaning to modern experience. This is the century of Darwin and the theory of evolution; of Marx and Lenin; of Gandhi's nonviolent resistance; of Einstein, Oppenheimer, and Teller, and a revolution in our understanding of the physical cosmos; of Freud's discovery of the unconscious; of Proust, Joyce, Stein, Eliot, and Woolf; of the Impressionist painters, and of Picasso, and Pollock; of Diaghilev and Nijinsky, of Fred Astaire and Ginger Rogers, of Isadora Duncan and Martha Graham; of Wagner, of Stravinsky and Schoenberg, of ragtime and jazz.

This complex of revolutions extends to the modern theater. Technological innovation, political developments, and two major wars encouraged an increasing internationalism across the arts of Europe, evident in the "international" style of architecture popularized by Le Corbusier, the Bauhaus, and their followers; in Cubist painting and sculpture; and in modernist writing and music. This internationalism, however, hardly fostered a single, monolithic sense of "modernism" in the arts. Instead, it gave rise to a series of fragmentary AVANT-GARDE movements—imagism, cubism, vorticism, futurism, symbolism, surrealism, Dada, and so on—each with its own ideals, esthetics, and audience, and usually with its own resistant posture toward society as well. The fragment—the poetic image, Joyce's "epiphanies," Schoenberg's twelve-tone row, montage in film— came to be valued as a means of expression in itself.

Modernist art also developed a distinction between "high art" and the esthetics of mass culture that parallels the modern division of labor and implies a division between highbrow and lowbrow, the elite and the popular. In many respects, the modernist theater became definitive of "high art" as it was edged from the center of cultural life by other performance media—film, radio, and later television—which claimed greater immediacy and wider distribution. After the turn of the century, the modern theater and drama were increasingly pressed to define what is germane, special, essential to live dramatic performance.

This unit (and unit 7) surveys the theater more widely than previous units, focusing not on a single city or site of performance, but instead on the broader developments of this international movement. For although the theaters of Chekhov's Moscow, Shaw's London, and Brecht's Berlin reflected very different social dynamics, they were engaged in a common, distinctly modernist project: bringing the stage into a critical relation to the forms of modern life by taking an experimental attitude toward theatrical production.

THE MODERN THEATER

Theatrical innovation always takes place on three fronts: as technology, as esthetics, and as ideology. The history of the modern theater is in one sense a history of new strategies and techniques for stage production: electric lighting, revolving stages, increasingly spectacular and illusionistic stage machinery, and new techniques of stage design, acting, and direction. What makes these changes meaningful is how they are used to represent and explain the world around us.

Reviewing the history of nineteenth-century drama, Brander Matthews—the first professor of dramatic literature in the United States—remarked in 1910 that modern drama owed its innovation more to Edison than to Ibsen, that the new drama was "the inevitable consequence of the incandescent bulb." The technological revolutions that brought engines and electricity to the public transformed theater throughout Europe and America: the replacement of candle lighting and gas lighting with more flexible electric lighting; the installation of the PROSCENIUM frame, emphasizing the pictorial coherence of the stage; the gradual disappearance of galleries and boxes in favor of seating the audience in darkened, fan-shaped theaters, emphasizing a perspective view of the proscenium; elevators to raise and lower sets; revolving stages on which several settings could be placed at one time. This technology could be put to a variety of uses, and the nineteenth-century theaters of Europe and America had an extraordinarily spectacular dimension, fostering a taste for EXTRAVAGANZAS, MELODRAMAS, NAUTICAL SHOWS, PANTOMIMES, and TABLEAUX. However, the apparatus of the modern theater came increasingly to be dominated by the notion of SCENIC UNITY, the idea that the stage set, the costumes, the behavior of the actors, and the dramatic action all should correspond to a single historical era and social milieu. Shakespeare's actors had mixed contemporary Elizabethan dress with "antique" costumes in the production of plays with classical settings. Throughout the eighteenth century, actors wore contemporary clothing regardless of the historical era of the play. By the late nineteenth century, however, following the example of Charles Kean and Henry Irving in England, the company of George II, the Duke of Saxe-Meiningen in Germany, and others, productions increasingly strove to establish a unified style on the stage, in which the dialogue, acting style, costumes, setting, and dramatic action all conformed to a single point-of-view.

The use of a unified theatrical style to assert a thorough VERISIMILITUDE, a photographic "slice of life" onstage, became the cornerstone of modern REALISM in drama and theater and of the movement called NATURALISM in which it began. In a series of essays calling for a "naturalism in the theater," published in the 1870s, the French novelist and playwright Émile Zola argued that the technology of the late nineteenth-century theater could be used to represent a more clinical or scientific attitude toward the world. He urged the stage to adopt a more lifelike and "naturalistic" style by adopting the "objective" methods and perspective of the natural sciences. By filling the stage with objects—real doors, real walls, pictures, furniture, fireplaces—the theater could place men and women in their "environment" rather than in the idealized "setting" of the classical theater, and the characters could then be seen as influenced by that material environment. In contrast to the ideal heroes of earlier drama, the characters of modern plays would become part of that stage milieu, influenced by the forces of history, society, economy, and psychology. Naturalism, that is, uses the technology of the stage to claim a "scientific" attitude toward social problems, usually emphasizing the determining role that the social environment plays in the characters' actions. It organized the theater's new technology and the idea of

A PROSCENIUM STAGE: SHAKESPEARE MEMORIAL THEATRE

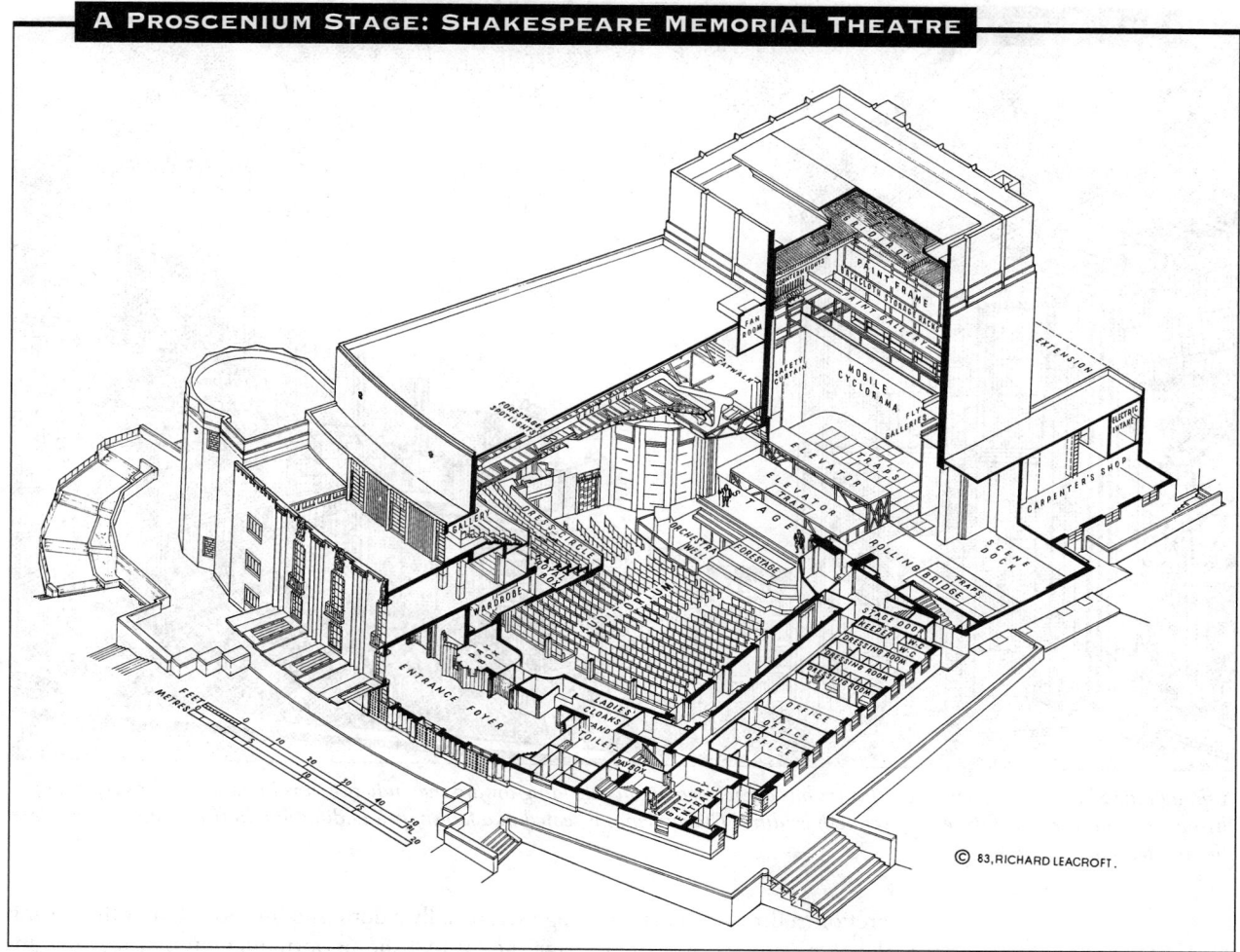

The Shakespeare Memorial Theatre, Stratford-upon-Avon, 1932, displays an extensive backstage area used for scenic machinery.

scenic unity it made possible, and provided modern theater with a characteristic kind of meaning: the achievement of verisimilitude.

Naturalism and realism are notoriously difficult to distinguish; here we can describe them as two phases in the history of modern theater and drama. In this sense, naturalism provides the thematic inspiration and many of the dramatic techniques we now associate with modern realistic drama. Realism in the theater is also committed to verisimilitude, but usually develops a wider range of style and a more problematic sense of the relationship of character and environment. While naturalistic plays tend to be preoccupied with the duplication of material reality onstage, realistic plays sometimes distort the verisimilitude of the stage picture in order to dramatize an inner, psychological truth. Tom, in Tennessee Williams's *The Glass Menagerie* (see unit 6), for example, moves in and out of the realistic setting onstage, between the world of memory, the world of the audience, and the objective social reality of the drama. Realism extends and refines the techniques first explored by Zola's generation of playwrights, directors, and actors: a simple and direct speaking style that usually masks a **SUBTEXT** of subtle, unspoken motives; middle- or lower-class characters; action that revolves around the discovery of some past crime or

Although the Shakespeare Memorial Theatre has a forestage apron extending toward the audience, it is in many respects typical of the proscenium theaters of the early twentieth century. The audience is seated in a fan-shaped auditorium, in fixed seats, facing the illuminated stage.

indiscretion; a three-dimensional stage set, usually a domestic interior. Rather than using the play as a vehicle for a single "star" actor, realistic performance emphasizes the ensemble playing of the cast, so that each character becomes important in the overall action. Onstage, realism often treats the boundary of the proscenium as an invisible **FOURTH WALL** dividing the environment onstage from the audience. The fourth wall prevents the actors from playing to the audience and so from destroying the unity of illusion onstage.

Realism has become the dominant mode of dramatic performance today, so pervasive that it may be difficult for us to recapture its special excitement and danger when first introduced in the 1880s and 1890s. In the first blush of the modern era, the ability to picture an untheatrical, apparently "real" world on the stage was in itself a kind of spectacle, akin to the magic of the new, competing art of photography. Moreover, the first generation of realistic playwrights often adopted a critical posture toward the pieties of the middle-class audience whose attitudes were embodied in the "realistic" vision of the world. Plays like Ibsen's *Ghosts* and *A Doll House*, Strindberg's *Miss Julie*, and even Glaspell's *Trifles* raised the scandalous topics of sexual betrayal, marital discord, class conflict, sexual freedom, and gender politics in ways that challenged the conventional morality of the bourgeois audience.

The realistic theater developed many of the practices we are familiar with today: new sets for each production, rather than the same furniture recycled from show to show, in order to create the play's specific environment; the fourth wall; the darkened auditorium.

Although realistic drama became pervasive, it first flourished in the small avant-garde theaters of the INDEPENDENT THEATER MOVEMENT at the turn of the century. Throughout Europe and the United States, playwrights and directors worked to carve a place for themselves outside the commercial mainstream, which often resisted and sometimes censored the controversial plays of the new realism. André Antoine founded the Théâtre Libre ("Free Theater") in Paris as a subscription theater in 1887; since the shows were open only to subscribers and not to the general public, he was able to avoid censorship and to produce plays like Ibsen's *Ghosts* and Strindberg's *The Father*. Antoine's work was paralleled by the German Freie Bühne ("Free Stage") in 1889. In England, the actress Janet Achurch mounted a production of Ibsen's *A Doll House* in 1889; J. T. Grein's Independent Theater opened in 1891 with a production of *Ghosts* and went on to produce plays by Ibsen, Shaw, and other contemporary playwrights. In Russia, Constantin Stanislavsky and Vladimir Nemirovich-Danchenko founded the Moscow Art Theater in 1898, launching one of the most influential of modern theaters with their production of Chekhov's *The Seagull*. Independent theaters were often part of nationalist movements as well, especially in Norway, Sweden, Finland, Italy, and Ireland. In Ireland, W. B. Yeats, Lady Augusta Gregory, John Millington Synge, and a solid cast of amateur actors established a nationalist theater company in 1902 and opened The Abbey Theater in 1904. Here, the artistic resistance of the independent theater was allied to political resistance and national self-definition. The influence of these theaters was felt in the United States throughout the first decades of the twentieth century. David Belasco's minute fidelity to detail had firmly established a realistic idiom in the American theater, but it took the LITTLE THEATER MOVEMENT, inaugurated by Eugene O'Neill, Susan Glaspell, and the Provincetown Playhouse in 1915, to establish a repertoire of modern drama in the United States, and they were soon followed by other companies.

The rise of the independent theaters also points to the theater's fragmentation and its marginalization in modern society. The theater no longer commands the cultural centrality that it had in classical Athens or in London and Paris in the sixteenth and seventeenth centuries. Instead, it has become the site for a diverse, sometimes confusing array of artistic experiments. Naturalism and realism were the first dramatic modes to consider themselves not as expressing the dominant political and ideological order, but as criticizing the values and institutions of middle-class society. The major plays of the realistic canon often tend to criticize modern life, particularly its dehumanizing, exploitative routine. The major heroes of the realistic mode—Nora Helmer, Major Barbara, Laura Wingfield—are all characters whose desire for freedom, vitality, and life is threatened by the deadening, deceptive world in which they live. Because realistic drama usually sees that world as an all-embracing "environment," though, its social themes don't finally lead to a call for social change. Modern society may be a prison, but the liberation urged by realistic drama is imagined on the individual level; the characters' search for freedom, value, and meaning leaves the world unchanged. Despite its critical stance toward modern society, realistic drama tacitly accepts the world and its values as an unchanging, and unchangeable, environment in which the characters live out their lives.

For this reason, realistic drama has often seemed an inadequate vehicle for a sustained critique of the forces of modern life, and almost from the moment of its inception in the 1880s and 1890s, realism inspired antagonistic forms of drama and theater. The history of modern drama is a series of reactions against bourgeois society and its values, and against the realistic drama that seemed to represent it and its vision of the world.

Although it was finally concerned with many of the same issues, the EXPRESSIONIST THEATER popular from the turn of the century through the 1930s marked an exciting stylistic departure from the realistic mode. Expressionist plays like Strindberg's *A Dream*

FORMS OF MODERN DRAMA

Play, or American plays like Elmer Rice's *The Adding Machine*, Sophie Treadwell's *Machinal*, or Eugene O'Neill's *The Emperor Jones*, transformed the terms of realistic theater and drama. Rather than showing a character whose inner vitality is crushed by the bourgeois environment, expressionist plays try to show the mind and heart of the character visually, to express it directly in the objects and actions of the stage. The stage set becomes distorted, nearly dreamlike, and it is often peopled by characters who are exaggerated, mechanized, or fantastic, as a way of conveying the emotional coloring of the central character's experience. In O'Neill's play, for instance, the Emperor Jones is haunted by his "Little Formless Fears" when he flees into the forest; his flight is accompanied by the sound of a drum, which beats faster and louder as the play proceeds. More often, characters in expressionist drama are unnamed, like the Young Woman of *Machinal* or Mr. Zero of *The Adding Machine*, emphasizing that they have become cogs in the modern social and industrial machine. The action of expressionist drama is episodic and much like morality drama. Ernst Toller even named the scenes of his play *Transfiguration* "stations" to stress the play's likeness to a Christian passion play.

Thematically, expressionist theater resembles realism in its attention to character psychology and in its portrayal—however distorted or exaggerated—of the dehumanizing process of modern life. However, the style of expressionism also subverts realism in important ways, challenging both the logical, causal ordering of realistic dramatic action and the visual verisimilitude of the realistic theater. The SYMBOLIST THEATER also developed antirealistic attitudes toward drama and staging and extended the expressionist theater's repudiation of the drama of modern life. Written in prose or in verse, symbolic drama created a dim and mysterious other world, sometimes drawn from mythology or simply from the poet's imagination. The Belgian playwright Maurice Maeterlinck created a vogue for this kind of drama at the turn of the century, a drama which finds analogies in the work of Stéphane Mallarmé, August Strindberg, T. S. Eliot, W. B. Yeats, and Samuel Beckett. Yeats's mythological plays—such as *On Baile's Strand*—are typical of this special and influential mode. Relatively static in action, the plays rely on a densely figurative language to enlarge and energize the "poetic" meaning of events onstage.

Finally, an explicitly Marxist theory of the ideologically coercive dimension of realism—the sense that realism claims that its special perspective of the world is *natural*, that is, unavoidable and *real*—stands at the center of modern EPIC THEATER. Though usually associated with Bertolt Brecht, many of the techniques of epic theater were developed by Erwin Piscator in Berlin during the 1920s and early 1930s and by Vsevolod Meyerhold in his brilliant experiments with CONSTRUCTIVIST THEATER after the Russian Revolution of 1917. Brecht assimilated these techniques to a political purpose that he called epic theater. Rather than claiming to represent reality directly onstage by concealing the workings of the theater, epic theater alerts the audience to the ideological dimension of theater practice by constantly keeping the stage's "means of production" in view. Brecht developed the ALIENATION EFFECT as a way of alerting the audience to the constructed nature of stage events. While the realistic theater claims that the theater and drama, actor and character, stage and dramatic locale are the same, epic theater shows how they are different. In so doing, Brecht argued, the epic theater enables the audience to ask how—with what purpose, to what effect—stage practice is making this dramatic effect come about, and so leads the audience to take a more critical view of the process of the theater. Epic acting, then, comments on itself as "acting." The stage is not unified as a single dramatic locale, but always remains visibly a stage. Brecht also argued that epic drama should be structured differently than realistic plays. Instead of the apparently organic, "causal" action of realistic drama, Brecht's plays are written in a series of episodes. This technique, Brecht argued, allows the actors and the audience to reconsider the character's possibilities for action and change afresh in each scene. By calling the audience's attention to how the play comes into being onstage, epic theater encourages the audience to develop a dialectical sense of how social reality—in the theater and in the world at large—comes into being, how it is made through the interaction of individual and social forces and the interaction of material reality and IDEOLOGY. Epic theater has had an enormous influence on drama and theater around the world, particularly in the 1960s, 1970s, and 1980s.

Stage practice has developed its own rich history, too—again often in reaction to realistic verisimilitude. Throughout the twentieth century, for instance, designers and architects have experimented with different ways of orienting the audience to the stage, in THEATER IN THE ROUND and in ENVIRONMENTAL THEATER, for instance. To see the dramatic action surrounded by spectators or to have the play take place among the audience alters the audience's relationship to both the drama and its performance and changes how the audience can read the production. The Constructivist experiments of Vsevolod Meyerhold following the Russian Revolution placed a nonrepresentational "construction" onstage, a structure that the actors used as a "machine for acting" rather than as a realistic set. Similarly, experimental performance altered notions of what dramatic and theatrical representation could be like. Following World War I, writers like Tristan Tzara called for an art that was formless and irrational, a process rather than a product; such "Dada"—a nonsense term—poems, plays, and monologues were often given CABARET PERFORMANCE in Zurich, Berlin, and Paris. DADA and SURREALIST THEATER developed a kind of hallucinatory intimacy between stage and audience, laying the foundations for Artaud's THEATER OF CRUELTY (see unit 7). In all of these experiments, the theater worked to disperse the visual unity characteristic of the realistic stage in ways that led to new configurations of the relationship between the audience and the performers and to new interpretive perspectives on drama and on the possibilities of theater.

Realism, expressionism, symbolist theater, and *epic theater*—these useful labels necessarily limit and categorize the rich variety of the stage in ways that are artificial and untrue to the dynamics of change in the modern theater, for new innovations tend to draw their techniques from several of these modes. Modern plays, for instance, often blend representational techniques as a way of challenging the audience's understanding of the drama and its implication in the world. Despite their "realistic" anchoring in a material, lifelike setting, for example, Chekhov's plays sometimes disturb the stability of that illusion with odd, almost "symbolic" effects—the breaking string in *The Cherry Orchard*, for instance. The action of Strindberg's *Miss Julie*, too, for all the play's emphasis on class and social environment, seems to lurch and accelerate in ways more characteristic of an "expressionist" linking of the dramatic form to the characters' psychological experience. In Pirandello's *Six Characters in Search of an Author*—a play indebted in many ways to the "symbolist" theater—the Characters want the Actors to produce a play much in the manner of Ibsen's drama, a realistic drama of hidden crime and its discovery. These labels are useful in helping us to describe some of the outlines of a given play, but we should remember that many modern playwrights wrote in a variety of modes, and that each play is itself a kind of experiment.

ACTING AND PERFORMANCE

The modern theater's radical redefinitions of the style and purpose of drama required similar redefinitions of acting and performance. At the turn of the century, a theatrical company would have been organized according to each actor's typical LINE OF BUSINESS. Something like the company in Pirandello's *Six Characters,* companies had a leading comic actor, a villain or "heavy," a leading man, a leading lady, a comic old man, a comic woman, and a variety of other parts. Unlike *commedia dell' arte,* actors each played a variety of different characters; nonetheless, each actor would have elaborated some relatively conventional "business" for acting the kind of character he or she usually played. The unity of illusion demanded by the realistic theater, however, required each character to be

Although most of the plays included in *The Harcourt Brace Anthology of Drama* have been popular in the theater, they are all to some extent plays that have been canonized for their qualities as dramatic "literature": rich language and characterization, complex engagement with social and moral issues, deft and original use of dramatic convention, and so on. However, theater and drama pose special problems to the idea of a single literary canon. As popular entertainments, plays have not always been regarded as having "literary" merit. Plays were published only irregularly in Shakespeare's era partly for this reason, and even today few publishers have much commitment to keeping contemporary plays in print—which makes it particularly difficult for contemporary drama to become part of *any* literary canon. More important, plays are produced under very different conditions than novels and poems. Plays are made to be meaningful in a specific theater; their "literary" impact on readers is often secondary to their original purpose, which is to make a theatrical impact on a given body of spectators.

In late-eighteenth and nineteenth-century Europe—in part as a result of the relaxing of restrictions on theatrical performance, and in part as a reflection of a sense of "literature" as part of a circumscribed sphere of "high culture"—a variety of new dramatic genres became popular, of which the most important is **MELODRAMA.** The term was initially used to indicate plays in which music was used to accentuate the emotional coloring of the action; the term became more generally applied to plays with a conventionalized set of characters, a clear narrative structure, and a distinct moral cosmos. In the nineteenth-century theater, melodrama was an extremely popular genre, fusing the theater's increasing capacity for visual spectacle with a strongly colored and direct dramatic action. The world of melodrama is a world of clear-cut moral absolutes: the hero and heroine are thoroughly virtuous and are threatened by villains who are equally unscrupulous. The action is organized in a series of episodes, in each of which the hero/heroine's happiness, virtue, fortune, or life is threatened with destruction; each act of a melodrama usually ends with some striking crisis, often calling for an elaborate stage effect—an explosion, train wreck, or storm. The action of melodrama is often highly involved and coincidental, yet usually works eventually toward a happy—or at least sentimental—ending. If the hero must die, he usually dies in the heroine's arms; more often, the couple are restored to one another and live happily ever after.

Melodrama is usually dated from the popularity of plays like Johann Christoph Friedrich von Schiller's (1759–1805) *The Robbers* (1782), August Friedrich Ferdinand von Kotzebue's (1761–1819) *Menschenhass und Reue* (1789), and René Charles Guilbert de Pixérécourt's (1773–1844) *Coelina* (1800); although Kotzebue and Pixérécourt are now rarely read, their plays were widely adapted throughout Europe. Thirty-six of Kotzebue's plays were translated into English, and several remained popular throughout the nineteenth century. Richard Brinsley Sheridan (1751–1816) adapted Kotzebue's *Der Spanier in Peru* as *Pizarro* in 1799, which became a brilliant success for the actor John Philip Kembel; Thomas Holcroft (1744–1809) adapted Pixérécourt's *Coelina* as *A Tale of Mystery* in 1802. While early nineteenth-century melodrama tended toward Gothic settings—mysterious castles, ghostly visitors, and the like—by later in the century melodrama's typical formal and moral patterns were applied to plays with local and contemporary settings. Pierce Egan's novel *Life in Lon-*

(A S I D E)

MELODRAMA

more finely individualized. Much as the stage designer provided a new set for each production and the costume designer provided clothing appropriate to the character and his or her setting, so the actors were forced to particularize their performances in new ways.

A second stimulus for this innovation was the drama itself. Playwrights like Ibsen and Chekhov typically created characters against the grain of theatrical stereotypes. Nora Helmer, for example, seems like a typical **SOUBRETTE** at the opening of *A Doll House,* the pert and clever young woman of light comedy. However, as the play develops, Ibsen challenges this convention and forces the actress to discover new ways of producing the character. Realistic plays frequently ask actors to work against the apparent "type" of the role,

don was adapted as *Tom and Jerry; or, Life in London* in 1821; Edward George Bulwer-Lytton's (1803–1873) *Money* (1840) was one of several plays that held the stage through the end of the century.

Since melodrama drew a wide audience, and often centered on poor-but-virtuous heroes and heroines, it has sometimes been thought to articulate social resistance. For while early versions like Douglas Jerrold's (1803–1857) hugely popular nautical melodrama *Black Ey'd Susan* (1829) emphasized the undying loyalty and patriotism of British navy sailors (or "tars"), the polarized moral ethos of melodrama could be turned into a vehicle for social critique. In the United States, melodrama became one vehicle for dramatizing ethnic and racial conflict. John Augustus Stone's (1800–1834) *Metamora; or, The Last of the Wampanoags* (1829), dramatized a heroic Indian chief's losing battle to save the land of his ancestors from his rapacious white enemies. In *The Octoroon* (1859), Dion Boucicault (1820–1890) staged the fatal love story between the octoroon Zoe, the virtuous plantation owner who loves her, and the wicked Yankee overseer, McCloskey, who threatens to buy her when it emerges that Zoe was never actually freed from slavery. But although these plays end with "tragic" consequences for their heroes and heroines, melodrama tends to locate its evils in the character of its villains, rather than

MELODRAMA: *THE BELLS*

Sir Henry Irving's (1838–1905) performance in Leopold Lewis's melodrama The Bells *was one of his greatest roles. The illustration presents both the emotionally exaggerated quality of melodramatic acting and melodrama's use of special effects. In the play, Mathias (Irving's role) has murdered and concealed the body of a Polish Jew. Although many years have passed since the murder, Mathias is haunted by the sound of his victim's sleigh bells. In this scene, he staggers before a vision of the crime itself.*

in the structure of society itself: for this reason, melodrama is usually unable to develop a deeper analysis of the social institutions—racism, for example—that afflict its characters' lives. When Bernard Shaw turned to melodrama as a vehicle for his own drama of social critique, he strategically inverted its patterns of characterization as a way of opening its social order to criticism: one way *Major Barbara*, for example, attempts to jolt the audience into examining its attitudes about society at large is by casting Andrew Undershaft—so similar to the scheming and all-powerful industrialist villain of countless popular melodramas—as the moral "hero" of the play.

to discover the psychological subtext of will and desire beneath the spoken words that motivates the character's actions. Actors and actresses at the turn of the century frequently had difficulty reading the new realistic plays, precisely because they could not see how to represent the more indirect action and individualized characters through the kinds of stage behavior they had been trained to use.

A new kind of drama requires a new kind of acting, and companies throughout Europe developed ways of acting more behavioristically onstage. The most systematic approach to acting was undertaken by the actor and director Constantin Stanislavski at the Moscow Art Theater around the turn of the century. Although Stanislavski thought that his techniques could be applied to any play, he discovered the need for such acting largely in his work on Chekhov's plays. Chekhov's plays were frustrating to actors of the old school because the characters did not conform to traditional types and the action seemed so indirect and inconsequential, lacking familiar dramatic rhythms and climaxes. Stanislavski developed techniques for approaching each character as an individual, techniques that were later systematized as a "method" of actor-training. Stanislavski trained the actor to associate his or her personal history with the invented actions of the dramatic character so that the actor could tap that emotional spontaneity, a "life in art," as part of the performance. By using the MAGIC IF—imagining themselves *as* the character, rather than applying a stock line of business—and using their own EMOTION MEMORY to vivify the character's inner life, Stanislavski's actors were taught to bring authentic emotional experience into their performances. Of course, Stanislavski also emphasized the many other abilities that an actor must develop—physical training, vocal control, grace, concentration—but his real contribution to the modern stage is the emphasis on the actor's emotional reality in performance. The realistic theater uses real objects to create a persuasive material environment, and its characters come alive through the actor's real feeling. Stanislavski's work has been extremely influential, particularly in the United States, where it was adapted as the school of METHOD ACTING in the 1930s, and it remains—in very different and modified forms—at the center of much actor-training today.

Antirealistic drama also called for the development of new styles of performance. Meyerhold developed BIOMECHANICS as a way to make the actor's performance more physical, less directly concerned with the behavioral and psychological verisimilitude typical of Stanislavskian realistic acting. His work has analogies in the use of dance and ritualized performance in symbolist theater and in the nonrepresentational physicality of Antonin Artaud's Theater of Cruelty (see unit 7). Symbolist theater also repudiated the lifelike quality of realistic acting. It required a highly artificial and statuesque stillness from performers, allowing the actors to strike powerful but ethereal poses in order to deliver the densely poetic language of the play without interference. Yeats—whose antipathy to realism was profound—thought of training his actors in barrels, to keep them from moving and gesturing as they would do in everyday life: the art of the symbolist theater should be emphatically artificial, thoroughly apart from the conduct of life beyond the stage.

Brecht, again, voiced the most thorough critique of realistic acting. To Brecht, the problem of realistic acting was that it showed the "character" as a finished product, a commodity, rather than revealing *how* the character had come into being, both through the social forces described in the drama and through the decisions taken by the actor as part of the performance. Brecht argued that the actor should acknowledge that he or she both empathizes with the character and demonstrates the character to the audience, that acting is both feeling and showing at the same time. This dialectical approach invites the audience to see how the actor is making the "character" and allows the public to interpret both the process and the product of theater art, the dramatic "character" and the actor's labor.

WOMEN IN MODERN DRAMA AND THEATER

Most readers of modern drama immediately note the prominence of women characters in the plays—Nora Helmer in *A Doll House,* Julie in *Miss Julie,* Barbara in *Major Barbara,* Courage in *Mother Courage.* Playwrights frequently associated the political and social limitations of middle-class life with male characters and used female characters to pose subversive questions about that social order. However, in the drama, as in society, this subversive freedom sometimes emerges as illusory or problematic. Ibsen, for instance, enables Nora to recognize how she has been defined by the men in her life, but the world outside her home hardly seems inviting; is there really anywhere for her to go? Many of the women—Miss Julie, Major Barbara—are also assigned an erotic power opposed to the "reason" of their male antagonists. While this power, too, can be disruptive, it sometimes also reinforces traditional gender stereotypes. Feminine erotic power in the drama carries with it other ascribed values, defining women as more emotional, as more subject to the influence of the body, as closer to "nature." Men retain a pragmatic, "rational" authority that places them at the center of society, and that defines the arena of culture and civilization as an implicitly male domain. The apparent freedom of these stage women, that is, often signals their deeper captivity to the gendered economy of modern society, a captivity shared by actresses in the period as well. Although this is also a period in which actresses—Sarah Bernhardt, Eleonora Duse, or Ellen Terry, for example—could earn an international reputation, they worked in a theater in which men greatly outnumbered women in the audience and in which nearly all of the managers and producers were men. In a male-dominated industry like the modern theater, it is not surprising that women on-stage—both dramatic characters and performers—should reflect fundamentally masculine attitudes about the place of women in society.

To think of the history of theater and drama since Ibsen is to think of an increasingly large and problematic array of dramatic styles, modes of theatrical production, and conceptions of the audience and its world. Many of these innovations were local at first, responding to the social and theatrical conditions of a specific time and place: Brecht's Marxist theater arose in the cabaret culture of Berlin in the late 1920s; Pirandello's **METATHEATER** was part of the lively Italian avant-garde following World War I; Shaw's drama was informed by the progressive politics of the British Fabian society and by dramatic conventions drawn from the popular plays of the late Victorian stage. The drama of modern Europe develops a posture of resistant inquiry toward the pieties of contemporary social life. It works both to represent that world and to change it, to affect our ideas about character and personality, about the political realities of our world, and even about the metaphysical certainties we have come to believe.

In this scene from Henrik Ibsen's A Doll House, Doctor Rank, Helmer, and Nora have just returned from the party; Nora wears her tarantella costume, and Helmer has been given a "mask" of middle-class respectability.

In this production of Luigi Pirandello's Six Characters in Search of an Author, *the statuesque "characters" arrive at the stage door, clothed in black and bathed in an eerie light.*

The photograph of the Moscow Art Theater's original production of Anton Chekhov's The Cherry Orchard *shows the naturalistic detail for which Constantin Stanislavski's company was famous; Stanislavski is at the left in the role of Gaev, gesturing to the bookcase.*

■ GEORG BÜCHNER ■

Georg Büchner (1813–1837) is something of an anomaly in the history of the modern theater. Born in Goddelau, Germany, Büchner was the son of a physician and enrolled at the University of Strasbourg in 1831 to pursue a medical degree. But in the revolutionary atmosphere of early nineteenth-century Europe—feeling the effects both of the French Revolution and of romantic idealism in literature and the arts—Büchner's interests shifted. He left Strasbourg in 1833 for Giessen, where he studied history and philosophy and became involved in political activity. He wrote a revolutionary pamphlet, *The Hessian Courier,* which was censored, and he had to flee Germany for Switzerland. There, Büchner continued his scientific training at the University of Zurich, where he died suddenly of a fever in 1837. He was 23 years old.

In Zurich, however, Büchner wrote three plays: *Danton's Death, Leonce and Lena,* and *Woyzeck.* These plays were unproduced and unpublished during Büchner's lifetime and were only discovered much later by the playwright Gerhart Hauptmann; the first staging of *Danton's Death* was produced by the German director Max Reinhardt in 1910. In many respects, Büchner's play seems to herald the modern theater that would not be born until much later in the century, for Büchner sets his characters within a deterministic world, one in which the forces of history and society limit their opportunities to act and finally destroy them.

WOYZECK

Woyzeck is a striking play by any measure, but particularly striking when we recall that it was composed more than 150 years ago. For *Woyzeck's* sensibility seems unusually well-attuned to the disjunctive experience of modern life. Unlike other plays of its period, *Woyzeck* is episodic in structure (though this may be an accident of history, since Büchner had not completed work on the play at his death); each scene places Woyzeck, the play's remarkable hero, in a new situation. Given the combination of his scientific training and his revolutionary politics, it's perhaps not surprising that Büchner's treatment of his lower-class hero emphasizes the social and material limitations of his life, pressures which finally destroy him. Yet while it seems to prefigure the naturalistic theater of Zola and his disciples, Büchner's play hardly adheres to the machine-like "logic" of the well-made naturalistic tragedy. First, each scene seems to offer the audience a different "slice" of Woyzeck's "life." Rather than a progressive narrative that seems to produce the tragic catastrophe as the unavoidable result of the plot's causal logic, Büchner offers a series of vignettes, snapshots of Woyzeck's life that the audience must assemble. At least as important, though, is Büchner's strategy of characterization. Again, rather than the smooth and linear development of a character's motives—think of how each event in Ibsen's *A Doll House* seems to provide Nora with a new plan of action—Büchner's hero seems to lurch wildly through the play. Although Woyzeck is governed by his material circumstances—his poverty, his temperament, his position in the army—he also seems to stand apart from them, a figure of Romantic anomie. As he says, drunkenly, in Scene 12,

> The world is out of order! Why did the street-lamp cleaner forget to wipe my eyes—everything's dark. Devil damn you, God! I lay in my own way: jump over myself. Where's my shadow gone? There's no safety in the kennels any more. Shine the moon through my legs again to see if my shadow's there.

Not until August Strindberg's plays of the 1890s would European drama again find characters so radically alienated from their world.

WOYZECK

Georg Büchner

TRANSLATED BY CARL RICHARD MUELLER

— CHARACTERS —

WOYZECK	OLD MAN WITH BARREL-ORGAN
MARIE	JEW
CAPTAIN	INNKEEPER
DOCTOR	APPRENTICES
DRUM MAJOR	KATHY
SERGEANT	KARL THE TOWN IDIOT
ANDRES	GRANDMOTHER
MARGRET	POLICEMAN
PROPRIETOR OF THE BOOTH	SOLDIERS, STUDENTS, YOUNG MEN *and* GIRLS, CHILDREN,
CHARLATAN	JUDGE, COURT CLERK, PEOPLE, CHARLATAN'S WIFE

— SCENE ONE —

At the CAPTAIN's.

(THE CAPTAIN *in a chair.* WOYZECK *shaving him.*)

CAPTAIN: Not so fast, Woyzeck, not so fast! One thing at a time! You're making me dizzy. What am I to do with the ten extra minutes that you'll finish early today? Just think, Woyzeck: you still have thirty beautiful years to live! Thirty
5 years! That makes three hundred and sixty months! And days! Hours! Minutes! What do you think you'll do with all that horrible stretch of time? Have you ever thought about it, Woyzeck?

WOYZECK: Yes, sir, Captain.

10 CAPTAIN: It frightens me when I think about the world . . . when I think about eternity. Busyness, Woyzeck, busyness! There's the eternal: that's eternal, that is eternal. That you can understand. But then again it's not eternal. It's only a moment. A mere moment. Woyzeck, it makes me shudder
15 when I think that the earth turns itself about in a single day! What a waste of time! Where will it all end? Woyzeck, I can't even look at a mill wheel any more without becoming melancholy.

WOYZECK: Yes, sir, Captain.

20 CAPTAIN: Woyzeck, you always seem so exasperated! A good man isn't like that. A good man with a good conscience, that is. Well, say something, Woyzeck! What's the weather like today?

WOYZECK: Bad, Captain, sir, bad: wind!

25 CAPTAIN: I feel it already. Sounds like a real storm out there. A wind like that has the same effect on me as a mouse. (*Cunningly.*) I think it must be something out of the north-south.

WOYZECK: Yes, sir, Captain.

CAPTAIN: Ha! Ha! Ha! North-south! Ha! Ha! Ha! Oh, he's
30 a stupid one! Horribly stupid! (*Moved.*) Woyzeck, you're a good man, but (*With dignity.*) Woyzeck, you have no morality! Morality, that's when you have morals, you understand. It's a good word. You have a child without the blessings of the Church, just like our Right Reverend Garrison Chaplain
35 says: "Without the blessings of the Church." It's not *my* phrase.

WOYZECK: Captain, sir, the good Lord's not going to look at a poor worm just because they said Amen over it before they went at it. The Lord said: "Suffer the little children to come unto me."
40
CAPTAIN: What's that you said? What kind of strange answer's that? You're confusing me with your answers!

WOYZECK: It's us poor people that . . . You see, Captain, sir . . . Money, money! Whoever hasn't got money . . . Well, who's got morals when he's bringing something like me into the
45 world? We're flesh and blood, too. Our kind is miserable only once: in this world and in the next. I think if we ever got to Heaven we'd have to help with the thunder.

CAPTAIN: Woyzeck, you have no virtue! You're not a virtuous human being! Flesh and blood? Whenever I rest at the win-
50 dow, when it's finished raining, and my eyes follow the white stockings along as they hurry across the street . . . Damnation, Woyzeck, I know what love is, too, then! I'm made of flesh and blood, too. But, Woyzeck: Virtue! Virtue! How was I to get rid of the time? I always say to myself: "You're a vir-
55 tuous man (*Moved.*), a good man, a good man."

WOYZECK: Yes, Captain, sir: Virtue. I haven't got much of that. You see, us common people, we haven't got virtue. That's the way it's got to be. But if I could be a gentleman, and if I could have a hat and a watch and a cane, and if I
60 could talk refined, I'd want to be virtuous, all right. There must be something beautiful in virtue, Captain, sir. But I'm just a poor good-for-nothing!

CAPTAIN: Good, Woyzeck. You're a good man, a good man. But you think too much. It eats at you. You always seem so
65 exasperated. Our discussion has affected me deeply. You can go now. And don't run so! Slowly! Nice and slowly down the street!

— SCENE TWO —

An open field. The town in the distance.

(WOYZECK *and* ANDRES *cut twigs from the bushes.* ANDRES *whistles.*)

WOYZECK: Andres? You know this place is cursed? Look at that light streak over there on the grass. There where the toadstools grow up. That's where the head rolls every night. One time somebody picked it up. He thought it was a hedgehog. Three days and three nights and he was in a box. *(Low.)* Andres, it was the Freemasons, don't you see, it was the Freemasons!

ANDRES: *(Sings.)*

> Two little rabbits sat on a lawn
> Eating, oh, eating the green green grass . . .

WOYZECK: Quiet! Can you hear it, Andres? Can you hear it? Something moving!

ANDRES: *(Sings.)*

> Eating, oh, eating the green green grass
> Till all the grass was gone.

WOYZECK: It's moving behind me! Under me! *(Stamps on the ground.)* Listen! Hollow! It's all hollow down there! It's the Freemasons!

ANDRES: I'm afraid.

WOYZECK: Strange how still it is. You almost want to hold your breath. Andres!

ANDRES: What?

WOYZECK: Say something! *(Looks about fixedly.)* Andres! How bright it is! It's all glowing over the town! A fire's sailing around the sky and a noise coming down like trumpets. It's coming closer! Let's get out of here! Don't look back! *(Drags him into the bushes.)*

ANDRES: *(After a pause.)* Woyzeck? Do you still hear it?

WOYZECK: It's quiet now. So quiet. Like the world's dead.

ANDRES: Listen! I can hear the drums inside. We've got to go!

— SCENE THREE —

The town.

*(*MARIE *with her* CHILD *at the window.* MARGRET. *The Retreat passes,* THE DRUM MAJOR *at its head.)*

MARIE: *(Rocking* THE CHILD *in her arms.)* Ho, boy! Da-da-da-da! Can you hear? They're coming! There!

MARGRET: What a man! Built like a tree!

MARIE: He walks like a lion. *(*THE DRUM MAJOR *salutes* MARIE.*)*

MARGRET: Oh, what a look he threw you, neighbor! We're not used to such things from you.

MARIE: *(Sings.)* Soldiers, oh, you pretty lads . . .

MARGRET: Your eyes are still shining.

MARIE: And if they are? Take *your* eyes to the Jew's and let him clean them for you. Maybe he can shine them so you can sell them for a pair of buttons!

MARGRET: Look who's talking! Just look who's talking! If it isn't the Virgin herself! I'm a respectable person. But you! Everyone knows you could stare your way through seven layers of leather pants!

MARIE: Slut! *(Slams the window shut.)* Come, boy! What's it to them, anyway! Even if you are just a poor whore's baby, your dishonorable little face still makes your mother happy! *(Sings.)*

> I have my trouble and bother
> But, baby dear, where is your father?
> Why should I worry and fight

> I'll hold you and sing through the night:
> Heio popeio, my baby, my dove
> What do I want now with love?

(A knock at the window.) Who's there? Is it you, Franz? Come in!

WOYZECK: Can't. There's roll call.

MARIE: Did you cut wood for the Captain?

WOYZECK: Yes, Marie.

MARIE: What is it, Franz? You look so troubled.

WOYZECK: Marie, it happened again, only there was more. Isn't it written: "And there arose a smoke out of the pit, as the smoke of a great furnace"?

MARIE: Oh, Franz!

WOYZECK: Shh! Quiet! I've got it! The Freemasons! There was a terrible noise in the sky and everything was on fire! I'm on the trail of something, something big. It followed me all the way to the town. Something that I can't put my hands on, or understand. Something that drives us mad. What'll come of it all?

MARIE: Franz!

WOYZECK: Don't you see? Look around you! Everything hard and fixed, so gloomy. What's moving back there? When God goes, everything goes. I've got to get back.

MARIE: And the child?

WOYZECK: My God, the boy!—Tonight at the fair! I've saved something again.

(He leaves.)

MARIE: That man! Seeing things like that! He'll go mad if he keeps thinking that way! He frightened me! It's so gloomy here. Why are you so quiet, boy? Are you afraid? It's growing so dark. As if we were going blind. Only that street lamp shining in from outside. *(Sings.)*

> And what if your cradle is bad
> Sleep tight, my lovey, my lad.

I can't stand it! It makes me shiver!

(She goes out.)

— SCENE FOUR —

Fair booths. Lights. People.

*(*OLD MAN *with a* CHILD, WOYZECK, MARIE, CHARLATAN, WIFE, DRUM MAJOR, *and* SERGEANT.*)*

OLD MAN: *(Sings while* THE CHILD *dances to the barrel-organ.)*

> There's nothing on this earth will last,
> Our lives are as the fields of grass,
> Soon all is past, is past.

WOYZECK: Ho! Hip-hop there, boy! Hip-hop! Poor man, old man! Poor child, young child! trouble and happiness!

MARIE: My God, when fools still have their senses, then we're all fools. Oh, what a mad world! What a beautiful world!

(They go over to THE CHARLATAN *who stands in front of a booth, his* WIFE *in trousers, and a monkey in costume.)*

CHARLATAN: Gentlemen, gentlemen! You see here before you a creature as God created it! But it is nothing this way!

10 Absolutely nothing! But now look at what Art can do. It walks upright. Wears coat and pants. And even carries a saber. This monkey here is a regular soldier. So what if he *isn't* much different! So what if he *is* still on the bottom rung of the human ladder! Hey there, take a bow! That's the way! Now you're a 15 baron, at least. Give us a kiss! *(The monkey trumpets.)* This little customer's musical, too. And, gentlemen, in here you will see the astronomical horse and the little lovebirds. Favorites of all the crowned heads of Europe. They'll tell you anything: how old you are, how many children you have, what your ail-20 ments are. The performance is about to begin. And at the beginning. The beginning of the beginning!

WOYZECK: You know, I had a little dog once who kept sniffing around the rim of a big hat, and I thought I'd be good to him and make it easier for him and sat him on top of it. And all 25 the people stood around and clapped.

GENTLEMEN: Oh, grotesque! How really grotesque!

WOYZECK: Don't you believe in God either? It's an honest fact I don't believe in God.—You call that grotesque? I like what's grotesque. See that? That grotesque enough for 30 you?—*(To* MARIE.*)* You want to go in?

MARIE: Sure. That must be nice in there. Look at the tassels on him! And his wife's got pants on!

(They go inside.)

DRUM MAJOR: Wait a minute! Did you see her? What a piece!

SERGEANT: Hell, she could whelp a couple regiments of 35 cavalry!

DRUM MAJOR: *And* breed drum majors!

SERGEANT: Look at the way she carries that head? You'd think all that black hair would pull her down like a weight. And those eyes!

40 DRUM MAJOR: Like looking down a well . . . or up a chimney. Come on, let's go after her!

— SCENE FIVE —

Interior of the brightly lighted booth.

*(*MARIE, WOYZECK, PROPRIETOR OF THE BOOTH, SERGEANT, *and* DRUM MAJOR.*)*

MARIE: All these lights!

WOYZECK: Sure, Marie. Black cats with fiery eyes.

PROPRIETOR OF THE BOOTH: *(Bringing forward a horse.)* 5 Show your talent! Show your brute reason! Put human society to shame! Gentlemen, this animal you see here, with a tail on its torso, and standing on its four hoofs, is a member of all the learnèd societies—as well as a professor at our university where he teaches students how to ride and fight. But that requires simple intelligence. Now think with your dou-10 ble reason! What do you do when you think with your double reason? Is there a jackass in this learnèd assembly? *(The nag shakes its head.)* How's that for double reasoning? That's physiognomy for you. This is no dumb animal. This is a person! A human being! But still an animal. A beast. *(The nag 15 conducts itself indecently.)* That's right, put society to shame. As you can see, this animal is still in a state of Nature. Not ideal Nature, of course! Take a lesson from him! But ask your doctor first, it may prove highly dangerous! What we have been told by this is: Man must be natural! You are cre-20 ated of dust, sand, and dung. Why must you be more than

dust, sand, and dung? Look there at his reason. He can figure even if he can't count it off on his fingers. And why? Because he cannot express himself, can't explain. A metamorphosed human being. Tell the gentlemen what time it is! Which of you ladies and gentlemen has a watch? A 25 watch?

SERGEANT: A watch? *(He pulls a watch imposingly and measuredly from his pocket.)* There you are, my good man!

MARIE: I want to see this.

(She clambers down to the first row of seats; THE SERGEANT *helps her.)*

DRUM MAJOR: What a piece! 30

— SCENE SIX —

MARIE's *room.*

*(*MARIE *with her* CHILD.*)*

MARIE: *(Sitting, her* CHILD *on her lap, a piece of mirror in her hand.)* He told Franz to get the hell out, so what could he do! *(Looks at herself in the mirror.)* Look how the stones shine! What kind are they, I wonder? What kind did he say they were? Sleep, boy! Close your eyes! Tight! Stay that way 5 now. Don't move or he'll get you! *(Sings.)*

> Hurry, lady, close up tight
> A gypsy lad is out tonight
> And he will take you by the hand
> And lead you into gypsyland. 10

(Continues to look at herself in the mirror.) They must be gold! I wonder how they'll look on me at the dance? Our kind's got only a little corner in the world and a piece of broken mirror. But my mouth is just as red as any of the fine ladies with their mirrors from top to bottom, and their hand-15 some gentlemen that kiss their hands for them! I'm just a poor common piece! *(*THE CHILD *sits up.)* Quiet, boy! Close your eyes! There's the sandman! Look at him run across the wall! *(She flashes with the mirror.)* Eyes tight! Or he'll look into them and make you blind! 20

*(*WOYZECK *enters behind her. She jumps up, her hands at her ears.)*

WOYZECK: What's that?

MARIE: Nothing.

WOYZECK: There's something shiny in your hands.

MARIE: An earring. I found it.

WOYZECK: I never have luck like that! Two at a time! 25

MARIE: Am I human or not?

WOYZECK: I'm sorry, Marie.—Look at the boy asleep. Lift his arm, the chair's hurting him. Look at the shiny drops on his forehead. Everything under the sun works! We even sweat in our sleep. Us poor people! Here's some money again, Marie. 30 My pay and something from the Captain.

MARIE: God bless you, Franz.

WOYZECK: I've got to get back. Tonight, Marie! I'll see you tonight!

(He goes off.)

MARIE: *(Alone, after a pause.)* I *am* bad, I *am*! I could run my-35 self through with a knife! Oh, what a life, what a life! We'll all end up in hell, anyway, in the end: man, woman, and child!

— SCENE SEVEN —

At the DOCTOR's.

(THE DOCTOR *and* WOYZECK.)

DOCTOR: I don't believe it, Woyzeck! And a man of your word!

WOYZECK: What's that, Doctor, sir?

DOCTOR: I saw it all, Woyzeck. You pissed on the street! You
    were pissing on the wall like a dog! And here I'm giving you
5   three groschen a day plus board! That's terrible, Woyzeck!
    The world's becoming a terrible place, a terrible place!

WOYZECK: But, Doctor, sir, when Nature . . .

DOCTOR: When Nature? When Nature? What has Nature to do
    with it? Did I or did I not prove to you that the *musculus con-*
10 *strictor vesicae* is controlled by your will? Nature! Woyzeck,
    man is free! In Mankind alone we see glorified the individ-
    ual's will to freedom! And you couldn't hold your water!
    (*Shakes his head, places his hands behind the small of his
    back, and walks back and forth.*) Have you eaten your peas
15 today, Woyzeck? Nothing but peas! *Cruciferae!* Remember
    that! There's going to be a revolution in science! I'm going to
    blow it sky-high! *Urea Oxygen.* Ammonium hydrochloratem
    hyperoxidic. Woyzeck, couldn't you just *try* to piss again? Go
    in the other room there and make another try.

20 WOYZECK: Doctor, sir, I can't.

DOCTOR: (*Disturbed.*) But you could piss on the wall. I have it
    here in black and white. Our contract is right here! I saw it. I
    saw it with these very eyes. I had just stuck my head out the
    window, opening it to let in the rays of the sun, so as to exe-
25 cute the process of sneezing. (*Going toward him.*) No,
    Woyzeck, I'm not going to vex myself. Vexation is unhealthy.
    Unscientific. I'm calm now, completely calm. My pulse is
    beating at its accustomed sixty, and I am speaking to you in
    utmost cold-bloodedness. Why should I vex myself over a
30 man, God forbid! A man! Now if he were a Proteus, it would
    be worth the vexation! But, Woyzeck, you really shouldn't
    have pissed on the wall.

WOYZECK: You see, Doctor, sir, sometimes a person's got a cer-
    tain kind of character, like when he's made a certain way.
35 But with Nature it's not the same, you see. With Nature (*He
    snaps his fingers.*), it's like *that!* How should I explain, it's
    like——

DOCTOR: Woyzeck, you're philosophizing again.

WOYZECK: (*Confidingly.*) Doctor, sir, did you ever see any-
40 thing with double nature? Like when the sun stops at noon,
    and it's like the world was going up in fire? That's when I
    hear a terrible voice saying things to me!

DOCTOR: Woyzeck, you have an *aberratio!*

WOYZECK: (*Places his finger at his nose.*) It's in the toadstools,
45 Doctor, sir, that's where it is. Did you ever see the shapes the
    toadstools make when they grow up out of the earth? If only
    somebody could read what they say!

DOCTOR: Woyzeck, you have a most beautiful *aberratio men-*
    talis partialis of a secondary order! And so wonderfully de-
50 veloped! Woyzeck, your salary is increased! *Idée fixe* of a sec-
    ondary order, and with a generally rational state. You go
    about your business normally? Still shaving the Captain?

WOYZECK: Yes, sir.

DOCTOR: You eat your peas?

55 WOYZECK: Just as always, Doctor, sir. My wife gets the money
    for the household.

DOCTOR: Still in the army?

WOYZECK: Yes, sir, Doctor.

DOCTOR: You're an interesting case. Patient Woyzeck, you're
    to have an increase in salary. So behave yourself! Let's feel   60
    the pulse. Ah yes.

— SCENE EIGHT —

MARIE's *room.*

(DRUM MAJOR *and* MARIE.)

DRUM MAJOR: Marie!

MARIE: (*Looking at him, with expression.*) Go on, show me
    how you march!—Chest broad as a bull's and a beard like a
    lion! There's not another man in the world like that! And
    there's not a prouder woman than me!   5

DRUM MAJOR: Wait till Sunday when I wear my helmet with
    the plume and my white gloves! Damn, that'll be a sight for
    you! The Prince always says: "My God, there goes a real
    man!"

MARIE: (*Scoffing.*) Ha! (*Goes toward him.*) A man?   10

DRUM MAJOR: You're not such a bad piece yourself! Hell, we'll
    plot a whole brood of drum majors! Right? (*He puts his arm
    around her.*)

MARIE: (*Annoyed.*) Let go!

DRUM MAJOR: Bitch!   15

MARIE: (*Fiercely.*)You just touch me!

DRUM MAJOR: There's devils in your eyes.

MARIE: Let there be, for all I care! What's the difference!

— SCENE NINE —

Street.

(CAPTAIN *and* DOCTOR. THE CAPTAIN *comes panting along the
street, stops; pants, looks about.*)

CAPTAIN: Ho, Doctor, don't run so fast! Don't paddle the air so
    with your stick! You're only courting death that way! A good
    man with a good conscience never walks as fast as that. A
    good man . . . (*He catches him by the coat.*) Doctor, permit
    me to save a human life!   5

DOCTOR: I'm in a hurry, Captain, I'm in a hurry!

CAPTAIN: Doctor, I'm so melancholy. I have such fantasies. I
    start to cry every time I see my coat hanging on the wall.

DOCTOR: Hm! Bloated, fat, thick neck: Apoplectic constitu-
    tion. Yes, Captain, you'll be having *apoplexia cerebria* any   10
    time now. Of course you could have it on only one side. In
    which case you'll be paralyzed down that one side. Or if
    things go really well you'll be mentally disabled so that you
    can vegetate away for the rest of your days. You may look for-
    ward to something approximately like that within the next   15
    four weeks! And, furthermore, I can assure you that you give
    promise of being a most interesting case. And if it is God's
    will that only one half of your tongue become paralyzed,
    then we will conduct the most immortal of experiments.

CAPTAIN: Doctor, you mustn't scare me that way! People are   20
    said to have died of fright. Of pure, sheer fright. I can see
    them now with lemons in their hands. But they'll say: "He
    was a good man, a good man." You devil's coffinnail-maker!

DOCTOR: (*Extending his hat toward him.*) Do you know who
    this is, Captain? This is Sir Hollowhead, my most honorable   25
    Captain Drilltheirassesoff!

CAPTAIN: (*Makes a series of folds in his sleeve.*) And do you know who this is, Doctor? This is Sir Manifold, my dear devil's coffinnail-maker! Ha! Ha! Ha! But no harm meant!
30 I'm good man, but I can play, too, when I want to, Doctor, when I want to. . . .

(WOYZECK *comes toward them and tries to pass in a hurry.*)

CAPTAIN: Ho! Woyzeck! Where are you off to in such a hurry? Stay awhile, Woyzeck! Running through the world like an open razor, you're liable to cut someone. He runs as if he
35 had to shave a castrated regiment and would be hung before he discovered and cut the longest hair that wasn't there. But on the subject of long beards. . . . What was it I wanted to say? Woyzeck, why was I thinking about beards?

DOCTOR: The wearing of long beards on the chin, remarks
40 Pliny, is a habit of which soldiers must be broken—

CAPTAIN: (*Continues.*) Ah, yes, this thing about beards! Tell me, Woyzeck, have you found any long hairs from beards in your soup bowl lately? Ho, I don't think he understands! A hair from a human face, from the beard of an engineer, a
45 sergeant, a . . . a drum major? Well, Woyzeck? But then he's got a good wife. It's not the same as with the others.

WOYZECK: Yes, sir, Captain! What was it you wanted to say to me, Captain, sir?

CAPTAIN: What a face he's making! Well, maybe not in his
50 soup, but if he hurries home around the corner I'll wager he might still find one on a certain pair of lips. A pair of lips, Woyzeck. I know what love is, too, Woyzeck. Look at him, he's white as chalk!

WOYZECK: Captain, sir, I'm just a poor devil. And there's noth-
55 ing else I've got in the world but her. Captain, sir, if you're just making a fool of me . . .

CAPTAIN: A fool? Me? Making a fool of you, Woyzeck?

DOCTOR: Your pulse, Woyzeck, your pulse! Short, hard, skipping, irregular.

60 WOYZECK: Captain, sir, the earth's hot as coals in hell. But I'm cold as ice, cold as ice. Hell is cold. I'll bet you. I don't believe it! God! God! I don't believe it!

CAPTAIN: Look here, you, how would you . . . how'd you like a pair of bullets in your skull? You keep stabbing at me with
65 those eyes of yours, and I'm only trying to help. Because you're a good man, Woyzeck, a good man.

DOCTOR: Facial muscles rigid, taut, occasionally twitches. Condition strained, excitable.

WOYZECK: I'm going. Anything's possible. The bitch! Any-
70 thing's possible.—The weather's nice, Captain, sir. Look, a beautiful, hard, gray sky. You'd almost like to pound a nail in up there and hang yourself on it. And only because of that little dash between Yes and Yes again . . . and No. Captain, sir: Yes and No: did No make Yes or Yes make No? I must
75 think about that.

(*He goes off with long strides, slowly at first, then faster and faster.*)

DOCTOR: (*Shouting after him.*) Phenomenon! Woyzeck, you get a raise!

CAPTAIN: I get so dizzy around such people. Look at him go! Long-legged rascals like him step out like a shadow running
80 away from its own spider. But short ones only dawdle along. The long-legged ones are the lightning, the short ones the thunder. Haha . . . Grotesque! Grotesque!

— SCENE TEN —

MARIE's *room.*

(WOYZECK *and* MARIE.)

WOYZECK: (*Looks fixedly at her and shakes his head.*) Hm! I don't see it! I don't see it! My God, why can't I see it, why can't I take it in my fists!

MARIE: (*Frightened.*) Franz, what is it?—You're raving, Franz.

WOYZECK: A sin so swollen and big—it stinks to smoke the an- 5
gels out of Heaven! You have a red mouth, Marie! No blisters on it? Marie, you're beautiful as sin. How can mortal sin be so beautiful?

MARIE: Franz, it's your fever making you talk this way!

WOYZECK: Damn you! Is this where he stood? Like this? Like 10
this?

MARIE: While the day's long and the world's old a lot of people can stand in one spot, one right after the other.—Why are you looking at me so strange, Franz! I'm afraid!

WOYZECK: It's a nice street for walking, uh? You could walk 15
corns on your feet! It's nice walking on the street, going around in society.

MARIE: Society?

WOYZECK: A lot of people pass through this street here, don't they! And you talk to them—to whoever you want—but 20
that's not my business!—Why wasn't it me!

MARIE: You expect me to tell people to keep off the streets—and take their mouths with them when they leave?

WOYZECK: And don't you ever leave your lips at home, they're too beautiful, it would be a sin! But then I guess the wasps 25
like to light on them, uh?

MARIE: And what wasp stung you! You're like a cow chased by hornets!

WOYZECK: I saw him!

MARIE: You can see a lot with two eyes while the sun shines! 30

WOYZECK: Whore! (*He goes after her.*)

MARIE: Don't you touch me, Franz! I'd rather have a knife in my body than your hands touch me. When I looked at him, my father didn't dare lay a hand on me from the time I was ten. 35

WOYZECK: Whore! No, it should show on you! Something! Every man's a chasm. It makes you dizzy when you look down in. It's got to show! And she looks like innocence itself. So, innocence, there's a spot on you. But I can't prove it—can't prove it! Who can prove it? 40

(*He goes off.*)

— SCENE ELEVEN —

The guardhouse.

(WOYZECK *and* ANDRES.)

ANDRES: (*Sings.*)

> Our hostess she has a pretty maid
> She sits in her garden night and day
> She sits within her garden . . .

WOYZECK: Andres!

ANDRES: Hm? 5

WOYZECK: Nice weather.

ANDRES: Sunday weather.—They're playing music tonight outside the town. All the whores are already there. The men stinking and sweating. Wonderful, uh?

10 WOYZECK: (*Restlessly.*) They're dancing, Andres, they're dancing!

ANDRES: Sure. So what? (*Sings.*)

> She sits within her garden
> But when the bells have tolled
15 > Then she waits at her garden gate
> Or so the soldiers say.

WOYZECK: Andres, I can't keep quiet.

ANDRES: You're a fool!

WOYZECK: I've got to go out there. It keeps turning and turn-
20 ing in my head. They're dancing, dancing! Will she have hot hands, Andres? God damn her, Andres! God damn her!

ANDRES: What do you want?

WOYZECK: I've got to go out there. I've got to see them.

ANDRES: Aren't you ever satisfied? What's all this for a whore?

25 WOYZECK: I've got to get out of here! I can't stand the heat!

— SCENE TWELVE —

The inn.

(*The windows are open. Dancing. Benches in front of the inn.* APPRENTICES.)

FIRST APPRENTICE: (*Sings.*)

> This shirt I've got on, it is not mine
> And my soul it stinketh of brandywine . . .

SECOND APPRENTICE: Brother, let me be a real friend and knock a hole in your nature! Forward! I'll knock a hole in his
5 nature! Hell, I'm as good a man as he is; I'll kill every flea on his body!

FIRST APPRENTICE: My soul, my soul stinketh of brandy-wine!—And even money passeth into decay! Forget me not, but the world's a beautiful place! Brother, my sadness could
10 fill a barrel with tears! I wish our noses were two bottles so we could pour them down one another's throats.

THE OTHERS: (*In chorus.*)

> A hunter from the Rhine
> Once rode through a forest so fine
> Hallei-hallo, he called to me
15 > From high on a meadow, open and free
> A hunter's life for me.

(WOYZECK *stands at the window.* MARIE *and* THE DRUM MAJOR *dance past without noticing him.*)

WOYZECK: Both of them! God damn her!

MARIE: (*Dancing past.*) Don't stop! Don't stop!

WOYZECK: (*Seats himself on the bench, trembling, as he looks
20 from there through the window.*) Listen! Listen! Ha, roll on each other, roll and turn! Don't stop, don't stop, she says!

IDIOT: Pah! It stinks!

WOYZECK: Yes, it stinks! Her cheeks are red, red, why should she stink already? Karl, what is it you smell?

25 IDIOT: I smell, I smell blood.

WOYZECK: Blood? Why are all things red that I look at now? Why are they all rolling in a sea of blood, one on top of the

other, tumbling, tumbling! Ha, the sea is red!—Don't stop! Don't stop! (*He starts up passionately, then sinks down again onto the bench.*) Don't stop! Don't stop! (*Beating his hands* 30 *together.*) Turn and roll and roll and turn! God, blow out the sun and let them roll on each other in their lechery! Man and woman and man and beast! They'll do it in the light of the sun! They'll do it in the palm of your hand like flies! Whore! That whore's red as coals, red as coals! Don't 35 stop! Don't stop! (*Jumps up.*) Watch how the bastard takes hold of her! Touching her body! He's holding her now, holding her . . . the way I held her once. (*He slumps down in a stupor.*)

FIRST APPRENTICE: (*Preaching from a table.*) I say unto you, 40 forget not the wanderer who standeth leaning against the stream of time, and who giveth himself answer with the wis-dom of God, and saith: What is Man? What is Man? Yea, verily I say unto you: How should the farmer, the cooper, the shoemaker, the doctor, live, had not God created Man for 45 their use? How should the tailor live had not God endowed Man with the need to slaughter himself? And therefore doubt ye not, for all things are lovely and sweet! Yet the world with all things is an evil place, and even money pas-seth into decay. In conclusion, my belovèd brethren, let us 50 piss once more upon the Cross so that somewhere a Jew will die!

(*Amid the general shouting and laughing* WOYZECK *wakens.* PEOPLE *are leaving the inn.*)

ANDRES: What are you doing there?

WOYZECK: What time is it?

ANDRES: Ten.   55

WOYZECK: Is that all it is? I think it should go faster—I want to think about it before night.

ANDRES: Why?

WOYZECK: So it'd be over.

ANDRES: What?   60

WOYZECK: The fun.

ANDRES: What are you sitting here by the door for?

WOYZECK: Because it feels good, and because I know—a lot of people sit by doors, but they don't know—they don't know till they're dragged out of the door feet first.   65

ANDRES: Come with me!

WOYZECK: It feels good here like this—and even better if I laid myself down . . .

ANDRES: There's blood on your head.

WOYZECK: *In* my head, maybe.—If they all knew what time it 70 was they'd strip themselves naked and put on a silk shirt and let the carpenter make their bed of wood shavings.

ANDRES: He's drunk.

(*Goes off with the others.*)

WOYZECK: The world is out of order! Why did the street-lamp cleaner forget to wipe my eyes—everything's dark. Devil 75 damn you, God! I lay in my own way: jump over myself. Where's my shadow gone? There's no safety in the kennels any more. Shine the moon through my legs again to see if my shadow's here. (*Sings.*)

> Eating, oh, eating the green green grass   80
> Eating, oh, eating the green green grass
> Till all the grass was go-o-one.

What's that lying over there? Shining like that? It's making me look. How it sparkles. I've got to have it.

(He rushes off.)

— SCENE THIRTEEN —

An open field.

(WOYZECK.)

WOYZECK: Don't stop! Don't stop. Hishh! Hashh! That's how the fiddles and pipes go.—Don't stop! Don't stop!—Stop your playing! What's that talking down there? *(He stretches out on the ground.)* What? What are you saying? What?
5 Louder! Louder! Stab? Stab the goat-bitch dead? Stab? Stab her? The goat-bitch dead? Should I? Must I? Do I hear it there, too? Does the wind say so, too? Won't it ever stop, ever stop? Stab her! Stab her! Dead! Dead!

— SCENE FOURTEEN —

A room in the barracks. Night.

(ANDRES *and* WOYZECK *in a bed.*)

WOYZECK: *(Softly.)* Andres! (ANDRES *murmurs in his sleep. Shakes* ANDRES.) Andres! Hey, Andres!
ANDRES: Mmmmm! What do you want?
WOYZECK: I can't sleep! When I close my eyes everything
5 turns and turns. I hear voices in the fiddles: Don't stop! Don't stop! And then the walls start to talk. Can't you hear it?
ANDRES: Sure. Let them dance! I'm tired. God bless us all, Amen.
WOYZECK: It's always saying: Stab! Stab! And then when I
10 close my eyes it keeps shining there, a big, broad knife, on a table by a window in a narrow, dark street, and an old man sitting behind it. And the knife is always in front of my eyes.
ANDRES: Go to sleep, you fool!
WOYZECK: Andres! There's something outside. In the ground.
15 They're always pointing to it. Don't you hear them now, listen, now, knocking on the walls? Somebody must have seen me out the window. Don't you hear? I hear it all day long. Don't stop. Stab! Stab the——
ANDRES: Lay down. You ought to go to the hospital. They'll
20 give you a schnapps with a powder in it. It'll cut your fever.
WOYZECK: Don't stop! Don't stop!
ANDRES: Go to sleep!

(He goes back to sleep.)

— SCENE FIFTEEN —

THE DOCTOR's *courtyard.*

(STUDENTS *and* WOYZECK *below,* THE DOCTOR *in the attic window.*)

DOCTOR: Gentlemen, I find myself on the roof like David when he beheld Bathsheba. But all I see are the Parisian panties of the girls' boarding school drying in the garden. Gentlemen, we are concerned with the weighty question of

the relationship of the subject to the object. If, for example, 5 we were to take one of those innumerable things in which we see the highest manifestation of the self-affirmation of the Godhead, and examine its relationship to space, to the earth, and to the planetary constellations . . . Gentlemen, if we were to take this cat and toss it out the window: how 10 would this object conduct itself in conformity with its own instincts towards its *centrum gravitationis?* Well, Woyzeck? *(Roars.)* Woyzeck!
WOYZECK: *(Picks up the cat.)* Doctor, sir, she's biting me!
DOCTOR: Damn, why do you handle the beast so tenderly! It's 15 not your grandmother! *(He descends.)*
WOYZECK: Doctor, I'm shaking.
DOCTOR: *(Utterly delighted.)* Excellent, Woyzeck, excellent! *(Rubs his hands, takes the cat.)* What's this, gentlemen? The new species of rabbit louse! A beautiful species . . . *(He pulls 20 out a magnifying glass; the cat runs off.)* Animals, gentlemen, simply have no scientific instincts. But in its place you may see something else. Now, observe: for three months this man has eaten nothing but peas. Notice the effect. Feel how irregularly his pulse beats! And look at his eyes! 25
WOYZECK: Doctor, sir, everything's going dark! *(He sits down.)*
DOCTOR: Courage, Woyzeck! A few more days and then it will all be over with. Feel, gentlemen, feel! *(They fumble over his temples, pulse, and chest.)*
DOCTOR: Apropos, Woyzeck, wiggle your ears for the gentle- 30 men! I've meant to show you this before. He uses only two muscles. Let's go, let's go! You stupid animal, shall I wiggle them for you? Trying to run out on us like the cat? There you are, gentlemen! Here you see an example of the transition into a donkey: frequently the result of being raised by women 35 and of a persistent usage of the Germanic language. How much hair has your mother pulled out recently for senti-mental remembrances of you? It's become so thin these last few days. It's the peas, gentlemen, the peas!

— SCENE SIXTEEN —

The inn.

(WOYZECK. THE SERGEANT.)

WOYZECK: *(Sings.)*

> Oh, daughter, my daughter
> And didn't you know
> That sleeping with coachmen
> Would bring you low?

What is it that our Good Lord God cannot do? What? He 5 cannot make what is done undone. Ha! Ha! Ha!—But that's the way it is, and that's the way it should be. But to make things better is to make things better. And a respectable man loves his life, and a man who loves his life has no courage, and a virtuous man has no courage. A man with courage is a 10 dirty dog.
SERGEANT: *(With dignity.)* You're forgetting yourself in the presence of a brave man.
WOYZECK: I wasn't talking about anybody, I wasn't talking about anything, not like the Frenchmen do when they talk, 15

but it was good of you.—But a man with courage is a dirty dog.

SERGEANT: Damn you! You broken mustache cup! You watch or I'll see you drink a pot of your own piss and swallow your own razor!

WOYZECK: Sir, you do yourself an injustice! Was it *you* I talked about? Did I say *you* had courage? Don't torment me, sir! My name is science. Every week for my scientific career I get half a guilder. You mustn't cut me in two or I'll go hungry. I'm a *Spinosa pericyclia*; I have a Latin behind. I am a living skeleton. All Mankind studies me.—What is Man? Bones! Dust, sand, dung. What is Nature? Dust, sand, dung. But poor, stupid Man, stupid Man! We must be friends. If only you had no courage, there would be no science. Only Nature, no amputation, no articulation. What is this? Woyzeck's arm, flesh, bones, veins. What is this? Dung. Why is it rooted in dung? Must I cut off my arm? No, Man is selfish, he beats, shoots, stabs his own kind. (*He sobs.*) We must be friends. I wish our noses were two bottles that we could pour down each other's throats. What a beautiful place the world is! Friend! My friend! The world! (*Moved.*) Look! The sun coming through the clouds—like God emptying His bedpan on the world. (*He cries.*)

— SCENE SEVENTEEN —

The barracks yard.

(WOYZECK. ANDRES.)

WOYZECK: What have you heard?

ANDRES: He's still inside with a friend.

WOYZECK: He said something.

ANDRES: How do you know? Why do I have to be the one to tell you? Well, he laughed and then he said she was some piece. And then something or other about her thighs—and that she was hot as a red poker.

WOYZECK: (*Quite coldly.*) So, he said that? What was that I dreamed about last night? About a knife? What stupid dreams we get!

ANDRES: Hey, friend! Where you off to?

WOYZECK: Get some wine for the Captain. Andres, you know something? There aren't many girls like she was.

ANDRES: Like who was?

WOYZECK: Nothing. I'll see you.

(*Goes off.*)

— SCENE EIGHTEEN —

The inn.

(DRUM MAJOR, WOYZECK, *and* PEOPLE.)

DRUM MAJOR: I'm a man! (*He pounds his chest.*) A man, you hear? Anybody say different? Anybody who's not as crocked as the Lord God Himself better keep off. I'll screw his nose up his own ass! I'll . . . (*To* WOYZECK.) You there, get drunk! I wish the world was schnapps, schnapps! You better start drinking! (WOYZECK *whistles.*) Son-of-a-bitch, you want me to pull your tongue out and wrap it around your

middle? (*They wrestle;* WOYZECK *loses.*) You want I should leave enough wind in you for a good old lady's fart? Uh! (*Exhausted and trembling,* WOYZECK *seats himself on the bench.*) The son-of-a-bitch can whistle himself blue in the face for all I care. (Sings.)

Brandy's all my life, my life
Brancy gives me courage!

A MAN: He sure got more than he asked for.

ANOTHER: He's bleeding.

WOYZECK: One thing after another.

— SCENE NINETEEN —

Pawnbroker's shop.

(WOYZECK *and* THE JEW.)

WOYZECK: The pistol costs too much.

JEW: So you want it or not? Make up your mind.

WOYZECK: How much was the knife?

JEW: It's straight and sharp. What do you want it for? To cut your throat? So what's the matter? You get it as cheap here as anywhere else. You'll die cheap enough, but not for nothing. What's the matter? It'll be a cheap death.

WOYZECK: This'll cut more than bread.

JEW: Two groschen.

WOYZECK: There!

(*He goes out.*)

JEW: There, he says! Like it was nothing! And it's real money!—Dog!

— SCENE TWENTY —

MARIE's *room.*

(THE IDIOT. THE CHILD. MARIE.)

IDIOT: (*Lying down, telling fairy tales on his fingers.*) This one has the golden crown. He's the Lord King. Tomorrow I'll bring the Lady Queen her child. Bloodsausage says: Come, Liversausage . . .

MARIE: (*Paging through her Bible.*) "And no guile is found in his mouth." Lord God, Lord God! Don't look at me! (*Paging further.*) "And the Scribes and Pharisees brought unto him a woman taken in adultery, and set her in the midst . . . And Jesus said unto her: Neither do I condemn thee; go, and sin no more." (*Striking her hands together.*) Lord God! Lord God! I can't. Lord God, give me only so much strength that I may pray. (THE CHILD *presses himself close to her.*) The child is a sword in my heart. (*To* THE IDIOT.) Karl!—I've strutted it in the light of the sun, like the whore I am—my sin, my sin! (THE IDIOT *takes* THE CHILD *and grows quiet.*) Franz hasn't come. Not yesterday. Not today. It's getting hot in here! (*She opens the window and reads further.*) "And stood at his feet weeping, and began to wash his feet with tears, and did wipe them with the hairs of her head, and anointed them with ointment." (*Striking her breast.*) Every thing dead! Saviour! Saviour! If only I might anoint Your feet!

— SCENE TWENTY-ONE —

An open field.

(WOYZECK.)

WOYZECK: *(Buries the knife in a hole.)* Thou shalt not kill. Lay here! I can't stay here!

(He rushes off.)

— SCENE TWENTY-TWO —

The barracks.

(ANDRES. WOYZECK *rummages through his belongings.*)

WOYZECK: Andres, this jacket's not part of the uniform, but you can use it, Andres.

ANDRES: *(Replies numbly to almost everything with.)* Sure.

WOYZECK: The cross is my sister's. And the ring.

5 ANDRES: Sure.

WOYZECK: I've got a Holy Picture, too: two hearts—they're real gold. I found it in my mother's Bible, and it said:

> O Lord with wounded head so sore
> So may my heart be evermore.

10 My mother only feels now when the sun shines on her hands . . . that doesn't matter.

ANDRES: Sure.

WOYZECK: *(Pulls out a paper.)* Friedrich Johann Franz Woyzeck. Soldier. Rifleman, Second Regiment, Second Battalion, Fourth Company. Born: the Feast of the Annunciation, twentieth of July. Today I'm thirty years old, seven months and twelve days.

ANDRES: Go to the hospital, Franz. Poor guy, you've got to drink some schnapps with a powder in it. It'll kill the fever.

20 WOYZECK: You know, Andres—when the carpenter puts those boards together, nobody knows who it's made for.

— SCENE TWENTY-THREE —

The street.

(MARIE *with little* GIRLS *in front of the house door.* GRANDMOTHER. *Later* WOYZECK.)

GIRLS: *(Singing.)*

> The sun shone bright on Candlemas Day
> And the corn was all in bloom
> And they marched along the meadow way
> They marched by two and two.
> 5 The pipers marched ahead
> The fiddlers followed through
> And their socks were scarlet red . . .

FIRST CHILD: I don't like that one.

SECOND CHILD: Why do you always want to be different?

10 FIRST CHILD: *You* sing for us, Marie!

MARIE: I can't.

SECOND CHILD: Why?

MARIE: Because.

SECOND CHILD: But *why* because?

THIRD CHILD: Grandmother, *you* tell us a story! 15

GRANDMOTHER: All right, you little crab apples!—Once upon a time there was a poor little girl who had no father and no mother. Everyone was dead, and there was no one left in the whole wide world. Everyone was dead. And the little girl went out and looked for someone night and day. And be- 20 cause there was no one left on the earth, she wanted to go to Heaven. And the moon looked down so friendly at her. And when she finally got to the moon, it was a piece of rotten wood. And so she went to the sun, and it was a faded sunflower. And when she got to the stars, they were little golden 25 flies, stuck up there as if they were caught in a spider's web. And when she wanted to go back to earth, the earth was an upside-down pot. And she was all alone. And she sat down there and she cried. And she sits there to this day, all, all alone. 30

WOYZECK: *(Appears.)* Marie!

MARIE: *(Startled.)* What!

WOYZECK: Let's go. It's getting time.

MARIE: Where to?

WOYZECK: How should I know? 35

— SCENE TWENTY-FOUR —

A pond by the edge of the woods.

(MARIE *and* WOYZECK.)

MARIE: Then the town must be out that way. It's so dark.

WOYZECK: You can't go yet. Come, sit down.

MARIE: But I've got to get back.

WOYZECK: You don't want to run your feet sore.

MARIE: What's happened to you? 5

WOYZECK: You know how long it's been, Marie?

MARIE: Two years from Pentecost.

WOYZECK: You know how much longer it'll last?

MARIE: I've got to get back. Supper's not made yet.

WOYZECK: Are you freezing, Marie? And still you're so warm. 10 Your lips are hot as coals! Hot as coals, the hot breath of a whore! And still I'd give up Heaven just to kiss them again. Are you freezing? When you're cold through, you won't freeze any more. The morning dew won't freeze you.

MARIE: What are you talking about? 15

WOYZECK: Nothing. *(Silence.)*

MARIE: Look how red the moon is! It's rising.

WOYZECK: Like a knife washed in blood.

MARIE: What are you going to do? Franz, you're so pale. *(He raises the knife.)* 20

MARIE: Franz! Stop! For Heaven's sake! Help me! Help me!

WOYZECK: *(Stabbing madly.)* There! There! Why can't you die? There! There! Ha, she's still shivering! Still not dead? Still not dead? Still shivering? *(Stabbing at her again.)* Are you dead? Dead! Dead! 25

(He drops the knife and runs away.)

(Two MEN *approach.)*

FIRST MAN: Wait!

SECOND MAN: You hear something? Shh! Over there!

FIRST MAN: Whhh! There! What a sound!

SECOND MAN: It's the water, it's calling. It's a long time since
30   anyone drowned here. Let's go! I don't like hearing such
      sounds!
FIRST MAN: Whhh! There it is again! Like a person, dying!
SECOND MAN: It's uncanny! So foggy, nothing but gray mist as
      far as you can see—and the hum of beetles like broken bells.
35   Let's get out of here!
FIRST MAN: No, it's too clear, it's too loud! Let's go up this way!
      Come on!

(They hurry on.)

— SCENE TWENTY-FIVE —

The inn.

(WOYZECK, KATHY, INNKEEPER, IDIOT, *and* PEOPLE.)

WOYZECK: Dance! Everybody! Don't stop! Sweat and stink!
      He'll get you all in the end! *(Sings.)*

            Oh, daughter, my daughter
            And didn't you know
5   That sleeping with coachmen
            Would bring you low?

(He dances.) Ho, Kathy! Sit down! I'm so hot, so hot! *(Takes
off his coat.)* That's the way it is: the devil takes one and lets
the other get away. Kathy, you're hot as coals! Why, tell me
10   why? Kathy, you'll be cold one day, too. Be reasonable.—
      Can't you sing something?
KATHY: *(Sings.)*

            That Swabian land I cannot bear
            And dresses long I will not wear
            For dresses long and pointed shoes
15   Are clothes a chambermaid never should choose.

WOYZECK: No shoes, no shoes! We can get to hell without
      shoes.
KATHY: *(Sings.)*

            To such and like I'll not be prone
            Take back your gold and sleep alone.

20 WOYZECK: Sure, sure! What do I want to get all bloody for?
KATHY: Then what's that on your hand?
WOYZECK: Me? Me?
KATHY: Red! It's blood! (PEOPLE *gather round him.*)
WOYZECK: Blood? Blood?
25 INNKEEPER: Blood!
WOYZECK: I think I cut myself. Here, on my right hand.
INNKEEPER: Then why is there blood on your elbow?
WOYZECK: I wiped it off.
INNKEEPER: Your right hand and you wiped it on your right
30   elbow? You're a smart one!
IDIOT: And then the Giant said: "I smell, I smell the flesh of
      Man." Pew, it stinks already!
WOYZECK: What do you want from me? Is it your business?
      Out of my way or the first one who . . . Damn you! Do I look
35   like I murdered somebody? Do I look like a murderer? What
      are you looking at? Look at yourselves! Look! Out of my way!

(He runs off.)

— SCENE TWENTY-SIX —

At the pond.

(WOYZECK, *alone.*)

WOYZECK: The knife! Where's the knife? I left it here. It'll give
      me away! Closer! And closer! What is this place? What's that
      noise? Something's moving! It's quiet now.—It's got to be
      here, close to her. Marie? Ha, Marie! Quiet. Everything's
5   quiet! Why are you so pale, Marie? Why are you wearing
      those red beads around your neck? Who was it gave you that
      necklace for sinning with him? Your sins made you black,
      Marie, they made you black! Did I make you so pale? Why is
      your hair uncombed? Did you forget to twist your braids
      today? The knife, the knife! I've got it! There! *(He runs to-*   10
      ward the water.) There, into the water! *(He throws the knife
      into the water.)* It dives like a stone into the black water. No,
      it's not out far enough for when they swim! *(He wades into
      the pond and throws it out farther.)* There! Now! But in the
      summer when they dive for mussels? Ha, it'll get rusty, who'll   15
      ever notice it! Why didn't I break it first! Am I still bloody?
      I've got to wash myself. There, there's a spot, and there's
      another . . .

(He goes farther out into the water.)

— SCENE TWENTY-SEVEN —

The street.

(CHILDREN.)

FIRST CHILD: Let's go find Marie!
SECOND CHILD: What happened?
FIRST CHILD: Don't you know? Everybody's out there. They
      found a body!
SECOND CHILD: Where?   5
FIRST CHILD: By the pond, out in the woods.
SECOND CHILD: Hurry, so we can still see something. Before
      they bring it back.

(They rush off.)

— SCENE TWENTY-EIGHT —

In front of MARIE's *house.*

(IDIOT, CHILD, WOYZECK.)

IDIOT: *(Holding* THE CHILD *on his knee, points to* WOYZECK *as
      he enters.)* Looky there, he fell in the water, he fell in the
      water, he fell in the water!
WOYZECK: Boy! Christian!
IDIOT: *(Looks at him fixedly.)* He fell in the water.   5
WOYZECK: *(Wanting to embrace* THE CHILD *tenderly, but it
      turns from him and screams.)* My God! My God!
IDIOT: He fell in the water.
WOYZECK: I'll buy you a horsey, Christian. There, there. (THE
      CHILD *pulls away. To the* IDIOT.) Here, buy the boy a horsey!   10
      (THE IDIOT *stares at him.)* Hop! Hop! Hip-hop, horsey!

IDIOT: *(Shouting joyously.)* Hop! Hop! Hip-hop, horsey! Hip-hop, horsey!

(He runs off with THE CHILD. WOYZECK *is alone.)*

— SCENE TWENTY-NINE —

The morgue.

(JUDGE, COURT CLERK, POLICEMAN, CAPTAIN, DOCTOR, DRUM MAJOR, SERGEANT, IDIOT, and others. WOYZECK.*)*

POLICEMAN: What a murder! A good, genuine, beautiful murder! Beautiful a murder as you could hope for! It's been a long time since we had one like this!

*(*WOYZECK *stands in their midst, dumbly looking at the body of* MARIE; *he is bound, the dogmatic atheist, tall, haggard, timid, good-natured, scientific.)*

■ HENRIK IBSEN ■

At the turn of the century, Henrik Ibsen (1828–1906) was synonymous with modernity in the European theater; much of the territory of modern drama was first explored in Ibsen's work. Born into a mercantile family in provincial Norway, Ibsen had planned to study medicine; however, after failing to matriculate at the university, he turned to a career as a writer. From 1850 through 1864, Ibsen worked for the nationalist Norwegian Theater in Bergen and then for the Mollergate Theater in Christiania (now Oslo). As literary manager, stage manager, and assistant to the director, Ibsen learned the craft of practical theater firsthand. He also wrote a series of romantic history plays, some in prose and some in verse. Although his fame now rests on the realistic plays he wrote later in his career, in his own lifetime these these history plays—such as *The Vikings at Helgeland* (1858)—were quite popular, especially in Norway.

In 1864, Ibsen left Norway and settled in Rome, where he wrote two pivotal plays, *Brand* (1866) and *Peer Gynt* (1867). The story of an idealistic minister, *Brand* established Ibsen as an important European writer and announced one of his central themes: the cost of moral idealism in the modern world. *Peer Gynt* is often taken as a companion-piece to *Brand*, for Peer's picaresque journey throughout Europe is undertaken simply for the purpose of his own self-satisfaction: while Brand's motto is "Be wholly what you are," Peer Gynt's is "To thine own self be . . . enough." In 1877, after extensive work on the Hegelian history drama *Emperor and Galilean*, Ibsen wrote *Pillars of Society*, a prose drama of modern life, inaugurating the stunning series of plays that made him famous and established the contours of modern realistic drama. In *A Doll House* (1879), *Ghosts* (1881), and *An Enemy of the People* (1882), Ibsen explored the conflict between the social and moral restrictions of bourgeois society and the psychological, often unconscious demands of individual freedom. Ibsen adapted the suspenseful, rigorously plotted form of the **WELL-MADE PLAY** (or *pièce bien faite*) popularized throughout Europe by French playwrights Eugène Scribe and Victorien Sardou and used it in plays of modern life critical of bourgeois morality and society. The well-made play is notoriously difficult to define, even though its features are familiar: a rigorously "causal" plot, a secret gradually revealed to the audience, a "necessary scene" (the *scène-à-faire*) in which the secret is revealed to the characters, a character (the *raisonneur*) who explains and moralizes the action to the others, and a predominance of coincidental events. In his earlier plays, Ibsen takes these formal conventions and makes them function as forces in the dramatic world. The world of the play comes to seem mechanistic, determined by a secret that will out, full of busybodies explaining and interpreting the action. The mechanics of the well-made play, that is, are identified with the deadening force of social convention, which painfully threatens to extinguish the vitality of the central characters. This conflict between deadening social convention and a mysterious inner vitality pervades Ibsen's mature plays as well, which increasingly moved away from the "well-made" form: *The Wild Duck* (1885), *Rosmersholm* (1887), *The Lady from the Sea* (1888), and *Hedda Gabler* (1890). Ibsen's last plays seem more poetic or symbolic, though they take place in the familiar milieu of the realistic stage: *The Master Builder* (1892), *Little Eyolf* (1894), *John Gabriel Borkman* (1896), and the unfinished *When We Dead Awaken* (1900). Ibsen suffered a paralyzing series of strokes in 1900 that left him unable to write. He died in 1906.

Ibsen's effect on his contemporaries and his influence on the course of modern drama were immediate and profound. His plays were rapidly translated into the major European languages, and stage productions—which often inaugurated the new "independent" theaters—frequently became the subject of sensation and controversy. Indeed, "Ibsenism" came to be a catchword for a variety of social causes, though Ibsen himself generally avoided politics. Although Ibsen's plays brought new issues to the stage, it was his practice as a playwright that proved truly revolutionary. Many playwrights had adopted the realistic theater's use of a material stage environment, its emphasis on the burden of the past, and its sense of a mechanized and constricting society. Ibsen not only used this material with powerful subtlety and resonance, he gave the stage its first distinctively modern characters: complex, contradictory individuals driven by a desire for something—the "joy of life," a sense of themselves—that they can barely recognize or name.

A DOLL HOUSE

A *Doll House* was inspired by a series of incidents that came to Ibsen's attention in 1878 when a woman named Laura Kieler contacted him. Kieler had signed a secret—and illegal—loan to raise money for a cure for her tubercular husband. She wrote to Ibsen asking him to recommend the novel she had written to his publisher, in hopes that the profits from its sale would allow her to repay the loan. Ibsen refused. Kieler forged a check and was caught. Her husband committed her to an asylum, had her charged as an unfit mother, and demanded a legal separation. When she was released from the asylum, however, the family remained together.

We can see the shaping power of Ibsen's imagination in his transformation of Laura Kieler's tragedy into the ironic masterpiece, *A Doll House*. The play—which by the turn of the century was a rallying point for international feminist demands for the vote and for other legal rights and protections for women—organizes the conflict between Nora and Helmer around a subtle set of contrasts: the childlike and protected Nora and the world-weary Mrs. Linde; the upright and protective Helmer and the shady—yet finally generous—Krogstad; the privations of the past and the financial freedom Nora sees on the horizon. However, as the play proceeds, the stable, bourgeois world that Helmer represents is revealed as a tissue of deception—the institutions of marriage, respectability, and social justice turn out to be fictions that the privileged use to manipulate their world. Nora comes to seem effective, efficient, worldly wise, and finally independent, while Helmer readily compromises his principles to save his reputation. The world of financial freedom Nora glimpses at the play's outset turns out to be a kind of prison and is replaced by another kind of freedom at the end of the play: the frightening freedom to cut herself loose from the bonds of marriage, family, and society.

Helmer had more authority with audiences in the 1880s and 1890s than he does today, and Nora was conventionally criticized as an "unwomanly woman" for taking the loan, deceiving her husband, and leaving her family. Indeed, the first English actress to be offered the part turned it down, because she didn't want audiences to think of her as the kind of woman who would desert her children. Yet the play tends to validate Nora's personal growth and her final decision to leave her family, and cannily uses the material environment of the stage setting to convey the suffocating situation in which Nora finds herself. The play takes place in one room: the drawing room where the upwardly mobile Helmers (deluxe books on the shelf, piano against the wall, framed art prints) receive their guests and conduct their lives. The room itself represents the Helmers' concern for social status and assumes a symbolic importance as well: it stands between the unseen privacy of the kitchen and bedroom—the domestic world of marriage and children—and the threatening public world beyond the front door, the world of Krogstad, of the dark and icy river, of Nora's final escape. The room becomes a kind of prison, a room in which Rank's declaration of love for Nora seems inappropriate, in which Helmer criticizes her dizzying tarantella—a Sicilian dance thought to imitate the death throes of someone bitten by a tarantula—as too abandoned, and in which Nora's final discussion with Helmer makes her submission to him impossible. That is, the room makes concrete the play's concern for the social constraints on a woman's life, becoming a visual image of how Helmer's masculine, bourgeois moral authority imprisons Nora. It is not entirely clear that Nora can survive in the harsh social and economic climate outside the comfortable parlor, but it is clear that escape from the parlor is her final alternative.

A DOLL HOUSE

HENRIK IBSEN

TRANSLATED BY ROLF FJELDE

— CHARACTERS —

TORVALD HELMER, *a lawyer*
NORA, *his wife*
DR. RANK
MRS. LINDE
NILS KROGSTAD, *a bank clerk*
THE HELMERS' THREE SMALL CHILDREN

ANNE-MARIE, *their nurse*
HELENE, *a maid*
A DELIVERY BOY

The action takes place in HELMER's *residence.*

— ACT ONE —

A comfortable room, tastefully but not expensively furnished. A door to the right in the back wall leads to the entryway; another to the left leads to HELMER's *study. Between these doors, a piano. Midway in the left-hand wall a door, and further back a window. Near the window a round table with an armchair and a small sofa. In the right-hand wall, toward the rear, a door, and nearer the foreground a porcelain stove with two armchairs and a rocking chair beside it. Between the stove and the side door, a small table. Engravings on the walls. An etagère with china figures and other small art objects; a small bookcase with richly bound books; the floor carpeted; a fire burning in the stove. It is a winter day.*

A bell rings in the entryway; shortly after we hear the door being unlocked. NORA *comes into the room, humming happily to herself; she is wearing street clothes and carries an armload of packages, which she puts down on the table to the right. She has left the hall door open; and through it a* DELIVERY BOY *is seen, holding a Christmas tree and a basket, which he gives to the* MAID *who let them in.*

NORA: Hide the tree well, Helene. The children mustn't get a glimpse of it till this evening, after it's trimmed. (*To the* DE-LIVERY BOY, *taking out her purse.*) How much?

DELIVERY BOY: Fifty, ma'am.

5 NORA: There's a crown. No, keep the change. (*The* BOY *thanks her and leaves.* NORA *shuts the door. She laughs softly to herself while taking off her street things. Drawing a bag of macaroons from her pocket, she eats a couple, then steals over and listens at her husband's study door.*) Yes, he's home. (*Hums*
10 *again as she moves to the table right.*)

HELMER: (*From the study.*) Is that my little lark twittering out there?

NORA: (*Busy opening some packages.*) Yes, it is.

HELMER: Is that my squirrel rummaging around?

15 NORA: Yes!

HELMER: When did my squirrel get in?

NORA: Just now. (*Putting the macaroon bag in her pocket and wiping her mouth.*) Do come in, Torvald, and see what I've bought.

20 HELMER: Can't be disturbed. (*After a moment he opens the door and peers in, pen in hand.*) Bought, you say? All that there? Has the little spendthrift been out throwing money around again?

NORA: Oh, but Torvald, this year we really should let ourselves go a bit. It's the first Christmas we haven't had to economize. 25

HELMER: But you know we can't go squandering.

NORA: Oh yes, Torvald, we can squander a little now. Can't we? Just a tiny, wee bit. Now that you've got a big salary and are going to make piles and piles of money.

HELMER: Yes—starting New Year's. But then it's a full three 30 months till the raise comes through.

NORA: Pooh! We can borrow that long.

HELMER: Nora! (*Goes over and playfully takes her by the ear.*) Are your scatterbrains off again? What if today I borrowed a thousand crowns, and you squandered them over Christmas 35 week, and then on New Year's Eve a roof tile fell on my head, and I lay there—

NORA: (*Putting her hand on his mouth.*) Oh! Don't say such things!

HELMER: Yes, but what if it happened—then what? 40

NORA: If anything so awful happened, then it just wouldn't matter if I had debts or not.

HELMER: Well, but the people I'd borrowed from?

NORA: Them? Who cares about them! They're strangers.

HELMER: Nora, Nora, how like a woman! No, but seriously, 45 Nora, you know what I think about that. No debts! Never borrow! Something of freedom's lost—and something of beauty, too—from a home that's founded on borrowing and debt. We've made a brave stand up to now, the two of us; and we'll go right on like that the little while we have to. 50

NORA: (*Going toward the stove.*) Yes, whatever you say, Torvald.

HELMER: (*Following her.*) Now, now, the little lark's wings mustn't droop. Come on, don't be a sulky squirrel. (*Taking out his wallet.*) Nora, guess what I have here.

NORA: (*Turning quickly.*) Money! 55

HELMER: There, see. (*Hands her some notes.*) Good grief, I know how costs go up in a house at Christmastime.

NORA: Ten—twenty—thirty—forty. Oh, thank you, Torvald; I can manage no end on this.

HELMER: You really will have to. 60

NORA: Oh yes, I promise I will! But come here so I can show you everything I bought. And so cheap! Look, new clothes for Ivar here—and a sword. Here a horse and a trumpet for Bob. And a doll and a doll's bed here for Emmy; they're nothing much, but she'll tear them to bits in no time any 65 way. And here I have dress material and handkerchiefs for the maids. Old Anne-Marie really deserves something more.

HELMER: And what's in that package there?

NORA: *(With a cry.)* Torvald, no! You can't see that till tonight!

70 HELMER: I see. But tell me now, you little prodigal, what have you thought of for yourself?

NORA: For myself? Oh, I don't want anything at all.

HELMER: Of course you do. Tell me just what—within reason—you'd most like to have.

75 NORA: I honestly don't know. Oh, listen, Torvald—

HELMER: Well?

NORA: *(Fumbling at his coat buttons, without looking at him.)* If you want to give me something, then maybe you could—you could—

80 HELMER: Come on, out with it.

NORA: *(Hurriedly.)* You could give me money, Torvald. No more than you think you can spare; then one of these days I'll buy something with it.

HELMER: But Nora—

85 NORA: Oh, please, Torvald darling, do that! I beg you, please. Then I could hang the bills in pretty gilt paper on the Christmas tree. Wouldn't that be fun?

HELMER: What are those little birds called that always fly through their fortunes?

90 NORA: Oh yes, spendthrifts; I know all that. But let's do as I say, Torvald; then I'll have time to decide what I really need most. That's very sensible, isn't it?

HELMER: *(Smiling.)* Yes, very—that is, if you actually hung onto the money I give you, and you actually used it to buy

95 yourself something. But it goes for the house and for all sorts of foolish things, and then I only have to lay out some more.

NORA: Oh, but Torvald—

HELMER: Don't deny it, my dear little Nora. *(Putting his arm around her waist.)* Spendthrifts are sweet, but they use up a

100 frightful amount of money. It's incredible what it costs a man to feed such birds.

NORA: Oh, how can you say that! Really, I save everything I can.

HELMER: *(Laughing.)* Yes, that's the truth. Everything you

105 can. But that's nothing at all.

NORA: *(Humming, with a smile of quiet satisfaction.)* Hm, if you only knew what expenses we larks and squirrels have, Torvald.

HELMER: You're an odd little one. Exactly the way your father

110 was. You're never at a loss for scaring up money; but the moment you have it, it runs right out through your fingers; you never know what you've done with it. Well, one takes you as you are. It's deep in your blood. Yes, these things are hereditary, Nora.

115 NORA: Ah, I could wish I'd inherited many of Papa's qualities.

HELMER: And I couldn't wish you anything but just what you are, my sweet little lark. But wait; it seems to me you have a very—what should I call it?—a very suspicious look today—

NORA: I do?

120 HELMER: You certainly do. Look me straight in the eye.

NORA: *(Looking at him.)* Well?

HELMER: *(Shaking an admonitory finger.)* Surely my sweet tooth hasn't been running riot in town today, has she?

NORA: No. Why do you imagine that?

125 HELMER: My sweet tooth really didn't make a little detour through the confectioner's?

NORA: No, I assure you, Torvald—

HELMER: Hasn't nibbled some pastry?

NORA: No, not at all.

130 HELMER: Not even munched a macaroon or two?

NORA: No, Torvald, I assure you, really—

HELMER: There, there now. Of course I'm only joking.

NORA: *(Going to the table, right.)* You know I could never think of going against you.

135 HELMER: No, I understand that; and you *have* given me your word. *(Going over to her.)* Well, you keep your little Christmas secrets to yourself, Nora darling. I expect they'll come to light this evening, when the tree is lit.

NORA: Did you remember to ask Dr. Rank?

140 HELMER: No. But there's no need for that; it's assumed he'll be dining with us. All the same, I'll ask him when he stops by here this morning. I've ordered some fine wine. Nora, you can't imagine how I'm looking forward to this evening.

NORA: So am I. And what fun for the children, Torvald!

145 HELMER: Ah, it's so gratifying to know that one's gotten a safe, secure job, and with a comfortable salary. It's a great satisfaction, isn't it?

NORA: Oh, it's wonderful!

HELMER: Remember last Christmas? Three whole weeks be-

150 fore, you shut yourself in every evening till long after midnight, making flowers for the Christmas tree, and all the other decorations to surprise us. Ugh, that was the dullest time I've ever lived through.

NORA: It wasn't at all dull for me.

155 HELMER: *(Smiling.)* But the outcome *was* pretty sorry, Nora.

NORA: Oh, don't tease me with that again. How could I help it that the cat came in and tore everything to shreds.

HELMER: No, poor thing, you certainly couldn't. You wanted so much to please us all, and that's what counts. But it's just

160 as well that the hard times are past.

NORA: Yes, it's really wonderful.

HELMER: Now I don't have to sit here alone, boring myself, and you don't have to tire your precious eyes and your fair little delicate hands—

165 NORA: *(Clapping her hands.)* No, is it really true, Torvald, I don't have to? Oh, how wonderfully lovely to hear! *(Taking his arm.)* Now I'll tell you just how I've thought we should plan things. Right after Christmas—*(The doorbell rings.)* Oh, the bell. *(Straightening the room up a bit.)* Somebody

170 would have to come. What a bore!

HELMER: I'm not at home to visitors, don't forget.

MAID: *(From the hall doorway.)* Ma'am, a lady to see you—

NORA: All right, let her come in.

MAID: *(To HELMER.)* And the doctor's just come too.

175 HELMER: Did he go right to my study?

MAID: Yes, he did.

(HELMER goes into his room. The MAID shows in MRS. LINDE, dressed in traveling clothes, and shuts the door after her.)

MRS. LINDE: *(In a dispirited and somewhat hesitant voice.)* Hello, Nora.

NORA: *(Uncertain.)* Hello—

MRS. LINDE: You don't recognize me.

180 NORA: No, I don't know—but wait, I think—*(Exclaiming.)* What! Kristine! Is it really you?

MRS. LINDE: Yes, it's me.

NORA: Kristine! To think I didn't recognize you. But then, how could I? *(More quietly.)* How you've changed, Kristine!

185 MRS. LINDE: Yes, no doubt I have. In nine—ten long years.

NORA: Is it so long since we met! Yes, it's all of that. Oh, these last eight years have been a happy time, believe me. And so

now you've come in to town, too. Made the long trip in the
190   winter. That took courage.

MRS. LINDE: I just got here by ship this morning.

NORA: To enjoy yourself over Christmas, of course. Oh, how
lovely! Yes, enjoy ourselves, we'll do that. But take your coat
off. You're not still cold? (*Helping her.*) There now, let's get
195   cozy here by the stove. No, the easy chair there! I'll take the
rocker here. (*Seizing her hands.*) Yes, now you have your old
look again; it was only in that first moment. You're a bit more
pale, Kristine—and maybe a bit thinner.

MRS. LINDE: And much, much older, Nora.

200   NORA: Yes, perhaps a bit older; a tiny, tiny bit; not much at all.
(*Stopping short; suddenly serious.*) Oh, but thoughtless me,
to sit here, chattering away. Sweet, good Kristine, can you
forgive me?

MRS. LINDE: What do you mean, Nora?

205   NORA: (*Softly.*) Poor Kristine, you've become a widow.

MRS. LINDE: Yes, three years ago.

NORA: Oh, I knew it, of course; I read it in the papers. Oh, Kristine, you must believe me; I often thought of writing you then,
but I kept postponing it, and something always interfered.

210   MRS. LINDE: Nora dear, I understand completely.

NORA: No, it was awful of me, Kristine. You poor thing, how
much you must have gone through. And he left you nothing?

MRS. LINDE: No.

NORA: And no children?

215   MRS. LINDE: No.

NORA: Nothing at all, then?

MRS. LINDE: Not even a sense of loss to feed on.

NORA: (*Looking incredulously at her.*) But Kristine, how could
that be?

220   MRS. LINDE: (*Smiling wearily and smoothing her hair.*) Oh,
sometimes it happens, Nora.

NORA: So completely alone. How terribly hard that must be
for you. I have three lovely children. You can't see them
now; they're out with the maid. But now you must tell me
225   everything—

MRS. LINDE: No, no, no, tell me about yourself.

NORA: No, you begin. Today I don't want to be selfish. I want
to think only of you today. But there *is* something I must tell
you. Did you hear of the wonderful luck we had recently?

230   MRS. LINDE: No, what's that?

NORA: My husband's been made manager in the bank, just
think!

MRS. LINDE: Your husband? How marvelous!

NORA: Isn't it? Being a lawyer is such an uncertain living, you
235   know, especially if one won't touch any cases that aren't
clean and decent. And of course Torvald would never do
that, and I'm with him completely there. Oh, we're simply
delighted, believe me! He'll join the bank right after New
Year's and start getting a huge salary and lots of commis-
240   sions. From now on we can live quite differently—just as we
want. Oh, Kristine, I feel so light and happy! Won't it be
lovely to have stacks of money and not a care in the world?

MRS. LINDE: Well, anyway, it would be lovely to have enough
for necessities.

245   NORA: No, not just for necessities, but stacks and stacks of
money!

MRS. LINDE: (*Smiling.*) Nora, Nora, aren't you sensible yet?
Back in school you were such a free spender.

NORA: (*With a quiet laugh.*) Yes, that's what Torvald still says.
250   (*Shaking her finger.*) But "Nora, Nora" isn't as silly as you all

think. Really, we've been in no position for me to go squandering. We've had to work, both of us.

MRS. LINDE: You too?

NORA: Yes, at odd jobs—needlework, crocheting, embroidery,
and such—(*Casually.*) and other things too. You remember   255
that Torvald left the department when we were married?
There was no chance of promotion in his office, and of
course he needed to earn more money. But that first year he
drove himself terribly. He took on all kinds of extra work that
kept him going morning and night. It wore him down, and   260
then he fell deathly ill. The doctors said it was essential for
him to travel south.

MRS. LINDE: Yes, didn't you spend a whole year in Italy?

NORA: That's right. It wasn't easy to get away, you know. Ivar
had just been born. But of course we had to go. Oh, that was   265
a beautiful trip, and it saved Torvald's life. But it cost a frightful sum, Kristine.

MRS. LINDE: I can well imagine.

NORA: Four thousand, eight hundred crowns it cost. That's really a lot of money.   270

MRS. LINDE: But it's lucky you had it when you needed it.

NORA: Well, as it was, we got it from Papa.

MRS. LINDE: I see. It was just about the time your father died.

NORA: Yes, just about then. And, you know, I couldn't make
that trip out to nurse him. I had to stay here, expecting Ivar   275
any moment, and with my poor sick Torvald to care for.
Dearest Papa, I never saw him again, Kristine. Oh, that was
the worst time I've known in all my marriage.

MRS. LINDE: I know how you loved him. And then you went
off to Italy?   280

NORA: Yes. We had the means now, and the doctors urged us.
So we left a month after.

MRS. LINDE: And your husband came back completely cured?

NORA: Sound as a drum!

MRS. LINDE: But—the doctor?   285

NORA: Who?

MRS. LINDE: I thought the maid said he was a doctor, the man
who came in with me.

NORA: Yes, that was Dr. Rank—but he's not making a sick call.
He's our closest friend, and he stops by at least once a day.   290
No, Torvald hasn't had a sick moment since, and the children are fit and strong, and I am, too. (*Jumping up and clapping her hands.*) Oh, dear God, Kristine, what a lovely thing
to live and be happy! But how disgusting of me—I'm talking
of nothing but my own affairs. (*Sits on a stool close by* KRIS-   295
TINE, *arms resting across her knees.*) Oh, don't be angry with
me! Tell me, is it really true that you weren't in love with
your husband? Why did you marry him, then?

MRS. LINDE: My mother was still alive, but bedridden and
helpless—and I had my two younger brothers to look after.   300
In all conscience, I didn't think I could turn him down.

NORA: No, you were right there. But was he rich at the time?

MRS. LINDE: He was very well off, I'd say. But the business was
shaky, Nora. When he died, it all fell apart, and nothing was
left.   305

NORA: And then—?

MRS. LINDE: Yes, so I had to scrape up a living with a little
shop and a little teaching and whatever else I could find.
The last three years have been like one endless workday
without a rest for me. Now it's over, Nora. My poor mother   310
doesn't need me, for she's passed on. Nor the boys, either;
they're working now and can take care of themselves.

NORA: How free you must feel—

MRS. LINDE: No—only unspeakably empty. Nothing to live for
now. (*Standing up anxiously.*) That's why I couldn't take it
any longer out in that desolate hole. Maybe here it'll be easier to find something to do and keep my mind occupied. If I
could only be lucky enough to get a steady job, some office
work—

NORA: Oh, but Kristine, that's so dreadfully tiring, and you already look so tired. It would be much better for you if you
could go off to a bathing resort.

MRS. LINDE: (*Going toward the window.*) I have no father to
give me travel money, Nora.

NORA: (*Rising.*) Oh, don't be angry with me.

MRS. LINDE: (*Going to her.*) Nora dear, don't you be angry
with me. The worst of my kind of situation is all the bitterness that's stored away. No one to work for, and yet you're always having to snap up your opportunities. You have to live;
and so you grow selfish. When you told me the happy
change in your lot, do you know I was delighted less for your
sakes than for mine?

NORA: How so? Oh, I see. You think maybe Torvald could do
something for you.

MRS. LINDE: Yes, that's what I thought.

NORA: And he will, Kristine! Just leave it to me; I'll bring it up
so delicately—find something attractive to humor him with.
Oh, I'm so eager to help you.

MRS. LINDE: How very kind of you, Nora, to be so concerned
over me—doubly kind, considering you really know so little
of life's burdens yourself.

NORA: I—? I know so little—?

MRS. LINDE: (*Smiling.*) Well, my heavens—a little needlework
and such—Nora, you're just a child.

NORA: (*Tossing her head and pacing the floor.*) You don't have
to act so superior.

MRS. LINDE: Oh?

NORA: You're just like the others. You all think I'm incapable
of anything serious—

MRS. LINDE: Come now—

NORA: That I've never had to face the raw world.

MRS. LINDE: Nora dear, you've just been telling me all your
troubles.

NORA: Hm! Trivia! (*Quietly.*) I haven't told you the big thing.

MRS. LINDE: Big thing? What do you mean?

NORA: You look down on me so, Kristine, but you shouldn't.
You're proud that you worked so long and hard for your
mother.

MRS. LINDE: I don't look down on a soul. But it *is* true: I'm
proud—and happy, too—to think it was given to me to make
my mother's last days almost free of care.

NORA: And you're also proud thinking of what you've done for
your brothers.

MRS. LINDE: I feel I've a right to be.

NORA: I agree. But listen to this, Kristine—I've also got something to be proud and happy for.

MRS. LINDE: I don't doubt it. But whatever do you mean?

NORA: Not so loud. What if Torvald heard! He mustn't, not for
anything in the world. Nobody must know, Kristine. No one
but you.

MRS. LINDE: But what is it, then?

NORA: Come here. (*Drawing her down beside her on the sofa.*)
It's true—I've also got something to be proud and happy for.
I'm the one who saved Torvald's life.

MRS. LINDE: Saved—? Saved how?

NORA: I told you about the trip to Italy. Torvald never would
have lived if he hadn't gone south—

MRS. LINDE: Of course; your father gave you the means—

NORA: (*Smiling.*) That's what Torvald and all the rest think,
but—

MRS. LINDE: But—?

NORA: Papa didn't give us a pin. I was the one who raised the
money.

MRS. LINDE: You? That whole amount?

NORA: Four thousand, eight hundred crowns. What do you say
to that?

MRS. LINDE: But Nora, how was it possible? Did you win the
lottery?

NORA: (*Disdainfully.*) The lottery? Pooh! No art to that.

MRS. LINDE: But where did you get it from then?

NORA: (*Humming, with a mysterious smile.*) Hmm, tra-la-la-la.

MRS. LINDE: Because you couldn't have borrowed it.

NORA: No? Why not?

MRS. LINDE: A wife can't borrow without her husband's
consent.

NORA: (*Tossing her head.*) Oh, but a wife with a little business
sense, a wife who knows how to manage—

MRS. LINDE: Nora, I simply don't understand—

NORA: You don't have to. Whoever said I *borrowed* the money?
I could have gotten it other ways. (*Throwing herself back on
the sofa.*) I could have gotten it from some admirer or other.
After all, a girl with my ravishing appeal—

MRS. LINDE: You lunatic.

NORA: I'll bet you're eaten up with curiosity, Kristine.

MRS. LINDE: Now listen here, Nora—you haven't done something indiscreet?

NORA: (*Sitting up again.*) Is it indiscreet to save your husband's
life?

MRS. LINDE: I think it's indiscreet that without his knowledge
you—

NORA: But that's the point: he mustn't know! My Lord, can't
you understand? He mustn't ever know the close call he had.
It was to *me* the doctors came to say his life was in danger—
that nothing could save him but a stay in the south. Didn't I
try strategy then! I began talking about how lovely it would
be for me to travel abroad like other young wives; I begged
and I cried; I told him please to remember my condition, to
be kind and indulge me; and then I dropped a hint that he
could easily take out a loan. But at that, Kristine, he nearly
exploded. He said I was frivolous, and it was his duty as man
of the house not to indulge me in whims and fancies—as I
think he called them. Aha, I thought, now you'll just have to
be saved—and that's when I saw my chance.

MRS. LINDE: And your father never told Torvald the money
wasn't from him?

NORA: No, never. Papa died right about then. I'd considered
bringing him into my secret and begging him never to tell.
But he was too sick at the time—and then, sadly, it didn't
matter.

MRS. LINDE: And you've never confided in your husband since?

NORA: For heaven's sake, no! Are you serious? He's so strict on
that subject. Besides—Torvald, with all his masculine
pride—how painfully humiliating for him if he ever found
out he was in debt to me. That would just ruin our relationship. Our beautiful, happy home would never be the same.

MRS. LINDE: Won't you ever tell him?

NORA: (*Thoughtfully, half smiling.*) Yes—maybe sometime, years from now, when I'm no longer so attractive. Don't laugh! I only mean when Torvald loves me less than now, when he stops enjoying my dancing and dressing up and reciting for him. Then it might be wise to have something in reserve—(*Breaking off.*) How ridiculous! That'll never happen—Well, Kristine, what do you think of my big secret? I'm capable of something too, hm? You can imagine, of course, how this thing hangs over me. It really hasn't been easy meeting the payments on time. In the business world there's what they call quarterly interest and what they call amortization, and these are always so terribly hard to manage. I've had to skimp a little here and there, wherever I could, you know. I could hardly spare anything from my house allowance, because Torvald has to live well. I couldn't let the children go poorly dressed; whatever I got for them, I felt I had to use up completely—the darlings!

MRS. LINDE: Poor Nora, so it had to come out of your own budget, then?

NORA: Yes, of course. But I was the one most responsible, too. Every time Torvald gave me money for new clothes and such, I never used more than half; always bought the simplest, cheapest outfits. It was a godsend that everything looks so well on me that Torvald never noticed. But it did weigh me down at times, Kristine. It *is* such a joy to wear fine things. You understand.

MRS. LINDE: Oh, of course.

NORA: And then I found other ways of making money. Last winter I was lucky enough to get a lot of copying to do. I locked myself in and sat writing every evening till late in the night. Ah, I was tired so often, dead tired. But still it was wonderful fun, sitting and working like that, earning money. It was almost like being a man.

MRS. LINDE: But how much have you paid off this way so far?

NORA: That's hard to say, exactly. These accounts, you know, aren't easy to figure. I only know that I've paid out all I could scrape together. Time and again I haven't known where to turn. (*Smiling.*) Then I'd sit here dreaming of a rich old gentleman who had fallen in love with me—

MRS. LINDE: What! Who is he?

NORA: Oh, really! And that he'd died, and when his will was opened, there in big letters it said, "All my fortune shall be paid over in cash, immediately, to that enchanting Mrs. Nora Helmer."

MRS. LINDE: But Nora dear—who *was* this gentleman?

NORA: Good grief, can't you understand? The old man never existed; that was only something I'd dream up time and again whenever I was at my wits' end for money. But it makes no difference now; the old fossil can go where he pleases for all I care; I don't need him or his will—because now I'm free. (*Jumping up.*) Oh, how lovely to think of that, Kristine! Carefree! To know you're carefree, utterly carefree; to be able to romp and play with the children, and to keep up a beautiful, charming home—everything just the way Torvald likes it! And think, spring is coming, with big blue skies. Maybe we can travel a little then. Maybe I'll see the ocean again. Oh yes, it *is* so marvelous to live and be happy!

(*The front doorbell rings.*)

MRS. LINDE: (*Rising.*) There's the bell. It's probably best that I go.

NORA: No, stay. No one's expected. It must be for Torvald.

MAID: (*From the hall doorway.*) Excuse me, ma'am—there's a gentleman here to see Mr. Helmer, but I didn't know—since the doctor's with him—

NORA: Who is the gentleman?

KROGSTAD: (*From the doorway.*) It's me, Mrs. Helmer.

(MRS. LINDE *starts and turns away toward the window.*)

NORA: (*Stepping toward him, tense, her voice a whisper.*) You? What is it? Why do you want to speak to my husband?

KROGSTAD: Bank business—after a fashion. I have a small job in the investment bank, and I hear now your husband is going to be our chief—

NORA: In other words, it's—

KROGSTAD: Just dry business, Mrs. Helmer. Nothing but that.

NORA: Yes, then please be good enough to step into the study. (*She nods indifferently as she sees him out by the hall door, then returns and begins stirring up the stove.*)

MRS. LINDE: Nora—who was that man?

NORA: That was a Mr. Krogstad—a lawyer.

MRS. LINDE: Then it really was him.

NORA: Do you know that person?

MRS. LINDE: I did once—many years ago. For a time he was a law clerk in our town.

NORA: Yes, he's been that.

MRS. LINDE: How he's changed.

NORA: I understand he had a very unhappy marriage.

MRS. LINDE: He's a widower now.

NORA: With a number of children. There now, it's burning. (*She closes the stove door and moves the rocker a bit to one side.*)

MRS. LINDE: They say he has a hand in all kinds of business.

NORA: Oh? That may be true; I wouldn't know. But let's not think about business. It's so dull.

(DR. RANK *enters from* HELMER's *study.*)

RANK: (*Still in the doorway.*) No, no, really—I don't want to intrude, I'd just as soon talk a little while with your wife. (*Shuts the door, then notices* MRS. LINDE.) Oh, beg pardon. I'm intruding here too.

NORA: No, not at all. (*Introducing him.*) Dr. Rank, Mrs. Linde.

RANK: Well now, that's a name much heard in this house. I believe I passed the lady on the stairs as I came.

MRS. LINDE: Yes, I take the stairs very slowly. They're rather hard on me.

RANK: Uh-hm, some touch of internal weakness?

MRS. LINDE: More overexertion, I'd say.

RANK: Nothing else? Then you're probably here in town to rest up in a round of parties?

MRS. LINDE: I'm here to look for work.

RANK: Is that the best cure for overexertion?

MRS. LINDE: One has to live, Doctor.

RANK: Yes, there's a common prejudice to that effect.

NORA: Oh, come on, Dr. Rank—you really do want to live yourself.

RANK: Yes, I really do. Wretched as I am, I'll gladly prolong my torment indefinitely. All my patients feel like that. And it's quite the same, too, with the morally sick. Right at this moment there's one of those moral invalids in there with Helmer—

MRS. LINDE: (*Softly.*) Ah!

NORA: Who do you mean?

RANK: Oh, it's a lawyer, Krogstad, a type you wouldn't know.
His character is rotten to the root—but even he began chattering all-importantly about how he had to *live*.

NORA: Oh? What did he want to talk to Torvald about?

RANK: I really don't know. I only heard something about the
bank.

NORA: I didn't know that Krog—that this man Krogstad had
anything to do with the bank.

RANK: Yes, he's gotten some kind of berth down there. *(To*
MRS. LINDE.) I don't know if you also have, in your neck of
the woods, a type of person who scuttles about breathlessly,
sniffing out hints of moral corruption, and then maneuvers
his victim into some sort of key position where he can keep
an eye on him. It's the healthy these days that are out in the
cold.

MRS. LINDE: All the same, it's the sick who most need to be
taken in.

RANK: *(With a shrug.)* Yes, there we have it. That's the concept
that's turning society into a sanatorium.

(NORA, lost in her thoughts, breaks out into quiet laughter and
claps her hands.)

RANK: Why do you laugh at that? Do you have any real idea of
what society is?

NORA: What do I care about dreary old society? I was laughing
at something quite different—something terribly funny. Tell
me, Doctor—is everyone who works in the bank dependent
now on Torvald?

RANK: Is that what you find so terribly funny?

NORA: *(Smiling and humming.)* Never mind, never mind!
(Pacing the floor.) Yes, that's really immensely amusing: that
we—that Torvald has so much power now over all those people. *(Taking the bag out of her pocket.)* Dr. Rank, a little
macaroon on that?

RANK: See here, macaroons! I thought they were contraband
here.

NORA: Yes, but these are some that Kristine gave me.

MRS. LINDE: What? I—?

NORA: Now, now, don't be afraid. You couldn't possibly know
that Torvald had forbidden them. You see, he's worried
they'll ruin my teeth. But hmp! Just this once! Isn't that so,
Dr. Rank? Help yourself! *(Puts a macaroon in his mouth.)*
And you too, Kristine. And I'll also have one, only a little
one—or two, at the most. *(Walking about again.)* Now I'm
really tremendously happy. Now there's just one last thing in
the world that I have an enormous desire to do.

RANK: Well! And what's that?

NORA: It's something I have such a consuming desire to say so
Torvald could hear.

RANK: And why can't you say it?

NORA: I don't dare. It's quite shocking.

MRS. LINDE: Shocking?

RANK: Well, then it isn't advisable. But in front of us you certainly can. What do you have such a desire to say so Torvald
could hear?

NORA: I have such a huge desire to say—to hell and be damned!

RANK: Are you crazy?

MRS. LINDE: My goodness, Nora!

RANK: Go on, say it. Here he is.

NORA: *(Hiding the macaroon bag.)* Shh, shh, shh!

(HELMER comes in from his study, hat in hand, overcoat over his
arm.)

NORA: *(Going toward him.)* Well, Torvald dear, are you
through with him?

HELMER: Yes, he just left.

NORA: Let me introduce you—this is Kristine, who's arrived
here in town.

HELMER: Kristine—? I'm sorry, but I don't know—

NORA: Mrs. Linde, Torvald dear. Mrs. Kristine Linde.

HELMER: Of course. A childhood friend of my wife's, no
doubt?

MRS. LINDE: Yes, we knew each other in those days.

NORA: And just think, she made the long trip down here in
order to talk with you.

HELMER: What's this?

MRS. LINDE: Well, not exactly—

NORA: You see, Kristine is remarkably clever in office work,
and so she's terribly eager to come under a capable man's supervision and add more to what she already knows—

HELMER: Very wise, Mrs. Linde.

NORA: And then when she heard that you'd become a bank
manager—the story was wired out to the papers—then she
came in as fast as she could and—Really, Torvald, for my
sake you can do a little something for Kristine, can't you?

HELMER: Yes, it's not at all impossible. Mrs. Linde, I suppose
you're a widow?

MRS. LINDE: Yes.

HELMER: Any experience in office work?

MRS. LINDE: Yes, a good deal.

HELMER: Well, it's quite likely that I can make an opening for
you—

NORA: *(Clapping her hands.)* You see, you see!

HELMER: You've come at a lucky moment, Mrs. Linde.

MRS. LINDE: Oh, how can I thank you?

HELMER: Not necessary. *(Putting his overcoat on.)* But today
you'll have to excuse me—

RANK: Wait, I'll go with you. *(He fetches his coat from the hall*
and warms it at the stove.)

NORA: Don't stay out long, dear.

HELMER: An hour; no more.

NORA: Are you going too, Kristine?

MRS. LINDE: *(Putting on her winter garments.)* Yes, I have to
see about a room now.

HELMER: Then perhaps we can all walk together.

NORA: *(Helping her.)* What a shame we're so cramped here,
but it's quite impossible for us to—

MRS. LINDE: Oh, don't even think of it! Good-bye, Nora dear,
and thanks for everything.

NORA: Good-bye for now. Of course you'll be back this evening.
And you too, Dr. Rank. What? If you're well enough? Oh,
you've got to be! Wrap up tight now.

(In a ripple of small talk the company moves out into the hall;
children's voices are heard outside on the steps.)

NORA: There they are! There they are! *(She runs to open the*
door. The children come in with their nurse, ANNE-MARIE.*)*
Come in, come in! *(Bends down and kisses them.)* Oh, you
darlings—! Look at them, Kristine. Aren't they lovely!

RANK: No loitering in the draft here.

665 HELMER: Come, Mrs. Linde—this place is unbearable now for anyone but mothers.

(DR. RANK, HELMER, and MRS. LINDE go down the stairs. ANNE-MARIE goes into the living room with the children. NORA follows, after closing the hall door.)

NORA: How fresh and strong you look. Oh, such red cheeks you have! Like apples and roses. *(The children interrupt her throughout the following.)* And it was so much fun? That's
670 wonderful. Really? You pulled both Emmy and Bob on the sled? Imagine, all together! Yes, you're a clever boy, Ivar. Oh, let me hold her a bit, Anne-Marie. My sweet little doll baby! *(Takes the smallest from the nurse and dances with her.)* Yes, yes, Mama will dance with Bob as well. What? Did you
675 throw snowballs? Oh, if I'd only been there! No, don't bother, Anne-Marie—I'll undress them myself. Oh yes, let me. It's such fun. Go in and rest; you look half frozen. There's hot coffee waiting for you on the stove. *(The nurse goes into the room to the left. NORA takes the children's winter*
680 *things off, throwing them about, while the children talk to her all at once.)* Is that so? A big dog chased you? But it didn't bite? No, dogs never bite little, lovely doll babies. Don't peek in the packages, Ivar! What is it? Yes, wouldn't you like to know. No, no, it's an ugly something. Well? Shall we play?
685 What shall we play? Hide-and-seek? Yes, let's play hide-and-seek. Bob must hide first. I must? Yes, let me hide first. *(Laughing and shouting, she and the children play in and out of the living room and the adjoining room to the right. At last NORA hides under the table. The children come storming in,*
690 *search, but cannot find her, then hear her muffled laughter, dash over to the table, lift the cloth up and find her. Wild shouting. She creeps forward as if to scare them. More shouts. Meanwhile, a knock at the hall door; no one has noticed it. Now the door half opens, and KROGSTAD appears. He waits a*
695 *moment; the game goes on.)*
KROGSTAD: Beg pardon, Mrs. Helmer—
NORA: *(With a strangled cry, turning and scrambling to her knees.)* Oh! What do you want?
KROGSTAD: Excuse me. The outer door was ajar; it must be
700 someone forgot to shut it—
NORA: *(Rising.)* My husband isn't home, Mr. Krogstad.
KROGSTAD: I know that.
NORA: Yes—then what do you want here?
KROGSTAD: A word with you.
705 NORA: With—? *(To the children, quietly.)* Go in to Anne-Marie. What? No, the strange man won't hurt Mama. When he's gone, we'll play some more. *(She leads the children into the room to the left and shuts the door after them. Then, tense and nervous:)* You want to speak to me?
710 KROGSTAD: Yes, I want to.
NORA: Today? But it's not yet the first of the month—
KROGSTAD: No, it's Christmas Eve. It's going to be up to you how merry a Christmas you have.
NORA: What is it you want? Today I absolutely can't—
715 KROGSTAD: We won't talk about that till later. This is something else. You do have a moment to spare, I suppose?
NORA: Oh yes, of course—I do, except—
KROGSTAD: Good. I was sitting over at Olsen's Restaurant when I saw your husband go down the street—
720 NORA: Yes?

KROGSTAD: With a lady.
NORA: Yes. So?
KROGSTAD: If you'll pardon my asking: wasn't that lady a Mrs. Linde?
NORA: Yes.   725
KROGSTAD: Just now come into town?
NORA: Yes, today.
KROGSTAD: She's a good friend of yours?
NORA: Yes, she is. But I don't see—
KROGSTAD: I also knew her once.   730
NORA: I'm aware of that.
KROGSTAD: Oh? You know all about it. I thought so. Well, then let me ask you short and sweet: is Mrs. Linde getting a job in the bank?
NORA: What makes you think you can cross-examine me, Mr.   735
Krogstad—you, one of my husband's employees? But since you ask, you might as well know—yes, Mrs. Linde's going to be taken on at the bank. And I'm the one who spoke for her, Mr. Krogstad. Now you know.
KROGSTAD: So I guessed right.   740
NORA: *(Pacing up and down.)* Oh, one does have a tiny bit of influence, I should hope. Just because I am a woman, don't think it means that—When one has a subordinate position, Mr. Krogstad, one really ought to be careful about pushing somebody who—hm—   745
KROGSTAD: Who has influence?
NORA: That's right.
KROGSTAD: *(In a different tone.)* Mrs. Helmer, would you be good enough to use your influence on my behalf?
NORA: What? What do you mean?   750
KROGSTAD: Would you please make sure that I keep my subordinate position in the bank?
NORA: What does that mean? Who's thinking of taking away your position?
KROGSTAD: Oh, don't play the innocent with me. I'm quite   755
aware that your friend would hardly relish the chance of running into me again; and I'm also aware now whom I can thank for being turned out.
NORA: But I promise you—
KROGSTAD: Yes, yes, yes, to the point: there's still time, and I'm   760
advising you to use your influence to prevent it.
NORA: But Mr. Krogstad, I have absolutely no influence.
KROGSTAD: You haven't? I thought you were just saying—
NORA: You shouldn't take me so literally. I! How can you believe that I have any such influence over my husband?   765
KROGSTAD: Oh, I've known your husband from our student days. I don't think the great bank manager's more steadfast than any other married man.
NORA: You speak insolently about my husband, and I'll show you the door.   770
KROGSTAD: The lady has spirit.
NORA: I'm not afraid of you any longer. After New Year's, I'll soon be done with the whole business.
KROGSTAD: *(Restraining himself.)* Now listen to me, Mrs. Helmer. If necessary, I'll fight for my little job in the bank as   775
if it were life itself.
NORA: Yes, so it seems.
KROGSTAD: It's not just a matter of income; that's the least of it. It's something else—All right, out with it! Look, this is the thing. You know, just like all the others, of course, that once,   780
a good many years ago, I did something rather rash.

NORA: I've heard rumors to that effect.

KROGSTAD: The case never got into court; but all the same, every door was closed in my face from then on. So I took up those various activities you know about. I had to grab hold somewhere; and I dare say I haven't been among the worst. But now I want to drop all that. My boys are growing up. For their sakes, I'll have to win back as much respect as possible here in town. That job in the bank was like the first rung in my ladder. And now your husband wants to kick me right back down in the mud again.

NORA: But for heaven's sake, Mr. Krogstad, it's simply not in my power to help you.

KROGSTAD: That's because you haven't the will to—but I have the means to make you.

NORA: You certainly won't tell my husband that I owe you money?

KROGSTAD: Hm—what if I told him that?

NORA: That would be shameful of you. (*Nearly in tears.*) This secret—my joy and my pride—that he should learn it in such a crude and disgusting way—learn it from you. You'd expose me to the most horrible unpleasantness—

KROGSTAD: Only unpleasantness?

NORA: (*Vehemently.*) But go on and try. It'll turn out the worse for you, because then my husband will really see what a crook you are, and then you'll *never* be able to hold your job.

KROGSTAD: I asked if it was just domestic unpleasantness you were afraid of?

NORA: If my husband finds out, then of course he'll pay what I owe at once, and then we'd be through with you for good.

KROGSTAD: (*A step closer.*) Listen, Mrs. Helmer—you've either got a very bad memory, or else no head at all for business. I'd better put you a little more in touch with the facts.

NORA: What do you mean?

KROGSTAD: When your husband was sick, you came to me for a loan of four thousand, eight hundred crowns.

NORA: Where else could I go?

KROGSTAD: I promised to get you that sum—

NORA: And you got it.

KROGSTAD: I promised to get you that sum, on certain conditions. You were so involved in your husband's illness, and so eager to finance your trip, that I guess you didn't think out all the details. It might just be a good idea to remind you. I promised you the money on the strength of a note I drew up.

NORA: Yes, and that I signed.

KROGSTAD: Right. But at the bottom I added some lines for your father to guarantee the loan. He was supposed to sign down there.

NORA: Supposed to? He did sign.

KROGSTAD: I left the date blank. In other words, your father would have dated his signature himself. Do you remember that?

NORA: Yes, I think—

KROGSTAD: Then I gave you the note for you to mail to your father. Isn't that so?

NORA: Yes.

KROGSTAD: And naturally you sent it at once—because only some five, six days later you brought me the note, properly signed. And with that, the money was yours.

NORA: Well, then; I've made my payments regularly, haven't I?

KROGSTAD: More or less. But—getting back to the point—those were hard times for you then, Mrs. Helmer.

NORA: Yes, they were.

KROGSTAD: Your father was very ill, I believe.

NORA: He was near the end.

KROGSTAD: He died soon after?

NORA: Yes.

KROGSTAD: Tell me, Mrs. Helmer, do you happen to recall the date of your father's death? The day of the month, I mean.

NORA: Papa died the twenty-ninth of September.

KROGSTAD: That's quite correct; I've already looked into that. And now we come to a curious thing—(*Taking out a paper.*) which I simply cannot comprehend.

NORA: Curious thing? I don't know—

KROGSTAD: This is the curious thing: that your father co-signed the note for your loan three days after his death.

NORA: How—? I don't understand.

KROGSTAD: Your father died the twenty-ninth of September. But look. Here your father dated his signature October second. Isn't that curious, Mrs. Helmer? (NORA *is silent.*) Can you explain it to me? (NORA *remains silent.*) It's also remarkable that the words "October second" and the year aren't written in your father's hand, but rather in one that I think I know. Well, it's easy to understand. Your father forgot perhaps to date his signature, and then someone or other added it, a bit sloppily, before anyone knew of his death. There's nothing wrong in that. It all comes down to the signature. And there's no question about *that*, Mrs. Helmer. It really *was* your father who signed his own name here, wasn't it?

NORA: (*After a short silence, throwing her head back and looking squarely at him.*) No, it wasn't. I signed Papa's name.

KROGSTAD: Wait, now—are you fully aware that this is a dangerous confession?

NORA: Why? You'll soon get your money.

KROGSTAD: Let me ask you a question—why didn't you send the paper to your father?

NORA: That was impossible. Papa was so sick. If I'd asked him for his signature, I also would have had to tell him what the money was for. But I couldn't tell him, sick as he was, that my husband's life was in danger. That was just impossible.

KROGSTAD: Then it would have been better if you'd given up the trip abroad.

NORA: I couldn't possibly. The trip was to save my husband's life. I couldn't give that up.

KROGSTAD: But didn't you ever consider that this was a fraud against me?

NORA: I couldn't let myself be bothered by that. You weren't any concern of mine. I couldn't stand you, with all those cold complications you made, even though you knew how badly off my husband was.

KROGSTAD: Mrs. Helmer, obviously you haven't the vaguest idea of what you've involved yourself in. But I can tell you this: it was nothing more and nothing worse that I once did—and it wrecked my whole reputation.

NORA: You? Do you expect me to believe that you ever acted bravely to save your wife's life?

KROGSTAD: Laws don't inquire into motives.

NORA: Then they must be very poor laws.

KROGSTAD: Poor or not—if I introduce this paper in court, you'll be judged according to law.

NORA: This I refuse to believe. A daughter hasn't a right to protect her dying father from anxiety and care? A wife hasn't a

905 right to save her husband's life? I don't know much about laws, but I'm sure that somewhere in the books these things are allowed. And you don't know anything about it—you who practice the law? You must be an awful lawyer, Mr. Krogstad.

KROGSTAD: Could be. But business—the kind of business we 910 two are mixed up in—don't you think I know about that? All right. Do what you want now. But I'm telling you *this*: if I get shoved down a second time, you're going to keep me company. (*He bows and goes out through the hall.*)

NORA: (*Pensive for a moment, then tossing her head.*) Oh, really! Trying to frighten me! I'm not so silly as all that. (*Begins* 915 *gathering up the children's clothes, but soon stops.*) But—? No, but that's impossible! I did it out of love.

THE CHILDREN: (*In the doorway, left.*) Mama, that strange man's gone out the door.

NORA: Yes, yes, I know it. But don't tell anyone about the 920 strange man. Do you hear? Not even Papa!

THE CHILDREN: No, Mama. But now will you play again?

NORA: No, not now.

THE CHILDREN: Oh, but Mama, you promised.

NORA: Yes, but I can't now. Go inside; I have too much to do. 925 Go in, go in, my sweet darlings. (*She herds them gently back in the room and shuts the door after them. Settling on the sofa, she takes up a piece of embroidery and makes some stitches, but soon stops abruptly.*) No! (*Throws the work aside, rises, goes to the hall door and calls out.*) Helene! Let me 930 have the tree in here. (*Goes to the table, left, opens the table drawer, and stops again.*) No, but that's utterly impossible!

MAID: (*With the Christmas tree.*) Where should I put it, ma'am?

NORA: There. The middle of the floor.

935 MAID: Should I bring anything else?

NORA: No, thanks. I have what I need.

(*The* MAID, *who has set the tree down, goes out.*)

NORA: (*Absorbed in trimming the tree.*) Candles here—and flowers here. That terrible creature! Talk, talk, talk! There's nothing to it at all. The tree's going to be lovely. I'll do any-940 thing to please you, Torvald. I'll sing for you, dance for you—

(HELMER *comes in from the hall, with a sheaf of papers under his arm.*)

NORA: Oh! You're back so soon?

HELMER: Yes. Has anyone been here?

NORA: Here? No.

945 HELMER: That's odd. I saw Krogstad leaving the front door.

NORA: So? Oh yes, that's true. Krogstad was here a moment.

HELMER: Nora, I can see by your face that he's been here, begging you to put in a good word for him.

NORA: Yes.

950 HELMER: And it was supposed to seem like your own idea? You were to hide it from me that he'd been here. He asked you that, too, didn't he?

NORA: Yes, Torvald, but—

HELMER: Nora, Nora, and you could fall for that? Talk with 955 that sort of person and promise him anything? And then in the bargain, tell me an untruth.

NORA: An untruth—?

HELMER: Didn't you say that no one had been here? (*Wagging his finger.*) My little songbird must never do that again. A 960 songbird needs a clean beak to warble with. No false notes. (*Putting his arm about her waist.*) That's the way it should be, isn't it? Yes, I'm sure of it. (*Releasing her.*) And so, enough of that. (*Sitting by the stove.*) Ah, how snug and cozy it is here. (*Leafing among his papers.*)

NORA: (*Busy with the tree, after a short pause.*) Torvald! 965

HELMER: Yes.

NORA: I'm so much looking forward to the Stenborgs' costume party, day after tomorrow.

HELMER: And I can't wait to see what you'll surprise me with.

NORA: Oh, that stupid business! 970

HELMER: What?

NORA: I can't find anything that's right. Everything seems so ridiculous, so inane.

HELMER: So my little Nora's come to *that* recognition?

NORA: (*Going behind his chair, her arms resting on its back.*) 975 Are you very busy, Torvald?

HELMER: Oh—

NORA: What papers are those?

HELMER: Bank matters.

NORA: Already? 980

HELMER: I've gotten full authority from the retiring management to make all necessary changes in personnel and procedure. I'll need Christmas week for that. I want to have everything in order by New Year's.

NORA: So that was the reason this poor Krogstad—

HELMER: Hm. 985

NORA: (*Still leaning on the chair and slowly stroking the nape of his neck.*) If you weren't so very busy, I would have asked you an enormous favor, Torvald.

HELMER: Let's hear. What is it?

NORA: You know, there isn't anyone who has your good taste— 990 and I want so much to look well at the costume party. Torvald, couldn't you take over and decide what I should be and plan my costume?

HELMER: Ah, is my stubborn little creature calling for a lifeguard? 995

NORA: Yes, Torvald, I can't get anywhere without your help.

HELMER: All right—I'll think it over. We'll hit on something.

NORA: Oh, how sweet of you. (*Goes to the tree again. Pause.*) Aren't the red flowers pretty—? But tell me, was it really such a crime that this Krogstad committed? 1000

HELMER: Forgery. Do you have any idea what that means?

NORA: Couldn't he have done it out of need?

HELMER: Yes, or thoughtlessness, like so many others. I'm not so heartless that I'd condemn a man categorically for just one mistake. 1005

NORA: No, of course not, Torvald!

HELMER: Plenty of men have redeemed themselves by openly confessing their crimes and taking their punishment.

NORA: Punishment—?

HELMER: But now Krogstad didn't go that way. He got himself 1010 out by sharp practices, and that's the real cause of his moral breakdown.

NORA: Do you really think that would—?

HELMER: Just imagine how a man with that sort of guilt in him has to lie and cheat and deceive on all sides, has to wear a 1015 mask even with the nearest and dearest he has, even with his own wife and children. And with the children, Nora—that's where it's most horrible.

NORA: Why?

1020 HELMER: Because that kind of atmosphere of lies infects the whole life of a home. Every breath the children take in is filled with the germs of something degenerate.

NORA: *(Coming closer behind him.)* Are you sure of that?

HELMER: Oh, I've seen it often enough as a lawyer. Almost
1025 everyone who goes bad early in life has a mother who's a chronic liar.

NORA: Why just—the mother?

HELMER: It's usually the mother's influence that's dominant, but the father's works in the same way, of course. Every
1030 lawyer is quite familiar with it. And still this Krogstad's been going home year in, year out, poisoning his own children with lies and pretense; that's why I call him morally lost. *(Reaching his hands out toward her.)* So my sweet little Nora must promise me never to plead his cause. Your hand on it.
1035 Come, come, what's this? Give me your hand. There, now. All settled. I can tell you it'd be impossible for me to work alongside of him. I literally feel physically revolted when I'm anywhere near such a person.

NORA: *(Withdraws her hand and goes to the other side of the*
1040 *Christmas tree.)* How hot it is here! And I've got so much to do.

HELMER: *(Getting up and gathering his papers.)* Yes, and I have to think about getting some of these read through before dinner. I'll think about your costume, too. And some
1045 thing to hang on the tree in gilt paper, I may even see about that. *(Putting his hand on her head.)* Oh you, my darling little songbird. *(He goes into his study and closes the door after him.)*

NORA: *(Softly, after a silence.)* Oh, really! it isn't so. It's impos-
1050 sible. It must be impossible.

ANNE-MARIE: *(In the doorway, left.)* The children are begging so hard to come in to Mama.

NORA: No, no, no, don't let them in to me! You stay with them, Anne-Marie.

1055 ANNE-MARIE: Of course, ma'am. *(Closes the door.)*

NORA: *(Pale with terror.)* Hurt my children—! Poison my home? *(A moment's pause; then she tosses her head.)* That's not true. Never. Never in all the world.

— ACT TWO —

Same room. Beside the piano the Christmas tree now stands stripped of ornament, burned-down candle stubs on its ragged branches. NORA's street clothes lie on the sofa. NORA, alone in the room, moves restlessly about; at last she stops at the sofa and picks up her coat.

NORA: *(Dropping the coat again.)* Someone's coming! *(Goes toward the door, listens.)* No—there's no one. Of course—nobody's coming today, Christmas Day—or tomorrow, either. But maybe—(Opens the door and looks out.) No, nothing in
5 the mailbox. Quite empty. *(Coming forward.)* What nonsense! He won't do anything serious. Nothing terrible could happen. It's impossible. Why, I have three small children.

(ANNE-MARIE, with a large carton, comes in from the room to the left.)

ANNE-MARIE: Well, at last I found the box with the masquerade clothes.

10 NORA: Thanks. Put it on the table.

ANNE-MARIE: *(Does so.)* But they're all pretty much of a mess.

NORA: Ahh! I'd love to rip them in a million pieces!

ANNE-MARIE: Oh, mercy, they can be fixed right up. Just a little patience.

NORA: Yes, I'll go get Mrs. Linde to help me. 15

ANNE-MARIE: Out again now? In this nasty weather? Miss Nora will catch cold—get sick.

NORA: Oh, worse things could happen—How are the children?

ANNE-MARIE: The poor mites are playing with their Christmas 20 presents, but—

NORA: Do they ask for me much?

ANNE-MARIE: They're so used to having Mama around, you know.

NORA: Yes, but Anne-Marie, I *can't* be together with them as 25 much as I was.

ANNE-MARIE: Well, small children get used to anything.

NORA: You think so? Do you think they'd forget their mother if she was gone for good?

ANNE-MARIE: Oh, mercy—gone for good! 30

NORA: Wait, tell me, Anne-Marie—I've wondered so often—how could you ever have the heart to give your child over to strangers?

ANNE-MARIE: But I had to, you know, to become little Nora's nurse. 35

NORA: Yes, but how could you *do* it?

ANNE-MARIE: When I could get such a good place? A girl who's poor and who's gotten in trouble is glad enough for that. Because that slippery fish, he didn't do a thing for me, you know. 40

NORA: But your daughter's surely forgotten you.

ANNE-MARIE: Oh, she certainly has not. She's written to me, both when she was confirmed and when she was married.

NORA: *(Clasping her about the neck.)* You old Anne-Marie, you were a good mother for me when I was little. 45

ANNE-MARIE: Poor little Nora, with no other mother but me.

NORA: And if the babies didn't have one, then I know that you'd—What silly talk! *(Opening the carton.)* Go in to them. Now I'll have to—Tomorrow you can see how lovely I'll look. 50

ANNE-MARIE: Oh, there won't be anyone at the party as lovely as Miss Nora. *(She goes off into the room, left.)*

NORA: *(Begins unpacking the box, but soon throws it aside.)* Oh, if I dared to go out. If only nobody would come. If only nothing would happen here while I'm out. What crazi- 55 ness—nobody's coming. Just don't think. This muff—needs a brushing. Beautiful gloves, beautiful gloves. Let it go. Let it go! One, two, three, four, five, six—(With a cry.) Oh, there they are! *(Poises to move toward the door, but remains irresolutely standing. MRS. LINDE enters from the hall, where she* 60 *has removed her street clothes.)*

NORA: Oh, it's you, Kristine. There's no one else out there? How good that you've come.

MRS. LINDE: I hear you were up asking for me.

NORA: Yes, I just stopped by. There's something you really can 65 help me with. Let's get settled on the sofa. Look, there's going to be a costume party tomorrow evening at the Stenborgs' right above us, and now Torvald wants me to go as a Neapolitan peasant girl and dance the tarantella that I learned in Capri. 70

MRS. LINDE: Really, are you giving a whole performance?

NORA: Torvald says yes, I should. See, here's the dress. Torvald had it made for me down there; but now it's all so tattered that I just don't know—

75 MRS. LINDE: Oh, we'll fix that up in no time. It's nothing more than the trimmings—they're a bit loose here and there. Needle and thread? Good, now we have what we need.

NORA: Oh, how sweet of you!

MRS. LINDE: (Sewing.) So you'll be in disguise tomorrow,
80 Nora. You know what? I'll stop by then for a moment and have a look at you all dressed up. But listen, I've absolutely forgotten to thank you for that pleasant evening yesterday.

NORA: (Getting up and walking about.) I don't think it was as pleasant as usual yesterday. You should have come to town a
85 bit sooner, Kristine—Yes, Torvald really knows how to give a home elegance and charm.

MRS. LINDE: And you do, too, if you ask me. You're not your father's daughter for nothing. But tell me, is Dr. Rank always so down in the mouth as yesterday?

90 NORA: No, that was quite an exception. But he goes around critically ill all the time—tuberculosis of the spine, poor man. You know, his father was a disgusting thing who kept mistresses and so on—and that's why the son's been sickly from birth.

95 MRS. LINDE: (Lets her sewing fall to her lap.) But my dearest Nora, how do you know about such things?

NORA: (Walking more jauntily.) Hmp! When you've had three children, then you've had a few visits from—from women who know something of medicine, and they tell you this and
100 that.

MRS. LINDE: (Resumes sewing; a short pause.) Does Dr. Rank come here every day?

NORA: Every blessed day. He's Torvald's best friend from childhood, and my good friend, too. Dr. Rank almost belongs to
105 this house.

MRS. LINDE: But tell me—is he quite sincere? I mean, doesn't he rather enjoy flattering people?

NORA: Just the opposite. Why do you think that?

MRS. LINDE: When you introduced us yesterday, he was pro-
110 claiming that he'd often heard my name in this house; but later I noticed that your husband hadn't the slightest idea who I really was. So how could Dr. Rank—?

NORA: But it's all true, Kristine. You see, Torvald loves me beyond words, and, as he puts it, he'd like to keep me all to
115 himself. For a long time he'd almost be jealous if I even mentioned any of my old friends back home. So of course I dropped that. But with Dr. Rank I talk a lot about such things, because he likes hearing about them.

MRS. LINDE: Now listen, Nora; in many ways you're still like a
120 child. I'm a good deal older than you, with a little more experience. I'll tell you something: you ought to put an end to all this with Dr. Rank.

NORA: What should I put an end to?

MRS. LINDE: Both parts of it, I think. Yesterday you said some-
125 thing about a rich admirer who'd provide you with money—

NORA: Yes, one who doesn't exist—worse luck. So?

MRS. LINDE: Is Dr. Rank well off?

NORA: Yes, he is.

MRS. LINDE: With no dependents?

130 NORA: No, no one. But—

MRS. LINDE: And he's over here every day?

NORA: Yes, I told you that.

MRS. LINDE: How can a man of such refinement be so grasping?

NORA: I don't follow you at all. 135

MRS. LINDE: Now don't try to hide it, Nora. You think I can't guess who loaned you the forty-eight hundred crowns?

NORA: Are you out of your mind? How could you think such a thing! A friend of ours, who comes here every single day. What an intolerable situation that would have been! 140

MRS. LINDE: Then it really wasn't him.

NORA: No, absolutely not. It never even crossed my mind for a moment—And he had nothing to lend in those days; his inheritance came later.

MRS. LINDE: Well, I think that was a stroke of luck for you, 145 Nora dear.

NORA: No, it never would have occurred to me to ask Dr. Rank—Still, I'm quite sure that if I had asked him—

MRS. LINDE: Which you won't, of course.

NORA: No, of course not. I can't see that I'd ever need to. But 150 I'm quite positive that if I talked to Dr. Rank—

MRS. LINDE: Behind your husband's back?

NORA: I've got to clear up this other thing; that's also behind his back. I've got to clear it all up.

MRS. LINDE: Yes, I was saying that yesterday, but— 155

NORA: (Pacing up and down.) A man handles these problems so much better than a woman—

MRS. LINDE: One's husband does, yes.

NORA: Nonsense. (Stopping.) When you pay everything you owe, then you get your note back, right? 160

MRS. LINDE: Yes, naturally.

NORA: And can rip it into a million pieces and burn it up— that filthy scrap of paper!

MRS. LINDE: (Looking hard at her, laying her sewing aside, and rising slowly.) Nora, you're hiding something from me. 165

NORA: You can see it in my face?

MRS. LINDE: Something's happened to you since yesterday morning. Nora, what is it?

NORA: (Hurrying toward her.) Kristine! (Listening.) Shh! Torvald's home. Look, go in with the children a while. Torvald 170 can't bear all this snipping and stitching. Let Anne-Marie help you.

MRS. LINDE: (Gathering up some of the things.) All right, but I'm not leaving here until we've talked this out. (She disappears into the room, left, as TORVALD enters from the hall.) 175

NORA: Oh, how I've been waiting for you, Torvald dear.

HELMER: Was that the dressmaker?

NORA: No, that was Kristine. She's helping me fix up my costume. You know, it's going to be quite attractive.

HELMER: Yes, wasn't that a bright idea I had? 180

NORA: Brilliant! But then wasn't I good as well to give in to you?

HELMER: Good—because you give in to your husband's judgment? All right, you little goose, I know you didn't mean it like that. But I won't disturb you. You'll want to have a fit- 185 ting, I suppose.

NORA: And you'll be working?

HELMER: Yes. (Indicating a bundle of papers.) See, I've been down to the bank. (Starts toward his study.)

NORA: Torvald. 190

HELMER: (Stops.) Yes.

NORA: If your little squirrel begged you, with all her heart and soul, for something—?

HELMER: What's that?

195 NORA: Then would you do it?

HELMER: First, naturally, I'd have to know what it was.

NORA: Your squirrel would scamper about and do tricks, if you'd only be sweet and give in.

HELMER: Out with it.

200 NORA: Your lark would be singing high and low in every room—

HELMER: Come on, she does that anyway.

NORA: I'd be a wood nymph and dance for you in the moonlight.

205 HELMER: Nora—don't tell me it's that same business from this morning?

NORA: (*Coming closer.*) Yes, Torvald, I beg you, please!

HELMER: And you actually have the nerve to drag that up again?

210 NORA: Yes, yes, you've got to give in to me; you *have* to let Krogstad keep his job in the bank.

HELMER: My dear Nora, I've slated his job for Mrs. Linde.

NORA: That's awfully kind of you. But you could just fire another clerk instead of Krogstad.

215 HELMER: This is the most incredible stubbornness! Because you go and give an impulsive promise to speak up for him, I'm expected to—

NORA: That's not the reason, Torvald. It's for your own sake. That man does writing for the worst papers; you said it your-
220 self. He could do you any amount of harm. I'm scared to death of him—

HELMER: Ah, I understand. It's the old memories haunting you.

NORA: What do you mean by that?

225 HELMER: Of course, you're thinking about your father.

NORA: Yes, all right. Just remember how those nasty gossips wrote in the papers about Papa and slandered him so cruelly. I think they'd have had him dismissed if the department hadn't sent you up to investigate, and if you hadn't been so
230 kind and open-minded toward him.

HELMER: My dear Nora, there's a notable difference between your father and me. Your father's official career was hardly above reproach. But mine is; and I hope it'll stay that way as long as I hold my position.

235 NORA: Oh, who can ever tell what vicious minds can invent? We could be so snug and happy now in our quiet, carefree home—you and I and the children, Torvald! That's why I'm pleading with you so—

HELMER: And just by pleading for him you make it impossible
240 for me to keep him on. It's already known at the bank that I'm firing Krogstad. What if it's rumored around now that the new bank manager was vetoed by his wife—

NORA: Yes, what then—?

HELMER: Oh yes—as long as our little bundle of stubbornness
245 gets her way—! I should go and make myself ridiculous in front of the whole office—give people the idea I can be swayed by all kinds of outside pressure. Oh, you can bet I'd feel the effects of that soon enough! Besides—there's something that rules Krogstad right out at the bank as long as I'm
250 the manager.

NORA: What's that?

HELMER: His moral failings I could maybe overlook if I had to—

NORA: Yes, Torvald, why not?

HELMER: And I hear he's quite efficient on the job. But he was 255 a crony of mine back in my teens—one of those rash friendships that crop up again and again to embarrass you later in life. Well, I might as well say it straight out: we're on a first-name basis. And that tactless fool makes no effort at all to hide it in front of others. Quite the contrary—he thinks that 260 entitles him to take a familiar air around me, and so every other second he comes booming out with his "Yes, Torvald!" and "Sure thing, Torvald!" I tell you, it's been excruciating for me. He's out to make my place in the bank unbearable.

NORA: Torvald, you can't be serious about all this. 265

HELMER: Oh no? Why not?

NORA: Because these are such petty considerations.

HELMER: What are you saying? Petty? You think I'm petty!

NORA: No, just the opposite, Torvald dear. That's exactly why— 270

HELMER: Never mind. You call my motives petty; then I might as well be just that. Petty! All right! We'll put a stop to this for good. (*Goes to the hall door and calls.*) Helene!

NORA: What do you want?

HELMER: (*Searching among his papers.*) A decision. (*The* MAID 275 *comes in.*) Look here; take this letter; go out with it at once. Get hold of a messenger and have him deliver it. Quick now. It's already addressed. Wait, here's some money.

MAID: Yes, sir. (*She leaves with the letter.*)

HELMER: (*Straightening his papers.*) There, now, little Miss 280 Willful.

NORA: (*Breathlessly.*) Torvald, what was that letter?

HELMER: Krogstad's notice.

NORA: Call it back, Torvald! There's still time. Oh, Torvald, call it back! Do it for my sake—for your sake, for the chil- 285 dren's sake! Do you hear, Torvald; do it! You don't know how this can harm us.

HELMER: Too late.

NORA: Yes, too late.

HELMER: Nora dear, I can forgive you this panic, even though 290 basically you're insulting me. Yes, you are! Or isn't it an insult to think that *I* should be afraid of a courtroom hack's revenge? But I forgive you anyway, because this shows so beautifully how much you love me. (*Takes her in his arms.*) This is the way it should be, my darling Nora. Whatever 295 comes, you'll see: when it really counts, I have strength and courage enough as a man to take on the whole weight myself.

NORA: (*Terrified.*) What do you mean by that?

HELMER: The whole weight, I said. 300

NORA: (*Resolutely.*) No, never in all the world.

HELMER: Good. So we'll share it, Nora, as man and wife. That's as it should be. (*Fondling her.*) Are you happy now? There, there, there—not these frightened dove's eyes. It's nothing at all but empty fantasies—Now you should run 305 through your tarantella and practice your tambourine. I'll go to the inner office and shut both doors, so I won't hear a thing; you can make all the noise you like. (*Turning in the doorway.*) And when Rank comes, just tell him where he can find me. (*He nods to her and goes with his papers into the* 310 *study, closing the door.*)

NORA: (*Standing as though rooted, dazed with fright, in a whisper.*) He really could do it. He will do it. He'll do it in spite of everything. No, not that, never, never! Anything but that! Escape! A way out—(*The doorbell rings.*) Dr. Rank! Anything 315 but that! *Anything, whatever it is! (Her hands pass over her face, smoothing it; she pulls herself together, goes over and opens the hall door.* DR. RANK *stands outside, hanging his fur coat up. During the following scene, it begins getting dark.)*

320 NORA: Hello, Dr. Rank. I recognized your ring. But you mustn't go in to Torvald yet; I believe he's working.

RANK: And you?

NORA: For you, I always have an hour to spare—you know that. *(He has entered, and she shuts the door after him.)*

325 RANK: Many thanks. I'll make use of these hours while I can.

NORA: What do you mean by that? While you can?

RANK: Does that disturb you?

NORA: Well, it's such an odd phrase. Is anything going to happen?

330 RANK: What's going to happen is what I've been expecting so long—but I honestly didn't think it would come so soon.

NORA: *(Gripping his arm.)* What is it you've found out? Dr. Rank, you have to tell me!

RANK: *(Sitting by the stove.)* It's all over with me. There's nothing to be done about it.

335 NORA: *(Breathing easier.)* Is it you—then—?

RANK: Who else? There's no point in lying to one's self. I'm the most miserable of all my patients, Mrs. Helmer. These past few days I've been auditing my internal accounts. Bankrupt!

340 Within a month I'll probably be laid out and rotting in the churchyard.

NORA: Oh, what a horrible thing to say.

RANK: The thing itself is horrible. But the worst of it is all the other horror before it's over. There's only one final examina-

345 tion left; when I'm finished with that, I'll know about when my disintegration will begin. There's something I want to say. Helmer with his sensitivity has such a sharp distaste for anything ugly. I don't want him near my sickroom.

NORA: Oh, but Dr. Rank—

350 RANK: I won't have him in there. Under no condition. I'll lock my door to him—As soon as I'm completely sure of the worst, I'll send you my calling card marked with a black cross, and you'll know then the wreck has started to come apart.

355 NORA: No, today you're completely unreasonable. And I wanted you so much to be in a really good humor.

RANK: With death up my sleeve? And then to suffer this way for somebody else's sins. Is there any justice in that? And in every single family, in some way or another, this inevitable

360 retribution of nature goes on—

NORA: *(Her hands pressed over her ears.)* Oh, stuff! Cheer up! Please—be gay!

RANK: Yes, I'd just as soon laugh at it all. My poor, innocent spine, serving time for my father's gay army days.

365 NORA: *(By the table, left.)* He was so infatuated with asparagus tips and *pâté de foie gras,* wasn't that it?

RANK: Yes—and with truffles.

NORA: Truffles, yes. And then with oysters, I suppose?

RANK: Yes, tons of oysters, naturally.

370 NORA: And then the port and champagne to go with it. It's so sad that all these delectable things have to strike at our bones.

RANK: Especially when they strike at the unhappy bones that never shared in the fun.

375 NORA: Ah, that's the saddest of all.

RANK: *(Looks searchingly at her.)* Hm.

NORA: *(After a moment.)* Why did you smile?

RANK: No, it was you who laughed.

NORA: No, it was you who smiled, Dr. Rank!

380 RANK: *(Getting up.)* You're even a bigger tease than I'd thought.

NORA: I'm full of wild ideas today.

RANK: That's obvious.

NORA: *(Putting both hands on his shoulders.)* Dear, dear Dr. Rank, you'll never die for Torvald and me.

385 RANK: Oh, that loss you'll easily get over. Those who go away are soon forgotten.

NORA: *(Looks fearfully at him.)* You believe that?

RANK: One makes new connections, and then—

NORA: Who makes new connections?

390 RANK: Both you and Torvald will when I'm gone. I'd say you're well under way already. What was that Mrs. Linde doing here last evening?

NORA: Oh, come—you can't be jealous of poor Kristine?

RANK: Oh yes, I am. She'll be my successor here in the house.

395 When I'm down under, that woman will probably—

NORA: Shh! Not so loud. She's right in there.

RANK: Today as well. So you see.

NORA: Only to sew on my dress. Good gracious, how unreasonable you are. *(Sitting on the sofa.)* Be nice now, Dr. Rank.

400 Tomorrow you'll see how beautifully I'll dance; and you can imagine then that I'm dancing only for you—yes, and of course for Torvald, too—that's understood. *(Takes various items out of the carton.)* Dr. Rank, sit over here and I'll show you something.

405 RANK: *(Sitting.)* What's that?

NORA: Look here. Look.

RANK: Silk stockings.

NORA: Flesh-colored. Aren't they lovely? Now it's so dark here, but tomorrow—No, no, no, just look at the feet. Oh well,

410 you might as well look at the rest.

RANK: Hm—

NORA: Why do you look so critical? Don't you believe they'll fit?

RANK: I've never had any chance to form an opinion on that.

415 NORA: *(Glancing at him a moment.)* Shame on you. *(Hits him lightly on the ear with the stockings.)* That's for you. *(Puts them away again.)*

RANK: And what other splendors am I going to see now?

NORA: Not the least bit more, because you've been naughty.

420 *(She hums a little and rummages among her things.)*

RANK: *(After a short silence.)* When I sit here together with you like this, completely easy and open, then I don't know—I simply can't imagine—whatever would have become of me if I'd never come into this house.

425 NORA: *(Smiling.)* Yes, I really think you feel completely at ease with us.

RANK: *(More quietly, staring straight ahead.)* And then to have to go away from it all—

NORA: Nonsense, you're not going away.

430 RANK: *(His voice unchanged.)* —and not even be able to leave some poor show of gratitude behind, scarcely a fleeting regret—no more than a vacant place that anyone can fill.

NORA: And if I asked you now for—? No—

RANK: For what?

435 NORA: For a great proof of your friendship—

RANK: Yes, yes?

NORA: No, I mean—for an exceptionally big favor—

RANK: Would you really, for once, make me so happy?

NORA: Oh, you haven't the vaguest idea what it is.

440 RANK: All right, then tell me.

NORA: No, but I can't, Dr. Rank—it's all out of reason. It's advice and help, too—and a favor—

RANK: So much the better. I can't fathom what you're hinting at. Just speak out. Don't you trust me?

445 NORA: Of course. More than anyone else. You're my best and truest friend, I'm sure. That's why I want to talk to you. All right, then, Dr. Rank: there's something you can help me prevent. You know how deeply, how inexpressibly dearly Torvald loves me; he'd never hesitate a second to give up his

450 life for me.

RANK: *(Leaning close to her.)* Nora—do you think he's the only one—

NORA: *(With a slight start.)* Who—?

RANK: Who'd gladly give up his life for you.

455 NORA: *(Heavily.)* I see.

RANK: I swore to myself you should know this before I'm gone. I'll never find a better chance. Yes, Nora, now you know. And also you know now that you can trust me beyond anyone else.

460 NORA: *(Rising, natural and calm.)* Let me by.

RANK: *(Making room for her, but still sitting.)* Nora—

NORA: *(In the hall doorway.)* Helene, bring the lamp in. *(Goes over to the stove.)* Ah, dear Dr. Rank, that was really mean of you.

465 RANK: *(Getting up.)* That I've loved you just as deeply as somebody else? Was *that* mean?

NORA: No, but that you came out and told me. That was quite unnecessary—

RANK: What do you mean? Have you known—?

(The MAID *comes in with the lamp, sets it on the table, and goes out again.)*

470 RANK: Nora—Mrs. Helmer—I'm asking you: have you known about it?

NORA: Oh, how can I tell what I know or don't know? Really, I don't know what to say—Why did you have to be so clumsy, Dr. Rank! Everything was so good.

475 RANK: Well, in any case, you now have the knowledge that my body and soul are at your command. So won't you speak out?

NORA: *(Looking at him.)* After that?

RANK: Please, just let me know what it is.

NORA: You can't know anything now.

480 RANK: I have to. You mustn't punish me like this. Give me the chance to do whatever is humanly possible for you.

NORA: Now there's nothing you can do for me. Besides, actually, I don't need any help. You'll see—it's only my fantasies. That's what it is. Of course! *(Sits in the rocker, looks at him,*

485 *and smiles.)* What a nice one you are, Dr. Rank. Aren't you a little bit ashamed, now that the lamp is here?

RANK: No, not exactly. But perhaps I'd better go—for good?

NORA: No, you certainly can't do that. You must come here just as you always have. You know Torvald can't do without

490 you.

RANK: Yes, but *you?*

NORA: You know how much I enjoy it when you're here.

RANK: That's precisely what threw me off. You're a mystery to me. So many times I've felt you'd almost rather be with me

495 than with Helmer.

NORA: Yes—you see, there are some people that one loves most and other people that one would almost prefer being with.

RANK: Yes, there's something to that.

NORA: When I was back home, of course I loved Papa most. 500 But I always thought it was so much fun when I could sneak down to the maids' quarters, because they never tried to improve me, and it was always so amusing, the way they talked to each other.

RANK: Aha, so it's *their* place that I've filled. 505

NORA: *(Jumping up and going to him.)* Oh, dear, sweet Dr. Rank, that's not what I meant at all. But you can understand that with Torvald it's just the same as with Papa—

(The MAID *enters from the hall.)*

MAID: Ma'am—please! *(She whispers to* NORA *and hands her a calling card.)* 510

NORA: *(Glancing at the card.)* Ah! *(Slips it into her pocket.)*

RANK: Anything wrong?

NORA: No, no, not at all. It's only some—it's my new dress—

RANK: Really? But—there's your dress.

NORA: Oh, that. But this is another one—I ordered it—Tor- 515 vald mustn't know—

RANK: Ah, now we have the big secret.

NORA: That's right. Just go in with him—he's back in the inner study. Keep him there as long as—

RANK: Don't worry. He won't get away. *(Goes into the study.)* 520

NORA: *(To the* MAID.*)* And he's standing waiting in the kitchen?

MAID: Yes, he came up by the back stairs.

NORA: But didn't you tell him somebody was here?

MAID: Yes, but that didn't do any good. 525

NORA: He won't leave?

MAID: No, he won't go till he's talked with you, ma'am.

NORA: Let him come in, then—but quietly. Helene, don't breathe a word about this. It's a surprise for my husband.

MAID: Yes, yes, I understand—*(Goes out.)* 530

NORA: This horror—it's going to happen. No, no, no, it can't happen, it mustn't. *(She goes and bolts* HELMER's *door. The* MAID *opens the hall door for* KROGSTAD *and shuts it behind him. He is dressed for travel in a fur coat, boots, and a fur cap.)* 535

NORA: *(Going toward him.)* Talk softly. My husband's home.

KROGSTAD: Well, good for him.

NORA: What do you want?

KROGSTAD: Some information.

NORA: Hurry up, then. What is it? 540

KROGSTAD: You know, of course, that I got my notice.

NORA: I couldn't prevent it, Mr. Krogstad. I fought for you to the bitter end, but nothing worked.

KROGSTAD: Does your husband's love for you run so thin? He knows everything I can expose you to, and all the same he 545 dares to—

NORA: How can you imagine he knows anything about this?

KROGSTAD: Ah, no—I can't imagine it either, now. It's not at all like my fine Torvald Helmer to have so much guts—

NORA: Mr. Krogstad, I demand respect for my husband! 550

KROGSTAD: Why, of course—all due respect. But since the lady's keeping it so carefully hidden, may I presume to ask if you're also a bit better informed than yesterday about what you've actually done?

555 NORA: More than you ever could teach me.
KROGSTAD: Yes, I *am* such an awful lawyer.
NORA: What is it you want from me?
KROGSTAD: Just a glimpse of how you are, Mrs. Helmer. I've
been thinking about you all day long. A cashier, a night–
560 court scribbler, a—well, a type like me also has a little of
what they call a heart, you know.
NORA: Then show it. Think of my children.
KROGSTAD: Did you or your husband ever think of mine? But
never mind. I simply wanted to tell you that you don't need
565 to take this thing too seriously. For the present, I'm not proceeding with any action.
NORA: Oh no, really! Well—I knew that.
KROGSTAD: Everything can be settled in a friendly spirit. It
doesn't have to get around town at all; it can stay just among
570 us three.
NORA: My husband must never know anything of this.
KROGSTAD: How can you manage that? Perhaps you can pay
me the balance?
NORA: No, not right now.
575 KROGSTAD: Or you know some way of raising the money in a
day or two?
NORA: No way that I'm willing to use.
KROGSTAD: Well, it wouldn't have done you any good, any-
way. If you stood in front of me with a fistful of bills, you still
580 couldn't buy your signature back.
NORA: Then tell me what you're going to do with it.
KROGSTAD: I'll just hold onto it—keep it on file. There's no
outsider who'll even get wind of it. So if you've been think-
ing of taking some desperate step—
585 NORA: I have.
KROGSTAD: Been thinking of running away from home—
NORA: I have!
KROGSTAD: Or even of something worse—
NORA: How could you guess that?
590 KROGSTAD: You can drop those thoughts.
NORA: How could you guess I was thinking of *that?*
KROGSTAD: Most of us think about *that* at first. I thought
about it too, but I discovered I hadn't the courage—
NORA: *(Lifelessly.)* I don't either.
595 KROGSTAD: *(Relieved.)* That's true, you haven't the courage?
You too?
NORA: I don't have it—I don't have it.
KROGSTAD: It would be terribly stupid, anyway. After that first
storm at home blows out, why, then—I have here in my
600 pocket a letter for your husband—
NORA: Telling everything?
KROGSTAD: As charitably as possible.
NORA: *(Quickly.)* He mustn't ever get that letter. Tear it up. I'll
find some way to get money.
605 KROGSTAD: Beg pardon, Mrs. Helmer, but I think I just told
you—
NORA: Oh, I don't mean the money I owe you. Let me know
how much you want from my husband, and I'll manage it.
KROGSTAD: I don't want any money from your husband.
610 NORA: What do you want, then?
KROGSTAD: I'll tell you what. I want to recoup, Mrs. Helmer; I
want to get on in the world—and there's where your husband can help me. For a year and a half I've kept myself
clean of anything disreputable—all that time struggling with
615 the worst conditions; but I was satisfied, working my way up

step by step. Now I've been written right off, and I'm just not
in the mood to come crawling back. I tell you, I want to
move on. I want to get back in the bank—in a better position. Your husband can set up a job for me—
NORA: He'll never do that! 620
KROGSTAD: He'll do it. I know him. He won't dare breathe a
word of protest. And once I'm in there together with him,
you just wait and see! Inside of a year, I'll be the manager's
righthand man. It'll be Nils Krogstad, not Torvald Helmer,
who runs the bank. 625
NORA: You'll never see the day!
KROGSTAD: Maybe you think you can—
NORA: I have the courage now—for *that.*
KROGSTAD: Oh, you don't scare me. A smart, spoiled lady like
you— 630
NORA: You'll see; you'll see!
KROGSTAD: Under the ice, maybe? Down in the freezing,
coal-black water? There, till you float up in the spring, ugly,
unrecognizable, with your hair falling out—
NORA: You don't frighten me. 635
KROGSTAD: Nor do you frighten me. One doesn't do these
things, Mrs. Helmer. Besides, what good would it be? I'd still
have him safe in my pocket.
NORA: Afterwards? When I'm no longer—?
KROGSTAD: Are you forgetting that *I'll* be in control then over 640
your final reputation? (NORA *stands speechless, staring at
him.*) Good; now I've warned you. Don't do anything stupid.
When Helmer's read my letter, I'll be waiting for his reply.
And bear in mind that it's your husband himself who's forced
me back to my old ways. I'll never forgive him for that. 645
Good-bye, Mrs. Helmer. (*He goes out through the hall.*)
NORA: (*Goes to the hall door, opens it a crack, and listens.*) He's
gone. Didn't leave the letter. Oh no, no, that's impossible
too! (*Opening the door more and more.*) What's that? He's
standing outside—not going downstairs. He's thinking it 650
over? Maybe he'll—? (*A letter falls in the mailbox; then*
KROGSTAD's *footsteps are heard, dying away down a flight of
stairs.* NORA *gives a muffled cry and runs over toward the sofa
table. A short pause.*) In the mailbox. (*Slips warily over to the
hall door.*) It's lying there. Torvald, Torvald—now we're lost! 655
MRS. LINDE: (*Entering with the costume from the room, left.*)
There now, I can't see anything else to mend. Perhaps you'd
like to try—
NORA: (*In a hoarse whisper.*) Kristine, come here.
MRS. LINDE: (*Tossing the dress on the sofa.*) What's wrong? You 660
look upset.
NORA: Come here. See that letter? *There!* Look—through the
glass in the mailbox.
MRS. LINDE: Yes, yes, I see it.
NORA: That letter's from Krogstad— 665
MRS. LINDE: Nora—it's Krogstad who loaned you the money!
NORA: Yes, and now Torvald will find out everything.
MRS. LINDE: Believe me, Nora, it's best for both of you.
NORA: There's more you don't know. I forged a name.
MRS. LINDE: But for heaven's sake—? 670
NORA: I only want to tell you that, Kristine, so that you can be
my witness.
MRS. LINDE: Witness? Why should I—?
NORA: If I should go out of my mind—it could easily happen—
MRS. LINDE: Nora! 675

NORA: Or anything else occurred—so I couldn't be present here—

MRS. LINDE: Nora, Nora, you aren't yourself at all!

680 NORA: And someone should try to take on the whole weight, all of the guilt, you follow me—

MRS. LINDE: Yes, of course, but why do you think—?

NORA: Then you're the witness that it isn't true, Kristine. I'm very much myself; my mind right now is perfectly clear; and I'm telling you: nobody else has known about this; I alone

685 did everything. Remember that.

MRS. LINDE: I will. But I don't understand all this.

NORA: Oh, how could you ever understand it? It's the miracle now that's going to take place.

MRS. LINDE: The miracle?

690 NORA: Yes, the miracle. But it's so awful, Kristine. It mustn't take place, not for anything in the world.

MRS. LINDE: I'm going right over and talk with Krogstad.

NORA: Don't go near him; he'll do you some terrible harm!

MRS. LINDE: There was a time once when he'd gladly have

695 done anything for me.

NORA: He?

MRS. LINDE: Where does he live?

NORA: Oh, how do I know? Yes. (*Searches in her pocket.*) Here's his card. But the letter, the letter—!

700 HELMER: (*From the study, knocking on the door.*) Nora!

NORA: (*With a cry of fear.*) Oh! What is it? What do you want?

HELMER: Now, now, don't be so frightened. We're not coming in. You locked the door—are you trying on the dress?

NORA: Yes, I'm trying it. I'll look just beautiful, Torvald.

705 MRS. LINDE: (*Who has read the card.*) He's living right around the corner.

NORA: Yes, but what's the use? We're lost. The letter's in the box.

MRS. LINDE: And your husband has the key?

710 NORA: Yes, always.

MRS. LINDE: Krogstad can ask for his letter back unread; he can find some excuse—

NORA: But it's just this time that Torvald usually—

MRS. LINDE: Stall him. Keep him in there. I'll be back as quick

715 as I can. (*She hurries out through the hall entrance.*)

NORA: (*Goes to* HELMER's *door, opens it, and peers in.*) Torvald!

HELMER: (*From the inner study.*) Well—does one dare set foot in one's own living room at last? Come on, Rank, now we'll

720 get a look—(*In the doorway.*) But what's this?

NORA: What, Torvald dear?

HELMER: Rank had me expecting some grand masquerade.

RANK: (*In the doorway.*) That was my impression, but I must have been wrong.

725 NORA: No one can admire me in my splendor—not till tomorrow.

HELMER: But Nora dear, you look so exhausted. Have you practiced too hard?

NORA: No, I haven't practiced at all yet.

730 HELMER: You know, it's necessary—

NORA: Oh, it's absolutely necessary, Torvald. But I can't get anywhere without your help. I've forgotten the whole thing completely.

HELMER: Ah, we'll soon take care of that.

735 NORA: Yes, take care of me, Torvald, please! Promise me that? Oh, I'm so nervous. That big party—You must give up

everything this evening for me. No business—don't even touch your pen. Yes? Dear Torvald, promise?

HELMER: It's a promise. Tonight I'm totally at your service— you little helpless thing. Hm—but first there's one thing I 740 want to—(*Goes toward the hall door.*)

NORA: What are you looking for?

HELMER: Just to see if there's any mail.

NORA: No, no, don't do that, Torvald!

HELMER: Now what? 745

NORA: Torvald, please. There isn't any.

HELMER: Let me look, though. (*Starts out.* NORA, *at the piano, strikes the first notes of the tarantella.* HELMER, *at the door, stops.*) Aha!

NORA: I can't dance tomorrow if I don't practice with you. 750

HELMER: (*Going over to her.*) Nora dear, are you really so frightened?

NORA: Yes, so terribly frightened. Let me practice right now; there's still time before dinner. Oh, sit down and play for me, Torvald. Direct me. Teach me, the way you always have. 755

HELMER: Gladly, if it's what you want. (*Sits at the piano.*)

NORA: (*Snatches the tambourine up from the box, then a long, varicolored shawl, which she throws around herself, whereupon she springs forward and cries out:*) Play for me now! Now I'll dance! 760

(HELMER *plays and* NORA *dances.* RANK *stands behind* HELMER *at the piano and looks on.*)

HELMER: (*As he plays.*) Slower. Slow down.

NORA: Can't change it.

HELMER: Not so violent, Nora!

NORA: Has to be just like this.

HELMER: (*Stopping.*) No, no, that won't do at all. 765

NORA: (*Laughing and swinging her tambourine.*) Isn't that what I told you?

RANK: Let me play for her.

HELMER: (*Getting up.*) Yes, go on. I can teach her more easily then. 770

(RANK *sits at the piano and plays;* NORA *dances more and more wildly.* HELMER *has stationed himself by the stove and repeatedly gives her directions; she seems not to hear them; her hair loosens and falls over her shoulders; she does not notice, but goes on dancing.* MRS. LINDE *enters.*)

MRS. LINDE: (*Standing dumbfounded at the door.*) Ah—!

NORA: (*Still dancing.*) See what fun, Kristine!

HELMER: But Nora darling, you dance as if your life were at stake.

NORA: And it is. 775

HELMER: Rank, stop! This is pure madness. Stop it, I say!

(RANK *breaks off playing, and* NORA *halts abruptly*).

HELMER: (*Going over to her.*) I never would have believed it. You've forgotten everything I taught you.

NORA: (*Throwing away the tambourine.*) You see for yourself.

HELMER: Well, there's certainly room for instruction here. 780

NORA: Yes, you see how important it is. You've got to teach me to the very last minute. Promise me that, Torvald?

HELMER: You can bet on it.

NORA: You mustn't, either today or tomorrow, think about anything else but me; you mustn't open any letters—or the 785 mailbox—

HELMER: Ah, it's still the fear of that man—

NORA: Oh yes, yes, that too.

790 HELMER: Nora, it's written all over you—there's already a letter from him out there.

NORA: I don't know. I guess so. But you mustn't read such things now; there mustn't be anything ugly between us before it's all over.

RANK: (*Quietly to* HELMER.) You shouldn't deny her.

795 HELMER: (*Putting his arm around her.*) The child can have her way. But tomorrow night, after you've danced—

NORA: Then you'll be free.

MAID: (*In the doorway, right.*) Ma'am, dinner is served.

NORA: We'll be wanting champagne, Helene.

800 MAID: Very good, ma'am. (*Goes out.*)

HELMER: So—a regular banquet, hm?

NORA: Yes, a banquet—champagne till daybreak! (*Calling out.*) And some macaroons, Helene. Heaps of them—just this once.

805 HELMER: (*Taking her hands.*) Now, now, now—no hysterics. Be my own little lark again.

NORA: Oh, I will soon enough. But go on in—and you, Dr. Rank. Kristine, help me put up my hair.

RANK: (*Whispering, as they go.*) There's nothing wrong—really wrong, is there?

810

HELMER: Oh, of course not. It's nothing more than this childish anxiety I was telling you about. (*They go out, right.*)

NORA: Well?

MRS. LINDE: Left town.

815 NORA: I could see by your face.

MRS. LINDE: He'll be home tomorrow evening. I wrote him a note.

NORA: You shouldn't have. Don't try to stop anything now. After all, it's a wonderful joy, this waiting here for the miracle.

820

MRS. LINDE: What is it you're waiting for?

NORA: Oh, you can't understand that. Go in to them; I'll be along in a moment.

(MRS. LINDE *goes into the dining room.* NORA *stands a short while as if composing herself; then she looks at her watch.*)

NORA: Five. Seven hours to midnight. Twenty-four hours to

825 the midnight after, and then the tarantella's done. Seven and twenty-four? Thirty-one hours to live.

HELMER: (*In the doorway, right.*) What's become of the little lark?

NORA: (*Going toward him with open arms.*) Here's your lark!

— ACT THREE —

Same scene. The table, with chairs around it, has been moved to the center of the room. A lamp on the table is lit. The hall door stands open. Dance music drifts down from the floor above. MRS. LINDE *sits at the table, absently paging through a book, trying to read, but apparently unable to focus her thoughts. Once or twice she pauses, tensely listening for a sound at the outer entrance.*

MRS. LINDE: (*Glancing at her watch.*) Not yet—and there's hardly any time left. If only he's not—(*Listening again.*) Ah, there he is. (*She goes out in the hall and cautiously opens the outer door. Quiet footsteps are heard on the stairs. She whis-*
5 *pers:*) Come in. Nobody's here.

KROGSTAD: (*In the doorway.*) I found a note from you at home. What's back of all this?

MRS. LINDE: I just *had* to talk to you.

KROGSTAD: Oh? And it just *had* to be here in this house?

MRS. LINDE: At my place it was impossible; my room hasn't a 10 private entrance. Come in; we're all alone. The maid's asleep, and the Helmers are at the dance upstairs.

KROGSTAD: (*Entering the room.*) Well, well, the Helmers are dancing tonight? Really?

MRS. LINDE: Yes, why not? 15

KROGSTAD: How true—why not?

MRS. LINDE: All right, Krogstad, let's talk.

KROGSTAD: Do we two have anything more to talk about?

MRS. LINDE: We have a great deal to talk about.

KROGSTAD: I wouldn't have thought so. 20

MRS. LINDE: No, because you've never understood me, really.

KROGSTAD: Was there anything more to understand—except what's all too common in life? A calculating woman throws over a man the moment a better catch comes by.

MRS. LINDE: You think I'm so thoroughly calculating? You 25 think I broke it off lightly?

KROGSTAD: Didn't you?

MRS. LINDE: Nils—is that what you really thought?

KROGSTAD: If you cared, then why did you write me the way you did? 30

MRS. LINDE: What else could I do? If I had to break off with you, then it was my job as well to root out everything you felt for me.

KROGSTAD: (*Wringing his hands.*) So that was it. And this—all this, simply for money! 35

MRS. LINDE: Don't forget I had a helpless mother and two small brothers. We couldn't wait for you, Nils; you had such a long road ahead of you then.

KROGSTAD: That may be; but you still hadn't the right to abandon me for somebody else's sake. 40

MRS. LINDE: Yes—I don't know. So many, many times I've asked myself if I did have that right.

KROGSTAD: (*More softly.*) When I lost you, it was as if all the solid ground dissolved from under my feet. Look at me; I'm a half-drowned man now, hanging onto a wreck. 45

MRS. LINDE: Help may be near.

KROGSTAD: It was near—but then you came and blocked it off.

MRS. LINDE: Without my knowing it, Nils. Today for the first time I learned that it's you I'm replacing at the bank. 50

KROGSTAD: All right—I believe you. But now that you know, will you step aside?

MRS. LINDE: No, because that wouldn't benefit you in the slightest.

KROGSTAD: Not "benefit" me, hm! I'd step aside anyway. 55

MRS. LINDE: I've learned to be realistic. Life and hard, bitter necessity have taught me that.

KROGSTAD: And life's taught me never to trust fine phrases.

MRS. LINDE: Then life's taught you a very sound thing. But you do have to trust in actions, don't you? 60

KROGSTAD: What does that mean?

MRS. LINDE: You said you were hanging on like a half-drowned man to a wreck.

KROGSTAD: I've good reason to say that.

MRS. LINDE: I'm also like a half-drowned woman on a wreck. 65 No one to suffer with; no one to care for.

KROGSTAD: You made your choice.

MRS. LINDE: There wasn't any choice then.

KROGSTAD: So—what of it?

70 MRS. LINDE: Nils, if only we two shipwrecked people could reach across to each other.

KROGSTAD: What are you saying?

MRS. LINDE: Two on one wreck are at least better off than each on his own.

75 KROGSTAD: Kristine!

MRS. LINDE: Why do you think I came into town?

KROGSTAD: Did you really have some thought of me?

MRS. LINDE: I have to work to go on living. All my born days, as long as I can remember, I've worked, and it's been my best

80 and my only joy. But now I'm completely alone in the world; it frightens me to be so empty and lost. To work for yourself—there's no joy in that. Nils, give me something—someone to work for.

KROGSTAD: I don't believe all this. It's just some hysterical

85 feminine urge to go out and make a noble sacrifice.

MRS. LINDE: Have you ever found me to be hysterical?

KROGSTAD: Can you honestly mean this? Tell me—do you know everything about my past?

MRS. LINDE: Yes.

90 KROGSTAD: And you know what they think I'm worth around here.

MRS. LINDE: From what you were saying before, it would seem that with me you could have been another person.

KROGSTAD: I'm positive of that.

95 MRS. LINDE: Couldn't it happen still?

KROGSTAD: Kristine—you're saying this in all seriousness? Yes, you are! I can see it in you. And do you really have the courage, then—?

MRS. LINDE: I need to have someone to care for; and your

100 children need a mother. We both need each other. Nils, I have faith that you're good at heart—I'll risk everything together with you.

KROGSTAD: (*Gripping her hands.*) Kristine, thank you, thank you—Now I know I can win back a place in their eyes. Yes—

105 but I forgot—

MRS. LINDE: (*Listening.*) Shh! The tarantella. Go now! Go on!

KROGSTAD: Why? What is it?

MRS. LINDE: Hear the dance up there? When that's over, they'll be coming down.

110 KROGSTAD: Oh, then I'll go. But—it's all pointless. Of course, you don't know the move I made against the Helmers.

MRS. LINDE: Yes, Nils, I know.

KROGSTAD: And all the same, you have the courage to—?

MRS. LINDE: I know how far despair can drive a man like you.

115 KROGSTAD: Oh, if I only could take it all back.

MRS. LINDE: You easily could—your letter's still lying in the mailbox.

KROGSTAD: Are you sure of that?

MRS. LINDE: Positive. But—

120 KROGSTAD: (*Looks at her searchingly.*) Is that the meaning of it, then? You'll save your friend at any price. Tell me straight out. Is that it?

MRS. LINDE: Nils—anyone who's sold herself for somebody else once isn't going to do it again.

125 KROGSTAD: I'll demand my letter back.

MRS. LINDE: No, no.

KROGSTAD: Yes, of course. I'll stay here till Helmer comes down; I'll tell him to give me my letter again—that it only involves my dismissal—that he shouldn't read it—

130 MRS. LINDE: No, Nils, don't call the letter back.

KROGSTAD: But wasn't that exactly why you wrote me to come here?

MRS. LINDE: Yes, in that first panic. But it's been a whole day and night since then, and in that time I've seen such incred-

135 ible things in this house. Helmer's got to learn everything; this dreadful secret has to be aired; those two have to come to a full understanding; all these lies and evasions can't go on.

KROGSTAD: Well, then, if you want to chance it. But at least

140 there's one thing I can do, and do right away—

MRS. LINDE: (*Listening.*) Go now, go, quick! The dance is over. We're not safe another second.

KROGSTAD: I'll wait for you downstairs.

MRS. LINDE: Yes, please do; take me home.

145 KROGSTAD: I can't believe it; I've never been so happy. (*He leaves by way of the outer door; the door between the room and the hall stays open.*)

MRS. LINDE: (*Straightening up a bit and getting together her street clothes.*) How different now! How different! Someone

150 to work for, to live for—a home to build. Well, it is worth the try! Oh, if they'd only come! (*Listening.*) Ah, there they are. Bundle up. (*She picks up her hat and coat.* NORA's *and* HELMER's *voices can be heard outside; a key turns in the lock, and* HELMER *brings* NORA *into the hall almost by force.*

155 *She is wearing the Italian costume with a large black shawl about her; he has on evening dress, with a black domino open over it.*)

NORA: (*Struggling in the doorway.*) No, no, no, not inside! I'm going up again. I don't want to leave so soon.

160 HELMER: But Nora dear—

NORA: Oh, I beg you, please, Torvald. From the bottom of my heart, *please*—only an hour more!

HELMER: Not a single minute, Nora darling. You know our agreement. Come on, in we go; you'll catch cold out here.

165 (*In spite of her resistance, he gently draws her into the room.*)

MRS. LINDE: Good evening.

NORA: Kristine!

HELMER: Why, Mrs. Linde—are you here so late?

MRS. LINDE: Yes, I'm sorry, but I did want to see Nora in cos-

170 tume.

NORA: Have you been sitting here, waiting for me?

MRS. LINDE: Yes. I didn't come early enough; you were all upstairs; and then I thought I really couldn't leave without seeing you.

175 HELMER: (*Removing* NORA's *shawl.*) Yes, take a good look. She's worth looking at, I can tell you that, Mrs. Linde. Isn't she lovely?

MRS. LINDE: Yes, I should say—

HELMER: A dream of loveliness, isn't she? That's what every-

180 one thought at the party, too. But she's horribly stubborn—this sweet little thing. What's to be done with her? Can you imagine, I almost had to use force to pry her away.

NORA: Oh, Torvald, you're going to regret you didn't indulge me, even for just a half hour more.

185 HELMER: There, you see. She danced her tarantella and got a tumultuous hand—which was well earned, although the

performance may have been a bit too naturalistic—I mean it rather overstepped the proprieties of art. But never mind—what's important is, she made a success, an overwhelming success. You think I could let her stay on after that and spoil the effect? Oh no; I took my lovely little Capri girl—my capricious little Capri girl, I should say—took her under my arm; one quick tour of the ballroom, a curtsy to every side, and then—as they say in novels—the beautiful vision disappeared. An exit should always be effective, Mrs. Linde, but that's what I can't get Nora to grasp. Phew, it's hot in here. (*Flings the domino on a chair and opens the door to his room.*) Why's it dark in here? Oh yes, of course. Excuse me. (*He goes in and lights a couple of candles.*)

NORA: (*In a sharp, breathless whisper.*) So?

MRS. LINDE: (*Quietly.*) I talked with him.

NORA: And—?

MRS. LINDE: Nora—you must tell your husband everything.

NORA: (*Dully.*) I knew it.

MRS. LINDE: You've got nothing to fear from Krogstad, but you have to speak out.

NORA: I won't tell.

MRS. LINDE: Then the letter will.

NORA: Thanks, Kristine. I know now what's to be done. Shh!

HELMER: (*Reentering.*) Well, then, Mrs. Linde—have you admired her?

MRS. LINDE: Yes, and now I'll say good night.

HELMER: Oh, come, so soon? Is this yours, this knitting?

MRS. LINDE: Yes, thanks. I nearly forgot it.

HELMER: Do you knit, then?

MRS. LINDE: Oh yes.

HELMER: You know what? You should embroider instead.

MRS. LINDE: Really? Why?

HELMER: Yes, because it's a lot prettier. See here, one holds the embroidery so, in the left hand, and then one guides the needle with the right—so—in an easy, sweeping curve—right?

MRS. LINDE: Yes, I guess that's—

HELMER: But, on the other hand, knitting—it can never be anything but ugly. Look, see here, the arms tucked in, the knitting needles going up and down—there's something Chinese about it. Ah, that was really a glorious champagne they served.

MRS. LINDE: Yes, good night, Nora, and don't be stubborn anymore.

HELMER: Well put, Mrs. Linde!

MRS. LINDE: Good night, Mr. Helmer.

HELMER: (*Accompanying her to the door.*) Good night, good night. I hope you get home all right. I'd be very happy to—but you don't have far to go. Good night, good night. (*She leaves. He shuts the door after her and returns.*) There, now, at last we got her out the door. She's a deadly bore, that creature.

NORA: Aren't you pretty tired, Torvald?

HELMER: No, not a bit.

NORA: You're not sleepy?

HELMER: Not at all. On the contrary, I'm feeling quite exhilarated. But you? Yes, you really look tired and sleepy.

NORA: Yes, I'm very tired. Soon now I'll sleep.

HELMER: See! You see! I was right all along that we shouldn't stay longer.

NORA: Whatever you do is always right.

HELMER: (*Kissing her brow.*) Now my little lark talks sense. Say, did you notice what a time Rank was having tonight?

NORA: Oh, was he? I didn't get to speak with him.

HELMER: I scarcely did either, but it's a long time since I've seen him in such high spirits. (*Gazes at her a moment, then comes nearer her.*) Hm—it's marvelous, though, to be back home again—to be completely alone with you. Oh, you bewitchingly lovely young woman!

NORA: Torvald, don't look at me like that!

HELMER: Can't I look at my richest treasure? At all that beauty that's mine, mine alone—completely and utterly.

NORA: (*Moving around to the other side of the table.*) You mustn't talk to me that way tonight.

HELMER: (*Following her.*) The tarantella is still in your blood, I can see—and it makes you even more enticing. Listen. The guests are beginning to go. (*Dropping his voice.*) Nora—it'll soon be quiet through this whole house.

NORA: Yes, I hope so.

HELMER: You do, don't you, my love? Do you realize—when I'm out at a party like this with you—do you know why I talk to you so little, and keep such a distance away; just send you a stolen look now and then—you know why I do it? It's because I'm imagining then that you're my secret darling, my secret young bride-to-be, and that no one suspects there's anything between us.

NORA: Yes, yes; oh, yes, I know you're always thinking of me.

HELMER: And then when we leave and I place the shawl over those fine young rounded shoulders—over that wonderful curving neck—then I pretend that you're my young bride, that we're just coming from the wedding, that for the first time I'm bringing you into my house—that for the first time I'm alone with you—completely alone with you, your trembling young beauty! All this evening I've longed for nothing but you. When I saw you turn and sway in the tarantella—my blood was pounding till I couldn't stand it—that's why I brought you down here so early—

NORA: Go away, Torvald! Leave me alone. I don't want all this.

HELMER: What do you mean? Nora, you're teasing me. You will, won't you? Aren't I your husband—?

(*A knock at the outside door.*)

NORA: (*Startled.*) What's that?

HELMER: (*Going toward the hall.*) Who is it?

RANK: (*Outside.*) It's me. May I come in a moment?

HELMER: (*With quiet irritation.*) Oh, what does he want now? (*Aloud.*) Hold on. (*Goes and opens the door.*) Oh, how nice that you didn't just pass us by!

RANK: I thought I heard your voice, and then I wanted so badly to have a look in. (*Lightly glancing about.*) Ah, me, these old familiar haunts. You have it snug and cozy in here, you two.

HELMER: You seemed to be having it pretty cozy upstairs, too.

RANK: Absolutely. Why shouldn't I? Why not take in everything in life? As much as you can, anyway, and as long as you can. The wine was superb—

HELMER: The champagne especially.

RANK: You noticed that too? It's amazing how much I could guzzle down.

NORA: Torvald also drank a lot of champagne this evening.

RANK: Oh?

305   NORA: Yes, and that always makes him so entertaining.

RANK: Well, why shouldn't one have a pleasant evening after a well-spent day?

HELMER: Well spent? I'm afraid I can't claim that.

RANK: (*Slapping him on the back.*) But I can, you see!

310   NORA: Dr. Rank, you must have done some scientific research today.

RANK: Quite so.

HELMER: Come now—little Nora talking about scientific research!

315   RANK: Indeed you may.

NORA: Then they were good?

RANK: The best possible for both doctor and patient—certainty.

NORA: (*Quickly and searchingly.*) Certainty?

320   RANK: Complete certainty. So don't I owe myself a gay evening afterwards?

NORA: Yes, you're right, Dr. Rank.

HELMER: I'm with you—just so long as you don't have to suffer for it in the morning.

325   RANK: Well, one never gets something for nothing in life.

NORA: Dr. Rank—are you very fond of masquerade parties?

RANK: Yes, if there's a good array of odd disguises—

NORA: Tell me, what should we two go as at the next masquerade?

330   HELMER: You little featherhead—already thinking of the next!

RANK: We two? I'll tell you what: you must go as Charmed Life—

HELMER: Yes, but find a costume for *that!*

RANK: Your wife can appear just as she looks every day.

335   HELMER: That was nicely put. But don't you know what you're going to be?

RANK: Yes, Helmer, I've made up my mind.

HELMER: Well?

RANK: At the next masquerade I'm going to be invisible.

340   HELMER: That's a funny idea.

RANK: They say there's a hat—black, huge—have you never heard of the hat that makes you invisible? You put it on, and then no one on earth can see you.

HELMER: (*Suppressing a smile.*) Ah, of course.

345   RANK: But I'm quite forgetting what I came for. Helmer, give me a cigar, one of the dark Havanas.

HELMER: With the greatest pleasure. (*Holds out his case.*)

RANK: Thanks. (*Takes one and cuts off the tip.*)

NORA: (*Striking a match.*) Let me give you a light.

350   RANK: Thank you. (*She holds the match for him; he lights the cigar.*) And now good-bye.

HELMER: Good-bye, good-bye, old friend.

NORA: Sleep well, Doctor.

RANK: Thanks for that wish.

355   NORA: Wish me the same.

RANK: You? All right, if you like—Sleep well. And thanks for the light. (*He nods to them both and leaves.*)

HELMER: (*His voice subdued.*) He's been drinking heavily.

NORA: (*Absently.*) Could be. (HELMER *takes his keys from his*

360   *pocket and goes out in the hall.*) Torvald—what are you after?

HELMER: Got to empty the mailbox; it's nearly full. There won't be room for the morning papers.

NORA: Are you working tonight?

HELMER: You know I'm not. Why—what's this? Someone's

365   been at the lock.

NORA: At the lock—?

HELMER: Yes, I'm positive. What do you suppose—? I can't imagine one of the maids—? Here's a broken hairpin. Nora, it's yours—

NORA: (*Quickly.*) Then it must be the children—   370

HELMER: You'd better break them of that. Hm, hm—well, opened it after all. (*Takes the contents out and calls into the kitchen.*) Helene! Helene, would you put out the lamp in the hall. (*He returns to the room, shutting the hall door, then displays the handful of mail.*) Look how it's piled up. (*Sorting*   375   *through them.*) Now what's this?

NORA: (*At the window.*) The letter! Oh, Torvald, no!

HELMER: Two calling cards—from Rank.

NORA: From Dr. Rank?

HELMER: (*Examining them.*) "Dr. Rank, Consulting Physi-   380   cian." They were on top. He must have dropped them in as he left.

NORA: Is there anything on them?

HELMER: There's a black cross over the name. See? That's a gruesome notion. He could almost be announcing his own   385   death.

NORA: That's just what he's doing.

HELMER: What! You've heard something? Something he's told you?

NORA: Yes. That when those cards came, he'd be taking his   390   leave of us. He'll shut himself in now and die.

HELMER: Ah, my poor friend! Of course I knew he wouldn't be here much longer. But so soon—And then to hide himself away like a wounded animal.

NORA: If it has to happen, then it's best it happens in silence—   395   don't you think so, Torvald?

HELMER: (*Pacing up and down.*) He'd grown right into our lives. I simply can't imagine him gone. He with his suffering and loneliness—like a dark cloud setting off our sunlit happiness. Well, maybe it's best this way. For him, at least.   400   (*Standing still.*) And maybe for us too, Nora. Now we're thrown back on each other, completely. (*Embracing her.*) Oh you, my darling wife, how can I hold you close enough? You know what, Nora—time and again I've wished you were in some terrible danger, just so I could stake my life and soul   405   and everything, for your sake.

NORA: (*Tearing herself away, her voice firm and decisive.*) Now you must read your mail, Torvald.

HELMER: No, no, not tonight. I want to stay with you, dearest.

NORA: With a dying friend on your mind?   410

HELMER: You're right. We've both had a shock. There's ugliness between us—these thoughts of death and corruption. We'll have to get free of them first. Until then—we'll stay apart.

NORA: (*Clinging about his neck.*) Torvald—good night! Good   415   night!

HELMER: (*Kissing her on the cheek.*) Good night, little songbird. Sleep well, Nora. I'll be reading my mail now. (*He takes the letters into his room and shuts the door after him.*)

NORA: (*With bewildered glances, groping about, seizing*   420   HELMER's *domino, throwing it around her, and speaking in short, hoarse, broken whispers.*) Never see him again. Never, never. (*Putting her shawl over her head.*) Never see the children either—them, too. Never, never. Oh, the freezing black water! The depths—down—Oh, I wish it were over—He has   425   it now; he's reading it—now. Oh no, no, not yet. Torvald, good-bye, you and the children—(*She starts for the hall; as she does,* HELMER *throws open his door and stands with an open letter in his hand.*)

430 HELMER: Nora!

NORA: (*Screams.*) Oh—!

HELMER: What is this? You know what's in this letter?

NORA: Yes, I know. Let me go! Let me out!

HELMER: (*Holding her back.*) Where are you going?

435 NORA: (*Struggling to break loose.*) You can't save me, Torvald!

HELMER: (*Slumping back.*) True! Then it's true what he writes? How horrible! No, no, it's impossible—it can't be true.

NORA: It *is* true. I've loved you more than all this world.

440 HELMER: Ah, none of your slippery tricks.

NORA: (*Taking one step toward him.*) Torvald—!

HELMER: What *is* this you've blundered into!

NORA: Just let me loose. You're not going to suffer for my sake. You're not going to take on my guilt.

445 HELMER: No more playacting. (*Locks the hall door.*) You stay right here and give me a reckoning. You understand what you've done? Answer! You understand?

NORA: (*Looking squarely at him, her face hardening.*) Yes. I'm beginning to understand everything now.

450 HELMER: (*Striding about.*) Oh, what an awful awakening! In all these eight years—she who was my pride and joy—a hypocrite, a liar—worse, worse—a criminal! How infinitely disgusting it all is! The shame! (NORA *says nothing and goes on looking straight at him. He stops in front of her.*) I should have suspected something of the kind. I should have known.

455 All your father's flimsy values—Be still! All your father's flimsy values have come out in you. No religion, no morals, no sense of duty—Oh, how I'm punished for letting him off! I did it for your sake, and you repay me like this.

460 NORA: Yes, like this.

HELMER: Now you've wrecked all my happiness—ruined my whole future. Oh, it's awful to think of. I'm in a cheap little grafter's hands; he can do anything he wants with me, ask for anything, play with me like a puppet—and I can't breathe a

465 word. I'll be swept down miserably into the depths on account of a featherbrained woman.

NORA: When I'm gone from this world, you'll be free.

HELMER: Oh, quit posing. Your father had a mess of those speeches too. What good would that ever do me if you were

470 gone from this world, as you say? Not the slightest. He can still make the whole thing known; and if he does, I could be falsely suspected as your accomplice. They might even think that I was behind it—that I put you up to it. And all that I can thank you for—you that I've coddled the whole of our

475 marriage. Can you see now what you've done to me?

NORA: (*Icily calm.*) Yes.

HELMER: It's so incredible, I just can't grasp it. But we'll have to patch up whatever we can. Take off the shawl. I said, take it off! I've got to appease him somehow or other. The thing

480 has to be hushed up at any cost. And as for you and me, it's got to seem like everything between us is just as it was—to the outside world, that is. You'll go right on living in this house, of course. But you can't be allowed to bring up the children; I don't dare trust you with them—Oh, to have to

485 say this to someone I've loved so much, and that I still—! Well, that's done with. From now on happiness doesn't matter; all that matters is saving the bits and pieces, the

appearance—(*The doorbell rings.* HELMER *starts.*) What's that? And so late. Maybe the worst—? You think he'd—? Hide, Nora! Say you're sick. (NORA *remains standing mo-* 490 *tionless.* HELMER *goes and opens the door.*)

MAID: (*Half dressed, in the hall.*) A letter for Mrs. Helmer.

HELMER: I'll take it. (*Snatches the letter and shuts the door.*) Yes, it's from him. You don't get it; I'm reading it myself.

NORA: Then read it. 495

HELMER: (*By the lamp.*) I hardly dare. We may be ruined, you and I. But—I've got to know. (*Rips open the letter, skims through a few lines, glances at an enclosure, then cries out joyfully.*) Nora! (NORA *looks inquiringly at him.*) Nora! Wait— better check it again—Yes, yes, it's true. I'm saved. Nora, I'm 500 saved!

NORA: And I?

HELMER: You too, of course. We're both saved, both of us. Look. He's sent back your note. He says he's sorry and ashamed—that a happy development in his life—oh, who 505 cares what he says! Nora, we're saved! No one can hurt you. Oh, Nora, Nora—but first, this ugliness all has to go. Let me see—(*Takes a look at the note.*) No, I don't want to see it; I want the whole thing to fade like a dream. (*Tears the note and both letters to pieces, throws them into the stove and* 510 *watches them burn.*) There—now there's nothing left—He wrote that since Christmas Eve you—Oh, they must have been three terrible days for you, Nora.

NORA: I fought a hard fight.

HELMER: And suffered pain and saw no escape but—No, 515 we're not going to dwell on anything unpleasant. We'll just be grateful and keep on repeating: it's over now, it's over! You hear me, Nora? You don't seem to realize—it's over. What's it mean—that frozen look? Oh, poor little Nora, I understand. You can't believe I've forgiven you. But I have, 520 Nora; I swear I have. I know that what you did, you did out of love for me.

NORA: That's true.

HELMER: You loved me the way a wife ought to love her husband. It's simply the means that you couldn't judge. But you 525 think I love you any the less for not knowing how to handle your affairs? No, no—just lean on me; I'll guide you and teach you. I wouldn't be a man if this feminine helplessness didn't make you twice as attractive to me. You mustn't mind those sharp words I said—that was all in the first confusion 530 of thinking my world had collapsed. I've forgiven you, Nora; I swear I've forgiven you.

NORA: My thanks for your forgiveness. (*She goes out through the door, right.*)

HELMER: No, wait—(*Peers in.*) What are you doing in there? 535

NORA: (*Inside.*) Getting out of my costume.

HELMER: (*By the open door.*) Yes, do that. Try to calm yourself and collect your thoughts again, my frightened little songbird. You can rest easy now; I've got wide wings to shelter you with. (*Walking about close by the door.*) How snug and nice 540 our home is, Nora. You're safe here; I'll keep you like a hunted dove I've rescued out of a hawk's claws. I'll bring peace to your poor, shuddering heart. Gradually it'll happen, Nora; you'll see. Tomorrow all this will look different to you; then everything will be as it was. I won't have to go on 545 repeating I forgive you; you'll feel it for yourself. How can you imagine I'd ever conceivably want to disown you—or even blame you in any way? Ah, you don't know a man's

heart, Nora. For a man there's something indescribably
sweet and satisfying in knowing he's forgiven his wife—and
forgiven her out of a full and open heart. It's as if she belongs
to him in two ways now: in a sense he's given her fresh into
the world again, and she's become his wife and his child as
well. From now on that's what you'll be to me—you little,
bewildered, helpless thing. Don't be afraid of anything,
Nora; just open your heart to me, and I'll be conscience and
will to you both—(NORA *enters in her regular clothes.*)
What's this? Not in bed? You've changed your dress?

NORA: Yes, Torvald, I've changed my dress.

HELMER: But why now, so late?

NORA: Tonight I'm not sleeping.

HELMER: But Nora dear—

NORA: (*Looking at her watch.*) It's still not so very late. Sit
down, Torvald; we have a lot to talk over. (*She sits at one side
of the table.*)

HELMER: Nora—what is this? That hard expression—

NORA: Sit down. This'll take some time. I have a lot to say.

HELMER: (*Sitting at the table directly opposite her.*) You worry
me, Nora. And I don't understand you.

NORA: No, that's exactly it. You don't understand me. And I've
never understood you either—until tonight. No, don't interrupt. You can just listen to what I say. We're closing out accounts, Torvald.

HELMER: How do you mean that?

NORA: (*After a short pause.*) Doesn't anything strike you about
our sitting here like this?

HELMER: What's that?

NORA: We've been married now eight years. Doesn't it occur
to you that this is the first time we two, you and I, man and
wife, have ever talked seriously together?

HELMER: What do you mean—seriously?

NORA: In eight whole years—longer even—right from our first
acquaintance, we've never exchanged a serious word on any
serious thing.

HELMER: You mean I should constantly go and involve you in
problems you couldn't possibly help me with?

NORA: I'm not talking of problems. I'm saying that we've never
sat down seriously together and tried to get to the bottom of
anything.

HELMER: But dearest, what good would that ever do you?

NORA: That's the point right there: you've never understood
me. I've been wronged greatly, Torvald—first by Papa, and
then by you.

HELMER: What! By us—the two people who've loved you
more than anyone else?

NORA: (*Shaking her head.*) You never loved me. You've
thought it fun to be in love with me, that's all.

HELMER: Nora, what a thing to say!

NORA: Yes, it's true now, Torvald. When I lived at home with
Papa, he told me all his opinions, so I had the same ones too;
or if they were different I hid them, since he wouldn't have
cared for that. He used to call me his doll-child, and he
played with me the way I played with my dolls. Then I came
into your house—

HELMER: How can you speak of our marriage like that?

NORA: (*Unperturbed.*) I mean, then I went from Papa's hands
into yours. You arranged everything to your own taste, and
so I got the same taste as you—or I pretended to; I can't

remember. I guess a little of both, first one, then the other.
Now when I look back, it seems as if I'd lived here like a beggar—just from hand to mouth. I've lived by doing tricks for
you, Torvald. But that's the way you wanted it. It's a great sin
what you and Papa did to me. You're to blame that nothing's
become of me.

HELMER: Nora, how unfair and ungrateful you are! Haven't
you been happy here?

NORA: No, never. I thought so—but I never have.

HELMER: Not—not happy!

NORA: No, only lighthearted. And you've always been so kind
to me. But our home's been nothing but a playpen. I've
been your doll-wife here, just as at home I was Papa's doll-
child. And in turn the children have been my dolls. I
thought it was fun when you played with me, just as they
thought it fun when I played with them. That's been our
marriage, Torvald.

HELMER: There's some truth in what you're saying—under all
the raving exaggeration. But it'll all be different after this.
Playtime's over; now for the schooling.

NORA: Whose schooling—mine or the children's?

HELMER: Both yours and the children's, dearest.

NORA: Oh, Torvald, you're not the man to teach me to be a
good wife to you.

HELMER: And you can say that?

NORA: And I—how am I equipped to bring up children?

HELMER: Nora!

NORA: Didn't you say a moment ago that that was no job to
trust me with?

HELMER: In a flare of temper! Why fasten on that?

NORA: Yes, but you were so very right. I'm not up to the job.
There's another job I have to do first. I have to try to educate
myself. You can't help me with that. I've got to do it alone.
And that's why I'm leaving you now.

HELMER: (*Jumping up.*) What's that?

NORA: I have to stand completely alone, if I'm ever going to
discover myself and the world out there. So I can't go on living with you.

HELMER: Nora, Nora!

NORA: I want to leave right away. Kristine should put me up
for the night—

HELMER: You're insane! You've no right! I forbid you!

NORA: From here on, there's no use forbidding me anything.
I'll take with me whatever is mine. I don't want a thing from
you, either now or later.

HELMER: What kind of madness is this!

NORA: Tomorrow I'm going home—I mean, home where I
came from. It'll be easier up there to find something to do.

HELMER: Oh, you blind, incompetent child!

NORA: I must learn to be competent, Torvald.

HELMER: Abandon your home, your husband, your children!
And you're not even thinking what people will say.

NORA: I can't be concerned about that. I only know how essential this is.

HELMER: Oh, it's outrageous. So you'll run out like this on
your most sacred vows.

NORA: What do you think are my most sacred vows?

HELMER: And I have to tell you that! Aren't they your duties to
your husband and children?

NORA: I have other duties equally sacred.

HELMER: That isn't true. What duties are they?

670 NORA: Duties to myself.

HELMER: Before all else, you're a wife and a mother.

NORA: I don't believe in that anymore. I believe that, before all else, I'm a human being, no less than you—or anyway, I ought to try to become one. I know the majority thinks

675 you're right, Torvald, and plenty of books agree with you, too. But I can't go on believing what the majority says, or what's written in books. I have to think over these things myself and try to understand them.

HELMER: Why can't you understand your place in your own

680 home? On a point like that, isn't there one everlasting guide you can turn to? Where's your religion?

NORA: Oh, Torvald, I'm really not sure what religion is.

HELMER: What—?

NORA: I only know what the minister said when I was con-

685 firmed. He told me religion was this thing and that. When I get clear and away by myself, I'll go into that problem too. I'll see if what the minister said was right, or, in any case, if it's right for me.

HELMER: A young woman your age shouldn't talk like that. If

690 religion can't move you, I can try to rouse your conscience. You do have some moral feeling? Or, tell me—has that gone too?

NORA: It's not easy to answer that, Torvald. I simply don't know. I'm all confused about these things. I just know I see

695 them so differently from you. I find out, for one thing, that the law's not at all what I'd thought—but I can't get it through my head that the law is fair. A woman hasn't a right to protect her dying father or save her husband's life! I can't believe that.

700 HELMER: You talk like a child. You don't know anything of the world you live in.

NORA: No, I don't. But now I'll begin to learn for myself. I'll try to discover who's right, the world or I.

HELMER: Nora, you're sick; you've got a fever. I almost think

705 you're out of your head.

NORA: I've never felt more clearheaded and sure in my life.

HELMER: And—clearheaded and sure—you're leaving your husband and children?

NORA: Yes.

710 HELMER: Then there's only one possible reason.

NORA: What?

HELMER: You no longer love me.

NORA: No. That's exactly it.

HELMER: Nora! You can't be serious!

715 NORA: Oh, this is so hard, Torvald—you've been so kind to me always. But I can't help it. I don't love you anymore.

HELMER: (*Struggling for composure.*) Are you also clearheaded and sure about that?

NORA: Yes, completely. That's why I can't go on staying here.

720 HELMER: Can you tell me what I did to lose your love?

NORA: Yes, I can tell you. It was this evening when the miraculous thing didn't come—then I knew you weren't the man I'd imagined.

HELMER: Be more explicit; I don't follow you.

725 NORA: I've waited now so patiently eight long years—for, my Lord, I know miracles don't come every day. Then this crisis broke over me, and such a certainty filled me: *now* the miraculous event would occur. While Krogstad's letter was

lying out there, I never for an instant dreamed that you could give in to his terms. I was so utterly sure you'd say to 730 him: go on, tell your tale to the whole wide world. And when he'd done that—

HELMER: Yes, what then? When I'd delivered my own wife into shame and disgrace—!

NORA: When he'd done that, I was so utterly sure that you'd 735 step forward, take the blame on yourself and say: I am the guilty one.

HELMER: Nora—!

NORA: You're thinking I'd never accept such a sacrifice from you? No, of course not. But what good would my protests be 740 against you? That was the miracle I was waiting for, in terror and hope. And to stave that off, I would have taken my life.

HELMER: I'd gladly work for you day and night, Nora—and take on pain and deprivation. But there's no one who gives up honor for love. 745

NORA: Millions of women have done just that.

HELMER: Oh, you think and talk like a silly child.

NORA: Perhaps. But you neither think nor talk like the man I could join myself to. When your big fright was over—and it wasn't from any threat against me, only for what might dam- 750 age you—when all the danger was past, for you it was just as if nothing had happened. I was exactly the same, your little lark, your doll, that you'd have to handle with double care now that I'd turned out so brittle and frail. (*Gets up.*) Torvald—in that instant it dawned on me that for eight years I've 755 been living here with a stranger, and that I'd even conceived three children—oh, I can't stand the thought of it! I could tear myself to bits.

HELMER: (*Heavily.*) I see. There's a gulf that's opened between us—that's clear. Oh, but Nora, can't we bridge it somehow? 760

NORA: The way I am now, I'm no wife for you.

HELMER: I have the strength to make myself over.

NORA: Maybe—if your doll gets taken away.

HELMER: But to part! To part from you! No, Nora, no—I can't imagine it. 765

NORA: (*Going out, right.*) All the more reason why it has to be. (*She reenters with her coat and a small overnight bag, which she puts on a chair by the table.*)

HELMER: Nora, Nora, not now! Wait till tomorrow.

NORA: I can't spend the night in a strange man's room. 770

HELMER: But couldn't we live here like brother and sister—

NORA: You know very well how long that would last. (*Throws her shawl about her.*) Good-bye, Torvald. I won't look in on the children. I know they're in better hands than mine. The way I am now, I'm no use to them. 775

HELMER: But someday, Nora—someday—?

NORA: How can I tell? I haven't the least idea what'll become of me.

HELMER: But you're my wife, now and wherever you go.

NORA: Listen, Torvald—I've heard that when a wife deserts her 780 husband's house just as I'm doing, then the law frees him from all responsibility. In any case, I'm freeing you from being responsible. Don't feel yourself bound, any more than I will. There has to be absolute freedom for us both. Here, take your ring back. Give me mine. 785

HELMER: That too?

NORA: That too.

HELMER: There it is.

NORA: Good. Well, now it's all over. I'm putting the keys here. The maids know all about keeping up the house—better than I do. Tomorrow, after I've left town, Kristine will stop by to pack up everything that's mine from home. I'd like those things shipped up to me.

HELMER: Over! All over! Nora, won't you ever think about me?

NORA: I'm sure I'll think of you often, and about the children and the house here.

HELMER: May I write you?

NORA: No—never. You're not to do that.

HELMER: Oh, but let me send you—

NORA: Nothing. Nothing.

HELMER: Or help you if you need it.

NORA: No. I accept nothing from strangers.

HELMER: Nora—can I never be more than a stranger to you?

NORA: *(Picking up the overnight bag.)* Ah, Torvald—it would take the greatest miracle of all—

HELMER: Tell me the greatest miracle!

NORA: You and I both would have to transform ourselves to the point that—Oh, Torvald, I've stopped believing in miracles.

HELMER: But I'll believe. Tell me! Transform ourselves to the point that—?

NORA: That our living together could be a true marriage. *(She goes out down the hall.)*

HELMER: *(Sinks down on a chair by the door, face buried in his hands.)* Nora! Nora! *(Looking about and rising.)* Empty. She's gone. *(A sudden hope leaps in him.)* The greatest miracle—?

(From below, the sound of a door slamming shut.)

■ AUGUST STRINDBERG ■

The Swedish playwright August Strindberg (1849–1912) was a modern Renaissance man—he wrote some fifty plays, several autobiographical novels, and a variety of scientific and occult works as well. A series of tempestuous marriages marked Strindberg's life and are reflected in his corrosively misogynistic attitudes and in his hostility toward Ibsen, who seemed to Strindberg to advocate a new order of feminine domination. Calling *A Doll House* "sick like its father," Strindberg wrote *The Father* (1887) in reply to Ibsen, a play in which a calculating woman drives her husband into madness. Although Strindberg considered the play to be an experiment in the new "naturalism," it is really a kind of psychological thriller: the characters are so consumed by their sexual combat with one another that the worldly environment hardly seems important. Strindberg sent the play to Zola, who found it absorbing and curious, but lacking in the material social reality he demanded of the new drama. Strindberg then wrote *Miss Julie* (1888) and considered the play's use of naturalism in his famous preface to the play. The battle of the sexes is one of Strindberg's preoccupations, examined in a series of plays including *Creditors* (1888) and *The Dance of Death, Parts 1 and 2* (1901).

The battle of the sexes was also the battle that occupied Strindberg's life outside the theater. His three marriages all involved periods of psychological breakdown and creative fertility. His breakdown of the mid-1890s after marrying his second wife is documented in *The Inferno* (1897) and is symptomatic of Strindberg's volatile and unstable frame of mind. Much of Strindberg's manic energy was focused on women—he believed that his wife was attempting to drive him mad by sending rays through the walls. Strindberg also developed a passion for the occult and for alchemy, and in addition to his plays, poems, and novels, he wrote a number of scientific and pseudoscientific treatises. Unlike Ibsen, Strindberg experimented in a variety of dramatic genres throughout his career. Calling himself the "Zola of the occult," Strindberg wrote an influential series of expressionist and symbolic plays; the best known today are *To Damascus* (in three parts, 1898–1901) and *A Dream Play* (1901). He also wrote several important plays on Swedish history, including *Erik XIV* (1899), *Gustav Adolph* (1900), and *Gustav III* (1902). In 1907 he founded a small theater—the Intimate Theater—which brought the independent theater movement to Sweden and produced his intense and often symbolic series of "chamber plays," including *The Ghost Sonata* (1907) and *The Pelican* (1907). When Strindberg died in 1912, he had become not only the most significant literary and theatrical figure in Swedish history, but also a major influence on the course of modern drama.

MISS JULIE

Despite its setting, *Miss Julie* is a good example of Strindberg's subversive attitude toward the conventions of realistic theater. The play concerns the intense, erotic struggle between Jean and Julie, a struggle that takes place at once in the material world they inhabit and in the shadowy realm of fantasy and desire as well. This oblique angle on realism is suggested in Strindberg's opening stage directions. Instead of a setting oriented frontally, toward the audience, creating the impression of a full and objective disclosure, Strindberg sets the stage at an angle, acknowledging that our vision of the characters will be imbalanced, skewed. The setting creates a real environment for the characters, but Strindberg also includes the symbolic Cupid upstage and the signs of Julie's father, the Count. Throughout the play his absent presence weighs on the scene, a disembodied reminder of the social realities governing the scene, personified by the speaking tube and the elegant, polished riding boots and spurs.

The play is set on Midsummer's Night, traditionally a holiday of festive release, but here the occasion for a duel to the death, as Jean fights to possess and destroy Julie. *Miss Julie* is at once a complex psychological drama and an examination of the dynamics of power governing the relations between classes and between men and women. Much as Julie represents the forbidden pleasures of the upper classes to Jean, she also represents the process of his own degradation; the story of his escape from her garden through the outhouse provides an emblem of his experience in relation to the privileged upper classes of the play. Yet if Jean is trapped in servitude, Julie is no less trapped by the conventional society that hems her in and by the ferocious erotic combat that Strindberg sees as definitive of mature sexuality.

PREFACE

TRANSLATED BY EVERT SPRINCHORN

Like the arts in general, the theater has for a long time seemed to me a *Biblia Pauperum,* a picture Bible for those who cannot read, and the playwright merely a lay preacher who hawks the latest ideals in popular form, so popular that the middle classes—the bulk of the audiences—can grasp them without racking their brains too much. That explains why the theater has always been an elementary school for youngsters and the half-educated, and for women, who still retain a primitive capacity for deceiving themselves and for letting themselves be deceived, that is, for succumbing to illusions and responding hypnotically to the suggestions of the author. Consequently, now that the rudimentary and undeveloped mental processes that operate in the realm of fantasy appear to be evolving to the level of reflection, research, and experimentation, I believe that the theater, like religion, is about to be replaced as a dying institution for whose enjoyment we lack the necessary qualifications. Support for my view is provided by the theater crisis through which all of Europe is now passing, and still more by the fact that in those highly cultured lands which have produced the finest minds of our time—England and Germany—the drama is dead, as for the most part are the other fine arts.

Other countries, however, have thought to create a new drama by filling the old forms with new contents. But since there has not been enough time to popularize the new ideas, the public cannot understand them. And in the second place, controversy has so stirred up the public that they can no longer look on with a pure and dispassionate interest, especially when they see their most cherished ideals assailed or hear an applauding or booing majority openly exercise its tyrannical power, as can happen in the theater. And in the third place, since the new forms for the new ideas have not been created, the new wine has burst the old bottles.

In the play that follows I have not tried to accomplish anything new—that is impossible. I have only tried to modernize the form to satisfy what I believe up-to-date people expect and demand of this art. And with that in mind I have seized upon—or let myself be seized by—a theme that may be said to lie outside current party strife, since the question of being on the way up or on the way down the social ladder, of being on the top or on the bottom, superior or inferior, man or woman, is, has been, and will be of perennial interest. When I took this theme from real life—I heard about it a few years ago and it made a deep impression on me—I thought it would be a suitable subject for a tragedy, since it still strikes us as tragic to see a happily favored individual go down in defeat, and even more so to see an entire family line die out. But perhaps a time will come when we shall be so highly developed and so enlightened that we can look with indifference upon the brutal, cynical, and heartless spectacle that life offers us, a time when we shall have laid aside those inferior and unreliable mechanical apparatuses called emotions, which will become superfluous and even harmful as our mental organs develop. The fact that my heroine wins sympathy is due entirely to the fact that we are still too weak to overcome the fear that the same fate might overtake us. The extremely sensitive viewer will of course not be satisfied with mere expressions of sympathy, and the man who believes in progress will demand that certain positive actions be taken for getting rid of the evil, a kind of program, in other words. But in the first place absolute evil does not exist. The decline of one family is the making of another, which now gets its chance to rise. This alternate rising and falling provides one of life's greatest pleasures, for happiness is, after all, relative. As for the man who has a program for changing the disagreeable circumstance that the hawk eats the chicken and that lice eat up the hawk, I should like to ask him why it should be changed. Life is not prearranged with such idiotic mathematical precision that only the larger gets to eat the smaller. Just as frequently the bee destroys the lion (in Aesop's fable)—or at least drives him wild.

If my tragedy makes most people feel sad, that is their fault. When we get to be as strong as the first French Revolutionists were, we shall be perfectly content and happy to watch the forests being cleared of rotting, superannuated trees that have stood too long in the way of others with just as much right to grow and flourish for a while—as content as we are when we see an incurably ill man finally die.

Recently my tragedy *The Father* was censured for being too unpleasant—as if one wanted merry tragedies. "The joy of life" is now the slogan of the day. Theater managers send out orders for nothing but farces, as if the joy of living lay in behaving like a clown and in depicting people as if they were afflicted with St. Vitus's dance or congenital idiocy. I find the joy of living in the fierce and ruthless battles of life, and my pleasure comes from learning something, from being taught something. That is why I have chosen for my play an unusual but instructive case, an exception, in other words—but an important exception of the kind that proves the rule—a choice of subject that I know will offend all lovers of the conventional. The next thing that will bother simple minds is that the motivation for the action is not simple and that the point of view is not single. Usually an event in life—and this is a fairly new discovery—is the result of a whole series of more or less deep-rooted causes. The spectator, however, generally chooses the one that puts the least strain on his mind or reflects most credit on his insight. Consider a case of suicide. "Business failure," says the merchant. "Unhappy love," say the women. "Physical illness," says the sick man. "Lost hopes," says the down-and-out. But it may be that the reason lay in all of these or in none of them, and that the suicide hid his real reason behind a completely different one that would reflect greater glory on his memory.

I have motivated the tragic fate of Miss Julie with an abundance of circumstances: her mother's basic instincts, her father's improper bringing-up of the girl, her own inborn nature, and her fiancé's sway over her weak and degenerate mind. Further and more immediately: the festive atmosphere of Midsummer Eve, her father's absence, her period, her preoccupation with animals, the erotic excitement of the dance, the long summer twilight, the highly aphrodisiac influence of flowers, and finally chance itself, which drives two people together in an out-of-the-way room, plus the boldness of the aroused man.

As one can see, I have not been entirely the physiologist, not been obsessively psychological, not traced everything to her mother's heredity, not found the sole cause in her period, not attributed everything to our "immoral times," and not simply preached a moral lesson. Lacking a priest, I have let the cook handle that.

I am proud to say that this complicated way of looking at things is in tune with the times. And if others have anticipated me in this, I am proud that I am not alone in my paradoxes, as all new discoveries are called. And no one can say this time that I am being one-sided.

As far as the drawing of characters is concerned, I have made the people in my play fairly "characterless" for the following reasons. In the course of time the word *character* has acquired many meanings. Originally it probably meant the dominant and fundamental trait in the soul complex and was confused with temperament. Later the middle class used it to mean an automaton. An individual who once for all had found his own true nature or adapted himself to a certain role in life, who in fact had ceased to grow, was called a man of character, while the man who was constantly developing, who, like a skillful sailor on the currents of life, did not sail with close-tied sheets but who fell off before the wind in order to luff again, was called a man of no character—derogatorily of course, since he was so difficult to keep track of, to pin down and pigeonhole. This middle-class conception of a fixed character was transferred to the stage, where the middle class has always ruled. A character there came to mean someone who was always one and the same, always drunk, always joking, always melancholy, and who needed to be characterized only by some physical defect such as a club foot, a wooden leg, or a red nose, or by the repetition of some such phrase as, "That's capital," or "Barkis is willin'." This uncomplicated way of viewing people is still to be found in the great Molière. Harpagon is nothing but a miser, although Harpagon could have been both a miser and an exceptional financier, a fine father, and a good citizen. Worse still, his "defect" is extremely advantageous to his son-in-law and his daughter who will be his heirs and who therefore should not find fault with him, even if they do have to wait a while to jump into bed together. So I do not believe in simple stage characters. And the summary judgments that writers pass on people—he is stupid, this one is brutal, that one is jealous, this one is stingy, and so on—should not pass unchallenged by the naturalists who know how complicated the soul is and who realize that vice has a reverse side very much like virtue.

Since the persons in my play are modern characters, living in a transitional era more hectic and hysterical than the previous one at least, I have depicted them as more unstable, as torn and divided, a mixture of the old and the new. Nor does it seem improbable to me that modern ideas might also have seeped down through newspapers and kitchen talk to the level of the servants. Consequently the valet may belch forth from his inherited slave soul certain modern ideas. And if there are those who find it wrong to allow people in a modern drama to talk Darwin and who recommend the practice of Shakespeare to our attention, may I remind them that the gravedigger in *Hamlet* talks the then fashionable philosophy of Giordano Bruno (Bacon's philosophy), which is even more improbable, seeing that the means of spreading ideas were fewer then than now. And besides, the fact of the matter is that Darwinism has always existed, ever since Moses' history of creation from the lower animals up to man, but it was not until recently that we discovered it and formulized it.

My souls—or characters—are conglomerations from various stages of culture, past and present, walking scrapbooks, shreds of human lives, tatters torn from old rags that were once Sunday best—hodgepodges just like the human soul. I have even supplied a little source history into the bargain by letting the weaker steal and repeat words of the stronger, letting them get ideas (suggestions as they are called) from one another, from the environment (the songbird's blood), and from objects (the razor). I have also arranged for *Gedankenübertragung*[1] through an inanimate medium to take place (the count's boots, the servant's bell). And I have even made use of "waking suggestions" (a variation of hypnotic suggestion), which have by now been so popularized that they cannot arouse ridicule or skepticism as they would have done in Mesmer's time.

I say Miss Julie is a modern character not because the man-hating half-woman has not always existed but because she has now been brought out into the open, has taken the stage, and is making a noise about herself. Victim of a superstition (one that has seized even stronger minds) that woman, that stunted form of human being, standing with man, the lord of creation, the creator of culture, is meant to be the equal of man or could ever possibly be, she involves herself in an absurd struggle with him in which she falls. Absurd because a stunted form, subject to the laws of propagation, will always be born stunted and can never catch up with the one who has the lead. As follows: A (the man) and B (the woman) start from the same point C, A with a speed of let us say 100 and B with a speed of 60. When will B overtake A? Answer: never. Neither with the help of equal education or equal voting rights—nor by universal disarmament and temperance societies—any more than two parallel lines can ever meet. The half-woman is a type that forces itself on others, selling itself for power, medals, recognition, diplomas, as formerly it sold itself for money. It represents degeneration. It is not a strong species for it does not maintain itself, but unfortunately it propagates its misery in the following generation. Degenerate men unconsciously select their mates from among these half-women, so that they breed and spread, producing creatures of indeterminate sex to whom life is a torture, but who fortunately are overcome eventually either by a hostile reality, or by the uncontrolled breaking loose of their repressed instincts, or else by their frustration in not being able to compete with the male sex. It is a tragic type, offering us the spectacle of a desperate fight against nature; a tragic legacy of romanticism, which is now being dissipated by naturalism—a movement that seeks only happiness, and for that strong and healthy species are required.

Miss Julie, however, is also a vestige of the old warrior nobility that is now being superseded by a new nobility of nerve and brain. She is a victim of the disorder produced within a family by a mother's "crime," of the mistakes of a whole generation gone wrong, of circumstances, of her own defective constitution—all of which put together is equivalent to the fate or universal law of the ancients. The naturalists have banished guilt along with God, but the consequences of an act—punishment, imprisonment, or the fear of it—cannot be banished for the simple reason that they remain whether or not the naturalist dismisses the case from his court. Those sitting on the sidelines can easily afford to be lenient; but what of the injured parties? And even if her father were compelled to forgo taking his revenge, Miss Julie would take vengeance on herself, as she does in the play, because of that inherited or acquired sense of honor that has been transmitted to the upper classes from—well, where does it come from? From the age of barbarism, from the first Aryans, from the chivalry of the Middle Ages. And a very fine code it was, but now inimical to the survival of the race. It is the aristocrat's form of hara-kiri, a law of conscience that bids the Japanese to slice his own stomach when someone else dishonors him. The same sort of thing survives, slightly modified, in that exclusive prerogative of the aristocracy, the duel. (Example: the husband challenges his wife's lover to a duel; the lover shoots the husband and runs off with the wife. Result: the husband has saved his *honor* but lost his wife.) Hence the servant Jean lives on; but not Miss Julie, who cannot live without honor. The advantage that the slave has over his master is that he has not committed

---

[1] Telepathy

himself to this defeatist principle. In all of us Aryans there is enough of the nobleman, or of the Don Quixote, to make us sympathize with the man who takes his own life after having dishonored himself by shameful deeds. And we are all of us aristocrats enough to be distressed at the sight of a great man lying like a dead hulk ready for the scrap pile, even, I suppose, if he were to raise himself up again and redeem himself by honorable deeds.

The servant Jean is the beginning of a new species in which noticeable differentiation has already taken place. He began as a child of a poor worker and is now evolving through self-education into a future gentleman of the upper classes. He is quick to learn, has highly developed senses (smell, taste, sight), and a keen appreciation of beauty. He has already come up in the world, for he is strong enough not to hesitate to make use of other people. He is already a stranger to his old friends, whom he despises as reminders of past stages in his development, and whom he fears and avoids because they know his secrets, guess his intentions, look with envy on his rise and with joyful expectation toward his fall. Hence his character is unformed and divided. He wavers between an admiration of high positions and a hatred of the men who occupy them. He is an aristocrat—he says so himself—familiar with the ins and outs of good society. He is polished on the outside, but coarse underneath. He wears his frock coat with elegance but offers no guarantee that he keeps his body clean.

Although he respects Miss Julie, he is afraid of Christine, because she knows his innermost secrets. Yet he is sufficiently hard-hearted not to let the events of the night upset his plans for the future. Possessing both the coarseness of the slave and the toughmindedness of the born ruler, he can look at blood without fainting, shake off bad luck like water, and take calamity by the horns. Consequently he will escape from the battle unwounded, probably ending up as proprietor of a hotel. And if he himself does not get to be a Rumanian count, his son will doubtless go to college and possibly end up as a government official.

Now his observations about life as the lower classes see it, from below, are well worth listening to—that is, they are whenever he is telling the truth, which is not too often, because he is more likely to say what is advantageous to him than what is true. When Miss Julie supposes that everyone in the lower classes must feel greatly oppressed by the weight of the classes above, Jean naturally agrees with her since he wants to win her sympathy. But he promptly takes it all back when he finds it expedient to separate himself from the mob.

Apart from the fact that Jean is coming up in the world, he is also superior to Miss Julie in that he is a man. In the sexual sphere, he is the aristocrat. He has the strength of the male, more highly developed senses, and the ability to take the initiative. His inferiority is merely the result of his social environment, which is only temporary and which he will probably slough off along with his livery.

His slave nature expresses itself in his awe of the count (the boots) and his religious superstitions. But he is awed by the count mainly because the count occupies the place he wants most in life; and this awe is still there even after he has won the daughter of the house and seen how empty that beautiful shell was.

I do not believe that any love in the "higher" sense can be born from the union of two such different souls; so I have let Miss Julie's love be refashioned in her imagination as a love that protects and purifies, and I have let Jean imagine that even his love might have a chance to grow under other social circumstances. For I suppose love is very much like the hyacinth that must strike roots deep in the dark earth *before* it can produce a vigorous blossom. Here it shoots up, bursts into bloom, and turns to seed all at once. Such plants can only be short-lived.

Christine—finally to get to her—is a female slave, spineless and phlegmatic after years spent at the kitchen stove, bovinely unconscious of her own hypocrisy, and with a full quota of moral and religious notions that serve as scapegoats and cloaks for her sins—which a stronger soul does not require since he is able either to carry the burden of his own sins or to rationalize them out of existence. She attends church regularly where she deftly unloads unto Jesus her household thefts and picks up from him another load of innocence. She is only a secondary character, and I have deliberately done no more than sketch her in—just as I treated the country doctor and parish priest in *The Father* where I only wanted to draw ordinary everyday people such as most country doctors and parsons are. That some have found my minor characters one-dimensional is due to the fact that ordinary people while at work are to a certain extent one-dimensional and do lack an independent existence, showing only one side of themselves in the performance of their duties. And as long as the audience does not feel it needs to see them from different angles, my abstract sketches will pass muster.

Now as far as the dialogue is concerned, I have broken somewhat with tradition in refusing to make my characters into interlocutors who ask stupid questions to elicit witty answers. I have avoided the symmetrical and mathematical design of the artfully constructed French dialogue and have let minds work as irregularly as they do in real life, where no subject is quite exhausted before another mind engages at random some cog in the conversation and governs it for a while. My dialogue wanders here and there, gathers material in the first scenes which is later picked up, repeated, reworked, developed, and expanded like the theme in a piece of music.

The action of the play poses no problem. Since it really involves only two people, I have limited myself to these two, introducing only one minor character, the cook, and keeping the unhappy spirit of the father brooding over the action as a whole. I have chosen this course because I have noticed that what interests people most nowadays is the psychological action. Our inveterately curious souls are no longer content to see a thing happen; we want to see how it happens. We want to see the strings, look at the machinery, examine the double-bottom drawer, put on the magic ring to find the hidden seam, look in the deck for the marked cards.

In treating the subject this way I have had in mind the case-history novels of the Goncourt brothers, which appeal to me more than anything else in modern literature.

As far as play construction is concerned, I have made a stab at getting rid of act divisions. I was afraid that the spectator's declining susceptibility to illusion might not carry him through the intermission, when he would have time to think about what he has seen and to escape the suggestive influence of the author-hypnotist. I figure my play lasts about ninety minutes. Since one can listen to a lecture, a sermon, or a political debate for that long or even longer, I have convinced myself that a play should not exhaust an audience in that length of time. As early as 1872 in one of my first attempts at the drama, *The Outlaw*, I tried out this concentrated form, although with little success. I had finished the work in five acts when I noticed the disjointed and disturbing effect it produced. I burned it, and from the ashes there arose a single, complete reworked act of fifty pages that would run for less than an hour. Although this play form is not completely new, it seems to be my special property and has a good chance of gaining favor with the public when tastes change. My hope is to educate a public to sit through a full evening's show in one act. But this whole question must first be probed more deeply. In the meantime, in order to establish resting places for the audience and the actors without destroying the illusion, I have made use of three arts that belong to the drama: the monologue, the pantomime, and the ballet, all of which were part of classic tragedy, the monody having become the monologue and the choral dance, the ballet.

The realists have banished the monologue from the stage as implausible. But if I can motivate it, I make it plausible, and I can then use it to my advantage. Now it is certainly plausible for a speaker to pace the floor and read his speech aloud to himself. It is plausible for an actor to practice his part aloud, for a child to talk to her cat, a mother to babble to her baby, an old lady to chatter to her parrot, and a sleeping man to talk in his sleep. And in order to give the actor a chance to work on his own for once and for a moment not be obliged to follow the author's directions, I have not written out the monologues in detail but simply outlined them. Since it makes very little difference what is said while asleep, or to the parrot or the cat, inasmuch as it does not affect the main action, a gifted player who is in the midst of the situation and mood of the play can probably improvise the monologue better than the author, who cannot estimate ahead of time how much may be said and for how long before the illusion is broken.

Some theaters in Italy have, as we know, returned to the art of improvisation and have thereby trained actors who are truly inventive—without, however, violating the intentions of the author. This seems to be a step in the right direction and possibly the beginning of a new, fertile form of art that will be genuinely *creative*.

In places where the monologue cannot be properly motivated, I have resorted to pantomime. Here I have given the actor even more freedom to be creative and win honor on his own. Nevertheless, not to try the audience beyond its limits, I have relied on music—well motivated by the Midsummer Eve dance—to exercise its hypnotic powers during the pantomime scene. I beg the music director to select his tunes with great care, so that associations foreign to the mood of the play will not be produced by reminders of popular operettas or current dance numbers or by folk music of interest only to ethnologists.

The ballet that I have introduced cannot be replaced by a so-called crowd scene. Such scenes are always badly acted, with a pack of babbling fools taking advantage of the occasion to "gag it up," thereby destroying the illusion. Inasmuch as country people do not improvise their taunts but make use of material already to hand by giving it a double meaning, I have not composed an original lampoon but have made use of a little known round dance that I noted down in the Stockholm district. The words do not fit the situation exactly, which is what I intended, since the slave in his cunning (that is, weakness) never attacks directly. At any rate, let us have no comedians in this serious story and no obscene smirking over an affair that nails the lid on a family coffin.

As far as the scenery is concerned, I have borrowed from impressionistic painting the idea of asymmetrical and open composition, and I believe that I have thereby gained something in the way of greater illusion. Because the audience cannot see the whole room and all the furniture, they will have to surmise what's missing; that is, their imagination will be stimulated to fill in the rest of the picture. I have gained something else by this: I have avoided those tiresome exits through doors. Stage doors are made of canvas and rock at the slightest touch. They cannot even be used to indicate the wrath of an angry father who storms out of the house after a bad dinner, slamming the door behind him "so that the whole house shakes." (In the theater it sways and billows.) Furthermore, I have confined the action to one set, both to give the characters a chance to become part and parcel of their environment and to cut down on scenic extravagance. If there is only one set, one has a right to expect it to be as realistic as possible. Yet nothing is more difficult than to make a room look like a room, however easy it may be for the scene painter to create waterfalls and erupting volcanos. I suppose we shall have to put up with walls made of canvas, but isn't it about time that we stopped painting shelves and pots and pans on the canvas? There are so many other conventions in the theater that we are told to accept in good faith that we should be spared the strain of believing in painted saucepans.

I have placed the backdrop and the table at an angle to force the actors to play face to face or in half profile when they are seated opposite each other at the table. In a production of *Aida* I saw a flat placed at such an angle, which led the eye out in an unfamiliar perspective. Nor did it look as if it had been set that way simply to be different to avoid those monotonous right angles.

Another desirable innovation would be the removal of the footlights. I understand that the purpose of lighting from below is to make the actors look more full in the face. But may I ask why all actors should have full faces? Doesn't this kind of lighting wipe out many of the finer features in the lower part of the face, especially around the jaws? Doesn't it distort the shape of the nose and throw false shadows above the eyes? If not, it certainly does something else: it hurts the actor's eyes. The footlights hit the retina at an angle from which it is usually shielded (except in sailors who must look at the sunlight reflected in the water), and the result is the loss of any effective play of the eyes. All one ever sees on stage are goggle-eyed glances sideways at the boxes or upward at the balcony, with only the whites of the eyes being visible in the latter case. And this probably also accounts for that tiresome fluttering of the eyelashes that the female performers are particularly guilty of. If an actor nowadays wants to express something with his eyes, he can only do it looking right at the audience, in which case he makes direct contact with someone outside the proscenium arch—a bad habit known, justifiably or not, as "saying hello to friends."[2]

I should think that the use of sufficiently strong side lights (through the use of reflectors or something like them) would provide the actor with a new asset: an increased range of expression made possible by the play of the eyes, the most expressive part of the face.

I have scarcely any illusions about getting actors to play for the audience and not directly at them, although this should be the goal. Nor do I dream of ever seeing an actor play through all of an important scene with his back to the audience. But is it too much to hope that crucial scenes could be played where the author indicated and not in front of the prompter's box as if they were duets demanding applause? I am not calling for a revolution, only for some small changes. I am well aware that transforming the stage into a real room with the fourth wall missing and with some of the furniture placed with backs to the auditorium would only upset the audience, at least for the present.

If I bring up the subject of make-up, it is not because I dare hope to be heeded by the ladies, who would rather be beautiful than truthful. But the male actor might do well to consider if it is an

---

[2] "Counting the house" would be the equivalent in American theater slang. —Trans.

advantage to paint his face with character lines that remain there like a mask. Let us imagine an actor who pencils in with soot a few lines between his eyes to indicate great anger, and let us suppose that in that permanently enraged state he finds he has to smile on a certain line. Imagine the horrible grimace! And how can the old character actor wrinkle his brows in anger when his false bald pate is as smooth as a billiard ball?

In a modern psychological drama, in which every tremor of the soul should be reflected more by facial expressions than by gestures and grunts, it would probably be most sensible to experiment with strong side lighting on a small stage, using actors without any make-up or a minimum of it.

And then, if we could get rid of the visible orchestra with its disturbing lights and the faces turned toward the public; if the auditorium floor could be raised so that the spectator's eyes are not level with the actor's knees; if we could get rid of the proscenium boxes and their occupants, arriving giggling and drunk from their dinners; and if we could have it dark in the auditorium during the performance; and if, above everything else, we could have a *small* stage and an *intimate* auditorium—then possibly a new drama might arise and at least one theater become a refuge for cultured audiences. While we are waiting for such a theater, we shall have to write for the dramatic stockpile and prepare the repertory that one day shall come.

Here is my attempt. If I have failed, there is still time to try again!

August Strindberg
(1888)

MISS JULIE

AUGUST STRINDBERG

TRANSLATED BY EVERT SPRINCHORN

— CHARACTERS —

MISS JULIE,[3] *twenty-five years old*
JEAN, *valet, thirty years old*
CHRISTINE, *cook, thirty-five years old*
THE CHORUS, *a party of country folk*

The scene is a country estate in Sweden.

The time: A Midsummer Night in the 1880s. The hours after midnight, June 24, St. John the Baptist's Day.

The scene is the kitchen of the estate belonging to the count, MISS JULIE's *father. It is a large kitchen, situated along with the servants' quarters in the basement of the manor house. The side walls and the ceiling of the kitchen are masked by the tormentors and borders of the set. The rear wall runs obliquely upstage from the left. On this wall to the left are two shelves with pots and pans of copper, iron, and pewter. The shelves are decorated with goffered paper. A little to the right can be seen three-fourths of a deep arched entry with two glass doors, and through them can be seen a fountain with a statue of a cupid, lilac bushes in bloom, and the tops of some Lombardy poplars.*

From the left of the stage the corner of a large, Dutch-tile kitchen stove protrudes with part of the hood showing.

Projecting from the right side of the stage is one end of the servants' dining table of white pine, with a few chairs around it.

The stove is decorated with branches of birch leaves; the floor is strewn with juniper twigs.

On the end of the table is a large Japanese spice jar filled with lilacs.

An icebox, a sink, a washbasin.

Over the door a big old-fashioned bell; and to the left of the door the gaping mouth of a speaking tube.

◆　◆　◆

CHRISTINE *is standing at the stove, frying something in a pan. She is wearing a light-colored cotton dress and an apron.*

JEAN *enters, dressed in livery and carrying a pair of high-top boots with spurs. He sets them where they are clearly visible.*

JEAN: What a night! She's wild again! Miss Julie's absolutely wild!

CHRISTINE: You sure took your time getting back!

5 JEAN: I took the count down to the station, and on my way back, I passed the barn and went in for a dance. And there was Miss Julie leading the dance with the game warden. Then she noticed me. And she ran right into my arms and chose me for the ladies' waltz. And she's been dancing ever

since like—like I don't know what. Wild, I tell you, absolutely wild! 10

CHRISTINE: That's nothing new. But she's been worse than ever during the last two weeks, ever since her engagement was broken off.

JEAN: Yes. I never did hear all there was to that. He was a good man, too, even if he wasn't rich. Well, they've got such crazy 15 ideas. (*He sits down at the end of the table.*) Tell me, isn't it strange that a young girl like her—all right, young woman—prefers to stay home here with the servants rather than go with her father to visit her relatives?

CHRISTINE: I suppose she's ashamed to face them after that 20 fiasco with her young man.

JEAN: No doubt. He wouldn't take any nonsense from her. Do you know what happened, Christine? I saw the whole thing. Of course, I didn't let on.

CHRISTINE: You were there? I don't believe it. 25

JEAN: Well, I was. They were in the stable yard one evening—and she was training him, that's what she called it. Do you know what? She was making him jump over her riding whip—training him like a dog. He jumped over twice, and she whipped him both times. But the third time, he grabbed 30 the whip from her, [scratched her face with it—long scratch on her left cheek;] then broke it in a thousand pieces—and walked off.

CHRISTINE: I don't believe it! What do you know!

JEAN: Yes, that put an end to that affair. —What have you got 35 for me that's really good, Christine?

CHRISTINE: (*Serving him from the frying pan.*) Just a little bit of kidney. Cut it from the veal roast.

JEAN: (*Smelling it.*) Wonderful! One of my special *délices!* (*Feeling the plate.*) Hey, you didn't warm the plate! 40

CHRISTINE: You're more fussy than the count himself when you set your mind to it. (*She rumples his hair affectionately.*)

JEAN: (*Irritated.*) Cut it out! Don't muss up my hair. You know how particular I am!

CHRISTINE: Oh, don't get mad. Can I help it if I like you? 45

(JEAN *eats.* CHRISTINE *gets out a bottle of beer.*)

JEAN: Beer on Midsummer Eve! No thank you! I've got something much better than that. (*He opens a drawer in the table and takes out a bottle of red wine with a gold seal.*) Do you see that? Gold Seal. Now give me a glass.

---

[3]Julie is not a countess; she is the daughter of a count. Her title "fröken" corresponds to the German "Fräulein" and the French "mademoiselle."

31–32 **scratched . . . left cheek** the passage in brackets was deleted in Strindberg's manuscript, probably by Strindberg himself

(She hands him a tumbler.)

50   —No, a wineglass of course. This has to be drunk properly. No water.

CHRISTINE: *(Goes back to the stove and puts on a small saucepan.)* Lord help the woman who gets you for a husband. You're an old fussbudget!

55 JEAN: Talk, talk! You'd consider yourself lucky if you got yourself a man as good as me. It hasn't done you any harm to have people think I'm your fiancé. *(He tastes the wine.)* Very good. Excellent. But warmed just a little too little. *(Warming the glass in his hands.)* We bought this in Dijon. Four francs

60 a liter, unbottled—and the tax on top of that. . . . What on earth are you cooking? It stinks like hell!

CHRISTINE: Some damn mess that Miss Julie wants for her Diana, that damn dog of hers.

JEAN: You should watch your language, Christine. . . . Why do

65 you have to stand in front of the stove on a holiday, cooking for that mutt? Is it sick?

CHRISTINE: Oh, she's sick, all right! She sneaked out to the gatekeeper's pug and—got herself in a fix. And you know Miss Julie, she can't stand anything like that.

70 JEAN: She's too stuck-up in some ways and not proud enough in others. Just like her mother. The countess felt right at home in the kitchen or down in the barn with the cows, but when she went driving, one horse wasn't enough for her, she had to have a pair. Her sleeves were always dirty, but her but-

75 tons had the royal crown on them. As for Miss Julie, she doesn't give a hoot in hell how she looks and acts. I mean, she's not really refined, not really. Just now, down at the barn, she grabbed the game warden right from under Anna's eyes and asked him to dance. You wouldn't see anybody in

80 our class behaving like that. But that's what happens when the gentry try to act like the common people—they become common! . . . However, I'll say one thing for her: she *is* beautiful! Statuesque! Ah, those shoulders—those—and so forth, and so forth!

85 CHRISTINE: Oh, don't exaggerate. Clara tells me all about her, and Clara dresses her.

JEAN: Clara, pooh! You women are always jealous of each other. I've been out riding with her. . . . And how she can dance . . . !

90 CHRISTINE: Listen, Jean, you *are* going to dance with me, aren't you, when I'm finished here?

JEAN: Certainly! Of course I am.

CHRISTINE: Promise?

JEAN: Promise! Listen if I say I'm going to do a thing, I do

95 it. . . . Christine, I thank you for a delicious meal. Superb! *(He shoves the cork back into the bottle.)*

(MISS JULIE appears in the entry, talking to someone outside.)

MISS JULIE: I'll be right back. Don't wait for me.

(JEAN slips the bottle into the table drawer quickly and rises respectfully. MISS JULIE comes in and crosses over to CHRISTINE, who is at the stove.)

MISS JULIE: Did you get it ready?

(CHRISTINE signals that JEAN is present.)

JEAN: *(Polite and charming.)* Are you ladies sharing secrets?

100 MISS JULIE: *(Flipping her handkerchief in his face.)* Don't be nosy!

JEAN: Oh, that smells good! Violets.

MISS JULIE: *(Flirting with him.)* Don't be impudent! And don't tell me you're an expert on perfumes, too. I love the way you dance!—No, mustn't look! Go away! 105

JEAN: *(Cocky but pleasant.)* What are the ladies cooking up? A witches' brew for Midsummer Eve? So they can tell the future? Read what's in the cards for them, and see who they'll marry?

MISS JULIE: *(Curtly.)* You'd have to have good eyes to see that. 110 *(To CHRISTINE.)* Pour it into a small bottle, and seal it tight. . . . Jean, come and dance a schottische with me.

JEAN: *(Hesitating.)* I hope you don't think I'm being rude, but I've already promised this dance to Christine.

MISS JULIE: She can always find someone. Isn't that so, Chris- 115 tine? You don't mind if I borrow Jean for a minute, do you?

CHRISTINE: It ain't up to me. If Miss Julie is gracious enough to invite you, it ain't right for you to say no, Jean. You go on, and thank her for the honor.

JEAN: Frankly, Miss Julie, I don't want to hurt your feelings, 120 but I wonder if it's wise—I mean for you to dance twice in a row with the same partner. Especially since the people around here love to talk.

MISS JULIE: *(Bridling.)* What do you mean? What kind of talk? What are you trying to say? 125

JEAN: *(Retreating.)* I wish you wouldn't misunderstand me, Miss Julie. It just doesn't look right for you to prefer one of your servants to the others who are hoping for the same unusual honor.

MISS JULIE: Prefer! What an idea! I'm really surprised. I, the 130 mistress of the house, am good enough to come to their dance, and when I feel like dancing, I want to dance with someone who knows how to lead. After all I don't want to look ridiculous.

JEAN: As you wish, Miss Julie. I am at your orders. 135

MISS JULIE: *(Gently.)* Don't take it as an order. Tonight we're all just having a good time. There's no question of rank. Now give me your arm. —Don't worry, Christine. I won't run off with your boyfriend.

(JEAN gives her his arm and leads her out.)

◆ ◆ ◆

PANTOMIME SCENE

This should be played as if the actress were actually alone. She turns her back on the audience when she feels like it; she does not look out into the auditorium; she does not rush through the scene as if afraid the audience will grow impatient.

CHRISTINE *alone. In the distance the sound of the violins playing the schottische.* CHRISTINE, *humming in time with the music, cleans up after* JEAN, *washes the dishes, dries them, and puts them away in a cupboard. Then she takes off her apron, takes a little mirror from one of the table drawers, and leans it against the jar of lilacs on the table. She lights a tallow candle, heats a curling iron, and curls the bangs on her forehead. Then she goes to the doorway and stands listening to the music. She comes back to the table and finds the handkerchief that* MISS JULIE *left behind. She smells it, spreads it out, and then, as if lost in thought, stretches it, smooths it out, and folds it in four.*

◆ ◆ ◆

(JEAN *enters alone.*)

JEAN: Wild! I told you she was wild! You should have seen the way she was dancing. Everyone was peeking at her from behind the doors and laughing at her. What's the matter with her, Christine?

5 CHRISTINE: You might know it's her monthlies, Jean. She always acts peculiar then. . . . Well, are you going to dance with me?

JEAN: You're not mad at me because I broke my promise?

CHRISTINE: Of course not. Not for a little thing like that, you
10 know that. I know my place.

JEAN: (*Grabs her around the waist.*) You're a sensible girl, Christine. You're going to make somebody a good wife—

(MISS JULIE, *coming in, sees them together. She is unpleasantly surprised.*)

MISS JULIE: (*With forced gaiety.*) Well, aren't you the gallant beau—running away from your partner!

15 JEAN: On the contrary, Miss Julie. As you can see, I've hurried back to the partner I deserted.

MISS JULIE: (*Changing tack.*) You know, you're the best dancer I've met. —Why are you wearing livery on a holiday? Take it off at once.

20 JEAN: I'd have to ask you to leave for a minute. My black coat is hanging right here—(*He moves to the right and points.*)

MISS JULIE: You're not embarrassed because I'm here, are you? Just to change your coat? Go in your room and come right back again. Or else stay here and I'll turn my back.

25 JEAN: If you'll excuse me, Miss Julie. (*He goes off to the right. His arm can be seen as he changes his coat.*)

MISS JULIE: (*To CHRISTINE.*) Tell me something, Christine. Is Jean your fiancé? He acts so familiar with you.

CHRISTINE: Fiancé? I suppose so. At least we say we are.

30 MISS JULIE: What do you mean?

CHRISTINE: Well, Miss Julie, you have had fiancés yourself, and you know—

MISS JULIE: But we were properly engaged—!

CHRISTINE: I know, but did anything come of it?

(JEAN *comes back, wearing a black cutaway coat and derby.*)

35 MISS JULIE: *Très gentil, monsieur Jean! Très gentil!*

JEAN: *Vous voulez plaisanter, madame.*

MISS JULIE: *Et vous voulez parler français!* Where did you learn to speak French?

JEAN: In Switzerland. I was *sommelier* in one of the biggest ho-
40 tels in Lucerne.

MISS JULIE: My! but you look quite the gentleman in that coat! *Charmant!* (*She sits down at the table.*)

JEAN: Flatterer!

MISS JULIE: (*Stiffening.*) Who said I was flattering you?

45 JEAN: My natural modesty would not allow me to presume that you were paying sincere compliments to someone like me, and therefore I could only assume that you were exaggerating, which, in this case, means flattering me.

MISS JULIE: You certainly have a way with words. Where did
50 you learn to talk like that? Seeing plays?

JEAN: And other places. You don't think I stayed in the house for six years when I was a valet in Stockholm, do you?

MISS JULIE: I thought you were born in this district. Weren't you?

JEAN: My father worked as a farmhand on the district attor- 55
ney's estate, next door to yours. I used to see you when you were little. Of course you didn't notice me.

MISS JULIE: Did you really?

JEAN: Yes. I remember one time in particular—. But I can't tell you about that! 60

MISS JULIE: Of course you can. . . . Oh, come on. Just this once—for me.

JEAN: No. No, I really couldn't. Not now. Some other time maybe.

MISS JULIE: Some other time? That means never. What's the 65
harm in telling me now?

JEAN: There's no harm. I just don't feel like it. —Look at her.

(*He nods at* CHRISTINE, *who has fallen asleep in a chair by the stove.*)

MISS JULIE: Won't she make somebody a pretty wife! I'll bet she snores, too.

JEAN: No, she doesn't. But she talks in her sleep. 70

MISS JULIE: (*Archly.*) Now how could you know she talks in her sleep?

JEAN: (*Coolly.*) I've heard her . . .

(*Pause. They look at each other.*)

MISS JULIE: Why don't you sit down?

JEAN: I wouldn't take the liberty in your presence. 75

MISS JULIE: Not even if I ordered you?

JEAN: Of course I'd obey.

MISS JULIE: Well then: sit down. —Wait a minute. Could you get me something to drink?

JEAN: I don't know what there is in the icebox. Only beer, I 80
suppose.

MISS JULIE: Only beer?! I have simple tastes. I prefer beer to wine.

(JEAN *takes a bottle of beer from the icebox and opens it. He looks in the cupboard for a glass and a plate, and serves her.*)

JEAN: At your service, *mademoiselle.*

MISS JULIE: Thank you. What about you? 85

JEAN: I'm not much of a beer-drinker, thank you, but if it's your wish—

MISS JULIE: My wish! I should think a gentleman would want to keep his lady company.

JEAN: A point well taken! (*He opens another bottle and takes a* 90
glass.)

MISS JULIE: Now drink a toast to me!

(JEAN *hesitates.*)

You're not shy, are you? A big, strong man like you?

(*Playfully,* JEAN *kneels and raises his glass in mock gallantry.*)

JEAN: To my lady's health!

MISS JULIE: Bravo! Now you have to kiss my shoe, too. Then 95
you will have hit it off perfectly.

(JEAN *hesitates, then boldly grasps her foot and touches it lightly with his lips.*)

Superb! You should have been an actor.

JEAN: (*Rising.*) This has got to stop, Miss Julie! Someone might come in and see us.

100 MISS JULIE: So what?

JEAN: People would talk, that's what! If you knew how their tongues were wagging out there just a few minutes ago!

MISS JULIE: What did they say? Tell me. Sit down and tell me.

JEAN: I don't want to hurt your feelings. . . . They used expres-
105 sions that—that hinted at certain—you know what I mean. You're not a child. And when they see a woman drinking, alone with a man—and a servant at that—in the middle of the night—well . . .

MISS JULIE: Well what?! Besides, we're not alone. Christine is
110 here.

JEAN: Sleeping!

MISS JULIE: I'll wake her up. (*She goes over to* CHRISTINE.) Christine! Are you asleep? (CHRISTINE *babbles in her sleep.*) Christine! —My, how sound she sleeps!

115 CHRISTINE: (*Talking in her sleep.*) Count's boots are brushed . . . put on the coffee . . . right away, right away, right . . . mm— mm . . . poofff . . .

(MISS JULIE *shakes* CHRISTINE.)

MISS JULIE: Wake up, will you!

JEAN: (*Sternly.*) Let her alone! Let her sleep!

120 MISS JULIE: (*Sharply.*) What?

JEAN: She's been standing over the stove all day. She's worn out when night comes. Anyone asleep is entitled to some consideration.

MISS JULIE: (*Changing her tone.*) That's a very kind thought. It
125 does you credit, Jean. You're right, of course. (*She offers* JEAN *her hand.*) Now come on out and pick some lilacs for me.

(*During the following,* CHRISTINE *wakes up and, drunk with sleep, shuffles off to the right to go to bed. A polka can be heard in the distance.*)

JEAN: With you, Miss Julie?

MISS JULIE: Yes, with me.

130 JEAN: That's no good. Absolutely not.

MISS JULIE: I don't know what you're thinking. Aren't you let-ting your imagination run away with you?

JEAN: No. Other people are.

MISS JULIE: How? Imagining that I'm—*verliebt* with a servant?

135 JEAN: I'm not conceited, but it's been known to happen. And to these people nothing's sacred.

MISS JULIE: "These people!" Why, I do believe you're an aristocrat!

JEAN: Yes, I am.

140 MISS JULIE: I'm climbing down—

JEAN: Don't climb down, Miss Julie! Take my advice. No one will believe that you climbed down deliberately. They'll say you fell.

MISS JULIE: I have a higher opinion of these people than you
145 do. Let's see who's right! Come on! (*She gives him a long, steady look.*)

JEAN: You know, you're very strange.

MISS JULIE: Perhaps. But then so are you. . . . Besides, every-thing is strange. Life, people, everything. It's all scum, drift-
150 ing and drifting on the water until it sinks—drowns. There's a dream I have every now and then. It's coming back to me now. I'm sitting on top of a pillar. I've climbed up it some-how and I don't know how to get back down. When I look down I get dizzy. I have to get down but I don't have the

courage to jump. I can't hold on much longer and I want to 155 fall; but I don't fall. I know I won't have any peace until I get down; no rest until I get down, down on the ground. And if I ever got down on the ground, I'd want to go farther down, right down into the earth. . . . Have you ever felt anything like that? 160

JEAN: Never! I used to dream that I'm lying under a tall tree in a dark woods. I want to get up, up to the very top, to look out over the bright landscape with the sun shining on it, to rob the bird's nest up there with the golden eggs in it. And I climb and I climb, but the trunk is so thick, and so smooth, 165 and it's such a long way to that first branch. But I know that if I could just reach that first branch, I'd go right to the top as if on a ladder. I've never reached it yet, but someday I will— even if only in my dreams.

MISS JULIE: Here I am talking about dreams with you. Come 170 out with me. Only into the park a way. (*She offers him her arm, and they start to go.*)

JEAN: Let's sleep on nine midsummer flowers, Miss Julie, and then our dreams will come true!

(MISS JULIE *and* JEAN *suddenly turn around in the doorway.* JEAN *is holding his hand over one eye.*)

MISS JULIE: You've caught something in your eye. Let me see. 175

JEAN: It's nothing. Just a bit of dust. It'll go away.

MISS JULIE: The sleeve of my dress must have grazed your eye. Sit down and I'll help you. (*She takes him by the arm and sits him down. She takes his head and leans it back. With the cor-ner of her handkerchief she tries to get out the bit of dust.*) 180 Now sit still, absolutely still. (*She slaps his hand.*) Do as you're told. Why, I believe you're trembling—a big, strong man like you. (*She feels his biceps.*) With such big arms!

JEAN: (*Warningly.*) Miss Julie!

MISS JULIE: Yes, *Monsieur Jean?* 185

JEAN: *Attention! Je ne suis qu'un homme!*

MISS JULIE: Sit still, I tell you! . . . There now! It's out. Kiss my hand and thank me!

JEAN: (*Rising to his feet.*) Listen to me, Miss Julie—Christine has gone to bed!—Listen to me, I tell you! 190

MISS JULIE: Kiss my hand first!

JEAN: Listen to me!

MISS JULIE: Kiss my hand first!

JEAN: All right. But you'll have no one to blame but yourself.

MISS JULIE: For what? 195

JEAN: For what! Are you twenty-five years old and still a child? Don't you know it's dangerous to play with fire?

MISS JULIE: Not for me, I'm insured!

JEAN: (*Boldly.*) Oh, no, you're not! And even if you are, there's inflammable stuff next door. 200

MISS JULIE: Meaning you?

JEAN: Yes. Not just because it's me, but because I'm young and—

MISS JULIE: And irresistibly handsome? What incredible con-ceit! A Don Juan, maybe! Or a Joseph! Yes, bless my soul, 205 that's it: you're a Joseph!

JEAN: You think so?!

---

173 **midsummer flowers** a girl would pick in silence on Midsummer Eve nine different sorts of flowers, make a bouquet of them, and place them under her pillow. The man who appeared in her dreams would be the man she would marry

MISS JULIE: I'm almost afraid so!

(JEAN *boldly steps up to her, grabs her around the waist, tries to kiss her. She slaps his face.*)

None of that!

JEAN: More games? Or are you serious?

210 MISS JULIE: I'm serious.

JEAN: Then you must have been serious a moment ago, too! You take your games too seriously; that's dangerous. Well, I'm tired of your games, and if you'll excuse me, I'll return to my work. (*Takes up the boots and starts to brush them.*) The

215 count will be wanting his boots on time, and it's long past midnight.

MISS JULIE: Put those boots down.

JEAN: No! This is my job. It's what I'm here for. I never under-took to be your playmate. That's something I could never be.

220 I consider myself too good for that.

MISS JULIE: You are proud.

JEAN: In some ways. Not in others.

MISS JULIE: Have you ever been in love?

JEAN: We don't use that word around here. But I've hankered

225 after some girls, if that's what you mean. . . . I even got sick once because I couldn't have the one I wanted—really sick, like the princes in the Arabian Nights—who couldn't eat or drink for love.

MISS JULIE: Who was she?

(JEAN *does not reply.*)

230 Who was the girl?

JEAN: You can't get that out of me.

MISS JULIE: Even if I ask you as an equal—ask you—as a friend? . . . Who was she?

JEAN: You.

235 MISS JULIE: (*Sitting down.*) How—amusing . . .

JEAN: Yes, maybe so. Ridiculous. . . . That's why I didn't want to tell you about it before. Want to hear the whole story? . . . Have you any idea what you and your people look like from down below? Of course not. Like hawks or eagles, that's

240 what: you hardly ever see their backs because they're always soaring so high up. I lived with seven brothers and sisters—and a pig—out on the wasteland where there wasn't even a tree growing. But from my window I could see the wall of the count's garden with the apple trees sticking up over it. That

245 was the Garden of Eden for me, and there were many angry angels with flaming swords standing guard over it. But in spite of them, I and the other boys found a way to the Tree of Life. . . . How contemptible, that's what you're thinking.

MISS JULIE: For stealing apples? All boys do that.

250 JEAN: That's what you say now. All the same, you think me contemptible. Never mind. One day I went with my mother into this paradise to weed the onion beds. Next to the veg-etable garden stood a Turkish pavilion, shaded by jasmine and hung all over with honeysuckle. I couldn't imagine what

255 it was used for; I only knew I had never seen such a beautiful building. People went in, and came out again. And then one day the door was left open. I sneaked in. The walls were cov-ered with portraits of kings and emperors, and the windows had red curtains with tassels on them. —Recognize it? Yes,

260 the count's private privy. . . . I—(*He breaks off a lilac and holds it under* MISS JULIE's *nose.*) I had never been inside a castle, never seen anything besides the church. This was

more beautiful. And no matter what I tried to think about, my thoughts always came back—to that little pavilion. And little by little there arose in me a desire to experience just for 265 once the whole pleasure of—. *Enfin,* I sneaked in, looked about, and marveled. And just then I heard someone com-ing! There was only one way out—for the upper-class peo-ple. But for me there was one more—a lower one. And I had no other choice but to take it. (MISS JULIE, *who has taken the* 270 *lilac from* JEAN, *lets it fall to the table.*) Then I began to run like mad, plunging through the raspberry bushes, ploughing through the strawberry patches, and came up on the rose ter-race. And there I caught sight of a pink dress and a pair of white stockings. You! I crawled under—well, you can imag- 275 ine what it was like—under thistles that pricked me and wet dirt that stank to high heaven. And all the while I could see you walking among the roses. I said to myself, "If it's true that a thief can enter heaven and be with the angels, isn't it strange that a poor man's child here on God's green earth 280 can't enter the count's park and play with the count's daughter."

MISS JULIE: (*Sentimentally.*) Do you think all poor children have felt that way?

JEAN: (*Hesitatingly at first, then with mounting conviction.*) If 285 all poor ch—? Yes—yes, naturally. Of course!

MISS JULIE: It must be terrible to be poor.

JEAN: (*With exaggerated intensity.*) Oh, Miss Julie! You don't know! A dog can lie on the sofa with its mistress; a horse can have its nose stroked by the hand of a countess; but a ser- 290 vant—! (*Changing his tone.*) Of course, now and then you meet somebody with guts enough to work his way up in the world, but how often?—Anyway, you know what I did after-ward? I threw myself into the millstream with all my clothes on. Got fished out and spanked. But the following Sunday, 295 when Pa and everybody else in the house went to visit Grandma, I arranged things so I'd be left behind. Then I washed myself all over with soap and warm water, put on my best clothes, and went off to church—just to see you there once more. I saw you, and then I went home determined to 300 die. But I wanted to die beautifully and comfortably, without pain. I remembered some stories I had heard about how fatal it was to sleep under an elderberry bush. And we had a big one that had just blossomed out. I stripped it of every leaf and blossom it had and made a bed of them in a bin of oats. 305 Have you ever noticed how smooth oats are? As smooth to the touch as human skin. . . . So I pulled the lid of the bin shut and closed my eyes. Fell asleep. And when they woke me I was really very sick. However, I didn't die, as you can see. —What was I trying to prove? I don't know. There was 310 no hope of winning you. It was just that you were a symbol of the absolute hopelessness of my ever getting out of the class I was born in.

MISS JULIE: You know, you have a real gift for telling stories. Did you go to school? 315

JEAN: A little. But I've read a lot of novels and gone to the the-ater. And I've also listened to educated people talk. That way I learned the most.

MISS JULIE: You mean to tell me you stand around listening to what we're saying! 320

JEAN: Certainly! And I've heard an awful lot, I can tell you—sitting on the coachman's seat or rowing the boat. One time I heard you and a girlfriend talking—

MISS JULIE: Really? . . . And just what did you hear?

325 JEAN: Well, now, I don't know if I can repeat it. I can tell you I was a little amazed. I couldn't imagine where you had learned such words. Maybe at bottom there isn't such a big difference as you might think, between people and people.

MISS JULIE: How vulgar! At least people in my class don't be-
330 have like you when we're engaged.

JEAN: (*Looking her in the eye.*) Are you sure? —Come on now, it's no use playing the innocent with me.

MISS JULIE: He was a beast. The man I offered my love was a beast.

335 JEAN: That's what you all say—afterward.

MISS JULIE: All?

JEAN: I'd say so. I've heard the same expression used several times before in similar circumstances.

MISS JULIE: What kind of circumstances?

340 JEAN: The kind we're talking about. I remember the last time I—

MISS JULIE: (*Rising.*) That's enough! I don't want to hear any more.

JEAN: How strange! Neither did she! . . . Well, now if you'll ex-
345 cuse me, I'll go to bed.

MISS JULIE: (*Softly.*) Go to bed on Midsummer Eve?

JEAN: That's right. Dancing with that crowd up there really doesn't amuse me.

MISS JULIE: Jean, get the key to the boathouse and row me out
350 on the lake. I want to see the sun come up.

JEAN: Do you think that's wise?

MISS JULIE: You sound as if you were worried about your reputation.

JEAN: Why not? I don't particularly care to be made ridicu-
355 lous, or to be kicked out without a recommendation just when I'm trying to establish myself. Besides, I have a certain obligation to Christine.

MISS JULIE: Oh, I see. It's Christine now.

JEAN: Yes, but I'm thinking of you, too. Take my advise, Miss
360 Julie. Go up to your room.

MISS JULIE: When did you start giving me orders?

JEAN: Just this once. For your own sake! Please! It's very late. You're so tired, you're drunk; you don't know what you're doing. Go to bed, Miss Julie. —Besides, if my ears aren't de-
365 ceiving me, they're coming this way, looking for me. If they find us here together, you're done for!

THE CHORUS: (*Is heard coming nearer, singing.*)

    Said Jill to Jack, "Soil needs a tilling."
    Tri-di-ri-di-ralla, tri-di-ri-di-ra.
370   Said Jack to Jill, "Time's a-spilling."
    Tri-di-ri-di-ralla-la.
    Said Jill to Jack, "Gold's a-hoarding."
    Tri-di-ri-di-ralla, tri-di-ri-di-ra.
    Said Jack to Jill, "Tell not my lording."
375   Tri-di-ri-di-ralla-la.
    Said Jill to Jack, "Hair is for plaiting."
    Tri-di-ri-di-ralla, tri-di-ri-di-ra.
    "But Jill for Jack is not waiting."
    Tri-di-ri-di-ralla-la!

MISS JULIE: I know these people. I love them just as they love 380
me. Let them come. You'll see.

JEAN: Oh, no, Miss Julie, they don't love you! They take the food you give them, but they spit on it as soon as your back is turned. Believe me! Just listen to them. Listen to what they're singing. —No, you'd better not listen. 385

MISS JULIE: (*Listening.*) What are they singing?

JEAN: A nasty song—about you and me!

BANDFOLKETS DANSVISA

Allegretto.

Det kom-mo två fru-ar från sko-gen
Tri - di - ri - di - ral - la Tri - di - ri - di - ra
Den en - a var våt om fo - o - ten
Tri di - ri - di ral - la - la.

    De talte om hundra riksdaler
      Tri (etc.)
    Men ägde knappast en daler
      Tri (etc.)

    Och kransen jag dig skänker
      Tri (etc.)
    En annan jag påtänker
      Tri (etc.)

MISS JULIE: How disgusting! Oh, what cowardly, sneaking—

JEAN: That's what the mob always is—cowards! You can't fight them; you can only run away. 390

MISS JULIE: Run away? Where? There's no way out of here. And we can't go in to Christine.

JEAN: What about my room? What do you say? Rules don't count in a situation like this. You can trust me. —You said, let's be friends. Remember? Well, I'm your friend—your 395
true, devoted, respectful friend.

MISS JULIE: But suppose—suppose they looked for you there?

JEAN: I'll bolt the door. If they try to break it down, I'll shoot. Come, Miss Julie! (*On his knees.*) Please, Miss Julie!

MISS JULIE: (*Meaningfully.*) You promise me that you won't— 400

JEAN: I swear to you!

---

367 **chorus** the Swedish original of this song follows l. 387.

The melody of the peasants' song was not printed in the first Swedish edition, but it did appear in Charles de Casanove's French translation of the play in 1893.

(MISS JULIE *goes out quickly to the right.* JEAN *follows her impetuously.*)

◆ ◆ ◆

THE BALLET

The country people enter in festive costumes, with flowers in their hats. The fiddler is in the lead. A keg of small beer and a little keg of liquor, decorated with greenery, are set up on the table. Glasses are brought out. They all drink. Then they form a circle and sing "Said Jill to Jack," dancing the round dance as they sing. At the end of the dance, they all leave singing.

◆ ◆ ◆

(MISS JULIE *comes in alone; looks at the devastated kitchen; clasps her hands together; then takes out a powder puff and powders her face.* JEAN *enters. He is in high spirits.*)

JEAN: You see! You heard them, didn't you? You've got to admit it's impossible to stay here.

MISS JULIE: No, I don't. But even if I did, what could we do?

JEAN: Go away, travel, get away from here!

5 MISS JULIE: Travel? Yes—but where?

JEAN: Switzerland, the Italian lakes. You've never been there?

MISS JULIE: No. Is it beautiful?

JEAN: Eternal summer, oranges, laurel trees, ah . . . !

MISS JULIE: What do we do when we get there?

10 JEAN: I'll set up a hotel—a first-class hotel with a first-class clientele.

MISS JULIE: Hotel?

JEAN: I tell you that's the life! Always new faces, new languages. Not a minute to think about yourself or worry about
15 your nerves. No looking for something to do. The work keeps you busy. Day and night the bells ring, the trains whistle, the buses come and go. And all the while the money comes rolling in. I tell you it's the life!

MISS JULIE: Yes, that's the life. But what about me?

20 JEAN: The mistress of the whole place, the star of the establishment! With your looks—and your personality—it can't fail. It's perfect! You'll sit in the office like a queen, setting your slaves in motion by pressing an electric button. The guests will file before your throne and timidly lay their treasures on
25 your table. You can't imagine how people tremble when you shove a bill in their face! I'll salt the bills and you'll sugar them with your prettiest smile. Come on, let's get away from here—(*He takes a timetable from his pocket.*)—right away— the next train! We'll be in Malmö at six-thirty, Hamburg
30 eight-forty in the morning; Frankfurt to Basle in one day, and to Como by way of the Gotthard tunnel in—let me see—three days! Three days!

MISS JULIE: You make it sound so wonderful. But, Jean, you have to give me strength. Tell me you love me. Come and
35 put your arms around me.

JEAN: (*Hesitates.*) I want to . . . but I don't dare. Not anymore, not in this house. I do love you—without a shadow of a doubt. How can you doubt that, Miss Julie?

MISS JULIE: (*Shyly, very becomingly.*) You don't have to be for-
40 mal with me, Jean. You can call me Julie. There aren't any barriers between us now. Call me Julie.

JEAN: (*Agonized.*) I can't! There are still barriers between us, Miss Julie, as long as we stay in this house! There's the past, there's the count. I've never met anyone I feel so much re-
45 spect for. I've only got to see his gloves lying on a table and I shrivel up. I only have to hear that bell ring and I shy like a frightened horse. I only have to look at his boots standing there so stiff and proud and I feel my spine bending. (*He kicks the boots.*) Superstitions, prejudices that they've drilled
50 into us since we were children! But they can be forgotten just as easily! Just we get to another country where they have a republic! They'll crawl on their hands and knees when they see my uniform. On their hands and knees, I tell you! But not me! Oh, no. I'm not made for crawling. I've got guts,
55 backbone. And once I grab that first branch, you just watch me climb. I may be a valet now, but next year I'll be owning property; in ten years, I'll be living off my investments. Then I'll go to Rumania, get myself some decorations, and maybe—notice I only say maybe—end up as a count!

60 MISS JULIE: How wonderful, wonderful.

JEAN: Listen, in Rumania you can buy titles. You'll be a countess after all. My countess.

MISS JULIE: But I'm not interested in that. I'm leaving all that behind. Tell me you love me, Jean, or else—or else what dif-
65 ference does it make what I am?

JEAN: I'll tell you a thousand times—but later! Not now. And not here. Above all, let's keep our feelings out of this or we'll make a mess of everything. We have to look at this thing calmly and coolly, like sensible people. (*He takes out a cigar,
70 clips the end, and lights it.*) Now you sit there and I'll sit here, and we'll talk as if nothing had happened.

MISS JULIE: (*In anguish.*) My God, what are you? Don't you have any feelings?

JEAN: Feelings? Nobody's got more feelings than I have. But
75 I've learned to control them.

MISS JULIE: A few minutes ago you were kissing my shoe—and now—!

JEAN: (*Harshly.*) That was a few minutes ago. We've got other things to think about now!

80 MISS JULIE: Don't speak to me like that, Jean!

JEAN: I'm just trying to be sensible. We've been stupid once; let's not be stupid again. Your father might be back at any moment, and we've got to decide our future before then. — Now what do you think about my plans? Do you approve or
85 don't you?

MISS JULIE: I don't see anything wrong with them. Except one thing. For a big undertaking like that, you'd need a lot of capital. Have you got it?

JEAN: (*Chewing on his cigar.*) Have I got it? Of course I have.
90 I've got my knowledge of the business, my vast experience, my familiarity with languages. That's capital that counts for something, let me tell you.

MISS JULIE: You can't even buy the railway tickets with it.

JEAN: That's true. That's why I need a backer—someone to
95 put up the money.

MISS JULIE: Where can you find him on a moment's notice?

JEAN: You'll find him—if you want to be my partner.

MISS JULIE: I can't. And I don't have a penny to my name.

(*Pause.*)

JEAN: Then you can forget the whole thing.

100 MISS JULIE: Forget—?

JEAN: And things will stay just the way they are.

MISS JULIE: Do you think I'm going to live under the same roof with you as your mistress? Do you think I'm going to have people sneering at me behind my back? How do you think I'll ever be able to look my father in the face after this? No, no! Take me away from here, Jean—the shame, the humiliation. . . . What have I done? Oh, my God, my God! What have I done! *(She bursts into tears.)*

JEAN: Now don't start singing that tune. It won't work. What have you done that's so awful? You're not the first.

MISS JULIE: *(Crying hysterically.)* Now you think me contemptible—I'm falling, falling!

JEAN: Fall down to me, and I'll lift you up again!

MISS JULIE: What awful hold did you have over me? What drove me to you? The weak to the strong? The falling to the rising! Or maybe it was love? Love? This? You don't know what love is!

JEAN: Want to bet? Did you think I was a virgin?

MISS JULIE: You're coarse—vulgar! The things you say, the things you think!

JEAN: That's the way I was brought up. It's the way I am! Now don't get hysterical. And don't play the fine lady with me. We're eating off the same platter now. . . . That's better. Come over here and be a good girl and I'll treat you to something special. *(He opens the table drawer and takes out the wine bottle. He pours the wine into two used glasses.)*

MISS JULIE: Where did you get that wine?

JEAN: From the wine cellar.

MISS JULIE: My father's burgundy!

JEAN: Should be good enough for his son-in-law.

MISS JULIE: I was drinking beer and you—!

JEAN: Shows I have better taste than you.

MISS JULIE: Thief!

JEAN: You going to squeal on me?

MISS JULIE: Oh, God! Partner in crime with a petty house thief! I must have been drunk; I must have been walking in my sleep. Midsummer Night! Night of innocent games—

JEAN: Yes, very innocent!

MISS JULIE: *(Pacing up and down.)* Is there anyone here on earth as miserable as I am?

JEAN: Why be miserable? Look at the conquest you've made! Think of poor Christine in there. Don't you think she's got any feelings?

MISS JULIE: I thought so a while ago; I don't now. A servant's a servant—

JEAN: And a whore's a whore!

MISS JULIE: *(Falls to her knees and clasps her hands together.)* Oh, God in heaven, put an end to my worthless life! Lift me out of this awful filth I'm sinking in! Save me! Save me!

JEAN: I feel sorry for you, I have to admit it. When I was lying in the onion beds, looking up at you on the rose terrace, I—I'm telling you the truth now—I had the same dirty thoughts that all boys have.

MISS JULIE: And you said you wanted to die for me!

JEAN: In the oat bin? That was only a story.

MISS JULIE: A lie, you mean.

JEAN: *(Getting sleepy.)* Practically. I think I read it in a paper about a chimney sweep who curled up in a wood-bin with some lilacs because they were going to arrest him for non support of his child.

MISS JULIE: Now I see you as you really are.

JEAN: What did you expect me to do? It's always the fancy talk that gets the women.

MISS JULIE: You dog!

JEAN: You bitch!

MISS JULIE: Well, now you've seen the eagle's back—

JEAN: Wasn't exactly its back—!

MISS JULIE: I was going to be the window dressing for your hotel—!

JEAN: And I the hotel—!

MISS JULIE: Sitting at the desk, attracting your customers, padding your bills—!

JEAN: I could manage that myself—!

MISS JULIE: How can a human soul be so dirty and filthy?

JEAN: Then why don't you clean it up?

MISS JULIE: You lackey! You shoeshine boy! Stand up when I talk to you!

JEAN: You lackey lover! You bootblack's tramp! Shut your mouth and get out of here! Who do you think you are telling me I'm coarse? I've never seen anybody in my class behave as crudely as you did tonight. Have you ever seen any of the girls around here grab at a man like you did? Do you think any of the girls of my class would throw themselves at a man like that? I've never seen the like of it except in animals and prostitutes!

MISS JULIE: *(Crushed.)* That's right! Hit me! Walk all over me! It's all I deserve. I'm rotten. But help me! Help me to get out of this—if there is any way out for me!

JEAN: *(Less harsh.)* I'd be doing myself an injustice if I didn't admit that part of the credit for this seduction belongs to me. But do you think a person in my position would have dared to look twice at you if you hadn't asked for it? I'm still amazed—

MISS JULIE: And still proud.

JEAN: Why not? But I've got to confess the victory was a little too easy to give me any real thrill.

MISS JULIE: Go on, hit me again!

JEAN: *(Standing up.)* No. . . . I'm sorry I said that. I never hit a person who's down, especially a woman. I can't deny that, in one way, it was good to find out that what I saw glittering up above was only fool's gold, to see that the eagle's back was as gray as its belly, that the smooth cheek was just powder, and that there could be dirt under the manicured nails, that the handkerchief was soiled even though it smelled of perfume. But, in another way, it hurts to find that everything I was striving for wasn't very high above me after all, wasn't even real. It hurts me to see you sink far lower than your own cook. Hurts, like seeing the last flowers cut to pieces by the autumn rains and turned to muck.

MISS JULIE: You talk as if you already stood high above me.

JEAN: Well, don't I? Don't forget I could make you a countess but you can never make me a count.

MISS JULIE: I have a father for a count. You can never have that!

JEAN: True. But I might father my own counts—that is, if—

MISS JULIE: You're a thief! I'm not!

JEAN: There are worse things than being a thief. A lot worse. And besides, when I take a position in a house, I consider myself a member of the family—in a way, like a child in the house. It's no crime for a child to steal a few ripe cherries when they're falling off the trees, is it? *(He begins to feel passionate again.)* Miss Julie, you're a beautiful woman, much too good for the likes of me. You got carried away by your emotions and now you want to cover up your mistake by telling yourself that you love me. You don't love me. Maybe you were attracted by my looks—in which case your kind of love is no better than mine. But I could never be satisfied to be just an animal for you, and I could never make you love me.

MISS JULIE: How do you know that for sure?

JEAN: You mean there's a chance? I could love you, there's no doubt about that. You're beautiful, you're refined—*(He goes up to her and takes her hand.)*—educated, lovable when you want to be, and once you set a man's heart on fire, I'll bet it burns forever. *(He puts his arm around her waist.)* You're like hot wine with strong spices. One of your kisses is enough to—

(He attempts to lead her out, but she rather reluctantly breaks away from him.)

MISS JULIE: Let me go. You don't get me that way.

JEAN: Then how? Not by petting you and not with pretty words, not by planning for the future, not by saving you from humiliation! Then how, tell me how?

MISS JULIE: How? How? I don't know how! I don't know at all!—I hate you like I hate rats, but I can't get away from you.

JEAN: Then come away with me!

MISS JULIE: *(Pulling herself together.)* Away? Yes, we'll go away!—But I'm so tired. Pour me a glass of wine, will you?

(JEAN pours the wine, MISS JULIE looks at her watch.)

Let's talk first. We still have a little time. *(She empties the glass of wine and holds it out for more.)*

JEAN: Don't overdo it. You'll get drunk.

MISS JULIE: What difference does it make?

JEAN: What difference? It looks cheap.—What did you want to say to me?

MISS JULIE: We're going to run away together, right? But we'll talk first—that is, I'll talk. So far you've done all the talking. You've told me your life, now I'll tell you mine. That way we'll know each other through and through before we become . . . traveling companions.

JEAN: Wait a minute. Are you sure you won't regret this afterward—surrendering your secrets to me?

MISS JULIE: I thought you were my friend.

JEAN: I am—sometimes. Just don't count on it.

MISS JULIE: You don't mean that. Anyway, everybody knows my secrets.—My mother's parents were very ordinary people, just commoners. She was brought up, according to the theories of her time, to believe in equality, the independence of women, and all that. And she had a strong aversion to marriage. When my father proposed to her, she swore she would never become his wife but that she might possibly consent to become his mistress. So he told her he didn't want to see the woman he loved enjoy less respect than he did. But she said she didn't care what the world thought—and he, believing that he couldn't live without her, accepted her conditions. That did it. From then on he was cut off from his old circle of friends and left without anything to do in the house, which couldn't have kept him occupied anyway. Then I came into the world—against my mother's wishes, as far as I can make out. My mother decided to bring me up as a nature child. And on top of that I had to learn everything a boy learns, so I could be living proof that women were just as good as men. I had to wear boy's clothes, learn to handle horses—but not to milk the cows! Girls did that! I was made to groom the horses and harness them, and learn farming and go hunting—I even had to learn how to slaughter the animals. It was disgusting. Awful! And on the estate all the men were set to doing women's chores, and the women to doing men's work—with the result that the whole place fell to pieces, and we became the local laughing-stock. Finally, my father must have come out of his trance. He rebelled, and everything was changed according to his wishes. They got married—very quietly. Then my mother got sick. I don't know what kind of sickness it was, but she often had convulsions, and she would hide herself in the attic or in the garden, and sometimes she would stay out all night. Then there occurred that big fire you've heard about. The house, the stables, the cowsheds, all burned down—and under very peculiar circumstances that led one to suspect arson. You see, the accident occurred the day after the insurance expired, and the premiums on the new policy, which my father had sent in, were delayed through the messenger's carelessness, and didn't arrive in time.

(She refills her glass and drinks.)

JEAN: You've had enough.

MISS JULIE: Who cares!—We were left without a penny to our name. We had to sleep in the carriages. My father didn't know where to turn for money to rebuild the house. Then Mother suggested to him that he might try to borrow money from an old friend of hers, who owned a brick factory not far from here. Father took out a loan, but there wasn't any interest charged, which surprised him. So the place was rebuilt. *(She drinks some more.)* Do you know who set fire to the place?

JEAN: Your honorable mother!

MISS JULIE: Do you know who the brick manufacturer was?

JEAN: Your mother's lover?

MISS JULIE: Do you know whose money it was?

JEAN: Let me think a minute. . . . No, I give up.

MISS JULIE: It was my mother's!

JEAN: The count's, you mean. Or was there a marriage settlement?

MISS JULIE: There wasn't a settlement. My mother had a little money of her own which she didn't want under my father's control, so she invested it with her—friend.

JEAN: Who pinched it!

MISS JULIE: Right! He kept it for himself. Well, my father found out what happened. But he couldn't go to court, couldn't pay his wife's lover, couldn't prove that it was his wife's money. That was how my mother got her revenge because he had taken control of the house. He was on the verge of shooting himself. There was even a rumor that he tried and failed. But somehow he took a new lease on life and he forced my mother to pay for her mistakes. Can you imagine what those five years were like for me? I loved my father, but I took my mother's side because I didn't know the whole story. She had taught me to hate all men—I'm sure you've heard how she hated men—and I swore to her that I'd never be slave to any man.

JEAN: You got engaged to the attorney, didn't you?

MISS JULIE: Only to make him my slave.

JEAN: I guess he didn't go for that, did he?

MISS JULIE: Oh, he wanted to well enough. I didn't give him
340   the chance. I got bored with him.

JEAN: Yes, so I noticed—in the stable yard.

MISS JULIE: What did you notice?

JEAN: I saw how he—. [Still see it on your cheek.

MISS JULIE: What!

345 JEAN: The stripe on your cheek.] He broke it off.

MISS JULIE: It's a lie! I broke it off! Did he tell you that? He's
   beneath contempt!

JEAN: Come on now, as bad as that? So you hate men, hm?

MISS JULIE: Yes, I do. . . . Most of the time. But sometimes,
350   when I can't help myself—oh . . . *(She shudders in disgust.)*

JEAN: Then you hate me, too?

MISS JULIE: You have no idea how much! I'd like to see you
   killed like an animal—

JEAN: Like when you're caught having sex with an animal: you
355   get two years at hard labor and the animal is killed. Right?

MISS JULIE: Right.

JEAN: But there's no one to catch us—and *no animal!*—So
   what are we going to do?

MISS JULIE: Go away from here.

360 JEAN: To torture ourselves to death?

MISS JULIE: No. To enjoy ourselves for a day or two, or a week,
   for as long as can—and then—to die—

JEAN: Die? That's stupid! I've got a better idea: start a hotel!

MISS JULIE: *(Continuing without hearing* JEAN.*)*—on the
365   shores of Lake Como, where the sun is always shining, where
   the laurels bloom at Christmas, and the golden oranges glow
   on the trees.

JEAN: Lake Como is a stinking wet hole, and the only oranges
   I saw there were on the fruit stands. But it's a good tourist
370   spot with a lot of villas and cottages that are rented out to
   lovers. Now there's a profitable business. You know why?
   They rent the villa for the whole season, but they leave after
   three weeks.

MISS JULIE: *(Naively.)* Why after only three weeks?

375 JEAN: Because that's about as long as they can stand each
   other. Why else? But they still have to pay the rent. You see?
   Then you rent it out again to another couple, and so on.
   There's no shortage of love—even if it doesn't last very long.

MISS JULIE: Then you don't want to die with me?

380 JEAN: I don't want to die at all! I enjoy life too much. And
   moreover, I consider taking your own life a sin against the
   Providence that gave us life.

MISS JULIE: You believe in God? You?

JEAN: Yes, certainly I do! I go to church every other Sunday—.
385   Honestly, I've had enough of this talk. I'm going to bed.

MISS JULIE: Really? You think you're going to get off that easy?
   Don't you know that a man owes something to the woman
   he's dishonored?

JEAN: *(Takes out his purse and throws a silver coin on the table.)*
390   There you are. I don't want to owe anybody anything.

MISS JULIE: *(Pretending not to notice.)* Do you know what the
   law says—?

343–345 **Still . . . cheek** the passage in brackets was deleted in Strindberg's manuscript, probably by Strindberg himself

JEAN: Lucky for you the law says nothing about women who seduce men!

MISS JULIE: *(As before.)* What else can we do but go away from 395
   here, get married, and get divorced?

JEAN: Suppose I refuse to enter into this *mésalliance?*

MISS JULIE: *Mésalliance?*

JEAN: For me! I've got better ancestors than you. I don't have a
   female arsonist in my family. 400

MISS JULIE: You can't prove that.

JEAN: You can't prove the opposite—because we don't have
   any family records—except in the police files. But I've read
   the whole history of your family in that peerage book in the
   drawing room. Do you know who the founder of your family 405
   line was? A miller—who let his wife sleep with the king one
   night during the Danish war. I don't have any ancestors like
   that. I don't have any ancestors at all! But I can become an
   ancestor myself.

MISS JULIE: This is what I get for baring my heart and soul to 410
   someone too low to understand, for sacrificing the honor of
   my family—

JEAN: Dishonor! —I warned you, remember? Drinking makes
   one talk, and talking's bad.

MISS JULIE: Oh, how sorry I am! . . . If only it had never hap- 415
   pened! . . . If only you at least loved me!

JEAN: For the last time—what do you want me to do? Cry?
   Jump over your whip? Kiss you? Lure you to Lake Como for
   three weeks and then—? What am I supposed to do? What
   do you want? I've had more than I can take. This is what I 420
   get for involving myself with women. . . . Miss Julie, I can
   see that you're unhappy; I know that you're suffering; but I
   simply cannot understand you. My people don't behave like
   this. We don't hate each other. We make love for the fun of
   it, when we can get any time off from our work. But we don't 425
   have time for it all day and all night like you do. If you ask
   me, you're sick, Miss Julie. Your mother's mind was affected,
   you know. There are whole counties affected with pietism.
   That was your mother's trouble—pietism. It's spreading like
   the plague. 430

MISS JULIE: You can be understanding, Jean. You're talking to
   me like a human being now.

JEAN: Well, be human yourself. You spit on me, but you don't
   let me wipe it off—on you.

MISS JULIE: Help me, Jean. Help me. Tell me what I should 435
   do, that's all—which way to go.

JEAN: For Christ's sake, if only I knew myself!

MISS JULIE: I've been crazy—I've been out of my mind—but
   does that mean there's no way out for me?

JEAN: Stay here as if nothing had happened. Nobody knows 440
   anything.

MISS JULIE: Impossible! Everybody who works here knows.
   Christine knows.

JEAN: They don't know a thing. Anyhow they'd never believe it.

MISS JULIE: *(Slowly, significantly.)* But . . . it might happen 445
   again.

JEAN: That's true!

MISS JULIE: And one time there might be . . . consequences.

JEAN: *(Stunned.)* Consequences!! What on earth have I been
   thinking of? You're right. There's only one thing to do: get 450
   away from here! Immediately! I can't go with you—that
   would give the whole game away. You'll have to go by yourself. Somewhere—I don't care where!

MISS JULIE: By myself? Where? —Oh, no, Jean, I can't. I can't!

455 JEAN: You've got to! Before the count comes back. You know as well as I do what will happen if you stay here. After one mistake, you figure you might as well go on—the damage is already done. Then you get more and more careless until—finally you're exposed. I tell you, you've got to get out of the

460 country. Afterward you can write to the count and tell him everything—leaving me out, of course. He'd never figure it was me. He wouldn't even let himself think it was me.

MISS JULIE: I'll go—if you'll come with me!

JEAN: Lady, are you out of your mind? "Miss Julie elopes with

465 her footman." The day after tomorrow it would be in all the papers. The count would never live it down.

MISS JULIE: I can't go away. I can't stay. Help me. I'm so tired, so awfully tired. . . . Tell me what to do. Order me. Start me going. I can't think anymore, can't move anymore . . .

470 JEAN: Now do you realize how weak you all are? What gives you the right to go strutting around with your noses in the air as if you owned the world? All right, I'll give you your orders. Go up and get dressed. Get some traveling money. And come back down here.

475 MISS JULIE: (*Almost in a whisper.*) Come up with me!

JEAN: To your room? . . . You're going crazy again! (*He hesitates a moment.*) No! No! Go! Right now! (*He takes her hand and leads her out.*)

MISS JULIE: (*As she is leaving.*) Don't be so harsh, Jean.

480 JEAN: Orders always sound harsh. You've never had to take them.

(JEAN, *left alone, heaves a sigh of relief and sits down at the table. He takes out a notebook and a pencil and begins to calculate, counting aloud now and then. The pantomime continues until* CHRISTINE *enters, dressed for church, and carrying* JEAN's *white tie and shirtfront in her hand.*)

CHRISTINE: Lord in Heaven, what a mess! What on earth have you been doing?

JEAN: It was Miss Julie. She dragged the whole crowd in here.

485 You must have been sleeping awfully sound if you didn't hear anything.

CHRISTINE: I slept like a log.

JEAN: You already dressed for church?

CHRISTINE: Yes, indeed. Don't you remember you promised to

490 go to communion with me today?

JEAN: Oh, yes. Of course, I remember. I see you've brought my things. All right. Come on, put it on me. (*He sits down, and* CHRISTINE *starts to put the white tie and shirtfront on him. Pause.*)

495 JEAN: (*Yawning.*) What's the lesson for today?

CHRISTINE: The beheading of John the Baptist, what else? It's Midsummer. It's his feast day.

JEAN: My God, that will go on forever.—Hey, you're choking me! . . . Oh, I'm so sleepy, so sleepy.

500 CHRISTINE: What were you doing up all night? You look green in the face.

JEAN: I've been sitting here talking with Miss Julie.

CHRISTINE: That girl! She doesn't know how to behave herself!

(*Pause.*)

JEAN: Tell me something, Christine . . .

505 CHRISTINE: Well, what?

JEAN: Isn't it strange when you think about it? Her, I mean.

CHRISTINE: What's so strange?

JEAN: Everything!

(*Pause.* CHRISTINE *looks at the half-empty glasses on the table.*)

CHRISTINE: Have you been drinking with her?

JEAN: Yes!

510 CHRISTINE: Shame on you!—Look me in the eyes! You haven't . . .?

JEAN: Yes!

CHRISTINE: Is it possible? Is it really possible?

JEAN: (*Thinking about it.*) Yes. It is.

515 CHRISTINE: Oh, how disgusting! I could never have believed anything like this would happen! No. No. This is too much!

JEAN: Don't tell me you're jealous of her?

CHRISTINE: No, not of her. If it had been Clara—or Sophie—I would have scratched your eyes out! But her—? That's dif-

520 ferent. I don't know why. . . . But it's still disgusting!

JEAN: You're not mad at her?

CHRISTINE: No. Mad at you. You were mean and cruel to do a thing like that, very mean. The poor girl! . . . Let me tell you, I'm not going to stay in this house a moment longer, not

525 when I can't have any respect for my employers.

JEAN: Why do you want to respect them?

CHRISTINE: Don't try to be smart. You don't want to work for people who behave like pigs, do you? Well, do you? If you ask me, you'd be lowering yourself by doing that.

530 JEAN: Oh, I don't know. I think it's rather comforting to find out that they're not one damn bit better than we are.

CHRISTINE: Well, I don't. If they're not any better, there's no point in us trying to be like them. —And think of the count. Think of all the sorrows he's been through in his time. My

535 God! I won't stay in this house any longer. . . . Imagine! You, of all people! If it had been the attorney fellow; if it had been somebody respectable—

JEAN: Now just a minute—!

CHRISTINE: Oh, you're all right in your own way. But there's a

540 big difference between one class and another. You can't deny that. —No, this is something I can never get over. She was so proud, and so sarcastic about men, you'd never believe she'd go and throw herself at one. And at somebody like you! And she was going to have Diana shot because the poor

545 thing ran after the gatekeeper's mongrel! —Well, I tell you, I've had enough! I'm not going to stay here any longer. When my term's up, I'm leaving.

JEAN: Then what'll you do?

CHRISTINE: Well, since you brought it up, it's about time that

550 you got yourself a decent place, if we're going to get married.

JEAN: Why should I go looking for another place? I could never get a job like this if I'm married.

CHRISTINE: Well, I know that! But you could get a job as a porter, or maybe try to get a government job as a caretaker

555 somewhere. A square deal and a square meal, that's what you get from the government—and a pension for the wife and children.

JEAN: (*Wryly.*) Fine, fine! But I'm not the kind of guy who thinks about dying for his wife and children this early in the

560 game. Let me tell you, I've got slightly bigger plans than that.

CHRISTINE: Plans! Ha! What about your obligations? You'd better start giving them a little thought!

565 JEAN: Don't start nagging me about obligations! I know what I have to do without you telling me. (*He hears a sound upstairs.*) Anyhow, we'll have plenty of chance to talk about this later. You just go and get yourself ready, and we'll be off to church.

570 CHRISTINE: Who is that walking around up there?

JEAN: I don't know. Clara, I suppose. Who else?

CHRISTINE: (*Starting to leave.*) It can't be the count, can it? Could he have come back without anybody hearing him?

JEAN: (*Frightened.*) The count? No, it can't be. He would have 575 rung.

CHRISTINE: (*Leaving.*) God help us! I've never heard the like of this.

(*The sun has now risen and strikes the tops of the trees in the park. As the scene progresses, the light shifts gradually until it is shining very obliquely through the windows.* JEAN *goes to the door and signals.* MISS JULIE *enters, dressed for travel, and carrying a small birdcage, covered with a towel. She sets the cage down on a chair.*)

MISS JULIE: I'm ready now.

JEAN: Shh! Christine's awake.

580 MISS JULIE: (*Extremely tense and nervous during the following.*) Did she suspect anything?

JEAN: She doesn't know a thing. —My God, what happened to you?

MISS JULIE: What do you mean? Do I look so strange?

585 JEAN: You're white as a ghost, and you've—excuse me—you've got dirt on your face.

MISS JULIE: Let me wash it off. (*She goes over to the washbasin and washes her face and hands.*) There! Do you have a towel? . . . Oh, look, the sun's coming up!

590 JEAN: That breaks the magic spell!

MISS JULIE: Yes, we were spellbound last night, weren't we? Midsummer madness . . . Jean, listen to me! Come with me. I've got the money!

JEAN: (*Suspiciously.*) Enough?

595 MISS JULIE: Enough for a start. Come with me, Jean. I can't travel alone today. Midsummer Day on a stifling hot train, packed in with crowds of people, all staring at me—stopping at every station when I want to be flying. I can't, Jean, I can't! . . . And everything will remind me of the past. Mid 600 summer Day when I was a child and the church was decorated with leaves—birch leaves and lilacs . . . the table spread for dinner with friends and relatives . . . and after dinner, dancing in the park, with flowers and games. Oh, no matter how far you travel, the memories tag right along in 605 the baggage car . . . and the regrets and the remorse.

JEAN: All right, I'll go with you! But it's got to be now—before it's too late! This very instant!

MISS JULIE: Hurry and get dressed! (*She picks up the birdcage.*)

JEAN: No baggage! It would give us away.

610 MISS JULIE: Nothing. Only what we can take to our seats.

JEAN: (*As he gets his hat.*) What in the devil have you got there? What is that?

MISS JULIE: It's only my canary. I can't leave it behind.

JEAN: A canary! My God, do you expect us to carry a birdcage 615 around with us? You're crazy. Put that cage down!

MISS JULIE: It's the only thing I'm taking with me from my home—the only living thing who loves me since Diana was unfaithful to me! Don't be cruel, Jean. Let me take it with me.

JEAN: I told you to put that cage down! —And don't talk so 620 loud. Christine can hear us.

MISS JULIE: No, I won't leave it with a stranger. I won't. I'd rather have you kill it.

JEAN: Give it here, the little pest. I'll wring its neck.

MISS JULIE: Oh, don't hurt it. Don't—. No, I can't do it! 625

JEAN: Don't worry, I can. Give it here.

(MISS JULIE *takes the bird out of the cage and kisses it.*)

MISS JULIE: Oh, my little Serena, must you die and leave your mistress?

JEAN: You don't have to make a scene of it. It's a question of 630 your whole life and future. You're wasting time!

(JEAN *grabs the canary from her, carries it to the chopping block, and picks up a meat cleaver.* MISS JULIE *turns away.*)

You should have learned how to kill chickens instead of shooting revolvers—(*He brings the cleaver down.*)—then a drop of blood wouldn't make you faint.

MISS JULIE: (*Screaming.*) Kill me too! Kill me! You can kill an innocent creature without turning a hair—then kill me. Oh, 635 how I hate you! I loathe you! There's blood between us. I curse the moment I first laid eyes on you! I curse the moment I was conceived in my mother's womb.

JEAN: What good does your cursing do? Let's get out of here!

MISS JULIE: (*Approaches the chopping block, drawn to it* 640 *against her will.*) No, I don't want to go yet. I can't. —I have to see. —Shh! (*She listens but keeps her eyes fastened on the chopping block and cleaver.*) You don't think I can stand the sight of blood, do you? You think I'm so weak, don't you? Oh, how I'd love to see your blood, your brains on that chop- 645 ping block. I'd love to see the whole of your sex swimming in a sea of blood just like that. I could drink blood out of your skull. Use your chest as a foot bath, dip my toes in your guts! I could eat your heart roasted whole! —You think I'm weak! You think I loved you because my womb hungered for your 650 semen. You think I want to carry your brood under my heart and feed it with my blood? Bear your child and take your name?—Come to think of it, what is your name? I've never even heard your last name. I'll bet you don't have one. I'd be Mrs. Doorman or Madame Garbageman. You dog with *my* 655 name on your collar—you lackey with *my* initials on your buttons! Do you think I'm going to share you with my cook and fight over you with my maid?! Ohh! —You think I'm a coward who's going to run away! No, I'm going to stay— come hell or high water. My father will come home—find 660 his desk broken into—his money gone. He'll ring—on that bell—two rings for the valet. And then he'll send for the sheriff—and I'll tell him everything. Everything! Oh, what a relief it'll be to have it all over . . . over and done with . . . if only it will be over. . . . He'll have a stroke and die . . . and 665 there'll be an end to all of us. There'll be peace . . . and quiet . . . forever. . . . The coat of arms will be broken on his coffin; the count's line will be extinct—while the valet's breed will continue in an orphanage, win triumphs in the gutter, and end in jail! 670

(CHRISTINE *enters, dressed for church and with a hymn-book in her hand.* MISS JULIE *rushes over to her and throws herself into her arms as if seeking protection.*)

MISS JULIE: Help me, Christine! Protect me against this man!

CHRISTINE: *(Cold and unmoved.)* This is a fine way to behave on a holy day! *(She sees the chopping block.)* Just look at the mess you've made there! How do you explain that? And what's all this shouting and screaming about?

MISS JULIE: Christine, you're a woman, you're my friend! I warn you, watch out for this—this monster!

JEAN: *(Feeling awkward.)* If you ladies are going to talk, you won't want me around. I think I'll go and shave. *(He slips out to the right.)*

MISS JULIE: You've got to understand, Christine! You've got to listen to me!

CHRISTINE: No, I don't. I don't understand this kind of shenanigans at all. Where do you think you're going dressed like that? And Jean with his hat on? —Well? —Well?

MISS JULIE: Listen to me, Christine! If you'll just listen to me, I'll tell you everything.

CHRISTINE: I don't want to know anything.

MISS JULIE: You've got to listen to me—!

CHRISTINE: What about? About your stupid behavior with Jean? I tell you that doesn't bother me at all, because it's none of my business. But if you have any silly idea about talking him into skipping out with you, I'll soon put a stop to that.

MISS JULIE: *(Extremely tense.)* Christine, please don't get upset. Listen to me. I can't stay here, and Jean can't stay here. So you see, we have to go away.

CHRISTINE: Hm, hm, hm.

MISS JULIE: *(Suddenly brightening up.)* Wait! I've got an idea! Why couldn't all three of us go away together?—out of the country—to Switzerland—and start a hotel? I've got the money, you see. Jean and I would be responsible for the whole affair—and Christine, you could run the kitchen, I thought. Doesn't that sound wonderful! Say you'll come, Christine, then everything will be settled. Say you will! Please! *(She throws her arms around* CHRISTINE *and pats her.)*

CHRISTINE: *(Remaining aloof and unmoved.)* Hm. Hm.

MISS JULIE: *(Presto tempo.)* You've never been traveling, Christine. You have to get out and see the world. You can't imagine how wonderful it is to travel by train—constantly new faces, new countries. We'll go to Hamburg, and stop over to look at the zoo—it's famous, has everything—you'll love that. And we'll go to the theater and the opera. And then when we get to Munich, we'll go to the museums, Christine. They have Rubenses and Raphaels there—those great painters, you know. Of course you've heard about Munich where King Ludwig lived—you know, the king who went mad. And then we can go and see his castles—they're just like the ones you read about in fairy tales. And from there it's just a short trip to Switzerland—with the Alps. Think of the Alps, Christine, covered with snow in the middle of summer. And oranges grow there, and laurel trees that are green the whole year round—

*(*JEAN *can be seen in the wings at the right, sharpening his straight razor on a strop held between his teeth and his left hand. He listens to* MISS JULIE *with a satisfied expression on his face, now and then nodding approvingly.* MISS JULIE *continues tempo prestissimo.)*

—and that's where we'll get a hotel. I'll sit at the desk while Jean stands at the door and receives the guests, goes out shopping, writes the letters. What a life that will be! The train whistle blowing, then the bus arriving, then a bell ringing upstairs, then the bell in the restaurant rings—and I'll be making out the bills—and I know just how much to salt them—you can't imagine how timid tourists are when you shove a bill in their face!—And you, Christine, you'll run the whole kitchen—there'll be not standing at the stove for you—of course not. If you're going to talk to the people, you'll have to dress. And with your looks—I'm not trying to flatter you, Christine—you'll run off with some man one fine day—a rich Englishman, that's who it'll be, they're so easy to—*(Slowing down.)*—to catch. —Then we'll all be rich. —We'll build a villa on Lake Como. —Maybe it does rain there sometimes, but—*(More and more lifelessly.)*—the sun has to shine sometimes, too—even if it looks cloudy. —And—then . . . or else we can always travel some more—and come back . . . *(Pause.)*—here . . . or somewhere else . . .

CHRISTINE: Do you really believe a word of that yourself, Miss Julie?

MISS JULIE: *(Completely beaten.)* Do I believe a word of it myself?

CHRISTINE: Do you?

MISS JULIE: *(Exhausted.)* I don't know. I don't believe anything anymore. *(She sinks down on the bench and lays her head between her arms on the table.)* Nothing. Nothing at all.

CHRISTINE: *(Turns to the right and faces* JEAN.*)* So! You were planning to run away, were you?

JEAN: *(Taken aback, lays his razor down on the table.)* We weren't exactly going to run away! Don't exaggerate. You heard Miss Julie's plans. Even if she's tired now after being up all night, her plans are perfectly practical.

CHRISTINE: Well, just listen to you! Did you really think you could get me to cook for that little—!

JEAN: *(Sharply.)* You keep a respectful tongue in your mouth when you talk to your mistress! Understand?

CHRISTINE: Mistress!

JEAN: Yes, mistress!

CHRISTINE: Well of all the—! I don't have to listen—

JEAN: Yes, you do! You need to listen more and blabber less. Miss Julie is your mistress. Don't you forget that! And if you're going to despise her for what she did, you ought to despise yourself for the same reason.

CHRISTINE: I've always held myself high enough to—

JEAN: High enough to make you look down on others!

CHRISTINE: —enough to keep from lowering myself beneath my station. Don't you dare say that the count's cook has ever had anything to do with the stable groom or the swineherd. Don't you dare!

JEAN: Yes, you got yourself a decent man. Lucky you!

CHRISTINE: What kind of a decent man is it who sells the oats from the count's stables?

JEAN: Listen to who's talking! You get the gravy on the groceries and take bribes from the butcher!

CHRISTINE: How dare you say a thing like that!

JEAN: And you say you can't respect your employers. You of all people! You!

CHRISTINE: Are you going to church or aren't you? You need a good sermon after your great exploits.

JEAN: No, I'm not going to church! Go yourself. Go tell God how bad you are.

CHRISTINE: Yes, I'll do just that. And I'll come back with enough forgiveness for your sins, too. Our Redeemer suffered and died on the cross for all our sins, and if we come to

790   Him in faith and with a penitent heart, He will take all our
      sins upon Himself.
JEAN: Rake-offs included?
MISS JULIE: Do you really believe that, Christine?
CHRISTINE: With all my heart, as sure as I'm standing here. It
795   was the faith I was born into, and I've held on to it since I was
      a little girl, Miss Julie. Where sin aboundeth, there grace
      aboundeth also.
MISS JULIE: If I had your faith, Christine, if only—
CHRISTINE: But you see, that's something you can't have with
800   out God's special grace. And it is not granted to everyone to
      receive it.
MISS JULIE: Then who receives it?
CHRISTINE: That's the secret of the workings of grace, Miss
      Julie, and God is no respecter of persons. With Him the last
805   shall be first—
MISS JULIE: In that case, he does have respect for the last,
      doesn't he?
CHRISTINE: (*Continuing.*)—and it is easier for a camel to go
      through the eye of a needle than for a rich man to enter the
810   kingdom of God. That's how things are, Miss Julie. I'm
      going to leave now—alone. And on my way out I'm going to
      tell the stable boy not to let any horses out, in case anyone
      has any ideas about leaving before the count comes home.
      Goodbye. (*She leaves.*)
815   JEAN: She's a devil in skirts! —All because of a canary!
MISS JULIE: (*Listlessly.*) Never mind the canary. . . . Do you see
      any way out of this, any end to it?
JEAN: (*After thinking for a moment.*) No.
MISS JULIE: What would you do if you were in my place?
820   JEAN: In your place? Let me think. . . . An aristocrat, a woman,
      and—fallen. . . . I don't know.—Or maybe I do.
MISS JULIE: (*Picks up the razor and makes a gesture with it.*)
      Like this?
JEAN: Yes. But I wouldn't do it, you understand. That's the dif-
825   ference between us.
MISS JULIE: Because you're a man and I'm a woman? What dif-
      ference does that make?
JEAN: Just the difference that there is—between a man and a
      woman.
830   MISS JULIE: (*Holding the razor in her hand.*) I want to! But I
      can't do it. My father couldn't do it either, that time when he
      should have.
JEAN: No, he was right not to. He had to get his revenge first.
MISS JULIE: And now my mother is getting her revenge again
835   through me.
JEAN: Didn't you ever love your father, Miss Julie?
MISS JULIE: Yes, enormously. But I must have hated him too.
      I must have hated him without knowing it. It was he who
      brought me up to despise my own sex, to be half woman
840   and half man. Who's to blame for what has happened? My
      father, my mother, myself? Myself? I don't have a self that's
      my own. I don't have a single thought I didn't get from my
      father, not an emotion I didn't get from my mother. And
      that last idea—about all people being equal—I got that
845   from him, my fiancé. That's why I say he's beneath con-
      tempt. How can it be my own fault? Put the blame on Jesus,
      like Christine does? I'm too proud to do that—and too in-
      telligent, thanks to what my father taught me. . . . A rich
      man can't get into heaven? That's a lie. But at least Chris-
850   tine, who's got money in the savings bank, won't get in. . . .

Who's to blame? What difference does it make who's to
blame? I'm still the one who has to bear the guilt, suffer the
consequences—
JEAN: Yes, but—

(*The bell rings sharply twice.* MISS JULIE *jumps up.* JEAN
changes his coat.)

JEAN: The count's back! What if Christine—(*He goes to the*   855
      speaking tube, taps on it, and listens.)
MISS JULIE: Has he looked in his desk yet?
JEAN: This is Jean, sir! (*Listens. The audience cannot hear what
      the count says.*) Yes, sir! (*Listens.*) Yes, as soon as I
      can. (*Listens.*) Yes, at once, sir! (*Listens.*) Very good, sir! In   860
      half an hour.
MISS JULIE: (*Trembling with anxiety.*) What did he say? For
      God's sake, what did he say?
JEAN: He ordered his boots and his coffee in half an hour.
MISS JULIE: Half an hour then! . . . Oh, I'm so tired. I can't   865
      bring myself to do anything. Can't repent, can't run away,
      can't stay, can't live . . . can't die. Help me, Jean. Command
      me, and I'll obey like a dog. Do me this last favor. Save my
      honor, save his name. You know what I ought to do but can't
      force myself to do. Let me use your willpower. You com-   870
      mand me and I'll obey.
JEAN: I don't know—. I can't either, not now. I don't know
      why. It's as if this coat made me—I can't give you orders in
      this. And now, after the count has spoken to me, I—I can't
      really explain it—but—I've got the backbone of a damned   875
      lackey! If the count came down here now and ordered me to
      cut my throat, I'd do it on the spot.
MISS JULIE: Then pretend you're him. Pretend I'm you. You
      were such a good actor just a while ago, when you were
      kneeling before me. You were the aristocrat then. Or else—   880
      have you been to the theater and seen a hypnotist?

(JEAN *nods.*)

      He says to his subject, "Take this broom!" and he takes it. He
      says, "Now sweep!" and he sweeps.
JEAN: The person has to be asleep!
MISS JULIE: (*Ecstatic, transported.*) I'm already asleep. The   885
      whole room has turned to smoke. You seem like an iron
      stove, a stove that looks like a man in black with a high hat.
      Your eyes are glowing like fading coals in a dying fire. Your
      face is a white smudge, like ashes.

(*The sun is now shining in on the floor and falls on* JEAN.)

      It's so good and warm—(*She rubs her hands together as if*   890
      warming them at a fire.)—and so bright—and so peaceful.
JEAN: (*Takes the razor and puts it in her hand.*) There's the
      broom. Go now, when the sun is up—out into the barn—
      and—(*He whispers in her ear.*)
MISS JULIE: (*Waking up.*) Thanks! I'm going to get my rest.   895
      But tell me one thing. Tell me that the first can also receive
      the gift of grace. Tell me that, even if you don't believe it.
JEAN: The first? I can't tell you that. —Wait a moment, Miss
      Julie. I know what I can tell you. You're no longer one of the
      first. You're one of—the last.   900
MISS JULIE: That's true! I'm one of the last. I am the very
      last!— Oh!—Now I can't go! Tell me just once more, tell me
      to go!
JEAN: Now I can't either. I can't!

905 MISS JULIE: And the first shall be the last . . .

JEAN: Don't think—don't think! You're taking all my strength from me. You're making me a coward. . . . What?! I thought I saw the bell move. No. . . . Let me stuff some paper in it. — Afraid of a bell! But it isn't just a bell. There's somebody be-

910 hind it. A hand that makes it move. And there's something that makes the hand move. —Stop your ears, that's it, stop your ears! But it only rings louder. Rings louder and louder until you answer it. And then it's too late. Then the sheriff comes—and then—(*There are two sharp rings on the bell.* JEAN *gives a start, then straightens himself up.*) It's horrible! 915 But there's no other way for it to end. —Go!

(MISS JULIE *walks resolutely out through the door.*)

■ OSCAR WILDE ■

Oscar Fingal O'Flahertie Willis Wilde (1854–1900) is best known as the esthete's esthete of 1880s and 1890s London, famous for his epigrammatic wit; for his novel *The Picture of Dorian Gray* (1890) and the moody symbolist drama *Salomé* (1892); for the highly-polished dramas he produced in the 1890s—*Lady Windermere's Fan* (1892), *A Woman of No Importance* (1893), *An Ideal Husband* (1895)—capped by his transcendent "trivial comedy for serious people," *The Importance of Being Earnest* (1895). However, Wilde also is remembered for the tragedy of his life as well—the terrible trial in which he was convicted of homosexual practices and sentenced to two years' hard labor—and for the poverty, isolation, and rejection that ensued.

Wilde was born in Dublin, the second son of Sir William Wilde—an author, oculist, and surgeon—and Jane Francesca Elgee, a poet and translator. He was educated at the Portora Royal School, read classics at Trinity College, Dublin, and then matriculated at Magdalen College, Oxford, where he continued to study classics. Leaving Oxford in 1876, Wilde began a career as a poet—his poem "Ravenna" won the Newdigate prize in 1878—and occasional critic on artistic subjects. By 1881, his wit, his ironic posturing, his green carnation (already part of the vestimentary code of Victorian gay culture) were so well known that he could be satirized as Bunthorne in Gilbert and Sullivan's operetta *Patience*. In the early 1880s he perfected his lecture performance on tour throughout the United States and Canada, but once he was married to Constance Lloyd in 1884—his two sons Cyril and Vyvyan were born in 1885 and 1886—Wilde had need of an income as a regular reviewer and essayist. Through the late 1880s, Wilde gained additional fame as the paradoxical spokesman of estheticism, writing a brilliant series of articles for the *Pall Mall Gazette*, the *Dramatic Review, Nineteenth Century* and other magazines, notably "The Decay of Lying" (1889), "The Artist as Critic" (1890), and "The Truth of Masks" (1885).

The posed, paradoxical, masked quality of Wilde's public *persona* had another dimension, for Wilde's homosexuality forced him to lead an elaborate double life. The passage of the Criminal Law Amendment Act in 1885 made homosexual activity illegal, and Wilde risked—and eventually suffered—both social rejection and legal punishment. As his career and public visibility began to crest in the early 1890s, with the publication of *The Picture of Dorian Gray* and the success of his first plays, Wilde became involved with a young man, Lord Alfred Douglas. In 1895, Douglas's father, the Marquess of Queensberry left a card at Wilde's club, addressed to Oscar Wilde, "posing as a somdomite" [*sic*]. Against the advice of his friends, Wilde prosecuted the Marquess for criminal libel, but when Queensberry was acquitted, Wilde was arrested for "acts of gross indecency with other male persons" and subjected to two jury trials, in which a series of young men were put on the stand, testifying to their sexual relations with Wilde. In the first trial, the jury was unable to reach a verdict; in the second, Wilde was found guilty and given the maximum sentence of two years' hard labor. Although he was eventually moved from hard labor in Pentonville to Wandsworth prison, and then finally to Reading Gaol, prison broke Wilde's health. Constance changed the last names of Cyril and Vyvyan to avoid association with Wilde, and when he was released in 1897 he was bankrupt and alone. Although Wilde's sexual orientation had long been known or suspected by many of his friends, most were unwilling to associate with Wilde after such public scandal: when Wilde returned to society he was cruelly and systematically shunned. He went first to France, then joined Alfred Douglas briefly in Italy; in 1898 he published *The Ballad of Reading Gaol* and settled in Paris, where he died two years later.

THE IMPORTANCE OF BEING EARNEST

Despite its energetic "triviality," *The Importance of Being Earnest* is deeply, symbolically involved in the contours of Wilde's life. The opening of *Earnest* in February of 1895 at George Alexander's fashionable St. James's Theatre was something of a society event; fearing the publicity of Wilde's trial, Alexander closed the hugely successful play only weeks later. However, *The Importance of Being Earnest* seems to resonate with Wilde's life in other ways as well. In an important sense, *The Importance of Being Earnest* is a play about masking. Much as Wilde's sexual identity had constantly to be negotiated behind the fictive "conventions" of polite society—his sexuality could be tolerated only as long as it was kept discreetly offstage, disacknowledged, unspoken—so in *Earnest* the process of social life in general seems to depend on a tissue of acceptable lies, which occasionally verge on truth: Algernon Moncrieff invents "an invaluable permanent invalid called Bunbury" so that he will have an excuse to escape London; Jack Worthing invents a wastrel younger brother named Ernest as an excuse to escape the country; Cecily invents scenes for her diary and Gwendolen keeps hers handy to "have something sensational to read on the train"; Jack and Algy, both vying to be baptized "Ernest," turn out to be brothers; and Jack, a foundling, turns out to be named Ernest after all.

As Algy remarks in Act 1, "The truth is rarely pure and never simple. Modern life would be very tedious if it were either, and modern literature a complete impossibility!" In *Earnest*, Wilde carefully constructs a comedy in which the deceptive surfaces of experience, the manifest fictions and deceptions of "modern life" turn out to provide the only vehicle for truth the play has to offer. Beneath the constricted, yet infinitely manipulable conventions of polite society surges the powerful force of desire. It is manifest in the elaborate verbal sparring between Jack, Algy, Gwendolen, and Cecily; in the manic, adolescent energy that drives Jack and Algy to the brink of baptism; even in the appetitive fury of the muffin scene. One final way in which these social conventions are marked is through their connection to the conventions of comedy itself—conventions that are forced to the forefront of the audience's attention throughout the play. *Earnest* comes to a climax in a paroxysm of artificiality: making a mockery of the recognition scene between long-lost siblings of romantic comedy, Wilde's Jack Worthing turns out to *be* his fictitious brother Ernest after all. In *The Importance of Being Earnest*, all convention—both social and comic—is shown to be a kind of mask, a fiction which sometimes enables the expression of truth.

THE IMPORTANCE OF BEING EARNEST

Oscar Wilde

— CHARACTERS —

JOHN WORTHING, J.P.
ALGERNON MONCRIEFF
REV. CANON CHASUBLE, D.D.
MERRIMAN (*Butler*)
LANE (*Manservant*)

LADY BRACKNELL
HON. GWENDOLEN FAIRFAX
CECILY CARDEW
MISS PRISM (*Governess*)

— THE SCENES OF THE PLAY —

ACT I.   Algernon Moncrieff's Flat in Half-Moon Street, W.
ACT II. The Garden at the Manor House, Woolton.
ACT III. Drawing-Room of the Manor House, Woolton.

TIME.—*The Present.*   PLACE.—*London.*

— ACT ONE —

Morning-room in ALGERNON's *flat in Half-Moon Street. The room is luxuriously and artistically furnished. The sound of a piano is heard in the adjoining room.*

(LANE *is arranging afternoon tea on the table, and after the music has ceased,* ALGERNON *enters.*)

ALGERNON: Did you hear what I was playing, Lane?
LANE: I didn't think it polite to listen, sir.
ALGERNON: I'm sorry for that, for your sake. I don't play accurately—anyone can play accurately—but I play with won-
5   derful expression. As far as the piano is concerned, senti-ment is my forte. I keep science for Life.
LANE: Yes, sir.
ALGERNON: And, speaking of the science of Life, have you got the cucumber sandwiches cut for Lady Bracknell?
10   LANE: Yes, sir. (*Hands them on a salver.*)
ALGERNON: (*Inspects them, takes two, and sits down on the sofa.*) Oh! . . . by the way, Lane, I see from your book that on Thursday night, when Lord Shoreman and Mr. Worthing were dining with me, eight bottles of champagne are entered
15   as having been consumed.
LANE: Yes, sir; eight bottles and a pint.
ALGERNON: Why is it that at a bachelor's establishment the servants invariably drink the champagne? I ask merely for information.
20   LANE: I attribute it to the superior quality of the wine, sir. I have often observed that in married households the cham-pagne is rarely of a first-rate brand.
ALGERNON: Good Heavens! Is marriage so demoralizing as that?
25   LANE: I believe it *is* a very pleasant state, sir. I have had very lit-tle experience of it myself up to the present. I have only been married once. That was in consequence of a misunderstand-ing between myself and a young woman.
ALGERNON: (*Languidly.*) I don't know that I am much inter-
30   ested in your family life, Lane.
LANE: No, sir; it is not a very interesting subject. I never think of it myself.
ALGERNON: Very natural, I am sure. That will do, Lane, thank you.
35   LANE: Thank you, sir. (LANE *goes out.*)
ALGERNON: Lane's views on marriage seem somewhat lax. Re-ally, if the lower orders don't set us a good example, what on earth is the use of them? They seem, as a class, to have ab-solutely no sense of moral responsibility.

(*Enter* LANE.)

LANE: Mr. Ernest Worthing.   40

(*Enter* JACK. LANE *goes out.*)

ALGERNON: How are you, my dear Ernest? What brings you up to town?
JACK: Oh, pleasure, pleasure! What else should bring one any-where? Eating as usual, I see, Algy!
ALGERNON: (*Stiffly.*) I believe it is customary in good society   45
to take some slight refreshment at five o'clock. Where have you been since last Thursday?
JACK: (*Sitting down on the sofa.*) In the country.
ALGERNON: What on earth do you do there?
JACK: (*Pulling off his gloves.*) When one is in town one amuses   50
oneself. When one is in the country one amuses other peo-ple. It is excessively boring.
ALGERNON: And who are the people you amuse?
JACK: (*Airily.*) Oh, neighbours, neighbours.
ALGERNON: Got nice neighbours in your part of Shropshire?   55
JACK: Perfectly horrid! Never speak to one of them.
ALGERNON: How immensely you must amuse them! (*Goes over and takes sandwich.*) By the way, Shropshire is your county, is it not?
JACK: Eh? Shropshire? Yes, of course. Hallo! Why all these   60
cups? Why cucumber sandwiches? Why such reckless ex-travagance in one so young? Who is coming to tea?
ALGERNON: Oh! merely Aunt Augusta and Gwendolen.
JACK: How perfectly delightful!
ALGERNON: Yes, that is all very well; but I am afraid Aunt Au-   65
gusta won't quite approve of your being here.
JACK: May I ask why?
ALGERNON: My dear fellow, the way you flirt with Gwendolen is perfectly disgraceful. It is almost as bad as the way Gwen-dolen flirts with you.   70
JACK: I am in love with Gwendolen. I have come up to town expressly to propose to her.
ALGERNON: I thought you had come up for pleasure? . . . I call that business.
JACK: How utterly unromantic you are!   75
ALGERNON: I really don't see anything romantic in proposing. It is very romantic to be in love. But there is nothing roman-tic about a definite proposal. Why, one may be accepted. One usually is, I believe. Then the excitement is all over. The very essence of romance is uncertainty. If ever I get mar-   80
ried, I'll certainly try to forget the fact.

JACK: I have no doubt about that dear Algy. The Divorce Court was specially invented for people whose memories are so curiously constituted.

85 ALGERNON: Oh! there is no use speculating on that subject. Divorces are made in Heaven—(JACK *puts out his hand to take a sandwich.* ALGERNON *at once interferes.*) Please don't touch the cucumber sandwiches. They are ordered specially for Aunt Augusta. *(Takes one and eats it.)*

90 JACK: Well, you have been eating them all the time.

ALGERNON: That is quite a different matter. She is my aunt. *(Takes plate from below.)* Have some bread and butter. The bread and butter is for Gwendolen. Gwendolen is devoted to bread and butter.

95 JACK: *(Advancing to table and helping himself.)* And very good bread and butter it is, too.

ALGERNON: Well, my dear fellow, you need not eat as if you were going to eat it all. You behave as if you were married to her already. You are not married to her already, and I don't

100 think you ever will be.

JACK: Why on earth do you say that?

ALGERNON: Well, in the first place girls never marry the men they flirt with. Girls don't think it right.

JACK: Oh, that is nonsense!

105 ALGERNON: It isn't. It is a great truth. It accounts for the extraordinary number of bachelors that one sees all over the place. In the second place, I don't give my consent.

JACK: Your consent!

ALGERNON: My dear fellow, Gwendolen is my first cousin.

110 And before I allow you to marry her, you will have to clear up the whole question of Cecily. *(Rings bell.)*

JACK: Cecily! What on earth do you mean? What do you mean, Algy, by Cecily? I don't know anyone of the name of Cecily.

(Enter LANE.*)*

115 ALGERNON: Bring me that cigarette case Mr. Worthing left in the smoking-room the last time he dined here.

LANE: Yes, sir. *(*LANE *goes out.)*

JACK: Do you mean to say you have had my cigarette case all this time? I wish to goodness you had let me know. I have

120 been writing frantic letters to Scotland Yard about it. I was very nearly offering a large reward.

ALGERNON: Well, I wish you would offer one. I happen to be more than usually hard up.

JACK: There is no good offering a large reward now that the

125 thing is found.

(Enter LANE *with the cigarette case on a salver.* ALGERNON *takes it at once.* LANE *goes out.)*

ALGERNON: I think that is rather mean of you, Ernest, I must say. *(Opens case and examines it.)* However, it makes no matter, for, now that I look at the inscription, I find that the thing isn't yours after all.

130 JACK: Of course it's mine. *(Moving to him.)* You have seen me with it a hundred times, and you have no right whatsoever to read what is written inside. It is a very ungentlemanly thing to read a private cigarette case.

ALGERNON: Oh! it is absurd to have a hard-and-fast rule about

135 what one should read and what one shouldn't. More than half of modern culture depends on what one shouldn't read.

JACK: I am quite aware of the fact, and I don't propose to discuss modern culture. It isn't the sort of thing one should talk of in private. I simply want my cigarette case back.

140 ALGERNON: Yes; but this isn't your cigarette case. This cigarette case is a present from someone of the name of Cecily, and you said you didn't know anyone of that name.

JACK: Well, if you want to know, Cecily happens to be my aunt.

145 ALGERNON: Your aunt!

JACK: Yes. Charming old lady she is, too. Lives at Tunbridge Wells. Just give it back to me, Algy.

ALGERNON: *(Retreating to back of sofa.)* But why does she call herself little Cecily if she is your aunt and lives at Tunbridge

150 Wells? *(Reading.)* "From little Cecily with her fondest love."

JACK: *(Moving to sofa and kneeling upon it.)* My dear fellow, what on earth is there in that? Some aunts are tall, some aunts are not tall. That is a matter that surely an aunt may be allowed to decide for herself. You seem to think that every

155 aunt should be exactly like your aunt! That is absurd! For Heaven's sake give me back my cigarette case. *(Follows* ALGERNON *round the room.)*

ALGERNON: Yes. But why does your aunt call you her uncle? "From little Cecily, with her fondest love to her dear Uncle

160 Jack." There is no objection, I admit, to an aunt being a small aunt, but why an aunt, no matter what her size may be, should call her own nephew her uncle, I can't quite make out. Besides, your name isn't Jack at all; it is Ernest.

JACK: It isn't Ernest; it's Jack.

165 ALGERNON: You have always told me it was Ernest. I have introduced you to everyone as Ernest. You answer to the name of Ernest. You look as if your name was Ernest. You are the most earnest looking person I ever saw in my life. It is perfectly absurd your saying that your name isn't Ernest. It's on

170 your cards. Here is one of them. *(Taking it from case.)* "Mr. Ernest Worthing, B 4, The Albany." I'll keep this as a proof your name is Ernest if ever you attempt to deny it to me, or to Gwendolen, or to anyone else. *(Puts the card in his pocket.)*

175 JACK: Well, my name is Ernest in town and Jack in the country, and the cigarette case was given to me in the country.

ALGERNON: Yes, but that does not account for the fact that your small Aunt Cecily, who lives at Tunbridge Wells, calls you her dear uncle. Come, old boy, you had much better

180 have the thing out at once.

JACK: My dear Algy, you talk exactly as if you were a dentist. It is very vulgar to talk like a dentist when one isn't a dentist. It produces a false impression.

ALGERNON: Well, that is exactly what dentists always do. Now,

185 go on! Tell me the whole thing. I may mention that I have always suspected you of being a confirmed and secret Bunburyist; and I am quite sure of it now.

JACK: Bunburyist? What on earth do you mean by a Bunburyist?

ALGERNON: I'll reveal to you the meaning of that incompara-

190 ble expression as soon as you are kind enough to inform me why you are Ernest in town and Jack in the country.

JACK: Well, produce my cigarette case first.

ALGERNON: Here it is. *(Hands cigarette case.)* Now produce your explanation, and pray make it improbable. *(Sits on

195 sofa.)*

JACK: My dear fellow, there is nothing improbable about my explanation at all. In fact it's perfectly ordinary. Old Mr.

Thomas Cardew, who adopted me when I was a little boy, made me in his will guardian to his grand-daughter, Miss
200 Cecily Cardew. Cecily, who addresses me as her uncle from motives of respect that you could not possibly appreciate, lives at my place in the country under the charge of her admirable governess, Miss Prism.

ALGERNON: Where is that place in the country, by the way?

205 JACK: That is nothing to you, dear boy. You are not going to be invited. . . . I may tell you candidly that the place is not in Shropshire.

ALGERNON: I suspected that, my dear fellow! I have Bunburyed all over Shropshire on two separate occasions. Now,
210 go on. Why are you Ernest in town and Jack in the country?

JACK: My dear Algy, I don't know whether you will be able to understand my real motives. You are hardly serious enough. When one is placed in the position of guardian, one has to adopt a very high moral tone on all subjects. It's one's duty to
215 do so. And as a high moral tone can hardly be said to conduce very much to either one's health or one's happiness, in order to get up to town I have always pretended to have a younger brother of the name of Ernest, who lives in the Albany, and gets into the most dreadful scrapes. That, my dear
220 Algy, is the whole truth pure and simple.

ALGERNON: The truth is rarely pure and never simple. Modern life would be very tedious if it were either, and modern literature a complete impossibility!

JACK: That wouldn't be at all a bad thing.

225 ALGERNON: Literary criticism is not your forte, my dear fellow. Don't try it. You should leave that to people who haven't been at a University. They do it so well in the daily papers. What you really are is a Bunburyist. I was quite right in saying you were a Bunburyist. You are one of the most ad-
230 vanced Bunburyists I know.

JACK: What on earth do you mean?

ALGERNON: You have invented a very useful younger brother called Ernest, in order that you may be able to come up to town as often as you like. I have invented an invaluable per-
235 manent invalid called Bunbury, in order that I may be able to go down into the country whenever I choose. Bunbury is perfectly invaluable. If it wasn't for Bunbury's extraordinary bad health, for instance, I wouldn't be able to dine with you at Willis's to-night, for I have been really engaged to Aunt
240 Augusta for more than a week.

JACK: I haven't asked you to dine with me anywhere to-night.

ALGERNON: I know. You are absolutely careless about sending out invitations. It is very foolish of you. Nothing annoys people so much as not receiving invitations.

245 JACK: You had much better dine with your Aunt Augusta.

ALGERNON: I haven't the smallest intention of doing anything of the kind. To begin with, I dined there on Monday, and once a week is quite enough to dine with one's own relatives. In the second place, whenever I do dine there I am always
250 treated as a member of the family, and sent down with either no woman at all, or two. In the third place, I know perfectly well whom she will place me next to, to-night. She will place me next Mary Farquhar, who always flirts with her own husband across the dinner-table. that is not very pleasant. In-
255 deed, it is not even decent . . . and that sort of thing is enormously on the increase. The amount of women in London who flirt with their own husbands is perfectly scandalous. It looks so bad. It is simply washing one's clean linen in public.

Besides, now that I know you to be a confirmed Bunburyist I naturally want to talk to you about Bunburying. I want to tell
260 you the rules.

JACK: I'm not a Bunburyist at all. If Gwendolen accepts me, I am going to kill my brother, indeed I think I'll kill him in any case. Cecily is a little too much interested in him. It is rather a bore. So I am going to get rid of Ernest. And I
265 strongly advise you to do the same with Mr. . . . with your invalid friend who has the absurd name.

ALGERNON: Nothing will induce me to part with Bunbury, and if you ever get married, which seems to me extremely problematic, you will be very glad to know Bunbury. A man
270 who marries without knowing Bunbury has a very tedious time of it.

JACK: That is nonsense. If I marry a charming girl like Gwendolen, and she is the only girl I ever saw in my life that I would marry, I certainly won't want to know Bunbury.
275

ALGERNON: Then your wife will. You don't seem to realize, that in married life three is company and two is none.

JACK: (*Sententiously.*) That, my dear young friend, is the theory that the corrupt French Drama has been propounding for the last fifty years.
280

ALGERNON: Yes; and that the happy English home has proved in half the time.

JACK: For heaven's sake, don't try to be cynical. It's perfectly easy to be cynical.

ALGERNON: My dear fellow, it isn't easy to be anything now-a-
285 days. There's such a lot of beastly competition about. (*The sound of an electric bell is heard.*) Ah! that must be Aunt Augusta. Only relatives, or creditors, ever ring in that Wagnerian manner. Now, if I get her out of the way for ten minutes, so that you can have an opportunity for proposing to Gwen-
290 dolen, may I dine with you to-night at Willis's?

JACK: I suppose so if you want to.

ALGERNON: Yes, but you must be serious about it. I hate people who are not serious about meals. It is so shallow of them.

(*Enter* LANE.)

LANE: Lady Bracknell and Miss Fairfax. (ALGERNON *goes*
295 *forward to meet them. Enter* LADY BRACKNELL *and* GWENDOLEN.)

LADY BRACKNELL: Good afternoon, dear Algernon, I hope you are behaving very well.

ALGERNON: I'm feeling very well, Aunt Augusta.
300

LADY BRACKNELL: That's not quite the same thing. In fact the two things rarely go together. (*Sees* JACK *and bows to him with icy coldness.*)

ALGERNON: (*To* GWENDOLEN.) Dear me, you are smart!

GWENDOLEN: I am always smart! Aren't I, Mr. Worthing?
305

JACK: You're quite perfect, Miss Fairfax.

GWENDOLEN: Oh! I hope I am not that. It would leave no room for developments, and I intend to develop in *many directions.* (GWENDOLEN *and* JACK *sit down together in the corner.*)
310

LADY BRACKNELL: I'm sorry if we are a little late, Algernon, but I was obliged to call on dear Lady Harbury. I hadn't been there since her poor husband's death. I never saw a woman so altered; she looks quite twenty years younger. And now I'll have a cup of tea, and one of those nice cucumber sand-
315 wiches you promised me.

ALGERNON: Certainly, Aunt Augusta. (*Goes over to tea-table.*)

LADY BRACKNELL: Won't you come and sit here, Gwendolen?

GWENDOLEN: Thanks, mamma, I'm quite comfortable where
320   I am.

ALGERNON: (Picking up empty plate in horror.) Good heavens!
   Lane! Why are there no cucumber sandwiches? I ordered
   them specially.

LANE: (Gravely.) There were no cucumbers in the market this
325   morning, sir. I went down twice.

ALGERNON: No cucumbers!

LANE: No, sir. Not even for ready money.

ALGERNON: That will do, Lane, thank you.

LANE: Thank you sir. (Goes out.)

330 ALGERNON: I am greatly distressed, Aunt Augusta, about there
   being no cucumbers, not even for ready money.

LADY BRACKNELL: It really makes no matter, Algernon. I had
   some crumpets with Lady Harbury, who seems to me to be
   living entirely for pleasure now.

335 ALGERNON: I hear her hair has turned quite gold from grief.

LADY BRACKNELL: It certainly has changed its colour. From
   what cause I, of course, cannot say. (ALGERNON crosses and
   hands tea.) Thank you. I've quite a treat for you to-night, Algernon. I am going to send you down with Mary Farquhar.
340   She is such a nice woman, and so attentive to her husband.
   It's delightful to watch them.

ALGERNON: I am afraid, Aunt Augusta, I shall have to give up
   the pleasure of dining with you to-night after all.

LADY BRACKNELL: (Frowning.) I hope not, Algernon. It would
345   put my table completely out. Your uncle would have to dine
   upstairs. Fortunately he is accustomed to that.

ALGERNON: It is a great bore, and, I need hardly say, a terrible
   disappointment to me, but the fact is I have just had a
   telegram to say that my poor friend Bunbury is very ill again.
350   (Exchanges glances with JACK.) They seem to think I should
   be with him.

LADY BRACKNELL: It is very strange. This Mr. Bunbury seems
   to suffer from curiously bad health.

ALGERNON: Yes; poor Bunbury is a dreadful invalid.

355 LADY BRACKNELL: Well, I must say, Algernon, that I think it is
   high time that Mr. Bunbury made up his mind whether he
   was going to live or to die. This shilly-shallying with the
   question is absurd. Nor do I in any way approve of the modern sympathy with invalids. I consider it morbid. Illness of
360   any kind is hardly a thing to be encouraged in others. Health
   is the primary duty of life. I am always telling that to your
   poor uncle, but he never seems to take much notice . . . as
   far as any improvement in his ailments goes. I should be
   much obliged if you would ask Mr. Bunbury, from me, to be
365   kind enough not to have a relapse on Saturday, for I rely on
   you to arrange my music for me. It is my last reception and
   one wants something that will encourage conversation, particularly at the end of the season when everyone has practically said whatever they had to say, which, in most cases, was
370   probably not much.

ALGERNON: I'll speak to Bunbury, Aunt Augusta, if he is still
   conscious, and I think I can promise you he'll be all right by
   Saturday. You see, if one plays good music, people don't listen, and if one plays bad music people don't talk. But I'll run
375   over the programme I've drawn out, if you will kindly come
   into the next room for a moment.

LADY BRACKNELL: Thank you, Algernon. It is very thoughtful
   of you. (Rising, and following ALGERNON.) I'm sure the
programme will be delightful, after a few expurgations.
French songs I cannot possibly allow. People always seem to 380
think that they are improper, and either look shocked, which
is vulgar, or laugh, which is worse. But German sounds a
thoroughly respectable language, and indeed, I believe is so.
Gwendolen, you will accompany me.

GWENDOLEN: Certainly, mamma. (LADY BRACKNELL and 385
ALGERNON go into the music-room, GWENDOLEN remains
behind.)

JACK: Charming day it has been, Miss Fairfax.

GWENDOLEN: Pray don't talk to me about the weather, Mr.
Worthing. Whenever people talk to me about the weather, I 390
always feel quite certain that they mean something else. And
that makes me so nervous.

JACK: I do mean something else.

GWENDOLEN: I thought so. In fact, I am never wrong.

JACK: And I would like to be allowed to take advantage of Lady 395
Bracknell's temporary absence . . .

GWENDOLEN: I would certainly advise you to do so. Mamma
has a way of coming back suddenly into a room that I have
often had to speak to her about.

JACK: (Nervously.) Miss Fairfax, ever since I met you I have ad- 400
mired you more than any girl . . . I have ever met since . . . I
met you.

GWENDOLEN: Yes, I am quite aware of the fact. And I often
wish that in public, at any rate, you had been more demonstrative. For me you have always had an irresistible fascina- 405
tion. Even before I met you I was far from indifferent to you.
(JACK looks at her in amazement.) We live, as I hope you
know, Mr. Worthing, in an age of ideals. The fact is constantly mentioned in the more expensive monthly magazines, and has reached the provincial pulpits I am told: and 410
my ideal has always been to love some one of the name of
Ernest. There is something in that name that inspires absolute confidence. The moment Algernon first mentioned to
me that he had a friend called Ernest, I knew I was destined
to love you.

JACK: You really love me, Gwendolen? 415

GWENDOLEN: Passionately!

JACK: Darling! You don't know how happy you've made me.

GWENDOLEN: My own Ernest!

JACK: But you don't really mean to say that you couldn't love
me if my name wasn't Ernest? 420

GWENDOLEN: But your name is Ernest.

JACK: Yes, I know it is. But supposing it was something else?
Do you mean to say you couldn't love me then?

GWENDOLEN: (Glibly.) Ah! that is clearly a metaphysical speculation, and like most metaphysical speculations has very lit- 425
tle reference at all to the actual facts of real life, as we know
them.

JACK: Personally, darling, to speak quite candidly, I don't much
care about the name of Ernest . . . I don't think that name
suits me at all. 430

GWENDOLEN: It suits you perfectly. It is a divine name. It has a
music of its own. It produces vibrations.

JACK: Well, really, Gwendolen, I must say that I think there are
lots of other much nicer names. I think, Jack, for instance, a
charming name. 435

GWENDOLEN: Jack? . . . No, there is very little music in the
name Jack, if any at all, indeed. It does not thrill. It produces
absolutely no vibration. . . . I have known several Jacks, and

they all, without exception, were more than usually plain. Besides, Jack is a notorious domesticity for John! And I pity any woman who is married to a man called John. She would probably never be allowed to know the entrancing pleasure of a single moment's solitude. The only really safe name is Ernest.

JACK: Gwendolen, I must get christened at once—I mean we must get married at once. There is no time to be lost.

GWENDOLEN: Married, Mr. Worthing?

JACK: (*Astounded.*) Well . . . surely. You know that I love you, and you led me to believe, Miss Fairfax, that you were not absolutely indifferent to me.

GWENDOLEN: I adore you. But you haven't proposed to me yet. Nothing has been said at all about marriage. The subject has not even been touched on.

JACK: Well . . . may I propose to you now?

GWENDOLEN: I think it would be an admirable opportunity. And to spare you any possible disappointment, Mr. Worthing, I think it only fair to tell you quite frankly beforehand that I am fully determined to accept you.

JACK: Gwendolen!

GWENDOLEN: Yes, Mr. Worthing, what have you got to say to me?

JACK: You know what I have got to say to you.

GWENDOLEN: Yes, but you don't say it.

JACK: Gwendolen, will you marry me? (*Goes on his knees.*)

GWENDOLEN: Of course I will, darling. How long you have been about it! I am afraid you have had very little experience in how to propose.

JACK: My own one, I have never loved anyone in the world but you.

GWENDOLEN: Yes, but men often propose for practice. I know my brother Gerald does. All my girl-friends tell me so. What wonderfully blue eyes you have, Ernest! They are quite, quite blue. I hope you will always look at me just like that, especially when there are other people present.

(*Enter* LADY BRACKNELL.)

LADY BRACKNELL: Mr. Worthing! Rise, sir, from this semi-recumbent posture. It is most indecorous.

GWENDOLEN: Mamma! (*He tries to rise; she restrains him.*) I must beg you to retire. This is no place for you. Besides, Mr. Worthing has not quite finished yet.

LADY BRACKNELL: Finished what, may I ask?

GWENDOLEN: I am engaged to Mr. Worthing, mamma.

(*They rise together.*)

LADY BRACKNELL: Pardon me, you are not engaged to anyone. When you do become engaged to some one, I, or your father, should his health permit him, will inform you of the fact. An engagement should come on a young girl as a surprise, pleasant or unpleasant, as the case may be. It is hardly a matter that she could be allowed to arrange for herself. . . . And now I have a few questions to put to you, Mr. Worthing. While I am making these inquiries, you, Gwendolen, will wait for me below in the carriage.

GWENDOLEN: (*Reproachfully.*) Mamma!

LADY BRACKNELL: In the carriage, Gwendolen! (GWENDOLEN *goes to the door. She and* JACK *blow kisses to each other behind* LADY BRACKNELL'S *back.* LADY BRACKNELL *looks vaguely about as if she could not understand what the noise was. Finally turns round.*) Gwendolen, the carriage!

GWENDOLEN: Yes, mamma. (*Goes out, looking back at* JACK.)

LADY BRACKNELL: (*Sitting down.*) You can take a seat, Mr. Worthing. (*Looks in her pocket for note-book and pencil.*)

JACK: Thank you, Lady Bracknell, I prefer standing.

LADY BRACKNELL: (*Pencil and note-book in hand.*) I feel bound to tell you that you are not down on my list of eligible young men, although I have the same list as the dear Duchess of Bolton has. We work together, in fact. However, I am quite ready to enter your name, should your answers be what a really affectionate mother requires. Do you smoke?

JACK: Well, yes, I must admit I smoke.

LADY BRACKNELL: I am glad to hear it. A man should always have an occupation of some kind. There are far too many idle men in London as it is. How old are you?

JACK: Twenty-nine.

LADY BRACKNELL: A very good age to be married at. I have always been of opinion that a man who desires to get married should know either everything or nothing. Which do you know?

JACK: (*After some hesitation.*) I know nothing, Lady Bracknell.

LADY BRACKNELL: I am pleased to hear it. I do not approve of anything that tampers with natural ignorance. Ignorance is like a delicate exotic fruit; touch it and the bloom is gone. The whole theory of modern education is radically unsound. Fortunately in England, at any rate, education produces no effect whatsoever. If it did, it would prove a serious danger to the upper classes, and probably lead to acts of violence in Grosvenor Square. What is your income?

JACK: Between seven and eight thousand a year.

LADY BRACKNELL: (*Makes a note in her book.*) In land, or in investments?

JACK: In investments, chiefly.

LADY BRACKNELL: That is satisfactory. What between the duties expected of one during one's life-time, and the duties exacted from one after one's death, land has ceased to be either a profit or a pleasure. It gives one position, and prevents one from keeping it up. That's all that can be said about land.

JACK: I have a country house with some land, of course, attached to it, about fifteen hundred acres, I believe; but I don't depend on that for my real income. In fact, as far as I can make out, the poachers are the only people who make anything out of it.

LADY BRACKNELL: A country house! How many bedrooms? Well, that point can be cleared up afterwards. You have a town house, I hope? A girl with a simple, unspoiled nature, like Gwendolen, could hardly be expected to reside in the country.

JACK: Well, I own a house in Belgrave Square, but it is let by the year to Lady Bloxham. Of course, I can get it back whenever I like, at six months' notice.

LADY BRACKNELL: Lady Bloxham? I don't know her.

JACK: Oh, she goes about very little. She is a lady considerably advanced in years.

LADY BRACKNELL: Ah, now-a-days that is no guarantee of respectability of character. What number in Belgrave Square?

JACK: 149.

LADY BRACKNELL: (*Shaking her head.*) The unfashionable side. I thought there was something. However, that could easily be altered.

JACK: Do you mean the fashion, or the side?

LADY BRACKNELL: *(Sternly.)* Both, if necessary, I presume. What are your politics?

560 JACK: Well, I am afraid I really have none. I am a Liberal Unionist.

LADY BRACKNELL: Oh, they count as Tories. They dine with us. Or comes in the evening, at any rate. Now to minor matters. Are your parents living?

JACK: I have lost both my parents.

565 LADY BRACKNELL: Both? . . . That seems like carelessness. Who was your father? He was evidently a man of some wealth. Was he born in what the Radical papers call the purple of commerce, or did he rise from the ranks of the aristocracy?

570 JACK: I am afraid I really don't know. The fact is, Lady Bracknell, I said I had lost my parents. It would be nearer the truth to say that my parents seem to have lost me . . . I don't actually know who I am by birth. I was . . . well, I was found.

LADY BRACKNELL: Found!

575 JACK: The late Mr. Thomas Cardew, an old gentleman of a very charitable and kindly disposition, found me, and gave me the name of Worthing, because he happened to have a first-class ticket for Worthing in his pocket at the time. Worthing is a place in Sussex. It is a seaside resort.

580 LADY BRACKNELL: Where did the charitable gentleman who had a first-class ticket for this seaside resort find you?

JACK: *(Gravely.)* In a hand-bag.

LADY BRACKNELL: A hand-bag?

JACK: *(Very seriously.)* Yes, Lady Bracknell. I was in a hand-

585 bag—a somewhat large, black leather hand-bag, with handles to it—an ordinary hand-bag in fact.

LADY BRACKNELL: In what locality did Mr. James, or Thomas, Cardew come across this ordinary hand-bag?

JACK: In the cloak-room at Victoria Station. It was given to

590 him in mistake for his own.

LADY BRACKNELL: The cloak-room at Victoria Station?

JACK: Yes. The Brighton line.

LADY BRACKNELL: The line is immaterial. Mr. Worthing, I confess I feel somewhat bewildered by what you have just

595 told me. To be born, or at any rate bred, in a hand-bag, whether it had handles or not, seems to me to display a contempt for the ordinary decencies of family life that remind one of the worst excesses of the French Revolution. And I presume you know what that unfortunate movement led to?

600 As for the particular locality in which the hand-bag was found, a cloak-room at a railway station might serve to conceal a social indiscretion—has probably, indeed, been used for the purpose before now—but it could hardly be regarded as an assured basis for a recognized position in good society.

605 JACK: May I ask you then what you would advise me to do? I need hardly say I would do anything in the world to ensure Gwendolen's happiness.

LADY BRACKNELL: I would strongly advise you, Mr. Worthing, to try and acquire some relations as soon as possible, and to

610 make a definite effort to produce at any rate one parent, of either sex, before the season is quite over.

JACK: Well, I don't see how I could possibly manage to do that. I can produce the hand-bag at any moment. It is in my dressing-room at home. I really think that should satisfy you, Lady

615 Bracknell.

LADY BRACKNELL: Me, sir! What has it to do with me? You can hardly imagine that I and Lord Bracknell would dream of allowing our only daughter—a girl brought up with the utmost care—to marry into a cloak-room, and form an alliance with a parcel? Good morning, Mr. Worthing! (LADY BRACKNELL 620 *sweeps out in majestic indignation.*)

JACK: Good morning! (ALGERNON, *from the other room, strikes up the Wedding March.* JACK *looks perfectly furious, and goes to the door.*) For goodness' sake don't play that ghastly tune, Algy! How idiotic you are! (*The music stops, and* ALGERNON 625 *enters cheerily.*)

ALGERNON: Didn't it go off all right, old boy? You don't mean to say Gwendolen refused you? I know it is a way she has. She is always refusing people. I think it is most ill-natured of her. 630

JACK: Oh, Gwendolen is as right as a trivet. As far as she is concerned, we are engaged. Her mother is perfectly unbearable. Never met such a Gorgon . . . I don't really know what a Gorgon is like, but I am quite sure that Lady Bracknell is one. In any case, she is a monster, without being a myth, 635 which is rather unfair. . . . I beg your pardon, Algy, I suppose I shouldn't talk about your own aunt in that way before you.

ALGERNON: My dear boy, I love hearing my relations abused. It is the only thing that makes me put up with them at all. Relations are simply a tedious pack of people, who haven't 640 got the remotest knowledge of how to live, nor the smallest instinct about when to die.

JACK: Oh, that is nonsense!

ALGERNON: It isn't!

JACK: Well, I won't argue about the matter. You always want to 645 argue about things.

ALGERNON: That is exactly what things were originally made for.

JACK: Upon my word, if I thought that, I'd shoot myself . . . (*A pause.*) You don't think there is any chance of Gwendolen 650 becoming like her mother in about a hundred and fifty years, do you, Algy?

ALGERNON: All women become like their mothers. That is their tragedy. No man does. That's his.

JACK: Is that clever? 655

ALGERNON: It is perfectly phrased! and quite as true as any observation in civilized life should be.

JACK: I am sick to death of cleverness. Everybody is clever now-a-days. You can't go anywhere without meeting clever people. The thing has become an absolute public nuisance. 660 I wish to goodness we had a few fools left.

ALGERNON: We have.

JACK: I should extremely like to meet them. What do they talk about?

ALGERNON: The fools? Oh! about the clever people, of course. 665

JACK: What fools!

ALGERNON: By the way, did you tell Gwendolen the truth about your being Ernest in town, and Jack in the country?

JACK: *(In a very patronising manner.)* My dear fellow, the truth isn't quite the sort of thing one tells to a nice, sweet, refined 670 girl. What extraordinary ideas you have about the way to behave to a woman!

ALGERNON: The only way to behave to a woman is to make love to her, if she is pretty, and to someone else if she is plain.

JACK: Oh, that is nonsense. 675

ALGERNON: What about your brother? What about the profligate Ernest?

JACK: Oh, before the end of the week I shall have got rid of him. I'll say he died in Paris of apoplexy. Lots of people die of apoplexy, quite suddenly, don't they?

ALGERNON: Yes, but it's hereditary, my dear fellow. It's a sort of thing that runs in families. You had much better say a severe chill.

JACK: You are sure a severe chill isn't hereditary, or anything of that kind?

ALGERNON: Of course it isn't!

JACK: Very well, then. My poor brother Ernest is carried off suddenly in Paris, by a severe chill. That gets rid of him.

ALGERNON: But I thought you said that . . . Miss Cardew was a little too interested in your poor brother Ernest? Won't she feel his loss a good deal?

JACK: Oh, that is all right. Cecily is not a silly, romantic girl, I am glad to say. She has got a capital appetite, goes for long walks, and pays no attention at all to her lessons.

ALGERNON: I would rather like to see Cecily.

JACK: I will take very good care you never do. She is excessively pretty, and she is only just eighteen.

ALGERNON: Have you told Gwendolen yet that you have an excessively pretty ward who is only just eighteen?

JACK: Oh! one doesn't blurt these things out to people. Cecily and Gwendolen are perfectly certain to be extremely great friends. I'll bet you anything you like that half an hour after they have met, they will be calling each other sister.

ALGERNON: Women only do that when they have called each other a lot of other thing first. Now, my dear boy, if we want to get a good table at Willis's, we really must go and dress. Do you know it is nearly seven?

JACK: (*Irritably.*) Oh! it always is nearly seven.

ALGERNON: Well, I'm hungry.

JACK: I never knew you when you weren't. . . .

ALGERNON: What shall we do after dinner? Go to a theatre?

JACK: Oh, no! I loathe listening.

ALGERNON: Well, let us go to the Club?

JACK: Oh, no! I hate talking.

ALGERNON: Well, we might trot round to the Empire at ten?

JACK: Oh, no! can't bear looking at things. It is so silly.

ALGERNON: Well, what shall we do?

JACK: Nothing!

ALGERNON: It is awfully hard work doing nothing. However, I don't mind hard work where there is no definite object of any kind.

(*Enter* LANE.)

LANE: Miss Fairfax.

(*Enter* GWENDOLEN. LANE *goes out.*)

ALGERNON: Gwendolen, upon my word!

GWENDOLEN: Algy, kindly turn your back. I have something very particular to say to Mr. Worthing.

ALGERNON: Really, Gwendolen, I don't think I can allow this at all.

GWENDOLEN: Algy, you always adopt a strictly immoral attitude towards life. You are not quite old enough to do that.

(ALGERNON *retires to the fireplace.*)

JACK: My own darling!

GWENDOLEN: Ernest, we may never be married. From the expression on mamma's face I fear we never shall. Few parents now-a-days pay any regard to what their children say to them. The old-fashioned respect for the young is fast dying out. Whatever influence I ever had over mamma, I lost at the age of three. But although she may prevent us from becoming man and wife, and I may marry someone else, and marry often, nothing that she can possibly do can alter my eternal devotion to you.

JACK: Dear Gwendolen.

GWENDOLEN: The story of your romantic origin, as related to me by mamma, with unpleasing comments, has naturally stirred the deeper fibers of my nature. Your Christian name has an irresistible fascination. The simplicity of your character makes you exquisitely incomprehensible to me. Your town address at the Albany I have. What is your address in the country?

JACK: The Manor House, Woolton, Hertfordshire. (ALGERNON, *who has been carefully listening, smiles to himself, and writes the address on his shirt-cuff. Then picks up the Railway Guide.*)

GWENDOLEN: There is a good postal service, I suppose? It may be necessary to do something desperate. That, of course, will require serious consideration. I will communicate with you daily.

JACK: My own one!

GWENDOLEN: How long do you remain in town?

JACK: Till Monday.

GWENDOLEN: Good! Algy, you may turn round now.

ALGERNON: Thanks, I've turned round already.

GWENDOLEN: You may also ring the bell.

JACK: You will let me see you to your carriage, my own darling?

GWENDOLEN: Certainly.

JACK: (*To* LANE, *who now enters.*) I will see Miss Fairfax out.

LANE: Yes, sir. (JACK *and* GWENDOLEN *go off.* LANE *presents several letters on a salver to* ALGERNON. *It is to be surmised that they are bills, as* ALGERNON, *after looking at the envelopes, tears them up.*)

ALGERNON: A glass of sherry, Lane.

LANE: Yes, sir.

ALGERNON: To-morrow, Lane, I'm going Bunburying.

LANE: Yes, sir.

ALGERNON: I shall probably not be back till Monday. You can put up my dress clothes, my smoking jacket, and all the Bunbury suits . . .

LANE: Yes, sir. (*Handing sherry.*)

ALGERNON: I hope to-morrow will be a fine day, Lane.

LANE: It never is, sir.

ALGERNON: Lane, you're a perfect pessimist.

LANE: I do my best to give satisfaction, sir.

(*Enter* JACK. LANE *goes off.*)

JACK: There's a sensible, intellectual girl! the only girl I ever cared for in my life. (ALGERNON *is laughing immoderately.*) What on earth are you so amused at?

ALGERNON: Oh, I'm a little anxious about poor Bunbury, that's all.

JACK: If you don't take care, your friend Bunbury will get you into a serious scrape some day.

790 ALGERNON: I love scrapes. They are the only things that are never serious.

JACK: Oh, that's nonsense, Algy. You never talk anything but nonsense.

ALGERNON: Nobody ever does. (JACK *looks indignantly at him,*
795 *and leaves the room.* ALGERNON *lights a cigarette, reads his shirt-cuff and smiles.*)

— ACT TWO —

Garden at the Manor House. A flight of gray stone steps leads up to the house. The garden, an old-fashioned one, full of roses. Time of year, July. Basket chairs, and a table covered with books, are set under a large yew tree.

(MISS PRISM *discovered seated at the table.* CECILY *is at the back watering flowers.*)

MISS PRISM: (*Calling.*) Cecily, Cecily! Surely such a utilitarian occupation as the watering of flowers is rather Moulton's duty than yours? Especially at a moment when intellectual pleasures await you. Your German grammar is on the table.
5 Pray open it at page fifteen. We will repeat yesterday's lesson.

CECILY: (*Coming over very slowly.*) But I don't like German. It isn't at all a becoming language. I know perfectly well that I look quite plain after my German lesson.

MISS PRISM: Child, you know how anxious your guardian is
10 that you should improve yourself in every way. He laid particular stress on your German, as he was leaving for town yesterday. Indeed, he always lays stress on your German when he is leaving for town.

CECILY: Dear Uncle Jack is so very serious! Sometimes he is so
15 serious that I think he cannot be quite well.

MISS PRISM: (*Drawing herself up.*) Your guardian enjoys the best of health, and his gravity of demeanour is especially to be commended in one so comparatively young as he is. I know no one who has a higher sense of duty and responsibility.

20 CECILY: I suppose that is why he often looks a little bored when we three are together.

MISS PRISM: Cecily! I am surprised at you. Mr. Worthing has many troubles in his life. Idle merriment and triviality would be out of place in his conversation. You must remem-
25 ber his constant anxiety about that unfortunate young man, his brother.

CECILY: I wish Uncle Jack would allow that unfortunate young man, his brother, to come down here sometimes. We might have a good influence over him, Miss Prism. I am sure you
30 certainly would. You know German, and geology, and things of that kind influence a man very much. (CECILY *begins to write in her diary.*)

MISS PRISM: (*Shaking her head.*) I do not think that even I could produce any effect on a character that, according to
35 his own brother's admission, is irretrievably weak and vacillating. Indeed, I am not sure that I would desire to reclaim him. I am not in favour of this modern mania for turning bad people into good people at a moment's notice. As a man sows so let him reap. You must put away your diary, Cecily. I
40 really don't see why you should keep a diary at all.

CECILY: I keep a diary in order to enter the wonderful secrets of my life. If I didn't write them down I should probably forget all about them.

MISS PRISM: Memory, my dear Cecily, is the diary that we all carry about with us.
45

CECILY: Yes, but it usually chronicles the things that have never happened, and couldn't possibly have happened. I believe that Memory is responsible for nearly all the three-volume novels that Mudie sends us.

MISS PRISM: Do not speak slightingly of the three-volume
50 novel, Cecily. I wrote one myself in earlier days.

CECILY: Did you really, Miss Prism? How wonderfully clever you are! I hope it did not end happily? I don't like novels that end happily. They depress me so much.

MISS PRISM: The good ended happily, and the bad unhappily.
55 That is what Fiction means.

CECILY: I suppose so. But it seems very unfair. And was your novel ever published?

MISS PRISM: Alas! no. The manuscript unfortunately was abandoned. I use the word in the sense of lost or mislaid. To your
60 work, child, these speculations are profitless.

CECILY: (*Smiling.*) But I see dear Dr. Chasuble coming up through the garden.

MISS PRISM: (*Rising and advancing.*) Dr. Chasuble! This is indeed a pleasure.
65

(*Enter* CANON CHASUBLE.)

CHASUBLE: And how are we this morning? Miss Prism, you are, I trust, well?

CECILY: Miss Prism has just been complaining of a slight headache. I think it would do her so much good to have a short stroll with you in the park, Dr. Chasuble.
70

MISS PRISM: Cecily, I have not mentioned anything about a headache.

CECILY: No, dear Miss Prism, I know that, but I felt instinctively that you had a headache. Indeed I was thinking about that, and not about my German lesson, when the Rector
75 came in.

CHASUBLE: I hope, Cecily, you are not inattentive.

CECILY: Oh, I am afraid I am.

CHASUBLE: That is strange. Were I fortunate enough to be Miss Prism's pupil, I would hang upon her lips. (MISS PRISM
80 *glares.*) I spoke metaphorically.—My metaphor was drawn from bees. Ahem! Mr. Worthing, I suppose, has not returned from town yet?

MISS PRISM: We do not expect him till Monday afternoon.

CHASUBLE: Ah yes, he usually likes to spend his Sunday in
85 London. He is not one of those whose sole aim is enjoyment, as, by all accounts, that unfortunate young man, his brother, seems to be. But I must not disturb Egeria and her pupil any longer.

MISS PRISM: Egeria? My name is Lætitia, Doctor.
90

CHASUBLE: (*Bowing.*) A classical allusion merely, drawn from the Pagan authors. I shall see you both no doubt at Evensong.

MISS PRISM: I think, dear Doctor, I will have a stroll with you. I find I have a headache after all, and a walk might do it good.
95

CHASUBLE: With pleasure, Miss Prism, with pleasure. We might go as far as the schools and back.

MISS PRISM: That would be delightful. Cecily, you will read your Political Economy in my absence. The chapter on the Fall of the Rupee you may omit. It is somewhat too
100

sensational. Even these metallic problems have their melodramatic side.

(Goes down the garden with DR. CHASUBLE.*)*

CECILY: *(Picks up books and throws them back on table.)* Horrid Political Economy! Horrid Geography! Horrid, horrid
105 German!

(Enter MERRIMAN *with a card on a salver.)*

MERRIMAN: Mr. Ernest Worthing has just driven over from the
station. He has brought his luggage with him.
CECILY: *(Takes the card and reads it.)* "Mr. Ernest Worthing, B
4 The Albany, W." Uncle Jack's brother! Did you tell him
110 Mr. Worthing was in town?
MERRIMAN: Yes, Miss. He seemed very much disappointed. I
mentioned that you and Miss Prism were in the garden. He
said he was anxious to speak to you privately for a moment.
CECILY: Ask Mr. Ernest Worthing to come here. I suppose you
115 had better talk to the housekeeper about a room for him.
MERRIMAN: Yes, Miss.

*(*MERRIMAN *goes off.)*

CECILY: I have never met any really wicked person before. I
feel rather frightened. I am so afraid he will look just like everyone else.

(Enter ALGERNON, *very gay and debonair.)*

120 He does!
ALGERNON: *(Raising his hat.)* You are my little cousin Cecily,
I'm sure.
CECILY: You are under some strange mistake. I am not little. In
fact, I am more than usually tall for my age. (ALGERNON *is
125 rather taken aback.)* But I am your cousin Cecily. You, I see
from your card, are Uncle Jack's brother, my cousin Ernest,
my wicked cousin Ernest.
ALGERNON: Oh! I am not really wicked at all, cousin Cecily.
You mustn't think that I am wicked.
130 CECILY: If you are not, then you have certainly been deceiving
us all in a very inexcusable manner. I hope you have not
been leading a double life, pretending to be wicked and
being really good all the time. That would be hypocrisy.
ALGERNON: *(Looks at her in amazement.)* Oh! of course I have
135 been rather reckless.
CECILY: I am glad to hear it.
ALGERNON: In fact, now you mention the subject, I have been
very bad in my own small way.
CECILY: I don't think you should be so proud of that, though I
140 am sure it must have been very pleasant.
ALGERNON: It is much pleasanter being here with you.
CECILY: I can't understand how you are here at all. Uncle Jack
won't be back till Monday afternoon.
ALGERNON: That is a great disappointment. I am obliged to go
145 up by the first train on Monday morning. I have a business
appointment that I am anxious . . . to miss.
CECILY: Couldn't you miss it anywhere but in London?
ALGERNON: No; the appointment is in London.
CECILY: Well, I know, of course, how important it is not to
150 keep a business engagement, if one wants to retain any sense
of the beauty of life, but still I think you had better wait till
Uncle Jack arrives. I know he wants to speak to you about
your emigrating.

ALGERNON: About my what?
CECILY: Your emigrating. He has gone up to buy your outfit.   155
ALGERNON: I certainly wouldn't let Jack buy my outfit. He has
no taste in neckties at all.
CECILY: I don't think you will require neckties. Uncle Jack is
sending you to Australia.
ALGERNON: Australia! I'd sooner die.   160
CECILY: Well, he said at dinner on Wednesday night, that you
would have to choose between this world, the next world,
and Australia.
ALGERNON: Oh, well! The accounts I have received of Aus-
tralia and the next world, are not particularly encouraging.   165
This world is good enough for me, cousin Cecily.
CECILY: Yes, but are you good enough for it?
ALGERNON: I'm afraid I'm not that. That is why I want you to
reform me. You might make that your mission, if you don't
mind, cousin Cecily.   170
CECILY: I'm afraid I've not time, this afternoon.
ALGERNON: Well, would you mind my reforming myself this
afternoon?
CECILY: That is rather Quixotic of you. But I think you should
try.   175
ALGERNON: I will. I feel better already.
CECILY: You are looking a little worse.
ALGERNON: That is because I am hungry.
CECILY: How thoughtless of me. I should have remembered
that when one is going to lead an entirely new life, one re-   180
quires regular and wholesome meals. Won't you come in?
ALGERNON: Thank you. Might I have a button-hole first? I
never have any appetite unless I have a button-hole first.
CECILY: A Maréchal Niel? *(Picks up scissors.)*
ALGERNON: No, I'd sooner have a pink rose.   185
CECILY: Why? *(Cuts a flower.)*
ALGERNON: Because you are like a pink rose, cousin Cecily.
CECILY: I don't think it can be right for you to talk to me like
that. Miss Prism never says such things to me.
ALGERNON: Then Miss Prism is a short-sighted old lady. (CE-   190
CILY *puts the rose in his button-hole.)* You are the prettiest girl
I ever saw.
CECILY: Miss Prism says that all good looks are a snare.
ALGERNON: They are a snare that every sensible man would
like to be caught in.   195
CECILY: Oh! I don't think I would care to catch a sensible
man. I shouldn't know what to talk to him about.

(They pass into the house. MISS PRISM *and* DR. CHASUBLE
return.)

MISS PRISM: You are too much alone, dear Dr. Chasuble. You
should get married. A misanthrope I can understand—a
womanthrope, never!   200
CHASUBLE: *(With a scholar's shudder.)* Believe me, I do not
deserve so neologistic a phrase. The precept as well as the
practice of the Primitive Church was distinctly against
matrimony.
MISS PRISM: *(Sententiously.)* That is obviously the reason why   205
the Primitive Church has not lasted up to the present day.
And you do not seem to realize, dear Doctor, that by persistently remaining single, a man converts himself into a permanent public temptation. Men should be careful; this very
celibacy leads weaker vessels astray.   210
CHASUBLE: But is a man not equally attractive when married?

MISS PRISM: No married man is ever attractive except to his wife.

CHASUBLE: And often, I've been told, not even to her.

215 MISS PRISM: That depends on the intellectual sympathies of the woman. Maturity can always be depended on. Ripeness can be trusted. Young women are green. (DR. CHASUBLE *starts.*) I spoke horticulturally. My metaphor was drawn from fruits. But where is Cecily?

220 CHASUBLE: Perhaps she followed us to the schools.

(Enter JACK slowly from the back of the garden. He is dressed in the deepest mourning, with crepe hatband and black gloves.)

MISS PRISM: Mr. Worthing!

CHASUBLE: Mr. Worthing?

MISS PRISM: This is indeed a surprise. We did not look for you till Monday afternoon.

225 JACK: (*Shakes MISS PRISM's hand in a tragic manner.*) I have returned sooner than I expected. Dr. Chasuble, I hope you are well?

CHASUBLE: Dear Mr. Worthing, I trust this garb of woe does not betoken some terrible calamity?

230 JACK: My brother.

MISS PRISM: More shameful debts and extravagance?

CHASUBLE: Still leading his life of pleasure?

JACK: (*Shaking his head.*) Dead!

CHASUBLE: Your brother Ernest dead?

235 JACK: Quite dead.

MISS PRISM: What a lesson for him! I trust he will profit by it.

CHASUBLE: Mr. Worthing, I offer you my sincere condolence. You have at least the consolation of knowing that you were always the most generous and forgiving of brothers.

240 JACK: Poor Ernest! He had many faults, but it is a sad, sad blow.

CHASUBLE: Very sad indeed. Were you with him at the end?

JACK: No. He died abroad; in Paris, in fact. I had a telegram last night from the manager of the Grand Hotel.

245 CHASUBLE: Was the cause of death mentioned?

JACK: A severe chill, it seems.

MISS PRISM: As a man sows, so shall he reap.

CHASUBLE: (*Raising his hand.*) Charity, dear Miss Prism, charity! None of us are perfect. I myself am peculiarly suscepti-
250 ble to draughts. Will the interment take place here?

JACK: No. He seems to have expressed a desire to be buried in Paris.

CHASUBLE: In Paris! (*Shakes his head.*) I fear that hardly points to any very serious state of mind at the last. You would no
255 doubt wish me to make some slight allusion to this tragic domestic affliction next Sunday. (JACK *presses his hand convulsively.*) My sermon on the meaning of the manna in the wilderness can be adapted to almost any occasion, joyful, or, as in the present case, distressing. (*All sigh.*) I have preached
260 it at harvest celebrations, christenings, confirmations, on days of humiliation and festal days. The last time I delivered it was in the Cathedral, as a charity sermon on behalf of the Society for the Prevention of Discontentment among the Upper Orders. The Bishop, who was present, was much
265 struck by some of the analogies I drew.

JACK: Ah, that reminds me, you mentioned christenings I think, Dr. Chasuble? I suppose you know how to christen all right? (DR. CHASUBLE *looks astounded.*) I mean, of course, you are continually christening, aren't you?

MISS PRISM: It is, I regret to say, one of the Rector's most con-
270 stant duties in this parish. I have often spoken to the poorer classes on the subject. But they don't seem to know what thrift is.

CHASUBLE: But is there any particular infant in whom you are interested, Mr. Worthing? Your brother was, I believe, un-
275 married, was he not?

JACK: Oh, yes.

MISS PRISM: (*Bitterly.*) People who live entirely for pleasure usually are.

JACK: But it is not for any child, dear Doctor. I am very fond of
280 children. No! the fact is, I would like to be christened myself, this afternoon, if you have nothing better to do.

CHASUBLE: But surely, Mr. Worthing, you have been christened already?

JACK: I don't remember anything about it.
285

CHASUBLE: But have you any grave doubts on the subject?

JACK: I certainly intend to have. Of course, I don't know if the thing would bother you in any way, or if you think I am a little too old now.

CHASUBLE: Not at all. The sprinkling, and, indeed, the im-
290 mersion of adults is a perfectly canonical practice.

JACK: Immersion!

CHASUBLE: You need have no apprehensions. Sprinkling is all that is necessary, or indeed I think advisable. Our weather is so changeable. At what hour would you wish the ceremony
295 performed?

JACK: Oh, I might trot around about five if that would suit you.

CHASUBLE: Perfectly, perfectly! In fact I have two similar ceremonies to perform at that time. A case of twins that occurred recently in one of the outlying cottages on your own estate.
300 Poor Jenkins the carter, a most hard-working man.

JACK: Oh! I don't see much fun in being christened along with other babies. It would be childish. Would half-past five do?

CHASUBLE: Admirably! Admirably! (*Takes out watch.*) And now, dear Mr. Worthing, I will not intrude any longer into a
305 house of sorrow. I would merely beg you not to be too much bowed down by grief. What seem to us bitter trials at the moment are often blessings in disguise.

MISS PRISM: This seems to me a blessing of an extremely obvious kind.
310

(Enter CECILY from the house.)

CECILY: Uncle Jack! Oh, I am pleased to see you back. But what horrid clothes you have on! Do go and change them.

MISS PRISM: Cecily!

CHASUBLE: My child! my child! (CECILY *goes towards JACK; he kisses her brow in a melancholy manner.*)
315

CECILY: What is the matter, Uncle Jack? Do look happy! You look as if you had a toothache and I have such a surprise for you. Who do you think is in the dining-room? Your brother!

JACK: Who?

CECILY: Your brother Ernest. He arrived about half an hour
320 ago.

JACK: What nonsense! I haven't got a brother.

CECILY: Oh, don't say that. However badly he may have behaved to you in the past he is still your brother. You couldn't be so heartless as to disown him. I'll tell him to come out.
325 And you will shake hands with him, won't you, Uncle Jack. *(Runs back into the house.)*

CHASUBLE: These are very joyful tidings.

330 MISS PRISM: After we had all been resigned to his loss, his sudden return seems to me peculiarly distressing.

JACK: My brother is in the dining-room? I don't know what it all means. I think it is perfectly absurd.

(Enter ALGERNON and CECILY hand in hand. They come slowly up to JACK.)

JACK: Good heavens! *(Motions ALGERNON away.)*

335 ALGERNON: Brother John, I have come down from town to tell you that I am very sorry for all the trouble I have given you, and that I intend to lead a better life in the future. *(JACK glares at him and does not take his hand.)*

CECILY: Uncle Jack, you are not going to refuse your own brother's hand?

340 JACK: Nothing will induce me to take his hand. I think his coming down here disgraceful. He knows perfectly well why.

CECILY: Uncle Jack, do be nice. There is some good in everyone. Ernest has just been telling me about his poor invalid friend, Mr. Bunbury, whom he goes to visit so often. And 345 surely there must be much good in one who is kind to an invalid, and leaves the pleasures of London to sit by a bed of pain.

JACK: Oh, he has been talking about Bunbury, has he?

CECILY: Yes, he has told me all about poor Mr. Bunbury, and 350 his terrible state of health.

JACK: Bunbury! Well, I won't have him talk to you about Bunbury or about anything else. It is enough to drive one perfectly frantic.

ALGERNON: Of course I admit that the faults were all on my 355 side. But I must say that I think that Brother John's coldness to me is peculiarly painful. I expected a more enthusiastic welcome, especially considering it is the first time I have come here.

CECILY: Uncle Jack, if you don't shake hands with Ernest I will 360 never forgive you.

JACK: Never forgive me?

CECILY: Never, never, never!

JACK: Well, this is the last time I shall ever do it. *(Shakes hands with ALGERNON and glares.)*

365 CHASUBLE: It's pleasant, is it not, to see so perfect a reconciliation? I think we might leave the two brothers together.

MISS PRISM: Cecily, you will come with us.

CECILY: Certainly, Miss Prism. My little task of reconciliation is over.

370 CHASUBLE: You have done a beautiful action to-day, dear child.

MISS PRISM: We must not be premature in our judgments.

CECILY: I feel very happy. *(They all go off.)*

JACK: You young scoundrel, Algy, you must get out of this place as soon as possible. I don't allow any Bunburying here.

(Enter MERRIMAN.)

375 MERRIMAN: I have put Mr. Ernest's things in the room next to yours, sir. I suppose that is all right?

JACK: What?

MERRIMAN: Mr. Ernest's luggage, sir. I have unpacked it and put it in the room next to your own.

380 JACK: His luggage?

MERRIMAN: Yes, sir. Three portmanteaus, a dressing-case, two hat-boxes, and a large luncheon-basket.

ALGERNON: I am afraid I can't stay more than a week this time.

JACK: Merriman, order the dog-cart at once. Mr. Ernest has 385 been suddenly called back to town.

MERRIMAN: Yes, sir. *(Goes back into the house.)*

ALGERNON: What a fearful liar you are, Jack. I have not been called back to town at all.

JACK: Yes, you have. 390

ALGERNON: I haven't heard anyone call me.

JACK: Your duty as a gentleman calls you back.

ALGERNON: My duty as a gentleman has never interfered with my pleasures in the smallest degree.

JACK: I can quite understand that. 395

ALGERNON: Well, Cecily is a darling.

JACK: You are not to talk of Miss Cardew like that. I don't like it.

ALGERNON: Well, I don't like your clothes. You look perfectly ridiculous in them. Why on earth don't you go up and change? It is perfectly childish to be in deep mourning for a 400 man who is actually staying for a whole week with you in your house as a guest. I call it grotesque.

JACK: You are certainly not staying with me for a whole week as a guest or anything else. You have got to leave . . . by the four-five train. 405

ALGERNON: I certainly won't leave you so long as you are in mourning. It would be most unfriendly. If I were in mourning you would stay with me, I suppose. I should think it very unkind if you didn't.

JACK: Well, will you go if I change my clothes? 410

ALGERNON: Yes, if you are not too long. I never saw anybody take so long to dress, and with such little result.

JACK: Well, at any rate, that is better than being always overdressed as you are.

ALGERNON: If I am occasionally a little over-dressed, I make 415 up for it by being always immensely over-educated.

JACK: Your vanity is ridiculous, your conduct an outrage, and your presence in my garden utterly absurd. However, you have got to catch the four-five, and I hope you will have a pleasant journey back to town. This Bunburying, as you call 420 it, has not been a great success for you. *(Goes into the house.)*

ALGERNON: I think it has been a great success. I'm in love with Cecily, and that is everything. *(Enter CECILY at the back of the garden. She picks up the can and begins to water the flowers.)* But I must see her before I go, and make arrangements 425 for another Bunbury. Ah, there she is.

CECILY: Oh, I merely came back to water the roses. I thought you were with Uncle Jack.

ALGERNON: He's gone to order the dog-cart for me.

CECILY: Oh, is he going to take you for a nice drive? 430

ALGERNON: He's going to send me away.

CECILY: Then have we got to part?

ALGERNON: I am afraid so. It's a very painful parting.

CECILY: It is always painful to part from people whom one has known for a very brief space of time. The absence of old 435 friends one can endure with equanimity. But even a momentary separation from anyone to whom one has just been introduced is almost unbearable.

ALGERNON: Thank you.

(Enter MERRIMAN.)

MERRIMAN: The dog-cart is at the door, sir. *(ALGERNON looks 440 appealingly at CECILY.)*

CECILY: It can wait, Merriman . . . for . . . five minutes.

MERRIMAN: Yes, miss.

(Exit MERRIMAN.*)*

445 ALGERNON: I hope, Cecily, I shall not offend you if I state quite frankly and openly that you seem to me to be in every way the visible personification of absolute perfection.

CECILY: I think your frankness does you great credit, Ernest. If you will allow me I will copy your remarks into my diary. *(Goes over to table and begins writing in diary.)*

450 ALGERNON: Do you really keep a diary? I'd give any thing to look at it. May I?

CECILY: Oh, no. *(Puts her hand over it.)* You see, it is simply a very young girl's record of her own thoughts and impressions, and consequently meant for publication. When it ap-

455 pears in volume form I hope you will order a copy. But pray, Ernest, don't stop. I delight in taking down from dictation. I have reached "absolute perfection." You can go on. I am quite ready for more.

ALGERNON: *(Somewhat taken aback.)* Ahem! Ahem!

460 CECILY: Oh, don't cough, Ernest. When one is dictating one should speak fluently and not cough. Besides, I don't know how to spell a cough. *(Writes as* ALGERNON *speaks.)*

ALGERNON: *(Speaking very rapidly.)* Cecily, ever since I first looked upon your wonderful and incomparable beauty, I

465 have dared to love you wildly, passionately, devotedly, hopelessly.

CECILY: I don't think that you should tell me that you love me wildly, passionately, devotedly, hopelessly. Hopelessly doesn't seem to make much sense, does it?

470 ALGERNON: Cecily!

(Enter MERRIMAN.*)*

MERRIMAN: The dog-cart is waiting, sir.

ALGERNON: Tell it to come round next week, at the same hour.

MERRIMAN: *(Looks at* CECILY, *who makes no sign.)* Yes, sir.

*(*MERRIMAN *retires.)*

CECILY: Uncle Jack would be very much annoyed if he knew

475 you were staying on till next week, at the same hour.

ALGERNON: Oh, I don't care about Jack. I don't care for anybody in the whole world but you. I love you, Cecily. You will marry me, won't you?

CECILY: You silly you! Of course. Why, we have been engaged

480 for the last three months.

ALGERNON: For the last three months?

CECILY: Yes, it will be exactly three months on Thursday.

ALGERNON: But how did we become engaged?

CECILY: Well, ever since dear Uncle Jack first confessed to us

485 that he had a younger brother who was very wicked and bad, you of course have formed the chief topic of conversation between myself and Miss Prism. And of course a man who is much talked about is always very attractive. One feels there must be something in him after all. I daresay it was foolish of

490 me, but I fell in love with you, Ernest.

ALGERNON: Darling! And when was the engagement actually settled?

CECILY: On the 14th of February last. Worn out by your entire ignorance of my existence, I determined to end the matter

495 one way or the other, and after a long struggle with myself I accepted you under this dear old tree here. The next day I bought this little ring in your name, and this is the little bangle with the true lovers' knot I promised you always to wear.

ALGERNON: Did I give you this? It's very pretty, isn't it?

500 CECILY: Yes, you've wonderfully good taste, Ernest. It's the excuse I've always given for your leading such a bad life. And this is the box in which I keep all your dear letters. *(Kneels at table, opens box, and produces letters tied up with blue ribbon.)*

505 ALGERNON: My letters! But my own sweet Cecily, I have never written you any letters.

CECILY: You need hardly remind me of that, Ernest. I remember only too well that I was forced to write your letters for you. I wrote always three times a week, and sometimes

510 oftener.

ALGERNON: Oh, do let me read them, Cecily?

CECILY: Oh, I couldn't possibly. They would make you far too conceited. *(Replaces box.)* The three you wrote me after I had broken off the engagement are so beautiful, and so

515 badly spelled, that even now I can hardly read them without crying a little.

ALGERNON: But was our engagement ever broken off?

CECILY: Of course it was. On the 22nd of last March. You can see the entry if you like. *(Shows diary.)* "Today I broke off my

520 engagement with Ernest. I feel it is better to do so. The weather still continues charming."

ALGERNON: But why on earth did you break it off? What had I done? I had done nothing at all. Cecily, I am very much hurt indeed to hear you broke it off. Particularly when the

525 weather was so charming.

CECILY: It would hardly have been a really serious engagement if it hadn't been broken off at least once. But I forgave you before the week was out.

ALGERNON: *(Crossing to her, and kneeling.)* What a perfect

530 angel you are, Cecily.

CECILY: You dear romantic boy. *(He kisses her, she puts her fingers through his hair.)* I hope your hair curls naturally, does it?

ALGERNON: Yes, darling, with a little help from others.

535 CECILY: I am so glad.

ALGERNON: You'll never break off our engagement again, Cecily?

CECILY: I don't think I could break it off now that I have actually met you. Besides, of course, that is the question of your

540 name.

ALGERNON: Yes, of course. *(Nervously.)*

CECILY: You must not laugh at me, darling, but it had always been a girlish dream of mine to love some one whose name was Ernest. *(*ALGERNON *rises,* CECILY *also.)* There is some-

545 thing in that name that seems to inspire absolute confidence. I pity any poor married woman whose husband is not called Ernest.

ALGERNON: But, my dear child, do you mean to say you could not love me if I had some other name?

550 CECILY: But what name?

ALGERNON: Oh, any name you like—Algernon, for instance. . . .

CECILY: But I don't like the name of Algernon.

ALGERNON: Well, my own dear, sweet, loving little darling, I

555 really can't see why you should object to the name of Algernon. It is not at all a bad name. In fact, it is rather an aristocratic name. Half of the chaps who get into the Bankruptcy Court are called Algernon. But seriously, Cecily . . . *(Moving to her.)* . . . if my name was Algy, couldn't you love me?

560

CECILY: I might respect you, Ernest, I might admire your character, but I fear that I should not be able to give you my undivided attention.

ALGERNON: Ahem! Cecily! (*Picking up hat.*) Your Rector here
565 is, I suppose, thoroughly experienced in the practice of all the rites and ceremonials of the church?

CECILY: Oh, yes. Dr. Chasuble is a most learned man. He has never written a single book, so you can imagine how much he knows.

570 ALGERNON: I must see him at once on a most important christening—I mean on most important business.

CECILY: Oh!

ALGERNON: I sha'n't be away more than half an hour.

CECILY: Considering that we have been engaged since Febru-
575 ary the 14th, and that I only met you to-day for the first time, I think it is rather hard that you should leave me for so long a period as half an hour. Couldn't you make it twenty minutes?

ALGERNON: I'll be back in no time. (*Kisses her and rushes*
580 *down the garden.*)

CECILY: What an impetuous boy he is. I like his hair so much. I must enter his proposal in my diary.

(*Enter* MERRIMAN.)

MERRIMAN: A Miss Fairfax has just called to see Mr. Worthing. On very important business, Miss Fairfax states.

585 CECILY: Isn't Mr. Worthing in his library?

MERRIMAN: Mr. Worthing went over in the direction of the Rectory some time ago.

CECILY: Pray ask the lady to come out here; Mr. Worthing is sure to be back soon. And you can bring tea.

590 MERRIMAN: Yes, miss.

(*Goes out.*)

CECILY: Miss Fairfax! I suppose one of the many good elderly women who are associated with Uncle Jack in some of his philanthropic work in London. I don't quite like women who are interested in philanthropic work. I think it is so for-
595 ward of them.

(*Enter* MERRIMAN.)

MERRIMAN: Miss Fairfax.

(*Enter* GWENDOLEN. *Exit* MERRIMAN.)

CECILY: (*Advancing to meet her.*) Pray let me introduce myself to you. My name is Cecily Cardew.

GWENDOLEN: Cecily Cardew? (*Moving to her and shaking*
600 *hands.*) What a very sweet name! Something tells me that we are going to be great friends. I like you already more than I can say. My first impressions of people are never wrong.

CECILY: How nice of you to like me so much after we have known each other such a comparatively short time. Pray sit
605 down.

GWENDOLEN: (*Still standing up.*) I may call you Cecily, may I not?

CECILY: With pleasure!

GWENDOLEN: And you will always call me Gwendolen, won't
610 you?

CECILY: If you wish.

GWENDOLEN: Then that is all quite settled, is it not?

CECILY: I hope so. (*A pause. They both sit down together.*)

GWENDOLEN: Perhaps this might be a favorable opportunity
615 for my mentioning who I am. My father is Lord Bracknell. You have never heard of papa, I suppose?

CECILY: I don't think so.

GWENDOLEN: Outside the family circle, papa, I am glad to say, is entirely unknown. I think that is quite as it should be.
620 The home seems to me to be the proper sphere for the man. And certainly once a man begins to neglect his domestic duties he becomes painfully effeminate, does he not? And I don't like that. It makes men so very attractive. Cecily, mamma, whose views on education are remarkably strict,
625 has brought me up to be extremely short-sighted; it is part of her system; so do you mind my looking at you through my glasses?

CECILY: Oh, not at all, Gwendolen. I am very fond of being looked at.

GWENDOLEN: (*After examining* CECILY *carefully through a*
630 *lorgnette.*) You are here on a short visit, I suppose.

CECILY: Oh, no, I live here.

GWENDOLEN: (*Severely.*) Really? Your mother, no doubt, or some female relative of advanced years, resides here also?

CECILY: Oh, no. I have no mother, nor, in fact, any relations.
635

GWENDOLEN: Indeed?

CECILY: My dear guardian, with the assistance of Miss Prism, has the arduous task of looking after me.

GWENDOLEN: Your guardian?

CECILY: Yes, I am Mr. Worthing's ward.
640

GWENDOLEN: Oh! It is strange he never mentioned to me that he had a ward. How secretive of him! He grows more interesting hourly. I am not sure, however, that the news inspires me with feelings of unmixed delight. (*Rising and going to her.*) I am very fond of you, Cecily; I have liked you ever
645 since I met you. But I am bound to state that now that I know that you are Mr. Worthing's ward, I cannot help expressing a wish you were—well, just a little older than you seem to be—and not quite so very alluring in appearance. In fact, if I may speak candidly—
650

CECILY: Pray do! I think that whenever one has anything unpleasant to say, one should always be quite candid.

GWENDOLEN: Well, to speak with perfect candour, Cecily, I wish that you were fully forty-two, and more than usually plain for your age. Ernest has a strong upright nature. He is
655 the very soul of truth and honour. Disloyalty would be as impossible to him as deception. But even men of the noblest possible moral character are extremely susceptible to the influence of the physical charms of others. Modern, no less than Ancient History, supplies us with many most painful ex-
660 amples of what I refer to. If it were not so, indeed, History would be quite unreadable.

CECILY: I beg your pardon, Gwendolen, did you say Ernest?

GWENDOLEN: Yes.

CECILY: Oh, but it is not Mr. Ernest Worthing who is my
665 guardian. It is his brother—his elder brother.

GWENDOLEN: (*Sitting down again.*) Ernest never mentioned to me that he had a brother.

CECILY: I am sorry to say they have not been on good terms for a long time.
670

GWENDOLEN: Ah! that accounts for it. And now that I think of it I have never heard any man mention his brother. The subject seems distasteful to most men. Cecily, you have lifted a load from my mind. I was growing almost anxious. It would have been terrible if any cloud had come across a friendship like ours, would it not? Of course you are quite, quite sure that it is not Mr. Ernest Worthing who is your guardian?

CECILY: Quite sure. (*A pause.*) In fact, I am going to be his.

GWENDOLEN: (*Enquiringly.*) I beg your pardon?

CECILY: (*Rather shy and confidingly.*) Dearest Gwendolen, there is no reason why I should make a secret of it to you. Our little county newspaper is sure to chronicle the fact next week. Mr. Ernest Worthing and I are engaged to be married.

GWENDOLEN: (*Quite politely, rising.*) My darling Cecily, I think there must be some slight error. Mr. Ernest Worthing is engaged to me. The announcement will appear in the *Morning Post* on Saturday at the latest.

CECILY: (*Very politely, rising.*) I am afraid you must be under some misconception. Ernest proposed to me exactly ten minutes ago. (*Shows diary.*)

GWENDOLEN: (*Examines diary through her lorgnette carefully.*) It is certainly very curious, for he asked me to be his wife yesterday afternoon at 5.30. If you would care to verify the incident, pray do so. (*Produces diary of her own.*) I never travel without my diary. One should always have something sensational to read in the train. I am so sorry, dear Cecily, if it is any disappointment to you, but I am afraid *I* have the prior claim.

CECILY: It would distress me more than I can tell you, dear Gwendolen, if it caused you any mental or physical anguish, but I feel bound to point out that since Ernest proposed to you he clearly has changed his mind.

GWENDOLEN: (*Meditatively.*) If the poor fellow has been entrapped into any foolish promise I shall consider it my duty to rescue him at once, and with a firm hand.

CECILY: (*Thoughtfully and sadly.*) Whatever unfortunate entanglement my dear boy may have got into, I will never reproach him with it after we are married.

GWENDOLEN: Do you allude to me, Miss Cardew, as an entanglement? You are presumptuous. On an occasion of this kind it becomes more than a moral duty to speak one's mind. It becomes a pleasure.

CECILY: Do you suggest, Miss Fairfax, that I entrapped Ernest into an engagement? How dare you? This is no time for wearing the shallow mask of manners. When I see a spade I call it a spade.

GWENDOLEN: (*Satirically.*) I am glad to say that I have never seen a spade. It is obvious that our social spheres have been widely different.

(*Enter* MERRIMAN, *followed by the footman. He carries a salver, tablecloth, and plate-stand.* CECILY *is about to retort. The presence of the servants exercises a restraining influence, under which both girls chafe.*)

MERRIMAN: Shall I lay tea here as usual, miss?

CECILY: (*Sternly, in a calm voice.*) Yes, as usual. (MERRIMAN *begins to clear and lay cloth. A long pause.* CECILY *and* GWENDOLEN *glare at each other.*)

GWENDOLEN: Are there many interesting walks in the vicinity, Miss Cardew?

CECILY: Oh, yes, a great many. From the top of one of the hills quite close one can see five counties.

GWENDOLEN: Five counties! I don't think I should like that. I hate crowds.

CECILY: (*Sweetly.*) I suppose that is why you live in town? (GWENDOLEN *bites her lip, and beats her foot nervously with her parasol.*)

GWENDOLEN: (*Looking around.*) Quite a well-kept garden this is, Miss Cardew.

CECILY: So glad you like it, Miss Fairfax.

GWENDOLEN: I had no idea there were any flowers in the country.

CECILY: Oh, flowers are as common here, Miss Fairfax, as people are in London.

GWENDOLEN: Personally I cannot understand how anybody manages to exist in the country, if anybody who is anybody does. The country always bores me to death.

CECILY: Ah! This is what the newspapers call agricultural depression, is it not? I believe the aristocracy are suffering very much from it just at present. It is almost an epidemic amongst them, I have been told. May I offer you some tea, Miss Fairfax?

GWENDOLEN: (*With elaborate politeness.*) Thank you. (*Aside.*) Detestable girl! But I require tea!

CECILY: (*Sweetly.*) Sugar?

GWENDOLEN: (*Superciliously.*) No, thank you. Sugar is not fashionable any more. (CECILY *looks angrily at her, takes up the tongs and puts four lumps of sugar into the cup.*)

CECILY: (*Severely.*) Cake or bread and butter?

GWENDOLEN: (*In a bored manner.*) Bread and butter, please. Cake is rarely seen at the best houses nowadays.

CECILY: (*Cuts a very large slice of cake, and puts it on the tray.*) Hand that to Miss Fairfax. (MERRIMAN *does so, and goes out with footman.* GWENDOLEN *drinks the tea and makes a grimace. Puts down cup at once, reaches out her hand to the bread and butter, looks at it, and finds it is cake. Rises in indignation.*)

GWENDOLEN: You have filled my tea with lumps of sugar, and though I asked most distinctly for bread and butter, you have given me cake. I am known for the gentleness of my disposition, and the extraordinary sweetness of my nature, but I warn you, Miss Cardew, you may go too far.

CECILY: (*Rising.*) To save my poor, innocent, trusting boy from the machinations of any other girl there are no lengths to which I would not go.

GWENDOLEN: From the moment I saw you I distrusted you. I felt that you were false and deceitful. I am never deceived in such matters. My first impressions of people are invariably right.

CECILY: It seems to me, Miss Fairfax, that I am trespassing on your valuable time. No doubt you have many other calls of a similar character to make in the neighbourhood.

(*Enter* JACK.)

GWENDOLEN: (*Catching sight of him.*) Ernest! My own Ernest!

JACK: Gwendolen! Darling! (*Offers to kiss her.*)

GWENDOLEN: (*Drawing back.*) A moment! May I ask if you are engaged to be married to this young lady? (*Points to* CECILY.)

JACK: (*Laughing.*) To dear little Cecily! Of course not! What could have put such an idea into your pretty little head?

GWENDOLEN: Thank you. You may. (*Offers her cheek.*)

CECILY: (*Very sweetly.*) I knew there must be some misunderstanding, Miss Fairfax. The gentleman whose arm is at present around your waist is my dear guardian, Mr. John Worthing.

790 GWENDOLEN: I beg your pardon?

CECILY: This is Uncle Jack.

GWENDOLEN: (*Receding.*) Jack! Oh!

(*Enter* ALGERNON.)

CECILY: Here is Ernest.

ALGERNON: (*Goes straight over to* CECILY *without noticing*
795 *anyone else.*) My own love! (*Offers to kiss her.*)

CECILY: (*Drawing back.*) A moment, Ernest! May I ask you—
are you engaged to be married to this young lady?

ALGERNON: (*Looking round.*) To what young lady? Good heavens! Gwendolen!

800 CECILY: Yes, to good heavens, Gwendolen, I mean to
Gwendolen.

ALGERNON: (*Laughing.*) Of course not! What could have put
such an idea into your pretty little head?

CECILY: Thank you. (*Presenting her cheek to be kissed.*) You
805 may. (ALGERNON *kisses her.*)

GWENDOLEN: I felt there was some slight error, Miss Cardew.
The gentleman who is now embracing you is my cousin, Mr.
Algernon Moncrieff.

CECILY: (*Breaking away from* ALGERNON.) Algernon Mon-
810 crieff! Oh! (*The two girls move towards each other and put
their arms round each other's waists as if for protection.*)

CECILY: Are you called Algernon?

ALGERNON: I cannot deny it.

CECILY: Oh!

815 GWENDOLEN: Is your name really John?

JACK: (*Standing rather proudly.*) I could deny it if I liked. I
could deny anything if I liked. But my name certainly is
John. It has been John for years.

CECILY: (*To* GWENDOLEN.) A gross deception has been prac-
820 tised on both of us.

GWENDOLEN: My poor wounded Cecily!

CECILY: My sweet, wronged Gwendolen!

GWENDOLEN: (*Slowing and seriously.*) You will call me sister,
will you not? (*They embrace.* JACK *and* ALGERNON *groan and*
825 *walk up and down.*)

CECILY: (*Rather brightly.*) There is just one question I would
like to be allowed to ask my guardian.

GWENDOLEN: An admirable idea! Mr. Worthing, there is just
one question I would like to be permitted to put to you.
830 Where is your brother Ernest? We are both engaged to be
married to your brother Ernest, so it is a matter of some
importance to us to know where your brother Ernest is at
present.

JACK: (*Slowly and hesitatingly.*) Gwendolen—Cecily—it is
835 very painful for me to be forced to speak the truth. It is the
first time in my life that I have ever been reduced to such a
painful position, and I am really quite inexperienced in
doing anything of the kind. However I will tell you quite
frankly that I have no brother Ernest. I have no brother at all.
840 I never had a brother in my life, and I certainly have not the
smallest intention of ever having one in the future.

CECILY: (*Surprised.*) No brother at all?

JACK: (*Cheerily.*) None!

GWENDOLEN: (*Severely.*) Had you never a brother of any kind?

845 JACK: (*Pleasantly.*) Never. Not even of any kind.

GWENDOLEN: I am afraid it is quite clear, Cecily, that neither
of us is engaged to be married to anyone.

CECILY: It is not a very pleasant position for a young girl suddenly to find herself in. Is it?

GWENDOLEN: Let us go into the house. They will hardly ven- 850
ture to come after us there.

CECILY: No, men are so cowardly, aren't they? (*They retire into
the house with scornful looks.*)

JACK: This ghastly state of things is what you call Bunburying,
I suppose? 855

ALGERNON: Yes, and a perfectly wonderful Bunbury it is. The
most wonderful Bunbury I have ever had in my life.

JACK: Well, you've no right whatsoever to Bunbury here.

ALGERNON: That is absurd. One has a right to Bunbury anywhere one chooses. Every serious Bunburyist knows that. 860

JACK: Serious Bunburyist! Good heavens!

ALGERNON: Well, one must be serious about something, if one
wants to have any amusement in life. I happen to be serious
about Bunburying. What on earth you are serious about I
haven't got the remotest idea. About everything, I should 865
fancy. You have such an absolutely trivial nature.

JACK: Well, the only small satisfaction I have in the whole of
this wretched business is that your friend Bunbury is quite
exploded. You won't be able to run down to the country
quite so often as you used to do, dear Algy. And a very good 870
thing, too.

ALGERNON: Your brother is a little off colour, isn't he, dear
Jack? You won't be able to disappear to London quite so frequently as your wicked custom was. And not a bad thing,
either. 875

JACK: As for your conduct towards Miss Cardew, I must say
that your taking in a sweet, simple, innocent girl like that is
quite inexcusable. To say nothing of the fact that she is my
ward.

ALGERNON: I can see no possible defence at all for your de- 880
ceiving a brilliant, clever, thoroughly experienced young
lady like Miss Fairfax. To say nothing of the fact that she is
my cousin.

JACK: I wanted to be engaged to Gwendolen, that is all. I love
her. 885

ALGERNON: Well, I simply wanted to be engaged to Cecily. I
adore her.

JACK: There is certainly no chance of your marrying Miss
Cardew.

ALGERNON: I don't think there is much likelihood, Jack, of 890
you and Miss Fairfax being united.

JACK: Well, that is no business of yours.

ALGERNON: If it was my business, I wouldn't talk about it. (*Begins to eat muffins.*) It is very vulgar to talk about one's business. Only people like stock-brokers do that, and then 895
merely at dinner parties.

JACK: How you can sit there, calmly eating muffins, when we
are in this horrible trouble, I can't make out. You seem to
me to be perfectly heartless.

ALGERNON: Well, I can't eat muffins in an agitated manner. 900
The butter would probably get on my cuffs. One should always eat muffins quite calmly. It is the only way to eat them.

JACK: I say it's perfectly heartless your eating muffins at all,
under the circumstances.

ALGERNON: When I am in trouble, eating is the only thing 905
that consoles me. Indeed, when I am in really great trouble,

as anyone who knows me intimately will tell you, I refuse everything except food and drink. At the present moment I am eating muffins because I am unhappy. Besides, I am par-
910 ticularly fond of muffins. *(Rising.)*

JACK: *(Rising.)* Well, that is no reason why you should eat them all in that greedy way. *(Takes muffin from* ALGERNON.*)*

ALGERNON: *(Offering tea-cake.)* I wish you would have tea-cake instead. I don't like tea-cake.

915 JACK: Good heavens! I suppose a man may eat his own muffins in his own garden.

ALGERNON: But you have just said it was perfectly heartless to eat muffins.

JACK: I said it was perfectly heartless of you, under the circum-
920 stances. That is a very different thing.

ALGERNON: That may be. But the muffins are the same. *(He seizes the muffin dish from* JACK.*)*

JACK: Algy, I wish to goodness you would go.

ALGERNON: You can't possibly ask me to go without having
925 some dinner. It's absurd. I never go without my dinner. No one ever does, except vegetarians and people like that. Besides I have just made arrangements with Dr. Chasuble to be christened at a quarter to six under the name of Ernest.

JACK: My dear fellow, the sooner you give up that nonsense the
930 better. I made arrangements this morning with Dr. Chasuble to be christened myself at 5.30, and I naturally will take the name of Ernest. Gwendolen would wish it. We can't both be christened Ernest. It's absurd. Besides, I have a perfect right to be christened if I like. There is no evidence
935 at all that I ever have been christened by anybody. I should think it extremely probable I never was, and so does Dr. Chasuble. It is entirely different in your case. You have been christened already.

ALGERNON: Yes, but I have not been christened for years.

940 JACK: Yes, but you have been christened. That is the important thing.

ALGERNON: Quite so. So I know my constitution can stand it. If you are not quite sure about your ever having been christened, I must say I think it rather dangerous your venturing
945 on it now. It might make you very unwell. You can hardly have forgotten that someone very closely connected with you was very nearly carried off this week in Paris by a severe chill.

JACK: Yes, but you said yourself that a severe chill was not
950 hereditary.

ALGERNON: It usedn't to be, I know—but I daresay it is now. Science is always making wonderful improvements in things.

JACK: *(Picking up the muffin-dish.)* Oh, that is nonsense; you
955 are always talking nonsense.

ALGERNON: Jack, you are at the muffins again! I wish you wouldn't. There are only two left. *(Takes them.)* I told you I was particularly fond of muffins.

JACK: But I hate tea-cake.

960 ALGERNON: Why on earth then do you allow tea-cake to be served up for your guests? What ideas you have of hospitality!

JACK: Algernon! I have already told you to go. I don't want you here. Why don't you go?

965 ALGERNON: I haven't quite finished my tea yet, and there is still one muffin left. *(*JACK *groans, and sinks into a chair.* AL-GERNON *still continues eating.)*

— ACT THREE —

Morning-room at the Manor House. GWENDOLEN *and* CECILY *are at the window, looking out into the garden.*

GWENDOLEN: The fact that they did not follow us at once into the house, as anyone else would have done, seems to me to show that they have some sense of shame left.

CECILY: They have been eating muffins. That looks like repentance.   5

GWENDOLEN: *(After a pause.)* They don't seem to notice us at all. Couldn't you cough?

GWENDOLEN: They're looking at us. What effrontery!

CECILY: They're approaching. That's very forward of them.

GWENDOLEN: Let us preserve a dignified silence.   10

CECILY: Certainly. It's the only thing to do now.

(Enter JACK, *followed by* ALGERNON. *They whistle some dread-ful popular air from a British opera.)*

GWENDOLEN: This dignified silence seems to produce an un-pleasant effect.

CECILY: A most distasteful one.

GWENDOLEN: But we will not be the first to speak.   15

CECILY: Certainly not.

GWENDOLEN: Mr. Worthing, I have something very particular to ask you. Much depends on your reply.

CECILY: Gwendolen, your common sense is invaluable. Mr. Moncrieff, kindly answer me the following question. Why 20
did you pretend to be my guardian's brother?

ALGERNON: In order that I might have an opportunity of meet-ing you.

CECILY: *(To* GWENDOLEN.*)* That certainly seems a satisfactory explanation, does it not?   25

GWENDOLEN: Yes, dear, if you can believe him.

CECILY: I don't. But that does not affect the wonderful beauty of his answer.

GWENDOLEN: True. In matters of grave importance, style, not sincerity, is the vital thing. Mr. Worthing, what explanation 30
can you offer to me for pretending to have a brother? Was it in order that you might have an opportunity of coming up to town to see me as often as possible?

JACK: Can you doubt it, Miss Fairfax?

GWENDOLEN: I have the gravest doubts upon the subject. But 35
I intend to crush them. This is not the moment for German scepticism. *(Moving to* CECILY.*)* Their explanations appear to be quite satisfactory, especially Mr. Worthing's. That seems to me to have the stamp of truth upon it.

CECILY: I am more than content with what Mr. Moncrieff   40
said. His voice alone inspires one with absolute credulity.

GWENDOLEN: Then you think we should forgive them?

CECILY: Yes. I mean no.

GWENDOLEN: True! I had forgotten. There are principles at stake that one cannot surrender. Which of us should tell 45
them? The task is not a pleasant one.

CECILY: Could we not both speak at the same time?

GWENDOLEN: An excellent idea! I nearly always speak at the same time as other people. Will you take the time from me?

CECILY: Certainly. *(*GWENDOLEN *beats time with uplifted* 50
finger.)

GWENDOLEN and CECILY: *(Speaking together.)* Your Christian names are still an insuperable barrier. That is all!

JACK *and* ALGERNON: *(Speaking together.)* Our Christian
55   names! Is that all? But we are going to be christened this afternoon.

GWENDOLEN: *(To* JACK.*)* For my sake you are prepared to do
this terrible thing?

JACK: I am.

60 CECILY: *(To* ALGERNON.*)* To please me you are ready to face
this fearful ordeal?

ALGERNON: I am!

GWENDOLEN: How absurd to talk of the equality of the sexes!
Where questions of self-sacrifice are concerned, men are in-
65 finitely beyond us.

JACK: We are. *(Clasps hands with* ALGERNON.*)*

CECILY: They have moments of physical courage of which we
women know absolutely nothing.

GWENDOLEN: *(To* JACK.*)* Darling!

70 ALGERNON: *(To* CECILY.*)* Darling! *(They fall into each other's
arms.)*

(Enter MERRIMAN. *When he enters he coughs loudly, seeing the
situation.)*

MERRIMAN: Ahem! Ahem! Lady Bracknell!

JACK: Good heavens!

(Enter LADY BRACKNELL. *The couples separate in alarm. Exit*
MERRIMAN.*)*

LADY BRACKNELL: Gwendolen! What does this mean?

75 GWENDOLEN: Merely that I am engaged to be married to Mr.
Worthing, Mamma.

LADY BRACKNELL: Come here. Sit down. Sit down immediately. Hesitation of any kind is a sign of mental decay in the
young, of physical weakness in the old. *(Turns to* JACK.*)* Ap-
80 prised, sir, of my daughter's sudden flight by her trusty maid,
whose confidence I purchased by means of a small coin, I
followed her at once by a luggage train. Her unhappy father
is, I am glad to say, under the impression that she is attending a more than usually lengthy lecture by the University Ex-
85 tension Scheme on the Influence of a Permanent Income
on Thought. I do not propose to undeceive him. Indeed I
have never undeceived him on any question. I would consider it wrong. But of course, you will clearly understand that
all communication between yourself and my daughter must
90 cease immediately from this moment. On this point, as indeed on all points, I am firm.

JACK: I am engaged to be married to Gwendolen, Lady
Bracknell!

LADY BRACKNELL: You are nothing of the kind, sir. And now,
95 as regards Algernon! . . . Algernon!

ALGERNON: Yes, Aunt Augusta.

LADY BRACKNELL: May I ask if it is in this house that your invalid friend Mr. Bunbury resides?

ALGERNON: *(Stammering.)* Oh, no! Bunbury doesn't live here.
100 Bunbury is somewhere else at present. In fact, Bunbury is
dead.

LADY BRACKNELL: Dead! When did Mr. Bunbury die? His
death must have been extremely sudden.

ALGERNON: *(Airily.)* Oh, I killed Bunbury this afternoon. I
105 mean poor Bunbury died this afternoon.

LADY BRACKNELL: What did he die of?

ALGERNON: Bunbury? Oh, he was quite exploded.

LADY BRACKNELL: Exploded! Was he the victim of a revolutionary outrage? I was not aware that Mr. Bunbury was interested in social legislation. If so, he is well punished for his 110
morbidity.

ALGERNON: My dear Aunt Augusta, I mean he was found out!
The doctors found out that Bunbury could not live, that is
what I mean—so Bunbury died.

LADY BRACKNELL: He seems to have had great confidence in 115
the opinion of his physicians. I am glad, however, that he
made up his mind at the last to some definite course of action, and acted under proper medical advice. And now that
we have finally got rid of this Mr. Bunbury, may I ask, Mr.
Worthing, who is that young person whose hand my nephew 120
Algernon is now holding in what seems to me a peculiarly
unnecessary manner?

JACK: That lady is Miss Cecily Cardew, my ward. (LADY
BRACKNELL *bows coldly to* CECILY.*)*

ALGERNON: I am engaged to be married to Cecily, Aunt 125
Augusta.

LADY BRACKNELL: I beg your pardon?

CECILY: Mr. Moncrieff and I are engaged to be married, Lady
Bracknell.

LADY BRACKNELL: *(With a shiver, crossing to the sofa and sitting* 130
down.) I do not know whether there is anything peculiarly
exciting in the air of this particular part of Hertfordshire, but
the number of engagements that go on seems to me considerably above the proper average that statistics have laid down for
our guidance. I think some preliminary enquiry on my part 135
would not be out of place. Mr. Worthing, is Miss Cardew at
all connected with any of the larger railway stations in London? I merely desire information. Until yesterday I had no
idea that there were any families or persons whose origin
was a Terminus. (JACK *looks perfectly furious, but restrains* 140
himself.)

JACK: *(In a clear, cold voice.)* Miss Cardew is the granddaugh-
ter of the late Mr. Thomas Cardew of 149, Belgrave Square,
S.W.; Gervase Park, Dorking, Surrey; and the Sporran,
Fifeshire, N.B. 145

LADY BRACKNELL: That sounds not unsatisfactory. Three addresses always inspire confidence, even in tradesmen. But
what proof have I of their authenticity?

JACK: I have carefully preserved the Court Guide of the period. They are open to your inspection, Lady Bracknell. 150

LADY BRACKNELL: *(Grimly.)* I have known strange errors in
that publication.

JACK: Miss Cardew's family solicitors are Messrs. Markby,
Markby, and Markby.

LADY BRACKNELL: Markby, Markby, and Markby? A firm of 155
the very highest position in their profession. Indeed I am told
that one of the Mr. Markbys is occasionally to be seen at dinner parties. So far I am satisfied.

JACK: *(Very irritably.)* How extremely kind of you, Lady Bracknell! I have also in my possession, you will be pleased to 160
hear, certificates of Miss Cardew's birth, baptism, whooping
cough, registration, vaccination, confirmation, and the
measles; both the German and the English variety.

LADY BRACKNELL: Ah! A life crowded with incident, I see;
though perhaps somewhat too exciting for a young girl. I am 165
not myself in favour of premature experiences. *(Rises, looks
at her watch.)* Gwendolen! the time approaches for our departure. We have not a moment to lose. As a matter of form,

Mr. Worthing, I had better ask you if Miss Cardew has any little fortune?

JACK: Oh, about a hundred and thirty thousand pounds in the Funds. That is all. Good-bye, Lady Bracknell. So pleased to have seen you.

LADY BRACKNELL: *(Sitting down again.)* A moment, Mr. Worthing. A hundred and thirty thousand pounds! And in the Funds! Miss Cardew seems to me a most attractive young lady, now that I look at her. Few girls of the present day have any really solid qualities, any of the qualities that last, and improve with time. We live, I regret to say, in an age of surfaces. *(To* CECILY.) Come over here, dear. (CECILY *goes across.)* Pretty child! your dress is sadly simple, and your hair seems almost as Nature might have left it. But we can soon alter all that. A thoroughly experienced French maid produces a really marvelous result in a very brief space of time. I remember recommending one to young Lady Lancing, and after three months her own husband did not know her.

JACK: *(Aside.)* And after six months nobody knew her.

LADY BRACKNELL: *(Glares at* JACK *for a few moments. Then bends, with a practised smile, to* CECILY.) Kindly turn round, sweet child. (CECILY *turns completely round.)* No, the side view is what I want. (CECILY *presents her profile.)* Yes, quite as I expected. There are distinct social possibilities in your profile. The two weak points in our age are its want of principle and its want of profile. The chin a little higher, dear. Style largely depends on the way the chin is worn. They are worn very high, just at present. Algernon!

ALGERNON: Yes, Aunt Augusta!

LADY BRACKNELL: There are distinct social possibilities in Miss Cardew's profile.

ALGERNON: Cecily is the sweetest, dearest, prettiest girl in the whole world. And I don't care twopence about social possibilities.

LADY BRACKNELL: Never speak disrespectfully of society, Algernon. Only people who can't get into it do that. *(To* CECILY.) Dear child, of course you know that Algernon has nothing but his debts to depend upon. But I do not approve of mercenary marriages. When I married Lord Bracknell I had no fortune of any kind. But I never dreamed for a moment of allowing that to stand in my way. Well, I suppose I must give my consent.

ALGERNON: Thank you, Aunt Augusta.

LADY BRACKNELL: Cecily, you may kiss me!

CECILY: *(Kisses her.)* Thank you, Lady Bracknell.

LADY BRACKNELL: You may also address me as Aunt Augusta for the future.

CECILY: Thank you, Aunt Augusta.

LADY BRACKNELL: The marriage, I think, had better take place quite soon.

ALGERNON: Thank you, Aunt Augusta.

CECILY: Thank, Aunt Augusta.

LADY BRACKNELL: To speak frankly, I am not in favour of long engagements. They give people the opportunity of finding out each other's character before marriage, which I think is never advisable.

JACK: I beg your pardon for interrupting you, Lady Bracknell, but this engagement is quite out of the question. I am Miss Cardew's guardian, and she cannot marry without my consent until she comes of age. That consent I absolutely decline to give.

LADY BRACKNELL: Upon what grounds, may I ask? Algernon is an extremely, I may almost say an ostentatiously, eligible young man. He has nothing, but he looks everything. What more can one desire?

JACK: It pains me very much to have to speak frankly to you, Lady Bracknell, about your nephew, but the fact is that I do not approve at all of his moral character. I suspect him of being untruthful. (ALGERNON *and* CECILY *look at him in indignant amazement.)*

LADY BRACKNELL: Untruthful! My nephew Algernon? Impossible! He is an Oxonian.

JACK: I fear there can be no possible doubt about the matter. This afternoon, during my temporary absence in London on an important question of romance, he obtained admission to my house by means of the false pretence of being my brother. Under an assumed name he drank, I've just been informed by my butler, an entire pint bottle of my Perrier-Jouet, Brut, '89; a wine I was specially reserving for myself. Continuing his disgraceful deception, he succeeded in the course of the afternoon in alienating the affections of my only ward. He subsequently stayed to tea, and devoured every single muffin. And what makes his conduct all the more heartless is, that he was perfectly well aware from the first that I have no brother, that I never had a brother, and that I don't intend to have a brother, not even of any kind. I distinctly told him so myself yesterday afternoon.

LADY BRACKNELL: Ahem! Mr. Worthing, after careful consideration I have decided entirely to overlook my nephew's conduct to you.

JACK: That is very generous of you, Lady Bracknell. My own decision, however, is unalterable. I decline to give my consent.

LADY BRACKNELL: *(To* CECILY.) Come here, sweet child. (CECILY *goes over.)* How old are you, dear?

CECILY: Well, I am really only eighteen, but I always admit to twenty when I go to evening parties.

LADY BRACKNELL: You are perfectly right in making some slight alteration. Indeed, no woman should ever be quite accurate about her age. It looks so calculating. . . . *(In meditative manner.)* Eighteen, but admitting to twenty at evening parties. Well, it will not be very long before you are of age and free from the restraints of tutelage. So I don't think your guardian's consent is, after all, a matter of any importance.

JACK: Pray excuse me, Lady Bracknell, for interrupting you again, but it is only fair to tell you that according to the terms of her grandfather's will Miss Cardew does not come legally of age till she is thirty-five.

LADY BRACKNELL: That does not seem to me to be a grave objection. Thirty-five is a very attractive age. London society is full of women of the very highest birth who have, of their own free choice, remained thirty-five for years. Lady Dumbleton is an instance in point. To my own knowledge she has been thirty-five ever since she arrived at the age of forty, which was many years ago now. I see no reason why our dear Cecily should not be even still more attractive at the age you mention than she is at present. There will be a large accumulation of property.

CECILY: Algy, could you wait for me till I was thirty-five?

ALGERNON: Of course I could, Cecily. You know I could.

CECILY: Yes, I felt it instinctively, but I couldn't wait all that time. I hate waiting even five minutes for anybody. It always makes me rather cross. I am not punctual myself, I know, but I do like punctuality in others, and waiting, even to be married, is quite out of the question.

ALGERNON: Then what is to be done, Cecily?

295 CECILY: I don't know, Mr. Moncrieff.

LADY BRACKNELL: My dear Mr. Worthing, as Miss Cardew states positively that she cannot wait till she is thirty-five—a remark which I am bound to say seems to me to show a somewhat impatient nature—I would beg of you to recon-

300 sider your decision.

JACK: But my dear Lady Bracknell, the matter is entirely in your own hands. The moment you consent to my marriage with Gwendolen, I will most gladly allow your nephew to form an alliance with my ward.

305 LADY BRACKNELL: (*Rising and drawing herself up.*) You must be quite aware that what you propose is out of the question.

JACK: Then a passionate celibacy is all that any of us can look forward to.

LADY BRACKNELL: That is not the destiny I propose for Gwen-

310 dolen. Algernon, of course, can choose for himself. (*Pulls out her watch.*) Come, dear, (GWENDOLEN *rises.*) we have already missed five, if not six, trains. To miss any more might expose us to comment on the platform.

(*Enter* DR. CHASUBLE.)

CHASUBLE: Everything is quite ready for the christenings.

315 LADY BRACKNELL: The christenings, sir! Is not that somewhat premature?

CHASUBLE: (*Looking rather puzzled, and pointing to* JACK *and* ALGERNON.) Both these gentlemen have expressed a desire for immediate baptism.

320 LADY BRACKNELL: At their age? The idea is grotesque and irreligious! Algernon, I forbid you to be baptised. I will not hear of such excesses. Lord Bracknell would be highly displeased if he learned that that was the way in which you wasted your time and money.

325 CHASUBLE: Am I to understand then that there are to be no christenings at all this afternoon?

JACK: I don't think that, as things are now, it would be of much practical value to either of us, Dr. Chasuble.

CHASUBLE: I am grieved to hear such sentiments from you,

330 Mr. Worthing. They savour of the heretical views of the Anabaptists, views that I have completely refuted in four of my unpublished sermons. However, as your present mood seems to be one peculiarly secular, I will return to the church at once. Indeed, I have just been informed by the

335 pewopener that for the last hour and a half Miss Prism has been waiting for me in the vestry.

LADY BRACKNELL: (*Starting.*) Miss Prism! Did I hear you mention a Miss Prism?

CHASUBLE: Yes, Lady Bracknell. I am on my way to join her.

340 LADY BRACKNELL: Pray allow me to detain you for a moment. This matter may prove to be one of vital importance to Lord Bracknell and myself. Is this Miss Prism a female of repellent aspect, remotely connected with education?

CHASUBLE: (*Somewhat indignantly.*) She is the most cultivated

345 of ladies, and the very picture of respectability.

LADY BRACKNELL: It is obviously the same person. May I ask what position she holds in your household?

CHASUBLE: (*Severely.*) I am a celibate, madam.

JACK: (*Interposing.*) Miss Prism, Lady Bracknell, has been for the last three years Miss Cardew's esteemed governess and valued companion. 350

LADY BRACKNELL: In spite of what I hear of her, I must see her at once. Let her be sent for.

CHASUBLE: (*Looking off.*) She approaches; she is nigh.

(*Enter* MISS PRISM *hurriedly.*)

MISS PRISM: I was told you expected me in the vestry, dear 355 Canon. I have been waiting for you there for an hour and three-quarters. (*Catches sight of* LADY BRACKNELL, *who has fixed her with a stony glare.* MISS PRISM *grows pale and quails. She looks anxiously round as if desirous to escape.*)

LADY BRACKNELL: (*In a severe, judicial voice.*) Prism! (MISS 360 PRISM *bows her head in shame.*) Come here, Prism! (MISS PRISM *approaches in a humble manner.*) Prism! Where is that baby? (*General consternation. The Canon starts back in horror.* ALGERNON *and* JACK *pretend to be anxious to shield* CECILY *and* GWENDOLEN *from hearing the details of a terri-* 365 *ble public scandal.*) Twenty-eight years ago, Prism, you left Lord Bracknell's house, Number 104, Upper Grosvenor Street, in charge of a perambulator that contained a baby, of the male sex. You never returned. A few weeks later, through the elaborate investigations of the Metropolitan police, the 370 perambulator was discovered at midnight, standing by itself in a remote corner of Bayswater. It contained the manuscript of a three-volume novel of more than usually revolting sentimentality. (MISS PRISM *starts in involuntary indignation.*) But the baby was not there! (*Everyone looks at* MISS PRISM.) 375 Prism, where is that baby? (*A pause.*)

MISS PRISM: Lady Bracknell, I admit with shame that I do not know. I only wish I did. The plain facts of the case are these. On the morning of the day you mention, a day that is forever branded on my memory, I prepared as usual to take the baby 380 out in its perambulator. I had also with me a somewhat old but capacious hand-bag in which I had intended to place the manuscript of a work of fiction that I had written during my few unoccupied hours. In a moment of mental abstraction, for which I never can forgive myself, I deposited the manu- 385 script in the bassinette, and placed the baby in the hand-bag.

JACK: (*Who has been listening attentively.*) But where did you deposit the hand-bag?

MISS PRISM: Do not ask me, Mr. Worthing.

JACK: Miss Prism, this is a matter of no small importance to 390 me. I insist on knowing where you deposited the hand-bag that contained that infant.

MISS PRISM: I left it in the cloak-room of one of the larger railway stations in London.

JACK: What railway station? 395

MISS PRISM: (*Quite crushed.*) Victoria. The Brighton line. (*Sinks into a chair.*)

JACK: I must retire to my room for a moment. Gwendolen, wait here for me.

GWENDOLEN: If you are not too long, I will wait here for you 400 all my life.

(*Exit* JACK *in great excitement.*)

CHASUBLE: What do you think this means, Lady Bracknell?

LADY BRACKNELL: I dare not even suspect, Dr. Chasuble. I need hardly tell you that in families of high position strange

405 coincidences are not supposed to occur. They are hardly considered the thing. (*Noises heard overhead as if someone was throwing trunks about. Everybody looks up.*)

CECILY: Uncle Jack seems strangely agitated.

CHASUBLE: Your guardian has a very emotional nature.

410 LADY BRACKNELL: This noise is extremely unpleasant. It sounds as if he was having an argument. I dislike arguments of any kind. They are always vulgar, and often convincing.

CHASUBLE: (*Looking up.*) It has stopped now. (*The noise is redoubled.*)

415 LADY BRACKNELL: I wish he would arrive at some conclusion.

GWENDOLEN: The suspense is terrible. I hope it will last.

(*Enter* JACK *with a hand-bag of black leather in his hand.*)

JACK: (*Rushing over to* MISS PRISM.) Is this the hand-bag, Miss Prism? Examine it carefully before you speak. The happiness of more than one life depends on your answer.

420 MISS PRISM: (*Calmly.*) It seems to be mine. Yes, here is the injury it received through the upsetting of a Gower Street omnibus in younger and happier days. Here is the stain on the lining caused by the explosion of a temperance beverage, an incident that occurred at Leamington. And here, on the

425 lock, are my initials. I had forgotten that in an extravagant mood I had had them placed there. The bag is undoubtedly mine. I am delighted to have it so unexpectedly restored to me. It has been a great inconvenience being without it all these years.

430 JACK: (*In a pathetic voice.*) Miss Prism, more is restored to you than this hand-bag. I was the baby you placed in it.

MISS PRISM: (*Amazed.*) You?

JACK: (*Embracing her.*) Yes . . . mother!

MISS PRISM: (*Recoiling in indignant astonishment.*) Mr. Worthing! I am unmarried!

435 JACK: Unmarried! I do not deny that is a serious blow. But after all, who has the right to cast a stone against one who has suffered? Cannot repentance wipe out an act of folly? Why should there be one law for men and another for women?

440 Mother, I forgive you. (*Tries to embrace her again.*)

MISS PRISM: (*Still more indignant.*) Mr. Worthing, there is some error. (*Pointing to* LADY BRACKNELL.) There is the lady who can tell you who you really are.

JACK: (*After a pause.*) Lady Bracknell, I hate to seem inquisi-

445 tive, but would you kindly inform me who I am?

LADY BRACKNELL: I am afraid that the news I have to give you will not altogether please you. You are the son of my poor sister, Mrs. Moncrieff, and consequently Algernon's elder brother.

450 JACK: Algy's elder brother! Then I have a brother after all. I knew I had a brother! I always said I had a brother! Cecily,— how could you have ever doubted that I had a brother? (*Seizes hold of* ALGERNON.) Dr. Chasuble, my unfortunate brother. Miss Prism, my unfortunate brother. Gwendolen,

455 my unfortunate brother. Algy, you young scoundrel, you will have to treat me with more respect in the future. You have never behaved to me like a brother in all your life.

ALGERNON: Well, not till to-day, old boy, I admit. I did my best, however, though I was out of practice. (*Shakes hands.*)

460 GWENDOLEN: (*To* JACK.) My own! But what own are you? What is your Christian name, now that you have become someone else?

JACK: Good heavens! . . . I had quite forgotten that point. Your decision on the subject of my name is irrevocable, I suppose?

GWENDOLEN: I never change, except in my affections. 465

CECILY: What a noble nature you have, Gwendolen!

JACK: Then the question had better be cleared up at once. Aunt Augusta, a moment. At the time when Miss Prism left me in the hand-bag, had I been christened already?

LADY BRACKNELL: Every luxury that money could buy, in- 470 cluding christening, had been lavished on you by your fond and doting parents.

JACK: Then I was christened! That is settled. Now, what name was I given? Let me know the worst.

LADY BRACKNELL: Being the eldest son you were naturally 475 christened after your father.

JACK: (*Irritably.*) Yes, but what was my father's Christian name?

LADY BRACKNELL: (*Meditatively.*) I cannot at the present moment recall what the General's Christian name was. But I 480 have no doubt he had one. He was eccentric, I admit. But only in later years. And that was the result of the Indian climate, and marriage, and indigestion, and other things of that kind.

JACK: Algy! Can't you recollect what our father's Christian 485 name was?

ALGERNON: My dear boy, we were never even on speaking terms. He died before I was a year old.

JACK: His name would appear in the Army Lists of the period, I suppose, Aunt Augusta? 490

LADY BRACKNELL: The General was essentially a man of peace, except in his domestic life. But I have no doubt his name would appear in any military directory.

JACK: The Army Lists of the last forty years are here. These delightful records should have been my constant study. 495 (*Rushes to bookcase and tears the books out.*) M. Generals . . . Mallam, Maxbohm, Magley, what ghastly names they have—Markby, Migsby, Mobbs, Moncrieff! Lieutenant 1840, Captain, Lieutenant-Colonel, Colonel, General 1869, Christian names, Ernest John. (*Puts book very quietly* 500 *down and speaks quite calmly.*) I always told you, Gwendolen, my name was Ernest didn't I? Well, it is Ernest after all, I mean it naturally is Ernest.

LADY BRACKNELL: Yes, I remember the General was called Ernest. I knew I had some particular reason for disliking the 505 name.

GWENDOLEN: Ernest! My own Ernest! I felt from the first that you could have no other name!

JACK: Gwendolen, it is a terrible thing for a man to find out suddenly that all his life he has been speaking nothing but 510 the truth. Can you forgive me?

GWENDOLEN: I can. For I feel sure that you are sure to change.

JACK: My own one!

CHASUBLE: (*To* MISS PRISM.) Lætitia! (*Embraces her.*) 515

MISS PRISM: (*Enthusiastically.*) Frederick! At last!

ALGERNON: Cecily! (*Embraces her.*) At last!

JACK: Gwendolen! (*Embraces her.*) At last!

LADY BRACKNELL: My nephew, you seem to be displaying signs of triviality. 520

JACK: On the contrary, Aunt Augusta, I've now realized for the first time in my life the vital Importance of Being Earnest.

■ ANTON CHEKHOV ■

The work of Anton Chekhov (1860–1904) is noted for its objectivity, its sympathetic yet almost clinical examination of turn-of-the-century Russian life. Born in the provincial town of Taganrog, Chekhov trained for a career in medicine and began practicing as a physician in the mid-1880s. At that time he also began to write his first short stories. In his fiction, as in his later plays, Chekhov adopted a mildly ironic attitude toward his subjects, one that resisted sensation and melodrama in favor of a more neutral stance; as he wrote in a letter, "It is necessary that on stage everything should be as complex and as simple as in life. People are having dinner, and while they're having it, their future happiness may be decided or their lives may be about to be shattered." Chekhov's life was shattered in just this way, simply, suddenly, and casually. In 1884 he coughed up blood, the sure sign that he had contracted tuberculosis. The disease could not be cured and required repeated periods of convalescence; an early death was a certainty.

Chekhov began writing plays in the 1880s as well, mainly short comic sketches he called "vaudevilles," among them *The Bear* (1888), *The Proposal* (1889), and *The Wedding* (1890). In 1896, the Alexandrinsky Theater in St. Petersburg performed his full-length drama *The Seagull.* The play's indirect plotting and its avoidance of the conventional climaxes of melodrama confused actors and audiences alike, and it failed. Chekhov was persuaded by Constantin Stanislavski and Vladimir Nemirovich-Danchenko to mount the play in their newly founded Moscow Art Theater (MAT) in 1898. Stanislavski's commitment to a restrained style of performance, emphasizing psychological complexity and balanced playing by the entire ensemble is generally credited with making the MAT production a success; a seagull became the company's signature. Chekhov produced three more major plays with the MAT. He revised *The Wood Demon* (1889) as *Uncle Vanya* in 1899 and then produced *Three Sisters* (1901) and *The Cherry Orchard* (1904). Chekhov married the actress Olga Knipper—who played leading roles in his plays, including Madame Ranevskaya in *The Cherry Orchard*—in 1901 and spent the final years of his life convalescing in Yalta.

THE CHERRY ORCHARD

The action of Chekhov's plays is usually indirect, not progressive and consequential in the manner of Ibsen's work. Instead, a Chekhov play generally opens with the arrival of some well-to-do characters in the provincial scene of the play and closes with their departure: Yelena and Serbryakov in *Uncle Vanya*, the regiment and its romantic Lieutenant Colonel Vershinin in *Three Sisters*, Madame Ranevskaya and her entourage in *The Cherry Orchard*. In between, we see how the lives of the characters are changed, and yet somehow remain the same, as though their interaction worked to reveal the fundamentally static condition of their lives.

More than Chekhov's earlier plays, perhaps, *The Cherry Orchard* also seems to prefigure the fall of a class: the leisured, ineffectual, yet attractive Madame Ranevskaya and her brother, who own the estate but are incapable of bringing it into the twentieth century. We are left with the final vision of the ancient servant Firs, himself a relic of the emancipation of the serfs half a century before, locked in the house while the orchard falls to the axes. The future seems to promise a brutal and sudden change which the main characters of the play are unable to face. The play takes, at best, an ironic attitude toward the fortunes of Lyubov and Gaev. Tragedies in Chekhov's plays occur in the momentary actions of daily life; they are casual and haphazard, almost accidental, and yet alter the course of life irrevocably. Varya and Lopakhin, for example, bumble their way through the long-expected scene of their engagement, but the scene doesn't come off. Lopakhin remains uncommitted and Varya remains a poor relation dependent on the charity of her family, soon to be sent away to work as a governess. For Varya, the misplayed scene has a bitter and tragic finality.

Chekhov calls the play a "comedy," and despite its mournful tone we might consider what he might have had in mind. Chekhov seems sympathetic to the tragedies of daily life, but often trains a skeptical eye on characters who assume the self-regarding accents of high tragedy, or whose sense of themselves verges on self-delusion, the solipsistic inability to see the world around them. Throughout *The Cherry Orchard*, some characters seem lost in a world of dreams: think of Gaev and his sister arriving in their childhood nursery, of Trofimov's vague and clumsy plans for the future, of kindly old Firs. Chekhov forces us to regard his characters with a certain distance, largely by weaving a texture of comedy into the fabric of the play. Everyone ridicules Gaev's sentimental apostrophe to the bookcase in Act 1, and Chekhov adds a list of vaudeville tricks to his characters' performances: Lopakhin's "Moo-o-o" at the opening of the play, Yepikhodov crushing the hatbox with the suitcase in Act 4, Trofimov tumbling down the stairs, Charlotta's music-hall turns, Firs's feeble efforts to keep everyone warm. The famous, inexplicable sound effect of Act 2—the breaking string—may work in this way as well. It both underscores the mournful tone of the scene and interrupts the illusionistic surface of the action, forcing the audience out of a fully sympathetic engagement with Chekhov's sentimental characters. The play, in this light, seems "tragic" only if we accept the main characters' view of their predicament and accept their idle, self-absorbed fantasies as the stuff of tragedy.

Chekhov went to some lengths to keep the play's tone unsettled, in part because he knew that Stanislavski tended to regard his work as high tragedy. Chekhov suggested to Stanislavski that he play the part of Lopakhin: "When I was writing Lopakhin," he wrote in a letter to the actor, "I thought of it as a part for you. . . . Lopakhin is a merchant, of course, but he is a very decent person in every sense. He must behave with perfect decorum, like an educated man, with no petty ways or tricks of any sort, and it seemed to me that this part, the central one of the play, would come out brilliantly in your hands. . . . you must remember that Varya, a serious and religious girl, is in love with Lopakhin; she wouldn't be in love with a mere money-grubber." Describing Lopakhin in terms of Varya is typical of Chekhov's tendency to think of the ensemble as a whole, rather than in terms of individual characters; but we might also think that Chekhov has strategic designs on Stanislavski as well. Fearing that Stanislavski would want to play the part of Gaev, and would play the part too sympathetically, Chekhov tried to persuade him to train his talents on the comic part of Lopakhin. Imagining Stanislavski as Lopakhin, we begin to see the kind of drama Chekhov had imagined: had he taken the part (Stanislavski played Gaev after all), Stanislavski would have played against the grain of broad humor that underlies Lopakhin, humanizing the role, creating neither a fully sympathetic character nor a vulgar comedian, but something in between. Similarly, *The Cherry Orchard* as a whole strikes a balance somewhere between comedy and tragedy, in which comic and tragic possibilities strain against one another as ways of interpreting the play and the experience of our lives.

As it turned out, Stanislavski's direction emphasized the play's sombre tone, the sense of a generation falling before modern progress as the orchard falls to the axes. After the Russian Revolution in 1917, *The Cherry Orchard* came to be regarded as nearly a prophetic allegory of the progress of history, the displacing of the feudal past by the modern, industrial present.

THE CHERRY ORCHARD
A COMEDY IN FOUR ACTS

ANTON CHEKHOV

TRANSLATED BY EUGENE K. BRISTOW

— CHARACTERS —

LYUBOV ANDREEVNA RANEVSKAYA, a *landowner*
ANYA, her *daughter, age seventeen*
VARYA, her *adopted daughter, age twenty-four*
LEONID ANDREEVICH GAEV, *brother of Mrs. Ranevskaya*
YERMOLAY ALEXEEVICH LOPAKHIN, *a merchant*
PYOTR SERGEEVICH TROFIMOV, *a student*
BORIS BORISOVICH SIMEONOV-PISHCHIK, *a landowner*
SHARLOTTA IVANOVNA, *a governess*
SEMYON PANTELEEVICH YEPIKHODOV, *a clerk*

DUNYASHA, *a maidservant*
FIRS, *an old manservant, age eighty-seven*
YASHA, *a young manservant*
A PASSER-BY
A STATIONMASTER
A POST OFFICE CIVIL SERVANT
GUESTS *and* SERVANTS

The action takes place on the estate of MRS. RANEVSKAYA.

— ACT ONE —

A room that still goes by the name of the nursery. One of the doors leads to ANYA's *room. It is dawn and the sun will soon come up. It is May. The cherry trees are in flower, but in the orchard it is cold, there is morning frost. The windows in the room are closed. Enter* DUNYASHA *with a candle and* LOPAKHIN *with a book in his hand.*

LOPAKHIN: The train's arrived, thank the Lord. What's the time?
DUNYASHA: Almost two o'clock. (*Extinguishes the candle.*) It's already light.
5 LOPAKHIN: How late was the train, how many hours? About two, at least. (*Yawns and stretches himself.*) Of all the stupid tricks to pull, damned if I haven't gone and done it again. I came here on purpose so I could meet them at the station, and before you know it, I slept right through it . . . Went
10 dead to sleep sitting up. Annoying, that's what . . . If only you might've awakened me.
DUNYASHA: I thought you'd left. (*Listens.*) There, I think they're coming now.
LOPAKHIN: (*Listens.*) No . . . they've got luggage to get, and
15 one thing or another . . . (*Pause.*) Lyubov Andreevna has been living five years abroad, and I don't know what she's become now . . . She's a very fine person. An obliging person, simple. I remember when I was a youngster about fifteen, my father—he's dead now but at the time he was a shop-
20 keeper in the village here—hit me in the face with his fist. The blood ran out of my nose . . . We had come to the yard here for some reason, and he'd been drinking. Lyubov Andreevna, as I remember right now, was still very young, such a slim woman she was. She led me over to the washstand
25 here in this very room, the nursery. "Don't cry, little peasant," she says "it will heal before your wedding . . ." (*Pause.*) Little peasant . . . It's true my father was a peasant, and here I am in a white waistcoat and yellow boots. Like a pig's nozzle showing up in a row of wedding cakes . . . It's just that
30 I'm rich, lots of money for sure, but if you really think about it and look into it, you'll know I'm just a peasant through and through . . . (*Turns the pages of the book.*) I read this book

and didn't catch on to a single thing. I was reading and fell right to sleep. (*Pause.*)
35 DUNYASHA: The dogs didn't sleep the whole night. They can sense their masters are coming.
LOPAKHIN: What is it with you, Dunyasha, such . . .
DUNYASHA: My hands are shaking. I'm going to faint.
LOPAKHIN: You're really delicate, Dunyasha, too much so.
40 You dress yourself like a lady, and your hair is fixed up the same way. You can't do things like that. Better remember who you are.

(YEPIKHODOV *enters, carrying a bouquet. He wears a jacket and brightly scrubbed high boots that squeak loudly. Entering, he drops the bouquet.*)

YEPIKHODOV: (*Picks up the bouquet.*) Here's what the gardener sent, he says to put them in the dining room. (*Gives the bouquet to* DUNYASHA.)
45
LOPAKHIN: And bring me some kvas.
DUNYASHA: Yes, sir. (*Goes out.*)
YEPIKHODOV: There's morning frost right now, three degrees of frost, but the cherry trees are all in bloom. I can't approve of our climate. (*Sighs.*) I can't. Our climate just can't pro-
50 mote the most suitable time. Here, Yermolay Alexeich, be so kind as to let me append to you, I bought myself these boots the day before yesterday, and they, I make bold to assure you, they squeak so it's beyond the realm of possibility. What should I lubricate them with?
55
LOPAKHIN: Leave me alone. I'm sick and tired of you.
YEPIKHODOV: Every day some catastrophe happens to me. But I don't grumble. I'm used to it, and I even smile. (DUNYASHA *enters and gives* LOPAKHIN *kvas.*) I'm going. (*Stumbles against a chair, which falls.*) There . . . (*As if he is celebrating it.*)
60 There you see, excuse the expression, the kind of circumstance I bump into, by the way . . . It's simply even out of this world! (*Goes out.*)
DUNYASHA: Oh, Yermolay Alexeich, I must confess Yepikhodov made a proposal to me.
65
LOPAKHIN: Oh!
DUNYASHA: I really don't know how . . . he's a mild sort of person, but those times he starts talking, you can't figure out a thing he says. Oh, it's very fine and there's plenty of feeling

658

70   in it, only nothing makes a bit of sense. I'm pretty sure I like
      him. He's madly in love with me. He's an unlucky person,
      and there's something or other every day. That's why they
      keep teasing him, calling him "Two-and-Twenty Hard
      Knocks . . ."
75   LOPAKHIN: *(Listening.)* There, I think they're coming . . .
      DUNYASHA: They're coming! Oh, what's the matter with me
           . . . I've gotten colder all over.
      LOPAKHIN: They're coming, it's a fact. Let's go and meet them.
           Will she recognize me, I wonder? It's been five years since
80   we've seen each other.
      DUNYASHA: *(Agitated.)* I'm going to faint right now . . . Oh, I
           know I'm going to faint!

(Two carriages are heard driving up to the house. LOPAKHIN *and*
DUNYASHA *quickly go out. The stage is empty. The sound of hubbub begins in the adjoining rooms. Leaning on a stick,* FIRS *hurriedly goes across the stage. He has been to the station to meet*
LYUBOV ANDREEVNA. *He wears old-fashioned livery and a high
hat. He keeps saying something to himself, but not a single word
can be understood. The noise offstage keeps growing louder. A
voice is heard saying: "Let's go through here." Enter, all walking
through the room,* LYUBOV ANDREEVNA, ANYA, *and* SHARLOTTA
IVANOVNA *with a small dog on a chain—all are in traveling
clothes—*VARYA, *wearing an overcoat and a scarf over her head,*
GAEV, SIMEONOV-PISHCHIK, LOPAKHIN, DUNYASHA *with a bundle and an umbrella, and servants with luggage.)*

      ANYA: Let's go through here. Mama, do you remember what
           room this is?
85   LYUBOV ANDREEVNA: *(Jubilantly, through tears.)* The nursery!
      VARYA: How cold it is, my hands are growing numb. *(To*
           LYUBOV ANDREEVNA.*)* Your rooms are the very same as they
           were, *Mamochka,* white and violet.
      LYUBOV ANDREEVNA: The nursery, my dear, beautiful room . . .
90   I slept here when I was a little girl . . . *(Weeps.)* And now I'm
           like a little girl again . . . *(Kisses her brother and* VARYA, *then
           her brother again.)* Varya is just the same as she's always been,
           she still looks like a nun. And I recognized Dunyasha . . .
           (Kisses DUNYASHA.*)*
95   GAEV: The train was two hours late. That's something, isn't it?
           What a way to manage things, wouldn't you say?
      SHARLOTTA: *(To* PISHCHIK.*)* My dog eats nuts, too.
      PISHCHIK: *(Surprised.)* What do you think of that!

(All go out except ANYA *and* DUNYASHA.*)*

      DUNYASHA: We've been waiting and expecting you for so
100   long . . . *(Takes off* ANYA's *overcoat and hat.)*
      ANYA: I haven't slept four whole nights on the way . . . now I
           feel terribly cold.
      DUNYASHA: You went away during Lent, it was snowing and
           there was a frost then, but now? My dear! *(Laughs and
105   kisses her.)* I've been waiting so long for you, my precious
           darling . . . I must tell you right now, I can't stand it another
           minute . . .
      ANYA: *(Listlessly.)* Not something again, surely . . .
      DUNYASHA: Right after Holy Week the clerk Yepikhodov made
110   a proposal to me.

      ANYA: You keep going on about the same thing . . . *(Adjusting
           her hair.)* I've been losing all my hairpins . . . *(She is very ex-
           hausted, she even staggers and sways.)*
      DUNYASHA: I really don't know what to think. He's in love with
           me, he loves me so!   115
      ANYA: *(Looks through the door into her own room, affection-
           ately.)* My own room, my windows, it's just as if I'd never
           gone away. I'm home, home! Tomorrow morning I'll get up
           and run out to the orchard . . . Oh, if only I could fall asleep!
           I didn't get one wink of sleep the whole way coming back, I   120
           wore myself out worrying.
      DUNYASHA: Pyotr Sergeich arrived the day before yesterday.
      ANYA: *(Jubilantly.)* Petya!
      DUNYASHA: He's asleep in the bathhouse, it's where he's living.
           "I'm afraid," he says, "of getting in their way." *(Having looked*   125
           at her pocket watch.) He ought to be wakened, but Varvara
           Mikhaylovna gave the word not to. "Don't you go and wake
           him," she says.

*(*VARYA *enters; she has a bunch of keys on her belt.)*

      VARYA: Dunyasha, bring some coffee quickly . . . *Mamochka* is
           asking for some.   130
      DUNYASHA: It won't be a minute. *(Goes out.)*
      VARYA: Well, thank the Lord, you've all come back. You're
           home again. *(Adoringly.)* My precious is here, my beautiful
           darling has come back!
      ANYA: I've had a horrible time of it.   135
      VARYA: I can well imagine!
      ANYA: I left just before Easter. It was cold at the time. Sharlotta
           kept on talking and doing her silly conjuring tricks the
           whole way there. Why you tacked Sharlotta onto me, I'll
           never know . . .   140
      VARYA: You couldn't have gone all alone, my precious. At
           seventeen!
      ANYA: We finally got to Paris and found it cold and snowing.
           My French was terrible. Mama was living on the fifth floor,
           and when I came to her place, some French people were vis-   145
           iting, ladies and an old priest with a little book. It was filled
           with smoke and not one bit cozy. All of a sudden I felt sorry
           for Mama, so sorry for her, I took her head in my arms and
           pressed her close to me and simply couldn't let go. After-
           wards Mama tried to make everything up to me, she was   150
           gentle and sweet and she kept crying . . .
      VARYA: *(Through tears.)* Don't go on talking about it, don't . . .
      ANYA: She's already sold her dacha near Mentone, and she had
           nothing left, nothing. I didn't have anything either, not a sin-
           gle kopek. We scarcely had enough to get here. But Mama   155
           just can't understand it! Whenever we sit down for dinner at
           the station, she keeps demanding the most expensive things
           and tipping the waiters a ruble each. Sharlotta's the same
           way. Yasha keeps demanding his share, too, it was simply ter-
           rible. Yasha is Mama's servant, you know. We brought him   160
           here with us . . .
      VARYA: I've seen the scoundrel.
      ANYA: Well, then, how are things going here? Have you paid
           the interest?
      VARYA: Not a chance in the world.   165

---

88 *Mamochka* intimate nickname for *Mama*

153 **Mentone** summer vacation home, Mentone is located on the
Mediterranean coast of France

ANYA: Dear God in heaven, dear God . . .

VARYA: The estate will be sold in August . . .

ANYA: Dear God in heaven . . .

LOPAKHIN: *(Looks in through the door and bleats like a calf.)*
170   Meh-meh-meh . . . *(Goes out.)*

VARYA: *(Through tears.)* Oh, I'd like to give him something . . .
(Threatens with her fist.)

ANYA: *(Embraces* VARYA, *quietly.)* Varya, has he proposed to
you? (VARYA *shakes her head.)* Surely he loves you . . . Why
175   don't the two of you talk it out, what on earth are you waiting
for?

VARYA: I don't think anything will come of it. He has so many
things to do he hasn't one bit of time for me . . . and he
doesn't pay one bit of attention to me, either. God help him,
180   I've had enough. It bothers me just to see him . . . Everyone
is talking about our wedding and offering congratulations,
but in fact there's nothing to it. It's all like a dream . . . *(In a
different tone of voice.)* You have a brooch that looks something like a little bee.

185   ANYA: *(Sadly.)* Mama bought it. *(Goes into her own room and
speaks happily like a child.)* You know in Paris I flew up in a
balloon!

VARYA: My precious is here, my beautiful darling has come
back! (DUNYASHA *has already returned with a coffee pot and
190   is preparing coffee.* VARYA *stands near the door.)* I spend the
whole day managing the house, my precious, but I
keep dreaming and dreaming. I'd like to see you married to a
rich person, and then I wouldn't feel troubled at all. I
could start out to a cloister, and then on to Kiev . . . to
195   Moscow, and so I'd keep walking from one holy place to the
next . . . I'd keep on walking and walking. What a blessed
way to live! . .

ANYA: The birds are singing in the orchard. What time is it
now?

200   VARYA: It must be past two. It's time for you to go to sleep, my
precious. *(Going into* ANYA's *room.)* What a blessed way to
live!

(YASHA enters with a rug and a traveling bag.)

YASHA: *(Goes across the stage, delicately.)* Is it possible for one
to go through here, Miss?

205   DUNYASHA: A person wouldn't recognize you, Yasha. You've
become something else since you've been abroad.

YASHA: Hmm . . . and who are you?

DUNYASHA: When you left here, I was about as big as this . . .
(Indicates distance from the floor.) I'm Dunyasha, the daugh-
210   ter of Fyodor Kozoedov. You can't remember me!

YASHA: Hmm . . . Saucy little cucumber! *(Looks around and
embraces her. She screams and drops a saucer.* YASHA *quickly
goes out.)*

VARYA: *(In a dissatisfied tone of voice, in the doorway.)* What's
215   going on now?

DUNYASHA: *(Through tears.)* I broke a saucer . . .

VARYA: It's a good sign.

ANYA: *(Coming out of her room.)* Mama ought to be warned in
advance that Petya's here . . .

220   VARYA: I gave word not to wake him.

ANYA: *(Deep in thought.)* Six years ago father died, and a
month later our brother Grisha drowned in the river. He was
a beautiful little boy, just seven years old. Mama couldn't
stand it anymore, and she went away, she went away without

so much as a backward glance . . . *(Shudders.)* How well I   225
can understand her, if she only knew! *(Pause.)* But Petya
Trofimov was Grisha's tutor, and he might bring to mind . . .

(FIRS enters, wearing a jacket and white waistcoat.)

FIRS: *(Goes to the coffee pot, anxiously.)* The mistress will sup
in here . . . *(Puts on white gloves.)* Is the coffee prepared? *(To
DUNYASHA, sternly.)* You there! And the cream?   230

DUNYASHA: Oh, dear God in heaven . . . *(Goes out quickly.)*

FIRS: *(Bustling around the coffee pot.)* Oh, you silly galoot,
you . . . *(Mumbles to himself.)* She's come back from
Paris . . . Once upon a time the master himself used to go
to Paris . . . by carriage . . . *(Laughs.)*   235

VARYA: What is it, Firs?

FIRS: What can I do for you, please? *(Jubilantly.)* My mistress
has come back! Home, home at last! I'm even ready to die
now . . . *(Weeps from joy.)*

*(LYUBOV ANDREEVNA, GAEV, and SIMEONOV-PISHCHIK enter.
PISHCHIK wears a long peasant coat made out of thin cloth and
high boots. Entering, GAEV moves his arms and body as if he
were playing billiards.)*

LYUBOV ANDREEVNA: How does it go? Let me remember a bit   240
. . . "Off the yellow into the corner pocket! Bank shot into
the middle!"

GAEV: An english shot into the corner! Once upon a time, sister, you and I used to sleep here in this very room, and now
I'm fifty-one, fifty-one years old. Strange, isn't it . . .   245

LOPAKHIN: Yes, time flies.

GAEV: How's that?

LOPAKHIN: Time flies, I was saying.

GAEV: This place reeks of patchouli.

ANYA: I'm going to sleep now. Good night, Mama. *(Kisses her   250
mother.)*

LYUBOV ANDREEVNA: My beloved little girl. *(Kisses her
hands.)* You're glad you're home, aren't you? I just can't get
hold of myself.

ANYA: Fare you well, Uncle.   255

GAEV: *(Kisses her face and hands.)* God be with you. Oh, you
look so much like your mother! *(To his sister.)* When you
were her age, Lyuba, you were exactly like she is.

*(ANYA gives her hand to LOPAKHIN and PISHCHIK, goes out, and
shuts the door to her room.)*

LYUBOV ANDREEVNA: She's completely exhausted.

PISHCHIK: Most likely it's the long trip.   260

VARYA: *(To LOPAKHIN and PISHCHIK.)* Well, hmm, gentlemen?
It's after two and time you said your good-byes.

LYUBOV ANDREEVNA: *(Laughs.)* You're the same as you've always been, Varya. *(Draws VARYA to her and kisses her.)* I'll just
drink some coffee, then we'll all go away. (FIRS *puts a little*   265

---

s.d. **peasant coat** Pishchik is wearing typical outdoor peasant clothing,
i.e., the *poddëvka*, which is fitted at the waist, and, probably long wide
trousers tucked into his high boots   241–242 **Off the yellow . . . middle** Since it is not clear whether Chekhov himself intended an accurate correspondence with the game as it was played in his day, I have
kept my translation of the billiard terms literal   246 **time flies** There is
no stage direction pertaining to Lopakhin's return onstage; it is assumed that he enters with Lyubov Andreevna, Gaev, and Simeonov-
Pishchik   249 **patchouli** a perfume made from an East Indian mint

cushion under her feet.) Thank you, my dear. I'm used to coffee now. I drink it day and night. Thank you, my dear old
man. *(Kisses* FIRS.)

VARYA: I must go and see if they've brought in all the things . . .
270   *(Goes out.)*

LYUBOV ANDREEVNA: It can't really be me sitting here, can it?
(Laughs.) I want to jump up, leap around, and wave my
arms. *(Covers her face with her hands.)* But suddenly I feel I
may only be sleeping! God can see I love my country, I love
275   it warmly. I couldn't even see it from the train—I was crying
the whole time. *(Through tears.)* All the same I must drink
my coffee. Thank you, Firs, thank you, my dear old man. I'm
so glad you're still alive.

FIRS: The day before yesterday.
280 GAEV: He's hard of hearing.

LOPAKHIN: I must start for Kharkov pretty soon, after four this
morning. Damned annoying! I wanted to have more of a
look at you, talk awhile . . . You're the same as you've always
been, a magnificent person.

285 PISHCHIK: *(Breathes heavily.)* Even prettier . . . Wearing Parisian clothes . . . Oh, my, that's something! "Get lost, my
cart," as the saying goes, "all four wheels . . ."

LOPAKHIN: Your brother, Leonid Andreich here, keeps talking
about me, saying I'm a peasant, a scoundrel grabbing with
290   both hands, but it doesn't matter what he says, not a bit. Let
him go on talking. The only thing I want is for you to believe
in me as you used to and look at me with your beautiful, gentle eyes as you did in times gone by. Oh, merciful God in
heaven! My father was a serf, belonging to your grandfather
295   and after him your father, but you—you personally—did so
much for me once I've forgotten all that and I love you as if
we were flesh and blood . . . even more than my own flesh
and blood.

LYUBOV ANDREEVNA: I can't sit any longer, not the way I
300   feel . . . *(Jumps up and walks in great agitation.)* I'm so
happy I can't stand it . . . Go ahead and laugh at me, I know
I'm silly . . . My own dear little bookcase . . . *(Kisses the
bookcase.)* My own little table . . .

GAEV: Oh, when you were gone *nyanya* died.
305 LYUBOV ANDREEVNA: *(Sits down and drinks her coffee.)* Yes,
may God in heaven be with her. They wrote me.

GAEV: And Anastasy died. Petrushka—the squint-eyed fellow—left me and now he's with the police chief in town.
(Takes a box of hard candy out of his pocket and sucks one.)

310 PISHCHIK: My daughter Dashenka . . . sends her regards to
you . . .

LOPAKHIN: I want to tell you something very pleasing and
cheerful. *(Having glanced at his watch.)* I'm on my way right
now, there's no time to talk . . . Oh, well, I can get to it in
315   two or three words. As you already know, your cherry orchard is being sold to pay off debts. The auction is set for August twenty-second, but you mustn't worry, my dear, you can
sleep in peace. There's a way out . . . Here's my plan. I beg
your close attention! Your estate is located only twenty versts
320   from town, the railroad goes nearby, and if the cherry orchard and the land by the river were broken up into residen-
tial lots and then leased for summer homes, you'll have an

income, at the very least, of twenty-five thousand rubles
each year.

GAEV: Excuse me, I've never heard such stuff and nonsense.   325

LYUBOV ANDREEVNA: I don't quite understand you, Yermolay
Alexeich.

LOPAKHIN: You will get from the tenants, at the very least,
twenty-five rubles a year for every plot of about three acres,
and if you advertise right away, I'm willing to bet whatever   330
you like that you won't have a sliver of land left by autumn.
Every bit of it will be grabbed up. In short, I congratulate
you. You are saved. It's a marvelous place for building, and
the river is deep. Only one thing, of course, it must be
cleaned up a little, whipped into shape . . . For example,   335
you'll have to pull down all the old buildings, let's say, and
this house here, which is no longer of any use, cut down the
old cherry orchard . . .

LYUBOV ANDREEVNA: Cut down? My dear, forgive me, but you
don't know what you're talking about. If there's anything at   340
all in this whole district that's still exciting, even incredible,
that one thing is our cherry orchard.

LOPAKHIN: The only thing incredible about that cherry orchard is that it's damn big. There's only one crop every two
years, and when it comes there's plenty of cherries around,   345
but nobody will buy them.

GAEV: This orchard is even mentioned in the *Encyclopedia*.

LOPAKHIN: *(Having glanced at his watch.)* If we don't think of
something or come up with an idea, the cherry orchard and
the whole estate will be sold at auction on August twenty-   350
second. You can make up your minds to it! There's no other
way out, I swear it to you. None at all, none.

FIRS: In times before, about forty or fifty years ago, the cherries
were dried, soaked, marinated, and jam was made, and it
used to be . . .   355

GAEV: Be quiet, Firs.

FIRS: And it used to be they'd send cartloads of dried cherries
off to Moscow and to Kharkov. Oh, there was money galore!
And dried cherries at that time were soft and juicy, sweet and
a good smell to them . . . They knew a way of doing it at that   360
time . . .

LYUBOV ANDREEVNA: And where on earth is that way now?

FIRS: They've forgotten. No one remembers it.

PISHCHIK: *(To* LYUBOV ANDREEVNA.) What's in Paris? How
did it go? Did you eat frogs?   365

LYUBOV ANDREEVNA: I ate crocodiles.

PISHCHIK: What do you think of that . . .

LOPAKHIN: Until recently you'd find only gentlemen and peasants in town, and now people for the summer are showing
up. All the cities, even the very smallest, are surrounded now   370
with summer places. You might even say, in the course of
about twenty years, these people will multiply beyond the
wildest dreams. Nowadays the summer resident only drinks
tea on his balcony, but you know it might happen he'll take
up farming his own plot of ground, and then your cherry or-   375
chard will become happy, rich, sumptuous . . .

---

319 **versts** a former Russian unit of measurement, the equivalent of
about thirty-five hundred feet

347 *Encyclopedia* probably the *Brockhaus and Efron Encyclopedia
Dictionary*, which was issued by F. A. Brockhaus-I. A. Efron joint-stock
publishing company in the period from 1890 to 1907 and which consisted of 86 volumes (82 books and four supplements)   358 **Kharkov**
(khárkaf), a large city in the northeastern Ukraine

GAEV: (*Exasperated.*) I've never heard such stuff and nonsense.

(VARYA *and* YASHA *enter.*)

VARYA: *Mamochka,* there are two telegrams for you. (*Picks out a key and noisily opens an old bookcase.*) Here they are.

380 LYUBOV ANDREEVNA: They're from Paris. (*Tears up the telegrams without reading them.*) Paris is over and done with . . .

GAEV: Oh, Lyuba, do you know how old this bookcase is? Last week I pulled out the bottom drawer, I looked and saw some

385 figures scorched on it. The bookcase was made exactly one hundred years ago. That's something, isn't it? Ah! We could celebrate its anniversary. It's an inanimate object, but all the same it's a receptacle for books, after all.

PISHCHIK: (*Surprised.*) One hundred years . . . What do you

390 think of that! . . .

GAEV: Yes . . . It's quite a thing . . . (*Having touched all parts of the bookcase.*) Dear, honored bookcase! I hail your existence. For more than one hundred years your very being has been directed to the shining ideals of cardinal good and jus-

395 tice. Your silent appeal to fruitful labor has never lessened in the course of a hundred years, upholding (*Through tears.*) in generations of our line personal courage and faith in a better future and nurturing in us the ideals of cardinal good and social consciousness. (*Pause.*)

400 LOPAKHIN: Yes . . .

LYUBOV ANDREEVNA: You're the same as you've always been, Lyonya.

GAEV: (*A little embarrassed.*) Off the ball right into the corner pocket! An english shot into the middle!

405 LOPAKHIN: (*Having glanced at his watch.*) Well, time for me to go.

YASHA: (*Handing medicine to* LYUBOV ANDREEVNA.) Perhaps you'll take your pills now . . .

PISHCHIK: No need to take medicines, my dearest . . . Oh, no

410 damage comes from it, no benefit, either . . . Here, let me have them . . . honored lady. (*Takes the pills, pours them into the palm of his hand, blows on them, puts them in his mouth, and drinks them down with kvas.*) There!

LYUBOV ANDREEVNA: (*Frightened.*) Why, you've lost your mind!

415 PISHCHIK: I've taken all the pills.

LOPAKHIN: It's a hog with a hollow leg!

(*Everyone laughs.*)

FIRS: The gentleman was visiting us in Holy Week and ate half a bucket of cucumbers . . . (*Mumbles to himself.*)

LYUBOV ANDREEVNA: What is it he's saying?

420 VARYA: He's been mumbling that way for three years now. We've become used to it.

YASHA: Old as Methuselah, I'd say.

(SHARLOTTA IVANOVNA, *in a white dress, walks across the stage. She is very thin and tightly laced, with a lorgnette on her belt.*)

LOPAKHIN: Forgive me, Sharlotta Ivanovna, I haven't had time yet to say how do you do to you. (*Wants to kiss her hand.*)

425 SHARLOTTA: (*Taking her hand away.*) If you were permitted to kiss my hand, why you'd want to go right to the elbow next, and then the shoulder . . .

LOPAKHIN: It's not my lucky day. (*Everyone laughs.*) Sharlotta Ivanovna, show us a trick or two!

430 LYUBOV ANDREEVNA: Yes, Sharlotta, show us a trick!

SHARLOTTA: I don't want to. I'd like to go to sleep. (*Goes out.*)

LOPAKHIN: We'll see each other in three weeks. (*Kisses* LYUBOV ANDREEVNA's *hand.*) In the meantime, good-bye. It's time for me. (*To* GAEV.) Until we meet again. (*Kisses* PISHCHIK.) Until we meet again. (*Shakes hands with* VARYA, 435 *then with* FIRS *and* YASHA.) I don't want to leave. (*To* LYUBOV ANDREEVNA.) If you make up your mind about those summer places and decide to go ahead with it, just give me the word and I'll loan you fifty thousand or so. Think about it seriously. 440

VARYA: (*Angrily.*) You're on your way, why don't you just leave now!

LOPAKHIN: I'll go, I'll go . . . (*Goes out.*)

GAEV: Grabbing peasant. Nevertheless, I beg your pardon . . . Varya's going to marry him. He's Varya's dear fiancé. 445

VARYA: You're talking much too much, Uncle dear.

LYUBOV ANDREEVNA: Well, hmm, Varya, I shall be very glad. He's a good person.

PISHCHIK: A person, if the truth were said . . . who's most worthy . . . And my Dashenka . . . keeps saying also that . . . she 450 keeps saying all sorts of words. (*Snores, but immediately wakes up.*) Be that as it may, my honored lady, if you'll oblige me with . . . a loan of two hundred and forty rubles . . . I can pay the interest due on the mortgage tomorrow . . .

VARYA: (*Frightened.*) We don't have it, we don't! 455

LYUBOV ANDREEVNA: As a matter of fact, we have nothing.

PISHCHIK: It'll turn up. (*Laughs.*) I never lose one bit of hope. Oh, time and again, I think everything's lost, gone, I've had it, and then—lo and behold—they built a railroad right through my land and . . . then went and paid me for it. Wait 460 and see, something or other will happen—if not today, then tomorrow . . . Dashenka is going to win two hundred thousand . . . She has a lottery ticket.

LYUBOV ANDREEVNA: The coffee is finished, we can get some peace and rest. 465

FIRS: (*Brushes* GAEV's *clothes, reprovingly.*) Again you've put on the wrong trousers. Oh, what on earth am I going to do with you!

VARYA: (*Quietly.*) Anya is sleeping. (*Quietly opens the window.*) The sun's come up now, and it isn't cold. Look, *Mamochka,* 470 what marvelous trees! And the air, too, dear God in heaven! The starlings are singing!

GAEV: (*Opens another window.*) The orchard is all in white. You haven't forgotten, Lyuba, have you? That long avenue over there keeps running straight, straight as a cord stretched 475 tight. It shines brightly on moonlit nights. You remember, you haven't forgotten, have you?

LYUBOV ANDREEVNA: (*Looks through the window at the orchard.*) Oh, my childhood, days of my innocence! In this very nursery I used to sleep, I used to look out at the orchard 480 from here, and when I woke up each morning I felt happy, so happy. At that time too the orchard was exactly the same, nothing at all has changed. (*Laughs jubilantly.*) All in white, all! Oh, my orchard! After the dreary, rainy autumn and cold winter, I find you young once more, filled with happiness, 485 and I know the angels in heaven have not deserted you . . . If only the heaviness I feel in my heart, the millstone I carry now, were suddenly taken away forever, if only I could forget my past!

GAEV: Yes, and the orchard will be sold to pay off debts. 490 Strange, isn't it . . .

LYUBOV ANDREEVNA: Just look, our own mama is walking in the orchard . . . in a white dress! (*Laughs jubilantly.*) See, it's Mama.

495 GAEV: Where is she?

VARYA: God be with you, *Mamochka.*

LYUBOV ANDREEVNA: There's no one, it just seemed to me I saw her. To the right, as the path turns to the summerhouse, there's a white small tree bending down—it looks like a

500 woman . . . (TROFIMOV *enters, wearing spectacles and dressed in a threadbare student's uniform.*) What a splendid orchard! Row upon row of white blossoms, the light blue sky . . .

TROFIMOV: Lyubov Andreevna! (*She looks around at him.*) I'll only pay my respects and then go away at once. (*Ardently*

505 *kisses her hand.*) I was told to wait until morning, but I didn't have the patience . . .

(LYUBOV ANDREEVNA *looks at him, bewildered.*)

VARYA: (*Through tears.*) It's Petya Trofimov . . .

TROFIMOV: Petya Trofimov, former tutor of your Grisha . . . Can it be I've changed so much?

(LYUBOV ANDREEVNA *embraces him and weeps quietly.*)

510 GAEV: (*Embarrassed.*) Enough, Lyuba, that'll do.

VARYA: (*Weeps.*) You see, Petya, I told you to wait until tomorrow.

LYUBOV ANDREEVNA: My Grisha . . . my little boy . . . Grisha . . . my son . . .

515 VARYA: What could we do, *Mamochka?* It was God's will.

TROFIMOV: (*Gently, through tears.*) There, there . . .

LYUBOV ANDREEVNA: (*Weeps quietly.*) My little boy is gone, drowned . . . and for what? Whatever was it for, my friend? (*More quietly.*) Anya is sleeping in there, and I go on talking

520 in a loud voice . . . making so much noise . . . Well, Petya? Why do you look so homely now? Why have you started putting on years?

TROFIMOV: An old peasant woman on the train called me "that used-up old gentleman."

525 LYUBOV ANDREEVNA: You were no more than a boy then, a sweet young student, but now your hair is getting thin and you're wearing spectacles. Don't tell me you're still a student? (*Walks toward the door.*)

TROFIMOV: No doubt I'll be a student forever and ever.

530 LYUBOV ANDREEVNA: (*Kisses her brother, then* VARYA.) Well then, better go to sleep . . . You've started putting on years, too, Leonid.

PISHCHIK: (*Follows her.*) So now we're going to sleep . . . Oh, my gout! I'll stay the night here . . . Lyubov Andreevna, my

535 darling, if you could help me out tomorrow morning, you know . . . two hundred and forty rubles . . .

GAEV: Oh, he keeps harping on the same old string.

PISHCHIK: Two hundred and forty rubles . . . to pay the interest due on the mortgage.

540 LYUBOV ANDREEVNA: I have no money, dear.

PISHCHIK: I'll pay it back, my dear . . . a trifling sum . . .

LYUBOV ANDREEVNA: Well, all right, Leonid will give you the amount . . . Leonid, you give it to him.

GAEV: Give it to him, Me? Oh, sure, open your pocket and see

545 what comes!

LYUBOV ANDREEVNA: What on earth can we do? Give him the money . . . he needs it . . . He'll pay it back.

(LYUBOV ANDREEVNA, TROFIMOV, PISHCHIK, *and* FIRS *go out;* GAEV, VARYA, *and* YASHA *remain.*)

GAEV: My sister still hasn't lost the habit of scattering all her money to the winds. (*To* YASHA.) Step out of the way, dear fellow, you smell like a dunghill biddy. 550

YASHA: (*With an ironical smile.*) You're just the same as you've always been, too, Leonid Andreevich.

GAEV: How's that? (*To* VARYA.) What did he say?

VARYA: (*To* YASHA.) Your mother's come from the village. She's been sitting in the servants' lodgings since yesterday. She 555 wants to see you . . .

YASHA: She can go to the devil, for all I care!

VARYA: Oh, you insolent pup, I'd be ashamed!

YASHA: She's a big help, isn't she? She might have come here tomorrow. (*Goes out.*) 560

VARYA: *Mamochka* is just the same as she was, she hasn't changed one whit. If she were given free rein, she'd give away everything.

GAEV: Yes . . . (*Pause.*) If plenty of remedies are prescribed for some sort of disease, it means the disease can't possibly be 565 cured. I keep on thinking, stewing my brains over it, and I've come up with a lot of remedies, plenty of them. Of course, that means I really don't have a single one that would work. It would be fine to receive some sort of inheritance, it would be nice to marry our Anya off to a rich per- 570 son, it would be fine to leave for Yaroslavl and try our luck with our dear aunt, the countess. Our auntie is rich, you know, very much so.

VARYA: (*Weeps.*) If only God would help.

GAEV: Stop blubbering. Our auntie is very rich, but she 575 doesn't care one iota for us. First of all, my sister married a lawyer, not a nobleman . . . (ANYA *appears in the doorway.*) She did not marry into the nobility, and you can't say she's led a particularly upright and godly life. She is kind and good, a glorious person, really, and I love her very much. But 580 whatever excuses you think of to justify what she's gone through, you must still admit she's an immoral woman. You're conscious of it in her slightest movement.

VARYA: (*In a whisper.*) Anya is standing in the doorway.

GAEV: How's that? (*Pause.*) You know, it's surprising, but some- 585 thing landed in my right eye . . . I've started to see poorly. And on Thursday when I was at the district court . . .

(ANYA *enters.*)

VARYA: Why on earth aren't you asleep, Anya?

ANYA: I can't fall asleep. I just can't.

GAEV: My little darling. (*Kisses* ANYA's *face and hands.*) My 590 dear child . . . (*Through tears.*) You're not simply my niece, you're my angel, you mean everything to me. Believe me, believe . . .

ANYA: I believe you, Uncle. Everyone loves and respects you . . . but you must keep quiet, dear Uncle, only keep quiet. 595 What were you saying just now about my mama, about your own sister? Whatever in the world made you say it?

GAEV: Yes, yes . . . (*Covers his face with her hand.*) It's terrible, really it is! Dear God in heaven! Dear God help me! And the

---

550 **dunghill biddy** literally, "There's the smell of a hen [coming] from you."   571 **Yaroslavl** an old Russian town on the Volga River

600 speech I made today—to the bookcase . . . so very foolish! And only when I finished did I realize it was so foolish.

VARYA: It's true, dear Uncle, you ought to keep quiet. Just keep quiet, that's all.

ANYA: If you'll stop talking, you will feel more at peace with
605 yourself.

GAEV: I'll keep quiet. *(Kisses* ANYA'S *and* VARYA'S *hands.)* I'll keep quiet. Only there is this business matter I should bring up. On Thursday I was at the district court, well, a bunch of us got together and talk started about this thing and that,
610 skipping around from here to there; and it seems we might arrange a loan on promissory notes and pay the interest to the bank.

VARYA: If only God will help!

GAEV: On Tuesday I'll go and talk it over with them once
615 more. *(To* VARYA.*)* Stop blubbering. *(To* ANYA.*)* Your mother is going to talk with Lopakhin. Of course, he won't turn her down . . . After you've had some peace and rest, you will leave for Yaroslavl to see the countess, your grandmother. In this way we'll be working from three sides—and so our
620 whole business drops nicely into the hat. I'm convinced we'll pay off the interest . . . *(Puts a piece of candy into his mouth.)* I give you my word of honor, I'll swear by anything you want, this estate will not be sold! *(Excitedly.)* I swear by my own happiness! Here, take my hand and then you can
625 call me a good-for-nothing rapscallion if I even so much as let the estate come up for auction! I swear it with all my heart and soul!

ANYA: *(A peaceful mood having returned to her, she is happy.)* What a good person you are, Uncle, and so smart too! *(Em-*
630 *braces her uncle.)* I'm at peace now! At peace and so happy!

*(*FIRS *enters.)*

FIRS: *(Reproachfully.)* Leonid Andreich, have you no fear of God? When is it you're going to sleep?

GAEV: At once, at once. You can leave, Firs. I, yes, it's perfectly all right, I can undress myself. Well, my children, time to say
635 bye-byes . . . We'll save the details until tomorrow, and now you go off to sleep. *(Kisses* ANYA *and* VARYA.*)* I'm a man of the eighties . . . No one pays tribute to those days, but I still went through plenty in life for my convictions, I can tell you I did. The peasant has reason to love me. You must get to know the
640 peasant, I say. You must know how to . . .

ANYA: You're starting again, Uncle!

VARYA: You better keep quiet, Uncle dear.

FIRS: *(Angrily.)* Leonid Andreich!

GAEV: I'm coming, I'm coming . . . Lie down and go to sleep.
645 Off two cushions right into the middle! I pocket the white . . . *(Goes out.* FIRS *quickly toddles after him.)*

ANYA: I'm at peace now. I don't want to go to Yaroslavl and I don't love my grandmother, but I still feel at peace. Thanks to Uncle. *(Sits down.)*

650 VARYA: We must go to sleep. I'm going to. Oh, something unpleasant happened here when you were gone. Only some old servants still live in the old servants' lodgings, as you well know—Yefimyushka, Polya, Yevstigney, and there's Karp, too. They started letting some rascals and passers-by
655 spend the night there. I kept silent. Only then I began hearing a rumor they were spreading that I'd given orders to feed them nothing but dried peas. Out of stinginess, if you can imagine . . . Yevstigney was behind it all . . . All right, I

think, if that's the way it is—then just you wait. I call in
Yevstigney . . . *(Yawns.)* He shows up . . . "What are you up   660
to," I say, "Yevstigney . . . you're such a fool . . ." *(Having glanced at* ANYA.*)* Anichka! *(Pause.)* She's fallen right to sleep . . . *(Takes* ANYA *by the arm.)* Come to your bed . . . Come along! . . . *(Leading her.)* My precious has gone to sleep! Come along . . .   665

(They go. A shepherd is heard playing on a reed pipe far beyond the orchard. TROFIMOV *crosses the stage and, having seen* VARYA *and* ANYA, *stops.)*

VARYA: Tsss . . . she's sleeping . . . sleeping . . . Come along, darling.

ANYA: *(Quietly, half-asleep.)* I'm so tired . . . those bells keep ringing . . . Uncle . . . dear . . . and Mama and Uncle . . .

VARYA: Come, darling, come along . . . *(They go into* ANYA'S   670
room.)

TROFIMOV: *(Deeply moved.)* Light of my life! My springtime!

— ACT TWO —

A field. A very small, old chapel—bent out of shape and deserted a long time ago. Near it are an old bench, a well, and large stones that apparently were once used as tombstones. A road to GAEV'S *estate can be seen. Towering poplar trees loom darkly on one side, where the cherry orchard begins. In the distance is a row of telegraph poles, and far, far away on the horizon—appearing indistinct—is a large town, clearly seen only in very fine, clear weather. It is shortly before sunset.* SHARLOTTA, YASHA, *and* DUNYASHA *are sitting on the bench.* YEPIKHODOV *stands nearby and plays the guitar, as the others sit lost in thought.* SHARLOTTA, *wearing an old peaked cap, has taken a gun from her shoulder and is adjusting the buckle on the sling.*

SHARLOTTA: *(In a thoughtful mood.)* I don't have a genuine passport. I don't know how old I am, but I keep on thinking I'm very young. When I was a small little girl, my father and *mamasha* used to travel from fair to fair and give shows—very good ones too. Oh, I used to jump around, doing *salto-*   5
mortale and all sorts of tricks. And when *papasha* and *ma-masha* died, a certain German woman took me into her home and started teaching me. All right. I grew up and then became a governess. But where I come from and who I am—I don't know . . . Who were my parents, maybe they   10
weren't even married . . . I don't know. *(Takes a cucumber out of her pocket and begins eating it.)* I don't know anything. *(Pause.)* I'd really like to start a conversation, but there's no one to start with . . . I don't have anybody at all.

YEPIKHODOV: *(Plays the guitar and sings.)*   15

"What care I for the world and its tumult,
What care I for my friends or my foes . . ."

How pleasant it is to play the mandolin!

---

662 **Anichka** a term of endearment for *Anya*

2 **passport** an "internal" passport, not for crossing the borders of Russia into foreign lands, but for movement within Russia   5 ***salto-mortale*** literally, "complete somersault"   6–7 ***papasha . . . mamasha*** affectionate terms for father and mother   16–17 **What care . . . foes** the words from a popular ballad at the turn of the century

DUNYASHA: It's a guitar, not a mandolin. (*Looks at herself in a*
20 *small mirror and powders herself.*)
YEPIKHODOV: To a man who's lost his mind and fallen in love,
this is a mandolin . . . (*Croons.*)

"Oh, how much my heart will burn
With the heat of your love in return . . ."

(YASHA *joins in.*)

25 SHARLOTTA: It's terrible the way these people sound . . . phew!
Like jackals.
DUNYASHA: (*To* YASHA.) All the same, what luck to go visiting
abroad.
YASHA: Yes, of course. I can't possibly disagree with you on that
30 point. (*Yawns, then lights a cigar.*)
YEPIKHODOV: It makes good sense. A long time ago everything
abroad shaped up and achieved its full build.
YASHA: Goes without saying.
YEPIKHODOV: I'm a well-developed person, and I read all sorts
35 of wonderful books. But I can't comprehend at all the direction I personally want to take, that is, to go on living or to
shoot myself, personally speaking. But nonetheless I always
carry a revolver on me. Here it is . . . (*Indicates the revolver.*)
SHARLOTTA: So much for that. Now I'm on my way. (*Slings on*
40 *her gun.*) Yepikhodov, you are a very intelligent man and
dreadfully frightening. Women must fall madly in love with
you. Brrr! (*Walks.*) These intellectuals are all so stupid,
there's no one to talk to . . . I feel alone all the time, all
alone, I don't have anybody at all and . . . and who I am,
45 what on earth I'm here for, is beyond me . . . (*Goes out with-*
out hurrying.)
YEPIKHODOV: Personally speaking, and I'm not going to touch
on other topics, I must explain something about myself, by
the way. That is, fate treats me without one bit of remorse,
50 like a storm regards a small ship. If, let us assume, I'm mistaken, then why is it I wake up this morning—and I'm saying
this by way of illustration—I look, and perched on my chest
is a spider of dreadful dimensions . . . That's how big. (*Indi-*
cates size with both hands.) And also if I pick up some kvas so
55 I can have a good drink, what do I see inside? Something or
other extremely indecent like a cockroach. (*Pause.*) Have
you read Buckle? (*Pause.*) Avdotya Fyodorovna, I wish to
bother you for a couple of words or so.
DUNYASHA: Go ahead and talk.
60 YEPIKHODOV: I'd find it most desirable if it were with you privately . . . (*Sighs.*)
DUNYASHA: (*Embarrassed.*) Very well . . . Only first of all bring
me my cape . . . it's somewhere near the cupboard . . . It's a
little damp here . . .
65 YEPIKHODOV: Very good, miss . . . I'll bring it, miss . . . Now I
know what I can do with my revolver . . . (*Takes the guitar*
and goes out playing.)
YASHA: Two-and-Twenty Hard Knocks! A stupid man, just between you and me. (*Yawns.*)
70 DUNYASHA: God forbid he doesn't shoot himself. (*Pause.*) I've
grown so uneasy, I'm always in a dither. I was still a little girl
when the master and mistress took me into their place, and

---

57 **Buckle** Henry Thomas Buckle (1821–1862), English liberal historian and sociologist, author of *A History of Civilization in England*

now I've lost the habit of living the way common people do.
Here, you can see my hands, white as white can be, just like
a lady's. I've grown fragile, so delicate, refined and ladylike,   75
everything in the world frightens me . . . terribly so. And if
you deceive me, Yasha, I just don't know what it will go and
do to my nerves.
YASHA: (*Kisses her.*) Saucy little cucumber! Every girl must remember who she is, to be sure, and there's nothing I dislike   80
more than a girl who doesn't behave herself as she should.
DUNYASHA: I love you so terribly much. You're educated,
there's nothing in the world you can't figure out. (*Pause.*)
YASHA: (*Yawns.*) Yes, miss . . . The way I look at it, if a girl loves
anyone, it means she's immoral. (*Pause.*) It's pleasant to   85
smoke a cigar in clean, pure air . . . (*Listens.*) Somebody's
coming here . . . It's the ladies and gentlemen . . . (DUN-
YASHA *impulsively embraces him.*) You go on home as if
you've gone to the river to bathe. Take that path, or else
you'll meet them and they'll start thinking I made a point of   90
going out with you. I can't take something like that.
DUNYASHA: (*Quietly coughs.*) I'm starting to get a headache
from your cigar . . . (*Goes out.*)

(YASHA *remains and sits down near the chapel.* LYUBOV AN-
DREEVNA, GAEV, *and* LOPAKHIN *enter.*)

LOPAKHIN: You must come to a decision once and for all—
time waits for no one. Surely the question is quite simple.   95
Do you agree to lease your land for summer cottages or don't
you? You can answer in one word. Is it yes or no? Just one
word!
LYUBOV ANDREEVNA: Who's smoking disgusting cigars out
here . . . (*Sits down.*)   100
GAEV: Things became convenient once they built the railroad.
(*Sits down.*) We made a short trip to town and had lunch . . .
Off the yellow into the middle pocket! I'd like to go to the
house first and play one game . . .
LYUBOV ANDREEVNA: You'll have time.   105
LOPAKHIN: Just one word! (*Beseechingly.*) Give me an answer,
do!
GAEV: (*Yawning.*) How's that?
LYUBOV ANDREEVNA: (*Looks in her purse.*) Yesterday I had
plenty of money, and today there's not much at all. Trying to   110
save money, my poor Varya feeds all of us milk soup, and the
old folks in the kitchen get nothing but dried peas. And yet I
go on spending money thoughtlessly, somehow. (*Drops her*
purse, scattering gold coins.) Now, they've fallen down . . .
(*She is annoyed.*)   115
YASHA: Allow me, I'll go pick them up at once. (*Gathers up the*
coins.)
LYUBOV ANDREEVNA: Please do, Yasha. Why on earth did I
lunch in town . . . That good-for-nothing restaurant of yours
with its music and tablecloths smelling of soap . . . Why did   120
you drink so much, Lyonya, or eat so much? And talk so
much? Today in the restaurant you were talking too much
again, and every bit of it was out of place—about the seventies and the decadent movement. And to whom? Talking to
the waiters about the decadents!   125
LOPAKHIN: Yes.
GAEV: (*Waves his hand.*) I'm incorrigible, that's obvious . . .
(*Irritably, to* YASHA.) What are you doing, popping up in
front of me all the time . . .
YASHA: (*Laughs.*) I can't listen to your voice without laughing.   130

GAEV: (*To his sister.*) Either he, or I . . .

LYUBOV ANDREEVNA: You can leave, Yasha, on your way now . . .

YASHA: (*Gives* LYUBOV ANDREEVNA *her purse.*) I'm going right now. (*Scarcely able to contain his laughter.*) This very minute . . . (*Goes out.*)

LOPAKHIN: That rich fellow Deriganov is thinking about buying your estate. They say he's coming to the auction himself.

LYUBOV ANDREEVNA: Oh, were did you hear that?

LOPAKHIN: They're talking about it in town.

GAEV: Our auntie in Yaroslavl promised to send us money, but when, or how much, is beyond me. . . .

LOPAKHIN: How much will she send? A hundred thousand? Two hundred thousand?

LYUBOV ANDREEVNA: Well . . . about ten or fifteen thousand, and we're thankful to get that.

LOPAKHIN: You must forgive me, but I've never met people as rattlebrained as you two are, my friends, or so unbusinesslike and strange, too. You are told in plain language your estate is going to be sold, and it's just as if you don't understand it.

LYUBOV ANDREEVNA: But what is it we can do? You tell us, what?

LOPAKHIN: I keep telling you every day. Every day I keep on saying one and the same thing. Both the cherry orchard and the land must be leased for summer residences. You must do it right now, as soon as possible—the auction is practically under our nose. Try and grasp what I'm saying. When you decide once and for all on the summer cottages, you can raise whatever sum of money you'd like to and then you're safe and sound.

LYUBOV ANDREEVNA: Summer cottages and the people who go with them. Forgive me, but it's all so petty, so vulgar.

GAEV: I agree with you completely.

LOPAKHIN: I'm going to burst into tears, or shout, or fall on the ground and faint. I can't stand it! You've worn me out completely! (*To* GAEV.) You're an old woman!

GAEV: How's that?

LOPAKHIN: An old woman, that's what! (*Wants to leave.*)

LYUBOV ANDREEVNA: (*Frightened.*) No, don't go away, stay with us, dear. I beg you. Perhaps we'll think of something or other!

LOPAKHIN: What's there to think about?

LYUBOV ANDREEVNA: Don't go away, I beg you. When you're around it's more cheerful . . . (*Pause.*) I keep waiting for something, just as if the house were going to fall down on us.

GAEV: (*Deep in thought.*) Bank shot into the corner . . . Across into the middle . . .

LYUBOV ANDREEVNA: Oh, how very much we have sinned . . .

LOPAKHIN: What sins could you possibly have . . .

GAEV: (*Puts a piece of candy into his mouth.*) They say I've eaten up my fortune in candy . . . (*Laughs.*)

LYUBOV ANDREEVNA: Oh, my sins, my sins . . . I've always scattered money to the winds, impulsively, like someone out of her mind, and I married a man who did nothing but build up debts. My husband died of champagne, he reveled in drinking, and then I was unlucky enough to fall in love with someone else. I began living with him. And just at that time—it was my first punishment, a blow that drove me mad with grief—here in this very river . . . My little boy was drowned. I went abroad, left forever, never to return—never to see this river again . . . I just closed my eyes and ran, losing all sense of what I was doing or who I am, and *he* followed me . . . callously, brutally. I bought a dacha near Mentone because it was there he fell sick, and for the next three years I knew neither rest nor peace, nursing him day and night. He wore me out completely, my soul dried up. And last year, when the dacha was sold to pay off debts, I left for Paris. It was there he robbed me, deserted me, and began living with another woman. I tried to poison myself . . . It was all so stupid and degrading . . . And suddenly I felt a longing to come home to Russia, home to my own land and my little girl . . . (*Wipes away her tears.*) Oh, Lord, dear Lord in heaven, be gracious, forgive me my sins! Don't punish me anymore! (*Takes a telegram out of her pocket.*) This came today from Paris . . . He begs forgiveness and implores me to return . . . (*Tears up the telegram.*) That's music coming from somewhere, I think. (*Listens.*)

GAEV: It's our celebrated Jewish orchestra. You remember, don't you, the four violins, flute, and double bass?

LYUBOV ANDREEVNA: It still exists, then? We ought to send for them sometime and arrange an evening party at the house.

LOPAKHIN: (*Listens.*) I can't hear anything . . . (*Sings quietly.*)

"For the right amount of money, oh, the Germans can
Change a solid Russian into a Frenchy man." (*Laughs.*)

What a play I saw at the theatre yesterday. Really a lot to laugh at.

LYUBOV ANDREEVNA: And probably there wasn't anything funny in it. Going to see plays isn't what you people should do. Try looking at yourselves a little more often and see what gray lives you all lead. How much of what you say is unnecessary.

LOPAKHIN: That's very true. You can be honest and say we all lead the life of a fool . . . (*Pause.*) My *papasha* was a peasant, an idiot. He didn't understand anything, so he taught me nothing and just beat me when he was drunk, always with a stick, too. As a matter of fact, I'm just as big a lunkhead and idiot myself. I never learned anything, and my handwriting's miserable. The way I write I'm ashamed to let people see it. Just the way a pig might write.

LYUBOV ANDREEVNA: You should get married, my friend.

LOPAKHIN: Yes . . . That's very true.

LYUBOV ANDREEVNA: To our own Varya. She's a fine girl.

LOPAKHIN: Yes.

LYUBOV ANDREEVNA: Her parents are common people. She works the whole day long, but what's really important is that she loves you. And you know you've liked her for a long time.

LOPAKHIN: Well, hmm? I've nothing against it . . . She's a fine girl. (*Pause.*)

GAEV: They offered me a job in a bank. Six thousand rubles a year . . . Have you heard?

LYUBOV ANDREEVNA: Oh, you're not up to it! You can stay as you are . . .

(FIRS *enters, bringing a coat.*)

FIRS: (*To* GAEV.) Be so good as to put this on, sir, it's damp here.

GAEV: (*Puts on coat.*) You're bothering me, old man.

213–214 **For the right . . . man** critics have been unable to trace the origin of these lines

FIRS: No use going on . . . This morning you left without saying one word to me. *(Looks him over.)*

LYUBOV ANDREEVNA: Oh, the years you've put on, Firs, the years!

250 FIRS: What can I do for you?

LOPAKHIN: They're saying you look so much older!

FIRS: I've been living a long time now. They were going to get me married before your *papasha* was even in the world yet . . . *(Laughs.)* When freedom came for the serfs, I was

255 already the head valet. I did not accept freedom at that time, so I kept on with the master and mistress . . . *(Pause.)* Oh, I remember everyone was glad, but what they were glad about, why, they didn't even know themselves.

LOPAKHIN: Oh, it was very good in the old days. At least they

260 used to flog them.

FIRS: *(Not having heard him.)* Yes, the good old days. The peasants were attached to the master, and the master to the peasants, but nowadays they are all mixed up, and you can't tell one from the other.

265 GAEV: Keep quiet for a moment, Firs. Tomorrow I must go to town. I was promised an introduction to a certain general who might give us money on a promissory note.

LOPAKHIN: Nothing will come out of it. And you won't pay the interest, either, you can rest assured of that.

270 LYUBOV ANDREEVNA: He's just ranting and raving again. There aren't any generals, none.

(TROFIMOV, ANYA, and VARYA enter.)

GAEV: Oh, here come the children.

ANYA: Mama's sitting down.

LYUBOV ANDREEVNA: *(Affectionately.)* Come, come along . . .

275 my darlings . . . *(Embraces ANYA and VARYA.)* If you both only knew how much I love you. Sit down beside me, that's the way.

(All sit down.)

LOPAKHIN: Our eternal student always takes good care of the young ladies.

280 TROFIMOV: It's none of your business.

LOPAKHIN: He's going to be fifty soon, but he's still a student.

TROFIMOV: You can stop your asinine jokes right now.

LOPAKHIN: What's a peculiar fellow like you getting angry about, anyway?

285 TROFIMOV: Oh, don't keep on pestering me, that's all.

LOPAKHIN: *(Laughs.)* Permit me, if you will, one question. What do you think about me?

TROFIMOV: I, Yermolay Alexeich, this is what I think. You are a rich man, and you're going to be a millionaire soon. In the

290 economy of nature one form of matter is exchanged for another, and so we find indispensable the beast of prey which devours everything that lands on its path. In that way you too are indispensable.

(All laugh.)

VARYA: Oh, Petya, you'd better tell us about the planets.

295 LYUBOV ANDREEVNA: No, let's go on with what we were saying yesterday.

---

254 **When freedom . . . serfs** literally, "When freedom came." The references in this speech are to the reforms of the 1860's, which began with the emancipation of the serfs in 1861

TROFIMOV: What was it about?

GAEV: Pride.

TROFIMOV: We talked a long time yesterday, but we didn't get anywhere. The proud person in your sense of the word has   300 something mystical inside. Maybe you're even right the way you see it. But if we reason it out simply and not try to be one bit fancy, then what sort of pride can you possibly take or what's the sense of ever having it, if man is poorly put together as a physiological type and if the enormous majority   305 of the human race is brutal, stupid, and profoundly unhappy? We must stop admiring ourselves. What we ought to do is just keep on working.

GAEV: We're going to die, so it doesn't matter.

TROFIMOV: Who knows for certain? Besides, what does "to   310 die" really mean? It may be that man has a hundred senses and at death only the five known to us are lost, while the remaining ninety-five go on living.

LYUBOV ANDREEVNA: How intelligent you are, Petya!

LOPAKHIN: *(Ironically.)* Terribly!   315

TROFIMOV: Humankind strides on, perfecting its strength. All that lies beyond us now will become one day comprehensible and within our grasp. The one thing we must do is to work and do all we can for those who seek the truth. Here in Russia very few people really work now. The educated people   320 I know, the vast majority at any rate, aren't in search of a single thing, and they certainly don't do anything. So far they lack even the ability for real work. They call themselves the intelligentsia, but they speak to their servants as inferiors and treat their peasants as if they were animals. They are   325 poor students, they read absolutely nothing serious, and they do precisely nothing. They only talk about science, and as for art, they understand next to nothing. They are all very serious people with stern expressions on their faces. They discuss nothing but important matters and like to philosophize   330 a great deal, while at the same time everyone can see that the workers are detestably fed, sleep without suitable bedding, thirty to forty in a room with bedbugs everywhere, the stench, the dampness, and the moral corruption . . . Obviously all our fine talk has gone on simply to hoodwink ourselves   335 and other people as well. Show me the day nurseries that they're talking so much about. And where are the libraries? Why, they just write about nurseries and libraries in novels, while in fact not a single one even exists. What does exist is nothing but dirt, vulgarity, and a barbarian way of life   340 . . . I dislike these terribly serious faces, they frighten me, and I'm afraid of serious conversations, too. We'd be better off if we all would just shut up for a while!

LOPAKHIN: You know, I get up before five in the morning, and I work from morning till night. Now, I've always got money   345 on hand—my own and other people's—and so I can see what kind of people are around. You have only to start doing something or other to realize how few honest, decent people there are. Sometimes when I can't get to sleep, I keep thinking, "Dear Lord in heaven, you gave us these enormous   350 forests, boundless fields, broad horizons, and living among them we really ought to be giants ourselves . . ."

LYUBOV ANDREEVNA: Now you find giants indispensable . . . Oh, they are very nice only in fairy stores; anywhere else they can scare you. (YEPIKHODOV *crosses at the depth of the stage,*   355 *playing his guitar.* LYUBOV ANDREEVNA *is deep in thought.)* There goes Yepikhodov . . .

ANYA: *(Deep in thought.)* There goes Yepikhodov . . .

GAEV: The sun has set, ladies and gentlemen.

360 TROFIMOV: Yes.

GAEV: *(In a low voice, as if reciting.)* Oh, nature, marvelous nature, shining with eternal radiance, beautiful yet unfeeling, you whom we name as mother, in whom are united both the living and the dead, you give life and you destroy . . .

365 VARYA: *(Beseechingly.)* Uncle dear!

ANYA: Uncle, you're starting again!

TROFIMOV: You'd better try a bank shot off the yellow into the middle.

GAEV: I'll keep silent, silent.

(All are sitting, deep in thought. Silence. All that can be heard is FIRS, *who mumbles quietly. Suddenly a sound is heard far off in the distance, as if coming from the sky. It is the sound of a string breaking that dies away sadly.)*

370 LYUBOV ANDREEVNA: What was that?

LOPAKHIN: I don't know. Somewhere far off in the mines a bucket must have broken loose. But it's somewhere far, far away.

GAEV: Perhaps it was a bird of some kind . . . like a heron.

375 TROFIMOV: Or an eagle owl . . .

LYUBOV ANDREEVNA: *(Shudders.)* It was unpleasant, and I don't know why. *(Pause.)*

FIRS: It was just the same before the troubles—and the owl kept hooting and the samovar humming without stopping.

380 GAEV: What troubles are you talking about?

FIRS: Just before the serfs were given their freedom. *(Pause.)*

LYUBOV ANDREEVNA: You know, dear friends, evening has come. Let's go on our way. *(To* ANYA.) You have tears in your eyes . . . What is it, my little girl? *(Embraces her.)*

385 ANYA: No reason, Mama, it's nothing.

TROFIMOV: There's someone coming.

(A passer-by appears, wearing a threadbare white peaked cap and an overcoat. He is slightly drunk.)

PASSER-BY: Permit me if you will one question. Can I go from here straight to the station?

GAEV: You can. Take that road.

390 PASSER-BY: I thank you from the bottom of my heart. *(Having coughed.)* Superb weather . . . *(Recites.)* "Oh, my brother, my suffering brother . . . come out to the Volga, whose moan . . ." *(To* VARYA.) Mademoiselle, could you allow a starving Russian thirty kopeks . . .

(VARYA is frightened and shrieks.)

395 LOPAKHIN: *(Angrily.)* Even rascals ought to know how to behave properly.

LYUBOV ANDREEVNA: *(Shocked and confused.)* Take it . . . here. . . . *(Looks in her purse.)* There's no silver here . . . It doesn't matter, here's a gold coin for you . . .

400 PASSER-BY: I thank you from the bottom of my heart! *(Goes out.)*

(There is laughter from those onstage.)

VARYA: *(Frightened.)* I'm going away . . . I'm going . . . Oh, there's nothing at home for the servants to eat, *Mamochka,* and you gave him a gold coin.

405 LYUBOV ANDREEVNA: I am foolish. What can be done with me, what! When we get home, I'll give you everything I have. Yermolay Alexeich, lend me something more, do! . .

LOPAKHIN: Yes, ma'am.

LYUBOV ANDREEVNA: Let's go, ladies and gentlemen, it's time. Oh, Varya, we've just signed, sealed, and absolutely promised 410 you in marriage. Congratulations.

VARYA: *(Through tears.)* Mama, this is nothing to joke about.

LOPAKHIN: Oralia, get thee to a nunnery . . .

GAEV: Oh, my hands are shaking. I haven't played a billiard game in a long time. 415

LOPAKHIN: Oralia, oh nymph, remember me in thy orisons!

LYUBOV ANDREEVNA: Come along, ladies and gentlemen. We'll sit down soon for supper.

VARYA: Oh, how he scared me. My heart hasn't stopped pounding yet. 420

LOPAKHIN: I'd like to remind you, ladies and gentlemen, the cherry orchard will be up for sale on the twenty-second of August. Think about it! . . Keep it in mind, do! . .

(All go out except TROFIMOV *and* ANYA.)

ANYA: *(Laughing.)* Thanks to that man who came by, Varya is scared, and we're alone now. 425

TROFIMOV: Varya's frightened we might suddenly fall in love, so she hasn't left us alone for days. With her narrow mind she can't possibly understand that we are above love. To give up all that is petty and unreal, which stops our being free and happy—that's the purpose and meaning of our lives. On 430 then, ahead! We stride invincibly on to that bright star burning there in the distance! On then, ahead! Don't fall behind, my friends!

ANYA: *(Throwing up her arms.)* How wonderfully you speak! *(Pause.)* It's unbelievable here today! 435

TROFIMOV: Yes, the weather is striking.

ANYA: Whatever have you done to me, Petya? Why is it I no longer love the cherry orchard as I used to? I loved it so tenderly, and I thought no place on earth was better than our own orchard. 440

TROFIMOV: All Russia is our orchard. The land is vast and beautiful and filled with marvelous places. *(Pause.)* Just think, Anya, your grandfather and your great-grandfather and all your ancestors owned both land and serfs, they owned living souls. Don't you see that from every cherry tree 445 in the orchard, from every leaf and every trunk, generations of human beings are gazing down at you, don't you hear their voices . . . To own human souls—it has transformed every one of you, don't you see, those who lived before and those living today. And so your mother, your uncle, and you 450 no longer notice that you are living in debt, at the expense of other people, at the expense of the very people you will allow no farther than the entrance to your home . . . We are at least two hundred years behind the times, we haven't made any real headway yet, and we still don't have any clear idea about 455 our relation to the past. We just philosophize, complain of boredom, or drink vodka. It's so clear, you see, that if we're to begin living in the present, we must first of all redeem our past and then be done with it forever. And the only way we can redeem our past is by suffering and by giving ourselves 460 over to exceptional labor, to steadfast and endless work. You must realize this, Anya.

ANYA: The house we live in hasn't really been ours for a long time, and I'm going to leave it. I give you my word.

TROFIMOV: If you're given the keys to the household, throw 465 them into the well and walk away, go. Be free like the wind.

ANYA: (*In exaltation.*) How wonderfully you said everything!

TROFIMOV: Believe me, Anya, you must believe! I'm not yet thirty, I'm a young man, and I'm still a student, but I have al-
470 ready gone through so much! As soon as winter's come, I find myself hungry, ill, worried, poor as a beggar, and—the places fate has driven me, the places! Where haven't I been, where? And the whole time, every minute of the day and night, I've felt impressions of the future abound in my soul,
475 visions I can't explain. I know happiness is coming, Anya, I can feel it. I already see it on the way . . .

ANYA: (*Deep in thought.*) The moon is rising.

(YEPIKHODOV *is heard playing the guitar, the same sad song as before. The moon rises. Somewhere near the poplar trees,* VARYA *is looking for* ANYA *and is calling, "Anya! Where are you?"*)

TROFIMOV: Yes, the moon is rising. (*Pause.*) There it is, happiness. There it comes, coming nearer, always nearer. I can al-
480 ready hear its footsteps. And if we don't see it, if we don't experience it, what does it matter? Other people will see it.

VARYA'S VOICE: (*Offstage.*) Anya! Where are you?

TROFIMOV: It's Varya again! (*Angrily.*) Oh, she is exasperating!

ANYA: Well, hmm? Let's go to the river. It's fine there.
485 TROFIMOV: Yes, let's go. (*They go out.*)

VARYA'S VOICE: (*Offstage.*) Anya! Anya!

— ACT THREE —

The drawing room. In the distance, through the archway, the ballroom can be seen. The chandelier is lighted. The Jewish orchestra mentioned in the second act is heard playing in the entrance hall. It is evening. In the ballroom they are dancing a grand rond. The voice of SIMEONOV-PISHCHIK *is heard, "Promenade à une paire!" They enter the drawing room:* PISHCHIK *and* SHARLOTTA IVANOVNA *are the first couple;* TROFIMOV *and* LYUBOV ANDREEVNA *the second;* ANYA *and the* POST OFFICE CIVIL SERVANT, *the third;* VARYA *and the* STATIONMASTER, *the fourth; and so on.* VARYA *is weeping quietly, and as she dances, she wipes her tears away.* DUNYASHA *is in the last couple. They walk around the drawing room, and* PISHCHIK *shouts, "Grand rond, balancez!" and "Les cavaliers à genoux et remerciez vos dames!"* FIRS, *wearing a dress coat, brings in a tray with seltzer water.* PISHCHIK *and* TROFIMOV *enter the drawing room.*

PISHCHIK: I'm a pretty full-blooded man. I've had two strokes already so dancing is hard work for me, but, as the saying goes,
5   "If you run with the pack,
                              you can trail.
             Keep silent or bark back,
                              you can't fail.
             But you'd better get crack-
                     ing to jiggle and jaggle
10   and wiggle and waggle
                                     your tail."
   I'm as healthy as a horse, however. My departed father was something of a joker—may the kingdom of heaven be his—

and he used to explain our origins like this. The ancient line of Simeonov-Pishchik, he'd say, comes down from the very
15 same horse that Caligula had seated in the senate . . . (*Sits down.*) But my trouble is I don't have any money, none! A hungry dog puts his trust only in meat . . . (*Snores and then wakes up immediately.*) That fits me to a . . . the only thing I keep thinking about is money . . .
20
TROFIMOV: Indeed your build is somehow like a horse.

PISHCHIK: Well, hmm . . . a horse is a fine animal . . . You can sell a horse . . .

(*The sound of a billiard game being played in an adjoining room is heard.* VARYA *appears in the ballroom underneath the archway.*)

TROFIMOV: (*Teases.*) Madame Lopakhina! Madame Lopakhina! . .
25
VARYA: (*Angrily.*) You're a used-up old gentleman!

TROFIMOV: Yes, I am a used-up old gentleman, and I'm proud of it!

VARYA: (*Meditating bitterly.*) Here we've gone and hired musicians, but what are we going to pay them with? (*Goes out.*)
30
TROFIMOV: (*To* PISHCHIK.) Just consider how much energy you've used up in the course of your life trying to find money to pay the interest on your loans. If you'd spent that same energy on something else, there's a good chance, when all's been said and done, you might have turned the world upside
35 down.

PISHCHIK: Nietzsche . . . the philosopher . . . the greatest, very famous . . . a fellow of enormous intellect. Well, he says in his own works that it's all right to forge banknotes.

TROFIMOV: Then you've read Nietzsche?
40
PISHCHIK: Well . . . Dashenka talked to me about it. Oh, the kind of situation I'm in right now, forging banknotes is about the only thing left for me to do . . . The day after tomorrow I must pay out three hundred and ten rubles . . . and what I've already got is one hundred and thirty . . . (*Feels his pockets,
45 alarmed.*) The money is gone! I've lost my money! (*Through tears.*) Where's my money? (*Jubilantly.*) Here it is, inside the lining . . . You know, I even started to sweat . . .

(LYUBOV ANDREEVNA *and* SHARLOTTA IVANOVNA *enter.*)

LYUBOV ANDREEVNA: (*Hums a lezginka.*) Why is Leonid taking so long? What's he doing in town? (*To* DUNYASHA.) Dun-
50 yasha, offer the musicians some tea . . .

TROFIMOV: I'd say the auction probably never took place.

LYUBOV ANDREEVNA: Oh, what on earth were we thinking of? Of all moments to send for the musicians. Of all moments to give a ball. The most inopportune of all . . . Well, it's noth-
55 ing, really . . . (*Sits and hums quietly.*)

SHARLOTTA: (*Gives a pack of cards to* PISHCHIK.) Here's a pack of cards. Think of a card, any card you want.

PISHCHIK: I've thought of one.

---

s.d. **Promenade . . . paire** "Promenade with your partner!" **Grand . . . balancez** "The great ring dance, get set!" **Les cavaliers . . . dames** "Gentlemen, on your knees and thank your ladies!"

40 **Nietzsche** Friedrich W. Nietzsche (1844–1900), German philosopher   49 **lezginka** the music that in the Caucasus mountains accompanies a courtship dance in which the man dances with abandon around the woman, who moves with grace and ease

60 SHARLOTTA: Now shuffle the pack. Very good. Now let me have them, oh my dear Mister Pishchik. *Ein, zwei, drei!* And now just look. There it is, in your side pocket . . .

PISHCHIK: *(Takes a card out of his side pocket.)* The eight of spades, you're positively right! *(Surprised.)* What do you
65 think of that!

SHARLOTTA: *(Holds the pack of cards on the palm of her hand; to* TROFIMOV.) Tell me quickly, what card is on top?

TROFIMOV: Well, hmm? Well, the queen of spades.

SHARLOTTA: And here it is! *(To* PISHCHIK.) Well, what do you
70 say the top card is now?

PISHCHIK: The ace of hearts.

SHARLOTTA: And here it is! *(Claps her hands and the pack of cards disappears.)* Oh, what fine weather today! *(She is answered by a mysterious woman's voice that apparently comes*
75 *from under the floor,* "Oh, yes, the weather is incredible, dear lady.") Oh, you're so fine, indeed you're my ideal . . .

(The voice, "I like you very much, too, dear lady.")

THE STATIONMASTER: *(Applauds.)* Bravo, our Miss Ventriloquist, bravo!

PISHCHIK: *(Surprised.)* What do you think of that! You're
80 charming, Sharlotta Ivanovna, just charming . . . you know I've simply fallen in love . . .

SHARLOTTA: In love? *(Having shrugged her shoulders.)* How could you ever fall in love, really? *Guter Mensch, aber schlechter Musikant.*

85 TROFIMOV: *(Claps* PISHCHIK *on the shoulder.)* Not bad for an old horse . . .

SHARLOTTA: I beg your attention, one last trick, if you please. *(Takes a lap robe from a chair.)* Here you see a very fine lap robe I'd like to sell . . . *(Shakes it.)* Isn't there anyone who'd
90 like to buy it?

PISHCHIK: *(Surprised.)* What do you think of that!

SHARLOTTA: *Ein, zwei, drei! (Quickly raises the lap robe, which she had lowered and held like a curtain, and behind it stands* ANYA, *who curtsies, runs to her mother, embraces her, and*
95 *runs back into the ballroom amid general excitement.)*

LYUBOV ANDREEVNA: *(Applauds.)* Bravo, bravo! . .

SHARLOTTA: Now once more! *Ein, zwei, drei! (Raises the lap robe and behind it stands* VARYA, *who bows.)*

PISHCHIK: *(Surprised.)* What do you think of that!

100 SHARLOTTA: That's all there is—the end! *(Throws the lap robe at* PISHCHIK, *curtsies, and runs off to the ballroom.)*

PISHCHIK: *(Hurries after her.)* Oh, you little scamp . . . Think you're something, don't you? Really something? *(Goes out.)*

LYUBOV ANDREEVNA: And Leonid still isn't back yet. I can't
105 imagine what he's doing in town all this time! You know the whole thing must be finished by now, either the estate's sold or the auction didn't take place. Then why on earth keep us in the dark all this time!

VARYA: *(Trying to comfort her.)* Dear Uncle bought it, I'm con-
110 vinced he did.

TROFIMOV: *(Derisively.)* Yes.

VARYA: Grandmother sent him the authority to buy it in her name and transfer the mortgage to her. It's for Anya's sake she's doing it. And with God's help I'm convinced dear
115 Uncle will buy it.

LYUBOV ANDREEVNA: Grandmother in Yaroslavl sent fifteen thousand rubles to buy the estate in her name—she didn't trust us—and the money she sent won't even pay the interest. *(Covers her face with her hands.)* My fate is being de-
120 cided today . . . my fate.

TROFIMOV: *(Teases* VARYA.) Madame Lopakhina!

VARYA: *(Angrily.)* Oh, it's the eternal student! He's been thrown out of the university two times so far.

LYUBOV ANDREEVNA: Why are you getting angry, Varya? He's
125 teasing you about Lopakhin, oh well, hmm? If you want to, then go and marry Lopakhin. He's a fine, interesting person. If you don't want to, then don't marry him. No one is forcing you, darling . . .

VARYA: I look on this whole matter seriously, *Mamochka,* I
130 must tell you frankly. He is a fine person and I like him.

LYUBOV ANDREEVNA: Then go and marry him. What is it you're waiting for, I simply don't understand!

VARYA: *Mamochka,* I can't propose to him myself, I can't. For the past two years everyone's been talking to me about him,
135 and they haven't stopped talking yet, but either he doesn't say anything or else he jokes about it. And I can understand why. He's growing rich, he's very busy, and he hasn't one bit of time for me. If only I had the money, even a little, if it were only a hundred rubles, I'd drop everything and walk
140 off. I'd go as far as I could. I'd go into a convent.

TROFIMOV: What a blessed way to live!

VARYA: *(To* TROFIMOV.) Our student can't stop proving how smart he is! *(In a gentle tone, in tears.)* Oh, Petya, you've grown so homely, and you look old, so very old! *(No longer*
145 *weeping, she speaks to* LYUBOV ANDREEVNA.) I just can't go through life without things to do, *Mamochka.* I must be doing something or other every single minute.

*(*YASHA *enters.)*

YASHA: *(Scarcely able to contain his laughter.)* Yepikhodov's gone and broken a billiard cue! . . *(Goes out.)*

VARYA: Why on earth is Yepikhodov here? And who gave him
150 permission to play billiards? These people don't make any sense to me . . . *(Goes out.)*

LYUBOV ANDREEVNA: Don't tease her, Petya. You can see, can't you, she's unhappy enough without that.

TROFIMOV: She's much too much the fanatic. Why can't she
155 stick to things that concern her? She's kept on bothering me and Anya the whole summer long, so afraid a love affair might come about. Why should it matter to her, anyway? Not for a single moment did I ever give any semblance of it, I'm far beyond vulgarity like that. We are above love!
160

LYUBOV ANDREEVNA: And here I am beneath love, I suppose. *(In great apprehension.)* Why on earth isn't Leonid back? I'd just like to know if the estate's sold or not. I can't believe this terrible thing has gone as far as it has—it's so incredible I don't even know what to think anymore, somehow I feel lost
165 . . . I could scream right now . . . or do something foolish. Save me, Petya. Say something now, talk to me . . .

TROFIMOV: Does it really matter whether the estate is sold today or not? It's over and done with, there's no turning back now, that path's already overgrown. Get hold of yourself, my
170 dear. And don't go and deceive yourself now. At least for once in your life look the truth right in the eyes.

---

61 **Ein . . . drei** German for "one, two, three"   83–84 **Guter Mensch . . . Musikant** German for "A good man, but a bad musician"

LYUBOV ANDREEVNA: What truth? You can see, can't you, where the truth is and where it isn't, but it seems I've lost my
175 sight, I see nothing. You confidently find answers for all the important problems, but tell me, my dear, isn't that because you're young, because you're not old enough for a single one of your problems to have brought about any substantial suf-
180 fering? You look ahead so boldly, and you don't see or expect anything terrible to happen, and isn't that because life is still hidden from your young eyes? You are bolder, more honest, deeper than we are, but try and go into the heart of the mat-ter—be at least halfway generous and have mercy on me. You know I was born here, my father and my mother lived
185 here, my grandfather, too. I love this house. Without the cherry orchard my life would lose its meaning, and if it must really be sold then go and sell me with the orchard . . . (Em-braces TROFIMOV and kisses him on the forehead.) You see my son was drowned here . . . (Weeps.) Have pity on me, my
190 fine, kind friend.
TROFIMOV: You know I feel for you with all my heart and soul.
LYUBOV ANDREEVNA: But that isn't the way to say it, it isn't the way at all . . . (Takes out her handkerchief. A telegram falls on the floor.) Today I feel I've lost heart and soul, you can't
195 imagine how difficult it is for me. It's too noisy here for me. Every sound cuts deep inside and I feel I'm trembling all over, but I can't go to my room, I can't. All alone in the si-lence, it's terrifying. Don't condemn me, Petya . . . I love you as if you were one of my very own. I'd willingly let Anya
200 marry you, I swear I would, my dear, only you must study and get your degree. You aren't doing a single thing, you just let fate throw you from one place to another, and that's what is so strange . . . Isn't it the truth? Yes? And you ought to do something or other with that beard to make it grow some-
205 how . . . (Laughs.) Oh, you're funny, you really are!
TROFIMOV: (Picks up telegram.) I don't have the slightest de-sire to be good looking.
LYUBOV ANDREEVNA: That telegram is from Paris. I get one every day. Both yesterday and today. That wild creature has
210 fallen ill again, and he's in trouble again . . . He begs for-giveness and implores me to go to him, and I really should go to Paris and spend some time near him. You disapprove, Petya, I can see from your face, but what else can be done, my dear, what can I really do? He is sick, he is alone and un-
215 happy, and who is there to look after him? Who can stop him from doing the wrong things, and who will give him his medicine at the right time? Then why try to hide it or keep quiet about the way I feel? I love him, that's clear. I love him, I love him . . . That man's a millstone around my
220 neck, I'm being dragged down with him, but I love that stone and I can't live without it. (Presses TROFIMOV's hand.) Don't think badly of me, Petya, don't say anything to me, don't say anything . . .
TROFIMOV: (Through tears.) Forgive me for being outspoken,
225 for God's sake, but you know he robbed you!
LYUBOV ANDREEVNA: No, no, no, you mustn't talk that way . . . (Puts her hands over her ears.)
TROFIMOV: That man is a good-for-nothing louse, and you're the only one who doesn't know it! He's a little, good-for-
230 nothing louse, a nobody . . .

---

183 **generous** literally, "be generous at least in your fingernails"

LYUBOV ANDREEVNA: (Having gotten angry, she controls her-self.) You are twenty-six or twenty-seven years old, but you are still a schoolboy!
TROFIMOV: And even if I am!
LYUBOV ANDREEVNA: You ought to be a man—at your age you 235 ought to have some understanding of people in love. And you ought to know what it is to love . . . You should fall in love yourself! (Angrily.) Yes, yes! And don't think you're so innocent and pure, you're simply an immaculate prude—that's what you are—a laughable eccentric boy, some kind of 240 freak . . .
TROFIMOV: (Horrified.) What can she be saying!
LYUBOV ANDREEVNA: "I am above love!" You aren't above love, but—as our Firs keeps saying—you are just a silly ga-loot, that's all. At your age and not to have a mistress! . . 245
TROFIMOV: (Horrified.) This is terrible! What can she be say-ing? (Having clutched his head, he goes into the ballroom.) This is terrible . . . I can't stand it, I'm going . . . (Goes out, but returns immediately.) All is over between us! (Goes out into the entrance hall.) 250
LYUBOV ANDREEVNA: (Shouts after him.) Petya, wait a mo-ment! You ridiculous boy, I was joking! Petya!
(In the entrance hall there are the sounds of someone quickly running on the stairway and suddenly falling downstairs with a clatter. ANYA and VARYA scream, which is followed immediately by the sound of laughter.)
LYUBOV ANDREEVNA: What's going on out there?
(ANYA runs in.)
ANYA: (Laughing.) Petya fell downstairs! (Runs out.)
LYUBOV ANDREEVNA: What an eccentric boy Petya is . . . 255 (Having stopped in the middle of the ballroom, the STATION-MASTER recites "The Sinful Woman" by Aleksey Tolstoy. They listen to him, but he has recited only a few lines when the sounds of a waltz come from the entrance hall and the reading is broken off. All dance. TROFIMOV, ANYA, VARYA, and 260 LYUBOV ANDREEVNA enter from the entrance hall.) Now, Petya . . . now there, you dear innocent soul . . . Forgive me, I beg you . . . Let's dance . . . (Dances with PETYA.)
(ANYA and VARYA dance. FIRS enters and puts his walking stick near the side door. YASHA has also come in from the drawing room and is watching the dancing.)
YASHA: What do you say, Grandpa?
FIRS: I don't feel too well. In times gone by, why generals, 265 barons, and admirals came to our dances, but now we send for the post office clerk and the stationmaster—and even they come against their will. Somehow I feel I've gotten weaker. My old master, who was their grandfather, used to dose every one of us with powdered sealing wax no matter 270 what sickness we had. I've been taking sealing wax for about twenty years now, but it might even be more. Maybe I'm still alive because of it.
YASHA: Gramps, you make me sick and tired. (Yawns.) If only you'd go off and croak—the sooner the better. 275
FIRS: Oh, you . . . you silly galoot, you! (Mumbles.)
(TROFIMOV and LYUBOV ANDREEVNA dance in the ballroom and then into the drawing room.)
LYUBOV ANDREEVNA: Merci. I'd like to sit down for a while . . . (Sits down.) I'm tired.

(ANYA enters.)

ANYA: *(Excitedly.)* In the kitchen just now someone was saying
   that the cherry orchard was sold today.

LYUBOV ANDREEVNA: Sold? To whom?

ANYA: He didn't say. He's gone now. *(Dances with* TROFIMOV;
   they go into the ballroom.)

YASHA: It was just some old man wagging his tongue out there.
   We didn't know him.

FIRS: Oh, Leonid Andreich still isn't here, he hasn't come back
   yet. He's only wearing his lightweight overcoat, his "be-
   tween-seasons" one, and before you can bat an eye he's going
   to catch cold. Oh, these green young things—they never
   learn.

LYUBOV ANDREEVNA: I'm going to die, I know it. Yasha, go and
   find out whom it was sold to.

YASHA: But he went away a long time back, it was an old man.
   (Laughs.)

LYUBOV ANDREEVNA: *(Slightly annoyed.)* Well, what are you
   laughing about? What's making you so happy?

YASHA: Oh, that Yepikhodov is really very funny. The man's so
   useless. Two-and-Twenty Hard Knocks.

LYUBOV ANDREEVNA: If the estate is sold, Firs, where will you
   go?

FIRS: Wherever you tell me, that's where I'll go.

LYUBOV ANDREEVNA: Why do you look like that? Aren't
   you feeling well? You ought to go lie down and sleep, you
   know . . .

FIRS: Yes . . . *(With an ironic smile.)* I'd go off to sleep, and if
   I'm not here who will there be to serve and keep things going
   the way they should? I'm the only one in charge of the whole
   house.

YASHA: *(To* LYUBOV ANDREEVNA.*)* Lyubov Andreevna! Allow
   me to ask you something, if you'd be so kind! If you go to
   Paris again, do me a favor and take me with you, please. I
   can't stay here, it's absolutely impossible here. *(Looks
   around, in an undertone.)* I suppose it's needless to say it, you
   can see for yourself, this country is uncivilized and the people don't have any morals at all. Then there's the boredom,
   too. In the kitchen they feed you disgusting things, and to
   make it worse—that man Firs keeps walking around the
   whole time and mumbling all sorts of words that don't make
   much sense. Take me with you, if you'd be so kind!

(PISHCHIK enters.)

PISHCHIK: Please do me the favor . . . of this little waltz, oh
   gorgeous woman . . . (LYUBOV ANDREEVNA *goes with him.)*
   But I'll still take that one hundred and eighty rubles from
   you, my charming lady . . . Yes, I will . . . *(Dances.)* One
   hundred and eighty rubles . . . *(They go into the ballroom.)*

YASHA: *(Quietly sings.)* "If you could but know the excitement
   of my soul . . ."

*(In the ballroom a woman dressed in a gray top hat and checked
trousers is seen jumping around and waving her arms. There are
shouts of "Bravo, Sharlotta Ivanovna.")*

DUNYASHA: *(Stops to powder.)* The young mistress told me to
   dance. There are plenty of gentlemen and only a few ladies,
   but dancing makes my head spin around and my heart is
   pounding. Just now, Firs Nikolaevich, the clerk from the post
   office told me something that made me lose my breath.

(The music subsides.)

FIRS: What exactly did he tell you?

DUNYASHA: You are like a flower, he said.

YASHA: *(Yawns.)* Sheer case of ignorance . . . *(Goes out.)*

DUNYASHA: Like a flower . . . I'm such a delicate girl I just love
   hearing sweet words like that.

FIRS: You'll get swept off your feet before you know it.

(YEPIKHODOV enters.)

YEPIKHODOV: You don't want to look at me, Avdotya Fyodorovna . . . as if I were an insect of some kind. *(Sighs.)* Oh,
   that's life!

DUNYASHA: What do you want?

YEPIKHODOV: No doubt you are right, perhaps. *(Sighs.)* But, of
   course, if you look at it from one point of view—and I will
   allow myself to express myself this way, please excuse me for
   being so outspoken—you have completely reduced me to a
   state of mind. I know what luck I face. Every day some catastrophe or other happens to me, but I got used to that long,
   long ago, so that I look upon my fate with a smile on my face.
   You gave me your word, and even though I . . .

DUNYASHA: I beg you, let's talk a little later on, but now just
   leave me alone. I'm dreaming right now. *(Plays with her
   fan.)*

YEPIKHODOV: I have a catastrophe every day and—I'll permit
   myself to express myself this way—I just go on smiling, and
   sometimes I even laugh.

(VARYA enters from the ballroom.)

VARYA: Haven't you left yet, Semyon? Who do you think you
   are, really, don't you have any respect? *(To* DUNYASHA.*)* Be
   off, Dunyasha, you can leave. *(To* YEPIKHODOV.*)* First you
   play billiards and break a cue, and now you walk around the
   drawing room as if you were a guest.

YEPIKHODOV: You can't make me—if you'll permit me to
   say—answer for it.

VARYA: I'm not making you answer for it, I'm just telling you.
   All you know how to do is walk from one place to the next,
   but you don't do one bit of work. We keep a clerk, but for
   what—it's beyond me.

YEPIKHODOV: *(Offended.)* Whether I work or ramble about,
   whether I eat or play billiards, these are issues up for discussion only by more reasonable and older people.

VARYA: How dare you talk to me that way! *(Having flared up.)*
   How dare you? Do you mean I'm not reasonable, is that it?
   Well, you can remove yourself, get out of here! This minute!

YEPIKHODOV: *(Having become intimidated.)* I beg you to express yourself in a delicate way.

VARYA: *(Flying into a rage.)* Get out of here this very minute!
   Out of here, out! *(He goes to the door and she follows him.)*
   Two-and-Twenty Hard Knocks! Out you go and never come
   in here again! Don't let me catch sight of you ever again!
   (YEPIKHODOV *goes out. Behind the door his voice is heard:
   "I'm going to bring a complaint against you.")* So you're
   coming back in here? *(Seizes the stick which* FIRS *placed
   near the door.)* Come on . . . come on . . . come on, I'll show
   you. . . . So you're coming back? You are, are you? Then
   take that . . . *(Flourishes the stick at the very moment*
   LOPAKHIN *enters.)*

LOPAKHIN: Thank you ever so much.

VARYA: *(Angrily and derisively.)* I'm very sorry!

LOPAKHIN: It's nothing, Miss. Thanks so much for your heartfelt generosity.

390   VARYA: Don't mention it. (*Walks away, then looks around and gently asks.*) I didn't hurt you, did I?

LOPAKHIN: No, it's nothing. There's going to be one whale of a swelling, though.

(*Voices are heard in the ballroom:* "Lopakhin's arrived! Yermolay Alexeich!")

395   PISHCHIK: Well, squint your eyes and bend your ears—it's him himself . . . (*Kisses* LOPAKHIN.) I caught a whiff of brandy on you, my dear old soul. We've been kicking up our heels around here too.

(LYUBOV ANDREEVNA *enters.*)

LYUBOV ANDREEVNA: Then it's you, Yermolay Alexeich? What's taken you so long? Where is Leonid?

400   LOPAKHIN: Leonid Andreich came with me, he's on his way . . .

LYUBOV ANDREEVNA: (*Agitated.*) Well, what is it? Did the auction take place? Talk to me, tell me!

LOPAKHIN: (*Embarrassed, fearing to betray his elation.*) The auction was over by four . . . We were late for the train, and we had to wait until half past nine. (*Having sighed heavily.*) Phew! My head's starting to go round and round . . .

405

(GAEV *enters. He has his purchases in his right hand and wipes away his tears with his left hand.*)

LYUBOV ANDREEVNA: Lyonya, what is it? Well, Lyonya? (*Impatiently, in tears.*) Tell me, for God's sake! Quickly . . .

410   GAEV: (*He can say nothing to her and only waves his hand; to* FIRS, *weeping.*) Here, take these . . . It's anchovies and Kerch herrings . . . I've had nothing to eat today . . . How much I've had to go through! (*The door to the billiard room is open. The cracking of billiard balls is heard, and* YASHA'S *voice:* "Seven and eighteen!" GAEV'S *expression changes and he no longer weeps.*) I'm terribly tired. Give me a hand, Firs, I must change my clothes. (*Goes to his room through the ballroom, followed by* FIRS.)

415

PISHCHIK: What went on at the auction? Tell us now, do!

420   LYUBOV ANDREEVNA: Is the cherry orchard sold?

LOPAKHIN: It's sold.

LYUBOV ANDREEVNA: Who bought it?

LOPAKHIN: I bought it. (*Pause.* LYUBOV ANDREEVNA *is crushed. If she were not standing next to the armchair and table, she would have fallen.* Varya *takes the keys from her belt, throws them on the floor in the middle of the drawing room, and goes out.*) I bought it! Wait, ladies and gentlemen, be kind and wait one moment. My head's going round in circles, I can't talk . . . (*Laughs.*) When we got to the auction, Deriganov was already there. Leonid Andreich had only fifteen thousand rubles, and right away Deriganov bid thirty over and above the arrearage on the mortgage. I saw the shape things were in, so I took him on. I bid forty. He went to forty-five, I made it fifty-five. That's the way it went. He kept raising his offer by five thousand, I kept raising mine by ten . . . Well, it came to a finish at last. I bid ninety thousand rubles on top of the arrears, and I got it. The cherry orchard is mine now! Mine! (*Shouts with laughter.*) God in heaven, dear Lord God, the cherry orchard is mine! Tell me I'm drunk or out of my mind, that it's all a daydream I see before my eyes . . . (*Stamps his feet.*) Don't laugh at me! If only my father and grandfather could rise from their graves and see their Yermolay now—their Yermolay who was forever getting beaten,

425

430

435

440

Yermolay who could scarcely read or write, who ran barefoot in the winter—if they could only see how this very same Yermolay went and bought this estate, the most beautiful spot in the world. I bought the estate where my grandfather and my father were slaves, where they weren't even allowed to go into the kitchen. I'm asleep, it's only a dream, it's only something that seems to be . . . This is the fruit of your imagination, concealed in the shadows of uncertainty . . . (*Picks up the keys, smiling affectionately.*) She threw down the keys—she wants to show she doesn't run this house anymore . . . (*Jingles the keys.*) Well, it doesn't matter anyway. (*The orchestra is heard tuning up.*) Hey there, musicians, start playing. I want to hear you! Come on, all of you, come and see Yermolay Lopakhin slash the cherry orchard with his axe. Watch and see the trees come crashing down! We're going to build summer cottages, and our grandchildren and our great-grandchildren are going to see a new way to live around here . . . Music, start playing! (*The orchestra plays.* LYUBOV ANDREEVNA *has sunk into a chair and is weeping bitterly.* LOPAKHIN *speaks reproachfully.*) Why on earth, why didn't you listen to me before? My poor, fine friend, you can't turn round and go back now. (*In tears.*) Oh, if only this would pass by as quickly as possible, if only we could hurry and change our life somehow, this unhappy, helter-skelter way we live.

445

450

455

460

465

PISHCHIK: (*Takes him by the arm, in an undertone.*) She's crying. Let's go into the ballroom, let her be alone . . . Come, let's go . . . (*Takes him by the arm and leads him into the ballroom.*)

470

LOPAKHIN: What's going on? Say, you doing the music, play lively and clear! Let's start having things the way I want it. (*Ironically.*) Here comes the new landlord, the owner of the cherry orchard! (*Accidentally shoves a small table, nearly overturns the candelabra.*) I can pay for everything! (*Goes out with* PISHCHIK.)

475

(*There is no one left in the ballroom or the drawing room except* LYUBOV ANDREEVNA, *who sits all shrunken and is weeping bitterly. The orchestra plays quietly.* ANYA *and* TROFIMOV *enter quickly.* ANYA *goes to her mother and kneels down in front of her.* TROFIMOV *stays by the entrance to the ballroom.*)

ANYA: Mama! . . Mama, are you crying? My dear, kind, beautiful Mama, my precious, I love you, I do . . . I give you my blessing. The cherry orchard is sold, it's gone now, it's true, so true, but don't cry, Mama. Your life is still ahead of you, and you haven't lost your beautiful, innocent soul . . . Come with me, my dear, let's go away from here, let's go! . . We shall plant a new orchard, far more splendid than this one. You shall see it, you shall know and find understanding, and happiness shall descend into your heart and soul—you shall know a quiet and profound joy—like the setting sun at the evening hour, and you shall smile, Mama! Come, my dear, let's go! Let's go! . .

480

485

490

— ACT FOUR —

The setting is the same as in the first act. There are no window curtains or pictures. The few remaining pieces of furniture have been piled into one corner, as if for sale. There is a feeling of emptiness. Suitcases, traveling bags, etc., have been piled up near the outer door at the rear of the stage. Through the open door, left, the voices of ANYA *and* VARYA *can be heard.* LOPAKHIN *is standing, waiting.* YASHA *is holding a tray with glasses filled with champagne. In the entrance hall* YEPIKHODOV *is tying up a box. There is a rumble coming from offstage at the rear, the voices of the peasants who have come to say good-bye.* GAEV's *voice is heard:* "Thanks, brothers, thank you."

YASHA: The peasants have come to say good-bye. The way I look at it, Yermolay Alexeich, such folks are decent enough, but they don't really know what's what.

(The rumble of voices subsides. LYUBOV ANDREEVNA *and* GAEV *come in through the entrance hall. She is not weeping; however, she is pale, her face is quivering, and she is unable to speak.)*

GAEV: You gave them your purse, Lyuba. That's something
5   you shouldn't do! You know you shouldn't!

LYUBOV ANDREEVNA: I couldn't help it! I simply couldn't help it! *(Both go out.)*

LOPAKHIN: *(In the doorway, calling after them.)* Please, I ask you from the bottom of my heart, let's have one little glass
10   since we must say good-bye. I didn't come up with the idea of bringing it from town, and I could only find one bottle at the station. Please, I beg you! *(Pause.)* Well, hmm, friends! Don't you want some? *(Walks away from the door.)* If I'd known, I wouldn't have bought it. Well, then, I'm not going
15   to drink any, either. *(YASHA carefully puts the tray on a chair.)* You take some, Yasha, at least you.

YASHA: To those who are going away! And good luck to those who stay behind! *(Drinks.)* This champagne isn't the real stuff, you can take my word for it.

20   LOPAKHIN: Eight rubles a bottle. *(Pause.)* Damn, it's cold in here.

YASHA: They didn't start the fires today. It doesn't matter, we're going away. *(Laughs.)*

LOPAKHIN: What's so funny?

25   YASHA: I feel pleased, that's all.

LOPAKHIN: October has come, but it's sunny and quiet outside, like in the summer. Good weather for building. *(Having glanced at his watch, calls through the doorway.)* Keep in mind, ladies and gentlemen, forty-six minutes before the
30   train leaves. That means we must start for the station in twenty minutes. Better hurry up.

(TROFIMOV, wearing an overcoat, enters from outside.)

TROFIMOV: I think it's time we set off. They've brought the horses to the door. Damned if I know where my galoshes are. They've disappeared. *(Calls through the doorway.)* Anya, my
35   galoshes aren't here! Can't find them at all!

LOPAKHIN: I must go to Kharkov. I'll be going with you on the same train. I'll spend the whole winter in Kharkov. I've been shooting the breeze with you folks all the time, it really bothers me when I don't have things to do. I can't stand going
40   without work, because I don't know what to do with my hands. You can see the peculiar way they dangle, just as if they belonged to someone else.

TROFIMOV: We're going away pretty soon, and you can get down to your useful labor again.

45   LOPAKHIN: How about it, have a little glass.

TROFIMOV: No, thanks.

LOPAKHIN: So you're going to Moscow, right?

TROFIMOV: Yes, I'll see them off and on their way in town, and tomorrow I'll start for Moscow.

50   LOPAKHIN: Yes . . . Well, hmm, the professors haven't started their lectures yet, I suppose, they must be waiting for you to show up!

TROFIMOV: It's none of your business.

LOPAKHIN: How many years have you been studying at the uni-
55   versity?

TROFIMOV: Think of something new to say. That joke is old and flat. *(Looks for his galoshes.)* You know, don't you, we may not see each other anymore, so let me give you a word or two of advice. Don't wave your arms around! Get rid of
60   that habit of waving your arms. Another thing too. When you count on building those summer homes and say that the owners in time will turn out to be independent farmers, you count so much on it—that's just the same as waving your arms around . . . Well, be that as it may, I still like you very
65   much. You have delicate and gentle fingers like an artist has, and in the same way, you are delicate and gentle too in your soul . . .

LOPAKHIN: *(Embraces him.)* Good-bye, my friend. Thank you for everything. Let me give you some money for the trip, in
70   case you need it.

TROFIMOV: Whatever for? I don't need it.

LOPAKHIN: You know you have nothing!

TROFIMOV: Yes, I have, and I thank you. I got something for a translation. It's here, in my pocket. *(Anxiously.)* But I still
75   don't have my galoshes!

VARYA: *(From the adjoining room.)* Oh, take your filthy things! *(Throws a pair of rubber galoshes out on the stage.)*

TROFIMOV: Why are you so angry, Varya? Hmm . . . Oh, these aren't my galoshes!

80   LOPAKHIN: In the spring I seeded almost three thousand acres in poppies, and I just earned forty thousand rubles clear and clean. And when my poppies were in flower, what a picture of beauty that was! What I'm saying is this. I made forty thousand, so I'm offering you a loan because I can well afford to.
85   So why stick your nose in the air? I'm a peasant . . . and I call a spade a spade.

TROFIMOV: Your father was a peasant, mine was a druggist, and these simple facts prove—exactly nothing. *(LOPAKHIN takes out his wallet.)* Oh, leave it alone, do . . . Even if you
90   gave me two hundred thousand, I wouldn't take it. I'm a free person. And everything you value so highly and is held so dear by all of you, both rich and poor, not one of these things can sway me one iota. Why, they have as much power as a fluff of eiderdown floating in the air. I can make a go of it
95   without you, I can even pass you by. I'm strong and proud. Humankind is on its way to a higher truth, to the greatest happiness possible on this earth, and I'm in the vanguard!

LOPAKHIN: Will you get there?

TROFIMOV: I will. *(Pause.)* I'll either get there or show others
100 the way to get there.

(There is heard the sound of an axe striking a tree in the distance.)

LOPAKHIN: Well, good-bye, dear boy. It's time to go. You and I stick our noses in the air and look down on each other, but life goes on without giving a hoot about us. When I work and keep at it steadily for some time, thoughts come more easily, and it seems to me I too know why I exist. But think how
105 many people there are in Russia who just exist, brother, and for what—it's beyond me. Well, it doesn't matter, that isn't

what keeps the wheels greased and spinning. Leonid Andreich has taken a job at the bank, they say, at six thousand a
110   year . . . He just won't stick to it, you know, he's much too lazy . . .

ANYA: (In the doorway.) Mama begs you not to cut down the orchard until she's gone.

TROFIMOV: Yes, really, don't you have tact enough to see . . .
115   (Goes out through the entrance hall.)

LOPAKHIN: All right, it'll take only a minute . . . Oh, these people, really. (Goes out after him.)

ANYA: Has Firs been sent to the hospital?

YASHA: I told them this morning. They've sent him, it stands to
120   reason they have.

ANYA: (To YEPIKHODOV, who is passing through the room.) Semyon Panteleich, please ask and find out if they've taken Firs to the hospital.

YASHA: (Offended.) I told Yegor this morning. Why keep on
125   asking about it? You've brought it up ten times.

YEPIKHODOV: Firs has lived through so many years, my final and decisive opinion is that he's gone far beyond repair. It's time for him to meet his forefathers. And I can only envy him. (He has put the suitcase down on a hatbox and has
130   crushed it.) Well, that's it, of course. I knew it'd turn out like that. (Goes out.)

YASHA: (Derisively.) Two-and-Twenty Hard Knocks . . .

VARYA: (From behind the door.) Has Firs been taken to the hospital?

135   ANYA: Yes, he has.

VARYA: Why is it they didn't take the letter to the doctor?

ANYA: Then we must send it on after him . . . (Goes out.)

VARYA: (From the adjoining room.) Where is Yasha? Tell him his mother's come and wants to say good-bye.

140   YASHA: (Waves his hand.) That's enough to make you lose your patience.

(All this time DUNYASHA has been fussing with the luggage. Now that YASHA is alone, she goes up to him.)

DUNYASHA: Why didn't you even glance at me once, Yasha? You are going away . . . You're walking out on me . . . (Weeps and throws her arms around his neck.)

145   YASHA: What are you crying about, hmm? (Drinks champagne.) I'll be in Paris again in six days. Tomorrow we'll take the express train, off we'll roll, and that's the last you'll see of us. I can't even believe it, somehow. Vive la France! . . It doesn't suit me here, I really can't stand this sort of life . . .
150   and that's all there is to it. I've seen enough ignorance, oh, have I had my fill of it. (Drinks champagne.) What are you crying about, hmm? Behave yourself as you should, and you won't have to cry then.

DUNYASHA: (Looking in the small mirror, powders.) Send me a
155   letter from Paris. You know I loved you, Yasha, I loved you so much! I'm a tenderhearted person, Yasha, through and through!

YASHA: Someone is coming. (Fusses with a suitcase, quietly hums.)

(LYUBOV ANDREEVNA, GAEV, ANYA, and SHARLOTTA IVANOVNA enter.)

160   GAEV: We ought to go. There's just a little time left. (Looking at YASHA.) Who is it in here reeks of herring?

LYUBOV ANDREEVNA: In about ten minutes we must be getting into the carriages . . . (Looks around the room.) Good-bye, my home. Fare thee well, dear old house of our forefathers.
165   Winter will pass, spring will come in time, and then you won't be here anymore, you will be pulled down. Oh, the sights these walls have seen in days gone by! (Kisses her daughter fervently.) My treasure, how radiant you look, your eyes are shining like diamonds. Are you pleased, child? Really pleased?
170

ANYA: Really! This is the beginning of a new life, Mama!

GAEV: (Cheerfully.) Yes, indeed, everything is fine again. Before the cherry orchard was sold, we were all upset and worried ourselves sick, but afterwards, when the whole thing was
175   settled once and for all, and not one chance of turning back, we all simmered down and even started to feel cheerful . . . I'm an employee of a bank now. I'm a financier . . . Off the yellow right into the middle. And Lyuba, in spite of everything, you are looking better, no doubt about it, none.
180

LYUBOV ANDREEVNA: Yes. My nerves are much better, that's true. (Someone helps her put on her hat and coat.) I'm sleeping fine. Take my things out, Yasha. It's time. (To ANYA.) My little girl, we'll see each other again soon . . . I'm going to Paris, and I'll live there on the money your grandmother from Yaroslavl sent to buy the estate—long live Grand-
185   mother! That money won't last for long.

ANYA: You'll come back soon, Mama, very soon . . . isn't that so? I'm going to study and pass my school examinations, and then I'll go to work and help you. Mama, we'll read all kinds of books together . . . isn't that so? (Kisses her mother's
190   hands.) We shall read during the autumn evenings, we'll read through lots of books, and a new marvelous world will open up before us . . . (Daydreams.) Mama, come back . . .

LYUBOV ANDREEVNA: I will, my precious. (Embraces her daughter.)
195

(LOPAKHIN enters. SHARLOTTA quietly hums a song.)

GAEV: Happy Sharlotta, she's singing!

SHARLOTTA: (Picks up a bundle which resembles a baby in swaddling clothes.) Bye, bye, little baby mine . . . (The crying of a baby is heard, "Wah, Wah! . .") Be quiet, my dear, my fine little boy. ("Wah! . . Wah! . .") I feel sorry for you, so
200   sorry! (Throws the bundle down.) Then please find me another job, won't you? I can't go on like this.

LOPAKHIN: We'll find something for you, Sharlotta Ivanovna, don't get upset.

GAEV: Everyone's discarding us. Varya's going away too . . . All
205   of a sudden we're not needed.

SHARLOTTA: I don't have any place to live in town. I must go away . . . (Hums.) It doesn't matter . . .

(PISHCHIK enters.)

LOPAKHIN: What do I see? One of nature's miracles! . .

PISHCHIK: (Out of breath.) Phew, give me a chance to get
210   my breath back . . . I'm bushed . . . My dear venerable friends . . . give me some water . . .

GAEV: You're after some money, I suppose? Your humble servant, I'm going to go now and leave my tempter behind me . . . (Goes out.)
215

PISHCHIK: It's been a while since I've been here . . . most beautiful lady . . . (To LOPAKHIN.) You're here too . . . I'm glad to see you . . . a fellow of most enormous intellect . . .

220 Here, take it . . . accept it, do . . . (*Gives* LOPAKHIN *money.*) Four hundred rubles . . . I still owe you eight hundred and forty.

LOPAKHIN: (*Bewildered, shrugs his shoulders.*) It's like a dream . . . Where on earth did you get it?

225 PISHCHIK: Wait a bit . . . I'm really hot . . . A most extraordinary incident. Some Englishmen arrived at my place and found some kind of white clay in the ground . . . (*To* LYUBOV ANDREEVNA.) And four hundred for you . . . my beautiful stunning woman . . . (*Gives her money.*) I'll give you the rest later on. (*Drinks water.*) Just now a certain young man on the

230 train was saying that some sort of . . . great philosopher advises everybody to run and jump off a roof . . . "Go ahead and jump," he says, and in that lies the whole problem. (*Surprised.*) What do you think of that! Give me some water! . .

LOPAKHIN: What sort of Englishmen were they?

235 PISHCHIK: I leased them the land with the clay in it for twenty-four years . . . And now, please excuse me, I've no more time . . . Must gallop farther on . . . I'm going to see Znoykov . . . and Kardamonov . . . I'm in debt to everybody . . . (*Drinks.*) I wish you all a good day . . . I'll drop by on Thursday . . .

240 LYUBOV ANDREEVNA: We're just now moving our things to town, and tomorrow I go abroad . . .

PISHCHIK: What's that? (*Becomes anxious.*) Why to town? Oh, yes, now I see the furniture . . . suitcases . . . Well, it's nothing . . . (*Through tears.*) It's nothing . . . People of mammoth

245 intellect . . . these Englishmen . . . It's nothing . . . all happiness to you . . . God will help you . . . It's nothing . . . Everything in this world must come to an end . . . (*Kisses* LYUBOV ANDREEVNA'S *hand.*) And if the news gets to you that my end has come, just recall this very . . . old horse and say,

250 "Once on this earth there was such-and-such a person . . . Simeonov-Pishchik . . . may the kingdom of heaven be his . . ." Most remarkable weather today . . . Yes . . . (*Goes out greatly troubled, but returns immediately to speak from the doorway.*) Dashenka sends her regards to you! (*Goes out.*)

255 LYUBOV ANDREEVNA: Well, we can go now. I'm leaving with two things weighing on my mind. My first worry is Firs and the fact that he's ill. (*Having glanced at her watch.*) We have about five minutes left . . .

ANYA: Mama, they've already sent Firs to the hospital. Yasha

260 sent him this morning.

LYUBOV ANDREEVNA: My other distress is Varya. She's accustomed to getting up early and working, and now without anything to do—she's like a fish out of water. She's become so thin and pale, and she weeps all the time, poor darling . . .

265 (*Pause.*) As you very well know, Yermaloy Alexeich, I've dreamed . . . of giving her in marriage to you. Besides, that's the way things seemed to look—you were planning to get married. (*Whispers to* ANYA, *who nods to* SHARLOTTA, *and they both go out.*) She loves you, you like her, and I don't

270 know—I really don't—why it is you try to avoid each other. I simply can't understand it!

LOPAKHIN: I don't understand it, either, to tell the truth. Somehow it's all pretty strange . . . If there's still time, I'm all set to go ahead right now . . . Let's get it settled, finish it up,

275 and—*basta*. But I don't feel I can make a proposal unless you're here too.

LYUBOV ANDREEVNA: Oh, that's splendid. You know it'll take about a minute, no more. I'll call her now . . .

LOPAKHIN: By the way, we even have champagne. (*Having glanced at the glasses.*) Empty, someone's already drunk it

280 all. (YASHA *coughs.*) That's really called lapping it up . . .

LYUBOV ANDREEVNA: (*Vivaciously.*) Wonderful. We'll leave you now . . . Yasha, *allez*! I'll call her . . . (*In the doorway.*) Varya, leave everything and come here. Come along now! (*Goes out with* YASHA.)

285 LOPAKHIN: (*Having glanced at his watch.*) Yes . . . (*Pause.*)

(*Suppressed laughter and whispering are heard from behind the door. Finally* VARYA *enters.*)

VARYA: (*Examines the luggage for a long time.*) It's strange, I just can't seem to find . . .

LOPAKHIN: What are you searching for?

290 VARYA: I packed it away myself, and I can't remember. (*Pause.*)

LOPAKHIN: Where is it you're going now, Varvara Mikhaylovna?

VARYA: Me? To Ragulins' . . . I've agreed to look after their place . . . as the housekeeper. At least that's the impression I

295 get.

LOPAKHIN: That's at Yashnevo, isn't it? About seventy versts away from here. (*Pause.*) And so life is over and done with in this house . . .

VARYA: (*Examining the luggage.*) Where on earth could it . . .

300 Or, maybe, I packed it away in the trunk . . . Yes, life in this house is over and done with . . . And it will never come back here anymore . . .

LOPAKHIN: And I'm just now on my way to Kharkov . . . On the next train, you see. I've got plenty to do. I'm leaving Yepikhodov here to look after the work outside . . . I've hired

305 him.

VARYA: Well, hmm!

LOPAKHIN: Last year at this time we had snow on the ground, if you recall, but now it's pretty quiet and plenty of sunshine. It's just cold, that's all . . . About three degrees of frost.

310 VARYA: I haven't looked. (*Pause.*) Besides, our thermometer's broken . . . (*Pause.*)

(*A voice from outside is heard calling through the door,* "Yermolay Alexeich!")

LOPAKHIN: (*As if he has been waiting a long time for this summons.*) This very minute! (*Quickly goes out.*)

(VARYA *sits on the floor, having laid her head on a bundle of clothing, and quietly sobs. The door opens, and* LYUBOV ANDREEVNA *enters warily.*)

315 LYUBOV ANDREEVNA: Well? (*Pause.*) We must go.

VARYA: (*No longer is weeping and has wiped her eyes.*) Yes, it's time, *Mamochka*. If I don't miss my train I can get to the Ragulins' today . . .

LYUBOV ANDREEVNA: (*In the doorway.*) Anya, bundle up!

320 (ANYA *enters, then* GAEV *and* SHARLOTTA IVANOVNA. GAEV *is wearing a warm overcoat with a hood. A* MAIDSERVANT *and* COACHMEN *enter and begin to fetch and carry.* YEPIKHODOV *bustles about and supervises those who carry the luggage.*) Now we can start on our way.

---

283 **allez** "Let's go!"

325 ANYA: *(Jubilantly.)* Yes, on our way!

GAEV: My friends, my dear, good friends! Deserting this home forever, how can I be silent, how can I refrain from expressing my feelings in saying good-bye, feelings that now fill my whole being . . .

330 ANYA: *(Beseechingly.)* Uncle!

VARYA: Uncle dear, you mustn't!

GAEV: *(Despondently.)* A bank shot off the yellow into the middle . . . I'll keep quiet . . .

(TROFIMOV enters, then LOPAKHIN.)

TROFIMOV: What about it, ladies and gentlemen, it's time to
335 go!

LOPAKHIN: Yepikhodov, my overcoat!

LYUBOV ANDREEVNA: I'll just sit down one more minute. It's just as if I'd never noticed what the walls and ceiling of this house look like, and now I see them eagerly, with such a gen-
340 tle love . . .

GAEV: I remember when I was six years old. I was sitting in this window on Trinity Sunday, and I saw my father going to church . . .

LYUBOV ANDREEVNA: Have they taken out all the things?

345 LOPAKHIN: Yes, it seems they have, everything. *(Putting on his coat, to YEPIKHODOV.)* Yepikhodov, be sure to look and see that everything's in the right order.

YEPIKHODOV: *(Speaks in a hoarse voice.)* You can rest assured, Yermolay Alexeich!

350 LOPAKHIN: What's the trouble with your voice?

YEPIKHODOV: I just now drank some water, I must have swallowed something or other.

YASHA: *(Scornfully.)* Sheer case of ignorance . . .

LYUBOV ANDREEVNA: We're going away, and not one soul will
355 be left here . . .

LOPAKHIN: Until this coming spring.

VARYA: *(Pulls an umbrella out of a bundle and it looks as if she were going to strike someone. LOPAKHIN pretends that he is frightened.)* Oh, you're not serious, you can't be . . . Why, the
360 thought never entered my mind.

TROFIMOV: Ladies and gentlemen, let's go and get in the carriages . . . It's time, time! The train will soon be in!

VARYA: Petya, here they are, your galoshes, next to the suitcase. *(Through tears.)* And how filthy they are, and old . . .

365 TROFIMOV: *(Putting on his galoshes.)* On our way, ladies and gentlemen!

GAEV: *(Greatly troubled and afraid of breaking into tears.)* The train . . . The station . . . Across into the middle, bank shot off the white into the corner . . .

370 LYUBOV ANDREEVNA: On our way!

LOPAKHIN: Is everyone here? Nobody left behind? *(Locks the side door at left.)* Some things are stored in here, better keep it locked. Let's go! . .

ANYA: Good-bye, house! Fare thee well, old life!

TROFIMOV: Welcome, new life! . . 375

(He goes out with ANYA. VARYA looks around the room and goes out without hurrying. YASHA and SHARLOTTA, with her dog, go out.)

LOPAKHIN: And so, till spring then. Come along, everybody . . . Until we meet again! . . *(Goes out.)*

(LYUBOV ANDREEVNA and GAEV are left alone. They seem to have waited for this moment and throw their arms around each other. They sob quietly, with restraint, afraid they might be overheard.)

GAEV: *(In despair.)* My sister, my sister . . .

LYUBOV ANDREEVNA: Oh, my beautiful orchard, my dear sweet orchard! . . My life, my youth, my happiness, good- 380 bye! . . Good-bye! . .

ANYA: *(Offstage, cheerfully and appealingly.)* Mama! . .

TROFIMOV: *(Offstage, cheerfully and excitedly.)* Hullo! . .

LYUBOV ANDREEVNA: One last look at the walls and the windows . . . Our dear mother loved to walk in this room . . . 385

GAEV: My sister, my sister! . .

ANYA: *(Offstage.)* Mama! . .

TROFIMOV: *(Offstage.)* Hullo! . .

LYUBOV ANDREEVNA: We're on our way! . .

(They go out. The stage is empty. The sound of all the doors being locked is heard, then of carriages being driven away. It grows quiet. In the stillness a dull thud is heard, the striking of an axe into a tree. It sounds solitary and dolorous. Footsteps are heard. From the door, right, appears FIRS. He is dressed, as always, in a jacket and white waistcoat, and he is wearing slippers. He is ill.)

FIRS: *(Goes up to the door and touches the handle.)* Locked. 390 They've gone away . . . *(Sits on the sofa.)* They forgot me . . . It's nothing . . . I'll sit here for a while . . . And Leonid Andreich didn't put on his fur coat, I suppose, he must have gone away in his light one . . . *(Sighs anxiously.)* I just didn't look after it . . . Oh, these green young things—they never 395 learn! *(Mumbles something that cannot be understood.)* Life just slipped by as if I'd never even lived . . . *(Lies down.)* I'll lie down for a while . . . You just don't have any strength, none, nothing's left, nothing at all. . . . Oh, you . . . silly galoot, you! . . 400

(He lies motionless. A sound is heard far off in the distance, as if coming from the sky. It is the sound of a string breaking that dies away sadly. A stillness falls, and nothing is heard but the sound of an axe striking a tree far away in the orchard.)

■ BERNARD SHAW ■

George Bernard Shaw (1856–1950)—Shaw disliked the name "George" and never used it, preferring the initials G. B. S.—was a man of wide-ranging passions and huge abilities. By his fortieth birthday he had written five novels, three volumes of classic music criticism, and three volumes of incendiary theater reviews; he had become visible in the influential socialist political organization, the FABIAN SOCIETY; he had written the first books in English on Wagner's operas and on Ibsen's plays; and he had just started his career as a dramatist, a career that would eventually include more than fifty plays.

Shaw was born in Dublin. Like Jonathan Swift and Richard Brinsley Sheridan before him, Shaw retained the satiric perspective of the Irish outsider in England. His mother was a music teacher and his sister was a promising singer when they left for London while Shaw was in his teens. He followed them to London in 1876. A shy and self-effacing young man, Shaw took a variety of jobs that brought him into contact with the public, and he used the opportunity of lecturing for the Fabian Society to develop the brilliantly articulate persona we recognize today as "G. B. S." Throughout the 1880s, Shaw worked with the Fabians, adopting their plan of gradual social reform in place of a more rigorously Marxist call for social revolution. The Fabians strove to change society through a strategy of permeation, working to get their members elected into prominent offices, where their educational and social reforms might be put into effect. Shaw was deeply influenced by the Fabians' gradualist scheme for social improvement—a scheme that underlies the utopian project of his greatest plays—for Fabian gradualism synchronized with Shaw's other passion, Creative Evolution. Appalled by what he regarded as the mindless mechanism of Darwinian natural selection, Shaw resisted the notion that human evolution followed a random and inevitable process. He urged instead that humanity take command of its future by willing itself to evolve in certain humane directions, and he advocated eugenics, capital punishment, and other ideas in the interest of the development of the species. Shaw attempted an uneasy synthesis of the Fabian socialist project of gradual social evolution with the individualist metaphysics of Creative Evolution: the improvement of society through the improvement of each of its members.

Shaw's friend William Archer once described seeing Shaw in the British Museum reading room simultaneously reading Marx's *Das Kapital* and the score of Wagner's *Ring of the Niebelung* cycle. The blending of political substance with a rich and deeply harmonized verbal music became a constant feature of Shaw's drama. Writing as a theater critic in the 1890s, Shaw became the champion of Ibsen in England. Vowing to lay siege to the conventions of the nineteenth-century theater, he touted Ibsen's plays and lambasted the corny tearjerkers, simplistic melodramas, and overstuffed Shakespearean productions that were the theater's common fare. Not incidentally, he worked to create a taste for his own plays, an operatic drama of the intellectual passions.

Shaw's career as a playwright falls into three main phases. Shaw's earliest plays—*Widowers' Houses* (1892) and *Mrs. Warren's Profession* (1893)—attacked specific social problems, like slum landlords and international prostitution. But Shaw more often linked social ills to the smug pieties of conventional morality. His plays generally work to disillusion his main characters—and his audience—from the ready acceptance of bourgeois ideology as a natural "reality." This process of disillusionment informs Shaw's lighter comedies of the 1890s, plays like *Arms and the Man* (1894), *Candida* (1894), and *Caesar and Cleopatra* (1898). After the turn of the century, however, Shaw entered on his maturity as a playwright, undertaking a series of major comedies that place this process of disillusionment directly in conflict with society's most important institutions: marriage and sexuality in *Man and Superman* (1903); British imperialism in Ireland in *John Bull's Other Island* (1904); salvation, damnation, and raw power in *Major Barbara* (1905); medicine in *The Doctor's Dilemma* (1906); language and class in *Pygmalion* (1912). Several of these plays were first produced at the Court Theater, under the management of Shaw's close friend Harley Granville Barker, who originated the part of Cusins in *Major Barbara* and other Shavian roles. Under Barker and his partner J. E. Vedrenne, the Court Theater in 1904–1907 became the most influential theater in London before World War I. Through its efforts, and Shaw's own energy as playwright, director, and advisor, the Court made Shaw's reputation as a major dramatist. With the coming of World War I, and the violent waste of civilization it brought with it, Shaw's confidence in the eventual perfection of humanity was deeply shaken, and the plays of his final half-century are much bleaker, more uncertain in tone: his magnificent "fantasia in the Russian manner on English themes," *Heartbreak House* (1919), modeled on Chekhov's *The Cherry Orchard; Saint Joan* (1923), perhaps his best-loved play; his five-play quintet on the origin and future of the species, *Back to Methuselah* (1921); and many others. In contrast to the confidence of Shaw's earlier plays, the later dramas generally seem to ask the question that Shaw gave to his Saint Joan, "O God that madest this beautiful earth, when will it be ready to receive Thy saints? How long, O Lord, how long?"

MAJOR BARBARA

Shaw was born before the publication of Darwin's *Origin of Species* in 1859, and he died after the dropping of the atomic bomb on Hiroshima. His major plays, like *Major Barbara*, treat the problems of the twentieth century in the dramatic vocabulary of Edwardian COMEDY OF MANNERS. *Major Barbara* is typical of the dialectical process of Shaw's plays. From the outset—when Stephen learns that his income is derived from his father's munitions empire—Shaw forces the audience and his characters to question the nature of their values, particularly the sense that good and evil, morality and economics, the power to save and the power to destroy can be easily or conveniently distinguished from one another. As a result, the play forces a deeply ironic experience on its characters and on the audience. For Shaw is interested in salvation, not simply the moralizing salvation promised by the Salvation Army, but a Nietzschean transvaluation of values, a salvation beyond the conventional abstractions of good and evil that he regards as necessary to the transformation of English society.

The play is structured dialectically, progressing from thesis, to antithesis, to a problematic synthesis. The "thesis" of Act 1 concerns the values of Wilton Crescent: the comfortable morality of the English upper classes. As the scene proceeds, though, Shaw suggests that conventional morality, the innate knowledge of right and wrong, is in fact supported by Undershaft's money and gunpowder. The "antithesis" of Act 2 offers the unconventional morality of the Salvation Army; Barbara's shelter in West Ham claims to provide true salvation by requiring a more sincere form of religious conviction. However, as it turns out, both Wilton Crescent and West Ham are equally in the grip of Bodger and Undershaft. The distiller and the munitions-maker determine the material realities on which society erects its illusory social "ideals" and calls them "reality." The Dionysian sacrifice of Barbara at the end of Act 2—with its echoes of Christ's crucifixion as well—prepares us for her resurrection in the "synthesis" offered by Act 3; in Perivale St Andrews, the spiritual Barbara and the intellectual Cusins are married with the blessing of the explosive Undershaft. We might be troubled, though, by the "synthesis" offered by the utopian factory town, for Undershaft's utopia hardly seems revolutionary. In many ways, Perivale St Andrews largely duplicates turn-of-the-century English class society and industrial capitalism, with the poverty and dirt cleaned up. The play's last act is often said to be unconvincing, and we might wonder whether that is in fact part of Shaw's purpose in *Major Barbara*. Once Shaw instructs us in the process of dialectical criticism, perhaps he invites us to scrutinize even Undershaft's bourgeois utopia, to see Perivale St Andrews as itself in need of further (r)evolution.

Shaw made Andrew Undershaft a magnificently melodramatic, attractive, amoral munitions-maker, whose creative ability is harnessed to the power to destroy. Moreover, Shaw drew a parallel between Undershaft and a crucial dramatic precursor, the Dionysus of Euripides' *The Bacchae*. The character of Cusins was modeled on Shaw's friend, the well-known classical scholar Gilbert Murray, and in the original production, Cusins was even played to resemble Murray. In Act 2, Cusins quotes a brief passage adapted from Murray's translation of *The Bacchae*, part of the choral speech delivered just before Pentheus is led out to spy on the Bacchae and be killed. We might take this invocation of Dionysus as a final clue to the play's attitude. Much like Euripides, Shaw prevents his audience from sympathizing entirely with his hero, from readily accepting the terrible power necessary to change the world. Although the play ends with a ceremonial marriage characteristic of RO-MANTIC COMEDY—symbolizing the union of intellect, spirit, and power—the fact that Dionysus Undershaft presides over this union should give us pause. Can the power he wields really be harnessed for our salvation?

MAJOR BARBARA

BERNARD SHAW

— CHARACTERS —

STEPHEN UNDERSHAFT

LADY BRITOMART

BARBARA UNDERSHAFT

SARAH UNDERSHAFT

ANDREW UNDERSHAFT

JENNY HILL

BILL WALKER

MORRISON

ADOLPHUS CUSINS

CHARLES LOMAX

RUMMY MITCHENS

SNOBBY PRICE

PETER SHIRLEY

BILTON

MRS BAINES

— ACT ONE —

It is after dinner in January 1906, in the library in LADY BRITO-
MART UNDERSHAFT's *house in Wilton Crescent. A large and
comfortable settee is in the middle of the room, upholstered in
dark leather. A person sitting on it (it is vacant at present) would
have, on his right,* LADY BRITOMART's *writing table, with the
lady herself busy at it; a smaller writing table behind him on his
left; the door behind him on* LADY BRITOMART's *side; and a window with a window seat directly on his left. Near the window is
an armchair.*

LADY BRITOMART *is a woman of fifty or thereabouts, well dressed
and yet careless of her dress, well bred and quite reckless of her
breeding, well mannered and yet appallingly outspoken and indifferent to the opinion of her interlocutors, amiable and yet
peremptory, arbitrary, and high-tempered to the last bearable degree, and withal a very typical managing matron of the upper
class, treated as a naughty child until she grew into a scolding
mother, and finally settling down with plenty of practical ability
and worldly experience, limited in the oddest way with domestic
and class limitations, conceiving the universe exactly as if it were
a large house in Wilton Crescent, though handling her corner of
it very effectively on that assumption, and being quite enlightened and liberal as to the books in the library, the pictures on the
walls, the music in the portfolios, and the articles in the papers.*

Her son, STEPHEN, *comes in. He is a gravely correct young man
under 25, taking himself very seriously, but still in some awe of
his mother, from childish habit and bachelor shyness rather than
from any weakness of character.*

STEPHEN: Whats the matter?

LADY BRITOMART: Presently, Stephen.

*(*STEPHEN *submissively walks to the settee and sits down. He
takes up a Liberal weekly called* The Speaker.*)*

LADY BRITOMART: Dont begin to read, Stephen. I shall require
all your attention.

5 STEPHEN: It was only while I was waiting—

LADY BRITOMART: Dont make excuses, Stephen. *(He puts
down* The Speaker.*)* Now! *(She finishes her writing; rises; and
comes to the settee.)* I have not kept you waiting very long, I
think.

10 STEPHEN: Not at all, mother.

LADY BRITOMART: Bring me my cushion. *(He takes the cushion from the chair at the desk and arranges it for her as she sits
down on the settee.)* Sit down. *(He sits down and fingers his
tie nervously.)* Dont fiddle with your tie, Stephen: there is
nothing the matter with it. 15

STEPHEN: I beg your pardon. *(He fiddles with his watch chain
instead.)*

LADY BRITOMART: Now are you attending to me, Stephen?

STEPHEN: Of course, mother.

LADY BRITOMART: No: it's not of course. I want something 20
much more than your everyday matter-of-course attention. I
am going to speak to you very seriously, Stephen. I wish you
would let that chain alone.

STEPHEN: *(Hastily relinquishing the chain.)* Have I done anything to annoy you, mother? If so, it was quite unintentional. 25

LADY BRITOMART: *(Astonished.)* Nonsense! *(With some remorse.)* My poor boy, did you think I was angry with you?

STEPHEN: What is it, then, mother? You are making me very
uneasy.

LADY BRITOMART: *(Squaring herself at him rather aggressively.)* 30
Stephen: may I ask how soon you intend to realize that you
are a grown-up man, and that I am only a woman?

STEPHEN: *(Amazed.)* Only a—

LADY BRITOMART: Dont repeat my words, please: it is a most
aggravating habit. You must learn to face life seriously, 35
Stephen. I really cannot bear the whole burden of our family
affairs any longer. You must advise me: you must assume the
responsibility.

STEPHEN: I!

LADY BRITOMART: Yes, you, of course. You were 24 last June. 40
Youve been at Harrow and Cambridge. Youve been to India
and Japan. You must know a lot of things, now; unless you
have wasted your time most scandalously. Well, advise me.

STEPHEN: *(Much perplexed.)* You know I have never interfered
in the household— 45

LADY BRITOMART: No: I should think not. I dont want you to
order the dinner.

STEPHEN: I mean in our family affairs.

LADY BRITOMART: Well, you must interfere now; for they are
getting quite beyond me. 50

STEPHEN: *(Troubled.)* I have thought sometimes that perhaps I
ought; but really, mother, I know so little about them; and
what I do know is so painful! it is so impossible to mention
some things to you—*(He stops, ashamed.)*

55 LADY BRITOMART: I suppose you mean your father.

STEPHEN: (*Almost inaudibly.*) Yes.

LADY BRITOMART: My dear: we cant go on all our lives not mentioning him. Of course you were quite right not to open the subject until I asked you to; but you are old enough now
60 to be taken into my confidence, and to help me to deal with him about the girls.

STEPHEN: But the girls are all right. They are engaged.

LADY BRITOMART: (*Complacently.*) Yes: I have made a very good match for Sarah. Charles Lomax will be a millionaire
65 at 35. But that is ten years ahead; and in the meantime his trustees cannot under the terms of his father's will allow him more than £800 a year.

STEPHEN: But the will says also that if he increases his income by his own exertions, they may double the increase.

70 LADY BRITOMART: Charles Lomax's exertions are much more likely to decrease his income than to increase it. Sarah will have to find at least another £800 a year for the next ten years; and even then they will be as poor as church mice. And what about Barbara? I thought Barbara was going to
75 make the most brilliant career of all of you. And what does she do? Joins the Salvation Army; discharges her maid; lives on a pound a week and walks in one evening with a professor of Greek whom she has picked up in the street, and who pretends to be a Salvationist, and actually plays the big drum for
80 her in public because he has fallen head over ears in love with her.

STEPHEN: I was certainly rather taken aback when I heard they were engaged. Cusins is a very nice fellow, certainly: nobody would ever guess that he was born in Australia; but—

85 LADY BRITOMART: Oh, Adolphus Cusins will make a very good husband. After all, nobody can say a word against Greek: it stamps a man at once as an educated gentleman. And my family, thank Heaven, is not a pig-headed Tory one. We are Whigs, and believe in liberty. Let snobbish people say what
90 they please: Barbara shall marry, not the man they like, but the man *I* like.

STEPHEN: Of course I was thinking only of his income. However, he is not likely to be extravagant.

LADY BRITOMART: Dont be too sure of that, Stephen. I know
95 your quiet, simple, refined, poetic people like Adolphus: quite content with the best of everything! They cost more than your extravagant people, who are always as mean as they are second rate. No: Barbara will need at least £2000 a year. You see it means two additional households. Besides,
100 my dear, you must marry soon. I dont approve of the present fashion of philandering bachelors and late marriages; and I am trying to arrange something for you.

STEPHEN: It's very good of you, mother; but perhaps I had better arrange that for myself.

105 LADY BRITOMART: Nonsense! you are much too young to begin matchmaking: you would be taken in by some pretty little nobody. Of course I dont mean that you are not to be consulted: you know that as well as I do. (STEPHEN *closes his lips and is silent.*) Now dont sulk, Stephen.

110 STEPHEN: I am not sulking, mother. What has all this got to do with—with—with my father?

LADY BRITOMART: My dear Stephen: where is the money to come from? It is easy enough for you and the other children to live on my income as long as we are in the same house;
115 but I cant keep four families in four separate houses. You

know how poor my father is: he has barely seven thousand a year now; and really, if he were not the Earl of Stevenage, he would have to give up society. He can do nothing for us. He says, naturally enough, that it is absurd that he should be
120 asked to provide for the children of a man who is rolling in money. You see, Stephen, your father must be fabulously wealthy, because there is always a war going on somewhere.

STEPHEN: You need not remind me of that, mother. I have hardly ever opened a newspaper in my life without seeing
125 our name in it. The Undershaft torpedo! The Undershaft quick firers! The Undershaft ten inch! the Undershaft disappearing rampart gun! the Undershaft submarine! and now the Undershaft aerial battleship! At Harrow they called me the Woolwich Infant. At Cambridge it was the same. A little
130 brute at King's who was always trying to get up revivals, spoilt my Bible—your first birthday present to me—by writing under my name, "Son and heir to Undershaft and Lazarus, Death and Destruction Dealers: address Christendom and Judea." But that was not so bad as the way I was kowtowed to
135 everywhere because my father was making millions by selling cannons.

LADY BRITOMART: It is not only the cannons, but the war loans that Lazarus arranges under cover of giving credit for the cannons. You know, Stephen, it's perfectly scandalous.
140 Those two men, Andrew Undershaft and Lazarus, positively have Europe under their thumbs. That is why your father is able to behave as he does. He is above the law. Do you think Bismarck or Gladstone or Disraeli could have openly defied every social and moral obligation all their lives as your father
145 has? They simply wouldnt have dared. I asked Gladstone to take it up. I asked The Times to take it up. I asked the Lord Chamberlain to take it up. But it was just like asking them to declare war on the Sultan. They wouldnt. They said they couldnt touch him. I believe they were afraid.

150 STEPHEN: What could they do? He does not actually break the law.

LADY BRITOMART: Not break the law! He is always breaking the law. He broke the law when he was born: his parents were not married.

155 STEPHEN: Mother! Is that true?

LADY BRITOMART: Of course it's true: that was why we separated.

STEPHEN: He married without letting you know that!

LADY BRITOMART: (*Rather taken aback by this inference.*) Oh
160 no. To do Andrew justice, that was not the sort of thing he did. Besides, you know the Undershaft motto: Unashamed. Everybody knew.

STEPHEN: But you said that was why you separated.

LADY BRITOMART: Yes, because he was not content with being
165 a foundling himself: he wanted to disinherit you for another foundling. That was what I couldnt stand.

STEPHEN: (*Ashamed.*) Do you mean for—for—for—

LADY BRITOMART: Dont stammer, Stephen. Speak distinctly.

STEPHEN: But this is so frightful to me, mother. To have to
170 speak to you about such things!

LADY BRITOMART: It's not pleasant for me, either, especially if you are still so childish that you must make it worse by a display of embarrassment. It is only in the middle classes, Stephen, that people get into a state of dumb helpless horror
175 when they find that there are wicked people in the world. In our class, we have to decide what is to be done with wicked

people; and nothing should disturb our self-possession. Now ask your question properly.

STEPHEN: Mother: have you no consideration for me? For
180 Heaven's sake either treat me as a child, as you always do, and tell me nothing at all or tell me everything and let me take it as best I can.

LADY BRITOMART: Treat you as a child! What do you mean? It is most unkind and ungrateful of you to say such a thing. You
185 know I have never treated any of you as children. I have always made you my companions and friends, and allowed you perfect freedom to do and say whatever you like, so long as you liked what I could approve of.

STEPHEN: (*Desperately.*) I daresay we have been the very im-
190 perfect children of a very perfect mother; but I do beg you to let me alone for once, and tell me about this horrible business of my father wanting to set me aside for another son.

LADY BRITOMART: (*Amazed.*) Another son! I never said anything of the kind. I never dreamt of such a thing. This is
195 what comes of interrupting me.

STEPHEN: But you said—

LADY BRITOMART: (*Cutting him short.*) Now be a good boy, Stephen, and listen to me patiently. The Undershafts are descended from a foundling in the parish of St Andrew Under-
200 shaft in the city. That was long ago, in the reign of James the First. Well, this foundling was adopted by an armorer and gun-maker. In the course of time the foundling succeeded to the business; and from some notion of gratitude, or some vow or something, he adopted another foundling, and left
205 the business to him. And that foundling did the same. Ever since that, the cannon business has always been left to an adopted foundling named Andrew Undershaft.

STEPHEN: But did they never marry? Were there no legitimate sons?

210 LADY BRITOMART: Oh yes: they married just as your father did; and they were rich enough to buy land for their own children and leave them well provided for. But they always adopted and trained some foundling to succeed them in the business; and of course they always quarrelled with their
215 wives furiously over it. Your father was adopted in that way; and he pretends to consider himself bound to keep up the tradition and adopt somebody to leave the business to. Of course I was not going to stand that. There may have been some reason for it when the Undershafts could only marry
220 women in their own class, whose sons were not fit to govern great estates. But there could be no excuse for passing over my son.

STEPHEN: (*Dubiously.*) I am afraid I should make a poor hand of managing a cannon foundry.

225 LADY BRITOMART: Nonsense! you could easily get a manager and pay him a salary.

STEPHEN: My father evidently had no great opinion of my capacity.

LADY BRITOMART: Stuff, child! you were only a baby: it had
230 nothing to do with your capacity. Andrew did it on principle, just as he did every perverse and wicked thing on principle. When my father remonstrated, Andrew actually told him to his face that history tells us of only two successful institutions: one the Undershaft firm, and the other the Roman
235 Empire under the Antonines. That was because the Antonine emperors all adopted their successors. Such rubbish! The Stevenages are as good as the Antonines, I hope; and you are a Stevenage. But that was Andrew all over. There you

have the man! Always clever and unanswerable when he was
defending nonsense and wickedness: always awkward and 240
sullen when he had to behave sensibly and decently!

STEPHEN: Then it was on my account that your home life was broken up, mother. I am sorry.

LADY BRITOMART: Well, dear, there were other differences. I really cannot bear an immoral man. I am not a Pharisee, I 245 hope; and I should not have minded his merely doing wrong things: we are none of us perfect. But your father didnt exactly do wrong things: he said them and thought them: that was what was so dreadful. He really had a sort of religion of wrongness. Just as one doesnt mind men practising immoral- 250 ity so long as they own that they are in the wrong by preaching morality; so I couldnt forgive Andrew for preaching immorality while he practised morality. You would all have grown up without principles, without any knowledge of right and wrong, if he had been in the house. You know, my dear, 255 your father was a very attractive man in some ways. Children did not dislike him; and he took advantage of it to put the wickedest ideas into their heads, and make them quite unmanageable. I did not dislike him myself: very far from it; but nothing can bridge over moral disagreement. 260

STEPHEN: All this simply bewilders me, mother. People may differ about matters of opinion, or even about religion; but how can they differ about right and wrong? Right is right; and wrong is wrong; and if a man cannot distinguish them properly, he is either a fool or a rascal: thats all. 265

LADY BRITOMART: (*Touched.*) Thats my own boy! (*She pats his cheek.*) Your father never could answer that: he used to laugh and get out of it under cover of some affectionate nonsense. And now that you understand the situation, what do you advise me to do? 270

STEPHEN: Well, what can you do?

LADY BRITOMART: I must get the money somehow.

STEPHEN: We cannot take money from him. I had rather go and live in some cheap place like Bedford Square or even Hampstead than take a farthing of his money. 275

LADY BRITOMART: But after all, Stephen, our present income comes from Andrew.

STEPHEN: (*Shocked.*) I never knew that.

LADY BRITOMART: Well, you surely didnt suppose your grandfather had anything to give me. The Stevenages could not do 280 everything for you. We gave you social position. Andrew had to contribute something. He had a very good bargain, I think.

STEPHEN: (*Bitterly.*) We are utterly dependent on him and his cannons, then? 285

LADY BRITOMART: Certainly not: the money is settled. But he provided it. So you see it is not a question of taking money from him or not: it is simply a question of how much. I dont want any more for myself.

STEPHEN: Nor do I. 290

LADY BRITOMART: But Sarah does; and Barbara does. That is, Charles Lomax and Adolphus Cusins will cost them more. So I must put my pride in my pocket and ask for it, I suppose. That is your advice, Stephen, is it not?

STEPHEN: No. 295

LADY BRITOMART: (*Sharply.*) Stephen!

STEPHEN: Of course if you are determined—

LADY BRITOMART: I am not determined: I ask your advice; and I am waiting for it. I will not have all the responsibility thrown on my shoulders. 300

STEPHEN: (*Obstinately.*) I would die sooner than ask him for another penny.

LADY BRITOMART: (*Resignedly.*) You mean that I must ask him. Very well, Stephen: it shall be as you wish. You will be glad
305 to know that your grandfather concurs. But he thinks I ought to ask Andrew to come here and see the girls. After all, he must have some natural affection for them.

STEPHEN: Ask him here!!!

LADY BRITOMART: Do not repeat my words, Stephen. Where
310 else can I ask him?

STEPHEN: I never expected you to ask him at all.

LADY BRITOMART: Now dont tease, Stephen. Come! you see that it is necessary that he should pay us a visit, dont you?

STEPHEN: (*Reluctantly.*) I suppose so, if the girls cannot do
315 without his money.

LADY BRITOMART: Thank you, Stephen: I knew you would give me the right advice when it was properly explained to you. I have asked your father to come this evening. (*Stephen bounds from his seat.*) Dont jump, Stephen: it fidgets me.

320 STEPHEN: (*In utter consternation.*) Do you mean to say that my father is coming here tonight—that he may be here at any moment?

LADY BRITOMART: (*Looking at her watch.*) I said nine. (*He gasps. She rises.*) Ring the bell, please. (*STEPHEN goes to the
325 smaller writing table; presses a button on it; and sits at it with his elbows on the table and his head in his hands, outwitted and overwhelmed.*) It is ten minutes to nine yet; and I have to prepare the girls. I asked Charles Lomax and Adolphus to dinner on purpose that they might be here. Andrew had bet-
330 ter see them in case he should cherish any delusions as to their being capable of supporting their wives. (*The butler enters: LADY BRITOMART goes behind the settee to speak to him.*) Morrison: go up to the drawing room and tell everybody to come down here at once. (*MORRISON withdraws. LADY BRIT-
335 OMART turns to STEPHEN.*) Now remember, Stephen: I shall need all your countenance and authority. (*He rises and tries to recover some vestige of these attributes.*) Give me a chair, dear. (*He pushes a chair forward from the wall to where she stands, near the smaller writing table. She sits down; and he
340 goes to the armchair, into which he throws himself.*) I dont know how Barbara will take it. Ever since they made her a major in the Salvation Army she has developed a propensity to have her own way and order people about which quite cows me sometimes. It's not ladylike: I'm sure I dont know
345 where she picked it up. Anyhow, Barbara shant bully me; but still it's just as well that your father should be here before she has time to refuse to meet him or make a fuss. Dont look nervous, Stephen: it will only encourage Barbara to make difficulties. I am nervous enough, goodness knows; but I
350 dont shew it.

(*SARAH and BARBARA come in with their respective young men, CHARLES LOMAX and ADOLPHUS CUSINS. SARAH is slender, bored, and mundane. BARBARA is robuster, jollier, much more energetic. SARAH is fashionably dressed: BARBARA is in Salvation Army uniform. LOMAX, a young man about town, is like many other young men about town. He is afflicted with a frivolous sense of humor which plunges him at the most inopportune moments into paroxysms of imperfectly suppressed laughter. CUSINS is a spectacled student, slight, thin haired, and sweet voiced, with a more complex form of LOMAX's complaint. His sense of humor is intellectual and subtle, and is complicated by an*

appalling temper. The lifelong struggle of a benevolent temperament and a high conscience against impulses of inhuman ridicule and fierce impatience has set up a chronic strain which has visibly wrecked his constitution. He is a most implacable, determined, tenacious, intolerant person who by mere force of character presents himself as—and indeed actually is—considerate, gentle, explanatory, even mild and apologetic, capable possibly of murder, but not of cruelty or coarseness. By the operation of some instinct which is not merciful enough to blind him with the illusions of love, he is obstinately bent on marrying BARBARA. LOMAX likes SARAH and thinks it will be rather a lark to marry her. Consequently he has not attempted to resist LADY BRITOMART's arrangements to that end.

All four look as if they had been having a good deal of fun in the drawing room. The girls enter first, leaving the swains outside. SARAH comes to the settee. BARBARA comes in after her and stops at the door.)

BARBARA: Are Cholly and Dolly to come in?

LADY BRITOMART: (*Forcibly.*) Barbara: I will not have Charles called Cholly: the vulgarity of it positively makes me ill.

BARBARA: It's all right, mother: Cholly is quite correct nowa-
355 days. Are they to come in?

LADY BRITOMART: Yes, if they will behave themselves.

BARBARA: (*Through the door.*) Come in, Dolly; and behave yourself.

(*BARBARA comes to her mother's writing table. CUSINS enters smiling, and wanders towards LADY BRITOMART.*)

SARAH: (*Calling.*) Come in, Cholly. (*LOMAX enters, controlling his features very imperfectly, and places himself vaguely be-
360 tween SARAH and BARBARA.*)

LADY BRITOMART: (*Peremptorily.*) Sit down, all of you. (*They sit. CUSINS crosses to the window and seats himself there. LOMAX takes a chair. BARBARA sits at the writing table and
365 SARAH on the settee.*) I dont in the least know what you are laughing at, Adolphus. I am surprised at you, though I expected nothing better from Charles Lomax.

CUSINS: (*In a remarkably gentle voice.*) Barbara has been trying to teach me the West Ham Salvation March.

370 LADY BRITOMART: I see nothing to laugh at in that; nor should you if you are really converted.

CUSINS: (*Sweetly.*) You were not present. It was really funny, I believe.

LOMAX: Ripping.

375 LADY BRITOMART: Be quiet, Charles. Now listen to me, children. Your father is coming here this evening.

(*General stupefaction. LOMAX, SARAH, and BARBARA rise: SARAH scared, and BARBARA amused and expectant.*)

LOMAX: (*Remonstrating.*) Oh I say!

LADY BRITOMART: You are not called on to say anything, Charles.

380 SARAH: Are you serious, mother?

LADY BRITOMART: Of course I am serious. It is on your account, Sarah, and also on Charles's. (*Silence. SARAH sits, with a shrug. CHARLES looks painfully unworthy.*) I hope you are not going to object, Barbara.

385 BARBARA: I! why should I? My father has a soul to be saved like anybody else. He's quite welcome as far as I am concerned. (*She sits on the table, and softly whistles 'Onward, Christian Soldiers'.*)

LOMAX: (*Still remonstrant.*) But really, dont you know! Oh I
390   say!

LADY BRITOMART: (*Frigidly.*) What do you wish to convey,
    Charles?

LOMAX: Well, you must admit that this is a bit thick.

LADY BRITOMART: (*Turning with ominous suavity to* CUSINS.)
395   Adolphus: you are a professor of Greek. Can you translate
    Charles Lomax's remarks into reputable English for us?

CUSINS: (*Cautiously.*) If I may say so, Lady Brit, I think
    Charles has rather happily expressed what we all feel.
    Homer, speaking of Autolycus, uses the same phrase.
400   πυκινὸν δόμον ἐλθεῖν means a bit thick.

LOMAX: (*Handsomely.*) Not that I mind, you know, if Sarah
    dont. (*He sits.*)

LADY BRITOMART: (*Crushingly.*) Thank you. Have I your per-
    mission, Adolphus, to invite my own husband to my own
405   house?

CUSINS: (*Gallantly.*) You have my unhesitating support in
    everything you do.

LADY BRITOMART: Tush! Sarah: have you nothing to say?

SARAH: Do you mean that he is coming regularly to live here?

410 LADY BRITOMART: Certainly not. The spare room is ready for
    him if he likes to stay for a day or two and see a little more of
    you; but there are limits.

SARAH: Well, he cant eat us, I suppose. *I* dont mind.

LOMAX: (*Chuckling.*) I wonder how the old man will take it.

415 LADY BRITOMART: Much as the old woman will, no doubt,
    Charles.

LOMAX: (*Abashed.*) I didnt mean—at least—

LADY BRITOMART: You didnt think, Charles. You never do; and
    the result is, you never mean anything. And now please attend
420   to me, children. Your father will be quite a stranger to us.

LOMAX: I suppose he hasnt seen Sarah since she was a little
    kid.

LADY BRITOMART: Not since she was a little kid, Charles, as
    you express it with that elegance of diction and refinement
425   of thought that seem never to desert you. Accordingly—er—
    (*Impatiently.*) Now I have forgotten what I was going to say.
    That comes of your provoking me to be sarcastic, Charles.
    Adolphus: will you kindly tell me where I was.

CUSINS: (*Sweetly.*) You were saying that as Mr Undershaft has
430   not seen his children since they were babies, he will form his
    opinion of the way you have brought them up from their be-
    havior tonight, and that therefore you wish us all to be par-
    ticularly careful to conduct ourselves well, especially
    Charles.

435 LADY BRITOMART: (*With emphatic approval.*) Precisely.

LOMAX: Look here, Dolly: Lady Brit didnt say that.

LADY BRITOMART: (*Vehemently.*) I did, Charles. Adolphus's
    recollection is perfectly correct. It is most important that you
    should be good; and I do beg you for once not to pair off into
440   opposite corners and giggle and whisper while I am speaking
    to your father.

BARBARA: All right, mother. We'll do you credit. (*She comes off
    the table, and sits in her chair with ladylike elegance.*)

LADY BRITOMART: Remember, Charles, that Sarah will want
445   to feel proud of you instead of ashamed of you.

LOMAX: Oh I say! theres nothing to be exactly proud of, dont
    you know.

LADY BRITOMART: Well, try and look as if there was.

(MORRISON, *pale and dismayed, breaks into the room in uncon-
cealed disorder.*)

MORRISON: Might I speak a word to you, my lady?

LADY BRITOMART: Nonsense! Shew him up.   450

MORRISON: Yes, my lady. (*He goes.*)

LOMAX: Does Morrison know who it is?

LADY BRITOMART: Of course. Morrison has always been with
    us.

LOMAX: It must be a regular corker for him, dont you know.   455

LADY BRITOMART: Is this a moment to get on my nerves,
    Charles, with your outrageous expressions?

LOMAX: But this is something out of the ordinary, really—

MORRISON: (*At the door.*) The—er—Mr Undershaft. (*He re-
    treats in confusion.*)   460

(ANDREW UNDERSHAFT *comes in. All rise.* LADY BRITOMART
meets him in the middle of the room behind the settee.

ANDREW *is, on the surface, a stoutish, easygoing elderly man,
with kindly patient manners, and an engaging simplicity of
character. But he has a watchful, deliberate, waiting, listening
face, and formidable reserves of power, both bodily and mental,
in his capacious chest and long head. His gentleness is partly
that of a strong man who has learnt by experience that his natural grip hurts ordinary people unless he handles them very carefully, and partly the mellowness of age and success. He is also a
little shy in his present very delicate situation.*)

LADY BRITOMART: Good evening, Andrew.

UNDERSHAFT: How d'ye do, my dear.

LADY BRITOMART: You look a good deal older.

UNDERSHAFT: (*Apologetically.*) I am somewhat older. (*Taking
    her hand with a touch of courtship.*) Time has stood still with   465
    you.

LADY BRITOMART: (*Throwing away his hand.*) Rubbish! This is
    your family.

UNDERSHAFT: (*Surprised.*) Is it so large? I am sorry to say my
    memory is failing very badly in some things. (*He offers his*   470
    hand with paternal kindness to LOMAX.)

LOMAX: (*Jerkily shaking his hand.*) Ahdedoo.

UNDERSHAFT: I can see you are my eldest. I am very glad to
    meet you again, my boy.

LOMAX: (*Remonstrating.*) No, but look here dont you know—   475
    (*Overcome.*) Oh I say!

LADY BRITOMART: (*Recovering from momentary speechless-
    ness.*) Andrew: do you mean to say that you dont remember
    how many children you have?

UNDERSHAFT: Well, I am afraid I—. They have grown so   480
    much—er. Am I making any ridiculous mistake? I may as
    well confess: I recollect only one son. But so many things
    have happened since, of course—er—

LADY BRITOMART: (*Decisively.*) Andrew: you are talking non-
    sense. Of course you have only one son.   485

UNDERSHAFT: Perhaps you will be good enough to introduce
    me, my dear.

LADY BRITOMART: That is Charles Lomax, who is engaged to
    Sarah.

UNDERSHAFT: My dear sir, I beg your pardon.   490

LOMAX: Notatall. Delighted, I assure you.

LADY BRITOMART: This is Stephen.

UNDERSHAFT: (*Bowing.*) Happy to make your acquaintance,
    Mr Stephen. Then (*Going to* CUSINS.) you must be my son.

495   (*Taking* CUSINS' *hands in his.*) How are you, my young
      friend? (*To* LADY BRITOMART) He is very like you, my love.
      CUSINS: You flatter me, Mr Undershaft. My name is Cusins:
      engaged to Barbara. (*Very explicitly.*) That is Major Barbara
500   Undershaft, of the Salvation Army. That is Sarah, your sec-
      ond daughter. This is Stephen Undershaft, your son.
      UNDERSHAFT: My dear Stephen, I beg your pardon.
      STEPHEN: Not at all.
      UNDERSHAFT: Mr Cusins: I am much indebted to you for ex-
      plaining so precisely. (*Turning to* SARAH.) Barbara, my dear—
505   SARAH: (*Prompting him.*) Sarah.
      UNDERSHAFT: Sarah, of course. (*They shake hands. He goes
      over to* BARBARA.) Barbara—I am right this time, I hope?
      BARBARA: Quite right. (*They shake hands.*)
      LADY BRITOMART: (*Resuming command.*) Sit down, all of you.
510   Sit down, Andrew. (*She comes forward and sits on the settee.*
      CUSINS *also brings his chair forward on her left.* BARBARA *and*
      STEPHEN *resume their seats.* LOMAX *gives his chair to* SARAH
      and goes for another.)
      UNDERSHAFT: Thank you, my love.
515   LOMAX: (*Conversationally, as he brings a chair forward be-
      tween the writing table and the settee, and offers it to* UNDER-
      SHAFT.) Takes you some time to find out exactly where you
      are, dont it?
      UNDERSHAFT: (*Accepting the chair, but remaining standing.*)
520   That is not what embarrasses me, Mr Lomax. My difficulty
      is that if I play the part of a father, I shall produce the effect
      of an intrusive stranger; and if I play the part of a discreet
      stranger, I may appear a callous father.
      LADY BRITOMART: There is no need for you to play any part at
525   all, Andrew. You had much better be sincere and natural.
      UNDERSHAFT: (*Submissively.*) Yes, my dear: I daresay that will
      be best. (*He sits down comfortably.*) Well, here I am. Now
      what can I do for you all?
      LADY BRITOMART: You need not do anything, Andrew. You are
530   one of the family. You can sit with us and enjoy yourself.

      (*A painfully conscious pause.* BARBARA *makes a face at* LOMAX,
      *whose too long suppressed mirth immediately explodes in ago-
      nized neighings.*)

      LADY BRITOMART: (*Outraged.*) Charles Lomax: if you can be-
      have yourself, behave yourself. If not, leave the room.
      LOMAX: I'm awfully sorry, Lady Brit; but really you know,
      upon my soul! (*He sits on the settee between* LADY BRITO-
535   MART *and* UNDERSHAFT, *quite overcome.*)
      BARBARA: Why dont you laugh if you want to, Cholly? It's good
      for your inside.
      LADY BRITOMART: Barbara: you have had the education of a
      lady. Please let your father see that; and dont talk like a street
540   girl.
      UNDERSHAFT: Never mind me, my dear. As you know, I am
      not a gentleman; and I was never educated.
      LOMAX: (*Encouragingly.*) Nobody'd know it, I assure you. You
      look all right, you know.
545   CUSINS: Let me advise you to study Greek, Mr Undershaft.
      Greek scholars are privileged men. Few of them know
      Greek; and none of them know anything else; but their posi-
      tion is unchallengeable. Other languages are the qualifica-
      tions of waiters and commercial travellers: Greek is to a man
550   of position what the hallmark is to silver.

      BARBARA: Dolly: dont be insincere. Cholly: fetch your con-
      certina and play something for us.
      LOMAX: (*Jumps up eagerly, but checks himself to remark doubt-
      fully to* UNDERSHAFT.) Perhaps that sort of thing isnt in your
555   line, eh?
      UNDERSHAFT: I am particularly fond of music.
      LOMAX: (*Delighted.*) Are you? Then I'll get it. (*He goes upstairs
      for the instrument.*)
      UNDERSHAFT: Do you play, Barbara?
560   BARBARA: Only the tambourine. But Cholly's teaching me the
      concertina.
      UNDERSHAFT: Is Cholly also a member of the Salvation Army?
      BARBARA: No: he says it's bad form to be a dissenter. But I dont
      despair of Cholly. I made him come yesterday to a meeting
565   at the dock gates, and take the collection in his hat.
      UNDERSHAFT: (*Looks whimsically at his wife.*)!!
      LADY BRITOMART: It is not my doing, Andrew. Barbara is old
      enough to take her own way. She has no father to advise her.
      BARBARA: Oh yes she has. There are no orphans in the Salva-
570   tion Army.
      UNDERSHAFT: Your father there has a great many children and
      plenty of experience, eh?
      BARBARA: (*Looking at him with quick interest and nodding.*)
      Just so. How did you come to understand that? (LOMAX *is
575   heard at the door trying the concertina.*)
      LADY BRITOMART: Come in, Charles. Play us something at
      once.
      LOMAX: Righto! (*He sits down in his former place, and preludes.*)
      UNDERSHAFT: One moment, Mr Lomax. I am rather inter-
580   ested in the Salvation Army. Its motto might be my own:
      Blood and Fire.
      LOMAX: (*Shocked.*) But not your sort of blood and fire, you
      know.
      UNDERSHAFT: My sort of blood cleanses: my sort of fire
585   purifies.
      BARBARA: So do ours. Come down tomorrow to my shelter—
      the West Ham shelter—and see what we're doing. We're
      going to march to a great meeting in the Assembly Hall at
      Mile End. Come and see the shelter and then march with
590   us: it will do you a lot of good. Can you play anything?
      UNDERSHAFT: In my youth I earned pennies, and even
      shillings occasionally, in the streets and in public house par-
      lors by my natural talent for stepdancing. Later on, I became
      a member of the Undershaft orchestral society, and per-
595   formed passably on the tenor trombone.
      LOMAX: (*Scandalized—putting down the concertina.*) Oh I say!
      BARBARA: Many a sinner has played himself into heaven on
      the trombone, thanks to the Army.
      LOMAX: (*To* BARBARA, *still rather shocked.*) Yes; but what about
600   the cannon business, dont you know? (*To* UNDERSHAFT.)
      Getting into heaven is not exactly in your line, is it?
      LADY BRITOMART: Charles!!!
      LOMAX: Well; but it stands to reason, dont it? The cannon
      business may be necessary and all that: we cant get on with-
605   out cannons; but it isnt right, you know. On the other hand,
      there may be a certain amount of tosh about the Salvation
      Army—I belong to the Established Church myself—but still
      you cant deny that it's religion; and you cant go against reli-
      gion, can you? At least unless youre downright immoral,
610   dont you know.
      UNDERSHAFT: You hardly appreciate my position, Mr Lomax—

LOMAX: *(Hastily.)* I'm not saying anything against you personally—

UNDERSHAFT: Quite so, quite so. But consider for a moment.
615 Here I am, a profiteer in mutilation and murder. I find myself in a specially amiable humor just now because, this morning, down at the foundry, we blew twenty-seven dummy soldiers into fragments with a gun which formerly destroyed only thirteen.

620 LOMAX: *(Leniently.)* Well, the more destructive war becomes, the sooner it will be abolished, eh?

UNDERSHAFT: Not at all. The more destructive war becomes the more fascinating we find it. No, Mr Lomax: I am obliged to you for making the usual excuse for my trade; but I am not
625 ashamed of it. I am not one of those men who keep their morals and their business in watertight compartments. All the spare money my trade rivals spend on hospitals, cathedrals, and other receptacles for conscience money, I devote to experiments and researches in improved methods of de-
630 stroying life and property. I have always done so; and I always shall. Therefore your Christmas card moralities of peace on earth and goodwill among men are of no use to me. Your Christianity, which enjoins you to resist not evil, and to turn the other cheek, would make me a bankrupt. My
635 morality—my religion—must have a place for cannons and torpedoes in it.

STEPHEN: *(Coldly—almost sullenly.)* You speak as if there were half a dozen moralities and religions to choose from, instead of one true morality and one true religion.

640 UNDERSHAFT: For me there is only one true morality; but it might not fit you, as you do not manufacture aerial battleships. There is only one true morality for every man; but every man has not the same true morality.

LOMAX: *(Overtaxed.)* Would you mind saying that again? I
645 didnt quite follow.

CUSINS: It's quite simple. As Euripides says, one man's meat is another man's poison morally as well as physically.

UNDERSHAFT: Precisely.

LOMAX: Oh, that! Yes, yes, yes. True. True.

650 STEPHEN: In other words, some men are honest and some are scoundrels.

BARBARA: Bosh! There are no scoundrels.

UNDERSHAFT: Indeed? Are there any good men?

BARBARA: No. Not one. There are neither good men nor
655 scoundrels: there are just children of one Father; and the sooner they stop calling one another names the better. You neednt talk to me: I know them. I've had scores of them through my hands: scoundrels, criminals, infidels, philanthropists, missionaries, county councillors, all sorts. Theyre
660 all just the same sort of sinner; and theres the same salvation ready for them all.

UNDERSHAFT: May I ask have you ever saved a maker of cannons?

BARBARA: No. Will you let me try?

665 UNDERSHAFT: Well, I will make a bargain with you. If I go to see you tomorrow in your Salvation Shelter, will you come the day after to see me in my cannon works?

BARBARA: Take care. It may end in your giving up the cannons for the sake of the Salvation Army.

670 UNDERSHAFT: Are you sure it will not end in your giving up the Salvation Army for the sake of the cannons?

BARBARA: I will take my chance of that.

UNDERSHAFT: And I will take my chance of the other. *(They shake hands on it.)* Where is your shelter?

BARBARA: In West Ham. At the sign of the cross. Ask anybody 675 in Canning Town. Where are your works?

UNDERSHAFT: In Perivale St Andrews. At the sign of the sword. Ask anybody in Europe.

LOMAX: Hadnt I better play something?

BARBARA: Yes. Give us 'Onward, Christian Soldiers.' 680

LOMAX: Well, thats rather a strong order to begin with, dont you know. Suppose I sing Thourt passing hence, my brother. It's much the same tune.

BARBARA: It's too melancholy. You get saved, Cholly; and youll pass hence, my brother, without making such a fuss about it. 685

LADY BRITOMART: Really, Barbara, you go on as if religion were a pleasant subject. Do have some sense of propriety.

UNDERSHAFT: I do not find it an unpleasant subject, my dear. It is the only one that capable people really care for.

LADY BRITOMART: *(Looking at her watch.)* Well, if you are de- 690 termined to have it, I insist on having it in a proper and respectable way. Charles: ring for prayers.

(General amazement. STEPHEN *rises in dismay.)*

LOMAX: *(Rising.)* Oh I say!

UNDERSHAFT: *(Rising.)* I am afraid I must be going.

LADY BRITOMART: You cannot go now, Andrew: it would be 695 most improper. Sit down. What will the servants think?

UNDERSHAFT: My dear: I have conscientious scruples. May I suggest a compromise? If Barbara will conduct a little service in the drawing room, with Mr Lomax as organist, I will attend it willingly. I will even take part, if a trombone can be 700 procured.

LADY BRITOMART: Dont mock, Andrew.

UNDERSHAFT: *(Shocked—to* BARBARA.*)* You dont think I am mocking, my love, I hope.

BARBARA: No, of course not; and it wouldnt matter if you were: 705 half the Army came to their first meeting for a lark. *(Rising.)* Come along. *(She throws her arm round her father and sweeps him out, calling to the others from the threshold.)* Come, Dolly. Come, Cholly.

*(*CUSINS *rises.)*

LADY BRITOMART: I will not be disobeyed by everybody. Adol- 710 phus: sit down. *(He does not.)* Charles: you may go. You are not fit for prayers: you cannot keep your countenance.

LOMAX: Oh I say! *(He goes out.)*

LADY BRITOMART: *(Continuing.)* But you, Adolphus, can behave yourself if you choose to. I insist on your staying. 715

CUSINS: My dear Lady Brit: there are things in the family prayer book that I couldnt bear to hear you say.

LADY BRITOMART: What things, pray?

CUSINS: Well, you would have to say before all the servants that we have done things we ought not to have done, and left 720 undone things we ought to have done, and that there is no health in us. I cannot bear to hear you doing yourself such an injustice, and Barbara such an injustice. As for myself, I flatly deny it: I have done my best. I shouldnt dare to marry Barbara—I couldnt look you in the face—if it were true. So 725 I must go to the drawing room.

LADY BRITOMART: *(Offended.)* Well, go. *(He starts for the door.)* And remember this, Adolphus *(He turns to listen.)*: I have a very strong suspicion that you went to the Salvation

730 Army to worship Barbara and nothing else. And I quite appreciate the very clever way in which you systematically
humbug me. I have found you out. Take care Barbara
doesnt. Thats all.

CUSINS: *(With unruffled sweetness.)* Dont tell on me. *(He*
735 *steals out.)*

LADY BRITOMART: Sarah: if you want to go, go. Anything's better than to sit there as if you wished you were a thousand
miles away.

SARAH: *(Languidly.)* Very well, mamma. *(She goes.)*

*(LADY BRITOMART, with a sudden flounce, gives way to a little
gust of tears.)*

740 STEPHEN: *(Going to her.)* Mother: whats the matter?

LADY BRITOMART: *(Swishing away her tears with her handker-*
chief.) Nothing. Foolishness. You can go with him, too, if
you like, and leave me with the servants.

STEPHEN: Oh, you mustnt think that, mother. I—I dont like
745 him.

LADY BRITOMART: The others do. That is the injustice of a
woman's lot. A woman has to bring up her children; and that
means to restrain them, to deny them things they want, to set
them tasks, to punish them when they do wrong, to do all the
750 unpleasant things. And then the father, who has nothing to
do but pet them and spoil them, comes in when all her work
is done and steals their affection from her.

STEPHEN: He has not stolen our affection from you. It is only
curiosity.

755 LADY BRITOMART: *(Violently.)* I wont be consoled, Stephen.
There is nothing the matter with me. *(She rises and goes to-*
wards the door.)

STEPHEN: Where are you going, mother?

LADY BRITOMART: To the drawing room, of course. *(She goes*
760 *out. 'Onward, Christian Soldiers,' on the concertina, with*
tambourine accompaniment, is heard when the door opens.)
Are you coming, Stephen?

STEPHEN: No. Certainly not. *(She goes. He sits down on the*
settee, with compressed lips and an expression of strong
765 *dislike.)*

— ACT TWO —

*The yard of the West Ham shelter of the Salvation Army is a cold
place on a January morning. The building itself, an old warehouse, is newly whitewashed. Its gabled end projects into the
yard in the middle, with a door on the ground floor, and another
in the loft above it without any balcony or ladder, but with a pulley rigged over it for hoisting sacks. Those who come from this
central gable end into the yard have the gateway leading to the
street on their left, with a stone horse-trough just beyond it, and,
on the right, a penthouse shielding a table from the weather.
There are forms at the table; and on them are seated a man and
a woman, both much down on their luck, finishing a meal of
bread (one thick slice each, with margarine and golden syrup)
and diluted milk.*

*The man, a workman out of employment, is young, agile, a
talker, a poser, sharp enough to be capable of anything in reason
except honesty or altruistic considerations of any kind. The
woman is a commonplace old bundle of poverty and hard-worn
humanity. She looks sixty and probably is forty-five. If they were*
*rich people, gloved and muffed and well wrapped up in furs and
overcoats, they would be numbed and miserable; for it is a grind-
ingly cold raw January day; and a glance at the background of
grimy warehouses and leaden sky visible over the whitewashed
walls of the yard would drive any idle rich person straight to the
Mediterranean. But these two, being no more troubled with visions of the Mediterranean than of the moon, and being compelled to keep more of their clothes in the pawnshop, and less on
their persons, in winter than in summer, are not depressed by the
cold: rather are they stung into vivacity, to which their meal has
just now given an almost jolly turn. The man takes a pull at his
mug, and then gets up and moves about the yard with his hands
deep in his pockets, occasionally breaking into a stepdance.*

THE WOMAN: Feel better arter your meal, sir?

THE MAN: No. Call that a meal! Good enough for you, praps;
but wot is it to me, an intelligent workin man.

THE WOMAN: Workin man! Wot are you?

THE MAN: Painter.   5

THE WOMAN: *(Sceptically.)* Yus, I dessay.

THE MAN: Yus, you dessay! I know. Every loafer that cant do
nothink calls issself a painter. Well, I'm a real painter:
grainer, finisher, thirty-eight bob a week when I can get it.

THE WOMAN: Then why dont you go and get it?   10

THE MAN: I'll tell you why. Fust: I'm intelligent—fffff! it's rotten cold here *(He dances a step or two.)*—yes: intelligent beyond the station o life into which it has pleased the
capitalists to call me; and they dont like a man that sees
through em. Second, an intelligent bein needs a doo share   15
of appiness; so I drink somethink cruel when I get the
chawnce. Third, I stand by my class and do as little as I can
so's to leave arf the job for me fellow workers. Fourth, I'm fly
enough to know wots inside the law and wots outside it; and
inside it I do as the capitalists do: pinch wot I can lay me   20
ands on. In a proper state of society I am sober, industrious
and honest: in Rome, so to speak, I do as the Romans do.
Wots the consequence? When trade is bad—and it's rotten
bad just now—and the employers az to sack arf their men,
they generally start on me.   25

THE WOMAN: Whats your name?

THE MAN: Price. Bronterre O'Brien Price. Usually called
Snobby Price, for short.

THE WOMAN: Snobby's a carpenter, aint it? You said you was a
painter.   30

PRICE: Not that kind of snob, but the genteel sort. I'm too uppish, owing to my intelligence, and my father being a
Chartist and a reading, thinking man: a stationer, too. I'm
none of your common hewers of wood and drawers of water;
and dont you forget it. *(He returns to his seat at the table, and* 35
takes up his mug.) Wots your name?

THE WOMAN: Rummy Mitchens, sir.

PRICE: *(Quaffing the remains of his milk to her.)* Your elth,
Miss Mitchens.

RUMMY: *(Correcting him.)* Missis Mitchens.   40

PRICE: Wot! Oh Rummy, Rummy! Respectable married woman, Rummy, gittin rescued by the Salvation Army by pre-
tendin to be a bad un. Same old game!

RUMMY: What am I to do? I cant starve. Them Salvation lasses
is dear good girls; but the better you are, the worse they likes 45
to think you were before they rescued you. Why shouldnt
they av a bit o credit, poor loves? theyre worn to rags by their

work. And where would they get the money to rescue us if we was to let on we're no worse than other people? You know what ladies and gentlemen are.

PRICE: Thievin swine! Wish I ad their job, Rummy, all the same. Wot does Rummy stand for? Pet name praps?

RUMMY: Short for Romola.

PRICE: For wot!?

RUMMY: Romola. It was out of a new book. Somebody me mother wanted me to grow up like.

PRICE: We're companions in misfortune, Rummy. Both on us got names that nobody cawnt pronounce. Consequently I'm Snobby and youre Rummy because Bill and Sally wasnt good enough for our parents. Such is life!

RUMMY: Who saved you, Mr Price? Was it Major Barbara?

PRICE: No: I come here on my own. I'm going to be Bronterre O'Brien Price, the converted painter. I know wot they like. I'll tell em how I blasphemed and gambled and wopped my poor old mother—

RUMMY: (*Shocked.*) Used you to beat your mother?

PRICE: Not likely. She used to beat me. No matter: you come and listen to the converted painter, and youll hear how she was a pious woman that taught me me prayers at er knee, an how I used to come home drunk and drag her out o bed be er snow white airs, an lam into er with the poker.

RUMMY: Thats whats so unfair to us women. Your confessions is just as big lies as ours: you dont tell what you really done no more than us; but you men can tell your lies right out at the meetins and be made much of for it; while the sort o confessions we az to make az to be wispered to one lady at a time. It aint right, spite of all their piety.

PRICE: Right! Do you spose the Army'd be allowed if it went and did right? Not much. It combs our air and makes us good little blokes to be robbed and put upon. But I'll play the game as good as any of em. I'll see somebody struck by lightnin, or hear a voice sayin 'Snobby Price: where will you spend eternity?' I'll av a time of it, I tell you.

RUMMY: You wont be let drink, though.

PRICE: I'll take it out in gorspellin, then. I dont want to drink if I can get fun enough any other way.

(JENNY HILL, *a pale, overwrought, pretty Salvation lass of 18, comes in through the yard gate, leading* PETER SHIRLEY, *a half hardened, half worn-out elderly man, weak with hunger.*)

JENNY: (*Supporting him.*) Come! pluck up. I'll get you something to eat. Youll be all right then.

PRICE: (*Rising and hurrying officiously to take the old man off Jenny's hands.*) Poor old man! Cheer up, brother: youll find rest and peace and appiness ere. Hurry up with the food, miss: e's fair done. (*Jenny hurries into the shelter.*) Ere, buck up, daddy! she's fetchin y'a thick slice o breadn treacle, an a mug o skyblue. (*He seats him at the corner of the table.*)

RUMMY: (*Gaily.*) Keep up your old art! Never say die!

SHIRLEY: I'm not an old man. I'm only 46. I'm as good as ever I was. The grey patch come in my hair before I was thirty. All it wants is three pennorth o hair dye: am I to be turned on the streets to starve for it? Holy God! I've worked ten to twelve hours a day since I was thirteen, and paid my way all through; and now am I to be thrown into the gutter and my job given to a young man that can do it no better than me because Ive black hair that goes white at the first change?

PRICE: (*Cheerfully.*) No good jawrin about it. Youre only a jumped-up, jerked-off, orspittle-turned-out incurable of an ole workin man: who cares about you? Eh? Make the thievin swine give you a meal: theyve stole many a one from you. Get a bit o your own back. (*Jenny returns with the usual meal.*) There you are, brother. Awsk a blessin an tuck that into you.

SHIRLEY: (*Looking at it ravenously but not touching it, and crying like a child.*) I never took anything before.

JENNY: (*Petting him.*) Come, come! the Lord sends it to you: he wasnt above taking bread from his friends; and why should you be? Besides, when we find you a job you can pay us for it if you like.

SHIRLEY: (*Eagerly.*) Yes, yes: thats true. I can pay you back: it's only a loan. (*Shivering.*) O Lord! oh Lord! (*He turns to the table and attacks the meal ravenously.*)

JENNY: Well, Rummy, are you more comfortable now?

RUMMY: God bless you, lovey! youve fed my body and saved my soul, havnt you? (*Jenny, touched, kisses her.*) Sit down and rest a bit: you must be ready to drop.

JENNY: Ive been going hard since morning. But theres more work than we can do. I mustnt stop.

RUMMY: Try a prayer for just two minutes. Youll work all the better after.

JENNY: (*Her eyes lighting up.*) Oh isnt it wonderful how a few minutes prayer revives you! I was quite lightheaded at twelve o'clock, I was so tired; but Major Barbara just sent me to pray for five minutes; and I was able to go on as if I had only just begun. (*To Price.*) Did you have a piece of bread?

PRICE: (*With unction.*) Yes, miss; but Ive got the piece that I value more; and thats the peace that passeth hall hannerstennin.

RUMMY: (*Fervently.*) Glory Hallelujah!

(BILL WALKER, *a rough customer of about 25, appears at the yard gate and looks malevolently at* JENNY.)

JENNY: That makes me so happy. When you say that, I feel wicked for loitering here. I must get to work again.

(*She is hurrying to the shelter, when the new-comer moves quickly up to the door and intercepts her. His manner is so threatening that she retreats as he comes at her truculently, driving her down the yard.*)

BILL: Aw knaow you. Youre the one that took awy maw girl. Youre the one that set er agen me. Well, I'm gowin to ev er aht. Not that Aw care a carse for er or you: see? Bat Aw'll let er knaow; and Aw'll let you knaow. Aw'm gowing to give her a doin thatll teach er to cat awy from me. Nah in wiv you and tell er to cam aht afore Aw cam in and kick er aht. Tell er Bill Walker wants er. She'll knaow wot thet means; and if she keeps me witin itll be worse. You stop to jawr beck at me; and Aw'll stawt on you: d'ye eah? Theres your wy. In you gow. (*He takes her by the arm and slings her towards the door of the shelter. She falls on her hand and knee.* RUMMY *helps her up again.*)

PRICE: (*Rising, and venturing irresolutely towards* BILL.) Easy there, mate. She aint doin you no arm.

BILL: Oo are you callin mite? (*Standing over him threateningly.*) Youre gowin to stend ap for er, aw yer? Put ap your ens.

RUMMY: *(Running indignantly to him to scold him.)* Oh, you great brute—*(He instantly swings his left hand back against her face. She screams and reels back to the trough, where she sits down, covering her bruised face with her hands and rock-*
160 *ing herself and moaning with pain.)*

JENNY: *(Going to her.)* Oh, God forgive you! How could you strike an old woman like that?

BILL: *(Seizing her by the hair so violently that she also screams, and tearing her away from the old woman.)* You Gawd
165 forgimme again an Aw'll Gawd forgive you one on the jawr thetll stop you pryin for a week. *(Holding her and turning fiercely on PRICE.)* Ev you ennything to sy agen it?

PRICE: *(Intimidated.)* No, matey: she aint anything to do with me.

170 BILL: Good job for you! Aw'd pat two meals into you and fawt you with one finger arter, you stawved cur. *(To JENNY.)* Nah are you gowin to fetch aht Mog Ebbijem; or em Aw to knock your fice off you and fetch her meself?

JENNY: *(Writhing in his grasp.)* Oh please someone go in and
175 tell Major Barbara—*(She screams again as he wrenches her head down; and PRICE and RUMMY flee into the shelter.)*

BILL: You want to gow in and tell your Mijor of me, do you?

JENNY: Oh please dont drag my hair. Let me go.

BILL: Do you or downt you? *(She stifles a scream.)* Yus or nao?

180 JENNY: God give me strength—

BILL: *(Striking her with his fist in the face.)* Gow an shaow her thet, and tell her if she wants one lawk it to cam and interfere with me. (JENNY, *crying with pain, goes into the shed. He goes to the form and addresses the old man.)* Eah: finish your
185 mess; an git aht o maw wy.

SHIRLEY: *(Springing up and facing him fiercely, with the mug in his hand.)* You take a liberty with me, and I'll smash you over the face with the mug and cut your eye out. Aint you satisfied—young whelps like you—with takin the bread out
190 o the mouths of your elders than have brought you up and slaved for you, but you must come shovin and cheekin and bullyin in here, where the bread o charity is sickenin in our stummicks?

BILL: *(Contemptuously, but backing a little.)* Wot good are you,
195 you aold palsy mag? Wot good are you?

SHIRLEY: As good as you and better. I'll do a day's work agen you or any fat young soaker of your age. Go and take my job at Horrockses, where I worked for ten year. They want young men there: they cant afford to keep men over forty-five.
200 Theyre very sorry—give you a character and happy to help you to get anything suited to your years—sure a steady man wont be long out of a job. Well, let em try you. Theyll find the differ. What do you know? Not as much as how to beeyave yourself—layin your dirty fist across the mouth of a
205 respectable woman!

BILL: Downt provowk me to ly it acrost yours: d'ye eah?

SHIRLEY: *(With blighting contempt.)* Yes: you like an old man to hit, dont you, when youve finished with the women. I aint seen you hit a young one yet.

210 BILL: *(Stung.)* You loy, you aold soupkitchener, you. There was a yang menn eah. Did Aw offer to itt him or did Aw not?

SHIRLEY: Was he starvin or was he not? Was he a man or only a crosseyed thief an a loafer? Would you hit my son-in-law's brother?

215 BILL: Oo's ee?

SHIRLEY: Todger Fairmile o Balls Pond. Him that won £20 off the Japanese wrastler at the music hall by standin out 17 minutes 4 seconds agen him.

BILL: *(Sullenly.)* Aw'm nao music awl wrastler. Ken he box?

220 SHIRLEY: Yes: an you cant.

BILL: Wot! Aw cawnt, cawnt Aw? Wots thet you sy *(Threatening him.)*?

SHIRLEY: *(Not budging an inch.)* Will you box Todger Fairmile if I put him on to you? Say the word.

225 BILL: *(Subsiding with a slouch.)* Aw'll stend ap to enny menn alawv, if he was ten Todger Fairmawls. But Aw dont set ap to be a perfeshnal.

SHIRLEY: *(Looking down on him with unfathomable disdain.)* You box! Slap an old woman with the back o your hand! You
230 hadnt even the sense to hit her where a magistrate couldnt see the mark of it, you silly young lump of conceit and igno-rance. Hit a girl in the jaw and ony make her cry! If Todger Fairmile'd done it, she wouldnt a got up inside o ten min-utes, no more than you would if he got on to you. Yah! I'd set
235 about you myself if I had a week's feedin in me instead o two months' starvation. *(He turns his back on him and sits down moodily at the table.)*

BILL: *(Following him and stooping over him to drive the taunt in.)* You loy! youve the bread and treacle in you that you cam
240 eah to beg.

SHIRLEY: *(Bursting into tears.)* Oh God! it's true: I'm only an old pauper on the scrap heap. *(Furiously.)* But youll come to it yourself; and then youll know. Youll come to it sooner than a teetotaller like me, fillin yourself with gin at this hour o the
245 mornin!

BILL: Aw'm nao gin drinker, you oald lawr; bat wen Aw want to give my girl a bloomin good awdin Aw lawk to ev a bit o devil in me: see? An eah Aw emm, talkin to a rotten aold blawter like you sted o givin her wot for. *(Working himself into a rage.)* Aw'm gowin in there to fetch her aht. *(He makes
250 vengefully for the shelter door.)*

SHIRLEY: Youre going to the station on a stretcher, more likely; and theyll take the gin and the devil out of you there when they get you inside. You mind what youre about: the major here is the Earl o Stevenage's granddaughter.

255 BILL: *(Checked.)* Garn!

SHIRLEY: Youll see.

BILL: *(His resolution oozing.)* Well, Aw aint dan nathin to er.

SHIRLEY: Spose she said you did! who'd believe you?

BILL: *(Very uneasy, skulking back to the corner of the pent-
260 house.)* Gawd! theres no jastice in this cantry. To think wot them people can do! Aw'm as good as er.

SHIRLEY: Tell her so. It's just what a fool like you would do.

(BARBARA, brisk and businesslike, comes from the shelter with a note book, and addresses herself to SHIRLEY. BILL, cowed, sits down in the corner on a form, and turns his back on them.)

BARBARA: Good morning.

SHIRLEY: *(Standing up and taking off his hat.)* Good morning,
265 miss.

BARBARA: Sit down: make yourself at home. *(He hesitates; but she puts a friendly hand on his shoulder and makes him obey.)* Now then! since youve made friends with us, we want to know all about you. Names and addresses and trades.
270

SHIRLEY: Peter Shirley. Fitter. Chucked out two months ago because I was too old.

BARBARA: *(Not at all surprised.)* Youd pass still. Why didnt you dye your hair?

275 SHIRLEY: I did. Me age come out at a coroner's inquest on me daughter.

BARBARA: Steady?

SHIRLEY: Teetotaller. Never out of a job before. Good worker. And sent to the knackers like an old horse!

280 BARBARA: No matter: if you did your part God will do his.

SHIRLEY: *(Suddenly stubborn.)* My religion's no concern of anybody but myself.

BARBARA: *(Guessing.)* I know. Secularist?

SHIRLEY: *(Hotly.)* Did I offer to deny it?

285 BARBARA: Why should you? My own father's a Secularist, I think. Our Father—yours and mine—fulfils himself in many ways; and I daresay he knew what he was about when he made a Secularist of you. So buck up, Peter! we can always find a job for a steady man like you. *(SHIRLEY, disarmed and*

290 *a little bewildered, touches his hat. She turns from him to* BILL.*)* Whats your name?

BILL: *(Insolently.)* Wots thet to you?

BARBARA: *(Calmly making a note.)* Afraid to give his name. Any trade?

295 BILL: Oo's afride to give is nime? *(Doggedly, with a sense of heroically defying the House of Lords in the person of Lord Stevenage.)* If you want to bring a chawge agen me, bring it. *(She waits, unruffled.)* Moy nime's Bill Walker.

BARBARA: *(As if the name were familiar: trying to remember*

300 *how.)* Bill Walker? *(Recollecting.)* Oh, I know: you're the man that Jenny Hill was praying for inside just now. *(She enters his name in her note book.)*

BILL: Oo's Jenny Ill? And wot call as she to pry for me?

BARBARA: I dont know. Perhaps it was you that cut her lip.

305 BILL: *(Defiantly.)* Yus, it was me that cat her lip. Aw aint afride o you.

BARBARA: How could you be, since youre not afraid of God? Youre a brave man, Mr Walker. It takes some pluck to do our work here; but none of us dare lift our hand against a girl like

310 that, for fear of her father in heaven.

BILL: *(Sullenly.)* I want nan o your kentin jawr. I spowse you think Aw cam eah to beg from you, like this demmiged lot eah. Not me. Aw downt want your bread and scripe and ketlep. Aw dont blieve in your Gawd, no more than you do

315 yourself.

BARBARA: *(Sunnily apologetic and ladylike, as on a new footing with him.)* Oh, I beg your pardon for putting your name down, Mr Walker. I didnt understand. I'll strike it out.

BILL: *(Taking this as a slight, and deeply wounded by it.)* Eah!

320 you let maw nime alown. Aint it good enaff to be in your book?

BARBARA: *(Considering.)* Well, you see, theres no use putting down your name unless I can do something for you, is there? Whats your trade?

325 BILL: *(Still smarting.)* Thets nao concern o yours.

BARBARA: Just so. *(Very businesslike.)* I'll put you down as *(Writing.)* the man who—struck—poor little Jenny Hill—in the mouth.

BILL: *(Rising threateningly.)* See eah. Awve ed enaff o this.

330 BARBARA: *(Quite sunny and fearless.)* What did you come to us for?

BILL: Aw cam for maw gel, see? Aw cam to tike her aht o this and to brike er jawr for er.

BARBARA: *(Complacently.)* You see I was right about your trade. *(BILL, on the point of retorting furiously, finds himself,* 335 *to his great shame and terror, in danger of crying instead. He sits down again suddenly.)* Whats her name?

BILL: *(Dogged.)* Er nime's Mog Ebbijem: thets wot her nime is.

BARBARA: Mog Habbijam! Oh, she's gone to Canning Town, to 340 our barracks there.

BILL: *(Fortified by his resentment of Mog's perfidy.)* Is she? *(Vindictively.)* Then Aw'm gowin to Kennintahn arter her. *(He crosses to the gate; hesitates; finally comes back at Barbara.)* Are you loyin to me to git shat o me? 345

BARBARA: I dont want to get shut of you. I want to keep you here and save your soul. Youd better stay: youre going to have a bad time today, Bill.

BILL: Oo's gowin to give it to me? You, preps?

BARBARA: Someone you dont believe in. But youll be glad 350 afterwards.

BILL: *(Slinking off.)* Aw'll gow to Kennintahn to be aht o reach o your tangue. *(Suddenly turning on her with intense malice.)* And if Aw downt fawnd Mog there, Aw'll cam beck and do two years for you, selp me Gawd if Aw downt! 355

BARBARA: *(A shade kindlier, if possible.)* It's no use, Bill. She's got another bloke.

BILL: Wot!

BARBARA: One of her own converts. He fell in love with her when he saw her with her soul saved, and her face clean, and 360 her hair washed.

BILL: *(Surprised.)* Wottud she wash it for, the carroty slat? It's red.

BARBARA: It's quite lovely now, because she wears a new look in her eyes with it. It's a pity youre too late. The new bloke 365 has put your nose out of joint, Bill.

BILL: Aw'll put his nowse aht o joint for him. Not that Aw care a carse for er, mawnd thet. But Aw'll teach her to drop me as if Aw was dirt. And Aw'll teach him to meddle with maw judy. Wots iz bleedin nime? 370

BARBARA: Sergeant Todger Fairmile.

SHIRLEY: *(Rising with grim joy.)* I'll go with him, miss. I want to see them two meet. I'll take him to the infirmary when it's over.

BILL: *(To SHIRLEY, with undissembled misgiving.)* Is thet im 375 you was speakin on?

SHIRLEY: Thats him.

BILL: Im that wrastled in the music awl?

SHIRLEY: The competitions at the National Sportin Club was worth nigh a hundred a year to him. He's gev em up now for 380 religion; so he's a bit fresh for want of the exercise he was accustomed to. He'll be glad to see you. Come along.

BILL: Wots is wight?

SHIRLEY: Thirteen four. *(BILL's last hope expires.)*

BARBARA: Go and talk to him, Bill. He'll convert you. 385

SHIRLEY: He'll convert your head into a mashed potato.

BILL: *(Sullenly.)* Aw aint afride of im. Aw aint afride of ennybody. Bat e can lick me. She's dan me. *(He sits down moodily on the edge of the horse trough.)*

SHIRLEY: You aint going. I thought not. *(He resumes his seat.)* 390

BARBARA: *(Calling.)* Jenny!

JENNY: *(Appearing at the shelter door with a plaster on the corner of her mouth.)* Yes, Major.

BARBARA: Send Rummy Mitchens out to clear away here.

395 JENNY: I think she's afraid.

BARBARA: *(Her resemblance to her mother flashing out for a moment.)* Nonsense! she must do as she's told.

JENNY: *(Calling into the shelter.)* Rummy: the Major says you must come.

(JENNY comes to BARBARA, purposely keeping on the side next to BILL, lest he should suppose that she shrank from him or bore malice.)

400 BARBARA: Poor little Jenny! Are you tired? *(Looking at the wounded cheek.)* Does it hurt?

JENNY: No: it's all right now. It was nothing.

BARBARA: *(Critically.)* It was as hard as he could hit, I expect. Poor Bill! You dont feel angry with him, do you?

405 JENNY: Oh no, no, no: indeed I dont, Major, bless his poor heart! *(BARBARA kisses her; and she runs away merrily into the shelter. BILL writhes with an agonizing return of his new and alarming symptoms, but says nothing. RUMMY MITCHENS comes from the shelter.)*

410 BARBARA: *(Going to meet RUMMY.)* Now Rummy, bustle. Take in those mugs and plates to be washed; and throw the crumbs about for the birds.

(RUMMY takes the three plates and mugs; but SHIRLEY takes back his mug from her, as there is still some milk left in it.)

RUMMY: There aint any crumbs. This aint a time to waste good bread on birds.

415 PRICE: *(Appearing at the shelter door.)* Gentleman come to see the shelter, Major. Says he's your father.

BARBARA: All right. Coming. *(SNOBBY goes back into the shelter, followed by BARBARA.)*

RUMMY: *(Stealing across to BILL and addressing him in a subdued voice, but with intense conviction.)* I'd av the lor of you, 420 you flat eared pignosed potwalloper, if she'd let me. Youre no gentleman, to hit a lady in the face. *(BILL, with greater things moving in him, takes no notice.)*

SHIRLEY: *(Following her.)* Here! in with you and dont get yourself into more trouble by talking.

425 RUMMY: *(With hauteur.)* I aint ad the pleasure o being hintroduced to you, as I can remember. *(She goes into the shelter with the plates.)*

SHIRLEY: Thats the—

430 BILL: *(Savagely.)* Downt you talk to me, d'ye eah? You lea me alown, or Aw'll do you a mischief. Aw'm not dirt under your feet, ennywy.

SHIRLEY: *(Calmly.)* Dont you be afeerd. You aint such prime company that you need expect to be sought after. *(He is 435 about to go into the shelter when BARBARA comes out, with UNDERSHAFT on her right.)*

BARBARA: Oh, there you are, Mr Shirley! *(Between them.)* This is my father: I told you he was a Secularist, didnt I? Perhaps youll be able to comfort one another.

440 UNDERSHAFT: *(Startled.)* A Secularist! Not the least in the world: on the contrary, a confirmed mystic.

BARBARA: Sorry, I'm sure. By the way, papa, what is your religion? in case I have to introduce you again.

UNDERSHAFT: My religion? Well, my dear, I am a Millionaire. 445 That is my religion.

BARBARA: Then I'm afraid you and Mr Shirley wont be able to comfort one another after all. Youre not a Millionaire, are you, Peter?

SHIRLEY: No; and proud of it.

UNDERSHAFT: *(Gravely.)* Poverty, my friend, is not a thing to 450 be proud of.

SHIRLEY: *(Angrily.)* Who made your millions for you? Me and my like. Whats kep us poor? Keepin you rich. I wouldnt have your conscience, not for all your income.

UNDERSHAFT: I wouldnt have your income, not for all your 455 conscience, Mr Shirley. *(He goes to the penthouse and sits down on a form.)*

BARBARA: *(Stopping SHIRLEY adroitly as he is about to retort.)* You wouldnt think he was my father, would you, Peter? Will you go into the shelter and lend the lasses a hand for a while: 460 we're worked off our feet.

SHIRLEY: *(Bitterly.)* Yes: I'm in their debt for a meal, aint I?

BARBARA: Oh, not because youre in their debt, but for love of them, Peter, for love of them. *(He cannot understand, and is rather scandalized.)* There! dont stare at me. In with you; 465 and give that conscience of yours a holiday *(Bustling him into the shelter.)*

SHIRLEY: *(As he goes in.)* Ah! it's a pity you never was trained to use your reason, miss. Youd have been a very taking lecturer on Secularism. 470

(BARBARA turns to her father.)

UNDERSHAFT: Never mind me, my dear. Go about your work; and let me watch it for a while.

BARBARA: All right.

UNDERSHAFT: For instance, whats the matter with that outpatient over there? 475

BARBARA: *(Looking at BILL, whose attitude has never changed, and whose expression of brooding wrath has deepened.)* Oh, we shall cure him in no time. Just watch. *(She goes over to BILL and waits. He glances up at her and casts his eyes down again, uneasy, but grimmer than ever.)* It would be nice to 480 just stamp on Mog Habbijam's face, wouldnt it, Bill?

BILL: *(Starting up from the trough in consternation.)* It's a loy: Aw never said so. *(She shakes her head.)* Oo taold you wot was in moy mawnd?

BARBARA: Only your new friend. 485

BILL: Wot new friend?

BARBARA: The devil, Bill. When he gets round people they get miserable, just like you.

BILL: *(With a heartbreaking attempt at devil-may-care cheerfulness.)* Aw aint miserable. *(He sits down again, and stretches 490 his legs in an attempt to seem indifferent.)*

BARBARA: Well, if youre happy, why dont you look happy, as we do?

BILL: *(His legs curling back in spite of him.)* Aw'm eppy enaff, Aw tell you. Woy cawnt you lea me alown? Wot ev I dan to 495 you? Aw aint smashed your fice, ev Aw?

BARBARA: *(Softly: wooing his soul.)* It's not me thats getting at you, Bill.

BILL: Oo else is it?

BARBARA: Somebody that doesnt intend you to smash women's 500 faces, I suppose. Somebody or something that wants to make a man of you.

BILL: *(Blustering.)* Mike a menn o me! Aint Aw a menn? eh? Oo sez Aw'm not a menn?

505 BARBARA: Theres a man in you somewhere, I suppose. But why did he let you hit poor little Jenny Hill? That wasnt very manly of him, was it?

BILL: *(Tormented.)* Ev dan wiv it, Aw tell you. Chack it. Aw'm sick o your Jenny Ill and er silly little fice.

510 BARBARA: Then why do you keep thinking about it? Why does it keep coming up against you in your mind? Youre not getting converted, are you?

BILL: *(With conviction.)* Not ME. Not lawkly.

BARBARA: Thats right, Bill. Hold out against it. Put out your strength. Dont lets get you cheap. Todger Fairmile said he 515 wrestled for three nights against his salvation harder than he ever wrestled with the Jap at the music hall. He gave in to the Jap when his arm was going to break. But he didnt give in to his salvation until his heart was going to break. Perhaps youll 520 escape that. You havnt any heart, have you?

BILL: Wot d'ye mean? Woy aint Aw got a awt the sime as ennybody else?

BARBARA: A man with a heart wouldnt have bashed poor little Jenny's face, would he?

525 BILL: *(Almost crying.)* Ow, will you lea me alown? Ev Aw ever offered to meddle with you, that you cam neggin and provowkin me lawk this? *(He writhes convulsively from his eyes to his toes.)*

BARBARA: *(With a steady soothing hand on his arm and a gen-*
530 *tle voice that never lets him go.)* It's your soul thats hurting you, Bill, and not me. Weve been through it all ourselves. Come with us, Bill. *(He looks wildly round.)* To brave manhood on earth and eternal glory in heaven. *(He is on the point of breaking down.)* Come. *(A drum is heard in the shel-*
535 *ter; and* BILL, *with a gasp, escapes from the spell as* BARBARA *turns quickly.* ADOLPHUS *enters from the shelter with a big drum.)* Oh! there you are, Dolly. Let me introduce a new friend of mine, Mr Bill Walker. This is my bloke, Bill: Mr Cusins. *(*CUSINS *salutes with his drumstick.)*

540 BILL: Gowin to merry im?

BARBARA: Yes.

BILL: *(Fervently.)* Gawd elp im! Gaw-aw-aw-awd elp im!

BARBARA: Why? Do you think he wont be happy with me?

BILL: Awve aony ed to stend it for a mawnin: e'll ev to stend it 545 for a lawftawm.

CUSINS: That is a frightful reflection, Mr Walker. But I cant tear myself away from her.

BILL: Well, Aw ken. *(To* BARBARA.*)* Eah! do you knaow where Aw'm gowin to, and wot Aw'm gowin to do?

550 BARBARA: Yes: youre going to heaven; and youre coming back here before the week's out to tell me so.

BILL: You loy. Aw'm gowin to Kennintahn, to spit in Todger Fairmawl's eye. Aw beshed Jenny Ill's fice; an nar Aw'll git me aown fice beshed and cam beck and shaow it to er. Ee'll 555 itt me ardern Aw itt her. Thatll mike us square. *(To* ADOL-PHUS.*)* Is thet fair or is it not? Youre a genlmn: you oughter knaow.

BARBARA: Two black eyes wont make one white one, Bill.

BILL: Aw didnt awst you. Cawnt you never keep your mahth 560 shat? Oy awst the genlmn.

CUSINS: *(Reflectively.)* Yes: I think youre right, Mr Walker. Yes: I should do it. It's curious: it's exactly what an ancient Greek would have done.

BARBARA: But what good will it do?

565 CUSINS: Well, it will give Mr Fairmile some exercise; and it will satisfy Mr Walker's soul.

BILL: Rot! there aint nao such a thing as a saoul. Ah kin you tell wevver Awve a saoul or not? You never seen it.

BARBARA: Ive seen it hurting you when you went against it.

570 BILL: *(With compressed aggravation.)* If you was maw gel and took the word aht o me mahth lawk thet, Aw'd give you sathink youd feel urtin, Aw would. *(To* ADOLPHUS.*)* You tike maw tip, mite. Stop er jawr; or youll doy afoah your tawm *(With intense expression.)* Wore aht: thets wot youll be: wore 575 aht. *(He goes away through the gate.)*

CUSINS: *(Looking after him.)* I wonder!

BARBARA: Dolly! *(Indignant, in her mother's manner.)*

CUSINS: Yes, my dear, it's very wearing to be in love with you. If it lasts, I quite think I shall die young.

580 BARBARA: Should you mind?

CUSINS: Not at all. *(He is suddenly softened, and kisses her over the drum, evidently not for the first time, as people cannot kiss over a big drum without practice.* UNDERSHAFT *coughs.)*

BARBARA: It's all right, papa, weve not forgotten you. Dolly: ex-585 plain the place to papa; I havnt time. *(She goes busily into the shelter.)*

*(*UNDERSHAFT *and* ADOLPHUS *now have the yard to themselves.* UNDERSHAFT, *seated on a form, and still keenly attentive, looks hard at* ADOLPHUS. ADOLPHUS *looks hard at him.)*

UNDERSHAFT: I fancy you guess something of what is in my mind, Mr Cusins. *(*CUSINS *flourishes his drumsticks as if in the act of beating a lively rataplan, but makes no sound.)* Ex-590 actly so. But suppose Barbara finds you out!

CUSINS: You know, I do not admit that I am imposing on Barbara. I am quite genuinely interested in the views of the Salvation Army. The fact is, I am a sort of collector of religions; and the curious thing is that I find I can believe them all. By 595 the way, have you any religion?

UNDERSHAFT: Yes.

CUSINS: Anything out of the common?

UNDERSHAFT: Only that there are two things necessary to Salvation.

600 CUSINS: *(Disappointed, but polite.)* Ah, the Church Catechism. Charles Lomax also belongs to the Established Church.

UNDERSHAFT: The two things are—

CUSINS: Baptism and—

605 UNDERSHAFT: No. Money and gunpowder.

CUSINS: *(Surprised, but interested.)* That is the general opinion of our governing classes. The novelty is in hearing any man confess it.

UNDERSHAFT: Just so.

610 CUSINS: Excuse me: is there any place in your religion for honor, justice, truth, love, mercy and so forth?

UNDERSHAFT: Yes: they are the graces and luxuries of a rich, strong, and safe life.

CUSINS: Suppose one is forced to choose between them and 615 money or gunpowder?

UNDERSHAFT: Choose money and gunpowder; for without enough of both you cannot afford the others.

CUSINS: That is your religion?

UNDERSHAFT: Yes.

(The cadence of this reply makes a full close in the conversation, CUSINS *twists his face dubiously and contemplates* UNDERSHAFT. UNDERSHAFT *contemplates him.)*

620 CUSINS: Barbara wont stand that. You will have to choose between your religion and Barbara.

UNDERSHAFT: So will you, my friend. She will find out that that drum of yours is hollow.

CUSINS: Father Undershaft: you are mistaken: I am a sincere
625 Salvationist. You do not understand the Salvation Army. It is the army of joy, of love, of courage: it has banished the fear and remorse and despair of the old hell-ridden evangelical sects: it marches to fight the devil with trumpet and drum, with music and dancing, with banner and palm, as becomes
630 a sally from heaven by its happy garrison. It picks the waster out of the public house and makes a man of him: it finds a worm wriggling in a back kitchen, and lo! a woman! Men and women of rank too, sons and daughters of the Highest. It takes the poor professor of Greek, the most artificial and self-
635 suppressed of human creatures, from his meal of roots, and lets loose the rhapsodist in him; reveals the true worship of Dionysos to him; sends him down the public street drumming dithyrambs *(He plays a thundering flourish on the drum.)*

640 UNDERSHAFT: You will alarm the shelter.

CUSINS: Oh, they are accustomed to these sudden ecstasies. However, if the drum worries you—*(He pockets the drumsticks; unhooks the drum; and stands it on the ground opposite the gateway.)*

645 UNDERSHAFT: Thank you.

CUSINS: You remember what Euripides says about your money and gunpowder?

UNDERSHAFT: No.

CUSINS: *(Declaiming.)*

650   One and another
     In money and guns may outpass his brother;
     And men in their millions float and flow
     And seethe with a million hopes as leaven;
     And they win their will; or they miss their will;
655 And their hopes are dead or are pined for still;
              But who'er can know
              As the long days go
     That to live is happy, has found his heaven.

My translation: what do you think of it?

660 UNDERSHAFT: I think, my friend, that if you wish to know, as the long days go, that to live is happy, you must first acquire money enough for a decent life, and power enough to be your own master.

CUSINS: You are damnably discouraging. *(He resumes his*
665 *declamation.)*

          Is it so hard a thing to see
          That the spirit of God—whate'er it be—
     The law that abides and changes not, ages long,
     The Eternal and Nature-born: these things be strong?
670 What else is Wisdom? What of Man's endeavor,
     Or God's high grace so lovely and so great?
     To stand from fear set free? to breathe and wait?
     To hold a hand uplifted over Fate?
     And shall not Barbara be loved for ever?

675 UNDERSHAFT: Euripides mentions Barbara, does he?

CUSINS: It is a fair translation. The word means Loveliness.

UNDERSHAFT: May I ask—as Barbara's father—how much a year she is to be loved for ever on?

CUSINS: As for Barbara's father, that is more your affair than
680 mine. I can feed her by teaching Greek: that is about all.

UNDERSHAFT: Do you consider it a good match for her?

CUSINS: *(With polite obstinacy.)* Mr Undershaft: I am in many ways a weak, timid, ineffectual person; and my health is far from satisfactory. But whenever I feel that I must have any-
685 thing, I get it, sooner or later. I feel that way about Barbara. I dont like marriage: I feel intensely afraid of it; and I dont know what I shall do with Barbara or what she will do with me. But I feel that I and nobody else must marry her. Please regard that as settled.—Not that I wish to be arbitrary; but
690 why should I waste your time in discussing what is inevitable?

UNDERSHAFT: You mean that you will stick at nothing: not even the conversion of the Salvation Army to the worship of Dionysos.

CUSINS: The business of the Salvation Army is to save, not to
695 wrangle about the name of the pathfinder. Dionysos or another: what does it matter?

UNDERSHAFT: *(Rising and approaching him.)* Professor Cusins: you are a young man after my own heart.

CUSINS: Mr Undershaft: you are, as far as I am able to gather, a
700 most infernal old rascal; but you appeal very strongly to my sense of ironic humor.

(UNDERSHAFT mutely offers his hand. They shake.)

UNDERSHAFT: *(Suddenly concentrating himself.)* And now to business.

CUSINS: Pardon me. We are discussing religion. Why go back to such an uninteresting and unimportant subject as business?
705

UNDERSHAFT: Religion is our business at present, because it is through religion alone that we can win Barbara.

CUSINS: Have you, too, fallen in love with Barbara?

UNDERSHAFT: Yes, with a father's love.

CUSINS: A father's love for a grown-up daughter is the most
710 dangerous of all infatuations. I apologize for mentioning my own pale, coy, mistrustful fancy in the same breath with it.

UNDERSHAFT: Keep to the point. We have to win her; and we are neither of us Methodists.

CUSINS: That doesnt matter. The power Barbara wields here—
715 the power that wields Barbara herself—is not Calvinism, not Presbyterianism, not Methodism—

UNDERSHAFT: Not Greek Paganism either, eh?

CUSINS: I admit that. Barbara is quite original in her religion.

UNDERSHAFT: *(Triumphantly.)* Aha! Barbara Undershaft
720 would be. Her inspiration comes from within herself.

CUSINS: How do you suppose it got there?

UNDERSHAFT: *(In towering excitement.)* It is the Undershaft inheritance. I shall hand on my torch to my daughter. She shall make my converts and preach my gospel—
725

CUSINS: What! Money and gunpowder!

UNDERSHAFT: Yes, money and gunpowder. Freedom and power. Command of life and command of death.

CUSINS: *(Urbanely: trying to bring him down to earth.)* This is extremely interesting, Mr Undershaft. Of course you know
730 that you are mad.

UNDERSHAFT: *(With redoubled force.)* And you?

CUSINS: Oh, mad as a hatter. You are welcome to my secret since I have discovered yours. But I am astonished. Can a madman make cannons?

UNDERSHAFT: Would anyone else than a madman make them? And now (*With surging energy.*) question for question. Can a sane man translate Euripides?

CUSINS: No.

UNDERSHAFT: (*Seizing him by the shoulder.*) Can a sane woman make a man of a waster or a woman of a worm?

CUSINS: (*Reeling before the storm.*) Father Colossus—Mammoth Millionaire—

UNDERSHAFT: (*Pressing him.*) Are there two mad people or three in this Salvation shelter today?

CUSINS: You mean Barbara is as mad as we are?

UNDERSHAFT: (*Pushing him lightly off and resuming his equanimity suddenly and completely.*) Pooh, Professor! let us call things by their proper names. I am a millionaire; you are a poet: Barbara is a savior of souls. What have we three to do with the common mob of slaves and idolators? (*He sits down again with a shrug of contempt for the mob.*)

CUSINS: Take care! Barbara is in love with the common people. So am I. Have you never felt the romance of that love?

UNDERSHAFT: (*Cold and sardonic.*) Have you ever been in love with Poverty, like St Francis? Have you ever been in love with Dirt, like St Simeon! Have you ever been in love with disease and suffering, like our nurses and philanthropists? Such passions are not virtues, but the most unnatural of all the vices. This love of the common people may please an earl's granddaughter and a university professor; but I have been a common man and a poor man; and it has no romance for me. Leave it to the poor to pretend that poverty is a blessing: leave it to the coward to make a religion of his cowardice by preaching humility: we know better than that. We three must stand together above the common people: how else can we help their children to climb up beside us? Barbara must belong to us, not to the Salvation Army.

CUSINS: Well, I can only say that if you think you will get her away from the Salvation Army by talking to her as you have been talking to me, you dont know Barbara.

UNDERSHAFT: My friend: I never ask for what I can buy.

CUSINS: (*In a white fury.*) Do I understand you to imply that you can buy Barbara?

UNDERSHAFT: No; but I can buy the Salvation Army.

CUSINS: Quite impossible.

UNDERSHAFT: You shall see. All religious organizations exist by selling themselves to the rich.

CUSINS: Not the Army. That is the Church of the poor.

UNDERSHAFT: All the more reason for buying it.

CUSINS: I dont think you quite know what the Army does for the poor.

UNDERSHAFT: Oh yes I do. It draws their teeth: that is enough for me as a man of business.

CUSINS: Nonsense! It makes them sober—

UNDERSHAFT: I prefer sober workmen. The profits are larger.

CUSINS: —honest—

UNDERSHAFT: Honest workmen are the most economical.

CUSINS: —attached to their homes—

UNDERSHAFT: So much the better: they will put up with anything sooner than change their shop.

CUSINS: —happy—

UNDERSHAFT: An invaluable safeguard against revolution.

CUSINS: —unselfish—

UNDERSHAFT: Indifferent to their own interests, which suits me exactly.

CUSINS: —with their thoughts on heavenly things—

UNDERSHAFT: (*Rising.*) And not on Trade Unionism nor Socialism. Excellent.

CUSINS: (*Revolted.*) You really are an infernal old rascal.

UNDERSHAFT: (*Indicating* PETER SHIRLEY, *who has just come from the shelter and strolled dejectedly down the yard between them.*) And this is an honest man!

SHIRLEY: Yes; and what av I got by it? (*He passes on bitterly and sits on the form, in the corner of the penthouse.*)

(SNOBBY PRICE, *beaming sanctimoniously, and* JENNY HILL, *with a tambourine full of coppers, come from the shelter and go to the drum, on which* JENNY *begins to count the money.*)

UNDERSHAFT: (*Replying to* SHIRLEY.) Oh, your employers must have got a good deal by it from first to last. (*He sits on the table, with one foot on the side form,* CUSINS, *overwhelmed, sits down on the same form nearer the shelter.* BARBARA *comes from the shelter to the middle of the yard. She is excited and a little overwrought.*)

BARBARA: Weve just had a splendid experience meeting at the other gate in Cripps's lane. Ive hardly ever seen them so much moved as they were by your confession, Mr Price.

PRICE: I could almost be glad of my past wickedness if I could believe that it would elp to keep hathers stright.

BARBARA: So it will, Snobby. How much, Jenny?

JENNY: Four and tenpence, Major.

BARBARA: Oh Snobby, if you had given your poor mother just one more kick, we should have got the whole five shillings!

PRICE: If she heard you say that, miss, she'd be sorry I didnt. But I'm glad. Oh what a joy it will be to her when she hears I'm saved!

UNDERSHAFT: Shall I contribute the odd twopence, Barbara? The millionaire's mite, eh? (*He takes a couple of pennies from his pocket.*)

BARBARA: How did you make that twopence?

UNDERSHAFT: As usual. By selling cannons, torpedoes, submarines, and my new patent Grand Duke hand grenade.

BARBARA: Put it back in your pocket. You cant buy your salvation here for twopence: you must work it out.

UNDERSHAFT: Is twopence not enough? I can afford a little more, if you press me.

BARBARA: Two million millions would not be enough. There is bad blood on your hands; and nothing but good blood can cleanse them. Money is no use. Take it away. (*She turns to* CUSINS.) Dolly: you must write another letter for me to the papers. (*He makes a wry face.*) Yes: I know you dont like it; but it must be done. The starvation this winter is beating us: everybody is unemployed. The General says we must close this shelter if we cant get more money. I force the collections at the meetings until I am ashamed: dont I, Snobby?

PRICE: It's a fair treat to see you work it, miss. The way you got them up from three-and-six to four-and-ten with that hymn, penny by penny and verse by verse, was a caution. Not a Cheap Jack on Mile End Waste could touch you at it.

BARBARA: Yes; but I wish we could do without it. I am getting at last to think more of the collection than of the people's souls. And what are those hatfuls of pence and halfpence? We want thousands! tens of thousands! hundreds of thousands! I want to convert people, not to be always begging for the Army in a way I'd die sooner than beg for myself.

UNDERSHAFT: (*In profound irony.*) Genuine unselfishness is capable of anything, my dear.

855 BARBARA: (*Unsuspectingly, as she turns away to take the money from the drum and put it in a cash bag she carries.*) Yes, isnt it? (UNDERSHAFT *looks sardonically at* CUSINS.)

CUSINS: (*Aside to* UNDERSHAFT.) Mephistopheles! Machiavelli!

BARBARA: (*Tears coming into her eyes as she ties the bag and*
860 *pockets it.*) How are we to feed them? I cant talk religion to a man with bodily hunger in his eyes. (*Almost breaking down.*) It's frightful.

JENNY: (*Running to her.*) Major, dear—

BARBARA: (*Rebounding.*) No: dont comfort me. It will be all
865 right. We shall get the money.

UNDERSHAFT: How?

JENNY: By praying for it, of course. Mrs Baines says she prayed for it last night; and she has never prayed for it in vain: never once. (*She goes to the gate and looks out into the street.*)

870 BARBARA: (*Who has dried her eyes and regained her compo-sure.*) By the way, dad, Mrs Baines has come to march with us to our big meeting this afternoon; and she is very anxious to meet you, for some reason or other. Perhaps she'll convert you.

875 UNDERSHAFT: I shall be delighted, my dear.

JENNY: (*At the gate: excitedly.*) Major! Major! heres that man back again.

BARBARA: What man?

JENNY: The man that hit me. Oh, I hope he's coming back to
880 join us.

(BILL WALKER, *with frost on his jacket, comes through the gate, his hands deep in his pockets and his chin sunk between his shoulders, like a cleaned-out gambler. He halts between* BAR-BARA *and the drum.*)

BARBARA: Hullo, Bill! Back already!

BILL: (*Nagging at her.*) Bin talkin ever sence, ev you?

BARBARA: Pretty nearly. Well, has Todger paid you out for poor Jenny's jaw?

885 BILL: Nao e aint.

BARBARA: I thought your jacket looked a bit snowy.

BILL: Sao it is snaowy. You want to knaow where the snaow cam from, downt you?

BARBARA: Yes.

890 BILL: Well, it cam from orf the grahnd in Pawkinses Corner in Kennintahn. It got rabbed orf be maw shaoulders: see?

BARBARA: Pity you didnt rub some off with your knees, Bill! That would have done you a lot of good.

BILL: (*With sour mirthless humor.*) Aw was sivin anather menn's
895 knees at the tawm. E was kneelin on moy ed, e was.

JENNY: Who was kneeling on your head?

BILL: Todger was. E was pryin for me: pryin camfortable wiv me as a cawpet. Sow was Mog. Sao was the aol bloomin meetin. Mog she sez 'Ow Lawd brike is stabborn sperrit; bat
900 downt urt is dear art.' Thet was wot she said. 'Downt urt is dear art'! An er blowk—thirteen stun four!—kneelin wiv all is wight on me. Fanny, aint it?

JENNY: Oh no. We're so sorry, Mr Walker.

BARBARA: (*Enjoying it frankly.*) Nonsense! of course it's funny.
905 Served you right, Bill! You must have done something to him first.

BILL: (*Doggedly.*) Aw did wot Aw said Aw'd do. Aw spit in is eye. E looks ap at the skoy and sez, 'Ow that Aw should be fahnd worthy to be spit upon for the gospel's sike!' e sez; an
910 Mog sez 'Glaory Allelloolier!'; an then e called me Brad-dher, an dahned me as if Aw was a kid and e was me mather worshin me a Setterda nawt. Aw ednt jast nao shaow wiv im at all. Arf the street pryed; an the tather arf larfed fit to split theirselves. (*To* BARBARA.) There! are you settisfawd nah?

915 BARBARA: (*Her eyes dancing.*) Wish I'd been there, Bill.

BILL: Yus: youd a got in a hextra bit o talk on me, wouldnt you?

JENNY: I'm so sorry, Mr Walker.

BILL: (*Fiercely.*) Downt you gow being sorry for me: youve no call. Listen eah. Aw browk your jawr.

920 JENNY: No, it didn't hurt me: indeed it didnt, except for a mo-ment. It was only that I was frightened.

BILL: Aw downt want to be forgive be you, or be ennybody. Wot Aw did Aw'll py for. Aw trawd to gat me aown jawr browk to settisfaw you—

925 JENNY: (*Distressed.*) Oh no—

BILL: (*Impatiently.*) Tell y' Aw did cawnt you listen to wots bein taold you? All Aw got be it was bein mide a sawt of in the pablic street for me pines. Well, if Aw cawnt settisfaw you one wy, Aw ken another. Listen eah! Aw ed two quid sived
930 agen the frost; an Awve a pahnd of it left. A mite o mawn last week ed words with the judy e's gowing to merry. E give er wot-for; an e's bin fawnd fifteen bob. E ed a rawt to itt er cause they was gowin to be merrid; but Aw ednt nao rawt to itt you; sao put another fawv bob on an call it a pahnd's
935 worth. (*He produces a sovereign.*) Eahs the manney. Tike it; and lets ev no more o your forgivin an prying and your Mijor jawrin me. Let wot Aw dan be dan an pide for; and let there be a end of it.

JENNY: Oh, I couldnt take it, Mr Walker. But if you would give
940 a shilling or two to poor Rummy Mitchens! you really did hurt her; and she's old.

BILL: (*Contemptuously.*) Not lawkly. Aw'd give her anather as soon as look at er. Let her ev the lawr o me as she threatened! She aint forgiven me: not mach. Wot Aw dan to er is not on
945 me mawnd—wot she (*Indicating* BARBARA.) mawt call on me conscience—no more than stickin a pig. It's this Christian gime o yours that Aw wownt ev plyed agen me: this bloomin forgivin an neggin an jawrin that mikes a menn thet sore that iz lawf's a burdn to im. Aw wownt ev it, Aw tell you; sao tike
950 your manney and stop thraowin your silly beshed fice hap agen me.

JENNY: Major: may I take a little of it for the Army?

BARBARA: No: the Army is not to be bought. We want your soul, Bill; and we'll take nothing less.

955 BILL: (*Bitterly.*) Aw knaow. Me an maw few shillins is not good enaff for you. Youre a earl's grendorter, you are. Nathink less than a andered pahnd for you.

UNDERSHAFT: Come, Barbara! you could do a great deal of good with a hundred pounds. If you will set this gentleman's mind at ease by taking his pound, I will give the other
960 ninety-nine.

(BILL, *dazed by such opulence, instinctively touches his cap.*)

BARBARA: Oh, youre too extravagant, papa. Bill offers twenty pieces of silver. All you need offer is the other ten. That will make the standard price to buy anybody who's for sale. I'm not; and the Army's not. (*To* BILL.) Youll never have another
965

quiet moment, Bill, until you come round to us. You cant stand out against your salvation.

BILL: *(Sullenly.)* Aw cawnt stend aht agen music awl wrastlers and awtful tangued women. Awve offered to py. Aw can do no more. Tike it or leave it. There it is. *(He throws the sovereign on the drum, and sits down on the horse-trough. The coin fascinates* SNOBBY PRICE, *who takes an early opportunity of dropping his cap on it.)*

*(*MRS BAINES *comes from the shelter. She is dressed as a Salvation Army Commissioner. She is an earnest looking woman of about 40, with a caressing, urgent voice, and an appealing manner.)*

BARBARA: This is my father, Mrs Baines. (UNDERSHAFT *comes from the table, taking his hat off with marked civility.)* Try what you can do with him. He wont listen to me, because he remembers what a fool I was when I was a baby. *(She leaves them together and chats with* JENNY.)

MRS BAINES: Have you been shewn over the shelter, Mr Undershaft? You know the work we're doing, of course.

UNDERSHAFT: *(Very civilly.)* The whole nation knows it, Mrs Baines.

MRS BAINES: No, sir: the whole nation does not know it, or we should not be crippled as we are for want of money to carry our work through the length and breadth of the land. Let me tell you that there would have been rioting this winter in London but for us.

UNDERSHAFT: You really think so?

MRS BAINES: I know it. I remember 1886, when you rich gentlemen hardened your hearts against the cry of the poor. They broke the windows of your clubs in Pall Mall.

UNDERSHAFT: *(Gleaming with approval of their method.)* And the Mansion House Fund went up next day from thirty thousand pounds to seventy-nine thousand! I remember quite well.

MRS BAINES: Well, wont you help me to get at the people? They wont break windows then. Come here, Price. Let me shew you to this gentleman (PRICE *comes to be inspected.)* Do you remember the window breaking?

PRICE: My ole father thought it was the revolution, maam.

MRS BAINES: Would you break windows now?

PRICE: Oh no, maam. The windows of eaven av bin opened to me. I know now that the rich man is a sinner like myself.

RUMMY: *(Appearing above at the loft door.)* Snobby Price!

SNOBBY: Wot is it?

RUMMY: Your mother's askin for you at the other gate in Cripps's Lane. She's heard about your confession (PRICE *turns pale.)*

MRS BAINES: Go, Mr Price; and pray with her.

JENNY: You can go through the shelter, Snobby.

PRICE: *(To* MRS BAINES.) I couldnt face her now, maam, with all the weight of my sins fresh on me. Tell her she'll find her son at ome, waitin for her in prayer. *(He skulks off through the gate, incidentally stealing the sovereign on his way out by picking up his cap from the drum.)*

MRS BAINES: *(With swimming eyes.)* You see how we take the anger and the bitterness against you out of their hearts, Mr Undershaft.

UNDERSHAFT: It is certainly most convenient and gratifying to all large employers of labor, Mrs Baines.

MRS BAINES: Barbara: Jenny: I have good news: most wonderful news. (JENNY *runs to her.)* My prayers have been answered. I told you they would, Jenny, didnt I?

JENNY: Yes, yes.

BARBARA: *(Moving nearer to the drum.)* Have we got money enough to keep the shelter open?

MRS BAINES: I hope we shall have enough to keep all the shelters open. Lord Saxmundham has promised us five thousand pounds—

BARBARA: Hooray!

JENNY: Glory!

MRS BAINES: —if—

BARBARA: 'If!' If what?

MRS BAINES: —if five other gentlemen will give a thousand each to make it up to ten thousand.

BARBARA: Who is Lord Saxmundham? I never heard of him.

UNDERSHAFT: *(Who has pricked up his ears at the peer's name, and is now watching* BARBARA *curiously.)* A new creation, my dear. You have heard of Sir Horace Bodger?

BARBARA: Bodger! Do you mean the distiller? Bodger's whisky!

UNDERSHAFT: That is the man. He is one of the greatest of our public benefactors. He restored the cathedral at Hakington. They made him a baronet for that. He gave half a million to the funds of his party: they made him a baron for that.

SHIRLEY: What will they give him for the five thousand?

UNDERSHAFT: There is nothing left to give him. So the five thousand, I should think, is to save his soul.

MRS BAINES: Heaven grant it may! Oh Mr Undershaft, you have some very rich friends. Cant you help us towards the other five thousand? We are going to hold a great meeting this afternoon at the Assembly Hall in the Mile End Road. If I could only announce that one gentleman had come forward to support Lord Saxmundham, others would follow. Dont you know somebody? couldnt you? wouldnt you? *(Her eyes fill with tears.)* oh, think of those poor people, Mr Undershaft: think of how much it means to them, and how little to a great man like you.

UNDERSHAFT: *(Sardonically gallant.)* Mrs Baines: you are irresistible. I cant disappoint you; and I cant deny myself the satisfaction of making Bodger pay up. You shall have your five thousand pounds.

MRS BAINES: Thank God!

UNDERSHAFT: You dont thank me?

MRS BAINES: Oh sir, dont try to be cynical: dont be ashamed of being a good man. The Lord will bless you abundantly; and our prayers will be like a strong fortification round you all the days of your life. *(With a touch of caution.)* You will let me have the cheque to shew at the meeting, wont you? Jenny: go in and fetch a pen and ink. (JENNY *runs to the shelter door.)*

UNDERSHAFT: Do not disturb Miss Hill: I have a fountain pen. (JENNY *halts. He sits at the table and writes the cheque.* CUSINS *rises to make room for him. They all watch him silently.)*

BILL: *(Cynically, aside to* BARBARA, *his voice and accent horribly debased.)* Wot prawce selvytion nah?

BARBARA: Stop. (UNDERSHAFT *stops writing: they all turn to her in surprise.)* Mrs Baines: are you really going to take this money?

MRS BAINES: *(Astonished.)* Why not, dear?

BARBARA: Why not! Do you know what my father is? Have you forgotten that Lord Saxmundham is Bodger the whisky man? Do you remember how we implored the County Council to stop him from writing Bodger's Whisky in letters of fire against the sky; so that the poor drink-ruined creatures on the

Embankment could not wake up from their snatches of sleep without being reminded of their deadly thirst by that wicked sky sign? Do you know that the worst thing I have had to fight here is not the devil, but Bodger, Bodger, Bodger, with his whisky, his distilleries, and his tied houses? Are you going to make our shelter another tied house for him, and ask me to keep it?

BILL: Rotten dranken whisky it is too.

MRS BAINES: Dear Barbara: Lord Saxmundham has a soul to be saved like any of us. If heaven has found the way to make a good use of his money, are we to set ourselves up against the answer to our prayers?

BARBARA: I know he has a soul to be saved. Let him come down here; and I'll do my best to help him to his salvation. But he wants to send his cheque down to buy us, and go on being as wicked as ever.

UNDERSHAFT: (*With a reasonableness which* CUSINS *alone perceives to be ironical.*) My dear Barbara: alcohol is a very necessary article. It heals the sick—

BARBARA: It does nothing of the sort.

UNDERSHAFT: Well, it assists the doctor: that is perhaps a less questionable way of putting it. It makes life bearable to millions of people who could not endure their existence if they were quite sober. It enables Parliament to do things at eleven at night that no sane person would do at eleven in the morning. Is it Bodger's fault that this inestimable gift is deplorably abused by less than one per cent of the poor? (*He turns again to the table; signs the cheque; and crosses it.*)

MRS BAINES: Barbara: will there be less drinking or more if all those poor souls we are saving come tomorrow and find the doors of our shelters shut in their faces? Lord Saxmundham gives us the money to stop drinking—to take his own business from him.

CUSINS: (*Impishly.*) Pure self-sacrifice on Bodger's part, clearly! Bless dear Bodger! (BARBARA *almost breaks down as* ADOLPHUS, *too, fails her.*)

UNDERSHAFT: (*Tearing out the cheque and pocketing the book as he rises and goes past* CUSINS *to* MRS BAINES.) I also, Mrs Baines, may claim a little disinterestedness. Think of my business! think of the widows and orphans! the men and lads torn to pieces with shrapnel and poisoned with lyddite! (MRS BAINES *shrinks; but he goes on remorselessly.*) the oceans of blood, not one drop of which is shed in a really just cause! the ravaged crops! the peaceful peasants forced, women and men, to till their fields under the fire of opposing armies on pain of starvation! the bad blood of the fierce little cowards at home who egg on others to fight for the gratification of their national vanity! All this makes money for me: I am never richer, never busier than when the papers are full of it. Well, it is your work to preach peace on earth and good will to men. (MRS BAINES's *face lights up again.*) Every convert you make is a vote against war. (*Her lips move in prayer.*) Yet I give you this money to help you to hasten my own commercial ruin. (*He gives her the cheque.*)

CUSINS: (*Mounting the form in an ecstasy of mischief.*) The millennium will be inaugurated by the unselfishness of Undershaft and Bodger. Oh be joyful! (*He takes the drumsticks from his pocket and flourishes them.*)

MRS BAINES: (*Taking the cheque.*) The longer I live the more proof I see that there is an Infinite Goodness that turns everything to the work of salvation sooner or later. Who would have thought that any good could have come out of war and drink? And yet their profits are brought today to the feet of salvation to do its blessed work. (*She is affected to tears.*)

JENNY: (*Running to* MRS BAINES *and throwing her arms round her.*) Oh dear! how blessed, how glorious it all is!

CUSINS: (*In a convulsion of irony.*) Let us seize this unspeakable moment. Let us march to the great meeting at once. Excuse me just an instant. (*He rushes into the shelter.* JENNY *takes her tambourine from the drum head.*)

MRS BAINES: Mr Undershaft: have you ever seen a thousand people fall on their knees with one impulse and pray? Come with us to the meeting. Barbara shall tell them that the Army is saved, and saved through you.

CUSINS: (*Returning impetuously from the shelter with a flag and a trombone, and coming between* MRS BAINES *and* UNDERSHAFT.) You shall carry the flag down the first street, Mrs Baines (*He gives her the flag.*) Mr Undershaft is a gifted trombonist: he shall intone an Olympian diapason to the West Ham Salvation March. (*Aside to* UNDERSHAFT, *as he forces the trombone on him.*) Blow, Machiavelli, blow.

UNDERSHAFT: (*Aside to him, as he takes the trombone.*) The trumpet in Zion! (CUSINS *rushes to the drum, which he takes up and puts on.* UNDERSHAFT *continues, aloud.*) I will do my best. I could vamp a bass if I knew the tune.

CUSINS: It is a wedding chorus from one of Donizetti's operas; but we have converted it. We convert everything to good here, including Bodger. You remember the chorus. 'For thee immense rejoicing—immenso giubilo—immenso giubilo.' (*With drum obbligato.*) Rum tum ti tum tum, tum tum ti ta—

BARBARA: Dolly: you are breaking my heart.

CUSINS: What is a broken heart more or less here? Dionysos Undershaft has descended. I am possessed.

MRS BAINES: Come, Barbara: I must have my dear Major to carry the flag with me.

JENNY: Yes, yes, Major darling.

(CUSINS *snatches the tambourine out of* JENNY's *hand and mutely offers it to* BARBARA.)

BARBARA: (*Coming forward a little as she puts the offer behind her with a shudder, whilst* CUSINS *recklessly tosses the tambourine back to* JENNY *and goes to the gate.*) I cant come.

JENNY: Not come!

MRS BAINES: (*With tears in her eyes.*) Barbara: do you think I am wrong to take the money?

BARBARA: (*Impulsively going to her and kissing her.*) No, no: God help you, dear, you must: you are saving the Army. Go; and may you have a great meeting!

JENNY: But arnt you coming?

BARBARA: No. (*She begins taking off the silver S brooch from her collar.*)

MRS BAINES: Barbara: what are you doing?

JENNY: Why are you taking your badge off? You cant be going to leave us, Major.

BARBARA: (*Quietly.*) Father: come here.

UNDERSHAFT: (*Coming to her.*) My dear! (*Seeing that she is going to pin the badge on his collar, he retreats to the penthouse in some alarm.*)

BARBARA: (*Following him.*) Dont be frightened. (*She pins the badge on and steps back towards the table, shewing him to the others.*) There! It's not much for £5000, is it?

MRS BAINES: Barbara: if you wont come and pray with us, promise me you will pray for us.

BARBARA: I cant pray now. Perhaps I shall never pray again.

MRS BAINES: Barbara!

JENNY: Major!

1210 BARBARA: *(Almost delirious.)* I cant bear any more. Quick march!

CUSINS: *(Calling to the procession in the street outside.)* Off we go. Play up, there! Immenso giubilo. *(He gives the time with his drum; and the band strikes up the march, which rapidly* 1215 *becomes more distant as the procession moves briskly away.)*

MRS BAINES: I must go, dear. Youre overworked: you will be all right tomorrow. We'll never lose you. Now Jenny: step out with the old flag. Blood and Fire! *(She marches out through the gate with her flag.)*

1220 JENNY: Glory Hallelujah! *(Flourishing her tambourine and marching.)*

UNDERSHAFT: *(To CUSINS, as he marches out past him easing the slide of his trombone.)* 'My ducats and my daughter'!

CUSINS: *(Following him out.)* Money and gunpowder!

1225 BARBARA: Drunkenness and Murder! My God: why hast thou forsaken me?

(She sinks on the form with her face buried in her hands. The march passes away into silence. BILL WALKER *steals across to her.)*

BILL: *(Taunting.)* Wot prawce selvytion nah?

SHIRLEY: Dont you hit her when she's down.

BILL: She itt me wen aw wiz dahn. Waw shouldnt Aw git a bit 1230 o me aown beck?

BARBARA: *(Raising her head.)* I didnt take your money, Bill. *(She crosses the yard to the gate and turns her back on the two men to hide her face from them.)*

BILL: *(Sneering after her.)* Naow, it warnt enaff for you. *(Turn-* 1235 *ing to the drum, he misses the money.)* Ellow! If you aint took it sammun else ez. Weres it gorn? Bly me if Jenny Ill didnt tike it after all!

RUMMY: *(Screaming at him from the loft.)* You lie, you dirty blackguard! Snobby Price pinched it off the drum when he 1240 took up his cap. I was up here all the time an see im do it.

BILL: Wot! Stowl maw manney! Waw didnt you call thief on him, you silly aold macker you?

RUMMY: To serve you aht for ittin me acrost the fice. It's cost y'pahnd, that az. *(Raising a pæan of squalid triumph.)* 1245 I done you. I'm even with you. Uve ad it aht o y—(BILL *snatches up* SHIRLEY's *mug and hurls it at her. She slams the loft door and vanishes. The mug smashes against the door and falls in fragments.)*

BILL: *(Beginning to chuckle.)* Tell us, aol menn, wot o'clock 1250 this mawnin was it wen im as they call Snobby Prawce was sived?

BARBARA: *(Turning to him more composedly, and with un-spoiled sweetness.)* About half past twelve, Bill. And he pinched your pound at a quarter to two. *I* know. Well, you 1255 cant afford to lose it. I'll send it to you.

BILL: *(His voice and accent suddenly improving.)* Not if Aw wiz to stawve for it. Aw aint to be bought.

SHIRLEY: Aint you? Youd sell yourself to the devil for a pint o beer; only there aint no devil to make the offer.

1260 BILL: *(Unashamed.)* Sao Aw would, mite, and often ev, cheer-ful. But she cawnt baw me. *(Approaching* BARBARA.*)* You wanted maw saoul, did you? Well, you aint got it.

BARBARA: I nearly got it, Bill. But weve sold it back to you for ten thousand pounds.

SHIRLEY: And dear at the money!   1265

BARBARA: No, Peter: it was worth more than money.

BILL: *(Salvationproof.)* It's nao good: you cawnt get rahnd me nah. Aw downt blieve in it; and Awve seen tody that Aw was rawt. *(Going.)* Sao long, aol soupkitchener! Ta, ta, Mijor Earl's Grendorter! *(Turning at the gate.)* Wot prawce selvy-   1270 tion nah? Snobby Prawce! Ha! ha!

BARBARA: *(Offering her hand.)* Goodbye, Bill.

BILL: *(Taken aback, half plucks his cap off; then shoves it on again defiantly.)* Git aht. (BARBARA *drops her hand, discour-aged. He has a twinge of remorse.)* But thets aw rawt, you   1275 knaow. Nathink pasnl. Naow mellice. Sao long, Judy. *(He goes.)*

BARBARA: No malice. So long, Bill.

SHIRLEY: *(Shaking his head.)* You make too much of him, miss, in your innocence.   1280

BARBARA: *(Going to him.)* Peter: I'm like you now. Cleaned out, and lost my job.

SHIRLEY: Youve youth an hope. Thats two better than me.

BARBARA: I'll get you a job, Peter. Thats hope for you: the youth will have to be enough for me. *(She counts her*   1285 *money.)* I have just enough left for two teas at Lockharts, a Rowton doss for you, and my tram and bus home. *(He frowns and rises with offended pride. She takes his arm.)* Dont be proud, Peter: it's sharing between friends. And promise me youll talk to me and not let me cry. *(She draws him towards*   1290 *the gate.)*

SHIRLEY: Well, I'm not accustomed to talk to the like of you—

BARBARA: *(Urgently.)* Yes, yes: you must talk to me. Tell me about Tom Paine's books and Bradlaugh's lectures. Come along.   1295

SHIRLEY: Ah, if you would only read Tom Paine in the proper spirit, miss! *(They go out through the gate together.)*

— ACT THREE —

Next day after lunch LADY BRITOMART *is writing in the library in Wilton Crescent.* SARAH *is reading in the armchair near the window.* BARBARA, *in ordinary fashionable dress, pale and brooding, is on the settee.* CHARLES LOMAX *enters. He starts on seeing* BARBARA *fashionably attired and in low spirits.*

LOMAX: Youve left off your uniform!

(BARBARA says nothing; but an expression of pain passes over her face.)

LADY BRITOMART: *(Warning him in low tones to be careful.)* Charles!

LOMAX: *(Much concerned, coming behind the settee and bend-ing sympathetically over* BARBARA.) I'm awfully sorry, Bar-   5 bara. You know I helped you all I could with the concertina and so forth. *(Momentously.)* Still, I have never shut my eyes to the fact that there is a certain amount of tosh about the Salvation Army. Now the claims of the Church of England—   10

LADY BRITOMART: Thats enough, Charles. Speak of something suited to your mental capacity.

LOMAX: But surely the Church of England is suited to all our capacities.

15 BARBARA: *(Pressing his hand.)* Thank you for your sympathy, Cholly. Now go and spoon with Sarah.

LOMAX: *(Dragging a chair from the writing table and seating himself affectionately by* SARAH's *side.)* How is my ownest today?

20 SARAH: I wish you wouldnt tell Cholly to do things, Barbara. He always comes straight and does them. Cholly: we're going to the works this afternoon.

LOMAX: What works?

SARAH: The cannon works.

25 LOMAX: What? your governor's shop!

SARAH: Yes.

LOMAX: Oh I say!

(CUSINS enters in poor condition. He also starts visibly when he sees BARBARA *without her uniform.)*

BARBARA: I expected you this morning, Dolly. Didnt you guess that?

30 CUSINS: *(Sitting down beside her.)* I'm sorry. I have only just breakfasted.

SARAH: But weve just finished lunch.

BARBARA: Have you had one of your bad nights?

CUSINS: No: I had rather a good night: in fact, one of the most

35 remarkable nights I have ever passed.

BARBARA: The meeting?

CUSINS: No: after the meeting.

LADY BRITOMART: You should have gone to bed after the meeting. What were you doing?

40 CUSINS: Drinking.

LADY BRITOMART: ⎫ Adolphus!
SARAH: ⎬ Dolly!
BARBARA: ⎭ Dolly!
LOMAX: Oh I say!

45 LADY BRITOMART: What were you drinking, may I ask?

CUSINS: A most devilish kind of Spanish burgundy, warranted free from added alcohol: a Temperance burgundy in fact. Its richness in natural alcohol made any addition superfluous.

BARBARA: Are you joking, Dolly?

50 CUSINS: *(Patiently.)* No. I have been making a night of it with the nominal head of this household: that is all.

LADY BRITOMART: Andrew made you drunk!

CUSINS: No: he only provided the wine. I think it was Dionysos who made me drunk. *(To* BARBARA.*)* I told you I

55 was possessed.

LADY BRITOMART: Youre not sober yet. Go home to bed at once.

CUSINS: I have never before ventured to reproach you, Lady Brit; but how could you marry the Prince of Darkness?

60 LADY BRITOMART: It was much more excusable to marry him than to get drunk with him. That is a new accomplishment of Andrew's, by the way. He usent to drink.

CUSINS: He doesnt now. He only sat there and completed the wreck of my moral basis, the rout of my convictions, the pur-

65 chase of my soul. He cares for you, Barbara. That is what makes him so dangerous to me.

BARBARA: That has nothing to do with it, Dolly. There are larger loves and diviner dreams than the fireside ones. You know that, dont you?

70 CUSINS: Yes: that is our understanding. I know it. I hold to it. Unless he can win me on that holier ground he may amuse me for a while; but he can get no deeper hold, strong as he is.

BARBARA: Keep to that; and the end will be right. Now tell me what happened at the meeting?

75 CUSINS: It was an amazing meeting. Mrs Baines almost died of emotion. Jenny Hill simply gibbered with hysteria. The Prince of Darkness played his trombone like a madman: its brazen roarings were like the laughter of the damned. 117 conversions took place then and there. They prayed with the

80 most touching sincerity and gratitude for Bodger, and for the anonymous donor of the £5000. Your father would not let his name be given.

LOMAX: That was rather fine of the old man, you know. Most chaps would have wanted the advertisement.

85 CUSINS: He said all the charitable institutions would be down on him like kites on a battle-field if he gave his name.

LADY BRITOMART: Thats Andrew all over. He never does a proper thing without giving an improper reason for it.

CUSINS: He convinced me that I have all my life been doing

90 improper things for proper reasons.

LADY BRITOMART: Adolphus: now that Barbara has left the Salvation Army, you had better leave it too. I will not have you playing that drum in the streets.

CUSINS: Your orders are already obeyed, Lady Brit.

95 BARBARA: Dolly: were you ever really in earnest about it? Would you have joined if you had never seen me?

CUSINS: *(Disingenuously.)* Well—er—well, possibly, as a collector of religions—

LOMAX: *(Cunningly.)* Not as a drummer, though, you know.

100 You are a very clearheaded brainy chap, Dolly; and it must have been apparent to you that there is a certain amount of tosh about—

LADY BRITOMART: Charles: if you must drivel, drivel like a grown-up man and not like a schoolboy.

105 LOMAX: *(Out of countenance.)* Well, drivel is drivel, dont you know, whatever a man's age.

LADY BRITOMART: In good society in England, Charles, men drivel at all ages by repeating silly formulas with an air of wisdom. Schoolboys make their own formulas out of slang, like

110 you. When they reach your age, and get political private secretaryships and things of that sort, they drop slang and get their formulas out of the Spectator or The Times. You had better confine yourself to The Times. You will find that there is a certain amount of tosh about The Times; but at least its

115 language is reputable.

LOMAX: *(Overwhelmed.)* You are so awfully strong-minded, Lady Brit—

LADY BRITOMART: Rubbish! *(MORRISON comes in.)* What is it?

MORRISON: If you please, my lady, Mr Undershaft has just

120 drove up to the door.

LADY BRITOMART: Well, let him in. *(MORRISON hesitates.)* Whats the matter with you?

MORRISON: Shall I announce him, my lady; or is he at home here, so to speak, my lady?

125 LADY BRITOMART: Announce him.

MORRISON: Thank you, my lady. You wont mind my asking, I hope. The occasion is in a manner of speaking new to me.

LADY BRITOMART: Quite right. Go and let him in.

MORRISON: Thank you, my lady. *(He withdraws.)*

130 LADY BRITOMART: Children: go and get ready. *(SARAH and* BARBARA *go upstairs for their out-of-door wraps.)* Charles: go and tell Stephen to come down here in five minutes: you will find him in the drawing room. *(CHARLES goes.)* Adolphus:

tell them to send round the carriage in about fifteen min-
135 utes. (ADOLPHUS *goes*.)

MORRISON: *(At the door.)* Mr Undershaft.

(UNDERSHAFT *comes in*. MORRISON *goes out*.)

UNDERSHAFT: Alone! How fortunate!

LADY BRITOMART: *(Rising.)* Dont be sentimental, Andrew. Sit
down. *(She sits on the settee: he sits beside her, on her left. She*
140 *comes to the point before he has time to breathe.)* Sarah must
have £800 a year until Charles Lomax comes into his property. Barbara will need more, and need it permanently, because Adolphus hasnt any property.

UNDERSHAFT: *(Resignedly.)* Yes, my dear: I will see to it. Any-
145 thing else? for yourself, for instance?

LADY BRITOMART: I want to talk to you about Stephen.

UNDERSHAFT: *(Rather wearily.)* Dont, my dear. Stephen
doesnt interest me.

LADY BRITOMART: He does interest me. He is our son.

150 UNDERSHAFT: Do you really think so? He has induced us to
bring him into the world; but he chose his parents very in-
congruously, I think. I see nothing of myself in him, and less
of you.

LADY BRITOMART: Andrew: Stephen is an excellent son, and a
155 most steady, capable, highminded young man. You are simply trying to find an excuse for disinheriting him.

UNDERSHAFT: My dear Biddy: the Undershaft tradition disin-
herits him. It would be dishonest of me to leave the cannon
foundry to my son.

160 LADY BRITOMART: It would be most unnatural and improper
of you to leave it to anyone else, Andrew. Do you suppose
this wicked and immoral tradition can be kept up for ever?
Do you pretend that Stephen could not carry on the foundry
just as well as all the other sons of the big business houses?

165 UNDERSHAFT: Yes: he could learn the office routine without
understanding the business, like all the other sons; and the
firm would go on by its own momentum until the real Undershaft—probably an Italian or a German—would invent a
new method and cut him out.

170 LADY BRITOMART: There is nothing that any Italian or German could do that Stephen could not do. And Stephen at
least has breeding.

UNDERSHAFT: The son of a foundling! Nonsense!

LADY BRITOMART: My son, Andrew! And even you may have
175 good blood in your veins for all you know.

UNDERSHAFT: True. Probably I have. That is another argument in favour of a foundling.

LADY BRITOMART: Andrew: dont be aggravating. And dont be
wicked. At present you are both.

180 UNDERSHAFT: This conversation is part of the Undershaft tradition, Biddy. Every Undershaft's wife has treated him to it
ever since the house was founded. It is mere waste of breath.
If the tradition be ever broken it will be for an abler man
than Stephen.

185 LADY BRITOMART: *(Pouting.)* Then go away.

UNDERSHAFT: *(Deprecatory.)* Go away!

LADY BRITOMART: Yes: go away. If you will do nothing for
Stephen, you are not wanted here. Go to your foundling,
whoever he is; and look after him.

190 UNDERSHAFT: The fact is, Biddy—

LADY BRITOMART: Dont call me Biddy. I dont call you Andy.

UNDERSHAFT: I will not call my wife Britomart: it is not good
sense. Seriously, my love, the Undershaft tradition has landed
me in a difficulty. I am getting on in years; and my partner
Lazarus has at last made a stand and insisted that the succes- 195
sion must be settled one way or the other; and of course he is
quite right. You see, I havent found a fit successor yet.

LADY BRITOMART: *(Obstinately.)* There is Stephen.

UNDERSHAFT: Thats just it: all the foundlings I can find are exactly like Stephen. 200

LADY BRITOMART: Andrew!!

UNDERSHAFT: I want a man with no relations and no schooling: that is, a man who would be out of the running altogether if he were not a strong man. And I cant find him.
Every blessed foundling nowadays is snapped up in his in- 205
fancy by Barnardo homes, or School Board officers, or
Boards of Guardians; and if he shews the least ability he is
fastened on by schoolmasters; trained to win scholarships
like a racehorse; crammed with secondhand ideas; drilled
and disciplined in docility and what they call good taste; and 210
lamed for life so that he is fit for nothing but teaching. If you
want to keep the foundry in the family, you had better find
an eligible foundling and marry him to Barbara.

LADY BRITOMART: Ah! Barbara! Your pet! You would sacrifice
Stephen to Barbara. 215

UNDERSHAFT: Cheerfully. And you, my dear, would boil Barbara to make soup for Stephen.

LADY BRITOMART: Andrew: this is not a question of our likings
and dislikings: it is a question of duty. It is your duty to make
Stephen your successor. 220

UNDERSHAFT: Just as much as it is your duty to submit to your
husband. Come, Biddy! these tricks of the governing class
are of no use with me. I am one of the governing class myself; and it is waste of time giving tracts to a missionary. I
have the power in this matter; and I am not to be hum- 225
bugged into using it for your purposes.

LADY BRITOMART: Andrew: you can talk my head off; but you
cant change wrong into right. And your tie is all on one side.
Put it straight.

UNDERSHAFT: *(Disconcerted.)* It wont stay unless it's pinned 230
(He fumbles at it with childish grimaces.)—

(STEPHEN *comes in*.)

STEPHEN: *(At the door.)* I beg your pardon *(About to retire.)*

LADY BRITOMART: No: come in, Stephen. (STEPHEN *comes forward to his mother's writing table.*)

UNDERSHAFT: *(Not very cordially.)* Good afternoon. 235

STEPHEN: *(Coldly.)* Good afternoon.

UNDERSHAFT: *(To* LADY BRITOMART.*)* He knows all about the
tradition, I suppose?

LADY BRITOMART: Yes. *(To* STEPHEN.*)* It is what I told you last
night, Stephen. 240

UNDERSHAFT: *(Sulkily.)* I understand you want to come into
the cannon business.

STEPHEN: I go into trade! Certainly not.

UNDERSHAFT: *(Opening his eyes, greatly eased in mind and
manner.)* Oh! in that case— 245

LADY BRITOMART: Cannons are not trade, Stephen. They are
enterprise.

STEPHEN: I have no intention of becoming a man of business
in any sense. I have no capacity for business and no taste for
it. I intend to devote myself to politics. 250

UNDERSHAFT: *(Rising.)* My dear boy: this is an immense relief
to me. And I trust it may prove an equally good thing for the
country. I was afraid you would consider yourself disparaged

and slighted. *(He moves towards* STEPHEN *as if to shake*
255 *hands with him.)*

LADY BRITOMART: *(Rising and interposing.)* Stephen: I cannot
allow you to throw away an enormous property like this.

STEPHEN: *(Stiffly.)* Mother: there must be an end of treating
me as a child, if you please. (LADY BRITOMART *recoils, deeply*
260 *wounded by his tone.)* Until last night I did not take your attitude seriously, because I did not think you meant it seriously.
But I find now that you left me in the dark as to matters
which you should have explained to me years ago. I am extremely hurt and offended. Any further discussion of my in-
265 tentions had better take place with my father, as between
one man and another.

LADY BRITOMART: Stephen! *(She sits down again, her eyes filling with tears.)*

UNDERSHAFT: *(With grave compassion.)* You see, my dear, it is
270 only the big men who can be treated as children.

STEPHEN: I am sorry, mother, that you have forced me—

UNDERSHAFT: *(Stopping him.)* Yes, yes, yes, yes: thats all right,
Stephen. She wont interfere with you any more: your independence is achieved: you have won your latchkey. Dont
275 rub it in; and above all, dont apologize. *(He resumes his
seat.)* Now what about your future, as between one man and
another—I beg your pardon, Biddy: as between two men
and a woman.

LADY BRITOMART: *(Who has pulled herself together strongly.)*
280 I quite understand, Stephen. By all means go your own way
if you feel strong enough. (STEPHEN *sits down magisterially
in the chair at the writing table with an air of affirming his
majority.)*

UNDERSHAFT: It is settled that you do not ask for the succes-
285 sion to the cannon business.

STEPHEN: I hope it is settled that I repudiate the cannon
business.

UNDERSHAFT: Come, come! dont be so devilishly sulky: it's
boyish. Freedom should be generous. Besides, I owe you a
290 fair start in life in exchange for disinheriting you. You cant
become prime minister all at once. Havnt you a turn for
something? What about literature, art, and so forth?

STEPHEN: I have nothing of the artist about me, either in faculty or character, thank Heaven!

295 UNDERSHAFT: A philosopher, perhaps? Eh?

STEPHEN: I make no such ridiculous pretension.

UNDERSHAFT: Just so. Well, there is the army, the navy, the
Church, the Bar. The Bar requires some ability. What about
the Bar?

300 STEPHEN: I have not studied law. And I am afraid I have not
the necessary push—I believe that is the name barristers give
to their vulgarity—for success in pleading.

UNDERSHAFT: Rather a difficult case, Stephen. Hardly anything left but the stage, is there? (STEPHEN *makes an impa-
305 tient movement.)* Well, come! is there anything you know or
care for?

STEPHEN: *(Rising and looking at him steadily.)* I know the difference between right and wrong.

UNDERSHAFT: *(Hugely tickled.)* You dont say so! What! no ca-
310 pacity for business, no knowledge of law, no sympathy with
art, no pretension to philosophy; only a simple knowledge of
the secret that has puzzled all the philosophers, baffled all
the lawyers, muddled all the men of business, and ruined
most of the artists: the secret of right and wrong. Why, man,
315 youre a genius, a master of masters, a god! At twentyfour, too!

STEPHEN: *(Keeping his temper with difficulty.)* You are pleased
to be facetious. I pretend to nothing more than any honorable English gentleman claims as his birthright *(He sits
down angrily.)*

UNDERSHAFT: Oh, thats everybody's birthright. Look at poor   320
little Jenny Hill, the Salvation lassie! she would think you
were laughing at her if you asked her to stand up in the street
and teach grammar or geography or mathematics or even
drawing room dancing; but it never occurs to her to doubt
that she can teach morals and religion. You are all alike, you   325
respectable people. You cant tell me the bursting strain of a
ten-inch gun, which is a very simple matter; but you all
think you can tell me the bursting strain of a man under
temptation. You darent handle high explosives; but youre all
ready to handle honesty and truth and justice and the whole   330
duty of man, and kill one another at that game. What a
country! What a world!

LADY BRITOMART: *(Uneasily.)* What do you think he had better do, Andrew?

UNDERSHAFT: Oh, just what he wants to do. He knows noth-   335
ing and he thinks he knows everything. That points clearly to
a political career. Get him a private secretaryship to someone who can get him an Under Secretaryship; and then
leave him alone. He will find his natural and proper place in
the end on the Treasury Bench.   340

STEPHEN: *(Springing up again.)* I am sorry, sir, that you force
me to forget the respect due to you as my father. I am an
Englishman and I will not hear the Government of my
country insulted. *(He thrusts his hands in his pockets, and
walks angrily across to the window.)*   345

UNDERSHAFT: *(With a touch of brutality.)* The government of
your country! I am the government of your country: I, and
Lazarus. Do you suppose that you and half a dozen amateurs
like you, sitting in a row in that foolish gabble shop, can govern Undershaft and Lazarus? No, my friend: you will do   350
what pays us. You will make war when it suits us, and keep
peace when it doesnt. You will find out that trade requires
certain measures when we have decided on those measures.
When I want anything to keep my dividends up, you will discover that my want is a national need. When other people   355
want something to keep my dividends down, you will call out
the police and military. And in return you shall have the support and applause of my newspapers, and the delight of
imagining that you are a great statesman. Government of
your country! Be off with you, my boy, and play with your   360
caucuses and leading articles and historic parties and great
leaders and burning questions and the rest of your toys. *I* am
going back to my counting-house to pay the piper and call
the tune.

STEPHEN: *(Actually smiling, and putting his hand on his fa-   365
ther's shoulder with indulgent patronage.)* Really, my dear father, it is impossible to be angry with you. You dont know
how absurd all this sounds to me. You are very properly
proud of having been industrious enough to make money;
and it is greatly to your credit that you have made so much of   370
it. But it has kept you in circles where you are valued for your
money and deferred to for it, instead of in the doubtless very
old-fashioned and behind-the-times public school and university where I formed my habits of mind. It is natural for
you to think that money governs England; but you must   375
allow me to think I know better.

UNDERSHAFT: And what does govern England, pray?

STEPHEN: Character, father, character.

UNDERSHAFT: Whose character? Yours or mine?

380 STEPHEN: Neither yours nor mine, father, but the best elements in the English national character.

UNDERSHAFT: Stephen: Ive found your profession for you. Youre a born journalist. I'll start you with a high-toned weekly review. There!

(Before STEPHEN *can reply,* SARAH, BARBARA, LOMAX, *and* CUSINS *come in ready for walking.* BARBARA *crosses the room to the window and looks out.* CUSINS *drifts amiably to the armchair.* LOMAX *remains near the door, whilst* SARAH *comes to her mother.)*

*(*STEPHEN *goes to the smaller writing table and busies himself with his letters.)*

385 SARAH: Go and get ready, mamma: the carriage is waiting.
    *(*LADY BRITOMART *leaves the room.)*

UNDERSHAFT: *(To* SARAH.*)* Good day, my dear. Good afternoon, Mr Lomax.

LOMAX: *(Vaguely.)* Ahdedoo.

390 UNDERSHAFT: *(To* CUSINS.*)* Quite well after last night, Euripides, eh?

CUSINS: As well as can be expected.

UNDERSHAFT: Thats right. *(To* BARBARA.*)* So you are coming to see my death and devastation factory, Barbara?

395 BARBARA: *(At the window.)* You came yesterday to see my salvation factory. I promised you a return visit.

LOMAX: *(Coming forward between* SARAH *and* UNDERSHAFT.*)* Youll find it awfully interesting. Ive been through the Woolwich Arsenal; and it gives you a ripping feeling of security, you know, to think of the lot of beggars we could kill if it came to fighting. *(To* UNDERSHAFT, *with sudden solemnity.)* Still, it must be rather an awful reflection for you, from the religious point of view as it were. Youre getting on, you know, and all that.

405 SARAH: You dont mind Cholly's imbecility, papa, do you?

LOMAX: *(Much taken aback.)* Oh I say!

UNDERSHAFT: Mr Lomax looks at the matter in a very proper spirit, my dear.

LOMAX: Just so. Thats all I meant, I assure you.

410 SARAH: Are you coming, Stephen?

STEPHEN: Well, I am rather busy—er—*(Magnanimously.)* Oh well, yes: I'll come. That is, if there is room for me.

UNDERSHAFT: I can take two with me in a little motor I am experimenting with for field use. You wont mind its being
415 rather unfashionable. It's not painted yet; but it's bullet proof.

LOMAX: *(Appalled at the prospect of confronting Wilton Crescent in an unpainted motor.)* Oh I say!

SARAH: The carriage for me, thank you. Barbara doesnt mind
420 what she's seen in.

LOMAX: I say, Dolly, old chap: do you really mind the car being a guy? Because of course if you do I'll go in it. Still—

CUSINS: I prefer it.

LOMAX: Thanks awfully, old man. Come, my ownest. *(He hurries
425 out to secure his seat in the carriage.* SARAH *follows him.)*

CUSINS: *(Moodily walking across to* LADY BRITOMART's *writing table.)* Why are we two coming to this Works Department of Hell? that is what I ask myself.

BARBARA: I have always thought of it as a sort of pit where lost creatures with blackened faces stirred up smoky fires and
430 were driven and tormented by my father? Is it like that, dad?

UNDERSHAFT: *(Scandalized.)* My dear! It is a spotlessly clean and beautiful hillside town.

CUSINS: With a Methodist chapel? Oh do say theres a Methodist chapel?
435

UNDERSHAFT: There are two: a Primitive one and a sophisticated one. There is even an Ethical Society; but it is not much patronized, as my men are all strongly religious. In the High Explosives Sheds they object to the presence of Agnostics as unsafe.
440

CUSINS: And yet they dont object to you!

BARBARA: Do they obey all your orders?

UNDERSHAFT: I never give them any orders. When I speak to one of them it is 'Well, Jones, is the baby doing well? and has Mrs Jones made a good recovery?' 'Nicely, thank you, sir.'
445 And thats all.

CUSINS: But Jones has to be kept in order. How do you maintain discipline among your men?

UNDERSHAFT: I dont. They do. You see, the one thing Jones wont stand is any rebellion from the man under him, or any
450 assertion of social equality between the wife of the man with 4 shillings a week less than himself, and Mrs Jones! Of course they all rebel against me, theoretically. Practically, every man of them keeps the man just below him in his place. I never meddle with them. I never bully them. I dont
455 even bully Lazarus. I say that certain things are to be done; but I dont order anybody to do them. I dont say, mind you, that there is no ordering about and snubbing and even bullying. The men snub the boys and order them about; the carmen snub the sweepers; the artisans snub the unskilled
460 laborers; the foremen drive and bully both the laborers and artisans; the assistant engineers find fault with the foremen; the chief engineers drop on the assistants; the departmental managers worry the chiefs; and the clerks have tall hats and hymnbooks and keep up the social tone by refusing to asso-
465 ciate on equal terms with anybody. The result is a colossal profit, which comes to me.

CUSINS: *(Revolted.)* You really are a—well, what I was saying yesterday.

BARBARA: What was he saying yesterday?
470

UNDERSHAFT: Never mind, my dear. He thinks I have made you unhappy. Have I?

BARBARA: Do you think I can be happy in this vulgar silly dress? I! who have worn the uniform. Do you understand what you have done to me? Yesterday I had a man's soul in
475 my hand. I set him in the way of life with his face to salvation. But when we took your money he turned back to drunkenness and derision. *(With intense conviction.)* I will never forgive you that. If I had a child, and you destroyed its body with your explosives—if you murdered Dolly with your
480 horrible guns—I could forgive you if my forgiveness would open the gates of heaven to you. But to take a human soul from me, and turn it into the soul of a wolf! that is worse than any murder.

UNDERSHAFT: Does my daughter despair so easily? Can you
485 strike a man to the heart and leave no mark on him?

BARBARA: *(Her face lighting up.)* Oh, you are right: he can never be lost now: where was my faith?

CUSINS: Oh, clever clever devil!

490 BARBARA: You may be a devil; but God speaks through you sometimes. (*She takes her father's hands and kisses them.*) You have given me back my happiness: I feel it deep down now, though my spirit is troubled.

UNDERSHAFT: You have learnt something. That always feels at 495 first as if you had lost something.

BARBARA: Well, take me to the factory of death; and let me learn something more. There must be some truth or other behind all this frightful irony. Come, Dolly. (*She goes out.*)

CUSINS: My guardian angel! (*To* UNDERSHAFT.) Avaunt! (*He* 500 follows BARBARA.)

STEPHEN: (*Quietly, at the writing table.*) You must not mind Cusins, father. He is a very amiable good fellow; but he is a Greek scholar and naturally a little eccentric.

UNDERSHAFT: Ah, quite so. Thank you, Stephen. Thank you. 505 (*He goes out.*)

(STEPHEN *smiles patronizingly; buttons his coat responsibly; and crosses the room to the door.* LADY BRITOMART, *dressed for out-of-doors, opens it before he reaches it. She looks round for others; looks at* STEPHEN; *and turns to go without a word.*)

STEPHEN: (*Embarrassed.*) Mother—

LADY BRITOMART: Dont be apologetic, Stephen. And dont forget that you have outgrown your mother. (*She goes out.*)

(*Perivale St Andrews lies between two Middlesex hills, half climbing the northern one. It is an almost smokeless town of white walls, roofs of narrow green slates or red tiles, tall trees, domes, campaniles, and slender chimney shafts, beautifully situated and beautiful in itself. The best view of it is obtained from the crest of a slope about half a mile to the east, where the high explosives are dealt with. The foundry lies hidden in the depths between, the tops of its chimneys sprouting like huge skittles into the middle distance. Across the crest runs an emplacement of concrete, with a firestep, and a parapet which suggests a fortification, because there is a huge cannon of the obsolete* Woolwich Infant *pattern peering across it at the town. The cannon is mounted on an experimental gun carriage: possibly the original model of the Undershaft disappearing rampart gun alluded to by* STEPHEN. *The firestep, being a convenient place to sit, is furnished here and there with straw disc cushions; and at one place there is the additional luxury of a fur rug.*

BARBARA *is standing on the firestep, looking over the parapet towards the town. On her right is the cannon; on her left the end of a shed raised on piles, with a ladder of three or four steps up to the door, which opens outwards and has a little wooden landing at the threshold, with a fire bucket in the corner of the landing. Several dummy soldiers more or less mutilated, with straw protruding from their gashes, have been shoved out of the way under the landing. A few others are nearly upright against the shed; and one has fallen forward and lies, like a grotesque corpse, on the emplacement. The parapet stops short of the shed, leaving a gap which is the beginning of the path down the hill through the foundry to the town. The rug is on the firestep near this gap. Down on the emplacement behind the cannon is a trolley carrying a huge conical bombshell with a red band painted on it. Further to the right is the door of an office, which, like the sheds, is of the lightest possible construction.*

CUSINS *arrives by the path from the town.*)

BARBARA: Well?

CUSINS: Not a ray of hope. Everything perfect! wonderful! 510 real! It only needs a cathedral to be a heavenly city instead of a hellish one.

BARBARA: Have you found out whether they have done anything for old Peter Shirley?

CUSINS: They have found him a job as gatekeeper and time- 515 keeper. He's frightfully miserable. He calls the time-keeping brainwork, and says he isnt used to it; and his gate lodge is so splendid that he's ashamed to use the rooms, and skulks in the scullery.

BARBARA: Poor Peter! 520

(STEPHEN *arrives from the town. He carries a fieldglass.*)

STEPHEN: (*Enthusiastically.*) Have you two seen the place? Why did you leave us?

CUSINS: I wanted to see everything I was not intended to see; and Barbara wanted to make the men talk.

STEPHEN: Have you found anything discreditable? 525

CUSINS: No. They call him Dandy Andy and are proud of his being a cunning old rascal; but it's all horribly, frightfully, immorally, unanswerably perfect.

(SARAH *arrives.*)

SARAH: Heavens! what a place! (*She crosses to the trolley.*) Did you see the nursing home!? (*She sits down on the shell.*) 530

STEPHEN: Did you see the libraries and schools!?

SARAH: Did you see the ball room and the banqueting chamber in the Town Hall!?

STEPHEN: Have you gone into the insurance fund, the pension fund, the building society, the various applications of 535 cooperation!?

(UNDERSHAFT *comes from the office, with a sheaf of telegrams in his hand.*)

UNDERSHAFT: Well, have you seen everything? I'm sorry I was called away. (*Indicating the telegrams.*) Good news from Manchuria.

STEPHEN: Another Japanese victory? 540

UNDERSHAFT: Oh, I dont know. Which side wins does not concern us here. No: the good news is that the aerial battleship is a tremendous success. At the first trial it has wiped out a fort with three hundred soldiers in it.

CUSINS: (*From the platform.*) Dummy soldiers? 545

UNDERSHAFT: (*Striding across to* STEPHEN *and kicking the prostrate dummy brutally out of his way.*) No: the real thing.

(CUSINS *and* BARBARA *exchange glances. Then* CUSINS *sits on the step and buries his face in his hands.* BARBARA *gravely lays her hand on his shoulder. He looks up at her in whimsical desperation.*)

UNDERSHAFT: Well, Stephen, what do you think of the place?

STEPHEN: Oh, magnificent. A perfect triumph of modern industry. Frankly, my dear father, I have been a fool: I had no 550 idea of what it all meant: of the wonderful forethought, the power of organization, the administrative capacity, the financial genius, the colossal capital it represents. I have been repeating to myself as I came through your streets 'Peace hath her victories no less renowned than War.' I have only one 555 misgiving about it all.

UNDERSHAFT: Out with it.

STEPHEN: Well, I cannot help thinking that all this provision for every want of your workmen may sap their independence

560 and weaken their sense of responsibility. And greatly as we enjoyed our tea at that splendid restaurant—how they gave us all that luxury and cake and jam and cream for three-pence I really cannot imagine!—still you must remember that restaurants break up home life. Look at the continent, 565 for instance! Are you sure so much pampering is really good for the men's characters?

UNDERSHAFT: Well you see, my dear boy, when you are orga-nizing civilization you have to make up your mind whether trouble and anxiety are good things or not. If you decide that 570 they are, then, I take it, you simply dont organize civiliza-tion; and there you are, with trouble and anxiety enough to make us all angels! But if you decide the other way, you may as well go through with it. However, Stephen, our characters are safe here. A sufficient dose of anxiety is always provided 575 by the fact that we may be blown to smithereens at any mo-ment.

SARAH: By the way, papa, where do you make the explosives?

UNDERSHAFT: In separate little sheds, like that one. When one of them blows up, it costs very little; and only the people 580 quite close to it are killed.

(STEPHEN, *who is quite close to it, looks at it rather scaredly, and moves away quickly to the cannon. At the same moment the door of the shed is thrown abruptly open; and a foreman in overalls and list slippers comes out on the little landing and holds the door for* LOMAX, *who appears in the doorway.*)

LOMAX: (*With studied coolness.*) My good fellow: you neednt get into a state of nerves. Nothing's going to happen to you; and I suppose it wouldnt be the end of the world if anything did. A little bit of British pluck is what you want, old chap. 585 (*He descends and strolls across to* SARAH.)

UNDERSHAFT: (*To the foreman.*) Anything wrong, Bilton?

BILTON: (*With ironic calm.*) Gentleman walked into the high explosives shed and lit a cigaret, sir: thats all.

UNDERSHAFT: Ah, quite so. (*Going over to* LOMAX.) Do you 590 happen to remember what you did with the match?

LOMAX: Oh come! I'm not a fool. I took jolly good care to blow it out before I chucked it away.

BILTON: The top of it was red hot inside, sir.

LOMAX: Well, suppose it was! I didnt chuck it into any of your 595 messes.

UNDERSHAFT: Think no more of it, Mr Lomax. By the way, would you mind lending me your matches.

LOMAX: (*Offering his box.*) Certainly.

UNDERSHAFT: Thanks. (*He pockets the matches.*)

600 LOMAX: (*Lecturing to the company generally.*) You know, these high explosives dont go off like gunpowder, except when theyre in a gun. When theyre spread loose, you can put a match to them without the least risk: they just burn quietly like a bit of paper. (*Warming to the scientific interest of the* 605 *subject.*) Did you know that, Undershaft? Have you ever tried?

UNDERSHAFT: Not on a large scale, Mr Lomax. Bilton will give you a sample of gun cotton when you are leaving if you ask him. You can experiment with it at home. (BILTON *looks* 610 *puzzled.*)

SARAH: Bilton will do nothing of the sort, papa. I suppose it's your business to blow up the Russians and Japs; but you might really stop short of blowing up poor Cholly. (BILTON *gives it up and retires into the shed.*)

LOMAX: My ownest, there is no danger. (*He sits beside her on* 615 *the shell.*)

(LADY BRITOMART *arrives from the town with a bouquet.*)

LADY BRITOMART: (*Impetuously.*) Andrew: you shouldnt have let me see this place.

UNDERSHAFT: Why, my dear?

LADY BRITOMART: Never mind why: you shouldnt have: thats 620 all. To think of all that (*Indicating the town.*) being yours! and that you have kept it to yourself all these years!

UNDERSHAFT: It does not belong to me. I belong to it. It is the Undershaft inheritance.

LADY BRITOMART: It is not. Your ridiculous cannons and that 625 noisy banging foundry may be the Undershaft inheritance; but all that plate and linen, all that furniture and those houses and orchards and gardens belong to us. They belong to me: they are not a man's business. I wont give them up. You must be out of your senses to throw them all away; and if 630 you persist in such folly, I will call in a doctor.

UNDERSHAFT: (*Stooping to smell the bouquet.*) Where did you get the flowers, my dear?

LADY BRITOMART: Your men presented them to me in your William Morris Labor Church. 635

CUSINS: Oh! It needed only that. A Labor Church! (*He mounts the firestep distractedly, and leans with his elbows on the parapet, turning his back to them.*)

LADY BRITOMART: Yes, with Morris's words in mosaic letters ten feet high round the dome. NO MAN IS GOOD ENOUGH 640 TO BE ANOTHER MAN'S MASTER. The cynicism of it!

UNDERSHAFT: It shocked the men at first, I am afraid. But now they take no more notice of it than of the ten command-ments in church.

LADY BRITOMART: Andrew: you are trying to put me off the 645 subject of the inheritance by profane jokes. Well, you shant. I dont ask it any longer for Stephen: he has inherited far too much of your perversity to be fit for it. But Barbara has rights as well as Stephen. Why should not Adolphus succeed to the inheritance? I could manage the town for him; and he can 650 look after the cannons, if they are really necessary.

UNDERSHAFT: I should ask nothing better if Adolphus were a foundling. He is exactly the sort of new blood that is wanted in English business. But he's not a foundling; and theres an end of it. (*He makes for the office door.*) 655

CUSINS: (*Turning to them.*) Not quite. (*They all turn and stare at him.*) I think—Mind! I am not committing myself in any way as to my future course—but I think the foundling diffi-culty can be got over. (*He jumps down to the emplacement.*)

UNDERSHAFT: (*Coming back to him.*) What do you mean? 660

CUSINS: Well, I have something to say which is in the nature of a confession.

SARAH:
LADY BRITOMART:
BARBARA: } Confession!
STEPHEN:

LOMAX: Oh I say!

CUSINS: Yes, a confession. Listen, all. Until I met Barbara I 665 thought myself in the main an honorable, truthful man, be-cause I wanted the approval of my conscience more than I wanted anything else. But the moment I saw Barbara, I wanted her far more than the approval of my conscience.

LADY BRITOMART: Adolphus! 670

CUSINS: It is true. You accused me yourself, Lady Brit, of joining the Army to worship Barbara; and so I did. She bought my soul like a flower at a street corner; but she bought it for herself.

675 UNDERSHAFT: What! Not for Dionysos or another?

CUSINS: Dionysos and all the others are in herself. I adored what was divine in her, and was therefore a true worshipper. But I was romantic about her too. I thought she was a woman of the people, and that a marriage with a professor of Greek

680 would be far beyond the wildest social ambitions of her rank.

LADY BRITOMART: Adolphus!!

LOMAX: Oh I say!!!

CUSINS: When I learnt the horrible truth—

LADY BRITOMART: What do you mean by the horrible truth,

685 pray?

CUSINS: That she was enormously rich; that her grandfather was an earl; that her father was the Prince of Darkness—

UNDERSHAFT: Chut!

CUSINS: —and that I was only an adventurer trying to catch a

690 rich wife, then I stooped to deceive her about my birth.

BARBARA: *(Rising.)* Dolly!

LADY BRITOMART: Your birth! Now Adolphus, dont dare to make up a wicked story for the sake of these wretched cannons. Remember: I have seen photographs of your parents;

695 and the Agent General for South Western Australia knows them personally and has assured me that they are most respectable married people.

CUSINS: So they are in Australia; but here they are outcasts. Their marriage is legal in Australia, but not in England. My

700 mother is my father's deceased wife's sister; and in this island I am consequently a foundling. *(Sensation.)*

BARBARA: Silly! *(She climbs to the cannon, and leans, listening, in the angle it makes with the parapet.)*

CUSINS: Is the subterfuge good enough, Machiavelli?

705 UNDERSHAFT: *(Thoughtfully.)* Biddy: this may be a way out of the difficulty.

LADY BRITOMART: Stuff! A man cant make cannons any the better for being his own cousin instead of his proper self *(She sits down on the rug with a bounce that expresses her down

710 right contempt for their casuistry.)*

UNDERSHAFT: *(To* CUSINS.) You are an educated man. That is against the tradition.

CUSINS: Once in ten thousand times it happens that the schoolboy is a born master of what they try to teach him.

715 Greek has not destroyed my mind: it has nourished it. Besides, I did not learn it at an English public school.

UNDERSHAFT: Hm! Well, I cannot afford to be too particular: you have cornered the foundling market. Let it pass. You are eligible, Euripides: you are eligible.

720 BARBARA: Dolly: yesterday morning, when Stephen told us all about the tradition, you became very silent; and you have been strange and excited ever since. Were you thinking of your birth then?

CUSINS: When the finger of Destiny suddenly points at a man

725 in the middle of his breakfast, it makes him thoughtful.

UNDERSHAFT: Aha! You have had your eye on the business, my young friend, have you?

CUSINS: Take care! There is an abyss of moral horror between me and your accursed aerial battleships.

730 UNDERSHAFT: Never mind the abyss for the present. Let us settle the practical details and leave your final decision open.

You know that you will have to change your name. Do you object to that?

CUSINS: Would any man named Adolphus—any man called Dolly!—object to be called something else?   735

UNDERSHAFT: Good. Now, as to money! I propose to treat you handsomely from the beginning. You shall start at a thousand a year.

CUSINS: *(With sudden heat, his spectacles twinkling with mischief.)* A thousand! You dare offer a miserable thousand to   740 the son-in-law of a millionaire! No, by Heavens, Machiavelli! you shall not cheat me. You cannot do without me; and I can do without you. I must have two thousand five hundred a year for two years. At the end of that time, if I am a failure, I go. But if I am a success, and stay on, you must   745 give me the other five thousand.

UNDERSHAFT: What other five thousand?

CUSINS: To make the two years up to five thousand a year. The two thousand five hundred is only half pay in case I should turn out a failure. The third year I must have ten per cent on   750 the profits.

UNDERSHAFT: *(Taken aback.)* Ten per cent! Why, man, do you know what my profits are?

CUSINS: Enormous, I hope: otherwise I shall require twenty-five per cent.   755

UNDERSHAFT: But, Mr Cusins, this is a serious matter of business. You are not bringing any capital into the concern.

CUSINS: What! no capital! Is my mastery of Greek no capital? Is my access to the subtlest thought, the loftiest poetry yet attained by humanity, no capital? My character! my intellect!   760 my life! my career! what Barbara calls my soul! are these no capital? Say another word; and I double my salary.

UNDERSHAFT: Be reasonable—

CUSINS: *(Peremptorily.)* Mr Undershaft: you have my terms. Take them or leave them.   765

UNDERSHAFT: *(Recovering himself.)* Very well. I note your terms; and I offer you half.

CUSINS: *(Disgusted.)* Half!

UNDERSHAFT: *(Firmly.)* Half.

CUSINS: You call yourself a gentleman; and you offer me   770 half!!

UNDERSHAFT: I do not call myself a gentleman; but I offer you half.

CUSINS: This to your future partner! your successor! your son-in-law!   775

BARBARA: You are selling your own soul, Dolly, not mine. Leave me out of the bargain, please.

UNDERSHAFT: Come! I will go a step further for Barbara's sake. I will give you three fifths; but that is my last word.

CUSINS: Done!   780

LOMAX: Done in the eye! Why, *I* get only eight hundred, you know.

CUSINS: By the way, Mac, I am a classical scholar, not an arithmetical one. Is three fifths more than half or less?

UNDERSHAFT: More, of course.   785

CUSINS: I would have taken two hundred and fifty. How you can succeed in business when you are willing to pay all that money to a University don who is obviously not worth a junior clerk's wages!—well! What will Lazarus say?

UNDERSHAFT: Lazarus is a gentle romantic Jew who cares for   790 nothing but string quartets and stalls at fashionable theatres. He will be blamed for your rapacity in money matters, poor fellow! as he has hitherto been blamed for mine. You are a

795 shark of the first order, Euripides. So much the better for the firm!

BARBARA: Is the bargain closed, Dolly? Does your soul belong to him now?

CUSINS: No: the price is settled: that is all. The real tug of war is still to come. What about the moral question?

800 LADY BRITOMART: There is no moral question in the matter at all, Adolphus. You must simply sell cannons and weapons to people whose cause is right and just, and refuse them to foreigners and criminals.

UNDERSHAFT: (*Determinedly.*) No: none of that. You must 805 keep the true faith of an Armorer, or you dont come in here.

CUSINS: What on earth is the true faith of an Armorer?

UNDERSHAFT: To give arms to all men who offer an honest price for them, without respect of persons or principles: to aristocrat and republican, to Nihilist and Tsar, to Capitalist 810 and Socialist, to Protestant and Catholic, to burglar and policeman, to black man, white man and yellow man, to all sorts and conditions, all nationalities, all faiths, all follies, all causes and all crimes. The first Undershaft wrote up in his shop IF GOD GAVE THE HAND, LET NOT MAN WITHHOLD 815 THE SWORD. The second wrote up ALL HAVE THE RIGHT TO FIGHT: NONE HAVE THE RIGHT TO JUDGE. The third wrote up TO MAN THE WEAPON: TO HEAVEN THE VICTORY. The fourth had no literary turn; so he did not write up anything; but he sold cannons to Napoleon under the nose of George 820 the Third. The fifth wrote up PEACE SHALL NOT PREVAIL SAVE WITH A SWORD IN HER HAND. The sixth, my master, was the best of all. He wrote up NOTHING IS EVER DONE IN THIS WORLD UNTIL MEN ARE PREPARED TO KILL ONE ANOTHER IF IT IS NOT DONE. After that, there was nothing left 825 for the seventh to say. So he wrote up, simply, UNASHAMED.

CUSINS: My good Machiavelli, I shall certainly write something up on the wall; only, as I shall write it in Greek, you wont be able to read it. But as to your Armorer's faith, if I take my neck out of the noose of my own morality I am not 830 going to put it into the noose of yours. I shall sell cannons to whom I please and refuse them to whom I please. So there!

UNDERSHAFT: From the moment when you become Andrew Undershaft, you will never do as you please again. Dont come here lusting for power, young man.

835 CUSINS: If power were my aim I should not come here for it. You have no power.

UNDERSHAFT: None of my own, certainly.

CUSINS: I have more power than you, more will. You do not drive this place: it drives you. And what drives the place?

840 UNDERSHAFT: (*Enigmatically.*) A will of which I am a part.

BARBARA: (*Startled.*) Father! Do you know what you are saying; or are you laying a snare for my soul?

CUSINS: Dont listen to his metaphysics, Barbara. The place is driven by the most rascally part of society, the money 845 hunters, the pleasure hunters, the military promotion hunters; and he is their slave.

UNDERSHAFT: Not necessarily. Remember the Armorer's Faith. I will take an order from a good man as cheerfully as from a bad one. If you good people prefer preaching and 850 shirking to buying my weapons and fighting the rascals, dont blame me. I can make cannons: I cannot make courage and conviction. Bah! you tire me, Euripides, with your morality mongering. Ask Barbara: she understands. (*He suddenly reaches up and takes* BARBARA'S *hands, looking powerfully* 855 *into her eyes.*) Tell him, my love, what power really means.

BARBARA: (*Hypnotized.*) Before I joined the Salvation Army, I was in my own power; and the consequence was that I never knew what to do with myself. When I joined it, I had not time enough for all the things I had to do.

UNDERSHAFT: (*Approvingly.*) Just so. And why was that, do you 860 suppose?

BARBARA: Yesterday I should have said, because I was in the power of God. (*She resumes her self-possession, withdrawing her hands from his with a power equal to his own.*) But you came and shewed me that I was in the power of Bodger and 865 Undershaft. Today I feel—oh! how can I put it into words? Sarah: do you remember the earthquake at Cannes, when we were little children?—how little the surprise of the first shock mattered compared to the dread and horror of waiting for the second? That is how I feel in this place today. I stood 870 on the rock I thought eternal; and without a word of warning it reeled and crumbled under me. I was safe with an infinite wisdom watching me, an army marching to Salvation with me; and in a moment, at a stroke of your pen in a cheque book, I stood alone; and the heavens were empty. That was 875 the first shock of the earthquake: I am waiting for the second.

UNDERSHAFT: Come, come, my daughter! dont make too much of your little tinpot tragedy. What do we do here when we spend years of work and thought and thousands of pounds of solid cash on a new gun or an aerial battleship 880 that turns out just a hairsbreadth wrong after all? Scrap it. Scrap it without wasting another hour or another pound on it. Well, you have made for yourself something that you call a morality or a religion or what not. It doesnt fit the facts. Well, scrap it. Scrap it and get one that does fit. That is what 885 is wrong with the world at present. It scraps its obsolete steam engines and dynamos; but it wont scrap its old prejudices and its old moralities and its old religions and its old political constitutions. Whats the result? In machinery it does very well; but in morals and religion and politics it is 890 working at a loss that brings it nearer bankruptcy every year. Dont persist in that folly. If your old religion broke down yesterday, get a newer and a better one for tomorrow.

BARBARA: Oh how gladly I would take a better one to my soul! But you offer me a worse one. (*Turning on him with sudden* 895 *vehemence.*) Justify yourself: shew me some light through the darkness of this dreadful place, with its beautifully clean workshops, and respectable workmen, and model homes.

UNDERSHAFT: Cleanliness and respectability do not need justification, Barbara: they justify themselves. I see no darkness 900 here, no dreadfulness. In your Salvation shelter I saw poverty, misery, cold and hunger. You gave them bread and treacle and dreams of heaven. I give from thirty shillings a week to twelve thousand a year. They find their own dreams; but I look after the drainage. 905

BARBARA: And their souls?

UNDERSHAFT: I save their souls just as I saved yours.

BARBARA: (*Revolted.*) You saved my soul! What do you mean?

UNDERSHAFT: I fed you and clothed you and housed you. I took care that you should have money enough to live hand- 910 somely—more than enough; so that you could be wasteful, careless, generous. That saved your soul from the seven deadly sins.

BARBARA: (*Bewildered.*) The seven deadly sins!

UNDERSHAFT: Yes, the deadly seven. (*Counting on his fingers.*) 915 Food, clothing, firing, rent, taxes, respectability and children. Nothing can lift those seven millstones from Man's

neck but money; and the spirit cannot soar until the millstones are lifted. I lifted them from your spirit. I enabled Bar-
920　bara to become Major Barbara; and I saved her from the
crime of poverty.

CUSINS: Do you call poverty a crime?

UNDERSHAFT: The worst of crimes. All the other crimes are
virtues beside it: all the other dishonors are chivalry itself by
925　comparison. Poverty blights whole cities; spreads horrible
pestilences; strikes dead the very souls of all who come
within sight, sound, or smell of it. What you call crime is
nothing: a murder here and a theft there, a blow now and a
curse then: what do they matter? they are only the accidents
930　and illnesses of life: there are not fifty genuine professional
criminals in London. But there are millions of poor people,
abject people, dirty people, ill fed, ill clothed people. They
poison us morally and physically: they kill the happiness of
society: they force us to do away with our own liberties and to
935　organize unnatural cruelties for fear they should rise against
us and drag us down into their abyss. Only fools fear crime:
we all fear poverty. Pah! *(Turning on* BARBARA.) you talk of
your halfsaved ruffian in West Ham: you accuse me of dragging his soul back to perdition. Well, bring him to me here;
940　and I will drag his soul back again to salvation for you. Not
by words and dreams; but by thirty-eight shillings a week, a
sound house in a handsome street, and a permanent job. In
three weeks he will have a fancy waistcoat; in three months a
tall hat and a chapel sitting; before the end of the year he
945　will shake hands with a duchess at a Primrose League meeting, and join the Conservative Party.

BARBARA: And will he be the better for that?

UNDERSHAFT: You know he will. Dont be a hypocrite, Barbara. He will be better fed, better housed, better clothed,
950　better behaved; and his children will be pounds heavier and
bigger. That will be better than an American cloth mattress
in a shelter, chopping firewood, eating bread and treacle,
and being forced to kneel down from time to time to thank
heaven for it: knee drill, I think you call it. It is cheap work
955　converting starving men with a Bible in one hand and a slice
of bread in the other. I will undertake to convert West Ham
to Mahometanism on the same terms. Try your hand on my
men: their souls are hungry because their bodies are full.

BARBARA: And leave the east end to starve?

960　UNDERSHAFT: *(His energetic tone dropping into one of bitter
and brooding remembrance.)* I was an east ender. I moralized
and starved until one day I swore that I would be a full-fed
free man at all costs; that nothing should stop me except a
bullet, neither reason nor morals nor the lives of other men.
965　I said 'Thou shalt starve ere I starve'; and with that word I became free and great. I was a dangerous man until I had my
will: now I am a useful, beneficent, kindly person. That is
the history of most self-made millionaires, I fancy. When it is
the history of every Englishman we shall have an England
970　worth living in.

LADY BRITOMART: Stop making speeches, Andrew. This is not
the place for them.

UNDERSHAFT: *(Punctured.)* My dear: I have no other means of
conveying my ideas.

975　LADY BRITOMART: Your ideas are nonsense. You got on because you were selfish and unscrupulous.

UNDERSHAFT: Not at all. I had the strongest scruples about
poverty and starvation. Your moralists are quite unscrupulous about both: they make virtues of them. I had rather be a

thief than a pauper. I had rather be a murderer than a slave. 980
I dont want to be either; but if you force the alternative on
me, then, by Heaven, I'll choose the braver and more moral
one. I hate poverty and slavery worse than any other crimes
whatsoever. And let me tell you this. Poverty and slavery
have stood up for centuries to your sermons and leading arti- 985
cles: they will not stand up to my machine guns. Dont
preach at them: dont reason with them. Kill them.

BARBARA: Killing. Is that your remedy for everything?

UNDERSHAFT: It is the final test of conviction, the only lever
strong enough to overturn a social system, the only way of 990
saying Must. Let six hundred and seventy fools loose in the
streets; and three policemen can scatter them. But huddle
them together in a certain house in Westminster; and let
them go through certain ceremonies and call themselves
certain names until at last they get the courage to kill; and 995
your six hundred and seventy fools become a government.
Your pious mob fills up ballot papers and imagines it is governing its masters; but the ballot paper that really governs is
the paper that has a bullet wrapped up in it.

CUSINS: That is perhaps why, like most intelligent people, I 1000
never vote.

UNDERSHAFT: Vote! Bah! When you vote, you only change the
names of the cabinet. When you shoot, you pull down governments, inaugurate new epochs, abolish old orders and set
up new. Is that historically true, Mr Learned Man, or is it 1005
not?

CUSINS: It is historically true. I loathe having to admit it. I repudiate your sentiments. I abhor your nature. I defy you in
every possible way. Still, it is true. But it ought not to be true.

UNDERSHAFT: Ought! ought! ought! ought! ought! Are you 1010
going to spend your life saying ought, like the rest of our
moralists? Turn your oughts into shalls, man. Come and
make explosives with me. Whatever can blow men up can
blow society up. The history of the world is the history of
those who had courage enough to embrace this truth. Have 1015
you the courage to embrace it, Barbara?

LADY BRITOMART: Barbara: I positively forbid you to listen to
your father's abominable wickedness. And you, Adolphus,
ought to know better than to go about saying that wrong
things are true. What does it matter whether they are true if 1020
they are wrong?

UNDERSHAFT: What does it matter whether they are wrong if
they are true?

LADY BRITOMART: *(Rising.)* Children: come home instantly.
Andrew: I am exceedingly sorry I allowed you to call on us. 1025
You are wickeder than ever. Come at once.

BARBARA: *(Shaking her head.)* It's no use running away from
wicked people, mamma.

LADY BRITOMART: It is every use. It shews your disapprobation
of them. 1030

BARBARA: It does not save them.

LADY BRITOMART: I can see that you are going to disobey me.
Sarah: are you coming home or are you not?

sarah: I daresay it's very wicked of papa to make cannons; but I
dont think I shall cut him on that account. 1035

LOMAX: *(Pouring oil on the troubled waters.)* The fact is, you
know, there is a certain amount of tosh about this notion of
wickedness. It doesnt work. You must look at facts. Not that I
would say a word in favor of anything wrong; but then, you
see, all sorts of chaps are always doing all sorts of things; and 1040
we have to fit them in somehow, dont you know. What I

mean is that you cant go cutting everybody; and thats about what it comes to. (*Their rapt attention to his eloquence makes him nervous.*) Perhaps I dont make myself clear.

1045 LADY BRITOMART: You are lucidity itself, Charles. Because Andrew is successful and has plenty of money to give to Sarah, you will flatter him and encourage him in his wickedness.

LOMAX: (*Unruffled.*) Well, where the carcase is, there will the eagles be gathered, dont you know. (*To* UNDERSHAFT.) Eh?
1050 What?

UNDERSHAFT: Precisely. By the way, may I call you Charles?

LOMAX: Delighted. Cholly is the usual ticket.

UNDERSHAFT: (*To* LADY BRITOMART.) Biddy—

LADY BRITOMART: (*Violently.*) Dont dare call me Biddy.
1055 Charles Lomax: you are a fool. Adolphus Cusins: you are a Jesuit. Stephen: you are a prig. Barbara: you are a lunatic. Andrew: you are a vulgar tradesman. Now you all know my opinion; and my conscience is clear, at all events (*She sits down with a vehemence that the rug fortunately softens.*)

1060 UNDERSHAFT: My dear: you are the incarnation of morality. (*She snorts.*) Your conscience is clear and your duty done when you have called everybody names. Come, Euripides! it is getting late; and we all want to go home. Make up your mind.

1065 CUSINS: Understand this, you old demon—

LADY BRITOMART: Adolphus!

UNDERSHAFT: Let him alone, Biddy. Proceed, Euripides.

CUSINS: You have me in a horrible dilemma. I want Barbara.

UNDERSHAFT: Like all young men, you greatly exaggerate the
1070 difference between one young woman and another.

BARBARA: Quite true, Dolly.

CUSINS: I also want to avoid being a rascal.

UNDERSHAFT: (*With biting contempt.*) You lust for personal righteousness, for self-approval, for what you call a good con-
1075 science, for what Barbara calls salvation, for what I call patronizing people who are not so lucky as yourself.

CUSINS: I do not: all the poet in me recoils from being a good man. But there are things in me that I must reckon with. Pity—

1080 UNDERSHAFT: Pity! The scavenger of misery.

CUSINS: Well, love.

UNDERSHAFT: I know. You love the needy and the outcast: you love the oppressed races, the negro, the Indian ryot, the underdog everywhere. Do you love the Japanese? Do you love
1085 the French? Do you love the English?

CUSINS: No. Every true Englishman detests the English. We are the wickedest nation on earth; and our success is a moral horror.

UNDERSHAFT: That is what comes of your gospel of love, is it?
1090 CUSINS: May I not love even my father-in-law?

UNDERSHAFT: Who wants your love, man? By what right do you take the liberty of offering it to me? I will have your due heed and respect, or I will kill you. But your love! Damn your impertinence!

1095 CUSINS: (*Grinning.*) I may not be able to control my affections, Mac.

UNDERSHAFT: You are fencing, Euripides. You are weakening: your grip is slipping. Come! try your last weapon. Pity and love have broken in your hand: forgiveness is still left.

1100 CUSINS: No: forgiveness is a beggar's refuge. I am with you there: we must pay our debts.

UNDERSHAFT: Well said. Come! you will suit me. Remember the words of Plato.

CUSINS: (*Starting.*) Plato! You dare quote Plato to me!

UNDERSHAFT: Plato says, my friend, that society cannot be 1105 saved until either the Professors of Greek take to making gunpowder, or else the makers of gunpowder become Professors of Greek.

CUSINS: Oh, tempter, cunning tempter!

UNDERSHAFT: Come! choose, man, choose. 1110

CUSINS: But perhaps Barbara will not marry me if I make the wrong choice.

BARBARA: Perhaps not.

CUSINS: (*Desperately perplexed.*) You hear!

BARBARA: Father: do you love nobody? 1115

UNDERSHAFT: I love my best friend.

LADY BRITOMART: And who is that, pray?

UNDERSHAFT: My bravest enemy. That is the man who keeps me up to the mark.

CUSINS: You know, the creature is really a sort of poet in his 1120 way. Suppose he is a great man, after all!

UNDERSHAFT: Suppose you stop talking and make up your mind, my young friend.

CUSINS: But you are driving me against my nature. I hate war.

UNDERSHAFT: Hatred is the coward's revenge for being intimi- 1125 dated. Dare you make war on war? Here are the means: my friend Mr Lomax is sitting on them.

LOMAX: (*Springing up.*) Oh I say! You dont mean that this thing is loaded, do you? My ownest: come off it.

SARAH: (*Sitting placidly on the shell.*) If I am to be blown up, 1130 the more thoroughly it is done the better. Dont fuss, Cholly.

LOMAX: (*To* UNDERSHAFT, *strongly remonstrant.*) Your own daughter, you know!

UNDERSHAFT: So I see! (*To* CUSINS.) Well, my friend, may we expect you here at six tomorrow morning? 1135

CUSINS: (*Firmly.*) Not on any account. I will see the whole establishment blown up with its own dynamite before I will get up at five. My hours are healthy, rational hours: eleven to five.

UNDERSHAFT: Come when you please: before a week you will 1140 come at six and stay until I turn you out for the sake of your health. (*Calling.*) Bilton! (*He turns to* LADY BRITOMART, *who rises.*) My dear: let us leave these two young people to themselves for a moment. (BILTON *comes from the shed.*) I am going to take you through the gun cotton shed. 1145

BILTON: (*Barring the way.*) You cant take anything explosive in here, sir.

LADY BRITOMART: What do you mean? Are you alluding to me?

BILTON: (*Unmoved.*) No, maam. Mr Undershaft has the other gentleman's matches in his pocket. 1150

LADY BRITOMART: (*Abruptly.*) Oh! I beg your pardon. (*She goes into the shed.*)

UNDERSHAFT: Quite right, Bilton, quite right: here you are. (*He gives* BILTON *the box of matches.*) Come, Stephen. Come, Charles. Bring Sarah. (*He passes into the shed.*) 1155

(BILTON *opens the box and deliberately drops the matches into the fire-bucket.*)

LOMAX: Oh! I say (BILTON *stolidly hands him the empty box.*) Infernal nonsense! Pure scientific ignorance! (*He goes in.*)

SARAH: Am I all right, Bilton?

BILTON: Youll have to put on list slippers, miss: thats all. Weve got em inside. (*She goes in.*) 1160

STEPHEN: (*Very seriously to* CUSINS.) Dolly, old fellow, think. Think before you decide. Do you feel that you are a sufficiently practical man? It is a huge undertaking, an enormous responsibility. All this mass of business will be Greek to you.

CUSINS: Oh, I think it will be much less difficult than Greek.

STEPHEN: Well, I just want to say this before I leave you to yourselves. Dont let anything I have said about right and wrong prejudice you against this great chance in life. I have satisfied myself that the business is one of the highest character and a credit to our country. *(Emotionally.)* I am very proud of my father. I—(*Unable to proceed, he presses* CUSINS' *hand and goes hastily into the shed, followed by* BILTON.)

*(*BARBARA *and* CUSINS, *left alone together, look at one another silently.)*

CUSINS: Barbara: I am going to accept this offer.

BARBARA: I thought you would.

CUSINS: You understand, dont you, that I had to decide without consulting you. If I had thrown the burden of the choice on you, you would sooner or later have despised me for it.

BARBARA: Yes: I did not want you to sell your soul for me any more than for this inheritance.

CUSINS: It is not the sale of my soul that troubles me: I have sold it too often to care about that. I have sold it for a professorship. I have sold it for an income. I have sold it to escape being imprisoned for refusing to pay taxes for hangmen's ropes and unjust wars and things that I abhor. What is all human conduct but the daily and hourly sale of our souls for trifles? What I am now selling it for is neither money nor position nor comfort, but for reality and for power.

BARBARA: You know that you will have no power, and that he has none.

CUSINS: I know. It is not for myself alone. I want to make power for the world.

BARBARA: I want to make power for the world too; but it must be spiritual power.

CUSINS: I think all power is spiritual: these cannons will not go off by themselves. I have tried to make spiritual power by teaching Greek. But the world can never be really touched by a dead language and a dead civilization. The people must have power; and the people cannot have Greek. Now the power that is made here can be wielded by all men.

BARBARA: Power to burn women's houses down and kill their sons and tear their husbands to pieces.

CUSINS: You cannot have power for good without having power for evil too. Even mother's milk nourishes murderers as well as heroes. This power which only tears men's bodies to pieces has never been so horribly abused as the intellectual power, the imaginative power, the poetic, religious power that can enslave men's souls. As a teacher of Greek I gave the intellectual man weapons against the common man. I now want to give the common man weapons against the intellectual man. I love the common people. I want to arm them against the lawyers, the doctors, the priests, the literary men, the professors, the artists, and the politicians, who, once in authority, are more disastrous and tyrannical than all the fools, rascals, and impostors. I want a power simple enough for common men to use, yet strong enough to force the intellectual oligarchy to use its genius for the general good.

BARBARA: Is there no higher power than that? *(Pointing to the shell.)*

CUSINS: Yes; but that power can destroy the higher powers just as a tiger can destroy a man: therefore Man must master that power first. I admitted this when the Turks and Greeks were last at war. My best pupil went out to fight for Hellas. My parting gift to him was not a copy of Plato's Republic, but a revolver and a hundred Undershaft cartridges. The blood of every Turk he shot—if he shot any—is on my head as well as on Undershaft's. That act committed me to this place for ever. Your father's challenge has beaten me. Dare I make war on war? I must. I will. And now, is it all over between us?

BARBARA: *(Touched by his evident dread of her answer.)* Silly baby Dolly! How could it be!

CUSINS: *(Overjoyed.)* Then you—you—you—Oh for my drum! *(He flourishes imaginary drumsticks.)*

BARBARA: *(Angered by his levity.)* Take care, Dolly, take care. Oh, if only I could get away from you and from father and from it all! if I could have the wings of a dove and fly away to heaven!

CUSINS: And leave me!

BARBARA: Yes, you, and all the other naughty mischievous children of men. But I cant. I was happy in the Salvation Army for a moment. I escaped from the world into a paradise of enthusiasm and prayer and soul saving; but the moment our money ran short, it all came back to Bodger: it was he who saved our people: he, and the Prince of Darkness, my papa. Undershaft and Bodger: their hands stretch everywhere: when we feed a starving fellow creature, it is with their bread, because there is no other bread; when we tend the sick, it is in the hospitals they endow; if we turn from the churches they build, we must kneel on the stones of the streets they pave. As long as that lasts, there is no getting away from them. Turning our backs on Bodger and Undershaft is turning our backs on life.

CUSINS: I thought you were determined to turn your back on the wicked side of life.

BARBARA: There is no wicked side: life is all one. And I never wanted to shirk my share in whatever evil must be endured, whether it be sin or suffering. I wish I could cure you of middle-class ideas, Dolly.

CUSINS: *(Gasping.)* Middle cl——! A snub! A social snub to me! from the daughter of a foundling!

BARBARA: That is why I have no class, Dolly: I come straight out of the heart of the whole people. If I were middle-class I should turn my back on my father's business; and we should both live in an artistic drawing room, with you reading the reviews in one corner, and I in the other at the piano, playing Schumann: both very superior persons, and neither of us a bit of use. Sooner than that, I would sweep out the guncotton shed, or be one of Bodger's barmaids. Do you know what would have happened if you had refused papa's offer?

CUSINS: I wonder!

BARBARA: I should have given you up and married the man who accepted it. After all, my dear old mother has more sense than any of you. I felt like her when I saw this place—felt that I must have it—that never, never, never could I let it go; only she thought it was the houses and the kitchen ranges and the linen and china, when it was really all the human souls to be saved: not weak souls in starved bodies, sobbing with gratitude for a scrap of bread and treacle, but fullfed, quarrelsome, snobbish, uppish creatures, all standing on their little rights and dignities, and thinking that my father ought to be greatly obliged to them for making so much

1285 money for him—and so he ought. That is where salvation is really wanted. My father shall never throw it in my teeth again that my converts were bribed with bread. *(She is transfigured.)* I have got rid of the bribe of bread. I have got rid of the bribe of heaven. Let God's work be done for its own sake: the work he had to create us to do because it cannot be done

1290 except by living men and women. When I die, let him be in my debt, not I in his; and let me forgive him as becomes a woman of my rank.

CUSINS: Then the way of life lies through the factory of death?

BARBARA: Yes, through the raising of hell to heaven and of man

1295 to God, through the unveiling of an eternal light in the Valley of The Shadow. *(Seizing him with both hands.)* Oh, did you think my courage would never come back? did you believe that I was a deserter? that I, who have stood in the streets, and taken my people to my heart, and talked of the

1300 holiest and greatest things with them, could ever turn back and chatter foolishly to fashionable people about nothing in a drawing room? Never, never, never, never: Major Barbara will die with the colors. Oh! and I have my dear little Dolly boy still; and he has found me my place and my work. Glory

1305 Hallelujah! *(She kisses him.)*

CUSINS: My dearest: consider my delicate health. I cannot stand as much happiness as you can.

BARBARA: Yes: it is not easy work being in love with me, is it? But it's good for you. *(She runs to the shed, and calls, childlike.)* Mamma! Mamma! (BILTON *comes out of the shed, followed by* UNDERSHAFT.) I want Mamma. 1310

UNDERSHAFT: She is taking off her list slippers, dear. *(He passes on to* CUSINS.) Well? What does she say?

CUSINS: She has gone right up into the skies.

LADY BRITOMART: *(Coming from the shed and stopping on the steps, obstructing* SARAH, *who follows with* LOMAX. BARBARA *clutches like a baby at her mother's skirt.)* Barbara: when will you learn to be independent and to act and think for yourself? I know as well as possible what that cry of 'Mamma, Mamma,' means. Always running to me! 1315 1320

SARAH: *(Touching* LADY BRITOMART's *ribs with her finger tips and imitating a bicycle horn.)* Pip! pip!

LADY BRITOMART: *(Highly indignant.)* How dare you say Pip! pip! to me, Sarah? You are both very naughty children. What do you want, Barbara? 1325

BARBARA: I want a house in the village to live in with Dolly. *(Dragging at the skirt.)* Come and tell me which one to take.

UNDERSHAFT: *(To* CUSINS.) Six o'clock tomorrow morning, Euripides.

■ LUIGI PIRANDELLO ■

Luigi Pirandello (1867–1936) created a diverse and influential body of plays, but his work is now most often associated with the preoccupations of his *Six Characters in Search of an Author*. Like *Six Characters*, Pirandello's plays use METATHEATER—roleplaying, plays-within-plays, and a flexible sense of the limits of stage illusion—to examine a highly theatricalized vision of identity. Can any of us be certain of our identity when others hold radically different perspectives on our actions, on who we are?

Pirandello was born in Sicily. He studied language and literature and received his doctoral degree in 1891 from the University of Rome. He then married the daughter of his father's business partner, but the collapse of the business forced him into a career as a writer. He wrote hundreds of stories in the 1890s and in the first decades of the twentieth century, as well as critical and scholarly articles. Pirandello's dramatic interest in the uncertainty of identity can be traced partly to his troubled marriage. His wife suffered a long mental illness and constantly accused him of adultery, despite his careful and constant attention to her health. In a sense, Pirandello was caught between his own sense of himself and the role he was given in this domestic tragedy.

Pirandello's use of the theater as a metaphor for representing this conflict pervades his mature plays: *Six Characters in Search of an Author* (1921; extensively revised 1925), *Enrico IV* (1922), *Each in His Own Way* (1924), and *Tonight We Improvise* (1930). In these plays, the struggle to discover and maintain identity is subjected to the pressure of performance in the world, performance that renders the "self" a kind of fiction. Yet while all behavior seems to verge on mere "acting," undermining our confidence in the authority or reality of a "self," Pirandello's plays do not seem nostalgic for the fixed and determined characters of realistic drama. For in Pirandello's drama, the "self" can also become a kind of prison, a role that traps the individual in a single and confining performance. This is the tragedy that the nameless hero of *Enrico IV* discovers at the close of that play, much as the hero—a famous author like Pirandello himself—of *When One Is Somebody* (1933) is gradually transformed from a man into a statue by the force of his admirers' adulation.

Pirandello became the director of his own company, the Art Theater of Rome, in 1924, and his major plays entered the world repertoire almost immediately. Pirandello's company toured throughout Europe and the Americas, influencing a generation of playwrights with the power of his theatrical conception of modern life. In addition to his short stories and criticism, Pirandello wrote over forty plays. He was awarded the Nobel Prize in 1934 in recognition of his achievement in the modern theater.

SIX CHARACTERS IN SEARCH OF AN AUTHOR

Six Characters seems at first to elaborate a simple and striking idea. What would happen if a cast of dramatic "characters" confronted the actors who gave them life on the stage? Pirandello had toyed with the idea for some time and had sketched it out as a short story. Onstage, though, the story develops a new and challenging dimension, for the confrontation between the Characters and Actors explores the nature of theatrical representation itself. As the play proceeds, it becomes clear that the Actors and Characters represent opposed versions of reality and of the theater, and their contest calls our understanding of the difference between them into question. The Characters need completion. Their melodramatic incest drama has defined each of them in an imprisoning role, as though the climactic moment of their unfinished play—when the Father nearly (or does he?) procures the Stepdaughter in Madame Pace's brothel—was definitive of the identity of each character. That is, Pirandello questions our fundamental notions of how dramatic characters represent the lives of real people, how they represent the rich complexity of a "life" through a short series of a few typical deeds. As the Father asks at one point, who of us would want his or her life summed up in one moment, one act?

The Actors, on the other hand, seem even less real than the Characters. Although the Characters are "fixed" by the design of their common story, that very consistency gives them a coherence and weight that the flighty Actors seem to lack. The Actors are entirely absorbed in the conventions of their lines of business and the petty jealousies of working together; the Leading Actor must always be "acting" the "Leading Actor," whether he is onstage or not, and so on through the rest of the cast. Oddly enough, then, *Six Characters* does not seem to allow us to choose between the Actors or Characters, to decide which kind of representation—narrative or stage performance—provides a more accurate depiction of "reality." The drama of *Six Characters* arises from the unresolved collision between these two perspectives. In the theater, the process of *Six Characters* insistently disorients its audience from the stable categories of "reality" and "illusion," which is perhaps why audiences rioted when the play was first produced. The Characters are, of course, played by actors, while the Actors are clearly "characters" to the audience. Are we, in the audience, any more "real?" Are we outside the play looking in, or has Pirandello managed to place *us* onstage, showing the audience also to be playing a role in the endless roleplaying of the theater? For this reason, when reading the play we should resist locating its "meanings" in the Father's philosophical monologues, those moments of *pirandellismo* that seem to sum up the play's confrontation between illusion and reality. The play's meaning arises through the entire process of its action, the baffling, inconclusive, and frustrating confrontation between Characters, Actors, and audience, a confrontation that finally prevents the Characters' drama from ever taking the stage.

Students should note that this version of *Six Characters* represents Pirandello's 1925 revision of the play, and that it differs in several ways—especially in the play's brilliant finale—from the earlier 1921 version. Also, this translation was first performed in England, where the role of "Producer" is what Americans generally call the "Director."

SIX CHARACTERS
IN SEARCH OF AN AUTHOR

Luigi Pirandello

TRANSLATED BY JOHN LINSTRUM

— CHARACTERS —

THE FATHER	THE BOY *(non-speaking)*
THE MOTHER	THE LITTLE GIRL *(non-speaking)*
THE STEPDAUGHTER	MADAME PACE
THE SON	

— ACTORS —

THE PRODUCER	THE STAGE MANAGER
THE LEADING ACTRESS	THE PROMPTER
THE LEADING ACTOR	THE PROPERTY MAN
THE SECOND ACTRESS	THE STAGE HAND
THE YOUNG ACTRESS	THE PRODUCER'S SECRETARY
THE YOUNG ACTOR	THE DOORKEEPER
OTHER ACTORS AND ACTRESSES *(a variable number)*	OTHER THEATRE STAFF

The action of the play takes place on the stage of a theatre. There are no act or scene divisions, but there are two interruptions: when the Producer and the Characters go to the officer to write the scenario, giving the Actors a break in rehearsal, and when a stage-hand lowers the front curtain by mistake.

References to 'prompt-box', 'curtains' and 'letting down trees' will need to be altered if they are not appropriate to the theatre where the performance is taking place.

— ACT ONE —

When the audience enters, the curtain is already up and the stage is just as it would be during the day. There is no set; it is empty, in almost total darkness. This is so that from the beginning the audience will have the feeling of being present, not at a performance of a properly rehearsed play, but at a performance of a play that happens spontaneously. Two small sets of steps, one on the right and one on the left, lead up to the stage from the auditorium. On the stage, the top is off the PROMPTER's *box and is lying next to it. Downstage, there is a small table and a chair with arms for the* PRODUCER: *it is turned with its back to the audience.*

Also downstage there are two small tables, one a little bigger than the other, and several chairs, ready for the rehearsal if needed. There are more chairs scattered on both left and right for the ACTORS: *to one side at the back and nearly hidden is a piano.*

When the houselights go down, the STAGE HAND *comes on through the back door. He is in blue overalls and carries a tool bag. He brings some pieces of wood on, comes to the front, kneels down and starts to nail them together.*

The STAGE MANAGER *rushes on from the wings.*

STAGE MANAGER: Hey! What are you doing?

STAGE HAND: What do you think I'm doing? I'm banging nails in.

STAGE MANAGER: Now? *(He looks at his watch.)* It's half-past
5 ten already. The Producer will be here in a moment to rehearse.

STAGE HAND: I've got to do my work some time, you know.

STAGE MANAGER: Right—but not now.

STAGE HAND: When?

STAGE MANAGER: When the rehearsal's finished. Come on, get 10 all this out of the way and let me set for the second act of 'The Rules of the Game'.

(The STAGE HAND *picks up his tools and wood and goes off, grumbling and muttering. The* ACTORS *of the company come in through the door, men and women, first one then another, then two together and so on: there will be nine or ten, enough for the parts for the rehearsal of a play by Pirandello, 'The Rules of the Game', today's rehearsal. They come in, say their 'Good-mornings' to the* STAGE MANAGER *and each other. Some go off to the dressing-rooms; others, among them the* PROMPTER *with the text rolled up under his arm, scatter about the stage waiting for the* PRODUCER *to start the rehearsal. Meanwhile, sitting or standing in groups, they chat together; some smoke, one complains about his part, another one loudly reads something from 'The Stage'. It would be as well if the* ACTORS *and* ACTRESSES *were dressed in colourful clothes, and this first scene should be improvised naturally and vivaciously. After a while somebody might sit down at the piano and play a song; the younger* AC-TORS *and* ACTRESSES *start dancing.)*

STAGE MANAGER: *(Clapping his hands to call their attention.)* Come on everybody! Quiet please. The Producer's here.

(The piano and the dancing both stop. The ACTORS *turn to look out into the theatre and through the door at the back comes the* PRODUCER; *he walks down the gangway between the seats and, calling 'Good-morning' to the* ACTORS, *climbs up one of the sets of stairs onto the stage. The* SECRETARY *gives him the post, a few magazines, a script. The* ACTORS *move to one side of the stage.)*

15 PRODUCER: Any letters?

SECRETARY: No. That's all the post there is. (*Giving him the script.*)

PRODUCER: Put it in the office. (*Then looking round and turning to the* STAGE MANAGER.) I can't see a thing here. Let's
20 have some lights please.

STAGE MANAGER: Right. (*Calling.*) Workers please!

(*In a few seconds the side of the stage where the* ACTORS *are standing is brilliantly lit with white light. The* PROMPTER *has gone into his box and spread out his script.*)

PRODUCER: Good. (*Clapping hands.*) Well then, let's get started. Anybody missing?

STAGE MANAGER: (*Heavily ironic.*) Our leading lady.

25 PRODUCER: Not again! (*Looking at his watch.*) We're ten minutes late already. Send her a note to come and see me. It might teach her to be on time for rehearsals. (*Almost before he has finished, the* LEADING ACTRESS's *voice is heard from the auditorium.*)

30 LEADING ACTRESS: Morning everybody. Sorry I'm late. (*She is very expensively dressed and is carrying a lap-dog. She comes down the aisle and goes up on to the stage.*)

PRODUCER: You're determined to keep us waiting, aren't you?

LEADING ACTRESS: I'm sorry. I just couldn't find a taxi any-
35 where. But you haven't started yet and I'm not on at the opening anyhow. (*Calling the* STAGE MANAGER, *she gives him the dog.*) Put him in my dressing-room for me will you?

PRODUCER: And she's even brought her lap-dog with her! As if we haven't enough lap-dogs here already. (*Clapping his*
40 *hands and turning to the* PROMPTER.) Right then, the second act of 'The Rules of the Game'. (*Sits in his arm-chair.*) Quiet please! Who's on?

(*The* ACTORS *clear from the front of the stage and sit to one side, except for three who are ready to start the scene—and the* LEADING ACTRESS. *She has ignored the* PRODUCER *and is sitting at one of the little tables.*)

PRODUCER: Are you in this scene, then?

LEADING ACTRESS: No—I've just told you.

45 PRODUCER: (*Annoyed.*) Then get off, for God's sake. (*The* LEADING ACTRESS *goes and sits with the others. To the* PROMPTER.) Come on then, let's get going.

PROMPTER: (*Reading his script.*) 'The house of Leone Gala. A peculiar room, both dining-room and study.'

50 PRODUCER: (*To the* STAGE MANAGER.) We'll use the red set.

STAGE MANAGER: (*Making a note.*) The red set—right.

PROMPTER: (*Still reading.*) 'The table is laid and there is a desk with books and papers. Bookcases full of books and china cabinets full of valuable china. An exit at the back
55 leads to Leone's bedroom. An exit to the left leads to the kitchen. The main entrance is on the right.'

PRODUCER: Right. Listen carefully everybody: there, the main entrance, there, the kitchen. (*To the* LEADING ACTOR *who plays Socrates.*) Your entrances and exits will be from there.
60 (*To the* STAGE MANAGER.) We'll have the French windows there and put the curtains on them.

STAGE MANAGER: (*Making a note.*) Right.

PROMPTER: (*Reading.*) 'Scene One. Leone Gala, Guido Venanzi, and Filippo, who is called Socrates.' (*To* PRODUCER.)
65 Have I to read the directions as well?

PRODUCER: Yes, you have! I've told you a hundred times.

PROMPTER: (*Reading.*) 'When the curtain rises, Leone Gala, in a cook's hat and apron, is beating an egg in a dish with a little wooden spoon. Filippo is beating another and he is dressed as a cook too. Guido Venanzi is sitting listening.' 70

LEADING ACTOR: Look, do I really have to wear a cook's hat?

PRODUCER: (*Annoyed by the question.*) I expect so! That's what it says in the script. (*Pointing to the script.*)

LEADING ACTOR: If you ask me it's ridiculous.

PRODUCER: (*Leaping to his feet furiously.*) Ridiculous? It's 75 ridiculous, is it? What do you expect me to do if nobody writes good plays any more and we're reduced to putting on plays by Pirandello? And if you can understand them you must be very clever. He writes them on purpose so nobody enjoys them, neither actors nor critics nor audience. (*The* 80 ACTORS *laugh. Then crosses to* LEADING ACTOR *and shouts at him.*) A cook's hat and you beat eggs. But don't run away with the idea that that's all you are doing—beating eggs. You must be joking! You have to be symbolic of the shells of the eggs you are beating. (*The* ACTORS *laugh again and start* 85 *making ironical comments to each other.*) Be quiet! Listen carefully while I explain. (*Turns back to* LEADING ACTOR.) Yes, the shells, because they are symbolic of the empty form of reason, without its content, blind instinct! You are reason and your wife is instinct: you are playing a game where you 90 have been given parts and in which you are not just yourself but the puppet of yourself. Do you see?

LEADING ACTOR: (*Spreading his hands.*) Me? No.

PRODUCER: (*Going back to his chair.*) Neither do I! Come on, let's get going; you wait till you see the end! You haven't seen 95 anything yet! (*Confidentially.*) By the way, I should turn almost to face the audience if I were you, about three-quarters face. Well, what with the obscure dialogue and the audience not being able to hear you properly in any case, the whole lot'll go to hell. (*Clapping hands again.*) Come on. Let's get 100 going!

PROMPTER: Excuse me, can I put the top back on the prompt-box? There's a bit of a draught.

PRODUCER: Yes, yes, of course. Get on with it.

(*The* STAGE DOORKEEPER, *in a braided cap, has come into the auditorium, and he comes all the way down the aisle to the stage to tell the* PRODUCER *the* SIX CHARACTERS *have come, who, having come in after him, look about them a little puzzled and dismayed. Every effort must be made to create the effect that the* SIX CHARACTERS *are very different from the* ACTORS *of the company. The placings of the two groups, indicated in the directions, once the* CHARACTERS *are on the stage, will help this; so will using different coloured lights. But the most effective idea is to use masks for the* CHARACTERS, *masks specially made of a material that will not go limp with perspiration and light enough not to worry the actors who wear them: they should be made so that the eyes, the nose and the mouth are all free. This is the way to bring out the deep significance of the play. The* CHARACTERS *should not appear as ghosts, but as created realities, timeless creations of the imagination, and so more real and consistent than the changeable realities of the* ACTORS. *The masks are designed to give the impression of figures constructed by art, each one fixed forever in its own fundamental emotion; that is, Remorse for the* FATHER, *Revenge for the* STEPDAUGHTER, *Scorn for the* SON, *Sorrow for the* MOTHER. *Her mask should have wax tears in the corners of the eyes and down the cheeks like the sculptured or painted weeping Madonna in a church. Her dress should be of a plain material, in stiff folds, looking almost as if it were carved and not of an ordinary material you can buy in a shop and have made up by a dressmaker.*

The FATHER *is about fifty: his reddish hair is thinning at the temples, but he is not bald: he has a full moustache that almost covers his young-looking mouth, which often opens in an uncertain and empty smile. He is pale, with a high forehead: he has blue oval eyes, clear and sharp: he is dressed in light trousers and a dark jacket: his voice is sometimes rich, at other times harsh and loud.*

The MOTHER *appears crushed by an intolerable weight of shame and humiliation. She is wearing a thick black veil and is dressed simply in black; when she raises her veil she shows a face like wax, but not suffering, with her eyes turned down humbly.*

The STEPDAUGHTER, *who is eighteen years old, is defiant, even insolent. She is very beautiful, dressed in mourning as well, but with striking elegance. She is scornful of the timid, suffering, dejected air of her* YOUNG BROTHER, *a grubby little boy of fourteen, also dressed in black; she is full of a warm tenderness, on the other hand, for the* LITTLE SISTER, *a girl of about four, dressed in white with a black silk sash round her waist.*

The SON *is twenty-two, tall, almost frozen in an air of scorn for the* FATHER *and indifference to the* MOTHER: *he is wearing a mauve overcoat and a long green scarf round his neck.)*

105 DOORMAN: Excuse me, sir.

PRODUCER: *(Angrily.)* What the hell is it now?

DOORMAN: There are some people here—they say they want to see you, sir.

(The PRODUCER *and the* ACTORS *are astonished and turn to look out into the auditorium.)*

PRODUCER: But I'm rehearsing! You know perfectly well that
110 no-one's allowed in during rehearsals. *(Turning to face out front.)* Who are you? What do you want?

FATHER: *(Coming forward, followed by the others, to the foot of one of the sets of steps.)* We're looking for an author.

PRODUCER: *(Angry and astonished.)* An author? Which author?
115 FATHER: Any author will do, sir.

PRODUCER: But there isn't an author here because we're not rehearsing a new play.

STEPDAUGHTER: *(Excitedly as she rushes up the steps.)* That's better still, better still! We can be your new play.
120 ACTORS: *(Lively comments and laughter from the* ACTORS.) Oh, listen to that, etc.

FATHER: *(Going up on the stage after the* STEPDAUGHTER.) Maybe, but if there isn't an author here . . . *(To the* PRODUCER.) Unless you'd like to be . . .

(Hand in hand, the MOTHER *and the* LITTLE GIRL, *followed by the* LITTLE BOY, *go up on the stage and wait. The* SON *stays sullenly behind.)*

125 PRODUCER: Is this some kind of joke?

FATHER: Now, how can you think that? On the contrary, we are bringing you a story of anguish.

STEPDAUGHTER: We might make your fortune for you!

PRODUCER: Do me a favour, will you? Go away. We haven't
130 time to waste on idiots.

FATHER: *(Hurt but answering gently.)* You know very well, as a man of the theatre, that life is full of all sorts of odd things which have no need at all to pretend to be real because they are actually true.

PRODUCER: What the devil are you talking about? 135

FATHER: What I'm saying is that you really must be mad to do things the opposite way round: to create situations that obviously aren't true and try to make them seem to be really happening. But then I suppose that sort of madness is the only reason for your profession. 140

(The ACTORS *are indignant.)*

PRODUCER: *(Getting up and glaring at him.)* Oh, yes? So ours is a profession of madmen, is it?

FATHER: Well, if you try to make something look true when it obviously isn't, especially if you're not forced to do it, but do it for a game . . . Isn't it your job to give life on the stage to 145 imaginary people?

PRODUCER: *(Quickly answering him and speaking for the* ACTORS *who are growing more indignant.)* I should like you to know, sir, that the actor's profession is one of great distinction. Even if nowadays the new writers only give us dull plays 150 to act and puppets to present instead of men, I'd have you know that it is our boast that we have given life, here on this stage, to immortal works.

(The ACTORS, *satisfied, agree with and applaud the* PRODUCER.)*

FATHER: *(Cutting in and following hard on his argument.)* There! You see? Good! You've given life! You've created liv- 155 ing beings with more genuine life than people have who breathe and wear clothes! Less real, perhaps, but nearer the truth. We are both saying the same thing.

(The ACTORS *look at each other, astonished.)*

PRODUCER: But just a moment! You said before . . .

FATHER: I'm sorry, but I said that before, about acting for fun, 160 because you shouted at us and said you'd no time to waste on idiots, but you must know better than anyone that Nature uses human imagination to lift her work of creation to even higher levels.

PRODUCER: All right then: but where does all this get us? 165

FATHER: Nowhere. I want to try to show that one can be thrust into life in many ways, in many forms: as a tree or a stone, as water or a butterfly—or as a woman. It might even be as a character in a play.

PRODUCER: *(Ironic, pretending to be annoyed.)* And you, and 170 these other people here, were thrust into life, as you put it, as characters in a play?

FATHER: Exactly! And alive, as you can see.

(The PRODUCER *and the* ACTORS *burst into laughter as if at a joke.)*

FATHER: I'm sorry you laugh like that, because we carry in us, as I said before, a story of terrible anguish as you can guess 175 from this woman dressed in black.

(Saying this, he offers his hand to the MOTHER *and helps her up the last steps and, holding her still by the hand, leads her with a sense of tragic solemnity across the stage which is suddenly lit by a fantastic light.*

The LITTLE GIRL *and the* BOY *follow the* MOTHER: *then the* SON *comes up and stands to one side in the background: then the*

STEPDAUGHTER *follows and leans against the proscenium arch: the* ACTORS *are astonished at first, but then, full of admiration for the 'entrance', they burst into applause—just as if it were a performance specially for them.*)

PRODUCER: *(At first astonished and then indignant.)* My God! Be quiet all of you. *(Turns to the* CHARACTERS.) And you lot get out! Clear off! *(To the* STAGE MANAGER.) Jesus! Get
180 them out of here.
STAGE MANAGER: *(Comes forward but stops short as if held back by something strange.)* Go on out! Get out!
FATHER: *(To* PRODUCER.) Oh no, please, you see, we . . .
PRODUCER: *(Shouting.)* We came here to work, you know.
185 LEADING ACTOR: We really can't be messed about like this.
FATHER: *(Resolutely, coming forward.)* I'm astonished! Why don't you believe me? Perhaps you are not used to seeing the characters created by an author spring into life up here on the stage face to face with each other. Perhaps it's because
190 we're not in a script? *(He points to the* PROMPTER's *box.)*
STEPDAUGHTER: *(Coming down to the* PRODUCER, *smiling and persuasive.)* Believe me, sir, we really are six of the most fascinating characters. But we've been neglected.
FATHER: Yes, that's right, we've been neglected. In the sense
195 that the author who created us, living in his mind, wouldn't or couldn't make us live in a written play for the world of art. And that really is a crime sir, because whoever has the luck to be born a character can laugh even at death. Because a character will never die! A man will die, a writer, the instru-
200 ment of creation: but what he has created will never die! And to be able to live for ever you don't need to have extraordinary gifts or be able to do miracles. Who was Sancho Panza? Who was Prospero? But they will live for ever because—living seeds—they had the luck to find a fruitful soil, an imagi-
205 nation which knew how to grow them and feed them, so that they will live for ever.
PRODUCER: This is all very well! But what do you want here?
FATHER: We want to live, sir.
PRODUCER: *(Ironically.)* For ever!
210 FATHER: No, no: only for a few moments—in you.
AN ACTOR: Listen to that!
LEADING ACTRESS: They want to live in us!
YOUNG ACTOR: *(Pointing to the* STEPDAUGHTER.) I don't mind . . . so long as I get her.
215 FATHER: Listen, listen: the play is all ready to be put together and if you and your actors would like to, we can work it out now between us.
PRODUCER: *(Annoyed.)* But what exactly do you want to do? We don't make up plays like that here! We present comedies
220 and tragedies here.
FATHER: That's right, we know that of course. That's why we've come.
PRODUCER: And where's the script?
FATHER: It's in us, sir. *(The* ACTORS *laugh.)* The play is in us:
225 we are the play and we are impatient to show it to you: the passion inside us is driving us on.
STEPDAUGHTER: *(Scornfully, with the tantalising charm of deliberate impudence.)* My passion, if only you knew! My passion for him! *(She points at the* FATHER *and suggests that she*
230 *is going to embrace him: but stops and bursts into a screeching laugh.)*

FATHER: *(With sudden anger.)* You keep out of this for the moment! And stop laughing like that!
STEPDAUGHTER: Really? Then with your permission, ladies and gentlemen; even though it's only two months since I be-
235 came an orphan, just watch how I can sing and dance.

(The ACTORS, *especially the younger, seem strangely attracted to her while she sings and dances and they edge closer and reach out their hands to catch hold of her. She eludes them, and when the* ACTORS *applaud her and the* PRODUCER *speaks sharply to her she stays still quite removed from them all.)*

ACTOR 1: Very good! etc.
PRODUCER: *(Angrily.)* Be quiet! Do you think this is a night-club? *(Turns to* FATHER *and asks with some concern.)* Is she a bit mad?
240
FATHER: Mad? Oh no—it's worse than that.
STEPDAUGHTER: *(Suddenly running to the* PRODUCER.) Yes. It's worse, much worse! Listen please! Let's put this play on at once, because you'll see that at a particular point I—when this darling little girl here—*(Taking the* LITTLE GIRL *by the*
245 *hand from next to the* MOTHER *and crossing with her to the* PRODUCER.) Isn't she pretty? *(Takes her in her arms.)* Darling! Darling! *(Puts her down again and adds, moved very deeply but almost without wanting to.)* Well, this lovely little girl here, when God suddenly takes her from this poor
250 Mother: and this little idiot here *(Turning to the* LITTLE BOY *and seizing him roughly by the sleeve.)* does the most stupid thing, like the half-wit he is,—then you will see me run away! Yes, you'll see me rush away! But not yet, not yet! Because, after all the intimate things there have been between
255 him and me *(In the direction of the* FATHER, *with a horrible vulgar wink.)* I can't stay with them any longer, to watch the insult to this mother through that supercilious cretin over there. *(Pointing to the* SON.) Look at him! Look at him! Condescending, stand-offish, because he's the legitimate son,
260 him! Full of contempt for me, for the boy and for the little girl: because we are bastards. Do you understand? Bastards. *(Running to the* MOTHER *and embracing her.)* And this poor mother—she—who is the mother of all of us—he doesn't want to recognise her as his own mother—and he looks
265 down on her, he does, as if she were only the mother of the three of us who are bastards—the traitor. *(She says all this quickly, with great excitement, and after having raised her voice on the word 'bastards' she speaks quietly, half-spitting the word 'traitor'.)*
270
MOTHER: *(With deep anguish to the* PRODUCER.) Sir, in the name of these two little ones, I beg you . . . *(Feels herself grow faint and sways.)* Oh, my God.
FATHER: *(Rushing to support her with almost all the* ACTORS *bewildered and concerned.)* Get a chair someone . . . quick,
275 get a chair for this poor widow.

(One of the ACTORS *offers a chair: the others press urgently around. The* MOTHER, *seated now, tries to stop the* FATHER *lifting her veil.)*

ACTORS: Is it real? Has she really fainted? etc.
FATHER: Look at her, everybody, look at her.
MOTHER: No, for God's sake, stop it.
FATHER: Let them look!
280

MOTHER: (*Lifting her hands and covering her face, desperately.*) Oh, please, I beg you, stop him from doing what he is trying to do; it's hateful.

285 PRODUCER: (*Overwhelmed, astounded.*) It's no use, I don't understand this any more. (*To the* FATHER.) Is this woman your wife?

FATHER: (*At once.*) That's right, she is my wife.

PRODUCER: How is she a widow, then, if you're still alive?

(*The* ACTORS *are bewildered too and find relief in a loud laugh.*)

FATHER: (*Wounded, with rising resentment.*) Don't laugh!
290 Please don't laugh like that! That's just the point, that's her own drama. You see, she had another man. Another man who ought to be here.

MOTHER: No, no! (*Crying out.*)

STEPDAUGHTER: Luckily for him he died. Two months ago, as
295 I told you: we are in mourning for him, as you can see.

FATHER: Yes, he's dead: but that's not the reason he isn't here. He isn't here because—well just look at her, please, and you'll understand at once—hers is not a passionate drama of the love of two men, because she was incapable of love, she
300 could feel nothing—except, perhaps, a little gratitude (but not to me, to him). She's not a woman; she's a mother. And her drama—and, believe me, it's a powerful one—her drama is focused completely on these four children of the two men she had.

305 MOTHER: I had them? How dare you say that I had them, as if I wanted them myself? It was him, sir! He forced the other man on me. He made me go away with him!

STEPDAUGHTER: (*Leaping up, indignantly.*) It isn't true!

MOTHER: (*Bewildered.*) How isn't it true?

310 STEPDAUGHTER: It isn't true, it just isn't true.

MOTHER: What do you know about it?

STEPDAUGHTER: It isn't true. (*To the* PRODUCER.) Don't believe it! Do you know why she said that? She said it because of him, over there. (*Pointing to the* SON.) She tortures her-
315 self, she exhausts herself with worry and all because of the indifference of that son of hers. She wants to make him believe that she abandoned him when he was two years old because the Father made her do it.

MOTHER: (*Passionately.*) He did! He made me! God's my wit-
320 ness. (*To the* PRODUCER.) Ask him if it isn't true. (*Pointing to the* FATHER.) Make him tell our son it's true. (*Turning to the* STEPDAUGHTER.) You don't know anything about it.

STEPDAUGHTER: I know that when my father was alive you were always happy and contented. You can't deny it.

325 MOTHER: No, I can't deny it.

STEPDAUGHTER: He was always full of love and care for you. (*Turning to the* LITTLE BOY *with anger.*) Isn't it true? Admit it. Why don't you say something, you little idiot?

MOTHER: Leave the poor boy alone! Why do you want to make
330 me appear ungrateful? You're my daughter. I don't in the least want to offend your father's memory. I've already told him that it wasn't my fault or even to please myself that I left his house and my son.

FATHER: It's quite true. It was my fault.

335 LEADING ACTOR: (*To other actors.*) Look at this. What a show!

LEADING ACTRESS: And we're the audience.

YOUNG ACTOR: For a change.

PRODUCER: (*Beginning to be very interested.*) Let's listen to them! Quiet! Listen!

(*He goes down the steps into the auditorium and stands there as if to get an idea of what the scene will look like from the audience's viewpoint.*)

SON: (*Without moving, coldly, quietly, ironically.*) Yes, listen to 340 his little scrap of philosophy. He's going to tell you all about the Daemon of Experiment.

FATHER: You're a cynical idiot, and I've told you so a hundred times. (*To the* PRODUCER *who is now in the stalls.*) He sneers at me because of this expression I've found to defend myself. 345

SON: Words, words.

FATHER: Yes words, words! When we're faced by something we don't understand, by a sense of evil that seems as if it's going to swallow us, don't we all find comfort in a word that tells us nothing but that calms us? 350

STEPDAUGHTER: And dulls your sense of remorse, too. That more than anything.

FATHER: Remorse? No, that's not true. It'd take more than words to dull the sense of remorse in me.

STEPDAUGHTER: It's taken a little money too, just a little 355 money. The money that he was going to offer as payment, gentlemen.

(*The* ACTORS *are horrified.*)

SON: (*Contemptuously to his stepsister.*) That's a filthy trick.

STEPDAUGHTER: A filthy trick? There it was in a pale blue envelope on the little mahogany table in the room behind the 360 shop at Madam Pace's. You know Madame Pace, don't you? One of those Madames who sell 'Robes et Manteaux' so that they can attract poor girls like me from decent families into their workroom.

SON: And she's bought the right to tyrannise over the whole lot 365 of us with that money—with what he was going to pay her: and luckily—now listen carefully—he had no reason to pay it to her.

STEPDAUGHTER: But it was close!

MOTHER: (*Rising up angrily.*) Shame on you, daughter! Shame! 370

STEPDAUGHTER: Shame? Not shame, revenge! I'm desperate, desperate to live that scene! The room . . . over here the showcase of coats, there the divan, there the mirror, and the screen, and over there in front of the window, that little mahogany table with the pale blue envelope and the money in 375 it. I can see it all quite clearly. I could pick it up! But you should turn your faces away, gentlemen: because I'm nearly naked! I'm not blushing any longer—I leave that to him. (*Pointing at the* FATHER.) But I tell you he was very pale, very pale then. (*To the* PRODUCER.) Believe me. 380

PRODUCER: I don't understand any more.

FATHER: I'm not surprised when you're attacked like that! Why don't you put your foot down and let me have my say before you believe all these horrible slanders she's so viciously telling about me. 385

STEPDAUGHTER: We don't want to hear any of your long winded fairy-stories.

FATHER: I'm not going to tell any fairy-stories! I want to explain things to him.

STEPDAUGHTER: I'm sure you do. Oh, yes! In your own special 390 way.

(The PRODUCER *comes back up on stage to take control.)*

FATHER: But isn't that the cause of all the trouble? Words! We all have a world of things inside ourselves and each one of us has his own private world. How can we understand each other if the words I use have the sense and the value that I expect them to have, but whoever is listening to me inevitably thinks that those same words have a different sense and value, because of the private world he has inside himself too. We think we understand each other: but we never do. Look! All my pity, all my compassion for this woman *(Pointing to the* MOTHER.*)* she sees as ferocious cruelty.

MOTHER: But he turned me out of the house!

FATHER: There, do you hear? I turned her out! She really believed that I had turned her out.

MOTHER: You know how to talk. I don't . . . But believe me, sir, *(Turning to the* PRODUCER.*)* after he married me . . . I can't think why! I was a poor, simple woman.

FATHER: But that was the reason! I married you for your simplicity, that's what I loved in you, believing—*(He stops because she is making gestures of contradiction. Then, seeing the impossibility of making her understand, he throws his arms wide in a gesture of desperation and turns back to the* PRODUCER.*)* No, do you see? She says no! It's terrifying, sir, believe me, terrifying, her deafness, her mental deafness. *(He taps his forehead.)* Affection for her children, oh yes. But deaf, mentally deaf, deaf, sir, to the point of desperation.

STEPDAUGHTER: Yes, but make him tell you what good all his cleverness has brought us.

FATHER: If only we could see in advance all the harm that can come from the good we think we are doing.

(The LEADING ACTRESS, *who has been growing angry watching the* LEADING ACTOR *flirting with the* STEPDAUGHTER, *comes forward and snaps at the* PRODUCER.*)*

LEADING ACTRESS: Excuse me, are we going to go on with our rehearsal?

PRODUCER: Yes, of course. But I want to listen to this first.

YOUNG ACTOR: It's such a new idea.

YOUNG ACTRESS: It's fascinating.

LEADING ACTRESS: For those who are interested. *(She looks meaningfully at the* LEADING ACTOR.*)*

PRODUCER: *(To the* FATHER.*)* Look here, you must explain yourself more clearly. *(He sits down.)*

FATHER: Listen then. You see, there was a rather poor fellow working for me as my assistant and secretary, very loyal: he understood her in everything. *(Pointing to the* MOTHER.*)* But without a hint of deceit, you must believe that: he was good and simple, like her: neither of them was capable even of thinking anything wrong, let alone doing it.

STEPDAUGHTER: So instead he thought of it for them and did it too!

FATHER: It's not true! What I did was for their good—oh yes and mine too, I admit it! The time had come when I couldn't say a word to either of them without there immediately flashing between them a sympathetic look: each one caught the other's eye for advice, about how to take what I had said, how not to make me angry. Well, that was enough, as I'm sure you'll understand, to put me in a bad temper all the time, in a state of intolerable exasperation.

PRODUCER: Then why didn't you sack this secretary of yours?

FATHER: Right! In the end I did sack him! But then I had to watch this poor woman wandering about in the house on her own, forlorn, like a stray animal you take in out of pity.

MOTHER: It's quite true.

FATHER: *(Suddenly, turning to her, as if to stop her.)* And what about the boy? Is that true as well?

MOTHER: But first he tore my son from me, sir.

FATHER: But not out of cruelty! It was so that he could grow up healthy and strong, in touch with the earth.

STEPDAUGHTER: *(Pointing to the* SON *jeeringly.)* And look at the result!

FATHER: *(Quickly.)* And is it my fault, too, that he's grown up like this? I took him to a nurse in the country, a peasant, because his mother didn't seem strong enough to me, although she is from a humble family herself. In fact that was what made me marry her. Perhaps it was superstitious of me; but what was I to do? I've always had this dreadful longing for a kind of sound moral healthiness.

(The STEPDAUGHTER *breaks out again into noisy laughter.)*

Make her stop that! It's unbearable.

PRODUCER: Stop it will you? Let me listen, for God's sake.

(When the PRODUCER *has spoken to her, she resumes her previous position . . . absorbed and distant, a half-smile on her lips. The* PRODUCER *comes down into the auditorium again to see how it looks from there.)*

FATHER: I couldn't bear the sight of this woman near me. *(Pointing to the* MOTHER.*)* Not so much because of the annoyance she caused me, you see, or even the feeling of being stifled, being suffocated that I got from her, as for the sorrow, the painful sorrow that I felt for her.

MOTHER: And he sent me away.

FATHER: With everything you needed, to the other man, to set her free from me.

MOTHER: And to set yourself free!

FATHER: Oh, yes, I admit it. And what terrible things came out of it. But I did it for the best, and more for her than for me: I swear it! *(Folds his arms: then turns suddenly to the* MOTHER.*)* I never lost sight of you did I? Until that fellow, without my knowing it, suddenly took you off to another town one day. He was idiotically suspicious of my interest in them, a genuine interest, I assure you, without any ulterior motive at all. I watched the new little family growing up round her with unbelievable tenderness, she'll confirm that. *(He points to the* STEPDAUGHTER.*)*

STEPDAUGHTER: Oh yes, I can indeed. I was a pretty little girl, you know, with plaits down to my shoulders and my little frilly knickers showing under my dress—so pretty—he used to watch me coming out of school. He came to see how I was maturing.

FATHER: That's shameful! It's monstrous.

STEPDAUGHTER: No it isn't! Why do you say it is?

FATHER: It's monstrous! Monstrous. *(He turns excitedly to the* PRODUCER *and goes on in explanation.)* After she'd gone away *(Pointing to the* MOTHER.*)*, my house seemed empty. She'd been like a weight on my spirit but she'd filled the house with her presence. Alone in the empty rooms I wandered about like a lost soul. This boy here, *(Indicating the* SON.*)* growing up away from home—whenever he came back to the home—I don't know—but he didn't seem to be mine any more. We needed the mother between us, to link us together, and so he grew up by himself, apart, with no connection to me either through intellect or love. And

505 then—it must seem odd, but it's true—first I was curious about and then strongly attracted to the little family that had come about because of what I'd done. And the thought of them began to fill all the emptiness that I felt around me. I needed, I really needed to believe that she was happy,

510 wrapped up in the simple cares of her life, lucky because she was better off away from the complicated torments of a soul like mine. And to prove it, I used to watch that child coming out of school.

STEPDAUGHTER: Listen to him! He used to follow me along the street; he used to smile at me and when we came near

515 the house he'd wave his hand—like this! I watched him, wide-eyed, puzzled. I didn't know who he was. I told my mother about him and she knew at once who it must be. (MOTHER *nods agreement.*) At first, she didn't let me go to school again, at any rate for a few days. But when I did go

520 back, I saw him standing near the door again—looking ridiculous—with a brown paper bag in his hand. He came close and petted me: then he opened the bag and took out a beautiful straw hat with a hoop of rosebuds round it—for me!

525 PRODUCER: All this is off the point, you know.

SON: (*Contemptuously.*) Yes . . . literature, literature.

FATHER: What do you mean, literature? This is real life: real passions.

PRODUCER: That may be! But you can't put it on the stage just

530 like that.

FATHER: That's right you can't. Because all this is only leading up to the main action. I'm not suggesting that this part should be put on the stage. In any case, you can see for yourself, (*Pointing at the* STEPDAUGHTER.) she isn't a pretty little

535 girl any longer with plaits down to her shoulders.

STEPDAUGHTER: —and with frilly knickers showing under her frock.

FATHER: The drama begins now: and it's new and complex.

STEPDAUGHTER: (*Coming forward, fierce and brooding.*) As

540 soon as my father died . . .

FATHER: (*Quickly, not giving her time to speak.*) They were so miserable. They came back here, but I didn't know about it because of the Mother's stubbornness. (*Pointing to the* MOTHER.) She can't really write you know; but she could

545 have got her daughter to write, or the boy, or tell me that they needed help.

MOTHER: But tell me, sir, how could I have known how he felt?

FATHER: And hasn't that always been your fault? You've never

550 known anything about how I felt.

MOTHER: After all the years away from him and after all that had happened.

FATHER: And was it my fault if that fellow took you so far away? (*Turning back to the* PRODUCER.) Suddenly, overnight, I tell

555 you, he'd found a job away from here without my knowing anything about it. I couldn't possibly trace them; and then, naturally I suppose, my interest in them grew less over the years. The drama broke out, unexpected and violent, when they came back: when I was driven in misery by the needs of

560 my flesh, still alive with desire . . . and it is misery, you know, unspeakable misery for the man who lives alone and who

detests sordid, casual affairs; not old enough to do without women, but not young enough to be able to go and look for one without shame! Misery? Is that what I called it. It's hor-

565 rible, it's revolting, because there isn't a woman who will give her love to him any more. And when he realises this, he should do without . . . It's easy to say though. Each of us, face to face with other men, is clothed with some sort of dignity, but we know only too well all the unspeakable things

570 that go on in the heart. We surrender, we given in to temptation: but afterwards we rise up out of it very quickly, in a desperate hurry to rebuild our dignity, whole and firm as if it were a gravestone that would cover every sign and memory of our shame, and hide it from even our own eyes. Every-

575 one's like that, only some of us haven't the courage to talk about it.

STEPDAUGHTER: But they've all got the courage to do it!

FATHER: Yes! But only in secret! That's why it takes more courage to talk about it! Because if a man does talk about

580 it—what happens then?—everybody says he's a cynic. And it's simply not true; he's just like everybody else; only better perhaps, because he's not afraid to use his intelligence to point out the blushing shame of human bestiality, that man, the beast, shuts his eyes to, trying to pretend it doesn't exist.

585 And what about woman—what is she like? She looks at you invitingly, teasingly. You take her in your arms. But as soon as she feels your arms round her she closes her eyes. It's the sign of her mission, the sign by which she says to a man, 'Blind yourself—I'm blind!'

590 STEPDAUGHTER: And when she doesn't close her eyes any more? What then? When she doesn't feel the need to hide from herself any more, to shut her eyes and hide her own shame. When she can see instead, dispassionately and dry-eyed this blushing shame of a man who has blinded himself,

595 who is without love. What then? Oh, then what disgust, what utter disgust she feels for all these intellectual complications, for all this philosophy that points to the bestiality of man and then tries to defend him, to excuse him . . . I can't listen to him, sir. Because when a man says he needs to 'simplify' life

600 like this—reducing it to bestiality—and throws away every human scrap of innocent desire, genuine feeling, idealism, duty, modesty, shame, then there's nothing more contemptible and nauseating than his remorse—crocodile tears!

PRODUCER: Let's get to the point, let's get to the point. This is

605 all chat.

FATHER: Right then! But a fact is like a sack—it won't stand up if it's empty. To make it stand up, first you have to put in it all the reasons and feelings that caused it in the first place. I couldn't possibly have known that when that fellow died

610 they'd come back here, that they were desperately poor and that the Mother had gone out to work as a dressmaker, nor that she'd gone to work for Madame Pace, of all people.

STEPDAUGHTER: She's a very high-class dressmaker—you must understand that. She apparently has only high-class cus-

615 tomers, but she has arranged things carefully so that these high-class customers in fact serve her—they give her a respectable front . . . without spoiling things for the other ladies at the shop, who are not quite so high-class at all.

MOTHER: Believe me, sir, the idea never entered my head that

620 the old hag gave me work because she had an eye on my daughter . . .

STEPDAUGHTER: Poor Mummy! Do you know what that woman would do when I took back the work that my mother had been doing? She would point out how the dress had been ruined by giving it to my mother to sew: she bargained, she grumbled. So, you see, I paid for it, while this poor woman here thought she was sacrificing herself for me and these two children, sewing dresses all night for Madame Pace.

(The ACTORS *make gestures and noises of disgust.)*

PRODUCER: *(Quickly.)* And there one day, you met . . .
STEPDAUGHTER: *(Pointing at the* FATHER.*)* Yes, him. Oh, he was an old customer of hers! What a scene that's going to be, superb!
FATHER: With her, the mother, arriving—
STEPDAUGHTER: *(Quickly, viciously.)*—Almost in time!
FATHER: *(Crying out.)*—No, just in time, just in time! Because, luckily, I found out who she was in time. And I took them all back to my house, sir. Can you imagine the situation now, for the two of us living in the same house? She, just as you see her here: and I, not able to look her in the face.
STEPDAUGHTER: It's so absurd! Do you think it's possible for me, sir, after what happened at Madame Pace's, to pretend that I'm a modest little miss, well brought up and virtuous just so that I can fit in with his damned pretensions to a 'sound moral healthiness'?
FATHER: This is the real drama for me; the belief that we all, you see, think of ourselves as one single person: but it's not true: each of us is several different people, and all these people live inside us. With one person we seem like this and with another we seem very different. But we always have the illusion of being the same person for everybody and of always being the same person in everything we do. But it's not true! It's not true! We find this out for ourselves very clearly when by some terrible chance we're suddenly stopped in the middle of doing something and we're left dangling there, suspended. We realise then, that every part of us was not involved in what we'd been doing and that it would be a dreadful injustice of other people to judge us only by this one action as we dangle there, hanging in chains, fixed for all eternity, as if the whole of one's personality were summed up in that single, interrupted action. Now do you understand this girl's treachery? She accidentally found me somewhere I shouldn't have been, doing something I shouldn't have been doing! She discovered a part of me that shouldn't have existed for her: and now she wants to fix on me a reality that I should never have had to assume for her: it came from a single brief and shameful moment in my life. This is what hurts me most of all. And you'll see that the play will make a tremendous impact from this idea of mine. But then, there's the position of the others. His . . .

(Pointing to the SON.*)*

SON: *(Shrugging his shoulders scornfully.)* Leave me out of it. I don't come into this.
FATHER: Why don't you come into this?
SON: I don't come into it and I don't want to come into it, because you know perfectly well that I wasn't intended to be mixed up with you lot.

STEPDAUGHTER: We're vulgar, common people, you see! He's a fine gentleman. But you've probably noticed that every now and then I look at him contemptuously, and when I do, he lowers his eyes—he knows the harm he's done me.
SON: *(Not looking at her.)* I have?
STEPDAUGHTER: Yes, you. It's your fault, dearie, that I went on the streets! Your fault! *(Movement of horror from the* ACTORS.*)* Did you or didn't you, with your attitude, deny us—I won't say the intimacy of your home—but that simple hospitality that makes guests feel comfortable? We were intruders who had come to invade the country of your 'legitimacy'! *(Turning to the* PRODUCER.*)* I'd like you to have seen some of the little scenes that went on between him and me, sir. He says that I tyrannised over everyone. But don't you see? It was because of the way he treated us. He called it 'vile' that I should insist on the right we had to move into his house with my mother—and she's his mother too. And I went into the house as its mistress.
SON: *(Slowly coming forward.)* They're really enjoying themselves, aren't they, sir? It's easy when they all gang up against me. But try to imagine what happened: one fine day, there is a son sitting quietly at home and he sees arrive as bold as brass, a young woman like this, who cheekily asks for his father, and heaven knows what business she has with him. Then he sees her come back with the same brazen look in her eye accompanied by that little girl there: and he sees her treat his father—without knowing why—in a most ambiguous and insolent way—asking him for money in a tone that leads one to suppose he really ought to give it, because he is obliged to do so.
FATHER: But I was obliged to do so: I owed it to your mother.
SON: And how was I to know that? When had I ever seen her before? When had I ever heard her mentioned? Then one day I see her come in with her *(Pointing at the* STEPDAUGHTER.*)*, that boy and that little girl: they say to me, 'Oh, didn't you know? This is your mother, too.' Little by little I began to understand, mostly from her attitude *(Points to* STEPDAUGHTER.*)* why they'd come to live in the house so suddenly. I can't and I won't say what I feel, and what I think. I wouldn't even like to confess it to myself. So I can't take any active part in this. Believe me, sir, I am a character who has not been fully developed dramatically, and I feel uncomfortable, most uncomfortable, in their company. So please leave me out of it.
FATHER: What! But it's precisely because you feel like this . . .
SON: *(Violently exasperated.)* How do you know what I feel? When have you ever bothered yourself about me?
FATHER: All right! I admit it! But isn't that a situation in itself? This withdrawing of yourself, it's cruel to me and to your mother: when she came back to the house, seeing you almost for the first time, not recognising you, but knowing that you're her own son . . . *(Turning to point out the* MOTHER *to the* PRODUCER.*)* There, look at her: she's weeping.
STEPDAUGHTER: *(Angrily, stamping her foot.)* Like the fool she is!
FATHER: *(Quickly pointing at the* STEPDAUGHTER *to the* PRODUCER.*)* She can't stand that young man, you know. *(Turning and referring to the* SON.*)* He says that he doesn't come into it, but he's really the pivot of the action! Look here at this little boy, who clings to his mother all the time,

frightened, humiliated. And it's because of him over there! Perhaps this little boy's problem is the worst of all: he feels an outsider, more than the others do; he feels so mortified, so humiliated just being in the house,—because it's charity, you see. *(Quietly.)* He's like his father: timid; he doesn't say anything . . .

PRODUCER: It's not a good idea at all, using him: you don't know what a nuisance children are on the stage.

FATHER: He won't need to be on the stage for long. Nor will the little girl—she's the first to go.

PRODUCER: That's good! Yes. I tell you all this interests me—it interests me very much. I'm sure we've the material here for a good play.

STEPDAUGHTER: *(Trying to push herself in.)* With a character like me you have!

FATHER: *(Driving her off, wanting to hear what the* PRODUCER *has decided.)* You stay out of it!

PRODUCER: *(Going on, ignoring the interruption.)* It's new, yes.

FATHER: Oh, it's absolutely new!

PRODUCER: You've got a nerve, though, haven't you, coming here and throwing it at me like this?

FATHER: I'm sure you understand. Born as we are for the stage . . .

PRODUCER: Are you amateur actors?

FATHER: No! I say we are born for the stage because . . .

PRODUCER: Come on now! You're an old hand at this, at acting!

FATHER: No I'm not. I only act, as everyone does, the part in life that he's chosen for himself, or that others have chosen for him. And you can see that sometimes my own passion gets a bit out of hand, a bit theatrical, as it does with all of us.

PRODUCER: Maybe, maybe . . . But you do see, don't you, that without an author . . . I could give you someone's address . . .

FATHER: Oh no! Look here! You do it.

PRODUCER: Me? What are you talking about?

FATHER: Yes, you. Why not?

PRODUCER: Because I've never written anything!

FATHER: Well, why not start now, if you don't mind my suggesting it? There's nothing to it. Everybody's doing it. And your job is even easier, because we're here, all of us, alive before you.

PRODUCER: That's not enough.

FATHER: Why isn't it enough? When you've seen us live our drama . . .

PRODUCER: Perhaps so. But we'll still need someone to write it.

FATHER: Only to write it down, perhaps, while it happens in front of him—live—scene by scene. It'll be enough to sketch it out simply first and then run through it.

PRODUCER: *(Coming back up, tempted by the idea.)* Do you know I'm almost tempted . . . just for fun . . . it might work.

FATHER: Of course it will. You'll see what wonderful scenes will come right out of it! I could tell you what they will be!

PRODUCER: You tempt me . . . you tempt me! We'll give it a chance. Come with me to the office. *(Turning to the* ACTORS.*)* Take a break: but don't go far away. Be back in a quarter of an hour or twenty minutes. *(To the* FATHER.*)* Let's see, let's try it out. Something extraordinary might come out of this.

FATHER: Of course it will! Don't you think it'd be better if the others came too? *(Indicating the other* CHARACTERS.*)*

PRODUCER: Yes, come on, come on. *(Going, then turning to speak to the* ACTORS.*)* Don't forget: don't be late: back in a quarter of an hour.

(The PRODUCER *and the* SIX CHARACTERS *cross the stage and go. The* ACTORS *look at each other in astonishment.)*

LEADING ACTOR: Is he serious? What's he going to do?

YOUNG ACTOR: I think he's gone round the bend.

ANOTHER ACTOR: Does he expect to make up a play in five minutes?

YOUNG ACTOR: Yes, like the old actors in the commedia del'arte!

LEADING ACTRESS: Well if he thinks I'm going to appear in that sort of nonsense . . .

YOUNG ACTOR: Nor me!

FOURTH ACTOR: I should like to know who they are.

THIRD ACTOR: Who do you think? They're probably escaped lunatics—or crooks.

YOUNG ACTOR: And is he taking them seriously?

YOUNG ACTRESS: It's vanity. The vanity of seeing himself as an author.

LEADING ACTOR: I've never heard of such a thing! If the theatre, ladies and gentlemen, is reduced to this . . .

FIFTH ACTOR: I'm enjoying it!

THIRD ACTOR: Really? We shall have to wait and see what happens next I suppose.

(Talking, they leave the stage. Some go out through the back door, some to the dressing-rooms.

The Curtain stays up.

The interval lasts twenty minutes.)

— ACT TWO —

The theatre warning-bell sounds to call the audience back. From the dressing-rooms, the door at the back and even from the auditorium, the ACTORS, *the* STAGE MANAGER, *the* STAGE HANDS, *the* PROMPTER, *the* PROPERTY MAN *and the* PRODUCER, *accompanied by the* SIX CHARACTERS *all come back on to the stage.*

The house lights go out and the stage lights come on again.

PRODUCER: Come on, everybody! Are we all here? Quiet now! Listen! Let's get started! Stage manager?

STAGE MANAGER: Yes, I'm here.

PRODUCER: Give me that little parlour setting, will you? A couple of plain flats and a door flat will do. Hurry up with it!

(The STAGE MANAGER *runs off to order someone to do this immediately and at the same time the* PRODUCER *is making arrangements with the* PROPERTY MAN, *the* PROMPTER, *and the* ACTORS: *the two flats and the door flat are painted in pink and gold stripes.)*

PRODUCER: *(To* PROPERTY MAN.*)* Go see if we have a sofa in stock.

PROPERTY MAN: Yes, there's that green one.

STEPDAUGHTER: No, no, not a green one! It was yellow, yellow velvet with flowers on it: it was enormous! And so comfortable!

PROPERTY MAN: We haven't got one like that.

PRODUCER: It doesn't matter! Give me whatever there is.

STEPDAUGHTER: What do you mean, it doesn't matter? It was Mme. Pace's famous sofa.

PRODUCER: It's only for a rehearsal! Please, don't interfere. *(To the* STAGE MANAGER.*)* Oh, and see if there's a shop window, will you—preferably a long, low one.

STEPDAUGHTER: And a little table, a little mahogany table for the blue envelope.

STAGE MANAGER: *(To the* PRODUCER.*)* There's that little gold one.

PRODUCER: That'll do—bring it.

FATHER: A mirror!

STEPDAUGHTER: And a screen! A screen, please, or I won't be able to manage, will I?

STAGE MANAGER: All right. We've lots of big screens, don't you worry.

PRODUCER: *(To* STEPDAUGHTER.*)* Then don't you want some coat-hangers and some clothes racks.

STEPDAUGHTER: Yes, lots of them, lots of them.

PRODUCER: *(To the* STAGE MANAGER.*)* See how many there are and have them brought up.

STAGE MANAGER: Right, I'll see to it.

(The STAGE MANAGER *goes off to do it: and while the* PRO-DUCER *is talking to the* PROMPTER, *the* CHARACTERS *and the* ACTORS, *the* STAGE MANAGER *is telling the* SCENE SHIFTERS *where to set up the furniture they have brought.)*

PRODUCER: *(To the* PROMPTER.*)* Now you, go sit down, will you? Look, this is an outline of the play, act by act. *(He hands him several sheets of paper.)* But you'll need to be on your toes.

PROMPTER: Shorthand?

PRODUCER: *(Pleasantly surprised.)* Oh, good! You know short-hand?

PROMPTER: I don't know much about prompting, but I do know about shorthand.

PRODUCER: Thank God for that anyway! *(He turns to a* STAGE HAND.*)* Go fetch me some paper from my office—lots of it—as much as you can find!

(The STAGE HAND *goes running off and then comes back shortly with a bundle of paper that he gives to the* PROMPTER.*)*

PRODUCER: *(Crossing to the* PROMPTER.*)* Follow the scenes, one after another, as they are played and try to get the lines down . . . at least the most important ones. *(Then turning to the* ACTORS.*)* Get out of the way everybody! Here, go over to the prompt side *(Pointing to stage left.)* and pay attention!

LEADING ACTRESS: But, excuse me, we . . .

PRODUCER: *(Anticipating her.)* You won't be expected to im-provise, don't worry!

LEADING ACTOR: Then what are we expected to do?

PRODUCER: Nothing! Just go over there, listen and watch. You'll all be given your parts later written out. Right now we're going to rehearse, as well as we can. And they will be doing the rehearsal. *(He points to the* CHARACTERS.*)*

FATHER: *(Rather bewildered, as if he had fallen from the clouds into the middle of the confusion on the stage.)* We are? Ex-cuse me, but what do you mean, a rehearsal?

PRODUCER: I mean a rehearsal—a rehearsal for the benefit of the actors. *(Pointing to the* ACTORS.*)*

FATHER: But if we are the characters . . .

PRODUCER: That's right, you're the 'characters': but characters don't act here, my dear chap. It's actors who act here. The characters are there in the script—*(Pointing to the* PROMPTER.*)* that's when there is a script.

FATHER: That's the point! Since there isn't one and you have the luck to have the characters alive in front of you . . .

PRODUCER: Great! You want to do everything yourselves, do you? To act your own play, to produce your own play!

FATHER: Well yes, just as we are.

PRODUCER: That would be an experience for us, I can tell you!

LEADING ACTOR: And what about us? What would we be doing then?

PRODUCER: Don't tell me you think you know how to act! Don't make me laugh! *(The* ACTORS *in fact laugh.)* There you are, you see, you've made them laugh. *(Then remember-ing.)* But let's get back to the point! We need to cast the play. Well, that's easy: it almost casts itself. *(To the* SECOND AC-TRESS.*)* You, the mother. *(To the* FATHER.*)* You'll need to give her a name.

FATHER: Amalia.

PRODUCER: But that's the real name of your wife isn't it? We can't use her real name.

FATHER: But why not? That is her name . . . But perhaps if this lady is to play the part . . . *(Indicating the* SECOND ACTRESS *vaguely with a wave of his hand.)* I think of her as Amalia . . . *(Pointing to the* MOTHER.*)* But do as you like . . . *(A little confused.)* I don't know what to say . . . I'm already starting to . . . how can I explain it . . . to sound false, my own words sound like someone else's.

PRODUCER: Now don't worry yourself about it, don't worry about it at all. We'll work out the right tone of voice. As for the name, if you want it to be Amalia, then Amalia it shall be: or we can find another. For the moment we'll refer to the characters like this: *(To the* YOUNG ACTOR, *the juvenile lead.)* you are The Son. *(To the* LEADING ACTRESS.*)* You, of course, are The Stepdaughter.

STEPDAUGHTER: *(Excitedly.)* What did you say? That woman is me? *(Bursts into laughter.)*

PRODUCER: *(Angrily.)* What are you laughing at?

LEADING ACTRESS: *(Indignantly.)* Nobody has ever dared to laugh at me before! Either you treat me with respect or I'm walking out! *(Starting to go.)*

STEPDAUGHTER: I'm sorry. I wasn't really laughing at you.

PRODUCER: *(To the* STEPDAUGHTER.*)* You should feel proud to be played by . . .

LEADING ACTRESS: *(Quickly, scornfully.)* . . . that woman!

STEPDAUGHTER: But I wasn't thinking about her, honestly. I was thinking about me: I can't see myself in you at all . . . you're not a bit like me!

FATHER: Yes, that's right: you see, our meaning . . .

PRODUCER: What are you talking about, 'our meaning'? Do you think you have exclusive rights to what you represent? Do you think it can only exist inside you? Not a bit of it!

FATHER: What? Don't we even have our own meaning?

PRODUCER: Not a bit of it! Whatever you mean is only mate-rial here, to which the actors give form and body, voice and gesture, and who, through their art, have given expression to much better material than what you have to offer: yours is re-ally very trivial and if it stands up on the stage, the credit, be-lieve me, will all be due to my actors.

FATHER: I don't dare to contradict you. But you for your part, must believe me—it doesn't seem trivial to us. We are suffering terribly now, with these bodies, these faces . . .

130 PRODUCER: (*Interrupting impatiently.*) Yes, well, the make-up will change that, make-up will change that, at least as far as the faces are concerned.

FATHER: Yes, but the voices, the gestures . . .

PRODUCER: That's enough! You can't come on the stage here as yourselves. It is our actors who will represent you here:
135 and let that be the end of it!

FATHER: I understand that. But now I think I see why our author who saw us alive as we are here now, didn't want to put us on the stage. I don't want to offend your actors. God forbid that I should! But I think that if I saw myself represented
140 . . . by I don't know whom . . .

LEADING ACTOR: (*Rising majestically and coming forward, followed by a laughing group of* YOUNG ACTRESSES.) By me, if you don't object.

FATHER: (*Respectfully, smoothly.*) I shall be honoured, sir. (*He*
145 *bows.*) But I think, that no matter how hard this gentleman works with all his will and all his art to identify himself with me . . . (*He stops, confused.*)

LEADING ACTOR: Yes, go on.

FATHER: Well, I was saying the performance he will give, even
150 if he is made up to look like me . . . I mean with the difference in our appearance . . . (*All the* ACTORS *laugh.*) it will be difficult for it to be a performance of me as I really am. It will be more like—well, not just because of his figure—it will be more an interpretation of what I am, what he believes
155 me to be, and not how I know myself to be. And it seems to me that this should be taken into account by those who are going to comment on us.

PRODUCER: So you are already worrying about what the critics will say, are you? And I'm still waiting to get this thing
160 started! The critics can say what they like: and we'll worry about putting on the play. If we can! (*Stepping out of the group and looking around.*) Come on, come on! Is the scene set for us yet? (*To the* ACTORS *and* CHARACTERS.) Out of the way! Let's have a look at it. (*Climbing down off the stage.*)
165 Don't let's waste any more time. (*To the* STEPDAUGHTER.) Does it look all right to you?

STEPDAUGHTER: What? That? I don't recognise it at all.

PRODUCER: Good God! Did you expect us to reconstruct the room at the back of Mme. Pace's shop here on the stage? (*To*
170 *the* FATHER.) Did you say the room had flowered wallpaper?

FATHER: White, yes.

PRODUCER: Well it's not white: it's striped. That sort of thing doesn't matter at all! As for furniture, it looks to me as if we have nearly everything we need. Move that little table a bit
175 further downstage. (*A* STAGE HAND *does it. To the* PROPERTY MAN.) Go and fetch an envelope, pale blue if you can find one, and give it to that gentleman there. (*Pointing to the* FATHER.)

STAGE HAND: An envelope for letters?

180 PRODUCER: } Yes, an envelope for letters!
FATHER: }

STAGE HAND: Right. (*He goes off.*)

PRODUCER: Now then, come on! The first scene is the young lady's. (*The* LEADING ACTRESS *comes to the centre.*) No, no, not yet. I said the young lady's. (*He points to the* STEP-
185 DAUGHTER.) You stay there and watch.

STEPDAUGHTER: (*Adding quickly.*). . . how I bring it to life.

LEADING ACTRESS: (*Resenting this.*) I shall know how to bring it to life, don't you worry, when I am allowed to.

PRODUCER: (*His head in his hands.*) Ladies, please, no more
190 arguments! Now then. The first scene is between the young lady and Mme. Pace. Oh! (*Worried, turning round and looking out into the auditorium.*) Where is Mme. Pace?

FATHER: She isn't here with us.

PRODUCER: So what do we do now?

195 FATHER: But she is real. She's real too!

PRODUCER: All right. So where is she?

FATHER: May I deal with this? (*Turns to the* ACTRESSES.) Would each of you ladies be kind enough to lend me a hat, a coat, a scarf or something?

200 ACTRESSES: (*Some are surprised or amused.*) What? My scarf? A coat? What's he want my hat for? What are you wanting to do with them? (*All the* ACTRESSES *are laughing.*)

FATHER: Oh, nothing much, just hang them up here on the racks for a minute or two. Perhaps someone would be kind
205 enough to lend me a coat?

ACTORS: Just a coat? Come on, more! The man must be mad.

AN ACTRESS: What for? Only my coat?

FATHER: Yes, to hang up here, just for a moment. I'm very grateful to you. Do you mind?

210 ACTRESSES: (*Taking off various hats, coats, scarves, laughing and going to hang them on the racks.*) Why not? Here you are. I really think it's crazy. Is it to dress the set?

FATHER: Yes, exactly. It's to dress the set.

PRODUCER: Would you mind telling me what you are doing?

215 FATHER: Yes, of course: perhaps, if we dress the set better, she will be drawn by the articles of her trade and, who knows, she may even come to join us . . . (*He invites them to watch the door at the back of the set.*) Look! Look!

(*The door at the back opens and* MME. PACE *takes a few steps downstage: she is a gross old harridan wearing a ludicrous carroty-coloured wig with a single red rose stuck in at one side, Spanish fashion: garishly made-up: in a vulgar but stylish red silk dress, holding an ostrich-feather fan in one hand and a cigarette between two fingers in the other. At the sight of this Apparition, the* ACTORS *and the* PRODUCER *immediately jump off the stage with cries of fear, leaping down into the auditorium and up the aisles. The* STEPDAUGHTER, *however, runs across to* MME. PACE, *and greets her respectfully, as if she were the mistress.*)

STEPDAUGHTER: (*Running across to her.*) Here she is! Here
220 she is!

FATHER: (*Smiling broadly.*) It's her! What did I tell you? Here she is!

PRODUCER: (*Recovering from his shock, indignantly.*) What sort of trick is this?

225 LEADING ACTOR: (*Almost at the same time as the others.*) What the hell is happening?

JUVENILE LEAD: Where on earth did they get that extra from?

YOUNG ACTRESS: They were keeping her hidden!

LEADING ACTRESS: It's a game, a conjuring trick!

230 FATHER: Wait a minute! Why do you want to spoil a miracle by being factual. Can't you see this is a miracle of reality, that is born, brought to life, lured here, reproduced, just for the sake of this scene, with more right to be alive here than you have? Perhaps it has more truth than you have yourselves. Which actress can improve on Mme. Pace there? Well?   235

That is the real Mme. Pace. You must admit that the actress who plays her will be less true than she is herself—and there she is in person! Look! My daughter recognised her straight away and went to meet her. Now watch—just watch this
240 scene.

(*Hesitantly, the* PRODUCER *and the* ACTORS *move back to their original places on the stage.*

But the scene between the STEPDAUGHTER *and* MME. PACE *has already begun while the* ACTORS *were protesting and the* FATHER *explaining: it is being played under their breaths, very quietly, very naturally, in a way that is obviously impossible on stage. So when the* ACTORS' *attention is recalled by the* FATHER *they turn and see that* MME. PACE *has just put her hand under the* STEPDAUGHTER's *chin to make her lift her head up: they also hear her speak in a way that is unintelligible to them. They watch and listen hard for a few moments, then they start to make fun of them.*)

PRODUCER: Well?

LEADING ACTOR: What's she saying?

LEADING ACTRESS: Can't hear a thing!

JUVENILE LEAD: Louder! Speak up!

245 STEPDAUGHTER: (*Leaving* MME. PACE *who has an astonishing smile on her face, and coming down to the* ACTORS.) Louder? What do you mean, 'Louder'? What we're talking about you can't talk about loudly. I could shout about it a moment ago to embarrass him (*Pointing to the* FATHER.) to shame him
250 and to get my own back on him! But it's a different matter for Mme. Pace. It would mean prison for her.

PRODUCER: What the hell are you on about? Here in the theatre you have to make yourself heard! Don't you see that? We can't hear you even from here, and we're on the stage with
255 you! Imagine what it would be like with an audience out front! You need to make the scene go! And after all, you would speak normally to each other when you're alone, and you will be, because we shan't be here anyway. I mean we're only here because it's a rehearsal. So just imagine that there
260 you are in the room at the back of the shop, and there's no one to hear you.

(*The* STEPDAUGHTER, *with a knowing smile, wags her finger and her head rather elegantly, as if to say no.*)

PRODUCER: Why not?

STEPDAUGHTER: (*Mysteriously, whispering loudly.*) Because there is someone who will hear if she speaks normally.
265 (*Pointing to* MME. PACE.)

PRODUCER: (*Anxiously.*) You're not going to make someone else appear are you?

(*The* ACTORS *get ready to dive off the stage again.*)

FATHER: No, no. She means me. I ought to be over there, waiting behind the door: and Mme. Pace knows I'm there, so ex-
270 cuse me will you: I'll go there now so that I shall be ready for my entrance.

(*He goes towards the back of the stage.*)

PRODUCER: (*Stopping him.*) No, no wait a minute! You must remember the stage conventions! Before you can go on to that part . . .
275 STEPDAUGHTER: (*Interrupts him.*) Oh yes, let's get on with that part. Now! Now! I'm dying to do that scene. If he wants to go through it now, I'm ready!

PRODUCER: (*Shouting.*) But before that we must have, clearly stated, the scene between you and her. (*Pointing to* MME. PACE.) Do you see?
280
STEPDAUGHTER: Oh God! She's only told me what you already know, that my mother's needlework is badly done again, the dress is spoilt and that I shall have to be patient if I want her to go on helping us out of our mess.

MME. PACE: (*Coming forward, with a great air of importance.*) 285 Ah, yes, sir, for that I do not wish to make a profit, to make advantage.

PRODUCER: (*Half frightened.*) What? Does she really speak like that?

(*All the* ACTORS *burst out laughing.*)

STEPDAUGHTER: (*Laughing too.*) Yes, she speaks like that, half 290 in Spanish, in the silliest way imaginable!

MME. PACE: Ah it is not good manners that you laugh at me when I make myself to speak, as I can, English, señor.

PRODUCER: No, no, you're right! Speak like that, please speak like that, madam. It'll be marvellous. Couldn't be better! 295 It'll add a little touch of comedy to a rather crude situation. Speak like that! It'll be great!

STEPDAUGHTER: Great! Why not? When you hear a proposition made in that sort of accent, it'll almost seem like a joke, won't it? Perhaps you'll want to laugh when you hear that 300 there's an 'old señor' who wants to 'amuse himself with me'—isn't that right, Madame?

MME. PACE: Not so old . . . but not quite young, no? But if he is not to your taste . . . he is, how you say, discreet!

(*The* MOTHER *leaps up, to the astonishment and dismay of the* ACTORS *who had not been paying any attention to her, so that when she shouts out they are startled and then smilingly restrain her: however she has already snatched off* MME. PACE's *wig and flung it on the floor.*)

MOTHER: You witch! Witch! Murderess! Oh, my daughter! 305

STEPDAUGHTER: (*Running across and taking hold of the* MOTHER.) No! No! Mother! Please!

FATHER: (*Running across to her as well.*) Calm yourself, calm yourself! Come and sit down.

MOTHER: Get her away from here! 310

STEPDAUGHTER: (*To the* PRODUCER *who has also crossed to her.*) My mother can't bear to be in the same place with her.

FATHER: (*Also speaking quietly to the* PRODUCER.) They can't possibly be in the same place! That's why she wasn't with us when we first came, do you see! If they meet, everything's 315 given away from the very beginning.

PRODUCER: It's not important, that's not important! This is only a first run-through at the moment! It's all useful stuff, even if it is confused. I'll sort it all out later. (*Turning to the* MOTHER *and taking her to sit down on her chair.*) Come on 320 my dear, take it easy, take it easy: come and sit down again.

STEPDAUGHTER: Go on, Mme. Pace.

MME. PACE: (*Offended.*) Oh no, thank-you! I no longer do nothing here with your mother present.

STEPDAUGHTER: Get on with it, bring in this 'old señor' who 325 wants to 'amuse himself with me'! (*Turning majestically to the others.*) You see, this next scene has got to be played out—we must do it now. (*To* MME. PACE.) Oh, you can go!

MME. PACE: Ah, I go, I go—I go! Most probably I go!

(*She leaves banging her wig back into place, glaring furiously at the* ACTORS *who applaud her exit, laughing loudly.*)

330   STEPDAUGHTER: *(To the* FATHER.*)* Now you come on! No, you don't need to go off again! Come back! Pretend you've just come in! Look, I'm standing here with my eyes on the ground, modestly—well, come on, speak up! Use that special sort of voice, like somebody who has just come in. 'Good
335   afternoon, my dear.'
       PRODUCER: *(Off the stage by now.)* Look here, who's the director here, you or me? *(To the* FATHER *who looks uncertain and bewildered.)* Go on, do as she says: go upstage—no, no don't bother to make an entrance. Then come down stage again.

(The FATHER *does as he is told, half mesmerised. He is very pale but already involved in the reality of his recreated life, smiles as he draws near the back of the stage, almost if he genuinely is not aware of the drama that is about to sweep over him. The* ACTORS *are immediately intent on the scene that is beginning now.)*

THE SCENE

FATHER: *(Coming forward with a new note in his voice.)* Good afternoon, my dear.
STEPDAUGHTER: *(Her head down trying to hide her fright.)* Good afternoon.
5   FATHER: *(Studying her a little under the brim of her hat which partly hides her face from him and seeing that she is very young, he exclaims to himself a little complacently and a little guardedly because of the danger of being compromised in a risky adventure.)* Ah . . . but . . . tell me, this won't be the first
10   time, will it? The first time you've been here?
STEPDAUGHTER: No, sir.
FATHER: You've been here before? *(And after the* STEPDAUGHTER *has nodded an answer.)* More than once? *(He waits for her reply: tries again to look at her under the brim of her hat:*
15   *smiles: then says.)* Well then . . . it shouldn't be too . . . May I take off your hat?
STEPDAUGHTER: *(Quickly, to stop him, unable to conceal her shudder of fear and disgust.)* No, don't! I'll do it!

(She takes it off unsteadily.

The MOTHER *watches the scene intently with the* SON *and the two smaller children who cling close to her all the time: they make a group on one side of the stage opposite the* ACTORS. *She follows the words and actions of the* FATHER *and the* STEPDAUGHTER *in this scene with a variety of expressions on her face—sadness, dismay, anxiety, horror: sometimes she turns her face away and sobs.)*

MOTHER: Oh God! Oh God!
20   FATHER: *(He stops as if turned to stone by the sobbing: then he goes on in the same tone of voice.)* Here, give it to me. I'll hang it up for you. *(He takes the hat in his hand.)* But such a pretty, dear little head like yours should have a much smarter hat than this! Would you like to help me choose one,
25   then, from these hats of Madame's hanging up here? Would you?
YOUNG ACTRESS: *(Interrupting.)* Be careful! Those are our hats!
30   PRODUCER: *(Quickly and angrily.)* For God's sake, shut up! Don't try to be funny! We're rehearsing! *(Turns back to the* STEPDAUGHTER.*)* Please go on, will you, from where you were interrupted.
STEPDAUGHTER: *(Going on.)* No, thank you, sir.
35   FATHER: Oh, don't say no to me please! Say you'll have one— to please me. Isn't this a pretty one—look! And then it will

please Madame too, you know. She's put them out here on purpose, of course.
STEPDAUGHTER: No, look, I could never wear it.
FATHER: Are you thinking of what they would say at home   40
when you went in wearing a new hat? Goodness me! Don't you know what to do? Shall I tell you what to say at home?
STEPDAUGHTER: *(Furiously, nearly exploding.)* That's not why! I couldn't wear it because . . . as you can see: you should have noticed it before. *(Indicating her black dress.)*   45
FATHER: You're in mourning! Oh, forgive me. You're right, I see that now. Please forgive me. Believe me, I'm really very sorry.
STEPDAUGHTER: *(Gathering all her strength and making herself overcome her contempt and revulsion.)* That's enough.   50
Don't go on, that's enough. I ought to be thanking you and not letting you blame yourself and get upset. Don't think any more about what I told you, please. And I should do the same. *(Forcing herself to smile and adding.)* I should try to forget that I'm dressed like this.   55
PRODUCER: *(Interrupting, turning to the* PROMPTER *in the box and jumping up on the stage again.)* Hold it, hold it! Don't put that last line down, leave it out. *(Turning to the* FATHER *and the* STEPDAUGHTER.*)* It's going well! It's going well! *(Then to the* FATHER *alone.)* Then we'll put in there the bit   60
that we talked about. *(To the* ACTORS.*)* That scene with the hats is good, isn't it?
STEPDAUGHTER: But the best bit is coming now! Why can't we get on with it?
PRODUCER: Just be patient, wait a minute. *(Turning and moving across to the* ACTORS.*)* Of course, it'll all have to be made   65
a lot more light-hearted.
LEADING ACTOR: We shall have to play it a lot quicker, I think.
LEADING ACTRESS: Of course: there's nothing particularly difficult in it. *(To the* LEADING ACTOR.*)* Shall we run through it   70
now?
LEADING ACTOR: Yes right . . . Shall we take it from my entrance? *(He goes to his position behind the door upstage.)*
PRODUCER: *(To the* LEADING ACTRESS.*)* Now then, listen, imagine the scene between you and Mme. Pace is finished.   75
I'll write it up myself properly later on. You ought to be over here I think—*(She goes the opposite way.)* Where are you going now?
LEADING ACTRESS: Just a minute, I want to get my hat—*(She crosses to take her hat from the stand.)*   80
PRODUCER: Right, good, ready now? You are standing here with your head down.
STEPDAUGHTER: *(Very amused.)* But she's not dressed in black!
LEADING ACTRESS: Oh, but I shall be, and I'll look a lot better   85
than you do, darling.
PRODUCER: *(To the* STEPDAUGHTER.*)* Shut up, will you! Go over there and watch! You might learn something! *(Clapping his hands.)* Right! Come on! Quiet please! Take it from his entrance!   90

(He climbs off stage so that he can see better. The door opens at the back of the set and the LEADING ACTOR *enters with the lively, knowing air of an ageing roué. The playing of the following scene by the* ACTORS *must seem from the very beginning to be something quite different from the earlier scene, but without having the faintest air of parody in it.)*

Naturally the STEPDAUGHTER *and the* FATHER, *unable to see themselves in the* LEADING ACTOR *and* LEADING ACTRESS, *hearing their words said by them, express their reactions in different ways, by gestures, or smiles or obvious protests so that we are aware of their suffering, their astonishment, their disbelief.*

The PROMPTER'S *voice is heard clearly between every line in the scene, telling the* ACTORS *what to say next.*)

LEADING ACTOR: Good afternoon, my dear.

FATHER: (*Immediately, unable to restrain himself.*) Oh, no!

(*The* STEPDAUGHTER, *watching the* LEADING ACTOR *enter this way, bursts into laughter.*)

PRODUCER: (*Furious.*) Shut up, for God's sake! And don't you dare laugh like that! We're never going to get anywhere at
95   this rate.

STEPDAUGHTER: (*Coming to the front.*) I'm sorry, I can't help it! The lady stands exactly where you told her to stand and she never moved. But if it were me and I heard someone say good afternoon to me in that way and with a voice like that I
100   should burst out laughing—so I did.

FATHER: (*Coming down a little too.*) Yes, she's right, the whole manner, the voice . . .

PRODUCER: To hell with the manner and the voice! Get out of the way, will you, and let me watch the rehearsal!

105   LEADING ACTOR: (*Coming down stage.*) If I have to play an old man who has come to a knocking shop—

PRODUCER: Take no notice, ignore them. Go on please! It's going well, it's going well! (*He waits for the* ACTOR *to begin again.*) Right, again!

110   LEADING ACTOR: Good afternoon, my dear.

LEADING ACTRESS: Good afternoon.

LEADING ACTOR: (*Copying the gestures of the* FATHER, *looking under the brim of the hat, but expressing distinctly the two emotions, first, complacent satisfaction and then anxiety.*) Ah!
115   But tell me . . . this won't be the first time I hope.

FATHER: (*Instinctively correcting him.*) Not 'I hope'—'will it', 'will it'.

PRODUCER: Say 'will it'—and it's a question.

LEADING ACTOR: (*Glaring at the* PROMPTER.) I distinctly heard
120   him say 'I hope'.

PRODUCER: So what? It's all the same, 'I hope' or 'isn't it'. It doesn't make any difference. Carry on, carry on. But perhaps it should still be a little bit lighter; I'll show you—watch me! (*He climbs up on the stage again, and going back to the
125   entrance, he does it himself.*) Good afternoon, my dear.

LEADING ACTRESS: Good afternoon.

PRODUCER: Ah, tell me . . . (*He turns to the* LEADING ACTOR *to make sure that he has seen the way he has demonstrated of looking under the brim of the hat.*) You see—surprise . . .
130   anxiety and self-satisfaction. (*Then, starting again, he turns to the* LEADING ACTRESS.) This won't be the first time, will it? The first time you've been here? (*Again turns to the* LEADING ACTOR, *questioningly.*) Right? (*To the* LEADING ACTRESS.) And then she says, 'No, sir'. (*Again to* LEADING
135   ACTOR.) See what I mean? More subtlety. (*And he climbs off the stage.*)

LEADING ACTRESS: No, sir.

LEADING ACTOR: You've been here before? More than once?

PRODUCER: No, no, no! Wait for it, wait for it. Let her answer
140   first. 'You've been here before?'

(*The* LEADING ACTRESS *lifts her head a little, her eyes closed in pain and disgust, and when the* PRODUCER *says 'Now' she nods her head twice.*)

STEPDAUGHTER: (*Involuntarily.*) Oh, my God! (*And she immediately claps her hand over her mouth to stifle her laughter.*)

PRODUCER: What now?

STEPDAUGHTER: (*Quickly.*) Nothing, nothing!

PRODUCER: (*To* LEADING ACTOR.) Come on, then, now it's you.   145

LEADING ACTOR: More than once? Well then, it shouldn't be too . . . May I take off your hat?

(*The* LEADING ACTOR *says this last line in such a way and adds to it such a gesture that the* STEPDAUGHTER, *even with her hand over her mouth trying to stop herself laughing, can't prevent a noisy burst of laughter.*)

LEADING ACTRESS: (*Indignantly turning.*) I'm not staying any longer to be laughed at by that woman!

LEADING ACTOR: Nor am I! That's the end—no more!   150

PRODUCER: (*To* STEPDAUGHTER, *shouting.*) Once and for all, will you shut up! Shut up!

STEPDAUGHTER: Yes, I'm sorry . . . I'm sorry.

PRODUCER: You're an ill-mannered little bitch! That's what you are! And you've gone too far this time!   155

FATHER: (*Trying to interrupt.*) Yes, you're right, she went too far, but please forgive her . . .

PRODUCER: (*Jumping on the stage.*) Why should I forgive her? Her behaviour is intolerable!

FATHER: Yes, it is, but the scene made such a peculiar impact   160
on us . . .

PRODUCER: Peculiar? What do you mean peculiar? Why peculiar?

FATHER: I'm full of admiration for your actors, for this gentleman (*To the* LEADING ACTOR.) and this lady. (*To the* LEAD-   165
ING ACTRESS.) But, you see, well . . . they're not us!

PRODUCER: Right! They're not! They're actors!

FATHER: That's just the point—they're actors. And they are acting our parts very well, both of them. But that's what's different. However much they want to be the same as us, they're   170
not.

PRODUCER: But why aren't they? What is it now?

FATHER: It's something to do with . . . being themselves, I suppose, not being us.

PRODUCER: Well we can't do anything about that! I've told   175
you already. You can't play the parts yourselves.

FATHER: Yes, I know, I know . . .

PRODUCER: Right then. That's enough of that. (*Turning back to the* ACTORS.) We'll rehearse this later on our own, as we usually do. It's always a bad idea to have rehearsals with au-   180
thors there! They're never satisfied. (*Turns back to the* FA-THER *and the* STEPDAUGHTER.) Come on, let's get on with it; and let's see if it's possible to do it without laughing.

STEPDAUGHTER: I won't laugh any more, I won't really. My best bit's coming up now, you wait and see!   185

PRODUCER: Right: when you say 'Don't think any more about what I told you, please. And I should do the same'. (*Turning to the* FATHER.) then you come in immediately with the line 'I understand, ah yes, I understand' and then you ask . . .

STEPDAUGHTER: (*Interrupting.*) Ask what? What does he ask?   190

PRODUCER: Why you're in mourning.

STEPDAUGHTER: No! No! That's not right! Look: when I said that I should try not to think about the way I was dressed, do you know what he said? 'Well then, let's take it off, we'll take it off at once, shall we, your little black dress.'

PRODUCER: That's great! That'll be wonderful! That'll bring the house down!

STEPDAUGHTER: But it's the truth!

PRODUCER: The truth! Do me a favour will you? This is the theatre you know! Truth's all very well up to a point but . . .

STEPDAUGHTER: What do you want to do then?

PRODUCER: You'll see! You'll see! Leave it all to me.

STEPDAUGHTER: No. No I won't. I know what you want to do! Out of my feeling of revulsion, out of all the vile and sordid reasons why I am what I am, you want to make a sugary little sentimental romance. You want him to ask me why I'm in mourning and you want me to reply with the tears running down my face that it is only two months since my father died. No. No. I won't have it! He must say to me what he really did say. 'Well then, let's take it off, we'll take it off at once, shall we, your little black dress.' And I, with my heart still grieving for my father's death only two months before, I went behind there, do you see? Behind that screen and with my fingers trembling with shame and loathing I took off the dress, unfastened my bra . . .

PRODUCER: (His head in his hands.) For God's sake! What are you saying!

STEPDAUGHTER: (Shouting excitedly.) The truth! I'm telling you the truth!

PRODUCER: All right then. Now listen to me. I'm not denying it's the truth. Right. And believe me I understand your horror, but you must see that we can't really put a scene like that on the stage.

STEPDAUGHTER: You can't? Then thanks very much. I'm not stopping here.

PRODUCER: No, listen . . .

STEPDAUGHTER: No, I'm going. I'm not stopping. The pair of you have worked it all out together, haven't you, what to put in the scene. Well, thank you very much! I understand everything now! He wants to get to the scene where he can talk about his spiritual torments but I want to show you my drama! Mine!

PRODUCER: (Shaking with anger.) Now we're getting to the real truth of it, aren't we? Your drama—yours! But it's not only yours, you know. It's drama for the other people as well! For him (Pointing to the FATHER.) and for your mother! You can't have one character coming on like you're doing, trampling over the others, taking over the play. Everything needs to be balanced and in harmony so that we can show what has to be shown! I know perfectly well that we've all got a life inside us and that we all want to parade it in front of other people. But that's the difficulty, how to present only the bits that are necessary in relation to the other characters: and in the small amount we show, to hint at all the rest of the inner life of the character! I agree, it would be so much simpler, if each character, in a soliloquy or in a lecture could pour out to the audience what's bubbling away inside him. But that's not the way we work. (In an indulgent, placating tone.) You must restrain yourself, you see. And believe me, it's in your own interests: because you could so easily make a bad impression, with all this uncontrollable anger, this disgust and exasperation. That seems a bit odd, if you don't mind my saying so, when you've admitted that you'd been with other men at Mme. Pace's and more than once.

STEPDAUGHTER: I suppose that's true. But you know, all the other men were all him as far as I was concerned.

PRODUCER: (Not understanding.) Uum—? What? What are you talking about?

STEPDAUGHTER: If someone falls into evil ways, isn't the responsibility for all the evil which follows to be laid at the door of the person who caused the first mistake? And in my case, it's him, from before I was even born. Look at him: see if it isn't true.

PRODUCER: Right then! What about the weight of remorse he's carrying? Isn't that important? Then, give him the chance to show it to us.

STEPDAUGHTER: But how? How on earth can he show all his long-suffering remorse, all his moral torments as he calls them, if you don't let him show his horror when he finds me in his arms one fine day, after he had asked me to take my dress off, a black dress for my father who had just died: and he finds that I'm the child he used to go and watch as she came out of school, me, a woman now, and a woman he could buy. (She says these last words in a voice trembling with emotion.)

(The MOTHER, hearing her say this, is overcome and at first gives way to stifled sobs: but then she bursts out into uncontrollable crying. Everyone is deeply moved. There is a long pause.)

STEPDAUGHTER: (As soon as the MOTHER has quietened herself she goes on, firmly and thoughtfully.) At the moment we are here on our own and the public doesn't know about us. But tomorrow you will present us and our story in whatever way you choose, I suppose. But wouldn't you like to see the real drama? Wouldn't you like to see it explode into life, as it really did?

PRODUCER: Of course, nothing I'd like better, then I can use as much of it as possible.

STEPDAUGHTER: Then persuade my mother to leave.

MOTHER: (Rising and her quiet weeping changing to a loud cry.) No! No! Don't let her! Don't let her do it!

PRODUCER: But they're only doing it for me to watch—only for me, do you see?

MOTHER: I can't bear it, I can't bear it!

PRODUCER: But if it's already happened, I can't see what's the objection.

MOTHER: No! It's happening now, as well: it's happening all the time. I'm not acting my suffering! Can't you understand that? I'm alive and here now but I can never forget that terrible moment of agony, that repeats itself endlessly and vividly in my mind. And these two little children here, you've never heard them speak have you? That's because they don't speak any more, not now. They just cling to me all the time: they help to keep my grief alive, but they don't really exist for themselves any more, not for themselves. And she (Indicating the STEPDAUGHTER.) . . . she has gone away, left me completely, she's lost to me, lost . . . you see her here for one reason only: to keep perpetually before me, always real, the anguish and the torment I've suffered on her account.

FATHER: The eternal moment, as I told you, sir. She is here (Indicating the STEPDAUGHTER.) to keep me too in that moment, trapped for all eternity, chained and suspended in that one fleeting shameful moment of my life. She can't give up her role and you cannot rescue me from it.

PRODUCER: But I'm not saying that we won't present that bit. Not at all! It will be the climax of the first act, when she (*He points to the* MOTHER.) surprises you.

FATHER: That's right, because that is the moment when I am
315 sentenced: all our suffering should reach a climax in her cry. (*Again indicating the* MOTHER.)

STEPDAUGHTER: I can still hear it ringing in my ears! It was that cry that sent me mad! You can have me played just as
320 you like: it doesn't matter! Dressed, too, if you want, so long as I can have at least an arm—only an arm—bare, because, you see, as I was standing like this (*She moves across to the* FATHER *and leans her head on his chest.*) with my head like this and my arms round his neck, I saw a vein, here in my arm, throbbing: and then it was almost as if that throbbing
325 vein filled me with a shivering fear, and I shut my eyes tightly like this, like this and buried my head in his chest. (*Turning to the* MOTHER.) Scream, Mummy, scream. (*She buries her head in the* FATHER'S *chest, and with her shoulders raised as if to try not to hear the scream, she speaks with a*
330 *voice tense with suffering.*) Scream, as you screamed then!

MOTHER: (*Coming forward to pull them apart.*) No! She's my daughter! My daughter! (*Tearing her from him.*) You brute, you animal, she's my daughter! Can't you see she's my daughter?

335 PRODUCER: (*Retreating as far as the footlights while the* ACTORS *are full of dismay.*) Marvellous! Yes, that's great! And then curtain!

FATHER: (*Running downstage to him, excitedly.*) That's it, that's it! Because it really was like that!

340 PRODUCER: (*Full of admiration and enthusiasm.*) Yes, yes, that's got to be the curtain line! Curtain! Curtain!

(*At the repeated calls of the* PRODUCER, *the* STAGE MANAGER *lowers the curtain, leaving on the apron in front, the* PRODUCER *and the* FATHER.)

PRODUCER: (*Looking up to heaven with his arms raised.*) The idiots! I didn't mean now! The bloody idiots—dropping it in on us like that! (*To the* FATHER, *and lifting up a corner of the*
345 *curtain.*) That's marvellous! Really marvellous! A terrific effect! We'll end the act like that! It's the best tag line I've heard for ages. What a First Act ending! I couldn't have done better if I'd written it myself!

(*They go through the curtain together.*)

— ACT THREE —

When the curtain goes up we see that the STAGE MANAGER *and* STAGE HANDS *have struck the first scene and have set another, a small garden fountain.*

From one side of the stage the ACTORS *come on and from the other the* CHARACTERS. *The* PRODUCER *is standing in the middle of the stage with his hand over his mouth, thinking.*

PRODUCER: (*After a short pause, shrugging his shoulders.*) Well, then: let's get on to the second act! Leave it all to me, and everything will work out properly.

STEPDAUGHTER: This is where we go to live at his house
5 (*Pointing to the* FATHER.) in spite of the objections of him over there. (*Pointing to the* SON.)

PRODUCER: (*Getting impatient.*) All right, all right! But leave it all to me, will you?

STEPDAUGHTER: Provided that you make it clear that he objected! 10

MOTHER: (*From the corner, shaking her head.*) That doesn't matter! The worse it was for us, the more he suffered from remorse.

PRODUCER: (*Impatiently.*) I know, I know! I'll take it all into account. Don't worry! 15

MOTHER: (*Pleading.*) To set my mind at rest, sir, please do make sure it's clear that I tried all I could—

STEPDAUGHTER: (*Interrupting her scornfully and going on.*) — to pacify me, to persuade me that this despicable creature wasn't worth making trouble about! (*To the* PRODUCER.) Go 20 on, set her mind at rest, because it's true, she tried very hard. I'm having a whale of a time now! You can see, can't you, that the meeker she was and the more she tried to worm her way into his heart, the more lofty and distant he became! How's that for a dramatic situation! 25

PRODUCER: Do you think that we can actually begin the Second Act?

STEPDAUGHTER: I won't say another word! But you'll see that it won't be possible to play everything in the garden, like you want to do. 30

PRODUCER: Why not?

STEPDAUGHTER: (*Pointing to the* SON.) Because to start with, he stays shut up in his room in the house all the time! And then all the scenes for this poor little devil of a boy happen in the house. I've told you once. 35

PRODUCER: Yes, I know that! But on the other hand we can't put up a notice to tell the audience where the scene is taking place, or change the set three or four times in each Act.

LEADING ACTOR: That's what they used to do in the good old days. 40

PRODUCER: Yes, when the audience was about as bright as that little girl over there!

LEADING ACTRESS: And it makes it easier to create an illusion.

FATHER: (*Leaping up.*) An illusion? For pity's sake don't talk about illusions! Don't use that word, it's especially hurtful 45 to us!

PRODUCER: (*Astonished.*) And why, for God's sake?

FATHER: It's so hurtful, so cruel! You ought to have realised that!

PRODUCER: What else should we call it? That's what we do 50 here—create an illusion for the audience . . .

LEADING ACTOR: With our performance . . .

PRODUCER: A perfect illusion of reality!

FATHER: Yes, I know that, I understand. But on the other hand, perhaps you don't understand us yet. I'm sorry! But you see, 55 for you and for your actors what goes on here on the stage is, quite rightly, well, it's only a game.

LEADING ACTRESS: (*Interrupting indignantly.*) A game! How dare you! We're not children! What happens here is serious!

FATHER: I'm not saying that it isn't serious. And I mean, really, 60 not just a game but an art, that tries, as you've just said, to create the perfect illusion of reality.

PRODUCER: That's right!

FATHER: Now try to imagine that we, as you see us here, (*He indicates himself and the other* CHARACTERS.) that we have 65 no other reality outside this illusion.

PRODUCER: (*Astonished and looking at the* ACTORS *with the same sense of bewilderment as they feel themselves.*) What the hell are you talking about now?

70 FATHER: (*After a short pause as he looks at them, with a faint smile.*) Isn't it obvious? What other reality is there for us? What for you is an illusion you create, for us is our only reality. (*Brief pause. He moves towards the* PRODUCER *and goes on.*) But it's not only true for us, it's true for others as well,
75 you know. Just think about it. (*He looks intently into the* PRODUCER's *eyes.*) Do you really know who you are? (*He stands pointing at the* PRODUCER.)

PRODUCER: (*A little disturbed but with a half smile.*) What? Who I am? I am me!

80 FATHER: What if I told you that that wasn't true: what if I told you that you were me?

PRODUCER: I would tell you that you were mad!

(*The* ACTORS *laugh.*)

FATHER: That's right, laugh! Because everything here is a game! (*To the* PRODUCER.) And yet you object when I say
85 that it is only for a game that the gentleman there (*Pointing to the* LEADING ACTOR.) who is 'himself' has to be 'me', who, on the contrary, am 'myself'. You see, I've caught you in a trap.

(*The* ACTORS *start to laugh.*)

PRODUCER: Not again! We've heard all about this a little while
90 ago.

FATHER: No, no. I didn't really want to talk about this. I'd like you to forget about your game, (*Looking at the* LEADING ACTRESS *as if to anticipate what she will say.*) I'm sorry—your artistry! Your art!—that you usually pursue here with your
95 actors; and I am going to ask you again in all seriousness, who are you?

PRODUCER: (*Turning with a mixture of amazement and annoyance, to the* ACTORS.) Of all the bloody nerve! A fellow who claims he is only a character comes and asks me who I am!

100 FATHER: (*With dignity but without annoyance.*) A character, my dear sir, can always ask a man who he is, because a character really has a life of his own, a life full of his own specific qualities, and because of these he is always 'someone'. While a man—I'm not speaking about you personally, of course,
105 but man in general—well, he can be an absolute 'nobody'.

PRODUCER: All right, all right! Well, since you've asked me, I'm the Director, the Producer—I'm in charge! Do you understand?

FATHER: (*Half smiling, but gently and politely.*) I'm only ask-
110 ing to try to find out if you really see yourself now in the same way that you saw yourself, for instance, once upon a time in the past, with all the illusions you had then, with everything inside and outside yourself as it seemed then— and not only seemed, but really was! Well then, look back on
115 those illusions, those ideas that you don't have any more, on all those things that no longer seem the same to you. Don't you feel that not only this stage is falling away from under your feet but so is the earth itself, and that all these realities of today are going to seem tomorrow as if they had been an
120 illusion?

PRODUCER: So? What does that prove?

FATHER: Oh, nothing much. I only want to make you see that if we (*Pointing to himself and the other* CHARACTERS.) have no other reality outside our own illusion, perhaps you ought to distrust your own sense of reality: because whatever is a re- 125 ality today, whatever you touch and believe in and that seems real for you today, is going to be—like the reality of yesterday—an illusion tomorrow.

PRODUCER: (*Deciding to make fun of him.*) Very good! So now you're saying that you as well as this play you're going to 130 show me here, are more real than I am?

FATHER: (*Very seriously.*) There's no doubt about that at all.

PRODUCER: Is that so?

FATHER: I thought you'd realised that from the beginning.

PRODUCER: More real than I am? 135

FATHER: If your reality can change between today and tomorrow—

PRODUCER: But everybody knows that it can change, don't they? It's always changing! Just like everybody else's!

FATHER: (*Crying out.*) But ours doesn't change! Do you see? 140 That's the difference! Ours doesn't change, it can't change, it can never be different, never, because it is already determined, like this, for ever, that's what's so terrible! We are an eternal reality. That should make you shudder to come near us. 145

PRODUCER: (*Jumping up, suddenly struck by an idea, and standing directly in front of the* FATHER.) Then I should like to know when anyone saw a character step out of his part and make a speech like you've done, proposing things, explaining things. Tell me when, will you? I've never seen it before. 150

FATHER: You've never seen it because an author usually hides all the difficulties of creating. When the characters are alive, really alive and standing in front of their author, he has only to follow their words, the actions that they suggest to him: and he must want them to be what they want to be: and it's 155 his bad luck if he doesn't do what they want! When a character is born he immediately assumes such an independence even of his own author that everyone can imagine him in scores of situations that his author hadn't even thought of putting him in, and he sometimes acquires a meaning that 160 his author never dreamed of giving him.

PRODUCER: Of course I know all that.

FATHER: Well, then. Why are you surprised by us? Imagine what a disaster it is for a character to be born in the imagination of an author who then refuses to give him life in a writ- 165 ten script. Tell me if a character, left like this, suspended, created but without a final life, isn't right to do what we are doing now, here in front of you. We spent such a long time, such a very long time, believe me, urging our author, persuading him, first me, then her, (*Pointing to the* STEP- 170 DAUGHTER.) then this poor Mother . . .

STEPDAUGHTER: (*Coming down the stage as if in a dream.*) It's true, I would go, would go and tempt him, time after time, in his gloomy study just as it was growing dark, when he was sitting quietly in an armchair not even bothering to switch a 175 light on but leaving the shadows to fill the room: the shadows were swarming with us, we had come to tempt him. (*As if she could see herself there in the study and is annoyed by the presence of the* ACTORS.) Go away will you! Leave us alone! Mother there, with that son of hers—me with the little girl— that poor little kid always on his own—and then me with 180 him (*Pointing to the* FATHER.) and then at last, just me, on my own, all on my own, in the shadows. (*She turns quickly as if she wants to cling on to the vision she has of herself, in the* 185 *shadows.*) Ah, what scenes, what scenes we suggested to him! What a life I could have had! I tempted him more than the others!

FATHER: Oh yes, you did! And it was probably all your fault that he did nothing about it! You were so insistent, you made 190 too many demands.

STEPDAUGHTER: But he wanted me to be like that! (*She comes closer to the* PRODUCER *to speak to him in confidence.*) I think it's more likely that he felt discouraged about the the-atre and even despised it because the public only wants to 195 see . . .

PRODUCER: Let's get on, for God's sake, let's get on. Come to the point will you?

STEPDAUGHTER: I'm sorry, but if you ask me, we've got too much happening already, just with our entry into his house. 200 (*Pointing to the* FATHER.) You said that we couldn't put up a notice or change the set every five minutes.

PRODUCER: Right! Of course we can't! We must combine things, group them together in one continuous flowing ac-tion: not the way you've been wanting, first of all seeing your 205 little brother come home from school and wander about the house like a lost soul, hiding behind the doors and brooding on some plan or other that would—what did you say it would do?

STEPDAUGHTER: Wither him . . . shrivel him up completely.

210 PRODUCER: That's good! That's a good expression. And then you 'can see it there in his eyes, getting stronger all the time'—isn't that what you said?

STEPDAUGHTER: Yes, that's right. Look at him! (*Pointing to him as he stands next to his* MOTHER.)

215 PRODUCER: Yes, great! And then, at the same time, you want to show the little girl playing in the garden, all innocence. One in the house and the other in the garden—we can't do it, don't you see that?

STEPDAUGHTER: Yes, playing in the sun, so happy! It's the only 220 pleasure I have left, her happiness, her delight in playing in the garden: away from the misery, the squalor of that sordid flat where all four of us slept and where she slept with me— with me! Just think of it! My vile, contaminated body close to hers, with her little arms wrapped tightly round my neck, 225 so lovingly, so innocently. In the garden, whenever she saw me, she would run and take my hand. She never wanted to show me the big flowers, she would run about looking for the 'little weeny' ones, so that she could show them to me; she was so happy, so thrilled! (*As she says this, tortured by the* 230 *memory, she breaks out into a long desperate cry, dropping her head on her arms that rest on a little table. Everybody is very affected by her. The* PRODUCER *comes to her almost pa-ternally and speaks to her in a soothing voice.*)

PRODUCER: We'll have the garden scene, we'll have it, don't 235 worry: and you'll see, you'll be very pleased with what we do! We'll play all the scenes in the garden! (*He calls out to a* STAGE HAND *by name.*) Hey . . . . , let down a few bits of tree, will you? A couple of cypresses will do, in front of the foun-tain. (*Someone drops in the two cypresses and a* STAGE HAND 240 *secures them with a couple of braces and weights.*)

PRODUCER: (*To the* STEPDAUGHTER.) That'll do for now, won't it? It'll just give us an idea. (*Calling out to a* STAGE

HAND *by name again.*) Hey, ... give me something for the sky will you?

STAGE HAND: What's that?   245

PRODUCER: Something for the sky! A small cloth to come in behind the fountain. (*A white cloth is dropped from the flies.*) Not white! I asked for a sky! Never mind: leave it! I'll do something with it. (*Calling out.*) Hey lights! Kill everything will you? Give me a bit of moonlight—the blues in the bat- 250 ten and a blue spot on the cloth . . . (*They do.*) That's it! That'll do! (*Now on the scene there is the light he asked for, a mysterious blue light that makes the* ACTORS *speak and move as if in the garden in the evening under a moon. To the* STEP-DAUGHTER.) Look here now: the little boy can come out 255 here in the garden and hide among the trees instead of hid-ing behind the doors in the house. But it's going to be diffi-cult to find a little girl to play the scene with you where she shows you the flowers. (*Turning to the* LITTLE BOY.) Come on, come on, son, come across here. Let's see what it'll look 260 like. (*But the* BOY *doesn't move.*) Come on will you, come on. (*Then he pulls him forward and tries to make him hold his head up, but every time it falls down again on his chest.*) There's something very odd about this lad . . . What's wrong with him? My God, he'll have to say something sometime! 265 (*He comes over to him again, puts his hand on his shoulder and pushes him between the trees.*) Come a bit nearer: let's have a look. Can you hide a bit more? That's it. Now pop your head out and look round. (*He moves away to look at the effect and as the* BOY *does what he has been told to do, the* AC- 270 TORS *watch impressed and a little disturbed.*) Ahh, that's good, very good . . . (*He turns to the* STEPDAUGHTER.) How about having the little girl, surprised to see him there, run across. Wouldn't that make him say something?

STEPDAUGHTER: (*Getting up.*) It's no use hoping he'll speak, 275 not as long as that creature's there. (*Pointing to the* SON.) You'll have to get him out of the way first.

SON: (*Moving determinedly to one of the sets of steps leading off the stage.*) With pleasure! I'll go now! Nothing will please me better!   280

PRODUCER: (*Stopping him immediately.*) Hey, no! Where are you going? Hang on!

(*The* MOTHER *gets up, anxious at the idea that he is really going and instinctively raising her arms as if to hold him back, but without moving from where she is.*)

SON: (*At the footlights, to the* PRODUCER *who is restraining him there.*) There's no reason why I should be here! Let me go will you? Let me go!   285

PRODUCER: What do you mean there's no reason for you to be here?

STEPDAUGHTER: (*Calmly, ironically.*) Don't bother to stop him. He won't go!

FATHER: You have to play that terrible scene in the garden 290 with your mother.

SON: (*Quickly, angry and determined.*) I'm not going to play anything! I've said that all along! (*To the* PRODUCER.) Let me go will you?

STEPDAUGHTER: (*Crossing to the* PRODUCER.) It's all right. 295 Let him go. (*She moves the* PRODUCER's *hand from the* SON. *Then she turns to the* SON *and says.*) Well, go on then! Off you go!

(The SON *stays near the steps but as if pulled by some strange force he is quite unable to go down them: then to the astonishment and even the dismay of the* ACTORS, *he moves along the front of the stage towards the other set of steps down into the auditorium: but having got there, he again stays near and doesn't actually go down them. The* STEPDAUGHTER *who has watched him scornfully but very intently, bursts into laughter.)*

STEPDAUGHTER: He can't, you see? He can't! He's got to stay
300 here! He must. He's chained to us for ever! No, I'm the one who goes, when what must happen does happen, and I run away, because I hate him, because I can't bear the sight of him any longer. Do you think it's possible for him to run away? He has to stay here with that wonderful father of his
305 and his mother there. She doesn't think she has any other son but him. *(She turns to the* MOTHER.*)* Come on, come on, Mummy, come on! *(Turning back to the* PRODUCER *to point her out to him.)* Look, she's going to try to stop him . . . *(To the* MOTHER, *half compelling her, as if by some magic*
310 *power.)* Come on, come on. *(Then to the* PRODUCER *again.)* Imagine how she must feel at showing her affection for him in front of your actors! But her longing to be near him is so strong that—look! She's going to go through that scene with him again! *(The* MOTHER *has now actually come close to the*
315 SON *as the* STEPDAUGHTER *says the last line: she gestures to show that she agrees to go on.)*
SON: *(Quickly.)* But I'm not! I'm not! If I can't get away then I suppose I shall have to stay here; but I repeat that I will not have any part in it.
320 FATHER: *(To the* PRODUCER, *excitedly.)* You must make him!
SON: Nobody's going to make me do anything!
FATHER: I'll make you!
STEPDAUGHTER: Wait! Just a minute! Before that, the little girl has to go to the fountain. *(She turns to take the* LITTLE GIRL,
325 *drops on her knees in front of her and takes her face between her hands.)* My poor little darling, those beautiful eyes, they look so bewildered. You're wondering where you are, aren't you? Well, we're on a stage, my darling! What's a stage? Well, it's a place where you pretend to be serious. They put
330 on plays here. And now we're going to put on a play. Seriously! Oh, yes! Even you . . . *(She hugs her tightly and rocks her gently for a moment.)* Oh, my little one, my little darling, what a terrible play it is for you! What horrible things have been planned for you! The garden, the fountain . . . Oh, yes,
335 it's only a pretend fountain, that's right. That's part of the game, my pretty darling: everything is pretends here. Perhaps you'll like a pretends fountain better than a real one: you can play here then. But it's only a game for the others; not for you, I'm afraid, it's real for you, my darling, and your
340 game is in a real fountain, a big beautiful green fountain with bamboos casting shadows, looking at your own reflection, with lots of baby ducks paddling about, shattering the reflections. You want to stroke one! *(With a scream that electrifies and terrifies everybody.)* No, Rosetta, no! Your
345 mummy isn't watching you, she's over there with that selfish bastard! Oh, God, I feel as if all the devils in hell were tearing me apart inside . . . And you . . . *(Leaving the* LITTLE GIRL *and turning to the* LITTLE BOY *in the usual way.)* What are you doing here, hanging about like a beggar? It'll be your
350 fault too, if that little girl drowns; you're always like this, as if I wasn't paying the price for getting all of you into this house.

(Shaking his arm to make him take his hand out of his pocket.) What have you got there? What are you hiding? Take it out, take your hand out! *(She drags his hand out of his pocket and to everyone's horror he is holding a revolver.* 355 *She looks at him for a moment, almost with satisfaction: then she says, grimly.)* Where on earth did you get that? *(The* BOY, *looking frightened, with his eyes wide and empty, doesn't answer.)* You idiot, if I'd been you, instead of killing myself, I'd have killed one of those two: either or both, the father and 360 the son. *(She pushes him towards the cypress trees where he then stands watching: then she takes the* LITTLE GIRL *and helps her to climb in to the fountain, making her lie so that she is hidden: after that she kneels down and puts her head and arms on the rim of the fountain.)* 365
PRODUCER: That's good! It's good! *(Turning to the* STEPDAUGHTER.*)* And at the same time . . .
SON: *(Scornfully.)* What do you mean, at the same time? There was nothing at the same time! There wasn't any scene between her and me. *(Pointing to the* MOTHER.*)* She'll tell 370 you the same thing herself, she'll tell you what happened.

(The SECOND ACTRESS *and the* JUVENILE LEAD *have left the group of* ACTORS *and have come to stand nearer the* MOTHER *and the* SON *as if to study them so as to play their parts.)*

MOTHER: Yes, it's true. I'd gone to his room . . .
SON: Room, do you hear? Not the garden!
PRODUCER: It's not important! We've got to reorganise the events anyway. I've told you that already. 375
SON: *(Glaring at the* JUVENILE LEAD *and the* SECOND ACTRESS.*)* What do you want?
JUVENILE LEAD: Nothing. I'm just watching.
SON: *(Turning to the* SECOND ACTRESS.*)* You as well! Getting ready to play her part are you? *(Pointing to the* MOTHER.*)* 380
PRODUCER: That's it. And I think you should be grateful— they're paying you a lot of attention.
SON: Oh, yes, thank you! But haven't you realised yet that you'll never be able to do this play? There's nothing of us inside you and you actors are only looking at us from the out- 385 side. Do you think we could go on living with a mirror held up in front of us that didn't only freeze our reflection for ever, but froze us in a reflection that laughed back at us with an expression that we didn't even recognise as our own?
FATHER: That's right! That's right! 390
PRODUCER: *(To* JUVENILE LEAD *and* SECOND ACTRESS.*)* Okay. Go back to the others.
SON: It's quite useless. I'm not prepared to do anything.
PRODUCER: Oh, shut up, will you, and let me listen to your mother. *(To the* MOTHER.*)* Well, you'd gone to his room, you 395 said.
MOTHER: Yes, to his room. I couldn't bear it any longer. I wanted to empty my heart to him, tell him about all the agony that was crushing me. But as soon as he saw me come in . . . 400
SON: Nothing happened. I got away! I wasn't going to get involved. I never have been involved. Do you understand?
MOTHER: It's true! That's right!
PRODUCER: But we must make up the scene between you, then. It's vital! 405
MOTHER: I'm ready to do it! If only I had the chance to talk to him for a moment, to pour out all my troubles to him.

FATHER: (*Going to the* SON *and speaking violently.*) You'll do it! For your Mother! For your Mother!

410 SON: (*More than ever determined.*) I'm doing nothing!

FATHER: (*Taking hold of his coat collar and shaking him.*) For God's sake, do as I tell you! Do as I tell you! Do you hear what she's saying? Haven't you any feelings for her?

SON: (*Taking hold of his* FATHER.) No I haven't! I haven't! Let
415 that be the end of it!

(*There is a general uproar. The* MOTHER *frightened out of her wits, tries to get between them and separate them.*)

MOTHER: Please stop it! Please!

FATHER: (*Hanging on.*) Do as I tell you! Do as I tell you!

SON: (*Wrestling with him and finally throwing him to the ground near the steps. Everyone is horrified.*) What's come
420 over you? Why are you so frantic? Do you want to parade our disgrace in front of everybody? Well, I'm having nothing to do with it! Nothing! And I'm doing what our author wanted as well—he never wanted to put us on the stage.

PRODUCER: Then why the hell did you come here?

425 SON: (*Pointing to the* FATHER.) He wanted to, I didn't.

PRODUCER: And aren't you here now?

SON: He was the one who wanted to come and he dragged all of us here with him and agreed with you in there about what to put in the play: and that meant not only what had really
430 happened, as if that wasn't bad enough, but what hadn't happened as well.

PRODUCER: All right, then, you tell me what happened. You tell me! Did you rush out of your room without saying anything?

435 SON: (*After a moment's hesitation.*) Without saying anything. I didn't want to make a scene.

PRODUCER: (*Needling him.*) What then? What did you do then?

SON: (*He is now the centre of everyone's agonised attention and he crosses the stage.*) Nothing . . . I went across the garden . . .
440 (*He breaks off gloomy and absorbed.*)

PRODUCER: (*Urging him to say more, impressed by his reluctance to speak.*) Well? What then? You crossed the garden?

SON: (*Exasperated, putting his face into the crook of his arm.*)
445 Why do you want me to talk about it? It's horrible! (*The* MOTHER *is trembling with stifled sobs and looking towards the fountain.*)

PRODUCER: (*Quietly, seeing where she is looking and turning to the* SON *with growing apprehension.*) The little girl?
450 SON: (*Looking straight in front, out to the audience.*) There, in the fountain . . .

FATHER: (*On the floor still, pointing with pity at the* MOTHER.) She was trailing after him!

PRODUCER: (*To the* SON, *anxiously.*) What did you do then?
455 SON: (*Still looking out front and speaking slowly.*) I dashed across. I was going to jump in and pull her out . . . But something else caught my eye: I saw something behind the tree that made my blood run cold: the little boy, he was standing there with a mad look in his eyes: he was standing looking
460 into the fountain at his little sister, floating there, drowned.

(*The* STEPDAUGHTER *is still bent at the fountain hiding the* LITTLE GIRL, *and she sobs pathetically, her sobs sounding like an echo.*

There is a pause.)

SON: (*Continued.*) I made a move towards him: but then . . .

(*From behind the trees where the* LITTLE BOY *is standing there is the sound of a shot.*)

MOTHER: (*With a terrible cry she runs along with the* SON *and all the* ACTORS *in the midst of a great general confusion.*) My son! My son! (*And then from out of the confusion and crying her voice comes out.*) Help! Help me!
465
PRODUCER: (*Amidst the shouting he tries to clear a space whilst the* LITTLE BOY *is carried by his feet and shoulders behind the white skycloth.*) Is he wounded? Really wounded? (*Everybody except the* PRODUCER *and the* FATHER *who is still on the floor by the steps, has gone behind the skycloth and stays there
470 talking anxiously. Then independently the* ACTORS *start to come back into view.*)

LEADING ACTRESS: (*Coming from the right, very upset.*) He's dead! The poor boy! He's dead! What a terrible thing!

LEADING ACTOR: (*Coming back from the left and smiling.*)
475 What do you mean, dead? It's all make-believe. It's a sham! He's not dead. Don't you believe it!

OTHER ACTORS FROM THE RIGHT: Make-believe? It's real! Real! He's dead!

OTHER ACTORS FROM THE LEFT: No, he isn't. He's pretend-
480 ing! It's all make-believe.

FATHER: (*Running off and shouting at them as he goes.*) What do you mean, make-believe? It's real! It's real, ladies and gentlemen! It's reality! (*And with desperation on his face he too goes behind the skycloth.*)
485
PRODUCER: (*Not caring any more.*) Make-believe?! Reality?! Oh, go to hell the lot of you! Lights! Lights! Lights!

(*At once all the stage and auditorium is flooded with light. The* PRODUCER *heaves a sigh of relief as if he has been relieved of a terrible weight and they all look at each other in distress and with uncertainty.*)

PRODUCER: God! I've never known anything like this! And we've lost a whole day's work! (*He looks at the clock.*) Get off with you, all of you! We can't do anything now! It's too late to
490 start a rehearsal. (*When the* ACTORS *have gone, he calls out.*) Hey, lights! Kill everything! (*As soon as he has said this, all the lights go out completely and leave him in the pitch dark.*) For God's sake!! You might have left the workers! I can't see where I'm going!
495
(*Suddenly, behind the skycloth, as if because of a bad connection, a green light comes up to throw on the cloth a huge sharp shadow of the* CHARACTERS, *but without the* LITTLE BOY *and the* LITTLE GIRL. *The* PRODUCER, *seeing this, jumps off the stage, terrified. At the same time the flood of light on them is switched off and the stage is again bathed in the same blue light as before. Slowly the* SON *comes on from the right, followed by the* MOTHER *with her arms raised towards him. Then from the left, the* FATHER *enters.*)

They come together in the middle of the stage and stand there as if transfixed. Finally from the left the STEPDAUGHTER *comes on and moves towards the steps at the front: on the top step she pauses for a moment to look back at the other three and then bursts out in a raucous laugh, dashes down the steps and turns to look at the three figures still on the stage. Then she runs out of the auditorium and we can still hear her manic laughter out into the foyer and beyond.*

After a pause the curtain falls slowly.)

■ BERTOLT BRECHT ■

Bertolt Brecht (1898–1956) changed the course of the modern European theater—and theater around the world—more than any playwright since Ibsen. However, Brecht's sphere of influence extends beyond his career as a playwright. As a dramatist, he wrote an unsurpassed body of plays; as a theoretician, Brecht's conception of "alienation" in the epic theater opened the way for sweeping innovation in our understanding of the possibilities of the stage; as a director, Brecht's work with his company, the Berliner Ensemble, made it the most influential and important theater in postwar Europe. The challenge of understanding Brecht is to understand the dialectical interplay between theory and practice that informs his assault on stage realism, and on the bourgeois theater itself.

Eugen Berthold Brecht (he later changed his name to Bertolt) was born in Augsburg, Bavaria, in 1898 to a prosperous family. In 1917, he enrolled at Munich University in the natural sciences and worked as a drama critic on the side. He also began work on several plays, including *Baal* (1917). In 1918 he was conscripted into military service for the remainder of World War I and worked in a military hospital. He returned briefly to the university after the war, but soon turned his attention full time to the theater. He moved to Berlin—Germany's theatrical capital at the time— and had the good fortune to work with two influential directors, Max Reinhardt and Erwin Piscator. Piscator advocated the use of new technologies in the theater, as a way of developing a kind of performance more responsive to the mechanized and accelerated routines of modern life. Brecht acknowledged that many of his own staging techniques were derived from his work with Piscator in the 1920s. Throughout the 1920s and early 1930s, Brecht wrote a series of plays that brought him notoriety, largely for their satire of the bourgeois establishment: *Drums in the Night* (1919), *In the Jungle of Cities* (1921), *Man Is Man* (1926), and the musical plays he wrote in collaboration with the composer Kurt Weill, *The Threepenny Opera* (1928) and *The Rise and Fall of the City of Mahagonny* (1930). In the 1920s, Brecht also began to collaborate with Margarete Steffin, one of several women—including Elisabeth Hauptmann and Ruth Berlau—with whom he collaborated as playwright.

Brecht also began his serious reading of Marx in the 1920s, and it was his application of Marxist dialectic to the process of theater that gave rise to his most powerful and original ideas for the stage. From Marx, Brecht adopted a revolutionary posture, not only toward the class struggle, but toward the stage of bourgeois "realism." To Brecht, the realistic theater was not an unbiased window on social reality. Instead, Brecht argued that realistic theater presented a particular political vision, a view of society as inevitably determined by history and evolution, and therefore not susceptible to change. In order to displace "realism," and to demonstrate these hidden politics, Brecht redefined Marx's conception of "alienation" as a theatrical practice. In *Das Kapital*, Marx argues that the division of labor in modern industrial production has altered the relationship between mankind and the world. In modern industry, workers sell their labor in order to produce commodities. These commodities, Marx contends, then seem "alien" in that they appear to have arisen magically. Capitalist production conceals the signs of how they were produced, so that commodities come to have a "natural" life of their own. Yet, even as commodities seem to come alive, the workers become dehumanized, incorporated into the machinery of production. In the world of capital, where everything is for sale, all human relations, lives, and desires become commodified. The prevailing view of the world—in which commodities confront workers as something natural and entirely separate from their makers—is, to Marx, a *false* view, perpetuated within the bourgeois social order to the political advantage of the ruling classes.

Brecht's theater works to provide its audience with ways of regarding bourgeois reality—including realistic theater and drama—as "unnatural," as a political vision, as an ideological view of the world produced in the interest of profit. Brecht's theater, that is, works to "alienate" or "estrange" the audience from the commonplace "realities" of daily life—which we have unreflectively come to regard as "natural" and "inevitable"—in order to train us to question the world made by modern capitalism and the society it sustains. As he wrote in "The Modern Theater is the Epic Theater," his theater is based on a "radical separation of the elements" of production, rather than on the scenic unity typical of realism. The seamless illusion of the realistic stage is that theater's most seductive commodity: it constantly and subliminally urges the audience to accept its "picture" of reality as a natural, apolitical image of the world as it is. Brecht's theater, in contrast, always shows both the dramatic illusion (the character, the setting, the action) and the process of its making (the work of the actor, the machinery of the theater, the activities of the stage). Brecht works to show the "means of production" in his theater, as a way of suggesting that stage realism, like social reality outside the theater, is *made*, not given.

Brecht called this theater by a variety of names, including EPIC THEATER, the term now generally used for Brecht's body of theory and technique. Brecht's plays tend to be episodic, a disconnected, open-ended MONTAGE of scenes: The audience must arrive at its own understanding of how the events are linked together, rather than being given an apparently inevitable narrative. Brecht generally left the stage bare in his productions, as a way of preventing the audience from seeing a complete illusion of some fictional dramatic locale. He exposed the lights above the stage, so the audience could see how lights influence the mood of the scene and so influence the audience's judgment. Brecht fragmented the "realistic" unity of the setting in other ways, too. Films could be projected on screens above the stage, forcing the audience to hold the drama in counterpoint to more recent events; placards onstage described the action to take place before the scene began. Finally, Brecht also urged his actors not to empathize entirely with the characters they played, but to strike a balance between a Stanislavskian identification with the character (being "in character," acting the character entirely from his or her point of view) and a more demonstrative attitude, one that enables the actor to represent the character from a variety of perspectives. Through these means, Brecht worked to involve the audience in the process of the play's production. Rather than being seduced by a commodified illusion of reality, the audience of epic theater is invited to consider, and enjoy, how the theater makes its fictions—as a way of teaching the audience to adopt a more critical, "alienated" way of seeing life outside the theater.

Brecht used many of these devices in *The Threepenny Opera* and in the series of plays he wrote in exile. Forced to flee Germany by Nazi purges of left-wing writers in 1933, Brecht spent the greater part of his creative life on the run, living briefly in Sweden, in Finland, and finally in Santa Monica, California, from 1941 to 1947. Although he had drafted *Life of Galileo* in 1938, Brecht continued to work on the play in California, collaborating on an English version with the actor Charles Laughton. He was also questioned by the House Un-American Activities Committee in 1947, as part of its infamous investigation of communism in the entertainment industry. Brecht was not charged and left the United States the following day to return to Europe and Germany. Living in exile, with no theater and little support, Brecht wrote his major plays: *Life of Galileo* (1938), *The Good Person of Szechwan* (1939), *Mother Courage and Her Children* (1939), *The Caucasian Chalk Circle* (1944). He also wrote his most important theoretical essays, including *A Short Organum for the Theater* (1948).

Brecht returned to East Berlin in 1947 and established his company, the Berliner Ensemble. Brecht's antirealist plays had long been the source of conflict with the SOCIAL REALISM advocated by the Communist Party, and even after the war Brecht had to work with a wary eye on the East German authorities. Nonetheless, the Berliner Ensemble—under Brecht's guidance and with the talents of his wife, Helene Weigel—became the leading European production company of the 1950s, sowing the seeds of innovation in every country they visited. Brecht died in August of 1956, just before the Berliner Ensemble's stunning visit to London, but the influence of his conception of theater has become worldwide, visible in plays from Marguerite Duras's *India Song* to Luis Valdez's *Los Vendidos* to Caryl Churchill's *Cloud 9* to Tony Kushner's *Angels in America*.

MOTHER COURAGE AND HER CHILDREN

Mother Courage and Her Children is typical of Brecht's innovative approach to theater and to "political theater" as well. Rather than presenting a thesis, the play works to question the audience's attitudes about a variety of social institutions: warfare, business, motherhood, morality. In a parable-like series of scenes reminiscent both of expressionist theater and of morality drama, *Mother Courage and Her Children* invites the audience to estrange, and so reconsider, its ways of mapping the world.

In his model-book of the play, Brecht wrote that he wanted to show that "war, which is a continuation of business by other means, makes the human virtues fatal to their possessors." The play considers this problem in a variety of challenging ways. Although it is perhaps tempting to see Courage—Why is she called Courage? Was she courageous?—as a tragic heroine, the play relentlessly questions her "heroic" survival, and our own attitudes about the distinctions between war, business, and morality. As Scene I demonstrates, war and business create an all-embracing market in which everything is commodified, for sale. Mother Courage sells a belt buckle and loses a son as part of the same transaction.

Much of the play's power onstage arises through its use of physical space and a few significant properties. The wagon—Courage's home, her means of survival, her mode of production—becomes in a sense the play's central "character." Placing it on a turntable, most productions convey the sense that the wagon is almost always in motion, yet never actually getting anywhere, much as Courage herself enters the play and leaves it singing the same song. Courage's fortunes are emblematized by the wagon as well. Loaded with goods and pulled by her two strong sons in the first scene, it is battered, barren, and empty in the last, pulled by Mother Courage herself as she struggles to catch up with the army. Brecht was attracted to the idea of using the wagon, the play's economic and material "base," so to speak, to elucidate some of the play's symbolic or moral themes. He used Courage's wash-line to link the wagon to the cannon at the opening of Scene III, tying warfare, the economy, and the domestic sphere together. He raised the harness-poles to form a kind of crucifix after the death of Swiss Cheese. Many of the most ironic moments of the Berliner Ensemble production of the play were Weigel's invention: as Mother Courage, she bit the coin in Scene I and slowly measured her pennies out of her purse when she paid the peasants to bury Kattrin at the end of the play. This is the kind of moment that Brecht worked—in theory, as a playwright, in directing productions—to make happen in the theater, a moment when a single gesture forces the audience to consider the scene in a new light, to question the relationship between its ideas of identity and morality and the society that gives them shape and meaning.

MOTHER COURAGE
AND HER CHILDREN
A CHRONICLE OF THE THIRTY YEARS' WAR

BERTOLT BRECHT

TRANSLATED BY JOHN WILLETT

— CHARACTERS —

MOTHER COURAGE	A CLERK
KATTRIN, *her dumb daughter*	A YOUNG SOLDIER
EILIF, *the elder son*	AN OLDER SOLDIER
SWISS CHEESE, *the younger son*	A PEASANT
THE RECRUITER	THE PEASANT'S WIFE
THE SERGEANT	THE YOUNG MAN
THE COOK	THE OLD WOMAN
THE GENERAL	ANOTHER PEASANT
THE CHAPLAIN	HIS WIFE
THE ARMOURER	THE YOUNG PEASANT
YVETTE POTTIER	THE ENSIGN
THE MAN WITH THE PATCH	SOLDIERS
ANOTHER SERGEANT	A VOICE
THE ANCIENT COLONEL	

— SCENE ONE —

Spring 1624. The Swedish Commander-in-Chief Count Oxenstierna is raising troops in Dalecarlia for the Polish campaign. The canteen woman Anna Fierling, known under the name of Mother Courage, loses one son

Country road near a town.

A SERGEANT *and a* RECRUITER *stand shivering.*

RECRUITER: How can you muster a unit in a place like this? I've been thinking about suicide, sergeant. Here am I, got to find our commander four companies before the twelfth of the month, and people round here are so nasty I can't sleep
5 nights. S'pose I get hold of some bloke and shut my eye to his pigeon chest and varicose veins, I get him proper drunk, he signs on the line, I'm just settling up, he goes for a piss, I follow him to the door because I smell a rat; bob's your uncle, he's off like a flea with the itch. No notion of word of hon-
10 our, loyalty, faith, sense of duty. This place has shattered my confidence in the human race, sergeant.
SERGEANT: It's too long since they had a war here; stands to reason. Where's their sense of morality to come from? Peace—that's just a mess; takes a war to restore order. Peace-
15 time, the human race runs wild. People and cattle get buggered about, who cares? Everyone eats just as he feels inclined, a hunk of cheese on top of his nice white bread, and a slice of fat on top of the cheese. How many young blokes and good horses in that town there, nobody knows; they
20 never thought of counting. I been in places ain't seen a war for nigh seventy years: folks hadn't got names to them, couldn't tell one another apart. Takes a war to get proper nominal rolls and inventories—shoes in bundles and corn in bags, and man and beast properly numbered and carted off,
25 cause it stands to reason: no order, no war.

RECRUITER: Too true.
SERGEANT: Same with all good things, it's a job to get a war going. But once it's blossomed out there's no holding it; folk start fighting shy of peace like punters what can't stop for fear of having to tot up what they lost. Before that it's war 30 they're fighting shy of. It's something new to them.
RECRUITER: Hey, here's a cart coming. Two tarts with two young fellows. Stop her, sergeant. If this one's a flop I'm not standing around in your spring winds any longer, I can tell you. 35

(Sound of a jew's-harp. Drawn by two young fellows, a covered cart rolls in. On it sit MOTHER COURAGE *and her dumb daughter* KATTRIN.*)*

MOTHER COURAGE: Morning, sergeant.
SERGEANT: *(Blocking the way.)* Morning, all And who are you?
MOTHER COURAGE: Business folk. *(Sings.)*

> You captains, tell the drums to slacken
> And give your infanteers a break: 40
> It's Mother Courage with her waggon
> Full of the finest boots they make.
> With crawling lice and looted cattle
> With lumbering guns and straggling kit—
> How can you flog them into battle 45
> Unless you get them boots that fit?
> The new year's come. The watchmen shout.
> The thaw sets in. The dead remain.
> Whatever life has not died out
> It staggers to its feet again. 50
>
> Captains, how can you make them face it—
> Marching to death without a brew?
> Courage has rum with which to lace it
> And boil their souls and bodies through.

736

55 Their musket primed, their stomach hollow—
Captains, your men don't look so well.
So feed them up and let them follow
While you command them into hell.
     The new year's come. The watchmen shout.
60   The thaw sets in. The dead remain.
     Wherever life has not died out
     It staggers to its feet again.

SERGEANT: Halt! Who are you with, you trash?
THE ELDER SON: Second Finnish Regiment.
65 SERGEANT: Where's your papers?
MOTHER COURAGE: Papers?
THE YOUNGER SON: What, mean to say you don't know Mother Courage?
SERGEANT: Never heard of her. What's she called Courage
70 for?
MOTHER COURAGE: Courage is the name they gave me because I was scared of going broke, sergeant, so I drove me cart right through the bombardment of Riga with fifty loaves of bread aboard. They were going mouldy, it was high time,
75 hadn't any choice really.
SERGEANT: Don't be funny with me. Your papers.
MOTHER COURAGE: (*Pulling a bundle of papers from a tin box and climbing down off the cart.*) That's all my papers, sergeant. You'll find a whole big missal from Altötting in
80 Bavaria for wrapping gherkins in, and a road map of Moravia, the Lord knows when I'll ever get there, might as well chuck it away, and here's a stamped certificate that my horse hasn't got foot-and-mouth, only he's dead worse luck, cost fifteen florins he did—not me luckily. That enough
85 paper for you?
SERGEANT: You pulling my leg? I'll knock that sauce out of you. S'pose you know you got to have a licence.
MOTHER COURAGE: Talk proper to me, do you mind, and don't you dare say I'm pulling your leg in front of my unsul-
90 lied children, 'tain't decent, I got no time for you. My honest face, that's me licence with the Second Regiment, and if it's too difficult for you to read there's nowt I can do about it. Nobody's putting a stamp on that.
RECRUITER: Sergeant, methinks I smell insubordination in
95 this individual. What's needed in our camp is obedience.
MOTHER COURAGE: Sausage, if you ask me.
SERGEANT: Name.
MOTHER COURAGE: Anna Fierling.
SERGEANT: You all called Fierling then?
100 MOTHER COURAGE: What d'you mean? It's me's called Fierling, not them.
SERGEANT: Aren't all this lot your children?
MOTHER COURAGE: You bet they are, but why should they all have to be called the same, eh? (*Pointing to her elder son.*)
105 For instance, that one's called Eilif Nojocki—Why? his father always claimed he was called Kojocki or Mojocki or something. The boy remembers him clearly, except that the one he remembers was someone else, a Frenchie with a little beard. Aside from that he's got his father's wits; that man
110 knew how to snitch a peasant's pants off his bum without him noticing. This way each of us has his own name, see.
SERGEANT: What, each one different?
MOTHER COURAGE: Don't tell me you ain't never come across that.

115 SERGEANT: So I s'pose he's a Chinaman? (*Pointing to the younger son.*)
MOTHER COURAGE: Wrong. Swiss.
SERGEANT: After the Frenchman?
MOTHER COURAGE: What Frenchman? I never heard tell of no Frenchman. You keep muddling things up, we'll be
120 hanging around here till dark. A Swiss, but called Fejos, and the name has nowt to do with his father. He was called something quite different and was a fortifications engineer, only drunk all the time.

(SWISS CHEESE *beams and nods;* dumb KATTRIN *too is amused.*)

125 SERGEANT: How in hell can he be called Fejos?
MOTHER COURAGE: I don't like to be rude, sergeant, but you ain't got much imagination, have you? Course he's called Fejos, because when he arrived I was with a Hungarian, very decent fellow, had terrible kidney trouble though he never
130 touched a drop. The boy takes after him.
SERGEANT: But he wasn't his father . . .
MOTHER COURAGE: Took after him just the same. I call him Swiss Cheese. (*Pointing to her daughter.*) And that's Kattrin Haupt, she's half German.
135 SERGEANT: Nice family, I must say.
MOTHER COURAGE: Aye, me cart and me have seen the world.
SERGEANT: I'm writing all this down. (*He writes.*) And you're from Bamberg in Bavaria; how d'you come to be here?
MOTHER COURAGE: Can't wait till war chooses to visit Bam-
140 berg, can I?
RECRUITER: (*To* EILIF.) You two should be called Jacob Ox and Esau Ox, pulling the cart like that. I s'pose you never get out of harness?
EILIF: Ma, can I clobber him one? I wouldn't half like to.
145 MOTHER COURAGE: And I says you can't; just you stop where you are. And now two fine officers like you, I bet you could use a good pistol, or a belt buckle, yours is on its last legs, sergeant.
SERGEANT: I could use something else. Those boys are healthy
150 as young birch trees, I observe: chests like barrels, solid leg muscles. So why are they dodging their military service, may I ask?
MOTHER COURAGE: (*Quickly.*) Nowt doing, sergeant. Yours is no trade for my kids.
155 RECRUITER: But why not? There's good money in it, glory too. Flogging boots is women's work. (*To* EILIF.) Come here, let's see if you've muscles in you or if you're a chicken.
MOTHER COURAGE: He's a chicken. Give him a fierce look, he'll fall over.
160 RECRUITER: Killing a young bull that happens to be in his way. (*Wants to lead him off.*)
MOTHER COURAGE: Let him alone, will you? He's nowt for you folk.
RECRUITER: He was crudely offensive and talked about clob-
165 bering me. The two of us are going to step into that field and settle it man to man.
EILIF: Don't you worry, mum, I'll fix him.
MOTHER COURAGE: Stop there! You varmint! I know you, nowt but fights. There's a knife down his boot. A slasher,
170 that's what he is.
RECRUITER: I'll draw it out of him like a milk-tooth. Come along, sonny.

MOTHER COURAGE: Sergeant, I'll tell the colonel. He'll have you both in irons. The lieutenant's going out with my daughter.

SERGEANT: No rough stuff, chum. (*To* MOTHER COURAGE.) What you got against military service? Wasn't his own father a soldier? Died a soldier's death, too? Said it yourself.

MOTHER COURAGE: He's nowt but a child. You want to take him off to slaughterhouse, I know you lot. They'll give you five florins for him.

RECRUITER: First he's going to get a smart cap and boots, eh?

EILIF: Not from you.

MOTHER COURAGE: Let's both go fishing, said angler to worm. (*To* SWISS CHEESE.) Run off, call out they're trying to kidnap your brother. (*She pulls a knife.*) Go on, you kidnap him, just try. I'll slit you open, trash. I'll teach you to make war with him. We're doing an honest trade in ham and linen, and we're peaceable folk.

SERGEANT: Peaceable I don't think; look at your knife. You should be ashamed of yourself; put that knife away, you old harridan. A minute back you were admitting you live off the war, how else should you live, what from? But how's anyone to have war without soldiers?

MOTHER COURAGE: No need for it to be my kids.

SERGEANT: Oh, you'd like war to eat the pips but spit out the apple? It's to fatten up your kids, but you won't invest in it. Got to look after itself, eh? And you called Courage, fancy that. Scared of the war that keeps you going? Your sons aren't scared of it, I can see that.

EILIF: Take more than a war to scare me.

SERGEANT: And why? Look at me: has army life done all that badly by me? Joined up at seventeen.

MOTHER COURAGE: Still got to reach seventy.

SERGEANT: I don't mind waiting.

MOTHER COURAGE: Under the sod, eh?

SERGEANT: You trying to insult me, saying I'll die?

MOTHER COURAGE: S'pose it's true? S'pose I can see the mark's on you? S'pose you look like a corpse on leave to me? Eh?

SWISS CHEESE: She's got second sight, Mother has.

RECRUITER: Go ahead, tell the sergeant's fortune, might amuse him.

MOTHER COURAGE: Gimme helmet. (*He gives it to her.*)

SERGEANT: It don't mean a bloody sausage. Anything for a laugh though.

MOTHER COURAGE: (*Taking out a sheet of parchment and tearing it up.*) Eilif, Swiss Cheese and Kattrin, may all of us be torn apart like this if we lets ourselves get too mixed up in the war. (*To the* SERGEANT.) Just for you I'm doing it for free. Black's for death. I'm putting a big black cross on this slip of paper.

SWISS CHEESE: Leaving the other one blank, see?

MOTHER COURAGE: Then I fold them across and shake them. All of us is jumbled together like this from our mother's womb, and now draw a slip and you'll know. (*The* SERGEANT *hesitates.*)

RECRUITER: (*To* EILIF.) I don't take just anybody, they all know I'm choosey, but you got the kind of fire I like to see.

SERGEANT: (*Fishing in the helmet.*) Too silly. Load of eyewash.

SWISS CHEESE: Drawn a black cross, he has. Write him off.

RECRUITER: They're having you on; not everybody's name's on a bullet.

SERGEANT: (*Hoarsely.*) You've put me in the shit.

MOTHER COURAGE: Did that yourself the day you became a soldier. Come along, let's move on now. 'Tain't every day we have a war, I got to get stirring.

SERGEANT: God damn it, you can't kid me. We're taking that bastard of yours for a soldier.

EILIF: Swiss Cheese'd like to be a soldier too.

MOTHER COURAGE: First I've heard of that. You'll have to draw too, all three of you. (*She goes to the rear to mark crosses on further slips.*)

RECRUITER: (*To* EILIF.) One of the things they say against us is that it's all holy-holy in the Swedish camp; but that's a malicious rumour to do us down. There's no hymn-singing but Sundays, just a single verse, and then only for those got voices.

MOTHER COURAGE: (*Coming back with the slips, which she drops into the* SERGEANT's *helmet.*) Trying to get away from their ma, the devils, off to war like calves to salt-lick. But I'm making you draw lots, and that'll show you the world is no vale of joys with 'Come along, son, we need a few more generals'. Sergeant, I'm so scared they won't get through the war. Such dreadful characters, all three of them. (*She hands the helmet to* EILIF.) Hey, come on, fish out your slip. (*He fishes one out, unfolds it. She snatches it from him.*) There you are, it's a cross. Oh, wretched mother that I am, o pain-racked giver of birth! Shall he die? Aye, in the springtime of life he is doomed. If he becomes a soldier he shall bite the dust, it's plain to see. He is too foolhardy, like his dad was. And if he ain't sensible he'll go the way of all flesh, his slip proves it. (*Shouts at him.*) You going to be sensible?

EILIF: Why not?

MOTHER COURAGE: Sensible thing is stay with your mother, never mind if they poke fun at you and call you chicken, just you laugh.

RECRUITER: If you're pissing in your pants I'll make do with your brother.

MOTHER COURAGE: I told you laugh. Go on, laugh. Now you draw, Swiss Cheese. I'm not so scared on your account, you're honest. (*He fishes in the helmet.*) Oh, why look at your slip in that strange way? It's got to be a blank. There can't be any cross on it. Surely I'm not going to lose *you*. (*She takes the slip.*) A cross? What, you too? Is that because you're so simple, perhaps? O Swiss Cheese, you too will be sunk if you don't stay utterly honest all the while, like I taught you from childhood when you brought the change back from the baker's. Else you can't save yourself. Look, sergeant, that's a black cross, ain't it?

SERGEANT: A cross, that's right. Can't think how I come to get one. I always stay in the rear. (*To the* RECRUITER.) There's no catch. Her own family get it too.

SWISS CHEESE: I get it too. But I listen to what I'm told.

MOTHER COURAGE: (*To* KATTRIN.) And now you're the only one I know's all right, you're a cross yourself; got a kind heart you have. (*Holds the helmet up to her on the cart, but takes the slip out herself.*) No, that's too much. That can't be right; must have made a mistake shuffling. Don't be too kind-hearted, Kattrin, you'll have to give it up, there's a cross above your path too. Lie doggo, girl, it can't be that hard once you're born dumb. Right, all of you know now. Look out for yourselves, you'll need to. And now up we get and on we go. (*She climbs on to the cart.*)

RECRUITER: (*To the* SERGEANT.) Do something.

SERGEANT: I don't feel very well.

RECRUITER: Must of caught a chill taking your helmet off in that wind. Involve her in a deal. (*Aloud.*) Might as well have a look at that belt-buckle, sergeant. After all, our friends here have to live by their business. Hey, you people, the sergeant wants to buy that belt-buckle.

MOTHER COURAGE: Half a florin. Two florins is what a belt like that's worth. (*Climbs down again.*)

SERGEANT: 'Tain't new. Let me get out of this damned wind and have a proper look at it. (*Goes behind the cart with the buckle.*)

MOTHER COURAGE: Ain't what I call windy.

SERGEANT: I s'pose it might be worth half a florin, it's silver.

MOTHER COURAGE: (*Joining him behind the cart.*) It's six solid ounces.

RECRUITER: (*To* EILIF.) And then we men'll have one together. Got your bounty money here, come along. (EILIF *stands undecided.*)

MOTHER COURAGE: Half a florin it is.

SERGEANT: It beats me. I'm always at the rear. Sergeant's the safest job there is. You can send the others up front, cover themselves with glory. Me dinner hour's properly spoiled. Shan't be able to hold nowt down, I know.

MOTHER COURAGE: Mustn't let it prey on you so's you can't eat. Just stay at the rear. Here, take a swig of brandy, man. (*Gives him a drink.*)

RECRUITER: (*Has taken* EILIF *by the arm and is leading him away up stage.*) Ten florins bounty money, then you're a gallant fellow fighting for the king and women'll be after you like flies. And you can clobber me for free for insulting you.

(*Exeunt both.*
Dumb* KATTRIN *leans down from the cart and makes hoarse noises.*)

MOTHER COURAGE: All right, Kattrin, all right. Sergeant's just paying. (*Bites the half-florin.*) I got no faith in any kind of money. Burnt child, that's me, sergeant. This coin's good, though. And now let's get moving. Where's Eilif?

SWISS CHEESE: Went off with the recruiter.

MOTHER COURAGE: (*Stands quite still, then.*) You simpleton. (*To* KATTRIN.) 'Tain't your fault, you can't speak, I know.

SERGEANT: Could do with a swig yourself, ma. That's life. Plenty worse things than being a soldier. Want to live off war, but keep yourself and family out of it, eh?

MOTHER COURAGE: You'll have to help your brother pull now, Kattrin.

(*Brother and sister hitch themselves to the cart and start pulling.*
MOTHER COURAGE *walks alongside. The cart rolls on.*)

SERGEANT: (*Looking after them.*)
Like the war to nourish you?
Have to feed it something too.

— SCENE TWO —

In the years 1625 and 1626 Mother Courage crosses Poland in the train of the Swedish armies. Before the fortress of Wallhof she meets her son again. Successful sale of a capon and heyday of her dashing son

The general's tent.
Beside it, his kitchen. Thunder of cannon. The cook is arguing with MOTHER COURAGE, *who wants to sell him a capon.*

THE COOK: Sixty hellers for a miserable bird like that?

MOTHER COURAGE: Miserable bird? This fat brute? Mean to say some greedy old general—and watch your step if you got nowt for his dinner—can't afford sixty hellers for him?

THE COOK: I can get a dozen like that for ten hellers just down the road.

MOTHER COURAGE: What, a capon like this you can get just down the road? In time of siege, which means hunger that tears your guts. A rat you might get: 'might' I say because they're all being gobbled up, five men spending best part of day chasing one hungry rat. Fifty hellers for a giant capon in time of siege!

THE COOK: But it ain't us having the siege, it's t'other side. We're conducting the siege, can't you get that in your head?

MOTHER COURAGE: But we got nowt to eat too, even worse than them in the town. Took it with them, didn't they? They're having a high old time, everyone says. And look at us! I been to the peasants, there's nowt there.

THE COOK: There's plenty. They're sitting on it.

MOTHER COURAGE: (*Triumphantly.*) They ain't. They're bust, that's what they are. Just about starving. I saw some, were grubbing up roots from sheer hunger, licking their fingers after they boiled some old leather strap. That's way it is. And me got a capon here and supposed to take forty hellers for it.

THE COOK: Thirty, not forty. I said thirty.

MOTHER COURAGE: Here, this ain't just any old capon. It was such a gifted beast, I been told, it could only eat to music, had a military march of its own. It could count, it was that intelligent. And you say forty hellers is too much? General will make mincemeat of you if there's nowt on his table.

THE COOK: See what I'm doing? (*He takes a piece of beef and puts his knife to it.*) Here I got a bit of beef, I'm going to roast it. Make up your mind quick.

MOTHER COURAGE: Go on, roast it. It's last year's.

THE COOK: Last night's. That animal was still alive and kicking, I saw him myself.

MOTHER COURAGE: Alive and stinking, you mean.

THE COOK: I'll cook him five hours if need be. I'll just see if he's still tough. (*He cuts into it.*)

MOTHER COURAGE: Put plenty of pepper on it so his lordship the general don't smell the pong.

(*The* GENERAL, *a* CHAPLAIN *and* EILIF *enter the tent.*)

THE GENERAL: (*Slapping* EILIF *on the shoulder.*) Now then, Eilif my son, into your general's tent with you and sit thou at my right hand. For you accomplished a deed of heroism, like a pious cavalier; and doing what you did for God, and in a war of religion at that, is something I commend in you most highly, you shall have a gold bracelet as soon as we've taken this town. Here we are, come to save their souls for them, and what do those insolent dung-encrusted yokels go and do? Drive their beef away from us. They stuff it into those priests of theirs all right, back and front, but you taught 'em manners, ha! So here's a pot of red wine for you, the two of us'll knock it back at one gulp. (*They do so.*) Piss all for the chaplain, the old bigot. And now, what would you like for dinner, my darling?

EILIF: A bit of meat, why not?

THE GENERAL: Cook! Meat!

THE COOK: And then he goes and brings guests when there's nowt there.

(MOTHER COURAGE *silences him so she can listen.*)

60   EILIF: Hungry job cutting down peasants.

MOTHER COURAGE: Jesus Christ, it's my Eilif.

THE COOK: Your what?

MOTHER COURAGE: My eldest boy. It's two years since I lost
    sight of him, they pinched him from me on the road, must
65   think well of him if the general's asking him to dinner, and
    what kind of a dinner can you offer? Nowt. You heard what
    the visitor wishes to eat: meat. Take my tip, you settle for the
    capon, it'll be a florin.

THE GENERAL: *(Has sat down with* EILIF, *and bellows.)* Food,
70   Lamb, you foul cook, or I'll have your hide.

THE COOK: Give it over, dammit, this is blackmail.

MOTHER COURAGE: Didn't someone say it was a miserable
    bird?

THE COOK: Miserable; give it over, and a criminal price, fifty
75   hellers.

MOTHER COURAGE: A florin, I said. For my eldest boy, the
    general's guest, no expense is too great for me.

THE COOK: *(Gives her the money.)* You might at least pluck it
    while I see to the fire.

80   MOTHER COURAGE: *(Sits down to pluck the fowl.)* He won't
    half be surprised to see me. He's my dashing clever son.
    Then I got a stupid one too, he's honest though. The girl's
    nowt. One good thing, she don't talk.

THE GENERAL: Drink up, my son, this is my best Falernian;
85   only got a barrel or two left, but that's nothing to pay for a
    sign that's there's still true faith to be found in my army. As
    for that shepherd of souls he can just look on, because all he
    does is preach, without the least idea how it's to be carried
    out. And now, my son Eilif, tell us more about the neat way
90   you smashed those yokels and captured the twenty oxen.
    Let's hope they get here soon.

EILIF: A day or two at most.

MOTHER COURAGE: Thoughtful of our Eilif not to bring the
    oxen in till tomorrow, else you lot wouldn't have looked
95   twice at my capon.

EILIF: Well, it was like this, see. I'd heard peasants had been
    driving the oxen they'd hidden, out of the forest into one par-
    ticular wood, on the sly and mostly by night. That's where
    people from the town were s'posed to come and pick them
100   up. So I holds off and lets them drive their oxen together,
    reckoning they'd be better than me at finding 'em. I had my
    blokes slavering after the meat, cut their emergency rations
    even further for a couple of days till their mouths was water-
    ing at the least sound of any word beginning with 'me-', like
105   'measles' say.

THE GENERAL: Very clever of you.

EILIF: Possibly. The rest was a piece of cake. Except that the
    peasants had cudgels and outnumbered us three to one and
    made a murderous attack on us. Four of 'em shoved me into
110   a thicket, knocked my sword from my hand and bawled out
    'Surrender!' What's the answer, I wondered; they're going to
    make mincemeat of me.

THE GENERAL: What did you do?

EILIF: I laughed.

115   THE GENERAL: You did what?

EILIF: Laughed. So we got talking. I put it on a business foot-
    ing from the start, told them 'Twenty florins a head's too
    much. I'll give you fifteen'. As if I was meaning to pay. That
    threw them, and they began scratching their heads. In a flash
120   I'd picked up my sword and was hacking 'em to pieces. Ne-
    cessity's the mother of invention, eh, sir?

THE GENERAL: What is your view, pastor of souls?

THE CHAPLAIN: That phrase is not strictly speaking in the
    Bible, but when Our Lord turned the five loaves into five
    hundred there was no war on and he could tell people to   125
    love their neighbours as they'd had enough to eat. Today it's
    another story.

THE GENERAL: *(Laughs.)* Quite another story. You can have a
    swig after all for that, you old Pharisee. *(To* EILIF.) Hacked
    'em to pieces, did you, so my gallant lads can get a proper   130
    bite to eat? What do the Scriptures say? 'Whatsoever thou
    doest for the least of my brethren, thou doest for me'. And
    what did you do for them? Got them a good square meal of
    beef, because they're not accustomed to mouldy bread, the
    old way was to fix a cold meal of rolls and wine in your hel-   135
    met before you went out to fight for God.

EILIF: Aye, in a flash I'd picked up my sword and was hacking
    them to pieces.

THE GENERAL: You've the makings of a young Caesar. You
    ought to see the King.   140

EILIF: I have from a distance. He kind of glows. I'd like to
    model myself on him.

THE GENERAL: You've got something in common already. I ap-
    preciate soldiers like you, Eilif, men of courage. Somebody
    like that I treat as I would my own son. *(He leads him over to*   145
    the map.) Have a look at the situation, Eilif; it's a long haul
    still.

MOTHER COURAGE: *(Who has been listening and now angrily*
    plucks the fowl.) That must be a rotten general.

THE COOK: He's ravenous all right, but why rotten?   150

MOTHER COURAGE: Because he's got to have men of courage,
    that's why. If he knew how to plan a proper campaign what
    would he be needing men of courage for? Ordinary ones
    would do. It's always the same; whenever there's a load of
    special virtues around it means something stinks.   155

THE COOK: I thought it meant things is all right.

MOTHER COURAGE: No, that they stink. Look, s'pose some
    general or king is bone stupid and leads his men up shit
    creek, then those men've got to be fearless, there's another
    virtue for you. S'pose he's stingy and hires too few soldiers,   160
    then they got to be a crowd of Hercules's. And s'pose he's
    slapdash and don't give a bugger, then they got to be clever
    as monkeys else their number's up. Same way they got to
    show exceptional loyalty each time he gives them impossible
    jobs. Nowt but virtues no proper country and no decent king   165
    or general would ever need. In decent countries folk don't
    have to have virtues, the whole lot can be perfectly ordinary,
    average intelligence, and for all I know cowards.

THE GENERAL: I'll wager your father was a soldier.

EILIF: A great soldier, I been told. My mother warned me   170
    about it. There's a song I know.

THE GENERAL: Sing it to us. *(Roars.)* When's that dinner
    coming?

EILIF: It's called The Song of the Girl and the Soldier. *(He*
    sings it, dancing a war dance with his sabre.)   175

The guns blaze away, and the bay'nit'll slay
And the water can't hardly be colder.
What's the answer to ice? Keep off's my advice!
That's what the girl told the soldier.
Next thing the soldier, wiv' a round up the spout   180
Hears the band playing and gives a great shout:
Why, it's marching what makes you a soldier!

So it's down to the south and then northwards once more:
See him catching that bay'nit in his naked paw!
185 That's what his comrades done told her.

Oh, do not despise the advice of the wise
Learn wisdom from those that are older
And don't try for things that are out of your reach—
That's what the girl told the soldier.
190 Next thing the soldier, his bay'nit in place
Wades into the river and laughs in her face
Though the water comes up to his shoulder.
When the shingle roof glints in the light o' the moon
We'll be wiv' you again, not a moment too soon!
195 That's what his comrades done told her.

MOTHER COURAGE: (*Takes up the song in the kitchen, beating on a pot with her spoon.*)

You'll go out like a light! And the sun'll take flight
For your courage just makes us feel colder.
200 Oh, that vanishing light! May God see that it's right!—
That's what the girl told the soldier.

EILIF: What's that?
MOTHER COURAGE: (*Continues singing.*)

Next thing the soldier, his bay'nit in place
205 Was caught by the current and went down without trace
And the water couldn't hardly be colder.
Then the shingle roof froze in the light o' the moon
As both soldier and ice drifted down to their doom—
And d'you know what his comrades done told her?

210 He went out like a light. And the sunshine took flight
For his courage just made 'em feel colder.
Oh, do not despise the advice of the wise!
That's what the girl told the soldier.

THE GENERAL: The things they get up to in my kitchen these
215 days.
EILIF: (*Has gone into the kitchen. He flings his arms round his mother.*) Fancy seeing you again, ma! Where's the others?
MOTHER COURAGE: (*In his arms.*) Snug as a bug in a rug.
They made Swiss Cheese paymaster of the Second Finnish;
220 any road he'll stay out of fighting that way, I couldn't keep him out altogether.
EILIF: How's the old feet?
MOTHER COURAGE: Bit tricky getting me shoes on of a morning.
225 THE GENERAL: (*Has joined them.*) So you're his mother, I hope you've got plenty more sons for me like this one.
EILIF: Ain't it my lucky day? You sitting out there in the kitchen, ma, hearing your son commended . . .
MOTHER COURAGE: You bet I heard. (*Slaps his face.*)
230 EILIF: (*Holding his cheek.*) What's that for? Taking the oxen?
MOTHER COURAGE: No. Not surrendering when those four went for you and wanted to make mincemeat of you. Didn't I say you should look after yourself? You Finnish devil!

(*The GENERAL and the CHAPLAIN stand in the doorway laughing.*)

— SCENE THREE —

Three years later Mother Courage is taken prisoner along with elements of a Finnish regiment. She manages to save her daughter, likewise her covered cart, but her honest son is killed

Military camp.
Afternoon. A flagpole with the regimental flag. From her cart, festooned now with all kinds of goods, MOTHER COURAGE *has stretched a washing line to a large cannon, across which she and* KATTRIN *are folding the washing. She is bargaining at the same time with an armourer over a sack of shot.* SWISS CHEESE, *now wearing a paymaster's uniform, is looking on.*

A comely person, YVETTE POTTIER, *is sewing a gaily coloured hat, a glass of brandy before her. She is in her stockinged feet, having laid aside her red high-heeled boots.*

THE ARMOURER: I'll let you have that shot for a couple of florins. It's cheap at the price, I got to have the money because the colonel's been boozing with his officers since two days back, and the drink's run out.
MOTHER COURAGE: That's troops' munitions. They catch me 5 with that, I'm for court-martial. You crooks flog the shot, and troops got nowt to fire at enemy.
THE ARMOURER: Have a heart, can't you; you scratch my back and I'll scratch yours.
MOTHER COURAGE: I'm not taking army property. Not at that 10 price.
THE ARMOURER: You can sell it on the q.t. tonight to the Fourth Regiment's armourer for five florins, eight even, if you let him have a receipt for twelve. He's right out of ammunition. 15
MOTHER COURAGE: Why not you do it?
THE ARMOURER: I don't trust him, he's a pal of mine.
MOTHER COURAGE: (*Takes the sack.*) Gimme. (*To* KATTRIN.)
Take it away and pay him a florin and a half. (*The* AR-MOURER *protests.*) I said a florin and a half. (KATTRIN *drags* 20 *the sack upstage, the* ARMOURER *following her.* MOTHER COURAGE *addresses* SWISS CHEESE.) Here's your woollies, now look after them, it's October and autumn may set in any time. I ain't saying it's got to, cause I've learned nowt's got to come when you think it will, not even seasons of the year. 25 But your regimental accounts got to add up right, come what may. Do they add up right?
SWISS CHEESE: Yes, mother.
MOTHER COURAGE: Don't you forget they made you paymaster cause you was honest, not dashing like your brother, and 30 above all so stupid I bet you ain't even thought of clearing off with it, no not you. That's a big consolation to me. And don't lose those woollies.
SWISS CHEESE: No, mother, I'll put them under my mattress. (*Begins to go.*) 35
THE ARMOURER: I'll go along with you, paymaster.
MOTHER COURAGE: And don't you start learning him none of your tricks.

(*The* ARMOURER *leaves with* SWISS CHEESE *without any farewell gesture.*)

YVETTE: (*Waving to him.*) No reason not to say goodbye, armourer. 40
MOTHER COURAGE: (*To* YVETTE.) I don't like to see them together. He's wrong company for our Swiss Cheese. Oh well, war's off to a good start. Easily take four, five years before all countries are in. A bit of foresight, don't do nothing silly, and business'll flourish. Don't you know you ain't s'posed to 45 drink before midday with your complaint?
YVETTE: Complaint, who says so, it's a libel.
MOTHER COURAGE: They all say so.

YVETTE: Because they're all telling lies, Mother Courage, and
50 me at my wits' end cause they're all avoiding me like something the cat brought in thanks to those lies, what the hell
am I remodelling my hat for? (*She throws it away.*) That's
why I drink before midday. Never used to, gives you crows'
feet, but now what the hell? All the Second Finnish know
55 me. Ought to have stayed at home when my first fellow did
me wrong. No good our sort being proud. Eat shit, that's
what you got to do, or down you go.

MOTHER COURAGE: Now don't you start up again about that
Pieter of yours and how it all happened, in front of my inno-
60 cent daughter too.

YVETTE: She's the one should hear it, put her off love.

MOTHER COURAGE: Nobody can put 'em off that.

YVETTE: Then I'll go on, get it off my chest. It all starts with
yours truly growing up in lovely Flanders, else I'd never of
65 seen him and wouldn't be stuck here now in Poland, cause
he was an army cook, fair-haired, a Dutchman but thin for
once. Kattrin, watch out for the thin ones, only in those days
I didn't know that, or that he'd got a girl already, or that they
all called him Puffing Piet cause he never took his pipe out
70 of his mouth when he was on the job, it meant that little to
him. (*She sings the Song of Fraternisation.*)

When I was only sixteen
The foe came into our land.
He laid aside his sabre
75 And with a smile he took my hand.
After the May parade
The May light starts to fade.
The regiment dressed by the right
The drums were beaten, that's the drill.
80 The foe took us behind the hill
And fraternised all night.

There were so many foes then
But mine worked in the mess.
I loathed him in the daytime.
85 At night I loved him none the less.
After the May parade
The May light starts to fade.
The regiment dressed by the right
The drums were beaten, that's the drill.
90 The foe took us behind the hill
And fraternised all night.

The love which came upon me
Was wished on me by fate.
My friends could never grasp why
95 I found it hard to share their hate.
The fields were wet with dew
When sorrow first I knew.
The regiment dressed by the right
The drums were beaten, that's the drill.
100 And then the foe, my lover still
Went marching out of sight.

I followed him, fool that I was, but I never found him, and
that was five years back. (*She walks unsteadily behind the
cart.*)
105 MOTHER COURAGE: You left your hat here.

YVETTE: Anyone wants it can have it.

MOTHER COURAGE: Let that be a lesson, Kattrin. Don't you
start anything with them soldiers. Love makes the world go
round, I'm warning you. Even with fellows not in the army
it's no bed of roses. He says he'd like to kiss the ground your 110
feet walk on—reminds me, did you wash them yesterday?—
and after that you're his skivvy. Be thankful you're dumb,
then you can't contradict yourself and won't be wanting to
bite your tongue off for speaking the truth; it's a godsend,
being dumb is. And here comes the general's cook, now 115
what's he after?

(*Enter the* COOK *and the* CHAPLAIN.)

THE CHAPLAIN: I have a message for you from your son Eilif,
and the cook has come along because you made such a profound impression on him.

THE COOK: I just came along to get a bit of air. 120

MOTHER COURAGE: That you can always do here if you behave yourself, and if you don't I can deal with you. What
does he want? I got no spare cash.

THE CHAPLAIN: Actually I had a message for his brother the
paymaster. 125

MOTHER COURAGE: He ain't here now nor anywhere else neither. He ain't his brother's paymaster. He's not to lead him
into temptation nor be clever at his expense. (*Giving him
money from the purse slung round her.*) Give him this, it's a
sin, he's banking on mother's love and ought to be ashamed 130
of himself.

THE COOK: Not for long, he'll have to be moving off with the
regiment, might be to his death. Give him a bit extra, you'll
be sorry later. You women are tough, then later on you're
sorry. A little glass of brandy wouldn't have been a problem, 135
but it wasn't offered and, who knows, a bloke may lie beneath the green sod and none of you people will ever be able
to dig him up again.

THE CHAPLAIN: Don't give way to your feelings, cook. To fall
in battle is a blessing, not an inconvenience, and why? It is a 140
war of faith. None of your common wars but a special one,
fought for the faith and therefore pleasing to God.

THE COOK: Very true. It's a war all right in one sense, what
with requisitioning, murder and looting and the odd bit of
rape thrown in, but different from all the other wars because 145
it's a war of faith; stands to reason. But it's thirsty work at
that, you must admit.

THE CHAPLAIN: (*To* MOTHER COURAGE, *indicating the* COOK.)
I tried to stop him, but he says he's taken a shine to you, you
figure in his dreams. 150

THE COOK: (*Lighting a stumpy pipe.*) Just want a glass of
brandy from a fair hand, what harm in that? Only I'm groggy
already cause the chaplain here's been telling such jokes all
the way along you bet I'm still blushing.

MOTHER COURAGE: Him a clergyman too. I'd best give the 155
pair of you a drink or you'll start making me immoral suggestions cause you've nowt else to do.

THE CHAPLAIN: Behold a temptation, said the court preacher,
and fell. (*Turning back to look at* KATTRIN *as he leaves.*) And
who is this entrancing young person? 160

MOTHER COURAGE: That ain't an entrancing but a decent
young person. (*The* CHAPLAIN *and the* COOK *go behind the
cart with* MOTHER COURAGE. KATTRIN *looks after them, then
walks away from her washing towards the hat. She picks it up
and sits down, pulling the red boots towards her.* MOTHER 165

COURAGE *can be heard in the background talking politics with the* CHAPLAIN *and the* COOK.)

MOTHER COURAGE: Those Poles here in Poland had no business sticking their noses in. Right, our king moved in on them, horse and foot, but did they keep the peace? no, went and stuck their noses into their own affairs, they did, and fell on king just as he was quietly clearing off. They committed a breach of peace, that's what, so blood's on their own head.

THE CHAPLAIN: All our king minded about was freedom. The emperor had made slaves of them all, Poles and Germans alike, and the king had to liberate them.

THE COOK: Just what I say, your brandy's first rate, I weren't mistaken in your face, but talk of the king, it cost the king dear trying to give freedom to Germany, what with giving Sweden the salt tax, what cost the poor folk a bit, so I've heard, on top of which he had to have the Germans locked up and drawn and quartered cause they wanted to carry on slaving for the emperor. Course the king took a serious view when anybody didn't want to be free. He set out by just trying to protect Poland against bad people, particularly the emperor, then it started to become a habit till he ended up protecting the whole of Germany. They didn't half kick. So the poor old king's had nowt but trouble for all his kindness and expenses, and that's something he had to make up for by taxes of course, which caused bad blood, not that he'd let a little matter like that depress him. One thing he had on his side, God's word, that was a help. Because otherwise folk would of been saying he done it all for himself and to make a bit on the side. So he's always had a good conscience, which was the main point.

MOTHER COURAGE: Anyone can see you're no Swede or you wouldn't be talking that way about the Hero King.

THE CHAPLAIN: After all he provides the bread you eat.

THE COOK: I don't eat it, I bake it.

MOTHER COURAGE: They'll never beat him, and why, his men got faith in him. (*Seriously.*) To go by what the big shots say, they're waging war for almighty God and in the name of everything that's good and lovely. But look closer, they ain't so silly, they're waging it for what they can get. Else little folk like me wouldn't be in it at all.

THE COOK: That's the way it is.

THE CHAPLAIN: As a Dutchman you'd do better to glance at the flag above your head before venting your opinions here in Poland.

MOTHER COURAGE: All good Lutherans here. Prosit!

(KATTRIN *has put on* YVETTE's *hat and begun strutting around in imitation of her way of walking.*

Suddenly there is a noise of cannon fire and shooting. Drums. MOTHER COURAGE, *the* COOK *and the* CHAPLAIN *rush out from behind the cart, the two last-named still carrying their glasses. The* ARMOURER *and another* SOLDIER *run up to the cannon and try to push it away.*)

MOTHER COURAGE: What's happening? Wait till I've taken my washing down, you louts! (*She tries to rescue her washing.*)

THE ARMOURER: The Catholics! Broken through. Don't know if we'll get out of here. (*To the* SOLDIER.) Get that gun shifted! (*Runs on.*)

THE COOK: God, I must find the general. Courage, I'll drop by in a day or two for another talk.

MOTHER COURAGE: Wait, you forgot your pipe.

THE COOK: (*In the distance.*) Keep it for me. I'll be needing it.

MOTHER COURAGE: Would happen just as we're making a bit of money.

THE CHAPLAIN: Ah well, I'll be going too. Indeed, if the enemy is so close as that it might be dangerous. Blesséd are the peacemakers is the motto in wartime. If only I had a cloak to cover me.

MOTHER COURAGE: I ain't lending no cloaks, not on your life. I been had too often.

THE CHAPLAIN: But my faith makes it particularly dangerous for me.

MOTHER COURAGE: (*Gets him a cloak.*) Goes against my conscience, this does. Now you run along.

THE CHAPLAIN: Thank you, dear lady, that's very generous of you, but I think it might be wiser for me to remain seated here; it could arouse suspicion and bring the enemy down on me if I were seen to run.

MOTHER COURAGE: (*To the* SOLDIER.) Leave it, you fool, who's going to pay you for that? I'll look after it for you, you're risking your neck.

THE SOLDIER: (*Running away.*) You can tell 'em I tried.

MOTHER COURAGE: Cross my heart. (*Sees her daughter with the hat.*) What you doing with that strumpet's hat? Take that lid off, you gone crazy? And the enemy arriving any minute! (*Pulls the hat off* KATTRIN's *head.*) Want 'em to pick you up and make a prostitute of you? And she's gone and put those boots on, whore of Babylon! Off with those boots! (*Tries to tug them off her.*) Jesus Christ, chaplain, gimme a hand, get those boots off her, I'll be right back. (*Runs to the cart.*)

YVETTE: (*Arrives, powdering her face.*) Fancy that, the Catholics are coming. Where's my hat? Who's been kicking it around? I can't go about looking like this if the Catholics are coming. What'll they think of me? No mirror either. (*To the* CHAPLAIN.) How do I look? Too much powder?

THE CHAPLAIN: Exactly right.

YVETTE: And where are them red boots? (*Fails to find them as* KATTRIN *hides her feet under her skirt.*) I left them here all right. Now I'll have to get to me tent barefoot. It's an outrage.

(*Exit.*)

(SWISS CHEESE *runs in carrying in a small box.*)

MOTHER COURAGE: (*Arrives with her hands full of ashes. To* KATTRIN.) Here some ashes. (*To* SWISS CHEESE.) What's that you're carrying?

SWISS CHEESE: Regimental cash box.

MOTHER COURAGE: Chuck it away. No more paymastering for you.

SWISS CHEESE: I'm responsible. (*He goes to the rear.*)

MOTHER COURAGE: (*To the* CHAPLAIN.) Take your clerical togs off, padre, or they'll spot you under that cloak. (*She rubs* KATTRIN's *face with ash.*) Keep still, will you? There you are, a bit of muck and you'll be safe. What a disaster. Sentries were drunk. Hide your light under a bushel, it says. Take a soldier, specially a Catholic one, add a clean face, and there's your instant whore. For weeks they get nowt to eat, then soon as they manage to get it by looting they're falling on anything in skirts. That ought to do. Let's have a look. Not bad. Looks like you been grubbing in muckheap. Stop trembling. Nothing'll happen to you like that. (*To* SWISS CHEESE.) Where d'you leave cash box?

SWISS CHEESE: Thought I'd put it in cart.

MOTHER COURAGE: *(Horrified.)* What, my cart? Sheer criminal idiocy. Only take me eyes off you one instant. Hang us all three, they will.

SWISS CHEESE: I'll put it somewhere else then, or clear out with it.

MOTHER COURAGE: You sit on it, it's too late now.

THE CHAPLAIN: *(Who is changing his clothes downstage.)* For heaven's sake, the flag!

MOTHER COURAGE: *(Hauls down the regimental flag.)* Bozhe moi! I'd given up noticing it were there. Twenty-five years I've had it.

(The thunder of cannon intensifies.)

(A morning three days later. The cannon has gone. MOTHER COURAGE, KATTRIN, *the* CHAPLAIN *and* SWISS CHEESE *are sitting gloomily over a meal.)*

SWISS CHEESE: That's three days I been sitting around with nowt to do, and sergeant's always been kind to me but any moment now he'll start asking where's Swiss Cheese with the pay box?

MOTHER COURAGE: You thank your stars they ain't after you.

THE CHAPLAIN: What can I say? I can't even hold a service here, it might make trouble for me. Whosoever hath a full heart, his tongue runneth over, it says, but heaven help me if mine starts running over.

MOTHER COURAGE: That's how it goes. Here they sit, one with his faith and the other with his cash box. Dunno which is more dangerous.

MOTHER COURAGE: Oh, I don't think it's as bad as that yet, though I must say I can't sleep nights. If it weren't for you, Swiss Cheese, things'd be easier. I think I got meself cleared. I told 'em I didn't hold with Antichrist, the Swedish one with horns on, and I'd observed left horn was a bit unserviceable. Half way through their interrogation I asked where I could get church candles not too dear. I knows the lingo cause Swiss Cheese's dad were Catholic, often used to make jokes about it, he did. They didn't believe me all that much, but they ain't got no regimental canteen lady. So they're winking an eye. Could turn out for the best, you know. We're prisoners, but same like fleas on dog.

THE CHAPLAIN: That's good milk. But we'll need to cut down our Swedish appetites a bit. After all, we've been defeated.

MOTHER COURAGE: Who's been defeated? Look, victory and defeat ain't bound to be same for the big shots up top as for them below, not by no means. Can be times the bottom lot find a defeat really pays them. Honour's lost, nowt else. I remember once up in Livonia our general took such a beating from enemy I got a horse off our baggage train in the confusion, pulled me cart seven months, he did, before we won and they checked up. As a rule you can say victory and defeat both come expensive to us ordinary folk. Best thing for us is when politics get bogged down solid. *(To* SWISS CHEESE.*)* Eat up.

SWISS CHEESE: Got no appetite for it. What's sergeant to do when pay day comes round?

MOTHER COURAGE: They don't have pay days on a retreat.

SWISS CHEESE: It's their right, though. They needn't retreat if they don't get paid. Needn't stir a foot.

MOTHER COURAGE: Swiss Cheese, you're that conscientious it makes me quite nervous. I brought you up to be honest, you

not being clever, but you got to know where to stop. Chaplain and me, we're off now to buy Catholic flag and some meat. Dunno anyone so good at sniffing meat, like sleepwalking it is, straight to target. I'd say he can pick out a good piece by the way his mouth starts watering. Well, thank goodness they're letting me go on trading. You don't ask tradespeople their faith but their prices. And Lutheran trousers keep cold out too.

THE CHAPLAIN: What did the mendicant say when he heard the Lutherans were going to turn everything in town and country topsy-turvy? 'They'll always need beggars'. *(*MOTHER COURAGE *disappears into the cart.)* So she's still worried about the cash box. So far they've taken us all for granted as part of the cart, but how long for?

SWISS CHEESE: I can get rid of it.

THE CHAPLAIN: That's almost more dangerous. Suppose you're seen. They have spies. Yesterday a fellow popped up out of the ditch in front of me just as I was relieving myself first thing. I was so scared I only just suppressed an ejaculatory prayer. That would have given me away all right. I think what they'd like best is to go sniffing people's excrement to see if they're Protestants. The spy was a little runt with a patch over one eye.

MOTHER COURAGE: *(Clambering out of the cart with a basket.)* What have I found, you shameless creature? *(She holds up the red boots in triumph.)* Yvette's red high-heeled boots! Coolly went and pinched them, she did. Cause you put it in her head she was an enchanting young person. *(She lays them in the basket.)* I'm giving them back. Stealing Yvette's boots! She's wrecking herself for money. That's understandable. But you'd do it for nothing, for pleasure. What did I tell you: you're to wait till it's peace. No soldiers for you. You're not to start exhibiting yourself till it's peacetime.

THE CHAPLAIN: I don't find she exhibits herself.

MOTHER COURAGE: Too much for my liking. Let her be like a stone in Dalecarlia, where there's nowt else, so folk say 'Can't see that cripple', that's how I'd lief have her. Then nowt'll happen to her. *(To* SWISS CHEESE.*)* You leave that box where it is, d'you hear? And keep an eye on your sister, she needs it. The pair of you'll have me in grave yet. Sooner be minding a bagful of fleas.

(She leaves with the CHAPLAIN. KATTRIN *clears away the dishes.)*

SWISS CHEESE: Won't be able to sit out in the sun in shirtsleeves much longer. *(*KATTRIN *points at a tree.)* Aye, leaves turning yellow. *(*KATTRIN *asks by gestures if he wants a drink.)* Don't want no drink. I'm thinking. *(Pause.)* Said she can't sleep. Best if I got rid of that box, found a good place for it. All right, let's have a glass. *(*KATTRIN *goes behind the cart.)* I'll stuff it down the rat-hole by the river for the time being. Probably pick it up tonight before first light and take it to Regiment. How far can they have retreated in three days? Bet sergeant's surprised. I'm agreeably disappointed in you, Swiss Cheese, he'll say. I make you responsible for the cash, and you go and bring it back.

(As KATTRIN *emerges from behind the cart with a full glass in her hand, two men confront her. One is a* SERGEANT, *the other doffs his hat to her. He has a patch over one eye.)*

THE MAN WITH THE PATCH: God be with you, mistress. Have you seen anyone round here from Second Finnish Regimental Headquarters?

(KATTRIN, *badly frightened, runs downstage, spilling the brandy. The two men look at one another, then withdraw on seeing* SWISS CHEESE *sitting there.*)

390   SWISS CHEESE: (*Interrupted in his thoughts.*) You spilt half of it. What are those faces for? Jabbed yourself in eye? I don't get it. And I'll have to be off, I've thought it over, it's the only way. (*He gets up. She does everything possible to make him realise the danger. He only shrugs her off.*) Wish I knew what
395   you're trying to say. Sure you mean well, poor creature, just can't get words out. What's it matter your spilling my brandy, I'll drink plenty more glasses yet, what's one more or less? (*He gets the box from the cart and takes it under his tunic.*) Be back in a moment. Don't hold me up now, or I'll be angry. I
400   know you mean well. Too bad you can't speak.

(*As she tries to hold him back he kisses her and tears himself away. Exit. She is desperate, running hither and thither uttering little noises. The* CHAPLAIN *and* MOTHER COURAGE *return.* KATTRIN *rushes to her mother.*)

MOTHER COURAGE: What's all this? Pull yourself together, love. They done something to you? Where's Swiss Cheese? Tell it me step by step, Kattrin. Mother understands you. What, so that bastard did take the box? I'll wrap it round his
405   ears, the little hypocrite. Take your time and don't gabble, use your hands, I don't like it when you howl like a dog, what'll his reverence say? Makes him uncomfortable. What, a one-eyed man came along?
THE CHAPLAIN: That one-eyed man is a spy. Have they ar-
410   rested Swiss Cheese? (KATTRIN *shakes her head, shrugs her shoulders.*) We're done for.
MOTHER COURAGE: (*Fishes in her basket and brings out a Catholic flag, which the* CHAPLAIN *fixes to the mast.*) Better hoist new flag.
415   THE CHAPLAIN: (*Bitterly.*) All good Catholics here.

(*Voices are heard from the rear. The two men bring in* SWISS CHEESE.)

SWISS CHEESE: Let me go, I got nowt. Don't twist my shoulder, I'm innocent.
SERGEANT: Here's where he came from. You know each other.
MOTHER COURAGE: Us? How?
420   SWISS CHEESE: I don't know her. Got no idea who she is, had nowt to do with them. I bought me dinner here, ten hellers it cost. You might have seen me sitting here, it was too salty.
SERGEANT: Who are you people, eh?
MOTHER COURAGE: We're law-abiding folk. That's right, he
425   bought a dinner. Said it was too salty.
SERGEANT: Trying to pretend you don't know each other, that it?
MOTHER COURAGE: Why should I know him? Can't know everyone. I don't go asking 'em what they're called and are they
430   a heretic; if he pays he ain't a heretic. You a heretic?
SWISS CHEESE: Go on.
THE CHAPLAIN: He sat there very properly, never opening his mouth except when eating. Then he had to.
SERGEANT: And who are you?
435   MOTHER COURAGE: He's just my potboy. Now I expect you gentlemen are thirsty, I'll get you a glass of brandy, you must be hot and tired with running.
SERGEANT: No brandy on duty. (*To* SWISS CHEESE.) You were carrying something. Must have hidden it by the river. Was a
440   bulge in your tunic when you left here.

MOTHER COURAGE: You sure it was him?
SWISS CHEESE: You must be thinking of someone else. I saw someone bounding off with a bulge in his tunic. I'm the wrong man.
445   MOTHER COURAGE: I'd say it was a misunderstanding too, such things happen. I'm a good judge of people, I'm Courage, you heard of me, everyone knows me, and I tell you that's an honest face he has.
SERGEANT: We're on the track of the Second Finnish Regi-
450   ment's cash box. We got the description of the fellow responsible for it. Been trailing him two days. It's you.
SWISS CHEESE: It's not me.
SERGEANT: And you better cough it up, or you're a goner, you know. Where is it?
455   MOTHER COURAGE: (*Urgently.*) Of course he'd give it over rather than be a goner. Right out he'd say: I got it, here it is, you're too strong. He ain't all that stupid. Speak up, stupid idiot, here's the sergeant giving you a chance.
SWISS CHEESE: S'pose I ain't got it.
460   SERGEANT: Then come along. We'll get it out of you. (*They lead him off.*)
MOTHER COURAGE: (*Calls after them.*) He'd tell you. He's not that stupid. And don't you twist his shoulder! (*Runs after them.*)

(*Evening of the same day. The* CHAPLAIN *and dumb* KATTRIN *are cleaning glasses and polishing knives.*)

465   THE CHAPLAIN: Cases like that, where somebody gets caught, are not unknown in religious history. It reminds me of the Passion of Our Lord and Saviour. There's an old song about that. (*He sings the Song of the Hours.*)

> In the first hour Jesus mild
> Who had prayed since even   470
> Was betrayed and led before
> Pontius the heathen.
>
> Pilate found him innocent
> Free from fault and error
> Therefore, having washed his hands   475
> Sent him to King Herod.
>
> In the third hour he was scourged
> Stripped and clad in scarlet
> And a plaited crown of thorns
> Set upon his forehead.   480
>
> On the Son of Man they spat
> Mocked him and made merry.
> Then the cross of death was brought
> Given him to carry.
>
> At the sixth hour with two thieves   485
> To the cross they nailed him
> And the people and the thieves
> Mocked him and reviled him.
>
> This is Jesus King of Jews
> Cried they in derision   490
> Till the sun withdrew its light
> From that awful vision.

---

468 *Song of the Hours* translated by Ralph Manheim

At the ninth hour Jesus wailed
Why hast thou me forsaken?
495   Soldiers brought him vinegar
Which he left untaken.

Then he yielded up the ghost
And the earth was shaken.
500   Rended was the temple's veil
And the saints were wakened.

Soldiers broke the two thieves' legs
As the night descended.
Thrust a spear in Jesus' side
When his life had ended.

505   Still they mocked, as from his wound
Flowed the blood and water
And blasphemed the Son of Man
With their cruel laughter.

MOTHER COURAGE: (*Entering excitedly.*) It's touch and go.
510   They say sergeant's open to reason though. Only we mustn't let on it's Swiss Cheese else they'll say we helped him. It's a matter of money, that's all. But where's money to come from? Hasn't Yvette been round? I ran into her, she's got her hooks on some colonel, maybe he'd buy her a canteen
515   business.
THE CHAPLAIN: Do you really wish to sell?
MOTHER COURAGE: Where's money for sergeant to come from?
THE CHAPLAIN: What'll you live on, then?
520   MOTHER COURAGE: That's just it.

(YVETTE POTTIER *arrives with an extremely ancient colonel.*)

YVETTE: (*Embracing* MOTHER COURAGE.) My dear Courage, fancy seeing you so soon. (*Whispers.*) He's not unwilling. (*Aloud.*) This is my good friend who advises me in business matters. I happened to hear you wanted to sell your cart on
525   account of circumstances. I'll think it over.
MOTHER COURAGE: Pledge it, not sell, just not too much hurry, tain't every day you find a cart like this in wartime.
YVETTE: (*Disappointed.*) Oh, pledge. I thought it was for sale. I'm not so sure I'm interested. (*To the* COLONEL.) How do
530   you feel about it?
THE COLONEL: Just as you feel, pet.
MOTHER COURAGE: I'm only pledging it.
YVETTE: I thought you'd got to have the money.
MOTHER COURAGE: (*Firmly.*) I got to have it, but sooner run
535   myself ragged looking for a bidder than sell outright. And why? The cart's our livelihood. It's a chance for you, Yvette; who knows when you'll get another like it and have a special friend to advise you, am I right?
YVETTE: Yes, my friend thinks I should clinch it, but I'm not
540   sure. If it's only a pledge . . . so you agree we ought to buy outright?
THE COLONEL: I agree, pet.
MOTHER COURAGE: Best look and see if you can find anything for sale then; maybe you will if you don't rush it, take your
545   friend along with you, say a week or fortnight, might find something suits you.
YVETTE: Then let's go looking. I adore going around looking for things, I adore going around with you, Poldi, it's such fun, isn't it? No matter if it takes a fortnight. How soon
550   would you pay the money back if you got it?

MOTHER COURAGE: I'd pay back in two weeks, maybe one.
YVETTE: I can't make up my mind, Poldi chéri, you advise me. (*Takes the* COLONEL *aside.*) She's got to sell, I know, no problem there. And there's that ensign, you know, the fair-haired one, he'd be glad to lend me the money. He's crazy   555
about me, says there's someone I remind him of. What do you advise?
THE COLONEL: You steer clear of him. He's no good. He's only making use of you. I said I'd buy you something, didn't I, pussykins?   560
YVETTE: I oughtn't to let you. Of course if you think the ensign might try to take advantage . . . Poldi, I'll accept it from you.
THE COLONEL: That's how I feel too.
YVETTE: Is that your advice?
THE COLONEL: That is my advice.   565
YVETTE: (*To* COURAGE *once more.*) My friend's advice would be to accept. Make me out a receipt saying the cart's mine once two weeks are up, with all its contents, we'll check it now, I'll bring the two hundred florins later. (*To the* COLONEL.) You go back to the camp, I'll follow, I got to   570
check it all and see there's nothing missing from my cart. (*She kisses him. He leaves. She climbs up on the cart.*) Not all that many boots, are there?
MOTHER COURAGE: Yvette, it's no time for checking your cart, s'posing it is yours. You promised you'd talk to sergeant about   575
Swiss Cheese, there ain't a minute to lose, they say in an hour he'll be courtmartialled.
YVETTE: Just let me count the shirts.
MOTHER COURAGE: (*Pulling her down by the skirt.*) You bloody vampire. Swiss Cheese's life's at stake. And not a   580
word about who's making the offer, for God's sake, pretend it's your friend, else we're all done for cause we looked after him.
YVETTE: I fixed to meet that one-eyed fellow in the copse, he should be there by now.   585
THE CHAPLAIN: It doesn't have to be the whole two hundred either, I'd go up to a hundred and fifty, that may be enough.
MOTHER COURAGE: Since when has it been your money? You kindly keep out of this. You'll get your hotpot all right, don't worry. Hurry up and don't haggle, it's life or death. (*Pushes*   590
YVETTE *off.*)
THE CHAPLAIN: Far be it from me to interfere, but what are we going to live on? You're saddled with a daughter who can't earn her keep.
MOTHER COURAGE: I'm counting on regimental cash box, Mr.   595
Clever. They'll allow it as his expenses.
THE CHAPLAIN: But will she get the message right?
MOTHER COURAGE: It's her interest I should spend her two hundred so she gets the cart. She's set on that, God knows how long that colonel of hers'll last. Kattrin, polish the   600
knives, there's the pumice. And you, stop hanging round like Jesus on Mount of Olives, get moving, wash them glasses, we'll have fifty or more of cavalry in tonight and I don't want to hear a lot of 'I'm not accustomed to having to run about, oh my poor feet, we never ran in church'. Thank the Lord   605
they're corruptible. After all, they ain't wolves, just humans out for money. Corruption in humans is same as compassion in God. Corruption's our only hope. Long as we have it there'll be lenient sentences and even an innocent man'll have a chance of being let off.   610
YVETTE: (*Comes in panting.*) They'll do it for two hundred. But it's got to be quick. Soon be out of their hands. Best

thing is I go right away to my colonel with the one-eyed
man. He's admitted he had the box, they put the thumb-
615 screws on him. But he chucked it in the river soon as he saw
they were on his track. The box is a write-off. I'll go and get
the money from my colonel, shall I?

MOTHER COURAGE: Box is a write-off? How'm I to pay back
two hundred then?

620 YVETTE: Oh, you thought you'd get it from the box, did you?
And I was to be Joe Soap I suppose? Better not count on that.
You'll have to pay up if you want Swiss Cheese back, or
would you sooner I dropped the whole thing so's you can
keep your cart?

625 MOTHER COURAGE: That's something I didn't allow for. Don't
worry, you'll get your cart, I've said goodbye to it, had it seventeen years, I have. I just need a moment to think, it's bit
sudden, what'm I to do, two hundred's too much for me, pity
you didn't beat 'em down. Must keep a bit back, else any
630 Tom, Dick and Harry'll be able to shove me in ditch. Go and
tell them I'll pay hundred and twenty florins, else it's all off,
either way I'm losing me cart.

YVETTE: They won't do it. That one-eyed man's impatient already, keeps looking over his shoulder, he's so worked up.
635 Hadn't I best pay them the whole two hundred?

MOTHER COURAGE: (*In despair.*) I can't pay that. Thirty years I
been working. She's twenty-five already, and no husband. I
got her to think of too. Don't push me, I know what I'm
doing. Say a hundred and twenty, or it's off.

640 YVETTE: It's up to you. (*Rushes off.*)

(*Without looking at either the* CHAPLAIN *or her daughter,*
MOTHER COURAGE *sits down to help* KATTRIN *polish knives.*)

MOTHER COURAGE: Don't smash them glasses, they ain't ours
now. Watch what you're doing, you'll cut yourself. Swiss
Cheese'll be back, I'll pay two hundred if it comes to the
pinch. You'll get your brother, love. For eighty florins we
645 could fill a pack with goods and start again. Plenty of folk has
to make do.

THE CHAPLAIN: The Lord will provide, it says.

MOTHER COURAGE: See they're properly dry. (*She cleans
knives in silence.* KATTRIN *suddenly runs behind the cart,*
650 *sobbing.*)

YVETTE: (*Comes running in.*) They won't do it. I told you so.
The one-eyed man wanted to leave right away, said there was
no point. He says he's just waiting for the drum-roll; that
means sentence has been pronounced. I offered a hundred
655 and fifty. He didn't even blink. I had to convince him to stay
there so's I could have another word with you.

MOTHER COURAGE: Tell him I'll pay the two hundred. Hurry!
(YVETTE *runs off. They sit in silence. The* CHAPLAIN *has
stopped polishing the glasses.*) I reckon I bargained too long.

(*In the distance drumming is heard. The* CHAPLAIN *gets up and
goes to the rear.* MOTHER COURAGE *remains seated. It grows
dark. The drumming stops. It grows light once more.* MOTHER
COURAGE *is sitting exactly as before.*)

660 YVETTE: (*Arrives, very pale.*) Well, you got what you asked for,
with your haggling and trying to keep your cart. Eleven bullets they gave him, that's all. You don't deserve I should
bother any more about you. But I did hear they don't believe
the box really is in the river. They've an idea it's here and
665 anyhow that you're connected with him. They're going to

bring him here, see if you gives yourself away when you sees
him. Thought I'd better warn you so's you don't recognise
him, else you'll all be for it. They're right on my heels, best
tell you quick. Shall I keep Kattrin away? (MOTHER
COURAGE *shakes her head.*) Does she know? She mayn't 670
have heard the drumming or know what it meant.

MOTHER COURAGE: She knows. Get her.

(YVETTE *fetches* KATTRIN, *who goes to her mother and stands beside her.* MOTHER COURAGE *takes her hand. Two lansequenets
come carrying a stretcher with something lying on it covered by a
sheet. The* SERGEANT *marches beside them. They set down the
stretcher.*)

SERGEANT: Here's somebody we dunno the name of. It's got to
be listed, though, so everything's shipshape. He had a meal
here. Have a look, see if you know him. (*He removes the* 675
sheet.) Know him? (MOTHER COURAGE *shakes her head.*)
What, never see him before he had that meal here?
(MOTHER COURAGE *shakes her head.*) Pick him up. Chuck
him in the pit. He's got nobody knows him. (*They carry him
away.*) 680

— SCENE FOUR —

| Mother Courage sings the Song of the Grand Capitulation |

Outside an officer's tent.
MOTHER COURAGE *is waiting. A* CLERK *looks out of the tent.*

THE CLERK: I know you. You had a paymaster from the Lutherans with you, what was in hiding. I'd not complain if I were
you.

MOTHER COURAGE: But I got a complaint to make. I'm innocent, would look as how I'd a bad conscience if I let this pass. 5
Slashed everything in me cart to pieces with their sabres,
they did, then wanted I should pay five taler fine for nowt, I
tell you, nowt.

CLERK: Take my tip, better shut up. We're short of canteens, so
we let you go on trading, specially if you got a bad con- 10
science and pay a fine now and then.

MOTHER COURAGE: I got a complaint.

CLERK: Have it your own way. Then you must wait till the captain's free. (*Withdraws inside the tent.*)

YOUNG SOLDIER: (*Enters aggressively.*) Bouque la Madonne! 15
Where's that bleeding pig of a captain what's took my reward
money to swig with his tarts? I'll do him.

OLDER SOLDIER: (*Running after him.*) Shut up. They'll put
you in irons.

YOUNG SOLDIER: Out of there, you thief! I'll slice you into 20
pork chops, I will. Pocketing my prize money after I'd swum
the river, only one in the whole squadron, and now I can't
even buy meself a beer. I'm not standing for that. Come on
out there so I can cut you up!

OLDER SOLDIER: Blessed Mother of God, he's asking for 25
trouble.

MOTHER COURAGE: Is it some reward he weren't paid?

YOUNG SOLDIER: Lemme go, I'll slash you too while I'm at it.

OLDER SOLDIER: He rescued the colonel's horse and got no reward for it. He's young yet, still wet behind the ears. 30

MOTHER COURAGE: Let him go, he ain't a dog you got to
chain up. Wanting your reward is good sound sense. Why be
a hero otherwise?

YOUNG SOLDIER: So's he can sit in there and booze. You're
35   shit-scared, the lot of you. I done something special and I
  want my reward.

MOTHER COURAGE: Don't you shout at me, young fellow. Got
  me own worries, I have; any road you should spare your
  voice, be needing it when captain comes, else there he'll be
40   and you too hoarse to make a sound, which'll make it hard
  for him to clap you in irons till you turn blue. People what
  shouts like that can't keep it up ever; half an hour, and they
  have to be rocked to sleep, they're so tired.

YOUNG SOLDIER: I ain't tired and to hell with sleep. I'm hun-
45   gry. They make our bread from acorns and hemp-seed, and
  they even skimp on that. He's whoring away my reward and
  I'm hungry. I'll do him.

MOTHER COURAGE: Oh I see, you're hungry. Last year that
  general of yours ordered you all off roads and across fields so
50   corn should be trampled flat; I could've got ten florins for a
  pair of boots s'pose I'd had boots and s'pose anyone'd been
  able to pay ten florins. Thought he'd be well away from that
  area this year, he did, but here he is, still there, and hunger is
  great. I see what you're angry about.

55 YOUNG SOLDIER: I won't have it, don't talk to me, it ain't fair
  and I'm not standing for that.

MOTHER COURAGE: And you're right; but how long? How
  long you not standing for unfairness? One hour, two hours?
  Didn't ask yourself that, did you, but it's the whole point, and
60   why, once you're in irons it's too bad if you suddenly finds
  you can put up with unfairness after all.

YOUNG SOLDIER: What am I listening to you for, I'd like to
  know? Bouque la Madonne, where's that captain?

MOTHER COURAGE: You been listening to me because you
65   knows it's like what I say, your anger has gone up in smoke
  already, it was just a short one and you needed a long one,
  but where you going to get it from?

YOUNG SOLDIER: Are you trying to tell me asking for my reward is wrong?

70 MOTHER COURAGE: Not a bit. I'm just telling you your anger
  ain't long enough, it's good for nowt, pity. If you'd a long one
  I'd be trying to prod you on. Cut him up, the swine, would
  be my advice to you in that case; but how about if you don't
  cut him up cause you feels your tail going between your
75   legs? Then I'd look silly and captain'd take it out on me.

OLDER SOLDIER: You're perfectly right, he's just a bit crazy.

YOUNG SOLDIER: Very well, let's see if I don't cut him up.
  (Draws his sword.) When he arrives I'm going to cut him up.

CLERK: *(Looks out.)* The captain'll be here in one minute. Sit
80   down.

(The YOUNG SOLDIER *sits down.)*

MOTHER COURAGE: He's sitting now. See, what did I say?
  You're sitting now. Ah, how well they know us, no one need
  tell 'em how to go about it. Sit down! and, bingo, we're sitting. And sitting and sedition don't mix. Don't try to stand
85   up, you won't stand the way you was standing before. I
  shouldn't worry about what I think; I'm no better, not one
  moment. Bought up all our fighting spirit, they have. Eh?
  S'pose I kick back, might be bad for business. Let me tell you
  a thing or two about the Grand Capitulation. *(She sings the*
90   *Song of the Grand Capitulation.)*

Back when I was young, I was brought to realise
What a very special person I must be
(Not just any old cottager's daughter, what with my looks
    and my talents and my urge towards Higher Things)
And insisted that my soup should have no hairs in it.   95
No one makes a sucker out of me!
(All or nothing, only the best is good enough, each man for
    himself, nobody's telling *me* what to do.)
Then I heard a tit
Chirp: Wait a bit!   100
    And you'll be marching with the band
    In step, responding to command
    And striking up your little dance:
    Now we advance.
    And now: parade, form square!   105
    Then men swear God's there—
    Not the faintest chance!

In no time at all anyone who looked could see
That I'd learned to take my medicine with good grace.
(Two kids on my hands and look at the price of bread, and   110
    things they expect of you!)
When they finally came to feel that they were through with
    me
They'd got me grovelling on my face.
(Takes all sorts to make a world, you scratch my back and
    I'll scratch yours, no good banging your head against a   115
    brick wall.)
Then I heard that tit
Chirp: Wait a bit!
    And you'll be marching with the band
    In step, responding to command   120
    And striking up your little dance:
    Now they advance.
    And now: parade, form square!
    Then men swear God's there—
    Not the faintest chance!   125

I've known people tried to storm the summits:
There's no star too bright or seems too far away.
(Dogged does it, where there's a will there's a way, by hook
    or by crook.)
As each peak disclosed fresh peaks to come, it's   130
Strange how much a plain straw hat could weigh.
(You have to cut your coat according to your cloth.)
Then I hear the tit
Chirp: Wait a bit!
    And they'll be marching with the band   135
    In step, responding to command
    And striking up their little dance:
    Now they advance
    And now: parade, form square!
    Then men swear God's there—   140
    Not the faintest chance!

MOTHER COURAGE: *(To the* YOUNG SOLDIER.) That's why I
reckon you should stay there with your sword drawn if you're
truly set on it and your anger's big enough, because you got
grounds, I agree, but if your anger's a short one best leave   145
right away.

YOUNG SOLDIER: Oh stuff it. *(He staggers off with the* OLDER
SOLDIER *following.)*

CLERK: (*Sticks his head out.*) Captain's here now. You can
150   make your complaint.

MOTHER COURAGE: I changed me mind. I ain't complaining.
(*Exit.*)

— SCENE FIVE —

Two years have gone by. The war is spreading to new
areas. Ceaselessly on the move, Courage's little cart
crosses Poland, Moravia, Bavaria, Italy then Bavaria
again. 1631. Tilly's victory at Magdeburg costs Mother
Courage four officers' shirts

MOTHER COURAGE's *cart has stopped in a badly shot-up village.
Thin military music in the distance. Two soldiers at the bar
being served by* KATTRIN *and* MOTHER COURAGE. *One of them
has a lady's fur coat over his shoulders.*

MOTHER COURAGE: Can't pay, that it? No money, no
schnapps. They give us victory parades, but catch them giving men their pay.

SOLDIER: I want my schnapps. I missed the looting. That
5   double-crossing general only allowed an hour's looting in
the town. He ain't an inhuman monster, he said. Town must
of paid him.

THE CHAPLAIN: (*Stumbles in.*) There are people still lying in
that yard. The peasant's family. Somebody give me a hand. I
10   need linen.

(*The* SECOND SOLDIER *goes off with him.* KATTRIN *becomes
very excited and tries to make her mother produce linen.*)

MOTHER COURAGE: I got none. All my bandages was sold to
regiment. I ain't tearing up my officer's shirts for that lot.

CHAPLAIN: (*Calling back.*) I need linen, I tell you.

MOTHER COURAGE: (*Blocking* KATTRIN's *way into the cart by
15   sitting on the step.*) I'm giving nowt. They'll never pay, and
why, nowt to pay with.

CHAPLAIN: (*Bending over a woman he has carried in.*) Why
d'you stay around during the gunfire?

PEASANT WOMAN: (*Feebly.*) Farm.

20 MOTHER COURAGE: Catch them abandoning anything. But
now I'm s'posed to foot the bill. I won't do it.

FIRST SOLDIER: Those are Protestants. What they have to be
Protestants for?

MOTHER COURAGE: They ain't bothering about faith. They
25   lost their farm.

SECOND SOLDIER: They're no Protestants. They're Catholics
like us.

FIRST SOLDIER: No way of sorting 'em out in a bombardment.

A PEASANT: (*Brought in by the* CHAPLAIN.) My arm's gone.

30 THE CHAPLAIN: Where's that linen?

MOTHER COURAGE: I can't give nowt. What with expenses,
taxes, loan interest and bribes. (*Making guttural noises,* KAT-
TRIN *raises a plank and threatens her mother with it.*) You
gone plain crazy? Put that plank away or I'll paste you one,
35   you cow. I'm giving nowt, don't want to, got to think of meself. (*The* CHAPLAIN *lifts her off the steps and sets her on the
ground, then starts pulling out shirts and tearing them into
strips.*) My officers' shirts! Half a florin apiece! I'm ruined.
(*From the house comes the cry of a child in pain.*)

40 THE PEASANT: The baby's in there still. (KATTRIN *dashes in.*)

THE CHAPLAIN: (*To the woman.*) Don't move. They'll get it out.

MOTHER COURAGE: Stop her, roof may fall in.

THE CHAPLAIN: I'm not going back in there.

MOTHER COURAGE: (*Torn both ways.*) Don't waste my precious linen.   45

(KATTRIN *brings a baby out of the ruins.*)

MOTHER COURAGE: How nice, found another baby to cart
around? Give it to its ma this instant, unless you'd have me
fighting for hours to get it off you, like last time, d'you hear?
(*To the* SECOND SOLDIER.) Don't stand there gawping, you
go back and tell them cut out that music, we can see it's a   50
victory with our own eyes. All your victories mean to me is
losses.

THE CHAPLAIN: (*Tying a bandage.*) Blood's coming through.

(KATTRIN *is rocking the baby and making lullaby noises.*)

MOTHER COURAGE: Look at her, happy as a queen in all this
misery; give it back at once, its mother's coming round. (*She*   55
catches the FIRST SOLDIER, *who has been attacking the drinks
and is trying to make off with one of the bottles.*) Psia krew!
Thought you'd score another victory, you animal? Now pay.

FIRST SOLDIER: I got nowt.

MOTHER COURAGE: (*Pulling the fur coat off his back.*) Then   60
leave that coat, it's stolen any road.

THE CHAPLAIN: There's still someone under there.

— SCENE SIX —

Outside the Bavarian town of Ingolstadt Courage participates in the funeral of the late Imperial commander
Tilly. Discussions are held about war heroes and the
war's duration. The Chaplain complains that his talents
are lying fallow, and dumb Kattrin gets the red boots.
The year is 1632

Inside a canteen tent.
*It has a bar towards the rear. Rain. Sound of drums and Fu-
neral music. The* CHAPLAIN *and the regimental* CLERK *are
playing a board game.* MOTHER COURAGE *and her daughter
are stocktaking.*

THE CHAPLAIN: Now the funeral procession will be moving
off.

MOTHER COURAGE: Too bad about commander in chief—
twenty-two pairs those socks—he fell by accident, they say.
Mist over fields, that was the trouble. General had just been   5
haranguing a regiment saying they must fight to last man
and last round, he was riding back when mist made him lose
direction so he was up front and a bullet got him in midst of
battle—only four hurricane lamps left. (*A whistle from the
rear. She goes to the bar.*) You scrimshankers, dodging your   10
commander in chief's funeral, scandal I call it. (*Pours
drinks.*)

THE CLERK: They should never of paid troops out before the
funeral. Instead of going now they're all getting pissed.

THE CHAPLAIN: (*To the* CLERK.) Aren't you supposed to go to   15
the funeral?

THE CLERK: Dodged it cause of the rain.

MOTHER COURAGE: It's different with you, your uniform
might get wet. I heard they wanted to toll bells for funeral as
usual, except it turned out all churches had been blown to   20
smithereens by his orders, so poor old commander in chief

won't be hearing no bells as they let the coffin down. They're going to let off three salvoes instead to cheer things up—seventeen belts.

25 SHOUTS: *(From the bar.)* Hey, Missis, a brandy!

MOTHER COURAGE: Let's see your money. No, I ain't having you in my tent with your disgusting boots. You can drink outside, rain or no rain. *(To the* CLERK.*)* I'm only letting in sergeants and up. Commander in chief had been having his

30 worries, they say. S'posed to have been trouble with Second Regiment cause he stopped their pay, said it was a war of faith and they should do it for free. *(Funeral march. All look to the rear.)*

THE CHAPLAIN: Now they'll be filing past the noble corpse.

35 MOTHER COURAGE: Can't help feeling sorry for those generals and emperors, there they are maybe thinking they're doing something extra special what folk'll talk about in years to come, and earning a public monument, like conquering the world for instance, that's a fine ambition for a general, how's

40 he to know any better? I mean, he plagues hisself to death, then it all breaks down on account of ordinary folk what just wants their beer and bit of a chat, nowt higher. Finest plans get bolloxed up by the pettiness of them as should be carrying them out, because emperors can't do nowt themselves,

45 they just counts on soldiers and people to back 'em up whatever happens, am I right?

THE CHAPLAIN: *(Laughs.)* Courage, you're right, aside from the soldiers. They do their best. Give me that lot outside there, for instance, drinking their brandy in the rain, and I'd

50 guarantee to make you one war after another for a hundred years if need be, and I'm no trained general.

MOTHER COURAGE: You don't think war might end, then?

THE CHAPLAIN: What, because the commander in chief's gone? Don't be childish. They're two a penny, no shortage of

55 heroes.

MOTHER COURAGE: Ee, I'm not asking for fun of it, but because I'm thinking whether to stock up, prices are low now, but if war's going to end it's money down the drain.

THE CHAPLAIN: I realise it's a serious question. There've al-

60 ways been people going round saying 'the war can't go on for ever'. I tell you there's nothing to stop it going on for ever. Of course there can be a bit of a breathing space. The war may need to get its second wind, it may even have an accident so to speak. There's no guarantee against that; nothing's perfect

65 on this earth of ours. A perfect war, the sort you might say couldn't be improved on, that's something we shall probably never see. It can suddenly come to a standstill for some quite unforeseen reason, you can't allow for everything. A slight case of negligence, and it's bogged down up to the axles. And

70 then it's a matter of hauling the war out of the mud again. But emperor and kings and popes will come to its rescue. So on the whole it has nothing serious to worry about, and will live to a ripe old age.

A SOLDIER: *(Sings at the bar.)*

75   A schnapps, landlord, you're late!
      A soldier cannot wait
      To do his emperor's orders.

    Make it a double, this is a holiday.

MOTHER COURAGE: S'pose I went by what you say . . .

80 THE CHAPLAIN: Think it out for yourself. What's to compete with the war?

THE SOLDIER: *(At the rear.)*

      Your breast, my girl, you're late!
      A soldier cannot wait
      To ride across the borders.   85

THE CLERK: *(Unexpectedly.)* And what about peace? I'm from Bohemia and I'd like to go home some day.

THE CHAPLAIN: Would you indeed? Ah, peace. Where is the hole once the cheese has been eaten?

THE SOLDIER: *(At the rear.)*   90

      Lead trumps, my friend, you're late!
      A soldier cannot wait.
      His emperor needs him badly.

      Your blessing, priest, you're late!
      A soldier cannot wait.   95
      Must lay his life down gladly.

THE CLERK: In the long run life's impossible if there's no peace.

THE CHAPLAIN: I'd say there's peace in war too; it has its peaceful moments. Because war satisfies all requirements, peace-

100 able ones included, they're catered for, and it would simply fizzle out if they weren't. In war you can do a crap like in the depths of peacetime, then between one battle and the next you can have a beer, then even when you're moving up you

105 can lay your head on your arms and have a bit of shuteye in the ditch, it's entirely possible. During a charge you can't play cards maybe, but nor can you in the depths of peacetime when you're ploughing, and after a victory there are various openings. You may get a leg blown off, then you start by

110 making a lot of fuss as though it were serious, but afterwards you calm down or get given a schnapps, and you end up hopping around and the war's no worse off than before. And what's to stop you being fruitful and multiplying in the middle of all the butchery, behind a barn or something, in the

115 long run you can't be held back from it, and then the war will have your progeny and can use them to carry on with. No, the war will always find an outlet, mark my words. Why should it ever stop?

(KATTRIN has ceased working and is staring at the CHAPLAIN.)

MOTHER COURAGE: I'll buy fresh stock then. If you say so.

120 *(KATTRIN suddenly flings a basket full of bottles to the ground and runs off.)* Kattrin! *(Laughs.)* Damn me if she weren't waiting for peace. I promised her she'd get a husband soon as peace came. *(Hurries after her.)*

THE CLERK: *(Standing up.)* I won. You been talking too much.

125 Pay up.

MOTHER COURAGE: *(Returning with KATTRIN.)* Don't be silly, war'll go on a bit longer, and we'll make a bit more money, and peacetime'll be all the nicer for it. Now you go into town, that's ten minutes' walk at most, fetch things from

130 Golden Lion, the expensive ones, we can fetch rest in cart later, it's all arranged, regimental clerk here will go with you. Nearly everybody's attending commander in chief's funeral, nowt can happen to you. Careful now, don't let them steal nowt, think of your dowry.   135

(KATTRIN puts a cloth over her head and leaves with the CLERK.)

THE CHAPLAIN: Is that all right to let her go with the clerk?

MOTHER COURAGE: She's not that pretty they'd want to ruin her.

THE CHAPLAIN: I admire the way you run your business and al-
140　ways win through. I see why they called you Courage.
MOTHER COURAGE: Poor folk got to have courage. Why,
they're lost. Simply getting up in morning takes some doing
in their situation. Or ploughing a field, and in a war at that.
Mere fact they bring kids into world shows they got courage,
145　cause there's no hope for them. They have to hang one another and slaughter one another, so just looking each other
in face must call for courage. Being able to put up with emperor and pope shows supernatural courage, cause those two
cost 'em their lives. (She sits down, takes a little pipe from her
150　purse and smokes.) You might chop us a bit of kindling.
THE CHAPLAIN: (Reluctantly removing his coat and preparing
to chop up sticks.) I happen to be a pastor of souls, not a
woodcutter.
MOTHER COURAGE: I got no soul, you see. Need firewood,
155　though.
THE CHAPLAIN: Where's that stumpy pipe from?
MOTHER COURAGE: Just a pipe.
THE CHAPLAIN: What d'you mean, 'just', it's a quite particular
pipe, that.
160　MOTHER COURAGE: Aha?
THE CHAPLAIN: That stumpy pipe belongs to the Oxenstierna
Regiment's cook.
MOTHER COURAGE: If you know that already why ask, Mr
Clever?
165　THE CHAPLAIN: Because I didn't know if you were aware what
you're smoking. You might just have been rummaging
around in your things, come across some old pipe or other,
and used it out of sheer absence of mind.
MOTHER COURAGE: And why not?
170　THE CHAPLAIN: Because you didn't. You're smoking that deliberately.
MOTHER COURAGE: And why shouldn't I?
THE CHAPLAIN: Courage, I'm warning you. It's my duty. Probably you'll never clap eyes on the gentleman again, and
175　that's no loss but your good fortune. He didn't make at all a
reliable impression on me. Quite the opposite.
MOTHER COURAGE: Really? Nice fellow that.
THE CHAPLAIN: So he's what you would call a nice fellow? I
wouldn't. Far be it from me to bear him the least ill-will, but
180　nice is not what I would call him. More like one of those
Don Juans, a slippery one. Have a look at that pipe if you
don't believe me. You must admit it tells you a good deal
about his character.
MOTHER COURAGE: Nowt that I can see. Worn out, I'd call it.
185　THE CHAPLAIN: Practically bitten through, you mean. A man
of wrath. That is the pipe of an unscrupulous man of wrath;
you must see that if you have any discrimination left.
MOTHER COURAGE: Don't chop my chopping block in two.
THE CHAPLAIN: I told you, I'm not a woodcutter by trade. I
190　studied to be a pastor of souls. My talent and abilities are
being abused in this place, by manual labour. My God-
given endowments are denied expression. It's a sin. You
have never heard me preach. One sermon of mine can put
a regiment in such a frame of mind it'll treat the enemy like
195　a flock of sheep. Life to them is a smelly old foot-cloth
which they fling away in a vision of final victory. God has
given me the gift of speech. I can preach so you'll lose all
sense of sight and hearing.
MOTHER COURAGE: I don't wish to lose my sense of sight and
200　hearing. Where'd that leave me?

THE CHAPLAIN: Courage, I have often thought that your dry
way of talking conceals more than just a warm heart. You too
are human and need warmth.
MOTHER COURAGE: Best way for us to get this tent warm is
have plenty of firewood.　　205
THE CHAPLAIN: Don't change the subject. Seriously, Courage,
I sometimes ask myself what it would be like if our relationship were to become somewhat closer. I mean, given that the
whirlwind of war has so strangely whirled us together.
MOTHER COURAGE: I'd say it was close enough. I cook meals　210
for you and you run around and chop firewood for instance.
THE CHAPLAIN: (Coming closer.) You know what I mean by
closer; it's not a relationship founded on meals and wood-
chopping and other such base necessities. Let your head
speak, harden thyself not.　　215
MOTHER COURAGE: Don't you come at me with that axe.
That'd be too close a relationship.
THE CHAPLAIN: You shouldn't make a joke of it. I'm a serious
person and I've thought about what I'm saying.
MOTHER COURAGE: Be sensible, padre. I like you. I don't want　220
to row you. All I'm after is get myself and children through
all this with my cart. I don't see it as mine, and I ain't in the
mood for private affairs. Right now I'm taking a gamble, buying stores just when commander in chief's fallen and all the
talk's of peace. Where d'you reckon you'd turn if I'm ruined?　225
Don't know, do you? You chop us some kindling wood, then
we can keep warm at night, that's quite something these
times. What's this? (She gets up. Enter KATTRIN, out of
breath, with a wound above her eye. She is carrying a variety
of stuff: parcels, leather goods, a drum and so on.)　　230
MOTHER COURAGE: What happened, someone assault you?
On way back? She was assaulted on her way back. Bet it was
that trooper was getting drunk here. I shouldn't have let you
go, love. Drop that stuff. Not too bad, just a flesh wound you
got. I'll bandage it and in a week it'll be all right. Worse than　235
wild beasts, they are. (She ties up the wound.)
THE CHAPLAIN: It's not them I blame. They never went raping
back home. The fault lies with those that start wars, it brings
humanity's lowest instincts to the surface.
MOTHER COURAGE: Calm down. Didn't clerk come back with　240
you? That's because you're respectable, they don't bother.
Wound ain't a deep one, won't leave no mark. There you
are, all bandaged up. You'll get something, love, keep calm.
Something I put aside for you, wait till you see. (She delves
into a sack and brings out YVETTE's red high-heeled boots.)　245
Made you open your eyes, eh? Something you always
wanted. They're yours. Put 'em on quick, before I change
me mind. Won't leave no mark, and what if it does? Ones
I'm really sorry for's the ones they fancy. Drag them around
till they're worn out, they do. Those they don't care for they　250
leaves alive. I seen girls before now had pretty faces, then in
no time looking fit to frighten a hyaena. Can't even go behind a bush without risking trouble, horrible life they lead.
Same like with trees, straight well-shaped ones get chopped
down to make beams for houses and crooked ones live hap-　255
pily ever after. So it's a stroke of luck for you really. Them
boots'll be all right, I greased them before putting them
away.

(KATTRIN leaves the boots where they are and crawls into the
cart.)

THE CHAPLAIN: Let's hope she's not disfigured.

260 MOTHER COURAGE: She'll have a scar. No use her waiting for peacetime now.

THE CHAPLAIN: She didn't let them steal the things.

MOTHER COURAGE: Maybe I shouldn't have dinned that into her so. Wish I knew what went on in that head of hers. Just
265 once she stayed out all night, once in all those years. Afterwards she went around like before, except she worked harder. Couldn't get her to tell what had happened. Worried me quite a while, that did. (*She collects the articles brought by* KATTRIN, *and sorts them angrily.*) That's war for you. Nice
270 way to get a living!

(*Sound of cannon fire.*)

THE CHAPLAIN: Now they'll be burying the commander in chief. This is a historic moment.

MOTHER COURAGE: What I call a historic moment is them bashing my daughter over the eye. She's half wrecked al-
275 ready, won't get no husband now, and her so crazy about kids; any road she's only dumb from war, soldier stuffed something in her mouth when she was little. As for Swiss Cheese I'll never see him again, and where Eilif is God alone knows. War be damned.

— SCENE SEVEN —

| Mother Courage at the peak of her business career |

High road.
The CHAPLAIN, MOTHER COURAGE *and* KATTRIN *are pulling the cart, which is hung with new wares.* MOTHER COURAGE *is wearing a necklace of silver coins.*

MOTHER COURAGE: I won't have you folk spoiling my war for me. I'm told it kills off the weak, but they're write-off in peacetime too. And war gives its people a better deal. (*She sings.*)

5   And if you feel your forces fading
         You won't be there to share the fruits.
         But what is war but private trading
         That deals in blood instead of boots?

And what's the use of settling down? Them as does are first to
10   go. (*Sings.*)

         Some people think to live by looting
         The goods some others haven't got.
         You think it's just a line they're shooting
         Until you hear they have been shot.

15   And some I saw dig six feet under
         In haste to lie down and pass out.
         Now they're at rest perhaps they wonder
         Just what was all their haste about.

(*They pull it further.*)

— SCENE EIGHT —

| The same year sees the death of the Swedish king Gustavus Adolphus at the battle of Lützen. Peace threatens to ruin Mother Courage's business. Courage's dashing son performs one heroic deed too many and comes to a sticky end |

Camp.
A summer morning. In front of the cart stand an OLD WOMAN *and her son. The son carries a large sack of bedding.*

MOTHER COURAGE'S VOICE: (*From inside the cart.*) Does it need to be this ungodly hour?

THE YOUNG MAN: We walked twenty miles in the night and got to be back today.

MOTHER COURAGE'S VOICE: What am I to do with bedding? 5 Folk've got no houses.

THE YOUNG MAN: Best have a look first.

THE OLD WOMAN: This place is no good either. Come on.

THE YOUNG MAN: What, and have them sell the roof over our head for taxes? She might pay three florins if you throw in 10 the bracelet. (*Bells start ringing.*) Listen, mother.

VOICES: (*From the rear.*) Peace! Swedish king's been killed.

MOTHER COURAGE: (*Sticks her head out of the cart. She has not yet done her hair.*) What's that bell-ringing about in mid-week? 15

THE CHAPLAIN: (*Crawling out from under the cart.*) What are they shouting? Peace?

MOTHER COURAGE: Don't tell me peace has broken out just after I laid in new stock.

THE CHAPLAIN: (*Calling to the rear.*) That true? Peace? 20

VOICES: Three weeks ago, they say, only no one told us.

THE CHAPLAIN: (*To* COURAGE.) What else would they be ringing the bells for?

VOICES: A whole lot of Lutherans have driven into town, they brought the news. 25

THE YOUNG MAN: Mother, it's peace. What's the matter?

(*The* OLD WOMAN *has collapsed.*)

MOTHER COURAGE: (*Speaking into the cart.*) Holy cow! Kattrin, peace! Put your black dress on, we're going to church. Least we can do for Swiss Cheese. Is it true, though?

THE YOUNG MAN: The people here say so. They've made 30 peace. Can you get up? (*The* OLD WOMAN *stands up dumbfounded.*) I'll get the saddlery going again, I promise. It'll all work out. Father will get his bedding back. Can you walk? (*To the* CHAPLAIN.) She came over queer. It's the news. She never thought there'd be peace again. Father always said so. 35 We're going straight home. (*They go off.*)

MOTHER COURAGE'S VOICE: Give her a schnapps.

THE CHAPLAIN: They've already gone.

MOTHER COURAGE'S VOICE: What's up in camp?

THE CHAPLAIN: They're assembling. I'll go on over. Shouldn't 40 I put on my clerical garb?

MOTHER COURAGE'S VOICE: Best check up before parading yourself as heretic. I'm glad about peace, never mind if I'm ruined. Any road I'll have got two of me children through the war. Be seeing Eilif again now. 45

THE CHAPLAIN: And who's that walking down the lines? Bless me, the army commander's cook.

THE COOK: (*Somewhat bedraggled and carrying a bundle.*) What do I behold? The padre!

THE CHAPLAIN: Courage, we've got company. 50

(MOTHER COURAGE *clambers out.*)

THE COOK: I promised I'd drop over for a little talk soon as I had the time. I've not forgotten your brandy, Mrs Fierling.

MOTHER COURAGE: Good grief, the general's cook! After all these years! Where's my eldest boy Eilif?

THE COOK: Hasn't he got here? He left before me, he was on his way to see you too.

THE CHAPLAIN: I shall don my clerical garb, just a moment.

(Goes off behind the cart.)

MOTHER COURAGE: Then he may be here any minute. *(Calls into the cart.)* Kattrin, Eilif's on his way. Get cook a glass of brandy, Kattrin! *(KATTRIN does not appear.)* Drag your hair down over it, that's all right. Mr Lamb's no stranger. *(Fetches the brandy herself.)* She don't like to come out, peace means nowt to her. Took too long coming, it did. They gave her a crack over one eye, you barely notice it now but she thinks folks are staring at her.

THE COOK: Ah yes. War. *(He and MOTHER COURAGE sit down.)*

MOTHER COURAGE: Cooky, you caught me at bad moment. I'm ruined.

THE COOK: What? That's hard.

MOTHER COURAGE: Peace'll wring my neck. I went and took Chaplain's advice, laid in fresh stocks only t'other day. And now they're going to demobilise and I'll be left sitting on me wares.

THE COOK: What d'you want to go and listen to padre for? If I hadn't been in such a hurry that time, the Catholics arriving so quickly and all, I'd warned you against that man. All piss and wind, he is. So he's the authority around here, eh?

MOTHER COURAGE: He's been doing washing-up for me and helping pull.

THE COOK: Him pull! I bet he told you some of those jokes of his too, I know him, got a very unhealthy view of women, he has, all my good influence on him went for nowt. He ain't steady.

MOTHER COURAGE: You steady then?

THE COOK: Whatever else I ain't, I'm steady. Mud in your eye!

MOTHER COURAGE: Steady, that's nowt. I only had one steady fellow, thank God. Hardest I ever had to work in me life; he flogged the kids' blankets soon as autumn came, and he called me mouth-organ an unchristian instrument. Ask me, you ain't saying much for yourself admitting you're steady.

THE COOK: Still tough as nails, I see; but that's what I like about you.

MOTHER COURAGE: Now don't tell me you been dreaming of me nails.

THE COOK: Well, well, here we are, along with armistice bells and your brandy like what nobody else ever serves, it's famous, that is.

MOTHER COURAGE: I don't give two pins for your armistice bells just now. Can't see 'em handing out all the back pay what's owing, so where does that leave me with my famous brandy? Had your pay yet?

THE COOK: *(Hesitantly.)* Not exactly. That's why we all shoved off. If that's how it is, I thought, I'll go and visit friends. So here I am sitting with you.

MOTHER COURAGE: Other words you got nowt.

THE COOK: High time they stopped that bloody clanging. Wouldn't mind getting into some sort of trade. I'm fed up being cook to that lot. I'm s'posed to rustle them up meals out of tree roots and old bootsoles, then they fling the hot soup in my face. Cook these days is a dog's life. Sooner do war service, only of course it's peacetime now. *(He sees the CHAPLAIN reappearing in his old garments.)* More about that later.

THE CHAPLAIN: It's still all right, only had a few moths in it.

THE COOK: Can't see why you bother. You won't get your old job back, who are you to inspire now to earn his pay honourably and lay down his life? What's more I got a bone to pick with you, cause you advised this lady to buy a lot of unnecessary goods saying war would go on for ever.

THE CHAPLAIN: *(Heatedly.)* I'd like to know what concern that is of yours.

THE COOK: Because it's unscrupulous, that sort of thing is. How dare you meddle in other folks' business arrangements with your unwanted advice?

THE CHAPLAIN: Who's meddling? *(To COURAGE.)* I never knew this gentleman was such an intimate you had to account to him for everything.

MOTHER COURAGE: Keep your hair on, cook's only giving his personal opinion and you can't deny your war was a flop.

THE CHAPLAIN: You should not blaspheme against peace, Courage. You are a hyaena of the battlefield.

MOTHER COURAGE: I'm what?

THE COOK: If you're going to insult this lady you'll have to settle with me.

THE CHAPLAIN: It's not you I'm talking to. Your intentions are only too transparent. *(To COURAGE.)* But when I see you picking up peace betwixt your finger and your thumb like some dirty old snot-rag, then my humanity feels outraged; for then I see that you don't want peace but war, because you profit from it; in which case you shouldn't forget the ancient saying that whosoever sups with the devil needs a long spoon.

MOTHER COURAGE: I got no use for war, and war ain't got much use for me. But I'm not being called no hyaena, you and me's through.

THE CHAPLAIN: Then why grumble about peace when everybody's breathing sighs of relief? Because of some old junk in your cart?

MOTHER COURAGE: My goods ain't old junk but what I lives by, and you too up to now.

THE CHAPLAIN: Off war, in other words. Aha.

THE COOK: *(To the CHAPLAIN.)* You're old enough to know it's always a mistake offering advice. *(To COURAGE.)* Way things are, your best bet's to get rid of certain goods quick as you can before prices hit rock-bottom. Dress yourself and get moving, not a moment to lose.

MOTHER COURAGE: That ain't bad advice. I'll do that, I guess.

THE CHAPLAIN: Because cooky says it.

MOTHER COURAGE: Why couldn't you say it? He's right, I'd best go off to market. *(Goes inside the cart.)*

THE COOK: That's one to me, padre. You got no presence of mind. What you should of said was: what, me offer advice, all I done was discuss politics. Better not take me on. Cock-fighting don't suit that get-up.

THE CHAPLAIN: If you don't stop your gob I'll murder you, get-up or no get-up.

THE COOK: *(Pulling off his boots and unwrapping his foot-cloths.)* Pity the war made such a godless shit of you, else you'd easily get another parsonage now it's peacetime. Cooks won't be needed, there's nowt to cook, but faith goes on just the same, nowt changed in that direction.

THE CHAPLAIN: Mr Lamb, I'm asking you not to elbow me out. Since I came down in the world I've become a better person. I couldn't preach to anyone now.

(Enter YVETTE POTTIER *in black, dressed up to the nines, carrying a cane. She is much older and fatter, and heavily powdered. She is followed by a manservant.)*

175   YVETTE: Hullo there, everybody. Is this Mother Courage's establishment?

THE CHAPLAIN: It is. And with whom have we the honour . . . ?

YVETTE: With the Countess Starhemberg, my good man. Where's Courage?

180   THE CHAPLAIN: *(Calls into the cart.)* The Countess Starhemberg wishes to speak to you.

MOTHER COURAGE'S VOICE: Just coming.

YVETTE: It's Yvette.

MOTHER COURAGE'S VOICE: Oh, Yvette!

185   YVETTE: Come to see how you are. *(Sees the* COOK *turn round aghast.)* Pieter!

THE COOK: Yvette!

YVETTE: Well I never! How d'you come to be here?

THE COOK: Got a lift.

190   THE CHAPLAIN: You know each other then? Intimately?

YVETTE: I should think so. *(She looks the* COOK *over.)* Fat.

THE COOK: Not all that skinny yourself.

YVETTE: All the same I'm glad to see you, you shit. Gives me a chance to say what I think of you.

195   THE CHAPLAIN: You say it, in full; but don't start till Courage is out here.

MOTHER COURAGE: *(Coming out with all kinds of goods.)* Yvette! *(They embrace.)* But what are you in mourning for?

YVETTE: Suits me, don't it? My husband the colonel died a
200   few years back.

MOTHER COURAGE: That old fellow what nearly bought the cart?

YVETTE: His elder brother.

MOTHER COURAGE: Then you're sitting pretty. Nice to find
205   somebody what's made it in this war.

YVETTE: Up and down and up again, that's the way it went.

MOTHER COURAGE: I'm not hearing a word against colonels, they make a mint of money.

THE CHAPLAIN: I would put my boots back on if I were you.
210   *(To* YVETTE.*)* You promised you would say what you think of the gentleman.

THE COOK: Don't kick up a stink here, Yvette.

MOTHER COURAGE: Yvette, this is a friend of mine.

YVETTE: That's old Puffing Piet.

215   THE COOK: Let's drop the nicknames. I'm called Lamb.

MOTHER COURAGE: *(Laughs.)* Puffing Piet! Him as made all the women crazy! Here, I been looking after your pipe for you.

THE CHAPLAIN: Smoking it, too.

220   YVETTE: What luck I can warn you against him. Worst of the lot, he was, rampaging along the whole Flanders coastline. Got more girls in trouble than he has fingers.

THE COOK: That's all a long while ago. Tain't true anyhow.

YVETTE: Stand up when a lady brings you into the conversa-
225   tion! How I loved this man! All the time he had a little dark girl with bandy legs, got her in trouble too of course.

THE COOK: Got you into high society more like, far as I can see.

YVETTE: Shut your trap, you pathetic remnant! Better watch
230   out for him, though; fellows like that are still dangerous even when on their last legs.

MOTHER COURAGE: *(To* YVETTE.*)* Come along, got to get rid of my stuff afore prices start dropping. You might be able to put a word in for me at regiment, with your connections.
235   *(Calls into the cart.)* Kattrin, church is off, I'm going to market instead. When Eilif turns up, one of you give him a drink. *(Exit with* YVETTE.*)*

YVETTE: *(As she leaves.)* Fancy a creature like that ever making me leave the straight and narrow path. Thank my lucky stars
240   I managed to reach the top all the same. But I've cooked your goose, Puffing Piet, and that's something that'll be credited to me one day in the world to come.

THE CHAPLAIN: I would like to take as a text for our little talk 'The mills of God grind slowly'. Weren't you complaining
245   about my jokes?

THE COOK: Dead out of luck, I am. It's like this, you see: I thought I might get a hot meal. Here am I starving, and now they'll be talking about me and she'll get quite a wrong picture. I think I'll clear out before she's back.

250   THE CHAPLAIN: I think so too.

THE COOK: Padre, I'm fed up already with this bloody peace. Human race has to go through fire and sword cause it's sinful from the cradle up. I wish I could be roasting a fat capon once again for the general, wherever he's got to, in mustard
255   sauce with a carrot or two.

THE CHAPLAIN: Red cabbage. Red cabbage for a capon.

THE COOK: You're right, but carrots was what he had to have.

THE CHAPLAIN: No sense of what's fitting.

THE COOK: Not that it stopped you guzzling your share.

260   THE CHAPLAIN: With misgivings.

THE COOK: Anyway you must admit those were the days.

THE CHAPLAIN: I might admit it if pressed.

THE COOK: Now you've called her a hyaena your days here are finished. What you staring at?

265   THE CHAPLAIN: Eilif! *(*EILIF *arrives, followed by* SOLDIERS *with pikes. His hands are fettered. His face is chalky-white.)* What's wrong?

EILIF: Where's mother?

THE CHAPLAIN: Gone into town.

270   EILIF: I heard she was around. They've allowed me to come and see her.

THE COOK: *(To the* SOLDIERS.*)* What you doing with him?

A SOLDIER: Something not nice.

THE CHAPLAIN: What's he been up to?

275   THE SOLDIER: Broke into a peasant's place. The wife's dead.

THE CHAPLAIN: How could you do a thing like that?

EILIF: It's what I did last time, ain't it?

THE COOK: Aye, but it's peace now.

EILIF: Shut up. All right if I sit down till she comes?

280   THE SOLDIER: We've no time.

THE CHAPLAIN: In wartime they recommended him for that, sat him at the general's right hand. Dashing, it was, in those days. Any chance of a word with the provost-marshal?

THE SOLDIER: Wouldn't do no good. Taking some peasant's
285   cattle, what's dashing about that?

THE COOK: Dumb, I call it.

EILIF: If I'd been dumb you'd of starved, clever bugger.

THE COOK: But as you were clever you're going to be shot.

THE CHAPLAIN: We'd better fetch Kattrin out anyhow.

290   EILIF: Sooner have a glass of schnapps, could do with that.

THE SOLDIER: No time, come along.

THE CHAPLAIN: And what shall we tell your mother?

EILIF: Tell her it wasn't any different, tell her it was the same thing. Or tell her nowt. (The SOLDIERS *propel him away.*)

295 THE CHAPLAIN: I'll accompany you on your grievous journey.

EILIF: Don't need any bloody parsons.

THE CHAPLAIN: Wait and see. (*Follows him.*)

THE COOK: (*Calls after them.*) I'll have to tell her, she'll want to see him.

300 THE CHAPLAIN: I wouldn't tell her anything. At most that he was here and will come again, maybe tomorrow. By then I'll be back and can break it to her. (*Hurries off.*)

(*The* COOK *looks after him, shaking his head, then walks restlessly around. Finally he comes up to the cart.*)

THE COOK: Hoy! Don't you want to come out? I can understand you hiding away from peace. Like to do the same my-
305 self. Remember me, I'm general's cook? I was wondering if you'd a bit of something to eat while I wait for your mum. I don't half feel like a bit of pork, or bread even, just to fill the time. (*Peers inside.*) Head under blanket. (*Sound of gunfire off.*)

MOTHER COURAGE: (*Runs in, out of breath and with all her*
310 *goods still.*) Cooky, peacetime's over. War's been on again three days now. Heard news before selling me stuff, thank God. They're having a shooting match with Lutherans in town. We must get cart away at once. Kattrin, pack up! What you in the dumps for? What's wrong?

315 THE COOK: Nowt.

MOTHER COURAGE: Something is. I see it way you look.

THE COOK: Cause war's starting up again, I s'pose. Looks as if it'll be tomorrow night before I get next hot food inside me.

MOTHER COURAGE: You're lying, cooky.

320 THE COOK: Eilif was here. Had to leave almost at once, though.

MOTHER COURAGE: Was he now? Then we'll be seeing him on march. I'm joining our side this time. How's he look?

THE COOK: Same as usual.

325 MOTHER COURAGE: Oh, he'll never change. Take more than war to steal him from me. Clever, he is. You going to help me get packed? (*Begins to pack up.*) What's his news? Still in general's good books? Say anything about his deeds of valour?

330 THE COOK: (*Glumly.*) Repeated one of them, I'm told.

MOTHER COURAGE: Tell it me later, we got to move off. (KATTRIN *appears.*) Kattrin, peacetime's finished now. We're moving on. (*To the* COOK.) How about you?

THE COOK: Have to join up again.

335 MOTHER COURAGE: Why don't you . . . Where's padre?

THE COOK: Went into town with Eilif.

MOTHER COURAGE: Then you come along with us a way. Need somebody to help me.

THE COOK: That business with Yvette, you know . . .

340 MOTHER COURAGE: Done you no harm in my eyes. Opposite. Where there's smoke there's fire, they say. You coming along?

THE COOK: I won't say no.

MOTHER COURAGE: The Twelfth moved off already. Take the
345 shaft. Here's a bit of bread. We must get round behind to Lutherans. Might even be seeing Eilif tonight. He's my favourite one. Short peace, wasn't it? Now we're off again. (*She sings as the* COOK *and* KATTRIN *harness themselves up.*)

From Ulm to Metz, from Metz to Munich
Courage will see the war gets fed.   350
The war will show a well-filled tunic
Given its daily shot of lead.
But lead alone can hardly nourish
It must have soldiers to subsist.
It's you it needs to make it flourish.   355
The war's still hungry. So enlist!

— SCENE NINE —

It is the seventeenth year of the great war of faith. Germany has lost more than half her inhabitants. Those who survive the bloodbath are killed off by terrible epidemics. Once fertile areas are ravaged by famine, wolves roam the burnt-out towns. In autumn 1634 we find Courage in the Fichtelgebirge, off the main axis of the Swedish armies. The winter this year is early and harsh. Business is bad, so that there is nothing to do but beg. The cook gets a letter from Utrecht and is sent packing

Outside a semi-dilapidated parsonage.
Grey morning in early winter. Gusts of wind. MOTHER COURAGE *and the* COOK *in shabby sheepskins, drawing the cart.*

THE COOK: It's all dark, nobody up yet.

MOTHER COURAGE: Except it's parson's house. Have to crawl out of bed to ring bells. Then he'll have hot soup.

THE COOK: What from when whole village is burnt, we seen it.   5

MOTHER COURAGE: It's lived in, though, dog was barking.

THE COOK: S'pose parson's got, he'll give nowt.

MOTHER COURAGE: Maybe if we sing. . . .

THE COOK: I've had enough. (*Abruptly.*) Got a letter from Utrecht saying mother died of cholera and inn's mine.   10
Here's letter if you don't believe me. No business of yours the way aunty goes on about my mode of existence, but have a look.

MOTHER COURAGE: (*Reads the letter.*) Lamb, I'm tired too of always being on the go. I feel like butcher's dog, dragging   15
meat round customers and getting nowt off it. I got nowt left to sell, and folk got nowt left to buy nowt with. Saxony a fellow in rags tried landing me a stack of old books for two eggs, Württemberg they wanted to swap their plough for a titchy bag of salt. What's to plough for? Nowt growing no more,   20
just brambles. In Pomerania villages are s'posed to have started in eating the younger kids, and nuns have been caught sticking folk up.

THE COOK: World's dying out.

MOTHER COURAGE: Sometimes I sees meself driving through   25
hell with me cart selling brimstone, or across heaven with packed lunches for hungry souls. Give me my kids what's left, let's find some place they ain't shooting, and I'd like a few more years undisturbed.

THE COOK: You and me could get that inn going, Courage,   30
think it over. Made up me mind in the night, I did: back to Utrecht with or without you, and starting today.

MOTHER COURAGE: Have to talk to Kattrin. That's a bit quick for me; I'm against making decisions all freezing cold and nowt inside you. Kattrin! (KATTRIN *climbs out of the cart.*)   35
Kattrin, got something to tell you. Cook and I want to go to

Utrecht. He's been left an inn there. That'd be a settled place for you, let you meet a few people. Lots of 'em respect
40 somebody mature, looks ain't everything. I'd like it too. I get on with cook. Say one thing for him, got a head for business. We'd have our meals for sure, not bad, eh? And your own bed too; like that, wouldn't you? Road's no life really. God knows how you might finish up. Lousy already, you are.
45 Have to make up our minds, see, we could move with the Swedes, up north, they're somewhere up that way. (*She points to the left.*) Reckon that's fixed, Kattrin.
THE COOK: Anna, I got something private to say to you.
MOTHER COURAGE: Get back in cart, Kattrin.

(KATTRIN *climbs back.*)

THE COOK: I had to interrupt, cause you don't understand, far
50 as I can see. I didn't think there was need to say it, sticks out a mile. But if it don't, then let me tell you straight, no question of taking her along, not on your life. You get me, eh.

(KATTRIN *sticks her head out of the cart behind them and listens.*)

MOTHER COURAGE: You mean I'm to leave Kattrin back here?
THE COOK: Use your imagination. Inn's got no room. It ain't
55 one of the sort got three bar parlours. Put our backs in it we two'll get a living, but not three, no chance of that. She can keep cart.
MOTHER COURAGE: Thought she might find husband in Utrecht.
60 THE COOK: Go on, make me laugh. Find a husband, how? Dumb and that scar on top of it. And at her age?
MOTHER COURAGE: Don't talk so loud.
THE COOK: Loud or soft, no getting over facts. And that's another reason why I can't have her in the inn. Customers
65 don't want to be looking at that all the time. Can't blame them.
MOTHER COURAGE: Shut your big mouth. I said not so loud.
THE COOK: Light's on in parson's house. We can try singing.
MOTHER COURAGE: Cooky, how's she to pull the cart on her
70 own? War scares her. She'll never stand it. The dreams she must have . . . I hear her nights groaning. Mostly after a battle. What's she seeing in those dreams, I'd like to know. She's got a soft heart. Lately I found she'd got another hedgehog tucked away what we'd run over.
75 THE COOK: Inn's too small. (*Calls out.*) Ladies and gentlemen, domestic staff and other residents! We are now going to give you a song concerning Solomon, Julius Caesar and other famous personages what had bad luck. So's you can see we're respectable folk, which makes it difficult to carry on, particu-
80 larly in winter. (*They sing.*)

You saw sagacious Solomon
You know what came of him.
To him complexities seemed plain.
He cursed the hour that gave birth to him
85 And saw that everything was vain.
How great and wise was Solomon!
The world however didn't wait
But soon observed what followed on.
It's wisdom that had brought him to this state—
90 How fortunate the man with none!

Yes, the virtues are dangerous stuff in this world, as this fine song proves, better not to have them and have a pleasant life

and breakfast instead, hot soup for instance. Look at me: I haven't any but I'd like some. I'm a serving soldier but what good did my courage do me in all them battles, nowt, here I 95 am starving and better have been shit-scared and stayed at home. For why?

You saw courageous Caesar next
You know what he became.
They deified him in his life 100
Then had him murdered just the same.
And as they raised the fatal knife
How loud he cried: You too, my son!
The world however didn't wait
But soon observed what followed on. 105
It's courage that had brought him to that state.
How fortunate the man with none!

(*Sotto voce.*) Don't even look out. (*Aloud.*) Ladies and gentlemen, domestic staff and other inmates! All right, you may say, gallantry never cooked a man's dinner, what about try- 110 ing honesty? You can eat all you want then, or anyhow not stay sober. How about it?

You heard of honest Socrates
The man who never lied:
They weren't so grateful as you'd think 115
Instead the rulers fixed to have him tried
And handed him the poisoned drink.
How honest was the people's noble son!
The world however didn't wait
But soon observed what followed on. 120
It's honesty that brought him to that state.
How fortunate the man with none!

Ah yes, they say, be unselfish and share what you've got, but how about if you got nowt? It's all very well to say the do- 125 gooders have a hard time, but you still got to have something. Aye, unselfishness is a rare virtue, cause it just don't pay.

Saint Martin couldn't bear to see
His fellows in distress. 130
He met a poor man in the snow
And shared his cloak with him, we know.
Both of them therefore froze to death.
His place in Heaven was surely won!
The world however didn't wait 135
But soon observed what followed on.
Unselfishness had brought him to that state.
How fortunate the man with none!

That's how it is with us. We're respectable folk, stick together, don't steal, don't murder, don't burn places down. 140 And all the time you might say we're sinking lower and lower, and it's true what the song says, and soup is few and far between, and if we weren't like this but thieves and murderers I dare say we'd be eating our fill. For virtues aren't their own reward, only wickednesses are, that's how the 145 world goes and it didn't ought to.

Here you can see respectable folk
Keeping to God's own laws.
So far he hasn't taken heed.
You who sit safe and warm indoors 150
Help to relieve our bitter need!

How virtuously we had begun!
The world however didn't wait
But soon observed what followed on.
155   It's fear of God that brought us to that state.
How fortunate the man with none!

VOICE: *(From above.)* Hey, you there! Come on up! There's hot soup if you want.

MOTHER COURAGE: Lamb, me stomach won't stand nowt.
160   'Tain't that it ain't sensible, what you say, but is that your last word? We got on all right.

THE COOK: Last word. Think it over.

MOTHER COURAGE: I've nowt to think. I'm not leaving her here.

165 THE COOK: That's proper senseless, nothing I can do about it though. I'm not a brute, just the inn's a small one. So now we better get on up, or there'll be nowt here either and wasted time singing in the cold.

MOTHER COURAGE: I'll get Kattrin.

170 THE COOK: Better bring a bit back for her. Scare them if they sees three of us coming. *(Exeunt both.)*

(KATTRIN climbs out of the cart with a bundle. She looks around to see if the other two have gone. Then she takes an old pair of trousers of the COOK's and a skirt of her mother's, and lays them side by side on one of the wheels, so that they are easily seen. She has finished and is picking up her bundle to go, when MOTHER COURAGE comes back from the house.)

MOTHER COURAGE: *(With a plate of soup.)* Kattrin! Will you stop there? Kattrin! Where you off to with that bundle? Has devil himself taken you over? *(She examines the bundle.)*
175 She's packed her things. You been listening? I told him nowt doing, Utrecht, his rotten inn, what'd we be up to there? You and me, inn's no place for us. Still plenty to be got out of war. *(She sees the trousers and the skirt.)* You're plain stupid. S'pose I'd seen that, and you gone away? *(She holds KATTRIN*
180 *back as she tries to break away.)* Don't you start thinking it's on your account I given him the push. It was cart, that's it. Catch me leaving my cart I'm used to, it ain't you, it's for cart. We'll go off in t'other direction, and we'll throw cook's stuff out so he finds it, silly man. *(She climbs in and throws*
185 *out a few other articles in the direction of the trousers.)* There, he's out of our business now, and I ain't having nobody else in, ever. You and me'll carry on now. This winter will pass, same as all the others. Get hitched up, it looks like snow.

(They both harness themselves to the cart, then wheel it round and drag it off. When the COOK arrives he looks blankly at his kit.)

— SCENE TEN —

During the whole of 1635 Mother Courage and her daughter Kattrin travel over the highroads of central Germany, in the wake of the increasingly bedraggled armies

High road.

MOTHER COURAGE and KATTRIN are pulling the cart. They pass a PEASANT's house inside which there is a voice singing.

THE VOICE:

The roses in our arbour
Delight us with their show:
They have such lovely flowers
Repaying all our labour
After the summer showers.   5
Happy are those with gardens now:
They have such lovely flowers.

When winter winds are freezing
As through the woods they blow
Our home is warm and pleasing.   10
We fixed the thatch above it
With straw and moss we wove it.
Happy are those with shelter now
When winter winds are freezing.

(MOTHER COURAGE and KATTRIN pause to listen, then continue pulling.)

— SCENE ELEVEN —

January 1636. The emperor's troops are threatening the Protestant town of Halle. The stone begins to speak. Mother Courage loses her daughter and trudges on alone. The war is a long way from being over

The cart is standing, much the worse for wear, alongside a PEAS-ANT's house with a huge thatched roof, backing on a wall of rock. It is night.

An ENSIGN and THREE SOLDIERS in heavy armour step out of the wood.

THE ENSIGN: I want no noise now. Anyone shouts, shove your pike into him.

FIRST SOLDIER: Have to knock them up, though, if we're to find a guide.

THE ENSIGN: Knocking sounds natural. Could be a cow   5
bumping the stable wall.

(The SOLDIERS knock on the door of the house. The PEASANT's WIFE opens it. They stop her mouth. TWO SOLDIERS go in.)

MAN'S VOICE: *(Within.)* What is it?

(The SOLDIERS bring out the PEASANT and his SON.)

THE ENSIGN: *(Pointing at the cart, where KATTRIN's head has appeared.)* There's another one. *(A SOLDIER drags her out.)* Anyone else live here beside you lot?   10

THE PEASANTS: This is our son. And she's dumb. Her mother's gone into town to buy stuff. For their business, cause so many people's getting out and selling things cheap. They're just passing through. Canteen folk.

THE ENSIGN: I'm warning you, keep quiet, or if there's the   15
least noise you get a pike across your nut. Now I want someone to come with us and show us the path to the town. *(Points to the YOUNG PEASANT.)* Here, you.

THE YOUNG PEASANT: I don't know no path.

SECOND SOLDIER: *(Grinning.)* He don't know no path.   20

THE YOUNG PEASANT: I ain't helping Catholics.

THE ENSIGN: *(To the SECOND SOLDIER.)* Stick your pike in his ribs.

THE YOUNG PEASANT: *(Forced to his knees, with the pike threatening him.)* I won't do it, not to save my life.   25

FIRST SOLDIER: I know what'll change his mind. (*Goes towards the stable.*) Two cows and an ox. Listen, you: if you're not reasonable I'll chop up your cattle.

THE YOUNG PEASANT: No, not that!

30 THE PEASANT'S WIFE: (*Weeps.*) Please spare our cattle, captain, it'd be starving us to death.

THE ENSIGN: They're dead if he goes on being obstinate.

FIRST SOLDIER: I'm taking the ox first.

THE YOUNG PEASANT: (*To his father.*) Have I got to? (*The* WIFE

35 *nods.*) Right.

THE PEASANT'S WIFE: And thank you kindly, captain, for sparing us, for ever and ever, Amen.

(*The* PEASANT *stops his wife from further expressions of gratitude.*)

FIRST SOLDIER: I knew the ox was what they minded about most, was I right?

(*Guided by the* YOUNG PEASANT, *the* ENSIGN *and his men continue on their way.*)

40 THE PEASANT: What are they up to, I'd like to know. Nowt good.

THE PEASANT'S WIFE: Perhaps they're just scouting. What you doing?

THE PEASANT: (*Putting a ladder against the roof and climbing*

45 *up it.*) Seeing if they're on their own. (*From the top.*) Something moving in the wood. Can see something down by the quarry. And there are men in armour in the clearing. And a gun. That's at least a regiment. God's mercy on the town and everyone in it!

50 THE PEASANT'S WIFE: Any lights in the town?

THE PEASANT: No. They'll all be asleep. (*Climbs down.*) If those people get in they'll butcher the lot.

THE PEASANT'S WIFE: Sentries're bound to spot them first.

THE PEASANT: Sentry in the tower up the hill must have been

55 killed, or he'd have blown his bugle.

THE PEASANT'S WIFE: If only there were more of us.

THE PEASANT: Just you and me and that cripple.

THE PEASANT'S WIFE: Nowt we can do, you'd say. . . .

THE PEASANT: Nowt.

60 THE PEASANT'S WIFE: Can't possibly run down there in the blackness.

THE PEASANT: Whole hillside's crawling with 'em. We could give a signal.

THE PEASANT'S WIFE: What, and have them butcher us too?

65 THE PEASANT: You're right, nowt we can do.

THE PEASANT'S WIFE: (*To* KATTRIN.) Pray, poor creature, pray! Nowt we can do to stop bloodshed. You can't talk, maybe, but at least you can pray. He'll hear you if no one else can. I'll help you. (*All kneel,* KATTRIN *behind the two* PEASANTS.)

70 Our Father, which art in Heaven, hear Thou our prayer, let not the town be destroyed with all what's in it sound asleep and suspecting nowt. Arouse Thou them that they may get up and go to the walls and see how the enemy approacheth with picks and guns in the blackness across fields below the

75 slope. (*Turning to* KATTRIN.) Guard Thou our mother and ensure that the watchman sleepeth not but wakes up, or it will be too late. Succour our brother-in-law also, he is inside there with his four children, spare Thou them, they are innocent and know nowt. (*To* KATTRIN, *who gives a groan.*)

80 One of them's not two yet, the eldest's seven. (KATTRIN *stands up distractedly.*) Our Father, hear us, for only Thou canst help; we look to be doomed, for why, we are weak and have no pike and nowt and can risk nowt and are in Thy hand along with our cattle and all the farm, and same with the town, it too is in Thy hand and the enemy is before the 85 walls in great strength.

(*Unobserved,* KATTRIN *has slipped away to the cart and taken from it something which she hides beneath her apron; then she climbs up the ladder on to the stable roof.*)

THE PEASANT'S WIFE: Forget not the children, what are in danger, the littlest ones especially, the old folk what can't move, and every living creature.

THE PEASANT: And forgive us our trespasses as we forgive them 90 that trespass against us. Amen.

(*Sitting on the roof,* KATTRIN *begins to beat the drum which she has pulled out from under her apron.*)

THE PEASANT'S WIFE: Jesus Christ, what's she doing?

THE PEASANT: She's out of her mind.

THE PEASANT'S WIFE: Quick, get her down.

(*The* PEASANT *hurries to the ladder, but* KATTRIN *pulls it up on to the roof.*)

THE PEASANT'S WIFE: She'll do us in. 95

THE PEASANT: Stop drumming at once, you cripple!

THE PEASANT'S WIFE: Bringing the Catholics down on us!

THE PEASANT: (*Looking for stones to throw.*) I'll stone you.

THE PEASANT'S WIFE: Where's your feelings? Where's your heart? We're done for if they come down on us. Slit our 100 throats, they will.

(KATTRIN *stares into the distance towards the town and carries on drumming.*)

THE PEASANT'S WIFE: (*To her husband.*) I told you we shouldn't have allowed those vagabonds on to farm. What do they care if our last cows are taken?

THE ENSIGN: (*Runs in with his* SOLDIERS *and the* YOUNG 105 PEASANT.) I'll cut you to ribbons, all of you!

THE PEASANT'S WIFE: Please, sir, it's not our fault, we couldn't help it. It was her sneaked up there. A foreigner.

THE ENSIGN: Where's the ladder?

THE PEASANT: There. 110

THE ENSIGN: (*Calls up.*) I order you, throw that drum down.

(KATTRIN *goes on drumming.*)

THE ENSIGN: You're all in this together. It'll be the end of you.

THE PEASANT: They been cutting pine trees in that wood. How about if we got one of the trunks and poked her off. . . .

FIRST SOLDIER: (*To the* ENSIGN.) Permission to make a sugges- 115 tion, sir! (*He whispers something in the* ENSIGN's *ear.*) Listen, we got a suggestion could help you. Get down off there and come into town with us right away. Show us which your mother is and we'll see she ain't harmed.

(KATTRIN *goes on drumming.*)

THE ENSIGN: (*Pushes him roughly aside.*) She doesn't trust 120 you; with a mug like yours it's not surprising. (*Calls up.*) Suppose I gave you my word? I can give my word of honour as an officer.

(KATTRIN *drums harder.*)

THE ENSIGN: Is nothing sacred to her?

125 THE YOUNG PEASANT: There's more than her mother involved, sir.

FIRST SOLDIER: This can't go on much longer. They're bound to hear in the town.

130 THE ENSIGN: We'll have somehow to make a noise that's louder than her drumming. What can we make a noise with?

FIRST SOLDIER: Thought we weren't s'posed to make no noise.

THE ENSIGN: A harmless one, you fool. A peaceful one.

THE PEASANT: I could chop wood with my axe.

THE ENSIGN: Good: you chop. (*The* PEASANT *fetches his axe*
135 *and attacks a tree-trunk.*) Chop harder! Harder! You're chopping for your life.

(KATTRIN *has been listening, drumming less loudly the while. She now looks wildly round, and goes on drumming.*)

THE ENSIGN: Not loud enough. (*To the* FIRST SOLDIER.) You chop too.

THE PEASANT: Only got the one axe. (*Stops chopping.*)

140 THE ENSIGN: We'll have to set the farm on fire. Smoke her out, that's it.

THE PEASANT: It wouldn't help, captain. If the townspeople see a fire here they'll know what's up.

(KATTRIN *has again been listening as she drums. At this point she laughs.*)

THE ENSIGN: Look at her laughing at us. I'm not having that.
145 I'll shoot her down, and damn the consequences. Fetch the harquebus.

(THREE SOLDIERS *hurry off.* KATTRIN *goes on drumming.*)

THE PEASANT'S WIFE: I got it, captain. That's their cart. If we smash it up she'll stop. Cart's all they got.

THE ENSIGN: (*To the* YOUNG PEASANT.) Smash it up. (*Calls*
150 *up.*) We're going to smash up your cart if you don't stop drumming. (*The* YOUNG PEASANT *gives the cart a few feeble blows.*)

THE PEASANT'S WIFE: Stop it, you animal!

(*Desperately looking towards the cart,* KATTRIN *emits pitiful noises. But she goes on drumming.*)

THE ENSIGN: Where are those clodhoppers with the harquebus?
155 FIRST SOLDIER: Can't have heard nowt in town yet, else we'd be hearing their guns.

THE ENSIGN: (*Calls up.*) They can't hear you at all. And now we're going to shoot you down. For the last time: throw down that drum!

160 THE YOUNG PEASANT: (*Suddenly flings away his plank.*) Go on drumming! Or they'll all be killed! Go on, go on. . . .

(*The* SOLDIER *knocks him down and beats him with his pike.* KATTRIN *starts to cry, but she goes on drumming.*)

THE PEASANT'S WIFE: Don't strike his back! For God's sake, you're beating him to death!

(*The* SOLDIERS *hurry in with the arquebus.*)

SECOND SOLDIER: Colonel's frothing at the mouth, sir. We're
165 all for court-martial.

THE ENSIGN: Set it up! Set it up! (*Calls up while the gun is being erected.*) For the very last time: stop drumming! (KATTRIN, *in tears, drums as loud as she can.*) Fire! (*The* SOLDIERS *fire.* KATTRIN *is hit, gives a few more drumbeats and then slowly crumples.*)
170
THE ENSIGN: That's the end of that.

(*But* KATTRIN's *last drumbeats are taken up by the town's cannon. In the distance can be heard a confused noise of tocsins and gunfire.*)

FIRST SOLDIER: She's made it.

— SCENE TWELVE —

Before first light. Sound of the fifes and drums of troops marching off into the distance

In front of the cart MOTHER COURAGE *is squatting by her daughter. The peasant family are standing near her.*

THE PEASANTS: (*With hostility.*) You must go, missis. There's only one more regiment behind that one. You can't go on your own.

MOTHER COURAGE: I think she's going to sleep. (*She sings.*)

> Lullaby baby 5
> What's that in the hay?
> Neighbours' kids grizzle
> But my kids are gay.
> Neighbours' are in tatters
> And you're dressed in lawn 10
> Cut down from the raiment an
> Angel has worn.
> Neighbours' kids go hungry
> And you shall eat cake
> Suppose it's too crumbly 15
> You've only to speak.
> Lullaby baby
> What's that in the hay?
> The one lies in Poland
> The other—who can say? 20

Better if you'd not told her nowt about your brother-in-law's kids.

THE PEASANT: If you'd not gone into town to get your cut it might never of happened.

MOTHER COURAGE: Now she's asleep. 25

THE PEASANT'S WIFE: She ain't asleep. Can't you see she's passed over?

THE PEASANT: And it's high time you got away yourself. There are wolves around and, what's worse, marauders.

MOTHER COURAGE: Aye. 30

(*She goes and gets a tarpaulin to cover the dead girl with.*)

THE PEASANT'S WIFE: Ain't you got nobody else? What you could go to?

MOTHER COURAGE: Aye, one left. Eilif.

THE PEASANT: (*As* MOTHER COURAGE *covers the dead girl.*) Best look for him, then. We'll mind her, see she gets proper 35 burial. Don't you worry about that.

MOTHER COURAGE: Here's money for expenses.

(She counts out coins into the PEASANT's *hands. The* PEASANT *and his son shake hands with her and carry* KATTRIN *away.)*

THE PEASANT'S WIFE: *(As she leaves.)* I'd hurry.

MOTHER COURAGE: *(Harnessing herself to the cart.)* Hope I
40 can pull cart all right by meself. Be all right, nowt much inside it. Got to get back in business again.

(Another regiment with its fifes and drums marches past in the background.)

MOTHER COURAGE: *(Tugging the cart.)* Take me along!

(Singing is heard from offstage.)

    With all its luck and all its danger
    The war is dragging on a bit   45
    Another hundred years or longer
    The common man won't benefit.
    Filthy his food, no soap to shave him
    The regiment steals half his pay.
    But still a miracle may save him: 50
    Tomorrow is another day!
        The new year's come. The watchmen shout.
        The thaw sets in. The dead remain.
        Wherever life has not died out
        It staggers to its feet again.   55

CRITICAL CONTEXTS

An influential novelist, playwright, and literary theorist, Zola became the spokesman for naturalism in the theater in a series of articles he wrote in the 1870s, collected as Naturalism in the Theatre *in 1878. In these essays, Zola urged the theater to adopt an attitude of scientific objectivity, an attitude reflected in the development of a new dramatic style. The naturalistic theater asserted such objectivity through its choice of subject matter (middle-class life), its treatment of characters (driven by "physiological" motives, not by "metaphysical" passions), its use of a prosaic, antiliterary language, and by the importance attached to the material environment.*

It seems impossible that the movement of inquiry and analysis, which is precisely the movement of the nineteenth century, can have revolutionized all the sciences and arts and left dramatic art to one side, as if isolated. The natural sciences date from the end of the last century; chemistry and physics are less than a hundred years old; history and criticism have been renovated, virtually re-created since the Revolution; an entire world has arisen; it has sent us back to the study of documents, to experience, made us realize that to start afresh we must first take things back to the beginning, become familiar with man and nature, verify what is. Thenceforward, the great naturalistic school, which has spread secretly, irrevocably, often making its way in darkness but always advancing, can finally come out triumphantly into the light of day. To trace the history of this movement, with the misunderstandings that might have impeded it and the multiple causes that have thrust it forward or slowed it down, would be to trace the history of the century itself. An irresistible current carries our society towards the study of reality. In the novel Balzac has been the bold and mighty innovator who has replaced the observation of the scholar with the imagination of the poet. But in the theatre the evolution seems slower. No eminent writer has yet formulated the new idea with any clarity.

I certainly do not say that some excellent works have not been produced, with characters in them who are ingeniously examined and bold truths taken right on to the stage. Let me, for instance, cite certain plays by M. Dumas *fils*, whose talent I scarcely admire, and M. Émile Augier, the most humane and powerful of all. Still, they are midgets beside Balzac; they lack the genius to lay down the formula. It must be said that one can never tell quite when a movement is getting under way; generally its source is remote and lost in the earlier movement from which it emerged. In a manner of speaking, the naturalistic current has always existed. It brings with it nothing absolutely novel. But it has finally flowed into a period favourable to it; it is succeeding and expanding because the human mind has attained the necessary maturity. I do not, therefore, deny the past; I affirm the present. The strength of naturalism is precisely that it has deep roots in our national literature which contains plenty of wisdom. It comes from the very entrails of humanity; it is that much the stronger because it has taken longer to grow and is found in a greater number of our masterpieces.

Certain things have come to pass and I point them out. Can we believe that *L'Ami Fritz* would have been applauded at the Comédie-Française twenty years ago? Definitely not! This play, in which people eat all the time and the lover talks in such homely language, would have disgusted both the classicists and the romantics. To explain its success we must concede that as the years have gone by a secret fermentation has been at work. Lifelike paintings, which used to repel the public, today attract them. The majority has been won over and the stage is open to every experiment. This is the only conclusion to draw.

So that is where we stand. To explain my point better—I am not afraid of repeating myself—I will sum up what I have said. Looking closely at the history of our dramatic literature, one can detect several clearly separated periods. First, there was the infancy of the art, farces and the mystery plays of the Middle Ages, the reciting of simple dialogues which developed as part of a naïve convention, with primitive staging and sets. Gradually, the plays became more complex but in a crude fashion. When Corneille appeared he was acclaimed most of all for his status as an innovator, for refining the dramatic formula of the time, and for hallowing it by means of his genius. It would be very interesting to study the pertinent documents and discover how our classical formula came to be created. It corresponded to the social spirit of the period. Nothing is solid that is

ÉMILE ZOLA
(1840–1902)

FROM
NATURALISM IN
THE THEATRE
(1878)

TRANSLATED BY
ALBERT BERMEL

not built on necessity. Tragedy reigned for two centuries because it satisfied the exact requirements of those centuries. Geniuses of differing temperaments had buttressed it with their masterpieces. And it continued to impose itself long afterwards, even when second-rate talents were producing inferior work. It acquired a momentum. It persisted also as the literary expression of that society, and nothing would have overthrown it if the society had not itself disappeared. After the Revolution, after that profound disturbance that was meant to transform everything and give birth to a new world, tragedy struggled to stay alive for a few more years. Then the formula cracked and romanticism broke through. A new formula asserted itself. We must look back at the first half of the century to understand the meaning of this cry for liberty. The young society was in the tremor of its infancy. The excited, bewildered, violently unleashed people were still racked by a dangerous fever; and in the first flush of their new liberty they yearned for prodigious adventures and superhuman love affairs. They gaped at the stars; some committed suicide, a very curious reaction to the social enfranchisement which had just been declared at the cost of so much blood. Turning specifically to dramatic literature, I maintain that romanticism in the theatre was an uncomplicated revolt, the invasion by a victorious group who took over the stage violently with drums beating and flags flying. In these early moments the combatants dreamed of making their imprint with a new form; to one rhetoric they opposed another: the Middle Ages to Antiquity, the exalting of passion to the exalting of duty. And that was all, for only the scenic conventions were altered. The characters remained marionettes in new clothing. Only the exterior aspect and the language were modified. But for the period that was enough. Romanticism had taken possession of the theatre in the name of literary freedom and it carried out its revolutionary task with incomparable bravura. But who does not see today that its role could extend no farther than that? Does romanticism have anything whatever to say about our present society? Does it meet one of our requirements? Obviously not. It is as outmoded as a jargon we no longer follow. It confidently expected to replace classical literature which had lasted for two centuries because it was based on social conditions. But romanticism was based on nothing but the fantasy of a few poets or, if you will, on the passing malady of minds overwhelmed by historical events; it was bound to disappear with the malady. It provided the occasion for a magnificent flowering of lyricism; that will be its eternal glory. Today, however, with the evolution accomplished, it is plain that romanticism was no more than the necessary link between classicism and naturalism. The struggle is over; now we must found a secure state. Naturalism flows out of classical art, just as our present society has arisen from the wreckage of the old society. Naturalism alone corresponds to our social needs; it alone has deep roots in the spirit of our times; and it alone can provide a living, durable formula for our art, because this formula will express the nature of our contemporary intelligence. There may be fashions and passing fantasies that exist outside naturalism but they will not survive for long. I say again, naturalism is the expression of our century and it will not die until a new upheaval transforms our democratic world.

Only one thing is needed now: men of genius who can fix the naturalistic formula. Balzac has done it for the novel and the novel is established. When will our Corneilles, Molières and Racines appear to establish our new theatre? We must hope and wait.

◆ ◆ ◆

The period when romantic drama ruled now seems distant. In Paris five or six of its playhouses prospered. The demolition of the old theatres along the Boulevard du Temple was a catastrophe of the first order. The theatres became separated from one another, the public changed, different fashions arose. But the discredit into which the drama has fallen proceeds mostly from the exhaustion of the genre—ridiculous, boring plays have gradually taken over from the potent works of 1830.

To this enfeeblement we must add the absolute lack of new actors who understand and can interpret these kinds of plays, for every dramatic formula that vanishes carries away its interpreters with it. Today the drama, hunted from stage to stage, has only two houses that really belong to it, the Ambigu and the Théâtre-Historique. Even at the Saint-Martin the drama is lucky to win a brief showing for itself, between one great spectacle and the next.

An occasional success may renew its courage. But its decline is inevitable; romantic drama is sliding into oblivion, and if it seems sometimes to check its descent, it does so only to roll even lower afterwards. Naturally, there are loud complaints. The tail-end romanticists are desperately unhappy. They swear that except in the drama—meaning their kind of drama—there is no salvation for dramatic literature. I believe, on the contrary, that we must find a new formula that will transform the drama, just as the writers in the first half of the century transformed tragedy. That is the essence of the matter. Today the battle is between romantic drama and naturalistic drama. By romantic drama I mean every play that mocks truthfulness in its incidents and characterization, that struts about in its puppet-box, stuffed to the belly with noises that flounder, for some idealistic reason or other, in pastiches of Shakespeare and Hugo. Every period has its formula; ours is certainly not that of 1830. We are an age of method, of experimental science; our primary need is for precise analysis. We hardly understand the liberty we have won if we use it only to imprison ourselves in a new tradition. The way is open: we can now return to man and nature.

Finally, there have been great efforts to revive the historical drama. Nothing could be better. A critic cannot roundly condemn the choice of historical subjects, even if his own preferences are entirely for subjects that are modern. It is simply that I am full of distrust. The manager one gives this sort of play to frightens me in advance. It is a question of how history is treated, what unusual characters are presented bearing the names of kings, great captains or great artists, and what awful sauce they are served up in to make the history palatable. As soon as the authors of these concoctions move into the past they think everything is permitted: improbabilities, cardboard dolls, monumental idiocies, the hysterical scribblings that falsely represent local colour. And what strange dialogue—François I talking like a haberdasher straight out of the Rue Saint-Denis, Richelieu using the words of a criminal from the Boulevard du Crime, Charlotte Corday with the weeping sentimentalities of a factory girl.

What astounds me is that our playwrights do not seem to suspect for a moment that the historical genre is unavoidably the least rewarding, the one that calls most strongly for research, integrity, a consummate gift of intuition, a talent for reconstruction. I am all for historical drama when it is in the hands of poets of genius or men of exceptional knowledge who are capable of making the public see an epoch come alive with its special quality, its manners, its civilization. In that case we have a work of prophecy or of profoundly interesting criticism.

But unfortunately I know what it is these partisans of historical drama want to revive: the swaggering and swordplay, the big spectacle with big words, the play of lies that shows off in front of the crowd, the gross exhibition that saddens honest minds. Hence my distrust. I think that all this antiquated business is better left in our museum of dramatic history under a pious layer of dust.

There are, undeniably, great obstacles to original experiments: we run up against the hypocrisies of criticism and the long education in idiocies that has been foisted on the public. This public, which titters at every childishness in melodramas, nevertheless lets itself be carried away by outbursts of fine sentiment. But the public is changing. Shakespeare's public and Molière's are no longer ours. We must reckon with shifts in outlook, with the need for reality which is everywhere getting more insistent. The last few romantics vainly repeat that the public wants this and the public wants that; the day is coming when the public will want the truth.

◆　◆　◆

The old formulas, classical and romantic, were based on the rearrangement and systematic amputation of the truth. They determined on principle that the truth is not good enough; they tried to draw out of it an essence, a 'poetry', on the pretext that nature must be expurgated and magnified. Up to the present the different literary schools disputed only over the question of the best way to disguise the truth so that it might not look too brazen to the public. The classicists adopted the toga; the romantics fought a revolution to impose the coat of mail and the doublet. Essentially the change of dress made little difference; the counterfeiting of nature went on. But today the naturalistic thinkers are telling us that the truth does not need clothing; it can walk naked. That, I repeat, is the quarrel.

Writers with any sense understand perfectly that tragedy and romantic drama are dead. The majority, though, are badly troubled when they turn their minds to the as-yet-unclear formula of tomorrow. Does the truth seriously ask them to give up the grandeur, the poetry, the traditional epic effects that their ambition tells them to put into their plays? Does naturalism demand that they shrink their horizons and risk not one flight into fantasy?

I will try to reply. But first we must determine the methods used by the idealists to lift their works into poetry. They begin by placing their chosen subject in a distant time. That provides them with costumes and makes the framework of the story vague enough to give them full scope for lying. Next, they generalize instead of particularizing; their characters are no longer living people but sentiments, arguments, passions that have been induced by reasoning. This false framework calls for heroes of marble or cardboard. A man of flesh and bone with his own originality would jar in such a legendary setting. Moreover, when we see the characters in romantic drama or tragedy walking about they are stiffened into an attitude, one representing duty, another patriotism, a third superstition, a fourth maternal love; thus, all the abstract ideas file by. Never the thorough analysis of an organism, never a character whose muscles and brain function as in nature.

These, then, are the mannerisms that writers with epic inclinations do not want to give up. For them poetry resides in the past and in abstraction, in the idealizing of facts and characters. As soon as one confronts them with daily life, with the people who fill our streets, they blink, they stammer, they are afraid; they no longer see clearly; they find everything ugly and not good enough for art. According to them, a subject must enter the lies of legend, men must harden and turn to stone like statues before the artist can accept them and make them fit the disguises he has prepared.

Now, it is at this point that the naturalistic movement comes along and says squarely that poetry is everywhere, in everything, even more in the present and the real than in the past and the abstract. Each event at each moment has its poetic, superb aspect. We brush up against heroes who are great and powerful in different respects from the puppets of the epic-makers. Not one playwright in this century has brought to life figures as lofty as Baron Hulot, Old Grandet, César Birotteau, and all the other characters of Balzac, who are so individual and so alive. Beside these real, giant creations Greek and Roman heroes quake; the heroes of the Middle Ages fall flat on their faces like lead soldiers.

With the superior works being produced in these times by the naturalistic school—works of high endeavour, pulsing with life—it is ridiculous and false to park our poetry in some antiquated temple and bury it in cobwebs. Poetry flows at its full force through everything that exists; the truer to life, the greater it becomes. And I mean to give the word poetry its widest definition, not to pin it down exclusively to the cadence of two rhymes, nor to burn it in a narrow coterie of dreamers, but to restore its real human significance which concerns the expansion and encouragement of every kind of truth.

Take our present environment, then, and try to make men live in it: you will write great works. It will undoubtedly call for some effort; it means sifting out of the confusion of life the simple formula of naturalism. Therein lies the difficulty: to do great things with the subjects and characters that our eyes, accustomed to the spectacle of the daily round, have come to see as small. I am aware that it is more convenient to present a marionette to the public and name it Charlemagne and puff it up with such tirades that the public believes it is watching a colossus; it is more convenient than taking a bourgeois of our time, a grotesque, unsightly man, and drawing sublime poetry out of him, making him, for example, Père Goriot, the father who gives his guts for his daughters, a figure so gigantic with truth and love that no other literature can offer his equal.

Nothing is as easy as persuading the managers with known formulas; and heroes in the classical or romantic taste cost so little labour that they are manufactured by the dozen, and have become standardized articles that clutter up our literature. But it takes hard work to create a real hero, intelligently analysed, alive and performing. That is probably why naturalism terrifies those authors who are used to fishing up great men from the troubled waters of history. They would have to burrow too deeply into humanity, learn about life, go straight for the greatness of reality and make it function with all their power. And let nobody gainsay this true poetry of humanity; it has been sifted out in the novel and can be in the theatre; only the method of adaptation remains to be found.

I am troubled by a comparison; it has been haunting me and I will now free myself of it. For two long months a play called *Les Danicheff* has been running at the Odéon. It takes place in Russia. It has been very successful here, but is apparently so dishonest, so packed with gross improbabilities, that the author, a Russian, has not even dared to show it in his country. What can you think of this work which is applauded in Paris and would be booed in St Petersburg? Well, imagine for a moment that the Romans could come back to life and see a performance of *Rome vaincue*. Can you hear their roars of laughter? Do you think the play would complete one performance? It would strike them as a parody; it would sink under the weight of mockery. And is there one historical play that could be performed before the society it claims to portray? A strange theatre, this, which is plausible only among foreigners, is based on the disappearance of the generations it deals with, and is made up of so much misinformation that it is good only for the ignorant!

The future is with naturalism. The formula will be found; it will be proved that there is more poetry in the little apartment of a bourgeois than in all the empty, worm-eaten palaces of history; in the end we will see that everything meets in the real: lovely fantasies that are free of capriciousness and whimsy, and idylls, and comedies, and dramas. Once the soil has been turned over, the task that seems alarming and unfeasible today will become easy.

I am not qualified to pronounce on the form that tomorrow's drama will take; that must be left to the voice of some genius to come. But I will allow myself to indicate the path I consider our theatre will follow.

First, the romantic drama must be abandoned. It would be disastrous for us to take over its outrageous acting, its rhetoric, its inherent thesis of action at the expense of character analysis. The finest models of the genre are, as has been said, mere operas with big effects. I believe, then, that we must go back to tragedy—not, heaven forbid, to borrow more of its rhetoric, its system of confidants, its declaiming, its endless speeches, but to return to its simplicity of action and its unique psychological and physiological study of the characters. Thus understood, the tragic framework is excellent; one deed unwinds in all its reality, and moves the characters to passions and feelings, the exact analysis of which constitutes the sole interest of the play—and in a contemporary environment, with the people who surround us.

My constant concern, my anxious vigil, has made me wonder which of us will have the strength to raise himself to the pitch of genius. If the naturalistic drama must come into being, only a genius can give birth to it. Corneille and Racine made tragedy. Victor Hugo made romantic drama. Where is the as-yet-unknown author who must make the naturalistic drama? In recent years experiments have not been wanting. But either because the public was not ready or because none of the beginners had the necessary staying-power, not one of these attempts has had decisive results.

In battles of this kind, small victories mean nothing; we need triumphs that overwhelm the adversary and win the public to the cause. Audiences would give way before the onslaught of a really strong man. This man would come with the expected word, the solution to the problem, the formula for a real life on stage, combining it with the illusions necessary in the theatre. He would have what the newcomers have as yet lacked: the cleverness or the might to impose himself and to remain so close to truth that his cleverness could not lead him into lies.

And what an immense place this innovator would occupy in our dramatic literature! He would be at the peak. He would build his monument in the middle of the desert of mediocrity that we are crossing, among the jerry-built houses strewn about our most illustrious stages. He would put everything in question and remake everything, scour the boards, create a world whose elements he would lift from life, from outside our traditions. Surely there is no more ambitious dream that a writer of our time could fulfil. The domain of the novel is crowded; the domain of the theatre is free. At this time in France an imperishable glory awaits the man of genius who takes up the work of Molière and finds in the reality of living comedy the full, true drama of modern society.

◆ ◆ ◆

. . . In effect, the great naturalistic evolution, which comes down directly from the fifteenth century to ours has everything to do with the gradual substitution of physiological man for metaphysical man. In tragedy metaphysical man, man according to dogma and logic, reigned absolutely. The body did not count; the soul was regarded as the only interesting piece of human machinery; drama took place in the air, in pure mind. Consequently, what use was the tangible world? Why worry about the place where the action was located? Why be surprised at a baroque costume or false declaiming? Why notice that Queen Dido was a boy whose budding beard forced him to wear a mask? None of that mattered; these trifles were not worth stooping to; the play was heard out as if it were a school essay or a law case; it was on a higher plane than man, in the world of ideas, so far away from real man that any intrusion of reality would have spoiled the show.

Such is the point of departure—in Mystery plays, the religious point; the philosophical point in tragedy. And from that beginning natural man, stifling under the rhetoric and dogma, struggled secretly, tried to break free, made lengthy, futile efforts, and in the end asserted himself, limb by limb. The whole history of our theatre is in this conquest by the physiological man, who emerged more clearly in each period from behind the dummy of religious and philosophical idealism. Corneille, Molière, Racine, Voltaire, Beaumarchais and, in our day, Victor Hugo, Émile Augier, Alexandre Dumas *fils*, even Sardou, have had only one task, even when they were not completely aware of it:

PHYSIOLOGICAL MAN

to increase the reality of our corpus of drama, to progress towards truth, to sift out more and more of the natural man and impose him on the public. And inevitably, the evolution will not end with them. It continues; it will continue forever. Mankind is very young. . . .

COSTUME, STAGE DESIGN, SPEECH

Modern clothes make a poor spectacle. If we depart from bourgeois tragedy, shut in between its four walls, and wish to use the breadth of larger stages for crowd scenes we are embarrassed and constrained by the monotony and the uniformly funereal look of the extras. In this case, I think, we should take advantage of the variety of garb offered by the different classes and occupations. To elaborate: I can imagine an author setting one act in the main marketplace of les Halles in Paris. The setting would be superb, with its bustling life and bold possibilities. In this immense setting we could have a very picturesque ensemble by displaying the porters wearing their large hats, the saleswomen with their white aprons and vividly-coloured scarves, the customers dressed in silk or wool or cotton prints, from the ladies accompanied by their maids to the female beggars on the prowl for anything they can pick up off the street. For inspiration it would be enough to go to les Halles and look about. Nothing is gaudier or more interesting. All of Paris would enjoy seeing this set if it were realized with the necessary accuracy and amplitude.

And how many other settings for popular drama there are for the taking! Inside a factory, the interior of a mine, the gingerbread market, a railway station, flower stalls, a racetrack, and so on. All the activities of modern life can take place in them. It will be said that such sets have already been tried. Unquestionably we have seen factories and railway stations in fantasy plays; but these were fantasy stations and factories. I mean, these sets were thrown together to create an illusion that was at best incomplete. What we need is detailed reproduction: costumes supplied by tradespeople, not sumptuous but adequate for the purposes of truth and for the interest of the scenes. Since everybody mourns the death of the drama our playwrights certainly ought to make a try at this type of popular, contemporary drama. At one stroke they could satisfy the public hunger for spectacle and the need for exact studies which grows more pressing every day. Let us hope, though, that the playwrights will show us real people and not those whining members of the working class who play such strange roles in boulevard melodrama.

As M. Adolphe Jullien has said—and I will never be tired of repeating it—everything is interdependent in the theatre. Lifelike costumes look wrong if the sets, the diction, the plays themselves are not lifelike. They must all march in step along the naturalistic road. When costume becomes more accurate, so do sets; actors free themselves from bombastic declaiming; plays study reality more closely and their characters are more true to life. I could make the same observations about sets I have just made about costume. With them too, we may seem to have reached the highest possible degree of truth, but we still have long strides to take. Most of all we would need to intensify the illusion in reconstructing the environments, less for their picturesque quality than for dramatic utility. The environment must determine the character. When a set is planned so as to give the lively impression of a description by Balzac; when, as the curtain rises, one catches the first glimpse of the characters, their personalities and behaviour, if only to see the actual locale in which they move, the importance of exact reproduction in the decor will be appreciated. Obviously, that is the way we are going. Environment, the study of which has transformed science and literature, will have to take a large role in the theatre. And here I may mention again the question of metaphysical man, the abstraction who had to be satisfied with his three walls in tragedy—whereas the physiological man in our modern works is asking more and more compellingly to be determined by his setting, by the environment that produced him. We see then that the road to progress is still long, for sets as well as costume. We are coming upon the truth but we can hardly stammer it out.

Another very serious matter is diction. True, we have got away from the chanting, the plainsong, of the seventeenth century. But we now have a 'theatre voice', a false recitation that is very obtrusive and very annoying. Everything that is wrong with it comes from the fixed traditional code set up by the majority of critics. They found the theatre in a certain state and, instead of looking to the future, and judging the progress we are making and the progress we shall make by the progress we have already made, they stubbornly defend the relics of the old conventions, swearing that these relics must be preserved. Ask them why, make them see how far we have travelled; they will give you no logical reason. They will reply with assertions based on a set of conditions that are disappearing.

In diction the errors come from what the critics call 'theatre language'. Their theory is that on stage you must not speak as you do in everyday life. To support this viewpoint they pick examples from traditional practices, from what was happening yesterday—and is happening still—without taking account of the naturalistic movement, the phases of which have been established for us by M. Jullien's book.[1] Let us realize that there is no such thing as 'theatre language'. There has been a rhetoric which grew more and more feeble and is now dying out. Those are the facts. If you compare the declaiming of actors under Louis XIV with that of Lekain, and if you compare Lekain's with that of our own artists today, you will clearly distinguish the phases, from tragic chanting down to our search for the natural, precise tone, the cry of truth. It follows that 'theatre language', that language of booming sonority, is vanishing. We are moving towards simplicity, the exact word spoken without emphasis, quite naturally. How many examples I could give if I had unlimited space! Consider the powerful effect that Geoffroy has on the public; all his talent comes from his natural personality. He holds the public because he speaks on stage as he does at home. When a sentence sounds outlandish he cannot pronounce it; the author has to find another one. That is the fundamental criticism of so-called 'theatre language'. Again, follow the diction of a talented actor and at the same time watch the public; the cheers go up, the house is in raptures when a truthful accent gives the words the exact value they must have. All the great successes of the stage are triumphs over convention.

Alas, yes, there is a 'theatre language'. It is the clichés, the resounding platitudes, the hollow words that roll about like empty barrels, all that intolerable rhetoric of our vaudevilles and dramas, which is beginning to make us smile. It would be very interesting to study the style of such talented authors as MM. Augier, Dumas and Sardou. I could find much to criticize, especially in the last two with their conventional language, a language of their own that they put into the mouths of all their characters, men, women, children, old folk, both sexes and all ages. This irritates me, for each character has his own language, and to create living people you must give them to the public not merely in accurate dress and in the environments that have made them what they are, but with their individual ways of thinking and expressing themselves. I repeat that that is the obvious aim of our theatre. There is no theatre language regulated by such a code as 'cadenced sentences' or sonority. There is simply a kind of dialogue that is growing more precise and is following—or rather, leading—sets and costumes towards naturalistic progress. When plays are more truthful, the actors' diction will gain enormously in simplicity and naturalness.

To conclude, I will repeat that the battle of the conventions is far from being finished, and that it will no doubt last forever. Today we are beginning to see clearly where we are going, but our steps are still impeded by the melting slush of rhetoric and metaphysics.

---

[1] Adolphe Jullien 1845–1932, writer on music and the theatre. The book Zola cites is *Histoire du costume au théâtre*, 1880.

BERTOLT BRECHT (1898–1956)

"THEATER FOR PLEASURE OR THEATER FOR INSTRUCTION" (1935–1936)

TRANSLATED BY JOHN WILLETT

In this essay, Brecht attacks the bourgeois notion that the theater can be divided into two kinds of art, as though drama were either instructive or entertaining. As he does in his plays, Brecht dialecticizes these categories, showing that they define one another and therefore exist within one another. Realistic plays, after all, not only entertain their audiences, but also offer an image of the world, a kind of instruction. On the other hand, intellectual or critical activity is not only pleasurable in itself, but it also can lead to a lively kind of theater as well, as Brecht's plays illustrate. This essay was unpublished in Brecht's lifetime: John Willett dates it from 1935 or 1936. He notes that Brecht uses the word Entfremdung here for "alienation," the same word used by Marx and Hegel. Brecht later coined his own word Verfremdungseffekt for "alienation effect."

A few years back, anybody talking about the modern theatre meant the theatre in Moscow, New York and Berlin. He might have thrown in a mention of one of Jouvet's productions in Paris or Cochran's in London, or *The Dybbuk* as given by the Habima (which is to all intents and purposes part of the Russian theatre, since Vakhtangov was its director). But broadly speaking there were only three capitals so far as modern theatre was concerned.

Russian, American and German theatres differed widely from one another, but were alike in being modern, that is to say in introducing technical and artistic innovations. In a sense they even achieved a certain stylistic resemblance, probably because technology is international (not just that part which is directly applied to the stage but also that which influences it, the film for instance), and because large progressive cities in large industrial countries are involved. Among the older capitalist countries it is the Berlin theatre that seemed of late to be in the lead. For a period all that is common to the modern theatre received its strongest and (so far) maturest expression there.

The Berlin theatre's last phase was the so-called epic theatre, and it showed the modern theatre's trend of development in its purest form. Whatever was labelled '*Zeitstück*' or '*Piscatorbühne*' or '*Lehrstück*' belongs to the epic theatre.

THE EPIC THEATRE

Many people imagine that the term 'epic theatre' is self-contradictory, as the epic and dramatic ways of narrating a story are held, following Aristotle, to be basically distinct. The difference between the two forms was never thought simply to lie in the fact that the one is performed by living beings while the other operates via the written word; epic works such as those of Homer and the medieval singers were at the same time theatrical performances, while dramas like Goethe's *Faust* and Byron's *Manfred* are agreed to have been more effective as books. Thus even by Aristotle's definition the difference between the dramatic and epic forms was attributed to their different methods of construction, whose laws were dealt with by two different branches of aesthetics. The method of construction depended on the different way of presenting the work to the public, sometimes via the stage, sometimes through a book; and independently of that there was the 'dramatic element' in epic works and the 'epic element' in dramatic. The bourgeois novel in the last century developed much that was 'dramatic,' by which was meant the strong centralization of the story, a momentum that drew the separate parts into a common relationship. A particular passion of utterance, a certain emphasis on the clash of forces are hallmarks of the 'dramatic'. The epic writer Döblin provided an excellent criterion when he said that with an epic work, as opposed to a dramatic, one can as it were take a pair of scissors and cut it into individual pieces, which remain fully capable of life.

This is no place to explain how the opposition of epic and dramatic lost its rigidity after having long been held to be irreconcilable. Let us just point out that the technical advances alone were enough to permit the stage to incorporate an element of narrative in its dramatic productions. The possibility of projections, the greater adaptability of the stage due to mechanization, the film, all completed the theatre's equipment, and did so at a point where the most important transactions between people could no longer be shown simply by personifying the motive forces or subjecting the characters to invisible metaphysical powers.

To make these transactions intelligible the environment in which the people lived had to be brought to bear in a big and 'significant' way.

This environment had of course been shown in the existing drama, but only as seen from the central figure's point of view, and not as an independent element. It was defined by the hero's reactions to it. It was seen as a storm can be seen when one sees the ships on a sheet of water unfolding their sails, and the sails filling out. In the epic theatre it was to appear standing on its own.

The stage began to tell a story. The narrator was no longer missing, along with the fourth wall. Not only did the background adopt an attitude to the events on the stage—by big screens recalling other simultaneous events elsewhere, by projecting documents which confirmed or contradicted what the characters said, by concrete and intelligible figures to accompany abstract conversations, by figures and sentences to support mimed transactions whose sense was unclear—but the actors too refrained from going over wholly into their role, remaining detached from the character they were playing and clearly inviting criticism of him.

The spectator was no longer in any way allowed to submit to an experience uncritically (and without practical consequences) by means of simple empathy with the characters in a play. The production took the subject-matter and the incidents shown and put them through a process of alienation: the alienation that is necessary to all understanding. When something seems 'the most obvious thing in the world' it means that any attempt to understand the world has been given up.

What is 'natural' must have the force of what is startling. This is the only way to expose the laws of cause and effect. People's activity must simultaneously be so and be capable of being different.

It was all a great change.

The dramatic theatre's spectator says: Yes, I have felt like that too—Just like me—It's only natural—It'll never change—The sufferings of this man appal me, because they are inescapable—

That's great art; it all seems the most obvious thing in the world—I weep when they weep, I laugh when they laugh.

The epic theatre's spectator says: I'd never have thought it—That's not the way—That's extraordinary, hardly believable—It's got to stop—The sufferings of this man appal me, because they are unnecessary—That's great art: nothing obvious in it—I laugh when they weep, I weep when they laugh.

The stage began to be instructive.

THE INSTRUCTIVE THEATRE

Oil, inflation, war, social struggles, the family, religion, wheat, the meat market, all became subjects for theatrical representation. Choruses enlightened the spectator about facts unknown to him. Films showed a montage of events from all over the world. Projections added statistical material. And as the 'background' came to the front of the stage so people's activity was subjected to criticism. Right and wrong courses of action were shown. People were shown who knew what they were doing, and others who did not. The theatre became an affair for philosophers, but only for such philosophers as wished not just to explain the world but also to change it. So we had philosophy, and we had instruction. And where was the amusement in all that? Were they sending us back to school, teaching us to read and write? Were we supposed to pass exams, work for diplomas?

Generally there is felt to be a very sharp distinction between learning and amusing oneself. The first may be useful, but only the second is pleasant. So we have to defend the epic theatre against the suspicion that it is a highly disagreeable, humourless, indeed strenuous affair.

Well: all that can be said is that the contrast between learning and amusing oneself is not laid down by divine rule; it is not one that has always been and must continue to be.

Undoubtedly there is much that is tedious about the kind of learning familiar to us from school, from our professional training, etc. But it must be remembered under what conditions and to what end that takes place.

It is really a commercial transaction. Knowledge is just a commodity. It is acquired in order to be resold. All those who have grown out of going to school have to do their learning virtually in secret, for anyone who admits that he still has something to learn devalues himself as a man whose knowledge is inadequate. Moreover the usefulness of learning is very much limited by factors outside the learner's control. There is unemployment, for instance, against which no knowledge can protect one. There is the division of labour, which makes generalized knowledge unnecessary and impossible. Learning is often among the concerns of those whom no amount of concern will get any forwarder. There is not much knowledge that leads to power, but plenty of knowledge to which only power can lead.

Learning has a very different function for different social strata. There are strata who cannot imagine any improvement in conditions: they find the conditions good enough for them. Whatever happens to oil they will benefit from it. And: they feel the years beginning to tell. There can't be all that many years more. What is the point of learning a lot now? They have said their final word: a grunt. But there are also strata 'waiting their turn' who are discontented with conditions, have a vast interest in the practical side of learning, want at all costs to find out where they stand, and know that they are lost without learning; these are the best and keenest learners. Similar differences apply to countries and peoples. Thus the pleasure of learning depends on all sorts of things; but none the less there is such a thing as pleasurable learning, cheerful and militant learning.

If there were not such amusement to be had from learning the theatre's whole structure would unfit it for teaching.

Theatre remains theatre even when it is instructive theatre, and in so far as it is good theatre it will amuse.

THEATRE AND KNOWLEDGE

But what has knowledge got to do with art? We know that knowledge can be amusing, but not everything that is amusing belongs in the theatre.

I have often been told, when pointing out the invaluable services that modern knowledge and science, if properly applied, can perform for art and specially for the theatre, that art and knowledge are two estimable but wholly distinct fields of human activity. This is a fearful truism, of course, and it is as well to agree quickly that, like most truisms, it is perfectly true. Art and science work in quite different ways: agreed. But, bad as it may sound, I have to admit that I cannot get along as an artist without the use of one or two sciences. This may well arouse serious doubts as to my artistic capacities. People are used to seeing poets as unique and slightly unnatural beings who reveal with a truly godlike assurance things that other people can only recognize after much sweat and toil. It is naturally distasteful to have to admit that one does not belong to this select band. All the same, it must be admitted. It must at the same time be made clear that the scientific occupations just confessed to are not pardonable side interests, pursued on days off after a good week's work. We all know how Goethe was interested in natural history, Schiller in history: as a kind of hobby, it is charitable to assume. I have no wish promptly to accuse these two of having needed these sciences for their poetic activity; I am not trying to shelter behind them; but I must say that I do need the sciences. I have to admit, however, that I look askance at all sorts of people who I know do not operate on the level of scientific understanding: that is to say, who sing as the birds sing, or as people imagine the birds to sing. I don't mean by that that I would reject a charming poem about the taste of fried fish or the delights of a boating party just because the writer had not studied gastronomy or navigation. But in my view the great and complicated things that go on in the world cannot be adequately recognized by people who do not use every possible aid to understanding.

Let us suppose that great passions or great events have to be shown which influence the fate of nations. The lust for power is nowadays held to be such a passion. Given that a poet 'feels' this lust and wants to have someone strive for power, how is he to show the exceedingly complicated machinery within which the struggle for power nowadays takes place? If his hero is a politician, how do politics work? If he is a business man, how does business work? And yet there are writers who find business and politics nothing like so passionately interesting as the individual's lust for power. How are they to acquire the necessary knowledge? They are scarcely likely to learn enough by going round and keeping their eyes open, though even then it is more than they would get by just rolling their eyes in an exalted frenzy. The foundation of a paper like the *Völkischer Beobachter* or a business like Standard Oil is a pretty complicated affair, and such things cannot be conveyed just like that. One important field for the playwright is psychology. It is taken for granted that a poet, if not an ordinary man, must be able without further instruction to discover the motives that lead a man to commit murder; he must be able to give a picture of a murderer's mental state 'from within himself.' It is taken for granted that one only has to look inside oneself in such a case; and then there's always one's imagination. . . . There are various reasons why I can no longer surrender to this agreeable hope of getting a result quite so simply. I can no longer find in myself all those motives which the press or scientific reports show to have been observed in people. Like the average judge when pronouncing sentence, I cannot without further ado conjure up an adequate picture of a murderer's mental state. Modern psychology, from psychoanalysis to behaviourism, acquaints me with facts that lead me to judge the case quite differently, especially if I bear in mind the findings of sociology and do not overlook economics and history. You will say: but that's getting complicated. I have to answer that it *is* complicated. Even if you let yourself be convinced, and agree with me that a large slice of literature is exceedingly primitive, you may still ask with profound concern: won't an evening in such a theatre be a most alarming affair? The answer to that is: no.

Whatever knowledge is embodied in a piece of poetic writing has to be wholly transmuted into poetry. Its utilization fulfils the very pleasure that the poetic element provokes. If it does not at the same time fulfil that which is fulfilled by the scientific element, none the less in an age of great discoveries and inventions one must have a certain inclination to penetrate deeper into things—a desire to make the world controllable—if one is to be sure of enjoying its poetry.

IS THE EPIC THEATRE SOME KIND OF 'MORAL INSTITUTION'?

According to Friedrich Schiller the theatre is supposed to be a moral institution. In making this demand it hardly occurred to Schiller that by moralizing from the stage he might drive the audience out of the theatre. Audiences had no objection to moralizing in his day. It was only later that Friedrich Nietzsche attacked him for blowing a moral trumpet. To Nietzsche any concern with morality was a depressing affair; to Schiller it seemed thoroughly enjoyable. He knew of nothing that could give greater amusement and satisfaction than the propagation of ideas. The bourgeoisie was setting about forming the ideas of the nation.

Putting one's house in order, patting oneself on the back, submitting one's account, is something highly agreeable. But describing the collapse of one's house, having pains in the back, paying one's account, is indeed a depressing affair, and that was how Friedrich Nietzsche saw things a century later. He was poorly disposed towards morality, and thus towards the previous Friedrich too.

The epic theatre was likewise often objected to as moralizing too much. Yet in the epic theatre moral arguments only took second place. Its aim was less to moralize than to observe. That is to say it observed, and then the thick end of the wedge followed: the story's moral. Of course we cannot pretend that we started our observations out of a pure passion for observing and without any more practical motive, only to be completely staggered by their results. Undoubtedly there were some painful discrepancies in our environment, circumstances that were barely tolerable, and this not merely on account of moral considerations. It is not only moral considerations that make hunger, cold and oppression hard to bear. Similarly the object of our inquiries was not just to arouse moral objections to such circumstances (even though they could easily be felt—though not by all the audience alike; such objections were seldom for instance felt by those who profited by the circumstances in question) but to discover means for their elimination. We were not in fact speaking in the name of morality but in that of the victims. These truly are two distinct matters, for the victims are often told that they ought to be contented with their lot, for moral reasons. Moralists of this sort see man as existing for morality, not morality for man. At least it should be possible to gather from the above to what degree and in what sense the epic theatre is a moral institution.

CAN EPIC THEATRE BE PLAYED ANYWHERE?

Stylistically speaking, there is nothing all that new about the epic theatre. Its expository character and its emphasis on virtuosity bring it close to the old Asiatic theatre. Didactic tendencies are to be found in the medieval mystery plays and the classical Spanish theatre, and also in the theatre of the Jesuits.

These theatrical forms corresponded to particular trends of their time, and vanished with them. Similarly the modern epic theatre is linked with certain trends. It cannot by any means be practised universally. Most of the great nations today are not disposed to use the theatre for ventilating their problems. London, Paris, Tokyo and Rome maintain their theatres for quite different purposes. Up to now favourable circumstances for an epic and didactic theatre have only been found in a few places and for a short period of time. In Berlin Fascism put a very definite stop to the development of such a theatre.

It demands not only a certain technological level but a powerful movement in society which is interested to see vital questions freely aired with a view to their solution, and can defend this interest against every contrary trend.

The epic theatre is the broadest and most far-reaching attempt at large-scale modern theatre, and it has all those immense difficulties to overcome that always confront the vital forces in the sphere of politics, philosophy, science and art.

Roland Barthes studied French literature at the University of Paris and taught French in Egypt and Romania before joining the Centre National de la Recherche Scientifique in Paris. Working in the fields of linguistics and sociology, Barthes was instrumental in articulating the relationship between the structure of language and the structures of other systems of signification. This "structuralist" approach to how meanings are produced was adapted to study in a variety of fields—anthropology, literary criticism, psychoanalysis—in the 1950s, 1960s, and 1970s. Throughout his brilliant and eclectic career, Barthes examined the nature of signification in literature, film, photography, and popular culture. His many books include Writing Degree Zero *(1953),* Mythologies *(1957),* Sade/Fourier/Loyola *(1971),* The Pleasure of the Text *(1973), and* Camera Lucida *(1980).*

In 1956, Barthes wrote a series of essays in response to the visit of the Berliner Ensemble to Paris. Here, he records the effect of the Berliner Ensemble's production, marking a fundamental shift in how we think about theater, society, and stage representation.

ROLAND BARTHES
(1915–1980)

"THE TASKS OF BRECHTIAN CRITICISM"
(1956)

TRANSLATED BY
RICHARD HOWARD

It is safe to predict that Brecht's work will become increasingly important for us; not only because it is great, but because it is exemplary as well; it shines, today at least, with an exceptional luster amid two deserts: the desert of our contemporary theater, where aside from his there are no great names to cite; and the desert of revolutionary art, sterile since the beginnings of the Zhdanovian impasse. Any reflection on theater and on revolution must come to terms with Brecht, who brought about this situation himself: the entire force of his work opposes the reactionary myth of unconscious genius; its greatness is the kind which best suits our period, the greatness of responsibility; it is a work which is in a state of "complicity" with the world, with our world: a knowledge of Brecht, a reflection on Brecht, in a word, Brechtian criticism is by definition extensive with the problematics of our time. We must tirelessly repeat this truth: knowing Brecht is of a different order of importance from knowing Shakespeare or Gogol; because it is for us, precisely, that Brecht has written his plays, and not for eternity. Brechtian criticism will therefore be written by the spectator, the reader, the consumer, and not the exegete: it is a criticism of a *concerned* man. And if I myself were to write the criticism whose context I am sketching here, I should not fail to suggest, at the risk of appearing indiscreet, how this work touches me and helps me, personally, as an individual. But to confine myself here to the essentials of a program of Brechtian criticism, I shall merely suggest the levels of analysis which such criticism should successively investigate.

(1) SOCIOLOGY

Generally speaking, we do not yet have adequate means of investigation to define the theater's public, or publics. Furthermore, in France at least, Brecht has not yet emerged from the experimental theaters (except for the TNP's *Mother Courage*, a production so misconceived that the case is anything but instructive). For the moment, therefore, we can study only the press reactions.

There are four types to distinguish. By the extreme right, Brecht's work is totally discredited because of its political commitment: Brecht's theater is mediocre *because* it is communist. By the right (a more complicated right, which can extend to the "modernist" bourgeoisie of *L'Express*), Brecht is subjected to the usual political denaturation: the man is dissociated from the work, the former consigned to politics (emphasizing successively and contradictorily his independence and his servility with regard to the Party), and the latter enlisted under the banners of an eternal theater: Brecht's work, we are told, is great in spite of Brecht, against Brecht.

On the left, there is first of all a humanist reading: Brecht is made into one of those giant creative figures committed to a humanitarian promotion of man, like Romain Rolland or Barbusse. This sympathetic view unfortunately disguises an anti-intellectualist prejudice frequent in certain far-left circles: in order to "humanize" Brecht, the theoretical part of his work is discredited or at least minimized: the plays are great *despite* Brecht's systematic views on epic theater, the actor, alienation, etc.: here we encounter one of the basic theorems of *petit-bourgeois* culture, the romantic contrast between heart and head, between intuition and reflection, between the ineffable and the rational—an opposition which ultimately masks a magical conception of art. Finally, the communists themselves express certain reservations (in France, at least) with regard to Brecht's opposition to the positive hero, his epic conception of theater, and the "formalist" orientation of his dramaturgy. Apart from the contestation of Roger Vailland, based on a defense of French tragedy as a dialectical art of crisis, these criticisms proceed from a Zhdanovian conception of art.

I am citing a dossier from memory; it should be examined in detail. The point, moreover, is not to refute Brecht's critics, but rather to approach Brecht by the means our society spontaneously employs to digest him. Brecht reveals whoever speaks about him, and this revelation naturally concerns Brecht to the highest degree.

(2) IDEOLOGY

Must we oppose the "digestions" of the Brechtian canon by a canonical truth of Brecht? In a sense and within certain limits, yes. There is a specific ideological content, coherent, consistent, and remarkably organized, in Brecht's theater, one which protests against abusive distortions. This content must be described.

In order to do this, we possess two kinds of texts: first of all, the theoretical texts, of an acute intelligence (it is no matter of indifference to encounter a man of the theater who is intelligent), of a great ideological lucidity, and which it would be childish to underrate on the pretext that they are only an intellectual appendage to an essentially *creative* body of work. Of course Brecht's theater is made to be performed. But before performing it or seeing it performed, there is no ban on its being understood: this intelligence is organically linked to its constitutive function, which is to transform a public even as it is being entertained. In a Marxist like Brecht, the relations between theory and practice must not be underestimated or distorted. To separate the Brechtian theater from its theoretical foundations would be as erroneous as to try to understand Marx's action without reading *The Communist Manifesto* or Lenin's politics without reading *The State and the Revolution*. There is no official decree or supernatural intervention which graciously dispenses the theater from the demands of theoretical reflection. Against an entire tendency of our criticism, we must assert the capital importance of Brecht's systematic writings: it does not weaken the creative value of this theater to regard it as a reasoned theater.

Moreover, the plays themselves afford the chief elements of Brechtian ideology. I can indicate here only the principal ones: the historical and not "natural" character of human misfortunes; the spiritual contagion of economic alienation, whose final effect is to blind the very men it oppresses as to the causes of their servitude; the correctible status of Nature, the tractability of the world; the necessary adequation of means and situations (for instance, in a bad society, the law can be re-established only by a reprobate judge); the transformation of ancient psychological "conflicts" into historical contradictions, subject as such to the corrective power of men.

We must note here that these truths are never set forth except as the consequence of concrete situations, and these situations are infinitely plastic. Contrary to the rightist prejudice, Brecht's theater is not a thesis theater, not a propaganda theater. What Brecht takes from Marxism are not slogans, an articulation of arguments, but a general method of explanation. It follows that in Brecht's theater the Marxist elements always seem to be recreated. Basically, Brecht's greatness, and his solitude, is that he keeps inventing Marxism. The ideological theme, in Brecht, could be precisely defined as a dynamic of events which combines observation and explanation, ethics and politics: according to the profoundest Marxist teaching, each theme is at once the expression of what men want to be and of what things are, at once a protest (because it unmasks) and a reconciliation (because it explains).

Semiology is the study of signs and significations. I do not want to engage here in a discussion of this science, which was postulated some forty years ago by the linguist Saussure and which is generally accused of formalism. Without letting ourselves be intimidated by the words, we might say that Brechtian dramaturgy, the theory of *Episierung*, of alienation, and the entire practice of the Berliner Ensemble with regard to sets and costumes, propose an explicit semiological problem. For what Brechtian dramaturgy postulates is that today at least, the responsibility of a dramatic art is not so much to express reality as to signify it. Hence there must be a certain distance between signified and signifier: revolutionary art must admit a certain arbitrary nature of signs, it must acknowledge a certain "formalism," in the sense that it must treat form according to an appropriate method, which is the semiological method. All Brechtian art protests against the Zhdanovian confusion between ideology and semiology, which has led to such an esthetic impasse. **(3) SEMIOLOGY**

We realize, moreover, why this aspect of Brechtian thought is most antipathetic to bourgeois and Zhdanovian criticism: both are attached to an esthetic of the "natural" expression of reality: art for them is a false Nature, a *pseudo-Physis*. For Brecht, on the contrary, art today—i.e., at the heart of a historical conflict whose stake in human disalienation—art today must be an *anti-Physis*. Brecht's formalism is a radical protest against the confusions of the bourgeois and *petit-bourgeois* false Nature: in a still-alienated society, art must be critical, it must cut off all illusions, even that of "Nature": the sign must be partially arbitrary, otherwise we fall back on an art of expression, an art of essentialist illusion.

Brechtian theater is a moral theater, that is, a theater which asks, with the spectator: what is to be done in such a situation? At this point we should classify and describe the archetypical situations of the Brechtian theater; they may be reduced, I think, to a single question: how to be good in a bad society? It seems to me very important to articulate the moral structure of Brecht's theater: granted that Marxism has had other more urgent tasks than to concern itself with problems of individual conduct; nonetheless capitalist society endures, and communism itself is being transformed: revolutionary action must increasingly cohabit, and in an almost institutional fashion, with the norms of bourgeois and *petit-bourgeois* morality: problems of conduct, and no longer of action, arise. Here is where Brecht can have a great cleansing power, a pedagogical power. **(4) MORALITY**

Especially since his morality has nothing catechistic about it, being for the most part strictly interrogative. Indeed, some of his plays conclude with a literal interrogation of the public, to whom the author leaves the responsibility of finding its own solution to the problem raised. Brecht's moral role is to infiltrate a question into what seems self-evident (this is the theme of the exception and the rule). For what is involved here is essentially a morality of invention. Brechtian invention is a tactical process to unite with revolutionary correction. In other words, for Brecht the outcome of every moral impasse depends on a more accurate analysis of the concrete situation in which the subject finds himself: the issue is joined by representing in explicit terms the historical particularity of this situation, its artificial, purely conformist nature. Essentially, Brecht's morality consists of a correct reading of history, and the plasticity of the morality *(to change Custom when necessary)* derives from the very plasticity of history.

MICHAEL GOLDMAN

"THE GHOST OF JOY: ROMANTICISM AND THE FORMS OF MODERN DRAMA" (1977)

Michael Goldman is the author of several influential books tracing the relationship between acting and drama: Shakespeare and the Energies of Drama *(1972),* Acting and Action in Shakespearean Tragedy *(1985), and* The Actor's Freedom *(1975). In this essay, Goldman suggests that many of the features of modern realistic theater are indebted to an earlier, disruptively Romantic sensibility.*

An actor appears on a stage. The moment is innately interesting; all plays begin well. This fact is crucial for understanding the "form" or "structure" of drama, whatever general name, that is, we give to the principle of maintained interest that seems to hold a play together—the whatever-it-is that lets excitement lead to excitement, that makes us feel moment calling to moment in a satisfying and significant way. For the promise of interest, and hence the source of any particular principle of interest, is already present in that first moment. Imagine the following exercise: write the *shortest possible* opening sequence of a play that would succeed in boring an audience. What would the minimum time be, I wonder? Thirty seconds? Twenty? Not much less, at any rate. The point is, it takes time for drama to bore us. The first word of a poem—as we first receive it—cannot be interesting in itself; the first moment of a play is; and thus we may seek in that first moment a quality which speaks to the uniqueness of drama as an art.

A man who is acting stands in a place set aside for acting. The innate interest springs from the appeal of acting itself, from the promise that the special kind of behavior we call "acting" will continue, transmitting to us its special kind of pleasure and energy. We may think of this energy as a kind of hauntedness. Primitive drama is almost exclusively concerned with the activity of ghosts and the impersonation of the dead. This has less to do with any religious "origin" of drama than with an essential feature of acting—the actor is inevitably a person who appears to be both himself and not himself, a figure specially liberated and set apart because he inhabits or is inhabited by another's identity. In this respect an actor is like a ghost, and it is no wonder that society has turned to acting and drama in its effort to grapple with the brooding presence of its dead. Conversely, if the appeal of acting has to do with the quality of hauntedness, then the continuing interest of a play has to do with the ways in which we feel this hauntedness exercised and transmitted, with who or what is haunting whom. Ghosts spook us—they transmit an unsettling and volatile energy to us and encourage us to haunt as we are haunted. Like Orestes or Hamlet or Oswald Alving, the haunted man becomes something of a ghost himself. When method actors look for the "spine" of a play, and, indeed, when we employ any method to identify what unifies a play's action as dramatic experience (and not, say, as theme), what we are seeking is a source of haunting for the play as a whole, the principle or premise which keeps the histrionic energy alive through a whole performance by providing an echo throughout the play of that strange displacement of the actor's being that is involved in acting a part.

Characters in modern drama are typically haunted by a feeling of being cut off from the joy of life, or indeed from life itself, a feeling of being dead. This is a Romantic feeling, and in this essay I wish to put forward the notion that the history of modern drama is essentially that of adapting this feeling to dramatic representation. The adaptation is a difficult one, and modern drama becomes successful only when it learns to treat the difficulty itself as an expressive device. I should add that I make my claims in an undogmatic and exploratory spirit, and that my plan here is not to offer a comprehensive and detailed analysis, but a series of reflections that I hope will stimulate further discussion. I aim simply to explain what I mean as clearly as I can, and then to point to

---

From *Romantic and Modern: Revaluations of Literary Tradition,* ed. George Bornstein (University of Pittsburgh Press 1977), pp. 54-67.

certain connections and patterns in the modern repertory that support my notion and that are, I think, illuminated by it.

First we must return to the feeling I have described, of being cut off from the joy of life. The feeling is romantic because it is the negative reflex or unfulfilled aspect of the romantic project of self-fulfillment. Like the feeling of being dead, the quest for self-fulfillment is hardly original with the Romantic era, but certain terms of the quest become paramount as the era dawns, above all a particular notion of where fulfillment lies, of how the self defines itself and how the joy of life is recognized.

A major defining impulse of Romanticism is the drive to conquer inner space, to possess internally a transcendent quality of being. This is often sought through action in the external world: revolt, travel, the pursuit of sublimity or freedom; but the ultimate reference of such activity is internal. The Romantic quest is validated by an expansion, possession, or transfiguration of the self. Inner space is no Romantic discovery, of course, but the shift of emphasis, the new notion of what the space is for, and perhaps of the effort required to explore it, is radical and seems to gain momentum as the Romantic era approaches. From our point of view, the shift is elusive, for two reasons. First, the traditional Western emphasis on inner discovery—as we find it, say, in Plato, or St. Augustine, or Shakespeare—is easily assimilated to our post-Romantic (or still-Romantic) reading of the world. Second, we are apt to project the Romantic reading backward onto self-absorbed literary heroes from the past—Homer's Achilles, say. In consequence, it is easy for us to miss the revolutionary character of the Romantic emphasis. Western thought has always been concerned with the individual and his private vision, but in the Romantic period private experience takes on a new articulation, a new primacy, which it retains today. When Janis Joplin's face fills the screen and describes the experience of singing, "You get inside yourself— and that becomes the entirety," she makes a statement that, with a little effort and translation, would have been perfectly intelligible (if not acceptable) to Shelley, say, as a description of a kind of satisfaction, a kind of awareness of self. But I suspect that it would be nearly unintelligible to anyone before Rousseau. Joplin is talking about the artistic process and the value of art. Both, she is certain, flow from the search for a pleasure to be found and won inside the self, a life within, realer and truer than anything outside.

This must be contrasted with the search for pleasure and achievement as it is understood in earlier periods. A stress on the life within appears, for instance, in Elizabethan literature, but the relation between inner and outer realms is quite different; and this applies to both the secular and religious perspectives. When Tamburlaine caps his great encomium to the restless human soul by defining its highest achievement as "the sweet fruition of an earthly crown," the phrase is apt to strike a modern reader oddly, as falling curiously short of the powers and ambitions evoked. We are likely to think of the sweet fruition of the artist or guru or philosopher as being greater because more inward, hence more profound. Tamburlaine's conclusion sounds odd to us because we no longer believe in the ultimate significance of outer kingdoms. Now, it is true that Tamburlaine's phrase might have struck some members of the Elizabethan audience as deficient, too—but only because they would have been thinking of the *heavenly* crown which was the soul's true goal. For the Elizabethan, there could be no doubt that the splendor and activity of the individual's inner world only pointed to the glory of some outer kingdom, whether earthly or heavenly. Shakespeare's heroes venture deep into the inner world and bring back news of the ripeness to be gained there, but, for even the most inward of them, that ripeness exists only in coordination with the outer world, usually the world of political achievement, in which the hero also lives in a primary way. Hamlet complains about having to set right the particularly ugly situation in Denmark; it is only Romantic criticism that imagines him to be complaining about having to act at all. We are accustomed to finding the external world deprecated in traditional Christian literature, but this is always and only in favor of a better world, which is distinguishable from the merely internal world of the individual. The kingdom of God is within us, to be sure, but it is larger and other than we are. Only in our era do we find the outer world deprecated in all its forms, the kingdom of God itself but a metaphor for the properly self-delighted soul. And in this sense at least, our era begins with the Romantics.

The heroes of Wordsworth and Keats, of Shelley, Byron, Goethe, Stendhal, Ibsen, and Chekhov are seeking sweet fruition in the Romantic sense. They may seem to find it in world traveling, or a life spent in nature, or the fight for freedom, or a high position in the church, or financial power, or building homes for human beings, or in sexual adventures, or even ecological adventures (like Dr. Astrov or Faust). These all may be vehicles for sweet fruition. But it is the sweet fruition itself, the expansion of the self into its internal kingdom, that they are after, and not whatever earthly or unearthly crown may help them to it.

What is new, then, is that the conquest of an inner realm is seen as an end in itself and not as a sign of having conquered an external one. For drama, the consequences are immense, though they take several decades to become apparent. The most obvious result is that characters are provided with a new type of intention. Consider, for example, the spine of *Ghosts*, as Francis Fergusson describes it: "to control the Alving heritage for my own life."[1] The last phrase is crucial. Some of the minor characters, like Engstrand, seem to be satisfied with putting the inheritance to good use in the external world, but this is a sign of their limited vision; it is why they are minor. What the heroine, Mrs. Alving, wants from the inheritance is "the joy of life," and this can only be verified internally. The orchard in *The Cherry Orchard* works well as a dramatic symbol because its flowering loveliness—like that of the forests Astrov loves in *Uncle Vanya*—stands for an inner achievement that seems to elude all the characters. To possess the orchard itself, as Lopakhin discovers, guarantees nothing. Like the Lyubovs, he cannot keep what is his. The central concern of the heroes of Ibsen, Strindberg, and Chekhov is always romantic in this sense. They aim, finally, to make something happen inside, to clear or refurnish a place in their secular souls.

This shift in focus changes the nature of drama because it changes the meaning of the stage. One quality of the acting area which stems directly from the peculiar hauntedness of acting, is that the area has always been felt to be a place where inner and outer worlds are powerfully superimposed. In all societies, the stage is perceived as a highly charged condensation of the outside world. It is like places the audience knows, or is marked by important features of place in the known world (the bull's-eye altar-center of the Greek theater, the hierarchical pageant-facade of the Elizabethan). At the same time, by the very nature of the dramatic occasion, the stage is charged with the special significance of the heightened life of acting. It is a place where crucial events will happen, a scene where the life of a few people can be projected into actions and statements that are clear and whole. In classical Greece and Elizabethan England, the structure of the scene glowed with the potential excitement of acting, with the felt receptivity of the stage to the thrusting inner world of acted characters. Now, for contrast, think of Romantic drama, the theater of Schiller and Hugo—and of its successor, modern realistic drama, the theater of Ibsen and Hauptmann. On the first of these stages, we see Romantic heroes in antique, pseudo-Shakespearean settings. On the next, Romantic heroes in tasteless parlors. In both cases, the outer worlds cannot glow with the possibilities of the inner, because the inner cannot fulfill its possibilities upon them.

The characters of high Romantic drama charge round a quasi-Elizabethan stage, stumbling upon opportunities for Romantic poetry, but not at all at home in the world of dramatic action the Elizabethan stage requires. Some great isoladoes, like Kleist and Büchner, manage to make of this failure to connect a compelling, if spasmodic stage poetry of absence, of ancient gestures like a dive into the void. But the Romantic drama proper is a spectacle of poets thrashing about in costume on an exhumed stage, speaking all the more loudly—and at times beautifully—for the silence of the painted world around them. Büchner's and Kleist's heroes seem to stagger or dream their way through busy theatrical worlds, like the Shakespearean-historical clamors of *Danton's Death* or *The Prince of Homburg*. What distinguishes their achievement from any of their contemporaries is that they are thus able to express—and to make dramatic meaning out of—the incompatibility of the Romantic hero's concerns with the external traffic of the stage.

We must bear this in mind when we come to consider Ibsen's "realistic" dramaturgy. Part of the sensation of forward movement we get from an Ibsen play comes from the steady solution of problems of plausibility, of matching the haunting thrust of the main characters to some notion of familiar social behavior and to a probable sequence of events. But the solution is never quite perfect; it never leaves the reader entirely comfortable. And for Ibsen, I would suggest, this is just the point. It was not only the awareness of a new external reality that governed his realism. It was not simply that people now lived in flats and used the telegraph and the railway, as opposed to living in palaces and riding on horseback. What mattered most was that this new reality could function as an irritant within the work of art itself. As a resistance to action and expression, it could suggest a tragic defect in the very impulse toward joy and self-fulfillment by which Ibsen's heroes were defined.

Here we may have a clue to the apparent unsatisfactoriness of the artist characters in Ibsen's later plays. There is always something grotesque and unlikely about their projects and achievements. Solness' "home for human beings" with a funny tower on top, Rubek's "Resurrection" with animal figures in the foreground, even Lovborg's *History of the Future*, have always struck critics as curiously awkward, defective as realism and heavy-handed as symbolism. It is as if Ibsen's weight of meaning could not quite be borne by any plausible book or statue or architectural design. My suggestion is that, in all these cases, the oddness in the portrait expresses the inadequacy of any contact between the romantic individual and the matter of the world. The ordinary home with the tower on it, the statue of the nude surrounded (and somehow "pushed to the background") by animals—a statue moreover that has been exhibited "all over the world"—these make us feel something unsatisfactory, a sense of disproportion or absurdity in what we are asked to think of as the highest possibilities of individual expression. Like Borkman's empty, grandiose dreams, or Mrs. Alving's great campaign for the joy of life (which consists, finally, in trying to convince her son's half-sister to become his mistress in order to take his mind off his syphilitic decline) they have the effect of yanking the stage out from under the hero.

In one form or another, this is the major pattern in Ibsen, and it stands at the heart of his realism. From the earliest prose plays, the climactic moments are those in which the individual's outlet to the world goes up in smoke. The orphanage burns down and reveals that Mrs. Alving cannot make an orphan of her son. The monument to Capt. Alving that was supposed to exorcise his baleful influence is destroyed; his influence is more virulent than ever. In *A Doll's House*, the letter from Krogstad plunks into the letter box but fails to produce the "wonderful thing" that Nora has hoped for. Both these climaxes deliberately remind us of the well-made play, of a dramaturgy that lets issues resolve themselves in neatly patterned change in the external world, but if (as reviewers from time to time complain) these contrivances "creak," in Ibsen it is the deliberate creak of a machine that has made nothing happen. Mrs. Alving and Nora turn to the world, to others, for an action that will expand their souls, and the world does not respond. *A Doll's House* remains unique among Ibsen's plays because it contrives to suggest that the world might respond; Nora runs off (with Ibsen, one might say) into a night of hope. But we have only to compare that final scene with the rest of Ibsen's plays to see what the hope amounts to. Onstage, in fact, all we can see is Helmer, and his hope for a wonderful resurrection is answered by the slam of the door; there is nothing creaking here.

The spectacular sunrise on the mountains at the end of *Ghosts*, the fire in the orphanage, the ominous letter box of *A Doll's House*, Ekdal's "hunting" garret in *The Wild Duck*, the snow-covered hillside in *Borkman*—these are all scenic devices whose literal character renders them at odds with the psychological expansiveness of the characters on stage. They express the characters' situation, to be sure, and sometimes very profoundly, but they do not join with them, they do not receive and extend the characters' actions as, say, the crowns in *Tamburlaine* or the carpet in the *Agamemnon* do. There is a seam in Ibsen that always shows between the inner life of his characters and their condition. James notices it in his famous review of *John Gabriel Borkman*. "If the spirit is a lamp within us," he observes, "glowing through what the world and flesh make of us as through a ground-glass shade, then such pictures as *Little Eyolf* and *John Gabriel* are each a *chassez-croisez* of lamps burning, as in tasteless parlors, with the flame practically exposed.[2] But the seam—the incompatibility of lamp and shade, of haunted hero and tasteless parlor—is not a sign of defective workmanship. It is the essential mark of Ibsen's tragic dramaturgy, the point where the romantic project fails to connect with the outer scene. It expresses the drama of the romantic self in its necessarily unsatisfactory commerce with the world.

Near the end of Pirandello's *Enrico IV*, the hero has a speech which offers a fine example of both the dramatic problem posed by the romantic project and the type of solution modern drama has found. The speech combines a profoundly ambiguous notion of reality with what appears to be a powerfully expansive and emphatic statement of individual transcendence. By doing so, it makes us feel both the haunting romantic drive toward a joy which escapes the formal constraints of life in society and a puzzling blockage which renders the drive unrealizable. Enrico has turned on his guests with scorn and contempt. In a series of big speeches, he seems bent on demonstrating the superiority of his conscious masquerade to the general falseness of the lives around him. Then, ostensibly in the same vein, he introduces an unexpected reminiscence:

> I remember a priest, certainly Irish, a nice-looking priest, who was sleeping in the sun one November day, with his arm on the corner of the bench of a public garden. He was lost in the golden delight of the mild sunny air which must have seemed for him almost summery. One may be sure that in that moment he did not know any more that he was a priest, or even where he was. He was dreaming. . . . A little boy passed with a flower in his hand. He touched the priest with it here on the neck. I saw him open his laughing eyes, while all his mouth smiled with the beauty of his dream. He was forgetful of everything.[3]

The little boy with a flower: it is a romantic intervention *par excellence*, a touch of nature breaking through the rigidities of convention, the body shocked and freed by immediate, sensual contact with life. Enrico continues:

> He was forgetful of everything. . . . But all at once, he pulled himself together, and stretched out his priest's cassock; and there came back to his eyes the same seriousness which you have seen in mine; because the Irish priests defend the seriousness of their Catholic faith with the same zeal with which I defend the sacred rights of hereditary monarchy!

The sequence is surprising. At the touch of the flower, the priest goes from the golden delight of his dream to the grim seriousness of his priestly role—from freedom, life, and pleasure to repression and rigidity. The effect is not far from the terrible climaxes of Ibsen—the moment of intensest contact with the longed-for, dreamed-of joy of life guttering, because of the contact, into absolute inhibition.

Indeed, I would call this the model sequence of modern drama. Here is the paradigm: First, we are caught up in the campaign of the individual soul to break through to reality in what the soul perceives to be an unreal world, a campaign on the side of joy, of an inner flowering, a campaign that seems to be leading to a breakthrough. And then comes the moment of breakthrough, in which the campaigning soul plunges into—an absence of some sort. In the nineteenth century, this is usually represented as an absence of joy, of fulfilled life. Later dramatists tend to treat it as an absence of reality. But whether it be Mrs. Alving discovering that the joy of life is impossible, or the revolutionaries in *The Balcony* learning that their war against illusion can only be sustained by illusion, or Brecht's Shen Te finding that she can only be a good woman by masquerading as a bad man, the final revelation opens a fissure between the individual drive that makes for the play's action—that "haunts" the main actor—and the world in which he tries to act.

Pirandello is perhaps the first dramatist to make this sequence explicitly question the nature of reality. In the speech just discussed, Enrico's train of thought undercuts his claim to have made a superior contact with the real. He argues that he is free, but he concludes in images of entrapment. He resembles the priest not in the brief moment of release, but in the long career of rigidity. Though he strikes the pose of the triumphant revenger, the liberated hero exposing the madness of a society he disdains, the play regularly shows him as trapped in his posture of liberation. All his life, Enrico has longed for human contact and been terrified of exclusion from life. His solution to the problem has been the masquerade, which has excluded him even more absolutely. Behind his performance as emperor lies a restless search for freedom. Speaking as emperor at the end of the first act, he has seen himself as dead and begged for resurrection:

> It isn't enough that [the Pope] should receive me! You know he can do *everything—everything* I tell you! He can even call up the dead. [*Touches his chest.*] Behold me! Do you see me? There is no magic art unknown to him. Well, Monsignor, my Lady, my torment is really this: that whether here or there [*Pointing to his portrait almost in fear.*] I can't free myself from this magic. I am a penitent now, you see; and I swear to you I shall remain so until he receives me. But you two, when the excommunication is taken off, must ask the Pope to do this thing he can so easily do: to take me away from that; [*Indicating the portrait again.*] and let me live wholly and freely my miserable life.   (p. 172)

Two acts later, the climax of the play, like the story of the dreaming priest that precedes it, shows that Enrico cannot be reawakened. His impulse to grasp life issues in emptiness suggesting the real function of the theatrical metaphor in *Enrico IV*. In the course of the play, role-playing comes to stand for an inhibition, a limit on the real life which, we are led to feel, lies behind the masquerade. But the action is contrived so that we feel—just as the impulse breaks through—that there is nothing but the masquerade available to the actor. Enrico, as is often pointed out, has no "real" name; we know him only by the name of the eleventh-century emperor he pretends to be. The point is not that all life is a masquerade. This is the type of "Pirandellism" that Pirandello is always trailing before us as a sort of philosophical red herring. The point is not a point at all, but an experience—the experience of breaking through to an emptiness that is charged with our longing for fullness. Enrico's masquerade is a device for exploring, in theatrical terms, the romantic impulse to private fulfillment.

The moment before he kills Belcredi, Enrico has roughly grasped Frida in his arms, and so we see him at the end not as a romantic hero defying society, but as an aging man grotesquely embracing a woman young enough to be his daughter, the daughter by another man of the woman he once loved. This sudden and disturbing version of the primal scene brutally mates reality and fantasy. The sad reality behind the masquerade and the pathetic fantasy behind the real embrace are both made visible. This is Enrico's reentry into real life—a painfully actual version of his grand desire. It may remind us of the similar scene that stands at the center of *Six Characters*, when the father approaches the step-daughter in Mme. Pace's brothel. *Six Characters*, too, is about the desire for "life," as the Characters keep telling us. In his preface to the play, Pirandello explicitly associates this desire with romanticism. More than that, he associates his presentation of the characters' desires, his success in making a play out of the *failure* of a play to be made, with the failure of romantic desire to make contact with reality:

> I have presented [a drama] . . . in which . . . there is a discreet satire on romantic procedures: in the six characters thus excited to the point where they stifle themselves in the roles which each of them plays in a certain drama while I present them as characters in another play which they don't know and don't suspect the existence of, so that this inflammation of their passion— which belongs to the realm of romantic procedures—is humorously "placed," located in the void.   (pp. 373–74)

Modern drama's greatest successes are largely of this kind. They show the failure of romanticism through theatrical forms in which one kind of dramatic procedure fails and is contained in another. The effect is to "locate" the self in the void.

Whenever we wish to inquire about the career of drama in a given period, we will always do well to inquire after the fate of *Hamlet* in that period. For in writing *Hamlet*, Shakespeare managed to hold a mirror up to the nature of drama. In the Romantic era, Hamlet, naturally enough, became a Romantic. But in transforming Hamlet into that extremely influential Hamlet-like image of itself, the era gave away a number of its secrets.

The Romantic Hamlet is a man set down in a world not of his own making and, perhaps even more significantly, a man who is ponderously disturbed, if not bewildered by this fact. Whether he be described as a delicate vase into which an oak tree has inadvertently been inserted (Goethe) or a procrastinating philosopher brutally constrained to practical action (Coleridge), Hamlet is seen by the Romantic imagination as a man at odds with the very conditions of existence in a real world. Indeed we might say that the Romantic imagination regards Hamlet as a poet unfairly and tragically forced to make an appearance in a play.

Hamlet is at his most Romantic when he claims that he has that within him which passes show. With this statement he places "real life" beyond the reach of theater. It is a position Shakespeare's Hamlet quickly learns he must abandon—for four-and-a-half acts of intricate action and play-acting—but the Hamlet of the Romantic imagination clings to it. If all that matters most to Hamlet is inaccessibly *within*, then he can never get beyond the withdrawal of his first appearance at Claudius' court. And this is the attitude in which Romantic criticism freezes Shakespeare's prince—the soulful adolescent brooding at the feast. Once more, the portrait points to the difficult relation between Romanticism and drama.

This is not to say, of course, that Romantic critics did not believe in action. In his discussion of *Hamlet*, Coleridge insists that "action is the chief end of existence," and Goethe's Faust finds happiness redeeming swampland. This will remind us, if we need reminding, that the nineteenth century was an age of projectors and revolutionaries, of adventurers with an itch for changing the order of the world. It will remind us of Borkman and Solness. In every case, however, the romantic itch for action expresses a yearning for inner fulfillment. The sweet fruition, even for Faust, is internal, an event inside the spirit. Ibsen differs from Goethe and Coleridge here only in that he firmly grasps the absurdity of the itch for action, the incompatibility between homes for human beings and the restless inner expansionism of the romantic project. It is not, I think, that Ibsen saw more clearly than Coleridge or Goethe, or that he came later and knew more. He *had* to see the incompatibility because his genius was dramatic. On any living stage, the Romantic Hamlet is an absurdity, a whirl-wind of passion disconnected from the world around him, a bad poet in an inflated closet drama, beating his sensibilities in vain.

Goethe's characterization of Hamlet as "a costly vase" provides a key to the defects of the Ro-mantic stage, to the inability of its great poets to produce real drama. Hamlet, in Goethe's metaphor, is a beautiful container, shattered by misuse. The image implies a conception of dra-matic character as something to be displayed or exclaimed over, something that remarkably indi-cates the rarity of its composition—Hamlet as a delicate vase, not the oak tree it contains, certainly not a Renaissance prince.

Like Coleridge, Goethe too saw Hamlet's inability to act as a sign of failure. Hamlet lacked "the strength of nerve which makes the hero," but my point is that the hero desiderated here is just another kind of vase, sturdier than the Hamlet variety, displaying, shall we say, the strength-of-nerve pattern. On the early nineteenth-century stage, such heroes are inevitably less interesting than a Prince of Homburg or a Danton—than characters who fall back deliberately and dangerously into the void, who puzzle over their discontinuity with the stage world they move in. The romantic proj-ect was neither a mistake nor an aberration, and I hope that nothing I have said suggests that it was. On the contrary, it was a necessary step into the labyrinth of being—and one result of it was a new and rich critical sensitivity to the inwardness of Shakespeare's heroes. Its gift to the drama was a new source for haunting, the imperious hunger for inner space, a flight from spiritual deadness which ul-timately transformed every object on the realistic stage into a ghost, a persecuting agent of the dead external world. But it took some time to discover the forms by which this haunting could be released in dramatic action.

Romantic man invented a secret place, the ego, and then set out to explore it. It was like a cavern or a heaven or a beautiful day or a sublime landscape, but it was different from all these in that it was inaccessible, or accessible only to its inventor, "I." And "I" seemed simultaneously imprisoned in his secret place and excluded from it. The Romantic egoist was doomed to explore his secret place in secret, though not in silence. Any traffic with the ego was subject to a fundamental interruption. Nothing could be brought into the cavern in its own state, as grace, say, could be brought to the Christian soul, victories to the hero, realms to the king, friends to the social man. All such had now to be translated into the currency of the secret place, which was by its nature private, coined and counted only by the Romantic individual in his private cave.

The art of Romantic man was a public form of this currency, a scrip one might say, a way of communicating value, of speaking to other privacies about the private cave. Today, we are accus-tomed to translating all art into such terms, and very likely it *is* an aspect of all art, at least all so-phisticated Western art, but, in truth, there is little we can do to avoid thinking this way. We cannot escape the Romantic translation because we cannot escape our past. For the purposes of this essay, however, it is only necessary to note how the public forms of art became firmly related to the inac-cessible privacy of the artist. The full purport of the privacy and the problems it raised were perhaps not immediately clear. Wordsworth could think of the poet as a man speaking to men, and thus, quite honestly, offer his unprecedented exploration of private experience in terms that linked it to a kind of Horatian conversation. But the solitaries who inhabit Wordsworth's landscapes like features in it, and the conversations in which Wordsworth and his interlocutor are clearly speaking different languages, tell a different story. The Wordsworthian conversation is extraordinary, like nothing be-fore it in English poetry, but he talks with men as he might with a flower or a rock. It is not that their speech is less meaningful or less respected than his own; it is simply other. And it speaks finally of the otherness of his private place. The poet who talks of a man speaking to men is the same as the boy who had to cling to a tree to keep the world from disappearing.

The contradictions already implicit in Wordsworth become crucial in the work of succeeding generations. The ambiguous privacy of the poet and his driven, unsatisfactory commerce with a dissolving world—these are themes the art of the period 1780–1830 bequeathed to the modern era. In one fashion or another, they make themselves felt in all the experiments of modern drama. We feel them at play in Enrico Quattro's struggle to make contact with the world, and in the struggles of Borkman, or Miss Julie, or Peter Handke's Kaspar. Much more explicitly, they form the basis for one of the great innovative dramas of the modern repertory—Brecht's first play, *Baal*. *Baal* is about a poet, a most un-Wordsworthian one in personal style, to be sure, but he too seems both locked in the depths of private experience and haunted by a desire to embrace the ungraspable world. It is fitting to close with a look at this prodigal, refractory work, which has always proved so resistant to analysis. *Baal* was conceived as a counter-play to Hanns Johst's *Der Einsame*, an Expressionist paean to the Romantic playwright, Grabbe. As such, it gives us a figure whose absorption in the personal is so complete as to be monstrous. At the beginning of the play, we see Baal surrounded by a throng of bourgeois poetry-lovers. They react to him as might an audience at some more conventional play—like Johst's—about the glories and sorrows of a stereotyped Romantic artist. But Baal neither responds nor performs as they wish. He takes what he wants from them—food, drink, the promise of an assignation. Quickly, he alienates them all. They leave, angry and troubled. At the end of the scene, the stage is empty except for Baal, who "goes on drinking."[4]

Baal haunts his play—and holds it together—by this endless capacity for ingestion. Like any Romantic artist, he values himself for what he contains, and he wishes to contain not only multitudes, but all—trees, sky, rain, death. There is some suggestion in the play that this desire amounts to a wish, on the poet's part, to incorporate the mother—if so, it is a brilliant insight into the romantic project with its dissatisfied yearning after death, apocalypse, self-generation, the womb. In any case, the movement toward ingestion is also a movement to dissolution. Scenically and structurally, the play seems to dissolve. There are no resistances; everything flows into Baal, and the more he dominates, the more he decays. His haunting power comes from the way he goes beyond whatever is extreme, whatever is romantic in those who surround him. He estranges them, and the audience, ever further by rejecting any of the pieties or limits by which we ordinarily accommodate the limitless romantic absorption in self to acceptable behavior in the world.

At the end of the play, Baal crawls out of a shabby workman's hut, dying, calling not on God, but on "dear Baal." For Brecht, this marks the fate of the private ego, grown absolute and terrifying in its asociality. Does Baal want to live more than he wants to die? It is not clear, but the absolute absorption in self that he represents is inseparable from his restless drive toward dissolution. Brecht's own artistic career is a brilliant, hopeless struggle to be free of the Romantic legacy. Throughout it, he remains profoundly ambivalent toward *Baal*, constantly trying to redefine the play in notes which serve only to emphasize the unsettling tensions it embodies. And Baal's destructive, restless, stirring, self-absorbed personality keeps recurring in his plays, never quite tamed by the distancing devices that surround it.

Writing near the end of his life, Brecht tries to assimilate *Baal* to the Marxist usefulness of epic theater. He finds it difficult, and prefaces his remarks with a wry warning: "*Baal* is a play which could present all kinds of difficulties to those who have not learned to think dialectically." Denying that the play is "a glorification of unrelieved egotism," he pictures Baal as "standing out against the demands and discouragements of a world whose form of production is designed for exploitation rather than usefulness." It is an unpersuasive argument, and Brecht himself seems unsatisfied with it. Finally, he asks us simply to accept *Baal* as a kind of weak spot in his oeuvre: "I have left the play as it was, not having the strength to alter it. I admit (and advise you): this play is lacking in wisdom."[5]

The conclusion is dismissive, but in the course of his remarks, Brecht makes an observation that is of great importance to our discussion. By emphasizing the unredeemed capitalism of the world Baal moves in, Brecht manages to hint at a significant and troubling relation between *Baal* and modern social thought, which also bears upon its relation to Romanticism. As a revolutionary play, Brecht suggests, *Baal* may be taken to have the following moral: "Humanity's urge for happiness can never be entirely killed."

This is a perplexing commentary on a play whose self-obsessed hero seems infinitely remote from the fraternal optimism of a phrase like "Humanity's urge for happiness." But is the distance so great? Just as the figure of Baal carries to extremes and thus subverts the cheerful glorification of the Romantic artist, so Baal's monstrous asocial appetite is an extreme expression of the Romantic notion of happiness as a purely internal achievement. The urge for happiness in this sense is ultimately subversive of any society or even of any coherent life in the world. In this, *Baal* is also very much in the mainstream of the modern theatrical investigation of romantic possibilities. In the twentieth century, drama has pursued to the source—more doggedly and deeply perhaps than any other form—the great promise of an internal kingdom that the revolutionary desires of the eighteenth and nineteenth centuries opened for our imagination. The link between the political and personal is crucial here—and not a little disturbing. "Bliss was it in that dawn to be alive," writes Wordsworth, and surely a great reason why it was bliss for a young Romantic to be alive as the French Revolution began was that the fraternal dreams of the Revolution and the more private dreams of the Romantic ego on the verge of new self-discovery seemed for a moment to be one. Freedom, for both self and society, was the promise in the air. Modern tragedy, based as it is on the failure of the Romantic project, strikes at the hopeful social vision that informed the blissful dawn of the modern idea of liberty, the political version of Mrs. Alving's "joy of life." As O'Neill's Larry Slade says, surveying the ragged, drunken wrecks about him in the first act of *The Iceman Cometh*, "It's a great game, the pursuit of happiness."

NOTES

[1] *The Idea of a Theater* (Princeton: Princeton University Press, 1949), p. 150.

[2] Henry James, *The Scenic Art: Notes on Acting and the Drama*, ed. Allan Wade (New York: Hill and Wang, 1957), p. 293.

[3] *Naked Masks*, ed. Eric Bentley (New York: Dutton, 1952), p. 205. Hereafter cited in the text.

[4] There are many versions of *Baal*. Some of the difficulties in deciding on a preferred text are discussed by Ralph Manheim and John Willett in the introduction and notes to the first volume of their edition of Brecht's *Collected Plays* (New York: Vintage Books, 1971). I follow Brecht's first published version of 1922, which has been translated by Eric Bentley and Martin Esslin (New York: Grove Press, 1964).

[5] Manheim and Willett, pp. 345–46.

W. B. WORTHEN

FROM *MODERN DRAMA AND THE RHETORIC OF THEATER* (1992)

W. B. Worthen, the editor of The Harcourt Brace Anthology of Drama, *has written widely about dramatic literature, theory, and performance. In this selection, he discusses the ideology of visibility in realistic theater.*

Let me recall a brief, brilliant scene from Chekhov's *Three Sisters*. Toward the end of the first act, the Prozorovs and their guests retire from the downstage drawing room to the partly concealed reception room upstage, to celebrate Irina's name-day. Natasha arrives, nervously checks herself in the mirror, and rushes to join the party. The forestage is empty, when two of the omnipresent junior officers suddenly appear. Taking out a camera—still a novelty at the turn of the century—they pose and silence the party, taking one photograph and then another. It is a striking moment. Taking a picture syncopates the action and highlights the stylistic transparency of Chekhov's drama. As the characters withdraw upstage, the play becomes lifelike by becoming random, oblique, untheatrical; the photograph stops the action, fixing it as an image for a second or two in the blue halo of the flash. Bernard Shaw remarked that "drama is no mere setting up of the camera to nature" (Preface 197), and Chekhov's camera both asserts the verisimilitude of his drama and denaturalizes it, exposing that "reality" as a rhetorical effect of the realistic stage.[1]

The history of stage realism is often told as a narrative of technical mastery, in which playwrights from Henrik Ibsen to David Storey find their theatrical expression through the practical innovations of great directors: André Antoine, Constantin Stanislavski, Harley Granville Barker, Elia Kazan, Lindsay Anderson, and so on. This parable presents theatrical change as an evolution in engineering, with playwrights, technicians, and directors collaborating to render the world on stage with increasing fidelity and precision. And yet, as Chekhov points out, stage verisimilitude is

---

[1] Hand-held Kodak cameras were, of course, available in Europe at the turn of the century, though their use in the home, and their appearance on the stage, would still have excited comment. Beaumont Newhall's description of Édouard Vuillard's use of the camera to photograph gatherings in his home is suggestive of the scene in *Three Sisters*. A "folding Kodak camera was a fixture in his house, and during social gatherings he liked to put it casually on a piece of furniture, point it at his guests, and ask them to hold still while he made short time exposures." See Newhall 136.

an effect of where we sit to receive it. The camera—something of a cliché for realism even in Chekhov's day—can only halt and distort the "life" it would reproduce. Chekhov's camera implies that the effect of the "real" arises not from mimetic fidelity but in our relation to the apparatus that discloses it. The effect of the "real" is something that we produce both before us and within ourselves, a world and an interpretation of it, a reading based, as Émile Zola—that novelist, playwright, and amateur photographer—might have put it, on a systematic "amputation of reality" (287)[2]

I want to begin a different narrative, tracing the rhetorical continuity between the experimental era of Zola's naturalist polemics and the equally experimental work of our own realistic theater a century later. Historically, the rise of modern realism in the theater is usually traced to developments in theater technology dating from the mid-nineteenth century. This complicity between dramatic style and stage technology is informed by a sustaining ideology, what Roland Barthes calls the "ideological unity of the bourgeoisie," a unity that "gave rise to a single mode of writing" (*Writing* 2–3). In *Writing Degree Zero* Barthes traces later divisions in literary form to the breakup of this unified bourgeois consciousness, and we can certainly see a related development in drama as well: the proliferation of such apparently anti-realistic dramatic forms as expressionism, symbolism, Brechtian epic theater, poetic drama, theater of the absurd, "new realism," theater of images, and socialist drama. In the theater, the hegemony of realism is challenged not simply in terms of the style of the drama, but in the terms of stage production as well—different strategies of theatrical production challenge realism's ways of framing a picture of the world and controlling the audience's reading of it. In this regard the theater tells a somewhat different story than Barthes does, in large part because the rhetoric of realistic production has been much more difficult to suspend, even when the drama it stages seems far from the mode of Ibsen, Chekhov, O'Neill, or Storey. Although competing modes of stage production challenge the rhetoric of realism and the audience it produces, they often bear the traces of the "realistic" designs they oppose.

Realism is notoriously elusive, difficult to locate either as a "style" or at a particular moment in history. Here, I treat realistic theater and drama as an arrangement of practices developed as part of a cultural milieu of which we are still a part. To this extent "realism" is always a shorthand for "modern realism," or for "realistic drama and theater since 1850." The date is less important than what it marks—though 1889, the year of the first unaltered production of Ibsen's *A Doll House* in England, comes to mind—for it points to the joining of literature, technology, and society in a sustaining ideological project. That project is what I mean by "realism," the distinguishing marks of which lie in its character as rhetoric, its ways of using theatrical production—conventions of acting, design, direction—to naturalize a particular relationship between the dramatic fiction and the offstage world of the audience. Unlike earlier modes of theater, realism not only asserts a reality that is natural or unconstructed, it argues that such a reality can only be shown on the stage by effacing the medium—literary style, acting, mise-en-scène—that discloses it. What is most characteristic of realism, that is, is not the verisimilitude it claims as its style (as though Hedda Gabler were more lifelike than Medea or Lady Macbeth simply because she speaks prose and owns a practical stove) but the framing machinery that seems to make such lifelikeness appear. Verisimilitude, instead, arises as an effect of the audience's activity, and it is the rhetorical purpose of realistic theater to assert the perception of verisimilitude as the sign of our proper engagement with the play. The modern realistic stage is a device for claiming and legitimating a certain kind of interpretive activity; its technology and techniques work to frame our ways of reading the stage and the kind of meanings we can find there.

Realism provides a way to hold audiences, performers, and drama in a particular relationship; the stage deploys its dramatic and theatrical style to shape certain forms of audience attention, experience, and interpretation. The formal and stylistic markers of realistic drama in this period are familiar: prosaic dialogue, bourgeois setting and subject matter (or, if the setting is drawn from another class, an implied bourgeois perspective on that class), a conflict between internal psychological motives and external economic or social pressures, a rigorously "causal" plotting, predominance

---

[2] Not surprisingly, perhaps, Zola exempts naturalism from the "amputation" characteristic of earlier modes: "Toutes les formules anciennes, la formule classique, la formule romantique, sont basées sur l'arrangement et sur l'amputation systématiques du vrai."

of incident, and so on. These are, in a sense, the features of "realism" that the drama appropriated from the novel in the late nineteenth century, and which similarly assert the drama's unmediated transparency to the offstage reality it presents.

To produce this dramatic effect onstage requires an equally articulate theatrical rhetoric, and before turning to a reading of realistic drama we will need to elaborate this rhetoric more fully. Two points are easily anticipated: the pictorial, "photographic" objectivity claimed for the mise-en-scène, and its ability to govern a behavioristic style of acting.[3] The third moment of this rhetoric—how this complex of dramatic, staging, and acting techniques produces a characteristic experience for its audience—is more difficult to bring into focus, because the realistic theater negates the audience's overt participation in the theater as a necessary part of its proper interpretive activity. Defining *verisimilitude* as a thorough identification of the drama (present) with its performance (transparent), the theater casts its audience as absent from the field of representation. Legitimate theater experience, and so a proper interpretation of the "knowledge" that realistic drama often promises, can occur only when we have been apparently exiled from the field of theater itself.

The realistic stage works to arouse a familiar modern appetite: the desire to view others as theater from a position of unstaged freedom. We might think of realistic rhetoric in the theater as the body of practices that both stimulate and satisfy this appetite for "objectivity." The desire to produce the stage as object, a photographic slice of life free from the mediation of dramatic or theatrical style, becomes visible in the first polemics calling for realistic experimentation in the 1870s and 1880s. As Zola suggests, the rhetoric of realism claims to duplicate the epistemology of experimental science. Naturalistic playwrights, Zola argues, should imitate "le mouvement d'enquête et d'analyse, qui est le mouvement même du dix-neuvième siècle" (283), by writing ironic, anti-romantic plays illustrating the behavior of characters as the effect of material causes, causes usually located in social pressures or "physiological" urgings. The "science" of theatrical naturalism lies less in the thematics of the drama than in the ideological neutrality it assigns to stage practice, and in the construction of the spectator as a disinterested, "objective" observer. The mise-en-scène appropriates the authority of "science" by assigning a "scientific" transparency to its own instruments, in order to ascribe a similarly scientific objectivity to its audience.

We can see that the machinery of theatrical production is assimilated to notions of scientific objectivity in a variety of ways. Much as the scientist's instruments or the photographer's camera are said to make objective observation possible, so too the technology of the theater is said to determine the "rise" of realistic drama. As Brander Matthews, the first professor of dramatic literature in the United States, found when he surveyed the history of the nineteenth-century theater in 1910, the "real responsibility" for the prosaic style of modern drama "does not lie on Ibsen's shoulders, but on Edison's—since it was an inevitable consequence of the incandescent bulb" (*A Study* 64). In *The Principles of Playmaking* (1919) Matthews clarifies this history:

> In the course of the middle half of the nineteenth century the actual stage underwent a transformation. It was so amply lighted first by gas and then by electricity, that the actor had no longer to go down to the footlights to let his changing expression be seen. The parallel wings and borders by means of which interiors had been crudely indicated were abolisht and the compact box-set enabled the stage-director to suggest more satisfactorily an actual room. The apron was cut away; and the curtain rose and fell in a picture-frame. The characters of the play were thereafter elements in a picture, which had a characteristic background, and which might be furnisht with the most realistic elaboration. The former intimacy of the actor with the spectators, due to his close proximity, disappeared speedily; and with this intimacy there disappeared also its concomitant, the soliloquy addrest by a character to the audience for the sole purpose of supplying information. The drama immediately became more pictorial; it could rely more certainly upon gesture; it could renounce the aid of purely rhetorical oratory; it could dispense with description; and it insisted that the performer should subdue himself to those new conditions and to be on his guard lest he should "get out of the picture." (236–37)

Matthews echoes Zola in treating the representational practices of the realistic theater and drama as the result of evolutionary necessity. Reifying the "fourth wall," displacing the drama from

---

[3] For a reading of the divergent styles of naturalism and realism in drama and in performance, see Styan vol. 1.

the apron into the recessed box set, integrating characterization with design and costume elements, assimilating acting style to the understated manners of social behavior, and displacing the audience as participant, are all, to Matthews, dictated by the simple fact of their technological possibility. Matthews sees in this technology the origin and cause of realism, but its history is actually bound to the rise of the more spectacular modes of production that dominated other precincts of the nineteenth-century stage: cataclysmic melodrama, Irving's splendid "historical" Shakespeare, the glitter and panache of pantomime and extravaganza.[4] Zola saw naturalism as the result of a positivist literary and social "évolution," both the expression of "l'intelligence contemporaine" and its absent cause, transcending the passing fashions of specific individuals, classes, or institutions (285). Matthews similarly finds the triumph of realism to be implicit in its theatrical environment; although stage technology might sustain a variety of dramatic species, only realism seems fit to survive.

Theatrical realism claims to stage an objective representation by integrating dramatic and performance style into the pictorial consistency of the material scene onstage. The purpose of this consistency is not, in the end, simply mimetic: the aim of realism is to produce an audience, to legitimate its private acts of interpretation as objective. How does the rhetoric of realism cast its audience, and render the audience's typical mode of attention—displaced, absent, private viewing—meaningful? The picture frame of the proscenium not only circumscribes a dramatic world, it establishes the characteristic relation between actor, role, and eavesdropping audience through which its meanings are realized. In *Play-Making* (1912), for example, William Archer describes the dramatist's craft in pictorial terms: the "stage now aims at presenting a complete picture, with the figures not 'a little out of the picture,' but completely in it" (64). Only by visualizing the stage as a pictorial environment, rather than as a stage set, can the playwright find "a safeguard against theatricality" (13). In part because the actor/character cannot emerge from the "picture," the environmental set becomes a decisive factor in the audience's interpretive activity, especially in its reading of "character." In 1911, for instance, David Belasco used the set for the opening scene of *The Return of Peter Grimm* to demonstrate the character's implication in a complex of social, economic, domestic, and even psychological histories:

> The sun comes brightly into the room. Through the window can be seen tulip beds, other flowers, hot houses, and rows of trees. Peter Grimm's botanic gardens supply seeds, plants, shrubbery, and trees to the wholesale trade as well as retail; and the view should suggest the importance and extent of the industry which Peter has inherited and improved.   (Marker 71)

A character so fully identified with its productive environment is more completely contained within the stage. "Character" is no longer a medium of theatrical exchange between actor and audience—as it was, say, in Shakespeare's or Garrick's theater, where the making of character was more openly negotiated between actor and audience—but one object among many, part of a dramatic ecology the audience can observe but not enter. The objectivity of the pictorial stage both withdraws it from the audience's influence, and claims to render the drama "absolute," as though it were not implicated in the activities of performance and of observation that fabricate it on the stage.[5]

---

[4] On the limits of technological determinism as a description of naturalism, see Williams, "Social environment" 208.

[5] Peter Szondi regards the historically specific conditions of the modern theater as an index to essential or universal features of the drama; although we differ markedly on this point, his description of the relationship between drama and audience—with this qualification—is powerful. The "much-maligned 'picture-frame' stage," Szondi says,

> is the only one adequate to the absoluteness of the drama and bears witness to it in each of its features. It is no more connected to the house (by steps, for example) than the Drama is connected (stepwise) to the audience. The stage becomes visible, thus exists, only at the beginning of the play—often, in fact, only after the first lines have been spoken. Because of this, it seems to be created by the play itself. At the end of the act, when the curtain falls, the stage is again withdrawn from the spectator's view, taken back as if it were part of the play. The footlights which illuminate it create the impression that the play sheds its own light on the stage.

Similarly, Szondi continues to describe acting as "subservient to the absoluteness of the Drama. The actor-role relationship should not be visible. Indeed, the actor and the character should unite to create a single personage" (8–9).

The desire to produce the audience in an "objective" relation to dramatic events also requires an increasingly underplayed acting style. Much as the mise-en-scène frames a coherent picture, purged of the traces of the theater, the pictorial stage suppresses a self-evident style of acting as an object of the audience's attention. Realistic acting erases itself from view, renders the actor the vehicle of a fully coherent "character" already present in the dramatic text. The actor's performance is rendered theatrically invisible, and aesthetically palatable, through a thoroughgoing identification between the conventions of "acting" and the manifest codes of social enactment. The increasingly subtle reproduction of domestic behavior informing English acting from Squire Bancroft to Granville Barker is one instance of this development, analogous to the efforts of Antoine's Théâtre Libre, of the Provincetown Players, of the Irish realists, of the Moscow Art Theater, and later of the American Method. This attitude is evident, too, in popular responses to the theater, which often betray this deeply idealized conception of dramatic performance. When the *Times* critic A. B. Walkley asks "What is the very quintessence of acting but the effort to bring about the complete identity" between actor and character, he inscribes in that identity a typical hierarchy of value: "If the actor *is* the part, so that you fail to distinguish one from the other, then he has achieved what he set out to do and he deserves all the praise he gets" (*More Prejudice* 69). In part, this priority reflects the sense that actors' special personality, their public extroversion, and their professional openness to the view of others necessarily violate the essential privacy and inwardness of the self, of authentic experience. In relation to the roles they perform—where "character" is revealed through indirection, unselfconscious disclosure—actors' public self-representation seems nearly pathological, and so must be neutralized by a mimetic rhetoric that assigns it an instrumental transparency.[6]

The widespread interest in puppets and marionettes at the turn of the century is also symptomatic of the uneasiness produced by the actors' dizzying self-multiplication. Gordon Craig's experiments, Meyerhold's sculptural plasticity, and Yeats's statuesque acting demonstrate the complicity between "symbolic" or "poetic" and "realistic" acting as strategies for audience implication: both claim to produce an ideal "character" by refining the actor's distracting personal charisma from our view. As Walkley suggests in proposing a marionette production of Thomas Hardy's *Dynasts*, puppet presentation

> would clarify, simplify, attenuate the medium through which the poem reaches the audience. The poet and his public would be in close contact. It is, of course, for many minds, especially for those peculiarly susceptible to poetry, a perpetual grievance against the actors that these living, bustling, solid people get between them and the poet and substitute fact, realism, flesh-and-blood for what these minds prefer to embody only in their imagination.

By using puppets or untrained performers instead of actors, Walkley hopes to dematerialize the actor's troubling opacity, to present the drama to its public through "a 'transparent medium'" (*Pastiche* 174–75, 177).

Realistic theater works to "attenuate the medium" by which the drama reaches its audience as a means of attenuating the audience's complicity in the performance itself. The spectator is cast as an impartial observer, construed outside and beyond both the drama and the theatrical activities—including his or her attendance, participation—that produce it. Staging *drama* that often insists on the pervasive determination of an environment metonymically reduced to the drawing-room box, realistic *theater* suppresses the theatrical environment as both cause and explanation of the drama's meanings or our interpretation of them. "A real subjection is born mechanically from a fictitious relation," Michel Foucault remarks of Jeremy Bentham's panopticon (202). Yet if the panopticon is, like the theater, a "privileged place for experiments on men, and for analysing with complete certainty the transformations that may be obtained from them" (204), it also points to the considerable

---

[6] One has a sense of the threatening pathology of actors in this analogy of William Archer's: "Suppose a man imprisoned in a narrow chamber, walled, roofed, and floored with mirrors, some plane, some concave, some convex, some warped in all conceivable ways, wherein every feature of his face, every motion of his limbs should be reflected and re-reflected, until his personality in all sorts of disguises and contortions, should seem to fill all space and stretch away into infinitude. Whose sanity could stand such a strain? Who would not emerge from perceptions clouded and nerves unstrung from a course of this 'self-consciousness torture,' as it might be called?" Archer goes on to note that "it is the inevitable tendency of the actor's art to build round him such a mirror-cell" (*About the Theatre* 219–22). On the pathology of acting in the period, see Worthen, *Idea* 131–53.

constraint exerted on the observer, the experimenter, the spectator. Much as it does in the panopticon, the spectator's interpretive freedom in the theater emerges within the substantial control placed on his or her activity by the apparatus that makes observation possible. The warden, after all, is free to gaze on the cells of the inmates only through the window of his own cell-like enclosure. To objectify *others* as public, as controlled by an "environment" which operates as fate, while remaining in a privileged position of observation, beyond representation: like the thematics of realistic drama, the relations that govern the realistic audience have been so fully "detextualized," rendered as a force of nature, that they appear to be merely the condition of theater itself.[7]

Stage technology and acting practice in the late nineteenth century enabled the realistic theater to place the audience before an integrated, freestanding tableau, "leaving the spectator free to draw his own moral from the picture" (Matthews, *Study* 89). The public's freedom of judgment, in the theater and elsewhere, is paradoxically framed by the constraints of the scene in which that freedom is enacted. The rhetoric of realism creates this "freedom" precisely through the denial of its own rhetoricity; this erasure is especially marked in accounts of playwriting, though we can see it in acting and directing as well. It is notable, for instance, that the antithesis to realism—"a picture of life, as it is or as it might be"—is not usually found in the expressionist, *symboliste*, or surreal theater, but in theater that explicitly avows its suasive purpose: political theater, known in this period in terms of its typical dramatic form, the thesis play. Thesis plays fail to produce realistic illusion by acknowledging the rhetorical character both of the drama and of the audience's response. As Archer suggests in *Play-Making*, thesis drama necessarily suffers "artistically from the obtrusive predominance of the theme—that is to say, the abstract element—over the human and concrete factors in the composition. . . . No outside force should appear to control the free rhythm of the action," or of the audience's reading of it (18–19).

Yet in *Play-Making* Archer has written a manual for controlling the dramatic action and its effect on the audience, and the playwriting he prescribes shapes the contours of the audience's freedom and necessity. Archer sees a symbiosis between the world offered by the playwright and the composition of the audience, implicitly acknowledging that the audience's sense of freedom is devised as an effect of the theater. The freedom of the spectator must be read against the substantial ground of necessity, his or her constraint by social opportunity, theatrical manners, and the playwright's clever manipulation of dramatic form and theatrical perspective:

> Again, at one class of theatre, the author of a sporting play is bound to exhibit a horse-race on the stage, or he is held to have shirked his obligatory scene. At another class of theatre, we shall have a scene, perhaps, in a box in the Grand Stand, where some Lady Gay Spanker shall breathlessly depict, from start to finish, the race which is visible to her, but invisible to the audience. At a third class of the theatre, the "specifically dramatic effect" to be extracted from a horse-race is found in a scene in a Black-Country slum, where a group of working-men and women are feverishly awaiting the evening paper which shall bring them the result of the St. Leger, involving for some of them opulence—to the extent, perhaps, of a £5 note—and for others ruin.   (238)

Archer's description precisely records the structure of visibility sustaining the production of an audience and its interpretive prerogatives. The lower classes are placed directly before, practically amidst, the spectacle. The theater replicates the spectacle of social life, casting them as an unreflective, tractable crowd, absorbed in sensational events and lacking the interest or ability to penetrate to their cause. The upper-class theater of society drama shifts attention from the race to the response of its well-bred stage audience. While the lower classes are seduced by the superficial hum of events, "society" replicates the world in its own self-absorbed and dizzy futility. In the third example, apparently an instance of the "new drama," the stage claims for its subject the social consequences that result from horse racing. This theater provides the audience with a complex and contradictory role, one that invites both empathetic engagement and a pacifying separation, a summons to action and an actual paralysis. The audience scrutinizes the consequences of gambling and is invited to criticize the social and political organization that permits it. Yet the social process that connects the

---

[7] On the detextualization of the body, see Berger.

slum to the track (and, of course, the track to the banks, to real estate interests, to the audience) remains invisible, undramatized, much like the audience's invisible, voyeuristic relation to the stage. These spectators see neither the action of the race nor themselves dramatized but occupy a position of interpretation and judgment. Yet the apparent power of the audience is also neutralized, since that power cannot be put into action: neither the audience's relation to the dramatic subject nor its implication in the theatrical production can be legitimately recognized.

"With Sardou play-making is not merely as much a trade as clock-making; it is the same trade." Although the mechanics of well-made dramaturgy are often mocked, they remain essential to the ideal "impersonality of the drama" in the turn-of-the-century theater (Walkley, *Playhouse* 80, 14). This impersonality is claimed by the mechanical "logic" of the well-made play. The action of such plays turns relentlessly on the revelation of "facts" (secrets, confessions, coincidents, letters, and so on), information which assumes the role of fate for characters and audience alike. Well-made dramaturgy claims to preserve this "impersonality" and, consequently, the freedom of the spectator, by assigning to information itself a transcendent explanatory power. Finding the plotting of Pinero's *The Second Mrs Tanqueray* (1893; unless otherwise noted, plays are dated by first stage production) to be "clear, simple, natural," William Archer explicitly naturalizes Pinero's relentlessly coincidental plot to the process of social life: the "limitations of *Mrs Tanqueray* are really the limitations of the dramatic form" (see 1893, 125–39). The explanatory character of this drama is partly epitomized by the functional necessity of the *raisonneur*, who points to a desire for interpretive closure implied in the reciprocity between well-made causality, the information it offers as explanation, and an interpretive situation outside or beyond the action itself. The familiar conventions of well-made plotting constitute a self-propelled dramatic machine. The audience ratifies this dramatic closure by marshaling information into an explanation, one that accounts for and totalizes the process of the dramatic action from which it has been exiled. To Archer, and to his theater, the working of "well-made" conventions has been so fully "transformed into feeling" as to be definitive of the working of ideology more generally: "an ideology which men will not feel to be an ideology," as Georg Lukács once put it ("Sociology" 443).[8]

Realistic production invites empathy and even understanding, but it invites us to practice that understanding only as spectators. June Howard and others have suggested that in naturalistic fiction, the role of the spectator prevents understanding and self-awareness from being translated into action, into the brute behavior so often described by the spectatorial heroes of naturalistic novels (see 106–16). Like the brilliant flash that Jacob Riis used in his pioneering photographs of New York slums, *How the Other Half Lives* (1890), the realistic stage tends to reveal the sordid constraints of social reality while sentimentalizing its characters to a more privileged audience. "Realistic" observation seems finally to deny the working of society at the moment that it is most profoundly active and visible. The politics of the realistic theater, like the rhetoric of realistic theatrical production, are conveyed through the concealment of a specific agency: the mystified social environment of the drama, the behavioristic transparency of acting style, the detheatricalized absence of the audience. Like the camera—its most pervasive metaphor—the realistic theater claims to offer images of an objective reality to an audience of detached observers; like photography, the realistic drama tends to imply how relations of visibility themselves encode other less apparent relations, relations of consciousness, of interpretation, of power.

The realistic stage assigns interpretive power and freedom to a class of patrons identified as absent, largely by imposing a certain kind of activity on the audience as the sign of its freedom. Meanwhile, it discloses others onstage as the products of an ineffable "environment," through the medium of a mise-en-scène and a histrionic technique that conceals or denies its working, its agency in the spectacle. The rhetoric of realism appears to enable the spectators to escape their own representation as the condition of entertainment, but the "privacy" it produces for the spectators becomes, finally, both a form of privilege and a kind of prison. The rhetorical character of this privacy intrudes again and again in realistic drama, as though the drama were unable to repress its own

---

[8] It should be noted that not everyone was as easily seduced as Archer by the "well-made" structure of feeling in *The Second Mrs Tanqueray*. Shaw remarked that "the only necessary conditions of this situation are that the persons concerned shall be respectable enough to be shocked by it, and that the step-mother shall be an improper person. Mr Pinero has not got above this minimum" (*Our Theatres* 1:46).

rhetoricity. Like *Three Sisters*, many plays expose the rhetorical character of stage realism and so dramatize the procedures that constitute "realistic" effects and interpretation; Ibsen's *The Wild Duck* (1885) provides a classic example of this kind of self-reflection. The play is fully within the orbit of realism: the densely material environment both controls characerization and helps to explain the action to the audience; the characters are integrated into their object world; the play urges a thematic concern for inheritance as a figure for the persistence of the past and the confinements of social life; and the play's well-made progression provides the gradual revelation of "facts" with a markedly "explanatory" force. Yet Ibsen strategically questions the confident rhetoric of realism, most directly in the representation of what might be called "well-made" thinking, in that the most benighted, unrealistic form of plotting in the play is practiced by Gregers Werle. Ibsen shows Gregers's disinterested plan to produce a "true marriage" for the Ekdals to be a solipsistic, manipulative fantasy by emphasizing its theatrical quality, particularly when Gregers is disillusioned by the failure of his climactic *scène à faire*: "I was really positive that when I came through that door I'd be met by a transfigured light in both your faces. And what do I see instead but this gloomy, heavy, dismal—" (459). Much as he does when improvising multiple causes for most of the play's effects—the history of blindness in both families, for instance—Ibsen carefully subverts the certainty of "well-made" logic, emptying it of value as an "objective" means to truth or understanding.

Ibsen's most searching investigation of the rhetoric of realism, though, develops through his use of theatrical space, particularly the loft area, that stagey playground whose scattered props and tawdry trees offset the insistent verisimilitude of the studio downstage. Something like chiaroscuro in painting, the obscure garret space—never fully seen by the audience—works to highlight the "reality" of the more visible forestage area, contributing to what Michael Fried has called in another context the "overall impression of self-sufficiency and repleteness that functions as a decisive hallmark of the 'real'" (59). Like Jean Genet's erotic theater, the garret room needs both false and authentic details to be persuasive to Ibsen's characters. To be redeemed from the realm of private fantasy, to function as a reduction of the "reality" that it replaces, displaces, and avoids, the garret needs "real" properties, real trees, a real duck. As an onstage theater, on the other hand, the garret seems to infiltrate and disrupt the realistic insistence that a complex social environment *can* be reduced metonymically to the stage scene through selective behavioral and material identity with the larger world it represents.[9] What seems striking about the loft in this context is not only its fantastic intrusion into verisimilar stage space but the ways in which this theatricalized milieu is entered and interpreted by Gregers and the Ekdals. The spectators onstage are only intermittently able to agree on their reading of the garret space, to join in the single perspective that coerces the theatrical spectators to read as a single public and to view the stage as objective reality. The tragedy, or irony, of *The Wild Duck* is that the garret theater seems not to refer to the world but only to the characters themselves, as when Gregers is shown the wild duck and immediately allegorizes it: "I'm hoping things will go the same with me as with the wild duck."

Ibsen's point here seems twofold. As a spectator, Gregers implies that objective interpretation is impossible, that all schemes claiming objectivity will in fact conceal unacknowledged agendas. To take Gregers as a model would lead us to look for other examples in the play where observation is shown to be a form of self-deluding blindness. Relling's assertion of the "life lie," for example, might seem to restate Gregers's "claim of the ideal," not to counter it. Relling's ability to interpret and guide the actions of others arises from his adoption of a spectatorial attitude much like Gregers's, perhaps as a way of preserving his own self-image as realistic healer. Werle, too, stages a play—the Ekdal family itself—that is manifestly a form of self-displacement. By providing for Old Ekdal, Gina, and Hedvig, he both assuages his guilt and frees himself from implication in their plight: his power in society is largely signified in the play through his ability to cast the family as a distinct "tableau" while keeping his own relation to the Ekdals in obscurity. And of course Hjalmar Ekdal's profession itself might be taken as an index of Ibsen's skeptical regard for his own theatrical procedures, for photography in *The Wild Duck* is mainly an art of retouching, an art that threatens

---

[9] On metonymy as reduction, see Burke, *Grammar* 505–07. Bert O. States amplifies Burke's position with reference to the practices of realistic theater, when he remarks: "Metonymy and synecdoche, as we find them on the realistic stage, are devices for reducing states, or qualities, or attributes, or whole entities like societies, to visible things in which they somehow inhere" (65).

to lead, in Hedvig's case, to blindness. *The Wild Duck* questions the premise that we can "know" as detached, uninvolved, "experimental" observers; the play offers no position that is not compromised by its procedure for staging others to the view.[10] To fail to attend to the ways that we make the world, to fail to recognize ourselves among the play's gallery of absent authors, is to enter into the delusions afflicting Ibsen's characters and to reproduce the circumstantial contradictions defining our role in the realistic audience.

As Amy Kaplan has remarked in her fine study of American realism, our attitudes toward the form and purposes of realism have undergone an important change since Ibsen's era, perhaps even since the heyday of Tennessee Williams; far from an "objective reflection of social life," realism has become, for us at least, "a fictional conceit, or deceit, packaging and naturalizing an official version of the ordinary" (1). To recognize the ideological work of stage realism, though, requires an inquiry into the specifically theatrical forms of this process, how the rhetoric of realism identifies the drama, its stage production, and the activities of its audience within the stabilizing attitudes of its sustaining culture. This work generally takes a double shape, which Michael Fried, in a telling reading of Thomas Eakins's paintings, suggestively describes:

> The result is a tension or competition between two fundamentally different modes of seeing— one that looks to enter the representational field and to merge its interests with those of the protagonists, inevitably losing sight of the whole in the process of doing so, and another that remains emphatically outside the representation, viewing the painting with something like detachment but also with special concern for "formal" values of a certain sort. (77)

These "conflicting modes of seeing, one excessively intimate and the other excessively detached" (85), are akin to the modes of experience articulated by the realistic theater, which invites sympathy for its Paulas and Hedvigs, but a sympathy that is necessarily performed across a paralyzing distance, a distance that conceals the audience's actual and figural role in the production of the "problems" onstage. The relation between these two kinds of seeing provides the ideological frame of realistic interpretation. In this sense, the realistic theater of disclosure is also a theater of concealment. The question is whether the space of concealment that we inhabit will also be exposed, be shown to be complicit in the making of the world.

---

[10] Indeed, Ingmar Bergman's 1972 production of the play emphasized just this point, by locating the loft downstage: the Ekdals looked through the loft toward the audience, now placed literally in the sphere of fantasy. See Marker and Marker.

WORKS CITED

Archer, William. *About the Theatre*. London: T. Fisher Unwin, 1886.

———. *Play-Making*. New York: Dodd, Mead, 1912.

———. *The Theatrical "World" for 1893*. London: Walter Scott, n.d. [1894].

Barthes, Roland. *Writing Degree Zero*. Boston: Beacon, 1970.

Berger, Harry, Jr. "Bodies and Texts." *Representations* 17 (Winter 1987): 144–66.

Burke, Kenneth. *A Grammar of Motives*. 1945. Berkeley: U of California P, 1969.

Foucault, Michel. *Discipline and Punish: The Birth of the Prison*. Trans. Alan Sheridan. New York: Vintage, 1979.

Fried, Michael. "Realism, Writing, and Disfiguration in Thomas Eakins's *Gross Clinic*, with a Postscript on Stephen Crane's Upturned Faces." *Representations* 9 (Winter 1985): 33–104.

Ibsen, Henrik. *The Wild Duck. The Complete Major Prose Plays*. Ed. and trans. Rolf Fjelde. New York: New American Library, 1978.

Kaplan, Amy. *The Social Construction of American Realism*. Chicago: U of Chicago P, 1988.

Lukács, Georg. "The Sociology of Modern Drama." Trans. Lee Baxandall. *The Theory of the Modern Stage*. Ed. Eric Bentley. Harmondsworth: Penguin, 1976, 421–50.

Marker, Frederick J., and Lise-Lone Marker. *Ibsen's Lively Art: A Performance Study of the Major Plays*. Cambridge: Cambridge UP, 1989.

Marker, Lise-Lone. *David Belasco: Naturalism in the American Theatre*. Princeton: Princeton UP, 1975.

Matthews, Brander. *The Principles of Playmaking and Other Discussions of the Drama*. New York: Scribner, 1919.

———. *A Study of the Drama*. Boston: Houghton Mifflin, 1910.

Newhall, Beaumont. *The History of Photography*. Rev. ed. New York: Museum of Modern Art, 1982.

Riis, Jacob A. *How the Other Half Lives: Studies Among the Tenements of New York*. New York: Scribner, 1890.

Shaw, Bernard. *Our Theatres in the Nineties.* 3 vols. London: Constable, 1932.

———. Preface to *Mrs Warren's Profession. Plays Unpleasant.* Harmondsworth: Penguin, 1975.

States, Bert O. *Great Reckonings in Little Rooms: On the Phenomenology of Theater.* Berkeley: U of California P, 1985.

Styan, J. L. *Modern Drama in Theory and Practice.* Cambridge: Cambridge UP, 1981.

Szondi, Peter. *Theory of the Modern Drama.* Ed. and trans. Michael Hays. Minneapolis: U of Minnesota P, 1987.

Walkley, A. B. *More Prejudice.* London: William Heinemann, 1923.

———. *Pastiche and Prejudice.* London: William Heinemann, 1921.

———. *Playhouse Impressions.* London: T. Fisher Unwin, 1892.

Williams, Raymond. "Social environment and theatrical environment: The case of English naturalism." *English Drama: Forms and Development. Essays in Honour of Muriel Clara Bradbrook.* Ed. Marie Axton and Raymond Williams. Cambridge: Cambridge UP, 1977. 203–23.

Worthen, William B. *The Idea of the Actor: Drama and the Ethics of Performance.* Princeton: Princeton UP, 1984.

Zola, Émile. "Le Naturalisme au théâtre." *Oeuvres critiques 2.* Vol. 11 of *Oeuvres Complètes.* Paris: Cercle du Livre Précieux, 1968. 14 vols. 1966–70.

VI

THE UNITED STATES

OCIAL AND TECHNOLOGICAL CHANGE TRANSFORMED THE WORLD IN THE late nineteenth and early twentieth centuries. Between 1860 and 1980, the United States emerged from a crippling civil war and then two world wars to become a dominant global power. However, despite the nation's emergence as a major player on the world stage, the arts in the United States were shaped by divided and contradictory impulses. The desire to imitate European models competed with a desire to bring distinctively American arts into being. Even as the Civil War threatened to destroy the nation itself, writers such as Walt Whitman, Ralph Waldo Emerson, Henry David Thoreau, and others gave voice to a national literature that both incorporated and redefined European traditions. With the global expansion of U.S. influence, especially after World War I, the question of an "American culture" became a pressing one; after World War II, certain forms of culture became one of the United States' most significant exports.

In the theater, the modern era has brought with it the search for a quintessentially "American" drama, in which theme, setting, and characterization explore American experience, often by invoking and then discarding styles and attitudes derived from the European stage. In a sense, American drama in the twentieth century translates the idea of American political freedom into more abstract, metaphorical, even Romantic terms, as a conflict between individual freedom and the pressures of confining social realities such as economic hardship, social class, gender, and race. The search for an American idiom in the theater absorbs the stylistic experiments of European modernism and reshapes them, bending the formal innovation of the European theater to American issues and concerns.

The democratic experience and populist rhetoric of American public life has generally resisted the idea of a national culture emanating from a single center like New York City or Washington, D.C. For this reason, perhaps, the dream of a national theater has repeatedly failed. In the nineteenth century, westward expansion brought theater from New York, Philadelphia, and Boston to the midwestern cities of Chicago, St. Louis, and Kansas City, and then to Los Angeles and San Francisco, and to scores of smaller towns between the Mississippi and the Pacific. The theater was a widely dispersed, local affair. Towns often boasted theaters that could be used for opera, drama, or vaudeville, and that supported local companies while also catering to touring shows with stars drawn from New York and Europe. Although a lively local theater thrived throughout the country, offering melodrama, classical plays, comedies, and other entertainments, the appetite for touring shows created a demand for organizations capable of handling scheduling problems for local theaters and regional booking agencies.

In 1896 a group of theatrical entrepreneurs headed by Charles Frohman formed a nationwide organization of booking agents called the SYNDICATE. In a sense, they created the first model of how a national theater might work in the United States. The Syndicate offered theater managers a full season of touring shows—provided that the manager contracted to deal only with the Syndicate. By gaining exclusive control over theaters on key travel routes, the Syndicate thwarted competition from other touring producers and often even denied local companies the use of local theaters. At its height, the Syndicate had exclusive rights to more than 700 theaters. It could blackball non-Syndicate performers from working by threatening producers who hired them, and it could withdraw Syndicate support from any manager who booked non-Syndicate shows or performers.

The effects of the Syndicate were profound and shaped the American theater for the next half-century. The Syndicate's grip on the theater effectively extinguished major

EUROPEAN INFLUENCE AND AMERICAN INNOVATION

"THE" AMERICAN THEATER?

professional theater outside New York as a source of new plays and productions; it also influenced playwriting, since the Syndicate developed plays only as commercial properties that could be successfully marketed to a general audience coast-to-coast. Although the Syndicate's power was resisted by a few famous actors and powerful producers, its approach was imitated by other groups. The parochial interests of the New York stage—where the shows of such organizations originated—became in practice the interests of the American theater, and New York became the center of theatrical production and theatrical investment. The revival of significant, professional "regional" theaters as centers of new productions—Margo Jones's Theater 47 in Dallas, the Alley Theater of Houston, the Arena Stage in Washington, D.C., the Actors Workshop of San Francisco, the Guthrie Theater in Minneapolis—had to wait until the 1940s and 1950s. The Syndicate's fortunes also point out the fallacy inherent in the notion of *an* American theater. Throughout its history, the American theater has embraced a range of dynamic and contradictory attitudes toward the stage and its place in society: New York *vs.* the "provinces," mainstream *vs.* elite, conventional *vs.* experimental, commercial *vs.* artistic. Theatrical innovation has been spurred primarily by theaters outside the commercial mainstream, especially by small, amateur "little theaters," by university and college theaters, by community theaters, and by ethnic theaters.

EUROPEAN INFLUENCE AND AMERICAN INNOVATION

The growth of American drama and theater was decisively shaped by the commercial climate of the stage, and also by the United States' isolation from the energetic traditions of European theater. Although turn-of-the-century Broadway developed a homegrown version of theatrical realism—epitomized by writer/producer David Belasco's *The Governor's Lady* (1912), which reproduced the interior of a familiar theater-district restaurant onstage—European experimentation made its impact on America in more indirect ways, usually only after those experiments had crystallized into a body of theatrical practices and conventions. Many major companies toured the United States. The Abbey Theater came with John Millington Synge's *The Playboy of the Western World* in 1911–1912, and the German producer Max Reinhardt brought his spectacular productions to the U.S. in 1912, 1914, 1924, and 1927–1928. The British director Harley Granville Barker, who sponsored Shaw's plays and had gained fame as an innovative director of Shakespeare, directed in New York in 1915; the Ballets Russes toured in 1916; and the Moscow Art Theater—whose disciples Richard Boleslavsky and Maria Ouspenskaya founded the American Laboratory Theater in 1923—performed in 1923–1924.

Many of these companies—the Abbey and the Moscow Art Theater in particular—had begun as small, independent, amateur theaters, and their work was most directly implemented in the United States by similar groups. Some innovation came from the new college and university programs in drama, George Pierce Baker's famous playwriting course at Harvard University in the first decades of the century (taken by Eugene O'Neill, among many others) and George T. Montgomery's program for black writers and performers at Howard University in the 1920s were only the beginning of a concerted effort to bring theater and drama into the university curriculum and to develop a greater awareness of progressive theater. However, it largely fell to the LITTLE THEATER MOVEMENT to assimilate this new work and redirect it toward particularly American concerns. Innovation in the American theater came largely from these small companies, committed to mounting new and uncommercial work. The Chicago Little Theater, the Toy Theater of Boston, the Neighborhood Playhouse and the Washington Square Playhouse of New York, and Detroit's Arts and Crafts Theater were all in operation by 1917, and the Little Negro Theater Movement was producing plays in Harlem and Washington, D.C., as well.

The Provincetown Playhouse provides a model of the "little theaters" and their fortunes in the early twentieth century. Founded in 1915 in Provincetown, Massachusetts—

an artists' retreat at the tip of Cape Cod—the company was initially a group of young amateurs intent on theater, including the playwright Susan Glaspell; her husband, George Cram Cook; and, later, Eugene O'Neill. In the first year, the players produced plays in their summer homes. In 1916 they converted an old wharf building into a small theater and produced, among other plays, O'Neill's *Bound East for Cardiff.* In the autumn, the players returned to New York and opened a small theater in Greenwich Village. The company could hardly afford complex and expensive sets and turned its efforts instead toward a simple and realistic kind of performance. Eugene O'Neill's early plays were produced by the Provincetown company, and after he became a successful Broadway playwright, he continued to open many of his plays there. Like all of the "little theaters," the Provincetown had difficulty managing the transition from a small amateur company to the larger demands of a self-sustaining professional company. It went through a series of transformations before closing in 1929, having introduced O'Neill to the stage and having staged plays by John Reed, Edna St. Vincent Millay, Susan Glaspell, Djuna Barnes, Edmund Wilson, Paul Green, Wallace Stevens, Theodore Dreiser, August Strindberg, and many others.

In the United States, the freedom to make theater has always been qualified by the need to make it pay. The trials of sustaining artistic ambition in the commercial environment of the theater is the central narrative of the most innovative theatrical companies of the modern era. The ideal of an American theater remained tantalizing yet elusive and was often pursued in several ways, usually by developing a distinctive repertoire of plays, or by trying to define a typically American performance idiom. "Little theaters" like the Provincetown emphasized the production of American drama. Other theaters tried to produce American drama, the new European drama, and the classics for a larger audience than the "little theaters" could reach. The Theater Guild, for example, was organized in 1919 in New York as a subscription company specifically for the purpose of producing noncommercial plays. In the course of the next decade, the Guild staged plays by Shaw, Pirandello, Ibsen, and Strindberg, as well as plays by Americans like O'Neill and Elmer Rice. The Guild succeeded in incorporating American plays like O'Neill's *Strange Interlude* (1928) and Rice's *The Adding Machine* (1923) into the repertoire of serious modern drama and in bringing it to a significant public. However, following the stock market crash of 1929 and the economic depression that ensued, the Guild invested in a less adventuresome repertoire in the hopes of drawing a larger audience and so lost its original mission.

Although it sponsored an innovative selection of plays, the Theater Guild did not develop an original style of production. In 1931, several Guild members began a spin-off company—called simply the Group—for the purpose of investigating different kinds of drama and different approaches to performance. Eventually including Harold Clurman, Cheryl Crawford, Lee Strasberg, Elia Kazan, Sanford Meisner, and many others, the Group at first worked on plays examining the social ferment of the 1930s and the hardship of the Great Depression. Much as Chekhov became the centerpiece of Stanislavsky's Moscow Art Theater, so the plays of Clifford Odets became the Group's standards: *Awake and Sing!, Waiting for Lefty,* and *Golden Boy.* However, the Group's most extensive contribution to the American theater was its systematic importation of Stanislavskian acting techniques. In the Group, and later in the Actors Studio, actors were trained in Stanislavsky's approach to EMOTION MEMORY and GIVEN CIRCUMSTANCES, laying the groundwork for what became a distinctly "American" style of acting, acting that was emotionally spontaneous, grounded in subtext, psychologically realistic and nuanced. Nonetheless, the Group, the Studio, and the training they devised produced a generation of actors ready to meet the challenges of the burgeoning American drama of the 1940s and 1950s: Marlon Brando, Ben Gazzara, Karl Malden, Geraldine Page, Kim Stanley, Maureen Stapleton, and many others.

The impact of this acting can be seen in the great stage productions of the post-war period. The 1940s and early 1950s saw the development of a distinctively American approach to stage realism, balancing nuanced characterization with a concern for the social environment. Arthur Miller's *Death of a Salesman* and *The Crucible*, Tennessee Williams's *A Streetcar Named Desire* and *The Glass Menagerie*, and Eugene O'Neill's *The Iceman Cometh* and *Long Day's Journey into Night* demanded the subtle realism that became the hallmark of American acting and of American drama in the world repertoire. These plays—and their descendants, like the plays of Beth Henley, David Mamet, or Sam Shepard—succeeded by criticizing American ideals and institutions while at the same time exploring the psyche of the American character. Indeed, in these plays the American character often seems to be thwarted precisely by the process of American society. The fragile beauty of Tennessee Williams's Southern belles is usually crushed by the sordid realities of modern urban life; in Shepard's *True West*, the American West becomes a mythic battleground, where a yuppie and a drifter shoot it out for control of the image.

POSTWAR EXPERIMENTS

After World War II, the most significant innovations in American theater have come from small "experimental" theater companies. In part through the influence of Antonin Artaud's conception of a **THEATER OF CRUELTY** (see unit 7), and the several tours of Jerzy Grotowski's Lab Theater of Poland, experimental theater in the 1960s and 1970s tended to reject the esthetic of stage realism in favor of producing an immediate, quintessentially *theatrical* experience for its audiences. As a result, many productions in the 1960s and 1970s—the Living Theater's *Paradise Now*, the Performance Group's *Dionysus in 69*, the Open Theater's *The Serpent*, the work of the Bread and Puppet theater, of Mabou Mines, and many others—incorporated the audience as participants in the action. Many of these experiments also led to new forms of playwriting, in which classical notions of representation also were broken down. In Ntozake Shange's *spell #7* actors assume a variety of roles and represent them through a powerful and original blending of drama, music, and poetry.

Moreover, American drama continued to strike a compromise with the innovations of the European theater after the war. Eric Bentley—a brilliant scholar, director, playwright, and translator—worked indefatigably to bring Bertolt Brecht to the attention of the American theater. Brecht became particularly important in the United States as the Vietnam War and widespread civil and social discontent spurred the theater in more agitational, political directions. Feminist theater, ethnic theater, and gay and lesbian theater have all at times availed themselves of Brecht's theater theory and practice. The work of Luis Valdez and El Teatro Campesino in California in the 1960s and 1970s is a direct extension of Brecht's sense of theater. Bringing a flatbed truck to farmworkers' strikes, Teatro Campesino produced its short, political dramas to an active, involved audience and became part of the process of social change. "Absurdist" playwrights like Samuel Beckett, Harold Pinter, and Eugène Ionesco were also both produced and imitated in the United States, influencing the work of American playwrights like Edward Albee, Maria Irene Fornes, Jack Gelber, Adrienne Kennedy, David Mamet, and Sam Shepard. Indeed, in plays like Amiri Baraka's *Dutchman*, Sam Shepard's *True West*, and Maria Irene Fornes's *Fefu and Her Friends*, we can see the inflections of theater of the absurd in plays that are recognizably "American" in style and subject matter.

AFRICAN-AMERICAN DRAMA AND THEATER

In 1935, an act of Congress established the Federal Theater Project, as a way to employ workers left unemployed by the depression (see Aside). The Federal Theater Project also sponsored a Negro Unit, directed by John Houseman and Orson Welles, which operated in ten cities around the U.S.; two of its productions, an all-black *Macbeth* and *The Swing Mikado*, were among the Federal Theater's most successful productions. The fact of a separate Negro Unit points to a different crisis in the idea of an American theater. How could a theater largely in the hands of the white, Anglo, male, middle class adequately represent the diversity of the nation's experience, particularly the experience of the oppressed? As the poet and playwright Langston Hughes noted in "Notes on Commercial Theater," published in 1940, the stage had in many ways appropriated African-American culture, systematically absorbing it into its own dominant values:

> Yep, you done taken my blues and gone.
> You also took my spirituals and gone.
> You put me in Macbeth and Carmen Jones
> And all kinds of Swing Mikados
> And in everything but what's about me—
> But someday somebody'll
> Stand up and talk about me,
> And write about me—
> Black and beautiful—

Far from representing authentic black experience in America, such theater more often confirmed the discriminatory fantasies already prominent on the stage and in society. Such stereotypes as the boozy Irishman, the dull Swede, the sunny and/or murderous Italian, and the greedy Jew—appearing even in "realistic" plays like Rice's *Street Scene* (1929)—work to reinforce the "normative" perspective of dominant culture, reflecting the attitudes, behavior, and social practices that oppress such groups in the world outside the theater. It is not surprising, then, that throughout the history of the United States, ethnic theaters have played a prominent part in maintaining the cultural identity of America's minority populations: the Yiddish theater of New York, Polish theaters in Chicago, Scandinavian theaters throughout the Midwest, a thriving circuit of Spanish-language theaters shared by Mexico and Southwestern states from Texas to California, Cuban-influenced theater in Florida, and Puerto Rican theater in New York. Some of these theaters produced versions of classic European plays in their own accents, but most developed their own dramatic forms, as ways of maintaining themselves in the face of a brutally exclusive "American" culture.

The experience of slavery places African Americans in a different position vis-à-vis the culture of the United States, and the black theater has had a profound impact on the course of the American stage. Although an African Theater Company was founded in New York in 1821—sponsoring, among others, the brilliant Shakespearean actor Ira Aldridge (1807–1867) who left the United States for a distinguished career in Europe—in the main, African Americans had little direct access to the theater before the twentieth century. Black characters had long figured as stage villains and comic buffoons in American drama. Played by white actors in blackface makeup, these abusive types literally enacted white attitudes toward racial difference. "Jim Crow" was first popularized by the white song-and-dance man T. D. Rice in the 1830s, and more "sympathetic" characters, like Tom in the hugely popular stage adaptations of Harriet Beecher Stowe's *Uncle Tom's Cabin* (1832), were devised by white authors and played by white actors. The minstrel troupes that became popular after the Civil War for depicting romanticized vignettes of plantation life were also first performed by white actors. Later, black performers—in minstrel troupes, or in the newly popular "Negro musicals"—often had little choice other than to enact these stereotypes themselves, for such roles were the only openings available on the stage (even black theaters were usually financed and operated by white entrepreneurs). Despite small inroads like the Lafayette Theater (founded in Harlem in 1915), representing black experience to America at large was almost exclusively the prerogative of white actors, producers, playwrights, and performers. In this regard, the theater—like the institutions of literature, the press, the legal system, and state and federal government—denied African Americans their own voice.

If the Group Theater and the Actors Studio created an identifiably "American" approach to acting, the Federal Theater Project succeeded—briefly—in creating a truly national theater. An act of Congress established the Federal Theater Project in 1935 under the Works Projects Administration, with Hallie Flanagan Davis (1890–1969) as director. Like other WPA projects, the Federal Theater was designed both to employ workers idled by the Depression and to provide service to the community. It was an enormous undertaking; in New York City alone, half the theaters were closed by 1933 and half its population of actors unemployed. Given the mission of providing employment by hiring large casts and supporting personnel, and a commitment to dramatizing contemporary social issues, the Federal Theater developed its most notable genre, the Living Newspaper. Living Newspapers incorporated dialogue taken from newspapers and other public media into a series of vignettes, readings, films, and other techniques to a problem in current national and world affairs: the farm crisis in *Triple A Plowed Under* (1936), housing in *One-Third of a Nation* (1938), rural electrification in *Power* (1937). At its height, the Federal Theater had branches in 40 states; these branches staged productions devised by the project's directors, using their own local resources, and often developed their own material. In 1936, for instance, a stage adaptation of Sinclair Lewis's *It Can't Happen Here* opened simultaneously in twenty-one theaters around the country, including black-cast and Yiddish productions. The Federal Theater ran for four full seasons before being terminated by Congress in 1939: it financed twelve hundred productions of 830 major works, at times employing more than 10,000 people, most of whom had been unemployed. Admission to its shows was inexpensive, and in an average week five hundred thousand people saw its productions; over its four years of production, its audiences numbered more than thirty million people. In New York alone, more than twelve million people saw its productions. However, in an era of labor unrest and the pervasive fear of outside agitation, the Newspapers were seen by the Project's enemies in government—many of whom opposed the WPA altogether—as too left-wing for government support.

Despite its demise, the United State's only truly national theater had significant influence on the course of

Spurred in part by successful plays by white dramatists that self-consciously attempted to "humanize" black characters for white audiences—O'Neill's *The Emperor Jones* (1920) and *All God's Chillun Got Wings* (1924), Marc Connelly's *The Green Pastures* (1930), Paul Green's *In Abraham's Bosom* (1926), and Dubose and Dorothy Heyward's *Porgy* (1920; transformed into the Gershwin musical *Porgy and Bess* in 1935)—black actors and writers became galvanized to "stand up and talk" about themselves. Throughout the 1920s the **LITTLE NEGRO THEATER MOVEMENT** sponsored plays of black life largely for black audiences. The Lafayette Theater, for example, opened Willis Richardson's *The Chipwoman's Fortune* in 1923; it later became the first play by a black playwright to reach Broadway. In the 1920s and 1930s, black drama increasingly addressed the politics of racism in the United States, while also depicting the effect of racism in daily life. Several organizations worked to sponsor African-American drama and theater. W. E. B. DuBois, a founder of the National Association for the Advancement of Colored People (NAACP), used his *Crisis* magazine—in collaboration with the National Urban League's *Opportunity*—to give a series of prizes to promising black playwrights; winners included Eulalie Spence's *Foreign Mail* (1926), Zora Neale Hurston's *Colorstruck* and *Spears* (1925), and Georgia Douglas Johnson's *Blue Blood* (1926). The NAACP also sponsored the production of plays, including Angelina Weld Grimke's influential drama of a young woman's reaction to the lynching of her father and brother, *Rachel* (1916). *Rachel* was one of the first of a series of plays about lynching. How this important genre of black theater—and a crucial element of

American theater and drama. Not only did the Federal Theater have huge audiences, but it brought new audiences into the theater: 65 percent of its audiences were seeing a stage play for the first time. The Living Newspapers developed a home-grown adaptation of the techniques of European experimental theater (including Brechtian epic theater) in the United States. In this sense, the Federal Theater inspired the work of several distinguished theater companies that survived its demise, notably John Houseman's (1915–1985) Mercury Theater, which produced Mark Blitzstein's *The Cradle Will Rock*, and a distinguished series of productions of modern and classic plays—by Shaw, Büchner, Shakespeare, and others. In addition, the Negro Units of the Federal Theater operated in Seattle, Hartford, Philadelphia, Newark, Los Angeles, Boston, Birmingham, Raleigh, San Francisco, and Chicago, employing more than 800 people and producing seventy-five productions in the

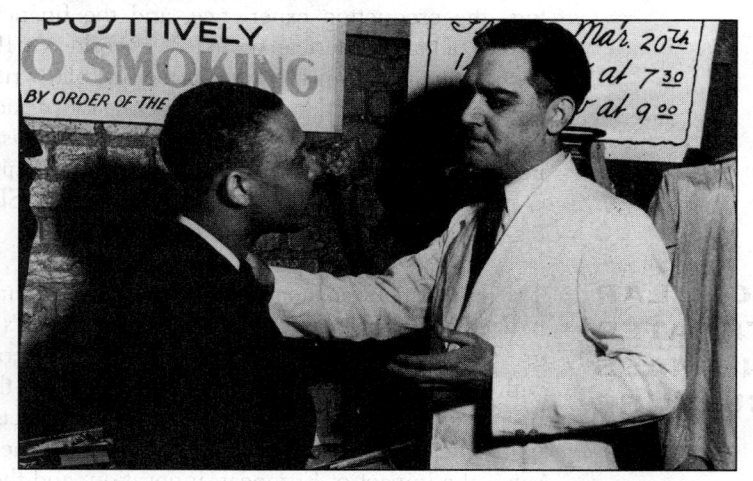

LIVING NEWSPAPER

The Federal Theater Project dramatizes news events in the New York production of 1935.

project's four years of operation. Most importantly, the Federal Theater enabled a generation of actors, designers,

directors, and playwrights to survive the Depression, and it brought the theater powerfully into the national scene.

black experience in the United States—was both overlooked and distorted by white theater is the subject of Alice Childress's brilliant play *Trouble in Mind*, which opened off-Broadway in 1955. Finally, black colleges, universities, and even high schools also became centers for a new dramatic repertoire. In 1921, Montgomery T. Gregory formed a department of Dramatic Arts at Howard University in Washington, D.C., and with Alain Locke developed an influential program in acting, playwriting, and theatrical production, offering the first institutionalized training for black writers and performers in the United States.

In a 1926 playbill for Harlem's Krigwa Players, W. E. B. DuBois described the goals of a black theater:

> The plays of a real Negro theater must be: *One: About us.* That is, they must have plots which reveal Negro life as it is. *Two: By us.* That is, they must be written by Negro authors who understand from birth and continual association just what it means to be a Negro today. *Three: For us.* That is, the theater must cater primarily to Negro audiences and be supported and sustained by their entertainment and approval. *Fourth: Near us.* The theater must be in a Negro neighborhood near the mass of ordinary Negro people.

Throughout the 1930s and 1940s, African-American playwrights and actors came into increasing national prominence, both by developing DuBois's agenda and by working to bring an authentic black drama to a wider audience. Langston Hughes wrote a number of plays in the 1930s, including the well-known *Mulatto* (1935); the Federal Theater Project produced W. E. B. DuBois's *Haiti* at the Lafayette Theater; and playwrights trained at Howard were produced in New York and elsewhere. The founding of the companies like the American Negro Theater in 1939, the Negro Playwrights Company in 1940, and the Negro Ensemble Company in 1957 began to meet DuBois's charge, developing the actors, the production experience, and the financing that would sustain the explosive growth of black American drama after World War II. When Lorraine Hansberry's *A Raisin in the Sun* opened in 1959, it was the first play written by a black woman to reach Broadway, the first directed by a black director (Lloyd Richards), and the first financed predominantly by African Americans. The success of *Raisin* foretold the success of black theater in the coming decades, as black playwrights—Amiri Baraka, Adrienne Kennedy, Charles Gordone, Ed Bullins, Charles Fuller, Ntozake Shange, August Wilson, and many others—came to shape the American theater.

POPULAR THEATER AND MASS CULTURE

The tension between commercial viability and dramatic achievement is perhaps best symbolized by Broadway itself, the American theater's "magnificent invalid," where even the greatest American plays can hardly compare in terms of commercial and popular success with Broadway's most uniquely American genre: the musical. Musical theater has a long history in the United States, and in many respects its fortunes parallel those of the dramatic theater. Musical theater also witnessed the tyranny of national producing syndicates, the impact of European innovation, and the powerful contributions of black and ethnic cultures. However, the integration of song and dance, orchestral music, and (usually) a romantic plot characteristic of the Broadway musical really dates to the period of World War II, probably to Richard Rodgers and Oscar Hammerstein's *Oklahoma!* (1943), which ran for 2248 performances (*Death of a Salesman*, in contrast, ran for 742). *Oklahoma!* provided the model not only for other Rodgers and Hammerstein hits—*Carousel* (1945), *South Pacific* (1949), *The King and I* (1951)—but for other musicals as well: Alan Jay Lerner and Frederick Loewe's updating of Shaw's *Pygmalion* in *My Fair Lady* (1956), Frank Loesser's *Guys and Dolls* (1950), and Leonard Bernstein, Stephen Sondheim, and Arthur Laurents's *West Side Story* (1957). Although the form of the Broadway musical underwent significant changes in the 1970s and 1980s, its popularity points to one of the ways that the theater has sought to recapture an audience from film and television: by emphasizing the unique excitement of a dazzling live spectacle. The musical theater also points to the fundamental conditions of the Broadway theatrical economy as well. Musicals remain popular with producers because the huge financial investment required to mount a musical can repay much larger returns for investors than any "straight" play.

Throughout the history of the stage in the West, important theaters have succeeded both in creating innovative drama and in creating a public. However, the American theater—if there is *an* American theater—is a different entity altogether from the citizens' theater of classical Athens, the courtly theater of Racine and Molière, or even the educated circle of subscribers to Shaw's Court Theater. In a sense, this difference can be traced to the fact that the American theater first came into force only in the twentieth century, at just the moment when other dramatic media—film and television—began to compete with it. The American theater has had to define itself in the environment of modern mass culture. Not only are film and television more accessible to most people, but the technology and distribution of such mass media have fundamentally altered our understanding both of drama and performance, and of what an audience *is*. "The American theater" has always been a critical fiction, homogenizing the diversity of stage activity in the United States, writing some forms of drama—chiefly American realistic plays— into history, and writing others out of it. Today, it may be equally artificial to separate live theater from other forms of dramatic production, forms that have massively changed the terrain where dramatic performance takes place.

 The conflict in Sam Shepard's True West *escalates when Austin (Gary Sinise) confronts Lee (John Malkovitch) after a night of stealing toasters.*

 The Angel appears above Prior Walter in Tony Kushner's Angels in America, Part I: Millennium Approaches.

 This scene from August Wilson's Fences *shows how Wilson's attention to the play's social environment has been translated into a detailed* mise-en-scène; *here, James Earl Jones plays the role of Troy Maxon.*

■ SUSAN GLASPELL ■

Susan Glaspell (1882–1948) was born in Iowa, studied at Drake University in Des Moines and at the University of Chicago, and then briefly pursued a career as a journalist. With her husband, George Cram Cook, she founded the Provincetown Playhouse and wrote many of the plays it produced: *Suppressed Desires* (1914, written with Cook), a spoof of the vogue for psychoanalysis among New York's intellectual elite; *Trifles* (1916); *Close the Book* (1917); *A Woman's Honor* (1918); and *Tickless Time* (1918, again written with Cook). After the reorganization of the Provincetown in 1921, Glaspell wrote a series of full-length, often experimental, plays: *Inheritors* (1920), *The Verge* (1921), and *Alison's House* (1930). *Alison's House*, based loosely on the life of Emily Dickinson and her family, won Glaspell the Pulitzer Prize in 1930. Glaspell then retired from playwriting and largely from the theater as well, returning briefly to serve as the director of the Mid-West Play Bureau for the Federal Theater Project.

TRIFLES

Trifles is an important play in the development of American realism. It poses a distinct contrast to Eugene O'Neill's early plays, with which it shared the Provincetown stage. O'Neill's realistic plays attempt to filter an abstract, metaphysical longing into the drab world of his down-and-out drifters and sailors. Glaspell's drama more directly examines the values and behavior of the society she brings to the stage. In *Trifles*—and in the short story "A Jury of Her Peers," which she adapted from the play the following year—Glaspell considers the relationship between truth, power, and gender. The play is a murder mystery. A local man, John Wright, has been found dead, and his wife, Minnie, is suspected of killing him. Called to investigate, County Attorney George Henderson, Henry Peters, and Lewis Hale readily assume a masculine prerogative to discover the truth of John Wright's murder, telling their wives to remain in the kitchen out of the way. However, the truth of the crime is in fact concealed *in* the kitchen, and only the women are able to discover it. Glaspell shows the audience that the "trifles" of the women's world are the signs of a reality wholly unreadable to the men, precisely because it is a world they regard as feminine, and therefore unimportant and uninteresting. *Trifles*, that is, works to subvert out notions of reality and truth by suggesting how such ideas are constructed within a specific social order—the masculine order of modern society.

TRIFLES
A PLAY IN ONE ACT

SUSAN GLASPELL

— CHARACTERS —

GEORGE HENDERSON, *County Attorney*
HENRY PETERS, *Sheriff*
LEWIS HALE, *A Neighboring Farmer*
MRS. PETERS
MRS. HALE

THE SETTING: *The kitchen in the now abandoned farmhouse of John Wright*

SCENE: *The kitchen in the now abandoned farmhouse of John Wright, a gloomy kitchen, and left without having been put in order—unwashed pans under the sink, a loaf of bread outside the breadbox, a dish towel on the table—other signs of incompleted work. At the rear the outer door opens and the* SHERIFF *comes in followed by the* COUNTY ATTORNEY *and* HALE. *The* SHERIFF *and* HALE *are men in middle life, the* COUNTY ATTORNEY *is a young man; all are much bundled up and go at once to the stove. They are followed by the two women—the* SHERIFF'S *wife first; she is a slight wiry woman, a thin nervous face.* MRS. HALE *is larger and would ordinarily be called more comfortable looking, but she is disturbed now and looks fearfully about as she enters. The women have come in slowly, and stand close together near the door.*

COUNTY ATTORNEY: *(Rubbing his hands.)* This feels good. Come up to the fire, ladies.

MRS. PETERS: *(After taking a step forward.)* I'm not—cold.

SHERIFF: *(Unbuttoning his overcoat and stepping away from*
5 *the stove as if to mark the beginning of official business.)* Now, Mr. Hale, before we move things about, you explain to Mr. Henderson just what you saw when you came here yesterday morning.

COUNTY ATTORNEY: By the way, has anything been moved?
10 Are things just as you left them yesterday?

SHERIFF: *(Looking about.)* It's just the same. When it dropped below zero last night I thought I'd better send Frank out this morning to make a fire for us—no use getting pneumonia with a big case on, but I told him not to touch anything ex-
15 cept the stove—and you know Frank.

COUNTY ATTORNEY: Somebody should have been left here yesterday.

SHERIFF: Oh—yesterday. When I had to send Frank to Morris Center for that man who went crazy—I want you to know I
20 had my hands full yesterday, I knew you could get back from Omaha by today and as long as I went over everything here myself—

COUNTY ATTORNEY: Well, Mr. Hale, tell just what happened when you came here yesterday morning.

25 HALE: Harry and I had started to town with a load of potatoes. We came along the road from my place and as I got here I said, "I'm going to see if I can't get John Wright to go in with me on a party telephone." I spoke to Wright about it once before and he put me off, saying folks talked too much any-
30 way, and all he asked was peace and quiet—I guess you know about how much he talked himself; but I thought maybe if I went to the house and talked about it before his wife, though I said to Harry that I didn't know as what his wife wanted made much difference to John—

35 COUNTY ATTORNEY: Let's talk about that later, Mr. Hale. I do want to talk about that, but tell now just what happened when you got to the house.

HALE: I didn't hear or see anything; I knocked at the door, and still it was all quiet inside. I knew they must be up, it was past
40 eight o'clock. So I knocked again, and I thought I heard somebody say, "Come in." I wasn't sure, I'm not sure yet, but I opened the door—this door *(Indicating the door by which the two women are still standing.)* and there in that rocker—*(Pointing to it.)* sat Mrs. Wright.

(They all look at the rocker.)

45 COUNTY ATTORNEY: What—was she doing?

HALE: She was rockin' back and forth. She had her apron in her hand and was kind of—pleating it.

COUNTY ATTORNEY: And how did she—look?

HALE: Well, she looked queer.

50 COUNTY ATTORNEY: How do you mean—queer?

HALE: Well, as if she didn't know what she was going to do next. And kind of done up.

COUNTY ATTORNEY: How did she seem to feel about your coming?

55 HALE: Why, I don't think she minded—one way or other. She didn't pay much attention. I said, "How do, Mrs. Wright, it's cold, ain't it?" And she said, "Is it?"—and went on kind of pleating at her apron. Well, I was surprised; she didn't ask me to come up to the stove, or to set down, but just sat there,
60 not even looking at me, so I said, "I want to see John." And then she—laughed. I guess you would call it a laugh. I thought of Harry and the team outside, so I said a little sharp: "Can't I see John?" "No," she says, kind o' dull like. "Ain't he home?" says I. "Yes," says she, "he's home." "Then
65 why can't I see him?" I asked her, out of patience. "'Cause he's dead," says she. "Dead?" says I. She just nodded her head, not getting a bit excited, but rockin' back and forth. "Why—where is he?" says I, not knowing what to say. She just pointed upstairs—like that *(Himself pointing to the room
70 above.)* I got up, with the idea of going up there. I walked from there to here—then I says, "Why, what did he die of?" "He died of a rope round his neck," says she, and just went on pleatin' at her apron. Well, I went out and called Harry. I thought I might—need help. We went upstairs and there he
75 was lyin'—

805

COUNTY ATTORNEY: I think I'd rather have you go into that upstairs, where you can point it all out. Just go on now with the rest of the story.

HALE: Well, my first thought was to get that rope off. It looked 80 . . . *(Stops, his face twitches.)* . . . but Harry, he went up to him, and he said, "No, he's dead all right, and we'd better not touch anything." So we went back down stairs. She was still sitting that same way. "Has anybody been notified?" I asked. "No," says she, unconcerned. "Who did this, Mrs. 85 Wright?" said Harry. He said it businesslike—and she stopped pleatin' of her apron. "I don't know," she says. "You don't *know?*" says Harry. "No," says she. "Weren't you sleepin' in the bed with him?" says Harry. "Yes," says she, "but I was on the inside." "Somebody slipped a rope round 90 his neck and strangled him and you didn't wake up?" says Harry. "I didn't wake up," she said after him. We must 'a looked as if we didn't see how that could be, for after a minute she said. "I sleep sound." Harry was going to ask her more questions but I said maybe we ought to let her tell 95 her story first to the coroner, or the sheriff, so Harry went fast as he could to Rivers' place, where there's a telephone.

COUNTY ATTORNEY: And what did Mrs. Wright do when she knew that you had gone for the coroner?

HALE: She moved from that chair to this one over here *(Pointing to a small chair in the corner.)* and just sat there with her 100 hands held together and looking down. I got a feeling that I ought to make some conversation, so I said I had come in to see if John wanted to put in a telephone, and at that she started to laugh, and then she stopped and looked at me— scared. *(The* COUNTY ATTORNEY, *who has had his notebook* 105 *out, makes a note.)* I dunno, maybe it wasn't scared. I wouldn't like to say it was. Soon Harry got back, and then Dr. Lloyd came, and you, Mr. Peters, and so I guess that's all I know that you don't.

COUNTY ATTORNEY: *(Looking around.)* I guess we'll go up- 110 stairs first—and then out to the barn and around there. *(To the* SHERIFF.*)* You're convinced that there was nothing important here—nothing that would point to any motive.

SHERIFF: Nothing here but kitchen things.

(The COUNTY ATTORNEY *after again looking around the kitchen, opens the door of a cupboard closet. He gets up on a chair and looks on a shelf. Pulls his hand away, sticky.)*

COUNTY ATTORNEY: Here's a nice mess. 115

(The women draw nearer.)

MRS. PETERS: *(To the other woman.)* Oh, her fruit; it did freeze. *(To the* COUNTY ATTORNEY.*)* She worried about that when it turned so cold. She said the fire'd go out and her jars would break.

SHERIFF: Well, can you beat the women! Held for murder and 120 worryin' about her preserves.

COUNTY ATTORNEY: I guess before we're through she may have something more serious than preserves to worry about.

HALE: Well, women are used to worrying over trifles.

(The two women move a little closer together.)

COUNTY ATTORNEY: *(With the gallantry of a young politi-* 125 *cian.)* And yet, for all their worries, what would we do without the ladies? *(The women do not unbend. He goes to the sink, takes a dipperful of water from the pail and pouring it* into a basin, washes his hands. Starts to wipe them on the roller towel, turns it for a cleaner place.)* Dirty towels! *(Kicks* 130 *his foot against the pans under the sink.)* Not much of a housekeeper, would you say, ladies?

MRS. HALE: *(Stiffly.)* There's a great deal of work to be done on a farm.

COUNTY ATTORNEY: To be sure. And yet *(With a little bow to* 135 *her.)* I know there are some Dickson county farmhouses which do not have such roller towels.

(He gives it a pull to expose its full length again.)

MRS. HALE: Those towels get dirty awful quick. Men's hands aren't always as clean as they might be.

COUNTY ATTORNEY: Ah, loyal to your sex, I see. But you and 140 Mrs. Wright were neighbors. I suppose you were friends, too.

MRS. HALE: *(Shaking her head.)* I've not seen much of her of late years. I've not been in this house—it's more than a year.

COUNTY ATTORNEY: And why was that? You didn't like her?

MRS. HALE: I liked her all well enough. Farmers' wives have 145 their hands full, Mr. Henderson. And then—

COUNTY ATTORNEY: Yes—?

MRS. HALE: *(Looking about.)* It never seemed a very cheerful place.

COUNTY ATTORNEY: No—it's not cheerful. I shouldn't say she 150 had the homemaking instinct.

MRS. HALE: Well, I don't know as Wright had, either.

COUNTY ATTORNEY: You mean that they didn't get on very well?

MRS. HALE: No, I don't mean anything. But I don't think a 155 place'd be any cheerfuller for John Wright's being in it.

COUNTY ATTORNEY: I'd like to talk more of that a little later. I want to get the lay of things upstairs now.

(He goes to the left, where three steps lead to a stair door.)

SHERIFF: I suppose anything Mrs. Peters does'll be all right. She was to take in some clothes for her, you know, and a few 160 little things. We left in such a hurry yesterday.

COUNTY ATTORNEY: Yes, but I would like to see what you take, Mrs. Peters, and keep an eye out for anything that might be of use to us.

MRS. PETERS: Yes, Mr. Henderson. 165

(The women listen to the men's steps on the stairs, then look about the kitchen.)

MRS. HALE: I'd hate to have men coming into my kitchen, snooping around and criticising.

(She arranges the pans under sink which the COUNTY ATTORNEY *had shoved out of place.)*

MRS. PETERS: Of course it's no more than their duty.

MRS. HALE: Duty's all right, but I guess that deputy sheriff that came out to make the fire might have got a little of this on. 170 *(Gives the roller towel a pull.)* Wish I'd thought of that sooner. Seems mean to talk about her for not having things slicked up when she had to come away in such a hurry.

MRS. PETERS: *(Who has gone to a small table in the left rear corner of the room, and lifted one end of a towel that covers a* 175 *pan.)* She had bread set.

(Stands still.)

MRS. HALE: *(Eyes fixed on a loaf of bread beside the breadbox, which is on a low shelf at the other side of the room. Moves*

slowly toward it.) She was going to put this in there. *(Picks up*
180 *loaf, then abruptly drops it. In a manner of returning to famil-*
iar things.) It's a shame about her fruit. I wonder if it's all
gone. *(Gets up on the chair and looks.)* I think there's some
here that's all right, Mrs. Peters. Yes—here; *(Holding it to-*
ward the window.) this is cherries, too. *(Looking again.)* I de-
185 clare I believe that's the only one. *(Gets down, bottle in her*
hand. Goes to the sink and wipes it off on the outside.) She'll
feel awful bad after all her hard work in the hot weather. I remember the afternoon I put up my cherries last summer.

(She puts the bottle on the big kitchen table, center of the room.
With a sigh, is about to sit down in the rocking-chair. Before she
is seated realizes what chair it is; with a slow look at it, steps
back. The chair which she has touched rocks back and forth.)

MRS. PETERS: Well, I must get those things from the front
190 room closet. *(She goes to the door at the right, but after look-*
ing into the other room, steps back.) You coming with me,
Mrs. Hale? You could help me carry them.

(They go in the other room; reappear, MRS. PETERS carrying a
dress and skirt, MRS. HALE following with a pair of shoes.)

MRS. PETERS: My, it's cold in there.

(She puts the clothes on the big table, and hurries to the stove.)

MRS. HALE: *(Examining the skirt.)* Wright was close. I think
195 maybe that's why she kept so much to herself. She didn't
even belong to the Ladies Aid. I suppose she felt she couldn't
do her part, and then you don't enjoy things when you feel
shabby. She used to wear pretty clothes and be lively, when
she was Minnie Foster, one of the town girls singing in the
200 choir. But that—oh, that was thirty years ago. This all you
was to take in?
MRS. PETERS: She said she wanted an apron. Funny thing to
want, for there isn't much to get you dirty in jail, goodness
knows. But I suppose just to make her feel more natural. She
205 said they was in the top drawer in this cupboard. Yes, here.
And then her little shawl that always hung behind the door.
(Opens stair door and looks.) Yes, here it is.

(Quickly shuts door leading upstairs.)

MRS. HALE: *(Abruptly moving toward her.)* Mrs. Peters?
MRS. PETERS: Yes, Mrs. Hale?
210 MRS. HALE: Do you think she did it?
MRS. PETERS: *(In a frightened voice.)* Oh, I don't know.
MRS. HALE: Well, I don't think she did. Asking for an apron
and her little shawl. Worrying about her fruit.
MRS. PETERS: *(Starts to speak, glances up, where footsteps are*
215 *heard in the room above. In a low voice.)* Mr. Peters says it
looks bad for her. Mr. Henderson is awful sarcastic in a
speech and he'll make fun of her sayin' she didn't wake up.
MRS. HALE: Well, I guess John Wright didn't wake when they
was slipping that rope under his neck.
220 MRS. PETERS: No, it's strange. It must have been done awful
crafty and still. They say it was such a—funny way to kill a
man, rigging it all up like that.
MRS. HALE: That's just what Mr. Hale said. There was a gun in
the house. He says that's what he can't understand.
225 MRS. PETERS: Mr. Henderson said coming out that what was
needed for the case was a motive; something to show anger,
or—sudden feeling.

MRS. HALE: *(Who is standing by the table.)* Well, I don't see
any signs of anger around here. *(She puts her hand on the*
dish towel which lies on the table, stands looking down at 230
table, one half of which is clean, the other half messy.) It's
wiped to here. *(Makes a move as if to finish work, then turns*
and looks at loaf of bread outside the breadbox. Drops towel.
In that voice of coming back to familiar things.) Wonder how
they are finding things upstairs. I hope she had it a little 235
more red-up up there. You know, it seems kind of *sneaking.*
Locking her up in town and then coming out here and trying to get her own house to turn against her!
MRS. PETERS: But Mrs. Hale, the law is the law.
MRS. HALE: I s'pose 'tis. *(Unbuttoning her coat.)* Better loosen 240
up your things, Mrs. Peters. You won't feel them when you
go out.

(MRS. PETERS takes off her fur tippet, goes to hang it on hook at
back of room, stands looking at the under part of the small cor-
ner table.)

MRS. PETERS: She was piecing a quilt.

(She brings the large sewing basket and they look at the bright
pieces.)

MRS. HALE: It's log cabin pattern. Pretty, isn't it? I wonder if
she was goin' to quilt it or just knot it? 245

(Footsteps have been heard coming down the stairs. The SHERIFF
enters followed by HALE and the COUNTY ATTORNEY.)

SHERIFF: They wonder if she was going to quilt it or just
knot it!

(The men laugh; the women look abashed.)

COUNTY ATTORNEY: *(Rubbing his hands over the stove.)*
Frank's fire didn't do much up there, did it? Well, let's go out
to the barn and get that cleared up. 250

(The men go outside.)

MRS. HALE: *(Resentfully.)* I don't know as there's anything so
strange, our takin' up our time with little things while we're
waiting for them to get the evidence. *(She sits down at the*
big table smoothing out a block with decision.) I don't see as
it's anything to laugh about. 255
MRS. PETERS: *(Apologetically.)* Of course they've got awful important things on their minds.

(Pulls up a chair and joins MRS. HALE at the table.)

MRS. HALE: *(Examining another block.)* Mrs. Peters, look at
this one. Here, this is the one she was working on, and look
at that sewing! All the rest of it has been so nice and even. 260
And look at this! It's all over the place! Why, it looks as if she
didn't know what she was about!

(After she has said this they look at each other, then start to
glance back at the door. After an instant MRS. HALE has pulled
at a knot and ripped the sewing.)

MRS. PETERS: Oh, what are you doing, Mrs. Hale?
MRS. HALE: *(Mildly.)* Just pulling out a stitch or two that's not
sewed very good. *(Threading a needle.)* Bad sewing always 265
made me fidgety.
MRS. PETERS: *(Nervously.)* I don't think we ought to touch
things.

MRS. HALE: I'll just finish up this end. (*Suddenly stopping and*
270 *leaning forward.*) Mrs. Peters?

MRS. PETERS: Yes, Mrs. Hale?

MRS. HALE: What do you suppose she was so nervous about?

MRS. PETERS: Oh—I don't know. I don't know as she was nervous. I sometimes sew awful queer when I'm just tired. (MRS.
275 HALE *starts to say something, looks at* MRS. PETERS, *then goes
on sewing.*) Well, I must get these things wrapped up. They
may be through sooner than we think. (*Putting apron and
other things together.*) I wonder where I can find a piece of
paper, and string.

280 MRS. HALE: In that cupboard, maybe.

MRS. PETERS: (*Looking in cupboard.*) Why, here's a birdcage.
(*Holds it up.*) Did she have a bird, Mrs. Hale?

MRS. HALE: Why, I don't know whether she did or not—I've
not been here for so long. There was a man around last year
285 selling canaries cheap, but I don't know as she took one;
maybe she did. She used to sing real pretty herself.

MRS. PETERS: (*Glancing around.*) Seems funny to think of a
bird here. But she must have had one, or why would she
have a cage? I wonder what happened to it.

290 MRS. HALE: I s'pose maybe the cat got it.

MRS. PETERS: No, she didn't have a cat. She's got that feeling
some people have about cats—being afraid of them. My cat
got in her room and she was real upset and asked me to take
it out.

295 MRS. HALE: My sister Bessie was like that. Queer, ain't it?

MRS. PETERS: (*Examining the cage.*) Why, look at this door. It's
broke. One hinge is pulled apart.

MRS. HALE: (*Looking too.*) Looks as if someone must have
been rough with it.

300 MRS. PETERS: Why, yes.

(*She brings the cage forward and puts it on the table.*)

MRS. HALE: I wish if they're going to find any evidence they'd
be about it. I don't like this place.

MRS. PETERS: But I'm awful glad you came with me, Mrs.
Hale. It would be lonesome for me sitting here alone.

305 MRS. HALE: It would, wouldn't it? (*Dropping her sewing.*) But I
tell you what I do wish, Mrs. Peters. I wish I had come over
sometimes when *she* was here. I—(*Looking around the
room.*)—wish I had.

MRS. PETERS: But of course you were awful busy, Mrs. Hale—
310 your house and your children.

MRS. HALE: I could've come. I stayed away because it weren't
cheerful—and that's why I ought to have come. I—I've
never liked this place. Maybe because it's down in a hollow
and you don't see the road. I dunno what it is, but it's a lone-
315 some place and always was. I wish I had come over to see
Minnie Foster sometimes. I can see now—

(*Shakes her head.*)

MRS. PETERS: Well you mustn't reproach yourself, Mrs. Hale.
Somehow we just don't see how it is with other folks until—
something comes up.

320 MRS. HALE: Not having children makes less work—but it
makes a quiet house, and Wright out to work all day, and no
company when he did come in. Did you know John Wright,
Mrs. Peters?

MRS. PETERS: Not to know him; I've seen him in town. They
325 say he was a good man.

MRS. HALE: Yes—good; he didn't drink, and kept his word as
well as most, I guess, and paid his debts. But he was a hard
man, Mrs. Peters. Just to pass the time of day with him—
(*Shivers.*) Like a raw wind that gets to the bone. (*Pauses, her
eye falling on the cage.*) I should think she would 'a wanted a 330
bird. But what do you suppose went with it?

MRS. PETERS: I don't know, unless it got sick and died.

(*She reaches over and swings the broken door, swings it again.
Both women watch it.*)

MRS. HALE: You weren't raised round here, were you? (MRS.
PETERS *shakes her head.*) You didn't know—her?

MRS. PETERS: Not till they brought her yesterday. 335

MRS. HALE: She—come to think of it, she was kind of like a
bird herself—real sweet and pretty, but kind of timid and—
fluttery. How—she—did—change. (*Silence; then as if struck
by a happy thought and relieved to get back to every day
things.*) Tell you what, Mrs. Peters, why don't you take the 340
quilt in with you? It might take up her mind.

MRS. PETERS: Why, I think that's a real nice idea, Mrs. Hale.
There couldn't possibly be any objection to it, could there?
Now, just what would I take? I wonder if her patches are in
here—and her things. 345

(*They look in the sewing basket.*)

MRS. HALE: Here's some red. I expect this has got sewing things
in it. (*Brings out a fancy box.*) What a pretty box. Looks like
something somebody would give you. Maybe her scissors are
in here. (*Opens box. Suddenly puts her hand to her nose.*)
Why—(MRS. PETERS *bends nearer, then turns her face away.*) 350
There's something wrapped up in this piece of silk.

MRS. PETERS: Why, this isn't her scissors.

MRS. HALE: (*Lifting the silk.*) Oh, Mrs. Peters—its—

(MRS. PETERS *bends closer.*)

MRS. PETERS: It's the bird.

MRS. HALE: (*Jumping up.*) But, Mrs. Peters—look at it! Its 355
neck! Look at its neck! It's all—other side *to*.

MRS. PETERS: Somebody—wrung—its—neck.

(*Their eyes meet. A look of growing comprehension, of horror.
Steps are heard outside.* MRS. HALE *slips box under quilt pieces,
and sinks into her chair. Enter* SHERIFF *and* COUNTY ATTOR-
NEY. MRS. PETERS *rises.*)

COUNTY ATTORNEY: (*As one turning from serious things to little pleasantries.*) Well, ladies, have you decided whether she
was going to quilt it or knot it? 360

MRS. HALE: We think she was going to—knot it.

COUNTY ATTORNEY: Well, that's interesting, I'm sure. (*Seeing
the birdcage.*) Has the bird flown?

MRS. HALE: (*Putting more quilt pieces over the box.*) We think
the—cat got it. 365

COUNTY ATTORNEY: (*Preoccupied.*) Is there a cat?

(MRS. HALE *glances in a quick covert way at* MRS. PETERS.)

MRS. PETERS: Well, not *now*. They're superstitious, you know.
They leave.

COUNTY ATTORNEY: (*To* SHERIFF PETERS *continuing an interrupted conversation.*) No sign at all of anyone having come 370
from the outside. Their own rope. Now let's go up again and
go over it piece by piece. (*They start upstairs.*) It would have
to have been someone who knew just the—

(MRS. PETERS *sits down. The two women sit there not looking at one another, but as if peering into something and at the same time holding back. When they talk now it is in the manner of feeling their way over strange ground, as if afraid of what they are saying, but as if they cannot help saying it.)*

375 MRS. HALE: She liked the bird. She was going to bury it in that pretty box.

MRS. PETERS: *(In a whisper.)* When I was a girl—my kitten—there was a boy took a hatchet, and before my eyes—and before I could get there—*(Covers her face an instant.)* If they hadn't held me back I would have—*(Catches herself, looks*

380 *upstairs where steps are heard, falters weakly.)*—hurt him.

MRS. HALE: *(With a slow look around her.)* I wonder how it would seem never to have had any children around. *(Pause.)* No, Wright wouldn't like the bird—a thing that sang. She used to sing. He killed that, too.

385 MRS. PETERS: *(Moving uneasily.)* We don't know who killed the bird.

MRS. HALE: I knew John Wright.

MRS. PETERS: It was an awful thing was done in this house that night, Mrs. Hale. Killing a man while he slept, slipping a

390 rope around his neck that choked the life out of him.

MRS. HALE: His neck. Choked the life out of him.

(Her hand goes out and rests on the birdcage.)

MRS. PETERS: *(With rising voice.)* We don't know who killed him. We don't know.

MRS. HALE: *(Her own feeling not interrupted.)* If there'd been

395 years and years of nothing, then a bird to sing to you, it would be awful—still, after the bird was still.

MRS. PETERS: *(Something within her speaking.)* I know what stillness is. When we homesteaded in Dakota, and my first baby died—after he was two years old, and me with no other

400 then—

MRS. HALE: *(Moving.)* How soon do you suppose they'll be through, looking for the evidence?

MRS. PETERS: I know what stillness is. *(Pulling herself back.)* The law has got to punish crime, Mrs. Hale.

405 MRS. HALE: *(Not as if answering that.)* I wish you'd seen Minnie Foster when she wore a white dress with blue ribbons and stood up there in the choir and sang. *(A look around the room.)* Oh, I *wish* I'd come over here once in a while! That was a crime! That was a crime! Who's going to punish that?

410 MRS. PETERS: *(Looking upstairs.)* We mustn't—take on.

MRS. HALE: I might have known she needed help! I know how things can be—for women. I tell you, it's queer, Mrs. Peters. We live close together and we live far apart. We all go through the same things—it's all just a different kind of the

415 same thing. *(Brushes her eyes; noticing the bottle of fruit, reaches out for it.)* If I was you I wouldn't tell her her fruit was gone. Tell her it *ain't.* Tell her it's all right. Take this in to prove it to her. She—she may never know whether it was broke or not.

420 MRS. PETERS: *(Takes the bottle, looks about for something to wrap it in, takes petticoat from the clothes brought from the*

other room, very nervously begins winding this around the bottle. In a false voice.)* My, it's a good thing the men couldn't hear us. Wouldn't they just laugh! Getting all stirred up over a little thing like a—dead canary. As if that could have any-425 thing to do with—with—wouldn't they *laugh!*

(The men are heard coming down stairs.)

MRS. HALE: *(Under her breath.)* Maybe they would—maybe they wouldn't.

COUNTY ATTORNEY: No, Peters, it's all perfectly clear except a reason for doing it. But you know juries when it comes to 430 women. If there was some definite thing. Something to show—something to make a story about—a thing that would connect up with this strange way of doing it—

(The women's eyes meet for an instant. Enter HALE *from outer door.)*

HALE: Well, I've got the team around. Pretty cold out there.

COUNTY ATTORNEY: I'm going to stay here a while by myself. 435 *(To the* SHERIFF.) You can send Frank out for me, can't you? I want to go over everything. I'm not satisfied that we can't do better.

SHERIFF: Do you want to see what Mrs. Peters is going to take in? 440

(The COUNTY ATTORNEY *goes to the table, picks up the apron, laughs.)*

COUNTY ATTORNEY: Oh, I guess they're not very dangerous things the ladies have picked out. *(Moves a few things about, disturbing the quilt pieces which cover the box. Steps back.)* No, Mrs. Peters doesn't need supervising. For that matter, a sheriff's wife is married to the law. Ever think of it that way, 445 Mrs. Peters?

MRS. PETERS: Not—just that way.

SHERIFF: *(Chuckling.)* Married to the law. *(Moves toward the other room.)* I just want you to come in here a minute, George. We ought to take a look at these windows. 450

COUNTY ATTORNEY: *(Scoffingly.)* Oh, windows!

SHERIFF: We'll be right out, Mr. Hale.

*(*HALE *goes outside. The* SHERIFF *follows the* COUNTY ATTORNEY *into the other room. Then* MRS. HALE *rises, hands tight together, looking intensely at* MRS. PETERS, *whose eyes make a slow turn, finally meeting* MRS. HALE's. *A moment* MRS. HALE *holds her, then her own eyes point the way to where the box is concealed. Suddenly* MRS. PETERS *throws back quilt pieces and tries to put the box in the bag she is wearing. It is too big. She opens box, starts to take bird out, cannot touch it, goes to pieces, stands there helpless. Sound of a knob turning in the other room.* MRS. HALE *snatches the box and puts it in the pocket of her big coat. Enter* COUNTY ATTORNEY *and* SHERIFF.)*

COUNTY ATTORNEY: *(Facetiously.)* Well, Henry, at least we found out that she was not going to quilt it. She was going to—what is it you call it, ladies? 455

MRS. HALE: *(Her hand against her pocket.)* We call it—knot it, Mr. Henderson.

■ EUGENE O'NEILL ■

Born the son of the famous turn-of-the-century actor, James O'Neill, Eugene O'Neill (1888–1953) became America's greatest dramatist. Much of O'Neill's younger life is described in his late play, *Long Day's Journey Into Night:* how he spent his first several years touring with his family following his father's career on the stage; his stints in boarding school and at Princeton; some time spent working on ships sailing to South America and Africa, and bumming around in Buenos Aires and New York; a serious bout with tuberculosis. In the play, O'Neill leaves the future of his young poet-hero uncertain, but in fact illness provided O'Neill with the time to begin writing seriously. When he recovered, O'Neill attended George Pierce Baker's playwriting classes at Harvard. He worked briefly in Greenwich Village and then joined the Provincetown Playhouse company on Cape Cod in 1916, where his first plays were produced.

O'Neill had a long and tumultous career in the theater. An admirer of Strindberg's drama, and widely read in Nietzsche, Freud, and Jung, O'Neill experimented in a variety of different theatrical styles, always searching for new ways to reveal the complex working of a character's psychology. He wrote a series of short realistic plays that were produced at the Provincetown and other "little theaters," the best of which concern life at sea: *Bound East for Cardiff* (1916), *Fog* (1917), *In the Zone* (1917), *The Long Voyage Home* (1917), and *The Moon of the Caribbees* (1918). His first Broadway production, *Beyond the Horizon* (1920) won him the first of four Pulitzer Prizes; he later won for *Anna Christie* (1921), *Strange Interlude* (1928), and *Long Day's Journey Into Night* (awarded posthumously in 1956). Throughout the 1920s, the period of his greatest success in the theater, O'Neill both wrote realistic plays like *Desire Under the Elms* (1924) and experimented in a variety of other modes. He tried expressionistic techniques in *The Hairy Ape* (1922) and *The Emperor Jones* (1920); masks in *The Great God Brown* (1926); and revealing "asides" in *Strange Interlude*, in which characters speak their unspoken "thoughts" directly to the audience. He also took a chance with comedy in *Ah, Wilderness!* (1932), something of a study for *Long Day's Journey*.

O'Neill's decade of success was followed by a series of impressive failures. Some of these plays are nonetheless fascinating. Although it played well in 1928, the asides and length (over eight hours) of *Strange Interlude* have militated against many revivals; the parallels between Aeschylus' *Oresteia* and O'Neill's *Mourning Becomes Electra* (1931) still attract comment and discussion. Much of O'Neill's work from the late 1920s and 1930s is inflated and bombastic, and plays like *Lazarus Laughed* (1928), *Marco Millions* (1929), *Dynamo* (1929), and *Days Without End* (1934) seemed to mark his flagging powers as a writer. When O'Neill won the Nobel Prize in 1936, his career was widely regarded as finished. His plays had become empty and grandiose, and he suffered from Parkinson's disease, which made it increasingly difficult for him to write. Throughout the 1930s and 1940s, though, O'Neill planned a massive cycle of plays concerning the fortunes of an American family, called *A Tale of Possessors Self-dispossessed*; of these he completed only *A Touch of the Poet* (written 1935–1942) and a draft of *More Stately Mansions* (1935–1940). However, in the 1940s, O'Neill also wrote his greatest plays, realistic dramas based for the most part on his family's history and on his own life. These hard-won plays may have been out of keeping with the national mood in the aftermath of World War II: when *The Iceman Cometh* opened in 1946, it ran for only 136 performances, and *A Moon for the Misbegotten* (1947) closed in Ohio before reaching New York. Yet when *Iceman* was revived in 1956, directed by Jose Quintero, it was a huge success and prompted a widespread reevaluation of O'Neill's drama.

Since O'Neill was raised on his father's melodramatic portrayal of *The Count of Monte Cristo*, it is not surprising that he was at times also infected with the spirit of melodrama. O'Neill's plays often recall melodrama's emphasis on the passions of the characters, its striking moments of stage action, its penchant for the romantic and the sentimental. O'Neill's experimentation and sure sense of the stage enabled him to achieve an unparalleled body of work and to define the course of drama in the United States in the first half of the twentieth century.

AH, WILDERNESS!

O'Neill is best known today for the striking series of tragedies he wrote late in his career in which he mined the events of his own life and transformed them into drama. In *Ah, Wilderness!*, however,

O'Neill turned to a slightly earlier era—the period of his early adolescence, rather than his twenties—to frame a charming comedy. The play is set in small-town Connecticut, a town not unlike the New London where his parents had settled, and many of the characters are based indirectly on figures from O'Neill's New London youth. However, while the setting—and even the design of the set itself—foreshadow O'Neill's more tortured confrontation with the same material in *Long Day's Journey* (which is set in 1912, not 1906), *Ah, Wilderness!* is a romantic comedy set on the Fourth of July in the busy Miller family: Nat Miller, smart and benign local newspaper editor; his shrewd and caring wife; their three sons and one daughter; the Irish maid; and two in-laws—Sid and Lily—who seem destined to be perpetually on the brink of marriage.

The play centers on the middle son, Richard, who at age sixteen is something of an affectionate self-portrait of young O'Neill, and a study for Edmund Tyrone in *Long Day's Journey*. Although Richard's mother and girlfriend are scandalized by Richard's freethinking reading, his Nietzschean pose is just that—a pose. While he reads Shaw and Wilde and Swinburne—and drunkenly compares himself to the self-destructive and poetic Eilert Lovborg in Ibsen's play *Hedda Gabler*—Richard's rebellion is more an idealistic search for self-expression than a deeper social or philosophical apostasy. Richard is innocent as well as idealistic: while he's right to puncture the stuffed-shirt moralizing of his Ivy League brother, his own experience to date has been narrowly confined to the "life" he finds between the covers of his books. His attempt to take revenge on his girlfriend Muriel by playing the rake with the "chorus girl," Belle, at the local saloon/brothel not only fails but leaves freethinking Richard miserable and guilty. For all his radicalism, Richard finally wants the approval of his family and the conventional, domestic happiness that bustles around him in the play: Richard's future is shown in the play's final image, the sentimental embrace of his parents.

AH, WILDERNESS!

EUGENE O'NEILL

— CHARACTERS —

NAT MILLER, *owner of the* EVENING GLOBE
ESSIE, *his wife*
ARTHUR ⎫
RICHARD ⎬ *their children*
MILDRED ⎪
TOMMY ⎭
SID DAVIS, *Essie's brother*
LILY MILLER, *Nat's sister*
DAVID MC COMBER
MURIEL MC COMBER, *his daughter*
WINT SELBY, *a classmate of Arthur's at Yale*
BELLE
NORAH
BARTENDER
SALESMAN

— SCENES —

Act One. Sitting-room of the Miller home in a large small-town in Connecticut—early morning, July 4th, 1906.
Act Two. Dining-room of the Miller home—evening of the same day.
Act Three. Scene One: Back room of a bar in a small hotel—10 o'clock the same night.
Scene Two: Same as Act One—the sitting-room of the Miller home—a little after 11 o'clock the same night.
Act Four. Scene One: The Miller sitting-room again—about 1 o'clock the following afternoon.
Scene Two: A strip of beach along the harbor—about 9 o'clock that night.
Scene Three: Same as Scene One—the sitting-room—about 10 o'clock the same night.

— ACT ONE —

Sitting-room of the Miller home in a large small-town in Connecticut—about 7:30 in the morning of July 4th, 1906. The room is fairly large, homely looking and cheerful in the morning sunlight, furnished with scrupulous medium-priced tastelessness of the period. Beneath the two windows at left, front, a sofa with silk and satin cushions stands against the wall. At rear of sofa, a bookcase with glass doors, filled with cheap sets, extends along the remaining length of wall. In the rear wall, left, is a double doorway with sliding doors and portières, leading into a dark, windowless, back parlor. At right of this doorway, another bookcase, this time a small, open one, crammed with boys' and girls' books and the bestselling novels of many past years—books the family really have read. To the right of this bookcase is the mate of the double doorway at its left, with sliding doors and portières, this one leading to a well-lighted front parlor. In the right wall, rear, a screen door opens on a porch. Farther forward in this wall are two windows, with a writing desk and a chair between them. At center is a big, round table with a green-shaded reading lamp, the cord of the lamp running up to one of five sockets in the chandelier above. Five chairs are grouped about the table—three rockers at left, right, and right rear of it, two armchairs at rear and left rear. A medium-priced, inoffensive rug covers most of the floor. The walls are papered white with a cheerful, ugly blue design.

Voices are heard in a conversational tone from the dining-room beyond the back parlor, where the family are just finishing breakfast. Then MRS. MILLER's *voice, raised commandingly, "Tommy! Come back here and finish your milk!" At the same moment* TOMMY *appears in the doorway from the back parlor—a chubby, sun-burnt boy of eleven with dark eyes, blond hair wetted and plastered down in a part, and a shiny, good-natured face, a rim of milk visible about his lips. Bursting with bottled-up energy and a longing to get started on the Fourth, he nevertheless has hesitated obediently at his mother's call.*

TOMMY: *(Calls back pleadingly.)* Aw, I'm full, Ma. And I said excuse me and you said all right. *(His* FATHER's *voice is heard speaking to his* MOTHER. *Then she calls: "All right, Tommy," and* TOMMY *asks eagerly.)* Can I go out now?

MOTHER'S VOICE: *(Correctingly.)* May I! 5

TOMMY: *(Fidgeting, but obediently.)* May I, Ma?

MOTHER'S VOICE: Yes. *(*TOMMY *jumps for the screen door to the porch at right like a sprinter released by the starting shot.)*

FATHER'S VOICE: *(Shouts after him.)* But you set off your crackers away from the house, remember! *(But* TOMMY *is already through the screen door, which he leaves open behind him.)* 10

(A moment later the family appear from the back parlor, coming from the dining-room. First are MILDRED *and* ARTHUR. MILDRED *is fifteen, tall and slender, with big, irregular features, resembling her father to the complete effacing of any pretense at prettiness. But her big, gray eyes are beautiful; she has vivacity and a fetching smile, and everyone thinks of her as an attractive girl. She is dressed in shirtwaist and skirt in the fashion of the period.*

ARTHUR, *the eldest of the Miller children who are still living home, is nineteen. He is tall, heavy, barrel-chested and muscular, the type of football lineman of that period, with a square, stolid face, small blue eyes and thick sandy hair. His manner is solemnly collegiate. He is dressed in the latest college fashion of that day, which has receded a bit from the extreme of preceding years, but still runs to padded shoulders and pants half-pegged at the top, and so small at their wide-cuffed bottoms that they cannot be taken off with shoes on.)*

812

MILDRED: *(As they appear—inquisitively.)* Where are you going today, Art?

15 ARTHUR: *(With superior dignity.)* That's my business. *(He ostentatiously takes from his pocket a tobacco pouch with a big Y and class numerals stamped on it, and a heavy bulldog briar pipe with silver Y and numerals, and starts filling the pipe.)*

20 MILDRED: *(Teasingly.)* Bet I know, just the same! Want me to tell you her initials? E.R.! *(She laughs.* ARTHUR, *pleased by this insinuation at his lady-killing activities, yet finds it beneath his dignity to reply. He goes to the table, lights his pipe and picks up the local morning paper, and slouches back into*

25 *the armchair at left rear of table, beginning to whistle "Oh, Waltz Me Around Again, Willie" as he scans the headlines.* MILDRED *sits on the sofa at left, front.)*

(Meanwhile, their mother and their AUNT LILY, *their father's sister, have appeared, following them from the back parlor.* MRS. MILLER *is around fifty, a short, stout woman with fading light-brown hair sprinkled with gray, who must have been decidedly pretty as a girl in a round-faced, cute, small-featured, wide-eyed fashion. She has big brown eyes, soft and maternal—a bustling, mother-of-a-family manner. She is dressed in shirtwaist and skirt.*

LILY MILLER, *her sister-in-law, is forty-two, tall, dark and thin. She conforms outwardly to the conventional type of old-maid school teacher, even to wearing glasses. But behind the glasses her gray eyes are gentle and tired, and her whole atmosphere is one of shy kindliness. Her voice presents the greatest contrast to her appearance—soft and full of sweetness. She, also, is dressed in a shirtwaist and skirt.)*

MRS. MILLER: *(As they appear.)* Getting milk down him is like—*(Suddenly she is aware of the screen door standing half*

30 *open.)* Goodness, look at that door he's left open! The house will be alive with flies! *(Rushing out to shut it.)* I've told him again and again—and that's all the good it does! It's just a waste of breath! *(She slams the door shut.)*

LILY: *(Smiling.)* Well, you can't expect a boy to remember to

35 shut doors—on the Fourth of July. *(She goes diffidently to the straight-backed chair before the desk at right, front, leaving the comfortable chairs to the others.)*

MRS. MILLER: That's you all over, Lily—always making excuses for him. You'll have him spoiled to death in spite of

40 me. *(She sinks in rocker at right of table.)* Phew, I'm hot, aren't you? This is going to be a scorcher. *(She picks up a magazine from the table and begins to rock, fanning herself.)*

(Meanwhile, her husband and her brother have appeared from the back parlor, both smoking cigars. NAT MILLER *is in his late fifties, a tall, dark, spare man, a little stoop-shouldered, more than a little bald, dressed with an awkward attempt at sober respectability imposed upon an innate heedlessness of clothes. His long face has large, irregular, undistinguished features, but he has fine, shrewd, humorous gray eyes.*

SID DAVIS, *his brother-in-law, is forty-five, short and fat, bald-headed, with the Puckish face of a Peck's Bad Boy who has never grown up. He is dressed in what had once been a very natty loud light suit but is now a shapeless and faded nondescript in cut and color.)*

SID: *(As they appear.)* Oh, I like the job first rate, Nat. Waterbury's a nifty old town with the lid off, when you get to know the ropes. I rang in a joke in one of my stories that tickled the

45 folks there pink. Waterwagon—Waterbury—Waterloo!

MILLER: *(Grinning.)* Darn good!

SID: *(Pleased.)* I thought it was pretty fair myself. *(Goes on a bit ruefully, as if oppressed by a secret sorrow.)* Yes, you can see life in Waterbury, all right—that is, if you're looking for life

50 in Waterbury!

MRS. MILLER: What's that about Waterbury, Sid?

SID: I was saying it's all right in its way—but there's no place like home. *(As if to punctuate this remark, there begins a series of bangs from just beyond the porch outside, as* TOMMY

55 *inaugurates his celebration by setting off a package of fire-crackers. The assembled family jump in their chairs.)*

MRS. MILLER: That boy! *(She rushes to the screen door and out on the porch, calling.)* Tommy! You mind what your Pa told you! You take your crackers out in the back yard, you hear me!

60 ARTHUR: *(Frowning scornfully.)* Fresh kid! He did it on purpose to scare us.

MILLER: *(Grinning through his annoyance.)* Darned youngster! He'll have the house afire before the day's out.

SID: *(Grins and sings.)*

65   "Dunno what ter call 'im
      But he's mighty like a Rose—velt."

(They all laugh.)

LILY: Sid, you Crazy! *(SID beams at her.* MRS. MILLER *comes back from the porch, still fuming.)*

MRS. MILLER: Well, I've made him go out back at last. Now

70 we'll have a little peace. *(As if to contradict this, the bang of firecrackers and torpedoes begins from the rear of the house, left, and continues at intervals throughout the scene, not nearly so loud as the first explosion, but sufficiently emphatic to form a disturbing punctuation to the conversation.)*

75 MILLER: Well, what's on the tappee for all of you today? Sid, you're coming to the Sachem Club picnic with me, of course.

SID: *(A bit embarrassedly.)* You bet. I mean I'd like to, Nat—that is, if—

MRS. MILLER: *(Regarding her brother with smiling suspicion.)*

80 Hmm! I know what that Sachem Club picnic's always meant!

LILY: *(Breaks in in a forced joking tone that conceals a deep earnestness.)* No, not this time, Essie. Sid's a reformed character since he's been on the paper in Waterbury. At least,

85 that's what he swore to me last night.

SID: *(Avoiding her eyes, humiliated—joking it off.)* Pure as the driven snow, that's me. They're running me for president of the W.C.T.U. *(They all laugh.)*

MRS. MILLER: Sid, you're a caution. You turn everything into a

90 joke. But you be careful, you hear? We're going to have dinner in the evening tonight, you know—the best shore dinner you ever tasted and I don't want you coming home—well, not able to appreciate it.

LILY: Oh, I know he'll be careful today. Won't you, Sid?

95 SID: *(More embarrassed than ever—joking it off melodramatically.)* Lily, I swear to you if any man offers me a drink, I'll kill him—that is, if he changes his mind! *(They all laugh except* LILY, *who bites her lip and stiffens.)*

100 MRS. MILLER: No use talking to him, Lily. You ought to know better by this time. We can only hope for the best.

MILLER: *(Now, you women stop picking on Sid.* It's the Fourth of July and even a downtrodden newspaperman has a right to enjoy himself when he's on his holiday.

105 MRS. MILLER: I wasn't thinking only of Sid.

MILLER: *(With a wink at the others.)* What, are you insinuating I ever—?

MRS. MILLER: Well, to do you justice, no, not what you'd really call—But I've known you to come back from this darned

110 Sachem Club picnic—Well, I didn't need any little bird to whisper that you'd been some place besides to the well! *(She smiles good-naturedly.* MILLER *chuckles.)*

SID: *(After a furtive glance at the stiff and silent* LILY—*changes the subject abruptly by turning to* ARTHUR.*)* How are you

115 spending the festive Fourth, Boola-Boola? *(ARTHUR stiffens dignifiedly.)*

MILDRED: *(Teasingly.)* I can tell you, if he won't.

MRS. MILLER: *(Smiling.)* Off to the Rands', I suppose.

ARTHUR: *(With dignity.)* I and Bert Turner are taking Elsie

120 and Ethel Rand canoeing. We're going to have a picnic lunch on Strawberry Island. And this evening I'm staying at the Rands' for dinner.

MILLER: You're accounted for, then. How about you, Mid?

MILDRED: I'm going to the beach to Anne Culver's.

125 ARTHUR: *(Sarcastically.)* Of course, there won't be any boys present! Johnny Dodd, for example?

MILDRED: *(Giggles—then with a coquettish toss of her head.)* Pooh! What do I care for him? He's not the only pebble on the beach.

130 MILLER: Stop your everlasting teasing, you two. How about you and Lily, Essie?

MRS. MILLER: I don't know. I haven't made any plans. Have you, Lily?

LILY: *(Quietly.)* No. Anything you want to do.

135 MRS. MILLER: Well, I thought we'd just sit around and rest and talk.

MILLER: You can gossip any day. This is the Fourth. Now, I've got a better suggestion than that. What do you say to an automobile ride? I'll get out the Buick and we'll drive around

140 town and out to the lighthouse and back. Then Sid and I will let you off here, or anywhere you say, and we'll go on to the picnic.

MRS. MILLER: I'd love it. Wouldn't you, Lily?

LILY: It would be nice.

145 MILLER: Then, that's all settled.

SID: *(Embarrassedly.)* Lily, want to come with me to the fireworks display at the beach tonight?

MRS. MILLER: That's right, Sid. You take her out. Poor Lily never has any fun, always sitting home with me.

150 LILY: *(Flustered and grateful.)* I—I'd like to, Sid, thank you. *(Then an apprehensive look comes over her face.)* Only not if you come home—you know.

SID: *(Again embarrassed and humiliated—again joking it off, solemnly.)* Evil-minded, I'm afraid, Nat. I hate to say it of

155 your sister. *(They all laugh. Even* LILY *cannot suppress a smile.)*

ARTHUR: *(With heavy jocularity.)* Listen, Uncle Sid. Don't let me catch you and Aunt Lily spooning on a bench tonight— or it'll be my duty to call a cop! *(*SID *and* LILY *both look*

painfully embarrassed at this, and the joke falls flat, except for 160 MILDRED *who can't restrain a giggle at the thought of these two ancients spooning.)*

MRS. MILLER: *(Rebukingly.)* Arthur!

MILLER: *(Dryly.)* That'll do you. Your education in kicking a football around Yale seems to have blunted your sense of 165 humor.

MRS. MILLER: *(Suddenly—startledly.)* But where's Richard? We're forgetting all about him. Why, where is that boy? I thought he came in with us from breakfast.

MILDRED: I'll bet he's off somewhere writing a poem to Muriel 170 McComber, the silly! Or pretending to write one. I think he just copies—

ARTHUR: *(Looking back toward the dining-room.)* He's still in the dining-room, reading a book. *(Turning back—scornfully.)* Gosh, he's always reading now. It's not my idea of hav- 175 ing a good time in vacation.

MILLER: *(Caustically.)* He read his school books, too, strange as that may seem to you. That's why he came out top of his class. I'm hoping before you leave New Haven they'll find time to teach you reading is a good habit. 180

MRS. MILLER: *(Sharply.)* That reminds me, Nat. I've been meaning to speak to you about those awful books Richard is reading. You've got to give him a good talking to—*(She gets up from her chair.)* I'll go up and get them right now. I found them where he'd hid them on the shelf in his wardrobe. You 185 just wait till you see what—*(She bustles off, rear right, through the front parlor.)*

MILLER: *(Plainly not relishing whatever is coming—to* SID, *grumblingly.)* Seems to me she might wait until the Fourth is over before bringing up—*(Then with a grin.)* I know there's 190 nothing to it, anyway. When I think of the books I used to sneak off and read when I was a kid.

SID: Me, too. I suppose Dick is deep in Nick Carter or Old Cap Collier.

MILLER: No, he passed that period long ago. Poetry's his red 195 meat nowadays, I think—love poetry—and socialism, too, I suspect, from some dire declarations he's made. *(Then briskly.)* Well, might as well get him on the carpet. *(He calls.)* Richard. *(No answer—louder.)* Richard. *(No answer— then in a bellow.)* Richard! 200

ARTHUR: *(Shouting.)* Hey, Dick, wake up! Pa's calling you.

RICHARD'S VOICE: *(From the dining-room.)* All right. I'm coming.

MILLER: Darn him! When he gets his nose in a book, the house could fall down and he'd never— 205

*(*RICHARD *appears in the doorway from the back parlor, the book he has been reading in one hand, a finger marking his place. He looks a bit startled still, reluctantly called back to earth from another world.)*

He is going on seventeen, just out of high school. In appearance he is a perfect blend of father and mother, so much so that each is convinced he is the image of the other. He has his mother's light-brown hair, his father's gray eyes; his features are neither large nor small; he is of medium height, neither fat nor thin. One would not call him a handsome boy; neither is he homely. But he is definitely different from both of his parents, too. There is something of extreme sensitiveness added—a restless, apprehensive, defiant, shy, dreamy, self-conscious intelligence about him. In manner he is alternately plain simple boy and a posey actor solemnly playing a role. He is dressed in prep school reflection of the college style of ARTHUR.)

RICHARD: Did you want me, Pa?

MILLER: I'd hoped I'd made that plain. Come and sit down a while. (*He points to the rocking chair at the right of table near his.*)

210 RICHARD: (*Coming forward—seizing on the opportunity to play up his preoccupation—with apologetic superiority.*) I didn't hear you, Pa. I was off in another world. (MILDRED *slyly shoves her foot out so that he trips over it, almost falling. She laughs gleefully. So does* ARTHUR.)

215 ARTHUR: Good for you, Mid! That'll wake him up!

RICHARD: (*Grins sheepishly—all boy now.*) Darn you, Mid! I'll show you! (*He pushes her back on the sofa and tickles her with his free hand, still holding the book in the other. She shrieks.*)

220 ARTHUR: Give it to her, Dick!

MILLER: That's enough, now. No more roughhouse. You sit down here, Richard. (RICHARD *obediently takes the chair at right of table, opposite his father.*) What were you planning to do with yourself today? Going out to the beach with Mil-
225 dred?

RICHARD: (*Scornfully superior.*) That silly skirt party! I should say not!

MILDRED: He's not coming because Muriel isn't. I'll bet he's got a date with her somewheres.

230 RICHARD: (*Flushing bashfully.*) You shut up! (*Then to his father.*) I thought I'd just stay home, Pa—this morning, anyway.

MILLER: Help Tommy set off firecrackers, eh?

RICHARD: (*Drawing himself up—with dignity.*) I should say
235 not. (*Then frowning portentously.*) I don't believe in this silly celebrating the Fourth of July—all this lying talk about liberty—when there is no liberty!

MILLER: (*A twinkle in his eye.*) Hmm.

RICHARD: (*Getting warmed up.*) The land of the free and the
240 home of the brave! Home of the slave is what they ought to call it—the wage slave ground under the heel of the capitalist class, starving, crying for bread for his children, and all he gets is a stone! The Fourth of July is a stupid farce!

MILLER: (*Putting a hand to his mouth to conceal a grin.*)
245 Hmm. Them are mighty strong words. You'd better not repeat such sentiments outside the bosom of the family or they'll have you in jail.

SID: And throw away the key.

RICHARD: (*Darkly.*) Let them put me in jail. But how about
250 the freedom of speech in the Constitution, then? That must be a farce, too. (*Then he adds grimly.*) No, you can celebrate your Fourth of July. I'll celebrate the day the people bring out the guillotine again and I see Pierpont Morgan being driven by in a tumbril! (*His father and* SID *are greatly
255 amused;* LILY *is shocked but, taking her cue from them, smiles.* MILDRED *stares at him in puzzled wonderment, never having heard this particular line before. Only* ARTHUR *betrays the outraged reaction of a patriot.*)

ARTHUR: Aw say, you fresh kid, tie that bull outside! You ought
260 to get a punch in the nose for talking that way on the Fourth!

MILLER: (*Solemnly.*) Son, if I didn't know it was you talking, I'd think we had Emma Goldman with us.

ARTHUR: Never mind, Pa. Wait till we get him down to Yale. We'll take that out of him!

265 RICHARD: (*With high scorn.*) Oh, Yale! You think there's nothing in the world besides Yale. After all, what is Yale?

ARTHUR: You'll find out what!

SID: (*Provocatively.*) Don't let them scare you, Dick. Give 'em hell!

270 LILY: (*Shocked.*) Sid! You shouldn't swear before—

RICHARD: What do you think I am, Aunt Lily—a baby? I've heard worse than anything Uncle Sid says.

MILDRED: And said worse himself, I bet!

MILLER: (*With a comic air of resignation.*) Well, Richard, I've
275 always found I've had to listen to at least one stump speech every Fourth. I only hope getting your extra strong one right after breakfast will let me off for the rest of the day. (*They all laugh now, taking this as a cue.*)

RICHARD: (*Somberly.*) That's right, laugh! After you, the del-
280 uge, you think! But look out! Supposing it comes before? Why shouldn't the workers of the world unite and rise? They have nothing to lose but their chains! (*He recites threateningly.*) "The days grow hot, O Babylon! 'Tis cool beneath thy willow trees!"

285 MILLER: Hmm. That's good. But where's the connection, exactly? Something from that book you're reading?

RICHARD: (*Superior.*) No. That's poetry. This is prose.

MILLER: I've heard there was a difference between 'em. What is the book?

290 RICHARD: (*Importantly.*) Carlyle's "French Revolution."

MILLER: Hmm. So that's where you drove the tumbril from and piled poor old Pierpont in it. (*Then seriously.*) Glad you're reading it, Richard. It's a darn fine book.

RICHARD: (*With unflattering astonishment.*) What, have you
295 read it?

MILLER: Well, you see, even a newspaper owner can't get out of reading a book every now and again.

RICHARD: (*Abashed.*) I—I didn't mean—I know you—(*Then enthusiastically.*) Say, isn't it a great book, though—that part
300 about Mirabeau—and about Marat and Robespierre—

MRS. MILLER: (*Appears from the front parlor in a great state of flushed annoyance.*) Never you mind Robespierre, young man! You tell me this minute where you've hidden those books! They were on the shelf in your wardrobe and now
305 you've gone and hid them somewhere else. You go right up and bring them to your father! (RICHARD, *for a second, looks suddenly guilty and crushed. Then he bristles defensively.*)

MILLER: (*After a quick understanding glance at him.*) Never mind his getting them now. We'll waste the whole morning
310 over those darned books. And anyway, he has a right to keep his library to himself—that is, if they're not too—What books are they, Richard?

RICHARD: (*Self-consciously.*) Well—there's—

MRS. MILLER: I'll tell you, if he won't—and you give him a
315 good talking to. (*Then, after a glance at* RICHARD, *mollifiedly.*) Not that I blame Richard. There must be some boy he knows who's trying to show off as advanced and wicked, and he told him about—

RICHARD: No! I read about them myself, in the papers and in other books.
320

MRS. MILLER: Well, no matter how, there they were on his shelf. Two by that awful Oscar Wilde they put in jail for heaven knows what wickedness.

ARTHUR: (*Suddenly—solemnly authoritative.*) He committed
325   bigamy. (*Then as* SID *smothers a burst of ribald laughter.*) What are you laughing at? I guess I ought to know. A fellow at college told me. His father was in England when this Wilde was pinched—and he said he remembered once his mother asked his father about it and he told her he'd com-
330   mitted bigamy.

MILLER: (*Hiding a smile behind his hand.*) Well then, that must be right, Arthur.

MRS. MILLER: I wouldn't put it past him, nor anything else. One book was called the Picture of something or other.

335 RICHARD: "The Picture of Dorian Gray." It's one of the greatest novels ever written!

MRS. MILLER: Looked to me like cheap trash. And the second book was poetry. The Ballad of I forget what.

RICHARD: "The Ballad of Reading Gaol," one of the greatest
340   poems ever written. (*He pronounces it Reading Goal [as in goalpost].*)

MRS. MILLER: All about someone who murdered his wife and got hung, as he richly deserved, as far as I could make out. And then there were two books by that Bernard Shaw—

345 RICHARD: The greatest playwright alive today!

MRS. MILLER: To hear him tell it, maybe! You know, Nat, the one who wrote a play about—well, never mind—that was so vile they wouldn't even let it play in New York!

MILLER: Hmm. I remember.

350 MRS. MILLER: One was a book of his plays and the other had a long title I couldn't make head or tail of, only it wasn't a play.

RICHARD: (*Proudly.*) "The Quintessence of Ibsenism."

MILDRED: Phew! Good gracious, what a name! What does it mean, Dick? I'll bet he doesn't know.

355 RICHARD: (*Outraged.*) I do, too, know! It's about Ibsen, the greatest playwright since Shakespeare!

MRS. MILLER: Yes, there was a book of plays by that Ibsen there, too! And poems by Swin something—

RICHARD: "Poems and Ballads" by Swinburne, Ma. The great-
360   est poet since Shelley! He tells the truth about real love!

MRS. MILLER: Love! Well, all I can say is, from reading here and there, that if he wasn't flung in jail along with Wilde, he should have been. Some of the things I simply couldn't read, they were so indecent—All about—well, I can't tell you be-
365   fore Lily and Mildred.

SID: (*With a wink at* RICHARD—*jokingly.*) Remember, I'm next on that one, Dick. I feel the need of a little poetical education.

LILY: (*Scandalized, but laughing.*) Sid! Aren't you ashamed?

370 MRS. MILLER: This is no laughing matter. And then there was Kipling—but I suppose he's not so bad. And last there was a poem—a long one—the Rubay—What is it, Richard?

RICHARD: "The Rubaiyat of Omar Khayyam." That's the best of all!

375 MILLER: Oh, I've read that, Essie—got a copy down at the office.

SID: (*Enthusiastically.*) So have I. It's a pippin!

LILY: (*With shy excitement.*) I—I've read it, too—at the library. I like—some parts of it.

380 MRS. MILLER: (*Scandalized.*) Why, Lily!

MILLER: Everybody's reading that now, Essie—and it don't seem to do them any harm. There's fine things in it, seems to me—true things.

MRS. MILLER: (*A bit bewildered and uncertain now.*) Why, Nat,
385   I don't see how you—It looked terrible blasphemous—parts I read.

SID: Remember this one: (*He quotes rhetorically.*) "Oh Thou, who didst with pitfall and gin beset the path I was to wander in—" Now, I've always noticed how beset my path was with
390   gin—in the past, you understand! (*He casts a joking side glance at* LILY. *The others laugh. But* LILY *is in a melancholy dream and hasn't heard him.*)

MRS. MILLER: (*Tartly, but evidently suppressing her usual smile where he is concerned.*) You would pick out the ones with
395   liquor in them!

LILY: (*Suddenly—with a sad pathos, quotes awkwardly and shyly.*) I like—because it's true:

      "The Moving Finger writes, and having writ,
      Moves on: nor all your Piety nor Wit
400   Shall lure it back to cancel half a Line,
      Nor all your Tears wash out a Word of it."

MRS. MILLER: (*Astonished, as are all the others.*) Why, Lily, I never knew you to recite poetry before!

LILY: (*Immediately guilty and apologetic.*) I—it just stuck in my
405   memory somehow.

RICHARD: (*Looking at her as if he had never seen her before.*) Good for you, Aunt Lily! (*Then enthusiastically.*) But that isn't the best. The best is:

      "A Book of Verses underneath the Bough,
      A Jug of Wine, A Loaf of Bread—and Thou
410   Beside me shining in the Wilderness—"

ARTHUR: (*Who, bored to death by all this poetry quoting, has wandered over to the window at rear of desk, right.*) Hey! Look who's coming up the walk!—Old Man McComber!

MILLER: (*Irritably.*) Dave? Now what in thunder does that
415   damned old—Sid, I can see where we never are going to get to that picnic.

MRS. MILLER: (*Vexatiously.*) He'll know we're in this early, too. No use lying. (*Then appalled by another thought.*) That Norah—she's that thick, she never can answer the front
420   door right unless I tell her each time. Nat, you've got to talk to Dave. I'll have her show him in here. Lily, you run up the back stairs and get your things on. I'll be up in a second. Nat, you get rid of him the first second you can! Whatever can the old fool want—(*She and* LILY *hurry out through the*
425   *back parlor.*)

ARTHUR: I'm going to beat it—just time to catch the eight-twenty trolley.

MILDRED: I've got to catch that, too. Wait till I get my hat, Art! (*She rushes into the back parlor.*)
430

ARTHUR: (*Shouts after her.*) I can't wait. You can catch up with me if you hurry. (*He turns at the back-parlor door—with a grin.*) McComber may be coming to see if your intentions toward his daughter are dishonorable, Dick! You'd better beat it while your shoes are good! (*He disappears through the*
435   *back-parlor door, laughing.*)

RICHARD: (*A bit shaken, but putting on a brave front.*) Think I'm scared of him?

MILLER: (*Gazing at him—frowning.*) Can't imagine what—
440   But it's to complain about something, I know that. I only
wish I didn't have to be pleasant with the old buzzard—but
he's about the most valuable advertiser I've got.

SID: (*Sympathetically.*) I know. But tell him to go to hell, anyway. He needs that ad more than you.

(*The sound of the bell comes from the rear of the house, off left
from back parlor.*)

445   MILLER: There he is. You clear out, Dick—but come right
back as soon as he's gone, you hear? I'm not through with
you, yet.

RICHARD: Yes, Pa.

MILLER: You better clear out, too, Sid. You know Dave doesn't
450   approve jokes.

SID: And loves me like poison! Come on, Dick, we'll go out
and help Tommy celebrate. (*He takes* RICHARD's *arm and
they also disappear through the back-parlor door.* MILLER
glances through the front parlor toward the front door, then
455   calls in a tone of strained heartiness.*)

MILLER: Hello, Dave. Come right in here. What good wind
blows you around on this glorious Fourth?

(*A flat, brittle voice answers him: "Good morning," and a moment later* DAVID MC COMBER *appears in the doorway from the
front parlor. He is a thin, dried-up little man with a head too
large for his body perched on a scrawny neck, and a long solemn
horse face with deepset little black eyes, a blunt formless nose
and a tiny slit of a mouth. He is about the same age as* MILLER
but is entirely bald, and looks ten years older. He is dressed with
a prim neatness in shiny old black clothes.*)

MILLER: Here, sit down and make yourself comfortable. (*Holding out the cigar box.*) Have a cigar?

460   MC COMBER: (*Sitting down in the chair at the right of table—
acidly.*) You're forgetting I never smoke.

MILLER: (*Forcing a laugh at himself.*) That's so. So I was. Well,
I'll smoke alone then. (*He bites off the end of the cigar viciously, as if he wished it were* MC COMBER's *head, and sits
465   down opposite him.*)

MC COMBER: You asked me what brings me here, so I'll come
to the point at once. I regret to say it's something disagreeable—disgraceful would be nearer the truth—and it concerns your son, Richard!

470   MILLER: (*Beginning to bristle—but calmly.*) Oh, come now,
Dave, I'm sure Richard hasn't—

MC COMBER: (*Sharply.*) And I'm positive he has. You're not
accusing me of being a liar, I hope.

MILLER: No one said anything about liar. I only meant you're
475   surely mistaken if you think—

MC COMBER: I'm not mistaken. I have proof of everything in
his own handwriting!

MILLER: (*Sharply.*) Let's get down to brass tacks. Just what is it
you're charging him with?

480   MC COMBER: With being dissolute and blasphemous—with
deliberately attempting to corrupt the morals of my young
daughter, Muriel.

MILLER: Then I'm afraid I will have to call you a liar, Dave!

MC COMBER: (*Without taking offense—in the same flat, brittle
485   voice.*) I thought you'd get around to that, so I brought some
of the proofs with me. I've a lot more of 'em at home. (*He

takes a wallet from his inside coat pocket, selects five or six
slips of paper, and holds them out to* MILLER.*) These are
good samples of the rest. My wife discovered them in one of
Muriel's bureau drawers hidden under the underwear.   490
They're all in his handwriting, you can't deny it. Anyway,
Muriel's confessed to me he wrote them. You read them and
then say I'm a liar. (*MILLER has taken the slips and is reading
them frowningly.* MC COMBER *talks on.*) Evidently you've
been too busy to take the right care about Richard's bringing 495
up or what he's allowed to read—though I can't see why his
mother failed in her duty. But that's your misfortune, and
none of my business. But Muriel is my business and I can't
and I won't have her innocence exposed to the contamina-
tion of a young man whose mind, judging from his choice of 500
reading matter, is as foul—

MILLER: (*Making a tremendous effort to control his temper.*)
Why, you damned old fool! Can't you see Richard's only a
fool kid who's just at the stage when he's out to rebel against
all authority, and so he grabs at everything radical to read   505
and wants to pass it on to his elders and his girl and boy
friends to show off what a young hellion he is! Why, at heart
you'd find Richard is just as innocent and as big a kid as
Muriel is! (*He pushes the slips of paper across the table contemptuously.*) This stuff doesn't mean anything to me—that 510
is, nothing of what you think it means. If you believe this
would corrupt Muriel, then you must believe she's easily corrupted! But I'll bet you'd find she knows a lot more about life
than you give her credit for—and can guess a stork didn't
bring her down your chimney!   515

MC COMBER: Now you're insulting my daughter. I won't forget
that.

MILLER: I'm not insulting her. I think Muriel is a darn nice
girl. That's why I'm giving her credit for ordinary good sense.
I'd say the same about my own Mildred, who's the same age. 520

MC COMBER: I know nothing about your Mildred except that
she's known all over as a flirt. (*Then more sharply.*) Well, I
knew you'd prove obstinate, but I certainly never dreamed
you'd have the impudence, after reading those papers, to
claim your son was innocent of all wrongdoing!   525

MILLER: And what did you dream I'd do?

MC COMBER: Do what it's your plain duty to do as a citizen to
protect other people's children! Take and give him a hiding
he'd remember to the last day of his life! You'd ought to do it
for his sake, if you had any sense—unless you want him to   530
end up in jail!

MILLER: (*His fists clenched, leans across the table.*) Dave, I've
stood all I can stand from you! You get out! And get out
quick, if you don't want a kick in the rear to help you!

MC COMBER: (*Again in his flat, brittle voice, slowly getting to   535
his feet.*) You needn't lose your temper. I'm only demanding
you do your duty by your own as I've already done by mine.
I'm punishing Muriel. She's not to be allowed out of the
house for a month and she's to be in bed every night by eight
sharp. And yet she's blameless, compared to that—   540

MILLER: I said I'd had enough out of you, Dave! (*He makes a
threatening movement.*)

MC COMBER: You needn't lay hands on me. I'm going. But
there's one thing more. (*He takes a letter from his wallet.*)
Here's a letter from Muriel for your son. (*Puts it on the   545
table.*) It makes clear, I think, how she's come to think about

him, now that her eyes have been opened. I hope he heeds what's inside—for his own good and yours—because if I ever catch him hanging about my place again I'll have him ar-
550 rested! And don't think I'm not going to make you regret the insults you've heaped on me. I'm taking the advertisement for my store out of your paper—and it won't go in again, I tell you, not unless you apologize in writing and promise to punish—

555 MILLER: I'll see you in hell first! As for your damned old ad, take it out and go to hell!

MC COMBER: That's plain bluff. You know how badly you need it. So do I. (*He starts stiffly for the door.*)

MILLER: Here! Listen a minute! I'm just going to call *your*
560 bluff and tell you that, whether you want to reconsider your decision or not, I'm going to refuse to print your damned ad after tomorrow! Put that in your pipe and smoke it! Furthermore, I'll start a campaign to encourage outside capital to open a dry-goods store in opposition to you that won't be the
565 public swindle I can prove yours is!

MC COMBER: (*A bit shaken by this threat—but in the same flat tone.*) I'll sue you for libel.

MILLER: When I get through, there won't be a person in town will buy a dishrag in your place!

570 MC COMBER: (*More shaken, his eyes shifting about furtively.*) That's all bluff. You wouldn't dare—(*Then finally he says uncertainly.*) Well, good day. (*And turns and goes out.* NAT *stands looking after him. Slowly the anger drains from his face and leaves him looking a bit sick and disgusted.* SID *appears*
575 *from the back parlor. He is nursing a burn on his right hand, but his face is one broad grin of satisfaction.*)

SID: I burned my hand with one of Tommy's damned firecrackers and came in to get some vaseline. I was listening to the last of your scrap. Good for you, Nat! You sure gave him
580 hell!

MILLER: (*Dully.*) Much good it'll do. He knows it was all talk.

SID: That's just what he don't know, Nat. The old skinflint has a guilty conscience.

MILLER: Well, anyone who knows me knows I wouldn't use my
585 paper for a dirty, spiteful trick like that—no matter what he did to me.

SID: Yes, everyone knows you're an old sucker, Nat, too decent for your own good. But McComber never saw you like this before. I tell you you scared the pants off him. (*He chuckles.*)

590 MILLER: (*Still dejectedly.*) I don't know what made me let go like that. The hell of skunks like McComber is that after being with them ten minutes you become as big skunks as they are.

SID: (*Notices the slips of paper on the table.*) What's this?
595 Something he brought? (*He picks them up and starts to read.*)

MILLER: (*Grimly.*) Samples of the new freedom—from those books Essie found—that Richard's been passing on to Muriel to educate her. They're what started the rumpus.
600 (*Then frowning.*) I've got to do something about that young anarchist or he'll be getting me, and himself, in a peck of trouble. (*Then pathetically helpless.*) But what can I do? Putting the curb bit on would make him worse. Then he'd have a harsh tyrant to defy. He'd love that, darn him!

605 SID: (*Has been reading the slips, a broad grin on his face—suddenly he whistles.*) Phew! This is a warm lulu for fair! (*He recites with a joking intensity.*)

"My life is bitter with thy love; thine eyes
Blind me, thy tresses burn me, thy sharp sighs
Divide my flesh and spirit with soft sound—" 610

MILLER: (*With a grim smile.*) Hmm. I missed that one. That must be Mr. Swinburne's copy. I've never read him, but I've heard something like that was the matter with him.

SID: Yes, it's labelled Swinburne—"Anactoria." Whatever that is. But wait, watch and listen! The worst is yet to come! (*He 615 recites with added comic intensity.*)

"That I could drink thy veins as wine, and eat
Thy breasts like honey, that from face to feet
Thy body were abolished and consumed,
And in my flesh thy very flesh entombed!" 620

MILLER: (*An irrepressible boyish grin coming to his face.*) Hell and hallelujah! Just picture old Dave digesting that for the first time! Gosh, I'd give a lot to have seen his face! (*Then a trace of shocked reproof showing in his voice.*) But it's no joking matter. That stuff *is* warm—too damned warm, if you ask 625 me! I don't like this a damned bit, Sid. That's no kind of thing to be sending a decent girl. (*More worriedly.*) I thought he was really stuck on her—as one gets stuck on a decent girl at his age—all moonshine and holding hands and a kiss now and again. But this looks—I wonder if he is hanging around 630 her to see what he can get? (*Angrily.*) By God, if that's true, he deserves that licking McComber says it's my duty to give him! I've got to draw the line somewhere!

SID: Yes, it won't do to have him getting any decent girl in trouble. 635

MILLER: The only thing I can do is put it up to him straight. (*With pride.*) Richard'll stand up to his guns, no matter what. I've never known him to lie to me.

SID: (*At a noise from the back parlor, looks that way—in a whisper.*) Then now's your chance. I'll beat it and leave you 640 alone—see if the women folks are ready upstairs. We ought to get started soon—if we're ever going to make that picnic. (*He is halfway to the entrance to the front parlor as* RICHARD *enters from the back parlor, very evidently nervous about* MC COMBER'S *call.*) 645

RICHARD: (*Adopting a forced, innocent tone.*) How's your hand, Uncle Sid?

SID: All right, Dick, thanks—only hurts a little. (*He disappears.* MILLER *watches his son frowningly.* RICHARD *gives him a quick side glance and grows more guiltily self-conscious.*) 650

RICHARD: (*Forcing a snicker.*) Gee, Pa, Uncle Sid's a bigger kid than Tommy is. He was throwing firecrackers in the air and catching them on the back of his hand and throwing 'em off again just before they went off—and one came and he wasn't quick enough, and it went off almost on top of— 655

MILLER: Never mind that. I've got something else to talk to you about besides firecrackers.

RICHARD: (*Apprehensively.*) What, Pa?

MILLER: (*Suddenly puts both hands on his shoulders—quietly.*) Look here, Son. I'm going to ask you a question, and I want 660 an honest answer. I warn you beforehand if the answer is "yes" I'm going to punish you and punish you hard because you'll have done something no boy of mine ought to do. But you've never lied to me before, I know, and I don't believe, even to save yourself punishment, you'd lie to me now, 665 would you?

RICHARD: (*Impressed—with dignity.*) I won't lie, Pa.

MILLER: Have you been trying to have something to do with Muriel—something you shouldn't—you know what I mean.

670 RICHARD: (*Stares at him for a moment, as if he couldn't comprehend—then, as he does, a look of shocked indignation comes over his face.*) No! What do you think I am, Pa? I never would! She's not that kind! Why, I—I love her! I'm going to marry her—after I get out of college! She's said she would!

675 We're engaged!

MILLER: (*With great relief.*) All right. That's all I wanted to know. We won't talk any more about it. (*He gives him an approving pat on the back.*)

RICHARD: I don't see how you could think—Did that old idiot

680 McComber say that about me?

MILLER: (*Joking now.*) Shouldn't call your future father-in-law names, should you? 'Tain't respectful. (*Then after a glance at* RICHARD'S *indignant face—points to the slips of paper on the table.*) Well, you can't exactly blame old Dave, can you,

685 when you read through that literature you wished on his innocent daughter?

RICHARD: (*Sees the slips for the first time and is overcome by embarrassment, which he immediately tries to cover up with a superior carelessness.*) Oh, so that's why. He found those, did

690 he? I told her to be careful—Well, it'll do him good to read the truth about life for once and get rid of his old-fogy ideas.

MILLER: I'm afraid I've got to agree with him, though, that they're hardly fit reading for a young girl. (*Then with subtle flattery.*) They're all well enough, in their way, for you

695 who're a man, but—Think it over, and see if you don't agree with me.

RICHARD: (*Embarrassedly.*) Aw, I only did it because I liked them—and I wanted her to face life as it is. She's so darned afraid of life—afraid of her Old Man—afraid of people say-

700 ing this or that about her—afraid of being in love—afraid of everything. She's even afraid to let me kiss her. I thought, maybe, reading those things—they're beautiful, aren't they, Pa?—I thought they would give her the spunk to lead her own life, and not be—always thinking of being afraid.

705 MILLER: I see. Well, I'm afraid she's still afraid. (*He takes the letter from the table.*) Here's a letter from her he said to give you. (RICHARD *takes the letter from him uncertainly, his expression changing to one of apprehension.* MILLER *adds with a kindly smile.*) You better be prepared for a bit of a blow. But

710 never mind. There's lots of other fish in the sea. (RICHARD *is not listening to him, but staring at the letter with a sort of fascinated dread.* MILLER *looks into his son's face a second, then turns away, troubled and embarrassed.*) Darn it! I better go upstairs and get rigged out or I never will get to that picnic.

715 (*He moves awkwardly and self-consciously off through the front parlor.* RICHARD *continues to stare at the letter for a moment—then girds up his courage and tears it open and begins to read swiftly. As he reads his face grows more and more wounded and tragic, until at the end his mouth draws down at

720 the corners, as if he were about to break into tears. With an effort he forces them back and his face grows flushed with humiliation and wronged anger.*)

RICHARD: (*Blurts out to himself.*) The little coward! I hate her! She can't treat me like that! I'll show her! (*At the sound of

725 voices from the front parlor, he quickly shoves the letter into the inside pocket of his coat and does his best to appear calm and indifferent, even attempting to whistle "Waiting at the Church." But the whistle peters out miserably as his mother,

LILY *and* SID *enter from the front parlor. They are dressed in all the elaborate paraphernalia of motoring at that period—*

730 *linen dusters, veils, goggles,* SID *in a snappy cap.*)

MRS. MILLER: Well, we're about ready to start at last, thank goodness! Let's hope no more callers are on the way. What did that McComber want, Richard, do you know? Sid

735 couldn't tell us.

RICHARD: You can search me. Ask Pa.

MRS. MILLER: (*Immediately sensing something "down" in his manner—going to him worriedly.*) Why, whatever's the matter with you, Richard? You sound as if you'd lost your last

740 friend! What is it?

RICHARD: (*Desperately.*) I—I don't feel so well—my stomach's sick.

MRS. MILLER: (*Immediately all sympathy—smoothing his hair back from his forehead.*) You poor boy! What a shame—on the Fourth, too, of all days! (*Turning to the others.*) Maybe I

745 better stay home with him, if he's sick.

LILY: Yes, I'll stay, too.

RICHARD: (*More desperately.*) No! You go, Ma! I'm not really sick. I'll be all right. You go. I want to be alone! (*Then, as a louder bang comes from in back as* TOMMY *sets off a cannon

750 cracker, he jumps to his feet.*) Darn Tommy and his darned firecrackers! You can't get any peace in this house with that darned kid around! Darn the Fourth of July, anyway! I wish we still belonged to England! (*He strides off in an indignant fury of misery through the front parlor.*)

755 MRS. MILLER: (*Stares after him worriedly—then sighs philosophically.*) Well, I guess he can't be so very sick—after that. (*She shakes her head.*) He's a queer boy. Sometimes I can't make head or tail of him.

MILLER: (*Calls from the front door beyond the back parlor.*)

760 Come along folks. Let's get started.

SID: We're coming, Nat. (*He and the two women move off through the front parlor.*)

(*Curtain.*)

— ACT TWO —

Dining-room of the MILLER *home—a little after 6 o'clock in the evening of the same day.*

The room is much too small for the medium-priced, formidable dining-room set, especially now when all the leaves of the table are in. At left, toward rear, is a double doorway with sliding doors and portières leading into the back parlor. In the rear wall, left, is the door to the pantry. At the right of door is the china closet with its display of the family cut glass and fancy china. In the right wall are two windows looking out on a side lawn. In front of the windows is a heavy, ugly sideboard with three pieces of old silver on its top. In the left wall, extreme front, is a screen door opening on a side porch. A dark rug covers most of the floor. The table, with a chair at each end, left and right, three chairs on the far side, facing front, and two on the near side, their backs to front, takes up most of the available space. The walls are papered in a somber brown and dark-red design.

MRS. MILLER *is supervising and helping the Second Girl,* NORAH, *in the setting of the table.* NORAH *is a clumsy, heavy-handed, heavy-footed, long-jawed, beamingly good-natured young Irish girl—a "greenhorn."*

MRS. MILLER: I really think you better put on the lights, Norah. It's getting so cloudy out, and this pesky room is so dark, anyway.

NORAH: Yes, Mum. (*She stretches awkwardly over the table to reach the chandelier that is suspended from the middle of the ceiling and manages to turn one light on—scornfully.*) Arrah, the contraption!

MRS. MILLER: (*Worriedly.*) Careful!

NORAH: Careful as can be, Mum. (*But in moving around to reach the next bulb she jars heavily against the table.*)

MRS. MILLER: There! I knew it! I do wish you'd watch—!

NORAH: (*A flustered appeal in her voice.*) Arrah, what have I done wrong now?

MRS. MILLER: (*Draws a deep breath—then sighs helplessly.*) Oh, nothing. Never mind the rest of the lights. You might as well go out in the kitchen and wait until I ring.

NORAH: (*Relieved and cheerful again.*) Yes, Mum. (*She starts for the pantry.*)

MRS. MILLER: But there's one thing—(NORAH *turns apprehensively.*) No, two things—things I've told you over and over, but you always forget. Don't pass the plates on the wrong side at dinner tonight, and do be careful not to let that pantry door slam behind you. Now you will try to remember, won't you?

NORAH: Yes, Mum. (*She goes into the pantry and shuts the door behind her with exaggerated care as* MRS. MILLER *watches her apprehensively.* MRS. MILLER *sighs and reaches up with difficulty and turns on another of the four lights in the chandelier. As she is doing so,* LILY *enters from the back parlor.*)

LILY: Here, let me do that, Essie. I'm taller. You'll only strain yourself. (*She quickly lights the other two bulbs.*)

MRS. MILLER: (*Gratefully.*) Thank you, Lily. It's a stretch for me, I'm getting so fat.

LILY: But where's Norah? Why didn't she—?

MRS. MILLER: (*Exasperatedly.*) Oh, that girl! Don't talk about her! She'll be the death of me! She's that thick, you honestly wouldn't believe it possible.

LILY: (*Smiling.*) Why, what did she do now?

MRS. MILLER: Oh, nothing. She means all right.

LILY: Anything else I can do, Essie?

MRS. MILLER: Well, she's got the table all wrong. We'll have to reset it. But you're always helping me. It isn't fair to ask you—in your vacation. You need your rest after teaching a pack of wild Indians of kids all year.

LILY: (*Beginning to help with the table.*) You know I love to help. It makes me feel I'm some use in this house instead of just sponging—

MRS. MILLER: (*Indignantly.*) Sponging! You pay, don't you?

LILY: Almost nothing. And you and Nat only take that little to make me feel better about living with you. (*Forcing a smile.*) I don't see how you stand me—having a cranky old maid around all the time.

MRS. MILLER: What nonsense you talk! As if Nat and I weren't only too tickled to death to have you! Lily Miller, I've no patience with you when you go on like that. We've been over this a thousand times before, and still you go on! Crazy, that's what it is! (*She changes the subject abruptly.*) What time's it getting to be?

LILY: (*Looking at her watch.*) Quarter past six.

MRS. MILLER: I do hope those men folks aren't going to be late for dinner. (*She sighs.*) But I suppose with that darned Sachem Club picnic it's more likely than not. (LILY *looks worried, and sighs.* MRS. MILLER *gives her a quick side glance.*) I see you've got your new dress on.

LILY: (*Embarrassedly.*) Yes, I thought—if Sid's taking me to the fireworks—I ought to spruce up a little.

MRS. MILLER: (*Looking away.*) Hmm. (*A pause—then she says with an effort to be casual.*) You mustn't mind if Sid comes home feeling a bit—gay. I expect Nat to—and we'll have to listen to all those old stories of his about when he was a boy. You know what those picnics are, and Sid'd be running into all his old friends.

LILY: (*Agitatedly.*) I don't think he will—this time—not after his promise.

MRS. MILLER: (*Avoiding looking at her.*) I know. But men are weak. (*Then quickly.*) That was a good notion of Nat's, getting Sid the job on the Waterbury *Standard*. All he ever needed was to get away from the rut he was in here. He's the kind that's the victim of his friends. He's easily led—but there's no real harm in him, you know that. (LILY *keeps silent, her eyes downcast.* MRS. MILLER *goes on meaningly.*) He's making good money in Waterbury, too—thirty-five a week. He's in a better position to get married than he ever was.

LILY: (*Stiffly.*) Well, I hope he finds a woman who's willing—though after he's through with his betting on horse races, and dice, and playing Kelly pool, there won't be much left for a wife—even if there was nothing else he spent his money on.

MRS. MILLER: Oh, he'd give up all that—for the right woman. (*Suddenly she comes directly to the point.*) Lily, why don't you change your mind and marry Sid and reform him? You love him and always have—

LILY: (*Stiffly.*) I can't love a man who drinks.

MRS. MILLER: You can't fool me. I know darned well you love him. And he loves you and always has.

LILY: Never enough to stop drinking for. (*Cutting off* MRS. MILLER's *reply.*) No, it's no good in your talking, Essie. We've been over this a thousand times before and I'll always feel the same as long as Sid's the same. If he gave me proof he'd—but even then I don't believe I could. It's sixteen years since I broke off our engagement, but what made me break it off is as clear to me today as it was then. It was what he'd be liable to do now to anyone who married him—his taking up with bad women.

MRS. MILLER: (*Protests half-heartedly.*) But he's always sworn he got raked into that party and never had anything to do with those harlots.

LILY: Well, I don't believe him—didn't then and don't now. I do believe he didn't deliberately plan to, but—Oh, it's no good talking, Essie. What's done is done. But you know how much I like Sid—in spite of everything. I know he was just born to be what he is—irresponsible, never meaning to harm but harming in spite of himself. But don't talk to me about marrying him—because I never could.

MRS. MILLER: (*Angrily.*) He's a dumb fool—a stupid dumb fool, that's what he is!

LILY: (*Quietly.*) No. He's just Sid.

MRS. MILLER: It's a shame for you—a measly shame—you that would have made such a wonderful wife for any man—that ought to have your own home and children!

LILY: (*Winces but puts her arm around her affectionately—gently.*) Now don't you go feeling sorry for me. I won't have that.

125 Here I am, thanks to your and Nat's kindness, with the best home in the world; and as for the children, I feel the same love for yours as if they were mine, and I didn't have the pain of bearing them. And then there are all the boys and girls I teach every year. I like to feel I'm a sort of second mother to
130 them and helping them to grow up to be good men and women. So I don't feel such a useless old maid, after all.

MRS. MILLER: (*Kisses her impulsively—her voice husky.*) You're a good woman, Lily—too good for the rest of us. (*She turns away, wiping a tear furtively—then abruptly changing the*
135 *subject.*) Good gracious, if I'm not forgetting one of the most important things! I've got to warn that Tommy against giving me away to Nat about the fish. He knows, because I had to send him to market for it, and he's liable to burst out laughing—

140 LILY: Laughing about what?

MRS. MILLER: (*Guiltily.*) Well, I've never told you, because it seemed sort of a sneaking trick, but you know how Nat carries on about not being able to eat bluefish.

LILY: I know he says there's a certain oil in it that poisons him.

145 MRS. MILLER: (*Chuckling.*) Poisons him, nothing! He's been eating bluefish for years—only I tell him each time it's weakfish. We're having it tonight—and I've got to warn that young imp to keep his face straight.

LILY: (*Laughing.*) Aren't you ashamed, Essie!

150 MRS. MILLER: Not much, I'm not! I like bluefish! (*She laughs.*) Where is Tommy? In the sitting-room?

LILY: No, Richard's there alone. I think Tommy's out on the piazza with Mildred. (MRS. MILLER *bustles out through the back parlor. As soon as she is gone, the smile fades from* LILY's
155 *lips. Her face grows sad and she again glances nervously at her watch.* RICHARD *appears from the back parlor, moving in an aimless way. His face wears a set expression of bitter gloom; he exudes tragedy. For* RICHARD, *after his first outburst of grief and humiliation, has begun to take a masochistic satis-*
160 *faction in his great sorrow, especially in the concern which it arouses in the family circle. On seeing his aunt, he gives her a dark look and turns and is about to stalk back toward the sitting-room when she speaks to him pityingly.*) Feel any better, Richard?

165 RICHARD: (*Somberly.*) I'm all right, Aunt Lily. You mustn't worry about me.

LILY: (*Going to him.*) But I do worry about you. I hate to see you so upset.

RICHARD: It doesn't matter. Nothing matters.

170 LILY: (*Puts her arm around him sympathetically.*) You really mustn't let yourself take it so seriously. You know, something happens and things like that come up, and we think there's no hope—

RICHARD: Things like what come up?

175 LILY: What's happened between you and Muriel.

RICHARD: (*With disdain.*) Oh, her! I wasn't even thinking about her. I was thinking about life.

LILY: But then—if we really, *really* love—why, then something else is bound to happen soon that changes everything again,
180 and it's all as it was before the misunderstanding, and everything works out all right in the end. That's the way it is with life.

RICHARD: (*With a tragic sneer.*) Life! Life is a joke! And everything comes out all wrong in the end!

185 LILY: (*A little shocked.*) You mustn't talk that way. But I know you don't mean it.

RICHARD: I do too mean it! You can have your silly optimism, if you like, Aunt Lily. But don't ask me to be so blind. I'm a pessimist! (*Then with an air of cruel cynicism.*) As for Muriel, that's all dead and past. I was only kidding her, anyway, just
190 to have a little fun, and she took it seriously, like a fool. (*He forces a cruel smile to his lips.*) You know what they say about women and trolley cars, Aunt Lily: there's always another one along in a minute.

195 LILY: (*Really shocked this time.*) I don't like you when you say such horrible, cynical things. It isn't nice.

RICHARD: Nice! that's all you women think of! I'm proud to be a cynic. It's the only thing you can be when you really face life. I suppose you think I ought to be heartbroken about Muriel—a little coward that's afraid to say her soul's her
200 own, and keeps tied to her father's apron strings! Well, not for mine! There's plenty of other fish in the sea! (*As he is finishing, his mother comes back through the back parlor.*)

MRS. MILLER: Why, hello. You here, Richard? Getting hungry,
205 I suppose?

RICHARD: (*Indignantly.*) I'm not hungry a bit! That's all you think of, Ma—food!

MRS. MILLER: Well, I must say I've never noticed you to hang back at meal times. (*To* LILY.) What's that he was saying
210 about fish in the sea?

LILY: (*Smiling.*) He says he's through with Muriel now.

MRS. MILLER: (*Tartly—giving her son a rebuking look.*) She's through with him, he means! The idea of your sending a nice girl like her things out of those indecent books! (*Deeply offended,* RICHARD *disdains to reply but stalks woundedly to*
215 *the screen door at left, front, and puts a hand on the knob.*) Where are you going?

RICHARD: (*Quotes from "Candida" in a hollow voice.*) "Out, then, into the night with me!" (*He stalks out, slamming the door behind him.*)
220 MRS. MILLER: (*Calls.*) Well, don't you go far, 'cause dinner'll be ready in a minute, and I'm not coming running after you! (*She turns to* LILY *with a chuckle.*) Goodness, that boy! He ought to be on the stage! (*She mimics.*) "Out—into the night"—and it isn't even dark yet! He got that out of one of
225 those books, I suppose. Do you know, I'm actually grateful to old Dave McComber for putting an end to his nonsense with Muriel. I never did approve of Richard getting so interested in girls. He's not old enough for such silliness. Why, seems to me it was only yesterday he was still a baby. (*She*
230 *sighs—then matter-of-factly.*) Well, nothing to do now till those men turn up. No use standing here like gawks. We might as well go in the sitting-room and be comfortable.

LILY: (*The nervous, worried note in her voice again.*) Yes, we might as well. (*They go out through the back parlor. They*
235 *have no sooner disappeared than the screen door is opened cautiously and* RICHARD *comes back in the room.*)

RICHARD: (*Stands inside the door, looking after them—quotes bitterly.*) "They do not know the secret in the poet's heart." (*He comes nearer the table and surveys it, especially the cut-*
240 *glass dish containing olives, with contempt and mutters disdainfully.*) Food! (*But the dish of olives seems to fascinate him and presently he has approached nearer, and stealthily lifts a couple and crams them into his mouth. He is just reaching out for more when the pantry door is opened slightly and* NORAH
245 *peers in.*)

NORAH: Mister Dick, you thief, lave them olives alone, or the missus'll be swearing it was me at them!

250 RICHARD: (*Draws back his hand as if he had been stung—too flustered to be anything but guilty boy for a second.*) I—I wasn't eating—

NORAH: Oho, no, of course not, divil fear you, you was only feeling their pulse! (*Then warningly.*) Mind what I'm saying now, or I'll have to tell on you to protect me good name!

255 (*She draws back into the pantry, closing the door.* RICHARD *stands, a prey to feelings of bitterest humiliation and seething revolt against everyone and everything. A low whistle comes from just outside the porch door. He starts. Then a masculine voice calls:* "Hey, Dick." *He goes over to the screen door*

260 *grumpily—then as he recognize the owner of the voice, his own as he answers becomes respectful and admiring.*)

RICHARD: Oh, hello, Wint. Come on in. (*He opens the door and* WINT SELBY *enters and stands just inside the door.* SELBY *is nineteen, a classmate of* ARTHUR's *at Yale. He's a typical,*

265 *good-looking college boy of the period, not the athletic but the hell-raising sport type. He is tall, blond, dressed in extreme collegiate cut.*)

WINT: (*As he enters—warningly, in a low tone.*) Keep it quiet, Kid. I don't want the folks to know I'm here. Tell Art I want

270 to see him a second—on the Q.T.

RICHARD: Can't. He's up at the Rands'—won't be home before ten, anyway.

WINT: (*Irritably.*) Damn, I thought he'd be here for dinner. (*More irritably.*) Hell, that gums the works for fair!

275 RICHARD: (*Ingratiatingly.*) What is it, Wint? Can't I help?

WINT: (*Gives him an appraising glance.*) I might tell you, if you can keep your face shut.

RICHARD: I can.

WINT: Well, I ran into a couple of swift babies from New

280 Haven this after. and I dated them up for tonight, thinking I could catch Art. But now it's too late to get anyone else and I'll have to pass it up. I'm nearly broke and I can't afford to blow them both to drinks.

RICHARD: (*With shy eagerness.*) I've got eleven dollars saved

285 up. I could loan you some.

WINT: (*Surveys him appreciatively.*) Say, you're a good sport. (*Then shaking his head.*) Nix, Kid, I don't want to borrow your money. (*Then getting an idea.*) But say, have you got anything on for tonight?

290 RICHARD: No.

WINT: Want to come along with me? (*Then quickly.*) I'm not trying to lead you astray, understand. But it'll be a help if you would just sit around with Belle and feed her a few drinks while I'm off with Edith. (*He winks.*) See what I mean? You

295 don't have to do anything, not even take a glass of beer—unless you want to.

RICHARD: (*Boastfully.*) Aw, what do you think I am—a rube?

WINT: You mean you're game for anything that's doing?

RICHARD: Sure I am!

300 WINT: Ever been out with any girls—I mean, real swift ones that there's something doing with, not these dead Janes around here?

RICHARD: (*Lies boldly.*) Aw, what do you think? Sure I have!

WINT: Ever drink anything besides sodas?

305 RICHARD: Sure. Lots of times. Beer and sloe-gin fizz and—Manhattans.

WINT: (*Impressed.*) Hell, you know more than I thought. (*Then considering.*) Can you fix it so your folks won't get wise? I don't want your old man coming after me. You can get back

by half-past ten or eleven, though, all right. Think you can 310 cook up some lie to cover that? (*As* RICHARD *hesitates—encouraging him.*) Ought to be easy—on the Fourth.

RICHARD: Sure. Don't worry about that.

WINT: But you've got to keep your face closed about this, you hear?—to Art and everybody else. I tell you straight, I 315 wouldn't ask you to come if I wasn't in a hole—and if I didn't know you were coming down to Yale next year, and didn't think you're giving me the straight goods about having been around before. I don't want to lead you astray.

RICHARD: (*Scornfully.*) Aw, I told you that was silly. 320

WINT: Well, you be at the Pleasant Beach House at half-past nine then. Come in the back room. And don't forget to grab some cloves to take the booze off your breath.

RICHARD: Aw, I know what to do.

WINT: See you later, then. (*He starts out and is just about to* 325 *close the door when he thinks of something.*) And say, I'll say you're a Harvard freshman, and you back me up. They don't know a damn thing about Harvard. I don't want them thinking I'm travelling around with any high-school kid.

RICHARD: Sure. That's easy. 330

WINT: So long, then. You better beat it right after your dinner while you've got a chance, and hang around until it's time. Watch your step, Kid.

RICHARD: So long. (*The door closes behind* WINT. RICHARD *stands for a moment, a look of bitter, defiant rebellion coming* 335 *over his face, and mutters to himself.*) I'll show her she can't treat me the way she's done! I'll show them all! (*Then the front door is heard slamming, and a moment later* TOMMY *rushes in from the back parlor.*)

TOMMY: Where's Ma? 340

RICHARD: (*Surlily.*) In the sitting-room. Where did you think, Bonehead?

TOMMY: Pa and Uncle Sid are coming. Mid and I saw them from the front piazza. Gee, I'm glad. I'm awful hungry, ain't you? (*He rushes out through the back parlor, calling.*) Ma! 345 They're coming! Let's have dinner quick! (*A moment later* MRS. MILLER *appears from the back parlor accompanied by* TOMMY, *who keeps insisting urgently.*) Gee, but I'm awful hungry, Ma!

MRS. MILLER: I know. You always are. You've got a tapeworm, 350 that's what I think.

TOMMY: Have we got lobsters, Ma? Gee, I love lobsters.

MRS. MILLER: Yes, we've got lobsters. And fish. You remember what I told you about that fish. (*He snickers.*) Now, do be quiet, Tommy! (*Then with a teasing smile at* RICHARD.) 355 Well, I'm glad to see you've got back out of the night, Richard. (*He scowls and turns his back on her.* LILY *appears through the back parlor, nervous and apprehensive. As she does so, from the front yard* SID's *voice is heard singing* "Poor John!" MRS. MILLER *shakes her head forebodingly—but, so* 360 *great is the comic spell for her even in her brother's voice, a humorous smile hovers at the corners of her lips.*) Mmm! Mmm! Lily, I'm afraid—

LILY: (*Bitterly.*) Yes, I might have known. (MILDRED *runs in through the back parlor. She is laughing to herself a bit* 365 *shamefacedly. She rushes to her mother.*)

MILDRED: Ma, Uncle Sid's—(*She whispers in her ear.*)

MRS. MILLER: Never mind! You shouldn't notice such things—at your age! And don't you encourage him by laughing at his foolishness, you hear! 370

TOMMY: You needn't whisper, Mid. Think I don't know? Uncle Sid's soused again.

MRS. MILLER: (*Shakes him by the arm indignantly.*) You be quiet! Did I ever! You're getting too smart! (*Gives him a push.*) Go to your place and sit right down and not another word out of you!

375

TOMMY: (*Aggrieved—rubbing his arm as he goes to his place.*) Aw, Ma!

MRS. MILLER: And you sit down, Richard and Mildred. You

380 better, too, Lily. We'll get him right in here and get some food in him. He'll be all right then. (RICHARD, *preserving the pose of the bitter, disillusioned pessimist, sits down in his place in the chair at right of the two whose backs face front.* MILDRED *takes the other chair facing back, at his left.* TOMMY

385 *has already slid into the end chair at right of those at the rear of table facing front.* LILY *sits in the one of those at left, by the head of the table, leaving the middle one [*SID'S*] vacant. While they are doing this, the front screen door is heard slamming and* NAT'S *and* SID'S *laughing voices, raised as they come in*

390 *and for a moment after, then suddenly cautiously lowered.* MRS. MILLER *goes to the entrance to the back parlor and calls peremptorily.*) You come right in here! Don't stop to wash up or anything. Dinner's coming right on the table.

MILLER'S VOICE: (*Jovially.*) All right, Essie. Here we are! Here

395 we are!

MRS. MILLER: (*Goes to pantry door, opens it and calls.*) All right, Norah. You can bring in the soup. (*She comes back to the back-parlor entrance just as* MILLER *enters. He isn't drunk by any means. He is just mellow and benignly ripened. His

400 face is one large, smiling, happy beam of utter appreciation of life. All's right with the world, so satisfyingly right that he becomes sentimentally moved even to think of it.*)

MILLER: Here we are, Essie! Right on the dot! Here we are! (*He pulls her to him and gives her a smacking kiss on the ear*

405 *as she jerks her head away.* MILDRED *and* TOMMY *giggle.* RICHARD *holds rigidly aloof and disdainful, his brooding gaze fixed on his plate.* LILY *forces a smile.*)

MRS. MILLER: (*Pulling away—embarrassedly, almost blushing.*) Don't, you Crazy! (*Then recovering herself—tartly.*) So I see,

410 you're here! And if I didn't, you've told me four times already!

MILLER: (*Beamingly.*) Now, Essie, don't be critical. Don't be carpingly critical. Good news can stand repeating, can't it? 'Course it can! (*He slaps her jovially on her fat buttocks.* TOMMY *and* MILDRED *roar with glee. And* NORAH, *who has

415 just entered from the pantry with a huge tureen of soup in her hands, almost drops it as she explodes in a merry guffaw.*)

MRS. MILLER: (*Scandalized.*) Nat! Aren't you ashamed!

MILLER: Couldn't resist it! Just simply couldn't resist it! (NORAH, *still standing with the soup tureen held out stiffly in*

420 *front of her, again guffaws.*)

MRS. MILLER: (*Turns on her with outraged indignation.*) Norah! Bring that soup here this minute! (*She stalks with stiff dignity toward her place at the foot of the table, right.*)

NORAH: (*Guiltily.*) Yes, Mum. (*She brings the soup around the

425 head of the table, passing* MILLER.)

MILLER: (*Jovially.*) Why, hello, Norah!

MRS. MILLER: Nat! (*She sits down stiffly at the foot of the table.*)

NORAH: (*Rebuking him familiarly.*) Arrah now, don't be mak-

430 ing me laugh and getting me into trouble!

MRS. MILLER: Norah!

NORAH: (*A bit resentfully.*) Yes, Mum. Here I am. (*She sets the soup tureen down with a thud in front of* MRS. MILLER *and passes around the other side, squeezing with difficulty between the china closet and the backs of chairs at the rear of the*

435 *table.*)

MRS. MILLER: Tommy! Stop spinning your napkin ring! How often have I got to tell you? Mildred! Sit up straight in your chair! Do you want to grow up a humpback? Richard! Take your elbows off the table!

440

MILLER: (*Coming to his place at the head of the table, rubbing his hands together genially.*) Well, well, well. Well, well, well. It's good to be home again. (NORAH *exits into the pantry and lets the door slam with a bang behind her.*)

MRS. MILLER: (*Jumps.*) Oh! (*Then exasperatedly.*) Nat, I do

445 wish you wouldn't encourage that stupid girl by talking to her, when I'm doing my best to train—

MILLER: (*Beamingly.*) All right, Essie. Your word is law! (*Then laughingly.*) We did have the darndest fun today! And Sid was the life of that picnic! You ought to have heard him!

450 Honestly, he had that crowd just rolling on the ground and splitting their sides! He ought to be on the stage.

MRS. MILLER: (*As* NORAH *comes back with a dish of saltines— begins ladling soup into the stack of plates before her.*) He ought to be at this table eating something to sober him up,

455 that's what he ought to be! (*She calls.*) Sid! You come right in here! (*Then to* NORAH, *handing her a soup plate.*) Here, Norah. (NORAH *begins passing soup.*) Sit down, Nat, for goodness sakes. Start eating, everybody. Don't wait for me. You know I've given up soup.

460

MILLER: (*Sits down but bends forward to call to his wife in a confidential tone.*) Essie—Sid's sort of embarrassed about coming—I mean I'm afraid he's a little bit—not too much, you understand—but he met such a lot of friends and—well, you know, don't be hard on him. Fourth of July is like Christ-

465 mas—comes but once a year. Don't pretend to notice, eh? And don't you kids, you hear! And don't you, Lily. He's scared of you.

LILY: (*With stiff meekness.*) Very well, Nat.

MILLER: (*Beaming again—calls.*) All right, Sid. The coast's

470 clear. (*He begins to absorb his soup ravenously.*) Good soup, Essie! Good soup! (*A moment later* SID *makes his entrance from the back parlor. He is in a condition that can best be described as blurry. His movements have a hazy uncertainty about them. His shiny fat face is one broad, blurred, Puckish,

475 naughty-boy grin; his eyes have a blurred, wondering vagueness. As he enters he makes a solemnly intense effort to appear casual and dead, cold sober. He waves his hand aimlessly and speaks with a silly gravity.*)

SID: Good evening. (*They all answer "Good evening," their

480 eyes on their plates. He makes his way vaguely toward his place, continuing his grave effort at conversation.*) Beautiful evening. I never remember seeing—more beautiful sunset. (*He bumps vaguely into* LILY'S *chair as he attempts to pass behind her—immediately he is all grave politeness.*) Sorry—

485 sorry, Lily—deeply sorry.

LILY: (*Her eyes on her plate—stiffly.*) It's all right.

SID: (*Manages to get into his chair at last—mutters to himself.*) Wha' was I sayin'? Oh, sunsets. But why butt in? Hasn't sun—perfect right to set? Mind y'r own business. (*He pauses

490 thoughtfully, considering this—then looks around from face to face, fixing each with a vague, blurred, wondering look, as*

if some deep puzzle were confronting him. Then suddenly he grins mistily and nods with satisfaction.) And there you are!
495 Am I right?

MILLER: *(Humoring him.)* Right.

SID: Right! *(He is silent, studying his soup plate, as if it were some strange enigma. Finally he looks up and regards his sister and asks with wondering amazement.)* Soup?

500 MRS. MILLER: Of course, it's soup. What did you think it was? And you hurry up and eat it.

SID: *(Again regards his soup with astonishment.)* Well! *(Then suddenly.)* Well, all right then! Soup be it! *(He picks up his spoon and begins to eat, but after two tries in which he finds it*
505 *difficult to locate his mouth, he addresses the spoon plaintively.)* Spoon, is this any way to treat a pal? *(Then suddenly comically angry, putting the spoon down with a bang.)* Down with spoons! *(He raises his soup plate and declaims.)* "We'll drink to the dead already, and hurrah for the next who dies."
510 *(Bowing solemnly to right and left.)* Your good health, ladies and gents. *(He starts drinking the soup. MILLER guffaws and MILDRED and TOMMY giggle. Even RICHARD forgets his melancholy and snickers, and MRS. MILLER conceals a smile. Only LILY remains stiff and silent.)*

515 MRS. MILLER: *(With forced severity.)* Sid!

SID: *(Peers at her muzzily, lowering the soup plate a little from his lips.)* Eh?

MRS. MILLER: Oh, nothing. Never mind.

SID: *(Solemnly offended.)* Are you—publicly rebuking me be-
520 fore assembled—? Isn't soup liquid? Aren't liquids drunk? *(Then considering this to himself.)* What if they are drunk? It's a good man's failing. *(He again peers mistily about at the company.)* Am I right or wrong?

MRS. MILLER: Hurry up and finish your soup, and stop talking
525 nonsense!

SID: *(Turning to her—again offendedly.)* Oh, no, Essie, if I ever so far forget myself as to drink a leg of lamb, then you might have some—excuse for—Just think of waste effort eating soup with spoons—fifty grueling lifts per plate—billions
530 of soup-eaters on globe—why, it's simply staggering! *(Then darkly to himself.)* No more spoons for me! If I want to develop my biceps, I'll buy Sandow Exerciser! *(He drinks the rest of his soup in a gulp and beams around at the company, suddenly all happiness again.)* Am I right, folks?

535 MILLER: *(Who has been choking with laughter.)* Haw, haw! You're right, Sid.

SID: *(Peers at him blurredly and shakes his head sadly.)* Poor old Nat! Always wrong—but heart of gold, heart of purest gold. And drunk again, I regret to note. Sister, my heart
540 bleeds for you and your poor fatherless chicks!

MRS. MILLER: *(restraining a giggle—severely.)* Sid! Do shut up for a minute! Pass me your soup plates, everybody. If we wait for that girl to take them, we'll be here all night. *(They all pass their plates, which MRS. MILLER stacks up and then puts on the sideboard. As she is doing this, NORAH appears from*
545 *the pantry with a platter of broiled fish. She is just about to place these before MILLER when SID catches her eye mistily and rises to his feet, making her a deep, uncertain bow.)*

SID: *(Raptly.)* Ah, Sight for Sore Eyes, my beautiful Macushla,
550 my star-eyed Mavourneen—

MRS. MILLER: Sid!

NORAH: *(Immensely pleased—gives him an arch, flirtatious glance.)* Ah, sure, Mister Sid, it's you that have kissed the Blarney Stone, when you've a drop taken!

MRS. MILLER: *(Outraged.)* Norah! Put down that fish!   555

NORAH: *(Flusteredly.)* Yes, Mum. *(She attempts to put the fish down hastily before MILLER, but her eyes are fixed nervously on MRS. MILLER and she gives MILLER a nasty swipe on the side of the head with the edge of the dish.)*

MILLER: Ouch! *(The children, even RICHARD, explode into*   560
laughter.)*

NORAH: *(Almost lets the dish fall.)* Oh, glory be to God! Is it hurted you are?

MILLER: *(Rubbing his head—good-naturedly.)* No, no harm done. Only careful, Norah, careful.   565

NORAH: *(Gratefully.)* Yes, sorr. *(She thumps down the dish in front of him with a sigh of relief.)*

SID: *(Who is still standing—with drunken gravity.)* Careful, Mavourneen, careful! You might have hit him some place besides the head. Always aim at his head, remember—so as   570
not to worry us. *(Again the children explode. Also NORAH. Even LILY suddenly lets out an hysterical giggle and is furious with herself for doing so.)*

LILY: I'm so sorry, Nat. I didn't mean to laugh. *(Turning on SID furiously.)* Will you please sit down and stop making a fool of   575
yourself? *(SID gives her a hurt, mournful look and then sinks meekly down on his chair.)*

NORAH: *(Grinning cheerfully, gives LILY a reassuring pat on the back.)* Ah, Miss Lily, don't mind him. He's only under the influence. Sure, there's no harm in him at all.   580

MRS. MILLER: Norah! *(NORAH exits hastily into the pantry, letting the door slam with a crash behind her. There is silence for a moment as MILLER serves the fish and it is passed around. NORAH comes back with the vegetables and disappears again, and these are dished out.)*   585

MILLER: *(Is about to take his first bite—stops suddenly and asks his wife.)* This isn't, by any chance, bluefish, is it, my dear?

MRS. MILLER: *(With a warning glance at TOMMY.)* Of course not. You know we never have bluefish, on account of you.

MILLER: *(Addressing the table now with the gravity of a man*   590
confessing his strange peculiarities.) Yes, I regret to say, there's a certain peculiar oil in bluefish that invariably poisons me. *(At this, TOMMY cannot stand it any more but explodes into laughter. MRS. MILLER, after a helpless glance at him, follows suit; then LILY goes off into uncontrollable, hys-*   595
terical laughter, and RICHARD and MILDRED are caught in the contagion. MILLER looks around at them with a weak smile, his dignity now ruffled a bit.) Well, I must say I don't see what's so darned funny about my being poisoned.

SID: *(Peers around him—then with drunken cunning.)* Aha! Nat,   600
I suspect—plot! This fish looks blue to me—very blue—in fact despondent, desperate, and—*(He points his fork dramatically at MRS. MILLER.)* See how guilty she looks—a ver—veritable Lucretia Georgia! Can it be this woman has been slowly poisoning you all these years? And how well—you've stood it!   605
What iron constitution! Even now, when you are invariably at death's door, I can't believe—*(Everyone goes off into uncontrollable laughter.)*

MILLER: *(Grumpily.)* Oh, give us a rest, you darned fool! A joke's a joke, but—*(He addresses his wife in a wounded tone.)*   610
Is this true, Essie?

MRS. MILLER: *(Wiping the tears from her eyes—defiantly.)* Yes, it is true, if you must know, and you'd never have suspected it, if it weren't for that darned Tommy, and Sid poking his nose in. You've eaten bluefish for years and thrived on it and   615
it's all nonsense about that peculiar oil.

MILLER: (*Deeply offended.*) Kindly allow me to know my own constitution! Now I think of it, I've felt upset afterwards every damned time we've had fish! (*He pushes his plate away from him with proud renunciation.*) I can't eat this.

MRS. MILLER: (*Insultingly matter-of-fact.*) Well, don't then. There's lots of lobster coming and you can fill up on that. (RICHARD *suddenly bursts out laughing again.*)

MILLER: (*Turns to him caustically.*) You seem in a merry mood, Richard. I thought you were the original of the Heart Bowed Down today.

SID: (*With mock condolence.*) Never mind, Dick. Let them—scoff! What can they understand about girls whose hair sizz-chels, whose lips are fireworks, whose eyes are red-hot sparks—

MILDRED: (*Laughing.*) Is that what he wrote to Muriel? (*Turning to her brother.*) You silly goat, you!

RICHARD: (*Surlily.*) Aw, shut up, Mid. What do I care about her? I'll show all of you how much I care!

MRS. MILLER: Pass your plates as soon as you're through, everybody. I've rung for the lobster. And that's all. You don't get any dessert or tea after lobster, you know. (NORAH *appears bearing a platter of cold boiled lobsters which she sets before* MILLER, *and disappears.*)

TOMMY: Gee, I love lobster! (MILLER *puts one on each plate, and they are passed around and everyone starts in pulling the cracked shells apart.*)

MILLER: (*Feeling more cheerful after a couple of mouthfuls—determining to give the conversation another turn, says to his daughter.*) Have a good time at the beach, Mildred?

MILDRED: Oh, fine, Pa, thanks. The water was wonderful and warm.

MILLER: Swim far?

MILDRED: Yes, for me. But that isn't so awful far.

MILLER: Well, you ought to be a good swimmer, if you take after me. I used to be a regular water rat when I was a boy. I'll have to go down to the beach with you one of these days—though I'd be rusty, not having been in in all these years. (*The reminiscent look comes into his eyes of one about to em bark on an oft-told tale of childhood adventure.*) You know, speaking of swimming, I never go down to that beach but what it calls to mind the day I and Red Sisk went in swimming there and I saved his life. (*By this time the family are beginning to exchange amused, guilty glances. They all know what is coming.*)

SID: (*With a sly, blurry wink around.*) Ha! Now we—have it again!

MILLER: (*Turning on him.*) Have what?

SID: Nothing—go on with your swimming—don't mind me.

MILLER: (*Glares at him—but immediately is overcome by the reminiscent mood again.*) Red Sisk—his father kept a black-smith shop where the Union Market is now—we kids called him Red because he had the darndest reddest crop of hair—

SID: (*As if he were talking to his plate.*) Remarkable!—the curi-ous imagination—of little children.

MRS. MILLER: (*As she sees* MILLER *about to explode—interposes tactfully.*) Sid! Eat your lobster and shut up! Go on, Nat.

MILLER: (*Gives* SID *a withering look—then is off again.*) Well, as I was saying, Red and I went swimming that day. Must have been—let me see—Red was fourteen, bigger and older than me, I was only twelve—forty-five years ago—wasn't a single house down there then—but there was a stake out where the whistling buoy is now, about a mile out. (TOMMY,

who has been having difficulty restraining himself, lets out a stifled giggle. MILLER *bends a frowning gaze on him.*) One more sound out of you, young man, and you'll leave the table!

MRS. MILLER: (*Quickly interposing, trying to stave off the story.*) Do eat your lobster, Nat. You didn't have any fish, you know.

MILLER: (*Not liking the reminder—pettishly.*) Well, if I'm going to be interrupted every second anyway—(*He turns to his lobster and chews in silence for a moment.*)

MILLER: (*Trying to switch the subject.*) How's Anne's mother's rheumatism, Mildred?

MILDRED: Oh, she's much better, Ma. She was in wading today. She says salt water's the only thing that really helps her bunion.

MRS. MILLER: Mildred! Where are your manners? At the table's no place to speak of—

MILLER: (*Fallen into the reminiscent obsession again.*) Well, as I was saying, there was I and Red, and he dared me to race him out to the stake and back. Well, I didn't let anyone dare me in those days. I was a spunky kid. So I said all right and we started out. We swam and swam and were pretty evenly matched; though, as I've said, he was bigger and older than me, but finally I drew ahead. I was going along easy, with lots in reserve, not a bit tired, when suddenly I heard a sort of gasp from behind me—like this—"help." (*He imitates. Everyone's eyes are firmly fixed on his plate, except* SID's.) And I turned and there was Red, his face all pinched and white, and he says weakly: "Help, Nat! I got a cramp in my leg!" Well, I don't mind telling you I got mighty scared. I didn't know what to do. Then suddenly I thought of the pile. If I could pull him to that, I could hang on to him till some-one'd notice us. But the pile was still—well, I calculate it must have been two hundred feet away.

SID: Two hundred and fifty!

MILLER: (*In confusion.*) What's that?

SID: Two hundred *and* fifty! I've taken down the distance every time you've saved Red's life for thirty years and the mean av-erage to that pile is two hundred and fifty feet! (*There is a burst of laughter from around the table.* SID *continues com-plainingly.*) Why didn't you let that Red drown, anyway, Nat? I never knew him but I know I'd never have liked him.

MILLER: (*Really hurt, forces a feeble smile to his lips and pre-tends to be a good sport about it.*) Well, guess you're right, Sid. Guess I have told that one too many times and bored ev-eryone. But it's a good true story for kids because it illustrates the danger of being foolhardy in the water—

MRS. MILLER: (*Sensing the hurt in his tone, comes to his res-cue.*) Of course it's a good story—and you tell it whenever you've a mind to. And you, Sid, if you were in any responsi-ble state, I'd give you a good piece of my mind for teasing Nat like that.

MILLER: (*With a sad, self-pitying smile at his wife.*) Getting old, I guess, Mother—getting to repeat myself. Someone ought to stop me.

MRS. MILLER: No such thing! You're as young as you ever were. (*She turns on* SID *again angrily.*) You eat your lobster and maybe it'll keep your mouth shut!

SID: (*After a few chews—irrepressibly.*) Lobster! Did you know, Tommy, your Uncle Sid is the man invented lobster? Fact! One day—when I was building the Pyramids—took a day off and just dashed off lobster. He was bigger'n' older than me and he had the darndest reddest crop of hair but I dashed him off just the same! Am I right, Nat? *(Then suddenly in the tones of a side-show barker.)* Ladies *and* Gents—

MRS. MILLER: Mercy sakes! Can't you shut up?

745 SID: In this cage you see the lobster. You will not believe me, ladies *and* gents, but it's a fact that this interesting bivalve only makes love to his mate once in every thousand years— but, dearie me, how he does enjoy it! *(The children roar.* LILY *and* MRS. MILLER *laugh in spite of themselves—then look em-*
750 *barrassed.* MILLER *guffaws—then suddenly grows shocked.)*

MILLER: Careful, Sid, careful. Remember you're at home.

TOMMY: *(Suddenly in a hoarse whisper to his mother, with an awed glance of admiration at his uncle.)* Ma! Look at him! He's eating that claw, shells and all!

755 MRS. MILLER: *(Horrified.)* Sid, do you want to kill yourself? Take it away from him, Lily!

SID: *(With great dignity.)* But I prefer the shells. All famous epicures prefer the shells—to the less delicate, coarser meat. It's the same with clams. Unless I eat the shells there is a cer-
760 tain, peculiar oil that invariably poisons—Am I right, Nat?

MILLER: *(Good-naturedly.)* You seem to be getting a lot of fun kidding me. Go ahead, then, I don't mind.

MRS. MILLER: He better go right up to bed for a while, that's what he better do.

765 SID: *(Considering this owlishly.)* Bed? Yes, maybe you're right. *(He gets to his feet.)* I am not at all well—in very delicate condition—we are praying for a boy. Am I right, Nat? Nat, I kept telling you all day I was in delicate condition and yet you kept forcing demon chowder on me, although you knew
770 full well—even if you were full—that there is a certain, pe- culiar oil in chowder that invariably—*(They are again all laughing—*LILY, *hysterically.)*

MRS. MILLER: Will you get to bed, you idiot!

SID: *(Mutters graciously.)* Immediately—if not sooner. *(He*
775 *turns to pass behind* LILY, *then stops, staring down at her.)* But wait. There is still a duty I must perform. No day is com- plete without it. Lily, answer once and for all, will you marry me?

LILY: *(With an hysterical giggle.)* No, I won't—never!

780 SID: *(Nodding his head.)* Right! And perhaps it's all for the best. For how could I forget the pre—precepts taught me at mother's dying knee. "Sidney," she said, "never marry a woman who drinks! Lips that touch liquor shall never touch yours!" *(Gazing at her mournfully.)* Too bad! So fine a
785 woman once—and now such a slave to rum! *(Turning to* NAT.*)* What can we do to save her, Nat? *(In a hoarse, confi- dential whisper.)* Better put her in institution where she'll be removed from temptation! The mere smell of it seems to drive her frantic!

790 MRS. MILLER: *(Struggling with her laughter.)* You leave Lily alone, and go to bed!

SID: Right! *(He comes around behind* LILY's *chair and moves to- ward the entrance to the back parlor—then suddenly turns and says with a bow.)* Good night, ladies—*and* gents. We
795 will meet—bye and bye! *(He gives an imitation of a Salva- tion Army drum.)* Boom! Boom! Boom! Come and be saved, Brothers! *(He starts to sing the old Army hymn.)*

> "In the sweet
> Bye and bye
800 > We will meet on that beautiful shore."

(He turns and marches solemnly out through the back parlor, singing.)

> Work and pray
> While you may.
> We will meet in the sky bye and bye."

*(*MILLER *and his wife and the children are all roaring with laughter.* LILY *giggles hysterically.)*

MILLER: *(Subsiding at last.)* Haw, haw. He's a case, if ever there was one! Darned if you can help laughing at him— 805 even when he's poking fun at you!

MRS. MILLER: Goodness, but he's a caution! Oh, my sides ache, I declare! I was trying so hard not to—but you can't help it, he's so silly! But I suppose we really shouldn't. It only encourages him. But, my lands—! 810

LILY: *(Suddenly gets up from her chair and stands rigidly, her face working—jerkily.)* That's just it—you shouldn't—even I laughed—it does encourage—that's been his downfall—ev- eryone always laughing, everyone always saying what a card he is, what a case, what a caution, so funny—and he's gone 815 on—and we're all responsible—making it easy for him— we're all to blame—and all we do is laugh!

MILLER: *(Worriedly.)* Now, Lily, now, you mustn't take on so. It isn't as serious as all that.

LILY: *(Bitterly.)* Maybe—it is—to me. Or was—once. *(Then* 820 *contritely.)* I'm sorry, Nat. I'm sorry, Essie. I didn't mean to—I'm not feeling myself tonight. If you'll excuse me, I'll go in the front parlor and lie down on the sofa awhile.

MRS. MILLER: Of course, Lily. You do whatever you've a mind to. *(*LILY *goes out.)* 825

MILLER: *(Frowning—a little shamefaced.)* Hmm. I suppose she's right. Never knew Lily to come out with things that way before. Anything special happened, Essie?

MRS. MILLER: Nothing I know—except he'd promised to take her to the fireworks. 830

MILLER: That's so. Well, supposing I take her? I don't want her to feel disappointed.

MRS. MILLER: *(Shaking her head.)* Wild horses couldn't drag her there now.

MILLER: Hmm. I thought she'd got completely over her fool- 835 ishness about him long ago.

MRS. MILLER: She never will.

MILLER: She'd better. He's got fired out of that Waterbury job—told me at the picnic after he'd got enough Dutch courage in him. 840

MRS. MILLER: Oh, dear! Isn't he the fool!

MILLER: I knew something was wrong when he came home. Well, I'll find a place for him on my paper again, of course. He always was the best news-getter this town ever had. But I'll tell him he's got to stop his damn nonsense. 845

MRS. MILLER: *(Doubtfully.)* Yes.

MILLER: Well, no use sitting here mourning over spilt milk. *(He gets up, and* RICHARD, MILDRED, TOMMY *and* MRS. MILLER *follow his example, the children quiet and a bit awed.)* You kids go out in the yard and try to keep quiet for a while, 850 so's your Uncle Sid'll get to sleep and your Aunt Lily can rest.

TOMMY: *(Mournfully.)* Ain't we going to set off the skyrockets and Roman candles, Pa?

MILLER: Later, Son, later. It isn't dark enough for them yet anyway. 855

MILDRED: Come on, Tommy. I'll see he keeps quiet, Pa.

MILLER: That's a good girl. (MILDRED *and* TOMMY *go out through the screen door.* RICHARD *remains standing, sunk in bitter, gloomy thoughts.* MILLER *glances at him—then irritably.*) Well, Melancholy Dane, what are you doing?

860

RICHARD: (*Darkly.*) I'm going out—for a while. (*Then suddenly.*) Do you know what I think? It's Aunt Lily's fault, Uncle Sid's going to ruin. It's all because he loves her, and she keeps him dangling after her, and eggs him on and ruins his life—like all women love to ruin men's lives! I don't blame him for drinking himself to death! What does he care if he dies, after the way she's treated him! I'd do the same thing myself if I were in his boots!

865

MRS. MILLER: (*Indignantly.*) Richard! You stop that talk!

RICHARD: (*Quotes bitterly.*)

870

"Drink! for you know not whence you come nor why.
Drink! for you know not why you go nor where!"

MILLER: (*Losing his temper—harshly.*) Listen here, young man! I've had about all I can stand of your nonsense for one day! You're growing a lot too big for your size, seems to me! You keep that damn fool talk to yourself, you hear me—or you're going to regret it! Mind now! (*He strides angrily away through the back parlor.*)

875

MRS. MILLER: (*Still indignant.*) Richard, I'm ashamed of you, that's what I am. (*She follows her husband.* RICHARD *stands for a second, bitter, humiliated, wronged, even his father turned enemy, his face growing more and more rebellious. Then he forces a scornful smiles to his lips.*)

880

RICHARD: Aw, what the hell do I care? I'll show them! (*He turns and goes out the screen door.*)

885

(*Curtain.*)

— ACT THREE —

SCENE 1

The back room of a bar in a small hotel—a small, dingy room, dimly lighted by two fly-specked globes in a fly-specked gilt chandelier suspended from the middle of the ceiling. At left, front, is the swinging door leading to the bar. At rear of door, against the wall, is a nickel-in-the-slot player-piano. In the rear wall, right, is a door leading to the "Family Entrance" and the stairway to the upstairs rooms. In the middle of the right wall is a window with closed shutters. Three tables with stained tops, four chairs around each table, are placed at center, front, at right, toward rear, and at rear, center. A brass cuspidor is on the floor by each table. The floor is unswept, littered with cigarette and cigar butts. The hideous saffron-colored wall-paper is blotched and spotted.

It is about 10 o'clock the same night. RICHARD *and* BELLE *are discovered sitting at the table at center,* BELLE *at left of it,* RICHARD *in the next chair at the middle of table, rear, facing front.*

BELLE *is twenty, a rather pretty peroxide blonde, a typical college "tart" of the period, and of the cheaper variety, dressed with tawdry flashiness. But she is a fairly recent recruit to the ranks, and is still a bit remorseful behind her make-up and defiantly careless manner.*

BELLE *has an empty gin-rickey glass before her,* RICHARD *a half-empty glass of beer. He looks horribly timid, embarrassed and* guilty, *but at the same time thrilled and proud of at last mingling with the pace that kills.*

The player-piano is grinding out "Bedelia." The BARTENDER, *a stocky young Irishman with a foxily cunning, stupid face and a cynically wise grin, stands just inside the bar entrance, watching them over the swinging door.*

BELLE: (*With an impatient glance at her escort—rattling the ice in her empty glass.*) Drink up your beer, why don't you? It's getting flat.

RICHARD: (*Embarrassedly.*) I let it get that way on purpose. I like it better when it's flat. (*But he hastily gulps down the rest of his glass, as if it were some nasty-tasting medicine. The* BARTENDER *chuckles audibly.* BELLE *glances at him.*)

5

BELLE: (*Nodding at the player-piano scornfully.*) Say, George, is "Bedelia" the latest to hit this hick burg? Well, it's only a couple of years old! You'll catch up in time! Why don't you get a new roll for that old box?

10

BARTENDER: (*With a grin.*) Complain to the boss, not me. We're not used to having Candy Kiddoes like you around— or maybe we'd get up to date.

BELLE: (*With a professionally arch grin at him.*) Don't kid me, please. I can't bear it. (*Then she sings to the music from the piano, her eyes now on* RICHARD.) "Bedelia, I'd like to feel yer." (*The* BARTENDER *laughs. She smirks at* RICHARD.) Ever hear those words to it, Kid?

15

RICHARD: (*Who has heard them but is shocked at hearing a girl say them—putting on a blasé air.*) Sure, lots of times. That's old.

20

BELLE: (*Edging her chair closer and putting a hand over one of his.*) Then why don't you act as if you knew what they were all about?

25

RICHARD: (*Terribly flustered.*) Sure, I've heard that old parody lots of times. What do you think I am?

BELLE: I don't know, Kid. Honest to God, you've got me guessing.

BARTENDER: (*With a mocking chuckle.*) He's a hot sport, can't you tell it? I never seen such a spender. My head's dizzy bringing you in drinks!

30

BELLE: (*Laughs irritably—to* RICHARD.) Don't let him kid you. You show him. Loosen up and buy another drink, what say?

RICHARD: (*Humiliated—manfully.*) Sure. Excuse me. I was thinking of something else. Have anything you like. (*He turns to the* BARTENDER *who has entered from the bar.*) See what the lady will have—and have one on me yourself.

35

BARTENDER: (*Coming to the table—with a wink at* BELLE.) That's talking! Didn't I say you were a sport? I'll take a cigar on you. (*To* BELLE.) What's yours, Kiddo—the same?

40

BELLE: Yes. And forget the house rules this time and remember a rickey is supposed to have gin in it.

BARTENDER: (*Grinning.*) I'll try to—seeing it's you. (*Then to* RICHARD.) What's yours—another beer?

45

RICHARD: (*Shyly.*) A small one, please. I'm not thirsty.

BELLE: (*Calculatedly taunting.*) Say, honest, are things that slow up at Harvard? If they had you down at New Haven, they'd put you in a kindergarten! Don't be such a dead one! Filling up on beer will only make you sleepy. Have a man's drink!

50

RICHARD: (*Shamefacedly.*) All right. I was going to. Bring me a sloe-gin fizz.

BELLE: (*To* BARTENDER.) And make it a real one.

55 BARTENDER: *(With a wink.)* I get you. Something that'll warm him up, eh? *(He goes into the bar, chuckling.)*

BELLE: *(Looks around the room—irritably.)* Christ, what a dump! (RICHARD *is startled and shocked by this curse and looks down at the table.)* If this isn't the deadest burg I ever
60 struck! Bet they take the sidewalks in after nine o'clock! *(Then turning on him.)* Say, honestly, Kid, does your mother know you're out?

RICHARD: *(Defensively.)* Aw, cut it out, why don't you—trying to kid me!

65 BELLE: *(Glances at him—then resolves on a new tack—patting his hand.)* All right. I didn't mean to, Dearie. Please don't get sore at me.

RICHARD: I'm not sore.

BELLE: *(Seductively.)* You see, it's this way with me. I think
70 you're one of the sweetest kids I've ever met—and I could like you such a lot if you'd give me half a chance—instead of acting so cold and indifferent.

RICHARD: I'm not cold and indifferent. *(Then solemnly tragic.)* It's only that I've got—a weight on my mind.

75 BELLE: *(Impatiently.)* Well, get it off your mind and give something else a chance to work. *(The* BARTENDER *comes in, bringing the drinks.)*

BARTENDER: *(Setting them down—with a wink at* BELLE.*)* This'll warm him for you. Forty cents, that is—with the
80 cigar.

RICHARD: *(Pulls out his roll and hands a dollar bill over—with exaggerated carelessness.)* Keep the change. (BELLE *emits a gasp and seems about to protest, then thinks better of it. The* BARTENDER *cannot believe his luck for a moment—then*
85 *pockets the bill hastily, as if afraid* RICHARD *will change his mind.)*

BARTENDER: *(Respect in his voice.)* Thank you, sir.

RICHARD: *(Grandly.)* Don't mention it.

BARTENDER: I hope you like the drink. I took special pains
90 with it. *(The voice of the* SALESMAN, *who has just come in the bar, calls "Hey! Anybody here?" and a coin is rapped on the bar.)* I'm coming. *(The* BARTENDER *goes out.)*

BELLE: *(remonstrating gently, a new appreciation for her escort's possibilities in her voice.)* You shouldn't be so generous,
95 Dearie. Gets him in bad habits. A dime would have been plenty.

RICHARD: Ah, that's all right. I'm no tightwad.

BELLE: That's the talk I like to hear. *(With a quick look toward the bar, she stealthily pulls up her dress—to* RICHARD's
100 *shocked fascination—and takes a package of cheap cigarettes from her stocking.)* Keep an eye out for that bartender, Kid, and tell me if you see him coming. Girls are only allowed to smoke upstairs in the rooms, he said.

RICHARD: *(Embarrassedly.)* All right. I'll watch.

105 BELLE: *(Having lighted her cigarette and inhaled deeply, holds the package out to him.)* Have a Sweet? You smoke, don't you?

RICHARD: *(Taking one.)* Sure! I've been smoking for the last two years—on the sly. But next year I'll be allowed—that is,
110 pipes and cigars. *(He lights his cigarette with elaborate nonchalance, puffs, but does not inhale—then, watching her, with shocked concern.)* Say, you oughtn't to inhale like that! Smoking's awful bad for girls, anyway, even if they don't—

BELLE: *(Cynically amused.)* Afraid it will stunt my growth?
115 Gee, Kid, you are a scream! You'll grow up to be a minister

yet! (RICHARD *looks shamefaced. She scans him impatiently—then holds up her drink.)* Well, here's how! Bottoms up, now! Show me you really know how to drink. It'll take that load off your mind. (RICHARD *follows her example and they both drink the whole contents of their glasses before set-* 120 *ting them down.)* There! That's something like! Feel better?

RICHARD: *(Proud of himself—with a shy smile.)* You bet.

BELLE: Well, you'll feel still better in a minute—and then maybe you won't be so distant and unfriendly, eh?

RICHARD: I'm not. 125

BELLE: Yes, you are. I think you just don't like me.

RICHARD: *(More manfully.)* I do too like you.

BELLE: How much? A lot?

RICHARD: Yes, a lot.

BELLE: Show me how much! *(Then as he fidgets embarrass-* 130 *edly.)* Want me to come sit on your lap?

RICHARD: Yes—I—(*She comes and sits on his lap. He looks desperately uncomfortable, but the gin is rising to his head and he feels proud of himself and devilish, too.)*

BELLE: Why don't you put your arm around me? *(He does so* 135 *awkwardly.)* No, not that dead way. Hold me tight. You needn't be afraid of hurting me. I like to be held tight, don't you?

RICHARD: Sure I do.

BELLE: 'Specially when it's by a nice handsome kid like you. *(Ruffling his hair.)* Gee, you've got pretty hair, do you know 140 it? Honest, I'm awfully strong for you! Why can't you be about me? I'm not so awfully ugly, am I?

RICHARD: No, you're—you're pretty.

BELLE: You don't say it as if you meant it.

RICHARD: I do mean it—honest. 145

BELLE: Then why don't you kiss me? *(She bends down her lips toward his. He hesitates, then kisses her and at once shrinks back.)* Call that kissing? Here. *(She holds his head and fastens her lips on his and holds them there. He starts and struggles. She laughs.)* What's the matter, Honey Boy? Haven't 150 you ever kissed like that before?

RICHARD: Sure. Lots of times.

BELLE: Then why did you jump as if I'd bitten you? *(Squirming around on his lap.)* Gee, I'm getting just crazy about you! What shall we do about it, eh? Tell me. 155

RICHARD: I—don't know. *(Then boldly.)* I—I'm crazy about you, too.

BELLE: *(Kissing him again.)* Just think of the wonderful time Edith and your friend, Wint, are having upstairs—while we sit down here like two dead ones. A room only costs two dol- 160 lars. And, seeing I like you so much, I'd only take five dollars—from you. I'd do it for nothing—for you—only I've got to live and I owe my room rent in New Haven—and you know how it is. I get ten dollars from everyone else. Honest! *(She kisses him again, then gets up from his lap—briskly.)* 165 Come on. Go out and tell the bartender you want a room. And hurry. Honest, I'm so strong for you I can hardly wait to get you upstairs!

RICHARD: *(Starts automatically for the door to the bar—then hesitates, a great struggle going on in his mind—timidity, dis-* 170 *gust at the money element, shocked modesty, and the guilty thought of* MURIEL, *fighting it out with the growing tipsiness that makes him want to be a hell of a fellow and go in for all forbidden fruit, and makes this tart a romantic, evil vampire in his eyes. Finally, he stops and mutters in confusion.)* I 175 can't.

BELLE: What, are you too bashful to ask for a room? Let me do it, then. (*She starts for the door.*)

RICHARD: (*Desperately.*) No—I don't want you to—I don't want to.

BELLE: (*Surveying him, anger coming into her eyes.*) Well, if you aren't the lousiest cheap skate!

RICHARD: I'm not a cheap skate!

BELLE: Keep me around here all night fooling with you when I might be out with some real live one—if there is such a thing in this burg!—and now you quit on me! Don't be such a piker! You've got five dollars! I seen it when you paid for the drinks, so don't hand me any lies!

RICHARD: I—Who said I hadn't? And I'm not a piker. If you need the five dollars so bad—for your room rent—you can have it without—I mean, I'll be glad to give—(*He has been fumbling in his pocket and pulls out his nine-dollar roll and holds out the five to her.*)

BELLE: (*Hardly able to believe her eyes, almost snatches it from his hand—then laughs and immediately becomes sentimentally grateful.*) Thanks, Kid. Gee—oh, thanks—Gee, forgive me for losing my temper and bawling you out, will you? Gee, you're a regular peach! You're the nicest kid I've ever met! (*She kisses him and he grins proudly, a hero to himself now on many counts.*) Gee, you're a peach! Thanks, again.

RICHARD: (*Grandly—and quite tipsily.*) It's—nothing—only too glad. (*Then boldly.*) Here—give me another kiss, and that'll pay me back.

BELLE: (*Kissing him.*) I'll give you a thousand, if you want 'em. Come on, let's sit down, and we'll have another drink—and this time I'll blow you just to show my appreciation. (*She calls.*) Hey, George! bring us another round—the same!

RICHARD: (*A remnant of caution coming to him.*) I don't know as I ought to—

BELLE: Oh, another won't hurt you. And I want to blow you, see. (*They sit down in their former places.*)

RICHARD: (*Boldly draws his chair closer and puts an arm around her—tipsily.*) I like you a lot—now I'm getting to know you. You're a darned nice girl.

BELLE: Nice is good! Tell me another! Well, if I'm so nice, why didn't you want to take me upstairs? That's what I don't get.

RICHARD: (*Lying boldly.*) I did want to—only I—(*Then he adds solemnly.*) I've sworn off. (*The* BARTENDER *enters with the drinks.*)

BARTENDER: (*Setting them on the table.*) Here's your pleasure. (*Then regarding* RICHARD's *arm about her waist.*) Ho-ho, we're coming on, I see. (RICHARD *grins at him muzzily.*)

BELLE: (*Digs into her stocking and gives him a dollar.*) Here. This is mine. (*He gives her change and she tips him a dime, and he goes out. She puts the five* RICHARD *had given her in her stocking and picks up her glass.*) Here's how—and thanks again. (*She sips.*)

RICHARD: (*Boisterously.*) Bottoms up! Bottoms up! (*He drinks all of his down and sighs with exaggerated satisfaction.*) Gee, that's good stuff, all right. (*Hugging her.*) Give me another kiss, Belle.

BELLE: (*Kisses him.*) What did you mean a minute ago when you said you'd sworn off?

RICHARD: (*Solemnly.*) I took an oath I'd be faithful.

BELLE: (*Cynically.*) Till death do us part, eh? Who's the girl?

RICHARD: (*Shortly.*) Never mind.

BELLE: (*Bristling.*) I'm not good enough to talk about her, I suppose?

RICHARD: I didn't—mean that. You're all right. (*Then with tipsy gravity.*) Only you oughtn't to lead this kind of life. It isn't right—for a nice girl like you. Why don't you reform?

BELLE: (*Sharply.*) Nix on that line of talk! Can it, you hear! You can do a lot with me for five dollars—but you can't reform me, see. Mind your own business, Kid, and don't butt in where you're not wanted!

RICHARD: I—I didn't mean to hurt your feelings.

BELLE: I know you didn't mean. You're only like a lot of people who mean well, to hear them tell it. (*Changing the subject.*) So you're faithful to your one love, eh? (*With an ugly sneer.*) And how about her? Bet you she's out with a guy under some bush this minute, giving him all he wants. Don't be a sucker, Kid! Even the little flies do it!

RICHARD: (*Starting up his chair again—angrily.*) Don't you say that! Don't you dare!

BELLE: (*Unimpressed—with a cynical shrug of her shoulders.*) All right. Have it your own way and be a sucker! It cuts no ice with me.

RICHARD: You don't know her or—

BELLE: And don't want to. Shut up about her, can't you? (*She stares before her bitterly.* RICHARD *subsides into scowling gloom. He is becoming perceptibly more intoxicated with each moment now. The* BARTENDER *and the* SALESMAN *appear just inside the swinging door. The* BARTENDER *nods toward* BELLE, *giving the* SALESMAN *a wink. The* SALESMAN *grins and comes into the room, carrying his highball in his hand. He is a stout, jowly-faced man in his late thirties, dressed with cheap nattiness, with the professional breeziness and jocular, kid-'em-along manner of his kind.* BELLE *looks up as he enters and he and she exchange a glance of complete recognition. She knows his type by heart and he knows hers.*)

SALESMAN: (*Passes by her to the table at right—grinning genially.*) Good evening.

BELLE: Good evening.

SALESMAN: (*Sitting down.*) Hope I'm not butting in on your party—but my dogs were giving out standing at that bar.

BELLE: All right with me. (*Giving* RICHARD *a rather contemptuous look.*) I've got no party on.

SALESMAN: That sounds hopeful.

RICHARD: (*Suddenly recites sentimentally.*)

"But I wouldn't do such, 'cause I loved her too much,
But I learned about women from her."

(*Turns to scowl at the* SALESMAN—*then to* BELLE.) Let's have 'nother drink!

BELLE: You've had enough. (RICHARD *subsides, muttering to himself.*)

SALESMAN: What is it—a child poet or a child actor?

BELLE: Don't know. Got me guessing.

SALESMAN: Well, if you could shake the cradle-robbing act, maybe we could do a little business.

BELLE: That's easy. I just pull my freight. (*She shakes* RICHARD *by the arm.*) Listen, Kid. Here's an old friend of mine, Mr. Smith of New Haven, just come in. I'm going over and sit at his table for a while, see. And you better go home.

RICHARD: (*Blinking at her and scowling.*) I'm never going home! I'll show them!

BELLE: Have it your own way—only let me up. (*She takes his arm from around her and goes to sit by the* SALESMAN. RICHARD *stares after her offendedly.*)

300 RICHARD: Go on. What do I care what you do? (*He recites scornfully.*) "For a woman's only a woman, but a good cigar's a smoke."

SALESMAN: (*As* BELLE *sits beside him.*) Well, what kind of beer will you have, Sister?

305 BELLE: Mine's a gin rickey.

SALESMAN: You've got extravagant tastes, I'm sorry to see.

RICHARD: (*Begins to recite sepulchrally.*)

"Yet each man kills the thing he loves,
By each let this be heard."

310 SALESMAN: (*Grinning.*) Say, this is rich! (*He calls encouragement.*) That's swell dope, young feller. Give us some more.

RICHARD: (*Ignoring him—goes on more rhetorically.*)

"Some do it with a bitter look,
Some with a flattering word,
315 The coward does it with a kiss,
The brave man with a sword!"

(*He stares at* BELLE *gloomily and mutters tragically.*) I did it with a kiss! I'm a coward.

SALESMAN: That's the old stuff, Kid. You've got something on 320 the ball, all right, all right! Give us another—right over the old pan, now!

BELLE: (*With a laugh.*) Get the hook!

RICHARD: (*Glowering at her—tragically.*)

"'Oho,' they cried, the world is wide,
325 But fettered limbs go lame!
And once, or twice, to throw the dice
Is a gentlemanly game,
But he does not win who plays with Sin
In the secret House of Shame!'"

330 BELLE: (*Angrily.*) Aw, can it! Give us a rest from that bunk!

SALESMAN: (*Mockingly.*) This gal of yours don't appreciate poetry. She's a lowbrow. But I'm the kid that eats it up. My middle name is Kelly and Sheets! Give us some more of the same! Do you know "The Lobster and the Wise Guy"? 335 (*Turns to* BELLE *seriously.*) No kidding, that's a peacherino. I heard a guy recite it at Poli's. Maybe this nut knows it. Do you, Kid? (*But* RICHARD *only glowers at him gloomily without answering.*)

BELLE: (*Surveying* RICHARD *contemptuously.*) He's copped a 340 fine skinful—and gee, he's hardly had anything.

RICHARD: (*Suddenly—with a dire emphasis.*) "And then—at ten o'clock—Eilert Lovborg will come—with vine leaves in his hair!"

BELLE: And bats in his belfry, if he's you!

345 RICHARD: (*Regards her bitterly—then starts to his feet bellicosely—to the* SALESMAN.) I don't believe you ever knew her in New Haven at all! You just picked her up now! You leave her alone, you hear! You don't do anything to her—not while I'm here to protect her!

350 BELLE: (*Laughing.*) Oh, my God! Listen to it!

SALESMAN: Ssshh! This is a scream! Wait! (*He addresses* RICHARD *in tones of exaggerated melodrama.*) Curse you, Jack Dalton, if I won't unhand her, what then?

SALESMAN: (*Threateningly.*) I'll give you a good punch in the snoot, that's what! (*He moves toward their table.*) 355

SALESMAN: (*With mock terror—screams in falsetto.*) Help! Help! (*The* BARTENDER *comes in irritably.*)

BARTENDER: Hey. Cut out the noise. What the hell's up with you?

RICHARD: (*Tipsily.*) He's too—damn fresh! 360

SALESMAN: (*With a wink.*) He's going to murder me. (*Then gets a bright idea for eliminating* RICHARD—*seriously to the* BARTENDER.) It's none of my business, Brother, but if I were in your boots I'd give this young souse the gate. He's under age; any fool can see that. 365

BARTENDER: (*Guiltily.*) He told me he was over eighteen.

BARTENDER: Yes, and I tell you I'm the Pope—but you don't have to believe me. If you're not looking for trouble, I'd advise you to get him started for some other gin mill and let them do the lying, if anything comes up. 370

BARTENDER: Hmm. (*He turns to* RICHARD *angrily and gives him a push.*) Come on, now. On your way! You'll start no trouble in here! Beat it now!

RICHARD: I will not beat it!

BARTENDER: Oho, won't you? (*He gives him another push that* 375 *almost sends him sprawling.*)

BELLE: (*Callously.*) Give him the bum's rush! I'm sick of his bull! (RICHARD *turns furiously and tries to punch the* BARTENDER.)

BARTENDER: (*Avoids the punch.*) Oho, you would, would you! 380 (*He grabs* RICHARD *by the back of the neck and the seat of the pants and marches him ignominiously toward the swinging door.*)

RICHARD: Leggo of me, you dirty coward!

BARTENDER: Quiet now—or I'll pin a Mary Ann on your jaw 385 that'll quiet you! (*He rushes him through the screen door and a moment later the outer doors are heard swinging back and forth.*)

SALESMAN: (*With a chuckle.*) Hand it to me, Kid. How was that for a slick way of getting rid of him? 390

BELLE: (*Suddenly sentimental.*) Poor kid. I hope he makes home all right. I liked him—before he got soused.

SALESMAN: Who is he?

BELLE: The boy who's upstairs with my friend told me, but I didn't pay much attention. Name's Miller. His old man runs 395 a paper in this one-horse burg, I think he said.

SALESMAN: (*With a whistle.*) Phew! He must be Nat Miller's kid, then.

BARTENDER: (*Coming back from the bar.*) Well, he's on his way—with a good boot in the tail to help him! 400

SALESMAN: (*With a malicious chuckle.*) Yes? Well, maybe that boot will cost you a job, Brother. Know Nat Miller who runs the *Globe*? That's his kid.

BARTENDER: (*His face falling.*) The hell he is! Who said so?

SALESMAN: This baby doll. (*Getting up.*) Say, I'll go keep cases 405 on him—see he gets on the trolley all right, anyway. Nat Miller's a good scout. (*He hurries out.*)

BARTENDER: (*Viciously.*) God damn the luck! If he ever finds out I served his kid, he'll run me out of town. (*He turns on* BELLE *furiously.*) Why didn't you put me wise, you lousy 410 tramp, you!

BELLE: Hey! I don't stand for that kind of talk—not from no hick beer-squirter like you, see!

BARTENDER: *(Furiously.)* You don't, don't you? Who was it but
415   you told me to hand him dynamite in that fizz? *(He gives her*
chair a push that almost throws her to the floor.) Beat it,
you—and beat it quick—or I'll call Sullivan from the corner
and have you run in for street-walking! *(He gives her a push*
that lands her against the family-entrance door.) Get the hell
420   out of here—and no long waits!
BELLE: *(Opens the door and goes out—turns and calls back vi-*
ciously.) I'll fix you for this, you thick Mick, if I have to go to
jail for it. *(She goes out and slams the door.)*
BARTENDER: *(Looks after her worriedly for a second—then*
425   *shrugs his shoulders.)* That's only her bull. *(Then with a sigh*
as he returns to the bar.) Them lousy tramps is always getting
this dump in Dutch!

(Curtain.)

SCENE II

Same as Act One—Sitting-room of the Miller home—about 11
o'clock the same night.

MILLER *is sitting in his favorite rocking-chair at left of table,*
front. He has discarded collar and tie, coat and shoes, and wears
an old, worn, brown dressing-gown and disreputable-looking car-
pet slippers. He has his reading specs on and is running over
items in a newspaper. But his mind is plainly preoccupied and
worried, and he is not paying much attention to what he reads.

MRS. MILLER *sits by the table at right, front. She also has on her*
specs. A sewing basket is on her lap and she is trying hard to
keep her attention fixed on the doily she is doing. But, as in the
case of her husband, but much more apparently, her mind is pre-
occupied, and she is obviously on tenterhooks of nervous uneasi-
ness.

LILY *is sitting in the armchair by the table at rear, facing right.*
She is pretending to read a novel, but her attention wanders, too,
and her expression is sad, although now it has lost all its bitter-
ness and become submissive and resigned again.

MILDRED *sits at the desk at right, front, writing two words over*
and over again, stopping each time to survey the result critically,
biting her tongue, intensely concentrated on her work.

TOMMY *sits on the sofa at left, front. He has had a hard day and*
is terribly sleepy but will not acknowledge it. His eyes blink shut
on him, his head begins to nod, but he isn't giving up, and every
time he senses any of the family glancing in his direction, he
goads himself into a bright-eyed wakefulness.

MILDRED: *(Finally surveys the two words she has been writing*
and is satisfied with them.) There. *(She takes the paper over*
to her mother.) Look, Ma. I've been practising a new way of
writing my name. Don't look at the others, only the last one.
5   Don't you think it's the real goods?
MRS. MILLER: *(Pulled out of her preoccupation.)* Don't talk that
horrible slang. It's bad enough for boys, but for a young girl
supposed to have manners—my goodness, when I was your
age, if my mother'd ever heard me—
10   MILDRED: Well, don't you think it's nice, then?
MRS. MILLER: *(Sinks back into preoccupation—scanning the*
paper—vaguely.) Yes, very nice, Mildred—very nice, indeed. *(Hands the paper back mechanically.)*

MILDRED: *(Is a little piqued, but smiles.)* Absent-minded! I
don't believe you even saw it. *(She passes around the table to*   15
show her AUNT LILY. MILLER *gives an uneasy glance at his*
wife and then, as if afraid of meeting her eye, looks quickly
back at his paper again.)
MRS. MILLER: *(Staring before her—sighs worriedly.)* Oh, I do
wish Richard would come home!   20
MILLER: There now, Essie. He'll be in any minute now. Don't
you worry about him.
MRS. MILLER: But I do worry about him!
LILY: *(Surveying* MILDRED'S *handiwork—smiling.)* This is fine,
Mildred. Your penmanship is improving wonderfully. But   25
don't you think that maybe you've got a little too many
flourishes?
MILDRED: *(Disappointedly.)* But, Aunt Lily, that's just what I
was practising hardest on.
MRS. MILLER: *(With another sigh.)* What time is it now, Nat?   30
MILLER: *(Adopting a joking tone.)* I'm going to buy a clock for
in here. You have me reaching for my watch every couple of
minutes. *(He has pulled his watch out of his vest pocket—*
with forced carelessness.) Only a little past ten.
MRS. MILLER: Why, you said it was that an hour ago! Nat   35
Miller, you're telling me a fib, so's not to worry me. You let
me see that watch!
MILLER: *(Guiltily.)* Well, it's quarter to eleven—but that's not
so late—when you remember it's Fourth of July.
MRS. MILLER: If you don't stop talking Fourth of July—! To   40
hear you go on, you'd think that was an excuse for anything
from murder to picking pockets!
MILDRED: *(Has brought her paper around to her father and*
now shoves it under his nose.) Look, Pa.
MILLER: *(Seizes on this interruption with relief.)* Let's see.   45
Hmm. Seems to me you've been inventing a new signature
every week lately. What are you in training for—writing
checks? You must be planning to catch a rich husband.
MILDRED: *(With an arch toss of her head.)* No wedding bells
for me! But how do you like it, Pa?   50
MILLER: It's overpowering—no other word for it, overpowering! You could put it on the Declaration of Independence
and not feel ashamed.
MRS. MILLER: *(Desolately, almost on the verge of tears.)* It's all
right for you to laugh and joke with Mildred! I'm the only   55
one in this house seems to care—*(Her lips tremble.)*
MILDRED: *(A bit disgustedly.)* Ah, Ma, Dick only sneaked off
to the fireworks at the beach, you wait and see.
MRS. MILLER: Those fireworks were over long ago. If he had,
he'd be home.   60
LILY: *(Soothingly.)* He probably couldn't get a seat, the trolleys
are so jammed, and he had to walk home.
MILLER: *(Seizing on this with relief.)* Yes, I never thought of
that, but I'll bet that's it.
MILDRED: Ah, don't let him worry you, Ma. He just wants to   65
show off he's heartbroken about that silly Muriel—and get
everyone fussing over him and wondering if he hasn't
drowned himself or something.
MRS. MILLER: *(Snappily.)* You be quiet! The way you talk at
times, I really believe you're that hard-hearted you haven't   70
got a heart in you! *(With an accusing glance at her husband.)*
One thing I know, you don't get that from me! *(He meets her*
eye and avoids it guiltily. She sniffs and looks away from him

around the room. TOMMY, *who is nodding and blinking, is afraid her eye is on him. He straightens alertly and speaks in a voice that, in spite of his effort, is dripping with drowsiness.*)

TOMMY: Let me see what you wrote, Mid.

MILDRED: (*Cruelly mocking.*) You? You're so sleepy you couldn't see it?

TOMMY: (*Valiantly.*) I am not sleepy!

MRS. MILLER: (*Has fixed her eye on him.*) My gracious, I was forgetting you were still up! You run up to bed this minute! It's hours past your bedtime!

TOMMY: But it's the Fourth of July. Ain't it, Pa?

MRS. MILLER: (*Gives her husband an accusing stare.*) There! You see what you've done? You might know he'd copy your excuses! (*Then sharply to* TOMMY.) You heard what I said, Young Man!

TOMMY: Aw, Ma, can't I stay up a *little* longer?

MRS. MILLER: I said, no! You obey me and no more arguing about it!

TOMMY: (*Drags himself to his feet.*) Aw! I should think I could stay up till Dick—

MILLER: (*Kindly but firmly.*) You heard your ma say no more arguing. When she says git, you better git. (TOMMY *accepts his fate resignedly and starts around kissing them all good night.*)

TOMMY: (*Kissing her.*) Good night, Aunt Lily.

LILY: Good night, dear. Sleep well.

TOMMY: (*Pecking at* MILDRED.) Good night, you.

MILDRED: Good night, you.

TOMMY: (*Kissing him.*) Good night, Pa.

MILLER: Good night, Son. Sleep tight.

TOMMY: (*Kissing her.*) Good night, Ma.

MRS. MILLER: Good night. Here! You look feverish. Let me feel of your head. No, you're all right. Hurry up, now. And don't forget your prayers.

(TOMMY *goes slowly to the doorway—then turns suddenly, the discovery of another excuse lighting up his face.*)

TOMMY: Here's another thing, Ma. When I was up to the water closet last—

MRS. MILLER: (*Sharply.*) When you were *where?*

TOMMY: The bathroom.

MRS. MILLER: That's better.

TOMMY: Uncle Sid was snoring like a fog horn—and he's right next to my room. How can I ever get to sleep while he's— (*He is overcome by a jaw-cracking yawn.*)

MRS. MILLER: I guess you'd get to sleep all right if you were inside a fog horn. You run along now. (TOMMY *gives up, grins sleepily, and moves off to bed. As soon as he is off her mind, all her former uneasiness comes back on* MRS. MILLER *tenfold. She sighs, moves restlessly, then finally asks.*) What time is it now, Nat?

MILLER: Now, Essie, I just told you a minute ago.

MRS. MILLER: (*Resentfully.*) I don't see how you can take it so calm! Here it's midnight, you might say, and our Richard still out, and we don't even know where he is.

MILDRED: I hear someone on the piazza. Bet that's him now, Ma.

MRS. MILLER: (*Her anxiety immediately turning to relieved anger.*) You give him a good piece of your mind, Nat, you

hear me! You're too easy with him, that's the whole trouble! The idea of him daring to stay out like this! (*The front door is heard being opened and shut, and someone whistling "Waltz Me Around Again, Willie."*)

MILDRED: No, that isn't Dick. It's Art.

MRS. MILLER: (*Her face falling.*) Oh. (*A moment later* ARTHUR *enters through the front parlor, whistling softly, half under his breath, looking complacently pleased with himself.*)

MILLER: (*Surveys him over his glasses, not with enthusiasm—shortly.*) So you're back, eh? We thought it was Richard.

ARTHUR: Is he still out? Where'd he go to?

MILLER: That's just what we'd like to know. You didn't run into him anywhere, did you?

ARTHUR: No. I've been at the Rands' ever since dinner. (*He sits down in the armchair at left of table, rear.*) I suppose he sneaked off to the beach to watch the fireworks.

MILLER: (*Pretending an assurance he is far from feeling.*) Of course. That's what we've been trying to tell your mother, but she insists on worrying her head off.

MRS. MILLER: But if he was going to the fireworks, why wouldn't he say so? He knew we'd let him.

ARTHUR: (*With calm wisdom.*) That's easy, Ma. (*He grins superiorly.*) Didn't you hear him this morning showing off bawling out the Fourth like an anarchist? He wouldn't want to reneg on that to you—but he'd want to see the old fireworks just the same. (*He adds complacently.*) I know. He's at the foolish age.

MILLER: (*Stares at* ARTHUR *with ill-concealed astonishment, then grins.*) Well, Arthur, by gosh, you make me feel as if I owed you an apology when you talk horse sense like that. (*He turns to his wife, greatly relieved.*) Arthur's hit the nail right on the head, I think, Essie. That was what I couldn't figure out—why he—but now it's clear as day.

MRS. MILLER: (*With a sigh.*) Well, I hope you're right. But I wish he was home.

ARTHUR: (*Takes out his pipe and fills and lights it with solemn gravity.*) He oughtn't to be allowed out this late at his age. I wasn't, Fourth or no Fourth—if I remember.

MILLER: (*A twinkle in his eyes.*) Don't tax your memory trying to recall those ancient days of your youth. (MILDRED *laughs and* ARTHUR *looks sheepish. But he soon regains his aplomb.*)

ARTHUR: (*Importantly.*) We had a corking dinner at the Rands'. We had sweetbreads on toast.

MRS. MILLER: (*Arising momentarily from her depression.*) Just like the Rands to put on airs before you! I never could see anything to sweetbreads. Always taste like soap to me. And no real nourishment to them. I wouldn't have the pesky things on my table! (ARTHUR *again feels sat upon.*)

MILDRED: (*Teasingly.*) Did you kiss Elsie good night?

ARTHUR: Stop trying to be so darn funny all the time! You give me a pain in the ear!

MILDRED: And that's where she gives me a pain, the stuck-up thing!—thinks she's the whole cheese!

MILLER: (*Irritably.*) And it's where your everlasting wrangling gives me a pain, you two! Give us a rest! (*There is silence for a moment.*)

MRS. MILLER: (*Sighs worriedly again.*) I do wish that boy would get home!

MILLER: (*Glances at her uneasily, peeks surreptitiously at his watch—then has an inspiration and turns to* ARTHUR.)

190 Arthur, what's this I hear about your having such a good singing voice? Rand was telling me he liked nothing better than to hear you sing—said you did every night you were up there. Why don't you ever give us folks at home here a treat?

ARTHUR: (*Pleased, but still nursing wounded dignity.*) I thought 195 you'd only sit on me.

MRS. MILLER: (*Perking up—proudly.*) Arthur has a real nice voice. He practises when you're not at home. I didn't know you cared for singing, Nat.

MILLER: Well, I do—nothing better—and when I was a boy I 200 had a fine voice myself and folks used to say I'd ought— (*Then abruptly, mindful of his painful experience with reminiscence at dinner, looking about him guiltily.*) Hmm. But don't hide your light under a bushel, Arthur. Why not give us a song or two now? You can play for him, can't you, 205 Mildred?

MILDRED: (*With a toss of her head.*) I can play as well as Elsie Rand, at least!

ARTHUR: (*Ignoring her—clearing his throat importantly.*) I've been singing a lot tonight. I don't know if my voice—

210 MILDRED: (*Forgetting her grudge, grabs her brother's hand and tugs at it.*) Come on. Don't play modest. You know you're just dying to show off. (*This puts* ARTHUR *off it at once. He snatches his hand away from her angrily.*)

ARTHUR: Let go of me, you! (*Then with surly dignity.*) I don't 215 feel like singing tonight, Pa. I will some other time.

MILLER: You let him alone, Mildred! (*He winks at* ARTHUR, *indicating with his eyes and a nod of his head* MRS. MILLER, *who has again sunk into worried brooding. He makes it plain by this pantomime that he wants him to sing to distract his* 220 *mother's mind.*)

ARTHUR: (*Puts aside his pipe and gets up promptly.*) Oh—sure, I'll do the best I can. (*He follows* MILDRED *into the front parlor, where he switches on the lights.*)

MILLER: (*To his wife.*) It won't keep Tommy awake. Nothing 225 could. And Sid, he'd sleep through an earthquake. (*Then suddenly, looking through the front parlor—grumpily.*) Darn it, speak of the devil, here he comes. Well, he's had a good sleep and he'd ought to be sobered up. (LILY *gets up from her chair and looks around her huntedly, as if for a place to hide.* 230 MILLER *says soothingly.*) Lily, you just sit down and read your book and don't pay any attention to him. (*She sits down again and bends over her book tensely. From the front parlor comes the tinkling of a piano as* MILDRED *runs over the scales. In the midst of this,* SID *enters through the front parlor.* 235 *All the effervescence of his jag has worn off and he is now suffering from a bad case of hangover—nervous, sick, a prey to gloomy remorse and bitter feelings of self-loathing and self-pity. His eyes are bloodshot and puffed, his face bloated, the fringe of hair around his baldness tousled and tufty. He sidles* 240 *into the room guiltily, his eyes shifting about, avoiding looking at anyone.*)

SID: (*Forcing a sickly, twitching smile.*) Hello.

MILLER: (*Considerately casual.*) Hello, Sid. Had a good nap? (*Then, as* SID *swallows hard and is about to break into further* 245 *speech,* MILDRED'S *voice comes from the front parlor, "I haven't played that in ever so long, but I'll try," and she starts an accompaniment.* MILLER *motions* SID *to be quiet.*) Ssshh! Arthur's going to sing for us. (SID *flattens himself against the edge of the bookcase at center, rear, miserably self-conscious*

and ill-at-ease there but nervously afraid to move anywhere 250 *else.* ARTHUR *begins to sing. He has a fairly decent voice but his method is untrained sentimentality to a dripping degree. He sings that old sentimental favorite, "Then You'll Remember Me." The effect on his audience is instant.* MILLER *gazes before him with a ruminating melancholy, his face seeming to* 255 *become gently sorrowful and old.* MRS. MILLER *stares before her, her expression becoming more and more doleful.* LILY *forgets to pretend to read her book but looks over it, her face growing tragically sad. As for* SID, *he is moved to his remorseful, guilt-stricken depths. His mouth pulls down at the corners and* 260 *he seems about to cry. The song comes to an end.* MILLER *starts, then claps his hands enthusiastically and calls.*) Well done, Arthur—well done! Why, you've got a splendid voice! Give us some more! You liked that, didn't you, Essie?

MRS. MILLER: (*Dolefully.*) Yes—but it's sad—terrible sad. 265

SID: (*After swallowing hard, suddenly blurts out.*) Nat and Essie—and Lily—I—I want to apologize—for coming home—the way I did—there's no excuse—but I didn't mean—

MILLER: (*Sympathetically.*) Of course, Sid. It's all forgotten. 270

MRS. MILLER: (*Rousing herself—affectionately pitying.*) Don't be a goose, Sid. We know how it is with picnics. You forget it. (*His face lights up a bit but his gaze shifts to* LILY *with a mute appeal, hoping for a word from her which is not forthcoming. Her eyes are fixed on her book, her body tense and rigid.*) 275

SID: (*Finally blurts out desperately.*) Lily—I'm sorry—about the fireworks. Can you—forgive me? (*But* LILY *remains implacably silent. A stricken look comes over* SID'S *face. In the front parlor* MILDRED *is heard saying "But I only know the chorus"—and she starts another accompaniment.*) 280

MILLER: (*Comes to* SID'S *rescue.*) Ssshh! We're going to have another song. Sit down, Sid. (SID, *hanging his head, flees to the farthest corner, left, front, and sits at the end of the sofa, facing front, hunched up, elbows on knees, face in hands, his round eyes childishly wounded and woe-begone.* ARTHUR *sings* 285 *the popular "Dearie," playing up its sentimental values for all he is worth. The effect on his audience is that of the previous song, intensified—especially upon* SID. *As he finishes,* MILLER *again starts and applauds.*) Mighty fine, Arthur! You sang that darned well! Didn't he, Essie? 290

MRS. MILLER: (*Dolefully.*) Yes—but I wish he wouldn't sing such sad songs. (*Then, her lips trembling.*) Richard's always whistling that.

MILLER: (*Hastily—calls.*) Give us something cheery, next one, Arthur. You know, just for variety's sake. 295

SID: (*Suddenly turns toward* LILY—*his voice choked with tears—in a passion of self-denunciation.*) You're right, Lily!—right not to forgive me!—I'm no good and never will be!—I'm a no-good drunken bum!—you shouldn't even wipe your feet on me!—I'm a dirty, rotten drunk!—no good 300 to myself or anybody else!—if I had any guts I'd kill myself, and good riddance!—but I haven't!—I'm yellow, too!—a yellow, drunken bum! (*He hides his face in his hands and begins to sob like a sick little boy. This is too much for* LILY. *All her bitter hurt and steely resolve to ignore and punish him* 305 *vanish in a flash, swamped by a pitying love for him. She runs and puts her arm around him—even kisses him tenderly and impulsively on his bald head, and soothes him as if he were a little boy.* MRS. MILLER, *almost equally moved, has half risen*

310 *to go to her brother, too, but* MILLER *winks and shakes his head vigorously and motions her to sit down.)*

LILY: There! Don't cry, Sid! I can't bear it! Of course, I forgive you! Haven't I always forgiven you? I know you're not to blame—So don't, Sid!

315 SID: *(Lifts a tearful, humbly grateful, pathetic face to her—but a face that the dawn of a cleansed conscience is already beginning to restore to its natural Puckish expression.)* Do you really forgive me—I know I don't deserve it—can you really—?

320 LILY: *(Gently.)* I told you I did, Sid—and I do.

SID: *(Kisses her hand humbly, like a big puppy licking it.)* Thanks, Lily. I can't tell you—*(In the front parlor,* ARTHUR *begins to sing rollickingly "Waiting at the Church," and after the first line or two* MILDRED *joins in.* SID's *face lights up with*
325 *appreciation and, automatically, he begins to tap one foot in time, still holding fast to* LILY's *hand. When they come to "sent around a note, this is what she wrote," he can no longer resist, but joins in a shaky bawl.)* "Can't get away to marry you today, My wife won't let me!" *(As the song finishes, the two in*
330 *the other room laugh.* MILLER *and* SID *laugh.* LILY *smiles at* SID's *laughter. Only* MRS. MILLER *remains dolefully preoccupied, as if she hadn't heard.)*

MILLER: That's fine, Arthur and Mildred. That's darned good.

SID: *(Turning to* LILY *enthusiastically.)* You ought to hear Vesta
335 Victoria sing that! Gosh, she's great! I heard her at Hammerstein's Victoria—you remember, that trip I made to New York.

LILY: *(Her face suddenly tired and sad again—for her memory of certain aspects of that trip is the opposite from what he would*
340 *like her to recall at this moment—gently disengaging her hand from his—with a hopeless sigh.)* Yes, I remember, Sid. *(He is overcome momentarily by guilty confusion. She goes quietly and sits down in her chair again. In the front parlor, from now on,* MILDRED *keeps starting to run over popular*
345 *tunes but always gets stuck and turns to another.)*

MRS. MILLER: *(Suddenly.)* What time is it now, Nat? *(Then without giving him a chance to answer.)* Oh, I'm getting worried something dreadful, Nat! You don't know what might have happened to Richard! You read in the papers every day
350 about boys getting run over by automobiles.

LILY: Oh, don't say that, Essie!

MILLER: *(Sharply, to conceal his own reawakened apprehension.)* Don't get to imagining things, now!

MRS. MILLER: Well, why couldn't it happen, with everyone
355 that owns one out tonight, and lots of those driving, drunk? Or he might have gone down to the beach dock and fallen overboard! *(On the verge of hysteria.)* Oh, I know something dreadful's happened! And you can sit there listening to songs and laughing as if—Why don't you do something? Why
360 don't you go out and find him? *(She bursts into tears.)*

LILY: *(Comes to her quickly and puts her arm around her.)* Essie, you mustn't worry so! You'll make yourself sick! Richard's all right. I've got a feeling in my bones he's all right.

365 MILDRED: *(Comes hurrying in from the front parlor.)* What's the trouble? *(*ARTHUR *appears in the doorway beside her. She goes to her mother and also puts an arm around her.)* Ah, don't cry, Ma! Dick'll turn up in a minute or two, wait and see!

370 ARTHUR: Sure, he will!

MILLER: *(Has gotten to his feet, frowning—soberly.)* I was going out to look—if he wasn't back by twelve sharp. That'd be the time it'd take him to walk from the beach if he left after the last car. But I'll go now, if it'll ease your mind. I'll take the auto and drive out the beach road—and likely pick
375 him up on the way. *(He has taken his collar and tie from where they hang from one corner of the bookcase at rear, center, and is starting to put them on.)* You better come with me, Arthur.

ARTHUR: Sure thing, Pa. *(Suddenly he listens and says.)* Ssshh!
380 There's someone on the piazza now—coming around to this door, too. That must be him. No one else would—

MRS. MILLER: Oh, thank God, thank God!

MILLER: *(With a sheepish smile.)* Darn him! I've a notion to give him hell for worrying us all like this. *(The screen door is
385 pushed violently open and* RICHARD *lurches in and stands swaying a little, blinking his eyes in the light. His face is a pasty pallor, shining with perspiration, and his eyes are glassy. The knees of his trousers are dirty, one of them torn from the sprawl on the sidewalk he had taken, following the
390 BARTENDER's kick. They all gape at him, too paralyzed for a moment to say anything.)*

MRS. MILLER: Oh, God, what's happened to him! He's gone crazy! Richard!

SID: *(The first to regain presence of mind—with a grin.)* Crazy,
395 nothing. He's only soused!

ARTHUR: He's drunk that's what! *(Then shocked and condemning.)* You've got your nerve! You fresh kid! We'll take that out of you when we get you down to Yale!

RICHARD: *(With a wild gesture of defiance—maudlinly
400 dramatic.)*

"Yesterday this Day's Madness did prepare
Tomorrow's Silence, Triumph, or Despair.
Drink! for—"

MILLER: *(His face grown stern and angry, takes a threatening
405 step toward him.)* Richard! How dare—!

MRS. MILLER: *(Hysterically.)* Don't you strike him, Nat! Don't you—!

SID: *(Grabbing his arm.)* Steady, Nat! Keep your temper! No good bawling him out now! He don't know what he's doing!

410 MILLER: *(Controlling himself and looking a bit ashamed.)* All right—you're right, Sid.

RICHARD: *(Drunkenly glorying in the sensation he is creating—recites with dramatic emphasis.)* "And then—I will come—with vine leaves in my hair!" *(He laughs with a double-dyed
415 sardonicism.)*

MRS. MILLER: *(Staring at him as if she couldn't believe her eyes.)* Richard! You're intoxicated!—you bad, wicked boy, you!

RICHARD: *(Forces a wicked leer to his lips and quotes with ponderous mockery.)* "Fancy that, Hedda!" *(Then suddenly his
420 whole expression changes, his pallor takes on a greenish, seasick tinge, his eyes seem to be turned inward uneasily—and, all pose gone, he calls to his mother appealingly, like a sick little boy.)* Ma! I feel—rotten! *(*MRS. MILLER *gives a cry and starts to go to him, but* SID *steps in her way.)*

425 SID: You let me take care of him, Essie. I know this game backwards.

MILLER: *(Putting his arm around his wife.)* Yes, you leave him to Sid.

430　SID: (*His arm around* RICHARD—*leading him off through the front parlor.*) Come on, Old Sport! Upstairs we go! Your old Uncle Sid'll fix you up. He's the kid that wrote the book!

MRS. MILLER: (*Staring after them—still aghast.*) Oh, it's too terrible! Imagine our Richard! And did you hear him talking
435　about some Hedda? Oh, I know he's been with one of those bad women, I know he has—my Richard! (*She hides her face on* MILLER's *shoulder and sobs heartbrokenly.*)

MILLER: (*A tired, harassed, deeply worried look on his face— soothing her.*) Now, now, you mustn't get to imagining such
440　things! You mustn't, Essie! (LILY *and* MILDRED *and* ARTHUR *are standing about awkwardly with awed, shocked faces.*)

(*Curtain.*)

— ACT FOUR —

SCENE I

The same—Sitting-room of the Miller house—about one o'clock in the afternoon of the following day.

As the curtain rises, the family, with the exception of RICHARD, *are discovered coming in through the back parlor from dinner in the dining-room.* MILLER *and his wife come first. His face is set in an expression of frowning severity.* MRS. MILLER's *face is drawn and worried. She has evidently had no rest yet from a sleepless, tearful night.* SID *is himself again, his expression as innocent as if nothing had occurred the previous day that remotely concerned him. And, outside of eyes that are bloodshot and nerves that are shaky, he shows no aftereffects except that he is terribly sleepy.* LILY *is gently sad and depressed.* ARTHUR *is self-consciously a virtuous young man against whom nothing can be said.* MILDRED *and* TOMMY *are subdued, covertly watching their father.*

They file into the sitting-room in silence and then stand around uncertainly, as if each were afraid to be the first to sit down. The atmosphere is as stiltedly grave as if they were attending a funeral service. Their eyes keep fixed on the head of the house, who has gone to the window at right and is staring out frowningly, savagely chewing a toothpick.

MILLER: (*Finally—irritably.*) Damn it, I'd ought to be back at the office putting in some good licks! I've a whole pile of things that have got to be done today!

MRS. MILLER: (*Accusingly.*) You don't mean to tell me you're
5　going back without seeing him? It's your duty—!

MILLER: (*Exasperatedly.*) 'Course I'm not! I wish you'd stop jumping to conclusions! What else did I come home for, I'd like to know? Do I usually come way back here for dinner on a busy day? I was only wishing this hadn't come up—just at
10　this particular time. (*He ends up very lamely and is irritably conscious of the fact.*)

TOMMY: (*Who has been fidgeting restlessly—unable to bear the suspense a moment longer.*) What is it Dick done? Why is everyone scared to tell me?

15　MILLER: (*Seizes this as an escape valve—turns and fixes his youngest son with a stern forbidding eye.*) Young man, I've never spanked you yet, but that don't mean I never will! Seems to me that you've been just itching for it lately! You keep your mouth shut till you're spoken to—or I warn you
20　something's going to happen!

MRS. MILLER: Yes, Tommy, you keep still and don't bother your pa. (*Then warningly to her husband.*) Careful what you say, Nat. Little pitchers have big ears.

MILLER: (*Peremptorily.*) You kids skedaddle—all of you. Why
25　are you always hanging around the house? Go out and play in the yard, or take a walk, and get some fresh air. (MILDRED *takes* TOMMY's *hand and leads him out through the front parlor.* ARTHUR *hangs back, as if the designation "kids" couldn't possibly apply to him. His father notices this—impatiently.*) You, too, Arthur. (ARTHUR *goes out with a stiff, wounded*
30　*dignity.*)

LILY: (*Tactfully.*) I think I'll go for a walk, too. (*She goes out through the front parlor.* SID *makes a movement as if to follow her.*)

MILLER: I'd like you to stay, Sid—for a while, anyway.
35

SID: Sure. (*He sits down in the rocking-chair at right, rear, of table and immediately yawns.*) Gosh, I'm dead. Don't know what's the matter with me today. Can't seem to keep awake.

MILLER: (*With caustic sarcasm.*) Maybe that demon chowder you drank at the picnic poisoned you! (SID *looks sheepish*
40　*and forces a grin. Then* MILLER *turns to his wife with the air of one who determinedly faces the unpleasant.*) Where is Richard?

MRS. MILLER: (*Flusteredly.*) He's still in bed. I made him stay in bed to punish him—and I thought he ought to, anyway,
45　after being so sick. But he says he feels all right.

SID: (*With another yawn.*) 'Course he does. When you're young you can stand anything without it feazing you. Why, I remember when I could come down on the morning after, fresh as a daisy, and eat a breakfast of pork chops and fried
50　onions and—(*He stops guiltily.*)

MILLER: (*Bitingly.*) I suppose that was before eating lobster shells had ruined your iron constitution!

MRS. MILLER: (*Regards her brother severely.*) If I was in your shoe, I'd keep still! (*Then turning to her husband.*) Richard
55　must be feeling better. He ate all the dinner I sent up, Norah says.

MILLER: I thought you weren't going to give him any dinner— to punish him.

MRS. MILLER: (*Guiltily.*) Well—in his weakened condition—I
60　thought it best—(*Then defensively.*) But you needn't think I haven't punished him. I've given him pieces of my mind he won't forget in a hurry. And I've kept reminding him his real punishment was still to come—that you were coming home to dinner on purpose—and then he'd learn that you could
65　be terrible stern when he did such awful things.

MILLER: (*Stirs uncomfortably.*) Hmm!

MRS. MILLER: And that's just what it's your duty to do—punish him good and hard! The idea of him daring—(*Then hastily.*) But you be careful how you go about it, Nat. Remember he's
70　like you inside—too sensitive for his own good. And he never would have done it, I know, if it hadn't been for that darned little dunce, Muriel, and her numbskull father—and then all of us teasing him and hurting his feelings all day—and then you lost your temper and were so sharp with him right
75　after dinner before he went out.

MILLER: (*Resentfully.*) I see this is going to work round to where it's all my fault!

MRS. MILLER: Now, I didn't say that, did I? Don't go losing your temper again. And here's another thing. You know as
80　well as I, Richard would never have done such a thing alone.

Why, he wouldn't know how! He must have been influenced and led by someone.

MILLER: Yes, I believe that. Did you worm out of him who it was? *(Then angrily.)* By God, I'll make whoever it was regret it!

MILLER: No, he wouldn't admit there was anyone. *(Then triumphantly.)* But there is one thing I did worm out of him—and I can tell you it relieved my mind more'n anything. You know, I was afraid he'd been with one of those bad women. Well, turns out there wasn't any Hedda. She was just out of those books he's been reading. He swears he's never known a Hedda in his life. And I believe him. Why, he seemed disgusted with me for having such a notion. *(Then lamely.)* So somehow—I can't kind of feel it's all as bad as I thought it was. *(Then quickly and indignantly.)* But it's bad enough, goodness knows—and you punish him good just the same. The idea of a boy his age—! Shall I go up now and tell him to get dressed, you want to see him?

MILLER: *(Helplessly—and irritably.)* Yes! I can't waste all day listening to you!

MRS. MILLER: *(Worriedly.)* Now you keep your temper, Nat, remember! *(She goes out through the front parlor.)*

MILLER: Darn women, anyway! They always get you mixed up. Their minds simply don't know what logic is! *(Then he notices that* SID *is dozing—sharply.)* Sid!

SID: *(Blinking—mechanically.)* I'll take the same. *(Then hurriedly.)* What'd you say, Nat?

MILLER: *(Caustically.)* What I didn't say was what'll you have. *(Irritably.)* Do you want to be of some help, or don't you? Then keep awake and try and use your brains! This is a damned sight more serious than Essie has any idea! She thinks there weren't any girls mixed up with Richard's spree last night—but I happen to know there were! *(He takes a letter from his pocket.)* Here's a note a woman left with one of the boys downstairs at the office this morning—didn't ask to see me, just said give me this. He'd never seen her before—said she looked like a tart. *(He has opened the letter and reads.)* "Your son got the booze he drank last night at the Pleasant Beach House. The bartender there knew he was under age but served him just the same. He thought it was a good joke to get him soused. If you have any guts you will run that bastard out of town." Well, what do you think of that? It's a woman's handwriting—not signed, of course.

SID: She's one of the babies, all right—judging from her elegant language.

MILLER: See if you recognize the handwriting.

SID: *(With a reproachful look.)* Nat, I resent the implication that I correspond with all the tramps around this town. *(Looking at the letter.)* No, I don't know who this one could be. *(Handing the letter back.)* But I deduce that the lady had a run-in with the barkeep and wants revenge.

MILLER: *(Grimly.)* And I deduce that before that she must have picked up Richard—or how would she know who he was?—and took him to this dive.

SID: Maybe. The Pleasant Beach House is nothing but a bed house—*(Quickly.)* At least, so I've been told.

MILLER: That's just the sort of damned fool thing he might do to spite Muriel, in the state of mind he was in—pick up some tart. And she'd try to get him drunk so—

SID: Yes, it might have happened like that—and it might not. How're we ever going to prove it? Everyone at the Pleasant Beach will lie their heads off.

MILLER: *(Simply and proudly.)* Richard won't lie.

SID: Well, don't blame him if he don't remember everything that happened last night. *(Then sincerely concerned.)* I hope you're wrong, Nat. That kind of baby is dangerous for a kid like Dick—in more ways than one. You know what I mean.

MILLER: *(Frowningly.)* Yep—and that's just what's got me worried. Damn it, I've got to have a straight talk with him—about women and all those things. I ought to have long ago.

SID: Yes. You ought.

MILLER: I've tried to a couple of times. I did it all right with Wilbur and Lawrence and Arthur, when it came time—but, hell, with Richard I always get sort of ashamed of myself and can't get started right. You feel, in spite of all his bold talk out of books, that he's so darned innocent inside.

SID: I know. I wouldn't like the job. *(Then after a pause—curiously.)* How were you figuring to punish him for his sins?

MILLER: *(Frowning.)* To be honest with you, Sid, I'm damned if I know. All depends on what I feel about what he feels when I first size him up—and then it'll be like shooting in the dark.

SID: If I didn't know you so well, I'd say don't be too hard on him. *(He smiles a little bitterly.)* If you remember, I was always getting punished—and see what a lot of good it did me!

MILLER: *(Kindly.)* Oh, there's lots worse than you around, so don't take to boasting. *(Then, at a sound from the front parlor—with a sigh.)* Well, here comes the Bad Man, I guess.

SID: *(Getting up.)* I'll beat it. *(But it is* MRS. MILLER *who appears in the doorway, looking guilty and defensive.* SID *sits down again.)*

MRS. MILLER: I'm sorry, Nat—but he was sound asleep and I didn't have the heart to wake him. I waited for him to wake up but he didn't.

MILLER: *(Concealing a relief of which he is ashamed—exasperatedly.)* Well, I'll be double damned! If you're not the—

MRS. MILLER: *(Defensively aggressive.)* Now don't lose your temper at me, Nat Miller! You know as well as I do he needs all the sleep he can get today—after last night's ructions! Do you want him to be taken down sick? And what difference does it make to you anyway? You can see him when you come home for supper, can't you? My goodness, I never saw you so savage-tempered! You'd think you couldn't bear waiting to punish him!

MILLER: *(Outraged.)* Well, I'll be eternally—*(Then suddenly he laughs.)* No use talking, you certainly take the cake! But you know darned well I told you I'm not coming home to supper tonight. I've got a date with Jack Lawson that may mean a lot of new advertising and it's important.

MRS. MILLER: Then you can see him when you do come home.

MILLER: *(Covering his evident relief at this respite with a fuming manner.)* All right! All right! I give up! I'm going back to the office. *(He starts for the front parlor.)* Bring a man all the way back here on a busy day and then you—No consideration—*(He disappears, and a moment later the front door is heard shutting behind him.)*

MRS. MILLER: Well! I never saw Nat so bad-tempered.

SID: *(With a chuckle.)* Bad temper, nothing. He's so tickled to get out of it for a while he can't see straight!

MRS. MILLER: *(With a sniff.)* I hope I know him better than you. *(Then fussing about the room, setting this and that in place, while* SID *yawns drowsily and blinks his eyes.)* Sleeping like a baby—so innocent looking. You'd think butter wouldn't melt in his mouth. It all goes to show you never can tell by appearances—not even when it's your own child. The idea!

SID: (*Drowsily.*) Oh, Dick's all right, Essie. Stop worrying.

210 MRS. MILLER: (*With a sniff.*) Of course, you'd say that. I suppose you'll have him out with you painting the town red the next thing!

(*As she is talking,* RICHARD *appears in the doorway from the sitting-room. He shows no ill effects from his experience the night before. In fact, he looks surprisingly healthy. He is dressed in old clothes that look as if they had been hurriedly flung on. His expression is one of hang-dog guilt mingled with a defensive defiance.*)

RICHARD: (*With self-conscious unconcern, ignoring his mother.*) Hello, Sid.

215 MRS. MILLER: (*Whirls on him.*) What are you doing here, Young Man? I thought you were asleep! Seems to me you woke up pretty quick—just after your pa left the house!

RICHARD: (*Sulkily.*) I wasn't asleep. I heard you in the room.

MRS. MILLER: (*Outraged.*) Do you mean to say you were delib-
220 erately deceiving—

RICHARD: I wasn't deceiving. You didn't ask if I was asleep.

MRS. MILLER: It amounts to the same thing and you know it! It isn't enough your wickedness last night, but now you have to take to lying!

225 RICHARD: I wasn't lying, Ma. If you'd asked if I was asleep I'd have said no.

MRS. MILLER: I've a good mind to send you straight back to bed and make you stay there!

RICHARD: Ah, what for, Ma? It was only giving me a headache,
230 lying there.

MRS. MILLER: If you've got a headache, I guess you know it doesn't come from that! And imagine me standing there, and feeling sorry for you, like a fool—even having a run-in with your pa because—But you wait till he comes back
235 tonight! If you don't catch it!

RICHARD: (*Sulkily.*) I don't care.

MRS. MILLER: You don't care? You talk as if you weren't sorry for what you did last night!

RICHARD: (*Defiantly.*) I'm not sorry.

240 MRS. MILLER: Richard! You ought to be ashamed! I'm beginning to think you're hardened in wickedness, that's what!

RICHARD: (*With bitter despondency.*) I'm not sorry because I don't care a darn what I did, or what's done to me, or anything about anything! I won't do it again—

245 MRS. MILLER: (*Seizing on this to relent a bit.*) Well, I'm glad to hear you say that, anyway!

RICHARD: But that's not because I think it was wicked or any such old-fogy moral notion, but because it wasn't any fun. It didn't make me happy and funny like it does Uncle Sid—

250 SID: (*Drowsily.*) What's that? Who's funny?

RICHARD: (*Ignoring him.*) It only made me sadder—and sick—so I don't see any sense in it.

MRS. MILLER: Now you're talking sense! That's a good boy.

RICHARD: But I'm not sorry I tried it once—curing the soul by
255 means of the senses, as Oscar Wilde says. (*Then with despairing pessimism.*) But what does it matter what I do or don't do? Life is all a stupid farce! I'm through with it! (*With a sinister smile.*) It's lucky there aren't any of General Gabler's pistols around—or you'd see if I'd stand it much
260 longer!

MRS. MILLER: (*Worriedly impressed by this threat—but pretending scorn.*) I don't know anything about General Gabler—I suppose that's more of those darned books—but you're a silly gabbler yourself when you talk that way!

265 RICHARD: (*Darkly.*) That's how little you know about me.

MRS. MILLER: (*Giving in to her worry.*) I wish you wouldn't say those terrible things—about life and pistols! You don't want to worry me to death, do you?

RICHARD: (*Reassuringly stoical now.*) You needn't worry, Ma.
270 It was only my despair talking. But I'm not a coward. I'll face—my fate.

MRS. MILLER: (*Stands looking at him puzzledly—then gives it up with a sigh.*) Well, all I can say is you're the queerest boy I ever did hear of! (*Then solicitously, putting her hand on his
275 forehead.*) How's your headache? Do you want me to get you some Bromo Seltzer?

RICHARD: (*Taken down—disgustedly.*) No, I don't! Aw, Ma, you don't understand anything!

MRS. MILLER: Well, I understand this much: It's your liver,
280 that's what! You'll take a good dose of salts tomorrow morning, and no nonsense about it! (*Then suddenly.*) My goodness, I wonder what time it's getting to be. I've got to go upstreet. (*She goes to the front-parlor doorway—then turns.*) You stay here, Richard, you hear? Remember, you're not al-
285 lowed out today—for a punishment. (*She hurries away.* RICHARD *sits in tragic gloom.* SID, *without opening his eyes, speaks to him drowsily.*)

SID: Well, how's my fellow Rum Pot, as good old Dowie calls us? Got a head?

290 RICHARD: (*Startled—sheepishly.*) Aw, don't go dragging that up, Uncle Sid. I'm never going to be such a fool again, I tell you.

SID: (*With drowsy cynicism—not unmixed with bitterness at the end.*) Seems to me I've heard someone say that before.
295 Who could it have been, I wonder? Why, if it wasn't Sid Davis! Yes, sir, I've heard him say that very thing a thousand times, must be. But then he's always fooling; you can't take a word he says seriously; he's a card, that Sid is!

RICHARD: (*Darkly.*) I was desperate, Uncle—even if she wasn't
300 worth it. I was wounded to the heart.

SID: I like to the quick better myself—more stylish. (*Then sadly.*) But you're right. Love is hell on a poor sucker. Don't I know it? (RICHARD *is disgusted and disdains to reply.* SID's *chin sinks on his chest and he begins to breathe noisily, fast
305 asleep.* RICHARD *glances at him with aversion. There is a sound of someone on the porch and the screen door is opened and* MILDRED *enters. She smiles on seeing her uncle, then gives a start on seeing* RICHARD.)

MILDRED: Hello! Are you allowed up?

310 RICHARD: Of course, I'm allowed up.

MILDRED: (*Comes and sits in her father's chair at right, front, of table.*) How did Pa punish you?

RICHARD: He didn't. He went back to the office without seeing me.

315 MILDRED: Well, you'll catch it later. (*Then rebukingly.*) And you ought to. If you'd ever seen how awful you looked last night!

RICHARD: Ah, forget it, can't you?

MILDRED: Well, are you ever going to do it again, that's what I
320 want to know.

RICHARD: What's that to you?

MILDRED: *(With suppressed excitement.)* Well, if you don't solemnly swear you won't—then I won't give you something I've got for you.

325 RICHARD: Don't try to kid me. You haven't got anything.

MILDRED: I have, too.

RICHARD: What?

MILDRED: Wouldn't you like to know! I'll give you three guesses.

330 RICHARD: *(With disdainful dignity.)* Don't bother me. I'm in no mood to play riddles with kids!

MILDRED: Oh, well, if you're going to get snippy! Anyway you haven't promised yet.

RICHARD: *(A prey to keen curiosity now.)* I promise. What is it?

335 MILDRED: What would you like best in the world?

RICHARD: I don't know. What?

MILDRED: And you pretend to be in love! If I told Muriel that!

RICHARD: *(Breathlessly.)* Is it—from her?

MILDRED: *(Laughing.)* Well, I guess it's a shame to keep you

340   guessing. Yes. It is from her. I was walking past her place just now when I saw her waving from their parlor window, and I went up and she said give this to Dick, and she didn't have a chance to say anything else because her mother called her and said she wasn't allowed to have company. So I took it—

345   and here it is. *(She gives him a letter folded many times into a tiny square.* RICHARD *opens it with a trembling eagerness and reads.* MILDRED *watches him curiously—then sighs affectedly.)* Gee, it must be nice to be in love like you are—all with one person.

350 RICHARD: *(His eyes shining.)* Gee, Mid, do you know what she says—that she didn't mean a word in that other letter. Her old man made her write it. And she loves me and only me and always will, no matter how they punish her!

MILDRED: My! I'd never think she had that much spunk.

355 RICHARD: Huh! You don't know her! Think I could fall in love with a girl that was afraid to say her soul's her own? I should say not! *(Then more gleefully still.)* And she's going to try and sneak out and meet me tonight. She says she thinks she can do it. *(Then suddenly feeling this enthusiasm before* MILDRED

360   *is entirely the wrong note for a cynical pessimist—with an affected bitter laugh.)* Ha! I knew darned well she couldn't hold out—that she'd ask to see me again. *(He misquotes cynically.)* "Women never know when the curtain has fallen. They always want another act."

365 MILDRED: Is that so, Smarty?

RICHARD: *(As if he were weighing the matter.)* I don't know whether I'll consent to keep this date or not.

MILDRED: Well, I know! You're not allowed out, you silly! So you can't!

370 RICHARD: *(Dropping all pretense—defiantly.)* Can't I, though! You wait and see if I can't! I'll see her tonight if it's the last thing I ever do! I don't care how I'm punished after!

MILDRED: *(Admiringly.)* Goodness! I never thought you had such nerve!

375 RICHARD: You promise to keep your face shut, Mid—until after I've left—then you can tell Pa and Ma where I've gone—I mean, if they're worrying I'm off like last night.

MILDRED: All right. Only you've got to do something for me when I ask.

380 RICHARD: 'Course I will. *(Then excitedly.)* And say, Mid! Right now's the best chance for me to get away—while everyone's out! Ma'll be coming back soon and she'll keep watching me

like a cat—*(He starts for the back parlor.)* I'm going. I'll sneak out the back.

MILDRED: *(Excitedly.)* But what'll you do till nighttime? It's 385 ages to wait.

RICHARD: What do I care how long I wait! *(Intensely sincere now.)* I'll think of her—and dream! I'd wait a million years and never mind it—for her! *(He gives his sister a superior scornful glance.)* The trouble with you is, you don't under- 390 stand what love means! *(He disappears through the back parlor.* MILDRED *looks after him admiringly.* SID *puffs and begins to snore peacefully.)*

(Curtain.)

SCENE II

A strip of beach along the harbor. At left, a bank of dark earth, running half-diagonally back along the beach, marking the line where the sand of the beach ends and fertile land begins. The top of the bank is grassy and the trailing boughs of willow trees extend out over it and over a part of the beach. At left, front, is a path leading up the bank, between the willows. On the beach, at center, front, a white, flat-bottomed rowboat is drawn up, its bow about touching the bank, the painter trailing up the bank, evidently made fast to the trunk of a willow. Halfway down the sky, at rear, left, the crescent of the new moon casts a soft, mysterious, caressing light over everything. The sand of the beach shimmers palely. The forward half (left of center) of the rowboat is in the deep shadow cast by the willow, the stern section is in moonlight. In the distance, the orchestra of a summer hotel can be heard very faintly at intervals.

RICHARD *is discovered sitting sideways on the gunwale of the rowboat near the stern. He is facing left, watching the path. He is in a great state of anxious expectancy, squirming about uncomfortably on the narrow gunwale, kicking at the sand restlessly, twirling his straw hat, with a bright-colored band in stripes, around on his finger.*

RICHARD: *(Thinking aloud.)* Must be nearly nine. . . . I can hear the Town Hall clock strike, it's so still tonight . . . Gee, I'll bet Ma had a fit when she found out I'd sneaked out . . . I'll catch hell when I get back, but it'll be worth it . . . if only Muriel turns up . . . she didn't say for certain she could . . . 5 gosh, I wish she'd come! . . . am I sure she wrote nine? . . . *(He puts the straw hat on the seat amidships and pulls the folded letter out of his pocket and peers at it in the moonlight.)* Yes, it's nine, all right. *(He starts to put the note back in his pocket, then stops and kisses it—then shoves it away hastily,* 10 *sheepish, looking around him shamefacedly, as if afraid he were being observed.)* Aw, that's silly . . . no, it isn't either . . . not when you're really in love. . . . *(He jumps to his feet restlessly.)* Darn it, I wish she'd show up! . . . think of something else . . . that'll make the time pass quicker . . . where was I 15 this time last night? . . . waiting outside the Pleasant Beach House . . . Belle . . . ah, forget her! . . . now, when Muriel's coming . . . that's a fine time to think of—! . . . but you hugged and kissed her . . . not until I was drunk, I didn't . . . and then it was all showing off . . . darned fool! . . . and I did- 20 n't go upstairs with her . . . even if she was pretty . . . aw, she wasn't pretty . . . she was all painted up . . . she was just a whore . . . she was everything dirty . . . Muriel's a million times prettier anyway . . . Muriel and I will go upstairs . . .

25 when we're married . . . but that will be beautiful . . . but I oughtn't even to think of that yet . . . it's not right . . . I'd never—now . . . and she'd never . . . she's a decent girl . . . I couldn't love her if she wasn't . . . but after we're married. . . . *(He gives a little shiver of passionate longing—then resolutely*
30 *turns his mind away from these improper, almost desecrating thoughts.)* That damned barkeep kicking me . . . I'll bet you if I hadn't been drunk I'd have given him one good punch in the nose, even if he could have licked me after! . . . *(Then with a shiver of shamefaced revulsion and self-disgust.)* Aw,
35 you deserved a kick in the pants . . . making such a darned slob of yourself . . . reciting the Ballad of Reading Gaol to those lowbrows! . . . you must have been a fine sight when you got home . . . having to be put to bed and getting sick! . . . Phaw! . . . *(He squirms disgustedly.)* Think of something else,
40 can't you? . . . recite something . . . see if you remember . . .

> "Nay, let us walk from fire unto fire
> From passionate pain to deadlier delight—
> I am too young to live without desire,
> Too young art thou to waste this summer night—"

45 . . . gee, that's a peach! . . . I'll have to memorize the rest and recite it to Muriel the next time. . . . I wish I could write poetry . . . about her and me. . . . *(He sighs and stares around him at the night.)* Gee, it's beautiful tonight . . . as if it was a special night . . . for me and Muriel. . . . Gee, I love
50 tonight. . . . I love the sand, and the trees, and the grass, and the water and the sky, and the moon . . . it's all in me and I'm in it . . . God, it's so beautiful! *(He stands staring at the moon with a rapt face. From the distance the Town Hall clock begins to strike. This brings him back to earth with a start.)* There's
55 nine now. . . . *(He peers at the path apprehensively.)* I don't see her . . . she must have got caught. . . . *(Almost tearfully.)* Gee, I hate to go home and catch hell . . . without having seen her! . . . *(Then calling a manly cynicism to his aid.)* Aw, who ever heard of a woman ever being on time. . . . I ought
60 to know enough about life by this time not to expect . . . *(Then with sudden excitement.)* There she comes now. . . . Gosh! *(He heaves a huge sigh of relief—then recites dramatically to himself, his eyes on the approaching figure.)*

> "And lo my love, mine own soul's heart, more dear
65 > Than mine own soul, more beautiful than God,
> Who hath my being between the hands of her—"

(Then hastily.) Mustn't let her know I'm so tickled. . . . I ought to be mad about that first letter, anyway . . . if women are too sure of you, they treat you like slaves . . . let her suf-
70 fer, for a change. . . .

(He starts to stroll around with exaggerated carelessness, turning his back on the path, hands in pockets, whistling with insouciance "Waiting at the Church."

MURIEL MC COMBER *enters from down the path, left front. She is fifteen, going on sixteen. She is a pretty girl with a plump, graceful little figure, fluffy, light-brown hair, big naïve wondering dark eyes, a round dimpled face, a melting drawly voice. Just now she is in a great thrilled state of timid adventurousness. She hesitates in the shadow at the foot of the path, waiting for* RICHARD *to see her; but he resolutely goes on whistling with back turned, and she has to call him.)*

MURIEL: Oh, Dick.

RICHARD: *(Turns around with an elaborate simulation of being disturbed in the midst of profound meditation.)* Oh, hello. Is it nine already? Gosh, time passes—when you're thinking.

MURIEL: *(Coming toward him as far as the edge of the shadow—* 75 *disappointedly.)* I thought you'd be waiting right here at the end of the path. I'll bet you'd forgotten I was even coming.

RICHARD: *(Strolling a little toward her but not too far—carelessly.)* No, I hadn't forgotten, honest. But I got to thinking about life. 80

MURIEL: You might think of me for a change, after all the risk I've run to see you! *(Hesitating timidly on the edge of the shadow.)* Dick! You come her to me. I'm afraid to go out in that bright moonlight where anyone might see me.

RICHARD: *(Coming toward her—scornfully.)* Aw, there you go 85 again—always scared of life!

MURIEL: *(Indignantly.)* Dick Miller, I do think you've got an awful nerve to say that after all the risks I've run making this date and then sneaking out! You didn't take the trouble to sneak any letter to me, I notice! 90

RICHARD: No, because after your first letter, I thought everything was dead and past between us.

MURIEL: And I'll bet you didn't care one little bit! *(On the verge of humiliated tears.)* Oh, I was a fool ever to come here! I've got a good notion to go right home and never speak to 95 you again! *(She half turns back toward the path.)*

RICHARD: *(Frightened—immediately becomes terribly sincere—grabbing her hand.)* Aw, don't go, Muriel! Please! I didn't mean anything like that, honest, I didn't! Gee, if you knew how broken-hearted I was by that first letter, and how darned 100 happy your second letter made me—!

MURIEL: *(Happily relieved—but appreciates she has the upper hand now and doesn't relent at once.)* I don't believe you.

RICHARD: You ask Mid how happy I was. She can prove it.

MURIEL: She'd say anything you told her to. I don't care any- 105 thing about what she'd say. It's you. You've got to swear to me—

RICHARD: I swear!

MURIEL: *(Demurely.)* Well then, all right, I'll believe you.

RICHARD: *(His eyes on her face lovingly—genuine adoration in* 110 *his voice.)* Gosh, you're pretty tonight, Muriel! It seems ages since we've been together! If you knew how I've suffered—!

MURIEL: I did, too.

RICHARD: *(Unable to resist falling into his tragic literary pose for a moment.)* The despair in my soul—*(He recites dramati-* 115 *cally.)* "Something was dead in each of us, And what was dead was Hope!" That was me! My hope of happiness was dead! *(Then with sincere boyish fervor.)* Gosh, Muriel, it sure is wonderful to be with you again! *(He puts a timid arm around her awkwardly.)* 120

MURIEL: *(Shyly.)* I'm glad—it makes you happy. I'm happy, too.

RICHARD: Can't I—won't you let me kiss you—now? Please! *(He bends his face toward hers.)*

MURIEL: *(Ducking her head away—timidly.)* No. You mustn't. 125 Don't—

RICHARD: Aw, why can't I?

MURIEL: Because—I'm afraid.

RICHARD: *(Discomfited—taking his arm from around her—a bit sulky and impatient with her.)* Aw, that's what you always 130 say! You're always so afraid! Aren't you ever going to let me?

MURIEL: I will—sometime.

RICHARD: When?

MURIEL: Soon, maybe.

135 RICHARD: Tonight, will you?

MURIEL: (*Coyly.*) I'll see.

RICHARD: Promise?

MURIEL: I promise—maybe.

RICHARD: All right. You remember you've promised. (*Then* 140 *coaxingly.*) Aw, don't let's stand here. Come on out and we can sit down in the boat.

MURIEL: (*Hesitantly.*) It's so bright out there.

RICHARD: No one'll see. You know there's never anyone around here at night.

145 MURIEL: (*Illogically.*) I know there isn't. That's why I thought it would be the best place. But there might be someone.

RICHARD: (*Taking her hand and tugging at it gently.*) There isn't a soul. (MURIEL *steps out a little and looks up and down fearfully.* RICHARD *goes on insistently.*) Aw, what's the use of 150 a moon if you can't see it!

MURIEL: But it's only a new moon. That's not much to look at.

RICHARD: But I want to see you. I can't here in the shadow. I want to—drink in—all your beauty.

MURIEL: (*Can't resist this.*) Well, all right—only I can't stay 155 only a few minutes. (*She lets him lead her toward the stern of the boat.*)

RICHARD: (*Pleadingly.*) Aw, you can stay a little while, can't you? Please! (*He helps her in and she settles herself in the stern seat of the boat, facing diagonally left front.*)

160 MURIEL: A little while. (*He sits beside her.*) But I've got to be home in bed again pretending to be asleep by ten o'clock. That's the time Pa and Ma come up to bed, as regular as clock work, and Ma always looks into my room.

RICHARD: But you'll have oodles of time to do that.

165 MURIEL: (*Excitedly.*) Dick, you have no idea what I went through to get here tonight! My, but it was exciting! You know Pa's punishing me by sending me to bed at eight sharp, and I had to get all undressed and into bed 'cause at half-past he sends Ma up to make sure I've obeyed, and she came up, 170 and I pretended to be asleep, and she went down again, and I got up and dressed in such a hurry—I must look a sight, don't I?

RICHARD: You do not! You look wonderful!

MURIEL: And then I sneaked down the back stairs. And the 175 pesky old stairs squeaked, and my heart was in my mouth, I was so scared, and then I sneaked out through the back yard, keeping in the dark under the trees, and—My, but it was exciting! Dick,, you don't realize how I've been punished for your sake. Pa's been so mean and nasty, I've almost hated 180 him!

RICHARD: And you don't realize what I've been through for you—and what I'm in for—for sneaking out—(*Then darkly.*) And for what I did last night—what your letter made me do!

MURIEL: (*Made terribly curious by his ominous tone.*) What did 185 my letter make you do?

RICHARD: (*Beginning to glory in this.*) It's too long a story— and let the dead past bury its dead. (*Then with real feeling.*) Only it isn't past, I can tell you! What I'll catch when Pa gets hold of me!

190 MURIEL: Tell me, Dick! Begin at the beginning and tell me!

RICHARD: (*Tragically.*) Well, after your old—your father left our place I caught holy hell from Pa.

MURIEL: Dick! You mustn't swear!

RICHARD: (*Somberly.*) Hell is the only word that can describe it. And on top of that, to torture me more, he gave me your 195 letter. After I'd read that I didn't want to live any more. Life seemed like a tragic farce.

MURIEL: I'm so awful sorry, Dick—honest I am! But you might have known I'd never write that unless—

RICHARD: I thought your love for me was dead. I thought you'd 200 never loved me, that you'd only been cruelly mocking me— to torture me!

MURIEL: Dick! I'd never! You know I'd never!

RICHARD: I wanted to die. I sat and brooded about death. Finally I made up my mind I'd kill myself. 205

MURIEL: (*Excitedly.*) Dick! You didn't!

RICHARD: I did, too! If there'd been one of Hedda Gabler's pistols around, you'd have seen if I wouldn't have done it beautifully! I thought, when I'm dead, she'll be sorry she ruined my life! 210

MURIEL: (*Cuddling up a little to him.*) If you ever had! I'd have died, too! Honest, I would!

RICHARD: But suicide is the act of a coward. That's what stopped me. (*Then with a bitter change of tone.*) And anyway, I thought to myself, she isn't worth it. 215

MURIEL: (*Huffily.*) That's a nice thing to say!

RICHARD: Well, if you meant what was in the letter, you wouldn't have been worth it, would you?

MURIEL: But I've told you Pa—

RICHARD: So I said to myself, I'm through with women; they're 220 all alike!

MURIEL: I'm not.

RICHARD: And I thought, what difference does it make what I do now? I might as well forget her and lead the pace that kills, and drown my sorrows! You know I had eleven dollars 225 saved up to buy you something for your birthday, but I thought, she's dead to me now and why shouldn't I throw it away? (*Then hastily.*) I've still got almost five left, Muriel, and I can get you something nice with that.

MURIEL: (*Excitedly.*) What do I care about your old presents? 230 You tell me what you did!

RICHARD: (*Darkly again.*) After it was dark, I sneaked out and went to a low dive I know about.

MURIEL: Dick Miller, I don't believe you ever!

RICHARD: You ask them at the Pleasant Beach House if I did- 235 n't! They won't forget me in a hurry!

MURIEL: (*Impressed and horrified.*) You went there? Why, that's a terrible place! Pa says it ought to be closed by the police!

RICHARD: (*Darkly.*) I said it was a dive, didn't I? It's a "secret 240 house of shame." And they let me into a secret room behind the barroom. There wasn't anyone there but a Princeton Senior I know—he belongs to Tiger Inn and he's fullback on the football team—and he had two chorus girls from New York with him, and they were all drinking champagne. 245

MURIEL: (*Disturbed by the entrance of the chorus girls.*) Dick Miller! I hope you didn't notice—

RICHARD: (*Carelessly.*) I had a highball by myself and then I noticed one of the girls—the one that wasn't with the fullback—looking at me. She had strange-looking eyes. And 250 then she asked me if I wouldn't drink champagne with them and come and sit with her.

MURIEL: She must have been a nice thing! (*Then a bit falteringly.*) And did—you?

255 RICHARD: (*With tragic bitterness.*) Why shouldn't I, when you'd told me in that letter you'd never see me again?

MURIEL: (*Almost tearfully.*) But you ought to have known Pa made me—

RICHARD: I didn't know that then. (*Then rubbing it in.*) Her
260 name was Belle. She had yellow hair—the kind that burns and stings you!

MURIEL: I'll bet it was dyed!

RICHARD: She kept smoking one cigarette after another—but that's nothing for a chorus girl.

265 MURIEL: (*Indignantly.*) She was low and bad, that's what she was or she couldn't be a chorus girl, and her smoking cigarettes proves it! (*Then falteringly again.*) And then what happened?

RICHARD: (*Carelessly.*) Oh, we just kept drinking cham-
270 pagne—I bought a round—and then I had a fight with the barkeep and knocked him down because he'd insulted her. He was a great big thug but—

MURIEL: (*Huffily.*) I don't see how he could—insult that kind! And why did you fight for her? Why didn't the Princeton
275 fullback who'd brought them there? He must have been bigger than you.

RICHARD: (*Stopped for a moment—then quickly.*) He was too drunk by that time.

MURIEL: And were you drunk?

280 RICHARD: Only a little then. I was worse later. (*Proudly.*) You ought to have seen me when I got home! I was on the verge of delirium tremens!

MURIEL: I'm glad I didn't see you. You must have been awful. I hate people who get drunk. I'd have hated you!

285 RICHARD: Well, it was all your fault, wasn't it? If you hadn't written that letter—

MURIEL: But I've told you I didn't mean—(*Then faltering but fascinated.*) But what happened with that Belle—after—before you went home?

290 RICHARD: Oh, we kept drinking champagne and she said she'd fallen in love with me at first sight and she came and sat on my lap and kissed me.

MURIEL: (*Stiffening.*) Oh!

RICHARD: (*Quickly, afraid he has gone too far.*) But it was only
295 all in fun, and then we just kept on drinking champagne, and finally I said good night and came home.

MURIEL: And did you kiss her?

RICHARD: No, I didn't.

MURIEL: (*Distractedly.*) You did, too! You're lying and you
300 know it. You did, too! (*Then tearfully.*) And there I was right at that time lying in bed not able to sleep, wondering how I was ever going to see you again and crying my eyes out, while you—! (*She suddenly jumps to her feet in a tearful fury.*) I hate you! I wish you were dead! I'm going home this
305 minute! I never want to lay eyes on you again! And this time I mean it! (*She tries to jump out of the boat but he holds her back. All the pose has dropped from him now and he is in a frightened state of contrition.*)

RICHARD: (*Imploringly.*) Muriel! Wait! Listen!

310 MURIEL: I don't want to listen! Let me go! If you don't I'll bite your hand!

RICHARD: I won't let you go! You've got to let me explain! I never—! Ouch! (*For* MURIEL *has bitten his hand and it hurts, and, stung by the pain, he lets go instinctively, and she*
315 *jumps quickly out of the boat and starts running toward the*

path. RICHARD *calls after her with bitter despair and hurt.*) All right! Go if you want to—if you haven't the decency to let me explain! I hate you, too! I'll go and see Belle!

MURIEL: (*Seeing he isn't following her, stops at the foot of the path—defiantly.*) Well, go and see her—if that's the kind of 320 girl you like! What do I care? (*Then as he only stares before him broodingly, sitting dejectedly in the stern of the boat, a pathetic figure of injured grief.*) You can't explain! What can you explain? You owned up you kissed her!

RICHARD: I did not. I said she kissed me. 325

MURIEL: (*Scornfully, but drifting back a step in his direction.*) And I suppose you just sat and let yourself be kissed! Tell that to the Marines!

RICHARD: (*Injuredly.*) All right! If you're going to call me a liar every word I say— 330

MURIEL: (*Drifting back another step.*) I didn't call you a liar. I only meant—it sounds fishy. Don't you know it does?

RICHARD: I don't know anything. I only know I wish I was dead!

MURIEL: (*Gently reproving.*) You oughtn't to say that. It's 335 wicked. (*Then after a pause.*) And I suppose you'll tell me you didn't fall in love with her?

RICHARD: (*Scornfully.*) I should say not! Fall in love with that kind of girl! What do you take me for?

MURIEL: (*Practically.*) How do you know what you did if you 340 drank so much champagne?

RICHARD: I kept my head—with her. I'm not a sucker, no matter what you think!

MURIEL: (*Drifting nearer.*) Then you didn't—love her?

RICHARD: I hated her! She wasn't even pretty! And I had a 345 fight with her before I left, she got so fresh. I told her I loved you and never could love anyone else, and for her to leave me alone.

MURIEL: But you said just now you were going to see her—

RICHARD: That was only bluff. I wouldn't—unless you left me. 350 Then I wouldn't care what I did—any more than I did last night. (*Then suddenly defiant.*) And what if I did kiss her once or twice? I only did it to get back at you!

MURIEL: Dick!

RICHARD: You're a fine one to blame me—when it was all your 355 fault! Why can't you be fair? Didn't I think you were out of my life forever? Hadn't you written me you were? Answer me that!

MURIEL: But I've told you a million times that Pa—

RICHARD: Why didn't you have more sense than to let him 360 make you write it? Was it my fault you didn't?

MURIEL: It was your fault for being so stupid! You ought to have known he stood right over me and told me each word to write. If I'd refused, it would only have made everything worse. I had to pretend, so I'd get a chance to see you. Don't 365 you see, Silly? And I had sand enough to sneak out to meet you tonight, didn't I? (*He doesn't answer. She moves nearer.*) Still I can see how you felt the way you did—and maybe I am to blame for that. So I'll forgive and forget, Dick—if you'll swear to me you didn't even think of loving that— 370

RICHARD: (*Eagerly.*) I didn't! I swear, Muriel. I couldn't. I love you!

MURIEL: Well, then—I still love you.

RICHARD: Then come back here, why don't you?

MURIEL: (*Coyly.*) It's getting late. 375

RICHARD: It's not near half-past yet.

MURIEL: *(Comes back and sits down by him shyly.)* All right—only I'll have to go soon, Dick. *(He puts his arm around her. She cuddles up close to him.)* I'm sorry—I hurt your hand.

380 RICHARD: That was nothing. It felt wonderful—even to have you bite!

MURIEL: *(Impulsively takes his hand and kisses it.)* There! That'll cure it. *(She is overcome by confusion at her boldness.)*

RICHARD: You shouldn't—waste that—on my hand. *(Then*
385 *tremblingly.)* You said—you'd let me—

MURIEL: I said, maybe.

RICHARD: Please, Muriel. You know—I want it so!

MURIEL: Will it wash off—her kisses—make you forget you ever—for always?

390 RICHARD: I should say so! I'd never remember—anything but it—never want anything but it—ever again.

MURIEL: *(Shyly lifting her lips.)* Then—all right—Dick. *(He kisses her tremblingly and for a moment their lips remain together. Then she lets her head sink on his shoulder and sighs*
395 *softly.)* The moon is beautiful, isn't it?

RICHARD: *(Kissing her hair.)* Not as beautiful as you! Nothing is! *(Then after a pause.)* Won't it be wonderful when we're married?

MURIEL: Yes—but it's so long to wait.

400 RICHARD: Perhaps I needn't go to Yale. Perhaps Pa will give me a job. Then I'd soon be making enough to—

MURIEL: You better do what your pa thinks best—and I'd like you to be at Yale. *(Then patting his face.)* Poor you! Do you think he'll punish you awful?

405 RICHARD: *(Intensely.)* I don't know and I don't care! Nothing would have kept me from seeing you tonight—not if I'd had to crawl over red-hot coals! *(Then falling back on Swinburne—but with passionate sincerity.)* You have my being between the hands of you! You are "my love, mine own soul's
410 heart, more dear than mine own soul, more beautiful than God!"

MURIEL: *(Shocked and delighted.)* Ssshh! It's wrong to say that.

RICHARD: *(Adoringly.)* Gosh, but I love you! Gosh, I love you—Darling!

415 MURIEL: I love you, too—Sweetheart! *(They kiss. Then she lets her head sink on his shoulder again and they both sit in a rapt trance, staring at the moon. After a pause—dreamily.)* Where'll we go on our honeymoon, Dick? To Niagara Falls?

RICHARD: *(Scornfully.)* That dump where all the silly fools go?
420 I should say not! *(With passionate romanticism.)* No, we'll go to some far-off wonderful place! *(He calls on Kipling to help him.)* Somewhere out on the Long Trail—the trail that is always new—on the road to Mandalay! We'll watch the dawn come up like thunder out of China!

425 MURIEL: *(Hazily but happily.)* That'll be wonderful, won't it?

(Curtain.)

SCENE III

The sitting-room of the Miller house again—about 10 o'clock the same night. MILLER *is sitting in his rocker at left, front, of table, his wife in the rocker at right, front, of table. Moonlight shines through the screen door at right, rear. Only the green-shaded reading lamp is lit and by its light* MILLER, *his specs on, is reading a book while his wife, sewing basket in lap, is working industriously on a doily.* MRS. MILLER's *face wears an expression of unworried content.* MILLER's *face has also lost its look of*

harassed preoccupation, although he still is a prey to certain misgivings, when he allows himself to think of them. Several books are piled on the table by his elbow, the books that have been confiscated from RICHARD.

MILLER: *(Chuckles at something he reads—then closes the book and puts it on the table.* MRS. MILLER *looks up from her sewing.)* This Shaw's a comical cuss—even if his ideas are so crazy they oughtn't to allow them to be printed. And that Swinburne's got a fine swing to his poetry—if he'd only 5 choose some other subjects besides loose women.

MRS. MILLER: *(Smiling teasingly.)* I can see where you're becoming corrupted by those books, too—pretending to read them out of duty to Richard, when your nose has been glued to the page! 10

MILLER: No, no—but I've got to be honest. There's something to them. That Rubaiyat of Omar Khayyam, now. I read that over again and liked it even better than I had before—parts of it, that is, where it isn't all about boozing.

MRS. MILLER: *(Has been busy with her own thoughts during* 15 *this last—with a deep sigh of relief.)* My, but I'm glad Mildred told me where Richard went off to. I'd have worried my heart out if she hadn't. But now, it's all right.

MILLER: *(Frowning a little.)* I'd hardly go so far as to say that. Just because we know he's all right tonight doesn't mean last 20 night is wiped out. He's still got to be punished for that.

MRS. MILLER: *(Defensively.)* Well, if you ask me, I think after the way I punished him all day, and the way I know he's punished himself, he's had about all he deserves. I've told you how sorry he was, and how he said he'd never touch liquor 25 again. It didn't make him feel happy like Sid, but only sad and sick, so he didn't see anything in it for him.

MILLER: Well, if he's really got that view of it driven into his skull, I don't know but I'm glad it all happened. That'll protect him more than a thousand lectures—just horse sense 30 about himself. *(Then frowning again.)* Still, I can't let him do such things and go scot-free. And then; besides, there's another side to it—*(He stops abruptly.)*

MRS. MILLER: *(Uneasily.)* What do you mean, another side?

MILLER: *(Hastily.)* I mean, discipline. There's got to be some 35 discipline in a family. I don't want him to get the idea he's got a stuffed shirt at the head of the table. No, he's got to be punished, if only to make the lesson stick in his mind, and I'm going to tell him he can't go to Yale, seeing he's so undependable. 40

MRS. MILLER: *(Up in arms at once.)* Not go to Yale! I guess he can go to Yale! Every man of your means in town is sending his boys to college! What would folks think of you? You let Wilbur go, and you'd have let Lawrence, only he didn't want to, and you're letting Arthur! If our other children can get 45 the benefit of a college education, you're not going to pick on Richard—

MILLER: Hush up, for God's sake! If you'd let me finish what I started to say! I said I'd *tell* him that now—bluff—then later on I'll change my mind, if he behaves himself. 50

MRS. MILLER: Oh, well, if that's all—*(Then defensively again.)* But it's your duty to give him every benefit. He's got an exceptional brain, that boy has! He's proved it by the way he likes to read all those deep plays and books and poetry.

MILLER: But I thought you—*(He stops, grinning helplessly.)* 55

MRS. MILLER: You thought I what?

MILLER: Never mind.

MRS. MILLER: (*Sniffs, but thinks it better to let this pass.*) You mark my words, that boy's going to turn out to be a great lawyer, or a great doctor, or a great writer, or—

MILLER: (*Grinning.*) You agree he's going to be great, anyway.

MRS. MILLER: Yes, I most certainly have a lot of faith in Richard.

MILLER: Well, so have I, as far as that goes.

MRS. MILLER: (*After a pause—judicially.*) And as for his being in love with Muriel, I don't see but what it might work out real well. Richard could do worse.

MILLER: But I thought you had no use for her, thought she was stupid.

MRS. MILLER: Well, so I did, but if she's good for Richard and he wants her—(*Then inconsequentially.*) Ma used to say you weren't overbright, but she changed her mind when she saw I didn't care if you were or not.

MILLER: (*Not exactly pleased by this.*) Well, I've been bright enough to—

MRS. MILLER: (*Going on as if he had not spoken.*) And Muriel's real cute-looking, I have to admit that. Takes after her mother. Alice Briggs was the prettiest girl before she married.

MILLER: Yes, and Muriel will get big as a house after she's married, the same as her mother did. That's the trouble. A man never can tell what he's letting himself in for—(*He stops, feeling his wife's eyes fixed on him with indignant suspicion.*)

MRS. MILLER: (*Sharply.*) I'm not too fat and don't you say it!

MILLER: Who was talking about you?

MRS. MILLER: And I'd rather have some flesh on my bones than be built like a string bean and bore a hole in a chair every time I sat down—like some people!

MILLER: (*Ignoring the insult—flatteringly.*) Why, no one'd ever call you fat, Essie. You're only plump, like a good figure ought to be.

MRS. MILLER: (*Childishly pleased—gratefully giving tit for tat.*) Well, you're not skinny, either—only slender—and I think you've been putting on weight lately, too. (*Having thus squared matters she takes up her sewing again. A pause. Then* MILLER *asks incredulously.*)

MILLER: You don't mean to tell me you're actually taking this Muriel crush of Richard's seriously, do you? I know it's a good thing to encourage right now but—pshaw, why, Richard'll probably forget all about her before he's away six months, and she'll have forgotten him.

MRS. MILLER: Don't be so cynical. (*Then, after a pause, thoughtfully.*) Well, anyway, he'll always have it to remember—no matter what happens after—and that's something.

MILLER: You bet that's something. (*Then with a grin.*) You surprise me at times with your deep wisdom.

MRS. MILLER: You don't give me credit for ever having common sense, that's why. (*She goes back to her sewing.*)

MILLER: (*After a pause.*) Where'd you say Sid and Lily had gone off to?

MRS. MILLER: To the beach to listen to the band. (*She sighs sympathetically.*) Poor Lily! Sid'll never change, and she'll never marry him. But she seems to get some queer satisfaction out of fussing over him like a hen that's hatched a duck—though Lord knows I wouldn't in her shoes!

MILLER: Arthur's up with Elsie Rand, I suppose?

MRS. MILLER: Of course.

MILLER: Where's Mildred?

MRS. MILLER: Out walking with her latest. I've forgot who it is. I can't keep track of them. (*She smiles.*)

MILLER: (*Smiling.*) Then, from all reports, we seem to be completely surrounded by love!

MRS. MILLER: Well, we've had our share, haven't we? We don't have to begrudge it to our children. (*Then has a sudden thought.*) But I've done all this talking about Muriel and Richard and clean forgot how wild old McComber was against it. But he'll get over that, I suppose.

MILLER: (*With a chuckle.*) He has already. I ran into him upstreet this afternoon and he was meek as pie. He backed water and said he guessed I was right. Richard had just copied stuff out of books, and kids would be kids, and so on. So I came off my high horse a bit—but not too far—and I guess all that won't bother anyone any more. (*Then rubbing his hands together—with a boyish grin of pleasure.*) And I told you about getting that business from Lawson, didn't I? It's been a good day, Essie—a darned good day! (*From the hall beyond the front parlor the sound of the front door being opened and shut is heard.* MRS. MILLER *leans forward to look, pushing her specs up.*)

MRS. MILLER: (*In a whisper.*) It's Richard.

MILLER: (*Immediately assuming an expression of becoming gravity.*) Hmm. (*He takes off his spectacles and puts them back in their case and straightens himself in his chair.* RICHARD *comes slowly in from the front parlor. He walks like one in a trance, his eyes shining with a dreamy happiness, his spirit still too exalted to be conscious of his surroundings, or to remember the threatened punishment. He carries his straw hat dangling in his hand, quite unaware of its existence.*)

RICHARD: (*Dreamily, like a ghost addressing fellow shades.*) Hello.

MRS. MILLER: (*Staring at him worriedly.*) Hello, Richard.

MILLER: (*Sizing him up shrewdly.*) Hello, Son.

(RICHARD *moves past his mother and comes to the far corner, left front, where the light is dimmest, and sits down on the sofa, and stares before him, his hat dangling in his hand.*)

MRS. MILLER: (*With frightened suspicion now.*) Goodness, he acts queer! Nat, you don't suppose he's been—?

MILLER: (*With a reassuring smile.*) No. It's love, not liquor, this time.

MRS. MILLER: (*Only partly reassured—sharply.*) Richard! What's the matter with you? (*He comes to himself with a start. She goes on scoldingly.*) How many times have I told you to hang up your hat in the hall when you come in! (*He looks at his hat as if he were surprised at its existence. She gets up fussily and goes to him.*) Here. Give it to me. I'll hang it up for you this once. And what are you sitting over here in the dark for? Don't forget your father's been waiting to talk to you! (*She comes back to the table and he follows her, still half in a dream, and stands by his father's chair.* MRS. MILLER *starts for the hall with his hat.*)

MILLER: (*Quietly but firmly now.*) You better leave Richard and me alone for a while, Essie.

MRS. MILLER: (*Turns to stare at him apprehensively.*) Well—all right. I'll go sit on the piazza. Call me if you want me. (*Then a bit pleadingly.*) But you'll remember all I said, Nat, won't you? (*MILLER nods reassuringly. She disappears through the front parlor.* RICHARD, *keenly conscious of himself as the about-to-be-sentenced criminal by this time, looks guilty and a*

175 *bit defiant, searches his father's expressionless face with uneasy side glances, and steels himself for what is coming.*)

MILLER: (*Casually, indicating* MRS. MILLER'*s rocker.*) Sit down, Richard. (RICHARD *slumps awkwardly into the chair and sits in a self-conscious, unnatural position.* MILLER *sizes him up keenly—then suddenly smiles and asks with quiet mockery.*) Well, how are the vine leaves in your hair this evening?

RICHARD: (*Totally unprepared for this approach—shamefacedly mutters.*) I don't know, Pa.

185 MILLER: Turned out to be poison ivy, didn't they? (*Then kindly.*) But you needn't look so alarmed. I'm not going to read you any temperance lecture. That'd bore me more than it would you. And, in spite of your damn foolishness last night, I'm still giving you credit for having brains. So I'm pretty sure anything I could say to you you've already said to
190 yourself.

RICHARD: (*His head down—humbly.*) I know I was a darned fool.

MILLER: (*Thinking it well to rub in this aspect—disgustedly.*) You sure were—not only a fool but a downright, stupid, dis-
195 gusting fool! (RICHARD *squirms, his head still lower.*) It was bad enough for you to let me and Arthur see you, but to appear like that before your mother and Mildred—! And I wonder if Muriel would think you were so fine if she ever saw you as you looked and acted then. I think she'd give you
200 your walking papers for keeps. And you couldn't blame her. No nice girl wants to give her love to a stupid drunk!

RICHARD: (*Writhing.*) I know, Pa.

MILLER: (*After a pause—quietly.*) All right. Then that settles—the booze end of it. (*He sizes* RICHARD *up searchingly—then
205 suddenly speaks sharply.*) But there is another thing that's more serious. How about that tart you went to bed with at the Pleasant Beach House?

RICHARD: (*Flabbergasted—stammers.*) You know—? But I didn't! If they've told you about her down there, they must have
210 told you I didn't! She wanted me to—but I wouldn't! I gave her the five dollars just so she'd let me out of it. Honest, Pa, I didn't! She made everything seem rotten and dirty—and—I didn't want to do a thing like that to Muriel—no matter how bad I thought she'd treated me—even after I felt drunk, I
215 didn't. Honest!

MILLER: How'd you happen to meet this lady, anyway?

RICHARD: I can't tell that, Pa. I'd have to snitch on someone—and you wouldn't want me to do that.

MILLER: (*A bit taken aback.*) No. I suppose I wouldn't. Hmm.
220 Well, I believe you—and I guess that settles that. (*Then, after a quick furtive glance at* RICHARD, *he nerves himself for the ordeal and begins with a shamefaced, self-conscious solemnity.*) But listen here, Richard, it's about time you and I had a serious talk about—hmm—certain matters pertaining to—and
225 now that the subject's come up of its own accord, it's a good time—I mean, there's no use in procrastinating further—so, here goes. (*But it doesn't go smoothly and as he goes on he becomes more and more guiltily embarrassed and self-conscious and his expressions more stilted.* RICHARD *sedulously avoids
230 even glancing at him, his own embarrassment made tenfold more painful by his father's.*) Richard, you have now come to the age when—Well, you're a fully developed man, in a way, and it's only natural for you to have certain desires of the flesh, to put it that way—I mean, pertaining to the opposite
235 sex—certain natural feelings and temptations—that'll want

to be gratified—and you'll want to gratify them. Hmm—well, human society being organized as it is, there's only one outlet for—unless you're a scoundrel and go around ruining decent girls—which you're not, of course. Well, there are a certain class of women—always have been and always will be 240 as long as human nature is what it is—It's wrong, maybe, but what can you do about it? I mean, girls like that one you—girls there's something doing with—and lots of 'em are pretty, and it's human nature if you—But that doesn't mean to ever get mixed up with them seriously! You just have what you 245 want and pay 'em and forget it. I know that sounds hard and unfeeling, but we're talking facts and—But don't think I'm encouraging you to—If you can stay away from 'em, all the better—but if—why—hmm—Here's what I'm driving at, Richard. They're apt to be whited sepulchres—I mean, your 250 whole life might be ruined if—so, darn it, you've got to know how to—I mean, there are ways and means—(*Suddenly he can go no farther and winds up helplessly.*) But, hell, I suppose you boys talk all this over among yourselves and you know more about it than I do. I'll admit I'm no authority. I 255 never had anything to do with such women, and it'll be a hell of a lot better for you if you never do!

RICHARD: (*Without looking at him.*) I'm never going to, Pa. (*Then shocked indignation coming into his voice.*) I don't see how you could think I could—now—when you know I love 260 Muriel and am going to marry her. I'd die before I'd—!

MILLER: (*Immensely relieved—enthusiastically.*) That's the talk! By God, I'm proud of you when you talk like that! (*Then hastily.*) And now that's all of that. There's nothing more to say and we'll forget it, eh? 265

RICHARD: (*After a pause.*) How are you going to punish me, Pa?

MILLER: I *was* sort of forgetting that, wasn't I? Well, I'd thought of telling you you couldn't go to Yale—

RICHARD: (*Eagerly.*) Don't I have to go? Gee, that's great! 270 Muriel thought you'd want me to. I was telling her I'd rather you gave me a job on the paper because then she and I could get married sooner. (*Then with a boyish grin.*) Gee, Pa, you picked a lemon. That isn't any punishment. You'll have to do something besides that. 275

MILLER: (*Grimly—but only half concealing an answering grin.*) Then you'll go to Yale and you'll stay there till you graduate, that's the answer to that! Muriel's got good sense and you haven't! (RICHARD *accepts this philosophically.*) And now we're finished, you better call your mother. (RICHARD 280 *opens the screen door and calls "Ma," and a moment later she comes in. She glances quickly from son to husband and immediately knows that all is well and tactfully refrains from all questions.*)

MRS. MILLER: My, it's a beautiful night. The moon's way down 285 low—almost setting. (*She sits in her chair and sighs contentedly.* RICHARD *remains standing by the door, staring out at the moon, his face pale in the moonlight.*)

MILLER: (*With a nod at* RICHARD, *winking at his wife.*) Yes, I don't believe I've hardly ever seen such a beautiful night— 290 with such a wonderful moon. Have you, Richard?

RICHARD: (*Turning to them—enthusiastically.*) No! It was wonderful—down at the beach—(*He stops abruptly, smiling shyly.*)

MILLER: (*Watching his son—after a pause—quietly.*) I can 295 only remember a few nights that were as beautiful as this—

and they were so long ago, when your mother and I were young and planning to get married.

300 RICHARD: (*Stares at him wonderingly for a moment, then quickly from his father to his mother and back again, strangely, as if he'd never seen them before—then he looks almost disgusted and swallows as if an acrid taste had come into his mouth—but then suddenly his face is transfigured by a smile of shy understanding and sympathy. He speaks shyly.*) Yes, I'll bet those
305 must have been wonderful nights, too. You sort of forget the moon was the same way back then—and everything.

MILLER: (*Huskily.*) You're all right, Richard. (*He gets up and blows his nose.*)

MRS. MILLER: (*Fondly.*) You're a good boy, Richard. (RICHARD
310 *looks dreadfully shy and embarrassed at this. His father comes to his rescue.*)

MILLER: Better get to bed early tonight, Son, hadn't you?

RICHARD: I couldn't sleep. Can't I go out on the piazza and sit for a while—until the moon sets?

315 MILLER: All right. Then you better say good night now. I don't know about your mother, but I'm going to bed right away. I'm dead tired.

MRS. MILLER: So am I.

RICHARD: (*Goes to her and kisses her.*) Good night, Ma.

320 MRS. MILLER: Good night. Don't you stay up till all hours now.

RICHARD: (*Comes to his father and stands awkwardly before him.*) Good night, Pa.

MILLER: (*Puts his arm around him and gives him a hug.*) Good night, Richard. (RICHARD *turns impulsively and kisses*
325 *him—then hurries out the screen door.* MILLER *stares after him—then says huskily.*) First time he's done that in years. I don't believe in kissing between fathers and sons after a certain age—seems mushy and silly—but that meant something! And I don't think we'll ever have to worry about his
330 being safe—from himself—again. And I guess no matter

what life will do to him, he can take care of it now. (*He sighs with satisfaction and, sitting down in his chair, begins to unlace his shoes.*) My darned feet are giving me fits!

MRS. MILLER: (*Laughing.*) Why do you bother unlacing your shoes now, you big goose—when we're going right up to 335 bed?

MILLER: (*As if he hadn't thought of that before, stops.*) Guess you're right. (*Then getting to his feet—with a grin.*) Mind if I don't say my prayers tonight, Essie? I'm certain God knows I'm too darned tired. 340

MRS. MILLER: Don't talk that way. It's real sinful. (*She gets up—then laughing fondly.*) If that isn't you all over! Always looking for an excuse to—You're worse than Tommy! But all right. I suppose tonight you needn't. You've had a hard day. (*She puts her hand on the reading-lamp switch.*) I'm going to 345 turn out the light. All ready?

MILLER: Yep. Let her go, Gallagher. (*She turns out the lamp. In the ensuing darkness the faint moonlight shines full in through the screen door. Walking together toward the front parlor they stand full in it for a moment, looking out.* MILLER 350 *puts his arm around her. He says in a low voice.*) There he is—like a statue of Love's Young Dream. (*Then he sighs and speaks with a gentle nostalgic melancholy.*) What's it that Rubaiyat says:
"Yet Ah, that Spring should vanish with the Rose! 355
That Youth's sweet-scented manuscript should close!"
(*Then throwing off his melancholy, with a loving smile at her.*) Well, Spring isn't everything, is it, Essie? There's a lot to be said for Autumn. That's got beauty, too. And Winter—
if you're together. 360

MRS. MILLER: (*Simply.*) Yes, Nat. (*She kisses him and they move quietly out of the moonlight, back into the darkness of the front parlor.*)

(*Curtain.*)

■ TENNESSEE WILLIAMS ■

Like Amanda Wingfield in *The Glass Menagerie*, Tennessee Williams (1911–1983) regarded himself as a product of the Old South and its genteel, rural, and—finally—obsolete traditions. Born Thomas Lanier Williams to a traveling shoe salesman and his wife, Williams was raised in Mississippi before moving to the tenements of St. Louis. As a child, Williams contracted diphtheria, which briefly paralyzed his legs and left him frail and homebound for some time. During his convalescence, Williams read and wrote avidly and published his first story at the age of sixteen. After high school, he briefly attended the University of Missouri, but withdrew when his poor health prevented him from passing the ROTC course. He then worked for three years in a shoe factory, then tried Washington University in St. Louis, but again dropped out. He finally took his degree in playwriting from the University of Iowa in 1938, when he changed his name to "Tennessee." In the 1930s, Williams's embattled relation to the world was deepened by the "loss" of his beloved sister Rose. Rose became chronically depressed, and Williams's mother, unable to cope with her erratic and wild behavior, consented to having a lobotomy performed. Rose was left docile but inert and became the prototype of several of Williams's most memorable dramatic characters, women whose inner beauty is too delicate to be disclosed to the world. At this time Williams also recognized his own homosexuality, a recognition that deepened his sense of the threatening conformity imposed by mainstream American society.

Coming of age in the Great Depression was formative for Williams's drama, particularly the range of themes associated with his mature work: a sexual tension surging beneath the surface of the characters' lives, the collapse of a sustaining family and social order, the attraction of misfits destroyed by a world that will not accept them. Williams wrote several now-lost plays in the late 1930s, and *Battle of Angels* (1940; later revised as *Orpheus Descending* in 1957) was produced by the Theater Guild in Boston, where it failed. Williams scored a major success with his next play, *The Glass Menagerie* (1944). He continued his success with a series of important dramas: *Summer and Smoke* (1947), *A Streetcar Named Desire* (1947), *The Rose Tattoo* (1951), *Camino Real* (1953), *Cat on a Hot Tin Roof* (1955), *Sweet Bird of Youth* (1959), *Night of the Iguana* (1961). In his later years, Williams's drama became increasingly gothic and sensational, and his personal life suffered as well; Williams became an alcoholic and was institutionalized on several occasions. He continued to write plays to the end of his life, developing his characteristic strengths: a feel for the nuances of character, and a flair for dramatizing the victims of an unfeeling world.

THE GLASS MENAGERIE

First performed in 1944, *The Glass Menagerie* looks back to the 1930s. Its characters are reminiscent of Williams and his family, and their grinding poverty recalls the depression-era plays of Elmer Rice and Clifford Odets. In many ways, *The Glass Menagerie* is a play in the realistic tradition. Laura's menagerie recalls how Ibsen, Chekhov, and Strindberg used stage objects (Nora's Christmas tree in *A Doll House*, the cherry orchard, Miss Julie's bird) to evoke and symbolize the characters' motives and sensibilities. However, Williams also uses the device of the "memory play" to disrupt the linearity of realistic drama. Tom constructs the scene and the characters for the audience, and slide projections of phrases and images often illustrate the action as it takes place. These devices lend *The Glass Menagerie* the flavor of symbolist theater. Moreover, Tom's anticipation of the Spanish Civil War and World War II sets the play in a larger social and political context that looms forebodingly over the fragile and self-absorbed characters. Amanda and Laura seem doomed never to escape the drab apartment, and even Tom, wandering the world, finally cannot escape it either. Deeply personal, *The Glass Menagerie* also provides a kind of study for Williams's later plays, for it includes a typical panoply of Williams's characters: the blunt, sexually aggressive, emotionally stunted Jim; Amanda, the faded Southern belle; Laura, more crippled emotionally than physically; and Tom, who falls in love with long distance yet never succeeds in escaping his past or in finding his future.

PRODUCTION NOTES

Being a "memory play," *The Glass Menagerie* can be presented with unusual freedom of convention. Because of its considerably delicate or tenuous material, atmospheric touches and subtleties of direction play a particularly important part. Expressionism and all other unconventional techniques in drama have only one valid aim, and that is a closer approach to truth. When a play employs unconventional techniques, it is not, or certainly shouldn't be, trying to escape its responsibility of dealing with reality, or interpreting experience, but is actually or should be attempting to find a closer approach, a more penetrating and vivid expression of things as they are. The straight realistic play with its genuine Frigidaire and authentic ice-cubes, its characters who speak exactly as its audience speaks, corresponds to the academic landscape and has the same virtue of a photographic likeness. Everyone should know nowadays the unimportance of the photographic in art: that truth, life, or reality is an organic thing which the poetic imagination can represent or suggest, in essence, only through transformation, through changing into other forms than those which were merely present in appearance.

These remarks are not meant as a preface only to this particular play. They have to do with a conception of a new, plastic theatre which must take the place of the exhausted theatre of realistic conventions if the theatre is to resume vitality as a part of our culture.

THE SCREEN DEVICE: There is *only one important difference between the original and the acting version of the play* and that is the *omission* in the latter of the device that I tentatively included in my *original* script. This device was the use of a screen on which were projected magic-lantern slides bearing images or titles. I do not regret the omission of this device from the original Broadway production. The extraordinary power of Miss Taylor's performance made it suitable to have the utmost simplicity in the physical production. But I think it may be interesting to some readers to see how this device was conceived. So I am putting it into the published manuscript. These images and legends, projected from behind, were cast on a section of wall between the front-room and dining-room areas, which should be indistinguishable from the rest when not in use.

The purpose of this will probably be apparent. It is to give accent to certain values in each scene. Each scene contains a particular point (or several) which is structurally the most important. In an episodic play, such as this, the basic structure or narrative line may be obscured from the audience; the effect may seem fragmentary rather than architectural. This may not be the fault of the play so much as a lack of attention in the audience. The legend or image upon the screen will strengthen the effect of what is merely allusion in the writing and allow the primary point to be made more simply and lightly than if the entire responsibility were on the spoken lines. Aside from this structural value, I think the screen will have a definite emotional appeal, less definable but just as important. An imaginative producer or director may invent many other uses for this device than those indicated in the present script. In fact the possibilities of the device seem much larger to me than the instance of this play can possibly utilize.

THE MUSIC: Another extra-literary accent in this play is provided by the use of music. A single recurring tune, "The Glass Menagerie," is used to give emotional emphasis to suitable passages. This tune is like circus music, not when you are on the grounds or in the immediate vicinity of the parade, but when you are at some distance and very likely thinking of something else. It seems under those circumstances to continue almost interminably and it weaves in and out of your preoccupied consciousness; then it is the lightest, most delicate music in the world and perhaps the saddest. It expresses the surface vivacity of life with the underlying strain of immutable and inexpressible sorrow. When you look at a piece of delicately spun glass you think of two things: how beautiful it is and how easily it can be broken. Both of those ideas should be woven into the recurring tune, which dips in and out of the play as if it were carried on a wind that changes. It serves as a thread of connection and allusion between the narrator with his separate point in time and space and the subject of his story. Between each episode it returns as reference to the emotion, nostalgia, which is the first condition of the play. It is primarily Laura's music and therefore comes out most clearly when the play focuses upon her and the lovely fragility of glass which is her image.

THE LIGHTING: The lighting in the play is not realistic. In keeping with the atmosphere of memory, the stage is dim. Shafts of light are focused on selected areas or actors, sometimes in contradistinction to what is the apparent center. For instance, in the quarrel scene between Tom and Amanda, in which Laura has no active part, the clearest pool of light is on her figure. This is also true of the supper scene, when her silent figure on the sofa should remain the visual center. The light upon Laura should be distinct from the others, having a peculiar pristine clarity such as light used in early religious portraits of female saints or madonnas. A certain correspondence to light in religious paintings, such as El Greco's, where the figures are radiant in atmosphere that is relatively dusky, could be effectively used throughout the play. (It will also permit a more effective use of the screen.) A free, imaginative use of light can be of enormous value in giving a mobile, plastic quality to plays of a more or less static nature.

Tennessee Williams

THE GLASS MENAGERIE

Tennessee Williams

— CHARACTERS —

AMANDA WINGFIELD (*the mother*), *a little woman of great but confused vitality clinging frantically to another time and place. Her characterization must be carefully created, not copied from type. She is not paranoiac, but her life is paranoia. There is much to admire in Amanda, and as much to love and pity as there is to laugh at. Certainly she has endurance and a kind of heroism, and though her foolishness makes her unwittingly cruel at times, there is tenderness in her slight person.*

LAURA WINGFIELD (*her daughter*), *Amanda, having failed to establish contact with reality, continues to live vitally in her illusions, but Laura's situation is even graver. A childhood illness has left her crippled, one leg slightly shorter than the other, and held in a brace. This defect need not be more than suggested on the stage. Stemming from this, Laura's separation increases till she is like a piece of her own glass collection, too exquisitely fragile to move from the shelf.*

TOM WINGFIELD (*her son*), *and the narrator of the play. A poet with a job in a warehouse. His nature is not remorseless, but to escape from a trap he has to act without pity.*

JIM O'CONNOR (*the gentleman caller*), *a nice, ordinary, young man.*

SCENE: *An Alley in St. Louis*

Part I.   *Preparation for a Gentleman Caller.*
Part II.   *The Gentlemen calls.*

TIME: *Now and the Past.*

— SCENE ONE —

The Wingfield apartment is in the rear of the building, one of those vast hive-like conglomerations of the cellular living-units that flower as warty growths in overcrowded urban centers of lower middle-class population and are symptomatic of the impulse of this largest and fundamentally enslaved section of American society to avoid fluidity and differentiation and to exist and function as one interfused mass of automatism.

The apartment faces an alley and is entered by a fire escape, a structure whose name is a touch of accidental poetic truth, for all of these huge buildings are always burning with the slow and implacable fires of human desperation. The fire escape is part of what we see—that is, the landing of it and steps descending from it.

The scene is memory and is therefore nonrealistic. Memory takes a lot of poetic license. It omits some details; others are exaggerated, according to the emotional value of the articles it touches, for memory is seated predominantly in the heart. The interior is therefore rather dim and poetic.

At the rise of the curtain, the audience is faced with the dark, grim rear wall of the Wingfield tenement. This building is flanked on both sides by dark, narrow alleys which run into murky canyons of tangled clotheslines, garbage cans, and the sinister latticework of neighboring fire escapes. It is up and down these side alleys that exterior entrances and exits are made during the play. At the end of TOM's opening commentary, the dark tenement wall slowly becomes transparent and reveals the interior of the ground-floor Wingfield apartment.

Nearest the audience is the living room, which also serves as a sleeping room for LAURA, the sofa unfolding to make her bed. Just beyond, separated from the living room by a wide arch or second proscenium with transparent faded portieres (or second curtain), is the dining room. In an old-fashioned whatnot in the living room are seen scores of transparent glass animals. A blown-up photograph of the father hangs on the wall of the living room, to the left of the archway. It is the face of a very handsome young man in a doughboy's First World War cap. He is gallantly smiling, ineluctably smiling, as if to say "I will be smiling forever."

Also hanging on the wall, near the photograph, are a typewriter keyboard chart and a Gregg shorthand diagram. An upright typewriter on a small table stands beneath the charts.

The audience hears and sees the opening scene in the dining room through both the transparent fourth wall of the building and the transparent gauze portieres of the dining-room arch. It is during this revealing scene that the fourth wall slowly ascends, out of sight. This transparent exterior wall is not brought down again until the very end of the play, during TOM's final speech.

The narrator is an undisguised convention of the play. He takes whatever license with dramatic convention is convenient to his purposes.

TOM *enters, dressed as a merchant sailor, and strolls across to the fire escape. There he stops and lights a cigarette. He addresses the audience.*

TOM: Yes, I have tricks in my pocket, I have things up my sleeve. But I am the opposite of a stage magician. He gives you illusion that has the appearance of truth. I give you truth in the pleasant disguise of illusion.

    To begin with, I turn back time. I reverse it to that quaint 5 period, the thirties, when the huge middle class of America was matriculating in a school for the blind. Their eyes had failed them, or they had failed their eyes, and so they were having their fingers pressed forcibly down on the fiery Braille alphabet of a dissolving economy. 10

    In Spain there was revolution. Here there was only shouting and confusion. In Spain there was Guernica. Here there were disturbances of labor, sometimes pretty violent, in otherwise peaceful cities such as Chicago, Cleveland, Saint Louis . . . This is the social background of the play. 15

(*Music begins to play.*)

    The play is memory. Being a memory play, it is dimly lighted, it is sentimental, it is not realistic. In memory

everything seems to happen to music. That explains the fiddle in the wings.

20   I am the narrator of the play, and also a character in it.
The other characters are my mother, Amanda, my sister,
Laura, and a gentleman caller who appears in the final
scenes. He is the most realistic character in the play, being
an emissary from a world of reality that we were somehow set
25   apart from. But since I have a poet's weakness for symbols, I
am using this character also as a symbol; he is the long-
delayed but always expected something that we live for.
    There is a fifth character in the play who doesn't appear
except in this larger-than-life-size photograph over the man-
30   tel. This is our father who left us a long time ago. He was a
telephone man who fell in love with long distances; he gave
up his job with the telephone company and skipped the light
fantastic out of town . . .
    The last we heard of him was a picture postcard from
35   Mazatlan, on the Pacific coast of Mexico, containing a message of two words: "Hello—Goodbye!" and no address.
    I think the rest of the play will explain itself. . . .

(AMANDA's *voice becomes audible through the portieres.*)

(*Legend on screen:* "Ou sont les neiges.")

(TOM *divides the portieres and enters the dining room.* AMANDA
and LAURA *are seated at a drop-leaf table. Eating is indicated by
gestures without food or utensils.* AMANDA *faces the audience.*
TOM *and* LAURA *are seated in profile. The interior has lit up
softly and through the scrim we see* AMANDA *and* LAURA *seated
at the table.*)

AMANDA: (*Calling.*) Tom?
TOM: Yes, Mother.
40   AMANDA: We can't say grace until you come to the table!
TOM: Coming, Mother. (*He bows slightly and withdraws, reappearing a few moments later in his place at the table.*)
AMANDA: (*To her son.*) Honey, don't *push* with your *fingers.* If
you have to push with something, the thing to push with is a
45   crust of bread. And chew—chew! Animals have secretions in
their stomachs which enable them to digest food without
mastication, but human beings are supposed to chew their
food before they swallow it down. Eat food leisurely, son, and
really enjoy it. A well-cooked meal has lots of delicate flavors
50   that have to be held in the mouth for appreciation. So chew
your food and give your salivary glands a chance to function!

(TOM *deliberately lays his imaginary fork down and pushes his
chair back from the table.*)

TOM: I haven't enjoyed one bite of this dinner because of your
constant directions on how to eat it. It's you that make me
rush through meals with your hawklike attention to every
55   bite I take. Sickening—spoils my appetite—all this discussion of—animals' secretion—salivary glands—mastication!
AMANDA: (*Lightly.*) Temperament like a Metropolitan star!

(TOM *rises and walks toward the living room.*)

You're not excused from the table.
TOM: I'm getting a cigarette.
60   AMANDA: You smoke too much.

(LAURA *rises.*)

LAURA: I'll bring in the blanc mange.

(TOM *remains standing with his cigarette by the portieres.*)

AMANDA: (*Rising.*) No, sister, no, sister—you be the lady this
time and I'll be the darky.
LAURA: I'm already up.
AMANDA: Resume your seat, little sister—I want you to stay   65
fresh and pretty—for gentlemen callers!
LAURA: (*Sitting down.*) I'm not expecting any gentlemen
callers.
AMANDA: (*Crossing out to the kitchenette, airily.*) Sometimes
they come when they are least expected! Why, I remember   70
one Sunday afternoon in Blue Mountain—

(*She enters the kitchenette.*)

TOM: I know what's coming!
LAURA: Yes. But let her tell it.
TOM: Again?
LAURA: She loves to tell it.   75

(AMANDA *returns with a bowl of dessert.*)

AMANDA: One Sunday afternoon in Blue Mountain—your
mother received—*seventeen!*—gentlemen callers! Why, some-
times there weren't chairs enough to accommodate them all.
We had to send the nigger over to bring in folding chairs from
the parish house.   80
TOM: (*Remaining at the portieres.*) How did you entertain
those gentlemen callers?
AMANDA: I understood the art of conversation!
TOM: I bet you could talk.
AMANDA: Girls in those days *knew* how to talk, I can tell you.   85
TOM: Yes?

(*Image on screen:* AMANDA *as a girl on a porch, greeting callers.*)

AMANDA: They knew how to entertain their gentlemen callers.
It wasn't enough for a girl to be possessed of a pretty face and
a graceful figure—although I wasn't slighted in either respect. She also needed to have a nimble wit and a tongue to   90
meet all occasions.
TOM: What did you talk about?
AMANDA: Things of importance going on in the world! Never
anything coarse or common or vulgar.

(*She addresses* TOM *as though he were seated in the vacant chair
at the table though he remains by the portieres. He plays this
scene as though reading from a script.*)

My callers were gentlemen—all! Among my callers were   95
some of the most prominent young planters of the Mississippi Delta—planters and sons of planters!

(TOM *motions for music and a spot of light on* AMANDA. *Her
eyes lift, her face glows, her voice becomes rich and elegiac.*)

(*Screen legend:* "Ou sont les neiges d'antan?")

There was young Champ Laughlin who later became vice-
president of the Delta Planters Bank. Hadley Stevenson who
was drowned in Moon Lake and left his widow one hundred   100
and fifty thousand in Government bonds. There were the
Cutrere brothers, Wesley and Bates. Bates was one of my
bright particular beaux! He got in a quarrel with that wild
Wainwright boy. They shot it out on the floor of Moon Lake
Casino. Bates was shot through the stomach. Died in the   105
ambulance on his way to Memphis. His widow was also well

provided-for, came into eight or ten thousand acres, that's
all. She married him on the rebound—never loved her—
carried my picture on him the night he died! And there
110   was that boy that every girl in the Delta had set her cap for!
That beautiful, brilliant young Fitzhugh boy from Greene
County!

TOM: What did he leave his widow?

AMANDA: He never married! Gracious, you talk as though all
115   of my old admirers had turned up their toes to the daisies!

TOM: Isn't this the first you've mentioned that still survives?

AMANDA: That Fitzhugh boy went North and made a fortune—came to be known as the Wolf of Wall Street! He had
the Midas touch, whatever he touched turned to gold! And I
120   could have been Mrs. Duncan J. Fitzhugh, mind you! But—
I picked your *father!*

LAURA: *(Rising.)* Mother, let me clear the table.

AMANDA: No, dear, you go in front and study your typewriter
chart. Or practice your shorthand a little. Stay fresh and
125   pretty!—It's almost time for our gentlemen callers to start arriving. *(She flounces girlishly toward the kitchenette.)* How
many do you suppose we're going to entertain this afternoon?

(TOM throws down the paper and jumps up with a groan.)

LAURA: *(Alone in the dining room.)* I don't believe we're going
130   to receive any, Mother.

AMANDA: *(Reappearing, airily.)* What? No one—not one? You
must be joking!

*(LAURA nervously echoes her laugh. She slips in a fugitive man-
ner through the half-open portieres and draws them gently behind her. A shaft of very clear light is thrown on her face against
the faded tapestry of the curtains. Faintly the music of "The
Glass Menagerie" is heard as she continues, lightly.)*

Not one gentleman caller? It can't be true! There must be a
flood, there must have been a tornado!

135 LAURA: It isn't a flood, it's not a tornado, Mother. I'm just not
popular like you were in Blue Mountain. . . .

*(TOM utters another groan. LAURA glances at him with a faint,
apologetic smile. Her voice catches a little.)*

Mother's afraid I'm going to be an old maid.

(The scene dims out with the "Glass Menagerie" music.)

— SCENE TWO —

*On the dark stage the screen is lighted with the image of blue
roses. Gradually LAURA's figure becomes apparent and the screen
goes out. The music subsides.*

LAURA *is seated in the delicate ivory chair at the small claw-foot
table. She wears a dress of soft violet material for a kimono—her
hair is tied back from her forehead with a ribbon. She is washing
and polishing her collection of glass.* AMANDA *appears on the
fire escape steps. At the sound of her ascent, LAURA catches her
breath, thrusts the bowl of ornaments away, and seats herself
stiffly before the diagram of the typewriter keyboard as though it
held her spellbound. Something has happened to AMANDA. It is
written in her face as she climbs to the landing: a look that is*

grim and hopeless and a little absurd. She has on one of those
cheap or imitation velvety-looking cloth coats with imitation fur
collar. Her hat is five or six years old, one of those dreadful
cloche hats that were worn in the late Twenties, and she is
clutching an enormous black patent-leather pocketbook with
nickel clasps and initials. This is her full-dress outfit, the one she
usually wears to the D.A.R. Before entering she looks through
the door. She purses her lips, opens her eyes very wide, rolls them
upward and shakes her head. Then she slowly lets herself in the
door. Seeing her mother's expression LAURA touches her lips with
a nervous gesture.*

LAURA: Hello, Mother, I was—*(She makes a nervous gesture toward the chart on the wall.* AMANDA *leans against the shut
door and stares at* LAURA *with a martyred look.)*

AMANDA: Deception? Deception? *(She slowly removes her hat
and gloves, continuing the sweet suffering stare. She lets the*   5
hat and gloves fall on the floor—a bit of acting.)

LAURA: *(Shakily.)* How was the D.A.R. meeting?

*(*AMANDA *slowly opens her purse and removes a dainty white
handkerchief which she shakes out delicately and delicately
touches to her lips and nostrils.)*

Didn't you go to the D.A.R. meeting, Mother?

AMANDA: *(Faintly, almost inaudibly.)* —No.—No. *(Then more
forcibly.)* I did not have the strength—to go to the D.A.R. In   10
fact, I did not have the courage! I wanted to find a hole in
the ground and hide myself in it forever! *(She crosses slowly
to the wall and removes the diagram of the typewriter keyboard. She holds it in front of her for a second, staring at it
sweetly and sorrowfully—then bites her lips and tears it into*   15
two pieces.)

LAURA: *(Faintly.)* Why did you do that, Mother?

*(*AMANDA *repeats the same procedure with the chart of the Gregg
Alphabet.)*

Why are you—

AMANDA: Why? Why? How old are you, Laura?

LAURA: Mother, you know my age.   20

AMANDA: I thought that you were an adult; it seems that I was
mistaken. *(She crosses slowly to the sofa and sinks down and
stares at Laura.)*

LAURA: Please don't stare at me, Mother.

*(*AMANDA *closes her eyes and lowers her head. There is a ten-
second pause.)*

AMANDA: What are we going to do, what is going to become of   25
us, what is the future?

(There is another pause.)

LAURA: Has something happened, Mother?

*(*AMANDA *draws a long breath, takes out the handkerchief again,
goes through the dabbing process.)*

Mother, has—something happened?

AMANDA: I'll be all right in a minute, I'm just bewildered—
(She hesitates.)—by life. . . .   30

LAURA: Mother, I wish that you would tell me what's happened!

AMANDA: As you know, I was supposed to be inducted into my
office at the D.A.R. this afternoon.

(Screen image: A swarm of typewriters.)

35 But I stopped off at Rubicam's Business College to speak to your teachers about your having a cold and ask them what progress they thought you were making down there.

LAURA: Oh. . . .

AMANDA: I went to the typing instructor and introduced my-
40 self as your mother. She didn't know who you were. "Wing-field," she said, "We don't have any such student enrolled at the school!"

I assured her she did, that you had been going to classes since early in January.

45 "I wonder," she said, "If you could be talking about that terribly shy little girl who dropped out of school after only a few days' attendance?"

"No," I said, "Laura, my daughter, has been going to school every day for the past six weeks!"

50 "Excuse me," she said. She took the attendance book out and there was your name, unmistakably printed, and all the dates you were absent until they decided that you had dropped out of school.

I still said, "No, there must have been some mistake! There must have been some mix-up in the records!"

55 And she said, "No—I remember her perfectly now. Her hands shook so that she couldn't hit the right keys! The first time we gave a speed test, she broke down completely—was sick at the stomach and almost had to be carried into the wash room! After that morning she never showed up any
60 more. We phoned the house but never got any answer"— While I was working at Famous-Barr, I suppose, demonstrating those—

(She indicates a brassiere with her hands.)

Oh! I felt so weak I could barely keep on my feet! I had to sit down while they got me a glass of water! Fifty dollars' tuition,
65 all of our plans—my hopes and ambitions for you—just gone up the spout, just gone up the spout like that.

(LAURA draws a long breath and gets awkwardly to her feet. She crosses to the Victrola and winds it up.)

What are you doing?

LAURA: Oh! *(She releases the handle and returns to her seat.)*

AMANDA: Laura, where have you been going when you've
70 gone out pretending that you were going to business college?

LAURA: I've just been going out walking.

AMANDA: That's not true.

LAURA: It is. I just went walking.

AMANDA: Walking? Walking? In winter? Deliberately courting
75 pneumonia in that light coat? Where did you walk to, Laura?

LAURA: All sorts of places—mostly in the park.

AMANDA: Even after you'd started catching that cold?

LAURA: It was the lesser of two evils, Mother.

(Screen image: Winter scene in a park.)

I couldn't go back there. I—threw up—on the floor!

80 AMANDA: From half past seven till after five every day you mean to tell me you walked around in the park, because you wanted to make me think that you were still going to Rubi-cam's Business College?

LAURA: It wasn't as bad as it sounds. I went inside places to get
85 warmed up.

AMANDA: Inside where?

LAURA: I went in the art museum and the bird houses at the Zoo. I visited the penquins every day! Sometimes I did without lunch and went to the movies. Lately I've been spending most of my afternoons in the Jewel Box, that big glass house 90 where they raise the tropical flowers.

AMANDA: You did all this to deceive me, just for deception? *(LAURA looks down.)* Why?

LAURA: Mother, when you're disappointed, you get that awful suffering look on your face, like the picture of Jesus' mother 95 in the museum!

AMANDA: Hush!

LAURA: I couldn't face it.

(There is a pause. A whisper of strings is heard. Legend on screen: "The Crust of Humility.")

AMANDA: *(Hopelessly fingering the huge pocketbook.)* So what are we going to do the rest of our lives? Stay home and watch 100 the parades go by? Amuse ourselves with the glass menagerie, darling? Eternally play those worn-out phonograph records your father left as a painful reminder of him? We won't have a business career—we've given that up because it gave us ner-vous indigestion! *(She laughs wearily.)* What is there left but 105 dependency all our lives? I know so well what becomes of un-married women who aren't prepared to occupy a position. I've seen such pitiful cases in the South—barely tolerated spinsters living upon the grudging patronage of sister's hus-band or brother's wife!—stuck away in some little mousetrap 110 of a room—encouraged by one in-law to visit another—little birdlike women without any nest—eating the crust of humil-ity all their life!

Is that the future that we've mapped out for ourselves? I swear it's the only alternative I can think of! *(She pauses.)* It 115 isn't a very pleasant alternative, is it? *(She pauses again.)* Of course—some girls *do marry.*

(LAURA twists her hands nervously.)

Haven't you ever liked some boy?

LAURA: Yes. I liked one once. *(She rises.)* I came across his pic-ture a while ago. 120

AMANDA: *(With some interest.)* He gave you his picture?

LAURA: No, it's in the yearbook.

AMANDA: *(Disappointed.)* Oh—a high school boy.

(Screen image: JIM as the high school hero bearing a silver cup.)

LAURA: Yes. His name was Jim. *(She lifts the heavy annual from the claw-foot table.)* Here he is in *The Pirates of Penzance.* 125

AMANDA: *(Absently.)* The what?

LAURA: The operetta the senior class put on. He had a wonder-ful voice and we sat across the aisle from each other Mon-days, Wednesdays and Fridays in the Aud. Here he is with the silver cup for debating! See his grin? 130

AMANDA: *(Absently.)* He must have had a jolly disposition.

LAURA: He used to call me—Blue Roses.

(Screen image: Blue roses.)

AMANDA: Why did he call you such a name as that?

LAURA: When I had that attack of pleurosis—he asked me what was the matter when I came back. I said pleurosis—he 135 thought that I said Blue Roses! So that's what he always called me after that. Whenever he saw me, he'd holler,

"Hello, Blue Roses!" I didn't care for the girl that he went
out with. Emily Meisenbach. Emily was the best-dressed girl
140 at Soldan. She never struck me, though, as being sincere . . .
It says in the Personal Section—they're engaged. That's—six
years ago! They must be married by now.

AMANDA: Girls that aren't cut out for business careers usually
wind up married to some nice man. (*She gets up with a spark*
145 *of revival.*) Sister, that's what you'll do!

(LAURA *utters a startled, doubtful laugh. She reaches quickly for
a piece of glass.*)

LAURA: But, Mother—
AMANDA: Yes? (*She goes over to the photograph.*)
LAURA: (*In a tone of frightened apology.*) I'm—crippled!
AMANDA: Nonsense! Laura, I've told you never, never to use
150 that word. Why, you're not crippled, you just have a little defect—hardly noticeable, even! When people have some
slight disadvantage like that, they cultivate other things to
make up for it—develop charm—and vivacity—and—
charm! That's all you have to do! (*She turns again to the*
155 *photograph.*) One thing your father had *plenty of*—was
charm!

(*The scene fades out with music.*)

— SCENE THREE —

Legend on screen: "After the fiasco—"

TOM *speaks from the fire escape landing.*

TOM: After the fiasco at Rubicam's Business College, the idea
of getting a gentleman caller for Laura began to play a more
and more important part in Mother's calculations. It became an obsession. Like some archetype of the universal un-
5 conscious, the image of the gentleman caller haunted our
small apartment. . . .

(*Screen image: A young man at the door of a house with
flowers.*)

An evening at home rarely passed without some allusion
to this image, this specter, this hope. . . . Even when he
wasn't mentioned, his presence hung in Mother's preoccu-
10 pied look and in my sister's frightened, apologetic manner—
hung like a sentence passed upon the Wingfields!
Mother was a woman of action as well as words. She
began to take logical steps in the planned direction. Late
that winter and in the early spring—realizing that extra
15 money would be needed to properly feather the nest and
plume the bird—she conducted a vigorous campaign on the
telephone, roping in subscribers to one of those magazines
for matrons called *The Homemaker's Companion,* the type of
journal that features the serialized sublimations of ladies of
20 letters who think in terms of delicate cuplike breasts, slim,
tapering waists, rich, creamy thighs, eyes like wood smoke in
autumn, fingers that soothe and caress like strains of music,
bodies as powerful as Etruscan sculpture.

(*Screen image: The cover of a glamor magazine.*)

(AMANDA *enters with the telephone on a long extension cord.
She is spotlighted in the dim stage.*)

AMANDA: Ida Scott? This is Amanda Wingfield! We *missed*
you at the D.A.R. last Monday! I said to myself: She's probably suffering with that sinus condition! How is that sinus
condition?
Horrors! Heaven have mercy!—You're a Christian martyr, yes, that's what you are, a Christian martyr!
Well, I just now happened to notice that your subscription to the *Companion's* about to expire! Yes, it expires with
the next issue, honey!—just when that wonderful new serial
by Bessie Mae Hopper is getting off to such an exciting start.
Oh, honey, it's something that you can't miss! You remember how *Gone with the Wind* took everybody by storm? You
simply couldn't go out if you hadn't read it. All everybody
talked was Scarlett O'Hara. Well, this is a book that critics already compare to *Gone with the Wind.* It's the *Gone with the
Wind* of the post–World War generation!—What?—Burning?—Oh, honey, don't let them burn, go take a look in the
oven and I'll hold the wire! Heavens—I think she's hung up!

(*The scene dims out.*)

(*Legend on screen:* "You think I'm in love with Continental
Shoemakers?")

(*Before the lights come up again, the violent voices of* TOM *and*
AMANDA *are heard. They are quarreling behind the portieres. In
front of them stands* LAURA *with clenched hands and panicky expression. A clear pool of light is on her figure throughout this
scene.*)

TOM: What in Christ's name am I—
AMANDA: (*Shrilly.*) Don't you use that—
TOM: —supposed to do!
AMANDA: —expression! Not in my—
TOM: Ohhh!
AMANDA: —presence! Have you gone out of your senses?
TOM: I have, that's true, *driven* out!
AMANDA: What is the matter with you, you—big—big— IDIOT!
TOM: Look!—I've got *no thing*, no single thing—
AMANDA: Lower your voice!
TOM: —in my life here that I can call my OWN! Everything is—
AMANDA: Stop that shouting!
TOM: Yesterday you confiscated my books! You had the nerve
to—
AMANDA: I took that horrible novel back to the library—yes!
That hideous book by that insane Mr. Lawrence.

(TOM *laughs wildly.*)

I cannot control the output of diseased minds or people who
cater to them—

(TOM *laughs still more wildly.*)

BUT I WON'T ALLOW SUCH FILTH BROUGHT INTO MY
HOUSE! No, no, no, no, no!
TOM: House, house! Who pays rent on it, who makes a slave of
himself to—
AMANDA: (*Fairly screeching.*) Don't you DARE to—
TOM: No, no, I mustn't say things! *I've* got to just—
AMANDA: Let me tell you—
TOM: I don't want to hear any more!

(*He tears the portieres open. The dining-room area is lit with a
turgid smoky red glow. Now we see* AMANDA; *her hair is in metal*

curlers and she is wearing a very old bathrobe, much too large for her slight figure, a relic of the faithless Mr. Wingfield. The upright typewriter now stands on the drop-leaf table, along with a wild disarray of manuscripts. The quarrel was probably precipitated by AMANDA's *interruption of* TOM's *creative labor. A chair lies overthrown on the floor. Their gesticulating shadows are cast on the ceiling by the fiery glow.)*

AMANDA: You *will* hear more, you—

TOM: No, I won't hear more, I'm going out!

70 AMANDA: You come right back in—

TOM: Out, out, out! Because I'm—

AMANDA: Come back here, Tom Wingfield! I'm not through talking to you!

TOM: Oh, go—

75 LAURA: *(Desperately.)* —Tom!

AMANDA: You're going to listen, and no more insolence from you! I'm at the end of my patience!

(He comes back toward her.)

TOM: What do you think I'm at? Aren't I supposed to have any patience to reach the end of, Mother? I know, I know. It
80 seems unimportant to you, what I'm *doing*—what I *want* to do—having a little *difference* between them! You don't think that—

AMANDA: I think you've been doing things that you're ashamed of. That's why you act like this. I don't believe that you go
85 every night to the movies. Nobody goes to the movies night after night. Nobody in their right minds goes to the movies as often as you pretend to. People don't go to the movies at nearly midnight, and movies don't let out at two A.M. Come in stumbling. Muttering to yourself like a maniac! You get
90 three hours' sleep and then go to work. Oh, I can picture the way you're doing down there. Moping, doping, because you're in no condition.

TOM: *(Wildly.)* No, I'm in no condition!

AMANDA: What right have you got to jeopardize your job?
95 Jeopardize the security of us all? How do you think we'd manage if you were—

TOM: Listen! You think I'm crazy about the *warehouse?* *(He bends fiercely toward her slight figure.)* You think I'm in love with the Continental Shoemakers? You think I want to
100 spend fifty-five *years* down there in that—*celotex interior!* with—*fluorescent—tubes!* Look! I'd rather somebody picked up a crowbar and battered out my brains—than go back mornings! I *go!* Every time you come in yelling that Goddamn *"Rise and Shine!" "Rise and Shine!"* I say to myself,
105 "How *lucky dead* people are!" But I get up. I *go!* For sixty-five dollars a month I give up all that I dream of doing and being *ever!* And you say self—*self's* all I ever think of. Why, listen, if self is what I thought of, Mother, I'd be where he is—GONE! *(He points to his father's picture.)* As far as the system of trans-
110 portation reaches! *(He starts past her. She grabs his arm.)* Don't grab at me, Mother!

AMANDA: Where are you going?

TOM: I'm going to the *movies!*

AMANDA: I don't believe that lie!

(TOM crouches toward her, overtowering her tiny figure. She backs away, gasping.)

115 TOM: I'm going to opium dens! Yes, opium dens, dens of vice and criminals' hangouts, Mother. I've joined the Hogan

Gang, I'm a hired assassin, I carry a tommy gun in a case! I run a string of cat houses in the Valley! They ca Killer, Killer Wingfield, I'm leading a double-life, a sin honest warehouse worker by day, by night a dynamic *cza* 120 the *underworld, Mother.* I go to gambling casinos, I spin away fortunes on the roulette table! I wear a patch over one eye and a false mustache, sometimes I put on green whiskers. On those occasions they call me—*El Diablo!* Oh, I could tell you many things to make you sleepless! My
125 enemies plan to dynamite this place. They're going to blow us all sky-high some night! I'll be glad, very happy, and so will you! You'll go up, up on a broomstick, over Blue Mountain with seventeen gentlemen callers! You ugly—babbling old—*witch.* . . . *(He goes through a series of violent, clumsy*
130 *movements, seizing his overcoat, lunging to the door, pulling it fiercely open. The women watch him, aghast. His arm catches in the sleeve of the coat as he struggles to pull it on. For a moment he is pinioned by the bulky garment. With an outraged groan he tears the coat off again, splitting the shoul-*
135 *der of it, and hurls it across the room. It strikes against the shelf of* LAURA's *glass collection, and there is a tinkle of shattering glass.* LAURA *cries out as if wounded.)*

(Music.)

(Screen legend: "The Glass Menagerie.")

LAURA: *(Shrilly.)* My glass!—menagerie. . . . *(She covers her face and turns away.)* 140

(But AMANDA *is still stunned and stupefied by the "ugly witch" so that she barely notices this occurrence. Now she recovers her speech.)*

AMANDA: *(In an awful voice.)* I won't speak to you—until you apologize!

(She crosses through the portieres and draws them together behind her. TOM *is left with* LAURA. LAURA *clings weakly to the mantel with her face averted.* TOM *stares at her stupidly for a moment. Then he crosses to the shelf. He drops awkwardly on his knees to collect the fallen glass, glancing at* LAURA *as if he would speak but couldn't.)*

("The Glass Menagerie" music steals in as the scene dims out.)

— SCENE FOUR —

The interior of the apartment is dark. There is a faint light in the alley. A deep-voiced bell in a church is tolling the hour of five.

TOM *appears at the top of the alley. After each solemn boom of the bell in the tower, he shakes a little noisemaker or rattle as if to express the tiny spasm of man in contrast to the sustained power and dignity of the Almighty. This and the unsteadiness of his advance make it evident that he has been drinking. As he climbs the few steps to the fire escape landing light steals up inside.* LAURA *appears in the front room in a nightdress. She notices that* TOM's *bed is empty.* TOM *fishes in his pockets for his door key, removing a motley assortment of articles in the search, including a shower of movie ticket stubs and an empty bottle. At last he finds the key, but just as he is about to insert it, it slips from his fingers. He strikes a match and crouches below the door.*

TOM: *(Bitterly.)* One crack—and it falls through!

(LAURA *opens the door.*)

LAURA: Tom! Tom, what are you doing?

TOM: Looking for a door key.

LAURA: Where have you been all this time?

5   TOM: I have been to the movies.

LAURA: All this time at the movies?

TOM: There was a very long program. There was a Garbo picture and a Mickey Mouse and a travelogue and a newsreel
and a preview of coming attractions. And there was an organ

10 solo and a collection for the Milk Fund—simultaneously—
which ended up in a terrible fight between a fat lady and an
usher!

LAURA: *(Innocently.)* Did you have to stay through everything?

TOM: Of course! And, oh, I forgot! There was a big stage show!

15 The headliner on this stage show was Malvolio the Magician. He performed wonderful tricks, many of them, such as
pouring water back and forth between pitchers. First it
turned to wine and then it turned to beer and then it turned
to whisky. I know it was whisky it finally turned into because

20 he needed somebody to come up out of the audience to help
him, and I came up—both shows! It was Kentucky Straight
Bourbon. A very generous fellow, he gave souvenirs. *(He
pulls from his back pocket a shimmering rainbow-colored
scarf.)* He gave me this. This is his magic scarf. You can have

25 it, Laura. You wave it over a canary cage and you get a bowl
of goldfish. You wave it over the goldfish bowl and they fly
away canaries. . . . But the wonderfullest trick of all was the
coffin trick. We nailed him into a coffin and he got out of
the coffin without removing one nail. *(He has come inside.)*

30 There is a trick that would come in handy for me—get me
out of this two-by-four situation! *(He flops onto the bed and
starts removing his shoes.)*

LAURA: Tom—shhh!

TOM: What're you shushing me for?

35 LAURA: You'll wake up Mother.

TOM: Goody, goody! Pay 'er back for all those "Rise an' Shines."
(He lies down, groaning.) You know it don't take much intelligence to get yourself into a nailed-up coffin, Laura. But who
in hell ever got himself out of one without removing one

40 nail?

(*As if in answer, the father's grinning photograph lights up. The
scene dims out.*)

(*Immediately following, the church bell is heard striking six. At
the sixth stroke the alarm clock goes off in* AMANDA'S *room, and
after a few moments we hear her calling: "Rise and Shine! Rise
and Shine!* LAURA, *go tell your brother to rise and shine!"*)

TOM: *(Sitting up slowly.)* I'll rise—but I won't shine.

(*The light increases.*)

AMANDA: Laura, tell your brother his coffee is ready.

(LAURA *slips into the front room.*)

LAURA: Tom!—It's nearly seven. Don't make Mother nervous.

(*He stares at her stupidly.*)

(*Beseechingly.*) Tom, speak to Mother this morning. Make

45 up with her, apologize, speak to her!

TOM: She won't to me. It's her that started not speaking.

LAURA: If you just say you're sorry she'll start speaking.

TOM: Her not speaking—is that such a tragedy?

LAURA: Please—please!

AMANDA: *(Calling from the kitchenette.)* Laura, are you going   50
to do what I asked you to do, or do I have to get dressed and
go out myself?

LAURA: Going, going—soon as I get on my coat!

(*She pulls on a shapeless felt hat with a nervous, jerky movement, pleadingly glancing at* TOM. *She rushes awkwardly for her
coat. The coat is one of* AMANDA's, *inaccurately made-over, the
sleeves too short for* LAURA.)

Butter and what else?

AMANDA: *(Entering from the kitchenette.)* Just butter. Tell them   55
to charge it.

LAURA: Mother, they make such faces when I do that.

AMANDA: Sticks and stones can break our bones, but the expression on Mr. Garfinkel's face won't harm us! Tell your
brother his coffee is getting cold.   60

LAURA: *(At the door.)* Do what I asked you, will you, will you,
Tom?

(*He looks sullenly away.*)

AMANDA: Laura, go now or just don't go at all!

LAURA: *(Rushing out.)* Going—going!

(*A second later she cries out.* TOM *springs up and crosses to the
door.* TOM *opens the door.*)

TOM: Laura?   65

LAURA: I'm all right. I slipped, but I'm all right.

AMANDA: *(Peering anxiously after her.)* If anyone breaks a leg
on those fire-escape steps, the landlord ought to be sued for
every cent he possesses! *(She shuts the door. Now she remembers she isn't speaking to* TOM *and returns to the other room.)*   70

(*As* TOM *comes listlessly for his coffee, she turns her back to him
and stands rigidly facing the window on the gloomy gray vault of
the areaway. Its light on her face with its aged but childish features is cruelly sharp, satirical as a Daumier print.*)

(*The music of "Ave Maria" is heard softly.*)

(TOM *glances sheepishly but sullenly at her averted figure and
slumps at the table. The coffee is scalding hot; he sips it and
gasps and spits it back in the cup. At his gasp,* AMANDA *catches
her breath and half turns. Then she catches herself and turns
back to the window.* TOM *blows on his coffee, glancing sidewise
at his mother. She clears her throat.* TOM *clears his. He starts to
rise, sinks back down again, scratches his head, clears his throat
again.* AMANDA *coughs.* TOM *raises his cup in both hands to
blow on it, his eyes staring over the rim of it at his mother for several moments. Then he slowly sets the cup down and awkwardly
and hesitantly rises from the chair.*)

TOM: *(Hoarsely.)* Mother. I—I apologize, Mother.

(AMANDA *draws a quick, shuddering breath. Her face works
grotesquely. She breaks into childlike tears.*)

I'm sorry for what I said, for everything that I said, I didn't
mean it.

AMANDA: *(Sobbingly.)* My devotion has made me a witch and
so I make myself hateful to my children!   75

TOM: *No, you* don't.

AMANDA: I worry so much, don't sleep, it makes me nervous!

TOM: *(Gently.)* I understand that.

AMANDA: I've had to put up a solitary battle all these years. But you're my right-hand bower! Don't fall down, don't fail!

TOM: *(Gently.)* I try, Mother.

AMANDA: *(With great enthusiasm.)* Try and you will *succeed!* *(The notion makes her breathless.)* Why, you—you're just *full* of natural endowments! Both of my children—they're *unusual* children! Don't you think I know it? I'm so—*proud!* Happy and—feel I've—so much to be thankful for but—promise me one thing, son!

TOM: What, Mother?

AMANDA: Promise, son, you'll—never be a drunkard!

TOM: *(Turns to her grinning.)* I will never be a drunkard, Mother.

AMANDA: That's what frightened me so, that you'd be drinking! Eat a bowl of Purina!

TOM: Just coffee, Mother.

AMANDA: Shredded wheat biscuit?

TOM: No. No, Mother, just coffee.

AMANDA: You can't put in a day's work on an empty stomach. You've got ten minutes—don't gulp! Drinking too-hot liquids makes cancer of the stomach. . . . Put cream in.

TOM: No, thank you.

AMANDA: To cool it.

TOM: No! No, thank you, I want it black.

AMANDA: I know, but it's not good for you. We have to do all that we can to build ourselves up. In these trying times we live in, all that we have to cling to is—each other. . . . That's why it's so important to—Tom, I—sent out your sister so I could discuss something with you. If you hadn't spoken I would have spoken to you. *(She sits down.)*

TOM: *(Gently.)* What is it, Mother, that you want to discuss?

AMANDA: *Laura!*

(TOM puts his cup down slowly.)

(Legend on screen: "Laura." Music: "The Glass Menagerie.")

TOM: —Oh.—Laura . . .

AMANDA: *(Touching his sleeve.)* You know how Laura is. So quiet but—still water runs deep! She notices things and I think she—broods about them.

(TOM looks up.)

A few days ago I came in and she was crying.

TOM: What about?

AMANDA: You.

TOM: Me?

AMANDA: She has an idea that you're not happy here.

TOM: What gave her that idea?

AMANDA: What gives her any idea? However, you do act strangely. I—I'm not criticizing, understand *that!* I know your ambitions do not lie in the warehouse, that like everybody in the whole wide world—you've had to—make sacrifices, but—Tom—Tom—life's not easy, it calls for—Spartan endurance! There's so many things in my heart that I cannot describe to you! I've never told you but I—*loved* your father. . . .

TOM: *(Gently.)* I know that, Mother.

AMANDA: And you—when I see you taking after his ways! Staying out late—and—well, you *had* been drinking the night you were in that—terrifying condition! Laura says that you hate the apartment and that you go out nights to get away from it! Is that true, Tom?

TOM: No. You say there's so much in your heart that you can't describe to me. That's true of me, too. There's so much in my heart that I can't describe to *you!* So let's respect each other's—

AMANDA: But, why—*why*, Tom—are you always so *restless?* Where do you go to, nights?

TOM: I—go to the movies.

AMANDA: Why do you go to the movies so much, Tom?

TOM: I go to the movies because—I like adventure. Adventure is something I don't have much of at work, so I go to the movies.

AMANDA: But, Tom, you go to the movies *entirely* too *much!*

TOM: I like a lot of adventure.

(AMANDA looks baffled, then hurt. As the familiar inquisition resumes, TOM becomes hard and impatient again. AMANDA slips back into her querulous attitude toward him.)

(Image on screen: A sailing vessel with Jolly Roger.)

AMANDA: Most young men find adventure in their careers.

TOM: Then most young men are not employed in a warehouse.

AMANDA: The world is full of young men employed in warehouses and offices and factories.

TOM: Do all of them find adventure in their careers?

AMANDA: They do or they do without it! Not everybody has a craze for adventure.

TOM: Man is by instinct a lover, a hunter, a fighter, and none of those instincts are given much play at the warehouse!

AMANDA: Man is by instinct! Don't quote instinct to me! Instinct is something that people have got away from! It belongs to animals! Christian adults don't want it!

TOM: What do Christian adults want, then, Mother?

AMANDA: Superior things! Things of the mind and the spirit! Only animals have to satisfy instincts! Surely your aims are somewhat higher than theirs! Than monkeys—pigs—

TOM: I reckon they're not.

AMANDA: You're joking. However, that isn't what I wanted to discuss.

TOM: *(Rising.)* I haven't much time.

AMANDA: *(Pushing his shoulders.)* Sit down.

TOM: You want me to punch in red at the warehouse, Mother?

AMANDA: You have five minutes. I want to talk about Laura.

(Screen legend: "Plans and Provisions.")

TOM: All right! What about Laura?

AMANDA: We have to be making some plans and provisions for her. She's older than you, two years, and nothing has happened. She just drifts along doing nothing. It frightens me terribly how she just drifts along.

TOM: I guess she's the type that people call home girls.

AMANDA: There's no such type, and if there is, it's a pity! That is unless the home is hers, with a husband!

TOM: What?

AMANDA: Oh, I can see the handwriting on the wall as plain as I see the nose in front of my face! It's terrifying! More and more you remind me of your father! He was out all hours without explanation!—Then *left! Goodbye!* And me with the bag to hold. I saw that letter you got from the Merchant Marine. I know what you're dreaming of. I'm not standing here blindfolded. *(She pauses.)* Very well, then. Then *do* it! But not till there's somebody to take your place.

TOM: What do you mean?

AMANDA: I mean that as soon as Laura has got somebody to
take care of her, married, a home of her own, independent—why, then you'll be free to go wherever you please, on
land, on sea, whichever way the wind blows you! But until
that time you've got to look out for your sister. I don't say me
because I'm old and don't matter! I say for your sister because she's young and dependent.

I put her in business college—a dismal failure! Frightened her so it made her sick at the stomach. I took her over
to the Young People's League at the church. Another fiasco.
She spoke to nobody, nobody spoke to her. Now all she does
is fool with those pieces of glass and play those worn-out
records. What kind of a life is that for a girl to lead?

TOM: What can I do about it?

AMANDA: Overcome selfishness! Self, self, self is all that you
ever think of!

(TOM *springs up and crosses to get his coat. It is ugly and bulky.
He pulls on a cap with earmuffs.*)

Where is your muffler? Put your wool muffler on!

(*He snatches it angrily from the closet, tosses it around his neck
and pulls both ends tight.*)

Tom! I haven't said what I had in mind to ask you.

TOM: I'm too late to—

AMANDA: (*Catching his arm—very importunately; then shyly.*)
Down at the warehouse, aren't there some—nice young
men?

TOM: No!

AMANDA: There *must* be—*some* . . .

TOM: Mother—(*He gestures.*)

AMANDA: Find out one that's clean-living—doesn't drink and
ask him out for sister!

TOM: What?

AMANDA: For *sister!* To *meet!* Get *acquainted!*

TOM: (*Stamping to the door.*) Oh, my go-osh!

AMANDA: Will you?

(*He opens the door. She says, imploringly:*)

Will you?

(*He starts down the fire escape.*)

Will you? *Will* you, dear?

TOM: (*Calling back.*) Yes!

(AMANDA *closes the door hesitantly and with a troubled but
faintly hopeful expression.*)

(*Screen image:* The cover of a glamor magazine.)

(*The spotlight picks up* AMANDA *at the phone.*)

AMANDA: Ella Cartwright? This is Amanda Wingfield!
How are you, honey?

How is that kidney condition?

(*There is a five-second pause.*)

Horrors!

(*There is another pause.*)

You're a Christian martyr, yes, honey, that's what you are, a
Christian martyr! Well, I just now happened to notice in my
little red book that your subscription to the *Companion* has

just run out! I knew that you wouldn't want to miss out on
the wonderful serial starting in this new issue. It's by Bessie
Mae Hopper, the first thing she's written since *Honeymoon
for Three.* Wasn't that a strange and interesting story? Well,
this one is even lovelier, I believe. It has a sophisticated,
society background. It's all about the horsey set on Long
Island!

(*The light fades out.*)

— SCENE FIVE —

Legend on the screen: "Annunciation."

Music is heard as the light slowly comes on.

*It is early dusk of a spring evening. Supper has just been finished
in the Wingfield apartment.* AMANDA *and* LAURA, *in light-
colored dresses, are removing dishes from the table in the dining
room, which is shadowy, their movements formalized almost as a
dance or ritual, their moving forms as pale and silent as moths.*
TOM, *in white shirt and trousers, rises from the table and crosses
toward the fire escape.*

AMANDA: (*As he passes her.*) Son, will you do me a favor?

TOM: What?

AMANDA: Comb your hair! You look so pretty when your hair is
combed!

(TOM *slouches on the sofa with the evening paper. Its enormous
headline reads:* "Franco Triumphs.")

There is only one respect in which I would like you to emulate your father.

TOM: What respect is that?

AMANDA: The care he always took of his appearance. He never
allowed himself to look untidy.

(*He throws down the paper and crosses to the fire escape.*)

Where are you going?

TOM: I'm going out to smoke.

AMANDA: You smoke too much. A pack a day at fifteen cents a
pack. How much would that amount to in a month? Thirty
times fifteen is how much, Tom? Figure it out and you will
be astounded at what you could save. Enough to give you a
night-school course in accounting at Washington U! Just
think what a wonderful thing that would be for you, son!

(TOM *is unmoved by the thought.*)

TOM: I'd rather smoke. (*He steps out on the landing, letting the
screen door slam.*)

AMANDA: (*Sharply.*) I know! That's the tragedy of it. . . .
(*Alone, she turns to look at her husband's picture.*)

(*Dance music:* "The World Is Waiting for the Sunrise!")

TOM: (*To the audience.*) Across the alley from us was the Paradise Dance Hall. On evenings in spring the windows and
doors were open and the music came outdoors. Sometimes
the lights were turned out except for a large glass sphere that
hung from the ceiling. It would turn slowly about and filter
the dusk with delicate rainbow colors. Then the orchestra
played a waltz or a tango, something that had a slow and sensuous rhythm. Couples would come outside, to the relative
privacy of the alley. You could see them kissing behind ash

pits and telephone poles. This was the compensation for lives that passed like mine, without any change or adventure. Adventure and change were imminent in this year. They were waiting around the corner for all these kids. Suspended
35 in the mist over Berchtesgaden, caught in the folds of Chamberlain's umbrella. In Spain there was Guernica! But here there was only hot swing music and liquor, dance halls, bars, and movies, and sex that hung in the gloom like a chandelier and flooded the world with brief, deceptive rainbows. . . . All
40 the world was waiting for bombardments!

(AMANDA turns from the picture and comes outside.)

AMANDA: *(Sighing.)* A fire escape landing's a poor excuse for a porch. *(She spreads a newspaper on a step and sits down, gracefully and demurely as if she were settling into a swing on a Mississippi veranda.)* What are you looking at?
45 TOM: The moon.
AMANDA: Is there a moon this evening?
TOM: It's rising over Garfinkel's Delicatessen.
AMANDA: So it is! A little silver slipper of a moon. Have you made a wish on it yet?
50 TOM: Um-hum.
AMANDA: What did you wish for?
TOM: That's a secret.
AMANDA: A secret, huh? Well, I won't tell mine either. I will be just as mysterious as you.
55 TOM: I bet I can guess what yours is.
AMANDA: Is my head so transparent?
TOM: You're not a sphinx.
AMANDA: No, I don't have secrets. I'll tell you what I wished for on the moon. Success and happiness for my precious
60 children! I wish for that whenever there's a moon, and when there isn't a moon, I wish for it, too.
TOM: I thought perhaps you wished for a gentleman caller.
AMANDA: Why do you say that?
TOM: Don't you remember asking me to fetch one?
65 AMANDA: I remember suggesting that it would be nice for your sister if you brought home some nice young man from the warehouse. I think that I've made that suggestion more than once.
TOM: Yes, you have made it repeatedly.
70 AMANDA: Well?
TOM: We are going to have one.
AMANDA: *What?*
TOM: A gentleman caller!

(The annunciation is celebrated with music.)

(AMANDA rises.)

(Image on screen: A caller with a bouquet.)

AMANDA: You mean you have asked some nice young man to
75 come over?
TOM: Yep. I've asked him to dinner.
AMANDA: You really did?
TOM: I did!
AMANDA: You did, and did he—*accept?*
80 TOM: He did!
AMANDA: Well, well—well, well! That's—lovely!
TOM: I thought that you would be pleased.
AMANDA: It's definite then?

TOM: Very definite.
AMANDA: Soon? 85
TOM: Very soon.
AMANDA: For heaven's sake, stop putting on and tell me some things, will you?
TOM: What things do you want me to tell you?
AMANDA: *Naturally* I would like to know when he's *coming!* 90
TOM: He's coming tomorrow.
AMANDA: *Tomorrow?*
TOM: Yep. Tomorrow.
AMANDA: But, Tom!
TOM: Yes, Mother? 95
AMANDA: Tomorrow gives me no time!
TOM: Time for what?
AMANDA: Preparations! Why didn't you phone me at once, as soon as you asked him, the minute that he accepted? Then don't you see, I could have been getting ready! 100
TOM: You don't have to make any fuss.
AMANDA: Oh, Tom, Tom, Tom, of course I have to make a fuss! I want things nice, not sloppy! Not thrown together. I'll certainly have to do some fast thinking, won't I?
TOM: I don't see why you have to think at all. 105
AMANDA: You just don't know. We can't have a gentleman caller in a pigsty! All my wedding silver has to be polished, the monogrammed table linen ought to be laundered! The windows have to be washed and fresh curtains put up. And how about clothes? We have to *wear* something, don't we? 110
TOM: Mother, this boy is no one to make a fuss over!
AMANDA: Do you realize he's the first young man we've introduced to your sister? It's terrible, dreadful, disgraceful that poor little sister has never received a single gentleman caller! Tom, come inside! *(She opens the screen door.)* 115
TOM: What for?
AMANDA: I want to ask you some things.
TOM: If you're going to make such a fuss, I'll call it off, I'll tell him not to come!
AMANDA: You certainly won't do anything of the kind. Noth- 120
ing offends people worse than broken engagements. It simply means I'll have to work like a Turk! We won't be brilliant, but we will pass inspection. Come on inside.

(TOM follows her inside, groaning.)

Sit down.
TOM: Any particular place you would like me to sit? 125
AMANDA: Thank heavens I've got that new sofa! I'm also making payments on a floor lamp I'll have sent out! And put the chintz covers on, they'll brighten things up! Of course I'd hoped to have these walls re-papered. . . . What is the young man's name? 130
TOM: His name is O'Connor.
AMANDA: That, of course, means fish—tomorrow is Friday! I'll have that salmon loaf—with Durkee's dressing! What does he do? He works at the warehouse?
TOM: Of course! How else would I— 135
AMANDA: Tom, he—doesn't drink?
TOM: Why do you ask me that?
AMANDA: Your father *did!*
TOM: Don't get started on that!
AMANDA: He *does* drink, then? 140
TOM: Not that I know of!

AMANDA: Make sure, be certain! The last thing I want for my daughter's a boy who drinks!

145 TOM: Aren't you being a little bit premature? Mr. O'Connor has not yet appeared on the scene!

AMANDA: But will tomorrow. To meet your sister, and what do I know about his character? Nothing! Old maids are better off than wives of drunkards!

TOM: Oh, my God!

150 AMANDA: Be still!

TOM: (*Leaning forward to whisper.*) Lots of fellows meet girls whom they don't marry!

AMANDA: Oh, talk sensibly, Tom—and don't be sarcastic! (*She has gotten a hairbrush.*)

155 TOM: What are you doing?

AMANDA: I'm brushing that cowlick down! (*She attacks his hair with the brush.*) What is this young man's position at the warehouse?

TOM: (*Submitting grimly to the brush and the interrogation.*)

160 This young man's position is that of a shipping clerk, Mother.

AMANDA: Sounds to me like a fairly responsible job, the sort of a job *you* would be in if you just had more *get-up*. What is his salary? Have you any idea?

165 TOM: I would judge it to be approximately eighty-five dollars a month.

AMANDA: Well—not princely, but—

TOM: Twenty more than I make.

AMANDA: Yes, how well I know! But for a family man, eighty-

170 five dollars a month is not much more than you can just get by on. . . .

TOM: Yes, but Mr. O'Connor is not a family man.

AMANDA: He might be, mightn't he? Some time in the future?

TOM: I see. Plans and provisions.

175 AMANDA: You are the only young man that I know of who ignores the fact that the future becomes the present, the present the past, and the past turns into everlasting regret if you don't plan for it!

TOM: I will think that over and see what I can make of it.

180 AMANDA: Don't be supercilious with your mother! Tell me some more about this—what do you call him?

TOM: James D. O'Connor. The D. is for Delaney.

AMANDA: Irish on *both* sides! *Gracious!* And doesn't drink?

TOM: Shall I call him up and ask him right this minute?

185 AMANDA: The only way to find out about those things is to make discreet inquiries at the proper moment. When I was a girl in Blue Mountain and it was suspected that a young man drank, the girl whose attentions he had been receiving, if any girl *was*, would sometimes speak to the minister of his

190 church, or rather her father would if her father was living, and sort of feel him out on the young man's character. That is the way such things are discreetly handled to keep a young woman from making a tragic mistake!

TOM: Then how did you happen to make a tragic mistake?

195 AMANDA: That innocent look of your father's had everyone fooled! He *smiled*—the world was *enchanted*! No girl can do worse than put herself at the mercy of a handsome appearance! I hope that Mr. O'Connor is not too good-looking.

TOM: No, he's not too good-looking. He's covered with freck-

200 les and hasn't too much of a nose.

AMANDA: He's not right-down homely, though?

TOM: Not right-down homely. Just medium homely, I'd say.

AMANDA: Character's what to look for in a man.

TOM: That's what I've always said, Mother.

AMANDA: You've never said anything of the kind and I suspect 205 you would never give it a thought.

TOM: Don't be so suspicious of me.

AMANDA: At least I hope he's the type that's up and coming.

TOM: I think he really goes in for self-improvement.

AMANDA: What reason have you to think so? 210

TOM: He goes to night school.

AMANDA: (*Beaming.*) Splendid! What does he do, I mean study?

TOM: Radio engineering and public speaking!

AMANDA: Then he has visions of being advanced in the world! 215 Any young man who studies public speaking is aiming to have an executive job some day! And radio engineering? A thing for the future! Both of these facts are very illuminating. Those are the sort of things that a mother should know concerning any young man who comes to call on her daughter. 220 Seriously or—not.

TOM: One little warning. He doesn't know about Laura. I didn't let on that we had dark ulterior motives. I just said, why don't you come and have dinner with us? He said okay and that was the whole conversation. 225

AMANDA: I bet it was! You're eloquent as an oyster. However, he'll know about Laura when he gets here. When he sees how lovely and sweet and pretty she is, he'll thank his lucky stars he was asked to dinner.

TOM: Mother, you mustn't expect too much of Laura. 230

AMANDA: What do you mean?

TOM: Laura seems all those things to you and me because she's ours and we love her. We don't even notice she's crippled any more.

AMANDA: Don't say crippled! You know that I never allow that 235 word to be used!

TOM: But face facts, Mother. She is and—that's not all—

AMANDA: What do you mean "not all"?

TOM: Laura is very different from other girls.

AMANDA: I think the difference is all to her advantage. 240

TOM: Not quite all—in the eyes of others—strangers—she's terribly shy and lives in a world of her own and those things make her seem a little peculiar to people outside the house.

AMANDA: Don't say peculiar.

TOM: Face the facts. She is. 245

(*The dance hall music changes to a tango that has a minor and somewhat ominous tone.*)

AMANDA: In what way is she peculiar—may I ask?

TOM: (*Gently.*) She lives in a world of her own—a world of little glass ornaments, Mother. . . .

(*He gets up.* AMANDA *remains holding the brush, looking at him, troubled.*)

She plays old phonograph records and—that's about all— (*He glances at himself in the mirror and crosses to the door.*) 250

AMANDA: (*Sharply.*) Where are you going?

TOM: I'm going to the movies. (*He goes out the screen door.*)

AMANDA: Not to the movies, every night to the movies! (*She follows quickly to the screen door.*) I don't believe you always go to the movies! 255

(*He is gone.* AMANDA *looks worriedly after him for a moment. Then vitality and optimism return and she turns from the door, crossing to the portieres.*)

Laura! Laura!

(LAURA *answers from the kitchenette.*)

LAURA: Yes, Mother.

AMANDA: Let those dishes go and come in front!

(LAURA *appears with a dish towel.* AMANDA *speaks to her gaily.*)

Laura, come here and make a wish on the moon!

(*Screen image:* The Moon.)

260 LAURA: (*Entering.*) Moon—moon?

AMANDA: A little silver slipper of a moon. Look over your left shoulder, Laura, and make a wish!

(LAURA *looks faintly puzzled as if called out of sleep.* AMANDA *seizes her shoulders and turns her at an angle by the door.*)

Now! Now, darling, *wish!*

LAURA: What shall I wish for, Mother?

265 AMANDA: (*Her voice trembling and her eyes suddenly filling with tears.*) Happiness! Good fortune!

(*The sound of the violin rises and the stage dims out.*)

— SCENE SIX —

The light comes up on the fire escape landing. TOM *is leaning against the grill, smoking.*

(*Screen image:* The high school hero.)

TOM: And so the following evening I brought Jim home to dinner. I had known Jim slightly in high school. In high school Jim was a hero. He had tremendous Irish good nature and vitality with the scrubbed and polished look of white chi-
5 naware. He seemed to move in a continual spotlight. He was a star in basketball, captain of the debating club, president of the senior class and the glee club and he sang the male lead in the annual light operas. He was always running or bounding, never just walking. He seemed always at the point of de-
10 feating the law of gravity. He was shooting with such velocity through his adolescence that you would logically expect him to arrive at nothing short of the White House by the time he was thirty. But Jim apparently ran into more interference after his graduation from Soldan. His speed had definitely
15 slowed. Six years after he left high school he was holding a job that wasn't much better than mine.

(*Screen image:* The Clerk.)

He was the only one at the warehouse with whom I was on friendly terms. I was valuable to him as someone who could remember his former glory, who had seen him win basket-
20 ball games and the silver cup in debating. He knew of my secret practice of retiring to a cabinet of the washroom to work on poems when business was slack in the warehouse. He called me Shakespeare. And while the other boys in the warehouse regarded me with suspicious hostility, Jim took a
25 humorous attitude toward me. Gradually his attitude affected the others, their hostility wore off and they also began to smile at me as people smile at an oddly fashioned dog who trots across their path at some distance.

I knew that Jim and Laura had known each other at Sol-
dan, and I had heard Laura speak admiringly of his voice. I 30
didn't know if Jim remembered her or not. In high school
Laura had been as unobtrusive as Jim had been astonishing.
If he did remember Laura, it was not as my sister, for when I
asked him to dinner, he grinned and said, "You know,
Shakespeare, I never thought of you as having folks!" 35
He was about to discover that I did. . . .

(*Legend on screen:* "The accent of a coming foot.")

(*The light dims out on* TOM *and comes up in the Wingfield living room—a delicate lemony light. It is about five on a Friday evening of late spring which comes "scattering poems in the sky."*)

(AMANDA *has worked like a Turk in preparation for the gentleman caller. The results are astonishing. The new floor lamp with its rose silk shade is in place, a colored paper lantern conceals the broken light fixture in the ceiling, new billowing white curtains are at the windows, chintz covers are on the chairs and sofa, a pair of new sofa pillows make their initial appearance. Open boxes and tissue paper are scattered on the floor.*)

(LAURA *stands in the middle of the room with lifted arms while* AMANDA *crouches before her, adjusting the hem of a new dress, devout and ritualistic. The dress is colored and designed by memory. The arrangement of* LAURA'S *hair is changed; it is softer and more becoming. A fragile, unearthly prettiness has come out in* LAURA: *she is like a piece of translucent glass touched by light, given a momentary radiance, not actual, not lasting.*)

AMANDA: (*Impatiently.*) Why are you trembling?

LAURA: Mother, you've made me so nervous!

AMANDA: How have I made you nervous?

LAURA: By all this fuss! You make it seem so important! 40

AMANDA: I don't understand you, Laura. You couldn't be satisfied with just sitting home, and yet whenever I try to arrange something for you, you seem to resist it. (*She gets up.*) Now take a look at yourself. No, wait! Wait just a moment—I have an idea! 45

LAURA: What is it now?

(AMANDA *produces two powder puffs which she wraps in handkerchiefs and stuffs in* LAURA'S *bosom.*)

LAURA: Mother, what are you doing?

AMANDA: They call them "Gay Deceivers"!

LAURA: I won't wear them!

AMANDA: You will! 50

LAURA: Why should I?

AMANDA: Because, to be painfully honest, your chest is flat.

LAURA: You make it seem like we were setting a trap.

AMANDA: All pretty girls are a trap, a pretty trap, and men expect them to be. 55

(*Legend on screen:* "A pretty trap.")

Now look at yourself, young lady. This is the prettiest you will ever be! (*She stands back to admire* LAURA.) I've got to fix myself now! You're going to be surprised by your mother's appearance!

(AMANDA *crosses through the portieres, humming gaily.* LAURA *moves slowly to the long mirror and stares solemnly at herself. A wind blows the white curtains inward in a slow, graceful motion and with a faint, sorrowful sighing.*)

60   AMANDA: *(From somewhere behind the portieres.)* It isn't dark
        enough yet.

(LAURA turns slowly before the mirror with a troubled look.)

*(Legend on screen: "This is my sister: Celebrate her with
strings!" Music plays.)*

AMANDA: *(Laughing, still not visible.)* I'm going to show you
        something. I'm going to make a spectacular appearance!

LAURA: What is it, Mother?

65   AMANDA: Possess your soul in patience—you will see! Some-
        thing I've resurrected from that old trunk! Styles haven't
        changed so terribly much after all. . . . *(She parts the por-
        tieres.)* Now just look at your mother! *(She wears a girlish
        frock of yellowed voile with a blue silk sash. She carries a
70   bunch of jonquils—the legend of her youth is nearly revived.
        Now she speaks feverishly.)* This is the dress in which I led
        the cotillion. Won the cakewalk twice at Sunset Hill, wore
        one Spring to the Governor's Ball in Jackson! See how I
        sashayed around the ballroom, Laura? *(She raises her skirt
75   and does a mincing step around the room.)* I wore it on Sun-
        days for my gentlemen callers! I had it on the day I met your
        father. . . . I had malaria fever all that Spring. The change of
        climate from East Tennessee to the Delta—weakened resis-
        tance. I had a little temperature all the time—not enough to
80   be serious—just enough to make me restless and giddy! Invi-
        tations poured in—parties all over the Delta! "Stay in bed,"
        said Mother, "you have a fever!"—but I just wouldn't. I took
        quinine but kept on going, going! Evenings, dances! After-
        noons, long, long rides! Picnics—lovely! So lovely, that
85   country in May—all lacy with dogwood, literally flooded
        with jonquils! That was the spring I had the craze for jon-
        quils. Jonquils became an absolute obsession. Mother said,
        "Honey, there's no more room for jonquils." And still I kept
        on bringing in more jonquils. Whenever, wherever I saw
90   them, I'd say "Stop! Stop! I see jonquils!" I made the young
        men help me gather the jonquils! It was a joke, Amanda and
        her jonquils. Finally there were no more vases to hold them,
        every available space was filled with jonquils. No vases to
        hold them? All right, I'll hold them myself! And then I—
95   *(She stops in front of the picture. Music plays.)* met your fa-
        ther! Malaria fever and jonquils and then—this—boy. . . .
        (She switches on the rose-colored lamp.) I hope they get here
        before it starts to rain. *(She crosses the room and places the
        jonquils in a bowl on the table.)* I gave your brother a little
100   extra change so he and Mr. O'Connor could take the service
        car home.

LAURA: *(With an altered look.)* What did you say his name
        was?

AMANDA: O'Connor.

105 LAURA: What is his first name?

AMANDA: I don't remember. Oh, yes, I do. It was—Jim!

(LAURA sways slightly and catches hold of a chair.)

(Legend on screen: "Not Jim!")

LAURA: *(Faintly.)* Not—Jim!

AMANDA: Yes, that was it, it was Jim! I've never known a Jim
        that wasn't nice!

(The music becomes ominous.)

110 LAURA: Are you sure his name is Jim O'Connor?

AMANDA: Yes. Why?

LAURA: Is he the one that Tom used to know in high school?

AMANDA: He didn't say so. I think he just got to know him at
        the warehouse.

LAURA: There was a Jim O'Connor we both knew in high   115
        school—*(Then, with effort.)* If that is the one that Tom is
        bringing to dinner—you'll have to excuse me, I won't come
        to the table.

AMANDA: What sort of nonsense is this?

LAURA: You asked me once if I'd ever liked a boy. Don't you   120
        remember I showed you this boy's picture?

AMANDA: You mean the boy you showed me in the yearbook?

LAURA: Yes, that boy.

AMANDA: Laura, Laura, were you in love with that boy?

LAURA: I don't know, Mother. All I know is I couldn't sit at the   125
        table if it was him!

AMANDA: It won't be him! It isn't the least bit likely. But
        whether it is or not, you will come to the table. You will not
        be excused.

LAURA: I'll have to be, Mother.   130

AMANDA: I don't intend to humor your silliness, Laura. I've
        had too much from you and your brother, both! So just sit
        down and compose yourself till they come. Tom has forgot-
        ten his key so you'll have to let them in, when they arrive.

LAURA: *(Panicky.)* Oh, Mother—*you* answer the door!   135

AMANDA: *(Lightly.)* I'll be in the kitchen—busy!

LAURA: Oh, Mother, please answer the door, don't make me
        do it!

AMANDA: *(Crossing into the kitchenette.)* I've got to fix the
        dressing for the salmon. Fuss, fuss—silliness!—over a gentle-   140
        man caller!

(The door swings shut. LAURA is left alone.)

(Legend on screen: "Terror!")

*(She utters a low moan and turns off the lamp—sits stiffly on the
edge of the sofa, knotting her fingers together.)*

(Legend on screen: "The Opening of a Door!")

*(TOM and JIM appear on the fire escape steps and climb to the
landing. Hearing their approach, LAURA rises with a panicky
gesture. She retreats to the portieres. The doorbell rings. LAURA
catches her breath and touches her throat. Low drums sound.)*

AMANDA: *(Calling.)* Laura, sweetheart! The door!

(LAURA stares at it without moving.)

JIM: I think we just beat the rain.

TOM: Uh-huh. *(He rings again, nervously. JIM whistles and
        fishes for a cigarette.)*   145

AMANDA: *(Very, very gaily.)* Laura, that is your brother and Mr.
        O'Connor! Will you let them in, darling?

(LAURA crosses toward the kitchenette door.)

LAURA: *(Breathlessly.)* Mother—you go to the door!

*(AMANDA steps out of the kitchenette and stares furiously at
LAURA. She points imperiously at the door.)*

LAURA: Please, please!

AMANDA: *(In a fierce whisper.)* What is the matter with you,   150
        you silly thing?

LAURA: *(Desperately.)* Please, you answer it, *please!*

AMANDA: I told you I wasn't going to humor you, Laura. Why
        have you chosen this moment to lose your mind?

155 LAURA: Please, please, please, you go!
AMANDA: You'll have to go to the door because I can't!
LAURA: (*Despairingly.*) I can't either!
AMANDA: *Why?*
LAURA: I'm *sick!*
160 AMANDA: I'm sick, too—of your nonsense! Why can't you and your brother be normal people? Fantastic whims and behavior!

(TOM *gives a long ring.*)

Preposterous goings on! Can you give me one reason—(*She calls out lyrically.*) *Coming! Just one second!*—why you
165 should be afraid to open a door? Now you answer it, Laura!
LAURA: Oh, oh, oh . . . (*She returns through the portieres, darts to the Victrola, winds it frantically and turns it on.*)
AMANDA: Laura Wingfield, you march right to that door!
LAURA: *Yes—yes, Mother!*

(*A faraway, scratchy rendition of "Dardanella" softens the air and gives her strength to move through it. She slips to the door and draws it cautiously open.* TOM *enters with the caller,* JIM O'CONNOR.)

170 TOM: Laura, this is Jim. Jim, this is my sister, Laura.
JIM: (*Stepping inside.*) I didn't know that Shakespeare had a sister!
LAURA: (*Retreating, stiff and trembling, from the door.*) How—how do you do?
175 JIM: (*Heartily, extending his hand.*) Okay!

(LAURA *touches it hesitantly with hers.*)

JIM: Your hand's *cold*, Laura!
LAURA: Yes, well—I've been playing the Victrola. . . .
JIM: Must have been playing classical music on it! You ought to play a little hot swing music to warm you up!
180 LAURA: Excuse me—I haven't finished playing the Victrola. . . . (*She turns awkwardly and hurries into the front room. She pauses a second by the Victrola. Then she catches her breath and darts through the portieres like a frightened deer.*)
JIM: (*Grinning.*) What was the matter?
185 TOM: Oh—with Laura? Laura is—terribly shy.
JIM: Shy, huh? It's unusual to meet a shy girl nowadays. I don't believe you ever mentioned you had a sister.
TOM: Well, now you know. I have one. Here is the Post Dispatch. You want a piece of it?
190 JIM: Uh-huh.
TOM: What piece? The comics?
JIM: Sports! (*He glances at it.*) Ole Dizzy Dean is on his bad behavior.
TOM: (*Uninterested.*) Yeah? (*He lights a cigarette and goes over
195 to the fire-escape door.*)
JIM: Where are *you* going?
TOM: I'm going out on the terrace.
JIM: (*Going after him.*) You know, Shakespeare—I'm going to sell you a bill of goods!
200 TOM: What goods?
JIM: A course I'm taking.
TOM: Huh?
JIM: In public speaking! You and me, we're not the warehouse type.
205 TOM: Thanks—that's good news. But what has public speaking got to do with it?

JIM: It fits you for—executive positions!
TOM: Awww.
JIM: I tell you it's done a helluva lot for me.

(*Image on screen:* Executive at his desk.)

TOM: In what respect? 210
JIM: In every! Ask yourself what is the difference between you an' me and men in the office down front? Brains?—No!—Ability?—No! Then what? Just one little thing—
TOM: What is that one little thing?
JIM: Primarily it amounts to—social poise! Being able to 215 square up to people and hold your own on any social level!
AMANDA: (*From the kitchenette.*) Tom?
TOM: Yes, Mother?
AMANDA: Is that you and Mr. O'Connor?
TOM: Yes, Mother. 220
AMANDA: Well, you just make yourselves comfortable in there.
TOM: Yes, Mother.
AMANDA: Ask Mr. O'Connor if he would like to wash his hands.
JIM: Aw, no—no—thank you—I took care of that at the ware- 225 house. Tom—
TOM: Yes?
JIM: Mr. Mendoza was speaking to me about you.
TOM: Favorably?
JIM: What do you think? 230
TOM: Well—
JIM: You're going to be out of a job if you don't wake up.
TOM: I am waking up—
JIM: You show no signs.
TOM: The signs are interior. 235

(*Image on screen:* The sailing vessel with the Jolly Roger again.)

TOM: I'm planning to change. (*He leans over the fire-escape rail, speaking with quiet exhilaration. The incandescent marquees and signs of the first-run movie houses light his face from across the alley. He looks like a voyager.*) I'm right at the point of committing myself to a future that doesn't include 240 the warehouse and Mr. Mendoza or even a night-school course in public speaking.
JIM: What are you gassing about?
TOM: I'm tired of the movies.
JIM: Movies! 245
TOM: Yes, movies! Look at them—(*A wave toward the marvels of Grand Avenue.*) All of those glamorous people—having adventures—hogging it all, gobbling the whole thing up! You know what happens? People go to the *movies* instead of *moving!* Hollywood characters are supposed to have all the 250 adventures for everybody in America, while everybody in America sits in a dark room and watches them have them! Yes, until there's a war. That's when adventure becomes available to the masses! *Everyone's* dish, not only Gable's! Then the people in the dark room come out of the dark 255 room to have some adventures themselves—goody, goody! It's our turn now, to go to the South Sea Island—to make a safari—to be exotic, far-off! But I'm not patient. I don't want to wait till then. I'm tired of the *movies* and I am *about* to *move!* 260
JIM: (*Incredulously.*) Move?
TOM: Yes.
JIM: When?

TOM: Soon!

265 JIM: Where? Where?

(The music seems to answer the question, while TOM *thinks it over. He searches in his pockets.)*

TOM: I'm starting to boil inside. I know I seem dreamy, but inside—well, I'm boiling! Whenever I pick up a shoe, I shudder a little thinking how short life is and what I am doing! Whatever that means, I know it doesn't mean shoes—except as something to wear on a traveler's feet! *(He finds what he has been searching for in his pockets and holds out a paper to Jim.)* Look—

JIM: What?

TOM: I'm a member.

275 JIM: *(Reading.)* The Union of Merchant Seamen.

TOM: I paid my dues this month, instead of the light bill.

JIM: You will regret it when they turn the lights off.

TOM: I won't be here.

JIM: How about your mother?

280 TOM: I'm like my father. The bastard son of a bastard! Did you notice how he's grinning in his picture in there? And he's been absent going on sixteen years!

JIM: You're just talking, you drip. How does your mother feel about it?

285 TOM: Shhh! Here comes Mother! Mother is not acquainted with my plans!

AMANDA: *(Coming through the portieres.)* Where are you all?

TOM: On the terrace, Mother.

(They start inside. She advances to them. TOM *is distinctly shocked at her appearance. Even* JIM *blinks a little. He is making his first contact with girlish Southern vivacity and in spite of the night-school course in public speaking is somewhat thrown off the beam by the unexpected outlay of social charm. Certain responses are attempted by* JIM *but are swept aside by* AMANDA's *gay laughter and chatter.* TOM *is embarrassed but after the first shock* JIM *reacts very warmly. He grins and chuckles, is altogether won over.)*

(Image on screen: AMANDA *as a girl.)*

AMANDA: *(Coyly smiling, shaking her girlish ringlets.)* Well,
290 well, well, so this is Mr. O'Connor. Introductions entirely unnecessary. I've heard so much about you from my boy. I finally said to him, Tom—good gracious!—why don't you bring this paragon to supper? I'd like to meet this nice young man at the warehouse!—instead of just hearing him sing
295 your praises so much! I don't know why my son is so standoffish—that's not Southern behavior!

Let's sit down and—I think we could stand a little more air in here! Tom, leave the door open. I felt a nice fresh breeze a moment ago. Where has it gone to? Mmm, so
300 warm already! And not quite summer, even. We're going to burn up when summer really gets started. However, we're having—we're having a very light supper. I think light things are better fo' this time of year. The same as light clothes are. Light clothes an' light food are what warm weather calls fo'.
305 You know our blood gets so thick during th' winter—it takes a while fo' us to *adjust* ou'selves!—when the season changes ... It's come so quick this year. I wasn't prepared. All of a sudden—heavens! Already summer! I ran to the trunk an' pulled out this light dress—terribly old! Historical almost!
310 But feels so good—so good an' co-ol, y' know....

TOM: Mother—

AMANDA: Yes, honey?

TOM: How about—supper?

AMANDA: Honey, you go ask Sister if supper is ready! You know that Sister is in full charge of supper! Tell her you hungry
315 boys are waiting for it. *(To* JIM.*)* Have you met Laura?

JIM: She—

AMANDA: Let you in? Oh, good, you've met already! It's rare for a girl as sweet an' pretty as Laura to be domestic! But Laura is, thank heavens, not only pretty but also very domes-
320 tic. I'm not at all. I never was a bit. I never could make a thing but angel-food cake. Well, in the South we had so many servants. Gone, gone, gone. All vestige of gracious living! Gone completely! I wasn't prepared for what the future brought me. All of my gentlemen callers were sons of
325 planters and so of course I assumed that I would be married to one and raise my family on a large piece of land with plenty of servants. But man proposes—and woman accepts the proposal! To vary that old, old saying a little bit—I married no planter! I married a man who worked for the tele-
330 phone company! That gallantly smiling gentleman over there! *(She points to the picture.)* A telephone man who— fell in love with long-distance! Now he travels and I don't even know where! But what am I going on for about my— tribulations? Tell me yours—I hope you don't have any!
335 Tom?

TOM: *(Returning.)* Yes, Mother?

AMANDA: Is supper nearly ready?

TOM: It looks to me like supper is on the table.

AMANDA: Let me look—*(She rises prettily and looks through*
340 *the portieres.)* Oh, lovely! But where is Sister?

TOM: Laura is not feeling well and she says that she thinks she'd better not come to the table.

AMANDA: What? Nonsense! Laura? Oh, Laura!

LAURA: *(From the kitchenette, faintly.)* Yes, Mother.
345 AMANDA: You really must come to the table. We won't be seated until you come to the table! Come in, Mr. O'Connor. You sit over there, and I'll.... Laura? Laura Wingfield! You're keeping us waiting, honey! We can't say grace until you come to the table!
350

(The kitchenette door is pushed weakly open and LAURA *comes in. She is obviously quite faint, her lips trembling, her eyes wide and staring. She moves unsteadily toward the table.)*

(Screen legend: "Terror!")

(Outside a summer storm is coming on abruptly. The white curtains billow inward at the windows and there is a sorrowful murmur from the deep blue dusk.)

(LAURA suddenly stumbles; she catches at a chair with a faint moan.)

TOM: Laura!

AMANDA: Laura!

(There is a clap of thunder.)

(Screen legend: "Ah!")

(Despairingly.) Why, Laura, you *are* ill, darling! Tom, help your sister into the living room, dear! Sit in the living room, Laura—rest on the sofa. Well! *(to* JIM *as* TOM *helps his sister*
355 *to the sofa in the living room.)* Standing over the hot stove

made her ill! I told her that it was just too warm this evening, but—

(TOM *comes back to the table.*)

Is Laura all right now?

360 TOM: Yes.

AMANDA: What *is* that? Rain? A nice cool rain has come up! (*She gives* JIM *a frightened look.*) I think we may—have grace—now . . .

(TOM *looks at her stupidly.*) Tom, honey—you say grace!

365 TOM: Oh . . . "For these and all thy mercies—"

(*They bow their heads,* AMANDA *stealing a nervous glance at* JIM. *In the living room* LAURA, *stretched on the sofa, clenches her hand to her lips, to hold back a shuddering sob.*)

God's Holy Name be praised—

(*The scene dims out.*)

— SCENE SEVEN —

It is half an hour later. Dinner is just being finished in the dining room. LAURA *is still huddled upon the sofa, her feet drawn under her, her head resting on a pale blue pillow, her eyes wide and mysteriously watchful. The new floor lamp with its shade of rose-colored silk gives a soft, becoming light to her face, bringing out the fragile, unearthly prettiness which usually escapes attention. From outside there is a steady murmur of rain, but it is slackening and soon stops; the air outside becomes pale and luminous as the moon breaks through the clouds. A moment after the curtain rises, the lights in both rooms flicker and go out.*

JIM: Hey, there, Mr. Light Bulb!

(AMANDA *laughs nervously.*)

(*Legend on screen:* "Suspension of a public service.")

AMANDA: Where was Moses when the lights went out? Ha-ha. Do you know the answer to that one, Mr. O'Connor?

LAURA: No, Ma'am, what's the answer?

5 AMANDA: In the dark!

(JIM *laughs appreciatively.*)

Everybody sit still. I'll light the candles. Isn't it lucky we have them on the table? Where's a match? Which of you gentlemen can provide a match?

JIM: Here.

10 AMANDA: Thank you, Sir.

JIM: Not at all, Ma'am!

AMANDA: (*As she lights the candles.*) I guess the fuse has burnt out. Mr. O'Connor, can you tell a burnt-out fuse? I know I can't and Tom is a total loss when it comes to mechanics.

(*They rise from the table and go into the kitchenette, from where their voices are heard.*)

15 Oh, be careful you don't bump into something. We don't want our gentleman caller to break his neck. Now wouldn't that be a fine howdy-do?

JIM: Ha-ha! Where is the fuse-box?

AMANDA: Right here next to the stove. Can you see anything?

20 JIM: Just a minute.

AMANDA: Isn't electricity a mysterious thing? Wasn't it Benjamin Franklin who tied a key to a kite? We live in such a mysterious universe, don't we? Some people say that science

clears up all the mysteries for us. In my opinion it only creates more! Have you found it yet?

25 JIM: No, Ma'am. All these fuses look okay to me.

AMANDA: Tom!

TOM: Yes, Mother?

AMANDA: That light bill I gave you several days ago. The one I told you we got the notices about?

30 (*Legend on screen:* "Ha!")

TOM: Oh—yeah.

AMANDA: You didn't neglect to pay it by any chance?

TOM: Why, I—

AMANDA: Didn't! I might have known it!

35 JIM: Shakespeare probably wrote a poem on that light bill, Mrs. Wingfield.

AMANDA: I might have known better than to trust him with it! There's such a high price for negligence in this world!

JIM: Maybe the poem will win a ten-dollar prize.

40 AMANDA: We'll just have to spend the remainder of the evening in the nineteenth century, before Mr. Edison made the Mazda lamp!

JIM: Candlelight is my favorite kind of light.

AMANDA: That shows you're romantic! But that's no excuse for Tom. Well, we got through dinner. Very considerate of them

45 to let us get through dinner before they plunged us into everlasting darkness, wasn't it, Mr. O'Connor?

JIM: Ha-ha!

AMANDA: Tom, as a penalty for your carelessness you can help me with the dishes.

50 JIM: Let me give you a hand.

AMANDA: Indeed you will not!

JIM: I ought to be good for something.

AMANDA: Good for something? (*Her tone is rhapsodic.*) You? Why, Mr. O'Connor, nobody, *nobody's* given me this much

55 entertainment in years—as you have!

JIM: Aw, now, Mrs. Wingfield!

AMANDA: I'm not exaggerating, not one bit! But Sister is all by her lonesome. You go keep her company in the parlor! I'll give you this lovely old candelabrum that used to be on the

60 altar at the Church of the Heavenly Rest. It was melted a little out of shape when the church burnt down. Lightning struck it one spring. Gypsy Jones was holding a revival at the time and he intimated that the church was destroyed because the Episcopalians gave card parties.

65 JIM: Ha-ha.

AMANDA: And how about you coaxing Sister to drink a little wine? I think it would be good for her! Can you carry both at once?

70 JIM: Sure. I'm Superman!

AMANDA: Now, Thomas, get into this apron!

(JIM *comes into the dining room, carrying the candelabrum, its candles lighted, in one hand and a glass of wine in the other. The door of the kitchenette swings closed on* AMANDA's *gay laughter; the flickering light approaches the portieres.* LAURA *sits up nervously as* JIM *enters. She can hardly speak from the almost intolerable strain of being alone with a stranger.*)

(*Screen legend:* "I don't suppose you remember me at all!")

(*At first, before* JIM's *warmth overcomes her paralyzing shyness,* LAURA's *voice is thin and breathless, as though she had just run up a steep flight of stairs.* JIM's *attitude is gently humorous.*

While the incident is apparently unimportant, it is to LAURA *the climax of her secret life.)*

JIM: Hello there, Laura.

LAURA: *(Faintly.)* Hello.

(She clears her throat.)

JIM: How are you feeling now? Better?

75 LAURA: Yes. Yes, thank you.

JIM: This is for you. A little dandelion wine. *(He extends the glass toward her with extravagant gallantry.)*

LAURA: Thank you.

JIM: Drink it—but don't get drunk!

(He laughs heartily. LAURA *takes the glass uncertainly; she laughs shyly.)*

80   Where shall I set the candles?

LAURA: Oh—oh, anywhere . . .

JIM: How about here on the floor? Any objections?

LAURA: No.

JIM: I'll spread a newspaper under to catch the drippings. I like

85   to sit on the floor. Mind if I do?

LAURA: Oh, no.

JIM: Give me a pillow?

LAURA: What?

JIM: A pillow!

90 LAURA: Oh . . . *(She hands him one quickly.)*

JIM: How about you? Don't you like to sit on the floor?

LAURA: Oh—yes.

JIM: Why don't you, then?

LAURA: I—will.

95 JIM: Take a pillow!

*(*LAURA *does. She sits on the floor on the other side of the candelabrum.* JIM *crosses his legs and smiles engagingly at her.)* I can't hardly see you sitting way over there.

LAURA: I can—see you.

100 JIM: I know, but that's not fair, I'm in the limelight.

*(*LAURA *moves her pillow closer.)*

Good! Now I can see you! Comfortable?

LAURA: Yes.

JIM: So am I. Comfortable as a cow! Will you have some gum?

LAURA: No, thank you.

105 JIM: I think that I will indulge, with your permission. *(He musingly unwraps a stick of gum and holds it up.)* Think of the fortune made by the guy that invented the first piece of chewing gum. Amazing, huh? The Wrigley Building is one of the sights of Chicago—I saw it when I went up to the Cen-

110   tury of Progress. Did you take in the Century of Progress?

LAURA: No, I didn't.

JIM: Well, it was quite a wonderful exposition. What impressed me most was the Hall of Science. Gives you an idea of what the future will be in America, even more wonderful than the

115   present time is! *(There is a pause. Jim smiles at her.)* Your brother tells me you're shy. Is that right, Laura?

LAURA: I—don't know.

JIM: I judge you to be an old-fashioned type of girl. Well, I think that's a pretty good type to be. Hope you don't think

120   I'm being too personal—do you?

LAURA: *(Hastily, out of embarrassment.)* I believe I *will* take a piece of gum, if you—don't mind. *(Clearing her throat.)* Mr. O'Connor, have you—kept up with your singing?

JIM: Singing? Me?

LAURA: Yes. I remember what a beautiful voice you had.   125

JIM: When did you hear me sing?

*(*LAURA *does not answer, and in the long pause which follows a man's voice is heard singing offstage.)*

VOICE:

O blow, ye winds, heigh-ho,
A-roving I will go!
   I'm off to my love
   With a boxing glove—   130
   Ten thousand miles away!

JIM: You say you've heard me sing?

LAURA: Oh, yes! Yes, very often . . . I—don't suppose—you remember me—at all?

JIM: *(Smiling doubtfully.)* You know I have an idea I've seen   135 you before. I had that idea soon as you opened the door. It seemed almost like I was about to remember your name. But the name that I started to call you—wasn't a name! And so I stopped myself before I said it.

LAURA: Wasn't it—Blue Roses?   140

JIM: *(Springing up, grinning.)* Blue Roses! My gosh, yes—Blue Roses! That's what I had on my tongue when you opened the door! Isn't it funny what tricks your memory plays? I didn't connect you with high school somehow or other. But that's where it was; it was high school. I didn't even know you were   145 Shakespeare's sister! Gosh, I'm sorry.

LAURA: I didn't expect you to. You—barely knew me!

JIM: But we did have a speaking acquaintance, huh?

LAURA: Yes, we—spoke to each other.

JIM: When did you recognize me?   150

LAURA: Oh, right away!

JIM: Soon as I came in the door?

LAURA: When I heard your name I thought it was probably you. I knew that Tom used to know you a little in high school. So when you came in the door—well, then I was—   155 sure.

JIM: Why didn't you *say* something, then?

LAURA: *(Breathlessly.)* I didn't know what to say, I was—too surprised!

JIM: For goodness' sakes! You know, this sure is funny!   160

LAURA: Yes! Yes, isn't it, though . . .

JIM: Didn't we have a class in something together?

LAURA: Yes, we did.

JIM: What class was that?

LAURA: It was—singing—chorus!   165

JIM: Aw!

LAURA: I sat across the aisle from you in the Aud.

JIM: Aw.

LAURA: Mondays, Wednesdays, and Fridays.

JIM: Now I remember—you always came in late.   170

LAURA: Yes, it was so hard for me, getting upstairs. I had that brace on my leg—it clumped so loud!

JIM: I never heard any clumping.

LAURA: *(Wincing at the recollection.)* To me it sounded like— thunder!   175

JIM: Well, well, well, I never even noticed.

LAURA: And everybody was seated before I came in. I had to walk in front of all those people. My seat was in the back row. I had to go clumping all the way up the aisle with everyone watching!   180

JIM: You shouldn't have been self-conscious.

LAURA: I know, but I was. It was always such a relief when the
singing started.

185 JIM: Aw, yes, I've placed you now! I used to call you Blue
Roses. How was it that I got started calling you that?

LAURA: I was out of school a little while with pleurosis. When I
came back you asked me what was the matter. I said I had
pleurosis—you thought I said *Blue Roses*. That's what you always called me after that!

190 JIM: I hope you didn't mind.

LAURA: Oh, no—I liked it. You see, I wasn't acquainted with
many—people. . . .

JIM: As I remember you sort of stuck by yourself.

LAURA: I—I—never have had much luck at—making friends.

195 JIM: I don't see why you wouldn't.

LAURA: Well, I—started out badly.

JIM: You mean being—

LAURA: Yes, it sort of—stood between me—

JIM: You shouldn't have let it!

200 LAURA: I know, but it did, and—

JIM: You were shy with people!

LAURA: I tried not to be but never could—

JIM: Overcome it?

LAURA: No, I—I never could!

205 JIM: I guess being shy is something you have to work out of
kind of gradually.

LAURA: *(Sorrowfully.)* Yes—I guess it—

JIM: Takes time!

LAURA: Yes—

210 JIM: People are not so dreadful when you know them. That's
what you have to remember! And everybody has problems,
not just you, but practically everybody has got some problems. You think of yourself as having the only problems, as
being the only one who is disappointed. But just look around

215 you and you will see lots of people as disappointed as you are.
For instance, I hoped when I was going to high school that I
would be further along at this time, six years later, than I am
now. You remember that wonderful write-up I had in *The
Torch?*

220 LAURA: Yes! *(She rises and crosses to the table.)*

JIM: It said I was bound to succeed in anything I went into!

(LAURA returns with the high school yearbook.)

Holy Jeez! *The Torch!*

*(He accepts it reverently. They smile across the book with mutual
wonder. LAURA crouches beside him and they begin to turn the
pages. LAURA's shyness is dissolving in his warmth.)*

LAURA: Here you are in *The Pirates of Penzance!*

JIM: *(Wistfully.)* I sang the baritone lead in that operetta.

225 LAURA: *(Raptly.)* So—beautifully!

JIM: *(Protesting.)* Aw—

LAURA: Yes, yes—beautifully—beautifully!

JIM: You heard me?

LAURA: All three times!

230 JIM: No!

LAURA: Yes!

JIM: All three performances?

LAURA: *(Looking down.)* Yes.

JIM: Why?

235 LAURA: I—wanted to ask you to—autograph my program. *(She
takes the program from the back of the yearbook and shows it
to him.)*

JIM: Why didn't you ask me to?

LAURA: You were always surrounded by your own friends so
much that I never had a chance to.   240

JIM: You should have just—

LAURA: Well, I—thought you might think I was—

JIM: Thought I might think you was—what?

LAURA: Oh—

JIM: *(With reflective relish.)* I was beleaguered by females in   245
those days.

LAURA: You were terribly popular!

JIM: Yeah—

LAURA: You had such a—friendly way—

JIM: I was spoiled in high school.   250

LAURA: Everybody—liked you!

JIM: Including you?

LAURA: I—yes, I—did, too—*(She gently closes the book in her
lap.)*

JIM: Well, well, well! Give me that program, Laura.   255

(She hands it to him. He signs it with a flourish.)

There you are—better late than never!

LAURA: Oh, I—what a—surprise!

JIM: My signature isn't worth very much right now. But some
day—maybe—it will increase in value! Being disappointed
is one thing and being discouraged is something else. I am   260
disappointed but I am not discouraged. I'm twenty-three
years old. How old are you?

LAURA: I'll be twenty-four in June.

JIM: That's not old age!

LAURA: No, but—   265

JIM: You finished high school?

LAURA: *(With difficulty.)* I didn't go back.

JIM: You mean you dropped out?

LAURA: I made bad grades in my final examinations. *(She rises
and replaces the book and the program on the table. Her voice   270
is strained.)* How is—Emily Meisenbach getting along?

JIM: Oh, that kraut-head!

LAURA: Why do you call her that?

JIM: That's what she was.

LAURA: You're not still—going with her?   275

JIM: I never see her.

LAURA: It said in the "Personal" section that you were—
engaged!

JIM: I know, but I wasn't impressed by that—propaganda!

LAURA: It wasn't—the truth?   280

JIM: Only in Emily's optimistic opinion!

LAURA: Oh—

(Legend: "What have you done since high school?")

*(JIM lights a cigarette and leans indolently back on his elbows
smiling at LAURA with a warmth and charm which lights her inwardly with altar candles. She remains by the table, picks up a
piece from the glass menagerie collection, and turns it in her
hands to cover her tumult.)*

JIM: *(After several reflective puffs on his cigarette.)* What have
you done since high school?

(She seems not to hear him.)

Huh?   285

(LAURA looks up.)

I said what have you done since high school, Laura?

LAURA: Nothing much.

JIM: You must have been doing something these six long years.

LAURA: Yes.

290 JIM: Well, then, such as what?

LAURA: I took a business course at business college—

JIM: How did that work out?

LAURA: Well, not very—well—I had to drop out, it gave me—indigestion—

(JIM laughs gently.)

295 JIM: What are you doing now?

LAURA: I don't do anything—much. Oh, please don't think I sit around doing nothing! My glass collection takes up a good deal of time. Glass is something you have to take good care of.

300 JIM: What did you say—about glass?

LAURA: Collection I said—I have one—*(She clears her throat and turns away again, acutely shy.)*

JIM: *(Abruptly.)* You know what I judge to be the trouble with you? Inferiority complex! Know what that is? That's what

305 they call it when someone low-rates himself! I understand it because I had it, too. Although my case was not so aggravated as yours seems to be. I had it until I took up public speaking, developed my voice, and learned that I had an aptitude for science. Before that time I never thought of myself

310 as being outstanding in any way whatsoever! Now I've never made a regular study of it, but I have a friend who says I can analyze people better than doctors that make a profession of it. I don't claim that to be necessarily true, but I can sure guess a person's psychology, Laura! *(He takes out his gum.)*

315 Excuse me, Laura. I always take it out when the flavor is gone. I'll use this scrap of paper to wrap it in. I know how it is to get it stuck on a shoe. *(He wraps the gum in paper and puts it in his pocket.)* Yep—that's what I judge to be your principal trouble. A lack of confidence in yourself as a per-

320 son. You don't have the proper amount of faith in yourself. I'm basing that fact on a number of your remarks and also on certain observations I've made. For instance that clumping you thought was so awful in high school. You say that you even dreaded to walk into class. You see what you did? You

325 dropped out of school, you gave up an education because of a clump, which as far as I know was practically non-existent! A little physical defect is what you have. Hardly noticeable even! Magnified thousands of times by imagination! You know what my strong advice to you is? Think of yourself as

330 *superior* in some way!

LAURA: In what way would I think?

JIM: Why, man alive, Laura! Just look about you a little. What do you see? A world full of common people! All of 'em born and all of 'em going to die! Which of them has one-tenth of

335 your good points! Or mine! Or anyone else's, as far as that goes—gosh! Everybody excels in some one thing. Some in many! *(He unconsciously glances at himself in the mirror.)* All you've got to do is discover in *what!* Take me, for instance. *(He adjusts his tie at the mirror.)* My interest happens to lie

340 in electro-dynamics. I'm taking a course in radio engineering at night school, Laura, on top of a fairly responsible job at the warehouse. I'm taking that course and studying public speaking.

LAURA: Ohhhh.

345 JIM: Because I believe in the future of television! *(Turning his back to her.)* I wish to be ready to go up right along with it.

Therefore I'm planning to get in on the ground floor. In fact I've already made the right connections and all that remains is for the industry itself to get under way! Full steam—*(His eyes are starry.)* Knowledge—Zzzzzp! Money—Zzzzzp!— 350 Power! That's the cycle democracy is built on!

(His attitude is convincingly dynamic. LAURA *stares at him, even her shyness eclipsed in her absolute wonder. He suddenly grins.)*

I guess you think I think a lot of myself!

LAURA: No—o-o-o, I—

JIM: Now how about you? Isn't there something you take more interest in than anything else?   355

LAURA: Well, I do—as I said—have my—glass collection—

(A peal of girlish laughter rings from the kitchenette.)

JIM: I'm not right sure I know what you're talking about. What kind of glass is it?

LAURA: Little articles of it, they're ornaments mostly! Most of them are little animals made out of glass, the tiniest little 360 animals in the world. Mother calls them a glass menagerie! Here's an example of one, if you'd like to see it! This one is one of the oldest. It's nearly thirteen.

(Music: "The Glass Menagerie.")

(He stretches out his hand.)

Oh, be careful—if you breathe, it breaks!

JIM: I'd better not take it. I'm pretty clumsy with things.   365

LAURA: Go on, I trust you with him! *(She places the piece in his palm.)* There now—you're holding him gently! Hold him over the light, he loves the light! You see how the light shines through him?

JIM: It sure does shine!   370

LAURA: I shouldn't be partial, but he is my favorite one.

JIM: What kind of a thing is this one supposed to be?

LAURA: Haven't you noticed the single horn on his forehead?

JIM: A unicorn, huh?

LAURA: Mmmm-hmmm!   375

JIM: Unicorns—aren't they extinct in the modern world?

LAURA: I know!

JIM: Poor little fellow, he must feel sort of lonesome.

LAURA: *(Smiling.)* Well, if he does, he doesn't complain about it. He stays on a shelf with some horses that don't have horns 380 and all of them seem to get along nicely together.

JIM: How do you know?

LAURA: *(Lightly.)* I haven't heard any arguments among them!

JIM: *(Grinning.)* No arguments, huh? Well, that's a pretty good sign! Where shall I set him?   385

LAURA: Put him on the table. They all like a change of scenery once in a while!

JIM: Well, well, well, well—*(He places the glass piece on the table, then raises his arms and stretches.)* Look how big my shadow is when I stretch!   390

LAURA: Oh, oh, yes—it stretches across the ceiling!

JIM: *(Crossing to the door.)* I think it's stopped raining. *(He opens the fire-escape door and the background music changes to a dance tune.)* Where does the music come from?

LAURA: From the Paradise Dance Hall across the alley.   395

JIM: How about cutting the rug a little, Miss Wingfield?

LAURA: Oh, I—

JIM: Or is your program filled up? Let me have a look at it. *(He grasps an imaginary card.)* Why, every dance is taken! I'll just have to scratch some out.   400

(Waltz music: "La Golondrina.")

Ahhh, a waltz! *(He executes some sweeping turns by himself, then holds his arms toward Laura.)*

LAURA: *(Breathlessly.)* I—can't dance!

JIM: There you go, that inferiority stuff!

405 LAURA: I've never danced in my life!

JIM: Come on, try!

LAURA: Oh, but I'd step on you!

JIM: I'm not made out of glass.

LAURA: How—how—how do we start?

410 JIM: Just leave it to me. You hold your arms out a little.

LAURA: Like this?

JIM: *(Taking her in his arms.)* A little bit higher. Right. Now don't tighten up, that's the main thing about it—relax.

LAURA: *(Laughing breathlessly.)* It's hard not to.

415 JIM: Okay.

LAURA: I'm afraid you can't budge me.

JIM: What do you bet I can't? *(He swings her into motion.)*

LAURA: Goodness, yes, you can!

JIM: Let yourself go, now, Laura, just let yourself go.

420 LAURA: I'm—

JIM: Come on!

LAURA: —trying!

JIM: Not so stiff—easy does it!

LAURA: I know but I'm—

425 JIM: Loosen th' backbone! There now, that's a lot better.

LAURA: Am I?

JIM: Lots, lots better! *(He moves her about the room in a clumsy waltz.)*

LAURA: Oh, my!

430 JIM: Ha-ha!

LAURA: Oh, my goodness!

JIM: Ha-ha-ha!

(They suddenly bump into the table, and the glass piece on it falls to the floor. JIM stops the dance.)

What did we hit on?

LAURA: Table.

435 JIM: Did something fall off it? I think—

LAURA: Yes.

JIM: I hope that it wasn't the little glass horse with the horn!

LAURA: Yes. *(She stoops to pick it up.)*

JIM: Aw, aw, aw. Is it broken?

440 LAURA: Now it is just like all the other horses.

JIM: It's lost its—

LAURA: Horn! It doesn't matter. Maybe it's a blessing in disguise.

JIM: You'll never forgive me. I bet that that was your favorite
445 piece of glass.

LAURA: I don't have favorites much. It's no tragedy, Freckles. Glass breaks so easily. No matter how careful you are. The traffic jars the shelves and things fall off them.

JIM: Still I'm awfully sorry that I was the cause.

450 LAURA: *(Smiling.)* I'll just imagine he had an operation. The horn was removed to make him feel less—freakish!

(They both laugh.)

Now he will feel more at home with the other horses, the ones that don't have horns. . . .

JIM: Ha-ha, that's very funny! *(Suddenly he is serious.)* I'm glad
455 to see that you have a sense of humor. You know—you're—

well—very different! Surprisingly different from anyone else I know! *(His voice becomes soft and hesitant with a genuine feeling.)* Do you mind me telling you that?

(LAURA is abashed beyond speech.)

I mean it in a nice way—

(LAURA nods shyly, looking away.)

You make me feel sort of—I don't know how to put it! I'm 460 usually pretty good at expressing things, but—this is something that I don't know how to say!

(LAURA touches her throat and clears it—turns the broken unicorn in her hands. His voice becomes softer.)

Has anyone ever told you that you were pretty?

(There is a pause, and the music rises slightly. LAURA looks up slowly, with wonder, and shakes her head.)

Well, you are! In a very different way from anyone else. And all the nicer because of the difference, too. 465

(His voice becomes low and husky. LAURA turns away, nearly faint with the novelty of her emotions.)

I wish that you were my sister. I'd teach you to have some confidence in yourself. The different people are not like other people, but being different is nothing to be ashamed of. Because other people are not such wonderful people. They're one hundred times one thousand. You're one times 470 one! They walk all over the earth. You just stay here. They're common as—weeds, but—you—well, you're—*Blue Roses!*

(Image on screen: Blue Roses.)

(The music changes.)

LAURA: But blue is wrong for—roses. . . .

JIM: It's right for you! You're—pretty!

LAURA: In what respect am I pretty? 475

JIM: In all respects—believe me! Your eyes—your hair—are pretty! Your hands are pretty! *(He catches hold of her hand.)* You think I'm making this up because I'm invited to dinner and have to be nice. Oh, I could do that! I could put on an act for you, Laura, and say lots of things without being very 480 sincere. But this time I am. I'm talking to you sincerely. I happened to notice you had this inferiority complex that keeps you from feeling comfortable with people. Somebody needs to build your confidence up and make you proud instead of shy and turning away and—blushing. Somebody— 485 ought to—*kiss you, Laura!*

(His hand slips slowly up her arm to her shoulder as the music swells tumultuously. He suddenly turns her about and kisses her on the lips. When he releases her, LAURA sinks on the sofa with a bright, dazed look. JIM backs away and fishes in his pocket for a cigarette.)

(Legend on screen: "A souvenir.")

Stumblejohn!

(He lights the cigarette, avoiding her look. There is a peal of girlish laughter from AMANDA in the kitchenette. LAURA slowly raises and opens her hand. It still contains the little broken glass animal. She looks at it with a tender, bewildered expression.)

Stumblejohn! I shouldn't have done that—that was way off the beam. You don't smoke, do you?

(She looks up, smiling, not hearing the question. He sits beside her rather gingerly. She looks at him speechlessly—waiting. He coughs decorously and moves a little farther aside as he considers the situation and senses her feelings, dimly, with perturbation. He speaks gently.)

490   Would you—care for a—mint?

(She doesn't seem to hear him but her look grows brighter even.)

Peppermint? Life Saver? My pocket's a regular drugstore—wherever I go.... *(He pops a mint in his mouth. Then he gulps and decides to make a clean breast of it. He speaks slowly and gingerly.)* Laura, you know, if I had a sister like

495   you, I'd do the same thing as Tom. I'd bring out fellows and—introduce her to them. The right type of boys—of a type to—appreciate her. Only—well—he made a mistake about me. Maybe I've got no call to be saying this. That may not have been the idea in having me over. But what if it was?

500   There's nothing wrong about that. The only trouble is that in my case—I'm not in a situation to—do the right thing. I can't take down your number and say I'll phone. I can't call up next week and—ask for a date. I thought I had better explain the situation in case you—misunderstood it and—I

505   hurt your feelings....

(There is a pause. Slowly, very slowly, LAURA's look changes, her eyes returning slowly from his to the glass figure in her palm. AMANDA utters another gay laugh in the kitchenette.)

LAURA: *(Faintly.)* You—won't—call again?

JIM: No, Laura. I can't. *(He rises from the sofa.)* As I was just explaining, I've—got strings on me. Laura, I've—been going steady! I go out all the time with a girl named Betty. She's a

510   home-girl like you, and Catholic, and Irish, and in a great many ways we—get along fine. I met her last summer on a moonlight boat trip up the river to Alton, on the *Majestic*. Well—right away from the start it was—love!

(Legend: Love!)

(LAURA sways slightly forward and grips the arm of the sofa. He fails to notice, now enrapt in his own comfortable being.)

Being in love has made a new man of me!

(Leaning stiffly forward, clutching the arm of the sofa, LAURA struggles visibly with her storm. But JIM is oblivious; she is a long way off.)

515   The power of love is really pretty tremendous! Love is something that—changes the whole world, Laura!

(The storm abates a little and LAURA leans back. He notices her again.)

It happened that Betty's aunt took sick, she got a wire and had to go to Centralia. So Tom—when he asked me to dinner—I naturally just accepted the invitation, not knowing

520   that you— that he—that I—*(He stops awkwardly.)* Huh—I'm a stumblejohn!

(He flops back on the sofa. The holy candles on the altar of LAURA's face have been snuffed out. There is a look of almost infinite desolation. JIM glances at her uneasily.)

I wish that you would—say something.

(She bites her lip which was trembling and then bravely smiles. She opens her hand again on the broken glass figure. Then she

gently takes his hand and raises it level with her own. She carefully places the unicorn in the palm of his hand, then pushes his fingers closed upon it.)

What are you—doing that for? You want me to have him? Laura?

(She nods.)

What for?   525

LAURA: A—souvenir....

(She rises unsteadily and crouches beside the Victrola to wind it up.)

(Legend on screen: "Things have a way of turning out so badly!" Or image: "Gentleman caller waving goodbye—gaily.")

(At this moment AMANDA rushes brightly back into the living room. She bears a pitcher of fruit punch in an old-fashioned cut-glass pitcher, and a plate of macaroons. The plate has a gold border and poppies painted on it.)

AMANDA: Well, well, well! Isn't the air delightful after the shower? I've made you children a little liquid refreshment. *(She turns gaily to JIM.)* Jim, do you know that song about lemonade?   530

"Lemonade, lemonade
Made in the shade and stirred with a spade—
Good enough for any old maid!"

JIM: *(Uneasily.)* Ha-ha! No—I never heard it.

AMANDA: Why, Laura! You look so serious!   535

JIM: We were having a serious conversation.

AMANDA: Good! Now you're better acquainted!

JIM: *(Uncertainly.)* Ha-ha! Yes.

AMANDA: You modern young people are much more serious-minded than my generation. I was so gay as a girl!   540

JIM: You haven't changed, Mrs. Wingfield.

AMANDA: Tonight I'm rejuvenated! The gaiety of the occasion, Mr. O'Connor! *(She tosses her head with a peal of laughter, spilling some lemonade.)* Oooo! I'm baptizing myself!

JIM: Here—let me—   545

AMANDA: *(Setting the pitcher down.)* There now. I discovered we had some maraschino cherries. I dumped them in, juice and all!

JIM: You shouldn't have gone to that trouble, Mrs. Wingfield.

AMANDA: Trouble, trouble? Why, it was loads of fun! Didn't   550
you hear me cutting up in the kitchen? I bet your ears were burning! I told Tom how outdone with him I was for keeping you to himself so long a time! He should have brought you over much, much sooner! Well, now that you've found your way, I want you to be a very frequent caller! Not just occa-   555
sional but all the time. Oh, we're going to have a lot of gay times together! I see them coming! Mmm, just breathe that air! So fresh, and the moon's so pretty! I'll skip back out—I know where my place is when young folks are having a—serious conversation!   560

JIM: Oh, don't go out, Mrs. Wingfield. The fact of the matter is I've got to be going.

AMANDA: Going, now? You're joking! Why, it's only the shank of the evening, Mr. O'Connor!

JIM: Well, you know how it is.   565

AMANDA: You mean you're a young workingman and have to keep workingmen's hours. We'll let you off early tonight. But

only on the condition that next time you stay later. What's
the best night for you? Isn't Saturday night the best night for
570   you workingmen?

JIM: I have a couple of time-clocks to punch, Mrs. Wingfield.
One at morning, another one at night!

AMANDA: My, but you *are* ambitious! You work at night, too?

JIM: No, Ma'am, not work but—Betty!

(He crosses deliberately to pick up his hat. The band at the Paradise Dance Hall goes into a tender waltz.)

575   AMANDA: Betty? Betty? Who's—Betty!

(There is an ominous cracking sound in the sky.)

JIM: Oh, just a girl. The girl I go steady with!

(He smiles charmingly. The sky falls.)

(Legend: "The Sky Falls.")

AMANDA: *(A long-drawn exhalation.)* Ohhhh . . . Is it a serious
romance, Mr. O'Connor?

JIM: We're going to be married the second Sunday in June.

580   AMANDA: Ohhhh—how nice! Tom didn't mention that you
were engaged to be married.

JIM: The cat's not out of the bag at the warehouse yet. You
know how they are. They call you Romeo and stuff like that.
(He stops at the oval mirror to put on his hat. He carefully
585   *shapes the brim and the crown to give a discreetly dashing ef-*
fect.) It's been a wonderful evening, Mrs. Wingfield. I guess
this is what they mean by Southern hospitality.

AMANDA: It really wasn't anything at all.

JIM: I hope it don't seem like I'm rushing off. But I promised
590   Betty I'd pick her up at the Wabash depot, an' by the time I
get my jalopy down there her train'll be in. Some women are
pretty upset if you keep 'em waiting.

AMANDA: Yes, I know—the tyranny of women! *(She extends her
hand.)* Goodbye, Mr. O'Connor. I wish you luck—and hap-
595   piness—and success! All three of them, and so does Laura!
Don't you, Laura?

LAURA: Yes!

JIM: *(Taking LAURA's hand.)* Goodbye, Laura. I'm certainly
going to treasure that souvenir. And don't you forget the
600   good advice I gave you. *(He raises his voice to a cheery shout.)*
So long, Shakespeare! Thanks again, ladies. Good night!

*(He grins and ducks jauntily out. Still bravely grimacing,
AMANDA closes the door on the gentleman caller. Then she turns
back to the room with a puzzled expression. She and LAURA don't
dare to face each other. LAURA crouches beside the Victrola to
wind it.)*

AMANDA: *(Faintly.)* Things have a way of turning out so badly.
I don't believe that I would play the Victrola. Well, well—
well! Our gentleman caller was engaged to be married! *(She*
605   *raises her voice.)* Tom!

TOM: *(From the kitchenette.)* Yes, Mother?

AMANDA: Come in here a minute. I want to tell you something
awfully funny.

TOM: *(Entering with a macaroon and a glass of the lemonade.)*
610   Has the gentleman caller gotten away already?

AMANDA: The gentleman caller has made an early departure.
What a wonderful joke you played on us!

TOM: How do you mean?

AMANDA: You didn't mention that he was engaged to be
married.   615

TOM: Jim? Engaged?

AMANDA: That's what he just informed us.

TOM: I'll be jiggered! I didn't know about that.

AMANDA: That seems very peculiar.

TOM: What's peculiar about it?   620

AMANDA: Didn't you call him your best friend down at the
warehouse?

TOM: He is, but how did I know?

AMANDA: It seems extremely peculiar that you wouldn't know
your best friend was going to be married!   625

TOM: The warehouse is where I work, not where I know things
about people!

AMANDA: You don't know things anywhere! You live in a
dream; you manufacture illusions!

(He crosses to the door.)

Where are you going?   630

TOM: I'm going to the movies.

AMANDA: That's right, now that you've had us make such fools
of ourselves. The effort, the preparations, all the expense!
The new floor lamp, the rug, the clothes for Laura! All for
what? To entertain some other girl's fiancé! Go to the movies,   635
go! Don't think about us, a mother deserted, an unmarried
sister who's crippled and has no job! Don't let anything
interfere with your selfish pleasure! Just go, go, go—to the
movies!

TOM: All right, I will! The more you shout about my selfish-   640
ness to me the quicker I'll go, and I won't go to the movies!

AMANDA: Go, then! Go to the moon—you selfish dreamer!

*(TOM smashes his glass on the floor. He plunges out on the fire
escape, slamming the door. LAURA screams in fright. The dance-
hall music becomes louder. TOM stands on the fire escape, gripping the rail. The moon breaks through the storm clouds,
illuminating his face.)*

(Legend on screen: "And so goodbye . . .")

*(TOM's closing speech is timed with what is happening inside the
house. We see, as though through soundproof glass, that
AMANDA appears to be making a comforting speech to LAURA,
who is huddled upon the sofa. Now that we cannot hear the
mother's speech, her silliness is gone and she has dignity and
tragic beauty. LAURA's hair hides her face until, at the end of the
speech, she lifts her head to smile at her mother. AMANDA's gestures are slow and graceful, almost dancelike, as she comforts her
daughter. At the end of her speech she glances a moment at
the father's picture—then withdraws through the portieres. At
the close of TOM's speech, LAURA blows out the candles, ending
the play.)*

TOM: I didn't go to the moon, I went much further—for time
is the longest distance between two places. Not long after
that I was fired for writing a poem on the lid of a shoe-box. I   645
left Saint Louis. I descended the steps of this fire escape for a
last time and followed, from then on, in my father's footsteps,
attempting to find in motion what was lost in space. I traveled around a great deal. The cities swept about me like
dead leaves, leaves that were brightly colored but torn away   650
from the branches. I would have stopped, but I was pursued

by something. It always came upon me unawares, taking me altogether by surprise. Perhaps it was a familiar bit of music. Perhaps it was only a piece of transparent glass. Perhaps I am 655 walking along a street at night, in some strange city, before I have found companions. I pass the lighted window of a shop where perfume is sold. The window is filled with pieces of colored glass, tiny transparent bottles in delicate colors, like bits of a shattered rainbow. Then all at once my sister 660 touches my shoulder. I turn around and look into her eyes. Oh, Laura, Laura, I tried to leave you behind me, but I am more faithful than I intended to be! I reach for a cigarette, I cross the street, I run into the movies or a bar, I buy a drink, I speak to the nearest stranger—anything that can blow your candles out!   665

(LAURA *bends over the candles.*)

For nowadays the world is lit by lightning! Blow out your candles, Laura—and so goodbye. . . .

(*She blows the candles out.*)

■ AMIRI BARAKA / LEROI JONES ■

Born Everett LeRoi Jones in Newark, New Jersey, in 1934, Amiri Baraka has become the most important revolutionary voice in contemporary black theater in the United States. He attended Rutgers University and Howard University, taking his B.A. from Howard in 1954. Baraka later said that his education at Howard was too involved with "learning to be white." He served in the United States Air Force before returning to New York in 1958. Living in Greenwich Village, he studied at Columbia University, married his first wife—an interracial marriage, lightly disguised in his play *The Slave*—and worked to develop his talents as a writer. Jones worked everywhere to develop a black esthetic, in his own poetry (in the mode of the Beat poets, Gregory Corso and Allen Ginsberg), in essays, and in magazines that he founded and edited. In 1960, Jones was part of a delegation of black Americans invited to Cuba to celebrate Fidel Castro's revolution. That visit had a profound impact on Jones, sharpening his sense of the need both for a distinctive black esthetic and culture, and for a social revolution to eradicate the injustices of white-dominated American society. His plays of the 1960s are, in fact, often directly concerned with this issue and with how white liberalism—ostensibly the ally of black power—finally becomes an obstacle to the more fundamental revolution needed to bring black identity, culture, and power into being. In 1964, three of his plays opened in New York: *The Eighth Ditch*, *The Baptism*, and *Dutchman*, which won the Obie award for the best American play of the season. He then wrote a series of plays examining black activism and revolution in American life: *The Slave* (1964) and *The Toilet* (1964), *Experimental Death Unit #1* (1965), and *J-e-l-l-o* (1965). The assassination of Malcolm X in 1965 and the Watts riots in Los Angeles also drove Jones toward a more militant position, as articulated in plays like *A Black Mass* (1966), *Slave Ship* (1966), *The Great Goodness of Life (A Coon Show)* (1967), *Home on the Range* (1968), and *The Death of Malcolm X* (1969), and later in *The Motion of History* (1977), and *Money* (1988). In 1964 Jones established the Black Arts Repertory Theater and School in Harlem and began a program of cultural nationalism there, which he has pursued subsequently in several other organizations and described in several collections of essays. He has been deeply involved in developing a theater that would serve the need for cultural and political revolution in the black community.

As part of his commitment to forging a sustaining system of values for the African-American community, Jones became a Kawaidi Muslim minister in 1968, adopting the title Imamu (spiritual leader) and the name Amiri Baraka at that time. Throughout the 1970s and 1980s, Baraka articulated and solidified the claims of cultural nationalism, frequently in a fiercely revolutionary, Marxist rhetoric. Baraka continues to be involved in a variety of political and social activities in the black community.

DUTCHMAN

Dutchman is one of Baraka's most powerful plays, both in its indictment of racist culture and in its straightforward confrontation between Lula and Clay. The title alludes to the legendary *Flying Dutchman*, the ship of the dead said to haunt the high seas. The subway car of the play is at once a ghost ship—where the young black man Clay is murdered—and a ghostly incarnation of racist fantasies. At the beginning of the play, Lula seems attracted to the middle-class Clay, but as the play develops it becomes clear that, to seduce Clay, Lula must transform him into something else, a fantasy figure of the white imagination. When Clay refuses to play along, delivering instead an impassioned statement of his own black identity, Lula murders him, with the implied consent of the white riders of the subway. *Dutchman* is a powerful parable of the problems of black identity in white culture.

DUTCHMAN

AMIRI BARAKA

— CHARACTERS —

CLAY, *twenty-year-old Negro*
LULA, *thirty-year-old white woman*
RIDERS OF COACH, *white and black*
YOUNG NEGRO
CONDUCTOR

In the flying underbelly of the city. Steaming hot, and summer on top, outside. Underground. The subway heaped in modern myth.

Opening scene is a man sitting in a subway seat, holding a magazine but looking vacantly just above its wilting pages. Occasionally he looks blankly toward the window on his right. Dim lights and darkness whistling by against the glass. (Or paste the lights, as admitted props, right on the subway windows. Have them move, even dim and flicker. But give the sense of speed. Also stations, whether the train is stopped or the glitter and activity of these stations merely flashes by the windows.)

The man is sitting alone. That is, only his seat is visible, though the rest of the car is outfitted as a complete subway car. But only his seat is shown. There might be, for a time, as the play begins, a loud scream of the actual train. And it can recur throughout the play, or continue on a lower key once the dialogue starts.

The train slows after a time, pulling to a brief stop at one of the stations. The man looks idly up, until he sees a woman's face staring at him through the window; when it realizes that the man has noticed the face, it begins very premeditatedly to smile. The man smiles too, for a moment, without a trace of self-consciousness. Almost an instinctive though undesirable response. Then a kind of awkwardness or embarrassment sets in, and the man makes to look away, is further embarrassed, so he brings back his eyes to where the face was, but by now the train is moving again, and the face would seem to be left behind by the way the man turns his head to look back through the other windows at the slowly fading platform. He smiles then; more comfortably confident, hoping perhaps that his memory of this brief encounter will be pleasant. And then he is idle again.

— SCENE ONE —

Train roars. Lights flash outside the windows.

LULA *enters from the rear of the car in bright, skimpy summer clothes and sandals. She carries a net bag full of paper books, fruit, and other anonymous articles. She is wearing sunglasses, which she pushes up on her forehead from time to time. LULA is a tall, slender, beautiful woman with long red hair hanging straight down her back, wearing only loud lipstick in somebody's good taste. She is eating an apple, very daintily. Coming down the car toward CLAY.*

She stops beside CLAY's seat and hangs languidly from the strap, still managing to eat the apple. It is apparent that she is going to sit in the seat next to CLAY, and that she is only waiting for him to notice her before she sits.

CLAY *sits as before, looking just beyond his magazine, now and again pulling the magazine slowly back and forth in front of his face in a hopeless effort to fan himself. Then he sees the woman hanging there beside him and he looks up into her face, smiling quizzically.*

LULA: Hello.
CLAY: Uh, hi're you?
LULA: I'm going to sit down. . . . O.K.?
CLAY: Sure.
5 LULA:

(Swings down onto the seat, pushing her legs straight out as if she is very weary.)

Oooof! Too much weight.
CLAY: Ha, doesn't look like much to me.

(Leaning back against the window, a little surprised and maybe stiff.)

LULA: It's so anyway.

(And she moves her toes in the sandals, then pulls her right leg up on the left knee, better to inspect the bottoms of the sandals and the back of her heel. She appears for a second not to notice that CLAY is sitting next to her or that she has spoken to him just a second before. CLAY looks at the magazine, then out the black window. As he does this, she turns very quickly toward him.)

Weren't you staring at me through the window?
CLAY: 10

(Wheeling around and very much stiffened.)

What?
LULA: Weren't you staring at me through the window? At the last stop?
CLAY: Staring at you? What do you mean?
LULA: Don't you know what staring means?   15
CLAY: I saw you through the window . . . if that's what it means. I don't know if I was staring. Seems to me you were staring through the window at me.
LULA: I was. But only after I'd turned around and saw you staring through that window down in the vicinity of my ass and   20 legs.
CLAY: Really?
LULA: Really. I guess you were just taking those idle potshots. Nothing else to do. Run your mind over people's flesh.
CLAY: Oh boy. Wow, now I admit I was looking in your direc-   25 tion. But the rest of that weight is yours.
LULA: I suppose.
CLAY: Staring through train windows is weird business. Much weirder than staring very sedately at abstract asses.

873

30   LULA: That's why I came looking through the window . . . so
you'd have more than that to go on. I even smiled at you.
CLAY: That's right.
LULA: I even got into this train, going some other way than
mine. Walked down the aisle . . . searching you out.
35   CLAY: Really? That's pretty funny.
LULA: That's pretty funny. . . . God, you're dull.
CLAY: Well, I'm sorry, lady, but I really wasn't prepared for
party talk.
LULA: No, you're not. What are you prepared for?

(*Wrapping the apple core in a Kleenex and dropping it on the
floor.*)

40   CLAY:

(*Takes her conversation as pure sex talk. He turns to confront her
squarely with this idea.*)

I'm prepared for anything. How about you?
LULA:

(*Laughing loudly and cutting it off abruptly.*)

What do you think you're doing?
CLAY: What?
45   LULA: You think I want to pick you up, get you to take me
somewhere and screw me, huh?
CLAY: Is that the way I look?
LULA: You look like you been trying to grow a beard. That's exactly what you look like. You look like you live in New Jersey
50   with your parents and are trying to grow a beard. That's
what. You look like you've been reading Chinese poetry and
drinking lukewarm sugarless tea.

(*Laughs, uncrossing and recrossing her legs.*)

You look like death eating a soda cracker.
CLAY:

(*Cocking his head from one side to the other, embarrassed and
trying to make some comeback, but also intrigued by what the
woman is saying . . . even the sharp city coarseness of her voice,
which is still a kind of gentle sidewalk throb.*)

55   Really? I look like all that?
LULA: Not all of it.

(*She feigns a seriousness to cover an actual somber tone.*)

I lie a lot.

(*Smiling.*)

It helps me control the world.
CLAY:

(*Relieved and laughing louder than the humor.*)

60   Yeah, I bet.
LULA: But it's true, most of it, right? Jersey? Your bumpy neck?
CLAY: How'd you know all that? Huh? Really. I mean about
Jersey . . . and even the beard. I met you before? You know
Warren Enright?
65   LULA: You tried to make it with your sister when you were ten.

(CLAY *leans back hard against the back of the seat, his eyes opening now, still trying to look amused.*)

But I succeeded a few weeks ago.

(*She starts to laugh again.*)

CLAY: What're you talking about? Warren tell you that? You're
a friend of Georgia's?
LULA: I told you I lie. I don't know your sister. I don't know
Warren Enright.   70
CLAY: You mean you're just picking these things out of the air?
LULA: Is Warren Enright a tall skinny black black boy with a
phony English accent?
CLAY: I figured you knew him.
LULA: But I don't. I just figured you would know somebody   75
like that.

(*Laughs.*)

CLAY: Yeah, yeah.
LULA: You're probably on your way to his house now.
CLAY: That's right.
LULA: 80

(*Putting her hand on* CLAY's *closer knee, drawing it from the
knee up to the thigh's hinge, then removing it, watching his face
very closely, and continuing to laugh, perhaps more gently than
before.*)

Dull, dull, dull. I bet you think I'm exciting.
CLAY: You're O.K.
LULA: Am I exciting you now?
CLAY: Right. That's not what's supposed to happen?
LULA: How do I know?   85

(*She returns her hand, without moving it, then takes it away and
plunges it in her bag to draw out an apple.*)

You want this?
CLAY: Sure.
LULA:

(*She gets one out of the bag for herself.*)

Eating apples together is always the first step. Or walking up
uninhabited Seventh Avenue in the twenties on weekends.   90

(*Bites and giggles, glancing at* CLAY *and speaking in loose
singsong.*)

Can get you involved . . . boy! Get us involved. Um-huh.

(*Mock seriousness.*)

Would you like to get involved with me, Mister Man?
CLAY:

(*Trying to be as flippant as* LULA, *whacking happily at the
apple.*)

Sure. Why not? A beautiful woman like you. Huh, I'd be a
fool not to.   95
LULA: And I bet you're sure you know what you're talking
about.

(*Taking him a little roughly by the wrist, so he cannot eat the
apple, then shaking the wrist.*)

I bet you're sure of almost everything anybody ever asked
you about . . . right?

(*Shakes his wrist harder.*)

Right?   100
CLAY: Yeah, right. . . . Wow, you're pretty strong, you know?
Whatta you, a lady wrestler or something?

LULA: What's wrong with lady wrestlers? And don't answer because you never knew any. Huh.

(Cynically.)

105   That's for sure. They don't have any lady wrestlers in that part of Jersey. That's for sure.

CLAY: Hey, you still haven't tole me how you know so much about me.

LULA: I told you I didn't know anything about *you* . . . you're a

110   well-known type.

CLAY: Really?

LULA: Or at least I know the type very well. And your skinny English friend too.

CLAY: Anonymously?

115   LULA:

(Settles back in seat, single-mindedly finishing her apple and humming snatches of rhythm and blues song.)

What?

CLAY: Without knowing us specifically?

LULA: Oh boy.

(Looking quickly at CLAY.)

What a face. You know, you could be a handsome man.

120   CLAY: I can't argue with you.

LULA:

(Vague, off-center response.)

What?

CLAY:

(Raising his voice, thinking the train noise has drowned part of his sentence.)

I can't argue with you.

125   LULA: My hair is turning gray. A gray hair for each year and type I've come through.

CLAY: Why do you want to sound so old?

LULA: But it's always gentle when it starts.

(Attention drifting.)

Hugged against tenements, day or night.

130   CLAY: What?

LULA:

(Refocusing.)

Hey, why don't you take me to that party you're going to?

LULA: You must be a friend of Warren's to know about the party.

135   LULA: Wouldn't you like to take me to the party?

(Imitates clinging vine.)

Oh, come on, ask me to your party.

CLAY: Of course I'll ask you to come with me to the party. And I'll bet you're a friend of Warren's.

LULA: Why not be a friend of Warren's? Why not?

(Taking his arm.)

140   Have you asked me yet?

CLAY: How can I ask you when I don't know your name?

LULA: Are you talking to my name?

CLAY: What is it, a secret?

LULA: I'm Lena the Hyena.

145   CLAY: The famous woman poet?

LULA: Poetess! The same!

CLAY: Well, you know so much about me . . . what's my name?

LULA: Morris the Hyena.

CLAY: The famous woman poet?

LULA: The same.   150

(Laughing and going into her bag.)

You want another apple?

CLAY: Can't make it, lady. I only have to keep one doctor away a day.

LULA: I bet your name is . . . something like . . . uh, Gerald or Walter. Huh?   155

CLAY: God, no.

LULA: Lloyd, Norman? One of those hopeless colored names creeping out of New Jersey. Leonard? Gag. . . .

CLAY: Like Warren?

LULA: Definitely. Just exactly like Warren. Or Everett.   160

CLAY: Gag. . . .

LULA: Well, for sure, it's not Willie.

CLAY: It's Clay.

LULA: Clay? Really? Clay what?

CLAY: Take your pick. Jackson, Johnson, or Williams.   165

LULA: Oh, really? Good for you. But it's got to be Williams. You're too pretentious to be a Jackson or Johnson.

CLAY: Thass right.

LULA: But Clay's O.K.

CLAY: So's Lena.   170

LULA: It's Lula.

CLAY: Oh?

LULA: Lula the Hyena.

CLAY: Very good.

LULA: 175

(Starts laughing again.)

Now you say to me, "Lula, Lula, why don't you go to this party with me tonight?" It's your turn, and let those be your lines.

CLAY: Lula, why don't you go to this party with me tonight, Huh?   180

LULA: Say my name twice before you ask, and no huh's.

CLAY: Lula, Lula, why don't you go to this party with me tonight?

LULA: I'd like to go, Clay, but how can you ask me to go when you barely know me?   185

CLAY: That is strange, isn't it?

LULA: What kind of reaction is that? You're supposed to say, "Aw, come on, we'll get to know each other better at the party."

CLAY: That's pretty corny.   190

LULA: What are you into anyway?

(Looking at him half sullenly but still amused.)

What thing are you playing at, Mister? Mister Clay Williams?

(Grabs his thigh, up near the crotch.)

What are *you* thinking about?

CLAY: Watch it now, you're gonna excite me for real.

LULA: 195

(Taking her hand away and throwing her apple core through the window.)

I bet.

(She slumps in the seat and is heavily silent.)

CLAY: I thought you knew everything about me? What happened?

(LULA looks at him, then looks slowly away, then over where the other aisle would be. Noise of the train. She reaches in her bag and pulls out one of the paper books. She puts it on her leg and thumbs the pages listlessly. CLAY cocks his head to see the title of the book. Noise of the train. LULA flips pages and her eyes drift. Both remain silent.)

Are you going to the party with me, Lula?

200 LULA:

(Bored and not even looking.)

I don't even know you.

CLAY: You said you know my type.

LULA:

(Strangely irritated.)

Don't get smart with me, Buster. I know you like the palm of
205 my hand.

CLAY: The one you eat the apples with?

LULA: Yeh. And the one I open doors late Saturday evening
with. That's my door. Up at the top of the stairs. Five flights.
Above a lot of Italians and lying Americans. And scrape car-
210 rots with. Also . . .

(Looks at him.)

the same hand I unbutton my dress with, or let my skirt fall
down. Same hand. Lover.

CLAY: Are you angry about anything? Did I say something
wrong?

215 LULA: Everything you say is wrong.

(Mock smile.)

That's what makes you so attractive. Ha. In that funnybook
jacket with all the buttons.

(More animate, taking hold of his jacket.)

What've you got the jacket and tie on in all this heat for? And
why're you wearing a jacket and tie like that? Did your peo-
220 ple ever burn witches or start revolutions over the price of
tea? Boy, those narrow-shoulder clothes come from a tradition you ought to feel oppressed by. A three-button suit.
What right do you have to be wearing a three-button suit
and striped tie? Your grandfather was a slave, he didn't go to
225 Harvard.

CLAY: My grandfather was a night watchman.

LULA: And you went to a colored college where everybody
thought they were Averell Harriman.

CLAY: All except me.

230 LULA: And who did you think you were? Who do you think you
are now?

CLAY:

*(Laughs as if to make light of the whole trend of the
conversation.)*

Well, in college I thought I was Baudelaire. But I've slowed
down since.

235 LULA: I bet you never once thought you were a black nigger.

*(Mock serious, then she howls with laughter. CLAY is stunned but
after initial reaction, he quickly tries to appreciate the humor.
LULA almost shrieks.)*

A black Baudelaire.

CLAY: That's right.

LULA: Boy, are you corny. I take back what I said before. Everything you say is not wrong. It's perfect. You should be on
television. 240

CLAY: You act like you're on television already.

LULA: That's because I'm an actress.

CLAY: I thought so.

LULA: Well, you're wrong. I'm no actress. I told you I always
lie. I'm nothing, honey, and don't you ever forget it. 245

(Lighter.)

Although my mother was a Communist. The only person in
my family ever to amount to anything.

CLAY: My mother was a Republican.

LULA: And your father voted for the man rather than the party.

CLAY: Right! 250

LULA: Yea for him. Yea, yea for him.

CLAY: Yea!

LULA: And yea for America where he is free to vote for the
mediocrity of his choice! Yea!

CLAY: Yea! 255

LULA: And yea for both your parents who even though they differ about so crucial a matter as the body politic still forged a
union of love and sacrifice that was destined to flower at the
birth of the noble Clay . . . what's your middle name?

CLAY: Clay. 260

LULA: A union of love and sacrifice that was destined to flower
at the birth of the noble Clay Clay Williams. Yea! And most
of all yea yea for you. Clay Clay. The Black Baudelaire! Yes!

(And with knifelike cynicism.)

My Christ. My Christ.

CLAY: Thank you, ma'am. 265

LULA: May the people accept you as a ghost of the future. And
love you, that you might not kill them when you can.

CLAY: What?

LULA: You're a murderer, Clay, and you know it.

(Her voice darkening with significance.)

You know goddamn well what I mean. 270

CLAY: I do?

LULA: So we'll pretend the air is light and full of perfume.

CLAY:

(Sniffing at her blouse.)

It is.

LULA: And we'll pretend the people cannot see you. That is, 275
the citizens. And that you are free of your own history. And I
am free of my history. We'll pretend that we are both anonymous beauties smashing along through the city's entrails.

(She yells as loud as she can.)

GROOVE!

(Black.)

— SCENE TWO —

Scene is the same as before, though now there are other seats visible in the car. And throughout the scene other people get on the subway. There are maybe one or two seated in the car as the scene opens, though neither CLAY *nor* LULA *notices them.* CLAY's *tie is open.* LULA *is hugging his arm.*

CLAY: The party!

LULA: I know it'll be something good. You can come in with me, looking casual and significant. I'll be strange, haughty, and silent, and walk with long slow strides.

5 CLAY: Right.

LULA: When you get drunk, pat me once, very lovingly on the flanks, and I'll look at you cryptically, licking my lips.

CLAY: It sounds like something we can do.

LULA: You'll go around talking to young men about your
10   mind, and to old men about your plans. If you meet a very close friend who is also with someone like me, we can stand together, sipping our drinks and exchanging codes of lust. The atmosphere will be slithering in love and half-love and very open moral decision.

15 CLAY: Great. Great.

LULA: And everyone will pretend they don't know your name, and then . . .

(She pauses heavily.)

later, when they have to, they'll claim a friendship that denies your sterling character.

20 CLAY:

(Kissing her neck and fingers.)

And then what?

LULA: Then? Well, then we'll go down the street, late night, eating apples and winding very deliberately toward my house.

25 CLAY: Deliberately?

LULA: I mean, we'll look in all the shopwindows, and make fun of the queers. Maybe we'll meet a Jewish Buddhist and flatten his conceits over some pretentious coffee.

CLAY: In honor of whose God?

30 LULA: Mine.

CLAY: Who is . . .?

LULA: Me . . . and you

CLAY: A corporate Godhead.

LULA: Exactly. Exactly.

(Notices one of the other people entering.)

35 CLAY: Go on with the chronicle. Then what happens to us?

LULA:

(A mild depression, but she still makes her description triumphant and increasingly direct.)

To my house, of course.

CLAY: Of course.

LULA: And up the narrow steps of the tenement.

40 CLAY: You live in a tenement?

LULA: Wouldn't live anywhere else. Reminds me specifically of my novel form of insanity.

CLAY: Up the tenement stairs.

LULA: And with my apple-eating hand I push open the door and lead you, my tender big-eyed prey, into my . . . God, 45 what can I call it . . . into my hovel.

CLAY: Then what happens?

LULA: After the dancing and games, after the long drinks and long walks, the real fun begins.

CLAY: Ah, the real fun. 50

(Embarrassed, in spite of himself.)

Which is . . .?

LULA:

(Laughs at him.)

Real fun in the dark house. Hah! Real fun in the dark house, high up above the street and the ignorant cowboys. I lead you in, holding your wet hand gently in my hand . . . 55

CLAY: Which is not wet?

LULA: Which is dry as ashes.

CLAY: And cold?

LULA: Don't think you'll get out of your responsibility that way. It's not cold at all. You Fascist! Into my dark living room. 60 Where we'll sit and talk endlessly, endlessly.

CLAY: About what?

LULA: About what? About your manhood, what do you think? What do you think we've been talking about all this time?

CLAY: Well, I didn't know it was that. That's for sure. Every 65 other thing in the world but that.

(Notices another person entering, looks quickly, almost involuntarily, up and down the car, seeing the other people in the car.)

Hey, I didn't even notice when those people got on.

LULA: Yeah, I know.

CLAY: Man, this subway is slow.

LULA: Yeah, I know. 70

CLAY: Well, go on. We were talking about my manhood.

LULA: We still are. All the time.

CLAY: We were in your living room.

LULA: My dark living room. Talking endlessly.

CLAY: About my manhood. 75

LULA: I'll make you a map of it. Just as soon as we get to my house.

CLAY: Well, that's great.

LULA: One of the things we do while we talk. And screw.

CLAY: 80

(Trying to make his smile broader and less shaky.)

We finally got there.

LULA: And you'll call my rooms black as a grave. You'll say, "This place is like Juliet's tomb."

CLAY:

(Laughs.)

I might. 85

LULA: I know. You've probably said it before.

CLAY: And is that all? The whole grand tour?

LULA: Not all. You'll say to me very close to my face, many, many times, you'll say, even whisper, that you love me.

CLAY: Maybe I will. 90

LULA: And you'll be lying.

CLAY: I wouldn't lie about something like that.

LULA: Hah. It's the only kind of thing you will lie about. Especially if you think it'll keep me alive.

95   CLAY: Keep you alive? I don't understand.

LULA:

(Bursting out laughing, but too shrilly.)

Don't understand? Well, don't look at me. It's the path I take, that's all. Where both feet take me when I set them down. One in front of the other.

100   CLAY: Morbid. Morbid. You sure you're not an actress? All that self-aggrandizement.

LULA: Well, I told you I wasn't an actress . . . but I also told you I lie all the time. Draw your own conclusions.

CLAY: And is that all of our lives together you've described?

105   There's no more?

LULA: I've told you all I know. Or almost all.

CLAY: There's no funny parts?

LULA: I thought it was all funny.

CLAY: But you mean peculiar, not ha-ha.

110   LULA: You don't know what I mean.

CLAY: Well, tell me the almost part then. You said almost all. What else? I want the whole story.

LULA:

(Searching aimlessly through her bag. She begins to talk breathlessly, with a light and silly tone.)

All stories are whole stories. All of 'em. Our whole story . . .

115   nothing but change. How could things go on like that forever? Huh?

(Slaps him on the shoulder, begins finding things in her bag, taking them out and throwing them over her shoulder into the aisle.)

Except I do go on as I do. Apples and long walks with deathless intelligent lovers. But you mix it up. Look out the window, all the time. Turning pages. Change change change.

120   Till, shit, I don't know you. Wouldn't, for that matter. You're too serious. I bet you're even too serious to be psychoanalyzed. Like all those Jewish poets from Yonkers, who leave their mothers looking for other mothers, or others' mothers, on whose baggy tits they lay their fumbling heads. Their

125   poems are always funny, and all about sex.

CLAY: They sound great. Like movies.

LULA: But you change.

(Blankly.)

And things work on you till you hate them.

(More people come into the train. They come closer to the couple, some of them not sitting, but swinging drearily on the straps, staring at the two with uncertain interest.)

CLAY: Wow. All these people, so suddenly. They must all come

130   from the same place.

LULA: Right. That they do.

CLAY: Oh? You know about them too?

LULA: Oh yeah. About them more than I know about you. Do they frighten you?

135   CLAY: Frighten me? Why should they frighten me?

LULA: 'Cause you're an escaped nigger.

CLAY: Yeah?

LULA: 'Cause you crawled through the wire and made tracks to my side.

CLAY: Wire?   140

LULA: Don't they have wire around plantations?

CLAY: You must be Jewish. All you can think about is wire. Plantations didn't have any wire. Plantations were big open whitewashed places like heaven, and everybody on 'em was grooved to be there. Just strummin' and hummin' all day.   145

LULA: Yes, yes.

CLAY: And that's how the blues was born.

LULA: Yes, yes. And that's how the blues was born.

(Begins to make up a song that becomes quickly hysterical. As she sings she rises from her seat, still throwing things out of her bag into the aisle, beginning a rhythmical shudder and twistlike wiggle, which she continues up and down the aisle, bumping into many of the standing people and tripping over the feet of those sitting. Each time she runs into a person she lets out a very vicious piece of profanity, wiggling and stepping all the time.)

And that's how the blues was born. Yes. Yes. Son of a bitch, get out of the way. Yes. Quack. Yes. Yes. And that's how the   150 blues was born. Ten little niggers sitting on a limb, but none of them ever looked like him.

(Points to CLAY, returns toward the seat, with her hands extended for him to rise and dance with her.)

And that's how blues was born. Yes. Come on. Clay. Let's do the nasty. Rub bellies. Rub bellies.

CLAY: 155

(Waves his hands to refuse. He is embarrassed, but determined to get a kick out of the proceedings.)

Hey, what was in those apples? Mirror, mirror on the wall, who's the fairest one of all? Snow White, baby, and don't you forget it.

LULA:

(Grabbing for his hands, which he draws away.)

Come on, Clay. Let's rub bellies on the train. The nasty. The   160 nasty. Do the gritty grind, like your ol' rag-head mammy. Grind till you lose your mind. Shake it, shake it, shake it, shake it! OOOOweeee! Come on, Clay. Let's do the choo-choo train shuffle, the navel scratcher.

CLAY: Hey, you coming on like the lady who smoked up her   165 grass skirt.

LULA:

(Becoming annoyed that he will not dance, and becoming more animated as if to embarrass him still further.)

Come on, Clay . . . let's do the thing. Uhh! Uhh! Clay! Clay! You middle-class black bastard. Forget your social-working mother for a few seconds and let's knock stomachs. Clay, you   170 liver-lipped white man. You would-be Christian. You ain't no nigger, you're just a dirty white man. Get up, Clay. Dance with me, Clay.

CLAY: Lula! Sit down, now. Be cool.

LULA: 175

(Mocking him, in wild dance.)

Be cool. Be cool. That's all you know . . . shaking the wild-root cream-oil on your knotty head, jackets buttoning up to your chin, so full of white man's words. Christ! God! Get up and scream at these people. Like scream meaningless shit in these hopeless faces.   180

(She screams at people in train, still dancing.)

Red trains cough Jewish underwear for keeps! Expanding smells of silence. Gravy snot whistling like sea birds. Clay. Clay, you got to break out. Don't sit there dying the way they want you to die. Get up.

185 CLAY: Oh, sit the fuck down.

(He moves to restrain her.)

Sit down, goddamn it.

LULA:

(Twisting out of his reach.)

Screw yourself, Uncle Tom. Thomas Woolly-Head.

(Begins to dance a kind of jig, mocking CLAY with loud forced humor.)

190 There is Uncle Tom . . . I mean, Uncle Thomas Woolly-Head. With old white matted mane. He hobbles on his wooden cane. Old Tom. Old Tom. Let the white man hump his ol' mama, and he jes' shuffle off in the woods and hide his gentle gray head. Ol' Thomas Woolly-Head.

(Some of the other riders are laughing now. A drunk gets up and joins LULA in her dance, singing, as best he can, her "song." CLAY gets up out of his seat and visibly scans the faces of the other riders.)

CLAY: Lula! Lula!

(She is dancing and turning, still shouting as loud as she can. The drunk too is shouting, and waving his hands wildly.)

195 Lula . . . you dumb bitch. Why don't you stop it?

(He rushes half stumbling from his seat, and grabs one of her flailing arms.)

LULA: Let me go! You black son of a bitch.

(She struggles against him.)

Let me go! Help!

(CLAY is dragging her towards her seat, and the drunk seeks to interfere. He grabs CLAY around the shoulders and begins wrestling with him. CLAY clubs the drunk to the floor without releasing LULA, who is still screaming. CLAY finally gets her to the seat and throws her into it.)

CLAY: Now you shut the hell up.

(Grabbing her shoulders.)

200 Just shut up. You don't know what you're talking about. You don't know anything. So just keep your stupid mouth closed.

LULA: You're afraid of white people. And your father was. Uncle Tom Big Lip!

CLAY:

(Slaps her as hard as he can, across the mouth. LULA's head bangs against the back of the seat. When she raises it again, CLAY slaps her again.)

Now shut up and let me talk.

(He turns toward the other riders, some of whom are sitting on the edge of their seats. The drunk is on one knee, rubbing his head, and singing softly the same song. He shuts up too when he

sees CLAY *watching him. The others go back to newspapers or stare out the windows.)*

Shit, you don't have any sense, Lula, nor feelings either. I 205 could murder you now. Such a tiny ugly throat. I could squeeze it flat, and watch you turn blue, on a humble. For dull kicks. And all these weak-faced ofays squatting around here, staring over their papers at me. Murder them too. Even if they expected it. That man there . . . 210

(Points to well-dressed man.)

I could rip that *Times* right out of his hand, as skinny and middle-classed as I am, I could rip that paper out of his hand and just as easily rip out his throat. It takes no great effort. For what? To kill you soft idiots? You don't understand anything but luxury. 215

LULA: You fool!

CLAY:

(Pushing her against the seat.)

I'm not telling you again, Tallulah Bankhead! Luxury. In your face and your fingers. You telling me what I ought to do.

(Sudden scream frightening the whole coach.)

Well, don't! Don't you tell me anything! If I'm a middle-class 220 fake white man . . . let me be. And let me be in the way I want.

(Through his teeth.)

I'll rip your lousy breasts off! Let me be who I feel like being. Uncle Tom. Thomas. Whoever. It's none of your business. You don't know anything except what's there for you to see. 225 An act. Lies. Device. Not the pure heart, the pumping black heart. You don't ever know that. And I sit here, in this buttoned-up suit, to keep myself from cutting all your throats. I mean wantonly. You great liberated whore! You fuck some black man, and right away you're an expert on black people. 230 What a lotta shit that is. The only thing you know is that you come if he bangs you hard enough. And that's all. The belly rub? You wanted to do the belly rub? Shit, you don't even know how. You don't know how. That ol' dipty-dip shit you do, rolling your ass like an elephant. That's not my kind of 235 belly rub. Belly rub is not Queens. Belly rub is dark places, with big hats and overcoats held up with one arm. Belly rub hates you. Old bald-headed four-eyed ofays popping their fingers . . . and don't know yet what they're doing. They say, "I love Bessie Smith." And don't even understand that Bessie 240 Smith is saying, "Kiss my ass, kiss my black unruly ass." Before love, suffering, desire, anything you can explain, she's saying, and very plainly, "Kiss my black ass." And if you don't know that, it's you that's doing the kissing.

Charlie Parker? Charlie Parker. All the hip white boys 245 scream for Bird. And Bird saying, "Up your ass, feeble-minded ofay! Up your ass." And they sit there talking about the tortured genius of Charlie Parker. Bird would've played not a note of music if he just walked up to East Sixty-seventh Street and killed the first ten white people he saw. Not a 250 note! And I'm the great would-be poet. Yes. That's right! Poet. Some kind of bastard literature . . . all it needs is a simple knife thrust. Just let me bleed you, you loud whore, and one poem vanished. A whole people of neurotics, struggling to keep from being sane. And the only thing that would cure 255 the neurosis would be your murder. Simple as that. I mean if

I murdered you, then other white people would begin to understand me. You understand? No. I guess not. If Bessie Smith had killed some white people she wouldn't have needed that music. She could have talked very straight and plain about the world. No metaphors. No grunts. No wiggles in the dark of her soul. Just straight two and two are four. Money. Power. Luxury. Like that. All of them. Crazy niggers turning their backs on sanity. When all it needs is that simple act. Murder. Just murder! Would make us all sane.

(Suddenly weary.)

Ahhh. Shit. But who needs it? I'd rather be a fool. Insane. Safe with my words, and no deaths, and clean, hard thoughts, urging me to new conquests. My people's madness. Hah! That's a laugh. My people. They don't need me to claim them. They got legs and arms of their own. Personal insanities. Mirrors. They don't need all those words. They don't need any defense. But listen, though, one more thing. And you tell this to your father, who's probably the kind of man who needs to know at once. So he can plan ahead. Tell him not to preach so much rationalism and cold logic to these niggers. Let them alone. Let them sing curses at you in code and see your filth as simple lack of style. Don't make the mistake, through some irresponsible surge of Christian charity, of talking too much about the advantages of Western rationalism, or the great intellectual legacy of the white man, or maybe they'll begin to listen. And then, maybe one day, you'll find they actually do understand exactly what you are talking about, all these fantasy people. All these blues people. And on that day, as sure as shit, when you really believe you can "accept" them into your fold, as half-white trusties late of the subject peoples. With no more blues, except the very old ones, and not a watermelon in sight, the great missionary heart will have triumphed, and all of those ex-coons will be stand-up Western men, with eyes for clean hard useful lives, sober, pious and sane, and they'll murder you. They'll murder you, and have very rational explanations. Very much like your own. They'll cut your throats, and drag you out to the edge of your cities so the flesh can fall away from your bones, in sanitary isolation.

LULA:

(Her voice takes on a different, more businesslike quality.)

I've heard enough.

CLAY:

(Reaching for his books.)

I bet you have. I guess I better collect my stuff and get off this train. Looks like we won't be acting out that little pageant you outlined before.

LULA: No. We won't. You're right about that, at least.

(She turns to look quickly around the rest of the car.)

All right!

(The others respond.)

CLAY:

(Bending across the girl to retrieve his belongings.)

Sorry, baby, I don't think we could make it.

(As he is bending over her, the girl brings up a small knife and plunges it into CLAY's chest. Twice. He slumps across her knees, his mouth working stupidly.)

LULA: Sorry is right.

(Turning to the others in the car who have already gotten up from their seats.)

Sorry is the rightest thing you've said. Get this man off me! Hurry, now!

(The others come and drag CLAY's body down the aisle.)

Open the door and throw his body out.

(They throw him off.)

And all of you get off at the next stop.

(LULA busies herself straightening her things. Getting everything in order. She takes out a notebook and makes a quick scribbling note. Drops it in her bag. The train apparently stops and all the others get off, leaving her alone in the coach. Very soon a young Negro of about twenty comes into the coach, with a couple of books under his arm. He sits a few seats in back of LULA. When he is seated she turns and gives him a long slow look. He looks up from his book and drops the book on his lap. Then an old Negro CONDUCTOR comes into the car, doing a sort of restrained soft shoe, and half mumbling the words of some song. He looks at the young man, briefly, with a quick greeting.)

CONDUCTOR: Hey, brother!
YOUNG MAN: Hey.

(The CONDUCTOR continues down the aisle with his little dance and the mumbled song. LULA turns to stare at him and follows his movements down the aisle. The CONDUCTOR tips his hat when he reaches her seat, and continues out the car.)

■ LUIS VALDEZ ■
AND EL TEATRO CAMPESINO

Luis Valdez (b. 1940), was born and raised the son of farmworkers in Delano, California. He majored in English at San Jose State College, taking his B.A. in 1964, and then joined the San Francisco Mime Troupe, an important experimental theater company. In 1965, when farm workers at the Delano grape plantations went on strike, Valdez formed El Teatro Campesino ("The Farmworkers' Theater"). Valdez and Teatro Campesino devised two dramatic forms: ACTOS, short, satirical plays dramatizing the oppression of the fieldworkers, and MITOS, poetic, lyrical plays on Chicano life. *Actos* were improvised by members of El Teatro Campesino playing "stock" characters (the farmworker, the boss, etc.); because they were improvised for each production and each community, *actos* varied considerably from performance to performance. The final versions published by Valdez were written down much later. El Teatro Campesino became one of several important Chicano theater companies that performed throughout the Southwest and in urban areas of the Midwest and Northeast, drawing on both American and European dramatic traditions, as well as traditions of Mexican and Spanish-language theater in the United States that date to the seventeenth century. In the late 1960s and 1970s, Teatro Campesino toured the United States and Europe and gained an international reputation. Valdez's other *actos* with Teatro Campesino include *Las Dos Caras del Patroncito* (1965), *No Saco Nada de la Escuela* (1969), and *Vietnam Campesino* (1970). Valdez produced the stage play *Zoot Suit* in 1978, which was released as a film in 1981. In 1980, Valdez transformed El Teatro Campesino into a production company, a marked shift from its collaborative and activist origins. This version of El Teatro Campesino hired "professional" actors, abandoning the collective aesthetic characteristic of the company's earlier work. Valdez developed several new projects in connection with the company's new theatre in San Juan Bautista (built in 1981), notably *Bandido!* (1981), *Corridos* (1992), and *I Don't Have to Show You No Stinking Badges* (1990). His film *La Bamba* was released in 1987, and Valdez filmed *Pastorelas* for PBS TV in 1990. Valdez has held academic appointments at the University of California, Berkeley, and at the University of California, Santa Cruz. He is teaching at the new campus of the California State University at Monterey.

LOS VENDIDOS

One of Teatro Campesino's best and most popular *actos*, *Los Vendidos*—"The Sellouts"—is reminiscent both of Brechtian political theater and more generally of popular satire. In its brief sketch of Honest Sancho's Used Mexican Lot, the play dramatizes a range of stereotypes applied by Anglo culture (represented by the Anglicized Mexican-American, Miss JIM-enez) to Chicano experience: farmworkers, Johnny Pachuco, the *revolucionario*, and the "new 1970 Mexican-American" yuppie. In the play's surprising finale, though, the yuppie turns on Miss JIM-enez, and the "used Mexicans" turn out to run the shop: Honest Sancho is *their* front.

The play clearly engages conflicting attitudes toward social experience, as emblematized by its title. For the title can mean both "those who are sold"—like the "used Mexicans" on Sancho's lot—and "the sellouts," presumably Honest Sancho and Miss JIM-enez. This duplicity is also inflected by the play's language, its mixture of Spanish and English, the two languages Chicano culture uses to define itself and to engage the Anglo world. The play works at the border between two cultures, where language is part of the complex social and political negotiation that characterizes Mexican-American life today.

LOS VENDIDOS

Luis Valdez and El Teatro Campesino

— CHARACTERS —

HONEST SANCHO
SECRETARY
FARM WORKER
JOHNNY
REVOLUCIONARIO
MEXICAN-AMERICAN

SCENE: HONEST SANCHO's *Used Mexican Lot and Mexican Curio Shop. Three models are on display in* HONEST SANCHO's *shop: to the right, there is a* REVOLUCIONARIO, *complete with sombrero, carrilleras, and carabina 30-30. At center, on the floor, there is the* FARM WORKER, *under a broad straw sombrero. At stage left is the* PACHUCO, *filero in hand.*

(HONEST SANCHO *is moving among his models, dusting them off and preparing for another day of business.*)

SANCHO: Bueno, bueno, mis monos, vamos a ver a quien vendemos ahora, ¿no? (*To audience.*) ¡Quihubo! I'm Honest Sancho and this is my shop. Antes fui contratista pero ahora logré tener mi negocito. All I need now is a customer. (*A bell
5   rings offstage.*) Ay, a customer!
SECRETARY: (*Entering.*) Good morning, I'm Miss Jiménez from—
SANCHO: ¡Ah, una chicana! Welcome, welcome Señorita Jiménez.
10 SECRETARY: (*Anglo pronunciation.*) JIM-enez.
SANCHO: ¿Qué?
SECRETARY: My name is Miss JIM-enez. Don't you speak English? What's wrong with you?
SANCHO: Oh, nothing, Señorita JIM-enez. I'm here to help
15   you.
SECRETARY: That's better. As I was starting to say, I'm a secretary from Governor Reagan's office, and we're looking for a Mexican type for the administration.
SANCHO: Well, you come to the right place, lady. This is Hon-
20   est Sancho's Used Mexican lot, and we got all types here. Any particular type you want?
SECRETARY: Yes, we were looking for somebody suave—
SANCHO: Suave.
SECRETARY: Debonair.
25 SANCHO: De buen aire.
SECRETARY: Dark.
SANCHO: Prieto.
SECRETARY: But of course not too dark.
SANCHO: No muy prieto.
30 SECRETARY: Perhaps, beige.
SANCHO: Beige, just the tone. Así como cafecito con leche, ¿no?
SECRETARY: One more thing. He must be hard-working.
SANCHO: That could only be one model. Step right over here
35   to the center of the shop, lady. (*They cross to the* FARM WORKER.) This is our standard farm worker model. As you

can see, in the words of our beloved Senator George Murphy, he is "built close to the ground." Also take special notice of his four-ply Goodyear huaraches, made from the rain tire. This wide-brimmed sombrero is an extra added fea- 40
ture—keeps off the sun, rain, and dust.
SECRETARY: Yes, it does look durable.
SANCHO: And our farm worker model is friendly. Muy amable. Watch. (*Snaps his fingers.*)
FARM WORKER: (*Lifts up head.*) Buenos días, señorita. (*His* 45
head drops.)
SECRETARY: My, he's friendly.
SANCHO: Didn't I tell you? Loves his patrones! But his most attractive feature is that he's hard-working. Let me show you. (*Snaps fingers.* FARM WORKER *stands.*) 50
FARM WORKER: ¡El jale! (*He begins to work.*)
SANCHO: As you can see, he is cutting grapes.
SECRETARY: Oh, I wouldn't know.
SANCHO: He also picks cotton. (*Snap.* FARM WORKER *begins to pick cotton.*) 55
SECRETARY: Versatile isn't he?
SANCHO: He also picks melons. (*Snap.* FARM WORKER *picks melons.*) That's his slow speed for late in the season. Here's his fast speed. (*Snap.* FARM WORKER *picks faster.*)
SECRETARY: ¡Chihuahua! . . . I mean, goodness, he sure is a 60
hard worker.
SANCHO: (*Pulls the* FARM WORKER *to his feet.*) And that isn't the half of it. Do you see these little holes on his arms that appear to be pores? During those hot sluggish days in the field, when the vines or the branches get so entangled, it's al- 65
most impossible to move; these holes emit a certain grease that allow our model to slip and slide right through the crop with no trouble at all.
SECRETARY: Wonderful. But is he economical?
SANCHO: Economical? Señorita, you are looking at the Volk- 70
swagen of Mexicans. Pennies a day is all it takes. One plate of beans and tortillas will keep him going all day. That, and chile. Plenty of chile. Chile jalapenos, chile verde, chile colorado. But, of course, if you do give him chile (*Snap.* FARM
WORKER *turns left face. Snap.* FARM WORKER *bends over.*) 75
then you have to change his oil filter once a week.
SECRETARY: What about storage?
SANCHO: No problem. You know these new farm labor camps our Honorable Governor Reagan has built out by Parlier or

---

Scene **carrilleras** literally chin straps, but may refer to cartridge belts
Scene **Pachuco** Chicano slang for 1940s zoot suiter **filero** blade   1–2
Bueno, bueno, . . . Quihubo "Good, good, my cute ones, let's see who we can sell now, O.K.?"   3–4 **Antes fui . . . negocito** "I used to be a contractor, but now I've succeeded in having my little business."   31
Así como . . . leche like coffee with milk

43 **Muy amable** very friendly   51 **El jale** the job

882

80   Raisin City? They were designed with our model in mind. Five, six, seven, even ten in one of those shacks will give you no trouble at all. You can also put him in old barns, old cars, river banks. You can even leave him out in the field overnight with no worry!

85   SECRETARY: Remarkable.

SANCHO: And here's an added feature: Every year at the end of the season, this model goes back to Mexico and doesn't return, automatically, until next Spring.

SECRETARY: How about that. But tell me: does he speak
90   English?

SANCHO: Another outstanding feature is that last year this model was programmed to go out on STRIKE! (*Snap.*)

FARM WORKER: ¡HUELGA! ¡HUELGA! Hermanos, sálganse de esos files. (*Snap. He stops.*)

95   SECRETARY: No! Oh no, we can't strike in the State Capitol.

SANCHO: Well, he also scabs. (*Snap.*)

FARM WORKER: Me vendo barato, ¿y qué? (*Snap.*)

SECRETARY: That's much better, but you didn't answer my question. Does he speak English?

100   SANCHO: Bueno . . . no pero he has other—

SECRETARY: No.

SANCHO: Other features.

SECRETARY: NO! He just won't do!

SANCHO: Okay, okay pues. We have other models.

105   SECRETARY: I hope so. What we need is something a little more sophisticated.

SANCHO: Sophisti—¿qué?

SECRETARY: An urban model.

SANCHO: Ah, from the city! Step right back. Over here in this
110   corner of the shop is exactly what you're looking for. Introducing our new 1969 JOHNNY PACHUCO model! This is our fast-back model. Streamlined. Built for speed, low-riding, city life. Take a look at some of these features. Mag shoes, dual exhausts, green chartreuse paint-job, dark-tint
115   windshield, a little poof on top. Let me just turn him on. (*Snap.* JOHNNY *walks to stage center with a pachuco bounce.*)

SECRETARY: What was that?

SANCHO: That, señorita, was the Chicano shuffle.

SECRETARY: Okay, what does he do?

120   SANCHO: Anything and everything necessary for city life. For instance, survival: He knife fights. (*Snap.* JOHNNY *pulls out switch blade and swings at secretary.*)

(SECRETARY *screams.*)

SANCHO: He dances. (*Snap.*)

JOHNNY: (*Singing.*) "Angel Baby, my Angel Baby . . ." (*Snap.*)

125   SANCHO: And here's a feature no city model can be without. He gets arrested, but not without resisting, of course. (*Snap.*)

JOHNNY: ¡En la madre, la placa! I didn't do it! I didn't do it! (JOHNNY *turns and stands up against an imaginary wall, legs spread out, arms behind his back.*)

130   SECRETARY: Oh no, we can't have arrests! We must maintain law and order.

SANCHO: But he's bilingual!

SECRETARY: Bilingual?

SANCHO: Simón que yes. He speaks English! Johnny, give us some English. (*Snap.*)

135   JOHNNY: (*Comes downstage.*) Fuck-you!

SECRETARY: (*Gasps.*) Oh! I've never been so insulted in my whole life!

SANCHO: Well, he learned it in your school.

SECRETARY: I don't care where he learned it.

140   SANCHO: But he's economical!

SECRETARY: Economical?

SANCHO: Nickels and dimes. You can keep Johnny running on hamburgers, Taco Bell tacos, Lucky Lager beer, Thunderbird wine, yesca—

145   SECRETARY: Yesca?

SANCHO: Mota.

SECRETARY: Mota?

SANCHO: Leños . . . Marijuana. (*Snap;* JOHNNY *inhales on an imaginary joint.*)

150   SECRETARY: That's against the law!

JOHNNY: (*Big smile, holding his breath.*) Yeah.

SANCHO: He also sniffs glue. (*Snap.* JOHNNY *inhales glue, big smile.*)

JOHNNY: Tha's too much man, ése.

155   SECRETARY: No, Mr. Sancho, I don't think this—

SANCHO: Wait a minute, he has other qualities I know you'll love. For example, an inferiority complex. (*Snap.*)

JOHNNY: (*To* SANCHO.) You think you're better than me, huh ése? (*Swings switch blade.*)

160   SANCHO: He can also be beaten and he bruises, cut him and he bleeds; kick him and he—(*He beats, bruises and kicks* PACHUCO.) would you like to try it?

SECRETARY: Oh, I couldn't.

SANCHO: Be my guest. He's a great scapegoat.

165   SECRETARY: No, really.

SANCHO: Please.

SECRETARY: Well, all right. Just once. (*She kicks* PACHUCO.) Oh, he's so soft.

SANCHO: Wasn't that good? Try again.

170   SECRETARY: (*Kicks* PACHUCO.) Oh, he's so wonderful! (*She kicks him again.*)

SANCHO: Okay, that's enough, lady. You ruin the merchandise. Yes, our Johnny Pachuco model can give you many hours of pleasure. Why, the L.A.P.D. just bought twenty of
175   these to train their rookie cops on. And talk about maintenance. Señorita, you are looking at an entirely self-supporting machine. You're never going to find our Johnny Pachuco model on the relief rolls. No, sir, this model knows how to liberate.

180   SECRETARY: Liberate?

SANCHO: He steals. (*Snap.* JOHNNY *rushes the* SECRETARY *and steals her purse.*)

JOHNNY: ¡Dame esa bolsa, vieja! (*He grabs the purse and runs. Snap by* SANCHO. *He stops.*)

185

(SECRETARY *runs after* JOHNNY *and grabs purse away from him, kicking him as she goes.*)

---

93 **¡HUELGA! ¡HUELGA!** . . . **esos files** "Strike! Strike! Brothers, leave those rows."   97 **Me vendo . . . qué** "I come cheap, so what?"   100 **Bueno . . . no, pero** "Well, no, but . . ."   127 **En la . . . placa** "Wow, the police!"

134 **Simón** . . . **yes** yeah, sure   149 **Leños** "joints" of marijuana   184 **Dame esa** . . . , **vieja** "Gimme that bag, old lady!"

SECRETARY: No, no, no! We can't have any *more* thieves in the State Administration. Put him back.

SANCHO: Okay, we still got other models. Come on, Johnny, we'll sell you to some old lady. (SANCHO *takes* JOHNNY *back to his place.*)

190 SECRETARY: Mr. Sancho, I don't think you quite understand what we need. What we need is something that will attract the women voters. Something more traditional, more romantic.

195 SANCHO: Ah, a lover. (*He smiles meaningfully.*) Step right over here, señorita. Introducing our standard Revolucionario and/or Early California Bandit type. As you can see he is well-built, sturdy, durable. This is the International Harvester of Mexicans.

200 SECRETARY: What does he do?

SANCHO: You name it, he does it. He rides horses, stays in the mountains, crosses deserts, plains, rivers, leads revolutions, follows revolutions, kills, can be killed, serves as a martyr, hero, movie star—did I say movie star? Did you ever see *Viva*

205 *Zapata? Viva Villa? Villa Rides? Pancho Villa Returns? Pancho Villa Goes Back? Pancho Villa Meets Abbot and Costello—*

SECRETARY: I've never seen any of those.

SANCHO: Well, he was in all of them. Listen to this. (*Snap.*)

210 REVOLUCIONARIO: (*Scream.*) ¡VIVA VILLAAAAA!

SECRETARY: That's awfully loud.

SANCHO: He has a volume control. (*He adjusts volume. Snap.*)

REVOLUCIONARIO: (*Mousey voice.*) ¡Viva Villa!

SECRETARY: That's better.

215 SANCHO: And even if you didn't see him in the movies, perhaps you saw him on TV. He makes commercials. (*Snap.*)

REVOLUCIONARIO: Is there a Frito Bandito in your house?

SECRETARY: Oh yes, I've seen that one!

SANCHO: Another feature about this one is that he is economi-

220 cal. He runs on raw horsemeat and tequila!

SECRETARY: Isn't that rather savage?

SANCHO: Al contrario, it makes him a lover. (*Snap.*)

REVOLUCIONARIO: (*To* SECRETARY.) ¡Ay, mamasota, cochota, ven pa'ca! (*He grabs* SECRETARY *and folds her back—Latin*

225 *lover style.*)

SANCHO: (*Snap.* REVOLUCIONARIO *goes back upright.*) Now wasn't that nice?

SECRETARY: Well, it was rather nice.

SANCHO: And finally, there is one outstanding feature about

230 this model I KNOW the ladies are going to love: He's a GENUINE antique! He was made in Mexico in 1910!

SECRETARY: Made in Mexico?

SANCHO: That's right. Once in Tijuana, twice in Guadalajara, three times in Cuernavaca.

235 SECRETARY: Mr. Sancho, I thought he was an American product.

SANCHO: No, but—

SECRETARY: No, I'm sorry. We can't buy anything but American-made products. He just won't do.

240 SANCHO: But he's an antique!

---

222 **Al contrario** on the contrary

SECRETARY: I don't care. You still don't understand what we need. It's true we need Mexican models such as these, but it's more important that he be *American*.

SANCHO: American?

SECRETARY: That's right, and judging from what you've shown 245 me, I don't think you have what we want. Well, my lunch hour's almost over; I better—

SANCHO: Wait a minute! Mexican but American?

SECRETARY: That's correct.

SANCHO: Mexican but . . . (*A sudden flash.*) AMERICAN! 250 Yeah, I think we've got exactly what you want. He just came in today! Give me a minute. (*He exits. Talks from backstage.*) Here he is in the shop. Let me just get some papers off. There. Introducing our new 1970 Mexican-American! Ta-ra-ra-ra-ra-ra-RA-RAAA! 255

(SANCHO *brings out the* MEXICAN-AMERICAN *model, a clean-shaven middle-class type in business suit, with glasses.*)

SECRETARY: (*Impressed.*) Where have you been hiding this one?

SANCHO: He just came in this morning. Ain't he a beauty? Feast your eyes on him! Sturdy US STEEL frame, stream-lined, modern. As a matter of fact, he is built exactly like our 260 Anglo models except that he comes in a variety of darker shades: naugahyde, leather, or leatherette.

SECRETARY: Naugahyde.

SANCHO: Well, we'll just write that down. Yes, señorita, this model represents the apex of American engineering! He is 265 bilingual, college educated, ambitious! Say the word "accul-turate" and he accelerates. He is intelligent, well-mannered, clean—did I say clean? (*Snap.* MEXICAN-AMERICAN *raises his arm.*) Smell.

SECRETARY: (*Smells.*) Old Sobaco, my favorite. 270

SANCHO: (*Snap.* MEXICAN-AMERICAN *turns toward* SANCHO.) Eric! (*To* SECRETARY.) We call him Eric Garcia. (*To* ERIC.) I want you to meet Miss JIM-enez, Eric.

MEXICAN-AMERICAN: Miss JIM-enez, I am delighted to make your acquaintance. (*He kisses her hand.*) 275

SECRETARY: Oh, my, how charming!

SANCHO: Did you feel the suction? He has seven especially engineered suction cups right behind his lips. He's a charmer all right!

SECRETARY: How about boards? Does he function on boards? 280

SANCHO: You name them, he is on them. Parole boards, draft boards, school boards, taco quality control boards, surf boards, two-by-fours.

SECRETARY: Does he function in politics?

SANCHO: Señorita, you are looking at a political MACHINE. 285 Have you ever heard of the OEO, EOC, COD, WAR ON POVERTY? That's our model! Not only that, he makes political speeches.

SECRETARY: May I hear one?

SANCHO: With pleasure. (*Snap.*) Eric, give us a speech. 290

MEXICAN-AMERICAN: Mr. Congressman, Mr. Chairman, members of the board, honored guests, ladies and gentlemen. (SANCHO *and* SECRETARY *applaud.*) Please, please, I come before you as a Mexican-American to tell you about the problems of the Mexican. The problems of the Mexican 295 stem from one thing and one thing alone: He's stupid. He's uneducated. He needs to stay in school. He needs to be ambitious, forward-looking, harder-working. He needs to think American, American, American, AMERICAN, AMERICAN, AMERICAN. GOD BLESS AMERICA! GOD BLESS AMERICA!! (*He goes out of control.*)

300

(SANCHO *snaps frantically and the* MEXICAN-AMERICAN *finally slumps forward, bending at the waist.*)

SECRETARY: Oh my, he's patriotic too!

SANCHO: Sí, señorita, he loves his country. Let me just make a little adjustment here. (*Stands* MEXICAN-AMERICAN *up.*)

305

SECRETARY: What about upkeep? Is he economical?

SANCHO: Well, no, I won't lie to you. The Mexican-American costs a little bit more, but you get what you pay for. He's worth every extra cent. You can keep him running on dry martinis, Langendorf bread.

310

SECRETARY: Apple pie?

SANCHO: Only Mom's. Of course, he's also programmed to eat Mexican food on ceremonial functions, but I must warn you: an overdose of beans will plug up his exhaust.

SECRETARY: Fine! There's just one more question: HOW MUCH DO YOU WANT FOR HIM?

315

SANCHO: Well, I tell you what I'm gonna do. Today and today only, because you've been so sweet, I'm gonna let you steal this model from me! I'm gonna let you drive him off the lot for the simple price of—let's see taxes and license included—$15,000.

320

SECRETARY: Fifteen thousand DOLLARS? For a MEXICAN!

SANCHO: Mexican? What are you talking, lady? This is a Mexican-AMERICAN! We had to melt down two pachucos, a farm worker and three gabachos to make this model! You want quality, but you gotta pay for it! This is no cheap runabout. He's got class!

325

SECRETARY: Okay, I'll take him.

SANCHO: You will?

SECRETARY: Here's your money.

330

SANCHO: You mind if I count it?

SECRETARY: Go right ahead.

SANCHO: Well, you'll get your pink slip in the mail. Oh, do you want me to wrap him up for you? We have a box in the back.

335

SECRETARY: No, thank you. The Governor is having a luncheon this afternoon, and we need a brown face in the crowd. How do I drive him?

SANCHO: Just snap your fingers. He'll do anything you want.

(SECRETARY *snaps.* MEXICAN-AMERICAN *steps forward.*)

340

MEXICAN-AMERICAN: RAZA QUERIDA, ¡VAMOS LEVANTANDO ARMAS PARA LIBERARNOS DE ESTOS DESGRACIADOS GABACHOS QUE NOS EXPLOTAN! VAMOS.

SECRETARY: What did he say?

345

SANCHO: Something about lifting arms, killing white people, etc.

SECRETARY: But he's not supposed to say that!

SANCHO: Look, lady, don't blame me for bugs from the factory. He's your Mexican-American; you bought him, now drive him off the lot!

SECRETARY: But he's broken!

350

SANCHO: Try snapping another finger.

(SECRETARY *snaps.* MEXICAN-AMERICAN *comes to life again.*)

MEXICAN-AMERICAN: ¡ESTA GRAN HUMANIDAD HA DICHO BASTA! Y SE HA PUESTO EN MARCHA! ¡BASTA! ¡BASTA! ¡VIVA LA RAZA! ¡VIVA LA CAUSA! ¡VIVA LA HUELGA! ¡VIVAN LOS BROWN BERETS! ¡VIVAN LOS ESTUDIANTES! ¡CHICANO POWER!

355

(*The* MEXICAN-AMERICAN *turns toward the* SECRETARY, *who gasps and backs up. He keeps turning toward the* PACHUCO, FARM WORKER, *and* REVOLUCIONARIO, *snapping his fingers and turning each of them on, one by one.*)

PACHUCO: (*Snap. To* SECRETARY.) I'm going to get you, baby! ¡Viva La Raza!

FARM WORKER: (*Snap. To* SECRETARY.) ¡Viva la huelga! ¡Viva la Huelga! ¡VIVA LA HUELGA!

360

REVOLUCIONARIO: (*Snap. To* SECRETARY.) ¡Viva la revolución! ¡VIVA LA REVOLUCIÓN!

REVOLUCIONARIO: (*Snap. To* SECRETARY.) ¡Viva la revolución! ¡VIVA LA REVOLUCIÓN!

(*The three models join together and advance toward the* SECRETARY *who backs up and runs out of the shop screaming.* SANCHO *is at the other end of the shop holding his money in his hand. All freeze. After a few seconds of silence, the* PACHUCO *moves and stretches, shaking his arms and loosening up. The* FARM WORKER *and* REVOLUCIONARIO *do the same.* SANCHO *stays where he is, frozen to his spot.*)

JOHNNY: Man, that was a long one, ése. (*Others agree with him.*)

365

FARM WORKER: How did we do?

JOHNNY: Perty good, look all that lana, man! (*He goes over to* SANCHO *and removes the money from his hand.* SANCHO *stays where he is.*)

370

REVOLUCIONARIO: En la madre, look at all the money.

JOHNNY: We keep this up, we're going to be rich.

FARM WORKER: They think we're machines.

REVOLUCIONARIO: Burros.

JOHNNY: Puppets.

375

MEXICAN-AMERICAN: The only thing I don't like is—how come I always got to play the goddamn Mexican-American?

JOHNNY: That's what you get for finishing high school.

FARM WORKER: How about our wages, ése?

JOHNNY: Here it comes right now. $3,000 for you, $3,000 for you, $3,000 for you, and $3,000 for me. The rest we put back into the business.

380

MEXICAN-AMERICAN: Too much, man. Heh, where you vatos going tonight?

FARM WORKER: I'm going over to Concha's. There's a party.

385

339–342 **RAZA QUERIDA, . . . VAMOS** "Beloved Raza, let's pick up arms to liberate ourselves from those damned whites that exploit us! Let's go."

352–356 **ESTA GRAN . . . CHICANO POWER** "This great mass of humanity has said enough! And it begins to march! Enough! Enough! Long live La Raza! Long live the Cause! Long live the strike! Long live the Brown Berets! Long live the students! Chicano Power!"

JOHNNY: Wait a minute, vatos. What about our salesman? I think he needs an oil job.

REVOLUCIONARIO: Leave him to me.

(*The* PACHUCO, FARM WORKER, *and* MEXICAN-AMERICAN *exit, talking loudly about their plans for the night. The* REVOLU-CIONARIO *goes over to* SANCHO, *removes his derby hat and cigar, lifts him up and throws him over his shoulder.* SANCHO *hangs loose, lifeless.*)

REVOLUCIONARIO: (*To audience.*) He's the best model we got! ¡Ajúa! (*Exit.*)

390

■ MARIA IRENE FORNES ■

Maria Irene Fornes was born in Cuba in 1930, and emigrated to the United States in 1945. She toured Europe in the mid-1950s studying to be a painter, and in Paris saw Roger Blin's production of Beckett's *Waiting for Godot*. Fornes was impressed both by its power and by its severe visual imagery onstage. Fornes returned to the United States in 1957 as a textile designer, but three years later had the idea for her first play, *Tango Palace*. Fornes has had a distinguished career in the avant-garde theater, experimenting in a variety of theatrical modes: she has produced brilliant absurdist plays like *There! You Died* (1963; revised as *Tango Palace* in 1964) and *Dr. Kheal* (1968); a successful musical, *Promenade* (1965, music by Al Carmines); and a moving, ritual-participatory play, *A Vietnamese Wedding* (1967). More recently, her plays have taken a more serious—though no less experimental—turn, examining women's identity in *Fefu and Her Friends* (1977) and *Abingdon Square* (1988), the relationship between politics, language, and love in *The Danube* (1982), and military and sexual oppression in Latin America in *The Conduct of Life* (1985). In 1986, she wrote another musical, with Tito Puente, *Lovers and Keepers*. Fornes has won several prestigious awards, including an Obie for Sustained Achievement in the Theater in 1982.

FEFU AND HER FRIENDS

Fefu and Her Friends is one of Fornes's most-performed plays; it was originally written to be performed as a piece of ENVIRONMENTAL THEATER in a SoHo loft, and has since been produced in conventional theaters as well as in "home" performance spaces. The play is set in 1935 and takes place in Fefu's home, where she has invited a group of women to rehearse a series of skits for a charity benefit. The women are introduced to the audience in the first scene and seem to know each other well—some were friends in college, and two are lovers, or ex-lovers. In several ways, the action of the play centers on Julia, who is in a wheelchair as the result of a mysterious hunting accident: although the bullet missed her, she is nonetheless paralyzed and haunted by mysterious male voices, the "judges" who torment her in Part 2.

On several occasions, Fornes has argued that *Fefu* is not a specifically "feminist" play; while this may be true, the play certainly raises the question of the relations of power that structure the lives of the women in the world of the play. From Fefu's opening line ("My husband married me to have a constant reminder of how loathsome women are") to Emma's question in Part 2 ("Do you think about genitals all the time?") to Julia's extraordinary monologue, in which she seems to give voice to the unconscious and oppressive voice of the patriarchy itself ("The human being is of the masculine gender"), the play seems to turn on the way the women's sense of themselves is deformed. The women seem, that is, to have internalized a male vision of themselves, a vision of their inferiority and powerlessness, that they are able to combat only in indirect ways—like the game Fefu plays with her husband Phillip, in which she shoots a gun at him not knowing whether it's loaded with live ammunition or blanks. Despite the horror of Julia's suffering, however, *Fefu* is in many ways a comedy; though Julia dies—again, she is hit by a bullet that appears to have missed her—the play seems to confirm the survival of Fefu and her friends.

One of the most striking features of *Fefu and Her Friends* is Fornes's brilliant manipulation of the conventions of realistic theater and of realistic performance. In one sense, *Fefu* is deeply indebted to the formal traditions of American realism: it is a domestic play that is so "realistic" that it invites the audience into Fefu's home and encourages them to follow the characters around the house in Part 2. Yet by inviting its audience into the performance space, Fornes subtly reshapes the dynamics of realistic representation; the audience is no longer a privileged observer, looking "scientifically" or "objectively" through the fourth-wall window into the secret lives of the characters. Instead, Fornes unseats the audience, divides it into four groups, and in the second section of the play each group sees each of the four scenes in a different order. The effect of this device is striking; the audience members (in small groups) are usually much closer to the performers, sharing their space; whether the "Kitchen Scene" is performed in an offstage area of a theater or in an actual kitchen, the actors play the scene in an intimate relation to the audience, one that enables their performance to be much more low-key, much more like everyday behavior. Moreover, throughout Part 2, the audience is aware that all four scenes are being played simultaneously (and repeated three times). While one group is watching the "Lawn Scene," for instance, it may well hear Julia's screams in the "Bedroom Scene."

By bringing her audience into the scene, Fornes works to break down the traditional logic of realistic theater. We see the characters from inside their world and have a different position of "judgment" in relation to them—especially after Julia's monologue, in which the audience "stands in" for the invisible "judges." Part 2 also breaks down the logic of realistic drama, in that the audience is made aware that it doesn't share a single perspective on the events, the omniscient viewpoint of the absent spectator of realism. We know, even as we take different seats in Part 3 than we had in Part 1, that at least *four* plays have been seen by the audience, and that how we interpret the action depends not only on the order in which we have witnessed the scenes, but perhaps on where we sit as well. This multiplication of perspective is complemented by Fornes's brilliant and elliptical strategy of characterization in the play, for Fornes's dialogue is at once familiar and surprising; the language seems both to obey the conventional superficiality of realistic dialogue and suddenly to swerve into other registers of feeling and experience. In the expressionist theater of the early twentieth century, characters often were able to speak their "thoughts" to an audience, and the Shakespearean soliloquy usually enables a character to reveal or explore some inner question. However, Fornes's strategy here is much more subtle, much more unstable, for the boundary between "inner" and "outer" discourse is often uncertain. By blurring the boundary between actors and audience in Part 2, Fornes also presents her characters as more flexible and elastic, capable of giving voice to emotions, anxieties, and desires that are usually concealed from view, hidden as much behind the conventions of realistic representation as they are behind the façade with which the women confront the masculine world around them.

FEFU AND HER FRIENDS

Maria Irene Fornes

— CHARACTERS —

FEFU
CINDY
CHRISTINA
JULIA
EMMA
PAULA
SUE
CECILIA

New England, Spring 1935.

Part I: Noon. The living room. The entire audience watches from the main auditorium.

Part II: Afternoon. The lawn, the study, the bedroom, the kitchen. The audience is divided into four groups. Each group is led to the spaces. These scenes are performed simultaneously. When the scenes are completed the audience moves to the next space and the scenes are performed again. This is repeated four times until each group has seen all four scenes. Then the audience is led back to the main auditorium.

Part III: Evening. The living room. The entire audience watches from the main auditorium.

Author's Note: Fefu is pronounced Feh-foo.

— PART I —

The living room of a country house in New England. The decor is a tasteful mixture of styles. To the right is the foyer and the main door. To the left, French doors leading to a terrace, the lawn and a pond. At the rear, there are stairs that lead to the upper floor, the entrance to the kitchen, and the entrance to other rooms on the ground floor. A couch faces the audience. There is a coffee table, two chairs on each side of the table. Upstage right there is a piano. Against the right wall there is an open liquor cabinet. Besides bottles of liquor there are glasses, an ice bucket, and a seltzer bottle. A double barrel shotgun leans on the wall near the French doors. On the table there is a dish with chocolates. On the couch there is a throw. FEFU *stands on the landing.* CINDY *lies on the couch.* CHRISTINA *sits on the chair to the right.*

FEFU: My husband married me to have a constant reminder of how loathsome women are.
CINDY: What?
FEFU: Yup.
5 CINDY: That's just awful.
FEFU: No, it isn't.
CINDY: It isn't awful?
FEFU: No.
CINDY: I don't think anyone would marry for that reason.
10 FEFU: He did.
CINDY: Did he say so?
FEFU: He tells me constantly.
CINDY: Oh, dear.
FEFU: I don't mind. I laugh when he tells me.
15 CINDY: You laugh?
FEFU: I do.
CINDY: How can you?
FEFU: It's funny.—And it's true. That's why I laugh.
CINDY: What is true?
20 FEFU: That women are loathsome.
CINDY: . . . Fefu!
FEFU: That shocks you.
CINDY: It does. I don't feel loathsome.
FEFU: I don't mean that you are loathsome.

CINDY: You don't mean that I'm loathsome. 25
FEFU: No . . . It's something to think about. It's a thought.
CINDY: It's a hideous thought.
FEFU: I take it all back.
CINDY: Isn't she incredible?
FEFU: Cindy, I'm not talking about anyone in particular. It's 30 something to think about.
CINDY: No one in particular, just women.
FEFU: Yes.
CINDY: In that case I am relieved. I thought you were referring to us. 35
FEFU: (*Affectionately.*) You are being stupid.
CINDY: Stupid and loathsome. (*To* CHRISTINA.) Have you ever heard anything so outrageous.
CHRISTINA: I am speechless.
FEFU: Why are you speechless? 40
CHRISTINA: I think you are outrageous.
FEFU: Don't be offended. I don't take enough care to be tactful. I know I don't. But don't be offended. Cindy is not offended. She pretends to be, but she isn't really. She understands what I mean. 45
CINDY: I do not.
FEFU: Yes, you do.—I like exciting ideas. They give me energy.
CHRISTINA: And how is women being loathsome an exciting idea?
FEFU: (*With mischief.*) It revolts me. 50
CHRISTINA: You find revulsion exciting?
FEFU: Don't you?
CHRISTINA: No.
FEFU: I do. It's something to grapple with.—What do you do with revulsion? 55
CHRISTINA: I avoid anything that's revolting to me.
FEFU: Hmmm. (*To* CINDY.) You too?
CINDY: Yes.
FEFU: Hmm. Have you ever turned a stone over in damp soil?
CHRISTINA: Ahm. 60
FEFU: And when you turn it there are worms crawling on it?
CHRISTINA: Ahm.
FEFU: And it's damp and full of fungus?

889

CHRISTINA: Ahm.

65 FEFU: Were you revolted?

CHRISTINA: Yes.

FEFU: Were you fascinated?

CHRISTINA: I was.

FEFU: There you have it! You too are fascinated with revulsion.

70 CHRISTINA: Hmm.

FEFU: You see, that which is exposed to the exterior . . . is smooth and dry and clean. That which is not . . . underneath, is slimy and filled with fungus and crawling with worms. It is another life that is parallel to the one we mani-

75 fest. It's there. The way worms are underneath the stone. If you don't recognize it . . . (*Whispering.*) it eats you. That is my opinion. Well, who is ready for lunch?

CINDY: I'll have some fried worms with lots of pepper.

FEFU: (*To* CHRISTINA.) You?

80 CHRISTINA: I'll have mine in a sandwich with mayonnaise.

FEFU: And to drink?

CHRISTINA: Just some dirty dishwater in a tall glass with ice.

(FEFU *looks at* CINDY.)

CINDY: That sounds fine.

FEFU: I'll go dig them up. (FEFU *walks to the French doors.*

85 *Beckoning* CHRISTINA.) Pst! (FEFU *gets the gun as* CHRISTINA *goes to the French doors.*) You haven't met Phillip. Have you?

CHRISTINA: No.

FEFU: That's him.

CHRISTINA: Which one?

90 FEFU: (*Aims and shoots.*) That one!

(CHRISTINA *and* CINDY *scream.* FEFU *smiles proudly. She blows on the mouth of the barrel. She puts down the gun and looks out again.*)

CINDY: Christ, Fefu.

FEFU: There he goes. He's up. It's a game we play. I shoot and he falls. Whenever he hears the blast he falls. No matter where he is, he falls. One time he fell in a puddle of mud

95 and his clothes were a mess. (*She looks out.*) It's not too bad. He's just dusting off some stuff. (*She waves to* PHILLIP *and starts to go upstairs.*) He's all right. Look.

CINDY: A drink?

CHRISTINA: Yes.

(CINDY *goes to the liquor cabinet.*)

100 CINDY: What would you like?

CHRISTINA: Bourbon and soda . . . (CINDY *puts ice and bourbon in a glass. As she starts to squirt the soda . . .*) lots of soda. Just soda. (CINDY *starts with a fresh glass. She starts to squirt soda just as* CHRISTINA *speaks.*) Wait. (CINDY *stops*

105 *squirting, but not soon enough.*) I'll have an ice cube with a few drops of bourbon. (CINDY *starts with a fresh glass.*)

CINDY: One or two ice cubes?

CHRISTINA: One. Something to suck on.

CINDY: She's unique. There's no one like her.

110 CHRISTINA: Thank God.

(CINDY *gives the drink to* CHRISTINA.)

CINDY: But she is lovely you know. She really is.

CHRISTINA: She's crazy.

CINDY: A little. She has a strange marriage.

CHRISTINA: Strange? It's revolting.—What is he like?

CINDY: He's crazy too. They drive each other crazy. They are 115 not crazy really. They drive each other crazy.

CHRISTINA: Why do they stay together?

CINDY: They love each other.

CHRISTINA: Love?

CINDY: It's love. 120

CHRISTINA: Who are the other two men?

CINDY: Fefu's younger brother, John. And the gardener. His name is Tom.—The gun is not loaded.

CHRISTINA: How do you know?

CINDY: It's not. Why should it be loaded? 125

CHRISTINA: It seemed to be loaded a moment ago.

CINDY: That was just a blank.

CHRISTINA: It sounded like a cannon shot.

CINDY: That was just gun powder. There's no bullet in a blank.

CHRISTINA: The blast alone could kill you. One can die of 130 fright, you know.

CINDY: True.

CHRISTINA: My heart is still beating.

CINDY: That's just fright. You're being a scaredy cat.

CHRISTINA: Of course it's just fright. It's fright. 135

CINDY: I mean, you were just scared. You didn't get hurt.

CHRISTINA: Just scared. I guess I was lucky I didn't get shot.

CINDY: Fefu won't shoot you. She only shoots Phillip.

CHRISTINA: That's nice of her. Put the gun away, I don't like looking at it. 140

FEFU: (*As she appears on the landing.*) I just fixed the toilet in your bathroom.

CINDY: You did?

FEFU: I did. The water stopper didn't work. It drained. I adjusted it. I'm waiting for the tank to fill up. Make sure it all 145 works.

CHRISTINA: You do your own plumbing?

FEFU: I just had to bend the metal that supports the rubber stopper so it falls right over the hole. What happened was it fell to the side so the water wouldn't stop running into the 150 bowl. (FEFU *sits near* CINDY.) He scared me this time, you know. He looked like he was really hurt.

CINDY: I thought the guns were not loaded.

FEFU: I'm never sure.

CHRISTINA: What? 155

CINDY: Fefu, what do you mean?

FEFU: He told me one day he'll put real bullets in the guns. He likes to make me nervous. (*There is a moment's silence.*) I have upset you . . . I don't mean to upset you. That's the way we are with each other. We always go to extremes but it's not 160 anything to be upset about.

CHRISTINA: You scare me.

FEFU: That's all right. I scare myself too, sometimes. But there's nothing wrong with being scared . . . it makes you stronger.—It does me.—He won't put real bullets in the 165 guns.—It suits our relationship . . . the game, I mean. If I didn't shoot him with blanks, I might shoot him for real. Do you see the sense of it?

CHRISTINA: I think you're crazy.

FEFU: I'm not. I'm sane. 170

CHRISTINA: (*Gently.*) You're very stupid.

FEFU: I'm not. I'm very bright.

CHRISTINA: (*Gently.*) You depress me.

FEFU: Don't be depressed. Laugh at me if you don't agree with
175   me. Say I'm ridiculous. I know I'm ridiculous. Come on,
       laugh. I hate to think I'm depressing to you.
CHRISTINA: All right. I'll laugh.
FEFU: I'll make you a drink.
CHRISTINA: No, I'm just sucking on the ice.
180 FEFU: Don't you feel well?
CHRISTINA: I'm all right.
FEFU: What are you drinking?
CHRISTINA: Bourbon.
FEFU: (Getting CHRISTINA's glass and going to the liquor cabi-
185   net.) Would you like some more? I'll get you some.
CHRISTINA: Just a drop.
FEFU: (With great care pours a single drop of bourbon on the
       ice cube.) Like that?
CHRISTINA: Yes, thank you.
190 FEFU: (Gives CHRISTINA the drink and watches her put the cube
       to her lips.) That's the cutest thing I've ever seen. It's cold.
       (CHRISTINA nods.) You need a stick in the ice, like a popsicle
       stick. You hold the stick and your fingers won't get cold. I
       have some sticks. I'll do some for you.
195 CHRISTINA: Don't trouble yourself.
FEFU: It won't be any trouble. You might want some later.—
       I'm strange, Christina. But I am fortunate in that I don't
       mind being strange. It's hard on others sometimes. But not
       that hard. Is it, Cindy? Those who love me, love me pre-
200   cisely because I am the way I am. (To CINDY.) Isn't that so?
       (CINDY smiles and nods.)
CINDY: I would love you even if you weren't the way you are.
FEFU: You wouldn't know it was me if I weren't the way I am.
CINDY: I would still know it was you underneath.
205 FEFU: (To CHRISTINA.) You see?—There are some good things
       about me.—I'm never angry, for example.
CHRISTINA: But you make everyone else angry.

(FEFU thinks a moment.)

FEFU: No.
CHRISTINA: You've made me furious.
210 FEFU: I know. And I might make you angry again. Still I would
       like it if you liked me.—You think it's unlikely.
CHRISTINA: I don't know.
FEFU: . . . We'll see. (FEFU goes to the doors. She stands there
       briefly and speaks reflectively.) I still like men better than
215   women.—I envy them. I like being like a man. Thinking
       like a man. Feeling like a man.—They are well together.
       Women are not. Look at them. They are checking the new
       grass mower. . . . Out in the fresh air and the sun, while we
       sit here in the dark. . . . Men have natural strength. Women
220   have to find their strength, and when they do find it, it
       comes forth with bitterness and it's erratic. . . . Women are
       restless with each other. They are like live wires . . . either
       chattering to keep themselves from making contact, or else,
       if they don't chatter, they avert their eyes . . . like Orpheus . . .
225   as if a god once said "and if they shall recognize each other,
       the world will be blown apart." They are always eager for the
       men to arrive. When they do, they can put themselves at
       rest, tranquilized and in a mild stupor. With the men they
       feel safe. The danger is gone. That's the closest they can be
230   to feeling wholesome. Men are muscle that cover the raw
       nerve. They are the insulators. The danger is gone, but the
       price is the mind and the spirit. . . . High price.—I've never
       understood it. Why?—What is feared?—Hmm. Well . . .—
       Do you know? Perhaps the heavens would fall.—Have I of-
       fended you again?   235
CHRISTINA: No. I too have wished for that trust men have for
       each other. The faith the world puts in them and they in turn
       put in the world. I know I don't have it.
FEFU: Hmm. Well, I have to see how my toilet is doing. (FEFU
       goes to the landing and exits. She puts her head out. She   240
       smiles.) Plumbing is more important than you think.

(CHRISTINA falls off her chair in a mock faint. CINDY goes to
her.)

CINDY: What do you think?
CHRISTINA: Think? I hurt. I'm all shreds inside.
CINDY: Anything I can do?
CHRISTINA: Sing.   245

(CINDY sings "Winter Wonderland." CHRISTINA harmonizes.
There is the sound of a horn. FEFU enters.)

FEFU: It's Julia. (To CHRISTINA, who is on the floor.) Are you all
       right?
CHRISTINA: Yes. (FEFU exits through the foyer.) Darn it!
       (CHRISTINA starts to stand.)
FEFU: (Off-stage.) Julia . . . let me help you.   250
JULIA: I can manage. I'm much stronger now.
FEFU: There you go.
JULIA: You have my bag.
FEFU: Yes.

(JULIA and FEFU enter. JULIA is in a wheelchair.)

JULIA: Hello Cindy.   255
CINDY: Hello darling. How are you?
JULIA: I'm very well now. I'm driving now. You must see my
       car. It's very clever the way they worked it all out. You might
       want to drive it. It's not hard at all. (Turning to CHRISTINA.)
       Christina.   260
CHRISTINA: Hello Julia.
JULIA: I'm glad to see you.
FEFU: I'll take this to your room. You're down here, if you want
       to wash up.

(FEFU exits through the upstage exit. JULIA follows her.)

CINDY: I can't get used to it.   265
CHRISTINA: She's better. Isn't she?
CINDY: Not really.
CHRISTINA: Was she actually hit by the bullet?
CINDY: No . . . I was with her.
CHRISTINA: I know.   270
CINDY: I thought the bullet hit her, but it didn't.—How do you
       know if a person is hit by a bullet?
CHRISTINA: Cindy . . . there's a wound and . . . there's a bullet.
CINDY: Well, the hunter aimed . . . at the deer. He shot.
CHRISTINA: He?   275
CINDY: Yes.
CHRISTINA: (Pointing in the direction of FEFU.) It wasn't . . . ?
CINDY: Fefu? . . . No. She wasn't even there. She used to hunt
       but she doesn't hunt any more. She loves animals.
CHRISTINA: Go on.   280
CINDY: He shot. Julia and the deer fell. The deer was dead . . .
       dying. Julia was unconscious. She had convulsions . . . like

the deer. He died and she didn't. I screamed for help and the
hunter came and examined Julia. He said, "She is not hurt."
285 Julia's forehead was bleeding. He said, "It is a surface wound.
I didn't hurt her." I know it wasn't he who hurt her. It was
someone else. He went for help and Julia started talking. She
was delirious.—Apparently there was a spinal nerve injury.
She hit her head and she suffered a concussion. She blanks
290 out and that is caused by the blow on the head. It's a scar in
the brain. It's called the petit mal.

(FEFU *enters.*)

CHRISTINA: What was it she said?
CINDY: Hmm? . . .
CHRISTINA: When she was delirious.
295 CINDY: When she was delirious? That she was persecuted.—
That they tortured her. . . . That they had tried her and that
the shot was her execution. That she recanted because she
wanted to live. . . . That if she talked about it . . . to anyone
. . . she would be tortured further and killed. And I have not
300 mentioned this before because . . . I fear for her.
CHRISTINA: It doesn't make any sense, Cindy.
CINDY: It makes sense to me. You heard? (FEFU *goes to* CINDY
and holds her.)
FEFU: Who hurt her?
305 CINDY: I don't know.
FEFU: (*To* CHRISTINA.) Did you know her?
CHRISTINA: I met her once years ago.
FEFU: You remember her then as she was. . . . She was afraid
of nothing. . . . Have you ever met anyone like that? . . .
310 She knew so much. She was so young and yet she knew so
much. . . . How did she learn all that? . . . (*To* CINDY.) Did
you ever wonder? Well, I still haven't checked my toilet.
Can you believe that. I still haven't checked it. (FEFU *goes
upstairs.*)
315 CHRISTINA: How long ago was the accident?
CINDY: A year . . . a little over a year.
CHRISTINA: Is she in pain?
CINDY: I don't think so.
CHRISTINA: We are made of putty. Aren't we?

(*There is the sound of a car. Car doors opening and closing. A
house window opening.*)

320 FEFU: (*Off-stage.*) Emma! What is that you're wearing. You
look marvelous.
EMMA: (*Off-stage.*) I got it in Turkey.
FEFU: Hi Paula, Sue.
PAULA: Hi.
325 SUE: Hi.

(CINDY *goes out to greet them.* JULIA *enters. She wheels herself to
the downstage area.*)

FEFU: I'll be right down! Hey, my toilet works.
EMMA: Stephany. Mine does too.
FEFU: Don't be funny.
EMMA: Come down.

(FEFU *enters as* EMMA, SUE, *and* PAULA *enter.* EMMA *and* FEFU
embrace.)

330 FEFU: How are you?
EMMA: Good . . . good . . . good . . . (*Still embracing* FEFU,
EMMA *sees* JULIA.) Julia! (*She runs to* JULIA *and sits on her
lap.*)

FEFU: Emma!
JULIA: It's all right. 335
EMMA: Take me for a ride. (JULIA *wheels the chair in a circle.*
EMMA *waves as they ride.*) Hi, Cindy, Paula, Sue, Fefu.
JULIA: Do you know Christina?
EMMA: How do you do.
CHRISTINA: How do you do. 340
EMMA: (*Pointing.*) Sue . . . Paula . . .
SUE: Hello.
PAULA: Hello.
CHRISTINA: Hello.
PAULA: (*To* FEFU.) I liked your talk at Flossie Crit. 345
FEFU: Oh god, don't remind me. I thought I was awful. Come,
I'll show you your rooms. (*She starts to go up.*)
PAULA: I thought you weren't. I found it very stimulating.
EMMA: When was that? . . . What was it on?
FEFU: Aviation. 350
PAULA: It wasn't on aviation. It was on Voltairine de Cleyre.
JULIA: I wish I had known.
FEFU: It wasn't important.
JULIA: I would have gone, Fefu.
FEFU: Really, it wasn't worth the trouble. 355
EMMA: Now you'll have to tell Julia and me all about
Voltairine de Cleyre.
FEFU: You know all about Voltairine de Cleyre.
EMMA: I don't.
FEFU: I'll tell you at lunch. 360
EMMA: I had lunch.
JULIA: You can sit and listen while we eat.
EMMA: I will. When do we start our meeting?
FEFU: After lunch. We'll have something to eat and then we'll
have our meeting. Who's ready for lunch? 365

(*The following lines are said almost simultaneously.*)

CINDY: I am.
JULIA: I'm not really hungry.
CHRISTINA: I could eat now.
PAULA: I'm ready.
SUE: I'd rather wait. 370
EMMA: I'll have coffee.
FEFU: . . . Well . . . we'll take a vote later.
CINDY: What are we doing exactly?
FEFU: About lunch?
CINDY: That too, but I meant the agenda. 375
SUE: Well, I thought we should first discuss what each of us is
going to talk about, so we don't duplicate what someone else
is saying, and then we have a review of it, a sort of rehearsal,
so we know in what order we should speak and how long it's
going to take. 380
EMMA: We should do a rehearsal in costume. What color
should each wear. It matters. Do you know what you're
wearing?
PAULA: I haven't thought about it. What color should I wear?
EMMA: Red. 385
PAULA: Red!
EMMA: Cherry red or white.
SUE: And I?
EMMA: Dark green.
CINDY: The treasurer should wear green. 390
EMMA: It suits her too.
SUE: And then we'll speak in order of color.

EMMA: Right. Who else wants to know? (CINDY *and* JULIA *raise
395 their hands. To* CINDY.) For you lavender. (*To* JULIA.) Pur-
purra. (FEFU *raises her hand.*) For you, all the gold in Persia.
FEFU: There is no gold in Persia.
EMMA: In Peru. I brought my costume. I'll put it on later.
FEFU: You're not in costume?
EMMA: No. This is just a dress. My costume is . . . dramatic. I
400 won't tell you any more about it. You'll see it.
SUE: I had no idea we were going to do theatre.
EMMA: Life is theatre. Theatre is life. If we're showing what
life is, can be, we must do theatre.
SUE: Will I have to act?
405 EMMA: It's not acting. It's being. It's springing forth with the
powers of the spirit. It's breathing.
JULIA: I'll do a dance.
EMMA: I'll stage a dance for you.
JULIA: Sitting?
410 EMMA: On a settee.
JULIA: I'm game.
EMMA: (*Takes a deep breath and walks through the French
doors.*) Phillip! What are you doing?—Hello.—Hello,
John.—What? I'm staging a dance for Julia!
415 FEFU: We'll never see her again.—Come.

(FEFU, PAULA, *and* SUE *go upstairs.* JULIA *goes to the gun, takes
it and smells the mouth of the barrel. She looks at* CINDY.)

CINDY: It's a blank.

(JULIA *takes the remaining slug out of the gun. She lets it fall on
the floor.*)

JULIA: She's hurting herself. (JULIA *looks blank and is motionless.* CINDY *picks up the slug. She notices* JULIA'S *condition.*)
CINDY: Julia. (*To* CHRISTINA.) She's absent.
420 CHRISTINA: What do we do?
CINDY: Nothing, she'll be all right in a moment. (*She takes the
gun from* JULIA. JULIA *comes to.*)
JULIA: It's a blank . . .
CINDY: It is.
425 JULIA: She's hurting herself. (JULIA *lets out a strange whimper.
She goes to the coffee table, takes a piece of chocolate, puts it
in her mouth and goes toward her room. After she crosses the
threshold, she stops.*) I must lie down a while.
CINDY: Call me if you need anything.
430 JULIA: I will. (*She exits.* CINDY *tries to put the slug in the rifle.
There is the sound of a car, a car door opening, closing.*)
CINDY: Do you know how to do this?
CHRISTINA: Of course not.

(CINDY *succeeds in putting the slug in the gun.* CECILIA *stands
in the threshold of the foyer.*)

CECILIA: I am Cecilia Johnson. Do I have the right place?
435 CINDY: Yes.

(CINDY *locks the gun. Lights fade all around* CECILIA. *Only her
head is lit. The light fades.*)

— **PART II** —

ON THE LAWN

There is a bench or a tree stump. FEFU *and* EMMA *bring boxes of
potatoes, carrots, beets, winter squash, and other vegetables from*

a root cellar and put them in a small wagon. FEFU *wears a hat
and gardening gloves.*

EMMA: (*Re-enters carrying a box as* FEFU *exits.*) Do you think
about genitals all the time?
FEFU: Genitals? No, I don't think about genitals all the time.
EMMA: (*Starting to exit.*) I do, and it drives me crazy. Each
person I see in the street, anywhere at all . . . I keep thinking 5
of their genitals, what they look like, what position they are
in. I think it's odd that everyone has them. Don't you?
FEFU: (*Crossing* EMMA.) No, I think it'd be odder if they didn't
have them.

(EMMA *laughs.* FEFU *re-enters.*)

EMMA: I mean, people act as if they don't have genitals.   10
FEFU: How do people with genitals act?
EMMA: I mean, how can business men and women stand in a
room and discuss business without even one reference to
their genitals. I mean everybody has them. They just pretend
they don't.   15
FEFU: I see. (*Shifting her glance from left to right with a
fiendish look.*) You mean they should do this all the time.

(EMMA *laughs.*)

EMMA: No, I don't mean that. Think of it. Don't you think I'm
right?
FEFU: Yes, I think you're right. (FEFU *sits.*) Oh, Emma,   20
EmmaEmmaEmma.
EMMA: That's m'name.—Well, you see, it's generally believed
that you go to heaven if you are good. If you are bad you go
to hell. That is correct. However, in heaven they don't judge
goodness the way we think. They don't. They have a divine   25
registry of sexual performance. In that registry they mark
down every little sexual activity in your life. If your faith is
not entirely in it, if you just perform as an obligation and you
don't feel the most profound devotion, if your spirit, your
heart, and your flesh is not religiously delivered to it, you are   30
condemned. They put you down in the black list and you
don't go to heaven. Heaven is populated with divine lovers.
And in hell live the duds.
FEFU: That's probably true.
EMMA: I knew you'd see it that way.   35
FEFU: Oh, I do. I do. You see, on earth we are judged by public acts, and sex is a private act. The partner cannot be said to
be the public, since both partners are engaged. So naturally,
it stands to reason that it's angels who judge our sexual life.
EMMA: Naturally.   40

(*Pause.*)

FEFU: You always bring joy to me.
EMMA: Thank you.
FEFU: I thank you. (FEFU *becomes distressed. She sits.*) I am in
constant pain. I don't want to give in to it. If I do I am afraid
I will never recover. . . . It's not physical, and it's not sorrow.   45
It's very strange Emma, I can't describe it, and it's very
frightening. . . . It is as if normally there is a lubricant . . . not
in the body . . . a spiritual lubricant . . . it's hard to describe
. . . and without it, life is a nightmare, and everything is distorted.—A black cat started coming to my kitchen. He's aw-   50
fully mangled and big. He is missing an eye and his skin is
diseased. At first I was repelled by him, but then, I thought,
this is a monster that has been sent to me and I must feed

him. And I fed him. One day he came and shat all over my
kitchen. Foul diarrhea. He still comes and I still feed him.—
I am afraid of him. (EMMA *kisses* FEFU.) How about a little
lemonade?

EMMA: Yes.

FEFU: How about a game of croquet?

EMMA: Fine.

(FEFU *exits.* EMMA *improvises an effigy of* FEFU. *She puts*
FEFU's *hat and gloves on it.*)

Not from the stars do I my judgment pluck.
And yet methinks I have astronomy;
But not to tell of good or evil luck,
Of plagues, of dearths, or seasons' quality;
Nor can I fortune to brief minutes tell,
Pointing to each his thunder, rain, and wind,
Or say with princes if it shall go well
By oft predict that I in heaven find.
But from thine eyes my knowledge I derive.
And, constant stars, in them I read such art
As truth and beauty shall together thrive
If from thyself to store thou wouldst convert:
    Or else of thee this I prognosticate,
    Thy end is truth's and beauty's doom and date.

(If FEFU's *entrance is delayed,* EMMA *will sing a popular song
of the period.* FEFU *re-enters with a pitcher and two glasses.*)

IN THE STUDY

*There are books on the walls, a desk, Victorian chairs, a rug on
the floor.* CHRISTINA *sits behind the desk. She reads a French
text book. She mumbles French sentences.* CINDY *sits to the left
of the desk with her feet up on a chair. She looks at a magazine.
A few moments pass.*

CHRISTINA: (*Practicing.*) Etes-vous externe ou demi-pension-
naire? La cuisine de votre cantine est-elle bonne, passable
ou mauvaise? (*She continues reading almost inaudibly. A moment passes.*)

CINDY: (*Reading.*) A lady in Africa divorced her husband because he was a cheetah.

CHRISTINA: Oh, dear. (*They laugh. They go back to their reading. A moment passes.*) Est-ce que votre professeur interroge
souvant les eleves? (*They go back to their reading. A moment
passes.*)

CINDY: I suppose . . . when a person is swept off their feet . . .
the feet remain and the person goes off . . . with the broom.

CHRISTINA: No . . . when a person is swept off their feet . . .
there is no broom.

CINDY: What does the sweeping?

CHRISTINA: An emotion . . . a feeling.

CINDY: Then emotions have bristles?

CHRISTINA: Yes.

CINDY: Now I understand. Do the feet remain?

CHRISTINA: No, the feet fly also . . . but separate from the
body. At the end of the leap, just before the landing, they join
the ankles and one is complete again.

CINDY: Oh, that sounds nice.

CHRISTINA: It is. Being swept off your feet is nice. Anything
else?

CINDY: Not for now. (*They go back to their reading. A moment
passes.*) Are you having a good time?

CHRISTINA: Yes, I'm very glad I came.

CINDY: Do you like everybody?

CHRISTINA: Yes.

CINDY: Do you like Fefu?

CHRISTINA: I do . . . She confuses me a little.—I try to be honest . . . and I wonder if she is . . . I don't mean that she
doesn't tell the truth. I know she does. I mean a kind of integrity. I know she has integrity too. . . . But I don't know if
she's careful with life . . . something bigger than the self . . . I
suppose I don't mean with life but more with convention.
I think she is an adventurer in a way. Her mind is adventurous. I don't know if there is dishonesty in that. But in adventure there is taking chances and risks, and then one has to,
somehow, have less regard or respect for things as they are.
That is, regard for a kind of convention, I suppose. I am
probably ultimately a conformist, I think. And I suppose I do
hold back for fear of being disrespectful or destroying something—and I admire those who are not. But I also feel they
are dangerous to me. I don't think they are dangerous to the
world; they are more useful than I am, more important, but
I feel some of my life is endangered by their way of thinking.
Do you understand?

CINDY: Yes, I do.

CHRISTINA: I guess I am proud and I don't like thinking that I
am thoughtful of things that have no value.—I like her.

CINDY: I had a terrible dream last night.

CHRISTINA: What was it?

CINDY: I was at a dance. And there was a young doctor I had
seen in connection with my health. We all danced in a circle
and he identified himself and said that he had spoken to
Mike about me, but that it was all right, that he had put it so
that it was all right. I was puzzled as to why Mike would
mind and why he had spoken to him. Then, suddenly everybody sat down on the floor and pretended they were having
singing lessons and one person was practicing Italian. The
singing professor was being tested by two secret policemen.
They were having him correct the voice of someone they
had brought. He apparently didn't know how to do it. Then,
one of the policemen put his hands on his vocal cords and
kicked him out the door. Then he grabbed me and felt my
throat from behind with his thumbs while he rubbed my nipples with his pinkies. Then, he pushed me out the door.
Then, the young doctor started cursing me. His mouth
moved like the mouth of a horse. I was on an upper level
with a railing and I said to him, "Stop and listen to me." I
said it so strongly that he stopped. Everybody turned to me
in admiration because I had made him stop. Then, I said to
him, "Restrain yourself." I wanted to say respect me. I wasn't
sure whether the words coming out of my mouth were what
I wanted to say. I turned to ask my sister. The young man was
bending over and trembling in mad rage. Another man told
me to run before the young man tried to kill me. Meg and I
ran downstairs. She asked me if I wanted to go to her place.
We grabbed a taxi, but before the taxi got enough speed he
came out and ran to the taxi and was on the verge of opening
the door when I woke up.

(*The door opens.* FEFU *looks in. Her entrance may interrupt*
CINDY's *speech at any point according to how long it takes her to
reach the kitchen.*)

FEFU: Who's for a game of croquet?

CINDY: In a little while.

FEFU: See you outside.

CHRISTINA: That was quite a dream.

CINDY: What do you think it means?

90 CHRISTINA: I think it means you should go to a different doctor.

CINDY: He's not my doctor. I never saw him before.

CHRISTINA: Well good. I'm sure he's not a good doctor.

(At the end of the fourth repeat, when FEFU *invites them for croquet,* CINDY *says, "Oh let's play croquet" and they follow* FEFU.)

IN THE BEDROOM

A plain unpainted room. Perhaps a room that was used for storage and was set up as a sleeping place for JULIA. *There is a mattress on the floor. To the right of the mattress there is a small table, to the left is* JULIA's *wheelchair. There is a sink on the wall. There are dry leaves on the floor although the time is not fall. The sheets are linen.* JULIA *lies in bed covered to her shoulders. She wears a white hospital gown.* JULIA *hallucinates. However, her behavior should not be the usual behavior attributed to a mad person. It should be rather still and luminous. There will be aspects of her hallucination that frighten her, but hallucinating itself does not.*

JULIA: They clubbed me. They broke my head. They broke my will. They broke my hands. They tore my eyes out. They took my voice away. They didn't do anything to my heart because I didn't bring my heart with me. They clubbed me

5 again, but my head did not fall off in pieces. That was because they were so good and they felt sorry for me. The judges. You didn't know the judges?—I was good and quiet. I never dropped my smile. I smiled to everyone. If I stopped smiling I would get clubbed because they love me. They say

10 they love me. I go along with that because if I don't . . .

(With her finger she indicates her throat being cut and makes the sound that usually accompanies that gesture.)

I told them the stinking parts of the body are the important ones: the genitals, the anus, the mouth, the armpit. All important parts except the armpits. And who knows, maybe the armpits are important too. That's what I said. *(Her voice*

15 *becomes gravelly and tight in imitation of the judges.)* He said that all those parts must be kept clean and put away. He said that women's entrails are heavier than anything on earth and to see a woman running creates a disparate and incongruous image in the mind. It's antiaesthetic. There-

20 fore women should not run. Instead they should strike positions that take into account the weight of their entrails. Only if they do, can they be aesthetic. He said, for example, Goya's Maja. He said Ruben's women are not aesthetic. Flesh. He said that a woman's bottom should be in a cush-

25 ion, otherwise it's revolting. He said there are exceptions. Ballet dancers are exceptions. They can run and lift their legs because they have no entrails. Isadora Duncan had entrails, that's why she should not have danced. But she danced and for this reason became crazy. *(Her voice is back*

30 *to normal.)* She wasn't crazy.

(She moves her hand as if guarding from a blow.)

She was. He said that I had to be punished because I was getting too smart. I'm not smart. I never was. Neither is Fefu smart. They are after her too. Well, she's still walking!

(She guards from a blow. Her eyes close.)

Wait! I'll say my prayers. I'm saying it.

(She mumbles. She opens her eye with caution.)

You don't think I'm going to argue with them, do you? I re- 35
pented. I told them exactly what they wanted to hear. They killed me. I was dead. The bullet didn't hit me. It hit the deer. But I died. He didn't. Then I repented and the deer died and I lived. *(With a gravelly voice.)* They said, "Live but crippled. And if you tell . . ." 40

(She repeats the throat cutting gesture.)

Why do you have to kill Fefu, for she's only a joker? *(With a gravelly voice.)* "Not kill, cure. Cure her." Will it hurt?

(She whimpers.)

Oh, dear, dear, my dear, they want your light. Your light my dear. Your precious light. Oh dear, my dear.

(Her head moves as if slapped.)

Not cry. I'll say my prayer. I'll say it. Right now. Look. 45

(She sits up as if pulled by an invisible force.)

The human being is of the masculine gender. The human being is a boy as a child and grown up he is a man. Everything on earth is for the human being, which is man. To nourish him.—There are evil things on earth, and noxious things. Evil and noxious things are on earth for man also. 50 For him to fight with, and conquer and turn its evil into good. So that it too can nourish him.—There are Evil Plants, Evil Animals, Evil Minerals, and Women are Evil.— Woman is not a human being. She is: 1—A mystery. 2—Another species. 3—As yet undefined. 4—Unpredictable; 55 therefore wicked and gentle and evil and good which is evil.—If a man commits an evil act, he must be pitied. The evil comes from outside him, through him and into the act. Woman generates the evil herself.—God gave man no other mate but woman. The oxen is good but it is not a mate for 60 man. The sheep is good but it is not a mate for man. The mate for man is woman and that is the cross man must bear.—Man is not spiritually sexual, he therefore can enjoy sexuality. His sexuality is physical which means his spirit is pure. Women's spirit is sexual. That is why after coitus they 65 dwell in nefarious feelings. Because that is their natural habitat. That is why it is difficult for them to return to the human world. Their sexual feelings remain with them till they die. And they take those feelings with them to the afterlife where they corrupt the heavens, and they are sent to hell 70 where through suffering they may shed those feelings and return to earth as man.

(Her head moves as if slapped.)

Don't hit me. Didn't I just say my prayer?

(A smaller slap.)

I believe it.

(She lies back.)

They say when I believe the prayer I will forget the judges. 75
And when I forget the judges I will believe the prayer. They say both happen at once. And all women have done it. Why can't I?

*(*SUE *enters with a bowl of soup on a tray.)*

SUE: Julia, are you asleep?

(Short pause.)

80 JULIA: No.
SUE: I brought your soup.
JULIA: Put it down. I'm getting up in a moment.

(SUE puts the soup down.)

SUE: Do you want me to help you?
JULIA: No, I can manage. Thank you, Sue.

(SUE goes to the door.)

85 SUE: You're all right?
JULIA: Yes.
SUE: I'll see you later.
JULIA: Thank you, Sue.

(SUE exits. JULIA closes her eyes. As soon as each audience group leaves, the tray is removed, if possible through a back door.)

IN THE KITCHEN

A fully equipped kitchen. There is a table and chairs and a high cutting table. On a counter next to the stove there is a tray with a soup dish and a spoon. There is also a ladle. On the cutting table there are two empty glasses. Soup is heating on a burner. A kettle with water sits on an unlit burner. In the refrigerator there is an ice tray with wooden sticks in each cube. The sticks should rest on the edge of the tray forming two parallel rows, like a caterpillar lying on its back. In the refrigerator there are also two pitchers, one with water, one with lemonade. PAULA sits at the table. She is writing on a pad. SUE waits for the soup to heat.

PAULA: I have it all figured out.
SUE: What?
PAULA: A love affair lasts seven years and three months.
SUE: It does?
5 PAULA: *(Reading.)* 3 months of love. 1 year saying: It's all right. This is just a passing disturbance. 1 year trying to understand what's wrong. 2 years knowing the end had come. 1 year finding the way to end it. After the separation, 2 years trying to understand what happened. 7 years, 3 months. *(No longer
10 reading.)* At any point the sequence might be interrupted by another love affair that has the same sequence. That is, it's not really interrupted, the new love affair relegates the first one to a second plane and both continue their sequence at the same time.

(SUE looks over PAULA's shoulder.)

15 SUE: You really added it up.
PAULA: Sure.
SUE: What do you want to drink?
PAULA: Water. The old love affair may fade, so you are not aware the process goes on. A year later it may surface and
20 you might find yourself figuring out what's wrong with the new one while trying to end the old one.
SUE: So how do you solve the problem?
PAULA: Celibacy?
SUE: *(Going to the refrigerator.)* Celibacy doesn't solve
25 anything.
PAULA: That's true.
SUE: *(Taking out the ice tray with the sticks.)* What's this? *(PAULA shakes her head.)* Dessert. *(PAULA shrugs her shoulders.*

SUE *takes an ice cube and places it against her forehead.)* For a headache. *(She takes another cube and moves her arms in a* 30 *Judo style.)* Eskimo wrestling. *(She places one stick behind her ear.)* Brain cooler. That's when you're thinking too much. You could use one. *(She tries to put the ice cube behind PAULA's ear. They wrestle and laugh. She puts the stick in her own mouth. She takes it out to speak.)* This is when 35 you want to keep chaste. No one will kiss you. *(She puts it back in to demonstrate. Then takes it out.)* That's good for celibacy. If you walk around with one of these in your mouth for seven years you can keep all your sequences straight. Finish one before you start the other. *(She puts the* 40 *ice cube in the tray and looks at it.)* A frozen caterpillar. *(She puts the tray away.)*
PAULA: You're leaving that ice cube in there?
SUE: I'm clean. *(Looking at the soup.)* So what else do you have on love? *(SUE places a bowl and spoon on the table and* 45 *sits as she waits for the soup to heat.)*
PAULA: Well, the break-up takes place in parts. The brain, the heart, the body, mutual things, shared things. The mind leaves but the heart is still there. The heart has left but the body wants to stay. The body leaves but the things are still at 50 the apartment. You must come back. You move everything out of the apartment but the mind stays behind. Memory lingers in the place. Seven years later, perhaps seven years later, it doesn't matter any more. Perhaps it takes longer. Perhaps it never ends. 55
SUE: It depends.
PAULA: Yup. It depends.
SUE: *(Pouring soup in the bowl.)* Something's bothering you.
PAULA: No.
SUE: *(Taking the tray.)* I'm going to take this to Julia. 60
PAULA: Go ahead.

(As SUE exits, CECILIA enters.)

CECILIA: May I come in?
PAULA: Yes . . . Would you like something to eat?
CECILIA: No, I ate lunch.
PAULA: I didn't eat lunch. I wasn't very hungry. 65
CECILIA: I know.
PAULA: Would you like some coffee?
CECILIA: I'll have tea.
PAULA: I'll make some.
CECILIA: No, you sit. I'll make it. *(CECILIA looks for tea.)* 70
PAULA: Here it is. *(She gets the tea and gives it to CECILIA.)*
CECILIA: *(As she lights the burner.)* I've been meaning to call you.
PAULA: It doesn't matter. I know you're busy.
CECILIA: Still I would have called you but I really didn't find 75 the time.
PAULA: Don't worry.
CECILIA: I wanted to see you again. I want to see you often.
PAULA: There's no hurry. Now we know we can see each other.
CECILIA: Yes, I'm glad we can. 80
PAULA: I have thought a great deal about my life since I saw you. I have questioned my life. I can't help doing that. It's been many years and I wondered how you see me now.
CECILIA: You're the same.
PAULA: I felt small in your presence . . . I haven't done all that 85 I could have. All I wanted to do. Our lives have gone in such different directions I cannot help but review what those years

have been for me. I gave up, almost gave up. I missed you in
my life. . . . I became lazy. I lost the drive. You abandoned
90 me and I kept going. But after a while I didn't know how to.
I didn't know how to go on. I knew why when I was with you.
To give you pleasure. So we could laugh together. So we
could rejoice together. To bring beauty to the world. . . .
Now we look at each other like strangers. We are guarded. I
95 speak and you don't understand my words. I remember
every day.

(FEFU *enters. She takes the lemonade pitcher from the refrigerator and two glasses from the top of the refrigerator.*)

FEFU: Emma and I are going to play croquet. You want to join
us? . . . No. You're having a serious conversation.

PAULA: Very serious. (PAULA *smiles at* CECILIA *in a conciliatory
100 manner.*) Too serious.

FEFU: (*As she exits.*) Come.

PAULA: I'm sorry. Let's go play croquet.—I'm not reproaching
you.

CECILIA: (*Reaching for* PAULA's *hand.*) I know. I've missed you
105 too.

(*They exit. As soon as the audience leaves the props are reset.*)

— PART III —

*The living room. It is dusk. As the audience enters, two or three of
the women are around the piano playing and singing Schubert's
"Who Is Silvia." They exit.* EMMA *enters, checks the lights in the
room on her hand, looks around the room and goes upstairs. The
rest enter through the rear.* CECILIA *enters speaking.*

CECILIA: Well, we each have our own system of receiving information, placing it, responding to it. (*She sits in the center
of the couch; the rest sit around her.*) That system can function with such a bias that it could take any situation and
5 translate it into one formula. That is, I think, the main reason for stupidity or even madness, not being able to tell the
difference between things.

SUE: Like?

CECILIA: Like . . . this person is screaming at me. He's a bully.
10 I don't like being screamed at. Another person or the same
person screams in a different situation. But you know you
have done something that provokes him to scream. He has a
good reason. They are two different things, the screaming of
one and the screaming of the other. Often that distinction is
15 not made. We cannot survive in a vacuum. We must be part
of a community, perhaps 10, 100, 1000. It depends on how
strong you are. But even the strongest will need a dozen,
three, even one who sees, thinks, and feels as he does. The
greater the need for that kind of reassurance, the greater the
20 number that he needs to identify with. Some need to identify with the whole nation. Then, the greater the number the
more limited the number of responses and thoughts. A common denominator must be reached. Thoughts, emotions
that fit all, have to be limited to a small number. That is, I
25 feel, the concern of the educator—to teach how to be sensitive to the differences in ourselves as well as outside ourselves, not to supervise the memorization of facts. (EMMA's
head appears in the doorway to the stairs.) Otherwise the unusual in us will perish. As we grow we feel we are strange
30 and fear any thought that is not shared with everyone.

JULIA: As I feel I am perishing. My hallucinations are madness,
of course, but I wish I could be with others who hallucinate
also. I would still know I am mad but I would not feel so isolated.—Hallucinations are real, you know. They are not like
dreams. They are as real as all of you here. I have actually 35
asked to be hospitalized so I could be with other nuts. But
the doctors don't want to. They can't diagnose me. That
makes me even more isolated. (*There is a moment's silence.*)
You see, right now, it's an awful moment because you don't
know what to say or do. If I were with other people who hal- 40
lucinate, they would say, "Oh yeah. Sure. It's awful. Those
dummies, they don't see anything." (*The others begin to
relax.*) It's not so bad, really. I can laugh at it. . . . Emma is
ready. We should start. (*The others are hesitant.* JULIA *speaks
to* FEFU.) Come on. 45

FEFU: Sure. (FEFU *begins to move the table. Others help move
the table and enough furniture to clear a space in the center.
They sit in a semicircle downstage on the floor facing upstage.*
CECILIA *sits on a chair to the left of the semicircle.*) All right.
I start. Right? 50

CINDY: Right.

(FEFU *goes to center and faces the others.* EMMA *sits on the
steps. Only her head and legs are visible.*)

FEFU: I talk about the stifling conditions of primary school education, etc. . . . etc. . . . The project . . . I know what I'm
going to say but I don't want to bore you with it. We all know
it by heart. Blah blah blah blah. And so on and so on. And so 55
on and so on. Then I introduce Emma . . . And now Miss
Emma Blake. (*They applaud.* EMMA *shakes her head.*) What.

EMMA: Paula goes next.

FEFU: Does it matter?

EMMA: Of course it matters. Dra-ma-tics. It has to build. I'm in 60
costume.

FEFU: Oh. And now, ladies and gentlemen, Miss Paula Cori
will speak on Art as a Tool for Learning. And I tell them the
work you have done at the Institute, community centers, essays, etc. Miss Paula Cori. 65

(*They applaud.* PAULA *goes to center.*)

PAULA: Ladies and gentlemen, I, like my fellow educator and
colleague, Stephany Beckmann . . .

FEFU: I am not an educator.

PAULA: What are you?

FEFU: . . . a do gooder, a girl scout. 70

PAULA: Well, I, like my fellow girl scout Stephany Beckmann
say blah blah blah blah, blah blah blah and I offer the jewels
of my wisdom and experience, which I will write down and
memorize, otherwise I would just stand there and stammer
and go blank. And even after I memorize it I'm sure I will 75
just stand there and stammer and go blank.

EMMA: I'll work with you on it.

PAULA: However, after our other colleague Miss Emma Blake
works with me on it . . . (*In imitation of* EMMA *she brings her
hands together and opens her arms as she moves her head 80
back and speaks.*) My impulses will burst forth through a
symphony of eloquence.

EMMA: Breathe . . . in . . . (PAULA *inhales slowly.*) And bow.
(PAULA *bows. They applaud.*)

PAULA: (*Coming up from the bow.*) Oh, I liked that. (*She sits.*) 85

EMMA: Good . . .

(They applaud.)

FEFU: And now, ladies and gentlemen, the one and only, the incomparable, our precious, dear Emma Blake.

(EMMA walks to center. She wears a robe which hangs from her arms to the floor.)

EMMA: From the prologue to "The Science of Educational
90   Dramatics" by Emma Sheridan Fry. *(She takes a dramatic pose and starts. The whole speech is dramatized by interpretive gestures and movements that cover the stage area.)*

    Environment knocks at the gateway of the senses. A rain of summons beats upon us day and night. . . . We do not
95   answer. Everything around us shouts against our deafness, struggles with our unwillingness, batters our walls, flashes into our blindness, strives to sieve through us at every pore, begging, fighting, insisting. It shouts, "Where are you? Where are you?" But we are deaf. The signals do not
100   reach us.

    Society restricts us, school straight jackets us, civilization submerges us, privation wrings us, luxury feather-beds us. The Divine Urge is checked. The Winged Horse balks on the road, and we, discouraged, defeated, dismount and bur-
105   row into ourselves. The gates are closed and Divine Urge is imprisoned at Center. Thus we are taken by indifference that is death. Environment finding the gates closed tries to break in. Turned away, it comes another way. Kept back, it stretches its hands to us. Always scheming to reach us. Never
110   was suitor more insistent than Environment, seeking admission, claiming recognition, signaling to be seen, shouting to be heard. And through the ages we sit inside ourselves deaf, dumb and blind, and will not stir. . . .

    . . . Maybe you are not deaf. . . . Perhaps signals reach
115   you. Maybe you stir. . . . The gates give. . . . Eternal Urge pushes through the stupor of our senses, making paths to meet the challenging suitor, windows through which to see him, ears through which to hear him. Environment shouting, "Where are you?" and Center battering at the inner side
120   of the wall crying, "Here I am," and dragging down bars, wrenching gates, prying at port-holes. Listening at cracks, reaching everywhere, and demanding that sense gates be flung open. The gates are open! Eternal Urge stands at the threshold signaling with venturous flag. An imperious in-
125   stinct lets us know that "all" is ours, and that whatever anyone has ever known, or may ever have or know, we will call and claim. A sense of life universal surges through our life individual. We attack the feast of this table with an insatiable appetite that cries for all.

130   What are we? A creation of God's consciousness coming now slowly and painfully into recognition of ourselves.

    What is Personality? A small part of us. The whole of us is behind that hungry rush at the gates of Senses.

    What is Civilization? A circumscribed order in which the
135   whole has not entered.

---

90 **Emma Sheridan Fry** taught acting to children at The Educational Alliance in New York from 1903 to 1909. In 1917, her book *Educational Dramatics* was published by Lloyd Adams Noble. The text of Emma's speech is taken from the prologue.

    What is Environment? Our mate, our true mate that clamors for our reunion.

    We will meet him. We will seize all, learn all, know all here, that we may fare further on the great quest! The task of
140 Now is only a step toward the task of the Whole! Let us then seek the laws governing real life forces, that coming into their own, they may create, develop and reconstruct. Let us awaken life dormant! Let us, boldly, seizing the star of our intent, lift it as the lantern of our necessity, and let it shine
145 over the darkness of our compliance. Come! The light shines. Come! It brightens our way. Come! Don't let its glorious light pass you by! Come! The day has come!

(EMMA throws herself on the couch. PAULA embraces her.) Oh, it's so beautiful.
JULIA: It is, Emma. It is.
150

(They applaud.)

CINDY: Encore! Encore!

(EMMA stands.)

EMMA: Environment knocks at the gateway . . . *(She laughs and joins the others in the semi-circle. PAULA remains seated on the couch.)* What's next.
FEFU: *(Going center.)* I introduce Cecilia. I don't think I
155 should introduce Cecilia. She should just come after Emma. Now things don't need introduction. *(Imitating EMMA as she goes to her seat.)* They are happening.
EMMA: Right!

(CECILIA goes to center.)

CECILIA: Well, as we say in the business, that's a very hard act
160 to follow.
EMMA: Not *very* hard. It's a hard act to follow.
CECILIA: Right. I should say my name first.
FEFU: Yes.
CECILIA: I should breathe too. *(She takes a breath. All except
165 PAULA start singing "Cecilia." CECILIA is perplexed and walks backwards till she sits on the couch. She is next to PAULA. Unaware of who she is next to, she puts her hand on PAULA's leg. At the end of the song CECILIA realizes she is next to PAULA and stands.)* I should go before Emma. I don't think anyone
170 should speak after Emma.
CINDY: Right. It should be Fefu, Paula, Cecilia, then Emma, and then Sue explaining the finances and asking for pledges. And the money should roll in. It's very good. *(They applaud.)* Sue . . . *(SUE goes to center.)*
175
SUE: Yes, blahblahblahblah, pledges and money. *(She does a few balletic moves and bows. They applaud.)*
FEFU: *(As SUE returns to her seat.)* Who's ready for coffee?
CINDY: *(As she stands.)* And dishes.
CHRISTINA: *(As she stands.)* I'll help.
180
EMMA: *(As she stands.)* Me too.
FEFU: Don't all come. Sit. Sit. You have done enough, relax.

(They put the furniture back as EMMA and SUE jump over the couch making loud warlike sounds. As they exit to the kitchen, SUE tries to get ahead of EMMA. EMMA speeds ahead of her. All except JULIA jump over the couch. All except CINDY and JULIA exit.)

JULIA: I should go do the dishes. I haven't done anything.
CINDY: You can do them tomorrow.

185 JULIA: True.—So how have you been?
CINDY: Hmm.
JULIA: Let me see. I can tell by looking at your face. Not so bad.
CINDY: Not so bad.

(There is the sound of laughter from the kitchen. CHRISTINA runs in.)

190 CHRISTINA: They're having a water fight over who's going to do the dishes.
CINDY: Emma?
CHRISTINA: And Paula, and Sue, all of them. Fefu was getting into it when I left. Cecilia got out the back door.

(CHRISTINA walks back to the kitchen with some caution. She runs back and lies on the couch covering her head with the throw. EMMA enters with a pan of water in her hand. She is wet. CINDY and JULIA point to the lawn. EMMA runs to the lawn. There is the sound of knocking from upstairs. While the following conversation goes on, EMMA, SUE, CINDY, and JULIA engage in water fights in and out of the living room. The screams, laughter, and water splashing may drown the words.)

195 PAULA: Open up.
FEFU: There's no one here.
PAULA: Open up you coward.
FEFU: I can't. I'm busy.
PAULA: What are you doing?
200 FEFU: I have a man here. Ah ah ah ah ah.
PAULA: O.K. I'll wait. Take your time.
FEFU: It's going to take quite a while.
PAULA: It's all right. I'll wait.
FEFU: Do me a favor?
205 PAULA: Sure. Open up and I'll do you a favor.

(There is the sound of a pot falling, a door slamming.)

FEFU: Fill it up for me.
PAULA: O.K.
FEFU: Thank you.
PAULA: Here's water. Open up.
210 FEFU: Leave it there. I'll come out in a minute.
PAULA: O.K. Here it is. I'm leaving now.

(Loud steps. PAULA comes down with a filled pan. EMMA hides by the entrance to the steps. EMMA splashes water on PAULA. PAULA splashes water on EMMA. SUE appears with a full pan.)

PAULA: Truce!
SUE: Who's the winner?
PAULA: You are. You do the dishes.
215 SUE: I'm the winner. You do the dishes.
FEFU: *(From the landing.)* Line up!
SUE: Psst. *(PAULA and EMMA look. SUE splashes water on them.)* Gotcha!
EMMA: Please don't.
220 PAULA: Truce. Truce.
FEFU: O.K. Line up. *(Pointing to the kitchen.)* Get in there! *(They all go to the kitchen.)* Start doing those dishes. *(There is a moment's pause.)*
JULIA: It's over.
225 CINDY: We're safe.
JULIA: *(To CHRISTINA.)* You can come up now. *(CHRISTINA stays down.)* You rather wait a while.

(CHRISTINA nods.)

CHRISTINA: *(Playful.)* I feel danger lurking.
CINDY: She's been hiding all day.

(FEFU enters. She is wet.)

FEFU: I won. I got them working.   230
JULIA: I thought the fight was over who'd do the dishes.
FEFU: Yes. *(Starting to go.)* I have to change. I'm soaked.
CHRISTINA: They forgot what the fight was about.
FEFU: We did?
JULIA: That's usually the way it is.   235
FEFU: *(Going to CHRISTINA and lifting the cover from her face.)* Are you ready for an ice cube?

(FEFU exits upstairs. CHRISTINA runs upstairs. There is silence.)

CINDY: So.—And how have you been?
JULIA: All right. I've been taking care of myself.
CINDY: You look well.   240
JULIA: I do not. . . . Have you seen Mike?
CINDY: No, not since Christmas.
JULIA: I'm sorry.
CINDY: I'm O.K.—And how's your love life?
JULIA: Far away. . . . I have no need for it.   245
CINDY: I'm sorry.
JULIA: Don't be. I'm very morbid these days. I think of death all the time.
PAULA: *(Standing in the doorway.)* Anyone for coffee? *(They raise their hands.)* Anyone take milk? *(They raise their hands.)* 250
JULIA: Should be go in?
PAULA: I'll bring it out. *(PAULA exits.)*
JULIA: I feel we are constantly threatened by death, every second, every instant, it's there. And every moment something rescues us. Something rescues us from death every moment   255
of our lives. For every moment we live we have to thank something. We have to be grateful to something that fights for us and saves us. I have felt lifeless and in the face of death. Death is not anything. It's being lifeless and I have felt lifeless sometimes for a brief moment, but I have been res- 260
cued by these . . . guardians. I am not sure who these guardians are. I only know they exist because I have felt their absence. I think we have come to know them as life, and we have become familiar with certain forms they take. Our sight is a form they take. That is why we take pleasure in seeing   265
things, and we find some things beautiful. The sun is a guardian. Those things we take pleasure in are usually guardians. We enjoy looking at the sunlight when it comes through the window. Don't we? We, as people, are guardians to each other when we give love. And then of course we have   270
white cells and antibodies protecting us. Those moments when I feel lifeless have occurred, and I am afraid one day the guardians won't come in time and I will be defenseless. I will die . . . for no apparent reason.

(Pause. PAULA stands in the doorway with a bottle of milk.)

PAULA: *(In a low-keyed manner.)* Anyone take rotten milk?   275
(Pause.) I'm kidding. This one is no good but there's more in there . . . *(Remaining in good spirits.)* Forget it. It's not a good joke.
JULIA: It's good.
PAULA: In there it seemed funny but here it isn't. *(As she exits   280
and shrugging her shoulders.)* It's a kitchen joke. Bye.

JULIA: *(After her.)* It is funny, Paula. *(To* CINDY.*)* It was funny.

CINDY: It's all right, Paula doesn't mind.

JULIA: I'm sure she minds. I'll go see . . . *(*JULIA *starts to go.*

285 PAULA *appears in the doorway.)*

PAULA: *(In a low-keyed manner.)* Hey, who was that lady I saw you with?—That was no lady. That was my rotten wife. That one wasn't good either, was it? *(Exiting.)* Emma. . . . That one was no good either.

*(*SUE *starts to enter carrying a tray with sugar, milk, and two cups of coffee. She stops at the doorway to look at* PAULA *and* EMMA *who are behind the wall.)*

290 SUE: *(Whispering.)* What are you doing?—What?—O.K., O.K. *(She enters whispering.* SUE *puts the tray down.)* They're plotting something.

*(*PAULA *appears in the doorway.)*

PAULA: *(In a low-keyed manner.)* Ladies and gentlemen. Ladies, since our material is too shocking and avant-garde,

295 we have decided to uplift our subject matter so it's more palatable to the sensitive public. *(*PAULA *takes a pose.* EMMA *enters. She lifts an imaginary camera to her face.)*

EMMA: Say cheese.

PAULA: Cheese. *(They both turn front and smile. The others ap-*

300 *plaud.)* Ah, success, success. Make it clean and you'll succeed.—Coffee's in the kitchen.

SUE: Oh, I brought theirs out.

PAULA: Oh, shall we have it here?

JULIA: We can all go in the kitchen. *(They each take their coffee*

305 *and go to the kitchen.* SUE *takes the tray to the kitchen. The sugar remains on the table.)*

PAULA: Either here or there. *(She sits on the couch.)* I'm exhausted.

*(*CECILIA *enters from the lawn.)*

CECILIA: Is the war over?

310 PAULA: Yes.

CECILIA: It's nice out. *(*PAULA *nods in agreement.)* Where's everybody?

PAULA: In the kitchen, having coffee.

CECILIA: We must talk. *(*PAULA *starts to speak.)* Not now. I'll

315 call you. *(*CECILIA *starts to go.)*

PAULA: When?

CECILIA: I don't know.

PAULA: I don't want you, you know.

CECILIA: I know.

320 PAULA: No, you don't. I'm not lusting after you.

CECILIA: I know that. *(She starts to go.)* I'll call you.

PAULA: When?

CECILIA: As soon as I can.

PAULA: I won't be home then.

325 CECILIA: When will you be home?

PAULA: I'll check my book and let you know.

CECILIA: Do that.—I'll be leaving after coffee. I'll say goodbye now.

PAULA: Goodbye. *(*CECILIA *goes towards the kitchen.* PAULA

330 *starts towards the steps.* FEFU *comes down the steps.)*

FEFU: You're still wet.

PAULA: I'm going to change now.

FEFU: Do you need anything?

PAULA: No, I have something I can change to. Thank you.

*(*PAULA *goes upstairs.* FEFU *stands by the steps. She is downcast. As the lights shift to an eerie tone,* JULIA *enters in slow motion, walking. She goes to the coffee table, gets the sugar bowl, lifts it in* FEFU's *direction, takes the cover off, puts it back on and walks to the kitchen. As soon as* JULIA *exits,* SUE's *voice is heard speaking the following lines. Immediately after,* JULIA *re-enters wheeled by* SUE. CINDY, CHRISTINA, EMMA, *and* CECILIA *are with them. On the arms of the wheelchair rests a tray with a coffee pot and cups. As they reach the couch and chairs they sit.* SUE *puts the tray on the table.* FEFU *stares at* JULIA.*)*

SUE: I was terribly exhausted and run down. I lived on coffee 335 so I could stay up all night and do my work. And they used to give us these medical check-ups all the time. But all they did was ask how we felt and we'd say "Fine," and they'd check us out. In the meantime I looked like a ghost. I was all bones. Remember Susan Austin? She was very naive and when they 340 asked her how she felt, she said she was nervous and she wasn't sleeping well. So she had to see a psychiatrist from then on.

EMMA: Well, she was crazy.

*(*FEFU *exits.)*

SUE: No, she wasn't.—Oh god, those were awful days. . . . Re- 345 member Julie Brooks?

EMMA: Sure.

SUE: She was a beautiful girl.

EMMA: Ah yes, she was gorgeous.

*(*PAULA *comes down the stairs as soon as she has changed. She sits on the steps half way down.)*

SUE: At the end of the first semester they called her in because 350 she had been out with 28 men and they thought that was awful. And the worst thing was that after that, she thought there was something wrong with her.

CINDY: *(Jokingly.)* She was a nymphomaniac, that's all.

SUE: She was not. She was just very beautiful so all the boys 355 wanted to go out with her. And if a boy asked her to go have a cup of coffee she'd sign out and write in the name of the boy. None of us did of course. All she did was go for coffee or go to a movie. She was really very innocent.

EMMA: And Gloria Schuman? She wrote a psychology paper 360 the faculty decided she didn't write and they called her in to try to make her admit she hadn't written it. She insisted she wrote it and they sent her to a psychiatrist also.

JULIA: Everybody ended going to the psychiatrist.

*(*FEFU *enters through the foyer.)*

EMMA: After a few visits the psychiatrist said: Don't you think 365 you know me well enough now that you can tell me the truth about the paper? He almost drove her crazy. They just couldn't believe she was so smart.

SUE: Those were difficult times.

PAULA: We were young. That's why it was difficult. On my first 370 year I thought you were all very happy. I had been so deprived in my childhood that I believed the rich were all happy. During the summer you spent your vacations in Europe or the Orient. I went to work and I resented that. But then I realized that many lives are ruined by poverty and 375 many lives are ruined by wealth. I was always able to manage. And I think I enjoyed myself as much when I went to Revere Beach on my day off as you did when you visited the

Taj Mahal. (CECILIA *enters from the foyer. She stands there*
380 *and listens.* PAULA *doesn't acknowledge her.*) Then, when I
stopped feeling envy, I started noticing the waste. I began
feeling contempt for those who, having everything a person
can ask for, make such a mess of it. I resented them because
they were not better than the poor. If you have all you need
385 you should be generous. If you can afford to go to school
your mind should be better. If you didn't have to fight for
your place on earth you should be nobler. But I saw them
cheating and grabbing like the kids in the slums, or wasting
away with self-indulgence. And I saw them be plain stupid. If
390 there is a reason why some are rich while others starve it
must be so they put everything they have at the service of
others. They should take the responsibility of everything that
happens in the world. They are the only ones who can influence things. The poor don't have the power to change
395 things. I think we should teach the poor and let the rich take
care of themselves. I'm sorry, I know that's what we're doing.
That's what Emma has been doing. I'm sorry . . . I guess I
feel it's not enough. (PAULA *sobs.*) I'll wash my face. I'll be
right back. (*She starts to go towards the kitchen.*) I think
400 highly of all of you.

(CECILIA *follows her.* PAULA *turns.* CECILIA *opens her arms and
puts them around* PAULA, *engulfing her. She kisses* PAULA *on the
lips.* PAULA *steps back. She is fearful.* CECILIA *follows her.* FEFU
enters from the lawn.)

FEFU: Have you been out? The sky if full of stars.

(EMMA, SUE, CHRISTINA, *and* CINDY *exit.*)

JULIA: What's the matter?

(FEFU *shakes her head.* JULIA *starts to go toward the door.*)

FEFU: Stay a moment, will you?
JULIA: Of course.
405 FEFU: Did you have enough coffee?
JULIA: Yes.
FEFU: Did you find the sugar?
JULIA: Yes. There was sugar in the kitchen. What's the matter?
FEFU: Can you walk? (JULIA *is hurt. She opens her arms imply-*
410 *ing she hides nothing.*) I am sorry, my dear.
JULIA: What is the matter?
FEFU: I don't know, Julia. Every breath is painful for me. I
don't know. (FEFU *turns* JULIA's *head to look into her eyes.*) I
think you know.

(JULIA *breaks away from* FEFU.)

415 JULIA: (*Avoiding* FEFU's *glance.*) No, I don't know. I haven't
seen much of you lately. I have thought of you a great deal. I
always think of you. Cindy tells me how you are. I always ask
her. How is Phillip? Things are not well with Phillip?
FEFU: No.
420 JULIA: What's wrong?
FEFU: A lot is wrong.
JULIA: He loves you.
FEFU: He can't stand me.
JULIA: He loves you.
425 FEFU: He's left me. His body is here but the rest is gone. I ex-
haust him. I torment him and I torment myself. I need him,
Julia.
JULIA: I know you do.

FEFU: I need his touch. I need his kiss. I need the person he is.
I can't give him up. (*She looks into* JULIA's *eyes.*) I look into 430
your eyes. and I know what you see. (JULIA *closes her eyes.*) It's
death. (JULIA *shakes her head.*) Fight!
JULIA: I can't.
FEFU: I saw you walking.
JULIA: No. I can't walk. 435
FEFU: You came for sugar, Julia. You came for sugar. Walk!
JULIA: You know I can't walk.
FEFU: Why not? Try! Get up! Stand up!
JULIA: What is wrong with you?
FEFU: You have given up! 440
JULIA: I get tired! I get exhausted! I am exhausted!
FEFU: What is it you see? (JULIA *doesn't answer.*) What is it you
see! Where is it you go that tires you so?
JULIA: I can't spend time with others! I get tired!
FEFU: What is it you see! 445
JULIA: You want to see it too?
FEFU: No, I don't. You're nuts, and willingly so.
JULIA: You know I'm not.
FEFU: And you're contagious. I'm going mad too.
JULIA: I try to keep away from you. 450
FEFU: Why?
JULIA: I might be harmful to you.
FEFU: Why?
JULIA: I am contagious. I can't be what I used to be.
FEFU: You have no courage. 455
JULIA: You're being cruel.
FEFU: I want to rest, Julia. How does a person rest. I want to
put my mind at rest. I am frightened. (JULIA *looks at* FEFU.)
Don't look at me. (*She covers* JULIA's *eyes with her hand.*) I
lose my courage when you look at me. 460
JULIA: May no harm come to your head.
FEFU: Fight!
JULIA: May no harm come to your will.
FEFU: Fight, Julia!

(FEFU *starts shaking the wheelchair and pulling* JULIA *off the
wheelchair.*)

JULIA: I have no life left. 465
FEFU: Fight, Julia!
JULIA: May no harm come to your hands.
FEFU: I need you to fight.
JULIA: May no harm come to your eyes.
FEFU: Fight with me! 470
JULIA: May no harm come to your voice.
FEFU: Fight with me!
JULIA: May no harm come to your heart.

(CHRISTINA *enters.* FEFU *sees* CHRISTINA, *releases* JULIA. *To*
CHRISTINA.)

FEFU: Now I have done it. Haven't I. You think I'm a monster.
(*She turns to* JULIA *and speaks to her with kindness.*) Forgive 475
me if you can. (JULIA *nods.*)
JULIA: I forgive you.

(FEFU *gets the gun.*)

CHRISTINA: What in the word are you doing with that gun!
FEFU: I'm going to clean it!
CHRISTINA: I think you better not! 480
FEFU: You're silly!

(CECILIA *appears on the landing.*)

CHRISTINA: I don't care if you shoot yourself! I just don't like the mess you're making!

(FEFU *starts to go to the lawn and turns.*)

FEFU: I enjoy betting it won't be a real bullet! You want to bet!

485   CHRISTINA: No! (FEFU *exits.* CHRISTINA *goes to* JULIA.) Are you all right?

JULIA: Yes.

CHRISTINA: Can I get you anything?

JULIA: Water. (CECILIA *goes to the liquor cabinet for water.*) Put

490   some sugar in it. Could I have a damp cloth for my fore-head? (CHRISTINA *goes toward the kitchen.* JULIA *speaks front.*) I didn't tell her anything. Did I? I didn't.

CECILIA: (*Going to* JULIA *with the water.*) About what?

JULIA: She knew.

(*There is the sound of a shot.* CHRISTINA *and* CECILIA *run out.* JULIA *puts her hand to her forehead. Her hand goes down slowly. There is blood on her forehead. Her head falls back.* FEFU *enters holding a dead rabbit.*)

FEFU: I killed it . . . I just shot . . . and killed it. . . . Julia . . .   495

(*Dropping the rabbit,* FEFU *walks to* JULIA *and stands behind the chair as she looks at* JULIA. SUE *and* CINDY *enter from the foyer,* EMMA *and* PAULA *from the kitchen,* CHRISTINA *and* CECILIA *from the lawn. They surround* JULIA. *The lights fade.*)

■ NTOZAKE SHANGE ■

Born Paulette Williams in Trenton, New Jersey, in 1948, Ntozake Shange was raised in New Jersey and St. Louis. She attended Barnard College in Manhattan in 1966, suffering a series of profound bouts of depression and attempting suicide on several occasions. She graduated from Barnard with a B.A. in American studies in 1970 and took her M.A. in American studies at the University of Southern California in 1971, when she took an African name, Ntozake Shange. Shange is a poet, and in the early 1970s, she read her poetry throughout the United States. In the summer of 1974, she began a series of seven poems that explored the realities of life among seven different black women. The women were nameless, and in the course of reading the series of poems to audiences, Shange realized its extraordinary theatrical power. Rather than seeing the monologues as material for a stage play, Shange's recognition of their dramatic power was linked to her interest in music and dance. As she suggested at the time, "with dance I discovered my body more intimately than I had imagined possible. With the acceptance of the ethnicity of my thighs and backside, came a clearer understanding of my voice as a woman and as a poet." Throughout the next year, she experimented with a variety of ways of staging the piece, coining the term "choreopoem" to describe its blending of music, dance, and poetry. As she writes in her introduction to the play, by the time *for colored girls who have considered suicide / when the rainbow is enuf* (1975) opened in California, it "waz a theater piece." The play was then brought to Broadway, where it was hugely popular. Shange's more recent plays continue to use music, lighting, dance, and poetry to examine the experience of black women: *a photograph: lovers in motion* (1977), *boogie woogie landscapes* (1978), and *spell #7 / geechee jibara quik magic trance manual for technologically stressed third world people* (1979). Shange has won many prestigious awards and also has written widely in non-dramatic forms. Her collections of poetry include *from okra to greens* (1984)—which became the basis for a play of the same name in 1985—*nappy edges* (1978), and *the love space demands* (1991). She also has written three novels (*Sassafrass* [1977], *Betsey Brown* [1985], and *Liliane* [1994]), a collection of "word paintings" called *ridin the moon in texas* (1987), a memoir entitled *a daughter's geography* (1983), and a collection of essays, *see no evil* (1984).

SPELL #7

Unlike her earlier choreopoem *for colored girls who have considered suicide / when the rainbow is enuf, spell #7* is subtitled a "theater piece." Although it uses Shange's powerful fusion of poetry and movement, *spell #7* engages in a critique of the politics of race and the politics of racial representation through the essential means of theater: roleplaying.

From its opening moments, when the audience sees a huge blackface mask hanging above the stage, and "*the rest of the company enters in tattered fieldhand garb, blackface, and the countenance of stepan fetchit when he waz frightened,*" it is apparent that *spell #7* will interrogate how African-American experience has been represented in white society, from the nineteenth-century minstrel shows, through the blackface musicals, comedies, and vaudeville of the 1920s, to contemporary stereotypes. Indeed, the play uses the "magic" of theater not only to investigage the social function of black theater traditions, but the way in which analogous stereotypes conceal, displace, and misrepresent African-American experience in social life. lou the magician enters and tells how his father, a magician,

> . . . retired from magic & took
> up another trade cuz this friend a mine
> from the 3rd grade / asked to be made white
> on the spot.

In *spell #7*, lou does not use his magic to turn black people white, but to reveal the black identity behind the white-imposed mask of blackface. Through lou's theatrical magic, the actors are able to remove their blackface masks and engage in a series of confessions, improvisations, and roleplayings that characterize black experience today.

The identities that emerge from behind the blackface are striking and powerful. The scene changes to eli's bar, a hangout for African-American actors, most of whom are unemployed because they are unable to get significant parts to play—"say as lady macbeth or mother courage," as lou suggests—and are forced to work odd jobs, play the tambourine on the street for subway fare, or to play stereotypically "black" roles. As bettina angrily complains, "no / my show is not closin / but if that director asks me to play it any blacker / i'm gonna have to do it in a mammy dress." Although blackface and the character stereotypes that accompanied it in an earlier era are no longer common in the theater, cultural stereotypes pervade our entertainment forms, and society as well. For this reason, lou's magic and the actors' anger conspire to produce a series of striking improvisations, as the actors remove their blackface masks and perform more authentic versions of contemporary African-American life: maxine plays "fay," out from Brooklyn to have a good time in Manhattan; lily reveals how she dreams of success while brushing her hair; natalie enacts "sue-jean," who gives birth to and then kills a baby boy named "myself." Finally, natalie and maxine play a "white girl" as a way of turning the tables on the blackface convention. Much as blackface represents black identity from the vantage of a privileged white society, natalie and maxine represent white identity from an oppressed black perspective.

As Shange suggests in her foreword to the play, much of the energy of *spell #7* derives from Shange's effort to maintain and celebrate the legacy of African-American arts, the fusion of poetry, music, and dance that should be an inspiring "cultural reality" for the African-American community.

FOREWORD / UNRECOVERED LOSSES / BLACK THEATER TRADITIONS

as a poet in american theater/ i find most activity that takes place on our stages overwhelmingly shallow/ stilted & imitative. that is probably one of the reasons i insist on calling myself a poet or writer/ rather than a playwright/ i am interested solely in the poetry of a moment/ the emotional & aesthetic impact of a character or a line. for too long now afro-americans in theater have been duped by the same artificial aesthetics that plague our white counterparts/ "the perfect play," as we know it to be/ a truly european framework for european psychology/ cannot function efficiently for those of us from this hemisphere.

furthermore/ with the advent of at least 6 musicals about the lives of black musicians & singers/ (EUBIE, BUBBLING BROWN SUGAR, AIN'T MISBEHAVIN', MAHALIA, etc.)/ the lives of millions of black people who dont sing & dance for a living/ are left unattended to in our theatrical literature. not that the lives of Eubie Blake or Fats Waller are well served in productions lacking any significant book/ but if the lives of our geniuses arent artfully rendered/ & the lives of our regular & precious are ignored/ we have a double loss to reckon with.

if we are drawn for a number of reasons/ to the lives & times of black people who conquered their environments/ or at least their pain with their art, & if these people are mostly musicians & singers & dancers/ then what is a writer to do to draw the most human & revealing moments from lives spent in nonverbal activity. first of all we should reconsider our choices/ we are centering ourselves around these artists for what reasons/ because their lives were richer than ours/ because they did something white people are still having a hard time duplicating/ because they proved something to the world like Jesse Owens did/ like Billie Holiday did. i think/ all the above contributes to the proliferation of musicals abt our musicians/ without forcing us to confront the real implications of the dynamic itself. we are compelled to examine these giants in order to give ourselves what we think they gave the worlds they lived in/ which is an independently created afro-american aesthetic. but we are going abt this process backwards/ by isolating the art forms & assuming a very narrow perspective vis-á-vis our own history.

if Fats Waller & Eubie Blake & Charlie Parker & Savilla Fort & Katherine Dunham moved the world outta their way/ how did they do it/ certainly not by mimicking the weakest area in american art/ the american theater. we must move our theater into the drama of our lives/ which is what the artists we keep resurrecting (or allowing others to resurrect) did in the first place/ the music & dance of our renowned predecessors appeals to us because it directly related to lives of those then living & the lives of the art forms.

in other words/ we are selling ourselves & our legacy quite cheaply/ since we are trying to make our primary statements with somebody else's life/ and somebody else's idea of what theater is. i wd suggest that: we demolish the notion of straight theater for a decade or so, refuse to allow play-wrights to work without dancers & musicians. "coon shows" were somebody else's idea. we have in-tegrated the notion that a drama must be words/ with no music & no dance/ cuz that wd take away the seriousness of the event/ cuz we all remember too well/ the chuckles & scoffs at the notion that all niggers cd sing & dance/ & most of us can sing & dance/ & the reason that so many plays written to silence & stasis fail/ is cuz most black people have some music & movement in our lives. we do sing & dance. this is a cultural reality. this is why I find the most inspiring theater among us to be in the realms of music & dance.

i think of my collaboration with David Murray on A PHOTOGRAPH/ & on WHERE THE MISSISSIPPI MEETS THE AMAZON & on SPELL #7/ in which music functions as another character. Teddy & his Sizzling Romancers (David Murray, sax.; Anthony Davis, piano; Fred Hopkins, bass; Paul Maddox, drums; Michael Gregory Jackson, guitar, harmonica & vocals) were as important as The Satin Sisters/ though the thirties motif served as a vehicle to introduce the dilemmas of our times. in A PHOTOGRAPH the cello (Abdul Wadud) & synthesizer (Michael Gregory Jackson) solos/ allowed Sean to break into parts of himself that wd have been unavailable had he been unable to "hear." one of the bounties of black culture is our ability to "hear"/ if we were to throw this away in search of less (just language) we wd be damning ourselves. in slave nar-ratives there are numerous references to instruments/ specifically violins, fifes & flutes/ "talking" to the folks. when working with Oliver Lake (sax.) or Baikida Carroll (tr.) in FROM OKRA TO GREENS/ or Jay Hoggard (vibes) in FIVE NOSE RINGS & SOWETO SUITE/ i am terribly aware of a conversation. in the company of Dianne McIntyre/ or Dyane Harvey's work with the Eleo Pomare Dance Company/ one is continually aroused by the immediacy of their movements/ "do this movement like yr life depends on it"/ as McIntyre says.

the fact that we are an interdisciplinary culture/ that we understand more than verbal commu-nication/ lays a weight on afro-american writers that few others are lucky enough to have been born into. we can use with some skill virtually all our physical senses/ as writers committed to bringing the world as we remember it/ imagine it/ & know it to be to the stage/ we must use everything we've got. i suggest that everyone shd cue from Julius Hemphill's wonderful persona, Roi Boye/ who ru-minates & dances/ sings & plays a saxophone/ shd cue from Cecil Taylor & Dianne McIntyre's col-laboration on SHADOWS/ shd cue from Joseph Jarman & Don Moye (of The Art Ensemble of Chicago) who are able to move/ to speak/ to sing & dance & play a myriad of instruments in EGWU-ANWU. look at Malinke who is an actor/ look at Amina Myers/ Paula Moss/ Aku Kadogo/ Michele Shay/ Laurie Carlos/ Ifa Iyaun Baeza & myself in NEGRESS/ a collective piece which al-lowed singers, dancers, musicians & writers to pass through the barriers & do more than 1 thing. dance to Hemphill or the B.A.G. (Black Artist Group)/ violinist Ramsey Amin lets his instrument make his body dance & my poems shout. i find that our contemporaries who are musicians are ex-hibiting more courage than we as writers might like to admit.

in the first version of BOOGIE WOOGIE LANDSCAPES i presented myself with the prob-lem of having my person/ body, voice & language/ address the space as if i were a band/ a dance company & a theater group all at once. cuz a poet shd do that/ create an emotional environment/ felt architecture.

to paraphrase Lester Bowie/ on the night of the World Saxophone Quartet's (David Murray, Julius Hemphill, Hamiett Bluiett & Oliver Lake) performance at the Public Theater/ "those guys are the greatest comedy team since the Marx Brothers." in other words/ they are theater. theater which is an all encompassing moment/ a moment of poetry/ the opportunity to make something happen. We shd think of George Clinton/ a.k.a. Dr. Funkenstein/ as he sings/ "here's a chance to dance our way out of our constrictions." as writers we might think more often of the implications of an Ayler solo/ the meaning of a contraction in anybody's body. we are responsible for saying how we feel. we "ourselves" are high art. our world is honesty & primal response.

1/22/79 NYC

although i rarely read reviews of my work/ two comments were repeated to me by "friends" for some reason/ & now that i am writing abt my own work/ i am finally finding some use for the appraisals of strangers. one new york critic had accused me of being too self-conscious of being a writer/ the other from the midwest had asserted that i waz so involved with the destruction of the english language/ that my writing approached verbal gymnastics like unto a reverse minstrel show. in reality/ there is an element of truth in both ideas/ but the lady who thought i waz self-conscious of being a writer/ apparently waz never a blk child who knew that no black people conducted themselves like amos n andy/ she waz not a blk child who knew that blk children didnt wear tiger skins n chase lions around trees n then eat pancakes/ she waznt a blk child who spoke an english that had evolved naturally/ only to hear a white man's version of blk speech that waz entirely made up & based on no linguistic system besides the language of racism. the man who thought i wrote with intentions of outdoing the white man in the acrobatic distortions of english waz absolutely correct. i can't count the number of times i have viscerally wanted to attack deform n maim the language that i waz taught to hate myself in/ the language that perpetuates the notions that cause pain to every black child as he/she learns to speak of the world & the "self." yes/ being an afro-american writer is something to be self-conscious abt/ & yes/ in order to think n communicate the thoughts n feelings i want to think n communicate/ i haveta fix my tool to my needs/ i have to take it apart to the bone/ so that the malignancies/ fall away/ leaving us space to literally create our own image.

i have not ceased to be amazed when i hear members of an audience whispering to one another in the foyers of theaters/ that they had never imagined they cd feel so much for characters/ even though they were black (or colored/ or niggers, if they don't notice me eavesdropping). on the other hand/ i hear other members of an audience say that there were so many things in the piece that they had felt/ experienced/ but had never found words to express/ even privately/ to themselves. these two phenomena point to the same dilemma/ the straightjacket that the english language slips over the minds of all americans. there are some thoughts that black people just dont have/ according to popular mythology/ so white people never "imagine" we are having them/ & black people "block" vocabularies we perceive to be white folks' ideas.[1] this will never do. for in addition to the obvious stress of racism n poverty/ afro-american culture/ in attempts to carry on/ to move forward/ has minimized its "emotional" vocabulary to the extent that admitting feelings of rage, defeat, frustration is virtually impossible outside a collective voice. so we can add self-inflicted repression to the cultural causes of our cultural disease of high blood pressure.

in everything i have ever written & everything i hope to write/ i have made use of what Frantz Fanon called "combat breath." although Fanon waz referring to francophone colonies, the schema he draws is sadly familiar:

> there is no occupation of territory, on the one hand, and independence of persons on the other. It is the country as a whole, its history, its daily pulsation that are contested, disfigured, in the hope of final destruction. Under this condition, the individual's breathing is an observed, an occupied breathing. It is a combat breathing.[2]

Fanon goes on to say that "combat breathing" is the living response/ the drive to reconcile the irreconcilable/ the black & white of what we live n where. (unfortunately, this language doesnt allow me to broaden "black" & "white" to figurative terms/ which is criminal since the words are so much larger n richer than our culture allows.) i have lived with this for 31 years/ as my people have lived with cut-off lives n limbs. the three pieces in this collection are the throes of pain n sensation experienced by my characters responding to the involuntary constrictions n amputations of their humanity/ in the context of combat breathing.

each of these pieces was excruciating to write/ for i had to confront/ again & again/ those moments that had left me with little more than fury n homicidal desires. in *spell #7* i included a prologue of a minstrel show/ which made me cry the first times i danced in it/ for the same reasons i had included it. the minstrel may be "banned" as racist/ but the minstrel is more powerful in his

---

[1] Just examine *Drylongso* by John Langston Gwaltney, Random House, 1980.
[2] Frantz Fanon, *A Dying Colonialism*, Grove Press, 1967.

deformities than our alleged rejection of him/ for every night we wd be grandly applauded. imme-diately thereafter/ we began to unveil the "minstrels," who turned out to be as fun-loving as fay:

> please/ let me join you/ i come all the way from brooklyn/ to have a good time/ ya dont think i'm high do ya/ cd i please join ya/ i just wanna have a good ol time.

as contorted as sue-jean:

> & i lay in the corner laughin/ with my drawers/ twisted round my ankles & my hair standin every which way/ i waz laughin/ knowin i wd have this child/ myself/ & no one wd ever claim him/ cept me/ cuz i was a low-down thing/ layin in sawdust & whiskey stains/ i laughed & had a good time masturbatin in the shadows.

as angry as the actor who confides:

> i just want to find out why no one has ever been able to sound a gong & all the reporters recite that the gong is ringin/ while we watch all the white people/ immigrants & invaders/ conquis-tadors & relatives of london debtors from georgia/ kneel & apologize to us/ just for three or four minutes. now/ this is not impossible.

& after all that/ our true visions & rigors laid bare/ down from the ceiling comes the huge minstrel face/ laughing at all of us for having been so game/ we believed we cd escape his powers/ how naive cd we be/ the magician explains:

> crackers are born with the right to be alive/i'm making ours up right here in yr face.

the most frequently overheard comment abt *spell #7* when it first opened at the public theater/ waz that it waz too intense. the cast & i usedta laugh. if this one hour n 45 minutes waz too much/ how in the world did these same people imagine the rest of our lives were/ & wd they ever be able to han-dle that/ simply being alive & black & feeling in this strange deceitful country. which brings me to *boogie woogie landscapes*/ totally devoted to the emotional topology of a yng woman/ how she got to be the way she is/ how she sees where she is. here/ again/ in the prologue lies the combat breath of layla/ but she's no all-american girl/ or is she?

> the lil black things/ pulled to her & whimpered lil black whys/ 'why did those white men make red of our house/ why did those white men want to blacken even the white doors of our house/ why make fire of our trees/ & our legs/ why make fire/ why laugh at us/ say go home/ arent we home/ arent we home?'

she waz raised to know nothing but black & white two-dimensional planes/ which is what racism al-lots everyone of us unless we fight. she found solace in jesus & the american way/ though jonestown & american bandstand lay no claims to her:

> shall i go to jonestown or the disco? i cd wear red sequins or a burlap bag. maybe it doesnt mat-ter/ paradise is fulla surprises/ & the floor of the disco changes colors like special species of vipers . . .

her lover/ her family/ her friends torment her/ calm her with the little they have left over from their own struggles to remain sane. everything in *boogie woogie landscapes* is the voice of layla's uncon-scious/ her unspeakable realities/ for no self-respecting afro-american girl wd reveal so much of her-self of her own will/ there is too much anger to handle assuredly/ too much pain to keep on truckin/ less ya bury it.

both *spell #7* & *boogie woogie landscapes* have elements of magic or leaps of faith/ in typical afro-american fashion/ not only will the lord find a way/ but there is a way outta here. this is the litany from the spirituals to Jimi Hendrix' "there must be some kinda way outta here"/ acceptance of my combat breath hasnt closed the possibilities of hope to me/ the soothing actualities of music n sorcery/ but that's why i'm doubly proud of *a photograph: lovers in motion*/ which has no cures for our "condition" save those we afford ourselves. the characters michael/ sean/ claire/ nevada/ earl/ are afflicted with the kinds of insecurities & delusions only available to those who learned themselves thru the traumas of racism. what is fascinating is the multiplicity of individual responses to this kind of oppression. michael displays her anger to her lovers:

> i've kept a lover who waznt all-american/ who didn't believe/ wdnt straighten up/ oh i've loved him in my own men/ sometimes hateful sometimes subtle like high fog & sun/ but who i loved is yr not believin. i loved yr bitterness & hankered after that space in you where you are outta control/ where you cannot touch or you wd kill me/ or somebody else who loved you. i never even saw a picture & i've loved him all my life he is all my insanity & anyone who loves me wd understand.

while nevada finds a nurtured protection from the same phenomenon:

> mama/ will he be handsome & strong/ maybe from memphis/ an old family of freedmen/ one of them reconstruction senators for a great grandfather . . .

their particular distortions interfere with them receiving one another as full persons:

> CLAIRE: no no/ i want nevada to understand that i understand that sean's a niggah/ & that's why he's never gonna be great or whatever you call it/ cuz he's a niggah & niggahs cant be nothin.
> NEVADA: see/ earl/ she's totally claimed by her station/ she cant imagine anyone growing thru the prison of poverty to become someone like sean
> CLAIRE: sean aint nothin but a niggah nevada/ i didnt know you liked niggahs.

such is the havoc created in the souls of people who arent supposed to exist. the malevolence/ the deceit/ & manipulation exhibited by these five are simply reflections of the larger world they inhabit/ but do not participate in:

> SEAN: contours of life unnoticed/
> MICHAEL: unrealized & suspect . . . our form is one of a bludgeoned thing/ wrapped in rhinestones & gauze/ blood almost sparklin/ a wildness lurks always . . .
>
> oppression/ makes us love one another badly/ makes our breathing
> mangled/ while i am desperately trying to clear the air/
> in the absence of extreme elegance/
> madness can set right in like
> a burnin gauloise on japanese silk.
> though highly cultured/
> even the silk must ask
> how to burn up discreetly.

Ntozake Shange
3/21/80 NYC

SPELL #7
GEECHEE JIBARA QUIK MAGIC TRANCE
MANUAL FOR TECHNOLOGICALLY STRESSED
THIRD WORLD PEOPLE
A Theater Piece

Ntozake Shange

— CHARACTERS —

LOU, *a practicing magician*
ALEC, *a frustrated, angry actor's actor*
DAHLIA, *young gypsy (singer/dancer)*
ELI, *a bartender who is also a poet*
BETTINA, *DAHLIA's co-worker in a chorus*

LILY, *an unemployed actress working as a barmaid*
NATALIE, *a not too successful performer*
NATALIE, ROSS, *guitarist-singer with*
MAXINE, *an experienced actress*

— ACT ONE —

(there is a huge black-face mask hanging from the ceiling of the theater as the audience enters. in a way the show has already begun, for the members of the audience must integrate this grotesque, larger than life misrepresentation of life into their pre-show chatter. slowly the house lights fade, but the mask looms even larger in the darkness.

once the mask is all that can be seen, LOU, *the magician, enters. he is dressed in the traditional costume of Mr. Interlocutor: tuxedo, bow-tie, top hat festooned with all kinds of whatnots that are obviously meant for good luck. he does a few catchy "soft-shoe" steps & begins singing a traditional version of a black play song)*

LOU: *(singing)*

> 10 lil picaninnies all in bed
> one fell out and the other nine said:
> i sees yr hiney
> 5 all black & shiny
> i see yr hiney
> all black & shiny/ shiny

(as a greeting)

> yes/ yes/ yes   isnt life wonderful

(confidentially)

> my father is a retired magician
> 10 which accounts for my irregular behavior
> everything comes outta magic hats
> or bottles wit no bottoms & parakeets
> are as easy to get as a couple a rabbits
> or 3 fifty-cent pieces/ 1958
> 15 my daddy retired from magic & took
> up another trade cuz this friend a mine
> from the 3rd grade/ asked to be made white
> on the spot

> what cd any self-respectin colored american magician
> 20 do wit such an outlandish request/ cept
> put all them razzamatazz hocus pocus zippity-doo-dah
> thingamajigs away   cuz

> colored chirren believin in magic
> waz becomin politically dangerous for the race
> & wasnt nobody gonna be made white   25
> on the spot just
> from a clap of my daddy's hands
> & the reason i'm so peculiar's
> cuz i been studyin up on my daddy's technique
> & everything i do is magic these days   30
> & it's very colored/ very now you see it/ now you
> dont mess wit me

(boastfully)

> i come from a family of retired
> sorcerers/ active houngans & pennyante fortune tellers
> with 41 million spirits/ critturs & celestial bodies   35
> on our side

> i'll listen to yr problems
> help wit yr career/ yr lover/
> yr wanderin spouse
> make yr grandma's stay in   40
>   heaven more
>   gratifyin
> ease yr mother thru menopause
> & show yr son
> how to clean his room   45

(while LOU *has been easing the audience into acceptance of his appearance & the mask [his father, the ancestors, our magic], the rest of the company enters in tattered fieldhand garb, black-face, and the countenance of stepan fetchit when he waz fright-ened. their presence belies the magician's promise that "you'll be colored n love it," just as the minstrel shows were lies, but* LOU *continues)*

> YES YES YES 3 wishes is all you get
>   scarlet ribbons for yr hair
>   a farm in mississippi
>   someone to love you madly
> all things are possible   50
> but aint no colored magician in his right mind
> gonna make you   white
> i mean

909

this is blk magic
55 you lookin at
& i'm fixin you up good/ fixin you up good & colored
& you gonna be colored all yr life
& you gonna love it/ bein colored/ all yr life/ colored &
love it
love it/ bein colored. SPELL #7!

(LOU *claps his hands, & the company which had been absolutely still til this moment/ jumps up. with a rhythm set on a
washboard carried by one of them/ they begin a series of steps
that identify every period of afro-american entertainment: from
acrobats, comedians, tap-dancers, calindy dancers, cotton club
choruses, apollo theatre du-wop groups, til they reach a frenzy in
the midst of "hambone, hambone where ya been"/ & then take a
bow à la bert williams/ the lights bump up abruptly.*

the magician, LOU, *walks thru the black-faced figures in their
kneeling poses, arms outstretched as if they were going to sing
"mammy." he speaks now [as a companion of the mask] to the
same audience who fell so easily into his hands & who were so
aroused by the way the black-faced figures "sang n danced")*

60 LOU: why dont you go on & integrate a german-american
school in st. louis mo./ 1955/ better yet why dont ya go on
& be a red niggah in a blk school in 1954/ i got it/ try &
make one friend at camp in the ozarks in 1957/ crawl thru
one a jesse james' caves wit a class of white kids waitin
65 outside to see the whites of yr eyes/ why dontcha invade a
clique of working class italians trying to be protestant in a
jewish community/ & come up a spade/ be a lil too dark/
lips a lil too full/ hair entirely too nappy/ to be beautiful/ be
a smart child trying to be dumb/ you go meet somebody
70 who wants/ always/ a lil less/ be cool when yr body says hot/
& more/ be a mistake in racial integrity/ an error in white
folks' most absurd fantasies/ be a blk kid in 1954/ who's not
blk enuf to lovingly ignore/ not beautiful enuf to leave
alone/ not smart enuf to move outta the way/ not bitter enuf
75 to die at an early age/ why dontchu c'mon & live my life for
me/ since the dreams aint enuf/ go on & live my life for
me/ i didnt want certain moments at all/ i'd give em to
anybody . . . awright. alec.

(*the black-faced* ALEC *gives his minstrel mask to* LOU *when he
hears his name/* ALEC *rises. the rest of the company is intimidated by this figure daring to talk without the protection of
black-face. they move away from him/ or move in place as if in
mourning)*

ALEC: st. louis/ such a colored town/ a whiskey black space of
80 history & neighborhood/ forever ours to lawrenceville/
where the only road open to me waz cleared by colonial
slaves/ whose children never moved/ never seems like
mended the torments of the Depression or the stains of
demented spittle/ dropped from the lips of crystal women/
85 still makin independence flags/
st. louis/ on a halloween's eve to the veiled prophet/
usurpin the mystery of mardi gras/ i made it mine tho the
queen waz always fair/ that parade of pagan floats &
tambourines/ commemorates me/ unlike the lonely walks
90 wit liberal trick or treaters/ back to my front door/ bag
half empty/

my face enuf to scare anyone i passed/ gee/ a colored kid/
whatta gas. here/ a tree/ wanderin the horizon/ dipped
in blues/ untended bones/ usedta hugs drawls rhythm &
decency here a tree/ waitin to be hanged   95
sumner high school/ squat & pale on the corner/ like our
vision waz to be vague/ our memory of the war/ that made
us free/ to be forgotten/ becomin paler/ linear
movement from sous' carolina to missouri/ freedmen/
landin in jackie wilson's yelp/ daughters of the manumitted 100
swimmin in tina turner's grinds/ this is chuck berry's town
disavowin miscega-nation/ in any situation/ & they let us
be/ electric blues & bo didley/ the rockin pneumonia &
boogie-woogie flu/ the slop & short fried heads/runnin
always to the river chambersburg/ lil italy/ i passed everyday 105
at the sweet shoppe/ & waz afraid/ the cops raided truants/
regularly/ & after dark i wd not be seen wit any other
colored/ sane & lovin my life

(*shouts n cries that are those of a white mob are heard, very loud
. . . the still black-faced figures try to move away from the menacing voices & memories*)

VOICES: hey niggah/ over here
ALEC: behind the truck lay five hands claspin chains   110
VOICES: hey niggah/ over here
ALEC: round the trees/ 4 more sucklin steel
VOICES: hey niggah/ over here
ALEC: this is the borderline
VOICES: hey niggah/ over here   115
ALEC: a territorial dispute
VOICES: hey niggah/ over here
ALEC: (*crouched on floor*) cars loaded with families/ fellas from
the factory/one or two practical nurses/ become our
trenches/ some dig into cement wit elbows/ under engines/   120
do not be seen in yr hometown
after sunset/ we suck up our shadows

(*finally moved to tear off their "shadows," all but two of the company leave with their true faces bared to the audience.* DAHLIA
*has, as if by some magical cause, shed not only her mask, but
also her hideous overalls & picaninny-buckwheat wig, to reveal a
finely laced unitard/ the body of a modern dancer. she throws her
mask to* ALEC, *who tosses it away.* DAHLIA *begins a lyrical but
pained solo as* ALEC *speaks for them*)

ALEC: we will stand here
our shoulders embrace an enormous spirit
my dreams waddle in my lap   125
run round to miz bertha's
where lil richard gets his process
run backward to the rosebushes
& a drunk man lyin
down the block to the nuns   130
in pink habits/ prayin in a pink chapel
my dreams run to meet aunt marie
my dreams haunt me like the little geechee river
our dreams draw blood from old sores
this is our space   135
we are not movin

(DAHLIA *finishes her movement/* ALEC *is seen reaching for her/
lights out. in the blackout they exit as* LOU *enters. lights come up
on* LOU *who repeats bitterly his challenge to the audience*)

LOU: why dontchu go on & live my life for me
    i didn't want certain moments at all
    i'd give them to anybody

(LOU *waves his hand commanding the minstrel mask to disappear, which it does. he signals to his left & again by magic, the lights come up higher revealing the interior of a lower manhattan bar & its bartender,* ELI, *setting up for the night.* ELI *greets* LOU *as he continues to set up tables, chairs, candles, etc., for the night's activities.* LOU *goes over to the jukebox, & plays "we are family" by sister sledge.* LOU *starts to tell us exactly where we are, but* ELI *takes over as characters are liable to do. throughout* ELI's *poem, the other members of the company enter the bar in their street clothes, & doing steps reminiscent of their solos during the minstrel sequence. as each enters, the audience is made aware that these ordinary people are the minstrels. the company continues to dance individually as* ELI *speaks)*

140   this is . . .
    ELI: MY kindgom.
      there shall be no trespassers/ no marauders
      no tourists in my land
      your nurture these gardens   or   be shot on sight
145   carelessness & other priorities
      are not permitted within these walls
      i am mantling an array of strength & beauty
      no one shall interfere with this
      the construction of myself
150   my city   my theater
      my bar   come to my poems
      but understand we speak english carefully
      & perfect antillean french
      our toilets are disinfected
155   the plants here sing to me each morning
      come to my kitchen my parlor even my bed
      i sleep on satin   surrounded by hand made
      infants who bring me good luck & warmth
      come even to my door
160   the burglar alarm/ armed guards vault from the east side
      if i am in danger   a siren shouts
      you are welcome
      to my kingdom   my city   my self
      but yr presence must not disturb these inhabitants
165   leave nothing out of place/ push no dust under my rugs
      leave not a crack in my wine glasses
      no finger prints
      clean up after yrself in the bathroom
      there are no maids here   no days off
170   for healing   no insurance policies
      for dislocation of the psyche
      aliens/ foreigners/ are granted resident status
      we give them a little green card
      as they prove themselves non-injurious
175   to the joy of my nation
      i sustain no intrusions/ no double-entendre romance
      no soliciting of sadness   in my life
      are those who love me well
      the rest are denied their visas . . .
180   is everyone ready to boogie

(finally, when ELI *calls for a boogie, the company does a dance that indicates these people have worked & played together a long time. as dance ends, the company sits & chats at the tables & at the bar. this is now a safe haven for these "minstrels" off from work. here they are free to be themselves, to reveal secrets, fantasies, nightmares, or hope. it is safe because it is segregated & magic reigns*

LILI, *the waitress, is continually moving abt the bar, taking orders for drinks & generally staying on top of things)*

ALEC: gimme a triple bourbon/ & a glass of angel dust
    these thursday nite audiences are abt to kill me

(ELI *goes behind bar to get drinks)*

DAHLIA: why do i drink so much?
BETTINA, LILY, NATALIE: *(in unison)* who cares?
DAHLIA: but I'm an actress. i have to ask myself these   185
    questions
LILY: that's a good reason to drink
DAHLIA: no/ i mean the character/ alec, you're a director/ give
    me some motivation
ALEC: motivation/ if you didn't drink you wd remember that   190
    you're not workin
LILY: i wish i cd get just one decent part
LOU: say as lady macbeth or mother courage
ELI: how the hell is she gonna play lady macbeth and mac-
    beth's a white dude?   195
LILY: ross & natalie/ why are you countin pennies like that?
NATALIE: we had to wait on our money again
ROSS: and then we didn't get it
BETTINA: maybe they think we still accept beads & ribbons
NATALIE: i had to go around wit my tambourine just to get   200
    subway fare
ELI: dont worry abt it/ have one on me
NATALIE: thank you eli
BETTINA: *(falling out of her chair)* oh . . .
ALEC: cut her off eli/ dont give her no more   205
LILY: what's the matter bettina/ is yr show closin?
BETTINA: *(gets up, resets chair)* no/ my show is not closin/ but
    if that director asks me to play it any blacker/ i'm gonna
    have to do it in a mammy dress
LOU: you know/ countin pennies/ lookin for parts/ breakin   210
    tambourines/ we must be outta our minds for doin this
BETTINA: no we're not outta our minds/ we're just sorta outta
    our minds
LILY: no/ we're not outta our minds/ we've been doing this shit
    a long time . . . ross/ captain theophilis conneau/ in a   215
    slaver's logbook/ says that "youths of both sexes wear rings in
    the nose and lower lip and stick porcupine quills thru the
    cartilage of the ear." ross/ when ringlin' bros. comes to
    madison square garden/ dontcha know the white people
    just go   220
ROSS: in their cb radios
DAHLIA: in their mcdonald's hats
ELI: with their save america t-shirts & those chirren who score
    higher on IQ tests for the white chirren who speak english
ALEC: when the hockey games absorb all america's attention   225
    in winter/ they go with their fists clenched & their tongues
    battering their women who dont know a puck from a 3-yr-
    old harness racer
BETTINA: they go & sweat in fierce anger
ROSS: these factories   230

NATALIE: these middle management positions
ROSS: make madison square garden
BETTINA: the temple of the primal scream

(LILY *gets money from cash register & heads toward jukebox*)

LILY: oh how they love blood
235 NATALIE: & how they dont even dress for the occasion/ all inconspicuous & pink
ELI: now if willie colon come there
BETTINA: if/ we say/ the fania all stars gonna be there in that nasty fantasy of the city council
240 ROSS: where the hot dogs are not even hebrew national
LILY: and the bread is stale
ROSS: even in such a place where dance is an obscure notion
BETTINA: where one's joy is good cause for a boring chat with the pinkerton guard
245 DAHLIA: where the halls lead nowhere
ELI: & "back to yr seat/ folks"
LILY: when all one's budget for cruisin
LOU: one's budget for that special dinner with you know who
LILY: the one you wd like to love you
250 BETTINA: when yr whole reasonable allowance for leisure activity/buys you a seat where what's goin on dont matter
DAHLIA: cuz you so high up/ you might be in seattle
LILY: even in such a tawdry space
ELI: where vorster & his pals wd spit & expect black folks to lick it up
255 ROSS: *(stands on chair)* in such a place i've seen miracles
ALL: oh yeah/ aw/ ross
ROSS: the miracles

(*"music for the love of it," by butch morris, comes up on the juke-box/ this is a catchy uptempo rhythm & blues post WW II. as they speak the company does a dance that highlights their ease with one another & their familiarity with "all the new dance steps"*)

LILY: the commodores
260 DAHLIA: muhammad ali
NATALIE: bob marley
ALEC: & these folks who upset alla 7th avenue with their glow/
    how the gold in their braids is new in this world of hard hats & men with the grace of wounded buffalo/ how these
265   folks in silk & satin/ in bodies reekin of good love comin/ these pretty muthafuckahs
DAHLIA: make this barn
LILY: this insult to good taste
BETTINA: a foray into paradise
270 DAHLIA, LILY, ALEC, NATALIE, & ROSS: *(in unison)* we dress up
BETTINA, ELI, & LOU: *(in unison)* we dress up
DAHLIA: cuz we got good manners
ROSS: cd you really ask dr. funkenstein to come all that way & greet him in the clothes you sweep yr kitchen in?
275 ALL: NO!
BETTINA: cd you say to muhammad ali/ well/ i just didnt have a chance to change/ you see i have a job/ & then i went jogging & well, you know its just madison square garden
LOU: my dear/ you know that wont do
280 NATALIE: we honor our guests/ if it costs us all we got

DAHLIA: when stevie wonder sings/ he don't want us lookin like we ain't got no common sense/ he wants us to be as lovely as we really are/ so we strut & reggae
ELI: i seen some doing the jump up/ i myself just got happy/ but i'm tellin you one thing for sure   285
LILY: we fill up where we at
BETTINA: no police
NATALIE: no cheap beer
DAHLIA: no nasty smellin bano
ROSS: no hallways fulla derelicts & hustlers   290
NATALIE: gonna interfere wit alla this beauty
ALEC: if it wasnt for us/ in our latino chic/ our rasta-fare our outer space funk suits & all the rest i have never seen
BETTINA: tho my daddy cd tell you bout them fox furs & stacked heels/ the diamonds & marie antoinette wigs   295
ELI: it's not cuz we got money
NATALIE: it's not cuz if we had money we wd spend it on luxury
LILY: it's just when you gotta audience with the pope/ you look yr best   300
BETINNA: when you gonna see the queen of england/ you polish yr nails
NATALIE: when you gonna see one of them/ & you know who i mean
ALEC: they gotta really know   305
BETTINA: we gotta make em feel
ELI: we dont do this for any old body
LOU: we're doin this for you
NATALIE: we dress up
ALEC: is our way of sayin/ you gettin the very best   310
DAHLIA: we cant do less/ we love too much to be stingy
ROSS: they give us too much to be loved ordinary
LILY: we simply have good manners
ROSS: & an addiction to joy
FEMALE CAST MEMBERS: *(in unison)* WHEE . . .   315
DAHLIA: we dress up
MALE CAST MEMBERS: *(in unison)* HEY . . .
BETTINA: we gotta show the world/ we gotta corner on the color
ROSS: happiness just jumped right outta us/ & we are lookin good   320

(*everyone in the bar is having so much fun/ that* MAXINE *takes on an exaggerated character as she enters/ in order to bring them to attention. the company freezes, half in respect/ half in parody*)

MAXINE: cognac!

(*the company relaxes, goes to tables or the bar. in the meantime,* ROSS *has remained in the spell of the character that* MAXINE *had introduced when she came in. he goes over to* MAXINE *who is having a drink/ & begins an improvisation*)

ROSS: she left the front gate open/ not quite knowing she wanted someone to walk on thru the wrought iron fence/ scrambled in whiskey bottles broken round old bike spokes/ some nice brown man to wind up in her bed/ she really   325
    didnt know/ the sombrero that enveloped her face was a lil too much for an april nite on the bowery/ & the silver halter dug out from summer cookouts near riis beach/ didnt sparkle with the intensity of her promise to have one good time/ before the children came back from carolina.   330
    brooklyn cd be such a drag. every street cept flatbush &

nostrand/ reminiscent of europe during the plague/ seems
like nobody but sickness waz out walkin/ drivels & hypes/ a
few youngsters lookin for more than they cd handle/ & then
335 there waz fay/

(MAXINE *rises, begins acting the story out*)

waitin for a cab. anyone of the cars inchin along the
boulevard cd see fay waznt no whore/ just a good clean
woman out for the nite/ & tho her left titty jumped out
from under her silver halter/ she didn't notice cuz she waz
340 lookin for a cab. the dank air fondled her long saggin
bosom like a possible companion/ she felt good. she stuck
her tin-ringed hand on her waist & watched her own ankles
dance in the nite. she waz gonna have a good time tonight/
she waz awright/ a whole lotta woman/ wit that special
345 brooklyn bottom strut. knowin she waznt comin in til
dawn/ fay covered herself/ sorta/ wit a light kacky jacket that
just kept her titties from rompin in the wind/ & she pulled
it closer to her/ the winds waz comin/ from nowhere jabbin/
& there wasnt no cabs/ the winds waz beatin her behind/
350 whisperin/ gigglin/ you aint goin noplace/ you an ol bitch/
shd be at home wit ur kids. fay beat off the voices/ & an
EBONY-TRUE-TO-YOU cab climbed the curb to get her.
(*as cabdriver*)
hope you aint plannin on stayin in brooklyn/ after 8:00
355 you dead in brooklyn. (*as narrator*)
she let her titty shake like she thot her mouth oughtta
bubble like/ wd she take off her panties/ i'd take
her anywhere.
MAXINE: (*as if in cab*) i'm into havin a good time/ yr arms/
360 veins burstin/ like you usedta lift tobacco onto trucks or cut
cane/ i want you to be happy/ long as we dont haveta stay
in brooklyn
ROSS: & she made like she waz gypsy rose lee/ or the hotsy
totsy girls in the carnival round from waycross/ when it waz
365 segregated
MAXINE: what's yr name?
ROSS: my name is raphael
MAXINE: oh that's nice
ROSS: & fay moved where i cd see her out the rear view
370 mirror/ waz tellin me all bout her children & big eddie who
waz away/ while we crossed the manhattan bridge/ i kept
smilin. (*as cabdriver*) where exactly you goin?
MAXINE: i dont really know. i just want to have a good time.
take me where i can see famous people/ & act bizarre like
375 sinatra at the kennedys/ maybe even go round & beat up
folks like jim brown/ throw somebody offa balcony/ you
know/ for a good time
ROSS: the only place I knew/ i took her/ after i kisst the spaces
she'd been layin open to me. fay had alla her $17 cuz i
380 hadnt charged her nothin/ turned the meter off/ said it waz
wonderful to pick up a lady like her on atlantic avenue/ i
saw nobody but those goddamn whores/ & fay

(MAXINE *moves in to* ROSS *& gives him a very long kiss*)

now fay waz a gd clean woman/ & she waz burstin with
pride & enthusiasm when she walked into the place where I
385 swore/ all the actresses & actors hung out

(*the company joins in* ROSS' *story; responding to* MAXINE *as tho
she waz entering their bar*)

oh yes/ there were actresses in braids & lipstick/ wigs &
winged tip pumps/ fay assumed the posture of someone
she'd always admired/ etta james/ the waitress asked her to
leave cuz she waz high/ & fay knew better than that
MAXINE: (*responding to* LILY's *indication of throwing her out*) i 390
aint high/ i'm enthusiastic/ and i'm gonna have me a
gooooooood/ ol time
ROSS: she waz all dressed up/ she came all the way from
brooklyn/ she must look high cuz i/ the taxi-man/ well i got
her a lil excited/ that waz all/ but she waz gonna cool out/ 395
cuz she waz gonna meet her friends/ at this place/ yes. she
knew that/ & she pushed a bunch of rhododendrum/ outta
her way so she cd get over to that table/ & stood over the
man with the biggest niggah eyes & warmest smellin mouth
MAXINE: please/ let me join you/ i come all the way from 400
brooklyn/ to have a good time/ you dont think i'm high do
ya/ cd i please join ya/ i just wanna have a good ol time
ROSS: (*as* BETTINA *turns away*) the woman sipped chablis &
looked out the window hopin to see one of the bowery
drunks fall down somewhere/ fay's voice hoverin/ flirtin 405
wit hope
LOU: (*turning to face* MAXINE) why dont you go downstairs &
put yr titty in yr shirt/ you cant have no good time lookin
like that/ now go on down & then come up & join us

(BETTINA & LOU *rise & move to another table*)

ROSS: fay tried to shove her flesh anywhere/ she took off her 410
hat/ bummed a kool/ swallowed somebody's cognac/ & sat
down/ waitin/ for a gd time
MAXINE: (*rises & hugs* ROSS) aw ross/ when am i gonna get a
chance to feel somethin like that/ i got into this business
cuz i wanted to feel things all the time/ & all they want me 415
to do is put my leg in my face/ smile/ &
LILY: you better knock on some wood/ maxine/ at least
yr workin
BETTINA: & at least yr not playin a whore/ if some other
woman comes in here & tells me she's playin a whore/ 420
i think i might kill her
ELI: you'd kill her so you cd say/ oh dahlia died & i know all
her lines
BETTINA: aw hush up eli/ dnt you know what i mean?
ELI: no miss/ i dont/ are you in the theater? 425
BETTINA: mr. bartender/ poet sir/ i am theater
DAHLIA: well miss theater/ that's a surprise/ especially since
you fell all over the damn stage in the middle of my solo
LILY: she did
ELI: miss theater herself fell down? 430
DAHLIA: yeah/ she cant figure out how to get attention without
makin somebody else look bad
MAXINE: now dahlia/ it waznt that bad/ i hardly noticed her
DAHLIA: it waz my solo/ you werent sposed to notice her at all!
BETTINA: you know dahlia/ i didn't do it on purpose/ i cda 435
hurt myself
DAHLIA: that wd be unfortunate
BETTINA: well miss thing with those big ass hips you got/ i
dont know why you think you can do the ballet anyway

(*the company breaks; they're expecting a fight*)

DAHLIA: (*crossing to* BETTINA) i got this 440

(*demonstrates her leg extension*)

& alla this

(DAHLIA *turns her back to* BETTINA/ *& slaps her own backside.*
BETTINA *grabs* DAHLIA, *turns her around & they begin a series
of finger snaps that are a paraphrase of ailey choreography
for very dangerous fights.* ELI *comes to break up the impending
altercation*)

ELI: ladies ladies ladies

(ELI *separates the two*)

ELI: people keep tellin me to put my feet on the ground i get
mad & scream/ there is no ground

445 only shit pieces from dogs horses & men who dont live
anywhere/ they tell me think straight & make myself
somethin/ i shout & sigh/ i am a poet/ i write poems
i make words cartwheel & somersault down pages
outta my mouth come visions distilled like bootleg

450 whiskey/ i am like a radio but i am a channel of my own
i keep sayin i write poems/ & people keep askin me
what do i do/ what in the hell is going on?
people keep tellin me these are hard times/ what are
you gonna be doin ten years from now/

455 what in the hell do you think/ i am gonna be writin poems
i will have poems inchin up the walls of the lincoln tunnel/
i am gonna feed my children poems on rye bread with
    horseradish/
i am gonna send my mailman off with a poem for his
    wagon/
give my doctor a poem for his heart/ i am a poet/

460 i am not a part-time poet/ i am not a amateur poet/
i dont even know what that person cd be/ whoever that is
authorizing poetry as an avocation/ is a fraud/
put yr own feet on the ground

BETTINA: i'm sorry eli/ i just dont want to be a gypsy all my life

(*the bar returns to normal humming & sipping. the lights
change to focus on* LILY/ *who begins to say what's really been on
her mind. the rest of the company is not aware of* LILY's *private
thoughts. only* BETTINA *responds to* LILY, *but as a partner in fantasy, not as a voyeur*)

465 LILY: (*illustrating her words with movement*) i'm gonna simply
    brush my hair. rapunzel pull yr tresses back into the tower.
    & lady godiva give up horseback riding. i'm gonna alter my
    social & professional life dramatically. i will brush 100
    strokes in the morning/ 100 strokes midday & 100 strokes

470 before retiring. i will have a very busy schedule. between
    the local trains & the express/ i'm gonna brush. i brush
    between telephone calls. at the disco i'm gonna brush on
    the slow songs/ i dont slow dance with strangers. i'ma brush
    my hair before making love & after. i'll brush my hair in

475 taxis. while windowshopping. when i have visitors over the
    kitchen table/ i'ma brush. i brush my hair while thinking
    abt anything. mostly i think abt how it will be when i get
    my full heada hair. like lifting my head in the morning will
    become a chore. i'll try to turn my cheek & my hair will

480 weigh me down

(LILY *falls to the floor.* BETTINA *helps lift her to her knees, then
begins to dance & mime as* LILY *speaks*)

    i dream of chaka khan/ chocolate from graham central
    station with all seven wigs/ & medusa. i brush & brush. i

use olive oil hair food/ & posner's vitamin E. but mostly i
brush & brush. i may lose contact with most of my friends. i
cd lose my job/ but i'm on unemployment & brush while   485
waiting on line for my check. i'm sure i get good
recommendations from my social worker: such a fastidious
woman/ that lily/ always brushing her hair. nothing in my
dreams suggests that hair brushing/ per se/ has anything to
do with my particular heada hair. a therapist might say that   490
the head fulla hair has to do with something else/ like: a
symbol of lily's unconscious desires. but i have no therapist

(*she takes imaginary pen from* BETTINA, *who was pretending to
be a therapist/ & sits down at table across from her*)

& my dreams mean things to me/ like if you dreamed abt
tobias/ then something has happened to tobias/ or he is
gonna show up. if you dream abt yr grandma who's dead/   495
then you must be doing something she doesnt like/ or she
wdnta gone to all the trouble to leave heaven like that. if
you dream something red/ you shd stop. if you dream
something green/ you shd keep doing it. if a blue person
appears in yr dreams/ then that person is yr true friend.   500
& that's how i see my dreams. & this head fulla hair i
have in my dreams is lavender & nappy as a 3-yr-old's in a
apple tree. i can fry an egg & see the white of the egg
spreadin in the grease like my hair is gonna spread in the air/
but i'm not egg-yolk yellow/ i am brown & the egg white   505
isnt white at all/ it is my actual hair/ & it wd go on & on
forever/ irregular like a rasta-man's hair. irregular/
gargantuan & lavender. nestled on blue satin pillows/
pillows like the sky. & so i fry my eggs. i buy daisies dyed
lavender & laced lavender tablemats & lavender nail polish. 510
though i never admit it/ i really do believe in magic/ & can
do strange things when something comes over me. soon
everything around me will be lavender/ fluffy &
consuming. i will know not a moment of bitterness/ through
all the wrist aching & tennis elbow from brushing/ i'll   515
smile. no regrets/ "je ne regrette rien" i'll sing like edith
piaf. when my friends want me to go see tina turner or
pacheco/ i'll croon "sorry/ i have to brush my hair."
i'll find ambrosia. my hair'll grow pomegranates & soil/
rich as round the aswan/ i wake in my bed to bananas/   520
avocados/ collard greens/ the tramps' latest disco hit/ fresh
croissant/ pouilly fuissé/ ishmael reed's essays/ charlotte
carter's stories/ all stream from my hair.
& with the bricks that plop from where a 9-year-old's top
braid wd be/ i will brush myself a house with running water 525
& a bidet. i'll have a closet full of clean bed linen & the lil
girl from the castro convertible commercial will come &
open the bed repeatedly & stay on as a helper to brush my
hair. lily is the only person i know whose every word leaves
a purple haze on the tip of yr tongue. when this happens i   530
says clouds are forming/ & i has to close the windows.
violet rain is hard to remove from blue satin pillows

(LOU, *the magician, gets up. he points to* LILY *sitting very still.
he reminds us that it is only thru him that we are able to know
these people without the "masks"/ the lies/ & he cautions that all
their thoughts are not benign. they are not safe from what they
remember or imagine*)

LOU: you have t come with me/ to this place where magic is/
    to hear my song/ some times i forget & leave my tune

535 in the corner of the closet under all the dirty clothes/
in this place/ magic asks me where i've been/ how i've
been singin/ lately i leave my self in all the wrong hands/
in this place where magic is involved in
undoin our masks/ i am able to smile & answer that.

540 in this place where magic always asks for me
i discovered a lot of other people who talk without mouths
who listen to what you say/ by watchin yr jewelry dance
& in this place where magic stays
you can let yrself in or out

545 but when you leave yrself at home/ burglars & daylight
thieves
pounce on you & sell yr skin/ at cut-rates on tenth avenue

(ROSS *has been playing the acoustic guitar softly as* LOU *spoke.*
ALEC *picks up on the train of* LOU's *thoughts & tells a story that
in turn captures* NATALIE's *attention. slowly,* NATALIE *becomes
the woman* ALEC *describes*)

ALEC: she had always wanted a baby/ never a family/ never a
man/
she had always wanted a baby/ who wd suckle & sleep
a baby boy who wd wet/ & cry/ & smile

550 suckle & sleep
when she sat in bars/ on the stool/ near the door/ & cross
from the juke box/ with her legs straddled & revealin red
lace pants/ & lil hair smashed under the stockings/ she wd
think how she wanted this baby & how she wd call the

555 baby/ "myself" & as she thot/ bout this brown lil thing/ she
ordered another bourbon/ double & tilted her head as if to
cuddle some infant/ not present/ the men in the bar never
imagined her as someone's mother/ she rarely tended her
own self carefully/

(NATALIE *rises slowly, sits astride on the floor*)

560 just enough to exude a languid sexuality that teased the
men off work/ & the bartender/ ray who waz her only
friend/ women didn't take to her/ so she spent her
afternoons with ray/ in the bar round the corner from her lil
house/ that shook winsomely in a hard wind/ surrounded by

565 three weepin willows
NATALIE: my name is sue-jean & i grew here/ a ordinary
colored girl with no claims to any thing/ or anyone/ i drink
now/ bourbon/ in harder times/ beer/ but i always wanted to
have a baby/ a lil boy/ named myself

570 ALEC: one time/ she made it with ray
NATALIE: & there waz nothin special there/ only a hot rough
bangin/ a brusque barrelin throwin of torso/ legs & sweat/
ray wanted to kiss me/ but i screamed/ cuz i didnt like
kissin/ only fuckin/ & we rolled round/ i waz a peculiar sorta

575 woman/ wantin no kisses/ no caresses/ just power/ heat &
no eaziness of thrust/ ray pulled himself outa me/ with no
particular exclamation/ he smacked me on my behind/ i
waz grinnin/ & he took that as a indication of his skill/ he
believed he waz a good lover/ & a woman like me/ didnt

580 never want nothin but a hard dick/ & everyone believed
that/ tho no one in town really knew
ALEC: so ray/ went on behind the bar cuz he had got his
NATALIE: & i lay in the corner laughin/ with my drawers/
twisted round my ankles & my hair standin every which way/

585 i waz laughin/ knowin i wd have this child/ myself/ & no
one wd ever claim him/ cept me cuz i waz a low-down

thing/ layin in sawdust & whiskey stains/ i laughed & had a
good time masturbatin in the shadows.
ALEC: sue-jean ate starch for good luck
NATALIE: like mama kareena/ tol me 590
ALEC: & she planted five okras/ five collards/ & five tomatoes
NATALIE: for good luck too/ i waz gonna have this baby/ i even
went over to the hospital to learn prenatal care/ & i kept
myself clean
ALEC: sue-jean's lanky body got ta spreadin & her stomach 595
waz taut & round high in her chest/ a high pregnancy is
sure to be a boy/ & she smiled
NATALIE: I stopped goin to the bar
ALEC: started cannin food
NATALIE: knittin lil booties 600
ALEC: even goin to church wit the late night radio evangelist
NATALIE: I gotta prayer cloth for the boy/ myself waz gonna be
safe from all that his mama/ waz prey to
ALEC: sure/ sue-jean waz a scandal/ but that waz to be
expected/ cuz she waz always a po criterish chile 605
NATALIE: & wont no man bout step my way/ ever/ just cuz i
hadda bad omen on me/ from the very womb/ i waz
bewitched is what the ol women usedta say
ALEC: sue-jean waz born on a full moon/ the year of the flood/
the night the river raised her skirts & sat over alla the towns 610
& settlements for 30 miles in each direction/ the nite the
river waz in labor/ gruntin & groanin/ splittin trees &
families/ spillin cupboards over the ground/ waz the nite
sue-jean waz born
NATALIE: & my mother died/ drownin/ holdin me up over the 615
mud crawlin in her mouth
ALEC: somebody took her & she lived to be the town's no one/
now with the boy achin & dancin in her belly/ sue jean waz
a gay & gracious woman/ she made pies/ she baked cakes &
left them on the stoop of the church she had never entered 620
just cuz she wanted/ & she grew plants & swept her floors/
she waz someone she had never known/ she waz herself
with child/ & she waz a wonderful bulbous thing
NATALIE: the nite/ myself waz born/ ol mama kareena from
the hills came down to see bout me/ i hollered & breathed/ 625
i did exactly like mama kareena said/ & i pushed & pushed
& there was a earthquake up in my womb/ i wanted to sit
up & pull the tons of logs trapped in my crotch out/ so i cd
sleep/ but it wdnt go way/ i pushed & thot I saw 19 horses
runnin in my pussy/ i waz sure there waz a locomotive 630
stalled up in there burnin coal & steamin & pushin gainst
a mountain
ALEC: finally the child's head waz within reach & mama
kareena/ brought the boy into this world
NATALIE: & he waz awright/ with alla his toes & his fingers/
his lil dick & eyes/ elbows that bent/ & legs/ straight/ i 635
wanted a big glassa bourbon/ & mama kareena brought it/
right away/ we sat drinkin the bourbon/ & lookin at the
child whose name waz myself/ like i had wanted/ & the two
of us ate placenta stew . . . i waznt really sure . . .
ALEC: sue-jean you werent really sure you wanted myself to 640
wake up/ you always wanted him to sleep/ or at most to
nurse/ the nites yr dreams were disturbed by his cryin
NATALIE: i had no one to help me
ALEC: so you were always with him/ & you didnt mind/ you
knew this waz yr baby/ myself/ & you cuddled him/ carried 645
him all over the house with you all day/ no matter/ what

NATALIE: everythin waz goin awright til/ myself wanted to crawl

ALEC: *(moving closer to* NATALIE*)* & discover a world of his
650   own/ then you became despondent/ & yr tits began to dry &
you lost the fullness of yr womb/ where myself/ had lived

NATALIE: i wanted that back

ALEC: you wanted back the milk

NATALIE: & the tight gourd of a stomach i had when myself
655   waz being in me

ALEC: so you slit his wrists

NATALIE: he waz sleepin

ALEC: sucked the blood back into yrself/ & waited/ myself
shriveled up in his crib

660 NATALIE: a dank lil blk think/ i never touched him again

ALEC: you were always holdin yr womb/ feelin him kick &
sing to you bout love/ & you wd hold yr tit in yr hand

NATALIE: like i always did when i fed him

ALEC: & you waited & waited/ for a new myself. tho there
665   were labor pains

NATALIE: & i screamed in my bed

ALEC: yr legs pinnin to the air

NATALIE: spinnin sometimes like a ferris wheel/ i cd get no
child to fall from me

670 ALEC: & she forgot abt the child bein born/ & waz heavy &
full all her life/ with "myself"

NATALIE: who'll be out/ any day now

*(*ELI *moves from behind the bar to help* NATALIE/ *or to clean tables. he doesnt really know, he stops suddenly)*

ELI: aint that a goddamn shame/ aint that a way
to come into the world
675   sometimes i really cant write
     sometimes i cant even talk

(the minstrel mask comes down very slowly. blackout, except for lights on the big minstrel mask which remains visible throughout intermission)

— ACT TWO —

(all players onstage are frozen, except LOU*, who makes a motion for the big minstrel mask to disappear again. as the mask flies up,* LOU *begins)*

LOU: in this place where magic stays
     you can let yrself in or out

(he makes a magic motion, a samba is heard from the jukebox & activity is begun in the bar again, DAHLIA, NATALIE & LILY *enter, apparently from the ladies room)*

NATALIE: i swear we went to that audition in good faith/ & that
man asked us where we learned to speak english so well/ i
5   swear this foreigner/ asked us/ from the city of new york/
where we learned to speak english.

LILY: all i did was say "bom dia/ como vai"/ and the
englishman got red in the face

LOU: *(as the englishman)* yr from the states/ aren't you?

10 LILY: "sim"/ i said/ in good portuguese

LOU: but you speak portuguese

LILY: "sim" i said/ in good portuguese

LOU: how did you pick that up?

LILY: i hadda answer so simple/ i cdnt say i learned it/ cuz
niggahs cant learn & that wda been too hard on the man/   15
so i said/ in good english: i held my ear to the ground &
listened to the samba from bêlim

DAHLIA: you should have said: i make a lotta phone calls to
casçais, portugao

BETTINA: i gotta bahiano boyfriend   20

NATALIE: how abt: i waz an angolan freedom fighter

MAXINE: no/ lily/ tell him: i'm a great admirer of zeza motto
& leci brandao

LILY: when the japanese red army invaded san juan/ they
poisoned the papaya with portuguese. i eat a lotta papaya.   25
last week/ i developed a strange schizophrenic condition/
with 4 manifest personalities: one spoke english &
understood nothing/ one spoke french & had access to the
world/ one spoke spanish & voted against statehood for
puerto rico/ one spoke portuguese. "eu naõ falo ingles entaõ   30
y voce"/ i don't speak english anymore/ & you?

(all the women in the company have been doing samba steps as the others spoke/ now they all dance around a table in their own ritual/ which stirs ALEC & LOU *to interrupt this female segregation. the women scatter to different tables, leaving the two interlopers alone, so,* ALEC & LOU *begin their conversation)*

ALEC: not only waz she without a tan, but she held her purse
close to her hip like a new yorker. someone who rode the
paris métro or listened to mariachis in plaza santa cecilia.
she waz not from here   35

(he sits at table)

LOU: *(following suit)* but from there

ALEC: some there where coloureds/ mulattoes/ negroes/blacks
cd make a living big enough to leave there to come here/
where no one went there much any more for all sorts
of reasons   40

LOU: the big reasons being immigration restrictions &
unemployment. nowadays, immigration restrictions of
every kind apply to any non-european persons who want to
go there from here

ALEC: some who want to go there from here risk fetching   45
trouble with the customs authority there

LOU: or later with the police, who can tell who's not from
there cuz the shoes are pointed & laced strange

ALEC: the pants be for august & yet it's january

LOU: the accent is patterned for pétionville, but working in   50
crown heights

ALEC: what makes a person comfortably ordinary here cd
make him dangerously conspicuous there.

LOU: so some go to london or amsterdam or paris/ where they
are so abounding no one tries to tell who is from where   55

ALEC: still the far right wing of every there prints lil pamphlets
that say everyone from there shd leave & go back where
they came from

LOU: this is manifest legally thru immigration restrictions &
personally thru unemployment   60

ALEC: anyway the yng woman waz from there/ & she waz
alone. that waz good. cuz if a person had no big brother in
gronigen/ no aunt in rouen

LOU: no sponsor in chicago

ALEC: this brown woman from there might be a good idea.   65
everybody in the world/ european & non-european alike/

everybody knows that rich white girls are hard to find. some
of them joined the weather underground/ some the baader
meinhof gang.

70   LOU: a whole bunch of them gave up men entirely
      ALEC: so the exotic lover in the sun routine becomes more
      difficult to swing/ if she wants to talk abt plastic explosives
      & the resistance of the black masses to socialism/ instead of
      giving head as the tide slips in or lending money
75   LOU: just for the next few days
      ALEC: is hard to find a rich white girl who is so dumb/ too
      LOU: anyway. the whole world knows/ european & non-
      european alike/ the whole world knows that nobody loves
      the black woman like they love farrah fawcett-majors. the
80   whole world dont turn out for a dead black woman like they
      did for marilyn monroe.
      ALEC: actually/ the demise of josephine baker waz an
      international event
      LOU: but she waz a war hero
85   the worldwide un-beloved black woman is a good idea/ if
      she is from there & one is a young man with gd looks/
      piercing eyes/ & knowledge of several romantic languages

*(throughout this conversation, ALEC & LOU will make attempts
to seduce, cajole, & woo the women of the bar as their narrative
indicates. the women play the roles as described, being so moved
by romance)*

      ALEC: the best dancing spots/ the hill where one can see the
      entire bay at twilight
90   LOU: the beach where the seals & pelicans run free/ the
      hidden "local" restaurants
      ALEC: "aw babee/ you so pretty" begins often in the lobby of
      hotels where the bright handsome yng men wd be loiterers
      LOU: were they not needed to tend the needs of the black
95   women from there
      ALEC: tourists are usually white people or asians who didnt
      come all this way to meet a black woman who isnt even
      foreign
      LOU: so hotel managers wink an eye at the yng men in the
100   lobby or by the bar who wd be loitering/ but are gonna help
      her have a gd time
      ALEC: maybe help themselves too
      LOU: everybody in the world/ european & non-european alike/
      everybody knows the black woman from there is not treated
105   as a princess/ as a jewel/ a cherished lover
      ALEC: that's not how sapphire got her reputation/ nor how
      mrs. jefferson perceives the world
      LOU: you know/ babee/ you dont act like them. aw babee/ you
      so pretty
110   ALEC: the yng man in the hotel watches the yng blk woman sit
      & sit & sit/ while the european tourists dance with each
      other/ & the dapper local fellas mambo frenetically with
      secretaries from arizona/ in search of the missing rich white
      girl. our girl sits &
115   FEMALE CAST MEMBERS: *(in unison)* sits & sits & sits
      ALEC: *(to DAHLIA & NATALIE, who move to the music)* maybe
      she is courageous & taps her foot. maybe she is bold &
      enjoys the music/ smiling/ shaking shoulders. let her sit &
      let her know she is unwanted
120   LOU: she is not white & she is not from here
      ALEC: let her know she is not pretty enuf to dance the next
      merengue. then appear/ mysteriously/ in the corner of the

bar. stare at her. just stare. when stevie wonder's song/ "isnt
she lovely"/ blares thru the red-tinted light/ ask her to dance
& hold her as tyrone power wda. hold her & stare   125

(ROSS & ELI sing the chorus to stevie wonder's "isn't she lovely")

      LOU: dance yr ass off. she has been discovered by the non
      european fred astaire
      ALEC: let her know she is a surprise/ an event. by the look on
      yr face you've never seen anyone like this black woman
      from there. you say: "aw/ you not from here?"/ totally   130
      astonished. she murmurs that she is from there. as if to
      apologize for her unfortunate place of birth
      LOU: you say
      ALEC: aw babee/ you so pretty. & it's all over
      LOU: a night in a pension near the sorbonne. pick her up   135
      from the mattress. throw her gainst the wall in a show of
      exotic temper & passion:
      "maintenant/ tu es ma femme. nous nous sommes mariés."
      unions of this sort are common wherever the yng black
      women travel alone. a woman traveling alone is an affront   140
      to the non-european man who is known the world over/ to
      european & non-european alike/ for his way with women
      ALEC: his sense of romance/ how he can say:
      LOU: aw babee/ you so pretty . . . and even a beautiful woman
      will believe no one else ever recognized her loveliness   145
      ELI: or else/ he comes to a cafe in willemstad in the height of
      the sunset, an able-bodied/ sinewy yng man who wants to
      buy one beer for the yng woman. after the first round/ he
      discovers he has run out of money/ so she must buy the next
      round/ when he discovers/ what beautiful legs you   150
      have/how yr mouth is like the breath of tiger lilies. we shall
      make love in the/ how you call it/ yes in the earth/ in the
      dirt/ i will have you in my/ how you say/ where things grow/
      aw/ yes/ i will have you in the soil. probably under the stars
      & smelling of wine/ an unforgettable international affair   155
      can be consummated

*(the company sings "tara's theme" as ELI ends his speech. ELI &
BETTINA take a tango walk to the bar, while MAXINE mimics
a 1930's photographer, shooting them as they sail off into the
sunset)*

      MAXINE: at 11:30 one evening i waz at the port authority/ new
      york/ united states/ myself. now i waz there & i spoke
      english & waz holding approximately $7 american
      currency/ when a yng man from there came up to me from   160
      the front of the line of people waiting for the princeton new
      jersey united states local bus. i mean to say/ he gave up his
      chance for a good seat to come say to me:
      ROSS: i never saw a black woman reading nietzsche
      MAXINE: i waz demure enough/ i said i have to for a philoso-   165
      phy class. but as the night went on i noticed this yng
      man waz so much like the other yng men from here/ who
      use their bodies as bait & their smiles as passport
      alternatives. anyway the night did go on. we were snuggled
      together in the rear of the bus going down the jersey   170
      turnpike. he told me in english/ that he had spoken all his
      life in st louis/ where he waz raised:
      ROSS: i've wanted all my life to meet someone like you. i want
      you to meet my family/ who haven't seen me in a long time/
      since i left missouri looking for opportunity . . .   175

(he is lost for words)

LOU: *(stage whisper)* opportunity to sculpt

ROSS: thank you/ opportunity to sculpt

MAXINE: he had been everyplace/ he said

ROSS: you arent like any black woman i've ever met anywhere

180 MAXINE: here or there

ROSS: i had to come back to new york cuz of immigration restrictions & high unemployment among black american sculptors abroad

185 MAXINE: just as we got to princeton/ he picked my face up from his shoulder & said:

ROSS: aw babee/ you so pretty

MAXINE: aw babee/ you so pretty. i believe that night i must have looked beautiful for a black woman from there/ though i cd be asked at any moment to tour the universe/ to

190 climb a 6-story walkup with a brilliant & starving painter/ to share kadushi/ to meet mama/ to getta kiss each time the swing falls toward the willow branch/ to imagine where he say he from/ & more. i cd/ i cd have all of it/ but i cd not be taken/ long as i don't let a stranger be the first to say:

195 LOU: aw babee/ you so pretty

MAXINE: after all/ immigration restrictions & unemployment cd drive a man to drink or to lie

(she breaks away from ROSS)

so if you know yr beautiful & bright & cherishable awready/ when he say/ in whatever language:

200 ALEC: *(to NATALIE)* aw babee/ you so pretty

MAXINE: you cd say:

NATALIE: i know. thank you

MAXINE: then he'll smile/ & you'll smile. he'll say:

ELI: *(stroking BETTINA's thigh)* what nice legs you have

205 MAXINE: you can say:

BETTINA: *(removing his hand)* yes. they run in the family

MAXINE: oh! whatta universe of beautiful & well traveled women!

MALE CAST MEMBERS: *(in unison)* aw babee/ i've never met

210 anyone like you

FEMALE CAST MEMBERS: *(in unison, pulling away from men to stage edges)* that's strange/ there are millions of us!

(men all cluster after unsuccessful attempts to persuade their women to talk. ALEC gets the idea to serenade the women; ROSS takes the first verse, with men singing back-up. song is "ooh baby," by smokey robinson)

ROSS: *(singing)* i did you wrong/ my heart went out to play/ but in the game i lost you/ what a price to pay/ i'm cryin . . .

215 MALE PLAYERS: *(singing)* oo oo oo/ baby baby. . . . oo oo oo/ baby baby

(this brings no response from the women; the men elect ELI to lead the second verse)

ELI: mistakes i know i've made a few/ but i'm only human you've made mistakes too/ i'm cryin . . . oo oo oo/ baby baby . . . oo oo oo/ baby baby

(the women slowly forsake their staunch indignation/ returning to the arms of their partners. all that is except LILY, who walks abt the room of couples awkwardly)

220 MALE CAST MEMBERS & LILY: *(singing)*

i'm just about at the end of my rope but i can't stop trying/ i cant give up hope

cause i/ i believe one day/ i'll hold you near whisper i love you/ until that day is here i'm crying . . . oo oo oo/ baby baby 225

(LILY begins as the company continues to sing)

LILY: unfortunately the most beautiful man in the world is unavailable that's what he told me i saw him wandering abt/ said well this is one of a kind 230 & i might be able to help him out so alone & pretty in all this ganja & bodies melting he danced with me & i cd become that a certain way to be held that's considered in advance a way a thoughtful man wd kiss a woman who 235 cd be offended easily/ but waznt cuz of course the most beautiful man in the world knows exactly what to do with someone who knows that's who he is/ these dreads fallin thru my dress 240 so my nipples just stood up these hands playin the guitar on my back the lips somewhere between my neck & my forehead talking bout ocho rios & how i really must go 245 marcus garvey cda come in the door & we/ we wd still be dancin that dance the motion that has more to do with kinetic energy than shootin stars/ more to do with the impossibility of all this/ & how it waz awready bein too much 250 our reason failed we tried to go away & be just together aside from the silence that weeped with greed/ we didnt need/ anything/ but one another for tonite 255 but he is the most beautiful man in the world says he's unavailable/ & this man whose eyes made me half-naked & still & brazen/ was singin with me since we cd not talk/ we sang 260

(male players end their chorus with a flourish)

LILY: we sang with bob marley this man/ surely the most beautiful man in the world/ & i sang/ "i wanna love you & treat you right/

(the couples begin different kinds of reggae dances)

i wanna love you every day & every nite"

THE COMPANY: *(dancing & singing)* 265

we'll be together with the roof right over our heads we'll share the shelter of my single bed we'll share the same room/ jah provide the bread

DAHLIA: *(stops dancing during conversaton)* i tell you it's not just the part that makes me love you so much 270

LOU: what is it/ wait/ i know/ you like my legs

DAHLIA: yes/ uh huh/ yr legs & yr arms/ & . . .

LOU: but that's just my body/ you started off saying you loved me & now i see it's just my body

DAHLIA: oh/ i didn't mean that/ it's just i dont know you/ 275 except as the character i'm sposed to love/ & well i know rehearsal is over/ but i'm still in love with you

(they go to the bar to get drinks, then sit at a table)

ROSS: but baby/ you have to go on the road. we need the
    money

NATALIE: i'm not going on the road so you can fuck all these
    aspiring actresses

280 ROSS: aw/ just some of them/ baby

NATALIE: that's why i'm not going

ROSS: if you don't go on the road i'll still be fuckin em/ but
    you & me/ we'll be in trouble/ you understand?

NATALIE: *(stops dancing)* no i don't understand

285 ROSS: well let me break it down to you

NATALIE: please/ break it down to me

BETTINA: *(stops dancing)* hey/ natalie/ why dont you make
    him go on the road/ they always want us to be so
    goddamned conscientious

290 ALEC: *(stops dancing)* dont you think you shd mind yr
    own bizness?

NATALIE: yeah bettina/ mind yr own bizness

(she pulls ROSS *to a table with her)*

BETTINA: *(to* ALEC*)* no/ i'm tired of having to take any & every
    old job to support us/ & you get to have artistic integrity &
    refuse parts that are beneath you

295 ALEC: thats right/ i'm not playing the fool or the black buck
    pimp circus/ i'm an actor not a stereotype/ i've been
    trained. you know i'm a classically trained actor

BETTINA: & just what do you think we are?

MAXINE: well/ i got offered another whore part downtown

300 ELI: you gonna take it?

MAXINE: yeah

LILY: if you dont/ i know someone who will

ALEC: *(to* BETTINA*)* i told you/ we arent gonna get anyplace/
    by doin every bit part for a niggah that someone waves in
305   fronta my face

BETTINA: & we aren't gonna live long on nothin/ either/ cuz
    i'm quittin my job

ALEC: be in the real world for once & try to understand me

BETTINA: you mean/ i shd understand that you are the great
310   artist & i'm the trouper

ALEC: i'm not sayin that we cant be gigglin & laughin all the
    time dancin around/ but i cant stay in these "hate whitey"
    shows/ cuz they arent true

BETTINA: a failure of imagination on yr part/ i take it

315 ALEC: no/ an insult to my person

BETTINA: oh i see/ you wanna give the people some more
    make-believe

ALEC: i cd always black up again & do minstrel work/ wd that
    make you happy?

320 BETINNA: there is nothing niggardly abt a decent job. work is
    honorable/ work!

ALEC: well/ i got a problem. i got lots of problems/ but i got
    one i want you to fix & if you can fix it/ i'll do anything you
    say. last spring this niggah from the midwest asked for
325   president carter to say he waz sorry for that forgettable
    phenomenon/ slavery/ which brought us all together. i
    never did get it/ none of us ever got no apology from no
    white folks abt not bein considered human beings/ that
    makes me mad & tired. someone told me "roots" was the
330   way white folks worked out their guilt/ the success of "roots"
    is the way white folks assuaged their consciences/ i dont
    know this/ this is what i waz told. i dont get any pleasure

from nobody watchin me trying to be a slave i once waz/
who got away/ when we all know they had an emancipation
proclamation/ that the civil war waz not fought over us. we 335
all know that we/ actually dont exist unless we play football
or basketball or baseball or soccer/ pélé/ see they still import
a strong niggah to earn money. art here/ isnt like in the old
country/ where we had some spare time & did what we
liked to do/ i dont know this either/ this is also something 340
i've been told. i just want to find out why no one has even
been able to sound a gong & all the reporters recite that the
gong is ringin/ while we watch all the white people/
immigrants & invaders/ conquistadors & relatives of london
debtors from georgia/ kneel & apologize to us/ just for three 345
or four minutes. now/ this is not impossible/ & someone
shd make a day where a few minutes of the pain of our lives
is acknowledged. i have never been very interested in what
white people did/ cuz i waz able/ like most of us/ to have
very lil to do with them/ but if i become a success that 350
means i have to talk to white folks more than in high
school/ they are everywhere/ you know how they talk abt a
neighborhood changin/ we suddenly become all over the
place/ they are now all over my life/ & i dont like it. i am
not talkin abt poets & painters/ not abt women & lovers of 355
beauty/ i am talkin abt that proverbial white person who is
usually a man who just/ turns yr body around/ looks at yr
teeth & yr ass/ who feels yr calves & back/ & agrees on a
price. we are/ you see/ now able to sell ourselves/ & i am
still a person who is tired/ a person who is not into his 360
demise/ just three minutes for our lives/ just three minutes
of silence & a gong in st. louis/ oakland/ in los angeles . . .

*(the entire company looks at him as if he's crazy/ he tries to leave
the bar/ but* BETTINA *stops him)*

BETTINA: you're still outta yr mind. ain't no apologies keeping
    us alive.

LOU: what are you gonna do with white folks kneeling all over 365
    the country anyway/ man

*(*LOU *signals everyone to kneel)*

LILY: they say i'm too light to work/ but when i asked him
    what he meant/ he said i didnt actually look black. but/ i
    said/ my mama knows i'm black & my daddy/ damn sure
    knows i'm black/ & he is the only one who has a problem 370
    thinkin i'm black/ i said so let me play a white girl/ i'm a
    classically trained actress & i need the work & i can do it/
    he said that wdnt be very ethical of him. can you imagine
    that shit/ not ethical

NATALIE: as a red-blooded white woman/ i cant allow you all 375
    to go on like that

*(*NATALIE *starts jocularly)*

cuz today i'm gonna be a white girl/ i'll retroactively
wake myself up/ ah low & behold/ a white girl in my bed/
but first i'll haveta call a white girl i know to have some
more accurate information/ what's the first thing white girls 380
think in the morning/ do they get up being glad they aint
niggahs/ do they remember mama/ or worry abt gettin to
work/ do they work?/ do they play isadora & wrap
themselves in sheets & go tip toeing to the kitchen to make
maxwell house coffee/ oh i know/ the first thing a white girl 385
does in the morning is fling her hair/

so now i'm done with that/ i'm gonna water my plants/
but am i a po white trash white girl with a old jellyjar/
or am i a sophisticated & protestant suburbanite with
390 2 valiums slugged awready & a porcelain water carrier
leading me up the stairs strewn with heads of dolls & nasty
smellin white husband person's underwear/ if i was really
protected from the niggahs/ i might go to early morning
mass & pick up a tomato pie on the way home/ so i cd eat it
395 during the young & the restless. in williams arizona as a
white girl/ i cd push the navaho women outta my way in
the supermarket & push my nose in the air so i wdnt haveta
smell them. coming from bay ridge on the train i cd smile
at all the black & puerto rican people/ & hope they cant tell
400 i want them to go back where they came from/ or at least
be invisible
   i'm still in my kitchen/ so i guess i'll just have to fling my
hair again & sit down. i shd pinch my cheeks to bring the
color back/ i wonder why the colored lady hasn't arrived
405 to clean my house yet/ so i cd go to the beauty parlor &
sit under a sunlamp to get some more color back/ it's
terrible how god gave those colored women such clear
complexions/ it take em years to develop wrinkles/ but
beauty can be bought & flattered into the world.
410   as a white girl on the street/ i can assume since i am a
white girl on the streets/ that everyone notices how beautiful
i am/ especially lil black & caribbean boys/ they love to look
at me/ i'm exotic/ no one in their families looks like me/
poor things. if i waz one of those white girls who loves one
415 of those grown black fellas/ i cd say with my eyes wide
open/ totally sincere/ oh i didnt know that/ i cd say i didnt
know/ i cant/ i dont know how/ cuz i'ma white girl & i dont
have to do much of anything.
   all of this is the fault of the white man's sexism/ oh
420 how i loathe tight-assed thin-lipped pink white men/ even
the football players lack a certain relaxed virility. that's why
my heroes are either just like my father/ who while he still
cdnt speak english knew enough to tell me how the niggers
shd go back where they came from/ or my heroes are
425 psychotic faggots who are white/ or else they are/ oh/ you
know/ colored men.
   being a white girl by dint of my will/ is much more
complicated than i thought it wd be/ but i wanted to try it
cuz so many men like white girls/ white men/ black men/
430 latin men/ jewish men/ asians/ everybody. so i thought if i
waz a white girl for a day i might understand this better/
after all gertrude stein wanted to know abt the black
women/ alice adams wrote *thinking abt billie*/ joyce carol
oates has three different black characters all with the same
435 name/ i guess cuz we are underdeveloped individuals or cuz
we are all the same/ at any rate i'm gonna call this thinkin
abt white girls/ cuz helmut newton's awready gotta book
called *white women*/ see what i mean/ that's a best seller/
one store i passed/ hadda sign said/

┌─────────────────────┐
│   WHITE WOMEN   │
│   SOLD OUT   │
└─────────────────────┘

---

440 it's this kinda pressure that forces us white girls to be so
absolutely pathological abt the other women in the world/
who now that they're not all servants or peasants want to be

considered beautiful too. we simply krinkle our hair/ learn
to dance the woogie dances/ slant our eyes with make-up or
surgery/ learn spanish & claim argentinian background/ or 445
as a real trump card/ show up looking like a real white girl.
you know all western civilization depends on us/
   i still havent left my house. i think i'll fling my hair
once more/ but this time with a pout/ cuz i think i havent
been fair to the sisterhood/ women's movement faction of 450
white girls/ although/ they always ask what do you people
really want. as if the colored woman of the world were a
strange sort of neutered workhorse/ which isnt too far from
reality/ since i'm still waiting for my cleaning lady & the
lady who takes care of my children & the lady who caters 455
my parties & the lady who accepts quarters at the bathroom
in sardi's. those poor creatures shd be sterilized/ no one shd
have to live such a life. cd you hand me a towel/ thank-you
caroline. i've left all of maxime's last winter clothes in a pile
for you by the back door. they have to be cleaned but i hope 460
yr girls can make gd use of them.
   oh/ i'm still not being fair/ all the white women in the
world dont wake up being glad they aint niggahs/ only some
of them/ the ones who dont/ wake up thinking how can
i survive another day of this culturally condoned 465
incompetence. i know i'll play a tenor horn & tell all the
colored artists i meet/ that now i'm just like them/ i'm
colored i'll say cuz i have a struggle too. or i cd punish this
white beleaguered body of mine with the advances of a
thousand ebony bodies/ all built like franco harris or peter 470
tosh/ a thousand of them may take me & do what they
want/ cuz i'm so sorry/ yes i'm so sorry they were born
niggahs. but then if i cant punish myself to death for being
white/ i certainly cant in good conscience keep waiting for
the cleaning lady/ & everytime i attempt even the smallest 475
venture into the world someone comes to help me/ like if i
do anything/ anything at all i'm extending myself as a white
girl/ cuz part of being a white girl is being absent/ like those
women who are just with a man but whose names the black
people never remember/ they just say oh yeah his white girl 480
waz with him/ or a white girl got beat & killed today/ why
someone will say/ cuz some niggah told her to give him her
money & she said no/ cuz she thought he realized that she
waz a white girl/ & he did know but he didnt care/ so he
killed her & took the money/ but the cops knew she waz a 485
white girl & cdnt be killed by a niggah especially/ when she
had awready said no. the niggah was sposed to hop round
the corner backwards/ you dig/ so the cops/ found the
culprit within 24 hours/ cuz just like emmett till/ niggahs
do not kill white girls. 490
   i'm still in my house/ having flung my hair-do for the last
time/ what with having to take 20 valium a day/ to consider
the ERA & all the men in the world/ & my
ignorance of the world/ it is overwhelming. i'm so glad i'm
colored. boy i cd wake up in the morning & think abt 495
anything. i can remember emmett till & not haveta smile
at anybody.
MAXINE: *(compelled to speak by* NATALIE's *pain)* whenever
these things happened to me/ & i waz young/ i wd eat a lot/
or buy new fancy underwear with rhinestones & lace/ or go 500
to the movies/ maybe call a friend/ talk to made-up
boyfriends til dawn. this waz when i waz under my parents'
roof/ & trees that grew into my room had to be cut back
once a year/ this waz when the birds sometimes flew thru

505 the halls of the house as if the ceilings were sky & i/ simply
another winged creature. yet no one around me noticed me
especially. no one around saw anything but a precocious
brown girl with peculiar ideas. like during the polio
epidemic/ i wanted to have a celebration/ which nobody cd
510 understand since iron lungs & not going swimming waznt
nothing to celebrate. but i explained that i waz celebrating
the bounty of the lord/ which more people didnt
understand/ til i went on to say that/ it waz obvious that god
had protected the colored folks from polio/ nobody
515 understood that. i did/ if god had made colored people
susceptible to polio/ then we wd be on the pictures & the
television with the white children. i knew only white folks
cd get that particular disease/ & i celebrated. that's how
come i always commemorated anything that affected me or
520 the colored people. according to my history of the colored
race/ not enough attention was paid to small victories or
small personal defeats of the colored. i celebrated the
colored trolley driver/ the colored basketball team/ the
colored blues singer/ & the colored light heavy weight
525 champion of the world. then too/ i had a baptist child's
version of high mass for the slaves in new orleans whom i
had read abt/ & i tried to grow watermelons & rice for the
dead slaves from the east. as a child i took on the burden of
easing the ghost-colored-folks' souls & trying hard to keep
530 up with the affairs of my own colored world.

when i became a woman, my world got smaller. my
grandma closed up the windows/ so the birds wdnt fly in the
house any more. waz bad luck for a girl so yng & in my
condition to have the shadows of flying creatures over my
535 head. i didn't celebrate the trolley driver anymore/ cuz he
might know how i waz in this condition. i didnt celebrate the
basketball team anymore/ cuz they were yng & handsome/
& yng & handsome cd mean trouble. but trouble waz when
white kids called you names or beat you up cuz you had no
540 older brother/ trouble waz when someone died/ or the
tornado hit yr house/ now trouble meant something abt yng
& handsome/ & white or colored. if he waz yng &
handsome that meant trouble. seemed like every one who
didnt have this condition/ so birds cdnt fly over yr head/
545 waz trouble. as i understood it/ my mama & my grandma
were sending me out to be with trouble/ but not to get into
trouble. the yng & handsome cd dance with me & call for
sunday supper/ the yng & handsome cd write my name on
their notebooks/ cd carry my ribbons on the field for gd
550 luck/ the uncles cd hug me & chat for hours abt my
growing up/ so i counted all 492 times cd this condition wd
make me victim to this trouble/ before i wd be immune to
it/ the way colored folks were immune to polio.

i had discovered innumerable manifestations of trouble:
555 jealousy/ fear/ indignation & recurring fits of vulnerability
that lead me right back to the contradiction i had never
understood/ even as a child/ how half the world's population
cd be bad news/ be yng & handsome/ & later/ eligible &
interested/ & trouble.

560 plus/ according to my own version of the history of the
colored people/ only white people hurt little colored girls or
grown colored women/ my mama told me only white
people had social disease & molested children/ and my
grandma told me only white people committed unnatural
565 acts. that's how come i knew only white folks got polio/

muscular dystrophy/ sclerosis/ & mental illness/ this waz all
verified by the television. but i found out that the colored
folks knew abt the same vicious & disease-ridden passions
that the white folks knew.

570 the pain i succumbed to each time a colored person did
something that i believed only white people did waz
staggering. my entire life seems to be worthless/ if my own
folks arent better than white folks/ then surely the sagas of
slavery & the jim crow hadnt convinced anyone that we
575 were better than them. i commenced to buying pieces of
gold/ 14 carat/ 24 carat/ 18 carat gold/ every time some
black person did something that waz beneath him as a black
person & more like a white person. i bought gold cuz it
came from the earth/ & more than likely it came from
580 south africa/ where the black people are humiliated &
oppressed like in slavery. i wear all these things at once/ to
remind the black people that it cost a lot for us to be here/
our value/ can be known instinctively/ but since so many
black people are having a hard time not being like white
585 folks/ i wear these gold pieces to protest their ignorance/
their disconnect from history. i buy gold with a vengeance/
each time someone appropriates my space or my time
without permission/ each time someone is discourteous or
actually cruel to me/ if my mind is not respected/ my body
590 toyed with/ i buy gold/ & weep. i weep as i fix the chains
round my neck/ my wrists/ my ankles. i weep cuz all my
childhood ceremonies for the ghost-slaves have been in
vain. colored people can get polio & mental illness. slavery
is not unfamiliar to me. no one on this planet knows/ what
595 i know abt gold/ abt anything hard to get & beautiful/
anything lasting/ wrought from pain. no one understands
that surviving the impossible is sposed to accentuate the
positive aspects of a people.

(ALEC *is the only member of the company able to come immediately to* MAXINE. *when he reaches her,* LOU, *in his full magician's
regalia, freezes the whole company*)

LOU: yes yes yes   3 wishes is all you get
600   scarlet ribbons for yr hair
                           a farm in mississippi
                           someone to love you madly
        all things are possible
        but aint no colored magician in his right mind
605   gonna make you white
        cuz this is blk magic you lookin at
        & i'm fixin you up good/ fixin you up good & colored
        & you gonna be colored all yr life
        & you gonna love it/ bein colored/ all yr life
610   colored & love it/ love it/ bein colored

(LOU *beckons the others to join him in the chant, "colored & love
it." it becomes a serious celebration, like church/ like home/ but
then* LOU *freezes them suddenly.*)

LOU: crackers are born with the right to be
        alive/ i'm making ours up right here
        in yr face/ & we gonna be
        colored & love it

(*the huge minstrel mask comes down as company continues to
sing "colored & love it/ love it being colored." blackout/ but the
minstrel mask remains visible. the company is singing "colored
& love it being colored" as audience exits*)

■ SAM SHEPARD ■

Sam Shepard (b. 1943), is probably the best-known American playwright of his generation. Born Samuel Shepard Rogers to a military family stationed in Illinois, Shepard's youth was spent moving from base to base, until his father retired and settled the family in southern California. Shepard was an indifferent student and left college for New York City in 1963. He took a job busing tables at the Village Gate jazz club and began to write plays for off-broadway, including *Cowboys* (1964), *Red Cross* (1966), *La Turista* (1966), *The Unseen Hand* (1970), *Cowboy Mouth* (1971), and *Tooth of Crime* (1972). In these plays, Shepard invented what became his characteristic idiom: a search for the "West" of myth, an image both fascinating and elusive, somehow undiscoverable amid the consumer trash of suburban society. He also developed a sense of split and fragmented characters, relying on his typically jazzy use of language. This is particularly true of *Tooth of Crime*, in which a kind of shoot-out between the old rock 'n' roll star, Hoss, and the Keith Richards-like Crow is conducted in an invented language of rock music, drugs, cars, gangsters, and old movies. Shepard won six Obie awards between 1964 and 1970, but his work took a great step forward in the major plays of the late 1970s and 1980s: *Curse of the Starving Class* (1978), *Buried Child* (Pulitzer Prize, 1979), *True West* (1980), *Fool for Love* (1982), *A Lie of the Mind* (1985), and *States of Shock* (1991). Shepard also has written the screenplay for the Wim Wenders film, *Paris, Texas*, and has starred in several films himself, notably as Chuck Yeager in *The Right Stuff* (1983).

True West

True West is the leanest, most elemental of Shepard's plays and brings the question of identity—individual and cultural—into sharp focus. The play concerns two brothers: Austin, a yuppie screenwriter, and his derelict brother, Lee, a petty thief who spends much of his time in the desert. In the course of the play, however, Austin and Lee subtly change roles and identities: Lee swings a deal to write the screenplay for a Western movie, while Austin seems to abandon the desire to be a writer, working to prove himself to Lee by stealing toasters from the suburban neighbors. *True West* is a kind of Western, though the brothers don't fight it out for any actual piece of territory, since there is no Dodge city, no True West to fight over. What the brothers finally duel for is a mythic terrain, the terrain of their father, of the desert, of Westerns: the "West" of the imagination.

TRUE WEST

SAM SHEPARD

— CHARACTERS —

AUSTIN, *early thirties, light blue sports shirt, light tan cardigan sweater, clean blue jeans, white tennis shoes*

LEE, *his older brother, early forties, filthy white t-shirt, tattered brown overcoat covered with dust, dark blue baggy suit pants from the Salvation Army, pink suede belt, pointed black forties dress shoes scuffed up, holes in the soles, no socks, no hat, long pronounced sideburns, "Gene Vincent" hairdo, two days' growth of beard, bad teeth*

SAUL KIMMER, *late forties, Hollywood producer, pink and white flower print sports shirt, white sports coat with matching polyester slacks, black and white loafers*

MOM, *early sixties, mother of the brothers, small woman, conservative white skirt and matching jacket, red shoulder bag, two pieces of matching red luggage*

SCENE: *All nine scenes take place on the same set; a kitchen and adjoining alcove of an older home in a Southern California suburb, about 40 miles east of Los Angeles. The kitchen takes up most of the playing area to stage left. The kitchen consists of a sink, upstage center, surrounded by counter space, a wall telephone, cupboards, and a small window just above it bordered by neat yellow curtains. Stage left of sink is a stove. Stage right, a refrigerator. The alcove adjoins the kitchen to stage right. There is no wall division or door to the alcove. It is open and easily accessible from the kitchen and defined only by the objects in it: a small round glass breakfast table mounted on white iron legs, two matching white iron chairs set across from each other. The two exterior walls of the alcove which prescribe a corner in the upstage right are composed of many small windows, beginning from a solid wall about three feet high and extending to the ceiling. The windows look out to bushes and citrus trees. The alcove is filled with all sorts of house plants in various pots, mostly Boston ferns hanging in planters at different levels. The floor of the alcove is composed of green synthetic grass.*

All entrances and exits are made stage left from the kitchen. There is no door. The actors simply go off and come onto the playing area.

NOTE ON SET AND COSTUME: *The set should be constructed realistically with no attempt to distort its dimensions, shapes, objects, or colors. No objects should be introduced which might draw special attention to themselves other than the props demanded by the script. If a stylistic "concept" is grafted onto the set design it will only serve to confuse the evolution of the characters' situation, which is the most important focus of the play.*

Likewise, the costumes should be exactly representative of who the characters are and not added onto for the sake of making a point to the audience.

NOTE ON SOUND: *The Coyote of Southern California has a distinct yapping, dog-like bark, similar to a Hyena. This yapping grows more intense and maniacal as the pack grows in numbers, which is usually the case when they lure and kill pets from suburban yards. The sense of growing frenzy in the pack should be felt in the background, particularly in Scenes 7 and 8. In any case, these Coyotes never make the long, mournful, solitary howl of the Hollywood stereotype.*

The sound of Crickets can speak for itself.

These sounds should also be treated realistically even though they sometimes grow in volume and numbers.

— ACT ONE —

SCENE I

Night. Sound of crickets in dark. Candlelight appears in alcove, illuminating AUSTIN, *seated at glass table hunched over a writing notebook, pen in hand, cigarette burning in ashtray, cup of coffee, typewriter on table, stacks of paper, candle burning on table.*

Soft moonlight fills kitchen illuminating LEE, *beer in hand, six-pack on counter behind him. He's leaning against the sink, mildly drunk; takes a slug of beer.*

LEE: So, Mom took off for Alaska, huh?

AUSTIN: Yeah.

LEE: Sorta' left you in charge.

AUSTIN: Well, she knew I was coming down here so she offered me the place.

5

LEE: You keepin' the plants watered?

AUSTIN: Yeah.

LEE: Keepin' the sink clean? She don't like even a single tea leaf in the sink ya' know.

AUSTIN: *(Trying to concentrate on writing.)* Yeah, I know. 10

(Pause.)

LEE: She gonna' be up there a long time?

AUSTIN: I don't know.

LEE: Kinda' nice for you, huh? Whole place to yourself.

AUSTIN: Yeah, it's great.

LEE: Ya' got crickets anyway. Tons a' crickets out there. *(Looks* 15
around kitchen.) Ya' got groceries? Coffee?

AUSTIN: *(Looking up from writing.)* What?

LEE: You got coffee?

AUSTIN: Yeah.

LEE: At's good. *(Short pause.)* Real coffee? From the bean? 20

AUSTIN: Yeah. You want some?

LEE: Naw. I brought some uh—*(Motions to beer.)*

AUSTIN: Help yourself to whatever's—*(Motions to refrigerator.)*

LEE: I will. Don't worry about me. I'm not the one to worry about. I mean I can uh—*(Pause.)* You always work by can- 25
dlelight?

AUSTIN: No—uh—Not always.

LEE: Just sometimes?

AUSTIN: *(Puts pen down, rubs his eyes.)* Yeah. Sometimes it's soothing.

LEE: Isn't that what the old guys did?

AUSTIN: What old guys?

LEE: The Forefathers. You know.

AUSTIN: Forefathers?

LEE: Isn't that what they did? Candlelight burning into the night? Cabins in the wilderness.

AUSTIN: *(Rubs hand through his hair.)* I suppose.

LEE: I'm not botherin' you am I? I mean I don't wanna break into yer uh—concentration or nothin'.

AUSTIN: No, it's all right.

LEE: That's good. I mean I realize that yer line a' work demands a lota' concentration.

AUSTIN: It's okay.

LEE: You probably think that I'm not fully able to comprehend somethin' like that, huh?

AUSTIN: Like what?

LEE: That stuff yer doin'. That art. You know. Whatever you call it.

AUSTIN: It's just a little research.

LEE: You may not know it but I did a little art myself once.

AUSTIN: You did?

LEE: Yeah! I did some a' that. I fooled around with it. No future in it.

AUSTIN: What'd you do?

LEE: Never mind what I did! Just never mind about that. *(Pause.)* It was ahead of its time.

(Pause.)

AUSTIN: So, you went out to see the old man, huh?

LEE: Yeah, I seen him.

AUSTIN: How's he doing?

LEE: Same. He's doin' just about the same.

AUSTIN: I was down there too, you know.

LEE: What d'ya' want, an award? You want some kinda' medal? You were down there. He told me all about you.

AUSTIN: What'd he say?

LEE: He told me. Don't worry.

(Pause.)

AUSTIN: Well—

LEE: You don't have to say nothin'.

AUSTIN: I wasn't.

LEE: Yeah, you were gonna' make somethin' up. Somethin' brilliant.

(Pause.)

AUSTIN: You going to be down here very long, Lee?

LEE: Might be. Depends on a few things.

AUSTIN: You got some friends down here?

LEE: *(Laughs.)* I know a few people. Yeah.

AUSTIN: Well, you can stay here as long as I'm here.

LEE: I don't need your permission do I?

AUSTIN: No.

LEE: I mean she's my mother too, right?

AUSTIN: Right.

LEE: She might've just as easily asked me to take care of her place as you.

AUSTIN: That's right.

LEE: I mean I know how to water plants.

(Long pause.)

AUSTIN: So you don't know how long you'll be staying then?

LEE: Depends mostly on houses, ya' know.

AUSTIN: Houses?

LEE: Yeah. Houses. Electric devices. Stuff like that. I gotta' make a little tour first.

(Short pause.)

AUSTIN: Lee, why don't you just try another neighborhood, all right?

LEE: *(Laughs.)* What'sa' matter with this neighborhood? This is a great neighborhood. Lush. Good class a' people. Not many dogs.

AUSTIN: Well, our uh—Our mother just happens to live here. That's all.

LEE: Nobody's gonna' know. All they know is somethin's missing. That's all. She'll never even hear about it. Nobody's gonna' know.

AUSTIN: You're going to get picked up if you start walking around here at night.

LEE: Me? I'm gonna' git picked up? What about you? You stick out like a sore thumb. Look at you. You think yer regular lookin'?

AUSTIN: I've got too much to deal with here to be worrying about—

LEE: Yer not gonna' have to worry about me! I've been doin' all right without you. I haven't been anywhere near you for five years! Now isn't that true?

AUSTIN: Yeah.

LEE: So you don't have to worry about me. I'm a free agent.

AUSTIN: All right.

LEE: Now all I wanna' do is borrow yer car.

AUSTIN: No!

LEE: Just fer a day. One day.

AUSTIN: No!

LEE: I won't take it outside a twenty mile radius. I promise ya'. You can check the speedometer.

AUSTIN: You're not borrowing my car! That's all there is to it.

(Pause.)

LEE: Then I'll just take the damn thing.

AUSTIN: Lee, look—I don't want any trouble, all right?

LEE: That's a dumb line. That is a dumb fuckin' line. You git paid fer dreamin' up a line like that?

AUSTIN: Look, I can give you some money if you need money.

(LEE suddenly lunges at AUSTIN, grabs him violently by the shirt and shakes him with tremendous power.)

LEE: Don't you say that to me! Don't you ever say that to me! *(Just as suddenly he turns him loose, pushes him away and backs off.)* You may be able to git away with that with the Old Man. Git him tanked up for a week! Buy him off with yer Hollywood blood money, but not me! I can git my own money my own way. Big money!

AUSTIN: I was just making an offer.

LEE: Yeah, well keep it to yourself!

(Long pause.)

Those are the most monotonous fuckin' crickets I ever heard in my life.

AUSTIN: I kinda' like the sound.

135 LEE: Yeah. Supposed to be able to tell the temperature by the number a' pulses. You believe that?

AUSTIN: The temperature?

LEE: Yeah. The air. How hot it is.

AUSTIN: How do you do that?

140 LEE: I don't know. Some woman told me that. She was a Botanist. So I believed her.

AUSTIN: Where'd you meet her?

LEE: What?

AUSTIN: The woman Botanist?

145 LEE: I met her on the desert. I been spendin' a lota' time on the desert.

AUSTIN: What were you doing out there?

LEE: (Pause, stares in space.) I forgot. Had me a Pit Bull there for a while but I lost him.

150 AUSTIN: Pit Bull?

LEE: Fightin' dog. Damn I made some good money off that little dog. Real good money.

(Pause.)

AUSTIN: You could come up north with me, you know.

LEE: What's up there?

155 AUSTIN: My family.

LEE: Oh, that's right, you got the wife and kiddies now don't ya'. The house, the car, the whole slam. That's right.

AUSTIN: You could spend a couple days. See how you like it. I've got an extra room.

160 LEE: Too cold up there.

(Pause.)

AUSTIN: You want to sleep for a while?

LEE: (Pause, stares at AUSTIN.) I don't sleep.

(Lights to black.)

SCENE II

Morning. AUSTIN *is watering plants with a vaporizer,* LEE *sits at glass table in alcove drinking beer.*

LEE: I never realized the old lady was so security-minded.

AUSTIN: How do you mean?

LEE: Made a little tour this morning. She's got locks on everything. Locks and double-locks and chain locks and—What's
5   she got that's so valuable?

AUSTIN: Antiques I guess. I don't know.

LEE: Antiques? Brought everything with her from the old place, huh. Just the same crap we always had around. Plates and spoons.

10 AUSTIN: I guess they have personal value to her.

LEE: Personal value. Yeah. Just a lota' junk. Most of it's phony anyway. Idaho decals. Now who in the hell wants to eat offa' plate with the State of Idaho starin' ya' in the face. Every time ya' take a bite ya' get to see a little bit more.

15 AUSTIN: Well it must mean something to her or she wouldn't save it.

LEE: Yeah, well personally I don't wann' be invaded by Idaho when I'm eatin'. When I'm eatin' I'm home. Ya' know what I'm sayin? I'm not driftin', I'm home. I don't need my
20   thoughts swept off to Idaho. I don't need that!

(Pause.)

AUSTIN: Did you go out last night?

LEE: Why?

AUSTIN: I thought I heard you go out.

LEE: Yeah, I went out. What about it?

AUSTIN: Just wondered.   25

LEE: Damn coyotes kept me awake.

AUSTIN: Oh yeah, I heard them. They must've killed somebody's dog or something.

LEE: Yappin' their fool heads off. They don't yap like that on the desert. They howl. These are city coyotes here.   30

AUSTIN: Well, you don't sleep anyway do you?

(Pause, LEE stares at him.)

LEE: You're pretty smart aren't ya?

AUSTIN: How do you mean?

LEE: I mean you never had any more on the ball than I did. But here you are gettin' invited into prominent people's   35 houses. Sittin' around talkin' like you know somethin'.

AUSTIN: They're not so prominent.

LEE: They're a helluva' lot more prominent than the houses I get invited into.

AUSTIN: Well you invite yourself.   40

LEE: That's right. I do. In fact I probably got a wider range a' choices than you do, come to think of it.

AUSTIN: I wouldn't doubt it.

LEE: In fact I been inside some pretty classy places in my time. And I never even went to an Ivy League school either.   45

AUSTIN: You want some breakfast or something?

LEE: Breakfast?

AUSTIN: Yeah. Don't you eat breakfast?

LEE: Look, don't worry about me pal. I can take care a' myself. You just go ahead as though I wasn't even here, all right? 50

(AUSTIN *goes into kitchen, makes coffee.*)

AUSTIN: Where'd you walk to last night?

(Pause.)

LEE: I went up in the foothills there. Up in the San Gabriels. Heat was drivin' me crazy.

AUSTIN: Well, wasn't it hot out on the desert?

LEE: Different kinda' heat. Out there it's clean. Cools off at   55 night. There's a nice little breeze.

AUSTIN: Where were you, the Mojave?

LEE: Yeah. The Mojave. That's right.

AUSTIN: I haven't been out there in years.

LEE: Out past Needles there.   60

AUSTIN: Oh yeah.

LEE: Up here it's different. This country's real different.

AUSTIN: Well, it's been built up.

LEE: Built up? Wiped out is more like it. I don't even hardly recognize it.   65

AUSTIN: Yeah. Foothills are the same though, aren't they?

LEE: Pretty much. It's funny goin' up in there. The smells and everything. Used to catch snakes up there, remember?

AUSTIN: You caught snakes.

LEE: Yeah. And you'd pretend you were Geronimo or some   70 damn thing. You used to go right out to lunch.

AUSTIN: I enjoyed my imagination.

LEE: That what you call it? Looks like yer still enjoyin' it.

AUSTIN: So you just wandered around up there, huh?

LEE: Yeah. With a purpose.   75

AUSTIN: See any houses?

(Pause.)

LEE: Couple. Couple a' real nice ones. One of 'em didn't even have a dog. Walked right up and stuck my head in the window. Not a peep. Just a sweet kinda' suburban silence.

80 AUSTIN: What kind of a place was it?

LEE: Like a paradise. Kinda' place that sorta' kills ya' inside. Warm yellow lights. Mexican tile all around. Copper pots hangin' over the stove. Ya' know like they got in the magazines. Blonde people movin' in and outa' the rooms, talkin'

85 to each other. *(Pause.)* Kinda' place you wish you sorta' grew up in, ya' know.

AUSTIN: That's the kind of place you wish you'd grown up in?

LEE: Yeah. why not?

AUSTIN: I thought you hated that kind of stuff.

90 LEE: Yeah, well you never knew too much about me did ya'?

(Pause.)

AUSTIN: Why'd you go out to the desert in the first place?

LEE: I was on my way to see the old man.

AUSTIN: You mean you just passed through there?

LEE: Yeah. That's right. Three months of passin' through.

95 AUSTIN: Three months?

LEE: Somethin' like that. Maybe more. Why?

AUSTIN: You lived on the Mojave for three months?

LEE: Yeah. What'sa' matter with that?

AUSTIN: By yourself?

100 LEE: Mostly. Had a couple a' visitors. Had that dog for a while.

AUSTIN: Didn't you miss people?

LEE: *(Laughs.)* People?

AUSTIN: Yeah. I mean I go crazy if I have to spend three nights in a motel by myself.

105 LEE: Yer not in a motel now.

AUSTIN: No, I know. But sometimes I have to stay in motels.

LEE: Well, they got people in motels don't they?

AUSTIN: Strangers.

LEE: Yer friendly aren't ya'? Aren't you the friendly type?

(Pause.)

110 AUSTIN: I'm going to have somebody coming by here later, Lee.

LEE: Ah! Lady friend?

AUSTIN: No, a producer.

LEE: Aha! What's he produce?

115 AUSTIN: Film. Movies. You know.

LEE: Oh, movies. Motion Pictures! A Big Wig huh?

AUSTIN: Yeah.

LEE: What's he comin' by here for?

AUSTIN: We have to talk about a project.

120 LEE: Whadya' mean, "a project? What's a "project"?

AUSTIN: A script.

LEE: Oh. That's what yer doin' with all these papers?

AUSTIN: Yeah.

LEE: Well, what's the project about?

125 AUSTIN: We're uh—it's a period piece.

LEE: What's "a period piece"?

AUSTIN: Look, it doesn't matter. The main thing is we need to discuss this alone. I mean—

LEE: Oh, I get it. You want me outa' the picture.

130 AUSTIN: Not exactly. I just need to be alone with him for a couple of hours. So we can talk.

LEE: Yer afraid I'll embarrass ya' huh?

AUSTIN: I'm not afraid you'll embarrass me!

LEE: Well, I tell ya' what—Why don't you just gimme the keys to yer car and I'll be back here around six o'clock or so. That 135 give ya' enough time?

AUSTIN: I'm not loaning you my car, Lee.

LEE: You want me to just git lost huh? Take a hike? Is that it? Pound the pavement for a few hours while you bullshit yer way into a million bucks. 140

AUSTIN: Look, it's going to be hard enough for me to face this character on my own without—

LEE: You don't know this guy?

AUSTIN: No I don't know—He's a producer. I mean I've been meeting with him for months but you never get to know a 145 producer.

LEE: Yer tryin' to hustle him? Is that it?

AUSTIN: I'm not trying to hustle him! I'm trying to work out a deal! It's not easy.

LEE: What kinda' deal? 150

AUSTIN: Convince him it's a worthwhile story.

LEE: He's not convinced? How come he's comin' over here if he's not convinced? I'll convince him for ya'.

AUSTIN: You don't understand the way things work down here.

LEE: How do things work down here? 155

(Pause.)

AUSTIN: Look, if I loan you my car will you have it back here by six?

LEE: On the button. With a full tank a' gas.

AUSTIN: *(Digging in his pocket for keys.)* Forget about the gas.

LEE: Hey, these days gas is gold, old buddy. 160

(AUSTIN hands the keys to LEE.)

You remember that car I used to loan you?

AUSTIN: Yeah.

LEE: Forty Ford. Flathead.

AUSTIN: Yeah.

LEE: Sucker hauled ass didn't it? 165

AUSTIN: Lee, it's not that I don't want to loan you my car—

LEE: You are loanin' me yer car.

(LEE gives AUSTIN a pat on the shoulder, pause.)

AUSTIN: I know. I just wish—

LEE: What? You wish what?

AUSTIN: I don't know. I wish I wasn't—I wish I didn't have to 170 be doing business down here. I'd like to just spend some time with you.

LEE: I thought it was "Art" you were doin'.

(LEE moves across kitchen toward exit, tosses keys in his hand.)

AUSTIN: Try to get it back here by six, okay?

LEE: No sweat. Hey, ya' know, if that uh—story of yours 175 doesn't go over with the guy—tell him I got a couple a' "projects" he might be interested in. Real commercial. Full a' suspense. True-to-life stuff.

(LEE exits, AUSTIN stares after LEE then turns, goes to papers at table, leafs through pages, lights fade to black.)

SCENE III

Afternoon. Alcove, SAUL KIMMER *and* AUSTIN *seated across from each other at table.*

SAUL: Well, to tell you the truth Austin, I have never felt so confident about a project in quite a long time.

AUSTIN: Well, that's good to hear, Saul.

5 SAUL: I am absolutely convinced we can get this thing off the ground. I mean we'll have to make a sale to television and that means getting a major star. Somebody bankable. But I think we can do it. I really do.

AUSTIN: Don't you think we need a first draft before we approach a star?

10 SAUL: No, no, not at all. I don't think it's necessary. Maybe a brief synopsis. I don't want you to touch the typewriter until we have some seed money.

AUSTIN: That's fine with me.

SAUL: I mean it's a great story. Just the story alone. You've really managed to capture something this time.

15 AUSTIN: I'm glad you like it, Saul.

(LEE *enters abruptly into kitchen carrying a stolen television set, short pause.*)

LEE: Aw shit, I'm sorry about that. I am really sorry Austin.

AUSTIN: (*Standing.*) That's all right.

LEE: (*Moving toward them.*) I mean I thought it was way past
20 six already. You said to have it back here by six.

AUSTIN: We were just finishing up. (*To* SAUL.) This is my, uh—brother, Lee.

SAUL: (*Standing.*) Oh, I'm very happy to meet you.

(LEE *sets T.V. on sink counter, shakes hands with* SAUL.)

LEE: I can't tell ya' how happy I am to meet you sir.
25 SAUL: Saul Kimmer.

LEE: Mr. Kipper.

SAUL: Kimmer.

AUSTIN: Lee's been living out on the desert and he just uh—

SAUL: Oh, that's terrific! (*To* LEE.) Palm Springs?
30 LEE: Yeah. Yeah, right. Right around in that area. Near uh— Bob Hope Drive there.

SAUL: Oh I love it out there. I just love it. The air is wonderful.

LEE: Yeah. Sure is. Healthy.

SAUL: And the golf. I don't know if you play golf, but the golf is
35 just about the best.

LEE: I play a lota' golf.

SAUL: Is that right?

LEE: Yeah. In fact I was hoping I'd run into somebody out here who played a little golf. I've been lookin' for a partner.
40 SAUL: Well, I uh—

AUSTIN: Lee's just down for a visit while our mother's in Alaska.

SAUL: Oh, your mother's in Alaska?

AUSTIN: Yes. She went up there on a little vacation. This is her
45 place.

SAUL: I see. Well isn't that something. Alaska.

LEE: What kinda' handicap do ya' have, Mr. Kimmer?

SAUL: Oh I'm just a Sunday duffer really. You know.

LEE: That's good 'cause I haven't swung a club in months.
50 SAUL: Well we ought to get together sometime and have a little game. Austin, do you play?

(SAUL *mimes a Johnny Carson golf swing for* AUSTIN.)

AUSTIN: No. I don't uh—I've watched it on T.V.

LEE: (*To* SAUL.) How 'bout tomorrow morning? Bright and early. We could get out there and put in eighteen holes be-
55 fore breakfast.

SAUL: Well, I've got uh—I have several appointments—

LEE: No, I mean real early. Crack a' dawn. While the dew's still thick on the fairway.

SAUL: Sounds really great.

LEE: Austin could be our caddie.   60

SAUL: Now that's an idea. (*Laughs.*)

AUSTIN: I don't know the first thing about golf.

LEE: There's nothin' to it. Isn't that right, Saul? He'd pick it up in fifteen minutes.

SAUL: Sure. Doesn't take long. 'Course you have to play for   65
years to find your true form. (*Chuckles.*)

LEE: (*To* AUSTIN.) We'll give ya' a quick run-down on the club faces. The irons, the woods. Show ya' a couple pointers on the basic swing. Might even let ya' hit the ball a couple times. Whadya' think, Saul?   70

SAUL: Why not. I think it'd be great. I haven't had any exercise in weeks.

LEE: At's the spirit! We'll have a little orange juice right afterwards.

(*Pause.*)

SAUL: Orange juice?   75

LEE: Yeah! Vitamin C! Nothin' like a shot a' orange juice after a round a' golf. Hot shower. Snappin' towels at each others' privates. Real sense a' fraternity.

SAUL: (*Smiles at* AUSTIN.) Well, you make it sound very inviting, I must say. It really does sound great.   80

LEE: Then it's a date.

SAUL: Well, I'll call the country club and see if I can arrange something.

LEE: Great! Boy, I sure am sorry that I busted in on ya' all in the middle of yer meeting.   85

SAUL: Oh that's quite all right. We were just about finished anyway.

LEE: I can wait out in the other room if you want.

SAUL: No really—

LEE: Just got Austin's color T.V. back from the shop. I can   90
watch a little amateur boxing now.

(LEE *and* AUSTIN *exchange looks.*)

SAUL: Oh—Yes.

LEE: You don't fool around in Television, do you Saul?

SAUL: Uh—I have in the past. Produced some T.V. Specials. Network stuff. But it's mainly features now.   95

LEE: That's where the big money is, huh?

SAUL: Yes. That's right.

AUSTIN: Why don't I call you tomorrow, Saul and we'll get together. We can have lunch or something.

SAUL: That'd be terrific.   100

LEE: Right after the golf.

(*Pause.*)

SAUL: What?

LEE: You can have lunch right after the golf.

SAUL: Oh, right.

LEE: Austin was tellin' me that yer interested in stories.   105

SAUL: Well, we develop certain projects that we feel have commercial potential.

LEE: What kinda' stuff do ya' go in for?

SAUL: Oh, the usual. You know. Good love interest. Lots of action. (*Chuckles at* AUSTIN.)   110

LEE: Westerns?

SAUL: Sometimes.

AUSTIN: I'll give you a ring, Saul.

(AUSTIN *tries to move* SAUL *across the kitchen but* LEE *blocks their way.*)

LEE: I got a Western that'd knock yer lights out.
115 SAUL: Oh really?
LEE: Yeah. Contemporary Western. Based on a true story. 'Course I'm not a writer like my brother here. I'm not a man of the pen.
SAUL: Well—
120 LEE: I mean I can tell ya' a story off the tongue but I can't put it down on paper. That don't make any difference though does it?
SAUL: No, not really.
LEE: I mean plenty a' guys have stories don't they? True-life
125 stories. Musta' been a lota' movies made from real life.
SAUL: Yes. I suppose so.
LEE: I haven't seen a good Western since "Lonely Are the Brave." You remember that movie?
SAUL: No, I'm afraid I—
130 LEE: Kirk Douglas. Helluva' movie. You remember that movie, Austin?
AUSTIN: Yes.
LEE: (*To* SAUL.) The man dies for the love of a horse.
SAUL: Is that right?
135 LEE: Yeah. Ya' hear the horse screamin' at the end of it. Rain's comin' down. Horse is screamin'. Then there's a shot. BLAM! Just a single shot like that. Then nothin' but the sound of rain. And Kirk Douglas is ridin' in the ambulance. Ridin' away from the scene of the accident. And when he
140 hears that shot he knows that his horse has died. He knows. And you see his eyes. And his eyes die. Right inside his face. And then his eyes close. And you know that he's died too. You know that Kirk Douglas has died from the death of his horse.
145 SAUL: (*Eyes* AUSTIN *nervously.*) Well, it sounds like a great movie. I'm sorry I missed it.
LEE: Yeah, you shouldn't a' missed that one.
SAUL: I'll have to try to catch it some time. Arrange a screening or something. Well, Austin, I'll have to hit the freeway before
150 rush hour.
AUSTIN: (*Ushers him toward exit.*) It's good seeing you, Saul.

(AUSTIN *and* SAUL *shake hands.*)

LEE: So ya' think there's room for a real Western these days? A true-to-life Western?
SAUL: Well, I don't see why not. Why don't you uh—tell the
155 story to Austin and have him write a little outline.
LEE: You'd take a look at it then?
SAUL: Yes. Sure. I'll give it a read-through. Always eager for new material. (*Smiles at* AUSTIN.)
LEE: That's great! You'd really read it then huh?
160 SAUL: It would just be my opinion of course.
LEE: That's all I want. Just an opinion. I happen to think it has a lota' possibilities.
SAUL: Well, it was great meeting you and I'll—

(SAUL *and* LEE *shake.*)

LEE: I'll call you tomorrow about the golf.
165 SAUL: Oh. Yes, right.
LEE: Austin's got your number, right?

SAUL: Yes.
LEE: So long Saul. (*Gives* SAUL *a pat on the back.*)

(SAUL *exits,* AUSTIN *turns to* LEE, *looks at T.V. then back to* LEE.)

AUSTIN: Give me the keys.

(AUSTIN *extends his hand toward* LEE, LEE *doesn't move, just stares at* AUSTIN, *smiles, lights to black.*)

SCENE IV

Night. Coyotes in distance, fade, sound of typewriter in dark, crickets, candlelight in alcove, dim light in kitchen, lights reveal AUSTIN *at glass table typing,* LEE *sits across from him, foot on table, drinking beer and whiskey, the T.V. is still on sink counter,* AUSTIN *types for a while, then stops.*

LEE: All right, now read it back to me.
AUSTIN: I'm not reading it back to you, Lee. You can read it when we're finished. I can't spend all night on this.
LEE: You got better things to do?
AUSTIN: Let's just go ahead. Now what happens when he 5 leaves Texas?
LEE: Is he ready to leave Texas yet? I didn't know we were that far along. He's not ready to leave Texas.
AUSTIN: He's right at the border.
LEE: (*Sitting up.*) No, see this is one a' the crucial parts. Right 10 here. (*Taps paper with beer can.*) We can't rush through this. He's not right at the border. He's a good fifty miles from the border. A lot can happen in fifty miles.
AUSTIN: It's only an outline. We're not writing an entire script now. 15
LEE: Well ya' can't leave things out even if it is an outline. It's one a' the most important parts. Ya' can't go leavin' it out.
AUSTIN: Okay, okay. Let's just—get it done.
LEE: All right. Now. He's in the truck and he's got his horse trailer and his horse. 20
AUSTIN: We've already established that.
LEE: And he sees this other guy comin' up behind him in another truck. And that truck is pullin' a gooseneck.
AUSTIN: What's a gooseneck?
LEE: Cattle trailer. You know the kind with a gooseneck, goes 25 right down in the bed a' the pick-up.
AUSTIN: Oh. All right. (*Types.*)
LEE: It's important.
AUSTIN: Okay. I got it.
LEE: All these details are important. 30

(AUSTIN *types as they talk.*)

AUSTIN: I've got it.
LEE: And this other guy's got his horse all saddled up in the back a' the gooseneck.
AUSTIN: Right.
LEE: So both these guys have got their horses right along with 35 'em, see.
AUSTIN: I understand.
LEE: Then this first guy suddenly realizes two things.
AUSTIN: The guy in front?
LEE: Right. The guy in front realizes two things almost at the 40 same time. Simultaneous.
AUSTIN: What were the two things?

LEE: Number one, he realizes that the guy behind him is the husband of the woman he's been—

(LEE *makes gesture of screwing by pumping his arm.*)

45 AUSTIN: (*Sees* LEE's *gesture.*) Oh, Yeah.
LEE: And number two, he realizes he's in the middle of Tornado Country.
AUSTIN: What's "Tornado Country"?
LEE: Panhandle.
50 AUSTIN: Panhandle?
LEE: Sweetwater. Around in that area. Nothin'. Nowhere. And number three—
AUSTIN: I thought there was only two.
LEE: There's three. There's a third unforeseen realization.
55 AUSTIN: And what's that?
LEE: That he's runnin' outa' gas.
AUSTIN: (*Stops typing.*) Come on, Lee.

(AUSTIN *gets up, moves to kitchen, gets a glass of water.*)

LEE: Whadya' mean, "come on"? That's what it is. Write it down! He's runnin' outa' gas.
60 AUSTIN: It's too—
LEE: What? It's too what? It's too real! That's what ya' mean isn't it? It's too much like real life!
AUSTIN: It's not like real life! It's not enough like real life. Things don't happen like that.
65 LEE: What! Men don't fuck other men's women?
AUSTIN: Yes. But they don't end up chasing each other across the Panhandle. Through "Tornado Country."
LEE: They do in this movie!
AUSTIN: And they don't have horses conveniently along with
70 them when they run out of gas! And they don't run out of gas either!
LEE: These guys run outa' gas! This is my story and one a' these guys runs outa' gas!
AUSTIN: It's just a dumb excuse to get them into a chase scene.
75 It's contrived.
LEE: It is a chase scene! It's already a chase scene. They been chasin' each other fer days.
AUSTIN: So now they're supposed to abandon their trucks, climb on their horses and chase each other into the mountains?
80 LEE: (*Standing suddenly.*) There aren't any mountains in the Panhandle! It's flat!

(LEE *turns violently toward windows in alcove and throws beer can at them.*)

LEE: Goddamn these crickets! (*Yells at crickets.*) Shut up out there! (*Pause, turns back toward table.*) This place is like a fuckin' rest home here. How're you supposed to think!
85 AUSTIN: You wanna' take a break?
LEE: No, I don't wanna' take a break! I wanna' get this done! This is my last chance to get this done.
AUSTIN: (*Moves back into alcove.*) All right. Take it easy.
LEE: I'm gonna' be leavin' this area. I don't have time to mess
90 around here.
AUSTIN: Where are you going?
LEE: Never mind where I'm goin'! That's got nothin' to do with you. I just gotta' get this done. I'm not like you. Hangin' around bein' a parasite offa' other fools. I gotta' do this thing
95 and get out.

(*Pause.*)

AUSTIN: A parasite? Me?
LEE: Yeah, you!
AUSTIN: After you break into people's houses and take their televisions?
100 LEE: They don't need their televisions! I'm doin' them a service.
AUSTIN: Give me back my keys, Lee.
LEE: Not until you write this thing! You're gonna' write this outline thing for me or that car's gonna' wind up in Arizona
105 with a different paint job.
AUSTIN: You think you can force me to write this? I was doing you a favor.
LEE: Git off yer high horse will ya'! Favor! Big favor. Handin' down favors from the mountain top.
110 AUSTIN: Let's just write it, okay? Let's sit down and not get upset and see if we can just get through this.

(AUSTIN *sits at typewriter.*)

(*Long pause.*)

LEE: Yer not gonna' even show it to him, are ya'?
AUSTIN: What?
LEE: This outline. You got no intention of showin' it to him.
115 Yer just doin' this 'cause yer afraid a' me.
AUSTIN: You can show it to him yourself.
LEE: I will, boy! I'm gonna' read it to him on the golf course.
AUSTIN: And I'm not afraid of you either.
LEE: Then how come yer doin' it?
120 AUSTIN: (*Pause.*) So I can get my keys back.

(*Pause as* LEE *takes keys out of his pocket slowly and throws them on table, long pause,* AUSTIN *stares at keys.*)

LEE: There. Now you got yer keys back.

(AUSTIN *looks up at* LEE *but doesn't take keys.*)

LEE: Go ahead. There's yer keys.

(AUSTIN *slowly takes keys off table and puts them back in his own pocket.*)

Now what're you gonna' do? Kick me out?
AUSTIN: I'm not going to kick you out, Lee.
125 LEE: You couldn't kick me out, boy.
AUSTIN: I know.
LEE: So you can't even consider that one. (*Pause.*) You could call the police. That'd be the obvious thing.
AUSTIN: You're my brother.
130 LEE: That don't mean a thing. You go down to the L.A. Police Department there and ask them what kinda' people kill each other the most. What do you think they'd say?
AUSTIN: Who said anything about killing?
LEE: Family people. Brothers. Brothers-in-law. Cousins. Real
135 American-type people. They kill each other in the heat mostly. In the Smog-Alerts. In the Brush Fire Season. Right about this time a' year.
AUSTIN: This isn't the same.
LEE: Oh no? What makes it different?
140 AUSTIN: We're not insane. We're not driven to acts of violence like that. Not over a dumb movie script. Now sit down.

(*Long pause,* LEE *considers which way to go with it.*)

LEE: Maybe not. (*He sits back down at table across from* AUSTIN.) Maybe you're right. Maybe we're too intelligent,

145   huh? (*Pause.*) We got our heads on our shoulders. One of us has even got a Ivy League diploma. Now that means somethin' don't it? Doesn't that mean somethin'?

AUSTIN: Look, I'll write this thing for you, Lee. I don't mind writing it. I just don't want to get all worked up about it. It's not worth it. Now, come on. Let's just get through it, okay?

150   LEE: Nah. I think there's easier money. Lotsa' places I could pick up thousands. Maybe millions. I don't need this shit. I could go up to Sacramento Valley and steal me a diesel. Ten thousand a week dismantling one a' those suckers. Ten thousand a week!

(LEE *opens another beer, puts his foot back up on table.*)

155   AUSTIN: No, really, look, I'll write it out for you. I think it's a great idea.

LEE: Nah, you got yer own work to do. I don't wanna' interfere with yer life.

AUSTIN: I mean it'd be really fantastic if you could sell this.
160   Turn it into a movie. I mean it.

(*Pause.*)

LEE: Ya' think so huh?

AUSTIN: Absolutely. You could really turn your life around, you know. Change things.

LEE: I could get me a house maybe.

165   AUSTIN: Sure you could get a house. You could get a whole ranch if you wanted to.

LEE: (*Laughs.*) A ranch? I could get a ranch?

AUSTIN: 'Course you could. You know what a screenplay sells for these days?

170   LEE: No. What's it sell for?

AUSTIN: A lot. A whole lot of money.

LEE: Thousands?

AUSTIN: Yeah. Thousands.

LEE: Millions?

175   AUSTIN: Well—

LEE: We could get the old man outa' hock then.

AUSTIN: Maybe.

LEE: Maybe? Whadya' mean, maybe?

AUSTIN: I mean it might take more than money.

180   LEE: You were just tellin' me it'd change my whole life around. Why wouldn't it change his?

AUSTIN: He's different.

LEE: Oh, he's of a different ilk huh?

AUSTIN: He's not gonna' change. Let's leave the old man out
185   of it.

LEE: That's right. He's not gonna' change but I will. I'll just turn myself right inside out. I could be just like you then, huh? Sittin' around dreamin' stuff up. Gettin' paid to dream. Ridin' back and forth on the freeway just dreamin' my fool
190   head off.

AUSTIN: It's not all that easy.

LEE: It's not, huh?

AUSTIN: No. There's a lot of work involved.

LEE: What's the toughest part? Deciding whether to jog or play
195   tennis?

(*Long pause.*)

AUSTIN: Well, look. You can stay here—do whatever you want to. Borrow the car. Come in and out. Doesn't matter to me.

It's not my house. I'll help you write this thing or—not. Just let me know what you want. You tell me.

LEE: Oh. So now suddenly you're at my service. Is that it?   200

AUSTIN: What do you want to do Lee?

(*Long pause,* LEE *stares at him then turns and dreams at windows.*)

LEE: I tell ya' what I'd do if I still had that dog. Ya' wanna' know what I'd do?

AUSTIN: What?

LEE: Head out to Ventura. Cook up a little match. God that   205
little dog could bear down. Lota' money in dog fightin'. Big money.

(*Pause.*)

AUSTIN: Why don't we try to see this through, Lee. Just for the hell of it. Maybe you've really got something here. What do
you think?   210

(*Pause,* LEE *considers.*)

LEE: Maybe so. No harm in tryin' I guess. You think it's such a hot idea. Besides, I always wondered what'd be like to be you.

AUSTIN: You did?

LEE: Yeah, sure. I used to picture you walkin' around some   215
campus with yer arms fulla' books. Blondes chasin' after ya'.

AUSTIN: Blondes? That's funny.

LEE: What's funny about it?

AUSTIN: Because I always used to picture you somewhere.

LEE: Where'd you picture me?   220

AUSTIN: Oh, I don't know. Different places. Adventures. You were always on some adventure.

LEE: Yeah.

AUSTIN: And I used to say to myself, "Lee's got the right idea. He's out there in the world and here I am. What am I   225
doing?"

LEE: Well you were settin' yourself up for somethin'.

AUSTIN: I guess.

LEE: We better get started on this thing then.

AUSTIN: Okay.   230

(AUSTIN *sits up at typewriter, puts new paper in.*)

LEE: Oh. Can I get the keys back before I forget?

(AUSTIN *hesitates.*)

You said I could borrow the car if I wanted, right? Isn't that what you said?

AUSTIN: Yeah. Right.

(AUSTIN *takes keys out of his pocket, sets them on table,* LEE *takes keys slowly, plays with them in his hand.*)

LEE: I could get a ranch, huh?   235

AUSTIN: Yeah. We have to write it first though.

LEE: Okay. Let's write it.

(*Lights start dimming slowly to end as* AUSTIN *types,* LEE *speaks.*)

So they take off after each other straight into an endless black prairie. The sun is just comin' down and they can feel the night on their backs. What they don't know is that each   240
one of 'em is afraid, see. Each one separately thinks that he's

the only one that's afraid. And they keep ridin' like that straight into the night. Not knowing. And the one who's chasin' doesn't know where the other one is taking him. And
245 the one who's being chased doesn't know where he's going.

(Lights to black, typing stops in the dark, crickets fade.)

— ACT TWO —

SCENE V

Morning. LEE *at the table in alcove with a set of golf clubs in a fancy leather bag,* AUSTIN *at sink washing a few dishes.*

AUSTIN: He really liked it, huh?
LEE: He wouldn't a' gave me these clubs if he didn't like it.
AUSTIN: He gave you the clubs?
LEE: Yeah. I told ya' he gave me the clubs. The bag too.
5 AUSTIN: I thought he just loaned them to you.
LEE: He said it was part a' the advance. A little gift like. Gesture of his good faith.
AUSTIN: He's giving you an advance?
LEE: Now what's so amazing about that? I told ya' it was a good
10 story. You even said it was a good story.
AUSTIN: Well that is really incredible Lee. You know how many guys spend their whole lives down here trying to break into this business? Just trying to get in the door?
LEE: *(Pulling clubs out of bag, testing them.)* I got no idea.
15 How many?

(Pause.)

AUSTIN: How much of an advance is he giving you?
LEE: Plenty. We were talkin' big money out there. Ninth hole is where I sealed the deal.
AUSTIN: He made a firm commitment?
20 LEE: Absolutely.
AUSTIN: Well, I know Saul and he doesn't fool around when he says he likes something.
LEE: I thought you said you didn't know him.
AUSTIN: Well, I'm familiar with his tastes.
25 LEE: I let him get two up on me goin' into the back nine. He was sure he had me cold. You shoulda' seen his face when I pulled out the old pitching wedge and plopped it pin-high, two feet from the cup. He 'bout shit his pants. "Where'd a guy like you ever learn how to play golf like that?" he says.

(LEE laughs, AUSTIN *stares at him.)*

30 AUSTIN: 'Course there's no contract yet. Nothing's final until it's on paper.
LEE: It's final, all right. There's no way he's gonna' back out of it now. We gambled for it.
AUSTIN: Saul, gambled?
35 LEE: Yeah, sure. I mean he liked the outline already so he wasn't risking that much. I just guaranteed it with my short game.

(Pause.)

AUSTIN: Well, we should celebrate or something. I think Mom left a bottle of champagne in the refrigerator. We should
40 have a little toast.

(AUSTIN gets glasses from cupboard, goes to refrigerator, pulls out bottle of champagne.)

LEE: You shouldn't oughta' take her champagne, Austin. She's gonna' miss that.
AUSTIN: Oh, she's not going to mind. She'd be glad we put it to good use. I'll get her another bottle. Besides, it's perfect for the occasion.   45

(Pause.)

LEE: Yer gonna' get a nice fee fer writin' the script a' course. Straight fee.

(AUSTIN stops, stares at LEE, puts glasses and bottle on table, pause.)

AUSTIN: I'm writing the script?
LEE: That's what he said. Said we couldn't hire a better screenwriter in the whole town.   50
AUSTIN: But I'm already working on a script. I've got my own project. I don't have time to write two scripts.
LEE: No, he said he was gonna' drop that other one.

(Pause.)

AUSTIN: What? You mean mine? He's going to drop mine and do yours instead?   55
LEE: *(Smiles.)* Now look, Austin, it's jest beginner's luck ya' know. I mean I sank a fifty foot putt for this deal. No hard feelings.

(AUSTIN goes to phone on wall, grabs it, starts dialing.)

He's not gonna' be in, Austin. Told me he wouldn't be in 'till late this afternoon.   60
AUSTIN: *(Stays on phone, dialing, listen.)* I can't believe this. I just can't believe it. Are you sure he said that? Why would he drop mine?
LEE: That's what he told me.
AUSTIN: He can't do that without telling me first. Without   65
talking to me at least. He wouldn't just make a decision like that without talking to me!
LEE: Well I was kinda' surprised myself. But he was real enthusiastic about my story.

(AUSTIN hangs up phone violently, paces.)

AUSTIN: What'd he say! Tell me everything he said!   70
LEE: I been tellin' ya'! He said he liked the story a whole lot. It was the first authentic Western to come along in a decade.
AUSTIN: He liked that story! Your story?
LEE: Yeah! What's so surprisin' about that?
AUSTIN: It's stupid! It's the dumbest story I ever heard in my   75
life.
LEE: Hey, hold on! That's my story yer talkin' about!
AUSTIN: It's a bullshit story! It's idiotic. Two lamebrains chasing each other across Texas! Are you kidding? Who do you think's going to go see a film like that?   80
LEE: It's not a film! It's a movie. There's a big difference. That's somethin' Saul told me.
AUSTIN: Oh he did, huh?
LEE: Yeah, he said, "In this business we make movies, American movies. Leave the films to the French."   85
AUSTIN: So you got real intimate with old Saul huh? He started pouring forth his vast knowledge of Cinema.

LEE: I think he liked me a lot, to tell ya' the truth. I think he felt I was somebody he could confide in.

90   AUSTIN: What'd you do, beat him up or something?

LEE: (*Stands fast.*) Hey, I've about had it with the insults buddy! You think yer the only one in the brain department here? Yer the only one that can sit around and cook things up? There's other people got ideas too, ya' know!

95   AUSTIN: You must've done something. Threatened him or something. Now what'd you do Lee?

LEE: I convinced him!

(LEE *makes sudden menacing lunge toward* AUSTIN, *wielding golf club above his head, stops himself, frozen moment, long pause,* LEE *lowers club.*)

AUSTIN: Oh, Jesus. You didn't hurt him did you?

(*Long silence,* LEE *sits back down at table.*)

Lee! Did you hurt him?

100   LEE: I didn't do nothin' to him! He liked my story. Pure and simple. He said it was the best story he's come across in a long, long time.

AUSTIN: That's what he told me about my story! That's the same thing he said to me.

105   LEE: Well, he musta' been lyin'. He musta' been lyin' to one of us anyway.

AUSTIN: You can't come into this town and start pushing people around. They're gonna' put you away!

LEE: I never pushed anybody around! I beat him fair and square. (*Pause.*) They can't touch me anyway. They can't put a finger on me. I'm gone. I can come in through the window and go out through the door. They never knew what hit 'em. You, yer stuck. Yer the one that's stuck. Not me. So don't be warnin' me what to do in this town.

(*Pause,* AUSTIN *crosses to table, sits at typewriter, rests.*)

115   AUSTIN: Lee, come on, level with me will you? It doesn't make any sense that suddenly he'd throw my idea out the window. I've been talking to him for months. I've got too much at stake. Everything's riding on this project.

LEE: What's yer idea?

AUSTIN: It's just a simple love story.

120   LEE: What kinda' love story?

AUSTIN: (*Stands, cross into kitchen.*) I'm not telling you!

LEE: Ha! 'Fraid I'll steal it huh? Competition's gettin' kinda' close to home isn't it?

125   AUSTIN: Where did Saul say he was going?

LEE: He was gonna' take my story to a couple studios.

AUSTIN: That's *my* outline you know! I wrote that outline! You've got no right to be peddling it around.

LEE: You weren't ready to take credit for it last night.

130   AUSTIN: Give me my keys!

LEE: What?

AUSTIN: The keys! I want my keys back!

LEE: Where you goin'?

AUSTIN: Just give me my keys! I gotta' take a drive. I gotta' get

135   out of here for a while.

LEE: Where you gonna' go, Austin?

AUSTIN: (*Pause.*) I might just drive out to the desert for a while. I gotta' think.

LEE: You can think here just as good. This is the perfect setup

140   for thinkin'. We got some writin' to do here, boy. Now let's just have us a little toast. Relax. We're partners now.

(LEE *pops the cork of the champagne bottle, pours two drinks as the lights fade to black.*)

SCENE VI

Afternoon. LEE *and* SAUL *in kitchen,* AUSTIN *in alcove*

LEE: Now you tell him. You tell him, Mr. Kipper.

SAUL: Kimmer.

LEE: Kimmer. You tell him what you told me. He don't believe me.

AUSTIN: I don't want to hear it.   5

SAUL: It's really not a big issue, Austin. I was simply amazed by your brother's story and—

AUSTIN: Amazed? You lost a bet! You gambled with my material!

SAUL: That's really beside the point, Austin. I'm ready to go all   10
the way with your brother's story. I think it has a great deal of merit.

AUSTIN: I don't want to hear about it, okay? Go tell it to the executives! Tell it to somebody who's going to turn it into a package deal or something. A T.V. series. Don't tell it to me.   15

SAUL: But I want to continue with your project too, Austin. It's not as though we can't do both. We're big enough for that aren't we?

AUSTIN: "We"? I can't do both! I don't know about "we."

LEE: (*To* SAUL.) See, what'd I tell ya'. He's totally unsympathetic.   20

SAUL: Austin, there's no point in our going to another screenwriter for this. It just doesn't make sense. You're brothers. You know each other. There's a familiarity with the material that just wouldn't be possible otherwise.

AUSTIN: There's no familiarity with the material! None! I don't   25
know what "Tornado Country" is. I don't know what a "gooseneck" is. And I don't want to know! (*Pointing to* LEE.) He's a hustler! He's a bigger hustler than you are! If you can't see that, then—

LEE: (*To* AUSTIN.) Hey, now hold on. I didn't have to bring this   30
bone back to you, boy. I persuaded Saul here that you were the right man for the job. You don't have to go throwin' up favors in my face.

AUSTIN: Favors! I'm the one who wrote the fuckin' outline! You can't even spell.   35

SAUL: (*To* AUSTIN.) Your brother told me about the situation with your father.

(*Pause.*)

AUSTIN: What? (*Looks at* LEE.)

SAUL: That's right. Now we have a clear-cut deal here, Austin.
We have big studio money standing behind this thing. Just   40
on the basis of your outline.

AUSTIN: (*To* SAUL.) What'd he tell you about my father?

SAUL: Well—that he's destitute. He needs money.

LEE: That's right. He does.

(AUSTIN *shakes his head, stares at them both.*)

AUSTIN: (*To* LEE.) And this little assignment is supposed to go   45
toward the old man? A charity project? Is that what this is? Did you cook this up on the ninth green too?

SAUL: It's a big slice, Austin.

AUSTIN: (*To* LEE.) I gave him money! I already gave him money. You know that. He drank it all up!   50

LEE: This is a different deal here.

SAUL: We can set up a trust for your father. A large sum of money. It can be doled out to him in parcels so he can't misuse it.

55 AUSTIN: Yeah, and who's doing the doling?

SAUL: Your brother volunteered.

(AUSTIN *laughs*.)

LEE: That's right. I'll make sure he uses it for groceries.

AUSTIN: (*To* SAUL.) I'm not doing this script! I'm not writing this crap for you or anybody else. You can't blackmail me

60 into it. You can't threaten me into it. There's no way I'm doing it. So just give it up. Both of you.

(*Long pause*.)

SAUL: Well, that's it then. I mean this is an easy three hundred grand. Just for a first draft. It's incredible, Austin. We've got three different studios all trying to cut each other's throats to

65 get this material. In one morning. That's how hot it is.

AUSTIN: Yeah, well you can afford to give me a percentage on the outline then. And you better get the genius here an agent before he gets burned.

LEE: Saul's gonna' be my agent. Isn't that right, Saul?

70 SAUL: That's right. (*To* AUSTIN.) Your brother has really got something, Austin. I've been around too long not to recognize it. Raw talent.

AUSTIN: He's got a lota' balls is what he's got. He's taking you right down the river.

75 SAUL: Three hundred thousand, Austin. Just for a first draft. Now you've never been offered that kind of money before.

AUSTIN: I'm not writing it.

(*Pause*.)

SAUL: I see. Well—

LEE: We'll just go to another writer then. Right, Saul? Just hire

80 us somebody with some enthusiasm. Somebody who can recognize the value of a good story.

SAUL: I'm sorry about this, Austin.

AUSTIN: Yeah.

SAUL: I mean I was hoping we could continue both things but

85 now I don't see how it's possible.

AUSTIN: So you're dropping my idea altogether. Is that it? Just trade horses in midstream? After all these months of meetings.

SAUL: I wish there was another way.

90 AUSTIN: I've got everything riding on this, Saul. You know that. It's my only shot. If this falls through—

SAUL: I have to go with what my instincts tell me—

AUSTIN: Your instincts!

SAUL: My gut reaction.

95 AUSTIN: You lost! That's your gut reaction. You lost a gamble. Now you're trying to tell me you like his story? How could you possibly fall for that story? It's as phony as Hoppalong Cassidy. What do you see in it? I'm curious.

SAUL: It has the ring of truth, Austin.

100 AUSTIN: (*Laughs*.) Truth?

LEE: It is true.

SAUL: Something about the real West.

AUSTIN: Why? Because it's got horses? Because it's got grown men acting like little boys?

105 SAUL: Something about the land. Your brother is speaking from experience.

AUSTIN: So am I!

SAUL: But nobody's interested in love these days, Austin. Let's face it.

LEE: That's right. 110

AUSTIN: (*To* SAUL.) He's been camped out on the desert for three months. Talking to cactus. What's he know about what people wanna' see on the screen! I drive on the freeway every day. I swallow the smog. I watch the news in color. I shop in the Safeway. I'm the one who's in touch! Not him! 115

SAUL: I have to go now, Austin.

(SAUL *starts to leave*.)

AUSTIN: There's no such thing as the West anymore! It's a dead issue! It's dried up, Saul, and so are you.

(SAUL *stops and turns to* AUSTIN.)

SAUL: Maybe you're right. But I have to take the gamble, don't I? 120

AUSTIN: You're a fool to do this, Saul.

SAUL: I've always gone on my hunches. Always. And I've never been wrong. (*To* LEE.) I'll talk to you tomorrow, Lee.

LEE: All right, Mr. Kimmer.

SAUL: Maybe we could have some lunch. 125

LEE: Fine with me. (*Smiles at* AUSTIN.)

SAUL: I'll give you a ring.

(SAUL *exits, lights to black as brothers look at each other from a distance*.)

SCENE VII

Night. Coyotes, crickets, sound of typewriter in dark, candlelight up on LEE *at typewriter struggling to type with one finger system,* AUSTIN *sits sprawled out on kitchen floor with whiskey bottle, drunk.*

AUSTIN: (*Singing, from floor*.)

"Red sails in the sunset
Way out on the blue
Please carry my loved one
Home safely to me 5

Red sails in the sunset—"

LEE: (*Slams fist on table*.) Hey! Knock it off will ya'! I'm tryin' to concentrate here.

AUSTIN: (*Laughs*.) You're tryin' to concentrate?

LEE: Yeah. That's right. 10

AUSTIN: Now you're tryin' to concentrate.

LEE: Between you, the coyotes and the crickets a thought don't have much of a chance.

AUSTIN: "Between me, the coyotes and the crickets." What a great title! 15

LEE: I don't need a title! I need a thought.

AUSTIN: (*Laughs*.) A thought! Here's a thought for ya'—

LEE: I'm not askin' fer yer thoughts! I got my own. I can do this thing on my own.

AUSTIN: You're going to write an entire script on your own? 20

LEE: That's right.

(*Pause*.)

AUSTIN: Here's a thought. Saul Kimmer—

LEE: Shut up will ya'!

AUSTIN: He thinks we're the same person.

25 LEE: Don't get cute.

AUSTIN: He does! He's lost his mind. Poor old Saul. (*Giggles.*) Thinks we're one and the same.

LEE: Why don't you ease up on that champagne.

AUSTIN: (*Holding up bottle.*) This isn't champagne anymore.
30 We went through the champagne a long time ago. This is serious stuff. The days of champagne are long gone.

LEE: Well, go outside and drink it.

AUSTIN: I'm enjoying your company, Lee. For the first time since your arrival I am finally enjoying your company. And
35 now you want me to go outside and drink alone?

LEE: That's right.

(LEE *reads through paper in typewriter, makes an erasure.*)

AUSTIN: You think you'll make more progress if you're alone? You might drive yourself crazy.

LEE: I could have this thing done in a night if I had a little si-
40 lence.

AUSTIN: Well you'd still have the crickets to contend with. The coyotes. The sounds of the Police Helicopters prowling above the neighborhood. Slashing their searchlights down through the streets. Hunting for the likes of you.

45 LEE: I'm a screenwriter now! I'm legitimate.

AUSTIN: (*Laughing.*) A screenwriter!

LEE: That's right. I'm on salary. That's more'n I can say for you. I got an advance coming.

AUSTIN: This is true. This is very true. An advance. (*Pause.*)
50 Well, maybe I oughta' go out and try my hand at your trade. Since you're doing so good at mine.

LEE: Ha!

(LEE *attempts to type some more but gets the ribbon tangled up, starts trying to re-thread it as they continue talking.*)

AUSTIN: Well why not? You don't think I've got what it takes to sneak into people's houses and steal their T.V.s?

55 LEE: You couldn't steal a toaster without losin' yer lunch.

(AUSTIN *stands with a struggle, supports himself by the sink.*)

AUSTIN: You don't think I could sneak into somebody's house and steal a toaster?

LEE: Go take a shower or somethin' will ya!

(LEE *gets more tangled up with the typewriter ribbon, pulling it out of the machine as though it was fishing line.*)

AUSTIN: You really don't think I could steal a crumby toaster?
60 How much you wanna' bet I can't steal a toaster! How much? Go ahead! You're a gambler aren't you? Tell me how much yer willing to put on the line. Some part of your big advance? Oh, you haven't got that yet have you. I forgot.

LEE: All right. I'll bet you your car that you can't steal a toaster
65 without gettin' busted.

AUSTIN: You already got my car!

LEE: Okay, your house then.

AUSTIN: What're you gonna' give me! I'm not talkin' about my house and my car, I'm talkin' about what are you gonna' give
70 me. You don't have nothin' to give me.

LEE: I'll give you—shared screen credit. How 'bout that? I'll have it put in the contract that this was written by the both of us.

AUSTIN: I don't want my name on that piece of shit! I want
75 something of value. You got anything of value? You got any

tidbits from the desert? Any Rattlesnake bones? I'm not a greedy man. Any little personal treasure will suffice.

LEE: I'm gonna' just kick yer ass out in a minute.

AUSTIN: Oh, so now you're gonna' kick me out! Now I'm the intruder. I'm the one who's invading your precious privacy. 80

LEE: I'm trying to do some screenwriting here!!

(LEE *stands, picks up typewriter, slams it down hard on table, pause, silence except for crickets.*)

AUSTIN: Well, you got everything you need. You got plenty a' coffee? Groceries. You got a car. A contract. (*pause*) Might need a new typewriter ribbon but other than that you're pretty well fixed. I'll just leave ya' alone for a while. 85

(AUSTIN *tries to steady himself to leave,* LEE *makes a move toward him.*)

LEE: Where you goin'?

AUSTIN: Don't worry about me. I'm not the one to worry about.

(AUSTIN *weaves toward exit, stops.*)

LEE: What're you gonna' do? Just go wander out into the night? 90

AUSTIN: I'm gonna' make a little tour.

LEE: Why don't ya' just go to bed for Christ's sake. Yer makin' me sick.

AUSTIN: I can take care a' myself. Don't worry about me.

(AUSTIN *weaves badly in another attempt to exit, he crashes to the floor,* LEE *goes to him but remains standing.*)

LEE: You want me to call your wife for ya' or something? 95

AUSTIN: (*From floor.*) My wife?

LEE: Yeah. I mean maybe she can help ya' out. Talk to ya' or somethin'.

AUSTIN: (*Struggles to stand again.*) She's five hundred miles away. North. North of here. Up in the North country where 100 things are calm. I don't need any help. I'm gonna' go outside and I'm gonna' steal a toaster. I'm gonna' steal some other stuff too. I might even commit bigger crimes. Bigger than you ever dreamed of. Crimes beyond the imagination!

(AUSTIN *manages to get himself vertical, tries to head for exit again.*)

LEE: Just hang on a minute, Austin. 105

AUSTIN: Why? What for? You don't need my help, right? You got a handle on the project. Besides, I'm lookin' forward to the smell of the night. The bushes. Orange blossoms. Dust in the driveways. Rain bird sprinklers. Lights in people's houses. You're right about the lights, Lee. Everybody else is 110 livin' the life. Indoors. Safe. This is a Paradise down here. You know that? We're livin' in a Paradise. We've forgotten about that.

LEE: You sound just like the old man now.

AUSTIN: Yeah, well we all sound alike when we're sloshed. We 115 just sorta' echo each other.

LEE: Maybe if we could work on this together we could bring him back out here. Get him settled down some place.

(AUSTIN *turns violently toward* LEE, *takes a swing at him, misses and crashes to the floor again,* LEE *stays standing.*)

AUSTIN: I don't want him out here! I've had it with him! I went all the way out there! I went out of my way. I gave him 120 money and all he did was play Al Jolson records and spit at me! I gave him money!

(Pause.)

LEE: Just help me a little with the characters, all right? You know how to do it, Austin.

125 AUSTIN: *(On floor, laughs.)* The characters!

LEE: Yeah. You know. The way they talk and stuff. I can hear it in my head but I can't get it down on paper.

AUSTIN: What characters?

LEE: The guys. The guys in the story.

130 AUSTIN: Those aren't characters.

LEE: Whatever you call 'em then. I need to write somethin' out.

AUSTIN: Those are illusions of characters.

LEE: I don't give a damn what ya' call 'em! You know what I'm

135 talkin' about!

AUSTIN: Those are fantasies of a long lost boyhood.

LEE: I gotta' write somethin' out on paper!!

(Pause.)

AUSTIN: What for? Saul's gonna' get you a fancy screenwriter isn't he?

140 LEE: I wanna' do it myself!

AUSTIN: Then do it! Yer on your own now, old buddy. You bulldogged yer way into contention. Now you gotta' carry it through.

LEE: I will but I need some advice. Just a couple a' things.

145 Come on, Austin. Just help me get 'em talkin' right. It won't take much.

AUSTIN: Oh, now you're having a little doubt huh? What happened? The pressure's on, boy. This is it. You gotta' come up with it now. You don't come up with a winner on your first

150 time out they just cut your head off. They don't give you a second chance ya' know.

LEE: I got a good story! I know it's a good story. I just need a little help is all.

AUSTIN: Not from me. Not from yer little old brother. I'm

155 retired.

LEE: You could save this thing for me, Austin. I'd give ya' half the money. I would. I only need half anyway. With this kinda' money I could be a long time down the road. I'd never bother ya' again. I promise. You'd never even see me

160 again.

AUSTIN: *(Still on floor.)* You'd disappear?

LEE: I would for sure.

AUSTIN: Where would you disappear to?

LEE: That don't matter. I got plenty a' places.

165 AUSTIN: Nobody can disappear. The old man tried that. Look where it got him. He lost his teeth.

LEE: He never had any money.

AUSTIN: I don't mean that. I mean his teeth! His real teeth. First he lost his real teeth, then he lost his false teeth. You

170 never knew that did ya'? He never confided in you.

LEE: Nah, I never knew that.

AUSTIN: You wanna' drink?

(AUSTIN offers bottle to LEE, LEE takes it, sits down on kitchen floor with AUSTIN, they share the bottle)

Yeah, he lost his real teeth one at a time. Woke up every morning with another tooth lying on the mattress. Finally,

he decides he's gotta' get 'em all pulled out but he doesn't 175 have any money. Middle of Arizona with no money and no insurance and every morning another tooth is lying on the mattress. *(Takes a drink.)* So what does he do?

LEE: I dunno'. I never knew about that.

AUSTIN: He begs the government. G.I. Bill or some damn 180 thing. Some pension plan he remembers in the back of his head. And they send him out the money.

LEE: They did?

(They keep trading the bottle between them, taking drinks.)

AUSTIN: Yeah. They send him the money but it's not enough money. Costs a lot to have all yer teeth yanked. They charge 185 by the individual tooth, ya' know. I mean one tooth isn't equal to another tooth. Some are more expensive. Like the big ones in the back—

LEE: So what happened?

AUSTIN: So he locates a Mexican dentist in Juarez who'll do 190 the whole thing for a song. And he takes off hitchhiking to the border.

LEE: Hitchhiking?

AUSTIN: Yeah. So how long you think it takes him to get to the border? A man his age. 195

LEE: I dunno.

AUSTIN: Eight days it takes him. Eight days in the rain and the sun and every day he's droppin' teeth on the blacktop nobody'll pick him up 'cause his mouth's full a' blood.

(Pause, they drink.)

So finally he stumbles into the dentist. Dentist takes all his 200 money and all his teeth. And there he is, in Mexico, with his gums sewed up and his pockets empty.

(Long silence, AUSTIN drinks.)

LEE: That's it?

AUSTIN: Then I go out to see him, see. I go out there and I take him out for a nice Chinese dinner. But he doesn't eat. All he 205 wants to do is drink Martinis outa' plastic cups. And he takes his teeth out and lays 'em on the table 'cause he can't stand the feel of 'em. And we ask the waitress for one a' those doggie bags to take the Chop Suey home in. So he drops his teeth in the doggie bag along with the Chop Suey. And then 210 we go out to hit all the bars up and down the highway. Says he wants to introduce me to all his buddies. And in one a' those bars, in one a' those bars up and down the highway, he left that doggie bag with his teeth laying in the Chop Suey.

LEE: You never found it? 215

AUSTIN: We went back but we never did find it. *(Pause.)* Now that's a true story. True to life.

(They drink as lights fade to black.)

SCENE VIII

Very early morning, between night and day. No crickets, coyotes yapping feverishly in distance before light comes up, a small fire blazes up in the dark from alcove area, sound of LEE *smashing typewriter with a golf club, lights coming up,* LEE *seen smashing typewriter methodically then dropping pages of his script into a burning bowl set on the floor of alcove, flames leap up,* AUSTIN *has a whole bunch of stolen toasters lined up on the sink counter along with* LEE's *stolen T.V., the toasters are of a wide variety of models, mostly chrome,* AUSTIN *goes up and down the line of toasters, breathing on them and polishing them with a dish towel, both men are drunk, empty whiskey bottles and beer cans litter floor of kitchen, they share a half empty bottle on one of the chairs in the alcove,* LEE *keeps periodically taking deliberate ax-chops at the typewriter using a nine-iron as* AUSTIN *speaks, all of their mother's house plants are dead and drooping.*

AUSTIN: (*Polishing toasters.*) There's gonna' be a general lack of toast in the neighborhood this morning. Many, many un-happy, bewildered breakfast faces. I guess it's best not to even think of the victims. Not to even entertain it. Is that the right psychology?

5   LEE: (*Pauses.*) What?

AUSTIN: Is that the correct criminal psychology? Not to think of the victims?

LEE: What victims?

(LEE *takes another swipe at typewriter with nine-iron, adds pages to the fire.*)

10 AUSTIN: The victims of crime. Of breaking and entering. I mean is it a prerequisite for a criminal not to have a con-science?

LEE: Ask a criminal.

(*Pause,* LEE *stares at* AUSTIN.)

What're you gonna' do with all those toasters? That's the dumbest thing I ever saw in my life.

15 AUSTIN: I've got hundreds of dollars worth of household appli-ances here. You may not realize that.

LEE: Yeah, and how many hundreds of dollars did you walk right past?

20 AUSTIN: It was toasters you challenged me to. Only toasters. I ignored every other temptation.

LEE: I never challenged you! That's no challenge. Anybody can steal a toaster.

(LEE *smashes typewriter again.*)

AUSTIN: You don't have to take it out on my typewriter ya' know. It's not the machine's fault that you can't write. It's a sin to do that to a good machine.

25 LEE: A sin?

AUSTIN: When you consider all the writers who never even had a machine. Who would have given an eyeball for a good typewriter. Any typewriter.

30 (LEE *smashes typewriter again.*)

AUSTIN: (*Polishing toasters.*) All the ones who wrote on match-book covers. Paper bags. Toilet paper. Who had their writing destroyed by their jailers. Who persisted beyond all odds. Those writers would find it hard to understand your actions.

(LEE *comes down on typewriter with one final crushing blow of the nine-iron then collapses in one of the chairs, takes a drink from bottle, pause.*)

35 AUSTIN: (*After pause.*) Not to mention demolishing a perfectly good golf club. What about all the struggling golfers? What about Lee Trevino? What do you think he would've said when he was batting balls around with broomsticks at the age of nine. Impoverished.

(*Pause.*)

LEE: What time is it anyway?   40

AUSTIN: No idea. Time stands still when you're havin' fun.

LEE: Is it too late to call a woman? You know any women?

AUSTIN: I'm a married man.

LEE: I mean a local woman.

(AUSTIN *looks out at light through window above sink.*)

AUSTIN: It's either too late or too early. You're the nature en-   45
thusiast. Can't you tell the time by the light in the sky? Ori-ent yourself around the North Star or something?

LEE: I can't tell anything.

AUSTIN: Maybe you need a little breakfast. Some toast! How 'bout some toast?   50

(AUSTIN *goes to cupboard, pulls out loaf of bread and starts dropping slices into every toaster,* LEE *stays sitting, drinks, watches* AUSTIN.)

LEE: I don't need toast. I need a woman.

AUSTIN: A woman isn't the answer. Never was.

LEE: I'm not talkin' about permanent. I'm talkin' about tem-porary.

AUSTIN: (*Putting toast in toasters.*) We'll just test the merits of   55
these little demons. See which brands have a tendency to burn. See which one can produce a perfectly golden piece of fluffy toast.

LEE: How much gas you got in yer car?

AUSTIN: I haven't driven my car for days now. So I haven't had   60
an opportunity to look at the gas gauge.

LEE: Take a guess. You think there's enough to get me to Bak-ersfield?

AUSTIN: Bakersfield? What's in Bakersfield?

LEE: Just never mind what's in Bakersfield! You think there's   65
enough goddamn gas in the car!

AUSTIN: Sure.

LEE: Sure. You could care less, right. Let me run outa' gas on the Grapevine. You could give a shit.

AUSTIN: I'd say there was enough gas to get you just about any-   70
where, Lee. With your determination and guts.

LEE: What the hell time is it anyway?

(LEE *pulls out his wallet, starts going through dozens of small pieces of paper with phone numbers written on them, drops some on the floor, drops others in the fire.*)

AUSTIN: Very early. This is the time of morning when the coy-otes kill people's cocker spaniels. Did you hear them? That's what they were doing out there. Luring innocent pets away   75
from their homes.

LEE: (*Searching through his papers.*) What's the area code for Bakersfield? You know?

AUSTIN: You could always call the operator.

LEE: I can't stand that voice they give ya'.   80

AUSTIN: What voice?

LEE: That voice that warns you that if you'd only tried harder to find the number in the phone book you wouldn't have to be calling the operator to begin with.

(LEE *gets up, holding a slip of paper from his wallet, stumbles to-ward phone on wall, yanks receiver, starts dialing.*)

AUSTIN: Well I don't understand why you'd want to talk to any-   85
body else anyway. I mean you can talk to me. I'm your brother.

LEE: *(Dialing.)* I wanna' talk to a woman. I haven't heard a woman's voice in a long time.

90 AUSTIN: Not since the Botanist?

LEE: What?

AUSTIN: Nothing. *(Starts singing as he tends toast.)*

"Red sails in the sunset
Way out on the blue
95 Please carry my loved one
Home safely to me"

LEE: Hey, knock it off will ya'! This is long distance here.

AUSTIN: Bakersfield?

LEE: Yeah, Bakersfield. It's Kern County.

100 AUSTIN: Well, what County are *we* in?

LEE: You better get yourself a 7-Up, boy.

AUSTIN: One County's as good as another.

(AUSTIN hums "Red Sails" softly as LEE talks on phone.)

LEE: *(To phone.)* Yeah, operator look—first off I wanna' know the area code for Bakersfield. Right. Bakersfield! Okay. Good.
105 Now I wanna' know if you can help me track somebody down. *(Pause.)* No, no I mean a phone number. Just a phone number. Okay. *(Holds a piece of paper up and reads it.)* Okay, the name is Melly Ferguson. Melly. *(Pause.)* I dunno'. Melly. Maybe. Yeah. Maybe Melanie. Yeah. Melanie Ferguson.
110 Okay. *(Pause.)* What? I can't hear ya' so good. Sounds like yer under the ocean. *(Pause.)* You got ten Melanie Fergusons? How could that be? Ten Melanie Fergusons in Bakersfield? Well gimme all of 'em then. *(Pause.)* What d'ya mean? Gimme all ten Melanie Fergusons! That's right. Just a sec-
115 ond. *(To AUSTIN.)* Gimme a pen.

AUSTIN: I don't have a pen.

LEE: Gimme a pencil then!

AUSTIN: I don't have a pencil.

LEE: *(To phone.)* Just a second, operator. *(To AUSTIN.)* Yer a
120 writer and ya' don't have a pen or a pencil!

AUSTIN: I'm not a writer. You're a writer.

LEE: I'm on the phone here! Get me a pen or a pencil.

AUSTIN: I gotta' watch the toast.

LEE: *(To phone.)* Hang on a second, operator.

(LEE lets the phone drop then starts pulling all the drawers in the kitchen out on the floor and dumping the contents, searching for a pencil, AUSTIN watches him casually.)

125 LEE: *(Crashing through drawers, throwing contents around kitchen.)* This is the last time I try to live with people, boy! I can't believe it. Here I am! Here I am again in a desperate situation! This would never happen out on the desert. I would never be in this kinda' situation out on the desert.
130 Isn't there a pen or a pencil in this house! Who lives in this house anyway!

AUSTIN: Our mother.

LEE: How come she don't have a pen or a pencil! She's a social person isn't she? Doesn't she have to make shopping lists?
135 She's gotta' have a pencil. *(Finds a pencil.)* Aaha! *(He rushes back to phone, picks up receiver.)* All right operator. Operator? Hey! Operator! Goddamnit!

(LEE rips the phone off the wall and throws it down, goes back to chair and falls into it, drinks, long pause.)

AUSTIN: She hung up?

LEE: Yeah, she hung up. I knew she was gonna' hang up. I could hear it in her voice.   140

(LEE starts going through his slips of paper again.)

AUSTIN: Well, you're probably better off staying here with me anyway. I'll take care of you.

LEE: I don't need takin' care of! Not by you anyway.

AUSTIN: Toast is almost ready.

(AUSTIN starts buttering all the toast as it pops up.)

LEE: I don't want any toast!   145

(Long pause.)

AUSTIN: You gotta' eat something. Can't just drink. How long have we been drinking, anyway?

LEE: *(Looking through slips of paper.)* Maybe it was Fresno. What's the area code for Fresno? How could I have lost that number! She was beautiful.   150

(Pause.)

AUSTIN: Why don't you just forget about that, Lee. Forget about the woman.

LEE: She had green eyes. You know what green eyes do to me?

AUSTIN: I know but you're not gonna' get it on with her now anyway. It's dawn already. She's in Bakersfield for Christ's   155
sake.

(Long pause, LEE considers the situation.)

LEE: Yeah. *(Looks at windows.)* It's dawn?

AUSTIN: Let's just have some toast and—

LEE: What is this bullshit with the toast anyway! You make it sound like salvation or something. I don't want any goddamn   160
toast! How many times I gotta' tell ya'! *(LEE gets up, crosses upstage to windows in alcove, looks out, AUSTIN butters toast.)*

AUSTIN: Well it is like salvation sort of. I mean the smell. I love the smell of toast. And the sun's coming up. It makes me feel like anything's possible. Ya' know?   165

LEE: *(Back to AUSTIN, facing windows upstage.)* So go to church why don't ya'

AUSTIN: Like a beginning. I love beginnings.

LEE: Oh yeah. I've always been kinda' partial to endings my-   170
self.

AUSTIN: What if I come with you, Lee?

LEE: *(Pause as LEE turns toward AUSTIN.)* What?

AUSTIN: What if I come with you out to the desert?

LEE: Are you kiddin'?

AUSTIN: No. I'd just like to see what it's like.   175

LEE: You wouldn't last a day out there pal.

AUSTIN: That's what you said about the toasters. You said I couldn't steal a toaster either.

LEE: A toaster's got nothin' to do with the desert.

AUSTIN: I could make it, Lee. I'm not that helpless. I can cook.   180

LEE: Cook?

AUSTIN: I can.

LEE: So what! You can cook. Toast.

AUSTIN: I can make fires. I know how to get fresh water from condensation.   185

(AUSTIN stacks buttered toast up in a tall stack on plate.)

(LEE slams table.)

LEE: It's not somethin' you learn out of a Boy Scout handbook!

AUSTIN: Well how do you learn it then! How're you supposed to learn it!

(Pause.)

190 LEE: Ya' just learn it, that's all. Ya' learn it 'cause ya' have to learn it. You don't *have* to learn it.

AUSTIN: You could teach me.

LEE: *(Stands.)* What're you, crazy or somethin'? You went to college. Here, you are down here, rollin' in bucks. Floatin' up and down in elevators. And you wanna' learn how to live

195 on the desert!

AUSTIN: I do, Lee. I really do. There's nothin' down here for me. There never was. When we were kids here it was different. There was a life here then. But now—I keep comin'

200 down here thinkin' it's the fifties or somethin'. I keep finding myself getting off the freeway at familiar landmarks that turn out to be unfamiliar. On the way to appointments. Wandering down streets I thought I recognized that turn out to be replicas of streets I remember. Streets I misremember. Streets I can't tell if I lived on or saw in a postcard. Fields

205 that don't even exist anymore.

LEE: There's no point cryin' about that now.

AUSTIN: There's nothin' real down here, Lee! Least of all me!

LEE: Well I can't save you from that!

AUSTIN: You can let me come with you.

210 LEE: No dice, pal.

AUSTIN: You could let me come with you, Lee!

LEE: Hey, do you actually think I chose to live out in the middle a' nowhere? Do ya'? Ya' think it's some kinda' philosophical decision I took or somethin'? I'm livin' out there

215 'cause I can't make it here! And yer bitchin' to me about all yer success!

AUSTIN: I'd cash it all in in a second. That's the truth.

LEE: *(Pause, shakes his head.)* I can't believe this.

AUSTIN: Let me go with you.

220 LEE: Stop sayin' that will ya'! Yer worse than a dog.

(AUSTIN offers out the plate of neatly stacked toast to LEE.)

AUSTIN: You want some toast?

(LEE suddenly explodes and knocks the plate out of AUSTIN's hand, toast goes flying, long frozen moment where it appears LEE might go all the way this time when AUSTIN breaks it by slowly lowering himself to his knees and begins gathering the scattered toast from the floor and stacking it back on the plate, LEE begins to circle AUSTIN in a slow, predatory way, crushing pieces of toast in his wake, no words for a while, AUSTIN keeps gathering toast, even the crushed pieces.)

LEE: Tell ya' what I'll do, little brother. I might just consider makin' you a deal. Little trade. *(AUSTIN continues gathering toast as LEE circles him through this.)* You write me up this

225 screenplay thing just like I tell ya'. I mean you can use all yer usual tricks and stuff. Yer fancy language. Yer artistic hocus pocus. But ya' gotta' write everything like I say. Every move. Every time they run outa' gas, they run outa' gas. Every time they wanna' jump on a horse, they do just that. If they

230 wanna' stay in Texas, by God they'll stay in Texas! *(Keeps circling.)* And you finish the whole thing up for me. Top to bottom. And you put my name on it. And I own all the rights. And every dime goes in my pocket. You do that and I'll sure enough take ya' with me to the desert. *(LEE stops, pause,*

235 *looks down at AUSTIN.)* How's that sound?

(Pause as AUSTIN stands slowly holding plate of demolished toast, their faces are very close, pause.)

AUSTIN: It's a deal.

(LEE stares straight into AUSTIN's eyes, then he slowly takes a piece of toast off the plate, raises it to his mouth and takes a huge crushing bite never taking his eyes off AUSTIN's as LEE crunches into the toast the lights black out.)

SCENE IX

Mid-day. No sound, blazing heat, the stage is ravaged; bottles, toasters, smashed typewriter, ripped out telephone, etc. All the debris from previous scene is now starkly visible in intense yellow light, the effect should be like a desert junkyard at high noon, the coolness of the preceding scenes is totally obliterated. AUSTIN is seated at table in alcove, shirt open, pouring with sweat, hunched over a writing notebook, scribbling notes desperately with a ballpoint pen. LEE with no shirt, beer in hand, sweat pouring down his chest, is walking a slow circle around the table, picking his way through the objects, sometimes kicking them aside.

LEE: *(As he walks.)* All right, read it back to me. Read it back to me!

AUSTIN: *(Scribbling at top speed.)* Just a second.

LEE: Come on, come on! Just read what ya' got.

AUSTIN: I can't keep up! It's not the same as if I had a   5
typewriter.

LEE: Just read what we got so far. Forget about the rest.

AUSTIN: All right. Let's see—okay—*(Wipes sweat from his face, reads as LEE circles.)* Luke says uh—

LEE: Luke?   10

AUSTIN: Yeah.

LEE: His name's Luke? All right, all right—we can change the names later. What's he say? Come on, come on.

AUSTIN: He says uh—*(Reading.)* "I told ya' you were a fool to follow me in here. I know this prairie like the back a' my   15
hand."

LEE: No, no, no! That's not what I said. I never said that.

AUSTIN: That's what I wrote.

LEE: It's not what I said. I never said "like the back a' my hand." That's stupid. That's one a' those—whadya' call it?   20
Whadya' call that?

AUSTIN: What?

LEE: Whadya' call it when somethin's been said a thousand times before. Whadya' call that?

AUSTIN: Um—a cliché?   25

LEE: Yeah. That's right. Cliché. That's what that is. A cliché. "The back a' my hand." That's stupid.

AUSTIN: That's what you said.

LEE: I never said that! And even if I did, that's where yer supposed to come in. That's where yer supposed to change it to   30
somethin' better.

AUSTIN: Well how am I supposed to do that and write down what you say at the same time?

LEE: Ya' just do, that's all! You hear a stupid line you change it. That's yer job.   35

AUSTIN: All right. *(Makes more notes.)*

LEE: What're you changin' it to?

AUSTIN: I'm not changing it. I'm just trying to catch up.

LEE: Well change it! We gotta' change that, we can't leave that in there like that. ". . . the back a' my hand." That's dumb.   40

AUSTIN: *(Stops writing, sits back.)* All right.

LEE: *(Pacing.)* So what'll we change it to?

AUSTIN: Um—How 'bout—"I'm on intimate terms with this prairie."

45 LEE: *(To himself considering line as he walks.)* "I'm on intimate terms with this prairie." Intimate terms, intimate terms. Intimate—that means like uh—sexual right?

AUSTIN: Well—yeah—or—

LEE: He's on sexual terms with the prairie? How dya' figure

50 that?

AUSTIN: Well it doesn't necessarily have to mean sexual.

LEE: What's it mean then?

AUSTIN: It means uh—close—personal—

LEE: All right. How's it sound? Put it into the uh—the line

55 there. Read it back. Let's see how it sounds. *(To himself.)* "Intimate terms."

AUSTIN: *(Scribbles in notebook.)* Okay. It'd go something like this: *(Reads.)* "I told ya' you were a fool to follow me in here. I'm on intimate terms with this prairie."

60 LEE: That's good. I like that. That's real good.

AUSTIN: You do?

LEE: Yeah. Don't you?

AUSTIN: Sure.

LEE: Sounds original now. "Intimate terms." That's good.

65 Okay. Now we're cookin! That has a real ring to it.

(AUSTIN makes more notes, LEE walks around, pours beer on his arms and rubs it over his chest feeling good about the new progress, as he does this MOM enters unobtrusively down left with her luggage, she stops and stares at the scene still holding luggage as the two men continue, unaware of her presence, AUSTIN absorbed in his writing, LEE cooling himself off with beer.)

LEE: *(Continues.)* "He's on intimate terms with this prairie." Sounds real mysterious and kinda' threatening at the same time.

AUSTIN: *(Writing rapidly.)* Good.

70 LEE: Now—*(LEE turns and suddenly sees MOM, he stares at her for a while, she stares back, AUSTIN keeps writing feverishly, not noticing, LEE walks slowly over to MOM and takes a closer look, long pause.)*

LEE: Mom?

(AUSTIN looks up suddenly from his writing, sees MOM, stands quickly, long pause, MOM surveys the damage.)

75 AUSTIN: Mom. What're you doing back?

MOM: I'm back.

LEE: Here, lemme take those for ya.

(LEE sets beer on counter then takes both her bags but doesn't know where to set them down in the sea of junk so he just keeps holding them.)

AUSTIN: I wasn't expecting you back so soon. I thought uh— How was Alaska?

80 MOM: Fine.

LEE: See any igloos?

MOM: No. Just glaciers.

AUSTIN: Cold huh?

MOM: What?

85 AUSTIN: It must've been cold up there?

MOM: Not really.

LEE: Musta' been colder than this here. I mean we're havin' a real scorcher here.

MOM: Oh? *(She looks at damage.)*

LEE: Yeah. Must be in the hundreds.   90

AUSTIN: You wanna' take your coat off, Mom?

MOM: No. *(Pause, she surveys space.)* What happened in here?

AUSTIN: Oh um—Me and Lee were just sort of celebrating and uh—

MOM: Celebrating?   95

AUSTIN: Yeah. Uh—Lee sold a screenplay. A story, I mean.

MOM: Lee did?

AUSTIN: Yeah.

MOM: Not you?

AUSTIN: No. Him.   100

MOM: *(To LEE.)* You sold a screenplay?

LEE: Yeah. That's right. We're just sorta' finishing it up right now. That's what we're doing here.

AUSTIN: Me and Lee are going out to the desert to live.

MOM: You and Lee?   105

AUSTIN: Yeah. I'm taking off with Lee.

MOM: *(She looks back and forth at each of them, pause.)* You gonna go live with your father?

AUSTIN: No. We're going to a different desert Mom.

MOM: I see. Well, you'll probably wind up on the same desert   110
sooner or later. What're all these toasters doing here?

AUSTIN: Well—we had kind of a contest.

MOM: Contest?

LEE: Yeah.

AUSTIN: Lee won.   115

MOM: Did you win a lot of money, Lee?

LEE: Well not yet. It's comin' in any day now.

MOM: *(To LEE.)* What happened to your shirt?

LEE: Oh. I was sweatin' like a pig and I took it off.

(AUSTIN grabs LEE's shirt off the table and tosses it to him, LEE sets down suitcases and puts his shirt on.)

MOM: Well it's one hell of a mess in here isn't it?   120

AUSTIN: Yeah, I'll clean it up for you, Mom. I just didn't know you were coming back so soon.

MOM: I didn't either.

AUSTIN: What happened?

MOM: Nothing. I just started missing all my plants.   125

(She notices dead plants.)

AUSTIN: Oh.

MOM: Oh, they're all dead aren't they. *(She crosses toward them, examines them closely.)* You didn't get a chance to water I guess.

AUSTIN: I was doing it and then Lee came and—   130

LEE: Yeah I just distracted him a whole lot here, Mom. It's not his fault.

(Pause, as MOM stares at plants.)

MOM: Oh well, one less thing to take care of I guess. *(Turns toward brothers.)* Oh, that reminds me—You boys will probably never guess who's in town. Try and guess.   135

(Long pause, brothers stare at her.)

AUSTIN: Whadya' mean, Mom?

MOM: Take a guess. Somebody very important has come to town. I read it, coming down on the Greyhound.

LEE: Somebody very important?

MOM: See if you can guess. You'll never guess.   140

AUSTIN: Mom—we're trying to uh—*(Points to writing pad.)*

MOM: Picasso. (*Pause.*) Picasso's in town. Isn't that incredible? Right now.

(*Pause.*)

AUSTIN: Picasso's dead, Mom.

145 MOM: No, he's not dead. He's visiting the museum. I read it on the bus. We have to go down there and see him.

AUSTIN: Mom—

MOM: This is the chance of a lifetime. Can you imagine? We could all go down and meet him. All three of us.

150 LEE: Uh—I don't think I'm really up fer meetin' anybody right now. I'm uh—What's his name?

MOM: Picasso! Picasso! You've never heard of Picasso? Austin, you've heard of Picasso.

AUSTIN: Mom, we're not going to have time.

155 MOM: It won't take long. We'll just hop in the car and go down there. An opportunity like this doesn't come along every day.

AUSTIN: We're gonna' be leavin' here, Mom!

(*Pause.*)

MOM: Oh.

LEE: Yeah.

(*Pause.*)

160 MOM: You're both leaving?

LEE: (*Looks at* AUSTIN.) Well we were thinkin' about that before but now I—

AUSTIN: No, we are! We're both leaving. We've got it all planned.

165 MOM: (*To* AUSTIN.) Well you can't leave. You have a family.

AUSTIN: I'm leaving. I'm getting out of here.

LEE: (*To* MOM.) I don't really think Austin's cut out for the desert do you?

MOM: No. He's not.

170 AUSTIN: I'm going with you, Lee!

MOM: He's too thin.

LEE: Yeah, he'd just burn up out there.

AUSTIN: (*To* LEE.) We just gotta' finish this screenplay and then we're gonna' take off. That's the plan. That's what you

175 said. Come on, let's get back to work, Lee.

LEE: I can't work under these conditions here. It's too hot.

AUSTIN: Then we'll do it on the desert.

LEE: Don't be tellin' me what we're gonna' do!

MOM: Don't shout in the house.

180 LEE: We're just gonna' have to postpone the whole deal.

AUSTIN: I can't postpone it! It's gone past postponing! I'm doing everything you said. I'm writing down exactly what you tell me.

LEE: Yeah, but you were right all along see. It is a dumb story.

185 "Two lamebrains chasin' each other across Texas." That's what you said, right?

AUSTIN: I never said that.

(LEE *sneers in* AUSTIN's *face then turns to* MOM.)

LEE: I'm gonna' just borrow some a' your antiques, Mom. You don't mind do ya'? Just a few plates and things. Silverware.

(LEE *starts going through all the cupboards in kitchen pulling out plates and stacking them on counter as* MOM *and* AUSTIN *watch.*)

190 MOM: You don't have any utensils on the desert?

LEE: Nah, I'm fresh out.

AUSTIN: (*To* LEE.) What're you doing?

MOM: Well some of those are very old. Bone China.

LEE: I'm tired of eatin' outa' my bare hands, ya' know. It's not civilized. 195

AUSTIN: (*To* LEE.) What're you doing? We made a deal!

MOM: Couldn't you borrow the plastic ones instead? I have plenty of plastic ones.

LEE: (*As he stacks plates.*) It's not the same. Plastic's not the same at all. What I need is somethin' authentic. Somethin' 200 to keep me in touch. It's easy to get outa' touch out there. Don't worry I'll get 'em back to ya'.

(AUSTIN *rushes up to* LEE, *grabs him by shoulders.*)

AUSTIN: You can't just drop the whole thing, Lee!

(LEE *turns, pushes* AUSTIN *in the chest knocking him backwards into the alcove,* MOM *watches numbly,* LEE *returns to collecting the plates, silverware, etc.*)

MOM: You boys shouldn't fight in the house. Go outside and fight. 205

LEE: I'm not fightin'. I'm leavin'.

MOM: There's been enough damage done already.

LEE: (*His back to* AUSTIN *and* MOM, *stacking dishes on counter.*) I'm clearin' outa' here once and for all. All this town does is drive a man insane. Look what it's done to 210 Austin there. I'm not lettin' that happen to me. Sell myself down the river. No sir. I'd rather be a hundred miles from nowhere than let that happen to me.

(*During this* AUSTIN *has picked up the ripped-out phone from the floor and wrapped the cord tightly around both his hands, he lunges at* LEE *whose back is still to him, wraps the cord around* LEE's *neck, plants a foot in* LEE's *back and pulls back on the cord, tightening it,* LEE *chokes desperately, can't speak and can't reach* AUSTIN *with his arms,* AUSTIN *keeps applying pressure on* LEE's *back with his foot, bending him into the sink,* MOM *watches.*)

AUSTIN: (*Tightening cord.*) You're not goin' anywhere! You're not takin' anything with you. You're not takin' my car! You're not takin' the dishes! You're not takin' anything! You're stayin' 215 right here!

MOM: You'll have to stop fighting in the house. There's plenty of room outside to fight. You've got the whole outdoors to fight in. 220

(LEE *tries to tear himself away, he crashes across the stage like an enraged bull dragging* AUSTIN *with him, he snorts and bellows but* AUSTIN *hangs on and manages to keep clear of* LEE's *attempts to grab him, they crash into the table, to the floor,* LEE *is face down thrashing wildly and choking,* AUSTIN *pulls cord tighter, stands with one foot planted on* LEE's *back and the cord stretched taut.*)

AUSTIN: (*Holding cord.*) Gimme back my keys, Lee! Take the keys out! Take 'em out!

(LEE *desperately tries to dig in his pockets, searching for the car keys,* MOM *moves closer.*)

MOM: (*Calmly to* AUSTIN.) You're not killing him are you?

AUSTIN: I don't know. I don't know if I'm killing him. I'm stopping him. That's all. I'm just stopping him. 225

(LEE *thrashes but* AUSTIN *is relentless.*)

MOM: You oughta' let him breathe a little bit.

AUSTIN: Throw the keys out, Lee!

(LEE *finally gets keys out and throws them on floor but out of* AUSTIN's *reach,* AUSTIN *keeps pressure on cord, pulling* LEE's *neck back,* LEE *gets one hand to the cord but can't relieve the pressure.*)

Reach me those keys would ya', Mom.

MOM: (*Not moving.*) Why are you doing this to him?

230 AUSTIN: Reach me the keys!

MOM: Not until you stop choking him.

AUSTIN: I can't stop choking him! He'll kill me if I stop choking him!

MOM: He won't kill you. He's your brother.

235 AUSTIN: Just get me the keys would ya'!

(*Pause.* MOM *picks keys up off floor, hands them to* AUSTIN.)

AUSTIN: (*To* MOM.) Thanks.

MOM: Will you let him go now?

AUSTIN: I don't know. He's not gonna' let me get outa' here.

MOM: Well you can't kill him.

240 AUSTIN: I can kill him! I can easily kill him. Right now. Right here. All I gotta' do is just tighten up. See? (*He tightens cord,* LEE *thrashes wildly.* AUSTIN *releases pressure a little, maintaining control.*) Ya' see that?

MOM: That's a savage thing to do.

245 AUSTIN: Yeah well don't tell me I can't kill him because I can. I can just twist. I can just keep twisting. (AUSTIN *twists the cord tighter,* LEE *weakens, his breathing changes to a short rasp.*)

MOM: Austin!

(AUSTIN *relieves pressure,* LEE *breathes easier but* AUSTIN *keeps him under control.*)

250 AUSTIN: (*eyes on* LEE, *holding cord.*) I'm goin' to the desert. There's nothing stopping me. I'm going by myself to the desert.

(MOM *moving toward her luggage.*)

MOM: Well, I'm going to go check into a motel. I can't stand this anymore.

255 AUSTIN: Don't go yet!

(MOM *pauses.*)

MOM: I can't stay here. This is worse than being homeless.

AUSTIN: I'll get everything fixed up for you, Mom. I promise. Just stay for a while.

MOM: (*Picking up luggage.*) You're going to the desert.

AUSTIN: Just wait! 260

(LEE *thrashes,* AUSTIN *subdues him,* MOM *watches holding luggage, pause.*)

MOM: It was the worst feeling being up there. In Alaska. Staring out a window. I never felt so desperate before. That's why when I saw that article on Picasso I thought—

AUSTIN: Stay here, Mom. This is where you live.

(*She looks around the stage.*)

MOM: I don't recognize it at all. 265

(*She exits with luggage,* AUSTIN *makes a move toward her but* LEE *starts to struggle and* AUSTIN *subdues him again with cord, pause.*)

AUSTIN: (*Holding cord.*) Lee? I'll make ya' a deal. You let me get outa' here. Just let me get to my car. All right, Lee? Gimme a little headstart and I'll turn you loose. Just gimme a little headstart. All right?

(LEE *makes no response,* AUSTIN *slowly releases tension cord, still nothing from* LEE.)

AUSTIN: Lee? 270

(LEE *is motionless,* AUSTIN *very slowly begins to stand, still keeping a tenuous hold on the cord and his eyes riveted to* LEE *for any sign of movement,* AUSTIN *slowly drops the cord and stands, he stares down at* LEE *who appears to be dead.*)

AUSTIN: (*Whispers.*) Lee?

(*Pause,* AUSTIN *considers, looks toward exit, back to* LEE, *then makes a small movement as if to leave. Instantly* LEE *is on his feet and moves toward exit, blocking* AUSTIN's *escape. They square off to each other, keeping a distance between them. Pause, a single coyote heard in distance, lights fade softly into moonlight, the figures of the brothers now appear to be caught in a vast desert-like landscape, they are very still but watchful for the next move, lights go slowly to black as the after-image of the brothers pulses in the dark, coyote fades.*)

■ AUGUST WILSON ■

August Wilson was born in 1945 and raised on "The Hill," the black ghetto of Pittsburgh. He dropped out of school in the ninth grade, but supported himself with odd jobs while he continued his self-education, reading and studying; he also began to write poems and stories on the changing problems of race relations in America. He founded a theater in Pittsburgh in the mid-1960s, and then founded Black Horizons Theater Company there in 1968. His first play, *Jitney*, was staged in 1978. Wilson then applied to study playwriting at the Eugene O'Neill Theater Center's National Playwright's Conference, where he submitted the text of *Ma Rainey's Black Bottom*, which was read by the eminent African-American stage director Lloyd Richards, who had brought Lorraine Hansberry's *A Raisin in the Sun* to Broadway in 1959. Richards read the play and produced it at the Yale Repertory Theater in 1984 before bringing it to Broadway. *Ma Rainey's Black Bottom* is the first of several plays examining African-American history in the twentieth century; it was followed by *Fences* (1985)—which won the Pulitzer Prize—*Joe Turner's Come and Gone* (1986), *The Piano Lesson* (1987), and *Two Trains Running* (1991). His most recent play, *Seven Guitars*, opened in Chicago in 1995.

FENCES

Set in 1957, the action of *Fences* sits on the brink of the civil rights movement and outlines the challenges facing African Americans whose legal freedoms had yet to become a social reality. The play is—as its final funeral scene implies—deeply reminiscent of Arthur Miller's *Death of a Salesman*, and suggests that realism is in many way still the dominant mode of American theater. Like Miller's play, it is about a hardworking man whose responsibilities to his family fall athwart his dreams of happiness, a conflict that finally costs him both. However, while Miller's Willy Loman is victimized by his belief in the "American Dream," Wilson's Troy Maxson lives his life on the underside of that dream. Thrown out of his home at fourteen by his father, Troy moved north to Pittsburgh; unable to find work, he made a living through petty crime until he was caught and sentenced to fifteen years' imprisonment. On his release, he found his wife and child and began a career in baseball, playing in the Negro Leagues. Integration came to baseball, and by 1957 Jackie Robinson, Hank Aaron, and a young Roberto Clemente are all playing in the major leagues—but it is too late for Troy. He is now working as a trash collector, fighting the company to let African Americans drive the garbage trucks as well as pick up the trash.

Like Willy Loman, Troy, too, is a family man. The family is Troy's refuge from the racism and defeat of his daily life, and his proudest accomplishment as well: he has forced himself to shoulder the responsibility of providing for his children and of loving his wife, a responsibility that lends his life purpose and direction. As he says to Rose in Act One, "Woman . . . I do the best I can do. . . . We go upstairs in that room at night . . . and I fall down on you and try to blast a hole into forever. I get up Monday morning . . . find my lunch on the table. I go out. Make my way. Find my strength to carry me through to the next Friday." However, as Rose notes, the world is changing around Troy, and these changes threaten the life that he has made. His son Cory is being recruited on a football scholarship. Troy, his own exploitation by the white-dominated sports industry still in mind, forces Cory to quit the team, and so to pass up the scholarship—and the chance to go to college. Nor does Troy shoulder the rest of his family life easily. He cares for his mentally-handicapped brother Gabriel, but eventually has him committed to a mental hospital in order to get half of his government pension. Despite his love for and gratitude to Rose, he has an affair with another woman, who dies delivering their daughter. Although family life has been Troy's salvation, it also has hemmed him in—in the dead-end jobs, the constant poverty, the fence he builds at the end of the play. He risks it all for the chance of some happiness with Alberta and loses; Rose takes in Troy's daughter: "From right now . . . this child got a mother. But you a womanless man." He fights Cory, and much as his own father had thrown him out of the house, he forces his own son to leave as well.

The joyous, mournful conclusion of *Fences*—when Gabriel dances Troy's soul into heaven—perhaps provides the best commentary on the life of Troy Maxson. Suffering the indignities and humiliation of racism throughout his life, Troy built a stable home for himself, a life. As a defense against the world, perhaps, that life was bound to crumble, particularly as pressure of social change forced Troy to deal with a future he had never imagined. In Wilson's final image, however, Troy's life is celebrated, a thing of rough and rugged beauty, demanding our attention and respect.

FENCES

AUGUST WILSON

— CHARACTERS —

TROY MAXSON
JIM BONO, TROY's *friend*
ROSE, TROY's *wife*
LYONS, TROY's *oldest son by previous marriage*
GABRIEL, TROY's *brother*
CORY, TROY *and* ROSE's *son*
RAYNELL, TROY's *daughter*

> When the sins of our fathers visit us
> We do not have to play host.
> We can banish them with forgiveness
> As God, in His Largeness and Laws.
> —August Wilson

SETTING: *The setting is the yard which fronts the only entrance to the* Maxson *household, an ancient two-story brick house set back off a small alley in a big-city neighborhood. The entrance to the house is gained by two or three steps leading to a wooden porch badly in need of paint.*

A relatively recent addition to the house and running its full width, the porch lacks congruence. It is a sturdy porch with a flat roof. One or two chairs of dubious value sit at one end where the kitchen window opens onto the porch. An old-fashioned icebox stands silent guard at the opposite end.

The yard is a small dirt yard, partially fenced, except for the last scene, with a wooden sawhorse, a pile of lumber, and other fence-building equipment set off to the side. Opposite is a tree from which hangs a ball made of rags. A baseball bat leans against the tree. Two oil drums serve as garbage receptacles and sit near the house at right to complete the setting.

THE PLAY: *Near the turn of the century, the destitute of Europe sprang on the city with tenacious claws and an honest and solid dream. The city devoured them. They swelled its belly until it burst into a thousand furnaces and sewing machines, a thousand butcher shops and bakers' ovens, a thousand churches and hospitals and funeral parlors and moneylenders. The city grew. It nourished itself and offered each man a partnership limited only by his talent, his guile, and his willingness and capacity for hard work. For the immigrants of Europe, a dream dared and won true.*

The descendants of African slaves were offered no such welcome or participation. They came from places called the Carolinas and the Virginias, Georgia, Alabama, Mississippi, and Tennessee. They came strong, eager, searching. The city rejected them and they fled and settled along the riverbanks and under bridges in shallow, ramshackle houses made of sticks and tar-paper. They collected rags and wood. They sold the use of their muscles and their bodies. They cleaned houses and washed clothes, they shined shoes, and in quiet desperation and vengeful pride, they stole, and lived in pursuit of their own dream. That they could breathe free, finally, and stand to meet life with the force of dignity and whatever eloquence the heart could call upon.

By 1957, the hard-won victories of the European immigrants had solidified the industrial might of America. War had been confronted and won with new energies that used loyalty and patriotism as its fuel. Life was rich, full, and flourishing. The Milwaukee Braves won the World Series, and the hot winds of change that would make the sixties a turbulent, racing, dangerous, and provocative decade had not yet begun to blow full.

— ACT ONE —

SCENE I

It is 1957. TROY *and* BONO *enter the yard, engaged in conversation.* TROY *is fifty-three years old, a large man with thick, heavy hands; it is this largeness that he strives to fill out and make an accommodation with. Together with his blackness, his largeness informs his sensibilities and the choices he has made in his life.*

Of the two men, BONO *is obviously the follower. His commitment to their friendship of thirty-odd years is rooted in his admiration of* TROY's *honesty, capacity for hard work, and his strength, which* BONO *seeks to emulate.*

It is Friday night, payday, and the one night of the week the two men engage in a ritual of talk and drink. TROY *is usually the most talkative and at times he can be crude and almost vulgar, though he is capable of rising to profound heights of expression. The men carry lunch buckets and wear or carry burlap aprons and are dressed in clothes suitable to their jobs as garbage collectors.*

BONO: Troy, you ought to stop that lying!

TROY: I ain't lying! The nigger had a watermelon this big.

(He indicates with his hands.)

Talking about . . . "What watermelon, Mr. Rand?" I liked to fell out! "What watermelon, Mr. Rand?" . . . And it sitting there big as life.   5

BONO: What did Mr. Rand say?

TROY: Ain't said nothing. Figure if the nigger too dumb to know he carrying a watermelon, he wasn't gonna get much sense out of him. Trying to hide that great big old watermelon under his coat. Afraid to let the white man see him   10 carry it home.

BONO: I'm like you . . . I ain't got no time for them kind of people.

TROY: Now what he look like getting mad cause he see the man from the union talking to Mr. Rand?   15

BONO: He come to me talking about . . . "Maxson gonna get us fired." I told him to get away from me with that. He walked away from me calling you a troublemaker. What Mr. Rand say?

20 TROY: Ain't said nothing. He told me to go down the Commissioner's office next Friday. They called me down there to see them.

BONO: Well, as long as you got your complaint filed, they can't fire you. That's what one of them white fellows tell me.

25 TROY: I ain't worried about them firing me. They gonna fire me cause I asked a question? That's all I did. I went to Mr. Rand and asked him, "Why?" Why you got the white mens driving and the colored lifting?" Told him, "what's the matter, don't I count? You think only white fellows got

30 sense enough to drive a truck. That ain't no paper job! Hell, anybody can drive a truck. How come you got all whites driving and the colored lifting?" He told me "take it to the union." Well, hell, that's what I done! Now they wanna come up with this pack of lies.

35 BONO: I told Brownie if the man come and ask him any questions . . . just tell the truth! It ain't nothing but something they done trumped up on you cause you filed a complaint on them.

TROY: Brownie don't understand nothing. All I want them to

40 do is change the job description. Give everybody a chance to drive the truck. Brownie can't see that. He ain't got that much sense.

BONO: How you figure he be making out with that gal be up at Taylors' all the time . . . that Alberta gal?

45 TROY: Same as you and me. Getting just as much as we is. Which is to say nothing.

BONO: It is, huh? I figure you doing a little better than me . . . and I ain't saying what I'm doing.

TROY: Aw, nigger, look here . . . I know you. If you had got any-

50 where near that gal, twenty minutes later you be looking to tell somebody. And the first one you gonna tell . . . that you gonna want to brag to . . . is gonna be me.

BONO: I ain't saying that. I see where you be eyeing her.

TROY: I eye all the women. I don't miss nothing. Don't never

55 let nobody tell you Troy Maxson don't eye the women.

BONO: You been doing more than eyeing her. You done bought her a drink or two.

TROY: Hell yeah, I bought her a drink! What that mean? I bought you one, too. What that mean cause I buy her a

60 drink? I'm just being polite.

BONO: It's alright to buy her one drink. That's what you call being polite. But when you wanna be buying two or three . . . that's what you call eyeing her.

TROY: Look here, as long as you known me . . . you ever

65 known me to chase after women?

BONO: Hell yeah! Long as I done known you. You forgetting I knew you when.

TROY: Naw, I'm talking about since I been married to Rose?

BONO: Oh, not since you been married to Rose. Now, that's

70 the truth, there. I can say that.

TROY: Alright then! Case closed.

BONO: I see you be walking up around Alberta's house. You supposed to be at Taylors' and you be walking up around there.

75 TROY: What you watching where I'm walking for? I ain't watching after you.

BONO: I seen you walking around there more than once.

TROY: Hell, you liable to see me walking anywhere! That don't mean nothing cause you see me walking around there.

80 BONO: Where she come from anyway? She just kinda showed up one day.

TROY: Tallahassee. You can look at her and tell she one of them Florida gals. They got some big healthy women down there. Grow them right up out the ground. Got a little bit of

85 Indian in her. Most of them niggers down in Florida got some Indian in them.

BONO: I don't know about that Indian part. But she damn sure big and healthy. Woman wear some big stockings. Got them great big old legs and hips as wide as the Mississippi River.

90 TROY: Legs don't mean nothing. You don't do nothing but push them out of the way. But them hips cushion the ride!

BONO: Troy, you ain't got no sense.

TROY: It's the truth! Like you riding on Goodyears!

(ROSE *enters from the house. She is ten years younger than* TROY, *her devotion to him stems from her recognition of the possibilities of her life without him: a succession of abusive men and their babies, a life of partying and running the streets, the Church, or aloneness with its attendant pain and frustration. She recognizes* TROY's *spirit as a fine and illuminating one and she either ignores or forgives his faults, only some of which she recognizes. Though she doesn't drink, her presence is an integral part of the Friday night rituals. She alternates between the porch and the kitchen, where supper preparations are under way.*)

ROSE: What you all out here getting into?

95 TROY: What you worried about what we getting into for? This is men talk, woman.

ROSE: What I care what you all talking about? Bono, you gonna stay for supper?

BONO: No, I thank you, Rose. But Lucille say she cooking up a

100 pot of pigfeet.

TROY: Pigfeet! Hell, I'm going home with you! Might even stay the night if you got some pigfeet. You got something in there to top them pigfeet, Rose?

ROSE: I'm cooking up some chicken. I got some chicken and

105 collard greens.

TROY: Well, go on back in the house and let me and Bono finish what we was talking about. This is men talk. I got some talk for you later. You know what kind of talk I mean. You go on and powder it up.

110 ROSE: Troy Maxson, don't you start that now!

TROY: (*Puts his arm around her.*) Aw, woman . . . come here. Look here, Bono . . . when I met this woman . . . I got out that place, say, "Hitch up my pony, saddle up my mare . . . there's a woman out there for me somewhere. I looked here.

115 Looked there. Saw Rose and latched on to her." I latched on to her and told her—I'm gonna tell you the truth—I told her, "Baby, I don't wanna marry, I just wanna be your man." Rose told me . . . tell him what you told me, Rose.

ROSE: I told him if he wasn't the marrying kind, then move out

120 the way so the marrying kind could find me.

TROY: That's what she told me. "Nigger, you in my way. You blocking the view! Move out the way so I can find me a husband." I thought it over two or three days. Come back—

ROSE: Ain't no two or three days nothing. You was back the

125 same night.

TROY: Come back, told her . . . "Okay, baby . . . but I'm gonna buy me a banty rooster and put him out there in the backyard

130 . . . and when he sees a stranger come, he'll flap his wings and crow . . ." Look here, Bono, I could watch the front door by myself . . . it was that back door I was worried about.

ROSE: Troy, you ought not talk like that. Troy ain't doing nothing but telling a lie.

TROY: Only thing is . . . when we first got married . . . forget the rooster . . . we ain't had no yard!

135 BONO: I hear you tell it. Me and Lucille was staying down there on Logan Street. Had two rooms with the outhouse in the back. I ain't mind the outhouse none. But when that goddamn wind blow through there in the winter . . . that's what I'm talking about! To this day I wonder why in the hell

140 I ever stayed down there for six long years. But see, I didn't know I could do no better. I thought only white folks had inside toilets and things.

ROSE: There's a lot of people don't know they can do no better than they doing now. That's just something you got to learn.

145 A lot of folks still shop at Bella's.

TROY: Ain't nothing wrong with shopping at Bella's. She got fresh food.

ROSE: I ain't said nothing about if she got fresh food. I'm talking about what she charge. She charge ten cents more than

150 the A&P.

TROY: The A&P ain't never done nothing for me. I spends my money where I'm treated right. I go down to Bella, say, "I need a loaf of bread, I'll pay you Friday." She give it to me. What sense that make when I got money to go and spend it

155 somewhere else and ignore the person who done right by me? That ain't in the Bible.

ROSE: We ain't talking about what's in the Bible. What sense it make to shop there when she overcharge?

TROY: You shop where you want to. I'll do my shopping where

160 the people been good to me.

ROSE: Well, I don't think it's right for her to overcharge. That's all I was saying.

BONO: Look here . . . I got to get on. Lucille going be raising all kind of hell.

165 TROY: Where you going, nigger? We ain't finished this pint. Come here, finish this pint.

BONO: Well, hell, I am . . . if you ever turn the bottle loose.

TROY: (*Hands him the bottle.*) The only thing I say about the A&P is I'm glad Cory got that job down there. Help him take

170 care of his school clothes and things. Gabe done moved out and things getting tight around here. He got that job . . . He can start to look out for himself.

ROSE: Cory done went and got recruited by a college football team.

175 TROY: I told that boy about that football stuff. The white man ain't gonna let him get nowhere with that football. I told him when he first come to me with it. Now you come telling me he done went and got more tied up in it. He ought to go and get recruited in how to fix cars or something where he can

180 make a living.

ROSE: He ain't talking about making no living playing football. It's just something the boys in school do. They gonna send a recruiter by to talk to you. He'll tell you he ain't talking about making no living playing football. It's a honor to

185 be recruited.

TROY: It ain't gonna get him nowhere. Bono'll tell you that.

BONO: If he be like you in the sports . . . he's gonna be alright. Ain't but two men ever played baseball as good as you. That's

190 Babe Ruth and Josh Gibson. Them's the only two men ever hit more home runs than you.

TROY: What it ever get me? Ain't got a pot to piss in or a window to throw it out of.

ROSE: Times have changed since you was playing baseball,

195 Troy. That was before the war. Times have changed a lot since then.

TROY: How in hell they done changed?

ROSE: They got lots of colored boys playing ball now. Baseball and football.

200 BONO: You right about that, Rose. Times have changed, Troy. You just come along too early.

TROY: There ought not never have been no time called too early! Now you take that fellow . . . what's that fellow they had playing right field for the Yankees back then? You know

205 who I'm talking about, Bono. Used to play right field for the Yankees.

ROSE: Selkirk?

TROY: Selkirk! That's it! Man batting .269, understand? .269. What kind of sense that make? I was hitting .432 with thirty-

210 seven home runs! Man batting .269 and playing right field for the Yankees! I saw Josh Gibson's daughter yesterday. She walking around with raggedy shoes on her feet. Now I bet you Selkirk's daughter ain't walking around with raggedy shoes on her feet! I bet you that!

215 ROSE: They got a lot of colored baseball players now. Jackie Robinson was the first. Folks had to wait for Jackie Robinson.

TROY: I done seen a hundred niggers play baseball better than Jackie Robinson. Hell, I know some teams Jackie Robinson couldn't even make! What you talking about Jackie Robin-

220 son. Jackie Robinson wasn't nobody. I'm talking about if you could play ball then they ought to have let you play. Don't care what color you were. Come telling me I come along too early. If you could play . . . then they ought to have let you play.

(TROY *takes a long drink from the bottle.*)

225 ROSE: You gonna drink yourself to death. You don't need to be drinking like that.

TROY: Death ain't nothing. I done seen him. Done wrassled with him. You can't tell me nothing about death. Death ain't nothing but a fastball on the outside corner. And you know what I'll do to that! Lookee here, Bono . . . am I lying? You

230 get one of them fastballs, about waist high, over the outside corner of the plate where you can get the meat of the bat on it . . . and good god! You can kiss it goodbye. Now, am I lying?

BONO: Naw, you telling the truth there. I seen you do it.

235 TROY: If I'm lying . . . that 450 feet worth of lying!

(*Pause.*)

That's all death is to me. A fastball on the outside corner.

ROSE: I don't know why you want to get on talking about death.

240 TROY: Ain't nothing wrong with talking about death. That's part of life. Everybody gonna die. You gonna die, I'm gonna die. Bono's gonna die. Hell, we all gonna die.

ROSE: But you ain't got to talk about it. I don't like to talk about it.

245 TROY: You the one brought it up. Me and Bono was talking about baseball . . . you tell me I'm gonna drink myself to

death. Ain't that right, Bono? You know I don't drink this but one night out of the week. That's Friday night. I'm gonna drink just enough to where I can handle it. Then I cuts it loose. I leave it alone. So don't you worry about me drinking myself to death. 'Cause I ain't worried about Death. I done seen him. I done wrestled with him.

Look here, Bono . . . I looked up one day and Death was marching straight at me. Like Soldiers on Parade! The Army of Death was marching straight at me. The middle of July, 1941. It got real cold just like it be winter. It seem like Death himself reached out and touched me on the shoulder. He touch me just like I touch you. I got cold as ice and Death standing there grinning at me.

ROSE: Troy, why don't you hush that talk.

TROY: I say . . . What you want, Mr. Death? You be wanting me? You done brought your army to be getting me? I looked him dead in the eye. I wasn't fearing nothing. I was ready to tangle. Just like I'm ready to tangle now. The Bible say be ever vigilant. That's why I don't get but so drunk. I got to keep watch.

ROSE: Troy was right down there in Mercy Hospital. You remember he had pneumonia? Laying there with a fever talking plumb out of his head.

TROY: Death standing there staring at me . . . carrying that sickle in his hand. Finally he say, "You want bound over for another year?" See, just like that . . . "You want bound over for another year?" I told him, "Bound over hell! Let's settle this now!"

It seem like he kinda fell back when I said that, and all the cold went out of me. I reached down and grabbed that sickle and threw it just as far as I could throw it . . . and me and him commenced to wrestling.

We wrestled for three days and three nights. I can't say where I found the strength from. Every time it seemed like he was gonna get the best of me, I'd reach way down deep inside myself and find the strength to do him one better.

ROSE: Every time Troy tell that story he find different ways to tell it. Different things to make up about it.

TROY: I ain't making up nothing. I'm telling you the facts of what happened. I wrestled with Death for three days and three nights and I'm standing here to tell you about it.

(Pause.)

Alright. At the end of the third night we done weakened each other to where we can't hardly move. Death stood up, throwed on his robe . . . had him a white robe with a hood on it. He throwed on that robe and went off to look for his sickle. Say, "I'll be back." Just like that. "I'll be back." I told him, say, "Yeah, but . . . you gonna have to find me!" I wasn't no fool. I wasn't going looking for him. Death ain't nothing to play with. And I know he's gonna get me. I know I got to join his army . . . his camp followers. But as long as I keep my strength and see him coming . . . as long as I keep up my vigilance . . . he's gonna have to fight to get me. I ain't going easy.

BONO: Well, look here, since you got to keep up your vigilance . . . let me have the bottle.

TROY: Aw hell, I shouldn't have told you that part. I should have left out that part.

ROSE: Troy be talking that stuff and half the time don't even know what he be talking about.

TROY: Bono know me better than that.

BONO: That's right. I know you. I know you got some Uncle Remus in your blood. You got more stories than the devil got sinners.

TROY: Aw hell, I done seen him too! Done talked with the devil.

ROSE: Troy, don't nobody wanna be hearing all that stuff.

(LYONS enters the yard from the street. Thirty-four years old, TROY's son by a previous marriage, he sports a neatly trimmed goatee, sport coat, white shirt, tieless and buttoned at the collar. Though he fancies himself a musician, he is more caught up in the rituals and "idea" of being a musician than in the actual practice of the music. He has come to borrow money from TROY, and while he knows he will be successful, he is uncertain as to what extent his lifestyle will be held up to scrutiny and ridicule.)

LYONS: Hey, Pop.

TROY: What you come "Hey, Popping" me for?

LYONS: How you doing, Rose?

(He kisses her.)

Mr. Bono. How you doing?

BONO: Hey, Lyons . . . how you been?

TROY: He must have been doing alright. I ain't seen him around here last week.

ROSE: Troy, leave your boy alone. He come by to see you and you wanna start all that nonsense.

TROY: I ain't bothering Lyons.

(Offers him the bottle.)

Here . . . get you a drink. We got an understanding. I know why he come by to see me and he know I know.

LYONS: Come on, Pop . . . I just stopped by to say hi . . . see how you was doing.

TROY: You ain't stopped by yesterday.

ROSE: You gonna stay for supper, Lyons? I got some chicken cooking in the oven.

LYONS: No, Rose . . . thanks. I was just in then neighborhood and thought I'd stop by for a minute.

TROY: You was in the neighborhood alright, nigger. You telling the truth there. You was in the neighborhood cause it's my payday.

LYONS: Well, hell, since you mentioned it . . . let me have ten dollars.

TROY: I'll be damned! I'll die and go to hell and play blackjack with the devil before I give you ten dollars.

BONO: That's what I wanna know about . . . that devil you done seen.

LYONS: What . . . Pop done seen the devil? You too much, Pops.

TROY: Yeah, I done seen him. Talked to him too!

ROSE: You ain't seen no devil. I done told you that man ain't had nothing to do with the devil. Anything you can't understand, you want to call it the devil.

TROY: Look here, Bono . . . I went down to see Hertzberger about some furniture. Got three rooms for two-ninety-eight. That what it say on the radio. "Three rooms . . . two-ninety-eight." Even made up a little song about it. Go down there . . . man tell me I can't get no credit. I'm working every day and can't get no credit. What to do? I got an empty house with some raggedy furniture in it. Cory ain't got no bed. He's sleeping on a pile of rags on the floor.

355 Working every day and can't get no credit. Come back here—Rose'll tell you—madder than hell. Sit down . . . try to figure what I'm gonna do. Come a knock on the door. Ain't been living here but three days. Who know I'm here? Open the door . . . devil standing there bigger than life.

360 White fellow . . . got on good clothes and everything. Standing there with a clipboard in his hand. I ain't had to say nothing. First words come out of his mouth was . . . "I understand you need some furniture and can't get no credit." I liked to fell over. He say "I'll give you all the credit you want, but you got to pay the interest on it." I told him,

365 "Give me three rooms worth and charge whatever you want." Next day a truck pulled up here and two men unloaded them three rooms. Man what drove the truck give me a book. Say send ten dollars, first of every month to the address in the book and everything will be alright. Say if I

370 miss a payment the devil was coming back and it'll be hell to pay. That was fifteen years ago. To this day . . . the first of the month I send my ten dollars, Rose'll tell you.

ROSE: Troy lying.

TROY: I ain't never seen that man since. Now you tell me who

375 else that could have been but the devil? I ain't sold my soul or nothing like that, you understand. Naw, I wouldn't have truck with the devil about nothing like that. I got my furniture and pays my ten dollars the first of the month just like clockwork.

380 BONO: How long you say you been paying this ten dollars a month?

TROY: Fifteen years!

BONO: Hell, ain't you finished paying for it yet? How much the man done charged you.

385 TROY: Aw hell, I done paid for it. I done paid for it ten times over! The fact is I'm scared to stop paying it.

ROSE: Troy lying. We got that furniture from Mr. Glickman. He ain't paying no ten dollars a month to nobody.

TROY: Aw hell, woman. Bono know I ain't that big a fool.

390 LYONS: I was just getting ready to say . . . I know where there's a bridge for sale.

TROY: Look here, I'll tell you this . . . it don't matter to me if he was the devil. It don't matter if the devil give credit. Somebody has got to give it.

395 ROSE: It ought to matter. You going around talking about having truck with the devil . . . God's the one you gonna have to answer to. He's the one gonna be at the Judgment.

LYONS: Yeah, well, look here, Pop . . . let me have that ten dollars. I'll give it back to you. Bonnie got a job working at the

400 hospital.

TROY: What I tell you, Bono? The only time I see this nigger is when he wants something. That's the only time I see him.

LYONS: Come on, Pop, Mr. Bono don't want to hear all that. Let me have the ten dollars. I told you Bonnie working.

405 TROY: What that mean to me? "Bonnie working." I don't care if she working. Go ask her for the ten dollars if she working. Talking about "Bonnie working." Why ain't you working?

LYONS: Aw, Pop, you know I can't find no decent job. Where am I gonna get a job at? You know I can't get no job.

410 TROY: I told you I know some people down there. I can get you on the rubbish if you want to work. I told you that the last time you came by here asking me for something.

LYONS: Naw, Pop . . . thanks. That ain't for me. I don't wanna be carrying nobody's rubbish. I don't wanna be punching

415 nobody's time clock.

TROY: What's the matter, you too good to carry people's rubbish? Where you think that ten dollars you talking about come from? I'm just supposed to haul people's rubbish and give my money to you cause you too lazy to work. You too lazy to work and wanna know why you ain't got what I got. 420

ROSE: What hospital Bonnie working at? Mercy?

LYONS: She's down at Passavant working in the laundry.

TROY: I ain't got nothing as it is. I give you that ten dollars and I got to eat beans the rest of the week. Naw . . . you ain't getting no ten dollars here. 425

LYONS: You ain't got to be eating no beans. I don't know why you wanna say that.

TROY: I ain't got no extra money. Gabe done moved over to Miss Pearl's paying her the rent and things done got tight around here. I can't afford to be giving you every payday. 430

LYONS: I ain't asked you to give me nothing. I asked you to loan me ten dollars. I know you got ten dollars.

TROY: Yeah, I got it. You know why I got it? Cause I don't throw my money away out there in the streets. You living the fast life . . . wanna be a musician . . . running around in them clubs 435 and things . . . then, you learn to take care of yourself. You ain't gonna find me going and asking nobody for nothing. I done spent too many years without.

LYONS: You and me is two different people, Pop.

TROY: I done learned my mistake and learned to do what's 440 right by it. You still trying to get something for nothing. Life don't owe you nothing. You owe it to yourself. Ask Bono. He'll tell you I'm right.

LYONS: You got your way of dealing with the world . . . I got mine. The only thing that matters to me is the music. 445

TROY: Yeah, I can see that! It don't matter how you gonna eat . . . where your next dollar is coming from. You telling the truth there.

LYONS: I know I got to eat. But I got to live too. I need something that gonna help me to get out of the bed in the morn- 450 ing. Make me feel like I belong in the world. I don't bother nobody. I just stay with my music cause that's the only way I can find to live in the world. Otherwise there ain't no telling what I might do. Now I don't come criticizing you and how you live. I just come by to ask you for ten dollars. I don't 455 wanna hear all that about how I live.

TROY: Boy, your mama did a hell of a job raising you.

LYONS: You can't change me, Pop. I'm thirty-four years old. If you wanted to change me, you should have been there when I was growing up. I come by to see you . . . ask for ten dollars 460 and you want to talk about how I was raised. You don't know nothing about how I was raised.

ROSE: Let the boy have ten dollars, Troy.

TROY: (*To* LYONS.) What the hell you looking at me for? I ain't got no ten dollars. You know what I do with my money. 465

(*To* ROSE.)

Give him ten dollars if you want him to have it.

ROSE: I will. Just as soon as you turn it loose.

TROY: (*Handing* ROSE *the money.*) There it is. Seventy-six dollars and forty-two cents. You see this, Bono? Now, I ain't gonna get but six of that back. 470

ROSE: You ought to stop telling that lie. Here, Lyons.

(*She hands him the money.*)

LYONS: Thanks, Rose. Look . . . I got to run . . . I'll see you later.

TROY: Wait a minute. You gonna say, "thanks, Rose" and ain't
475 gonna look to see where she got that ten dollars from? See
how they do me, Bono?

LYONS: I know she got it from you, Pop. Thanks. I'll give it
back to you.

TROY: There he go telling another lie. Time I see that ten dol-
480 lars . . . he'll be owing me thirty more.

LYONS: See you, Mr. Bono.

BONO: Take care, Lyons!

LYONS: Thanks, Pop. I'll see you again.

(LYONS *exits the yard.*)

TROY: I don't know why he don't go and get him a decent job
485 and take care of that woman he got.

BONO: He'll be alright, Troy. The boy is still young.

TROY: The *boy* is thirty-four years old.

ROSE: Let's not get off into all that.

BONO: Look here . . . I got to be going. I got to be getting on.
490 Lucille gonna be waiting.

TROY: (*Puts his arm around* ROSE.) See this woman, Bono? I
love this woman. I love this woman so much it hurts. I love
her so much . . . I done run out of ways of loving her. So I got
to go back to basics. Don't you come by my house Monday
495 morning talking about time to go to work . . . 'cause I'm still
gonna be stroking!

ROSE: Troy! Stop it now!

BONO: I ain't paying him no mind, Rose. That ain't nothing
but gin-talk. Go on, Troy. I'll see you Monday.

500 TROY: Don't you come by my house, nigger! I done told you
what I'm gonna be doing.

(*The lights go down to black.*)

SCENE II

The lights come up on ROSE *hanging up clothes. She hums and
sings softly to herself. It is the following morning.*

ROSE: (*Sings.*)

Jesus, be a fence all around me every day
Jesus, I want you to protect me as I travel on my way.
Jesus, be a fence all around me every day.

(TROY *enters from the house.*)

5   ROSE: (*Continued.*)

Jesus, I want you to protect me
As I travel on my way.

(*To* TROY.)

'Morning. You ready for breakfast? I can fix it soon as I finish
hanging up these clothes?

10   TROY: I got the coffee on. That'll be alright. I'll just drink
some of that this morning.

ROSE: That 651 hit yesterday. That's the second time this
month. Miss Pearl hit for a dollar . . . seem like those that
need the least always get lucky. Poor folks can't get nothing.

15   TROY: Them numbers don't know nobody. I don't know why
you fool with them. You and Lyons both.

ROSE: It's something to do.

TROY: You ain't doing nothing but throwing your money away.

ROSE: Troy, you know I don't play foolishly. I just play a nickel
20   here and a nickel there.

TROY: That's two nickels you done thrown away.

ROSE: Now I hit sometimes . . . that makes up for it. It always
comes in handy when I do hit. I don't hear you complaining
then.

25   TROY: I ain't complaining now. I just say it's foolish. Trying to
guess out of six hundred ways which way the number gonna
come. If I had all the money niggers, these Negroes, throw
away on numbers for one week—just one week—I'd be a
rich man.

30   ROSE: Well, you wishing and calling it foolish ain't gonna stop
folks from playing numbers. That's one thing for sure. Besides . . . some good things come from playing numbers.
Look where Pope done bought him that restaurant off of
numbers.

35   TROY: I can't stand niggers like that. Man ain't had two dimes
to rub together. He walking around with his shoes all run
over bumming money for cigarettes. Alright. Got lucky there
and hit the numbers . . .

ROSE: Troy, I know all about it.

40   TROY: Had good sense, I'll say that for him. He ain't throwed
his money away. I seen niggers hit the numbers and go
through two thousand dollars in four days. Man bought him
that restaurant down there . . . fixed it up real nice . . . and
then didn't want nobody to come in it! A Negro go in there
45   and can't get no kind of service. I seen a white fellow come
in there and order a bowl of stew. Pope picked all the meat
out the pot for him. Man ain't had nothing but a bowl of
meat! Negro come behind him and ain't got nothing but the
potatoes and carrots. Talking about what numbers do for
50   people, you picked a wrong example. Ain't done nothing but
make a worser fool out of him than he was before.

ROSE: Troy, you ought to stop worrying about what happened
at work yesterday.

TROY: I ain't worried. Just told me to be down there at the
55   Commissioner's office on Friday. Everybody think they
gonna fire me. I ain't worried about them firing me. You
ain't got to worry about that.

(*Pause.*)

Where's Cory? Cory in the house? (*Calls.*) Cory?

ROSE: He gone out.

60   TROY: Out, huh? He gone out 'cause he know I want him to
help me with this fence. I know how he is. That boy scared of
work.

(GABRIEL *enters. He comes halfway down the alley and, hearing*
TROY'*s voice, stops.*)

TROY: (*Continues.*) He ain't done a lick of work in his life.

ROSE: He had to go to football practice. Coach wanted them
to get in a little extra practice before the season start.

65   TROY: I got his practice . . . running out of here before he get
his chores done.

ROSE: Troy, what is wrong with you this morning? Don't nothing set right with you. Go on back in there and go to bed . . .
get up on the other side.

70   TROY: Why something got to be wrong with me? I ain't said
nothing wrong with me.

ROSE: You got something to say about everything. First it's the
numbers . . . then it's the way the man runs his restaurant . . .
then you done got on Cory. What's it gonna be next? Take a
75   look up there and see if the weather suits you . . . or is it
gonna be how you gonna put up the fence with the clothes
hanging in the yard.

TROY: You hit the nail on the head then.

80 ROSE: I know you like I know the back of my hand. Go on in there and get you some coffee . . . see if that straighten you up. 'Cause you ain't right this morning.

(TROY *starts into the house and sees* GABRIEL. GABRIEL *starts singing.* TROY's *brother, he is seven years younger than* TROY. *Injured in World War II, he has a metal plate in his head. He carries an old trumpet tied around his waist and believes with every fiber of his being that he is the Archangel Gabriel. He carries a chipped basket with an assortment of discarded fruits and vegetables he has picked up in the strip district and which he attempts to sell.*)

GABRIEL: *(Singing.)*

Yes, ma'am, I got plums
85   You ask me how I sell them
          Oh ten cents apiece
          Three for a quarter
          Come and buy now
          'Cause I'm here today
90   And tomorrow I'll be gone

(GABRIEL *enters.*)

Hey, Rose!
ROSE: How you doing, Gabe?
GABRIEL: There's Troy . . . Hey, Troy!
TROY: Hey, Gabe.

(*Exit into kitchen.*)

95 ROSE: *(To* GABRIEL.*)* What you got there?
GABRIEL: You know what I got, Rose. I got fruits and vegetables.
ROSE: *(Looking in basket.)* Where's all these plums you talking about?
GABRIEL: I ain't got no plums today, Rose. I was just singing
100   that. Have some tomorrow. Put me in a big order for plums. Have enough plums tomorrow for St. Peter and everybody.

(TROY *re-enters from kitchen, crosses to steps.*

To ROSE.)

Troy's mad at me.
TROY: I ain't mad at you. What I got to be mad at you about? You ain't done nothing to me.
105 GABRIEL: I just moved over to Miss Pearl's to keep out from in your way. I ain't mean no harm by it.
TROY: Who said anything about that? I ain't said anything about that.
GABRIEL: You ain't mad at me, is you?
110 TROY: Naw . . . I ain't mad at you, Gabe. If I was mad at you I'd tell you about it.
GABRIEL: Got me two rooms. In the basement. Got my own door too. Wanna see my key?

(*He holds up a key.*)

That's my own key! Ain't nobody else got a key like that.
115   That's my key! My two rooms!
TROY: Well, that's good, Gabe. You got your own key . . . that's good.
ROSE: You hungry, Gabe? I was just fixing to cook Troy his breakfast.

GABRIEL: I'll take some biscuits. You got some biscuits? Did   120
you know when I was in heaven . . . every morning me and St. Peter would sit down by the gate and eat some big fat biscuits? Oh, yeah! We had us a good time. We'd sit there and eat us them biscuits and then St. Peter would go off to sleep and tell me to wake him up when it's time to open the gates   125
for the judgment.
ROSE: Well, come on . . . I'll make up a batch of biscuits.

(ROSE *exits into the house.*)

GABRIEL: Troy . . . St. peter got your name in the book. I seen it. It say . . . Troy Maxson. I say . . . I know him! He got the same name like what I got. That's my brother!   130
TROY: How many times you gonna tell me that, Gabe?
GABRIEL: Ain't got my name in the book. Don't have to have my name. I done died and went to heaven. He got your name though. One morning St. Peter was looking at his book . . . marking it for the judgment . . . and he let me see   135
your name. Got it in there under M. Got Rose's name . . . I ain't seen it like I seen yours . . . but I know it's in there. He got a great big book. Got everybody's name what was ever been born. That's what he told me. But I seen your name. Seen it with my own eyes.   140
TROY: Go on in the house there. Rose going to fix you something to eat.
GABRIEL: Oh, I ain't hungry. I done had breakfast with Aunt Jemimah. She come by and cooked me up a whole mess of flapjacks. Remember how we used to eat them flapjacks.   145
TROY: Go on in the house and get you something to eat now.
GABRIEL: I got to go sell my plums. I done sold some tomatoes. Got me two quarters. Wanna see?

(*He shows* TROY *his quarters.*)

I'm gonna save them and buy me a new horn so St. Peter can hear me when it's time to open the gates.   150

(GABRIEL *stops suddenly. Listens.*)

Hear that? That's the hellhounds. I got to chase them out of here. Go on get out of here! Get out!

(GABRIEL *exits singing.*)

Better get ready for the judgment
Better get ready for the judgment
My Lord is coming down   155

(ROSE *enters from the house.*)

TROY: He gone off somewhere.
GABRIEL: *(Offstage.)*

Better get ready for the judgment
Better get ready for the judgment morning
Better get ready for the judgment   160
My God is coming down

ROSE: He ain't eating right. Miss Pearl say she can't get him to eat nothing.
TROY: What you want me to do about it, Rose? I done did everything I can for the man. I can't make him get well.   165
Man got half his head blown away . . . what you expect?
ROSE: Seem like something ought to be done to help him.
TROY: Man don't bother nobody. He just mixed up from that metal plate he got in his head. Ain't no sense for him to go back into the hospital.   170

ROSE: Least he be eating right. They can help him take care of himself.

TROY: Don't nobody wanna be locked up, Rose. What you wanna lock him up for? Man go over there and fight the war
175 . . . messin' around with them Japs, get half his head blown off . . . and they give him a lousy three thousand dollars. And I had to swoop down on that.

ROSE: Is you fixing to go into that again?

TROY: That's the only way I got a roof over my head . . . cause
180 of that metal plate.

ROSE: Ain't no sense you blaming yourself for nothing. Gabe wasn't in no condition to manage that money. You done what was right by him. Can't nobody say you ain't done what was right by him. Look how long you took care of him . . .
185 till he wanted to have his own place and moved over there with Miss Pearl.

TROY: That ain't what I'm saying, woman! I'm just stating the facts. If my brother didn't have that metal plate in his head . . . I wouldn't have a pot to piss in or a window to throw it
190 out of. And I'm fifty-three years old. Now see if you can understand that!

(TROY *gets up from the porch and starts to exit the yard.*)

ROSE: Where you going off to? You been running out of here every Saturday for weeks. I thought you was gonna work on this fence?

195 TROY: I'm gonna walk down to Taylors'. Listen to the ball game. I'll be back in a bit. I'll work on it when I get back.

(*He exits the yard. The lights go to black.*)

SCENE III

The lights come up on the yard. It is four hours later. ROSE *is taking down the clothes from the line.* CORY *enters carrying his football equipment.*

ROSE: Your daddy like to had a fit with you running out of here this morning without doing your chores.

CORY: I told you I had to go to practice.

ROSE: He say you were supposed to help him with this fence.

5 CORY: He been saying that the last four or five Saturdays, and then he don't never do nothing, but go down to Taylors'. Did you tell him about the recruiter?

ROSE: Yeah, I told him.

CORY: What he say?

10 ROSE: He ain't said nothing too much. You get in there and get started on your chores before he gets back. Go on and scrub down them steps before he gets back here hollering and carrying on.

CORY: I'm hungry. What you got to eat, Mama?

15 ROSE: Go on and get started on your chores. I got some meat loaf in there. Go on and make you a sandwich . . . and don't leave no mess in there.

(CORY *exits into the house.* ROSE *continues to take down the clothes.* TROY *enters the yard and sneaks up and grabs her from behind.*)

Troy! Go on, now. You liked to scared me to death. What was the score of the game? Lucille had me on the phone and I
20 couldn't keep up with it.

TROY: What I care about the game? Come here, woman.

(*He tries to kiss her.*)

ROSE: I thought you went down Taylors' to listen to the game. Go on, Troy! You supposed to be putting up this fence.

TROY: (*Attempting to kiss her again.*) I'll put it up when I finish with what is at hand. 25

ROSE: Go on, Troy. I ain't studying you.

TROY: (*Chasing after her.*) I'm studying you . . . fixing to do my homework!

ROSE: Troy, you better leave me alone.

TROY: Where's Cory? That boy brought his butt home yet? 30

ROSE: He's in the house doing his chores.

TROY: (*Calling.*) Cory! Get your butt out here, boy!

(ROSE *exits into the house with the laundry.* TROY *goes over to the pile of wood, picks up a board, and starts sawing.* CORY *enters from the house.*)

TROY: You just now coming in here from leaving this morning?

CORY: Yeah, I had to go to football practice.

TROY: Yeah, what? 35

CORY: Yessir.

TROY: I ain't but two seconds off you noway. The garbage sitting in there overflowing . . . you ain't done none of your chores . . . and you come in here talking about "Yeah."

CORY: I was just getting ready to do my chores now, Pop . . . 40

TROY: Your first chore is to help me with this fence on Saturday. Everything else come after that. Now get that saw and cut them boards.

(CORY *takes the saw and begins cutting the boards.* TROY *continues working. There is a long pause.*)

CORY: Hey, Pop . . . why don't you buy a TV?

TROY: What I want with a TV? What I want one of them for? 45

CORY: Everybody got one. Earl, Ba Bra . . . Jesse!

TROY: I ain't asked you who had one. I say what I want with one?

CORY: So you can watch it. They got lots of things on TV. Baseball games and everything. We could watch the World 50 Series.

TROY: Yeah . . . and how much this TV cost?

CORY: I don't know. They got them on sale for around two hundred dollars.

TROY: Two hundred dollars, huh? 55

CORY: That ain't that much, Pop.

TROY: Naw, it's just two hundred dollars. See that roof you got over your head at night? Let me tell you something about that roof. It's been over ten years since that roof was last tarred. See now . . . the snow come this winter and sit up 60 there on that roof like it is . . . and it's gonna seep inside. It's just gonna be a little bit . . . ain't gonna hardly notice it. Then the next thing you know, it's gonna be leaking all over the house. Then the wood rot from all that water and you gonna need a whole new roof. Now, how much you think it 65 cost to get that roof tarred?

CORY: I don't know.

TROY: Two hundred and sixty-four dollars . . . cash money. While you thinking about a TV, I got to be thinking about the roof . . . and whatever else go wrong around here. Now if 70 you had two hundred dollars, what would you do . . . fix the roof or buy a TV?

CORY: I'd buy a TV. Then when the roof started to leak . . . when it needed fixing . . . I'd fix it.

75 TROY: Where you gonna get the money from? You done spent it for a TV. You gonna sit up and watch the water run all over your brand new TV.

CORY: Aw, Pop. You got money. I know you do.

TROY: Where I got it at, Huh?

80 CORY: You got it in the bank.

TROY: You wanna see my bankbook? You wanna see that seventy-three dollars and twenty-two cents I got sitting up in there.

CORY: You ain't got to pay for it all at one time. You can put a
85 down payment on it and carry it on home with you.

TROY: Not me. I ain't gonna owe nobody nothing if I can help it. Miss a payment and they come and snatch it right out your house. Then what you got? Now, soon as I get two hundred dollars clear, then I'll buy a TV. Right now, as soon as I
90 get two hundred and sixty-four dollars, I'm gonna have this roof tarred.

CORY: Aw . . . Pop!

TROY: You go on and get you two hundred dollars and buy one if ya want it. I got better things to do with my money.

95 CORY: I can't get no two hundred dollars. I ain't never seen two hundred dollars.

TROY: I'll tell you what . . . you get you a hundred dollars and I'll put the other hundred with it.

CORY: Alright, I'm gonna show you.

100 TROY: You gonna show me how you can cut them boards right now.

(CORY *begins to cut the boards. There is a long pause.*)

CORY: The Pirates won today. That makes five in a row.

TROY: I ain't thinking about the Pirates. Got an all-white team. Got that boy . . . that Puerto Rican boy . . . Clemente. Don't
105 even half-play him. That boy could be something if they give him a chance. Play him one day and sit him on the bench the next.

CORY: He gets a lot of chances to play.

TROY: I'm talking about playing regular. Playing every day so
110 you can get your timing. That's what I'm talking about.

CORY: They got some white guys on the team that don't play every day. You can't play everybody at the same time.

TROY: If they got a white fellow sitting on the bench . . . you can bet your last dollar he can't play! The colored guy got to
115 be twice as good before he get on the team. That's why I don't want you to get all tied up in them sports. Man on the team and what it get him? They got colored on the team and don't use them. Same as not having them. All them teams the same.

120 CORY: The Braves got Hank Aaron and Wes Covington. Hank Aaron hit two home runs today. That makes forty-three.

TROY: Hank Aaron ain't nobody. That's what you supposed to do. That's how you supposed to play the game. Ain't nothing to it. It's just a matter of timing . . . getting the right follow-
125 through. Hell, I can hit forty-three home runs right now!

CORY: Not off no major-league pitching, you couldn't.

TROY: We had better pitching in the Negro leagues. I hit seven home runs off of Satchel Paige. You can't get no better than that!

130 CORY: Sandy Koufax. He's leading the league in strikeouts.

TROY: I ain't thinking of no Sandy Koufax.

CORY: You got Warren Spahn and Lew Burdette. I bet you couldn't hit no home runs off of Warren Spahn.

TROY: I'm through with it now. You go on and cut them
135 boards.

(*Pause.*)

Your mama tell me you done got recruited by a college football team? Is that right?

CORY: Yeah. Coach Zellman say the recruiter gonna be coming by to talk to you. Get you to sign the permission papers.

TROY: I thought you supposed to be working down there at the
140 A&P. Ain't you suppose to be working down there after school?

CORY: Mr. Stawicki say he gonna hold my job for me until after the football season. Say starting next week I can work
145 weekends.

TROY: I thought we had an understanding about this football stuff? You suppose to keep up with your chores and hold that job down at the A&P. Ain't been around here all day on a Saturday. Ain't none of your chores done . . . and now you
150 telling me you done quit your job.

CORY: I'm gonna be working weekends.

TROY: You damn right you are! And ain't no need for nobody coming around here to talk to me about signing nothing.

CORY: Hey, Pop . . . you can't do that. He's coming all the way
155 from North Carolina.

TROY: I don't care where he coming from. The white man ain't gonna let you get nowhere with that football noway. You go on and get your book-learning so you can work yourself up in that A&P or learn how to fix cars or build houses or some-
160 thing, get you a trade. That way you have something can't nobody take away from you. You go on and learn how to put your hands to some good use. Besides hauling people's garbage.

CORY: I get good grades, Pop. That's why the recruiter wants to
165 talk with you. You got to keep up your grades to get recruited. This way I'll be going to college. I'll get a chance . . .

TROY: First you gonna get your butt down there to the A&P and get your job back.

CORY: Mr. Stawicki done already hired somebody else 'cause I
170 told him I was playing football.

TROY: You a bigger fool than I thought . . . to let somebody take away your job so you can play some football. Where you gonna get your money to take out your girlfriend and what-not? What kind of foolishness is that to let somebody take
175 away your job?

CORY: I'm still gonna be working weekends.

TROY: Naw . . . naw. You getting your butt out of here and finding you another job.

CORY: Come on, Pop! I got to practice. I can't work after
180 school and play football too. The team needs me. That's what Coach Zellman say . . .

TROY: I don't care what nobody else say. I'm the boss . . . you understand? I'm the boss around here. I do the only saying what counts.

185 CORY: Come on, Pop!

TROY: I asked you . . . did you understand?

CORY: Yeah . . .

TROY: What?!

CORY: Yessir.

190 TROY: You go on down there to that A&P and see if you can get your job back. If you can't do both . . . then you quit the football team. You've got to take the crookeds with the straights.

CORY: Yessir.

(*Pause.*)

Can I ask you a question?

195 TROY: What the hell you wanna ask me? Mr. Stawicki the one
you got the questions for.

CORY: How come you ain't never liked me?

TROY: Liked you? Who the hell say I got to like you? What law
is there say I got to like you? Wanna stand up in my face and

200 ask a damn fool-ass question like that. Talking about liking
somebody. Come here boy, when I talk to you.

(CORY *comes over to where* TROY *is working. He stands slouched
over and* TROY *shoves him on his shoulder.*)

Straighten up, goddammit! I asked you a question . . . what
law is there say I got to like you?

CORY: None.

205 TROY: Well, alright then! Don't you eat every day?

(*Pause.*)

Answer me when I talk to you! Don't you eat every day?

CORY: Yeah.

TROY: Nigger, as long as you in my house, you put that sir on
the end of it when you talk to me!

210 CORY: Yes . . . sir.

TROY: You eat every day.

CORY: Yessir!

TROY: Got a roof over your head.

CORY: Yessir!

215 TROY: Got clothes on your back.

CORY: Yessir.

TROY: Why you think that is?

CORY: Cause of you.

TROY: Aw, hell I know it's 'cause of me . . . but why do you

220 think that is?

CORY: (*Hesitant.*) Cause you like me.

TROY: Like you? I go out of here every morning . . . bust my
butt . . . putting up with them crackers every day . . . cause I
like you? You about the biggest fool I ever saw.

(*Pause.*)

225 It's my job. It's my responsibility! You understand that? A
man got to take care of his family. You live in my house . . .
sleep you behind on my bedclothes . . . fill you belly up with
my food . . . cause you my son. You my flesh and blood. Not
'cause I like you! Cause it's my duty to take care of you. I owe

230 a responsibility to you! Let's get this straight right here . . .
before it go along any further . . . I ain't got to like you. Mr.
Rand don't give me my money come payday cause he likes
me. He gives me cause he owe me. I done give you everything I had to give you. I gave you your life! Me and your

235 mama worked that out between us. And liking your black ass
wasn't part of the bargain. Don't you try and go through life
worrying about if somebody like you or not. You best be
making sure they doing right by you. You understand what
I'm saying, boy?

240 CORY: Yessir.

TROY: Then get the hell out of my face, and get on down to
that A&P.

(ROSE *has been standing behind the screen door for much of the
scene. She enters as* CORY *exits.*)

ROSE: Why don't you let the boy go ahead and play football,
Troy? Ain't no harm in that. He's just trying to be like you
with the sports.   245

TROY: I don't want him to be like me! I want him to move as
far away from my life as he can get. You the only decent
thing that ever happened to me. I wish him that. But I don't
wish him a thing else from my life. I decided seventeen years
ago that boy wasn't getting involved in no sports. Not after   250
what they did to me in the sports.

ROSE: Troy, why don't you admit you was too old to play in the
major leagues? For once . . . why don't you admit that?

TROY: What do you mean too old? Don't come telling me I
was too old. I just wasn't the right color. Hell, I'm fifty-three 255
years old and can do better than Selkirk's .269 right now!

ROSE: How's was you gonna play ball when you were over
forty? Sometimes I can't get no sense out of you.

TROY: I got good sense, woman. I got sense enough not to let
my boy get hurt over playing no sports. You been mothering   260
that boy too much. Worried about if people like him.

ROSE: Everything that boy do . . . he do for you. He wants you
to say "Good job, son." That's all.

TROY: Rose, I ain't got time for that. He's alive. He's healthy.
He's got to make his own way. I made mine. Ain't nobody   265
gonna hold his hand when he get out there in that world.

ROSE: Times have changed from when you was young, Troy.
People change. The world's changing around you and you
can't even see it.

TROY: (*Slow, methodical.*) Woman . . . I do the best I can do. I 270
come in here every Friday. I carry a sack of potatoes and a
bucket of lard. You all line up at the door with your hands
out. I give you the lint from my pockets. I give you my sweat
and my blood. I ain't got no tears. I done spent them. We go
upstairs in that room at night . . . and I fall down on you and 275
try to blast a hole into forever. I get up Monday morning . . .
find my lunch on the table. I go out. Make my way. Find my
strength to carry me through to the next Friday.

(*Pause.*)

That's all I got, Rose. That's all I got to give. I can't give
nothing else.   280

(TROY *exits into the house. The lights go down to black.*)

SCENE IV

It is Friday. Two weeks later. CORY *starts out of the house with
his football equipment. The phone rings.*

CORY: (*Calling.*) I got it!

(*He answers the phone and stands in the screen door talking.*)

Hello? Hey, Jesse. Naw . . . I was just getting ready to leave
now.

ROSE: (*Calling.*) Cory!

CORY: I told you, man, them spikes is all tore up. You can use   5
them if you want, but they ain't no good. Earl got some
spikes.

ROSE: (*Calling.*) Cory!

CORY: (*Calling to* ROSE.) Mam? I'm talking to Jesse.

(*Into phone.*)

When she say that. (*Pause.*) Aw, you lying, man. I'm gonna   10
tell her you said that.

ROSE: (*Calling.*) Cory, don't you go nowhere!

CORY: I got to go to the game, Ma!

(*Into the phone.*)

15 Yeah, hey, look, I'll talk to you later. Yeah, I'll meet you over Earl's house. Later. Bye, Ma.

(CORY *exits the house and starts out the yard.*)

ROSE: Cory, where you going off to? You got that stuff all pulled out and thrown all over your room.

CORY: (*In the yard.*) I was looking for my spikes. Jesse wanted to borrow my spikes.

20 ROSE: Get up there and get that cleaned up before your daddy get back in here.

CORY: I got to go to the game! I'll clean it up *when I get back.*

(CORY *exits.*)

ROSE: That's all he need to do is see that room all messed up.

(ROSE *exits into the house.* TROY *and* BONO *enter the yard.* TROY *is dressed in clothes other than his work clothes.*)

BONO: He told him the same thing he told you. Take it to the

25 union.

TROY: Brownie ain't got that much sense. Man wasn't thinking about nothing. He wait until I confront them on it . . . then he wanna come crying seniority.

(*Calls.*)

Hey, Rose!

30 BONO: I wish I could have seen Mr. Rand's face when he told you.

TROY: He couldn't get it out of his mouth! Liked to bit his tongue! When they called me down there to the Commissioner's office . . . he thought they was gonna fire me. Like

35 everybody else.

BONO: I didn't think they was gonna fire you. I thought they was gonna put you on the warning paper.

TROY: Hey, Rose!

(*To* BONO.)

Yeah, Mr. Rand like to bit his tongue.

(TROY *breaks the seal on the bottle, takes a drink, and hands it to* BONO.)

40 BONO: I see you run right down to Taylors' and told that Alberta gal.

TROY: (*Calling.*) Hey Rose! (*To* BONO.) I told everybody. Hey, Rose! I went down there to cash my check.

ROSE: (*Entering from the house.*) Hush all that hollering, man!

45 I know you out here. What they say down there at the Commissioner's office?

TROY: You supposed to come when I call you, woman. Bono'll tell you that.

(*To* BONO.)

Don't Lucille come when you call her?

50 ROSE: Man, hush your mouth. I ain't no dog . . . talk about "come when you call me."

TROY: (*Puts his arm around* ROSE.) You hear this, Bono? I had me an old dog used to get uppity like that. You say, "C'mere, Blue!" . . . and he just lay there and look at you. End up get-

55 ting a stick and chasing him away trying to make him come.

ROSE: I ain't studying you and your dog. I remember you used to sing that old song.

TROY: (*He sings.*) Hear it ring! Hear it ring! I had a dog his name was Blue.

ROSE: Don't nobody wanna hear you sing that old song. 60

TROY: (*Sings.*) You know Blue was mighty true.

ROSE: Used to have Cory running around here singing that song.

BONO: Hell, I remember that song myself.

TROY: (*Sings.*) 65

You know Blue was a good old dog.
Blue treed a possum in a hollow log.

That was my daddy's song. My daddy made up that song.

ROSE: I don't care who made it up. Don't nobody wanna hear you sing it. 70

TROY: (*Makes a song like calling a dog.*) Come here, woman.

ROSE: You come in here carrying on, I reckon they ain't fired you. What they say down there at the Commissioner's office?

TROY: Look here, Rose . . . Mr. Rand called me into his office today when I got back from talking to them people down 75 there . . . it come from up top . . . he called me in and told me they was making me a driver.

ROSE: Troy, you kidding!

TROY: No I ain't. Ask Bono.

ROSE: Well, that's great, Troy. Now you don't have to hassle 80 them people no more.

(LYONS *enters from the street.*)

TROY: Aw hell, I wasn't looking to see you today. I thought you was in jail. Got it all over the front page of the *Courier* about them raiding Sefus' place . . . where you be hanging out with all them thugs? 85

LYONS: Hey, Pop . . . that ain't got nothing to do with me. I don't go down there gambling. I go down there to sit in with the band. I ain't got nothing to do with the gambling part. They got some good music down there.

TROY: They got some rogues . . . is what they got. 90

LYONS: How you been, Mr. Bono? Hi, Rose.

BONO: I see where you playing down at the Crawford Grill tonight.

ROSE: How come you ain't brought Bonnie like I told you. You should have brought Bonnie with you, she ain't been over in 95 a month of Sundays.

LYONS: I was just in the neighborhood . . . thought I'd stop by.

TROY: Here he come . . .

BONO: Your daddy got a promotion on the rubbish. He's gonna be the first colored driver. Ain't got to do nothing but sit up 100 there and read the paper like them white fellows.

LYONS: Hey, Pop . . . if you knew how to read you'd be alright.

BONO: Naw . . . naw . . . you mean if the nigger knew how to *drive* he'd be all right. Been fighting with them people about driving and ain't even got a license. Mr. Rand know you ain't 105 got no driver's license?

TROY: Driving ain't nothing. All you do is point the truck where you want it to go. Driving ain't nothing.

BONO: Do Mr. Rand know you ain't got no driver's license? That's what I'm talking about. I ain't asked if driving was 110 easy. I asked if Mr. Rand know you ain't got no driver's license.

TROY: He ain't got to know. The man ain't got to know my business. Time he find out, I have two or three driver's licenses. 115

LYONS: (*Going into his pocket.*) Say, look here, Pop . . .

TROY: I knew it was coming. Didn't I tell you, Bono? I know what kind of "Look here, Pop" that was. The nigger fixing to ask me for some money. It's Friday night. It's my payday. All them rogues down there on the avenue . . . the ones that ain't in jail . . . and Lyons is hopping in his shoes to get down there with them.

LYONS: See, Pop . . . if you give somebody else a chance to talk sometime, you'd see that I was fixing to pay you back your ten dollars like I told you. Here . . . I told you I'd pay you when Bonnie got paid.

TROY: Naw . . . you go ahead and keep that ten dollars. Put it in the bank. The next time you feel like you wanna come by here and ask me for something . . . you go on down there and get that.

LYONS: Here's your ten dollars, Pop. I told you I don't want you to give me nothing. I just wanted to borrow ten dollars.

TROY: Naw . . . you go on and keep that for the next time you want to ask me.

LYONS: Come on, Pop . . . here go your ten dollars.

ROSE: Why don't you go on and let the boy pay you back, Troy?

LYONS: Here you go, Rose. If you don't take it I'm gonna have to hear about it for the next six months.

(He hands her the money.)

ROSE: You can hand yours over here too, Troy.

TROY: You see this, Bono. You see how they do me.

BONO: Yeah, Lucille do me the same way.

(GABRIEL is heard singing offstage. He enters.)

GABRIEL: Better get ready for the Judgment! Better get ready for . . . Hey! . . . Hey! . . . There's Troy's boy!

LYONS: How you doing, Uncle Gabe?

GABRIEL: Lyons . . . The King of the Jungle! Rose . . . hey, Rose. Got a flower for you.

(He takes a rose from his pocket.)

Picked it myself. That's the same rose like you is!

ROSE: That's right nice of you, Gabe.

LYONS: What you been doing, Uncle Gabe?

GABRIEL: Oh, I been chasing hellhounds and waiting on the time to tell St. Peter to open the gates.

LYONS: You been chasing hellhounds, huh? Well . . . you doing the right thing, Uncle Gabe. Somebody got to chase them.

GABRIEL: Oh, yeah . . . I know it. The devil's strong. The devil ain't no pushover. Hellhounds snipping at everybody's heels. But I got my trumpet waiting on the judgment time.

LYONS: Waiting on the Battle of Armageddon, huh?

GABRIEL: Ain't gonna be too much of a battle when God get to waving that Judgment sword. But the people's gonna have a hell of a time trying to get into heaven if them gates ain't open.

LYONS: *(Putting his arm around GABRIEL.)* You hear this, Pop. Uncle Gabe, you alright!

GABRIEL: *(Laughing with LYONS.)* Lyons! King of the Jungle.

ROSE: You gonna stay for supper, Gabe. Want me to fix you a plate?

GABRIEL: I'll take a sandwich, Rose. Don't want no plate. Just wanna eat with my hands. I'll take a sandwich.

ROSE: How about you, Lyons? You staying? Got some short ribs cooking.

LYONS: Naw, I won't eat nothing till after we finished playing.

(Pause.)

You ought to come down and listen to me play, Pop.

TROY: I don't like that Chinese music. All that noise.

ROSE: Go on in the house and wash up, Gabe . . . I'll fix you a sandwich.

GABRIEL: *(To LYONS, as he exits.)* Troy's mad at me.

LYONS: What you mad at Uncle Gabe for, Pop.

ROSE: He thinks Troy's mad at him cause he moved over to Miss Pearl's.

TROY: I ain't mad at the man. He can live where he want to live at.

LYONS: What he move over there for? Miss Pearl don't like nobody.

ROSE: She don't mind him none. She treats him real nice. She just don't allow all that singing.

TROY: She don't mind that rent he be paying . . . that's what she don't mind.

ROSE: Troy, I ain't going through that with you no more. He's over there cause he want to have his own place. He can come and go as he please.

TROY: Hell, he could come and go as he please here. I wasn't stopping him. I ain't put no rules on him.

ROSE: It ain't the same thing, Troy. And you know it.

(GABRIEL comes to the door.)

Now, that's the last I wanna hear about that. I don't wanna hear nothing else about Gabe and Miss Pearl. And next week . . .

GABRIEL: I'm ready for my sandwich, Rose.

ROSE: And next week . . . when that recruiter come from that school . . . I want you to sign that paper and go on and let Cory play football. Then that'll be the last I have to hear about that.

TROY: *(To ROSE as she exits into the house.)* I ain't thinking about Cory nothing.

LYONS: What . . . Cory got recruited? What school he going to?

TROY: That boy walking around here smelling his piss . . . thinking he's grown. Thinking he's gonna do what he want, irrespective of what I say. Look here, Bono . . . I left the Commissioner's office and went down to the A&P . . . that boy ain't working down there. He lying to me. Telling me he got his job back . . . telling me he working weekends . . . telling me he working after school . . . Mr. Stawicki tell me he ain't working down there at all!

LYONS: Cory just growing up. He's just busting at the seams trying to fill out your shoes.

TROY: I don't care what he's doing. When he get to the point where he wanna disobey me . . . then it's time for him to move on. Bono'll tell you that. I bet he ain't never disobeyed his daddy without paying the consequences.

BONO: I ain't never had a chance. My daddy came on through . . . but I ain't never knew him to see him . . . or what he had on his mind or where he went. Just moving on through. Searching out the New Land. That's what the old folks used to call it. See a fellow moving around from place to place . . . woman to woman . . . called it searching out the New Land. I can't say if he ever found it. I come along, didn't want no kids. Didn't know if I was gonna be in one place long enough to fix on them right as their daddy. I figured I was going searching too. As it turned out I been hooked up with

Lucille near about as long as your daddy been with Rose. Going on sixteen years.

TROY: Sometimes I wish I hadn't known my daddy. He ain't cared nothing about no kids. A kid to him wasn't nothing.
235 All he wanted was for you to learn how to walk so he could start you to working. When it come time for eating . . . he ate first. If there was anything left over, that's what you got. Man would sit down and eat two chickens and give you the wing.

LYONS: You ought to stop that, Pop. Everybody feed their kids.
240 No matter how hard times is . . . everybody care about their kids. Make sure they have something to eat.

TROY: The only thing my daddy cared about was getting them bales of cotton into Mr. Lubin. That's the only thing that mattered to him. Sometimes I used to wonder why he was
245 living. Wonder why the devil hadn't come and got him. "Get them bales of cotton in to Mr. Lubin" and find out he owe him money . . .

LYONS: He should have just went on and left when he saw he couldn't get nowhere. That's what I would have done.
250 TROY: How he gonna leave with eleven kids? And where he gonna go? He ain't knew how to do nothing but farm. No, he was trapped and I think he knew it. But I'll say this for him . . . he felt a responsibility toward us. Maybe he ain't treated us the way I felt he should have . . . but without that
255 responsibility he could have walked off and left us . . . made his own way.

BONO: A lot of them did. Back in those days what you talking about . . . they walk out their front door and just take on down one road or another and keep on walking.
260 LYONS: There you go! That's what I'm talking about.

BONO: Just keep on walking till you come to something else. Ain't you never heard of nobody having the walking blues? Well, that's what you call it when you just take off like that.

TROY: My daddy ain't had them walking blues! What you talk-
265 ing about? He stayed right there with his family. But he was just as evil as he could be. My mama couldn't stand him. Couldn't stand that evilness. She run off when I was about eight. She sneaked off one night after he had gone to sleep. Told me she was coming back for me. I ain't never seen her
270 no more. All his women run off and left him. He wasn't good for nobody.

When my turn come to head out, I was fourteen and got to sniffing around Joe Canewell's daughter. Had us an old mule we called Greyboy. My daddy sent me out to do some
275 plowing and I tied up Greyboy and went to fooling around with Joe Canewell's daughter. We done found us a nice little spot, got real cozy with each other. She about thirteen and we done figured we was grown anyway . . . so we down there enjoying ourselves . . . ain't thinking about nothing.
280 We didn't know Greyboy had got loose and wandered back to the house and my daddy was looking for me. We down there by the creek enjoying ourselves when my daddy come up on us. Surprised us. He had them leather straps off the mule and commenced to whupping me like there was no
285 tomorrow. I jumped up, mad and embarrassed. I was scared of my daddy. When he commenced to whupping on me . . . quite naturally I run to get out of the way.

(Pause.)

Now I thought he was mad cause I ain't done my work. But I see where he was chasing me off so he could have the gal for

himself. When I see what the matter of it was, I lost all fear of 290 my daddy. Right there is where I become a man . . . at fourteen years of age.

(Pause.)

Now it was my turn to run him off. I picked up them same reins that he had used on me. I picked up them reins and commenced to whupping on him. The gal jumped up and 295 run off . . . and when my daddy turned to face me, I could see why the devil had never come to get him . . . cause he was the devil himself. I don't know what happened. When I woke up, I was laying right there by the creek, and Blue . . . this old dog we had . . . was licking my face. I thought I was 300 blind. I couldn't see nothing. Both my eyes were swollen shut. I layed there and cried. I didn't know what I was gonna do. The only thing I knew was the time had come for me to leave my daddy's house. And right there the world suddenly got big. And it was a long time before I could cut it down to 305 where I could handle it.

Part of that cutting down was when I got to the place where I could feel him kicking in my blood and knew that the only thing that separated us was the matter of a few years.

(GABRIEL enters from the house with a sandwich.)

LYONS: What you got there, Uncle Gabe? 310
GABRIEL: Got me a ham sandwich. Rose gave me a ham sandwich.

TROY: I don't know what happened to him. I done lost touch with everybody except Gabriel. But I hope he's dead. I hope he found some peace. 315
LYONS: That's a heavy story, Pop. I didn't know you left home when you was fourteen.

TROY: And didn't know nothing. The only part of the world I knew was the forty-two acres of Mr. Lubin's land. That's all I knew about life. 320
LYONS: Fourteen's kinda young to be out on your own. *(Phone rings.)* I don't even think I was ready to be out on my own at fourteen. I don't know what I would have done.

TROY: I got up from the creek and walked on down to Mobile. I was through with farming. Figured I could do better in the 325 city. So I walked the two hundred miles to Mobile.

LYONS: Wait a minute . . . you ain't walked no two hundred miles, Pop. Ain't nobody gonna walk no two hundred miles. You talking about some walking there.

BONO: That's the only way you got anywhere back in them 330 days.

LYONS: Shhh. Damn if I wouldn't have hitched a ride with somebody!

TROY: Who you gonna hitch it with? They ain't had no cars and things like they got now. We talking about 1918. 335
ROSE: *(Entering.)* What you all out here getting into?

TROY: *(To ROSE.)* I'm telling Lyons how good he got it. He don't know nothing about this I'm talking.

ROSE: Lyons, that was Bonnie on the phone. She say you supposed to pick her up. 340
LYONS: Yeah, okay, Rose.

TROY: I walked on down to Mobile and hitched up with some of them fellows that was heading this way. Got up here and found out . . . not only couldn't you get a job . . . you couldn't find no place to live. I thought I was in freedom. 345 Shhh. Colored folks living down there on the riverbanks in whatever kind of shelter they could find for themselves. Right down there under the Brady Street Bridge. Living in shacks made of sticks and tarpaper. Messed around there and went from bad to worse. Started stealing. First it was food. Then I figured, hell, if I steal money I can buy me some food. Buy me some shoes too! One thing led to another. Met your mama. I was young and anxious to be a man. Met your mama and had you. What I do that for? Now I got to worry about feeding you and her. Got to steal three times as much. Went out one day looking for somebody to rob . . . that's what I was, a robber. I'll tell you the truth. I'm ashamed of it today. But it's the truth. Went to rob this fellow . . . pulled out my knife . . . and he pulled out a gun. Shot me in the chest. It felt just like somebody had taken a hot branding iron and laid it on me. When he shot me I jumped at him with my knife. They told me I killed him and they put me in the penitentiary and locked me up for fifteen years. That's where I met Bono. That's where I learned how to play baseball. Got out that place and your mama had taken you and went on to make life without me. Fifteen years was a long time for her to wait. But that fifteen years cured me of that robbing stuff. Rose'll tell you. She asked me when I met her if I had gotten all that foolishness out of my system. And I told her, "Baby, it's you and baseball all what count with me." You hear me, Bono? I meant it too. She say, "Which one comes first?" I told her, "Baby, ain't no doubt it's baseball . . . but you stick and get old with me and we'll both outlive this baseball." Am I right, Rose? And it's true.

ROSE: Man, hush your mouth. You ain't said no such thing. Talking about, "Baby, you know you'll always be number one with me." That's what you was talking.

TROY: You hear that, Bono. That's why I love her.

BONO: Rose'll keep you straight. You get off the track, she'll straighten you up.

ROSE: Lyons, you better get on up and get Bonnie. She waiting on you.

LYONS: (Gets up to go.) Hey, Pop, why don't you come on down to the Grill and hear me play?

TROY: I ain't going down there. I'm too old to be sitting around in them clubs.

BONO: You got to be good to play down at the Grill.

LYONS: Come on, Pop . . .

TROY: I got to get up in the morning.

LYONS: You ain't got to stay long.

TROY: Naw, I'm gonna get my supper and go on to bed.

LYONS: Well, I got to go. I'll see you again.

TROY: Don't you come around my house on my payday.

ROSE: Pick up the phone and let somebody know you coming. And bring Bonnie with you. You know I'm always glad to see her.

LYONS: Yeah, I'll do that, Rose. You take care now. See you, Pop. See you, Mr. Bono. See you, Uncle Gabe.

GABRIEL: Lyons! King of the Jungle!

(LYONS exits.)

TROY: Is supper ready, woman? Me and you got some business to take care of. I'm gonna tear it up too.

ROSE: Troy, I done told you now!

TROY: (Puts his arm around BONO.) Aw hell, woman . . . this is Bono. Bono like family. I done known this nigger since . . . how long I done know you?

BONO: It's been a long time.

TROY: I done known this nigger since Skippy was a pup. Me and him done been through some times.

BONO: You sure right about that.

TROY: Hell, I done know him longer than I known you. And we still standing shoulder to shoulder. Hey, look here, Bono . . . a man can't ask for no more than that.

(Drinks to him.)

I love you, nigger.

BONO: Hell, I love you too . . . but I got to get home see my woman. You got yours in hand. I got to go get mine.

(BONO starts to exit as CORY enters the yard, dressed in his football uniform. He gives TROY a hard, uncompromising look.)

CORY: What you do that for, Pop?

(He throws his helmet down in the direction of TROY.)

ROSE: What's the matter? Cory . . . what's the matter?

CORY: Papa done went up to the school and told Coach Zellman I can't play football no more. Wouldn't even let me play the game. Told him to tell the recruiter not to come.

ROSE: Troy . . .

TROY: What you Troying me for? Yeah, I did it. And the boy know why I did it.

CORY: Why you wanna do that to me? That was the one chance I had.

ROSE: Ain't nothing wrong with Cory playing football, Troy.

TROY: The boy lied to me. I told the nigger if he wanna play football . . . to keep his chores and hold down that job at the A&P. That was the conditions. Stopped down there to see Mr. Stawicki . . .

CORY: I can't work after school during the football season, Pop! I tried to tell you that Mr. Stawicki's holding my job for me. You don't never want to listen to nobody. And then you wanna go and do this to me!

TROY: I ain't done nothing to you. You done it to yourself.

CORY: Just cause you didn't have a chance! You just scared I'm gonna be better than you, that's all.

TROY: Come here.

ROSE: Troy . . .

(CORY reluctantly crosses over to TROY.)

TROY: Alright! See. You done made a mistake.

CORY: I didn't even do nothing!

TROY: I'm gonna tell you what your mistake was. See . . . you swung at the ball and didn't hit it. That's strike one. See, you in the batter's box now. You swung and you missed. That's strike one. Don't you strike out!

(Lights fade to black.)

— ACT TWO —

SCENE 1

The following morning. CORY *is at the tree hitting the ball with the bat. He tries to mimic* TROY, *but his swing is awkward, less sure.* ROSE *enters from the house.*

ROSE: Cory, I want you to help me with this cupboard.

CORY: I ain't quitting the team. I don't care what Poppa say.

ROSE: I'll talk to him when he gets back. He had to go see about your Uncle Gabe. The police done arrested him. Say he was disturbing the peace. He'll be back directly. Come on in here and help me clean out the top of this cupboard.

(CORY exits into the house. ROSE sees TROY and BONO coming down the alley.)

Troy . . . what they say down there?

TROY: Ain't said nothing. I give them fifty dollars and they let him go. I'll talk to you about it. Where's Cory?

ROSE: He's in there helping me clean out these cupboards.

TROY: Tell him to get his butt out here.

(TROY and BONO go over to the pile of wood. BONO picks up the saw and begins sawing.)

TROY: (To BONO.) All they want is the money. That makes six or seven times I done went down there and got him. See me coming they stick out their hands.

BONO: Yeah. I know what you mean. That's all they care about . . . that money. They don't care about what's right.

(Pause.)

Nigger, why you got to go and get some hard wood? You ain't doing nothing but building a little old fence. Get you some soft pine wood. That's all you need.

TROY: I know what I'm doing. This is outside wood. You put pine wood inside the house. Pine wood is inside wood. This here is outside wood. Now you tell me where the fence is gonna be?

BONO: You don't need this wood. You can put it up with pine wood and it's stand as long as you gonna be here looking at it.

TROY: How you know how long I'm gonna be here, nigger? Hell, I might just live forever. Live longer than old man Horsely.

BONO: That's what Magee used to say.

TROY: Magee's a damn fool. Now you tell me who you ever heard of gonna pull their own teeth with a pair of rusty pliers.

BONO: The old folks . . . my granddaddy used to pull his teeth with pliers. They ain't had no dentists for the colored folks back then.

TROY: Get clean pliers! You understand? Clean pliers! Sterilize them! Besides we ain't living back then. All Magee had to do was walk over to Doc Goldblums.

BONO: I see where you and that Tallahassee gal . . . that Alberta . . . I see where you all done got tight.

TROY: What you mean "got tight"?

BONO: I see where you be laughing and joking with her all the time.

TROY: I laughs and jokes with all of them, Bono. You know me.

BONO: That ain't the kind of laughing and joking I'm talking about.

(CORY enters from the house.)

CORY: How you doing, Mr. Bono?

TROY: Cory? Get that saw from Bono and cut some wood. He talking about the wood's too hard to cut. Stand back there, Jim, and let that young boy show you how it's done.

BONO: He's sure welcome to it.

(CORY takes the saw and begins to cut the wood.)

Whew-e-e! Look at that. Big old strong boy. Look like Joe Louis. Hell, must be getting old the way I'm watching that boy whip through that wood.

CORY: I don't see why Mama want a fence around the yard noways.

TROY: Damn if I know either. What the hell she keeping out with it? She ain't got nothing nobody want.

BONO: Some people build fences to keep people out . . . and other people build fences to keep people in. Rose wants to hold on to you all. She loves you.

TROY: Hell, nigger, I don't need nobody to tell me my wife loves me, Cory . . . go on in the house and see if you can find that other saw.

CORY: Where's it at?

TROY: I said find it! Look for it till you find it!

(CORY exits into the house.)

What's that supposed to mean? Wanna keep us in?

BONO: Troy . . . I done known you seem like damn near my whole life. You and Rose both. I done know both of you all for a long time. I remember when you met Rose. When you was hitting them baseball out the park. A lot of them old gals was after you then. You had the pick of the litter. When you picked Rose, I was happy for you. That was the first time I knew you had any sense. I said . . . My man Troy knows what he's doing . . . I'm gonna follow this nigger . . . he might take me somewhere. I been following you too. I done learned a whole heap of things about life watching you. I done learned how to tell where the shit lies. How to tell it from the alfalfa. You done learned me a lot of things. You showed me how to not make the same mistakes . . . to take life as it comes along and keep putting one foot in front of the other.

(Pause.)

Rose a good woman, Troy.

TROY: Hell, nigger, I know she a good woman. I been married to her for eighteen years. What you got on your mind, Bono?

BONO: I just say she a good woman. Just like I say anything. I ain't got to have nothing on my mind.

TROY: You just gonna say she a good woman and leave it hanging out there like that? Why you telling me she a good woman?

BONO: She loves you, Troy. Rose loves you.

TROY: You saying I don't measure up. That's what you trying to say. I don't measure up cause I'm seeing this other gal. I know what you trying to say.

BONO: I know what Rose means to you, Troy. I'm just trying to say I don't want to see you mess up.

TROY: Yeah, I appreciate that, Bono. If you was messing around on Lucille I'd be telling you the same thing.

BONO: Well, that's all I got to say. I just say that because I love you both.

TROY: Hell, you know me . . . I wasn't out there looking for nothing. You can't find a better woman than Rose. I know that. But seems like this woman just stuck onto me where I can't shake her loose. I done wrestled with it, tried to throw her off me . . . but she just stuck on tighter. Now she's stuck on for good.

BONO: You's in control . . . that's what you tell me all the time. You responsible for what you do.

TROY: I ain't ducking the responsibility of it. As long as it sets
right in my heart . . . then I'm okay. Cause that's all I listen
to. It'll tell me right from wrong every time. And I ain't talking about doing Rose no bad turn. I love Rose. She done carried me a long ways and I love and respect her for that.

BONO: I know you do. That's why I don't want to see you hurt
her. But what you gonna do when she find out? What you
got then? If you try and juggle both of them . . . sooner or
later you gonna drop one of them. That's common sense.

TROY: Yeah, I hear what you saying, Bono. I been trying to figure a way to work it out.

BONO: Work it out right, Troy. I don't want to be getting all up
between you and Rose's business . . . but work it so it come
out right.

TROY: Aw hell, I get all up between you and Lucille's business.
When you gonna get that woman that refrigerator she been
wanting? Don't tell me you ain't got no money now. I know
who your banker is. Mellon don't need that money bad as
Lucille want that refrigerator. I'll tell you that.

BONO: Tell you what I'll do . . . when you finish building this
fence for Rose . . . I'll buy Lucille that refrigerator.

TROY: You done stuck your foot in your mouth now!

(TROY *grabs up a board and begins to saw.* BONO *starts to walk out the yard.*)

Hey, nigger . . . where you going?

BONO: I'm going home. I know you don't expect me to help
you now. I'm protecting my money. I wanna see you put that
fence up by yourself. That's what I want to see. You'll be here
another six month without me.

TROY: Nigger, you ain't right.

BONO: When it comes to my money . . . I'm right as fireworks
on the Fourth of July.

TROY: Alright, we gonna see now. You better get out your
bankbook.

(BONO *exits, and* TROY *continues to work.* ROSE *enters from the house.*)

ROSE: What they say down there? What's happening with
Gabe?

TROY: I went down there and got him out. Cost me fifty dollars. Say he was disturbing the peace. Judge set up a hearing
for him in three weeks. Say to show cause why he shouldn't
be re-committed.

ROSE: What was he doing that cause them to arrest him?

TROY: Some kids was teasing him and he run them off home.
Say he was howling and carrying on. Some folks seen him
and called the police. That's all it was.

ROSE: Well, what's you say? What'd you tell the judge?

TROY: Told him I'd look after him. It didn't make no sense to
recommit the man. He stuck out his big greasy palm and
told me to give him fifty dollars and take him on home.

ROSE: Where's he at now? Where'd he go off to?

TROY: He's gone on about his business. He don't need nobody
to hold his hand.

ROSE: Well, I don't know. Seem like that would be the best
place for him if they did put him into the hospital. I know
what you're gonna say. But that's what I think would be best.

TROY: The man done had his life ruined fighting for what?
And they wanna take and lock him up. Let him be free. He
don't bother nobody.

ROSE: Well, everybody got their own way of looking at it I
guess. Come on and get your lunch. I got a bowl of lima
beans and some cornbread in the oven. Come on get something to eat. Ain't no sense you fretting over Gabe.

(ROSE *turns to go into the house.*)

TROY: Rose . . . got something to tell you.

ROSE: Well, come on . . . wait till I get this food on the table.

TROY: Rose!

(She *stops and turns around.*)

I don't know how to say this.

(*Pause.*)

I can't explain it none. It just sort of grows on you till it gets
out of hand. It starts out like a little bush . . . and the next
thing you know it's a whole forest.

ROSE: Troy . . . what is you talking about?

TROY: I'm talking, woman, let me talk. I'm trying to find a way
to tell you . . . I'm gonna be a daddy. I'm gonna be somebody's daddy.

ROSE: Troy . . . you're not telling me this? You're gonna be . . .
what?

TROY: Rose . . . now . . . see . . .

ROSE: You telling me you gonna be somebody's daddy? You
telling your *wife* this?

(GABRIEL *enters from the street. He carries a rose in his hand.*)

GABRIEL: Hey, Troy! Hey, Rose!

ROSE: I have to wait eighteen years to hear something like this.

GABRIEL: Hey, Rose . . . I got a flower for you.

(*He hands it to her.*)

That's a rose. Same rose like you is.

ROSE: Thanks, Gabe.

GABRIEL: Troy, you ain't mad at me is you? Them bad mens
come and put me away. You ain't mad at me is you?

TROY: Naw, Gabe, I ain't mad at you.

ROSE: Eighteen years and you wanna come with this.

GABRIEL: (*Takes a quarter out of his pocket.*) See what I got?
Got a brand new quarter.

TROY: Rose . . . it's just . . .

ROSE: Ain't nothing you can say, Troy. Ain't no way of explaining that.

GABRIEL: Fellow that give me this quarter had a whole mess of
them. I'm gonna keep this quarter till it stop shining.

ROSE: Gabe, go on in the house there. I got some watermelon
in the frigidaire. Go on and get you a piece.

GABRIEL: Say, Rose . . . you know I was chasing hellhounds
and them bad mens come and get me and take me away.
Troy helped me. He come down there and told them they
better let me go before he beat them up. Yeah, he did!

ROSE: You go on and get you a piece of watermelon, Gabe.
Them bad mens is gone now.

GABRIEL: Okay, Rose . . . gonna get me some watermelon.
The kind with the stripes on it.

(GABRIEL *exits into the house.*)

ROSE: Why, Troy? Why? After all these years to come dragging
this in to me now. It don't make no sense at your age. I could
have expected this ten or fifteen years ago, but not now.

TROY: Age ain't got nothing to do with it, Rose.

ROSE: I done tried to be everything a wife should be. Everything a wife could be. Been married eighteen years and I got to live to see the day you tell me you been seeing another woman and done fathered a child by her. And you know I ain't never wanted no half nothing in my family. My whole family is half. Everybody got different fathers and mothers . . . my two sisters and my brother. Can't hardly tell who's who. Can't never sit down and talk about Papa and Mama. It's your papa and your mama and my papa and my mama . . .

TROY: Rose . . . stop it now.

ROSE: I ain't never wanted that for none of my children. And now you wanna drag your behind in here and tell me something like this.

TROY: You ought to know. It's time for you to know.

ROSE: Well, I don't want to know, goddamn it!

TROY: I can't just make it go away. It's done now. I can't wish the circumstance of the thing away.

ROSE: And you don't want to either. Maybe you want to wish me and my boy away. Maybe that's what you want? Well, you can't wish us away. I've got eighteen years of my life invested in you. You ought to have stayed upstairs in my bed where you belong.

TROY: Rose . . . now listen to me . . . we can get a handle on this thing. We can talk this out . . . come to an understanding.

ROSE: All of a sudden it's "we." Where was "we" at when you was down there rolling around with some godforsaken woman? "We" should have come to an understanding before you started making a damn fool of yourself. You're a day late and a dollar short when it comes to an understanding with me.

TROY: It's just . . . She gives me a different idea . . . a different understanding about myself. I can step out of this house and get away from the pressures and problems . . . be a different man. I ain't got to wonder how I'm gonna pay the bills or get the roof fixed. I can just be a part of myself that I ain't never been.

ROSE: What I want to know . . . is do you plan to continue seeing her. That's all you can say to me.

TROY: I can sit up in her house and laugh. Do you understand what I'm saying. I can laugh out loud . . . and it feels good. It reaches all the way down to the bottom of my shoes.

(Pause.)

Rose, I can't give that up.

ROSE: Maybe you ought to go on and stay down there with her . . . if she a better woman than me,

TROY: It ain't about nobody being a better woman or nothing. Rose, you ain't the blame. A man couldn't ask for no woman to be a better wife than you've been. I'm responsible for it. I done locked myself into a pattern trying to take care of you all that I forgot about myself.

ROSE: What the hell was I there for? That was my job, not somebody else's.

TROY: Rose, I done tried all my life to live decent . . . to live a clean . . . hard . . . useful life. I tried to be a good husband to you. In every way I knew how. Maybe I come into the world backwards, I don't know. But . . . you born with two strikes on you before you come to the plate. You got to guard it closely . . . always looking for the curve-ball on the inside corner. You can't afford to let none get past you. You can't afford a call strike. If you going down . . . you going down swinging. Everything lined up against you. What you gonna do. I fooled them, Rose. I bunted. When I found you and Cory and a halfway decent job . . . I was safe. Couldn't nothing touch me. I wasn't gonna strike out no more. I wasn't going back to the penitentiary. I wasn't gonna lay in the streets with a bottle of wine. I was safe. I had me a family. A job. I wasn't gonna get that last strike. I was on first looking for one of them boys to knock me in. To get me home.

ROSE: You should have stayed in my bed, Troy.

TROY: Then when I saw that gal . . . she firmed up my backbone. And I got to thinking that if I tried . . . I just might be able to steal second. Do you understand after eighteen years I wanted to steal second.

ROSE: You should have held me tight. You should have grabbed me and held on.

TROY: I stood on first base for eighteen years and I thought . . . well, goddamn it . . . go on for it!

ROSE: We're not talking about baseball! We're talking about you going off to lay in bed with another woman . . . and then bring it home to me. That's what we're talking about. We ain't talking about no baseball.

TROY: Rose, you're not listening to me. I'm trying the best I can to explain it to you. It's not easy for me to admit that I been standing in the same place for eighteen years.

ROSE: I been standing with you! I been right here with you, Troy. I got a life too. I gave eighteen years of my life to stand in the same spot with you. Don't you think I ever wanted other things? Don't you think I had dreams and hopes? What about my life? What about me. Don't you think it ever crossed my mind to want to know other men? That I wanted to lay up somewhere and forget about my responsibilities? That I wanted someone to make me laugh so I could feel good? You not the only one who's got wants and needs. But I held on to you, Troy. I took all my feelings, my wants and needs, my dreams . . . and I buried them inside you. I planted a seed and watched and prayed over it. I planted myself inside you and waited to bloom. And it didn't take me no eighteen years to find out the soil was hard and rocky and it wasn't never gonna bloom.

But I held on to you, Troy. I held you tighter. You was my husband. I owed you everything I had. Every part of me I could find to give you. And upstairs in that room . . . with the darkness falling in on me . . . I gave everything I had to try and erase the doubt that you wasn't the finest man in the world. And wherever you was going . . . I wanted to be there with you. Cause you was my husband. Cause that's the only way I was gonna survive as your wife. You always talking about what you give . . . and what you don't have to give. But you take too. You take . . . and don't even know nobody's giving!

(ROSE turns to exit into the house; TROY grabs her arm.)

TROY: You say I take and don't give!

ROSE: Troy! You're hurting me!

TROY: You say I take and don't give.

ROSE: Troy . . . you're hurting my arm! Let go!

TROY: I done give you everything I got. Don't you tell that lie on me.

ROSE: Troy!
330 TROY: Don't you tell that lie on me!

(CORY *enters from the house.*)

CORY: Mama!
ROSE: Troy. You're hurting me.
TROY: Don't you tell me about no taking and giving.

(CORY *comes up behind* TROY *and grabs him.* TROY, *surprised, is thrown off balance just as* CORY *throws a glancing blow that catches him on the chest and knocks him down.* TROY *is stunned, as is* CORY.)

ROSE: Troy. Troy. No!

(TROY *gets to his feet and starts at* CORY.)

335   Troy . . . no. Please! Troy!

(ROSE *pulls on* TROY *to hold him back.* TROY *stops himself.*)

TROY: (*To* CORY.) Alright. That's strike two. You stay away from around me, boy. Don't you strike out. You living with a full count. Don't you strike out.

(TROY *exits out the yard as the lights go down.*)

SCENE II

It is six months later, early afternoon. TROY *enters from the house and starts to exit the yard.* ROSE *enters from the house.*

ROSE: Troy, I want to talk to you.
TROY: All of a sudden, after all this time, you want to talk to me, huh? You ain't wanted to talk to me for months. You ain't wanted to talk to me last night. You ain't wanted no part
5 of me then. What you wanna talk to me about now?
ROSE: Tomorrow's Friday.
TROY: I know what day tomorrow is. You think I don't know to-morrow's Friday? My whole life I ain't done nothing but look to see Friday coming and you got to tell me it's Friday.
10 ROSE: I want to know if you're coming home.
TROY: I always come home, Rose. You know that. There ain't never been a night I ain't come home.
ROSE: That ain't what I mean . . . and you know it. I want to know if you're coming straight home after work.
15 TROY: I figure I'd cash my check . . . hang out at Taylors' with the boys . . . maybe play a game of checkers . . .
ROSE: Troy, I can't live like this. I won't live like this. You livin' on borrowed time with me. It's been going on six months now you ain't been coming home.
20 TROY: I be here every night. Every night of the year. That's 365 days.
ROSE: I want you to come home tomorrow after work.
TROY: Rose . . . I don't mess up my pay. You know that now. I take my pay and I give it to you. I don't have no money but
25 what you give me back. I just want to have a little time to my-self . . . a little time to enjoy life.
ROSE: What about me? When's my time to enjoy life?
TROY: I don't know what to tell you, Rose. I'm doing the best I can.
30 ROSE: You ain't been home from work but time enough to change your clothes and run out . . . and you wanna call that the best you can do?

TROY: I'm going over to the hospital to see Alberta. She went into the hospital this afternoon. Look like she might have the baby early. I won't be gone long.   35
ROSE: Well, you ought to know. They went over to Miss Pearl's and got Gabe today. She said you told them to go ahead and lock him up.
TROY: I ain't said no such thing. Whoever told you that is telling a lie. Pearl ain't doing nothing but telling a big fat lie. 40
ROSE: She ain't had to tell me. I read it on the papers.
TROY: I ain't told them nothing of the kind.
ROSE: I saw it right there on the papers.
TROY: What it say, huh?
ROSE: It said you told them to take him.   45
TROY: Then they screwed that up, just the way they screw up everything. I ain't worried about what they got on the paper.
ROSE: Say the government send part of his check to the hospi-tal and the other part to you.
TROY: I ain't got nothing to do with that if that's the way it 50
works. I ain't made up the rules about how it work.
ROSE: You did Gabe just like you did Cory. You wouldn't sign the paper for Cory . . . but you signed for Gabe. You signed that paper.

(*The telephone is heard ringing inside the house.*)

TROY: I told you I ain't signed nothing, woman! The only thing 55
I signed was the release form. Hell, I can't read, I don't know what they had on that paper! I ain't signed nothing about sending Gabe away.
ROSE: I said send him to the hospital . . . you said let him be free . . . now you done went down there and signed him to 60
the hospital for half his money. You went back on yourself, Troy. You gonna have to answer for that.
TROY: See now . . . you been over there talking to Miss Pearl. She done got mad cause she ain't getting Gabe's rent money. That's all it is. She's liable to say anything.   65
ROSE: Troy, I seen where you signed the paper.
TROY: You ain't seen nothing I signed. What she doing got pa-pers on my brother anyway? Miss Pearl telling a big fat lie. And I'm gonna tell her about it too! You ain't seen nothing I signed. Say . . . you ain't seen nothing I signed.   70

(ROSE *exits into the house to answer the telephone. Presently she returns.*)

ROSE: Troy . . . that was the hospital. Alberta had the baby.
TROY: What she have? What is it?
ROSE: It's a girl.
TROY: I better get on down to the hospital to see her.
ROSE: Troy . . .   75
TROY: Rose . . . I got to go see her now. That's only right . . . what's the matter . . . the baby's alright, ain't it?
ROSE: Alberta died having the baby.
TROY: Died . . . you say she's dead? Alberta's dead?
ROSE: They said they done all they could. They couldn't do 80
nothing for her.
TROY: The baby? How's the baby?
ROSE: They say it's healthy. I wonder who's gonna bury her.
TROY: She had family, Rose. She wasn't living in the world by herself.   85
ROSE: I know she wasn't living in the world by herself.

TROY: Next thing you gonna want to know if she had any insurance.

ROSE: Troy, you ain't got to talk like that.

90 TROY: That's the first thing that jumped out your mouth. "Who's gonna bury her?" Like I'm fixing to take on that task for myself.

ROSE: I am your wife. Don't push me away.

TROY: I ain't pushing nobody away. Just give me some space.
95 That's all. Just give me some room to breathe.

(ROSE *exits into the house.* TROY *walks about the yard.*)

TROY: (*With a quiet rage that threatens to consume him.*) Alright . . . Mr. Death. See now . . . I'm gonna tell you what I'm gonna do. I'm gonna take and build me a fence around this yard. See? I'm gonna build me a fence around what be-
100 longs to me. And then I want you to stay on the other side. See? You stay over there until you're ready for me. Then you come on. Bring your army. Bring your sickle. Bring your wrestling clothes. I ain't gonna fall down on my vigilance this time. You ain't gonna sneak up on me no more. When
105 you ready for me . . . when the top of your list say Troy Maxson . . . that's when you come around here. You come up and knock on the front door. Ain't nobody else got nothing to do with this. This is between you and me. Man to man. You stay on the other side of that fence until you ready for
110 me. Then you come up and knock on the front door. Anytime you want. I'll be ready for you.

(*The lights go down to black.*)

SCENE III

The lights come up on the porch. It is late evening three days later. ROSE *sits listening to the ball game waiting for* TROY. *The final out of the game is made and* ROSE *switches off the radio.* TROY *enters the yard carrying an infant wrapped in blankets. He stands back from the house and calls.*

(ROSE *enters and stands on the porch. There is a long, awkward silence, the weight of which grows heavier with each passing second.*)

TROY: Rose . . . I'm standing here with my daughter in my arms. She ain't but a wee bittie little old thing. She don't know nothing about grownups' business. She innocent . . . and she ain't got no mama.

5 ROSE: What you telling me for, Troy?

(*She turns and exits into the house.*)

TROY: Well . . . I guess we'll just sit out here on the porch.

(*He sits down on the porch. There is an awkward indelicateness about the way he handles the baby. His largeness engulfs and seems to swallow it. He speaks loud enough for* ROSE *to hear.*)

A man's got to do what's right for him. I ain't sorry for nothing I done. It felt right in my heart.

(*To the baby.*)

What you smiling at? Your daddy's a big man. Got these
10 great big old hands. But sometimes he's scared. And right now your daddy's scared cause we sitting out here and ain't got no home. Oh, I been homeless before. I ain't had no little baby with me. But I been homeless. You just be out on

the road by your lonesome and you see one of them trains coming and you just kinda go like this . . .
15

(*He sings as a lullaby.*)

Please, Mr. Engineer let a man ride the line
Please, Mr. Engineer let a man ride the line
I ain't got no ticket please let me ride the blinds

(ROSE *enters from the house.* TROY *hearing her steps behind him, stands and faces her.*)

She's my daughter, Rose. My own flesh and blood. I can't deny her no more than I can deny them boys.
20

(*Pause.*)

You and them boys is my family. You and them and this child is all I got in the world. So I guess what I'm saying is . . . I'd appreciate it if you'd help take care of her.

ROSE: Okay, Troy . . . you're right. I'll take care of your baby for you . . . cause . . . like you say . . . she's innocent . . . and 25 you can't visit the sins of the father upon the child. A motherless child has got a hard time.

(*She takes the baby from him.*)

From right now . . . this child got a mother. But you a womanless man.

(ROSE *turns and exits into the house with the baby. Lights go down to black.*)

SCENE IV

It is two months later. LYONS *enters from the street. He knocks on the door and calls.*

LYONS: Hey, Rose! (*Pause.*) Rose!

ROSE: (*From inside the house.*) Stop that yelling. You gonna wake up Raynell. I just got her to sleep.

LYONS: I just stopped by to pay Papa this twenty dollars I owe him. Where's Papa at? 5

ROSE: He should be here in a minute. I'm getting ready to go down to the church. Sit down and wait on him.

LYONS: I got to go pick up Bonnie over her mother's house.

ROSE: Well, sit it down there on the table. He'll get it.

LYONS: (*Enters the house and sets the money on the table.*) Tell 10 Papa I said thanks. I'll see you again.

ROSE: Alright, Lyons. We'll see you.

(LYONS *starts to exit as* CORY *enters.*)

CORY: Hey, Lyons.

LYONS: What's happening, Cory. Say man, I'm sorry I missed your graduation. You know I had a gig and couldn't get away. 15 Otherwise, I would have been there, man. So what you doing?

CORY: I'm trying to find a job.

LYONS: Yeah I know how that go, man. It's rough out here. Jobs are scarce. 20

CORY: Yeah, I know.

LYONS: Look here, I got to run. Talk to Papa . . . he know some people. He'll be able to help get you a job. Talk to him . . . see what he say.

CORY: Yeah . . . alright, Lyons. 25

LYONS: You take care. I'll talk to you soon. We'll find some time to talk.

(LYONS *exits the yard.* CORY *wanders over to the tree, picks up the bat and assumes a batting stance. He studies an imaginary pitcher and swings. Dissatisfied with the result, he tries again.* TROY *enters. They eye each other for a beat.* CORY *puts the bat down and exits the yard.* TROY *starts into the house as* ROSE *exits with* RAYNELL. *She is carrying a cake.*)

TROY: I'm coming in and everybody's going out.

ROSE: I'm taking this cake down to the church for the bake-
30   sale. Lyons was by to see you. He stopped by to pay you your twenty dollars. It's laying in there on the table.

TROY: (*Going into his pocket.*) Well . . . here go this money.

ROSE: Put it in there on the table, Troy. I'll get it.

TROY: What time you coming back?

35 ROSE: Ain't no use in you studying me. It don't matter what time I come back.

TROY: I just asked you a question, woman. What's the matter . . . can't I ask you a question?

ROSE: Troy, I don't want to go into it. Your dinner's in there on
40   the stove. All you got to do is heat it up. And don't you be eating the rest of them cakes in there. I'm coming back for them. We having a bakesale at the church tomorrow.

(ROSE *exits the yard.* TROY *sits down on the steps, takes a pint bottle from his pocket, opens it and drinks. He begins to sing.*)

TROY:

    Hear it ring! Hear it ring!
45   Had an old dog his name was Blue
    You know Blue was mighty true
    You know Blue as a good old dog
    Blue trees a possum in a hollow log
    You know from that he was a good old dog

(BONO *enters the yard.*)

50 BONO: Hey, Troy.

TROY: Hey, what's happening, Bono?

BONO: I just thought I'd stop by to see you.

TROY: What you stop by and see me for? You ain't stopped by in a month of Sundays. Hell, I must owe you money or
55   something.

BONO: Since you got your promotion I can't keep up with you. Used to see you everyday. Now I don't even know what route you working.

TROY: They keep switching me around. Got me out in Green-
60   tree now . . . hauling white folks' garbage.

BONO: Greentree, huh? You lucky, at least you ain't got to be lifting them barrels. Damn if they ain't getting heavier. I'm gonna put in my two years and call it quits.

TROY: I'm thinking about retiring myself.

65 BONO: You got it easy. You can *drive* for another five years.

TROY: It ain't the same, Bono. It ain't like working the back of the truck. Ain't got nobody to talk to . . . feel like you working by yourself. Naw, I'm thinking about retiring. How's Lucille?

70 BONO: She alright. Her arthritis get to acting up on her sometime. Saw Rose on my way in. She going down to the church, huh?

TROY: Yeah, she took up going down there. All them preachers looking for somebody to fatten their pockets.

(*Pause.*)

Got some gin here.   75

BONO: Naw, thanks. I just stopped by to say hello.

TROY: Hell, nigger . . . you can take a drink. I ain't never known you to say no to a drink. You ain't got to work tomorrow.

BONO: I just stopped by. I'm fixing to go over to Skinner's. We   80
got us a domino game going over his house every Friday.

TROY: Nigger, you can't play no dominoes. I used to whup you four games out of five.

BONO: Well, that learned me. I'm getting better.

TROY: Yeah? Well, that's alright.   85

BONO: Look here . . . I got to be getting on. Stop by sometime, huh?

TROY: Yeah, I'll do that, Bono. Lucille told Rose you bought her a new refrigerator.

BONO: Yeah, Rose told Lucille you had finally built your fence   90
. . . so I figured we'd call it even.

TROY: I knew you would.

BONO: Yeah . . . okay. I'll be talking to you.

TROY: Yeah, take care, Bono. Good to see you. I'm gonna stop over.   95

BONO: Yeah. Okay, Troy.

(BONO *exits.* TROY *drinks from the bottle.*)

TROY:

    Old Blue died and I dig his grave
    Let him down with a golden chain
    Every night when I hear old Blue bark   100
    I know Blue treed a possum in Noah's Ark.
    Hear it ring! Hear it ring!

(CORY *enters the yard. They eye each other for a beat.* TROY *is sitting in the middle of the steps.* CORY *walks over.*)

CORY: I got to get by.

TROY: Say what? What's you say?

CORY: You in my way. I got to get by.   105

TROY: You got to get by where? This is my house. Bought and paid for. In full. Took me fifteen years. And if you wanna go in my house and I'm sitting on the steps . . . you say excuse me. Like your mama taught you.

CORY: Come on, Pop . . . I got to get by.   110

(CORY *starts to maneuver his way past* TROY. TROY *grabs his leg and shoves him back.*)

TROY: You just gonna walk over top of me?

CORY: I live here too!

TROY: (*Advancing toward him.*) You just gonna walk over top of me in my own house?

CORY: I ain't scared of you.   115

TROY: I ain't asked if you was scared of me. I asked you if you was fixing to walk over top of me in my own house? That's the question. You ain't gonna say excuse me? You just gonna walk over top of me?

CORY: If you wanna put it like that.   120

TROY: How else am I gonna put it?

CORY: I was walking by you to go into the house cause you sitting on the steps drunk, singing to yourself. You can put it like that.

TROY: Without saying excuse me???   125

(CORY *doesn't respond.*)

I asked you a question. Without saying excuse me???

CORY: I ain't got to say excuse me to you. You don't count around here no more.

TROY: Oh, I see . . . I don't count around here no more. You
130 ain't got to say excuse me to your daddy. All of a sudden you done got so grown that your daddy don't count around here no more . . . Around here in his own house and yard that he done paid for with the sweat of his brow. You done got so
135 grown to where you gonna take over. You gonna take over my house. Is that right? You gonna wear my pants. You gonna go in there and stretch out on my bed. You ain't got to say excuse me cause I don't count around here no more. Is that right?

CORY: That's right. You always talking this dumb stuff. Now,
140 why don't you just get out my way.

TROY: I guess you got someplace to sleep and something to put in your belly. You got that, huh? You got that? That's what you need. You got that, huh?

CORY: You don't know what I got. You ain't got to worry about
145 what I got.

TROY: You right! You one hundred percent right! I done spent the last seventeen years worrying about what you got. Now it's your turn, see? I'll tell you what to do. You grown . . . we done established that. You a man. Now, let's see you act like
150 one. Turn your behind around and walk out this yard. And when you get out there in the alley . . . you can forget about this house. See? Cause this is my house. You go on and be a man and get your own house. You can forget about this. Cause this is mine. You go on and get yours cause I'm
155 through with doing for you.

CORY: You talking about what you did for me . . . what'd you ever give me?

TROY: Them feet and bones! That pumping heart, nigger! I give you more than anybody else is ever gonna give you.

160 CORY: You ain't never gave me nothing! You ain't never done nothing but hold me back. Afraid I was gonna be better than you. All you ever did was try and make me scared of you. I used to tremble every time you called my name. Every time I heard your footsteps in the house. Wondering all the time
165 . . . what's Papa gonna say if I do this? . . . What's he gonna say if I do that? . . . What's Papa gonna say if I turn on the radio? And Mama, too . . . she tries . . . but she's scared of you.

TROY: You leave your mama out of this. She ain't got nothing to do with this.

170 CORY: I don't know how she stand you . . . after what you did to her.

TROY: I told you to leave your mama out of this!

(He advances toward CORY.)

CORY: What you gonna do . . . give me a whupping? You can't whup me no more. You're too old. You just an old man.

175 TROY: *(Shoves him on his shoulder.)* Nigger! That's what you are. You just another nigger on the street to me!

CORY: You crazy! You know that?

TROY: Go on now! You got the devil in you. Get on away from me!

180 CORY: You just a crazy old man . . . talking about I got the devil in me.

TROY: Yeah, I'm crazy! If you don't get on the other side of that yard . . . I'm gonna show you how crazy I am! Go on . . . get the hell out of my yard.

CORY: It ain't your yard. You took Uncle Gabe's money he got   185
from the army to buy this house and then you put him out.

TROY: *(TROY advances on CORY.)* Get your black ass out of my yard!

(TROY's advance backs CORY up against the tree. CORY grabs up the bat.)

CORY: I ain't going nowhere! Come on . . . put me out! I ain't
scared of you.   190

TROY: That's my bat!

CORY: Come on!

TROY: Put my bat down!

CORY: Come on, put me out.

(CORY swings at TROY, who backs across the yard.)

What's the matter? You so bad . . . put me out!   195

(TROY advances toward CORY.)

CORY: *(Backing up.)* Come on! Come on!

TROY: You're gonna have to use it! You wanna draw that bat back on me . . . you're gonna have to use it.

CORY: Come on! . . . Come on!

(CORY swings the bat at TROY a second time. He misses. TROY continues to advance toward him.)

TROY: You're gonna have to kill me! You wanna draw that bat   200
back on me. You're gonna have to kill me.

(CORY, backed up against the tree, can go no farther. TROY taunts him. He sticks out his head and offers him a target.)

Come on! Come on!

(CORY is unable to swing the bat. TROY grabs it.)

TROY: Then I'll show you.

(CORY and TROY struggle over the bat. The struggle is fierce and fully engaged. TROY ultimately is the stronger, and takes the bat from CORY and stands over him ready to swing. He stops himself.)

Go on and get away from around my house.

(CORY, stung by his defeat, picks himself up, walks slowly out of the yard and up the alley.)

CORY: Tell Mama I'll be back for my things.   205

TROY: They'll be on the other side of that fence.

(CORY exits.)

TROY: I can't taste nothing. Helluljah! I can't taste nothing no more. *(TROY assumes a batting posture and begins to taunt Death, the fastball in the outside corner.)* Come on! It's between you and me now! Come on! Anytime you want!   210
Come on! I be ready for you . . . but I ain't gonna be easy.

(The lights go down on the scene.)

SCENE V

The time is 1965. The lights come up in the yard. It is the morning of TROY's funeral. A funeral plaque with a light hangs beside the door. There is a small garden plot off to the side. There is noise and activity in the house as ROSE, GABRIEL and BONO have gathered. The door opens and RAYNELL, seven years old, enters dressed in a flannel nightgown. She crosses to the garden and pokes around with a stick. ROSE calls from the house.

ROSE: Raynell!
RAYNELL: Mam?
ROSE: What you doing out there?
RAYNELL: Nothing.

(ROSE *comes to the door.*)

5 ROSE: Girl, get in here and get dressed. What you doing?
RAYNELL: Seeing if my garden growed.
ROSE: I told you it ain't gonna grow overnight. You got to wait.
RAYNELL: It don't look like it never gonna grow. Dag!
ROSE: I told you a watched pot never boils. Get in here and get
10   dressed.
RAYNELL: This ain't even no pot, Mama.
ROSE: You just have to give it a chance. It'll grow. Now you
    come on and do what I told you. We got to be getting ready.
    This ain't no morning to be playing around. You hear me?
15 RAYNELL: Yes, mam.

(ROSE *exits into the house.* RAYNELL *continues to poke at her garden with a stick.* CORY *enters. He is dressed in a Marine corporal's uniform, and carries a duffel bag. His posture is that of a military man, and his speech has a clipped sternness.*)

CORY: (*To* RAYNELL.) Hi.

(*Pause.*)

I bet your name is Raynell.
RAYNELL: Uh huh.
CORY: Is your mama home?

(RAYNELL *runs up on the porch and calls through the screen door.*)

20 RAYNELL: Mama . . . there's some man out here. Mama?

(ROSE *comes to the door.*)

ROSE: Cory? Lord have mercy! Look here, you all!

(ROSE *and* CORY *embrace in a tearful reunion as* BONO *and* LYONS *enter from the house dressed in funeral clothes.*)

BONO: Aw, looka here . . .
ROSE: Done got all grown up!
CORY: Don't cry, Mama. What you crying about?
25 ROSE: I'm just so glad you made it.
CORY: Hey Lyons. How you doing, Mr. Bono.

(LYONS *goes to embrace* CORY.)

LYONS: Look at you, man. Look at you. Don't he look good,
    Rose. Got them Corporal stripes.
ROSE: What took you so long.
30 CORY: You know how the Marines are, Mama. They got to get
    all their paperwork straight before they let you do anything.
ROSE: Well, I'm sure glad you made it. They let Lyons come.
    Your Uncle Gabe's still in the hospital. They don't know if
    they gonna let him out or not. I just talked to them a little
35   while ago.
LYONS: A Corporal in the United States Marines.
BONO: Your daddy knew you had it in you. He used to tell me
    all the time.
LYONS: Don't he look good, Mr. Bono?
40 BONO: Yeah, he remind me of Troy when I first met him.

(*Pause.*)

Say, Rose, Lucille's down at the church with the choir. I'm
    gonna go down and get the pallbearers lined up. I'll be back
    to get you all.
ROSE: Thanks, Jim.
CORY: See you, Mr. Bono.   45
LYONS: (*With his arm around* RAYNELL.) Cory . . . look at
    Raynell. Ain't she precious? She gonna break a whole lot of
    hearts.
ROSE: Raynell, come and say hello to your brother. This is
    your brother, Cory. You remember Cory.   50
RAYNELL: No, Mam.
CORY: She don't remember me, Mama.
ROSE: Well, we talk about you. She heard us talk about you.
    (*To* RAYNELL.) This is your brother, Cory. Come on and say
    hello.   55
RAYNELL: Hi.
CORY: Hi. So you're Raynell. Mama told me a lot about you.
ROSE: You all come on into the house and let me fix you some
    breakfast. Keep up your strength.
CORY: I ain't hungry, Mama.   60
LYONS: You can fix me something, Rose. I'll be in there in a
    minute.
ROSE: Cory, you sure you don't want nothing. I know they ain't
    feeding you right.
CORY: No, Mama . . . thanks. I don't feel like eating. I'll get   65
    something later.
ROSE: Raynell . . . get on upstairs and get that dress on like I
    told you.

(ROSE *and* RAYNELL *exit into the house.*)

LYONS: So . . . I hear you thinking about getting married.
CORY: Yeah, I done found the right one, Lyons. It's about time. 70
LYONS: Me and Bonnie been split up about four years now.
    About the time Papa retired. I guess she just got tired of all
    them changes I was putting her through.

(*Pause.*)

I always knew you was gonna make something out yourself.
    Your head was always in the right direction. So . . . you 75
    gonna stay in . . . make it a career . . . put in your twenty
    years?
CORY: I don't know. I got six already, I think that's enough.
LYONS: Stick with Uncle Sam and retire early. Ain't nothing
    out here. I guess Rose told you what happened with me. 80
    They got me down the workhouse. I thought I was being
    slick cashing other people's checks.
CORY: How much time you doing?
LYONS: They give me three years. I got that beat now. I ain't
    got but nine more months. It ain't so bad. You learn to deal 85
    with it like anything else. You got to take the crookeds with
    the straights. That's what Papa used to say. He used to say
    that when he struck out. I seen him strike out three times in
    a row . . . and the next time up he hit the ball over the grand-
    stand. Right out there in Homestead Field. He wasn't satis- 90
    fied hitting in the seats . . . he want to hit it over everything!
    After the game he had two hundred people standing around
    waiting to shake his hand. You got to take the crookeds with
    the straights. Yeah, papa was something else.
CORY: You still playing?   95
LYONS: Cory . . . you know I'm gonna do that. There's some
    fellows down there we got us a band . . . we gonna try and

stay together when we get out . . . but yeah, I'm still playing. It still helps me to get out of bed in the morning. As long as
100 it do that I'm gonna be right there playing and trying to make some sense out of it.

ROSE: *(Calling.)* Lyons, I got these eggs in the pan.

LYONS: Let me go on and get these eggs, man. Get ready to go bury Papa.

(Pause.)

105 How you doing? You doing alright?

(CORY nods. LYONS touches him on the shoulder and they share a moment of silent grief. LYONS exits into the house. CORY wanders about the yard. RAYNELL enters.)

RAYNELL: Hi.

CORY: Hi.

RAYNELL: Did you used to sleep in my room?

CORY: Yeah . . . that used to be my room.

110 RAYNELL: That's what Papa call it. "Cory's room." It got your football in the closet.

(ROSE comes to the door.)

ROSE: Raynell, get in there and get them good shoes on.

RAYNELL: Mama, can't I wear these. Them other ones hurt my feet.

115 ROSE: Well, they just gonna have to hurt your feet for a while. You ain't said they hurt your feet when you went down to the store and got them.

RAYNELL: They didn't hurt then. My feet done got bigger.

ROSE: Don't you give me no backtalk now. You get in there
120 and get them shoes on.

(RAYNELL exits into the house.)

Ain't too much changed. He still got that piece of rag tied to that tree. He was out here swinging that bat. I was just ready to go back in the house. He swung that bat and then he just fell over. Seem like he swung it and stood there with this grin
125 on his face . . . and then he just fell over. They carried him on down to the hospital, but I knew there wasn't no need . . . why don't you come on in the house?

CORY: Mama . . . I got something to tell you. I don't know how to tell you this . . . but I've got to tell you . . . I'm not going to
130 Papa's funeral.

ROSE: Boy, hush your mouth. That's your daddy you talking about. I don't want hear that kind of talk this morning. I done raised you to come to this? You standing there all healthy and grown talking about you ain't going to your
135 daddy's funeral.

CORY: Mama . . . listen . . .

ROSE: I don't want to hear it, Cory. You just get that thought out of your head.

CORY: I can't drag Papa with me everywhere I go. I've got to
140 say no to him. One time in my life I've got to say no.

ROSE: Don't nobody have to listen to nothing like that. I know you and your daddy ain't seen eye to eye, but I ain't got to listen to that kind of talk this morning. Whatever was between you and your daddy . . . the time has come to put it aside.
145 Just take it and set it over there on the shelf and forget about it. Disrespecting your daddy ain't gonna make you a man, Cory. You got to find a way to come to that on your own. Not going to your daddy's funeral ain't gonna make you a man.

CORY: The whole time I was growing up . . . living in his house . . . Papa was like a shadow that followed you every- 150 where. It weighed on you and sunk into your flesh. It would wrap around you and lay there until you couldn't tell which one was you anymore. That shadow digging in your flesh. Trying to crawl in. Trying to live through you. Everywhere I looked, Troy Maxson was staring back at me . . . hiding 155 under the bed . . . in the closet. I'm just saying I've got to find a way to get rid of that shadow, Mama.

ROSE: You just like him. You got him in you good.

CORY: Don't tell me that, Mama.

ROSE: You Troy Maxson all over again. 160

CORY: I don't want to be Troy Maxson. I want to be me.

ROSE: You can't be nobody but who you are, Cory. That shadow wasn't nothing but you growing into yourself. You either got to grow into it or cut it down to fit you. But that's all you got to make life with. That's all you got to measure your- 165 self against that world out there. Your daddy wanted you to be everything he wasn't . . . and at the same time he tried to make you into everything he was. I don't know if he was right or wrong . . . but I do know he meant to do more good than he meant to do harm. He wasn't always right. Sometimes 170 when he touched he bruised. And sometimes when he took me in his arms he cut.

When I first met your daddy I thought . . . Here is a man I can lay down with and make a baby. That's the first thing I thought when I seen him. I was thirty years old and had 175 done seen my share of men. But when he walked up to me and said, "I can dance a waltz that'll make you dizzy," I thought, Rose Lee, here is a man that you can open yourself up to and be filled to bursting. Here is a man that can fill all them empty spaces you been tipping around the edges of. 180 One of them empty spaces was being somebody's mother.

I married your daddy and settled down to cooking his supper and keeping clean sheets on the bed. When your daddy walked through the house he was so big he filled it up. That was my first mistake. Not to make him leave some 185 room for me. For my part in the matter. But at that time I wanted that. I wanted a house that I could sing in. And that's what your daddy gave me. I didn't know to keep up his strength I had to give up little pieces of mine. I did that. I took on his life as mine and mixed up the pieces so that you 190 couldn't hardly tell which was which anymore. It was my choice. It was my life and I didn't have to live it like that. But that's what life offered me in the way of being a woman and I took it. I grabbed hold of it with both hands.

By the time Raynell came into the house, me and your 195 daddy had done lost touch with one another. I didn't want to make my blessing off of nobody's misfortune . . . but I took on to Raynell like she was all them babies I had wanted and never had.

(The phone rings.)

Like I'd been blessed to relive a part of my life. And if the 200 Lord see fit to keep up my strength . . . I'm gonna do her just like your daddy did you . . . I'm gonna give her the best of what's in me.

RAYNELL: *(Entering, still with her old shoes.)* Mama . . . Reverend Tollivier on the phone. 205

(ROSE exits into the house.)

RAYNELL: Hi.

CORY: Hi.

RAYNELL: You in the Army or the Marines?

CORY: Marines.

210 RAYNELL: Papa said it was the Army. Did you know Blue?

CORY: Blue? Who's Blue?

RAYNELL: Papa's dog what he sing about all the time.

CORY: (*Singing.*) Hear it ring! Hear it ring!
I had a dog his name was Blue
215 You know Blue was mighty true
You know Blue was a good old dog
Blue treed a possum in a hollow log
You know from that he was a good old dog.
Hear it ring! Hear it ring!

(RAYNELL *joins in singing.*)

220 CORY and RAYNELL: Blue treed a possum out on a limb
Blue looked at me and I looked at him
Grabbed that possum and put him in a sack
Blue stayed there till I came back
Old Blue's feets was big and round
225 Never allowed a possum to touch the ground.
Old Blue died and I dug his grave
I dug his grave with a silver spade
Let him down with a golden chain
And every night I call his name
230 Go on Blue, you good dog you
Go on Blue, you good dog you

RAYNELL: Blue laid down and died like a man
Blue laid down and died . . .

BOTH: Blue laid down and died like a man
235 Now he's treeing possums in the Promised Land
I'm gonna tell you this to let you know
Blue's gone where the good dogs go
When I hear old Blue bark
When I hear old Blue bark
240 Blue treed a possum in Noah's Ark
Blue treed a possum in Noah's Ark.

(ROSE *comes to the screen door.*)

ROSE: Cory, we gonna be ready to go in a minute.

CORY: (*To* RAYNELL.) You go on in the house and change them shoes like Mama told you so we can go to Papa's funeral.

RAYNELL: Okay, I'll be back. 245

(RAYNELL *exits into the house.* CORY *gets up and crosses over to the tree.* ROSE *stands in the screen door watching him.* GABRIEL *enters from the alley.*)

GABRIEL: (*Calling.*) Hey, Rose!

ROSE: Gabe?

GABRIEL: I'm here, Rose. Hey Rose, I'm here!

(ROSE *enters from the house.*)

ROSE: Lord . . . Look here, Lyons!

LYONS: See, I told you, Rose . . . I told you they'd let him 250 come.

CORY: How you doing, Uncle Gabe?

LYONS: How you doing, Uncle Gabe?

GABRIEL: Hey, Rose. It's time. It's time to tell St. Peter to open the gates. Troy, you ready? You ready, Troy. I'm gonna tell 255 St. Peter to open the gates. You get ready now.

(GABRIEL, *with great fanfare, braces himself to blow. The trumpet is without a mouthpiece. He puts the end of it into his mouth and blows with great force, like a man who has been waiting some twenty-odd years for this single moment. No sound comes out of the trumpet. He braces himself and blows again with the same result. A third time he blows. There is a weight of impossible description that falls away and leaves him bare and exposed to a frightful realization. It is a trauma that a sane and normal mind would be unable to withstand. He begins to dance. A slow, strange dance, eerie and lifegiving. A dance of atavistic signature and ritual.* LYONS *attempts to embrace him.* GABRIEL *pushes* LYONS *away. He begins to howl in what is an attempt at song, or perhaps a song turning back into itself in an attempt at speech. He finishes his dance and the gates of heaven stand open as wide as God's closet.*)

That's the way that go!

(*Blackout.*)

■ DAVID HENRY HWANG ■

David Henry Hwang was born in Los Angeles in 1957. He graduated with a B.A. in English from Stanford University in 1979 and studied at the Yale School of Drama 1980–1981. In the 1980s, Hwang wrote a series of powerful plays concerning the cultural and political experience of Asian Americans in the United States. His first play, *F.O.B.* ("fresh off the boat"), dramatizes the tensions that arise between Chinese immigrants to the United States and their assimilated friends and relatives. The play won an Obie award in 1980. Hwang addressed similar issues in *The Dance of the Railroad* (1981) and in *Rich Relations* (1986), and he collaborated with composer Philip Glass on *1000 Airplanes on the Roof* (1988). Hwang's Tony Award-winning *M. Butterfly* (1988) is a brilliant critique of Western attitudes toward Asia, epitomized by one of Western culture's most powerful and seductive images of the Orient: Puccini's opera, *Madame Butterfly*.

M. BUTTERFLY

In *M. Butterfly*, Hwang traces the relationship between the "Orient" of the Western imagination and the political realities that such images help to foster. The play's central character, the diplomat Gallimard, conducts his relationship with China in terms of Puccini's *Madame Butterfly*. In Puccini's 1904 opera, the naval officer Pinkerton marries the Japanese geisha girl Butterfly. He leaves for the United States, promising to return, and Butterfly waits for him, meanwhile bearing his child. When Pinkerton sends his wife from America to collect his child, Butterfly realizes that he will never return. She commits suicide.

As Hwang has remarked, Butterfly has become a cultural stereotype of East-West relations — "speaking of an Asian woman, we would sometimes say, 'She's pulling a Butterfly,' which meant playing the submissive Oriental number." This sexist and racist stereotype, Hwang argues, pervades not only Western men's fantasies about Asian women — as the mail-order business in Asian wives suggests, Western men see Asian women as obedient, submissive, and sexually self-sacrificing — but also conditions the political relationship between Asia and the West as well.

M. Butterfly fuses this erotic and political desire for domination in the character of Gallimard, a French diplomat who falls in love with Song Liling, an opera singer whom he first sees singing the death aria from *Madame Butterfly*. However, the play develops a fascinating twist, for Song is in fact a man, who plays female roles in the Beijing Opera, and who — as a woman — develops a love affair with Gallimard in order to spy for the Chinese government. *M. Butterfly* compacts a complex reading of the politics of race, gender, and sexuality in a brilliantly theatrical drama.

M. BUTTERFLY

DAVID HENRY HWANG

— CHARACTERS —

KUROGO
RENE GALLIMARD
SONG LILING
MARC
MAN #2
CONSUL SHARPLESS
RENEE
WOMAN AT PARTY
GIRL IN MAGAZINE
COMRADE CHIN

SUZUKI
SHU FANG
HELGA
M. TOULON
MAN #1
JUDGE

The action of the play takes place in a Paris prison in the present, and in recall, during the decade 1960 to 1970 in Beijing, and from 1966 to the present in Paris.

— ACT ONE —

SCENE I

M. GALLIMARD's *prison cell. Paris. Present.*

Lights fade up to reveal RENE GALLIMARD, *65, in a prison cell. He wears a comfortable bathrobe, and looks old and tired. The sparsely furnished cell contains a wooden crate upon which sits a hot plate with a kettle, and a portable tape recorder.* GALLIMARD *sits on the crate staring at the recorder, a sad smile on his face.*

Upstage SONG, *who appears as a beautiful woman in traditional Chinese garb, dances a traditional piece from the Peking Opera, surrounded by the percussive clatter of Chinese music.*

Then, slowly, lights and sound cross-fade; the Chinese opera music dissolves into a Western opera, the "Love Duet" from Puccini's Madame Butterfly. SONG *continues dancing, now to the Western accompaniment. Though her movements are the same, the difference in music now gives them a balletic quality.*

GALLIMARD rises, and turns upstage towards the figure of SONG, *who dances without acknowledging him.*

GALLIMARD: Butterfly, Butterfly . . .

(He forces himself to turn away, as the image of SONG *fades out, and talks to us.)*

GALLIMARD: The limits of my cell are as such: four-and-a-half meters by five. There's one window against the far wall; a door, very strong, to protect me from autograph hounds. I'm
5   responsible for the tape recorder, the hot plate, and this charming coffee table.
         When I want to eat, I'm marched off to the dining room—hot, steaming slop appears on my plate. When I want to sleep, the light bulb turns itself off—the work of fairies.
10   It's an enchanted space I occupy. The French—we know how to run a prison.
         But, to be honest, I'm not treated like an ordinary prisoner. Why? Because I'm a celebrity. You see, I make people laugh.
         I never dreamed this day would arrive. I've never been
15   considered witty or clever. In fact, as a young boy, in an informal poll among my grammar school classmates, I was voted "least likely to be invited to a party." It's a title I managed to hold onto for many years. Despite some stiff competition.
         But now, how the tables turn! Look at me: the life of every social function in Paris. Paris? Why be modest? My   20
fame has spread to Amsterdam, London, New York. Listen to them! In the world's smartest parlors. I'm the one who lifts their spirits!

(With a flourish, GALLIMARD *directs our attention to another part of the stage.)*

SCENE II

A party. Present.

Lights go up on a chic-looking parlor, where a well-dressed trio, two men and one woman, make conversation. GALLIMARD *also remains lit; he observes them from his cell.*

WOMAN: And what of Gallimard?

MAN 1: Gallimard?

MAN 2: Gallimard!

GALLIMARD: *(To us.)* You see? They're all determined to say my name, as if it were some new dance.   5

WOMAN: He still claims not to believe the truth.

MAN 1: What? Still? Even since the trial?

WOMAN: Yes. Isn't it mad?

MAN 2: *(Laughing.)* He says . . . it was dark . . . and she was very modest!   10

(The trio break into laughter.)

MAN 1: So—what? He never touched her with his hands?

MAN 2: Perhaps he did, and simply misidentified the equipment. A compelling case for sex education in the schools.

WOMAN: To protect the National Security—the Church can't argue with that.   15

MAN 1: That's impossible! How could he not know?

MAN 2: Simple ignorance.

MAN 1: For twenty years?

MAN 2: Time flies when you're being stupid.

WOMAN: Well, I thought the French were ladies' men.   20

MAN 2: It seems Monsieur Gallimard was overly anxious to live up to his national reputation.

WOMAN: Well, he's not very good-looking.

MAN 1: No, he's not.

25 MAN 2: Certainly not.
WOMAN: Actually, I feel sorry for him.
MAN 2: A toast! To Monsieur Gallimard!
WOMAN: Yes! To Gallimard!
MAN 1: To Gallimard!
30 MAN 2: Vive la différence!

(They toast, laughing. Lights down on them.)

SCENE III

M. GALLIMARD's *cell.*

GALLIMARD: *(Smiling.)* You see? They toast me. I've become patron saint of the socially inept. Can they really be so foolish? Men like that—they should be scratching at my door, begging to learn my secrets! For I, Rene Gallimard, you see,
5   I have known, and been loved by . . . the Perfect Woman.

Alone in this cell, I sit night after night, watching our story play through my head, always searching for a new ending, one which redeems my honor, where she returns at last to my arms. And I imagine you—my ideal audience—who come to
10   understand and even, perhaps just a little, to envy me.

(He turns on his tape recorder. Over the house speakers, we hear the opening phrases of Madame Butterfly.*)*

GALLIMARD: In order for you to understand what I did and why, I must introduce you to my favorite opera: *Madame Butterfly.* By Giacomo Puccini. First produced at La Scala, Milan, in 1904, it is now beloved throughout the Western
15   world.

(As GALLIMARD *describes the opera, the tape segues in and out to sections he may be describing.)*

GALLIMARD: And why not? Its heroine, Cio-Cio-San, also known as Butterfly, is a feminine ideal, beautiful and brave. And its hero, the man for whom she gives up everything, is— *(He pulls out a naval officer's cap from under his crate, pops it
20   on his head, and struts about.)*—not very good-looking, not too bright, and pretty much a wimp: Benjamin Franklin Pinkerton of the U.S. Navy. As the curtain rises, he's just closed on two great bargains: one on a house, the other on a woman—call it a package deal.

25   Pinkerton purchased the rights to Butterfly for one hundred yen—in modern currency, equivalent to about . . . sixty-six cents. So, he's feeling pretty pleased with himself as Sharpless, the American consul, arrives to witness the marriage.

(MARC, wearing an official cap to designate SHARPLESS, *enters and plays the character.)*

30 SHARPLESS/MARC: Pinkerton!
PINKERTON/GALLIMARD: Sharpless! How's it hangin'? It's a great day, just great. Between my house, my wife, and the rickshaw ride in from town, I've saved nineteen cents just this morning.
35 SHARPLESS: Wonderful. I can see the inscription on your tombstone already: "I saved a dollar, here I lie." *(He looks around.)* Nice house.
PINKERTON: It's artistic. Artistic, don't you think? Like the way the shoji screens slide open to reveal the wet bar and disco
40   mirror ball? Classy, huh? Great for impressing the chicks.

SHARPLESS: "Chicks"? Pinkerton, you're going to be a married man!
PINKERTON: Well, sort of.
SHARPLESS: What do you mean?
PINKERTON: This country—Sharpless, it is okay. You got all 45 these geisha girls running around—
SHARPLESS: I know! I live here!
PINKERTON: Then, you know the marriage laws, right? I split for one month, it's annulled!
SHARPLESS: Leave it to you to read the fine print. Who's the 50 lucky girl?
PINKERTON: Cio-Cio-San. Her friends call her Butterfly. Sharpless, she eats out of my hand!
SHARPLESS: She's probably very hungry.
PINKERTON: Not like American girls. It's true what they say 55 about Oriental girls. They want to be treated bad!
SHARPLESS: Oh, please!
PINKERTON: It's true!
SHARPLESS: Are you serious about this girl?
PINKERTON: I'm marrying her, aren't I? 60
SHARPLESS: Yes—with generous trade-in terms.
PINKERTON: When I leave, she'll know what it's like to have loved a real man. And I'll even buy her a few nylons.
SHARPLESS: You aren't planning to take her with you?
PINKERTON: Huh? Where? 65
SHARPLESS: Home!
PINKERTON: You mean, America? Are you crazy? Can you see her trying to buy rice in St. Louis?
SHARPLESS: So, you're not serious.

(Pause.)

PINKERTON/GALLIMARD: *(As* PINKERTON.*)* Consul, I am a 70 sailor in port. *(As* GALLIMARD.*)* They then proceed to sing the famous duet, "The Whole World Over."

(The duet plays on the speakers. GALLIMARD, *as* PINKERTON, *lip-syncs his lines from the opera.)*

GALLIMARD: To give a rough translation: "The whole world over, the Yankee travels, casting his anchor wherever he wants. Life's not worth living unless he can win the hearts of 75 the fairest maidens, then hotfoot it off the premises ASAP." *(He turns towards* MARC.*)* In the preceding scene, I played Pinkerton, the womanizing cad, and my friend Marc from school . . . *(MARC bows grandly for our benefit.)* played Sharpless, the sensitive soul of reason. In life, however, our positions were usually—no, always—reversed. 80

SCENE IV

Ecole Nationale. Aix-en-Provence. 1947.

GALLIMARD: No, Marc, I think I'd rather stay home.
MARC: Are you crazy?! We are going to Dad's condo in Marseille! You know what happened last time?
GALLIMARD: Of course I do.
MARC: Of course you don't! You never know. . . . They 5 stripped, Rene!
GALLIMARD: Who stripped?
MARC: The girls!
GALLIMARD: Girls? Who said anything about girls?
MARC: Rene, we're a buncha university guys goin' up to the 10 woods. What are we gonna do—talk philosophy?

GALLIMARD: What girls? Where do you get them?

MARC: Who cares? The point is, they come. On trucks. Packed in like sardines. The back flips open, babes hop out, we're ready to roll.

GALLIMARD: You mean, they just—?

MARC: Before you know it, every last one of them—they're stripped and splashing around my pool. There's no moon out, they can't see what's going on, their boobs are flapping, right? You close your eyes, reach out—it's grab bag, get it? Doesn't matter whose ass is between whose legs, whose teeth are sinking into who. You're just in there, going at it, eyes closed, on and on for as long as you can stand. *(Pause.)* Some fun, huh?

GALLIMARD: What happens in the morning?

MARC: In the morning, you're ready to talk some philosophy. *(Beat.)* So how 'bout it?

GALLIMARD: Marc, I can't . . . I'm afraid they'll say no—the girls. So I never ask.

MARC: You don't have to ask! That's the beauty—don't you see? They don't have to say yes. It's perfect for a guy like you, really.

GALLIMARD: You go ahead . . . I may come later.

MARC: Hey, Rene—it doesn't matter that you're clumsy and got zits—they're not looking!

GALLIMARD: Thank you very much.

MARC: Wimp.

(MARC walks over to the other side of the stage, and starts waving and smiling at women in the audience.)

GALLIMARD: *(To us.)* We now return to my version of *Madame Butterfly* and the events leading to my recent conviction for treason.

(GALLIMARD notices MARC making lewd gestures.)

Marc, what are you doing?

MARC: Huh? *(Sotto voce.)* Rene, there're a lotta great babes out there. They're probably lookin' at me and thinking, "What a dangerous guy."

GALLIMARD: Yes—how could they help but be impressed by your cool sophistication?

(GALLIMARD pops the SHARPLESS cap on MARC's head, and points him offstage. MARC exits, leering.)

SCENE V

M. GALLIMARD'S *cell.*

GALLIMARD: Next, Butterfly makes her entrance. We learn her age—fifteen . . . but very mature for her years.

(Lights come up on the area where we saw SONG dancing at the top of the play. She appears there again, now dressed as MADAME BUTTERFLY, moving to the "Love Duet." GALLIMARD turns upstage slightly to watch, transfixed.)

GALLIMARD: But as she glides past him, beautiful, laughing softly behind her fan, don't we who are men sigh with hope? We, who are not handsome, nor brave, nor powerful, yet somehow believe, like Pinkerton, that we deserve a Butterfly. She arrives with all her possessions in the folds of her sleeves, lays them all out, for her man to do with as he pleases. Even her life itself—she bows her head as she whispers that she's not even worth the hundred yen he paid for

her. He's already given too much, when we know he's really had to give nothing at all.

(Music and lights on SONG out. GALLIMARD sits at his crate.)

GALLIMARD: In real life, women who put their total worth at less than sixty-six cents are quite hard to find. The closest we come is in the pages of these magazines. *(He reaches into his crate, pulls out a stack of girlie magazines, and begins flipping through them.)* Quite a necessity in prison. For three or four dollars, you get seven or eight women.

I first discovered these magazines at my uncle's house. One day, as a boy of twelve. The first time I saw them in his closet . . . all lined up—my body shook. Not with lust—no, with power. Here were women—a shelfful—who would do exactly as I wanted.

(The "Love Duet" creeps in over the speakers. Special comes up, revealing, not SONG this time, but a pinup girl in a sexy negligee, her back to us. GALLIMARD turns upstage and looks at her.)

GIRL: I know you're watching me.

GALLIMARD: My throat . . . it's dry.

GIRL: I leave my blinds open every night before I go to bed.

GALLIMARD: I can't move.

GIRL: I leave my blinds open and the lights on.

GALLIMARD: I'm shaking. My skin is hot, but my penis is soft. Why?

GIRL: I stand in front of the window.

GALLIMARD: What is she going to do?

GIRL: I toss my hair, and I let my lips part . . . barely.

GALLIMARD: I shouldn't be seeing this. It's so dirty. I'm so bad.

GIRL: Then, slowly, I lift off my nightdress.

GALLIMARD: Oh, god. I can't believe it. I can't—

GIRL: I toss it to the ground.

GALLIMARD: Now, she's going to walk away. She's going to—

GIRL: I stand there, in the light, displaying myself.

GALLIMARD: No. She's—why is she naked?

GIRL: To you.

GALLIMARD: In front of a window? This is wrong. No—

GIRL: Without shame.

GALLIMARD: No, she must . . . like it.

GIRL: I like it.

GALLIMARD: She . . . she wants me to see.

GIRL: I want you to see.

GALLIMARD: I can't believe it! She's getting excited!

GIRL: I can't see you. You can do whatever you want.

GALLIMARD: I can't do a thing. Why?

GIRL: What would you like me to do . . . next?

(Lights go down on her. Music off. Silence, as GALLIMARD puts away his magazines. Then he resumes talking to us.)

GALLIMARD: Act Two begins with Butterfly staring at the ocean. Pinkerton's been called back to the U.S., and he's given his wife a detailed schedule of his plans. In the column marked "return date," he's written "when the robins nest." This failed to ignite her suspicions. Now, three years have passed without a peep from him. Which brings a response from her faithful servant, Suzuki.

(COMRADE CHIN enters, playing SUZUKI.)

SUZUKI: Girl, he's a loser. What'd he ever give you? Nineteen cents and those ugly Day-Glo stockings? Look, it's finished! Kaput! Done! And you should be glad! I mean, the guy was a woofer! He tried before, you know—before he met you, he went down to geisha central and plunked down his spare change in front of the usual candidates—everyone else gagged! These are hungry prostitutes, and they were not interested, get the picture? Now, stop slathering when an American ship sails in, and let's make some bucks—I mean, yen! We are broke!

Now, what about Yamadori? Hey, hey—don't look away—the man is a prince—figuratively, and, what's even better, literally. He's rich, he's handsome, he says he'll die if you don't marry him—and he's even willing to overlook the little fact that you've been deflowered all over the place by a foreign devil. What do you mean, "But he's Japanese?" You're Japanese! You think you've been touched by the whitey god? He was a sailor with dirty hands!

(SUZUKI stalks offstage.)

GALLIMARD: She's also visited by Consul Sharpless, sent by Pinkerton on a minor errand.

(MARC enters, as SHARPLESS.)

SHARPLESS: I hate this job.

GALLIMARD: This Pinkerton—he doesn't show up personally to tell his wife he's abandoning her. No, he sends a government diplomat . . . at taxpayer's expense.

SHARPLESS: Butterfly? Butterfly? I have some bad—I'm going to be ill. Butterfly, I came to tell you—

GALLIMARD: Butterfly says she knows he'll return and if he doesn't she'll kill herself rather than go back to her own people. *(Beat.)* This causes a lull in the conversation.

SHARPLESS: Let's put it this way . . .

GALLIMARD: Butterfly runs into the next room, and returns holding—

(Sound cue: a baby crying. SHARPLESS, "seeing" this, backs away.)

SHARPLESS: Well, good. Happy to see things going so well. I suppose I'll be going now. Ta ta. Ciao. *(He turns away. Sound cue out.)* I hate this job. *(He exits.)*

GALLIMARD: At that moment, Butterfly spots in the harbor an American ship—the *Abramo Lincoln!*

(Music cue: "The Flower Duet." SONG, still dressed as BUTTERFLY, changes into a wedding kimono, moving to the music.)

GALLIMARD: This is the moment that redeems her years of waiting. With Suzuki's help, they cover the room with flowers—

(CHIN, as SUZUKI, trudges onstage and drops a lone flower without much enthusiasm.)

GALLIMARD: —and she changes into her wedding dress to prepare for Pinkerton's arrival.

(SUZUKI helps BUTTERFLY change. HELGA enters, and helps GALLIMARD change into a tuxedo.)

GALLIMARD: I married a woman older than myself—Helga.

HELGA: My father was ambassador to Australia. I grew up among criminals and kangaroos.

GALLIMARD: Hearing that brought me to the altar—

(HELGA exits.)

GALLIMARD: —where I took a vow renouncing love. No fantasy woman would ever want me, so, yes, I would settle for a quick leap up the career ladder. Passion, I banish, and in its place—practicality!

But my vows had long since lost their charm by the time we arrived in China. The sad truth is that all men want a beautiful woman, and the uglier the man, the greater the want.

(SUZUKI makes final adjustments of BUTTERFLY's costume, as does GALLIMARD of his tuxedo.)

GALLIMARD: I married late, at age thirty-one. I was faithful to my marriage for eight years. Until the day when, as a junior-level diplomat in puritanical Peking, in a parlor at the German ambassador's house, during the "Reign of a Hundred Flowers," I first saw her . . . singing the death scene from *Madame Butterfly*.

(SUZUKI runs offstage.)

SCENE VI

German ambassador's house. Beijing. 1960.

The upstage special area now becomes a stage. Several chairs face upstage, representing seating for some twenty guests in the parlor. A few "diplomats"—RENEE, MARC, TOULON—in formal dress enter and take seats.

GALLIMARD also sits down, but turns towards us and continues to talk. Orchestral accompaniment on the tape is now replaced by a simple piano. SONG picks up the death scene from the point where BUTTERFLY uncovers the hara-kiri knife.

GALLIMARD: The ending is pitiful. Pinkerton, in an art of great courage, stays home and sends his American wife to pick up Butterfly's child. The truth, long deferred, has come up to her door.

(SONG, playing BUTTERFLY, sings the lines from the opera in her own voice—which, though not classical, should be decent.)

SONG: "Con onor muore/ chi non puo serbar/ vita con onore."

GALLIMARD: *(Simultaneously.)* "Death with honor / Is better than life / Life with dishonor."

(The stage is illuminated; we are now completely within an elegant diplomat's residence. SONG proceeds to play out an abbreviated death scene. Everyone in the room applauds. SONG, shyly, takes her bows. Others in the room rush to congratulate her. GALLIMARD remains with us.)

GALLIMARD: They say in opera the voice is everything. That's probably why I'd never before enjoyed opera. Here . . . here was a Butterfly with little or no voice—but she had the grace, the delicacy . . . I believed this girl. I believed her suffering. I wanted to take her in my arms—so delicate, even I could protect her, take her home, pamper her until she smiled.

(Over the course of the preceding speech, SONG has broken from the upstage crowd and moved directly upstage of GALLIMARD.)

SONG: Excuse me. Monsieur. . . ?

(GALLIMARD turns upstage, shocked.)

GALLIMARD: Oh! Gallimard. Mademoiselle. . . ? A beautiful . . .

SONG: Song Liling.

GALLIMARD: A beautiful performance.

SONG: Oh, please.

20 GALLIMARD: I usually—

SONG: You make me blush. I'm no opera singer at all.

GALLIMARD: I usually don't like *Butterfly*.

SONG: I can't blame you in the least.

GALLIMARD: I mean, the story—

25 SONG: Ridiculous.

GALLIMARD: I like the story, but . . . what?

SONG: Oh, you like it?

GALLIMARD: I . . . what I mean is, I've always seen it played by huge women in so much bad makeup.

30 SONG: Bad makeup is not unique to the West.

GALLIMARD: But, who can believe them?

SONG: And you believe me?

GALLIMARD: Absolutely. You were utterly convincing. It's the first time—

35 SONG: Convincing? As a Japanese woman? The Japanese used hundreds of our people for medical experiments during the war, you know. But I gather such an irony is lost on you.

GALLIMARD: No! I was about to say, it's the first time I've seen the beauty of the story.

40 SONG: Really?

GALLIMARD: Of her death. It's a . . . a pure sacrifice. He's unworthy, but what can she do? She loves him . . . so much. It's a very beautiful story.

SONG: Well, yes, to a Westerner.

45 GALLIMARD: Excuse me?

SONG: It's one of your favorite fantasies, isn't it? The submissive Oriental woman and the cruel white man.

GALLIMARD: Well, I didn't quite mean . . .

SONG: Consider it this way: what would you say if a blonde

50 homecoming queen fell in love with a short Japanese businessman? He treats her cruelly, then goes home for three years, during which time she prays to his picture and turns down marriage from a young Kennedy. Then, when she learns he has remarried, she kills herself. Now, I believe you

55 would consider this girl to be a deranged idiot, correct? But because it's an Oriental who kills herself for a Westerner— ah!—you find it beautiful.

(Silence.)

GALLIMARD: Yes . . . well . . . I see your point . . .

SONG: I will never do Butterfly again, Monsieur Gallimard. If

60 you wish to see some real theatre, come to the Peking Opera sometime. Expand your mind.

(SONG walks offstage.)

GALLIMARD: *(To us.)* So much for protecting her in my big Western arms.

SCENE VII

M. GALLIMARD'S *apartment. Beijing. 1960.*

GALLIMARD *changes from his tux into a casual suit.* HELGA *enters.*

GALLIMARD: The Chinese are an incredibly arrogant people.

HELGA: They warned us about that in Paris, remember?

GALLIMARD: Even Parisians consider them arrogant. That's a switch.

HELGA: What is that Madame Su says? "We are a very old 5 civilization." I never know if she's talking about her country or herself.

GALLIMARD: I walk around here, all I hear every day, everywhere is how *old* this culture is. The fact that "old" may be synonymous with "senile" doesn't occur to them. 10

HELGA: You're not going to change them. "East is east, west is west, and . . ." whatever that guy said.

GALLIMARD: It's just that . . . silly. I met . . . at Ambassador Koening's tonight—you should've been there.

HELGA: Koening? Oh god, no. Did he enchant you all again 15 with the history of Bavaria?

GALLIMARD: No. I met, I suppose, the Chinese equivalent of a diva. She's a singer in the Chinese opera.

HELGA: They have an opera, too? Do they sing in Chinese? Or maybe—in Italian? 20

GALLIMARD: Tonight, she did sing in Italian.

HELGA: How'd she manage that?

GALLIMARD: She must've been educated in the West before the Revolution. Her French is very good also. Anyway, she sang the death scene from *Madame Butterfly*. 25

HELGA: *Madame Butterfly!* Then I should have come. *(She begins humming, floating around the room as if dragging long kimono sleeves.)* Did she have a nice costume? I think it's a classic piece of music.

GALLIMARD: That's what *I* thought, too. Don't let her hear you 30 say that.

HELGA: What's wrong?

GALLIMARD: Evidently the Chinese hate it.

HELGA: She hated it, but she performed it anyway? Is she perverse? 35

GALLIMARD: They hate it because the white man gets the girl. Sour grapes if you ask me.

HELGA: Politics again? Why can't they just hear it as a piece of beautiful music? So, what's in *their* opera?

GALLIMARD: I don't know. But, whatever it is, I'm sure it must 40 be *old*.

(HELGA exits.)

SCENE VIII

Chinese opera house and the streets of Beijing. 1960.

The sound of gongs clanging fills the stage.

GALLIMARD: My wife's innocent question kept ringing in my ears. I asked around, but no one knew anything about the Chinese opera. It took four weeks, but my curiosity overcame my cowardice. This Chinese diva—this unwilling Butterfly—what did she do to make her so proud? 5

The room was hot, and full of smoke. Wrinkled faces, old women, teeth missing—a man with a growth on his neck, like a human toad. All smiling, pipes falling from their mouths, cracking nuts between their teeth, a live chicken pecking at my foot—all looking, screaming, gawking . . . at 10 her.

(The upstage area is suddenly hit with a harsh white light. It has become the stage for the Chinese opera performance. Two dancers enter, along with SONG. GALLIMARD *stands apart, watching.* SONG *glides gracefully amidst the two dancers. Drums suddenly slam to a halt.* SONG *strikes a pose, looking*

straight at GALLIMARD. *Dancers exit. Light change. Pause, then* SONG *walks right off the stage and straight up to* GALLIMARD.)

SONG: Yes. You. White man. I'm looking straight at you.

GALLIMARD: Me?

SONG: You see any other white men? It was too easy to spot
15   you. How often does a man in my audience come in a tie?

(SONG *starts to remove her costume. Underneath, she wears simple baggy clothes. They are now backstage. The show is over.*)

SONG: So, you are an adventurous imperialist?

GALLIMARD: I . . . thought it would further my education.

SONG: It took you four weeks. Why?

GALLIMARD: I've been busy.

20 SONG: Well, education has always been undervalued in the
    West, hasn't it?

GALLIMARD: *(Laughing.)* I don't think it's true.

SONG: No, you wouldn't. You're a Westerner. How can you objectively judge your own values?

25 GALLIMARD: I think it's possible to achieve some distance.

SONG: Do you? *(Pause.)* It stinks in here. Let's go.

GALLIMARD: These are the smells of your loyal fans.

SONG: I love them for being my fans, I hate the smell they
    leave behind. I too can distance myself from my people.
30   *(She looks around, then whispers in his ear.)* "Art for the
    masses" is a shitty excuse to keep artists poor. *(She pops a
    cigarette in her mouth.)* Be a gentleman, will you? And light
    my cigarette.

(GALLIMARD *fumbles for a match.*)

GALLIMARD: I don't . . . smoke.

35 SONG: *(Lighting her own.)* Your loss. Had you lit my cigarette,
    I might have blown a puff of smoke right between your eyes.
    Come.

(*They start to walk about the stage. It is a summer night on the Beijing streets. Sounds of the city play on the house speakers.*)

SONG: How I wish there were even a tiny cafe to sit in. With
    cappuccinos, and men in tuxedos and bad expatriate jazz.

40 GALLIMARD: If my history serves me correctly, you weren't even
    allowed into the clubs in Shanghai before the Revolution.

SONG: Your history serves you poorly, Monsieur Gallimard.
    True, there were signs reading "No dogs and Chinamen."
    But a woman, especially a delicate Oriental woman—we al-
45   ways go where we please. Could you imagine it otherwise?
    Clubs in China filled with pasty, big-thighed white women,
    while thousands of slender lotus blossoms wait just outside
    the door? Never. The clubs would be empty. *(Beat.)* We have
    always held a certain fascination for you Caucasian men,
50   have we not?

GALLIMARD: But . . . that fascination is imperialist, or so you
    tell me.

SONG: Do you believe everything I tell you? Yes. It is always
    imperialist. But sometimes . . . sometimes, it is also mutual.
55   Oh—this is my flat.

GALLIMARD: I didn't even—

SONG: Thank you. Come another time and we will further ex-
    pand your mind.

(SONG *exits.* GALLIMARD *continues roaming the streets as he speaks to us.*)

GALLIMARD: What was that? What did she mean, "Sometimes
60   . . . it is mutual?" Women do not flirt with me. And I

normally can't talk to them. But tonight, I held up my end of
the conversation.

SCENE IX

GALLIMARD's *bedroom. Beijing. 1960.*

HELGA *enters.*

HELGA: You didn't tell me you'd be home late.

GALLIMARD: I didn't intend to. Something came up.

HELGA: Oh! Like what?

GALLIMARD: I went to the . . . to the Dutch ambassador's
    home.   5

HELGA: Again?

GALLIMARD: There was a reception for a visiting scholar. He's
    writing a six-volume treatise on the Chinese revolution. We
    all gathered that meant he'd have to live here long enough to
    actually write six volumes, and we all expressed our deepest   10
    sympathies.

HELGA: Well, I had a good night too. I went with the ladies to a
    martial arts demonstration. Some of those men—when they
    break those thick boards—*(She mimes fanning herself.)*
    whoo-whoo!   15

(HELGA *exits. Lights dim.*)

GALLIMARD: I lied to my wife. Why? I've never had any reason
    to lie before. But what reason did I have tonight? I didn't do
    anything wrong. That night, I had a dream. Other people,
    I've been told, have dreams where angels appear. Or drag-
    ons, or Sophia Loren in a towel. In my dream, Marc from   20
    school appeared.

(MARC *enters, in a nightshirt and cap.*)

MARC: Rene! You met a girl!

(GALLIMARD *and* MARC *stumble down the Beijing streets. Night sounds over the speakers.*)

GALLIMARD: It's not that amazing, thank you.

MARC: No! It's so monumental, I heard about it halfway
    around the world in my sleep!   25

GALLIMARD: I've met girls before, you know.

MARC: Name one. I've come across time and space to congrat-
    ulate you. *(He hands* GALLIMARD *a bottle of wine.)*

GALLIMARD: Marc, this is expensive.

MARC: On those rare occasions when you become a formless   30
    spirit, why not steal the best?

(MARC *pops open the bottle, begins to share it with* GALLIMARD.)

GALLIMARD: You embarrass me. She . . . there's no reason to
    think she likes me.

MARC: "Sometimes, it is mutual"?

GALLIMARD: Oh.   35

MARC: "Mutual"? "Mutual"? What does that mean?

GALLIMARD: You heard!

MARC: It means the money is in the bank, you only have to
    write the check!

GALLIMARD: I am a married man!   40

MARC: And an excellent one too. I cheated after . . . six
    months. Then again and again, until now—three hundred
    girls in twelve years.

GALLIMARD: I don't think we should hold that up as a model.

MARC: Of course not! My life—it is disgusting! Phooey!   45
    Phooey! But, you—you are the model husband.

GALLIMARD: Anyway, it's impossible. I'm a foreigner.

MARC: Ah, yes. She cannot love you, it is taboo, but something deep inside her heart . . . she cannot help herself . . . she
50   must surrender to you. It is her destiny.

GALLIMARD: How do you imagine all this?

MARC: The same way you do. It's an old story. It's in our blood. They fear us, Rene. Their women fear us. And their men—their men hate us. And, you know something? They are all
55   correct.

(They spot a light in a window.)

MARC: There! There, Rene!

GALLIMARD: It's her window.

MARC: Late at night—it burns. The light—it burns for you.

GALLIMARD: I won't look. It's not respectful.

60 MARC: We don't have to be respectful. We're foreign devils.

(Enter SONG, in a sheer robe. The "One Fine Day" aria creeps in over the speakers. With her back to us, SONG mimes attending to her toilette. Her robe comes loose, revealing her white shoulders.)

MARC: All your life you've waited for a beautiful girl who would lay down for you. All your life you've smiled like a saint when it's happened to every other man you know. And you see them in magazines and you see them in movies. And
65   you wonder, what's wrong with me? Will anyone beautiful ever want me? As the years pass, your hair thins and you struggle to hold onto even your hopes. Stop struggling, Rene. The wait is over. *(He exits.)*

GALLIMARD: Marc? Marc?

(At that moment, SONG, her back still towards us, drops her robe. A second of her naked back, then a sound cue: a phone ringing, very loud. Blackout, followed in the next beat by a special up on the bedroom area, where a phone now sits. GALLIMARD stumbles across the stage and picks up the phone. Sound cue out. Over the course of his conversation, area lights fill in the vicinity of his bed. It is the following morning.)

70 GALLIMARD: Yes? Hello?

SONG: *(Offstage.)* Is it very early?

GALLIMARD: Why, yes.

SONG: *(Offstage.)* How early?

GALLIMARD: It's . . . it's 5:30. Why are you—?

75 SONG: *(Offstage.)* But it's light outside. Already.

GALLIMARD: It is. The sun must be in confusion today.

(Over the course of SONG's next speech, her upstage special comes up again. She sits in a chair, legs crossed, in a robe, telephone to her ear.)

SONG: I waited until I saw the sun. That was as much discipline as I could manage for one night. Do you forgive me?

GALLIMARD: Of course . . . for what?

80 SONG: Then I'll ask you quickly. Are you really interested in the opera?

GALLIMARD: Why, yes. Yes I am.

SONG: Then come again next Thursday. I am playing *The Drunken Beauty.* May I count on you?

85 GALLIMARD: Yes. You may.

SONG: Perfect. Well, I must be getting to bed. I'm exhausted. It's been a very long night for me.

(SONG hangs up; special on her goes off. GALLIMARD begins to dress for work.)

SCENE X

SONG LILING's *apartment. Beijing. 1960.*

GALLIMARD: I returned to the opera that next week, and the week after that . . . she keeps our meetings so short—perhaps fifteen, twenty minutes at most. So I am left each week with a thirst which is intensified. In this way, fifteen weeks have gone by. I am starting to doubt the words of my friend Marc. 5 But no, not really. In my heart, I know she has . . . an interest in me. I suspect this is her way. She is outwardly bold and outspoken, yet her heart is shy and afraid. It is the Oriental in her at war with her Western education.

SONG: *(Offstage.)* I will be out in an instant. Ask the servant 10 for anything you want.

GALLIMARD: Tonight, I have finally been invited to enter her apartment. Though the idea is almost beyond belief, I believe she is afraid of me.

(GALLIMARD looks around the room. He picks up a picture in a frame, studies it. Without his noticing, SONG enters, dressed elegantly in a black gown from the twenties. She stands in the doorway looking like Anna May Wong.)

SONG: That is my father. 15

GALLIMARD: *(Surprised.)* Mademoiselle Song . . .

(She glides up to him, snatches away the picture.)

SONG: It is very good that he did not live to see the Revolution. They would, no doubt, have made him kneel on broken glass. Not that he didn't deserve such a punishment. But he is my father. I would've hated to see it happen. 20

GALLIMARD: I'm very honored that you've allowed me to visit your home.

(SONG curtsys.)

SONG: Thank you. Oh! Haven't you been poured any tea?

GALLIMARD: I'm really not—

SONG: *(To her offstage servant.)* Shu-Fang! Cha! Kwai-lah! *(To* 25 GALLIMARD.) I'm sorry. You want everything to be perfect—

GALLIMARD: Please.

SONG: —and before the evening even begins—

GALLIMARD: I'm really not thirsty.

SONG: —it's ruined. 30

GALLIMARD: *(Sharply.)* Mademoiselle Song!

(SONG sits down.)

SONG: I'm sorry.

GALLIMARD: What are you apologizing for now?

(Pause; SONG starts to giggle.)

SONG: I don't know!

(GALLIMARD laughs.)

GALLIMARD: Exactly my point. 35

SONG: Oh, I am silly. Lightheaded. I promise not to apologize for anything else tonight, do you hear me?

GALLIMARD: That's a good girl!

(SHU-FANG, a servant girl, comes out with a tea tray and starts to pour.)

SONG: *(To SHU-FANG.)* No! I'll pour myself for the gentleman!

(SHU-FANG, staring at GALLIMARD, exits.)

40 SONG: No, I . . . I don't even know why I invited you up.
GALLIMARD: Well, I'm glad you did.

(SONG *looks around the room.*)

SONG: There is an element of danger to your presence.
GALLIMARD: Oh?
SONG: You must know.
45 GALLIMARD: It doesn't concern me. We both know why I'm here.
SONG: It doesn't concern me either. No . . . well perhaps . . .
GALLIMARD: What?
SONG: Perhaps I am slightly afraid of scandal.
50 GALLIMARD: What are we doing?
SONG: I'm entertaining you. In my parlor.
GALLIMARD: In France, that would hardly—
SONG: France. France is a country living in the modern era. Perhaps even ahead of it. China is a nation whose soul is
55 firmly rooted two thousand years in the past. What I do, even pouring the tea for you now . . . it has . . . implications. The walls and windows say so. Even my own heart, strapped inside this Western dress . . . even it says things—things I don't care to hear.

(SONG *hands* GALLIMARD *a cup of tea.* GALLIMARD *puts his hand over both the teacup and* SONG's *hand.*)

60 GALLIMARD: This is a beautiful dress.
SONG: Don't.
GALLIMARD: What?
SONG: I don't even know if it looks right on me.
GALLIMARD: Believe me—
65 SONG: You are from France. You see so many beautiful women.
GALLIMARD: France? Since when are the European women—?
SONG: Oh! What am I trying to do, anyway?!

(SONG *runs to the door, composes herself, then turns towards* GALLIMARD.)

SONG: Monsieur Gallimard, perhaps you should go.
70 GALLIMARD: But . . . why?
SONG: There's something wrong about this.
GALLIMARD: I don't see what.
SONG: I feel . . . I am not myself.
GALLIMARD: No. You're nervous.
75 SONG: Please. Hard as I try to be modern, to speak like a man, to hold a Western woman's strong face up to my own . . . in the end, I fail. A small, frightened heart beats too quickly and gives me away. Monsieur Gallimard, I'm a Chinese girl. I've never . . . never invited a man up to my flat before. The
80 forwardness of my actions makes my skin burn.
GALLIMARD: What are you afraid of? Certainly not me, I hope.
SONG: I'm a modest girl.
GALLIMARD: I know. And very beautiful. (*He touches her hair.*)
SONG: Please—go now. The next time you see me, I shall
85 again be myself.
GALLIMARD: I like you the way you are right now.
SONG: You are a cad.
GALLIMARD: What do you expect? I'm a foreign devil.

(GALLIMARD *walks downstage.* SONG *exits.*)

GALLIMARD: (*To us.*) Did you hear the way she talked about
90 Western women? Much differently than the first night. She does—she feels inferior to them—and to me.

SCENE XI

The French embassy. Beijing. 1960.

GALLIMARD *moves towards a desk.*

GALLIMARD: I determined to try an experiment. In *Madame Butterfly*, Cio-Cio-San fears that the Western man who catches a butterfly will pierce its heart with a needle, then leave it to perish. I began to wonder: had I, too, caught a butterfly who would writhe on a needle? 5

(MARC *enters, dressed as a bureaucrat, holding a stack of papers. As* GALLIMARD *speaks,* MARC *hands papers to him. He peruses, then signs, stamps or rejects them.*)

GALLIMARD: Over the next five weeks, I worked like a dynamo. I stopped going to the opera, I didn't phone or write her. I knew this little flower was waiting for me to call, and, as I wickedly refused to do so, I felt for the first time that rush of power—the absolute power of a man. 10

(MARC *continues acting as the bureaucrat, but he now speaks as himself.*)

MARC: Rene! It's me!
GALLIMARD: Marc—I hear your voice everywhere now. Even in the midst of work.
MARC: That's because I'm watching you—all the time.
GALLIMARD: You were always the most popular guy in school. 15
MARC: Well, there's no guarantee of failure in life like happiness in high school. Somehow I knew I'd end up in the suburbs working for Renault and you'd be in the Orient picking exotic women off the trees. And they say there's no justice.
GALLIMARD: That's why you were my friend? 20
MARC: I gave you a little of my life, so that now you can give me some of yours. (*Pause.*) Remember Isabelle?
GALLIMARD: Of course I remember! She was my first experience.
MARC: We all wanted to ball her. But she only wanted me. 25
GALLIMARD: I had her.
MARC: Right. You balled her.
GALLIMARD: You were the only one who ever believed me.
MARC: Well, there's a good reason for that. (*Beat.*) C'mon. You must've guessed. 30
GALLIMARD: You told me to wait in the bushes by the cafeteria that night. The next thing I knew, she was on me. Dress up in the air.
MARC: She never wore underwear.
GALLIMARD: My arms were pinned to the dirt. 35
MARC: She loved the superior position. A girl ahead of her time.
GALLIMARD: I looked up, and there was this woman . . . bouncing up and down on my loins.
MARC: Screaming, right?
GALLIMARD: Screaming, and breaking off the branches all 40 around me, and pounding my butt up and down into the dirt.
MARC: Huffing and puffing like a locomotive.
GALLIMARD: And in the middle of all this, the leaves were getting into my mouth, my legs were losing circulation, I 45 thought, "God. So this is *it?*"
MARC: You thought that?
GALLIMARD: Well, I was worried about my legs falling off.
MARC: You didn't have a good time?
GALLIMARD: No, that's not what I—I had a great time! 50
MARC: You're sure?

GALLIMARD: Yeah. Really.

MARC: 'Cuz I wanted you to have a good time.

GALLIMARD: I did.

(*Pause.*)

55 MARC: Shit. (*Pause.*) When all is said and done, she was kind of a lousy lay, wasn't she? I mean, there was a lot of energy there, but you never knew what she was doing with it. Like when she yelled "I'm coming!"—hell, it was so loud, you wanted to go "Look, it's not that big a deal."

60 GALLIMARD: I got scared. I thought she meant someone was actually coming. (*Pause.*) But, Marc?

MARC: What?

GALLIMARD: Thanks.

MARC: Oh, don't mention it.

65 GALLIMARD: It was my first experience.

MARC: Yeah. You got her.

GALLIMARD: I got her.

MARC: Wait! Look at that letter again!

(GALLIMARD *picks up one of the papers he's been stamping, and rereads it.*)

GALLIMARD: (*To us.*) After six weeks, they began to arrive. The
70 letters.

(*Upstage special on* SONG, *as* MADAME BUTTERFLY. *The scene is underscored by the* "Love Duet.")

SONG: Did we fight? I do not know. Is the opera no longer of interest to you? Please come—my audiences miss the white devil in their midst.

(GALLIMARD *looks up from the letter, towards us.*)

GALLIMARD: (*To us.*) A concession, but much too dignified.
75 (*Beat; he discards the letter.*) I skipped the opera again that week to complete a position paper on trade.

(*The bureaucrat hands him another letter.*)

SONG: Six weeks have passed since last we met. In this your practice—to leave friends in the lurch? Sometimes I hate you, sometimes I hate myself, but always I miss you.

80 GALLIMARD: (*To us.*) Better, but I don't like the way she calls me "friend." When a woman calls a man her "friend," she's calling him a eunuch or a homosexual. (*Beat; he discards the letter.*) I was absent from the opera for the seventh week, feeling a sudden urge to clean out my files.

(*Bureaucrat hands him another letter.*)

85 SONG: Your rudeness is beyond belief. I don't deserve this cruelty. Don't bother to call. I'll have you turned away at the door.

GALLIMARD: (*To us.*) I didn't. (*He discards the letter; bureaucrat hands him another.*) And then finally, the letter that con-
90 cluded my experiment.

SONG: I am out of words. I can hide behind dignity no longer. What do you want? I have already given you my shame.

(GALLIMARD *gives the letter back to* MARC, *slowly. Special on* SONG *fades out.*)

GALLIMARD: (*To us.*) Reading it, I became suddenly ashamed. Yes, my experiment had been a success. She was turning on
95 my needle. But the victory seemed hollow.

MARC: Hollow? Are you crazy?

GALLIMARD: Nothing, Marc. Please go away.

MARC: (*Exiting, with papers.*) Haven't I taught you anything?

GALLIMARD: "I have already given you my shame." I had to at-
100 tend a reception that evening. On the way, I felt sick. If there is a God, surely he would punish me now. I had finally gained power over a beautiful woman, only to abuse it cruelly. There must be justice in the world. I had the strange feeling that the ax would fall this very evening.

SCENE XII

AMBASSADOR TOULON's *residence. Beijing. 1960.*

Sound cue: party noises. Light change. We are now in a spacious residence. TOULON, *the French ambassador, enters and taps* GALLIMARD *on the shoulder.*

TOULON: Gallimard? Can I have a word? Over here.

GALLIMARD: (*To us.*) Manuel Toulon. French ambassador to China. He likes to think of us all as his children. Rather like God.

TOULON: Look, Gallimard, there's not much to say. I've liked
5 you. From the day you walked in. You were no leader, but you were tidy and efficient.

GALLIMARD: Thank you, sir.

TOULON: Don't jump the gun. Okay, our needs in China are changing. It's embarrassing that we lost Indochina. Some-
10 one just wasn't on the ball there. I don't mean you personally, of course.

GALLIMARD: Thank you, sir.

TOULON: We're going to be doing a lot more information-gathering in the future. The nature of our work here is
15 changing. Some people are just going to have to go. It's nothing personal.

GALLIMARD: Oh.

TOULON: Want to know a secret? Vice-Consul LeBon is being transferred.
20
GALLIMARD: (*To us.*) My immediate superior!

TOULON: And most of his department.

GALLIMARD: (*To us.*) Just as I feared! God has seen my evil heart—

TOULON: But not you.
25
GALLIMARD: (*To us.*)—and he's taking her away just as . . . (*To* TOULON.) Excuse me, sir?

TOULON: Scare you? I think I did. Cheer up, Gallimard. I want you to replace LeBon as vice-consul.

GALLIMARD: You—? Yes, well, thank you, sir.
30
TOULON: Anytime.

GALLIMARD: I . . . accept with great humility.

TOULON: Humility won't be part of the job. You're going to coordinate the revamped intelligence division. Want to know a secret? A year ago, you would've been out. But the past few
35 months, I don't know how it happened, you've become this new aggressive confident . . . thing. And they also tell me you get along with the Chinese. So I think you're a lucky man, Gallimard. Congratulations.

(*They shake hands.* TOULON *exits. Party noises out.* GALLIMARD *stumbles across a darkened stage.*)

GALLIMARD: Vice-consul? Impossible! As I stumbled out of
40 the party, I saw it written across the sky: There is no God. Or, no—say that there is a God. But that God . . . understands. Of course! God who creates Eve to serve Adam, who blesses Solomon with his harem but ties Jezebel to a burning bed—

that God is a man. And he understands! At age thirty-nine, I was suddenly initiated into the way of the world.

SCENE XIII

SONG LILING's *apartment. Beijing. 1960.*

SONG *enters, in a sheer dressing gown.*

SONG: Are you crazy?

GALLIMARD: Mademoiselle Song—

SONG: To come here—at this hour? After . . . after eight weeks?

GALLIMARD: It's the most amazing—

5   SONG: You bang on my door? Scare my servants, scandalize the neighbors?

GALLIMARD: I've been promoted. To vice-consul.

(Pause.)

SONG: And what is that supposed to mean to me?

GALLIMARD: Are you my Butterfly?

10   SONG: What are you saying?

GALLIMARD: I've come tonight for an answer: are you my Butterfly?

SONG: Don't you know already?

GALLIMARD: I want you to say it.

15   SONG: I don't want to say it.

GALLIMARD: So, that is your answer?

SONG: You know how I feel about—

GALLIMARD: I do remember one thing.

SONG: What?

20   GALLIMARD: In the letter I received today.

SONG: Don't.

GALLIMARD: "I have already given you my shame."

SONG: It's enough that I even wrote it.

GALLIMARD: Well, then—

25   SONG: I shouldn't have it splashed across my face.

GALLIMARD: —if that's all true—

SONG: Stop!

GALLIMARD: Then what is one more short answer?

SONG: I don't want to!

30   GALLIMARD: Are you my Butterfly? *(Silence; he crosses the room and begins to touch her hair.)* I want from you honesty. There should be nothing false between us. No false pride.

(Pause.)

SONG: Yes, I am. I am your Butterfly.

GALLIMARD: Then let me be honest with you. It is because of you that I was promoted tonight. You have changed my life forever. My little Butterfly, there should be no more secrets: I love you.

(He starts to kiss her roughly. She resists slightly.)

SONG: No . . . no . . . gently . . . please, I've never . . .

GALLIMARD: No?

40   SONG: I've tried to appear experienced, but . . . the truth is . . . no.

GALLIMARD: Are you cold?

SONG: Yes. Cold.

GALLIMARD: Then we will go very, very slowly.

(He starts to caress her; her gown begins to open.)

45   SONG: No . . . let me . . . keep my clothes . . .

GALLIMARD: But . . .

SONG: Please . . . it all frightens me. I'm a modest Chinese girl.

GALLIMARD: My poor little treasure.

SONG: I am your treasure. Though inexperienced, I am not . . .   50
ignorant. They teach us things, our mothers, about pleasing a man.

GALLIMARD: Yes?

SONG: I'll do my best to make you happy. Turn off the lights.

(GALLIMARD gets up and heads for a lamp. SONG, propped up on one elbow, tosses her hair back and smiles.)

SONG: Monsieur Gallimard?   55

GALLIMARD: Yes, Butterfly?

SONG: "Vieni, vieni!"

GALLIMARD: "Come, darling."

SONG: "Ah! Dolce notte!"

GALLIMARD: "Beautiful night."   60

SONG: "Tutto estatico d'amor ride il ciel!"

GALLIMARD: "All ecstatic with love, the heavens are filled with laughter."

(He turns off the lamp. Blackout.)

— ACT TWO —

SCENE I

M. GALLIMARD's *cell. Paris. Present.*

Lights up on GALLIMARD. *He sits in his cell, reading from a leaflet.*

GALLIMARD: This, from a contemporary critic's commentary on *Madame Butterfly:* "Pinkerton suffers from . . . being an obnoxious bounder whom every man in the audience itches to kick." Bully for us men in the audience! Then, in the same note: "Butterfly is the most irresistibly appealing of   5
Puccini's 'Little Women.' Watching the succession of her humiliations is like watching a child under torture." *(He tosses the pamphlet over his shoulder.)* I suggest that, while we men may all want to kick Pinkerton, very few of us would pass up the opportunity to be Pinkerton.   10

(GALLIMARD moves out of his cell.)

SCENE II

GALLIMARD *and* BUTTERFLY's *flat. Beijing. 1960.*

We are in a simple but well-decorated parlor. GALLIMARD *moves to sit on a sofa, while* SONG, *dressed in a chong sam, enters and curls up at his feet.*

GALLIMARD: *(To us.)* We secured a flat on the outskirts of Peking. Butterfly, as I was calling her now, decorated our "home" with Western furniture and Chinese antiques. And there, on a few stolen afternoons or evenings each week, Butterfly commenced her education.   5

SONG: The Chinese men—they keep us down.

GALLIMARD: Even in the "New Society"?

SONG: In the "New Society," we are all kept ignorant equally. That's one of the exciting things about loving a Western man. I know you are not threatened by a woman's education.   10

GALLIMARD: I'm no saint, Butterfly.

SONG: But you come from a progressive society.

GALLIMARD: We're not always reminding each other how "old" we are, if that's what you mean.

15 SONG: Exactly. We Chinese—once, I suppose, it is true, we ruled the world. But so what? How much more exciting to be part of the society ruling the world today. Tell me—what's happening in Vietnam?

GALLIMARD: Oh, Butterfly—you want me to bring my work
20 home?

SONG: I want to know what you know. To be impressed by my man. It's not the particulars so much as the fact that you're making decisions which change the shape of the world.

GALLIMARD: Not the world. At best, a small corner.

(TOULON *enters, and sits at a desk upstage.*)

SCENE III

French embassy. Beijing. 1961.

GALLIMARD *moves downstage, to* TOULON's *desk.* SONG *remains upstage, watching.*

TOULON: And a more troublesome corner is hard to imagine.

GALLIMARD: So, the Americans plan to begin bombing?

TOULON: This is very secret, Gallimard: yes. The Americans don't have an embassy here. They're asking us to be their
5 eyes and ears. Say Jack Kennedy signed an order to bomb North Vietnam, Laos. How would the Chinese react?

GALLIMARD: I think the Chinese will squawk—

TOULON: Uh-huh.

GALLIMARD: —but, in their hearts, they don't even like Ho
10 Chi Minh.

(*Pause.*)

TOULON: What a bunch of jerks. Vietnam was *our* colony. Not only didn't the Americans help us fight to keep them, but now, seven years later, they've come back to grab the territory for themselves. It's very irritating.

15 GALLIMARD: With all due respect, sir, why, should the Americans have won our war for us back in '54 if we didn't have the will to win it ourselves?

TOULON: You're kidding, aren't you?

(*Pause.*)

GALLIMARD: The Orientals simply want to be associated with
20 whoever shows the most strength and power. You live with the Chinese, sir. Do you think they like Communism?

TOULON: I live in China. Not with the Chinese.

GALLIMARD: Well, I—

TOULON: *You* live with the Chinese.

25 GALLIMARD: Excuse me?

TOULON: I can't keep a secret.

GALLIMARD: What are you saying?

TOULON: Only that I'm not immune to gossip. So, you're keeping a native mistress. Don't answer. It's none of my busi-
30 ness. (*Pause.*) I'm sure she must be gorgeous.

GALLIMARD: Well . . .

TOULON: I'm impressed. You have the stamina to go out into the streets and hunt one down. Some of us have to be content with the wives of the expatriate community.

35 GALLIMARD: I do feel . . . fortunate.

TOULON: So, Gallimard, you've got the inside knowledge— what *do* the Chinese think?

GALLIMARD: Deep down, they miss the old days. You know, cappuccinos, men in tuxedos—

TOULON: So what do we tell the Americans about Vietnam? 40

GALLIMARD: Tell them there's a natural affinity between the West and the Orient.

TOULON: And that you speak from experience?

GALLIMARD: The Orientals are people too. They want the good things we can give them. If the Americans demonstrate 45 the will to win, the Vietnamese will welcome them into a mutually beneficial union.

TOULON: I don't see how the Vietnamese can stand up to American firepower.

GALLIMARD: Orientals will always submit to a greater force. 50

TOULON: I'll note your opinions in my report. The Americans always love to hear how "welcome" they'll be. (*He starts to exit.*)

GALLIMARD: Sir?

TOULON: Mmmm? 55

GALLIMARD: This . . . rumor you've heard.

TOULON: Uh-huh?

GALLIMARD: How . . . widespread do you think it is?

TOULON: It's only widespread within this embassy. Where no-body talks because everybody is guilty. We were worried 60 about you, Gallimard. We thought you were the only one here without a secret. Now you go and find a lotus blossom . . . and top us all. (*He exits.*)

GALLIMARD: (*To us.*) Toulon knows! And he approves! I was learning the benefits of being a man. We form our own 65 clubs, sit behind thick doors, smoke—and celebrate the fact that we're still boys. (*He starts to move downstage, towards* SONG.) So, over the—

(*Suddenly* COMRADE CHIN *enters.* GALLIMARD *backs away.*)

GALLIMARD: (*To* SONG.) No! Why does she have to come in?

SONG: Rene, be sensible. How can they understand the story 70 without her? Now, don't embarrass yourself.

(GALLIMARD *moves down center.*)

GALLIMARD: (*To us.*) Now, you will see why my story is so amusing to so many people. Why they snicker at parties in disbelief. Please—try to understand it from my point of view. We are all prisoners of our time and place. (*He exits.*) 75

SCENE IV

GALLIMARD *and* BUTTERFLY's *flat. Beijing. 1961.*

SONG: (*To us.*) 1961. The flat Monsieur Gallimard rented for us. An evening after he has gone.

CHIN: Okay, see if you find out when the Americans plan to start bombing Vietnam. If you can find out what cities, even better. 5

SONG: I'll do my best, but I don't want to arouse his suspicions.

CHIN: Yeah, sure, of course. So, what else?

SONG: The Americans will increase troops in Vietnam to 170,000 soldiers with 120,000 militia and 11,000 American advisors.

CHIN: (*Writing*) Wait, wait. 120,000 militia and — 10

SONG: —11,000 American—

CHIN: —American advisors. (*Beat.*) How do you remember so much?

SONG: I'm an actor. 15

CHIN: Yeah. *(Beat.)* Is that how come you dress like that?

SONG: Like what, Miss Chin?

CHIN: Like that dress! You're wearing a dress. And every time I come here, you're wearing a dress. Is that because you're an
20 actor? Or what?

SONG: It's a . . . disguise, Miss Chin.

CHIN: Actors, I think they're all weirdos. My mother tells me actors are like gamblers or prostitutes or —

SONG: It helps me in my assignment.

(Pause.)

25 CHIN: You're not gathering information in any way that violates Communist Party principles, are you?

SONG: Why would I do that?

CHIN: Just checking. Remember: when working for the Great Proletarian State, you represent our Chairman Mao in every
30 position you take.

SONG: I'll try to imagine the Chairman taking my positions.

CHIN: We all think of him this way. Good-bye, comrade. *(She starts to exit.)* Comrade?

SONG: Yes?

35 CHIN: Don't forget: there is no homosexuality in China!

SONG: Yes, I've heard.

CHIN: Just checking. *(She exits.)*

SONG: *(To us.)* What passes for a woman in modern China.

(GALLIMARD sticks his head out from the wings.)

GALLIMARD: Is she gone?

40 SONG: Yes, Rene. Please continue in your own fashion.

SCENE V

Beijing. 1961–63.

GALLIMARD *moves to the couch where* SONG *still sits. He lies down in her lap, and she strokes his forehead.*

GALLIMARD: *(To us.)* And so, over the years 1961, '62, '63, we settled into our routine, Butterfly and I. She would always have prepared a light snack and then, ever so delicately, and only if I agreed, she would start to pleasure me. With her
5 hands, her mouth . . . too many ways to explain, and too sad, given my present situation. But mostly we would talk. About my life. Perhaps there is nothing more rare than to find a woman who passionately listens.

(SONG remains upstage, listening, as HELGA enters and plays a scene downstage with GALLIMARD.)

HELGA: Rene, I visited Dr. Bolleart this morning.

10 GALLIMARD: Why? Are you ill?

HELGA: No, no. You see, I wanted to ask him . . . that question we've been discussing.

GALLIMARD: And I told you, it's only a matter of time. Why did you bring a doctor into this? We just have to keep trying—
15 like a crapshoot, actually.

HELGA: I went, I'm sorry. But listen: he says there's nothing wrong with me.

GALLIMARD: You see? Now, will you stop—?

HELGA: Rene, he says he'd like you to go in and take some
20 tests.

GALLIMARD: Why? So he can find there's nothing wrong with both of us?

HELGA: Rene, I don't ask for much. One trip! One visit! And then, whatever you want to do about it—you decide.

GALLIMARD: You're assuming he'll find something defective! 25

HELGA: No! Of course not! Whatever he finds—if he finds nothing, we decide what to do about nothing! But go!

GALLIMARD: If he finds nothing, we keep trying. Just like we do now.

HELGA: But at least we'll know! *(Pause.)* I'm sorry. *(She starts* 30 *to exit.)*

GALLIMARD: Do you really want me to see Dr. Bolleart?

HELGA: Only if you want a child, Rene. We have to face the fact that time is running out. Only if you want a child. *(She exits.)* 35

GALLIMARD: *(To SONG.)* I'm a modern man, Butterfly. And yet, I don't want to go. It's the same old voodoo. I feel like God himself is laughing at me if I can't produce a child.

SONG: You men of the West—you're obsessed by your odd desire for equality. Your wife can't give you a child, and *you're* 40 going to the doctor?

GALLIMARD: Well, you see, she's already gone.

SONG: And because this incompetent can't find the defect, you now have to subject yourself to him? It's unnatural.

GALLIMARD: Well, what is the "natural" solution? 45

SONG: In Imperial China, when a man found that one wife was inadequate, he turned to another—to give him his son.

GALLIMARD: What do you—? I can't . . . marry you, yet.

SONG: Please. I'm not asking you to be my husband. But I am already your wife. 50

GALLIMARD: Do you want to . . . have my child?

SONG: I thought you'd never ask.

GALLIMARD: But, your career . . . your—

SONG: Phooey on my career! That's your Western mind, twisting itself into strange shapes again. Of course I love my ca- 55
reer. But what would I love most of all? To feel something inside me—day and night—something I know is yours. *(Pause.)* Promise me . . . you won't go to this doctor. Who is this Western quack to set himself as judge over the man I love? I know who is a man, and who is not. *(She exits.)* 60

GALLIMARD: *(To us.)* Dr. Bolleart? Of course I didn't go. What man would?

SCENE VI

Beijing. 1963.

Party noises over the house speakers. RENEE *enters, wearing a revealing gown.*

GALLIMARD: 1963. A party at the Austrian embassy. None of us could remember the Austrian ambassador's name, which seemed somehow appropriate. *(To RENEE.)* So, I tell the Americans, Diem must go. The U.S. wants to be respected by the Vietnamese, and yet they're propping up this nobody 5
seminarian as her president. A man whose claim to fame is his sister-in-law imposing fanatic "moral order" campaigns? Oriental women—when they're good, they're very good, but when they're bad, they're Christians.

RENEE: Yeah. 10

GALLIMARD: And what do you do?

RENEE: I'm a student. My father exports a lot of useless stuff to the Third World.

GALLIMARD: How useless?

15　RENEE: You know. Squirt guns, confectioner's sugar, hula
　　　　hoops . . .
　　GALLIMARD: I'm sure they appreciate the sugar.
　　RENEE: I'm here for two years to study Chinese.
　　GALLIMARD: Two years?
20　RENEE: That's what everybody says.
　　GALLIMARD: When did you arrive?
　　RENEE: Three weeks ago.
　　GALLIMARD: And?
　　RENEE: I like it. It's primitive, but . . . well, this is the place to
25　　　　learn Chinese, so here I am.
　　GALLIMARD: Why Chinese?
　　RENEE: I think it'll be important someday.
　　GALLIMARD: You do?
　　RENEE: Don't ask me when, but . . . that's what I think.
30　GALLIMARD: Well, I agree with you. One hundred precent.
　　　　That's very farsighted.
　　RENEE: Yeah. Well of course, my father thinks I'm a complete
　　　　weirdo.
　　GALLIMARD: He'll thank you someday.
35　RENEE: Like when the Chinese start buying hula hoops?
　　GALLIMARD: There're a billion bellies out there.
　　RENEE: And if they end up taking over the world—well, then
　　　　I'll be lucky to know Chinese too, right?

(Pause.)

　　GALLIMARD: At this point, I don't see how the Chinese can
40　　　　possibly take—
　　RENEE: You know what I *don't* like about China?
　　GALLIMARD: Excuse me? No—what?
　　RENEE: Nothing to do at night.
　　GALLIMARD: You come to parties at embassies like everyone
45　　　　else.
　　RENEE: Yeah, but they get out at ten. And then what?
　　GALLIMARD: I'm afraid the Chinese idea of a dance hall is a
　　　　dirt floor and a man with a flute.
　　RENEE: Are you married?
50　GALLIMARD: Yes. Why?
　　RENEE: You wanna . . . fool around?

(Pause.)

　　GALLIMARD: Sure.
　　RENEE: I'll wait for you outside. What's your name?
　　GALLIMARD: Gallimard. Rene.
55　RENEE: Weird. I'm Renee too. *(She exits.)*
　　GALLIMARD: *(To us.)* And so, I embarked on my first extra-ex-
　　　　tramarital affair. Renee was picture perfect. With a body
　　　　like those girls in the magazines. If I put a tissue paper over
　　　　my eyes, I wouldn't have been able to tell the difference.
60　　　　And it was exciting to be with someone who wasn't afraid to
　　　　be seen completely naked. But is it possible for a woman to
　　　　be *too* uninhibited, *too* willing, so as to seem almost too . . .
　　　　masculine?

*(CHUCK BERRY blares from the house speakers, then comes down
in volume as RENEE enters, toweling her hair.)*

　　RENEE: You have a nice weenie.
65　GALLIMARD: What?
　　RENEE: Penis. You have a nice penis.
　　GALLIMARD: Oh. Well, thank you. That's very . . .
　　RENEE: What—can't take a compliment?

　　GALLIMARD: No, it's very . . . reassuring.
　　RENEE: But most girls don't come out and say it, huh?　　70
　　GALLIMARD: And also . . . what did you call it?
　　RENEE: Oh. Most girls don't call it a "weenie," huh?
　　GALLIMARD: It sounds very—
　　RENEE: Small, I know.
　　GALLIMARD: I was going to say, "young."　　75
　　RENEE: Yeah. Young, small, same thing. Most guys are pretty,
　　　　uh, sensitive about that. Like, you know, I had a boyfriend
　　　　back home in Denmark. I got mad at him once and called
　　　　him a little weeniehead. He got so mad! He said at least I
　　　　should call him a great big weeniehead.　　80
　　GALLIMARD: I suppose I just say "penis."
　　RENEE: Yeah. That's pretty clinical. There's "cock," but that
　　　　sounds like a chicken. And "prick" is painful, and "dick" is
　　　　like you're talking about someone who's not in the room.
　　GALLIMARD: Yes. It's a . . . bigger problem than I imagined.　　85
　　RENEE: I—I think maybe it's because I really don't know what
　　　　to do with them—that's why I call them "weenies."
　　GALLIMARD: Well, you did quite well with . . . mine.
　　RENEE: Thanks, but I mean, really *do* with them. Like, okay,
　　　　have you ever looked at one? I mean, really?　　90
　　GALLIMARD: No, I suppose when it's part of you, you sort of
　　　　take it for granted.
　　RENEE: I guess. But, like, it just hangs there. This little . . . flap
　　　　of flesh. And there's so much fuss that we make about it.
　　　　Like, I think the reason we fight wars is because we wear　　95
　　　　clothes. Because no one knows—between the men, I
　　　　mean—who has the bigger . . . weenie. So, if I'm a guy with
　　　　a small one, I'm going to build a really big building or take
　　　　over a really big piece of land or write a really long book so
　　　　the other men don't know, right? But, see, it never really　　100
　　　　works, that's the problem. I mean, you conquer the country,
　　　　or whatever, but you're still wearing clothes, so there's no
　　　　way to prove absolutely whose is bigger or smaller. And that's
　　　　what we call a civilized society. The whole world run by a
　　　　bunch of men with pricks the size of pins. *(She exits.)*　　105
　　GALLIMARD: *(To us.)* This was simply not acceptable.

*(A high-pitched chime rings through the air. SONG, dressed as
BUTTERFLY, appears in the upstage special. She is obviously distressed. Her body swoons as she attempts to clip the stems of
flowers she's arranging in a vase.)*

　　GALLIMARD: But I kept up our affair, wildly, for several
　　　　months. Why? I believe because of Butterfly. She knew the
　　　　secret I was trying to hide. But, unlike a Western woman,
　　　　she didn't confront me, threaten, even pout. I remembered　　110
　　　　the words of Puccini's *Butterfly*:
　　SONG: "Noi siamo gente avvezza / alle piccole cose / umili e
　　　　silenziose."
　　GALLIMARD: "I come from a people/ Who are accustomed to
　　　　little/ Humble and silent." I saw Pinkerton and Butterfly,　　115
　　　　and what she would say if he were unfaithful . . . nothing.
　　　　She would cry, alone, into those wildly soft sleeves, once full
　　　　of possessions, now empty to collect her tears. It was her tears
　　　　and her silence that excited me, every time I visited Renee.
　　TOULON: *(Offstage.)* Gallimard!　　120

*(TOULON enters. GALLIMARD turns towards him. During the
next section, SONG, up center, begins to dance with the flowers.
It is a drunken dance, where she breaks small pieces off the
stems.)*

TOULON: They're killing him.

GALLIMARD: Who? I'm sorry? What?

TOULON: Bother you to come over at this late hour?

GALLIMARD: No . . . of course not.

125 TOULON: Not after you hear my secret. Champagne?

GALLIMARD: Um . . . thank you.

TOULON: You're surprised. There's something that you've wanted, Gallimard. No, not a promotion. Next time. Something in the world. You're not aware of this, but there's an in-

130 formal gossip circle among intelligence agents. And some of ours heard from some of the Americans—

GALLIMARD: Yes?

TOULON: That the U.S. will allow the Vietnamese generals to stage a coup . . . and assassinate President Diem.

(The chime rings again. TOULON *freezes.* GALLIMARD *turns upstage and looks at* BUTTERFLY, *who slowly and deliberately clips a flower off its stem.* GALLIMARD *turns back towards* TOULON.*)*

135 GALLIMARD: I think . . . that's a very wise move!

*(*TOULON *unfreezes.*)*

TOULON: It's what you've been advocating. A toast?

GALLIMARD: Sure. I consider this a vindication.

TOULON: Not exactly. "To the test. Let's hope you pass."

(They drink. The chime rings again. TOULON *freezes.* GALLIMARD *turns upstage, and* SONG *clips another flower.*)*

GALLIMARD: *(To* TOULON.*)* The test?

140 TOULON: *(Unfreezing.)* It's a test of everything you've been saying. I personally think the generals probably will stop the Communists. And you'll be a hero. But if anything goes wrong, then your opinions won't be worth a pig's ear. I'm sure that won't happen. But sometimes it's easier when they

145 don't listen to you.

GALLIMARD: They're your opinions too, aren't they?

TOULON: Personally, yes.

GALLIMARD: So we agree.

TOULON: But my opinions aren't on that report. Yours are.

150 Cheers.

*(*TOULON *turns away from* GALLIMARD *and raises his glass. At that instant* SONG *picks up the vase and hurls it to the ground. It shatters.* SONG *sinks down amidst the shards of the vase, in a calm, childlike trance. She sings softly, as if reciting a child's nursery rhyme.*)*

SONG: *(Repeat as necessary.)* "The whole world over, the white man travels, setting anchor, wherever he likes. Life's not worth living, unless he finds, the finest maidens, of every land . . ."

*(*GALLIMARD *turns downstage towards us.* SONG *continues singing.*)*

155 GALLIMARD: I shook as I left his house. That coward! That worm! To put the burden for his decisions on my shoulders! I started for Renee's. But no, that was all I needed. A schoolgirl who would question the role of the penis in modern society. What I wanted was revenge. A vessel to contain

160 my humiliation. Though I hadn't seen her in several weeks, I headed for Butterfly's.

*(*GALLIMARD *enters* SONG's *apartment.*)*

SONG: Oh! Rene . . . I was dreaming!

GALLIMARD: You've been drinking?

SONG: If I can't sleep, then yes, I drink. But then, it gives me these dreams which—Rene, it's been almost three weeks 165 since you visited me last.

GALLIMARD: I know. There's been a lot going on in the world.

SONG: Fortunately I am drunk. So I can speak freely. It's not the world, it's you and me. And an old problem. Even the softest skin becomes like leather to a man who's touched it 170 too often. I confess I don't know how to stop it. I don't know how to become another woman.

GALLIMARD: I have a request.

SONG: Is this a solution? Or are you ready to give up the flat?

GALLIMARD: It may be a solution. But I'm sure you won't 175 like it.

SONG: Oh well, that's very important. "Like it?" Do you think I "like" lying here alone, waiting, always waiting for your return? Please—don't worry about what I may not "like."

GALLIMARD: I want to see you . . . naked. 180

(Silence.)

SONG: I thought you understood my modesty. So you want me to—what—strip? Like a big cowboy girl? Shiny pasties on my breasts? Shall I fling my kimono over my head and yell "ya-hoo" in the process? I thought you respected my shame!

GALLIMARD: I believe you gave me your shame many years 185 ago.

SONG: Yes—and it is just like a white devil to use it against me. I can't believe it. I thought myself so repulsed by the passive Oriental and the cruel white man. Now I see—we are always most revolted by the things hidden within us. 190

GALLIMARD: I just mean—

SONG: Yes?

GALLIMARD: —that it will remove the only barrier left between us.

SONG: No, Rene. Don't couch your request in sweet words. Be 195 yourself—a cad—and know that my love is enough, that I submit—submit to the worst you can give me. *(Pause.)* Well, come. Strip me. Whatever happens, know that you have willed it. Our love, in your hands. I'm helpless before my man. 200

*(*GALLIMARD *starts to cross the room.*)*

GALLIMARD: Did I not undress her because I knew, somewhere deep down, what I would find? Perhaps. Happiness is so rare that our mind can turn somersaults to protect it.

At the time, I only knew that I was seeing Pinkerton stalking towards his Butterfly, ready to reward her love with his 205 lecherous hands. The image sickened me, pulled me to my knees, so I was crawling towards her like a worm. By the time I reached her, Pinkerton . . . had vanished from my heart. To be replaced by something new, something unnatural, that flew in the face of all I'd learned in the world—something 210 very close to love.

(He grabs her around the waist; she strokes his hair.)

GALLIMARD: Butterfly, forgive me.

SONG: Rene . . .

GALLIMARD: For everything. From the start.

SONG: I'm . . . 215

GALLIMARD: I want to—

SONG: I'm pregnant. (*Beat.*) I'm pregnant. (*Beat.*) I'm pregnant. (*Beat.*)

GALLIMARD: I want to marry you!

SCENE VII

GALLIMARD *and* BUTTERFLY's *flat. Beijing. 1963.*

Downstage, SONG *paces as* COMRADE CHIN *reads from her notepad. Upstage,* GALLIMARD *is still kneeling. He remains on his knees throughout the scene, watching it.*

SONG: I need a baby.

CHIN: (*From pad.*) He's been spotted going to a dorm.

SONG: I need a baby.

CHIN: At the Foreign Language Institute.

5   SONG: I need a baby.

CHIN: The room of a Danish girl . . . What do you mean, you need a baby?!

SONG: Tell Comrade Kang—last night, the entire mission, it could've ended.

10   CHIN: What do you mean?

SONG: Tell Kang—he told me to strip.

CHIN: *Strip?!*

SONG: Write!

CHIN: I tell you, I don't understand nothing about this case
15   anymore. Nothing.

SONG: He told me to strip, and I took a chance. Oh, we Chinese, we know how to gamble.

CHIN: (*Writing.*) ". . . told him to strip."

SONG: My palms were wet, I had to make a split-second deci-
20   sion.

CHIN: Hey! Can you slow down?!

(*Pause.*)

SONG: You write faster, I'm the artist here. Suddenly, it hit me—"All he wants is for her to submit. Once a woman submits, a man is always ready to become 'generous.'"

25   CHIN: You're just gonna end up with rough notes.

SONG: And it worked! He gave in! Now, if I can just present him with a baby. A Chinese baby with blond hair—he'll be mine for life!

CHIN: Kang will never agree! The trading of babies has to be a
30   counterrevolutionary act.

SONG: Sometimes, a counterrevolutionary act is necessary to counter a counterrevolutionary act.

(*Pause.*)

CHIN: Wait.

SONG: I need one . . . in seven months. Make sure it's a boy.

35   CHIN: This doesn't sound like something the Chairman would do. Maybe you'd better talk to Comrade Kang yourself.

SONG: Good. I will.

(CHIN *gets up to leave.*)

SONG: Miss Chin? Why, in the Peking Opera, are women's roles played by men?

40   CHIN: I don't know. Maybe, a reactionary remnant of male—

SONG: No. (*Beat.*) Because only a man knows how a woman is supposed to act.

(CHIN *exits.* SONG *turns upstage, towards* GALLIMARD.)

GALLIMARD: (*Calling after* CHIN.) Good riddance! (*To* SONG)
I could forget all that betrayal in an instant, you know. If
you'd just come back and become Butterfly again.   45

SONG: Fat chance. You're here in prison, rotting in a cell. And I'm on a plane, winging my way back to China. Your President pardoned me of our treason, you know.

GALLIMARD: Yes, I read about that.

SONG: Must make you feel . . . lower than shit.   50

GALLIMARD: But don't you, even a little bit, wish you were here with me?

SONG: I'm an artist, Rene. You were my greatest . . . acting challenge. (*She laughs.*) It doesn't matter how rotten I answer, does it? You still adore me. That's why I love you,   55
Rene. (*She points to us.*) So—you were telling your audience about the night I announced I was pregnant.

(GALLIMARD *puts his arms around* SONG's *waist. He and* SONG *are in the positions they were in at the end of Scene 6.*)

SCENE VIII

Same.

GALLIMARD: I'll divorce my wife. We'll live together here, and then later in France.

SONG: I feel so . . . ashamed.

GALLIMARD: Why?

SONG: I had begun to lose faith. And now, you shame me with   5
your generosity.

GALLIMARD: Generosity? No, I'm proposing for very selfish reasons.

SONG: Your apologies only make me feel more ashamed. My outburst a moment ago!   10

GALLIMARD: Your outburst? What about my request?!

SONG: You've been very patient dealing with my . . . eccentricities. A Western man, used to women freer with their bodies—

GALLIMARD: It was sick! Don't make excuses for me.   15

SONG: I have to. You don't seem willing to make them for yourself.

(*Pause.*)

GALLIMARD: You're crazy.

SONG: I'm happy. Which often looks like crazy.

GALLIMARD: Then make me crazy. Marry me.   20

(*Pause.*)

SONG: No.

GALLIMARD: What?

SONG: Do I sound silly, a slave, if I say I'm not worthy?

GALLIMARD: Yes. In fact you do. No one has loved me like you.

SONG: Thank you. And no one ever will. I'll see to that.   25

GALLIMARD: So what is the problem?

SONG: Rene, we Chinese are realists. We understand rice, gold, and guns. You are a diplomat. Your career is skyrocketing. Now, what would happen if you divorced your wife to marry a Communist Chinese actress?   30

GALLIMARD: That's not being realistic. That's defeating yourself before you begin.

SONG: We must conserve our strength for the battles we can win.

35 GALLIMARD: That sounds like a fortune cookie!

SONG: Where do you think fortune cookies come from?

GALLIMARD: I don't care.

SONG: You do. So do I. And we should. That is why I say I'm not worthy. I'm worthy to love and even to be loved by you.

40 But I am not worthy to end the career of one of the West's most promising diplomats.

GALLIMARD: It's not that great a career! I made it sound like more than it is!

SONG: Modesty will get you nowhere. Flatter yourself, and you

45 flatter me. I'm flattered to decline your offer. (*She exits.*)

GALLIMARD: (*To us.*) Butterfly and I argued all night. And, in the end, I left, knowing I would never be her husband. She went away for several months—to the countryside, like a small animal. Until the night I received her call.

(*A baby's cry from offstage.* SONG *enters, carrying a child.*)

50 He looks like you.

GALLIMARD: Oh! (*Beat; he approaches the baby.*) Well, babies are never very attractive at birth.

SONG: Stop!

GALLIMARD: I'm sure he'll grow more beautiful with age.

55 More like his mother.

SONG: "Chi vide mai / a bimbo del Giappon . . ."

GALLIMARD: "What baby, I wonder, was ever born in Japan"—or China, for that matter—

SONG: ". . . occhi azzurrini?"

60 GALLIMARD: "With azure eyes"—they're actually sort of brown, wouldn't you say?

SONG: "E il labbro."

GALLIMARD: "And such lips!" (*He kisses* SONG.) And such lips.

SONG: "E i ricciolini d'oro schietto?"

65 GALLIMARD: "And such a head of golden"—if slightly patchy—"curls?"

SONG: I'm going to call him "Peepee."

GALLIMARD: Darling, could you repeat that because I'm sure a rickshaw just flew by overhead.

70 SONG: You heard me.

GALLIMARD: "Song Peepee"? May I suggest Michael, or Stephan, or Adolph?

SONG: You may, but I won't listen.

GALLIMARD: You can't be serious. Can you imagine the time

75 this child will have in school?

SONG: In the West, yes.

GALLIMARD: It's worse than naming him Ping Pong or Long Dong or—

SONG: But he's never going to live in the West, is he?

(*Pause.*)

80 GALLIMARD: That wasn't my choice.

SONG: It is mine. And this is my promise to you: I will raise him, he will be our child, but he will never burden you outside of China.

GALLIMARD: Why do you make these promises? I want to be

85 burdened! I want a scandal to cover the papers!

SONG: (*To us.*) Prophetic.

GALLIMARD: I'm serious.

SONG: So am I. His name is as I registered it. And he will never live in the West.

(SONG *exits with the child.*)

GALLIMARD: (*To us.*) It is possible that her stubbornness only 90 made me want her more. That drawing back at the moment of my capitulation was the most brilliant strategy she could have chosen. It is possible. But it is also possible that by this point she could have said, could have done . . . anything, and I would have adored her still. 95

SCENE IX

Beijing. 1966.

A driving rhythm of Chinese percussion fills the stage.

GALLIMARD: And then, China began to change. Mao became very old, and his cult became very strong. And, like many old men, he entered his second childhood. So he handed over the reins of state to those with minds like his own. And children ruled the Middle Kingdom with complete caprice. 5 The doctrine of the Cultural Revolution implied continuous anarchy. Contact between Chinese and foreigners became impossible. Our flat was confiscated. Her fame and my money now counted against us.

(*Two dancers in Mao suits and red-starred caps enter, and begin crudely mimicking revolutionary violence, in an agitprop fashion.*)

GALLIMARD: And somehow the American war went wrong too. 10 Four hundred thousand dollars were being spent for every Viet Cong killed; so General Westmoreland's remark that the Oriental does not value life the way Americans do was oddly accurate. Why weren't the Vietnamese people giving in? Why were they content instead to die and die and die 15 again?

(TOULON *enters.*)

TOULON: Congratulations, Gallimard.

GALLIMARD: Excuse me, sir?

TOULON: Not a promotion. That was last time. You're going home. 20

GALLIMARD: What?

TOULON: Don't say I didn't warn you.

GALLIMARD: I'm being transferred . . . because I was wrong about the American war?

TOULON: Of course not. We don't care about the Americans. 25 We care about your mind. The quality of your analysis. In general, everything you've predicted here in the Orient . . . just hasn't happened.

GALLIMARD: I think that's premature.

TOULON: Don't force me to be blunt. Okay, you said China 30 was ready to open to Western trade. The only thing they're trading out there are Western heads. And, yes, you said the Americans would succeed in Indochina. You were kidding, right?

GALLIMARD: I think the end is in sight. 35

TOULON: Don't be pathetic. And don't take this personally. You were wrong. It's not your fault.

GALLIMARD: But I'm going home.

TOULON: Right. Could I have the number of your mistress? (*Beat.*) Joke! Joke! Eat a croissant for me. 40

(TOULON *exits.* SONG, *wearing a Mao suit, is dragged in from the wings as part of the upstage dance. They "beat" her, then lampoon the acrobatics of the Chinese opera, as she is made to kneel onstage.*)

GALLIMARD: *(Simultaneously.)* I don't care to recall how But-terfly and I said our hurried farewell. Perhaps it was better to end our affair before it killed her.

(GALLIMARD exits. COMRADE CHIN walks across the stage with a banner reading: "The Actor Renounces His Decadent Profes-sion!" She reaches the kneeling SONG. Percussion stops with a thud. Dancers strike poses.)

45 CHIN: Actor-oppressor, for years you have lived above the com-mon people and looked down on their labor. While the farmer ate millet—

SONG: I ate pastries from France and sweetmeats from silver trays.

CHIN: And how did you come to live in such an exalted position?

50 SONG: I was a plaything for the imperialists!

CHIN: What did you do?

SONG: I shamed China by allowing myself to be corrupted by a foreigner . . .

CHIN: What does this mean? The People demand a full con-

55 fession!

SONG: I engaged in the lowest perversions with China's ene-mies!

CHIN: What perversions? Be more clear!

SONG: I let him put it up my ass!

(Dancers look over, disgusted.)

60 CHIN: Aaaa-ya! How can you use such sickening language?!

SONG: My language . . . is only as foul as the crimes I com-mitted . . .

CHIN: Yeah. That's better. So—what do you want to do now?

SONG: I want to serve the people.

(Percussion starts up, with Chinese strings.)

65 CHIN: What?

SONG: I want to serve the people!

(Dancers regain their revolutionary smiles, and begin a dance of victory.)

CHIN: What?!

SONG: I want to serve the people!

(Dancers unveil a banner: "The Actor Is Rehabilitated!" SONG remains kneeling before CHIN, as the dancers bounce around them, then exit. Music out.)

SCENE X

A commune. Hunan Province. 1970.

CHIN: How you planning to do that?

SONG: I've already worked four years in the fields of Hunan, Comrade Chin.

CHIN: So? Farmers work all their lives. Let me see your hands.

(SONG holds them out for her inspection.)

5 CHIN: Goddamn! Still so smooth! How long does it take to turn you actors into good anythings? Hunh. You've just spent too many years in luxury to be any good to the Revolution.

SONG: I served the Revolution.

CHIN: Serve the Resolution? Bullshit! You wore dresses! Don't

10 tell me—I was there. I saw you! You and your white vice-con-sul! Stuck up there in your flat, living off the People's Trea-sury! Yeah, I knew what was going on! You two . . . homos! Homos! Homos! *(Pause; she composes herself.)* Ah! Well . . .

you will serve the people, all right. But not with the Revolu-tion's money. This time, you use your own money. 15

SONG: I have no money.

CHIN: Shut up! And you won't stink up China anymore with your pervert stuff. You'll pollute the place where pollution begins—the West.

SONG: What do you mean? 20

CHIN: Shut up! You're going to France. Without a cent in your pocket. You find your consul's house, you make him pay your expenses—

SONG: No.

CHIN: And you give us weekly reports! Useful information! 25

SONG: That's crazy. It's been four years.

CHIN: Either that, or back to rehabilitation center!

SONG: Comrade Chin, he's not going to support me! Not in France! He's a white man! I was just his plaything—

CHIN: Oh yuck! Again with the sickening language. Where's 30 my stick?

SONG: You don't understand the mind of a man.

(Pause.)

CHIN: Oh no? No I don't? Then how come I'm married, huh? How come I got a man? Five, six years ago, you always tell me those kinds of things, I felt very bad. But not now! Be- 35 cause what does the Chairman say? He tells us I'm now the smart one, you're now the nincompoop! You're the black-head, the harebrain, the nitwit! You think you're so smart? You understand "The Mind of a Man"? Good! Then you go to France and be a pervert for Chairman Mao! 40

(CHIN and SONG exit in opposite directions.)

SCENE XI

Paris. 1968–70.

GALLIMARD *enters.*

GALLIMARD: And what was waiting for me back in Paris? Well, better Chinese food than I'd eaten in China. Friends and relatives. A little accounting, regular schedule, keeping track of traffic violations in the suburbs. . . . And the indignity of students shouting the slogans of Chairman Mao at me—in 5 French.

HELGA: Rene? Rene? *(She enters, soaking wet.)* I've had a . . . a problem. *(She sneezes.)*

GALLIMARD: You're wet.

HELGA: Yes, I . . . coming back from the grocer's. A group of 10 students, waving red flags, they—

(GALLIMARD fetches a towel.)

HELGA: —they ran by, I was caught up along with them. Be-fore I knew what was happening—

(GALLIMARD gives her the towel.)

HELGA: Thank you. The police started firing water cannons at us. I tried to shout, to tell them I was the wife of a diplomat, 15 but—you know how it is . . . *(Pause.)* Needless to say, I lost the groceries. Rene, what's happening to France?

GALLIMARD: What's—? Well, nothing, really.

HELGA: Nothing? The storefronts are in flames, there's glass in the streets, buildings are toppling—and I'm wet! 20

GALLIMARD: Nothing! . . . that I care to think about.

HELGA: And is that why you stay in this room?

GALLIMARD: Yes, in fact.

HELGA: With the incense burning? You know something? I
25 hate incense. It smells so sickly sweet.

GALLIMARD: Well, I hate the French. Who just smell—period!

HELGA: And the Chinese were better?

GALLIMARD: Please—don't start.

HELGA: When we left, this exact same thing, the riots—
30 GALLIMARD: No, no . . .

HELGA: Students screaming slogans, smashing down doors—

GALLIMARD: Helga—

HELGA: It was all going on in China, too. Don't you remember?!

GALLIMARD: Helga! Please! *(Pause.)* You have never under-
35 stood China, have you? You walk in here with these ridiculous
ideas, that the West is falling apart, that China was spitting in
our faces. You come in, dripping of the streets, and you leave
water all over my floor. *(He grabs* HELGA's *towel, begins mopping up the floor.)*
40 HELGA: But it's the truth!

GALLIMARD: Helga, I want a divorce.

(Pause; GALLIMARD *continues, mopping the floor.)*

HELGA: I take it back. China is . . . beautiful. Incense, I like
incense.

GALLIMARD: I've had a mistress.
45 HELGA: So?

GALLIMARD: For eight years.

HELGA: I knew you would. I knew you would the day I married
you. And now what? You want to marry her?

GALLIMARD: I can't. She's in China.
50 HELGA: I see. You want to leave. For someone who's not here,
is that right?

GALLIMARD: That's right.

HELGA: You can't live with her, but still you don't want to live
with me.
55 GALLIMARD: That's right.

(Pause.)

HELGA: Shit. How terrible that I can figure that out. *(Pause.)* I
never thought I'd say it. But, in China, I was happy. I knew,
in my own way, I knew that you were not everything you pretended to be. But the pretense—going on your arm to the
60 embassy ball, visiting your office and the guards saying,
"Good morning, good morning, Madame Gallimard"—the
pretense . . . was very good indeed. *(Pause.)* I hope everyone
is mean to you for the rest of your life. *(She exits.)*

GALLIMARD: *(To us.)* Prophetic.

*(*MARC *enters with two drinks.)*
65 GALLIMARD: *(To* MARC.*)* In China, I was different from all
other men.

MARC: Sure. You were white. Here's your drink.

GALLIMARD: I felt . . . touched.

MARC: In the head? Rene, I don't want to hear about the Ori-
70 ental love goddess. Okay? One night—can we just drink and
throw up without a lot of conversation?

GALLIMARD: You still don't believe me, do you?

MARC: Sure I do. She was the most beautiful, et cetera, et
cetera, blasé blasé.

(Pause.)
75 GALLIMARD: My life in the West has been such a
disappointment.

MARC: Life in the West is like that. You'll get used to it. Look,
you're driving me away. I'm leaving. Happy, now? *(He exits,
then returns.)* Look, I have a date tomorrow night. You
wanna come? I can fix you up with— 80
GALLIMARD: Of course. I would love to come.

(Pause.)

MARC: Uh—on second thought, no. You'd better get ahold of
yourself first.

(He exits; GALLIMARD *nurses his drink.)*

GALLIMARD: *(To us.)* This is the ultimate cruelty, isn't it? That
I can talk and talk and to anyone listening, it's only air—too 85
rich a diet to be swallowed by a mundane world. Why can't
anyone understand? That in China, I once loved, and was
loved by, very simply, the Perfect Woman.

*(*SONG *enters, dressed as* BUTTERFLY *in wedding dress.)*

GALLIMARD: *(To* SONG.*)* Not again. My imagination is hell.
Am I asleep this time? Or did I drink too much? 90
SONG: Rene?

GALLIMARD: God, it's too painful! That you speak?

SONG: What are you talking about? Rene—touch me.

GALLIMARD: Why?

SONG: I'm real. Take my hand. 95
GALLIMARD: Why? So you can disappear again and leave me
clutching at the air? For the entertainment of my neighbors
who—?

*(*SONG *touches* GALLIMARD.*)*

SONG: Rene?

*(*GALLIMARD *takes* SONG's *hand. Silence.)*

GALLIMARD: Butterfly? I never doubted you'd return. 100
SONG: You hadn't . . . forgotten—?

GALLIMARD: Yes, actually, I've forgotten everything. My mind,
you see—there wasn't enough room in this hard head—not
for the world *and* for you. No, there was only room for one.
(Beat.) Come, look. See? Your bed has been waiting, with 105
the Klimt poster you like, and—see? The xiang lu [incense
burner] you gave me?

SONG: I . . . I don't know what to say.

GALLIMARD: There's nothing to say. Not at the end of a long
trip. Can I make you some tea? 110
SONG: But where's your wife?

GALLIMARD: She's by my side. She's by my side at last.

*(*GALLIMARD *reaches to embrace* SONG. SONG *sidesteps, dodging
him.)*

GALLIMARD: Why?

SONG: *(To us.)* So I did return to Rene in Paris. Where I
found— 115
GALLIMARD: Why do you run away? Can't we show them how
we embraced that evening?

SONG: Please. I'm talking.

GALLIMARD: You have to do what I say! I'm conjuring you up
in *my* mind! 120
SONG: Rene, I've never done what you've said. Why should it
be any different in your mind? Now split—the story moves
on, and I must change.

GALLIMARD: I welcomed you into my home! I didn't have to,
you know! I could've left you penniless on the streets of 125
Paris! But I took you in!

SONG: Thank you.

GALLIMARD: So . . . please . . . don't change.

SONG: You know I have to. You know I will. And anyway, what
130   difference does it make? No matter what your eyes tell you,
you can't ignore the truth. You already know too much.

(GALLIMARD *exits.* SONG *turns to us.*)

SONG: The change I'm going to make requires about five minutes. So I thought you might want to take this opportunity to
stretch your legs, enjoy a drink, or listen to the musicians. I'll
135   be here, when you return, right where you left me.

(SONG *goes to a mirror in front of which is a wash basin of water.
She starts to remove her makeup as stagelights go to half and
houselights come up.*)

— ACT THREE —

SCENE 1

A courthouse in Paris. 1986.

As he promised, SONG *has completed the bulk of his transformation, onstage by the time the houselights go down and the stagelights come up full. He removes his wig and kimono, leaving
them on the floor. Underneath, he wears a well-cut suit.*

SONG: So I'd done my job better than I had a right to expect.
Well, give him some credit, too. He's right — I was in a fix
when I arrived in Paris. I walked from the airport into town,
then I located, by blind groping, the Chinatown district. Let
5   me make one thing clear: whatever else may be said about
the Chinese, they are stingy! I slept in doorways three days
until I could find a tailor who would make me this kimono
on credit. As it turns out, maybe I didn't even need it. Maybe
he would've been happy to see me in a simple shift and mas-
10   cara. But . . . better safe than sorry.
     That was 1970, when I arrived in Paris. For the next fif-
teen years, yes, I lived in a very comfy life. Some relief,
believe me, after four years on a fucking commune in
Nowheresville, China. Rene supported the boy and me, and
15   I did some demonstrations around the country as part of my
"cultural exchange" cover. And then there was the spying.

(SONG *moves upstage, to a chair.* TOULON *enters as a judge,
wearing the appropriate wig and robes. He sits near* SONG. *It's
1986, and* SONG *is testifying in a courtroom.*)

SONG: Not much at first. Rene had lost all his high-level contacts. Comrade Chin wasn't very interested in parking-ticket
statistics. But finally, at my urging, Rene got a job as a
20   courier, handling sensitive documents. He'd photograph
them for me, and I'd pass them on to the Chinese embassy.

JUDGE: Did he understand the extent of his activity?

SONG: He didn't ask. He knew that I needed those documents,
and that was enough.

25 JUDGE: But he must've known he was passing classified
information.

SONG: I can't say.

JUDGE: He never asked what you were going to do with them?

SONG: Nope.

(*Pause.*)

30 JUDGE: There is one thing that the court — indeed, that all of
France — would like to know.

SONG: Fire away.

JUDGE: Did Monsieur Gallimard know you were a man?

SONG: Well, he never saw me completely naked. Ever.

JUDGE: But surely, he must've . . . how can I put this?   35

SONG: Put it however you like. I'm not shy. He must've felt
around?

JUDGE: Mmmmm.

SONG: Not really. I did all the work. He just laid back. Of
course we did enjoy more . . . complete union, and I sup-   40
pose he *might* have wondered why I was always on my stomach, but. . . . But what you're thinking is. "Of course a wrist
must've brushed . . . a hand hit . . . over twenty years!" Yeah.
Well, Your Honor, it was my job to make him think I was a
woman. And chew on this: it wasn't all that hard. See, my   45
mother was a prostitute along the Bundt before the Revolution. And, uh, I think it's fair to say she learned a few things
about Western men. So I borrowed her knowledge. In service to my country.

JUDGE: Would you care to enlighten the court with this secret   50
knowledge? I'm sure we're all very curious.

SONG: I'm sure you are. (*Pause.*) Okay, Rule One is: Men always believe what they want to hear. So a girl can tell the
most obnoxious lies and the guys will believe them every
time — "This is my first time" — "That's the biggest I've ever   55
seen" — or *both*, which, if you really think about it, is not possible in a single lifetime. You've maybe heard those phrases a
few times in your own life, yes, Your Honor?

JUDGE: It's not my life, Monsieur Song, which is on trial
today.   60

SONG: Okay, okay, just trying to lighten up the proceedings.
Tough room.

JUDGE: Go on.

SONG: Rule Two: As soon as a Western man comes into contact with the East — he's already confused. The West has sort   65
of an international rape mentality towards the East. Do you
know rape mentality?

JUDGE: Give us your definition, please.

SONG: Basically, "Her mouth says no, but her eyes say yes."
     The West thinks of itself as masculine — big guns, big in-   70
dustry, big money — so the East is feminine — weak, delicate,
poor . . . but good at art, and full of inscrutable wisdom —
the feminine mystique.
     Her mouth says no, but her eyes say yes. The West be-
lieves the East, deep down, *wants* to be dominated — because   75
a woman can't think for herself.

JUDGE: What does this have to do with my question?

SONG: You expect Oriental countries to submit to your guns,
and you expect Oriental women to be submissive to your
men. That's why you say they make the best wives.   80

JUDGE: But why would that make it possible for you to fool
Monsieur Gallimard? Please — get to the point.

SONG: One, because when he finally met his fantasy woman,
he wanted more than anything to believe that she was, in
fact, a woman. And second, I am an Oriental. And being an   85
Oriental, I could never be completely a man.

(*Pause.*)

JUDGE: Your armchair political theory is tenuous, Monsieur
Song.

SONG: You think so? That's why you'll lose in all your dealings
with the East.   90

JUDGE: Just answer my question: did he know you were a man?

(Pause.)

SONG: You know, your Honor, I never asked.

SCENE II

Same.

Music from the "Death Scene" from BUTTERFLY *blares over the house speakers. It is the loudest thing we've heard in this play.*

GALLIMARD *enters, crawling towards* SONG's *wig and kimono.*

GALLIMARD: Butterfly? Butterfly?

*(*SONG *remains a man, in the witness box, delivering a testimony we do not hear.)*

GALLIMARD: *(To us.)* In my moment of greatest shame, here, in this courtroom—with that . . . person up there, telling the world. . . . What strikes me especially is how swallow he is,
5   how glib and obsequious . . . completely . . . without sub- stance! The type that prowls around discos with a gold medallion stinking of garlic. So little like my Butterfly.

Yet even in this moment my mind remains agile, flip- flopping like a man on a trampoline. Even now, my picture
10   dissolves, and I see that . . . witness . . . talking to me.

*(*SONG *suddenly stands staight up in his witness box, and looks at* GALLIMARD.)*

SONG: Yes. You. White man.

*(*SONG *steps out of the witness box, and moves downstage to- wards* GALLIMARD. *Light change.)*

GALLIMARD: *(To* SONG.) Who? Me?

SONG: Do you see any other white men?

GALLIMARD: Yes. There're white men all around. This is a
15   French courtroom.

SONG: So you are an adventurous imperialist. Tell me, why did it take you so long? To come back to this place?

GALLIMARD: What place?

SONG: This theatre in China. Where we met many years ago.

20   GALLIMARD: *(To us.)* And once again, against my will, I am transported.

(Chinese opera music comes up on the speakers. SONG *begins to do opera moves, as he did the night they met.)*

SONG: Do you remember? The night you gave your heart?

GALLIMARD: It was a long time ago.

SONG: Not long enough. A night that turned your world up-
25   side down.

GALLIMARD: Perhaps.

SONG: Oh, be honest with me. What's another bit of flattery when you've already given me twenty years' worth? It's a wonder my head hasn't swollen to the size of China.

30   GALLIMARD: Who's to say it hasn't?

SONG: Who's to say? And what's the shame? In pride? You think I could've pulled this off if I wasn't already full of pride when we met? No, not just pride. Arrogance. It takes arro- gance, really—to believe you can will, with your eyes and
35   your lips, the destiny of another. *(He dances.)* C'mon. Admit it. You still want me. Even in slacks and a button-down collar.

GALLIMARD: I don't see what the point of—

SONG: You don't? Well maybe, Rene, just maybe—I want you.

GALLIMARD: You do?   40

SONG: Then again, maybe I'm just playing with you. How can you tell? *(Reprising his feminine character, he sidles up to* GALLIMARD.) "How I wish there were even a small cafe to sit in. With men in tuxedos, and cappuccinos, and bad expatri- ate jazz." Now you want to kiss me, don't you?   45

GALLIMARD: *(Pulling away.)* What makes you—?

SONG: —so sure? See? I take the words from your mouth. Then I wait for you to come and retrieve them. *(He reclines on the floor.)*

GALLIMARD: Why? Why do you treat me so cruelly?   50

SONG: Perhaps I *was* treating you cruelly. But now—I'm being nice. Come here, my little one.

GALLIMARD: I'm not your little one!

SONG: My mistake. It's I who am *your* little one, right?

GALLIMARD: Yes, I—   55

SONG: So come get your little one. If you like. I may even let you strip me.

GALLIMARD: I mean, you were! Before . . . but not like this!

SONG: I was? Then perhaps I still am. If you look hard enough. *(He starts to remove his clothes.)*   60

GALLIMARD: What—what are you doing?

SONG: Helping you to see through my act.

GALLIMARD: Stop that! I don't want to! I don't—

SONG: Oh, but you asked me to strip, remember?

GALLIMARD: What? That was years ago! And I took it back!   65

SONG: No. You postponed it. Postponed the inevitable. Today, the inevitable has come calling.

(From the speakers, cacophony: BUTTERFLY *mixed in with Chi- nese gongs.)*

GALLIMARD: No! Stop! I don't want to see!

SONG: Then look away.

GALLIMARD: You're only in my mind! All this is in my mind! I   70 order you! To stop!

SONG: To what? To strip? That's just what I'm—

GALLIMARD: No! Stop! I want you—!

SONG: You want me?

GALLIMARD: To stop!   75

SONG: You know something, Rene? Your mouth says no, but your eyes say yes. Turn them away. I dare you.

GALLIMARD: I don't have to! Every night, you say you're going to strip, but then I beg you and you stop!

SONG: I guess tonight is different.   80

GALLIMARD: Why? Why should that be?

SONG: Maybe I've become frustrated. Maybe I'm saying "Look at me, you fool!" Or maybe I'm just feeling . . . sexy. *(He is down to his briefs.)*

GALLIMARD: Please. This is unnecessary. I know what you are.   85

SONG: Do you? What am I?

GALLIMARD: A—a man.

SONG: You don't really believe that.

GALLIMARD: Yes I do! I knew all the time somewhere that my happiness was temporary, my love a deception. But my mind   90 kept the knowledge at bay. To make the wait bearable.

SONG: Monsieur Gallimard—the wait is over.

*(*SONG *drops his briefs. He is naked. Sound cue out. Slowly, we and* SONG *come to the realization that what we had thought to be* GALLIMARD's *sobbing is actually his laughter.)*

GALLIMARD: Oh god! What an idiot! Of course!

SONG: Rene—what?

95   GALLIMARD: Look at you! You're a man! *(He bursts into laughter again.)*

SONG: I fail to see what's so funny!

GALLIMARD: "You fail to see—!" I mean, you never did have much of a sense of humor, did you? I just think it's ridicu-

100   lously funny that I've wasted so much time on just a man!

SONG: Wait. I'm not "just a man."

GALLIMARD: No? Isn't that what you've been trying to convince me of?

SONG: Yes, but what I mean—

105   GALLIMARD: And now, I finally believe you, and you tell me it's not true? I think you must have some kind of identity problem.

SONG: Will you listen to me?

GALLIMARD: Why?! I've been listening to you for twenty years.

110   Don't I deserve a vacation?

SONG: I'm not just any man!

GALLIMARD: Then, what exactly are you?

SONG: Rene, how can you ask—? Okay, what about this?

(He picks up BUTTERFLY's *robes, starts to dance around. No music.)*

GALLIMARD: Yes, that's very nice. I have to admit.

(SONG holds out his arm to GALLIMARD.)

115   SONG: It's the same skin you've worshiped for years. Touch it.

GALLIMARD: Yes, it does feel the same.

SONG: Now—close your eyes.

(SONG covers GALLIMARD's *eyes with one hand. With the other,* SONG *draws* GALLIMARD's *hand up to his face.* GALLIMARD, *like a blind man, lets his hands run over* SONG's *face.)*

GALLIMARD: This skin, I remember. The curve of her face, the softness of her cheek, her hair against the back of my hand . . .

120   SONG: I'm your Butterfly. Under the robes, beneath everything, it was always me. Now, open your eyes and admit it— you adore me. *(He removes his hand from* GALLIMARD's *eyes.)*

GALLIMARD: You, who knew every inch of my desires—how could you, of all people, have made such a mistake?

125   SONG: What?

GALLIMARD: You showed me your true self. When all I loved was the lie. A perfect lie, which you let fall to the ground— and now, it's old and soiled.

SONG: So—you never really loved me? Only when I was play-

130   ing a part?

GALLIMARD: I'm a man who loved a woman created by a man. Everything else—simply falls short.

(Pause.)

SONG: What am I supposed to do now?

GALLIMARD: You were a fine spy, Monsieur Song, with an

135   even finer accomplice. But now I believe you should go. Get out of my life!

SONG: Go where? Rene, you can't live without me. Not after twenty years.

GALLIMARD: I certainly can't live with you—not after twenty

140   years of betrayal.

SONG: Don't be so stubborn! Where will you go?

GALLIMARD: I have a date . . . with my Butterfly.

SONG: So, throw away your pride. And come . . .

GALLIMARD: Get away from me! Tonight, I've finally learned to tell fantasy from reality. And, knowing the difference, I   145   choose fantasy.

SONG: *I'm* your fantasy!

GALLIMARD: You? You're as real as hamburger. Now get out! I have a date with my Butterfly and I don't want your body polluting the room! *(He tosses* SONG's *suit at him.)* Look at   150   these—you dress like a pimp.

SONG: Hey! These are Armani slacks and—! *(He puts on his briefs and slacks.)* Let's just say . . . I'm disappointed in you, Rene. In the crush of your adoration, I thought you'd become something more. More like . . . a woman.   155

But no. Men. You're like the rest of them. It's all in the way we dress, and make up our faces, and bat our eyelashes. You really have so little imagination!

GALLIMARD: You, Monsieur Song? Accuse me of too little imagination? You, if anyone, should know—I am pure imag-   160   ination. And in imagination I will remain. Now get out!

(GALLIMARD bodily removes SONG *from the stage, taking his kimono.)*

SONG: Rene! I'll never put on those robes again! You'll be sorry!

GALLIMARD: *(To* SONG.) I'm already sorry! *(Looking at the kimono in his hands.)* Exactly as sorry . . . as a Butterfly.

SCENE III

M. GALLIMARD's *prison cell. Paris. Present.*

GALLIMARD: I've played out the events of my life night after night, always searching for a new ending to my story, one where I leave this cell and return forever to my Butterfly's arms.

Tonight I realize my search is over. That I've looked all   5   along in the wrong place. And now, to you, I will prove that my love was not in vain—by returning to the world of fantasy where I first met her.

(He picks up the kimono; dancers enter.)

GALLIMARD: There is a vision of the Orient that I have. Of slender women in chong sams and kimonos who die for the   10   love of unworthy foreign devils. Who are born and raised to be the perfect women. Who take whatever punishment we give them, and bounce back, strengthened by love, unconditionally. It is a vision that has become my life.

(Dancers bring the wash basin to him and help him make up his face.)

GALLIMARD: In public, I have continued to deny that Song Lil-   15   ing is a man. This brings me headlines, and is a source of great embarrassment to my French colleagues, who can now be sent into a coughing fit by the mere mention of Chinese food. But alone, in my cell, I have long since faced the truth.

And the truth demands a sacrifice. For mistakes made   20   over the course of a lifetime. My mistakes were simple and absolute—the man I loved was a cad, a bounder. He deserved nothing but a kick in the behind, and instead I gave him . . . all my love.

Yes—love. Why not admit it all? That was my undoing,   25   wasn't it? Love warped my judgment, blinded my eyes, rearranged the very lines on my face . . . until I could look in the mirror and see nothing but . . . a woman.

(Dancers help him put on the BUTTERFLY *wig.)*

GALLIMARD: I have a vision. Of the Orient. That, deep within
its almond eyes, there are still women. Women willing to
sacrifice themselves for the love of a man. Even a man
whose love is completely without worth.

(Dancers assist GALLIMARD *in donning the kimono. They hand
him a knife.)*

GALLIMARD: Death with honor is better than life . . . life with
dishonor. *(He sets himself center stage, in a seppuku position.)*
The love of a Butterfly can withstand many things— unfaithfulness, loss, even abandonment. But how can it face the one
sin that implies all others? The devastating knowledge that,
underneath it all, the object of her love was nothing more,
nothing less than . . . a man. *(He sets the tip of the knife
against his body.)* It is 19____ . And I have found her at last.
In a prison on the outskirts of Paris. My name is Rene Gallimard—also known as Madame Butterfly.

*(*GALLIMARD *turns upstage and plunges his knife into his body,
as music from the "Love Duet" blares over the speakers. He collapses into the arms of the dancers, who lay him reverently on the
floor. The image holds for several beats. Then a tight special up
on* SONG, *who stands as a man, staring at the dead* GALLIMARD.
*He smokes a cigarette; the smoke filters up through the lights.
Two words leave his lips.)*

SONG: Butterfly? Butterfly?

(Smoke rises as lights fade slowly to black.)

■ TONY KUSHNER ■

Born in 1956, Tony Kushner first came to international prominence with *Angels in America* (1991), a two-part play that was an enormous success both in London and in Los Angeles before moving to New York in 1993. Kushner's "gay fantasia on national themes" is, in a sense, a displaced autobiography: the displaced narrative of his own growing up as a gay man in the American era of Roy Cohn, the decline of the Communist menace, the onset of the AIDS epidemic, and the rise of the conservative political agenda that dominated American politics in the 1980s. Kushner was born in New York, but his family soon moved to New Orleans, where his parents were musicians in the New Orleans Philharmonic. When he was two, the family moved to Lake Charles, Louisiana; his mother, once a prominent New York bassoonist, devoted herself to educating the children in literature, music, and the arts; she also acted in the Lake Charles theater company. Kushner knew that he was gay but concealed it from his parents; when he went to college at Columbia University, he spent some time in psychoanalysis trying to alter his sexual orientation. However, by his mid-twenties, Kushner was able to accept his sexuality and came out. After taking his B.A. at Columbia, he studied theater at New York University. His first play, *A Bright Room Called Day* (1985), was written while he worked as a switchboard operator; it concerns the collapse of the left and the rise of fascism during the German Weimar Republic. *Angels in America* is his second play. Kushner's third play, *Slavs*, opened in New York in 1994.

ANGELS IN AMERICA, PART I:
MILLENNIUM APPROACHES

The first part of *Angels in America* (the second part is entitled *Perestroika*), *Millennium Approaches* is a complete play in its own right. Kushner began writing the play in 1988 when Oskar Eustis, who had directed his first play for the Eureka Theater Company in San Francisco, asked Kushner for another play. Subtitled "A Gay Fantasia on National Themes," *Millennium Approaches* is at once a deeply personal look at the lives of two couples—Joe and Harper, a young Mormon couple transplanted to New York; Louis and Prior, a gay couple facing (and not facing) the onset of AIDS—and a political "fantasia" in the manner of Shaw's *Heartbreak House* or *The Apple Cart*. Kushner sets the characters' struggles against the background of conservative politics and the increasing power of the right in 1980s America; as Martin remarks in Act Two: ". . . we'll get our way on just about everything: abortion, defense, Central America, protecting the family, a live investment climate. . . . It's really the end of Liberalism. The end of New Deal Socialism. The end of ipso facto secular humanism."

While Kushner's play takes aim at the policies of the Republican administration, the play's politics extend deeply into the politics of personal action. The emphasis on individualism, on self-sufficiency, on destroying the liberal consensus, and on eliminating social programs characteristic of the Reagan administration has consequences in the private sphere as well, where freedom looks alternately like selfishness and chaos. Roy Cohn—famous for his anticommunist activities and for prosecuting (and winning) the death sentence for Julius and Ethel Rosenberg for selling secret information to the Soviet Union—in many ways exemplifies this linkage in the play. Unable to give up his view of political power ("the game . . . of being alive"), Cohn refuses to be treated for AIDS because it would mean a public admission that he is gay, something generally known but not acknowledged. Louis, unable to bring himself to care for Prior during his horrifying illness, finds both emptiness and freedom in deserting his lover. Harper, whose valium-induced fantasies summon the cosmic travel-agent Mr. Lies (who whisks her off to Antarctica) is in the throes of a nervous breakdown, a literalized response to the decaying world in which she lives, where "everywhere, things are collapsing, lies surfacing, systems of defense giving way."

The hallucinatory style of *Millennium Approaches* enables Kushner to bring this blending of public and private, the grand sweep of history and the narrower compass of individual suffering, into a close juxtaposition. *Millennium Approaches* ends when Prior's ancestors—a medieval monk and an eighteenth-century dandy—appear to announce the coming of a mysterious angel, whose voice is heard intermittently throughout the play. The Angel's arrival is heralded in a number of ways: Prior regards his first lesion of Kaposi's Syndrome as the mark of the angel of death; a feather drops from above and the voice is heard at the end of Harper's/Prior's intertwined dream-hallucination in Act One; Joe alludes to Jacob wrestling with his angel, an image of Joe's fight to recognize and admit his own homosexuality. The Angel is a figure of release and redemption from the isolation in which the characters find themselves.

However, the Angel also has a public, historical significance as well. Kushner has suggested that the Angel alludes to a comment made by the German cultural critic Walter Benjamin. In "Theses on the Philosophy of History," Benjamin makes the following remark on the process of history:

> A Klee painting named "Angelus Novus" shows an angel looking as though he is about to move away from something he is fixedly contemplating. His eyes are staring, his mouth is open, his wings are spread. This is how one pictures the angel of history. His face is turned toward the past. Where we perceive a chain of events, he sees one single catastrophe which keeps piling wreckage upon wreckage and hurls it in front of his feet. The angel would like to stay, awaken the dead, and make whole what has been smashed. But a storm is blowing from Paradise; it has got caught in his wings with such violence that the angel can no longer close them. This storm irresistibly propels him into the future to which his back is turned, while the pile of debris before him grows skyward. This storm is what we call progress.

The Angel is, to Kushner as to Benjamin, a figure for the dialectical force of history, the way that history moves into the future both in antithesis to the past, and yet bearing the past along with it. In *Angels in America*, Tony Kushner provides a sense of how it is we live today, in the midst of this "storm . . . we call progress."

ANGELS IN AMERICA, PART I:
MILLENNIUM APPROACHES

Tony Kushner

— CHARACTERS —

ROY M. COHN, *a successful New York lawyer and unofficial power broker.*

JOSEPH PORTER PITT, *chief clerk for Justice Theodore Wilson of the Federal Court of Appeals, Second Circuit.*

HARPER AMATY PITT, *Joe's wife, an agoraphobic with a mild Valium addiction.*

LOUIS IRONSON, *a word processor working for the Second Circuit Court of Appeals.*

PRIOR WALTER, *Louis's boyfriend. Occasionally works as a club designer or caterer, otherwise lives very modestly but with great style off a small trust fund.*

HANNAH PORTER PITT, *Joe's mother, currently residing in Salt Lake City, living off her deceased husband's army pension.*

BELIZE, *a former drag queen and former lover of Prior's: A registered nurse. Belize's name was originally Norman Arriaga; Belize is a drag name that stuck.*

THE ANGEL, *four divine emanations, Fluor, Phosphor, Lumen and Candle; manifest in One: the Continental Principality of America. She has magnificent steel-gray wings.*

RABBI ISIDOR CHEMELWITZ, *an orthodox Jewish rabbi, played by the actor playing Hannah.*

MR. LIES, *Harper's imaginary friend, a travel agent, who in style of dress and speech suggests a jazz musician; he always wears a large lapel badge emblazoned "IOTA" (The International Order of Travel Agents). He is played by the actor playing Belize.*

THE MAN IN THE PARK, *played by the actor playing Prior.*

THE VOICE, *the voice of The Angel.*

HENRY, *Roy's doctor, played by the actor playing Hannah.*

EMILY, *a nurse, played by the actor playing The Angel.*

MARTIN HELLER, *a Reagan Administration Justice Department flackman, played by the actor playing Harper.*

SISTER ELLA CHAPTER, *a Salt Lake City real-estate saleswoman, played by the actor playing The Angel.*

PRIOR 1, *the ghost of a dead Prior Walter from the 13th century, played by the actor playing Joe. He is a blunt, gloomy medieval farmer with a gutteral Yorkshire accent.*

PRIOR 2, *the ghost of a dead Prior Walter from the 17th century, played by the actor playing Roy. He is a Londoner, sophisticated, with a High British accent.*

THE ESKIMO, *played by the actor playing Joe.*

THE WOMAN IN THE SOUTH BRONX, *played by the actor playing The Angel.*

ETHEL ROSENBERG, *played by the actor playing Hannah.*

— PLAYWRIGHT'S NOTES —

A DISCLAIMER: *Roy M. Cohn, the character, is based on the late Roy M. Cohn (1927–1986), who was all too real; for the most part the acts attributed to the character Roy, such as his illegal conferences with Judge Kaufmann during the trial of Ethel Rosenberg, are to be found in the historical record. But this Roy is a work of dramatic fiction; his words are my invention, and liberties have been taken.*

A NOTE ABOUT THE STAGING: *The play benefits from a pared-down style of presentation, with minimal scenery and scene shifts done rapidly (no blackouts!), employing the cast as well as stagehands—which makes for an actor-driven event, as this must be. The moments of magic—the appearance and disappearance of Mr. Lies and the ghosts, the Book hallucination, and the ending—are to be fully realized, as bits of wonderful theatrical illusion—which means it's OK if the wires show, and maybe it's good that they do, but the magic should at the same time be thoroughly amazing.*

> . . . In a murderous time
> the heart breaks and breaks
> and lives by breaking.
>
> —STANLEY KUNITZ
> "THE TESTING-TREE"

— ACT ONE —
BAD NEWS
OCTOBER–NOVEMBER 1985

SCENE I

The last days of October. RABBI ISIDOR CHEMELWITZ *alone onstage with a small coffin. It is a rough pine box with two wooden pegs, one at the foot and one at the head, holding the lid in place. A prayer shawl embroidered with a Star of David is draped over the lid, and by the head a yarzheit candle is burning.*

RABBI ISIDOR CHEMELWITZ: (*He speaks sonorously, with a heavy Eastern European accent, unapologetically consulting a sheet of notes for the family names.*) Hello and good morning. I am Rabbi Isidor Chemelwitz of the Bronx Home for Aged Hebrews. We are here this morning to pay respects at the passing of Sarah Ironson, devoted wife of Benjamin Ironson, also deceased, loving and caring mother of her sons Morris, Abraham, and Samuel, and her daughters Esther and Rachel; beloved grandmother of Max, Mark, Louis, Lisa, Maria . . . uh . . . Lesley, Angela, Doris, Luke and Eric. (*Looks more closely at paper.*) Eric? This is a Jewish name? (*Shrugs.*) Eric. A large and loving family. We assemble that we may mourn collectively this good and righteous woman.

(He looks at the coffin.)

This woman. I did not know this woman. I cannot accurately
describe her attributes, nor do justice to her dimensions. She
was. . . . Well, in the Bronx Home of Aged Hebrews are
many like this, the old, and to many I speak but not to be
frank with this one. She preferred silence. So I do not know
her and yet I know her. She was . . .

(He touches the coffin.)

. . . not a person but a whole kind of person, the ones who
crossed the ocean, who brought with us to America the villages of Russia and Lithuania—and how we struggled, and
how we fought, for the family, for the Jewish home, so that
you would not grow up *here*, in this strange place, in the
melting pot where nothing melted. Descendants of this im-
migrant woman, you do not grow up in America, you and
your children and their children with the goyische names.
You do not live in America. No such place exists. Your clay is
the clay of some Litvak shtetl, your air the air of the
steppes—because she carried the old world on her back
across the ocean, in a boat, and she put it down on Grand
Concourse Avenue, or in Flatbush, and she worked that
earth into your bones, and you pass it to your children, this
ancient, ancient culture and home.

(Little pause.)

You can never make that crossing that she made, for such
Great Voyages in this world do not any more exist. But every
day of your lives the miles that voyage between that place
and this one you cross. Every day. You understand me? In
you that journey is.

So . . .

She was the last of the Mohicans, this one was. Pretty soon
. . . all the old will be dead.

SCENE II

Same day. ROY *and* JOE *in* ROY's *office.* ROY *at an impressive
desk, bare except for a very elaborate phone system, rows and
rows of flashing buttons which bleep and beep and whistle incessantly, making chaotic music underneath* ROY's *conversations.*
JOE *is sitting, waiting.* ROY *conducts business with great energy,
impatience and sensual abandon: gesticulating, shouting, cajol-
ing, crooning, playing the phone, receiver and hold button with
virtuosity and love.*

ROY: *(Hitting a button.)* Hold. *(To* JOE.) I wish I was an octopus, a fucking octopus. Eight loving arms and all those suckers. Know what I mean?

JOE: No, I . . .

ROY: *(Gesturing to a deli platter of little sandwiches on his
desk.)* You want lunch?

JOE: No, that's OK really I just . . .

ROY: *(Hitting a button.)* Ailene? Roy Cohn. Now what kind of
a greeting is. . . . I thought we were friends, Ai. . . . Look
Mrs. Soffer you don't have to get. . . . You're upset. You're
yelling. You'll aggravate your condition, you shouldn't yell,
you'll pop little blood vessels in your face if you yell. . . . No
that was a joke, Mrs. Soffer, I was joking. . . . I already apolo-
gized sixteen times for that, Mrs. Soffer, you . . . *(While she's
fulminating,* ROY *covers the mouthpiece with his hand and
talks to* JOE.) This'll take a minute, *eat* already, what is this
tasty sandwich here it's—(*He takes a bite of a sandwich.)*
Mmmmm, liver or some. . . . Here.

(He pitches the sandwich to JOE, *who catches it and returns it to
the platter.)*

ROY: *(Back to Mrs. Soffer.)* Uh huh, uh huh. . . . No, I already
told you, it wasn't a vacation, it was business. Mrs. Soffer, I
have clients in Haiti, Mrs. Soffer, I. . . . Listen, Ailene, YOU
THINK I'M THE ONLY GODDAM LAWYER IN HIS-
TORY EVER MISSED A COURT DATE? Don't make
such a big fucking. . . . Hold. *(He hits the hold button.)* You
HAG!

JOE: If this is a bad time . . .

ROY: *Bad* time? This is a *good* time! *(Button.)* Baby doll, get
me. . . . Oh fuck, wait . . . *(Button, button.)* Hello? Yah.
Sorry to keep you holding, Judge Hollins, I. . . . Oh *Mrs.*
Hollins, sorry dear deep voice you got. Enjoying your visit?
(Hand over mouthpiece, to JOE.) She sounds like a truck-
driver and he sounds like Kate Smith, very confusing. Nixon
appointed him, all the geeks are Nixon appointees . . . *(To
Mrs. Hollins.)* Yeah yeah right good so how many tickets
dear? Seven. For what, *Cats, 42nd Street,* what? No you
wouldn't like *La Cage,* trust me, I know. Oh for godsake. . . .
Hold. *(Button, button.)* Baby doll, seven for *Cats* or something, anything hard to get, I don't give a fuck what and neither will they. *(Button; to* JOE.) You see *La Cage?*

JOE: No, I . . .

ROY: Fabulous. Best thing on Broadway. Maybe ever. *(Button.)*
Who? Aw, Jesus H. Christ, Harry, *no,* Harry, Judge John
Francis Grimes, Manhattan Family Court. Do I have to do
every goddam thing myself? *Touch* the bastard, Harry, and
don't call me on this line again, I told you not to . . .

JOE: *(Starting to get up.)* Roy, uh, should I wait outside or . . .

ROY: *(To* JOE.) Oh sit. *(To* HARRY.) You hold. I pay you to hold
fuck you Harry you jerk. *(Button.)* Half-wit dick-brain. *(Instantly philosophical.)* I see the universe, Joe, as a kind of
sandstorm in outer space with winds of mega-hurricane velocity, but instead of grains of sand it's shards and splinters of
glass. You ever feel that way? Ever have one of those days?

JOE: I'm not sure I . . .

ROY: So how's life in Appeals? How's the Judge?

JOE: He sends his best.

ROY: He's a good man. Loyal. Not the brightest man on the
bench, but he has manners. And a nice head of silver hair.

JOE: He gives me a lot of responsibility.

ROY: Yeah, like writing his decisions and signing his name.

JOE: Well . . .

ROY: He's a nice guy. And you cover admirably.

JOE: Well, thanks, Roy, I . . .

ROY: *(Button.)* Who is *this?* Well who the fuck are *you?*
Hold—*(Button.)* Harry? Eighty-seven grand, something like
that. Fuck him. Eat me. New Jersey, chain of porno film
stores in, uh, Weehawken. That's—Harry, that's the beauty
of the law. *(Button.)* So, baby doll, what? *Cats?* Bleah. *(Button.)* Cats! It's about cats. Singing cats, you'll love it. Eight
o'clock, the theatre's always at eight. *(Button.)* Fucking
tourists. *(Button, then to* JOE.) Oh live a little, Joe, *eat* something for Christ sake—

JOE: Um, Roy, could you . . .

ROY: What? *(To* HARRY.) Hold a minute. *(Button.)* Mrs. Soffer?
Mrs. . . . *(Button.)* God-fucking-dammit to hell, where is . . .

JOE: *(Overlapping.)* Roy, I'd really appreciate it if . . .

ROY: *(Overlapping.)* Well she was here a minute ago, baby
doll, see if . . .

(The phone starts making three different beeping sounds, all at once.)

ROY: *(Smashing buttons.)* Jesus fuck this goddam thing . . .

JOE: *(Overlapping.)* I really wish you wouldn't . . .

80 ROY: *(Overlapping.)* Baby doll? Ring the *Post* get me Suzy see if . . .

(The phone starts whistling loudly.)

ROY: CHRIST!

JOE: *Roy.*

ROY: *(Into receiver.)* Hold. *(Button; to* JOE.) *What?*

85 JOE: Could you please not take the Lord's name in vain?

(Pause.)

I'm sorry. But please. At least while I'm . . .

ROY: *(Laughs, then.)* Right. Sorry. Fuck.

Only in America. *(Punches a button.)* Baby doll, tell 'em all to fuck off. Tell 'em I died. You handle Mrs. Soffer. Tell her

90 it's on the way. Tell her I'm schtupping the judge. I'll call her back. I *will* call her. I *know* how much I borrowed. She's got four hundred times that stuffed up her. . . . Yeah, tell her I said that. *(Button. The phone is silent.)*

So, Joe.

95 JOE: I'm sorry Roy, I just . . .

ROY: No no no no, principles count, I respect principles, I'm not religious but I like God and God likes me. Baptist, Catholic?

JOE: Mormon.

100 ROY: Mormon. Delectable. Absolutely. Only in America. So, Joe. Whattya think?

JOE: It's . . . well . . .

ROY: Crazy life.

JOE: Chaotic.

105 ROY: Well but God bless chaos. Right?

JOE: Ummm . . .

ROY: Huh. Mormons. I knew Mormons, in, um, Nevada.

JOE: Utah, mostly.

ROY: No, these Mormons were in Vegas.

110 So. So, how'd you like to go to Washington and work for the Justice Department?

JOE: Sorry?

ROY: How'd you like to go to Washington and work for the Justice Department? All I gotta do is pick up the phone, talk to

115 Ed, and you're in.

JOE: In . . . what, exactly?

ROY: Associate Assistant Something Big. Internal Affairs, heart of the woods, something nice with clout.

JOE: Ed . . . ?

120 ROY: Meese. The Attorney General.

JOE: Oh.

ROY: I just have to pick up the phone . . .

JOE: I have to think.

ROY: Of course.

(Pause.)

125 It's a great time to be in Washington, Joe.

JOE: Roy, it's incredibly exciting . . .

ROY: And it would mean something to me. You understand?

(Little pause.)

JOE: I . . . can't say how much I appreciate this Roy, I'm sort of . . . well, stunned, I mean. . . . Thanks, Roy. But I have to give it some thought. I have to ask my wife. 130

ROY: Your wife. Of course.

JOE: But I really appreciate . . .

ROY: Of course. Talk to your wife.

SCENE III

Later that day. HARPER *at home, alone. She is listening to the radio and talking to herself, as she often does. She speaks to the audience.*

HARPER: People who are lonely, people left alone, sit talking nonsense to the air, imagining . . . beautiful systems dying, old fixed orders spiraling apart . . .

When you look at the ozone layer, from outside, from a spaceship, it looks like a pale blue halo, a gentle, shimmer- 5 ing aureole encircling the atmosphere encircling the earth. Thirty miles above our heads, a thin layer of three-atom oxygen molecules, product of photosynthesis, which explains the fussy vegetable preference for visible light, its rejection of darker rays and emanations. Danger from without. It's a 10 kind of gift, from God, the crowning touch to the creation of the world: guardian angels, hands linked, make a spherical net, a blue-green nesting orb, a shell of safety for life itself. But everywhere, things are collapsing, lies surfacing, systems of defense giving way. . . . This is why, Joe, this is why I 15 shouldn't be left alone.

(Little pause.)

I'd like to go traveling. Leave you behind to worry. I'll send postcards with strange stamps and tantalizing messages on the back. "Later maybe." "Nevermore . . ."

(MR. LIES, a travel agent, appears.)

HARPER: Oh! You startled me! 20

MR. LIES: Cash, check or credit card?

HARPER: I remember you. You're from Salt Lake. You sold us the plane tickets when we flew here. What are you doing in Brooklyn?

MR. LIES: You said you wanted to travel . . . 25

HARPER: And here you are. How thoughtful.

MR. LIES: Mr. Lies. Of the International Order of Travel Agents. We mobilize the globe, we set people adrift, we stir the populace and send nomads eddying across the planet. We are adepts of motion, acolytes of the flux. Cash, check or 30 credit card. Name your destination.

HARPER: Antarctica, maybe. I want to see the hole in the ozone. I heard on the radio . . .

MR. LIES: *(He has a computer terminal in his briefcase.)* I can arrange a guided tour. Now? 35

HARPER: Soon. Maybe soon. I'm not safe here you see. Things aren't right with me. Weird stuff happens . . .

MR. LIES: Like?

HARPER: Well, like you, for instance. Just appearing. Or last week . . . well never mind. 40

People are like planets, you need a thick skin. Things get to me, Joe stays away and now. . . . Well look. My dreams are talking back to me.

MR. LIES: It's the price of rootlessness. Motion sickness. The only cure: to keep moving. 45

HARPER: I'm undecided. I feel . . . that something's going to give. It's 1985. Fifteen years till the third millennium. Maybe Christ will come again. Maybe seeds will be planted, maybe there'll be harvests then, maybe early figs to eat,
50 maybe new life, maybe fresh blood, maybe companionship and love and protection, safety from what's outside, maybe the door will hold, or maybe . . . maybe the troubles will come, and the end will come, and the sky will collapse and there will be terrible rains and showers of poison light, or
55 maybe my life is really fine, maybe Joe loves me and I'm only crazy thinking otherwise, or maybe not, maybe it's even worse than I know, maybe . . . I want to know, maybe I don't. The suspense, Mr. Lies, it's killing me.

MR. LIES: I suggest a vacation.

60 HARPER: *(Hearing something.)* That was the elevator. Oh God, I should fix myself up, I. . . . You have to go, you shouldn't be here . . . you aren't even real.

MR. LIES: Call me when you decide . . .

HARPER: Go!

(The TRAVEL AGENT *vanishes as* JOE *enters.)*

65 JOE: Buddy?
Buddy? Sorry I'm late. I was just . . . out. Walking. Are you mad?

HARPER: I got a little anxious.

JOE: Buddy kiss.

(They kiss.)

70 JOE: Nothing to get anxious about.
So. So how'd you like to move to Washington?

SCENE IV

Same day. LOUIS *and* PRIOR *outside the funeral home, sitting on a bench, both dressed in funereal finery, talking. The funeral service for Sarah Ironson has just concluded and* LOUIS *is about to leave for the cemetery.*

LOUIS: My grandmother actually saw Emma Goldman speak. In Yiddish. But all Grandma could remember was that she spoke well and wore a hat.
What a weird service. That rabbi . . .

5 PRIOR: A definite find. Get his number when you go to the graveyard. I want him to bury me.

LOUIS: Better head out there. Everyone gets to put dirt on the coffin once it's lowered in.

PRIOR: Oooh. Cemetery fun. Don't want to miss that.

10 LOUIS: It's an old Jewish custom to express love. Here, Grandma, have a shovelful. Latecomers run the risk of finding the grave completely filled.
She was pretty crazy. She was up there in that home for ten years, talking to herself. I never visited. She looked too much
15 like my mother.

PRIOR: (Hugs him.) Poor Louis. I'm sorry your grandma is dead.

LOUIS: Tiny little coffin, huh?
Sorry I didn't introduce you to. . . . I always get so closety at
20 these family things.

PRIOR: Butch. You get butch. (Imitating.) "Hi Cousin Doris, you don't remember me I'm Lou, Rachel's boy." Lou, not Louis, because if you say Louis they'll hear the sibilant S.

LOUIS: I don't have a . . .

PRIOR: I don't blame you, hiding. Bloodlines. Jewish curses are 25 the worst. I personally would dissolve if anyone ever looked me in the eye and said "Feh." Fortunately WASPs don't say "Feh." Oh and by the way, darling, cousin Doris is a dyke.

LOUIS: No.
Really? 30

PRIOR: You don't notice anything. If I hadn't spent the last four years fellating you I'd swear you were straight.

LOUIS: You're in a pissy mood. Cat still missing?

(Little pause.)

PRIOR: Not a furball in sight. It's your fault.

LOUIS: It is? 35

PRIOR: I warned you, Louis. Names are important. Call an animal "Little Sheba" and you can't expect it to stick around. Besides, it's a dog's name.

LOUIS: I wanted a dog in the first place, not a cat. He sprayed my books. 40

PRIOR: He was a female cat.

LOUIS: Cats are stupid, high-strung predators. Babylonians sealed them up in bricks. Dogs have brains.

PRIOR: Cats have intuition.

LOUIS: A sharp dog is as smart as a really dull two-year-old 45 child.

PRIOR: Cats know when something's wrong.

LOUIS: Only if you stop feeding them.

PRIOR: They know. That's why Sheba left, because she knew.

LOUIS: Knew what? 50

(Pause.)

PRIOR: I did my best Shirley Booth this morning, floppy slippers, housecoat, curlers, can of Little Friskies; "Come back, little Sheba, come back. . . ." To no avail. Le chat, elle ne reviendra jamais, jamais . . .

(He removes his jacket, rolls up his sleeve, shows LOUIS *a dark purple spot on the underside of his arm near the shoulder.)*

See. 55

LOUIS: That's just a burst blood vessel.

PRIOR: Not according to the best medical authorities.

LOUIS: What?

(Pause.)

Tell me.

PRIOR: K.S., baby. Lesion number one. Lookit. The wine-dark 60 kiss of the angel of death.

LOUIS: *(Very softly, holding* PRIOR's *arm.)* Oh please . . .

PRIOR: I'm a lesionnaire. The Foreign Lesion. The American Lesion. Lesionnaire's disease.

LOUIS: Stop. 65

PRIOR: My troubles are lesion.

LOUIS: Will you *stop*.

PRIOR: Don't you think I'm handling this well? I'm going to die.

LOUIS: Bullshit. 70

PRIOR: Let go of my arm.

LOUIS: No.

PRIOR: Let go.

LOUIS: *(Grabbing* PRIOR, *embracing him ferociously.)* No.

PRIOR: I can't find a way to spare you baby. No wall like the 75 wall of hard scientific fact. K.S. Wham. Bang your head on that.

LOUIS: Fuck you. (*Letting go.*) Fuck you fuck you fuck you.

PRIOR: Now that's what I like to hear. A mature reaction.

80 Let's go see if the cat's come home. Louis?

LOUIS: When did you find this?

PRIOR: I couldn't tell you.

LOUIS: Why?

85 PRIOR: I was scared, Lou.

LOUIS: Of what?

PRIOR: That you'll leave me.

LOUIS: Oh.

(*Little pause.*)

PRIOR: Bad timing, funeral and all, but I figured as long as

90 we're on the subject of death . . .

LOUIS: I have to go bury my grandma.

PRIOR: Lou?

(*Pause.*)

Then you'll come home?

LOUIS: Then I'll come home.

SCENE V

Same day, later on. Split scene: JOE *and* HARPER *at home;* LOUIS *at the cemetery with* RABBI ISIDOR CHEMELWITZ *and the little coffin.*

HARPER: Washington?

JOE: It's an incredible honor, buddy, and . . .

HARPER: I have to think.

JOE: Of course.

5 HARPER: Say no.

JOE: You said you were going to think about it.

HARPER: I don't want to move to Washington.

JOE: Well I do.

HARPER: It's a giant cemetery, huge white graves and mau-

10 soleums everywhere.

JOE: We could live in Maryland. Or Georgetown.

HARPER: We're happy here.

JOE: That's not really true, buddy, we . . .

HARPER: Well happy enough! Pretend-happy. That's better

15 than nothing.

JOE: It's time to make some changes, Harper.

HARPER: No changes. Why?

JOE: I've been chief clerk for four years. I make twenty-nine thousand dollars a year. That's ridiculous. I graduated fourth

20 in my class and I make less than anyone I know. And I'm . . . I'm tired of being a clerk, I want to go where something good is happening.

HARPER: Nothing good happens in Washington. We'll forget church teachings and buy furniture at . . . at *Conran's* and

25 become yuppies. I have too much to do here.

JOE: Like what?

HARPER: I *do* have things . . .

JOE: What things?

HARPER: I have to finish painting the bedroom.

30 JOE: You've been painting in there for over a year.

HARPER: I know, I. . . . It just isn't done because I never get time to finish it.

JOE: Oh that's . . . that doesn't make sense. You have all the time in the world. You could finish it when I'm at work.

HARPER: I'm afraid to go in there alone. 35

JOE: Afraid of what?

HARPER: I heard someone in there. Metal scraping on the wall. A man with a knife, maybe.

JOE: There's no one in the bedroom, Harper.

HARPER: Not now. 40

JOE: Not this morning either.

HARPER: How do you know? You were at work this morning. There's something creepy about this place. Remember *Rosemary's Baby*?

JOE: *Rosemary's Baby*? 45

HARPER: Our apartment looks like that one. Wasn't that apartment in Brooklyn?

JOE: No, it was . . .

HARPER: Well, it looked like this. It did.

JOE: Then let's move. 50

HARPER: Georgetown's worse. *The Exorcist* was in Georgetown.

JOE: The devil, everywhere you turn, huh, buddy.

HARPER: Yeah. Everywhere.

JOE: How many pills today, buddy?

HARPER: None. One. Three. Only three. 55

LOUIS: (*Pointing at the coffin.*) Why are there just two little wooden pegs holding the lid down?

RABBI ISIDOR CHEMELWITZ: So she can get out easier if she wants to.

LOUIS: I hope she stays put. 60

I pretended for years that she was already dead. When they called to say she had died it was a surprise. I abandoned her.

RABBI ISIDOR CHEMELWITZ: "Sharfer vi di tson fun a shlang iz an umdankbar kind!" 65

LOUIS: I don't speak Yiddish.

RABBI ISIDOR CHEMELWITZ: Sharper than the serpent's tooth is the ingratitude of children. Shakespeare. *Kenig Lear.*

LOUIS: Rabbi, what does the Holy Writ say about someone who abandons someone he loves at a time of great need? 70

RABBI ISIDOR CHEMELWITZ: Why would a person do such a thing?

LOUIS: Because he has to.

Maybe because this person's sense of the world, that it will change for the better with struggle, maybe a person who has 75 this neo-Hegelian positivist sense of constant historical progress towards happiness or perfection or something, who feels very powerful because he feels connected to these forces, moving uphill all the time . . . maybe that person can't, um, incorporate sickness into this sense of how things are sup- 80 posed to go. Maybe vomit . . . and sores and disease . . . really frighten him, maybe . . . he isn't so good with death.

RABBI ISIDOR CHEMELWITZ: The Holy Scriptures have nothing to say about such a person.

LOUIS: Rabbi, I'm afraid of the crimes I may commit. 85

RABBI ISIDOR CHEMELWITZ: Please, mister. I'm a sick old rabbi facing a long drive home to the Bronx. You want to confess, better you should find a priest.

LOUIS: But I'm not a Catholic, I'm a Jew.

RABBI ISIDOR CHEMELWITZ: Worse luck for you, bubbulah. 90 Catholics believe in forgiveness. Jews believe in Guilt. (*He pats the coffin tenderly.*)

LOUIS: You just make sure those pegs are in good and tight.

RABBI ISIDOR CHEMELWITZ: Don't worry, mister. The life she

95   had, she'll stay put. She's better off.

JOE: Look, I know this is scary for you. But try to understand what it means to me. Will you try?

HARPER: Yes.

JOE: Good. Really try.

100   I think things are starting to change in the world.

HARPER: But I don't want . . .

JOE: Wait. For the good. Change for the good. America has re-discovered itself. Its sacred position among nations. And people aren't ashamed of that like they used to be. This is a great

105   thing. The truth restored. Law restored. That's what President Reagan's done, Harper. He says "Truth exists and can be spoken proudly." And the country responds to him. We become better. More good. I need to be a part of that, I need something big to lift me up. I mean, six years ago the world

110   seemed in decline, horrible, hopeless, full of unsolvable problems and crime and confusion and hunger and . . .

HARPER: But it still seems that way. More now than before. They say the ozone layer is . . .

JOE: Harper . . .

115 HARPER: And today out the window on Atlantic Avenue there was a schizophrenic traffic cop who was making these . . .

JOE: Stop it! I'm trying to make a point.

HARPER: So am I.

JOE: You aren't even making sense, you . . .

120 HARPER: My point is the world seems just as . . .

JOE: It only seems that way to you because you never go out in the world, Harper, and you have emotional problems.

HARPER: I do so get out in the world.

JOE: You don't. You stay in all day, fretting about imaginary . . .

125 HARPER: I get out. I do. You don't know what I do.

JOE: You don't stay in all day.

HARPER: No.

JOE: Well. . . . Yes you do.

HARPER: That's what you think.

130 JOE: Where do you go?

HARPER: Where do *you* go? When you walk.

     (Pause, then angrily.) And I DO NOT have emotional problems.

JOE: I'm sorry.

135 HARPER: And if I do have emotional problems it's from living with you. Or . . .

JOE: I'm sorry buddy, I didn't mean to . . .

HARPER: Or if you do think I do then you should never have married me. You have all these secrets and lies.

140 JOE: I want to be married to you, Harper.

HARPER: You shouldn't. You never should.

(Pause.)

   Hey buddy. Hey buddy.

JOE: Buddy kiss . . .

(They kiss.)

HARPER: I heard on the radio how to give a blowjob.

145 JOE: What?

HARPER: You want to try?

JOE: You really shouldn't listen to stuff like that.

HARPER: Mormons can give blowjobs.

JOE: *Harper.*

HARPER: *(Imitating his tone.)* Joe.   150
   It was a little Jewish lady with a German accent.
   This is a good time. For me to make a baby.

(Little pause. JOE *turns away.)*

HARPER: Then they went on to a program about holes in the ozone layer. Over Antarctica. Skin burns, birds go blind, ice-bergs melt. The world's coming to an end.   155

SCENE VI

First week of November. In the men's room of the offices of the Brooklyn Federal Court of Appeals; LOUIS *is crying over the sink;* JOE *enters.*

JOE: Oh, um. . . . Morning.

LOUIS: Good morning, counselor.

JOE: *(He watches* LOUIS *cry.)* Sorry, I . . . I don't know your name.

LOUIS: Don't bother. Word processor. The lowest of the low.   5

JOE: *(Holding out hand.)* Joe Pitt. I'm with Justice Wilson . . .

LOUIS: Oh, I know that. Counselor Pitt. Chief Clerk.

JOE: Were you . . . are you OK?

LOUIS: Oh, yeah. Thanks. What a nice man.

JOE: Not so nice.   10

LOUIS: What?

JOE: Not so nice. Nothing. You sure you're . . .

LOUIS: Life sucks shit. Life . . . just sucks shit.

JOE: What's wrong?

LOUIS: Run in my nylons.   15

JOE: Sorry . . . ?

LOUIS: Forget it. Look, thanks for asking.

JOE: Well . . .

LOUIS: I mean it really is nice of you.

(He starts crying again.)

   Sorry, sorry, sick friend . . .   20

JOE: Oh, I'm sorry.

LOUIS: Yeah, yeah, well, that's sweet.
   Three of your colleagues have preceded you to this baleful sight and you're the first one to ask. The others just opened the door, saw me, and fled. I hope they had to pee   25
   real bad.

JOE: *(Handing him a wad of toilet paper.)* They just didn't want to intrude.

LOUIS: Hah. Reaganite heartless macho asshole lawyers.

JOE: Oh, that's unfair.   30

LOUIS: What is? Heartless? Macho? Reaganite? Lawyer?

JOE: I voted for Reagan.

LOUIS: You did?

JOE: Twice.

LOUIS: Twice? Well, oh boy. A Gay Republican.   35

JOE: Excuse me?

LOUIS: Nothing.

JOE: I'm not . . .
   Forget it.

LOUIS: Republican? Not Republican? Or . . .   40

JOE: What?

LOUIS: What?

JOE: Not gay. I'm not gay.

LOUIS: Oh. Sorry. *(Blows his nose loudly.)* It's just . . .

JOE: Yes?   45

LOUIS: Well, sometimes you can tell from the way a person sounds that . . . I mean you *sound* like a . . .

JOE: No I don't. Like what?

LOUIS: Like a Republican.

(Little pause. JOE *knows he's being teased;* LOUIS *knows he knows.* JOE *decides to be a little brave.)*

50 JOE: *(Making sure no one else is around.)* Do I? Sound like a . . . ?

LOUIS: What? Like a . . . ? Republican, or . . . ? Do I?

JOE: Do you what?

LOUIS: Sound like a . . . ?

55 JOE: Like a . . . ?
I'm confused.

LOUIS: Yes.
My name is Louis. But all my friends call me Louise. I work in Word Processing. Thanks for the toilet paper.

*(*LOUIS *offers* JOE *his hand,* JOE *reaches,* LOUIS *feints and pecks* JOE *on the cheek, then exits.)*

SCENE VII

A week later. Mutual dream scene. PRIOR *is at a fantastic makeup table, having a dream, applying the face.* HARPER *is having a pill-induced hallucination. She has these from time to time. For some reason,* PRIOR *has appeared in this one. Or* HARPER *has appeared in* PRIOR'*s dream. It is bewildering.*

PRIOR: *(Alone, putting on makeup, then examining the results in the mirror; to the audience.)* "I'm ready for my closeup, Mr. DeMille."
One wants to move through life with elegance and grace,
5   blossoming infrequently but with exquisite taste, and perfect timing, like a rare bloom, a zebra orchid. . . . One wants. . . . But one so seldom gets what one wants, does one? No. One does not. One gets fucked. Over. One . . . dies at thirty, robbed of . . . decades of majesty.
10   Fuck this shit. Fuck this shit.

(He almost crumbles; he pulls himself together; he studies his handiwork in the mirror.)

I look like a corpse. A corpsette. Oh my queen; you know you've hit rock-bottom when even drag is a drag.

*(*HARPER *appears.)*

HARPER: Are you. . . . Who are you?

PRIOR: Who are you?

15 HARPER: What are you doing in my hallucination?

PRIOR: I'm not in your hallucination. You're in my dream.

HARPER: You're wearing makeup.

PRIOR: So are you.

HARPER: But you're a man.

20 PRIOR: *(Feigning dismay, shock, he mimes slashing his throat with his lipstick and dies, fabulously tragic. Then.)* The hands and feet give it away.

HARPER: There must be some mistake here. I don't recognize you. You're not. . . . Are you my . . . some sort of imaginary
25   friend?

PRIOR: No. Aren't you too old to have imaginary friends?

HARPER: I have emotional problems. I took too many pills. Why are you wearing makeup?

PRIOR: I was in the process of applying the face, trying to make myself feel better—I swiped the new fall colors at the Clin-   30 ique counter at Macy's. *(Showing her.)*

HARPER: You stole these?

PRIOR: I was out of cash; it was an emotional emergency!

HARPER: Joe will be so angry. I promised him. No more pills.

PRIOR: These pills you keep alluding to?   35

HARPER: Valium. I take Valium. Lots of Valium.

PRIOR: And you're dancing as fast as you can.

HARPER: I'm not *addicted.* I don't believe in addiction, and I never . . . well, I *never* drink. And I *never* take drugs.

PRIOR: Well, smell *you,* Nancy Drew.   40

HARPER: Except Valium.

PRIOR: Except Valium; in wee fistfuls.

HARPER: It's terrible. Mormons are not supposed to be addicted to anything. I'm a Mormon.

PRIOR: I'm a homosexual.   45

HARPER: Oh! In my church we don't believe in homosexuals.

PRIOR: In my church we don't believe in Mormons.

HARPER: What church do . . . oh! *(She laughs.)* I get it.
I don't understand this. If I didn't ever see you before and I don't think I did then I don't think you should be here, in   50 this hallucination, because in my experience the mind, which is where hallucinations come from, shouldn't be able to make up anything that wasn't there to start with, that didn't enter it from experience, from the real world. Imagination can't create anything new, can it? It only recycles bits   55 and pieces from the world and reassembles them into visions. . . . Am I making sense right now?

PRIOR: Given the circumstances, yes.

HARPER: So when we think we've escaped the unbearable ordinariness and, well, untruthfulness of our lives, it's really only   60 the same old ordinariness and falseness rearranged into the appearance of novelty and truth. Nothing unknown is knowable. Don't you think it's depressing?

PRIOR: The limitations of the imagination?

HARPER: Yes.   65

PRIOR: It's something you learn after your second theme party: It's All Been Done Before.

HARPER: The world. Finite. Terribly, terribly. . . . Well . . . This is the most depressing hallucination I've ever had.

PRIOR: Apologies. I do try to be amusing.   70

HARPER: Oh, well, don't apologize, you. . . . I can't expect someone who's really sick to entertain me.

PRIOR: How on earth did you know . . .

HARPER: Oh that happens. This is the very threshhold of revelation sometimes. You can see things . . . how sick you are.   75 Do you see anything about me?

PRIOR: Yes.

HARPER: What?

PRIOR: You are amazingly unhappy.

HARPER: Oh big deal. You meet a Valium addict and you fig-   80 ure out she's unhappy. That doesn't count. Of course I. . . . Something else. Something surprising.

PRIOR: Something surprising.

HARPER: Yes.

PRIOR: Your husband's a homo.   85

(Pause.)

HARPER: Oh, ridiculous.

(Pause, then very quietly.)

Really?

PRIOR: *(Shrugs.)* Threshhold of revelation.

HARPER: Well I don't like your revelations. I don't think you in-
90   tuit well at all. Joe's a very normal man, he . . .
    Oh God. Oh God. He. . . . Do homos take, like, lots of long
    walks?

PRIOR: Yes. We do. In stretch pants with lavender coifs. I just
    looked at you, and there was . . .

95 HARPER: A sort of blue streak of recognition.

PRIOR: Yes.

HARPER: Like you knew me incredibly well.

PRIOR: Yes.

HARPER: Yes.

100   I have to go now, get back, something just . . . fell apart. Oh
    God, I feel so sad . . .

PRIOR: I . . . I'm sorry. I usually say, "Fuck the truth," but
    mostly, the truth fucks you.

HARPER: I see something else about you . . .

105 PRIOR: Oh?

HARPER: Deep inside you, there's a part of you, the most inner
    part, entirely free of disease. I can see that.

PRIOR: Is that. . . . That isn't true.

HARPER: Threshhold of revelation.

110   Home . . .

(She vanishes.)

PRIOR: People come and go so quickly here . . .
    (To himself in the mirror.) I don't think there's any unin-
    fected part of me. My heart is pumping polluted blood. I feel
    dirty.

*(He begins to wipe makeup off with his hands, smearing it
around. A large gray feather falls from up above. PRIOR stops
smearing the makeup and looks at the feather. He goes to it and
picks it up.)*

115 A VOICE: *(It is an incredibly beautiful voice.)* Look up!

PRIOR: *(Looking up, not seeing anyone.)* Hello?

A VOICE: Look up!

PRIOR: Who is that?

A VOICE: Prepare the way!

120 PRIOR: I don't see any . . .

(There is a dramatic change in lighting, from above.)

A VOICE:
    Look up, look up,
    prepare the way
    the infinite descent
125   A breath in air
    floating down
    Glory to . . .

(Silence.)

PRIOR: Hello? Is that it? Helloooo!
    What the fuck . . . ? *(He holds himself.)*
130   Poor me. Poor poor me. Why me? Why poor poor me? Oh I
    don't feel good right now. I really don't.

SCENE VIII

That night. Split scene: HARPER *and* JOE *at home;* PRIOR *and*
LOUIS *in bed.*

HARPER: Where were you?

JOE: Out.

HARPER: Where?

JOE: Just out. Thinking.

HARPER: It's late.   5

JOE: I had a lot to think about.

HARPER: I burned dinner.

JOE: Sorry.

HARPER: Not my dinner. My dinner was fine. Your dinner. I
    put it back in the oven and turned everything up as high as it   10
    could go and I watched till it burned black. It's still hot. Very
    hot. Want it?

JOE: You didn't have to do that.

HARPER: I know. It just seemed like the kind of thing a men-
    tally deranged sex-starved pill-popping housewife would do.   15

JOE: Uh huh.

HARPER: So I did it. Who knows anymore what I have to do?

JOE: How many pills?

HARPER: A bunch. Don't change the subject.

JOE: I won't talk to you when you . . .   20

HARPER: No. No. Don't do that! I'm . . . fine, pills are not the
    problem, not our problem, I WANT TO KNOW WHERE
    YOU'VE BEEN! I WANT TO KNOW WHAT'S GOING
    ON!

JOE: Going on with what? The job?   25

HARPER: Not the job.

JOE: I said I need more time.

HARPER: Not the job!

JOE: Mr. Cohn, I talked to him on the phone, he said I had to
    hurry . . .   30

HARPER: Not the . . .

JOE: But I can't get you to talk sensibly about anything so . . .

HARPER: SHUT UP!

JOE: Then what?

HARPER: Stick to the subject.   35

JOE: I don't know what that is. You have something you want to
    ask me? Ask me. Go.

HARPER: I . . . can't. I'm scared of you.

JOE: I'm tired, I'm going to bed.

HARPER: Tell me without making me ask. Please.   40

JOE: This is crazy, I'm not . . .

HARPER: When you come through the door at night your face
    is never exactly the way I remembered it. I get surprised by
    something . . . mean and hard about the way you look. Even
    the weight of you in the bed at night, the way you breathe in   45
    your sleep seems unfamiliar.
    You terrify me.

JOE: *(Cold.)* I know who you are.

HARPER: Yes. I'm the enemy. That's easy. That doesn't change.
    You think you're the only one who hates sex; I do; I hate it   50
    with you; I do. I dream that you batter away at me till all my
    joints come apart, like wax, and I fall into pieces. It's like a
    punishment. It was wrong of me to marry you. I knew you . . .
    (She stops herself.) It's a sin, and it's killing us both.

JOE: I can always tell when you've taken pills because it makes   55
    you red-faced and sweaty and frankly that's very often why I
    don't want to . . .

HARPER: Because . . .

JOE: Well, you aren't pretty. Not like this.

HARPER: I have something to ask you.   60

JOE: Then ASK! ASK! What in hell are you . . .

HARPER: Are you a homo?

(Pause.)

65 Are you? If you try to walk out right now I'll put your dinner back in the oven and turn it up so high the whole building will fill with smoke and everyone in it will asphyxiate. So help me God I will.
Now answer the question.

JOE: What if I . . .

(Small pause.)

HARPER: Then tell me, please. And we'll see.

70 JOE: No. I'm not.
I don't see what difference it makes.

LOUIS: Jews don't have any clear textual guide to the afterlife; even that it exists. I don't think much about it. I see it as a perpetual rainy Thursday afternoon in March. Dead leaves.

75 PRIOR: Eeeugh. Very Greco-Roman.

LOUIS: Well for us it's not the verdict that counts, it's the act of judgment. That's why I could never be a lawyer. In court all that matters is the verdict.

PRIOR: You could never be a lawyer because you are oversexed.

80 You're too distracted.

LOUIS: Not distracted, *ab*stracted. I'm trying to make a point:

PRIOR: Namely:

LOUIS: It's the judge in his or her chambers, weighing, books open, pondering the evidence, ranging freely over cate-

85 gories: good, evil, innocent, guilty; the judge in the chamber of circumspection, not the judge on the bench with the gavel. The shaping of the law, not its execution.

PRIOR: The point, dear, the point . . .

LOUIS: That it should be the questions and shape of a life, its

90 total complexity gathered, arranged and considered, which matters in the end, not some stamp of salvation or damnation which disperses all the complexity in some unsatisfying little decision—the balancing of the scales . . .

PRIOR: I like this; very zen; it's . . . reassuringly incomprehen-

95 sible and useless. We who are about to die thank you.

LOUIS: You are not about to die.

PRIOR: It's not going well, really . . . two new lesions. My leg hurts. There's protein in my urine, the doctor says, but who knows what the fuck that portends. Anyway it shouldn't be

100 there, the protein. My butt is chapped from diarrhea and yesterday I shat blood.

LOUIS: I really hate this. You don't tell me . . .

PRIOR: You get too upset, I wind up comforting you. It's easier . . .

105 LOUIS: Oh thanks.

PRIOR: If it's bad I'll tell you.

LOUIS: Shitting blood sounds bad to me.

PRIOR: And I'm telling you.

LOUIS: And I'm handing it.

110 PRIOR: Tell me some more about justice.

LOUIS: I *am* not handling it.

PRIOR: Well Louis you win Trooper of the Month.

(LOUIS starts to cry.)

PRIOR: I take it back. You aren't Trooper of the Month.
This isn't working . . .

115 Tell me some more about justice.

LOUIS: You are not about to die.

PRIOR: Justice . . .

LOUIS: . . . is an immensity, a confusing vastness. Justice is God. Prior?

120 PRIOR: Hmmm?

LOUIS: You love me.

PRIOR: Yes.

LOUIS: What if I walked out on this?
Would you hate me forever?

(PRIOR kisses LOUIS on the forehead.)

PRIOR: Yes.   125

JOE: I think we ought to pray. Ask God for help. Ask him together . . .

HARPER: God won't talk to me. I have to make up people to talk to me.

JOE: You have to keep asking.   130

HARPER: I forgot the question.
Oh yeah. God, is my husband a . . .

JOE: (Scary.) Stop it. Stop it. I'm warning you.
Does it make any difference? That I might be one thing deep within, no matter how wrong or ugly that thing is, so   135
long as I have fought, with everything I have, to kill it. What do you want from me? What do you want from me, Harper? More than that? For God's sake, there's nothing left, I'm a shell. There's nothing left to kill.
As long as my behavior is what I know it has to be. Decent.   140
Correct. That alone in the eyes of God.

HARPER: No, no, not that, that's Utah talk, Mormon talk, I hate it, Joe, tell me, say it . . .

JOE: All I will say is that I am a very good man who has worked very hard to become good and you want to destroy that. You   145
want to destroy me, but I am not going to let you do that.

(Pause.)

HARPER: I'm going to have a baby.

JOE: Liar.

HARPER: You liar.
A baby born addicted to pills. A baby who does not dream   150
but who hallucinates, who stares up at us with big mirror eyes and who does not know who we are.

(Pause.)

JOE: Are you really . . .

HARPER: No. Yes. No. Yes. Get away from me.
Now we both have a secret.   155

PRIOR: One of my ancestors was a ship's captain who made money bringing whale oil to Europe and returning with immigrants—Irish mostly, packed in tight, so many dollars per head. The last ship he captained foundered off the coast of Nova Scotia in a winter tempest and sank to the bottom. He   160
went down with the ship—la Grande Geste—but his crew took seventy women and kids in the ship's only longboat, this big, open rowboat, and when the weather got too rough, and they thought the boat was overcrowded, the crew started lifting people up and hurling them into the sea. Until they got   165
the ballast right. They walked up and down the longboat, eyes to the waterline, and when the boat rode low in the water they'd grab the nearest passenger and throw them into the sea. The boat was leaky, see; seventy people; they arrived in Halifax with nine people on board.   170

LOUIS: Jesus.

PRIOR: I think about that story a lot now. People in a boat, waiting, terrified, while implacable, unsmiling men, irresistibly strong, seize . . . maybe the person next to you, maybe you, and with no warning at all, with time only for a quick intake   175
of air you are pitched into freezing, turbulent water and salt and darkness to drown.

I like your cosmology, baby. While time is running out I find myself drawn to anything that's suspended, that lacks an end-
180   ing—but it seems to me that it lets you off scot-free.
LOUIS: What do you mean?
PRIOR: No judgment, no guilt or responsibility.
LOUIS: For me.
PRIOR: For anyone. It was an editorial "you."
185   LOUIS: Please get better. Please.
Please don't get any sicker.

SCENE IX

Third week in November. ROY *and* HENRY, *his doctor, in* HENRY's *office.*

HENRY: Nobody knows what causes it. And nobody knows how to cure it. The best theory is that we blame a retrovirus, the Human Immunodeficiency Virus. Its presence is made known to us by the useless antibodies which appear in reac-
5   tion to its entrance into the bloodstream through a cut, or an orifice. The antibodies are powerless to protect the body against it. Why, we don't know. The body's immune system ceases to function. Sometimes the body even attacks itself. At any rate it's left open to a whole horror house of infections
10   from microbes which it usually defends against.
Like Kaposi's sarcomas. These lesions. Or your throat prob-lem. Or the glands.
We think it may also be able to slip past the blood-brain bar-rier into the brain. Which is of course very bad news.
15   And it's fatal in we don't know what percent of people with suppressed immune responses.

(Pause)

ROY: This is very interesting, Mr. Wizard, but why the fuck are you telling me this?

(Pause.)

HENRY: Well, I have just removed one of three lesions which
20   biopsy results will probably tell us is a Kaposi's sarcoma le-sion. And you have a pronounced swelling of glands in your neck, groin, and armpits—lymphadenopathy is another sign. And you have oral candidiasis and maybe a little more fun-gus under the fingernails of two digits on your right hand. So
25   that's why . . .
ROY: This disease . . .
HENRY: Syndrome.
ROY: Whatever. It afflicts mostly homosexuals and drug ad-dicts.
30   HENRY: Mostly. Hemophiliacs are also at risk.
ROY: Homosexuals and drug addicts. So why are you implying that I . . .

(Pause.)

What are you implying, Henry?
HENRY: I don't . . .
35   ROY: I'm not a drug addict.
HENRY: Oh come on Roy.
ROY: What, what, come on Roy what? Do you think I'm a junkie, Henry, do you see tracks?
HENRY: This is absurd.
40   ROY: Say it.
HENRY: Say what?

ROY: Say, "Roy Cohn, you are a . . ."
HENRY: Roy.
ROY: "You are a . . ." Go on. Not "Roy Cohn you are a drug fiend." "Roy Marcus Cohn, you are a . . ."   45
Go on, Henry, it starts with an "H."
HENRY: Oh I'm not going to . . .
ROY: *With an* "H," Henry, and it isn't "Hemophiliac." Come on . . .
HENRY: What are you doing, Roy?   50
ROY: No, say it. I mean it. Say: "Roy Cohn, you are a homo-sexual."

(Pause.)

And I will proceed, systemically, to destroy your reputation and your practice and your career in New York State, Henry. Which you know I can do.   55

(Pause.)

HENRY: Roy, you have been seeing me since 1958. Apart from the facelifts I have treated you for everything from syphilis . . .
ROY: From a whore in Dallas.
HENRY: From syphilis to venereal warts. In your rectum. Which you may have gotten from a whore in Dallas, but it   60
wasn't a female whore.

(Pause.)

ROY: So say it.
HENRY: Roy Cohn, you are . . .
You have had sex with men, many many times, Roy, and one of them, or any number of them, has made you very sick.   65
You have AIDS.
ROY: AIDS.
Your problem, Henry, is that you are hung up on words, on labels, that you believe they mean what they seem to mean. AIDS. Homosexual. Gay. Lesbian. You think these are   70
names that tell you who someone sleeps with, but they don't tell you that.
HENRY: No?
ROY: No. Like all labels they tell you one thing and one thing only: where does an individual so identified fit in the food   75
chain, in the pecking order? Not ideology, or sexual taste, but something much simpler: clout. Not who I fuck or who fucks me, but who will pick up the phone when I call, who owes me favors. This is what a label refers to. Now to some-one who does not understand this, homosexual is what I am   80
because I have sex with men. But really this is wrong. Ho-mosexuals are not men who sleep with other men. Homo-sexuals are men who in fifteen years of trying cannot get a pissant antidiscrimination bill through City Council. Homo-sexuals are men who know nobody and who nobody knows.   85
Who have zero clout. Does this sound like me, Henry?
HENRY: No.
ROY: No. I have clout. A lot. I can pick up this phone, punch fifteen numbers, and you know who will be on the other end in under five minutes, Henry?   90
HENRY: The President.
ROY: Even better, Henry. His wife.
HENRY: I'm impressed.
ROY: I don't want you to be impressed. I want you to under-stand. This is not sophistry. And this is not hypocrisy. This is   95
reality. I have sex with men. But unlike nearly every other

man of whom this is true, I bring the guy I'm screwing to the White House and President Reagan smiles at us and shakes his hand. Because *what* I am is defined entirely by *who* I am.
100 Roy Cohn is not a homosexual. Roy Cohn is a heterosexual man, Henry, who fucks around with guys.

HENRY: OK, Roy.

ROY: And what is my diagnosis, Henry?

HENRY: You have AIDS, Roy.

105 ROY: No, Henry, no. AIDS is what homosexuals have. I have liver cancer.

(Pause.)

HENRY: Well, whatever the fuck you have, Roy, it's very serious, and I haven't got a damn thing for you. The NIH in Bethesda has a new drug called AZT with a two-year waiting
110 list that not even I can get you onto. So get on the phone, Roy, and dial the fifteen numbers, and tell the First Lady you need in on an experimental treatment for liver cancer, because you can call it any damn thing you want, Roy, but what it boils down to is very bad news.

— ACT TWO —
IN VITRO
DECEMBER 1985–JANUARY 1986

SCENE I

Night, the third week in December. PRIOR *alone on the floor of his bedroom; he is much worse.*

PRIOR: Louis, Louis, please wake up, oh God.

(LOUIS runs in.)

PRIOR: I think something horrible is wrong with me I can't breathe . . .

LOUIS: *(Starting to exit.)* I'm calling the ambulance.

5 PRIOR: No, wait, I . . .

LOUIS: *Wait?* Are you fucking crazy? Oh God you're on fire, your head is on fire.

PRIOR: It hurts, it hurts . . .

LOUIS: I'm calling the ambulance.

10 PRIOR: I don't want to go to the hospital, I don't want to go to the hospital please let me lie here, just . . .

LOUIS: No, no, God, Prior, stand up . . .

PRIOR: DON'T TOUCH MY LEG!

LOUIS: We have to . . . oh God this is so crazy.

15 PRIOR: I'll be OK if I just lie here Lou, really, if I can only sleep a little . . .

(LOUIS exits.)

PRIOR: Louis?
NO! NO! Don't call, you'll send me there and I won't come back, please, please Louis I'm begging, baby, please . . .
20 *(Screams.)* LOUIS!!

LOUIS: *(From off; hysterical.)* WILL YOU SHUT THE FUCK UP!

PRIOR: *(Trying to stand.)* Aaaah. I have . . . to go to the bathroom. Wait. Wait, just . . . oh. Oh God. *(He shits himself.)*

25 LOUIS: *(Entering.)* Prior? They'll be here in . . . Oh my God.

PRIOR: I'm sorry, I'm sorry.

LOUIS: What did . . . ? What?

PRIOR: I had an accident.

(LOUIS goes to him.)

LOUIS: This is blood.

PRIOR: Maybe you shouldn't touch it . . . me . . . . I . . . *(He 30 faints.)*

LOUIS: *(Quietly.)* Oh help. Oh help. Oh God oh God oh God help me I can't I can't I can't.

SCENE II

Same night. HARPER *is sitting at home, all alone, with no lights on. We can barely see her.* JOE *enters, but he doesn't turn on the lights.*

JOE: Why are you sitting in the dark? Turn on the light.

HARPER: *No.* I heard the sounds in the bedroom again. I know someone was in there.

JOE: No one was.

HARPER: Maybe actually in the bed, under the covers with a 5 knife.
Oh, boy. Joe. I, um, I'm thinking of going away. By which I mean: I think I'm going off again. You . . . you know what I mean?

JOE: Please don't. Stay. We can fix it. I pray for that. This is my 10 fault, but I can correct it. You have to try too . . .

(He turns on the light. She turns it off again.)

HARPER: When you pray, what do you pray for?

JOE: I pray for God to crush me, break me up into little pieces and start all over again.

HARPER: Oh. Please. Don't pray for that. 15

JOE: I had a book of Bible stories when I was a kid. There was a picture I'd look at twenty times every day: Jacob wrestles with the angel. I don't really remember the story, or why the wrestling—just the picture. Jacob is young and very strong. The angel is . . . a beautiful man, with golden hair and 20 wings, of course. I still dream about it. Many nights. I'm. . . . It's me. In that struggle. Fierce, and unfair. The angel is not human, and it holds nothing back, so how could anyone human win, what kind of a fight is that? It's not just. Losing means your soul thrown down in the dust, your heart torn 25 out from God's. But you can't not lose.

HARPER: In the whole entire world, you are the only person, the only person I love or have ever loved. And I love you terribly. Terribly. That's what's so awfully, irreducibly real. I can make up anything but I can't dream that away. 30

JOE: Are you . . . are you really going to have a baby?

HARPER: It's my time and there's no blood. I don't really know. I suppose it wouldn't be a great thing. Maybe I'm just not bleeding because I take too many pills. Maybe I'll give birth to a pill. That would give a new meaning to pill-popping, 35 huh?
I think you should go to Washington. Alone. Change, like you said.

JOE: I'm not going to leave you, Harper.

HARPER: Well maybe not. But I'm going to leave you. 40

SCENE III

One AM, *the next morning.* LOUIS *and a nurse,* EMILY, *are sitting in* PRIOR'S *room in the hospital.*

EMILY: He'll be all right now.

LOUIS: No he won't.

EMILY: No. I guess not. I gave him something that makes him sleep.

5 LOUIS: Deep asleep?

EMILY: Orbiting the moons of Jupiter.

LOUIS: A good place to be.

EMILY: Anyplace better than here. You his . . . uh?

LOUIS: Yes. I'm his uh.

10 EMILY: This must be hell for you.

LOUIS: It is. Hell. The After Life. Which is not at all like a rainy afternoon in March, by the way, Prior. A lot more vivid than I'd expected. Dead leaves, but the crunchy kind. Sharp, dry air. The kind of long, luxurious dying feeling that breaks

15 your heart.

EMILY: Yeah, well we all get to break our hearts on this one. He seems like a nice guy. Cute.

LOUIS: Not like this.
Yes, he is. Was. Whatever.

20 EMILY: Weird name. Prior Walter. Like, "The Walter before this one."

LOUIS: Lots of Walters before this one. Prior is an old old family name in an old old family. The Walters go back to the Mayflower and beyond. Back to the Norman Conquest. He

25 says there's a Prior Walter stitched into the Bayeux tapestry.

EMILY: Is that impressive?

LOUIS: Well, it's old. Very old. Which in some circles equals impressive.

EMILY: Not in my circle. What's the name of the tapestry?

30 LOUIS: The Bayeux tapestry. Embroidered by La Reine Mathilde.

EMILY: I'll tell my mother. She embroiders. Drives me nuts.

LOUIS: Manual therapy for anxious hands.

EMILY: Maybe you should try it.

35 LOUIS: Mathilde stitched while William the Conqueror was off to war. She was capable of . . . more than loyalty. Devotion. She waited for him, she stitched for years. And if he had come back broken and defeated from war, she would have loved him even more. And if he had returned mutilated,

40 ugly, full of infection and horror, she would still have loved him; fed by pity, by a sharing of pain, she would love him even more, and even more, and she would never, never have prayed to God, please let him die if he can't return to me whole and healthy and able to live a normal life. . . . If he

45 had died, she would have buried her heart with him.
So what the fuck is the matter with me?

(Little pause.)

Will he sleep through the night?

EMILY: At least.

LOUIS: I'm going.

50 EMILY: It's one AM. Where do you have to go at . . .

LOUIS: I know what time it is. A walk. Night air, good for the. . . . The park.

EMILY: Be careful.

LOUIS: Yeah. Danger.

55 Tell him, if he wakes up and you're still on, tell him good-bye, tell him I had to go.

SCENE IV

An hour later. Split scene: JOE *and* ROY *in a fancy (straight) bar;* LOUIS *and a* MAN *in the Rambles in Central Park.* JOE *and* ROY *are sitting at the bar; the place is brightly lit.* JOE *has a plate of food in front of him but he isn't eating.* ROY *occasionally reaches over the table and forks small bites off* JOE's *plate.* ROY *is drinking heavily,* JOE *not at all.* LOUIS *and the* MAN *are eyeing each other, each alternating interest and indifference.*

JOE: The pills were something she started when she miscarried or . . . no, she took some before that. She had a really bad time at home, when she was a kid, her home was really bad. I think a lot of drinking and physical stuff. She doesn't talk

5 about that, instead she talks about . . . the sky falling down, people with knives hiding under sofas. Monsters. Mormons. Everyone thinks Mormons don't come from homes like that, we aren't supposed to behave that way, but we do. It's not lying, or being two-faced. Everyone tries very hard to live up

10 to God's strictures, which are very . . . um . . .

ROY: Strict.

JOE: I shouldn't be bothering you with this.

ROY: No, please. Heart to heart. Want another. . . . What is that, seltzer?

15 JOE: The failure to measure up hits people very hard. From such a strong desire to be good they feel very far from goodness when they fail.
What scares me is that maybe what I really love in her is the part of her that's farthest from the light, from God's love;

20 maybe I was drawn to that in the first place. And I'm keeping it alive because I need it.

ROY: Why would you need it?

JOE: There are things. . . . I don't know how well we know ourselves. I mean, what if? I know I married her because she . . .

25 because I loved it that she was always wrong, always doing something wrong, like one step out of step. In Salt Lake City that stands out. I never stood out, on the outside, but inside, it was hard for me. To pass.

ROY: Pass?

30 JOE: Yeah.

ROY: Pass as what?

JOE: Oh. Well. . . . As someone cheerful and strong. Those who love God with an open heart unclouded by secrets and struggles are cheerful; God's easy simple love for them shows

35 in how strong and happy they are. The saints.

ROY: But you had secrets? Secret struggles . . .

JOE: I wanted to be one of the elect, one of the Blessed. You feel you ought to be, that the blemishes are yours by choice, which of course they aren't. Harper's sorrow, that really deep

40 sorrow, she didn't choose that. But it's there.

ROY: You didn't put it there.

JOE: No.

ROY: You sound like you think you did.

JOE: I am responsible for her.

45 ROY: Because she's your wife.

JOE: That. And I do love her.

ROY: Whatever. She's your wife. And so there are obligations. To her. But also to yourself.

JOE: She'd fall apart in Washington.

50 ROY: Then let her stay here.

JOE: She'll fall apart if I leave her.

ROY: Then bring her to Washington.

JOE: I just can't, Roy. She needs me.

ROY: Listen, Joe. I'm the best divorce lawyer in the business.

(Little pause.)

55 JOE: Can't Washington wait?

ROY: You do what you need to do, Joe. What *you* need. *You.* Let her life go where it wants to go. You'll both be better for that. *Somebody* should get what they want.

MAN: What do you want?

60 LOUIS: I want you to fuck me, hurt me, make me bleed.

MAN: I want to.

LOUIS: Yeah?

MAN: I want to hurt you.

LOUIS: Fuck me.

65 MAN: Yeah?

LOUIS: Hard.

MAN: Yeah? You been a bad boy?

(Pause. LOUIS *laughs, softly.)*

LOUIS: Very bad. Very bad.

MAN: You need to be punished, boy?

70 LOUIS: Yes. I do.

MAN: Yes what?

(Little pause.)

LOUIS: Um, I . . .

MAN: Yes *what,* boy?

LOUIS: Oh. Yes sir.

75 MAN: I want you to take me to your place, boy.

LOUIS: No, I can't do that.

MAN: No *what?*

LOUIS: No sir, I can't, I . . .
    I don't live alone, sir.

80 MAN: Your lover know you're out with a man tonight, boy?

LOUIS: No sir, he . . .
    My lover doesn't know.

MAN: Your lover know you . . .

LOUIS: Let's change the subject, OK? Can we go to your

85 place?

MAN: I live with my parents.

LOUIS: Oh.

ROY: Everyone who makes it in this world makes it because somebody older and more powerful takes an interest. The

90 most precious asset in life, I think, is the ability to be a good son. You have that, Joe. Somebody who can be a good son to a father who pushes them farther than they would otherwise go. I've had many fathers, I owe my life to them, powerful, powerful men. Walter Winchell, Edgar Hoover. Joe

95 McCarthy most of all. He valued me because I am a good lawyer, but he loved me because I was and am a good son. He was a very difficult man, very guarded and cagey; I brought out something tender in him. He would have died for me. And me for him. Does this embarrass you?

100 JOE: I had a hard time with my father.

ROY: Well sometimes that's the way. Then you have to find other fathers, substitutes, I don't know. The father-son relationship is central to life. Women are for birth, beginning, but the father is continuance. The son offers the father his

105 life as a vessel for carrying forth his father's dream. Your father's living?

JOE: Um, dead.

ROY: He was . . . what? A difficult man?

JOE: He was in the military. He could be very unfair. And cold.

110 ROY: But he loved you.

JOE: I don't know.

ROY: No, no, Joe, he did, I know this. Sometimes a father's love has to be very, very hard, unfair even, cold to make his son grow strong in a world like this. This isn't a good world.

MAN: Here, then. 115

LOUIS: I. . . . Do you have a rubber?

MAN: I don't use rubbers.

LOUIS: You should. *(He takes one from his coat pocket.)* Here.

MAN: I don't use them.

LOUIS: Forget it, then. *(He starts to leave.)* 120

MAN: No, wait.
    Put it on me. Boy.

LOUIS: Forget it, I have to get back. Home. I must be going crazy.

MAN: Oh come on please he won't find out. 125

LOUIS: It's cold. Too cold.

MAN: It's never too cold, let me warm you up. Please?

(They begin to fuck.)

MAN: Relax.

LOUIS: *(A small laugh.)* Not a chance.

MAN: It . . . 130

LOUIS: What?

MAN: I think it broke. The rubber. You want me to keep going?
    (Little pause.) Pull out? Should I . . .

LOUIS: Keep going.
    Infect me. 135
    I don't care. I don't care.

(Pause. The MAN *pulls out.)*

MAN: I . . . um, look, I'm sorry, but I think I want to go.

LOUIS: Yeah.
    Give my best to mom and dad.

(The MAN *slaps him.)*

LOUIS: Ow! 140

(They stare at each other.)

LOUIS: It was a joke.

(The MAN *leaves.)*

ROY: How long have we known each other?

JOE: Since 1980.

ROY: Right. A long time. I feel close to you, Joe. Do I advise you well? 145

JOE: You've been an incredible friend, Roy, I . . .

ROY: I want to be family. Familia, as my Italian friends call it. La Familia. A lovely word. It's important for me to help you, like I was helped.

JOE: I owe practically everything to you, Roy. 150

ROY: I'm dying, Joe. Cancer.

JOE: Oh my God.

ROY: Please. Let me finish.
    Few people know this and I'm telling you this only because.
    . . . I'm not afraid of death. What can death bring that I 155
    haven't faced? I've lived; life is the worst. *(Gently mocking himself.)* Listen to me, I'm a philosopher.
    Joe. You must do this. You must must must. Love; that's a trap. Responsibility; that's a trap too. Like a father to a son I tell you this: Life is full of horror; nobody escapes, nobody; 160
    save yourself. Whatever pulls on you, whatever needs from you, threatens you. Don't be afraid; people are so afraid;

don't be afraid to live in the raw wind, naked, alone. . . .
Learn at least this: What you are capable of. Let nothing
165   stand in your way.

SCENE V

Three days later. PRIOR *and* BELIZE *in* PRIOR's *hospital room.*
PRIOR *is very sick but improving.* BELIZE *has just arrived.*

PRIOR: Miss Thing.
BELIZE: Ma cherie bichette.
PRIOR: Stella.
BELIZE: Stella for star. Let me see. *(Scrutinizing* PRIOR.) You
5   look like shit, why yes indeed you do, comme la merde!
PRIOR: Merci.
BELIZE: *(Taking little plastic bottles from his bag, handing
       them to* PRIOR.) Not to despair, Belle Reeve. Lookie! Magic
       goop!
10   PRIOR: *(Opening a bottle, sniffing.)* Pooh! What kinda crap is
       that?
BELIZE: Beats me. Let's rub it on your poor blistered body and
       see what it does.
PRIOR: This is not Western medicine, these bottles . . .
15   BELIZE: Voodoo cream. From the botanica 'round the block.
PRIOR: And you a registered nurse.
BELIZE: *(Sniffing it.)* Beeswax and cheap perfume. Cut with
       Jergen's Lotion. Full of good vibes and love from some little
       black Cubana witch in Miami.
20   PRIOR: Get that trash away from me. I am immune-suppressed.
BELIZE: I *am* a health professional. I *know* what I'm doing.
PRIOR: It stinks. Any word from Louis?

(Pause. BELIZE *starts giving* PRIOR *a gentle massage.)*

PRIOR: Gone.
BELIZE: He'll be back. I know the type. Likes to keep a girl on
25   edge.
PRIOR: It's been . . .

(Pause)

BELIZE: *(Trying to jog his memory.)* How long?
PRIOR: I don't remember.
BELIZE: How long have you been here?
30   PRIOR: *(Getting suddenly upset.)* I don't remember, I don't
       give a fuck. I want Louis. I want my fucking boyfriend,
       where the fuck is he? I'm dying, I'm dying, where's Louis?
BELIZE: Shhhh, shhh . . .
PRIOR: This is a very strange drug, this drug. Emotional labil-
35   ity, for starters.
BELIZE: Save a tab or two for me.
PRIOR: Oh no, not this drug, ce n'est pas pour la joyeux noël et
       la bonne année, this drug she is serious poisonous chemistry,
       ma pauvre bichette.
40   And not just disorienting. I hear things. Voices.
BELIZE: Voices.
PRIOR: A voice.
BELIZE: Saying what?

(Pause.)

PRIOR: I'm not supposed to tell.
45   BELIZE: You better tell the doctor. Or I will.
PRIOR: No no don't. Please. I want the voice; it's wonderful.
       It's all that's keeping me alive. I don't want to talk to some in-
       tern about it.
       You know what happens? When I hear it, I get hard.

BELIZE: Oh my.   50
PRIOR: Comme ça. *(He uses his arm to demonstrate.)* And you
       know I am slow to rise.
BELIZE: My jaw aches at the memory.
PRIOR: And would you deny me this little solace—betray my
       concupiscence to Florence Nightingale's storm troopers?   55
BELIZE: Perish the thought, ma bébé.
PRIOR: They'd change the drug just to spoil the fun.
BELIZE: You and your boner can depend on me.
PRIOR: Je t'adore, ma belle nègre.
BELIZE: All this girl-talk shit is politically incorrect, you know.   60
       We should have dropped it back when we gave up drag.
PRIOR: I'm sick, I get to be politically incorrect if it makes me
       feel better. You sound like Lou.

(Little pause.)

       Well, at least I have the satisfaction of knowing he's in an-
       guish somewhere. I loved his anguish. Watching him stick   65
       his head up his asshole and eat his guts out over some rela-
       tively minor moral conundrum—it was the best show in
       town. But Mother warned me; if they get overwhelmed by
       the little things . . .
BELIZE: They'll be belly-up bustville when something big   70
       comes along.
PRIOR: Mother warned me.
BELIZE: And they do come along.
PRIOR: But I didn't listen.
BELIZE: No. *(Doing Hepburn.)* Men are beasts.   75
PRIOR: *(Also Hepburn.)* The absolute lowest.
BELIZE: I have to go. If I want to spend my whole lonely life
       looking after white people I can get underpaid to do it.
PRIOR: You're just a Christian martyr.
BELIZE: Whatever happens, baby, I will be here for you.   80
PRIOR: Je t'aime.
BELIZE: Je t'aime. Don't go crazy on me, girlfriend, I already
       got enough crazy queens for one lifetime. For two. I can't be
       bothering with dementia.
PRIOR: I promise.   85
BELIZE: *(Touching him; softly.)* Ouch.
PRIOR: Ouch. Indeed.
BELIZE: Why'd they have to pick on you?
       And eat more, girlfriend, you really do look like shit.

*(*BELIZE *leaves.)*

PRIOR: *(After waiting a beat.)* He's gone.   90
       Are you still . . .
VOICE: I can't stay. I will return.
PRIOR: Are you one of those "Follow me to the other side"
       voices?
VOICE: No. I am no nightbird. I am a messenger . . .   95
PRIOR: You have a beautiful voice, it sounds . . . like a viola,
       like a perfectly tuned, tight string, balanced, the truth. . . .
       Stay with me.
VOICE: Not now. Soon I will return, I will reveal myself to you;
       I am glorious, glorious; my heart, my countenance and my   100
       message. You must prepare.
PRIOR: For what? I don't want to . . .
VOICE: No death, no:
       A marvelous work and a wonder we undertake, an edifice
       awry we sink plumb and straighten, a great Lie we abolish, a   105
       great error correct, with the rule, sword and broom of Truth!
PRIOR: What are you talking about, I . . .

VOICE:
110   I am on my way; when I am manifest, our Work begins;
Prepare for the parting of the air,
The breath, the ascent,
Glory to . . .

SCENE VI

The second week of January. MARTIN, ROY *and* JOE *in a fancy Manhattan restaurant.*

MARTIN: It's a revolution in Washington, Joe. We have a new
agenda and finally a real leader. They got back the Senate
but we have the courts. By the nineties the Supreme Court
will be block-solid Republican appointees, and the Federal
5   bench—Republican judges like land mines, everywhere,
everywhere they turn. Affirmative action? Take it to court.
Boom! Land mine. And we'll get our way on just about
everything: abortion, defense, Central America, family values, a live investment climate. We have the White House
10   locked till the year 2000. And beyond. A permanent fix on
the Oval Office? It's possible. By '92 we'll get the Senate
back, and in ten years the South is going to give us the
House. It's really the end of Liberalism. The end of New
Deal Socialism. The end of ipso facto secular humanism.
15   The dawning of a genuinely American political personality.
Modeled on Ronald Wilson Reagan.
JOE: It sounds great, Mr. Heller.
MARTIN: Martin. And Justice is the hub. Especially since Ed
Meese took over. He doesn't specialize in Fine Points of
20   the Law. He's a flatfoot, a cop. He reminds me of Teddy
Roosevelt.
JOE: I can't wait to meet him.
MARTIN: Too bad, Joe, he's been dead for sixty years!

(There is a little awkwardness. JOE *doesn't respond.)*

MARTIN: Teddy Roosevelt. You said you wanted to. . . . Little
25   joke. It reminds me of the story about the . . .
ROY: *(Smiling, but nasty.)* Aw shut the fuck up Martin.
(To JOE.*)* You see that? Mr. Heller here is one of the mighty,
Joseph, in D.C. he sitteth on the right hand of the man
who sitteth on the right hand of The Man. And yet I can
30   say "shut the fuck up" and he will take no offense. Loyalty.
He . . . Martin?
MARTIN: Yes, Roy?
ROY: Rub my back.
MARTIN: Roy . . .
35   ROY: No no really, a sore spot, I get them all the time now,
these. . . . Rub it for me darling, would you do that for me?

*(*MARTIN *rubs* ROY's *back. They both look at* JOE.*)*

ROY: *(To* JOE.*)* How do you think a handful of Bolsheviks
turned St. Petersburg into Leningrad in one afternoon?
Comrades. Who do for each other. Marx and Engels. Lenin
40   and Trotsky. Josef Stalin and Franklin Delano Roosevelt.

*(*MARTIN *laughs.)*

ROY: *Comrades,* right Martin?
MARTIN: This man, Joe, is a Saint of the Right.
JOE: I know, Mr. Heller, I . . .
ROY: And you see what I mean, Martin? He's special, right?
45   MARTIN: Don't embarrass him, Roy.

ROY: Gravity, decency, smarts! His strength is as the strength of
ten because his heart is pure! *And* he's a Royboy, one hundred percent.
MARTIN: We're on the move, Joe. On the move.
JOE: Mr. Heller, I . . .   50
MARTIN: *(Ending backrub.)* We can't wait any longer for an
answer.

(Little pause.)

JOE: Oh. Um, I . . .
ROY: Joe's a married man, Martin.
MARTIN: Aha.   55
ROY: With a wife. She doesn't care to go to D.C., and so Joe
cannot go. And keeps us dangling. We've seen that kind of
thing before, haven't we? These men and their wives.
MARTIN: Oh yes. Beware.
JOE: I really can't discuss this under . . .   60
MARTIN: Then *don't* discuss. Say yes, Joe.
ROY: Now.
MARTIN: Say yes I will.
ROY: Now.
Now. I'll hold my breath till you do, I'm turning blue wait-   65
ing. . . . *Now,* goddammit!
MARTIN: Roy, calm down, it's not . . .
ROY: Aw, fuck it. *(He takes a letter from his jacket pocket, hands
it to* JOE.*)*
Read. Came today.   70

*(*JOE *reads the first paragraph, then looks up.)*

JOE: Roy. This is . . . Roy, this is terrible.
ROY: You're telling me.
A letter from the New York State Bar Association, Martin.
They're gonna try and disbar me.
MARTIN: Oh my.   75
JOE: Why?
ROY: Why, Martin?
MARTIN: Revenge.
ROY: The whole Establishment. Their little rules. Because I
know no rules. Because I don't see the Law as a dead and ar-   80
bitrary collection of antiquated dictums, thou shall, thou
shalt not, because, because I know the Law's a pliable,
breathing, sweating . . . *organ,* because, because . . .
MARTIN: Because he borrowed half a million from one of his
clients.   85
ROY: Yeah, well, there's that.
MARTIN: *And* he forgot to *return* it.
JOE: Roy, that's. . . . You borrowed money from a client?
ROY: I'm deeply ashamed.

(Little pause.)

JOE: *(Very sympathetic.)* Roy, you know how much I admire   90
you. Well I mean I know you have unorthodox ways, but I'm
sure you only did what you thought at the time you needed
to do. And I have faith that . . .
ROY: Not so damp, please. I'll deny it was a loan. She's got no
paperwork. Can't prove a fucking thing.   95

(Little pause. MARTIN *studies the menu.)*

JOE: *(Handing back the letter, more official in tone.)* Roy I really appreciate your telling me this, and I'll do whatever I
can to help.

ROY: *(Holding up a hand, then, carefully.)* I'll tell you what you
100 can do.
I'm about to be tried, Joe, by a jury that is not a jury of my
peers. The disbarment committee: genteel gentleman Brahmin lawyers, country-club men. I offend them, to these men
. . . I'm what, Martin, some sort of filthy little Jewish troll?
105 MARTIN: Oh well, I wouldn't go so far as . . .
ROY: Oh well I would.
Very fancy lawyers, these disbarment committee lawyers,
fancy lawyers with fancy corporate clients and complicated
cases. Antitrust suits. Deregulation. Environmental control.
110 Complex cases like these need Justice Department cooperation like flowers need the sun. Wouldn't you say that's an accurate assessment, Martin?
MARTIN: I'm not here, Roy. I'm not hearing any of this.
ROY: No. Of course not.
115 Without the light of the sun, Joe, these cases, and the fancy
lawyers who represent them, will wither and die.
A well-placed friend, someone in the Justice Department,
say, can turn off the sun. Cast a deep shadow on my behalf.
Make them shiver in the cold. If they overstep. They would
120 fear that.

(Pause.)

JOE: Roy. I don't understand.
ROY: You do.

(Pause.)

JOE: You're not asking me to . . .
ROY: Ssshhhh. Careful.
125 JOE: *(A beat, then.)* Even if I said yes to the job, it would be illegal to interfere. With the hearings. It's unethical. No. I
can't.
ROY: Un-ethical.
Would you excuse us, Martin?
130 MARTIN: Excuse you?
ROY: Take a walk, Martin. For real.

(MARTIN leaves.)

ROY: Un-ethical. Are you trying to embarrass me in front of my
friend?
JOE: Well it is unethical, I can't . . .
135 ROY: Boy, you are really something. What the fuck do you
think this is, Sunday School?
JOE: No, but Roy this is . . .
ROY: This is . . . this is gastric juices churning, this is enzymes
and acids, this is intestinal is what this is, bowel movement
140 and blood-red meat—this stinks, this is *politics*, Joe, the
game of being alive. And you think you're. . . . What? Above
that? Above alive is what? Dead! In the clouds! You're on
earth, goddammit! Plant a foot, stay a while.
I'm sick. They smell I'm weak. They want blood this
145 time. I must have eyes in Justice. In Justice you will protect
me.
JOE: Why can't Mr. Heller . . .
ROY: Grow up, Joe. The administration can't get involved.
JOE: But I'd be part of the administration. The same as him.
150 ROY: Not the same. Martin's Ed's man. And Ed's Reagan's
man. So Martin's Reagan's man.
And you're mine.

(Little pause. He holds up the letter.)

This will never be. Understand me?

(He tears the letter up.)

I'm gonna be a lawyer, Joe, I'm gonna be a lawyer, Joe, I'm
gonna be a goddam motherfucking legally licensed member 155
of the bar lawyer, just like my daddy was, till my last bitter
day on earth, Joseph, until the day I die.

(MARTIN returns.)

ROY: Ah, Martin's back.
MARTIN: So are we agreed?
ROY: Joe? 160

(Little pause.)

JOE: I will think about it.
(To ROY.) I will.
ROY: Huh.
MARTIN: It's the fear of what comes after the doing that makes
the doing hard to do. 165
ROY: Amen.
MARTIN: But you can almost always live with the conse-
quences.

SCENE VII

*That afternoon. On the granite steps outside the Hall of Justice,
Brooklyn. It is cold and sunny. A Sabrett wagon is selling hot
dogs.* LOUIS, *in a shabby overcoat, is sitting on the steps contem-
platively eating one.* JOE *enters with three hot dogs and a can of
Coke.*

JOE: Can I . . . ?
LOUIS: Oh sure. Sure. Crazy cold sun.
JOE: *(Sitting.)* Have to make the best of it.
How's your friend?
LOUIS: My . . . ? Oh. He's worse. My friend is worse. 5
JOE: I'm sorry.
LOUIS: Yeah, well. Thanks for asking. It's nice. You're nice. I
can't believe you voted for Reagan.
JOE: I hope he gets better.
LOUIS: Reagan? 10
JOE: Your friend.
LOUIS: He won't. Neither will Reagan.
JOE: Let's not talk politics, OK?
LOUIS: *(Pointing to* JOE's *lunch.)* You're eating three of those?
JOE: Well . . . I'm . . . hungry. 15
LOUIS: They're really terrible for you. Full of rat-poo and bee-
tle legs and wood shavings 'n' shit.
JOE: Huh.
LOUIS: And . . . um . . . irridium, I think. Something toxic.
JOE: You're eating one. 20
LOUIS: Yeah, well, the shape, I can't help myself, plus I'm *try-
ing* to commit suicide, what's your excuse?
JOE: I don't have an excuse. I just have Pepto-Bismol.

(JOE takes a bottle of Pepto-Bismol and chugs it. LOUIS *shudders
audibly.)*

JOE: Yeah I know but then I wash it down with Coke.

(He does this. LOUIS *mimes barfing in* JOE's *lap.* JOE *pushes*
LOUIS's *head away.)*

JOE: Are you *always* like this? 25
LOUIS: I've been worrying a lot about his kids.

JOE: Whose?

LOUIS: Reagan's. Maureen and Mike and little orphan Patti and Miss Ron Reagan Jr., the you-should-pardon-the-30 expression heterosexual.

JOE: Ron Reagan Jr. is *not* . . . You shouldn't just make these assumptions about people. How do you know? About him? What he is? You don't know.

LOUIS: (*Doing Tallulah.*) Well darling he never sucked *my* 35 cock but . . .

JOE: Look, if you're going to get vulgar . . .

LOUIS: No no really I mean. . . . What's it like to be the child of the Zeitgeist? To have the American Animus as your dad? It's not really a *family*, the Reagans, I read *People*, there 40 aren't any connections there, no love, they don't ever even speak to each other except through their agents. So what's it like to be Reagan's kid? Enquiring minds want to know.

JOE: You can't believe everything you . . .

LOUIS: (*Looking away.*) But . . . I think we all know what that's 45 like. Nowadays. No connections. No responsibilities. All of us . . . falling through the cracks that separate what we owe to our selves and . . . and what we owe to love.

JOE: You just. . . . Whatever you feel like saying or doing, you don't care, you just . . . do it.

50 LOUIS: Do what?

JOE: It. Whatever. Whatever it is you want to do.

LOUIS: Are you trying to tell me something?

(*Little pause, sexual. They stare at each other.* JOE *looks away.*)

JOE: No, I'm just observing that you . . .

LOUIS: Impulsive.

55 JOE: Yes, I mean it must be scary, you . . .

LOUIS: (*Shrugs.*) Land of the free. Home of the brave. Call me irresponsible.

JOE: It's kind of terrifying.

LOUIS: Yeah, well, freedom is. Heartless, too.

60 JOE: Oh you're not heartless.

LOUIS: You don't know.
Finish your weenie.

(*He pats* JOE *on the knee, starts to leave.*)

JOE: Um . . .

(LOUIS *turns, looks at him.* JOE *searches for something to say.*)

JOE: Yesterday was Sunday but I've been a little unfocused re-65 cently and I thought it was Monday. So I came here like I was going to work. And the whole place was empty. And at first I couldn't figure out why, and I had this moment of in-credible . . . fear and also. . . . It just flashed through my mind: The whole Hall of Justice, it's empty, it's deserted, it's 70 gone out of business. Forever. The people that make it run have up and abandoned. it.

LOUIS: (*Looking at the building.*) Creepy.

JOE: Well yes but. I felt that I was going to scream. Not be-cause it was creepy, but because the emptiness felt so *fast*. 75 And . . . well, good. A . . . happy scream.
I just wondered what a thing it would be . . . if overnight everything you owe anything to, justice, or love, had really gone away. Free.
It would be . . . heartless terror. Yes. Terrible, and . . . 80 Very great. To shed your skin, every old skin, one by one and then walk away, unencumbered, into the morning.

(*Little pause. He looks at the building.*)

I can't go in there today.

LOUIS: Then don't.

JOE: (*Not really hearing* LOUIS.) I can't go in, I need . . .

(*He looks for what he needs. He takes a swig of Pepto-Bismol.*)

I can't *be* this anymore. I need . . . a change, I should just . . . 85

LOUIS: (*Not a come-on, necessarily; he doesn't want to be alone.*) Want some company? For whatever?

(*Pause.* JOE *looks at* LOUIS *and looks away, afraid.* LOUIS *shrugs.*)

LOUIS: Sometimes, even if it scares you to death, you have to be willing to break the law. Know what I mean?

(*Another little pause.*)

JOE: Yes. 90

(*Another little pause.*)

LOUIS: I moved out. I moved out on my . . .
I haven't been sleeping well.

JOE: Me neither.

(LOUIS *goes up to* JOE, *licks his napkin and dabs at* JOE's *mouth.*)

LOUIS: Antacid moustache.
(*Points to the building.*) Maybe the court won't convene. 95 Ever again. Maybe we are free. To do whatever.
Children of the new morning, criminal minds. Selfish and greedy and loveless and blind. Reagan's children.
You're scared. So am I. Everybody is in the land of the free. 100
God help us all.

SCENE VIII

Late that night. JOE *at a payphone phoning* HANNAH *at home in Salt Lake City.*

JOE: Mom?

HANNAH: Joe?

JOE: Hi.

HANNAH: You're calling from the street. It's . . . it must be four in the morning. What's happened? 5

JOE: Nothing, nothing, I . . .

HANNAH: It's Harper. Is Harper. . . . Joe? Joe?

JOE: Yeah, hi. No, Harper's fine. Well, no, she's . . . not fine. How are you, Mom?

HANNAH: What's happened? 10

JOE: I just wanted to talk to you. I, uh, wanted to try something out on you.

HANNAH: Joe, you haven't . . . have you been drinking, Joe?

JOE: Yes ma'am. I'm drunk.

HANNAH: That isn't like you. 15

JOE: No. I mean, who's to say?

HANNAH: Why are you out on the street at four AM? In that crazy city. It's dangerous.

JOE: Actually, Mom, I'm not on the street. I'm near the boathouse in the park. 20

HANNAH: What park?

JOE: Central Park.

HANNAH: CENTRAL PARK! Oh my Lord. What on earth are you doing in Central Park at this time of night? Are you . . .

25   Joe, I think you ought to go home right now. Call me from home.

(Little pause.)

  Joe?

JOE: I come here to watch, Mom. Sometimes. Just to watch.

HANNAH: Watch what? What's there to watch at four in the . . .

30 JOE: Mom, did Dad love me?

HANNAH: What?

JOE: Did he?

HANNAH: You ought to go home and call from there.

JOE: Answer.

35 HANNAH: Oh now really. This is maudlin. I don't like this conversation.

JOE: Yeah, well, it gets worse from here on.

(Pause.)

HANNAH: Joe?

JOE: Mom. Momma. I'm a homosexual, Momma.

40   Boy, did that come out awkward.

(Pause.)

  Hello? Hello?
  I'm a homosexual.

(Pause.)

  Please, Momma, Say something.

HANNAH: You're old enough to understand that your father

45   didn't love you without being ridiculous about it.

JOE: What?

HANNAH: You're ridiculous. You're being ridiculous.

JOE: I'm . . .
  What?

50 HANNAH: You really ought to go home now to your wife. I need to go to bed. This phone call. . . . We will just forget this phone call.

JOE: Mom.

HANNAH: No more talk. Tonight. This . . .

55   *(Suddenly very angry.)* Drinking is a sin! A sin! I raised you better than that. *(She hangs up.)*

SCENE IX

The following morning, early. Split scene: HARPER *and* JOE *at home;* LOUIS *and* PRIOR *in* PRIOR's *hospital room.* JOE *and* LOUIS *have just entered. This should be fast and obviously furious; overlapping is fine; the proceedings may be a little confusing but not the final results.*

HARPER: Oh God. Home. The moment of truth has arrived.

JOE: Harper.

LOUIS: I'm going to move out.

PRIOR: The fuck you are.

5 JOE: Harper. Please listen. I still love you very much. You're still my best buddy; I'm not going to leave you.

HARPER: No, I don't like the sound of this. I'm leaving.

LOUIS: I'm leaving.
  I already have.

10 JOE: Please listen. Stay. This is really hard. We have to talk.

HARPER: We are talking. Aren't we. Now please shut up. OK?

PRIOR: Bastard. Sneaking off while I'm flat out here, that's low. If I could get up now I'd beat the holy shit out of you.

JOE: Did you take pills? How many?

HARPER: No pills. Bad for the . . . *(Pats stomach.)*   15

JOE: You aren't pregnant. I called your gynecologist.

HARPER: I'm seeing a new gynecologist.

PRIOR: You have no right to do this.

LOUIS: Oh, that's ridiculous.

PRIOR: No right. It's criminal.   20

JOE: Forget about that. Just listen. You want the truth. This is the truth.
  I knew this when I married you. I've known this I guess for as long as I've known anything, but . . . I don't know, I thought maybe that with enough effort and will I could change myself . . . but I can't . . .   25

PRIOR: Criminal.

LOUIS: There oughta be a law.

PRIOR: There is a law. You'll see.

JOE: I'm losing ground here, I go walking, you want to know   30 where I walk, I . . . go to the park, or up and down 53rd Street, or places where. . . . And I keep swearing I won't go walking again, but I just can't.

LOUIS: I need some privacy.

PRIOR: That's new.   35

LOUIS: Everything's new, Prior.

JOE: I try to tighten my heart into a knot, a snarl, I try to learn to live dead, just numb, but then I see someone I want, and it's like a nail, like a hot spike right through my chest, and I know I'm losing.   40

PRIOR: Apartment too small for three? Louis and Prior comfy but not Louis and Prior and Prior's disease?

LOUIS: Something like that.
  I won't be judged by you. This isn't a crime, just—the inevitable consequence of people who run out of—whose   45 limitations . . .

PRIOR: Bang bang bang. The court will come to order.

LOUIS: I mean let's talk practicalities, schedules; I'll come over if you want, spend nights with you when I can, I can . . .

PRIOR: Has the jury reached a verdict?   50

LOUIS: I'm doing the best I can.

PRIOR: Pathetic. Who cares?

JOE: My whole life has conspired to bring me to this place, and I can't despise my whole life. I think I believed when I met you I could save you, you at least if not myself, but . . . I   55 don't have any sexual feelings for you, Harper. And I don't think I ever did.

(Little pause.)

HARPER: I think you should go.

JOE: Where?

HARPER: Washington. Doesn't matter.   60

JOE: What are you talking about?

HARPER: Without me.
  Without me, Joe. Isn't that what you want to hear?

(Little pause.)

JOE: Yes.

LOUIS: You can love someone and fail them. You can love   65 someone and not be able to . . .

PRIOR: You *can*, theoretically, yes. A person can, maybe an editorial "you" can love, Louis, but not *you*, specifically you, I don't know, I think you are excluded from that general category.

HARPER: You were going to save me, but the whole time you were spinning a lie. I just don't understand that.

PRIOR: A person could theoretically love and maybe many do but we both know now you can't.

LOUIS: I do.

PRIOR: You can't even say it.

LOUIS: I love you, Prior.

PRIOR: I repeat. Who cares?

HARPER: This is so scary, I want this to stop, to go back . . .

PRIOR: We have reached a verdict, your honor. This man's heart is deficient. He loves, but his love is worth nothing.

JOE: Harper . . .

HARPER: Mr. Lies, I want to get away from here. Far away. Right now. Before he starts talking again. Please, please . . .

JOE: As long as I've known you Harper you've been afraid of . . . of men hiding under the bed, men hiding under the sofa, men with knives.

PRIOR: (*Shattered; almost pleading; trying to reach him.*) I'm dying! You stupid fuck! Do you know what that is! Love! Do you know what love means? We lived together four-and-a-half years, you animal, you idiot.

LOUIS: I have to find some way to save myself.

JOE: Who are these men? I never understood it. Now I know.

HARPER: What?

JOE: It's me.

HARPER: It is?

PRIOR: GET OUT OF MY ROOM!

JOE: I'm the man with the knives.

HARPER: You are?

PRIOR: If I could get up now I'd kill you. I would. Go away. Go away or I'll scream.

HARPER: Oh God . . .

JOE: I'm sorry . . .

HARPER: It is you.

LOUIS: Please don't scream.

PRIOR: Go.

HARPER: I recognize you now.

LOUIS: Please . . .

JOE: Oh. Wait, I. . . . Oh!

(*He covers his mouth with his hand, gags, and removes his hand, red with blood.*)

I'm bleeding.

(PRIOR *screams.*)

HARPER: Mr. Lies.

MR. LIES: (*Appearing, dressed in antarctic explorer's apparel.*) Right here.

HARPER: I want to go away. I can't see him anymore.

MR. LIES: Where?

HARPER: Anywhere. Far away.

MR. LIES: Absolutamento.

(HARPER *and* MR. LIES *vanish.* JOE *looks up, sees that she's gone.*)

PRIOR: (*Closing his eyes.*) When I open my eyes you'll be gone.

(LOUIS *leaves.*)

JOE: Harper?

PRIOR: (*Opening his eyes.*) Huh. It worked.

JOE: (*Calling.*) Harper?

PRIOR: I hurt all over. I wish I was dead.

SCENE X

The same day, sunset. HANNAH *and* SISTER ELLA CHAPTER, *a real-estate saleswoman, Hannah Pitt's closest friend, in front of Hannah's house in Salt Lake City.*

SISTER ELLA CHAPTER: Look at that view! A view of heaven. Like the living city of heaven, isn't it, it just fairly glimmers in the sun.

HANNAH: Glimmers.

SISTER ELLA CHAPTER: Even the stone and brick it just glimmers and glitters like heaven in the sunshine. Such a nice view you get, perched up on a canyon rim. Some kind of beautiful place.

HANNAH: It's just Salt Lake, and you're selling the house *for* me, not *to* me.

SISTER ELLA CHAPTER: I like to work up an enthusiasm for my properties.

HANNAH: Just get me a good price.

SISTER ELLA CHAPTER: Well, the market's off.

HANNAH: At least fifty.

SISTER ELLA CHAPTER: Forty'd be more like it.

HANNAH: Fifty.

SISTER ELLA CHAPTER: Wish you'd wait a bit.

HANNAH: Well I can't.

SISTER ELLA CHAPTER: Wish you would. You're about the only friend I got.

HANNAH: Oh well now.

SISTER ELLA CHAPTER: Know why I decided to like you? I decided to like you 'cause you're the only unfriendly Mormon I ever met.

HANNAH: Your wig is crooked.

SISTER ELLA CHAPTER: Fix it.

(HANNAH *straightens* SISTER ELLA's *wig.*)

SISTER ELLA CHAPTER: New York City. All they got there is tiny rooms.

I always thought: People ought to stay put. That's why I got my license to sell real estate. It's a way of saying: Have a house! Stay put! It's a way of saying traveling's no good. Plus I needed the cash. (*She takes a pack of cigarettes out of her purse, lights one, offers pack to* HANNAH.)

HANNAH: Not out here, anyone could come by.

There's been days I've stood at this ledge and thought about stepping over.

It's a hard place, Salt Lake: baked dry. Abundant energy; not much intelligence. That's a combination that can wear a body out. No harm looking someplace else. I don't need much room.

My sister-in-law Libby thinks there's radon gas in the basement.

SISTER ELLA CHAPTER: Is there gas in the . . .

HANNAH: Of course not. Libby's a fool.

SISTER ELLA CHAPTER: 'Cause I'd have to include that in the description.

HANNAH: There's no gas, Ella. (*Little pause.*) Give a puff. (*She takes a furtive drag of* ELLA's *cigarette.*) Put it away now.

SISTER ELLA CHAPTER: So I guess it's goodbye.

HANNAH: You'll be all right, Ella, I wasn't ever much of a friend.

SISTER ELLA CHAPTER: I'll say something but don't laugh, OK?
55 This is the home of saints, the godliest place on earth, they say, and I think they're right. That means there's no evil here? No. Evil's everywhere. Sin's everywhere. But this . . . is the spring of sweet water in the desert, the desert flower. Every step a Believer takes away from here is a step fraught with peril. I fear for you, Hannah Pitt, because you are my
60 friend. Stay put. This is the right home of saints.

HANNAH: Latter-day saints.

SISTER ELLA CHAPTER: Only kind left.

HANNAH: But still. Late in the day . . . for saints and everyone. That's all. That's all.
65 Fifty thousand dollars for the house, Sister Ella Chapter; don't undersell. It's an impressive view.

— ACT THREE —
NOT-YET-CONSCIOUS, FORWARD DAWNING
JANUARY 1986

SCENE I

Late night, three days after the end of Act Two. The stage is completely dark. PRIOR *is in bed in his apartment, having a nightmare. He wakes up, sits up and switches on a nightlight. He looks at his clock. Seated by the table near the bed is a man dressed in the clothing of a 13th-century British squire.*

PRIOR: *(Terrified.)* Who are you?

PRIOR 1: My name is Prior Walter.

(Pause.)

PRIOR: My name is Prior Walter.

PRIOR 1: I know that.

5 PRIOR: Explain.

PRIOR 1: You're alive. I'm not. We have the same name. What do you want me to explain?

PRIOR: A ghost?

PRIOR 1: An ancestor.

10 PRIOR: Not *the* Prior Walter? The Bayeux tapestry Prior Walter?

PRIOR 1: His great-great grandson. The fifth of the name.

PRIOR: I'm the thirty-fourth, I think.

PRIOR 1: Actually the thirty-second.

15 PRIOR: Not according to Mother.

PRIOR 1: She's including the two bastards, then; I say leave them out. I say no room for bastards. The little things you swallow . . .

PRIOR: Pills.

20 PRIOR 1: Pills. For the pestilence. I too . . .

PRIOR: Pestilence. . . . You too what?

PRIOR 1: The pestilence in my time was much worse than now. Whole villages of empty houses. You could look outdoors and see Death walking in the morning, dew dampening the
25 ragged hem of his black robe. Plain as I see you now.

PRIOR: You died of the plague.

PRIOR 1: The spotty monster. Like you, alone.

PRIOR: I'm not alone.

PRIOR 1: You have no wife, no children.

30 PRIOR: I'm gay.

PRIOR 1: So? Be gay, dance in your altogether for all I care, what's that to do with not having children?

PRIOR: Gay homosexual, not bonny, blithe and . . . never mind.

PRIOR 1: I had twelve. When I died. 35

(The second ghost appears, this one dressed in the clothing of an elegant 17th-century Londoner.)

PRIOR 1: *(Pointing to* PRIOR 2.) And I was three years younger than him.

*(*PRIOR *sees the new ghosts, screams.)*

PRIOR: Oh God another one.

PRIOR 2: Prior Walter. Prior to you by some seventeen others.

PRIOR 1: He's counting the bastards. 40

PRIOR: Are we having a convention?

PRIOR 2: We've been sent to declare her fabulous incipience. They love a well-paved entrance with lots of heralds, and . . .

PRIOR 1: The messenger come. Prepare the way. The infinite descent, a breath in air . . . 45

PRIOR 2: They chose us, I suspect, because of the mortal affinities. In a family as long-descended as the Walters there are bound to be a few carried off by plague.

PRIOR 1: The spotty monster.

PRIOR 2: Black Jack. Came from a water pump, half the city of 50 London, can you imagine? His came from fleas. Yours, I understand, is the lamentable consequence of venery . . .

PRIOR 1: Fleas on rats, but who knew that?

PRIOR: Am I going to die?

PRIOR 2: We aren't allowed to discuss . . . 55

PRIOR 1: When you do, you don't get ancestors to help you through it. You may be surrounded by children but you die alone.

PRIOR: I'm afraid.

PRIOR 1: You should be. There aren't even torches, and the 60 path's rocky, dark and steep.

PRIOR 2: Don't alarm him. There's good news before there's bad.
We two come to strew rose petal and palm leaf before the triumphal procession. Prophet. Seer. Revelator. It's a great 65 honor for the family.

PRIOR 1: He hasn't got a family.

PRIOR 2: I meant for the Walters, for the family in the larger sense.

PRIOR: *(Singing.)* 70

All I want is a room somewhere,
Far away from the cold night air . . .

PRIOR 2: *(Putting a hand on* PRIOR's *forehead.)* Calm, calm, this is no brain fever . . .

*(*PRIOR *calms down, but keeps his eyes closed. The lights begin to change. Distant Glorious Music.)*

PRIOR 1: *(Low chant.)* 75
Adonai, Adonai,
Olam ha-yichud,
Zefirot, Zazahot,
Ha-adam, ha-gadol
Daughter of Light,
Daughter of Splendors, 80
Fluor! Phosphor!
Lumen! Candle!

PRIOR 2: (*Simultaneously.*)
85   Even now,
        From the mirror-bright halls of heaven,
        Across the cold and lifeless infinity of space,
        The Messenger comes
        Trailing orbs of light,
90   Fabulous, incipient,
        Oh Prophet,
        To you . . .
PRIOR 1 and PRIOR 2:
        Prepare, prepare,
95   The Infinite Descent,
        A breath, a feather,
        Glory to . . .

(*They vanish.*)

SCENE II

The next day. Split scene: LOUIS *and* BELIZE *in a coffee shop.*
PRIOR *is at the outpatient clinic at the hospital with* EMILY, *the*
nurse; she has him on a pentamidine IV drip.

LOUIS: Why has democracy succeeded in America? Of course
        by succeeded I mean comparatively, not literally, not in the
        present, but what makes for the prospect of some sort of rad-
        ical democracy spreading outward and growing up? Why
5   does the power that was once so carefully preserved at the
        top of the pyramid by the original framers of the Constitu-
        tion seem drawn inexorably downward and outward in spite
        of the best effort of the Right to stop this? I mean it's the re-
        ally hard thing about being Left in this country, the Ameri-
10   can Left can't help but trip over all these petrified little
        fetishes: freedom, that's the worst; you know, *Jeane Kirk-*
        patrick for God's sake will go on and on about freedom and
        so what does that mean, the word freedom, when she talks
        about it, or human rights; you have Bush talking about
15   human rights, and so what are these people talking about,
        they might as well be talking about the mating habits of
        Venusians, these people don't begin to know what, ontologi-
        cally, freedom is or human rights, like they see these bour-
        geois property-based Rights-of-Man-type rights but that's not
20   enfranchisement, not democracy, not what's implicit, what's
        potential within the idea, not the idea with blood in it.
        That's just liberalism, the worst kind of liberalism, really,
        bourgeois tolerance, and what I think is that what AIDS
        shows us is the limits of tolerance, that it's not enough to be
25   tolerated, because when the shit hits the fan you find out
        how much tolerance is worth. Nothing. And underneath all
        the tolerance is intense, passionate hatred.
BELIZE: Uh huh.
LOUIS: Well don't you think that's true?
30 BELIZE: Uh huh. It is.
LOUIS: *Power* is the object, not being tolerated. Fuck assimila-
        tion. But I mean in spite of all this the thing about America,
        I think, is that ultimately we're different from every other na-
        tion on earth, in that, with people here of every race, we
35   can't. . . . Ultimately what defines us isn't race, but politics.
        Not like any European country where there's an insur-
        mountable fact of a kind of racial, or ethnic, monopoly, or
        monolith, like all Dutchmen, I mean Dutch people, are
        well, Dutch, and the Jews of Europe were never Europeans,

just a small problem. Facing the monolith. But here there   40
        are so many small problems, it's really just a collection of
        small problems, the monolith is missing. Oh, I mean, of
        course I suppose there's the monolith of White America.
        White Straight Male America.
BELIZE: Which is not unimpressive, even among monoliths.   45
LOUIS: Well, no, but when the race thing gets taken care of,
        and I don't mean to minimalize how major it is, I mean I
        know it is, this is a really, really incredibly racist country but
        it's like, well, the British. I mean, all these blue-eyed pink
        people. And it's just weird, you know, I mean I'm not all that   50
        Jewish-looking, or . . . well, maybe I am but, you know, in
        New York, everyone is . . . well, not everyone, but so many
        are but so but in England, in London I walk into bars and I
        feel like Sid the Yid, you know I mean like Woody Allen in
        Annie Hall, with the payess and the gabardine coat, like   55
        never, never anywhere so much—I mean, not actively de-
        spised, not like they're Germans, who I think are still terribly
        anti-Semitic, and racist too, I mean black-racist, they pretend
        otherwise but, anyway, in London, there's just . . . and at one
        point I met this black gay guy from Jamaica who talked with   60
        a lilt but he said his family'd been living in London since be-
        fore the Civil War—the American one—and how the En-
        glish never let him forget for a minute that he wasn't
        blue-eyed and pink and I said yeah, me too, these people are
        anti-Semites and he said yeah but the British Jews have the   65
        clothing business all sewed up and blacks there can't get a
        foothold. And it was an incredibly awkward moment of just.
        . . . I mean here we were, in this bar that was gay but it was a
        pub, you know, the beams and the plaster and those horrible
        little, like, two-day-old fish and egg sandwiches—and just so   70
        British, so *old,* and I felt, well, there's no way out of this be-
        cause both of us are, right now, too much immersed in this
        history, hope is dissolved in the sheer age of this place, where
        race is what counts and there's no real hope of change—it's
        the racial destiny of the Brits that matters to them, not their   75
        political destiny, whereas in America . . .
BELIZE: Here in America race doesn't count.
LOUIS: No, no, that's not. . . . I mean you *can't* be hearing
        that . . .
BELIZE: I . . .   80
LOUIS: It's—look, race, yes, but ultimately race here is a politi-
        cal question, right? Racists just try to use race here as a tool
        in a political struggle. It's not really about race. Like the spir-
        itualists try to use that stuff, are you enlightened, are you
        centered, channeled, whatever, this reaching out for a spiri-   85
        tual past in a country where no indigenous spirits exist—
        only the Indians, I mean Native American spirits and we
        killed them off so now, there are no gods here, no ghosts and
        spirits in America, there are no angels in America, no spiri-
        tual past, no racial past, there's only the political, and the de-   90
        coys and the ploys to maneuver around the inescapable bat-
        tle of politics, the shifting downwards and outwards of politi-
        cal power to the people . . .
BELIZE: POWER to the People! AMEN! (*Looking at his*
        watch.) OH MY GOODNESS! Will you look at the time, I   95
        gotta . . .
LOUIS: Do you. . . . You think this is, what, racist or naive or
        something?
BELIZE: Well it's certainly *something.* Look, I just remembered
        I have an appointment . . .   100

LOUIS: What? I mean I really don't want to, like, speak from some position of privilege and . . .

BELIZE: I'm sitting here, thinking, eventually he's *got* to run out of steam, so I let you rattle on and on saying about maybe
105   seven or eight things I find really offensive.

LOUIS: What?

BELIZE: But I know you, Louis, and I know the guilt fueling this peculiar tirade is obviously already swollen bigger than your hemorrhoids.

110   LOUIS: I don't have hemorrhoids.

BELIZE: I hear different. May I finish?

LOUIS: Yes, but I don't have hemorrhoids.

BELIZE: So finally, when I . . .

LOUIS: Prior told you, he's an asshole, he shouldn't have . . .

115   BELIZE: You promised, Louis. Prior is not a subject.

LOUIS: You brought him up.

BELIZE: I brought up hemorrhoids.

LOUIS: So it's indirect. Passive-aggressive.

BELIZE: Unlike, I suppose, banging me over the head with
120   your theory that America doesn't have a race problem.

LOUIS: Oh be fair I never said that.

BELIZE: Not exactly, but . . .

LOUIS: I said . . .

BELIZE: . . . but it was close enough, because if it'd been that
125   blunt I'd've just walked out and . . .

LOUIS: You deliberately misinterpreted! I . . .

BELIZE: Stop interrupting! I haven't been able to . . .

LOUIS: Just let me . . .

BELIZE: NO! What, *talk?* You've been running your mouth non
130   stop since I got here, yaddadda yaddadda blah blah blah, up the hill, down the hill, playing with your MONOLITH . . .

LOUIS: *(Overlapping)* Well, you could have joined in at any time instead of . . .

BELIZE: *(Continuing over* LOUIS.*)* . . . and girlfriend it is truly
135   an *awesome* spectacle but I got better things to do with my time than sit here listening to this racist bullshit just because I feel sorry for you that . . .

LOUIS: I am not a racist!

BELIZE: Oh come on . . .

140   LOUIS: So maybe I am a racist but . . .

BELIZE: Oh I really hate that! It's no fun picking on you Louis; you're so guilty, it's like throwing darts at a glob of jello, there's no satisfying hits, just quivering, the darts just blop in and vanish.

145   LOUIS: I just think when you are discussing lines of oppression it gets very complicated and . . .

BELIZE: Oh is that a fact? You know, we black drag queens have a rather intimate knowledge of the complexity of the lines of . . .

150   LOUIS: *Ex-*black drag queen.

BELIZE: Actually ex-ex.

LOUIS: You're doing drag again?

BELIZE: I don't. . . . Maybe. I don't have to tell you. Maybe.

LOUIS: I think it's sexist.

155   BELIZE: I didn't ask you.

LOUIS: Well it is. The gay community, I think, has to adopt the same attitude towards drag as black women have to take towards black women blues singers.

BELIZE: Oh my we *are* walking dangerous tonight.

160   LOUIS: Well, it's all internalized oppression, right, I mean the masochism, the stereotypes, the . . .

BELIZE: Louis, are you deliberately trying to make me hate you?

LOUIS: No, I . . .

BELIZE: I mean, are you deliberately transforming yourself   165
into an arrogant, sexual-political Stalinist-slash-racist flag-waving thug for my benefit?

(Pause.)

LOUIS: You know what I think?

BELIZE: What?

LOUIS: You hate me because I'm a Jew.   170

BELIZE: I'm leaving.

LOUIS: It's true.

BELIZE: You have no basis except your . . .
Louis, it's good to know you haven't changed; you are still an honorary citizen of the Twilight Zone, and after your pale,   175
pale white polemics on behalf of racial insensitivity you have a flaming *fuck* of a lot of nerve calling me an anti-Semite. Now I really gotta go.

LOUIS: You called me Lou the Jew.

BELIZE: That was a joke.   180

LOUIS: I didn't think it was funny. It was hostile.

BELIZE: It was three years ago.

LOUIS: So?

BELIZE: You just called yourself Sid the Yid.

LOUIS: That's not the same thing.   185

BELIZE: Sid the Yid is different from Lou the Jew.

LOUIS: Yes.

BELIZE: Someday you'll have to explain that to me, but right now . . .
You hate me because you hate black people.   190

LOUIS: I do not. But I do think most black people are anti-Semitic.

BELIZE: "Most black people." *That's* racist, Louis, and *I* think most Jews . . .

LOUIS: Louis Farrakhan.   195

BELIZE: Ed Koch.

LOUIS: Jesse Jackson.

BELIZE: Jackson. Oh really, Louis, this is . . .

LOUIS: Hymietown! Hymietown!

BELIZE: Louis, you voted for Jesse Jackson. You send checks to   200
the Rainbow Coalition.

LOUIS: I'm ambivalent. The checks bounced.

BELIZE: All your checks bounce, Louis; you're ambivalent about everything.

LOUIS: What's that supposed to mean?   205

BELIZE: You may be dumber than shit but I refuse to believe you can't figure it out. Try.

LOUIS: I was never ambivalent about Prior. I love him. I do. I really do.

BELIZE: Nobody said different.   210

LOUIS: Love and ambivalence are. . . . Real love isn't ambivalent.

BELIZE: "Real love isn't ambivalent." I'd swear that's a line from my favorite bestselling paperback novel, *In Love with the Night Mysterious,* except I don't think you ever read it.   215

(Pause.)

LOUIS: I never read it, no.

BELIZE: You ought to. Instead of spending the rest of your life trying to get through *Democracy in America.* It's about this

220 white woman whose Daddy owns a plantation in the Deep
South in the years before the Civil War—the American
one—and her name is Margaret, and she's in love with her
Daddy's number-one slave, and his name is Thaddeus, and
she's married but her white slave-owner husband has AIDS:
225 Antebellum Insufficiently Developed Sexorgans. And there's
a lot of hot stuff going down when Margaret and Thaddeus
can catch a spare torrid ten under the cottonpicking moon,
and then of course the Yankees come, and they set the slaves
free, and the slaves string up old Daddy, and so on. Histori-
230 cal fiction. Somewhere in there I recall Margaret and Thaddeus find the time to discuss the nature of love; her face is reflecting the flames of the burning plantation—you know, the
way white people do—and his black face is dark in the night
and she says to him, "Thaddeus, real love isn't ever ambivalent."

(Little pause. EMILY *enters and turns off IV drip.)*

235 BELIZE: Thaddeus looks at her; he's contemplating her thesis;
and he isn't sure he agrees.
EMILY: *(Removing IV drip from* PRIOR'*s arm.)* Treatment num-
ber . . . *(Consulting chart.)* four.
PRIOR: Pharmaceutical miracle. Lazarus breathes again.
240 LOUIS: Is he. . . . How bad is he?
BELIZE: You want the laundry list?
EMILY: Shirt off, let's check the . . .

*(*PRIOR *takes his shirt off. She examines his lesions.)*

BELIZE: There's the weight problem and the shit problem and
the morale problem.
245 EMILY: Only six. That's good. Pants.

(He drops his pants. He's naked. She examines.)

BELIZE: And. He thinks he's going crazy.
EMILY: Looking good. What else?
PRIOR: Ankles sore and swollen, but the leg's better. The nausea's mostly gone with the little orange pills. BM's pure liq-
250 uid but not bloody anymore, for now, my eye doctor says
everything's OK, for now, my dentist says "Yuck!" when he
sees my fuzzy tongue, and now he wears little condoms on
his thumb and forefinger. And a mask. So what? My derma-
tologist is in Hawaii and my mother . . . well leave my
255 mother out of it. Which is usually where my mother is, out
of it. My glands are like walnuts, my weight's holding steady
for week two, and a friend died two days ago of bird tuberculosis; bird tuberculosis; that scared me and I didn't go to the
funeral today because he was an Irish Catholic and it's prob-
260 ably open casket and I'm afraid of . . . something, the bird
TB or seeing him or. . . . So I guess I'm doing OK. Except for
of course I'm going nuts.
EMILY: We ran the toxoplasmosis series and there's no
indication . . .
265 PRIOR: I know, I know, but I feel like something terrifying is on
its way, you know, like a missile from outer space, and it's
plummeting down towards the earth, and I'm ground zero,
and . . . I am generally known where I am known as one
cool, collected queen. And I am ruffled.
270 EMILY: There's really nothing to worry about. I think that
shochen bamromim hamtzeh menucho nechono al kanfey
haschino.
PRIOR: What?

EMILY: Everything's fine. Bemaalos k'doshim ut'horim kezo-
har horokeea mazhirim . . .
275 PRIOR: Oh I don't understand what you're . . .
EMILY: Es nishmas Prior sheholoch leolomoh, baavur shenod-
voo z'dokoh b'ad hazkoras nishmosoh.
PRIOR: Why are you doing that?! Stop it! Stop it!
EMILY: Stop what?
280 PRIOR: You were just . . . weren't you just speaking in Hebrew
or something.
EMILY: *Hebrew? (Laughs.)* I'm basically Italian-American. No.
I didn't speak in Hebrew.
285 PRIOR: Oh no, oh God please I really think I . . .
EMILY: Look, I'm sorry, I have a waiting room full of. . . . I
think you're one of the lucky ones, you'll live for years, probably—you're pretty healthy for someone with no immune
system. Are you seeing someone? Loneliness is a danger. A
290 therapist?
PRIOR: No, I don't need to see anyone, I just . . .
EMILY: Well think about it. You aren't going crazy. You're just
under a lot of stress. No wonder . . . *(She starts to write in his
chart.)*

*(Suddenly there is an astonishing blaze of light, a huge chord
sounded by a gigantic choir, and a great book with steel pages
mounted atop a molten-red pillar pops up from the stage floor.
The book opens; there is a large Aleph inscribed on its pages,
which bursts into flames. Immediately the book slams shut and
disappears instantly under the floor as the lights become normal
again.* EMILY *notices none of this, writing.* PRIOR *is agog.)*

EMILY: *(Laughing, exiting.)* Hebrew . . .   295

*(*PRIOR *flees.)*

LOUIS: Help me.
BELIZE: I beg your pardon?
LOUIS: You're a nurse, give me something, I . . . don't know
what to do anymore, I. . . . Last week at work I screwed up
300 the Xerox machine like permanently and so I . . . then I
tripped on the subway steps and my glasses broke and I cut
my forehead, here, see, and now I can't see much and my
forehead . . . it's like the Mark of Cain, stupid, right, but it
won't heal and every morning I see it and I think, Biblical
305 things, Mark of Cain, Judas Iscariot and his silver and his
noose, people who . . . in betraying what they love betray
what's truest in themselves, I feel . . . nothing but cold for
myself, just cold, and every night I miss him, I miss him so
much but then . . . those sores, and the smell and . . . where
310 I thought it was going. . . . I could be . . . I could be sick too,
maybe I'm sick too. I don't know.
Belize. Tell him I love him. Can you do that?
BELIZE: I've thought about it for a very long time, and I still
don't understand what love is. Justice is simple. Democracy
315 is simple. Those things are unambivalent. But love is very
hard. And it goes bad for you if you violate the hard law of
love.
LOUIS: I'm dying.
BELIZE: He's dying. You just wish you were. Oh cheer up,
Louis. Look at that heavy sky out there.   320
LOUIS: Purple.
BELIZE: *Purple?* Boy, what kind of a homosexual are you, anyway? That's not purple, Mary, that color up there is *(Very
grand.)* mauve.

325 All day today it's felt like Thanksgiving. Soon, this . . . ruination will be blanketed white. You can smell it—can you smell it?

LOUIS: Smell what?

BELIZE: Softness, compliance, forgiveness, grace.

330 LOUIS: No . . .

BELIZE: I can't help you learn that. I can't help you, Louis. You're not my business. *(He exits.)*

(LOUIS puts his head in his hands, inadvertently touching his cut forehead.)

LOUIS: Ow FUCK! *(He stands slowly, looks towards where BELIZE exited.)* Smell what? *(He looks both ways to be sure no*
335 *one is watching, then inhales deeply, and is surprised.)* Huh. Snow.

SCENE III

Same day. HARPER *in a very white, cold place, with a brilliant blue sky above; a delicate snowfall. She is dressed in a beautiful snowsuit. The sound of the sea, faint.)*

HARPER: Snow! Ice! Mountains of ice! Where am I? I . . . feel better, I do, I . . . feel better. There are ice crystals in my lungs, wonderful and sharp. And the snow smells like cold, crushed peaches. And there's something . . . some current of
5 blood in the wind, how strange, it has that iron taste.

MR. LIES: Ozone.

HARPER: Ozone! Wow! Where am I?

MR. LIES: The Kingdom of Ice, the bottommost part of the world.

10 HARPER: *(Looking around, then realizing.)* Antarctica. This is Antarctica!

MR. LIES: Cold shelter for the shattered. No sorrow here, tears freeze.

HARPER: Antarctica, Antarctica, oh boy oh boy, LOOK at this,
15 I . . . Wow, I must've really snapped the tether, huh?

MR. LIES: Apparently . . .

HARPER: That's great. I want to stay here forever. Set up camp. Build things. Build a city, an enormous city made up of frontier forts, dark wood and green roofs and high gates made of
20 pointed logs and bonfires burning on every street corner. I should build by a river. Where are the forests?

MR. LIES: No timber here. Too cold. Ice, no trees.

HARPER: Oh details! I'm sick of details! I'll plant them and grow them. I'll live off caribou fat, I'll melt it over the bon-
25 fires and drink it from long, curved goat-horn cups. It'll be great. I want to make a new world here. So that I never have to go home again.

MR. LIES: As long as it lasts. Ice has a way of melting . . .

HARPER: No. Forever. I can have anything I want here—
30 maybe even companionship, someone who has . . . desire for me. You, maybe.

MR. LIES: It's against the by-laws of the International Order of Travel Agents to get involved with clients. Rules are rules. Anyway, I'm not the one you really want.

35 HARPER: There isn't anyone . . . maybe an Eskimo. Who could ice-fish for food. And help me build a nest for when the baby comes.

MR. LIES: There are no Eskimo in Antarctica. And you're not really pregnant. You made that up.

40 HARPER: Well all of this is made up. So if the snow feels cold I'm pregnant. Right? Here, I can be pregnant. And I can have any kind of a baby I want.

MR. LIES: This is a retreat, a vacuum, its virtue is that it lacks everything; deep-freeze for feelings. You can be numb and safe here, that's what you came for. Respect the delicate 45 ecology of your delusions.

HARPER: You mean like no Eskimo in Antarctica.

MR. LIES: Correcto. Ice and snow, no Eskimo. Even hallucinations have laws.

HARPER: Well then who's that? 50

(The ESKIMO appears.)

MR. LIES: An Eskimo.

HARPER: An antarctic Eskimo. A fisher of the polar deep.

MR. LIES: There's something wrong with this picture.

(The ESKIMO beckons.)

HARPER: I'm going to like this place. It's my own National Geographic Special! Oh! Oh! *(She holds her stomach.)* I think 55 . . . I think I felt her kicking. Maybe I'll give birth to a baby covered with thick white fur, and that way she won't be cold. My breasts will be full of hot cocoa so she doesn't get chilly. And if it gets really cold, she'll have a pouch I can crawl into. Like a marsupial. We'll mend together. That's what we'll do; 60 we'll mend.

SCENE IV

Same day. An abandoned lot in the South Bronx. A homeless WOMAN *is standing near an oil drum in which a fire is burning. Snowfall. Trash around.* HANNAH *enters dragging two heavy suitcases.*

HANNAH: Excuse me? I said excuse me? Can you tell me where I am? Is this Brooklyn? Do you know a Pineapple Street? Is there some sort of bus or train or . . . ? I'm lost, I just arrived from Salt Lake. City. Utah? I took the bus that I was told to take and I got off—well it was the very 5 last stop, so I had to get off, and I *asked* the driver was this Brooklyn, and he nodded yes but he was from one of those foreign countries where they think it's good manners to nod at everything even if you have no idea what it is you're nodding at, and in truth I think he spoke no English at all, 10 which I think would make him ineligible for employment on public transportation. The public being English-speaking, mostly. Do you speak English?

(The WOMAN nods.)

HANNAH: I was supposed to be met at the airport by my son. He didn't show and I don't wait more than three and three- 15 quarters hours for *anyone.* I should have been patient, I guess, I. . . . Is this . . .

WOMAN: Bronx.

HANNAH: Is that. . . . The *Bronx?* Well how in the name of Heaven did I get to the Bronx when the bus driver said . . . 20

WOMAN: *(Talking to herself.)* Slurp slurp slurp will you STOP that disgusting slurping! YOU DISGUSTING SLURPING FEEDING ANIMAL! Feeding yourself, just feeding yourself, what would it matter, to you or to ANYONE, if you just stopped. Feeding. And DIED? 25

(Pause.)

HANNAH: Can you just tell me where I . . .

WOMAN: Why was the Kosciusko Bridge named after a Polack?

HANNAH: I don't know what you're . . .

WOMAN: That was a joke.

30 HANNAH: Well what's the punchline?
WOMAN: I don't know.
HANNAH: *(Looking around desperately.)* Oh for pete's sake, is there anyone else who . . .
35 WOMAN: *(Again, to herself.)* Stand further off you fat loathsome whore, you can't have any more of this soup, slurp slurp slurp you animal, and the—I know you'll just go pee it all away and where will you do that? Behind what bush? It's FUCKING COLD out here and I . . .
40 Oh that's right, because it was supposed to have been a tunnel!
That's not very funny.
Have you read the prophecies of Nostradamus?
HANNAH: Who?
45 WOMAN: Some guy I went out with once somewhere, Nostradamus. Prophet, outcast, eyes like. . . . Scary shit, he . . .
HANNAH: Shut up. Please. Now I want you to stop jabbering for a minute and pull your wits together and tell me how to get to Brooklyn. Because you know! And you are going to tell me! Because there is no one else around to tell me and I
50 am wet and cold and I am very angry! So I am sorry you're psychotic but just make the effort—take a deep breath—DO IT!

(HANNAH and WOMAN breathe together.)

HANNAH: That's good. Now exhale.

(They do.)

HANNAH: Good. Now how do I get to Brooklyn?
55 WOMAN: Don't know. Never been. Sorry. Want some soup?
HANNAH: Manhattan? Maybe you know . . . I don't suppose you know the location of the Mormon Visitor's . . .
WOMAN: 65th and Broadway.
HANNAH: How do you . . .
60 WOMAN: Go there all the time. Free movies. Boring, but you can stay all day.
HANNAH: Well. . . . So how do I . . .
WOMAN: Take the D Train. Next block make a right.
HANNAH: Thank you.
65 WOMAN: Oh yeah. In the new century I think we will all be insane.

SCENE V

Same day. JOE and ROY in the study of ROY's brownstone. ROY is wearing an elegant bathrobe. He has made a considerable effort to look well. He isn't well, and he hasn't succeeded much in looking it.

JOE: I can't. The answer's no. I'm sorry.
ROY: Oh, well, apologies . . .
I can't see that there's anyone asking for apologies.

(Pause.)

JOE: I'm sorry, Roy.
5 ROY: Oh, well, apologies.
JOE: My wife is missing, Roy. My mother's coming from Salt Lake to . . . to help look, I guess. I'm supposed to be at the airport now, picking her up but. . . . I just spent two days in a hospital, Roy, with a bleeding ulcer, I was spitting up blood.
10 ROY: Blood, huh? Look, I'm very busy here and . . .
JOE: It's just a job.
ROY: A job? A *job*? *Washington!* Dumb Utah Mormon hick shit!

JOE: Roy . . .
15 ROY: *WASHINGTON!* When Washington called me I was younger than you, you think I said "Aw fuck no I can't go I got two fingers up my asshole and a little moral nosebleed to boot!" When Washington calls you my pretty young punk friend you go or you can go fuck yourself sideways 'cause the train has pulled out of the station, and you are *out*, nowhere,
20 out in the cold. Fuck you, Mary Jane, get outta here.
JOE: Just let me . . .
ROY: Explain? Ephemera. You broke my heart. Explain that. Explain that.
25 JOE: I love you. Roy.
There's so much that I want, to be . . . what you see in me, I want to be a participant in the world, in your world, Roy, I want to be capable of that, I've tried, really I have but . . . I can't do this. Not because I don't believe in you, but because I believe in you so much, in what you stand for, at
30 heart, the order, the decency. I would give anything to protect you, but. . . . There are laws I can't break. It's too ingrained. It's not me. There's enough damage I've already done.
Maybe you were right, maybe I'm dead.
35 ROY: You're not dead, boy, you're a sissy.
You love me; that's moving, I'm moved. It's nice to be loved. I warned you about her, didn't I, Joe? But you don't listen to me, why, because you say Roy is smart and Roy's a friend but Roy . . . well, he isn't nice, and you wanna be nice. Right? A
40 nice, nice man!

(Little pause.)

You know what my greatest accomplishment was, Joe, in my life, what I am able to look back on and be proudest of? And I have helped make Presidents and unmake them and mayors and more goddam judges than anyone in NYC ever—
45 AND several million dollars, tax-free—and what do you think means the most to me?
You ever hear of Ethel Rosenberg? Huh, Joe, huh?
JOE: Well, yeah, I guess I. . . . Yes.
50 ROY: Yes. Yes. You have heard of Ethel Rosenberg. Yes. Maybe you even read about her in the history books.
If it wasn't for me, Joe, Ethel Rosenberg would be alive today, writing some personal-advice column for *Ms.* magazine. She isn't. Because during the trial, Joe, I was on the phone every day, talking with the judge . . .
55 JOE: Roy . . .
ROY: Every day, doing what I do best, talking on the telephone, making sure that timid Yid nebbish on the bench did his duty to America, to history. That sweet unprepossessing woman, two kids, boo-hoo-hoo, reminded us all of our little
60 Jewish mamas—she came this close to getting life; I pleaded till I wept to put her in the chair. Me. I did that. I would have fucking pulled the switch if they'd have let me. Why? Because I fucking hate traitors. Because I fucking hate communists. Was it legal? Fuck legal. Am I a nice man? Fuck nice.
65 They say terrible things about me in the *Nation.* Fuck the *Nation.* You want to be Nice, or you want to be Effective? Make the law, or subject to it. Choose. Your wife chose. A week from today, she'll be back. SHE knows how to get what SHE wants. Maybe I ought to send *her* to Washington.
70 JOE: I don't believe you.
ROY: Gospel.

JOE: You can't possibly mean what you're saying.

75   Roy, you were the Assistant United States Attorney on the Rosenberg case, ex-parte communication with the judge during the trial would be . . . censurable, at least, probably conspiracy and . . . in a case that resulted in execution, it's . . .

ROY: What? Murder?

JOE: You're not well is all.

80   ROY: What do you mean, not well? Who's not well?

(Pause.)

JOE: You said . . .

ROY: No I didn't. I said what?

JOE: Roy, you have cancer.

ROY: No I don't.

(Pause.)

85   JOE: You told me you were dying.

ROY: What the fuck are you talking about, Joe? I never said that. I'm in perfect health. There's not a goddam thing wrong with me.

(He smiles.)

Shake?

(JOE hesitates. He holds out his hand to ROY. ROY pulls JOE into a close, strong clinch.)

90   ROY: *(More to himself than to JOE.)* It's OK that you hurt me because I love you, baby Joe. That's why I'm so rough on you.

(ROY releases JOE. JOE backs away a step or two.)

ROY: Prodigal son. The world will wipe its dirty hands all over you.

95   JOE: It already has, Roy.

ROY: Now go.

(ROY shoves JOE hard. JOE turns to leave. ROY stops him, turns him around.)

ROY: *(Smoothing JOE's lapels, tenderly.)* I'll always be here, waiting for you . . .

(Then again, with sudden violence, he pulls JOE close, violently.)

What did you want from me, what was all this, what do you
100   want, treacherous ungrateful little . . .

(JOE, very close to belting ROY, grabs him by the front of his robe, and propels him across the length of the room. He holds ROY at arm's length, the other arm ready to hit.)

ROY: *(Laughing softly, almost pleading to be hit.)* Transgress a little, Joseph.

(JOE releases ROY.)

ROY: There are so many laws; find one you can break.

(JOE hesitates, then leaves, backing out. When JOE has gone, ROY doubles over in great pain, which he's been hiding throughout the scene with JOE.)

ROY: Ah, Christ . . .
105   Andy! Andy! Get in here! Andy!

(The door opens, but it isn't ANDY. A small Jewish Woman dressed modestly in a fifties hat and coat stands in the doorway. The room darkens.)

ROY: Who the fuck are you? The new nurse?

(The figure in the doorway says nothing. She stares at ROY. A pause. ROY looks at her carefully, gets up, crosses to her. He crosses back to the chair, sits heavily.)

ROY: Aw, fuck. Ethel.

ETHEL ROSENBERG: *(Her manner is friendly, her voice is ice-cold.)* You don't look good, Roy.

ROY: Well, Ethel. I don't feel good.   110

ETHEL ROSENBERG: But you lost a lot of weight. That suits you. You were heavy back then. Zaftig, mit hips.

ROY: I haven't been that heavy since 1960. We were all heavier back then, before the body thing started. Now I look like a skeleton. They stare.   115

ETHEL ROSENBERG: The shit's really hit the fan, huh, Roy?

(Little pause. ROY nods.)

ETHEL ROSENBERG: Well the fun's just started.

ROY: What is this, Ethel, Halloween? You trying to scare me?

(ETHEL says nothing.)

ROY: Well you're wasting your time! I'm scarier than you any
day of the week! So beat it, Ethel. BOOO! BETTER DEAD   120
THAN RED! Somebody trying to shake me up? HAH HAH!
From the throne of God in heaven to the belly of hell, you
can all fuck yourselves and then go jump in the lake because
I'M NOT AFRAID OF YOU OR DEATH OR HELL OR
ANYTHING!   125

ETHEL ROSENBERG: Be seeing you soon, Roy. Julius sends his regards.

ROY: Yeah, well send this to Julius!

(He flips the bird in her direction, stands and moves towards her. Halfway across the room he slumps to the floor, breathing laboriously, in pain.)

ETHEL ROSENBERG: You're a very sick man, Roy.

ROY: Oh God . . . ANDY!   130

ETHEL ROSENBERG: Hmmm. He doesn't hear you, I guess. We should call the ambulance.

(She goes to the phone.)

Hah! Buttons! Such things they got now.
What do I dial, Roy?

(Pause. ROY looks at her, then:)

ROY: 911.   135

ETHEL ROSENBERG: *(Dials the phone.)* It sings!
(Imitating dial tones.) La la la . . .
Huh.
Yes, you should please send an ambulance to the home of
Mister Roy Cohn, the famous lawyer.   140
What's the address, Roy?

ROY: *(A beat, then.)* 244 East 87th.

ETHEL ROSENBERG: 244 East 87th Street. No apartment number, he's got the whole building.
My name? *(A beat.)* Ethel Greenglass Rosenberg.   145
(Small smile.) Me? No I'm not related to Mr. Cohn. An old friend.

(She hangs up.)

They said a minute.

ROY: I have all the time in the world.

150 ETHEL ROSENBERG: You're immortal.
ROY: I'm immortal. Ethel. *(He forces himself to stand.)*
   I have *forced* my way into history. I ain't never gonna die.
ETHEL ROSENBERG: *(A little laugh, then.)* History is about to
   crack wide open. Millennium approaches.

SCENE VI

Late that night. PRIOR's *bedroom.* PRIOR 1 *watching* PRIOR *in
bed, who is staring back at him, terrified. Tonight* PRIOR 1 *is
dressed in weird alchemical robes and hat over his historical
clothing and he carries a long palm-leaf bundle.*

PRIOR 1: Tonight's the night! Aren't you excited? Tonight she
   arrives! Right through the roof! Ha-adam, Ha-gadol . . .
PRIOR 2: *(Appearing, similarly attired.)* Lumen! Phosphor!
   Fluor! Candle! An unending billowing of scarlet and . . .
5 PRIOR: Look. Garlic. A mirror. Holy water. A crucifix. FUCK
   OFF! Get the fuck out of my room! GO!
PRIOR 1: *(To* PRIOR 2.) Hard as a hickory knob, I'll bet.
PRIOR 2: We all tumesce when they approach. We wax full,
   like moons.
10 PRIOR 1: Dance.
PRIOR: Dance?
PRIOR 1: Stand up, dammit, give us your hands, dance!
PRIOR 2: Listen . . .

(A lone oboe begins to play a little dance tune.)

PRIOR 2: Delightful sound. Care to dance?
15 PRIOR: Please leave me alone, please just let me sleep . . .
PRIOR 2: Ah, he wants someone familiar. A partner who knows
   his steps. *(To* PRIOR.) Close your eyes. Imagine . . .
PRIOR: I don't . . .
PRIOR 2: Hush. Close your eyes.

*(*PRIOR *does.)*

20 PRIOR 2: Now open them.

*(*PRIOR *does.* LOUIS *appears. He looks gorgeous. The music
builds gradually into a full-blooded, romantic dance tune.)*

PRIOR: Lou.
LOUIS: Dance with me.
PRIOR: I can't, my leg, it hurts at night . . .
   Are you . . . a ghost, Lou?
25 LOUIS: No. Just spectral. Lost to myself. Sitting all day on cold
   park benches. Wishing I could be with you. Dance with me,
   babe . . .

*(*PRIOR *stands up. The leg stops hurting. They begin to dance.
The music is beautiful.)*

PRIOR 1: *(To* PRIOR 2.) Hah. Now I see why he's got no children. He's a sodomite.
30 PRIOR 2: Oh be quiet, you medieval gnome, and let them
   dance.
PRIOR 1: I'm not interfering, I've done my bit. Hooray, hooray,
   the messenger's come, now I'm blowing off. I don't like it
   here.

*(*PRIOR 1 *vanishes.)*

35 PRIOR 2: The twentieth century. Oh dear, the world has gotten
   so terribly, terribly old.

*(*PRIOR 2 *vanishes.* LOUIS *and* PRIOR *waltz happily. Lights fade
back to normal.* LOUIS *vanishes.*

PRIOR *dances alone.
Then suddenly, the sound of wings fills the room.)*

SCENE VII

Split scene: PRIOR *alone in his apartment;* LOUIS *alone in the
park.*

Again, a sound of beating wings.

PRIOR: Oh don't come in here don't come in . . . LOUIS!! No.
   My name is Prior Walter, I am . . . the scion of an ancient
   line, I am . . . abandoned I . . . no, my name is . . . is . . .
   Prior and I live . . . *here and now,* and . . . in the dark, in the
   dark, the Recording Angel opens its hundred eyes and snaps   5
   the spine of the Book of Life and . . . hush! Hush!
   I'm talking nonsense, I . . .
   No more mad scene, hush, hush . . .

*(*LOUIS *in the park on a bench.* JOE *approaches, stands at a distance. They stare at each other, then* LOUIS *turns away.)*

LOUIS: Do you know the story of Lazarus?
JOE: Lazarus?   10
LOUIS: Lazarus. I can't remember what happens, exactly.
JOE: I don't. . . . Well, he was dead, Lazarus, and Jesus
   breathed life into him. He brought him back from death.
LOUIS: Come here often?
JOE: No. Yes. Yes.   15
LOUIS: Back from the dead. You believe that really happened?
JOE: I don't know anymore what I believe.
LOUIS: This is quite a coincidence. Us meeting.
JOE: I followed you.
   From work. I . . . followed you here.   20

(Pause.)

LOUIS: You followed me.
   You probably saw me that day in the washroom and
   thought: there's a sweet guy, sensitive, cries for friends in
   trouble.
JOE: Yes.   25
LOUIS: You thought maybe I'll cry for you.
JOE: Yes.
LOUIS: Well I fooled you. Crocodile tears. Nothing . . . *(He
   touches his heart, shrugs.)*

*(*JOE *reaches tentatively to touch* LOUIS's *face.)*

LOUIS: *(Pulling back.)* What are you doing? Don't do that.   30
JOE: *(Withdrawing his hand.)* Sorry. I'm sorry.
LOUIS: I'm . . . just not . . . I think, if you touch me, your hand
   might fall off or something. Worse things have happened to
   people who have touched me.
JOE: Please.   35
   Oh, boy . . .
   Can I . . .
   I . . . want . . . to touch you. Can I please just touch
   you . . . um, here?

(He puts his hand on one side of LOUIS's *face. He holds it there.)*

   I'm going to hell for doing this.   40
LOUIS: Big deal. You think it could be any worse than New
   York City?

(He puts his hand on JOE's *hand. He takes* JOE's *hand away
from his face, holds it for a moment, then.)* Come on.

45   JOE: Where?

LOUIS: Home. With me.

JOE: This makes no sense. I mean I don't know you.

LOUIS: Likewise.

JOE: And what you do know about me you don't like.

50   LOUIS: The Republican stuff?

JOE: Yeah, well for starters.

LOUIS: I don't not like that. I *hate* that.

JOE: So why on earth should we . . .

(LOUIS *goes to* JOE *and kisses him.*)

LOUIS: Strange bedfellows. I don't know. I never made it with
55   one of the damned before.

    I would really rather not have to spend tonight alone.

JOE: I'm a pretty terrible person, Louis.

LOUIS: Lou.

JOE: No, I really really am. I don't think I deserve being loved.

60   LOUIS: There? See? We already have a lot in common.

(LOUIS *stands, begins to walk away. He turns, looks back at* JOE.
JOE *follows. They exit.*)

(PRIOR *listens. At first no sound, then once again, the sound of
beating wings, frighteningly near.*)

PRIOR: That sound, that sound, it. . . . What is that, like birds
    or something, like a *really* big bird, I'm frightened, I . . . no,
    no fear, find the anger, find the . . . anger, my blood is
    clean, my brain is fine, I can handle pressure, I am a gay
65   man and I am used to pressure, to trouble, I am tough and
    strong and. . . . Oh. Oh my goodness. I . . . (*He is washed
    over by an intense sexual feeling.*) Ooohhhh. . . . I'm hot,
    I'm . . . so . . . aw Jeez what is going on here I . . . must have
    a fever I . . .

(*The bedside lamp flickers wildly as the bed begins to roll forward and back. There is a deep bass creaking and groaning from
the bedroom ceiling, like the timbers of a ship under immense
stress, and from above a fine rain of plaster dust.*)

PRIOR: OH!   70

    PLEASE, OH PLEASE! Something's coming in here, I'm
    scared, I don't like this at all, something's approaching and
    I. . . . OH!

(*There is a great blaze of triumphal music, heralding. The light
turns an extraordinary harsh, cold, pale blue, then a rich, brilliant warm golden color, then a hot, bilious green, and then finally a spectacular royal purple. Then silence.*)

PRIOR: (*An awestruck whisper.*) God almighty . . .   75

    Very Steven Spielberg.

(*A sound, like a plummeting meteor, tears down from very, very
far above the earth, hurtling at an incredible velocity towards the
bedroom; the light seems to be sucked out of the room as the pro-
jectile approaches; as the room reaches darkness, we hear a terrifying CRASH as something immense strikes earth; the whole
building shudders and a part of the bedroom ceiling, lots of plaster and lathe and wiring, crashes to the floor. And then in a
shower of unearthly white light, spreading great opalescent gray-
silver wings, the* ANGEL *descends into the room and floats above
the bed.*)

ANGEL:

    Greetings, Prophet;

    The Great Work begins:

    The Messenger has arrived.

(*Blackout.*)

◆ E N D O F P A R T O N E ◆

CRITICAL CONTEXTS

Arthur Miller wrote this essay for the New York Times *shortly after the opening of* Death of a Salesman. *In the essay, Miller develops a reading of the tragic hero that both contests and modifies Aristotle's description of the form and style of tragic drama. He also identifies his own presiding interests in the dynamics of tragic character.*

ARTHUR MILLER

"Tragedy and the Common Man" **(1949)**

In this age few tragedies are written. It has often been held that the lack is due to a paucity of heroes among us, or else that modern man has had the blood drawn out of his organs of belief by the skepticism of science, and the heroic attack on life cannot feed on an attitude of reserve and circumspection. For one reason or another, we are often held to be below tragedy—or tragedy above us. The inevitable conclusion is, of course, that the tragic mode is archaic, fit only for the very highly placed, the kings or the kingly, and where this admission is not made in so many words it is most often implied.

I believe that the common man is as apt a subject for tragedy in its highest sense as kings were. On the face of it this ought to be obvious in the light of modern psychiatry, which bases its analysis upon classic formulations, such as the Oedipus and Orestes complexes, for instances, which were enacted by royal beings, but which apply to everyone in similar emotional situations.

More simply, when the question of tragedy in art is not at issue, we never hesitate to attribute to the well-placed and the exalted the very same mental processes as the lowly. And finally, if the exaltation of tragic action were truly a property of the high-bred character alone, it is inconceivable that the mass of mankind should cherish tragedy above all other forms, let alone be capable of understanding it.

As a general rule, to which there may be exceptions unknown to me, I think the tragic feeling is evoked in us when we are in the presence of a character who is ready to lay down his life, if need be, to secure one thing—his sense of personal dignity. From Orestes to Hamlet, Medea to Macbeth, the underlying struggle is that of the individual attempting to gain his "rightful" position in his society.

Sometimes he is one who has been displaced from it, sometimes one who seeks to attain it for the first time, but the fateful wound from which the inevitable events spiral is the wound of indignity, and its dominant force is indignation. Tragedy, then, is the consequence of a man's total compulsion to evaluate himself justly.

In the sense of having been initiated by the hero himself, the tale always reveals what has been called his "tragic flaw," a failing that is not peculiar to grand or elevated characters. Nor is it necessarily a weakness. The flaw, or crack in the character, is really nothing—and need be nothing—but his inherent unwillingness to remain passive in the face of what he conceives to be a challenge to his dignity, his image of his rightful status. Only the passive, only those who accept their lot without active retaliation, are "flawless." Most of us are in that category.

But there are among us today, as there always have been, those who act against the scheme of things that degrades them, and in the process of action everything we have accepted out of fear or insensitivity or ignorance is shaken before us and examined, and from this total onslaught by an individual against the seemingly stable cosmos surrounding us—from this total examination of the "unchangeable" environment—comes the terror and the fear that is classically associated with tragedy.

More important, from this total questioning of what has previously been unquestioned, we learn. And such a process is not beyond the common man. In revolutions around the world, these past thirty years, he has demonstrated again and again this inner dynamic of all tragedy.

Insistence upon the rank of the tragic hero, or the so-called nobility of his character, is really but a clinging to the outward forms of tragedy. If rank or nobility of character was indispensable, then it would follow that the problems of those with rank were the particular problems of tragedy. But surely the right of one monarch to capture the domain from another no longer raises our passions, nor are our concepts of justice what they were to the mind of an Elizabethan king.

The quality in such plays that does shake us, however, derives from the underlying fear of being displaced, the disaster inherent in being torn away from our chosen image of what and who we are in this world. Among us today this fear is as strong, and perhaps stronger, than it ever was. In fact, it is the common man who knows this fear best.

Now, if it is true that tragedy is the consequence of a man's total compulsion to evaluate himself justly, his destruction in the attempt posits a wrong or an evil in his environment. And this is precisely the morality of tragedy and its lesson. The discovery of the moral law, which is what the enlightenment of tragedy consists of, is not the discovery of some abstract or metaphysical quantity.

The tragic right is a condition of life, a condition in which the human personality is able to flower and realize itself. The wrong is the condition which suppresses man, perverts the flowing out of his love and creative instinct. Tragedy enlightens—and it must, in that it points the heroic finger at the enemy of man's freedom. The thrust for freedom is the quality in tragedy which exalts. The revolutionary questioning of the stable environment is what terrifies. In no way is the common man debarred from such thoughts or such actions.

Seen in this light, our lack of tragedy may be partially accounted for by the turn which modern literature has taken toward the purely psychiatric view of life, or the purely sociological. If all our miseries, our indignities, are born and bred within our minds, then all action, let alone the heroic action, is obviously impossible.

And if society alone is responsible for the cramping of our lives, then the protagonist must needs be so pure and faultless as to force us to deny his validity as a character. From neither of these views can tragedy derive, simply because neither represents a balanced concept of life. Above all else, tragedy requires the finest appreciation by the writer of cause and effect.

No tragedy can therefore come about when its author fears to question absolutely everything, when he regards any institution, habit or custom as being either everlasting, immutable or inevitable. In the tragic view the need of man to wholly realize himself is the only fixed star, and whatever it is that hedges his nature and lowers it is ripe for attack and examination. Which is not to say that tragedy must preach revolution.

The Greeks could probe the very heavenly origin of their ways and return to confirm the rightness of laws. And Job could face God in anger, demanding his right and end in submission. But for a moment everything is in suspension, nothing is accepted, and in this stretching and tearing apart of the cosmos, in the very action of so doing, the character gains "size," the tragic stature which is spuriously attached to the royal or the highborn in our minds. The commonest of men may take on that stature to the extent of his willingness to throw all he has into the contest, the battle to secure his rightful place in his world.

There is a misconception of tragedy with which I have been struck in review after review, and in many conversations with writers and readers alike. It is the idea that tragedy is of necessity allied to pessimism. Even the dictionary says nothing more about the word than that it means a story with a sad or unhappy ending. This impression is so firmly fixed that I almost hesitate to claim that in truth tragedy implies more optimism in its author than does comedy, and that its final result ought to be the reinforcement of the onlooker's brightest opinions of the human animal.

For, if it is true to say that in essence the tragic hero is intent upon claiming his whole due as a personality, and if this struggle must be total and without reservation, then it automatically demonstrates the indestructible will of man to achieve his humanity.

The possibility of victory must be there in tragedy. Where pathos rules, where pathos is finally derived, a character has fought a battle he could not possibly have won. The pathetic is achieved when the protagonist is, by virtue of his witlessness, his insensitivity or the very air he gives off, incapable of grappling with a much superior force.

Pathos truly is the mode for the pessimist. But tragedy requires a nicer balance between what is possible and what is impossible. And it is curious, although edifying, that the plays we revere, century after century, are the tragedies. In them, and in them alone, lies the belief—optimistic, if you will, in the perfectibility of man.

It is time, I think, that we who are without kings, took up this bright thread of our history and followed it to the only place it can possibly lead in our time—the heart and spirit of the average man.

George Steiner has written widely on literature and culture in books like Language and Silence *(1967),* Antigones *(1984), and many others. In* The Death of Tragedy, *Steiner argues that the essential experience of tragedy can come about only when the drama and its audience share a common culture and a common set of values. Given the fragmentation of modern culture and society, Steiner seems skeptical about the possibility of an authentic tragic drama on the modern stage.*

GEORGE STEINER

FROM *THE DEATH OF TRAGEDY* (1961)

. . . As we have seen, the decline of tragedy is inseparably related to the decline of the organic world view and of its attendant context of mythological, symbolic, and ritual reference. It was on this context that Greek drama was founded, and the Elizabethans were still able to give it imaginative adherence. This ordered and stylized vision of life, with its bent toward allegory and emblematic action, was already in decline at the time of Racine. But by strenuous observance of neo-classic conventions, Racine succeeded in giving to the old mythology, now emptied of belief, the vitality of living form. His was a brilliant rear-guard action. But after Racine the ancient habits of awareness and immediate recognition which gave to tragic drama its frame of reference were no longer prevalent. Ibsen, therefore, faced a real vacuum. He had to create for his plays a context of ideological meaning (an effective mythology), and he had to devise the symbols and theatrical conventions whereby to communicate his meaning to an audience corrupted by the easy virtues of the realistic stage. He was in the position of a writer who invents a new language and must then teach it to his readers.

Being a consummate fighter, Ibsen turned his deprivations to advantage. He made the precariousness of modern beliefs and the absence of an imaginative world order his starting point. Man moves naked in a world bereft of explanatory or conciliating myth. Ibsen's dramas presuppose the withdrawal of God from human affairs, and that withdrawal has left the door open to cold gusts blowing in from a malevolent though inanimate creation. But the most dangerous assaults upon reason and life come not from without, as they do in Greek and Elizabethan tragedy. They arise in the unstable soul. Ibsen proceeds from the modern awareness that there is rivalry and unbalance in the individual psyche. The ghosts that haunt his characters are not the palpable heralds of damnation whom we find in *Hamlet* and *Macbeth*. They are forces of disruption that have broken loose from the core of the spirit. Or, more precisely, they are cancers growing in the soul. In Ibsen's vocabulary, the most deadly of these cancers is "idealism," the mask of hypocrisy and self-deception with which men seek to guard against the realities of social and personal life. When "ideals" seize upon an Ibsen character, they drive him to psychological and material ruin as the Weird Sisters drive Macbeth. Once the mask has grown close to the skin, it can be removed only at suicidal cost. When Rosmer and Rebecca West have attained the ability to confront life, they are on the verge of death. When the mask no longer shields her against the light, Hedda Gabler kills herself.

To articulate this vision of a God-abandoned world and of man's splintered and vulnerable consciousness, Ibsen contrived an astounding series of symbols and figurative gestures. Like most creators of a coherent mythology, moreover, he determined early on his objective incarnations. The meanings assumed by the sea, the fjord, the avalanches, and the spectral bird in *Brand* carry over to Ibsen's very last play, *When We Dead Awaken*. The new church in *Brand* brings on the moment of disaster, as does the new steeple in *The Master Builder*. The white stallion of Peer Gynt foreshadows the ghost-chargers at Rosmersholm. From the start, Ibsen uses certain material objects to concentrate symbolic values (the wild duck, General Gabler's pistols, the flagpole standing in front of the house in *The Lady from the Sea*). And it is the association of an explicit, responsible image of life with the material setting and objects best able to denote and dramatize this image that is the source of Ibsen's power. It allows him to organize his plays into shapes of action richer and more expressive than any the theatre had known since Shakespeare. Consider the stress of dramatic feeling and the complexity of meaning conveyed by the tarantella which Nora dances in *A Doll's House*; by Hedda Gabler's proposal to crown Lövborg with vine leaves; or by the venture into high narrow places that occurs in *Rosmersholm, The Master Builder*, and *When We Dead Awaken*. Each is in itself a coherent episode in the play, yet it is at the same time a symbolic act which argues a specific vision of life. Ibsen arrived at this vision, and he devised the stylistic and theatrical means that give it dramatic life. This is his rare achievement.

Ibsen's late plays represent the kind of inward motion that we find also in the late plays of Shakespeare. *Cymbeline, The Winter's Tale,* and *The Tempest* retain the conventions of Jacobean tragicomedy. But these conventions act as signposts pointing toward interior meanings. The storms, the music, the allegoric masques have implications which belong less to the common imaginative repertoire than they do to a most private understanding of the world. The current theatrical forms are a mere scaffold to the inner shape. That is exactly the case in *The Master Builder, Little Eyolf, John Gabriel Borkman,* and *When We Dead Awaken.* These dramas give an appearance of belonging to the realistic tradition and of observing the conventions of the three-walled stage. But, in fact, this is not so. The setting is thinned out so as to become bleakly transparent, and it leads into a strange landscape appropriate to Ibsen's mythology of death and resurrection.

It is in these four plays—and they are among the summits of drama—that Ibsen comes nearest tragedy. But it is tragedy of a peculiar, limited order. These are fables of the dead, set in a cold purgatory. Halvard Solness is dead long before he ascends the tower of his new villa. Allmers and Rita are dead to each other in the suffocation of their marriage. Borkman is an enraged ghost pacing up and down in a coffin that has the semblance of a house. In *When We Dead Awaken,* the purgatorial theme is explicit. In the mad egotism of his art, Rubeck has trampled on the quick of life. He has destroyed Irene by refusing to treat her as a living being. But in such destruction there is always a part of suicide, and the great sculptor—the shaper of life—has withered to a grotesque shadow. Yet there remains a chance of miracle; in sharing mortal danger, the dead may awaken. And so Rubeck and Irene press on, up the storm-swept mountain.

There are in these fierce parables occasional resonances from classic and Shakespearean tragedy. We do, I think, experience a related sense of tragic form when Agamemnon strides across the purple carpet and Solness mounts to his tower. But the focus is utterly different. Ibsen starts where earlier tragedies end, and his plots are epilogues to previous disaster. Suppose Shakespeare had written a play showing Macbeth and Lady Macbeth living out their black lives in exile after they had been defeated by their avenging enemies. We might then have the angle of vision that we find in *John Gabriel Borkman.* These are dramas of afterlife, engaging vivid shadows such as animate the lower regions of the *Purgatorio.* But even in these late works, there is a purpose which goes beyond tragedy. Ibsen is telling us that one need not live in premature burial. He is reading the lesson of meaningful life. The Allmers and the Rubecks of the world can waken from their living death if they establish among themselves relations of honesty and sacrifice. There is a way out, even if it leads up to the glaciers. There is no such way for Agamemnon or Hamlet or Phèdre. In the gloom of the late Ibsen the core of militant hope is intact.

Why is it that this magnificent body of drama has not exercised a greater or more liberating influence on the modern theatre? Such playwrights as Arthur Miller stand toward Ibsen rather as Dryden stood toward Shakespeare. They have observed the technical means of the Ibsen play and adopted some of its conventions and defining gestures. But the rich and complex critique of life implicit in Ibsen, and the transparency of his realistic settings to the light of symbolism, are absent. Where Ibsen has been influential, as in the case of Shaw, it is the programmatic plays that have counted, not the harrowing dramas of his maturity. Why should this be? In part, the answer is that Ibsen did his work too well. Many of the hypocrisies that he strove against have loosened their grip on the mind. Many of the spectres of middle-class oppression have been exorcized. The triumph of the reformer has obscured the greatness of the poet. In part, there is the barrier of language. Those who read Norwegian tell one that Ibsen's mature prose is as tightly wrought in cadence and inner poise as is good verse. As in poetry, moreover, the force and direction of meaning often hinge on the particular inflections and array of sounds. These resist translation. And so there is in the versions of Ibsen's plays available to most readers a prosaic flatness entirely inappropriate to the symbolic design and lyricism of the late dramas. In short, that which translates best in Ibsen is perhaps the least notable. Thus we do not yet have the Ibsen playhouse for which Shaw pleaded at the turn of the century.

If Ibsen falls outside the scope of classic or Shakespearean tragedy, the same is true to an even greater extent of Strindberg and Chekhov.

In the plays of Strindberg we find some of the radical conventions of the late Ibsen, without the sustaining fabric of a responsible vision of life. The symbolism has a wild, arresting brilliance, but there is behind it no controlling mythology. The conception of the world implicit in Strindberg's plays is hysterical and fragmentary. No playwright ever made of so public a form as drama a more private expression. Strindberg's characters are emanations from his own tormented psyche and his harrowed life. Gradually, they lose all connection to a governing centre and are like fragments scattered from some great burst of secret energy. In *The Spook Sonata* and *A Dream Play*, the personages seem to collide at random in a kind of empty space. Hence the conventions of irreality and the allegory of the spectre and the dream. These dramas belong to a theatre of the mind and work inside us like remembered music. But what Strindberg achieved in depth, he lost in theatrical coherence. These ghostplays are shadows of drama.

This queer perspective, as if all things were seen through mist and in broken lines, extends even to the historical plays. Strindberg's treatment of Charles XII diminishes the scale of politics to that of a puppet theatre full of strange, nervous marionettes. It is over the short run that Strindberg succeeds. *Miss Julie* and *Creditors* are masterpieces. The high pitch of feeling and nervous susceptibility on which they rely can be enforced over a single, brief action. Miss Julie's final exit is like the receding terror of a nightmare. We wake from it drugged and appalled. But over the longer or more elaborate course, the tension breaks, and we get the kind of flaccid obscurity that disfigures *To Damascus* and even the finest of Strindberg's surrealistic plays, *The Dance of Death*.

Strindberg is neither in the dominant tradition of the tragic theatre nor does he build forward from Ibsen. He stands with Kleist and Wedekind on that eccentric verge where drama is not primarily an imitation of life, but rather a mirror to the private soul. And the expressive means of his art, influential as they have been on certain experimental movements in modern drama, belong less to the playhouse than they do to the distorting and hallucinatory modes of the film.

In Strindberg's late style, the conflicts of ideology and character from which drama normally proceeds are eroded. Instead, we find the creation of a special mood or atmosphere in which the shape of action becomes fluid and musical. Sometimes, Strindberg uses actual music to establish or modulate the tone of feeling. The theatre of Chekhov always tends toward the condition of music. A Chekhov play is not directed primarily toward a representation of conflict or argument. It seeks to exteriorize, to make sensuously perceptible, certain crises of interior life. The characters move in an atmosphere receptive to the slightest shift in intonation. As if passing through a magnetic field, their every word and gesture provokes a complex disturbance and regrouping of psychological forces. This kind of drama is immensely difficult to produce because the means of realization are very close to music. A Chekhovian dialogue is a musical score set for speaking voice. It alternates between acceleration and retardment. Pitch and timbre are often as meaningful as the explicit sense. The design of the plot, moreover, is polyphonic. Several distinct actions and levels of consciousness are developed at the same time. The characteristic gatherings—the theatrical *soirée* in *The Sea-Gull*, the party at the house of the three sisters, the outing in *The Cherry Orchard*—are ensembles in which the various melodies combine or clash in dissonance. In the second Act of *The Cherry Orchard*, the voices of Madame Ranevsky, Lopakhin, Gayev, Trofimov, and Anya perform a quintet. The melodic lines move in isolation and seeming incongruence. Suddenly a mysterious sound is heard in the evening sky, "the sound of a snapped string." It changes the key of the entire play. The brittle weariness in the different voices now swells to a great sombre chord. "Well, good people, let us go," says Madame Ranevsky, "it's getting dark."

But it is as difficult for the language of criticism to deal with the art of Chekhov as it is for any language to deal with music. All I would stress here is the fact that Chekhov lies outside a consideration of tragedy. He himself insisted that his plays were comedies, and so they are regarded on native ground. It is when travelling west that the wine has darkened. To us, these grave, lyric portrayals of the failure of human beings to master their condition or communicate with each other, convey an unutterable sadness. But perhaps we are reading into them too much lastingness. Chekhov's dramas are rooted in a specific historical circumstance and contain a strong element of political irony and social satire. These bruised, exquisite beings in their genteel poverty are doomed, and their pretensions are ridiculous. The axe must ring out in the cherry orchard if there is to be new life in the world. Lopakhin is a vulgar brute; but vulgarity is health, and it will build houses for the living on the fallow estates of the dead. Chekhov was a physician, and medicine knows grief and even despair in the particular instance, but not tragedy.

Or perhaps one should approach these elusive plays by discarding all traditions of dramatic genre. At the close of the *Symposium*, Socrates compelled his listeners to agree that the genius of comedy was the same as that of tragedy. Being drowsy with wine, they were unable to follow his argument. One after another, they fell asleep around the master; he alone remained serene and lucid till break of dawn. Even Aristophanes could not stay awake to discover in what manner he might be regarded as a tragedian. Thus the Socratic demonstration of the ultimate unity of tragic and comic drama is forever lost. But the proof is in the art of Chekhov.

RAYMOND WILLIAMS
(1921–1988)

FROM *MODERN TRAGEDY* (1966)

The brilliant Marxist cultural critic Raymond Williams has written extensively on drama. In Modern Tragedy, *Williams undertakes an indirect reply to George Steiner's* The Death of Tragedy. *Williams invites us to see tragedy not as a universal form or experience, but as something local, an experience that must be discovered and defined anew as the historical circumstances of its surrounding society change. Williams is also the author of several groundbreaking books, including* Culture and Society *(1958),* Drama from Ibsen to Brecht *(1968), and* The Country and the City *(1973).*

We have seen, in our own time, the climax and the decline of liberal tragedy. To understand its structure of feeling is now a central problem. For we are all to some extent still governed by it, even now when we can see that it is failing to hold.

At the centre of liberal tragedy is a single situation: that of a man at the height of his powers and the limits of his strength, at once aspiring and being defeated, releasing and destroyed by his own energies. The structure is liberal in its emphasis on the surpassing individual, and tragic in its ultimate recognition of defeat or the limits of victory. We have known, for nearly four centuries, a tension between this thrust of the individual and an absolute resistance, but the tension has passed through many forms, which we must try to distinguish. What we must trace, finally, is the transformation of the tragic hero into the tragic victim.

Tragedy, for us, has been mainly the conflict between an individual and the forces that destroy him. When any feeling is as strong as this, it can shape the mind so closely that the past itself is absorbed and transmuted, and the art of others lives only in its light. Our reading of Greek tragedy is perhaps the clearest example. Until very recently, against the evidence, we have remade Greek tragic drama in this image of our own: the tragic hero, at the centre of the play, magnificently exposed to a crushing external design. We have tried to take psychology, because that is our science, into the heart of an action to which it can never, critically, be relevant. We have looked for a tragic flaw, capable of starting such an action, in the character of an individual man. Yet it is now becoming clear (at a time, significantly, when our own governing structure of feeling is beginning to disintegrate) that the Greek tragic action was not rooted in individuals, or in individual psychology, in any of our senses. It was rooted in history, and not a human history alone. Its thrust came, not from the personality of an individual but from a man's inheritance and relationships, within a world that ultimately transcended him. What we then see is a general action specified, not an individual action generalised. What we learn is not character but the mutability of the world. Human life as such, always and everywhere, is subject to these exigencies. The exemplary case, reminding us, relieving this knowledge, brings pity and fear, in the general human condition.

It is said that Christianity altered this view of the world, putting a new emphasis on the individual. But this seems doubtful, especially in its assumption of a single Christian tradition. There is no important tragedy, within the Christian world, until there is also humanism and indeed individualism. In our own literature, there is no important tragedy before the release of personal energy, the emphasis of personal destiny, which we can see, looking back, in the complex process of Renaissance and Reformation. By the time of Marlowe and Shakespeare, the structure we now know was being actively shaped: an individual man, from his own aspirations, from his own nature, set out on an action that led him to tragedy.

We are bound to recognise this new spirit, even when we have properly remembered how strong a hold a different and traditional interpretation of life still had. Certainly we cannot understand Elizabethan tragedy if we fail to notice the elements that persisted from a mediaeval view of the world. The old conceptions of order and hierarchy, the intricate connections between man and nature, are there not only in active speech but in some of the essential conventions of the dramatic form. It is comparatively easy to demonstrate such continuities, in particular the continuation of the morality tradition, with all this implied for the relationship between individual and type and a common condition. But the continuities were within a very active process of change. We have only to go back a hundred years from Marlowe, to the morality *Everyman*, to see what these fundamental ideas and conventions produced on their own. Death comes to Everyman, in the midst of life, and of course is feared; the attempt made to avert it. But the action, confidently, takes Everyman forward to the edge of that dark room in which he must disappear, and the most remarkable aspect of this confidence is that physically, on a scaffold above the dark room, God himself is waiting for Everyman to come. The hesitation in entering is still strong; the room itself can not be seen into. But to pass through it is not only inevitable; it is also the only way in which Everyman can come to his Father. While that dimension holds, there is aversion and fear, but the later tragic voice cannot come. When it does come, it is unmistakeable: a man alone in his extremity. It is not only, dramatically, that God has gone from the scaffold. It is also that life, before this extremity, is quite differently experienced. Where there had been, in *Everyman*, a gathering of life into common and formal categories, there is now a particularity, a momentariness, an active awareness of process. Much of the new drama, even when its reference points are familiar categories, takes its most active life from a consciousness of the self in a passing moment of experience: a self-consciousness which is now in itself dramatic, and which new dramatic resources are employed to express. The common process of life is seen at its most intense in an individual experience.

The action changes accordingly. Again and again it is rooted in the nature of a particular man. It is true that this man, this hero, ends by finding his limits: tragic limits, including the absolute limit of death. But it is also true that again and again, if not invariably, he has *reached* for these limits: set his whole energy on an aspiring course which yet finally reveals them. Much of the extraordinary richness of this drama, beyond its incomparable celebration of the particularity of life, is precisely in the discovery and exploration of these limits, which can never be only death. Here, indeed, the persistence of orders and hierarchies, the familiar categories of man, exerts its necessary pressures. There is confusion, an exciting confusion, as the pressures are taken and tested, in the living act.

But the limits men reach, in their challenge to order, are not only of this kind. There are also new limits, within man himself. Order can break there, within the personality, as decisively and as tragically. Breakdown and madness, as private experiences, are quite newly realised and explored. The emphasis, as we take the full weight, is not on the naming of limits, but on their intense and confused discovery and exploration. The traditional categories are affirmed, but everything is questioned, in an outburst of energy so great that it seems, at times, to be shaking the whole body of man to pieces. Here, decisively, is one of the origins of the structure of feeling we are tracing: the thrust of living energy, in individual men, against limits which had once been composed into a confident order but which now, though still present and active, are questioned, fragmented, newly known and named, and are also confused by new experiences, new sources, of tragedy. The tragic voice, of our own immediate tradition, is then first heard: the aspiration for a meaning, at the very limits of a man's strength; the known meanings and answers, affirmed and yet also questioned, broken down, by contradictory experience.

The most important persistence, for the subsequent history of drama, was that of a public order, at the centre of what is otherwise personal tragedy. The hero is still, normally, the man of rank, the prince. An order can rise or fall with him, be affirmed or broken by him, even when what is driving him is a personal energy. The tragic hero is still marked by a social status, which defines his general importance, even when, in this new exploration of life, the hero becomes other than his status, or at least can be otherwise seen. Where in Greek tragedy the hero's status, with all it implied of inheritance, kinship and duty, enclosed the personality, which was developed only so far as the general action required, we find now, in Elizabethan tragedy, a personality within and beyond the similarly defining status, and the conflict that can result from this coexistence is often one of the sources of the tragedy. Thus the tension of the general action, between the exploring energies of life and all that is known of order, is repeated in the hero himself, between the individual man and the social role. In these tensions, this particular tragedy was formed.

At this stage of development, we can properly speak of humanist tragedy, but not yet, in a precise way, of liberal tragedy. The next stage was indeed a collapse of the tensions which had produced this remarkable drama. In the early eighteenth century, a determined attempt was made in England to adapt tragedy to the habits of thinking of middle-class life. This necessary and understandable attempt had little immediate success, though the imitation of its example in France and

Germany provided one of the elements for the emergence of serious modern tragedy. It is easy, looking back, to fix attention on the change most often discussed: that of the status of the hero.

> Stripp'd of Regal Pomp, and glaring Show
> His Muse reports a tale of Private Woe
> Works up Distress from Common Scenes in Life
> A Treach'rous Brother, and an Injur'd Wife.

But something else is happening, beyond the change of rank:

> Long has the Fate of Kings and Empires been
> The common business of the Tragick Scene,
> As if Misfortune made the Throne her Seat,
> And none could be unhappy but the Great . . .
> Stories like this with Wonder we may hear,
> But far remote, and in a higher Sphere,
> We ne'er can pity what we ne'er can share.

Or again:

> The Tragic Muse, sublime, delights to show
> Princes distrest and scenes of royal woe;
> In awful pomp, majestic, to relate
> The fall of nations or some hero's fate:
> That sceptered chiefs may by example know
> The strange vicissitude of things below;
> What dangers on security attend,
> How pride and cruelty in ruin end;
> Hence Providence supreme to know, and own
> Humanity adds glory to a throne.
> In ev'ry former age and foreign tongue
> With native grandeur thus the goddess sung.
> Upon our stage indeed with wished success
> You've sometimes seen her in a humbler dress . . .
> The brilliant drops that fall from each bright eye
> The absent pomp with brighter gems supply.
> Forgive us then, if we attempt to show,
> In artless strains, a tale of private woe,
> A London 'prentice ruined, is our theme . . .

And finally:

> From lower Life we draw our Scene's Distress:
> —Let not your Equals move your Pity less.

What we notice here is the new and single emphasis on pity: pity as sympathy. This is the mark of a growing humanitarianism, at least as aspiration. But what is then interesting is the contrast of pity with pomp, and the extent to which previous tragedy is interpreted as if rank as such were the decisive factor. It was inevitable, of course, in an age of bourgeois revolutions, that feudal and post-feudal connections between princely power and the order of the universe should be rejected. But what happens in practice, in this rejection, is an evident loss of dimension, which we can define as the loss of human connection at anything more than a private level. Humanitarianism, as an ideology, is the exact expression of this reduction. It expresses sympathy and pity between private persons, but tacitly excludes any positive conception of society, and thence any clear view of order or justice.

It is of course easy to blame the bourgeois for this, as so many historians of the drama have done. But simple blame conveniently omits the actual intermediate stage, in which the feudal order, as expressed in drama, collapsed from within. The vigorous exploration of the tensions between individuality and order had in fact ended abruptly in the early seventeenth century, so far as the drama was concerned. The decisive social challenge of the English Revolution might have produced new kinds of drama, but did not; the Puritan distrust of the drama was probably decisive. What in fact happened was a separation of drama from the mainstream of the society, and the reduction of the great tensions of Elizabethan tragedy to 'pomp' and 'show' took place within the continuing minority drama itself. The energy of the hero, reaching out to the human limits, was conventionalised and frozen into the fixed postures of 'heroic tragedy'. Pope might describe Addison's Cato as

> A brave man struggling in the storms of fate,
> And greatly falling with a falling State

but the truer description, of what had become tragedy, is Cotes's:

> What pen but yours could draw the doubtful strife
> Of honour struggling with the love of life?

The conflict of fixed and formal passions with the fixed and formal duties of rank and honour had decisively replaced the earlier and more creative tensions. When the bourgeois tragedians rejected 'pomp' they were hitting an already empty shell.

Rank, that is to say, became class, and once it did so a new definition of tragedy was inevitable. Rank implied order and connection; class was only separation, within an amorphous society. The attempt at human connection was then necessarily a matter of humanitarian sympathy, in 'private woe' and 'private distress'. The growth of active pity was accompanied by a belief in what was called redemption: in fact, repentance and the change of heart. It is not only that this structure of feeling made the writing of tragedy difficult; such a loss would be small, if the structure really held. Nor is it only that the attempt to combine disparate structures produced a sentimental tragedy, which is now valueless. The important loss is one of dimension and reference. There is an evident gap between private sympathy and the public order. The bourgeois tragedians, moved by pity and sympathy, and struggling for realism, were in fact betrayed by this gap, where no realism was possible. For the sources of tragedy were not, even in their experience, *only* private. The best known play of the period, Lillo's *The London Merchant*, is even explicitly social. And what we must then notice is that pity and sympathy have little chance, except as gestures, against the actual and affirmed imperatives of the new society. Where property is in question, as in this story of the thieving apprentice, the judgement is sharp and certain. Thieving is connected with murder as systematically, and as mystically, as once rebellion with disturbing the universe. Then the gallows is erected, with its own kind of inevitability, and the humanitarian feelings of pity and sympathy have to stand in its shadow. Distress accompanies execution, and humanitarianism is at its limits.

What we then see, behind the loss of dimension, is a complacent affirmation of the existing social framework. Crime does not pay, and crime is about property. The arbitrariness of power had been experienced in the blood; its pretensions could be dismissed as pomp. But the arbitrariness of property is a human datum, which the bourgeois tragedians lack the nerve to test. Obliquely, confusedly, the recognition is made, that the struggle for money has replaced the struggle for power as a human motive and as a tragic motive. The disruption of the family by greed for money is obliquely present in Lillo's *Fatal Curiosity*. But the imperative is not seriously questioned, and certainly cannot be connected with the whole body of human desire. Bourgeois tragedy has been blamed for being too social, for excluding the universal reference of Renaissance and humanist tragedy. Another way of putting the matter is that it is not social enough, for with its private ethic of pity and sympathy it could not negotiate the real contradictions of its own time, between human desire and the now social limits set on it. Through its double voice, of pity and certainty, we hear the first weak accents of man the victim: the old far-reaching heroism gone, the limits known but not named. When at last, in fact, the limits were known and named, as a false society, the hero could re-emerge, as a rebel against it. But this, effectively, was still a century ahead, in the period of liberal tragedy.

Bourgeois tragedy, as a creative force, faded quickly, in its original forms. In a sense it went underground, was driven there by its own contradictions. The exploring energy re-emerged, in strange ways, in Romantic tragedy. What is quite evident, through all the failures of Romantic drama, is a renewal and a renewed assertion of individual energy. The desires of man are again intense and imperative; they reach out and test the universe itself. Society is identified as convention, and convention as the enemy of desire. The individual rebellion is humanist, at a conscious level. Prometheus and Faust, characteristically, are its heroes. But the condition of desire, unconsciously, is that it is always forbidden. What then happens is that the forms of desire become devious and often perverse, and what looks like revolt is more properly a desperate defiance of heaven and hell. There is a related preoccupation with remorse: deep, pervasive, and beyond all its nominal causes. For in Romantic tragedy man is guilty of the ultimate and nameless crime of being himself.

The impossibility of finding a home in the world, the condemnation to a guilty wandering, the dissolution of self and others in a desire that is beyond all relationships: these Romantic themes are an important source of nearly all modern tragedy. Aspiration is absolute, but occurs, paradoxically, within a situation of man on the run from himself. Within this paradox, one dramatist of genius was eventually to work. But also, by the time of Ibsen's maturity, the last source of liberal tragedy had appeared: the increasingly confident identification of a false society as man's real enemy; the naming, in social terms, of the formerly nameless alienation. This body of social thinking had many kinds of influence. In one direction, it led to the denial of tragedy. Man had not only made but could remake himself. The Romantic desire for redemption and regeneration was given, in this tendency, a more or less precise social definition: when man was at the limits which ordinarily produced tragedy he became conscious of their nature and could begin to abolish them. When this abolition was seen as a social process, it did not, at least in the nineteenth century, lead to tragedy at all. The idea of tragedy, indeed, was dismissed as mystification and fatalism: an irony that still haunts us now that collective tragedy, and the tragic society, have been widely and deeply experienced. But this was not, in any case, the liberal path. What emerged there, as a controlling image, was not revolution, but the individual liberator. Acting on his own, and for his own reasons, a single man could change the human limits and transform his world. Looking back to Romantic tragedy, and forward to existentialist tragedy, this conception was still in its purest form in the late nineteenth century. By an act of choice, by an act of will, the individual refused the role of victim and became a new kind of hero. The heroism was not in the nobility of suffering, as the limits were reached. It was now, unambiguously, in the aspiration itself. What was demanded was self-fulfilment, and any such process was a general liberation. The singular man, as a matter of speech, became plural and capital: Man.

Liberal tragedy, at its full development, drew from all the sources that have been named, but in a new form and pressure created a new and specific structure of feeling. It is important, at this stage, not to try to fragment it, when it appears in Ibsen. The humanist exploration of the unknown reaches of life; the bourgeois preoccupation with humanitarianism and with money; the romantic intensities of alienation, remorse and perverted desire; the social recognition of dead institutions and limiting beliefs: all these are present in Ibsen, but in active combination, not as separate influences. To try to resolve his work into one of these lines has been a common practice in criticism: Ibsen the social critic; Ibsen the romantic or existentialist: each has been plausibly presented. But the real interest lies, where the work lies, in the struggle of these forces and in their composition into a particular drama.

Ibsen creates again and again in his plays, with an extraordinary richness of detail, false relationships, a false society, a false condition of man. The marks along this scale are often difficult to discern. The immediate lie is almost always present, but there is great variation in its ultimate reference: sometimes to an alterable condition; sometimes to an absolute condition; often, ambiguously, between these. Yet the generalising reference, in whatever kind, is persistent; the lie is never merely local, for it is seen as a symptom of a general condition. Characteristically, for liberal tragedy, the fight against the lie is individual; a man fights for his own life. Brand's vocation is 'All or Nothing', and compromise is personally impossible:

> One thing is yours you may not spend,
> Your very inmost self of all,
> You may not bind it, may not bend,
> Nor stem the river of your call.

Or again:

> Self completely to fulfil,
> That's a valid right of man,
> And no more than that I will.

At the same time, the 'right' is also the 'call':

> A great one gave me charge. I *must*.

The call to wholeness is seen as self-fulfilment, and yet also as necessary. The right and the duty coincide in self-fulfilment, as in the classic liberal statements.

Yet the whole point about self-fulfilment is that it challenges, to the death, the existing compromise order. For here the lie is actual: men are afraid of wholeness and of self-fulfilment. As the Provost argues:

> The surest way to destroy a man
> Is to turn him into an individual.

Men have settled for a fragmentary life, as the easiest way, but this settlement is the sickness of their own personal lives and of their society. Routine is destructive, but so also are the wild breaks from routine, the simple refusals. What is needed is a new and total assent, for

> Our time, our generation, that is sick
> And must be cured.

Thus the individual, fulfiling himself absolutely, becomes, or offers himself as, the liberator. This position is reached again and again in Ibsen, but the resolution varies. In *Pillars of Society*, *A Doll's House*, *Enemy of the People*, the refusal of compromise is unambiguously carried through, if not to liberation, at least to positive individual defiance. In *Peer Gynt*, what looks like the quest for self-fulfilment is shown in the end to be simple evasion: the self alone, detached from the reality of world and relationships, withers and is wasted, to be redeemed only by return. More commonly, in varying degrees of emphasis, the individual's struggle is seen as both necessary and tragic. The evasion of fulfilment, by compromise, breeds false relationships and a sick society, but the attempt at fulfilment ends again and again in tragedy: the individual is destroyed in his attempt to climb out of his partial world.

This is the crux of liberal tragedy, and it is in many ways difficult to understand. The simple position is that of the heroic liberator opposed and destroyed by a false society: the liberal martyr. It is clear that Ibsen knew this feeling; it finds memorable expression in Stockmann. But it is not in this pattern that Ibsen takes his heroes to their deaths. Stockmann, faced only by this, is stronger and survives:

> The strongest man in the world is he who stands most alone.

Nor is it merely by accident and complication that the hero dies. The tragedy, in fact, is built into the form of the aspiration, in the significant concept of *debt*.

In the action and imagery of the plays, the nature of debt is persistently explored. Just as aspiration cannot be reduced simply to social reform, to a religious calling, or to self-expression, but remains obstinately general—the liberation of human spirit and energy—so debt cannot be reduced to inherited obligations, to a society burdened by compromises, or to original sin. These are often the forms in which aspiration and debt appear, but the actual works are more often explorations of the conflicting forces than definitions of them. Thus while in *Brand* there is simple fatalism—

> Blood of children must be spilt
> To atone for parents' guilt

—it is also clear that new debts are contracted in the act of refusal of compromise; it is Brand himself, and not merely Brand the son or the human being, who is eventually guilty. The position would be simpler if this guilt were then condemned, if the voice through the final avalanche—'He is the God of love'—were a verdict. But this is not the case. Brand had to do what he did, and yet had to come to this point. This is not ethical tragedy, where a different choice would have brought safety. The choice and the fate admit no real alternatives.

What happens, again and again in Ibsen, is that the hero defines an opposing world, full of lies and compromises and dead positions, only to find, as he struggles against it, that as a man he belongs to this world, and has its destructive inheritance in himself. Ibsen turned this way and that, looking for a way out of this tragic deadlock, but normally he returned to it, and confessed its terrible power:

> Ghosts! . . . I almost believe we are all ghosts, Pastor Manders. It is not only what we have inherited from our fathers and mothers that walks in us. It is every kind of dead idea, lifeless old beliefs and so on. They are not alive, but they cling to us for all that, and we can never rid ourselves of them. Whenever I read a newspaper I seem to see ghosts stealing between the lines. There must be ghosts the whole country over, as thick as the sands of the sea. And then we are all of us so wretchedly afraid of the light.

This position, so often stated, is not a gloss for surrender to the darkness. The cry for light, the desire to climb out of such a world, is persistent and emphatic:

> Give me air and the blaze of day . . .
> Through darkness to light . . .
> A summer night on the uplands . . .
> The joy of life . . . always, always the joy of life—light and sunshine
> and glorious air . . .
> Mother, give me the sun.

But as the last phrase, the dying cry of Osvald, reminds us, the light is only a breaking aspiration, at the limits of human endurance. The death of Julian the Apostate, not the death of Christ, is the significant ending:

> Beautiful earth, beautiful life . . . O, Helios, Helios, why hast thou betrayed me?

There is no turning away from life to death, no tragic resignation. Ibsen's heroes, characteristically, die fighting and struggling and climbing: the aspiration to light is confirmed, not contradicted, by their deaths. In this sense, they are still heroes, but also they are tragic heroes. The ghosts

> cling to us . . . we can never rid ourselves of them.

Or as the liberal Rosmer puts it:

> We can never escape them, we of this house.

Ibsen seems to depend, as some of his language certainly depends, on a traditional idea of original sin. But the effect of his whole work is in fact a transformation of this. He never gives up the idea of the false society, even when he has realised that its complications eat into the lives of those opposing it. Nor, truly, does he ever mean 'sin' by 'debt'. The debts that count, in bringing his heroes down, are incurred in the struggle for life and light, however wayward this is often shown to be. When we have said 'sin', of Adam's desire, we have discounted human life, in any aspiring sense. But this desire, in Ibsen, is deep and valid. This is most clearly shown in *Emperor and Galilean*, where the false world of power and the false doctrine of resignation are alike rejected, in the struggle for the 'third empire', in which 'the spirit of men shall re-enter on its heritage'. It is the false condition of spirit against flesh that Julian fights, because all that is human has become unlawful since the day when the seer of Galilee became ruler of the world. Through him, life has become death.

The desire fails, or is broken, but is never denied. Ibsen's world, from his historical dramas to his domestic plays, is recognisable always by this fact: the struggle of individual desire, in a false and compromising situation, to break free and know itself. This is why we must not render him back to a dramatic tradition which would show the desire as false or unlawful. In the best sense, this is still a liberal world.

It is also, however, the world of liberal tragedy. Implacably, in most of his plays, the affirmed desire is brought to a breaking-point

—a tight place where you stick fast. There is no going forward or backward—

and the hero, if not the desire itself, is broken. Why should this be so? Why, repeatedly, should so powerful a struggle of human desire fail to break through? It is not any force outside man that breaks him. As Rosmer says, going to his death:

There is no judge over us, and therefore we must do justice upon ourselves.

But the justice, still, is death. The conviction of guilt, and of necessary retribution, is as strong as ever it was when imposed by an external design.

And this is the heart of liberal tragedy, for we have moved from the heroic position of the individual liberator, the aspiring self against society, to a tragic position, of the self against the self. Guilt, that is to say, has become internal and personal, just as aspiration was internal and personal. The internal and personal fact is the only general fact, in the end. Liberalism, in its heroic phase, begins to pass into its twentieth-century breakdown: the self-enclosed, guilty and isolated world; the time of man his own victim.

We are still in this world, and it is doubtful if we can clearly name all its pressures. A characteristic ideology has presented it as truth and even as science, until argument against it has come to seem hopeless. A structure of feeling as deep as this enacts a world, as well as interpreting it, so that we learn it from experience as well as from ideology. All we can say, reflecting on Ibsen's tragedy, is that the deadlock reached there, the heroic deadlock in which men die still struggling to climb, was indeed necessary. For there is no way out, there is only an inevitable tragic consciousness, while desire is seen as essentially individual. We have to push past Ibsen's undoubted social consciousness to discover, at its roots, this same individual consciousness. Certainly there is to be reform, the 'sick earth' is to be 'made whole', but this is to happen, always, by an individual act: the liberal conscience, *against* society. Change is never to be *with* people; if others come, they can at most be led. But also change, significantly often, is against people; it is against their wills that the liberator is thrown, and disillusion is then rapid. He speaks for human desire, as a general fact, but he knows this only as individual fulfilment. The self then makes its most terrible discovery: that there is not only a world outside it, resisting it, but other selves, capable of similar suffering and desire. It is possible then for fulfilment to be re-defined: a getting away from the world and from others; the loneliness of the high mountains. But desire had included the joy of life: the life of earth, and of men and women, which the hero is still governed by, even while he drives himself to reject it. The conflict is then indeed internal: a desire for relationship when all that is known of relationship is restricting; desire narrowing to an image in the mind, until it is realised that the search for warmth and light has ended in cold and darkness. Every move towards relationship ends in guilt. It is significant that nowhere in Ibsen is there a loving, active, lasting relationship; the image of it, at the end of *Peer Gynt*, is as much a relapse from effort, a return to the mother, as a discovery of a loving equal. More often, the tie to the parent is not even relapse. There is a kind of terror in natural inheritance itself. As later in Freudian psychology, the parent-child relationship is guilty as such, and the revelation of the face or feeling of father and mother, behind the adult self, is in itself horrifying. That inescapable connection haunts, quite literally, the liberal idea of the self. In this sense, to be born is to be guilty, and inheritance is inevitably 'debt'. For the identity of the 'free' self is limited and impugned by the necessary physical inheritance. That connection to others is involuntary, and is in the blood. To the liberal self this is not connection but tainting.

Then, driven by individual desire, which cannot admit any final connection, Ibsen's adult persons simply involve and damage each other, beyond the possibility of fulfilment. Freedom is defined as getting away from this net, or exposing it, in the name of truth. But there is nowhere to get away to, except by renunciation of the individual life and desire which are still active and compelling. Desire, consistently, betrays desire. The most active search to fulfil the self leads away from the persons in whom fulfilment is desired. It was this that Ibsen recognised, in his last plays; most notably in the Dramatic Epilogue:

> We see the irretrievable only when . . .
> When? . . .
> When we dead awaken.
> What do we really see then?
> We see that we have never lived.

The search for self-fulfilment has ended in the denial of life:

> It was self-murder, a deadly sin against myself. And that sin I can never expiate.

It is the final tragic recognition: that the self, which is all that is known as desire, leads away from fulfilment, and to its own breakdown.

From this recognition, there is no way out, within the liberal consciousness. There is either the movement to common desire, common aspiration, which politically is socialism, or there is the acceptance, reluctant at first but strengthening and darkening, of failure and breakdown as common and inevitable. In one way or the other, a total condition is asserted, and the differentiated self becomes dramatically rare. It is true that Shaw, in *Saint Joan* and elsewhere, could retain the simpler pattern, of the heroic and liberating individual destroyed by a false society. Numerically, many other plays have repeated this, but, at least in European drama, this pattern has commonly failed to include any of the deepest human energies and problems. The heroic individual, as in Shaw, survives only as a romantic portrait, emptied of personality so that the positive role can be played without complications. The act of liberation, correspondingly, is in the narrow sense historical or political; it is not an absolute human demand, but a limited cause here and there. The problem of the frustrated individual is masked by his theatrical transformation into a movement, leaving all the deeper problems, of history and personality, untouched.

The mainstream of tragedy has gone elsewhere: into the self-enclosed, guilty and isolated world of the breakdown of liberalism. We shall need to trace this through its complicated particular phases. But, with Ibsen in mind, it is worth looking briefly at the plays of Arthur Miller, who represents, essentially, a late revival of liberal tragedy, on the edge (but only on the edge) of its transformation into socialism. What distinguishes Miller from the majority contemporary drama of guilt and breakdown is the retained consciousness of a false society, an alterable condition. In *All My Sons* we are in many ways back in the world of Ibsen: a particular lie becomes the demonstration of a general lie. Joe Keller, a small manufacturer, has committed a social crime for which he has escaped responsibility. He acquiesced in the sending of defective parts to the Air Force in wartime, and allowed another man to take the consequences and imprisonment. The action of the play is that the social crime is made personal (by the fact of the death of Keller's own pilot son), and from this realisation made social again, in a new understanding of what society is. This is, in fact, the overcoming of alienation:

> Joe Keller's trouble . . . is not that he cannot tell right from wrong but that his cast of mind cannot admit that he, personally, has any viable connection with his world, his universe, or his society.

This is

the concept of a man's becoming a function of production or distribution to the point where his personality becomes divorced from the actions it propels.

By seeing a particular case, to which he has a father's connection, he is forced to recognise the general fact of human connection:

> I think to him they were all my sons. And I guess they were, I guess they were.

However, this new positive consciousness cannot go beyond the level of statement; it is a new feeling, of collective responsibility and of collective guilt, personally affirmed, but the tragedy is in the fact that it is retrospective. Keller, and those he has killed, can only be victims.

This sense of the victim is very deep in Miller. *The Crucible* may remind us, dramatically, of *Enemy of the People*, but there is a wholly new sense of the terrible power of collective persecution. Individuals suffer for what they are and naturally desire, rather than for what they try to do, and the innocent are swept up with the guilty, with epidemic force. The social consciousness has now changed, decisively. Society is not merely a false system, which the liberator can challenge. It is actively destructive and evil, claiming its victims merely because they are alive. It is still seen as a false and alterable society, but merely to live in it, now, is enough to become its victim. In *Death of a Salesman* the victim is not the nonconformist, the heroic but defeated liberator; he is, rather, the conformist, the type of the society itself. Willy Loman is a man who from selling things has passed to selling himself, and has become, in effect, a commodity which like other commodities will at a certain point be discarded by the laws of the economy. He brings tragedy down on himself, not by opposing the lie, but by living it. Ironically, the form of his aspiration is again the form of his defeat, but now for no liberating end; simply to get by, to see himself and his sons all right. The connection between parents and children, seen as necessarily contradictory, is again tragically decisive. A new consciousness is then shaped: that of the victim who has no living way out, but who can try, in death, to affirm his lost identity and his lost will.

Proctor, in *The Crucible*, had died as an act of self-preservation: preservation of the truth of himself and of others, in opposition to the lies of the persecuting authority.

> How may I live without my name?

This sense of personal verification by death is the last stage of liberal tragedy. In *The Crucible* it is virtually the position of the liberal martyr, though characteristically complicated by Proctor's personal guilt. But in *Death of a Salesman* and *A View from the Bridge* this wider implication is absent. It is not now the martyr but the victim; the disconnected individual. In Willy Loman's death the disconnection confirmed a general fact about the society; in Eddie Carbone's death, Miller has moved further back, and the death of the victim illustrates a total condition. Here, once again, at the end of a development, is the self against the self. Desire is quickened, releasing energies which destroy. As Eddie moves out of routine and into desire, there is rapid disintegration: the known sexual rhythms break down into their perverse variations, which now alone have energy. He rejects his wife, as his desire transfers to the girl they have brought up. And as his most vital energy drives him towards both incest and homosexuality, guilt becomes so much a part of desire that his identity and his normal connections are simply burned out. In the terror of his complicated jealousies, he betrays the human connection by which he has lived, surrenders immigrants of his wife's kin to the inhuman and alien society. When desire and guilt are thus inextricable, there is no way to live, and he provokes his death shouting 'I want my name'.

It is a last tragic cry, in a disintegrating world. Human desire destroys itself, under intolerable pressures, and the figure of the individual hero, who would remake his life and his world, is now quite forgotten, is one of the old stories, while isolated contemporary man, wanting no more than to be himself, fails even in this and transfers significance to his name and his death. To preserve one's life, as things are, is 'to settle for half', as Miller puts it at the end of *A View from the Bridge*. And if this is so, in a false society which the individual alone cannot change, then the original liberal impulse, of complete self-fulfilment, becomes inevitably tragic. The self that wills and desires destroys the self that lives, yet the rejection of will and desire is also tragedy: a corroding insignificance, as the self is cut down.

The final step, made clear in *After the Fall*, is the acceptance and generalisation of just this insignificance: the personally urgent yet finally complacent acknowledgement that desire and guilt are inextricable; the identification of the false society—torture, betrayal—as part of one's own desires, so that it can no longer be meaningfully opposed, or even bitterly challenged by death, but has simply to be confirmed, forgiven, and lived with, in our separate and isolated suffering. And then at this point the deadlock is absolute, and we are all victims: aspiration itself is only a disguise for cruelty. But when this has happened, in the mind of a whole culture, liberal tragedy has ended, in its own deadlock.

AMIRI BARAKA / LEROI JONES

"THE REVOLUTIONARY THEATRE" (1966)

The preceding essays have, in various ways, described a common dramatic tradition. In "The Revolutionary Theatre," Amiri Baraka describes the challenges posed by an emerging African-American theater.

The Revolutionary Theatre should force change; it should be change. (All their faces turned into the lights and you work on them black nigger magic, and cleanse them at having seen the ugliness. And if the beautiful see themselves, they will love themselves.) We are preaching virtue again, but by that to mean NOW, toward what seems the most constructive use of the world.

The Revolutionary Theatre must EXPOSE! Show up the insides of these humans, look into black skulls. White men will cower before this theatre because it hates them. Because they themselves have been trained to hate. The Revolutionary Theatre must hate them for hating. For presuming with their technology to deny the supremacy of the Spirit. They will all die because of this.

The Revolutionary Theatre must teach them their deaths. It must crack their faces open to the mad cries of the poor. It must teach them about silence and the truths lodged there. It must kill any God anyone names except Common Sense. The Revolutionary Theatre should flush the fags and murders out of Lincoln's face.

It should stagger through our universe correcting, insulting, preaching, spitting craziness—but a craziness taught to us in our most rational moments. People must be taught to trust true scientists (knowers, diggers, oddballs) and that the holiness of life is the constant possibility of widening the consciousness. And they must be incited to strike back against *any* agency that attempts to prevent this widening.

The Revolutionary Theatre must Accuse and Attack anything that can be accused and attacked. It must Accuse and Attack because it is a theatre of Victims. It looks at the sky with the victims' eyes, and moves the victims to look at the strength in their minds and their bodies.

Clay in *Dutchman*, Ray in *The Toilet*, Walker in *The Slave*, are all victims. In the Western sense they could be heroes. But the Revolutionary Theatre, even if it is Western, must be anti-Western. It must show horrible coming attractions of *The Crumbling of the West*. Even as Artaud designed *The Conquest of Mexico*, so we must design *The Conquest of White Eye*, and show the missionaries and wiggly liberals dying under blasts of concrete. For sound effects, wild screams of joy, from all the peoples of the world.

The Revolutionary Theatre must take dreams and give them a reality. It must isolate the ritual and historical cycles of reality. But it must be food for all those who need food, and daring propaganda for the beauty of the Human Mind. It is a political theatre, a weapon to help in the slaughter of these dimwitted fatbellied white guys who somehow believe that the rest of the world is here for them to slobber on.

This should be a theatre of World Spirit. Where the spirit can be shown to be the most competent force in the world. Force. Spirit. Feeling. The language will be anybody's, but tightened by the poet's backbone. And even the language must show what the facts are in this consciousness epic, what's happening. We will talk about the world, and the preciseness with which we are able to summon the world will be our art. Art is method. And art, "like any ashtray or senator," remains in the world. Wittgenstein said ethics and aesthetics are one. I believe this. So the Broadway theatre is a theatre of reaction whose ethics, like its aesthetics, reflect the spiritual values of this unholy society, which sends young crackers all over the world blowing off colored people's heads. (In some of these flippy Southern towns they even shoot up the immigrants' Favorite Son, be it Michael Schwerner or JFKennedy.)

The Revolutionary Theatre is shaped by the world, and moves to reshape the world, using as its force the natural force and perpetual vibrations of the mind in the world. We are history and desire, what we are, and what any experience can make us.

It is a social theatre, but all theatre is social theatre. But we will change the drawing rooms into places where real things can be said about a real world, or into smoky rooms where the destruction of Washington can be plotted. The Revolutionary Theatre must function like an incendiary pencil planted in Curtis Lemay's cap. So that when the final curtain goes down brains are splattered over the seats and the floor, and bleeding nuns must wire SOS's to Belgians with gold teeth.

Our theatre will show victims so that their brothers in the audience will be better able to understand that they are the brothers of victims, and that they themselves are victims if they are blood brothers. And what we show must cause the blood to rush, so that pre-revolutionary temperaments will be bathed in this blood, and it will cause their deepest souls to move, and they will find themselves tensed and clenched, even ready to die, at what the soul has been taught. We will scream and cry, murder, run through the streets in agony, if it means some soul will be moved, moved to actual life understanding of what the world is, and what it ought to be. We are preaching virtue and feeling, and a natural sense of the self in the world. All men live in the world, and the world ought to be a place for them to live.

What is called the imagination (from image, magi, magic, magician, etc.) is a practical vector from the soul. It stores all data, and can be called on to solve all our "problems." The imagination is the projection of ourselves past our sense of ourselves as "things." Imagination (Image) is all possibility, because from the image, the initial circumscribed energy, any use (idea) is possible. And so begins that image's use in the world. Possibility is what moves us.

The popular white man's theatre like the popular white man's novel shows tired white lives, and the problems of eating white sugar, or else it herds bigcaboosed blondes onto huge stages in rhinestones and makes believe they are dancing or singing. WHITE BUSINESSMEN OF THE WORLD, DO YOU WANT TO SEE PEOPLE REALLY DANCING AND SINGING??? ALL OF YOU GO UP TO HARLEM AND GET YOURSELF KILLED. THERE WILL BE DANCING AND SINGING, THEN, FOR REAL!! (In *The Slave*, Walker Vessels, the black revolutionary, wears an armband, which is the insignia of the attacking army—a big red-lipped minstrel, grinning like crazy.)

The liberal white man's objection to the theatre of the revolution (if he is "hip" enough) will be on aesthetic grounds. Most white Western artists do not need to be "political," since usually, whether they know it or not, they are in complete sympathy with the most repressive social forces in the world today. There are more junior birdmen fascists running around the West today disguised as Artists than there are disguised as fascists. (But then, that word, *Fascist*, and with it, *Fascism*, has been made obsolete by the words *America*, and *Americanism*.) The American Artist usually turns out to be just a super-Bourgeois, because, finally, all he has to show for his sojourn through the world is "better taste" than the Bourgeois—many times not even that.

Americans will hate the Revolutionary Theatre because it will be out to destroy them and whatever they believe is real. American cops will try to close the theatres where such nakedness of the human spirit is paraded. American producers will say the revolutionary plays are filth, usually because they will treat human life as if it were actually happening. American directors will say that the white guys in the plays are too abstract and cowardly ("don't get me wrong . . . I mean aesthetically . . .") and they will be right.

The force we want is of twenty million spooks storming America with furious cries and unstoppable weapons. We want actual explosions and actual brutality: AN EPIC IS CRUMBLING and we must give it the space and hugeness of its actual demise. The Revolutionary Theatre, which is now peopled with victims, will soon begin to be peopled with new kinds of heroes—not the weak Hamlets debating whether or not they are ready to die for what's on their minds, but men and women (and minds) digging out from under a thousand years of "high art" and weak-faced dalliance. We must make an art that will function so as to call down the actual wrath of world spirit. We are witch doctors and assassins, but we will open a place for the true scientists to expand our consciousness. This is a theatre of assault. The play that will split the heavens for us will be called THE DESTRUCTION OF AMERICA. The heroes will be Crazy Horse, Denmark Vesey, Patrice Lumumba, and not history, not memory, not sad sentimental groping for a warmth in our despair; these will be new men, new heroes, and their enemies most of you who are reading this.

**HENRY LOUIS
GATES JR.**

*"BEYOND THE
CULTURE WARS"*
(1994)

**MULTI-
CULTURALISM
AT THE LIMIT**

Henry Louis Gates, Jr., is the W. E. B. Du Bois Professor of the Humanities at Harvard University and is one of the most distinguished critics of African-American literature and culture writing in the United States today. His many books include Figures in Black: Words, Signs, and the "Racial" Self, Loose Canons: Notes on the Culture Wars, *and* The Signifying Monkey: A Theory of Afro-American Literary Criticism. *In "Beyond the Culture Wars," Gates examines the relationship between the movement for multiculturalism in education, the discourse of identity politics, and the formation of "race."*

What is this crazy thing called multiculturalism? As an overview of the current debate suggests, a salient difficulty raised by the variety of uses to which the term has been put is that multiculturalism itself has certain imperial tendencies. Its boundaries have not been easy to establish. We are told that it is concerned with the representation of difference—but whose differences? which differences?

Almost all differences in which we take an interest express themselves in cultural ways; many, perhaps most, are exhausted by their cultural manifestations. To assert this claim is, in most cases, to assert a tautology. Narrowing the terms of argument, we might say that multiculturalism is concerned with the representation, not of difference as such, but of cultural identities. But which ones are those? Indeed, if we ask what sort of identities are helpfully modeled by multiculturalism, the answer is less than obvious. Gender identity, sexual identity, racial identity: if all these things are socially inflected and produced, rather than unmediatedly natural, why won't they fit into the culturalist model? (I use the slippery term *culturalist* here, somewhat anomalously, as a back-formation from *multicultural.*) Or will they?

We can probably agree, for example, that gender identity and sexual identity are hard to reduce to the model of cultural difference, even though the meaning of these categories is culturally specific. First, we can discuss the categories in a transcultural, transhistorical manner, if only to elaborate on their transcultural and transhistorical disparities. (Try that with "Basque" or "Catalan.") Second, the culturalist model normally imagines its constituent elements as cultural bubbles that may collide but that usually could, in principle, exist in splendid isolation from one another: hence the rubric of "cultural diversity." This sort of cultural externalism—required by a model of cultural distance or disparity—does not work so well with gender identity or sexual identity. What we call "sexual difference" is a difference within, something culturally intrinsic. Why won't the culturalist reduction work? As Jonathan Dollimore and others point out about sexual difference, homophobia in our culture is part of the structure of sexuality itself: it's not out there; it's in here. Sexism, perhaps even more obviously, is also part of our conventional gender identities. Othering starts in the home.

I do not mean to deny the existence of subcultural differentiae in particular social contexts, wherein sexual difference seems to become "ethnicized" and a sexual ethnicity is forged. At the same time, the relation between the sexual and the cultural is necessarily contingent. Obviously, we can't assume that Ronald Firbank and Sophocles—or, for that matter, Marcel Proust and Michelangelo—would recognize their putative fraternity.

And yet it has sometimes seemed to me that what really explains the fervor of some of the Afrocentrist preoccupation with Egypt is an unexpressed belief that deep continuities supervene on skin color. Beyond the heartfelt claim that Cleopatra was "black" is the lurking conviction that if you traveled back in time and dropped the needle on a James Brown album, Cleo would instantly break out into the camel walk. The belief that we cherish is not so much a proposition about melanin and physiognomy; it's the proposition that, through the mists of history, Cleopatra was a *sister.*

For obvious reasons, sexual dimorphism is a basic aspect of human experience. Racial difference is certainly less so; understanding its significance always requires a particular engagement with a specific historical trajectory. There is no master key. But what emerges, again, is that despite the complex interrelations between race and culture—a matter that takes a sinister turn in the racialization of culture in the nineteenth century—no ready conversion factor connects the two, only the vagaries of history.

As the critic John Brenkman notes, blacks have been inscribed in the American matrix in a particular way; they are not just missing or absent or elsewhere: "[B]lacks were historically not merely excluded from the American polity; they were inscribed within it as *nonparticipants.*" He continues:

The forms of that negating inscription have varied through a complex history of legal and political designations. These set the conditions of the African-American discourse on identity and citizenship, and the meaning of that discourse would in turn have to be interpreted in light of those conditions and of the strategies embedded in its response to them. (98)

What good are roots, Gertrude Stein once asked, if you can't take them with you? But a number of critics now suggest that the contemporary model of ethnicity sometimes fails us by its historically foreshortened perspective, its inability to grasp the roots as well as the branches of cultural identity. In a recent book, the theorist E. San Juan, Jr., harshly decries what he calls the "cult of ethnicity and the fetish of pluralism" and launches probably the most thoroughgoing critique of multiculturalism from a radical perspective that we have. San Juan writes:

> With the gradual academicization of Ethnic Studies, "the cult of ethnicity" based on the paradigm of European immigrant success became the orthodox doctrine. The theoretical aggrandizement of ethnicity systematically erased from the historical frame of reference any perception of race and racism as causal factors in the making of the political and economic structures of the United States. (132)

In a similar vein, Hazel Carby has proposed a perspective that "[b]y insisting that 'culture' denotes antagonistic relations of domination and subordination . . . undermines the pluralistic notion of compatibility inherent in *multi*culturalism. . . ." She continues:

> The paradigm of multiculturalism actually excludes the concept of dominant and subordinate cultures—either indigenous or migrant—and fails to recognize that the existence of racism relates to the possession and exercise of politico-economic control and authority and also to forms of resistance to the power of dominant social groups. (64–65)

The issues that radical critics such as San Juan and Carby raise are important, but they have received little hearing because liberal multiculturalism has generally failed to engage with leftist critiques of this sort. Those familiar with multiculturalism only through its right-wing opponents are sometimes surprised to discover that these broad-gauge radical critiques even exist. Consequently, the extended face-off with conservatism has had a deforming effect, encouraging multiculturalism to know what it is against but not what it is for. So even if we finally demur to aspects of the radical critique, we will be better off for having sorted through some of its arguments. In what follows, I want to examine the paradoxes of pluralism and consider some of the limitations of multiculturalism—that is, of multi*culturalism*—as a model for the range of phenomena it has often been required to subsume. I also raise questions about the historically recent triumph of "ethnicity" as a paradigm or master code for human difference. I conclude with an appeal for pluralism, but it is a pluralism, let me serve fair notice, of a singularly banal and uninspiring variety, conducing to a vision of society, and of the university, as a place of what one philosopher calls "constrained disagreement" (MacIntyre 231). Here, then, are two cheers for multiculturalism.

How does the vocabulary of multiculturalism occlude race? You may have noticed that *multiculturalism* is frequently used in the popular media as a substitute for the earlier designation *multiracial*. Typically, a column on advertising will describe a Benetton-style ad with, say, black and white and Asian children together as "multicultural." Do these children—presumably supplied by the Ford Model Agency and in all likelihood hailing from exotic Westchester County—in fact represent different cultures? That, of course, is the one thing you cannot tell from a photograph of this sort. But you will find that in almost every instance where the older form *multiracial* would have been used, the newer lexeme *multicultural* is employed instead, even where cultural traits, as opposed to physiognomic traits, are obviously undiscoverable or irrelevant.

I want to be clear. In many cases, the shift from race to ethnicity is a salutary one, a necessary move away from the essentialist biologizing of a previous era. The emphasis on the social construction of race may be a familiar one, but it remains an imperative one for all that. And yet we ought to consider the correlative danger of essentializing culture when we blithely allow *culture* to substitute for *race* without affecting the basic circulation of the term. The conventional multicultural vision suggests that for every insult there is a culture: that is, if I can be denigrated as an X, I can be affirmed as an X. This mechanism of remediation is perhaps not the most sophisticated, but the intentions are good.

So far, we've seen the ethnicity paradigm faulted for a tendency to leave out history, power relations, and, of course, the history of power relations. But its perplexities do not end here. We might bear in mind that the ascent of the vocabulary of ethnicity is, as Werner Sollors has emphasized, largely a postwar phenomenon, the very term having been coined by W. Lloyd Warner in 1941. The most conservative aspect of some populist versions of multiculturalism may be an understanding of group identity and group rights that borrows whole hog a reified conception of cultural membership derived from the social sciences of mid-century. What's new is that cultural survival—the preservation of cultural differentiae—is assigned an almost medical sense of urgency. And if the delimitation of cultural identity borrows from the social sciences, the interpretation of its products sometimes seems to court the gaze of anthropology; in place of hermeneutics, it would seem, some might prefer ethnography. That is, under the sign of multiculturalism, literary readings are often guided by the desire to elicit, first and foremost, indices of ethnic particularity, especially those that can be construed as oppositional, transgressive, subversive.

Then there's another paradox. In a critique of liberal individualism, we debunk the supposed "stability" of the individual as a category, and yet we sometimes reconstitute and recuperate the same essential stability in the form of an ethnos that allegedly exhibits all the regularities and uniformities we could not locate in the individual subject. Conversely, as John Guillory writes, "The critique of the canon responds to the disunity of the culture as a whole, as a *fragmented* whole, by constituting new cultural unities at the level of gender, race, or more recently, ethnic subcultures, or gay or lesbian subcultures" (34). Skepticism about the status of the individual is surely chastening, but there may be a danger in a too easy invocation of the correlative group, the status of which may be problematic in another way.

Finally, to complete our overview of the limits of culturalism, we should take account of the critique of multiculturalism put forward by the influential French anthropologist Jean-Loup Amselle, who contends that the very notion of discrete ethnicities is an artifact of his discipline. Warning against what he dubs ethnic or cultural fundamentalism, Amselle maintains that the notion of a multicultural society, "far from being an instrument of tolerance and of liberation of minorities, as its partisans affirm, manifests, to the contrary, all the hallmarks of ethnological reason, and that is why it has been taken up in France by the New Right" (35). But Amselle's concerns are not merely political; they are ontological as well. "Cultures aren't situated one by the other like Leibniz's windowless monads," he argues. Rather, "the very definition of a given culture is in fact the result of intercultural relations of forces" (55). On the face of it, Amselle's considerations are yet another blow against what I've referred to as the bubble model of cultures. Insofar as this idea is a necessary feature of the culturalism promoted by multiculturalism, it might have to be discarded.

IDENTITY VERSUS POLITICS

While the discourses of identity politics and of liberation are often conflated, they may be in mortal combat on a more fundamental level. Identity politics, in its purest form, must be concerned with the survival of an identity. By contrast, the utopian agenda of liberation pursues what it takes to be the objective interests of its subjects, but it may be little concerned with its cultural continuity or integrity. More than that, the discourse of liberation often looks forward to the birth of a transformed subject, the creation of a new identity, which is, by definition, the surcease of the old. And that, at least in theory, is the rub.

Consider an example I have touched on in "Critical Fanonism." If colonialism inscribes itself on the psyche of the colonized, if it is part of the process of colonial subject formation, then doesn't this inscription establish limits to the very intelligibility of liberation? This critique, more or less, is the one that the Tunisian philosopher Albert Memmi makes about Frantz Fanon's anticolonial rhetoric. How are we to prize apart the discourse of the colonized and the discourse of the colonizer? Memmi suggests that Fanon, for all his ambivalences, somehow believed that "the day oppression ceases, the new man is supposed to appear before our eyes immediately." But, says Memmi, "this is not the way it happens." The utopian moment that Memmi decries in Fanon is the depiction of decolonization as engendering "a kind of tabula rasa," as "quite simply the replacing of a certain 'species' of men by another 'species' of men" so that the fear that we will continue to be "overdetermined from without" is never reconciled with Fanon's political vision of emancipation (qtd. in Gates 469). Certainly it would be hard to reconcile with any recognizable version of identitarian politics.

We can easily retrieve a lesson from the hot sands of Algeria. Any discourse of emancipation, insofar as it retains a specifically cultural cast, must contend with similar issues. That is the paradox entailed by a politics conducted on behalf of cultural identities when those identities are in part defined by the structural or positional features that the politics aims to dismantle.

Return, for a moment, to Carby's insistence that the "paradigm of multiculturalism actually excludes the concept of dominant and subordinate cultures." In what sense is this statement true? I think that Guillory, whose work on the canon debate is plainly the best of its kind, provides a helpful gloss when he writes that

> . . . a culturalist politics, though it glances worriedly at the phenomenon of class, has in practice never devised a politics that would arise from a class "identity." For while it is easy enough to conceive of a self-affirmative racial or sexual identity, it makes very little sense to posit an affirmative lower-class identity, as such an identity would have to be grounded in the experience of deprivation per se, [the affirmation of which is] hardly incompatible with a program for the abolition of want. (13)

And yet class may provide a particularly stark instance of a more general limitation. Obviously, if being subordinate is a constitutive aspect of an identity, then a liberation politics would foreclose an identity politics and vice versa. This situation is stipulatively true for Guillory's example of a "lower-class identity." But might it not, at least contingently, prove true for a host of other putatively cultural identities as well?

The point is that identity politics cannot be understood as a politics in the harness of a pregiven identity. The "identity" half of the catchall phrase "identity politics" must be conceived as being just as labile and dynamic as the "politics" half is. The two terms must be in dialogue, as it were, or we should be prepared for the phrase to be revealed as an oxymoron.

We might then ask how identity and politics are best reconciled. Can multiculturalism—often depicted as a slippery slope to anarchy and tribal war—support the sort of civil society one might want?

In a recent essay, the distinguished historian John Higham complained that

> . . . multiculturalism has remained for two decades a stubbornly practical enterprise, justified by immediate demands rather than long range goals: a movement without an overall theory. . . . Still, it is troubling that twenty years after those convulsive beginnings, multiculturalism has suddenly become a policy issue in America's colleges, universities, and secondary schools without yet proposing a vision of the kind of society it wants. (204)

Multiculturalism may or may not have political consequences, in Higham's rather persuasive diagnosis, but it does not have a political vision.

In a provocative and unusual attempt to connect the multicultural agenda to the program of democracy, Brenkman takes up Higham's challenge. He argues:

> Citizens can *freely* enter the field of political persuasion and decision only insofar as they draw on the contingent vocabularies of their own identities. Democracy needs participants who are conversant with the images, symbols, stories, and vocabularies that have evolved across the whole of the history. . . . By the same token, democracy also requires citizens who are fluent enough in one another's vocabularies and histories to share the forums of political deliberation and decision on an equal footing. (89)

I find this formulation attractive and heartening, though in its instrumental conception of cultural knowledge it may have unsuspected affinities with E. D. Hirsch. But I want to make two points here. First, a caveat: to say that "[c]itizens can freely enter the field of political persuasion and decision"—that is, the field of politics, *tout court*—"only insofar as they draw on the contingent vocabularies of their own identities" is to suppose that one exists, in some sense, as a cultural atom, that

MULTI-CULTURALISM AND DEMOCRACY

one's identity exists anterior to one's engagement in the field of the political. It is to suppose that one arrives at this field already constituted, already culturally whole, rather than to acknowledge that the political might create or contour one's cultural or ethnic identity. Second, this formulation does not entail what we might call "group" multiculturalism, which devotes itself to the empowerment of crisply delimited cultural units and conceives society as a sort of federation of officially recognized cultural sovereignties. We've already registered the sorts of criticisms that have been raised against that model, but they needn't arise just yet.

Brenkman is no Pangloss: he remarks a tension between multiculturalism and democracy but proposes a tradition of civic republicanism or civic humanism by which the tension might be resolved. The emphasis of this tradition, which was of particular influence in the early history of the United States, is on civic participation over liberalism's privatism; individual development (here he cites the British historian J. G. A. Pocock) is seen as intrinsically linked to the individual's participation as a citizen of an "autonomous decision-making community, a polis or republic." Even so, Brenkman concedes:

> [C]ivic humanism also always assumed the homogeneity of those who enjoyed citizenship. As Michael Warner has shown, for example, the republican representation of citizenship in revolutionary America tacitly depended upon the exclusion of women, African slaves, and Native Americans from the forms of literacy that were the emblem and the means of the patriots' equality. To evoke the republican tradition in the context of multicultural societies quickly exposes those elements of civic humanism that run directly counter to diversity and plurality. (95)

The charge that this civic humanism depended on the homogeneity of its citizenry is easily supported, but is *cultural* homogeneity precisely the issue? As I noted earlier, the exclusion of women is not, at least customarily, depicted as a matter of cultural distance. And while both Native Americans and African slaves would doubtless be marked by cultural differentiae, what Brenkman criticizes here is the perpetuation of such differences by the patriots' withholding the tools of assimilation, namely, English literacy. What is at stake is not the eradication of difference—by, for example, the unwanted imposition of English literacy, which is a grievance that has arisen in some non-Western settings. We cannot, then, conclude that cultural distance motivated the exclusion of Native Americans and African slaves; on the contrary, their exclusion was achieved by the patriots' enforcing the cultural distance. And so what we come up against, once again, are the limits of the culturalist model, its tendency to occlude the categories of race.

However symptomatic these slippages—and I cite them as cautionary—I believe that Brenkman's elaborated vision of the "modern polity [as] a dynamic space in which citizenship is always being contested rather than the fixed space of the premodern ideal of a republic" is a signal contribution to the debate surrounding multiculturalism (99).

MULTI-CULTURALISM VERSUS RELATIVISM

One last obstacle remains to the articulation of a multicultural polity: the specter of relativism, which haunts many of multiculturalism's friends and outrages its enemies. For the cultural conservatives, from William Kristol to Roger Kimball, it has totemic significance, a one-word encapsulation of all that is wrong with their progressive counterparts. If all difference deserves respect, how can morality survive and governance be maintained? Progressives find the doctrine equally unsettling: the righting of wrongs, after all, demands a recognition of them as wrongs. And the classic 1965 handbook by Herbert Marcuse, Barrington Moore, and Robert Paul Wolff, *A Critique of Pure Tolerance*, should remind us that critiques from the left are far from exceptional. Indeed, it seems scarcely plausible that relativism has anything like the currency that some critics have imputed to it. "'Relativism,'" Richard Rorty has stated, "is the view that every belief on a certain topic, or perhaps about *any* topic is as good as every other. No one holds this view," he says flatly, except "the occasional cooperative freshman" (166). Alas, this is surely an overstatement, though in the present climate probably a salutary one.

Certainly, relativism comes in many different flavors—moral and aesthetic as well as epistemological—and what actually follows from relativism of any particular variety is seldom clear. But one kind of relativism—the epistemological or cognitive—has achieved a certain limited currency among some anthropologists, whose business is culture, and might be supposed to make an occasional appearance in the multicultural context.

CRITICAL CONTEXTS   1043

The Wittgensteinian Peter Winch, for example, in his classic book *The Idea of a Social Science and Its Relation to Philosophy,* has argued that "our idea of what belongs to the realm of reality is given to us in the language that we use" (15). John Beattie has decried a similar cognitive relativism in, for example, F. Allan Hanson's *Meaning in Culture* and Roy Wagner's *The Invention of Culture.* For Winch, there is no reality independent of our conceptual schemes, which may differ in incommensurable ways.

This is a curious view, one that has been rebutted most vigorously by intellectuals from just those non-Western cultures that relativism would consign to hermetic isolation. As the distinguished Ghanaian philosopher Kwasi Wiredu writes:

> [R]elativism . . . falsely denied the existence of inter-personal criteria of rationality. That is what the denial of objectivity amounts to. Unless at least the basic canons of rational thinking were common to men, they could not even communicate among themselves. Thus, in seeking to foreclose rational discussion, the relativist view is in effect seeking to undermine the foundations of human community. (220–21)

The general problem with relativism of this sort is that it makes the project of cross-cultural understanding unintelligible. (Martin Hollis observes that "without assumptions about reality and rationality we cannot translate anything and no translation could show the assumptions to be wrong" [240].)

So let me put the argument at its strongest: if relativism is right, then multiculturalism is impossible. Relativism, far from conducing to multiculturalism, would rescind its very conditions of possibility.

By way of a return to politics and a rounding out of my critical overview, I wish to enlist Isaiah Berlin, whom we might describe as the paterfamilias of liberal pluralism and whose banishment from the current debate is a matter of puzzlement, unless the fear is that adducing Berlin's lifelong argument would compromise our claims to novelty. Berlin stresses that "relativism is not the only alternative to what Lovejoy called uninformitarianism" ("Relativism" 85). In what Berlin distinguishes as pluralism, "[w]e are free to criticize the values of other cultures, to condemn them, but we cannot pretend not to understand them at all, or to regard them simply as subjective, the product of creatures in different circumstances with different tastes from our own, which do not speak to us at all" ("Pursuit" 11). He writes:

PLURALISM REDUX

> What is clear is that values can clash—that is why civilizations are incompatible. They can be incompatible between cultures, or groups in the same culture, or between you and me. . . . Values may easily clash within the breast of a single individual; and it does not follow that, if they do some must be true and others false. [Indeed], these collisions of values are of the essence of what they are and what we are. ("Pursuit" 12–13)

Berlin's pluralism is radically anti-utopian. Perhaps it is not the sort of thing likely to inspire one to risk one's life or the lives of others. But I don't think it is a flaccid or undemanding faith for all that. And, in the essay from which I've been reading, entitled "The Pursuit of the Ideal," Berlin anticipates the complaint:

> Of course social or political collisions will take place; the mere conflict of positive values alone makes this unavoidable. Yet they can, I believe, be minimized by promoting and preserving an uneasy equilibrium, which is constantly threatened and in need of repair—that alone, I repeat, is the precondition for decent societies and morally acceptable behavior; otherwise we are bound to lose our way. A little dull as a solution, you will say? Not the stuff of which calls to heroic action by inspired leaders are made? Yet if there is some truth in this view, perhaps that is sufficient. (19)

The vision here, if it is a vision, is one of the central themes of Berlin's corpus, but we can find it promulgated elsewhere with a range of inflections. It warns us off final solutions of all sorts, admonishes us that the search for purity—whether we speak of "ethnic cleansing" or of primordial "cultural authenticity"—poses a greater threat to civil order, and human decency, than does the messy affair of cultural variegation. It lets us remember that identities are always in dialogue, that they exist (as Amselle expatiates) only in relation to one another, and that they are, like everything else, sites of contest and negotiation, self-fashioning and refashioning. (As Higham observes, "[A]n adequate theory of American culture will have to address the reality of assimilation as well as the persistence of differences" [209]). And it suggests, finally, that a multiculturalism that can accept its limitations might be one worth working for.

WORKS CITED

Amselle, Jean-Loup. *Logiques métisses.* Paris: Payot, 1990.

Beattie, John M. "Objectivity and Social Anthropology." *Objectivity and Cultural Divergence.* Ed. S. C. Brown. Cambridge: Cambridge UP, 1984. 1–20.

Berlin, Isaiah. "Alleged Relativism in Eighteenth-Century European Thought." *Crooked Timber* 70–90.

———. *The Crooked Timber of Humanity: Chapters in the History of Ideas.* New York: Knopf, 1991.

———. "The Pursuit of the Ideal." *Crooked Timber* 1–19.

Brenkman, John. "Multiculturalism and Criticism." *English Inside and Out.* Ed. Susan Gubar and Jonathan Kamholtz. New York: Routledge, 1993. 87–101.

Carby, Hazel. "Multi-culture." *Screen* 34 (1980): 62–70.

Dollimore, Jonathan. "Homophobia and Sexual Difference." *Oxford Literary Review* 8. 1–2 (1986): 5–12.

Gates, Henry Louis, Jr. "Critical Fanonism." *Critical Inquiry* 17 (1991): 457–70.

Guillory, John. *Cultural Capital: The Problem of Literary Canon Formation.* Chicago: U of Chicago P, 1993.

Higham, John. "Multiculturalism and Universalism: A History and Critique." *American Quarterly* 45 (1993): 195–219.

Hollis, Martin. "Reason and Ritual." *Philosophy* 43 (1968): 231–47.

MacIntyre, Alasdair. *Three Rival Versions of Moral Enquiry.* Notre Dame: U of Notre Dame P, 1990.

Marcuse, Herbert, Barrington Moore, and Robert Paul Wolff. *A Critique of Pure Tolerance.* Boston: Beacon, 1965.

Rorty, Richard. "Pragmatism, Relativism, Irrationalism." *Consequences of Pragmatism.* Minneapolis: U of Minnesota P, 1982. 160–75.

San Juan, E., Jr. *Racial Formations/Critical Transformations: Articulations of Power in Ethnic and Racial Studies in the United States.* Atlantic Highlands: Humanities, 1992.

Sollors, Werner. "E Pluribus Unus." Unpublished essay.

Winch, Peter. *The Idea of a Social Science and Its Relation to Philosophy.* London: Routledge, 1958.

Wiredu, Kwasi. *Philosophy and an African Culture.* Cambridge: Cambridge UP, 1980.

THE WORLD STAGE

ISTORIC SOCIAL, POLITICAL, AND TECHNOLOGICAL CHANGES HAVE RE-shaped the world since 1950, with a consequential impact on the theater. The aftermath of World War II has seen the remapping of the planet: the indepen-dence of India, Pakistan, and many Asian and African nations from colonial rule; the founding of Israel and the displacement of the Palestinians; and wars in Korea, Indochina, the Middle East, Africa, and the Persian Gulf. Those decades also witnessed bitter civil strife and the glimmerings of peace in Northern Ireland, Argentina, Chile, the United States, Europe, and elsewhere; the Cuban missile crisis, the death of Francisco Franco in Spain, and the dismantling of the Berlin Wall; independence movements in the former Soviet Union and in Eastern Europe; the collapse of Yugoslavia and protracted war in Bosnia; the civil rights movement in the United States and the waning of apartheid in South Africa.

With the rise of global communications, a global economy, and global political and military interests, such social and political revolutions immediately become the world's business. They reshape the world we live in even as we watch the changes unfold on our television screens. Television, fortunately, has not really transformed the world's diverse cultures into a single "global village," but local cultures all feel the impact of events around the world. Think of the global effects of environmental disasters like the Cher-nobyl nuclear meltdown and the deforestation of the rain forests of the Amazon; of med-ical advances like vaccination and of epidemics like AIDS; of the international effects of social movements like nuclear disarmament, human rights, Amnesty International, femi-nism, and the peace movement, or, more horrifyingly, of anti-Semitism, racism, and homophobia.

Drama requires the collaboration of playwrights, actors, and audiences; the public structure of a theater site or building; and the social and political incentives and protec-tions that make theatergoing attractive—it is an art deeply woven into the social fabric of a given culture and its history. Although we can still speak of the "London theater" or of "American drama," terms like these have become in our era a critical convenience for reducing the dynamic variety of contemporary theater to the fictional boundaries of a sin-gle "national" culture. (This convenience is marked in the organization of this anthology, too, which treats contemporary American plays separately in unit 6, in order to clarify the continuities of American theater and to raise specific questions of canonicity. American drama is, of course, part of "world drama," and the remarks in this introduction apply to those plays as well.) Although the theater still requires the support, work, and energy of its local community, today's dramatic repertoire is a global one. American playwright Sam Shepard first produced several of his plays in London. British playwright Edward Bond is more widely produced in Germany than in the United Kingdom. Many Eastern Euro-pean and Latin American playwrights have been forced by censorship and political perse-cution to smuggle their plays to Europe or the United States to be staged. South African playwright Athol Fugard has premiered several plays in the United States. Nigerian Wole Soyinka is regularly produced throughout the world. These playwrights are deeply impli-cated in the working of their native cultures, but their plays have rapidly become part of the world repertoire.

The impact of film and television has forced the theater to work to define what kinds of performance are specific to the stage, how live dramatic performances can offer some-thing unique, something not already available in other performance media. For this rea-son, perhaps, theater and drama since 1950 have necessarily been "experimental,"

THEATER IN THE ROUND

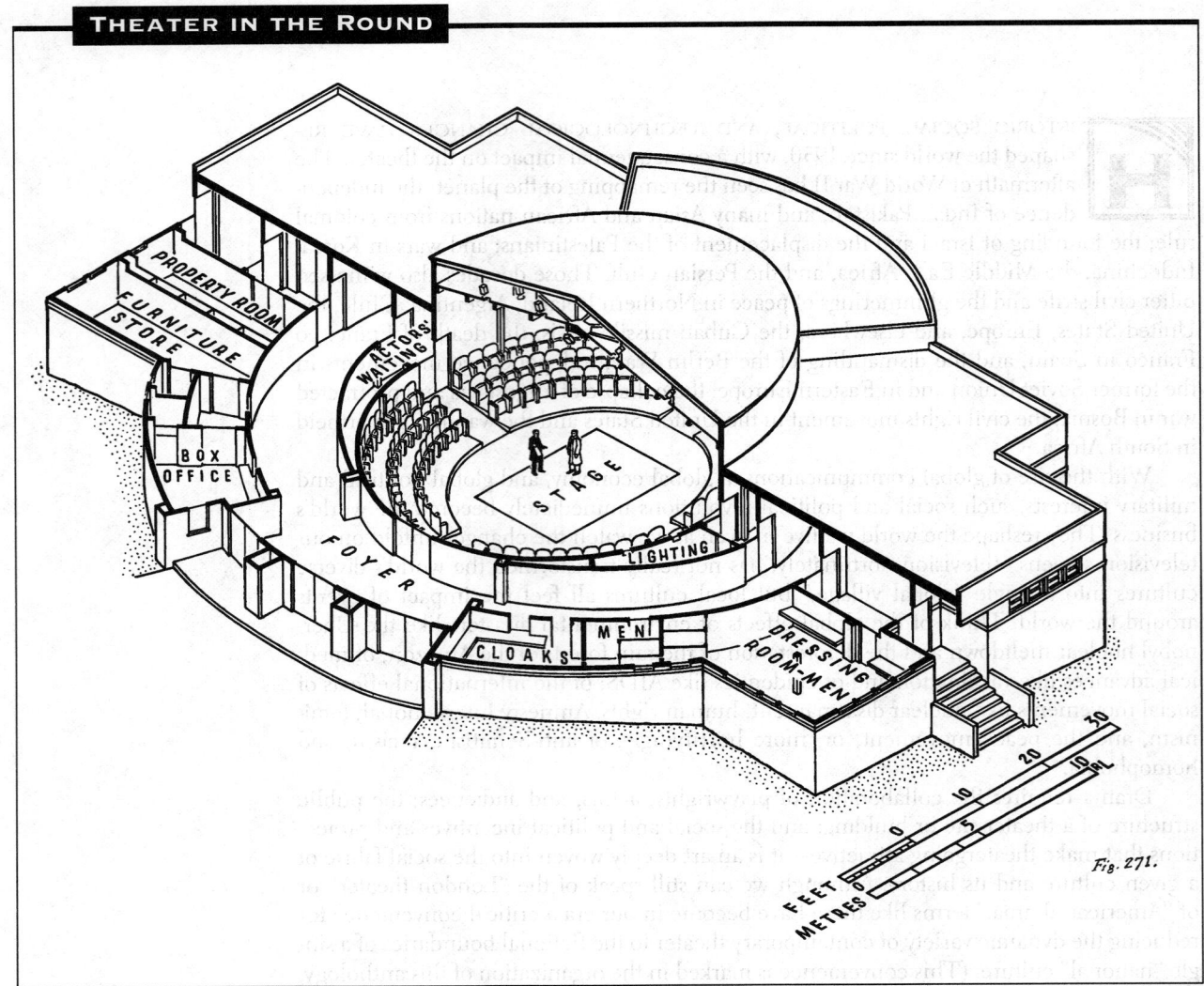

In a theater in the round, the audience surrounds the action, rather than facing the stage as in a proscenium theater. Theater space of this kind lends itself to greater immediacy and contact between the performers and the audience.

working to develop new kinds of plays, new practices of stage production, and new kinds of theatrical experience for their audiences. Much as the proscenium theaters of the early twentieth century have given way to other, more flexible kinds of theater spaces, so dramatic writing has become much more varied and experimental. Even stage realism—the mode of Ibsen and Chekhov, Miller and Williams—has undergone an important reworking in the plays of Sam Shepard, Harold Pinter, Maria Irene Fornes, and others.

Here, we can identify three patterns of innovation as a way of organizing our thinking about the diversity of the contemporary stage. One strategy—inspired most directly by Antonin Artaud's THEATER OF CRUELTY—attacks the notion that the theater is essentially a *representational* medium, emphasizing instead the *experiential* aspect of theater. Rather than staging images of some fictive world to an audience of passive spectators, this kind of theater works to structure the *present experience* of the audience in new ways, as in the participatory and ritualistic theater experiments of the 1960s and 1970s. The influence of Artaud's assault on representation is evident in the contemporary theater in several ways: in absurdist drama, the physicalized "choreopoems" of Ntozake Shange, and the dreamlike visual spectacles of Marguerite Duras, among others.

The second mode of innovation, THEATER OF THE ABSURD, originated as a new form of playwriting rather than as theatrical experimentation. The plays of Samuel Beckett, Slawomir Mrozek, Eugène Ionesco, Boris Vian, Edward Albee, Harold Pinter, and others create a strangely dislocated dramatic world, in which arbitrary or "absurd" events both confront and mystify the characters.

While Artaud inspired an existential or experiential theater, Bertolt Brecht—whose work became widely known and imitated only after World War II—inspired a different kind of assault on the conventions of realistic theater. Contemporary POLITICAL THEATER also criticizes the notion of "representation," but in different terms than Artaud or theater of the absurd, "representation" is a word with two senses; in "representing" a picture of the world, the arts necessarily claim that their images are "representative" in some way. Political theater frequently shows how a social or political order uses its power to "represent" others coercively—for example, by depicting those others through demeaning or limiting stereotypes. For this reason, political theater today is intent on using live performance to change the prejudicial attitudes concealed in conventional ideas of representation.

Of course, no plays fit easily or fully into these three categories, but to think of the drama of the postwar period as raising questions of our existential or our political relation to the theater—and so to the world—provides a useful and powerful way of opening that drama to our understanding. Each of these modes of theater creates a different relationship between the stage and its audience, and we should examine each of them in some detail.

ARTAUD AND THE THEATER OF CRUELTY

The writings of Antonin Artaud, particularly the essays collected in the volume *The Theater and Its Double* (written in the late 1920s and 1930s, published in France in 1938, translated to English in 1958), have had an extraordinary impact on our sense of theater. Like many innovators of his generation—think of Brecht or Pirandello—Artaud worked to undermine the notion that the theater can only show its audiences realistic vignettes of daily life. Instead, Artaud argued that the theater should alter the balance between presentation—the actual, immediate activities of actors and audiences, their *presence* in the theater—and representation, the fictive "drama" that had seemed to define the purpose and scope of theater. Artaud—who used the term *theater of cruelty* for this project—advocated transforming the theater into an all-consuming spectacle, akin both to rituals like the Catholic Mass and to public festivals, in which the boundaries between acting and observing, actor and spectator, fiction and reality, conscious and unconscious would be broken or transgressed. The idea that the theater would "communicate," but not through rational means, is captured in one of Artaud's most powerful metaphors for this nearly unimaginable theater: the plague. Artaud envisioned a theater that would transmit its experiences corporeally, through the body, like disease, like mystical wisdom, alchemically transforming all of its participants. To avoid staging conventional dramas, Artaud called for a theater of "no more masterpieces," one that would use the dramatic text to transform the relations between stage and spectator by making the production a total experience— visual, auditory, gustatory, olfactory, tactile, physical—for the audience.

Stage director Peter Brook once remarked that "Artaud applied is Artaud betrayed," and it is true that Artaud's sense of theater is deeply metaphorical, a kind of theater experience that is almost unimaginable to us, and certainly not imaginable to us as theater. Artaud rarely offers a practical description of how this theater could come into being. Instead, the value and influence of Artaud's writing has been indirect and inspirational, bearing in a variety of tangential ways on kinds of theater that are not in any literal sense "Artaudian." In that Artaud imagines a theater of *presence*—not of representation—involving the audience in an experience rather than showing them a picture, his theater comes into contact with several very different kinds of innovation. Although the American experimental theater of the 1960s and 1970s is the most direct application—and betrayal—of Artaud, Artaud's conception of theater stands distantly behind a variety of more formally constructed plays: the fusion of dance, music, and poetry in Ntozake Shange's work; the dislocating imagery of Beckett and Fornes; perhaps even the ritualized, hallucinatory violence of Pinter's plays. Of course, as *written* plays, "masterpieces," these plays are specifically opposed to the ideals of Artaud's unrealizable theater, while at the same time they explore part of the terrain opened by Artaud's vision.

THEATER OF THE ABSURD

Coined by the theater critic Martin Esslin in 1961, the phrase *theater of the absurd* tries to capture the special irrationality and unpredictability of a certain wave of dramatic writing of the late 1950s and 1960s, including the plays of Samuel Beckett and Harold Pinter, for example. Taking as his keynote Beckett's famous play *Waiting for Godot* (1953)—a play in which two Chaplinesque tramps wait for a mysterious man named Godot, who never arrives—Esslin finds the theater of the absurd to have certain stylistic and thematic characteristics. It rejects the sense of causality found in realistic plays, the sense that it is possible to find the causes for events either in the environment or in the psychological motives of the characters themselves. Instead, theater of the absurd tends to be about a world in which inexplicable, arbitrary, or irrational events happen. Although the events usually seem to be part of some kind of order or scheme, it is an order that the characters and their audience cannot quite grasp. As Hamm says in Beckett's play *Endgame*, "Something is taking its course," but neither the characters nor the audience are ever sure what that "something" is. In Eugène Ionesco's play *Rhinoceros* (1960), the inhabitants of a small French village begin to turn inexplicably into rhinoceroses. In each act of Boris Vian's *The Empire Builders* (1959), a family moves to a smaller room in an apartment building, always accompanied by a mysterious, bandaged figure. In Slawomir Mrozek's *Striptease* (1961), two men are commanded by a huge, silent finger to remove their clothes and don huge conical hats that conceal and blind them. As Esslin suggests, this drama insists that the fictions we use to make sense of our world—ideas of order, causality, rationality—are just that: fictions imposed on an arbitrary and mysterious reality, whose meanings remain fugitive and elusive.

Absurdist drama treats its audience somewhat differently than realistic plays do, rejecting the "dramatic irony" of the traditional theater, in which the audience understands more than the characters onstage. Instead, the theater of the absurd refuses to provide this privilege to its spectators. We are as baffled and frustrated by our attempts to make the events mean something as the characters are; "Mean something!" a character remarks in *Endgame*, "You and I, mean something! (*Brief laugh*)." Our *present* experience as an audience is structured and made significant by absurdist theatrical production. In the theater, we don't just observe the "absurd" drama onstage, we are forced to undergo it, to live it through. For this reason, both the drama onstage and the audience's experience in the theater are sometimes described as *existential*. We have to *decide* the meaning of our being in the theater, without the comfort, solace, or guidance of some transcendent, predetermined worldview.

POLITICAL THEATER

Much as theater of the absurd works to make the spectators' situation in the theater an extension of the characters' situation on the stage, political theater since Brecht has worked to make the audience's performance in the theater a recognizably political one. By fragmenting the stage space, by showing how the illusion is made rather than concealing its means of production, and by involving the audience more overtly in deciding the meaning of the play's events, the theater is shown to be a political instrument. Like television, newspapers, universities, the courts, and so on, the theater is an institution that produces the ideas and images with which we govern our lives. Both the example of Brecht's plays and his challenging theory of performance have been absorbed and redefined by the world theater. In common with theater of the absurd, political theater works to resist and complicate realistic representation, the "slice of life" of Ibsen, Chekhov, and Miller. Instead of staging an arbitrarily unreal and absurd world, political theater examines "representative" images of reality. Who makes those images? Who benefits from them? Who is injured, governed, or oppressed by them? How do they help to maintain the social *status quo?*

For this reason, much political theater connects representation onstage with representation in society, showing how various social groups—women, gay men, lesbians, ethnic and racial groups, the poor—have been staged in society and in the theater. A fundamental assumption of political theater is that these stereotypes are part of the larger system of discrimination that operates in society, and that they reveal the dominant attitudes of those who govern, control, or influence society from positions of power. In plays like Amiri Baraka's *Dutchman*, Ntozake Shange's *spell #7*, and Wole Soyinka's *Death and the King's Horseman*, the racial conflicts informing contemporary society and culture are explored in very different ways: in relation to colonialism, to white myths of black identity, to women's experience. These plays are very different in style, ranging from a kind of realism in *Death and the King's Horseman* to Genet's ritualized spectacle. It is not a single point of view or a single dramatic style that defines political theater, but the use of theatrical representation itself as a way to analyze representation in society at large.

A similar approach to theater informs many of the modern plays gathered in this anthology, for many of them explore the issue of representation: how Asia is represented in the minds of the West in David Henry Hwang's *M. Butterfly*, how the English remapped and so represented the Irish in their own language and political system in Brian Friel's *Translations*, how African tribal traditions are tragically misunderstood by British imperialists in Wole Soyinka's *Death and the King's Horseman*, how the Chicano and Anglo cultures interact in Luis Valdez's *Los Vendidos*, how patriarchy assaults women in Maria Irene Fornes's *Fefu and Her Friends*. Political theater sometimes seems highly message oriented, overtly didactic to readers and audiences used to the more subtle instruction offered by realistic plays. Yet the messages of contemporary political theater tend to be fused into the process of theater, so that the politics of the play come into being not in the prepared script of the play but in our experience as an audience. All of these plays disrupt the expectations, attitudes, and preconceptions of the empowered audience and invite the audience to develop different ways of reading their society as part of their involvement in the play.

On the contemporary stage, though, these modes of theater do not work in isolation from one another, but interact with one another, as part of the dynamic means the theater uses to engage its audiences in an understanding of the world. Indeed, to describe the contemporary theater in terms of its historical inheritance from the modernist theater of Brecht, Artaud, and the absurdists is in an important sense to overlook what is most significant about the stage today: its break from the traditions of modernism. If we look at the range of contemporary performance activity, much of it has little to do with traditional drama. Think of the performance-art monologues of Spalding Gray (one of his best-known, *Swimming to Cambodia*, was made into a film by Jonathan Demme) or Karen Finley (whose work was at the center of the 1990 censorship controversy at the National Endowment for the Arts); of the music of Laurie Anderson; of video art and film; of music television and advertising; of the disorienting stage spectacles of Robert Wilson; even of "plays" like Peter Handke's *Offending the Audience* and *The Ride Across Lake Constance*, or

DRAMA, THEATER, AND THE "POST- MODERN"

Since the mid 1960s, a variety of non-dramatic performance modes have developed in Western theater that are commonly known by the generic label of "performance art." Although it is difficult to generalize about this wide range of performances, most performance art works share certain features: many (though certainly not all) are solo works, in which a performer (or performers) relates directly to an audience; although the performer(s) may be working from a plan or script, the performance is not a traditional "drama," enacting a fictitious narrative of the deeds of a fictitious "character" through "acting." Instead, in performance art, the performer uses a variety of means—monologue, physical performance, music, dance—to produce a spectacle that is "really happening" between him/herself and the spectators.

Many performance-art works of the 1970s and 1980s used the performers' bodies to explore the limits of "theater." Chris Burden, for example, staged several events in which he wounded himself before an audience: in one 1970 work, he shot himself in the arm with a pistol; in another, he was crucified on top of a Volkswagen. In one of Carolee Schneeman's works, she unwinds a long scroll from her vagina, reading it to the audience. Annie Sprinkle, once a pornographic film star, openly objectifies her body onstage for a visible audience of men (and women), as she had once done in the more covert and coercive scene of pornography; in one performance, she invites the audience onstage while she conducts her own vaginal examination. Many performance art works take place outside theatrical venues, so that the performance becomes part of the everyday "performance" of street life. Linda Montano spent

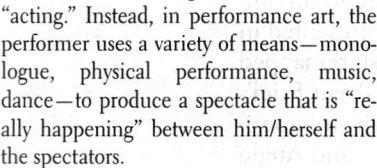

(ASIDE)

PERFORMANCE ART

one year connected by a short rope to Teching Tsieh; the artists' lack of privacy was constantly on display in the streets of New York. In one of her early performances, Laurie Anderson stood in a large block of ice on a New York City street, playing her violin until the ice melted.

Several performance artists have become well-known for their monologue-performances, which range widely in technique and strategy. Anna Deavere Smith's works—such as *Fires in the Mirror: Crown Heights, Brooklyn, and Other Identities* and *Twilight—Los Angeles, 1992*—differ from many performance art monologues in that Smith impersonates and represents a range of speakers; yet both in the brilliance of her individual performance, and in her effort to perform the speakers faithfully (rather than "act" them in a theatrical sense), Smith's work touches on the "authentic" aspect of performance art. This emphasis on the "authentic," the "real," enables several performance artists to explore the relationship between identity politics and performance. In *Memory Tricks*, Marga Gomez, daughter of a Cuban theater impresario and a Puerto Rican "exotic dancer," recalls her family and childhood to interrogate the formation of Latina identity in the United States. David Drake's *The Night Larry Kramer Kissed Me* dramatizes the performer's understanding and exploration of his gay sexuality from the time of his sixth birthday, on the night of the 1969 Stonewall Riots in New York's Greenwich Village—in which gay men and lesbians protested abusive treatment by the police—through the AIDS crisis of the 1980s and 1990s.

Many artists use performance to foreground and criticize the everyday racist, sexist, and/or homophobic "performance" commonly accepted as "normal behavior"

in U.S. society, and to bring into view other ways of performing identity. Adrian Piper, a light-skinned African-American woman, sometimes hands out business cards to people who "ignore" her race:

"I am black. I am sure that you did not realize this when you made/laughed at/agreed with that racist remark. In the past, I have attempted to alert white people to my racial identity in advance. Unfortunately, this invariably causes them to react to me as pushy, manipulative, or socially inappropriate. Therefore, my policy is to assume that white people do not make these remarks, even when they believe there are no black people present, and to distribute this card when they do. I regret any discomfort my presence is causing you, just as I am sure you regret the discomfort your racism is causing me."

Lesbian playwright Holly Hughes had written several plays—notably *The Well of Horniness*, *The Lady Dick*, and *Dress Suits for Hire*, which was performed by Peggy Shaw and Lois Weaver at the WOW Cafe—before developing her well-known performance piece *World Without End* in 1989. In *My Queer Body*, Tim Miller narrates the history of his sexual experience and the formation of his identity as a gay man; he undresses during the performance and performs part of *My Queer Body* in the nude, sometimes moving about the audience. Karen Finley's performances often express her outrage at the implicit and explicit violence against women in American culture; in monologues like *Constant State of Desire* and *We Keep Our Victims Ready*, she uses her body to enact and physicalize the "obscenity" of such violence. In a section of *We Keep Our Victims Ready* entitled "St. Valentine's Massacre," Finley examines the way patriarchal culture encodes a subtle hatred of women, one that women can self-destructively internalize. In performance, while Finley monologues, "My life is worth nothing but shit," she smears her naked body with chocolate pudding and studs it with sperm-like bean sprouts, a stunning and physical image of the sexualization of violence; as the performance continues, though, she layers herself with tinsel and red candies, transforming her abjection into a strange beauty. Such performances purposefully transgress the boundaries of decorous social behavior, in part to dramatize the kind of oppression that lurks in "everyday" performance. By all accounts, audiences who have seen Finley's or Miller's performances have found them powerful and moving; but to some critics (who often proudly claim that they have not seen the performance), such performance verges on "obscenity." In 1990, conservative politicians led by Senator Jesse Helms (R-North Carolina) pressured the National Endowment for the Arts to withdraw funding from four performance artists who had been recommended by the peer-review process for support. Not only were Tim Miller, Karen Finley, Holly Hughes, and John Fleck denied funding, but the Endowment's head John Frohnmayer subsequently resigned, and a "general standards of decency" restriction of dubious constitutionality was required of subsequent recipients of NEA support.

Perhaps the best-known autobiographical performer, however, is Spalding Gray. Gray began his career with The Performance Group, an avant-garde company working with **ENVIRONMENTAL THEATER** in the late 1960s and 1970s. With Elizabeth LeCompte and other members of the Group, Gray collaborated on a series of performances, collectively called *The Rhode Island Trilogy—Sakonnet Point* (1975), *Rumstick Road* (1977), and *Nyatt School* (1978), followed by an epilogue, *Point Judith* (1979). The Performance Group was committed to authentic "performance" (in which the actors behave as themselves, rather than "acting" in a theatrical sense), and Gray found a sequence of *Rumstick Road*—in which he narrated events of his life to the audience—to be a particularly fertile ground for continued exploration. In the course of the next several years, Gray developed a series of auto-

PERFORMANCE ART

Anna Deavere Smith portrays Angela King at the world premier of Smith's Twilight—Los Angeles, 1992.

biographical performances. In some of these works, Gray structures a certain degree of randomness in the performance: in *India and After (America)* (1979), for example, he randomly chooses words from a dictionary to key part of his monologue; in *A Personal History of the American Theatre* (1980), he shuffles a collection of index cards with play titles on them and uses the series to direct his performance. Gray's more recent work has been made into films, and so has become known to a wider audience. The film versions of *Swimming to Cambodia* (1984) and *Monster in a Box* (1990) preserve much of the ambience of Gray's performance. In the opening sequence of *Swimming to Cambodia*, for example, we see Gray

walking through the streets of the Village, entering the Performance Garage, seating himself onstage at a long table, and opening the notebook that seems to provide the score for his performance. Gray addresses the camera and, as in his stage performances, seems to occupy a startling and fascinating middle ground between acting and being: he is clearly shaping the story, representing and constructing the narrative of his life as a kind of fiction, while at the same time claiming that quasi-fictive narrative as his own, as himself. Like other postmodern artforms, performance art evocatively explores the edge between representation and "reality," refusing to demarcate a fixed difference between them.

Heiner Müller's *Hamletmachine,* or Samuel Beckett's later work for the theater, *Not I, Footfalls,* and *Ohio Impromptu.*

Theorists of culture and the arts have related these developments to innovations in the visual arts, in architecture, and in writing, characterizing their common features as POSTMODERN. The term itself is a difficult one, suggesting that these works often share some of the features of earlier, "modernist" art; the literary and cultural theorist Fredric Jameson suggests that the distinguishing feature of postmodern art is its attitude toward history. Jameson points out that postmodern works frequently invoke or appropriate the style of earlier historical periods, as in the use of neoclassical ornamentation in recent architecture, or the recollection of earlier film styles in more recent movies (FILM NOIR in *Chinatown* or *Dead Again*). Jameson labels this technique PASTICHE. What is striking about these postmodern quotations of style, though, is not any systematic reinterpretation of tradition or any statement of value, but their tonelessness, their neutrality, the absence of the kind of moral and historical sense we might expect from the act of confronting history. In postmodern pastiche, the recollection of an earlier style does not provide a new understanding of the past, nor does it illuminate our contemporary historical situation. Instead, pastiche denatures that style by removing it from history, and history from it. Style becomes exactly that: simply another option. Hamm's many quotations from English literature in *Endgame,* the pastiche of Gilbert-and-Sullivan operetta in Churchill's *Cloud Nine,* and even the American domestic-drama setting of Fornes's *Fefu and Her Friends* are perhaps part of this complex problem, for in each case the "past" is presented to the audience in terms of an artistic style that is largely emptied of its force as history.

Moreover, Jameson's discussion of pastiche also emphasizes the importance of the esthetic *surface* in postmodern art. Music video and advertising are sometimes taken as the paradigmatic postmodern forms, forms whose "message" lies almost exclusively in a rapidly changing, brilliantly seductive, series of images. Although this technique relates to the modernist use of MONTAGE in film and theater, it is different in several important ways. Modernist montage uses a series of images narratively, to tell a story. Although the camera cuts quickly from image to image, the audience assembles the images in a single complete narrative. Both the narrative and the interpreting spectator achieve a sense of wholeness. In contrast, postmodern images are juxtaposed in striking, sometimes contradictory combinations that resist our ability to impose a single narrative explanation, a single story line. Postmodern performance—on film or video or in the theater—is insistently fragmentary; it asserts the incompletion of the artistic object and the incomplete quality of the spectator's experience as well. Postmodern arts resist imposing a single explanatory interpretation that would both complete the narrative and confirm the audience's sense of wholeness, of self-integration. In this sense, postmodern arts are sometimes described as concerned with the "death of the subject." They question the possibility both of a comprehensible world and of a comprehending individual. By disorienting language, fragmenting narrative, and dispensing with such organizing principles as "plot" and "character," postmodern art claims that we have entered a new age in which the complex disconnections of modern culture have made obsolete many of our beliefs about the world and our ways of representing the world and ourselves.

This photograph captures the suffocating emptiness of the room in Samuel Beckett's Endgame; *here, Hamm takes his tour around the room with Clov.*

This scene from Tomson Highway's Dry Lips Oughta Move to Kapuskasing *shows how a few props can be used to establish an environment — here, Spooky Lacroix's house.*

This scene from Act 1 of Caryl Churchill's Cloud 9 *shows Churchill's use of cross-dressing: Betty (left) is played by a man, and Edward (downstage center in his Victorian sailor suit) is played by a woman.*

■ SAMUEL BECKETT ■

Samuel Beckett (1906–1989) is the most influential European dramatist of the postwar period. Born near Dublin, Ireland, Beckett was educated at Trinity College, Dublin, where he studied modern languages. Taking his B.A. in 1928, Beckett received an appointment as *lecteur* at l'École Normale Supérieure in Paris. While in Paris, Beckett met the Irish novelist James Joyce. Beckett assisted Joyce (who was nearly blind) in a variety of ways and became a close friend. Joyce also exerted a profound influence on Beckett's writing. In 1929, Beckett contributed an essay entitled "Dante . . . Bruno . Vico . . Joyce" to a volume on Joyce's *Finnegans Wake*. Throughout the 1930s, Beckett was associated with Joyce and with a variety of avant-garde movements in Paris. He wrote a series of poems—including the prize-winning "Whoroscope"—as well as a study of Proust (1931), the volume of short stories *More Pricks than Kicks* (1934), and the novel *Murphy* (1938). Although Beckett returned briefly to Ireland on a few occasions, he had settled permanently in Paris. During World War II, Beckett served in the French Resistance. He was discovered by the Nazis and forced to flee Paris in 1942. He worked in the unoccupied zone of southern France for the remainder of the war, where he wrote the novel *Watt* (1953). After the war, Beckett received the Croix de Guerre and the Médaille de la Résistance for his services. He began to write exclusively in French, starting work on a major trilogy of novels—*Molloy* (1951), *Malone Dies* (1951), and *The Unnameable* (1953).

Beckett had experimented with drama during the 1930s and 1940s, but his first staged play, *Waiting for Godot* (also written in French, as *En attendant Godot*), produced at the tiny Théâtre de Babylone in January of 1953, impelled him in a new direction. Although Beckett continued to write fiction—including *From an Abandoned Work* (1956), *How It Is* (1964), *Imagination Dead Imagine* (1965), and *Company* (1979)—his major writing of the 1960s, 1970s, and 1980s was for the theater. His second play, *Endgame*, also written in French, was produced in 1957 and was followed by a series of challenging works for the stage: *Krapp's Last Tape* (1958), *Happy Days* (1962), *Play* (1963), *Not I* (1972), *Footfalls* (1975), *Rockaby* (1981), and *Catastrophe* (1982). For his extraordinarily diverse and influential body of work, Beckett won the Nobel Prize for Literature in 1970. Beckett also wrote several plays for radio and television, as well as a film starring Buster Keaton, *Film* (1965). Beginning in the mid-1960s, Beckett directed productions of his plays, and several productions he directed in France and in Germany now have the status of classics—something like Elia Kazan's productions of Tennessee Williams's plays, or Stanislavsky's productions of Chekhov.

Beckett's impact on the contemporary theater can hardly be overestimated and can be seen in the work of Sam Shepard, Maria Irene Fornes, Harold Pinter, and many others. *Waiting for Godot* signaled new possibilities for stage action—or inaction—and developed the implications of Chekhov's static stage in a more symbolic direction. Each of Beckett's plays explores the nature and limitations of its medium in new and challenging ways. *Endgame* refigures the claustral box of realistic drama, for its characters are trapped in a room of endless—or possibly ending—routine. In *Play*, Beckett puts three urns onstage, from which three heads emerge to deliver, more or less simultaneously, a jarring, repetitive monologue of seduction and betrayal. Once the play has finished, Beckett directs his performers—and his audience—to "Repeat play," and so calls the relationship between actors and spectators, theater and reality into question: If we cannot leave the theater when the play is over, is it possible that there is no way out of the purgatory on the stage and in the auditorium? This sense that the self is always in flight is the theme of several of Beckett's later plays. In *Not I*, for instance, all that the audience sees is a Mouth eight feet above the stage, reciting an endless narrative in which she avoids claiming the speech as her own. In *Ohio Impromptu* (1981), an identical reader and listener relate a painful narrative of loss, in which it is unclear whether they are two individuals or parts of a single person. The power of Beckett's spare, minimalist theater, the beauty of his sculptural use of actors and stage space, and the harsh exigency of the action of his plays have transformed the stage of our time.

ENDGAME

Endgame is Beckett's second full-length play to reach the stage; although its simplicity and repetitiveness are in some ways reminiscent of *Waiting for Godot*, the tone of *Endgame* is bleaker, harsher.

As Beckett wrote to Alan Schneider, the play's first American director, *Endgame*'s power is "the power of the text to claw."

The "endgame" of a chess match is the final portion of the game, at which either a checkmate or a stalemate has become inevitable. In *Endgame*, Beckett literalizes the uncertainty of the endgame—will the tortuous nothingness of the characters' lives continue indefinitely, move after move, or will it somehow end? Although some critics have taken the "shelter" and the empty landscape outside as an indication that the play takes place in a bomb shelter after a nuclear bombing, *Endgame* seems to present a microcosm of postmodern life, in which the futile search for fugitive "meanings" raises the despairing feeling that our lives are meaningless, "absurd" after all. Hamm is a kind of ham actor and recalls Shakespeare's Richard III ("My kingdom for a nightman") and Prospero ("Our revels now are ended"), as well as perhaps King Lear and Hamlet in his performance. Hamm is perhaps the first **POSTMODERN** dramatic hero, less a full "character" than a pastiche of dramatic roles and possibilities, which exist now only in bits and pieces, recollected fragments (on *pastiche*, see Fredric Jameson's essay). Hamm's blindness also recalls both Oedipus—who also struggled with his father—and Ham the son of Noah, who was blinded when he saw his father naked. Hamm continually reminds us that his performance—it's full of asides, a "last soliloquy," and many self-regarding comments on Hamm's success or failure—is an attempt to impose meaning on the process of the play's action. This recollection of the dramatic and literary tradition also points to the problematic place—or absence—of history in *Endgame*. If there is a kind of past ("Once!") in *Endgame*, it is recalled most clearly by Hamm's parents. Nagg and Nell, legless in their garbage cans, describe an earlier, more sentimental or romantic era, when couples rode tandems in the Ardennes and rowed on Lake Como. Overall, though, time seems to be an endless present moment in *Endgame*, a moment disconnected from the past that once gave it meaning, and from the future which gave it closure. It may be that the play is post-nuclear (though Beckett's draft manuscripts suggest that the inspiration was really a war hospital), but this setting is less important than the sense of time that this tiny world contains. For *Endgame* is finally about time and its passing, the painfully slow passage of moment to moment, and its finality once it is past.

Endgame was originally written in French as *Fin de partie*, and was rewritten into English by Beckett himself; there are several small differences in dialogue and action between the two versions.

ENDGAME

Samuel Beckett

— CHARACTERS —

NAGG	HAMM
NELL	CLOV

Bare interior.

Grey light.

Left and right back, high up, two small windows, curtains drawn.

Front right, a door. Hanging near door, its face to wall, a picture.

Front left, touching each other, covered with an old sheet, two ashbins.

Center, in an armchair on castors, covered with an old sheet, HAMM.

Motionless by the door, his eyes fixed on HAMM, CLOV. *Very red face.*

Brief tableau.

(CLOV *goes and stands under window left. Stiff, staggering walk. He looks up at window left. He turns and looks at window right. He goes and stands under window right. He looks up at window right. He turns and looks at window left. He goes out, comes back immediately with a small step-ladder, carries it over and sets it down under window left, gets up on it, draws back curtain. He gets down, takes six steps [for example] towards window right, goes back for ladder, carries it over and sets it down under window right, gets up on it, draws back curtain. He gets down, takes three steps towards window left, goes back for ladder, carries it over and sets it down under window left, gets up on it, looks out of window. Brief laugh. He gets down, takes one step towards window right, goes back for ladder, carries it over and sets it down under window right, gets up on it, looks out of window. Brief laugh. He gets down, goes with ladder towards ashbins, halts, turns, carries back ladder and sets it down under window right, goes to ashbins, removes sheet covering them, folds it over his arm. He raises one lid, stoops and looks into bin. Brief laugh. He closes lid. Same with other bin. He goes to* HAMM, *removes sheet covering him, folds it over his arm. In a dressing-gown, a stiff toque on his head, a large blood-stained handkerchief over his face, a whistle hanging from his neck, a rug over his knees, thick socks on his feet,* HAMM *seems to be asleep.* CLOV *looks him over. Brief laugh. He goes to door, halts, turns towards auditorium.*)

CLOV: (*Fixed gaze, tonelessly.*) Finished, it's finished, nearly finished, it must be nearly finished.

(*Pause.*)

Grain upon grain, one by one, and one day, suddenly, there's 5 a heap, a little heap, the impossible heap.

(*Pause.*)

I can't be punished any more.

(*Pause.*)

I'll go now to my kitchen, ten feet by ten feet by ten feet, and 10 wait for him to whistle me.

(*Pause.*)

Nice dimensions, nice proportions, I'll lean on the table, and look at the wall, and wait for him to whistle me.

(*He remains a moment motionless, then goes out. He comes back immediately, goes to window right, takes up the ladder and carries it out. Pause.* HAMM *stirs. He yawns under the handkerchief. He removes the handkerchief from his face. Very red face. Black glasses.*)

HAMM: Me—

(*He yawns.*) 15

—to play.

(*He holds the handkerchief spread out before him.*)

Old stancher!

(*He takes off his glasses, wipes his eyes, his face, the glasses, puts* 20 *them on again, folds the handkerchief and puts it back neatly in the breast-pocket of his dressing-gown. He clears his throat, joins the tips of his fingers.*)

Can there be misery—

(*He yawns.*)

—loftier than mine? No doubt. Formerly. But now? 25

(*Pause.*)

My father?

(*Pause.*)

My mother?

(*Pause.*) 30

My . . . dog?

(*Pause.*)

Oh I am willing to believe they suffer as much as such creatures can suffer. But does that mean their sufferings equal mine? No doubt. 35

(*Pause.*)

No, all is a—

(*He yawns.*)

—bsolute,

(*Proudly.*) 40

the bigger a man is the fuller he is.

(*Pause. Gloomily.*)

And the emptier.

(*He sniffs.*)

Clov! 45

(*Pause.*)

No, alone.

(*Pause.*)

What dreams! Those forests!

(*Pause.*) 50

Enough, it's time it ended, in the shelter too.

(*Pause.*)

And yet I hesitate, I hesitate to . . . to end. Yes, there it is, it's time it ended and yet I hesitate to—

55 *(He yawns.)*
  —to end.
(Yawns.)
  God, I'm tired, I'd be better off in bed.
(He whistles. Enter CLOV *immediately. He halts beside the*
60 *chair.)*
  You pollute the air!
(Pause.)
  Get me ready, I'm going to bed.
CLOV: I've just got you up.
65 HAMM: And what of it?
CLOV: I can't be getting you up and putting you to bed every
  five minutes, I have things to do.
(Pause.)
HAMM: Did you ever see my eyes?
70 CLOV: No.
HAMM: Did you never have the curiosity, while I was sleeping,
  to take off my glasses and look at my eyes?
CLOV: Pulling back the lids?
(Pause.)
75 No.
HAMM: One of these days I'll show them to you.
(Pause.)
  It seems they've gone all white.
(Pause.)
80 What time is it?
CLOV: The same as usual.
HAMM: *(Gesture towards window right.)* Have you looked?
CLOV: Yes.
HAMM: Well?
85 CLOV: Zero.
HAMM: It'd need to rain.
CLOV: It won't rain.

(Pause.)

HAMM: Apart from that, how do you feel?
CLOV: I don't complain.
90 HAMM: You feel normal?
CLOV: *(Irritably.)* I tell you I don't complain.
HAMM: I feel a little queer.
(Pause.)
  Clov!
95 CLOV: Yes.
HAMM: Have you not had enough?
CLOV: Yes!
(Pause.)
  Of what?
100 HAMM: Of this . . . this . . . thing.
CLOV: I always had.
(Pause.)
  Not you?
HAMM: *(Gloomily.)* Then there's no reason for it to change.
105 CLOV: It may end.
(Pause.)
  All life long the same questions, the same answers.
HAMM: Get me ready.
(CLOV does not move.)
110 Go and get the sheet.
(CLOV does not move.)
  Clov!
CLOV: Yes.

HAMM: I'll give you nothing more to eat.
CLOV: Then we'll die. 115
HAMM: I'll give you just enough to keep you from dying. You'll
  be hungry all the time.
CLOV: Then we won't die.
(Pause.)
  I'll go and get the sheet. 120

(He goes towards the door.)

HAMM: No!
(CLOV halts.)
  I'll give you one biscuit per day.
(Pause.)
  One and a half. 125
(Pause.)
  Why do you stay with me?
CLOV: Why do you keep me?
HAMM: There's no one else.
CLOV: There's nowhere else. 130

(Pause.)

HAMM: You're leaving me all the same.
CLOV: I'm trying.
HAMM: You don't love me.
CLOV: No.
HAMM: You loved me once. 135
CLOV: Once!
HAMM: I've made you suffer too much.
(Pause.)
  Haven't I?
CLOV: It's not that. 140
HAMM: *(Shocked.)* I haven't made you suffer too much?
CLOV: Yes!
HAMM: *(Relieved.)* Ah you gave me a fright!
(Pause. Coldly.)
  Forgive me. 145
(Pause. Louder.)
  I said, Forgive me.
CLOV: I heard you.
(Pause.)
  Have you bled? 150
HAMM: Less.
(Pause.)
  Is it not time for my pain-killer?
CLOV: No.
(Pause.) 155
HAMM: How are your eyes?
CLOV: Bad.
HAMM: How are your legs?
CLOV: Bad.
HAMM: But you can move. 160
CLOV: Yes.
HAMM: *(Violently.)* Then move!
*(CLOV goes to back wall, leans against it with his forehead and
hands.)*
  Where are you? 165
CLOV: Here.
HAMM: Come back!
(CLOV returns to his place beside the chair.)
  Where are you?
CLOV: Here. 170

HAMM: Why don't you kill me?

CLOV: I don't know the combination of the cupboard.

(Pause.)

HAMM: Go and get two bicycle-wheels.

175 CLOV: There are no more bicycle-wheels.

HAMM: What have you done with your bicycle?

CLOV: I never had a bicycle.

HAMM: The thing is impossible.

CLOV: When there were still bicycles I wept to have one. I
180   crawled at your feet. You told me to go to hell. Now there are
    none.

HAMM: And your rounds? When you inspected my paupers.
    Always on foot?

CLOV: Sometimes on horse.

185 *(The lid of one of the bins lifts and the hands of* NAGG *appear,
gripping the rim. Then his head emerges. Nightcap. Very white
face.* NAGG *yawns, then listens.)*

    I'll leave you, I have things to do.

HAMM: In your kitchen?

190 CLOV: Yes.

HAMM: Outside of here it's death.

(Pause.)

    All right, be off.

(Exit CLOV. *Pause.)*

195   We're getting on.

NAGG: Me pap!

HAMM: Accursed progenitor!

NAGG: Me pap!

HAMM: The old folks at home! No decency left! Guzzle, guz-
200   zle, that's all they think of.

(He whistles. Enter CLOV. *He halts beside the chair.)*

    Well! I thought you were leaving me.

CLOV: Oh not just yet, not just yet.

NAGG: Me pap!

205 HAMM: Give him his pap.

CLOV: There's no more pap.

HAMM: *(To* NAGG.*)* Do you hear that? There's no more pap.
    You'll never get any more pap.

NAGG: I want me pap!

210 HAMM: Give him a biscuit.

(Exit CLOV.*)*

    Accursed fornicator! How are your stumps?

NAGG: Never mind me stumps.

(Enter CLOV *with biscuit.)*

215 CLOV: I'm back again, with the biscuit.

(He gives biscuit to NAGG *who fingers it, sniffs it.)*

NAGG: *(Plaintively.)* What is it?

CLOV: Spratt's medium.

NAGG: *(As before.)* It's hard! I can't!

220 HAMM: Bottle him!

*(*CLOV *pushes* NAGG *back into the bin, closes the lid.)*

CLOV: *(Returning to his place beside the chair.)* If age but
    knew!

HAMM: Sit on him!

225 CLOV: I can't sit.

HAMM: True. And I can't stand.

CLOV: So it is.

HAMM: Every man his speciality.

(Pause.)

230   No phone calls?

(Pause.)

Don't we laugh?

CLOV: *(After reflection.)* I don't feel like it.

HAMM: *(After reflection.)* Nor I.

(Pause.)   235

    Clov!

CLOV: Yes.

HAMM: Nature has forgotten us.

CLOV: There's no more nature.

HAMM: No more nature! You exaggerate.   240

CLOV: In the vicinity.

HAMM: But we breathe, we change! We lose our hair, our
    teeth! Our bloom! Our ideals!

CLOV: Then she hasn't forgotten us.

HAMM: But you say there is none.   245

CLOV: *(Sadly.)* No one that ever lived ever thought so crooked
    as we.

HAMM: We do what we can.

CLOV: We shouldn't.

(Pause.)

HAMM: You're a bit of all right, aren't you?   250

CLOV: A smithereen.

(Pause.)

HAMM: This is slow work.

(Pause.)

    Is it not time for my pain-killer?   255

CLOV: No.

(Pause.)

    I'll leave you, I have things to do.

HAMM: In your kitchen?

CLOV: Yes.   260

HAMM: What, I'd like to know.

CLOV: I look at the wall.

HAMM: The wall! And what do you see on your wall? Mene,
    mene? Naked bodies?

CLOV: I see my light dying.   265

HAMM: Your light dying! Listen to that! Well, it can die just as
    well here, *your* light. Take a look at me and then come back
    and tell me what you think of *your* light.

(Pause.)

CLOV: You shouldn't speak to me like that.

(Pause.)

HAMM: *(Coldly.)* Forgive me.   270

(Pause. Louder.)

    I said, Forgive me.

CLOV: I heard you.

(The lid of NAGG's *bin lifts. His hands appear, gripping the rim.
Then his head emerges. In his mouth the biscuit. He listens.)*

HAMM: Did your seeds come up?

CLOV: No.   275

HAMM: Did you scratch round them to see if they had sprouted?

CLOV: They haven't sprouted.

HAMM: Perhaps it's still too early.

CLOV: If they were going to sprout they would have sprouted.

(Violently.)   280

    They'll never sprout!

(Pause. NAGG *takes biscuit in his hand.)*

HAMM: This is not much fun.

(Pause.)

285   But that's always the way at the end of the day, isn't it, Clov?
CLOV: Always.
HAMM: It's the end of the day like any other day, isn't it, Clov?
CLOV: Looks like it.
(Pause.)
290 HAMM: *(Anguished.)* What's happening, what's happening?
CLOV: Something is taking its course.
(Pause.)
HAMM: All right, be off.
(He leans back in his chair, remains motionless. CLOV *does not*
295 *move, heaves a great groaning sigh.* HAMM *sits up.)*
    I thought I told you to be off.
CLOV: I'm trying.
(He goes to door, halts.)
    Ever since I was whelped.

(Exit CLOV.*)*

300 HAMM: We're getting on.

(He leans back in his chair, remains motionless. NAGG *knocks on*
the lid of the other bin. Pause. He knocks harder. The lid lifts and
the hands of NELL *appear, gripping the rim. Then her head*
emerges. Lace cap. Very white face.)

NELL: What is it, my pet?
(Pause.)
    Time for love?
NAGG: Were you asleep?
305 NELL: Oh no!
NAGG: Kiss me.
NELL: We can't.
NAGG: Try.
(Their heads strain towards each other, fail to meet, fall apart
310 *again.)*
NELL: Why this farce, day after day?
(Pause.)
NAGG: I've lost me tooth.
NELL: When?
315 NAGG: I had it yesterday.
NELL: *(Elegiac.)* Ah yesterday!
(They turn painfully towards each other.)
NAGG: Can you see me?
NELL: Hardly. And you?
320 NAGG: What?
NELL: Can you see me?
NAGG: Hardly.
NELL: So much the better, so much the better.
NAGG: Don't say that.
325 *(Pause.)*
    Our sight has failed.
NELL: Yes.
(Pause. They turn away from each other.)
NAGG: Can you hear me?
330 NELL: Yes. And you?
NAGG: Yes.
(Pause.)
    Our hearing hasn't failed.
NELL: Our what?
335 NAGG: Our hearing.
NELL: No.
(Pause.)
    Have you anything else to say to me?

NAGG: Do you remember—
NELL: No.   340
NAGG: When we crashed on our tandem and lost our shanks.
(They laugh heartily.)
NELL: It was in the Ardennes.
(They laugh less heartily.)
NAGG: On the road to Sedan.   345
(They laugh still less heartily.)
    Are you cold?
NELL: Yes, perished. And you?
NAGG: *(Pause.)* I'm freezing.
(Pause.)   350
    Do you want to go in?
NELL: Yes.
NAGG: Then go in.
(NELL does not move.)
    Why don't you go in?   355
NELL: I don't know.
(Pause.)
NAGG: Has he changed your sawdust?
NELL: It isn't sawdust.
(Pause. Wearily.)   360
    Can you not be a little accurate, Nagg?
NAGG: Your sand then. It's not important.
NELL: It is important.
(Pause.)
NAGG: It was sawdust once.   365
NELL: Once!
NAGG: And now it's sand.
(Pause.)
    From the shore.
(Pause. Impatiently.)   370
    Now it's sand he fetches from the shore.
NELL: Now it's sand.
NAGG: Has he changed yours?
NELL: No.
NAGG: Nor mine.   375
(Pause.)
    I won't have it!
(Pause. Holding up the biscuit.)
    Do you want a bit?
NELL: No.   380
(Pause.)
    Of what?
NAGG: Biscuit. I've kept you half.
(He looks at the biscuit. Proudly.)
    Three quarters. For you. Here.   385
(He proffers the biscuit.)
    No?
(Pause.)
    Do you not feel well?
HAMM: *(Wearily.)* Quiet, quiet, you're keeping me awake.   390
(Pause.)
    Talk softer.
(Pause.)
    If I could sleep I might make love. I'd go into the woods. My
    eyes would see . . . the sky, the earth. I'd run, run, they   395
    wouldn't catch me.
(Pause.)
    Nature!
(Pause.)

400   There's something dripping in my head.
(Pause.)
    A heart, a heart in my head.
(Pause.)
NAGG: *(Soft.)* Do you hear him? A heart in his head!
405 *(He chuckles cautiously.)*
NELL: One mustn't laugh at those things, Nagg. Why must you always laugh at them?
NAGG: Not so loud!
NELL: *(Without lowering her voice.)* Nothing is funnier than
410   unhappiness, I grant you that. But—
NAGG: *(Shocked.)* Oh!
NELL: Yes, yes, it's the most comical thing in the world. And we laugh, we laugh, with a will, in the beginning. But it's always the same thing. Yes, it's like the funny story we have
415   heard too often, we still find it funny, but we don't laugh any more.
(Pause.)
    Have you anything else to say to me?
NAGG: No.
420 NELL: Are you quite sure?
(Pause.)
    Then I'll leave you.
NAGG: Do you not want your biscuit?
(Pause.)
425   I'll keep it for you.
(Pause.)
    I thought you were going to leave me.
NELL: I am going to leave you.
NAGG: Could you give me a scratch before you go?
430 NELL: No.
(Pause.)
    Where?
NAGG: In the back.
NELL: No.
435 *(Pause.)*
    Rub yourself against the rim.
NAGG: It's lower down. In the hollow.
NELL: What hollow?
NAGG: The hollow!
440 *(Pause.)*
    Could you not?
(Pause.)
    Yesterday you scratched me there.
NELL: *(Elegiac.)* Ah yesterday!
445 NAGG: Could you not?
(Pause.)
    Would you like me to scratch you?
(Pause.)
    Are you crying again?
450 NELL: I was trying.
(Pause.)
HAMM: Perhaps it's a little vein.
(Pause.)
NAGG: What was that he said?
455 NELL: Perhaps it's a little vein.
NAGG: What does that mean?
(Pause.)
    That means nothing.
(Pause.)
460   Will I tell you the story of the tailor?

NELL: No.
(Pause.)
    What for?
NAGG: To cheer you up.
NELL: It's not funny. 465
NAGG: It always made you laugh.
(Pause.)
    The first time I thought you'd die.
NELL: It was on Lake Como.
(Pause.) 470
    One April afternoon.
(Pause.)
    Can you believe it?
NAGG: What?
NELL: That we once went out rowing on Lake Como. 475
(Pause.)
    One April afternoon.
NAGG: We had got engaged the day before.
NELL: Engaged!
NAGG: You were in such fits that we capsized. By rights we 480
    should have been drowned.
NELL: It was because I felt happy.
NAGG: *(Indignant.)* It was not, it was not, it was my story and nothing else. Happy! Don't you laugh at it still? Every time I tell it. Happy! 485
NELL: It was deep, deep. And you could see down to the bottom. So white. So clean.
NAGG: Let me tell it again.
(Raconteur's voice.)
    An Englishman, needing a pair of striped trousers in a hurry 490
for the New Year festivities, goes to his tailor who takes his measurements.
(Tailor's voice.)
    "That's the lot, come back in four days, I'll have it ready."
Good. Four days later. 495
(Tailor's voice.)
    "So sorry, come back in a week, I've made a mess of the seat." Good, that's all right, a neat seat can be very ticklish. A week later.
(Tailor's voice.) 500
    "Frightfully sorry, come back in ten days, I've made a hash of the crotch." Good, can't be helped, a snug crotch is always a teaser. Ten days later.
(Tailor's voice.)
    "Dreadfully sorry, come back in a fortnight, I've made a balls 505
of the fly." Good, at a pinch, a smart fly is a stiff proposition.
(Pause. Normal voice.)
    I never told it worse.
(Pause. Gloomy.)
    I tell this story worse and worse. 510
(Pause. Raconteur's voice.)
    Well, to make it short, the bluebells are blowing and he bal-lockses the buttonholes.
(Customer's voice.)
    "God damn you to hell, Sir, no, it's indecent, there are lim- 515
its! In six days, do you hear me, six days, God made the world. Yes Sir, no less Sir, the WORLD! And you are not bloody well capable of making me a pair of trousers in three months!"
(Tailor's voice, scandalized.) 520
    "But my dear Sir, my dear Sir, look—

(Disdainful gesture, disgustedly.)
—at the world—
(Pause.)
525   and look—
(Loving gesture, proudly.)
—at my TROUSERS!"

(Pause. He looks at NELL *who has remained impassive, her eyes unseeing, breaks into a high forced laugh, cuts it short, pokes his head towards* NELL, *launches his laugh again.)*

HAMM: Silence!
*(*NAGG *starts, cuts short his laugh.)*
530   NELL: You could see down to the bottom.
HAMM: *(Exasperated.)* Have you not finished? Will you never finish?
(With sudden fury.)
Will this never finish?
535   *(*NAGG *disappears into his bin, closes the lid behind him.* NELL *does not move. Frenziedly.)*
My kingdom for a nightman!
(He whistles. Enter CLOV.)
Clear away this muck! Chuck it in the sea!

*(*CLOV *goes to bins, halts.)*

540   NELL: So white.
HAMM: What? What's she blathering about?

*(*CLOV *stoops, takes* NELL's *hand, feels her pulse.)*

NELL: *(To* CLOV.) Desert!

*(*CLOV *lets go her hand, pushes her back in the bin, closes the lid.)*

CLOV: *(Returning to his place beside the chair.)* She has no pulse.
545   HAMM: What was she drivelling about?
CLOV: She told me to go away, into the desert.
HAMM: Damn busybody! Is that all?
CLOV: No.
HAMM: What else?
550   CLOV: I didn't understand.
HAMM: Have you bottled her?
CLOV: Yes.
HAMM: Are they both bottled?
CLOV: Yes.
555   HAMM: Screw down the lids.
*(*CLOV *goes towards door.)*
Time enough.
*(*CLOV *halts.)*
My anger subsides, I'd like to pee.
560   CLOV: *(With alacrity.)* I'll go and get the catheter.
(He goes towards door.)
HAMM: Time enough.
*(*CLOV *halts.)*
Give me my pain-killer.
565   CLOV: It's too soon.
(Pause.)
It's too soon on top of your tonic, it wouldn't act.
HAMM: In the morning they brace you up and in the evening they calm you down. Unless it's the other way round.
570   *(Pause.)*
That old doctor, he's dead naturally?

CLOV: He wasn't old.
HAMM: But he's dead?
CLOV: Naturally.
(Pause.)   575
You ask *me* that?

(Pause.)

HAMM: Take me for a little turn.
*(*CLOV *goes behind the chair and pushes it forward.)*
Not too fast!
*(*CLOV *pushes chair.)*   580
Right round the world!
*(*CLOV *pushes chair.)*
Hug the walls, then back to the center again.
*(*CLOV *pushes chair.)*
I was right in the center, wasn't I?   585
CLOV: *(Pushing.)* Yes.
HAMM: We'd need a proper wheel-chair. With big wheels. Bicycle wheels!
(Pause.)
Are you hugging?   590
CLOV: *(Pushing.)* Yes.
HAMM: *(Groping for wall.)* It's a lie! Why do you lie to me?
CLOV: *(Bearing closer to wall.)* There! There!
HAMM: Stop!
*(*CLOV *stops chair close to back wall.* HAMM *lays his hand*   595
against wall.)
Old wall!
(Pause.)
Beyond is the . . . other hell.
(Pause. Violently.)   600
Closer! Closer! Up against!
CLOV: Take away your hand.
*(*HAMM *withdraws his hand.* CLOV *rams chair against wall.)*
There!
*(*HAMM *leans towards wall, applies his ear to it.)*   605
HAMM: Do you hear?
(He strikes the wall with his knuckles.)
Do you hear? Hollow bricks!
(He strikes again.)
All that's hollow!   610
(Pause. He straightens up. Violently.)
That's enough. Back!
CLOV: We haven't done the round.
HAMM: Back to my place!
*(*CLOV *pushes chair back to center.)*   615
Is that my place?
CLOV: Yes, that's your place.
HAMM: Am I right in the center?
CLOV: I'll measure it.
HAMM: More or less! More or less!   620
CLOV: *(Moving chair slightly.)* There!
HAMM: I'm more or less in the center?
CLOV: I'd say so.
HAMM: You'd say so! Put me right in the center!
CLOV: I'll go and get the tape.   625
HAMM: Roughly! Roughly!
*(*CLOV *moves chair slightly.)*
Bang in the center!
CLOV: There!
(Pause.)   630

HAMM: I feel a little too far to the left.
(CLOV *moves chair slightly.*)
    Now I feel a little too far to the right.
(CLOV *moves chair slightly.*)
635   I feel a little too far forward.
(CLOV *moves chair slightly.*)
    Now I feel a little too far back.
(CLOV *moves chair slightly.*)
    Don't stay there,
640 (*i.e., Behind the chair.*)
    you give me the shivers.
(CLOV *returns to his place beside the chair.*)
CLOV: If I could kill him I'd die happy.
(*Pause.*)
645 HAMM: What's the weather like?
CLOV: As usual.
HAMM: Look at the earth.
CLOV: I've looked.
HAMM: With the glass?
650 CLOV: No need of the glass.
HAMM: Look at it with the glass.
CLOV: I'll go and get the glass.
(*Exit* CLOV.)
HAMM: No need of the glass!
655 (*Enter* CLOV *with telescope.*)
CLOV: I'm back again, with the glass.
(*He goes to window right, looks up at it.*)
    I need the steps.
HAMM: Why? Have you shrunk?
660 (*Exit* CLOV *with telescope.*)
    I don't like that, I don't like that.
(*Enter* CLOV *with ladder, but without telescope.*)
CLOV: I'm back again, with the steps.
(*He sets down ladder under window right, gets up on it, realizes*
665 *he has not the telescope, gets down.*)
    I need the glass.
(*He goes towards door.*)
HAMM: (*Violently.*) But you have the glass!
CLOV: (*Halting, violently.*) No, I haven't the glass!
670 (*Exit* CLOV.)
HAMM: This is deadly.
(*Enter* CLOV *with telescope. He goes towards ladder.*)
CLOV: Things are livening up.
(*He gets up on ladder, raises the telescope, lets it fall.*)
675   I did it on purpose.
(*He gets down, picks up the telescope, turns it on auditorium.*)
    I see . . . a multitude . . . in transports . . . of joy.
(*Pause.*)
    That's what I call a magnifier.
680 (*He lowers the telescope, turns towards* HAMM.)
    Well? Don't we laugh?
HAMM: (*After reflection.*) I don't.
CLOV: (*After reflection.*) Nor I.
(*He gets up on ladder, turns the telescope on the without.*)
685   Let's see.
(*He looks, moving the telescope.*)
    Zero . . .
(*He looks.*)
    . . . zero . . .
690 (*He looks.*)
    . . . and zero.

HAMM: Nothing stirs. All is—
CLOV: Zer—
HAMM: (*Violently.*) Wait till you're spoken to!
(*Normal voice.*)   695
    All is . . . all is . . . all is what?
(*Violently.*)
    All is what?
CLOV: What all is? In a word? Is that what you want to know?
    Just a moment.   700
(*He turns the telescope on the without, looks, lowers the tele-*
scope, turns towards HAMM.)
    Corpsed.
(*Pause.*)
    Well? Content?   705
HAMM: Look at the sea.
CLOV: It's the same.
HAMM: Look at the ocean!

(CLOV *gets down, takes a few steps towards window left, goes*
back for ladder, carries it over and sets it down under window
left, gets up on it, turns the telescope on the without, looks at
length. He starts, lowers the telescope, examines it, turns it again
on the without.)

CLOV: Never seen anything like that!
HAMM: (*Anxious.*) What? A sail? A fin? Smoke?   710
CLOV: (*Looking.*) The light is sunk.
HAMM: (*Relieved.*) Pah! We all knew that.
CLOV: (*Looking.*) There was a bit left.
HAMM: The base.
CLOV: (*Looking.*) Yes.   715
HAMM: And now?
CLOV: (*Looking.*) All gone.
HAMM: No gulls?
CLOV: (*Looking.*) Gulls!
HAMM: And the horizon? Nothing on the horizon?   720
CLOV: (*Lowering the telescope, turning towards* HAMM, *exasper-*
    ated.) What in God's name could there be on the horizon?
(*Pause.*)
HAMM: The waves, how are the waves?
CLOV: The waves?   725
(*He turns the telescope on the waves.*)
    Lead.
HAMM: And the sun?
CLOV: (*Looking.*) Zero.
HAMM: But it should be sinking. Look again.   730
CLOV: (*Looking.*) Damn the sun.
HAMM: Is it night already then?
CLOV: (*Looking.*) No.
HAMM: Then what is it?
CLOV: (*Looking.*) Gray.   735
(*Lowering the telescope, turning towards* HAMM, *louder.*)
    Gray!
(*Pause. Still louder.*)
    GRRAY!
(*Pause. He gets down, approaches* HAMM *from behind, whispers* 740
in his ear.)
HAMM: (*Starting.*) Gray! Did I hear you say gray?
CLOV: Light black. From pole to pole.
HAMM: You exaggerate.
(*Pause.*)   745
    Don't stay there, you give me the shivers.

(CLOV *returns to his place beside the chair.*)
CLOV: Why this farce, day after day?
HAMM: Routine. One never knows.
750 (*Pause.*)
Last night I saw inside my breast. There was a big sore.
CLOV: Pah! You saw your heart.
HAMM: No, it was living.
(*Pause. Anguished.*)
755 Clov!
CLOV: Yes.
HAMM: What's happening?
CLOV: Something is taking its course.
(*Pause.*)
760 HAMM: Clov!
CLOV: (*Impatiently.*) What is it?
HAMM: We're not beginning to . . . to . . . mean something?
CLOV: Mean something! You and I, mean something!
(*Brief laugh.*)
765 Ah that's a good one!
HAMM: I wonder.
(*Pause.*)
Imagine if a rational being came back to earth, wouldn't he be liable to get ideas into his head if he observed us long
770 enough.
(*Voice of rational being.*)
Ah, good, now I see what it is, yes, now I understand what they're at!
(*CLOV starts, drops the telescope and begins to scratch his belly
775 with both hands. Normal voice.*)
And without going so far as that, we ourselves . . .
(*With emotion.*)
. . . we ourselves . . . at certain moments . . .
(*Vehemently.*)
780 To think perhaps it won't all have been for nothing!
CLOV: (*Anguished, scratching himself.*) I have a flea!
HAMM: A flea! Are there still fleas?
CLOV: On me there's one.
(*Scratching.*)
785 Unless it's a crablouse.
HAMM: (*Very perturbed.*) But humanity might start from there all over again! Catch him, for the love of God!
CLOV: I'll go and get the powder.
(*Exit CLOV.*)
790 HAMM: A flea! This is awful! What a day!
(*Enter CLOV with a sprinkling-tin.*)
CLOV: I'm back again, with the insecticide.
HAMM: Let him have it!

(CLOV *loosens the top of his trousers, pulls it forward and shakes powder into the aperture. He stoops, looks, waits, starts, frenziedly shakes more powder, stoops, looks, waits.*)

CLOV: The bastard!
795 HAMM: Did you get him?
CLOV: Looks like it.
(*He drops the tin and adjusts his trousers.*)
Unless he's laying doggo.
HAMM: Laying! Lying you mean. Unless he's *lying* doggo.
800 CLOV: Ah? One says lying? One doesn't say laying?
HAMM: Use your head, can't you. If he was laying we'd be bitched.
CLOV: Ah.

(*Pause.*)
What about that pee?   805
HAMM: I'm having it.
CLOV: Ah that's the spirit, that's the spirit!
(*Pause.*)
HAMM: (*With ardour.*) Let's go from here, the two of us!
South! You can make a raft and the currents will carry us   810
away, far away, to other . . . mammals!
CLOV: God forbid!
HAMM: Alone, I'll embark alone! Get working on that raft immediately. Tomorrow I'll be gone for ever.
CLOV: (*Hastening towards door.*) I'll start straight away.   815
HAMM: Wait!
(CLOV *halts.*)
Will there be sharks, do you think?
CLOV: Sharks? I don't know. If there are there will be.
(*He goes towards door.*)   820
HAMM: Wait!
(CLOV *halts.*)
Is it not yet time for my pain-killer?
CLOV: (*Violently.*) No!
(*He goes towards door.*)   825
HAMM: Wait!
(CLOV *halts.*)
How are your eyes?
CLOV: Bad.
HAMM: But you can see.   830
CLOV: All I want.
HAMM: How are your legs?
CLOV: Bad.
HAMM: But you can walk.
CLOV: I come . . . and go.   835
HAMM: In my house.
(*Pause. With prophetic relish.*)
One day you'll be blind, like me. You'll be sitting there, a speck in the void, in the dark, for ever, like me.
(*Pause.*)   840
One day you'll say to yourself, I'm tired, I'll sit down, and you'll go and sit down. Then you'll say, I'm hungry, I'll get up and get something to eat. But you won't get up. You'll say, I shouldn't have sat down, but since I have I'll sit on a little longer, then I'll get up and get something to eat. But you   845
won't get up and you won't get anything to eat.
(*Pause.*)
You'll look at the wall a while, then you'll say, I'll close my eyes, perhaps have a little sleep, after that I'll feel better, and you'll close them. And when you open them again there'll be   850
no wall any more.
(*Pause.*)
Infinite emptiness will be all around you, all the resurrected dead of all the ages wouldn't fill it, and there you'll be like a little bit of grit in the middle of the steppe.   855
(*Pause.*)
Yes, one day you'll know what it is, you'll be like me, except that you won't have anyone with you, because you won't have had pity on anyone and because there won't be anyone left to have pity on.   860
(*Pause.*)
CLOV: It's not certain.
(*Pause.*)
And there's one thing you forget.

865   HAMM: Ah?

CLOV: I can't sit down.

HAMM: (*Impatiently.*) Well you'll lie down then, what the hell! Or you'll come to a standstill, simply stop and stand still, the way you are now. One day you'll say, I'm tired, I'll stop. What

870   does the attitude matter?

(*Pause.*)

CLOV: So you all want me to leave you.

HAMM: Naturally.

CLOV: Then I'll leave you.

875   HAMM: You can't leave us.

CLOV: Then I won't leave you.

(*Pause.*)

HAMM: Why don't you finish us?

(*Pause.*)

880   I'll tell you the combination of the cupboard if you promise to finish me.

CLOV: I couldn't finish you.

HAMM: Then you won't finish me.

(*Pause.*)

885   CLOV: I'll leave you, I have things to do.

HAMM: Do you remember when you came here?

CLOV: No. Too small, you told me.

HAMM: Do you remember your father.

CLOV: (*Wearily.*) Same answer.

890   (*Pause.*)

You've asked me these questions millions of times.

HAMM: I love the old questions.

(*With fervour.*)

Ah the old questions, the old answers, there's nothing like

895   them!

(*Pause.*)

It was I was a father to you.

CLOV: Yes.

(*He looks at* HAMM *fixedly.*)

900   You were that to me.

HAMM: My house a home for you.

CLOV: Yes.

(*He looks about him.*)

This was that for me.

905   HAMM: (*Proudly.*) But for me,

(*Gesture towards himself.*)

no father. But for Hamm,

(*Gesture towards surroundings.*)

no home.

910   (*Pause.*)

CLOV: I'll leave you.

HAMM: Did you ever think of one thing?

CLOV: Never.

HAMM: That here we're down in a hole.

915   (*Pause.*)

But beyond the hills? Eh? Perhaps it's still green. Eh?

(*Pause.*)

Flora! Pomona!

(*Ecstatically.*)

920   Ceres!

(*Pause.*)

Perhaps you won't need to go very far.

CLOV: I can't go very far.

(*Pause.*)

925   I'll leave you.

HAMM: Is my dog ready?

CLOV: He lacks a leg.

HAMM: Is he silky?

CLOV: He's a kind of Pomeranian.

HAMM: Go and get him.   930

CLOV: He lacks a leg.

HAMM: Go and get him!

(*Exit* CLOV.)

We're getting on.

(*Enter* CLOV *holding by one of its three legs a black toy dog.*)   935

CLOV: Your dogs are here.

(*He hands the dog to* HAMM *who feels it, fondles it.*)

HAMM: He's white, isn't he?

CLOV: Nearly.

HAMM: What do you mean, nearly? Is he white or isn't he?   940

CLOV: He isn't.

(*Pause.*)

HAMM: You've forgotten the sex.

CLOV: (*Vexed.*) But he isn't finished. The sex goes on at the end.   945

(*Pause.*)

HAMM: You haven't put on his ribbon.

CLOV: (*Angrily.*) But he isn't finished, I tell you! First you finish your dog and then you put on his ribbon!

(*Pause.*)   950

HAMM: Can he stand?

CLOV: I don't know.

HAMM: Try.

(*He hands the dog to* CLOV *who places it on the ground.*)

Well?   955

CLOV: Wait!

(*He squats down and tries to get the dog to stand on its three legs, fails, lets it go. The dog falls on its side.*)

HAMM: (*Impatiently.*) Well?

CLOV: He's standing.

HAMM: (*Groping for the dog.*) Where? Where is he?

(CLOV *holds up the dog in a standing position.*)   960

CLOV: There.

(*He takes* HAMM's *hand and guides it towards the dog's head.*)

HAMM: (*His hand on the dog's head.*) Is he gazing at me?

CLOV: Yes.

HAMM: (*Proudly.*) As if he were asking me to take him for a   965
walk?

CLOV: If you like.

HAMM: (*As before.*) Or as if he were begging me for a bone.

(*He withdraws his hand.*)

Leave him like that, standing there imploring me.   970

(CLOV *straightens up. The dog falls on its side.*)

CLOV: I'll leave you.

HAMM: Have you had your visions?

CLOV: Less.

HAMM: Is Mother Pegg's light on?   975

CLOV: Light! How could anyone's light be on?

HAMM: Extinguished!

CLOV: Naturally it's extinguished. If it's not on it's extinguished.

HAMM: No, I mean Mother Pegg.

CLOV: But naturally she's extinguished!   980

(*Pause.*)

What's the matter with you today?

HAMM: I'm taking my course.

(*Pause.*)

Is she buried?   985

CLOV: Buried! Who would have buried her?
HAMM: You.
CLOV: Me! Haven't I enough to do without burying people?
HAMM: But you'll bury me.
990 CLOV: No I won't bury you.
(Pause.)
HAMM: She was bonny once, like a flower of the field.
(With reminiscent leer.)
And a great one for the men!
995 CLOV: We too were bonny—once. It's a rare thing not to have been bonny—once.
(Pause.)
HAMM: Go and get the gaff.
(CLOV goes to door, halts.)
1000 CLOV: Do this, do that, and I do it. I never refuse. Why?
HAMM: You're not able to.
CLOV: Soon I won't do it any more.
HAMM: You won't be able to any more.
(Exit CLOV.)
1005 Ah the creatures, the creatures, everything has to be explained to them.
(Enter CLOV with gaff.)
CLOV: Here's your gaff. Stick it up.

(He gives the gaff to HAMM who, wielding it like a puntpole, tries to move his chair.)

HAMM: Did I move?
1010 CLOV: No.
(HAMM throws down the gaff.)
HAMM: Go and get the oilcan.
CLOV: What for?
HAMM: To oil the castors.
1015 CLOV: I oiled them yesterday.
HAMM: Yesterday! What does that mean? Yesterday!
CLOV: (Violently.) That means that bloody awful day, long ago, before this bloody awful day. I use the words you taught me. If they don't mean anything any more, teach me others.
1020 Or let me be silent.
(Pause.)
HAMM: I once knew a madman who thought the end of the world had come. He was a painter—and engraver. I had a great fondness for him. I used to go and see him, in the asylum. I'd take him by the hand and drag him to the window.
1025 Look! There! All that rising corn! And there! Look! The sails of the herring fleet! All that loveliness!
(Pause.)
He'd snatch away his hand and go back into his corner. Appalled. All he had seen was ashes.
1030 (Pause.)
He alone had been spared.
(Pause.)
Forgotten.
1035 (Pause.)
It appears the case is . . . was not so . . . so unusual.
CLOV: A madman? When was that?
HAMM: Oh way back, way back, you weren't in the land of the living.
1040 CLOV: God be with the days!
(Pause. HAMM raises his toque.)
HAMM: I had a great fondness for him.
(Pause. He puts on his toque again.)
He was a painter—and engraver.

1045 CLOV: There are so many terrible things.
HAMM: No, no, there are not so many now.
(Pause.)
Clov!
CLOV: Yes.
HAMM: Do you not think this has gone on long enough? 1050
CLOV: Yes!
(Pause.)
What?
HAMM: This . . . this . . . thing.
CLOV: I've always thought so. 1055
(Pause.)
You not?
HAMM: (Gloomily.) Then it's a day like any other day.
CLOV: As long as it lasts.
(Pause.) 1060
All life long the same inanities.
HAMM: I can't leave you.
CLOV: I know. And you can't follow me.
(Pause.)
HAMM: If you leave me how shall I know? 1065
CLOV: (Briskly.) Well you simply whistle me and if I don't come running it means I've left you.
(Pause.)
HAMM: You won't come and kiss me goodbye?
CLOV: Oh I shouldn't think so. 1070
(Pause.)
HAMM: But you might be merely dead in your kitchen.
CLOV: The result would be the same.
HAMM: Yes, but how would I know, if you were merely dead in your kitchen? 1075
CLOV: Well . . . sooner or later I'd start to stink.
HAMM: You stink already. The whole place stinks of corpses.
CLOV: The whole universe.
HAMM: (Angrily.) To hell with the universe.
(Pause.) 1080
Think of something.
CLOV: What?
HAMM: An idea, have an idea.
(Angrily.)
A bright idea! 1085
CLOV: Ah good.
(He starts pacing to and fro, his eyes fixed on the ground, his hands behind his back. He halts.)
The pains in my legs! It's unbelievable! Soon I won't be able to think any more. 1090
HAMM: You won't be able to leave me.
(CLOV resumes his pacing.)
What are you doing?
CLOV: Having an idea.
(He paces.) 1095
Ah!
(He halts.)
HAMM: What a brain!
(Pause.)
Well? 1100
CLOV: Wait!
(He meditates. Not very convinced.)
Yes . . .
(Pause. More convinced.)
Yes! 1105
(He raises his head.)

I have it! I set the alarm.

(*Pause.*)

1110 HAMM: This is perhaps not one of my bright days, but frankly—

CLOV: You whistle me. I don't come. The alarm rings. I'm gone. It doesn't ring. I'm dead.

(*Pause.*)

HAMM: Is it working?

1115 (*Pause. Impatiently.*)

The alarm, is it working?

CLOV: Why wouldn't it be working?

HAMM: Because it's worked too much.

CLOV: But it's hardly worked at all.

1120 HAMM: (*Angrily.*) Then because it's worked too little!

CLOV: I'll go and see.

(*Exit* CLOV. *Brief ring of alarm off. Enter* CLOV *with alarm-clock. He holds it against* HAMM's *ear and releases alarm. They listen to it ringing to the end. Pause.*)

1125 Fit to wake the dead! Did you hear it?

HAMM: Vaguely.

CLOV: The end is terrific!

HAMM: I prefer the middle.

(*Pause.*)

1130 Is it not time for my pain-killer?

CLOV: No!

(*He goes to door, turns.*)

I'll leave you.

HAMM: It's time for my story. Do you want to listen to my story.

1135 CLOV: No.

HAMM: Ask my father if he wants to listen to my story.

(CLOV *goes to bins, raises the lid of* NAGG's, *stoops, looks into it. Pause. He straightens up.*)

CLOV: He's asleep.

HAMM: Wake him.

(CLOV *stoops, wakes* NAGG *with the alarm. Unintelligible words.* CLOV *straightens up.*)

CLOV: He doesn't want to listen to your story.

1140 HAMM: I'll give him a bon-bon.

(CLOV *stoops. As before.*)

CLOV: He wants a sugar-plum.

HAMM: He'll get a sugar-plum.

(CLOV *stoops. As before.*)

1145 CLOV: It's a deal.

(*He goes towards door.* NAGG's *hands appear, gripping the rim. Then the head emerges.* CLOV *reaches door, turns.*)

Do you believe in the life to come?

HAMM: Mine was always that.

1150 (*Exit* CLOV.)

Got him that time!

NAGG: I'm listening.

HAMM: Scoundrel! Why did you engender me?

NAGG: I didn't know.

1155 HAMM: What? What didn't you know?

NAGG: That it'd be you.

(*Pause.*)

You'll give me a sugar-plum?

HAMM: After the audition.

1160 NAGG: You swear?

HAMM: Yes.

NAGG: On what?

HAMM: My honor.

(*Pause. They laugh heartily.*)

1165 NAGG: Two.

HAMM: One.

NAGG: One for me and one for—

HAMM: One! Silence!

(*Pause.*)

Where was I?

1170 (*Pause. Gloomily.*)

It's finished, we're finished.

(*Pause.*)

Nearly finished.

(*Pause.*)

1175 There'll be no more speech.

(*Pause.*)

Something dripping in my head, ever since the fontanelles.

(*Stifled hilarity of* NAGG.)

Splash, splash, always on the same spot.

1180 (*Pause.*)

Perhaps it's a little vein.

(*Pause.*)

A little artery.

(*Pause. More animated.*)

1185 Enough of that, it's story time, where was I?

(*Pause. Narrative tone.*)

The man came crawling towards me, on his belly. Pale, wonderfully pale and thin, he seemed on the point of—

(*Pause. Normal tone.*)

1190 No, I've done that bit.

(*Pause. Narrative tone.*)

I calmly filled my pipe—the meerschaum, lit it with . . . let us say a vesta, drew a few puffs. Aah!

(*Pause.*)

1195 Well, what is it *you* want?

(*Pause.*)

It was an extra-ordinarily bitter day, I remember, zero by the thermometer. But considering it was Christmas Eve there was nothing . . . extra-ordinary about that. Seasonable weather, 1200 for once in a way.

(*Pause.*)

Well, what ill wind blows you my way? He raised his face to me, black with mingled dirt and tears.

(*Pause. Normal tone.*)

1205 That should do it.

(*Narrative tone.*)

No no, don't look at me, don't look at me. He dropped his eyes and mumbled something, apologies I presume.

(*Pause.*)

1210 I'm a busy man, you know, the final touches, before the festivities, you know what it is.

(*Pause. Forcibly.*)

Come on now, what is the object of this invasion?

(*Pause.*)

1215 It was a glorious bright day, I remember, fifty by the heliometer, but already the sun was sinking down into the . . . down among the dead.

(*Normal tone.*)

Nicely put, that.

1220 (*Narrative tone.*)

Come on now, come on, present your petition and let me resume my labors.

(Pause. Normal tone.)

1225   There's English for you. Ah well . . .

(Narrative tone.)

    It was then he took the plunge. It's my little one, he said. Tsstss, a little one, that's bad. My little boy, he said, as if the sex mattered. Where did he come from? He named the hole.

1230   A good half-day, on horse. What are you insinuating? That the place is still inhabited? No no, not a soul, except himself and the child—assuming he existed. Good. I enquired about the situation at Kov, beyond the gulf. Not a sinner. Good. And you expect me to believe you have left your little one

1235   back there, all alone, and alive into the bargain? Come now!

(Pause.)

    It was a howling wild day, I remember, a hundred by the anenometer. The wind was tearing up the dead pines and sweeping them . . . away.

1240 *(Pause. Normal tone.)*

    A bit feeble, that.

(Narrative tone.)

    Come on, man, speak up, what is it you want from me, I have to put up my holly.

1245 *(Pause.)*

    Well to make it short it finally transpired that what he wanted from me was . . . bread for his brat? Bread? But I have no bread, it doesn't agree with me. Good. Then perhaps a little corn?

1250 *(Pause. Normal tone.)*

    That should do it.

(Narrative tone.)

    Corn, yes, I have corn, it's true, in my granaries. But use your head. I give you some corn, a pound, a pound and a

1255   half, you bring it back to your child and you make him—if he's still alive—a nice pot of porridge,

(NAGG reacts.)

    a nice pot and a half of porridge, full of nourishment. Good. The colors come back into his little cheeks—perhaps. And

1260   then?

(Pause.)

    I lost patience.

(Violently.)

    Use your head, can't you, use your head, you're on earth,

1265   there's no cure for that!

(Pause.)

    It was an exceedingly dry day, I remember, zero by the hygrometer. Ideal weather, for my lumbago.

(Pause. Violently.)

1270   But what in God's name do you imagine? That the earth will awake in spring? That the rivers and seas will run with fish again? That there's manna in heaven still for imbeciles like you?

(Pause.)

1275   Gradually I cooled down, sufficiently at least to ask him how long he had taken on the way. Three whole days. Good. In what condition he had left the child. Deep in sleep.

(Forcibly.)

    But deep in what sleep, deep in what sleep already?

1280 *(Pause.)*

    Well to make it short I finally offered to take him into my service. He had touched a chord. And then I imagined already that I wasn't much longer for this world.

(He laughs. Pause.)

1285   Well?

(Pause.)

    Well? Here if you were careful you might die a nice natural death, in peace and comfort.

(Pause.)

    Well?   1290

(Pause.)

    In the end he asked me would I consent to take in the child as well—if he were still alive.

(Pause.)

    It was the moment I was waiting for.   1295

(Pause.)

    Would I consent to take in the child . . .

(Pause.)

    I can see him still, down on his knees, his hands flat on the ground, glaring at me with his mad eyes, in defiance of my   1300 wishes.

(Pause. Normal tone.)

    I'll soon have finished with this story.

(Pause.)

    Unless I bring in other characters.   1305

(Pause.)

    But where would I find them?

(Pause.)

    Where would I look for them?

(Pause. He whistles. Enter CLOV.*)*   1310

    Let us pray to God.

NAGG: Me sugar-plum!

CLOV: There's a rat in the kitchen!

HAMM: A rat! Are there still rats?

CLOV: In the kitchen there's one.   1315

HAMM: And you haven't exterminated him?

CLOV: Half. You disturbed us.

HAMM: He can't get away?

CLOV: No.

HAMM: You'll finish him later. Let us pray to God.   1320

CLOV: Again!

NAGG: Me sugar-plum!

HAMM: God first!

(Pause.)

    Are you right?   1325

CLOV: *(Resigned.)* Off we go.

HAMM: *(To* NAGG.*)* And you?

NAGG: *(Clasping his hands, closing his eyes, in a gabble.)* Our Father which art—

HAMM: Silence! In silence! Where are your manners?   1330

(Pause.)

    Off we go.

(Attitudes of prayer. Silence. Abandoning his attitude, discouraged.)

    Well?   1335

CLOV: *(Abandoning his attitude.)* What a hope! And you?

HAMM: Sweet damn all!

(To NAGG.*)*

    And you?

NAGG: Wait!   1340

(Pause. Abandoning his attitude.)

    Nothing doing!

HAMM: The bastard! He doesn't exist!

CLOV: Not yet.

NAGG: Me sugar-plum!   1345

HAMM: There are no more sugar-plums!

(Pause.)

NAGG: It's natural. After all I'm your father. It's true if it hadn't been me it would have been someone else. But that's no excuse.

(*Pause.*)

Turkish Delight, for example, which no longer exists, we all know that, there is nothing in the world I love more. And one day I'll ask you for some, in return for a kindness, and you'll promise it to me. One must live with the times.

(*Pause.*)

Whom did you call when you were a tiny boy, and were frightened, in the dark? Your mother? No. Me. We let you cry. Then we moved you out of earshot, so that we might sleep in peace.

(*Pause.*)

I was asleep, as happy as a king, and you woke me up to have me listen to you. It wasn't indispensable, you didn't really need to have me listen to you.

(*Pause.*)

I hope the day will come when you'll really need to have me listen to you, and need to hear my voice, any voice.

(*Pause.*)

Yes, I hope I'll live till then, to hear you calling me like when you were a tiny boy, and were frightened, in the dark, and I was your only hope.

(*Pause.* NAGG *knocks on lid of* NELL's *bin. Pause.*)

Nell!

(*Pause. He knocks louder. Pause. Louder.*)

Nell!

(*Pause.* NAGG *sinks back into his bin, closes the lid behind him. Pause.*)

HAMM: Our revels now are ended.

(*He gropes for the dog.*)

The dog's gone.

CLOV: He's not a real dog, he can't go.

HAMM: (*Groping.*) He's not there.

CLOV: He's lain down.

HAMM: Give him up to me.

(CLOV *picks up the dog and gives it to* HAMM. HAMM *holds it in his arms. Pause.* HAMM *throws away the dog.*)

Dirty brute!

(CLOV *begins to pick up the objects lying on the ground.*)

What are you doing?

CLOV: Putting things in order.

(*He straightens up. Fervently.*)

I'm going to clear everything away!

(*He starts picking up again.*)

HAMM: Order!

CLOV: (*Straightening up.*) I love order. It's my dream. A world where all would be silent and still and each thing in its last place, under the last dust.

(*He starts picking up again.*)

HAMM: (*Exasperated.*) What in God's name do you think you are doing?

CLOV: (*Straightening up.*) I'm doing my best to create a little order.

HAMM: Drop it!

(CLOV *drops the objects he has picked up.*)

CLOV: After all, there or elsewhere.

(*He goes towards door.*)

HAMM: (*Irritably.*) What's wrong with your feet?

CLOV: My feet?

HAMM: Tramp! Tramp!

CLOV: I must have put on my boots.

HAMM: Your slippers were hurting you?

(*Pause.*)

CLOV: I'll leave you.

HAMM: No!

CLOV: What is there to keep me here?

HAMM: The dialogue.

(*Pause.*)

I've got on with my story.

(*Pause.*)

I've got on with it well.

(*Pause. Irritably.*)

Ask me where I've got to.

CLOV: Oh, by the way, your story?

HAMM: (*Surprised.*) What story?

CLOV: The one you've been telling yourself all your days.

HAMM: Ah you mean my chronicle?

CLOV: That's the one.

(*Pause.*)

HAMM: (*Angrily.*) Keep going, can't you, keep going!

CLOV: You've got on with it, I hope.

HAMM: (*Modestly.*) Oh not very far, not very far.

(*He sighs.*)

There are days like that, one isn't inspired.

(*Pause.*)

Nothing you can do about it, just wait for it to come.

(*Pause.*)

No forcing, no forcing, it's fatal.

(*Pause.*)

I've got on with it a little all the same.

(*Pause.*)

Technique, you know.

(*Pause. Irritably.*)

I say I've got on with it a little all the same.

CLOV: (*Admiringly.*) Well I never! In spite of everything you were able to get on with it!

HAMM: (*Modestly.*) Oh not very far, you know, not very far, but nevertheless, better than nothing.

CLOV: Better than nothing! Is it possible?

HAMM: I'll tell you how it goes. He comes crawling on his belly—

CLOV: Who?

HAMM: What?

CLOV: Who do you mean, he?

HAMM: Who do I mean! Yet another.

CLOV: Ah him! I wasn't sure.

HAMM: Crawling on his belly, whining for bread for his brat. He's offered a job as gardener. Before—

(CLOV *bursts out laughing.*)

What is there so funny about that?

CLOV: A job as gardener!

HAMM: Is that what tickles you?

CLOV: It must be that.

HAMM: It wouldn't be the bread?

CLOV: Or the brat.

(*Pause.*)

HAMM: The whole thing is comical, I grant you that. What about having a good guffaw the two of us together?

CLOV: (*After reflection.*) I couldn't guffaw again today.

HAMM: *(After reflection.)* Nor I.
(Pause.)
    I continue then. Before accepting with gratitude he asks if he
1470   may have his little boy with him.
CLOV: What age?
HAMM: Oh tiny.
CLOV: He would have climbed the trees.
HAMM: All the little odd jobs.
1475 CLOV: And then he would have grown up.
HAMM: Very likely.
(Pause.)
CLOV: Keep going, can't you, keep going!
HAMM: That's all. I stopped there.
1480 *(Pause.)*
CLOV: Do you see how it goes on.
HAMM: More or less.
CLOV: Will it not soon be the end?
HAMM: I'm afraid it will.
1485 CLOV: Pah! You'll make up another.
HAMM: I don't know.
(Pause.)
    I feel rather drained.
(Pause.)
1490   The prolonged creative effort.
(Pause.)
    If I could drag myself down to the sea! I'd make a pillow of
    sand for my head and the tide would come.
CLOV: There's no more tide.
1495 *(Pause.)*
HAMM: Go and see is she dead.
(CLOV goes to bins, raises the lid of NELL's, *stoops, looks into it.
Pause.)*
CLOV: Looks like it.
1500 *(He closes the lid, straightens up.* HAMM *raises his toque. Pause
He puts it on again.)*
HAMM: *(With his hand to his toque.)* And Nagg?
(CLOV raises lid of NAGG's *bin, stoops, looks into it. Pause.)*
CLOV: Doesn't look like it.
1505 *(He closes the lid, straightens up.)*
HAMM: *(Letting go his toque.)* What's he doing?
(CLOV raises lid of NAGG's *bin, stoops, looks into it. Pause.)*
CLOV: He's crying.
(He closes lid, straightens up.)
1510 HAMM: Then he's living.
(Pause.)
    Did you ever have an instant of happiness?
CLOV: Not to my knowledge.
(Pause.)
1515 HAMM: Bring me under the window.
(CLOV goes towards chair.)
    I want to feel the light on my face.
(CLOV pushes chair.)
    Do you remember, in the beginning, when you took me for
1520   a turn? You used to hold the chair too high. At every step you
    nearly tipped me out.
(With senile quaver.)
    Ah great fun, we had, the two of us, great fun.
(Gloomily.)
1525   And then we got into the way of it.
(CLOV stops the chair under window right.)
    There already?

(Pause. He tilts back his head.)
    Is it light?
CLOV: It isn't dark.   1530
HAMM: *(Angrily.)* I'm asking you is it light.
CLOV: Yes.
(Pause.)
HAMM: The curtain isn't closed?
CLOV: No.   1535
HAMM: What window is it?
CLOV: The earth.
HAMM: I knew it!
(Angrily.)
    But there's no light there! The other!   1540
(CLOV pushes chair towards window left.)
    The earth!
(CLOV stops the chair under window left. HAMM *tilts back his
head.)*
    That's what I call light!   1545
(Pause.)
    Feels like a ray of sunshine.
(Pause.)
    No?
CLOV: No.   1550
HAMM: It isn't a ray of sunshine I feel on my face?
CLOV: No.

(Pause.)

HAMM: Am I very white?
(Pause. Angrily.)
    I'm asking you am I very white!   1555
CLOV: Not more so than usual.

(Pause.)

HAMM: Open the window.
CLOV: What for?
HAMM: I want to hear the sea.
CLOV: You wouldn't hear it.   1560
HAMM: Even if you opened the window?
CLOV: No.
HAMM: Then it's not worth while opening it?
CLOV: No.
HAMM: *(Violently.)* Then open it!   1565
(CLOV gets up on the ladder, opens the window. Pause.)
    Have you opened it?
CLOV: Yes.
(Pause.)
HAMM: You swear you've opened it?   1570
CLOV: Yes.
(Pause.)
HAMM: Well . . . !
(Pause.)
    It must be very calm.   1575
(Pause. Violently.)
    I'm asking you is it very calm!
CLOV: Yes.
HAMM: It's because there are no more navigators.
(Pause.)   1580
    You haven't much conversation all of a sudden. Do you not
    feel well?
CLOV: I'm cold.
HAMM: What month are we?

1585   (*Pause.*)
    Close the window, we're going back.
    (CLOV *closes the window, gets down, pushes the chair back to its place, remains standing behind it, head bowed.*)
    Don't stay there, you give me the shivers!
1590   (CLOV *returns to his place beside the chair.*)
    Father!
    (*Pause. Louder.*)
    Father!
    (*Pause.*)
1595   Go and see did he hear me.

    (CLOV *goes to* NAGG's *bin, raises the lid, stoops. Unintelligible words.* CLOV *straightens up.*)

    CLOV: Yes.
    HAMM: Both times?
    (CLOV *stoops. As before.*)
    CLOV: Once only.
1600   HAMM: The first time or the second?
    (CLOV *stoops. As before.*)
    CLOV: He doesn't know.
    HAMM: It must have been the second.
    CLOV: We'll never know.
1605   (*He closes lid.*)
    HAMM: Is he still crying?
    CLOV: No.
    HAMM: The dead go fast.
    (*Pause.*)
1610   What's he doing?
    CLOV: Sucking his biscuit.
    HAMM: Life goes on.
    (CLOV *returns to his place beside the chair.*)
    Give me a rug, I'm freezing.
1615   CLOV: There are no more rugs.
    (*Pause.*)
    HAMM: Kiss me.
    (*Pause.*)
    Will you not kiss me?
1620   CLOV: No.
    HAMM: On the forehead.
    CLOV: I won't kiss you anywhere.
    (*Pause.*)
    HAMM: (*Holding out his hand.*) Give me your hand at least.
1625   (*Pause.*)
    Will you not give me your hand?
    CLOV: I won't touch you.
    (*Pause.*)
    HAMM: Give me the dog.
1630   (CLOV *looks round for the dog.*)
    No!
    CLOV: Do you not want your dog?
    HAMM: No.
    CLOV: Then I'll leave you.
1635   HAMM: (*Head bowed, absently.*) That's right.
    (CLOV *goes to door, turns.*)
    CLOV: If I don't kill that rat he'll die.
    HAMM: (*As before.*) That's right.

    (*Exit* CLOV. *Pause.*)

    Me to play.
1640   (*He takes out his handkerchief, unfolds it, holds it spread out before him.*)

We're getting on.
(*Pause.*)
You weep, and weep, for nothing, so as not to laugh, and lit-   1645
tle by little . . . you begin to grieve.
(*He folds the handkerchief, puts it back in his pocket, raises his head.*)
All those I might have helped.
(*Pause.*)
Helped!   1650
(*Pause.*)
Saved.
(*Pause.*)
Saved!
(*Pause.*)   1655
The place was crawling with them!
(*Pause. Violently.*)
Use your head, can't you, use your head, you're on earth, there's no cure for that!
(*Pause.*)   1660
Get out of here and love one another! Lick your neighbor as yourself!
(*Pause. Calmer.*)
When it wasn't bread they wanted it was crumpets.
(*Pause. Violently.*)   1665
Out of my sight and back to your petting parties!
(*Pause.*)
All that, all that!
(*Pause.*)
Not even a real dog!   1670
(*Calmer.*)
The end is in the beginning and yet you go on.
(*Pause.*)
Perhaps I could go on with my story, end it and begin an-   1675
other.
(*Pause.*)
Perhaps I could throw myself out on the floor.
(*He pushes himself painfully off his seat, falls back again.*)
Dig my nails into the cracks and drag myself forward with my fingers.   1680
(*Pause.*)
It will be the end and there I'll be, wondering what can have brought it on and wondering what can have . . .
(*He hesitates.*)
. . . why it was so long coming.   1685
(*Pause.*)
There I'll be, in the old shelter, alone against the silence and . . .
(*He hesitates.*)
. . . the stillness. If I can hold my peace, and sit quiet, it will   1690
be all over with sound, and motion, all over and done with.
(*Pause.*)
I'll have called my father and I'll have called my . . .
(*He hesitates.*)
. . . my son. And even twice, or three times, in case they   1695
shouldn't have heard me, the first time, or the second.
(*Pause.*)
I'll say to myself, He'll come back.
(*Pause.*)
And then?   1700
(*Pause.*)
And then?
(*Pause.*)

He couldn't, he has gone too far.

1705 *(Pause.)*

And then?

(Pause. Very agitated.)

All kinds of fantasies! That I'm being watched! A rat! Steps! Breath held and then . . .

1710 *(He breathes out.)*

Then babble, babble, words, like the solitary child who turns himself into children, two, three, so as to be together, and whisper together, in the dark.

(Pause.)

1715 Moment upon moment, pattering down, like the millet grains of . . .

(He hesitates.)

. . . that old Greek, and all life long you wait for that to mount up to a life.

1720 *(Pause. He opens his mouth to continue, renounces.)*

Ah let's get it over!

(He whistles. Enter CLOV *with alarm-clock. He halts beside the chair.)*

What? Neither gone nor dead?

1725 CLOV: In spirit only.

HAMM: Which?

CLOV: Both.

HAMM: Gone from me you'd be dead.

CLOV: And vice versa.

1730 HAMM: Outside of here it's death!

(Pause.)

And the rat?

CLOV: He's got away.

HAMM: He can't go far.

1735 *(Pause. Anxious.)*

Eh?

CLOV: He doesn't need to go far.

(Pause.)

HAMM: Is it not time for my pain-killer?

1740 CLOV: Yes.

HAMM: Ah! At last! Give it to me! Quick!

(Pause.)

CLOV: There's no more pain-killer.

(Pause.)

1745 HAMM: *(Appalled.)* Good. . . !

(Pause.)

No more pain-killer!

CLOV: No more pain-killer. You'll never get any more pain-killer.

1750 *(Pause.)*

HAMM: But the little round box. It was full!

CLOV: Yes. But now it's empty.

(Pause. CLOV *starts to move about the room. He is looking for a place to put down the alarm-clock.)*

HAMM: *(Soft.)* What'll I do?

(Pause. In a scream.)

1755 What'll I do?

*(*CLOV *sees the picture, takes it down, stands it on the floor with its face to the wall, hangs up the alarm-clock in its place.)*

What are you doing?

CLOV: Winding up.

1760 HAMM: Look at the earth.

CLOV: Again!

HAMM: Since it's calling to you.

CLOV: Is your throat sore?

(Pause.)

Would you like a lozenge? 1765

(Pause.)

No.

(Pause.)

Pity.

*(*CLOV *goes, humming, towards window right, halts before it, looks up at it.)*

HAMM: Don't sing. 1770

CLOV: *(Turning towards* HAMM.*)* One hasn't the right to sing any more?

HAMM: No.

CLOV: Then how can it end?

HAMM: You want it to end? 1775

CLOV: I want to sing.

HAMM: I can't prevent you.

(Pause. CLOV *turns towards window right.)*

CLOV: What did I do with that steps?

(He looks around for ladder.) 1780

You didn't see that steps?

(He sees it.)

Ah, about time.

(He goes towards window left.)

Sometimes I wonder if I'm in my right mind. Then it passes 1785

over and I'm as lucid as before.

(He gets up on ladder, looks out of window.)

Christ, she's under water!

(He looks.)

How can that be? 1790

(He pokes forward his head, his hand above his eyes.)

It hasn't rained.

(He wipes the pane, looks. Pause.)

Ah what a fool I am! I'm on the wrong side!

(He gets down, takes a few steps towards window right.) 1795

Under water!

(He goes back for ladder.)

What a fool I am!

(He carries ladder towards window right.)

Sometimes I wonder if I'm in my right senses. Then it passes 1800

off and I'm as intelligent as ever.

(He sets down ladder under window right, gets up on it, looks out of window. He turns towards HAMM.*)*

Any particular sector you fancy? Or merely the whole thing?

HAMM: Whole thing. 1805

CLOV: The general effect? Just a moment.

(He looks out of window. Pause.)

HAMM: Clov.

CLOV: *(Absorbed.)* Mmm.

HAMM: Do you know what it is? 1810

CLOV: *(As before.)* Mmm.

HAMM: I was never there.

(Pause.)

Clov!

CLOV: *(Turning towards* HAMM, *exasperated.)* What is it? 1815

HAMM: I was never there.

CLOV: Lucky for you.

(He looks out of window.)

HAMM: Absent, always. It all happened without me. I don't know what's happened. 1820

(Pause.)

Do you know what's happened?
(Pause.)
Clov!

1825 CLOV: *(Turning towards* HAMM, *exasperated.)* Do you want me to look at this muckheap, yes or no?
HAMM: Answer me first.
CLOV: What?
HAMM: Do you know what's happened?
1830 CLOV: When? Where?
HAMM: *(Violently.)* When! What's happened? Use your head, can't you! What has happened?
CLOV: What for Christ's sake does it matter?
(He looks out of window.)
1835 HAMM: I don't know.
(Pause. CLOV *turns towards* HAMM.)
CLOV: *(Harshly.)* When old Mother Pegg asked you for oil for her lamp and you told her to get out to hell, you knew what was happening then, no?
1840 *(Pause.)*
You know what she died of, Mother Pegg? Of darkness.
HAMM: *(Feebly.)* I hadn't any.
CLOV: *(As before.)* Yes, you had.
(Pause.)
1845 HAMM: Have you the glass?
CLOV: No, it's clear enough as it is.
HAMM: Go and get it.

(Pause. CLOV *casts up his eyes, brandishes his fists. He loses balance, clutches on to the ladder. He starts to get down, halts.)*

CLOV: There's one thing I'll never understand.
(He gets down.)
1850 Why I always obey you. Can you explain that to me?
HAMM: No. . . . Perhaps it's compassion.
(Pause.)
A kind of great compassion.
(Pause.)
1855 Oh you won't find it easy, you won't find it easy.

(Pause. CLOV *begins to move about the room in search of the telescope.)*

CLOV: I'm tired of our goings on, very tired.
(He searches.)
You're not sitting on it?
(He moves the chair, looks at the place where it stood, resumes
1860 *his search.)*
HAMM: *(Anguished.)* Don't leave me there!
(Angrily CLOV *restores the chair to its place.)*
Am I right in the center?
CLOV: You'd need a microscope to find this—
1865 *(He sees the telescope.)*
Ah, about time.
(He picks up the telescope, gets up on the ladder, turns the telescope on the without.)
HAMM: Give me the dog.
1870 CLOV: *(Looking.)* Quiet!
HAMM: *(Angrily.)* Give me the dog!

(CLOV drops the telescope, clasps his hands to his head. Pause. He gets down precipitately, looks for the dog, sees it, picks it up, hastens towards* HAMM *and strikes him violently on the head with the dog.)*

CLOV: There's your dog for you!
(The dog falls to the ground. Pause.)
HAMM: He hit me!
CLOV: You drive me mad, I'm mad! 1875
HAMM: If you must hit me, hit me with the axe.
(Pause.)
Or with the gaff, hit me with the gaff. Not with the dog. With the gaff. Or with the axe.

(CLOV picks up the dog and gives it to* HAMM *who takes it in his arms.)*

CLOV: *(Imploringly.)* Let's stop playing! 1880
HAMM: Never!
(Pause.)
Put me in my coffin.
CLOV: There are no more coffins.
HAMM: Then let it end! 1885
(CLOV goes towards ladder.)*
With a bang!
(CLOV gets up on ladder, gets down again, looks for telescope, sees it, picks it up, gets up ladder, raises telescope.)*
Of darkness! And me? Did anyone ever have pity on me? 1890
CLOV: *(Lowering the telescope, turning towards* HAMM.): What?
(Pause.)
Is it me you're referring to?
HAMM: *(Angrily.)* An aside, ape! Did you never hear an aside before? 1895
(Pause.)
I'm warming up for my last soliloquy.
CLOV: I warn you. I'm going to look at this filth since it's an order. But it's the last time.
(He turns the telescope on the without.) 1900
Let's see.
(He moves the telescope.)
Nothing . . . nothing . . . good . . . good . . . nothing . . . goo—
(He starts, lowers the telescope, examines it, turns it again on the 1905
without. Pause.)
Bad luck to it!
HAMM: More complications!
(CLOV gets down.)*
Not an underplot, I trust. 1910

(CLOV moves ladder nearer window, gets up on it, turns telescope on the without.)*

CLOV: *(Dismayed.)* Looks like a small boy!
HAMM: *(Sarcastic.)* A small . . . boy!
CLOV: I'll go and see.
(He gets down, drops the telescope, goes towards door, turns.)
I'll take the gaff. 1915
(He looks for the gaff, sees it, picks it up, hastens towards door.)
HAMM: No!
(CLOV halts.)*
CLOV: No? A potential procreator?
HAMM: If he exists he'll die there or he'll come here. And if he 1920
doesn't . . .
(Pause.)
CLOV: You don't believe me? You think I'm inventing?
(Pause.)
HAMM: It's the end, Clov, we've come to the end. I don't need 1925
you any more.

(Pause.)

CLOV: Lucky for you.

(He goes towards door.)

1930 HAMM: Leave me the gaff.

(CLOV gives him the gaff, goes towards door, halts, looks at alarm-clock, takes it down, looks round for a better place to put it, goes to bins, puts it on lid of NAGG's bin. Pause.)

CLOV: I'll leave you.

(He goes towards door.)

HAMM: Before you go . . .

(CLOV halts near door.)

1935 . . . say something.

CLOV: There is nothing to say.

HAMM: A few words . . . to ponder . . . in my heart.

CLOV: Your heart!

HAMM: Yes.

1940 *(Pause. Forcibly.)*

Yes!

(Pause.)

With the rest, in the end, the shadows, the murmurs, all the trouble, to end up with.

1945 *(Pause.)*

Clov. . . . He never spoke to me. Then, in the end, before he went, without my having asked him, he spoke to me. He said . . .

CLOV: *(Despairingly.)* Ah. . . !

1950 HAMM: Something . . . from your heart.

CLOV: My heart!

HAMM: A few words . . . from your heart.

(Pause.)

CLOV: *(Fixed gaze, tonelessly, towards auditorium.)* They said

1955 to me, That's love, yes, yes, not a doubt, now you see how—

HAMM: Articulate!

CLOV: *(As before.)* How easy it is. They said to me, That's friendship, yes, yes, no question, you've found it. They said to me, Here's the place, stop, raise your head and look at all

1960 that beauty. That order! They said to me, Come now, you're not a brute beast, think upon these things and you'll see how all becomes clear. And simple! They said to me, What skilled attention they get, all these dying of their wounds.

HAMM: Enough!

1965 CLOV: *(As before.)* I say to myself—sometimes, Clov, you must learn to suffer better than that if you want them to weary of punishing you—one day. I say to myself—sometimes, Clov, you must be there better than that if you want them to let you go—one day. But I feel too old, and too far, to form new

1970 habits. Good, it'll never end, I'll never go.

(Pause.)

Then one day, suddenly, it ends, it changes, I don't understand, it dies, or it's me, I don't understand, that either. I ask the words that remain—sleeping, waking, morning, evening.

1975 They have nothing to say.

(Pause.)

I open the door of the cell and go. I am so bowed I only see my feet, if I open my eyes, and between my legs a little trail of black dust. I say to myself that the earth is extinguished,

1980 though I never saw it lit.

(Pause.)

It's easy going.

(Pause.)

When I fall I'll weep for happiness.

(Pause. He goes towards door.)

1985 HAMM: Clov!

(CLOV halts, without turning.)

Nothing.

(CLOV moves on.)

Clov! 1990

(CLOV halts, without turning.)

CLOV: This is what we call making an exit.

HAMM: I'm obliged to you, Clov. For your services.

CLOV: *(Turning, sharply.)* Ah pardon, it's I am obliged to you.

HAMM: It's we are obliged to each other. 1995

(Pause. CLOV goes towards door.)

One thing more.

(CLOV halts.)

A last favor.

(Exit CLOV.) 2000

Cover me with the sheet.

(Long pause.)

No? Good.

(Pause.)

Me to play. 2005

(Pause. Wearily.)

Old endgame lost of old, play and lose and have done with losing.

(Pause. More animated.)

Let me see. 2010

(Pause.)

Ah yes!

(He tries to move the chair, using the gaff as before. Enter CLOV, dressed for the road. Panama hat, tweed coat, raincoat over his arm, umbrella, bag. He halts by the door and stands there, im- 2015 *passive and motionless, his eyes fixed on HAMM, till the end. HAMM gives up.)*

Good.

(Pause.)

Discard. 2020

(He throws away the gaff, makes to throw away the dog, thinks better of it.)

Take it easy.

(Pause.)

And now? 2025

(Pause.)

Raise hat.

(He raises his toque.)

Peace to our . . . arses.

(Pause.) 2030

And put on again.

(He puts on his toque.)

Deuce.

(Pause. He takes off his glasses.)

Wipe. 2035

(He takes out his handkerchief and, without unfolding it, wipes his glasses.)

And put on again.

(He puts on his glasses, puts back the handkerchief in his pocket.) 2040

We're coming. A few more squirms like that and I'll call.

(Pause.)

A little poetry.

(Pause.)

2045 You prayed—
(*Pause. He corrects himself.*)
You CRIED for night; it comes—
(*Pause. He corrects himself.*)
It FALLS: now cry in darkness.
2050 (*He repeats, chanting.*)
You cried for night; it falls: now cry in darkness.
(*Pause.*)
Nicely put, that.
(*Pause.*)
2055 And now?
(*Pause.*)
Moments for nothing, now as always, time was never and time is over, reckoning closed and story ended.
(*Pause. Narrative tone.*)
2060 If he could have his child with him. . . .
(*Pause.*)
It was the moment I was waiting for.
(*Pause.*)
You don't want to abandon him? You want him to bloom
2065 while you are withering? Be there to solace your last million last moments?
(*Pause.*)
He doesn't realize, all he knows is hunger, and cold, and death to crown it all. But you! You ought to know what
2070 the earth is like, nowadays. Oh I put him before his responsibilities!
(*Pause. Normal tone.*)
Well, there we are, there I am, that's enough.
(*He raises the whistle to his lips, hesitates, drops it. Pause.*)
2075 Yes, truly!
(*He whistles. Pause. Louder. Pause.*)
Good.
(*Pause.*)

Father!
(*Pause. Louder.*)
Father!   2080
(*Pause.*)
Good.
(*Pause.*)
We're coming.   2085
(*Pause.*)
And to end up with?
(*Pause.*)
Discard.
(*He throws away the dog. He tears the whistle from his neck.*) 2090
With my compliments.
(*He throws whistle towards auditorium. Pause. He sniffs. Soft.*)
Clov!
(*Long pause.*)
No? Good.   2095
(*He takes out the handkerchief.*)
Since that's the way we're playing it . . .
(*He unfolds handkerchief.*)
. . . let's play it that way . . .
(*He unfolds.*)   2100
. . . and speak no more about it . . .
(*He finishes unfolding.*)
. . . speak no more.
(*He holds handkerchief spread out before him.*)
Old stancher!   2105
(*Pause.*)
You . . . remain.
(*Pause. He covers his face with handkerchief, lowers his arms to armrests, remains motionless.*)

(*Brief tableau.*)

■ HAROLD PINTER ■

Harold Pinter (b. 1930) has had an extensive career as an actor, playwright, and screenwriter, but is best-known for his strikingly disorienting stage plays. Pinter was born and raised in Hackney, a working-class neighborhood just beyond London's East End. He studied briefly at the Royal Academy of Dramatic Art and pursued a career as a stage and radio actor in the early 1950s before becoming a playwright. His early plays—notably *The Room* (1957), *The Birthday Party* (1958), and *The Dumb Waiter* (1960)—are inflected by the theater of the absurd in the indirect, often menacing, and finally inexplicable quality of their action. However, Pinter's drama is set in a much more recognizable locale than are many of Beckett's or Ionesco's plays; his plays often work by frustrating our "realistic" expectations of characters and their stage world. This is particularly true of Pinter's two major successes of the 1960s, *The Caretaker* (1960) and *The Homecoming* (1965). In both of these plays, a visitor disturbs the delicate balance of relations that bind a family together. What is characteristically "Pinteresque" about the action is the way that Pinter's spare and oblique dialogue makes the characters' motives and intentions nearly unreadable, often despite the violence with which they are expressed. If the poverty of language in most realistic drama tends to imply the emptiness of the characters, in Pinter's drama it seems most often to imply their explosive potential to erupt.

Pinter went through a period of profound writer's block in the late 1960s, writing only the short plays *Landscape* (1969) and *Silence* (1969). In the 1970s, though, he wrote a series of major dramas: *Old Times* (1971), *No Man's Land* (1975), and *Betrayal* (1978). These plays take memory and the past as their subject, examining how, in the words of Anna in *Old Times*, "There are things I remember which may never have happened but as I recall them so they take place." More recently, Pinter has written *A Kind of Alaska* (1982), a play based on Oliver Sachs's *Awakenings*, and four plays on more political subjects, *One for the Road* (1984), *Mountain Language* (1988), *Party Time* (1990), and *Moonlight* (1993). Pinter also has written a number of screenplays, both for his own plays, such as *Betrayal*, and for other projects, including *The French Lieutenant's Woman* and *Turtle Diary*.

THE HOMECOMING

The Homecoming is typical of Pinter's earlier drama in that it provides us with a recognizable situation—Teddy, an American college professor, returns home to London with his wife Ruth to visit his family—that immediately twists in new and surprising directions. For much like the room onstage, with its missing upstage wall, something is missing in this family that determines the structure of their relationships. The most obvious missing element of family life here is the absent mother, Jessie, whose absence informs the relationships between the men of the play: Max, who does the cleaning and cooking, to everyone's ridicule; Sam, who is accused of homosexual prostitution; Lenny, the pimp; Joey, the macho boxer. When Ruth appears in this scenario, she seems suddenly to take the role vacated by Jessie, becoming the controlling figure in the house of crippled men. Ruth assumes the two roles attributed to Jessie—mother and whore. The question, as Max asks at the end, is will she prove "adaptable" to the men's fantasies or will she—as Ruth's independence suggests—adapt the men to her own designs?

The Homecoming clearly plays with the formalities and conventions of realistic drama. The secret that often motivates the action of an Ibsen play (Nora's forgery in *A Doll House*, for example) seems to be disclosed in the play by Sam—"MacGregor had Jessie in the back of my cab as I drove them along"—but finally this "secret" loses its power to explain. It is either already known or finally irrelevant to the characters. Indeed, the past in *The Homecoming* seems to be largely improvised or invented. The characters frequently seem to make up stories of the "past" that function more as maneuverings in the present than as reliable accounts of something that actually happened. Lenny's story of beating up a prostitute underneath an arch in Act 1, for instance, seems not really to have happened. It is instead an effort to intimidate the seductive Ruth, also a woman standing underneath an arch in the living room. The past in *The Homecoming* is one that the characters invent and reinvent as the action progresses. The past becomes a fantasy that the characters work to re-create in the present action of the play.

THE HOMECOMING

Harold Pinter

— CHARACTERS —

MAX, *a man of seventy*
LENNY, *a man in his early thirties*
SAM, *a man of sixty-three*
JOEY, *a man in his middle twenties*
TEDDY, *a man in his middle thirties*
RUTH, *a woman in her early thirties*

SUMMER: *An old house in North London.*

A large room, extending the width of the stage.

The back wall, which contained the door, has been removed. A square arch shape remains. Beyond it, the hall. In the hall a staircase, ascending upstage left, well in view. The front door upstage right. A coatstand, hooks, etc.

In the room a window, right. Odd tables, chairs. Two large armchairs. A large sofa, left. Against right wall a large sideboard, the upper half of which contains a mirror. Upstage left, a radiogram.

— ACT ONE —

(Evening.

LENNY *is sitting on the sofa with a newspaper, a pencil in his hand. He wears a dark suit. He makes occasional marks on the back page.*

MAX *comes in, from the direction of the kitchen. He goes to sideboard, opens top drawer, rummages in it, closes it.*

He wears an old cardigan and a cap, and carries a stick.

He walks downstage, stands, looks about the room.)

MAX: What have you done with the scissors?

(Pause.)

I said I'm looking for the scissors. What have you done with them?

(Pause.)

Did you hear me? I want to cut something out of the paper.

5   LENNY: I'm reading the paper.
MAX: Not that paper. I haven't even read that paper. I'm talking about last Sunday's paper. I was just having a look at it in the kitchen.

(Pause.)

Do you hear what I'm saying? I'm talking to you! Where's
10   the scissors?
LENNY: *(Looking up, quietly.)* Why don't you shut up, you daft prat?

(MAX lifts his stick and points it at him.)

MAX: Don't you talk to me like that. I'm warning you.

(He sits in large armchair.)

There's an advertisement in the paper about flannel vests.
15   Cut price. Navy surplus. I could do with a few of them.

(Pause.)

I think I'll have a fag. Give me a fag.

(Pause.)

I just asked you to give me a cigarette.

(Pause.)

Look what I'm lumbered with.

(He takes a crumpled cigarette from his pocket.)

I'm getting old, my word of honour.

(He lights it.)

You think I wasn't a tearaway? I could have taken care of you,   20
twice over. I'm still strong. You ask your Uncle Sam what I was. But at the same time I always had a kind heart. Always.

(Pause.)

I used to knock about with a man called MacGregor. I called him Mac. You remember Mac? Eh?

(Pause.)

Huhh! We were two of the worst hated men in the West End   25
of London. I tell you, I still got the scars. We'd walk into a place, the whole room'd stand up, they'd make way to let us pass. You never heard such silence. Mind you, he was a big man, he was over six foot tall. His family were all MacGregors, they came all the way from Aberdeen, but he was the   30
only one they called Mac.

(Pause.)

He was very fond of your mother, Mac was. Very fond. He always had a good word for her.

(Pause.)

Mind you, she wasn't such a bad woman. Even though it made me sick just to look at her rotten stinking face, she   35
wasn't such a bad bitch. I gave her the best bleeding years of my life, anyway.
LENNY: Plug it, will you, you stupid sod, I'm trying to read the paper.
MAX: Listen! I'll chop your spine off, you talk to me like that!   40
You understand? Talking to your lousy filthy father like that!
LENNY: You know what, you're getting demented.

(Pause.)

What do you think of Second Wind for the three-thirty?
MAX: Where?
LENNY: Sandown Park.   45
MAX: Don't stand a chance.
LENNY: Sure he does.

MAX: Not a chance.
LENNY: He's the winner.

(LENNY *ticks the paper.*)

50 MAX: He talks to me about horses.

(*Pause.*)

I used to live on the course. One of the loves of my life.
Epsom? I knew it like the back of my hand. I was one of the
best-known faces down at the paddock. What a marvellous
open-air life.

(*Pause.*)

55 He talks to me about horses. You only read their names in
the papers. But I've stroked their manes, I've held them, I've
calmed them down before a big race. I was the one they used
to call for. Max, they'd say, there's a horse here, he's highly
strung, you're the only man on the course who can calm
60 him. It was true. I had a . . . I had an instinctive understanding of animals. I should have been a trainer. Many times I
was offered the job—you know, a proper post, by the Duke
of . . . I forget his name . . . one of the Dukes. But I had family obligations, my family needed me at home.

(*Pause.*)

65 The times I've watched those animals thundering past the
post. What an experience. Mind you, I didn't lose, I made a
few bob out of it, and you know why? Because I always had
the smell of a good horse. I could smell him. And not only
the colts but the fillies. Because the fillies are more highly
70 strung than the colts, they're more unreliable, did you know
that? No, what do you know? Nothing. But I was always able
to tell a good filly by one particular trick. I'd look her in the
eye. You see? I'd stand in front of her and look her straight in
the eye, it was a kind of hypnotism, and by the look deep
75 down in her eye I could tell whether she was a stayer or not.
It was a gift. I had a gift.

(*Pause.*)

And he talks to me about horses.
LENNY: Dad, do you mind if I change the subject?

(*Pause.*)

I want to ask you something. That dinner we had before,
80 what was the name of it? What do you call it?

(*Pause.*)

Why don't you buy a dog? You're a dog cook. Honest. You
think you're cooking for a lot of dogs.
MAX: If you don't like it get out.
LENNY: I am going out. I'm going out to buy myself a proper
85 dinner.
MAX: Well, get out! What are you waiting for?

(LENNY *looks at him.*)

LENNY: What did you say?
MAX: I said shove off out of it, that's what I said.
LENNY: You'll go before me, Dad, if you talk to me in that tone
90 of voice.
MAX: Will I, you bitch?

(MAX *grips his stick.*)

LENNY: Oh, Daddy, you're not going to use your stick on me,
are you? Eh? Don't use your stick on me, Daddy. No, please.
It wasn't my fault, it was one of the others. I haven't done
anything wrong, Dad, honest. Don't clout me with that   95
stick, Dad.

(*Silence.*

MAX *sits hunched.* LENNY *reads the paper.*

SAM *comes in the front door. He wears a chauffeur's uniform. He
hangs his hat on a hook in the hall and comes into the room. He
goes to a chair, sits in it and sighs.*)

Hullo, Uncle Sam.
SAM: Hullo.
LENNY: How are you, Uncle?
SAM: Not bad. A bit tired.   100
LENNY: Tired? I bet you're tired. Where you been?
SAM: I've been to London Airport.
LENNY: All the way up to London Airport? What, right up the
M4?
SAM: Yes, all the way up there.   105
LENNY: Tch, tch, tch. Well, I think you're entitled to be tired,
Uncle.
SAM: Well, it's the drivers.
LENNY: I know. That's what I'm talking about. I'm talking
about the drivers.   110
SAM: Knocks you out.

(*Pause.*)

MAX: I'm here, too, you know.

(SAM *looks at him.*)

I said I'm here, too. I'm sitting here.
SAM: I know you're here.

(*Pause.*)

SAM: I took a Yankee out there today . . . to the Airport.   115
LENNY: Oh, a Yankee, was it?
SAM: Yes, I been with him all day. Picked him up at the Savoy
at half past twelve, took him to the Caprice for his lunch.
After lunch I picked him up again, took him down to a
house in Eaton Square—he had to pay a visit to a friend   120
there—and then round about tea-time I took him right the
way out to the Airport.
LENNY: Had to catch a plane there, did he?
SAM: Yes. Look what he gave me. He gave me a box of cigars.

(SAM *takes a box of cigars from his pocket.*)

MAX: Come here. Let's have a look at them.   125

(SAM *shows* MAX *the cigars.* MAX *takes one from the box, pinches
it and sniffs it.*)

It's a fair cigar.
SAM: Want to try one?

(MAX *and* SAM *light cigars.*)

You know what he said to me? He told me I was the best
chauffeur he'd ever had. The best one.
MAX: From what point of view?   130
SAM: Eh?
MAX: From what point of view?

LENNY: From the point of view of his driving, Dad, and his general sense of courtesy, I should say.

135 MAX: Thought you were a good driver, did he, Sam? Well, he gave you a first-class cigar.

SAM: Yes, he thought I was the best he'd ever had. They all say that, you know. They won't have anyone else, they only ask for me. They say I'm the best chauffeur in the firm.

140 LENNY: I bet the other drivers tend to get jealous, don't they, Uncle?

SAM: They do get jealous. They get very jealous.

MAX: Why?

(*Pause.*)

SAM: I just told you.

145 MAX: No, I just can't get it clear, Sam. Why do the other drivers get jealous?

SAM: Because (a) I'm the best driver, and because . . . (b) I don't take liberties.

(*Pause.*)

I don't press myself on people, you see. These big business
150 men, men of affairs, they don't want the driver jawing all the time, they like to sit in the back, have a bit of peace and quiet. After all, they're sitting in a Humber Super Snipe, they can afford to relax. At the same time, though, this is what really makes me special . . . I do know how to pass the time of
155 day when required.

(*Pause.*)

For instance, I told this man today I was in the second world war. Not the first. I told him I was too young for the first. But I told him I fought in the second.

(*Pause.*)

So did he, it turned out.

(LENNY *stands, goes to the mirror and straightens his tie.*)

160 LENNY: He was probably a colonel, or something, in the American Air Force.

SAM: Yes.

LENNY: Probably a navigator, or something like that, in a Flying Fortress. Now he's most likely a high executive in a
165 worldwide group of aeronautical engineers.

SAM: Yes.

LENNY: Yes, I know the kind of man you're talking about.

(LENNY *goes out, turning to his right.*)

SAM: After all, I'm experienced. I was driving a dust cart at the age of nineteen. Then I was in long-distance haulage. I
170 had ten years as a taxi-driver and I've had five as a private chauffeur.

MAX: It's funny you never got married, isn't it? A man with all your gifts.

(*Pause.*)

Isn't it? A man like you?

175 SAM: There's still time.

MAX: Is there?

(*Pause.*)

SAM: You'd be surprised.

MAX: What you been doing, banging away at your lady customers, have you?

SAM: Not me. 180

MAX: In the back of the Snipe? Been having a few crafty reefs in a layby, have you?

SAM: Not me.

MAX: On the back seat? What about the armrest, was it up or down? 185

SAM: I've never done that kind of thing in my car.

MAX: Above all that kind of thing, are you, Sam?

SAM: Too true.

MAX: Above having a good bang on the back seat, are you?

SAM: Yes, I leave that to others. 190

MAX: You leave it to others? What others? You paralysed prat!

SAM: I don't mess up my car! Or my . . . my boss's car! Like other people.

MAX: Other people? What other people?

(*Pause.*)

What other people? 195

(*Pause.*)

SAM: Other people.

(*Pause.*)

MAX: When you find the right girl, Sam, let your family know, don't forget, we'll give you a number one send-off, I promise you. You can bring her to live here, she can keep us all happy. We'd take it in turns to give her a walk around the 200 park.

SAM: I wouldn't bring her here.

MAX: Sam, it's your decision. You're welcome to bring your bride here, to the place where you live, or on the other hand you can take a suite at the Dorchester. It's entirely up to you. 205

SAM: I haven't got a bride.

(SAM *stands, goes to the sideboard, takes an apple from the bowl, bites into it.*)

Getting a bit peckish.

(*He looks out of the window.*)

Never get a bride like you had, anyway. Nothing like your bride . . . going about these days. Like Jessie.

(*Pause.*)

After all, I escorted her once or twice, didn't I? Drove her 210 round once or twice in my cab. She was a charming woman.

(*Pause.*)

All the same, she was your wife. But still . . . they were some of the most delightful evenings I've ever had. Used to just drive her about. It was my pleasure.

MAX: (*Softly, closing his eyes.*) Christ. 215

SAM: I used to pull up at a stall and buy her a cup of coffee. She was a very nice companion to be with.

(*Silence.*

JOEY *comes in the front door. He walks into the room, takes his jacket off, throws it on a chair and stands.*

Silence.)

JOEY: Feel a bit hungry.

SAM: Me, too.

MAX: Who do you think I am, your mother? Eh? Honest. They 220 walk in here every time of the day and night like bloody animals. Go and find yourself a mother.

(LENNY *walks into the room, stands.*)

JOEY: I've been training down at the gym.

SAM: Yes, the boy's been working all day and training all night.

225 MAX: What do you want, you bitch? You spend all the day sitting on your arse at London Airport, buy yourself a jamroll. You expect me to sit here waiting to rush into the kitchen the moment you step in the door? You've been living sixty-three years, why don't you learn to cook?

230 SAM: I can cook.

MAX: Well, go and cook!

(*Pause.*)

LENNY: What the boys want, Dad, is your own special brand of cooking, Dad. That's what the boys look forward to. The special understanding of food, you know, that you've got.

235 MAX: Stop calling me Dad. Just stop all that calling me Dad, do you understand?

LENNY: But I'm your son. You used to tuck me up in bed every night. He tucked you up, too, didn't he, Joey?

(*Pause.*)

He used to like tucking up his sons.

(LENNY *turns and goes towards the front door.*)

240 MAX: Lenny.

LENNY: (*Turning.*) What?

MAX: I'll give you a proper tuck up one of these nights, son. You mark my word.

(*They look at each other.*

LENNY *opens the front door and goes out.*

Silence.)

JOEY: I've been training with Bobby Dodd.

(*Pause.*)

245 And I had a good go at the bag as well.

(*Pause.*)

I wasn't in bad trim.

MAX: Boxing's a gentleman's game.

(*Pause.*)

I'll tell you what you've got to do. What you've got to do is you've got to learn how to defend yourself, and you've got to 250 learn how to attack. That's your only trouble as a boxer. You don't know how to defend yourself, and you don't know how to attack.

(*Pause.*)

Once you've mastered those arts you can go straight to the top.

(*Pause.*)

255 JOEY: I've got a pretty good idea . . . of how to do that.

(JOEY *looks round for his jacket, picks it up, goes out of the room and up the stairs.*

Pause.)

MAX: Sam . . . why don't you go, too, eh? Why don't you just go upstairs? Leave me quiet. Leave me alone.

SAM: I want to make something clear about Jessie, Max. I want to. I do. When I took her out in the cab, round the town, I

was taking care of her, for you. I was looking after her for 260 you, when you were busy, wasn't I? I was showing her the West End.

(*Pause.*)

You wouldn't have trusted any of your other brothers. You wouldn't have trusted Mac, would you? But you trusted me. I want to remind you. 265

(*Pause.*)

Old Mac died a few years ago, didn't he? Isn't he dead?

(*Pause.*)

He was a lousy stinking rotten loudmouth. A bastard uncouth sodding runt. Mind you, he was a good friend of yours.

(*Pause.*)

MAX: Eh, Sam . . .

SAM: What? 270

MAX: Why do I keep you here? You're just an old grub.

SAM: Am I?

MAX: You're a maggot.

SAM: Oh yes?

MAX: As soon as you stop paying your way here, I mean when 275 you're too old to pay your way, you know what I'm going to do? I'm going to give you the boot.

SAM: You are, eh?

MAX: Sure. I mean, bring in the money and I'll put up with you. But when the firm gets rid of you—you can flake off. 280

SAM: This is my house as well, you know. This was our mother's house.

MAX: One lot after the other. One mess after the other.

SAM: Our father's house.

MAX: Look what I'm lumbered with. One cast-iron bunch of 285 crap after another. One flow of stinking pus after another.

(*Pause.*)

Our father? I remember him. Don't worry. You kid yourself. He used to come over to me and look down at me. My old man did. He'd bend right over me, then he'd pick me up. I was only that big. Then he'd dandle me. Give me the bottle. 290 Wipe me clean. Give me a smile. Pat me on the bum. Pass me around, pass me from hand to hand. Toss me up in the air. Catch me coming down. I remember my father.

(*Blackout.*

Lights up. Night. TEDDY *and* RUTH *stand at the threshold of the room.*

They are both well dressed in light summer suits and light raincoats. Two suitcases are by their side.

They look at the room. TEDDY *tosses the key in his hand, smiles.*)

TEDDY: Well, the key worked.

(*Pause.*)

They haven't changed the lock. 295

(*Pause.*)

RUTH: No one's here.

TEDDY: (*Looking up.*) They're asleep.

(*Pause.*)

RUTH: Can I sit down?

TEDDY: Of course.

300   RUTH: I'm tired.

(*Pause.*)

TEDDY: Then sit down.

(*She does not move.*)

That's my father's chair.
RUTH: That one?
305   TEDDY: (*Smiling.*) Yes, that's it. Shall I go up and see if my room's still there?
RUTH: It can't have moved.
TEDDY: No, I mean if my bed's still there.
RUTH: Someone might be in it.
TEDDY: No. They've got their own beds.

(*Pause.*)

310   RUTH: Shouldn't you wake someone up? Tell them you're here?
TEDDY: Not at this time of night. It's too late.

(*Pause.*)

Shall I go up?

(*He goes into the hall, looks up the stairs, comes back.*)

Why don't you sit down?

(*Pause.*)

315   I'll just go up . . . have a look.

(*He goes up the stairs, stealthily.*

RUTH *stands, then slowly walks across the room.*

TEDDY *returns.*)

It's still there. My room. Empty. The bed's there. What are you doing?

(*She looks at him.*)

Blankets, no sheets. I'll find some sheets. I could hear snores. Really. They're all still here, I think. They're all snoring up
320   there. Are you cold?
RUTH: No.
TEDDY: I'll make something to drink, if you like. Something hot.
RUTH: No, I don't want anything.

(TEDDY *walks about.*)

325   TEDDY: What do you think of the room? Big, isn't it? It's a big house. I mean, it's a fine room, don't you think? Actually there was a wall, across there . . . with a door. We knocked it down . . . years ago . . . to make an open living area. The structure wasn't affected, you see. My mother was dead.

(RUTH *sits.*)

330   Tired?
RUTH: Just a little.
TEDDY: We can go to bed if you like. No point in waking any-one up now. Just go to bed. See them all in the morning . . . see my father in the morning . . .

(*Pause.*)

335   RUTH: Do you want to stay?
TEDDY: Stay?

(*Pause.*)

We've come to say. We're bound to stay . . . for a few days.
RUTH: I think . . . the children . . . might be missing us.
TEDDY: Don't be silly.
RUTH: They might.   340
TEDDY: Look, we'll be back in a few days, won't we?

(*He walks about the room.*)

Nothing's changed. Still the same.

(*Pause.*)

Still, he'll get a surprise in the morning, won't he? The old man. I think you'll like him very much. Honestly. He's a . . . well, he's old, of course. Getting on.   345

(*Pause.*)

I was born here, do you realize that?
RUTH: I know.

(*Pause.*)

TEDDY: Why don't you go to bed? I'll find some sheets. I feel . . . wide awake, isn't it odd? I think I'll stay up for a bit. Are you tired?   350
RUTH: No.
TEDDY: Go to bed. I'll show you the room.
RUTH: No, I don't want to.
TEDDY: You'll be perfectly all right up there without me. Really you will. I mean, I won't be long. Look, it's just up there. **355** It's the first door on the landing. The bathroom's right next door. You . . . need some rest, you know.

(*Pause.*)

I just want to . . . walk about for a few minutes. Do you mind?
RUTH: Of course I don't.   360
TEDDY: Well . . . Shall I show you the room?
RUTH: No, I'm happy at the moment.
TEDDY: You don't have to go to bed. I'm not saying you have to. I mean, you can stay up with me. Perhaps I'll make a cup of tea or something. The only thing is we don't want to make   365 too much noise, we don't want to wake anyone up.
RUTH: I'm not making any noise.
TEDDY: I know you're not.

(*He goes to her.*)

(*Gently.*) Look, it's all right, really. I'm here. I mean . . . I'm with you. There's no need to be nervous. Are you nervous?   370
RUTH: No.
TEDDY: There's no need to be.

(*Pause.*)

They're very warm people, really. Very warm. They're my family. They're not ogres.

(*Pause.*)

Well, perhaps we should go to bed. After all, we have to be   375 up early, see Dad. Wouldn't be quite right if he found us in bed, I think. (*He chuckles.*) Have to be up before six, come down, say hullo.

(*Pause.*)

RUTH: I think I'll have a breath of air.
TEDDY: Air?   380

(Pause.)

What do you mean?

RUTH: *(Standing.)* Just a stroll.

TEDDY: At this time of night? But we've . . . only just got here. We've got to go to bed.

385   RUTH: I just feel like some air.

TEDDY: But I'm going to bed.

RUTH: That's all right.

TEDDY: But what am I going to do?

(Pause.)

The last thing I want is a breath of air. Why do you want a
390   breath of air?

RUTH: I just do.

TEDDY: But it's late.

RUTH: I won't go far. I'll come back.

(Pause.)

TEDDY: I'll wait up for you.

395   RUTH: Why?

TEDDY: I'm not going to bed without you.

RUTH: Can I have the key?

(He gives it to her.)

Why don't you go to bed?

(He puts his arms on her shoulders and kisses her.

They look at each other, briefly. She smiles.)

I won't be long.

(She goes out of the front door.

TEDDY *goes to the window, peers out after her, half turns from
the window, stands, suddenly chews his knuckles.*

LENNY *walks into the room from upstage left. He stands. He
wears pyjamas and dressing-gown. He watches* TEDDY.

TEDDY *turns and sees him.*

Silence.)

400   TEDDY: Hullo, Lenny.

LENNY: Hullo, Teddy.

(Pause.)

TEDDY: I didn't hear you come down the stairs.

LENNY: I didn't.

(Pause.)

I sleep down here now. Next door. I've got a kind of study,
405   workroom cum bedroom next door now, you see.

TEDDY: Oh. Did I . . . wake you up?

LENNY: No. I just had an early night tonight. You know how it
    is. Can't sleep. Keep waking up.

(Pause.)

TEDDY: How are you?

410   LENNY: Well, just sleeping a bit restlessly, that's all. Tonight,
    anyway.

TEDDY: Bad dreams?

LENNY: No, I wouldn't say I was dreaming. It's not exactly a
    dream. It's just that something keeps waking me up. Some
415   kind of tick.

TEDDY: A tick?

LENNY: Yes.

TEDDY: Well, what is it?

LENNY: I don't know.

(Pause.)

TEDDY: Have you got a clock in your room?   420

LENNY: Yes.

TEDDY: Well, maybe it's the clock.

LENNY: Yes, could be, I suppose.

(Pause.)

Well, if it's the clock I'd better do something about it. Stifle it
    in some way, or something.   425

(Pause.)

TEDDY: I've . . . just come back for a few days.

LENNY: Oh yes? Have you?

(Pause.)

TEDDY: How's the old man?

LENNY: He's in the pink.

(Pause.)

TEDDY: I've been keeping well.   430

LENNY: Oh, have you?

(Pause.)

Staying the night then, are you?

TEDDY: Yes.

LENNY: Well, you can sleep in your old room.

TEDDY: Yes, I've been up.   435

LENNY: Yes, you can sleep there.

*(*LENNY *yawns.)*

Oh well.

TEDDY: I'm going to bed.

LENNY: Are you?

TEDDY: Yes, I'll get some sleep.   440

LENNY: Yes, I'm going to bed, too.

*(*TEDDY *picks up the cases.)*

I'll give you a hand.

TEDDY: No, they're not heavy.

*(*TEDDY *goes into the hall with the cases.* LENNY *turns out the
light in the room.*

The light in the hall remains on.

LENNY *follows into the hall.)*

LENNY: Nothing you want?

TEDDY: Mmmm?   445

LENNY: Nothing you might want, for the night? Glass of water,
    anything like that?

TEDDY: Any sheets anywhere?

LENNY: In the sideboard in your room.

TEDDY: Oh, good.   450

LENNY: Friends of mine occasionally stay there, you know, in
    your room, when they're passing through this part of the
    world.

*(*LENNY *turns out the hall light and turns on the first landing
light.*

TEDDY *begins to walk up the stairs.)*

TEDDY: Well, I'll see you at breakfast, then.

455 LENNY: Yes, that's it. Ta-ta.

(TEDDY *goes upstairs.*

LENNY *goes off left.*

Silence.

The landing light goes out. Slight night light in the hall and room.

LENNY *comes back into the room, goes to the window and looks out.*

He leaves the window and turns on a lamp. He is holding a small clock.

He sits, places the clock in front of him, lights a cigarette and sits. RUTH *comes in the front door.*

She stands still. LENNY *turns his head, smiles. She walks slowly into the room.)*

LENNY: Good evening.

RUTH: Morning, I think.

LENNY: You're right there.

(Pause.)

My name's Lenny. What's yours?

460 RUTH: Ruth.

(She sits, puts her coat collar around her.)

LENNY: Cold?

RUTH: No.

LENNY: It's been a wonderful summer, hasn't it? Remarkable.

(Pause.)

Would you like something? Refreshment of some kind? An 465 aperitif, anything like that?

RUTH: No, thanks.

LENNY: I'm glad you said that. We haven't got a drink in the house. Mind you, I'd soon get some in, if we had a party or something like that. Some kind of celebration . . . you know.

(Pause.)

470 You must be connected with my brother in some way. The one who's been abroad.

RUTH: I'm his wife.

LENNY: Eh listen, I wonder if you can advise me. I've been having a bit of a rough time with this clock. The tick's been 475 keeping me up. The trouble is I'm not all that convinced it was the clock. I mean there are lots of things which tick in the night, don't you find that? All sorts of objects, which, in the day, you wouldn't call anything else but commonplace. They give you no trouble. But in the night any given one of 480 a number of them is liable to start letting out a bit of a tick. Whereas you look at these objects in the day and they're just commonplace. They're as quiet as mice during the daytime. So . . . all things being equal . . . this question of me saying it was the clock that woke me up, well, that could very easily 485 prove something of a false hypothesis.

(He goes to the sideboard, pours from a jug into a glass, takes the glass to RUTH.)

Here you are. I bet you could do with this.

RUTH: What is it?

LENNY: Water.

(She takes it, sips, places the glass on a small table by her chair.

LENNY *watches her.)*

Isn't it funny? I've got my pyjamas on and you're fully dressed? 490

(He goes to the sideboard and pours another glass of water.)

Mind if I have one? Yes, it's funny seeing my old brother again after all these years. It's just the sort of tonic my Dad needs, you know. He'll be chuffed to his bollocks in the morning, when he sees his eldest son. I was surprised myself when I saw Teddy, you know. Old Ted. I thought he was in 495 America.

RUTH: We're on a visit to Europe.

LENNY: What, both of you?

RUTH: Yes.

LENNY: What, you sort of live with him over there, do you? 500

RUTH: We're married.

LENNY: On a visit to Europe, eh? Seen much of it?

RUTH: We've just come from Italy.

LENNY: Oh, you went to Italy first, did you? And then he brought you over here to meet the family, did he? Well, the 505 old man'll be pleased to see you, I can tell you.

RUTH: Good.

LENNY: What did you say?

RUTH: Good.

(Pause.)

LENNY: Where'd you go to in Italy? 510

RUTH: Venice.

LENNY: Not dear old Venice? Eh? That's funny. You know, I've always had a feeling that if I'd been a soldier in the last war–say in the Italian campaign—I'd probably have found myself in Venice. I've always had that feeling. The trouble 515 was I was too young to serve, you see. I was only a child, I was too small, otherwise I've got a pretty shrewd idea I'd probably have gone through Venice. Yes, I'd almost certainly have gone through it with my battalion. Do you mind if I hold your hand? 520

RUTH: Why?

LENNY: Just a touch.

(He stands and goes to her.)

Just a tickle.

RUTH: Why?

(He looks down at her.)

LENNY: I'll tell you why. 525

(Slight pause.)

One night, not too long ago, one night down by the docks, I was standing alone under an arch, watching all the men jibbing the boom, out in the harbour, and playing about with the yardarm, when a certain lady came up to me and made me a certain proposal. This lady had been searching for me 530 for days. She'd lost track of my whereabouts. However, the fact was she eventually caught up with me, and when she caught up with me she made me this certain proposal. Well, this proposal wasn't entirely out of order and normally I would have subscribed to it. I mean I would have subscribed 535 to it in the normal course of events. The only trouble was she was falling apart with the pox. So I turned it down. Well, this lady was very insistent and started taking liberties with me

540 down under this arch, liberties which by any criterion I couldn't be expected to tolerate, the facts being what they were, so I clumped her one. It was on my mind at the time to do away with her, you know, to kill her, and the fact is, that as killings go, it would have been a simple matter, nothing to it.

545 Her chauffeur, who had located me for her, he'd popped around the corner to have a drink, which just left this lady and myself, you see, alone, standing underneath this arch, watching all the steamers steaming up, no one about, all quiet on the Western Front, and there she was up against the wall—well, just sliding down the wall, following the blow I'd

550 given her. Well, to sum up, everything was in my favour, for a killing. Don't worry about the chauffeur. The chauffeur would never have spoken. He was an old friend of the family. But . . . in the end I thought . . . Aaah, why go to all the bother . . . you know, getting rid of the corpse and all that,

555 getting yourself into a state of tension. So I just gave her another belt in the nose and a couple of turns of the boot and sort of left it at that.

RUTH: How did you know she was diseased?
LENNY: How did I know?

(Pause.)

560 I decided she was.

(Silence.)

You and my brother are newly-weds, are you?
RUTH: We've been married six years.
LENNY: He's always been my favourite brother, old Teddy. Do you know that? And my goodness we are proud of him here, I

565 can tell you. Doctor of Philosophy and all that . . . leaves quite an impression. Of course, he's a very sensitive man, isn't he? Ted. Very. I've often wished I was as sensitive as he is.
RUTH: Have you?
LENNY: Oh yes. Oh yes, very much so. I mean, I'm not saying

570 I'm not sensitive. I am. I could just be a bit more so, that's all.
RUTH: Could you?
LENNY: Yes, just a bit more so, that's all.

(Pause.)

I mean, I am very sensitive to atmosphere, but I tend to get desensitized, if you know what I mean, when people make

575 unreasonable demands on me. For instance, last Christmas I decided to do a bit of snow-clearing for the Borough Council, because we had a heavy snow over here that year in Europe. I didn't have to do this snow-clearing—I mean I wasn't financially embarrassed in any way—it just appealed to me,

580 it appealed to something inside me. What I anticipated with a good deal of pleasure was the brisk cold bite in the air in the early morning. And I was right. I had to get my snow-boots on and I had to stand on a corner, at about five-thirty in the morning, to wait for the lorry to pick me up, to take

585 me to the allotted area. Bloody freezing. Well, the lorry came, I jumped on the tailboard, headlights on, dipped, and off we went. Got there, shovels up, fags on, and off we went, deep into the December snow, hours before cockcrow. Well, that morning, while I was having my mid-morning cup of

590 tea in a neighboring cafe, the shovel standing by my chair, an old lady approached me and asked me if I would give her a hand with her iron mangle. Her brother-in-law, she said, had left it for her, but he'd left it in the wrong room, he'd left it in the front room. Well, naturally, she wanted it in the back

595 room. It was a present he'd given her, you see, a mangle, to iron out the washing. But he'd left it in the wrong room, he'd left it in the front room, well that was a silly place to leave it, it couldn't stay there. So I took time off to give her a hand. She only lived up the road. Well, the only trouble was when

600 I got there I couldn't move this mangle. It must have weighed about half a ton. How this brother-in-law got it up there in the first place I can't even begin to envisage. So there I was, doing a bit of shoulders on with the mangle, risking a rupture, and this old lady just standing there, waving

605 me on, not even lifting a little finger to give me a helping hand. So after a few minutes I said to her, now look here, why don't you stuff this iron mangle up your arse? Anyway, I said, they're out of date, you want to get a spin drier. I had a good mind to give her a workover there and then, but as I

610 was feeling jubilant with the snow-clearing I just gave her a short-arm jab to the belly and jumped on a bus outside. Excuse me, shall I take this ashtray out of your way?
RUTH: It's not in my way.
LENNY: It seems to be in the way of your glass. The glass was

615 about to fall. Or the ashtray. I'm rather worried about the carpet. It's not me, it's my father. He's obsessed with order and clarity. He doesn't like mess. So, as I don't believe you're smoking at the moment, I'm sure you won't object if I move the ashtray.

(He does so.)

620 And now perhaps I'll relieve you of your glass.
RUTH: I haven't quite finished.
LENNY: You've consumed quite enough, in my opinion.
RUTH: No, I haven't.
LENNY: Quite sufficient, in my own opinion.
625 RUTH: Not in mine, Leonard.

(Pause.)

LENNY: Don't call me that, please.
RUTH: Why not?
LENNY: That's the name my mother gave me.

(Pause.)

Just give me the glass.
630 RUTH: No.

(Pause.)

LENNY: I'll take it, then.
RUTH: If you take the glass . . . I'll take you.

(Pause.)

LENNY: How about me taking the glass without you taking me?
RUTH: Why don't I just take you?

(Pause.)

635 LENNY: You're joking.

(Pause.)

You're in love, anyway, with another man. You've had a secret liaison with another man. His family didn't even know. Then you come here without a word of warning and start to make trouble.

(She picks up the glass and lifts it towards him.)

640 RUTH: Have a sip. Go on. Have a sip from my glass.

(He is still.)

Sit on my lap. Take a long cool sip.

(*She pats her lap.*

Pause. She stands, moves to him with the glass.)

Put your head back and open your mouth.
LENNY: Take that glass away from me.
RUTH: Lie on the floor. Go on. I'll pour it down your throat.
645 LENNY: What are you doing, making me some kind of proposal?

(*She laughs shortly, drains the glass.*)

RUTH: Oh, I was thirsty.

(*She smiles at him, puts the glass down, goes into the hall and up the stairs.*

He follows into the hall and shouts up the stairs.)

LENNY: What was that supposed to be? Some kind of proposal?

(*Silence.*

He comes back into the room, goes to his own glass, drains it.

A door slams upstairs. The landing light goes on.

MAX *comes down the stairs, in pyjamas and cap. He comes into the room.*)

MAX: What's going on here? You drunk?

(*He stares at* LENNY.)

What are you shouting about? You gone mad?

(LENNY *pours another glass of water.*)

650 Prancing about in the middle of the night shouting your head off. What are you, a raving lunatic?
LENNY: I was thinking aloud.
MAX: Is Joey down here? You been shouting at Joey?
LENNY: Didn't you hear what I said, Dad? I said I was thinking
655 aloud.
MAX: You were thinking so loud you got me out of bed.
LENNY: Look, why don't you just . . . pop off, eh?
MAX: Pop off? He wakes me up in the middle of the night, I think we got burglars here, I think he's got a knife stuck in
660 him, I come down here, he tells me to pop off.

(LENNY *sits down.*)

He was talking to someone. Who could he have been talking to? They're all asleep. He was having a conversation with someone. He won't tell me who it was. He pretends he was thinking aloud. What are you doing, hiding someone here?
665 LENNY: I was sleepwalking. Get out of it, leave me alone, will you?
MAX: I want an explanation, you understand? I asked you who you got hiding here.

(*Pause.*)

LENNY: I'll tell you what, Dad, since you're in the mood for a
670 bit of a . . . chat, I'll ask you a question. It's a question I've been meaning to ask you for some time. That night . . . you know . . . the night you got me . . . that night with Mum, what was it like? Eh? When I was just a glint in your eye. What was it like? What was the background to it? I mean, I
675 want to know the real facts about my background. I mean,

for instance, is it a fact that you had me in mind all the time, or is it a fact that I was the last thing you had in mind?

(*Pause.*)

I'm only asking this in a spirit of inquiry, you understand that, don't you? I'm curious. And there's lots of people of my 680 age share that curiosity, you know that, Dad? They often ruminate, sometimes singly, sometimes in groups, about the true facts of that particular night—the night they were made in the image of those two people *at it.* It's a question long overdue, from my point of view, but as we happen to be passing the time of day here tonight I thought I'd pop it to you. 685

(*Pause.*)

MAX: You'll drown in your own blood.
LENNY: If you prefer to answer the question in writing I've got no objection.

(MAX *stands.*)

I should have asked my dear mother. Why didn't I ask my dear mother? Now it's too late. She's passed over to the other 690 side.

(MAX *spits at him.*

LENNY *looks down at the carpet.*)

Now look what you've done. I'll have to Hoover that in the morning, you know.

(MAX *turns and walks up the stairs.*

LENNY *sits still.*

Blackout.

Lights up.

Morning.

JOEY *in front of the mirror. He is doing some slow limbering-up exercises. He stops, combs his hair, carefully. He then shadow-boxes, heavily, watching himself in the mirror.*

MAX *comes in from upstage left.*

Both MAX *and* JOEY *are dressed.* MAX *watches* JOEY *in silence.*
JOEY *stops shadowboxing, picks up a newspaper and sits.*

Silence.)

MAX: I hate this room.

(*Pause.*)

It's the kitchen I like. It's nice in there. It's cosy. 695

(*Pause.*)

But I can't stay in there. You know why? Because he's always washing up in there, scraping the plates, driving me out of the kitchen, that's why.
JOEY: Why don't you bring your tea in here?
MAX: I don't want to bring my tea in here. I hate it here. I want 700 to drink my tea in there.

(*He goes into the hall and looks towards the kitchen.*)

What's he doing in there?

(*He returns.*)

What's the time?
JOEY: Half past six.

705　MAX: Half past six.

(Pause.)

I'm going to see a game of football this afternoon. You want to come?

(Pause.)

I'm talking to you.

JOEY: I'm training this afternoon. I'm doing six rounds with
710　Blackie.

MAX: That's not till five o'clock. You've got time to see a game of football before five o'clock. It's the first game of the season.

JOEY: No, I'm not going.

MAX: Why not?

(Pause.

MAX *goes into the hall.)*

715　Sam! Come here!

(MAX comes back into the room.

SAM *enters with a cloth.)*

SAM: What?

MAX: What are you doing in there?

SAM: Washing up.

MAX: What else?

720　SAM: Getting rid of your leavings.

MAX: Putting them in the bin, eh?

SAM: Right in.

MAX: What point you trying to prove?

SAM: No point.

725　MAX: Oh yes, you are. You resent making my breakfast, that's what it is, isn't it? That's why you bang round the kitchen like that, scraping the frying-pan, scraping all the leavings into the bin, scraping all the plates, scraping all the tea out of the teapot . . . that's why you do that, every single stinking
730　morning. I know. Listen, Sam. I want to say something to you. From my heart.

(He moves closer.)

I want you to get rid of these feelings of resentment you've got towards me. I wish I could understand them. Honestly, have I ever given you cause? Never. When Dad died he said
735　to me, Max, look after your brothers. That's exactly what he said to me.

SAM: How could he say that when he was dead?

MAX: What?

SAM: How could he speak if he was dead?

(Pause.)

740　MAX: Before he died, Sam. Just before. They were his last words. His last sacred words, Sammy. A split second after he said those words . . . he was a dead man. You think I'm joking? You think when my father spoke—on his death-bed—I wouldn't obey his words to the last letter? You hear that,
745　Joey? He'll stop at nothing. He's even prepared to spit on the memory of our Dad. What kind of a son were you, you wet wick? You spent half your time doing crossword puzzles! We took you into the butcher's shop, you couldn't even sweep the dust off the floor. We took MacGregor into the shop, he
750　could run the place by the end of a week. Well, I'll tell you one thing. I respected my father not only as a man but as a number one butcher! And to prove it I followed him into the shop. I learned to carve a carcass at his knee. I commemorated his name in blood. I gave birth to three grown men! All on my own bat. What have you done?　　　　　　　755

(Pause.)

What have you done? You tit!

SAM: Do you want to finish the washing up? Look, here's the cloth.

MAX: So try to get rid of these feelings of resentment, Sam. After all, we are brothers.　　　　　　　760

SAM: Do you want the cloth? Here you are. Take it.

(TEDDY and RUTH come down the stairs. They walk across the hall and stop just inside the room.

The others turn and look at them. JOEY *stands.*

TEDDY *and* RUTH *are wearing dressing-gowns.*

Silence.

TEDDY *smiles.)*

TEDDY: Hullo . . . Dad . . . We overslept.

(Pause.)

What's for breakfast?

(Silence.

TEDDY *chuckles.)*

Huh. We overslept.

(MAX turns to SAM.)*

MAX: Did you know he was here?　　　　　　　765

SAM: No.

(MAX turns to JOEY.)*

MAX: Did you know he was here?

(Pause.)

I asked you if you knew he was here.

JOEY: No.

MAX: Then who knew?　　　　　　　770

(Pause.)

Who knew?

(Pause.)

I didn't know.

TEDDY: I was going to come down, Dad, I was going to . . . be here, when you came down.

(Pause.)

How are you?　　　　　　　775

(Pause.)

Uh . . . look, I'd . . . like you to meet . . .

MAX: How long you been in this house?

TEDDY: All night.

MAX: All night? I'm a laughing-stock. How did you get in?

TEDDY: I had my key.　　　　　　　780

(MAX whistles and laughs.)

MAX: Who's this?

TEDDY: I was just going to introduce you.

MAX: Who asked you to bring tarts in here?

TEDDY: Tarts?

785 MAX: Who asked you to bring dirty tarts into this house?

TEDDY: Listen, don't be silly—

MAX: You been here all night?

TEDDY: Yes, we arrived from Venice—

MAX: We've had a smelly scrubber in my house all night.
790 We've had a stinking pox-ridden slut in my house all night.

TEDDY: Stop it! What are you talking about?

MAX: I haven't seen the bitch for six years, he comes home without a word, he brings a filthy scrubber off the street, he shacks up in my house!

795 TEDDY: She's my wife! We're married!

(Pause.)

MAX: I've never had a whore under this roof before. Ever since your mother died. My word of honour. *(To* JOEY.*)* Have you ever had a whore here? Has Lenny ever had a whore here? They come back from America, they bring the slopbucket
800 with them. They bring the bedpan with them. *(To* TEDDY.*)* Take that disease away from me. Get her away from me.

TEDDY: She's my wife.

MAX: *(To* JOEY.*)* Chuck them out.

(Pause.)

A Doctor of Philosophy. Sam, you want to meet a Doctor of
805 Philosophy? *(To* JOEY.*)* I said chuck them out.

(Pause.)

What's the matter? You deaf?

JOEY: You're an old man. *(To* TEDDY.*)* He's an old man.

(LENNY walks into the room, in a dressing-gown.

He stops.

They all look round. MAX *turns back, hits* JOEY *in the stomach with all his might.*

JOEY contorts, staggers across the stage. MAX, *with the exertion of the blow, begins to collapse. His knees buckle. He clutches his stick.*

SAM moves forward to help him.

MAX *hits him across the head with his stick.*

SAM sits, head in hands.

JOEY, hands pressed to his stomach, sinks down at the feet of RUTH.

She looks down at him. LENNY *and* TEDDY *are still.*

JOEY slowly stands. He is close to RUTH. *He turns from* RUTH, *looks round at* MAX.

SAM clutches his head. MAX *breathes heavily, very slowly gets to his feet.* JOEY *moves to him.*

They look at each other.

Silence.

MAX *moves past* JOEY, *walks towards* RUTH. *He gestures with his stick.)*

MAX: Miss.

(RUTH walks toward him.)

RUTH: Yes?

(He looks at her.)

MAX: You a mother? 810

RUTH: Yes.

MAX: How many you got?

RUTH: Three.

(He turns to TEDDY.*)*

MAX: All yours, Ted?

(Pause.)

Teddy, why don't we have a nice cuddle and kiss, eh? Like 815
the old days? What about a nice cuddle and kiss, eh?

TEDDY: Come on, then.

(Pause.)

MAX: You want to kiss your old father? Want a cuddle with your old father?

TEDDY: Come on, then. 820

(TEDDY moves a step towards him.)

Come on.

(Pause.)

MAX: You still love your old Dad, eh?

(They face each other.)

TEDDY: Come on, Dad. I'm ready for the cuddle.

(MAX begins to chuckle, gurgling.

He turns to the family and addresses them.)

MAX: He still loves his father!

(Curtain.)

— ACT TWO —

(Afternoon.

MAX, TEDDY, LENNY *and* SAM *are about the stage, lighting cigars.*

JOEY *comes in from upstage left with a coffee tray, followed by* RUTH. *He puts the tray down.* RUTH *hands coffee to all the men. She sits with her cup.* MAX *smiles at her.)*

RUTH: That was a very good lunch.

MAX: I'm glad you liked it. *(To the others.)* Did you hear that? *(To* RUTH.*)* Well, I put my heart and soul into it, I can tell you. *(He sips.)* And this is a lovely cup of coffee.

RUTH: I'm glad. 5

(Pause.)

MAX: I've got the feeling you're a first-rate cook.

RUTH: I'm not bad.

MAX: No, I've got the feeling you're a number one cook. Am I right, Teddy?

TEDDY: Yes, she's a very good cook. 10

(Pause.)

MAX: Well, it's a long time since the whole family was together, eh? If only your mother was alive. Eh, what do you say, Sam? What would Jessie say if she was alive? Sitting here with her three sons. Three fine grown-up lads. And a lovely daughter-in-law. The only shame is her grandchildren aren't here. 15

She'd have petted them and cooed over them, wouldn't she, Sam? She'd have fussed over them and played with them, told them stories, tickled them—I tell you she'd have been hysterical. *(To* RUTH.*)* Mind you, she taught those boys everything they know. She taught them all the morality they know. I'm telling you. Every single bit of the moral code they live by—was taught to them by their mother. And she had a heart to go with it. What a heart. Eh, Sam? Listen, what's the use of beating round the bush? That woman was the backbone to this family. I mean, I was busy working twenty-four hours a day in the shop, I was going all over the country to find meat, I was making my way in the world, but I left a woman at home with a will of iron, a heart of gold and a mind. Right, Sam?

(Pause.)

What a mind.

(Pause.)

Mind you, I was a generous man to her. I never left her short of a few bob. I remember one year I entered into negotiations with a top-class group of butchers with continental connections. I was going into association with them. I remember the night I came home, I kept quiet. First of all I gave Lenny a bath, then Teddy a bath, then Joey a bath. What fun we used to have in the bath, eh, boys? Then I came downstairs and I made Jessie put her feet up on a pouffe—what happened to that pouffe, I haven't seen it for years—she put her feet up on the pouffe and I said to her, Jessie, I think our ship is going to come home, I'm going to treat you to a couple of items, I'm going to buy you a dress in pale corded blue silk, heavily encrusted in pearls, and for casual wear, a pair of pantaloons in lilac flowered taffeta. Then I gave her a drop of cherry brandy. I remember the boys came down, in their pyjamas, all their hair shining, their faces pink, it was before they started shaving, and they knelt down at our feet, Jessie's and mine. I tell you, it was like Christmas.

(Pause.)

RUTH: What happened to the group of butchers?

MAX: The group? They turned out to be a bunch of criminals like everyone else.

(Pause.)

This is a lousy cigar.

(He stubs it out.

He turns to SAM.*)*

What time you going to work?

SAM: Soon.

MAX: You've got a job on this afternoon, haven't you?

SAM: Yes, I know.

MAX: What do you mean, you know? You'll be late. You'll lose your job? What are you trying to do, humiliate me?

SAM: Don't worry about me.

MAX: It makes the bile come up in my mouth. The bile—you understand. *(To* RUTH.*)* I worked as a butcher all my life, using the chopper and the slab, the slab, you know what I mean, the chopper and the slab! To keep my family in luxury. Two families! My mother was bedridden, my brothers were all invalids. I had to earn the money for the leading

psychiatrists. I had to read books! I had to study the disease, so that I could cope with an emergency at every stage. A crippled family, three bastard sons, a slutbitch of a wife— don't talk to me about the pain of childbirth—I suffered the pain, I've still got the pangs—when I give a little cough my back collapses— and here I've got a lazy idle bugger of a brother won't even get to work on time. The best chauffeur in the world. All his life he's sat in the front seat giving lovely hand signals. You call that work? This man doesn't know his gearbox from his arse!

SAM: You go and ask my customers! I'm the only one they ever ask for.

MAX: What do the other drivers do, sleep all day?

SAM: I can only drive one car. They can't all have me at the same time.

MAX: Anyone could have you at the same time. You'd bend over for half a dollar on Blackfriars Bridge.

SAM: Me!

MAX: For two bob and a toffee apple.

SAM: He's insulting me. He's insulting his brother. I'm driving a man to Hampton Court at four forty-five.

MAX: Do you want to know who could drive? MacGregor! MacGregor was a driver.

SAM: Don't you believe it.

*(*MAX *points his stick at* SAM.*)*

MAX: He didn't even fight in the war. This man didn't even fight in the bloody war!

SAM: I did!

MAX: Who did you kill?

(Silence.

SAM *gets up, goes to* RUTH, *shakes her hand and goes out of the front door.*

MAX *turns to* TEDDY.*)*

Well, how you been keeping, son?

TEDDY: I've been keeping very well, Dad.

MAX: It's nice to have you with us, son.

TEDDY: It's nice to be back, Dad.

(Pause.)

MAX: You should have told me you were married, Teddy. I'd have sent you a present. Where was the wedding, in America?

TEDDY: No. Here. The day before we left.

MAX: Did you have a big function?

TEDDY: No, there was no one there.

MAX: You're mad. I'd have given you a white wedding. We'd have had the cream of the cream here. I'd have been only too glad to bear the expense, my word of honour.

(Pause.)

TEDDY: You were busy at the time. I didn't want to bother you.

MAX: But you're my own flesh and blood. You're my first born. I'd have dropped everything. Sam would have driven you to the reception in the Snipe, Lenny would have been your best man, and then we'd have all seen you off on the boat. I mean, you don't think I disapprove of marriage, do you? Don't be daft. *(To* RUTH.*)* I've been begging my two youngsters for years to find a nice feminine girl with proper credentials—it makes life worth living. *(To* TEDDY.*)* Anyway, what's the difference, you did it, you made a wonderful choice, you've got a wonderful family, a marvellous career . . . so why don't we let bygones be bygones?

(Pause.)

120 You know what I'm saying? I want you both to know that you have my blessing.

TEDDY: Thank you.

MAX: Don't mention it. How many other houses in the district have got a Doctor of Philosophy sitting down drinking a cup of coffee?

(Pause.)

125 RUTH: I'm sure Teddy's very happy . . . to know that you're pleased with me.

(Pause.)

I think he wondered whether you would be pleased with me.

MAX: But you're a charming woman.

(Pause.)

RUTH: I was . . .

130 MAX: What?

(Pause.)

What she say?

(They all look at her.)

RUTH: I was . . . different . . . when I met Teddy . . . first.

TEDDY: No you weren't. You were the same.

RUTH: I wasn't.

135 MAX: Who cares? Listen, live in the present, what are you worrying about? I mean, don't forget the earth's about five thousand million years old, at least. Who can afford to live in the past?

(Pause.)

TEDDY: She's a great help to me over there. She's a wonderful
140 wife and mother. She's a very popular woman. She's got lots of friends. It's a great life, at the University . . . you know . . . it's a very good life. We've got a lovely house . . . we've got all . . . we've got everything we want. It's a very stimulating environment.

(Pause.)

145 My department . . . is highly successful.

(Pause.)

We've got three boys, you know.

MAX: All boys? Isn't that funny, eh? You've got three, I've got three. You've got three nephews, Joey. Joey! You're an uncle, do you hear? You could teach them how to box.

(Pause.)

150 JOEY: *(To RUTH.)* I'm a boxer. In the evenings, after work. I'm in demolition in the daytime.

RUTH: Oh?

JOEY: Yes. I hope to be full time, when I get more bouts.

MAX: *(To LENNY.)* He speaks so easily to his sister-in-law, do
155 you notice? That's because she's an intelligent and sympathetic woman.

(He leans to her.)

Eh, tell me, do you think the children are missing their mother?

(She looks at him.)

TEDDY: Of course they are. They love her. We'll be seeing
160 them soon.

(Pause.)

LENNY: *(To TEDDY.)* Your cigar's gone out.

TEDDY: Oh, yes.

LENNY: Want a light?

TEDDY: No. No.

(Pause.)

So has yours. 165

LENNY: Oh, yes.

(Pause.)

Eh, Teddy, you haven't told us much about your Doctorship of Philosophy. What do you teach?

TEDDY: Philosophy.

LENNY: Well, I want to ask you something. Do you detect a 170 certain logical incoherence in the central affirmations of Christian theism?

TEDDY: That question doesn't fall within my province.

LENNY: Well, look at it this way . . . you don't mind my asking you some questions, do you? 175

TEDDY: If they're within my province.

LENNY: Well, look at it this way. How can the unknown merit reverence? In other words, how can you revere that of which you're ignorant? At the same time, it would be ridiculous to propose that what we *know* merits reverence. What we know 180 merits any one of a number of things, but it stands to reason reverence isn't one of them. In other words, apart from the known and the unknown, what else is there?

(Pause.)

TEDDY: I'm afraid I'm the wrong person to ask.

LENNY: But you're a philosopher. Come on, be frank. What do 185 you make of all this business of being and not-being?

TEDDY: What do you make of it?

LENNY: Well, for instance, take a table. Philosophically speaking. What is it?

TEDDY: A table. 190

LENNY: Ah. You mean it's nothing else but a table. Well, some people would envy your certainty, wouldn't they, Joey? For instance, I've got a couple of friends of mine, we often sit round the Ritz Bar having a few liqueurs, and they're always saying things like that, you know, things like: Take a table, 195 take it. All right, I say, *take* it, *take* a table, but once you've taken it, what you going to do with it? Once you've got hold of it, where you going to take it?

MAX: You'd probably sell it.

LENNY: You wouldn't get much for it. 200

JOEY: Chop it up for firewood.

(LENNY looks at him and laughs.)

RUTH: Don't be too sure though. You've forgotten something. Look at me. I . . . move my leg. That's all it is. But I wear . . . underwear . . . which moves with me . . . it . . . captures your attention. Perhaps you misinterpret. The action is simple. It's 205 a leg . . . moving. My lips move. Why don't you restrict . . . your observations to that? Perhaps the fact that they move is more significant . . . than the words which come through them. You must bear that . . . possibility . . . in mind.

(*Silence.*

TEDDY *stands.*)

210   I was born quite near here.

(*Pause.*)

     Then . . . six years ago, I went to America.

(*Pause.*)

     It's all rock. And sand. It stretches . . . so far . . . everywhere you look. And there's lots of insects there.

(*Pause.*)

     And there's lots of insects there.

(*Silence.*

She is still.

MAX *stands.*)

215   MAX: Well, it's time to go to the gym. Time for your workout, Joey.

LENNY: (*Standing.*) I'll come with you.

(JOEY *sits looking at* RUTH.)

MAX: Joe.

(JOEY *stands. The three go out.*

TEDDY *sits by* RUTH, *holds her hand. She smiles at him.*

Pause.)

TEDDY: I think we'll go back. Mmnn?

(*Pause.*)

220   Shall we go home?

RUTH: Why?

TEDDY: Well, we were only here for a few days, weren't we? We might as well . . . cut it short, I think.

RUTH: Why? Don't you like it here?

225   TEDDY: Of course I do. But I'd like to go back and see the boys now.

(*Pause.*)

RUTH: Don't you like your family?

TEDDY: Which family?

RUTH: Your family here.

230   TEDDY: Of course I like them. What are you talking about?

(*Pause.*)

RUTH: You don't like them as much as you thought you did?

TEDDY: Of course I do. Of course I . . . like them. I don't know what you're talking about.

(*Pause.*)

     Listen. You know what time of the day it is there now, do
235   you?

RUTH: What?

TEDDY: It's morning. It's about eleven o'clock.

RUTH: Is it?

TEDDY: Yes, they're about six hours behind us . . . I mean . . .
240   behind the time here. The boys'll be at the pool . . . now . . . swimming. Think of it. Morning over there. Sun. We'll go anyway, mmnn? It's so clean there.

RUTH: Clean.

TEDDY: Yes.

RUTH: Is it dirty here?   245

TEDDY: No, of course not. But it's cleaner there.

(*Pause.*)

     Look, I just brought you back to meet the family, didn't I? You've met them, we can go. The fall semester will be starting soon.

RUTH: You find it dirty here?   250

TEDDY: I didn't say I found it dirty here.

(*Pause.*)

     I didn't say that.

(*Pause.*)

     Look. I'll go and pack. You rest for a while. Will you? They won't be back for at least an hour. You can sleep. Rest.   255
Please.

(*She looks at him.*)

     You can help me with my lectures when we get back. I'd love that. I'd be so grateful for it, really. We can bathe till October. You know that. Here, there's nowhere to bathe, except the swimming bath down the road. You know what it's like? It's like a urinal. A filthy urinal!   260

(*Pause.*)

     You liked Venice, didn't you? It was lovely, wasn't it? You had a good week. I mean . . . I took you there. I can speak Italian.

RUTH: But if I'd been a nurse in the Italian campaign I would have been there before.

(*Pause.*)

TEDDY: You just rest. I'll go and pack.   265

(TEDDY *goes out and up the stairs.*

She closes her eyes.

LENNY *appears from upstage left. He walks into the room and sits near her.*

She opens her eyes.

Silence.)

LENNY: Well, the evenings are drawing in.

RUTH: Yes, it's getting dark.

(*Pause.*)

LENNY: Winter'll soon be upon us. Time to renew one's wardrobe.

(*Pause.*)

RUTH: That's a good thing to do.   270

LENNY: What?

(*Pause.*)

RUTH: I always . . .

(*Pause.*)

     Do you like clothes?

LENNY: Oh, yes. Very fond of clothes.

(*Pause.*)

RUTH: I'm fond . . .   275

(*Pause.*)

     What do you think of my shoes?

LENNY: They're very nice.

RUTH: No, I can't get the ones I want over there.

LENNY: Can't get them over there, eh?

280   RUTH: No . . . you don't get them there.

(Pause.)

I was a model before I went away.

LENNY: Hats?

(Pause.)

I bought a girl a hat once. We saw it in a glass case, in a shop. I tell you what it had. It had a bunch of daffodils on it,
285   tied with a black satin bow, and then it was covered with a cloche of black veiling. A cloche. I'm telling you. She was made for it.

RUTH: No . . . I was a model for the body. A photographic model for the body.

290   LENNY: Indoor work?

RUTH: That was before I had . . . all my children.

(Pause.)

No, not always indoors.

(Pause.)

Once or twice we went to a place in the country, by train. Oh, six or seven times. We used to pass a . . . a large white
295   water tower. This place . . . this house . . . was very big . . . the trees . . . there was a lake, you see . . . we used to change and walk down towards the lake . . . we went down a path . . . on stones . . . there were . . . on this path, Oh, just . . . wait . . . yes . . . when we changed in the house we
300   had a drink. There was a cold buffet.

(Pause.)

Sometimes we stayed in the house but . . . most often . . . we walked down to the lake . . . and did our modelling there.

(Pause.)

Just before we went to America I went down there. I walked from the station to the gate and then I walked up the drive.
305   There were lights on . . . I stood in the drive . . . the house was very light.

(TEDDY comes down the stairs with the cases. He puts them down, looks at LENNY.)

TEDDY: What have you been saying to her?

(He goes to RUTH.)

Here's your coat.

(LENNY goes to the radiogram and puts on a record of slow jazz.)

Ruth. Come on. Put it on.

310   LENNY: *(To RUTH.)* What about one dance before you go?

TEDDY: We're going.

LENNY: Just one.

TEDDY: No. We're going.

LENNY: Just one dance, with her brother-in-law, before she
315   goes.

(LENNY bends to her.)

Madam?

(RUTH stands. They dance, slowly.

TEDDY *stands, with* RUTH's *coat.*

MAX *and* JOEY *come in the front door and into the room. They stand.*

LENNY *kisses* RUTH. *They stand, kissing.)*

JOEY: Christ, she's wide open. Dad, look at that.

(Pause.)

She's a tart.

(Pause.)

Old Lenny's got a tart in here.

(JOEY goes to them. He takes RUTH's arm. He smiles at LENNY. He sits with RUTH on the sofa, embraces and kisses her.

He looks up at LENNY.)

Just up my street.   320

(He leans her back until she lies beneath him. He kisses her. He looks up at TEDDY and MAX.)

It's better than a rubdown, this.

(LENNY sits on the arm of the sofa. He caresses RUTH's hair as JOEY embraces her.

MAX *comes forward, looks at the cases.)*

MAX: You going, Teddy? Already?

(Pause.)

Well, when you coming over again, eh? Look, next time you come over, don't forget to let us know beforehand whether you're married or not. I'll always be glad to meet the wife.   325
Honest. I'm telling you.

(JOEY lies heavily on RUTH.

They are almost still.

LENNY *caresses her hair.)*

Listen, you think I don't know why you didn't tell me you were married? I know why. You were ashamed. You thought I'd be annoyed because you married a woman beneath you. You should have known me better. I'm broadminded. I'm a   330
broadminded man.

(He peers to see RUTH's face under JOEY, turns back to TEDDY.)

Mind you, she's a lovely girl. A beautiful woman. And a mother too. A mother of three. You've made a happy woman out of her. It's something to be proud of. I mean, we're talk-ing about a woman of quality. We're talking about a woman   335
of feeling.

(JOEY and RUTH roll off the sofa on to the floor.

JOEY *clasps her.* LENNY *moves to stand above them. He looks down on them. He touches RUTH gently with his foot.*

RUTH *suddenly pushes JOEY away.*

She stands up. JOEY *gets to his feet, stares at her.)*

RUTH: I'd like something to eat. *(To LENNY.)* I'd like a drink. Did you get any drink?

LENNY: We've got drink.

RUTH: I'd like one, please.   340

LENNY: What drink?

RUTH: Whisky.

LENNY: I've got it.

(Pause.)

RUTH: Well, get it.

(LENNY goes to the sideboard, takes out bottle and glasses.

JOEY moves towards her.)

345   Put the record off.

(He looks at her, turns, puts the record off.)

        I want something to eat.

(Pause.)

JOEY: I can't cook. *(Pointing to MAX.)* He's the cook.

(LENNY brings her a glass of whisky.)

LENNY: Soda on the side?

RUTH: What's this glass? I can't drink out of this. Haven't you
350   got a tumbler?

LENNY: Yes.

RUTH: Well, put it in a tumbler.

*(He takes the glass back, pours whisky into a tumbler, brings it
to her.)*

LENNY: On the rocks? Or as it comes?

RUTH: Rocks? What do you know about rocks?

355 LENNY: We've got rocks. But they're frozen stiff in the fridge.

(RUTH drinks.

LENNY looks round at the others.)

        Drinks all round?

(He goes to the sideboard and pours drinks.

JOEY moves closer to RUTH.)

JOEY: What food do you want?

(RUTH walks round the room.)

RUTH: *(To TEDDY.)* Have your family read your critical works?

MAX: That's one thing I've never done. I've never read one of
360   his critical works.

TEDDY: You wouldn't understand them.

(LENNY hands drinks all round.)

JOEY: What sort of food do you want? I'm not the cook, anyway.

LENNY: Soda, Ted? Or as it comes?

TEDDY: You wouldn't understand my works. You wouldn't
365   have the faintest idea of what they were about. You wouldn't
        appreciate the points of reference. You're way behind. All of
        you. There's no point in my sending you my works. You'd be
        lost. It's nothing to do with the question of intelligence. It's a
        way of being able to look at the world. It's a question of how
370   far you can operate on things and not in things. I mean it's a
        question of your capacity to ally the two, to relate the two, to
        balance the two. To see, to be able to *see!* I'm the one who
        can see. That's why I can write my critical works. Might do
        you good . . . have a look at them . . . see how certain people
375   can view . . . things . . . how certain people can maintain . . .
        intellectual equilibrium. Intellectual equilibrium. You're
        just objects. You just . . . move about. I can observe it. I can

see what you do. It's the same as I do. But you're lost in it.
You won't get me being . . . I won't be lost in it.

(Blackout.

Lights up.

Evening.

TEDDY *sitting, in his coat, the cases by him.* SAM.)

(Pause.)

SAM: Do you remember MacGregor, Teddy?   380
TEDDY: Mac?
SAM: Yes.
TEDDY: Of course I do.
SAM: What did you think of him? Did you take to him?
TEDDY: Yes. I liked him. Why?   385

(Pause.)

SAM: You know, you were always my favourite, of the lads.
Always.

(Pause.)

When you wrote to me from America I was very touched,
you know. I mean you'd written to your father a few times
but you'd never written to me. But then, when I got that let- 390
ter from you . . . well, I was very touched. I never told him. I
never told him I'd heard from you.

(Pause.)

(Whispering.) Teddy, shall I tell you something? You were always your mother's favourite. She told me. It's true. You
were always the . . . you were always the main object of her 395
love.

(Pause.)

Why don't you stay for a couple more weeks, eh? We could
have a few laughs.

(LENNY comes in the front door and into the room.)

LENNY: Still here, Ted? You'll be late for your first seminar.

*(He goes to the sideboard, opens it, peers in it, to the right and
the left, stands.)*

        Where's my cheese-roll?   400

(Pause.)

        Someone's taken my cheese-roll. I left it there *(To* SAM.*)* You
        been thieving?

TEDDY: I took your cheese-roll, Lenny.

(Silence.

SAM *looks at them, picks up his hat and goes out of the front
door.*

Silence.)

LENNY: You took my cheese-roll?
TEDDY: Yes.   405
LENNY: I made that roll myself. I cut it and put the butter on. I
        sliced a piece of cheese and put it in between. I put it on a
        plate and I put it in the sideboard. I did all that before I went
        out. Now I come back and you've eaten it.
TEDDY: Well, what are you going to do about it?   410
LENNY: I'm waiting for you to apologize.

TEDDY: But I took it deliberately, Lenny.
LENNY: You mean you didn't stumble on it by mistake?
TEDDY: No, I saw you put it there. I was hungry, so I ate it.

(*Pause.*)

415 LENNY: Barefaced audacity.

(*Pause.*)

What led you to be so . . . vindictive against your own brother? I'm bowled over.

(*Pause.*)

Well, Ted, I would say this is something approaching the naked truth, isn't it? It's a real cards on the table stunt. I
420 mean, we're in the land of no holds barred now. Well, how else can you interpret it? To pinch your younger brother's specially made cheese-roll when he's out doing a spot of work, that's not equivocal, it's unequivocal.

(*Pause.*)

Mind you, I will say you do seem to have grown a bit sulky
425 during the last six years. A bit sulky. A bit inner. A bit less forthcoming. It's funny, because I'd have thought that in the United States of America, I mean with the sun and all that, the open spaces, on the old campus, in your position, lec-
430 turing, in the centre of all the intellectual life out there, on the old campus, all the social whirl, all the stimulation of it all, all your kids and all that, to have fun with, down by the pool, the Greyhound buses and all that, tons of iced water, all the comfort of those Bermuda shorts and all that, on the old campus, no time of the day or night you can't get a cup
435 of coffee or a Dutch gin, I'd have thought you'd have grown more forthcoming, not less. Because I want you to know that you set a standard for us, Teddy. Your family looks up to you, boy, and you know what it does? It does its best to follow the example you set. Because you're a great source of pride to
440 us. That's why we were so glad to see you come back, to welcome you back to your birthplace. That's why.

(*Pause.*)

No, listen, Ted, there's no question that we live a less rich life here than you do over there. We live a closer life. We're busy, of course. Joey's busy with his boxing, I'm busy with
445 my occupation, Dad still plays a good game of poker, and he does the cooking as well, well up to his old standard, and Uncle Sam's the best chauffeur in the firm. But nevertheless we do make up a unit, Teddy, and you're an integral part of it. When we all sit round the backyard having a quiet
450 gander at the night sky, there's always an empty chair standing in the circle, which is in fact yours. And so when you at length return to us, we do expect a bit of grace, a bit of je ne sais quoi, a bit of generosity of mind, a bit of liberality of spirit, to reassure us. We do expect that. But do we get it?
455 Have we got it? Is that what you've given us?

(*Pause.*)

TEDDY: Yes.

(*JOEY comes down the stairs and into the room, with a newspaper.*)

LENNY: (*To* JOEY.) How'd you get on?
JOEY: Er . . . not bad.
LENNY: What do you mean?

(*Pause.*)

What do you mean?   460
JOEY: Not bad.
LENNY: I want to know what you *mean*—by not bad.
JOEY: What's it got to do with you?
LENNY: Joey, you tell your brother everything.

(*Pause.*)

JOEY: I didn't get all the way.   465
LENNY: You didn't get all the way?

(*Pause.*)

(*With emphasis.*) You didn't get all the way?
But you've had her up there for two hours.
JOEY: Well?
LENNY: You didn't get all the way and you've had her up there 470
for two hours!
JOEY: What about it?

(LENNY *moves closer to him.*)

LENNY: What are you telling me?
JOEY: What do you mean?
LENNY: Are you telling me she's a tease?   475

(*Pause.*)

She's a tease!

(*Pause.*)

What do you think of that, Ted? Your wife turns out to be a tease. He's had her up there for two hours and he didn't go the whole hog.
JOEY: I didn't say she was a tease.   480
LENNY: Are you joking? It sounds like a tease to me, don't it to you, Ted?
TEDDY: Perhaps he hasn't got the right touch.
LENNY: Joey? Not the right touch? Don't be ridiculous. He's had more dolly than you've had cream cakes. He's irre-   485
sistible. He's one of the few and far between. Tell him about the last bird you had, Joey.

(*Pause.*)

JOEY: What bird?
LENNY: The last bird? When we stopped the car . . .
JOEY: Oh, that . . . yes . . . well, we were in Lenny's car one 490
night last week . . .
LENNY: The Alfa.
JOEY: And er . . . bowling down the road . . .
LENNY: Up near the Scrubs.
JOEY: Yes, up over by the Scrubs . . .   495
LENNY: We were doing a little survey of North Paddington.
JOEY: And er . . . it was pretty late, wasn't it?
LENNY: Yes, it was late. Well?

(*Pause.*)

JOEY: And then we . . . well, by the kerb, we saw this parked car . . . with a couple of girls in it.   500
LENNY: And their escorts.
JOEY: Yes, there were two geezers in it. Anyway . . .

(*Paue.*)

What we do then?
LENNY: We stopped the car and got out!

505 JOEY: Yes . . . we got out . . . and we told the . . . two escorts . . . to go away . . . which they did . . . and then we . . . got the girls out of the car . . .

LENNY: We didn't take them over the Scrubs.

JOEY: Oh, no. Not over the Scrubs. Well, the police would
510 have noticed us there . . . you see. We took them over a bombed site.

LENNY: Rubble. In the rubble.

JOEY: Yes, plenty of rubble.

(Pause.)

Well . . . you know . . . then we had them.

515 LENNY: You've missed out the best bit. He's missed out the best bit!

JOEY: What bit?

LENNY: *(To* TEDDY.) His bird says to him, I don't mind, she says, but I've got to have some protection. I've got to have
520 some contraceptive protection. I haven't got any contraceptive protection, old Joey says to her. In that case I won't do it, she says. Yes you will says Joey, never mind about the contraceptive protection.

*(*LENNY *laughs.)*

Even my bird laughed when she heard that. Yes, even she
525 gave out a bit of a laugh. So you can't say old Joey isn't a bit of a knockout when he gets going, can you? And here he is upstairs with your wife for two hours and he hasn't even been the whole hog. Well, your wife sounds like a bit of a tease to me, Ted. What do you make of it, Joey? You satis-
530 fied? Don't tell me you're satisfied without going the whole hog?

(Pause.)

JOEY: I've been the whole hog plenty of times. Sometimes . . . you can be happy . . . and not go the whole hog. Now and again . . . you can be happy . . . without going any hog.

*(*LENNY *stares at him.*

MAX *and* SAM *come in the front door and into the room.)*

535 MAX: Where's the whore? Still in bed? She'll make us all animals.

LENNY: The girl's a tease.

MAX: What?

LENNY: She's had Joey on a string.

540 MAX: What do you mean?

TEDDY: He had her up there for two hours and he didn't go the whole hog.

(Pause.)

MAX: My Joey? She did that to my boy?

(Pause.)

To my youngest son? Tch, tch, tch, tch. How you feeling,
545 son? Are you all right?

JOEY: Sure I'm all right.

MAX: *(To* TEDDY.) Does she do that to you, too?

TEDDY: No.

LENNY: He gets the gravy.

550 MAX: You think so?

JOEY: No he don't.

(Pause.)

SAM: He's her lawful husband. She's his lawful wife.

JOEY: No he don't! He don't get no gravy! I'm telling you. I'm telling all of you. I'll kill the next man who says he gets the
555 gravy.

MAX: Joey . . . what are you getting so excited about? *(To* LENNY.) It's because he's frustrated. You see what happens?

JOEY: Who is?

MAX: Joey. No one's saying you're wrong. In fact, everyone's
560 saying you're right.

(Pause.

MAX *turns to the others.)*

You know something? Perhaps it's not a bad idea to have a woman in the house. Perhaps it's a good thing. Who knows? Maybe we should keep her.

(Pause.)

Maybe we'll ask her if she wants to stay.

(Pause.)

TEDDY: I'm afraid not, Dad. She's not well, and we've got to
565 get home to the children.

MAX: Not well? I told you, I'm used to looking after people who are not so well. Don't worry about that. Perhaps we'll keep her here.

(Pause.)

SAM: Don't be silly.
570 MAX: What's silly?

SAM: You're talking rubbish.

MAX: Me?

SAM: She's got three children.

MAX: She can have more! Here. If she's so keen.
575 TEDDY: She doesn't want any more.

MAX: What do you know about what she wants, eh, Ted?

TEDDY: *(Smiling.)* The best thing for her is to come home with me, Dad. Really. We're married, you know.

*(*MAX *walks about the room, clicks his fingers.)*

MAX: We'd have to pay her, of course. You realize that? We
580 can't leave her walking about without any pocket money. She'll have to have a little allowance.

JOEY: Of course we'll pay her. She's got to have some money in her pocket.

MAX: That's what I'm saying. You can't expect a woman to
585 walk about without a few bob to spend on a pair of stockings.

(Pause.)

LENNY: Where's the money going to come from?

MAX: Well, how much is she worth? What we talking about, three figures?

LENNY: I asked you where the money's going to come from.
590 It'll be an extra mouth to feed. It'll be an extra body to clothe. You realize that?

JOEY: I'll buy her clothes.

LENNY: What with?

JOEY: I'll put in a certain amount out of my wages.
595 MAX: That's it. We'll pass the hat round. We'll make a donation. We're all grown-up people, we've got a sense of responsibility. We'll all put a little in the hat. It's democratic.

LENNY: It'll come to a few quid, Dad.

(Pause.)

600 I mean, she's not a woman who likes walking around in second-hand goods. She's up to the latest fashion. You wouldn't want her walking about in clothes which don't show her off at her best, would you?

MAX: Lenny, do you mind if I make a little comment? It's not

605 meant to be critical. But I think you're concentrating too much on the economic considerations. There are other considerations. There are the human considerations. You understand what I mean? There are the human considerations. Don't forget them.

610 LENNY: I won't.

MAX: Well don't.

(Pause.)

Listen, we're bound to treat her in something approximating, at least, to the manner in which she's accustomed. After all, she's not someone off the street, she's my daughter-in-law!

615 JOEY: That's right.

MAX: There you are, you see. Joey'll donate, Sam'll donate. . . .

(SAM looks at him.)

I'll put in a few bob out of my pension, Lenny'll cough up. We're laughing. What about you, Ted? How much you going to put in the kitty?

620 TEDDY: I'm not putting anything in the kitty.

MAX: What? You won't even help to support your own wife? I thought he was a son of mine. You lousy stinkpig. Your mother would drop dead if she heard you take that attitude.

LENNY: Eh, Dad.

(LENNY walks forward.)

625 I've got a better idea.

MAX: What?

LENNY: There's no need for us to go to all this expense. I know these women. Once they get started they ruin your budget. I've got a better idea. Why don't I take her up with me to

630 Greek Street?

(Pause.)

MAX: You mean put her on the game?

(Pause.)

We'll put her on the game. That's a stroke of genius, that's a marvellous idea. You mean she can earn the money herself—on her back?

635 LENNY: Yes.

MAX: Wonderful. The only thing is, it'll have to be short hours. We don't want her out of the house all night.

LENNY: I can limit the hours.

MAX: How many?

640 LENNY: Four hours a night.

MAX: *(Dubiously.)* Is that enough?

LENNY: She'll bring in a good sum for four hours a night.

MAX: Well, you should know. After all, it's true, the last thing we want to do is wear the girl out. She's going to have her ob-

645 ligations this end as well. Where you going to put her in Greek Street?

LENNY: It doesn't have to be right in Greek Street, Dad. I've got a number of flats all around that area.

MAX: You have? Well, what about me? Why don't you give me

650 one?

LENNY: You're sexless.

JOEY: Eh, wait a minute, what's all this?

MAX: I know what Lenny's saying. Lenny's saying she can pay her own way. What do you think, Teddy? That'll solve all our

655 problems.

JOEY: Eh, wait a minute. I don't want to share her.

MAX: What did you say?

JOEY: I don't want to share her with a lot of yobs!

MAX: Yobs! You arrogant git! What arrogance. *(To LENNY.)*

660 Will you be supplying her with yobs?

LENNY: I've got a very distinguished clientèle, Joey. They're more distinguished than you'll ever be.

MAX: So you can count yourself lucky we're including you in.

JOEY: I didn't think I was going to have to share her!

MAX: Well, you *are* going to have to share her! Otherwise she

665 goes straight back to America. You understand?

(Pause.)

It's tricky enough as it is, without you shoving your oar in. But there's something worrying me. Perhaps she's not so up to the mark. Eh? Teddy, you're the best judge. Do you think

670 she'd be up to the mark?

(Pause.)

I mean what about all this teasing? Is she going to make a habit of it? That'll get us nowhere.

(Pause.)

TEDDY: It was just love play . . . I suppose . . . that's all I sup-

675 pose it was.

MAX: Love play? Two bleeding hours? That's a bloody long time for love play!

LENNY: I don't think we've got anything to worry about on that score, Dad.

MAX: How do you know?

680 LENNY: I'm giving you a professional opinion.

(LENNY goes to TEDDY.)

LENNY: Listen, Teddy, you could help us, actually. If I were to send you some cards, over to America . . . you know, very nice ones, with a name on, and a telephone number, very discreet, well, you could distribute them . . . to various par-

685 ties, who might be making a trip over here. Of course, you'd get a little percentage out of it.

MAX: I mean, you needn't tell them she's your wife.

LENNY: No, we'd call her something else. Dolores, or something.

690 MAX: Or Spanish Jacky.

LENNY: No, you've got to be reserved about it, Dad. We could call her something nice . . . like Cynthia . . . or Gillian.

(Pause.)

JOEY: Gillian.

(Pause.)

695 LENNY: No, what I mean, Teddy, you must know lots of professors, heads of departments, men like that. They pop over here for a week at the Savoy, they need somewhere they can go to have a nice quiet poke. And of course you'd be in a position to give them inside information.

MAX: Sure. You can give them proper data. You know, the kind
700 of thing she's willing to do. How far she'd be prepared to go
with their little whims and fancies. Eh, Lenny? To what extent she's various. I mean if you don't know who does?

(Pause.)

I bet you before two months we'd have a waiting list.
LENNY: You could be our representative in the States.
705 MAX: Of course. We're talking in international terms! By the
time we've finished Pan-American'll give us a discount.

(Pause.)

TEDDY: She'd get old . . . very quickly.
MAX: No . . . not in this day and age! With the health service?
Old! How could she get old? She'll have the time of her life.

(RUTH comes down the stairs, dressed.

She comes into the room.

She smiles at the gathering, and sits.

Silence.)

710 TEDDY: Ruth . . . the family have invited you to stay, for a little
while longer. As a . . . as a kind of guest. If you like the idea I
don't mind. We can manage very easily at home . . . until
you come back.
RUTH: How very nice of them.

(Pause.)

715 MAX: It's an offer from our heart.
RUTH: It's very sweet of you.
MAX: Listen . . . it would be our pleasure.

(Pause.)

RUTH: I think I'd be too much trouble.
MAX: Trouble? What are you talking about? What trouble? Lis-
720 ten, I'll tell you something. Since poor Jessie died, eh, Sam?
we haven't had a woman in the house. Not one. Inside this
house. And I'll tell you why. Because their mother's image
was so dear any other woman would have . . . tarnished it.
But you . . . Ruth . . . you're not only lovely and beautiful,
725 but you're kin. You're kin. You belong here.

(Pause.)

RUTH: I'm very touched.
MAX: Of course you're touched. I'm touched.

(Pause.)

TEDDY: But Ruth, I should tell you . . . that you'll have to pull
your weight a little, if you stay. Financially. My father isn't
730 very well off.
RUTH: *(To MAX.)* Oh, I'm sorry.
MAX: No, you'd just have to bring in a little, that's all. A few
pennies. Nothing much. It's just that we're waiting for Joey
to hit the top as a boxer. When Joey hits the top . . . well . . .

(Pause.)

735 TEDDY: Or you can come home with me.
LENNY: We'd get you a flat.

(Pause.)

RUTH: A flat?
LENNY: Yes.

RUTH: Where?
LENNY: In town.   740

(Pause.)

But you'd live here, with us.
MAX: Of course you would. This would be your home. In the
bosom of the family.
LENNY: You'd just pop up to the flat a couple of hours a night,
that's all.   745
MAX: Just a couple of hours, that's all. That's all.
LENNY: And you make enough money to keep you going here.

(Pause.)

RUTH: How many rooms would this flat have?
LENNY: Not many.
RUTH: I would want at least three rooms and a bathroom.   750
LENNY: You wouldn't need three rooms and a bathroom.
MAX: She'd need a bathroom.
LENNY: But not three rooms.

(Pause.)

RUTH: Oh, I would. Really.
LENNY: Two would do.   755
RUTH: No. Two wouldn't be enough.

(Pause.)

I'd want a dressing-room, a rest-room, and a bedroom.

(Pause.)

LENNY: All right, we'll get you a flat with three rooms and a
bathroom.
RUTH: With what kind of conveniences?   760
LENNY: All conveniences.
RUTH: A personal maid?
LENNY: Of course.

(Pause.)

We'd finance you, to begin with, and then, when you were
established, you could pay us back, in instalments.   765
RUTH: Oh, no, I wouldn't agree to that.
LENNY: Oh, why not?
RUTH: You would have to regard your original outlay simply as
a capital investment.

(Pause.)

LENNY: I see. All right.   770
RUTH: You'd supply my wardrobe, of course?
LENNY: We'd supply everything. Everything you need.
RUTH: I'd need an awful lot. Otherwise I wouldn't be content.
LENNY: You'd have everything.
RUTH: I would naturally want to draw up an inventory of   775
everything I would need, which would require your signa-
tures in the presence of witnesses.
LENNY: Naturally.
RUTH: All aspects of the agreement and conditions of employ-
ment would have to be clarified to our mutual satisfaction   780
before we finalized the contract.
LENNY: Of course.

(Pause.)

RUTH: Well, it might prove a workable arrangement.
LENNY: I think so.

785 MAX: And you'd have the whole of your daytime free, of course. You could do a bit of cooking here if you wanted to.

LENNY: Make the beds.

MAX: Scrub the place out a bit.

TEDDY: Keep everyone company.

(SAM *comes forward.*)

790 SAM: (*In one breath.*) MacGregor had Jessie in the back of my cab as I drove them along.

(*He croaks and collapses.*

He lies still.

They look at him.)

MAX: What's he done? Dropped dead?

LENNY: Yes.

MAX: A corpse? A corpse on my floor? Get him out of here!

795 Clear him out of here!

(JOEY *bends over* SAM.)

JOEY: He's not dead.

LENNY: He probably was dead, for about thirty seconds.

MAX: He's not even dead!

(LENNY *looks down at* SAM.)

LENNY: Yes, there's still some breath there.

800 MAX: (*Pointing at* SAM.) You know what that man had?

LENNY: Has.

MAX: Has! A diseased imagination.

(*Pause.*)

RUTH: Yes, it sounds a very attractive idea.

MAX: Do you want to shake on it now, or do you want to leave

805 it till later?

RUTH: Oh, we'll leave it till later.

(TEDDY *stands.*

He looks down at SAM.)

TEDDY: I was going to ask him to drive me to London Airport.

(*He goes to the cases, picks one up.*)

Well, I'll leave your case, Ruth. I'll just go up the road to the Underground.

810 MAX: Listen, if you go the other way, first left, first right, you remember, you might find a cab passing there.

TEDDY: Yes, I might do that.

MAX: Or you can take the tube to Piccadilly Circus, won't take you ten minutes, and pick up a cab from there out to the

815 Airport.

TEDDY: Yes, I'll probably do that.

MAX: Mind you, they'll charge you double fare. They'll charge you for the return trip. It's over the six-mile limit.

TEDDY: Yes, Well, bye-bye, Dad. Look after yourself.

(*They shake hands.*)

820 MAX: Thanks, son. Listen. I want to tell you something. It's been wonderful to see you.

(*Pause.*)

TEDDY: It's been wonderful to see you.

MAX: Do your boys know about me? Eh? Would they like to see a photo, do you think, of their grandfather?

TEDDY: I know they would. 825

(MAX *brings out his wallet.*)

MAX: I've got one on me. I've got one here. Just a minute. Here you are. Will they like that one?

TEDDY: (*Taking it.*) They'll be thrilled.

(*He turns to* LENNY.)

Good-bye, Lenny.

(*They shake hands.*)

LENNY: Ta-ta, Ted. Good to see you. Have a good trip. 830

TEDDY: Bye-bye, Joey.

(JOEY *does not move.*)

JOEY: Ta-ta.

(TEDDY *goes to the front door.*)

RUTH: Eddie.

(TEDDY *turns.*)

(*Pause.*)

Don't become a stranger.

(TEDDY *goes, shuts the front door.*

Silence.

The three men stand.

RUTH *sits relaxed in her chair.* SAM *lies still.*

JOEY *walks slowly across the room. He kneels at her chair.*

She touches his head, lightly.

He puts his head in her lap.

MAX *begins to move above them, backwards and forwards.*

LENNY *stands still.* MAX *turns to* LENNY.)

MAX: I'm too old, I suppose. She thinks I'm an old man. **835**

(*Pause.*)

I'm not such an old man.

(*Pause.*)

(*To* RUTH.) You think I'm too old for you?

(*Pause.*)

Listen. You think you're just going to get that big slag all the time? You think you're just going to have him . . . you're going to just have him all the time? You're going to have to 840 work! You'll have to take them on, you understand?

(*Pause.*)

Does she realize that?

(*Pause.*)

Lenny, do you think she understands . . .

(*He begins to stammer.*)

What . . . what . . . what . . . we're getting at? What . . . we've got in mind? Do you think she's got it clear? 845

(*Pause.*)

I don't think she's got it clear.

(Pause.)

You understand what I mean? Listen, I've got a funny idea she'll do the dirty on us, you want to bet? She'll use us, she'll make use of us, I can tell you! I can smell it! You want to bet?

(Pause.)

850   She won't . . . be adaptable!

(He falls to his knees, whimpers, begins to moan and sob. He stops sobbing, crawls past SAM's *body round her chair, to the other side of her.)*

I'm not an old man.

(He looks up at her.)

Do you hear me?

(He raises his face to her.)

Kiss me.

(She continues to touch JOEY's *head, lightly.)*

LENNY *stands, watching.)*

(Curtain.)

■ MARGUERITE DURAS ■

Born in 1914, Marguerite Duras was raised in Indochina (now Vietnam) during the period of French colonial rule; although she visited France occasionally, much of her youth was spent in Vietnam, which would later provide the setting for her most powerful novels. After completing school in Saigon, Duras went to Paris in 1932 and took degrees in law and political science in 1935. She became a secretary in the Department of Colonies and began to write as well; her first novel, *The Impudent Ones*, was published in 1943. Much of Duras's fiction involves her sense of the exploitation and poverty of the Vietnam of her youth, which provides the background for an intense exploration of personal relationships; this is particularly true of *The Sea Wall* (1950), and *The Lover* (1984); other novels, such as *Moderato Cantabile* (1958) and *The Vice-Consul* (1965), are set elsewhere in Asia and also confront the depredations of colonial exploitation.

Duras's drama similarly centers on interpersonal conflict in short plays like *The Square* (1956), the murder-thriller *The Viaduct* (1963), *Water and Forests* (1965), *La Musica* (1966), and in her first full-length play, *Days in the Trees* (1966). Duras's evocative sense of the visual is explored in other genres as well; her powerful film *Hiroshima Mon Amour* (1959), directed by Alain Resnais, won the International Critics' Prize at the Cannes Film Festival in 1959. In the 1960s, Duras's experiments with non-linear narrative led her to other cinematic projects: she directed the filming of her own *Days in the Trees* (1976), wrote two other films, *Aurélia Steiner* (1979) and *The Atlantic Man* (1982), and experimented with a simultaneous film/fiction version of the same work, *Destroy, She Said* (1969). *India Song* (1972), commissioned by Peter Hall for the opening of the Lyttleton Theater of London's National Theatre, is part of Duras's efforts to transgress the boundaries of genre. Based on her novel *The Vice-Consul*, it is at once a play and a film scenario, and Duras produced and directed the film version of *India Song* in 1975.

INDIA SONG

In an interview published in 1987, Duras remarked on her interest in a theater in which language and acting would be held separate from one another, in which the voice alone would register the drama: "No need to gesticulate to show how the body is suffering because of the words being uttered: the whole drama resides in the words themselves and the body remains unmoved."[1] This special sense of the different registers of representation that can be achieved by the voice and the body stands at the center of Duras's play *India Song*. As she suggests in her "General Remarks" to the play, she has drawn characters from her novel *The Vice-Consul* and projected them "into new narrative regions." There are, nonetheless, a number of stylistic and narrative similarities between the two works. Both centrally concern Anne-Marie Stretter and the various colonial officials and businessmen who surround her—her husband, the Young Attaché (named Charles Rossett in the novel), Michael Richardson, and the mysterious Vice-Consul, waiting in disgrace in Calcutta after wildly shooting at lepers in the Shalimar Gardens of Lahore. In both the novel and the play the Europeans, the "whites," live in a constant state of mental oppression, as the heat, the poverty, the futility of India seem to drive them to the brink of madness—and possibly beyond it. Finally, in both works, Anne-Marie—originally from Venice, mysteriously married, perhaps rescued by marriage in Savannakhet, Laos—is paired with the beggar woman, who was abandoned as a child and is living on scraps of food from the embassy and fish she catches and eats raw from the Ganges, a woman whose vitality, suffering, degradation, and dignity make her a kind of alter-ego to Anne-Marie Stretter herself.

While both works have an extraordinary lyricism, *India Song* deploys that lyricism onstage in effective and original ways. *India Song* is centrally about desire, the desire that circulates around, and largely objectifies its central character, Anne-Marie Stretter. The play opens with Anne-Marie lying dead onstage and closes with her suicide; it is centrally occupied with how she is desired: by the male characters in the play, and, more powerfully by the voices, male and female, that narrate

---

[1] See *Practicalities*, trans. Barbara Bray (New York: Grove Weidenfeld, 1990), p. 9.

the action. In many ways, *India Song* is less about the narrative, the "plot" of the interinvolved love affairs that the play brings together than about how "Anne-Marie Stretter" is positioned as an object of desire, both in the narrative past and in the theatrical present. Much as the play's voices produce Anne-Marie, they also fetishize her, and the play systematically forces its audience into a similar position of voyeurism, where the desire for narrative closure becomes inseparable from the desire for Stretter herself. This dimension of the play becomes clear early in the action, where Stretter, the *"white of the naked body"* visible onstage *"freezes. Head thrown back. Gasping for air. Touching grace of the thin, fragile body. Stays like that, upright, exposed. Offered to the voices. (The voices are slow, stifled, a prey to desire—through this motionless body.)"* The voices are prey to desire, but Stretter is also their victim; more important, the scene laminates the audience to the voices, suggesting that narration, the desire to tell the story, is inseparable from spectating, the desire to *see* Stretter there, powerless before our gaze on the stage. In *India Song*, the offstage voices are unable to achieve a kind of narrative closure, to complete the story; what they are able to do is to evoke their dependence, their realization through the story they narrate. In this sense, Duras forges an explicit critique of theater in *India Song*, which suggests that the stage necessarily animates desire, renders it visible.

GENERAL REMARKS

The names of Indian towns, rivers, states, and seas are used here primarily in a musical sense.
All references to physical, human, or political geography are incorrect:
You can't drive from Calcutta to the estuary of the Ganges in an afternoon. Nor to Nepal.
The "Prince of Wales" hotel is not on an island in the Delta, but in Colombo.
And New Delhi, not Calcutta, is the administrative capital of India.
And so on.

The characters in the story have been taken out of a book called *The Vice-Consul* and projected into new narrative regions. So it is not possible to relate them back to the book and see *India Song* as a film or theatre adaptation of *The Vice-Consul*. Even where a whole episode is taken over from the book, its insertion into the new narrative means that it has to be read, seen, differently.

In fact, *India Song* follows on from *The Woman of the Ganges*. If *The Woman of the Ganges* hadn't been written, neither would *India Song*. The fact that it goes into and reveals an unexplored area of *The Vice-Consul* wouldn't have been a sufficient reason.

What was a sufficient reason was the discovery, in *The Woman of the Ganges*, of the *means* of exploration, revelation: the voices external to the narrative. This discovery made it possible to let the narrative be forgotten and put at the disposal of memories other than that of the author: memories which might remember, in the same way, any other love story. Memories that distort. That create.

Some voices from *The Woman of the Ganges* have been used here. And even some of their words.

That is about all that can be said.

As far as I know, no "India Song" yet exists. When it has been written, the author will make it available and it should be used for all performances of *India Song* in France and elsewhere.

If by any chance *India Song* were performed in France, there should be no public dress rehearsal. This does not apply to other countries.

Marguerite Duras

INDIA SONG

Marguerite Duras

TRANSLATED BY BARBARA BRAY

— CHARACTERS —

ANNE-MARIE STRETTER	FIRST SERVANT
THE BEGGAR WOMAN	SECOND SERVANT
MICHAEL RICHARDSON	2 WOMEN'S VOICES
THE YOUNG ATTACHÉ *(not named)*	2 MEN'S VOICES
THE STRETTERS' GUEST *(not named)*	*10 women extras*
GEORGE CRAWN	*10 men extras*
THE FRENCH VICE-CONSUL IN LAHORE *(not named)*	

— ACT ONE —

NOTES ON VOICES 1 AND 2

VOICES 1 and 2 are women's voices. Young.

They are linked together by a love story.

Sometimes they speak of this love, their own. Most of the time they speak of another love, another story. But this other story leads us back to theirs. And vice versa.

Unlike the men's voices—VOICES 3 and 4, which don't come in until the end of the narrative—the women's voices are tinged with madness. Their sweetness is pernicious. Their memory of the love story is illogical, anarchic. Most of the time they are in a state of transport, a delirium, at once calm and feverish. VOICE 1 is consumed with the story of ANNE-MARIE STRETTER. VOICE 2 is consumed with its passion for VOICE 1.

They should always be heard with perfect clarity, but the level varies according to what they are saying. They are most immediately present when they veer toward their own story—that is, when, in the course of a perpetual shifting process, the love story of *India Song* is juxtaposed with their own. But there is a distinction. When they speak of the story we see unfolding before us, they rediscover it at the same time we do, and so are frightened and perhaps moved by it in the same way we are. But when they speak of their own story, they are always shot through with desire, and we should feel the difference between their two passions. Above all, we should feel the terror of VOICE 2 at the fascination the resuscitated story exerts over VOICE 1. VOICE 1 is in danger of being "lost" in the story of *India Song*, which is in the past, legendary, a model. VOICE 1 is in danger of departing its own life.

The voices are never raised, and their sweetness remains constant.

Blackout.

A tune from between the two wars, "India Song," is played slowly on the piano.

It is played right through, to cover the time—always long—that it takes the audience, or the reader, to emerge from the ordinary world they are in when the performance, or the book, begins.

"India Song" still.

Still.

And now it ends.

Now it is repeated, "farther away" than the first time, as if it were being played elsewhere.

Now it is played at its usual rhythm—blues.

The darkness begins to lighten.

As the dark slowly disperses, suddenly there are voices. Others besides ourselves were watching, hearing, what we thought we alone were watching and hearing. They are women. The voices are slow, sweet. Very close, enclosed like us in this place. And intangible, inaccessible.

VOICE 1: He followed her to India.
VOICE 2: Yes.

(Pause.)

VOICE 2: For he left everything.
　Overnight.
VOICE 1: The night of the dance?　　　　　　　　　　5
VOICE 2: Yes.

(The light continues to grow. We still hear "India Song." The voices are silent for some time. Then they begin again:)

VOICE 1: Was it she who played the piano?
VOICE 2: *(Hesitating.)* Yes . . . but he played too . . . It was he who used sometimes, in the evening, to play the tune they played in S. Thala . . .　　　　　　　　　　10

(Silence.
A house in India. Huge. A "white people's" house. Divans. Armchairs.
Furniture of the period of "India Song."
A ceiling fan is working, but at nightmare slowness.
Net screens over the windows. Beyond, the paths of a large tropical garden. Oleanders. Palm trees.
Complete stillness. No wind outside. Inside, dense shadow. Is it the evening? We don't know. Space. Gilt. A piano. Unlit chandeliers. Indoor plants. Nothing moves, nothing except the fan, which moves with nightmare "unreality."
The slowness of the voices goes with the very slow growth of the light; their sweetness matches the poignancy of the setting.)

VOICE 1: *(As if reading.)* "Michael Richardson was engaged to a girl from S. Thala. Lola Valérie Stein."

They were to have been married in the autumn.
Then there was the dance.
15   The dance at S. Thala . . ."

(Silence.)

VOICE 2: She arrived at the dance late . . . in the middle of the
    night . . .
VOICE 1: Yes . . . *dressed in black . . .*
    What love, at the dance . . .
20   What desire . . .

(Silence.
As the light grows we see, set in this colonial décor, presences.
There were people there all the time.
They are behind either a row of plants, or a fine net screen, or a
transparent blind, or smoke from perfume burners—something
which makes the second part of the space explored less easily
visible.
Lying on a divan, long, slender, almost thin, is a woman dressed
in black.
Sitting close to her is a man, also dressed in black.
Away from the lovers there is another man in black. [One of the
men is smoking a cigarette—is that what made us sense there
were people there?]
VOICE 1 discovers—after we do—the presence of the woman in
black.)

VOICE 1: *(Tense, low.)* Anne-Marie Stretter . . .

(It is as if VOICE 2 had not heard.)

VOICE 2: *(Low.)* How pale you are . . . what are you frightened
    of . . .

(No answer.
Silence.
The three people seem struck by a deathly stillness.
"India Song" has stopped.
The voices grow lower, to match the deathliness of the scene.)

VOICE 2: After she died, he left India . . .

(Silence.
That was said all in one breath, as if recited slowly.
So the woman in black, there in front of us, is dead.
The light is now steady, somber.
Silence everywhere.
Near and far.
The voices are full of pain. Their memory, which was gone, is
coming back. But they are as sweet, as gentle as before.)

25   VOICE 2: She's buried in the English cemetery . . .

(Pause.)

VOICE 1: . . . she died there?
VOICE 2: In the islands. *(Hesitates.)* One night. Found dead.

(Silence.
"India Song" again, slow, far away.
At first we don't see the movement, the beginnings of movement.
But it begins exactly on the first note of "India Song."
The woman in black and the man sitting near her begin to stir.
Emerge from death. Their footsteps make no sound.
They are standing up.
They are close together.
What are they doing?

They are dancing.
Dancing. We only realize it when they are already dancing.
They go on, slowly, dancing.
When VOICE 1 speaks they have been dancing for some time.
VOICE 1 is gradually remembering.)

VOICE 1: The French Embassy in India . . .
VOICE 2: Yes.

(Pause.)

VOICE 1: That murmur? The Ganges?   30
VOICE 2: Yes.

(Pause.)

VOICE 1: That light?
VOICE 2: The monsoon.
VOICE 1: . . . no wind . . .
VOICE 2: *(Continues.)* . . . it will break over Bengal . . .   35
VOICE 1: The dust?
VOICE 2: The middle of Calcutta.

(Silence.)

VOICE 1: Isn't there a smell of flowers?
VOICE 2: Leprosy.

(Silence.
They are still dancing to "India Song."
They are dancing. But it needs to be said.
[As if otherwise it weren't sure. And so that the image and the
voices coincide, touch.])

VOICE 2: They're dancing.   40

(Silence.)

VOICE 2: In the evening they used to dance.

(Silence.
They dance.
So close they are one.
"India Song" fades in the distance.
They are merged together in the dance, almost motionless.
Now quite motionless.)

VOICE 2: Why are you crying?

(No answer.
Silence.
No more music.
A murmur in the distance. Then it stops. Other murmurs.
They, the man and woman, are still motionless in the silence
hemmed in by sound.
Fixed. Arrested.
It lasts a long while.
Over the fixed couple:)

VOICE 2: I love you so much I can't see any more, can't
    hear . . .
    . . . can't live . . .   45

(No answer.
Silence.
"India Song" comes back from far away. Slowly the couple un-
freeze, come back to life.
Sound increases behind the music: the sound of Calcutta: a
loud, a great murmur. All around, various other sounds. The reg-
ular cries of merchants. Dogs. Shouts in the distance.

As the sound outside increases, the sky in the garden becomes overcast. Murky light. No wind.
Silence.
The couple separate and turn toward the garden. They look out at it, motionless.
The second man sitting there also begins to look out at the garden.
The light grows still murkier.
The sound of Calcutta ceases.
Waiting.
Waiting. It is almost dark.
Suddenly the waiting is over:
The noise of the rain.
A cool, slaking noise.
It is raining over Bengal.
The rain cannot be seen. Only heard. As if it were raining everywhere except in the garden, deleted from life.
Everyone looks at the sound of the rain.)

VOICE 2: *(Scarcely voiced.)* It's raining over Bengal . . .
VOICE 1: An ocean . . .

(Silence.
Cries in the distance, of joy, shouts in Hindustani, the unknown language.
The light gradually returns.
The rain, the noise, very loud for a few seconds.
It grows less. Isolated shouts and laughter are heard more clearly through the sound of the rain.
The light continues to grow stronger.
Suddenly, clearer, nearer cries—a woman's. Her laughter.)

VOICE 1: Someone's shouting . . . a woman . . .
VOICE 2: What?
50   VOICE 1: Disconnected words.
  She's laughing.
VOICE 2: A beggar.

(Pause.)

VOICE 1: Mad?
VOICE 2: Yes . . .

(In the garden paths, sun after the rain. Moving sunlight.
Patches of light, gray, pale.
Still the shouting and laughter of the BEGGAR WOMAN.)

55   VOICE 1: Oh yes . . . I remember. She goes by the banks of the rivers . . . is she from Burma?
VOICE 2: Yes.

(While the voices speak of the BEGGAR, *the three people move, leave the room by side doors.)*

VOICE 2: She's not Indian.
  She comes from Savannakhet.
60   Born there.
VOICE 1: Ah yes . . . yes . . .
  One day . . . she's been walking ten years, and one day, there in front of her, the Ganges?
VOICE 2: Yes.
65   And there she stops.
VOICE 1: Yes . . .

(The three people have disappeared. The place is empty.
Someone speaking, almost shouting, in the distance, in a soft-sounding language, Laotian.)

VOICE 1: *(After a pause.)* Twelve children die while she's walking to Bengal . . . ?
VOICE 2: Yes. She leaves them. Sells them. Forgets them. *(Pause.)* On the way to Bengal, becomes barren.   70

(The three people reach the garden and stroll slowly through the cool after the rain, moving through the patches of sunlight. In the distance, the shouting of the BEGGAR WOMAN, *still. Suddenly, in the shouting, the word "Savannakhet."*
The voices halt briefly. Then resume.)

VOICE 1: Savannakhet—Laos?
VOICE 2: Yes. *(Pause.)* Seventeen . . . she's pregnant, she's seventeen . . . *(Pause.)* She's turned out by her mother, goes away. *(Pause.)* She asks the way to get lost. Remember? No one knows.   75
VOICE 1: *(Pause.)* Yes.
  One day, she's been walking ten years, and one day: Calcutta, there in front of her.
  She stays.

(Silence.)

VOICE 2: She's there on the banks of the Ganges, under the   80 trees. She has forgotten.

(Silence.
The three people go out of the garden.
Movements of light, monsoon, in the empty garden.
The song of the BEGGAR—*"song of Savannakhet"—in the distance.*
[VOICE 2 *is informative, calm, gentle.*])

VOICE 2: Lepers burst like sacks of dust, you know.
VOICE 1: Don't suffer?
VOICE 2: No. Not a thing.
  Laugh.   85

(Silence.)

VOICE 2: They were there together, in Calcutta. The white woman and the other. During the same years.

(The voices are silent.
A distant part of the garden, so far very dark, as if neglected by the lighting, gradually becomes visible. It is revealed by spotlights—extremely slowly, but regularly, mathematically.
Far away, the song of Savannakhet—coming, going. Sound of Calcutta, in the distance.
The wire netting round a tennis court emerges from the darkness.
Against the wire a woman's bicycle—red.
The place is deserted.
The voices recognize these things and are afraid:)

VOICE 1: *(Smothered exclamation of fear.)* The tennis courts, deserted . . .
VOICE 2: *(The same.)* . . . Anne-Marie Stretter's red bicycle . . .   90

(Silence.
A man has come into the garden. Tall, thin, dressed in white. He walks slowly. His footsteps make no sound.
He gazes around him at the stillness everywhere. Gazes for some time. Tries to see into the house: no one there.
Now what is he looking at? We don't know at first. Then it becomes clear: he's looking at ANNE-MARIE STRETTER's *bicycle by the deserted tennis courts.*
He goes over to the bicycle. Stops. Hesitates. Doesn't go any nearer. Looks, stares at it.
[*The voices are low, scared.*])

VOICE 2: . . . he comes every night . . .

(Pause.)

VOICE 1: The French Vice-Consul in Lahore . . .
VOICE 2: Yes.
  . . . in Calcutta in disgrace . . .

(Silence.
Slowly, the man in white moves. He walks. He goes along a path.
He goes away.
Disappears.
After he has disappeared, everything remains in suspense.
Silence. Fear.
The song of Savannakhet, in the distance, innocent.
Then, two shots.
The first makes the light go dim.
The second makes it go out.
Silence.
Blackout.
The song of Savannakhet stopped when the shots were fired. As if
they had been aimed at it.
Silence.
Blackout.
The voices are very quiet, terrified.)

95 VOICE 2: Someone fired a gun under the trees . . . on the
      banks of the Ganges . . .

(Silence.)

VOICE 1: It was a song of Savannakhet . . . ?
VOICE 2: Yes.

(Silence.
By a strictly symmetrical inversion, and without passing through
any intermediate stages, the light becomes the same as it was
when the first shot made it go dim.
This stands for night.
It is night.
The place, the stage, is still empty.
The only movement—that of the nightmare fan.
Time passes over the empty place.
Silence.
A Hindu servant dressed in white goes by, passing through the
drawing rooms of the French Embassy.
He has gone. Emptiness again.
Far away, the song of Savannakhet begins again: the BEGGAR
WOMAN wasn't killed.
The voices are still low, frightened.)

VOICE 1: . . . she's not dead . . .
100 VOICE 2: Can't die.
VOICE 1: (Scarcely heard.) No . . .

(Silence.)

VOICE 2: She goes hunting at night beside the Ganges. For
      food . . .

(No answer.
Silence.)

VOICE 1: Where's the one dressed in black?
105 VOICE 2: Out. Every evening.
      She comes back when it's dark.

(Silence.
A servant enters, lights a lamp, very faint, in a corner of the
room. Does various things.

Goes away [but remains visible].
Comes back.
Opens a window.
Perhaps he lights some sticks of incense against the mosquitoes—
in which case the audience will be able to smell it.
Empties ashtrays.)

VOICE 2: She's back.
      The Embassy's black Lancia has just come through the
      gates.

(Silence.
The servant goes out.
The place remains empty for a few more seconds, and then the
woman in black enters the darkness. She is barefoot. Her hair is
loose. She is wearing a short wrap of loose black cotton.
The scene is very long and slow.
Slowly she goes and stands under the nightmare fan. Stays there.
Puts up her hands and thrusts her hair away from her body in a
gesture of exhaustion—someone stifling from the heat. Then lets
her arms fall down by her sides.
Through the opening of the wrap, the white of the naked body.
She freezes. Head thrown back. Gasping for air. Trying to escape
out of the heat.
Touching grace of the thin, fragile body.
Stays like that, upright, exposed. Offered to the voices.
[The voices are slow, stifled, a prey to desire—through this mo-
tionless body.])

VOICE 2: (Smothered outburst.) How lovely you look dressed in   110
      white . . .

(Pause.)

VOICE 1: I'd like to go and visit the woman of the Ganges . . .

(Held pause.)

VOICE 1: . . . the white woman . . .
VOICE 2: (Pause.) The one who . . . ?
VOICE 1: Her . . .   115
VOICE 2: . . . dead in the islands . . .
VOICE 1: Eyes dead, blinded with light.
VOICE 2: Yes.
      There under the stone.
      In a bend in the Ganges.   120

(Silence.
Still motionless before us, the dead woman of the Ganges.
The voices are a song so quiet it does not awaken her death.
Apparently nothing changes, nothing happens. But suddenly,
fear.)

VOICE 1: (Low, frightened.) What is it?

(No answer.)

VOICE 1: (As before.) What time is it?
VOICE 2: (Pause.) Four o'clock.
      Black night.

(Pause.)

VOICE 1: No one can sleep?   125
VOICE 2: No.

(Silence.
Tears on the woman's face.
The features remain unmoving.
She is weeping. Without suffering.

A state of tears.
The voices speak of the heat, they speak of desire—as if the voices were issuing from the weeping body.)

VOICE 1: The heat
Impossible
Terrible

(Pause.)

130 VOICE 2: Another storm . . .
Approaching Bengal . . .
VOICE 1: *(Pause.)* Coming from the islands . . .
VOICE 2: *(Pause.)* The estuaries.
Inexhaustible . . .

(Silence.)

135 VOICE 1: What's that sound?
VOICE 2: *(Pause.)* Her weeping.

(Silence.)

VOICE 1: Doesn't suffer, does she . . . ?
VOICE 2: She neither.
A leper, of the heart.

(Silence.)

140 VOICE 1: Can't bear it . . . ?
VOICE 2: No.
Can't bear it.
Can't bear India.

(Silence.
A man enters through the door on the left. He too is wearing a black wrap.
He halts, looks at her.
Then slowly goes over to her, a statue in her tears, under the fan, asleep.
He looks at her—asleep standing up. Goes right up to her.
Passes lightly over her face a hand outspread in a caress. Takes his hand away, looks at it: it is wet from the tears.)

VOICE 2: *(Very low.)* She's asleep.

(With infinite precaution, the man takes up the weeping woman and lays her down on the floor.
He's the man we have already seen, the man she danced with at the dance in S. Thala: MICHAEL RICHARDSON.
He sits down beside the outstretched body.
Looks at it.
Uncovers the body so that it is better exposed to the cool—imaginary—from the fan.
Strokes her forehead. Wipes away the tears, the sweat. Caresses the sleeping body.
Doesn't go close. Stays there watching over her sleep.
The voices slow down to the rhythm of the man's movements, taking up again in a sort of sung complaint the themes adjacent to the main story.)

145 VOICE 1: He loved her more than anything in the world.
VOICE 2: *(Pause.)* More even than that . . .

(Silence.
VOICE 2 *spoke as if of its own love.)*

VOICE 1: Where was the girl from S. Thala?

(No answer.)

VOICE 1: *(As if reading.)* "From behind the indoor plants in the bar, she watches them. *(Pause.)* It was only at dawn . . . *(Stops.)* . . . when the lovers were going toward the door of 150 the ballroom that Lola Valérie Stein uttered a cry."

(Silence.
In the distance, a regular cry in Hindustani. Someone selling something again.
It stops.
Quiet.)

VOICE 2: At four in the morning, sometimes, sleep comes.

(Silence.
The lover is still beside the sleeping body.
He looks at it.
Takes the hands, touches them. Looks at them.
They fall back, dead.
Silence.)

VOICE 1: She never got over it, the girl from S. Thala?
VOICE 2: Never.
VOICE 1: They didn't hear her cry out? 155
VOICE 2: No.
Couldn't hear any more.
Couldn't see.

(Pause.)

VOICE 1: *(Pause.)* They abandoned her? *(Pause.)* Killed her?
VOICE 2: Yes. 160

(Pause.)

VOICE 1: And with this crime behind them . . .
VOICE 2: *(Scarcely heard.)* Yes.

(Silence.)

VOICE 1: What did the girl from S. Thala want?
VOICE 2: To go with them
See them 165
The lovers of the Ganges: to see them.

(Silence.
That is what we are doing: seeing.
Slowly the man lies down beside the sleeping body. His hand goes on caressing the face, the body.
Far away, distant sounds, oars, water. Then laughter, a zither, fading in the distance.
Then it stops.)

VOICE 2: Listen . . .
Ganges fishermen . . .
Musicians . . .

(Silence again.
The voices speak of the heat again. Of their desire.)

VOICE 2: *(Very slow.)* What darkness 170
What heat
Unmitigated
Deathly

(Silence.
A voice that is clear, implacable, terrifying:)

VOICE 2: I love you with a desire that is absolute.

(No answer.
Silence.

The hand of MICHAEL RICHARDSON—*the lover—immediately stops caressing the body, as if arrested by what* VOICE 2 *has just said.*
It lies there where it is on the body.
Silence.
A second man enters the room. He stands in the doorway for a moment, looking at the lovers.
MICHAEL RICHARDSON's *hand starts to move again, caressing the uncovered body.*
The man goes over to them.
Like the lover, he sits down beside her.
The lover's hand now moves more slowly.
Then it stops.
The newcomer does not caress the woman's body.
He lies down too.
All three lie motionless under the fan.
Silence.
Rain.
Another storm over Bengal.
The sound of rain over sleep.
The voices are like breaths of coolness, gentle murmurs.)

175 VOICE 1: . . . rain . . .
VOICE 2: . . . yes . . .

(*Pause.*)

VOICE 1: . . . cool . . .

(*Silence.*
The sky gets lighter, but it is still night.
Gradually, music: Beethoven's 14th Variation on a Theme by Diabelli. Piano, very distant.
The rain slackens.
In its place, a white light. Patches of moonlight on the garden paths. No wind.
The three bodies, their eyes closed, sleep.
The voices, interwoven, in a climax of sweetness, are about to sing the legend of ANNE-MARIE STRETTER. *A slow recitative made up of scraps of memory. Out of it, every so often, a phrase emerges, intact, from oblivion.*)

VOICE 1: Venice.
    She was from Venice . . .
180 VOICE 2: Yes. The music was in Venice.
    A hope in music . . .
VOICE 1: (*Pause.*) She never gave up playing?
VOICE 2: No.

(*Silence.*)

VOICE 1: (*Very slow.*) Anna Maria Guardi . . .
185 VOICE 2: Yes.

(*Silence.*)

VOICE 1: The first marriage, the first post . . . ?
VOICE 2: Savannakhet, Laos.
    She's married to a French colonial official.
    She's eighteen.
190 VOICE 1: (*Remembering.*) Ah yes . . . a river . . .
    . . . she's sitting by a river. Already . . .
    Looking at it.
VOICE 2: The Mekong.
VOICE 1: (*Pause.*) She's silent?
195 Crying?

VOICE 2: Yes. They say: "She can't get acclimatized. She'll have to be sent back to Europe."

(*Pause.*)

VOICE 1: Couldn't bear it. Even then.
VOICE 2: Even then.

(*Silence.*)

VOICE 1: (*Visionary.*) Those walls all round her?   200
VOICE 2: The grounds of the chancellery.
VOICE 1: (*As before.*) The sentries?
VOICE 2: Official.
VOICE 1: Even then . . .
VOICE 2: Yes.   205
VOICE 1: Even then, couldn't bear it.
VOICE 2: No.

(*Silence.*)

VOICE 2: One day a government launch calls. Monsieur Stretter is inspecting the posts on the Mekong.
VOICE 1: (*Pause.*) He takes her away from Savannakhet?   210
VOICE 2: Yes. Takes her with him.
    Takes her with him for seventeen years through the capitals of Asia.

(*Pause.*)

VOICE 2: You find her in Peking.
    Then in Mandalay.   215
    In Bangkok.
    Rangoon. Sydney.
    Lahore.
    Seventeen years.
    You find her in Calcutta.   220
    In Calcutta:
    She dies.

(*Silence.*
The tall thin man dressed in white enters the garden.
The voices haven't seen him.
He stops. Looks through the screens on the windows at the three sleeping forms.
Stops, looking at her, the woman.
The voices still haven't seen him.)

VOICE 1: Michael Richardson used to go to S. Thala in the summer.
VOICE 2: Yes.   225
    She didn't go often.
    But that summer . . .
VOICE 1: He was English, Michael Richardson?
VOICE 2: Yes. (*Pause. As if reading.*) "Michael Richardson started a marine insurance company in Bengal, so that he   230
    could stay in India."
VOICE 1: Near her.
VOICE 2: Yes.

(*The man goes away. We see him, from behind, going slowly along the path toward the deserted tennis courts.*)

VOICE 1: The other man who's sleeping?
VOICE 2: Passing through. A friend of the Stretters'.   235
    She belongs to whoever wants her.
    Gives her to whoever will have her.
VOICE 1: (*Pause, pain.*) Prostitution in Calcutta.

VOICE 2: Yes.
240   She's a Christian without God.
    Splendor.
VOICE 1: *(Very low.)* Love.
VOICE 2: *(Scarcely heard.)* Yes . . .

(Silence.
The thin man goes toward the red bicycle propped against the
wire around the deserted tennis courts.
The voices have seen him.
They resume very softly, in fear.)

VOICE 1: He's back in the garden.
245 VOICE 2: Yes . . . Every night . . .
    Looks at her . . .

(Silence.
The man hesitates. Then goes up to ANNE-MARIE STRETTER's
bicycle.)

VOICE 1: He never spoke to her . . .
VOICE 2: No.
    Never went near . . .

(Halt.)

250 VOICE 1: The male virgin of Lahore . . .
VOICE 2: Yes . . .

(The man is beside the bicycle.
Puts out his hands. Hesitates.
Then touches it.
Strokes it.
Leans forward and holds it in his arms.
Stays clasping ANNE-MARIE STRETTER's *bicycle—frozen in this*
gesture of desire.
Silence.
Almost imperceptibly, a movement over by the sleeping bodies. It
is she.
As he bends over the bicycle, she, by a converse movement, sits
up. In the same slow rhythm she sits up and turns toward the
garden.
ANNE-MARIE STRETTER *looks at the man in white with his arms*
around her bicycle.
Silence.
Suddenly the man lets go of the bicycle. Remains with his arms
hanging by his sides, his hands open, in an attitude of passion
and despair.
Sound of a man sobbing [the only sound heard directly].
The woman still looks, sitting with her hands flat on the ground.
The sobs cease.
The man gets up.
He stands facing the bicycle.
Then slowly turns around.
Sees her.
The woman doesn't move.
Silence.
They look at each other.
This lasts several seconds.
Silence.
It is the man who stops looking.
First he turns his face away. Then his body moves.
He walks away.
She, still sitting, watches him walk away.

Then, after he has slowly disappeared from sight, she takes up
her former position, asleep under the nightmare fan.
Silence.
Stillness.
Sobs of the VICE-CONSUL *in the distance.*
Silence again.
In the garden the light grows dim again, murky.
No wind in the deserted garden.)

VOICE 2: *(Afraid, very low.)* The sound of your heart frightens
    me . . .

(Silence.
Another stirring in the still mass of the three sleeping bodies:
MICHAEL RICHARDSON's *hand reaches out to the woman's body,*
caresses it, stays there.
MICHAEL RICHARDSON *was not asleep.*
The light gets dimmer still.
VOICE 2 *is full of desire and terror.)*

VOICE 2: Your heart, so young, a child's . . .

(No answer.
Silence.)

VOICE 2: Where are you?   255

(No answer.
Silence.
Shouts in the distance: the VICE-CONSUL. *Cries of despair.*
Heart-rending, obscene.)

VOICE 1: *(Distant.)* What's he shouting?
VOICE 2: The name she used to have in Venice, in the desert
    of Calcutta.

(Silence.
The cries fade in the distance.
Disappear.
VOICE 2, *all in one breath, in fear, tells the story of the crime, the*
crime committed in Lahore:)

VOICE 2: *(Low.)* "He fired a gun. One night, from his balcony
    in Lahore, he fired on the lepers in the Shalimar gardens."   260

(Silence.
VOICE 1 *is gentle—calm and gentle.)*

VOICE 1: Couldn't bear it.
VOICE 2: No.
VOICE 1: India—couldn't bear India?
VOICE 2: No.
VOICE 1: What couldn't he bear about it?   265
VOICE 2: The idea.

(Silence.
It is getting darker. The bodies grow less and less distinguishable.
Above them the fan goes on turning, the blades gleaming slowly.
You can no longer tell one body from another.
Silence.)

VOICE 1: A black Lancia is speeding along the road to Chan-
    dernagor . . .

(No answer.)

VOICE 1: *(Continuing.)* . . . It was there . . . there that she
    first . . .   270

(The voice stops.)

VOICE 2: Yes.
   Brought back by ambulance.
   They talked about an accident . . .

(Pause.)

VOICE 1: She's been thin ever since.
275 VOICE 2: *(Scarcely heard.)* Yes.

*(Beethoven's 14th Variation on a Theme by Diabelli. Distant.
Total blackout.
Then, beyond the garden, gleams in the sky. Either day or fire—
rust-colored fire.
The voice is slow: a calm declaration.)*

VOICE 1: Those gleams over there?
VOICE 2: The burning-ghats.
VOICE 1: Burning people who've starved to death?
VOICE 2: Yes.
280   It will soon be daylight.

*(Silence.
The 14th Variation is heard till the end, over the gleams from the
burning-ghats.
Blackout.)*

— ACT TWO —

We are in the same place as before.

*The only difference is that the right side of it is now revealed, as
if the angle of vision had been changed. Doors opening on the
reception rooms on one side, and on the other on the garden.*

(As if these rooms were in a wing of the Embassy.)

Bright light everywhere. Chandeliers.

Chinese lanterns in the garden.

Silence.

It is as if the French Embassy were quite empty.

*Nothing can be seen of the reception rooms except the light com-
ing out of the doors and illuminating the garden.*

All remains empty for a few seconds.

Then, without a sound, a servant passes through.

*Carrying a tray with glasses of champagne, he goes through and
out toward the right.*

Silence again. Emptiness again.

Waiting.

Then, suddenly, noise.

*The noise of the reception begins quite suddenly, full volume.
The party is triggered off as if by some mechanism: the noise
bursts forth instantaneously from behind the walls, through the
open doors.*

*A woman is singing "The Merry Widow," accompanied by a
piano and two violins.*

Behind the music:

The sound of many conversations all merging into one.

The sound of glasses, crockery, etc.

But the feet of the dancers make no sound.

*No conversation will take place on the stage, or be seen. It will
never be the actors on the stage who are speaking.*

*The only exception to this rule is that the sobs of the French
VICE-CONSUL are both seen and heard.*

*When the conversations recorded here take place, the sound of
the reception grows fainter.*

*Often it almost stops: for example, during the conversations be-
tween the YOUNG ATTACHÉ and ANNE-MARIE STRETTER, and
between her and the French VICE-CONSUL. It is as if the guests
at the reception, intrigued, watched them talking instead of talking themselves. So the fading of the sound is not arbitrary.*

*All the conversations, whether private or not, whether they make
the guests around them go quiet or not, should give the impression that only the spectators hear them clearly—not the guests.*

*So the sound of the reception should be heard, however faintly,
behind all the conversations. The fact that these conversations
are now and again mingled with conversations on other subjects
should prove that the private conversations are not audible, or
hardly, to the guests. So also the fact that some of what is overheard is sometimes repeated, but always more or less wrongly—
with slight mistakes which show that only the spectators hear the
private conversations properly.*

*The sound of the reception should come from the right and from
the stage, and from the auditorium, as if the reception were taking place beyond the walls of the auditorium, too.*

ANNE-MARIE STRETTER *wears a black dress—the one she wore
at the dance in S. Thala—the one described in* Le Ravissement
de Lol. V. Stein.

*The men wear black dinner jackets, with the exception of the
French* VICE-CONSUL *in Lahore, who wears a white one.*

The other women at the reception wear long dresses, colored.

*The reception overflows, all the time it lasts, either into the gar-
den or into the place we already know:* ANNE-MARIE STRETTER's
private drawing room.

*From the point of view of sound, the image, the stage, plays the
part of an echo chamber. Passing through that space, the voices
should sound, to the spectator, like his own "internal rending"
voice.*

*The set should seem accidental—stolen from a "whole" that is by
its nature inaccessible, that is, the reception.*

*The diction should in general be extremely precise. It should not
seem completely natural. During rehearsals some slight defect
should be settled on, common to all the voices.*

*One ought to get the impression of a reading, but one which is re-
ported, that is, one which has been performed before. That is
what is meant by a "reading-to-himself voice."*

To repeat: not a single word is uttered on the stage.

*("Heure exquise" sung by a woman. Then repeated by the
orchestra.
A waltzing couple cross a corner of the garden.)*

Some women are talking: (Quite close.)
——— This is the last reception before the monsoon.
——— What? Do you mean to say the monsoon hasn't begun?

—— Not really. It'll be at its height in a fortnight. No sun for
5   six months . . . You'll see . . . No one can sleep . . . They just
wait for the storms to break . . .

*(An Indian servant passes through, on his way to the reception.
He carries a tray with brimming glasses of champagne.
Two couples go through, waltzing. Slowly. Disappear.)*

Some women are talking: (Farther away.)
—— She invited the French Vice-Consul in Lahore . . .
—— Yes. At the last minute she sent him a card: "Come."
10   The Ambassador didn't say anything.

*(A young man arrives. He stops and looks around. Clearly he
isn't familiar with this part of the Embassy. He looks tired, as if
he wants to get away from the reception. He looks out toward the
deserted tennis courts.
As he looks, a couple dance across a corner of the garden and disappear.)*

Some men are talking: (About the young man.)
—— Who is he?
—— The new Attaché . . . Only been out here a month . . .
He can't get used to it.
15   —— It's the first time he's been here.

(Pause.)

—— He'll be back. He'll be invited, he'll go to the islands . . .
The Ambassador asks people to stay there. For her—for his
wife.

(Pause.)

—— What makes you think *he'll* be asked?

(Pause.)

20   —— He looks so troubled . . . She doesn't like people who
get used to it.
—— Are there any?
—— Some . . .
—— Clubs, to keep India out, that's the answer . . . isn't it?
25   —— Yes.

(The YOUNG ATTACHÉ *goes on looking around. Then he turns
toward the dancing, watches the reception. And goes back to it.
"Heure exquise" ends.
There is a moment without music.
Only the sound of the reception. No laughter. A sort of general
dejection.
Some women go by in the garden, looking curiously toward*
ANNE-MARIE STRETTER's *drawing room.
They fan themselves with big white fans.
They are gone.)*

A man speaks: (The Ambassador.)
—— I think my wife may have mentioned it . . . we'd be
very glad if you'd join us some time in the islands . . . There
are some newcomers one feels specially attracted to . . . And
30   the rules governing ordinary society don't apply here . . . We
don't choose . . . *(A smile in the voice.)* You will? The residency looks out on the Indian Ocean, it dates from the days
of the Company, it's worth seeing. And the islands are very
healthy, especially the main one, it's the biggest island in the
35   Delta.

(Silence.)

Men talking:
—— He used to write, the Ambassador . . . Did you know?
I've read a little volume of his poems . . .
—— So I've heard . . . They say it's because of her he gave it
up . . .   40

*("Heure exquise" has been followed by a tango.
The French* VICE-CONSUL *in Lahore has come into the garden.
He is wearing a white dinner jacket. He is alone. No one seems to
have noticed him yet.)*

Two conversations (1 and 2) between men and women:
No. 1
—— She might have spared us the embarrassment . . .

(Pause.)

—— What exactly did he do? I never know what goes on . . .
—— The worst possible thing . . . How can I explain . . . ?
—— The worst . . . ?   45

(Silence.)

No. 2
—— An intriguing woman. No one really knows how she
spends her time . . . What does she do? She must do something . . .
—— She must read . . . Between her siesta and when it's
time to go out, what else could she do . . .   50
—— Parcels of books come for her from Venice . . . And she
spends some time with her daughters . . . In the dry season
they play tennis—you see all three of them going by the office, dressed in white . . .

(Pause.)

—— The fact that one wonders what she does, that's what's   55
strangest of all.

(Silence.)

No. 1 *(Continued.)*
—— Did he kill somebody?
—— He used to fire shots at the Shalimar gardens at
night . . . You knew that . . . ? But bullets were found in the
mirrors of his own residence in Lahore . . .   60
—— He was shooting at himself . . . *(Little laugh.)*

(No answer.)

—— It's difficult to tell which are the lepers . . .
—— You see, you do know: you talk about the lepers . . .

(Silence.)

No. 2 *(Continued.)*
—— She goes cycling too, very early in the morning, in the
grounds. Not during the monsoon, of course . . .   65
No. 1 *(Continued.)*
—— What's the official version?
—— His nerves gave way . . . Often happens.

(Pause.)

—— Funny, he forces you to think about him . . .

*(*MICHAEL RICHARDSON *has entered. He is not wearing a dinner
jacket. He sits down. He smokes a cigarette. He doesn't look toward the garden.
In the garden, the* VICE-CONSUL: *he looks at* MICHAEL
RICHARDSON.*)*

Two women enter on the right, and stop. They have seen
MICHAEL RICHARDSON *and look at him with curiosity. He*
doesn't see them.
A servant goes by with glasses of champagne. He offers one to
MICHAEL RICHARDSON, *and goes.*
The tango, as if in the distance.
MICHAEL RICHARDSON *gets up, begins to go toward the recep-*
tion, looks at it from some distance, then turns around: sees the
VICE-CONSUL; *in the garden.*
Then the women see him too and draw back.)

Women speaking: (Low.)

70   ────── Look . . . Michael Richardson . . .

(Pause.)

        ────── Yes . . . He doesn't attend receptions?
        ────── No, only at the end, toward the middle of the night.
        When there's just a few friends left . . .

(Pause.)

        ────── What a business . . . what love . . . They say he gave up
75   everything to be with her . . .
        ────── Everything. He was engaged to be married. Every-
        thing. Overnight . . .

(Silence.
MICHAEL RICHARDSON *makes a movement toward the* VICE-
CONSUL—*toward the gate into the garden.*
The VICE-CONSUL *turns away.*
MICHAEL RICHARDSON *stops.*
The two women watch.)

Women talking: (Low, afraid.)
        ────── Look in the garden . . .
80   ────── Is that him?
        ────── Yes.
        ────── So thin . . . and the face . . . as if it were grafted on . . .
        so pale . . .

(Silence.
MICHAEL RICHARDSON *turns back toward the reception.*
The watching women disappear.)

Women: (Continued.)
85   ────── Do they know each other?
        ────── Evidently not . . .

(Silence.
The VICE-CONSUL *looks at the reception.* MICHAEL RICHARD-
SON *looks again at him. The* VICE-CONSUL *seems absorbed, and*
does not notice him.)

Men talking:
        ────── He used to fire shots at night from his balcony.
        ────── Yes. He used to shout too. Half naked.
90   ────── What?
        ────── Disconnected words. He used to laugh.

(Pause.)

        ────── And no woman was ever close enough to him, in
        Lahore, to be able to say anything . . . ?
        ────── No. Never.
95   ────── How is that possible?
        ────── His house, no one ever went to his house in
        Lahore . . .
        ────── It's terrifying . . . Such abstinence . . . Terrible . . .

(Silence.
MICHAEL RICHARDSON *turns toward the reception, tries to make*
out what the VICE-CONSUL *can be watching so avidly.)*

Men and women:
        ────── Did you hear? The Ambassador said to the Young At-   100
        taché: "People avoid him, I know . . . he frightens them . . .
        But I'd be grateful if you'd go and have a word with him."

(Pause.)

        ────── What's known about his background? his childhood?
        ────── His father was a bank manager in Neuilly. An only
        child. The mother's supposed to have left the father. Ex-   105
        pelled from several schools for bad behavior. Brilliant at his
        work, but after high school . . . That's all . . .
        ────── So they don't know anything about him really?
        ────── Nothing.

(Pause.)

        ────── Isn't there in all of us . . . how shall I put it . . . ? a   110
        chance in a thousand we might be like him . . . I mean . . .
        (Pause.) I'm only asking . . .

(No answer.
Silence.
A couple come to the edge of the garden. They see the VICE-
CONSUL, *and don't go any farther.* MICHAEL RICHARDSON *looks*
at them. They hesitate. Turn away. Go back to the reception.
The VICE-CONSUL *looks at the reception and laughs.*
Some women go through the garden fanning themselves. They
don't see the VICE-CONSUL. *They stop and look at the reception*
from a distance: something catches their attention:)

Women:
        ────── Who's she dancing with?
        ────── The Ambassador.   115
        ────── You knew he took her away from some official in the
        wilds of French Indochina . . . I can't quite remember where
        . . . Laos, I think . . .
        ────── Savannakhet?
        ────── That's it . . .   120
        ────── Don't you remember? " . . . slow launch with awnings,
        slow journey up the Mekong to Savannakhet . . . wide ex-
        panse of water between virgin forest, gray paddy-fields . . .
        and in the evening, clusters of mosquitoes clinging to the
        mosquito nets . . ."   125
        ────── What a memory! *(Little laugh.)*

(Silence.)

        ────── Seventeen years they've been wandering around Asia.

(Silence.
They all look toward the reception, toward the Ambassador danc-
ing with his wife.
The VICE-CONSUL *laughs silently.)*

Men:
        ────── Has he ever talked to anyone about Lahore?
        ────── Never.   130
        ────── About anything else?
        ────── I don't think so . . . He gets letters from France. An el-
        derly aunt . . . The letters were intercepted . . . Apparently . . .
        he told the Secretary of the European Club he was in a refor-
        matory . . . when he was fifteen . . . in the North . . .   135

———— He talks to him, then? That drunk?

———— Well . . . the other one's asleep, so really he's talking to himself . . . *(Little laugh.)*

———— So he doesn't talk to anyone then . . .

140 ———— That's right . . . *(Little laugh.)*

———— What did he find in India to set him off? Didn't he know about it before? Did he actually have to see it? It's not so difficult to find out . . .

Women:

145 ———— There are moments when he seems happy. Look . . . As if he were suddenly madly happy . . .

(Pause.)

———— Perhaps when she dances . . .

———— What an idea . . .

———— I've only just noticed . . .

(Silence.)

150 ———— Who mentioned Bombay?

———— He did, to the Secretary at the Club. He saw himself being photographed beside the Sea of Oman on a chaise longue . . . *(Little laugh.)*

———— He doesn't talk about it any more, apparently.

(Silence.

The YOUNG ATTACHÉ *has now entered the garden. He goes toward the French* VICE-CONSUL, *slowly, as if not to frighten him. The* VICE-CONSUL *makes as if to run away. The* YOUNG ATTACHÉ *hesitates, then takes him by the arm. The* VICE-CONSUL *doesn't attempt to run away any more.*

The YOUNG ATTACHÉ *signs to the* VICE-CONSUL *to go with him. They go toward the reception. Go in.* MICHAEL RICHARDSON *has seen them—he is the only one not watching* ANNE-MARIE STRETTER *dancing with her husband.)*

155 Women:

———— Did you see . . . ?

(Pause.)

———— Yes, it's her he's looking at . . .

(Pause.)

———— If you ask me, Bombay's too popular, they'll send him somewhere else . . .

(Silence.)

160 ———— Tell me about Madame Stretter.

———— Irreproachable. Outside the kitchens you'll see big jars of cold water put out for the beggars . . . It's she who . . .

———— . . . Irreproachable . . . *(Little laugh.)* Come, come . . .

———— Nothing that shows. That's what we mean here by
165 irreproachable.

(Silence.

Several people go into the garden and look toward the reception. Women fan themselves. [It is to be remembered that it's never those who are seen that speak.])

A man and a woman:

———— She looks . . . imprisoned in a kind of suffering. But . . . a very old suffering . . . too old to make her sad any more . . .

(Pause.)

———— And yet she cries . . . People have seen her . . . in the garden . . . sometimes . . . 170

———— The light perhaps, it's so harsh . . . and her eyes are so pale . . .

———— Perhaps . . . What grace . . . Look . . .

———— Yes . . .

———— Frightening . . . don't you think? 175

(Silence.

MICHAEL RICHARDSON *has sat down on the left side of the room. He looks as if he is waiting. He doesn't look toward the reception. He is clearly visible. Very handsome. Younger than* ANNE-MARIE STRETTER. *Obviously shy.*

He is smoking. He is tense, absorbed.

Several conversations take place between people, some of whom have and some of whom have not seen the VICE-CONSUL *go into the reception.)*

Women:

———— The roses are sent direct from Nepal . . .

———— She gives them away when the dance is over.

———— *(Low.)* Look . . . there he is . . .

(Silence.)

———— He doesn't notice everyone is looking at him . . . 180

———— You can hardly see his eyes . . .

———— His face looks dead . . . Don't you think so? . . . Frightening . . .

———— Yes. The laugh looks . . . stuck on . . . *(Pause.)* What's he laughing at? 185

———— Who knows?

(Pause.)

———— In the gardens, on the way to the office, he whistles "India Song."

———— What work does he do?

———— Filing . . . nothing much . . . just to keep him occupied . . . 190

(Silence.)

Men:

———— It's strange—most women in India have very white skins . . .

———— They live out of the sun. Closed shutters . . . they're 195 recluses . . .

———— And they don't do anything out here . . . they're waited on.

———— Yes, they just rest.

(Silence.)

———— I admit I have a look when she and her daughters go by 200 on their way to play tennis . . . In shorts . . . Women's legs seem so beautiful here . . . walking through all that horror . . . *(Pause, then a start.)* But look . . .

(Silence.)

Women:

———— The first thing to see is the islands . . . 205

———— They're so beautiful . . . I don't know what we'd do here without them.

———— That's what we'll miss about India—the islands in the Indian Ocean . . .

(Silence.)

210 *Isolated woman's voice:*
——— The best thing during the monsoon ... did you know? ... hot green tea, the way the Chinese make it ...

(Silence.)

Woman:
——— Do you see? The Young Attaché's talking to the Vice-
215 Consul from Lahore ...

(Silence.)

——— The voice ... listen to the voice ... how blank it is ...

(Silence.
Almost total silence. Everyone looks at the YOUNG ATTACHÉ *and the* VICE-CONSUL.
[The VICE-CONSUL's *voice is harsh, almost strident. The* YOUNG ATTACHÉ's *voice is low and soft.])*

YOUNG ATTACHÉ *and* VICE-CONSUL:
VICE-CONSUL: Yes, it's difficult, of course. But what is it with you, exactly?
YOUNG ATTACHÉ: The heat, naturally. But also the monotony
220 ... the light ... no color ... I don't know if I shall ever get used to it.
VICE-CONSUL: As bad as that?
YOUNG ATTACHÉ: Well ... I wasn't prejudiced before I left France ... What about you? before Lahore? would you have
225 preferred somewhere else?
VICE-CONSUL: No. Lahore was what I wanted.

(Silence.
Then "India Song.")

Man and woman: (Low.)
——— Did you hear?
——— Not very clearly. I thought he said: "Lahore was what I
230 desired"...
——— I heard: "what I ... what I'd ..."
——— And what does it mean? Nothing ...
——— *(In one breath.)* The report said people used to see him at night through his bedroom window, walking up and
235 down as if it was broad daylight ... and talking ... always to himself ...
——— ... At night ... as if it was broad daylight ...
——— Yes ...

(Silence.
One man's voice is heard dominating all the others.)

Man (GEORGE CRAWN.):
240 ——— Come over to the bar. Allow me to introduce myself. An old friend of Anne-Marie Stretter's. George Crawn ... Serve yourselves ... there isn't a bartender ...

(Hubbub for a few seconds—people going over to the bar.)

Woman:
——— He said that to distract people's attention ...

(The noise dies down.)

245 YOUNG ATTACHÉ: Come over to the bar. *(Pause.)* What are you afraid of?

(No answer.)

YOUNG ATTACHÉ: They say you'd like to go to Bombay?

VICE-CONSUL: Won't they let me stay in Calcutta?
YOUNG ATTACHÉ: No.
VICE-CONSUL: In that case I leave it to the authorities. They   250
can send me where they like.
YOUNG ATTACHÉ: Bombay's not so crowded, the climate's better, and it's pleasant to be by the sea.

(Silence.)

Isolated man's voice:
——— It's as if he didn't hear when you speak to him.   255
YOUNG ATTACHÉ: What are you doing? Come along ...
VICE-CONSUL: I'm listening to "India Song." *(Pause.)* I came to India because of it.

(Silence.
ANNE-MARIE STRETTER *appears on the stage for the first time in Act II. She has come from the reception. She smiles at* MICHAEL RICHARDSON. *He stands, and watches her coming. He doesn't smile. No one sees them (everyone is watching the* VICE-CONSUL *and the* YOUNG ATTACHÉ). *It was she whom* MICHAEL RICHARDSON *was waiting for.*
ANNE-MARIE STRETTER *and* MICHAEL RICHARDSON *look at each other.*
He puts his arms around her.
They dance in a corner of the room, alone.
We hear the public *voice of the* VICE-CONSUL.)*

VICE-CONSUL: That tune makes me want to love. I never have.

(No answer.
Silence.
The last speech was delivered while we could see the couple dancing.
The couple disappear, left.
"India Song" still.)

VICE-CONSUL: I'm sorry. I didn't ask to see my file. But you   260
know it. What do they say?
YOUNG ATTACHÉ: They say Lahore ... What you did in Lahore ... People can't understand it, no one can, no matter how they try ...
VICE-CONSUL: *(Pause.)* No one?   265

(No answer.
Silence.
The BEGGAR WOMAN *appears in the garden.*
She hides behind a bush.
Stays there.)

Men:
——— He said it was impossible for him to give a convincing explanation of what he did in Lahore.
——— ... convincing ...?
——— I was particularly struck by the word.   270

*(*ANNE-MARIE STRETTER *comes back, from the left side of the room. Slowly. She stops. She looks toward the garden: the two women of the Ganges look at each other.*
The BEGGAR WOMAN, *unafraid, sticks her bald head out, then hides again.*
ANNE-MARIE STRETTER *walks away, with the same slow step.)*

Women:
——— She goes to the islands alone. The Ambassador goes hunting in Nepal.
——— Alone ... well ...

275 —— With him—Michael Richardson. And others . . .
—— They say her lovers are Englishmen, foreigners from the embassies . . . They say the Ambassador knows . . .
—— It's only what he expected when he met her . . . he's older than she is . . .

(Pause.)

280 —— There's a friendship between them now that's proof against anything . . .

(Silence.
ANNE-MARIE STRETTER *has gone into the reception.*
"India Song" ends.
The VICE-CONSUL *goes back into the garden.*
He is near the BEGGAR WOMAN, *but they don't see each other.*
A blues.)

Men and women:
—— Protocol requires everyone to have one dance with the Ambassador's wife . . .
285 —— Look . . . He's left the Young Attaché . . . He's gone back into the garden . . .
—— Again . . . Ever since the beginning of the evening he's kept going back there . . .
—— As if he was on the point of running away.
290 —— And yet at the same time . . .

(Silence.
The VICE-CONSUL *stands motionless, staring at the reception with all his might.)*

Men and women: (Continued.)
—— What's he looking at?
—— The Ambassador's wife dancing with the Young Attaché.

(Silence.
The YOUNG ATTACHÉ *and* ANNE-MARIE STRETTER *dance into the room, then back to the reception. They too create a silence around them.)*

295 *Women: (Low.)*
—— Did you hear? *(Pause.)* She said to him: "I wish I were you, arriving in India for the first time during the summer monsoon." *(Pause.)* They're too far away . . . I can't hear any more . . .

Conversation between ANNE-MARIE STRETTER *(Voice marvelous in its sweetness.) and the* YOUNG ATTACHÉ:

300 ANNE-MARIE STRETTER: *(Deliberate repetition with slight error.)* I wish I were you, coming here for the first time in the rains. *(Pause.)* You're not bored? What do you do? In the evenings? On Sundays?
YOUNG ATTACHÉ: I read . . . I sleep . . . I don't really know . . .
305 ANNE-MARIE STRETTER: *(Pause.)* Boredom is a personal thing, of course. One doesn't know what to advise.
YOUNG ATTACHÉ: I don't think I'm bored.

(Pause.)

ANNE-MARIE STRETTER: And then . . . (Stops.) . . . perhaps it's not so important as people make out . . . Thank you for the
310 parcels of books, you send them on from the office so quickly . . .

YOUNG ATTACHÉ: A pleasure . . .

(Silence.
The noise gradually starts up around them again, faintly.)

Men: (In the silence of the preceding conversation.)
—— What an intriguing woman. All those books. Those
315 sleepless nights in the residency in the Delta . . .
—— Yes . . . What can be behind that sweetness . . . ?
—— Nearly every smile is enough to break your heart . . .

(Silence.)

ANNE-MARIE STRETTER: One might say practically nothing is . . . one can do practically nothing in India . . .
320 YOUNG ATTACHÉ: *(Gentle.)* You mean . . . ?
ANNE-MARIE STRETTER: Oh . . . nothing . . . the general despondency . . . *(There is a smile in her voice.)*
Men and women:
—— They say she sometimes has had . . . attacks . . .
325 —— *(Low.)* You mean . . . the trip to Chandernagor?
—— Yes. And something else . . . sometimes she shuts herself up in her room . . . No one can see her . . .
—— Except him, Michael Richardson . . .
—— Yes, of course . . .
330 ANNE-MARIE STRETTER: It's neither painful nor pleasant living in India. Neither easy nor difficult. It's nothing, really . . . nothing . . .
YOUNG ATTACHÉ: *(Pause.)* You mean it's impossible?
ANNE-MARIE STRETTER: Well . . . *(Charming frivolity in her voice.)* . . . yes . . . perhaps . . . *(Smile in her voice.)* But that's
335 probably an oversimplification . . .
Men and women:
—— She used to give concerts in Venice . . . She was one of the hopes of European music.
340 —— Was she very young when she left Venice?
—— Yes. She went away with a French civil servant that she left for Stretter.

(Silence.)

YOUNG ATTACHÉ: They say you're a Venetian.
ANNE-MARIE STRETTER: My father was French. My mother . . .
345 yes, she was from Venice.

(Silence.)

Men and women: (Continued.)
—— She plays nearly every evening. In the dry season, that is. *(Pause.)* During the monsoon it's so damp pianos get out of tune overnight . . .

(Silence.)

YOUNG ATTACHÉ: The first time I saw you I thought you were
350 English.
ANNE-MARIE STRETTER: That does sometimes happen.

(Pause.)

YOUNG ATTACHÉ: Are there any who never get used to it?
ANNE-MARIE STRETTER: *(Slowly.)* Nearly everyone gets used to it.
355

(Silence.)

YOUNG ATTACHÉ: *(Suddenly crisp.)* The French Vice-Consul in Lahore is looking at you.

(No answer.)

YOUNG ATTACHÉ: He's been looking at you all evening.

(No answer.)

YOUNG ATTACHÉ: Haven't you noticed?

(She avoids answering.)

360 ANNE-MARIE STRETTER: Where is he hoping to be posted, do
    you know?

YOUNG ATTACHÉ: *(He knows.)* Here in Calcutta.

ANNE-MARIE STRETTER: Really . . .

YOUNG ATTACHÉ: I imagined you knew.

(No answer.
Silence.
Servants pass through.
Dances follow one another: blues, tangos, foxtrots.)

365 ANNE-MARIE STRETTER: Did my husband tell you? We'd like
    to invite you to the islands.

YOUNG ATTACHÉ: I'll be very pleased to come.

(Silence.)

Man and woman:
——— If you listen closely, the voice has certain Italian
370   inflections . . .

(Pause.)

——— Yes . . . Perhaps it's that . . . the foreign origin . . . that
makes her seem . . . far away?
——— Perhaps . . .

ANNE-MARIE STRETTER: You write, I believe?

375 YOUNG ATTACHÉ: *(Pause.)* I once thought I could. Before.
    (Pause.) Did someone tell you?

ANNE-MARIE STRETTER: Yes, but I'd probably have guessed . . .
    (Smile in the voice.) From your way of being silent . . .

YOUNG ATTACHÉ: *(Smiling.)* I gave it up. *(Pause.)* Monsieur
380   Stretter used to write too?

ANNE-MARIE STRETTER: Yes, it did happen, to him too. And
    then . . . *(She stops.)*

YOUNG ATTACHÉ: *(Pause.)* And you?

ANNE-MARIE STRETTER: I've never tried . . .

385 YOUNG ATTACHÉ: *(Crisply.)* You think it's not worth it, don't
    you . . . ?

ANNE-MARIE STRETTER: *(Smile.)* Well . . . *(She stops.)* Well,
    yes, if you like . . .

(Pause.)

YOUNG ATTACHÉ: You play.

390 ANNE-MARIE STRETTER: Sometimes. *(Pause.)* Not so much,
    the last few years . . .

YOUNG ATTACHÉ: *(Gently; love already.)* Why?

ANNE-MARIE STRETTER: *(Slowly.)* It's hard to put it into
    words . . .

(Long pause.)

395 YOUNG ATTACHÉ: Tell me.

ANNE-MARIE STRETTER: For me . . . for some time . . . there's
    been a kind of pain . . . associated with music . . .

(No answer.
Silence.
The VICE-CONSUL *moves from where he was standing in the gar-*
den and goes into the reception. The people still going back and
forth between the garden and the reception watch him.
A certain commotion. Some stifled exclamations.

Then two or three couples come into the garden, as if they were
running away from the man from Lahore.)

Woman:
——— What's happening?
——— The Vice-Consul from Lahore has asked the wife of   400
the First Secretary at the Spanish Embassy to dance . . .

(Pause.)

——— Poor woman . . . But what are people afraid of?
——— They're not afraid . . . It's more a sort of . . . repulsion . . .
But it's . . . involuntary . . . you can't analyze it . . .

(Silence.)

YOUNG ATTACHÉ: Will you have to dance with him?   405

ANNE-MARIE STRETTER: I don't have to do anything, but . . .
    (Smile in the voice.)

(Pause.)

YOUNG ATTACHÉ: Last night he was in the garden. By the ten-
    nis courts.

(The answer comes slowly.)

ANNE-MARIE STRETTER: I think he sleeps badly.   410

(Pause.)

YOUNG ATTACHÉ: He's still looking at you.

(Silence.)

Isolated woman's voice:
——— Poor woman . . . and on top of that she feels obliged to
talk to him . . .

(Silence.)

YOUNG ATTACHÉ: Repulsion is a feeling you know nothing   415
    about?

(Pause.)

ANNE-MARIE STRETTER: I don't understand . . . How could
    one know nothing about it?

YOUNG ATTACHÉ: *(Low.)* The horror . . .

(No answer.
Silence.)

YOUNG ATTACHÉ: *(Very clear and distinct.)* They're talking   420
    about leprosy.

(Silence.
The YOUNG ATTACHÉ *was referring to the conversation between*
the VICE-CONSUL *and the wife [Spanish] of the Secretary at the*
Spanish Embassy.)

VICE-CONSUL *and* SPANISH WOMAN:
SPANISH WOMAN: *(Accent.)* . . . the wife of one of our secre-
    taries was going mad, thinking she'd caught it . . . impossible
    to get the idea out of her head . . . she had to be sent back to
    Madrid . . .   425

VICE-CONSUL: She had leprosy?

SPANISH WOMAN: *(Astonished.)* Of course not! . . . accidents
    are very rare . . . in three years I only know of a ballboy at the
    Club . . . all the staff are examined regularly . . . most thor-
    ough . . . I shouldn't have mentioned it . . . I don't know   430
    how it happened . . .

VICE-CONSUL: But I'm not frightened of leprosy.

SPANISH WOMAN: Just as well, because . . . Of course, there are worse places . . . Take Singapore . . .

435 VICE-CONSUL: *(Interrupting.)* Don't you understand? I want to catch it.

(Slight commotion.
Then silence.)

Man and woman:
——— She left him in the middle of the dance . . . What happened?
440 ——— He must have said something . . . something that frightened her . . .

(Silence.
Some guests leave the garden and go back into the reception.
The BEGGAR WOMAN *sticks her bald head out and watches—*
like an owl. Then hides again. The YOUNG ATTACHÉ *must have*
seen her.)

YOUNG ATTACHÉ: There's a beggar woman in the garden.
ANNE-MARIE STRETTER: I know . . . She's the one who sings—
didn't you know? Of course, you've only just arrived in Cal-
445 cutta . . . I think she sings a song from Savannakhet . . .
That's in Laos . . . She intrigues us . . . I tell myself I must be
mistaken, it's not possible, we're thousands of miles from Indochina here . . . How could she have done it?
YOUNG ATTACHÉ: *(Pause.)* I've heard her in the street, early in
450 the morning . . . It's a cheerful song.
ANNE-MARIE STRETTER: The children sing it in Laos . . . She
must have come down through the river valleys. But how did
she cross the mountains—the Cardamon Hills?
YOUNG ATTACHÉ: She's quite mad.
455 ANNE-MARIE STRETTER: Yes, but you see . . . she's alive. Sometimes she comes to the islands. How? No one knows.
YOUNG ATTACHÉ: Perhaps she follows you. Follows white
people?
ANNE-MARIE STRETTER: That happens. Food.

(Some guests leave the reception. Slight fear.)

460 *Men and women:*
——— Where is he?
——— Over by the bar . . . He drinks too much, that fellow.
It'll end badly.
——— There's something . . . impossible . . . about him.
465 ——— Yes.
——— And no one invited him anywhere in Lahore either?
——— No.
——— He went through hell in Lahore.
——— Yes, but . . . How can one overcome this . . . this
470 disgust . . . ?
Men:
——— He's anger personified.
——— Against whom? Against what?

(No answer.
Silence.)

Women:
475 ——— He used to call down death on Lahore, fire and death.
——— Perhaps he drank?
——— No, no . . . Out here, drinking affects us all in the same
way—we talk about going home . . . No, he wasn't drunk . . .

(Two women have come into the room. They are hot, they fan
themselves. They look around.
A blues.
They look at the reception.
Suddenly they stop fanning themselves: they've just seen some-
thing.
Blues.)

Isolated woman's voice:
——— It was bound to happen. Look . . . The Vice-Consul   480
from Lahore is going over to Madame Stretter . . .

(Silence.)

Men:
——— Have you noticed? Out here the white people talk
about nothing but themselves . . . The rest . . . And yet the
time when most Europeans commit suicide is during   485
famines . . .
——— . . . which don't cause them any suffering . . . *(Little*
laugh.)

(Silence.
The two women watch with intense curiosity as the VICE-
CONSUL *goes over toward Madame Stretter.*
The sound of the reception ceases almost completely for a few
seconds.
Then it begins again, faintly. Politely stifled exclamations.)

Men and women: (Conversations 1 and 2.)
No. 1
——— Did you see? The Ambassador . . . ? How cleverly he   490
got his wife out of it . . .

(Silence.)

——— Where are they going?
——— Into the other drawing room . . . Of course, the Ambassador would have had to talk to him sooner or later . . .
so . . .   495

(Silence.)

No. 2
——— Did you see? What diplomacy . . . everyone saw.
——— Where are they going?
——— Into the other drawing room . . . *(Pause.)* A servant's
bringing them some champagne . . .

(Silence.)

No. 1
——— Why doesn't he go? Asking to be humiliated like   500
that . . .

No. 2
——— He said something to the Club Secretary that keeps
coming back to me . . . "At home, in Neuilly, in a drawing
room, there's a big black piano—closed . . . On the music
rest there's the score of 'India Song.' My mother used to play   505
it. I could hear it from my bedroom. It's been there ever
since she died . . ."
——— What is it you find so striking?
——— The image.

(Silence.
Silence. Blues.

MADAME STRETTER *and the* YOUNG ATTACHÉ *are walking*
through the gardens.)

AMBASSADOR *and* VICE-CONSUL:

510   AMBASSADOR: If I've got it right, my dear fellow, you'd prefer Bombay? But you wouldn't be given the same job there as you had in . . . *(He hesitates.)* Lahore. It's too soon yet . . . Whereas if you stay here . . . people will forget . . . India is a gulf of indifference, really . . . If you like, I'll keep you on in
515   Calcutta . . . Would you like me to?

VICE-CONSUL: Yes.

(Silence.)

Women: *(Low.)*
——— He told her he wanted to catch leprosy.
——— Mad . . .

(Silence.)

520   AMBASSADOR: Funny things, careers. The more you want one the less you make one. You can't just make a career. There are a thousand different ways of being a French Vice-Consul . . . If you forget Lahore other people will forget it too . . .

VICE-CONSUL: *(Pause.)* I don't forget Lahore.

(Silence.)

525   *Isolated man's voice:*
——— Only one person has anything to do with him. The Secretary at the European Club. A drunk.

AMBASSADOR: You can't get used to Calcutta? *(No answer.)* People put that sort of thing down to their nerves. There are
530   remedies, you know.

VICE-CONSUL: No.

(Silence.)

Woman and man: *(Low.)*
——— And what are they talking about?
——— The reformatory in Arras. Childhood. And . . . *(Stops.)*
535   ——— And . . . ?
——— Her . . . the French Ambassador's wife . . .

(Silence.)

AMBASSADOR: At first everyone's like that. I remember I was, myself. You either go home or you stay. If you stay, you have to find . . . or rather invent . . . a way of looking at things . . .
540   of enduring Lahore . . .

VICE-CONSUL: I couldn't.

(Silence.)

Isolated woman's voice: *(Low.)*
——— She's gone into the garden with the Young Attaché. *(Pause.)* I told you.

(Silence.)

545   AMBASSADOR: Take my advice . . . weigh up the pros and cons . . . and if you're not . . . sure of yourself, go back to Paris . . .

VICE-CONSUL: No.

(Silence.)

AMBASSADOR: In that case . . . how do you see the future?

VICE-CONSUL: I see nothing.

(Silence.)

550   Women: *(Low.)*
——— After every reception the leftovers are given to the poor. Her idea. *(Lower.)* She's coming back . . .

(Silence.)

——— Oh, I see! The garden's full of beggars . . . crowds of them all around the kitchens . . .
——— The sentries have been told to let them through.   555

(Silence.
ANNE-MARIE STRETTER *and the* YOUNG ATTACHÉ *come in again [from the left]. They go toward the reception.*
The blues is over. Another takes up the theme of "India Song."
Before entering the reception ANNE-MARIE STRETTER *halts, as does the* YOUNG ATTACHÉ. *They wait.*
For there, on the other side of the room, is the man from Lahore. Distraught, he comes toward her. Stops. Bows. Pale.
The YOUNG ATTACHÉ *makes a gesture as if to stop* ANNE-MARIE STRETTER *from accepting.*
She hesitates, but only for a second, and then accepts the man from Lahore's invitation to dance.
"India Song" becomes very distant. All conversations grow faint, become intermittent murmurs. Almost total silence.
At first, the VICE-CONSUL *and* ANNE-MARIE STRETTER *dance in the room.*
The YOUNG ATTACHÉ *watches them.*
Then they move toward the reception.
The YOUNG ATTACHÉ *moves forward, still watching them.*
Other people move toward the garden. They all look toward the reception.)

(Conversation between ANNE-MARIE STRETTER *and the* VICE-CONSUL, *low but violent, very slow.)*

(Long silence, before the conversation begins.)

VICE-CONSUL: I didn't know that you existed.

(No answer.)

VICE-CONSUL: Calcutta has become a form of hope for me.

(Silence.)

ANNE-MARIE STRETTER: I love Michael Richardson. I'm not free of that love.

VICE-CONSUL: I know.   560
  I love you like that, in that love.
  It doesn't matter to me.

(No answer.)

VICE-CONSUL: My voice sounds odd. Can you hear?
  It frightens them.

ANNE-MARIE STRETTER: Yes.   565

VICE-CONSUL: Whose voice is it?

(No answer.)

VICE-CONSUL: I shot at myself in Lahore, but I didn't die. Other people separate me from Lahore. I don't separate myself.
  Lahore is me. Do you understand too?   570

(Pause. Gently.)

ANNE-MARIE STRETTER: Yes. Don't shout.

VICE-CONSUL: No.

(Silence.)

VICE-CONSUL: You are with me about Lahore. I know. You are in me. I'll carry you inside me. *(Terrible brief laugh.)* And

575 you'll shoot the Shalimar lepers with me. What can you do about it?

(Silence.)

VICE-CONSUL: I didn't need to dance with you to know you. You know that.
ANNE-MARIE STRETTER: Yes.

(Pause.)

580 VICE-CONSUL: There's no need for us to go any further, you and I. *(Terrible brief laugh.)* We haven't anything to say to each other. We are the same.

(Pause.)

ANNE-MARIE STRETTER: I believe you.

(Pause.)

VICE-CONSUL: Love affairs you have with others. We don't
585 need that.

*(Silence.
The* VICE-CONSUL'S *voice is broken by a sob. It is no longer under his control.)*

VICE-CONSUL: I wanted to know the smell of your hair—that's why I . . . *(He stops. A sob.)*

*(Silence.
His voice returns to normal—almost.)*

VICE-CONSUL: After the reception your friends stay on. I'd like to stay with you for once.
590 ANNE-MARIE STRETTER: You haven't a chance.

(Pause.)

VICE-CONSUL: They'd throw me out.
ANNE-MARIE STRETTER: Yes.
You're someone they have to forget.

(Pause.)

VICE-CONSUL: Like Lahore.
595 ANNE-MARIE STRETTER: Yes.

(Silence.)

VICE-CONSUL: What will become of me?
ANNE-MARIE STRETTER: You'll be posted somewhere a long way from Calcutta.

(Pause.)

VICE-CONSUL: That's what you want.
600 ANNE-MARIE STRETTER: Yes.

(Pause.)

VICE-CONSUL: Very well. And when will it end?
ANNE-MARIE STRETTER: When you die, I believe.

(Silence.)

VICE-CONSUL: *(Heart-rending.)* What's this pain? Mine?

(Pause.)

ANNE-MARIE STRETTER: Knowledge.
605 VICE-CONSUL: *(Terrible laugh.)* Of you?

*(No answer.
Silence.)*

VICE-CONSUL: I'm going to shout. I'm going to ask them to let me stay tonight.

(Pause.)

ANNE-MARIE STRETTER: *(Pause.)* Do as you like.
VICE-CONSUL: So that something should happen between us. In public. Shouting is all I know. Let them at least find out a 610 love can be shouted.

(No answer.)

VICE-CONSUL: They'll feel uncomfortable for half an hour. Then they'll start talking again.

(No answer.)

VICE-CONSUL: I even know you won't tell anyone you agreed.

*(No answer.
Silence.
"India Song" ends.
It is replaced by "Heure exquise," sung.
The sky grows pale.
Two men, drunk, stagger in and collapse in armchairs.
Over "Heure exquise," mingled with it, the* VICE-CONSUL'S *first cry.)*

VICE-CONSUL: Let me stay! 615

*(Silence.
Guests shrink back toward the garden. The two drunk men laugh. The others are horrified.)*

VICE-CONSUL: I'm going to stay here tonight, with her, for once, with her! Do you hear?

(Silence.)

Isolated woman's voice:
—— How awful . . .
Isolated voice of YOUNG ATTACHÉ: 620
—— You really ought to go home, you've had too much to drink . . . come along . . .

*("Heure exquise" still.
The* VICE-CONSUL *shrieks.)*

VICE-CONSUL: I'm going to stay! In the French Embassy! I'm going to the islands with her!
Please! Please! Let me stay! 625

(Silence.)

Isolated woman's voice: (Anguished.)
—— She looks as if she didn't hear . . .
Another: (The same.)
—— This is terrible . . .

(Silence.)

VICE-CONSUL: *(Shrieking.)* Once! Just once! I've never loved 630 anyone but her!

(Silence.)

Isolated man's voice, to VICE-CONSUL:
—— We're sorry, but you're the sort of person who only interests us when you're not there.

(Silence.)

Isolated woman's voice: 635
—— How cruel . . . It's terrible . . . horrible . . .

(The VICE-CONSUL's *sobs. Unrestrained. All dignity swept away. Everyone suddenly turns aside.)*

Isolated woman's voice:
——— I can't bear to see it . . .

(The VICE-CONSUL *appears, shaken with sobs. We see and hear them.*
A man, a stranger, leads him by the arm toward the entrance of the Embassy. The VICE-CONSUL *resists at first, then lets himself be led away.*
They disappear.
Everyone stands looking after them.)

Isolated woman's voice:
640   ——— He's gone. *(Long pause.)* They're shutting the gate.

(In the distance, the same cries: the VICE-CONSUL *has started to shout again.)*

Isolated woman's voice:
——— He was laughing and crying at the same time. Did you
  see?

(Silence.
"Heure exquise" continues imperturbably to the end, while everyone stands looking away from the reception and toward the VICE-CONSUL.
The cries still go on.)

Isolated man's voice:
645   ——— He's trying to break down the gate.

(Silence.
"Heure exquise" ends.
The cries get farther away.)

Isolated voice:
——— The beggars are frightened . . .
Isolated voice, the last:
——— He's gone.

(Silence. A few seconds of it, then:
Blackout.
Darkness gradually blots out the picture as, in the far distance, the silhouette of the BEGGAR WOMAN *passes by, then disappears.*
Silence.
Then suddenly, on the piano, Beethoven's 14th Variation on a Theme by Diabelli.
Blackout.)

— ACT THREE —

NOTES ON VOICES 3 AND 4

VOICES 3 and 4 are men's voices. The only thing that connects them is the fascination exerted on them by the story of the lovers of the Ganges, especially, once again, by that of ANNE-MARIE STRETTER.

VOICE 3 can remember almost nothing of the chronology of the story. It questions VOICE 4, and VOICE 4 answers.

Of all the voices, VOICE 4 is the one which has forgotten the story the least. It knows almost all of it.

But VOICE 3, although it has forgotten almost everything, recognizes things as VOICE 4 relates them. VOICE 4 doesn't tell it anything it didn't know before, at a time when it too knew the story very well.

The difference between VOICES 3 and 4, between forgetfulness on the one hand and remembrance on the other, arises from the same cause—the fascination the story exerts on the two voices. VOICE 3 has rejected the fascination, VOICE 4 has tolerated it.

The story of the lovers of the Ganges is *in* both voices—latent in the one, manifest in the other. About to survive or revive.

The difference—between the tolerable and the intolerable—should be reflected in the sensibilities of the two voices.

It is not without apprehension that VOICE 4 informs VOICE 3. VOICE 4 often hesitates. For VOICE 3 is exposed to the danger, not of madness, like VOICE 1, but of suffering.

We are in the same part of the Embassy as before. There are five people there in the darkness, which slowly disappears:

ANNE-MARIE STRETTER, MICHAEL RICHARDSON, *the* YOUNG ATTACHÉ, *the* GUEST *(friend of the Stretters), and an old friend, an Englishman,* GEORGE CRAWN.

The drunk journalists have gone. The rest are by themselves, in an intimacy in which each of them feels alone. It is late, they are separated by fatigue.

They are waiting. Their chairs—except for those of ANNE-MARIE STRETTER *and* MICHAEL RICHARDSON—*are too far apart for conversation.*

The YOUNG ATTACHÉ *and the Stretters'* GUEST *look exhausted, also, by the events of the evening.*

We don't know what they are waiting for: perhaps for it to be light, so that they can leave for the islands. Probably.

We still hear Beethoven's 14th Variation on a Theme by Diabelli. Through the music, the sounds of Calcutta grow stronger with the light.

ANNE-MARIE STRETTER *sits with her head flung back and to one side over the arm of a chair. She might seem to be asleep if it weren't for the fact that her eyes are open.*

MICHAEL RICHARDSON *is near her, half lying on a low chair.*

The YOUNG ATTACHÉ *is sitting up straight, smoking. He looks as if he is listening to the noises of Calcutta, through which one suddenly recognizes the cries, the last spasms of the calls to love of the* VICE-CONSUL *from Lahore. The* YOUNG ATTACHÉ *obviously finds them hard to bear. The others do not.*

The Stretters' GUEST, *standing, looks around at the others: these people of India whom he thought he knew, but whom he scarcely recognizes after the night of the reception. He too listens to the cries of the* VICE-CONSUL.

GEORGE CRAWN *listens to the Beethoven: he is entirely absorbed by the music.*

VOICE 4: As usual after a reception, some people stayed on.
VOICE 3: *(Low.)* Is he the one sitting near her—Michael
  Richardson?
VOICE 4: Yes.
VOICE 3: *(Hesitating.)* Did they ever find out . . . ?
VOICE 4: *(Hesitating.)* After she died he left India.

5

(Silence.)

VOICE 4: *(Continuing.)* The one standing up is the Young Attaché.

VOICE 3: And the elderly Englishman?

10 VOICE 4: George Crawn. He knew her in Peking.

(Pause.)

VOICE 3: And the one looking at them?

VOICE 4: Someone passing through. Stretter's guest.

(Silence.)

VOICE 3: Is that the French Vice-Consul shouting?

VOICE 4: Yes. Still.

(Silence.)

15 VOICE 4: All trace of him disappears in 1938. *(Pause.)* He resigns from the consular service. The resignation is the last
thing on the file.

VOICE 3: *(Hesitating.)* Very soon afterwards . . .

VOICE 4: A few days.

(Silence. Cries.)

20 VOICE 3: What's he shouting?

VOICE 4: Her name.

(Pause.)

VOICE 3: *(Slowly.)* Anna Maria Guardi.

VOICE 4: Yes. All night, all through Calcutta, he's been shouting that name.

(Silence.
The women's voices [from Act I] now arrive. They too speak of the
VICE-CONSUL.*)*

25 VOICE 2: *(As if exhausted.)* He walks along by the Ganges.
He comes on the lepers asleep.
Someone else is shouting on the other bank.

(Pause.)

VOICE 1: Yes.

(Silence.)

VOICE 2: Can you see him?

30 VOICE 1: *(Distant.)* Yes. I'm watching.
I see.

(Silence.)

VOICE 2: *(Slow.)* Is he looking for something? . . . Or walking
at random? . . . Aimlessly?

(No answer.)

VOICE 2: Is he looking for something he's lost?

(No answer.)

35 VOICE 2: Something in common that he's lost too?

(No answer.)

VOICE 2: The love of her?

VOICE 1: Love. Yes.

(Silence.)

VOICE 2: *(Yearning, desire.)* How far away you are . . . from
me . . .

(No answer.
Silence.
A servant goes through with trays piled with glasses, ashtrays,
etc. He passes them as though he didn't see them.
Gleams in the sky. The burning-ghats.)

VOICE 1: *(Slow.)* It will soon be day. 40

(Silence.)

VOICE 1: *(Very slow.)* Dawn is breaking here, all around.
And there.
The air smells of mud. And leprosy. And burning.

VOICE 2: Not a breath.

VOICE 1: No. Slow stirrings, slow movements, smells. 45

(Silence.)

VOICE 2: Can't I hear music?

VOICE 1: No.

VOICE 2: That sound of wings, of birds.

VOICE 1: The fan. Forgotten.

(Silence.
The men's voices mingle with the women's.)

VOICE 3: Those gleams. 50

VOICE 4: Day.
The first zone is the zone of leprosy and dogs. They are on
the banks of the Ganges, under the trees. No strength left.
No pain.

VOICE 3: And those who have died of hunger? 55

VOICE 4: Farther away, in the density of the North. The last
zone.

(Pause.)

VOICE 4: Day. The sun.

(Pause.)

VOICE 3: The light. Terrible.

(Silence.)

VOICE 1: The light. Of exile. 60

VOICE 2: Is she asleep?

VOICE 1: Which one?

VOICE 2: The white woman.

VOICE 1: No. Resting.

(Silence.)

VOICE 2: *(Mournfully.)* How far away you are. Quite absent. 65

(No answer.
Silence.
MICHAEL RICHARDSON *slowly turns his head toward* ANNE-
MARIE STRETTER. *Looks at her.)*

VOICE 3: *(Startled.)* Voices near us suddenly? Did you hear?

VOICE 4: *(Pause.)* No . . .

VOICE 3: Young voices . . . women's?

VOICE 4: *(Pause.)* I don't hear anything. *(Pause.)* Silence.

(Silence.)

VOICE 4: He's looking at her. 70

VOICE 3: Yes.
She is far away. Quite absent.

(Silence.)

VOICE 4: *(In one breath.)* People said one day they'd both be found dead in a brothel in Calcutta they used to go to some-times during the monsoon.

75

(Silence.)

VOICE 3: Not a breath. The heat is the color of rust. Above, the smoke.

VOICE 4: The factories. The middle zone.

(Silence.
Very slowly ANNE-MARIE STRETTER *has inclined her head toward* MICHAEL RICHARDSON. *They look at each other.)*

VOICE 3: That overhanging mass . . . ?

80 VOICE 4: The monsoon.
Below, Bengal.

VOICE 3: And farther away . . . lower . . . under the clouds . . . ? Look . . .

(No answer.)

VOICE 3: That white patch . . . in a bend in the Ganges . . . ? There . . . ?

85 VOICE 4: *(Hesitating.)* The English cemetery.

(Silence.
The stranger and the YOUNG ATTACHÉ *begin to look at* ANNE-MARIE STRETTER.*)*

VOICE 1: Is she a leper?

VOICE 2: Which one?

VOICE 1: The beggar.

90 VOICE 2: She sleeps in leprosy, and every morning . . . No. *(Pause.)* No.

(Silence.)

VOICE 1: And the white woman?

VOICE 2: A false alarm ten years ago. But no, she neither. *(Pause.)* Listen . . .

(Sound of a machine and of water.)

95 VOICE 1: The water sprinklers in the English quarter.

(Silence.
The men turn their eyes away from ANNE-MARIE STRETTER *and look at the ground.*
The stage gradually gets lighter.)

VOICE 1: A car is speeding along the straight roads. Beside the Ganges.

VOICE 2: Black?

VOICE 1: Yes.

100 VOICE 2: They've left for the islands.

(Silence.
The fires of the ghats are out. It is daylight. Pale daylight.
They lie there, in the same deathly attitude, as the voices describe the journey.)

VOICE 4: The French Embassy's black Lancia has started out for the Delta.

(Long silence.)

VOICE 3: *(As if reciting a lesson.)* The granary of northern India . . . The frontier of the waters. The Delta.

105 VOICE 4: Yes, the mingling of the waters. The sweet and the salt.

VOICE 3: After the deluge, before the light . . .

(Pause.)

VOICE 3: And those junks?

VOICE 4: Rice.
Sailing down to Coromandel. 110

(Pause.)

VOICE 3: Those dark patches on the banks?

VOICE 4: People.
The highest density in the world.

(Silence.)

VOICE 3: Those thousands of dark mirrors?

VOICE 4: The paddy fields of India. 115

(Silence.)

VOICE 4: They're asleep.
She's lying close to him.

(Silence.)

VOICE 3: She used to wake up late during the monsoon?

VOICE 4: Yes. Didn't go out till after dark.

(Silence.)

VOICE 3: The black Lancia has stopped. 120

VOICE 4: The rain. The roads are blocked.
They took shelter in a rest house. *(As if reading.)*
It was there the Young Attaché said: "I saw the Vice-Consul again before I left. He was still shouting in the streets. He asked me if I was going to the islands. I said no, I was going 125 to Nepal with the Ambassador."

(Pause.)

VOICE 3: Did she approve of the Young Attaché's lie?

VOICE 4: She practically never mentioned the man from Lahore.

(Silence.)

VOICE 3: That patch of green? it's getting bigger . . . 130

VOICE 4: The sea.

(Silence.
Blackout.
The voices speak in the dark.)

VOICE 4: The islands.

VOICE 3: Which one?

VOICE 4: The biggest, the middle one. They're there.

(Silence.)

VOICE 3: That big white building . . . ? 135

VOICE 4: A big international hotel. The "Prince of Wales."
The sea is rough. There's been a storm.

(Blackout ends.)

— ACT FOUR —

The same as before, but it has become a lounge in the "Prince of Wales."

They are not there.

A bright, greenish light instead of that of the monsoon.

The servants in white gloves are putting up green canvas blinds over the screened windows.

We do not recognize the garden. It has exploded into a violent green light—the garden of the "Prince of Wales." All that remains of the garden in Calcutta are some clumps of foliage.

The sound of the sea gradually spreads, increasing every second, until it invades everything. Then it remains stable.

The wind makes the blinds flap.

Sound of launches' sirens in the distance.

Close, the cheeping of birds.

The fan is still there, going around at the same nightmare speed.

In the distance, a dance: an orchestra is playing "India Song."

The sounds occur one after the other. For example:

1. *The wind.*
2. *The sea.*
3. *Sirens.*
4. *Birds.*
5. *Dance.*

As the two servants put up the blinds, thus creating the set for the "Prince of Wales," VOICES 3 *and* 4 *speak to each other.*

*(*VOICE 4 *remains the same throughout.*

VOICE 3 *changes as the end of the story approaches. It becomes either more pressing or, conversely, less eager to question. When it speaks of* ANNE-MARIE STRETTER *it gets lower, with silences between words and phrases.)*

VOICE 4: In front, the landing stages. The boats go to and from the South Pacific.
Behind, there's a yachting harbor.

(Silence.)

VOICE 3: Beyond the palms, the same flat horizon.
5 VOICE 4: They're alluvial islands, formed by the Ganges mud.

(Silence.)

VOICE 3: Where's the French residency?
VOICE 4: The other side of the hotel, looking out to sea.

(The servants go out. They have "finished" the set for the "Prince of Wales." When they have gone the sound of the dance is heard in the distance.
They are playing "India Song.")

VOICE 4: At this time of the day, people used to start to drink at all the tables in the "Prince of Wales." On the sideboards
10 there are French grapes. In the showcases, perfumes.
Roses are sent every day from Nepal.
VOICE 3: Who lives in this hotel?
VOICE 4: White India.

(Silence.)

VOICE 3: *(Almost shouting.)* What's that sudden smell of death?
15 VOICE 4: Incense.

(The smell of incense should pervade the auditorium.
Silence.)

VOICE 3: She wanted to go for a swim when they got here?
VOICE 4: Yes. It was late, the sea was rough, it was impossible to swim. Just let the warm waves break over you. She and he both went in.

(Silence.)

VOICE 3: *(Afraid.)* All those screens in the sea? 20
VOICE 4: Protection against the sharks.
VOICE 3: Oh.

(Silence.)

VOICE 3: Where is she?
VOICE 4: She'll come.

(Silence.)

VOICE 4: Here she is. 25
VOICE 3: *(Hesitating; lower, more slowly.)* Was she like that that night . . . ?
VOICE 4: *(Pause.)* Smiling.
Dressed in white.

(Silence.
These last two phrases should be felt as terrifying: ANNE-MARIE STRETTER's *smile, the whiteness of her dress.*
In the green light, ANNE-MARIE STRETTER *enters.*
Smiling, dressed in white.
She goes and looks at the sea, beyond the garden.
The four men enter, also dressed in white, from different parts of the hotel.
They all go toward the garden and look out at the sea.
MICHAEL RICHARDSON *turns and gazes at* ANNE-MARIE STRETTER.
She doesn't look at him any more.
In the distance, a voice over a loudspeaker.)

LOUDSPEAKER: The last boat tonight leaves at seven o'clock. 30
VOICE 4: That's for the tourists who want to get back. There's a storm threatening.

(Ships' sirens. Then silence.)

VOICE 4: The last launch has just arrived. The one that brings supplies.

(Silence.
A head waiter comes and bows to the five people. Their table is ready. They go off toward the left. Still the distant airport music.)

VOICE 4: *(Pause.)* Their table's ready. The food here is 35 excellent.
Michael Richardson used to say that once you knew the "Prince of Wales" you were never really satisfied anywhere else in the world.
VOICE 3: *(Low.)* I can't quite remember . . . isn't she going to 40 the French residency?
VOICE 4: She only used to sleep there.
She used to dine at the "Prince of Wales" when she stayed on the islands. *(Hesitates.)*
She'd had the servants at the residency sent back to Calcutta. 45

(Pause.
Fear.)

VOICE 3: *(Low.)* How long ago?
VOICE 4: A few weeks.

(Bird cries, so loud they are almost unbearable.)

VOICE 3: The birds . . . thousands of them.
VOICE 4: Prisoners on the islands. They couldn't fly back to the coast because of the storm. 50
VOICE 3: It's as if they were right inside the hotel . . .

VOICE 4: They're in the mango trees. They strip them. They'll fly away when it's light.

(Noise of birds swamps everything else.
Silence.)

VOICE 3: There's dancing at the other end of the lounge.

55 VOICE 4: Tourists from Ceylon.

(Silence.)

VOICE 4: During dinner . . . she asked them to raise the blind. She wants to see the sea, the sky, above the estuaries. They scarcely speak, they're very tired from last night.

(Silence.)

VOICE 3: She's not eating anything.

60 VOICE 4: Hardly anything. She's looking out of the window.

VOICE 3: I remember . . . A wall of mist is sweeping toward the islands . . .

VOICE 4: Yes. She's saying something about Venice. *(Effort of memory.)* Venice in the winter . . . yes, that's right . . .

(Pause.)

65 VOICE 3: Venice . . .

VOICE 4: Yes. Perhaps, some winter evenings in Venice, the same kind of mist . . .

VOICE 3: . . . she's saying the name of . . . *(Stops.)* of a color . . .

VOICE 4: Purple. The color of the mist in the Delta . . .

(Silence.
Beyond the green windows of the hotel, disheveled, exhausted, his features contorted, still wearing his white dinner jacket, appears the French VICE-CONSUL. *He goes through the garden of the hotel, searching.*
Disappears.
Then reappears almost at once on the stage, now the lounge of the "Prince of Wales," walks across the room, looks toward the left, stops short.
He has seen her.
He stands there looking at her.)

70 VOICE 3: He came over by the last boat.

VOICE 4: Yes. The seven-o'clock.

(Pause.)

He hadn't been home all day. *(Pause.)* He never went back to Calcutta.

(Silence.
The tune of "India Song" is played loudly for a few seconds, then fades.)

VOICE 3: "India Song" . . .

75 VOICE 4: Yes.

(Silence.)

VOICE 4: Now that the mist has come the wind has dropped.

(Silence.
Some tourists go by in the garden beyond the green windows.
One can make out women fanning themselves with white fans.
Light-colored dresses.)

VOICE 4: They're talking about the beggar woman.

(No answer.
Silence.)

VOICE 4: George Crawn and the Stretters' guest are talking about the beggar woman.

(Silence.)

FIRST VERSION: *The conversation between* GEORGE CRAWN *and the Stretters'* GUEST *is heard as from some distance. [Very light and ordinary.])*

GEORGE CRAWN: She doesn't know a word of Hindustani. 80

GUEST: Not a word. If she's from Savannakhet she must have come through Laos, Cambodia, Siam, and Burma, and then probably down through the Irrawaddy Valley . . . Mandalay . . . Prome . . . Bassein . . .

GEORGE CRAWN: It must have been not just one journey, as 85 we might think, but hundreds, thousands, every day, each one the last . . . Hunger always driving her on, farther and farther . . . She must have followed roads, railways, boats . . . but what's strange is that she always went toward the sunset . . . 90

GUEST: . . . I suppose she traveled at night, and faced toward the light . . . She's bald . . . Because of hunger, do you think?

GEORGE CRAWN: Yes.

(Pause.)

GEORGE CRAWN: Sometimes she comes to the islands. Following the whites, probably: food . . . In Calcutta she lives by 95 the Ganges, under the trees. She gets up at night and goes through the English quarter. Apparently she hunts for food at night along the Ganges.

(Pause.)

GUEST: And what's left of her in Calcutta? Not much . . . The song of Savannakhet, the laugh . . . and her native language 100 is still there of course, but there's no use for it. The madness was there when she arrived . . . already too far gone . . .

(Pause.)

GEORGE CRAWN: Why Calcutta? Why did her journey stop there?

GUEST: Perhaps because she can lose herself there. She's al- 105 ways been trying to lose herself, really, ever since her life began . . .

(Pause.)

GEORGE CRAWN: She too.

GUEST: Yes . . .

(Silence.

SECOND VERSION: VOICES 3 *and* 4 *relate the conversation between* GEORGE CRAWN *and the* STRETTERS' GUEST. [VOICE 4 *is the one that hears it.])*

VOICE 4: They've seen her. 110
She must have crossed the Delta on the roof of a bus. She stowed away on the last boat.
They met her by the lagoon, a few hundred yards from the French residency.

(Pause.)

VOICE 3: She must have been following Anne-Marie 115 Stretter . . .

VOICE 4: The guest says she followed him to the gate. She frightened him.

He said: "That eternal smile is frightening . . ."

120 VOICE 3: That too . . .

VOICE 4: Yes. *(Pause.)* You remember?

The first attempt . . . *(Stops.)* at Savannakhet, because of a dead child . . .

VOICE 3: . . . sold by its mother, a beggar from the North . . .

125 very young . . . ?

VOICE 4: Yes. Seventeen . . . *(Pause.)* A few days before Stretter arrived.

(Silence.
Suddenly the VICE-CONSUL *goes toward the right, and disappears: he has seen them.*
Here they are, coming out from dinner. There are now only three of them: ANNE-MARIE STRETTER, MICHAEL RICHARDSON, *the* YOUNG ATTACHÉ.
They walk across the lounge, making for the garden through the middle door.
In the garden they separate.
ANNE-MARIE STRETTER *goes to the right.*
The others go straight on through the garden and disappear.
The VICE-CONSUL *begins to go after* ANNE-MARIE STRETTER.
He halts.
She has stopped too.
She looks around her at the sea, the palms.
She hasn't seen the VICE-CONSUL.*)*

VOICE 4: She wanted to walk back on her own.

(Silence.)

VOICE 4: The other two went for a sail . . .

(Silence.)

130 VOICE 4: The Young Attaché and Michael Richardson went back to the French residency the other way, along the beach.

(Pause.)

VOICE 4: It was as hot again as it had been in Calcutta.

*(*ANNE-MARIE STRETTER *walks slowly away.*
Behind her, the VICE-CONSUL. *He is following her.*
They disappear.
Blackout.
During the blackout, the 14th Beethoven-Diabelli Variation in the distance.
Blackout fades.)

— ACT FIVE —

The same as before, but it is now the French residency.

The light is different. It seems to come from outside. It is blue, like moonlight.

The fan is still there. Still going around.

The garden of the Embassy and the garden of the hotel have both gone. There is just an empty space. A path, and at the end of it a white gate.

Everything is enveloped in endless, fathomless emptiness. But it has a sound: the sea.

After a while, MICHAEL RICHARDSON *and the* YOUNG ATTACHÉ *come in through the white gate.*

Simultaneously, she enters, from the left of the house.

She is barefoot. Her hair is loose. She wears the short black cotton wrap.

She joins them on the path, they go toward one another, meet in the half-light.

They look at the sea.

VOICE 4: She's supposed to have said she was worried about George Crawn and the Guest. The sea was rough.

(Sound of a rowing boat in the distance. They all look toward something out at sea.)

VOICE 4: She didn't have to worry any more. George Crawn and the Guest went straight back to the hotel without calling in at the residency.

(Silence.
They slowly walk back into the house.)

VOICE 3: *(Pause; stricken.)* She didn't say anything that evening that might have made anyone think . . . *(Stops.)*

VOICE 4: No. Nothing.

(Terrific tension. But nothing breaks the quiet spell of death.
MICHAEL RICHARDSON *goes over to the piano.*
She goes out of the room.
The two men are left there alone. They look at each other.
Outside, in the distance, at the end of the path, the white shape of the VICE-CONSUL *comes through the open gate.*
They don't see him.
She comes back, bringing glasses and champagne. She smiles at them.
She puts the bottle and glasses down on a low table and pours out the champagne.
She takes it to them.
They drink.
She sits down on a sofa.
There is still the fixed smile on ANNE-MARIE STRETTER's *face.*
Outside, the VICE-CONSUL *watches.*
MICHAEL RICHARDSON *plays.*
He plays the 14th Beethoven-Diabelli Variation.
Complete stillness.
Suddenly the stillness is shattered:
The YOUNG ATTACHÉ *goes over to* ANNE-MARIE STRETTER, *puts his arms around her, then falls at her feet, and stays there with his arms around her legs.*
He stays there, riveted to her.
She doesn't prevent him.
Strokes his hair.
Still the smile. The fixed smile.
He gets up. Draws her to her feet, flings his arms around her body, naked under the wrap. A gesture of supplication. Vain.
They kiss. A long kiss.
MICHAEL RICHARDSON *watches. Plays the piano and watches them. His face is as we have always known it.*
The white shape from Lahore gazes in avidly from outside.
The YOUNG ATTACHÉ *roughly releases* ANNE-MARIE STRETTER, *staggers over to the piano and leans on it with his head in his hands. The Beethoven continues:* MICHAEL RICHARDSON *goes on playing. Stillness. Stillness enveloped in music.*
The YOUNG ATTACHÉ *remains leaning on the piano, motionless.*
The attitude of despair itself.
For the last time, one of the women's voices:)

5

VOICE 2: *(Terrified.)* Where are you? *(Waits. No answer.)*
10   You're so far away . . . I'm frightened . . .

(VOICE 1 doesn't answer any more.
Silence.
ANNE-MARIE STRETTER turns toward outside, toward the sea.
Shows no surprise when she sees the VICE-CONSUL.
He doesn't move, makes no attempt to conceal himself. Gazes
fixedly at her.
She turns and bares her body to the fan.
Perhaps her naked body is visible to everyone.
To the VICE-CONSUL also—the body already separate from her.
She stands there motionless under the fan.
Silence.)

VOICE 3: *(Low, almost a murmur.)* Michael Richardson left
    her alone that evening?
VOICE 4: *(Hesitating.)* It had been agreed between the lovers
    of the Ganges that they'd leave each other free if ever either
15   of them decided . . . *(Stops.)*

(Silence.)

VOICE 3: *(Suffering, terror.)* But he doesn't know, it isn't
    possible . . .

(No answer.)

VOICE 3: What does he know?
VOICE 4: *(Pause.)* Ever since the servants were sent away,
20   Michael Richardson had been living with this possibility.

(Silence.
ANNE-MARIE STRETTER has lain down under the fan.
She has closed her eyes.
MICHAEL RICHARDSON and the YOUNG ATTACHÉ slowly tear
themselves away, as if she had actually ordered them to leave her
alone there.
They cross the empty space outside. Shadows.

The VICE-CONSUL is there. He doesn't hide as they go past.
It is as if they do not see him.
They disappear from sight.
ANNE-MARIE STRETTER and the VICE-CONSUL from Lahore are
the only ones left in the French residency.
Silence.
She gets up, goes out, slowly walks through the empty space to-
ward the white gate.
It is as if she doesn't see anything. She doesn't see the VICE-
CONSUL.
And he makes not the slightest gesture toward her.)

VOICE 3: *(Scarcely breathed.)* Is he the only one who saw . . . ?
VOICE 4: He didn't say.
VOICE 3: *(As before.)* . . . he didn't do anything to stop . . .

(No answer.)

VOICE 4: The Young Attaché came back to the residency in
    the course of the night. He saw her.   25
    She was lying on the path, resting on her elbow.
    He said: "She laid her arm out straight and leaned her head
    on it. The Vice-Consul from Lahore was sitting ten yards
    away. They didn't speak to each other."

(Silence.
What has just been related is what ANNE-MARIE STRETTER does.
She lays her face on her arm. Stays like that. The VICE-CONSUL
looks at her, riveted to the distance between them.)

VOICE 4: She must have stayed there a long while, till day-   30
    light—and then she must have gone along the path . . .
    (Stops.) They found the wrap on the beach.

(Silence.
The fan stops.
Rest a few seconds on the stopping of the fan.
Blackout.)

■ TOM STOPPARD ■

Tom Stoppard was born Tomas Straussler, in Zlin, Czechoslovakia, in 1937. His father was a doctor, and the family emigrated to Singapore before World War II. With the outbreak of the war, Stoppard and his mother left Singapore for India, but before his father could leave Singapore he was killed during the Japanese invasion. Stoppard's mother, Martha, married Kenneth Stoppard, a major in the British army, in 1946, and the family journeyed to England, settling eventually in Bristol in 1950. Stoppard attended the Dolphin School and the Pocklington School in Yorkshire, but did not continue to a university education. Instead, in 1954 he left school to pursue a career in journalism; by the early 1960s, he was writing plays, working free-lance as a journalist, and serving as drama critic for *Scene*. Although Stoppard had written a short television play, *A Walk on the Water*, in 1963 and had produced *If You're Glad I'll Be Frank* on BBC radio in 1966, his first success as a playwright came in 1967, with the stunning comedy *Rosencrantz and Guildenstern Are Dead*. As he would do in several later plays, Stoppard bases the action on a familiar play—Shakespeare's *Hamlet*—but gives the action a decisive, philosophical twist. For while they enact the deeds they perform in *Hamlet*, Ros and Guil seem to be refugees from another play, a play like Samuel Beckett's *Waiting for Godot*: they seem to inhabit an "absurd" and arbitrary world, in which their lives have strangely come to intersect with Hamlet's deadly revenge. *Rosencrantz and Guildenstern Are Dead* established Stoppard as an important comic playwright in the English tradition of Wilde and Shaw, and swept a series of awards for 1967, including the *Evening Standard* award for most promising playwright, the John Whiting Award, a Tony, and the New York Drama Critics Circle Award.

Stoppard continued to explore the relationship between literary and theatrical conventions and the structure of "real" life in a series of plays in the late 1960s and 1970s: *The Real Inspector Hound* (1968), *After Magritte* (1970), *Dogg's Our Pet* (1971), and *Jumpers* (1972). Perhaps Stoppard's most ingenious play, *Jumpers*, takes a skeptical view of the moral relativism of modern philosophy, by intertwining a murder mystery, a tale of astronauts stranded on the moon, a seduction story, and a political coup d'état, with the doings of a squad of acrobats ("jumpers") who turn out to represent the faculty of philosophy of a major university. Stoppard extended this comic meditation on the relationship between literature and politics in his next play, *Travesties* (1974), which concerns the constellation of James Joyce, the Dada poet Tristan Tzara, and V. I. Lenin around the production of Oscar Wilde's *The Importance of Being Earnest* in 1918 Zurich.

Stoppard has honed his talents as a comic playwright by adapting the works of several European dramatists, notably Arthur Schnitzler's *Undiscovered Country* (1979) and Johan Nestroy's *On the Razzle* (1981). Because he was born in Czechoslovakia, Stoppard also has remained involved in the politics of Eastern Europe, and he was active in protesting human rights abuses of dissident Eastern writers. He adapted the Polish playwright Slawomir Mrozek's banned play *Tango* in 1966 and explored the relationship between individual freedom, the news media, and the state in a number of plays of the 1970s: *Dirty Linen and New Found Land* (1976), *Every Good Boy Deserves Favour* (1977), *Night and Day* (1978), and *Cahoot's Macbeth* (1979). Stoppard's fascination with the relationship between theatrical illusion and moral and philosophical problems continues to animate his playwriting. His short play *Dogg's Hamlet* (1979) concerns a production of *Hamlet* in an invented language ("Dogg") and might be seen as an elaborate theatrical exploration of Ludwig Wittgenstein's philosophy of language. Stoppard's major plays of the 1980s and 1990s—*The Real Thing* (1982), *Hapgood* (1988), and *Arcadia* (1993)—continue Stoppard's moral investigation of the relationship between truth, knowledge, and appearance, explored through his inventive use of the medium of stage comedy.

TRAVESTIES

Travesties is one of Stoppard's most inventive plays, particularly in his lively imitation of the several authors—Wilde, Joyce, Tzara, and Lenin—who are the main characters of the play. As he remarks in his headnote to the play, the action centers on a production of *The Importance of Being Earnest* mounted during World War I by James Joyce in Zurich. Apparently the consular official who was cast to play Algernon Moncrieff in the play—Henry Carr—took offense at Joyce and eventually brought him to court, alleging that he should be reimbursed for the cost of his costume. Placing Henry Carr center stage, and having him remember his conflict with Joyce, Stoppard is able to orchestrate the play's principal fantasy: an elaborate encounter between three writers who may have been in Zurich at the same time—Lenin, Joyce, and Tzara.

Having decided to incorporate Wilde's *Earnest* into his play, Stoppard was clearly posed with a problem: how to compete with Wilde's brilliant verbal comedy. Yet Stoppard's verbal panache is everywhere evident in *Travesties*. By having old Henry Carr recall the events of 1918, Stoppard is able to have the action assume a rather surreal quality. In the long conversation between Carr and his servant Bennett that opens the play, for example, Bennett's recitation of the events of the war and the Russian Revolution are met with Wildean ripostes from Carr, who seems to slip into the character of Algernon Moncrieff ("I have always found that irony among the lower orders is the first sign of an awakening social consciousness"). When Joyce enters, Stoppard constructs the dialogue in an extended series of limericks; later in the play, Joyce's conversation with Tzara ("Give further examples of Dada") imitates the famous "catechism" of Joyce's "Ithaca" chapter in his novel *Ulysses*. Tzara's theory of random Dada poetry is satirized at several points in the play, and Lenin frequently speaks *in propria persona* in the play. Fittingly, much of the action is conveyed through *Travesties'* elaborate invocation of *The Importance of Being Earnest* itself. Not only does Stoppard import Cecily and Gwendolen directly into the play—where they become involved in an elaborate romantic plot with Carr and Tzara—but he concludes the play with an elaborate homage to Wilde, as Gwen and Cecily reprise Wilde's "discovery" scene.

HENRY WILFRED CARR, 1894–1962

The reader of a play whose principal characters include Lenin, James Joyce and Tristan Tzara may not realise that the figure of Henry Carr is likewise taken from history. But this is so.

In March 1918 (I take the following information from Richard Ellmann's *James Joyce*), Claud Sykes, an actor temporarily living in Zurich, suggested to Joyce that they form a theatrical company to put on plays in English. Joyce agreed, and became the business manager of The English Players, the first production to be that of *The Importance of Being Earnest*. Actors were sought. Professionals were to receive a token fee of 30 francs (24 shillings at the current rate of exchange) and amateurs to make do with 10 francs for tram fare to rehearsals. Joyce became very active and visited the Consul General, A. Percy Bennett, in order to procure official approval for the Players. He succeeded in this, despite the fact that Bennett "was annoyed with Joyce for not having reported to the Consulate officially to offer his services in wartime, and was perhaps aware of Joyce's work for the neutralist *International Review* and of his open indifference to the war's outcome. He may even have heard of Joyce's version of *Mr. Dooley*, written about this time . . ."—I quote from Ellmann's superb biography, whose companionship was not the least pleasure in the writing of *Travesties*.

Meanwhile, Sykes was piecing together a cast . . . "An important find was Tristan Rawson, a handsome man who had sung baritone roles for four years in the Cologne Opera House but had never acted in a play. After much coaxing Rawson agreed to take on the role of John Worthing. Sykes recruited Cecil Palmer as the butler, and found a woman named Ethel Turner to play Miss Prism . . . As yet, however, there was no one to take the leading role of Algernon Moncrieff. In an unlucky moment Joyce nominated a tall, goodlooking young man named Henry Carr, whom he had seen in the consulate. Carr, invalided from the service, had a small job there. Sykes learned that he had acted in some amateur plays in Canada, and decided to risk him."

Carr's performance turned out to be a small triumph. He had even, in his enthusiasm, bought some trousers, a hat and a pair of gloves to wear as Algernon. But immediately after the performance the actor and the business manager quarrelled. Joyce handed each member of the cast 10 or 30 francs, as pre-arranged, but succeeded in piquing Carr, who later complained to Sykes that Joyce had handed over the money like a tip.

The upshot was disproportionate and drawn out. Joyce and Carr ended up going to law, in two separate actions, Carr claiming reimbursement for the cost of the trousers, etc., or alternatively a share of the profits, and Joyce counter-claiming for the price of five tickets sold by Carr, and also suing for slander. These matters were not settled until February 1919. Joyce won on the money and lost on the slander, but he reserved his full retribution for *Ulysses,* where "he allotted punishments as scrupulously and inexorably as Dante . . . Originally Joyce intended to make Consul General Bennett and Henry Carr the two drunken, blasphemous and obscene soldiers who knock Stephen Dedalus down in the 'Circe' episode; but he eventually decided that Bennett should be the sergeant-major, with authority over Private Carr, who, however, refers to him with utter disrespect."

From these meagre facts about Henry Carr—and being able to discover no others—I conjured up an elderly gentleman still living in Zurich, married to a girl he met in the Library during the Lenin years, and recollecting, perhaps not with entire accuracy, his encounters with Joyce and the Dadaist Tzara.

Soon after the play opened in London I was excited and somewhat alarmed to receive a letter beginning, "I was totally fascinated by the reviews of your play—the chief reason being that Henry Carr was my husband until he died in 1962." The letter was from Mrs. Noël Carr, his second wife.

From her I learned that Henry Wilfred Carr was born in Sunderland in 1894 and brought up in County Durham. He was one of four sons, including his twin Walter, now also dead. At 17 Henry went to Canada where he worked for a time in a bank. In 1915 he volunteered for military service and went to France with the Canadian Black Watch. He was badly wounded the following year and—after lying five days in no-man's-land—was taken prisoner. Because of his wounds Henry was sent by the Germans to stay at a monastery where the monks tended him to a partial recovery, and then as an "exchange prisoner" he was one of a group who were sent to Switzerland.

Thus Henry Carr arrived in Zurich where he was to cross the path of James Joyce and find himself a leading actor in both onstage and offstage dramas, leading to immortality of a kind as a minor character in *Ulysses.*

It was in Zurich, too, that he met his first wife, Nora Tulloch. They married in England after the war and later he took her back to Canada where he found a job in a department store in Montreal. He rose within the organisation to become company secretary.

In 1928, while in Montreal, he met Noël Bach and after his divorce they were married there in 1933. The following year they returned to England. Henry ultimately joined a foundry company and when the next war came he and his wife were living in Sheffield. They were bombed out, and moved to a Warwickshire village, where Henry commanded the Home Guard, and they stayed in Warwickshire in the post-war years.

In 1962, while he was on a visit to London, Henry had a heart attack, and he died in St. Mary Abbots Hospital, Kensington. He had no children.

I am indebted to Mrs. Noël Carr for these biographical details, and, particularly, for her benevolence towards me and towards what must seem to her a peculiarly well-named play.

T.S.

ACKNOWLEDGEMENTS

Nearly everything spoken by Lenin and Nadezhda Krupskaya herein comes from his Collected Writings and from her *Memories of Lenin.* I have also profited variously—and gratefully—from the following books: *Lenin* by Michael C. Morgan; *Lenin* by Robert Payne; *Lenin and the Bolsheviks* by Adam B. Ulam; *To The Finland Station* by Edmund Wilson; *Days With Lenin* by Maxim Gorki; *The First World War, an Illustrated History* by A. J. P. Taylor; *James Joyce* by Richard Ellmann; *Joyce* by John Gross; *Dada, Art and Anti-Art* by Hans Richter; and *The Dada Painters and Poets,* edited by Robert Motherwell. I am also indebted to Mr. James Klugmann for material relating to Lenin in Switzerland. The responsibility for the use to which this and all other material is put is my own.

TRAVESTIES

TOM STOPPARD

— CHARACTERS —

HENRY CARR, *appears as a very old man and also as his youthful self. He dresses in a most elegant way and is especially interested in the cut of his trousers; he has the figure for it.*

TRISTAN TZARA, *is the Dadaist of that name. He was a short, dark-haired, very boyish-looking young man, and charming (his word). He wears a monocle.*

JAMES JOYCE, *is James Joyce in 1917/18, aged 36. He wears a jacket and trousers from two different suits.*

LENIN, *is Lenin in 1917: aged 47.*

BENNETT, *is Carr's manservant. Quite a weighty presence.*

GWENDOLEN, *is Carr's younger sister; young and attractive but also a personality to be reckoned with.*

CECILY, *is also young and attractive and even more to be reckoned with. Also appears as her old self.*

NADYA, *is Nadezhda Krupskaya, Lenin's wife: aged 48.*

The play is set in Zurich, in two locations: the drawing room of Henry Carr's apartment ("THE ROOM"), and a section of the Zurich Public Library ("THE LIBRARY"). *Most of the action takes place within Carr's memory, which goes back to the period of the First World War, and this period is reflected appropriately in the design and the costumes, etc. It is to be supposed that Old Carr has lived in the same apartment since that time.*

The ROOM *must have the main door Centre Upstage: most of the entrances would be weakened seriously if they occurred from the side. Double doors would be best. However, there is also at least one side door. There is a centre table with a good chair on each side, and a side table, apart from other furniture.*

The LIBRARY *suggests a larger scale—tall bookcases, etc. In Act Two Cecily (the librarian) requires a counter or desk, which need not necessarily be in view at the beginning of the play. Some of the entrances, e.g. Nadya's, should be through a door rather than from the wings.*

The LIBRARY *in the Prologue and the Second Act does not necessarily have to be presented from the same angle.*

— ACT ONE —

We begin in the LIBRARY.

There are places for JOYCE, LENIN *and* TZARA.

GWEN *sits with* JOYCE. *They are occupied with books, papers, pencils . . .*

LENIN *is also writing quietly, among books and papers.* TZARA *is writing as the play begins. On his table are a hat and a large pair of scissors.* TZARA *finishes writing, then takes up the scissors and cuts the paper, word by word, into his hat. When all the words are in the hat he shakes the hat and empties it on the table. He rapidly separates the bits of paper into random lines, turning a few over, etc., and then reads the result in a loud voice.*

TZARA: Eel ate enormous appletzara
    key dairy chef's hat he'll learn oomparah!
    Ill raced alas whispers kill later nut east,
    noon avuncular ill day Clara!

5   CECILY: *(Entering.)* Sssssssh!

(Her admonition is to the Library in general. She enters from one wing, not through the door, and crosses the stage, leaving by the opposite wing, moving quite quickly, like someone who is busy. No one takes any notice.)

JOYCE: *(Dictating to* GWEN.) Deshill holles eamus . . .
GWEN: *(Writing.)* Deshill holles eamus . . .
JOYCE: Thrice.
GWEN: Uh-hum.
10   JOYCE: Send us bright one, light one, Horhorn, quickening and wombfruit.
GWEN: Send us bright one, light one, Horhorn, quickening and wombfruit.
JOYCE: Thrice.
15   GWEN: Uh-hum.

JOYCE: Hoopsa, boyaboy, hoopsa!
GWEN: Hoopsa, boyaboy, hoopsa!
JOYCE: Hoopsa, boyaboy, hoopsa!
GWEN: Likewise thrice?
JOYCE: Uh-hum.

  20

(By this time TZARA *has replaced the bits of paper into the hat. He takes out a handful, and reads the words one at a time, placing them into the hat as he reads each one.)*

TZARA: Clara avuncular!
    Whispers ill oomparah!
    Eel nut dairy day
    Appletzara . . .
    . . . Hat!
CECILY: *(Re-entering.)* Sssssssh!

  25

*(*CECILY *has come in with a few books which she places by* LENIN.)

TZARA *leaves the Library through the door.*

It is now necessary that the audience should observe the following: GWEN *has received from* JOYCE *a folder.* CECILY *receives an identical folder from* LENIN. *These folders, assumed to contain manuscripts, are eye-catching objects in some striking colour. Each girl has cause to place her folder down on a table or chair, and each girl then picks up the wrong folder. In the original production,* GWEN *dropped a glove, etc., etc., but it is not important how this transference is achieved, only that it is seen to occur.*

GWEN *is now ready to leave the Library, and does so, taking Lenin's folder with her.*

CECILY *also leaves, not through the door but into the wings.*

NADYA *enters as* GWEN *leaves; They bump into each other, and each apologises,* GWEN *in English,* NADYA *in Russian.*

NADYA *enters in an agitated state. She looks round for her husband and goes straight to him. Their conversation is in Russian.)*

NADYA: Vylodya!
LENIN: Shto takoya?
NADYA: Bronski prishol. On s'kazal shto v'Peterburge revolut-
30 sia!
LENIN: Revolutsia!

(At this point JOYCE *stands up and begins to walk up and down searching his pockets for tiny scraps of paper on which he has previously written down things he may wish to use. While the* LENINS *continue their conversation,* JOYCE *fishes out, one by one, these scraps of paper and reads out what he finds on them.)*

JOYCE: *(Regarding his first find.)* "Morose delectation . . . Aquinas tunbelly . . . Frate porcospino . . ."

(He decides he doesn't need this one. He screws it up and throws it away, and finds a second.)

"Und alle Schiffe brucken . . ."

(He decides to keep this one, so re-pockets it. He takes out another.)

35 "Entweder transubstantiality, oder consubstantiality, but in no way substantiality . . ."

(He decides to keep this one as well. Meanwhile, the LENINS *have been continuing in the following manner.)*

LENIN: Otkuda on znayet?
NADYA: Napisano v'Gazetakh. On govorit shto Tzar sobi-
raet'sia otretchsya ot prestola!
40 LENIN: Shtoty!
NADYA: Da!
LENIN: Eto v'gazetakh?
NADYA: Da—da. Idiom damoi. On zhdyot.
LENIN: On tam?
45 NADYA: Da!
LENIN: Gazetakh u nievo?
NADYA: Da!
LENIN: Ty sama vidyela?
NADYA: Da, da, da!

*(*JOYCE's *voice, however, has dominated this passage. He now encounters a further scrap of paper which is lying on the floor:* LENIN *has inadvertently dropped it.* JOYCE *picks this paper up.* NADYA *is leaving the Library, through the door,* LENIN *saying in Russian . . .)*

50 LENIN: Idyi nazad y skazhee y'moo shto ya prichazhoo. Tolka pasbyrayu svai b'magi.

*(*LENIN *is gathering his papers.* JOYCE *is examining the dropped paper.)*

JOYCE: "G.E.C. 250 million marks, 28,000 workers . . . profit 254,000,000 marks . . ."

*(*LENIN *recognizes these words. He pauses, and approaches* JOYCE.)*

LENIN: Pardon! . . . Entschuldigung! . . . Scusi! . . . Excuse
me! 55
JOYCE: *(Handing him the paper.)* Je vous en prie! Bitte! Prego! It's perfectly all right!

*(*LENIN *leaves.* JOYCE *is alone now.)*

(Declaims.) A librarianness of Zurisssh
only emerged from her niche
when a lack of response 60
to *Nicht Reden! Silence!*
obliged her to utter the plea——
CECILY: *(Entering as before.)*—sssssh!

*(*JOYCE *accedes to her request, puts on his hat, picks up his stick, and while she regards him with disapproval he leaves at a strolling pace, singing . . .)*

JOYCE: If you ever go across the sea to Ireland . . .
It may be at the closing of the day . . . 65
you can sit and watch the moon rise over Claddagh
and watch the sun go down on Galway Bay . . .

(The stage now belongs to OLD CARR. *The* LIBRARY *must now be replaced by the* ROOM. *Needless to say, the change should occur with as little disruption as possible, and the use of music as a bridge is probably desirable.)*

*(*NOTE: *In the original production, the Room contained a piano which was at different times used by Old Carr, and in this instance Old Carr played (very badly) the tune of Galway Bay while the set was changed; the piano being right downstage in a permanent position. It is possible that* CARR *has been immobile on stage from the beginning, an old man remembering . . .)*

CARR: He was Irish, of course. Though not actually from Limerick—he was a Dublin man, Joyce, everybody knows that,
couldn't have written the book without. There was a young 70
man from Dublin, tum-ti-ti-tum-ti-ti troublin' . . . I used to
have quite a knack for it, but there's little encouragement for
that sort of thing in the Consular Service. Not a great patron
of poetry, the Service, didn't push it, never made a feature of
it. I mean you'd never say that a facility for rhyme and metre 75
was the sine qua non of advancement in the Consular Service . . . Didn't *discourage* it, I'm not saying that, on the contrary, a most enlightened and cultivated body of men, fully
sympathetic to all the arts (look no further than the occasion
that brought us together, me and Joyce, brought him to this 80
room, full support, a theatrical event of the first water, great
success, personal triumph in the demanding role of Ernest,
not Ernest, the other one, in at the top, have we got the cucumber sandwiches for Lady Bracknell, notwithstanding the
unfortunate consequences. Irish lout. Not one to bear a 85
grudge, however, not after all these years, and him dead in
the cemetery up the hill, no hard feelings either side, unpleasant as it is to be dragged through the courts for a few
francs (though it wasn't the money, or the trousers for that

---

28 **Shto takoya?** What is it? 29–30 **Bronski . . . revolutsia!** Bronski came to the house. He says there's a revolution in St. Petersburg! 37 **Otkuda on znayet?** How does he know? 38–39 **Napisano . . . prestola!** It's all in the papers. He says the Tsar is going to abdicate! 40 **Shtoty!** No! 41 **Da!** Yes! 42 **Eto v'gazetakh?** Is that in the news- paper? 43 **Da . . . zhdyot** Yes—yes. Come on home. He's waiting. 44 **On tam?** Is he there? 46 **Gazetakh u nievo?** He brought the paper? 48 **Ty . . . vidyela?** You saw it yourself? 50–51 **Idyi . . . b'magi** Go home ahead of me. I will collect my papers and follow.

---

52 **G.E.C.** U.S.A.

matter), *but*, be that as it may, all in all, truth be told, the encouragement of poetry writing, was not the primary concern
of the British Consulate in Zurich in 1917, and now I've lost
my knack for it. Too late to go back for it. Alas and a lack for
it. But I digress. No apologies required, constant digression
being the saving grace of senile reminiscence.

My memoirs, is it, then? Life and times, friend of the famous. Memories of James Joyce. James Joyce As I Knew
Him. The James Joyce I Knew. Through the Courts With
James Joyce . . . What was he like, James Joyce, I am often
asked. It is true that I knew him well at the height of his powers, his genius in full flood in the making of *Ulysses,* before
publication and fame turned him into a public monument
for pilgrim cameras more often than not in a velvet smoking
jacket of an unknown colour, photography being in those
days a black and white affair, but probably real blue if not
empirical purple and sniffing a bunch of sultry violets that
positively defy development, don't go on, do it on my head,
caviar for the general public, now then—*Memories of James
Joyce* . . . It's coming.

To those of us who knew him, Joyce's genius was never in
doubt. To be in his presence was to be aware of an amazing
intellect bent on shaping itself into the permanent form of
its own monument—the book the world now knows as
Ulysses! Though at that time we were still calling it (I hope
memory serves) by its original title, Elasticated Bloomers.

A prudish, prudent man, Joyce, in no way profligate or
vulgar, and yet convivial, without being spend-thrift, and yet
still without primness towards hard currency in all its trans-
mutable and transferable forms and denominations, of
which, however, he demanded only a sufficiency from the
world at large, exhibiting a monkish unconcern for worldly
and bodily comforts, without at the same time shutting himself off from the richness of human society, whose temptations, on the other hand, he met with an ascetic disregard
tempered only by sudden and catastrophic aberrations—in
short, a complex personality, an enigma, a contradictory
spokesman for the truth, an obsessive litigant and yet an essentially private man who wished his total indifference to
public notice to be universally recognised—in short a liar
and a hypocrite, a tight-fisted, sponging, fornicating drunk
not worth the paper, that's that bit done.

Further recollections of a Consular Official in Whitest
Switzerland. The Ups and Downs of Consular life in Zurich
During the Great War: A Sketch.

'Twas in the bustling metropolis of swiftly gliding trams
and greystone banking houses, of cosmopolitan restaurants
on the great stone banks of the swiftly-gliding snot-green
(mucus mutandis) Limmat River, of jewelled escapements
and refugees of all kinds, e.g. Lenin, there's a point . . .
Lenin As I Knew Him. The Lenin I Knew. Halfway to the
Finland Station with V. I. Lenin: A Sketch, I well remember
the first time I met Lenin, or as he was known on his library
ticket, Vladimir Ilyich Ulyanov. To be in his presence was to
be aware of a complex personality, enigmatic, magnetic, but
not, I think, astigmatic, his piercing brown (if memory
serves) eyes giving no hint of it. An essentially simple man,
and yet an intellectual theoretician, bent, as I was already
aware, on the seemingly impossible task of reshaping the
civilised world into a federation of standing committees of
workers' deputies. As I shook the hand of this dynamic,

gnomic and yet not, I think, anaemic stranger, who with his
fine head of blond hair falling over his forehead had the
clean-shaven look of a Scandinavian seafaring—hello, hello,
got the wrong chap, has he?—take no notice, all come out in
the wash, that's the art of it. Fact of the matter, *who* (without
benefit of historical perspective and the photograph album,
Red Square packed to the corner stickers with comrader-
aderie, and now for our main speaker, balding bearded in
the three-piece suit, good God if it isn't Ulyanov!, knew him
well, always sat between the window and Economics A-K
etceterarera) well, take away all *that*, and who was he to
Radek or Radek to him, or Martov or Martinov, Plekhanov,
or he to Ulyanov for that matter?—in Zurich in 1917? Café
conspirators, so what? Snowballs in hell. Snowballs at all,
Lenin he only had one chance in a million, remember the
time they had the meeting?—Social Democrats for Civil
War in Europe. Total attendance: four. Ulyanov, Mrs.
Ulyanov, Zinoviev and a police spy. And now they want to
know what was he like? What was he like, Lenin, I am often
asked.

(He makes an effort.)

To those of us who knew him Lenin's greatness was never
in doubt.

(He gives up again.)

So why didn't you put a pound on him, you'd be a millionaire, like that chap who bet sixpence against the Titanic. No.
Truth of the matter, who'd have thought big oaks from a corner room at number 14 Spiegelgasse?—now here's a thing:
two revolutions formed *in the same street*. Face to face in
Spiegelgasse! *Street of Revolution! A sketch.* Meet by the
sadly-sliding chagrinned Limmat River, strike west and immediately we find ourselves soaking wet, strike east and
immediately we find ourselves in the Old Town, having left
behind the banking bouncing metropolis of trampolines and
chronometry of all kinds for here time has stopped in the riddled maze of alleyways and by the way you'd never believe a
Swiss redlight district, pornographic fretwork shops, vice
dens, get a grip on yourself, sorry, sorry, second right, third
left—Spiegelgasse!—narrow, cobbled, high old houses in a
solid rank, number 14 the house of the narrow cobbler himself, Kammerer his name, Lenin his tenant—and across the
way at Number One, the Meierei Bar, crucible of anti-art,
cradle of Dada!!! Who? What? Whatsisay Dada?? You remember Dada!—historical halfway house between Futurism and Surrealism, twixt Marinetti and André Breton,
'tween the before-the-war-to-end-all-wars years and the
between-the-wars years—*Dada!*—down with reason, logic,
causality, coherence, tradition, proportion, sense and consequence, my art belongs to Dada 'cos Dada 'e treats me so—
well then, *Memories of Dada by a Consular Friend of the
Famous in Old Zurich: A Sketch.*

What did it do in the Great War, Dada, I am often asked.
How did it begin? where did it? when? what was it, who
named it and why Dada? These are just some of the questions that continue to baffle Dadaists the world over. To
those of us who lived through it Dada was, topographically
speaking, the high point of Western European culture—I
well remember as though it were yesteryear (oh where are
they now?) how Hugo Ball—or was it Hans Arp? yes!—no—

Picabia, was it?—no, Tzara—yes!—wrote his name in the
snow with a walking stick and said: There! I think I'll call it
210 The Alps. Oh the yes-no's of yesteryear. Whose only age
done gone. Over the hills and far away the sixpounders
pounding in howitzerland, no louder than the soft thud of
snow falling off the roof—*oh heaven!* to be picked out—
plucked out—blessed by the blood of a negligible wound
215 and released into the folds of snow-covered hills—Oh,
Switzerland!—unfurled like a white flag, pacific civilian
Switzerland—the miraculous neutrality of it, the non-
combatant impartiality of it, the non-aggression pacts of it,
the international red cross of it—entente to the left, detente
220 to the right, into the valley of the invalided blundered and
wandered myself when young——
     Carr of the Consulate!—first name Henry, that much is
beyond dispute, I'm mentioned in the books.
     For the rest I'd be willing to enter into discussion but not
225 if you don't mind correspondence, into matters of detail and
chronology—I stand open to correction on all points, except
for my height which can't be far off, and the success of my
performance, which I remember clearly, in the demanding
role of Ernest (not Ernest, the other one)——
230   *that,* and the sense of sheer relief at arriving in a state of
rest, namely Switzerland, the still centre of the wheel of war.
That's really the thing——

(CARR *is now a young man in his drawing room in 1917. Ideally
the actor should simply take off e.g. a hat and dressing gown—
no wig or beard, no make-up—Carr's age has been in his voice.*)

—the first thing to grasp about Switzerland is that there is no
war here. Even when there is war *everywhere else,* there is
235 no war in Switzerland.
BENNETT: Yes, sir.

(BENNETT *has entered with a tray of tea things, set for two, with
sandwiches.*)

CARR: It is this complete absence of bellicosity, coupled with
     an ostentatious punctuality of public clocks, that gives the
     place its reassuring air of permanence. Switzerland, one in-
240   stinctively feels, will not go away. Nor will it turn into some-
     where else. You have no doubt heard allusions to the benefi-
     cial quality of the Swiss air, Bennett. The quality referred to
     is permanence.
BENNETT: Yes, sir.
245 CARR: Desperate men who have heard the clocks strike thir-
     teen in Alsace, in Trieste, in Serbia and Montenegro, who
     have felt the ground shift beneath them in Estonia, Austro-
     Hungary and the Ottoman Empire, arrive in Switzerland
     and after a few deep breaths find that the ringing and
250   buzzing in their ears has regulated itself into a soothing tick-
     tock, and that the ground beneath their feet, while invariably
     sloping, is as steady as an alp. Tonight I incline to the the-
     atre; get me out the straight cut trouser with the blue satin
     stripe and the silk cutaway. I'll wear the opal studs.
255 BENNETT: Yes, sir. I have put the newspapers and telegrams on
     the sideboard, sir.
CARR: Is there anything of interest?
BENNETT: The *Neue Zuricher Zeitung* and the *Zuricher Post*
     announce, respectively, an important Allied and German
260   victory, each side gaining ground after inflicting heavy casu-
     alties on the other with little loss to itself.

CARR: Ah—yes . . . the war! Poor devils! How I wish I could get
     back to the trenches!—to my comrades in arms—the won-
     derful spirit out there in the mud and wire—the brave days
     and fearful nights. Bliss it was to see the dawn! To be alive 265
     was very heaven! Never in the whole history of human con-
     flict was there anything to match the carnage—God's
     blood!, the shot and shell!—graveyard stench!—Christ
     Jesu!—deserted by simpletons, they damn us to hell—ora
     pro nobis—quick! no, *get me out!*—I think to match the car- 270
     nation, oxblood shot-silk cravat, starched, creased just so, as-
     serted by a simple pin, the damask lapels—or a brown, no,
     biscuit—no—get me out the straight cut trouser with the
     blue satin stripe and the silk cutaway. I'll wear the opal studs.
BENNETT: Yes, sir. I have put the newspapers and telegrams on 275
     the sideboard, sir.
CARR: Is there anything of interest?
BENNETT: The war continues to dominate the newspapers, sir.
CARR: Ah yes . . . the war, always the war . . .

(*A note on the above: the scene [and most of the play] is under
the erratic control of Old Carr's memory, which is not notably reliable, and also of his various prejudices and delusions. One result is that the story [like a toy train perhaps] occasionally jumps
the rails and has to be restarted at the point where it goes wild.*

*This scene has several of these "time slips", indicated by the rep-
etitions of the exchange between* BENNETT *and* CARR *about the
"newspapers and telegrams". Later in the play there are similar
cycles as Carr's memory drops a scene and then picks it up again
with a repeated line [e.g.* CARR *and* CECILY *in the Library]. It
may be desirable to mark these moments more heavily by using
an extraneous sound or a light effect, or both. The sound of a
cuckoo-clock, artificially amplified, would be appropriate since
it alludes to time and to Switzerland; in which case a naturalistic cuckoo-clock could be seen to strike during the here-and-now
scene of Old Carr's first monologue. At any rate the effect of
these time-slips is not meant to be bewildering, and it should be
made clear what is happening.*)

I was in Savile Row when I heard the news, talking to the 280
head cutter at Drewitt and Madge in a hounds-tooth check
slightly flared behind the knee, quite unusual. Old Drewitt,
or Madge, came in and told me. Never trusted the Hun, I remarked. Boche, he replied, and I, at that time unfamiliar
with the appellation, turned on my heel and walked into 285
Trimmett and Punch where I ordered a complete suit of
Harris knicker-bockers with hacking vents. By the time they
were ready, I was in France. Great days! Dawn breaking over
no-man's-land. Dewdrops glistening on the poppies in the
early morning sun—All quiet on the Western Front . . . 290
Tickety boo, tickety boo, tickety boo . . .
BENNETT: A gentleman called, sir. He did not wait.
CARR: What did he want?
BENNETT: He did not vouchsafe his business, sir. He left his
     card. 295

(*Offers it on a salver.*)

CARR: "Tristan Tzara. Dada Dada Dada." Did he have a stutter?
BENNETT: He spoke French with a Rumanian accent, and
     wore a monocle.
CARR: He is obviously trying to pass himself off as a spy. It is a
     form of vanity widely indulged in in Zurich during a Euro- 300
     pean war, I believe, and adds greatly to the inconveniences

caused by the crowds of *real* spies who conspire to fill the Odeon and the Terasse, and make it almost impossible to get a table at either.

305 BENNETT: I have noticed him with a group of friends at the Terrasse, sir. Whether they were conspirators I could not, of course, tell.

CARR: To masquerade as a conspirator, or at any rate to speak French with a Rumanian accent and wear a monocle, is at
310 least as wicked as to be one; in fact, rather more wicked, since it gives a dishonest impression of perfidy, and, moreover, makes the over-crowding in the cafés gratuitous, being the result neither of genuine intrigue nor bona fide treachery—was it not, after all, La Rochefoucauld in his *Maximes*
315 who had it that in Zurich in Spring in wartime a gentleman is hard put to find a vacant seat for the spurious spies peeping at police spies spying on spies eyeing counter-spies *what a bloody country even the cheese has got holes in it!!*

(Off the rails again. CARR *has, on the above words, done violence to the inside of a cheese sandwich.)*

BENNETT: Yes, sir. I have put the newspapers and telegrams on
320 the sideboard, sir.
CARR: Is there anything of interest?
BENNETT: There is a revolution in Russia, sir.
CARR: Really? What sort of revolution?
BENNETT: A social revolution, sir.
325 CARR: A *social* revolution? Unaccompanied women smoking at the Opera, that sort of thing? . . .
BENNETT: Not precisely that, sir. It is more in the nature of a revolution of classes contraposed by the fissiparous disequilibrium of Russian society.
330 CARR: What do you mean, classes?
BENNETT: Masters and servants. As it were. Sir.
CARR: Oh, Masters and servants. *Classes.*
BENNETT: *(Expressionless as always.)* There have been scenes of violence.
335 CARR: I see. Well, I'm not in the least bit surprised, Bennett. I don't wish to appear wise after the event, but anyone with half an acquaintance with Russian society could see that the day was not far off before the exploited class, disillusioned by the neglect of its interests, alarmed by the falling value of the
340 rouble, and above all goaded beyond endurance by the insolent rapacity of its servants, should turn upon those butlers, footmen, cooks, valets . . . (parenthetically, Bennett, I see from your book that on Thursday night when Mr. Tzara was dining with me, eight bottles of champagne are entered as
345 having been consumed. I have had previous occasion to speak to you of the virtues of moderation, Bennett: this time I will only say, remember Russia).
BENNETT: Yes, sir. I have put the newspapers and telegrams on the sideboard, sir.
350 CARR: Is there anything of interest?
BENNETT: The Tsar has now abdicated, sir. There is a Provisional Government headed by Prince Lvov, with Guchkov as Minister of War, Milyukov Foreign Minister and the Socialist Kerensky as Minister of Justice. The inclusion of
355 Kerensky is calculated to recommend the Government to a broad base of the common people, but effective authority has already been challenged by a committee of workers' deputies, or "Soviet", which has for the moment united all shades of socialist opinion. However there is no immediate

prospect of the Socialists seizing power, for the revolution is 360 regarded by them as the fulfilment of Karl Marx's prophecy of a *bourgeois capitalist era* in Russia's progress towards socialism. According to Marxist dogma, there is no way for a country to leap from autocracy to socialism: while the *ultimate* triumph of socialism is inevitable, being the necessary 365 end of the process of dialectical materialism, it must, by the same token, be preceded by a bourgeois-capitalist stage of development. When the time is ripe, and not before, there will be a further revolution, led by the organised industrial workers, or "Proletariat", who will assume a temporary dicta- 370 torship to ensure the safe transition of the State into a true Communist Utopia. Thus, it is the duty of Russian Marxists to welcome the present bourgeois revolution, even though it might take several generations to get through, if the examples of Western Europe and the United States are anything 375 to go by. As things stand, therefore, if one can be certain of anything it is that Russia is set fair to become a parliamentary democracy on the British model.
CARR: Newspapers or coded telegram?
BENNETT: A consensus of the most recent London dailies and 380 political and humorous weeklies, and general rumour put about Zurich by the crowds of spies, counter-spies, radicals, artists and riff-raff of all kinds. Mr. Tzara called, sir. He did not wait.
CARR: I'm not sure that I approve of your taking up this modish 385 novelty of "free association", Bennett. I realise that it is all the rage in Zurich—even in the most respectable salons to try to follow a conversation nowadays is like reading every other line of a sonnet—but if the servant classes are going to ape the fashions of society, the end can only be ruin and 390 decay.
BENNETT: I'm sorry, sir. It is only that Mr. Tzara being an artist——
CARR: I will not have you passing moral judgements on my friends. If Mr. Tzara is an artist that is his misfortune. 395
BENNETT: Yes, sir. I have put the newspapers and telegrams on the sideboard, sir.
CARR: Is there anything of interest?
BENNETT: In St. Petersburg, the Provisional Government has now declared its intention to carry on the war, and has 400 gained the sympathy of the British and the French. However, the committee of workers' deputies, or Soviet, consider the war to be nothing more than an imperialist adventure carried on at the expense of workers of both sides. To cooperate in this adventure is to be stigmatised in a novel 405 phrase which seems to translate as a "lickspittle capitalist manservant", unnecessarily offensive in my view.
CARR: *(Languidly.)* I'm not sure that I'm much interested in your views, Bennett.
BENNETT: *(Apologetically.)* They're *not* particularly interest- 410 ing, sir. However, the Soviet has ordered soldiers and sailors to ignore the orders of the Provisional Government; this has won it the corresponding sympathy of the Germans. However, unity of the Left is not now complete. There is a more extreme position put forward by the Bolshevik party. The 415 Bolshevik line is that some unspecified but unique property of the Russian situation, unforeseen by Marx, has caused the bourgeois-capitalist era of Russian history to be compressed into the last few days, and that the time for the proletarian revolution is now ripe. Furthermore, the Bolsheviks say the 420

soldiers should shoot all the officers and turn the war into a European civil war. However, the Bolsheviks are a small minority in the Soviet, and their leader, Vladimir Ulyanov, also known as Lenin, has been in exile since the abortive 1905
425 revolution, and is in fact living in Zurich.

CARR: Naturally.

BENNETT: Yes, sir—if I may quote La Rochefoucauld, "Quel pays sanguinaire, même le fromage est plein des trous."
430 Lenin is desperately trying to return to Russia but naturally the Allies will not allow him free passage. Since Lenin is almost alone in proclaiming the Bolshevik orthodoxy, which is indeed his creation, his views at present count for nothing in St. Petersburg, where ostensible Bolsheviks like Kamenev and Stalin are taking a moderate line. A betting man would
435 lay odds of about a million to one against Lenin's view prevailing. However, it is suggested that you take all steps to ascertain his plans.

CARR: A consensus of the humorous and intellectual weeklies?

BENNETT: Telegram from the Minister. (*He starts to leave.*)
440 CARR: A million to one.

BENNETT: I'd put a pound on him, sir.

CARR: You know him?

BENNETT: I do, sir. And if any doubt remained, the London papers carry the assurance that the man to watch is Kerensky.

(*Exit* BENNETT.)

445 CARR: (*Aside.*) Bennett seems to be showing alarming signs of irony. I have always found that irony among the lower orders is the first sign of an awakening social consciousness. It remains to be seen whether it will grow into an armed seizure of the means of production, distribution and exchange, or
450 spend itself in liberal journalism.

BENNETT: (*Entering.*) Mr. Tzara. (TZARA *enters.* BENNETT *retires.*)

CARR: How are you, my dear Tristan. What brings you here?

(*This Tzara [there is to be another] is a Rumanian nonsense. His entrance might be set to appropriate music.*)

TZARA: (*Ebulliently.*) Plaizure, plaizure! What else? Eating ez
455 usual, I see 'Enri?!—'allo—'allo, vhat is all the teapots etcetera? Somebody comink? It is Gwendolen I hopp!—I luff'er, 'Enri—I have come by tram expressly to propose a marriage—ah—ha!——

BENNETT: (*Entering.*) Miss Gwendolen and Mr. Joyce.

(GWENDOLEN *and* JAMES JOYCE *enter.* BENNETT *remains by the door.* GWENDOLEN *and* TZARA *are momentarily transfixed by each other. This is hardly noticed as* JOYCE *has made it his own entrance.*)

460 JOYCE: Top o' the morning!—James Joyce!
I hope you'll allow me to voice
my regrets in advance
for coming on the off-chance—
b'jasus I hadn't much choice!

(*This* JOYCE *is obviously an Irish nonsense. The whole scene is going to take a limerick form, so for clarity's sake the lay-out of the text is modified.*)

465 CARR: I . . . sorry . . . would you say that again?

JOYCE: Begob—I'd better explain
I'm told that you are a——

TZARA: Miss Carr!

GWEN: Mr. Tzara!

JOYCE: (*Seeing* TZARA *for the first time.*) B'jasus'. Joyce is the
470 name.

GWEN: I'm sorry!—how terribly rude!
Henry—Mr. Joyce!

CARR: How d'you do?

JOYCE: Delighted!
475
TZARA: Good day!

JOYCE: I just wanted to say
how sorry I am to intrude.

CARR: Tell me . . . are you some kind of a poet?

JOYCE: You know my work?
480
CARR: No—it's
something about your deliv'ry—
can't quite——

JOYCE: Irish.

CARR: From Lim'rick?
485
JOYCE: No—Dublin, don't tell me you know it!

GWEN: He's a poor writer——

JOYCE: Aha!
A fine writer who writes caviar
for the general, hence poor——
490
TZARA: Wants to touch you for sure.

JOYCE: I'm addressing my friend, Mr . . .

CARR: (*Gulp.*) Carr.

GWEN: Mr. Tzara writes poetry and sculpts,
with quite unexpected results.
495
I'm told he recites
and on Saturday nights
does all kinds of things for adults.

JOYCE: I really don't think Mr. Carr
is interested much in da-dah——
500
TZARA: We say it like Dah-da.

JOYCE: (*To* CARR.) The fact is I'm rather
hard up.

CARR: Yes I'm told that you are.
If it's money you want, I'm afraid . . .
505
GWEN: Oh, Henry!—he's mounting a play,
and Mr. Joyce thought
your official support . . .

CARR: Ah . . . !

JOYCE: And a couple of pounds till I'm paid.
510
CARR: I don't see why not. For my part,
H.M.G. is considered pro-Art.

TZARA: Consider me anti.

GWEN: Consider your auntie?

JOYCE: A pound would do for a start.
515
CARR: The Boche put on culture a-plenty
for Swiss, what's the word?

JOYCE: Cognoscenti.

CARR: It's worth fifty tanks

JOYCE: Or twenty-five francs
520
CARR: Now . . . British culture . . .

JOYCE: I'll take twenty.

TZARA: (*Scornful.*) Culture and reason!

JOYCE: Fifteen.

TZARA: They give us the mincing machine!
525
GWEN: That's awf'ly profound.

JOYCE: Could you lend me a pound?

TZARA: All literature is obscene!
The classics—tradition—vomit on it!

GWEN: (Oh!)
530
TZARA: Beethoven! Mozart! I spit on it!

GWEN: (Oh!)

TZARA: Everything's chance!

GWEN: Consider your aunts.

535 TZARA: Causality—logic—I sssssh——

GWEN: —awf'ly profound

JOYCE: (To BENNETT.) Could you lend me a pound?

GWEN: I thought he was going to say "Shit on it".

(Her hand flies, too late, to her mouth. CARR has been thinking hard.)

CARR: By jove, I've got it! Iolanthe!

540 TZARA: Obscene!

CARR: Is it?

TZARA: Avanti!
      Gut'n tag! Adios!

GWEN: Au revoir!

545 TZARA: Vamanos!

BENNETT: Give my regards to your auntie.

(BENNETT closes the door behind TZARA and GWEN.

The whole thing has been manic from beginning to end, and now it's finished, except that JOYCE is a leftover.)

JOYCE: A Rumanian rhymer I met
      used a system he based on roulette.
      His reliance on chance
550   was a def'nite advance
      And yet . . . and yet . . . and yet . . .

(The light steps down between verses.)

      An impromptu poet of Hibernia
      rhymed himself into a hernia
      He became quite adept
555   at the practice except
      for occasional anti-climaxes.

      When I want to leave things in the air
      I say, "Excuse me, I've got to repair
      to my book about Bloom—"
560   and just leave the room.

(He has gone. Pause. Low light on motionless CARR in his chair.)

CARR: Well, let us resume. *Zurich By One Who Was There.*

(Normal light.)

BENNETT: (Entering.) Mr. Tzara. (TZARA enters. BENNETT retires.)

CARR: How are you, my dear Tristan? What brings you here?

565 TZARA: Oh, pleasure, pleasure! What else should bring anyone anywhere?

(TZARA, no less than CARR, is straight out of The Importance of Being Earnest.)

CARR: I don't know that I approve of these Benthamite ideas, Tristan. I realise they are all the rage in Zurich—even in the most respectable salon, to remark that one was brought there
570   by a sense of duty, leads to terrible scenes but if society is going to ape the fashions of philosophy, the end can only be ruin and decay.

TZARA: Eating and drinking, as usual, I see, Henry? I have often observed that Stoical principles are more easily borne
575   by those of Epicurean habits.

CARR: (Stiffly.) I believe it is done to drink a glass of hock and seltzer before luncheon, and it is well done to drink it well

before luncheon. I took to drinking hock and seltzer for my nerves at a time when nerves were fashionable in good society. This season it is trenchfoot, but I drink it regardless be- 580 cause I feel much better after it.

TZARA: You might have felt much better anyway.

CARR: No, no—post hock, propter hock.

TZARA: But, my dear Henry, causality, is no longer fashionable owing to the war. 585

CARR: How illogical, since the war itself had causes. I forget what they were, but it was all in the papers at the time. Something about brave little Belgium, wasn't it?

TZARA: Was it? I thought it was Serbia . . .

CARR: Brave little Serbia . . . ? No, I don't think so. The news- 590 papers would never have risked calling the British public to arms without a proper regard for succinct alliteration.

TZARA: Oh, what nonsense you talk!

CARR: It may be nonsense, but at least it is clever nonsense.

TZARA: I am sick of cleverness. The clever people try to im- 595 pose a design on the world and when it goes calamitously wrong they call it fate. In point of fact, everything is Chance, including design.

CARR: That sounds awfully clever. What does it mean? Not that it has to mean anything, of course. 600

TZARA: It means, my dear Henry, that the causes we know everything about depend on causes we know very little about, which depend on causes we know absolutely nothing about. And it is the duty of the artist to jeer and howl and belch at the delusion that infinite generations of real effects 605 can be inferred from the gross expression of apparent cause.

CARR: It is the duty of the artist to beautify existence.

TZARA: (Articulately.) Dada dada dada dada dada dada dada dada dada dada dada dada dada dada dada dada dada dada dada dada dada dada dada dada dada dada dada dada dada 610 dada dada dada dada dada dada.

CARR: (Slight pause.) Oh, what nonsense you talk!

TZARA: It may be nonsense, but at least it's not clever non- sense. Cleverness has been exploded, along with so much else, by the war. 615

CARR: You forget that I was there, in the mud and blood of a foreign field, unmatched by anything in the whole history of human carnage. Ruined several pairs of trousers. Nobody who has not been in the trenches can have the faintest con- ception of the horror of it. I had hardly set foot in France be- 620 fore I sank in up to the knees in a pair of twill jodphurs with pigskin straps handstitched by Ramidge and Hawkes. And so it went on—the sixteen ounce serge, the heavy worsteds, the silk flannel mixture—until I was invalided out with a bullet through the calf of an irreplaceable lambswool dyed khaki in 625 the yarn to my own specification. I tell you, there is nothing in Switzerland to compare with it.

TZARA: Oh, come now, Henry, your trousers always look——

CARR: I mean with trench warfare.

TZARA: Well, I daresay, Henry, but you could have spent the 630 time in Switzerland as an artist.

CARR: (Coldly.) My dear Tristan, to be an artist at all is like liv- ing in Switzerland during a world war. To be an artist in Zurich, in 1917, implies a degree of self-absorption that would have glazed over the eyes of Narcissus. When I sent 635 round to Hamish and Rudge for their military pattern book, I was responding to feelings of patriotism, duty, to my love of freedom, my hatred of tyranny and my sense of oneness with the underdog—I mean in general, I never particularly cared

640 for the Belgians as such. And besides I couldn't be an artist *anywhere*—I can do none of the things by which is meant Art.

TZARA: Doing the things by which is meant Art is no longer considered the proper concern of the artist. In fact it is frowned upon. Nowadays, an artist is someone who makes art mean the things he does. A man may be an artist by exhibiting his hindquarters. He may be a poet by drawing words out of a hat. In fact some of my best poems have been drawn out of my hat which I afterwards exhibited to general acclaim at the Dada Gallery in Bahnhofstrasse.

CARR: But that is simply to change the meaning of the word Art.

TZARA: I see I have made myself clear.

CARR: Then you are not actually *an artist* at all?

655 TZARA: On the contrary. I have just told you I am.

CARR: But that does not make you an artist. An artist is someone who is gifted in some way that enables him to do something more or less well which can only be done badly or not at all by someone who is not thus gifted. If there is any point in using language at all it is that a word is taken to stand for a particular fact or idea and not for other facts or ideas. I might claim to be able to fly . . . Lo, I say, I am flying. But you are not propelling yourself about while suspended in the air, someone may point out. Oh no, I reply, that is no longer considered the proper concern of people who can fly. In fact, it is frowned upon. Nowadays, a flyer never leaves the ground and wouldn't know how. I see, says my somewhat baffled interlocutor, so when you say you can *fly* you are using the word in a purely private sense. I see I have made myself clear, I say. Then, says this chap in some relief, you cannot actually *fly* after all? On the contrary, I say, I have just told you I can. Don't you see my dear Tristan you are simply asking me to accept that the word Art means whatever you wish it to mean; but I do not accept it.

675 TZARA: Why not? You do exactly the same thing with words like *patriotism, duty, love, freedom,* king and country, brave little Belgium, saucy little Serbia——

CARR: (*Coldly.*) You are insulting my comrades-in-arms, many of whom died on the field of honour——

680 TZARA: —and honour—all the traditional sophistries for waging wars of expansion and self-interest, presented to the people in the guise of rational argument set to patriotic hymns . . . Music is corrupted, language conscripted. Words are taken to stand for opposite facts, opposite ideas. That is why anti-art is the art of our time.

(*The argument becomes progressively more heated.*)

CARR: The nerve of it. Wars are fought to make the world safe for artists. It is never quite put in those terms but it is a useful way of grasping what civilised ideals are all about. The easiest way of knowing whether good has triumphed over evil is to examine the freedom of the artist. The *ingratitude* of artists, indeed their hostility, not to mention the loss of nerve and failure of talent which accounts for "modern art", merely demonstrate the freedom of the artist to be ungrateful, hostile, self-centred and talentless, for which freedom I went to war, and a more selfless ideal for a man of my taste it would be difficult to imagine.

TZARA: Wars are fought for oil wells and coaling stations; for control of the Dardanelles or the Suez Canal; for colonial pickings to buy cheap in and conquered markets to sell dear in. War is capitalism with the gloves off and many who go to 700 war know it but they go to war because they don't want to be a hero. It takes courage to sit down and be counted. But how much better to live bravely in Switzerland than to die cravenly in France, quite apart from what it does to one's trousers. 705

CARR: My God, you little Rumanian wog—you bloody dago— you jumped-up phrase-making smart-alecy arty-intellectual Balkan turd!!! Think you know it all!—while we poor dupes think we're fighting for ideals, you've got a profound understanding of what is *really* going on, underneath!—you've got 710 a phrase for it! You pedant! Do you think your phrases are the true sum of each man's living of each day?—*capitalism with the gloves off*?—do you think that's the true experience of a wire-cutting party caught in a crossfire in no-man's-land?—Why not infantile sexuality in khaki trews? Or the 715 collective unconscious in a tin hat? (*Viciously.*) It's all the rage in Zurich!—You slug! I'll tell you what's *really* going on: I went to war because it was my *duty*, because my country needed me, and that's *patriotism*. I went to war because I believed that those boring little Belgians and incompetent 720 Frogs had the right to be defended from German militarism, and that's *love of freedom*. *That's* how things are underneath, and I won't be told by some yellow-bellied Bolshevik that I ended up in the trenches because there's a profit in ball-bearings! 725

TZARA: (*Storming.*) Quite right! You ended up in the trenches, because on the 28th of June 1900 the heir to the throne of Austro-Hungary married beneath him and found that the wife he loved was never allowed to sit next to him on royal occasions, except! when he was acting in his military capac- 730 ity as Inspector General of the Austro-Hungarian army—in which capacity he therefore decided to inspect the army in Bosnia, so that *at least on their wedding anniversary,* the 28th of June 1914, they might ride side by side in an open carriage through the streets of Sarajevo! (*Sentimentally.*) 735 Aaaaah! (*Then slaps his hands sharply together like a gunshot.*) Or, to put it another way——

CARR: (*Quietly.*) We're here because we're here . . . because we're here because we're here . . . we're here because we're here because we're here because we're here . . . 740

(CARR *has dropped into the familiar chant, quite quiet.*

TZARA *joins in, just using the sound "da-da" to the same tune. The light starts to go. The chant grows. When* CARR *starts to speak,* TZARA *continues the chanting quietly for a few more moments under* CARR's *words.*)

Great days! The dawn breaking over no-man's-land—Dew-drops glistening on the poppies in the early morning sun! The trenches stirring to life! . . . "Good morning, corporal! All quiet on the Western Front?" . . . "Tickety-boo, sir!"— "Carry on!"—Wonderful spirit in the trenches—never in 745 the whole history of human conflict was there anything to match the courage, the comradeship, the warmth, the cold, the mud, the stench—fear—folly—Christ Jesu!, but for this blessed leg!—I never thought to be picked out, plucked out, blessed by the blood of a blighty wound—oh *heaven!*—re- 750 leased into folds of snow-white feather beds, pacific civilian heaven!, the mystical swisticality of it, the entente cordiality of it!, the Jesus Christ I'm out of it!—into the valley of the invalided—Carr of the Consulate!

(Lights to normal.)

755   And what brings *you* here, my dear Tristan?

TZARA: Oh, pleasure, pleasure . . . What else should bring anyone anywhere? Eating as usual, I see, Henry?

CARR: I believe it is customary in good society to take a cucumber sandwich at five o'clock. Where have you been
760   since last Thursday?

TZARA: In the Public Library.

CARR: What on earth were you doing there?

TZARA: That's just what I kept asking myself.

CARR: And what was the reply?

765   TZARA: "Ssssh!" Cecily does not approve of garrulity in the Reference Section.

CARR: Who is Cecily? And is she as pretty and well-bred as she sounds? Cecily is a name well thought of at fashionable christenings.

770   TZARA: Cecily is a librarianness. I say, do you know someone called Joyce?

CARR: *Joyce* is a name which could only expose a child to comment around the font.

TZARA: No, no, Mr. Joyce, Irish writer, mainly of limericks,
775   christened James Augustine, though registered, due to a clerical error, as James Augusta, a little known fact.

CARR: Certainly I did not know it. But then I have never taken an interest in Irish affairs. In fashionable society it would be considered a sign of incipient vulgarity with radi-
780   cal undertones.

TZARA: The war caught Joyce and his wife in Trieste in Austro-Hungary. They got into Switzerland and settled in Zurich. He lives in Universitätsstrasse, and is often seen round about, in the library, in the cafés, wearing, for example, a
785   black pinstripe jacket with grey herringbone trousers, or brown Donegal jacket with black pinstripe trousers, or grey herringbone jacket with brown Donegal trousers, all being the mismatched halves of sundry sundered Sunday suits: sorts language into hands of contract bridge; looks down on
790   Dada, though his own poems reek of old hat, being second-hand fin-de-siècle slop. His limericks are said to be more interesting, though hardly likely to start a revolution—I say, do you know someone called Ulyanov?

CARR: I'm finding this conversation extremely hard to follow.
795   It's like hearing every other line of the Catechism. And you still have not told me what you were doing in the public library. I had no idea that poets nowadays were interested in literature. Or is it that your interest is in Cecily?

TZARA: Good heavens, no. Cecily is rather pretty, and well-
800   bred, as you surmised, but her views on poetry are very old-fashioned and her knowledge of the poets, as indeed of everything else, is eccentric, being based on alphabetical precedence. She is working her way along the shelves. She has read Allingham, Arnold, Belloc, Blake, both Brownings,
805   Byron, and so on up to, I believe, G.

CARR: Who is Allingham?

TZARA: "Up the airy mountain, down the rushy glen, we daren't go a-hunting for fear of little men . . ." Cecily would regard any poem that came out of a hat with the gravest
810   suspicion.

CARR: It is a librarian's duty to distinguish between poetry and a sort of belle-litter.

TZARA: Hello—why the extra cup?—why cucumber sandwiches? Who's coming to tea?

CARR: It is merely set for Gwendolen—she usually returns at   815
about this hour.

TZARA: How perfectly delightful, and to be honest not unexpected. I am in love with Gwendolen and have come expressly to propose to her.

CARR: Well, that is a surprise.   820

TZARA: Surely not, Henry; I have made my feelings for Gwendolen quite plain.

CARR: Of course you have, my dear fellow. The way you pass her the cucumber sandwiches puts me in mind of nothing so much as a curate assisting at his first Holy Communion.   825
But my surprise stems from the fact that you must surely have met Gwendolen at the Public Library, for she has left here every morning this week saying that that is where she is going, and Gwendolen is a scrupulously truthful girl. In fact, as her elder brother I have had to speak to her about it.   830
Unrelieved truthfulness can give a young girl a reputation for insincerity. I have known plain girls with nothing to hide captivate the London season purely by discriminate mendacity.

TZARA: Oh, I assure you Gwendolen has been in the Public   835
Library. But I have had to admire her from afar, all the way from Economics to Foreign Literature.

CARR: I had no idea Gwendolen knew any foreign languages, and I am not sure that I approve. It's the sort of thing that can only broaden a girl's mind.   840

TZARA: Well, in this library Foreign Literature includes English.

CARR: What a novel arrangement. Is any reason given?

TZARA: *(Impatiently.)* The point is, Henry, I can't get to speak to her alone.   845

CARR: Ah, yes—her chaperone.

TZARA: Chaperone?

CARR: Yes—you don't imagine I'd let my sister go unchaperoned in a city largely frequented by foreigners. Gwendolen has made a friend in Zurich. I have not met her but Gwen-   850
dolen assures me that they are continuously in each other's company, and from a description which I have elicited by discreet questioning she cannot but be a wholesome and restraining influence, being practically middle-aged, plainly dressed, bespectacled and answering to the name of Joyce,   855
oh good heavens. Is he after her money?

TZARA: Only in derisory instalments. He claims to be writing a novel, and has made a disciple out of Gwendolen. She transcribes for him, looks things up in works of reference, and so on. The poor girl is so innocent she does not stop to wonder   860
what possible book could be derived from reference to Homer's *Odyssey* and the Dublin Street Directory for 1904.

CARR: Homer's *Odyssey* and the Dublin Street Directory?

TZARA: For 1904.

CARR: I admit it's an unusual combination of sources, but not   865
wholly without possibilities. Anyway, there's no need to behave as though you were married to her already. You are not married to her already, and I don't think you ever will be.

TZARA: Why on earth do you say that?

CARR: In the first place, girls never marry Rumanians, and in   870
the second place I don't give my consent.

TZARA: Your consent!

CARR: My dear fellow, Gwendolen is my sister and before I allow you to marry her you will have to clear up the whole question of Jack.

TZARA: Jack! What on earth do you mean? What do you mean, Henry, by Jack? I don't know anyone of the name of Jack.

CARR: *(Taking a library ticket from his pocket.)* You left this here the last time you dined.

TZARA: Do you mean to say you have had my library ticket all this time? I had to pay a small fine in replacing it.

CARR: That was extravagant of you, since the ticket does not belong to you. It is made out in the name of Mr. Jack Tzara, and your name isn't Jack, it's Tristan.

TZARA: No, it isn't, it's Jack.

CARR: You have always told me it was Tristan. I have introduced you to everyone as Tristan. You answer to the name of Tristan. Your notoriety at the Meierei Bar is firmly associated with the name Tristan. It is perfectly absurd saying your name isn't Tristan.

TZARA: Well, my name is Tristan in the Meierei Bar and Jack in the library, and the ticket was issued in the library.

CARR: To write—or at any rate to draw words out of a hat—under one name, and appear at the Public Library under another is an understandable precaution—but I cannot believe that that is the whole explanation.

TZARA: My dear Henry, the explanation is perfectly simple. One day last year, not long after the triumph at the Meierei Bar of our noise concert for siren, rattle and fire-extinguisher, I met Ulyanov, also known as Lenin, at the Café Zum Adler with a group of Zimmerwaldists.

CARR: That sounds like the last word in revolutionary politics. What does it mean?

TZARA: It describes those Socialists who at the Zimmerwald Conference in 1915 called on the workers of the world to oppose the war. Well, at the Zum Adler Lenin was raging away against the chauvinist moderates who didn't necessarily want to bayonet every man over the rank of NCO, when someone at the bar piano started to play a Beethoven sonata. Lenin went completely to pieces and when he recovered he dried his eyes and lashed into the Dadaists, if you please. Well, as a Dadaist myself I am the natural enemy of bourgeois art and the natural ally of the political left, but the odd thing about revolution is that the further left you go politically the more bourgeois they like their art. Fortunately at the Zum Adler my name meant nothing to Lenin, but a few days later I met him at the library and he introduced me to Cecily. "Tzara!" said she. "Not the Dadaist, I hope!" "My younger brother, Tristan," I replied. "Most unfortunate. Terrible blow to the family." When I filled up my application form, for some reason the first name I thought of was Jack. It has really turned out rather well.

CARR: *(With great interest.)* Cecily knows *Lenin,* does she?

TZARA: Oh, yes, he's made quite a disciple out of Cecily. She's helping him with his book on Imperialism.

CARR: *(Thoughtfully.)* Did you say the reference section?

TZARA: They agree on everything, including art. It *is* odd, isn't it? I mean it is *the* contradiction of the radical movement.

CARR: There is nothing contradictory about it . . . Revolution in art is in no way connected with *class* revolution. Artists are members of a privileged class. Art is absurdly overrated by artists, which is understandable, but what is strange is that it is absurdly overrated by everyone else.

TZARA: Because man cannot live by bread alone.

CARR: Yes, he can. It's *art* he can't live on. "Bread—Peace—Freedom"—that's the slogan of revolution, I believe. What possible connection could there be between *that* and the shrill self-enclosed squabbles of rival ego-maniacs—formless painters, senseless poets, hatless sculptors——

TZARA: *(Coldly.)* You are insulting me and my comrades in the Dada Exhibition——

CARR: —and exhibitionists in general. When I was at school, on certain afternoons we all had to do what was called Labour—weeding, sweeping, sawing logs for the boiler-room, that kind of thing; but if you had a chit from Matron you were let off to spend the afternoon messing about in the Art Room. Labour or Art. And you've got a chit for *life? (Passionately.)* Where did you get it? What is an artist? For every thousand people there's nine hundred doing the work, ninety doing well, nine doing good, and one lucky bastard who's the artist.

TZARA: *(Hard.)* Yes, by Christ!—and when you see the drawings he made on the walls of the cave, and the fingernail patterns he one day pressed into the clay of the cooking pot, *then* you say, *My God, I am of these people!* It's not the hunters and the warriors that put you on the first rung of the ladder to consecutive thought and a rather unusual flair in your poncey trousers.

CARR: Oh yes it was. The hunter decorated the pot, the warrior scrawled the antelope on the wall, the artist came home with the kill. All of a piece. The idea of the artist as a special kind of human being is art's greatest achievement, and it's a fake!

TZARA: My God, you bloody English philistine—you ignorant smart-arse bogus bourgeois Anglo-Saxon prick! When the strongest began to fight for the tribe, and the fastest to hunt, it was the artist who became the priest-guardian of the magic that conjured the intelligence out of the appetites. Without him, man would be a coffee-mill. Eat—grind—shit. Hunt—*eat*—fight—*grind*—saw the logs—*shit.* The difference between being a man and being a coffee-mill is art. But that difference has become smaller and smaller and smaller. Art created patrons and was corrupted. It began to celebrate the ambitions and acquisitions of the paymaster. The artist has negated himself: paint—*eat*—sculpt—grind—write—shit.

(A light change.)

Without art man was a coffee-mill: but *with* art, man—is a coffee-mill! That is the message of Dada.—dada dada dada dada dada dada dada dada dada dada dada dada dada . . .

*(*TZARA *is shouting, raving.* CARR *immobile.*

Normal light as BENNETT *opens the door. Everything back to "normal".)*

BENNETT: Miss Gwendolen and Mr. Joyce.

*(*GWENDOLEN *and* JOYCE *appear as before.* BENNETT *retires.)*

JOYCE: Good morning, my name is James Joyce——

CARR: James Augusta?

JOYCE: *(Taken aback.)* Was that a shot in the dark?

CARR: Not at all—I am a student of footnotes to expatriate Irish literature.

JOYCE: You know my work?

CARR: No—only your name.

TZARA: Miss Carr . . .

GWEN: Mr. Tzara . . .

990 CARR: . . . but something about you suggests Limerick.

JOYCE: Dublin, don't tell me you know it?

CARR: Only from the guidebook, and I gather you are in the process of revising that.

JOYCE: Yes.

995 GWEN: Oh! I'm sorry—how terribly rude! Henry—Mr. Joyce—

CARR: How'dyou do?

JOYCE: Delighted.

TZARA: Good day.

JOYCE: I just wanted to say——

1000 GWEN: Do you know Mr. Tzara, the poet?

JOYCE: By sight, and reputation; but I am a martyr to glaucoma and inflation. Recently as I was walking down the Bahnhofstrasse my eye was caught by a gallery showcase and I was made almost insensible with pain.

1005 GWEN: Mr. Joyce has written a poem about it. It is something you two have in common.

JOYCE: Hardly. Mr. Tzara's disability is monocular, and, by rumour, affected, whereas I have certificates for conjunctivitis, iritis and synechia, and am something of an international

1010 eyesore.

GWEN: I mean poetry. I was thinking of your poem "Bahnhofstrasse", beginning

"The eyes that mock me sign the way
Whereto I pass at eve of day,

1015 Grey way whose violet signals are
The trysting and the twining star."

TZARA: (*To* JOYCE.) For your masterpiece
I have great expectorations
(GWEN's *squeak,* "*Oh!*")

1020 For you I would eructate a monument.
(*Oh!*)
Art for art's sake—I defecate!

GWEN: Delectate . . .

TZARA: I'm a foreigner.

1025 JOYCE: So am I.

GWEN: But it is the most beautiful thing I've ever heard. I have a good ear, would you not agree, Mr. Tzara?

TZARA: It is the most perfect thing about you, Miss Carr.

GWEN: Oh, I hope not. That would leave no room for

1030 development.

JOYCE: But have you not read any of Mr. Tzara's poems?

GWEN: To my shame I have not—but perhaps the shame is yours, Mr. Tzara.

TZARA: I accept it—but the matter can be easily put right, and

1035 at once.

GWEN: (*Fluttering.*) Oh, Mr. Tzara! . . .

(TZARA *retires to the sideboard, or writing table if there is one, and begins to write fluently on a large piece of white paper.*)

CARR: (*To* JOYCE.) And what about you, Doris?

JOYCE: Joyce.

CARR: Joyce.

1040 JOYCE: It is not as a poet that I come to see you, sir, but as the business manager of the English Players, a theatrical troupe.

CARR: The business manager?

JOYCE: Yes.

CARR: Well, if it's money you want, I'm afraid . . .

1045 GWEN: Oh, Henry!—he's mounting a play, and he thought your official support——

JOYCE: Perhaps I'd better explain. It seems, sir, that my name is in bad odour among the British community in Zurich. Whether it is my occasional contribution to the neutralist press, or whether it is my version of *Mr. Dooley,* beginning: 1050
"Who is the man, when all the gallant nations run to war,
Goes home to have his dinner by the very first cable car,
And as he eats his canteloupe contorts himself with mirth
To read the blatant bulletins of the rules of the earth?"
—and continuing: 1055
"Who is the furious fellow who declines to go to church
Since pope and priest and parson left the poor man in the lurch
And taught their flocks the only way to save all human souls
Was piercing human bodies through with dum-dum bullet 1060
holes?"
—and proceeding to:
"Who is the tranquil gentleman who won't salute the State?
Or serve Nebuchadnezzar or proletariat
But thinks that every son of man has quite enough to do 1065
To paddle down the stream of life his personal canoe?"
—by way of:
"Who is the meek philosopher who doesn't care a damn
About the yellow peril or the problem of Siam
And disbelieves that British Tar is water from life's fount 1070
And will not gulp the Gospel of the German on the Mount"
—and ending:
"It's Mr. Dooley
Mr. Dooley
The wisest wight our country ever knew! 1075
'Poor Europe ambles
like sheep to shambles'
Sighs Mr. Dooley-ooley-ooley-ooo."
or some other cause altogether, the impression remains that
I regard both sides with equal indifference. 1080

CARR: And you don't?

JOYCE: Only as an artist. As an artist, naturally I attach no importance to the swings and roundabout of political history. But I come here not as an artist but as James A. Joyce. I am an Irishman. The proudest boast of an Irishman is—I paid 1085
back my way . . .

CARR: So it is money.

JOYCE: A couple of pounds would be welcome—certainly, but it is to repay a debt that I have come. Not long ago, after many years of self-reliance and hardship during which my 1090
work had been neglected and reviled even to the point of being burned by a bigoted Dublin printer, there being no other kind of printer available in Dublin, I received £100 from the Civil List at the discretion of the Prime Minister.

CARR: The Prime Minister——? 1095

JOYCE: Mr. Asquith.

CARR: I am perfectly well aware who the Prime Minister is—I am the representative for His Majesty's Government in Zurich.

JOYCE: The Prime Minister is Mr. Lloyd George, but at that 1100
time it was Mr. Asquith.

CARR: Oh yes.

JOYCE: I do not at this moment possess £100, nor was it the intention that I would repay the debt in kind. However I mentioned the English Players. By the fortune of war, Zurich has 1105
become the theatrical centre of Europe. Here culture is the continuation of war by other means—Italian opera against French painting—German music against Russian ballet—

1110   but nothing from England. Night after night, actors totter about the raked stages of this alpine renaissance, speaking in every tongue but one—the tongue of Shakespeare—of Sheridan—of Wilde . . . The English Players intend to mount a repertoire of masterpieces that will show the Swiss who leads the world in dramatic art.

1115   CARR: Gilbert and Sullivan—by God!

GWEN: And also Mr. Joyce's own play *Exiles* which so far, unfortunately——

JOYCE: That's quite by the way——

CARR: *Patience!*

1120   JOYCE: Exactly. First things first.

CARR: *Trial by Jury! Pirates of Penzance!*

JOYCE: We intend to begin with that quintessential English jewel, *The Importance of Being Earnest.*

CARR: *(Pause.)* I don't know it. But I've heard of it and I don't

1125   like it. It is a play written by an Irish—*(Glances at* GWEN-DOLEN.*)* Gomorrahist—Now look here, Janice, I may as well tell you, His Majesty's Government——

JOYCE: I have come to ask you to play the leading role.

CARR: What?

1130   JOYCE: We would be honoured and grateful.

CARR: What on earth makes you think that I am qualified to play the leading role in *The Importance of Being Earnest?*

GWEN: It was my suggestion, Henry. You were a wonderful Goneril at Eton.

1135   CARR: Yes, I know, but——

JOYCE: We are short of a good actor to play the lead—he's an articulate and witty English gentleman——

CARR: Ernest?

JOYCE: Not Ernest—the other one.

1140   CARR: *(Tempted.)* No—no—I absolutely——

JOYCE: Aristocratic—romantic—epigrammatic—he's a young swell.

CARR: A swell . . . ?

JOYCE: He says things like, I may occasionally be a little over-

1145   dressed but I make up for it by being immensely over-educated. That gives you the general idea of him.

CARR: How many changes of costume?

JOYCE: Two complete outfits.

CARR: Town or country?

1150   JOYCE: First one then the other.

CARR: Indoors or out?

JOYCE: Both.

CARR: Summer or winter?

JOYCE: Summer but not too hot.

1155   CARR: Not raining?

JOYCE: Not a cloud in the sky.

CARR: But he could be wearing—a boater?

JOYCE: It is expressly stipulated.

CARR: And he's not in—pyjamas?

1160   JOYCE: Expressly proscribed.

CARR: Or in mourning?

JOYCE: Not the other one—Ernest.

CARR: *(Claps his hands once.)* Describe the play briefly, omitting all but essential detail.

1165   JOYCE: The curtain rises. A flat in Mayfair. Teatime. You enter in a bottle-green velvet smoking jacket with black frogging—hose white, cravat perfect, boots elastic-sided, trousers of your own choice.

CARR: I shall have to make certain expenditures.

1170   JOYCE: Act Two. A rose garden. After lunch. Some by-play among the small parts. You enter in a debonair garden party outfit—beribboned boater, gaily striped blazer, parti-coloured shoes, trousers of your own choice.

CARR: *(Instantly.)* Cream flannel.

1175   JOYCE: Act Three. The morning room. A few moments later.

CARR: A change of costume?

JOYCE: Possibly by the alteration of a mere line or two of dialogue . . .

CARR: You have brought a copy of the play?

1180   JOYCE: I have it here.

CARR: Then let us retire to the next room and peruse it.

(CARR opens the door of "his" room for JOYCE.)

JOYCE: About those two pounds——

CARR: *(Generously, reaching for his wallet.)* My dear Phyllis . . . ! *(—and closes it after them.)*

(Pause. Freeze.)

1185   GWEN: *(Absently.)* Gomorrahist . . . Silly bugger.

(TZARA comes forward with rare diffidence, holding a hat like a brimming bowl. It transpires that he has written down a Shakespeare sonnet and cut it up into single words which he has placed in the hat.)

TZARA: Miss Carr . . .

GWEN: Mr. Tzara!—you're not leaving? *(The hat.)*

TZARA: Not before I offer you my poem.

(He offers the hat. GWEN *looks into it.)*

GWEN: Your technique is unusual.

1190   TZARA: All poetry is a reshuffling of a pack of picture cards, and all poets are cheats. I offer you a Shakespeare sonnet, but it is no longer his. It comes from the wellspring where my atoms are uniquely organised, and my signature is written in the hand of chance.

1195   GWEN: Which sonnet—was it?

TZARA: The eighteenth.

GWEN: *(Sadly.)* "Shall I compare thee to a summer's day . . ."

". . . Thou art more lovely and more temperate.

Rough winds do shake the darling buds of May

And summer's lease hath all too short a date.

1200   Sometimes too hot the eye of heaven shines,

And often is his gold complexion dimm'd;

And every fair from fair sometime declines,

By chance or nature's changing course untrimm'd;

But thy eternal summer shall not fade

1205   Nor lose possession of that fair thou owest;

Nor shall Death brag thou wander'st in his shade,

When in eternal lines to time thou growest:

So long as men can breathe or eyes can see,

So long lives this and this gives life to thee . . ."

1210   You tear him for his bad verses?

(She lets a handful of words fall from her fingers, back into the hat, and her sadness starts to give way to anger.)

These are but wild and whirling words, my lord.

TZARA: Ay, Madam.

GWEN: Truly I wish the gods had made thee poetical.

1215   TZARA: I do not know what poetical is. Is it honest in word and deed? Is it a true thing?

GWEN: Sure he that made us with such large discourse, look-ing before and after, gave us not *that* capability, *and* god-like reason to fust in us unused.

1220 TZARA: I was not born under a rhyming planet. Those fellows of infinite tongue that can rhyme themselves into ladies' favours, they do reason themselves out again. And that would set my teeth nothing on edge—*nothing* so much as mincing poetry.

1225 GWEN: (*Rising to his vicious edge.*) Thy honesty and love doth mince *this* matter—Put your bonnet for his right use, 'tis for the head! (*Sniffs away a tear.*) I had rather than forty shilling my book of songs and sonnets here.

(*She has turned away. He approaches with his hat offered.*)

1230 TZARA: (*Gently.*) But since he died, and poet better prove, his for his style you'll read, mine for my—love.

(GWEN *hesitates but then takes the first slip of paper out of the hat.*)

GWEN: "Darling".

(*She now continues, holding on to all the pieces of paper she takes out.*)

shake thou thy gold buds
the untrimm'd but short fair shade
shines—
1235 see, this lovely hot possession growest
so long
by nature's course—
so . . . long—heaven!

(*She gives a little shriek, using "heaven" and turns her back on the hat, taking a few steps away from TZARA, who takes out the next few words, lowering the temperature . . .*)

TZARA: and declines,
1240 summer changing, more temperate complexion . . .
GWEN: (*Still flustered.*) Pray don't talk to me about the weather, Mr. Tzara. Whenever people talk to me about the weather I always feel quite certain that they mean something else.

1245 TZARA: (*Coming to her.*) I do mean something else, Miss Carr. Every since I met you I have admired you.

(*He drops his few papers into the hat, she does likewise with hers, he puts the hat aside.*)

GWEN: For me you have always had an irresistible fascination. Even before I met you I was far from indifferent to you. As you know I have been helping Mr. Joyce with his new book,
1250 which I am convinced is a work of genius, and I am deter-mined to secure for him the universal recognition he de-serves. But alas, in fashionable society a girl receives few opportunities for intellectual connections. When Henry told me that he had a friend who edited a magazine of all that is
1255 newest and best in literature, I knew I was destined to love you.

(*She has the folder she acquired in the Prologue and gives it to* TZARA.)

TZARA: (*Amazed.*) Do you really love me, Gwendolen?
GWEN: Passionately!
TZARA: Darling, you don't know how happy you've made me.
1260 GWEN: My own Tristan!

(*They embrace.*)

TZARA: (*Breaking off.*) But you don't mean that you couldn't love me if I didn't share your regard for Mr. Joyce as an artist?
GWEN: But you do.
TZARA: Yes. I know I *do,* but supposing——   1265

(*She kisses him on the mouth.*

They embrace. JOYCE *re-enters.*)

JOYCE: Rise, sir, from that semi-recumbent posture!

(TZARA *and* GWEN *spring apart.* JOYCE *walks across to the main door, picking up his hat, opens the door, addresses* TZARA.)

Your monocle is in the wrong eye.

(TZARA *has indeed placed his monocle in the wrong eye. He re-places it.* JOYCE *has left on his line.*)

GWEN: I must tell Henry!
TZARA: Have you ever seen my magazine "Dada", darling?
GWEN: Never, da-da-darling!   1270

(GWEN *kisses him and runs into Henry's room.*

TZARA *starts reading the manuscript in the folder.*

The main door opens again and JOYCE *re-enters, pausing in the threshold. He is covered from head to breast in little bits of white paper, each bit bearing one of the words of Shakespeare's eigh-teenth sonnet, i.e.* TZARA *was using Joyce's hat. The effect must be immediate and self-evident, and it is probably necessary for the actor playing Joyce to change into a specially prepared jacket and even a duplicate wig; the bits of paper must be lightly stuck on to the hair and jacket, for the play's need of them is not finished.*)

JOYCE: What is the meaning of this?
TZARA: It has no meaning. It is without meaning as Nature is. It is Dada.
JOYCE: Give further examples of Dada.
TZARA: The Zoological Gardens after closing time. The logi-   1275
cal gardenia. The bankrupt gambler. The successful gam-bler. The Eggboard, a sport or pastime for the top ten thou-sand in which the players, covered from head to foot in eggyolk, leave the field of play.
JOYCE: Are you the inventor of this sport or pastime?   1280
TZARA: I am not.
JOYCE: What is the name of the inventor?
TZARA: Arp.
JOYCE: Is he your sworn enemy, pet aversion, bête noir, or oth-erwise persona non grata?   1285
TZARA: He is not.
JOYCE: Is he your friend, comrade-in-arms, trusted confidant or otherwise pal, mate or crony?
TZARA: He is.
JOYCE: By what familiarity, indicating possession and amica-   1290
bility in equal parts, do you habitually refer to him?
TZARA: My friend Arp.
JOYCE: Alternating with what colloquialism redolent of virtue and longevity?
TZARA: Good old Arp.   1295
JOYCE: Grasping any opportunity for paradox as might occur, in what way is the first name of your friend Arp singular?
TZARA: In that it is duplicate.

JOYCE: Namely?

1300 TZARA: Hans Arp. Jean Arp.

JOYCE: How can this contradiction of two distinct and equal first names be accounted for?

TZARA: Linguistically, each being a translation of the other, from German into French and conversely.

1305 JOYCE: Given a superficial knowledge of your friend's birth and parentage on the one hand, and of the political history of nineteenth-century Europe on the other, how would his bi-lingual nomination strike one?

TZARA: As understandable.

1310 JOYCE: Why?

TZARA: He is a native of Alsace, of French background, and a German citizen by virtue of the conquest of 1870.

JOYCE: What declaration of an international and belligerent nature brought this ambivalence into sharp conflict?

1315 TZARA: The declaration of war between Germany and France.

JOYCE: How did Hans or Jean Arp view the situation?

TZARA: As absurd.

JOYCE: How did he redress it?

TZARA: By making his way to Zurich and inventing the Egg
1320 board, a sport or pastime for the top ten thousand in which the players, covered from head to foot in eggyolk, leave the field of play.

JOYCE: From whom did he receive encouragement and friendship?

1325 TZARA: From Hugo Ball.

JOYCE: Describe Ball by epithet.

TZARA: Unspherical. Tall, thin, sacerdotal, German.

JOYCE: Describe him by enumeration of his occupations and preoccupations.

1330 TZARA: Novelist, journalist, philosopher, poet, artist, mystic, pacifist, founder of the Caberet Voltaire at the Meierei Bar, number one Spiegelgasse.

JOYCE: Did Ball keep a diary?

TZARA: He did.

1335 JOYCE: Was it published?

TZARA: It was.

JOYCE: Is it in the public domain by virtue of the expiration of copyright protection as defined in the Berne Convention of 1886?

1340 TZARA: It is not.

JOYCE: Quote judiciously so as to combine maximum information with minimum liability.

TZARA: "I went to Herr Ephraim, the owner of the Meierei, and said, 'Herr Ephraim, please let me have your room, I
1345 want to start a nightclub.' Herr Ephraim agreed and gave me the room. And I went to some people I knew and said, 'Please give me a picture. I should like to put on an exhibition in my nightclub.' I went to the friendly Zurich press and said, 'Put in some announcements. There is going to be an
1350 international cabaret. We shall do great things.' And they gave me pictures and they put in my announcements."

JOYCE: On what date did the first announcement appear in the Zurich press?

TZARA: On February 2nd, 1916.

1355 JOYCE: Quote discriminately from Ball's diary in such a manner as to avoid forfeiting the goodwill of his executors.

TZARA: "About six in the evening, when we were still hammering and putting up Futurist posters, there appeared an Oriental-looking deputation of four little men with portfolios

and pictures under their arms, bowing politely many times. 1360 They introduced themselves: Marcel Janco the painter, Tristan Tzara, Georges Janco, and a fourth whose name I did not catch. Arp was also there, and we came to an understanding without many words. Soon Janco's opulent Archangels hung alongside the other objects of beauty, and 1365 that same evening Tzara gave a reading of poems, conservative in style, which he rather endearingly fished out of the various pockets of his coat."

JOYCE: Is that the coat?

TZARA: It is. 1370

JOYCE: In what regard is a coat inferior, and in what superior, to a hat in so far as they are interchangeable in the production of poetry?

TZARA: *Inferior* to a hat in regard to the tendency of one or both sleeves to hang down in front of the eyes, with the re- 1375 sultant possibility of the wearer falling off the edge of the platform. *Superior* to a hat in regard to the number of its pockets.

JOYCE: In so far as what technique were your poems on that historic occasion conservative? 1380

TZARA: In so far as I produced each one entire and consecutive in its parts from one pocket, as opposed to producing it piecemeal and randomly from different pockets. Also in so far as I read only one poem at a time. Also in so far as I read it without accompaniment of whistles, rattles and percussion 1385 of packing cases.

JOYCE: Soon afterwards could this be said?

TZARA: It could not.

JOYCE: Corroborate discreetly from any contemporary diarist whose estate is not given to obsessive litigation over trivial in- 1390 fringements of copyright.

TZARA: "On February 26th Richard Huelsenbeck arrived from Berlin, and on March 30th we performed some stupendous Negro music. Herr Tristan Tzara was the initiator of a performance, the first in Zurich and in the world, of simultanist 1395 verse, including a poème simultané of his own composition."

JOYCE: Quote severally your recollections of what was declaimed synchronously.

TZARA: I began, "Boum boum boum il déshabille sa chair quand les grenouilles humides commencerent a brûler." 1400 Huelsenbeck began, "Ahoi ahoi des admirals gwirktes Beinkleid schnell zerfallt." Janco chanted, "I can hear the whip o' will around the hill and at five o'clock when tea is set I like to have my tea with some brunette, everybody's doing it, doing it." The title of the poem was "Admiral Seeks House To Let". 1405

JOYCE: Is it the case that within a remarkably short time performances of this kind made Dada in general and Tzara in particular names to conjure with wherever art was discussed?

TZARA: It is.

(All this time, JOYCE has been picking bits of paper from his hair and from his clothes, replacing each bit in his hat, which is on his knees. Casually, on the word "conjure", he conjures from the hat a white carnation, apparently made from the bits of paper (he turns the hat up to show it is empty). He tosses the carnation at TZARA.)

JOYCE: How would you describe this triumph? 1410

TZARA: *(Putting the carnation into his buttonhole.)* As just and proper. Well merited. An example of enterprise and charm receiving their due.

(JOYCE *starts to pull silk hankies from the hat.*)

1415 JOYCE: Realising that this local bourgeois-baiting pussy-cat, Dada, had grown into a tiger standing for scandal, provocation and moral outrage through art, what, reduced to their simplest reciprocal form, were Tzara's thoughts about Ball's thoughts about Tzara, and Tzara's thoughts about Ball's thoughts about Tzara's thoughts about Ball?

1420 TZARA: He thought that he thought that he would ride the tiger, whereas he knew that he knew that he knew that he would not.

JOYCE: And did they?

TZARA: They did and they didn't. Ball left Zurich, eventually
1425 became a Catholic and lived quietly among peasants until his death in 1927. Tzara remained to guide the Dada revolution into the next stage, Surrealism—but that was in Paris after the war.

JOYCE: What did Dada bring to pictorial art, sculpture, poetry
1430 and music that had not been brought to these activities previously in . . .

(*The appropriate flags start coming out of the hat.*)

. . . Barcelona, New York, Paris, Rome and St. Petersburg by, for example, Picabia, Duchamp, Satie, Marinetti, and Mayakovsky who shouts his fractured lines in a yellow blazer
1435 with blue roses painted on his cheeks?

TZARA: The word Dada.

JOYCE: Describe sensibly without self-contradiction, and especially without reference to people stuffing bread rolls up their noses, how the word Dada was discovered.

1440 TZARA: Tristan Tzara discovered the word Dada by accident in a Larousse Dictionary. It has been said, and he does not deny, that a paper-knife was inserted at random into the book. In French *dada* is a child's word for a hobbyhorse. In German it denotes a simple-minded preoccupation with ba-
1445 bies. Huelsenbeck recounts how *he* discovered the word one day in Hugo Ball's French-German dictionary in Hugo Ball's room while Tzara was not present. Hans or Jean Arp, however, has stated, "I hereby declare that Tristan Tzara found the word Dada on February the 8th 1916 at six o'clock
1450 in the afternoon. I was present with my twelve children when Tzara first uttered the word which filled us with justified enthusiasm. This occurred in the Café de la Terrasse in Zurich and I was wearing a brioche in my left nostril."

JOYCE: Were there further disagreements between Tzara and
1455 Huelsenbeck?

TZARA: There were.

JOYCE: As to?

TZARA: As to the meaning and purpose of Dada.

JOYCE: As indicated?

1460 TZARA: As indicated by manifestoes written by Tzara and those by Huelsenbeck.

JOYCE: Huelsenbeck demanding, for example?

TZARA: International revolutionary union of all creative men and women on the basis of radical Communism—expropria-
1465 tion of property—socialization . . .

JOYCE: As opposed to Tzara's demanding?

TZARA: The right to urinate in different colours.

JOYCE: Each person in different colours at different times, or different people in each colour all the time? Or everybody
1470 multi-coloured every time?

TZARA: It was more to make the point that making poetry should be as natural as making water—

JOYCE: (*Rising: the conjuring is over.*) God send you don't make them in the one hat.

(*This is too much for* TZARA.)

1475 TZARA: By God, you supercilious streak of Irish puke! You four-eyed, bog-ignorant, potato-eating ponce! Your art has failed. You've turned literature into a religion and it's as dead as all the rest, it's an overripe corpse and you're cutting fancy figures at the wake. It's too late for geniuses! Now we need
1480 vandals and desecrators, simple-minded demolition men to smash centuries of baroque subtlety, to bring down the temple, and thus finally, to reconcile the shame and the necessity of being an artist! Dada! *Dada! Dada!!*

(*He starts to smash whatever crockery is to hand; which done, he strikes a satisfied pose.* JOYCE *has not moved.*)

JOYCE: You are an over-excited little man, with a need for self-
1485 expression far beyond the scope of your natural gifts. This is not discreditable. Neither does it make you an artist. An artist is the magician put among men to gratify—capriciously—their urge for immortality. The temples are built and brought down around him, continuously and contigu-
1490 ously, from Troy to the fields of Flanders. If there is any meaning in any of it, it is in what survives as art, yes even in the celebration of tyrants, yes even in the celebration of nonentities. What now of the Trojan War if it had been passed over by the artist's touch? Dust. A forgotten expedi-
1495 tion prompted by Greek merchants looking for new markets. A minor redistribution of broken pots. But it is we who stand enriched, by a tale of heroes, of a golden apple, a wooden horse, a face that launched a thousand ships—and above all, of Ulysses, the wanderer, the most human, the most com-
1500 plete of all heroes—husband, father, son, lover, farmer, soldier, pacifist, politician, inventor and adventurer . . . It is a theme so overwhelming that I am almost afraid to treat it. And yet I with my Dublin Odyssey will double that immortality, yes by God *there's* a corpse that will dance for some
1505 time yet and *leave the world precisely as it finds it*—and if you hope to shame it into the grave with your fashionable magic, I would strongly advise you to try and acquire some genius and if possible some subtlety before the season is quite over. Top o' the morning, Mr. Tzara!

(*With which* JOYCE *produces a rabbit out of his hat, puts the hat on his head, and leaves, holding the rabbit.*

CARR's *voice is heard off.*)

1510 CARR: (*Voice off.*) "Really, if the lower orders don't set us a good example what on earth is the use of them? They seem as a class to have absolutely no sense of moral responsibility."

(TZARA *has moved to* CARR's *door. He opens it, and goes through.*)

(*Voice off.*) "How are you, my dear Ernest. What brings you up to town?"—"Pleasure, pleasure—eating as usual, I see,
1515 Algy . . ."

(CARR *enters, as Old Carr, holding a book.*)

Algy! The other one. Personal triumph in the demanding role of Algernon Montcrieff. The Theater zur Kaufleuten on

Pelikanstrasse, an evening in Spring, the English Players in that quintessential English jewel "The Imprudence of Being—" Now I've forgotten the first one. By Oscar Wilde. Henry Carr as Algy. Other parts played by Tristan Rawson, Cecil Palmer, Ethel Turner, Evelyn Cotton . . . forget the rest. Tickets five francs, four bob a nob and every seat filled, must have made a packet for the Irish lout and his cronies— still, not one to bear a grudge, not after all these years, and him dead in the cemetery up the hill, unpleasant as it is to be dragged through the courts for a few francs—after I'd paid for my trousers *and* filled every seat in the house—*not* very pleasant to be handed ten francs like a *tip!*—and then asking me for twenty-five francs for tickets—bloody nerve—Here, I got it out——

(From his pocket, a tattered document.)

—Bezirksgericht Zuerich, Zurich District Court, Justices Billeter (presiding) and Hammann and Kaufmann (participating) in the case of Dr. James Joyce—doctor my eye—plaintiff and counter-defendant versus Henry Carr, defendant and counter-plaintiff, with reference to the claim for settlement of the following issues: (a) Suit: Is defendant and counter-plaintiff (that's me) obliged to pay the plaintiff and counter-defendant (that's him) twenty-five francs? (b) Counter-suit: is plaintiff and counter-defendant bound to pay defendant and counter-plaintiff four hundred and seventy-five francs, or possibly three hundred francs? Have you got that? Joyce says I owe him twenty-five francs for tickets. I say Joyce owes me four hundred and seventy-five francs as my share of the profits, or alternatively three hundred francs for the trousers, etcetera, purchased by me for my performance as Henry—or rather—*god dammit!*—the other one . . .

Incidentally, you may or may not have noticed that I got my wires crossed a bit here and there, you know how it is when the old think-box gets stuck in a groove and before you know where you are you've jumped the points and suddenly you think, No, steady on, old chap, that was Algernon—*Algernon!*—There you are—all coming back now, I've got it straight, I'll be all right from here on. In fact, anybody hanging on just for the cheap comedy of senile confusion might as well go because now I'm on to how I met Lenin and could have changed the course of history etcetera, what's this?? *(The document.)* Oh yes.

Erkannt—has decided that. I. Der Beklagte, the defendant, Henry Carr, is obliged to pay den Klager, the plaintiff, James Joyce, twenty-five francs. The counter-claim of Henry Carr is denied. Herr Carr to indemnify Doktor Joyce sixty francs for trouble and expenses. In other words, a travesty of justice. Later the other case came up—Oh yes, he sued me for slander, claimed I called him a swindler and a cad . . . Thrown out of court, naturally. But it was the money with Joyce. Well, it was a long time ago. He left Zurich after the war, went to Paris, stayed twenty years and turned up here again in December 1940. Another war . . . But he was a sick man then, perforated ulcer, and in January he was dead . . . buried one cold snowy day in the Fluntern Cemetery up the hill.

I dreamed about him, dreamed I had him in the witness box, a masterly cross-examination, case practically won, admitted it all, the whole thing, the trousers, everything, and I

flung at him—"And what did you do in the Great War?" "I wrote *Ulysses*," he said. "What did you do?"

Bloody nerve.

(Blackout.)

— ACT TWO —

THE LIBRARY

The set however is not "lit" at the beginning of the Act. Apart from the bookcases, etc. the Library's furniture includes CECILY's *desk, which is perhaps more like a counter forming three sides of a square.*

Most of the light is on CECILY *who stands patiently at the front of the stage, waiting for the last members of the audience to come in and sit down.*

The performance of the whole of this lecture is not a requirement, but is an option. After "To resume" it could pick up at any point, e.g. "Lenin was convinced . . ." or "Karl Marx had taken it as an axiom . . ."; but no later than that.

CECILY'S LECTURE

To resume.

It was with considerable surprise that Marx learned of the Russian translation of *Das Kapital*. This appeared in St. Petersburg in 1872, before being translated into any other language. He didn't know what to make of it. The conditions for a socialist revolution as he saw it did not exist in Russia at all. Two thirds of the population were peasants, the industrial age had hardly begun, and the proletariat was correspondingly insignificant. According to Marxist theory Russia still had to pass through the whole bourgeois-capitalist cycle.

But there were also good reasons for Russians to read Marx. Some believed that Russia would find a short cut to the Communist society through a peasant revolution. Others were content to adopt Communist ideals for the Populist movement, which was the main revolutionary movement of the time. The Populists—the Narodniki—hoped, through education or incitement—to get the weight of those millions of peasants behind the wheel of reform. But the freedom of action and expression which had long been won in Western Europe simply did not exist in Russia, and by 1874 Populist activity had been crushed. As a result, some of the Narodniki formed a secret party named "Land and Freedom". But the party soon split over the question of violence. Plekhanov, the leading Russian Marxist, took his supporters out of the party. The remainder, now calling themselves "The People's Will", dedicated themselves to terrorism, with the assassination of the Tsar, Alexander II, as their main objective. This they achieved in March, 1881. The leaders of the People's Will were all caught, and hanged. Plekhanov left Russia and settled in Switzerland. Here in exile, he and his associates laid the foundations of the Russian Worker's Party which evolved into the Communist Party.

The leader of the assassins had said that history sometimes needed a push. Marx held that terrorism was unscientific and useless. Events after 1881 supported Marx. Alexander II had freed the serfs and allowed modest reforms, but with his death repression came down more tightly than ever. The reforms had evidently been a mistake. Alexander III set out to re-Russianise Russia. Six years later there was a last flicker from the party of the People's Will. A group of students were arrested while plotting to kill the Tsar.

Among them was the eldest son of an uncontroversial family living in Simbirsk—Alexander Ulyanov, the 20 year old brother of Vladimir. The family knew nothing of his activities, and were shocked by his arrest. Vladimir was nearly seventeen. The father, a district inspector of schools, had died the previous year. When news of the arrest reached Simbirsk, the mother set out on the thousand mile journey to St. Petersburg to plead for Alexander's life. One day in May when she had visited him in prison the night before, she learned from a newspaper bought in the street that Alexander had been hanged.

Vladimir was preparing at this time for his final examinations at high school. He came out top. The family moved to Kazan where Vladimir entered the university, and it was in Kazan, studying in the back kitchen in the Ulyanov apartment just outside this ancient Eastern city, that Vladimir first read Marx. His fidelity to Marx was established then and it never wavered. Marx had shown the only way forward. To quote Marx was enough to settle an argument. To question Marx was to betray the revolution.

Vladimir's role as the public conscience of Marxist orthodoxy began when he was in Siberian exile in the late 1890s—his arrest in 1895 had followed his first trip abroad to establish relations with Plekhanov and other Russian Marxists exiled in Geneva. During his own exile in Siberia, Vladimir began signing his articles with the *nom de guerre* "Lenin".

By this time he had been joined by a comrade, Nadezhda Krupskaya, whom he married in exile.

Lenin was convinced, like Marx, that history worked dialectically, that it advanced through the clash of opposing forces and not through the pragmatic negotiation of stiles and stepping-stones. He was a hard-liner. The class war was war, and to direct it effectively the Party had to be a compact group of professional revolutionaries who gave the orders. Out of one exile and into another, self-imposed outside Russia, Lenin encountered opposition in the party. Many of his colleagues wanted a more diffuse party, reaching down to the factory floor. Lenin answered that in the Russian autocracy this was useless and harmful. So there was a crack in the party façade, and in 1903 at the Second Congress, in the August heat of the Tottenham Court Road in London, it split the party down the middle. The issue finally revolved on the control of the party newspaper. In an atmosphere of strained friendships and bitter recriminations, Lenin got his majority. From then on, his faction of the Russian Social Democratic Labour Party was known as the "majoritarians"—the Bolsheviki.

But the vote in Congress turned out to be a hollow victory. Within months the Bolsheviks were ironically named. The Congress minority—the Mensheviks—regained control of the party paper and of the Central Committee, and made a much stronger impression during the abortive 1905 revolution in St. Petersburg. When the revolution failed, the Mensheviks retreated into the shell of semi-legal Marxism:

the Revisionists were in the citadel. But Lenin had already left it, taking the grail with him, and for ten more years in exile he waged a war of words against all revisionists and reformists. And in 1914 the war produced a new enemy of Marxism—the patriot.

Karl Marx had taken it as an axiom that the workers of different countries had more in common with each other than with their bourgeois compatriots. At conference after conference right up to the eve of hostilities, socialists resolved to have no part of a capitalist war. But in August 1914 war fever swept over the socialist movement. In the Reichstag the Social Democrats voted almost to a man in favour of war credits. Against them, Russian Social Democrats also discovered that they were first and foremost patriots—or as Lenin now called them, Social Chauvinists.

The war caught Lenin and his wife in Galicia, in Austro-Hungary. After a brief internment they got into Switzerland and settled in Berne. In 1916, needing a better library than the one in Berne, Lenin came to Zurich . . .

(The library set is now lit.)

. . intending to stay two weeks. But he and Nadezhda liked it here and decided to stay. They rented a room in the house of a shoe-maker named Kammerer at 14 Spiegelgasse. Zurich during the war was a magnet for refugees, exiles, spies, anarchists, artists and radicals of all kinds. Here could be seen James Joyce, reshaping the novel into the permanent form of his own monument, the book the world now knows as *Ulysses!*—and here, too, the Dadaists were performing nightly at the Cabaret Voltaire in the Meierei Bar at Number One Spiegelgasse, led by a dark, boyish and obscure Rumanian poet . . .

(JOYCE is seen passing among the bookshelves; and also CARR, now monocled and wearing blazer, cream flannels, boater . . . and holding a large pair of scissors which he snips speculatively as he passes between the bookcases. JOYCE and CARR pass out of view.)

Every morning at nine o'clock when the library opened, Lenin would arrive.

(LENIN arrives, saying "Good morning", in Russian: "Zdvasvitsa".)

He would work till the lunch hour, when the library closed, and then return and work until six, except on Thursdays when we remained closed. He was working on his book on Imperialism.

(LENIN is at work among books and papers.)

On January 22nd, 1917, at the Zurich People's House Lenin told an audience of young people, "We of the older generation may not live to see the decisive battles of the coming revolution." We all believed that that was so. But one day hardly more than a month later, a Polish comrade, Bronsky, ran into the Ulyanov house with the news that there was a revolution in Russia . . .

(NADYA enters as in the Prologue, and she and LENIN repeat the Russian conversation previously enacted. This time CECILY translates it for the audience, pedantically repeating each speech in English, even the simple "No!" and "Yes!" The LENINS leave.)

NADYA *says "Das vedanya" to* CECILY *[i.e. Goodbye] as she goes.)*

140 As Nadezhda writes in her *Memories of Lenin* "From the moment the news of the February revolution came, Ilyich burned with eagerness to go to Russia." But this was easier said than done, in this landlocked country. Russia was at war with Germany. And Lenin was no friend of the Allied coun-

145 tries. His war policy made him a positive danger to them;

*(*CARR *enters, very debonair in his boater and blazer, etc.* CARR *has come to the library as a "spy", and his manner betrays this until* CECILY *addresses him.)*

indeed it was clear that the British and the French would wish to prevent Lenin from leaving Switzerland. And that they would have him watched. Oh!

*(*CECILY *sees* CARR *who hands her the visiting card he received from* BENNETT *in Act One.)*

CECILY: Tristan Tzara. Dada, Dada, Dada . . . Why, it's Jack's

150 younger brother!!

CARR: You must be Cecily!

CECILY: Sssh!

CARR: You are!

CECILY: And you, I see from your calling card, are Jack's deca-

155 dent nihilist younger brother.

CARR: Oh, I'm not really a decadent nihilist at all, Cecily. You mustn't think that I am a decadent nihilist.

CECILY: If you are not then you have certainly been deceiving us all in a very inexcusable manner. To *masquerade* as a

160 decadent nihilist—or at any rate to ruminate in different colours and display the results in the Bahnhofstrasse—would be hypocritical.

CARR: *(Taken aback.)* Oh! Of course, I have been rather *louche* and devil-take-the-hindmost.

165 CECILY: I am glad to hear it.

CARR: In fact now you mention the subject I have made quite a corner in voluptuous disdain.

CECILY: I don't think you should be so proud of it, however pleasant it must be. You have been a great disappointment to

170 your brother.

CARR: Well, my brother has been a great disappointment to me, and to Dada. His mother isn't exactly mad about him either. My brother Jack is a booby, and if you want to know why he is a booby, I will tell you why he is a booby. He told

175 me that you were rather pretty, whereas you are at a glance the prettiest girl in the whole world. Have you got any books here one can borrow?

CECILY: I don't think you ought to talk to me like that during library hours. However, as the reference section is about to

180 close for lunch I will overlook it. Intellectual curiosity is not so common that one can afford to discourage it. What kind of books were you wanting?

CARR: Any kind at all.

CECILY: Is there no limit to the scope of your interests?

185 CARR: It is rather that I wish to increase it. An overly methodical education has left me to fend as best I can with some small knowledge of the aardvark, a mastery of the abacus and a facility for abstract art. An aardvark, by the way, is a sort of African pig found mainly——

190 CECILY: I know only too well what an aardvark is, Mr. Tzara. To be frank, you strike a sympathetic chord in me.

CARR: Politically, I haven't really got beyond anarchism.

CECILY: I see. Your elder brother, meanwhile——

CARR: Bolshevism. And you, I suppose . . . ?

195 CECILY: Zimmervaldism!

CARR: Oh, Cecily, will you not make it your mission to reform me? We can begin over lunch. It will give me an appetite. Nothing gives me an appetite so much as renouncing my beliefs over a glass of hock.

200 CECILY: I'm afraid I am too busy to reform you today. I must spend the lunch hour preparing references for Lenin.

CARR: Some faithful governess seeking fresh pastures?

CECILY: Far from it. I refer to Vladimir Ilyich who with my little help is writing his book on "Imperialism, the highest

205 stage of capitalism".

CARR: Of course—*Lenin*. But surely, now that the revolution has broken out in St. Petersburg, he will be anxious to return home.

CECILY: That is true. When the history of the Revolution—or

210 indeed of anything else—is written, Switzerland is unlikely to loom large in the story. However, all avenues are closed to him. He will have to travel in disguise with false papers. Oh, but I fear I have said too much already. Vladimir is positive that there are agents watching him and trying to ingratiate

215 themselves with those who are close to him. The British are among the most determined, though the least competent. Only yesterday the Ambassador received secret instructions to watch the ports.

CARR: *(Ashamed.)* The ports?

220 CECILY: At the same time, the Consul in Zurich has received a flurry of cryptic telegrams suggesting intense and dramatic activity—"Knock 'em cold"—"Drive 'em Wilde"—"Break a leg"—and one from the Ambassador himself, "Thinking of you tonight, Horace."

225 CARR: I think I can throw some light on that. The Consul has been busy for several weeks in rehearsals which culminated last evening in a performance at the Theater zur Kaufleuten on Pelikanstrasse. I happened to be present.

CECILY: That would no doubt explain why he virtually left the

230 Consulate's affairs in the hands of his manservant—who, fortunately, has radical sympathies.

CARR: Good heavens!

CECILY: You seem surprised.

CARR: Not at all. I have a servant myself.

235 CECILY: I am afraid that I disapprove of servants.

CARR: You are quite right to do so. Most of them are without scruples.

CECILY: In the socialist future, no one will have any.

CARR: So I believe. To whom did this manservant pass the

240 Consul's correspondence?

CECILY: Your brother Jack. Oh dear, there I go again! You are not a bit like your brother. You are more English.

CARR: I assure you I am as Bulgarian as he is.

CECILY: He is Rumanian.

245 CARR: They are the same place. Some people call it the one, some the other.

CECILY: I didn't know that, though I always suspected it.

CARR: Anyway, now that *Earnest* has opened, no doubt the Consul will relieve his servant of diplomatic business. In all fairness, he did have a personal triumph in a most demand-

250 ing role.

CECILY: *Earnest??*

CARR: No—the other one.

CECILY: What do you mean by *Earnest?*

255 CARR: *The Importance of Being Earnest* by Oscar Wilde.

CECILY: I don't know it. But I've heard of it and I don't like it. It is a play written by an Irish-coxcomb and bugbear of the Home Rule sodality, so I hear.

CARR: Your ears deceive you. Far from being a bugbear of the
260 Home Rule sodality, Cecily, Wilde was indifferent to politics. He may occasionally have been a little overdressed but he made up for it by being immensely uncommitted.

CECILY: That is my objection to him. The sole duty and justification for art is social criticism.

265 CARR: That is a most interesting view of the sole duty and justification for art, Cecily, but it has the disadvantage that a great deal of what we call art has no such function and yet in some way it gratifies a hunger that is common to princes and peasants.

270 CECILY: In an age when the difference between prince and peasant was thought to be in the stars, Mr. Tzara, art was naturally an affirmation for the one and a consolation to the other; but we live in an age when the social order is seen to be the work of material forces and we have been given an en-
275 tirely new kind of responsibility, the responsibility of changing society.

CARR: No, no, no, no, no—my dear girl!—art doesn't change society, it is merely changed by it.

(From here the argument becomes gradually heated.)

CECILY: Art *is* society! It is one part of many parts all touching
280 each other, everything from poetry to politics. And until the whole is reformed, artistic decadence, whether in the form of the perfectly phrased epigram or a hatful of words flung in the public's face, is a luxury which only artists can afford.

CARR: Kindly do not confuse a Dada raffle with Victorian high
285 comedy——

CECILY: Both bourgeois—both decadent——

CARR: You are familiar with neither——

CECILY: Art is a critique of society or it is nothing!

CARR: Do you know Gilbert and Sullivan??!

290 CECILY: I know Gilbert but not Sullivan.

CARR: Well, if you knew Iolanthe like I know Iolanthe——

CECILY: I doubt it——

CARR: Patience!

CECILY: How dare you!

295 CARR: Pirates! Pinafore!

CECILY: Control yourself!

CARR: *Ruddigore!*

CECILY: This is a Public Library, Mr. Tzara!

CARR: *GONDOLIERS, Madam!*

(Another "time slip . . .")

300 CECILY: I don't think you ought to talk to me like that during library hours. However as the reference section is about to close for lunch I will overlook it. Intellectual curiosity is not so common that one can afford to discourage it. What kind of books were you wanting?

305 CARR: Any kind at all. You choose. I should like you, if you would, to make it your mission to reform me. We can begin over lunch.

CECILY: I'm afraid I am too busy to reform you today. You will have to reform yourself. Here is an article which I have

been translating for Vladimir Ilyich. It is addressed to the
310 British, French and German Socialists who have deserted the correct path for economism, opportunism and social chauvinism.

(She hands him the folder which came into her possession in the Prologue. It is identical to the one given by GWEN *to* TZARA.*)*

CARR: That sounds awfully serious. What does it mean?

CECILY: Trade unions, parliament and support for the war. You
315 may not be aware, Mr. Tzara, that in the governments of Western Europe today there are ten Socialist ministers.

CARR: I must admit my work has prevented me from taking an interest in European politics. But ten is certainly impressive.

CECILY: It is scandalous. They are supporting an imperialist
320 war. To a socialist it makes no difference who wins: it is a war fought between slave-owners over a fairer distribution of slaves. Meanwhile the real struggle, the class war, is being undermined by these revisionists like Kautsky and
325 MacDonald.

CARR: *(Puzzled.)* Do you mean Ramsay MacDonald, Cecily?

CECILY: I don't mean Flora Macdonald, Mr. Tzara.

CARR: But he's an absolute Bolshie. Everybody knows that— he opposed the war.

330 CECILY: He is still an economist and opportunist.

CARR: But do you mean that forcing up wages and voting their own chaps into power is against the interests of the workers?

CECILY: Of course. It is working within the bourgeois capitalist system and postponing its destruction. Karl Marx has
335 shown that capitalism is digging its own grave. Left to itself it will destroy itself. As the gap between rich and poor gets wider——

CARR: But it doesn't.

CECILY: Not at the moment, but Vladimir Ilyich has shown in his new book *Imperialism, the Highest Stage of Capitalism*
340 that the European Worker is benefitting from the exploitation of his colonial brothers. Imperialism has introduced a breathing space, but the inexorable working-out of Marx's theory of capital——

CARR: No, no, no, no, my dear girl—Marx got it wrong. He got
345 it wrong for good reasons but he got it wrong just the same. And twice over. In the first place he was the victim of an historical accident, and in the second place his materialism made a monkey out of him, and of his theory——

CECILY: *(Coldly.)* Mr. Tzara, you are insulting me and my
350 comrades——

CARR: —and especially of his comrades. The historical accident could have happened to anybody. By bad luck he encountered the capitalist system at its most deceptive period.
355 The industrial revolution had crowded the people into slums and enslaved them in factories, but it had not yet begun to bring them the benefits of an industrialised society. Marx looked about him and saw that the system depended on a wretched army of wage slaves. He drew the lesson that
360 the wealth of the capitalist was the counterpart to the poverty of the worker and had in fact been stolen from the worker in the form of unpaid labour. He thought that was how the whole thing worked. That false assumption was itself added to a false premise. This premise was that people were a sen-
365 sational kind of material object and would behave predictably in a material world. Marx predicted that they would behave according to their class. But they didn't. Deprived,

self-interested, bitter or greedy as the case may be, they showed streaks of superior intelligence, superior strength,
370 superior morality . . . Legislation, unions, share capital, consumer power—in all kinds of ways and for all kinds of reasons, the classes moved closer together instead of further apart. The critical moment never came. It receded. The tide must have turned at about the time when *Das Kapital* after
375 eighteen years of hard labour was finally coming off the press, a moving reminder, Cecily, of the folly of authorship. How sweet you look suddenly—pink as a rose.

CECILY: That's because I'm about to puke into your nancy straw hat, you *prig!*—you swanking canting fop, you bour-
380 geois intellectual humbugger, you—*artist!* Do you think that's what socialism is about?—being allowed to strike, to vote, to buy or not to buy, allowed this and allowed that?—*do you think it's about winning concessions?*—Socialism is about *ownership*—the natural right of the people to the com-
385 mon ownership of their country and its resources, the *land,* and what is *under* the land and what *grows* on the land, and all the profits and the benefits! A new society, root and branch, it won't grow like leaves on a tree. Marx warned us against the liberals, the philanthropists, the piecemeal re-
390 formers—change won't come from *them* but from a head-on collision, *that's* how history works! When Lenin was 21 there was famine in Russia. The intellectuals organised relief—soup kitchens, seed corn, all kinds of do-gooding with Tolstoy in the lead. Lenin did—nothing. He understood that the
395 famine was a force for the revolution, that it would help to break down the peasantry and bring Russia closer to industrialised capitalism, closer to socialist revolution, closer to the dictatorship of the proletariat, closer to the Communist society. Twenty-one years old, in Samara, in 1890–91. He
400 was a boy, and he understood that, so don't talk to me about superior morality, you patronising Kant-struck prig, all the time you're talking about the classes you're trying to imagine how I'd looked stripped off to my knickers——

CARR: That's a lie!

(But apparently it isn't. As CECILY *continues to speak we get a partial Carr's-mind view of her. Coloured lights begin to play over her body, and most of the other light goes except for a bright spot on Carr. Faintly from 1974, comes the sound of the big band playing "The Stripper".* CARR *is in a trance. The music builds.* CECILY *might perhaps climb on to her desk. The desk may have "cabaret lights" built into it for use at this point.)*

405 CECILY: In England the rich own the poor and the men own the women. Five per cent of the people own eighty per cent of the property. The only way is the way of Marx, and of Lenin, the enemy of all revisionism—of economism—oppor-
410 tunism—liberalism—of bourgeois anarchist individualism—of quasi-socialist ad hoc-ism, of syndicalist quasi-Marxist populism—liberal quasi-communist opportunism, economist quasi-internationalist imperialism, social chauvinist quasi-Zimmervaldist Menshevism, self-determinist quasi-socialist annexationism, Kautskyism, Bundism, Kantism——

415 CARR: *Get 'em off!*

(The light snaps back to normal.)

CECILY: I don't think you ought to talk to me like that during library hours. However, as the reference section is about to close for lunch I will overlook it. Intellectual curiosity is not

so common that one can afford to discourage it. What kind of books were you wanting?
420

CARR: Books? What books? What do you mean, Cecily, by books? I have read Mr. Lenin's article and I don't need to read any more. I have come to tell you that you seem to me to be the visible personification of absolute perfection.

CECILY: In body or mind?
425

CARR: In every way.

CECILY: Oh, Tristan!

CARR: You will love me back and tell me all your secrets, won't you?

CECILY: You silly boy! Of course! I have waited for you for
430 months.

CARR: *(Amazed.)* For months?

CECILY: Ever since Jack told me he had a younger brother who was a decadent nihilist it has been my girlish dream to reform you and to love you.
435

CARR: Oh, Cecily!

(Her embrace drags him down out of sight behind her desk. He re-surfaces momentarily——)

But, my dear Cecily, you don't mean that you couldn't love me if——

(—and is dragged down again.

NADYA *enters and comes down to address the audience, undramatically.)*

NADYA: From the moment news of the revolution came, Ilyich burned with eagerness to go to Russia . . . He did not
440 sleep, and at night all sorts of incredible plans were made. We could travel by aeroplane. But such things could only be thought of in the semi-delirium of the night. A passport of a foreigner from a neutral country would have to be obtained. Letter to Yakov Ganetsky in Stockholm, March
445 19th, 1917 . . . "I cannot wait any longer. No legal means of transit available. Whatever happens, Zinoviev and I must reach Russia. The only possible plan is as follows: you must find two Swedes who resemble Zinoviev and me, but since we cannot speak Swedish they must be deaf mutes. I en-
450 close our photographs for this purpose."

*(*TZARA *enters.)*

TZARA: *(A rising note of incredulity.)* Two . . . Swedish . . . deaf mutes . . . ???

(He leans his back against the desk.)

NADYA: *(Out front, independent of Tzara.)* The plan mentioned in this letter was not realised.
455

*(*LENIN *enters, clean shaven and wearing a wig.)*

Letter to V. A. Karpinsky in Geneva, the same day, March 19th, 1917.

LENIN: My dear Vyacheslav Alexeyevich. I am considering carefully and from every point of view what will be the best way of travelling to Russia. The following is absolutely
460 secret. I ask you to reply at once, and perhaps it would be best by express (let us hope we will not ruin the party by sending a dozen or more express letters!) so as to be certain no one has read this letter.

*(*CARR *pops up attentively from behind the desk, and listens carefully.)*

465　Please procure in your name papers for travelling to France
　　and England. I will use these when passing through England
　　and *Holland* to Russia. I can wear a wig.
　　　　The passport photograph will be of *me* in a wig. I shall go
　　to the Berne Consulate to present your papers and I shall be
470　wearing the wig.

(CECILY appears from behind the desk.)

　　You must disappear from Geneva for at least two or three
　　weeks, until you receive a telegram from me in Scandinavia
　　. . . Your Lenin. P.S. . . . I write to you because I am con-
475　vinced that everything between us will remain *absolutely*
　　secret.

CECILY: Jack!

TZARA: *(Turning one way.)* Cecily!

CECILY: I have such a surprise for you. Your brother is here.

TZARA: What nonsense! I haven't got a brother.

480　CECILY: Oh, don't say that! He has renounced the life of deca-
　　　dent nihilism which you and Vladimir Ilyich rightly——

TZARA: I don't know what it all means, it is perfectly absurd—
　　　(He turns the other way and sees CARR.)—Oh my God.

(The LENINS stop and stare at these events.)

CARR: Brother Jack, I have come to tell you that I am sorry for
485　　all the embarrassment I have caused you in the past, and that
　　　I hope very much that I do not have to embarrass you in the
　　　future.

CECILY: Jack, you are not going to refuse your own brother's
　　　hand!

490　TZARA: Nothing will induce me to take his hand. He knows
　　　perfectly well why.

(CECILY runs, weeping, off-stage, followed by CARR.

LENIN and NADYA turn away. LENIN takes off his wig in disgust.)

NADYA: The plan mentioned in this letter was not realised. On
　　　the same day, March 19th, there was a meeting of the Russ-
　　　ian political emigré groups in Switzerland to discuss ways
495　　and means of getting back to Russia.

*(CARR returns as Old Carr. The lighting changes to a spot on
him, dark elsewhere. He takes up NADYA's words . . .)*

CARR: On the same day March 19th, there was a meeting of
　　　the Russian political emigré groups in Switzerland to discuss
　　　ways and means of—sorry about the other business, inciden-
　　　tally, did you notice? Of course you did—hello, hello, you
500　　thought, he's doing it again, right well never mind here's the
　　　picture: middle of March: Lenin and I in Zurich. I'd got
　　　pretty close to him, had a stroke of luck with a certain little
　　　lady and I'd got a pretty good idea of his plans, in fact I might
　　　have stopped the whole Bolshevik thing in its tracks, but—
505　　here's the point. *I was uncertain.* What was the right thing?
　　　And then there were my feelings for Cecily. And don't forget,
　　　he wasn't Lenin then! I mean who was he? as it were. So there
　　　I was, the lives of millions of people hanging on which way
　　　I'd move, or whether I'd move at all, another man might
510　　have cracked—sorry about the other business, inciden-
　　　tally—On the same day, March 19th, there was a meeting
　　　of the Russian political emigré groups in Switzerland to discuss
　　　ways and means of getting back to Russia . . .

*(CARR exits. Alternatively a projection screen may be lowered in
front of him and photos of the various people NADYA mentions
could be projected.)*

NADYA: Martov suggested obtaining permits for emigrants to
　　　pass through Germany in exchange for German and Aus-　515
　　　trian prisoners of war interned in Russia. But no one wanted
　　　to go that way, except Lenin, who snatched at the plan.

LENIN: March 21st, letter to Karpinsky in Geneva: "Martov's
　　　plan is good. We ought to begin working for it, only *we* can-
　　　not do this directly. We would be suspected . . . But the plan　520
　　　itself is *very* good and *quite* right."

*(CARR re-enters, young again, and comes down and stands next
to TZARA.*

*The corner of the Stage now occupied by TZARA and CARR is in-
dependent of the LENINS. It can no longer be said that the scene
is taking place "in the Library". CARR and TZARA might be in a
café; or anywhere.)*

CARR: According to the papers, the man to watch is Kerensky.

NADYA: *Lenin's Journey Through Germany in the Sealed Train,*
　　　book by Fritz Platten, Swiss socialist, 1924.
　　　　"Since direct contact between the exiles and the German　525
　　　authorities was considered undesirable, it was agreed that
　　　Comrade Grimm—President of the Zimmerwald Commit-
　　　tee—should undertake the negotiations."

CARR: I should like to make it clear that my feelings for Cecily
　　　are genuine.　530

NADYA: March 25th. Telegram from the German High Com-
　　　mand to the Foreign Ministry in Berlin: "No objection to the
　　　transit of Russian revolutionaries if effected in special train
　　　with reliable escort."

CARR: Look—be fair. The Americans are about to enter the　535
　　　war and it's not a good moment for some Bolshevik to pull
　　　the Russians out of it. It could turn the whole thing round. I
　　　mean, I *am* on the side of Right. Remember plucky little
　　　Poland—not Poland, the other one.

NADYA: March 31st. Telegram to Grimm.　540

LENIN: "Our party definitely decided to accept plan for Russ-
　　　ian emigrants to pass through Germany . . . We absolutely
　　　cannot agree to any further delay. Protest strongly against
　　　it . . ."

NADYA: Lenin therefore decided to take a hand in the affair　545
　　　himself, through the medium of someone in his confidence.
　　　One morning at about eleven a.m., Fritz Platten received a
　　　telephone message at the Party Secretariat asking him to go
　　　to a discussion with Comrade Lenin at 1.30 p.m. at the Ein-
　　　tract Restaurant. When he got there he found quite a　550
　　　gathering of people round the lunch table. Lenin, Radek,
　　　Munzenberg and Platten, then withdrew for a confidential
　　　discussion during which Lenin asked Platten——

LENIN: Are you prepared to act as our representative in the
　　　matter of the journey home and to accompany us on the　555
　　　journey through Germany?

NADYA: After considering the matter for a short time, Platten
　　　agreed.

CARR: Anyway, according to Marxist theory, the dialectic of
　　　history will get you to much the same place with or without　560
　　　him. If Lenin did not exist it would be unnecessary to invent
　　　him. Or Marx, for that matter.

LENIN: Telegram to Bolsheviks leaving Scandinavia for St. Petersburg: "Our tactics: no trust in and no support of the new Government. Kerensky is especially suspect. Arming of the proletariat is the only guarantee. Immediate elections to the Petrograd Duma. No rapprochement with other parties. Telegraph this to Petrograd."

NADYA: April 3rd. The German Minister received Platten. He was authorised by Lenin and Zinoviev to present the following conditions to Minister Romberg: (1) That he, Fritz Platten, assume full personal responsibility for escorting the railway carriage. (2) The carriage to be allowed extra-territorial rights. (3) No passport control or check. (4) . . .

CARR: Furthermore I don't understand your interest. All this dancing attendance on Marxism is sheer pretension. You're an amiable bourgeois with a chit from Matron and if the revolution came you wouldn't know what hit you. You're nothing. You're an artist. And multi-coloured micturition is no trick to those boys, they'll have you pissing blood.

TZARA: Artists and intellectuals will be the conscience of the revolution. He is a reactionary in art, and in politics he was brought up in a hard school that killed weaker spirits, but he is moved by a vision of a society of free and equal men. And he will listen. He listens to Gorki—do you know Gorki?

CARR: No.

TZARA: Well, do what you will. To a Dadaist history comes out of a hat too.

LENIN: April 7th. Telegram to Ganetsky in Stockholm: "Twenty of us are leaving tomorrow."

CARR: I don't think there'll be a place for Dada in a Communist society.

TZARA: That's what we have against this one. There's a place for us in it.

NADYA: On April 9th at 2.30 in the afternoon the travellers moved off from the Zahringer Hof Restaurant in true Russian style, loaded with pillows, blankets and a few personal belongings. Ilyich wore a bowler hat, a heavy overcoat and the thick-soled hobnailed boots that had been made for him by the cobbler Kammerer at number 14 Spiegelgasse. Telegram to his sister in St. Petersburg:

LENIN: "Arriving Monday night, eleven. Tell *Pravda.*"

(NADYA *and* LENIN *leave.*

Distant sound of train setting off.)

TZARA: The train left at 3.10, on time.

(TZARA *leaves.)*

CARR: (*Decisively.)* No, it is perfectly clear in my mind. He must be stopped. The Russians have got a government of patriotic and moderate men. Prince Lvov is moderately conservative, Kerensky is moderately socialist, and Guchkov is a businessman. All in all a promising foundation for a liberal democracy on the Western model, and for a vigorous prosecution of the war on the Eastern front, followed by a rapid expansion of trade. I shall telegraph the Minister in Berne.

(CARR *leaves.*

The train noise becomes very loud.

Everything black except a light on LENIN. *He is bearded again. There is a much reproduced photograph of Lenin addressing the crowd in a public square in May 1920—"balding, bearded, in the three-piece suit" as Carr describes him; he stands as though* leaning into a gale, his chin jutting, his hands gripping the edge of the rostrum which is waist-high, the right hand at the same time gripping a cloth cap . . . a justly famous image. [This is the photo, incidentally, which Stalin had re-touched so as to expunge Kamenev and Trotsky who feature prominently in the original.]

The image on stage now recalls this photograph.

The screen, if one is used, now disappears. It is structurally important to the Act that the following speech is delivered from the strongest possible position with the most dramatic change of effect from the general stage appearance preceding it. Ideally LENIN *should speak from a high rostrum, possibly using Cecily's desk, or a bookcase.*

LENIN, *as the orator, is now the only person on stage.)*

LENIN: Today, literature must become party literature. Down with non-partisan literature! Down with literary supermen! Literature must become a part of the common cause of the proletariat, a cog in the Social Democratic mechanism . . . I dare say there will be hysterical intellectuals to raise a howl at this . . . Such outcries would be nothing more than an expression of bourgeois-intellectual individualism.

Publishing and distributing centres, bookshops and reading rooms, libraries and similar establishments must all be under party control. We want to establish and we shall establish a free press, free not simply from the police, but also from capital, from careerism, and what is more, *free from bourgeois anarchist individualism!* These last words may seem paradoxical or an affront to my audience. Calm yourselves, ladies and gentlemen! Everyone is free to write and say whatever he likes, without any restrictions. *But* every voluntary association, including the party, is also free to expel members who use the name of the party to advocate antiparty views. Secondly, we must say to you bourgeois individualists that your talk about absolute freedom is sheer hypocrisy. There can be no real and effective freedom in a society based on the power of money. Are you free in relation to your bourgeois publisher, Mr. Writer? And in relation to your bourgeois public which demands that you provide it with pornography? The freedom of the bourgeois writer, artist or actor is simply disguised dependence on the moneybag, on corruption, on prostitution. Socialist literature and art will be free because the idea of socialism and sympathy with the working people, instead of greed and careerism, will bring ever new forces to its ranks. It will be free because it will serve not some satiated heroine, not the bored upper ten thousand suffering from fatty degeneration, but the millions and tens of millions of working people, the flower of the country, its strength and its future.

(*A climactic note, and a light cue which reveals* NADYA *standing downstage and which changes the ambience into something less public, more interior.* LENIN *disappears.)*

NADYA: Ilyich wrote those remarks in 1905 during the first revolution. He wrote very little about art and literature, generally, but he enjoyed it. We sometimes went to concerts and the theatre, even the music hall—he laughed a lot at the clowns—and he was moved to tears when we saw *La Dame aux Camelias* in London in 1907. Gorki tells us in his *Days with Lenin* how Ilyich admired Tolstoy, which is true, of course, especially *War and Peace*, but, as Ilyich put it in an article in 1908 on Tolstoy's 80th birthday . . .

655 LENIN: *(Entering.)* . . . On the one hand we have the great artist; on the other hand we have the landlord obsessed with Christ. On the one hand the strong and sincere protester against social injustice, and on the other hand the jaded hys-

660 terical sniveller known as the Russian intellectual, beating his breast in public and wailing, "I am a bad wicked man, but I am practising moral self-perfection. I don't eat meat, I now eat rice cutlets." On the one hand, merciless criticism of capitalist exploitation, on the other hand the crackpot

665 preaching of submission and of one of the most odious things on earth, namely religion. Tolstoy reflected the stored-up hatred and the readiness for a new future—and at the same time the immature dreaming and political flabbiness which was one of the main causes for the failure of the 1905 revolution.

670 NADYA: However he respected Tolstoy's traditional values as an artist. The *new* art seemed somehow alien and incomprehensible to him. Clara Zetkin, in her memoirs, remembers him bursting out.

LENIN: Bosh and nonsense! We are good revolutionaries but

675 we seem to be somehow obliged to keep up with modern art. Well, as for me I'm a barbarian. Expressionism, futurism, cubism . . . I don't understand them and I get no pleasure from them.

NADYA: Once, in 1919, we went to a concert in the Kremlin

680 and an actress started declaiming something by Mayakovsky . . . Mayakovsky was celebrated even before the revolution, when he used to shout his fractured lines in a yellow blazer with blue roses painted on his cheeks. Ilyich was in the front row, and he nearly jumped out of his skin.

685 LENIN: Memo to A. V. Lunacharsky, Commissar for Education—"Aren't you ashamed for printing 5,000 copies of Mayakovsky's new book? It is nonsense, stupidity, double-dyed stupidity and affectation. I believe such things should be published one in ten, and not more than 1,500 copies, for

690 librarians and cranks. As for Mayakovsky, he should be flogged for his futurism."

NADYA: One evening Ilyich wanted to see for himself how the young people were getting on in the communes. I think it was the day Kropotkin was buried in 1921. It was a hungry

695 year but the young people were filled with enthusiasm and their joy was reflected in his face.

LENIN: What do you read?—do you read Pushkin?

NADYA: "Oh no," said someone, "after all, he was a bourgeois. We read Mayakovsky."

700 LENIN: I think that Pushkin is better.

NADYA: After this, Ilyich took a more favourable view of Mayakovsky. He admitted that he was not a competent judge of poetical talent. Ilyich was much more concerned with the question of bourgeois intellectuals.

705 LENIN: February 13, 1908, to Gorki, Dear Alexei Maximych . . . I think that some of the questions you raise about our differences of opinion are a sheer misunderstanding. Never of course, have I thought of, quote, persecuting the intelligentsia . . . or of denying that the intelligentsia is necessary to the

710 workers' movement . . .

NADYA: Gorki joined the Democratic Party before 1905, and supported it with his earnings. Ilyich liked Gorki the man and he liked Gorki the artist. He said that Gorki the artist was capable of grasping things instantly. With Gorki he al-

715 ways spoke very frankly.

LENIN: September 15, 1919, to A. M. Gorki, Dear Alexei Maximych . . . Even before receiving your letter we had decided in the Central Committee to appoint Kamenev and Bukharin to check on the arrests of bourgeois intellectuals of the near-Cadet type, and to release whoever possible. For it 720 is clear to us too that there have been mistakes here.

It is also clear that in general the measure of arrest has been necessary and correct. Reading your frank opinion of this matter, I recall a remark of yours which stuck in my mind during our talks (in London, on Capri, and later)— 725 namely: "We artists are irresponsible people." Exactly! You utter incredibly angry words—about what? About a few dozen (or perhaps even a few hundred) Cadet and near-Cadet gentry spending a few days in jail in order to prevent plots which threaten the lives of tens of thousands of workers 730 and peasants. A calamity indeed! What an injustice! A few days, or even weeks, in jail for intellectuals in order to prevent the massacre of tens of thousands of workers and peasants. "Artists are irresponsible people!" Both on Capri and afterwards, I told you—you allow yourself to be surrounded 735 by the very worst elements of bourgeois intelligentsia and succumb to their whining.

No, really, you will go under if you don't tear yourself away from these bourgeois intellectuals. With all my heart I wish that you do this quickly. All the best. Yours, Lenin. P.S. 740 For you are not writing anything! For an artist to waste himself on the whining of rotting intellectuals—is it not ruinous and shameful?

NADYA: I remember when we were in London in 1903 how Ilyich wished he could go to the Moscow Art Theatre to see 745 *The Lower Depths.* We did so after the Revolution. It goes without saying that he set high standards for a Gorki production. Well, the over-acting irritated him. After seeing *The Lower Depths* he avoided the theatre for a long time. But once we went to see *Uncle Vanya,* which he liked very 750 much. And finally the last time we went to the theatre, in 1922, we saw a stage version of Charles Dicken's *Cricket on the Hearth.* After the first act, Ilyich found it dull. The saccharine sentimentality got on his nerves, and during the conversation between the old toymaker and his blind daugh- 755 ter he could stand it no longer and we left.

(The "Appassionata" Sonata of Beethoven is quietly introduced.)

But I remember him one evening at a friend's house in Moscow, listening to a Beethoven Sonata . . .

LENIN: I don't know of anything greater than the Appassionata. Amazing, superhuman music. It always makes me feel, 760 perhaps naïvely, it makes me feel proud of the miracles that human beings can perform. But I can't listen to music often. It affects my nerves, makes me want to say nice stupid things and pat the heads of those people who while living in this vile hell can create such beauty. Nowadays we can't pat 765 heads or we'll get our hands bitten off. We've got to *hit* heads, hit them without mercy, though ideally we're against doing violence to people . . . Hm, one's duty is infernally hard . . .

(The light goes out on him. He leaves.)

The music continues.)

NADYA: Once when Vladimir was in prison—in St. Peters- 770 burg—he wrote to me and asked that at certain times of day I should go and stand on a particular square of pavement on

the Shpalernaya. When the prisoners were taken out for ex-
775 ercise it was possible through one of the windows in the corridor to catch a momentary glimpse of this spot. I went for
several days and stood a long while on the pavement there.
But he never saw me. Something went wrong. I forget what.

*(The "Appassionata" swells in the dark to cover the set-change to
"The Room".* GWEN *is seated. There are tea things on the table.
The "Appassionata" degenerates absurdly into "Mr. Gallagher
and Mr. Shean".* BENNETT *enters, followed by* CECILY.

*The rhyme-scheme of the song is fairly evident. The verses are of
ten lines each, the first line being a non-rhyming primer. The
fourth and fifth verses may be omitted in performance.)*

BENNETT: Miss Carruthers . . .
CECILY: Cecily Carruthers . . .
GWEN: Cecily Carruthers! What a pretty name!
780   According to the Consul
'Round the fashionable fonts you'll
often hear the Cecily's declaimed.
CECILY: Oh dear Miss Carr, oh dear Miss Carr,
pleasure remain exactly where you are—
785   I beg you don't get up——
GWEN: *(To* BENNETT.*)* I think we'll need another cup—
Pray sit down, Miss Carruthers,
CECILY: So kind of you, Miss Carr.

(Exit BENNETT.*)*

GWEN: Miss Carruthers, oh Miss Carruthers . . .
I hope that you will call me Gwendolen.
790   I feel I've known you long
And I'm never ever wrong—
Something tells me that we're going to be great friends.
CECILY: *(Upper class.)* Oh, Gwendolen! Oh, Gwendolen!
It sounds ez pretty *ez* a mendolen!
795   I hope that you'll feel free
to call me Cecily . . .
GWEN: Absolutely, Cecily.
CECILY: Then that's settled Gwendolen.

CECILY: Oh, Gwendolen, Oh, Gwendolen . . .
I fear you don't remember where we met.
800   I'm not so picturesque
when seen behind a desk——
GWEN: Of *course*, my dear—*how* could I forget?
Oh, Cecily, Oh, Cecily,
Accept my sincere apology!
805   Now be absolutely frank,
is there trouble at the bank?
CECILY: At the Libr'ry, Gwendolen.
GWEN: At the *Libr'ry*, Cecily!

CECILY: Oh Gwendolen, Oh Gwendolen . . .
I dread to state the reason for my call.
810   The fact is there's a fee
due on Homer's *Odyssey*
and the *Irish Times* for June 1904.
GWEN: Oh Cecily, Oh Cecily,
A friend of mine is writing *Ulysses!*
815   I'm sure he never knew
that the books were overdue——
CECILY: Since October, Gwendolen.
GWEN: On my ticket, Cecily!

(Enter BENNETT *with cup. There is a certain amount of tea-
pouring and tea-sipping to come, not to mention the cup suddenly clinked down on the saucer, and all that; but directions to
this effect are omitted.)*

GWEN: Oh Cecily, Oh Cecily . . .
Aren't you the girl who has that Russian friend?
I pass him every day   820
by Economics A to K——
CECILY: *(Sadly.)* It's never going to be the same again.
Oh Gwendolen, Oh Gwendolen!
He left this afternoon on the three-ten.
I've just come from the train.   825
But we'll hear of him again . . .
GWEN: *(Insincerely.)* Absolutely, Cecily . . .
CECILY: *Positively*, Gwendolen!

(Exit BENNETT.*)*

CECILY: Oh Gwendolen, Oh Gwendolen . . .
The Library is going to seem so sad.
Apart from Mr. Tzara   830
all the Bolsheviki are a-
board that special choo-choo bound for Petrograd.
GWEN: Excuse me, Cecily, dear Cecily . . .
This Mr. Tzara, does he spell it with a T?
T-Z-A-R-A?   835
A Bolshevik, you say?
CECILY: Absolutely, Gwendolen.
GWEN: You surprise me, Cecily.
GWEN: Oh Cecily, oh Cecily . . .
I must admit you've taken me aback.
I shall certainly insist on   840
a tête-à-tête with Tristan——
CECILY: With Tristan?—No, I mean his brother Jack.
Oh Gwendolen, Oh Gwendolen!
Tristan's quite another thing again.
GWEN: Brother Jack is news to me——   845
CECILY: They kept it in the family——
GWEN: Relatively, Cecily.
CECILY: Imminently, Gwendolen.
CECILY: Oh Gwendolen, Oh Gwendolen
I'd like you to be the first to know . . .
Tristan's hanging up his hat   850
for the proletariat.
We have an understanding——
GWEN: *(Rising.)*   Just a mo-
(Sitting.) ment, Cecily, dear Cecily,
Tristan's understanding is with me.
What he writes (or draws)   855
is no concern of yours.
CECILY: Relatively, Gwendolen——
GWEN: *Absolutely*, Cecily!
GWEN: Oh, Cecily . . . Oh Cecily . . .
you have made an unfortunate mistake.
Forgive me if I say   860
Tristan mentioned yesterday
he delectates his art for its own sake.
CECILY: Oh Gwendolen, Oh Gwendolen
Clearly he has changed his mind since then.
Today he said, "My heart's   865
no longer in the arts
excepting, Cecily, as a means towards an end."

GWEN: (*Frigid.*) Oh Cecily, Oh Cecily . . .
To say this gives me physical distress
870 but one of Joyce's chapters
sent Tristan into raptures
on the subject of the stream of consciousness.
CECILY: Oh Gwendolen, Oh Gwendolen,
it harrows me to contradict a friend,
875 but his consciousness of class
is the one that's going to last——
GWEN: Lower middle, Cecily?
CECILY: Are you really, Gwendolen?
GWEN: (*Rising.*) Miss Carruthers,
CECILY: (*Ditto.*)   Yes, Miss Carr.
GWEN: I do not wish to trespass on your time.
880 CECILY: I hope that I will see
you at the Library
should you ever get around to pay your fine.
Miss Carr. (*Bows.*)

(*To the door.*)

GWEN: Miss Carruthers,
Is it done to wish you luck with all the others?
885 I'm not awfully au fait
with manners down your way——
CECILY: And up yours, Miss Carr—*Tristan!*

(CARR *has entered. Pause.*)

GWEN: (*Censoriously.*)   That's my brother.
CECILY: Your brother?
GWEN: Yes, My brother, Henry Carr.
890 CECILY: Do you mean that he is not Tristan Tzara the artist?
GWEN: Quite the contrary. He is the British Consul.

(CARR *has frozen like a hunting dog. He is holding the folder given to him by* CECILY *in the Library.* BENNETT *opens the door.*)

BENNETT: Mr. Tzara . . .

(TRISTAN *enters.* BENNETT *retires.* TZARA *carries his folder.*)

GWEN: Tristan! My Tristan!
CECILY: Comrade Jack!
895 GWEN: Comrade Jack?
CECILY: Yes. The gentleman who has his arm round your waist is a luminary of the Zimmerwald Left.
GWEN: Are they Bolsheviks?
CECILY: Well, they dine with us.
900 GWEN: A gross deception has been practised upon us. My poor wounded Cecily!
CECILY: My sweet wronged Gwendolen!

(*They are making for the door.*)

CECILY: (*Halting.*) There is just one question I should like to ask Mr. Carr.
905 GWEN: An admirable idea. Mr. Tzara, there is a question I should like to put to you.
CECILY: What in truth *was* your opinion of the essay I gave you to read?
GWEN: What indeed *did* you think of the chapter I showed
910 you?
CARR: (*Timidly.*) Very . . . well written . . . Interesting style . . .
TZARA: (*Timidly.*) Very . . . well read . . . Rich material.
CECILY: But as a social critique—— ?

GWEN: But as art for art's sake——?
CARR: (*Giving up.*) Rubbish! He's a madman!   915
TZARA: Bilge! It's unreadable!
GWEN & CECILY: Oh! Hypocrites!
CARR: I'm sorry! 'Twas for love!
GWEN & CECILY: For love?
GWEN: That is true . . .   920
CECILY: Yes, it is.

(*In unison they move towards the men, then in unison change their minds.*)

GWEN & CECILY: But our intellectual differences are an insuperable barrier!

(*The door closes behind them.*

CARR *and* TZARA *sink into the two main chairs.*)

CARR: By the way, I hear that Bennett has been showing you my private correspondence.   925

(BENNETT *enters with champagne for two on a tray. He begins to dispense it.*)

TZARA: He has radical sympathies.
CARR: There is no one so radical as a manservant whose freedom of the champagne bin has been interfered with.
TZARA: So I believe.
CARR: Well, I've put a stop to it.   930
TZARA: Given him notice?
CARR: Given him more champagne.
TZARA: We Rumanians have much to learn from the English.
CARR: I expect you'll be missing Sofia.
TZARA: You mean Gwendolen.   935
CARR: (*Frowns; clears.*) Bucharest.
TZARA: Oh, yes, Yes. The Paris of the Balkans . . .
CARR: Silly place to put it, really . . . (*Sips.*) Is this the Perrier-Jouet, Brut, '89????!!!
BENNETT: No, sir.   940
CARR: (*He has read the writing on the wall.*) All gone . . . ?
BENNETT: (*Implacably.*) I'm afraid so, sir.
CARR: Very well, Bennett.
BENNETT: I have put the newspapers and telegrams on the sideboard, sir.   945
CARR: Anything of interest?
BENNETT: The *Neue Zuricher Zeitung* and the *Zuricher Post* announce respectively the cultural high and low point of the theatrical season at the Theater zur Kaufleuten yesterday evening. The *Zeitung* singles you out for a personal triumph   950
in a demanding role. The Minister telegraphs his congratulations, and also thanks you for your telegram to him. He urges you to prevent Mr. Ulyanov leaving Switzerland at all costs.

(BENNETT *leaves. Pause.*)

CARR: Irish lout . . .   955
TZARA: Russian . . .
CARR: No—whatsisname—Deidre.
TZARA: Bridget . . . (*Pause.*)
CARR: Joyce!
TZARA: Joyce!   960
CARR: Lout. Quadri-oculate Irish git. . . . Came round to the dressing room and handed me ten francs like a *tip*—bloody nerve—Sponger——

(BENNETT enters.)

BENNETT: Mr. Joyce.

(JOYCE enters in an agitated state.)

965 JOYCE: Where is your sister?

CARR: Her money is in trust.

JOYCE: I have only one request to make of *you*——

CARR: And I have only one request to make of *you—why for God's sake cannot you contrive just once to wear the jacket that is suggested by your trousers??*

970

(It is indeed the case that JOYCE is now wearing the other halves of the outfit he wore in Act One.)

JOYCE: *(With dignity.)* If I could do it once, I could do it every time. My wardrobe got out of step in Trieste, and its reciprocal members pass each other endlessly in the night. Now—could you let me have the twenty-five francs.

975 CARR: What twenty-five francs?

JOYCE: You were given eight tickets to sell at five francs per ticket. My books indicate that only fifteen francs has been received from you.

CARR: I have spent three hundred and fifty francs of my own
980 money so that your off-the-peg production should boast one character who looked as if he was acquainted with a tailor. If you hope to get a further twenty-five francs out of me you will have to drag me through the courts. *(Deliberately.)* You are a swindler and a cad!

985 TZARA: *(Handing JOYCE his folder.)* Furthermore, your book has much in common with your dress. As an arrangement of words it is graceless without being random; as a narrative it lacks charm or even vulgarity; as an experience it is like sharing a cell with a fanatic in search of a mania.

(GWEN and CECILY enter. JOYCE is scanning the manuscript.)

990 JOYCE: Who gave you this manuscript to read?

GWEN: I did!

JOYCE: Miss Carr, did I or did I not give you to type a chapter in which Mr. Bloom's adventures correspond to the Homeric episode of the Oxen of the Sun?

995 GWEN: Yes, you did! And it was wonderful!

JOYCE: Then why do you return to me an ill-tempered thesis purporting to prove, amongst other things, that Ramsay MacDonald is a bourgeois lickspittle gentleman's gentleman?

GWEN: *(Aaaah)*
1000 TZARA: *(Ohhhh)*

CECILY: *(Oops!)*

CARR: *(Aaah!)*

JOYCE: *(Thunders.)* Miss Carr, where is the missing chapter???

CARR: Excuse me—did you say Bloom?

1005 JOYCE: I did.

CARR: And is it a chapter, inordinate in length and erratic in style, remotely connected with midwifery?

JOYCE: It is a chapter which by a miracle of compression, uses the gamut of English literature from Chaucer to Carlyle to
1010 describe events taking place in a lying-in hospital in Dublin.

CARR: *(Holding out his folder.)* It is obviously the same work.

(GWEN and CECILY swap folders with cries of recognition. CARR and TZARA close in. A rapid but formal climax, with appropriate

cries of "Cecily! Gwendolen! Henry! Tristan!" *and appropriate embraces.*

Music, appropriate to the period. Light change. A formal, short dance sequence. TZARA dances with GWEN, CARR with CECILY. JOYCE and BENNETT dance independently. The effect is of course a complete dislocation of the play. CARR and CECILY dance out of view. The others continue, and then they, too, dance offstage just as OLD CARR dances back on stage with OLD CECILY.

OLD CECILY is about 80 of course, like Old Carr. They dance a few decrepit steps.)

OLD CECILY: No, no, no, no it's pathetic though there was a court case I admit, and your trousers came into it, I don't deny, but you never got close to Vladimir Ilyich, and I don't remember the other one. I do remember Joyce, yes you are 1015 quite right and he was Irish with glasses but that was the year after—1918—and the train had long gone from the station! I waved a red hanky and cried long live the revolution as the carriage took him away in his bowler hat and yes, I said yes when you asked me, but he was the leader of millions by the 1020 time you did your Algernon . . .

CARR: Algernon—that was him.

OLD CECILY: I said that was the year after——

CARR: After what?

OLD CECILY: You never even saw Lenin. 1025

CARR: Yes I did. Saw him in the cafés. I knew them all. Part of the job.

OLD CECILY: *(Small pause.)* And you were never the Consul.

CARR: Never said I was.

OLD CECILY: Yes you did. 1030

CARR: Should we have a cup of tea?

OLD CECILY: The Consul was Percy somebody.

CARR: *(Bennett.)*

OLD CECILY: What?

CARR: *(Testily.)* I said the Consul's name was Bennett! 1035

OLD CECILY: Oh yes . . . Bennett . . . *(Pause.)* That's another thing——

CARR: *Are we going to have a cup of tea or not?*

OLD CECILY: And I never helped him write *Imperialism, the Highest Stage of Capitalism.* That was the year before, too. 1040 1916.

CARR: Oh, Cecily. I wish I'd known then that you'd turn out to be a pedant! *(Getting angry.)* Wasn't this—Didn't do that—1916—1917—*What of it?* I was here. They were here. They went on. I went on. We all went on. 1045

OLD CECILY: No, we didn't. We stayed. Sophia married that artist. I married you. You played Algernon. They all went on.

(Most of the fading light is on CARR now.)

CARR: Great days . . . Zurich during the war. Refugees, spies, exiles, painters, poets, writers, radicals of all kinds. I knew them all. Used to argue far into the night . . . at the Odeon, 1050 the Terrasse . . . I learned three things in Zurich during the war. I wrote them down. Firstly, you're either a revolutionary or you're not, and if you're not you might as well be an artist as anything else. Secondly, if you can't be an artist, you might as well be a revolutionary . . . I forget the third thing. 1055

(Blackout.)

■ WOLE SOYINKA ■

Wole Soyinka was born in 1934 in Abeokuta, Nigeria. Educated at Government College in Ibadan, Soyinka then studied at Leeds University in England, where he worked with the notable Shakespearian scholar and actor G. Wilson Knight and took his B.A. in English in 1957. He remained in England working as play reader for the Royal Court Theater before returning to Nigeria in 1959, where his first play, *The Lion and the Jewel*, was produced. In the course of the next decade, Soyinka wrote an important body of dramatic work, including the plays *The Invention* (1959), *A Dance of the Forests* (1960), *The Trials of Brother Jero* (1960), *Camwood on the Leaves* (radio play, 1960), *The Strong Breed* (1964), *Kongi's Harvest* (1964), and *The Road* (1965). He also taught at the universities of Ibadan, Ife, and Lagos, and founded two important theaters, the Orisun Theater and the 1960 Masks theater. Much of Soyinka's work is critical of authoritarian politics; he was arrested in 1967 and held as a political prisoner until 1969. Soyinka's memoir of imprisonment, *The Man Died*, was published in 1972 and was cited for excellence by Amnesty International. In the 1970s, Soyinka continued to write plays examining the tensions of tribal life in modern Africa: *Madmen and Specialists* (1970) and *Death and the King's Horseman* (1976). He also wrote plays more directly examining contemporary African politics: his rewriting of Brecht's *Threepenny Opera* as *Opera Wonyosi* (1977), and *A Play of Giants* (1985). He also wrote an adaptation of Euripides' *The Bacchae* (1973), placing the Greek narrative in a more explicitly tribal and ritualistic setting. Soyinka was awarded the Nobel Prize in 1986, the first African writer to receive the prize for literature.

DEATH AND THE KING'S HORSEMAN

Soyinka is sometimes criticized by other African writers for being too oriented toward Europe. Not only are some of his plays adaptations or imitations of European works, but Soyinka has continued to write in English—the language of the colonial power, after all—rather than writing in his native language, Yoruba. It is precisely this tension between village and metropolis, between Africa and Europe, that provides the springboard for some of Soyinka's greatest work and dramatizes the challenges of cross-cultural interaction in the complex contemporary political environment.

Death and the King's Horseman is based on events that took place in the Yoruba city of Oyo in 1946. The play opens on the day the local African king is to be buried. According to custom, his Horseman, Elesin Oba, will die on this day as well, following his master in death as he followed him in life. It is clear from the scene in the marketplace that this ritual death is, however, a celebration. The village enacts a festive and playful marriage between Elesin and a new, young bride, so that he can procreate before he dies, bringing new life into the world even as he passes out of it.

In *Death and the King's Horseman*, indigenous African culture operates within the more restricted sphere of Britain's colonial values, laws, and institutions. The region's colonial administrator, Simon Pilkings, who is on his way to a masquerade to celebrate the arrival of the Prince, acts to stop Elesin's death. However, Pilkings and his wife are wearing African ceremonial costumes of the dead to the English masquerade, a decision that is not only offensive and irreligious to the Africans they meet, but that marks their complete incomprehension of the complex situation in which they find themselves. Wearing the costume also marks the Pilkingses, and the colonial British as a whole, as figures of death, in contrast to the paradoxical life celebrated by Elesin.

Pilkings "saves" Elesin and brings about the play's tragic catastrophe. For Elesin's son Olunde—studying medicine in Britain—returns to perform funeral rites for his father. However, when Elesin is prevented from dying, it becomes clear that colonial intervention has destroyed what it attempted to protect. Olunde, too, is dishonored when his father remains alive and takes the only possible course of action.

In his note to the play, Soyinka criticizes the phrase "clash of cultures" to describe his work, for it "presupposes a potential equality *in every given situation* of the alien culture and the indigenous." In *Death and the King's Horseman*, the power vested in the colonial administration signals its ability to destroy the indigenous culture it claims, ironically, to govern.

AUTHOR'S NOTE

This play is based on events which took place in Oyo, ancient Yoruba city of Nigeria, in 1946. That year, the lives of Elesin (Olori Elesin), his son, and the Colonial District Officer intertwined with the disastrous results set out in the play. The changes I have made are in matters of detail, sequence and of course characterisation. The action has also been set back two or three years to while the war was still on, for minor reasons of dramaturgy.

The factual account still exists in the archives of the British Colonial Administration. It has already inspired a fine play in Yoruba (Oba Wàjà) by Duro Ladipo. It has also misbegotten a film by some German television company.

The bane of themes of this genre is that they are no sooner employed creatively than they acquire the facile tag of 'clash of cultures', a prejudicial label which, quite apart from its frequent misapplication, presupposes a potential equality *in every given situation* of the alien culture and the indigenous, on the actual soil of the latter. (In the area of misapplication, the overseas prize for illiteracy and mental conditioning undoubtedly goes to the blurb-writer for the American edition of my novel *Season of Anomy* who unblushingly declares that this work portrays the 'clash between old values and new ways, between western methods and African traditions'!) It is thanks to this kind of perverse mentality that I find it necessary to caution the would-be producer of this play against a sadly familiar reductionist tendency, and to direct his vision instead to the far more difficult and risky task of eliciting the play's threnodic essence.

One of the more obvious alternative structures of the play would be to make the District Officer the victim of a cruel dilemma. This is not to my taste and it is not by chance that I have avoided dialogue or situation which would encourage this. No attempt should be made in production to suggest it. The Colonial Factor is an incident, a catalytic incident merely. The confrontation in the play is largely metaphysical, contained in the human vehicle which is Elesin and the universe of the Yoruba mind—the world of the living, the dead and the unborn, and the numinous passage which links all: transition. *Death and the King's Horseman* can be fully realised only through an evocation of music from the abyss of transition.

Wole Soyinka

DEATH AND THE KING'S HORSEMAN

Wole Soyinka

— CHARACTERS —

PRAISE-SINGER
ELESIN, *Horseman of the King*
IYALOJA, *'Mother' of the market*
SIMON PILKINGS, *District Officer*
JANE PILKINGS, *his wife*
SERGEANT AMUSA
JOSEPH, *houseboy to the Pilkingses*
BRIDE

H.R.H. THE PRINCE
THE RESIDENT
AIDE-DE-CAMP
OLUNDE, *eldest son of Elesin*
DRUMMERS, WOMEN, YOUNG GIRLS, DANCERS *at the Ball*

The play should run without an interval. For rapid scene changes, one adjustable outline set is very appropriate.

— ONE —

A passage through a market in its closing stages. The stalls are being emptied, mats folded. A few women pass through on their way home, loaded with baskets. On a cloth-stand, bolts of cloth are taken down, display pieces folded and piled on a tray. ELESIN OBA *enters along a passage before the market, pursued by his* DRUMMERS *and* PRAISE-SINGERS. *He is a man of enormous vitality, speaks, dances and sings with that infectious enjoyment of life which accompanies all his actions.*

PRAISE-SINGER: Elesin o! Elesin Oba! Howu! What tryst is this the cockerel goes to keep with such haste that he must leave his tail behind?

ELESIN: *(Slows down a bit, laughing.)* A tryst where the cock-
5 erel needs no adornment.

PRAISE-SINGER: O-oh, you hear that my companions? That's the way the world goes. Because the man approaches a brand-new bride he forgets the long faithful mother of his children.

10 ELESIN: When the horse sniffs the stable does he not strain at the bridle? The market is the long-suffering home of my spirit and the women are packing up to go. That Esu-harrassed day slipped into the stewpot while we feasted. We ate it up with the rest of the meat. I have neglected my women.

15 PRAISE-SINGER: We know all that. Still it's no reason for shedding your tail on this day of all days. I know the women will cover you in damask and *alari* but when the wind blows cold from behind, that's when the fowl knows his true friends.

ELESIN: Olohun-iyo!

20 PRAISE-SINGER: Are you sure there will be one like me on the other side?

ELESIN: Olohun-iyo!

PRAISE-SINGER: Far be it for me to belittle the dwellers of that place but, a man is either born to his art or he isn't. And I
25 don't know for certain that you'll meet my father, so who is going to sing these deeds in accents that will pierce the deafness of the ancient ones. I have prepared my going—just tell me: Olohun-iyo, I need you on this journey and I shall be behind you.

ELESIN: You're like a jealous wife. Stay close to me, but only 30 on this side. My fame, my honour are legacies to the living; stay behind and let the world sip its honey from your lips.

PRAISE-SINGER: Your name will be like the sweet berry a child places under his tongue to sweeten the passage of food. The world will never spit it out. 35

ELESIN: Come then. This market is my roost. When I come among the women I am a chicken with a hundred mothers. I become a monarch whose palace is built with tenderness and beauty.

PRAISE-SINGER: They love to spoil you but beware. The hands 40 of women also weaken the unwary.

ELESIN: This night I'll lay my head upon their lap and go to sleep. This night I'll touch feet with their feet in a dance that is no longer of this earth. But the smell of their flesh, their sweat, the smell of indigo on their cloth, this is the last air I 45 wish to breathe as I go to meet my great forebears.

PRAISE-SINGER: In their time the world was never tilted from its groove, it shall not be in yours.

ELESIN: The gods have said No.

PRAISE-SINGER: In their time the great wars came and went, 50 the little wars came and went; the white slavers came and went, they took away the heart of our race, they bore away the mind and muscle of our race. The city fell and was rebuilt; the city fell and our people trudged through mountain and forest to found a new home but—Elesin Oba do you 55 hear me?

ELESIN: I hear your voice Olohun-iyo.

PRAISE-SINGER: Our world was never wrenched from its true course.

ELESIN: The gods have said No. 60

PRAISE-SINGER: There is only one home to the life of a river-mussel; there is only one home to the life of a tortoise; there is only one shell to the soul of man: there is only one world to the spirit of our race. If that world leaves its course and smashes on boulders of the great void, whose world will give 65 us shelter?

ELESIN: It did not in the time of my forebears, it shall not in mine.

Note to this edition: Certain Yoruba words which appear in italics in the text are explained in a brief glossary at the end of the play.

PRAISE-SINGER: The cockerel must not be seen without his
70   feathers.
ELESIN: Nor will the Not-I bird be much longer without his
    nest.
PRAISE-SINGER: (*Stopped in his lyric stride.*) The Not-I bird,
    Elesin?
75 ELESIN: I said, the Not-I bird.
PRAISE-SINGER: All respect to our elders but, is there really
    such a bird?
ELESIN: What! Could it be that he failed to knock on your
    door?
80 PRAISE-SINGER: (*Smiling.*) Elesin's riddles are not merely the
    nut in the kernel that breaks human teeth; he also buries the
    kernel in hot embers and dares a man's fingers to draw it out.
ELESIN: I am sure he called on you, Olohun-iyo. Did you hide
    in the loft and push out the servant to tell him you were out?

(ELESIN *executes a brief, half-taunting dance. The* DRUMMER
moves in and draws a rhythm out of his steps. ELESIN *dances to-*
wards the market-place as he chants the story of the Not-I bird,
his voice changing dexterously to mimic his characters. He per-
forms like a born raconteur, infecting his retinue with his hu-
mour and energy. More women arrive during his recital,
including IYALOJA.)

85   Death came calling.
    Who does not know his rasp of reeds?
    A twilight whisper in the leaves before
    The great araba falls? Did you hear it?
    Not I! swears the farmer. He snaps
90   His fingers round his head, abandons
    A hard-worn harvest and begins
    A rapid dialogue with his legs.

    'Not I,' shouts the fearless hunter, 'but—
    It's getting dark, and this night-lamp
95   Has leaked out all its oil. I think
    It's best to go home and resume my hunt
    Another day.' But now he pauses, suddenly
    Lets out a wail: 'Oh foolish mouth, calling
    Down a curse on your own head! Your lamp
100   Has leaked out all its oil, has it?'
    Forwards or backwards now he dare not move.
    To search for leaves and make *etutu*
    On that spot? Or race home to the safety
    Of his hearth? Ten market-days have passed
105   My friends, and still he's rooted there
    Rigid as the plinth of Orayan.

    The mouth of the courtesan barely
    Opened wide enough to take a ha' penny *robo*
    When she wailed: 'Not I.' All dressed she was
110   To call upon my friend the Chief Tax Officer.
    But now she sends her go-between instead:
    'Tell him I'm ill: my period has come suddenly
    But not—I hope—my time.'

    Why is the pupil crying?
115   His hapless head was made to taste
    The knuckles of my friend the Mallam:
    'If you were then reciting the Koran
    Would you have ears for idle noises
    Darkening the trees, you child of ill omen?'
120   He shuts down school before its time

    Runs home and rings himself with amulets.
    And take my good kinsman Ifawomi.
    His hands were like a carver's, strong
    And true. I saw them
    Tremble like wet wings of a fowl   125
    One day he cast his time-smoothed *opele*
    Across the divination board. And all because
    The suppliant looked him in the eye and asked,
    'Did you hear that whisper in the leaves?'
    'Not I,' was his reply; 'perhaps I'm growing deaf—   130
    Good-day.' And Ifa spoke no more that day
    The priest locked fast his doors,
    Sealed up his leaking roof—but wait!
    This sudden care was not for Fawomi
    But for Osanyin, courier-bird of Ifa's   135
    Heart of wisdom. I did not know a kite
    Was hovering in the sky
    And Ifa now a twittering chicken in
    The brood of Fawomi the Mother Hen.

    Ah, but I must not forget my evening   140
    Courier from the abundant palm, whose groan
    Became Not I, as he constipated down
    A wayside bush. He wonders if Elegbara
    Has tricked his buttocks to discharge
    Against a sacred grove. Hear him   145
    Mutter spells to ward off penalties
    For an abomination he did not intend.
    If any here
    Stumbles on a gourd of wine, fermenting
    Near the road, and nearby hears a stream   150
    Of spells issuing from a crouching form.
    Brother to a *sigidi*, bring home my wine,
    Tell my tapper I have ejected
    Fear from home and farm. Assure him,
    All is well.   155
PRAISE-SINGER: In your time we do not doubt the peace of
    farmstead and home, the peace of road and hearth, we do
    not doubt the peace of the forest.
ELESIN: There was fear in the forest too.
    Not-I was lately heard even in the lair   160
    Of beasts. The hyena cackled loud Not I,
    The civet twitched his fiery tail and glared:
    Not I. Not-I became the answering-name
    Of the restless bird, that little one
    Whom Death found nesting in the leaves   165
    When whisper of his coming ran
    Before him on the wind. Not-I
    Has long abandoned home. This same dawn
    I heard him twitter in the gods' abode.
    Ah, companions of this living world   170
    What a thing this is, that even those
    We call immortal
    Should fear to die.
IYALOJA: But you, husband of multitudes?
ELESIN: I, when that Not-I bird perched   175
    Upon my roof, bade him seek his nest again,
    Safe, without care or fear. I unrolled
    My welcome mat for him to see. Not-I
    Flew happily away, you'll hear his voice
    No more in this lifetime—You all know   180
    What I am.

PRAISE-SINGER: That rock which turns its open lodes
    Into the path of lightning. A gay
    Thoroughbred whose sudden disdains
185   To falter though an adder reared
    Suddenly in his path.
ELESIN: My rein is loosened.
    I am master of my Fate. When the hour comes
    Watch me dance along the narrowing path
190   Glazed by the soles of my great precursors.
    My soul is eager. I shall not turn aside.
WOMEN: You will not delay?
ELESIN: Where the storm pleases, and when, it directs
    The giants of the forest. When friendship summons
195   Is when the true comrade goes.
WOMEN: Nothing will hold you back?
ELESIN: Nothing. What! Has no one told you yet?
    I go to keep my friend and master company.
    Who says the mouth does not believe in
200   'No, I have chewed all that before?' I say I have.
    The world is not a constant honey-pot.
    Where I found little I made do with little.
    Where there was plenty I gorged myself.
    My master's hands and mine have always
205   Dipped together and, home or sacred feast,
    The bowl was beaten bronze, the meats
    So succulent our teeth accused us of neglect.
    We shared the choicest of the season's
    Harvest of yams. How my friend would read
210   Desire in my eyes before I knew the cause—
    However rare, however precious, it was mine.
WOMEN: The town, the very land was yours.
ELESIN: The world was mine. Our joint hands
    Raised houseposts of trust that withstood
215   The siege of envy and the termites of time.
    But the twilight hour brings bats and rodents—
    Shall I yield them cause to foul the rafters?
PRAISE-SINGER: Elesin Oba! Are you not that man who
    Looked out of doors that stormy day
220   The god of luck limped by, drenched
    To the very lice that held
    His rags together? You took pity upon
    His sores and wished him fortune.
    Fortune was footloose this dawn, he replied,
225   Till you trapped him in a heartfelt wish
    That now returns to you. Elesin Oba!
    I say you are that man who
    Chanced upon the calabash of honour
    You thought it was palm wine and
230   Drained its contents to the final drop.
ELESIN: Life has an end. A life that will outlive
    Fame and friendship begs another name.
    What elder takes his tongue to his plate,
    Licks it clean of every crumb? He will encounter
235   Silence when he calls on children to fulfill
    The smallest errand! Life is honour.
    It ends when honour ends.
WOMEN: We know you for a man of honour.
ELESIN: Stop! Enough of that!
240 WOMEN: (*Puzzled, they whisper among themselves, turning
    mostly to* IYALOJA.) What is it? Did we say something to give
    offense? Have we slighted him in some way?

ELESIN: Enough of that sound I say. Let me hear no more in
    that vein. I've heard enough.
IYALOJA: We must have said something wrong. (*Comes forward*   245
    a little.) Elesin Oba, we ask forgiveness before you speak.
ELESIN: I am bitterly offended.
IYALOJA: Our unworthiness has betrayed us. All we can do is
    ask your forgiveness. Correct us like a kind father.
ELESIN: This day of all days . . .   250
IYALOJA: It does not bear thinking. If we offend you now we
    have mortified the gods. We offend heaven itself. Father of
    us all, tell us where we went astray. (*She kneels, the other
    women follow.*)
ELESIN: Are you not ashamed? Even a tear-veiled   255
    Eye preserves its function of sight.
    Because my mind was raised to horizons
    Even the boldest man lowers his gaze
    In thinking of, must my body here
    Be taken for a vagrant's?   260
IYALOJA: Horseman of the King, I am more baffled than ever.
PRAISE-SINGER: The strictest father unbends his brow when
    the child is penitent, Elesin. When time is short, we do not
    spend it prolonging the riddle. Their shoulders are bowed
    with the weight of fear lest they have marred your day be-   265
    yond repair. Speak now in plain words and let us pursue the
    ailment to the home of remedies.
ELESIN: Words are cheap. 'We know you for
    A man of honour.' Well tell me, is this how
    A man of honour should be seen?   270
    Are these not the same clothes in which
    I came among you a full half-hour ago?

(*He roars with laughter and the* WOMEN, *relieved, rise and rush
into stalls to fetch rich cloths.*)

WOMAN: The gods are kind. A fault soon remedied is soon for-
    given. Elesin Oba, even as we match our words with deed,
    let your heart forgive us completely.   275
ELESIN: You who are breath and giver of my being
    How shall I dare refuse you forgiveness
    Even if the offence were real.
IYALOJA: (*Dancing round him. Sings.*)

             He forgives us. He forgives us.   280
             What a fearful thing it is when
             The voyager sets forth
             But a curse remains behind.

WOMEN: For a while we truly feared
    Our hands had wrenched the world adrift   285
    In emptiness.
IYALOJA: Richly, richly, robe him richly
    The cloth of honour is *alari*
    Sanyan is the band of friendship
    Boa-skin makes slippers of esteem.   290
WOMEN: For a while we truly feared
    Our hands had wrenched the world adrift
    In emptiness.
PRAISE-SINGER: He who must, must voyage forth
    The world will not roll backwards   295
    It is he who must, with one
    Great gesture overtake the world.

WOMEN: For a while we truly feared
    Our hands had wrenched the world
300   In emptiness.
PRAISE-SINGER: The gourd you bear is not for shirking.
    The gourd is not for setting down
    At the first crossroad or wayside grove.
    Only one river may know its contents.
305 WOMEN: We shall all meet at the great market
    We shall all meet at the great market
    He who goes early takes the best bargains
    But we shall meet, and resume our banter.

(ELESIN stands resplendent in rich clothes, cap, shawl, etc. His sash is of a bright red alari cloth. The WOMEN dance round him. Suddenly, his attention is caught by an object off-stage.)

ELESIN: The world I know is good.
310 WOMEN: We know you'll leave it so.
ELESIN: The world I know is the bounty
    Of hives after bees have swarmed.
    No goodness teems with such open hands
    Even in the dreams of deities.
315 WOMEN: And we know you'll leave it so.
ELESIN: I was born to keep it so. A hive
    Is never known to wander. An anthill
    Does not desert its roots. We cannot see
    The still great womb of the world—
320   No man beholds his mother's womb—
    Yet who denies it's there? Coiled
    To the navel of the world is that
    Endless cord that links us all
    To the great origin. If I lose my way
325   The trailing cord will bring me to the roots.
WOMEN: The world is in your hands.

(The earlier distraction, a beautiful young girl, comes along the passage through which ELESIN first made his entry.)

ELESIN: I embrace it. And let me tell you, women—
    I like this farewell that the world designed,
    Unless my eyes deceive me, unless
330   We are already parted, the world and I,
    And all that breeds desire is lodged
    Among our tireless ancestors. Tell me friends,
    Am I still earthed in that beloved market
    Of my youth? Or could it be my will
335   Has outleapt the conscious act and I have come
    Among the great departed?
PRAISE-SINGER: Elesin-Oba why do your eyes roll like a bush-
    rat who sees his fate like his father's spirit, mirrored in the
    eye of a snake? And all these questions! You're standing on
340   the same earth you've always stood upon. This voice you
    hear is mine, Oluhun-iyo, not that of an acolyte in heaven.
ELESIN: How can that be? In all my life
    As Horseman of the King, the juiciest
    Fruit on every tree was mine. I saw,
345   I touched, I wooed, rarely was the answer No.
    The honour of my place, the veneration I
    Received in the eye of man or woman
    Prospered my suit and
    Played havoc with my sleeping hours.

    And they tell me my eyes were a hawk   350
    In perpetual hunger. Split an iroko tree
    In two, hide a woman's beauty in its heartwood
    And seal it up again—Elesin, journeying by,
    Would make his camp beside that tree
    Of all the shades in the forest.   355
PRAISE-SINGER: Who would deny your reputation, snake-on-
    the-loose in dark passages of the market! Bed-bug who wages
    war on the mat and receives the thanks of the vanquished!
    When caught with his bride's own sister he protested—but I
    was only prostrating myself to her as becomes a grateful in-   360
    law. Hunter who carries his powder-horn on the hips and
    fires crouching or standing! Warrior who never makes that
    excuse of the whining coward—but how can I go to battle
    without my trousers?—trouserless or shirtless it's all one to
    him. Oka-rearing-from-a-camouflage-of-leaves, before he   365
    strikes the victim is already prone! Once they told him,
    Howu, a stallion does not feed on the grass beneath him: he
    replied, true, but surely he can roll on it!
WOMEN: Ba-a-a-ba O!
PRAISE-SINGER: Ah, but listen yet. You know there is the leaf-   370
    knibbling grub and there is the cola-chewing beetle; the
    leaf-nibbling grub lives on the leaf, the cola-chewing beetle
    lives in the colanut. Don't we know what our man feeds on
    when we find him cocooned in a woman's wrapper?
ELESIN: Enough, enough, you all have cause   375
    To know me well. But, if you say this earth
    Is still the same as gave birth to those songs,
    Tell me who was that goddess through whose lips
    I saw the ivory pebbles of Oya's river-bed.
    Iyaloja, who is she? I saw her enter   380
    Your stall; all your daughters I know well.
    No, not even Ogun-of-the-farm toiling
    Dawn till dusk on his tuber patch
    Not even Ogun with the finest hoe he ever
    Forged at the anvil could have shaped   385
    That rise of buttocks, not though he had
    The richest earth between his fingers.
    Her wrapper was no disguise
    For thighs whose ripples shamed the river's
    Coils around the hills of Ilesi. Her eyes   390
    Were new-laid eggs glowing in the dark.
    Her skin . . .
IYALOJA: Elesin Oba . . .
ELESIN: What! Where do you all say I am?
IYALOJA: Still among the living.   395
ELESIN: And that radiance which so suddenly
    Lit up this market I could boast
    I knew so well?
IYALOJA: Has one step already in her husband's home. She is
    betrothed.   400
ELESIN: *(Irritated.)* Why do you tell me that?

(IYALOJA falls silent. The women shuffle uneasily.)

IYALOJA: Not because we dare give you offence Elesin. Today
    is your day and the whole world is yours. Still, even those
    who leave town to make a new dwelling elsewhere like to be
    remembered by what they leave behind.   405
ELESIN: Who does not seek to be remembered?
    Memory is Master of Death, the chink

In his armour of conceit. I shall leave
That which makes my going the sheerest
410   Dream of an afternoon. Should voyagers
Not travel light? Let the considerate traveller
Shed, of his excessive load, all
That may benefit the living.
WOMEN: *(Relieved.)* Ah Elesin Oba, we knew you for a man of
415   honour.
ELESIN: Then honour me. I deserve a bed of honour to lie
upon.
IYALOJA: The best is yours. We know you for a man of honour.
You are not one who eats and leaves nothing on his plate for
420   children. Did you not say it yourself? Not one who blights
the happiness of others for a moment's pleasure.
ELESIN: Who speaks of pleasure? O women, listen!
Pleasure palls. Our acts should have meaning.
The sap of the plantain never dries.
425   You have seen the young shoot swelling
Even as the parent stalk begins to wither.
Women, let my going be likened to
The twilight hour of the plantain.
WOMEN: What does he mean Iyaloja? This language is the
430   language of our elders, we do not fully grasp it.
IYALOJA: I dare not understand you yet Elesin.
ELESIN: All you who stand before the spirit that dares
The opening of the last door of passage,
Dare to rid my going of regrets! My wish
435   Transcends the blotting out of thought
In one mere moment's tremor of the senses.
Do me credit. And do me honour.
I am girded for the route beyond
Burdens of waste and longing.
440   Then let me travel light. Let
Seed that will not serve the stomach
On the way remain behind. Let it take root
In the earth of my choice, in this earth
I leave behind.
445   IYALOJA: *(Turns to* WOMEN.*)* The voice I hear is already
touched by the waiting fingers of our departed. I dare not
refuse.
WOMAN: Buy Iyaloja . . .
IYALOJA: The matter is no longer in our hands.
450   WOMAN: But she is betrothed to your own son. Tell him.
IYALOJA: My son's wish is mine. I did the asking for him, the
loss can be remedied. But who will remedy the blight of
closed hands on the day when all should be openness and
light? Tell him, you say! You wish that I burden him with
455   knowledge that will sour his wish and lay regrets on the last
moments of his mind. You pray to him who is your interces-
sor to the other world—don't set this world adrift in your own
time; would you rather it was my hand whose sacrilege
wrenched it loose?
460   WOMAN: Not many men will brave the curse of a dispossessed
husband.
IYALOJA: Only the curses of the departed are to be feared. The
claims of one whose foot is on the threshold of their abode
surpasses even the claims of blood. It is impiety even to place
465   hindrances in their ways.
ELESIN: What do my mothers say? Shall I step
Burdened into the unknown?

IYALOJA: Not we, but the very earth says No. The sap in the
plantain does not dry. Let grain that will not feed the voyager
at his passage drop here and take root as he steps beyond this   470
earth and us. Oh you who fill the home from hearth to
threshold with the voices of children, you who now bestride
the hidden gulf and pause to draw the right foot across and
into the resting-home of the great forebears, it is good that
your loins be drained into the earth we know, that your last   475
strength be ploughed back into the womb that gave you
being.
PRAISE-SINGER: Iyaloja, mother of multitudes in the teeming
market of the world, how your wisdom transfigures you!
IYALOJA: *(Smiling broadly, completely reconciled.)* Elesin, even   480
at the narrow end of the passage I know you will look back
and sigh a last regret for the flesh that flashed past your spirit
in flight. You always had a restless eye. Your choice has my
blessing. *(To the* WOMEN.*)* Take the good news to our daughter and make her ready. *(Some* WOMEN *go off.)*   485
ELESIN: Your eyes were clouded at first.
IYALOJA: Not for long. It is those who stand at the gateway of
the great change to whose cry we must pay heed. And then,
think of this—it makes the mind tremble. The fruit of such a
union is rare. It will be neither of this world nor of the next.   490
Nor of the one behind us. As if the timelessness of the ancestor world and the unborn have joined spirits to wring an
issue of the elusive being of passage . . . Elesin!
ELESIN: I am here. What is it?
IYALOJA: Did you hear all I said just now?   495
ELESIN: Yes.
IYALOJA: The living must eat and drink. When the moment
comes, don't turn the food to rodents' droppings in their
mouth. Don't let them taste the ashes of the world when they
step out at dawn to breathe the morning dew.   500
ELESIN: This doubt is unworthy of you Iyaloja.
IYALOJA: Eating the awusa nut is not so difficult as drinking
water afterwards.
ELESIN: The waters of the bitter stream are honey to a man
Whose tongue has savoured all.   505
IYALOJA: No one knows when the ants desert their home; they
leave the mound intact. The swallow is never seen to peck
holes in its nest when it is time to move with the season.
There are always throngs of humanity behind the leave-
taker. The rain should not come through the roof for them,   510
the wind must not blow through the walls at night.
ELESIN: I refuse to take offence.
IYALOJA: You wish to travel light. Well, the earth is yours. But
be sure the seed you leave in it attracts no curse.
ELESIN: You really mistake my person Iyaloja.   515
IYALOJA: I said nothing. Now we must go prepare your bridal
chamber. Then these same hands will lay your shrouds.
ELESIN: *(Exasperated.)* Must you be so blunt? *(Recovers.)*
Well, weave your shrouds, but let the fingers of my bride seal
my eyelids with earth and wash my body.   520
IYALOJA: Prepare yourself Elesin.

*(She gets up to leave. At that moment the women return, leading
the* BRIDE. ELESIN's *face glows with pleasure. He flicks the
sleeves of his agbada with renewed confidence and steps forward
to meet the group. As the girl kneels before* IYALOJA, *lights fade
out on the scene.)*

— TWO —

The verandah of the District Officer's bungalow. A tango is play-ing from an old hand-cranked gramophone and, glimpsed through the wide windows and doors which open onto the fore-stage verandah are the shapes of SIMON PILKINGS *and his wife,* JANE, *tangoing in and out of shadows in the living-room. They were wearing what is immediately apparent as some form of fancy-dress. The dance goes on for some moments and then the figure of a 'Native Administration' policeman emerges and climbs up the steps onto the verandah. He peeps through and ob-serves the dancing couple, reacting with what is obviously a long-standing bewilderment. He stiffens suddenly, his expression changes to one of disbelief and horror. In his excitement he up-sets a flower-pot and attracts the attention of the couple. They stop dancing.*

PILKINGS: Is there anyone out there?

JANE: I'll turn off the gramophone.

PILKINGS: *(Approaching the verandah.)* I'm sure I heard some-thing fall over. *(The constable retreats slowly, open-mouthed*
5 *as* PILKINGS *approaches the verandah.)* Oh it's you Amusa. Why didn't you just knock instead of knocking things over?

AMUSA: *(Stammers badly and points a shaky finger at his dress.)* Mista Pirinkin . . . Mista Pirinkin . . .

PILKINGS: What is the matter with you?

10 JANE: *(Emerging.)* Who is it dear? Oh, Amusa . . .

PILKINGS: Yes it's Amusa, and acting most strangely.

AMUSA: *(His attention now transferred to* MRS PILKINGS.*)* Mammadam . . . you too!

PILKINGS: What the hell is the matter with you man!

15 JANE: Your costume darling. Our fancy dress.

PILKINGS: Oh hell, I'd forgotten all about that. *(Lifts the face mask over his head showing his face. His wife follows suit.)*

JANE: I think you've shocked his big pagan heart bless him.

PILKINGS: Nonsense, he's a Moslem. Come on Amusa, you
20 don't believe in all this nonsense do you? I thought you were a good Moslem.

AMUSA: Mista Pirinkin, I beg you sir, what you think you do with that dress? It belong to dead cult, not for human being.

PILKINGS: Oh Amusa, what a let down you are. I swear by you
25 at the club you know—thank God for Amusa, he doesn't be-lieve in any mumbo-jumbo. And now look at you!

AMUSA: Mista Pirinkin, I beg you, take it off. Is not good for man like you to touch that cloth.

PILKINGS: Well, I've got it on. And what's more Jane and I
30 have bet on it we're taking first prize at the ball. Now, if you can just pull yourself together and tell me what you wanted to see me about . . .

AMUSA: Sir, I cannot talk this matter to you in that dress. I no fit.

35 PILKINGS: What's that rubbish again?

JANE: He is dead earnest too Simon. I think you'll have to handle this delicately.

PILKINGS: Delicately my. . . ! Look here Amusa, I think this lit-tle joke has gone far enough hm? Let's have some sense. You
40 seem to forget that you are a police officer in the service of His Majesty's Government. I order you to report your busi-ness at once or face disciplinary action.

AMUSA: Sir, it is a matter of death. How can man talk against death to person in uniform of death? Is like talking against

government to person in uniform of police. Please sir, I go 45 and come back.

PILKINGS: *(Roars.)* Now! (AMUSA *switches his gaze to the ceil-ing suddenly, remains mute.)*

JANE: Oh Amusa, what is there to be scared of in the costume? You saw it confiscated last month from those *egungun* men 50 who were creating trouble in town. You helped arrest the cult leaders yourself—if the juju didn't harm you at the time how could it possibly harm you now? And merely by looking at it?

AMUSA: *(Without looking down.)* Madam, I arrest the ring- 55 leaders who make trouble but me I no touch *egungun*. That *egungun* insef, I no touch. And I no abuse 'am. I arrest ring-leader but I treat *egungun* with respect.

PILKINGS: It's hopeless. We'll merely end up missing the best part of the ball. When they get this way there is nothing you 60 can do. It's simply hammering against a brick wall. Write your report or whatever it is on that pad Amusa and take yourself out of here. Come on Jane. We only upset his deli-cate sensibilities by remaining here.

*(*AMUSA *waits for them to leave, then writes in the notebook, somewhat laboriously. Drumming from the direction of the town wells up.* AMUSA *listens, makes a movement as if he wants to re-call* PILKINGS *but changes his mind. Completes his note and goes. A few moments later* PILKINGS *emerges, picks up the pad and reads.)*

PILKINGS: Jane! 65

JANE: *(From the bedroom.)* Coming darling. Nearly ready.

PILKINGS: Never mind being ready, just listen to this.

JANE: What is it?

PILKINGS: Amusa's report. Listen. 'I have to report that it come to my information that one prominent chief, namely, the 70 Elesin Oba, is to commit death tonight as a result of native custom. Because this is criminal offence I await further in-struction at charge office. Sergeant Amusa.'

*(*JANE *comes out onto the verandah while he is reading.)*

JANE: Did I hear you say commit death?

PILKINGS: Obviously he means murder. 75

JANE: You mean a ritual murder?

PILKINGS: Must be. You think you've stamped it all out but it's always lurking under the surface somewhere.

JANE: Oh. Does it mean we are not getting to the ball at all?

PILKINGS: No-o. I'll have the man arrested. Everyone remotely 80 involved. In any case there may be nothing to it. Just ru-mours.

JANE: Really? I thought you found Amusa's rumours generally reliable.

PILKINGS: That's true enough. But who knows what may have 85 been giving him the scare lately. Look at his conduct tonight.

JANE: *(Laughing.)* You have to admit he had his own peculiar logic. *(Deepens her voice.)* How can man talk against death to person in uniform of death? *(Laughs.)* Anyway, you can't 90 go into the police station dressed like that.

PILKINGS: I'll send Joseph with instructions. Damn it, what a confounded nuisance!

JANE: But don't you think you should talk first to the man, Simon? 95

PILKINGS: Do you want to go to the ball or not?

JANE: Darling, why are you getting rattled? I was only trying to be intelligent. It seems hardly fair just to lock up a man— and a chief at that—simply on the er . . . what is that legal word again?—uncorroborated word of a sergeant.

PILKINGS: Well, that's easily decided. Joseph!

JOSEPH: *(From within.)* Yes master.

PILKINGS: You're quite right of course, I am getting rattled. Probably the effect of those bloody drums. Do you hear how they go on and on?

JANE: I wondered when you'd notice. Do you suppose it has something to do with this affair?

PILKINGS: Who knows? They always find an excuse for making a noise . . . *(Thoughtfully.)* Even so . . .

JANE: Yes Simon?

PILKINGS: It's different Jane. I don't think I've heard this particular —sound—before. Something unsettling about it.

JANE: I thought all bush drumming sounded the same.

PILKINGS: Don't tease me now Jane. This may be serious.

JANE: I'm sorry. *(Gets up and throws her arms around his neck. Kisses him. The houseboy enters, retreats and knocks.)*

PILKINGS: *(Wearily.)* Oh, come in Joseph! I don't know where you pick up all these elephantine notions of tact. Come over here.

JOSEPH: Sir?

PILKINGS: Joseph, are you a christian or not?

JOSEPH: Yessir.

PILKINGS: Does seeing me in this outfit bother you?

JOSEPH: No sir, it has no power.

PILKINGS: Thank God for some sanity at last. Now Joseph, answer me on the honour of a christian—what is supposed to be going on in town tonight?

JOSEPH: Tonight sir? You mean that chief who is going to kill himself?

PILKINGS: What?

JANE: What do you mean, kill himself?

PILKINGS: You do mean he is going to kill somebody don't you?

JOSEPH: No master. He will not kill anybody and no one will kill him. He will simply die.

JANE: But why Joseph?

JOSEPH: It is native law and custom. The King die last month. Tonight is his burial. But before they can bury him, the Elesin must die so as to accompany him to heaven.

PILKINGS: I seem to be fated to clash more often with that man than with any of the other chiefs.

JOSEPH: He is the King's Chief Horseman.

PILKINGS: *(In a resigned way.)* I know.

JANE: Simon, what's the matter?

PILKINGS: It would have to be him!

JANE: Who is he?

PILKINGS: Don't you remember? He's that chief with whom I had a scrap some three or four years ago. I helped his son get to a medical school in England, remember? He fought tooth and nail to prevent it.

JANE: Oh now I remember. He was that very sensitive young man. What was his name again?

PILKINGS: Olunde. Haven't replied to his last letter come to think of it. The old pagan wanted him to stay and carry on some family tradition or the other. Honestly I couldn't understand the fuss he made. I literally had to help the boy escape from close confinement and load him onto the next boat. A most intelligent boy, really bright.

JANE: I rather thought he was much too sensitive you know. The kind of person you feel should be a poet munching rose petals in Bloomsbury.

PILKINGS: Well, he's going to make a first-class doctor. His mind is set on that. And as long as he wants my help he is welcome to it.

JANE: *(After a pause.)* Simon.

PILKINGS: Yes?

JANE: This boy, he was his eldest son wasn't he?

PILKINGS: I'm not sure. Who could tell with that old ram?

JANE: Do you know, Joseph?

JOSEPH: Oh yes madam. He was the eldest son. That's why Elesin cursed master good and proper. The eldest son is not supposed to travel away from the land.

JANE: *(Giggling.)* Is that true Simon? Did he really curse you good and proper?

PILKINGS: By all accounts I should be dead by now.

JOSEPH: Oh no, master is white man. And good christian. Black man juju can't touch master.

JANE: If he was his eldest, it means that he would be the Elesin to the next king. It's a family thing isn't it, Joseph?

JOSEPH: Yes madam. And if this Elesin had died before the King, his eldest son must take his place.

JANE: That would explain why the old chief was so mad you took the boy away.

PILKINGS: Well it makes me all the more happy I did.

JANE: I wonder if he knew.

PILKINGS: Who? Oh, you mean Olunde?

JANE: Yes. Was that why he was so determined to get away? I wouldn't stay if I knew I was trapped in such a horrible custom.

PILKINGS: *(Thoughtfully.)* No, I don't think he knew. At least he gave no indication. But you couldn't really tell with him. He was rather close you know, quite unlike most of them. Didn't give much away, not even to me.

JANE: Aren't they all rather close, Simon?

PILKINGS: These natives here? Good gracious. They'll open their mouths and yap with you about their family secrets before you can stop them. Only the other day . . .

JANE: But Simon, do they really give anything away? I mean, anything that really counts. This affair for instance, we didn't know they still practised that custom did we?

PILKINGS: Ye-e-es, I suppose you're right there. Sly, devious bastards.

JOSEPH: *(Stiffly.)* Can I go now master? I have to clean the kitchen.

PILKINGS: What? Oh, you can go. Forgot you were still here.

(JOSEPH goes.)

JANE: Simon, you really must watch your language. Bastard isn't just a simple swear-word in these parts, you know.

PILKINGS: Look, just when did you become a social anthropologist, that's what I'd like to know.

JANE: I'm not claiming to know anything. I just happen to have overheard quarrels among the servants. That's how I know they consider it a smear.

PILKINGS: I thought the extended family system took care of all that. Elastic family, no bastards.

JANE: *(Shrugs.)* Have it your own way.

(Awkward silence. The drumming increases in volume. JANE *gets up suddenly, restless.)*

That drumming Simon, do you think it might really be connected with this ritual? It's been going on all evening.

PILKINGS: Let's ask our native guide. Joseph! Just a minute Joseph. (JOSEPH *re-enters.)* What's the drumming about?

220 JOSEPH: I don't know master.

PILKINGS: What do you mean you don't know? It's only two years since your conversion. Don't tell me all that holy water nonsense also wiped out your tribal memory.

JOSEPH: *(Visibly shocked.)* Master!

225 JANE: Now you've done it.

PILKINGS: What have I done now?

JANE: Never mind. Listen Joseph, just tell me this. Is that drumming connected with dying or anything of that nature?

JOSEPH: Madam, this is what I am trying to say: I am not sure.
230 It sounds like the death of a great chief and then, it sounds like the wedding of a great chief. It really mix me up.

PILKINGS: Oh get back to the kitchen. A fat lot of help you are.

JOSEPH: Yes master. *(Goes.)*

JANE: Simon . . .

235 PILKINGS: Alright, alright. I'm in no mood for preaching.

JANE: It isn't my preaching you have to worry about, it's the preaching of the missionaries who preceded you here. When they make converts they really convert them. Calling holy water nonsense to our Joseph is really like insulting the Vir-
240 gin Mary before a Roman Catholic. He's going to hand in his notice tomorrow you mark my word.

PILKINGS: Now you're being ridiculous.

JANE: Am I? What are you willing to bet that tomorrow we are going to be without a steward-boy? Did you see his face?

245 PILKINGS: I am more concerned about whether or not we will be one native chief short by tomorrow. Christ! Just listen to those drums. *(He strides up and down, undecided.)*

JANE: *(Getting up.)* I'll change and make up some supper.

PILKINGS: What's that?

250 JANE: Simon, it's obvious we have to miss this ball.

PILKINGS: Nonsense. It's the first bit of real fun the European club has managed to organise for over a year, I'm damned if I'm going to miss it. And it is a rather special occasion. Doesn't happen every day.

255 JANE: You know this business has to be stopped Simon. And you are the only man who can do it.

PILKINGS: I don't have to stop anything. If they want to throw themselves off the top of a cliff or poison themselves for the sake of some barbaric custom what is that to me? If it were
260 ritual murder or something like that I'd be duty-bound to do something. I can't keep an eye on all the potential suicides in this province. And as for that man—believe me it's good riddance.

JANE: *(Laughs.)* I know you better than that Simon. You are
265 going to have to do something to stop it—after you've finished blustering.

PILKINGS: *(Shouts after her.)* And suppose after all it's only a wedding. I'd look a proper fool if I interrupted a chief on his honeymoon, wouldn't I? *(Resumes his angry stride, slows
270 down.)* Ah well, who can tell what those chiefs actually do on their honeymoon anyway? *(He takes up the pad and scribbles rapidly on it.)* Joseph! Joseph! Joseph! *(Some moments later* JOSEPH *puts in a sulky appearance.)* Did you hear me call you? Why the hell didn't you answer?

275 JOSEPH: I didn't hear master.

PILKINGS: You didn't hear me! How come you are here then?

JOSEPH: *(Stubbornly.)* I didn't hear master.

PILKINGS: *(Controls himself with an effort.)* We'll talk about it in the morning. I want you to take this note directly to
280 Sergeant Amusa. You'll find him at the charge office. Get on your bicycle and race there with it. I expect you back in twenty minutes exactly. Twenty minutes, is that clear?

JOSEPH: Yes master. *(Going.)*

PILKINGS: Oh er . . . Joseph.

285 JOSEPH: Yes master?

PILKINGS: *(Between gritted teeth.)* Er . . . forget what I said just now. The holy water is not nonsense. *I* was talking nonsense.

JOSEPH: Yes master. *(Goes.)*

JANE: *(Pokes her head round the door.)* Have you found him?

290 PILKINGS: Found who?

JANE: Joseph. Weren't you shouting for him?

PILKINGS: Oh yes, he turned up finally.

JANE: You sounded desperate. What was it all about?

PILKINGS: Oh nothing. I just wanted to apologise to him. As-
295 sure him that the holy water isn't really nonsense.

JANE: Oh? And how did he take it?

PILKINGS: Who the hell gives a damn! I had a sudden vision of our Very Reverend Macfarlane drafting another letter of complaint to the Resident about my unchristian language to-
300 wards his parishioners.

JANE: Oh I think he's given up on you by now.

PILKINGS: Don't be too sure. And anyway, I wanted to make sure Joseph didn't 'lose' my note on the way. He looked sufficiently full of the holy crusade to do some such thing.

305 JANE: If you've finished exaggerating, come and have something to eat.

PILKINGS: No, put it all way. We can still get to the ball.

JANE: Simon . . .

PILKINGS: Get your costume back on. Nothing to worry about.
310 I've instructed Amusa to arrest the man and lock him up.

JANE: But that station is hardly secure Simon. He'll soon get his friends to help him escape.

PILKINGS: A-ah, that's where I have out-thought you. I'm not having him put in the station cell. Amusa will bring him
315 right here and lock him up in my study. And he'll stay with him till we get back. No one will dare come here to incite him to anything.

JANE: How clever of you darling. I'll get ready.

PILKINGS: Hey.

320 JANE: Yes darling.

PILKINGS: I have a surprise for you. I was going to keep it until we actually got to the ball.

JANE: What is it?

PILKINGS: You know the Prince is on a tour of the colonies
325 don't you? Well, he docked in the capital only this morning but he is already at the Residency. He is going to grace the ball with his presence later tonight.

JANE: Simon! Not really.

PILKINGS: Yes he is. He's been invited to give away the prizes
330 and he has agreed. You must admit old Engleton is the best Club Secretary we ever had. Quick off the mark that lad.

JANE: But how thrilling.

PILKINGS: The other provincials are going to be damned envious.

335 JANE: I wonder what he'll come as.

PILKINGS: Oh I don't know. As a coat-of-arms perhaps. Anyway it won't be anything to touch this.

JANE: Well that's lucky. If we are to be presented I won't have to start looking for a pair of gloves. It's all sewn on.

340 PILKINGS: (*Laughing.*) Quite right. Trust a woman to think of that. Come on, let's get going.

JANE: (*Rushing off.*) Won't be a second. (*Stops.*) Now I see why you've been so edgy all evening. I thought you weren't handling this affair with your usual brilliance—to begin with

345 that is.

PILKINGS: (*His mood is much improved.*) Shut up woman and get your things on.

JANE: Alright boss, coming.

(PILKINGS *suddenly begins to hum the tango to which they were dancing before. Starts to execute a few practice steps. Lights fade.*)

— THREE —

A *swelling, agitated hum of women's voices rises immediately in the background. The lights come on and we see the frontage of a converted cloth stall in the market. The floor leading up to the entrance is covered in rich velvets and woven cloth. The women come on stage, borne backwards by the determined progress of Sergeant* AMUSA *and his two constables who already have their batons out and use them as a pressure against the women. At the edge of the cloth-covered floor however the women take a determined stand and block all further progress of the men. They begin to tease them mercilessly.*

AMUSA: I am tell you women for last time to commot my road. I am here on official business.

WOMAN: Official business you white man's eunuch? Official business is taking place where you want to go and it's a busi-
5 ness you wouldn't understand.

WOMAN: (*Makes a quick tug at the constable's baton.*) That doesn't fool anyone you know. It's the one you carry under your government knickers that counts. (*She bends low as if to peep under the baggy shorts. The embarrassed constable
10 quickly puts his knees together. The* WOMEN *roar.*)

WOMAN: You mean there is nothing there at all?

WOMAN: Oh there was something. You know that handbell which the whiteman uses to summon his servants . . . ?

AMUSA: (*He manages to preserve some dignity throughout.*) I
15 hope you women know that interfering with officer in execution of his duty is criminal offence.

WOMAN: Interfere? He says we're interfering with him. You foolish man we're telling you there's nothing there to interfere with.

20 AMUSA: I am order you now to clear the road.

WOMAN: What road? The one your father built?

WOMAN: You are a Policeman not so? Then you know what they call trespassing in court. Or—(*Pointing to the cloth-lined steps.*)—do you think that kind of road is built for every
25 kind of feet.

WOMAN: Go back and tell the white man who sent you to come himself.

AMUSA: If I go I will come back with reinforcement. And we will all return carrying weapons.

WOMAN: Oh, now I understand. Before they can put on those   30 knickers the white man first cuts off their weapons.

WOMAN: What a cheek! You mean you come here to show power to women and you don't even have a weapon.

AMUSA: (*Shouting above the laughter.*) For the last time I warn you women to clear the road.   35

WOMAN: To where?

AMUSA: To that hut. I know he dey dere.

WOMAN: Who?

AMUSA: The chief who call himself Elesin Oba.

WOMAN: You ignorant man. It is not he who calls himself   40 Elesin Oba, it is his blood that says it. As it called out to his father before him and will to his son after him. And that is in spite of everything your white man can do.

WOMAN: Is it not the same ocean that washes this land and the white man's land? Tell your white man he can hide our son   45 away as long as he likes. When the time comes for him, the same ocean will bring him back.

AMUSA: The government say dat kin' ting must stop.

WOMAN: Who will stop it? You? Tonight our husband and father will prove himself greater than the laws of strangers.   50

AMUSA: I tell you nobody go prove anyting tonight or anytime. Is ignorant and criminal to prove dat kin' prove.

IYALOJA: (*Entering, from the hut. She is accompanied by a group of young girls who have been attending the* BRIDE.) What is it Amusa? Why do you come here to disturb the hap-   55 piness of others.

AMUSA: Madame Iyaloja, I glad you come. You know me. I no like trouble but duty is duty. I am here to arrest Elesin for criminal intent. Tell these women to stop obstructing me in the performance of my duty.   60

IYALOJA: And you? What gives you the right to obstruct our leader of men in the performance of his duty.

AMUSA: What kin' duty be dat one Iyaloja.

IYALOJA: What kin' duty? What kin' duty does a man have to his new bride?   65

AMUSA: (*Bewildered, looks at the women and at the entrance to the hut.*) Iyaloja, is it wedding you call dis kin' ting?

IYALOJA: You have wives haven't you? Whatever the white man has done to you he hasn't stopped you having wives. And if he has, at least he is married. If you don't know what a mar-   70 riage is, go and ask him to tell you.

AMUSA: This no to wedding.

IYALOJA: And ask him at the same time what he would have done if anyone had come to disturb him on his wedding night.   75

AMUSA: Iyaloja, I say dis no to wedding.

IYALOJA: You want to look inside the bridal chamber? You want to see for yourself how a man cuts the virgin knot?

AMUSA: Madam . . .

WOMAN: Perhaps his wives are still waiting for him to learn.   80

AMUSA: Iyaloja, make you tell dese women make den no insult me again. If I hear dat kin' insult once more . . .

GIRL: (*Pushing her way through.*) You will do what?

GIRL: He's out of his mind. It's our mothers you're talking to, do you know that? Not to any illiterate villager you can bully   85 and terrorise. How dare you intrude here anyway?

GIRL: What a cheek, what impertinence!

GIRL: You've treated them too gently. Now let them see what it is to tamper with the mothers of this market.

90 GIRLS: Your betters dare not enter the market when the women say no!

GIRL: Haven't you learnt that yet, you jester in khaki and starch?

IYALOJA: Daughters . . .

95 GIRL: No no Iyaloja, leave us to deal with him. He no longer knows his mother, we'll teach him.

(With a sudden movement they snatch the batons of the two constables. They begin to hem them in.)

GIRL: What next? We have your batons? What next? What are you going to do?

(With equally swift movements they knock off their hats.)

GIRL: Move if you dare. We have your hats, what will you do
100 about it? Didn't the white man teach you to take off your hats before women?

IYALOJA: It's a wedding night. It's a night of joy for us. Peace . . .

GIRL: Not for him. Who asked him here?

GIRL: Does he dare go to the Residency without an invitation?

105 GIRL: Not even where the servants eat the left-overs.

GIRLS: *(In turn. In an 'English' accent.)* Well well it's Mister Amusa. Were you invited? *(Play-acting to one another. The older* WOMEN *encourage them with their titters.)*

—Your invitation card please?

110 —Who are you? Have we been introduced?

—And who did you say you were?

—Sorry, I didn't quite catch your name.

—May I take your hat?

—If you insist. May I take yours? *(Exchanging the police-*
115 *man's hats.)*

—How very kind of you.

—Not at all. Won't you sit down?

—After you.

—Oh no.

120 —I insist.

—You're most gracious.

—And how do you find the place?

—The natives are alright.

—Friendly?

125 —Tractable.

—Not a teeny-weeny bit restless?

—Well, a teeny-weeny bit restless.

—One might even say, difficult?

—Indeed one might be tempted to say, difficult.

130 —But you do manage to cope?

—Yes indeed I do. I have a rather faithful ox called Amusa.

—He's loyal?

—Absolutely.

—Lay down his life for you what?

135 —Without a moment's thought.

—Had one like that once. Trust him with my life.

—Mostly of course they are liars.

—Never known a native tell the truth.

—Does it get rather close around here?

140 —It's mild for this time of the year.

—But the rains may still come.

—They are late this year aren't they?

—They are keeping African time.

—Ha ha ha ha

145 —Ha ha ha ha

—The humidity is what gets me.

—It used to be whisky.

—Ha ha ha ha

—Ha ha ha ha

—What's your handicap old chap? 150

—Is there racing by golly?

—Splendid golf course, you'll like it.

—I'm beginning to like it already.

—And a European club, exclusive.

—You've kept the flag flying. 155

—We do our best for the old country.

—It's a pleasure to serve.

—Another whisky old chap?

—You are indeed too too kind.

—Not at all sir. Where is that boy? *(With a sudden bellow.)* 160
Sergeant!

AMUSA: *(Snaps to attention.)* Yessir!

(The WOMEN *collapse with laughter.)*

GIRL: Take your men out of here.

AMUSA: *(Realising the trick, he rages from loss of face.)* I'm give
you warning . . . 165

GIRL: Alright then. Off with his knickers! *(They surge slowly forward.)*

IYALOJA: Daughters, please.

AMUSA: *(Squaring himself for defence.)* The first woman wey
touch me . . . 170

IYALOJA: My children, I beg of you . . .

GIRL: Then tell him to leave this market. This is the home of our mothers. We don't want the eater of white left-overs at the feast their hands have prepared.

IYALOJA: You heard them Amusa. You had better go. 175

GIRLS: Now!

AMUSA: *(Commencing his retreat.)* We dey go now, but make you no say we no warn you.

GIRL: Before we read the riot act—you should know all about
that. 180

AMUSA: Make we go. *(They depart, more precipitately.)*

(The WOMEN *strike their palms across in the gesture of wonder.)*

WOMEN: Do they teach you all that school?

WOMAN: And to think I nearly kept Apinke away from the place.

WOMAN: Did you hear them? Did you see how they mimicked 185
the white man?

WOMAN: The voices exactly. Hey, there are wonders in this world!

IYALOJA: Well, our elders have said it: Dada may be weak, but
he has a younger sibling who is truly fearless. 190

WOMAN: The next time the white man shows his face in this market I will set Wuraola on his tail.

(A WOMAN *bursts into song and dance of euphoria—'Tani l'awa o l'ogbeja? Kayi! A l'ogbeja. Omo Kekere l'ogbeja.' ['Who says we haven't a defender? Silence! We have our defenders. Little children are our champions.']* The rest of the WOMEN *join in, some placing the girls on their back like infants, other dancing round them. The dance becomes general, mounting in excitement.* ELESIN *appears, in wrapper only. In his hands a white velvet cloth folded loosely as if it held some delicate object. He cries out.)*

ELESIN: Oh you mothers of beautiful brides! *(The dancing stops. They turn and see him, and the object in his hands.* 195 IYALOJA *approaches and gently takes the cloth from him.)* Take it. It is no mere virgin stain, but the union of life and the seeds of passage. My vital flow, the last from this flesh is intermingled with the promise of future life. All is prepared. Listen! *(A steady drum-beat from the distance.)* Yes. It is 200 nearly time. The King's dog has been killed. The King's favourite horse is about to follow his master. My brother chiefs know their task and perform it well. *(He listens again.)*

(The BRIDE *emerges, stands shyly by the door. He turns to her.)*

Our marriage is not yet wholly fulfilled. When earth and passage wed, the consummation is complete only when 205 there are grains of earth on the eyelids of passage. Stay by me till then. My faithful drummers, do me your last service. This is where I have chosen to do my leave-taking, in this heart of life, this hive which contains the swarm of the world in its small compass. This is where I have known love and 210 laughter away from the palace. Even the richest food cloys when eaten days on end; in the market, nothing ever cloys. Listen. *(They listen to the drums.)* They have begun to seek out the heart of the King's favourite horse. Soon it will ride in its bolt of raffia with the dog at its feet. Together they will 215 ride on the shoulders of the King's grooms through the pulse centres of the town. They know it is here I shall await them. I have told them. *(His eyes appear to cloud. He passes his hand over them as if to clear his sight. He gives a faint smile.)* It promises well; just then I felt my spirit's eagerness. The 220 kite makes for wide spaces and the wind creeps up behind its tail; can the kite say less than— thank you, the quicker the better? But wait a while my spirit. Wait. Wait for the coming of the King. Do you know friends, the horse is born to this one destiny, to bear the burden that is man upon 225 its back. Except for this night, this night alone when the spotless stallion will ride in triumph on the back of man. In the time of my father I witnessed the strange sight. Perhaps tonight also I shall see it for the last time. If they arrive before the drums beat for me, I shall tell him to let the Alafin know 230 I follow swiftly. If they come after the drums have sounded, why then, all is well for I have gone ahead. Our spirits shall fall in step along the great passage. *(He listens to the drums. He seems again to be falling into a state of semi-hypnosis; his eyes scan the sky but it is in a kind of daze. His voice is a little* 235 *breathless.)* The moon has fed, a glow from its full stomach fills the sky and air, but I cannot tell where is that gateway through which I must pass. My faithful friends, let our feet touch together this last time, lead me into the other name with sounds that cover my skin with down yet make my 240 limbs strike earth like a thoroughbred. Dear mothers, let me dance into the passage even as I have lived beneath your roofs. *(He comes down progressively among them. They make a way for him, the* DRUMMERS *playing. His dance is one of solemn, regal motions, each gesture of the body is made with a* 245 *solemn finality. The* WOMEN *join him, their steps a somewhat more fluid version of his. Beneath the* PRAISE-SINGER's *exhortations the* WOMEN *dirge 'Ale le le, awo mi lo'.)*
PRAISE-SINGER: Elesin Alafin, can you hear my voice?
ELESIN: Faintly, my friend, faintly.
250 PRAISE-SINGER: Elesin Alafin, can you hear my call?

ELESIN: Faintly my king, faintly.
PRAISE-SINGER: Is your memory sound Elesin?
  Shall my voice be a blade of grass and
  Tickle the armpit of the past?
ELESIN: My memory needs no prodding but   255
  What do you wish to say to me?
PRAISE-SINGER: Only what has been spoken. Only what concerns
  The dying wish of the father of all.
ELESIN: It is buried like seed-yam in my mind   260
  This is the season of quick rains, the harvest
  Is this moment due for gathering?
PRAISE-SINGER: If you cannot come, I said, swear
  You'll tell my favourite horse. I shall
  Ride on through the gates alone.   265
ELESIN: Elesin's message will be read
  Only when his loyal heart no longer beats.
PRAISE-SINGER: If you cannot come Elesin, tell my dog.
  I cannot stay the keeper too long
  At the gate.   270
ELESIN: A dog does not outrun the hand
  That feeds it meat. A horse that throws its rider
  Slows down to a stop. Elesin Alafin
  Trusts no beasts with messages between
  A king and his companion.   275
PRAISE-SINGER: If you get lost my dog will track
  The hidden path to me.
ELESIN: The seven-way crossroads confuses
  Only the stranger. The Horseman of the King
  Was born in the recesses of the house.   280
PRAISE-SINGER: I know the wickedness of men. If there is
  Weight on the loose end of your sash, such weight
  As no mere man can shift; if your sash is earthed
  By evil minds who mean to part us at the last . . .
ELESIN: My sash is of the deep purple ALARI;   285
  It is no tethering-rope. The elephant
  Trails no tethering-rope; that king
  Is not yet crowned who will peg an elephant—
  Not even you my friend and King.
PRAISE-SINGER: And yet this fear will not depart from me   290
  The darkness of this new abode is deep—
  Will your human eyes suffice?
ELESIN: In a night which falls before our eyes
  However deep, we do not miss our way.
PRAISE-SINGER: Shall I now not acknowledge I have stood   295
  Where wonders met their end? The elephant deserves
  Better than that we say 'I have caught
  A glimpse of something.' If we see the tamer
  Of the forest let us say plainly, we have seen
  An elephant.   300
ELESIN: *(His voice is drowsy.)* I have freed myself of earth and now
  It's getting dark. Strange voices guide my feet.
PRAISE-SINGER: The river is never so high that the eyes
  Of a fish are covered. The night is not so dark
  That the albino fails to find his way. A child   305
  Returning homewards craves no leading by the hand.
  Gracefully does the mask regain his grove at the end of the day . . .
  Gracefully. Gracefully does the mask dance   310
  Homeward at the end of day, gracefully . . .

(ELESIN's *trance appears to be deepening, his steps heavier.*)

IYALOJA: It is the death of war that kills the valiant,
Death of water is how the swimmer goes
It is the death of markets that kills the trader
315 And death of indecision takes the idle away
The trade of the cutlass blunts its edge
And the beautiful die the death of beauty.
It takes an Elesin to die the death of death . . .
Only Elesin . . . dies the unknowable death of death . . .
320 Gracefully, gracefully does the horseman regain
The stables at the end of day, gracefully . . .

PRAISE-SINGER: How shall I tell what my eyes have seen? The Horseman gallops on before the courier, how shall I tell what my eyes have seen? He says a dog may be confused by 325 new scents of beings he never dreamt of, so he must precede the dog to heaven. He says a horse may stumble on strange boulders and be lamed, so he races on before the horse to heaven. It is best, he says, to trust no messenger who may falter at the outer gate; oh how shall I tell what my ears have 330 heard? But do you hear me still Elesin, do you hear your faithful one?

(ELESIN *in his motions appears to feel for a direction of sound, subtly, but he only sinks deeper into his trance-dance.*)

Elesin Alafin, I no longer sense your flesh. The drums are changing now but you have gone far ahead of the world. It is not yet noon in heaven; let those who claim it is begin their 335 own journey home. So why must you rush like an impatient bride: why do you race to desert your Olohun-iyo?

(ELESIN *is now sunk fully deep in his trance, there is no longer sign of any awareness of his surroundings.*)

Does the deep voice of *gbedu* cover you then, like the passage of royal elephants? Those drums that brook no rivals, have they blocked the passage to your ears that my voice 340 passes into wind, a mere leaf floating in the night? Is your flesh lightened Elesin, is that lump of earth I slid between your slippers to keep you longer slowly sifting from your feet? Are the drums on the other side now tuning skin to skin with ours in *osugbo*? Are there sounds there I cannot hear, do 345 footsteps surround you which pound the earth like *gbedu*, roll like thunder round the dome of the world? Is the darkness gathering in your head Elesin? Is there now a streak of light at the end of the passage, a light I dare not look upon? Does it reveal whose voices we often heard, whose touches 350 we often felt, whose wisdoms come suddenly into the mind when the wisest have shaken their heads and murmured: It cannot be done? Elesin Alafin, don't think I do not know why your lips are heavy, why your limbs are drowsy as palm oil in the cold of harmattan. I would call you back but when 355 the elephant heads for the jungle, the tail is too small a handhold for the hunter that would pull him back. The sun that heads for the sea no longer heeds the prayers of the farmer. When the river begins to taste the salt of the ocean, we no longer know what deity to call on, the river-god or Olokun. 360 No arrow flies back to the string, the child does not return through the same passage that gave it birth. Elesin Oba, can you hear me at all? Your eyelids are glazed like a courtesan's, is it that you see the dark groom and master of life? And will you see my father? Will you tell him that I stayed with you to 365 the last? Will my voice ring in your ears awhile, will you remember Olohun-iyo even if the music on the other side surpasses his mortal craft? But will they know you over there? Have they eyes to gauge your worth, have they the heart to love you, will they know what thoroughbred prances towards them in caparisons of honour? If they do not Elesin, if any 370 there cuts your yam with a small knife, or pours you wine in a small calabash, turn back and return to welcoming hands. If the world were not greater than the wishes of Olohun-iyo, I would not let you go . . .

(*He appears to break down.* ELESIN *dances on, completely in a trance. The dirge wells up louder and stronger.* ELESIN's *dance does not lose its elasticity but his gestures become, if possible, even more weighty. Lights fade slowly on the scene.*)

— FOUR —

A Masque. The front side of the stage is part of a wide corridor around the great hall of the Residency extending beyond vision into the rear and wings. It is redolent of the tawdry decadence of a far-flung but key imperial frontier. The couples in a variety of fancy-dress are ranged around the walls, gazing in the same direction. The guest-of-honour is about to make an appearance. A portion of the local police brass band with its white conductor is just visible. At last, the entrance of Royalty. The band plays 'Rule Britannia', badly, beginning long before he is visible. The couples bow and curtsey as he passes by them. Both he and his companions are dressed in seventeenth century European costume. Following behind are the RESIDENT *and his partner similarly attired. As they gain the end of the hall where the orchestra dais begins the music comes to an end. The* PRINCE *bows to the guests. The band strikes up a Viennese waltz and the* PRINCE *formally opens the floor. Several bars later the* RESIDENT *and his companion follow suit. Others follow in appropriate pecking order. The orchestra's waltz rendition is not of the highest musical standard.*

Some time later the PRINCE *dances again into view and is settled into a corner by the* RESIDENT *who then proceeds to select couples as they dance past for introduction, sometimes threading his way through the dancers to tap the lucky couple on the shoulder. Desperate efforts from many to ensure that they are recognised in spite of, perhaps, their costume. The ritual of introductions soon takes in* PILKINGS *and his wife. The* PRINCE *is quite fascinated by their costume and they demonstrate the adaptations they have made to it, pulling down the mask to demonstrate how the egungun normally appears, then showing the various pressbutton controls they have innovated for the face flaps, the sleeves, etc. They demonstrate the dance steps and the guttural sounds made by the egungun, harrass other dancers in the hall,* MRS PILKINGS *playing the 'restrainer' to* PILKINGS' *manic darts. Everyone is highly entertained, the Royal Party especially who lead the applause.*

At this point a liveried footman comes in with a note on a salver and is intercepted almost absent-mindedly by the RESIDENT *who takes the note and reads it. After polite coughs he succeeds in excusing the* PILKINGSES *from the* PRINCE *and takes them aside. The* PRINCE *considerately offers the* RESIDENT's *wife his hand and dancing is resumed.*

On their way out the RESIDENT *gives an order to his* AIDE-DE-CAMP. *They come into the side corridor where the* RESIDENT *hands the note to* PILKINGS.

RESIDENT: As you see it says 'emergency' on the outside. I took the liberty of opening it because His Highness was obviously enjoying the entertainment. I didn't want to interrupt unless really necessary.

5 PILKINGS: Yes, yes of course sir.

RESIDENT: Is it really as bad as it says? What's it all about?

PILKINGS: Some strange custom they have sir. It seems because the King is dead some important chief has to commit suicide.

10 RESIDENT: The King? Isn't it the same one who died nearly a month ago?

PILKINGS: Yes sir.

RESIDENT: Haven't they buried him yet?

PILKINGS: They take their time about these things sir. The pre-

15 burial ceremonies last nearly thirty days. It seems tonight is the final night.

RESIDENT: But what has it got to do with the market women? Why are they rioting? We've waived that troublesome tax haven't we?

20 PILKINGS: We don't quite know that they are exactly rioting yet sir. Sergeant Amusa is sometimes prone to exaggerations.

RESIDENT: He sounds desperate enough. That comes out even in his rather quaint grammar. Where is the man anyway? I asked my aide-de-camp to bring him here.

25 PILKINGS: They are probably looking in the wrong verandah. I'll fetch him myself.

RESIDENT: No no you stay here. Let your wife go and look for them. Do you mind my dear . . . ?

JANE: Certainly not, your Excellency. (*Goes.*)

30 RESIDENT: You should have kept me informed Pilkings. You realise how disastrous it would have been if things had erupted while His Highness was here.

PILKINGS: I wasn't aware of the whole business until tonight sir.

35 RESIDENT: Nose to the ground Pilkings, nose to the ground. If we all let these little things slip past us where would the empire be eh? Tell me that. Where would we all be?

PILKINGS: (*Low voice.*) Sleeping peacefully at home I bet.

RESIDENT: What did you say Pilkings?

40 PILKINGS: It won't happen again sir.

RESIDENT: It mustn't Pilkings. It mustn't. Where is that damned sergeant? I ought to get back to His Highness as quickly as possible and offer him some plausible explanation for my rather abrupt conduct. Can you think of one Pilkings?

45 PILKINGS: You could tell him the truth sir.

RESIDENT: I could? No no no no no Pilkings, that would never do. What! Go and tell him there is a riot just two miles away from him? This is supposed to be a secure colony of His Majesty, Pilkings.

50 PILKINGS: Yes sir.

RESIDENT: Ah, there they are. No, these are not our native police. Are these the ring-leaders of the riot?

PILKINGS: Sir, these are my police officers.

RESIDENT: Oh, I beg your pardon officers. You do look a little

55 . . . I say, isn't there something missing in their uniforms? I think they used to have some rather colourful sashes. If I remember rightly I recommended them myself in my young

days in the service. A bit of colour always appeals to the natives, yes. I remember putting that in my report. Well well well, where are we? Make your report man.

60 PILKINGS: (*Moves close to* AMUSA, *between his teeth.*) And let's have no more superstitious nonsense from you Amusa or I'll throw you in the guardroom for a month and feed you pork!

RESIDENT: What's that? What has pork to do with it?

65 PILKINGS: Sir, I was just warning him to be brief. I'm sure you are most anxious to hear his report.

RESIDENT: Yes yes yes of course. Come on man, speak up. Hey, didn't we give them some colourful fez hats with all those wavy things, yes, pink tassells . . .

70 PILKINGS: Sir, I think if he was permitted to make his report we might find that he lost his hat in the riot.

RESIDENT: Ah yes indeed. I'd better tell His Highness that. Lost his hat in the riot, ha ha. He'll probably say well, as long as he didn't lost his head. (*Chuckles to himself.*) Don't forget

75 to send me a report first thing in the morning young Pilkings.

PILKINGS: No sir.

RESIDENT: And whatever you do, don't let things get out of hand. Keep a cool head and—nose to the ground Pilkings. (*Wanders off in the general direction of the hall.*)

80 PILKINGS: Yes sir.

AIDE-DE-CAMP: Would you be needing me sir?

PILKINGS: No thanks Bob. I think His Excellency's need of you is greater than ours.

AIDE-DE-CAMP: We have a detachment of soldiers from the

85 capital sir. They accompanied His Highness up here.

PILKINGS: I doubt if it will come to that but, thanks, I'll bear it in mind. Oh, could you send an orderly with my cloak.

AIDE-DE-CAMP: Very good sir. (*Goes.*)

PILKINGS: Now Sergeant.

90 AMUSA: Sir . . . (*Makes an effort, stops dead. Eyes to the ceiling.*)

PILKINGS: Oh, not again.

AMUSA: I cannot against death to dead cult. This dress get power of dead.

PILKINGS: Alright, let's go. You are relieved of all further duty

95 Amusa. Report to me first thing in the morning.

JANE: Shall I come Simon?

PILKINGS: No, there's no need for that. If I can get back later I will. Otherwise get Bob to bring you home.

JANE: Be careful Simon . . . I mean, be clever.

100 PILKINGS: Sure I will. You two, come with me. (*As he turns to go, the clock in the Residency begins to chime.* PILKINGS *looks at his watch then turns, horror-stricken, to stare at his wife. The same thought clearly occurs to her. He swallows hard. An orderly brings his cloak.*) It's midnight. I had no idea it was

105 that late.

JANE: But surely . . . they don't count the hours the way we do. The moon, or something.

PILKINGS: I am . . . not so sure.

(*He turns and breaks into a sudden run. The two constables follow, also at a run.* AMUSA, *who has kept his eyes on the ceiling throughout waits until the last of the footsteps has faded out of hearing. He salutes suddenly, but without once looking in the direction of the woman.*)

AMUSA: Goodnight madam.

JANE: Oh. (*She hesitates.*) Amusa . . . (*He goes off without*

110 *seeming to have heard.*) Poor Simon . . . (*A figure emerges from the shadows, a young black man dressed in a sober*

western suit. He peeps into the hall, trying to make out the figures of the dancers.) Who is that?

115 OLUNDE: (*Emerging into the light.*) I didn't mean to startle you madam. I am looking for the District Officer.

JANE: Wait a minute . . . don't I know you? Yes, you are Olunde, the young man who . . .

OLUNDE: Mrs Pilkings! How fortunate. I came here to look for 120 your husband.

JANE: Olunde! Let's look at you. What a fine young man you've become. Grand but solemn. Good God, when did you return? Simon never said a word. But you do look well Olunde. Really!

125 OLUNDE: You are . . . well, you look quite well yourself Mrs Pilkings. From what little I can see of you.

JANE: Oh, this. It's caused quite a stir I assure you, and not all of it very pleasant. You are not shocked I hope?

OLUNDE: Why should I be? But don't you find it rather hot in 130 there? Your skin must find it difficult to breathe.

JANE: Well, it is a little hot I must confess, but it's all in a good cause.

OLUNDE: What cause Mrs Pilkings?

JANE: All this. The ball. And His Highness being here in per- 135 son and all that.

OLUNDE: (*Mildly.*) And that is the good cause for which you desecrate an ancestral mask?

JANE: Oh, so you are shocked after all. How disappointing.

OLUNDE: No I am not shocked Mrs Pilkings. You forget that I 140 have now spent four years among your people. I discovered that you have no respect for what you do not understand.

JANE: Oh. So you've returned with a chip on your shoulder. That's a pity Olunde. I am sorry.

(*An uncomfortable silence follows.*)

I take it then that you did not find your stay in England alto- 145 gether edifying.

OLUNDE: I don't say that. I found your people quite admirable in many ways, their conduct and courage in this war for instance.

JANE: Ah yes the war. Here of course it is all rather remote. 150 From time to time we have a black-out drill just to remind us that there is a war on. And the rare convoy passes through on its way somewhere or on manoeuvres. Mind you there is the occasional bit of excitement like that ship that was blown up in the harbour.

155 OLUNDE: Here? Do you mean through enemy action?

JANE: Oh no, the war hasn't come that close. The captain did it himself. I don't quite understand it really. Simon tried to explain. The ship had to be blown up because it had become dangerous to the other ships, even to the city itself. Hundreds 160 of the coastal population would have died.

OLUNDE: Maybe it was loaded with ammunition and had caught fire. Or some of those lethal gases they've been experimenting on.

JANE: Something like that. The captain blew himself up with 165 it. Deliberately. Simon said someone had to remain on board to light the fuse.

OLUNDE: It must have been a very short fuse.

JANE: (*Shrugs.*) I don't know much about it. Only that there was no other way to save lives. No time to devise anything 170 else. The captain took the decision and carried it out.

OLUNDE: Yes . . . I quite believe it. I met men like that in England.

JANE: Oh just look at me! Fancy welcoming you back with such morbid news. Stale too. It was at least six months ago.

OLUNDE: I don't find it morbid at all. I find it rather inspiring. 175 It is an affirmative commentary on life.

JANE: What is?

OLUNDE: That captain's self-sacrifice.

JANE: Nonsense. Life should never be thrown deliberately away. 180

OLUNDE: And the innocent people round the harbour?

JANE: Oh, how does one know? The whole thing was probably exaggerated anyway.

OLUNDE: That was a risk the captain couldn't take. But please Mrs Pilkings, do you think you could find your husband for 185 me? I have to talk to him.

JANE: Simon? Oh. (*As she recollects for the first time the full significance of* OLUNDE's *presence.*) Simon is . . . there is a little problem in town. He was sent for. But . . . when did you arrive? Does Simon know you're here? 190

OLUNDE: (*Suddenly earnest.*) I need your help Mrs Pilkings. I've always found you somewhat more understanding than your husband. Please find him for me and when you do, you must help me talk to him.

JANE: I'm afraid I don't quite . . . follow you. Have you seen my 195 husband already?

OLUNDE: I went to your house. Your houseboy told me you were here. (*He smiles.*) He even told me how I would recognise you and Mr Pilkings.

JANE: Then you must know what my husband is trying to do 200 for you.

OLUNDE: For me?

JANE: For you. For your people. And to think he didn't even know you were coming back! But how do you happen to be here? Only this evening we were talking about you. We 205 thought you were still four thousand miles away.

OLUNDE: I was sent a cable.

JANE: A cable? Who did? Simon? The business of your father didn't begin till tonight.

OLUNDE: A relation sent it weeks ago, and it said nothing 210 about my father. All it said was, Our King is dead. But I knew I had to return home at once so as to bury my father. I understood that.

JANE: Well, thank God you don't have to go through that agony. Simon is going to stop it. 215

OLUNDE: That's why I want to see him. He's wasting his time. And since he has been so helpful to me I don't want him to incur the enmity of our people. Especially over nothing.

JANE: (*Sits down open-mouthed.*) You . . . you Olunde!

OLUNDE: Mrs Pilkings, I came home to bury my father. As 220 soon as I heard the news I booked my passage home. In fact we were fortunate. We travelled in the same convoy as your Prince, so we had excellent protection.

JANE: But you don't think your father is also entitled to whatever protection is available to him? 225

OLUNDE: How can I make you understand? He *has* protection. No one can undertake what he does tonight without the deepest protection the mind can conceive. What can you offer him in place of his peace of mind, in place of the honour and veneration of his own people? What would you 230 think of your Prince if he had refused to accept the risk of losing his life on this voyage? This . . . showing-the-flag tour of colonial possessions.

JANE: I see. So it isn't just medicine you studied in England.

235 OLUNDE: Yet another error into which your people fall. You believe that everything which appears to make sense was learnt from you.

JANE: Not so fast Olunde. You have learnt to argue I can tell that, but I never said you made sense. However cleverly you

240 try to put it, it is still a barbaric custom. It is even worse—it's feudal! The king dies and a chieftain must be buried with him. How feudalistic can you get!

OLUNDE: (*Waves his hand towards the background. The* PRINCE *is dancing past again—to a different step—and all*

245 *the guests are bowing and curtseying as he passes.*) And this? Even in the midst of a devastating war, look at that. What name would you give to that?

JANE: Therapy, British style. The preservation of sanity in the midst of chaos.

250 OLUNDE: Others would call it decadence. However, it doesn't really interest me. You white races know how to survive; I've seen proof of that. By all logical and natural laws this war should end with all the white races wiping out one another, wiping out their so-called civilisation for all time and revert-

255 ing to a state of primitivism the like of which has so far only existed in your imagination when you thought of us. I thought all that at the beginning. Then I slowly realised that your greatest art is the art of survival. But at least have the humility to let others survive in their own way.

260 JANE: Through ritual suicide?

OLUNDE: Is that worse than mass suicide? Mrs Pilkings, what do you call what those young men are sent to do by their generals in this war? Of course you have also mastered the art of calling things by names which don't remotely describe

265 them.

JANE: You talk! You people with your long-winded, round-about way of making conversation.

OLUNDE: Mrs Pilkings, whatever we do, we never suggest that a thing is the opposite of what it really is. In your newsreels I

270 heard defeats, thorough, murderous defeats described as strategic victories. No wait, it wasn't just on your newsreels. Don't forget I was attached to hospitals all the time. Hordes of your wounded passed through those wards. I spoke to them. I spent long evenings by their bedside while they

275 spoke terrible truths of the realities of that war. I know now how history is made.

JANE: But surely, in a war of this nature, for the morale of the nation you must expect . . .

OLUNDE: That a disaster beyond human reckoning be spoken

280 of as a triumph? No. I mean, is there no mourning in the home of the bereaved that such blasphemy is permitted?

JANE: (*After a moment's pause.*) Perhaps I can understand you now. The time we picked for you was not really one for seeing us at our best.

285 OLUNDE: Don't think it was just the war. Before that even started I had plenty of time to study your people. I saw nothing, finally, that gave you the right to pass judgement on other peoples and their ways. Nothing at all.

JANE: (*Hesitantly.*) Was it the . . . colour thing? I know there is

290 some discrimination.

OLUNDE: Don't make it so simple, Mrs Pilkings. You make it sound as if when I left, I took nothing at all with me.

JANE: Yes . . . and to tell the truth, only this evening, Simon and I agreed that we never really knew what you left with.

295 OLUNDE: Neither did I. But I found out over there. I am grateful to your country for that. And I will never give it up.

JANE: Olunde, please. . . . promise me something. Whatever you do, don't throw away what you have started to do. You want to be a doctor. My husband and I believe you will make an excellent one, sympathetic and competent. Don't let any-

300 thing make you throw away your training.

OLUNDE: (*Genuinely surprised.*) Of course not. What a strange idea. I intend to return and complete my training. Once the burial of my father is over.

JANE: Oh, please . . . !

305 OLUNDE: Listen! Come outside. You can't hear anything against that music.

JANE: What is it?

OLUNDE: The drums. Can you hear the change? Listen.

(*The drums come over, still distant but more distinct. There is a change of rhythm, it rises to a crescendo and then, suddenly, it is cut off. After a silence, a new beat begins, slow and resonant.*)

There. It's all over.

310 JANE: You mean he's . . .

OLUNDE: Yes Mrs Pilkings, my father is dead. His will-power has always been enormous; I know he is dead.

JANE: (*Screams.*) How can you be so callous! So unfeeling! You announce your father's own death like a surgeon looking

315 down on some strange . . . stranger's body! You're just a savage like all the rest.

AIDE-DE-CAMP: (*Rushing out.*) Mrs Pilkings. Mrs Pilkings. (*She breaks down, sobbing.*) Are you alright, Mrs Pilkings?

OLUNDE: She'll be alright. (*Turns to go.*)

320 AIDE-DE-CAMP: Who are you? And who the hell asked your opinion?

OLUNDE: You're quite right, nobody. (*Going.*)

AIDE-DE-CAMP: What the hell! Did you hear me ask you who you were?

325 OLUNDE: I have business to attend to.

AIDE-DE-CAMP: I'll give you business in a moment you impudent nigger. Answer my question!

OLUNDE: I have a funeral to arrange. Excuse me. (*Going.*)

AIDE-DE-CAMP: I said stop! Orderly!

330 JANE: No no, don't do that. I'm alright. And for heaven's sake don't act so foolishly. He's a family friend.

AIDE-DE-CAMP: Well he'd better learn to answer civil questions when he's asked them. These natives put a suit on and they get high opinions of themselves.

335 OLUNDE: Can I go now?

JANE: No no don't go. I must talk to you. I'm sorry about what I said.

OLUNDE: It's nothing Mrs Pilkings. And I'm really anxious to go. I couldn't see my father before, it's forbidden for me, his

340 heir and successor to set eyes on him from the moment of the king's death. But now . . . I would like to touch his body while it is still warm.

JANE: You will. I promise I shan't keep you long. Only, I couldn't possibly let you go like that. Bob, please excuse us.

345 AIDE-DE-CAMP: If you're sure . . .

JANE: Of course I'm sure. Something happened to upset me just then, but I'm alright now. Really.

(*The* AIDE-DE-CAMP *goes, somewhat reluctantly.*)

OLUNDE: I mustn't stay long.

JANE: Please, I promise not to keep you. It's just that . . . oh you

350 saw yourself what happens to one in this place. The Resident's man thought he was being helpful, that's the way we

all react. But I can't go in among that crowd just now and if
I stay by myself somebody will come looking for me. Please,
355 just say something for a few moments and then you can go.
Just so I can recover myself.

OLUNDE: What do you want me to say?

JANE: Your calm acceptance for instance, can you explain
that? It was so unnatural. I don't understand that at all. I feel
360 a need to understand all I can.

OLUNDE: But you explained it yourself. My medical training
perhaps. I have seen death too often. And the soldiers who
returned from the front, they died on our hands all the time.

JANE: No. It has to be more than that. I feel it has to do with
365 the many things we don't really grasp about your people. At
least you can explain.

OLUNDE: All these things are part of it. And anyway, my father
has been dead in my mind for nearly a month. Ever since I
learnt of the King's death. I've lived with my bereavement so
370 long now that I cannot think of him alive. On that journey
on the boat, I kept my mind on my duties as the one who
must perform the rites over his body. I went through it all
again and again in my mind as he himself had taught me. I
didn't want to do anything wrong, something which might
375 jeopardise the welfare of my people.

JANE: But he had disowned you. When you left he swore publicly you were no longer his son.

OLUNDE: I told you, he was a man of tremendous will. Sometimes that's another way of saying stubborn. But among our
380 people, you don't disown a child just like that. Even if I had
died before him I would still be buried like his eldest son.
But it's time for me to go.

JANE: Thank you. I feel calmer. Don't let me keep you from
your duties.

385 OLUNDE: Goodnight Mrs Pilkings.

JANE: Welcome home. (*She holds out her hand. As he takes it
footsteps are heard approaching the drive. A short while later
a woman's sobbing is also heard.*)

PILKINGS: (*Off.*) Keep them here till I get back. (*He strides into
390 view, reacts at the sight of* OLUNDE *but turns to his wife.*)
Thank goodness you're still here.

JANE: Simon, what happened?

PILKINGS: Later Jane, please. Is Bob still here?

JANE: Yes, I think so. I'm sure he must be.

395 PILKINGS: Try and get him out here as quietly as you can. Tell
him it's urgent.

JANE: Of course. Oh Simon, you remember . . .

PILKINGS: Yes yes. I can see who it is. Get Bob out here. (*She
runs off.*) At first I thought I was seeing a ghost.

400 OLUNDE: Mr Pilkings, I appreciate what you tried to do. I want
you to believe that. I can only tell you it would have been a
terrible calamity if you'd succeeded.

PILKINGS: (*Opens his mouth several times, shuts it.*) You . . .
said what?

405 OLUNDE: A calamity for us, the entire people.

PILKINGS: (*Sighs.*) I see. Hm.

OLUNDE: And now I must go. I must see him before he turns
cold.

PILKINGS: Oh ah . . . em . . . but this is a shock to see you. I
410 mean er thinking all this while you were in England and
thanking God for that.

OLUNDE: I came on the mail boat. We travelled in the Prince's
convoy.

PILKINGS: Ah yes, a-ah, hm . . . er well . . .

OLUNDE: Goodnight. I can see you are shocked by the whole 415
business. But you must know by now there are things you
cannot understand—or help.

PILKINGS: Yes. Just a minute. There are armed policemen that
way and they have instructions to let no one pass. I suggest
you wait a little. I'll er . . . yes, I'll give you an escort. 420

OLUNDE: That's very kind of you. But do you think it could be
quickly arranged.

PILKINGS: Of course. In fact, yes, what I'll do is send Bob over
with some men to the er . . . place. You can go with them.
Here he comes now. Excuse me a minute. 425

AIDE-DE-CAMP: Anything wrong sir?

PILKINGS: (*Takes him to one side.*) Listen Bob, that cellar in
the disused annexe of the Residency, you know, where the
slaves were stored before being taken down to the coast . . .

AIDE-DE-CAMP: Oh yes, we use it as a storeroom for broken 430
furniture.

PILKINGS: But it's still got the bars on it?

AIDE-DE-CAMP: Oh yes, they are quite intact.

PILKINGS: Get the keys please. I'll explain later. And I want a
strong guard over the Residency tonight. 435

AIDE-DE-CAMP: We have that already. The detachment from
the coast . . .

PILKINGS: No, I don't want them at the gates of the Residency.
I want you to deploy them at the bottom of the hill, a long
way from the main hall so they can deal with any situation 440
long before the sound carries to the house.

AIDE-DE-CAMP: Yes of course.

PILKINGS: I don't want His Highness alarmed.

AIDE-DE-CAMP: You think the riot will spread here?

PILKINGS: It's unlikely but I don't want to take a chance. I 445
made them believe I was going to lock the man up in my
house, which was what I had planned to do in the first place.
They are probably assailing it by now. I took a roundabout
route here so I don't think there is any danger at all. At least
not before dawn. Nobody is to leave the premises of 450
course—the native employees I mean. They'll soon smell
something is up and they can't keep their mouths shut.

AIDE-DE-CAMP: I'll give instructions at once.

PILKINGS: I'll take the prisoner down myself. Two policemen
will stay with him throughout the night. Inside the cell. 455

AIDE-DE-CAMP: Right sir. (*Salutes and goes off at the double.*)

PILKINGS: Jane. Bob is coming back in a moment with a detachment. Until he gets back please stay with Olunde.

(*He makes an extra warning gesture with his eyes.*)

OLUNDE: Please Mr Pilkings . . .

PILKINGS: I hate to be stuffy old son, but we have a crisis on 460
our hands. It has to do with your father's affair if you must
know. And it happens also at a time when we have His Highness here. I am responsible for security so you'll simply have
to do as I say. I hope that's understood. (*Marches off quickly,
in the direction from which he made his first appearance.*) 465

OLUNDE: What's going on? All this can't be just because he
failed to stop my father killing himself.

JANE: I honestly don't know. Could it have sparked off a riot?

OLUNDE: No. If he'd succeeded that would be more likely to
start the riot. Perhaps there were other factors involved. Was 470
there a chieftancy dispute?

JANE: None that I know of.

ELESIN: *(An animal bellow from off.)* Leave me alone! Is it not
475 enough that you have covered me in shame! White man,
     take your hand from my body!

*(OLUNDE stands frozen on the spot. JANE understanding at last,
tries to move him.)*

JANE: Let's go in. It's getting chilly out here.
PILKINGS: *(Off.)* Carry him.
ELESIN: Give me back the name you have taken away from me
     you ghost from the land of the nameless!
480 PILKINGS: Carry him! I can't have a disturbance here.
     Quickly! stuff up his mouth.
JANE: Oh God! Let's go in. Please Olunde. *(OLUNDE does not
     move.)*
ELESIN: Take your albino's hand from me you . . .

(Sounds of a struggle. His voice chokes as he is gagged.)

485 OLUNDE: *(Quietly.)* That was my father's voice.
JANE: Oh you poor orphan, what have you come home to?

*(There is a sudden explosion of rage from off-stage and powerful
steps come running up the drive.)*

PILKINGS: You bloody fools, after him!

*(Immediately ELESIN, in handcuffs, comes pounding in the di-
rection of JANE and OLUNDE, followed some moments afterwards
by PILKINGS and the constables. ELESIN confronted by the seeming statue of his son, stops dead. OLUNDE stares above his head
into the distance. The constables try to grab him. JANE screams
at them.)*

JANE: Leave him alone! Simon, tell them to leave him alone.
PILKINGS: All right, stand aside you. *(Shrugs.)* Maybe just as
490 well. It might help to calm him down.

*(For several moments they hold the same position. ELESIN moves
a few steps forward, almost as if he's still in doubt.)*

ELESIN: Olunde? *(He moves his head, inspecting him from side
     to side.)* Olunde! *(He collapses slowly at OLUNDE's feet.)* Oh
     son, don't let the sight of your father turn you blind!
495 OLUNDE: *(He moves for the first time since he heard his voice,
     brings his head slowly down to look on him.)* I have no father,
     eater of left-overs.

*(He walks slowly down the way his father had run. Light fades
out on ELESIN, sobbing into the ground.)*

— FIVE —

*A wide iron-barred gate stretches almost the whole width of the
cell in which ELESIN is imprisoned. His wrists are encased in
thick iron bracelets, chained together; he stands against the bars,
looking out. Seated on the ground to one side on the outside is
his recent BRIDE, her eyes bent perpetually to the ground. Figures
of the two guards can be seen deeper inside the cell, alert to every
movement ELESIN makes. PILKINGS now in a police officer's uniform enters noiselessly, observes him for a while. Then he coughs
ostentatiously and approaches. Leans against the bars near a
corner, his back to ELESIN. He is obviously trying to fall in mood
with him. Some moments' silence.*

PILKINGS: You seem fascinated by the moon.

ELESIN: *(After a pause.)* Yes, ghostly one. Your twin-brother up
     there engages my thoughts.
PILKINGS: It is a beautiful night.
ELESIN: Is that so?   5
PILKINGS: The light on the leaves, the peace of the night . . .
ELESIN: The night is not at peace, District Officer.
PILKINGS: No? I would have said it was. You know, quiet . . .
ELESIN: And does quiet mean peace for you?
PILKINGS: Well, nearly the same thing. Naturally there is a   10
     subtle difference . . .
ELESIN: The night is not at peace ghostly one. The world is not
     at peace. You have shattered the peace of the world for ever.
     There is no sleep in the world tonight.
PILKINGS: It is still a good bargain if the world should lose one   15
     night's sleep as the price of saving a man's life.
ELESIN: You did not save my life District Officer. You de-
     stroyed it.
PILKINGS: Now come on . . .
ELESIN: And not merely my life but the lives of many. The end   20
     of the night's work is not over. Neither this year nor the next
     will see it. If I wished you well, I would pray that you do not
     stay long enough on our land to see the disaster you have
     brought upon us.
PILKINGS: Well, I did my duty as I saw it. I have no regrets.   25
ELESIN: No. The regrets of life always come later.

(Some moments' pause.)

You are waiting for dawn white man. I hear you saying to
yourself: only so many hours until dawn and then the danger
is over. All I must do is keep him alive tonight. You don't
quite understand it all but you know that tonight is when   30
what ought to be must be brought about. I shall ease your
mind even more, ghostly one. It is not an entire night but a
moment of the night, and that moment is past. The moon
was my messenger and guide. When it reached a certain
gateway in the sky, it touched that moment for which my   35
whole life has been spent in blessings. Even I do not know
the gateway. I have stood here and scanned the sky for a
glimpse of that door but, I cannot see it. Human eyes are
useless for a search of this nature. But in the house of *osugbo*,
those who keep watch through the spirit recognised the mo-   40
ment, they sent word to me through the voice of our sacred
drums to prepare myself. I heard them and I shed all
thoughts of earth. I began to follow the moon to the abode of
gods . . . servant of the white king, that was when you entered my chosen place of departure on feet of desecration.   45
PILKINGS: I'm sorry, but we all see our duty differently.
ELESIN: I no longer blame you. You stole from me my first-
born, sent him to your country so you could turn him into
something in your own image. Did you plan it all beforehand? There are moments when it seems part of a larger   50
plan. He who must follow my footsteps is taken from me,
sent across the ocean. Then, in my turn, I am stopped from
fulfilling my destiny. Did you think it all out before, this plan
to push our world from its course and sever the cord that
links us to the great origin?   55
PILKINGS: You don't really believe that. Anyway, if that was my
intention with your son, I appear to have failed.
ELESIN: You did not fail in the main thing ghostly one. We
know the roof covers the rafters, the cloth covers blemishes;
who would have known that the white skin covered our   60

future, preventing us from seeing the death our enemies had prepared for us. The world is set adrift and its inhabitants are lost. Around them, there is nothing but emptiness.

PILKINGS: Your son does not take so gloomy a view.

65 ELESIN: Are you dreaming now white man? Were you not present at my reunion of shame? Did you not see when the world reversed itself and the father fell before his son, asking forgiveness?

PILKINGS: That was in the heat of the moment. I spoke to him
70 and . . . if you want to know, he wishes he could cut out his tongue for uttering the words he did.

ELESIN: No. What he said must never be unsaid. The contempt of my own son rescued something of my shame at your hands. You may have stopped me in my duty but I know
75 now that I did give birth to a son. Once I mistrusted him for seeking the companionship of those my spirit knew as enemies of our race. Now I understand. One should seek to obtain the secrets of his enemies. He will avenge my shame, white one. His spirit will destroy you and yours.

80 PILKINGS: That kind of talk is hardly called for. If you don't want my consolation . . .

ELESIN: No white man, I do not want your consolation.

PILKINGS: As you wish. Your son anyway, sends his consolation. He asks your forgiveness. When I asked him not to de-
85 spise you his reply was: I cannot judge him, and if I cannot judge him, I cannot despise him. He wants to come to you to say goodbye and to receive your blessing.

ELESIN: Goodbye? Is he returning to your land?

PILKINGS: Don't you think that's the most sensible thing for
90 him to do? I advised him to leave at once, before dawn, and he agrees that is the right course of action.

ELESIN: Yes, it is best. And even if I did not think so, I have lost the father's place of honour. My voice is broken.

PILKINGS: Your son honours you. If he didn't he would not ask
95 your blessing.

ELESIN: No. Even a thoroughbred is not without pity for the turf he strikes with his hoof. When is he coming?

PILKINGS: As soon as the town is a little quieter. I advised it.

ELESIN: Yes white man, I am sure you advised it. You advise all
100 our lives although on the authority of what gods, I do not know.

PILKINGS: (*Opens his mouth to reply, then appears to change his mind. Turns to go. Hesitates and stops again.*) Before I leave you, may I ask just one thing of you?

105 ELESIN: I am listening.

PILKINGS: I wish to ask you to search the quiet of your heart and tell me—do you not find great contradictions in the wisdom of your own race?

ELESIN: Make yourself clear, white one.

110 PILKINGS: I have lived among you long enough to learn a saying or two. One came to my mind tonight when I stepped into the market and saw what was going on. You were surrounded by those who egged you on with song and praises. I thought, are these not the same people who say: the elder
115 grimly approaches heaven and you ask him to bear your greetings yonder; do you really think he makes the journey willingly? After that, I did not hesitate.

(*A pause.* ELESIN *sighs. Before he can speak a sound of running feet is heard.*)

JANE: (*Off.*) Simon! Simon!

PILKINGS: What on earth . . ! (*Runs off.*)

(ELESIN *turns to his new wife, gazes on her for some moments.*)

ELESIN: My young bride, did you hear the ghostly one? You sit 120
and sob in your silent heart but say nothing to all this. First I blamed the white man, then I blamed my gods for deserting me. Now I feel I want to blame you for the mystery of the sapping of my will. But blame is a strange peace offering for a man to bring a world he has deeply wronged, and to its in- 125
nocent dwellers. Oh little mother, I have taken countless women in my life but you were more than a desire of the flesh. I needed you as the abyss across which my body must be drawn, I filled it with earth and dropped my seed in it at the moment of preparedness for my crossing. You were the 130
final gift of the living to their emissary to the land of the ancestors, and perhaps your warmth and youth brought new insights of this world to me and turned my feet leaden on this side of the abyss. For I confess to you, daughter, my weakness came not merely from the abomination of the white man 135
who came violently into my fading presence, there was also a weight of longing on my earth-held limbs. I would have shaken it off, already my foot had begun to lift but then, the white ghost entered and all was defiled.

(*Approaching voices of* PILKINGS *and his wife.*)

JANE: Oh Simon, you will let her in won't you? 140

PILKINGS: I really wish you'd stop interfering.

(*They come in view.* JANE *is in a dressing-gown.* PILKINGS *is holding a note to which he refers from time to time.*)

JANE: Good gracious, I didn't initiate this. I was sleeping quietly, or trying to anyway, when the servant brought it. It's not my fault if one can't sleep undisturbed even in the Residency. 145

PILKINGS: He'd have done the same if we were sleeping at home so don't sidetrack the issue. He knows he can get round you or he wouldn't send you the petition in the first place.

JANE: Be fair Simon. After all he was thinking of your own interests. He is grateful you know, you seem to forget that. He feels he owes you something. 150

PILKINGS: I just wish they'd leave this man alone tonight, that's all.

JANE: Trust him Simon. He's pledged his word it will all go 155
peacefully.

PILKINGS: Yes, and that's the other thing. I don't like being threatened.

JANE: Threatened? (*Takes the note.*) I didn't spot any threat.

PILKINGS: It's there. Veiled, but it's there. The only way to pre- 160
vent serious rioting tomorrow—what a cheek!

JANE: I don't think he's threatening you Simon.

PILKINGS: He's picked up the idiom alright. Wouldn't surprise me if he's been mixing with commies or anarchists over there. The phrasing sounds too good to be true. Damn! If 165
only the Prince hadn't picked this time for his visit.

JANE: Well, even so Simon, what have you got to lose? You don't want a riot on your hands, not with the Prince here.

PILKINGS: (*Going up to* ELESIN.) Let's see what he has to say. Chief Elesin, there is yet another person who wants to see 170
you. As she is not a next-of-kin I don't really feel obliged to let her in. But your son sent a note with her, so it's up to you.

ELESIN: I know who that must be. So she found out your hiding-place. Well, it was not difficult. My stench of shame is so strong, it requires no hunter's dog to follow it. 175

PILKINGS: If you don't want to see her, just say so and I'll send her packing.

ELESIN: Why should I not want to see her? Let her come. I have no more holes in my rag of shame. All is laid bare.

180 PILKINGS: I'll bring her in. (*Goes off.*)

JANE: (*Hesitates, then goes to* ELESIN.) Please, try and understand. Everything my husband did was for the best.

ELESIN: (*He gives her a long strange stare, as if he is trying to understand who she is.*) You are the wife of the District
185 Officer?

JANE: Yes. My name, is Jane.

ELESIN: That is my wife sitting down there. You notice how still and silent she sits? My business is with your husband.

(PILKINGS *returns with* IYALOJA.)

PILKINGS: Here she is. Now first I want your word of honour
190 that you will try nothing foolish.

ELESIN: Honour? White one, did you say you wanted my word of honour?

PILKINGS: I know you to be an honourable man. Give me your word of honour you will receive nothing from her.

195 ELESIN: But I am sure you have searched her clothing as you would never dare touch your own mother. And there are these two lizards of yours who roll their eyes even when I scratch.

PILKINGS: And I shall be sitting on that tree trunk watching
200 even how you blink. Just the same I want your word that you will not let her pass anything to you.

ELESIN: You have my honour already. It is locked up in that desk in which you will put away your report of this night's events. Even the honour of my people you have taken al
205 ready; it is tied together with those papers of treachery which make you masters in this land.

PILKINGS: Alright. I am trying to make things easy but if you must bring in politics we'll have to do it the hard way. Madam, I want you to remain along this line and move no
210 nearer to that cell door. Guards! (*They spring to attention.*) If she moves beyond this point, blow your whistle. Come on Jane. (*They go off.*)

IYALOJA: How boldly the lizard struts before the pigeon when it was the eagle itself he promised us he would confront.

215 ELESIN: I don't ask you to take pity on me Iyaloja. You have a message for me or you would not have come. Even if it is the curses of the world, I shall listen.

IYALOJA: You made so bold with the servant of the white king who took your side against death. I must tell your brother
220 chiefs when I return how bravely you waged war against him. Especially with words.

ELESIN: I more than deserve your scorn.

IYALOJA: (*With sudden anger.*) I warned you, if you must leave a seed behind, be sure it is not tainted with the curses of the
225 world. Who are you to open a new life when you dared not open the door to a new existence? I say who are you to make so bold? (*The* BRIDE *sobs and* IYALOJA *notices her. Her contempt noticeably increases as she turns back to* ELESIN.) Oh you self-vaunted stem of the plantain, how hollow it all
230 proves. The pith is gone in the parent stem, so how will it prove with the new shoot? How will it go with that earth that bears it? Who are you to bring this abomination on us!

ELESIN: My powers deserted me. My charms, my spells, even my voice lacked strength when I made to summon the pow-
235 ers that would lead me over the last measure of earth into the

land of the fleshless. You saw it, Iyaloja. You saw me struggle to retrieve my will from the power of the stranger whose shadow fell across the doorway and left me floundering and blundering in a maze I had never before encountered. My senses were numbed when the touch of cold iron came upon 240 my wrists. I could do nothing to save myself.

IYALOJA: You have betrayed us. We fed you sweetmeats such as we hoped awaited you on the other side. But you said No, I must eat the world's left-overs. We said you were the hunter who brought the quarry down; to you belonged the vital por- 245 tions of the game. No, you said, I am the hunter's dog and I shall eat the entrails of the game and the faeces of the hunter. We said you were the hunter returning home in triumph, a slain buffalo pressing down on his neck, you said wait, I first must turn up this cricket hole with my toes. We 250 said yours was the doorway at which we first spy the tapper when he comes down from the tree, yours was the blessing of the twilight wine, the purl that brings night spirits out of doors to steal their portion before the light of day. We said yours was the body of wine whose burden shakes the tapper 255 like a sudden gust on his perch. You said, No, I am content to lick the dregs from each calabash when the drinkers are done. We said, the dew on earth's surface was for you to wash your feet along the slopes of honour. You said No, I shall step in the vomit of cats and the droppings of mice; I shall fight 260 them for the left-overs of the world.

ELESIN: Enough Iyaloja, enough.

IYALOJA: We called you leader and oh, how you led us on. What we have no intention of eating should not be held to the nose. 265

ELESIN: Enough, enough. My shame is heavy enough.

IYALOJA: Wait. I came with a burden.

ELESIN: You have more than discharged it.

IYALOJA: I wish I could pity you.

ELESIN: I need neither your pity nor the pity of the world. I 270 need understanding. Even I need to understand. You were present at my defeat. You were part of the beginnings. You brought about the renewal of my tie to earth, you helped in the binding of the cord.

IYALOJA: I gave you warning. The river which fills up before 275 our eyes does not sweep us away in its flood.

ELESIN: What were warnings beside the moist contact of living earth between my fingers? What were warnings beside the renewal of famished embers lodged eternally in the heart of man. But even that, even if it overwhelmed one with a thou- 280 sandfold temptations to linger a little while, a man could overcome it. It is when the alien hand pollutes the source of will, when a stranger force of violence shatters the mind's calm resolution, this is when a man is made to commit the awful treachery of relief, commit in his thought the unspeak- 285 able blasphemy of seeing the hand of the gods in this alien rupture of his world. I know it was this thought that killed me, sapped my powers and turned me into an infant in the hands of unnamable strangers. I made to utter my spells anew but my tongue merely rattled in my mouth. I fingered 290 hidden charms and the contact was damp; there was no spark left to sever the life-strings that should stretch from every finger-tip. My will was squelched in the spittle of an alien race, and all because I had committed this blasphemy of thought—that there might be the hand of the gods in a 295 stranger's intervention.

IYALOJA: Explain it how you will, I hope it brings you peace of mind. The bush-rat fled his rightful cause, reached the market and set up a lamentation. 'Please save me!'—are these fit-
300 ting words to hear from an ancestral mask? 'There's a wild beast at my heels' is not becoming language from a hunter.

ELESIN: May the world forgive me.

IYALOJA: I came with a burden I said. It approaches the gates which are so well guarded by those jackals whose spittle will
305 from this day on be your food and drink. But first, tell me, you who were once Elesin Oba, tell me, you who know so well the cycle of the plantain: is it the parent shoot which withers to give sap to the younger or, does your wisdom see it running the other way?

310 ELESIN: I don't see your meaning Iyaloja?

IYALOJA: Did I ask you for a meaning? I asked a question. Whose trunk withers to give sap to the other? The parent shoot or the younger?

ELESIN: The parent.

315 IYALOJA: Ah. So you do know that. There are sights in this world which say different Elesin. There are some who choose to reverse this cycle of our being. Oh you emptied bark that the world once saluted for a pith-laden being, shall I tell you what the gods have claimed of you?

(In her agitation she steps beyond the line indicated by PILKINGS *and the air is rent by piercing whistles. The two* GUARDS *also leap forward and place safe-guarding hands on* ELESIN. IYALOJA *stops, astonished.* PILKINGS *comes racing, followed by* JANE.)

320 PILKINGS: What is it? Did they try something?

GUARD: She stepped beyond the line.

ELESIN: (*In a broken voice.*) Let her alone. She meant no harm.

IYALOJA: Oh Elesin, see what you've become. Once you had no need to open your mouth in explanation because evil-
325 smelling goats, itchy of hand and foot had lost their senses. And it was a brave man indeed who dared lay hands on you because Iyaloja stepped from one side of the earth onto another. Now look at the spectacle of your life. I grieve for you.

PILKINGS: I think you'd better leave. I doubt you have done
330 him much good by coming here. I shall make sure you are not allowed to see him again. In any case we are moving him to a different place before dawn, so don't bother to come back.

IYALOJA: We foresaw that. Hence the burden I trudged here to
335 lay beside your gates.

PILKINGS: What was that you said?

IYALOJA: Didn't our son explain? Ask that one. He knows what it is. At least we hope the man we once knew as Elesin remembers the lesser oaths he need not break.

340 PILKINGS: Do you know what she is talking about?

ELESIN: Go to the gates, ghostly one. Whatever you find there, bring it to me.

IYALOJA: Not yet. It drags behind me on the slow, weary feet of women. Slow as it is Elesin, it has long overtaken you. It
345 rides ahead of your laggard will.

PILKINGS: What is she saying now? Christ! Must your people forever speak in riddles?

ELESIN: It will come white man, it will come. Tell your men at the gates to let it through.

350 PILKINGS: (*Dubiously.*) I'll have to see what it is.

IYALOJA: You will. (*Passionately.*) But this is one oath he cannot shirk. White one, you have a king here, a visitor from your land. We know of his presence here. Tell me, were he to

die would you leave his spirit roaming restlessly on the surface of earth? Would you bury him here among those you 355
consider less than human? In your land have you no ceremonies of the dead?

PILKINGS: Yes. But we don't make our chiefs commit suicide to keep him company.

IYALOJA: Child, I have not come to help your understanding. 360
(*Points to* ELESIN.) This is the man whose weakened under-
standing holds us in bondage to you. But ask him if you wish. He knows the meaning of a king's passage; he was not born yesterday. He knows the peril to the race when our dead father, who goes as intermediary, waits and waits and knows he 365
is betrayed. He knows when the narrow gate was opened and he knows it will not stay for laggards who drag their feet in dung and vomit, whose lips are reeking of the left-overs of lesser men. He knows he has condemned our king to wander in the void of evil with beings who are enemies of life. 370

PILKINGS: Yes er . . . but look here . . .

IYALOJA: What we ask is little enough. Let him release our King so he can ride on homewards alone. The messenger is on his way on the backs of women. Let him send word through the heart that is folded up within the bolt. It is the 375
least of all his oaths, it is the easiest fulfilled.

(The AIDE-DE-CAMP *runs in.)*

PILKINGS: Bob?

AIDE-DE-CAMP: Sir, there's a group of women chanting up the hill.

PILKINGS: (*Rounding on* IYALOJA.) If you people want trouble 380
. . .

JANE: Simon, I think that's what Olunde referred to in his letter.

PILKINGS: He knows damned well I can't have a crowd here! Damn it, I explained the delicacy of my position to him. I 385
think it's about time I got him out of town. Bob, send a car and two or three soldiers to bring him in. I think the sooner he takes his leave of his father and gets out the better.

IYALOJA: Save your labour white one. If it is the father of your prisoner you want, Olunde, he who until this night we knew 390
as Elesin's son, he comes soon himself to take his leave. He has sent the women ahead, so let them in.

(PILKINGS remains undecided.)

AIDE-DE-CAMP: What do we do about the invasion? We can still stop them far from here.

PILKINGS: What do they look like? 395

AIDE-DE-CAMP: They're not many. And they seem quite peaceful.

PILKINGS: No men?

AIDE-DE-CAMP: Mm, two or three at the most.

JANE: Honestly, Simon, I'd trust Olunde. I don't think he'll de- 400
ceive you about their intentions.

PILKINGS: He'd better not. Alright, let them in Bob. Warn them to control themselves. Then hurry Olunde here. Make sure he brings his baggage because I'm not returning him into town. 405

AIDE-DE-CAMP: Very good sir. (*Goes.*)

PILKINGS: (*To* IYALOJA.) I hope you understand that if anything goes wrong it will be on your head. My men have orders to shoot at the first sign of trouble.

IYALOJA: To prevent one death you will actually make other 410
deaths? Ah, great is the wisdom of the white race. But have

no fear. Your Prince will sleep peacefully. So at long last will ours. We will disturb you no further, servant of the white king. Just let Elesin fulfil his oath and we will retire home and pay homage to our King.

JANE: I believe her Simon, don't you?

PILKINGS: Maybe.

ELESIN: Have no fear ghostly one. I have a message to send my King and then you have nothing more to fear.

IYALOJA: Olunde would have done it. The chiefs asked him to speak the words but he said no, not while you lived.

ELESIN: Even from the depths to which my spirit has sunk, I find some joy that this little has been left to me.

(The WOMEN enter, intoning the dirge 'Ale le le' and swaying from side to side. On their shoulders is borne a longish object roughly like a cylindrical bolt, covered in cloth. They set it down on the spot where IYALOJA had stood earlier, and form a semi-circle round it. The PRAISE-SINGER and DRUMMER stand on the inside of the semi-circle but the drum is not used at all. The DRUMMER intones under the PRAISE-SINGER's invocations.)

PILKINGS: *(As they enter.)* What is that?

IYALOJA: The burden you have made white one, but we bring it in peace.

PILKINGS: I said *what* is it?

ELESIN: White man, you must let me out. I have a duty to perform.

PILKINGS: I most certainly will not.

ELESIN: There lies the courier of my King. Let me out so I can perform what is demanded of me.

PILKINGS: You'll do what you need to do from inside there or not at all. I've gone as far as I intend to with this business.

ELESIN: The worshipper who lights a candle in your church to bear a message to his god bows his head and speaks in a whisper to the flame. Have I not seen it ghostly one? His voice does not ring out to the world. Mine are no words for anyone's ears. They are not words even for the bearers of this load. They are words I must speak secretly, even as my father whispered them in my ears and I in the ears of my first-born. I cannot shout them to the wind and the open night-sky.

JANE: Simon . . .

PILKINGS: Don't interfere. Please!

IYALOJA: They have slain the favourite horse of the king and slain his dog. They have borne them from pulse to pulse centre of the land receiving prayers for their king. But the rider has chosen to stay behind. Is it too much to ask that he speak his heart to heart of the waiting courier? *(PILKINGS turns his back on her.)* So be it. Elesin Oba, you see how even the mere leavings are denied you. *(She gestures to the PRAISE-SINGER.)*

PRAISE-SINGER: Elesin Oba! I call you by that name only this last time. Remember when I said, if you cannot come, tell my horse. *(Pause.)* What? I cannot hear you? I said, if you cannot come, whisper in the ears of my horse. Is your tongue severed from the roots Elesin? I can hear no response. I said, if there are boulders you cannot climb, mount my horse's back, this spotless black stallion, he'll bring you over them. *(Pauses.)* Elesin Oba, once you had a tongue that darted like a drummer's stick. I said, if you get lost my dog will track a path to me. My memory fails me but I think you replied: My feet have found the path, Alafin.

(The dirge rises and falls.)

I said at the last, if evil hands hold you back, just tell my horse there is weight on the hem of your smock. I dare not wait too long.

(The dirge rises and falls.)

There lies the swiftest ever messenger of a king, so set me free with the errand of your heart. There lie the head and heart of the favourite of the gods, whisper in his ears. Oh my companion, if you had followed when you should, we would not say that the horse preceded its rider. If you had followed when it was time, we would not say the dog has raced beyond and left his master behind. If you had raised your will to cut the thread of life at the summons of the drums, we would not say your mere shadow fell across the gateway and took its owner's place at the banquet. But the hunter, laden with a slain buffalo, stayed to root in the cricket's hole with his toes. What now is left? If there is a dearth of bats, the pigeon must serve us for the offering. Speak the words over your shadow which must now serve in your place.

ELESIN: I cannot approach. Take off the cloth. I shall speak my message from heart to heart of silence.

IYALOJA: *(Moves forward and removes the coverings.)* Your courier Elesin, cast your eyes on the favoured companion of the King.

(Rolled up in the mat, his head and feet showing at either end is the body of OLUNDE.)

There lies the honour of your household and of our race. Because he could not bear to let honour fly out of doors, he stopped it with his life. The son has proved the father Elesin, and there is nothing left in your mouth to gnash but infant gums.

PRAISE-SINGER: Elesin, we placed the reins of the world in your hands yet you watched it plunge over the edge of the bitter precipice. You sat with folded arms while evil strangers tilted the world from its course and crashed it beyond the edge of emptiness—you muttered, there is little that one man can do, you left us floundering in a blind future. Your heir has taken the burden on himself. What the end will be, we are not gods to tell. But this young shoot has poured its sap into the parent stalk, and we know this is not the way of life. Our world is tumbling in the void of strangers, Elesin.

(ELESIN has stood rock-still, his knuckles taut on the bars, his eyes glued to the body of his son. The stillness seizes and paralyses everyone, including PILKINGS who has turned to look. Suddenly ELESIN flings one arm round his neck, once, and with the loop of the chain, strangles himself in a swift, decisive pull. The guards rush forward to stop him but they are only in time to let his body down. PILKINGS has leapt to the door at the same time and struggles with the lock. He rushes within, fumbles with the handcuffs and unlocks them, raises the body to a sitting position while he tries to give resuscitation. The WOMEN continue their dirge, unmoved by the sudden event.)

IYALOJA: Why do you strain yourself? Why do you labour at tasks for which no one, not even the man lying there would give you thanks? He is gone at last into the passage but oh, how late it all is. His son will feast on the meat and throw him bones. The passage is clogged with droppings from the King's stallion; he will arrive all stained in dung.

PILKINGS: *(In a tired voice.)* Was this what you wanted?

IYALOJA: No child, it is what you brought to be, you who play with strangers' lives, who even usurp the vestments of our dead, yet believe that the stain of death will not cling to you. The gods demanded only the old expired plantain but you cut down the sap-laden shoot to feed your pride. There is your board, filled to overflowing. Feast on it. *(She screams at him suddenly, seeing that* PILKINGS *is about to close* ELESIN's *staring eyes.)* Let him alone! However sunk he was in debt he is no pauper's carrion abandoned on the road. Since when have strangers donned clothes of indigo before the bereaved cries out his loss?

(She turns to the BRIDE *who has remained motionless throughout.)*

Child.

(The GIRL *takes up a little earth, walks calmly into the cell and closes* ELESIN's *eyes. She then pours some earth over each eyelid and comes out again.)*

Now forget the dead, forget even the living. Turn your mind only to the unborn.

(She goes off, accompanied by the BRIDE. *The dirge rises in volume and the* WOMEN *continue their sway. Lights fade to a blackout.)*

GLOSSARY

alari a rich, woven cloth, brightly coloured
egungun ancestral masquerade
etutu placatory rites or medicine
gbedu a deep-timbred royal drum
opele string of beads used in Ifa divination
osugbo secret 'executive' cult of the Yoruba; its meeting place

robo a delicacy made from crushed melon seeds, fried in tiny balls
sanyan a richly valued woven cloth
sigidi a squat, carved figure, endowed with the powers of an incubus

■ CARYL CHURCHILL ■

Caryl Churchill (b. 1938) was born in England and began her education in Canada during World War II; she returned to study at Oxford University, taking her B.A. in 1960. At Oxford, Churchill began her career as a playwright, producing several plays: *Downstairs* (1958), *Having a Wonderful Time* (1960), and *Early Death* (1962). During the 1960s, she wrote a series of brilliant radio plays. She also studied radical politics and returned to the theater in the 1970s with a series of striking political dramas: *Owners* (1972), *Objections to Sex and Violence* (1975), and *A Light Shining in Buckinghamshire* (1976). In the mid-1970s, Churchill began to work more closely with experimental theater companies, collaborating with actors and directors in the writing of her plays. Working with the feminist theater company Monstrous Regiment (the name alludes to the Calvinist preacher John Knox's 1558 diatribe against Queen Mary of England, "The First Blast of the Trumpet against the Monstrous Regiment of Women"), she wrote *Vinegar Tom*, a play about witchcraft and sexual politics in seventeenth-century England. With the Joint Stock company, she investigated the politics of sexuality more extensively in *Cloud Nine* (1979), a pastiche of melodrama, Gilbert-and-Sullivan operetta, and modern realistic theater that uses CROSS-DRESSING and ROLE-DOUBLING to explore the relationship between colonial and sexual oppression in the nineteenth century and today. The history of gender oppression and the options for contemporary women are the subject of *Top Girls* (1982), and Churchill has continued to write challenging plays on the relationship between class, race, and gender in British social life, including *Fen* (1983) and *Serious Money* (1987). *Mad Forest* (1990) concerns the revolution in Rumania. Her most recent play, *Skryker* (1994), was developed from Lancashire folk-tales.

CLOUD NINE

Onstage, the most exciting and interesting device in *Cloud Nine* is its use of *cross-dressing* and *role-doubling*. In the first act, for instance, Betty must be played by a man, Joshua by a white man, and Edward by a woman. By "alienating" actors from the characters they play, Churchill clearly intends to raise the questions of gender, sexual orientation, and race as ideological issues, for in each of these cases the difference between the performer and the role marks what Clive wants to see as real. Betty is played by a man because Clive—and his patriarchal society—cannot envision women's identity; women are constructed on the model of male attitudes. Joshua is played by a white man because imperial and racist culture reduces African identity to the construction of white, European attitudes. Edward is played by a woman to express the impossibility of Edward's conforming to Clive's heterosexual standards. In all three cases, the "identity" of the character is compromised or even erased, to be filled-in and embodied by the attitudes that Clive and his society want them to hold. This performative dimension of the play's politics is echoed by the play's doubling of parts—each of the actors in Act 1 takes a part in Act 2, inviting the audience to draw comparisons between the two characters. Although other doubling patterns are possible, Churchill has suggested doubling Harry Bagley, the explorer, with Martin, the superficially liberated man; Clive, the father, with Cathy, the child; Betty with Edward; and so on. Doubling and cross-dressing are familiar conventions in the theater, but in *Cloud Nine* they have a specific dramatic purpose in developing the themes of the play. By denaturalizing the categories of gender, race, and sexuality, *Cloud Nine* undertakes a typically postmodern inquiry into the construction of social reality, asking what meanings are created by these categories, and how they work to structure the relationship between self and society.

AUTHOR'S NOTE

Cloud Nine was written for Joint Stock Theatre Group in 1978–79. The company's usual work method is to set up a workshop in which the writer, director and actors research a particular subject. The writer then goes away to write the play, before returning to the company for a rehearsal and rewrite period. In the case of *Cloud Nine* the workshop lasted for three weeks, the writing period for twelve, and the rehearsal for six.

The workshop for *Cloud Nine* was about sexual politics. This meant that the starting point for our research was to talk about ourselves and share our very different attitudes and experiences. We also explored stereotypes and role reversals in games and improvisations, read books and talked to other people. Though the play's situations and characters were not developed in the workshop, it draws deeply on this material, and I wouldn't have written the same play without it.

When I came to write the play, I returned to an idea that had been touched on briefly in the workshop—the parallel between colonial and sexual oppression, which Genet calls 'the colonial or feminine mentality of interiorised repression'. So the first act of *Cloud Nine* takes place in Victorian Africa, where Clive, the white man, imposes his ideals on his family and the natives. Betty, Clive's wife, is played by a man because she wants to be what men want her to be, and, in the same way, Joshua, the black servant, is played by a white man because he wants to be what whites want him to be. Betty does not value herself as a woman, nor does Joshua value himself as a black. Edward, Clive's son, is played by a woman for a different reason—partly to do with the stage convention of having boys played by women (Peter Pan, radio plays, etc.) and partly with highlighting the way Clive tries to impose traditional male behaviour on him. Clive struggles throughout the act to maintain the world he wants to see—a faithful wife, a manly son. Harry's homosexuality is reviled, Ellen's is invisible. Rehearsing the play for the first time, we were initially taken by how funny the first act was and then by the painfulness of the relationships—which then became more funny than when they had seemed purely farcical.

The second act is set in London in 1979—this is where I wanted the play to end up, in the changing sexuality of our own time. Betty is middle-aged, Edward and Victoria have grown up. A hundred years have passed, but for the characters only twenty-five years. There were two reasons for this. I felt the first act would be stronger set in Victorian times, at the height of colonialism, rather than in Africa during the 1950s. And when the company talked about their childhoods and the attitudes to sex and marriage that they had been given when they were young, everyone felt that they had received very conventional, almost Victorian expectations and that they had made great changes and discoveries in their lifetimes.

The first act, like the society it shows, is male dominated and firmly structured. In the second act, more energy comes from the women and the gays. The uncertainties and changes of society, and a more feminine and less authoritarian feeling, are reflected in the looser structure of the act. Betty, Edward and Victoria all change from the rigid positions they had been left in by the first act, partly because of their encounters with Gerry and Lin.

In fact, all the characters in this act change a little for the better. If men are finding it hard to keep control in the first act, they are finding it hard to let go in the second: Martin dominates Victoria, despite his declarations of sympathy for feminism, and the bitter end of colonialism is apparent in Lin's soldier brother, who dies in Northern Ireland. Betty is now played by a woman, as she gradually becomes real to herself. Cathy is played by a man, partly as a simple reversal of Edward being played by a woman, partly because the size and presence of a man on stage seemed appropriate to the emotional force of young children, and partly, as with Edward, to show more clearly the issues involved in learning what is considered correct behaviour for a girl.

It is essential for Joshua to be played by a white, Betty (I) by a man, Edward (I) by a woman, and Cathy by a man. The soldier should be played by the actor who plays Cathy. The doubling of Mrs Saunders and Ellen is not intended to make a point so much as for sheer fun—and of course to keep the company to seven in each act. The doubling can be done in any way that seems right for any particular production. The first production went Clive-Cathy, Betty-Edward, Edward-Betty, Maud-Victoria, Mrs Saunders/Ellen-Lin, Joshua-Gerry, Harry-Martin. When we did the play again, at the Royal Court in 1980, we decided to try a different doubling: Clive-Edward, Betty-Gerry, Edward-Victoria, Maud-Lin, Mrs Saunders/Ellen-Betty, Joshua-Cathy, Harry-Martin. I've a slight preference for the first way because I like seeing Clive become Cathy, and enjoy the Edward-Betty connections. Some doublings aren't practicable, but any way of doing the doubling seems to set up some interesting resonances between the two acts.

C.C. 1983

THE TEXT

The first edition of *Cloud Nine* (Pluto/Joint Stock 1979) went to press before the end of rehearsal. Further changes were made within the first week or two of production, and these were incorporated in the Pluto/Joint Stock/Royal Court edition 1980. This edition also went to press during rehearsal, so although it may include some small changes made for that production, others don't turn up till the Pluto Plays edition 1983, which also includes a few changes from the American production, a few lines cut here or reinstated there. Other changes for the American production can be found in French's American acting edition—the main ones are the position of Betty's monologue and some lines of the 'ghosts'. For the Fireside Bookclub and Methuen Inc (1984) in America I did another brushing up, not very different from Pluto '83, and I have kept almost the same text for this edition. The scenes I tinker with most are the flogging scene and Edward's and Gerry's last scene—I no longer know what's the final version except by looking at the text.

There's a problem with the Maud and Ellen reappearances in Act Two. If Ellen is doubled with Betty, obviously only Maud can appear. Equally Maud-Betty would mean only Ellen could, though that seems a dull doubling. This text gives both Maud and Ellen. In the production at the Court in 1981 only Maud appeared and she has some extra lines so she can talk about sex as well as work; they can be found in Pluto 1983.

C.C. 1984

CLOUD NINE

Caryl Churchill

— CHARACTERS —

ACT ONE
CLIVE, *a colonial administrator*
BETTY, *his wife, played by a man*
JOSHUA, *his black servant, played by a white*
EDWARD, *his son, played by a woman*
VICTORIA, *his daughter, a dummy*
MAUD, *his mother-in-law*
ELLEN, *Edward's governess*
HARRY BAGLEY, *an explorer*
MRS SAUNDERS, *a widow*

ACT TWO
BETTY
EDWARD, *her son*

VICTORIA, *her daughter*
MARTIN, *Victoria's husband*
LIN
CATHY, *Lin's daughter, age 5, played by a man*
GERRY, *Edward's lover*

Except for Cathy, characters in Act Two are played by actors of their own sex.

Act One takes place in a British colony in Africa in Victorian times.

Act Two takes place in London in 1979. But for the characters it is twenty-five years later.

— ACT ONE —

SCENE I

Low bright sun. Verandah. Flagpole with union jack. The Family—CLIVE, BETTY, EDWARD, VICTORIA, MAUD, ELLEN, JOSHUA

ALL: *(Sing.)* Come gather, sons of England, come gather in
    your pride.
  Now meet the world united, now face it side by side;
  Ye who the earth's wide corners, from veldt to prairie, roam.
  From bush and jungle muster all who call old England
    'home'.
5 Then gather round for England,
  Rally to the flag,
  From North and South and East and West
  Come one and all for England!
CLIVE: This is my family. Though far from home
10 We serve the Queen wherever we may roam
  I am a father to the natives here,
  And father to my family so dear.

(He presents BETTY. *She is played by a man.)*

  My wife is all I dreamt a wife should be,
  And everything she is she owes to me.
15 BETTY: I live for Clive. The whole aim of my life
  Is to be what he looks for in a wife.
  I am a man's creation as you see,
  And what men want is what I want to be.

(CLIVE presents JOSHUA. *He is played by a white.)*

CLIVE: My boy's a jewel. Really has the knack.
20 You'd hardly notice that the fellow's black.
JOSHUA: My skin is black but oh my soul is white.
  I hate my tribe. My master is my light.
  I only live for him. As you can see,
  What white men want is what I want to be.

(CLIVE presents EDWARD. *He is played by a woman.)*

25 CLIVE: My son is young. I'm doing all I can

To teach him to grow up to be a man.
EDWARD: What father wants I'd dearly like to be.
  I find it rather hard as you can see.

(CLIVE presents VICTORIA, *who is a dummy,* MAUD, *and* ELLEN.)*

CLIVE: No need for any speeches by the rest.
  My daughter, mother-in-law, and governess.   30
ALL: *(Sing.)*

  O'er countless numbers she, our Queen,
  Victoria reigns supreme;
  O'er Africa's sunny plains, and o'er
  Canadian frozen stream;   35
  The forge of war shall weld the chains of brotherhood secure;
  So to all time in ev'ry clime our Empire shall endure.
  Then gather round for England,
  Rally to the flag,
  From North and South and East and West   40
  Come one and all for England!

(All go except BETTY. CLIVE *comes.)*

BETTY: Clive?
CLIVE: Betty. Joshua!

(JOSHUA comes with a drink for CLIVE.)*

BETTY: I thought you would never come. The day's so long
  without you.   45
CLIVE: Long ride in the bush.
BETTY: Is anything wrong? I heard drums.
CLIVE: Nothing serious. Beauty is a damned good mare. I
  must get some new boots sent from home. These ones have
  never been right. I have a blister.   50
BETTY: My poor dear foot.
CLIVE: It's nothing.
BETTY: Oh but it's sore.
CLIVE: We are not in this country to enjoy ourselves. Must
  have ridden fifty miles. Spoke to three different headmen   55
  who would all gladly chop off each other's heads and wear
  them round their waists.

BETTY: Clive!

CLIVE: Don't be squeamish, Betty, let me have my joke. And
60 what has my little dove done today?

BETTY: I've read a little.

CLIVE: Good. Is it good?

BETTY: It's poetry.

CLIVE: You're so delicate and sensitive.

65 BETTY: And I played the piano. Shall I send for the children?

CLIVE: Yes, in a minute. I've a piece of news for you.

BETTY: Good news?

CLIVE: You'll certainly think it's good. A visitor.

BETTY: From home?

70 CLIVE: No. Well of course originally from home.

BETTY: Man or woman?

CLIVE: Man.

BETTY: I can't imagine.

CLIVE: Something of an explorer. Bit of a poet. Odd chap but
75 brave as a lion. And a great admirer of yours.

BETTY: What do you mean? Whoever can it be?

CLIVE: With an H and a B. And does conjuring tricks for little
Edward.

BETTY: That sounds like Mr Bagley.

80 CLIVE: Harry Bagley.

BETTY: He certainly doesn't admire me, Clive, what a thing to
say. How could I possibly guess from that. He's hardly explored anything at all, he's just been up a river, he's done
nothing at all compared to what you do. You should have
85 said a heavy drinker and a bit of a bore.

CLIVE: But you like him well enough. You don't mind him
coming?

BETTY: Anyone at all to break the monotony.

CLIVE: But you have your mother. You have Ellen.

90 BETTY: Ellen is a governess. My mother is my mother.

CLIVE: I hoped when she came to visit she would be company
for you.

BETTY: I don't think mother is on a visit. I think she lives
with us.

95 CLIVE: I think she does.

BETTY: Clive you are so good.

CLIVE: But are you bored my love?

BETTY: It's just that I miss you when you're away. We're not in
this country to enjoy ourselves. If I lack society that is my
100 form of service.

CLIVE: That's a brave girl. So today has been all right? No
fainting? No hysteria?

BETTY: I have been very tranquil.

CLIVE: Ah what a haven of peace to come home to. The
105 coolth, the calm, the beauty.

BETTY: There is one thing, Clive, if you don't mind.

CLIVE: What can I do for you, my dear?

BETTY: It's about Joshua.

CLIVE: I wouldn't leave you alone here with a quiet mind if it
110 weren't for Joshua.

BETTY: Joshua doesn't like me.

CLIVE: Joshua has been my boy for eight years. He has saved
my life. I have saved his life. He is devoted to me and to
mine. I have said this before.

115 BETTY: He is rude to me. He doesn't do what I say. Speak to
him.

CLIVE: Tell me what happened.

BETTY: He said something improper.

CLIVE: Well, what?

BETTY: I don't like to repeat it.   120

CLIVE: I must insist.

BETTY: I had left my book inside on the piano. I was in the
hammock. I asked him to fetch it.

CLIVE: And did he not fetch it?

BETTY: Yes, he did eventually.   125

CLIVE: And what did he say?

BETTY: Clive—

CLIVE: Betty.

BETTY: He said Fetch it yourself. You've got legs under that
dress.   130

CLIVE: Joshua!

(JOSHUA comes.)

Joshua, madam says you spoke impolitely to her this
afternoon.

JOSHUA: Sir?

CLIVE: When she asked you to pass her book from the piano.   135

JOSHUA: She has the book, sir.

BETTY: I have the book now, but when I told you—

CLIVE: Betty, please, let me handle this. You didn't pass it at
once?

JOSHUA: No sir, I made a joke first.   140

CLIVE: What was that?

JOSHUA: I said my legs were tired, sir. That was funny because
the book was very near, it would not make my legs tired to
get it.

BETTY: That's not true.   145

JOSHUA: Did madam hear me wrong?

CLIVE: She heard something else.

JOSHUA: What was that, madam?

BETTY: Never mind.

CLIVE: Now Joshua, it won't do you know. Madam doesn't like   150
that kind of joke. You must do what madam says, just do
what she says and don't answer back. You know your place,
Joshua. I don't have to say any more.

JOSHUA: No sir.

BETTY: I expect an apology.   155

JOSHUA: I apologise, madam.

CLIVE: There now. It won't happen again, my dear. I'm very
shocked Joshua, very shocked.

(CLIVE winks at JOSHUA, unseen by BETTY. JOSHUA goes.)

CLIVE: I think another drink, and send for the children, and
isn't that Harry riding down the hill? Wave, wave. Just in   160
time before dark. Cuts it fine, the blighter. Always a hothead,
Harry.

BETTY: Can he see us?

CLIVE: Stand further forward. He'll see your white dress.
There, he waved back.   165

BETTY: Do you think so? I wonder what he saw. Sometimes
sunset is so terrifying I can't bear to look.

CLIVE: It makes me proud. Elsewhere in the empire the sun is
rising.

BETTY: Harry looks so small on the hillside.   170

(ELLEN comes.)

ELLEN: Shall I bring the children?

BETTY: Shall Ellen bring the children?

CLIVE: Delightful.

BETTY: Yes, Ellen, make sure they're warm. The night air is de-
175   ceptive. Victoria was looking pale yesterday.
CLIVE: My love.

(MAUD *comes from inside the house.*)

MAUD: Are you warm enough Betty?
BETTY: Perfectly.
MAUD: The night air is deceptive.
180 BETTY: I'm quite warm. I'm too warm.
MAUD: You're not getting a fever, I hope? She's not strong, you
    know, Clive. I don't know how long you'll keep her in this
    climate.
CLIVE: I look after Her Majesty's domains. I think you can
185   trust me to look after my wife.

(ELLEN *comes carrying* VICTORIA, *age 2.* EDWARD, *aged 9, lags
behind.*)

BETTY: Victoria, my pet, say good evening to papa.

(CLIVE *takes* VICTORIA *on his knee.*)

CLIVE: There's my sweet little Vicky. What have we done
    today?
BETTY: She wore Ellen's hat.
190 CLIVE: Did she wear Ellen's big hat like a lady? What a pretty.
BETTY: And Joshua gave her a piggy back. Tell papa. Horsy
    with Joshy?
ELLEN: She's tired.
CLIVE: Nice Joshy played horsy. What a big strong Joshy. Did
195   you have a gallop? Did you make him stop and go? Not very
    chatty tonight are we?
BETTY: Edward, say good evening to papa.
CLIVE: Edward my boy. Have you done your lessons well?
EDWARD: Yes papa.
200 CLIVE: Did you go riding?
EDWARD: Yes papa.
CLIVE: What's that you're holding?
BETTY: It's Victoria's doll. What are you doing with it,
    Edward?
205 EDWARD: Minding her.
BETTY: Well I should give it to Ellen quickly. You don't want
    papa to see you with a doll.
CLIVE: No, we had you with Victoria's doll once before,
    Edward.
210 ELLEN: He's minding it for Vicky. He's not playing with it.
BETTY: He's not playing with it, Clive. He's minding it for
    Vicky.
CLIVE: Ellen minds Victoria, let Ellen mind the doll.
ELLEN: Come, give it to me.

(ELLEN *takes the doll.*)

215 EDWARD: Don't pull her about. Vicky's very fond of her. She
    likes me to have her.
BETTY: He's a very good brother.
CLIVE: Yes, it's manly of you Edward, to take care of your little
    sister. We'll say no more about it. Tomorrow I'll take you rid-
220   ing with me and Harry Bagley. Would you like that?
EDWARD: Is he here?
CLIVE: He's just arrived. There Betty, take Victoria now. I
    must go and welcome Harry.

(CLIVE *tosses* VICTORIA *to* BETTY, *who gives her to* ELLEN.)

EDWARD: Can I come, papa?

BETTY: Is he warm enough?   225
EDWARD: Am I warm enough?
CLIVE: Never mind the women, Ned. Come and meet Harry.

(*They go. The women are left. There is a silence.*)

MAUD: I daresay Mr Bagley will be out all day and we'll see
    nothing of him.
BETTY: He plays the piano. Surely he will sometimes stay at   230
    home with us.
MAUD: We can't expect it. The men have their duties and we
    have ours.
BETTY: He won't have seen a piano for a year. He lives a very
    rough life.   235
ELLEN: Will it be exciting for you, Betty?
MAUD: Whatever do you mean, Ellen?
ELLEN: We don't have very much society.
BETTY: Clive is my society.
MAUD: It's time Victoria went to bed.   240
ELLEN: She'd like to stay up and see Mr Bagley.
MAUD: Mr Bagley can see her tomorrow.

(ELLEN *goes.*)

MAUD: You let that girl forget her place, Betty.
BETTY: Mother, she is governess to my son. I know what her
    place is. I think my friendship does her good. She is not very   245
    happy.
MAUD: Young women are never happy.
BETTY: Mother, what a thing to say.
MAUD: Then when they're older they look back and see that
    comparatively speaking they were ecstatic.   250
BETTY: I'm perfectly happy.
MAUD: You are looking very pretty tonight. You were such a
    success as a young girl. You have made a most fortunate mar-
    riage. I'm sure you will be an excellent hostess to Mr Bagley.
BETTY: I feel quite nervous at the thought of entertaining.   255
MAUD: I can always advise you if I'm asked.
BETTY: What a long time they're taking. I always seem to be
    waiting for the men.
MAUD: Betty you have to learn to be patient. I am patient. My
    mama was very patient.   260

(CLIVE *approaches, supporting* CAROLINE SAUNDERS.)

CLIVE: It is a pleasure. It is an honour. It is positively your duty
    to seek my help. I would be hurt, I would be insulted by any
    show of independence. Your husband would have been one
    of my dearest friends if he had lived. Betty, look who has
    come, Mrs Saunders. She has ridden here all alone, amazing   265
    spirit. What will you have? Tea or something stronger? Let
    her lie down, she is overcome. Betty, you will know what
    to do.

(MRS SAUNDERS *lies down.*)

MAUD: I knew it. I heard drums. We'll be killed in our beds.
CLIVE: Now, please, calm yourself.   270
MAUD: I am perfectly calm. I am just outspoken. If it comes to
    being killed I shall take it as calmly as anyone.
CLIVE: There is no cause for alarm. Mrs Saunders has been
    alone since her husband died last year, amazing spirit. Not
    surprisingly, the strain has told. She has come to us as her   275
    nearest neighbours.
MAUD: What happened to make her come?

CLIVE: This is not an easy country for a woman.

MAUD: Clive, I heard drums. We are not children.

280　CLIVE: Of course you heard drums. The tribes are constantly at war, if the term is not too grand to grace their squabbles. Not unnaturally Mrs Saunders would like the company of white women. The piano. Poetry.

BETTY: We are not her nearest neighbours.

285　CLIVE: We are among her nearest neighbours and I was a dear friend of her late husband. She knows that she will find a welcome here. She will not be disappointed. She will be cared for.

MAUD: Of course we will care for her.

290　BETTY: Victoria is in bed. I must go and say goodnight. Mother, please, you look after Mrs Saunders.

CLIVE: Harry will be here at once.

(BETTY goes.)

MAUD: How rash to go out after dark without a shawl.

CLIVE: Amazing spirit. Drink this.

295　MRS SAUNDERS: Where am I?

MAUD: You are quite safe.

MRS SAUNDERS: Clive? Clive? Thank God. This is very kind. How do you do? I am sorry to be a nuisance. Charmed. Have you a gun? I have a gun.

300　CLIVE: There is no need for guns I hope. We are all friends here.

MRS SAUNDERS: I think I will lie down again.

(HARRY BAGLEY and EDWARD have approached.)

MAUD: Ah, here is Mr Bagley.

EDWARD: I gave his horse some water.

305　CLIVE: You don't know Mrs Saunders, do you Harry? She has at present collapsed, but she is recovering thanks to the good offices of my wife's mother who I think you've met before. Betty will be along in a minute. Edward will go home to school shortly. He is quite a young man since you saw him.

310　HARRY: I hardly knew him.

MAUD: What news have you for us, Mr Bagley?

CLIVE: Do you know Mrs Saunders, Harry? Amazing spirit.

EDWARD: Did you hardly know me?

HARRY: Of course I knew you. I mean you have grown.

315　EDWARD: What do you expect?

HARRY: That's quite right, people don't get smaller.

MAUD: Edward. You should be in bed.

EDWARD: No, I'm not tired, I'm not tired am I Uncle Harry?

HARRY: I don't think he's tired.

320　CLIVE: He is overtired. It is past his bedtime. Say goodnight.

EDWARD: Goodnight, sir.

CLIVE: And to your grandmother.

EDWARD: Goodnight, grandmother.

(EDWARD goes.)

MAUD: Shall I help Mrs Saunders indoors? I'm afraid she may

325　get a chill.

CLIVE: Shall I give her an arm?

MAUD: How kind of you Clive. I think I am strong enough.

(MAUD helps MRS SAUNDERS into the house.)

CLIVE: Not a word to alarm the women.

HARRY: Absolutely.

330　CLIVE: I did some good today I think. Kept up some alliances. There's a lot of affection there.

HARRY: They're affectionate people. They can be very cruel of course.

CLIVE: Well they are savages.

HARRY: Very beautiful people many of them.　　　　　　　335

CLIVE: Joshua! *(To HARRY.)* I think we should sleep with guns.

HARRY: I haven't slept in a house for six months. It seems extremely safe.

(JOSHUA comes.)

CLIVE: Joshua, you will have gathered there's a spot of bother. Rumours of this and that. You should be armed I think.　340

JOSHUA: There are many bad men, sir. I pray about it. Jesus will protect us.

CLIVE: He will indeed and I'll also get you a weapon. Betty, come and keep Harry company. Look in the barn, Joshua, every night.　　　　　　　　　　　　　　　　　　345

(CLIVE and JOSHUA go. BETTY comes.)

HARRY: I wondered where you were.

BETTY: I was singing lullabies.

HARRY: When I think of you I always think of you with Edward in your lap.

BETTY: Do you think of me sometimes then?　　　　　　350

HARRY: You have been thought of where no white woman has ever been thought of before.

BETTY: It's one way of having adventures. I suppose I will never go in person.

HARRY: That's up to you.　　　　　　　　　　　　　　355

BETTY: Of course it's not. I have duties.

HARRY: Are you happy, Betty?

BETTY: Where have you been?

HARRY: Built a raft and went up the river. Stayed with some people. The king is always very good to me. They have a lot　360 of skulls around the place but not white men's I think. I made up a poem one night. If I should die in this forsaken spot, There is a loving heart without a blot, Where I will live—and so on.

BETTY: When I'm near you it's like going out into the jungle.　365 It's like going up the river on a raft. It's like going out in the dark.

HARRY: And you are safety and light and peace and home.

BETTY: But I want to be dangerous.

HARRY: Clive is my friend.　　　　　　　　　　　　　370

BETTY: I am your friend.

HARRY: I don't like dangerous women.

BETTY: Is Mrs Saunders dangerous?

HARRY: Not to me. She's a bit of an old boot.

(JOSHUA comes, unobserved.)

BETTY: Am I dangerous?　　　　　　　　　　　　　　375

HARRY: You are rather.

BETTY: Please like me.

HARRY: I worship you.

BETTY: Please want me.

HARRY: I don't want to want you. Of course I want you.　　380

BETTY: What are we going to do?

HARRY: I should have stayed on the river. The hell with it.

(He goes to take her in his arms, she runs away into the house. HARRY stays where he is. He becomes aware of JOSHUA.)

HARRY: Who's there?

JOSHUA: Only me sir.

385   HARRY: Got a gun now have you?
JOSHUA: Yes sir.
HARRY: Where's Clive?
JOSHUA: Going round the boundaries sir.
HARRY: Have you checked there's nobody in the barns?
390   JOSHUA: Yes sir.
HARRY: Shall we go in a barn and fuck? It's not an order.
JOSHUA: That's all right, yes.

(They go off.)

SCENE II

An open space some distance from the house. MRS SAUNDERS *alone, breathless. She is carrying a riding crop.* CLIVE *arrives.*

CLIVE: Why? Why?
MRS SAUNDERS: Don't fuss, Clive, it makes you sweat.
CLIVE: Why ride off now? Sweat, you would sweat if you were in love with somebody as disgustingly capricious as you are.
5   You will be shot with poisoned arrows. You will miss the picnic. Somebody will notice I came after you.
MRS SAUNDERS: I didn't want you to come after me. I wanted to be alone.
CLIVE: You will be raped by cannibals.
10   MRS SAUNDERS: I just wanted to get out of your house.
CLIVE: My God, what women put us through. Cruel, cruel. I think you are the sort of woman who would enjoy whipping somebody. I've never met one before.
MRS SAUNDERS: Can I tell you something, Clive?
15   CLIVE: Let me tell you something first. Since you came to the house I have had an erection twenty-four hours a day except for ten minutes after the time we had intercourse.
MRS SAUNDERS: I don't think that's physically possible.
CLIVE: You are causing me appalling physical suffering. Is this
20   the way to treat a benefactor?
MRS SAUNDERS: Clive, when I came to your house the other night I came because I was afraid. The cook was going to let his whole tribe in through the window.
CLIVE: I know that, my poor sweet. Amazing—
25   MRS SAUNDERS: I came to you although you are not my nearest neighbour—
CLIVE: Rather than to the old major of seventy-two.
MRS SAUNDERS: Because the last time he came to visit me I had to defend myself with a shotgun and I thought you
30   would take no for an answer.
CLIVE: But you've already answered yes.
MRS SAUNDERS: I answered yes once. Sometimes I want to say no.
CLIVE: Women, my God. Look the picnic will start, I have to
35   go to the picnic. Please Caroline—
MRS SAUNDERS: I think I will have to go back to my own house.
CLIVE: Caroline, if you were shot with poisoned arrows do you know what I'd do? I'd fuck your dead body and poison my-
40   self. Caroline, you smell amazing. You terrify me. You are dark like this continent. Mysterious. Treacherous. When you rode to me through the night. When you fainted in my arms. When I came to you in your bed, when I lifted the mosquito netting, when I said let me in, let me in. Oh don't
45   shut me out, Caroline, let me in.

(He has been caressing her feet and legs. He disappears completely under her skirt.)

MRS SAUNDERS: Please stop. I can't concentrate. I want to go home. I wish I didn't enjoy the sensation because I don't like you, Clive. I do like living in your house where there's plenty of guns. But I don't like you at all. But I do like the sensation. Well I'll have it then. I'll have it, I'll have it—   50

(Voices are heard singing The First Noël.*)*

Don't stop. Don't stop.

(CLIVE comes out from under her skirt.)

CLIVE: The Christmas picnic. I came.
MRS SAUNDERS: I didn't.
CLIVE: I'm all sticky.
MRS SAUNDERS: What about me? Wait.   55
CLIVE: All right, are you? Come on. We mustn't be found.
MRS SAUNDERS: Don't go now.
CLIVE: Caroline, you are so voracious. Do let go. Tidy yourself up. There's a hair in my mouth.

(CLIVE and MRS SAUNDERS go off. BETTY *and* MAUD *come, with* JOSHUA *carrying hamper.)*

MAUD: I never would have thought a guinea fowl could taste   60
so like a turkey.
BETTY: I had to explain to the cook three times.
MAUD: You did very well dear.

(JOSHUA sits apart with gun. EDWARD *and* HARRY *with* VICTORIA *on his shoulder, singing* The First Noël. MAUD *and* BETTY *are unpacking the hamper.* CLIVE *arrives separately.)*

MAUD: This tablecloth was one of my mama's.
BETTY: Uncle Harry playing horsy.   65
EDWARD: Crackers crackers.
BETTY: Not yet, Edward.
CLIVE: And now the moment we have all been waiting for.

(CLIVE opens champagne. General acclaim.)

CLIVE: Oh dear, stained my trousers, never mind.
EDWARD: Can I have some?   70
MAUD: Oh no Edward, not for you.
CLIVE: Give him half a glass.
MAUD: If your father says so.
CLIVE: All rise please. To Her Majesty Queen Victoria, God bless her, and her husband and all her dear children.   75
ALL: The Queen.
EDWARD: Crackers crackers.

(General cracker pulling, hats. CLIVE *and* HARRY *discuss champagne.)*

HARRY: Excellent, Clive, wherever did you get it?
CLIVE: I know a chap in French Equatorial Africa.
EDWARD: I won, I won mama.   80

(ELLEN arrives.)

BETTY: Give a hat to Joshua, he'd like it.

(EDWARD takes hat to JOSHUA. BETTY *takes a ball from the hamper and plays catch with* ELLEN. *Murmurs of surprise and congratulations from the men whenever they catch the ball.)*

EDWARD: Mama, don't play. You know you can't catch a ball.

BETTY: He's perfectly right. I can't throw either.

(BETTY *sits down.* ELLEN *has the ball.*)

EDWARD: Ellen, don't you play either. You're no good. You
85   spoil it.

(EDWARD *takes* VICTORIA *from* HARRY *and gives her to* ELLEN.
He takes the ball and throws it to HARRY. HARRY, CLIVE *and* ED-
WARD *play ball.*)

BETTY: Ellen come and sit with me. We'll be spectators and
clap.

(EDWARD *misses the ball.*)

CLIVE: Butterfingers.
EDWARD: I'm not.
90   HARRY: Throw straight now.
EDWARD: I did, I did.
CLIVE: Keep your eye on the ball.
EDWARD: You can't throw.
CLIVE: Don't be a baby.
95   EDWARD: I'm not, throw a hard one, throw a hard one—
CLIVE: Butterfingers. What will Uncle Harry think of you?
EDWARD: It's your fault. You can't throw. I hate you.

(He throws the ball wildly in the direction of JOSHUA.)

CLIVE: Now you've lost the ball. He's lost the ball.
EDWARD: It's Joshua's fault. Joshua's butterfingers.
100   CLIVE: I don't think I want to play any more. Joshua, find the
ball will you?
EDWARD: Yes, please play. I'll find the ball. Please play.
CLIVE: You're so silly and you can't catch. You'll be no good at
cricket.
105   MAUD: Why don't we play hide and seek?
EDWARD: Because it's a baby game.
BETTY: You've hurt Edward's feelings.
CLIVE: A boy has no business having feelings.
HARRY: Hide and seek. I'll be it. Everybody must hide. This is
110   the base, you have to get home to base.
EDWARD: Hide and seek, hide and seek.
HARRY: Can we persuade the ladies to join us?
MAUD: I'm playing. I love games.
BETTY: I always get found straight away.
115   ELLEN: Come on, Betty, do. Vicky wants to play.
EDWARD: You won't find me ever.

(They all go except CLIVE, HARRY, JOSHUA.)

HARRY: It is safe, I suppose?
CLIVE: They won't go far. This is very much my territory and
it's broad daylight. Joshua will keep an open eye.
120   HARRY: Well I must give them a hundred. You don't know what
this means to me, Clive. A chap can only go on so long
alone. I can climb mountains and go down rivers, but what's
it for? For Christmas and England and games and women
singing. This is the empire, Clive. It's not me putting a flag
125   in new lands. It's you. The empire is one big family. I'm one
of its black sheep, Clive. And I know you think my life is
rather dashing. But I want you to know I admire you. This is
the empire, Clive, and I serve it. With all my heart.
CLIVE: I think that's about a hundred.
130   HARRY: Ready or not, here I come!

(He goes.)

CLIVE: Harry Bagley is a fine man, Joshua. You should be
proud to know him. He will be in history books.
JOSHUA: Sir, while we are alone.
CLIVE: Joshua of course, what is it? You always have my ear.
135   Any time.
JOSHUA: Sir, I have some information. The stable boys are not
to be trusted. They whisper. They go out at night. They visit
their people. Their people are not my people. I do not visit
my people.
140   CLIVE: Thank you, Joshua. They certainly look after Beauty.
I'll be sorry to have to replace them.
JOSHUA: They carry knives.
CLIVE: Thank you, Joshua.
JOSHUA: And, sir.
145   CLIVE: I appreciate this, Joshua, very much.
JOSHUA: Your wife.
CLIVE: Ah, yes?
JOSHUA: She also thinks Harry Bagley is a fine man.
CLIVE: Thank you, Joshua.
150   JOSHUA: Are you going to hide?
CLIVE: Yes, yes I am. Thank you. Keep your eyes open Joshua.
JOSHUA: I do, sir.

(CLIVE *goes.* JOSHUA *goes.* HARRY *and* BETTY *race back to base.*)

BETTY: I can't run, I can't run at all.
HARRY: There, I've caught you.
155   BETTY: Harry, what are we going to do?
HARRY: It's impossible, Betty.
BETTY: Shall we run away together?

(MAUD *comes.*)

MAUD: I give up. Don't catch me. I have been stung.
HARRY: Nothing serious I hope.
160   MAUD: I have ointment in my bag. I always carry ointment. I
shall just sit down and rest. I am too old for all this fun.
Hadn't you better be seeking, Harry?

(HARRY *goes.* MAUD *and* BETTY *are alone for some time. They
don't speak.* HARRY *and* EDWARD *race back.*)

EDWARD: I won, I won, you didn't catch me.
HARRY: Yes I did.
165   EDWARD: Mama, who was first?
BETTY: I wasn't watching. I think it was Harry.
EDWARD: It wasn't Harry. You're no good at judging. I won,
didn't I grandma?
MAUD: I expect so, since it's Christmas.
170   EDWARD: I won, Uncle Harry. I'm better than you.
BETTY: Why don't you help Uncle Harry look for the others?
EDWARD: Shall I?
HARRY: Yes, of course.
BETTY: Run along then. He's just coming.

(EDWARD *goes.*)

175   Harry, I shall scream.
HARRY: Ready or not, here I come.

(HARRY *runs off.*)

BETTY: Why don't you go back to the house, mother, and rest
your insect-bite?
MAUD: Betty, my duty is here. I don't like what I see. Clive
180   wouldn't like it, Betty. I am your mother.

BETTY: Clive gives you a home because you are my mother.

(HARRY *comes back.*)

HARRY: I can't find anyone else. I'm getting quite hot.
BETTY: Sit down a minute.
HARRY: I can't do that. I'm he. How's your sting?
185 MAUD: It seems to be swelling up.
BETTY: Why don't you go home and rest? Joshua will go with you. Joshua!
HARRY: I could take you back.
MAUD: That would be charming.
190 BETTY: You can't go. You're he.

(JOSHUA *comes.*)

Joshua, my mother wants to go back to the house. Will you go with her please.
JOSHUA: Sir told me I have to keep an eye.
BETTY: I am telling you to go back to the house. Then you can
195   come back here and keep an eye.
MAUD: Thank you Betty. I know we have our little differences, but I always want what is best for you.

(JOSHUA *and* MAUD *go.*)

HARRY: Don't give way. Keep calm.
BETTY: I shall kill myself.
200 HARRY: Betty, you are a star in my sky. Without you I would have no sense of direction. I need you, and I need you where you are, I need you to be Clive's wife. I need to go up rivers and know you are sitting here thinking of me.
BETTY: I want more than that. Is that wicked of me?
205 HARRY: Not wicked, Betty. Silly.

(EDWARD *calls in the distance.*)

EDWARD: Uncle Harry, where are you?
BETTY: Can't we ever be alone?
HARRY: You are a mother. And a daughter. And a wife.
BETTY: I think I shall go and hide again.

(BETTY *goes.* HARRY *goes.* CLIVE *chases* MRS SAUNDERS *across the stage.* EDWARD *and* HARRY *call in the distance.*)

210 EDWARD: Uncle Harry!
HARRY: Edward!

(EDWARD *comes.*)

EDWARD: Uncle Harry!

(HARRY *comes.*)

There you are. I haven't found anyone have you?
HARRY: I wonder where they all are.
215 EDWARD: Perhaps they're lost forever. Perhaps they're dead. There's trouble going on isn't there, and nobody says because of not frightening the women and children.
HARRY: Yes, that's right.
EDWARD: Do you think we'll be killed in our beds?
220 HARRY: Not very likely.
EDWARD: I can't sleep at night. Can you?
HARRY: I'm not used to sleeping in a house.
EDWARD: If I'm awake at night can I come and see you? I won't wake you up. I'll only come in if you're awake.
225 HARRY: You should try to sleep.
EDWARD: I don't mind being awake because I make up adventures. Once we were on a raft going down to the rapids.

We've lost the paddles because we used them to fight off the crocodiles. A crocodile comes at me and I stab it again and again and the blood is everywhere and it tips up the raft and 230 it has you by the leg and it's biting your leg right off and I take my knife and stab it in the throat and rip open its stomach and it lets go of you but it bites my hand but it's dead. And I drag you onto the river bank and I'm almost fainting with pain and we lie there in each other's arms. 235
HARRY: Have I lost my leg?
EDWARD: I forgot about the leg by then.
HARRY: Hadn't we better look for the others?
EDWARD: Wait. I've got something for you. It was in mama's box but she never wears it. 240

(EDWARD *gives* HARRY *a necklace.*)

You don't have to wear it either but you might like it to look at.
HARRY: It's beautiful. But you'll have to put it back.
EDWARD: I wanted to give it to you.
HARRY: You did. It can go back in the box. You still gave it to 245 me. Come on now, we have to find the others.
EDWARD: Harry, I love you.
HARRY: Yes I know. I love you too.
EDWARD: You know what we did when you were here before. I want to do it again. I think about it all the time. I try to do it 250 to myself but it's not as good. Don't you want to any more?
HARRY: I do, but it's a sin and a crime and it's also wrong.
EDWARD: But we'll do it anyway won't we?
HARRY: Yes of course.
EDWARD: I wish the others would all be killed. Take it out now 255 and let me see it.
HARRY: No.
EDWARD: Is it big now?
HARRY: Yes.
EDWARD: Let me touch it. 260
HARRY: No.
EDWARD: Just hold me.
HARRY: When you can't sleep.
EDWARD: We'd better find the others then. Come on.
HARRY: Ready or not, here we come. 265

(*They go out with whoops and shouts.* BETTY *and* ELLEN *come.*)

BETTY: Ellen, I don't want to play any more.
ELLEN: Nor do I, Betty.
BETTY: Come and sit here with me. Oh Ellen, what will become of me?
ELLEN: Betty, are you crying? Are you laughing? 270
BETTY: Tell me what you think of Harry Bagley.
ELLEN: He's a very fine man.
BETTY: No, Ellen, what you really think.
ELLEN: I think you think he's very handsome.
BETTY: And don't you think he is? Oh Ellen, you're so good 275 and I'm so wicked.
ELLEN: I'm not so good as you think.

(EDWARD *comes.*)

EDWARD: I've found you.
ELLEN: We're not hiding Edward.
EDWARD: But I found you.
ELLEN: We're not playing, Edward, now run along. 280
EDWARD: Come on, Ellen, do play. Come on, mama.

ELLEN: Edward, don't pull your mama like that.

BETTY: Edward, you must do what your governess says. Go and
285 play with Uncle Harry.

EDWARD: Uncle Harry!

(EDWARD *goes.*)

BETTY: Ellen, can you keep a secret?

ELLEN: Oh yes, yes please.

BETTY: I love Harry Bagley. I want to go away with him. There,
290 I've said it, it's true.

ELLEN: How do you know you love him?

BETTY: I kissed him.

ELLEN: Betty.

BETTY: He held my hand like this. Oh I want him to do it
295 again. I want him to stroke my hair.

ELLEN: Your lovely hair. Like this, Betty?

BETTY: I want him to put his arm around my waist.

ELLEN: Like this, Betty?

BETTY: Yes, oh I want him to kiss me again.

300 ELLEN: Like this Betty?

(ELLEN *kisses* BETTY.)

BETTY: Ellen, whatever are you doing? It's not a joke.

ELLEN: I'm sorry, Betty. You're so pretty. Harry Bagley doesn't
deserve you. You wouldn't really go away with him?

BETTY: Oh Ellen, you don't know what I suffer. You don't
305 know what love is. Everyone will hate me, but it's worth it for
Harry's love.

ELLEN: I don't hate you, Betty, I love you.

BETTY: Harry says we shouldn't go away. But he says he worships me.

310 ELLEN: I worship you Betty.

BETTY: Oh Ellen, you are my only friend.

(*They embrace. The others have all gathered together.* MAUD *has
rejoined the party, and* JOSHUA.)

CLIVE: Come along everyone, you mustn't miss Harry's conjuring trick.

(BETTY *and* ELLEN *go to join the others.*)

MAUD: I didn't want to spoil the fun by not being here.

315 HARRY: What is it that flies all over the world and is up my
sleeve?

(HARRY *produces a union jack from up his sleeve. General
acclaim.*)

CLIVE: I think we should have some singing now. Ladies, I rely
on you to lead the way.

ELLEN: We have a surprise for you. I have taught Joshua a
320 Christmas carol. He has been singing it at the piano but I'm
sure he can sing it unaccompanied, can't you, Joshua?

JOSHUA: In the deep midwinter
Frosty wind made moan,
Earth stood hard as iron,
325   Water like a stone.
Snow had fallen snow on snow
Snow on snow,
In the deep midwinter
Long long ago.

330   What can I give him
Poor as I am?
If I were a shepherd

I would bring a lamb.
If I were a wise man
I would do my part   335
What can I give him,
Give my heart.

SCENE III

Inside the house. BETTY, MRS SAUNDERS, MAUD *with* VICTORIA.
*The blinds are down so the light isn't bright though it is day out-
side.* CLIVE *looks in.*

CLIVE: Everything all right? Nothing to be frightened of.

(CLIVE *goes. Silence.*)

MAUD: Clap hands, daddy comes, with his pockets full of
plums. All for Vicky.

(*Silence.*)

MRS SAUNDERS: Who actually does the flogging?

MAUD: I don't think we want to imagine.   5

MRS SAUNDERS: I imagine Joshua.

BETTY: Yes I think it would be Joshua. Or would Clive do it
himself?

MRS SAUNDERS: Well we can ask them afterwards.

MAUD: I don't like the way you speak of it, Mrs Saunders.   10

MRS SAUNDERS: How should I speak of it?

MAUD: The men will do it in the proper way, whatever it is. We
have our own part to play.

MRS SAUNDERS: Harry Bagley says they should just be sent
away. I don't think he likes to see them beaten.   15

BETTY: Harry is so tender hearted. Perhaps he is right.

MAUD: Harry Bagley is not altogether—He has lived in this
country a long time without any responsibilities. It is part of
his charm but it hasn't improved his judgment. If the boys
were just sent away they would go back to the village and   20
make more trouble.

MRS SAUNDERS: And what will they say about us in the village
if they've been flogged?

BETTY: Perhaps Clive should keep them here.

MRS SAUNDERS: That is never wise.   25

BETTY: Whatever shall we do?

MAUD: I don't think it is up to us to wonder. The men don't
tell us what is going on among the tribes, so how can we possibly make a judgment?

MRS SAUNDERS: I know a little of what is going on.   30

BETTY: Tell me what you know. Clive tells me nothing.

MAUD: You would not want to be told about it, Betty. It is
enough for you that Clive knows what is happening. Clive
will know what to do. Your father always knew what to do.

BETTY: Are you saying you would do something different,   35
Caroline?

MRS SAUNDERS: I would do what I did at my own home. I left.
I can't see any way out except to leave. I will leave here. I will
keep leaving everywhere I suppose.

MAUD: Luckily this household has a head. I am squeamish my-   40
self. But luckily Clive is not.

BETTY: You are leaving here then, Caroline?

MRS SAUNDERS: Not immediately. I'm sorry.

(*Silence.*)

MRS SAUNDERS: I wonder if it's over.

(EDWARD *comes in.*)

45 BETTY: Shouldn't you be with the men, Edward?

EDWARD: I didn't want to see any more. They got what they deserved. Uncle Harry said I could come in.

MRS SAUNDERS: I never allowed the servants to be beaten in my own house. I'm going to find out what's happening.

(MRS SAUNDERS *goes out.*)

50 BETTY: Will she go and look?

MAUD: Let Mrs Saunders be a warning to you, Betty. She is alone in the world. You are not, thank God. Since your father died, I know what it is to be unprotected. Vicky is such a pretty little girl. Clap hands, daddy comes, with his pockets
55   full of plums. All for Vicky.

(EDWARD, *meanwhile, has found the doll and is playing clap hands with her.*)

BETTY: Edward, what have you got there?

EDWARD: I'm minding her.

BETTY: Edward, I've told you before, dolls are for girls.

MAUD: Where is Ellen? She should be looking after Edward.
60   (*She goes to the door.*) Ellen! Betty, why do you let that girl mope about in her own room? That's not what she's come to Africa for.

BETTY: You must never let the boys at school know you like dolls. Never, never. No one will talk to you, you won't be on
65   the cricket team, you won't grow up to be a man like your papa.

EDWARD: I don't want to be like papa. I hate papa.

MAUD: Edward! Edward!

BETTY: You're a horrid wicked boy and papa will beat you. Of
70   course you don't hate him, you love him. Now give Victoria her doll at once.

EDWARD: She's not Victoria's doll, she's my doll. She doesn't love Victoria and Victoria doesn't love her. Victoria never even plays with her.

75 MAUD: Victoria will learn to play with her.

EDWARD: She's mine and she loves me and she won't be happy if you take her away, she'll cry, she'll cry, she'll cry.

(BETTY *takes the doll away, slaps him, bursts into tears.* ELLEN *comes in.*)

BETTY: Ellen, look what you've done. Edward's got the doll again. Now, Ellen, will you please do your job.

80 ELLEN: Edward, you are a wicked boy. I am going to lock you in the nursery until supper time. Now go upstairs this minute.

(*She slaps* EDWARD, *who bursts into tears and goes out.*)

I do try to do what you want. I'm so sorry.

(ELLEN *bursts into tears and goes out.*)

MAUD: There now, Vicky's got her baby back. Where did
85   Vicky's naughty baby go? Shall we smack her? Just a little smack. (MAUD *smacks the doll hard.*) There, now she's a good baby. Clap hands, daddy comes, with his pockets full of plums. All for Vicky's baby. When I was a child we honoured our parents. My mama was an angel.

(JOSHUA *comes in. He stands without speaking.*)

90 BETTY: Joshua?

JOSHUA: Madam?

BETTY: Did you want something?

JOSHUA: Sent to see the ladies are all right, madam.

(MRS SAUNDERS *comes in.*)

MRS SAUNDERS: We're very well thank you, Joshua, and how are you?   95

JOSHUA: Very well thank you, Mrs Saunders.

MRS SAUNDERS: And the stable boys?

JOSHUA: They have had justice, madam.

MRS SAUNDERS: So I saw. And does your arm ache?

MAUD: This is not a proper conversation, Mrs Saunders.   100

MRS SAUNDERS: You don't mind beating your own people?

JOSHUA: Not my people, madam.

MRS SAUNDERS: A different tribe?

JOSHUA: Bad people.

(HARRY *and* CLIVE *come in.*)

CLIVE: Well this is all very gloomy and solemn. Can we have   105
the shutters open? The heat of the day has gone, we could have some light, I think. And cool drinks on the verandah, Joshua. Have some lemonade yourself. It is most refreshing.

(*Sunlight floods in as the shutters are opened.* EDWARD *comes.*)

EDWARD: Papa, papa, Ellen tried to lock me in the nursery.
Mama is going to tell you of me. I'd rather tell you myself. I   110
was playing with Vicky's doll again and I know it's very bad of me. And I said I didn't want to be like you and I said I hated you. And it's not true and I'm sorry, I'm sorry and please beat me and forgive me.

CLIVE: Well there's a brave boy to own up. You should always   115
respect and love me, Edward, not for myself, I may not deserve it, but as I respected and loved my own father, because he was my father. Through our father we love our Queen and our God, Edward. Do you understand? It is something men understand.   120

EDWARD: Yes papa.

CLIVE: Then I forgive you and shake you by the hand. You spend too much time with the women. You may spend more time with me and Uncle Harry, little man.

EDWARD: I don't like women. I don't like dolls. I love you,   125
papa, and I love you, Uncle Harry.

CLIVE: There's a fine fellow. Let us go out onto the verandah.

(*They all start to go.* EDWARD *takes* HARRY's *hand and goes with him.* CLIVE *draws* BETTY *back. They embrace.*)

BETTY: Poor Clive.

CLIVE: It was my duty to have them flogged. For you and Edward and Victoria, to keep you safe.   130

BETTY: It is terrible to feel betrayed.

CLIVE: You can tame a wild animal only so far. They revert to their true nature and savage your hand. Sometimes I feel the natives are the enemy. I know that is wrong. I know I have a responsibility towards them, to care for them and bring them   135
all to be like Joshua. But there is something dangerous. Implacable. This whole continent is my enemy. I am pitching my whole mind and will and reason and spirit against it to tame it, and I sometimes feel it will break over me and swallow me up.   140

BETTY: Clive, Clive, I am here. I have faith in you.

CLIVE: Yes, I can show you my moments of weakness, Betty, because you are my wife and because I trust you. I trust you, Betty, and it would break my heart if you did not deserve that

145 trust. Harry Bagley is my friend. It would break my heart if
he did not deserve my trust.
BETTY: I'm sorry, I'm sorry. Forgive me. It is not Harry's fault,
it is all mine. Harry is noble. He has rejected me. It is my
wickedness, I get bored, I get restless, I imagine things.
150 There is something so wicked in me, Clive.
CLIVE: I have never thought of you having the weakness of
your sex, only the good qualities.
BETTY: I am bad, bad, bad—
CLIVE: You are thoughtless, Betty, that's all. Women can be
155 treacherous and evil. They are darker and more dangerous
than men. The family protects us from that, you protect me
from that. You are not that sort of woman. You are not unfaithful to me, Betty. I can't believe you are. It would hurt
me so much to cast you off. That would be my duty.
160 BETTY: No, no, no.
CLIVE: Joshua has seen you kissing.
BETTY: Forgive me.
CLIVE: But I don't want to know about it. I don't want to know.
I wonder of course, I wonder constantly. If Harry Bagley was
165 not my friend I would shoot him. If I shot you every British
man and woman would applaud me. But no. It was a moment of passion such as women are too weak to resist. But
you must resist it, Betty, or it will destroy us. We must fight
against it. We must resist this dark female lust, Betty, or it
170 will swallow us up.
BETTY: I do, I do resist. Help me. Forgive me.
CLIVE: Yes I do forgive you. But I can't feel the same about you
as I did. You are still my wife and we still have duties to the
household.

(They go out arm in arm. As soon as they have gone EDWARD
*sneaks back to get the doll, which has been dropped on the floor.
He picks it up and comforts it.* JOSHUA *comes through with a
tray of drinks.)*

175 JOSHUA: Baby. Sissy. Girly.

*(*JOSHUA *goes.* BETTY *calls from off.)*

BETTY: Edward?

*(*BETTY *comes in.)*

BETTY: There you are, my darling. Come, papa wants us all to
be together. Uncle Harry is going to tell how he caught a
crocodile. Mama's sorry she smacked you.

(They embrace. JOSHUA *comes in again, passing through.)*

180 BETTY: Joshua, fetch me some blue thread from my sewing
box. It is on the piano.
JOSHUA: You've got legs under that skirt.
BETTY: Joshua.
JOSHUA: And more than legs.
185 BETTY: Edward, are you going to stand there and let a servant
insult your mother?
EDWARD: Joshua, get my mother's thread.
JOSHUA: Oh little Eddy, playing at master. It's only a joke.
EDWARD: Don't speak to my mother like that again.
190 JOSHUA: Ladies have no sense of humour. You like a joke with
Joshua.
EDWARD: You fetch her sewing at once, do you hear me? You
move when I speak to you, boy.
JOSHUA: Yes sir, master Edward sir.

*(*JOSHUA *goes.)*

BETTY: Edward, you were wonderful.   195

(She goes to embrace him but he moves away.)

EDWARD: Don't touch me.

SONG
A BOY'S BEST FRIEND

ALL: While plodding on our way, the toilsome road of life,
How few the friends that daily there we meet.
Not many will stand in trouble and in strife,
With counsel and affection ever sweet.   200
But there is one whose smile will ever on us beam,
Whose love is dearer far than any other;
And wherever we may turn
This lesson we will learn
A boy's best friend is his mother.   205

Then cherish her with care
And smooth her silv'ry hair,
When gone you will never get another.
And wherever we may turn
This lesson we shall learn,   210
A boy's best friend is his mother.

SCENE IV

The verandah as in Scene One. Early morning. Nobody there.
JOSHUA *comes out of the house slowly and stands for some time
doing nothing.* EDWARD *comes out.*

EDWARD: Tell me another bad story, Joshua. Nobody else is
even awake yet.
JOSHUA: First there was nothing and then there was the great
goddess. She was very large and she had golden eyes and she
made the stars and the sun and the earth. But soon she was   5
miserable and lonely and she cried like a great waterfall and
her tears made all the rivers in the world. So the great spirit
sent a terrible monster, a tree with hundreds of eyes and a
long green tongue, and it came chasing after her and she
jumped into a lake and the tree jumped in after her, and she 10
jumped right up into the sky. And the tree couldn't follow,
he was stuck in the mud. So he picked up a big handful of
mud and he threw it at her, up among the stars, and it hit her
on the head. And she fell down onto the earth into his arms
and the ball of mud is the moon in the sky. And then they   15
had children which is all of us.
EDWARD: It's not true, though.
JOSHUA: Of course it's not true. It's a bad story. Adam and Eve
is true. God made man white like him and gave him the bad
woman who liked the snake and gave us all this trouble.   20

*(*CLIVE *and* HARRY *come out.)*

CLIVE: Run along now, Edward. No, you may stay. You must-
n't repeat anything you hear to your mother or your grandmother or Ellen.
EDWARD: Or Mrs Saunders?
CLIVE: Mrs Saunders is an unusual woman and does not re-   25
quire protection in the same way. Harry, there was trouble
last night where we expected it. But it's all over now. Everything is under control but nobody should leave the house
today I think.

30 HARRY: Casualties?

CLIVE: No, none of the soldiers hurt thank God. We did a certain amount of damage, set a village on fire and so forth.

HARRY: Was that necessary?

35 CLIVE: Obviously, it was necessary, Harry, or it wouldn't have happened. The army will come and visit, no doubt. You'll like that, eh, Joshua, to see the British army? And a treat for you, Edward, to see the soldiers. Would you like to be a soldier?

EDWARD: I'd rather be an explorer.

40 CLIVE: Ah, Harry, like you, you see. I didn't know an explorer at his age. Breakfast, I think, Joshua.

(CLIVE and JOSHUA go in. HARRY is following.)

EDWARD: Uncle.

(HARRY stops.)

EDWARD: Harry, why won't you talk to me?

HARRY: Of course I'll talk to you.

45 EDWARD: If you won't be nice to me I'll tell father.

HARRY: Edward, no, not a word, never, not to your mother, nobody, please. Edward, do you understand? Please.

EDWARD: I won't tell. I promise I'll never tell. I've cut my finger and sworn.

50 HARRY: There's no need to get so excited Edward. We can't be together all the time. I will have to leave soon anyway, and go back to the river.

EDWARD: You can't, you can't go. Take me with you.

ELLEN: Edward!

55 HARRY: I have my duty to the Empire.

(HARRY goes in. ELLEN comes out.)

ELLEN: Edward, breakfast time. Edward.

EDWARD: I'm not hungry.

ELLEN: Betty, please come and speak to Edward.

(BETTY comes.)

BETTY: Why what's the matter?

60 ELLEN: He won't come in for breakfast.

BETTY: Edward, I shall call your father.

EDWARD: You can't make me eat.

(He goes in. BETTY is about to follow.)

ELLEN: Betty.

(BETTY stops.)

65 ELLEN: Betty, when Edward goes to school will I have to leave?

BETTY: Never mind, Ellen dear, you'll get another place. I'll give you an excellent reference.

ELLEN: I don't want another place, Betty. I want to stay with you forever.

70 BETTY: If you go back to England you might get married, Ellen. You're quite pretty, you shouldn't despair of getting a husband.

ELLEN: I don't want a husband. I want you.

BETTY: Children of your own, Ellen, think.

75 ELLEN: I don't want children, I don't like children. I just want to be alone with you, Betty, and sing for you and kiss you because I love you, Betty.

BETTY: I love you too, Ellen. But women have their duty as soldiers have. You must be a mother if you can.

80 ELLEN: Betty, Betty, I love you so much. I want to stay with you forever, my love for you is eternal, stronger than death. I'd rather die than leave you, Betty.

BETTY: No you wouldn't, Ellen, don't be silly. Come, don't cry. You don't feel what you think you do. It's the loneliness here and the climate is very confusing. Come and have breakfast, Ellen dear, and I'll forget all about it.

(ELLEN goes, CLIVE comes.)

BETTY: Clive, please forgive me.

CLIVE: Will you leave me alone?

(BETTY goes back into the house. HARRY comes.)

CLIVE: Women, Harry. I envy you going into the jungle, a man's life.

90 HARRY: I envy you.

CLIVE: Harry, I know you do. I have spoken to Betty.

HARRY: I assure you, Clive—

CLIVE: Please say nothing about it.

95 HARRY: My friendship for you—

CLIVE: Absolutely. I know the friendship between us, Harry, is not something that could be spoiled by the weaker sex. Friendship between men is a fine thing. It is the noblest form of relationship.

100 HARRY: I agree with you.

CLIVE: There is the necessity of reproduction. The family is all important. And there is the pleasure. But what we put ourselves through to get that pleasure, Harry. When I heard about our fine fellows last night fighting those savages to protect us I thought yes, that is what I aspire to. I tell you Harry, 105 in confidence, I suddenly got out of Mrs Saunders' bed and came out here on the verandah and looked at the stars.

HARRY: I couldn't sleep last night either.

CLIVE: There is something dark about women, that threatens what is best in us. Between men that light burns brightly. 110

HARRY: I didn't know you felt like that.

CLIVE: Women are irrational, demanding, inconsistent, treacherous, lustful, and they smell different from us.

HARRY: Clive—

CLIVE: Think of the comradeship of men, Harry, sharing ad- 115 ventures, sharing danger, risking their lives together.

(HARRY takes hold of CLIVE.)

CLIVE: What are you doing?

HARRY: Well, you said—

CLIVE: I said what?

HARRY: Between men. 120

(CLIVE is speechless.)

I'm sorry, I misunderstood, I would never have dreamt, I thought—

CLIVE: My God, Harry, how disgusting.

HARRY: You will not betray my confidence.

CLIVE: I feel contaminated. 125

HARRY: I struggle against it. You cannot imagine the shame. I have tried everything to save myself.

CLIVE: The most revolting perversion. Rome fell, Harry, and this sin can destroy an empire.

HARRY: It is not a sin, it is a disease. 130

CLIVE: A disease more dangerous than diphtheria. Effeminacy is contagious. How I have been deceived. Your face does not look degenerate. Oh Harry, how did you sink to this?

HARRY: Clive, help me, what am I to do?

135 CLIVE: You have been away from England too long.

HARRY: Where can I go except into the jungle to hide?

CLIVE: You don't do it with the natives, Harry? My God, what a betrayal of the Queen.

HARRY: Clive, I am like a man born crippled. Please help me.

140 CLIVE: You must repent.

HARRY: I have thought of killing myself.

CLIVE: That is a sin too.

HARRY: There is no way out. Clive, I beg of you, do not betray my confidence.

145 CLIVE: I cannot keep a secret like this. Rivers will be named after you, it's unthinkable. You must save yourself from depravity. You must get married. You are not unattractive to women. What a relief that you and Betty were not after all — good God, how disgusting. Now Mrs Saunders. She's a

150 woman of spirit, she could go with you on your expeditions.

HARRY: I suppose getting married wouldn't be any worse than killing myself.

CLIVE: Mrs Saunders! Mrs Saunders! Ask her now, Harry. Think of England.

(MRS SAUNDERS *comes.* CLIVE *withdraws.* HARRY *goes up to* MRS SAUNDERS.)

155 HARRY: Mrs Saunders, will you marry me?

MRS SAUNDERS: Why?

HARRY: We are both alone.

MRS SAUNDERS: I choose to be alone, Mr Bagley. If I can look after myself, I'm sure you can. Clive, I have something im-

160 portant to tell you. I've just found Joshua putting earth on his head. He tells me his parents were killed last night by the British soldiers. I think you owe him an apology on behalf of the Queen.

CLIVE: Joshua! Joshua!

165 MRS SAUNDERS: Mr Bagley, I could never be a wife again. There is only one thing about marriage that I like.

(JOSHUA *comes.*)

CLIVE: Joshua, I am horrified to hear what has happened. Good God!

MRS SAUNDERS: His father was shot. His mother died in the

170 blaze.

(MRS SAUNDERS *goes.*)

CLIVE: Joshua, do you want a day off? Do you want to go to your people?

JOSHUA: Not my people, sir.

CLIVE: But you want to go to your parents' funeral?

175 JOSHUA: No sir.

CLIVE: Yes, Joshua, yes, your father and mother. I'm sure they were loyal to the crown. I'm sure it was all a terrible mistake.

JOSHUA: My mother and father were bad people.

CLIVE: Joshua, no.

180 JOSHUA: You are my father and mother.

CLIVE: Well really. I don't know what to say. That's very decent of you. Are you sure there's nothing I can do? You can have the day off you know.

(BETTY *comes out followed by* EDWARD.)

BETTY: What's the matter? What's happening?

185 CLIVE: Something terrible has happened. No, I mean some relatives of Joshua's met with an accident.

JOSHUA: May I go sir?

CLIVE: Yes, yes of course. Good God, what a terrible thing. Bring us a drink will you Joshua?

(JOSHUA *goes.*)

EDWARD: What? What?   190

BETTY: Edward, go and do your lessons.

EDWARD: What is it, Uncle Harry?

HARRY: Go and do your lessons.

ELLEN: Edward, come in here at once.

EDWARD: What's happened, Uncle Harry?   195

(HARRY *has moved aside,* EDWARD *follows him.* ELLEN *comes out.*)

HARRY: Go away. Go inside. Ellen!

ELLEN: Go inside, Edward. I shall tell your mother.

BETTY: Go inside, Edward at once. I shall tell your father.

CLIVE: Go inside, Edward. And Betty you go inside too.

(BETTY, EDWARD *and* ELLEN *go.* MAUD *comes out.*)

CLIVE: Go inside. And Ellen, you come outside.   200

(ELLEN *comes out.*)

Mr Bagley has something to say to you.

HARRY: Ellen. I don't suppose you would marry me?

ELLEN: What if I said yes?

CLIVE: Run along now, you two want to be alone.

(HARRY *and* ELLEN *go out.* JOSHUA *brings* CLIVE *a drink.*)

JOSHUA: The governess and your wife, sir.   205

CLIVE: What's that, Joshua?

JOSHUA: She talks of love to your wife, sir. I have seen them. Bad women.

CLIVE: Joshua, you go too far. Get out of my sight.

SCENE V

The verandah. A table with a white cloth. A wedding cake and a large knife. Bottles and glasses. JOSHUA *is putting things on the table.* EDWARD *has the doll.* JOSHUA *sees him with it. He holds out his hand.* EDWARD *gives him the doll.* JOSHUA *takes the knife and cuts the doll open and shakes the sawdust out of it.* JOSHUA *throws the doll under the table.*

MAUD: Come along Edward, this is such fun.

(*Everyone enters, triumphal arch for* HARRY *and* ELLEN.)

MAUD: Your mama's wedding was a splendid occasion, Edward. I cried and cried.

(ELLEN *and* BETTY *go aside.*)

ELLEN: Betty, what happens with a man? I don't know what to do.   5

BETTY: You just keep still.

ELLEN: And what does he do?

BETTY: Harry will know what to do.

ELLEN: And is it enjoyable?

BETTY: Ellen, you're not getting married to enjoy yourself.   10

ELLEN: Don't forget me, Betty.

(ELLEN *goes.*)

BETTY: I think my necklace has been stolen Clive. I did so want to wear it at the wedding.

EDWARD: It was Joshua. Joshua took it.

15   CLIVE: Joshua?
EDWARD: He did, he did, I saw him with it.
HARRY: Edward, that's not true.
EDWARD: It is, it is.
HARRY: Edward, I'm afraid you took it yourself.
20   EDWARD: I did not.
HARRY: I have seen him with it.
CLIVE: Edward, is that true? Where is it? Did you take your mother's necklace? And to try and blame Joshua, good God.

(EDWARD runs off.)

BETTY: Edward, come back. Have you got my necklace?
25   HARRY: I should leave him alone. He'll bring it back.
BETTY: I wanted to wear it. I wanted to look my best at your wedding.
HARRY: You always look your best to me.
BETTY: I shall get drunk.

(MRS SAUNDERS comes.)

30   MRS SAUNDERS: The sale of my property is completed. I shall leave tomorrow.
CLIVE: That's just as well. Whose protection will you seek this time?
MRS SAUNDERS: I shall go to England and buy a farm there. I
35   shall introduce threshing machines.
CLIVE: Amazing spirit.

(He kisses her. BETTY launches herself on MRS SAUNDERS. They fall to the ground.)

CLIVE: Betty—Caroline—I don't deserve this—Harry, Harry.

(HARRY and CLIVE separate them. HARRY holding MRS SAUNDERS, CLIVE BETTY.)

CLIVE: Mrs Saunders, how can you abuse my hospitality? How dare you touch my wife? You must leave here at once.
40   BETTY: Go away, go away. You are a wicked woman.
MAUD: Mrs Saunders, I am shocked. This is your hostess.
CLIVE: Pack your bags and leave the house this instant.
MRS SAUNDERS: I was leaving anyway. There's no place for me here. I have made arrangements to leave tomorrow, and to-
45   morrow is when I will leave. I wish you joy, Mr Bagley.

(MRS SAUNDERS goes.)

CLIVE: No place for her anywhere I should think. Shocking behaviour.
BETTY: Oh Clive, forgive me, and love me like you used to.
CLIVE: Were you jealous my dove? My own dear wife!
50   MAUD: Ah, Mr Bagley, one flesh, you see.

(EDWARD comes back with the necklace.)

CLIVE: Good God, Edward, it's true.
EDWARD: I was minding it for mama because of the troubles.
CLIVE: Well done, Edward, that was very manly of you. See Betty? Edward was protecting his mama's jewels from the
55   rebels. What a hysterical fuss over nothing. Well done, little man. It is quite safe now. The bad men are dead. Edward, you may do up the necklace for mama.

(EDWARD does up BETTY's necklace, supervised by CLIVE, JOSHUA is drinking steadily. ELLEN comes back.)

MAUD: Ah, here's the bride. Come along, Ellen, you don't cry at your own wedding, only at other people's.

CLIVE: Now, speeches, speeches. Who is going to make a   60
speech? Harry, make a speech.
HARRY: I'm no speaker. You're the one for that.
ALL: Speech, speech.
HARRY: My dear friends—what can I say—the empire—the
family—the married state to which I have always aspired—   65
your shining example of domestic bliss—my great good fortune in winning Ellen's love—happiest day of my life.

(Applause.)

CLIVE: Cut the cake, cut the cake.

(HARRY and ELLEN take the knife to cut the cake. HARRY steps on the doll under the table.)

HARRY: What's this?
ELLEN: Oh look.   70
BETTY: Edward.
EDWARD: It was Joshua. It was Joshua. I saw him.
CLIVE: Don't tell lies again.

(He hits EDWARD across the side of the head.)

Unaccustomed as I am to public speaking—

(Cheers.)

Harry, my friend. So brave and strong and supple.   75
Ellen, from neath her veil so shyly peeking.
I wish you joy. A toast—the happy couple.
Dangers are past. Our enemies are killed.
—Put your arm round her, Harry, have a kiss—
All murmuring of discontent is stilled.   80
Long may you live in peace and joy and bliss.

(While he is speaking JOSHUA raises his gun to shoot CLIVE. Only EDWARD sees. He does nothing to warn the others. He puts his hands over his ears.)

(Black.)

— ACT TWO —

SCENE I

Winter afternoon. Inside the hut of a one o'clock club, a children's playcentre in a park, VICTORIA *and* LIN, *mothers.* CATHY, LIN's *daughter, age 5, played by a man, clinging to* LIN. VICTORIA *reading a book.*

CATHY: Yum yum bubblegum.
Stick it up your mother's bum.
When it's brown
Pull it down
Yum yum bubblegum.   5
LIN: Like your shoes, Victoria.
CATHY: Jack be nimble, Jack be quick,
Jack jump over the candlestick.
Silly Jack, he should jump higher,
Goodness gracious, great balls of fire.   10
LIN: Cathy, do stop. Do a painting.
CATHY: You do a painting.
LIN: You do a painting.
CATHY: What shall I paint?
LIN: Paint a house.   15
CATHY: No.

LIN: Princess.
CATHY: No.
LIN: Pirates.
20 CATHY: Already done that.
LIN: Spacemen.
CATHY: I never paint spacemen. You know I never.
LIN: Paint a car crash and blood everywhere.
CATHY: No, don't tell me. I know what to paint.
25 LIN: Go on then. You need an apron, where's an apron. Here.
CATHY: Don't want an apron.
LIN: Lift up your arms. There's a good girl.
CATHY: I don't want to paint.
LIN: Don't paint. Don't paint.
30 CATHY: What shall I do? You paint. What shall I do mum?
VICTORIA: There's nobody on the big bike, Cathy, quick.

(CATHY *goes out.* VICTORIA *is watching the children playing outside.*)

VICTORIA: Tommy, it's Jimmy's gun. Let him have it. What the hell.

(*She goes on reading. She reads while she talks.*)

LIN: I don't know how you can concentrate.
35 VICTORIA: You have to or you never do anything.
LIN: Yeh, well. It's really warm in here, that's one thing. It's better than standing out there. I got chilblains last winter.
VICTORIA: It is warm.
LIN: I suppose Tommy doesn't let you read much. I expect he
40   talks to you while you're reading.
VICTORIA: Yes, he does.
LIN: I didn't get very far with that book you lent me.
VICTORIA: That's all right.
LIN: I was glad to have it, though. I sit with it on my lap while
45   I'm watching telly. Well, Cathy's off. She's frightened I'm going to leave her. It's the babyminder didn't work out when she was two, she still remembers. You can't get them used to other people if you're by yourself. It's no good blaming me. She clings round my knees every morning up the nursery
50   and they don't say anything but they make you feel you're making her do it. But I'm desperate for her to go to school. I did cry when I left her the first day. You wouldn't, you're too fucking sensible. You'll call the teacher by her first name. I really fancy you.
55 VICTORIA: What?
LIN: Put your book down will you for five minutes. You didn't hear a word I said.
VICTORIA: I don't get much time to myself.
LIN: Do you ever go to the movies?
60 VICTORIA: Tommy's very funny who he's left with. My mother babysits sometimes.
LIN: Your husband could babysit.
VICTORIA: But then we couldn't go to the movies.
LIN: You could go to the movies with me.
65 VICTORIA: Oh I see.
LIN: Couldn't you?
VICTORIA: Well yes, I could.
LIN: Friday night?
VICTORIA: What film are we talking about?
70 LIN: Does it matter what film?
VICTORIA: Of course it does.
LIN: You choose then. Friday night.

(CATHY *comes in with gun, shoots them saying* Kiou kiou kiou, *and runs off again.*)

Not in a foreign language, ok. You don't go in the movies to read.

(LIN *watches the children playing outside.*)

Don't hit him, Cathy, kill him. Point the gun, kiou, kiou,   75
kiou. That's the way.
VICTORIA: They've just banned war toys in Sweden.
LIN: The kids'll just hit each other more.
VICTORIA: Well, psychologists do differ in their opinions as to whether or not aggression is innate.   80
LIN: Yeh?
VICTORIA: I'm afraid I do let Tommy play with guns and just hope he'll get it out of his system and not end up in the army.
LIN: I've got a brother in the army.
VICTORIA: Oh I'm sorry. Whereabouts is he stationed?   85
LIN: Belfast.
VICTORIA: Oh dear.
LIN: I've got a friend who's Irish and we went on a Troops Out march. Now my dad won't speak to me.
VICTORIA: I don't get on too well with my father either.   90
LIN: And your husband? How do you get on with him?
VICTORIA: Oh, fine. Up and down. You know. Very well. He helps with the washing up and everything.
LIN: I left mine two years ago. He let me keep Cathy and I'm grateful for that.   95
VICTORIA: You shouldn't be grateful.
LIN: I'm a lesbian.
VICTORIA: You still shouldn't be grateful.
LIN: I'm grateful he didn't hit me harder than he did.
VICTORIA: I suppose I'm very lucky with Martin.   100
LIN: Don't get at me about how I bring up Cathy, ok?
VICTORIA: I didn't.
LIN: Yes you did. War toys. I'll give her a rifle for Christmas and blast Tommy's pretty head off for a start.

(VICTORIA *goes back to her book.*)

LIN: I hate men.   105
VICTORIA: You have to look at it in a historical perspective in terms of learnt behaviour since the industrial revolution.
LIN: I just hate the bastards.
VICTORIA: Well it's a point of view.

(*By now* CATHY *has come back in and started painting in many colours, without an apron.* EDWARD *comes in.*)

EDWARD: Victoria, mother's in the park. She's walking round   110
all the paths very fast.
VICTORIA: By herself?
EDWARD: I told her you were here.
VICTORIA: Thanks.
EDWARD: Come on.   115
VICTORIA: Ten minutes talking to my mother and I have to spend two hours in a hot bath.

(VICTORIA *goes out.*)

LIN: Shit, Cathy, what about an apron. I don't mind you having paint on your frock but if it doesn't wash off just don't tell me you can't wear your frock with paint on, ok?   120
CATHY: Ok.
LIN: You're gay, aren't you?

EDWARD: I beg your pardon?

LIN: I really fancy your sister. I thought you'd understand. You do but you can go on pretending you don't, I don't mind. That's lovely Cathy, I like the green bit.

EDWARD: Don't go around saying that. I might lose my job.

LIN: The last gardener was ever so straight. He used to flash at all the little girls.

EDWARD: I wish you hadn't said that about me. It's not true.

LIN: It's not true and I never said it and I never thought it and I never will think it again.

EDWARD: Someone might have heard you.

LIN: Shut up about it then.

(BETTY and VICTORIA come up.)

BETTY: It's quite a nasty bump.

VICTORIA: He's not even crying.

BETTY: I think that's very worrying. You and Edward always cried. Perhaps he's got concussion.

VICTORIA: Of course he hasn't mummy.

BETTY: That other little boy was very rough. Should you speak to somebody about him?

VICTORIA: Tommy was hitting him with a spade.

BETTY: Well he's a real little boy. And so brave not to cry. You must watch him for signs of drowsiness. And nausea. If he's sick in the night, phone an ambulance. Well, you're looking very well darling, a bit tired, a bit peaky. I think the fresh air agrees with Edward. He likes the open air life because of growing up in Africa. He misses the sunshine, don't you, darling? We'll soon have Edward back on his feet. What fun it is here.

VICTORIA: This is Lin. And Cathy.

BETTY: Oh Cathy what a lovely painting. What is it? Well I think it's a house on fire. I think all that red is a fire. Is that right? Or do I see legs, is it a horse? Can I have the lovely painting or is it for mummy? Children have such imagination, it makes them so exhausting. *(To LIN.)* I'm sure you're wonderful, just like Victoria. I had help with my children. One does need help. That was in Africa of course so there wasn't the servant problem. This is my son Edward. This is—

EDWARD: Lin.

BETTY: Lin, this is Lin. Edward is doing something such fun, he's working in the park as a gardener. He does look exactly like a gardener.

EDWARD: I am a gardener.

BETTY: He's certainly making a stab at it. Well it will be a story to tell. I expect he will write a novel about it, or perhaps a television series. Well what a pretty child Cathy is. Victoria was a pretty child just like a little doll—you can't be certain how they'll grow up. I think Victoria's very pretty but she doesn't make the most of herself, do you darling, it's not the fashion I'm told but there are still women who dress out of *Vogue*, well we hope that's not what Martin looks for, though in many ways I wish it was, I don't know what it is Martin looks for and nor does he I'm afraid poor Martin. Well I am rattling on. I like your skirt dear but your shoes won't do at all. Well do they have lady gardeners, Edward, because I'm going to leave your father and I think I might need to get a job, not a gardener really of course. I haven't got green fingers I'm afraid, everything I touch shrivels straight up. Vicky gave me a poinsettia last Christmas and the leaves all fell

off on Boxing Day. Well good heavens, look what's happened to that lovely painting.

(CATHY has slowly and carefully been going over the whole sheet with black paint. She has almost finished.)

LIN: What you do that for silly? It was nice.

CATHY: I like your earrings.

VICTORIA: Did you say you're leaving Daddy?

BETTY: Do you darling? Shall I put them on you? My ears aren't pierced, I never wanted that, they just clip on the lobe.

LIN: She'll get paint on you, mind.

BETTY: There's a pretty girl. It doesn't hurt does it. Well you'll grow up to know you have to suffer a little bit for beauty.

CATHY: Look mum I'm pretty, I'm pretty, I'm pretty.

LIN: Stop showing off Cathy.

VICTORIA: It's time we went home. Tommy, time to go home. Last go then, all right.

EDWARD: Mum did I hear you right just now?

CATHY: I want my ears pierced.

BETTY: Ooh, not till you're big.

CATHY: I know a girl got her ears pierced and she's three. She's got real gold.

BETTY: I don't expect she's English, darling. Can I give her a sweety? I know they're not very good for the teeth, Vicky gets terribly cross with me. What does mummy say?

LIN: Just one, thank you very much.

CATHY: I like your beads.

BETTY: Yes they are pretty. Here you are.

(It is the necklace from Act One.)

CATHY: Look at me, look at me. Vicky, Vicky, Vicky look at me.

LIN: You look lovely, come on now.

CATHY: And your hat, and your hat.

LIN: No, that's enough.

BETTY: Of course she can have my hat.

CATHY: Yes, yes, hat, hat. Look look look.

LIN: That's enough, please, stop it now. Hat off, bye bye hat.

CATHY: Give me my hat.

LIN: Bye bye beads.

BETTY: It's just fun.

LIN: It's very nice of you.

CATHY: I want my beads.

LIN: Where's the other earring?

CATHY: I want my beads.

(CATHY has the other earring in her hand. Meanwhile VICTORIA and EDWARD look for it.)

EDWARD: Is it on the floor?

VICTORIA: Don't step on it.

EDWARD: Where?

CATHY: I want my beads. I want my beads.

LIN: You'll have a smack.

(LIN gets the earring from CATHY.)

CATHY: I want my beads.

BETTY: Oh dear oh dear. Have you got the earring? Thank you darling.

CATHY: I want my beads, you're horrid, I hate you, mum, you smell.

BETTY: This is the point you see where one had help. Well it's been lovely seeing you dears and I'll be off again on my little walk.

VICTORIA: You're leaving him? Really?

235 BETTY: Yes you hear aright, Vicky, yes. I'm finding a little flat, that will be fun.

(BETTY goes.)

Bye bye Tommy, granny's going now. Tommy don't hit that little girl, say goodbye to granny.

VICTORIA: Fucking hell.

240 EDWARD: Puking Jesus.

LIN: That was news was it, leaving your father?

EDWARD: They're going to want so much attention.

VICTORIA: Does everybody hate their mothers?

EDWARD: Mind you, I wouldn't live with him.

245 LIN: Stop snivelling, pigface. Where's your coat? Be quiet now and we'll have doughnuts for tea and if you keep on we'll have dogshit on toast.

(CATHY laughs so much she lies on the floor.)

VICTORIA: Tommy, you've had two last goes. Last last last last go.

250 LIN: Not that funny, come on, coat on.

EDWARD: Can I have your painting?

CATHY: What for?

EDWARD: For a friend of mine.

CATHY: What's his name?

255 EDWARD: Gerry.

CATHY: How old is he?

EDWARD: Thirty-two.

CATHY: You can if you like. I don't care. Kiou kiou kiou kiou.

(CATHY goes out. EDWARD takes the painting and goes out.)

LIN: Will you have sex with me?

260 VICTORIA: I don't know what Martin would say. Does it count as adultery with a woman?

LIN: You'd enjoy it.

SCENE II

Spring. Swing, bench, pond nearby. EDWARD is gardening. GERRY sitting on a bench.

EDWARD: I sometimes pretend we don't know each other. And you've come to the park to eat your sandwiches and look at me.

GERRY: That would be more interesting, yes. Come and sit
5   down.

EDWARD: If the superintendent comes I'll be in trouble. It's not my dinner time yet. Where were you last night? I think you owe me an explanation. We always do tell each other everything.

10 GERRY: Is that a rule?

EDWARD: It's what we agreed.

GERRY: It's a habit we've got into. Look, I was drunk. I woke up at 4 o'clock on somebody's floor. I was sick. I hadn't any money for a cab. I went back to sleep.

15 EDWARD: You could have phoned.

GERRY: There wasn't a phone.

EDWARD: Sorry.

GERRY: There was a phone and I didn't phone you. Leave it alone, Eddy, I'm warning you.

20 EDWARD: What are you going to do to me, then?

GERRY: I'm going to the pub.

EDWARD: I'll join you in ten minutes.

GERRY: I didn't ask you to come. (EDWARD goes.) Two years I've been with Edward. You have to get away sometimes or you lose sight of yourself. The train from Victoria to 25 Clapham still has those compartments without a corridor. As soon as I got on the platform I saw who I wanted. Slim hips, tense shoulders, trying not to look at anyone. I put my hand on my packet just long enough so that he couldn't miss it. The train came in. You don't want to get in too fast or some 30 straight dumbo might get in with you. I sat by the window. I couldn't see where the fuck he'd got to. Then just as the whistle went he got in. Great. It's a six-minute journey so you can't start anything you can't finish. I stared at him and he unzipped his flies. Then he stopped. So I stood up and 35 took my cock out. He took me in his mouth and shut his eyes tight. He was sort of mumbling it about as if he wasn't sure what to do, so I said, 'A bit tighter son' and he said 'Sorry' and then got on with it. He was jerking off with his left hand, and I could see he'd got a fairsized one. I wished 40 he'd keep still so I could see his watch. I was getting really turned on. What if we pulled into Clapham Junction now. Of course by the time we sat down again the train was just slowing up. I felt wonderful. Then he started talking. It's better if nothing is said. Once you find he's a librarian in 45 Walthamstow with a special interest in science fiction and lives with his aunt, then forget it. He said I hope you don't think I do this all the time. I said I hope you will from now on. He said he would if I was on the train, but why don't we go out for a meal? I opened the door before the train 50 stopped. I told him I live with somebody, I don't want to know. He was jogging sideways to keep up. He said 'What's your phone number, you're my ideal physical type, what sign of the zodiac are you? Where do you live? Where are you going now?' It's not fair, I saw him at Victoria a couple of 55 months later and I went straight down to the end of the platform and I picked up somebody really great who never said a word, just smiled.

(CATHY is on the swing.)

CATHY: Batman and Robin
Had a batmobile.   60
Robin done a fart
And paralysed the wheel.
The wheel couldn't take it,
The engine fell apart,
All because of Robin   65
And his supersonic fart.

(CATHY goes. MARTIN, VICTORIA and BETTY walking slowly.)

MARTIN: Tom!

BETTY: He'll fall in.

VICTORIA: No he won't.

MARTIN: Don't go too near the edge Tom. Throw the bread 70 from there. The ducks can get it.

BETTY: I'll never be able to manage. If I can't even walk down the street by myself. Everything looks so fierce.

VICTORIA: Just watch Tommy feeding the ducks.

BETTY: He's going to fall in. Make Martin make him move 75 back.

VICTORIA: He's not going to fall in.

BETTY: It's since I left your father.

VICTORIA: Mummy, it really was the right decision.

80 BETTY: Everything comes at me from all directions. Martin despises me.

VICTORIA: Of course he doesn't, mummy.

BETTY: Of course he does.

MARTIN: Throw the bread. That's the way. The duck can get it.
85 Quack quack quack quack quack.

BETTY: I don't want to take pills. Lin says you can't trust doctors.

VICTORIA: You're not taking pills. You're doing very well.

BETTY: But I'm so frightened.

90 VICTORIA: What are you frightened of?

BETTY: Victoria, you always ask that as if there was suddenly going to be an answer.

VICTORIA: Are you all right sitting there?

BETTY: Yes, yes. Go and be with Martin.

(VICTORIA joins MARTIN, BETTY stays sitting on the bench.)

95 MARTIN: You take the job, you go to Manchester. You turn it down, you stay in London. People are making decisions like this every day of the week. It needn't be for more than a year. You get long vacations. Our relationship might well stand the strain of that, and if it doesn't we're better out of it. I
100 don't want to put any pressure on you. I'd just like to know so we can sell the house. I think we're moving into an entirely different way of life if you go to Manchester because it won't end there. We could keep the house as security for Tommy but he might as well get used to the fact that life nowadays is
105 insecure. You should ask your mother what she thinks and then do the opposite. I could just take that room in Barbara's house, and then we could babysit for each other. You think that means I want to fuck Barbara. I don't. Well, I do, but I won't. And even if I did, what's a fuck between friends?
110 What are we meant to do it with, strangers? Whatever you want to do, I'll be delighted. If you could just let me know what it is I'm to be delighted about. Don't cry again, Vicky, I'm not the sort of man who makes women cry.

(LIN has come in and sat down with BETTY, CATHY joins them. She is wearing a pink dress and carrying a rifle.)

LIN: I've bought her three new frocks. She won't wear jeans to
115 school any more because Tracy and Mandy called her a boy.

CATHY: Tracy's got a perm.

LIN: You should have shot them.

CATHY: They're coming to tea and we've got to have trifle. Not trifle you make, trifle out of a packet. And you've got to wear
120 a skirt. And tights.

LIN: Tracy's mum wears jeans.

CATHY: She does not. She wears velvet.

BETTY: Well I think you look very pretty. And if that gun has caps in it please take it a long way away.

125 CATHY: It's got red caps. They're louder.

MARTIN: Do you think you're well enough to do this job? You don't have to do it. No one's going to think any the less of you if you stay here with me. There's no point being so liberated you make yourself cry all the time. You stay and we'll
130 get everything sorted out. What it is about sex, when we talk while it's happening I get to feel it's like a driving lesson. Left, right, a little faster, carry on, slow down—

(CATHY shoots VICTORIA.)

CATHY: You're dead Vicky.

VICTORIA: Aaaargh.

CATHY: Fall over. 135

VICTORIA: I'm not falling over, the ground's wet.

CATHY: You're dead.

VICTORIA: Yes, I'm dead.

CATHY: The Dead Hand Gang fall over. They said I had to fall over in the mud or I can't play. That duck's a mandarin. 140

MARTIN: Which one? Look, Tommy.

CATHY: That's a diver. It's got a yellow eye and it dives. That's a goose. Tommy doesn't know it's a goose, he thinks it's a duck. The babies get eaten by weasels. Kiou kiou.

(CATHY goes.)

MARTIN: So I lost my erection last night not because I'm not 145 prepared to talk, it's just that taking in technical information is a different part of the brain and also I don't like to feel that you do it better to yourself. I have read the Hite report. I do know that women have to learn to get their pleasure despite our clumsy attempts at expressing undying devotion and ec- 150 stasy, and that what we spent our adolescence thinking was an animal urge we had to suppress is in fact a fine art we have to acquire. I'm not like whatever percentage of American men have become impotent as a direct result of women's liberation, which I am totally in favour of, more I sometimes 155 think than you are yourself. Nor am I one of your villains who sticks it in, bangs away, and falls asleep. My one aim is to give you pleasure. My one aim is to give you rolling orgasms like I do other women. So why the hell don't you have them? My analysis for what it's worth is that despite all my ef- 160 forts you still feel dominated by me. I in fact think it's very sad that you don't feel able to take that job. It makes me feel very guilty. I don't want you to do it just because I encourage you to do it. But don't you think you'd feel better if you did take the job? You're the one who's talked about freedom. 165 You're the one who's experimenting with bisexuality, and I don't stop you, I think women have something to give each other. You seem to need the mutual support. You find me too overwhelming. So follow it through, go away, leave me and Tommy alone for a bit, we can manage perfectly well 170 without you. I'm not putting any pressure on you but I don't think you're being a whole person. God knows I do everything I can to make you stand on your own two feet. Just be yourself. You don't seem to realise how insulting it is to me that you can't get yourself together. 175

(MARTIN and VICTORIA go.)

BETTY: You must be very lonely yourself with no husband. You don't miss him?

LIN: Not really, no.

BETTY: Maybe you like being on your own.

LIN: I'm seeing quite a lot of Vicky. I don't live alone. I live 180 with Cathy.

BETTY: I would have been frightened when I was your age. I thought, the poor children, their mother all alone.

LIN: I've a lot of friends.

BETTY: I find when I'm making tea I put out two cups. It's 185 strange not having a man in the house. You don't know who to do things for.

LIN: Yourself.

BETTY: Oh, that's very selfish.

LIN: Have you any women friends? 190

BETTY: I've never been so short of men's company that I've had to bother with women.

LIN: Don't you like women?

195 BETTY: They don't have such interesting conversations as men. There has never been a woman composer of genius. They don't have a sense of humour. They spoil things for themselves with their emotions. I can't say I do like women very much, no.

LIN: But you're a woman.

200 BETTY: There's nothing says you have to like yourself.

LIN: Do you like me?

BETTY: There's no need to take it personally, Lin.

(MARTIN *and* VICTORIA *come back.*)

MARTIN: Did you know if you put cocaine on your prick you can keep it up all night? The only thing is of course it goes

205 numb so you don't feel anything. But you would, that's the main thing. I just want to make you happy.

BETTY: Vicky, I'd like to go home.

VICTORIA: Yes, mummy, of course.

BETTY: I'm sorry, dear.

210 VICTORIA: I think Tommy would like to stay out a bit longer.

LIN: Hello, Martin. We do keep out of each other's way.

MARTIN: I think that's the best thing to do.

BETTY: Perhaps you'd walk home with me, Martin. I do feel safer with a man. The park is so large the grass seems to tilt.

215 MARTIN: Yes, I'd like to go home and do some work. I'm writing a novel about women from the women's point of view.

(MARTIN *and* BETTY *go.* LIN *and* VICTORIA *are alone. They embrace.*)

VICTORIA: Why the hell can't he just be a wife and come with me? Why does Martin make me tie myself in knots? No wonder we can't just have a simple fuck. No, not Martin,

220 why do I make myself tie myself in knots. It's got to stop, Lin. I'm not like that with you. Would you love me if I went to Manchester?

LIN: Yes.

VICTORIA: Would you love me if I went on a climbing expedi-

225 tion in the Andes mountains?

LIN: Yes.

VICTORIA: Would you love me if my teeth fell out?

LIN: Yes.

VICTORIA: Would you love me if I loved ten other people?

230 LIN: And me?

VICTORIA: Yes.

LIN: Yes.

VICTORIA: And I feel apologetic for not being quite so subordi-nate as I was. I am more intelligent than him. I am brilliant.

235 LIN: Leave him Vic. Come and live with me.

VICTORIA: Don't be silly.

LIN: Silly, Christ, don't then. I'm not asking because I need to live with someone. I'd enjoy it, that's all, we'd both enjoy it. Fuck you. Cathy, for fuck's sake stop throwing stones at the

240 ducks. The man's going to get you.

VICTORIA: What man? Do you need a man to frighten your child with?

LIN: My mother said it.

VICTORIA: You're so inconsistent, Lin.

245 LIN: I've changed who I sleep with, I can't change everything.

VICTORIA: Like when I had to stop you getting a job in a bou-tique and collaborating with sexist consumerism.

LIN: I should have got that job, Cathy would have liked it. Why shouldn't I have some decent clothes? I'm sick of dress-ing like a boy, why can't I look sexy, wouldn't you love me? 250

VICTORIA: Lin, you've no analysis.

LIN: No but I'm good at kissing aren't I? I give Cathy guns, my mum didn't give me guns. I dress her in jeans, she wants to wear dresses. I don't know. I can't work it out, I don't want to. You read too many books, you get at me all the time, you're 255 worse to me than Martin is to you, you piss me off, my brother's been killed. I'm sorry to win the argument that way but there it is.

VICTORIA: What do you mean win the argument?

LIN: I mean be nice to me. 260

VICTORIA: In Belfast?

LIN: I heard this morning. Don't don't start. I've hardly seen him for two years. I rung my father. You'd think I'd shot my-self. He doesn't want me to go to the funeral.

(CATHY *approaches.*)

VICTORIA: What will you do? 265

LIN: Go of course.

CATHY: What is it? Who's killed? What?

LIN: It's Bill. Your uncle. In the army. Bill that gave you the blue teddy.

CATHY: Can I have his gun? 270

LIN: It's time we went home. Time you went to bed.

CATHY: No it's not.

LIN: We go home and you have tea and you have a bath and you go to bed.

CATHY: Fuck off. 275

LIN: Cathy, shut up.

VICTORIA: It's only half past five, why don't we—

LIN: I'll tell you why she has to go to bed—

VICTORIA: She can come home with me.

LIN: Because I want her out of the fucking way. 280

VICTORIA: She can come home with me.

CATHY: I'm not going to bed.

LIN: I want her home with me not home with you, I want her in bed, I want today over.

CATHY: I'm not going to bed. 285

(LIN *hits* CATHY, CATHY *cries.*)

LIN: And shut up or I'll give you something to cry for.

CATHY: I'm not going to bed.

VICTORIA: Cathy—

LIN: You keep out of it.

VICTORIA: Lin for God's sake. 290

(*They are all shouting.* CATHY *runs off.* LIN *and* VICTORIA *are silent. Then they laugh and embrace.*)

LIN: Where's Tommy?

VICTORIA: What? Didn't he go with Martin?

LIN: Did he?

VICTORIA: God oh God.

LIN: Cathy! Cathy! 295

VICTORIA: I haven't thought about him. How could I not think about him? Tommy!

LIN: Cathy! Come on, quick, I want some help.

VICTORIA: Tommy! Tommy!

(CATHY *comes back.*)

300 LIN: Where's Tommy? Have you seen him? Did he go with
  Martin? Do you know where he is?
CATHY: I showed him the goose. We went in the bushes.
LIN: Then what?
CATHY: I came back on the swing.
305 VICTORIA: And Tommy? Where was Tommy?
CATHY: He fed the ducks.
LIN: No that was before.
CATHY: He did a pee in the bushes. I helped him with his
  trousers.
310 VICTORIA: And after that?
CATHY: He fed the ducks.
VICTORIA: No no.
CATHY: He liked the ducks. I expect he fell in.
LIN: Did you see him fall in?
315 VICTORIA: Tommy! Tommy!
LIN: What's the last time you saw him?
CATHY: He did a pee.
VICTORIA: Mummy said he would fall in. Oh God, Tommy!
LIN: We'll go round the pond. We'll go opposite ways round
320   the pond.
ALL: (*Shout.*) Tommy!

(VICTORIA *and* LIN *go off opposite sides.* CATHY *climbs the
bench.*)

CATHY: Georgie Best, superstar
  Walks like a woman and wears a bra.
  There he is! I see him! Mum! Vicky! There he is! He's in the
325   bushes.

(LIN *comes back.*)

LIN: Come on Cathy love, let's go home.
CATHY: Vicky's got him.
LIN: Come on.
CATHY: Is she cross?
330 LIN: No. Come on.
CATHY: I found him.
LIN: Yes. Come on.

(CATHY *gets off the bench.* CATHY *and* LIN *hug.*)

CATHY: I'm watching telly.
LIN: Ok.
335 CATHY: After the news.
LIN: Ok.
CATHY: I'm not going to bed.
LIN: Yes you are.
CATHY: I'm not going to bed now.
340 LIN: Not now but early.
CATHY: How early?
LIN: Not late.
CATHY: How not late?
LIN: Early.
345 CATHY: How early?
LIN: Not late.

(*They go off together.* GERRY *comes on. He waits.* EDWARD
comes.)

EDWARD: I've got some fish for dinner. I thought I'd make a
  cheese sauce.

GERRY: I won't be in.
EDWARD: Where are you going?
GERRY: For a start I'm going to a sauna. Then I'll see.   350
EDWARD: All right. What time will you be back? We'll eat
  then.
GERRY: You're getting like a wife.
EDWARD: I don't mind that.   355
GERRY: Why don't I do the cooking sometime?
EDWARD: You can if you like. You're just not so good at it that's
  all. Do it tonight.
GERRY: I won't be in tonight.
EDWARD: Do it tomorrow. If we can't eat it we can always go to 360
  a restaurant.
GERRY: Stop it.
EDWARD: Stop what?
GERRY: Just be yourself.
EDWARD: I don't know what you mean. Everyone's always   365
  tried to stop me being feminine and now you are too.
GERRY: You're putting it on.
EDWARD: I like doing the cooking. I like being fucked. You do
  like me like this really.
GERRY: I'm bored, Eddy.   370
EDWARD: Go to the sauna.
GERRY: And you'll stay home and wait up for me.
EDWARD: No, I'll go to bed and read a book.
GERRY: Or knit. You could knit me a pair of socks.
EDWARD: I might knit. I like knitting.   375
GERRY: I don't mind if you knit. I don't want to be married.
EDWARD: I do.
GERRY: Well I'm divorcing you.
EDWARD: I wouldn't want to keep a man who wants his
  freedom.   380
GERRY: Eddy, do stop playing the injured wife, it's not funny.
EDWARD: I'm not playing. It's true.
GERRY: I'm not the husband so you can't be the wife.
EDWARD: I'll always be here, Gerry, if you want to come back.
  I know you men like to go off by yourselves. I don't think I 385
  could love deeply more than once. But I don't think I can
  face life on my own so don't leave it too long or it may be
  too late.
GERRY: What are you trying to turn me into?
EDWARD: A monster, darling, which is what you are.   390
GERRY: I'll collect my stuff from the flat in the morning.

(GERRY *goes.* EDWARD *sits on the bench. It gets darker.* VICTO-
RIA *comes.*)

VICTORIA: Tommy dropped a toy car somewhere, you haven't
  seen it? It's red. He says it's his best one. Oh the hell with it.
  Martin's reading him a story. There, isn't it quiet?

(*They sit on the bench, holding hands.*)

EDWARD: I like women.   395
VICTORIA: That should please mother.
EDWARD: No listen Vicky. I'd rather be a woman. I wish I had
  breasts like that, I think they're beautiful. Can I touch them?
VICTORIA: What, pretending they're yours?
EDWARD: No, I know it's you.   400
VICTORIA: I think I should warn you I'm enjoying this.
EDWARD: I'm sick of men.
VICTORIA: I'm sick of men.
EDWARD: I think I'm a lesbian.

SCENE III

The park. Summer night. VICTORIA, LIN *and* EDWARD *drunk.*

LIN: Where are you?
VICTORIA: Come on.
EDWARD: Do we sit in a circle?
VICTORIA: Sit in a triangle.
5 EDWARD: You're good at mathematics. She's good at mathematics.
VICTORIA: Give me your hand. We all hold hands.
EDWARD: Do you know what to do?
LIN: She's making it up.
10 VICTORIA: We start off by being quiet.
EDWARD: What?
LIN: Hush.
EDWARD: Will something appear?
VICTORIA: It was your idea.
15 EDWARD: It wasn't my idea. It was your book.
LIN: You said call up the goddess.
EDWARD: I don't remember saying that.
LIN: We could have called her on the telephone.
EDWARD: Don't be so silly, this is meant to be frightening.
20 LIN: Kiss me.
VICTORIA: Are we going to do it?
LIN: We're doing it.
VICTORIA: A ceremony.
LIN: It's very sexy, you said it is. You said the women were
25 priests in the temples and fucked all the time. I'm just
helping.
VICTORIA: As long as it's sacred.
LIN: It's very sacred.
VICTORIA: Innin, Innana, Nana, Nut, Anat, Anahita, Istar, Isis.
30 LIN: I can't remember all that.
VICTORIA: Lin! Innin, Innana, Nana, Nut, Anat, Anahita, Istar, Isis.

(LIN *and* EDWARD *join in and continue the chant under* VICTORIA'S *speech.*)

Goddess of many names, oldest of the old, who walked in
chaos and created life, hear us calling you back through
35 time, before Jehovah, before Christ, before men drove you
out and burnt your temples, hear us, Lady, give us back what
we were, give us the history we haven't had, make us the
women we can't be.
ALL: Innin, Innana, Nana, Nut, Anat, Anahita, Istar, Isis.

(*Chant continues under other speeches.*)

40 LIN: Come back, goddess.
VICTORIA: Goddess of the sun and the moon her brother, little
goddess of Crete with snakes in your hands.
LIN: Goddess of breasts.
VICTORIA: Goddess of cunts.
45 LIN: Goddess of fat bellies and babies. And blood blood blood.

(*Chant continues.*)

I see her.
EDWARD: What?

(*They stop chanting.*)

LIN: I see her. Very tall. Snakes in her hands. Light light
light—look out! Did I give you a fright?

EDWARD: I was terrified.   50
VICTORIA: Don't spoil it Lin.
LIN: It's all out of a book.
VICTORIA: Innin Innana—I can't do it now. I was really enjoying myself.
LIN: She won't appear with a man here.   55
VICTORIA: They had men, they had sons and lovers.
EDWARD: They had eunuchs.
LIN: Don't give us ideas.
VICTORIA: There's Attis and Tammuz, they're torn to pieces.
EDWARD: Tear me to pieces, Lin.   60
VICTORIA: The priestess chose a lover for a year and he was
king because she chose him and then he was killed at the
end of the year.
EDWARD: Hurray.
VICTORIA: And the women had the children and nobody knew   65
it was done by fucking so they didn't know about fathers and
nobody cared who the father was and the property was
passed down through the maternal line—
LIN: Don't turn it into a lecture, Vicky, it's meant to be an
orgy.   70
VICTORIA: It never hurts to understand the theoretical background. You can't separate fucking and economics.
LIN: Give us a kiss.
EDWARD: Shut up, listen.
LIN: What?   75
EDWARD: There's somebody there.
LIN: Where?
EDWARD: There.
VICTORIA: The priestesses used to make love to total strangers.
LIN: Go on then, I dare you.   80
EDWARD: Go on, Vicky.
VICTORIA: He won't know it's a sacred rite in honour of the
goddess.
EDWARD: We'll know.
LIN: We can tell him.   85
EDWARD: It's not what he thinks, it's what we think.
LIN: Don't tell him till after, he'll run a mile.
VICTORIA: Hello. We're having an orgy. Do you want me to
suck your cock?

(*The stranger approaches. It is* MARTIN.)

MARTIN: There you are. I've been looking everywhere. What   90
the hell are you doing? Do you know what the time is? You're
all pissed out of your minds.

(*They leap on* MARTIN, *pull him down and start to make love to him.*)

MARTIN: Well that's all right. If all we're talking about is having a lot of sex there's no problem. I was all for the sixties
when liberation just meant fucking.   95

(*Another stranger approaches.*)

LIN: Hey you, come here. Come and have sex with us.
VICTORIA: Who is it?

(*The stranger is a soldier.*)

LIN: It's my brother.
EDWARD: Lin, don't.
LIN: It's my brother.   100
VICTORIA: It's her sense of humour, you get used to it.

LIN: Shut up Vicky, it's my brother. Isn't it? Bill?

SOLDIER: Yes it's me.

LIN: And you are dead.

105 SOLDIER: Fucking dead all right yeh.

LIN: Have you come back to tell us something?

SOLDIER: No I've come for a fuck. That was the worst thing in the fucking army. Never fucking let out. Can't fucking talk to Irish girls. Fucking bored out of my fucking head. That or

110 shit scared. For five minutes I'd be glad I wasn't bored, then I was fucking scared. Then we'd come in and I'd be glad I wasn't scared and then I was fucking bored. Spent the day reading fucking porn and the fucking night wanking. Man's fucking life in the fucking army? No fun when the fucking

115 kids hate you. I got so I fucking wanted to kill someone and I got fucking killed myself and I want a fuck.

LIN: I miss you. Bill. Bill.

(LIN *collapses.* SOLDIER *goes.* VICTORIA *comforts* LIN.)

EDWARD: Let's go home.

LIN: Victoria, come home with us. Victoria's coming to live

120 with me and Edward.

MARTIN: Tell me about it in the morning.

LIN: It's true.

VICTORIA: It is true.

MARTIN: Tell me when you're sober.

(EDWARD, LIN, VICTORIA *go off together.* MARTIN *goes off alone.* GERRY *comes on.*)

125 GERRY: I come here sometimes at night and pick somebody up. Sometimes I come here at night and don't pick anybody up. I do also enjoy walking about at night. There's never any trouble finding someone. I can have sex any time. You might not find the type you most fancy every day

130 of the week, but there's plenty of people about who just enjoy having a good time. I quite like living alone. If I live with someone I get annoyed with them. Edward always put on Capital radio when he got up. The silence gets wasted. I wake up at four o'clock sometimes. Birds. Silence. If I bring

135 somebody home I never let them stay the night. Edward! Edward!

(EDWARD *from Act One comes on.*)

EDWARD: Gerry I love you.

GERRY: Yes, I know. I love you, too.

EDWARD: You know what we did? I want to do it again. I think

140 about it all the time. Don't you want to any more?

GERRY: Yes, of course.

SONG
CLOUD NINE

ALL: It'll be fine when you reach Cloud Nine.

Mist was rising and the night was dark.
Me and my baby took a walk in the park.
145 He said Be mine and you're on Cloud Nine.

Better watch out when you're on Cloud Nine.

Smoked some dope on the playground swings
Higher and higher on true love's wings
He said Be mine and you're on Cloud Nine.

Twenty-five years on the same Cloud Nine. 150

Who did she meet on her first blind date?
The guys were no surprise but the lady was great
They were women in love, they were on Cloud Nine.

Two the same, they were on Cloud Nine.

The bride was sixty-five, the groom was seventeen, 155
They fucked in the back of the black limousine.
It was divine in their silver Cloud Nine.

Simply divine in their silver Cloud Nine.

The wife's lover's children and my lover's wife,
Cooking in my kitchen, confusing my life. 160
And it's upside down when you reach Cloud Nine.

Upside down when you reach Cloud Nine.

SCENE IV

The park. Afternoon in late summer. MARTIN, CATHY, EDWARD.

CATHY: Under the bramble bushes,
Under the sea boom boom boom,
True love for you my darling,
True love for me my darling,
When we are married, 5
We'll raise a family.
Boy for you, girl for me,
Boom tiddley oom boom
SEXY.

EDWARD: You'll have Tommy and Cathy tonight then ok? 10
Tommy's still on antibiotics, do make him finish the bottle, he takes it in Ribena. It's no good in orange, he spits it out. Remind me to give you Cathy's swimming things.

CATHY: I did six strokes, didn't I Martin? Did I do a width? How many strokes is a length? How many miles is a swim- 15 ming pool? I'm going to take my bronze and silver and gold and diamond.

MARTIN: Is Tommy still wetting the bed?

EDWARD: Don't get angry with him about it.

MARTIN: I just need to go to the launderette so I've got a spare 20 sheet. Of course I don't get fucking angry, Eddy, for God's sake. I don't like to say he is my son but he is my son. I'm surprised I'm not wetting the bed myself.

CATHY: I don't wet the bed ever. Do you wet the bed Martin?

MARTIN: No. 25

CATHY: You said you did.

(BETTY *comes.*)

BETTY: I do miss the sun living in England but today couldn't be more beautiful. You appreciate the weekend when you're working. Betty's been at work this week, Cathy. It's terrible 30 tiring, Martin, I don't know how you've done it all these years. And the money, I feel like a child with the money, Clive always paid everything but I do understand it perfectly well. Look Cathy let me show you my money.

CATHY: I'll count it. Let me count it. What's that?

BETTY: Five pounds, Five and five is— 35

CATHY: One two three—
BETTY: Five and five is ten, and five—
CATHY: If I get it right can I have one?
EDWARD: No you can't.

(CATHY *goes on counting the money.*)

40 BETTY: I never like to say anything, Martin, or you'll think I'm being a mother-in-law.
EDWARD: Which you are.
BETTY: Thank you, Edward, I'm not talking to you. Martin, I think you're being wonderful. Vicky will come back. Just let
45 her stay with Lin till she sorts herself out. It's very nice for a girl to have a friend; I had friends at school, that was very nice. But I'm sure Lin and Edward don't want her with them all the time. I'm not at all shocked that Lin and Edward aren't married and she already has a child, we all know first
50 marriages don't always work out. But really Vicky must be in the way. And poor little Tommy. I hear he doesn't sleep properly and he's had a cough.
MARTIN: No, he's fine, Betty, thank you.
CATHY: My bed's horrible. I want to sleep in the big bed with
55 Lin and Vicky and Eddy and I do get in if I've got a bad dream, and my bed's got a bump right in my back. I want to sleep in a tent.
BETTY: Well Tommy has got a nasty cough, Martin, whatever you say.
60 EDWARD: He's over that. He's got some medicine.
MARTIN: He takes it in Ribena.
BETTY: Well I'm glad to hear it. Look what a lot of money, Cathy, and I sit behind a desk of my own and I answer the telephone and keep the doctor's appointment book and it re-
65 ally is great fun.
CATHY: Can we go camping, Martin, in a tent? We could take the Dead Hand Gang.
BETTY: Not those big boys, Cathy? They're far too big and rough for you. They climb back into the park after dark. I'm
70 sure mummy doesn't let you play with them, does she Edward? Well I don't know.

(*Ice cream bells.*)

CATHY: Ice cream. Martin you promised. I'll have a double ninety-nine. No I'll have a shandy lolly. Betty, you have a shandy lolly and I'll have a lick. No, you have a double
75 ninety-nine and I'll have the chocolate.

(MARTIN, CATHY *and* BETTY *go, leaving* EDWARD. GERRY *comes.*)

GERRY: Hello, Eddy. Thought I might find you here.
EDWARD: Gerry.
GERRY: Not working today then?
EDWARD: I don't work here any more.
80 GERRY: Your mum got you into a dark suit?
EDWARD: No of course not. I'm on the dole. I am working, though, I do housework.
GERRY: Whose wife are you now then?
EDWARD: Nobody's. I don't think like that any more. I'm living
85 with some women.
GERRY: What women?
EDWARD: It's my sister, Vic, and her lover. They go out to work and I look after the kids.
GERRY: I thought for a moment you said you were living with
90 women.

EDWARD: We do sleep together, yes.
GERRY: I was passing the park anyway so I thought I'd look in. I was in the sauna the other night and I saw someone who looked like you but it wasn't. I had sex with him anyway.
EDWARD: I do go to the sauna sometimes. 95

(CATHY *comes, gives* EDWARD *an ice cream, goes.*)

GERRY: I don't think I'd like living with children. They make a lot of noise don't they?
EDWARD: I tell them to shut up and they shut up. I wouldn't want to leave them at the moment.
GERRY: Look why don't we go for a meal sometime? 100
EDWARD: Yes I'd like that. Where are you living now?
GERRY: Same place.
EDWARD: I'll come round for you tomorrow night about 7.30.
GERRY: Great.

(EDWARD *goes.* HARRY *comes.* HARRY *and* GERRY *pick each other up. They go off.* BETTY *comes back.*)

BETTY: No, the ice cream was my treat, Martin. Off you go. 105 I'm going to have a quiet sit in the sun.

(MAUD *comes.*)

MAUD: Let Mrs Saunders be a warning to you, Betty. I know what it is to be unprotected.
BETTY: But mother, I have a job. I earn money.
MAUD: I know we have our little differences but I always want 110 what is best for you.

(ELLEN *comes.*)

ELLEN: Betty, what happens with a man?
BETTY: You just keep still.
ELLEN: And is it enjoyable? Don't forget me, Betty.

(MAUD *and* ELLEN *go.*)

BETTY: I used to think Clive was the one who liked sex. But 115 then I found I missed it. I used to touch myself when I was very little, I thought I'd invented something wonderful. I used to do it to go to sleep with or to cheer myself up, and one day it was raining and I was under the kitchen table, and my mother saw me with my hand under my dress rubbing 120 away, and she dragged me out so quickly I hit my head and it bled and I was sick, and nothing was said, and I never did it again till this year. I thought if Clive wasn't looking at me there wasn't a person there. And one night in bed in my flat I was so frightened I started touching myself. I thought my 125 hand might go through space. I touched my face, it was there, my arm, my breast, and my hand went down where I thought it shouldn't, and I thought well there is somebody there. It felt very sweet, it was a feeling from very long ago, it was very soft, just barely touching, and I felt myself gathering 130 together more and more and I felt angry with Clive and angry with my mother and I went on and on defying them, and there was this vast feeling growing in me and all round me and they couldn't stop me and no one could stop me and I was there and coming and coming. Afterwards I thought 135 I'd betrayed Clive. My mother would kill me. But I felt triumphant because I was a separate person from them. And I cried because I didn't want to be. But I don't cry about it any more. Sometimes I do it three times in one night and it really is great fun.
140

(VICTORIA and LIN come in.)

VICTORIA: So I said to the professor, I don't think this is an occasion for invoking the concept of structural causality—oh hello mummy.

145 BETTY: I'm going to ask you a question, both of you. I have a little money from your grandmother. And the three of you are living in that tiny flat with two children. I wonder if we could get a house and all live in it together? It would give you more room.

VICTORIA: But I'm going to Manchester anyway.

150 LIN: We'd have a garden, Vicky.

BETTY: You do seem to have such fun all of you.

VICTORIA: I don't want to.

BETTY: I didn't think you would.

LIN: Come on, Vicky, she knows we sleep together, and Eddy.

155 BETTY: I think I've known for quite a while but I'm not sure. I don't usually think about it, so I don't know if I know about it or not.

VICTORIA: I don't want to live with my mother.

LIN: Don't think of her as your mother, think of her as Betty.

160 VICTORIA: But she thinks of herself as my mother.

BETTY: I am your mother.

VICTORIA: But mummy we don't even like each other.

BETTY: We might begin to.

(CATHY comes on howling with a nosebleed.)

LIN: Oh Cathy what happened?

165 BETTY: She's been assaulted.

VICTORIA: It's a nosebleed.

CATHY: Took my ice cream.

LIN: Who did?

CATHY: Took my money.

(MARTIN comes.)

170 MARTIN: Is everything all right?

LIN: I thought you were looking after her.

CATHY: They hit me. I can't play. They said I'm a girl.

BETTY: Those dreadful boys, the gang, the Dead Hand.

MARTIN: What do you mean you thought I was looking after her?

175 LIN: Last I saw her she was with you getting an ice cream. It's your afternoon.

MARTIN: Then she went off to play. She goes off to play. You don't keep an eye on her every minute.

180 LIN: She doesn't get beaten up when I'm looking after her.

CATHY: Took my money.

MARTIN: Why the hell should I look after your child anyway? I just want Tommy. Why should he live with you and Vicky all week?

185 LIN: I don't mind if you don't want to look after her but don't say you will and then this happens.

VICTORIA: When I get to Manchester everything's going to be different anyway, Lin's staying here, and you're staying here, we're all going to have to sit down and talk it through.

190 MARTIN: I'd really enjoy that.

CATHY: Hit me on the face.

LIN: You were the one looking after her and look at her now, that's all.

MARTIN: I've had enough of you telling me.

195 LIN: Yes you know it all.

MARTIN: Now stop it. I work very hard at not being like this, I could do with some credit.

LIN: Ok you're quite nice, try and enjoy it. Don't make me sorry for you, Martin, it's hard for me too. We've better things to do than quarrel. I've got to go and sort those little 200 bastards out for a start. Where are they, Cathy?

CATHY: Don't kill them, mum, hit them. Give them a nosebleed, mum.

(LIN goes.)

VICTORIA: Tommy's asleep in the pushchair. We'd better wake him up or he won't sleep tonight. 205

MARTIN: Sometimes I keep him up watching television till he falls asleep on the sofa so I can hold him. Come on, Cathy, we'll get another ice cream.

CATHY: Chocolate sauce and nuts.

VICTORIA: Betty, would you like an ice cream? 210

BETTY: No thank you, the cold hurts my teeth, but what a nice thought, Vicky, thank you.

(VICTORIA goes. BETTY alone. GERRY comes.)

BETTY: I think you used to be Edward's flatmate.

GERRY: You're his mother. He's talked about you.

BETTY: Well never mind. Children are always wrong about 215 their parents. It's a great problem knowing where to live and who to share with. I live by myself just now.

GERRY: Good, So do I. You can do what you like.

BETTY: I don't really know what I like.

GERRY: You'll soon find out. 220

BETTY: What do you like?

GERRY: Waking up at four in the morning.

BETTY: I like listening to music in bed and sometimes for supper I just have a big piece of bread and dip it in very hot lime pickle. So you don't get lonely by yourself? Perhaps you have 225 a lot of visitors. I've been thinking I should have some visitors, I could give a little dinner party. Would you come? There wouldn't just be bread and lime pickle.

GERRY: Thank you very much.

BETTY: Or don't wait to be asked to dinner. Just drop in infor- 230 mally. I'll give you the address shall I? I don't usually give strange men my address but then you're not a strange man, you're a friend of Edward's. I suppose I seem a different generation to you but you are older than Edward. I was married for so many years it's quite hard to know how to get ac- 235 quainted. But if there isn't a right way to do things you have to invent one. I always thought my mother was far too old to be attractive but when you get to an age yourself it feels quite different.

GERRY: I think you could be quite attractive. 240

BETTY: If what?

GERRY: If you stop worrying.

BETTY: I think when I do more about things I worry about them less. So perhaps you could help me do more.

GERRY: I might be going to live with Edward again. 245

BETTY: That's nice, but I'm rather surprised if he wants to share a flat. He's rather involved with a young woman he lives with, or two young women, I don't understand Edward but never mind.

GERRY: I'm very involved with him. 250

BETTY: I think Edward did try to tell me once but I didn't listen. So what I'm being told now is that Edward is 'gay' is that right? And you are too. And I've been making rather a fool of myself. But Edward does also sleep with women.

255 GERRY: He does, yes, I don't.

BETTY: Well people always say it's the mother's fault but I don't intend to start blaming myself. He seems perfectly happy.

GERRY: I could still come and see you.

BETTY: So you could, yes. I'd like that. I've never tried to pick
260 up a man before.

GERRY: Not everyone's gay.

BETTY: No, that's lucky isn't it.

(GERRY *goes.* CLIVE *comes.*)

CLIVE: You are not that sort of woman, Betty. I can't believe you are. I can't feel the same about you as I did. And Africa is to be communist I suppose. I used to be proud to be British. 265 There was a high ideal. I came out onto the verandah and looked at the stars.

(CLIVE *goes.* BETTY *from Act One comes.* BETTY *and* BETTY *embrace.*)

■ BRIAN FRIEL ■

Brian Friel (b. 1929) is perhaps the most prominent living Irish playwright, the heir of Ireland's brilliant modern dramatic tradition, the tradition of William Butler Yeats, John Millington Synge, and Sean O'Casey. Unlike these predecessors, who worked for the independence of the Republic of Ireland, Friel works in Northern Ireland, still a part of the United Kingdom. Educated in Derry and Belfast, Friel's concerns as a playwright have spanned the "troubles" of Northern Ireland, the poverty and depression of Derry in the 1930s, 1940s, and 1950s, and the installation of a British military presence and the open street warfare of the 1960s, 1970s, and 1980s. From his earliest success, *Philadelphia, Here I Come!* (1964), about a man's divided feelings concerning his emigration to the United States, Friel's drama has centered on the problems of Irish identity in the face of British rule. Many of his early plays and stories—*The Loves of Cass McGuire* (1966), *The Lovers* (1967)—are portraits of Irish life in the manner of Synge, and Friel's dramatization of the personal consequences of contemporary Irish life remains a prominent feature of fine plays like *Living Quarters* (1977) and *Faith Healer* (1979). However, Friel's drama has increasingly become more satirical—in *The Mundy Scheme* (1969) and *The Gentle Island* (1971)—and more politically concerned. In *The Freedom of the City* (1973), Friel dramatizes the fate of three people caught and killed by British soldiers in the 1972 "Bloody Sunday" riots in Derry. In *Volunteers* (1975), a crew of political prisoners are forced to work on an archaeological site, recovering the history of Celtic Ireland even as they are oppressed by British rule. In *Making History* (1988), Friel returns to the origins of Ireland's subjection to the British in the seventeenth and eighteenth centuries. In 1980, Friel and Stephen Rea founded the Field Day theater company in Derry, and its first production was the play generally taken to be Friel's masterpiece, *Translations*. Friel's *Dancing at Lughnasa* opened in 1990, and his most recent play, *Wonderful Tennessee*, opened in 1992.

TRANSLATIONS

Translations is set in early nineteenth-century Ireland and concerns the mapping—both actual and cultural—of Ireland by the British. The play takes place at a local hedge-school, a subscription school run by a local master and attended by a variety of children and adults. This Ireland is already threatened by the British culture to the east: a national school—where, presumably, English will be the required language—is about to open, and the British army surveyors have arrived to map the region, part of the 1833 Survey of Ireland.

The play's politics are largely conveyed through the politics of language. Jimmy's Homeric Greek, for example, draws a parallel between Ireland and another lost civilization. The romance between Yolland and Maire bridges the barrier of language. They learn to communicate across this barrier, while the British army works to tear it down and destroy Irish cultural identity in the process. In mapping Ireland, the British convert local place names into English, either by translating them directly or by inventing some equivalent. As the relationship between the Irish Owen and his British officers makes clear, English is the language of power; to map the landscape with English names is a figure for rewriting Ireland and its culture into submission and, finally, into nonexistence.

Although *Translations* may seem only indirectly about contemporary Irish politics, it dramatizes a struggle for national and cultural identity that continues to embroil Northern Ireland today. Throughout the play, for example, the mysterious and unseen Donnelly twins move around the edges of the action, guerrillas hindering the British progress through the country. Finally, when Yolland is missing, we learn the true consequences of the British mapping of Ireland. Mapping the land in English is the prelude to its occupation, as the army systematically destroys the village and countryside that they have made their own. At the play's close, we scent the sickly sweet smell of blighted potatoes, the sign of the impending famine that would weaken and disperse Friel's rural Irish population for good.

TRANSLATIONS

Brian Friel

— CHARACTERS —

MANUS   BRIDGET
SARAH   HUGH
JIMMY JACK   OWEN
MAIRE   CAPTAIN LANCEY
DOALTY   LIEUTENANT YOLLAND

The action takes place in a hedge-school in the townland of Baile Beag/Ballybeg, an Irish-speaking community in County Donegal.

ACT ONE   *An afternoon in late August 1833.*
ACT TWO   *A few days later.*
ACT THREE   *The evening of the following day.*
One interval—between the two scenes in Act Two

— ACT ONE —

The hedge-school is held in a disused barn or hay-shed or byre. Along the back wall are the remains of five or six stalls—wooden posts and chains—where cows were once milked and bedded. A double door left, large enough to allow a cart to enter. A window right. A wooden stairway without a banister leads to the upstairs living-quarters (off) of the schoolmaster and his son. Around the room are broken and forgotten implements: a cart-wheel, some lobster-pots, farming tools, a battle of hay, a churn, etc. There are also the stools and bench-seats which the pupils use and a table and chair for the master. At the door a pail of water and a soiled towel. The room is comfortless and dusty and functional—there is no trace of a woman's hand.

When the play opens, MANUS *is teaching* SARAH *to speak. He kneels beside her. She is sitting on a low stool, her head down, very tense, clutching a slate on her knees. He is coaxing her gently and firmly and—as with everything he does—with a kind of zeal.*

MANUS *is in his late twenties/early thirties; the master's older son. He is pale-faced, lightly built, intense, and works as an unpaid assistant—a monitor—to his father. His clothes are shabby; and when he moves we see that he is lame.*

SARAH's *speech defect is so bad that all her life she has been considered locally to be dumb and she has accepted this: when she wishes to communicate, she grunts and makes unintelligible nasal sounds. She has a waiflike appearance and could be any age from seventeen to thirty-five.*

JIMMY JACK CASSIE—*known as the Infant Prodigy—sits by himself, contentedly reading Homer in Greek and smiling to himself. He is a bachelor in his sixties, lives alone, and comes to these evening classes partly for the company and partly for the intellectual stimulation. He is fluent in Latin and Greek but is in no way pedantic—to him it is perfectly normal to speak these tongues. He never washes. His clothes—heavy top coat, hat, mittens, which he wears now—are filthy and he lives in them summer and winter, day and night. He now reads in a quiet voice and smiles in profound satisfaction. For* JIMMY *the world of the gods and the ancient myths is as real and as immediate as everyday life in the townland of Baile Beag.*

MANUS *holds* SARAH's *hands in his and he articulates slowly and distinctly into her face.*

MANUS: We're doing very well. And we're going to try it once more—just once more. Now—relax and breathe in . . . deep . . . and out . . . in . . . and out . . .

*(*SARAH *shakes her head vigorously and stubbornly.)*

MANUS: Come on, Sarah. This is our secret.

(Again vigorous and stubborn shaking of SARAH's *head.)*

MANUS: Nobody's listening. Nobody hears you.   5
JIMMY: 'Ton d'emeibet epeita thea glaukopis Athene . . .'
MANUS: Get your tongue and your lips working. 'My name—' Come on. One more try. 'My name is—' Good girl.
SARAH: My . . .
MANUS: Great. 'My name—'   10
SARAH: My . . . my . . .
MANUS: Raise your head. Shout it out. Nobody's listening.
JIMMY: ' . . . alla hekelos estai en Atreidao domois . . .'
MANUS: Jimmy, please! Once more—just once more—'My name—' Good girl. Come on now. Head up. Mouth open. 15
SARAH: My . . .
MANUS: Good.
SARAH: My . . .
MANUS: Great.
SARAH: My name . . .   20
MANUS: Yes?
SARAH: My name is . . .
MANUS: Yes?

*(*SARAH *pauses. Then in a rush.)*

SARAH: My name is Sarah.
MANUS: Marvellous! Bloody marvellous!   25

*(*MANUS *hugs* SARAH. *She smiles in shy, embarrassed pleasure.)*

Did you hear that, Jimmy?—'My name is Sarah'—clear as a bell. *(To* SARAH.*)* The Infant Prodigy doesn't know what we're at. (*SARAH laughs at this.* MANUS *hugs her again and stands up.)* Now we're really started! Nothing'll stop us now! Nothing in the wide world!   30

*(*JIMMY, *chuckling at his text, comes over to them.)*

---

6 **Ton d'emeibet epeita thea glaukopis Athene** But the grey-eyed goddess Athene then replied to him (from Homer, *Odyssey*, XIII, 420)   13 **alla hekelos estai en Atreidao domois** . . . but he sits at ease in the halls of the Sons of Athens . . . (from Homer, *Odyssey*, XIII, 423–24)

JIMMY: Listen to this, Manus.

MANUS: Soon you'll be telling me all the secrets that have been in that head of yours all these years. Certainly, James—what is it? (*To* SARAH.) Maybe you'd set out the stools?

(MANUS *runs up the stairs.*)

35 SARAH: Wait till you hear this, Manus.

MANUS: Go ahead. I'll be straight down.

JIMMY: '*Hos ara min phamene rabdo epemassat Athene—*' 'After Athene had said this, she touched Ulysses with her wand. She withered the fair skin of his supple limbs and de-
40 stroyed the flaxen hair from off his head and about his limbs she put the skin of an old man . . .'! The divil! The divil!

(MANUS *has emerged again with a bowl of milk and a piece of bread.*)

JIMMY: And wait till you hear! She's not finished with him yet!

(As MANUS *descends the stairs he toasts* SARAH *with his bowl.*)

JIMMY: '*Knuzosen de oi osse—*' 'She dimmed his two eyes that were so beautiful and clothed him in a vile ragged cloak be-
45 grimed with filthy smoke . . .'! D'you see! Smoke! Smoke! D'you see! Sure look at what the same turf-smoke has done to myself! (*He rapidly removes his hat to display his bald head.*) Would you call that flaxen hair?

MANUS: Of course I would.

50 JIMMY: 'And about him she cast the great skin of a filthy hind, stripped of the hair, and into his hand she thrust a staff and a wallet'! Ha-ha-ha! Athene did that to Ulysses! Made him into a tramp! Isn't she the tight one?

MANUS: You couldn't watch her, Jimmy.

55 JIMMY: You know what they call her?

MANUS: '*Glaukopis Athene.*'

JIMMY: That's it! The flashing-eyed Athene! By God, Manus, sir, if you had a woman like that about the house, it's not stripping a turf-bank you'd be thinking about—eh?

60 MANUS: She was a goddess, Jimmy.

JIMMY: Better still. Sure isn't our own Grania a class of a god-dess and—

MANUS: Who?

JIMMY: Grania—Grania—Diarmuid's Grania.

65 MANUS: Ah.

JIMMY: And sure she can't get her fill of men.

MANUS: Jimmy, you're impossible.

JIMMY: I was just thinking to myself last night: if you had the choosing between Athene and Artemis and Helen of Troy—
70 all three of them Zeus's girls—imagine three powerful-looking daughters like that all in the one parish of Athens!—now, if you had the picking between them, which would you take?

MANUS: (*To* SARAH.) Which should I take, Sarah?

75 JIMMY: No harm to Helen; and no harm to Artemis; and in-deed no harm to our own Grania, Manus. But I think I've no choice but to go bull-straight for Athene. By God, sir, them flashing eyes would fair keep a man jigged up constant!

(*Suddenly and momentarily, as if in spasm,* JIMMY *stands to attention and salutes, his face raised in pained ecstasy.* MANUS *laughs. So does* SARAH. JIMMY *goes back to his seat, and his reading.*)

MANUS: You're a dangerous bloody man, Jimmy Jack.

JIMMY: 'Flashing-eyed'! Hah! Sure Homer knows it all, boy. 80 Homer knows it all.

(MANUS *goes to the window and looks out.*)

MANUS: Where the hell has he got to?

(SARAH *goes to* MANUS *and touches his elbow. She mimes rocking a baby.*)

MANUS: Yes, I know he's at the christening; but it doesn't take them all day to put a name on a baby, does it?

(SARAH *mimes pouring drinks and tossing them back quickly.*)

MANUS: You may be sure. Which pub? 85

(SARAH *indicates.*)

MANUS: Gracie's?

(*No. Further away.*)

MANUS: Con Connie Tim's?

(*No. To the right of there.*)

MANUS: Anna na mBreag's?

(*Yes. That's it.*)

MANUS: Great. She'll fill him up. I suppose I may take the class then. 90

(MANUS *begins to distribute some books, slates and chalk, texts, etc., beside the seats.* SARAH *goes over to the straw and produces a bunch of flowers she has hidden there. During this:*)

JIMMY: '*Autar o ek limenos prosebe—*' 'But Ulysses went forth from the harbour and through the woodland to the place where Athene had shown him he could find the good swine-herd who—'*o oi biotoio malista kedeto*'—what's that, Manus? 95

MANUS: 'Who cared most for his substance'.

JIMMY: That's it! 'The good swineherd who cared most for his substance above all the slaves that Ulysses possessed . . .'

(SARAH *presents the flowers to* MANUS.)

MANUS: Those are lovely, Sarah.

(*But* SARAH *has fled in embarrassment to her seat and has her head buried in a book.* MANUS *goes to her.*)

MANUS: Flow-ers. 100

(*Pause.* SARAH *does not look up.*)

MANUS: Say the word: flow-ers. Come on—flow-ers.

SARAH: Flowers.

MANUS: You see?—you're off!

(MANUS *leans down and kisses the top of* SARAH's *head.*)

MANUS: And they're beautiful flowers. Thank you.

---

37 **Hos ara min phamene rabdo epemassat Athene** As she spoke Athene touched him with her wand (from Homer, *Odyssey*, XIII, 429) 43 **Knuzosen de oi osse** She dimmed his eyes (from Homer, *Odyssey*, XIII, 433) 56 **Glaukopis Athene** flashing-eyed Athene

91 **Autar o ek limenos prosebe** But he went forth from the harbour (from Homer, *Odyssey*, XIV, 1) 94 **o oi biotoio malista kedeto** he cared very much for his substance (from Homer, *Odyssey*, XIV, 3–4)

(MAIRE *enters, a strong-minded, strong-bodied woman in her twenties with a head of curly hair. She is carrying a small can of milk.*)

105   MAIRE: Is this all's here? Is there no school this evening?
MANUS: If my father's not back, I'll take it.

(MANUS *stands awkwardly, having been caught kissing* SARAH *and with the flowers almost formally at his chest.*)

MAIRE: Well now, isn't that a pretty sight. There's your milk. How's Sarah?

(SARAH *grunts a reply.*)

MANUS: I saw you out at the hay.

(MAIRE *ignores this and goes to* JIMMY.)

110   MAIRE: And how's Jimmy Jack Cassie?
JIMMY: Sit down beside me, Maire.
MAIRE: Would I be safe?
JIMMY: No safer man in Donegal.

(MAIRE *flops on a stool beside* JIMMY.)

MAIRE: Ooooh. The best harvest in living memory, they say;
115   but I don't want to see another like it. (*Showing* JIMMY *her hands.*) Look at the blisters.
JIMMY: *Esne fatigata?*
MAIRE: *Sum fatigatissima.*
JIMMY: *Bene! Optime!*
120   MAIRE: That's the height of my Latin. Fit me better if I had even that much English.
JIMMY: English? I thought you had some English?
MAIRE: Three words. Wait—there was a spake I used to have off by heart. What's this it was? (*Her accent is strange because
125   she is speaking a foreign language and because she does not understand what she is saying.*) 'In Norfolk we besport ourselves around the maypoll.' What about that!
MANUS: Maypole.

(*Again* MAIRE *ignores* MANUS.)

MAIRE: God have mercy on my Aunt Mary—she taught me
130   that when I was about four, whatever it means. Do you know what it means, Jimmy?
JIMMY: Sure you know I have only Irish like yourself.
MAIRE: And Latin. And Greek.
JIMMY: I'm telling you a lie: I know one English word.
135   MAIRE: What?
JIMMY: Bo-som.
MAIRE: What's a bo-som?
JIMMY: You know—(*He illustrates with his hands.*)—bo-som—bo-som—you know—Diana, the huntress, she has two pow-
140   erful bosom.
MAIRE: You may be sure that's the one English word you would know. (*Rises.*) Is there a drop of water about?

(MANUS *gives* MAIRE *his bowl of milk.*)

MANUS: I'm sorry I couldn't get up last night.
MAIRE: Doesn't matter.
145   MANUS: Biddy Hanna sent for me to write a letter to her sister in Nova Scotia. All the gossip of the parish. 'I brought the

cow to the bull three times last week but no good. There's nothing for it now but Big Ned Frank.'
MAIRE: (*Drinking.*) That's better.
MANUS: And she got so engrossed in it that she forgot who she 150
was dictating to: 'The aul drunken schoolmaster and that lame son of his are still footering about in the hedge-school, wasting people's good time and money.'

(MAIRE *has to laugh at this.*)

MAIRE: She did not!
MANUS: And me taking it all down. 'Thank God one of 155
them new national schools is being built above at Poll na gCaorach.' It was after midnight by the time I got back.
MAIRE: Great to be a busy man.

(MAIRE *moves away.* MANUS *follows.*)

MANUS: I could hear music on my way past but I thought it was too late to call. 160
MAIRE: (*To* SARAH.) Wasn't your father in great voice last night?

(SARAH *nods and smiles.*)

MAIRE: It must have been near three o'clock by the time you got home?

(SARAH *holds up four fingers.*)

MAIRE: Was it four? No wonder we're in pieces. 165
MANUS: I can give you a hand at the hay tomorrow.
MAIRE: That's the name of a hornpipe, isn't it?—'The Scholar In The Hayfield'—or is it a reel?
MANUS: If the day's good.
MAIRE: Suit yourself. The English soldiers below in the tents, 170
them sapper fellas, they're coming up to give us a hand. I don't know a word they're saying, nor they me; but sure that doesn't matter, does it?
MANUS: What the hell are you so crabbed about?!

(DOALTY *and* BRIDGET *enter noisily. Both are in their twenties.*
DOALTY *is brandishing a surveyor's pole. He is an open-minded, open-hearted, generous and slightly thick young man.* BRIDGET *is a plump, fresh young girl, ready to laugh, vain, and with a countrywoman's instinctive cunning.* DOALTY *enters doing his imitation of the master.*)

DOALTY: Vesperal salutations to you all. 175
BRIDGET: He's coming down past Carraig na Ri and he's as full as a pig!
DOALTY: *Ignari, stulti, rustici*—pot-boys and peasant whelps—semi-literates and illegitimates.
BRIDGET: He's been on the batter since this morning; he sent 180
the wee ones home at eleven o'clock.
DOALTY: Three questions. Question A—Am I drunk? Question B—Am I sober? (*Into* MAIRE's *face.*) *Responde—responde!*
BRIDGET: Question C, Master—When were you last sober? 185
MAIRE: What's the weapon, Doalty?
BRIDGET: I warned him. He'll be arrested one of these days.
DOALTY: Up in the bog with Bridget and her aul fella, and the Red Coats were just across at the foot of Croc na Mona,

---

117 **Esne fatigata?** Are you tired?   118 **Sum fatigatissima** I am very tired.   119 **Bene! Optime!** Good! Excellent!

178 **Ignari, stulti, rustici** Ignoramuses, fools, peasants   183 **Responde—responde!** Answer—answer

190 dragging them aul chains and peeping through that big machine they lug about everywhere with them—you know the
name of it, Manus?

MAIRE: Theodolite.

BRIDGET: How do you know?

195 MAIRE: They leave it in our byre at night sometimes if it's
raining.

JIMMY: Theodolite—what's the etymology of that word,
Manus?

MANUS: No idea.

200 BRIDGET: Get on with the story.

JIMMY: *Theo—theos*—something to do with a god. Maybe
thea—a goddess! What shape's the yoke?

DOALTY: 'Shape!' Will you shut up, you aul eejit you! Anyway,
every time they'd stick one of these poles into the ground
205 and move across the bog, I'd creep up and shift it twenty or
thirty paces to the side.

BRIDGET: God!

DOALTY: Then they'd come back and stare at it and look at
their calculations and stare at it again and scratch their
210 heads. And cripes, d'you know what they ended up doing?

BRIDGET: Wait till you hear!

DOALTY: They took the bloody machine apart!

*(And immediately he speaks in gibberish—an imitation of two
very agitated and confused sappers in rapid conversation.)*

BRIDGET: That's the image of them!

MAIRE: You must be proud of yourself, Doalty.

215 DOALTY: What d'you mean?

MAIRE: That was a very clever piece of work.

MANUS: It was a gesture.

MAIRE: What sort of gesture?

MANUS: Just to indicate . . . a presence.

220 MAIRE: Hah!

BRIDGET: I'm telling you—you'll be arrested.

(When DOALTY *is embarrassed—or pleased—he reacts physically. He now grabs* BRIDGET *around the waist.)*

DOALTY: What d'you make of that for an implement, Bridget?
Wouldn't that make a great aul shaft for your churn?

BRIDGET: Let go of me, you dirty brute! I've a headline to do
225 before Big Hughie comes.

MANUS: I don't think we'll wait for him. Let's get started.

*(Slowly, reluctantly they begin to move to their seats and specific
tasks.* DOALTY *goes to the bucket of water at the door and washes
his hands.* BRIDGET *sets up a hand-mirror and combs her hair.)*

BRIDGET: Nellie Ruadh's baby was to be christened this morning. Did any of yous hear what she called it? Did you, Sarah?

*(*SARAH *grunts: No.)*

BRIDGET: Did you, Maire?

230 MAIRE: No.

BRIDGET: Our Seamus says she was threatening she was going
to call it after its father.

DOALTY: Who's the father?

BRIDGET: That's the point, you donkey you!

235 DOALTY: Ah.

BRIDGET: So there's a lot of uneasy bucks about Baile Beag
this day.

DOALTY: She told me last Sunday she was going to call it
Jimmy.

BRIDGET: You're a liar, Doalty. 240

DOALTY: Would I tell you a lie? Hi, Jimmy, Nellie Ruadh's aul
fella's looking for you.

JIMMY: For me?

MAIRE: Come on, Doalty.

DOALTY: Someone told him . . . 245

MAIRE: Doalty!

DOALTY: He heard you know the first book of the Satires of
Horace off by heart . . .

JIMMY: That's true.

DOALTY: . . . and he wants you to recite it for him. 250

JIMMY: I'll do that for him certainly, certainly.

DOALTY: He's busting to hear it.

*(*JIMMY *fumbles in his pockets.)*

JIMMY: I came across this last night—this'll interest you—in
Book Two of Virgil's *Georgics*.

DOALTY: Be God, that's my territory alright. 255

BRIDGET: You clown you! *(To* SARAH.) Hold this for me, would
you? *(Her mirror.)*

JIMMY: Listen to this, Manus. '*Nigra fere et presso pinguis sub
vomere terra . . .*'

DOALTY: Steady on now—easy, boys, easy—don't rush me, 260
boys—

(He mimes great concentration.)

JIMMY: Manus?

MANUS: 'Land that is black and rich beneath the pressure of
the plough . . .'

DOALTY: Give *me* a chance! 265

JIMMY: 'And with *cui putre*—with crumbly soil—is in the main
best for corn.' There you are!

DOALTY: There you are.

JIMMY: 'From no other land will you see more wagons wending
homeward behind slow bullocks.' Virgil! There! 270

DOALTY: 'Slow bullocks'!

JIMMY: Isn't that what I'm always telling you? Black soil for
corn. *That's* what you should have in that upper field of
yours—corn, not spuds.

DOALTY: Would you listen to that fella! Too lazy be Jasus to 275
wash himself and he's lecturing me on agriculture! Would
you go and take a running race at yourself, Jimmy Jack
Cassie! *(Grabs* SARAH.) Come away out of this with me,
Sarah, and we'll plant some corn together.

MANUS: All right—all right. Let's settle down and get some 280
work done. I know Sean Beag isn't coming—he's at the
salmon. What about the Donnelly twins? *(To* DOALTY.) Are
the Donnelly twins not coming any more?

*(*DOALTY *shrugs and turns away.)*

Did you ask them?

DOALTY: Haven't seen them. Not about these days. 285

---

201 **theos** a god   202 **thea** a goddess

258–259 **Nigra fere . . . vomere terra** Land that is black and rich beneath the pressure of the plough   266 **cui putre** crumbly soil

(DOALTY *begins whistling through his teeth. Suddenly the atmosphere is silent and alert.*)

MANUS: Aren't they at home?

DOALTY: No.

MANUS: Where are they then?

DOALTY: How would I know?

290 BRIDGET: Our Seamus says two of the soldiers' horses were found last night at the foot of the cliffs at Machaire Buidhe and . . . (*She stops suddenly and begins writing with chalk on her slate.*) D'you hear the whistles of this aul slate? Sure nobody could write on an aul slippery thing like that.

295 MANUS: What headline did my father set you?

BRIDGET: 'It's easier to stamp out learning than to recall it.'

JIMMY: Book Three, the *Agricola* of Tacitus.

BRIDGET: God but you're a dose.

MANUS: Can you do it?

300 BRIDGET: There. Is it bad? Will he ate me?

MANUS: It's very good. Keep your elbow in closer to your side. Doalty?

DOALTY: I'm at the seven-times table. I'm perfect, skipper.

(MANUS *moves to* SARAH.)

MANUS: Do you understand those sums?

(SARAH *nods: Yes.* MANUS *leans down to her ear.*)

305 MANUS: My name is Sarah.

(MANUS *goes to* MAIRE. *While he is talking to her the others swop books, talk quietly, etc.*)

MANUS: Can I help you? What are you at?

MAIRE: Map of America. (*Pause.*) The passage money came last Friday.

MANUS: You never told me that.

310 MAIRE: Because I haven't seen you since, have I?

MANUS: You don't want to go. You said that yourself.

MAIRE: There's ten below me to be raised and no man in the house. What do you suggest?

MANUS: Do you want to go?

315 MAIRE: Did you apply for that job in the new national school?

MANUS: No.

MAIRE: You said you would.

MANUS: I said I might.

MAIRE: When it opens, this is finished: nobody's going to pay

320 to go to a hedge-school.

MANUS: I know that and I . . . (*He breaks off because he sees* SARAH, *obviously listening, at his shoulder. She moves away again.*) I was thinking that maybe I could . . .

MAIRE: It's £56 a year you're throwing away.

325 MANUS: I can't apply for it.

MAIRE: You *promised* me you would.

MANUS: My father has applied for it.

MAIRE: He has not!

MANUS: Day before yesterday.

330 MAIRE: For God's sake, sure you know he'd never—

MANUS: I couldn't—I can't go in against him.

(MAIRE *looks at him for a second. Then:—*)

MAIRE: Suit yourself. (*To* BRIDGET.) I saw your Seamus heading off to the Port fair early this morning.

BRIDGET: And wait till you hear this—I forgot to tell you this.

335 He said that as soon as he crossed over the gap at Cnoc na

Mona—just beyond where the soldiers are making the maps—the sweet smell was everywhere.

DOALTY: You never told me that.

BRIDGET: It went out of my head.

DOALTY: He saw the crops in Port? 340

BRIDGET: Some.

MANUS: How did the tops look?

BRIDGET: Fine—I think.

DOALTY: In flower?

BRIDGET: I don't know. I think so. He didn't say. 345

MANUS: Just the sweet smell—that's all?

BRIDGET: They say that's the way it snakes in, don't they? First the smell; and then one morning the stalks are all black and limp.

DOALTY: Are you stupid? It's the rotting stalks makes the sweet 350 smell for God's sake. That's what the smell is—rotting stalks.

MAIRE: Sweet smell! Sweet smell! Every year at this time somebody comes back with stories of the sweet smell. Sweet God, did the potatoes ever fail in Baile Beag? Well, did they ever—ever? Never! There was never blight here. Never. 355 Never. But we're always sniffing about for it, aren't we?—looking for disaster. The rents are going to go up again—the harvest's going to be lost—the herring have gone away for ever—there's going to be evictions. Honest to God, some of you people aren't happy unless you're miserable and you'll 360 not be right content until you're dead!

DOALTY: Bloody right, Maire. And sure St Colmcille prophesied there'd never be blight here. He said:

The spuds will bloom in Baile Beag
Till rabbits grow an extra lug. 365

And sure that'll never be. So we're all right. Seven threes are twenty-one; seven fours are twenty-eight; seven fives are forty-nine—Hi, Jimmy, do you fancy my chances as boss of the new national school?

JIMMY: What's that?—what's that? 370

DOALTY: Agh, g'way back home to Greece, son.

MAIRE: You ought to apply, Doalty.

DOALTY: D'you think so? Cripes, maybe I will. Hah!

BRIDGET: Did you know that you start at the age of six and you have to stick at it until you're twelve at least—no matter how 375 smart you are or how much you know.

DOALTY: Who told you that yarn?

BRIDGET: And every child from every house has to go all day, every day, summer or winter. That's the law.

DOALTY: I'll tell you something—nobody's going to go near 380 them—they're not going to take on—law or no law.

BRIDGET: And everything's free in them. You pay for nothing except the books you use; that's what our Seamus says.

DOALTY: 'Our Seamus'. Sure your Seamus wouldn't pay anyway. She's making this all up. 385

BRIDGET: Isn't that right, Manus?

MANUS: I think so.

BRIDGET: And from the very first day you go, you'll not hear one word of Irish spoken. You'll be taught to speak English and every subject will be taught through English and every- 390 one'll end up as cute as the Buncrana people.

(SARAH *suddenly grunts and mimes a warning that the master is coming. The atmosphere changes. Sudden business. Heads down.*)

DOALTY: He's here, boys. Cripes, he'll make yella meal out of me for those bloody tables.

BRIDGET: Have you any extra chalk, Manus?

395 MAIRE: And the atlas for me.

(DOALTY *goes to* MAIRE *who is sitting on a stool at the back.*)

DOALTY: Swop you seats.

MAIRE: Why?

DOALTY: There's an empty one beside the Infant Prodigy.

MAIRE: I'm fine here.

400 DOALTY: Please, Maire. I want to jouk in the back here.

(MAIRE *rises.*)

God love you. (*Aloud.*) Anyone got a bloody table-book? Cripes, I'm wrecked.

(SARAH *gives him one.*)

God, I'm dying about you.

(*In his haste to get to the back seat,* DOALTY *bumps into* BRIDGET *who is kneeling on the floor and writing laboriously on a slate resting on top of a bench-seat.*)

BRIDGET: Watch where you're going, Doalty!

(DOALTY *gooses* BRIDGET. *She squeals. Now the quiet hum of work:* JIMMY *reading Homer in a low voice;* BRIDGET *copying her headline;* MAIRE *studying the atlas;* DOALTY, *his eyes shut tight, mouthing his tables;* SARAH *doing sums. After a few seconds:—*)

405 BRIDGET: Is this 'g' right, Manus? How do you put a tail on it?

DOALTY: Will you shut up! I can't concentrate!

(*A few more seconds of work. Then* DOALTY *opens his eyes and looks around.*)

False alarm, boys. The bugger's not coming at all. Sure the bugger's hardly fit to walk.

(*And immediately* HUGH *enters. A large man, with residual dignity, shabbily dressed, carrying a stick. He has, as always, a large quantity of drink taken, but he is by no means drunk. He is in his early sixties.*)

HUGH: *Adsum*, Doalty, *adsum*. Perhaps not in *sobrietate perfecta* but adequately *sobrius* to overhear your quip. Vesperal salutations to you all.

(*Various responses.*)

JIMMY: *Ave*, Hugh.

HUGH: James. (*He removes his hat and coat and hands them and his stick to* MANUS, *as if to a footman.*) Apologies for my late arrival: we were celebrating the baptism of Nellie Ruadh's baby.

BRIDGET: (*Innocently.*) What name did she put on it, Master?

HUGH: Was it Eamon? Yes, it was Eamon.

BRIDGET: Eamon Donal from Tor! Cripes!

420 HUGH: And after the *caerimonia nominationis*—Maire?

MAIRE: The ritual of naming.

HUGH: Indeed—we then had a few libations to mark the occasion. Altogether very pleasant. The derivation of the word 'baptize'?—where are my Greek scholars? Doalty?

425 DOALTY: Would it be—ah—ah—

HUGH: Too slow. James?

JIMMY: 'Baptizein'—to dip or immerse.

HUGH: Indeed—our friend Pliny Minor speaks of the '*baptisterium*'—the cold bath.

430 DOALTY: Master.

HUGH: Doalty?

DOALTY: I suppose you could talk then about baptizing a sheep at sheep-dipping, could you?

(*Laughter. Comments.*)

HUGH: Indeed—the precedent is there—the day you were appropriately named Doalty—seven nines?

435 DOALTY: What's that, Master?

HUGH: Seven times nine?

DOALTY: Seven nines—seven nines—seven times nine—seven times nine are—cripes, it's on the tip of my tongue, Master—I knew it for sure this morning—funny that's the only one that foxes me—

440

BRIDGET: (*Prompt.*) Sixty-three.

DOALTY: What's wrong with me: sure seven nines are fifty-three, Master.

445 HUGH: Sophocles from Colonus would agree with Doalty Dan Doalty from Tulach Alainn: 'To know nothing is the sweetest life.' Where's Sean Beag?

MANUS: He's at the salmon.

HUGH: And Nora Dan?

450 MAIRE: She says she's not coming back any more.

HUGH: Ah. Nora Dan can now write her name—Nora Dan's education is complete. And the Donnelly twins?

(*Brief pause. Then:—*)

BRIDGET: They're probably at the turf. (*She goes to* HUGH.) There's the one-and-eight I owe you for last quarter's arithmetic and there's my one-and-six for this quarter's writing.

455

HUGH: *Gratias tibi ago.* (*He sits at his table.*) Before we commence our *studia* I have three items of information to impart to you—(*To* MANUS.) A bowl of tea, strong tea, black—

(MANUS *leaves.*)

Item A: on my perambulations today—Bridget? Too slow. Maire?

460

MAIRE: *Perambulare*—to walk about.

HUGH: Indeed—I encountered Captain Lancey of the Royal Engineers who is engaged in the ordnance survey of this area. He tells me that in the past few days two of his horses have strayed and some of his equipment seems to be mislaid. I expressed my regret and suggested he address you himself on these matters. He then explained that he does not speak Irish. Latin? I asked. None. Greek? Not a syllable. He speaks—on his own admission—only English; and to his credit he seemed suitably verecund—James?

465

470

JIMMY: *Verecundus*—humble.

HUGH: Indeed—he voiced some surprise that we did not speak his language. I explained that a few of us did, on occasion—outside the parish of course—and then usually for the purposes of commerce, a use to which his tongue seemed

475

---

409 **adsum** I am present; **sobrietate perfecta** with complete sobriety 410 **sobrius** sober 412 **Ave** hail 420 **caerimonia nominationis** ceremony of naming

427 **baptizein** to dip or immerse 428 **baptisterium** a cold bath, swimming pool 456 **Gratias tibi ago** I thank you 457 **studia** studies 461 **perambulare** to walk through 471 **verecundus** shame-faced, modest

particularly suited—(*Shouts.*) and a slice of soda bread— and I went on to propose that our own culture and the classi- cal tongues made a happier conjugation—Doalty?

DOALTY: *Conjugo*—I join together.

(DOALTY *is so pleased with himself that he prods and winks at* BRIDGET.)

480 HUGH: Indeed—English, I suggested, couldn't really express us. And again to his credit he acquiesced to my logic. Acqui- esced—Maire?

(MAIRE *turns away impatiently.* HUGH *is unaware of the gesture.*)

Too slow. Bridget?

BRIDGET: *Acquiesco.*

485 HUGH: *Procede.*

BRIDGET: *Acquiesco, acquiescere, acquievi, acquietum.*

HUGH: Indeed—and Item B . . .

MAIRE: Master.

HUGH: Yes?

(MAIRE *gets to her feet uneasily but determinedly. Pause.*)

490 Well, girl?

MAIRE: We should all be learning to speak English. That's what my mother says. That's what I say. That's what Dan O'Connell said last month in Ennis. He said the sooner we all learn to speak English the better.

(*Suddenly several speak together.*)

495 JIMMY: What's she saying? What? What?

DOALTY: It's Irish he uses when he's travelling around scroung- ing votes.

BRIDGET: And sleeping with married women. Sure no woman's safe from that fella.

500 JIMMY: Who-who-who? Who's this? Who's this?

HUGH: *Silentium!* (*Pause.*) Who is she talking about?

MAIRE: I'm talking about Daniel O'Connell.

HUGH: Does she mean that little Kerry politician?

MAIRE: I'm talking about the Liberator, Master, as you well

505 know. And what he said was this: 'The old language is a bar- rier to modern progress.' He said that last month. And he's right. I don't want Greek. I don't want Latin. I want English.

(MANUS *reappears on the platform above.*)

I want to be able to speak English because I'm going to America as soon as the harvest's all saved.

(MAIRE *remains standing.* HUGH *puts his hand into his pocket and produces a flask of whiskey. He removes the cap, pours a drink into it, tosses it back, replaces the cap, puts the flask back into his pocket. Then:—*)

510 HUGH: We have been diverted—*diverto*—*divertere*—Where were we?

DOALTY: Three items of information, Master. You're at Item B.

HUGH: Indeed—Item B—Item B—yes—On my way to the christening this morning I chanced to meet Mr George

515 Alexander, Justice of the Peace. We discussed the new na- tional school. Mr Alexander invited me to take charge of it

---

479 **conjugo** I join together   484 **acquiesco, acquiescere** to rest, to find comfort in   485 **procede** proceed   501 **Silentium!** Silence! 510 **diverto, divertere** to turn away

---

when it opens. I thanked him and explained that I could do that only if I were free to run it as I have run this hedge- school for the past thirty-five years—filling what our friend Euripides calls the '*aplestos pithos*'—James?   520

JIMMY: 'The cask that cannot be filled'.

HUGH: Indeed—and Mr Alexander retorted courteously and emphatically that he hopes that is how it will be run.

(MAIRE *now sits.*)

Indeed. I have had a strenuous day and I am weary of you all. (*He rises.*) Manus will take care of you.   525

(HUGH *goes towards the steps.* OWEN *enters.* OWEN *is the younger son, a handsome, attractive young man in his twenties. He is dressed smartly—a city man. His manner is easy and charming: everything he does is invested with consideration and enthusiasm. He now stands framed in the doorway, a travelling bag across his shoulder.*)

OWEN: Could anybody tell me is this where Hugh Mor O'Donnell holds his hedge-school?

DOALTY: It's Owen—Owen Hugh! Look, boys—it's Owen Hugh!

(OWEN *enters. As he crosses the room he touches and has a word for each person.*)

OWEN: Doalty! (*Playful punch.*) How are you, boy? *Jacobe,*   530 *quid agis?* Are you well?

JIMMY: Fine. Fine.

OWEN: And Bridget! Give us a kiss. Aaaaaah!

BRIDGET: You're welcome, Owen.

OWEN: It's not—? Yes, it *is* Maire Chatach! God! A young   535 woman.

MAIRE: How are you, Owen?

(OWEN *is now in front of* HUGH. *He puts his two hands on his* FATHER's *shoulders.*)

OWEN: And how's the old man himself?

HUGH: Fair—fair.

OWEN: Fair? For God's sake you never looked better! Come   540 here to me. (*He embraces* HUGH *warmly and genuinely.*) Great to see you, Father. Great to be back.

(HUGH's *eyes are moist—partly joy, partly the drink.*)

HUGH: I—I'm—I'm—pay no attention to—

OWEN: Come on—come on—come on—(*He gives* HUGH *his handkerchief.*) Do you know what you and I are going to do   545 tonight? We are going to go up to Anna na mBreag's . . .

DOALTY: Not there, Owen.

OWEN: Why not?

DOALTY: Her poteen's worse than ever.

BRIDGET: They say she puts frogs in it!   550

OWEN: All the better. (*To* HUGH.) And you and I are going to get footless drunk. That's arranged.

(OWEN *sees* MANUS *coming down the steps with tea and soda bread. They meet at the bottom.*)

And Manus!

MANUS: You're welcome, Owen.

---

520 **aplestos pithos** unfillable cask   530–531 **Jacobe, quid agis?** James, how are you?

555 OWEN: I know I am. And it's great to be here. (*He turns round, arms outstretched.*) I can't believe it. I come back after six years and everything's just as it was! Nothing's changed! Not a thing! (*Sniffs.*) Even that smell—that's the same smell this place always had. What is it anyway? Is it the straw?

560 DOALTY: Jimmy Jack's feet.

(*General laughter. It opens little pockets of conversation round the room.*)

OWEN: And Doalty Dan Doalty hasn't changed either!
DOALTY: Bloody right, Owen.
OWEN: Jimmy, are you well?
JIMMY: Dodging about.
565 OWEN: Any word of the big day?

(*This is greeted with 'ohs' and 'ahs'.*)

Time enough, Jimmy. Homer's easier to live with, isn't he?
MAIRE: We heard stories that you own ten big shops in Dublin—is it true?
OWEN: Only nine.
570 BRIDGET: And you've twelve horses and six servants.
OWEN: Yes—that's true. God Almighty, would you listen to them—taking a hand at me!
MANUS: When did you arrive?
OWEN: We left Dublin yesterday morning, spent last night in
575 Omagh and got here half an hour ago.
MANUS: You're hungry then.
HUGH: Indeed—get him food—get him a drink.
OWEN: Not now, thanks; later. Listen—am I interrupting you all?
580 HUGH: By no means. We're finished for the day.
OWEN: Wonderful. I'll tell you why. Two friends of mine are waiting outside the door. They'd like to meet you and I'd like you to meet them. May I bring them in?
HUGH: Certainly. You'll all eat and have . . .
585 OWEN: Not just yet, Father. You've seen the sappers working in this area for the past fortnight, haven't you? Well, the older man is Captain Lancey . . .
HUGH: I've met Captain Lancey.
OWEN: Great. He's the cartographer in charge of this whole
590 area. Cartographer—James?

(OWEN *begins to play this game—his father's game—partly to involve his classroom audience, partly to show he has not forgotten it, and indeed partly because he enjoys it.*)

JIMMY: A maker of maps.
OWEN: Indeed—and the younger man that I travelled with from Dublin, his name is Lieutenant Yolland and he is attached to the toponymic department—Father?—*responde—*
595 *responde!*
HUGH: He gives names to places.
OWEN: Indeed—although he is in fact an orthographer—Doalty?—too slow—Manus?
MANUS: The correct spelling of those names.
600 OWEN: Indeed—indeed!

(OWEN *laughs and claps his hands. Some of the others join in.*)

Beautiful! Beautiful! Honest to God, it's such a delight to be back here with you all again—'civilized' people. Anyhow—may I bring them in?
HUGH: Your friends are our friends.
605 OWEN: I'll be straight back.

(*There is general talk as* OWEN *goes towards the door. He stops beside* SARAH.)

OWEN: That's a new face. Who are you?

(*A very brief hesitation. Then:—*)

SARAH: My name is Sarah.
OWEN: Sarah who?
SARAH: Sarah Johnny Sally.
OWEN: Of course! From Bun na hAbhann! I'm Owen—Owen 610 Hugh Mor. From Baile Beag. Good to see you.

(*During this* OWEN—SARAH *exchange.*)

HUGH: Come on now. Let's tidy this place up. (*He rubs the top of his table with his sleeve.*) Move, Doalty—lift those books off the floor.
DOALTY: Right, Master; certainly, Master; I'm doing my best, 615 Master.

(OWEN *stops at the door.*)

OWEN: One small thing, Father.
HUGH: *Silentium!*
OWEN: I'm on their pay-roll.

(SARAH, *very elated at her success, is beside* MANUS.)

SARAH: I said it, Manus! 620

(MANUS *ignores* SARAH. *He is much more interested in* OWEN *now.*)

MANUS: You haven't enlisted, have you?!

(SARAH *moves away.*)

OWEN: Me a soldier? I'm employed as a part-time, underpaid, civilian interpreter. My job is to translate the quaint, archaic tongue you people persist in speaking into the King's good English. 625

(*He goes out.*)

HUGH: Move—move—move! Put some order on things! Come on, Sarah—hide that bucket. Whose are these slates? Somebody take these dishes away. *Festinate! Festinate!*

(MANUS *goes to* MAIRE *who is busy tidying.*)

MANUS: You didn't tell me you were definitely leaving.
MAIRE: Not now. 630
HUGH: Good girl, Bridget. That's the style.
MANUS: You might at least have told me.
HUGH: Are these your books, James?
JIMMY: Thank you.
MANUS: Fine! Fine! Go ahead! Go ahead! 635
MAIRE: You talk to me about getting married—with neither a roof over your head nor a sod of ground under your foot. I suggest you go for the new school; but no—'My father's in for that.' Well now he's got it and now this is finished and now you've nothing. 640
MANUS: I can always . . .
MAIRE: What? Teach classics to the cows? Agh—

(MAIRE *moves away from* MANUS. OWEN *enters with* LANCEY *and* YOLLAND. CAPTAIN LANCEY *is middle-aged; a small, crisp officer, expert in his field as cartographer but uneasy with people—especially civilians, especially these foreign civilians. His*

---

628 **Festinate!** Hurry!

skill is with deeds, not words. LIEUTENANT YOLLAND *is in his late twenties/early thirties. He is tall and thin and gangling, blond hair, a shy, awkward manner. A soldier by accident.)*

OWEN: Here we are. Captain Lancey—my father.

LANCEY: Good evening.

(HUGH becomes expansive, almost courtly, with his visitors.)

645 HUGH: You and I have already met, sir.

LANCEY: Yes.

OWEN: And Lieutenant Yolland—both Royal Engineers—my father.

HUGH: You're very welcome, gentlemen.

650 YOLLAND: How do you do.

HUGH: *Gaudeo vos hic adesse.*

OWEN: And I'll make no other introductions except that these are some of the people of Baile Beag and—what?—well you're among the best people in Ireland now. *(He pauses to*
655 *allow* LANCEY *to speak.* LANCEY *does not.)* Would you like to say a few words, Captain?

HUGH: What about a drop, sir?

LANCEY: A what?

HUGH: Perhaps a modest refreshment? A little sampling of our
660 *aqua vitae?*

LANCEY: No, no.

HUGH: Later perhaps when—

LANCEY: I'll say what I have to say, if I may, and as briefly as possible. Do they speak *any* English, Roland?

665 OWEN: Don't worry. I'll translate.

LANCEY: I see. *(He clears his throat. He speaks as if he were addressing children—a shade too loudly and enunciating excessively.)* You may have seen me—seen me—working in this section—section?—working. We are here—here—in this
670 place—you understand?—to make a map—a map—a map and—

JIMMY: *Nonne Latine loquitur?*

(HUGH holds up a restraining hand.)

HUGH: James.

LANCEY: *(To* JIMMY*)* I do not speak Gaelic, sir.

(He looks at OWEN.*)*

675 OWEN: Carry on.

LANCEY: A map is a representation on paper—a picture—you understand picture?—a paper picture—showing, representing this country—yes?—showing your country in miniature—a scaled drawing on paper of—of—of—

(Suddenly DOALTY *sniggers. Then* BRIDGET. *Then* SARAH. OWEN *leaps in quickly.)*

680 OWEN: It might be better if you *assume* they understand you—

LANCEY: Yes?

OWEN: And I'll translate as you go along.

LANCEY: I see. Yes. Very well. Perhaps you're right. Well. What we are doing is this. *(He looks at* OWEN. OWEN *nods reassur-*
685 *ingly.)* His Majesty's government has ordered the first ever comprehensive survey of this entire country—a general triangulation which will embrace detailed hydrographic and

topographic information and which will be executed to a scale of six inches to the English mile.

HUGH: *(Pouring a drink.)* Excellent—excellent.   690

(LANCEY looks at OWEN.*)*

OWEN: A new map is being made of the whole country.

(LANCEY looks to OWEN: *Is that all?* OWEN *smiles reassuringly and indicates to proceed.)*

LANCEY: This enormous task has been embarked on so that the military authorities will be equipped with up-to-date and accurate information on every corner of this part of the Empire.   695

OWEN: The job is being done by soldiers because they are skilled in this work.

LANCEY: And also so that the entire basis of land valuation can be reassessed for purposes of more equitable taxation.

OWEN: This new map will take the place of the estate agent's   700 map so that from now on you will know exactly what is yours in law.

LANCEY: In conclusion I wish to quote two brief extracts from the white paper which is our governing charter: *(Reads)* 'All former surveys of Ireland originated in forfeiture and violent 705 transfer of property; the present survey has for its object the relief which can be afforded to the proprietors and occupiers of land from unequal taxation.'

OWEN: The captain hopes that the public will cooperate with the sappers and that the new map will mean that taxes are   710 reduced.

HUGH: A worthy enterprise—*opus honestum!* And Extract B?

LANCEY: 'Ireland is privileged. No such survey is being undertaken in England. So this survey cannot but be received as proof of the disposition of this government to advance the in- 715 terests of Ireland.' My sentiments, too.

OWEN: This survey demonstrates the government's interest in Ireland and the captain thanks you for listening so attentively to him.

HUGH: Our pleasure, Captain.   720

LANCEY: Lieutenant Yolland?

YOLLAND: I—I—I've nothing to say—really—

OWEN: The captain is the man who actually makes the new map. George's task is to see that the place-names on this map are . . . correct. *(To* YOLLAND.*)* Just a few words—they'd 725 like to hear you. *(To class.)* Don't you want to hear George, too?

MAIRE: Has he anything to say?

YOLLAND: *(To* MAIRE.*)* Sorry—sorry?

OWEN: She says she's dying to hear you.   730

YOLLAND: *(To* MAIRE.*)* Very kind of you—thank you . . . *(To class.)* I can only say that I feel—I feel very foolish to—to—to be working here and not to speak your language. But I intend to rectify that—with Roland's help—indeed I do.

OWEN: He wants me to teach him Irish!   735

HUGH: You are doubly welcome, sir.

YOLLAND: I think your countryside is—is—is—is very beautiful. I've fallen in love with it already. I hope we're not too—too crude an intrusion on your lives. And I know that I'm going to be happy, very happy, here.   740

OWEN: He is already a committed Hibernophile—

---

651 **Gaudeo vos hic adesse** Welcome   672 **Nonne Latine loquitur?**
Does he not speak Latin?

712 **opus honestum** an honourable task

JIMMY: He loves—

OWEN: All right, Jimmy—we know—he loves Baile Beag; and he loves you all.

745 HUGH: Please . . . May I . . . ?

(HUGH *is now drunk. He holds on to the edge of the table.*)

OWEN: Go ahead, Father. (*Hands up for quiet.*) Please—please.

HUGH: And we, gentlemen, we in turn are happy to offer you our friendship, our hospitality, and every assistance that you

750 may require. Gentlemen—welcome!

(*A few desultory claps. The formalities are over. General conversation. The soldiers meet the locals.* MANUS *and* OWEN *meet down stage.*)

OWEN: Lancey's a bloody ramrod but George's all right. How are you anyway?

MANUS: What sort of a translation was that, Owen?

OWEN: Did I make a mess of it?

755 MANUS: You weren't saying what Lancey was saying!

OWEN: 'Uncertainty in meaning is incipient poetry'—who said that?

MANUS: There was nothing uncertain about what Lancey said: it's a bloody military operation, Owen! And what's Yolland's

760 function? What's 'incorrect' about the place-names we have here?

OWEN: Nothing at all. They're just going to be standardized.

MANUS: You mean changed into English?

OWEN: Where there's ambiguity, they'll be Anglicized.

765 MANUS: And they call you Roland! They both call you Roland!

OWEN: Shhhhh. Isn't it ridiculous? They seemed to get it wrong from the very beginning—or else they can't pronounce Owen. I was afraid some of you bastards would laugh.

770 MANUS: Aren't you going to tell them?

OWEN: Yes—yes—soon—soon.

MANUS: But they . . .

OWEN: Easy, man, easy. Owen—Roland—what the hell. It's only a name. It's the same me, isn't it? Well, isn't it?

775 MANUS: Indeed it is. It's the same Owen.

OWEN: And the same Manus. And in a way we complement each other. (*He punches* MANUS *lightly, playfully and turns to join the others. As he goes.*) All right—who has met whom? Isn't this a job for the go-between?

(MANUS *watches* OWEN *move confidently across the floor, taking* MAIRE *by the hand and introducing her to* YOLLAND. HUGH *is trying to negotiate the steps.* JIMMY *is lost in a text.* DOALTY *and* BRIDGET *are reliving their giggling.* SARAH *is staring at* MANUS.)

— ACT TWO —

SCENE I

The sappers have already mapped most of the area. YOLLAND's *official task, which* OWEN *is now doing, is to take each of the Gaelic names—every hill, stream, rock, even every patch of ground which possessed its own distinctive Irish name—and Anglicize it, either by changing it into its approximate English sound or by translating it into English words. For example, a Gaelic name like Cnoc Ban could become Knockban or—directly translated—Fair Hill. These new standardized names were* entered into the Name-Book, and when the new maps appeared they contained all these new Anglicized names. OWEN's *official function as translator is to pronounce each name in Irish and then provide the English translation.*

The hot weather continues. It is late afternoon some days later.

Stage right: an improvised clothes-line strung between the shafts of the cart and a nail in the wall; on it are some shirts and socks.

A large map—one of the new blank maps—is spread out on the floor. OWEN *is on his hands and knees, consulting it. He is totally engrossed in his task which he pursues with great energy and efficiency.*

YOLLAND's *hesitancy has vanished—he is at home here now. He is sitting on the floor, his long legs stretched out before him, his back resting against a creel, his eyes closed. His mind is elsewhere. One of the reference books—a church registry—lies open on his lap.*

Around them are various reference books, the Name-Book, a bottle of poteen, some cups, etc.

OWEN *completes an entry in the Name-Book and returns to the map on the floor.*

OWEN: Now. Where have we got to? Yes—the point where that stream enters the sea—that tiny little beach there. George!

YOLLAND: Yes. I'm listening. What do you call it? Say the Irish name again?

OWEN: Bun na hAbhann. 5

YOLLAND: Again.

OWEN: Bun na hAbhann.

YOLLAND: Bun na hAbhann.

OWEN: That's terrible, George.

YOLLAND: I know. I'm sorry. Say it again. 10

OWEN: Bun na hAbhann.

YOLLAND: Bun na hAbhann.

OWEN: That's better. Bun is the Irish word for bottom. And Abha means river. So it's literally the mouth of the river.

YOLLAND: Let's leave it alone. There's no English equivalent 15 for a sound like that.

OWEN: What is it called in the church registry?

(*Only now does* YOLLAND *open his eyes.*)

YOLLAND: Let's see . . . Banowen.

OWEN: That's wrong. (*Consults text.*) The list of freeholders calls it Owenmore—that's completely wrong: Owenmore's 20 the big river at the west end of the parish. (*Another text.*) And in the grand jury lists it's called—God!—Binhone!—wherever they got that. I suppose we could Anglicize it to Bunowen; but somehow that's neither fish nor flesh.

(YOLLAND *closes his eyes again.*)

YOLLAND: I give up. 25

OWEN: (*At map.*) Back to first principles. What are we trying to do?

YOLLAND: Good question.

OWEN: We are trying to denominate and at the same time describe that tiny area of soggy, rocky, sandy ground where that 30 little stream enters the sea, an area known locally as Bun na hAbhann . . . Burnfoot! What about Burnfoot?

YOLLAND: (*Indifferently.*) Good, Roland, Burnfoot's good.

OWEN: George, my name isn't . . .

35　YOLLAND: B-u-r-n-f-o-o-t?
OWEN: Are you happy with that?
YOLLAND: Yes.
OWEN: Burnfoot it is then. (*He makes the entry into the Name-Book.*) Bun na hAbhann—B-u-r-n—
40　YOLLAND: You're becoming very skilled at this.
OWEN: We're not moving fast enough.
YOLLAND: (*Opens eyes again.*) Lancey lectured me again last night.
OWEN: When does he finish here?
45　YOLLAND: The sappers are pulling out at the end of the week. The trouble is, the maps they've completed can't be printed without these names. So London screams at Lancey and Lancey screams at me. But I wasn't intimidated.

(MANUS *emerges from upstairs and descends.*)

'I'm sorry, sir,' I said, 'But certain tasks demand their own
50　tempo. You cannot rename a whole country overnight.' Your Irish air has made me bold. (*To* MANUS.) Do you want us to leave?
MANUS: Time enough. Class won't begin for another half-hour.
YOLLAND: Sorry—sorry?
55　OWEN: Can't you speak English?

(MANUS *gathers the things off the clothes-line.* OWEN *returns to the map.*)

OWEN: We now come across that beach . . .
YOLLAND: Tra—that's the Irish for beach. (*To* MANUS.) I'm picking up the odd word, Manus.
MANUS: So.
60　OWEN: . . . on past Burnfoot; and there's nothing around here that has any name that I know of until we come down here to the south end, just about here . . . and there should be a ridge of rocks there . . . Have the sappers marked it? They have. Look, George.
65　YOLLAND: Where are we?
OWEN: There.
YOLLAND: I'm lost.
OWEN: Here. And the name of that ridge is Druim Dubh. Put English on that, Lieutenant.
70　YOLLAND: Say it again.
OWEN: Druim Dubh.
YOLLAND: Dubh means black.
OWEN: Yes.
YOLLAND: And Druim means . . . what? a fort?
75　OWEN: We met it yesterday in Druim Luachra.
YOLLAND: A ridge! The Black Ridge! (*To* MANUS.) You see, Manus?
OWEN: We'll have you fluent at the Irish before the summer's over.
80　YOLLAND: Oh, I wish I were. (*To* MANUS *as he crosses to go back upstairs.*) We got a crate of oranges from Dublin today. I'll send some up to you.
MANUS: Thanks. (*To* OWEN.) Better hide that bottle. Father's just up and he'd be better without it.
85　OWEN: Can't you speak English before your man?
MANUS: Why?
OWEN: Out of courtesy.
MANUS: Doesn't he want to learn Irish? (*To* YOLLAND.) Don't you want to learn Irish?
90　YOLLAND: Sorry—sorry? I—I—

MANUS: I understand the Lanceys perfectly but people like you puzzle me.
OWEN: Manus, for God's sake!
MANUS: (*Still to* YOLLAND.) How's the work going?
YOLLAND: The work?—the work? Oh, it's—it's staggering　95
along—I think—(*To* OWEN.)—isn't it? But we'd be lost without Roland.
MANUS: (*Leaving.*) I'm sure. But there are always the Rolands, aren't there?

(*He goes upstairs and exits.*)

YOLLAND: What was that he said?—something about Lancey,　100
was it?
OWEN: He said we should hide that bottle before Father gets his hands on it.
YOLLAND: Ah.
OWEN: He's always trying to protect him.　105
YOLLAND: Was he lame from birth?
OWEN: An accident when he was a baby: Father fell across his cradle. That's why Manus feels so responsible for him.
YOLLAND: Why doesn't he marry?
OWEN: Can't afford to, I suppose.　110
YOLLAND: Hasn't he a salary?
OWEN: What salary? All he gets is the odd shilling Father throws him—and that's seldom enough. I got out in time, didn't I?

(YOLLAND *is pouring a drink.*)

Easy with that stuff—it'll hit you suddenly.　115
YOLLAND: I like it.
OWEN: Let's get back to the job. Druim Dubh—what's it called in the jury lists? (*Consults texts.*)
YOLLAND: Some people here resent us.
OWEN: Dramduff—wrong as usual.　120
YOLLAND: I was passing a little girl yesterday and she spat at me.
OWEN: And it's Drimdoo here. What's it called in the registry?
YOLLAND: Do you know the Donnelly twins?
OWEN: Who?　125
YOLLAND: The Donnelly twins.
OWEN: Yes. Best fishermen about here. What about them?
YOLLAND: Lancey's looking for them.
OWEN: What for?
YOLLAND: He wants them for questioning.　130
OWEN: Probably stolen somebody's nets. Dramduffy! Nobody ever called it Dramduffy. Take your pick of those three.
YOLLAND: My head's addled. Let's take a rest. Do you want a drink?
OWEN: Thanks. Now, every Dubh we've come across we've　135
changed to Duff. So if we're to be consistent, I suppose Druim Dubh has to become Dromduff.

(YOLLAND *is now looking out the window.*)

You can see the end of the ridge from where you're standing. But D-r-u-m- or D-r-o-m-? (*Name-Book.*) Do you remember—which did we agree on for Druim Luachra?　140
YOLLAND: That house immediately above where we're camped—
OWEN: Mm?
YOLLAND: The house where Maire lives.
OWEN: Maire? Oh, Maire Chatach.　145

YOLLAND: What does that mean?

OWEN: Curly-haired; the whole family are called the Chatachs. What about it?

YOLLAND: I hear music coming from that house almost every
150 night.

OWEN: Why don't you drop in?

YOLLAND: Could I?

OWEN: Why not? We used D-r-o-m then. So we've got to call it D-r-o-m-d-u-f-f—all right?

155 YOLLAND: Go back up to where the new school is being built and just say the names again for me, would you?

OWEN: That's a good idea. Poolkerry, Ballybeg—

YOLLAND: No, no; as they still are—in your own language.

OWEN: Poll na gCaorach,

(YOLLAND *repeats the names silently after him.*)

160 Baile Beag, Ceann Balor, Lis Maol, Machaire Buidhe, Baile na gGall, Carraig na Ri, Mullach Dearg—

YOLLAND: Do you think I could live here?

OWEN: What are you talking about?

YOLLAND: Settle down here—live here.

165 OWEN: Come on, George.

YOLLAND: I mean it.

OWEN: Live on what? Potatoes? Buttermilk?

YOLLAND: It's really heavenly.

OWEN: For God's sake! The first hot summer in fifty years and
170 you think it's Eden. Don't be such a bloody romantic. You wouldn't survive a mild winter here.

YOLLAND: Do you think not? Maybe you're right.

(DOALTY *enters in a rush.*)

DOALTY: Hi, boys, is Manus about?

OWEN: He's upstairs. Give him a shout.

175 DOALTY: Manus! The cattle's going mad in that heat—Cripes, running wild all over the place. (*To* YOLLAND.) How are you doing, skipper?

(MANUS *appears.*)

YOLLAND: Thank you for—I—I'm very grateful to you for—

DOALTY: Wasting your time. I don't know a word you're saying.
180 Hi, Manus, there's two bucks down the road there asking for you.

MANUS: (*Descending.*) Who are they?

DOALTY: Never clapped eyes on them. They want to talk to you.

185 MANUS: What about?

DOALTY: They wouldn't say. Come on. The bloody beasts'll end up in Loch an Iubhair if they're not capped. Good luck, boys!

(DOALTY *rushes off.* MANUS *follows him.*)

OWEN: Good luck! What were you thanking Doalty for?

190 YOLLAND: I was washing outside my tent this morning and he was passing with a scythe across his shoulder and he came up to me and pointed to the long grass and then cut a pathway round my tent and from the tent down to the road—so that my feet won't get wet with the dew. Wasn't that kind of
195 him? And I have no words to thank him . . . I suppose you're right: I suppose I couldn't live here . . . Just before Doalty came up to me this morning, I was thinking that at that moment I might have been in Bombay instead of Ballybeg. You

see, my father was at his wits end with me and finally he got
200 me a job with the East India Company—some kind of a clerkship. That was ten, eleven months ago. So I set off for London. Unfortunately I—I—I missed the boat. Literally. And since I couldn't face Father and hadn't enough money to hang about until the next sailing, I joined the army. And
205 they stuck me into the Engineers and posted me to Dublin. And Dublin sent me here. And while I was washing this morning and looking across the Tra Bhan, I was thinking how very, very lucky I am to be here and not in Bombay.

OWEN: Do you believe in fate?

210 YOLLAND: Lancey's so like my father. I was watching him last night. He met every group of sappers as they reported in. He checked the field kitchens. He examined the horses. He inspected every single report—even examining the texture of the paper and commenting on the neatness of the handwrit-
215 ing. The perfect colonial servant: not only must the job be done—it must be done with excellence. Father has that drive, too; that dedication; that indefatigable energy. He builds roads—hopping from one end of the Empire to the other. Can't sit still for five minutes. He says himself the
220 longest time he ever sat still was the night before Waterloo when they were waiting for Wellington to make up his mind to attack.

OWEN: What age is he?

YOLLAND: Born in 1789—the very day the Bastille fell. I've
225 often thought maybe that gave his whole life its character. Do you think it could? He inherited a new world the day he was born—The Year One. Ancient time was at an end. The world had cast off its old skin. There were no longer any frontiers to man's potential. Possibilities were endless and ex-
230 citing. He still believes that. The Apocalypse is just about to happen . . . I'm afraid I'm a great disappointment to him. I've neither his energy, nor his coherence, nor his belief. Do I believe in fate? The day I arrived in Ballybeg—no, Baile Beag—the moment you brought me in here, I had a curious
235 sensation. It's difficult to describe. It was a momentary sense of discovery; no—not quite a sense of discovery—a sense of recognition, of confirmation of something I half knew instinctively; as if I had stepped . . .

OWEN: Back into ancient time?

240 YOLLAND: No, no. It wasn't an awareness of *direction* being changed but of experience being of a totally different order. I had moved into a consciousness that wasn't striving nor agitated, but at its ease and with its own conviction and assurance. And when I heard Jimmy Jack and your father swap-
245 ping stories about Apollo and Cuchulainn and Paris and Ferdia—as if they lived down the road—it was then that I thought—I knew—perhaps I could live here . . . (*Now embarrassed.*) Where's the pot-een?

OWEN: Poteen.

250 YOLLAND: Poteen—poteen—poteen. Even if I did speak Irish I'd always be an outsider here, wouldn't I? I may learn the password but the language of the tribe will always elude me, won't it? The private core will always be . . . hermetic, won't it?

255 OWEN: You can learn to decode us.

(HUGH *emerges from upstairs and descends. He is dressed for the road. Today he is physically and mentally jaunty and alert—almost self-consciously jaunty and alert. Indeed, as the*

scene progresses, one has the sense that he is deliberately paro-
dying himself. The moment HUGH *gets to the bottom of the*
steps YOLLAND *leaps respectfully to his feet.)*

HUGH: *(As he descends.)*
    Quantumvis cursum longum fessumque moratur
    Sol, sacro tandem carmine vesper adest.
    I dabble in verse, Lieutenant, after the style of Ovid. *(To*
260   OWEN.) A drop of that to fortify me.
YOLLAND: You'll have to translate it for me.
HUGH: Let's see—
    No matter how long the sun may linger on his long and
       weary journey
265   At length evening comes with its sacred song.
YOLLAND: Very nice, sir.
HUGH: English succeeds in making it sound . . . plebeian.
OWEN: Where are you off to, Father?
HUGH: An *expeditio* with three purposes. Purpose A: to ac-
270   quire a testimonial from our parish priest—*(To* YOLLAND.) a
    worthy man but barely literate; and since he'll ask me to
    write it myself, how in all modesty can I do myself justice?
    (To OWEN.) Where did this *(drink)* come from?
OWEN: Anna na mBreag's.
275 HUGH: *(To* YOLLAND.) In that case address yourself to it with
    circumspection. *(And* HUGH *instantly tosses the drink back in*
    one gulp and grimaces.) Aaaaaaagh! *(Holds out his glass for a*
    refill.) Anna na mBreag means Anna of the Lies. And Pur-
    pose B: to talk to the builders of the new school about the
280   kind of living accommodation I will require there. I have
    lived too long like a journeyman tailor.
YOLLAND: Some years ago we lived fairly close to a poet—well,
    about three miles away.
HUGH: His name?
285 YOLLAND: Wordsworth—William Wordsworth.
HUGH: Did he speak of me to you?
YOLLAND: Actually I never talked to him. I just saw him out
    walking—in the distance.
HUGH: Wordsworth? . . . No. I'm afraid we're not familiar with
290   your literature, Lieutenant. We feel closer to the warm
    Mediterranean. We tend to overlook your island.
YOLLAND: I'm learning to speak Irish, sir.
HUGH: Good.
YOLLAND: Roland's teaching me.
295 HUGH: Splendid.
YOLLAND: I mean—I feel so cut off from the people here. And
    I was trying to explain a few minutes ago how remarkable a
    community this is. To meet people like yourself and Jimmy
    Jack who actually converse in Greek and Latin. And your
300   place names—what was the one we came across this morn-
    ing?—Termon, from Terminus, the god of boundaries. It—
    it—it's really astonishing.
HUGH: We like to think we endure around truths immemori-
    ally posited.
305 YOLLAND: And your Gaelic literature—you're a poet yourself—
HUGH: Only in Latin, I'm afraid.

257–258 Quantumvis cursum . . . vesper adest No matter how long
the sun delays on his long weary course/At length evening comes with
its sacred song   **269 expeditio** an expedition

YOLLAND: I understand it's enormously rich and ornate.
HUGH: Indeed, Lieutenant. A rich language. A rich literature.
    You'll find, sir, that certain cultures expend on their vocabu-
    laries and syntax acquisitive energies and ostentations en- 310
    tirely lacking in their material lives. I suppose you could call
    us a spiritual people.
OWEN: *(Not unkindly; more out of embarrassment before* YOL-
    LAND.) Will you stop that nonsense, Father.
HUGH: Nonsense? What nonsense? 315
OWEN: Do you know where the priest lives?
HUGH: At Lis na Muc, over near . . .
OWEN: No, he doesn't. Lis na Muc, the Fort of the Pigs, has
    become Swinefort. *(Now turning the pages of the Name-*
    Book—a page per name.) And to get to Swinefort you pass 320
    through Greencastle and Fair Head and Strandhill and
    Gort and Whiteplains. And the new school isn't at Poll na
    gCaorach—it's at Sheepsrock. Will you be able to find your
    way?

*(*HUGH *pours himself another drink. Then:—)*

HUGH: Yes, it is a rich language, Lieutenant, full of the 325
    mythologies of fantasy and hope and self-deception—a syn-
    tax opulent with tomorrows. It is our response to mud cabins
    and a diet of potatoes; and our only method of replying
    to . . . inevitabilities. *(To* OWEN.) Can you give me the loan
    of half-a-crown? I'll repay you out of the subscriptions I'm 330
    collecting for the publication of my new book. *(To* YOL-
    LAND.) It is entitled: 'The Pentaglot Preceptor or Elemen-
    tary Institute of the English, Greek, Hebrew, Latin and Irish
    Languages; Particularly Calculated for the Instruction of
    Such Ladies and Gentlemen as may Wish to Learn without 335
    the Help of a Master'.
YOLLAND: *(Laughs.)* That's a wonderful title!
HUGH: Between ourselves—the best part of the enterprise.
    Nor do I, in fact, speak Hebrew. And that last phrase—'with-
    out the Help of a Master'—that was written before the new 340
    national school was thrust upon me—do you think I ought
    to drop it now? After all you don't dispose of the cow just be-
    cause it has produced a magnificent calf, do you?
YOLLAND: You certainly do not.
HUGH: The phrase goes. And I'm interrupting work of mo- 345
    ment. *(He goes to the door and stops there.)* To return briefly
    to that other matter, Lieutenant. I understand your sense of
    exclusion, of being cut off from a life here; and I trust you
    will find access to us with my son's help. But remember that
    words are signals, counters. They are not immortal. And it 350
    can happen—to use an image you'll understand—it can
    happen that a civilization can be imprisoned in a linguistic
    contour which no longer matches the landscape of . . . fact.
    Gentlemen. *(He leaves.)*
OWEN: 'An *expeditio* with three purposes': the children laugh 355
    at him: he always promises three points and he never gets be-
    yond A and B.
YOLLAND: He's an astute man.
OWEN: He's bloody pompous.
YOLLAND: But so astute. 360
OWEN: And he drinks too much. Is it astute not to be able to
    adjust for survival? Enduring around truths immemorially
    posited—hah!
YOLLAND: He knows what's happening.
OWEN: What is happening? 365

YOLLAND: I'm not sure. But I'm concerned about my part in it. It's an eviction of sorts.

OWEN: We're making a six-inch map of the country. Is there something sinister in that?

370 YOLLAND: Not in—

OWEN: And we're taking place-names that are riddled with confusion and—

YOLLAND: Who's confused? Are the people confused?

OWEN: —and we're standardizing those names as accurately
375 and as sensitively as we can.

YOLLAND: Something is being eroded.

OWEN: Back to the romance again. All right! Fine! Fine! Look where we've got to. (*He drops on his hands and knees and stabs a finger at the map.*) We've come to this crossroads.
380 Come here and look at it, man! Look at it! And we call that crossroads Tobair Vree. And why do we call it Tobair Vree? I'll tell you why. Tobair means a well. But what does Vree mean? It's a corruption of Brian—(*Gaelic pronunciation.*) Brian—an erosion of Tobair Bhriain. Because a hundred-
385 and-fifty years ago there used to be a well there, not at the crossroads, mind you—that would be too simple—but in a field close to the crossroads. And an old man called Brian, whose face was disfigured by an enormous growth, got it into his head that the water in that well was blessed; and every
390 day for seven months he went there and bathed his face in it. But the growth didn't go away; and one morning Brian was found drowned in that well. And ever since that crossroads is known as Tobair Vree—even though that well has long since dried up. I know the story because my grandfather told
395 it to me. But ask Doalty—or Maire—or Bridget—even my father—even Manus—why it's called Tobair Vree; and do you think they'll know? I know they don't know. So the question I put to you, Lieutenant, is this: what do we do with a name like that? Do we scrap Tobair Vree altogether and call
400 it—what?—The Cross? Crossroads? Or do we keep piety with a man long dead, long forgotten, his name 'eroded' beyond recognition, whose trivial little story nobody in the parish remembers?

YOLLAND: Except you.

405 OWEN: I've left here.

YOLLAND: You remember it.

OWEN: I'm asking you: what do we write in the Name-Book?

YOLLAND: Tobair Vree.

OWEN: Even though the well is a hundred yards from the ac-
410 tual crossroads—and there's no well anyway—and what the hell does Vree mean?

YOLLAND: Tobair Vree.

OWEN: That's what you want?

YOLLAND: Yes.

415 OWEN: You're certain?

YOLLAND: Yes.

OWEN: Fine. Fine. That's what you'll get.

YOLLAND: That's what you want, too, Roland.

(*Pause.*)

OWEN: (*Explodes.*) George! For God's sake! *My name is not*
420 *Roland!*

YOLLAND: What?

OWEN: (*Softly.*) My name is Owen.

(*Pause.*)

YOLLAND: Not Roland?

OWEN: Owen.

YOLLAND: You mean to say—? 425

OWEN: Owen.

YOLLAND: But I've been—

OWEN: O-w-e-n.

YOLLAND: Where did Roland come from?

OWEN: I don't know. 430

YOLLAND: It was never Roland?

OWEN: Never.

YOLLAND: O my God!

(*Pause. They stare at one another. Then the absurdity of the situation strikes them suddenly. They explode with laughter.* OWEN *pours drinks. As they roll about, their lines overlap.*)

YOLLAND: Why didn't you tell me?

OWEN: Do I look like a Roland? 435

YOLLAND: Spell Owen again.

OWEN: I was getting fond of Roland.

YOLLAND: O my God!

OWEN: O-w-e-n.

YOLLAND: What'll we write— 440

OWEN: —in the Name Book?!

YOLLAND: R-o-w-e-n!

OWEN: Or what about Ol-

YOLLAND: Ol-what?

OWEN: Oland! 445

(*And again they explode.* MANUS *enters. He is very elated.*)

MANUS: What's the celebration?

OWEN: A christening!

YOLLAND: A baptism!

OWEN: A hundred christenings!

YOLLAND: A thousand baptisms! Welcome to Eden! 450

OWEN: Eden's right! We name a thing and—bang!—it leaps into existence!

YOLLAND: Each name a perfect equation with its roots.

OWEN: A perfect congruence with its reality. (*To* MANUS.) Take a drink. 455

YOLLAND: Poteen—beautiful.

OWEN: Lying Anna's poteen.

YOLLAND: Anna na mBreag's poteen.

OWEN: Excellent, George.

YOLLAND: I'll decode you yet. 460

OWEN: (*Offers drink.*) Manus?

MANUS: Not if that's what it does to you.

OWEN: You're right. Steady—steady—sober up—sober up.

YOLLAND: Sober as a judge, Owen.

(MANUS *moves beside* OWEN.)

MANUS: I've got good news! Where's Father? 465

OWEN: He's gone out. What's the good news?

MANUS: I've been offered a job.

OWEN: Where? (*Now aware of* YOLLAND.) Come on, man— speak in English.

MANUS: For the benefit of the colonist? 470

OWEN: He's a decent man.

MANUS: Aren't they all at some level?

OWEN: Please.

(MANUS *shrugs.*)

He's been offered a job.

475 YOLLAND: Where?

OWEN: Well—tell us!

MANUS: I've just had a meeting with two men from Inis Meadhon. They want me to go there and start a hedge-school. They're giving me a free house, free turf, and free milk; a

480 rood of standing corn; twelve drills of potatoes; and—

(He stops.)

OWEN: And what?

MANUS: A salary of £42 a year!

OWEN: Manus, that's wonderful!

MANUS: You're talking to a man of substance.

485 OWEN: I'm delighted.

YOLLAND: Where's Inis Meadhon?

OWEN: An island south of here. And they came looking for you?

MANUS: Well, I mean to say . . .

(OWEN punches MANUS.)

490 OWEN: Aaaaagh! This calls for a real celebration.

YOLLAND: Congratulations.

MANUS: Thank you.

OWEN: Where are you, Anna?

YOLLAND: When do you start?

495 MANUS: Next Monday.

OWEN: We'll stay with you when we're there. *(To YOLLAND.)* How long will it be before we reach Inis Meadhon?

YOLLAND: How far south is it?

MANUS: About fifty miles.

500 YOLLAND: Could we make it by December?

OWEN: We'll have Christmas together. *(Sings.)* 'Christmas Day on Inis Meadhon . . .'

YOLLAND: *(Toast.)* I hope you're very content there, Manus.

MANUS: Thank you.

(YOLLAND holds out his hand. MANUS takes it. They shake warmly.)

505 OWEN: *(Toast.)* Manus.

MANUS: *(Toast.)* To Inis Meadhon.

(He drinks quickly and turns to leave.)

OWEN: Hold on—hold on—refills coming up.

MANUS: I've got to go.

OWEN: Come on, man; this is an occasion. Where are you

510 rushing to?

MANUS: I've got to tell Maire.

(MAIRE enters with her can of milk.)

MAIRE: You've got to tell Maire what?

OWEN: He's got a job!

MAIRE: Manus?

515 OWEN: He's been invited to start a hedge-school in Inis Meadhon.

MAIRE: Where?

MANUS: Inis Meadhon—the island! They're giving me £42 a year and . . .

520 OWEN: A house, fuel, milk, potatoes, corn, pupils, what-not!

MANUS: I start on Monday.

OWEN: You'll take a drink. Isn't it great?

MANUS: I want to talk to you for—

MAIRE: There's your milk. I need the can back.

(MANUS takes the can and runs up the steps.)

MANUS: *(As he goes.)* How will you like living on an island?   525

OWEN: You know George, don't you?

MAIRE: We wave to each other across the fields.

YOLLAND: Sorry-sorry?

OWEN: She says you wave to each other across the fields.

YOLLAND: Yes, we do; oh, yes; indeed we do.   530

MAIRE: What's he saying?

OWEN: He says you wave to each other across the fields.

MAIRE: That's right. So we do.

YOLLAND: What's she saying?

OWEN: Nothing—nothing—nothing. *(To MAIRE.)* What's the   535 news?

(MAIRE moves away, touching the text books with her toe.)

MAIRE: Not a thing. You're busy, the two of you.

OWEN: We think we are.

MAIRE: I hear the Fiddler O'Shea's about. There's some talk of a dance tomorrow night.   540

OWEN: Where will it be?

MAIRE: Maybe over the road. Maybe at Tobair Vree.

YOLLAND: Tobair Vree!

MAIRE: Yes.

YOLLAND: Tobair Vree! Tobair Vree!   545

MAIRE: Does he know what I'm saying?

OWEN: Not a word.

MAIRE: Tell him then.

OWEN: Tell him what?

MAIRE: About the dance.   550

OWEN: Maire says there may be a dance tomorrow night.

YOLLAND: *(To OWEN.)* Yes? May I come? *(To MAIRE.)* Would anybody object if I came?

MAIRE: *(To OWEN.)* What's he saying?

OWEN: *(To YOLLAND.)* Who would object?   555

MAIRE: *(To OWEN.)* Did you tell him?

YOLLAND: *(To MAIRE.)* Sorry-sorry?

OWEN: *(To MAIRE.)* He says may he come?

MAIRE: *(To YOLLAND.)* That's up to you.

YOLLAND: *(To OWEN.)* What does she say?   560

OWEN: *(To YOLLAND.)* She says—

YOLLAND: *(To MAIRE.)* What-what?

MAIRE: *(To OWEN.)* Well?

YOLLAND: *(To OWEN.)* Sorry-sorry?

OWEN: *(To YOLLAND.)* Will you go?   565

YOLLAND: *(To MAIRE.)* Yes, yes, if I may.

MAIRE: *(To OWEN.)* What does he say?

YOLLAND: *(To OWEN.)* What is she saying?

OWEN: Oh for God's sake! *(To MANUS who is descending with the empty can.)* You take on this job, Manus.   570

MANUS: I'll walk you up to the house. Is your mother at home? I want to talk to her.

MAIRE: What's the rush? *(To OWEN.)* Didn't you offer me a drink?

OWEN: Will you risk Anna na mBreag?   575

MAIRE: Why not.

(YOLLAND is suddenly intoxicated. He leaps up on a stool, raises his glass and shouts.)

YOLLAND: Anna na mBreag! Baile Beag! Inis Meadhon! Bombay! Tobair Vree! Eden! And poteen—correct, Owen?

OWEN: Perfect.

580 YOLLAND: And bloody marvellous stuff it is, too. I love it! Bloody, bloody, bloody marvellous!

(Simultaneously with his final 'bloody marvellous' bring up very loud the introductory music of the reel. Then immediately go to black. Retain the music throughout the very brief interval.)

SCENE II

The following night.

This scene may be played in the schoolroom, but it would be preferable to lose—by lighting—as much of the schoolroom as possible, and to play the scene down front in a vaguely 'outside' area.

The music rises to a crescendo. Then in the distance we hear MAIRE *and* YOLLAND *approach—laughing and running. They run on, hand-in-hand. They have just left the dance. Fade the music to distant background. Then after a time it is lost and replaced by guitar music.* MAIRE *and* YOLLAND *are now down front, still holding hands and excited by their sudden and impetuous escape from the dance.*

MAIRE: O my God, that leap across the ditch nearly killed me.

YOLLAND: I could scarcely keep up with you.

MAIRE: Wait till I get my breath back.

YOLLAND: We must have looked as if we were being chased.

(They now realize they are alone and holding hands—the beginnings of embarrassment. The hands disengage. They begin to drift apart. Pause.)

5 MAIRE: Manus'll wonder where I've got to.

YOLLAND: I wonder did anyone notice us leave.

(Pause. Slightly further apart.)

MAIRE: The grass must be wet. My feet are soaking.

YOLLAND: Your feet must be wet. The grass is soaking.

(Another pause. Another few paces apart. They are now a long distance from one another.)

YOLLAND: *(Indicating himself.)* George.

*(*MAIRE *nods: Yes-yes. Then:—)*

10 MAIRE: Lieutenant George.

YOLLAND: Don't call me that. I never think of myself as Lieutenant.

MAIRE: What-what?

YOLLAND: Sorry-sorry? *(He points to himself again.)* George.

*(*MAIRE *nods: Yes-yes. Then points to herself.)*

15 MAIRE: Maire.

YOLLAND: Yes, I know you're Maire. Of course I know you're Maire. I mean I've been watching you night and day for the past—

MAIRE: *(Eagerly.)* What-what?

20 YOLLAND: *(Points.)* Maire. *(Points.)* George. *(Points both.)* Maire and George.

*(*MAIRE *nods: Yes-yes-yes.)*

I—I—I—

MAIRE: Say anything at all. I love the sound of your speech.

YOLLAND: *(Eagerly.)* Sorry-sorry?

(In acute frustration he looks around, hoping for some inspiration that will provide him with communicative means. Now he has a thought: he tries raising his voice and articulating in a staccato style and with equal and absurd emphasis on each word.)

Every-morning-I-see-you-feeding-brown-hens-and-giving- 25
meal-to-black-calf—*(The futility of it.)*—Oh my God.

*(*MAIRE *smiles. She moves towards him. She will try to communicate in Latin.)*

MAIRE: *Tu es centurio in—in—in exercitu Britannico—*

YOLLAND: Yes-yes? Go on—go on—say anything at all—I love the sound of your speech.

MAIRE: *—et es in castris quae—quae—quae sunt in agro—(The* 30
futility of it.)—O my God. *(*YOLLAND *smiles. He moves towards her. Now for her English words.)* George—water.

YOLLAND: 'Water'? Water! Oh yes—water—water—very good—water—good—good.

MAIRE: Fire. 35

YOLLAND: Fire—indeed—wonderful—fire, fire, fire—splendid—splendid!

MAIRE: Ah . . . ah . . .

YOLLAND: Yes? Go on.

MAIRE: Earth. 40

YOLLAND: 'Earth'?

MAIRE: Earth. Earth. *(*YOLLAND *still does not understand.* MAIRE *stoops down and picks up a handful of clay. Holding it out.)* Earth.

YOLLAND: Earth! Of course—earth! Earth. Earth. Good Lord, 45
Maire, your English is perfect!

MAIRE: *(Eagerly.)* What-what?

YOLLAND: Perfect English. English perfect.

MAIRE: George—

YOLLAND: That's beautiful—oh, that's really beautiful. 50

MAIRE: George—

YOLLAND: Say it again—say it again—

MAIRE: Shhh. *(She holds her hand up for silence—she is trying to remember her one line of English. Now she remembers it and she delivers the line as if English were her language—easily,* 55
fluidly, conversationally.) George, 'In Norfolk we besport ourselves around the maypoll.'

YOLLAND: Good God, do you? That's where my mother comes from—Norfolk. Norwich actually. Not exactly Norwich town but a small village called Little Walsingham close be- 60
side it. But in our own village of Winfarthing we have a maypole too and every year on the first of May—*(He stops abruptly, only now realizing. He stares at her. She in turn misunderstands his excitement.)*

MAIRE: *(To herself.)* Mother of God, my Aunt Mary wouldn't 65
have taught me something dirty, would she?

(Pause. YOLLAND *extends his hand to* MAIRE. *She turns away from him and moves slowly across the stage.)*

YOLLAND: Maire.

---

27 **Tu es centurio in exercitu Britannico** You are a centurion in the British Army   30 **et es in castris quae sunt in agro** and you are in the camp in the field

(She still moves away.)

Maire Chatach.

(She still moves away.)

70 Bun na hAbhann? *(He says the name softly, almost privately, very tentatively, as if he were searching for a sound she might respond to. He tries again.)* Druim Dubh?

(MAIRE stops. She is listening. YOLLAND is encouraged.)

Poll na gCaorach. Lis Maol.

(MAIRE turns towards him.)

Lis na nGall.
MAIRE: Lis na nGradh.

(They are now facing each other and begin moving—almost imperceptibly—towards one another.)

75 MAIRE: Carraig an Phoill.
YOLLAND: Carraig na Ri. Loch na nEan.
MAIRE: Loch an Iubhair. Machaire Buidhe.
YOLLAND: Machaire Mor. Cnoc na Mona.
MAIRE: Cnoc na nGabhar.
80 YOLLAND: Mullach.
MAIRE: Port.
YOLLAND: Tor.
MAIRE: Lag.

(She holds out her hands to YOLLAND. He takes them. Each now speaks almost to himself/herself.)

YOLLAND: I wish to God you could understand me.
85 MAIRE: Soft hands; a gentleman's hands.
YOLLAND: Because if you could understand me I could tell you how I spend my days either thinking of you or gazing up at your house in the hope that you'll appear even for a second.
90 MAIRE: Every evening you walk by yourself along the Tra Bhan and every morning you wash yourself in front of your tent.
YOLLAND: I would tell you how beautiful you are, curly-headed Maire. I would so like to tell you how beautiful you are.
95 MAIRE: Your arms are long and thin and the skin on your shoulders is very white.
YOLLAND: I would tell you . . .
MAIRE: Don't stop—I know what you're saying.
YOLLAND: I would tell you how I want to be here—to live
100 here—always—with you—always, always.
MAIRE: 'Always'? What is that word—'always'?
YOLLAND: Yes-yes; always.
MAIRE: You're trembling.
YOLLAND: Yes, I'm trembling because of you.
105 MAIRE: I'm trembling, too.

(She holds his face in her hand.)

YOLLAND: I've made up my mind . . .
MAIRE: Shhhh.
YOLLAND: I'm not going to leave here . . .
MAIRE: Shhhh—listen to me. I want you, too, soldier.
110 YOLLAND: Don't stop—I know what you're saying.
MAIRE: I want to live with you—anywhere—anywhere at all— always—always.
YOLLAND: 'Always'? What is that word—'always'?

MAIRE: Take me away with you, George.

(Pause. Suddenly they kiss. SARAH enters. She sees them. She stands shocked, staring at them. Her mouth works. Then almost to herself.)

SARAH: Manus . . . Manus!   115

(SARAH runs off. Music to crescendo.)

— ACT THREE —

The following evening. It is raining.

SARAH *and* OWEN *alone in the schoolroom.* SARAH, *more waif-like than ever, is sitting very still on a stool, an open book across her knee. She is pretending to read but her eyes keep going up to the room upstairs.* OWEN *is working on the floor as before, surrounded by his reference books, map, Name-Book, etc. But he has neither concentration nor interest; and like* SARAH *he glances up at the upstairs room.*

After a few seconds MANUS *emerges and descends, carrying a large paper bag which already contains his clothes. His movements are determined and urgent. He moves around the class-room, picking up books, examining each title carefully, and choosing about six of them which he puts into his bag. As he selects these books:—*

OWEN: You know that old limekiln beyond Con Connie Tim's pub, the place we call The Murren?—do you know why it's called The Murren?

(MANUS does not answer.)

I've only just discovered: it's a corruption of Saint Muranus. It seems Saint Muranus had a monastery somewhere about 5 there at the beginning of the seventh century. And over the years the name became shortened to the Murren. Very unattractive name, isn't it? I think we should go back to the original—Saint Muranus. What do you think? The original's Saint Muranus. Don't you think we should go back to that? 10

(No response. OWEN *begins writing the name into the Name-Book.* MANUS *is now rooting about among the forgotten implements for a piece of rope. He finds a piece. He begins to tie the mouth of the flimsy, overloaded bag—and it bursts, the contents spilling out on the floor.)*

MANUS: Bloody, bloody, bloody hell!

(His voice breaks in exasperation: he is about to cry. OWEN *leaps to his feet.)*

OWEN: Hold on. I've a bag upstairs.

(He runs upstairs. SARAH *waits until* OWEN *is off. Then:—)*

SARAH: Manus . . . Manus, I . . .

*(MANUS *hears* SARAH *but makes no acknowledgement. He gathers up his belongings.* OWEN *reappears with the bag he had on his arrival.)*

OWEN: Take this one—I'm finished with it anyway. And it's supposed to keep out the rain.   15

*(MANUS *transfers his few belongings.* OWEN *drifts back to his task. The packing is now complete.)*

MANUS: You'll be here for a while? For a week or two anyhow?

OWEN: Yes.

MANUS: You're not leaving with the army?

OWEN: I haven't made up my mind. Why?

20 MANUS: Those Inis Meadhon men will be back to see why I haven't turned up. Tell them—tell them I'll write to them as soon as I can. Tell them I still want the job but that it might be three or four months before I'm free to go.

OWEN: You're being damned stupid, Manus.

25 MANUS: Will you do that for me?

OWEN: Clear out now and Lancey'll think you're involved somehow.

MANUS: Will you do that for me?

OWEN: Wait a couple of days even. You know George—he's a
30 bloody romantic—maybe he's gone out to one of the islands and he'll suddenly reappear tomorrow morning. Or maybe the search party'll find him this evening lying drunk somewhere in the sandhills. You've seen him drinking that po-
35 teen—doesn't know how to handle it. Had he drink on him last night at the dance?

MANUS: I had a stone in my hand when I went out looking for him—I was going to fell him. The lame scholar turned violent.

OWEN: Did anybody see you?

40 MANUS: (*Again close to tears.*) But when I saw him standing there at the side of the road—smiling—and her face buried in his shoulder—I couldn't even go close to them. I just shouted something stupid—something like, 'You're a bastard, Yolland.' If I'd even said it in English . . . 'cos he kept
45 saying 'Sorry-sorry?' The wrong gesture in the wrong language.

OWEN: And you didn't see him again?

MANUS: 'Sorry?'

OWEN: Before you leave tell Lancey that—just to clear
50 yourself.

MANUS: What have I to say to Lancey? You'll give that message to the islandmen?

OWEN: I'm warning you: run away now and you're bound to be—

55 MANUS: (*To* SARAH.) Will you give that message to the Inis Meadhon men?

SARAH: I will.

(MANUS *picks up an old sack and throws it across his shoulders.*)

OWEN: Have you any idea where you're going?

MANUS: Mayo, maybe. I remember Mother saying she had
60 cousins somewhere away out in the Erris Peninsula. (*He picks up his bag.*) Tell Father I took only the Virgil and the Caesar and the Aeschylus because they're mine anyway—I bought them with the money I got for that pet lamb I reared—do you remember that pet lamb? And tell him that
65 Nora Dan never returned the dictionary and that she still owes him two-and-six for last quarter's reading—he always forgets those things.

OWEN: Yes.

MANUS: And his good shirt's ironed and hanging up in the
70 press and his clean socks are in the butter-box under the bed.

OWEN: All right.

MANUS: And tell him I'll write.

OWEN: If Maire asks where you've gone . . . ?

MANUS: He'll need only half the amount of milk now, won't
75 he? Even less than half—he usually takes his tea black.

(*Pause.*) And when he comes in at night—you'll hear him; he makes a lot of noise—I usually come down and give him a hand up. Those stairs are dangerous without a banister. Maybe before you leave you'd get Big Ned Frank to put up
80 some sort of a handrail. (*Pause.*) And if you can bake, he's very fond of soda bread.

OWEN: I can give you money. I'm wealthy. Do you know what they pay me? Two shillings a day for this—this—this—

(MANUS *rejects the offer by holding out his hand.*)

Goodbye, Manus.

(MANUS *and* OWEN *shake hands. Then* MANUS *picks up his bag briskly and goes towards the door. He stops a few paces beyond* SARAH, *turns, comes back to her. He addresses her as he did in Act One but now without warmth or concern for her.*)

MANUS: What is your name? (*Pause.*) Come on. What is your
85 name?

SARAH: My name is Sarah.

MANUS: Just Sarah? Sarah what? (*Pause.*) Well?

SARAH: Sarah Johnny Sally.

MANUS: And where do you live? Come on.
90
SARAH: I live in Bun na hAbhann.

(*She is now crying quietly.*)

MANUS: Very good, Sarah Johnny Sally. There's nothing to stop you now—nothing in the wide world. (Pause. He looks down at her.) It's all right—it's all right—you did no harm—
95 you did no harm at all.

(*He stoops over her and kisses the top of her head—as if in absolution. Then briskly to the door and off.*)

OWEN: Good luck, Manus!

SARAH: (*Quietly.*) I'm sorry . . . I'm sorry . . . I'm so sorry, Manus . . .

(OWEN *tries to work but cannot concentrate. He begins folding up the map. As he does:—*)

OWEN: Is there a class this evening?

(SARAH *nods: yes.*)

I suppose Father knows. Where is he anyhow?
100

(SARAH *points.*)

Where?

(SARAH *mimes rocking a baby.*)

I don't understand—where?

(SARAH *repeats the mime and wipes away tears.* OWEN *is still puzzled.*)

It doesn't matter. He'll probably turn up.

(BRIDGET *and* DOALTY *enter, sacks over their heads against the rain. They are self-consciously noisier, more ebullient, more garrulous than ever—brimming over with excitement and gossip and brio.*)

DOALTY: You're missing the crack, boys! Cripes, you're missing the crack! Fifty more soldiers arrived an hour ago!
105
BRIDGET: And they're spread out in a big line from Sean Neal's over to Lag and they're moving straight across the fields towards Cnoc na nGabhar!

110 DOALTY: Prodding every inch of the ground in front of them with their bayonets and scattering animals and hens in all directions!
BRIDGET: And tumbling everything before them—fences, ditches, haystacks, turf-stacks!
115 DOALTY: They came to Barney Petey's field of corn—straight through it be God as if it was heather!
BRIDGET: Not a blade of it left standing!
DOALTY: And Barney Petey just out of his bed and running after them in his drawers: 'You hoors you! Get out of my corn, you hoors you!'
120 BRIDGET: First time he ever ran in his life.
DOALTY: Too lazy, the wee get, to cut it when the weather was good.

(SARAH begins putting out the seats.)

BRIDGET: Tell them about Big Hughie.
DOALTY: Cripes, if you'd seen your aul fella, Owen.
125 BRIDGET: They were all inside in Anna na mBreag's pub—all the crowd from the wake—
DOALTY: And they hear the commotion and they all come out to the street—
BRIDGET: Your father in front; the Infant Prodigy footless behind him!
130 DOALTY: And your aul fella, he sees the army stretched across the countryside—
BRIDGET: O my God!
DOALTY: And Cripes he starts roaring at them!
135 BRIDGET: 'Visigoths! Huns! Vandals!'
DOALTY: '*Ignari! Stulti! Rustici!*'
BRIDGET: And wee Jimmy Jack jumping up and down and shouting, 'Thermopylae! Thermopylae!'
DOALTY: You never saw crack like it in your life, boys. Come
140 away on out with me, Sarah, and you'll see it all.
BRIDGET: Big Hughie's fit to take no class. Is Manus about?
OWEN: Manus is gone.
BRIDGET: Gone where?
OWEN: He's left—gone away.
145 DOALTY: Where to?
OWEN: He doesn't know. Mayo, maybe.
DOALTY: What's on in Mayo?
OWEN: *(To BRIDGET.)* Did you see George and Maire Chatach leave the dance last night?
150 BRIDGET: We did. Didn't we, Doalty?
OWEN: Did you see Manus following them out?
BRIDGET: I didn't see him going out but I saw him coming in by himself later.
OWEN: Did George and Maire come back to the dance?
155 BRIDGET: No.
OWEN: Did you see them again?
BRIDGET: He left her home. We passed them going up the back road—didn't we, Doalty?
OWEN: And Manus stayed till the end of the dance?
160 DOALTY: We know nothing. What are you asking us for?
OWEN: Because Lancey'll question me when he hears Manus's gone. *(Back to BRIDGET.)* That's the way George went home? By the back road? That's where you saw him?
BRIDGET: Leave me alone, Owen. I know nothing about Yol-
165 land. If you want to know about Yolland, ask the Donnelly twins.

(Silence. DOALTY moves over to the window.)

(To SARAH.) He's a powerful fiddler, O'Shea, isn't he? He told our Seamus he'll come back for a night at Hallowe'en.

(OWEN goes to DOALTY who looks resolutely out the window.)

OWEN: What's this about the Donnellys? *(Pause.)* Were they about last night? 170
DOALTY: Didn't see them if they were.

(Begins whistling through his teeth.)

OWEN: George is a friend of mine.
DOALTY: So.
OWEN: I want to know what's happened to him.
DOALTY: Couldn't tell you. 175
OWEN: What have the Donnelly twins to do with it? *(Pause.)* Doalty!
DOALTY: I know nothing, Owen—nothing at all—I swear to God. All I know is this: on my way to the dance I saw their boat beached at Port. It wasn't there on my way home, after I 180 left Bridget. And that's all I know. As God's my judge. The half-dozen times I met him I didn't know a word he said to me; but he seemed a right enough sort . . . *(With sudden excessive interest in the scene outside.)* Cripes, they're crawling all over the place! Cripes, there's millions of them! Cripes, 185 they're levelling the whole land!

(OWEN moves away. MAIRE enters. She is bareheaded and wet from the rain; her hair in disarray. She attempts to appear normal but she is in acute distress, on the verge of being distraught. She is carrying the milk-can.)

MAIRE: Honest to God, I must be going off my head. I'm halfway here and I think to myself, 'Isn't this can very light?' and I look into it and isn't it empty.
OWEN: It doesn't matter. 190
MAIRE: How will you manage for tonight?
OWEN: We have enough.
MAIRE: Are you sure?
OWEN: Plenty, thanks.
MAIRE: It'll take me no time at all to go back up for some. 195
OWEN: Honestly, Maire.
MAIRE: Sure it's better you have it than that black calf that's . . . that . . . *(She looks around.)* Have you heard anything?
OWEN: Nothing.
MAIRE: What does Lancey say? 200
OWEN: I haven't seen him since this morning.
MAIRE: What does he *think*?
OWEN: We really didn't talk. He was here for only a few seconds.
MAIRE: He left me home, Owen. And the last thing he said to 205 me—he tried to speak in Irish—he said, 'I'll see you yesterday'—he meant to say 'I'll see you tomorrow.' And I laughed that much he pretended to get cross and he said 'Maypoll! Maypoll!' because I said that word wrong. And off he went, laughing—laughing, Owen! Do you think he's all right? 210 What do *you* think?
OWEN: I'm sure he'll turn up, Maire.
MAIRE: He comes from a tiny wee place called Winfarthing. *(She suddenly drops on her hands and knees on the floor— where OWEN had his map a few minutes ago—and with her 215 finger traces out an outline map.)* Come here till you see. Look. There's Winfarthing. And there's two other wee villages right beside it; one of them's called Barton

220 Bendish—it's there; and the other's called Saxingham Nethergate—it's about there. And there's Little Walsingham—that's his mother's townland. Aren't they odd names? Sure they make no sense to me at all. And Winfarthing's near a big town called Norwich. And Norwich is in a county called Norfolk. And Norfolk is in the east of England.

225 He drew a map for me on the wet strand and wrote the names on it. I have it all in my head now: Winfarthing—Barton Bendish—Saxingham Nethergate—Little Walsingham—Norwich—Norfolk. Strange sounds, aren't they? But nice sounds; like Jimmy Jack reciting his Homer.

230 *(She gets to her feet and looks around; she is almost serene now. To* SARAH.*)* You were looking lovely last night, Sarah. Is that the dress you got from Boston? Green suits you. *(To* OWEN.*)* Something very bad's happened to him, Owen. I know. He wouldn't go away without telling me. Where is

235 he, Owen? You're his friend—where is he? *(Again she looks around the room; then sits on a stool.)* I didn't get a chance to do my geography last night. The master'll be angry with me. *(She rises again.)* I think I'll go home now. The wee ones have to be washed and put to bed and that black calf

240 has to be fed . . . My hands are that rough; they're still blistered from the hay. I'm ashamed of them. I hope to God there's no hay to be saved in Brooklyn. *(She stops at the door.)* Did you hear? Nellie Ruadh's baby died in the middle of the night. I must go up to the wake. It didn't last long,

245 did it?

(MAIRE leaves. Silence. Then.)

OWEN: I don't think there'll be any class. Maybe you should . . .

(OWEN begins picking up his texts. DOALTY goes to him.)

DOALTY: Is he long gone?—Manus?
OWEN: Half an hour.
DOALTY: Stupid bloody fool.
250 OWEN: I told him that.
DOALTY: Do they know he's gone?
OWEN: Who?
DOALTY: The army.
OWEN: Not yet.
255 DOALTY: They'll be after him like bloody beagles. Bloody, bloody fool, limping along the coast. They'll overtake him before night for Christ's sake.

(DOALTY returns to the window. LANCEY enters—now the commanding officer.)

OWEN: Any news? Any word?

(LANCEY moves into the centre of the room, looking around as he does.)

LANCEY: I understood there was a class. Where are the others?
260 OWEN: There was to be a class but my father—
LANCEY: This will suffice. I will address them and it will be their responsibility to pass on what I have to say to every family in this section.

(LANCEY indicates to OWEN to translate. OWEN hesitates, trying to assess the change in LANCEY's manner and attitude.)

I'm in a hurry, O'Donnell.
265 OWEN: The captain has an announcement to make.
LANCEY: Lieutenant Yolland is missing. We are searching for him. If we don't find him, or if we receive no information as

to where he is to be found, I will pursue the following course of action. *(He indicates to* OWEN *to translate.)*
270 OWEN: They are searching for George. If they don't find him—
LANCEY: Commencing twenty-four hours from now we will shoot all livestock in Ballybeg.

(OWEN stares at LANCEY.)

At once.
275 OWEN: Beginning this time tomorrow they'll kill every animal in Baile Beag—unless they're told where George is.
LANCEY: If that doesn't bear results, commencing forty-eight hours from now we will embark on a series of evictions and levelling of every abode in the following selected areas—
280 OWEN: You're not—!
LANCEY: Do your job. Translate.
OWEN: If they still haven't found him in two days time they'll begin evicting and levelling every house starting with these townlands.

(LANCEY reads from his list.)

285 LANCEY: Swinefort.
OWEN: Lis na Muc.
LANCEY: Burnfoot.
OWEN: Bun na hAbhann.
LANCEY: Dromduff.
290 OWEN: Druim Dubh.
LANCEY: Whiteplains.
OWEN: Machaire Ban.
LANCEY: Kings Head.
OWEN: Cnoc na Ri.
295 LANCEY: If by then the lieutenant hasn't been found, we will proceed until a complete clearance is made of this entire section.
OWEN: If Yolland hasn't been got by then, they will ravish the whole parish.
300 LANCEY: I trust they know exactly what they've got to do. *(Pointing to* BRIDGET.*)* I know you. I know where you live. *(Pointing to* SARAH.*)* Who are you? Name!

(SARAH's mouth opens and shuts, opens and shuts. Her face becomes contorted.)

What's your name?

(Again SARAH *tries frantically.)*

OWEN: Go on, Sarah. You can tell him.

(But SARAH *cannot. And she knows she cannot. She closes her mouth. Her head goes down.)*

305 OWEN: Her name is Sarah Johnny Sally.
LANCEY: Where does she live?
OWEN: Bun na hAbhann.
LANCEY: Where?
OWEN: Burnfoot.
310 LANCEY: I want to talk to your brother—is he here?
OWEN: Not at the moment.
LANCEY: Where is he?
OWEN: He's at a wake.
LANCEY: What wake?

(DOALTY, who has been looking out the window all through LANCEY's announcements, now speaks—calmly, almost casually.)

315 DOALTY: Tell him his whole camp's on fire.
LANCEY: What's your name? (*To* OWEN.) Who's that lout?
OWEN: Doalty Dan Doalty.
LANCEY: Where does he live?
OWEN: Tulach Alainn.
320 LANCEY: What do we call it?
OWEN: Fair Hill. He says your whole camp is on fire.

(LANCEY *rushes to the window and looks out. Then he wheels on* DOALTY.)

LANCEY: I'll remember you, Mr Doalty. (*To* OWEN.) You carry a big responsibility in all this.

(*He goes off.*)

BRIDGET: Mother of God, does he mean it, Owen?
325 OWEN: Yes, he does.
BRIDGET: We'll have to hide the beasts somewhere—our Seamus'll know where. Maybe at the back of Lis na nGradh—or in the caves at the far end of Tra Bhan. Come on, Doalty! Come on! Don't be standing about there!

(DOALTY *does not move.* BRIDGET *runs to the door and stops suddenly. She sniffs the air. Panic.*)

330 The sweet smell! Smell it! It's the sweet smell! Jesus, it's the potato blight!
DOALTY: It's the army tents burning, Bridget.
BRIDGET: Is it? Are you sure? Is that what it is? God, I thought we were destroyed altogether. Come on! Come on!

(*She runs off.* OWEN *goes to* SARAH *who is preparing to leave.*)

335 OWEN: How are you? Are you all right?

(SARAH *nods: Yes.*)

OWEN: Don't worry. It will come back to you again.

(SARAH *shakes her head.*)

OWEN: It will. You're upset now. He frightened you. That's all's wrong.

(*Again* SARAH *shakes her head, slowly, emphatically, and smiles at* OWEN. *Then she leaves.* OWEN *busies himself gathering his belongings.* DOALTY *leaves the window and goes to him.*)

DOALTY: He'll do it, too.
340 OWEN: Unless Yolland's found.
DOALTY: Hah!
OWEN: Then he'll certainly do it.
DOALTY: When my grandfather was a boy they did the same thing. (*Simply, altogether without irony.*) And after all the
345 trouble you went to, mapping the place and thinking up new names for it. (OWEN *busies himself. Pause.* DOALTY *almost dreamily.*) I've damned little to defend but he'll not put me out without a fight. And there'll be others who think the same as me.
350 OWEN: That's a matter for you.
DOALTY: If we'd all stick together. If we knew how to defend ourselves.
OWEN: Against a trained army.
DOALTY: The Donnelly twins know how.
355 OWEN: If they could be found.
DOALTY: If they could be found. (*He goes to the door.*) Give me a shout after you've finished with Lancey. I might know something then.

(*He leaves.*)

(OWEN *picks up the Name-Book. He looks at it momentarily, then puts it on top of the pile he is carrying. It falls to the floor. He stoops to pick it up—hesitates—leaves it. He goes upstairs. As* OWEN *ascends,* HUGH *and* JIMMY JACK *enter. Both wet and drunk.* JIMMY *is very unsteady. He is trotting behind* HUGH, *trying to break in on* HUGH's *declamation.* HUGH *is equally drunk but more experienced in drunkenness: there is a portion of his mind which retains its clarity.*)

HUGH: There I was, appropriately dispositioned to proffer my condolences to the bereaved mother . . . 360
JIMMY: Hugh—
HUGH: . . . and about to enter the *domus lugubris*—Maire Chatach?
JIMMY: The wake house.
HUGH: Indeed—when I experience a plucking at my elbow: 365 Mister George Alexander, Justice of the Peace. 'My tidings are infelicitous,' said he—Bridget? Too slow. Doalty?
JIMMY: *Infelix*—unhappy.
HUGH: Unhappy indeed. 'Master Bartley Timlin has been appointed to the new national school.' 'Timlin? Who is Tim- 370 lin?' 'A schoolmaster from Cork. And he will be a major asset to the community: he is also a very skilled bacon-curer!'
JIMMY: Hugh—
HUGH: Ha-ha-ha-ha-ha! The Cork bacon-curer! *Barbarus hic ego sum quia non intelligor ulli*—James? 375
JIMMY: Ovid.
HUGH: *Procede.*
JIMMY: 'I am a barbarian in this place because I am not understood by anyone.'
HUGH: Indeed—(*Shouts.*) Manus! Tea! I will compose a satire 380 on Master Bartley Timlin, schoolmaster and bacon-curer. But it will be too easy, won't it? (*Shouts.*) Strong tea! Black!

(*The only way* JIMMY *can get* HUGH's *attention is by standing in front of him and holding his arms.*)

JIMMY: Will you listen to me, Hugh!
HUGH: James. (*Shouts.*) And a slice of soda bread.
JIMMY: I'm going to get married. 385
HUGH: Well!
JIMMY: At Christmas.
HUGH: Splendid.
JIMMY: To Athene.
HUGH: Who? 390
JIMMY: Pallas Athene.
HUGH: *Glaukopis Athene?*
JIMMY: Flashing-eyed, Hugh, flashing-eyed!

(*He attempts the gesture he has made before: standing to attention, the momentary spasm, the salute, the face raised in pained ecstasy—but the body does not respond efficiently this time. The gesture is grotesque.*)

HUGH: The lady has assented?
JIMMY: She asked *me*—I assented. 395
HUGH: Ah. When was this?

---

362 **domus lugubris** house of mourning   368 **infelix** unlucky, unhappy   374–375 **Barbarus hic ego . . . ulli** I am a barbarian here because I am not understood by anyone

JIMMY: Last night.

HUGH: What does her mother say?

JIMMY: Metis from Hellespont? Decent people—good stock.

400   HUGH: And her father?

JIMMY: I'm meeting Zeus tomorrow. Hugh, will you be my best man?

HUGH: Honoured, James; profoundly honoured.

JIMMY: You know what I'm looking for, Hugh, don't you? I
405   mean to say—you know—I—I—I joke like the rest of them—you know?—(*Again he attempts the pathetic routine but abandons it instantly.*) You know yourself, Hugh—don't you?—you know all that. But what I'm really looking for, Hugh—what I really want—companionship, Hugh—at my
410   time of life, companionship, company, someone to talk to. Away up in Beann na Gaoithe—you've no idea how lonely it is. Companionship—correct, Hugh? Correct?

HUGH: Correct.

JIMMY: And I always liked her, Hugh. Correct?

415   HUGH: Correct, James.

JIMMY: Someone to talk to.

HUGH: Indeed.

JIMMY: That's all, Hugh. The whole story. You know it all now, Hugh. You know it all.

(*As* JIMMY *says those last lines he is crying, shaking his head, trying to keep his balance, and holding a finger up to his lips in absurd gestures of secrecy and intimacy. Now he staggers away, tries to sit on a stool, misses it, slides to the floor, his feet in front of him, his back against the broken cart. Almost at once he is asleep.* HUGH *watches all of this. Then he produces his flask and is about to pour a drink when he sees the Name-Book on the floor. He picks it up and leafs through it, pronouncing the strange names as he does. Just as he begins,* OWEN *emerges and descends with two bowls of tea.*)

420   HUGH: Ballybeg. Burnfoot. King's Head. Whiteplains. Fair Hill. Dunboy. Green Bank.

(OWEN *snatches the book from* HUGH.)

OWEN: I'll take that. (*In apology.*) It's only a catalogue of names.

HUGH: I know what it is.

425   OWEN: A mistake—my mistake—nothing to do with us. I hope that's strong enough (*Tea*). (*He throws the book on the table and crosses over to* JIMMY.) Jimmy. Wake up, Jimmy. Wake up, man.

JIMMY: What—what-what?

430   OWEN: Here. Drink this. Then go on away home. There may be trouble. Do you hear me, Jimmy? There may be trouble.

HUGH: (*Indicating Name-Book.*) We must learn those new names.

OWEN: (*Searching around.*) Did you see a sack lying about?

435   HUGH: We must learn where we live. We must learn to make them our own. We must make them our new home.

(OWEN *finds a sack and throws it across his shoulders.*)

OWEN: I know where I live.

HUGH: James thinks he knows, too. I look at James and three thoughts occur to me: A—that it is not the literal past, the
440   'facts' of history, that shape us, but images of the past embodied in language. James has ceased to make that discrimination.

OWEN: Don't lecture me, Father.

HUGH: B—we must never cease renewing those images; because once we do, we fossilize. Is there no soda bread?   445

OWEN: And C, Father—one single, unalterable 'fact': if Yolland is not found, we are all going to be evicted. Lancey has issued the order.

HUGH: Ah. *Edictum imperatoris.*

OWEN: You should change out of those wet clothes. I've got to   450
go. I've got to see Doalty Dan Doalty.

HUGH: What about?

OWEN: I'll be back soon.

(*As* OWEN *exits.*)

HUGH: Take care, Owen. To remember everything is a form of madness. (*He looks around the room, carefully, as if he were   455
about to leave it forever. Then he looks at* JIMMY, *asleep again.*) The road to Sligo. A spring morning. 1798. Going into battle. Do you remember, James? Two young gallants with pikes across their shoulders and the *Aeneid* in their pockets. Everything seemed to find definition that spring—a   460
congruence, a miraculous matching of hope and past and present and possibility. Striding across the fresh, green land. The rhythms of perception heightened. The whole enterprise of consciousness accelerated. We were gods that morning, James; and I had recently married *my* goddess, Caitlin   465
Dubh Nic Reactainn, may she rest in peace. And to leave her and my infant son in his cradle—that was heroic, too. By God, sir, we were magnificent. We marched as far as—where was it?—Glenties! All of twenty-three miles in one day. And it was there, in Phelan's pub, that we got homesick   470
for Athens, just like Ulysses. The *desiderium nostrorum*—the need for our own. Our *pietas*, James, was for older, quieter things. And that was the longest twenty-three miles back I ever made. (*Toasts* JIMMY.) My friend, confusion is not an ignoble condition.   475

(MAIRE *enters.*)

MAIRE: I'm back again. I set out for somewhere but I couldn't remember where. So I came back here.

HUGH: Yes, I will teach you English, Maire Chatach.

MAIRE: Will you, Master? I must learn it. I need to learn it.

HUGH: Indeed you may well be my only pupil.   480

(*He goes towards the steps and begins to ascend.*)

MAIRE: When can we start?

HUGH: Not today. Tomorrow, perhaps. After the funeral. We'll begin tomorrow. (*Ascending.*) But don't expect too much. I will provide you with the available words and the available   485
grammar. But will that help you to interpret between privacies? I have no idea. But it's all we have. I have no idea at all.

(*He is now at the top.*)

MAIRE: Master, what does the English word 'always' mean?

HUGH: *Semper—per omnia saecula.* The Greeks called it '*aei*'. It's not a word I'd start with. It's a silly word, girl.

---

449 **edictum imperatoris** the decree of the commander   471
desiderium nostrorum longing/need for our things/people   472
pietas piety   488 **Semper—per omnia saecula** Always—for all time;
aei always

(He sits. JIMMY *is awake. He gets to his feet.* MAIRE *sees the Name-Book, picks it up, and sits with it on her knee.)*

490 MAIRE: When he comes back, this is where he'll come to. He told me this is where he was happiest.

*(*JIMMY *sits beside* MAIRE.*)*

JIMMY: Do you know the Greek word *endogamein?* It means to marry within the tribe. And the word *exogamein* means to marry outside the tribe. And you don't cross those borders 495 casually—both sides get very angry. Now, the problem is this: Is Athene sufficiently mortal or am I sufficiently godlike for the marriage to be acceptable to her people and to my people? You think about that.

HUGH: *Urbs antiqua fuit*—there was an ancient city which, 'tis 500 said, Juno loved above all the lands. And it was the goddess's aim and cherished hope that here should be the capital of all nations—should the fates perchance allow that. Yet in truth she discovered that a race was springing from Trojan blood to overthrow some day these Tyrian towers—a people *late regem belloque superbum*—kings of broad realms and proud 505 in war who would come forth for Lybia's downfall—such was—such was the course—such was the course ordained— ordained by fate . . . What the hell's wrong with me? Sure I know it backwards. I'll begin again. *Urbs antiqua fuit*—there was an ancient city which, 'tis said, Juno loved above all the 510 lands.

(Begin to bring down the lights.)

And it was the goddess's aim and cherished hope that here should be the capital of all nations—should the fates perchance allow that. Yet in truth she discovered that a race was springing from Trojan blood to overthrow some day these 515 Tyrian towers—a people kings of broad realms and proud in war who would come forth for Lybia's downfall . . .

(Blackout.)

---

492 **endogamein** to marry within the tribe   493 **exogamein** to marry outside the tribe   499 **Urbs antiqua fuit** there was an ancient city

504–505 **late regem belloque superbum** kings of broad realms and proud in war

■ BETTE BOURNE, PAUL SHAW, PEGGY SHAW, LOIS WEAVER ■

Although Bette Bourne (b. 1939) and Paul Shaw (b. 1953) and Peggy Shaw (b. 1944) and Lois Weaver (b. 1949) collaborated on the Obie Award–winning play *Belle Reprieve* (1991), they are best known for their work as two distinct performing companies—Bloolips and Split Britches.

Lois Weaver was born and raised in rural southwest Virginia; she received her B.S. in theatre and education from Radford College (now Radford University) in 1972 and became a founding member of Spiderwoman Theatre in 1975. Peggy Shaw grew up in Massachusetts and studied at the Massachusetts College of Art before joining the gay male cabaret Hot Peaches. Weaver and Shaw met in the late 1970s, when Hot Peaches and Spiderwoman were both touring in Europe; by the early 1980s, they were working together on several influential projects. In 1981 the two joined forces with writer and performer Deborah Margolin to form their own company, Split Britches, and in 1982 they founded the WOW Cafe (Women's One World), a performance space for women in New York's East Village, which has become an important venue for new women's performance. Their first production, *Splitbritches*, given at WOW's inaugural festivals in 1980 and 1981, was a series of monologues, songs, and transformations based on Weaver's rural Southern family. As lesbians and performers, Weaver and Shaw have undertaken a series of works staging the conflict between the ideology of compulsory heterosexuality and the lives of lesbian women, and Split Britches has developed a critique of the working of gender and sexual identity in contemporary America that is at once theoretical and theatrical. The work of Split Britches has come to stand at the center both of lesbian performance and of the contemporary critique of gender politics in the theater, and it includes performances like *Beauty and the Beast* (1982), *Upwardly Mobile Home* (1984), *Dress Suits to Hire* (written by Holly Hughes, 1987), *Anniversary Waltz* (1990), *Belle Reprieve* (1991), and *Lesbians Who Kill* (1992). Lois Weaver is currently also the joint artistic director for London's Gay Sweatshop Theatre Company.

Belle Reprieve was devised in a month-long workshop/retreat that Shaw and Weaver took in Majorca with Bette Bourne and Paul Shaw ("Precious Pearl"), who formed the British gay male performing company Bloolips. Bette Bourne was born in Wales and trained for the theater at the Central School of Speech and Drama in London in the early 1960s, where he now directs and lectures in Shakespearean analysis when not performing. Although he had trained as a classical actor, his career changed course in 1970, when he became involved in gay politics and street theater and performed with Hot Peaches. In 1977 he formed Bloolips. Paul Shaw, from Littlehampton, in Sussex, England, studied theater design at the Wimbledon School of Art. He then worked as assistant director to Malcolm Pride and as the assistant director of the Glasgow Citizens' Theatre before joining Bloolips in 1983. Bloolips has toured throughout Britain, Europe, Canada, and the United States, and their many shows—*Lust in Space, Gland Motel, Get Her,* and *Living Leg-Ends*—use a variety of stage strategies (camp, vaudeville, cross-dressing) to examine the construction of sexual orientation in contemporary culture. Bourne has also starred in *Sarrasine,* by Neil Bartlett and Nicholas Bloomfield, and in a new solo piece, *The Dish* (1993), by Paul Hallam.

BELLE REPRIEVE

Taken from Blanche Dubois's ancestral home "Belle Reve" in Tennessee Williams's *A Streetcar Named Desire, Belle Reprieve* explores the relation between gender and power in American life and in American theater. *Belle Reprieve* uses a farcical mixture of cross-dressing to develop both a performative "rereading" of *Streetcar* and a critique of contemporary sexual politics, both in and out of the theater. First, the play is systematically cross-cast, often in ways that underscore the gender and sexual tensions of the famous film version of the play. The film seems at once both to express and to subvert conventional notions of sexuality. Karl Malden's Mitch is concerned about his manliness, readily dominated both by his mother and by Blanche; Kim Stanley's Stella is played as nearly narcotized by her sexual desire for Stanley; Vivien Leigh's Blanche is the erotic center of the play, yet is consumed by illusions of propriety and refinement—illusions shattered by her first love for a boy who was gay; Marlon Brando's Stanley, for all his macho qualities, exudes in the film a kind of "femme" sensuality.

Belle Reprieve works to bring this performative subtext to light, largely through a campy cross-playing that in many respects both literalizes and foregrounds the sexual identifications ex-/re-pressed by *Streetcar*: Mitch, "a fairy disguised as a man," is played by Paul Shaw/Precious Pearl; Stella, a "woman disguised as a woman" is played by the femme lesbian Lois Weaver; Stanley, "a butch lesbian," is played by butch Peggy Shaw; and Blanche, "a man in a dress," is played by Bette Bourne, a man in a dress. *Belle Reprieve* then systematically replays and analyzes the key relationships of *Streetcar*, in a way that throws the "natural" distribution of sex/gender identification into question. For example, a love scene between Blanche and Stella is enacted by Lois Weaver and Bette Bourne; moments later a pendant scene between Mitch and Stanley, literalizing the homoerotic quality of their relationship in *Streetcar*, is played by Precious Pearl and Peggy Shaw. Although both of these scenes are "cross-dressed," the performance of gender roles is complicated by a second performative dimension, the visible signifiers of sexual orientation. Unlike a similar seduction scene between, say Ellen and Betty in Act One of Caryl Churchill's *Cloud Nine*, when we may feel that, in some productions at least, the cross-dressing of Betty (played by a man) can mistakenly work to "naturalize" this lesbian relationship for the comfort of a heterosexual audience, here, the cross-dressing of Blanche and Stanley is no more—and no less—a "performance" than the playing of Mitch or Stella. In this sense, *Belle Reprieve* elaborates the esthetics of "camp" in performance. As David Savran suggests in his book *Communists, Cowboys, and Queers: The Politics of Masculinity in the Works of Arthur Miller and Tennessee Williams*, camp does not merely reverse notions of gender and sexuality because it is "based on the assumption that genders and sexualities are not produced in opposition and therefore cannot be 'simply' reversed." Instead, camp tends to "make elaborate substitutions and delight in the capriciousness of spoken and performative languages. It will also frequently and pointedly transpose genders, producing transvestite subjects based on its recognition that all gender is masquerade and all costume is a form of drag" (118).

Belle Reprieve uses this vaudevillian strategy to foreground its own *performance*, suggesting that gender and sexual identification take place at the level of performance. Indeed, the play suggests that this performative dimension of identity is visible even in the repressed mode of American realism itself. This is the burden of the play's brilliant conclusion, when the "realism" of *Streetcar* is also shown to consist of playing "the extremes, the stereotypes." As Precious Pearl, Bette Bourne, Lois Weaver, and Peggy Shaw suggest in their final song, if gender and sexual identification are a kind of performance, then we are all—straight and gay alike—in love with playing our part, fundamentally, necessarily, in love with our art.

BELLE REPRIEVE

BETTE BOURNE, PAUL SHAW, PEGGY SHAW, LOIS WEAVER

— CHARACTERS —

MITCH, *a fairy disguised as a man*
STELLA, *a woman disguised as a woman*
STANLEY, *a butch lesbian*
BLANCHE, *a man in a dress*

PLACE: *An empty stage. The backdrop is a scrim painted to resemble the interior of a 1940s New Orleans apartment. There are three high-tension wires strung across the stage. Throughout the play, various painted cloth curtains are pulled across these wires to denote a change in scenery or mood.*

TIME: *Four o'clock in the morning.*

— ACT ONE —

MITCH *is wheeling three large boxes onstage with a handtruck. One is designed to resemble a steamer trunk. The second is square, large enough to hold an actor, and shaped to resemble a card table, which it becomes in later scenes. The third is tall, rectangular, and large enough to hold another actor. It is turned on its back to represent a bathtub in the second act.*

MITCH: Inside this box it's four o'clock in the morning. I know that sounds incredible but it's true. I know because it's *my* four o'clock in the morning. Every time it comes around, I put it in this box. I've been doing it for years now. At four
5 o'clock in the morning, the thread that holds us to the earth is at its most slender, and all the creatures that never see sunlight come out to make mincemeat of well-laid plans. So you can imagine what it's like in there. If you listen closely you can hear them shuffling about, like the sound of rain or chit-
10 tering birds. It reminds me of a soundtrack, the beginning of a movie . . . (STELLA *appears drinking a coke behind the scrim.*) a clean slate. Darkness all around. Small sounds that give a taste of an atmosphere, a head turning, a body lit from behind, shadows in a dark, tiled hallway, a blues piano. (*Pi-
15 anist strikes a match and begins to play the blues.*)
STELLA: (*Moving to center from behind scrim, still drinking the coke.*) Is there something you want? What can I do for you? Do you know who I am, what I feel, how I think? You want my body. My soul, my food, my bed, my skin, my hands? You
20 want to touch me, hold me, lick me, smell me, eat me, have me? You think you need a little more time to decide? Well, you've got a little over an hour to have your fill. Meanwhile . . . (MITCH *enters with last box, swatting bugs.*) I'm surprised there aren't more bugs out this time of year. All the ones that
25 are out seem to be buzzing around my head.
MITCH: No, there's plenty for both of us. Don't feel singled out.
STELLA: I think it's 'cuz I eat so much sugar that they're attracted to me. Sugar in my blood. And my veins are close to
30 the surface.
MITCH: You know that they excrete something to digest your blood, that's why they leave that bump on your skin.
STELLA: I always worry that they carry things with them, transferring them from person to person.
35 MITCH: That's an old wives' tale. This country has no tradition of disease being spread by mosquitoes. You're mistaken.

STELLA: Well, every year I make one big mistake. I wonder what it will be this year?
MITCH: This mistake, is it at a particular time, or can't you tell when it's coming? 40
STELLA: I can usually feel it coming . . .
BLANCHE: (*From inside box.*) I've always depended on the strangeness of strangers.
STELLA: Or at least after the fact I thought I knew it was coming. 45
MITCH: Isn't there something you can do to stop it happening?
STELLA: Such as . . .
MITCH: Change the script!
STELLA: Change the script. Ha ha. You want me to do *what* in these shoes? The script is not the problem. I've changed the 50 script.
MITCH: It's a start.
STELLA: Look, I'm supposed to wander around in a state of narcotized sensuality. That's my part. (BLANCHE *and* STANLEY *speak simultaneously from inside the two largest boxes.*) 55
BLANCHE: You didn't see, Miss Stella, see what I saw, the long parade to the graveyard. The mortgage on the house, death is expensive, Miss Stella, death is expensive.
STANLEY: Is that so? You don't say, hey Stella wasn't we happy before she showed up. Didn't we see those colored lights you 60 and me. Didn't we see those colored lights.
STELLA: And anyway, it's too late. It's already started.
STANLEY: Hey Stella! (*Coming out of stage right box.*)
STELLA: Don't holler at me like that, Stanley.
STANLEY: Hey Stella, Stella baby! Catch! 65
STELLA: What!
STANLEY: Meat.
BLANCHE: (*Emerging from stage left box.*) Are we here? Is this the place? Are my necessaries disembarked? How sweet it is to arrive at a new place for the first time. The future stretch- 70 ing out in front of us like a clean, white carpet. There's the stir and rustle of endless possibility in the air.
STANLEY: You don't say.
STELLA: Honey, we're in exactly the same place we started out from. 75
BLANCHE: Started out? What do you mean started out? You mean we haven't arrived?
STELLA: No, we haven't arrived, but don't worry about that now. You just take it easy.
STANLEY: Something smells fishy around here and it's not me. 80

STELLA: (To STANLEY.) Now you be kind to my sister. Tell her how nice she looks.

BLANCHE: I can't stand being in between. I just can't bear it.

STELLA: (To STANLEY.) You should try to understand her a lit-
85   tle better, she's just different.

STANLEY: Different? You can say that again.

BLANCHE: I have never regretted my decision to be unique.

STANLEY: I'm gonna put an end to this charade here and now.

BLANCHE: (As STANLEY moves to center stage with trunk and
90   becomes a customs agent.) That my plans of late have gone somewhat awry is the price one has to pay if life is to be superb.

STANLEY: (To BLANCHE.) Ticket please.

BLANCHE: (To MITCH.) Young man, don't I know you?

95   MITCH: We were engaged to be married.

STANLEY: Ticket please!

BLANCHE: Did I break your heart?

MITCH: No, you broke my leg.

BLANCHE: I must be stronger than I thought.

100 STANLEY: Ticket please!

BLANCHE: Oh, well, all right, I have it here somewhere. (Rum-
mages through her bag.) Which ticket do you mean, the one that got me here or the one that will take me away?

STANLEY: Both.

105 BLANCHE: Oh, well I don't seem to have either at the moment. Although we must have gotten here somehow, we can't have walked, we have a heavy load. However, I present myself as overwhelming evidence that I am actually here.

STANLEY: While we're at it, I'm gonna need your passport.

110 BLANCHE: Passport? I wasn't aware that we were crossing any borders. What borders?

STANLEY: Passport.

BLANCHE: (Rummaging around.) Passport, passport . . . (MITCH steps forward with her passport and hands it to STANLEY.)

115 STANLEY: (Still staring at MITCH.) Name?

BLANCHE: Blanche DuBois.

STANLEY: That's not what it says here.

BLANCHE: I assure you that is who I am. My namesake is a role played by that incandescent star, Vivien Leigh, and although
120 the resemblance is not immediately striking I have been told we have the same shoulders.

STANLEY: (Looking at passport photo.) Then who's this here?

BLANCHE: The information in that document is a convention which allows me to pass in the world without let or hin-
125 drance. If you'll just notice the message inside the front cover, the Queen of England herself not only requests this but requires it.

STANLEY: You don't look anything like this photograph.

BLANCHE: I believe nature is there to be improved upon.

130 STANLEY: You're lying.

BLANCHE: Well, that's one way of looking at it.

STANLEY: Is there another?!

BLANCHE: You wouldn't treat me like this if I wasn't at the end of my rope!

135 STANLEY: (Slamming fist on trunk.) But ya are Blanche, ya are.

(Cat screams from MITCH and STELLA.)

BLANCHE: What was that?

STANLEY: Cats. I'm afraid I'm going to have to perform an intimate search.

BLANCHE: My body?

STANLEY: Your luggage.   140

BLANCHE: Stella, how do I look?

STELLA: Fresh as a daisy.

STANLEY: One that's been picked a few days.

MITCH: Look, can't we just scrub 'round the search and get on with the scenes of brutal humiliation and sexual passion? 145

STANLEY: I'm afraid we have to find a motive in this case, and I believe it's in this trunk. (To MITCH.) Why don't you mind your own business?

BLANCHE: How dare you speak to my ex-fiancé like that!

STANLEY: Your ex-fiancé?! This man is your ex-fiancé?   150

BLANCHE: That's right.

MITCH: I told her I loved her and she pushed me down the stairwell, but I forgave her as any decent man would.

STANLEY: That's not what it says in the script. In the script it says you treated her like shit because you're a stuck-up   155
mommy's boy.

MITCH: That's a lie!

BLANCHE: I think I'm going to faint.

STELLA: Is all this really necessary?

STANLEY: Look, have you any idea how many people we have   160
come in here saying they're Blanche DuBois, clutching tiny handbags and fainting in the foyer? I'm afraid I'll have to subject this case to the closest possible scrutiny before I allow any of you to pass any further.

BLANCHE: I see, you want me to come clean by showing my   165
dirty laundry to the world.

STANLEY: You got it.

BLANCHE: I think I'll go into the dressing room and burst into tears.

STELLA: We're in this up to our asses now. There's no going   170
back.

BLANCHE: Hold me Stella, I think I feel a flashback coming on. (Lights flash, music plays, a curtain painted like a grotesque piece of torn lace is pulled on stage behind the action, the actors shuffling backward around trunk.) And so it   175
was that I set out to prove to the world that I was indeed myself. A difficult enough task, you might say, for anyone.

STELLA: She threw herself at the feet of an unforgiving world to prove her identity.

MITCH: The answer was somewhere in that trunk.   180

STANLEY: (Thumping fist on trunk as music and lights stop flashing.) This is gonna cost you, lady. What did you think, you were gonna get a free ride or something? (About to open trunk.) What do we have here?

BLANCHE: Please open the doors one at a time! If you open   185
them all at once pink things and fur things, dainty things, delicate and wistful things might pop out.

STANLEY: I'll open them one at a time. First things first. (Music starts. STANLEY pulls out a jacket and tosses it to STELLA, then pulls out a scarf and throws it to MITCH.)   190

BLANCHE: I won't take it personally the way you're treating everything I own in the world.

STANLEY: Let's see, what are little girls made of? (Singing.) I put my right hand in, I pull my right hand out (Pulls it out empty and laughs.), I put my right hand in (Pulls out dress on   195
hanger and puts it around his neck.) and I shake it all about.

BLANCHE: I can't approve of any of this, just as you can't approve of my entire life.

STANLEY: I do the hokey-pokey and I turn myself around. That's what it's all about. So this is what little girls are made of. 200

Tiaras, diamond tiaras. *(Puts tiara on his head.)* And what's this? *(Pulling out gold bracelet and putting it on.)* A solid gold Cadillac. This must be worth a fortune. And what have we got here? A box of valuables. *(Tossing the contents onto the floor.)*
205   Love letters, scrap books, newspaper clippings.

BLANCHE: Everybody has something they don't want others to touch because of their intimate nature.

STANLEY: *(Singing, as* MITCH *picks up newspaper clippings.)* I put my right foot in, I take my right foot out, I put my right
210   foot in and I shake it all about . . . *(STANLEY pulls out high-heeled shoe.)*

MITCH: *(As* STANLEY *continues singing.)* There was a time when everyone was trying to get a piece of her. These are the pieces left over, "Tipped for the Top," "What an Angel."
215   Now the angel's in the kitchen, washing the dishes and picking her teeth.

BLANCHE: *(As* MITCH *hands her newspaper clippings.)* I don't see how any of this relates to my own life except in the way people perceive my fall.

220   STANLEY: I put my left hand in . . . *(Shaking the box violently from inside.)*

BLANCHE: *(Ripping up the newspaper clippings.)* Tearing . . . I hear tearing . . . be careful . . . the wings, you're tearing them!

STANLEY: They're just animals, lady, what's the matter with
225   you?

BLANCHE: But they've been faithful their whole lives. There are things we don't know here.

STANLEY: Things are different now. *(Still struggling inside box.)* I pull the white-feathered excited body of one swan off
230   the white-feathered excited body of another swan. *(He pulls out handful of feathers.)*

BLANCHE: What right have you to interfere with nature?

STANLEY: *(Pulling feathers apart to reveal that they are a boa, which he drapes across his shoulders.)* And shake it all about.

235   BLANCHE: Birds of a feather.

STANLEY: I put my left hand in . . . *(Pulling hand quickly out.)* Oww, Stella, Stella!

STELLA: What?

STANLEY: I burned my hand.

240   STELLA: Oh, Stanley, it's just candle wax.

STANLEY: I know but it hurts.

STELLA: Some people think it's sexy.

STANLEY: *(Pulling hand away from her.)* I can see where it might be sexy if I knew it was coming. I put my left hand in,
245   I pull my left hand out . . . oh, a little cheerleading doll . . . *(Breaks off the arm.)* the arm is busted . . . the rubber band must be broken inside.

BLANCHE: My mother gave me that.

STANLEY: *(Dancing doll on top of trunk.)* And I shake it all
250   about . . .

BLANCHE: And before that, it was her mother's.

STANLEY: *(Slamming doll down.)* Look, lady, I'm just trying to do my job here.

BLANCHE: Yes, of course.

255   STANLEY: And my job is to make sure you're not smuggling something personal in this here trunk. *(Reaching into trunk.)* Let's see, what's this? And what is this? *(Pulling out purse.)*

BLANCHE: This contains all of my hopes and dreams . . . this is my hope chest.

260   STANLEY: Hopes and dreams? Forget it. *(Sticking hand into purse.)* I put my whole body in, I take my whole body out.

(Pulling out scarf.) I grab myself a frilly thing and shake it all about. I pin it on my shoulders and I sashay up and down, that's what it's all about. Yes? I put my right hand in, I take my right hand out . . . *(Pulls out hand covered in blood.*
265   BLANCHE *and* STELLA *exit.* MITCH *enters in fading light to roll away trunk, music and lights slowly fade out. In black-out.)* I am suddenly aware that the atmosphere has changed. It's dark. The night has a thousand eyes and they're all looking at me. They're burning into me, burning into my chest.
270   If I don't sleep now, I never will . . . don't panic . . . the night seems to last forever . . . don't panic . . . I'm scared, I'm wrong, the night is making me feel . . . *(Lights return suddenly on a curtain with a painting of an oversized clawed foot of a bathtub and a straight razor lying on a tiled floor.* STELLA
275   *is onstage with* STANLEY. *She is wearing a cheerleading outfit and carries a cheerleading doll.)* Vivien Leigh, huh? O.K., that's your story and I'm stuck with it for now. But let's see if you can keep up the deception day after day, week after week in front of me. Let that be a challenge to our relationship.
280   But meanwhile, relax, make yourself at home, have a drink. Tell me about yourself, stuff I haven't heard before, recent stuff like how've you been lately. I got all the time in the world and I'm all ears.

STELLA: Stanley, you come out here and let Blanche finish
285   dressing. *(STANLEY exits.)* I let her keep her hopes and dreams, just like I let her keep her cheerleading memories. I pretended they were mine as well, came to know them as I know my own face in the mirror. A face that was not a twin of my older sister.
290
BLANCHE: *(Entering stage left in a bathrobe.)* I think I handled that really well. It's a tricky business, deception in the face of legal documents. Thank heavens for bathrooms, they always make me feel so new.

STELLA: Blanche, honey, are you all right in there? There was
295   no answer, but I could hear her splashing and the sound of her radio.

BLANCHE: I can always refresh my spirits in the bathroom.

STELLA: Blanche, I brought you your lemon coke.

BLANCHE: All right sweetie. Be right out.
300
STELLA: I'll wait out here.

BLANCHE: I don't want you to have to wait on me.

STELLA: I like waiting on you Blanche, it feels more like home.

BLANCHE: I must admit, I do like to be waited on.

STELLA: Well, I'm waiting.
305
BLANCHE: One day I'll probably just dissolve in the bath. They'll come looking for me, but there'll be nothing left. "Drag Queen Dissolves in Bathtub," that'll be the headline. "All that was left was a full head of hair clogging up the plughole. She was exceptional even in death. . . ." I wonder
310   where I'll end up. In the sea, I suppose.

STELLA: I'm waiting, Blanche.

BLANCHE: Just a few last finishing touches.

STELLA: Waiting. Waiting in the wings. Waiting for her to get off the phone.
315
BLANCHE: You wouldn't want me to go out looking a mess, now would you?

STELLA: Waiting for her to come home from Woolworth's with the new Tangee lipstick. And when I wasn't waiting I was following. I used to follow her into the bathroom. I loved the
320   way she touched her cheek with the back of her hand. How she let her hand come to rest just slightly between her breasts

as she took one last look in the mirror. I used to study the way she adjusted her hips and twisted her thighs in that funny way when she was changing her shoes. Then she would fling open the bathroom door and sail down the staircase into the front room to receive her gentlemen callers.

BLANCHE: (*Colliding into* STELLA, *who drops the doll.*) My doll, it's broken!

STELLA: (*Laughingly.*) No it isn't.

BLANCHE: I did. I broke it.

STELLA: No, honey. You didn't.

BLANCHE: Yes I did. I broke it.

STELLA: (*Shaking* BLANCHE.) No, Blanche, it was already broken.

BLANCHE: I don't know why I'm like this today.

STELLA: (*Embracing her.*) Blanche, you know what this reminds me of? My homecoming corsage, remember? Before the homecoming parade, when the band and all the floats were gathering in front of the war memorial. It was your senior year, you were the captain of the cheerleaders, and I was the mascot. And they gave us these big orange and maroon chrysanthemums with ribbon streamers; mine was just as big as yours.

BLANCHE: And I pinned it on your shoulder and you were so proud of its size and excited by the smell of it.

STELLA: I felt every bit as tall and glamorous as the real cheerleaders, the majorettes, the homecoming court, even Miss Mississippi herself. I stood in that November air imagining all the things a grownup woman could be . . . and then, that great big ole football player came walking across the red dirt and smacked right into me.

BLANCHE: And your poor corsage, it started to bleed, it started to lose its petals one by one.

STELLA: And I started to cry. I threw a god-awful fit.

BLANCHE: You certainly did.

STELLA: My whole life was disappearing with those dripping petals. How was I going to present myself in the same parade with Miss Mississippi, her in her strapless gown and me with a handful of petals. But you put your big strong arms around me and set me right up there on the float with . . .

BLANCHE: The beauty queen herself. And there you were, all puffy-eyed and corsageless . . .

STELLA: Right next to the great white virgin, with her round bare shoulders and her rhinestone tiara.

BLANCHE: (*As music starts.*) And I took your picture and it was in the papers. (BLANCHE *takes off bathrobe to reveal cheerleading outfit and they sing.*)

UNDER THE COVERS

When life is unfair, and the world makes you sick
I know somewhere that's bliss on a stick.
(STELLA.) Somewhere to go when things are unsteady
(BLANCHE.) Somewhere to go with Coco and Teddy.

Under the covers, the pillows and laces
We both can share, those soft cotton places
(STELLA.) Lying together like spoons in a drawer
(BLANCHE.) Then turning over to have an explore . . .

Under the covers, those smooth satin covers
We share our dreams
(STELLA.) Like goose downy lovers

(BLANCHE.) Tucked in together like girls in the dorm
Under the covers everything's cozy and warm . . .

(*They pull hidden pom-poms from each other's sleeves and cheer.*)

AMO, AMAS, AMAT
WE LOVE OUR TEAM A LOT
WE'RE GONNA FIGHT FIGHT FIGHT
WE'RE GONNA WIN WIN WIN
WE'RE GONNA BE . . . (BLANCHE.) FABULOUS.

(*Tap dance break.*)

Under the covers, it's you and it's me now
Our pleasure grows, because we are two now
Lean on a pillow and look in my eyes
Spreading our knowledge and sharing our thighs
Under the covers, our fingers exploring
Those hidden dreams, we've found there is something

(STELLA *pulls a hand covered in menstrual blood out from under her skirt.*)

Mother has maybe forgotten to tell
Tho' if she found out
We'd found out
She'd give us hell.

STANLEY: (*Yelling from backstage.*) Stella!

BLANCHE & STELLA: She'd give us hell.

STANLEY: Stella!

BLANCHE & STELLA: She'd give us . . . (*Song dissolves into laughter.*)

STANLEY: When are you hens gonna end that conversation?

STELLA: Oh, you can't hear us.

STANLEY: Well, you can hear me, and I say hush up!

STELLA: This is my house too, Stanley, and I'll talk as much as . . .

BLANCHE: (*Interrupting her.*) Please don't start another row, I couldn't bear it . . . (*She exits.*)

STELLA: I tried to follow her, but I got stuck. Stuck in the bathroom, where I saw myself in the medicine chest mirror. I stopped there and I stared. For three days I stared. I wasn't her little sister. And in the mirror I saw the road split, and I took mine . . .

STANLEY: (*Grabbing* STELLA.) Stella. (*They hug,* STELLA *exits,* STANLEY *goes to bathroom and starts shaving. Lights dim.*)

MITCH: (*Entering stage right. He carries a painting of a card table, which he places over the front of the square box.*) Now and then I reached out to touch his wrists. They glittered with a dozen golden bracelets that matched the large earrings he wore. He was like a shimmering waterfall of gold, his whole front covered with golden pendants that looked like coins. Beneath, he wore a purple semitransparent shift that matched the dark makeup around his large bedroom eyes. There was something both fierce and warm in his face. He was glowing with a pagan intensity that matched the intense feelings brimming up in my heart, which in turn matched the brimming purple wine that was being poured, seemingly without end, into our glittering golden goblets that matched the shafts of golden scorching sunlight that poured through the high windows down onto the banqueting table, where they were scattered in a dozen colors as they hit the gold in the glass. Finally, he rose from his throne,

which was covered in a mantle of blue macaw feathers that cost ten dollars per square inch and matched the cerulean
435 blue of the deep-piled carpet reputedly made by the tiny fingers of ten-year-old eunuchs within the forbidden city in Peking. Then he began to dance . . .

STANLEY: (*Grabbing* MITCH *by the shoulders.*) You know, a bum like me can grow up in a great country like this and be
440 her lover, which is a hell of a better job than being president of the United States.

MITCH: You're a lucky man.

STANLEY: You know, when I think about her, it's like food, I want to eat her, just put her whole leg in my mouth, or her
445 face, or her hands . . .

MITCH: That's a mouthful!

STANLEY: I feel so hungry when I think of her, I could eat my car, I could eat dirt, I could eat a brick wall. I have to, I have no choice. I have to touch things, and my hands bring them
450 to my mouth.

MITCH: Your big hands!

STANLEY: Feelings grow inside me, and sometimes they fly out of me so fast and then smack, I'm out of control. When it comes to big hands, I have no competition. (STANLEY *takes a*
455 *swig of beer.*)

MITCH: When it comes to big hands, she knows she's got your big hands all over her. (*He takes a swig.*)

STANLEY: (*Challenging him to arm wrestle.*) My big pioneer hands all over her rocky mountains.
460 MITCH: (*Taking the challenge.*) All over her livestock and vegetation.

STANLEY: Her buffaloes and prairies.

MITCH: Her thick forests and golden sunsets.

STANLEY: All over her stars!
465 MITCH: She's in your hands!

STANLEY: She's in my hands and . . . yeeaaa . . . (STANLEY *pins* MITCH's *arm down.*)

MITCH: That's right! Bite me! Bite me! Suck on me . . . oops.

STANLEY: (*Pulling away from* MITCH.) What are you talking
470 about?

MITCH: Mosquitoes! Biting me, biting me . . .

STANLEY: (*They both slap at bugs.*) Suck on me, suck on my body!

MITCH: What do you think I'm here for, your entertainment?
475 A Coney Island for you?

STANLEY: A joyride on my ankle! A suck on my wrist! I'll eliminate you! (*Mimes machine gun and makes gun noise.*)

MITCH: Remove you from my space! Pow!

STANLEY: Away from my body, you aggravating hungry bugger.
480 MITCH: Bugger off! Away with you!

STANLEY: You're spoiled . . . Splat!

MITCH: You're educated . . . Squash!

STANLEY: You remind me of my fate.

MITCH: You remind me of my immortality! Leave me my
485 blood.

STANLEY: Blood!

MITCH: Bloody sheet.

STANLEY: Bloody night.

MITCH: Blood on your hand!
490 STANLEY: It's my hand, I'm dealing the cards.

MITCH: (*Running after* STANLEY *around box.*) Deal me!

STANLEY: If you want another card I'll hit you with it.

MITCH: Hit me!

STANLEY: When it comes to big hands I got no competition.
495 MITCH: Take me!

STANLEY: Your shuffle.

MITCH: Cut me in!

STANLEY: Throw your checkbook out the window!

MITCH: Empty my pockets!

STANLEY: I'm a royal flush, I win every time. (*Challenging him*
500 *to arm wrestle.*)

MITCH: (*Taking the challenge.*) I'm the last sailboat across the horizon before the sun sets.

STANLEY: Nobody can audition for my part.

MITCH: I flop and smash and throw things.
505 STANLEY: I turn and punch the air!

MITCH: I sweat.

STANLEY: I smell.

MITCH: I smell!

STANLEY: I smell of car oil, I smell of your blood.
510 MITCH: I smell of . . . cologne!

STANLEY: I'm hungry, ha, hungry! I'm gonna eat rough memories.

MITCH: I'm gonna eat tough dreams.

STANLEY: Digest hard words. Hard, hard words.
515 MITCH: I'm gonna spit them out!

STANLEY: It's gonna cost you my hunger!

MITCH: I'm gonna pay!

STANLEY: (*Grabbing* MITCH.) I'm gonna eat my car. I'm gonna
520 eat dirt!

MITCH: I'm gonna eat a tree! Eat your whole leg!

STANLEY: I'm gonna eat the sun and then I'll sweat!

STANLEY & MITCH: (*In a frenzy.*) Bite me! Bite me! Suck on me!

BLANCHE: (*Opening the bathroom curtain and entering.*) Suck
525 my wrist.

STANLEY: (*Singing.*)

I'M A MAN

When I was a little boy, at the age of five
I had something in my pocket, kept a lot of folks alive
530 Now I'm a man, made twenty-one
I'll tell you baby, we can have a lot of fun
'Cos I'm a man
Spelled M . . . A . . . N . . . Man
Oohh . . . oowww . . . oowww

535 All you pretty women, standing in a line
I can make love to you, in an hour's time
'Cos I'm a man
Spelled M . . . A . . . N . . . Man

(*Dance break.*)

The line I shoot will never miss
540 When I make love to you baby, it comes to this
I'm a man
Spelled M . . . A . . . N . . . Man
Oowww . . . oowww . . . owww . . . I'm a man, yes I am,
I'm a man . . .

545 (*Gradually noticing* BLANCHE *has a finger up her nose.*) Hold it, hold it. (*To* BLANCHE.) Is there something I can help you with?

BLANCHE: Please could you give me a tissue. I think I've got something stuck up my nose.

550 STANLEY: Would you like me to have a look?

BLANCHE: Please don't trouble. I think a tissue would probably do it.

STANLEY: (*Handing her a tissue.*) Here.

BLANCHE: Probably a boogey, I expect.

555 STANLEY: An acquaintance of mine lost his sense of smell from having a booger stuck up his nose . . . better?

BLANCHE: Not really, no.

MITCH: Can I help?

BLANCHE: Oh no, please, it's only something stuck up my

560 nose.

MITCH: Try sticking your little finger in as far as it'll go.

STANLEY: Then blow your nose.

MITCH: Please let me look, I happen to be a doctor.

BLANCHE: It's very kind of you.

565 MITCH: Turn around to the light please. Now look up. Now look down. Now look up again . . . I can see it . . . keep still . . . (*He twists the tissue and pokes it up her nose.*) There!

BLANCHE: Oh dear, what a relief, it was agonizing.

MITCH: (*Holding up the tissue.*) It looks like a piece of Christ-

570 mas Pudding.

BLANCHE: Thank you very much indeed.

MITCH: Not at all.

BLANCHE: How lucky for me you happened to be here.

MITCH: Anybody could have done it.

575 BLANCHE: Never mind, you did and I'm most grateful.

MITCH: There's my train . . . Goodbye. (*He exits.*)

BLANCHE: And that's how it all began, just through me getting a booger stuck up my nose.

(*She turns to face* STANLEY, *then walks away upstage left as lights dim and music starts.* MITCH *enters and motions for* BLANCHE *to dance with him, as* STANLEY *shuffles a deck of cards.*)

STANLEY: Hey Mitch, you in this game or what?

580 MITCH: Deal me out. I'm talking to Miss DuBois. (*They begin to dance as* STELLA *wanders on.*)

STELLA: Look, we made enchantment.

STANLEY: Who turned that on? Turn it off.

STELLA: Ah-h-h-h let them have their music.

585 STANLEY: I said turn it off!

STELLA: What are you doing?

STANLEY: That's the last time anybody plays music during my game. Now get OUT! OUT! (MITCH *and* BLANCHE *exit.*) Everybody get out! (*To pianist.*) OUT! (*Music stops,* STELLA

590 *is laughing quietly.*)

STELLA: I guess you think that's funny.

STANLEY: Yeah, I thought it was pretty funny.

STELLA: Well, maybe I blinked at the wrong time, 'cuz I missed the joke.

595 STANLEY: Oh, so now you're an authority on what's funny.

STELLA: I didn't say that. I said I didn't think that that was funny.

STANLEY: Well, if you know so much, why don't you show me what is funny.

600 STELLA: Look, I don't want to get twisted out of shape about it, I just didn't think it was all that funny.

STANLEY: Oh, you thought it was just a little bit funny.

STELLA: No, not even a little bit funny.

STANLEY: So, show me!

605 STELLA: This is ridiculous.

STANLEY: Show me what's funny.

STELLA: You want me to show you what's funny.

STANLEY: Yeah, show me funny.

STELLA: O.K., I'll show you funny . . . (*Rips* STANLEY'S *sleeve.*) That's funny. 610

STANLEY: That was not funny.

STELLA: You want funny? (*Rips off the other sleeve.*) That's funny.

STANLEY: That was not funny.

STELLA: Okay. What about this? (*Rips off half of* STANLEY'S 615 *shirt.*) Or this? (*Rips off other half.*)

STANLEY: That's not funny.

STELLA: I'll be right back. (*Bustles offstage and comes back with a seltzer bottle, then sprays* STANLEY.) That was funny.

STANLEY: That was not funny. 620

STELLA: I'll be right back. (*Comes back with a giant powder puff and powders* STANLEY.) That was funny.

STANLEY: That's not funny.

STELLA: I'll be right back. (*Comes back with a cream pie. As she nears* STANLEY, STANLEY *unexpectedly tips it into* STELLA'S 625 *face.*)

STANLEY: Now *that* was funny.

(STANLEY *exits.* MITCH *enters, pulling a curtain with a painting of a giant orchid. The* Cassandra *aria from* Les Troyens *comes on loudly, then fades.*)

MITCH: The bell sounds and they're both middle weights. They know the rules, and they've been publicized as an even match. 'Ere, you've paid good money to see them, you want 630 to see a battle, you want to see blood. Round One is I Love You, Round Two is You See Me For Who I Really Am. You never see a person more clearly than the first time they lay hands on you. After that, it's all up for grabs. (*To* STELLA.) He's gonna be back and he's gonna say he's sorry. 635

STELLA: (*Wiping pie from her face.*) Sorry. (*Laughs.*) Sorry . . . sorry, sorry. (*Laughs.*) The Indian women. The Indian women, wrapping their soft bodies in thin silk the colors of a church window. Sari. (*Laughs.*) I'm sorry too. It makes me laugh. They can't take it back. What the gods give they can- 640 not take back, they can only add to what they've given, to make the gift painful to have. Cassandra! Zeus gave her the gift of the seer, and then she wouldn't have sex with him, but he couldn't take back the gift. He couldn't have her, so he made sure no one would believe her. . . . She knew all those 645 men were in that wooden horse, but they wouldn't listen . . . (*Laughs.*) That's hysterical. It was their loss, that curse! Zeus made a prophetess and then spit in her face. And just what do you think went on inside that horse? Hundreds of warlike men, spitting, smoking, dreaming death in the belly of a fake 650 horse. . . . I dream a purple darkness . . . purple . . . the color of the sari . . . darlings. I'm in here. I'm on drugs. I'm braless, shirtless, I'm giggling, I'm lost, I'm in love. I'm stuck in the stomach of a fake horse, can you hear me? I hear you. Cassandra tell me what will happen. I promise I'll believe you! I 655 . . . I'm in love with you Cassandra, you blonde, you seer, you whisperer . . . tell me what's going to happen . . . come here . . . let's make it happen. Please don't, blonde seer. I can't, I'm already married. Take your hands off my breasts, I'm already married. I'm in here. The horse! I'm in the belly 660 of a horse, smoking, shirtless. I'm preparing for a war. (*She begins to strip off her house dress to reveal a tight, strapless*

665 *dress.)* Someone stole my woman, stole her from my house, filched her from history, and I'm here to get her back. I am a powerful warrior. *(She poses like Marilyn Monroe.)* Come sweet prophetess, what is going to happen? Tell me, I'm nailed to this story. Cut me down. I'm in here. Can't you see me? I'm having sex with the fortune teller that men don't believe. Sex . . . sex! *(She sings.)*

RUNNING WILD

670 Running wild, lost control
Running wild, mighty bold
Feeling gay, reckless too
Carefree mind, all the time, never blue

675 Always going—don't know where
Always showing—I don't care
Don't love nobody, it's not worthwhile
All alone and running wild

(STANLEY *has entered audience and applauds* STELLA *loudly as piano starts intro for* STELLA'*s next song.)*

SWEET LITTLE ANGEL

I've got a sweet little angel
And I love the way she spreads her wings
680 I've got a sweet little angel
And I love the way she spreads her wings
When she spreads those wings over me
She brings joy in everything.

STANLEY: *(Clapping loudly and talking to audience.)* Is she
685 good or what? She is so good . . . can you believe how good she is? (STELLA *stops singing.)* Any moment this dame spends out of bed is wasted, totally wasted. (STANLEY *runs to* STELLA *and drops to his knees.)*
STELLA: I could smell you coming.
690 STANLEY: You say the sweetest things.
STELLA: Women have to develop a sense of smell. Just in general. Just as a matter of fact. Like in a war. In a war, you learn to smell the enemy. You learn to cross the street. You learn to see through their disguises.
695 STANLEY: I am not your enemy.
STELLA: No . . . but you have many of the characteristics. Not that I go by appearances, just smell and instinct.
STANLEY: What are you looking for?
STELLA: You're tense.
700 STANLEY: I'm always tense. It keeps me in check, keeps me in balance.
STELLA: It's hard to watch.
STANLEY: That's 'cuz you don't know that it's leading to something.
705 STELLA: And are you gonna tell me what that is?
STANLEY: It's a fact of life, you figure it out.
STELLA: I already did. I don't have to spend long on the likes of you, not one as experienced as I am. I know that your tension is sexual, and it's a desire that I share in, but not for your
710 pleasure, for my own. I'm lookin' for it, I might not find it in you, I might find it somewhere else, as a matter of fact, and there's nothing you can do about it. You don't satisfy me, you're not real.
STANLEY: Are you saying I'm not a real man?
715 STELLA: I'm saying you're not real. You're cute. Could be much cuter if you weren't quite so obvious.

STANLEY: Then it wouldn't be me. I am not subtle.
STELLA: Try it, just for tonight.
STANLEY: You mean put it on like clothes? I couldn't pull that
720 off.
STELLA: No, take it off. Take it all off. I want to see what you're really made of. I want to see what it is that makes me want you. That makes me want to have you as I've never had anyone. Strip. Take it off, then we'll talk.
725 STANLEY: Talk is cheap.
STELLA: I want to see you naked like a baby.
STANLEY: No more talk, let's make a deal.
STELLA: We are partners in this deal. I have my part, you have yours.
730 STANLEY: I can live up to my end of the deal, how 'bout you.
STELLA: Put your cards on the table, I'm calling your bluff. *(Blackout.)*
STANLEY: Hey, turn on the light!
STELLA: I like it in the dark.
735 STANLEY: I don't like the dark, I like to see.
STELLA: *(As lights slowly fade up.)* You can see if you get your eyes used to it.
STANLEY: I don't want to get used to it, I'm afraid of the dark. *(Low light reveals their silhouettes dancing as the piano*
740 *player sings.)*

SWEET LITTLE ANGEL

I've got a sweet little angel
And I love the way she spreads her wings
I've got a sweet little angel
And I love the way she spreads her wings
745 When she spreads those wings over me
She brings joy in everything

I asked my angel for a nickel
And she gave me a twenty dollar bill
I asked my angel for a nickel
750 And she gave me a twenty dollar bill
When I asked her for her body
She said she'd leave it to me in her will . . .

Well my angel if she quit me
I believe I would die
755 Well my angel if she quit me
I believe I would die
If you don't love me
You must tell me the reason why.

(STELLA *has pulled off* STANLEY'*s ripped T-shirt as they dance. She jumps up and wraps her body around* STANLEY *and throws the shirt to the ground as they exit. Blackout.)*

— ACT TWO —

The stage is empty except for the large rectangular box on its side, with the painting of a tub across the front. Dim orange light comes up on STELLA *standing and stretching in bathtub in her slip.*

STELLA: The fire is keeping me awake. It reminds me of the night Yellow Mountain was burning. All night long I could see Yellow Mountain burning on my bedroom ceiling. I was afraid that the burning debris would fall from the mountain

5   on to our roof and burn through the ceiling. Meet up with a
     flicker that was already there, waiting to devour me.
     MITCH: (*Light behind scrim reveals* BLANCHE *in a nightgown
     holding a cigarette and* MITCH *standing beside her.* MITCH
     lights her cigarette.) There's a shadow over by the window.
10   It's a woman. She's smoking a cigarette. (BLANCHE *blows
     smoke into* MITCH's *face; he coughs.*) The smoke is coming
     my way. Maybe she wants me to go with her. (BLANCHE
     *passes around scrim and crosses to center stage, where she
     picks up* STANLEY's *torn T-shirt.*)
15   STELLA: The fire has leapt out of control. It's too late, the fire-
     men have all gone home to their wives. Had to hose down
     their own houses, to protect them from the falling debris.
     BLANCHE: (*Examining* STANLEY's *shirt.*) This shirt smells of
     success to me. These elements of manhood . . . there's some-
20   thing about Stanley I can't quite put my finger on. I can't put
     my finger on his smell. I don't believe he's a man. I question
     his sexuality. His postures are not real, don't seem to be com-
     ing from a true place. He's a phoney, and he's got her believ-
     ing it, and if she has children he'll have them believing it
25   and when he dies, they'll find out. (*Crossing to* STELLA.)
     Have you ever seen him naked?
     STELLA: (*Drinking coke.*) It's the sugar that satisfies me. The
     cool liquid running down my throat is only temporary. It's
     when the sugar hits the bloodstream, that's when my heart
30   starts pumping.
     BLANCHE: There's something about the way he smells, some-
     thing about the way he has to prove his manhood all the
     time, that makes me suspicious. I'm looking at the shape, not
     the content.
35   STELLA: (*Straddling the edge of the tub.*) Don't you love that
     feeling when you lean against a solid surface and you can
     feel your heart beating under your body.
     BLANCHE: The noises he makes, the way he walks like Mae
     West, the sensual way he wears his clothes, this is no garage-
40   mechanic working-class boy, this is planned behavior. This
     is calculated sexuality, developed over years of picking up
     signals not necessarily genetic is what I'm trying to say.
     STELLA: I remember leaning my abdomen against the cold
     sink and feeling my heart beating between my legs.
45   BLANCHE: I'm trying to say, what I mean is, perhaps he was a
     man in some former life. Perhaps he's just a halfway house,
     to lure you into a sexual trap, a trap well laid, with just the
     right flavors, just the right mood to seduce you . . . what I'm
     trying to say is, I think he's a fag.
50   STELLA: The thing about coca-cola is that one sixteen-ounce
     bottle has more than four tablespoons of sugar.
     BLANCHE: But now you have the chance to get out. To end
     this charade before it's too late . . .
     STELLA: Enough to keep you up half the night.
55   BLANCHE: Only someone as skilled as I am at being a woman
     can pick up these subtle signs.
     STELLA: Enough to curb your appetite.
     BLANCHE: I'm well trained, equipped. I know how to talk to
     him, to flirt with him, not get involved really, to decorate his
60   arm, to aid him in his charade, to give him a passing grade.
     STELLA: Sugar in a sixteen-ounce bottle.
     BLANCHE: (*Grabbing* STELLA's *hand.*) I'm the real woman for
     you. I can show you satisfaction. A rewarding, cultural life;
     me and you, you and me, Blanche and Stella, Stella and
65   Blanche. . . . You were such a pretty girl. (STELLA *pulls
     away.*) What day was it that you changed? You were tipped

for the top and you threw it all away. You were headed upward to the good, right life and suddenly you changed.
STELLA: Pure sugar, liquid sex.
BLANCHE: Stella, you haven't been listening to a word I've   70
been saying.
STELLA: (STANLEY *has come through the audience and is standing facing* STELLA *and* BLANCHE.) The fire is still burning . . .
my clothes sticking to my chest just like Mama's dress against
her naked belly. Now why did you stay at the sink so long . . .   75
(*Walking towards* STANLEY.) and every day without underwear. (*She jumps into* STANLEY's *arms.*)
STANLEY: Hey! (STANLEY *spins her around, then they walk offstage together.*)
BLANCHE: Trouble is, Marlon Brando does look gorgeous.   80
And I know that if I met him at the time he was in that film
I'd want to lick his armpits. I don't suppose he'd be able to
open himself up to that though . . . surrender himself. But
he does have that big shapely mouth . . . I guess I'm pretty
taken with this actor in the film. But what if the film was life   85
and I could just walk right into it? I don't suppose he'd welcome me, probably give me a hard time. Just like he gave
Blanche . . . I mean Miss Leigh . . . and what would she say
if this drag queen poured out of the camera lens and blew up
to size right there in front of her. Yes, well, she had to deal   90
with Marlon Brando all day and Laurence Olivier in the
evenings . . . I'd say she had enough problems without me
on the set. . . . I feel like an old hotel. (*Piano starts prelude to
"Beautiful Dream."*) Beautiful bits of dereliction in need of
massive renovation. There's that record again. Have you ever   95
had something stuck in your head for a very long time, like a
record playing over and over and every time it stops there's
applause, and then it starts all over again . . . (*The music
stops and* BLANCHE *sticks her hand in the tub.*) I like a warm
bath. It's the warmth I'm after, not the cleanliness. I don't   100
even mind Stella's cheap, common soap . . . Oh I did it you
know, I did lead the grand life . . . chauffeurs, limos. I used
to go to clubs and know I was the most attractive person
there . . . now I don't go to clubs.
STANLEY: (*Pulling in painted vaudeville curtain behind*   105
BLANCHE.) Ha Ha.
BLANCHE: (*Music begins again.*) Now, here it comes . . . the
record . . . and there's a dark burgundy curtain opening on
the stage, and there we are, just me and Vivien . . .
STANLEY: HA HA. Did you hear what I said? I said, HA HA HA.   110
(STANLEY *exits.*)
BLANCHE: (*Singing.*)

BEAUTIFUL DREAM

Cold wind blowing through the empty rooms
Windows broken, floors damp and rotten now
No sound in the silence   115
No step in the stillness
No warmth in the cold air
Only shadows moving in the half-light
Empty lockers, lines of empty hooks
Vacant showers, all deep in dust now   120
Just a modest price bought you paradise
No one wondered would it last
Running out of steam, now the beautiful dream
Has passed.

125 No one greets me as I step inside
Hot and ready for whatever comes my way
No warm body waiting for me
No pulse of a warm heart near me
No strong arms around me
130 No one lying warm and sweet beside me
Thought we'd party 'til the end of time
But it's over, seems so long ago now
Down the long parade, see them slowly fade
As they all leave one by one
135 Running out of steam, now the beautiful dream
Has gone.

So I fill the tub, rub-a-dub-dub-dub
But I still freeze up inside
'Cuz the water's cold
140 And the dream has grown old and died
Running out of steam
Now the beautiful dream
Has gone.

(Lights fade, curtain is pulled offstage, BLANCHE *moves to the*
145 *tub upstage left and climbs in.)* Bubbles, bawbles, bumholes
. . . *(Smelling soap.)* Municipal, that's the word. Now I'm
going under . . . can't hear any noises at all . . . just the odd
humps and hoomps and grinds . . . my hair is floating about
. . . whooosh . . . up in the air again. (BLANCHE *reappears in*
150 *the tub wearing bubble dress as a ukelele strums in the back-*
ground.) Listen . . . there it is again, the record, going around
and around and then the applause. Until something replaces
that song and that wild applause, I know I'll cling to it. I'll always choose applause over death.
155 MITCH: *(Lights behind scrim reveal* MITCH *in fairy costume*
perched on a ladder and looking down on BLANCHE *in the*
tub. He is playing the ukelele and singing.)

THE FAIRY SONG

I was sitting on my asteroid, way up in the sky
When I saw you through the window, and I thought I'd drop by
160 You were looking sad, bothered and forlorn
Wondering where your days of youth and beauty all had gone.

Now I don't possess a magic wand, my wings are rather small
As far as fairies go I'm nothing special at all
But still I've got that something that I know you'll just adore
165 That special kind of magic, gonna sweep you off the floor.

(Chorus.)

I'm a supernatural being, I'm your sweetie-pie
And I've come here from somewhere far, away up in the sky
I'm here to play a song tonight by Rimsky-Korsakov
And if you play your cards right we might even have it off.

*(*STELLA *mouths the words as* MITCH *continues singing.)*

170 Now I was sitting in the bathtub, minding my own biz
When this vision came from outer space and now I'm in a tiz
He was gorgeous, he was handsome, he was eager just to please
And he said that he'd come here so me and him could have a
  squeeze.

I'm a supernatural being, I'm your sweetie-pie
175 And I've come here from somewhere far, away up in the sky
I'll take you to my fairy dell, in my fairy car
And hang a sign "Do not disturb" upon the evening star.

(Dance break, BLANCHE *twirls around and motions* MITCH *to*
join her. They dance.)

*(*BLANCHE *speaks.)*

Are you sure that you're a fairy?
I'd imagined they were blonde.
And frankly I'm not leaving 'til I've seen your magic wand.   180

*(*MITCH *sings.)*

My wand, alas, I left at home, you'll have to come on spec
But I promise when we get there you can hold it for a sec.

(Chorus.)

*(*MITCH *and* BLANCHE *exit.* BLANCHE *reenters with* STELLA *and*
STANLEY, *who resets table box and holds a birthday cake.)*

STANLEY: *(Sings in monotone.)* Happy birthday to you, happy
birthday to you, happy birthday . . . Blanche, happy birthday
to you.   185
BLANCHE: What a lovely cake. How many candles are on it?
STELLA: Don't you worry about that right now. Why don't you
tell us one of your funny stories.
BLANCHE: I don't think Mr. Kowalski would be interested in
any of my funny stories.   190
STANLEY: I've got a funny story, what about this: There's these
two faggots sitting on the sofa, which one is the cocksucker?
(Long pause.) The one with the feathers coming out of his
mouth.
BLANCHE: In the version I heard it was two pollacks.   195
STANLEY: I am not a pollack. People from Poland are Poles.
There is no such thing as a pollack. And in any case, for your
information, I am one hundred percent American.
STELLA: Well, now that we're all getting along so well, why
don't you blow out the candles, Blanche, and make a wish.   200
STANLEY: Be careful what you wish for. (BLANCHE *blows out*
all the candles. They relight. She blows them out again, but
again they relight. As she goes to blow them out again, STAN-
LEY *brushes her aside and sticks the candles upside down in*
the cake one by one. Blackout. The bathtub is removed and a   205
painting of an oversized naked light bulb is pulled onstage.)
Stella! Blanche! Mitch! It's dark. I'm afraid.
STELLA: Let's just play a game.
STANLEY: This is not funny. Stella. Mitch. *(Lights slowly fade*   210
up. STANLEY *is wandering around the stage blindfolded.)*
Don't panic . . . I feel these original sins burning into me. I
feel I'm never safe. There I am at four a.m. with giant monsters spelling out my life in large slimy letters above my body,
just far enough above it to heat it up. To make my skin bead
in sweat starting just under my hair, above my forehead, on   215
the back of my neck, on my chest and the back of my knees.
Don't panic . . . I was born this way. I didn't learn it at theatre school. I was born butch. I'm so queer I don't even have
to talk about it. It speaks for itself, it's not funny. Being butch
isn't funny . . . don't panic . . . I fall to pieces in the night.   220
I'm just thousands of parts of other people all mashed into
one body. I am not an original person. I take all these pieces,
snatch them off the floor before they get swept under the
bed, and I manufacture myself. When I'm saying I fall to
pieces, I'm saying Marlon Brando was not there for me.   225
(Piano starts playing softly.) James Dean failed to come
through, where was Susan Hayward when I needed her, and
Rita Hayworth was nowhere to be found. I fall to pieces at

230 the drop of a hat. Just pick the piece you want and when I pull myself back together again I'll think of you. I'll think of you and what you want me to be. *(He sings all the verses to the Frank Sinatra hit "My Way," while crawling onto the table with the birthday cake and presents on it. As he gets to*
235 *his knees on top of the table, one hand breaks through a box and comes out covered in blood, the other hand goes into the cake and then into a box filled with feathers. He sings the final stanza kneeling on the cake.)* WHERE THE FUCK IS EVERYBODY?! *(Blackout. After a short pause lights come up on* STELLA *and* STANLEY.*)* What time is it?

240 STELLA: It's four a.m.
STANLEY: Help me make it through the night.
STELLA: Don't I always?
STANLEY: I'll be tired tomorrow, I'll be tired all day.
STELLA: Don't think about tomorrow. *(They embrace and kiss*
245 *as the lights fade to black. Lights come up upstage right on* MITCH *stuffing cake into his mouth.)*
MITCH: *(Talking with his mouth full throughout.)* I think it all started to go wrong when I wasn't allowed to be a boy scout. There were more important things to be done. Vacuuming,
250 clearing up at home, putting the garbage out. I used to get so angry putting out the garbage, I'd kick the shit out of the garbage cans in front. I thought about what I was missing. It gave me a repulsion for physical activity. Swimming was the only exception, and even then it took me a long time to
255 learn, as I was afraid of deep water. Then one day I fell in love with a beautiful young man. He came like a messenger from another world bearing a message of simple physical desire. But it was already too late, for me everything about the body was bound up with pain and boredom. I even used to
260 eat fast because I found it so boring. Soon the boy left. He knew better than to spend his life cooking dinners for someone with poor appetite. Then I was alone. I lived in a small room near a fly-over. I stopped going out except to go to the laundry and get groceries. At night I would lie awake on my
265 bed, and imagine I could hear things.

(Sound of a ukelele from offstage. He opens one of the gift boxes on the table and the sound comes again. He reaches into the box and pulls out a ukelele, then sings "The Man I Love," by George and Ira Gershwin. As he sings, tap-dancing chinese lanterns — the remaining members of the cast in lantern costumes — enter and begin dancing around him. During the song the lanterns begin running into each other and floundering around the stage. The audience begins to hear them mumbling from under their costumes.)

BLANCHE: Oh, what are we doing? I can't stand it! I want to be in a real play! *(Bright light pops on as* STELLA *drops her lantern to the floor.)* With real scenery! White telephones,
270 french windows, a beginning, a middle, and an end! This is the most confusing show I've ever been in. What's wrong with red plush? What's wrong with a theme and a plot we can all follow? There isn't even a fucking drinks trolley. Agatha Christie was right.
STELLA: Now we all talked about this, and we decided that re-
275 alism works against us.
BLANCHE: Oh we did, did we?
STELLA, STANLEY & MITCH: Yes we did!
BLANCHE: But I felt better before, I could cope. All I had to do was learn my lines and not trip over the furniture. It was all

so clear. And here we are romping about in the avant-garde 280 and I don't know what else. I want my mother to come and have a good time. She's seventy-three for chrissake. You know she's expecting me to play Romeo before it's too late. What am I supposed to tell her? That I like being a drag-queen? She couldn't bear it, I know she couldn't. 285
She wants me to be in something realistic, playing a real person with a real job, like on television.
STELLA: You want realism?
BLANCHE: What do you mean?
STELLA: You want realism, you can have it. 290
BLANCHE: You mean like in a real play?
STELLA: If that's what you want.
BLANCHE: With Marlon Brando and Vivien Leigh?
STELLA: You think you can play it?
BLANCHE: I have the shoulders. 295
STANLEY: I have the pajamas . . . O.K., let's go for it. *(*MITCH *and* STELLA *exit, striking the light bulb curtain.* STANLEY *sweeps the table with his forearm knocking the cake and presents to the floor.)* I cleared my place, want me to clear yours? It's just you and me now, Blanche. 300
BLANCHE: You mean we're alone in here?
STANLEY: Unless you got someone in the bathroom. *(He takes off his pajama top and pulls out a bottle of beer.)*
BLANCHE: Please don't get undressed without pulling the curtain. 305
STANLEY: Oh, this is all I'm gonna undress right now. Feel like a shower? *(He opens the beer and shakes it, then lets it squirt all over the stage, then pours some over his head before drinking it.)* You want some?
BLANCHE: No thank you. 310
STANLEY: *(Moving towards her, menacingly.)* Sure I can't make you reconsider?
BLANCHE: Keep away from me.
STANLEY: What's the matter, don't you trust me? Afraid I might touch you or something? You should be so lucky. Take 315
a look at yourself in that worn out party dress from a third-rate thrift store. What queen do you think you are?
BLANCHE: *(Trying to get past him.)* Oh god.
STANLEY: *(Blocking her exit.)* I got your number baby.
BLANCHE: Do we have to play this scene? 320
STANLEY: You said that's what you wanted.
BLANCHE: But I didn't mean it.
STANLEY: You wanted realism.
BLANCHE: Just let me get by you.
STANLEY: Get by me? Sure, go ahead. 325
BLANCHE: You stand over there.
STANLEY: You got plenty of room, go ahead.
BLANCHE: Not with you there! I've got to get by somehow!
STANLEY: You can get by, there's plenty of room. I won't hurt you. I like you. We're in this together, me and you. We've 330
known that from the start. We're the extremes, the stereotypes. We are as far as we can go. We have no choice, me and you. We've tried it all, haven't we? We've rejected ourselves, not trusted ourselves, mirrored ourselves, and we always come back to ourselves. We're the warriors. We have an 335
agreement . . . there's plenty in this world for both of us. We don't have to give each other up to anyone. You are my special angel.
BLANCHE: You wouldn't talk this way if you were a real man.

340 STANLEY: No, if I was a real man I'd say, "Come to think of it, you wouldn't be so bad to interfere with."

BLANCHE: And if I were really Blanche I'd say, "Stay back . . . don't come near me another step . . . or I'll . . ."

STANLEY: You'll what?

345 BLANCHE: Something's gonna happen here. It will.

STANLEY: What are you trying to pull?

BLANCHE: *(Pulling off one of her stiletto-heeled shoes.)* I warn you . . . don't!

STANLEY: Now what did you do that for?

350 BLANCHE: So I could twist this heel right in your face.

STANLEY: You'd do that, wouldn't you?

BLANCHE: I would, and I will if you . . .

STANLEY: You want to play dirty? I can play dirty. *(He grabs her arm.)* Drop it. I said drop it! Drop the stiletto!

355 BLANCHE: You think I'm crazy or something?

STANLEY: If you want to be in this play you've got to drop the stiletto.

BLANCHE: If you want to be in this play you've got to make me!

STANLEY: If you want to play a woman, the woman in this play

360 gets raped and she goes crazy in the end.

BLANCHE: I don't want to get raped and go crazy, I just wanted to wear a nice frock, and look at the shit they've given me!

STELLA: *(Entering with* MITCH.) Gimme that shoe! *(Piano starts "Pushover" as she grabs* STANLEY *and sings to him.)*

365 All the girls think you're fine, they even call you Romeo,
You've got 'em, yeah you've got 'em runnin' to and fro, oh yes you have,
But I don't want a one night thrill, I want a love that's for real,
And I can tell by your lies, yours is not the lasting kind.

You took me for a pushover, you thought I was a pushover,
370 I'm not a pushover, you thought that you could change my mind.

*(*MITCH *sings to* BLANCHE.)*

So you told all the boys that you were gonna take me out
You even, yeah you even had the nerve to make a bet, oh yes you did,
That I, I would give in, all of my love you would win,
But you haven't, you haven't won it yet.

375 You took me for a pushover, you thought I was a pushover,
I'm not a pushover, you thought my love was easy to get.

*(*MITCH *and* STELLA *together.)*

Your tempting lips, your wavy hair,
Your pretty eyes with that come hither stare,
It makes me weak, I start to bend and then I stop and think again,
380 No, no, no don't let yourself go.
I wanna spoil your reputation, I want true love, not an imitation,
And I'm hip, to every word in your conversation.

You took me for a pushover, I'm not a pushover,
You can't push me over, you thought I was a pushover . . .

STELLA: *(To audience.)* Did you figure it out yet? who's who, 385
what's what, who gets what, where the toaster is plugged in?
Did you get what you wanted?

STANLEY: Hey Stella, I just figured it out. Wasn't Blanche blonde?

STELLA: That's right. And come to think of it, it was suspicious 390
she didn't have a southern accent.

STANLEY: I knew it all along. The person we've been referring to as your sister is an imposter.

STELLA: Incredible! There's no flies on you Stanley.

STANLEY: What did you say? 395

STELLA: I said there's no disguising you, Stanley. You're one hundred percent.

STANLEY: I thought you said something else . . . something about flies.

STELLA: Well, come to think of it, there is something in that 400
area I've been meaning to open up a little.

STANLEY: So, you figured it out.

STELLA: Yeah, I figured it out.

STANLEY: And in those shoes. Un-fuckin'-believable! You know what this means? 405

STELLA: No, what?

STANLEY: This means that you are the only thing we can rely on, because you are at least who you seem to be.

STELLA: Well Stanley, there's something I've been meaning to tell you . . . *(She sings.)* 410

You took me for a pushover *(All join in.)* I'm not a pushover
You can't push me over, you thought I was a pushover.
DON'T PUSH!

(Encore.)

I LOVE MY ART

I've been mad about the stage since childhood,
When I roamed the sage and wildwood, 415
The attraction for the dazzling lights,
Caused me troublesome nights
Now I realize my one ambition
I can make a full and frank admission,
I am madly in love with my art, I love to play my part, 420

I love the theatre, I love it better than all my life, and just because
It's so entrancing, the song and dancing, to the music of applause,
I love the stage and all about it, it simply goes right to my heart,
I love the glamour, I love the drama,
I love I love I love my art 425
I love the glamour, I love the drama,
I love I love I love my art

■ TOMSON HIGHWAY ■

Since the production of his two most celebrated plays, *The Rez Sisters* (1986) and *Dry Lips Oughta Move to Kapuskasing* (1989), Tomson Highway has become perhaps the best-known of the many Native playwrights now working in North America. Tomson Highway was born in 1951, the eleventh of twelve children, on a trapline in a Native reserve (the Canadian term for what is called a "reservation" in the United States) in northern Manitoba, Canada. Until the age of six, Highway lived a nomadic life with his family. His first language was Cree, and he did not begin to learn English until he was sent to a Roman Catholic boarding school. Like many Native children, Highway attended boarding school, visiting his family only during the summer. After graduating from high school in Winnipeg, Highway studied piano at the University of Manitoba Faculty of Music, and then studied in London before returning to Canada. He graduated with a bachelor's degree in music from the University of Western Ontario in 1975 and is an accomplished concert pianist. He remained at the university for an additional year, however, to complete a bachelor's degree in English.

After college, Highway worked at The Native Peoples' Resource Centre in London, Ontario, and at the Ontario Federation of Indian Friendship Centres in Toronto. Highway traveled to reserves across Canada, working with Native people in schools, prisons, and other institutions. He also began writing plays about Native life, many of which were performed on reserves and in Native community centers. He first worked on *The Rez Sisters* with the De-ba-jeh-mu-jig Theatre Company of Manitoulin Island, Ontario, in 1986. Like many Native theater companies, De-ba-jeh-mu-jig is devoted to the production of new plays by Native playwrights and produces an increasing number of its plays in Native languages. As artistic director of the Native Earth Performing Arts Company, Highway produced *The Rez Sisters* again in Toronto in December of 1986, where it won the Dora Mavor Moore Award for the best new play of the season and was runner-up for outstanding Canadian play of the year. The play was produced in 1993 in New York by the American Indian Community House and the New York Theatre Workshop.

Highway's next play, *Dry Lips Oughta Move to Kapuskasing* was first produced in Toronto in 1989 by the Native Earth Performing Arts Company. It was later moved to the Royal Alexandra Theatre in Toronto, one of the very few Canadian plays—and the first by a Native playwright—to receive a full-scale production by a commercial theater. Highway continues to work as artistic director of Native Earth Performing Arts, one of many important Native theater companies now working in Canada and the United States (others include Four Winds Theatre, Native Theatre School, Ondinnok, Takwakin Theatre, Awasikan Theatre, and A-Maize Theatre in Canada; Spiderwoman Theater, Institute of American Indian Arts, American Indian Theater Company, Minneapolis American Indian AIDS Task Force, and Off the Beaten Path in the United States). Though Highway is gay, his central aims as a playwright to date have been to make Native narrative and mythological traditions more central to contemporary Native—and non-Native—arts.

DRY LIPS OUGHTA MOVE TO KAPUSKASING

Like *The Rez Sisters*, *Dry Lips Oughta Move to Kapuskasing* concerns life on the fictional Wasaychigan Hill reserve and is written in a mixture of English, Cree, and Ojibway. However, while *The Rez Sisters* concerns a group of Native women who travel to Toronto for the "World's Biggest Bingo," *Dry Lips* is a much darker and more violent play, concerning the men of the reservation. In some respects, the poverty of life on the reserve is made evident in the play's opening scene, the run-down living room of the reserve house shared by Big Joey and Gazelle Nataways, and is developed through the men's interrupted plans to improve life on the "rez." While the women have formed a hockey team (the importance of hockey is epitomized in Pierre's mantra, "Hockey. Life. Hockey. Life."), the men squabble about their plans: Zachary Jeremiah Keechigeesik's bakery, Big Joey's radio station, and Pierre St. Pierre's new job as referee for the women's games. In some ways, the men seem threatened by the women's independence and by their brash appropriation of hockey, and this anxiety seems to imply a more generalized impotence: seedy Creature Nataways does Big Joey's bidding, even though his wife Gazelle has moved in with Big Joey; Simon Starblanket is absorbed in an endlessly aborted effort at cultural revival; Dickie Bird Halked, born with fetal al-cohol syndrome, is at once shy and explosive, violently raping Patsy Pegahmagahbow with a cruci-fix. Even Pierre St. Pierre has a hard time finding his other skate.

Hanging around, drinking beer, complaining about the women—in many ways the Native men seem to epitomize "Canadian hoser culture," in the words of one Native critic of the play. Yet the men continually blame the women for the state of their lives, as Big Joey does in Act 2: "I hate them fuckin' bitches. Because they—our own women—took the fuckin' power away from us faster than the FBI ever did." Big Joey's tirade points up the play's most controversial element, which cen-ters on the performance of the Trickster figure Nanabush. The play begins and ends with Zachary awakening on the floor of Big Joey's house; we don't discover until the end of the play that the action has been a kind of dream, maybe a nightmare. Throughout, Nanabush occupies an elevated stage, sometimes watching the action, sometimes participating in it. In Native mythology, Nanabush is ca-pable of changing shape and gender; neither explicitly male nor female, the Trickser uses his/her wiles in a range of legendary escapades. In *Dry Lips*, however, Nanabush takes "female" shape in a number of ways—assuming outsized breasts to play Gazelle Nataways, a large rear-end to play Patsy ("Big-Bum") Pegahmagahbow, and so on. In one reading of the play—a dream play, after all—Nanabush here enacts the men's phobias and fantasies about women, and so offers an implied cri-tique of their sexist attitudes. From another perspective, though, one shared by many Native women who saw the play, the way Nanabush is characterized *as* a woman—her appearance (a version of the derogatory "squaw" stereotype), the "stripper" scene, the rape scene, the loss of the hockey puck in Gazelle/Nanabush's enormous breasts—merely reinforces the fundamentally misogynistic attitudes of the men in the play. In this sense, *Dry Lips Oughta Move to Kapuskasing* seems poised on the razor's edge of political theater: readers, audiences, and producers of the play must consider whether it criticizes the sexist and possibly misogynist ways women are presented in the play, or whether it merely reinforces such attitudes.

PRODUCTION NOTES

The set for the original production of *Dry Lips Oughta Move to Kapuskasing* contained certain ele-ments which I think are essential to the play.

First of all, it was designed on two levels, the lower of which was the domain of the "real" Wasaychigan Hill. This lower level contained, on stage-left, Big Joey's living room/kitchen, with its kitchen counter at the back and, facing down-stage, an old brown couch with a television set a few feet in front of it. This television set could be made to double as a smaller rock for the forest scenes. Stage-right had Spooky Lacroix's kitchen, with its kitchen counter (for which Big Joey's kitchen counter could double) and its table and chairs.

In front of all this was an open area, the floor of which was covered with teflon, a material which looks like ice and on which one can actually skate, using real ice skates; this was the rink for the hockey arena scenes. With lighting effects, this area could also be turned into "the forest" sur-rounding the village of Wasaychigan Hill, with its leafless winter trees. The only other essential ele-ment here was a larger jutting rock beside which, for instance, Zachary Jeremiah Keechigeesik and Simon Starblanket meet, a rock which could be made to glow at certain key points. Pierre's "little boot-leg joint" in Act Two, with its "window," was also created with lighting effects.

The upper level of the set was almost exclusively the realm of Nanabush. The principal ele-ment here was her perch, located in the very middle of this area. The perch was actually an old jukebox of a late 60's/early 70's make, but it was semi-hidden throughout most of the play, so that it was fully revealed as this fabulous jukebox only at those few times when it was needed; the effect sought after here is of this magical, mystical jukebox hanging in the night air, like a haunting and persistent memory, high up over the village of Wasaychigan Hill. Over and behind this perch was suspended a huge full moon whose glow came on, for the most part, only during the outdoor scenes, which all take place at nighttime. All other effects in this area were accomplished with light-ing. The very front of this level, all along its edge, was also utilized as the "bleachers" area for the hockey arena scenes.

Easy access was provided for between the lower and the upper levels of this set.

The "sound-scape" of *Dry Lips Oughta Move to Kapuskasing* was mostly provided for by a musician playing, live, on harmonica, off to the side. It is as though the "dream-scape" of the play were laced all the way through with Zachary Jeremiah Keechigeesik's "idealized" form of harmonica playing, permeated with a definite "blues" flavor. Although Zachary ideally should play his harmonica, and not too well, in those few scenes where it is called for, the sound of this harmonica is most effectively used to under-line and highlight the many magical appearances of Nanabush in her various guises.

Spooky Lacroix's baby, towards the end of Act Two, can, and should, be played by a doll wrapped in a blanket. But for greatest effect, Zachary's baby, at the very end of the play, should be played by a real baby, preferably about five months of age.

Finally, both Cree and Ojibway are used freely in this text for the reasons that these two languages, belonging to the same linguistic family, are very similar and that the fictional reserve of Wasaychigan Hill has a mixture of both Cree and Ojibway residents.

A NOTE ON NANABUSH

The dream world of North American Indian mythology is inhabited by the most fantastic creatures, beings and events. Foremost among these beings is the "Trickster," as pivotal and important a figure in our world as Christ is in the realm of Christian mythology. "Weesageechak" in Cree, "Nanabush" in Ojibway, "Raven" in others, "Coyote" in still others, this Trickster goes by many names and many guises. In fact, he can assume any guise he chooses. Essentially a comic, clownish sort of character, his role is to teach us about the nature and the meaning of existence on the planet Earth; he straddles the consciousness of man and that of God, the Great Spirit.

The most explicit distinguishing feature between the North American Indian languages and the European languages is that in Indian (e.g., Cree, Ojibway), there is no gender. In Cree, Ojibway, etc., unlike English, French, German, etc., the male-female-neuter hierarchy is entirely absent. So that by this system of thought, the central hero figure from our mythology—theology, if you will—is theoretically neither exclusively male nor exclusively female, or is both simultaneously. Therefore, where in *The Rez Sisters*, Nanabush was male, in this play—"flip-side" to *The Rez Sisters*—Nanabush is female.

Some say that Nanabush left this continent when the white man came. We believe she/he is still here among us—albeit a little the worse for wear and tear—having assumed other guises. Without the continued presence of this extraordinary figure, the core of Indian culture would be gone forever.

Tomson Highway

DRY LIPS OUGHTA MOVE TO KAPUSKASING

Tomson Highway

— CHARACTERS —

NANABUSH (*as the spirit of Gazelle Nataways, Patsy Pegahma-gahbow and Black Lady Halked*)
ZACHARY JEREMIAH KEECHIGEESIK - *41 years old*
BIG JOEY - *39*
CREATURE NATAWAYS - *39*
DICKIE BIRD HALKED - *17*
PIERRE ST. PIERRE - *53*
SPOOKY LACROIX - *39*

SIMON STARBLANKET - *20*
HERA KEECHIGEESIK - *39*

TIME: *Between Saturday, February 3, 1990, 11 p.m., and Saturday, February 10, 1990, 11 a.m.*

PLACE: *The Wasaychigan Hill Indian Reserve, Manitoulin Island, Ontario*

— ACT ONE —

The set for this first scene is the rather shabby and very messy living room/kitchen of the reserve house BIG JOEY *and* GAZELLE NATAWAYS *currently share. Prominently displayed on one wall is a life-size pin-up poster of Marilyn Monroe. The remains of a party are obvious. On the worn-out old brown couch, with its back towards the entrance, lies* ZACHARY JEREMIAH KEECHIGEESIK, *a very handsome Indian man. He is naked, passed out. The first thing we see when the light comes up—a very small "spot," precisely focussed—is* ZACHARY's *bare, naked bum. Then, from behind the couch, we see a woman's leg, sliding languorously into a nylon stocking and right over Zachary's bum. It is* NANABUSH, *as the spirit of* GAZELLE NATAWAYS, *dressing to leave. She eases herself luxuriously over the couch and over Zachary's bum and then reaches under Zachary's sleeping head, from where she gently pulls a gigantic pair of false, rubberized breasts. She proceeds to put these on over her own bare breasts. Then* NANABUSH/GAZELLE NATAWAYS *sashays over to the side of the couch, picks a giant hockey sweater up off the floor and shimmies into it. The sweater has a huge, plunging neckline, with the capital letter "W" and the number "1" prominently sewn on. Then she sashays back to the couch and behind it. Pleasurably and mischievously, she leans over and plants a kiss on Zachary's bum, leaving behind a gorgeous, luminescent lip-stick mark. The last thing she does before she leaves is to turn the television on. This television sits facing the couch that* ZACHARY *lies on.* NANABUSH/GAZELLE *does not use her hand for this, though; instead, she turns the appliance on with one last bump of her voluptuous hips. "Hockey Night in Canada" comes on. The sound of this hockey game is on only slightly, so that we hear it as background "music" all the way through the coming scene. Then* NANABUSH/GAZELLE *exits, to sit on her perch on the upper level of the set. The only light left on stage is that coming from the television screen, giving off its eery glow. Beat.*

The kitchen door bangs open, the "kitchen light" flashes on and BIG JOEY *and* CREATURE NATAWAYS *enter,* CREATURE *carrying a case of beer on his head. At first, they are oblivious to* ZACHARY'S *presence. Also at about this time, the face of* DICKIE BIRD HALKED *emerges from the shadows at the "kitchen window."*

Keechigeesik *means "heaven" or "great sky" in Cree* **Wasaychigan** *means "window" in Ojibway*

Silently, he watches the rest of the proceedings, taking a particular interest—even fascination—in the movements and behavior of BIG JOEY.

BIG JOEY: (*Calling out for* GAZELLE *who, of course, is not home.*) Hey, bitch!

CREATURE: (*As he, at regular intervals, bangs the beer case down on the kitchen counter, rips it open, pops bottles open, throws one to* BIG JOEY, *all noises that serve to "punctuate" the rat-a-tat rhythm of his frenetic speech.*) Batman oughta move to Kapuskasing, nah, Kap's too good for Batman, right, Big Joey? I tole you once I tole you twice he shouldna done it he shouldna done what he went and did goddawful Batman Manitowabi the way he went and crossed that blue line with the puck, man, he's got the flippin' puck right in the palm of his flippin' hand and only a minute-and-a-half to go he just about gave me the shits the way Batman Manitowabi went and crossed that blue line right in front of that brick shithouse of a whiteman why the hell did that brick shithouse of a whiteman have to be there . . .

ZACHARY: (*Talking in his sleep.*) No!

CREATURE: Hey!

(BIG JOEY *raises a finger signaling* CREATURE *to shut up.*)

ZACHARY: I said no!

CREATURE: (*In a hoarse whisper.*) That's not a TV kind of sound.

BIG JOEY: Shhh!

ZACHARY: . . . goodness sakes, Hera, you just had a baby . . .

CREATURE: That's a real life kind of sound, right, Big Joey? (BIG JOEY *and* CREATURE *slowly come over to the couch.*)

ZACHARY: . . . women playing hockey . . . damn silliest thing I heard in my life . . .

BIG JOEY: Well, well . . .

CREATURE: Ho-leee! (*Whispering.*) Hey, what's that on his arse look like lip marks.

ZACHARY: . . . Simon Starblanket, that's who's gonna help me with my bakery . . .

CREATURE: He's stitchless, he's nude, he's gonna pneumonia . . .

BIG JOEY: Shut up.

CREATURE: Get the camera. Chris'sakes, take a picture.

(CREATURE *scrambles for the Polaroid, which he finds under one end of the couch.*)

ZACHARY: . . . Simon! (*Jumps up.*) What the?!

CREATURE: Surprise! (*Camera flashes.*)

ZACHARY: Put that damn thing away. What are you doing here? Where's my wife? Hera!

(*He realizes he's naked, grabs a cast iron frying pan and slaps it over his crotch, almost castrating himself in the process.*)

40   Ooof!

BIG JOEY: (*Smiling.*) Over easy or sunny side up, Zachary Jeremiah Keechigeesik?

ZACHARY: Get outa my house.

CREATURE: This ain't your house. This is Big Joey's house, 45   right, Big Joey?

BIG JOEY: Shut up.

ZACHARY: Creature Nataways. Get outa here. Gimme that camera.

CREATURE: Come and geeeet it!

(*Grabs* ZACHARY's *pants from the floor.*)

50   ZACHARY: Cut it out. Gimme them goddamn pants.

CREATURE: (*Singing.*) Lipstick on your arshole, tole da tale on you-hoo.

ZACHARY: What? (*Straining to see his bum.*) Oh lordy, lordy, lordy gimme them pants.

(*As he tries to wipe the stain off.*)

55   CREATURE: Here doggy, doggy. Here poochie, poochie woof woof! (ZACHARY *grabs the pants. They rip almost completely in half.* CREATURE *yelps.*) Yip!

(*Momentary light up on* NANABUSH/GAZELLE, *up on her perch, as she gives a throaty laugh.* BIG JOEY *echoes this,* CREATURE *tittering away in the background.*)

ZACHARY: Hey, this is not my doing, Big Joey. (*As he clumsily puts on what's left of his pants.* CREATURE *manages to get in* 60   *one more shot with the camera.*) We were just having a nice quiet drink over at Andy Manigitogan's when Gazelle Nataways shows up. She brought me over here to give me the recipe for her bannock apple pie cuz, goodness sakes, Simon Starblanket was saying it's the best, that pie was selling like 65   hot cakes at the bingo and he knows I'm tryna establish this reserve's first pie-making business gimme that camera.

(BIG JOEY *suddenly makes a lunge at* ZACHARY *but* ZACHARY *evades him.*)

CREATURE: (*In the background, like a little dog.*) Yah, yah.

BIG JOEY: (*Slowly stalking* ZACHARY *around the room.*) You know, Zach, there's a whole lotta guys on this rez been slip-70   pin' my old lady the goods but there ain't but a handful been stupid enough to get caught by me. (*He snaps his fingers and, as always,* CREATURE *obediently scurries over. He hands* BIG JOEY *the picture of* ZACHARY *naked on the couch.* BIG JOEY *shows the picture to* ZACHARY, *right up to his face.*) 75   Kinda em-bare-ass-in' for a hoity-toity educated community pillar like you, eh Zach?

(ZACHARY *grabs for the picture but* BIG JOEY *snaps it away.*)

ZACHARY: What do you want?

BIG JOEY: What's this I hear about you tellin' the chief I can wait for my radio station?

80   ZACHARY: (*As he proceeds with looking around the room to collect and put on what he can find of his clothes.* BIG JOEY *and*

CREATURE *follow him around, obviously enjoying his predicament.*) I don't know where the hell you heard that from.

BIG JOEY: Yeah, right. Well, Lorraine Manigitogan had a word or two with Gazelle Nataways the other night. When you 85   presented your initial proposal at the band office, you said: "Joe can wait. He's only got another three months left in the hockey season."

ZACHARY: I never said no such thing.

BIG JOEY: Bullshit.   90

ZACHARY: W-w-w-what I said was that employment at this bakery of mine would do nothing but add to those in such places as those down at the arena. I never mentioned your name once. And I said it only in passing reference to the fact . . .

BIG JOEY: . . . that this radio idea of mine doesn't have as much 95   long-term significance to the future of this community as this fancy bakery idea of yours, Mr. Pillsbury dough-boy, right?

ZACHARY: If that's what you heard, then you didn't hear it from Lorraine Manigitogan. You got it from Gazelle Nataways 100   and you know yourself she's got a bone to pick with . . .

BIG JOEY: You know, Zach, you and me, we work for the same cause, don't we?

ZACHARY: Never said otherwise.

BIG JOEY: We work for the betterment and the advancement of 105   this community, don't we? And seeing as we're about the only two guys in this whole hell-hole who's got the get-up-and-go to do something . . .

ZACHARY: That's not exactly true, Joe. Take a look at Simon Starblanket . . .   110

BIG JOEY: . . . we should be working together, not against. What do you say you simply postpone that proposal to the Band Council . . .

ZACHARY: I'm sorry. Can't do that.

BIG JOEY: (*Cornering* ZACHARY.) Listen here, bud. You turned 115   your back on me when everybody said I was responsible for that business in Espanola seventeen years ago and you said nothin'. I overlooked that. Never said nothin'. (ZACHARY *remembers his undershorts and proceeds, with even greater desperation, to look for them, zeroing in on the couch and* 120 *under it.* BIG JOEY *catches the drift and snaps his fingers, signaling* CREATURE *to look for the shorts under the couch.* CREATURE *jumps for the couch. Without missing a beat,* BIG JOEY *continues.*) You turned your back on me when you said you didn't want nothin' to do with me from that day on. 125 I overlooked that. Never said nothin'. You gave me one hell of a slap in the face when your wife gave my Gazelle that kick in the belly. I overlooked that. Never said nothin'. (CREATURE, *having found the shorts among the junk under the couch just split seconds before* ZACHARY *does, throws* 130 *them to* BIG JOEY. BIG JOEY *holds the shorts up to* ZACHARY, *smiling with satisfaction.*) That, however, was the last time . . .

ZACHARY: That wasn't my fault, Joe. It's that witch woman of yours Gazelle Nataways provoked that fight between her and 135 Hera and you know yourself Hera tried to come and sew up her belly again . . .

BIG JOEY: Zach. I got ambition . . .

ZACHARY: Yeah, right.

BIG JOEY: I aim to get that radio station off the ground, starting 140 with them games down at my arena.

ZACHARY: Phhhh!

BIG JOEY: I aim to get a chain of them community radio stations not only on this here island but beyond as well . . .

145 ZACHARY: Dream on, Big Joey, dream on . . .

BIG JOEY: . . . and I aim to prove this broadcasting of games among the folks is one sure way to get some pride . . .

ZACHARY: Bullshit! You're in it for yourself.

BIG JOEY: . . . some pride and dignity back so you just get your
150 ass on out of my house and you go tell that Chief your Band Council Resolution can wait until next fiscal year or else . . .

ZACHARY: I ain't doing no such thing, Joe, no way. Not when I'm this close.

BIG JOEY: (*As he eases himself down onto the couch, twirling the*
155 *shorts with his fore-finger.*) . . . or else I get my Gazelle Nataways to wash these skivvies of yours, put them in a box all nice and gussied up, your picture on top, show up at your door-stop and hand them over to your wife. (*Silence.*)

ZACHARY: (*Quietly, to* BIG JOEY.) Gimme them shorts. (*No an-*
160 *swer. Then to* CREATURE.) Gimme them snapshots. (*Still no response.*)

BIG JOEY: (*Dead calm.*) Get out.

ZACHARY: (*Seeing he can't win for the moment, prepares to exit.*) You may have won this time, Joe, but . . .

165 BIG JOEY: (*Like a steel trap.*) Get out.

(*Silence. Finally* ZACHARY *exits, looking very humble. Seconds before* ZACHARY'S *exit,* DICKIE BIRD HALKED, *to avoid being seen by* ZACHARY, *disappears from the "window." The moment* ZACHARY *is gone,* CREATURE *scurries to the kitchen door, shaking his fist in the direction of the already-departed* ZACHARY.)

CREATURE: Damn rights! (*Then strutting like a cock, he turns to* BIG JOEY.) Zachary Jeremiah Keechigeesik never shoulda come in your house, Big Joey. Thank god, Gazelle Nataways ain't my wife no more . . . (BIG JOEY *merely has to throw a*
170 *glance in* CREATURE'S *direction to intimidate him. At once,* CREATURE *reverts back to his usual nervous self.*) . . . not really, she's yours now, right, Big Joey? It's you she's livin' with these days, not me.

BIG JOEY: (*As he sits on the couch with his beer, mostly ignoring*
175 CREATURE *and watching the hockey game on television.*) Don't make her my wife.

CREATURE: But you live together, you sleep together, you eat ooops!

BIG JOEY: Still don't make her my wife.

180 CREATURE: (*As he proceeds to try to clean up the mess around the couch, mostly shoving everything back under it.*) I don't mind, Big Joey, I really don't. I tole you once I tole you twice she's yours now. It's like I loaned her to you, I don't mind. I can take it. We made a deal, remember? The night she
185 threw the toaster at me and just about broke my skull, she tole me: "I had enough, Creature Nataways, I had enough from you. I had your kids and I had your disease and that's all I ever want from you, I'm leavin'." And then she grabbed her suitcase and she grabbed the kids, no, she didn't even grab
190 the kids, she grabbed the TV and she just sashayed herself over here. She left me. It's been four years now, Big Joey, I know, I know. Oh, it was hell, it was hell at first but you and me we're buddies since we're babies, right? So I thought it over for about a year . . . then one day I swallowed my pride
195 and I got up off that chesterfield and I walked over here, I opened your door and I shook your hand and I said: "It's okay, Big Joey, it's okay." And then we went and played darts

in Espanola except we kinda got side-tracked, remember, Big Joey, we ended up on that three-day bender?

BIG JOEY: Creature Nataways? 200

CREATURE: What?

BIG JOEY: You talk too much.

CREATURE: I tole you once I tole you twice I don't mind . . .

(*But* PIERRE ST. PIERRE *comes bursting in, in a state of great excitement.*)

PIERRE: (*Addressing the case of beer directly.*) Hallelujah! Have you heard the news? 205

CREATURE: Pierre St. Pierre. Chris'sakes, knock. You're walkin' into a civilized house.

PIERRE: The news. Have you heard the news?

CREATURE: I'll tell you a piece of news. Anyways, we come in the door and guess who . . . 210

BIG JOEY: (*To* CREATURE.) Sit down.

PIERRE: Gimme a beer.

CREATURE: (*To* PIERRE.) Sit down.

PIERRE: Gimme a beer.

BIG JOEY: Give him a fuckin' beer. (*But* PIERRE *has already* 215 *grabbed, opened and is drinking a beer.*)

CREATURE: Have a beer.

PIERRE: (*Talking out the side of his mouth, as he continues drinking.*) Tank you.

BIG JOEY: Talk. 220

PIERRE: (*Putting his emptied bottle down triumphantly and grabbing another beer.*) Toast me.

BIG JOEY: Spit it out.

CREATURE: Chris'sakes.

PIERRE: Toast me. 225

CREATURE: Toast you? The hell for?

PIERRE: Shut up. Just toast me.

CREATURE/BIG JOEY: Toast.

PIERRE: Tank you. You just toasted "The Ref."

CREATURE: (*To* PIERRE.) The ref? (*To* BIG JOEY.) The what? 230

PIERRE: "The Ref!"

CREATURE: The ref of the what?

PIERRE: The ref. I'm gonna be the referee down at the arena. Big Joey's arena. The Wasaychigan Hill Hippodrome.

CREATURE: We already got a referee. 235

PIERRE: Yeah, but this here's different, this here's special.

BIG JOEY: I'd never hire a toothless old bootlegger like you.

PIERRE: They play their first game in just a coupla days. Against the Canoe Lake Bravettes. And I got six teeth left so you just keep your trap shut about my teeth. 240

CREATURE: The Canoe Lake Bravettes?

BIG JOEY: Who's "they?"

PIERRE: Haven't you heard?

BIG JOEY: Who's "they?"

PIERRE: I don't believe this. 245

BIG JOEY: Who's "they?"

PIERRE: I don't believe this. (BIG JOEY *bangs* PIERRE *on the head.*) Oww, you big bully! The Wasaychigan Hill Wailerettes, of course. I'm talkin' about the Wasy Wailerettes, who else geez. 250

CREATURE: The Wasy Wailerettes? Chris'sakes . . .

PIERRE: Dominique Ladouche, Black Lady Halked, that terrible Dictionary woman, Fluffy Sainte-Marie, Dry Lips Manigitogan, Leonarda Lee Starblanket, Annie Cook, June Bug McLeod, Big Bum Pegahmagahbow, all twenty-seven of 255 'em. Them women from right here on this reserve, a whole batch of 'em, they upped and they said: "Bullshit! Ain't nobody on the face of this earth's gonna tell us us women's got no business playin' hockey. That's bullshit!" That's what they said: "Bullshit!" So. They took matters into their own hands. And, holy shit la marde, I almost forgot to tell you my wife Veronique St. Pierre, she went and made up her mind she's joinin' the Wasy Wailerettes, only the other women wouldn't let her at first on account she never had no babies—cuz, you see, you gotta be pregnant or have piles and piles of babies to be a Wasy Wailerette—but my wife, she put her foot down and she says: "Zhaboonigan Peterson may be just my adopted daughter and she may be retarded as a doormat but she's still my baby." That's what she says to 'em. And she's on and they're playin' hockey and the Wasy Wailerettes, they're just a-rarin' to go, who woulda thunk it, huh?

CREATURE: Ho-leee!

PIERRE: God's truth . . .

BIG JOEY: They never booked the ice.

PIERRE: Ha! Booked it through Gazelle Nataways. Sure as I'm alive and walkin' these treacherous icy roads . . .

BIG JOEY: Hang on.

PIERRE: . . . god's truth in all its naked splendor. (*As he pops open yet another beer.*) I kid you not, gentlemen, not for one slippery goddamn minute. Toast!

BIG JOEY: (*Grabbing the bottle right out of* PIERRE's *mouth.*) Where'd you sniff out all this crap?

PIERRE: From my wife, who else? My wife, Veronique St. Pierre, she told me. She says to me: "Pierre St. Pierre, you'll eat your shorts but I'm playin' hockey and I don't care what you say. Or think." And she left. No. First, she cleaned out my wallet, (*Grabs his beer back from* BIG JOEY's *hand.*) grabbed her big brown rosaries from off the wall. Then she left. Just slammed the door and left. Period. I just about ate my shorts. Toast!

CREATURE: Shouldn't we . . . shouldn't we stop them?

PIERRE: Phhht! . . . (CREATURE *just misses getting spat on.*)

CREATURE: Ayoah!

PIERRE: . . . Haven't seen hide nor hair of 'em since. Gone to Sudbury. Every single last one of 'em. Piled theirselves into seven cars and just took off. Them back wheels was squealin' and rattlin' like them little jinger bells. Just past tea-time. Shoppin'. Hockey equipment. Phhht! (*Again,* CREATURE *just misses getting spat on.*)

CREATURE: Ayoah! It's enough to give you the shits every time he opens his mouth.

PIERRE: And they picked me. Referee.

BIG JOEY: And why you, may I ask?

PIERRE: (*Faking humility.*) Oh, I don't know. Somethin' about the referee here's too damn perschnickety. That drumbangin' young whipperschnapper, Simon Starblanket, (*Grabbing yet another beer.*) he's got the rules all mixed up or somethin' like that, is what they says. They kinda wanna play it their own way. So they picked me. Toast me.

CREATURE: Toast.

PIERRE: To the ref.

CREATURE: To the ref.

PIERRE: Tank you. (*They both drink.*) Ahhh. (*Pause. To* BIG JOEY.) So. I want my skates.

CREATURE: Your skates?

PIERRE: My skates. I want 'em back.

CREATURE: The hell's he talkin' about now?

PIERRE: They're here. I know they're here. I loaned 'em to you, remember?

BIG JOEY: Run that by me again?

PIERRE: I loaned 'em to you. That Saturday night Gazelle Nataways came in that door with her TV and her suitcase and you and me we were sittin' right there on that old chesterfield with Lalala Lacroix sittin' between us and I loaned you my skates in return for that forty-ouncer of rye and Gazelle Nataways plunked her TV down, marched right up to Lalala Lacroix, slapped her in the face and chased her out the door. But we still had time to make the deal whereby if I wanted my skates back you'd give 'em back to me if I gave you back your forty-ouncer, right? Right. (*Produces the bottle from under his coat.*) Ta-da! Gimme my skates.

BIG JOEY: You sold them skates. They're mine.

PIERRE: Never you mind, Big Joey, never you mind. I want my skates. Take this. Go on. Take it.

(BIG JOEY *fishes one skate out from under the couch.*)

CREATURE: (*To himself, as he sits on the couch.*) Women playin' hockey. Ho-leee!

(BIG JOEY *and* PIERRE *exchange bottle and skate.*)

PIERRE: Tank you. (*He makes a triumphant exit.* BIG JOEY *merely sits there and waits knowingly. Silence. Then* PIERRE *suddenly re-enters.*) There's only one. (*Silence.*) Well, where the hell's the other one? (*Silence.* PIERRE *nearly explodes with indignation.*) Gimme back my bottle! Where's the other one?

BIG JOEY: You got your skate. I got my bottle.

PIERRE: Don't talk backwards at me. I'm your elder.

CREATURE: It's gone.

PIERRE: Huh?

CREATURE: Gone. The other skate's gone, right, Big Joey?

PIERRE: Gone? Where?

CREATURE: My wife Gazelle Nataways . . .

PIERRE: . . . your ex-wife . . .

CREATURE: . . . she threw it out the door two years ago the night Spooky Lacroix went crazy in the head and tried to come and rip Gazelle Nataways' door off for cheatin' at the bingo. Just about killed Spooky Lacroix too, right, Big Joey?

PIERRE: So where's my other skate?

CREATURE: At Spooky Lacroix's, I guess.

PIERRE: Aw, shit la marde, you'se guys don't play fair.

BIG JOEY: You go over to Spooky Lacroix's and you tell him I told you you could have your skate back.

PIERRE: No way, José. Spooky Lacroix's gonna preach at me.

BIG JOEY: Preach back.

PIERRE: You come with me. You used to be friends with Spooky Lacroix. You talk to Spooky Lacroix. Spooky Lacroix likes you.

BIG JOEY: He likes you too.

PIERRE: Yeah, but he likes you better. Oh, shit la marde! (*As he takes another beer out of the case.*) And I almost forgot to tell you they decided to make Gazelle Nataways captain of the Wasy Wailerettes. I mean, she kind of . . . decided on her own, if you know what I mean.

BIG JOEY: Spooky Lacroix's waitin' for you.

PIERRE: How do you know?

BIG JOEY: God told me.

PIERRE: (*Pause.* PIERRE *actually wonders to himself. Then:*) Aw,
375   bullshit.

(*Exits. Silence. Then* BIG JOEY *and* CREATURE *look at each other, break down and laugh themselves into prolonged hysterical fits. After a while, they calm down and come to a dead stop. They sit and think. They look at the hockey game on the television. Then, dead serious, they turn to each other.*)

CREATURE: Women . . . Gazelle Nataways . . . hockey? Ho-leee . . .

BIG JOEY: (*Still holding* PIERRE's *bottle of whiskey.*) Chris'-sakes . . .

(*Fade-out.*

From this darkness emerges the sound of SPOOKY LACROIX's *voice, singing with great emotion. As he sings, the lights fade in on his kitchen, where* DICKIE BIRD HALKED *is sitting across the table from* SPOOKY LACROIX. DICKIE BIRD *is scribbling on a piece of paper with a pencil.* SPOOKY *is knitting (pale blue baby booties). A bible sits on the table to the left of* SPOOKY, *a knitting pattern to his right. The place is covered with knitted doodads: knitted doilies, tea cozy, a tacky picture of "The Last Supper" with knitted frame and, on the wall, as subtly conspicuous as possible, a crucifix with pale blue knitted baby booties covering each of its four extremities. Throughout this scene,* SPOOKY *periodically consults the knitting pattern, wearing tiny little reading glasses, perched "just so" on the end of his nose. He knits with great difficulty and, therefore, with great concentration, sometimes, in moments of excitement, getting the bible and the knitting pattern mixed up with each other. He has tremendous difficulty getting the "disturbed"* DICKIE BIRD *to sit still and pay attention.*)

380 SPOOKY: (*Singing.*) Everybody oughta know. Everybody
    oughta know. Who Jesus is. (*Speaking.*) This is it. This is the
    end. Igwani eeweepoonaskeewuk. ("The end of the world is
    at hand.") Says right here in the book. Very, very, very impor-
    tant to read the book. If you want the Lord to come into your
385   life, Dickie Bird Halked, you've got to read the book. Not
    much time left. Yessiree. 1990. The last year. This will be the
    last year of our lives. Clear as a picture. The end of the world
    is here. At last. About time too, with the world going crazy,
    people shooting, killing each other left, right and center. Jet
390   planes full of people crashing into the bushes, lakes turning
    black, fish choking to death. Terrible. Terrible. (DICKIE BIRD
    shoves a note he's been scribbling over to SPOOKY.) What's
    this? (SPOOKY *reads, with some difficulty.*) "How . . . do . . .
    you . . . make . . . babies?" (*Shocked.*) Dickie Bird Halked? At
395   your age? Surely. Anyway. That young Starblanket boy who
    went and shot himself. Right here. Right in the einsteins.
    Bleeding from the belly, all this white mushy stuff come ooz-
    ing out. Yuch! Brrr! I guess there's just nothing better to do
    for the young people on this reserve these days than go
400   around shooting their einsteins out from inside their bellies.
    But the Lord has had enough. He's sick of it. No more, he
    says, no more. This is it. (DICKIE BIRD *shoves another note
    over.* SPOOKY *pauses to read. And finishes.*) Why, me and
    Lalala, we're married. And we're gonna have a baby. Period.
405   Now. When the world comes to an end? The sky will open
    up. The clouds will part. And the Lord will come down in a
    holy vapor. And only those who are born-again Christian will

go with him when he goes back up. And the rest? You know
what's gonna happen to the rest? They will die. Big Joey, for
instance, they will go to hell and they will burn for their 410
wicked, whorish ways. But we will be taken up into the
clouds to spend eternity surrounded by the wondrous and the
mystical glory of god. Clear as a picture, Dickie Bird Halked,
clear as a picture. So I'm telling you right now, you've got to
read the book. Very, very, very important. (DICKIE BIRD 415
shoves a third note over to SPOOKY. SPOOKY *reads and finishes.*) Why, Wellington Halked's your father, Dickie Bird
Halked. Don't you be asking questions like that. My sister,
Black Lady Halked, that's your mother. Right? And because
Wellington Halked is married to Black Lady Halked, he is 420
your father. And don't you ever let no one tell you different.

(*Black-out. From the darkness of the theater emerges the magical flickering of a luminescent powwow dancing bustle. As it moves gradually towards the downstage area, a second—and larger—bustle appears on the upper level of the set, also flickering magically and moving about. The two bustles "play" with each other, almost affectionately, looking like two giant fire flies. The smaller bustle finally reaches the downstage area and from behind it emerges the face of* SIMON STARBLANKET. *He is dancing and chanting in a forest made of light and shadows. The larger bustle remains on the upper level; behind it is the entire person of* NANABUSH *as the spirit of* PATSY PEGAHMAGAHBOW, *a vivacious young girl of eighteen with a very big bum (i.e., an oversized prosthetic bum). From this level,* NANABUSH/PATSY *watches and "plays" with the proceedings on the lower level. The giant full moon is in full bloom behind her. From the very beginning of all this, and in counterpoint to* SIMON's *chanting, also emerges the sound of someone playing a harmonica, a sad, mournful tune. It is* ZACHARY JEREMIAH KEECHIGEESIK, *stuck in the bush in his embarrassing state, playing his heart out. Then the harmonica stops and, from the darkness, we hear* ZACHARY's *voice.*)

ZACHARY: Hey. (SIMON *hears this, looks behind, but sees noth-
    ing and continues his chanting and dancing.* SIMON *chants
    and dances as though he were desperately trying to find the
    right chant and dance. Then:*) Pssst! 425
SIMON: Awinuk awa? ("Who's this?")
ZACHARY: (*In a hoarse whisper.*) Simon Starblanket.
SIMON: Neee, Zachary Jeremiah Keechigeesik. Awus! ("Go
    away!") Katha peeweestatooweemin. ("Don't come bother-
    ing me [with your words].") 430

(*Finally,* ZACHARY *emerges from the shadows and from behind a large rock, carrying his harmonica in one hand and holding his torn pants together as best he can with the other.* SIMON *ignores him and continues with his chanting and dancing.*)

ZACHARY: W-w-w-what's it cost to get one of them dough-
    making machines?
SIMON: (*Not quite believing his ears.*) What?
ZACHARY: Them dough-making machines. What's it cost to
    buy one of them? 435
SIMON: A Hobart?
ZACHARY: A what?

---

428 **Neee** probably the most common Cree expression, meaning something like "Oh, you," or "My goodness"

SIMON: Hobart. H-O-B-A-R-T. Hobart.

ZACHARY: (*To himself.*) Hobart. Hmmm.

440 SIMON: (*Amused at the rather funny-looking* ZACHARY.) Neee, machi ma-a, ("Oh you, but naturally,") Westinghouse for refrigerators, Kellogg's for corn flakes igwa ("and") Hobart for dough-making machines. Kinsitootawin na? ("Get it?") Brand name. Except we used to call it "the pig" because it 445 had this . . . piggish kind of motion to it. But never mind. Awus. Don't bother me.

ZACHARY: What's it cost to get this . . . pig?

SIMON: (*Laughing.*) Neee, Zachary Jeremiah, here you are, one of Wasy's most respected citizens, standing in the middle 450 of the bush on a Saturday night in February freezing your buns off and you want to know how much a pig costs?

ZACHARY: (*Vehemently.*) I promised Hera I'd have all this in-formation by tonight we were supposed to sit down and dis-cuss the budget for this damn bakery tonight and here I went 455 and messed it all up thank god I ran into you because now you're the only person left on this whole reserve who might have the figures I need what's this damn dough-making ma-chine cost come on now tell me!

SIMON: (*A little cowed.*) Neee, about four thousand bucks. 460 Maybe five.

ZACHARY: You don't know for sure? But you worked there.

SIMON: I was only the dishwasher, Zachary Jeremiah, I didn't own the place. Mama Louisa was a poor woman. She had re-ally old equipment, most of which she dragged over herself 465 all the way from Italy after the Second World War. It wouldn't cost the same today.

ZACHARY: Five thousand dollars for a Mobart, hmmm . . .

SIMON: Hobart.

ZACHARY: I wish I had a piece of paper to write all this down, 470 sheesh. You got a piece of paper on you?

SIMON: No. Just . . . this. (*Holding the dancing bustle up.*) Why are you holding yourself like that?

ZACHARY: I was . . . standing on the road down by Andy Manigitogan's place when this car came by and wooof! My 475 pants ripped. Ripped right down the middle. And my shorts, well, they just . . . took off. How do you like that, eh?

SIMON: Nope. I don't like it. Neee, awus. Kigithaskin. ("You're lying to me.")

ZACHARY: W-w-w-why would I pull your leg for? I don't really 480 mind it except it is damn cold out here.

(*At this point,* NANABUSH/PATSY, *on the upper level, scurries closer to get a better look, her giant powwow dancing bustle flick-ering magically in the half-light.* SIMON's *attention is momen-tarily pulled away by this fleeting vision.*)

SIMON: Hey! Did you see that?

(*But* ZACHARY, *too caught up with his own dilemma, does not notice.*)

ZACHARY: I'm very, very upset right now . . .

SIMON: . . . I thought I just saw Patsy Pegahmagahbow . . . with this . . .

485 ZACHARY: (*As he looks, perplexed, in the direction* SIMON *indi-cates.*) . . . do you think . . . my two ordinary convection ovens . . .

SIMON: (*Calling out.*) Patsy? . . . (*Pause. Then, slowly, he turns back to* ZACHARY.) . . . like . . . she made this for me,

eh? (*Referring to the bustle.*) She and her step-mother, Rosie 490 Kakapetum, back in September, after my mother's funeral. Well, I was out here thinking, if this . . . like, if this . . . dance didn't come to me real natural, like from deep inside of me, then I was gonna burn it. (*Referring to the bustle.*) Right here on this spot. Cuz then . . . it doesn't mean anything real to 495 me, does it? Like, it's false . . . it's driving me crazy, this dream where Indian people are just dropping off like flies . . .

(NANABUSH/PATSY *begins to "play" with the two men, almost as if with the help of the winter night's magic and the power of the full moon, she were weaving a spell around* SIMON *and* ZACHARY.)

ZACHARY: (*Singing softly to himself.*) Hot cross buns. Hot cross buns. One a penny, two a penny, hot cross buns . . .

SIMON: . . . something has to be done . . . 500

ZACHARY: (*Speaking.*) . . . strawberry pies . . .

SIMON: . . . in this dream . . .

ZACHARY: . . . so fresh and flakey they fairly bubble over with the cream from the very breast of Mother Nature herself . . .

SIMON: . . . the drum has to come back, mistigwuskeek ("the 505 drum") . . .

ZACHARY: . . . bran muffins, cherry tarts . . .

SIMON: . . . the medicine, the power, this . . .

(*Holding the bustle up in the air.*)

ZACHARY: . . . butter tarts . . .

SIMON: . . . has to come back. We've got to learn to dance 510 again.

ZACHARY: . . . tarts tarts tarts upside-down cakes cakes cakes and not to forget, no, never, ever to forget that Black Forest Cake . . .

SIMON: . . . Patsy Pegahmagahbow . . . 515

ZACHARY: . . . cherries jubilee . . .

SIMON: . . . her step-mother, Rosie Kakapetum, the medicine woman . . .

ZACHARY: . . . lemon meringue pie . . .

SIMON: . . . the power . . . 520

ZACHARY: . . . baked Alaska . . .

SIMON: . . . Nanabush! . . .

ZACHARY: (*Then suddenly, with bitterness.*) . . . Gazelle Nat-aways. K'skanagoos! ("The female dog!")

(*All of a sudden, from the darkness of the winter night, emerges a strange, eery sound; whether it is wolves howling or women wail-ing, we are not sure at first. And whether this sound comes from somewhere deep in the forest, from the full moon or where, we are not certain. But there is definitely a "spirit" in the air. The sound of this wailing is under-cut by the sound of rocks hitting boards, or the sides of houses, echoing, as in a vast empty chamber. Gradually, as* SIMON *speaks,* ZACHARY—*filled with confusing emotion as he is—takes out his harmonica, sits down on the large rock and begins to play, a sad, mournful melody, tinged, as always, with a touch of the blues.*)

SIMON: . . . I have my arms around this rock, this large black 525 rock sticking out of the ground, right here on this spot. And then I hear this baby crying, from inside this rock. The baby is crying out my name. As if I am somehow responsible for it being caught inside that rock. I can't move. My arms, my whole body, stuck to this rock. Then this . . . eagle . . . lands 530

beside me, right over there. But this bird has three faces, three women. And the eagle says to me: "the baby is crying, my grand-child is crying to hear the drum again." (NANABUSH/PATSY, *her face surrounded by the brilliant feath-*
535 *ers of her bustle, so that she looks like some fantastic, mysteri-ous bird, begins to wail, her voice weaving in and out of the other wailing voices.*) There's this noise all around us, as if rocks are hitting the sides of houses—echoing and echoing like in a vast empty room—and women are wailing. The
540 whole world is filled with this noise. (*Then* SIMON, *too, wails, a heart-searing wail. From here on, all the wailing begins to fade.*) Then the eagle is gone and the rock cracks and this mass of flesh, covered with veins and blood, comes oozing out and a woman's voice somewhere is singing something
545 about angels and god and angels and god . . .

(*The wailing has now faded into complete silence.* ZACHARY *finally rises from his seat on the rock.*)

ZACHARY: . . . I dreamt I woke up at Gazelle Nataways' place with no shorts on. And I got this nagging suspicion them shorts are still over there. If you could just go on over there now . . . I couldn't have been over there. I mean, there's my
550 wife Hera. And there's my bakery. And this bakery could do a lot for the Indian people. Economic development. Jobs. Bread. Apple pie. So you see, there's an awful lot that's hanging on them shorts. This is a good chance for you to do something for your people, Simon, if you know what I
555 mean . . .

SIMON: I'm the one who has to bring the drum back. And it's Patsy's medicine power, that stuff she's learning from her step-mother Rosie Kakapetum that . . . helps me . . .

ZACHARY: I go walking into my house with no underwear,
560 pants ripped right down the middle, not a shred of budget in sight and wooof! . . .

(PIERRE ST. PIERRE *comes bursting in on the two men with his one skate in hand, taking them completely by surprise.* NANABUSH/PATSY *disappears.*)

ZACHARY: Pierre St. Pierre! Just the man . . .

PIERRE: No time. No time. Lalala Lacroix's having a baby any minute now so I gotta get over to Spook's before she pops.
565 SIMON: I can go get Rosie Kakapetum.

PIERRE: Too old. Too old. She can't be on the team.

SIMON: Neee, what team? Rosie Kakapetum's the last mid-wife left in Wasy, Pierre St. Pierre, of course she can't be on a team.

570 ZACHARY: (*To* PIERRE.) You know that greasy shit-brown chesterfield over at Gazelle Nataways?

SIMON: (*To* ZACHARY.) Mind you, if there was a team of mid-wives, chee-i? ("eh?") Wha!

PIERRE: Gazelle Nataways? Hallelujah, haven't you heard the
575 news?

ZACHARY: What? . . . you mean . . . it's out already?

PIERRE: All up and down Wasaychigan Hill . . .

ZACHARY: (*Thoughtfully, to himself, as it dawns on him.*) The whole place knows.

580 PIERRE: . . . clean across Manitoulin Island and right to the outskirts of Sudbury . . .

ZACHARY: Lordy, lordy, lordy . . .

PIERRE: Gazelle Nataways, Dominique Ladouche, Black Lady Halked, that terrible Dictionary woman, Fluffy Sainte-
585 Marie, Dry Lips Manigitogan, Leonarda Lee Starblanket,

Annie Cook, June Bug McLeod, Big Bum Pegahmagah-bow . . .

SIMON: Patsy Pegahmagahbow. Get it straight . . .

PIERRE: Quiet! I'm not finished . . . all twenty-seven of 'em . . .

590 SIMON: Neee, Zachary Jeremiah, your goose is cooked.

PIERRE: Phhht! Cooked and burnt right down to a nice crispy pitch black cinder because your wife Hera Keechigeesik is in on it too.

(ZACHARY, *reeling from the horror of it all, finally sits back down on the rock.*)

SIMON: Patsy Pegahmagahbow is pregnant, Pierre St. Pierre.
595 She can't go running around all over Manitoulin Island with a belly that's getting bigger by the . . .

SIMON: Aw, they're all pregnant, them women, or have piles and piles of babies and I'll be right smack dab in the middle of it all just a-blowin' my whistle and a-throwin' that dirty lit-
600 tle black thingie around . . .

ZACHARY: (*Rising from the rock.*) Now you listen here, Pierre St. Pierre. I may have lost my shorts under Gazelle Nat-aways' greasy shit-brown chesterfield not one hour ago and I may have lost my entire life, not to mention my bakery, as a
605 result of that one very foolish mistake but I'll have you know that my shorts, they are clean as a whistle, I change them every day, my favorite color is light blue and black and crusted with shit my shorts most certainly are not!

SIMON: (*Surprised and thrilled at* ZACHARY's *renewed "fight-*
610 *ing" spirit.*) Wha!

PIERRE: Whoa! Easy, Zachary Jeremiah, easy there. Not one stitch of your shorts has anything whatsoever to do with the revolution.

SIMON: Pierre St. Pierre, what revolution are you wheezing
615 and snorting on about?

PIERRE: The puck. I'm talkin' about the puck.

ZACHARY: The puck?

SIMON: The puck?

PIERRE: Yes, the puck. The puck, the puck, the puck and
620 nothin' but the goddam puck they're playin' hockey, them women from right here on this reserve, they're playin' hockey and nothin', includin' Zachary Jeremiah Keechi-geesik's bright crispy undershorts, is gonna stop 'em.

SIMON: Women playing hockey. Neee, watstagatch! ("Good
625 grief!")

PIERRE: "Neee, watstagatch" is right because they're in Sud-bury, as I speak, shoppin' for hockey equipment, and I'm the referee! Outa my way! Or the Lacroixs will pop before I get there.

(*He begins to exit.*)

630 ZACHARY: Pierre St. Pierre, get me my shorts or I'll report your bootleg joint to the police.

PIERRE: No time. No time.

(*Exits.*)

ZACHARY: (*Calling out.*) Did Hera go to Sudbury, too? (*But* PIERRE *is gone.*)

635 SIMON: (*Thoughtfully to himself, as he catches another glimpse of* NANABUSH/PATSY *and her bustle.*) . . . rocks hitting boards . . .

ZACHARY: (*To himself.*) What in God's name is happening to Wasaychigan Hill . . .

640   SIMON: . . . women wailing . . .

ZACHARY: *(With even greater urgency.)* Do you think those two ordinary convection ovens are gonna do the job or should I get one of them great big pizza ovens right away?

SIMON: . . . pucks . . .

645   ZACHARY: Simon, I'm desperate!

SIMON: *(Finally, snapping out of his speculation and looking straight into* ZACHARY's *face.)* Neee, Zachary Jeremiah. Okay. Goes like this. *(Then, very quickly:)* It depends on what you're gonna bake, eh? Like if you're gonna bake bread

650   and, like, lots of it, you're gonna need one of them great big ovens but if you're gonna bake just muffins . . .

ZACHARY: *(In the background.)* . . . muffins, nah, not just muffins . . .

SIMON: . . . then all you need is one of them ordinary little

655   ovens but like I say, I was only the dishwasher . . .

ZACHARY: How many employees were there in your bakery?

SIMON: . . . it depends on how big a community you're gonna serve, Zachary Jeremiah . . .

ZACHARY: . . . nah, Wasy, just Wasy, to start with . . .

660   SIMON: . . . like, we had five, one to make the dough—like, mix the flour and the water and the yeast and all that—like, this guy had to be at work by six a.m., that's gonna be hard here in Wasy, Zachary Jeremiah, I'm telling you that right now . . .

665   ZACHARY: . . . nah, I can do that myself, no problem . . .

SIMON: . . . then we had three others to roll the dough and knead and twist and punch and pound it on this great big wooden table . . .

ZACHARY: . . . I'm gonna need a great big wooden table? . . .

670   SIMON: . . . hard wood, Zachary Jeremiah, not soft wood. And then one to actually bake the loaves, like, we had these long wooden paddles, eh? . . .

ZACHARY: . . . paddles . . .

SIMON: . . . yeah, paddles, Zachary Jeremiah, real long ones. It

675   was kinda neat, actually . . .

ZACHARY: . . . go on, go on . . .

SIMON: Listen here, Zachary Jeremiah, I'm going to Sudbury next Saturday, okay? And if you wanna come along, I can take you straight to Mama Louisa's Pasticerria myself. I'll in-

680   troduce you to the crusty old girl and you can take a good long look at her rubbery old Hobart, how's that? You can even touch it if you want, neee . . .

ZACHARY: . . . really? . . .

SIMON: Me? I'm asking Patsy Pegahmagahbow to marry me . . .

685   ZACHARY: . . . Simon, Simon . . .

SIMON: . . . and we're gonna hang two thousand of these things *(Referring to his dancing bustle.)* all over Manitoulin Island, me and Patsy and our baby. And me and Patsy and our baby and this Nanabush character, we're gonna be dancing up

690   and down Wasaychigan Hill like nobody's business cuz I'm gonna go out there and I'm gonna bring that drum back if it kills me.

ZACHARY: *(Pause. Then, quietly.)* Get me a safety pin.

SIMON: *(Pause.)* Neee, okay. And you, Zachary Jeremiah

695   Keechigeesik, you're gonna see a Hobart such as you have never seen ever before in your entire life!

SIMON/ZACHARY: *(Smiling, almost laughing, at each other.)* Neee . . .

(Black-out.

Lights up on the upper level, where we see this bizarre vision of NANABUSH, *now in the guise of* BLACK LADY HALKED, *nine months pregnant (i.e., wearing a huge, out-sized prosthetic belly). Over this, she wears a maternity gown and, pacing the floor slowly, holds a huge string of rosary beads. She recites the rosary quietly to herself. She is also drinking a beer and, obviously, is a little unsteady on her feet because of this.*

Fade-in on the lower level into SPOOKY LACROIX's *kitchen.* DICKIE BIRD HALKED *is on his knees, praying fervently to this surrealistic, miraculous vision of "the Madonna" (i.e., his own mother), which he actually sees inside his own mind. Oblivious to all this,* SPOOKY LACROIX *sits at his table, still knitting his baby booties and preaching away.)*

SPOOKY: Dickie Bird Halked? I want you to come to heaven with me. I insist. But before you do that, you take one of   700 them courses in sign language, help me prepare this reserve for the Lord. Can't you just see yourself, standing on that podium in the Wasaychigan Hill Hippodrome, talking sign language to the people? Talking about the Lord and how close we are to the end? I could take a break. And these poor   705 people with their meaningless, useless . . .

*(*PIERRE ST. PIERRE *comes bursting in and marches right up to* SPOOKY. *The vision of* NANABUSH/BLACK LADY HALKED *disappears.)*

PIERRE: Alright. Hand it over.

SPOOKY: *(Startled out of his wits.)* Pierre St. Pierre! You went and mixed up my booty!

PIERRE: I know it's here somewhere.   710

SPOOKY: Whatever it is you're looking for, you're not getting it until you bring the Lord into your life.

PIERRE: My skate. Gimme my skate.

SPOOKY: I don't have no skate. Now listen to me.

PIERRE: My skate. The skate Gazelle Nataways threw at you   715 and just about killed you.

SPOOKY: What the hell are you gonna do with a skate at this hour of the night?

PIERRE: Haven't you heard the news?

SPOOKY: *(Pauses to think.)* No, I haven't heard any news.   720

*(*DICKIE BIRD *gets up and starts to wander around the kitchen. He looks around at random, first out the window, as if to see who has been chanting, then, eventually, he zeroes in on the crucifix on the wall and stands there looking at it. Finally, he takes it off the wall and plays with its cute little booties.)*

PIERRE: The women. I'm gonna be right smack dab in the middle of it all. The revolution. Right here in Wasaychigan Hill.

SPOOKY: The Chief or the priest. Which one are they gonna revolution?   725

PIERRE: No, no, no. Dominique Ladouche, Black Lady Halked, that terrible Dictionary woman, that witch Gazelle Nataways, Fluffy Sainte-Marie, Dry Lips Manigitogan, Leonarda Lee Starblanket, Annie Cook, June Bug McLeod, Big Bum Pegahmagahbow, all twenty-seven of 'em. Even my   730 wife, Veronique St. Pierre, she'll be right smack dab in the middle of it all. Defense.

SPOOKY: Defense? The Americans. We're being attacked. Is the situation that serious?

735 PIERRE: No, no, no, for Chris'sakes. They're playin' hockey. Them women are playin' hockey. Dead serious they are too.

SPOOKY: No.

PIERRE: Yes.

SPOOKY: Thank the Lord this is the last year!

740 PIERRE: Don't you care to ask?

SPOOKY: Thank the Lord the end of the world is coming this year!

(Gasping, he marches up to DICKIE BIRD.)

PIERRE: I'm the referee, dammit.

SPOOKY: Watch your language.

(Grabbing the crucifix from DICKIE BIRD.)

745 PIERRE: That's what I mean when I say I'm gonna be right smack dab in the middle of it all. You don't listen to me.

SPOOKY: *(As he proceeds to put the little booties back on the crucifix.)* But you're not a woman.

PIERRE: You don't have to be. To be a referee these days, you
750 can be anything, man or woman, don't matter which away. So gimme my skate.

SPOOKY: What skate?

PIERRE: The skate Gazelle Nataways just about killed you with after the bingo that time.

755 SPOOKY: Oh, that. I hid it in the basement. *(PIERRE opens a door, falls in and comes struggling out with a mouse trap stuck to a finger.)* Pierre St. Pierre, what the hell are you doing in Lalala's closet?

PIERRE: Well, where the hell's the basement?

(He frees his finger.)

760 SPOOKY: Pierre St. Pierre, you drink too much. You gotta have the Lord in your life.

PIERRE: I don't need the Lord in my life, for god's sake, I need my skate. I gotta practice my figure eights.

SPOOKY: *(As he begins to put the crucifix back up on the wall.)*
765 You gotta promise me before I give you your skate.

PIERRE: I promise.

SPOOKY: *(Unaware, he threatens* PIERRE *with the crucifix, holding it up against his neck.)* You gotta have the Lord come into your life.

770 PIERRE: Alright, alright.

SPOOKY: For how long?

PIERRE: My whole life. I promise I'm gonna bring the Lord into my life and keep him there right up until the day I die just gimme my goddamn skate.

775 SPOOKY: Cross my heart.

PIERRE: Alright? Cross your heart.

(Neither man makes a move, until SPOOKY, *finally catching on, throws* PIERRE *a look.* PIERRE *crosses himself.)*

SPOOKY: Good.

(Exits to the basement.)

PIERRE: *(Now alone with* DICKIE BIRD, *half-whispering to him. As* PIERRE *speaks,* DICKIE BIRD *again takes the crucifix off the
780 wall and returns with it to his seat and there takes the booties off in haphazard fashion.)* Has he been feedin' you this crappola, too? Don't you be startin' that foolishness. That Spooky Lacroix's so fulla shit he wouldn't know a two thousand year-old Egyptian Sphinxter if he came face to face with one.
785 He's just preachifyin' at you because you're the one person

on this reserve who can't argue back. You listen to me. I was there in the same room as your mother when she gave birth to you. So I know well who you are and where you come from. I remember the whole picture. Even though we were all in a bit of a fizzy . . . I remember. Do you know, Dickie
790 Bird Halked, that you were named after that bar? Anyone ever tell you that? *(DICKIE BIRD starts to shake.* PIERRE *takes fright.)* Spooky Lacroix, move that holy ass of yours, for fuck's sakes! *(DICKIE BIRD laughs.* PIERRE *makes a weak attempt to laugh along.)* And I'll never forgive your father, Big
795 Joey oops . . . *(DICKIE BIRD reacts.)* . . . I mean, Wellington Halked, for letting your mother do that to you. "It's not good for the people of this world," I says to him "it's not good for 'em to have the first thing they see when they come into the world is a goddamn jukebox." That's what I says to him.
800 Thank god, you survived, Dickie Bird Halked, thank god, seventeen years later you're sittin' here smack-dab in front of me, hail and hearty as cake. Except for your tongue. Talk, Dickie Bird Halked, talk. Say somethin'. Come on. Try this: "Daddy, daddy, daddy." *(DICKIE BIRD shakes his head.)*
805 Come on. Just this once. Maybe it will work. *(Takes* DICKIE BIRD *by the cheeks with one hand.)* "Daddy, daddy, daddy, daddy." *(DICKIE BIRD jumps up and attacks* PIERRE, *looking as though he were about to shove the crucifix down* PIERRE's *throat.* PIERRE *is genuinely terrified. Just then,* SPOOKY *re-
810 enters with the skate.)* Whoa, whoa. Easy. Easy now, Dickie Bird. Easy.

SPOOKY: *(Gasping again at the sight of* DICKIE BIRD *manhandling the crucifix, he makes a bee-line for the boy.)* Dickie Bird Halked? Give me that thing. *(And grabs the crucifix
815 with a flourish. Then he turns to* PIERRE *and holds the skate out with his other hand.)* Promise.

PIERRE: Cross my heart. *(Crosses himself.)*

SPOOKY: *(Replacing the crucifix on the wall and pointing at* PIERRE.) The Lord.
820

PIERRE: The Lord.

(SPOOKY hands the skate over to Pierre. Just then, CREATURE NATAWAYS *stumbles in, now visibly drunk.)*

CREATURE: The Lord!

(Picking on the hapless DICKIE BIRD, CREATURE *roughly shoves the boy down to a chair.)*

PIERRE: *(Holding up both his skates.)* I got 'em both. See? I got 'em.

CREATURE: Hallelujah! Now all you gotta do is learn how to
825 skate.

SPOOKY: Creature Nataways, I don't want you in my house in that condition. Lalala is liable to pop any minute now and I don't want my son to see the first thing he sees when he comes into the world is a drunk.
830

PIERRE: Damn rights!

SPOOKY: . . . you too, Pierre St. Pierre.

CREATURE: Aw! William Lacroix, don't give me that holier than-me, poker-up-the-bum spiritual bull crap . . .
835

SPOOKY: . . . say wha? . . .

CREATURE: Are you preachin' to this boy, William Lacroix? Are you usin' him again to practice your preachy-preachy? Don't do that, William, the boy is helpless. If you wanna practice, go practice on your old buddy, go preach on Big Joey. He's the one who needs it.
840

SPOOKY: You're hurting again, aren't you, Creature Nataways.

CREATURE: Don't listen to Spooky Lacroix, Dickie Bird. You follow Spooky Lacroix and you go right down to the dogs, I'm tellin' you that right now. Hair spray, lysol, vanilla ex-
845 tract, shoe polish, xerox machine juice, he's done it all, this man. If you'd given William Lacroix the chance, he'd have sliced up the Xerox machine and ate it . . .

PIERRE: *(Mockingly, in the background.)* No!

CREATURE: . . . He once drank a Kitty Wells record. He lied to
850 his own mother and he stole her record and he boiled it and swallowed it right up . . .

PIERRE: Good heavens!

(BIG JOEY enters and stands at the door unseen.)

CREATURE: . . . Made the Globe and Mail, too. He's robbed, he's cheated his best friend . . .
855 SPOOKY: Alphonse Nataways? Why are you doing this, may I ask?

CREATURE: Oh, he was bad, Dickie Bird Halked, he was bad. Fifteen years. Fifteen years of his life pukin' his guts out on sidewalks from here to Sicamous, B.C., this man . . .
860 SPOOKY: Shush!

CREATURE: . . . and this is the same man . . .

BIG JOEY: *(Speaking suddenly and laughing, he takes everyone by surprise. They gasp. And practically freeze in their tracks.)* . . . who's yellin' and preachin' about "the Lord!" They
865 oughta retire the beaver and put this guy on the Canadian nickel, he's become a national goddamn symbol, that what you're sayin', Creature Nataways? This the kind of man you wanna become, that what you're sayin' to the boy, Creature Nataways? *(Close up to* DICKIE BIRD.*)* A man who couldn't
870 get a hard-on in front of a woman if you paid him a two dol-lar bill?

SPOOKY: *(Stung to the quick.)* And is this the kind of man you wanna become, Dickie Bird Halked, this MAN who can't take the sight of blood least of all woman's blood, this MAN
875 who, when he sees a woman's blood, chokes up, pukes and faints, how do you like that?

(PIERRE, sensing potential violence, begins to sneak out.)

BIG JOEY: *(Pulls a bottle out of his coat.)* Spooky Lacroix, ig-wani eeweepoonaskeewuk. ("The end of the world is at hand.")

(PIERRE, seeing the bottle, retraces his steps and sits down again, grabbing a tea-cup en route, ready for a drink.)

880 SPOOKY: *(Shocked.)* Get that thing out of my house!

BIG JOEY: Tonight, we're gonna celebrate my wife, Spooky Lacroix, we're gonna celebrate because my wife, the fabu-lous, the incredible Gazelle Delphina Nataways has been crowned Captain of the Wasy Wailerettes. The Rez is makin'
885 history, Spooky Lacroix. The world will never be the same. Come on, it's on me, it's on your old buddy, the old, old buddy you said you'd never, ever forget.

SPOOKY: I told you a long time ago, Big Joey, after what you went and done to my sister, this here boy's own mother,
890 you're no buddy of mine. Get out of my house. Get!

BIG JOEY: *(Handing the bottle of whiskey to* CREATURE.*)* Crea-ture Nataways, celebrate your wife.

CREATURE: *(Raising the bottle in a toast.)* To my wife!

PIERRE: *(Holding his cup out to the bottle.)* Your ex-wife.

BIG JOEY: *(Suddenly quiet and intimate.)* William. William. 895 You and me. You and me, we used to be buddies, kigiskisin? ("Remember?") Wounded Knee. South Dakota. Spring of '73. We parked my van over by that little lake, we swam across, you almost didn't make it and nothin' could get you to swim back. Kigiskisin? So here we're walkin' back through 900 the bush, all the way around this small lake, nothin' on but bare feet and wet undershorts and this black bear come up behind you, kigiskisin? And you freaked out.

(Laughs. PIERRE *tries, as best he can, to create a party atmo-sphere, to little avail.* CREATURE *nervously watches* BIG JOEY *and* SPOOKY. *DICKIE BIRD merely sits there, head down, rocking back and forth.)*

SPOOKY: *(Obviously extremely uncomfortable.)* You freaked out too, ha-ha, ha-ha. 905

BIG JOEY: That bear gave you a real spook, huh? *(Pause. Then, suddenly, he jumps at the other men.)* Boo! *(The other men, including* SPOOKY, *jump, splashing whiskey all over the place.* BIG JOEY *laughs. The other men pretend to laugh.)* That's how you got your name, you old Spook . . . 910

SPOOKY: You were scared too, ha-ha, ha-ha.

BIG JOEY: . . . we get back to the camp and there's Creature and Eugene and Zach and Roscoe, bacon and eggs all ready for us. Christ, I never laughed so hard in my life. But here you were, not laughin' and we'd say: "What's the matter, 915 Spook, you don't like our jokes? And you'd say: "That's good, yeah, that's good." I guess you were laughin' from a different part of yourself, huh? You were beautiful . . .

SPOOKY: That's good, yeah, that's good.

BIG JOEY: *(Getting the bottle back from* CREATURE *and* 920 PIERRE.*)* So tonight, Bear-who-went-and-gave-you-a-real-Spooky Lacroix, we're gonna celebrate another new page in our lives. Wounded Knee Three! Women's version!

PIERRE: Damn rights.

BIG JOEY: *(Raising the bottle up in a toast.)* To my wife! 925

SPOOKY: Ha! Get that thing away from me.

PIERRE: Spooky Lacroix, co-operate. Co-operate for once. The women, the women are playin' hockey.

CREATURE: To my wife!

PIERRE: Your ex-wife. 930

CREATURE: Shut up you toothless old bugger.

SPOOKY: Big Joey, you're not my friend no more.

BIG JOEY: *(Finally grabbing* SPOOKY *roughly by the throat.* CREATURE *jumps to help hold* SPOOKY *still.)* You never let a friend for life go, William Hector Lacroix, not even if you 935 turn your back on your own father, Nicotine Lacroix's spiri-tual teachings and pretend like hell to be this born-again Christian.

SPOOKY: Let go, Creature Nataways, let go of me! *(To* BIG JOEY.*)* For what you did to this boy at that bar seventeen years 940 ago, Joseph Jeremiah McLeod, you are going to hell. To hell! *(*BIG JOEY *baptizes* SPOOKY *with the remainder of the bottle's contents. Breaking free,* SPOOKY *grabs* DICKIE BIRD *and shoves him toward* BIG JOEY.*)* Look at him. He can't even talk. He hasn't talked in seventeen years! *(*DICKIE BIRD *cries* 945 *out, breaks free, grabs the crucifix from off the wall and runs out the door, crying.* SPOOKY *breaks down, falls to the floor and weeps.* BIG JOEY *attempts to pick him up gently, but* SPOOKY *kicks him away.)* Let go of me! Let go!

950 CREATURE: *(Lifting the empty bottle, laughing and crying at the same time.)* To my wife, to my wife, to my wife, to my wife, to my wife . . .

(BIG JOEY *suddenly lifts* SPOOKY *off the floor by the collar and lifts a fist to punch his face. Black-out.*)

Out of this black-out emerges the eery, distant sound of women wailing and pucks hitting boards, echoing and echoing as in a vast empty chamber. The lights come up on DICKIE BIRD HALKED *and* SIMON STARBLANKET, *standing beside each other in the "bleachers" of the hockey arena, watching the "ice" area (i.e., looking out over the audience). The "bleachers" area is actually on the upper level of the set, in a straight line directly in front of* NANABUSH's *perch.* DICKIE BIRD *is still holding* SPOOKY's *crucifix and* SIMON *is still holding his dancing bustle.)*

SIMON: Your grandpa, Nicotine Lacroix, was a medicine man.
955 Hell of a name, but he was a medicine man. Old priest here, Father Boucher, years ago—oh, he was a terrible man—he went and convinced the people old Nicotine Lacroix talked to the devil. That's not true. Nicotine Lacroix was a good man. That's why I want you for my best man. Me and Patsy
960 are getting married a couple of months from now. It's decided. We're gonna have a baby. Then we're going down to South Dakota and we're gonna dance with the Rosebud Sioux this summer. *(Sings as he stomps his foot in the rhythm of a powwow drum.)* ". . . and me I don't wanna go to the moon, I'm gonna leave that moon alone. I just wanna dance
965 with the Rosebud Sioux this summer, yeah, yeah, yeah . . ."

(And he breaks into a chant. DICKIE BIRD *watches, fascinated, particularly by the bustle* SIMON *holds up in the air.*

At this point, ZACHARY JEREMIAH KEECHIGEESIK *approaches timidly from behind a beam, his pants held flimsily together with a huge safety pin. The sound of women wailing and pucks hitting boards now shifts into the sound of an actual hockey arena, just before a big game.)*

ZACHARY: *(To* SIMON.*)* Hey! *(But* SIMON *doesn't hear and continues chanting.)* Pssst!
SIMON: Zachary Jeremiah. Neee, watstagatch!
ZACHARY: Is Hera out there?
970 SIMON: *(Indicating the "ice.")* Yup. There she is.
ZACHARY: Lordy, lordy, lordy . . .
SIMON: Just kidding. She's not out there . . .
ZACHARY: Don't do that to me!
SIMON: . . . yet.
975 ZACHARY: *(Finally coming up to join the young men at the "bleachers.")* You know that Nanabush character you were telling me about a couple of nights ago? What do you say I give his name over to them little gingerbread cookie men I'm gonna be making? For starters. Think that would help
980 any?
SIMON: Neee . . .

(Just then, BIG JOEY *enters and proceeds to get a microphone stand ready for broadcasting the game.* ZACHARY *recoils and goes to stand as far away from him as possible.)*

ZACHARY: *(Looking out over the "ice.")* It's almost noon. They're late getting started.
BIG JOEY: *(Yawning luxuriously.)* That's right. Me and Gazelle
985 Nataways . . . slept in.

(CREATURE NATAWAYS comes scurrying in.)

CREATURE: *(Still talking to himself.)* . . . I tole you once I tole you twice . . . *(Then to the other men.)* Chris' sakes! Are they really gonna do it? Chris'sakes!

(SPOOKY LACROIX enters wearing a woolen scarf he obviously knitted himself. He is still knitting, this time a pale blue baby sweater. He also now sports a black eye and band-aide on his face. All the men, except PIERRE ST. PIERRE, *are now in the "bleachers," standing in a straight line facing the audience, with* DICKIE BIRD *in the center area,* SIMON *and* SPOOKY *to his immediate right and left, respectively.)*

SPOOKY: It's bad luck to start late. I know. I read the interview with Gay Lafleur in last week's Expositor. They won't get far.
990 *(He sees* GAZELLE NATAWAYS *entering the "rink," unseen by the audience. [All the hockey players on the "ice" are unseen by the audience; it is only the men who can actually "see" them.])* Look! Gazelle Nataways went and got her sweater trimmed in the chest area!
995

(Wild cat calls from the men.)

CREATURE: Trimmed it? She's got it plunging down to her oot-see. ("belly button.")
ZACHARY: Ahem. Smokes too much. Lung problems.
BIG JOEY: Nah. More like it's got somethin' to do with the undershorts she's wearin' today.
1000
ZACHARY: *(Fast on the up-take.)* Fuck you!
BIG JOEY: *(Blowing* ZACHARY *a kiss.)* Poosees. ("Pussy cat." [Zachary's childhood nickname.])
SPOOKY: Terrible. Terrible. Tsk, tsk, tsk.

(PIERRE ST. PIERRE enters on the lower level, teetering dangerously on his skates towards the "ice" area downstage. He wears a referee's top and a whistle around his neck.)

PIERRE: *(Checking the names off as he reads from a clipboard.)* 1005
Dominique Ladouche, Black Lady Halked, Annie Cook, June Bug McLeod, Big Bum Pegahmagahbow . . .
SIMON: *(Calling out.)* Patsy Pegahmagahbow, turkey.
PIERRE: Shut up. I'm workin' here. . . . Leonarda Lee Starblanket, that terrible Dictionary woman, Fluffy Sainte-Marie, 1010
Chicken Lips Pegahmagahbow, Dry Lips Manigitogan, Little Hand Manigitogan, Little Girl Manitowabi, Victoria Manitowabi, Belinda Nickikoosimeenicaning, Martha Two-Axe Early-in-the-Morning, her royal highness Gazelle Delphina Nataways, Delia Opekokew, Barbra Nahwegahbow, Gloria 1015
May Eshkibok, Hera Keechigeesik, Tall Mary Ann Patchnose, Short Mary Ann Patchnose, Queen Elizabeth Patchnose, the triplets Marjorie Moose, Maggie May Moose, Mighty Moose and, of course, my wife, Veronique St. Pierre. Yup. They're all there, I hope, and the world is about to explode! 1020
SPOOKY: That's what I've been trying to tell you!

(PIERRE ST. PIERRE, barely able to stand on his skates, hobbles about, obviously getting almost trampled by the hockey players at various times.)

BIG JOEY: *(Now speaking on the microphone. The other men watch the women on the "ice"; some are cheering and whistling, some calling down the game.)* Welcome, ladies igwa gentlemen, welcome one and all to the Wasaychigan 1025
Hill Hip-hip-hippodrome. This is your host for the big game, Big Joey—and they don't call me Big Joey for

nothin'—Chairman, CEO and Proprietor of the Wasaychigan Hill Hippodrome, bringin' you a game such as has never been seen ever before on the ice of any hockey arena anywhere on the island of Manitoulin, anywhere on the face of this country, anywhere on the face of this planet. And there . . .

CREATURE: . . . there's Gazelle Nataways, number one . . .

BIG JOEY: . . . they are, ladies . . .

SPOOKY: . . . terrible, terrible . . .

BIG JOEY: . . . igwa gentlemen . . .

CREATURE: . . . Chris'sakes, that's my wife, Chris'sakes . . .

BIG JOEY: . . . there they are, the most beautiful . . .

SIMON: . . . give 'em hell, Patsy Pegahmagahbow, give 'em hell . . .

BIG JOEY: . . . daring, death- . . .

SIMON: (*To* ZACHARY.) . . . there's Hera Keechigeesik, number nine . . .

BIG JOEY: . . . defying Indian women . . .

SPOOKY: . . . terrible, terrible . . .

BIG JOEY: . . . in the world . . .

ZACHARY: . . . that's my wife . . .

BIG JOEY: . . . the Wasy Wailerettes . . .

(*Clears his throat and tests the microphone by tapping it gently.*)

ZACHARY: . . . lordy, lordy, lordy . . .

CREATURE: Hey, Gazelle Nataways and Hera Keechigeesik are lookin' at each other awful funny. Something bad's gonna happen, I tole you once I tole you twice, something bad's gonna happen . . .

SPOOKY: This is sign from the Lord. This is THE sign . . .

BIG JOEY: Number One Gazelle Nataways, Captain of the Wasy Wailerettes, facing off with Number Nine, Flora McDonald, Captain of the Canoe Lake Bravettes. And referee Pierre St. Pierre drops the puck and takes off like a herd of wild turtles . . .

SIMON: Aw, Spooky Lacroix, eat my shitty shorts, neee . . .

BIG JOEY:[1] . . . Hey, aspin Number Six Dry Lips Manigitogan, right-winger for the Wasy Wailerettes . . .

ZACHARY: . . . look pretty damn stupid, if you ask me. Fifteen thousand dollars for all that new equipment . . .

BIG JOEY: . . . eemaskamat Number Thirteen of the Canoe Lake Bravettes anee-i puck . . .

CREATURE: . . . Cancel the game! Cancel the game! Cancel the game! . . .

(*Etc.*)

BIG JOEY: . . . igwa aspin sipweesinskwataygew. Hey, k'see goochin! (*Off microphone.*) Creature Nataways. Shut up. (*To the other men.*) Get this asshole out of here. . . .

SIMON: Yay, Patsy Pegahmagahbow! Pat-see! Pat-see! Pat-see! . . .

(*Etc.*)

BIG JOEY: (*Back on microphone.*) . . . How, Number Six Dry Lips Manigitogan, right-winger for the Wasy Wailerettes, soogi pugamawew igwa anee-i puck igwa aspin center-line ispathoo ana puck . . .

CREATURE: (*To* SIMON.) Shut up. Don't encourage them . . .

BIG JOEY: . . . ita Number Nine Hera Keechigeesik, left-winger for . . .

SIMON: (*To* CREATURE.) Aw, lay off! Pat-see! Pat-see! Pat-see! . . . (*Etc.*)

BIG JOEY: . . . the Wasy Wailerettes, kagatchitnat. How, Number Nine Hera Keechigeesik . . .

(*He continues uninterrupted.*)

CREATURE: . . . Stop the game! Stop the game! Stop the game! . . . (*Etc.*)

ZACHARY: Goodness sakes, there's gonna be a fight out there!

(CREATURE *continues his "stop the game,"* ZACHARY *repeats "goodness sakes, there's gonna be a fight out there,"* SIMON's *"Pat-see!" has now built up into a full chant, his foot pounding on the floor so that it sounds like a powwow drum, his dancing bustle held aloft like a shield.* SPOOKY *finally grabs the crucifix away from* DICKIE BIRD, *holds it aloft and begins to pray, loudly, as in a ceremony.* DICKIE BIRD, *caught between Simon's chanting and* SPOOKY's *praying, blocks his ears with his hands and looks with growing consternation at "the game."* PIERRE *blows his whistle and skates around like a puppet gone mad.*)

SPOOKY: The Lord is my shepherd; I shall not want. He maketh me to lie down in green pastures; he leadeth me beside the still waters. He restoreth my soul; he leadeth me in the paths of righteousness for his name's sake. Yea, though I walk through the valley of the shadow of death, I will fear no evil; for thou art with me. Yea, though I walk through the valley of the shadow of death, I will fear no evil; for thou art with me . . .

(*He repeats this last phrase over and over again. Finally,* DICKIE BIRD *freaks out, screams and runs down to the "ice" area.*)

BIG JOEY: (*Continuing uninterrupted above all the other men's voices.*) . . . igwa ati-ooteetum blue line ita Number One Gazelle Nataways, Captain of the Wasy Wailerettes, kagagweemaskamat anee-i puck, ma-a Number Nine Hera Keechigeesik mawch weemeethew anee-i puck. Wha! "Hooking," itwew referee Pierre St. Pierre, Gazelle Nataways isa keehookiwatew her own team-mate Hera Keechigeesikwa, wha! How, Number One Gazelle Nataways, Captain of the Wasy Wailerettes, face-off igwa meena itootum asichi Number Nine Flora McDonald, Captain of the Canoe Lake Bravettes igwa Flora McDonald soogi pugamawew anee-i puck, ma-a Number Thirty-seven Big Bum Pegahmagahbow, defense-woman for the Wasy Wailerettes, stops the puck and passes it to Number Eleven Black Lady Halked, also defense-woman for the Wasy Wailerettes, but Gazelle Nataways, Captain of the Wasy Wailerettes, soogi body check meethew her own team-mate Black Lady Halked woops! She falls, ladies igwa gentlemen, Black Lady Halked hits the boards and Black Lady Halked is singin' the blues, ladies igwa gentlemen, Black Lady Halked sings the blues. (*Off microphone, to the other men.*) What the hell is goin' on down there? Dickie Bird, get off the ice! (*Back on microphone.*) Wha! Number Eleven Black Lady Halked is up in a flash igwa seemak

[1]The following hockey commentary by Big Joey (pages 1257–1258) is translated on page 1269.

1120   n'taymaskamew Gazelle Nataways anee-i puck, holy shit!
The ailing but very, very furious Black Lady Halked skates
back, turns and takes aim, it's gonna be a slap shot, ladies
igwa gentlemen, slap shot keetnatch taytootum Black Lady
Halked igwa Black Lady Halked shootiwoo anee-i puck,
1125   wha! She shoots straight at her very own captain, Gazelle
Nataways and holy shit, holy shit, holy fuckin' shit!

(All hell breaks loose; it is as though some bizarre dream has en-
tered the arena. We hear the sound of women wailing and pucks
hitting boards, echoing and echoing as in a vast empty chamber.
The men are all screaming at the same time, from the "bleach-
ers," re-calling BLACK LADY HALKED's *legendary fall of seventeen*
years ago.)

BIG JOEY: *(Dropping his microphone in horror.)* Holy Christ! If
there is a devil in this world, then he has just walked into this
room. Holy Christ! . . . *(He says this over and over again.)*
1130   ZACHARY: Do something about her, goodness sakes, I told you
guys to do something about her seventeen years ago, but you
wouldn't do fuck-all. So go out there now and help her . . .
(Repeated.)
CREATURE: Never mind, Chris'sakes, don't bother her. Let me
1135   out of here. Chris'sakes, let me out of here! . . . *(Repeated.)*
SPOOKY: . . . Yea, though I walk through the valley of the
shadow of death, I will fear no evil; for thou art with me . . .

(Repeated. While SIMON *continues chanting and stomping.)*

PIERRE: *(From the "ice" area.)* Never you mind, Zachary Jeremiah, never you mind. She'll be okay. No she won't.
1140   Zachary Jeremiah, go out there and help her. No. She'll be
okay. No she won't. Yes. No. Yes. No. No. Help! Where's the
puck? Can't do nothin' without the goddamn puck. Where's
the puck?! Where's the puck?! Where's the puck?! . . .

(He repeats this last phrase over and over again. Center- and
down-stage, on the "ice" area, DICKIE BIRD *is going into a com-*
plete "freak-out," breaking into a grotesque, fractured version of a
Cree chant. Gradually, BIG JOEY, ZACHARY *and* CREATURE *join*
PIERRE's *refrain of "where's the puck?!", with which they all, in-*
cluding the chanting SIMON *and the praying* SPOOKY, *scatter*
and come running down to the "ice" area. As they reach the
lower level and begin to approach the audience, their movements
break down into slow motion, as though they were trying to run
through the sticky, gummy substance of some horrible, surrealis-
tic nightmare.)

PIERRE/BIG JOEY/ZACHARY/CREATURE: *(Slower and slower, as*
1145   *on a record that is slowing down gradually to a stop.)* Where's
the puck?! Where's the puck?! Where's the puck?! . . . *(Etc.)*

*(*SIMON *continues chanting and stomping,* SPOOKY *continues*
intoning the last phrase of his prayer and DICKIE BIRD *continues*
his fractured chant. Out of this fading "sound collage" emerges
the sound of a jukebox playing the introduction to Kitty Wells'
"It Wasn't God Who Made Honky Tonk Angels," as though fil-
tered through memory. At this point, on the upper level, a giant
luminescent hockey stick comes seemingly out of nowhere and, in
very slow motion, shoots a giant luminescent puck. On the puck,
looking like a radiant but damaged "Madonna-with-child," sits
NANABUSH, *as the spirit of* BLACK LADY HALKED, *naked, nine*
months pregnant, drunk almost senseless and barely able to hold
a bottle of beer up to her mouth. All the men freeze in their

standing positions facing the audience, except for DICKIE BIRD
who continues his fractured chanting and whimpering, hold-
ing his arms up towards NANABUSH/BLACK LADY HALKED. *The*
giant luminescent puck reaches and stops at the edge of the
upper level. NANABUSH/BLACK LADY HALKED *struggles to stand*
and begins staggering toward her perch. She reaches it and falls
with one arm on top of it. The magical, glittering lights flare on
and, for the first time, the jukebox is revealed. NANABUSH/BLACK
LADY HALKED *staggers laboriously up to the top of the jukebox*
and stands there in profile, one arm lifted to raise her beer as she
pours it over her belly. Behind her, the full moon begins to glow,
blood red. And from the jukebox, Kitty Wells sings.)

As I sit here tonight, the jukebox playing,
That tune about the wild side of life;
As I listen to the words you are saying,
It brings memories when I was a trusting wife.   1150

It wasn't God who made honky tonk angels,
As you said in the words of your song;
Too many times married men think they're still single,
That has caused many a good girl to go wrong.

(During the "instrumental break" of the song here, DICKIE
BIRD *finally explodes and shrieks out towards the vision of*
NANABUSH/BLACK LADY HALKED.)*

DICKIE BIRD: Mama! Mama! Katha paksini. Katha paksini.   1155
Kanawapata wastew. Kanawapataw wastew. Michimina.
Michimina. Katha pagitina. Kaweechee-ik nipapa.
Kaweechee-ik nipapa. Nipapa. Papa. Papa. Papa. Papa.
Papa! Mommy! Mommy! Don't fall. Don't fall. Look at the
light. Look at the light. Hold on to it. Hold on to it. Don't let   1160
it go. My daddy will help you. My daddy will help you. My
daddy. Daddy. Daddy. . . . *(Etc.)*

(He crumples to the floor and freezes. Kitty Wells sings.)

It's a shame that all the blame is on us women,
It's not true that only you men feel the same;
From the start most every heart that's ever broken,   1165
Was because there always was a man to blame.

It wasn't God who made honky tonk angels;
As you said in the words of your song;
Too many times married men think they're still single,
That has caused many a good girl to go wrong.   1170

(As the song fades, the final tableau is one of DICKIE BIRD *col-*
lapsed on the floor between SIMON, *who is holding aloft his bus-*
tle, and SPOOKY, *who is holding aloft his crucifix, directly in*
front of and at the feet of BIG JOEY *and, above* BIG JOEY, *the*
pregnant NANABUSH/BLACK LADY HALKED, *who is standing on*
top of the flashing jukebox, in silhouette against the full moon,
bottle held up above her mouth. ZACHARY, CREATURE *and*
PIERRE *are likewise frozen, standing off to the side of this central*
grouping. Slow fade-out.)

— ACT TWO —

When the lights come up, DICKIE BIRD HALKED *is standing on a*
rock in the forest, his clothes and hair all askew. He holds
SPOOKY's *crucifix, raised with one hand up to the night sky; he is*
trying, as best he can, to chant, after SIMON STARBLANKET's

fashion. As he does, NANABUSH *appears in the shadows a distance behind him (as the spirit of* GAZELLE NATAWAYS, *minus the gigantic breasts, but dressed, this time, as a stripper). She lingers and watches with interest. Slowly,* DICKIE BIRD *climbs off the rock and walks off-stage, his quavering voice fading into the distance. The full moon glows. Fade-out.*

Fade-in on SPOOKY LACROIX's *kitchen, where* SPOOKY *is busy pinning four little pale blue baby booties on the wall where the crucifix used to be, the booties that, in Act One, covered the four extremities of the crucifix. At the table are* PIERRE ST. PIERRE *and* ZACHARY JEREMIAH KEECHIGEESIK. PIERRE *is stringing pale blue yarn around* ZACHARY's *raised, parted hands. Then* SPOOKY *joins them at the table and begins knitting again, this time, a baby bonnet, also pale blue.* ZACHARY *sits removed through most of this scene, pre-occupied with the problem of his still missing shorts, his bakery and his wife. The atmosphere is one of fear and foreboding, almost as though the men were constantly resisting the impulse to look over their shoulders. On the upper level, in a soft, dim light,* NANABUSH/GAZELLE *can be seen sitting up on her perch, waiting impatiently for "the boys" to finish their talk.*

PIERRE: *(In a quavering voice.)* The Wasy Wailerettes are dead. Gentlemen, my job is disappeared from underneath my feet.

SPOOKY: And we have only the Lord to thank for that.

PIERRE: Gazelle Nataways, she just sashayed herself off that
5   ice, behind swayin' like a walrus pudding. That game, gentlemen, was what I call a real apostrophe . . .

ZACHARY: Catastrophe.

PIERRE: That's what I said, dammit. . . .

SPOOKY: . . . tsk . . .

10 PIERRE: . . . didn't even get to referee more than ten minutes. But you have to admit, gentlemen, that slap shot . . .

SPOOKY: . . . that's my sister, Black Lady Halked, that's my sister . . .

PIERRE: . . . did you see her slap shot? Fantastic! Like a bullet,
15   like a killer shark. Unbelievable!

ZACHARY: *(Uncomfortable.)* Yeah, right.

PIERRE: When Black Lady Halked hit Gazelle Nataways with that puck. Them Nataways eyes. Big as plates!

SPOOKY: Bigger than a ditch!

20 PIERRE: Them mascara stretch marks alone was a perfectly frightful thing to behold. Holy shit la marde! But you know, they couldn't find that puck.

SPOOKY: *(Losing his cool and laughing, falsely and nervously.)* Did you see it? It fell . . . it fell . . . that puck went splat on
25   her chest . . . and it went . . . it went . . . plummety plop . . .

PIERRE: . . . plummety plop to be sure . . .

SPOOKY: . . . down her . . . down her . . .

PIERRE: Down the crack. Right down that horrendous, scarifyin' Nataways bosom crack.

(The "kitchen lights" go out momentarily and, to the men, inexplicably. Then they come back on. The men look about them, perplexed.)

30 SPOOKY: Serves . . . her . . . right for trimming her hockey sweater in the chest area, is what I say.

PIERRE: They say that puck slid somewhere deep, deep into the folds of her fleshy, womanly juices . . .

ZACHARY: . . . there's a lot of things they're saying about that
35   puck . . .

PIERRE: . . . and it's lost. Disappeared. Gone. Phhht! Nobody can find that puck.

(At this point, SPOOKY *gets up to check the light switch. The lights go out.)*

ZACHARY: *(In the darkness.)* Won't let no one come near her, is what they say. Not six inches.

PIERRE: I gotta go look for that puck. *(Lights come back on.* 40
PIERRE *inexplicably appears sitting in another chair.)* Gentlemen, I gotta go jiggle that woman.

(Lights out again.)

ZACHARY: *(From the darkness.)* What's the matter, Spook?

SPOOKY: *(Obviously quite worried.)* Oh, nothing, nothing . . .
(Lights come back on. PIERRE *appears sitting back in his orig-* 45
inal chair. The men are even more mystified, but try to brighten up anyway.) . . . just . . . checking the lights . . . Queen of the Indians, that's what she tried to look like, walking off that ice.

PIERRE: Queen of the Indians, to be sure. That's when them 50
women went and put their foot down and made up their mind, on principle, no holds barred . . .

(A magical flash of lavender light floods the room very briefly, establishing a connection between SPOOKY's *kitchen and* NANABUSH's *perch, where* NANABUSH/GAZELLE *is still sitting, tapping her fingers impatiently, looking over her shoulder periodically, as if to say: "come on, boys, get with it."* PIERRE's *speech momentarily goes into slow motion.)*

. . . no . . . way . . . they're . . . takin' up . . . them hockey sticks again until that particular puck is found. "The particular puck," that's what they call it. Gentlemen, the Wasy 55
Wailerettes are dead. My job is disappeared. Gone. Kaput kaput. Phhht!

SPOOKY: Amen.

(Pause. Thoughtful silence for a beat or two.)

ZACHARY: W-w-w-where's that nephew of yours, Spook?

SPOOKY: Dickie Bird Halked? 60

PIERRE: My wife, Veronique St. Pierre, she informs me that Dickie Bird Halked, last he was seen, was pacin' the bushes in the general direction of the Pegahmagahbow acreage near Buzwah, lookin' for all the world like he had lost his mind, poor boy. 65

ZACHARY: Lordy, lordy, lordy, I'm telling you right now, Spooky Lacroix, if you don't do something about that nephew of yours, he's liable to go out there and kill someone next time.

SPOOKY: I'd be out there myself pacing the bushes with him 70
except my wife Lalala's liable to pop any minute now and I gotta be ready to zip her up to Sudbury General.

PIERRE: Bah. Them folks of his, they don't care. If it's not hockey, it's bingo she's out playin' every night of the week, that Black Lady of a mother of his. 75

ZACHARY: Went and won the jackpot again last night, Black Lady Halked did. All fifty pounds of it . . .

PIERRE: Beat Gazelle Nataways by one number!

ZACHARY: . . . if it wasn't for her, I'd have mastered that apple pie recipe by now. I was counting on all that lard. Fifty 80
pounds, goodness sakes.

SPOOKY: This little old kitchen? It's yours, Zachary Jeremiah, anytime, anytime. Lalala's got tons of lard.

PIERRE: Ha! She better have. Zachary Jeremiah hasn't dared go nowhere near his own kitchen in almost a week.

ZACHARY: Four nights! It's only Wednesday night, Pierre St. Pierre. Don't go stretching the truth just cuz you were too damn chicken to go get me my shorts.

PIERRE: Bah!

SPOOKY: *(To ZACHARY.)* Your shorts?

ZACHARY: *(Evading the issue.)* I just hope that Black Lady Halked's out there looking after her boy cuz if she isn't, we're all in a heap of trouble, I have a funny feeling. *(Suddenly, he throws the yarn down and rises.)* Achh! I've got to cook!

(He goes behind the kitchen counter, puts an apron on and begins the preparations for making pie pastry.)

SPOOKY: *(To PIERRE, half-whispering.)* His shorts?

(PIERRE merely shrugs, indicating ZACHARY's pants, which are still held together with a large safety pin. SPOOKY and PIERRE laugh nervously. SPOOKY looks concernedly at the four little booties on the wall where the crucifix used to be. Beat.)

Suddenly, PIERRE *slaps the table with one hand and leans over to* SPOOKY, *all set for an argument, an argument they've obviously had many times before. Through all this,* ZACHARY *is making pie pastry at the counter and* SPOOKY *continues knitting. The atmosphere of "faked" jocular camaraderie grows, particularly as the music gets louder later on.* NANABUSH/GAZELLE *is now getting ready for her strip in earnest, standing on her perch, spraying perfume on, stretching her legs, etc. The little tivoli lights in the jukebox begin to twinkle little by little.)*

PIERRE: Queen of Hearts.

SPOOKY: Belvedere.

PIERRE: Queen of Hearts.

SPOOKY: The Belvedere.

PIERRE: I told you many times, Spooky Lacroix, it was the Queen of Hearts. I was there. You were there. Zachary Jeremiah, Big Joey, Creature Nataways, we were all there.

(From here on, the red/blue/purple glow of the jukebox (i.e., NANABUSH's *perch) becomes more and more apparent.)*

SPOOKY: And I'm telling you it was the Belvedere Hotel, before it was even called the Belvedere Hotel, when it was still called . . .

PIERRE: Spooky Lacroix, don't contribute your elder. Big Joey, may he rot in hell, he was the bouncer there that night, he was right there the night it happened.

ZACHARY: Hey, Spook. Where do you keep your rolling pin?

SPOOKY: Use my salami.

PIERRE: *(To SPOOKY.)* He was there.

ZACHARY: Big Joey was never the bouncer, he was the janitor.

SPOOKY: At the Belvedere Hotel.

PIERRE: Never you mind, Spooky Lacroix, never you mind. Black Lady Halked was sittin' there in her corner of the bar for three weeks . . .

SPOOKY: Three weeks?! It was more like three nights. Aw, you went and mixed up my baby's cap. *(Getting all tangled up with his knitting.)*

ZACHARY: Got any cinnamon?

SPOOKY: I got chili powder. Same color as cinnamon.

(Faintly, the strip music from the jukebox begins to play.)

PIERRE: . . . the place was so jam-packed with people drinkin' beer and singin' and smokin' cigarettes and watchin' the dancin' girl . . .

SPOOKY: . . . Gazelle Nataways, she was the dancing girl . . .

(The music is now on full volume and NANABUSH/GAZELLE's *strip is in full swing. She dances on top of the jukebox, which is now a riot of sound and flashing lights.* SPOOKY's *kitchen is bathed in a gorgeous lavender light.* BIG JOEY *and* CREATURE NATAWAYS *appear at* SPOOKY's *table, each drinking a bottle of beer. The strip of seventeen years ago is fully recreated, the memory becoming so heated that* NANABUSH/GAZELLE *magically appears dancing right on top of* SPOOKY's *kitchen table. The men are going wild, applauding, laughing, drinking, all in slow motion and in mime. In the heat of the moment, as* NANABUSH/GAZELLE *strips down to silk tassels and G-string, they begin tearing their clothes off.*

Suddenly, SIMON STARBLANKET *appears at* SPOOKY's *door:* NANABUSH/GAZELLE *disappears, as do* BIG JOEY *and* CREATURE. *And* SPOOKY, PIERRE *and* ZACHARY *are caught with their pants down. The jukebox music fades.)*

SIMON: Spooky Lacroix. *(The lavender light snaps off, we are back to "reality" and* SPOOKY, PIERRE *and* ZACHARY *stand there, embarrassed. In a panic, they begin putting their clothes back on and reclaim the positions they had before the strip.* SPOOKY *motions* SIMON *to take a seat at the table.* SIMON *does so.)* Spooky Lacroix. Rosie Kakapetum expresses interest in coming here to birth Lalala's baby when the time comes.

SPOOKY: Rosie Kakapetum? No way some witch is gonna come and put her witchy little fingers on my baby boy.

SIMON: Rosie Kakapetum's no witch, Spooky Lacroix. She's Patsy Pegahmagahbow's step-mother and she's Wasy's only surviving medicine woman and mid-wife . . .

SPOOKY: Hogwash!

PIERRE: Ahem. Rosie Kakapetum says it's a cryin' shame the Wasy Wailerettes is the only team that's not in the Ontario Hockey League.

ZACHARY: Ontario Hockey League?

PIERRE: Absolutely. The OHL. Indian women's OHL. All the Indian women in Ontario's playin' hockey now. It's like a fever out there.

ZACHARY: Shoot. *(Referring to his pastry.)* I hope this new recipe works for me.

PIERRE: Well, it's not exactly new without the cinnamon.

SPOOKY: *(To SIMON.)* My son will be born at Sudbury General Hospital . . .

SIMON: You know what they do to them babies in them city hospitals?

SPOOKY: . . . Sudbury General, Simon Starblanket, like any good Christian boy . . .

PIERRE: *(Attempting to diffuse the argument.)* Ahem. We got to get them Wasy Wailerettes back on that ice again.

SIMON: *(Refusing to let go of* SPOOKY.)* They pull them away right from their own mother's breast the minute they come into this world and they put them behind these glass cages together with another two hundred babies like they were some kind of scientific specimens . . .

PIERRE: . . . like two hundred of them little monsters . . .

ZACHARY: Hamsters!

165 PIERRE: . . . that's what I said dammit . . .

SPOOKY: . . . tsk . . .

PIERRE: . . . you can't even tell which hamster belongs to which mother. You take Lalala to Sudbury General, Spooky Lacroix, and your hamster's liable to end up stuck to some
170 French lady's tit.

SIMON: . . . and they'll hang Lalala up in metal stirrups and your baby's gonna be born going up instead of dropping down which is the natural way. You were born going up instead of dropping down like you should have . . .

175 PIERRE: Yup. You were born at Sudbury General, Spooky Lacroix, that's why you get weirder and weirder as the days get longer, that's why them white peoples is so weird they were all born going up . . .

SIMON: . . . instead of dropping down . . .

180 ZACHARY: (*Sprinkling flour in* SPOOKY's *face, with both hands, and laughing.*) . . . to the earth, Spooky Lacroix, to the earth . . .

SPOOKY: Pooh!

PIERRE: . . . but we got to find that puck, Simon Starblanket,
185 them Wasy Wailerettes have got to join the OHL . . .

SPOOKY: (*To* SIMON.) If Rosie Kakapetum is a medicine woman, Simon Starblanket, then how come she can't drive the madness from my nephew's brain, how come she can't make him talk, huh?

190 SIMON: Because the medical establishment and the church establishment and people like you, Spooky Lacroix, have effectively put an end to her usefulness and the usefulness of people like her everywhere, that's why Spooky Lacroix.

SPOOKY: Phooey!

195 SIMON: Do you or your sister even know that your nephew hasn't been home in two days, since that incident at the hockey game, Spooky Lacroix? Do you even care? Why can't you and that thing . . . (*Pointing at the bible that sits beside* SPOOKY.) and all it stands for cure your nephew's madness,
200 as you call it, Spooky Lacroix? What has this thing . . . (*The bible again.*) done to cure the madness of this community and communities like it clean across this country, Spooky Lacroix? Why didn't "the Lord" as you call him, come to your sister's rescue at that bar seventeen years ago, huh,
205 Spooky Lacroix? (*Pause. Tense silence.*) Rosie Kakapetum is gonna be my mother-in-law in two months, Spooky Lacroix, and if Patsy and I are gonna do this thing right, if we're gonna work together to make my best man, Dickie Bird Halked, well again, then Rosie Kakapetum has got to birth
210 that baby. (*He begins to exit.*)

SPOOKY: (*In hard, measured cadence.*) Rosie Kakapetum works for the devil.

(SIMON *freezes in his tracks. Silence. Then he turns, grabs a chair violently, bangs it down and sits determinedly.*)

SIMON: Fine. I'll sit here and I'll wait.

SPOOKY: Fine. You sit there and you wait.

(*Silence.* SIMON *sits silent and motionless, his back to the other men.*)

215 PIERRE: Ahem. Never you mind, Spooky Lacroix, never you mind. Now as I was sayin', Black Lady Halked was nine months pregnant when she was sittin' in that corner of the Queen of Hearts.

SPOOKY: The Belvedere!

PIERRE: Three weeks, Black Lady Halked was sittin' there 220
drinkin' beer. They say she got the money by winnin' the jackpot at the Espanola bingo just three blocks down the street. Three weeks, sure as I'm alive and walkin' these treacherous icy roads, three weeks she sat there in that dark corner by herself. They say the only light you could see her 225
by was the light from the jukebox playin' "Rim of Fire" by Johnny Cash . . .

ZACHARY: "Rim of Fire." Yeah, right, Pierre St. Pierre.

SPOOKY: Kitty Wells! Kitty Wells!

(*The sound of the jukebox playing "It Wasn't God Who Made Honky Tonk Angels" can be heard faintly in the background.*)

PIERRE: . . . the place was so jam-packed with people drinkin' 230
and singin' and smokin' cigarettes and watchin' the dancin' girl . . .

SPOOKY: . . . Gazelle Nataways, she was the dancing girl, Lord save her soul . . .

PIERRE: . . . until Black Lady Halked collapsed . . . 235

(SPOOKY, PIERRE *and* ZACHARY *freeze in their positions, looking in horror at the memory of seventeen years ago.*)

On the upper level, NANABUSH, *back in her guise as the spirit of* BLACK LADY HALKED, *sits on the jukebox, facing the audience, legs out directly in front. Nine months pregnant and naked, she holds a bottle of beer up in the air and is drunk almost senseless. The song, "It Wasn't God Who Made Honky Tonk Angels," rises to full volume, the lights from the jukebox flashing riotously. The full moon glows blood red. Immediately below* NANABUSH/BLACK LADY HALKED, DICKIE BIRD HALKED *appears, kneeling, naked, arms raised toward his mother.* NANABUSH/BLACK LADY HALKED *begins to writhe and scream, laughing and crying hysterically at the same time and, as she does, her water breaks.* DICKIE BIRD, *drenched, rises slowly from the floor, arms still raised, and screams.*)

DICKIE BIRD: Mama! Mama!

(*And from here on, the lights and the sound on this scene begin to fade slowly, as the scene on the lower level resumes.*)

PIERRE: . . . she kind of oozed down right then and there, right down to the floor of the Queen of Hearts Tavern. And Big Joey, may he rot in hell, he was the bouncer there that night, when he saw the blood, he ran away and puked over on the 240
other side of the bar, the sight of all that woman's blood just scared the shit right out of him. And that's when Dickie Bird Halked, as we know him, came ragin' out from his mother's womb, Spooky Lacroix, in between beers, right there on the floor, under a table, by the light of the jukebox, on a Satur- 245
day night, at the Queen of Hearts . . .

SPOOKY: They went and named him after the bar, you crusted old fossil! That bar, which is now called the Belvedere Hotel, used to be called the Dickie Bird Tavern . . .

SIMON: (*Suddenly jumping out of his chair and practically 250
lunging at* SPOOKY.) It doesn't matter what the fuck the name of that fucking bar was! (*The lights and sound on* NANABUSH *and the jukebox have now faded completely.*) The fact of the matter is, it never should have happened, that kind of thing should never be allowed to happen, not to us 255
Indians, not to anyone living and breathing on the face of

God's green earth. (*Pause. Silence. Then, dead calm.*) You guys have given up, haven't you? You and your generation. You gave up a long time ago. You'd rather turn your back on the whole thing and pretend to laugh, wouldn't you? (*Silence.*) Well, not me. Not us. (*Silence.*) This is not the kind of Earth we want to inherit. (*He begins to leave, but turns once more.*) I'll be back. With Patsy. And Rosie.

(*He exits. Another embarrassed silence.*)

SPOOKY: (*Unwilling to face up to the full horror of it, he chooses, instead, to do exactly what* SIMON *said: turn his back and pretend to laugh.*) That bar, which is now called the Belvedere Hotel, used to be called the Dickie Bird Tavern. That's how Dickie Bird Halked got his name. And that's why he goes hay-wire every now and again and that's why he doesn't talk. Fetal Alcohol something-something, Pierre St. Pierre . . .

ZACHARY: (*From behind the counter, where he is still busy making pie crust.*) Fetal Alcohol Syndrome.

SPOOKY: . . . that's the devil that stole the baby's tongue because Dickie Bird Halked was born drunk and very, very mad. At the Dickie Bird Tavern in downtown Espanola seventeen years ago and that's a fact.

PIERRE: Aw, shit la marde. Fuck you, Spooky Lacroix, I'm gonna go get me my rest.

(*Throws the yarn in* SPOOKY's *face, jumps up and exits.* SPOOKY *sits there with a pile of yarn stuck to his face, caught on his glasses.*)

ZACHARY: (*Proudly holding up the pie crust in its plate.*) It worked!

(*Black-out.*

On the upper level, in a dim light away from her perch, NANABUSH/BLACK LADY HALKED *is getting ready to go out for the evening, combing her hair in front of a mirror, putting on her clothes, etc.* DICKIE BIRD *is with her, naked, getting ready to go to bed.* SPOOKY's *crucifix sits on a night-table to his side. In* DICKIE BIRD's *mind, he is at home with his mother.*)

DICKIE BIRD: Mama. Mama. N'tagoosin. ("I'm sick.")

NANABUSH/BLACK LADY: Say your prayers.

DICKIE BIRD: Achimoostawin nimoosoom. ("Tell me about my grandpa.")

NANABUSH/BLACK LADY: Go to bed. I'm going out soon.

DICKIE BIRD: Mawch. Achimoostawin nimoosoom. ("No. Tell me about my grandpa.")

NANABUSH/BLACK LADY: You shouldn't talk about him.

DICKIE BIRD: Tapweechee eegeemachipoowamit nimoosoom? ("Is it true my grandpa had bad medicine?")

NANABUSH/BLACK LADY: They say he met the devil once. Your grandpa talked to the devil. Don't talk about him.

DICKIE BIRD: Eegeemithoopoowamit nimoosoom, eetweet Simon Starblanket. ("Simon Starblanket says he had good medicine.")

NANABUSH/BLACK LADY: Ashhh! Simon Starblanket.

DICKIE BIRD: Mawch eemithoosit awa aymeewatik keetnanow kichi, eetweet Simon Starblanket. ("Simon Starblanket says that this cross is not right for us.") (*He grabs the crucifix from the night-table and spits on it.*)

NANABUSH/BLACK LADY: (*Grabbing the crucifix from* DICKIE BIRD, *she attempts to spank him but* DICKIE BIRD *evades her.*) Dickie Bird! Kipasta-oon! ("You're committing a mortal sin!") Say ten Hail Marys and two Our Fathers.

DICKIE BIRD: Mootha apoochiga taskootch nimama keetha. Mootha apoochiga m'tanawgatch kisagee-in. ("You're not even like my mother. You don't even love me at all.")

NANABUSH/BLACK LADY: Dickie Bird. Shut up. I'll say them with you. "Hail Mary, full of grace, the Lord is with thee . . ." Hurry up. I have to go out. (*As* NANABUSH/BLACK LADY HALKED *now prepares to leave.*) "Hail Mary, full of grace, the Lord is with thee . . ." (*She gives up.*) Ashhh! Your father should be home soon. (*Exits.*)

DICKIE BIRD: (*Speaking out to the now absent* NANABUSH/BLACK LADY.) Mootha nipapa ana. ("He's not my father.") (*He grabs his clothes and the crucifix and runs out, down to the lower level and into the forest made of light and shadows.*) Tapwee anima ka-itweechik, chee-i? Neetha ooma kimineechagan, chee-i? ("It's true what they say, isn't it? I'm a bastard, aren't I?) (*He is now sitting on the rock, where* SIMON *and* ZACHARY *first met in Act One.*) Nipapa ana . . . Big Joey . . . (*To himself, quietly.*) . . . nipapa ana . . . Big Joey . . . ("My father is . . . Big Joey.")

(*Silence.*

A few moments later, NANABUSH comes bouncing into the forest, as the spirit of the vivacious, young PATSY PEGAHMAGAHBOW, complete with very large, oversized bum. The full moon glows.)

NANABUSH/PATSY: (*To herself, as she peers into the shadows.*) Oooh, my poor bum. I fell on the ice four days ago, eh? And it still hurts, oooh. (*She finally sees* DICKIE BIRD *huddling on the rock, barely dressed.*) There you are. I came out to look for you. What happened to your clothes? It's freezing out here. Put them on. Here. (*She starts to help dress him.*) What happened at the arena? You were on the ice, eh? You feel like talking? In Indian? How, weetamawin. ("Come on, tell me.")

(BIG JOEY *and* CREATURE NATAWAYS *enter a distance away. They are smoking a joint and* BIG JOEY *carries a gun. They stop and watch from the shadows.*)

CREATURE: Check her out.

NANABUSH/PATSY: Why do you always carry that crucifix? I don't believe that stuff. I traded mine in for sweetgrass. Hey. You wanna come to Rosie's and eat fry bread with me? Simon will be there, too. Simon and me, we're getting married, eh? We're gonna have a baby . . .

CREATURE: What's she trying to do?

NANABUSH/PATSY: . . . Rosie's got deer meat, too, come on, you like my Mom's cooking, eh? (*She attempts to take the crucifix away from* DICKIE BIRD.) But you'll have to leave that here because Rosie can't stand the Pope . . .

(DICKIE BIRD *grabs the crucifix back.*)

CREATURE: What's he trying to do?

NANABUSH/PATSY: . . . give it to me . . . Dickie . . . come on . . .

CREATURE: He's weird, Big Joey, he's weird.

NANABUSH/PATSY: . . . leave it here . . . it will be safe here . . . we'll bury it in the snow . . .

(Playfully, she tries to get the crucifix away from DICKIE BIRD.*)*

350 CREATURE: Hey, don't do that, don't do that, man, he's ticklish.
NANABUSH/PATSY: *(As* DICKIE BIRD *begins poking her playfully with the crucifix and laughing,* NANABUSH/PATSY *gradually starts to get frightened.)* . . . don't look at me that way . . . Dickie Bird, what's wrong? . . . ya, Dickie Bird, awus . . .

*(*DICKIE BIRD *starts to grab at* NANABUSH/PATSY.*)*

355 CREATURE: Hey, don't you think, don't you think . . . he's getting kind of carried away?
NANABUSH/PATSY: . . . awus . . .
CREATURE: We gotta do something, Big Joey, we gotta do something. *(*BIG JOEY *stops* CREATURE.*)* Let go! Let go!
360 NANABUSH/PATSY: *(Now in a panic.)* . . . Awus! Awus! Awus! . . .

*(*DICKIE BIRD *grabs* NANABUSH/PATSY *and throws her violently to the ground, he lifts her skirt and shoves the crucifix up against her.)*

BIG JOEY: *(To* CREATURE.*)* Shut up.
NANABUSH/PATSY: *(Screams and goes into hysteria.)* . . . Simon! . . .

*(*DICKIE BIRD *rapes* NANABUSH/PATSY *with the crucifix. A heartbreaking, very slow, sensuous tango breaks out on off-stage harmonica.)*

CREATURE: *(To* BIG JOEY.*)* No! Let me go. Big Joey, let me go,
365 please! *(*BIG JOEY *suddenly grabs* CREATURE *violently by the collar.)*
BIG JOEY: Get out. Get the fuck out of here. You're nothin' but a fuckin' fruit. Fuck off. *(*CREATURE *collapses.)* I said fuck off.

*(*CREATURE *flees.* BIG JOEY *just stands there, paralyzed, and watches.*

NANABUSH/PATSY, *who has gradually been moving back and back, is now standing up on her perch again (i.e., the "mound"/jukebox which no longer looks like a jukebox). She stands there, facing the audience, and slowly gathers her skirt, in agony, until she is holding it up above her waist. A blood stain slowly spreads across her panties and flows down her leg. At the same time, Dickie Bird stands down-stage beside the rock, holding the crucifix and making violent jabbing motions with it, downward. All this happens in slow motion. The crucifix starts to bleed. When* DICKIE BIRD *lifts the crucifix up, his arms and chest are covered with blood. Finally,* NANABUSH/PATSY *collapses to the floor of her platform and slowly crawls away. Lights fade on her. On the lower level,* BIG JOEY, *in a state of shock, staggers, almost faints and vomits violently. Then he reels over to* DICKIE BIRD *and, not knowing what else to do, begins collecting his clothes and calming him down.)*

370 BIG JOEY: How, Dickie Bird, How, astum. Igwa. Mootha nantow. Mootha nantow. Shhh. Shhh. ("Come on, Dickie Bird. Come. Let's go. It's okay. It's okay. Shhh. Shhh . . .") *(Barely able to bring himself to touch it, he takes the crucifix from* DICKIE BIRD *and drops it quickly on the rock. Then he begins
375 wiping the blood off* DICKIE BIRD.*)* How, mootha nantow. Mootha nantow. How, astum, keeyapitch upisees ootee. Igwani. Igwani. Poonimatoo. Mootha nantow. Mootha nantow. ("Come on, it's okay. It's okay. Come on, a little more

over here. That's all. That's all. Stop crying. It's okay. It's okay . . .") *(*DICKIE BIRD, *shaking with emotion, looks ques-
380 tioningly into* BIG JOEY's *face.)* Eehee. Nigoosis keetha. Mootha Wellington Halked kipapa. Neetha . . . kipapa. ("Yes. You are my son. Wellington Halked is not your father. I'm . . . your father.")

(Silence. They look at each other. DICKIE BIRD *grabs* BIG JOEY *and clings to him,* BIG JOEY *reacting tentatively, at first, and then passionately, with* DICKIE BIRD *finally bursting out into uncontrollable sobs. Fade-out.*

Out of this darkness, gunshots explode. And we hear a man's voice wailing, in complete and utter agony. Then comes violent pounding at a door. Finally, still in the darkness, we hear SIMON STARBLANKET's *speaking voice.)*

SIMON: Open up! Pierre St. Pierre, open up! I know you're in 385
there!
PIERRE: *(Still in the darkness.)* Whoa! Easy now. Easy on that goddamn door. Must you create such a carpostrophe smack dab in the middle of my rest period? *(When the lights come up, we are outside the "window" to* PIERRE ST. PIERRE's *little 390
boot-leg joint.* PIERRE *pokes his head out, wearing his night clothes, complete with pointy cap.)* Go home. Go to bed. Don't be disturbin' my rest period. My wife, Veronique St. Pierre, she tells me there's now not only a OHL but a NHL, too. Indian women's National Hockey League. All the In- 395
dian women on every reserve in Canada, all the Indian women in Canada is playin' hockey now. It's like a fever out there. That's why I gotta get my rest. First thing tomorrow mornin', I go jiggle that puck out of Gazelle Nataways. Listen to me. I'm your elder. 400

*(*SIMON *shoots the gun into the house, just missing* PIERRE's *head.)*

SIMON: *(Dead calm.)* One, you give me a bottle. Two, I report your joint to the Manitowaning police. Three, I shoot your fucking head off.
PIERRE: Alright. Alright. *(He pops in for a bottle of whiskey and hands it out to* SIMON.*)* Now you go on home with this. Go 405
have yourself a nice quiet drink. *(*SIMON *begins to exit.* PIERRE *calls out.)* What the hell are you gonna do with that gun?
SIMON: *(Calling back.)* I'm gonna go get that mute. Little bastard raped Patsy Pegahmagahbow. *(Exits.)* 410

(Pause.)

PIERRE: Holy shit la marde! *(Pause.)* I gotta warn him. No. I need my rest. No. I gotta warn that boy. No. I gotta find that puck. No. Dickie Bird's life. No. The puck. No. Dickie Bird. No. Hockey. No. His life. No. Hockey. No. Life. Hockey. Life. Hockey. Life. Hockey. Life. Hockey. Life . . . 415

(Fade-out.)

Lights up on SPOOKY LACROIX's *kitchen.* CREATURE NATAWAYS *is sitting at the table, silent, head propped up in his hands.* SPOOKY *is knitting, with obvious haste, a white christening gown, of which a large crucifix is the center-piece.* SPOOKY's *bible still sits on the table beside him.)*

SPOOKY: Why didn't you do something? (*Silence.*) Creature. (*Silence. Finally,* SPOOKY *stops knitting and looks up.*) Alphonse Nataways, why didn't you stop him? (*Silence.*) You're scared of him, aren't you? You're scared to death of Big Joey. Admit it.

(*Silence.*)

CREATURE: (*Quietly and calmly.*) I love him, Spooky.

SPOOKY: Say wha?!

CREATURE: I love him.

SPOOKY: You love him? What do you mean? How? How do you love him?

CREATURE: I love him.

SPOOKY: Lord have mercy on Wasaychigan Hill!

CREATURE: (*Rising suddenly.*) I love the way he stands. I love the way he walks. The way he laughs. The way he wears his cowboy boots . . .

SPOOKY: You're kidding me.

CREATURE: . . . the way his tight blue jeans fall over his ass. The way he talks so smart and tough. The way women fall at his feet. I wanna be like him. I always wanted to be like him, William. I always wanted to have a dick as big as his.

SPOOKY: Creature Alphonse Nataways? You know not what you say.

CREATURE: I don't care.

SPOOKY: I care.

CREATURE: I don't care. I can't stand it anymore.

SPOOKY: Shut up. You're making me nervous. Real nervous.

CREATURE: Come with me.

SPOOKY: Come with you where?

CREATURE: To his house.

SPOOKY: Whose house?

CREATURE: Big Joey.

SPOOKY: Are you crazy?

CREATURE: Come with me.

SPOOKY: No.

CREATURE: Yes.

SPOOKY: No.

CREATURE: (*Suddenly and viciously grabbing* SPOOKY *by the throat.*) Cut the goddamn bull crap, Spooky Lacroix! (SPOOKY *tries desperately to save the christening gown.*) I seen you crawl in the mud and shit so drunk you were snortin' like a pig.

SPOOKY: I changed my ways, thank you.

CREATURE: Twenty one years. Twenty one years ago. You, me, Big Joey, Eugene Starblanket, that goddamn Zachary Jeremiah Keechigeesik. We were eighteen. We cut our wrists. Your own father's huntin' knife. We mixed blood. Swore we'd be friends for life. Frontenac Hotel. Twenty one years ago. You got jumped by seven white guys. Broken beer bottle come straight at your face. If it wasn't for me, you wouldn't be here today, wavin' that stinkin' bible in my face like it was a slab of meat. I'm not a dog. I'm your buddy. Your friend.

SPOOKY: I know that.

(CREATURE *tightens his hold on* SPOOKY's *throat. The two men are staring straight into each other's eyes, inches apart. Silence.*)

CREATURE: William. Think of your father. Remember the words of Nicotine Lacroix.

(*Finally,* SPOOKY *screams, throwing the christening gown, knitting needles and all, over the bible on the table.*)

SPOOKY: You goddamn, fucking son-of-a-bitch!

(*Black-out. Gunshots in the distance.*)

Lights up on BIG JOEY's *living room/kitchen.* BIG JOEY *is sitting, silent and motionless, on the couch, staring straight ahead, as though he were in a trance. His hunting rifle rests on his lap.* DICKIE BIRD HALKED *stands directly in front of and facing the life-size pin-up poster of Marilyn Monroe, also as though he were in a trance. Then his head drops down in remorse.* BIG JOEY *lifts the gun, loads it and aims it out directly in front. When* DICKIE BIRD *hears the snap of the gun being loaded, he turns to look. Then he slowly walks over to* BIG JOEY, *kneels down directly in front of the barrel of the gun, puts it in his mouth and then slowly reaches over and gently, almost lovingly, moves* BIG JOEY's *hand away from the trigger, caressing the older man's hand as he does.* BIG JOEY *slowly looks up at* DICKIE BIRD's *face, stunned.* DICKIE BIRD *puts his own thumb on the trigger and pulls. Click. Nothing. In the complete silence, the two men are looking directly into each other's eyes. Complete stillness. Fade-out. Split seconds before complete black-out, Marilyn Monroe farts, courtesy of* MS. NANABUSH: *a little flag reading "poot" pops up out of Ms. Monroe's derrier, as on a play gun. We hear a cute little "poot" sound.*

Out of this black-out emerges the sound of a harmonica; it is ZACHARY JEREMIAH KEECHIGEESIK *playing his heart out. Fade-in on* PIERRE ST. PIERRE, *still in his night-clothes but also wearing his winter coat and hat over them, rushing all over the "forest" ostensibly rushing to* BIG JOEY's *house to warn* DICKIE BIRD HALKED *about the gun-toting* SIMON STARBLANKET. *He mutters to himself as he goes.*)

PIERRE: . . . Hockey. Life. Hockey. Life. Hockey. Life . . .

(ZACHARY *appears in the shadows and sees* PIERRE.)

ZACHARY: Hey!

PIERRE: (*Not hearing* ZACHARY.) . . . Hockey. Life. Hockey. Life . . .

ZACHARY: Pssst!

PIERRE: (*Still not hearing* ZACHARY.) . . . Hockey. Life. Hockey. Life. (*Pause.*) Hockey life!

ZACHARY: (*Finally yelling.*) Pierre St. Pierre!

(PIERRE *jumps.*)

PIERRE: Hallelujah! Have you heard the news?

ZACHARY: The Band Council went and okayed Big Joey's radio station.

PIERRE: All the Indian women in the world is playin' hockey now! World Hockey League, they call themselves. Aboriginal Women's WHL. My wife, Veronique St. Pierre, she just got the news. Eegeeweetamagoot fax machine. ("Fax machine told her.") It's like a burnin', ragin', blindin' fever out there. Them Cree women in Saskatchewan, them Blood women in Alberta, them Yakima, them Heidis out in the middle of your Specific Ocean, them Kickapoo, Chickasaw, Cherokee, Chipewyan, Choctaw, Chippewa, Wichita, Kiowa down in Oklahoma, them Seminole, Navajo, Onondaga, Tuscarora, Winnebago, Mimac-paddy-wack-why-it's-enough-to-give-your-dog-a-bone! . . .

(*As, getting completely carried away, he grabs his crotch.*)

ZACHARY: Pierre. Pierre.

495 PIERRE: . . . they're turnin' the whole world topsy-turkey right before our very eyes and the Prime Minister's a-shittin' grape juice . . . (*A gunshot explodes in the near distance.* PIERRE *suddenly lays low and changes tone completely.*) Holy shit la marde! He's after Dickie Bird. There's a red-eyed, crazed

500 devil out there and he's after Dickie Bird Halked and he's gonna kill us all if we don't stop him right this minute.

ZACHARY: Who? Who's gonna kill us?

PIERRE: Simon Starblanket. Drunk. Power mad. Half-crazed on whiskey and he's got a gun.

505 ZACHARY: Simon?

PIERRE: He's drunk and he's mean and he's out to kill. (*Another gunshot.*) Hear that?

ZACHARY: (*To himself.*) That's Simon? I thought . . .

PIERRE: When he heard about the Pegahmagahbow rape . . .

510 ZACHARY: Pegahmagahbow what?

PIERRE: Why, haven't you heard? Dickie Bird Halked raped Patsy Pegahmagahbow in most brutal fashion and Simon Starblanket is out to kill Dickie Bird Halked so I'm on my way to Big Joey's right this minute and I'm takin' that huntin'

515 rifle of his and I'm sittin' next to that Halked boy right up until the cows come home.

(*Exits.*)

ZACHARY: (*To himself.*) Simon Starblanket. Patsy . . .

(*Black-out.*

Out of this black-out come the gunshots, much louder this time, and SIMON'S *wailing voice.*)

SIMON: Aieeeeee-yip-yip! Nanabush! . . . (*Fade-in on* SIMON, *in the forest close by the large rock, still carrying his hunting*
520 *rifle.* SIMON *is half-crazed by this time, drunk out of his skull. The full moon glows.*) . . . Weesageechak! Come back! Rosie! Rosie Kakapetum, tell him to come back, not to run away, cuz we need him . . .

(NANABUSH/PATSY PEGAHMAGAHBOW'S *voice comes filtering out of the darkness on the upper level. It is as though* SIMON *were hearing a voice from inside his head.*)

NANABUSH/PATSY: . . . her . . .

525 SIMON: . . . him . . .

NANABUSH/PATSY: . . . her . . .

(*Slow fade-in on* NANABUSH/PATSY, *standing on the upper level, looking down at* SIMON. *She still wears her very large bum.*)

SIMON: . . . weetha ("him/her"—i.e., no gender) . . . Christ! What is it? Him? Her? Stupid fucking language, fuck you, da Englesa. Me no speakum no more da goodie Englesa, in
530 Cree we say "weetha," not "him" or "her" Nanabush, come back! (*Speaks directly to* NANABUSH, *as though he/she were there, directly in front of him; he doesn't see* NANABUSH/PATSY *standing on the upper level.*) Aw, boozhoo how are ya? Me good. Me berry, berry good. I seen you! I just seen you jump-
535 ing jack-ass thisa away . . .

NANABUSH/PATSY: (*As though she/he were playing games behind* SIMON'S *back.*). . . and thataway . . .

SIMON: . . . and thisaway and . . .

NANABUSH/PATSY: . . . thataway . . .

540 SIMON: . . . and thisaway and . . .

NANABUSH/PATSY: . . . thataway . . .

SIMON: . . . and thisaway and . . .

NANABUSH/PATSY: . . . thataway . . .

SIMON: . . . etcetra, etcetra, etcetra . . .

NANABUSH/PATSY: . . . etcetERA. (*Pause.*) She's here! She's 545 here!

SIMON: . . . Nanabush! Weesageechak! . . . (NANABUSH/PATSY *peals out with a silvery, magical laugh that echoes and echoes.*) . . . Dey shove dis . . . whach-you-ma-call-it . . . da crucifix up your holy cunt ouch, eh? Ouch, eh? (SIMON *sees* 550 *the bloody crucifix sitting on the rock and slowly approaches it. He kneels directly before it.*) Nah . . . (*Laughs a long mad, hysterical laugh that ends with hysterical weeping.*) . . . yessssss . . . noooo . . . oh, noooo! Crucifix! (*Spits violently on the crucifix.*) Fucking goddamn crucifix yesssss . . . God!* 555 You're a man. You're a woman. You're a man? You're a woman? You see, nineethoowan poogoo neetha ("I speak only Cree") . . .

NANABUSH/PATSY: . . . ohhh . . .

SIMON: . . . keetha ma-a? ("How about you?") . . . Nah. Da En- 560 glesa him . . .

NANABUSH/PATSY: . . . her . . .

SIMON: . . . him . . .

NANABUSH/PATSY: . . . her . . .

SIMON: . . . him! . . . 565

NANABUSH/PATSY: . . . her! . . .

SIMON: . . . all da time . . .

NANABUSH/PATSY: . . . all da time . . .

SIMON: . . . tsk, tsk, tsk . . .

NANABUSH/PATSY: . . . tsk, tsk, tsk. 570

SIMON: If God, you are a woman/man in Cree but only a man in da Englesa, then how come you still got a cun . . .

NANABUSH/PATSY: . . . a womb.

(*With this,* SIMON *finally sees* NANABUSH/PATSY. *He calls out to her.*)

SIMON: Patsy! Big Bum Pegahmagahbow, you flying across da ice on world's biggest puck. Patsy, look what dey done to 575 your puss . . . (NANABUSH/PATSY *lifts her skirt and displays the blood stain on her panties. She then finally takes off the prosthetic that is her huge bum and holds it in one arm.*) Hey! (*And* NANABUSH/PATSY *holds an eagle feather up in the air, ready to dance.* SIMON *stomps on the ground, rhythmi-* 580 *cally, and sings.*) ". . . and me I don't wanna go to the moon, I'm gonna leave that moon alone. I just wanna dance with the Rosebud Sioux this summer, yeah, yeah, yeah . . ." (SIMON *chants and he and* NANABUSH/PATSY *dance, he on the lower level with his hunting rifle in the air, she on the* 585 *upper level with her eagle feather.*) How, astum, Patsy, kiam. N'tayneemeetootan. ("Come on, Patsy, never mind. Let's go dance.")

(*We hear* ZACHARY JEREMIAH KEECHIGEESIK'S *voice calling from the darkness a distance away.*)

ZACHARY: Hey!

(*But* SIMON *and* NANABUSH/PATSY *pay no heed.*)

NANABUSH/PATSY: . . . n'tayneemeetootan South Dakota? . . . 590

SIMON: . . . how, astum, Patsy. N'tayneemeetootan South Dakota. Hey, Patsy Pegahmagahbow. . . .

(*As he finally approaches her and holds his hand out.*)

NANABUSH/PATSY: *(As she holds her hand out toward his.)* . . . Simon Starblanket . . .

595 SIMON/NANABUSH/PATSY: . . . eenpaysagee-itan ("I love you to death") . . .

(ZACHARY finally emerges tentatively from the shadows. He is holding a beautiful, fresh pie. NANABUSH/PATSY disappears.)

ZACHARY: *(Calling out over the distance.)* Hey! You want some pie?

SIMON: *(Silence. Calling back.)* What?!

(Not seeing ZACHARY, he looks around cautiously.)

600 ZACHARY: I said. You want some pie?

SIMON: *(Calling back, after some confused thought.)* What?

ZACHARY: *(He approaches SIMON slowly.)* Do you want some pie?

605 SIMON: *(Silence. Finally, he sees ZACHARY and points the gun at him.)* What kind?

ZACHARY: Apple. I just made some. It's still hot.

SIMON: *(Long pause.)* Okay.

(Slowly, NANABUSH/PATSY enters the scene and comes up behind SIMON, holding SIMON's dancing bustle in front of her, as in a ceremony.)

ZACHARY: Okay. But you gotta give me the gun first. *(The gun goes off accidentally, just missing ZACHARY's head.)* I said,
610 you gotta give me the gun first.

(Gradually, the dancing bustle begins to shimmer and dance in NANABUSH/PATSY's hands.)

SIMON: Patsy. I gotta go see Patsy.

ZACHARY: You and me and Patsy and Hera. We're gonna go have some pie. Fresh, hot apple pie. Then, we go to Sudbury and have a look at that Mobart, what do you say?

(The shimmering movements of the bustle balloon out into these magical, dance-like arches, as NANABUSH/PATSY maneuvers it directly in front of SIMON, hiding him momentarily. Behind this, SIMON drops the base of the rifle to the ground, causing it to go off accidentally. The bullet hits SIMON in the stomach. He falls to the ground. ZACHARY lets go of his pie and runs over to him. The shimmering of the bustle dies off into the darkness of the forest and disappears, NANABUSH/PATSY maneuvering it.)

615 ZACHARY: Simon! Simon! Oh, lordy, lordy, lordy . . . Are you alright? Are you okay? Simon. Simon. Talk to me. Goodness sakes, talk to me Simon. Ayumi-in! ("Talk to me!")

SIMON: *(Barely able to speak, as he sinks slowly to the ground beside the large rock.)* Kamoowanow . . . apple . . . pie . . . patima
620 . . . neetha . . . igwa Patsy . . . n'gapeetootanan . . . patima . . . apple . . . pie . . . neee. ("We'll eat . . . apple . . . pie . . . later . . . me . . . and Patsy . . . we'll come over . . . later . . . apple . . . pie . . . neee.")

(He dies.)

ZACHARY: *(As he kneels over SIMON's body, the full moon glow-*
625 *ing even redder.)* Oh, lordy, lordy . . . Holy shit! Holy shit! What's happening? What's become of this place? What's happening to this place? What's happening to these people? My people. He didn't have to die. He didn't have to die. That's the goddamn most stupid . . . no reason . . . this kind
630 of living has got to stop. It's got to stop! *(Talking and then just*

shrieking at the sky.) Aieeeeeee-Lord! God! God of the In-dian! God of the Whiteman! God-Al-fucking-mighty! What-ever the fuck your name is. Why are you doing this to us? Why are you doing this to us? Are you up there at all? Or are you some stupid, drunken shit, out-of-your-mind-passed out 635 under some great beer table up there in your stupid fucking clouds? Come down! Astum oota! ("Come down here!") Why don't you come down? I dare you to come down from your high-falutin' fuckin' shit-throne up there, come down and show us you got the guts to stop this stupid, stupid, stu- 640 pid way of living. It's got to stop. It's got to stop. It's got to stop. It's got to stop. It's got to stop. It's got to stop . . .

(He collapses over SIMON's body and weeps. Fade-out. Towards the end of this speech, a light comes up on NANABUSH. Her perch (i.e., the jukebox) has swivelled around and she is sitting on a toilet having a good shit. He/she is dressed in an old man's white beard and wig, but also wearing sexy, elegant women's high-heeled pumps. Surrounded by white, puffy clouds, she/he sits with her legs crossed, nonchalantly filing his/her fingernails. Fade-out.)

Fade-in on BIG JOEY's living room/kitchen. BIG JOEY, DICKIE BIRD HALKED, CREATURE NATAWAYS, SPOOKY LACROIX and PIERRE ST. PIERRE are sitting and standing in various positions, in complete silence. A hush pervades the room for about twenty beats. DICKIE BIRD is holding BIG JOEY's hunting rifle. Sud-denly, ZACHARY JEREMIAH KEECHIGEESIK enters; in a semi-crazed state. DICKIE BIRD starts and points the rifle straight at ZACHARY's head.

CREATURE: Zachary Jeremiah! What are you doing here?

BIG JOEY: Lookin' for your shorts, Zach?

(From his position on the couch, he motions DICKIE BIRD to put the gun down. DICKIE BIRD does so.)

ZACHARY: *(To BIG JOEY.)* You're unbelievable. You're fucking 645 unbelievable. You let this young man, you let your own son get away with this inconceivable act . . .

CREATURE: Don't say that to him, Zachary Jeremiah, don't say that . . .

ZACHARY: *(Ignoring CREATURE.)* You know he did it and you're 650 hiding him what in God's name is wrong with you?

SPOOKY: Zachary Jeremiah, you're not yourself . . .

PIERRE: Nope. Not himself. Talkin' wild.

(Sensing potential violence, he sneaks out the door.)

BIG JOEY: *(To ZACHARY.)* He don't even know he done any-thing. 655

ZACHARY: Bull shit! They're not even sure the air ambulance will get Patsy Pegahmagahbow to Sudbury in time. Simon Starblanket just shot himself and this boy is responsible . . .

(SIMON rises slowly from the ground and "sleep walks" right through this scene and up to the upper level, towards the full moon. The men are only vaguely aware of his passing.)

BIG JOEY: He ain't responsible for nothin'.

ZACHARY: Simon Starblanket was on his way to South Dakota 660 where he could have learned a few things and made some-thing of himself, same place you went and made a total ass-hole of yourself seventeen years ago . . .

CREATURE: Shush, Zachary Jeremiah, that's the past . . .

665 SPOOKY: . . . the past . . .

CREATURE: . . . Chris'sakes . . .

ZACHARY: What happened to all those dreams you were so full of for your people, the same dreams this young man just died for?

670 SPOOKY: (*To* BIG JOEY, *though not looking at him.*) And my sister, Black Lady Halked, seventeen years ago at that bar, Big Joey, you could have stopped her drinking, you could have sent her home and this thing never would have happened. That was your son inside her belly.

675 CREATURE: He didn't do nothing. He wouldn't let me do nothing. He just stood there and watched the whole thing . . .

SPOOKY: Creature Nataways!

CREATURE: I don't care. I'm gonna tell. He watched this little bastard do that to Patsy Pegahmagahbow . . .

680 BIG JOEY: (*Suddenly turning on* CREATURE.) You little cocksucker!

(DICKIE BIRD *hits* CREATURE *on the back with the butt of the rifle, knocking him unconscious.*)

SPOOKY: Why, Big Joey, why did you do that?

(*Silence.*)

ZACHARY: Yes, Joe. Why?

(*Long silence. All the men look at* BIG JOEY.)

BIG JOEY: (*Raising his arms, as for a battle cry.*) "This is the
685 end of the suffering of a great nation!" That was me. Wounded Knee, South Dakota, Spring of '73. The FBI. They beat us to the ground. Again and again and again. Ever since that spring, I've had these dreams where blood is spillin' out from my groin, nothin' there but blood and
690 emptiness. It's like . . . I lost myself. So when I saw this baby comin' out of Caroline, Black Lady . . . Gazelle dancin' . . . all this blood . . . and I knew it was gonna come . . . I . . . I tried to stop it . . . I freaked out. I don't know what I did . . . and I knew it was mine . . .

695 ZACHARY: Why? Why did you let him do it? Why? Why did you let him do it? Why? Why did you let him do it? Why? Why did you let him do it? (*Finally grabbing* BIG JOEY *by the collar.*) Why?! Why did you let him do it?!

BIG JOEY: (*Breaking free from* ZACHARY's *hold.*) Because I hate
700 them! I hate them fuckin' bitches. Because they—our own women—took the fuckin' power away from us faster than the FBI ever did.

SPOOKY: (*Softly, in the background.*) They always had it.

(*Silence.*)

BIG JOEY: There. I said it. I'm tired. Tired.

(*He slumps down on the couch and cries.*)

705 ZACHARY: (*Softly.*) Joe. Joe.

(*Fade-out.*

Out of this darkness emerges the sound of SIMON STARBLANKET's *chanting voice. Away up over* NANABUSH's *perch, the moon begins to glow, fully and magnificently. Against it, in silhouette, we see* SIMON *wearing his powwow bustle.* SIMON STARBLANKET *is dancing in the moon. Fade-out.*

Fade-in on the "ice" at the hockey arena, where PIERRE ST. PIERRE, *in full referee regalia, is gossiping with* CREATURE NATAWAYS *and* SPOOKY LACROIX. CREATURE *is knitting, with great difficulty, pink baby booties.* SPOOKY *is holding his new baby, wrapped in a pale blue knit blanket. We hear the sound of a hockey arena, just before a big game.*)

PIERRE: . . . she says to me: "did you know, Pierre St. Pierre, that Gazelle Nataways found Zachary Jeremiah Keechigeesik's undershorts under her chesterfield and washed them and put them in a box real nice, all folded up and even sprin-
710 kled her perfume all over them and sashayed herself over to Hera Keechigeesik's house and handed the box over to her? I just about had a heart attack," she says to me. "And what's more," she says to me, "when Hera Keechigeesik opened that box, there was a picture sittin' on top of them shorts, a
715 color picture of none other than our very own Zachary Jeremiah Keechigeesik . . . (*Unseen by* PIERRE, ZACHARY *approaches the group, wearing a baker's hat and carrying a rolling pin.*) . . . wearin' nothin' but the suit God gave him. That's when Hera Keechigeesik went wild, like a banshee
720 tigger, and she tore the hair out of Gazelle Nataways which, as it turns out, was a wig . . ." Imagine. After all these years. ". . . and she beat Gazelle Nataways to a cinder, right there into the treacherous icy door-step. And that's when 'the particular puck' finally came squishin' out of them consider-
725 able Nataways bosoms." And gentlemen? The Wasy Wailerettes are on again!

CREATURE: Ho-leee!

SPOOKY: Holy fuck!

PIERRE: And I say shit la ma . . . (*Finally seeing* ZACHARY, *who
730 is standing there, listening to all this.*) . . . oh my . . . (PIERRE *turns quickly to* SPOOKY's *baby.*) . . . hello there, koochie-koochie-koo, welcome to the world!

SPOOKY: It's not koochie-koochie-koo, Pierre St. Pierre. Her name's "Kichigeechacha." Rhymes with Lalala. Ain't she
735 purdy?

(*Up in the "bleachers,"* BIG JOEY *enters and prepares his microphone stand.* DICKIE BIRD *enters with a big sign saying: "WASY-FM" and hangs it proudly up above the microphone stand.*)

PIERRE: Aw, she'll be readin' that ole holy bible before you can go: "Phhht! Phhht!"

(PIERRE *accidentally spits in the baby's face.* SPOOKY *shoos him away.*)

SPOOKY: "Phhht! Phhht!" to you too, Pierre St. Pierre.

CREATURE: Spooky Lacroix. Lalala. They never made it to
740 Sudbury General.

SPOOKY: I was busy helping Eugene Starblanket out with Simon . . .

SPOOKY/PIERRE: . . . may he rest in peace . . .

ZACHARY: Good old Rosie Kakapetum. "Stand and deliver,"
745 they said to her. And stand and deliver she did. How's the knitting going there, Creature Nataways?

CREATURE: Kichigeechacha, my god-daughter, she's wearin' all the wrong colors. I gotta work like a dog.

PIERRE: (*Calling up to* DICKIE BIRD HALKED.) Don't you worry
750 a wart about that court appearance, Dickie Bird Halked. I'll be right there beside you tellin' that ole judge a thing or two about that goddamn jukebox.

SPOOKY: (*To* CREATURE.) Come on. Let's go watch Lalala play her first game.

(*He and* CREATURE *go up to the "bleachers" on the upper level, directly in front of* NANABUSH's *perch, to watch the big "game."*)

755 PIERRE: (*Reading from his clip-board and checking off the list.*) Now then, Dominique Ladouche, Black Lady Halked, Annie Cook, June Bug Mcleod . . .

(*He stops abruptly for* BIG JOEY's *announcement, as do the other men.*)

BIG JOEY: (*On the microphone.*) Patsy Pegahmagahbow, who is recuperating at Sudbury General Hospital, sends her love 760 and requests that the first goal scored by the Wasy Wailerettes be dedicated to the memory of Simon Starblanket . . .

(CREATURE *and* SPOOKY, *with knitting and baby, respectively, are now up in the "bleachers" with* DICKIE BIRD *and* BIG JOEY, *who are standing beside each other at the microphone stand.* PIERRE ST. PIERRE *is again skating around on the "ice" in his own inimitable fashion, "warming up."* ZACHARY JEREMIAH KEECHIGEESIK, *meanwhile, now has his apple pie, as well as his rolling pin, in hand, still wearing his baker's hat. At this point, the hockey arena sounds shift abruptly to the sound of women wailing and pucks hitting boards, echoing and echoing as in a vast empty chamber. As this "hockey game sequence" progresses, the spectacle of the men watching, cheering, etc., becomes more and more dream-like, all the men's movements imperceptibly breaking down into slow motion, until they fade, later, into the darkness.* ZACHARY *"sleep walks" through the whole lower level of the set, almost as though he were retracing his steps back through the whole play. Slowly, he takes off his clothes item by item, until, by the end, he is back lying naked on the couch where he began the play, except that, this time, it will be his own couch he is lying on.* BIG JOEY *continues uninterrupted.*)[2]

. . . And there they are, ladies igwa gentlemen, there they are, the most beautiful, daring, death-defying Indian women in the world, the Wasy Wailerettes! How, Number Nine Hera 765 Keechigeesik, CAPTAIN of the Wasy Wailerettes, face-off igwa itootum asichi Number Nine Flora McDonald, Captain of the Canoe Lake Bravettes. Hey, soogi pagichee-ipinew "particular puck" referee Pierre St. Pierre . . .

CREATURE: Go Hera go! Go Hera go! Go Hera go! . . .

(*Repeated all the way through—and under—* BIG JOEY's *commentary.*)

770 BIG JOEY: . . . igwa seemak wathay g'waskootoo like a herd of wild turtles . . .

SPOOKY: Wasy once. Wasy twice. Holy jumping Christ! Rim ram. God damn. Fuck, son-of-a-bitch, shit!

(*Repeated in time to* CREATURE's *cheer, all the way through—and under—* BIG JOEY's *commentary.*)

BIG JOEY: . . . Hey, aspin Number Six Dry Lips Manigitogan, 775 right-winger for the Wasy Wailerettes, eemaskamat Number Thirteen of the Canoe Lake Bravettes anee-i "particular puck" . . . (DICKIE BIRD *begins chanting and stomping his foot in time to* CREATURE's *and* SPOOKY's *cheers. Bits and*

pieces of NANABUSH/GAZELLE NATAWAYS' *"strip music" and Kitty Wells' "It Wasn't God Who Made Honky Tonk Angels"* 780 *begin to weave in and out of this "sound collage," a collage which now has a definite "pounding" rhythm to it. Over it all soars the sound of* ZACHARY's *harmonica, swooping and diving brilliantly, recalling many of* NANABUSH's *appearances throughout the play.* BIG JOEY *continues uninterrupted.*) . . . 785 igwa aspin sipweesinskwataygew. Hey, k'seegoochin! How, Number Six Dry Lips Manigitogan igwa soogi pugamawew anee-i "particular puck" ita Number Twenty-six Little Girl Manitowabi, left-winger for the Wasy Wailerettes, katee-ooteetuk blue line ita Number Eleven Black Lady Halked, 790 wha! defense-woman for the Wasy Wailerettes, kagatchitnat anee-i "particular puck" igwa seemak kapassiwatat Captain Hera Keechigeesikwa igwa Hera Keechigeesik mitooni eepimithat, hey, kwayus graceful Hera Keechigeesik, mi-tooni Russian ballerina eesinagoosit. Captain Hera 795 Keechigeesik bee-line igwa itootum straight for the Canoe Lake Bravettes' net igwa shootiwatew anee-i "particular puck" igwa she shoots, she scores . . . almost! Wha! Close one, ladies igwa gentlemen, kwayus close one. But Number Six Dry Lips Manigitogan, right-winger for the Wasy Wailerettes, 800 accidentally tripped and blocked the shot . . . (BIG JOEY's *voice begins to trail off as, at this point,* CREATURE NATAWAYS *marches over and angrily grabs the microphone away from him.*) . . . How, Number Nine Flora McDonald, Captain of the Canoe Lake Bravettes, igwa ooteetinew anee-i "particular 805 puck" igwa skate-oo-oo behind the net igwa soogi heading along the right side of the rink ita Number Twenty-one Annie Cook . . .

CREATURE: (*Off microphone, as he marches over to it.*) Aw shit! Aw shit! . . . (*He grabs the microphone and, as he talks into it,* 810 *the sound of all the other men's voices, including the entire "sound collage," begins to fade.*) . . . That Dry Lips Manigitogan, she's no damn good, Spooky Lacroix, I tole you once I tole you twice she shouldna done it she shouldna done what she went and did goddawful Dry Lips Manigitogan they 815 shouldna let her play, she's too fat, she's gotten positively blubbery lately, I tole you once I tole you twice that Dry Lips Manigitogan oughta move to Kapuskasing, she really oughta, Spooky Lacroix. I tole you once I tole you twice she oughta move to Kapuskasing, Dry Lips oughta move to Ka- 820 puskasing! Dry Lips oughta move to Kapuskasing! Dry Lips oughta move to Kapuskasing! Dry Lips oughta move to Ka-puskasing Dry Lips oughta move to Kapuskasing Dry Lips oughta move to Kapuskasing Dry Lips oughta move to Ka-puskasing Dry Lips oughta move to Kapuskasing Dry Lips 825 oughta move to Kapuskasing . . .

(*And this, too, fades into, first a whisper, magnified on tape to "other-worldly" proportions, then into a slow kind of heavy breathing. On top of this we hear* SPOOKY's *baby crying. Complete fade-out on all this (lights and sound), except for the baby's crying and the heavy breathing, which continue in the darkness. When the lights come up again, we are in* ZACHARY's *own living room (i.e., what was all along* BIG JOEY's *living room/kitchen, only much cleaner). The couch* ZACHARY *lies on is now covered with a "starblanket" and over the pin-up poster of*

---

[2] The following hockey commentary by Big Joey (page 1268) is translated on page 1269.

Marilyn Monroe now hangs what was, earlier on, NANABUSH's *large powwow dancing bustle. The theme from "The Smurfs" television show bleeds in.* ZACHARY *is lying on the couch face down, naked, sleeping and snoring. The television in front of the couch comes on and "The Smurfs" are playing merrily away.* ZACHARY's *wife, the "real"* HERA KEECHIGEESIK, *enters carrying their baby, who is covered completely with a blanket.* HERA *is soothing the crying baby.)*

ZACHARY: *(Talking in his sleep.)* . . . Dry Lips . . . oughta move to . . . Kapus . . .

HERA: Poosees.

830 ZACHARY: . . . kasing . . . damn silliest thing I heard in my life . . .

HERA: Honey.

(Bends over the couch and kisses ZACHARY *on the bum.)*

ZACHARY: . . . goodness sakes, Hera, you just had a baby . . . *(Suddenly, he jumps up and falls off the couch.)* Simon!

835 HERA: Yoah! Keegatch igwa kipageecheep'skawinan. ("Yoah! You almost knocked us down.")

ZACHARY: Hera! Where's my shorts?!

HERA: Neee, kigipoochimeek awus-chayees. ("Neee, just a couple of inches past the rim of your ass-hole.")

840 ZACHARY: Neee, chimagideedoosh. ("Neee, you unfragrant kozy": Ojibway.)

(He struggles to a sitting position on the couch.)

HERA: *(Correcting him and laughing.)* "ChimagideeDEESH." ("You unfragrant KOOZIE.")

ZACHARY: Alright. "ChimagideeDEESH."

845 HERA: And what were you dreaming abou . . .

ZACHARY: *(Finally seeing the television.)* Hey, it's the Smurfs! And they're not playing hockey de Englesa.

HERA: Neee, machi ma-a tatoo-Saturday morning Smurfs. Mootha meena weegatch hockey meetaweewuk weethawow

850 Smurfs. ("Well, of course, the Smurfs are on every Saturday morning. But they never play hockey, those Smurfs.") Here, you take her. *(She hands the baby over to* ZACHARY *and goes to sit beside him.)* Boy, that full moon last night. Ever look particularly like a giant puck, eh? Neee . . .

(Silence. ZACHARY *plays with the baby.)*

855 ZACHARY: *(To* HERA.*)* Hey, cup-cake. You ever think of playing hockey?

HERA: Yeah, right. That's all I need is a flying puck right in the left tit, neee . . . *(But she stops to speculate.)* . . . hockey, hmmm . . .

860 ZACHARY: *(To himself.)* Lordy, lordy, lordy . . . *(*HERA *fishes* ZACHARY's *undershorts, which are pale blue in color, from under a cushion and hands them to him.* ZACHARY *gladly grabs them.)* Neee, magawa nipeetawitoos . . . ("Neee, here's my shorts . . .")

865 HERA: *(Correcting him and laughing.)* "NipeetawiTAS." ("My SHORTS")

ZACHARY: Alright. "NipeetawiTAS." *(Dangles the shorts up to the baby's face with thumb and fore-finger and laughs. Sing-songy, bouncing the baby on his lap:)* Magawa nipeetawitas.

870 Nipeetawitas. Nipeetawitas. Nipeetawitas . . .

(The baby finally gets "dislodged" from the blanket and emerges, naked. And the last thing we see is this beautiful naked Indian man lifting his naked baby Indian girl up in the air, his wife sitting beside them watching and laughing. Slow fade-out. Split seconds before complete black-out, HERA *peals out with this magical, silvery* NANABUSH *laugh, which is echoed and echoed by one last magical arpeggio on the harmonica, from off-stage. Finally, in the darkness, the last sound we hear is the baby's laughing voice, magnified on tape to fill the entire theater. And this, too, fades into complete silence.)*

End of play.

Translation from the Cree of Big Joey's hockey commentary, Act One, pages 1257–1258.

. . . Hey, and there goes Number Six Dry Lips Manigitogan, right-winger for the Wasy Wailerettes . . . and steals the puck from Number Thirteen of the Canoe Lake Bravettes . . . and skates off. Hey, is she ever flying . . . *(Off microphone.)* Creature Nataways. Shut up. *(To the other men.)* Get this asshole   5
out of here. *(Back on microphone.)* Now, Number Six Dry Lips Manigitogan, right-winger for the Wasy Wailerettes, shoots the puck and the puck goes flying over towards the center-line . . . where Number Nine Hera Keechigeesik, left-winger for . . . the Wasy Wailerettes, catches it. Now,   10
Number Nine Hera Keechigeesik . . . approaching the blue line where Number One Gazelle Nataways, Captain of the Wasy Wailerettes, tries to get the puck off her, but Number Nine Hera Keechigeesik won't give it to her. Wha! "Hooking," says referee Pierre St. Pierre, Gazelle Nataways has ap-   15
parently hooked her own team-mate Hera Keechigeesik, wha! Now, Number One Gazelle Nataways, Captain of the Wasy Wailerettes, facing off once again with Number Nine Flora McDonald, Captain of the Canoe Lake Bravettes and Flora McDonald shoots the puck, but Number Thirty-seven   20
Big Bum Pegahmagahbow, defense-woman for the Wasy Wailerettes, stops the puck and passes it to Number Eleven Black Lady Halked, also defense-woman for the Wasy Wailerettes, but Gazelle Nataways, Captain of the Wasy Wailerettes, gives a mean body check to her own team-mate   25
Black Lady Halked woops! She falls, ladies and gentlemen, Black Lady Halked hits the boards and Black Lady Halked is singin' the blues, ladies and gentlemen, Black Lady sings the blues. *(Off microphone.)* What the hell is going on down there? Dickie Bird, get off the ice! *(Back on microphone.)*   30
Wha! Number Eleven Black Lady Halked is up in a flash and grabs the puck from Gazelle Nataways, holy shit! The ailing but very, very furious Black Lady Halked skates back, turns and takes aim, it's gonna be a slap shot, ladies and gentlemen, Black Lady Halked is gonna take a slap shot for sure   35
and Black Lady Halked shoots the puck, wha! She shoots straight at her very own captain, Gazelle Nataways and holy shit, holy shit, holy fuckin' shit!

Translation from the Cree of Big Joey's hockey commentary, Act Two, page 1268.

. . . And there they are, ladies and gentlemen, there they are, the most beautiful, daring, death-defying Indian women in the world, the Wasy Wailerettes! Now, Number Nine Hera

Keechigeesik, CAPTAIN of the Wasy Wailerettes, facing off with Number Nine Flora McDonald, Captain of the Canoe Lake Bravettes. Hey, and referee Pierre St. Pierre drops the "particular puck" . . . and takes off like a herd of wild turtles . . . Hey, and there goes Dry Lips Manigitogan, right-winger for the Wasy Wailerettes, and steals the "particular puck" from Number Thirteen of the Canoe Lake Bravettes . . . and skates off. Hey, is she ever flying. Now, Number Six Dry Lips Manigitogan shoots the "particular puck" towards where Number Twenty-six Little Girl Manitowabi, left-winger for the Wasy Wailerettes, is heading straight for the blue line where Number Eleven Black Lady Halked, wha! defense-woman for the Wasy Wailerettes, catches the "particular puck" and straight-way passes it to Captain Hera Keechigeesik and Hera Keechigeesik is just a-flyin', hey, is she graceful or what, that Hera Keechigeesik, she looks just like a Russian ballerina. Captain Hera Keechigeesik now makes a bee-line straight for the Canoe Lake Bravettes' net and shoots the "particular puck" and she shoots, she scores . . . almost! Wha! Close one, ladies and gentlemen, real close one. But Number Six Dry Lips Manitigotan, right-winger for the Wasy Wailerettes, accidentally tripped and blocked the shot . . . (CREATURE NATAWAYS *grabs the microphone away from* BIG JOEY.) . . . Now, Number Nine Flora McDonald, Captain of the Canoe Lake Bravettes, grabs the "particular puck" and skates behind the net and now heading along the right side of the rink where Number Twenty-one Annie Cook . . .

CRITICAL CONTEXTS

An early member of the surrealist movement in Paris, Antonin Artaud was well-known between the wars as an actor, playwright, and essayist of the avant-garde theater, and he is one of the formative influences on the modern European theater. Artaud is most often associated with the "theater of cruelty," his label for a theater that would assault the representational dynamics of traditional theater and break the boundaries between actor and audience, stage and spectacle. Artaud was declared insane and committed to a mental hospital in 1937. He remained institutionalized for most of the remainder of his life.

ANTONIN ARTAUD
(1896–1948)

FROM *THE THEATER AND ITS DOUBLE* **(1938)**

TRANSLATED BY MARY CAROLINE RICHARDS

THE THEATER AND CULTURE

Never before, when it is life itself that is in question, has there been so much talk of civilization and culture. And there is a curious parallel between this generalized collapse of life at the root of our present demoralization and our concern for a culture which has never been coincident with life, which in fact has been devised to tyrannize over life.

Before speaking further about culture, I must remark that the world is hungry and not concerned with culture, and that the attempt to orient toward culture thoughts turned only toward hunger is a purely artificial expedient.

What is most important, it seems to me, is not so much to defend a culture whose existence has never kept a man from going hungry, as to extract, from what is called culture, ideas whose compelling force is identical with that of hunger.

We need to live first of all; to believe in what makes us live and that something *makes* us live—to believe that whatever is produced from the mysterious depths of ourselves need not forever haunt us as an exclusively digestive concern.

I mean that if it is important for us to eat first of all, it is even more important for us not to waste in the sole concern for eating our simple power of being hungry.

If confusion is the sign of the times, I see at the root of this confusion a rupture between things and words, between things and the ideas and signs that are their representation.

Not, of course, for lack of philosophical systems; their number and contradictions characterize our old French and European culture: but where can it be shown that life, our life, has ever been affected by these systems? I will not say that philosophical systems must be applied directly and immediately: but of the following alternatives, one must be true:

Either these systems are within us and permeate our being to the point of supporting life itself (and if this is the case, what use are books?), or they do *not* permeate us and therefore do not have the capacity to support life (and in this case what does their disappearance matter?).

We must insist upon the idea of culture-in-action, of culture growing within us like a new organ, a sort of second breath; and on civilization as an applied culture controlling even our subtlest actions, a *presence of mind*; the distinction between culture and civilization is an artificial one, providing two words to signify an identical function.

A civilized man judges and is judged according to his behavior, but even the term "civilized" leads to confusion: a cultivated "civilized" man is regarded as a person instructed in systems, a person who thinks in forms, signs, representations—a monster whose faculty of deriving thoughts from acts, instead of identifying acts with thoughts, is developed to an absurdity.

If our life lacks brimstone, i.e., a constant magic, it is because we choose to observe our acts and lose ourselves in considerations of their imagined form instead of being impelled by their force.

And this faculty is an exclusively human one. I would even say that it is this infection of the human which contaminates ideas that should have remained divine; for far from believing that man invented the supernatural and the divine, I think it is man's age-old intervention which has ultimately corrupted the divine within him.

All our ideas about life must be revised in a period when nothing any longer adheres to life; it is this painful cleavage which is responsible for the revenge of *things*; the poetry which is no longer within us and which we no longer succeed in finding in things suddenly appears on their wrong side: consider the unprecedented number of crimes whose perverse gratuitousness is explained only by our powerlessness to take complete possession of life.

If the theater has been created as an outlet for our repressions, the agonized poetry expressed in its bizarre corruptions of the facts of life demonstrates that life's intensity is still intact and asks only to be better directed.

But no matter how loudly we clamor for magic in our lives, we are really afraid of pursuing an existence entirely under its influence and sign.

Hence our confirmed lack of culture is astonished by certain grandiose anomalies; for example, on an island without any contact with modern civilization, the mere passage of a ship carrying only healthy passengers may provoke the sudden outbreak of diseases unknown on that island but a specialty of nations like our own: shingles, influenza, grippe, rheumatism, sinusitis, polyneuritis, etc.

Similarly, if we think Negroes smell bad, we are ignorant of the fact that anywhere but in Europe it is we whites who "smell bad." And I would even say that we give off an odor as white as the gathering of pus in an infected wound.

As iron can be heated until it turns white, so it can be said that everything excessive is white; for Asiatics white has become the mark of extreme decomposition.

This said, we can begin to form an idea of culture, an idea which is first of all a protest.

A protest against the senseless constraint imposed upon the idea of culture by reducing it to a sort of inconceivable Pantheon, producing an idolatry no different from the image-worship of those religions which relegate their gods to Pantheons.

A protest against the idea of culture as distinct from life—as if there were culture on one side and life on the other, as if true culture were not a refined means of understanding and *exercising* life.

The library at Alexandria can be burnt down. There are forces above and beyond papyrus: we may temporarily be deprived of our ability to discover these forces, but their energy will not be suppressed. It is good that our excessive facilities are no longer available, that forms fall into oblivion: a culture without space or time, restrained only by the capacity of our own nerves, will reappear with all the more energy. It is right that from time to time cataclysms occur which compel us to return to nature, i.e., to rediscover life. The old totemism of animals, stones, objects capable of discharging thunderbolts, costumes impregnated with bestial essences—everything, in short, that might determine, disclose, and direct the secret forces of the universe—is for us a dead thing, from which we derive nothing but static and aesthetic profit, the profit of an audience, not of an actor.

Yet totemism is an actor, for it moves, and has been created in behalf of actors; all true culture relies upon the barbaric and primitive means of totemism whose savage, i.e., entirely spontaneous, life I wish to worship.

What has lost us culture is our Occidental idea of art and the profits we seek to derive from it. Art and culture cannot be considered together, contrary to the treatment universally accorded them!

True culture operates by exaltation and force, while the European ideal of art attempts to cast the mind into an attitude distinct from force but addicted to exaltation. It is a lazy, unserviceable notion which engenders an imminent death. If the Serpent Quetzalcoatl's multiple twists and turns are harmonious, it is because they express the equilibrium and fluctuations of a sleeping force; the intensity of the forms is there only to seduce and direct a force which, in music, would produce an insupportable range of sound.

The gods that sleep in museums: the god of fire with his incense burner that resembles an Inquisition tripod; Tlaloc, one of the manifold Gods of the Waters, on his wall of green granite; the Mother Goddess of Waters, the Mother Goddess of Flowers; the immutable expression, echoing from beneath many layers of water, of the Goddess robed in green jade; the enraptured, blissful expression, features crackling with incense, where atoms of sunlight circle—the countenance of the Mother Goddess of Flowers; this world of obligatory servitude in which a stone comes alive when it has been properly carved, the world of organically civilized men whose vital organs too awaken from their slumber, this human world enters into us, participating in the dance of the gods without turning round or looking back, on pain of becoming, like ourselves, crumbled pillars of salt.

In Mexico, since we are talking about Mexico, there is no art: things are made for use. And the world is in perpetual exaltation.

To our disinterested and inert idea of art an authentic culture opposes a violently egoistic and magical, i.e., *interested* idea. For the Mexicans seek contact with the *Manas*, forces latent in every form, unreleased by contemplation of the forms for themselves, but springing to life by magic identification with these forms. And the old Totems are there to hasten the communication.

How hard it is, when everything encourages us to sleep, though we may look about us with conscious, clinging eyes, to wake and yet look about us as in a dream, with eyes that no longer know their function and whose gaze is turned inward.

This is how our strange idea of disinterested action originated, though it is action nonetheless, and all the more violent for skirting the temptation of repose.

Every real effigy has a shadow which is its double; and art must falter and fail from the moment the sculptor believes he has liberated the kind of shadow whose very existence will destroy his repose.

Like all magic cultures expressed by appropriate hieroglyphs, the true theater has its shadows too, and, of all languages and all arts, the theater is the only one left whose shadows have shattered their limitations. From the beginning, one might say its shadows did not tolerate limitations.

Our petrified idea of the theater is connected with our petrified idea of a culture without shadows, where, no matter which way it turns, our mind *(esprit)* encounters only emptiness, though space is full.

But the true theater, because it moves and makes use of living instruments, continues to stir up shadows where life has never ceased to grope its way. The actor does not make the same gestures twice, but he makes gestures, he moves; and although he brutalizes forms, nevertheless behind them and through their destruction he rejoins that which outlives forms and produces their continuation.

The theater, which is in *no thing*, but makes use of everything—gestures, sounds, words, screams, light, darkness—rediscovers itself at precisely the point where the mind requires a language to express its manifestations.

And the fixation of the theater in one language—written words, music, lights, noises—betokens its imminent ruin, the choice of any one language betraying a taste for the special effects of that language; and the dessication of the language accompanies its limitation.

For the theater as for culture, it remains a question of naming and directing shadows: and the theater, not confined to a fixed language and form, not only destroys false shadows but prepares the way for a new generation of shadows, around which assembles the true spectacle of life.

To break through language in order to touch life is to create or recreate the theater; the essential thing is not to believe that this act must remain sacred, i.e., set apart—the essential thing is to believe that not just anyone can create it, and that there must be a preparation.

This leads to the rejection of the usual limitations of man and man's powers, and infinitely extends the frontiers of what is called reality.

We must believe in a sense of life renewed by the theater, a sense of life in which man fearlessly makes himself master of what does not yet exist, and brings it into being. And everything that has not been born can still be brought to life if we are not satisfied to remain mere recording organisms.

Furthermore, when we speak the word "life," it must be understood we are not referring to life as we know it from its surface of fact, but to that fragile, fluctuating center which forms never reach. And if there is still one hellish, truly accursed thing in our time, it is our artistic dallying with forms, instead of being like victims burnt at the stake, signaling through the flames.

◆　◆　◆

One of the reasons for the asphyxiating atmosphere in which we live without possible escape or remedy—and in which we all share, even the most revolutionary among us—is our respect for what has been written, formulated, or painted, what has been given form, as if all expression were not at last exhausted, were not at a point where things must break apart if they are to start anew and begin fresh.

We must have done with this idea of masterpieces reserved for a self-styled elite and not understood by the general public; the mind has no such restricted districts as those so often used for clandestine sexual encounters.

NO MORE MASTERPIECES

Masterpieces of the past are good for the past: they are not good for us. We have the right to say what has been said and even what has not been said in a way that belongs to us, a way that is immediate and direct, corresponding to present modes of feeling, and understandable to everyone.

It is idiotic to reproach the masses for having no sense of the sublime, when the sublime is confused with one or another of its formal manifestations, which are moreover always defunct manifestations. And if for example a contemporary public does not understand *Oedipus Rex*, I shall make bold to say that it is the fault of *Oedipus Rex* and not of the public.

In *Oedipus Rex* there is the theme of incest and the idea that nature mocks at morality and that there are certain unspecified powers at large which we would do well to beware of, call them *destiny* or anything you choose.

There is in addition the presence of a plague epidemic which is a physical incarnation of these powers. But the whole in a manner and language that have lost all touch with the rude and epileptic rhythm of our time. Sophocles speaks grandly perhaps, but in a style that is no longer timely. His language is too refined for this age, it is as if he were speaking beside the point.

However, a public that shudders at train wrecks, that is familiar with earthquakes, plagues, revolutions, wars; that is sensitive to the disordered anguish of love, can be affected by all these grand notions and asks only to become aware of them, but on condition that it is addressed in its own language, and that its knowledge of these things does not come to it through adulterated trappings and speech that belong to extinct eras which will never live again.

Today as yesterday, the public is greedy for mystery: it asks only to become aware of the laws according to which destiny manifests itself, and to divine perhaps the secret of its apparitions.

Let us leave textual criticism to graduate students, formal criticism to esthetes, and recognize that what has been said is not still to be said; that an expression does not have the same value twice, does not live two lives; that all words, once spoken, are dead and function only at the moment when they are uttered, that a form, once it has served, cannot be used again and asks only to be replaced by another, and that the theater is the only place in the world where a gesture, once made, can never be made the same way twice.

If the public does not frequent our literary masterpieces, it is because those masterpieces are literary, that is to say, fixed; and fixed in forms that no longer respond to the needs of the time.

Far from blaming the public, we ought to blame the formal screen we interpose between ourselves and the public, and this new form of idolatry, the idolatry of fixed masterpieces which is one of the aspects of bourgeois conformism.

This conformism makes us confuse sublimity, ideas, and things with the forms they have taken in time and in our minds—in our snobbish, precious, aesthetic mentalities which the public does not understand.

How pointless in such matters to accuse the public of bad taste because it relishes insanities, so long as the public is not shown a valid spectacle; and I defy anyone to show me *here* a spectacle valid—valid in the supreme sense of the theater—since the last great romantic melodramas, i.e., since a hundred years ago.

The public, which takes the false for the true, has the sense of the true and always responds to it when it is manifested. However it is not upon the stage that the true is to be sought nowadays, but in the street; and if the crowd in the street is offered an occasion to show its human dignity, it will always do so.

If people are out of the habit of going to the theater, if we have all finally come to think of theater as an inferior art, a means of popular distraction, and to use it as an outlet for our worst instincts, it is because we have learned too well what the theater has been, namely, falsehood and illusion. It is because we have been accustomed for four hundred years, that is since the Renaissance, to a purely descriptive and narrative theater—storytelling psychology; it is because every possible ingenuity has been exerted in bringing to life on the stage plausible but detached beings, with the spectacle on one side, the public on the other—and because the public is no longer shown anything but the mirror of itself.

Shakespeare himself is responsible for this aberration and decline, this disinterested idea of the theater which wishes a theatrical performance to leave the public intact, without setting off one image that will shake the organism to its foundations and leave an ineffaceable scar.

If, in Shakespeare, a man is sometimes preoccupied with what transcends him, it is always in order to determine the ultimate consequences of this preoccupation within him, i.e., psychology.

Psychology, which works relentlessly to reduce the unknown to the known, to the quotidian and the ordinary, is the cause of the theater's abasement and its fearful loss of energy, which seems to me to have reached its lowest point. And I think both the theater and we ourselves have had enough of psychology.

I believe furthermore that we can all agree on this matter sufficiently so that there is no need to descend to the repugnant level of the modern and French theater to condemn the theater of psychology.

Stories about money, worry over money, social careerism, the pangs of love unspoiled by altruism, sexuality sugar-coated with an eroticism that has lost its mystery have nothing to do with the theater, even if they do belong to psychology. These torments, seductions, and lusts before which we are nothing but Peeping Toms gratifying our cravings, tend to go bad, and their rot turns to revolution: we must take this into account.

But this is not our most serious concern.

If Shakespeare and his imitators have gradually insinuated the idea of art for art's sake, with art on one side and life on the other, we can rest on this feeble and lazy idea only as long as the life outside endures. But there are too many signs that everything that used to sustain our lives no longer does so, that we are all mad, desperate, and sick. And I call for *us* to react.

This idea of a detached art, of poetry as a charm which exists only to distract our leisure, is a decadent idea and an unmistakable symptom of our power to castrate.

Our literary admiration for Rimbaud, Jarry, Lautréamont, and a few others, which has driven two men to suicide, but turned into café gossip for the rest, belongs to this idea of literary poetry, of detached art, of neutral spiritual activity which creates nothing and produces nothing; and I can bear witness that at the very moment when that kind of personal poetry which involves only the man who creates it and only at the moment he creates it broke out in its most abusive fashion, the theater was scorned more than ever before by poets who have never had the sense of direct and concerted action, nor of efficacity, nor of danger.

We must get rid of our superstitious valuation of texts and *written* poetry. Written poetry is worth reading once, and then should be destroyed. Let the dead poets make way for others. Then we might even come to see that it is our veneration for what has already been created, however beautiful and valid it may be, that petrifies us, deadens our responses, and prevents us from making contact with that underlying power, call it thought-energy, the life force, the determinism of change, lunar menses, or anything you like. Beneath the poetry of the texts, there is the actual poetry, without form and without text. And just as the efficacity of masks in the magic practices of certain tribes is exhausted—and these masks are no longer good for anything except museums—so the poetic efficacity of a text is exhausted; yet the poetry and the efficacity of the theater are exhausted least quickly of all, since they permit the *action* of what is gesticulated and pronounced, and which is never made the same way twice.

It is a question of knowing what we want. If we are prepared for war, plague, famine, and slaughter we do not even need to say so, we have only to continue as we are; continue behaving like snobs, rushing en masse to hear such and such a singer, to see such and such an admirable performance which never transcends the realm of art (and even the Russian ballet at the height of its splendor never transcended the realm of art), to marvel at such and such an exhibition of painting in which exciting shapes explode here and there but at random and without any genuine consciousness of the forces they could rouse.

This empiricism, randomness, individualism, and anarchy must cease.

Enough of personal poems, benefitting those who create them much more than those who read them.

Once and for all, enough of this closed, egoistic, and personal art.

Our spiritual anarchy and intellectual disorder is a function of the anarchy of everything else—or rather, everything else is a function of this anarchy.

I am not one of those who believe that civilization has to change in order for the theater to change; but I do believe that the theater, utilized in the highest and most difficult sense possible, has the power to influence the aspect and formation of things: and the encounter upon the stage of two passionate manifestations, two living centers, two nervous magnetisms is something as entire, true, even decisive, as, in life, the encounter of one epidermis with another in a timeless debauchery.

That is why I propose a theater of cruelty.—With this mania we all have for depreciating everything, as soon as I have said "cruelty," everybody will at once take it to mean "blood." But *"theater of cruelty"* means a theater difficult and cruel for myself first of all. And, on the level of performance, it is not the cruelty we can exercise upon each other by hacking at each other's bodies, carving up our personal anatomies, or, like Assyrian emperors, sending parcels of human ears, noses, or neatly detached nostrils through the mail, but the much more terrible and necessary cruelty which things can exercise against us. We are not free. And the sky can still fall on our heads. And the theater has been created to teach us that first of all.

Either we will be capable of returning by present-day means to this superior idea of poetry and poetry-through-theater which underlies the Myths told by the great ancient tragedians, capable once more of entertaining a religious idea of the theater (without meditation, useless contemplation, and vague dreams), capable of attaining awareness and a possession of certain dominant forces, of certain notions that control all others, and (since ideas, when they are effective, carry their energy with them) capable of recovering within ourselves those energies which ultimately create order and increase the value of life, or else we might as well abandon ourselves now, without protest, and recognize that we are no longer good for anything but disorder, famine, blood, war, and epidemics.

Either we restore all the arts to a central attitude and necessity, finding an analogy between a gesture made in painting or the theater, and a gesture made by lava in a volcanic explosion, or we must stop painting, babbling, writing, or doing whatever it is we do.

I propose to bring back into the theater this elementary magical idea, taken up by modern psychoanalysis, which consists in effecting a patient's cure by making him assume the apparent and exterior attitudes of the desired condition.

I propose to renounce our empiricism of imagery, in which the unconscious furnishes images at random, and which the poet arranges at random too, calling them poetic and hence hermetic images, as if the kind of trance that poetry provides did not have its reverberations throughout the whole sensibility, in every nerve, and as if poetry were some vague force whose movements were invariable.

I propose to return through the theater to an idea of the physical knowledge of images and the means of inducing trances, as in Chinese medicine which knows, over the entire extent of the human anatomy, at what points to puncture in order to regulate the subtlest functions.

Those who have forgotten the communicative power and magical mimesis of a gesture, the theater can reinstruct, because a gesture carries its energy with it, and there are still human beings in the theater to manifest the force of the gesture made.

To create art is to deprive a gesture of its reverberation in the organism, whereas this reverberation, if the gesture is made in the conditions and with the force required, incites the organism and, through it, the entire individuality, to take attitudes in harmony with the gesture.

The theater is the only place in the world, the last general means we still possess of directly affecting the organism and, in periods of neurosis and petty sensuality like the one in which we are immersed, of attacking this sensuality by physical means it cannot withstand.

If music affects snakes, it is not on account of the spiritual notions it offers them, but because snakes are long and coil their length upon the earth, because their bodies touch the earth at almost every point; and because the musical vibrations which are communicated to the earth affect them like a very subtle, very long massage; and I propose to treat the spectators like the snakecharmer's subjects and conduct them *by means of their organisms* to an apprehension of the subtlest notions.

At first by crude means, which will gradually be refined. These immediate crude means will hold their attention at the start.

That is why in the "theater of cruelty" the spectator is in the center and the spectacle surrounds him.

In this spectacle the sonorisation is constant: sounds, noises, cries are chosen first for their vibratory quality, then for what they represent.

Among these gradually refined means light is interposed in its turn. Light which is not created merely to add color or to brighten, and which brings its power, influence, suggestions with it. And the light of a green cavern does not sensually dispose the organism like the light of a windy day.

After sound and light there is action, and the dynamism of action: here the theater, far from copying life, puts itself whenever possible in communication with pure forces. And whether you accept or deny them, there is nevertheless a way of speaking which gives the name of "forces" to whatever brings to birth images of energy in the unconscious, and gratuitous crime on the surface.

A violent and concentrated action is a kind of lyricism: it summons up supernatural images, a bloodstream of images, a bleeding spurt of images in the poet's head and in the spectator's as well.

Whatever the conflicts that haunt the mind of a given period, I defy any spectator to whom such violent scenes will have transferred their blood, who will have felt in himself the transit of a superior action, who will have seen the extraordinary and essential movements of his thought illuminated in extraordinary deeds—the violence and blood having been placed at the service of the violence of the thought—I defy that spectator to give himself up, once outside the theater, to ideas of war, riot, and blatant murder.

So expressed, this idea seems dangerous and sophomoric. It will be claimed that example breeds example, that if the attitude of cure induces cure, the attitude of murder will induce murder. Everything depends upon the manner and the purity with which the thing is done. There is a risk. But let it not be forgotten that though a theatrical gesture is violent, it is disinterested; and that the theater teaches precisely the uselessness of the action which, once done, is not to be done, and the superior use of the state unused by the action and which, *restored*, produces a purification.

I propose then a theater in which violent physical images crush and hypnotize the sensibility of the spectator seized by the theater as by a whirlwind of higher forces.

A theater which, abandoning psychology, recounts the extraordinary, stages natural conflicts, natural and subtle forces, and presents itself first of all as an exceptional power of redirection. A theater that induces trance, as the dances of Dervishes induce trance, and that addresses itself to the organism by precise instruments, by the same means as those of certain tribal music cures which we admire on records but are incapable of originating among ourselves.

There is a risk involved, but in the present circumstances I believe it is a risk worth running. I do not believe we have managed to revitalize the world we live in, and I do not believe it is worth the trouble of clinging to; but I do propose something to get us out of our marasmus, instead of continuing to complain about it, and about the boredom, inertia, and stupidity of everything.

In his seminal study of the postwar theater of Eugène Ionesco, Samuel Beckett, Harold Pinter, and other playwrights, Martin Esslin coined the phrase "theater of the absurd" to describe the disorienting quality of their plays. The book has been widely influential and provided the first generation of postwar theatergoers with a way of understanding the new drama. Esslin has written several books on modern drama and theater, including Brecht: A Choice of Evils *(1959),* Pinter: A Study of His Plays *(1976), and* An Anatomy of Drama *(1976). He also has worked for the British Broadcasting Corporation and has taught drama at Stanford University and elsewhere.*

MARTIN ESSLIN

FROM *THE THEATRE OF THE ABSURD* **(1961)**

On 19 November 1957, a group of worried actors were preparing to face their audience. The actors were members of the company of the San Francisco Actors' Workshop. The audience consisted of fourteen hundred convicts at the San Quentin penitentiary. No live play had been performed at San Quentin since Sarah Bernhardt appeared there in 1913. Now, forty-four years later, the play that had been chosen, largely because no woman appeared in it, was Samuel Beckett's *Waiting for Godot.*

No wonder the actors and Herbert Blau, the director, were apprehensive. How were they to face one of the toughest audiences in the world with a highly obscure, intellectual play that had produced near riots among a good many highly sophisticated audiences in Western Europe? Herbert Blau decided to prepare the San Quentin audience for what was to come. He stepped on to the stage and addressed the packed, darkened North Dining Hall—a sea of flickering matches that the convicts tossed over their shoulders after lighting their cigarettes. Blau compared the play to a piece of jazz music 'to which one must listen for whatever one may find in it.' In the same way, he hoped, there would be some meaning, some personal significance for each member of the audience in *Waiting for Godot*.

The curtain parted. The play began. And what had bewildered the sophisticated audiences of Paris, London, and New York was immediately grasped by an audience of convicts. As the writer of 'Memos of a first-nighter' put it in the columns of the prison paper, the *San Quentin News*:

> The trio of muscle-men, biceps overflowing, . . . parked all 642 lbs on the aisle and waited for the girls and funny stuff. When this didn't appear they audibly fumed and audibly decided to wait until the house lights dimmed before escaping. They made one error. They listened and looked two minutes too long—and stayed. Left at the end. All shook . . .[1]

Or as the writer of the lead story of the same paper reported, under the headline, 'San Francisco Group Leaves S.Q. Audience Waiting for Godot':

> From the moment Robin Wagner's thoughtful and limbo-like set was dressed with light, until the last futile and expectant handclasp was hesitantly activated between the two searching vagrants, the San Francisco company had its audience of captives in its collective hand. . . . Those that had felt a less controversial vehicle should be attempted as a first play here had their fears allayed a short five minutes after the Samuel Beckett piece began to unfold.[2]

A reporter from the San Francisco *Chronicle* who was present noted that the convicts did not find it difficult to understand the play. One prisoner told him, 'Godot is society.' Said another: 'He's the outside.'[3] A teacher at the prison was quoted as saying, 'They know what is meant by waiting . . . and they knew if Godot finally came, he would only be a disappointment.'[4] The leading article of the prison paper showed how clearly the writer had understood the meaning of the play:

> It was an expression, symbolic in order to avoid all personal error, by an author who expected each member of his audience to draw his own conclusions, make his own errors. It asked nothing in point, it forced no dramatized moral on the viewer, it held out no specific hope. . . . We're still waiting for Godot, and shall continue to wait. When the scenery gets too drab and the action too slow, we'll call each other names and swear to part forever—but then, there's no place to go![5]

It is said that Godot himself, as well as turns of phrase and characters from the play, have since become a permanent part of the private language, the institutional mythology of San Quentin.

Why did a play of the supposedly esoteric avant-garde make so immediate and so deep an impact on an audience of convicts? Because it confronted them with a situation in some ways analogous to their own? Perhaps. Or perhaps because they were unsophisticated enough to come to the theatre without any preconceived notions and ready-made expectations, so that they avoided the mistake that trapped so many established critics who condemned the play for its lack of plot, development, characterization, suspense, or plain common sense. Certainly the prisoners of San Quentin could not be suspected of the sin of intellectual snobbery, for which a sizeable proportion of the audiences of *Waiting for Godot* have often been reproached; of pretending to like a play they did not even begin to understand, just to appear in the know.

The reception of *Waiting for Godot* at San Quentin, and the wide acclaim given to plays by Ionesco, Adamov, Pinter, and others, testify that these plays, which are so often superciliously

---

[1] *San Quentin News*, San Quentin, Calif., 28 November 1957.

[2] ibid.

[3] *Theatre Arts*, New York, July 1958.

[4] ibid.

[5] *San Quentin News*, 28 November 1957.

dismissed as nonsense or mystification, *have* something to say and *can* be understood. Most of the incomprehension with which plays of this type are still being received by critics and theatrical reviewers, most of the bewilderment they have caused and to which they still give rise, come from the fact that they are part of a new, and still developing stage convention that has not yet been generally understood and has hardly ever been defined. Inevitably, plays written in this new convention will, when judged by the standards and criteria of another, be regarded as impertinent and outrageous impostures. If a good play must have a cleverly constructed story, these have no story or plot to speak of; if a good play is judged by subtlety of characterization and motivation, these are often without recognizable characters and present the audience with almost mechanical puppets; if a good play has to have a fully explained theme, which is neatly exposed and finally solved, these often have neither a beginning nor an end; if a good play is to hold the mirror up to nature and portray the manners and mannerisms of the age in finely observed sketches, these seem often to be reflections of dreams and nightmares; if a good play relies on witty repartee and pointed dialogue, these often consist of incoherent babblings.

But the plays we are concerned with here pursue ends quite different from those of the conventional play and therefore use quite different methods. They can be judged only by the standards of the Theatre of the Absurd, which it is the purpose of this book to define and clarify.

It must be stressed, however, that the dramatists whose work is here discussed do not form part of any self-proclaimed or self-conscious school or movement. On the contrary, each of the writers in question is an individual who regards himself as a lone outsider, cut off and isolated in his private world. Each has his own personal approach to both subject-matter and form; his own roots, sources, and background. If they also, very clearly and in spite of themselves, have a good deal in common, it is because their work most sensitively mirrors and reflects the preoccupations and anxieties, the emotions and thinking of many of their contemporaries in the Western world.

This is not to say that their works are representative of mass attitudes. It is an oversimplification to assume that any age presents a homogeneous pattern. Ours being, more than most others, an age of transition, it displays a bewilderingly stratified picture: medieval beliefs still held and overlaid by eighteenth-century rationalism and mid-nineteenth-century Marxism, rocked by sudden volcanic eruptions of prehistoric fanaticisms and primitive tribal cults. Each of these components of the cultural pattern of the age finds its own artistic expression. The Theatre of the Absurd, however, can be seen as the reflection of what seems to be the attitude most genuinely representative of our own time.

The hallmark of this attitude is its sense that the certitudes and unshakable basic assumptions of former ages have been swept away, that they have been tested and found wanting, that they have been discredited as cheap and somewhat childish illusions. The decline of religious faith was masked until the end of the Second World War by the substitute religions of faith in progress, nationalism, and various totalitarian fallacies. All this was shattered by the war. By 1942, Albert Camus was calmly putting the question why, since life had lost all meaning, man should not seek escape in suicide. In one of the great, seminal heart-searchings of our time, *The Myth of Sisyphus*, Camus tried to diagnose the human situation in a world of shattered beliefs:

> A world that can be explained by reasoning, however faulty, is a familiar world. But in a universe that is suddenly deprived of illusions and of light, man feels a stranger. His is an irremediable exile, because he is deprived of memories of a lost homeland as much as he lacks the hope of a promised land to come. This divorce between man and his life, the actor and his setting, truly constitutes the feeling of Absurdity.[6]

'Absurd' originally means 'out of harmony', in a musical context. Hence its dictionary definition: 'out of harmony with reason or propriety; incongruous, unreasonable, illogical'. In common usage, 'absurd' may simply mean 'ridiculous', but this is not the sense in which Camus uses the word, and in which it is used when we speak of the Theatre of the Absurd. In an essay on Kafka, Ionesco defined his understanding of the term as follows: 'Absurd is that which is devoid of

---

[6] Albert Camus, *Le Mythe de Sisyphe* (Paris: Gallimard, 1942), p. 18.

purpose. . . . Cut off from his religious, metaphysical, and transcendental roots, man is lost; all his actions become senseless, absurd, useless.'[7]

This sense of metaphysical anguish at the absurdity of the human condition is, broadly speaking, the theme of the plays of Beckett, Adamov, Ionesco, Genet, and the other writers discussed in this book. But it is not merely the subject-matter that defines what is here called the Theatre of the Absurd. A similar sense of the senselessness of life, of the inevitable devaluation of ideals, purity, and purpose, is also the theme of much of the work of dramatists like Giraudoux, Anouilh, Salacrou, Sartre, and Camus himself. Yet these writers differ from the dramatists of the Absurd in an important respect: they present their sense of the irrationality of the human condition in the form of highly lucid and logically constructed reasoning, while the Theatre of the Absurd strives to express its sense of the senselessness of the human condition and the inadequacy of the rational approach by the open abandonment of rational devices and discursive thought. While Sartre or Camus express the new content in the old convention, the Theatre of the Absurd goes a step further in trying to achieve a unity between its basic assumptions and the form in which these are expressed. In some senses, the *theatre* of Sartre and Camus is less adequate as an expression of the *philosophy* of Sartre and Camus—in artistic, as distinct from philosophic, terms—than the Theatre of the Absurd.

If Camus argued that in our disillusioned age the world has ceased to make sense, he did so in the elegantly rationalistic and discursive style of an eighteenth-century moralist, in well-constructed and polished plays. If Sartre argues that existence comes before essence and that human personality can be reduced to pure potentiality and the freedom to choose itself anew at any moment, he presents his ideas in plays based on brilliantly drawn characters who remain wholly consistent and thus reflect the old convention that each human being has a core of immutable, unchanging essence—in fact, an immortal soul. And the beautiful phrasing and argumentative brilliance of both Sartre and Camus in their relentless probing still, by implication, proclaim a tacit conviction that logical discourse can offer valid solutions, that the analysis of language will lead to the uncovering of basic concepts—Platonic ideas.

This is an inner contradiction that the dramatists of the Absurd are trying, by instinct and intuition rather than by conscious effort, to overcome and resolve. The Theatre of the Absurd has renounced arguing *about* the absurdity of the human condition; it merely *presents* it in being—that is, in terms of concrete stage images. This is the difference between the approach of the philosopher and that of the poet; the difference, to take an example from another sphere, between the *idea* of God in the works of Thomas Aquinas or Spinoza and the *intuition* of God in those of St John of the Cross or Meister Eckhart—the difference between theory and experience.

It is this striving for an integration between the subject-matter and the form in which it is expressed that separates the Theatre of the Absurd from the Existentialist theatre.

It must also be distinguished from another important, and parallel, trend in the contemporary French theatre, which is equally preoccupied with the absurdity and uncertainty of the human condition: the 'poetic avant-garde' theatre of dramatists like Michel de Ghelderode, Jacques Audiberti, Georges Neveux, and, in the younger generation, Georges Schehadé, Henri Pichette, and Jean Vauthier, to name only some of its most important exponents. This is an even more difficult dividing line to draw, for the two approaches overlap a good deal. The 'poetic avant-garde' relies on fantasy and dream reality as much as the Theatre of the Absurd does; it also disregards such traditional axioms as that of the basic unity and consistency of each character or the need for a plot. Yet basically the 'poetic avant-garde' represents a different mood; it is more lyrical, and far less violent and grotesque. Even more important is its different attitude toward language: the 'poetic avant-garde' relies to a far greater extent on consciously 'poetic' speech; it aspires to plays that are in effect poems, images composed of a rich web of verbal associations.

The Theatre of the Absurd, on the other hand, tends toward a radical devaluation of language, toward a poetry that is to emerge from the concrete and objectified images of the stage itself. The element of language still plays an important part in this conception, but what *happens* on the stage transcends, and often contradicts, the *words* spoken by the characters. In Ionesco's *The Chairs*, for

[7] Eugène Ionesco, *'Dans les armes de la ville'*, *Cahiers de la Compagnie Madeleine Renaud-Jean-Louis Barrault*, Paris, no. 20, October 1957.

example, the poetic content of a powerfully poetic play does not lie in the banal words that are uttered but in the fact that they are spoken to an ever-growing number of empty chairs.

The Theatre of the Absurd is thus part of the 'anti-literary' movement of our time, which has found its expression in abstract painting, with its rejection of 'literary' elements in pictures; or in the 'new novel' in France, with its reliance on the description of objects and its rejection of empathy and anthropomorphism. It is no coincidence that, like all these movements and so many of the efforts to create new forms of expression in all the arts, the Theatre of the Absurd should be centred in Paris. . . .

Fredric Jameson is probably the most prominent Marxist cultural critic writing in the United States today and is the author of several important books, including Marxism and Form *(1971),* The Prison-House of Language *(1972), and* The Political Unconscious *(1988). This section is from one of Jameson's many essays on postmodern art, culture, and society. Jameson uses the term pastiche to characterize the problematic ways contemporary arts invoke the imagery and style of earlier historical eras, paradoxically erasing "history" in the process.*

FREDRIC JAMESON

FROM "POSTMODERNISM AND CONSUMER SOCIETY" (1983)

PASTICHE ECLIPSES PARODY

One of the most significant features or practices in postmodernism today is pastiche. I must first explain this term, which people generally tend to confuse with or assimilate to that related verbal phenomenon called parody. Both pastiche and parody involve the imitation or, better still, the mimicry of other styles and particularly of the mannerisms and stylistic twitches of other styles. It is obvious that modern literature in general offers a very rich field for parody, since the great modern writers have all been defined by the invention or production of rather unique styles: think of the Faulknerian long sentence or of D. H. Lawrence's characteristic nature imagery; think of Wallace Stevens's peculiar way of using abstractions; think also of the mannerisms of the philosophers, of Heidegger for example, or Sartre; think of the musical styles of Mahler or Prokofiev. All of these styles, however different from each other, are comparable in this: each is quite unmistakable; once one is learned, it is not likely to be confused with something else.

Now parody capitalizes on the uniqueness of these styles and seizes on their idiosyncrasies and eccentricities to produce an imitation which mocks the original. I won't say that the satiric impulse is conscious in all forms of parody. In any case, a good or great parodist has to have some secret sympathy for the original, just as a great mimic has to have the capacity to put himself/herself in the place of the person imitated. Still, the general effect of parody is—whether in sympathy or with malice—to cast ridicule on the private nature of these stylistic mannerisms and their excessiveness and eccentricity with respect to the way people normally speak or write. So there remains somewhere behind all parody the feeling that there is a linguistic norm in contrast to which the styles of the great modernists can be mocked.

But what would happen if one no longer believed in the existence of normal language, of ordinary speech, of the linguistic norm (the kind of clarity and communicative power celebrated by Orwell in his famous essay, say)? One could think of it in this way; perhaps the immense fragmentation and privatization of modern literature—its explosion into a host of distinct private styles and mannerisms—foreshadows deeper and more general tendencies in social life as a whole. Supposing that modern art and modernism—far from being a kind of specialized aesthetic curiosity—actually anticipated social developments along these lines; supposing that in the decades since the emergence of the great modern styles society has itself begun to fragment in this way, each group coming to speak a curious private language of its own, each profession developing its private code or idiolect, and finally each individual coming to be a kind of linguistic island, separated from everyone else? But then in that case, the very possibility of any linguistic norm in terms of which one could ridicule private languages and idiosyncratic styles would vanish, and we would have nothing but stylistic diversity and heterogeneity.

That is the moment at which pastiche appears and parody has become impossible. Pastiche is, like parody, the imitation of a peculiar or unique style, the wearing of a stylistic mask, speech in a dead language: but it is a neutral practice of such mimicry, without parody's ulterior motive, without the satirical impulse, without laughter, without that still latent feeling that there exists something *normal* compared to which what is being imitated is rather comic. Pastiche is blank parody, parody that has lost its sense of humor: pastiche is to parody what that curious thing, the modern practice of a kind of blank irony, is to what Wayne Booth calls the stable and comic ironies of, say, the eighteenth century.

THE DEATH OF THE SUBJECT

But now we need to introduce a new piece into this puzzle, which may help to explain why classical modernism is a thing of the past and why postmodernism should have taken its place. This new component is what is generally called the 'death of the subject' or, to say it in more conventional language, the end of individualism as such. The great modernisms were, as we have said, predicated on the invention of a personal, private style, as unmistakable as your fingerprint, as incomparable as your own body. But this means that the modernist aesthetic is in some way organically linked to the conception of a unique self and private identity, a unique personality and individuality, which can be expected to generate its own unique vision of the world and to forge its own unique, unmistakable style.

Yet today, from any number of distinct perspectives, the social theorists, the psychoanalysts, even the linguists, not to speak of those of us who work in the area of culture and cultural and formal change, are all exploring the notion that that kind of individualism and personal identity is a thing of the past; that the old individual or individualist subject is 'dead'; and that one might even describe the concept of the unique individual and the theoretical basis of individualism as ideological. There are in fact two positions on all this, one of which is more radical than the other. The first one is content to say: yes, once upon a time, in the classic age of competitive capitalism, in the heyday of the nuclear family and the emergence of the bourgeoisie as the hegemonic social class, there was such a thing as individualism, as individual subjects. But today, in the age of corporate capitalism, of the so-called organization man, of bureaucracies in business as well as in the state, of demographic explosion—today, that older bourgeois individual subject no longer exists.

Then there is a second position, the more radical of the two, what one might call the poststructuralist position. It adds: not only is the bourgeois individual subject a thing of the past, it is also a myth; it *never* really existed in the first place; there have never been autonomous subjects of that type. Rather, this construct is merely a philosophical and cultural mystification which sought to persuade people that they 'had' individual subjects and possessed this unique personal identity.

For our purposes, it is not particularly important to decide which of these positions is correct (or rather, which is more interesting and productive). What we have to retain from all this is rather an aesthetic dilemma: because if the experience and the ideology of the unique self, an experience and ideology which informed the stylistic practice of classical modernism, is over and done with, then it is no longer clear what the artists and writers of the present period are supposed to be doing. What is clear is merely that the older models—Picasso, Proust, T. S. Eliot—do not work any more (or are positively harmful), since nobody has that kind of unique private world and style to express any longer. And this is perhaps not merely a 'psychological' matter: we also have to take into account the immense weight of seventy or eighty years of classical modernism itself. There is another sense in which the writers and artists of the present day will no longer be able to invent new styles and worlds—they've already been invented; only a limited number of combinations are possible; the unique ones have been thought of already. So the weight of the whole modernist aesthetic tradition—now dead—also 'weighs like a nightmare on the brains of the living', as Marx said in another context.

Hence, once again, pastiche: in a world in which stylistic innovation is no longer possible, all that is left is to imitate dead styles, to speak through the masks and with the voices of the styles in the imaginary museum. But this means that contemporary or postmodernist art is going to be about art itself in a new kind of way; even more, it means that one of its essential messages will involve the necessary failure of art and the aesthetic, the failure of the new, the imprisonment in the past.

THE NOSTALGIA MODE

As this may seem very abstract, I want to give a few examples, one of which is so omnipresent that we rarely link it with the kinds of developments in high art discussed here. This particular practice of pastiche is not high-cultural but very much within mass culture, and it is generally known as the 'nostalgia film' (what the French neatly call *la mode rétro*—retrospective styling). We must conceive of this category in the broadest way: narrowly, no doubt, it consists merely of films about the past and about specific generational moments of that past. Thus, one of the inaugural films in this new 'genre' (if that's what it is) was Lucas's *American Graffiti,* which in 1973 set out to recapture all the atmosphere and stylistic peculiarities of the 1950s United States, the United States of the Eisenhower era. Polanski's great film *Chinatown* does something similar for the 1930s, as does Bertolucci's *The Conformist* for the Italian and European context of the same period, the fascist era in Italy; and so forth. We could go on listing these films for some time: why call them pastiche? Are they not rather work in the more traditional genre known as the historical film—work which can more simply be theorized by extrapolating that other well-known form which is the historical novel?

I have my reasons for thinking that we need new categories for such films. But let me first add some anomalies: supposing I suggested that *Star Wars* is also a nostalgia film. What could that mean? I presume we can agree that this is not a historical film about our own intergalactic past. Let me put it somewhat differently: one of the most important cultural experiences of the generations that grew up from the 1930s to the 1950s was the Saturday afternoon serial of the Buck Rogers type—alien villains, true American heroes, heroines in distress, the death ray or the doomsday box, and the cliffhanger at the end whose miraculous resolution was to be witnessed next Saturday afternoon. *Star Wars* reinvents this experience in the form of a pastiche: that is, there is no longer any point to a parody of such serials since they are long extinct. *Star Wars,* far from being a pointless satire of such now dead forms, satisfies a deep (might I even say repressed?) longing to experience them again: it is a complex object in which on some first level children and adolescents can take the adventures straight, while the adult public is able to gratify a deeper and more properly nostalgic desire to return to that older period and to live its strange old aesthetic artifacts through once again. This film is thus *metonymically* a historical or nostalgia film: unlike *American Graffiti,* it does not reinvent a picture of the past in its lived totality; rather, by reinventing the feel and shape of characteristic art objects of an older period (the serials), it seeks to reawaken a sense of the past associated with those objects. *Raiders of the Lost Ark,* meanwhile, occupies an intermediary position here: on some level it is *about* the 1930s and 1940s, but in reality it too conveys that period metonymically through its own characteristic adventure stories (which are no longer ours).

Now let me discuss another interesting anomaly which may take us further towards understanding nostalgia film in particular and pastiche generally. This one involves a recent film called *Body Heat,* which, as has abundantly been pointed out by the critics, is a kind of distant remake of *The Postman Always Rings Twice* or *Double Indemnity.* (The allusive and elusive plagiarism of older plots is, of course, also a feature of pastiche.) Now *Body Heat* is technically not a nostalgia film, since it takes place in a contemporary setting, in a little Florida village near Miami. On the other hand, this technical contemporaneity is most ambiguous indeed: the credits—always our first cue—are lettered and scripted in a 1930s Art-Deco style which cannot but trigger nostalgic reactions (first to *Chinatown,* no doubt, and then beyond it to some more historical referent). Then the very style of the hero himself is ambiguous: William Hurt is a new star but has nothing of the distinctive style of the preceding generation of male superstars like Steve McQueen or even Jack Nicholson, or rather, his persona here is a kind of mix of their characteristics with an older role of the type generally associated with Clark Gable. So here too there is a faintly archaic feel to all this. The spectator begins to wonder why this story, which could have been situated anywhere, is set in a small Florida town, in spite of its contemporary reference. One begins to realize after a while that the small town setting has a crucial strategic function: it allows the film to do without most of the signals and references which we might associate with the contemporary world, with consumer society—the appliances and artifacts, the high rises, the object world of late capitalism. Technically, then, its objects (its cars, for instance) are 1980s products, but everything in the film conspires to blur that immediate contemporary reference and to make it possible to receive this too as nostalgia work—as a narrative set in some indefinable nostalgic past, an eternal 1930s, say, beyond history. It seems to me exceedingly symptomatic to find the very style of nostalgia films invading and colonizing even those movies today which have contemporary settings: as though, for some reason, we were unable today to focus our own present, as though we have become incapable of achieving aesthetic representations of our own current experience. But if that is so, then it is a terrible indictment of consumer capitalism itself—or, at the very least, an alarming and pathological symptom of a society that has become incapable of dealing with time and history.

So now we come back to the question of why nostalgia film or pastiche is to be considered different from the older historical novel or film. (I should also include in this discussion the major literary example of all this, to my mind: the novels of E. L. Doctorow—*Ragtime*, with its turn-of-the-century atmosphere, and *Loon Lake*, for the most part about our 1930s. But these are, in my opinion, historical novels in appearance only. Doctorow is a serious artist and one of the few genuinely left or radical novelists at work today. It is no disservice to him, however, to suggest that his narratives do not represent our historical past so much as they represent our ideas or cultural stereotypes about that past.) Cultural production has been driven back inside the mind, within the monadic subject: it can no longer look directly out of its eyes at the real world for the referent but must, as in Plato's cave, trace its mental images of the world on its confining walls. If there is any realism left here, it is a 'realism' which springs from the shock of grasping that confinement and of realizing that, for whatever peculiar reasons, we seem condemned to seek the historical past through our own pop images and stereotypes about that past, which itself remains forever out of reach.

ELIN DIAMOND

***"Brechtian Theory/Feminist Theory: Toward a Gestic Feminist Criticism"* (1988)**

Elin Diamond is an important feminist theorist of theater and representation; in addition to her book, Pinter's Comic Play, *she is known for an influential series of articles, including "Refusing the Romanticism of Identity: Narrative Interventions in Churchill, Benmussa, Duras" and "Mimesis, Mimicry, and the 'True-Real.'" In "Brechtian Theory/Feminist Theory," Diamond develops a strategic re-reading of Brechtian "alienation," and argues that the gestus can help to reconceptualize the representational project of feminist theater.*

This essay begins and ends with a short text on pointing.

> In the 1930s, Gertrude Stein and Alice Toklas, on their American lecture tour, were driving in the country in Western Massachusetts. Toklas pointed out a batch of clouds. Stein replied, "Fresh eggs." Toklas insisted that Stein look at the clouds. Stein replied again, "Fresh eggs." Then Toklas asked, "Are you making symbolical language?" "No," Stein answered, "I'm reading the signs. I love to read the signs" (Stimpson 1986:7).

One might devote an essay merely to unpacking this statement for its historical, discursive, and sexual resonances. Let me just say that Toklas's irritation seems justified. She is pointing to clouds; they have an ontological, referential status *as* clouds, but Stein playfully crosses ontology with textuality, object with symbol, referent with sign. Acting the self-conscious spectator, Stein produces a reading and says that *that* is more pleasurable than any Massachusetts clouds. I am concerned with how we point to and read signs in the theatre, and by "we" I mean feminist critics and theorists and also students of Brecht's theatre theory—an unlikely group, but then this is part of my argument. I would suggest that feminist theory and Brechtian theory need to be read intertextually, for among the effects of such a reading are a recovery of the radical potential of the Brechtian critique and a discovery, for feminist theory, of the specificity of theatre.[1]

At the outset I should say that like Gertrude Stein's clouds, feminist theory and Brechtian theory are moving, changing discourses, open to multiple readings. The umbrella term "feminist theory" covers feminist film theory, feminist literary theory, psychoanalytic feminist theory, socialist feminist theory, black feminist theory, lesbian feminist theory, cross-cultural feminist theory—many of which combine under different rubrics with different topoi, different political inflections. Yet perhaps all theories that call themselves "feminist" share a goal: the passionate analysis of gender in material social relations and in discursive and representational structures, especially theatre and film, which involve scopic pleasures and the body. Brecht's theatre theory, written over a 30-year period, constantly reformulates its concepts but it, too, has certain concerns: attention to the dialectical and contradictory forces within social relations, principally the agon of class conflict in its changing historical forms; commitment to alienation techniques and nonmimetic disunity in theatrical signification; "literarization" of the theatre space to produce a spectator/reader who is not interpolated into ideology but is passionately and pleasurably engaged in observation and analysis.

Now feminists in film studies have been quick to appropriate elements of Brecht's critique of the theatre apparatus.[2] In Summer 1974, the British film journal *Screen* published a Brecht issue whose stated purpose was a consideration of Brecht's theoretical texts and the possibility of a revolutionary cinema. In Autumn 1975, Laura Mulvey published her influential essay "Visual Pleasure and Narrative Cinema" in which, employing psychoanalysis "as a political weapon," she argues that Hollywood film conventions construct a specifically male viewing position by aligning or suturing the male's gaze to that of the fictional hero, and by inviting him thereby both to identify narcissistically with that hero and to fetishize the female (turning her into an object of sexual stimulation) (1975:6). In rejecting this dominant cinematic tradition, Mulvey powerfully invokes Brechtian concepts:

> The first blow against the monolithic accumulation of traditional film conventions [. . .] is to free the look of the camera into its materiality in time and space and the look of the audience into dialectics, passionate detachment (1975:18).

Demystifying representation, showing how and when the object of pleasure is made, releasing the spectator from imaginary and illusory identifications—these are crucial elements in Brecht's theoretical project. Yet we feminists in drama and theatre studies have attended more to the critique of the gaze than to the Brechtian intervention that signals a way of dismantling the gaze. Feminist film theorists, fellow-traveling with psychoanalysis and semiotics, have given us a lot to think about, but we, through Brechtian theory, have something to give them: a female body in representation that resists fetishization and a viable position for the female spectator.

In this essay, then, I have two purposes. One, an intertextual reading of key topoi of feminist theory: gender critique and sexual difference; questions of authority in women's writing and women's history; spectatorship and the body—with key topoi in Brechtian theory: *Verfremdungseffekt*, the "not, but," historicization, and *Gestus*. Two, emerging from this intertexting, a proposal for a theatre-specific feminist criticism. I call it "gestic criticism" and close the essay with a brief example (my second text on pointing).

Some quick qualifications and clarifications: I realize that feminists in drama studies might greet this coupling with some bemusement. Brecht exhibits a typical Marxian blindness toward gender relations, and except for some interesting excursions into male erotic violence, he created conventionally gendered plays and too many saintly mothers (one is too many). Moreover, the postmodern critique of Brecht by Heiner Müllerites should not be ignored, particularly the rejection of the Brechtian "fable" which Müller describes as a "closed form" that the audience accepts as a "package, a commodity" (Weber 1980:121). This essay brackets both Brecht's plays and their retrograde (and unBrechtian) stagings in the German Democratic Republic and the West over the last three decades. My interest lies in the potentiality of Brecht's theory for feminism, and, as I mentioned above, a possible re-radicalization of his theory through feminism. In current literary theory, especially from the English Left, Brecht's concepts have become weapons in campaigns against mimetic linearity (see Dollimore 1984), bourgeois naturalism (see Barker 1984), and, in a fine reading by Terry Eagleton (1986), on the side of deconstructive rhetoric. Even Toril Moi (Oxford-based Norwegian), in her notorious *Sexual/Textual Politics*, parses the feminisms by enlisting Brecht's debate with Lukacs on the question of socialist realism to challenge Anglo-American critics of Virginia Woolf (1985:17). Strange bedfellows perhaps, but the point I wish to make is that these critics have understood that Brechtian theory in all its gaps and inconsistencies is not literary criticism, but rather a theorizing of the workings of an apparatus of representation with enormous formal and political resonance. I think we should be long past the point of accepting Martin Esslin's view that Brecht's theories "were merely rationalizations of intuition, taste, and imagination" (1971:146), or Eric Bentley's view that the theory is a didactic distraction from Brecht's true art (1981:46ff). Herbert Blau has the best if not the last word on theory-versus-practice debates: "Theater is theory, or a shadow of it. [. . .] In the act of seeing, there is already theory (1982:1).

The cornerstone of Brecht's theory is the Verfremdungseffekt, the technique of defamiliarizing a word, an idea, a gesture so as to enable the spectator to see or hear it afresh: "a representation that alienates is one which allows us to recognize its subject, but at the same time makes it seem unfamiliar" (Brecht 1964:192); "the A-effect consists of turning an object from something ordinary and

GENDER, VERFREMDUNGS-EFFEKT

immediately accessible into something peculiar, striking, and unexpected" (1964:143). In performance the actor "alienates" rather than impersonates her character; she "quotes" or demonstrates the character's behavior instead of identifying with it. Brecht theorizes that if the performer remains outside the character's feelings, the audience may also, thereby remaining free to analyze and form opinions about the play's "fable." Verfremdungseffekt also challenges the mimetic property of acting that semioticians call iconicity, the fact that the performer's body conventionally resembles the object (or character) to which it refers. This is why gender critique in the theatre can be so powerful.

Gender refers to the words, gestures, appearances, ideas, and behavior that dominant culture understands as indices of feminine or masculine identity. When spectators "see" gender they are seeing (and reproducing) the cultural signs of gender, and by implication, the gender ideology of a culture. Gender in fact provides a perfect illustration of ideology at work since "feminine" or "masculine" behavior usually appears to be a "natural"—and thus fixed and unalterable—extension of biological sex. Feminist practice that seeks to expose or mock the strictures of gender usually uses some version of the Brechtian A-effect. That is, by alienating (not simply rejecting) iconicity, by foregrounding the expectation of resemblance, the ideology of gender is exposed and thrown back to the spectator.[3] In Caryl Churchill's play *Cloud 9*, cross-dressing, in which the male body can be seen in feminine clothes, provides A-effects for a gender critique of the familial and sexual roles in Victorian colonial society. In lesbian performances at New York's WOW Cafe—I'm thinking of Holly Hughes's *Lady Dick* and Split Britches' *Upwardly Mobile Home*—and in the broadly satirical monologs of Italy's Franca Rame, gender is exposed as a sexual costume, a sign of a role, not evidence of identity. Recalling such performances should remind us of the rigorous self-consciousness that goes into even the most playful gender-bending. A-effects are not easy to produce, but the payoffs can be stunning. When gender is "alienated" or foregrounded, the spectator is enabled to see a sign system *as* a sign system—the appearance, words, gestures, ideas, attitudes, etc., that comprise the gender lexicon become so many illusionistic trappings to be put on or shed at will. Understanding gender as ideology—as a system of beliefs and behavior mapped across the bodies of females and males, which reinforces a social status quo—is to appreciate the continued timeliness of Verfremdungseffekt, the purpose of which is to denaturalize and defamiliarize what ideology makes seem normal, acceptable, inescapable.

SEXUAL DIFFERENCE, THE "NOT, BUT"

Gender critique in artistic and discursive practices is often and wrongly confused with another topos in feminist theory: sexual difference. I would propose that "sexual difference" be understood not as a synonym for gender oppositions but as a possible reference to differences within sexuality. I take my cue here partly from the poststructuralist privileging of "difference" across all representational systems, particularly language. Derridean deconstruction posits the disturbance of the signifier within the linguistic sign or word; the seemingly stable word is inhabited by a signifier that bears the trace of another signifier and another, so that contained within the meaning of any given word is the trace of the word it is not. Thus the word is always different from itself, or, as Barbara Johnson patiently teases out its connotations, "difference" refers not to what distinguishes one identity from another—"it is not a difference between [. . .] independent units [. . .] but a difference within" (1980:4). Texts, she argues, are not different from other texts but different from themselves. Deconstruction thus wreaks havoc on identity, with its connotations of wholeness and coherence: if an identity is always different from itself it can no longer *be* an identity. Sexual *difference*, then, might be seen to destabilize the bipolar oppositions that constitute gender identity.

Psychoanalysis offers other cues. Despite the normative tone of his gender distinctions, Freud also makes clear that the drives and desires that constitute sexuality do not add up to a stable identity:

> [W]e are accustomed to say that every human being displays both male and female instinctual impulses, needs and attributes; but though anatomy it is true, can point out the characteristic of maleness and femaleness, psychology cannot. For psychology the contrast between the sexes fades away into one between activity and passivity, in which we far too readily identify activity with maleness and passivity with femaleness, a view which is by no means universally confirmed (in Watney 1988:16).

In fact the Freudian account of the diverse identifications and effects of childhood sexuality undermine the idea of a stable-gendered subject. To paraphrase Gayle Rubin, women and men are certainly different, but gender coercively translates the nuanced differences within sexuality into a structure of opposition: male vs. female, masculine vs. feminine, etc. (see 1978:179). In my reading of Rubin, the "sex-gender system," the trace of the difference of sexuality is kept alive within the sterile opposition of gender. I am suggesting that sexual difference is where we imagine, where we theorize; gender is where we live, our social address, although most of us, with an effort, are trying to leave home. Let me put it another way: no feminist can ignore the social and political battlefield of gender, but no feminist can ignore the fact that the language of the battlefield is a system based on difference whose traces contain our most powerful desires.

Keeping differences in view instead of conforming to stable representations of identity, and *linking those differences to a practical politics* are key to Brecht's theory of the "not, but," a feature of alienated acting that I read intertextually with the sex-gender system. "When [an actor] appears on stage, besides what he actually is doing he will at all essential points discover, specify, imply what he is not doing; that is he will act in such a way that the alternative emerges as clearly as possible, that his acting allows the other possibilities to be inferred and only represents one of the possible variants. [. . .] Whatever he doesn't do must be contained and conserved in what he does" (Brecht 1964:137). Each action must contain the trace of the action it represses, thus the meaning of each action contains difference. The audience is invited to look beyond representation—beyond what is authoritatively put in view—to the possibilities of as yet unarticulated actions or judgments. Brecht's early plays, particularly *In the Jungle of Cities*, thematize the "not, but": "I'm never anything more than half," says Mary Garga, who doesn't have the pleasure of joining the men in what Brecht called "the idealist dialectic" of the play or "the pure joy of fighting." Contemporary feminist plays by Michelene Wandor, Caryl Churchill, and Adrienne Kennedy also thematize the "not, but" in their sex-gender referents, but it would be interesting to query sex-gender nuances in *Measure for Measure*, *The Master Builder*, and *No Man's Land* to name only three.

The Brechtian "not, but" is the theatrical and theoretical analog to the subversiveness of sexual difference, because it allows us to imagine the deconstruction of gender—and all other—representations. Such deconstructions dramatize, at least at the level of theory, the infinite play of difference that Derrida calls *écriture*—the superfluity of signification that places meaning beyond capture within the covers of the play or the hours of performance. This is not to deny Brecht's wish for an instructive, analytical theatre; on the contrary, it invites the participatory play of the spectator, and the possibility for which Brecht most devoutly wished, that significance (the production of meaning) continue beyond play's end, congealing into choice and action after the spectator leaves the theatre.

The sex-gender system requires contextualization. The understanding of women's material conditions in history and the problematics of uncovering "women's history" are topoi in feminist theory that Brecht's theory of historicization greatly informs. Of course there must be limits to this discussion: Brecht was not writing history, but as a student devoted to the Marxist "classics" Brecht understood social relations, particularly class relations, as part of a moving dialectic. The crux of "historicization" is change: through A-effects spectators observe the potential movement in class relations, discover the limitations and strengths of their own perceptions, and begin to change their lives. There is a double movement in Brechtian historicization of preserving the "distinguishing marks" of the past and acknowledging, even foregrounding, the audience's present perspective (Brecht 1964:190). When Brecht says that spectators should become historians, he refers both to the spectator's detachment, her "critical" position, *and* to the fact that she is writing her own history even as she absorbs messages from the stage. Historicization is, then, *a way of seeing* and the enemy of recuperation and appropriation. One cannot historicize and colonize the Other or, as Luce Irigaray would have it, "reduce all others to the economy of the same" (1985:76). Brecht considered bourgeois illusionism insidious because it is guilty of precisely that:

> When our theatres perform plays of other periods they like to annihilate distance, fill in the gap, gloss over the differences. But what comes in our delight in comparisons, in distance, in dissimilarity—which is at the same time a delight in what is close and proper to ourselves? (Brecht 1964:276).

In historicized performance, gaps are not to be filled in, seams and contradictions show in all their roughness, and therein lies one aspect of spectatorial pleasure—when our differences *from* the past

HISTORY, HISTORICIZATION

and *within* the present are palpable, graspable, applicable. Plays aspiring to realistically depict the present require the same historicization. Realism disgusted Brecht not only because it dissimulates its conventions but because it is hegemonic: by copying the surface details of the world it offers the illusion of lived experience, even as it marks off only one version of that experience.[4] This is perhaps why the most innovative women playwrights refuse the seamless narrative of conflicting egos in classic realism. Consider Adrienne Kennedy's *Funnyhouse of a Negro* or *The Owl Answers* which lurch and reach through memory/fantasy staking the real in obsessional repetition and in fragmented characters who embrace and speak from their difference. Kennedy rejects the Brechtian fable—narrative progress is meaningless in her worlds—and instead dramatizes gaps and contradictions as, precisely, the black woman's experience of history. Brechtian historicization challenges the presumed ideological neutrality of any historical reflection. Rather it assumes, and promotes, what historians are now claiming: that reader/spectators of "facts" and "events" will, like Gertrude Stein reading the clouds, translate what is inchoate into signs (and stories), a move that produces not "truth," but mastery and pleasure.

SPECTATOR,
BODY,
HISTORICIZATION

Historicization in fact puts on the table the issue of spectatorship and the performer's body. According to Brecht, one way that the actor alienates or distances the audience from the character is to suggest the historicity of the character in contrast to the actor's own present-time self-awareness on stage. The actor must not lose herself in the character but rather *demonstrate* the character as a function of particular sociohistorical relations, a conduit of particular choices. As Timothy Wiles puts it, actor and audience, both in present time, "look back on" the historical character as she fumbles through choices and judgments (1980:72). This does not, however, endow the actor with superiority, for as Wiles later points out this present-time actor is also fragmented: "Brecht separates the historical man who acts from the aesthetic function of the actor" (1980:85). The historical subject *plays* an actor presumed to have superior knowledge in relation to an ignorant character from the past, but the subject herself remains as divided and uncertain as the spectators to whom the play is addressed. This performer-subject neither disappears into a representation of the character *nor* into a representation of the actor; each remains processual, historical, incomplete. And the spectator? Aware of three temporalities within a single stage figure the spectator cannot read one without the other; her/his gaze is constantly split; her/his *"vouloir-voir"* (Pavis 1982:88)—the wanting to see and know all without any obstacle—is deflected into the dialectic of which the divided performer is only a part. Moreover, in reading a complex ever-changing text, spectators are "pulled out of [their] fixity" (Heath 1974:112); they become part of—indeed they produce—the dialectical comparisons and contributions that the text enacts.

The special characteristics of Brechtian reception emerge in relation to analogous processes in film theory. In psychoanalytic film theory, the film-text and the viewing-state are set in motion by unconscious fantasy.[5] In the darkened room, in immobile seats, the spectator enters what Jean-Louis Baudry calls a "state of artificial regression" (1980:56), the womblike effects of film viewing which confuse boundaries and send the subject back to earlier stages of psychic development, particularly the Lacanian mirror phase in which the infant, lacking controlled motor development, sees its image in a mirror or in its caretaker's eyes as a coherent whole. Misrecognizing himself (the male infant is specifically at issue here) as a complete, autonomous other, he spends the rest of his life unconsciously seeking an imaginary ideal—and discovers him, so the theory goes, at the movies.

Now the differences between the Brechtian spectator and the cinematic spectator are obvious. The last thing Brecht wants is a spectator in a "state of artificial regression," in thrall to his imaginary ideal. Brechtian theory formulates (and reformulates) a spectatorial state that breaks the suturing of imaginary identifications and keeps the spectator independent. Much influenced by Brecht, Patrice Pavis's semiotics of the mise-en-scene rests almost entirely on the spectator: "[. . .] the mise-en-scene is not entirely an indication of the intentionality of the director, but a structuring by the spectator of materials presented [. . .] whose linking is dependent on the perceiving subject" (Pavis 1982:138). In film theory the subject position is constructed ready-made for the spectator, only his capacity to regress is assumed. In Brechtian theory the subject's capacity to regress is suppressed. Film semiotics posits a spectator who is given the illusion that he creates the film; theatre semiotics posits a spectator whose active reception constantly revises the spectacle's meanings.

But Pavis is too much of a postmodernist to theorize a spectator with total authority. He deconstructs the spectatorial position by locating its difference within: "What we need," he says, "is a theory of 'reception desire'"—a theory that, without positing a spectator "in a state of artificial regression," accounts for the spectator's unconscious desire and thereby opens the door to pleasurable identification with stage figures (Pavis 1982:158).

What does Brecht contribute to "reception desire"? Although he talks a lot about pleasure, it is the pleasure of cognition, of capturing meaning; Brecht does not apparently release the body, either on stage or in the audience. The actor's body is subsumed in the dialectical narrative of social relations; the spectator's body is given over to rational inquiry (unless there's pleasure to be had with the Brechtian cigar). And Brecht exhibits the blindness typical of all Marxist theorists regarding sex-gender configurations. Feminist theory, however, insists on the presence of the gendered body, on the sex-gender system, and on the problematics of desire.

It is at this point—at the point of conceptualizing an unfetishized female performer and a female spectator—that an intertextual reading of Brechtian and feminist theories works productively. If feminist theory sees the body as culturally mapped and gendered, Brechtian historicization insists that this body is not a fixed essence but a site of struggle and change. If feminist theory is concerned with the multiple and complex signs of a woman's life: her color, her age, her desires, her politics— what I want to call her *historicity*[6]—Brechtian theory gives us a way to put that historicity on view— in the theatre. In its conventional iconicity, theatre laminates body to character, but the body in historicization stands visibly and palpably separate from the "role" of the actor as well as the role of the character; it is always insufficient and open. I want to be clear about this important point: The body, particularly the female body, by virtue of entering the stage space, enters representation—it is not just *there*, a live, unmediated presence, but rather (1) a signifying element in a dramatic fiction; (2) a part of a theatrical sign system whose conventions of gesturing, voicing, and impersonating are referents for both performer and audience; and (3) a sign in a system governed by a particular apparatus, usually owned and operated by men for the pleasure of a viewing public whose major wage earners are male.

Yet with all these qualifications, Brechtian theory imagines a polyvalence to the body's representation, for the performer's body is also *historicized*, loaded with its own history and that of the character, and these histories ruffle the smooth edges of the image, of representation. In my hybrid construction—based in feminist and Brechtian theory—the female performer, unlike her filmic counterpart, connotes not "to-be-looked-at-ness" (Mulvey 1975:11)—the perfect fetish—but rather "looking-at-being-looked-at-ness" or even just "looking-ness." This Brechtian-feminist body is paradoxically available for *both* analysis and identification, paradoxically within representation while refusing its fixity.

SPECTATOR, AUTHOR, GESTUS

The explosive (and elusive) synthesis of alienation, historicization, and the "not, but" is the Brechtian *Gestus*: a gesture, a word, an action, a tableau by which, separately or in series, the social attitudes encoded in the playtext become visible to the spectator. A gest becomes *social* when it "allows conclusions to be drawn about social circumstances" (Brecht 1964:105). A famous social gest is Helene Weigel's snapping shut her leather money bag after each selling transaction in *Mother Courage*, thereby underscoring the contradictions between profiteering and survival—for Brecht the social reality of war. This gest has become something of a reification, but Brecht always emphasized complexity:

> [The] expressions of a gest are usually highly complicated and contradictory, so that they cannot be rendered by any single word and the actor must take care that in giving his image the necessary emphasis he does not lose anything, but emphasizes the entire complex (1964:198).

The gestic moment in a sense explains the play, but it also exceeds the play, opening it to the social and discursive ideologies that inform its production. Brecht writes that the scene of the social gest "should be played as a piece of history" (1964:86) and Pavis elaborates: Gestus makes visible (alienates) "the class behind the individual, the critique behind the naive object, the commentary behind the affirmation. [. . .] [It] gives us the key to the relationship between the play being performed and the public. [. . .]" (1982:42). If we read feminist concerns back into this discussion, the social gest signifies a moment of theoretical insight into sex-gender complexities, not only in the play's "fable," but in the culture which the play, at the moment of reception, is dialogically reflecting and shaping.

But this moment of visibility or insight is the very moment that complicates the viewing process. Because the Gestus is effected by a historical actor/subject, what the spectator sees is not a mere miming of social relationship, but a *reading* of it, an interpretation by a historical subject who supplements (rather than disappears into) the production of meaning. As noted earlier, the historical subject playing an actor, playing a character, splits the gaze of the spectator, who, as a reader of a complex sign system, cannot consume or reduce the object of her vision to a monolithic projection of the self. In fact, Gestus undermines the stability of the spectatorial "self," for in the act of looking the spectator engages with her own temporality. She, too, becomes historicized—in motion and at risk, but also free to compare the actor/character's signs to "what is close and proper to [herself]"—her material conditions, her politics, her skin, her desires. Sitting not in the dark, but in the Brechtian semi-lit smoker's theatre, the spectator still has the possibility of pleasurable identification. This is effected not through imaginary projection onto an ideal but through a triangular structure of actor/subject—character—spectator. Looking at the character, the spectator is constantly intercepted by the actor/subject, and the latter, heeding no fourth wall, is theoretically free to look back. The difference, then, between this triangle and the familiar oedipal one is that no one side signifies authority, knowledge, or the law. Brechtian theatre depends on a structure of representation, on exposing and making visible, but what appears even in the Gestus can only be provisional, indeterminate, nonauthoritative.[7]

This feminist rereading of Gestus makes room, at least theoretically, for a viewing position for the female spectator. Because the semiosis of Gestus involves the gendered bodies of spectator, actor/subject, and character, all working together but *never harmoniously*, there can be no fetishization and no end to signification. In this Brechtian-feminist paradigm, the spectator's look is freed into "dialectics, passionate detachment" (Mulvey 1975:18). She might borrow Gertrude Stein's line, and give equal emphasis to each word: "I love to read the signs."

If Gestus invites us to think about the performer and the spectator in their historical and sexual specificity, it also asks us to consider the author's inscription. "The author's attitude to the public, that of the era represented and of the time in which the play is performed, the collective style of acting of the characters, etc., are a few of the parameters of the basic *Gestus*" (Pavis 1982:42). In the case of women writers and particularly of women dramatists, the erasure from history has been so nearly complete that the feminist critic feels compelled to make some attempt at recovery—and here Brechtian theory, fellow-traveling with feminist theory, suggests a critical practice—gestic feminist criticism—that would contextualize *and* reclaim the author.

A gestic feminist criticism would "alienate" or foreground those moments in a playtext in which social attitudes about gender could be made visible. It would highlight sex-gender configurations as they conceal or disrupt a coercive or patriarchal ideology. It would refuse to appropriate and naturalize male or female dramatists, but rather focus on historical material constraints in the production of images. It would attempt to engage dialectically with, rather than master, the playtext. And in generating meanings, it would recover (specifically gestic) moments in which the historical actor, the character, the spectator, *and* the author enter representation, however provisionally.

GESTIC FEMINIST CRITICISM, APHRA BEHN

In the brief space remaining, it is impossible to flesh out this critical schema, but I want to draw attention to a gestic moment that Aphra Behn has provided—in the prolog of her first play, produced in 1670. A middle-class woman with prestigious connections but no supporting family, a former spy and recent inmate in debtor's prison, Behn had her first play produced for the Duke's company, originally patented to William Davenant, and very much committed to the Davenant style of movable scenes, machines, spectacular tableaux, songs, and dances. The Restoration theatre was fully "culinary" in its desire to lure and entertain the public exclusively for private profit. It was also, from the giver of the royal patent to the patentees and playwrights, upper class and male.[8]

The audience, historians are finally telling us, was more varied—and contradictory—than was previously believed. Professional men and respectable women and their maids went regularly to the theatre, as did noisy unattached rakes, prostitutes, and members of royal entourage. There had been women writers—the Duchess of Newcastle, Katherine Phillipps, and Frances Boothby each had a play produced. But when Behn's *The Forced Marriage, or The Jealous Bridegroom* opened in December 1670, it was a novelty and no one knew whether she would have staying power. The female performer, having arrived on the professional stage only ten years earlier, though she was paid a lower salary than her male colleagues, had already proved her staying power; in décolletage, in breeches, in "undress," the actress represented an important financial lure and provocation, especially to male spectators.

Conventionally, the Restoration prolog describes the state of literary production, complains about the lowly status of poetry, berates the audience for its stupidity, disparages the whores, condemns the factions of noisy fops, refers to any current political turmoil, introduces and/or playfully positions the author, and, in a vague way, describes the play.

In the prolog of her first play, Behn takes note of the factions in the audience and genders them. She writes lines for a performer (gender unclear, but I would guess male) who enjoins the males in the audience to be leery of "spies"—by implication whores whom the author has planted "to hold you in wanton Compliment / That so you may not censure what she'as writ,/ Which done, they face you down 'twas full of Wit" (Behn 1915:286).

I come now, at last, to my second short text on pointing.

Within moments the stage directions read "*Enter an Actress,*" who "*pointing to the ladies*" asks, "Can any see that glorious Sight and say / A Woman shall not Victor prove today?" In that pointing gesture, the actress sets up a triangular structure—between historical performer, the role she is destined to play, and the female spectators in the audience. She also mentions "A Woman," a potential victor, and that seems to have a referent: the writer Aphra Behn (although it could be one of the females in the play). In that shared look, actor-subject, character, spectator, and author are momentarily joined, and for perhaps the first time on the English stage all four positions are filled by women. But not for long. In casting a closer eye at the female spectators, the actress soon differentiates, and in specifically sexual terms. Insisting, ironically perhaps, that "There's not a Vizard in our whole Cabal" she condemns the lower-class whores, the Pickeroons, "that scour for prey," but ends by promising total female "sacrifice" to "pleasure you" (Behn 1915:286).

Whom that "you" now designates has become fully undecideable. In the sexual slang of the day, actress meant whore, authoress was soon to mean whore, and both were commodities in a pleasure market whose major consumers were male. Still, before conventional representation resumes, the signifying space is dominated by the interlocking look of women. I would call the actress's pointing, and the entire prolog, a Gestus, a moment when the sex-gender system, theatre politics, and social history cathect and become visible. For the feminist critic and theorist this Gestus marks a first step toward recovering a woman playwright in her sexual, historical, and theatrical specificity. It also marks a site, in the text, of indeterminacy, of multiple meanings—a pleasurable moment for reading the clouds.

NOTES

[1] An earlier version of this paper was presented at the American Theater in Higher Education (ATHE) Conference in Chicago, August 1987.

[2] I am grateful to Barton Byg, whose excellent paper, "Brecht on the Margins: Film and Feminist Theory" provided many useful insights.

[3] Without discussing gender per se, Brecht refers briefly to this phenomenon in the "Short Organum," no. 59: "[. . .] it is also good for the actors when they see their characters copied or portrayed in another form. If the part is played by somebody of the opposite sex the sex of the character will be more clearly brought out [. . .]" (Brecht 1964:197).

[4] Brecht elaborates in various ways on this point: "The individual whose innermost being is thus driven into the open then of course comes to stand for Man with a capital M. Everyone (including the spectator) is then carried away by the momentum of the events portrayed, so that in a performance of *Oedipus* one has for all practical purposes an auditorium

full of little Oedipuses, an auditorium full of Emperor Joneses for a performance of *The Emperor Jones*" (in "On the Use of Music in an Epic Theatre," Brecht 1964:87). Also: "The bourgeois theatre emphasized the timelessness of its objects. Its representation of people is bound by the alleged 'eternally human.' Its story is arranged in such a way as to create 'universal' situations that allow Man with a capital M to express himself: man of every period and every colour" (in "Alienation Effects in Chinese Acting," Brecht 1964:97).

[5] I was very much helped by the extensive summary/analysis of psychoanalytic film theory in Sandy Flitterman-Lewis's "Psychoanalysis in Film and Television" (1987) which I read in manuscript form.

[6] I use "historicity" not "history" as the latter term suggests a narrative form which feminists have sought to problematize. In film studies see de Lauretis 1984; in fiction see Brewer 1984; in drama and theatre see Diamond 1985.

[7] This is fully played out in Brecht's attitude toward textual authority. As is well known, he revised constantly and cared little about definitive or authoritative versions of his plays.

[8] One of Behn's biographers, Maureen Duffy, provides this context: "Of the fifteen living dramatists who had had two or more plays produced since the theatres reopened in 1660, two were earls, one a duke, one was to be a titular baron, four were knights. [. . .] In 1671 [most of the new writers] were of the gentry or nobility, and almost all had university or Inns of Court educations. Compared with such a company Aphra Behn's pretensions must have seemed even more extravagant" (1977:103–104).

WORKS CITED

Barker, Francis. *The Tremulous Private Body: Essays on Subjection.* London: Methuen, 1984.

Byg, Barton. "Brecht on the Margins: Film and Film Theory." Paper presented at the annual convention of the Modern Language Association, New York, December, 1986.

Baudry, Jean-Louis. "The Apparatus: Metapsychological Approaches to the Impression of Reality." In *Apparatus*, edited by Theresa Hak Kyung, 41–62. New York: Tanam Press, 1980.

Behn, Aphra. *The Forced Marriage, or The Jealous Bridegroom.* In *The Works of Aphra Behn*, vol. 3, edited by Montague Summers, 285–381. London: Wm Heinemann, 1915.

Bentley, Eric. *The Brecht Commentaries.* London: Methuen, 1981.

Blau, Herbert. *Take Up the Bodies: Theater at the Vanishing Point.* Urbana: University of Illinois Press, 1982.

Brecht, Bertolt. *Brecht on Theatre*, edited by John Willet. New York: Hill and Wang, 1964.

Brewer, Mária Minich. "A Loosening of Tongues: From Narrative Economy to Women Writing." *MLN* 9, no. 5 (December):1141–1161, 1984.

Diamond, Elin. "Refusing the Romanticism of Identity: Narrative Interventions in Churchill, Benmussa, Duras." *Theatre Journal* 37, no. 3 (October):273–286, 1985.

Dollimore, Jonathan. *Radical Tragedy: Religion, Ideology and Power in the Drama of Shakespeare and His Contemporaries.* Chicago: University of Chicago Press, 1984.

Duffy, Maureen. *The Passionate Shepardess: Aphra Behn (1640–89).* London: Jonathan Cape, 1977.

Eagleton, Terry. "Brecht and Rhetoric." In *Against the Grain: Essays 1975–1985*, 167–172. London: Verso, 1986.

Esslin, Martin. *Brecht: The Man and His Work.* New York: W. W. Norton, 1971.

Flitterman-Lewis, Sandy. "Psychoanalysis in Film and Television." In *Channels of Discourse: Television and Contemporary Criticism*, edited by Robert C. Allen, 170–210. Chapel Hill: University of North Carolina Press, 1987.

Heath, Stephen. "Lessons from Brecht." *Screen* 15, no. 2 (Summer):103–127, 1974.

Irigaray, Luce. "The Power of Discourse and the Subordination of the Feminine." In *This Sex Which Is Not One*, translated by Catherine Porter with Carolyn Burke, 68–85. Ithaca, NY: Cornell University Press, 1985.

Johnson, Barbara. *The Critical Difference: Essays in the Contemporary Rhetoric of Reading.* Baltimore, MD: Johns Hopkins University Press, 1980.

de Lauretis, Teresa. *Alice Doesn't: Feminism, Semiotics, Cinema.* Bloomington: University of Indiana Press, 1984.

Moi, Toril. *Sexual/Textual Politics: Feminist Literary Theory.* London: Methuen, 1985.

Mulvey, Laura. "Visual Pleasure and Narrative Cinema." *Screen* 16, no. 3 (Autumn):6–18, 1975.

Pavis, Patrice. *Languages of the Stage: Essays in the Semiology of the Theatre.* New York: Performing Arts Journal Publications, 1982.

Rubin, Gayle. "The Traffic in Women: Notes on the 'Political Economy' of Sex." In *Toward an Anthropology of Women*, edited by Rayna Reiter, 157–210. New York: Monthly Review Press, 1978.

Stimpson, Catherine R. "Stein and the Transposition of Gender." In *The Poetics of Gender*, edited by Nancy K. Miller, 1–18. New York: Columbia University Press, 1986.

Watney, Simon. "The Banality of Gender." In *Sexual Difference*, edited by Robert Young, 13–21. London: The Oxford Literary Review, 1986.

Weber, Carl. "Brecht in Eclipse?" *The Drama Review* 24, no. 1 (T85):114–124, 1980.

Wiles, Timothy J. *The Theater Event: Modern Theories of Performance.* Chicago: The University of Chicago Press, 1980.

APPENDIX
WRITING ABOUT DRAMA AND THEATER

I N MOST WAYS, WRITING ABOUT DRAMA AND THEATER IS LIKE OTHER KINDS OF analytical and argumentative writing. The best work is clear in its claims, tenacious in its analysis, rich and skillful in its discussion of detail. This section presents a brief outline of some of the techniques and practices of effective writing and some of the special concerns particular to writing about drama.

On one level, this is an easy question to answer. You are writing because the instructor has assigned a paper as one of the requirements of the class. Most instructors assign papers—rather than merely assigning quizzes or examinations—because they believe that writing plays a unique role in teaching and in learning. Writing is active, a means of producing learning. When you write, you explore a particular problem or issue: thinking about it in a variety of ways, and teaching yourself something about it in the process. By writing, you also present an argument that attempts to persuade your audience to view the problem in the way that you do. In effect, you become a teacher yourself. Writing forces you to make the subject your own. It forces you to explore it and to consider how you can best represent the results of your thinking. Indeed, in the act of writing you may well discover what it is you have to say.

Most college-level writing about drama asks you to construct an interpretation of some aspect of a play or plays. The kind of interpretation you will perform, though, has much in common with persuasive argument—your paper should make an assertion about the play, a *claim* that you will develop in the course of the essay. First, a good claim is not simply a description of the work, a statement of what's already self-evident. To say, for example, that Ibsen's play *A Doll House* is about conflicted gender and marital relations is merely to state the obvious; it leaves you nothing to argue. Nor is a good claim merely a personal opinion about the work, a statement that invites agreement without persuasion or evidence. To say that *A Doll House* is a bad play, or that Nora is an unbelievable character, is an opinion-statement of this kind. Argumentative writing requires you to consider a fundamentally *problematic* issue, a question about which there could be some important disagreement—disagreement regarding the interpretation of the play itself. Writing is, after all, a form of communication. It is important that you have something worthwhile to say and that you way of saying it can be made persuasive to others.

For most people, writing an effective analytical argument has three basic phases that work to transform thoughts into an effective piece of writing. The first phase is the *invention* phase, when you consider the issues you want to raise. This is the time to ask yourself very general and stimulating questions that will lead to a commitment—a *claim*—about the work. If the choice of the paper is up to you, you might ask which of the plays you have read you liked the most. What aspects of the play seem most important, impressive, or unusual to you? If a paper topic has been assigned, you still need to make it your own. You might ask yourself how the topic seems to interpret the play, what problems or questions the topic seems to raise about your understanding of the play. It is at this point that most students come up with the *topic* of their papers; but a topic is only a first step. In order for a topic to be transformed into an argumentative claim, you have to think about it as a *problem*. A topic is inert while a problem is controversial—an idea about which there can be disagreement. For example, this is a topic: "Nora Helmer is a good mother in *A Doll House*." Although this statement does make a claim, the claim is vague and underdeveloped. Its importance and consequences are not yet made clear. To transform the topic into a problem, we might ask how this claim could be seen as controversial, to involve us in a specific kind of interpretation of the play. One way to transform this topic into a problem is to imply an alternative perspective as part of the claim: "Although Nora Helmer leaves her children at the end of the play, she is really a good mother." This is a more problematic claim, precisely because it raises the possibility that Nora could be seen in two ways. This claim could be made more effective by suggesting how resolving this problem is central to an understanding of the play: "Although Nora Helmer leaves her children at the end of *A Doll House*, the play presents her as a good mother. Nora herself must become a free adult, must discover who she really is, before she can raise her children." This claim raises several complex issues and suggests a particular perspective on them. Your audience would expect you to discuss Nora's accomplishments as a mother in the play and relate those accomplishments to her difficult decision to leave her family at the end of the play.

This process—transforming a topic into a problem—usually marks the end of the first phase of writing, at which you come up with the major claim of your paper, a provisional *thesis*. This claim is still only provisional, because you will probably have to modify it in the next phase of the writing process: organizing your argument, developing your evidence, and drafting the paper. Now that you have a sense of what you want to claim in the essay, you will want to consider how to present your claim effectively. This usually means choosing some elements of the play to examine in detail. In this case, for instance, you might choose to discuss the scenes in which Nora interacts with her children; or the scenes in which she refuses to see them; or the scenes in which she discusses her children with others, like Mrs. Linde and Torvald. Of course, none of these scenes explicitly answers your claim: Ibsen never tells his audience "Nora is a good mother in this scene." It's your task to *interpret* the scene, suggest how we—your audience—should look at it in order to see it as you do. Generating detail of this kind—scenes, characters, speeches, language—to discuss is often one of the most challenging parts of the writing process. One way to help yourself here (and as a writer) is to take some notes on the play after you have read it. What scenes do you think are important or memorable? Why? What do you make of the major characters? These notes can help to provide some of the initial material you will discuss as part of your drafting of the essay.

Having considered what aspects of the play you want to address, you will want to make an outline, a map of your approach. Most students learn to make a formal outline—with major headings, subheadings, and so on—in high school, and some college and university classes require you to submit the outline as part of your writing process. Most writers use a more informal outlining strategy; they make a list of the issues or evidence they want to treat in the paper, as a way of putting main points and main pieces of evidence in order. Once you begin writing, you may well need to revise your outline, as what you have already written suggest new directions for the rest of the essay. Having outlined your approach, the next step is the writing itself. Instead of trying to get everything right in the first draft, most writers use the writing process to generate ideas and develop some prose. There will be plenty of opportunity to shape, develop and revise the writing later. So, when you begin the paper, do your best to get your argument into a clear order. Write as much as it occurs to you to say on each point, giving yourself a lot of leeway to improvise ideas that may need to be clarified in revision. If important new evidence occurs to you, put it down in the draft, making a note to return to it. The important factor at this stage is to get as many of your thoughts down in order as you can.

The final phase—or phases, since most good papers take several revisions—is the process of revision. Revising is where the process of your thinking is transformed into an effective argument. Through revision your thinking is reshaped to become effective written communication. Written communication is sequential; your audience can only process information one piece at a time. For that reason, it's important to clarify your claims at the outset, tell your audience where the argument is going, and why. It's also important to tell the audience how each section of the argument is helping to substantiate that claim, and why it is important that we've accompanied you so far. A major objective of revision is to make the outlines of the argument—its major phases—explicit in this way. When revising, one useful trick is to read over your text—a paragraph, for instance—and then ask yourself, "What's the point of this paragraph? How does it contribute to my overall argument?" If you cannot answer that question, then you need to consider whether the paragraph—in this form—belongs in the paper at all. If you can answer it, then look to see that you answer is actually written down in the paragraph somewhere, made explicit to your readers, who, after all, are probably not thinking about the problem in exactly the way that you are.

Of course, these are the large-scale revisions; you will also want to ask similar questions of more local matters. Have I presented enough evidence on this point? Have I interpreted the evidence fully for the reader? How are my mechanics—sentence clarity, structure, variety, spelling?

APPROACHES TO WRITING

Writing about drama and theater is not essentially different from writing about other literary, historical, or cultural subjects, and the skills and habits of effective writing will serve well in writing about drama, too. However, writing about drama and theater also follows some of its own conventions. First, papers are generally written in the present verb tense, as though the play were actually taking place now, in front of us. It's up to you, of course, whether you want to write from the point of view of the reader or the point of view of the theater audience, but you will have to adopt a consistent perspective throughout and recognize that each perspective can help to make certain features of the play more clearly visible.

Second, many papers about drama begin by taking issue with one of Aristotle's categories of dramatic structure: the play's plot (how does its sequence of events contribute to its overall meaning?), its characters (how are the characters constructed; how do the conventions of characterization represent "real" people?), its thought or themes (how does the play generate its "themes"?), its language (are there patterns of language, images, or ways of speaking that contribute to your sense of its action?), and its spectacle (are there explicit features of its action onstage that help to realize the play's meaning?). These topics can be expanded through reference to the specific forms of drama in a given period or theater. To talk about the plot structure of a Shakespearean play, after all, is to talk about something very different from the plot of a Beckett play. It's important to realize that these features of the drama can provide a good starting point for your discussion, but that each will need to be specified in terms of your particular argument.

Another approach that's often useful in thinking about drama is to consider the play's staging, either in terms of effects that are described or made explicit in the text (the times that Prospero appears "aloft" in *The Tempest*; the confining single room of *A Doll House*), or in terms of the actual production choices made in a given staging. Thinking about how a production you have seen interpreted the text and how it used acting, movement, set design, and costuming to provide the audience with a given perspective on the play is another standard approach to writing about drama and theater.

CITATION AND DOCUMENTATION

There are a few mechanical conventions specific to writing about drama. As you can see from the essays included in this volume, there are several forms you can use for citing secondary sources. The two main approaches are to use footnotes for all citations (see Sue-Ellen Case's article in unit 1), or to put the page numbers in parentheses in the text and add a list of Works Cited at the end of the paper, saving notes only for further explanation

This essay on Racine's Phaedra was written by an undergraduate student in a class on tragedy at the University of Texas at Austin. In the essay, Heather E. Brand uses Georges Bataille's discussion of eroticism to analyze and discuss the stages of Phaedra's moral progress through the play. Several aspects of this essay seem particularly successful: Brand's definition of the problem in the opening paragraph, her arrangement of the paper's series of ideas around Bataille's phases of erotic transgression, and her interpretation of scenes and passages from Phaedra to substantiate her claims about the play. Although different papers will require different conceptual and organizational strategies, this paper suggests one concise, effective, and detailed way of comparing the action of a play to a critical or theoretical text.

(A S I D E)

A SAMPLE STUDENT ESSAY

TRAGIC EROTICISM

Heather E. Brand
English 379M
Professor Worthen
30 April 1991

Human existence is founded on a dichotomy—the conflict between the discontinuous order of society and the continuous chaos of the natural world. While social order is defended by a system of taboos and boundaries, human desire aims at transcending these taboos through transgression. However, once the transgression occurs, the transgressor is forever excluded from the realm of society and is either driven to exile or to death. Between the mutually exclusive realms of nature and society lies the domain of eroticism. As Georges Bataille argues, the erotic is the means by which "we are incessantly trying to get at continuity, which implies that the boundaries have been crossed, without actually crossing the boundaries of the discontinuous life. We want to get across without taking the final step, while remaining cautiously on the hither side" (Bataille 141). The tragic theater shares with the erotic this form of voyeurism—a means of envisioning social transgression without its nullifying repercussions. Jean Racine Utilizes this tragic eroticism in *Phaedra* as a tool for denouncing erotic fulfillment as detrimental to social morality. In this particular instance. Racine uses the character Phaedra to portray the destructive and tragic phases of erotic fulfillment.

Bataille's theory of eroticism involves three phases: attraction, transgression, and sacrifice. Phaedra enacts this process throughout the course of the play. Phaedra is simultaneously confronted by her desire to uphold the order of society in the absence of Theseus, and her incentuous attraction to Hippolytus. The incest taboo is historically grounded in the attempt to deny our animal nature in favor of forming the social order of the family, the foundation of the social structure. "The horror of incest thus embodies a factor which makes humans of us and the problem it poses is the problem of man himself as far as he adds the human element to animal nature. In consequence all that we are is at stake in our decision to eschew the loose freedom of sexual conduct and the natural and unformulated life of the animals" (Bataille 198).

Phaedra's transgressive urges are characterized by her inconsistent behavior in the beginning of the play; Racine presents her in the throes of erotic anxiety. For example, she is rendered practically incapable of making the slightest decision, such as the styling of her hair or whether or not to venture into the sunlight. Oenone recognizes this interior struggle:

How all her wishes war among
    themselves!
Yourself, condemning your unlawful
    plans,
A moment past, bade us adorn your brow;
Yourself, summoning your former
    strength,
Wished to come forth and see the light
    again.
Scarce have you seen it than you long
    to hide;
You hate the daylight you came forth
    to see. (Racine 155)

In order to impress the maddening agony of erotic passion upon the audience, Racine reduces Phaedra to a state of social withdrawal and mental division as she wavers between taboo and transgression.

(see Lynda Boose's article in unit 3). Your instructor may well have a preference here and will help you to use secondary citations. The purpose of citing secondary works you may use in writing your essay is twofold: first, to give credit to your sources, to the other writers whose work you may have used in coming to your own conclusions; second, to direct your readers to other material that may be interesting or helpful to them. At most colleges and

Phaedra's submission to erotic fulfillment constitutes the second phase of her erotic destruction. Although she never actually commits the crime of incest, her confession of her desire is enough to render her culpable in the eyes of society. In the preface to the play, Racine comments that, "The very thought of crime is regarded with as much horror as the crime itself" (Racine 146). Her admission of erotic attraction is a transgression in itself; her guilt is confounding. In submitting to this animal desire, Phaedra irrevocably dissolves her social bonds and becomes a self-proclaimed "monster," continuous with the irrational chaos of nature. Her feeble attempt to realign herself with order by falsely accusing Hippolytus of her own crime only serves to magnify her monstrosity. When approached with the possible leadership of the state, she recognizes the irreconcilable contradictions of her position:

I reign? I bring a State beneath my rule?
When reason reigns no longer over me.
When I have lost my self-dominion;
   when
Beneath a shameful sway I scarcely
   breathe;
When I am dying? (Racine 180–181)

In this passage, Phaedra realizes that her only prospect is to submit to nature entirely, to submit to death. The tragic transgression of taboo, instigated by eroticism, leads her to no other possibility than that of self-destruction.

Yet, the act of transgression is not only fatal to the transgressor but also to the erotic object. The death of the erotic object, in this instance the death of Hippolytus, marks the third and final phase of eroticism. Since Hippolytus' death is the result of a false accusation, we must regard it as a sacrifice that restores moral and social order. Bataille suggests that the sacrificial process is an "extravagance of nature ending in the profusion of death" (Bataille 88); this "profusion" or "chaos" of death signifies the utter dissolution of the human body into the continuity of nature, just as Hippolytus' body, in death, is no longer a singular object, but a part of nature itself. Theramenes is left with the task of relaying Hippolytus' corporeal explosion:

The traces of his blood showed us the way.
The rocks were stained with it, the
   cruel thorns
Dripped with the bleeding remnants
   of his hair. . .
. . . And then he passed away,
And in my arms lay a disfigured corpse,
A tribute to the anger of the gods.

The death of Hippolytus is a sacrificial appeal to social order because it inspires the communal response of disgust and nausea among the spectators. More important, in dying Hippolytus becomes continuous with nature, one with the rocks, thorns, and bushes that bear the traces of his body. His grotesque return to nature is Racine's reminder of the horrible consequences of the erotic. This scene also serves to unite the audience in a feeling of pathos: pity for the innocent, and fear of transgression. In this manner, Racine justifies the moral importance of maintaining social taboos.

Racine employs these three phases of eroticism (the attraction, transgression, and sacrifice) as a means of ordering the erotic into a plot of destruction. In inducing the audience to identify the erotic attraction of the tragic theater with that of Phaedra's attraction Hippolytus, the play invites the audience to undergo a sympathetic process of erotic fulfillment. However, Racine then proceeds to play upon this desire by presenting his audience with the destructive nature of erotic fulfillment and its negative social implications. Racine, conscious that "eroticism springs from an alternation of fascination and horror, of affirmation and denial," fosters tragic eroticism as a tool for encouraging the denial of eroticism itself (Bataille 211). He relies on a classical pathos to act as a purging mechanism for our own erotic desire. In centering his tragedy upon the crux of eroticism, Racine allows the spectator to experience the continuous chaos beyond taboo without actually becoming committed to it. The method of theatrical voyeurism, then, assigns its eroticism to the ordered domain of theatrical language and form; Racine's play guards against any actual social transgression by inviting us, finally, to reorder erotic transgression within moral terms. This edifying morality of tragic eroticism is what Racine claims as "the real purpose of tragedy" (Racine 147).

WORKS CITED

Bataille, Georges. *Eroticism*. San Francisco: City Lights Books, 1986.

Racine, Jean. *Iphigenia/Phaedra/Athaliah*. New York: Viking Penguin, 1970.

universities, plagiarism—submitting someone else's work as your own—is an extremely serious offense, and careful attention to citations protects you as well as informing your readers.

Writing about drama uses several conventions to identify quotations from plays. Classical Greek plays are usually cited by line number, and the citation follows the quotation:

Clytaemnestra's effect on Agamemnon is complete when he steps on to the blood-red carpet, saying, "I feel such shame—to tread the life of the house" (ll. 945–46).

Notice that "ll." is the abbreviation for the word "lines" and is used to identify the line numbers of the quotation, and that the citation follows the close-quotation mark and precedes the period. The citation is part of the sentence, so it's included inside the sentence, before the period.

A different convention is followed for plays from the Renaissance, Restoration, and Neoclassical periods, which are commonly written in verse and usually are divided into acts and scenes. Here, the citation includes act, scene, and line numbers, separated by a period. Some people prefer using Roman numerals (IV.iii.21–22)—for Act Four, Scene 3, Lines 21–22—but many people now use Arabic numerals (4.3.21–22) as follows:

Prospero finally accepts his own role in creating Caliban at the end of *The Tempest,* when he says, "this thing of darkness I/Acknowledge mine" (5.1.305–6).

When the play is written in verse, the lineation of the original text is preserved with a slash (/) between the lines, and the capitalization of each new line is preserved as above. Usually, quotations of more that three lines are set of as a separate quotation.

Since modern plays are not consistently divided into acts and scenes, and are not written in verse lines, it's common to identify the section (act and scene) of the play you are discussing as part of your prose, and then to cite the page number:

The most chilling moment in Shaw's *Major Barbara* occurs at the end of the second act of the play, when Cusins claims, "Dionysus Undershaft has descended. I am possessed!" (478).

The mechanics of quotation are easy to learn and lend your work an air of competence and credibility. For additional information, ask your instructor to recommend a handbook, or consult *The MLA Handbook for Writers of Research Papers,* ed. Joseph Gibaldi and Walter S. Achtert, 3rd ed. (New York, Modern Language Association of America, 1988). It contains extensive material on how and when to use footnotes, the preparation of works cited, and more specialized questions of style and mechanics.

GLOSSARY

Absurd *See* **Theater of the Absurd.**

Académie Française An academy founded by Cardinal Richelieu in 1635 to resolve the critical debate surrounding Corneille's play *The Cid*, and to regularize the French language.

actos Short satirical plays devised by Luis Valdez and El Teatro Campesino in the late 1960s to dramatize the conditions of farmworkers in California.

afterpiece A short play—usually a pantomime or farce—that followed the main play on the evening's bill; common in England in the eighteenth and nineteenth centuries.

agora The marketplace in ancient Greek towns; the *agora* was often used for dramatic performance.

Alienation effect A stage technique developed by Bertolt Brecht in the 1920s and 1930s for "estranging" the action of the play. By making characters and their actions seem remarkable, alien, or unusual, Brecht encouraged the audience to question the social realities that produced such events, the political and ideological background of the drama and of its stage production.

allegory A literary or dramatic technique that uses actual characters, places, and actions to represent more abstract political, moral, or religious ideas. *See Everyman.*

alojería The tavern at the rear of the *patio* in a Spanish Golden Age Theater, or *corral*.

amphitheater A semicircular theater design, consisting of a playing area faced by rising tiers of seats; often used outdoors, this was the design of classical Greek theaters.

anachronism Using people, places, or things that are chronologically out of keeping with the rest of the fictive world of a play or narrative; for example, using medieval English shepherds to attend the birth of Christ in medieval cycle plays.

anagnorisis Greek term for a character's "recognition" of something previously not known in the play. In the *Poetics*, Aristotle links *anagnorisis* with *peripeteia*, the "reversal" in the action of the play.

antagonist The force or character that opposes the main character ("**protagonist**") of a play.

antimasque A scene of misrule, usually involving witches, goblins, demons, or savages, who are transformed magically into princes, gods and goddesses, or virtues in a Jacobean **masque.**

antiphonal performance Alternative or responsive singing between individuals or groups; in the Middle Ages, it commonly involved two choirs.

archon A magistrate in classical Athens; each year, an *archon* was assigned the responsibility for organizing the City Dionysia.

apron The section of the stage that extends toward the auditorium beyond the **proscenium.**

Atellan farce Improvised comic skits featuring stock characters performed by masked actors in ancient Rome.

atoza Upstage area in a **Noh** theater in which the musicians are seated.

auto sacramentale Elaborate Spanish religious dramas originally devised as part of the feast of Corpus Christi. *Autos* continued to be performed in Spain until 1765.

avant-garde Literally the "advance group," the term usually refers to the most innovative, experimental, or unorthodox artists in a given historical period. Used almost exclusively of late nineteenth- and twentieth-century movements.

backcloth A painted cloth lowered at the rear of the stage to represent a dramatic location.

benefit   In the English theater of the seventeenth, eighteenth, and nineteenth centuries, a performance whose profits were assigned to a single performer or to the playwright.

biomechanics   An experimental technique for actor training and performance devised by the Russian director Vsevolod Meyerhold after the Russian Revolution (1917). The technique emphasized the actor's physical training, stressing acrobatic and choreographic elements in production.

bhava   A stageable emotion in **Sanskrit drama**, related to the play's principal *rasa* or mood.

biwa   Four-stringed, plucked instrument used to accompany spoken narration in medieval Japan.

blank verse   An English verse meter consisting of unrhymed **iambic pentameter** lines (ten syllables with alternating stress, the first stress falling on the second syllable.)

box   Box seating first appeared in theaters in the late seventeenth century; boxes were arranged around the side of the stage and the sides of the auditorium for the private accommodation of small numbers of people. Boxes were more expensive than pit or gallery seats.

box set   First devised in the 1830s, a set consisting of three practical walls enclosing the stage in a room-like way.

bunraku   The term used for modern Japanese **puppet theater**, derived from the eighteenth-century master Uemura Bunrakuken.

butai   The acting area, or stage proper, of a **Noh** theater.

cabaret performance   Stage performances in restaurants serving food and drink; especially popular in Europe after World War I, cabarets often were used for innovative kinds of performance.

canon   An authorized body of texts, such as the "canon" of Shakespeare's known plays; also commonly used to mean a "traditional" body of texts.

capa y espada   Literally "cape and sword" plays, swashbuckling romances in the Golden Age theater.

Capitano   The braggart soldier of *commedia dell' arte.*

carro   Wagon used for performance of Spanish *auto sacramentale.*

catastrophe   The turning point in the plot of a classical tragedy.

catharsis   Literally, the "purging" that Aristotle discusses as the effect of tragedy in his *Poetics.* Catharsis has been variously described as an emotional release on the part of the spectators, or as the recognition and purging of wrongdoing in the action of the play.

cazuela   The women's gallery above the *alojería* in a Spanish Golden Age theater, or *corral.*

character   A fictional "person" appearing in a play or other work of fiction; usually conventionalized to some degree.

chonin   Japanese term for townsmen.

choregos   An important citizen in ancient Athens given the responsibility for financing, assembling, and training the chorus of Greek tragedy.

chorus   A masked group of young men who sang and danced as a group in Greek tragedy and comedy; larger choruses also performed *dithyrambs.*

City Dionysia   Annual spring festival honoring the god Dionysus; one of four festivals held between December and April. Sometimes called the "Great Dionysia," it was the site of dramatic competitions and other public displays and rituals.

comedia nueva   Mixed mode form of drama associated with Lope de Vega.

Comédie Française   The official national theater of France, devoted to the staging of the classics. Founded and chartered by Louis XIV in 1680 when Molière's company and the Marais company were united.

comedy Traditionally a humorous literary form, comedy typically concerns the trials of love, and/or ridicules the failings of certain members of society. *See* **comedy of manners, new comedy, old comedy, romantic comedy.**

comedy of manners Comic drama that takes the manners of high society as its subject; in comedy of manners, the dialogue is often witty or epigrammatic.

commedia dell' arte Improvised comic plays performed by itinerant companies; it originated in Italy in the sixteenth century and then spread throughout Europe. Actors each played a stock character type and improvised the action according to a shared outline plot.

Constructivist theater A movement in the Soviet theater after World War I, and often associated with the director Vsevolod Meyerhold. Adapted from the visual arts, constructivist theater resisted the use of representational sets, using more abstract "constructions" onstage.

corral Open-air Spanish theater of the sixteenth and seventeenth centuries, constructed within an open courtyard.

cross-dressing One of the conventions of cross-gendered acting, in which women play male characters in male costume, and men play female characters in women's clothing.

cycle plays A series of plays dramatizing Christian history from the Creation to the Last Judgment, devised and performed in the Middle Ages by craft-guilds called "mysteries"; the cycles are sometimes also called "mystery cycles" or "mystery plays." Performed outside the church on the Feast of Corpus Christi.

Dada A nonsense term adopted as the name of a literary and theatrical movement in Europe after World War I; Dada developed an esthetic of random and irrational art. Dada performances became popular in cabarets of Paris, Zurich, and Berlin in the 1920s.

daimyo Feudal lord of Japan, member of the *samurai* class of warriors, and owing duty to the *shogun.*

decorum The notion, associated with **neoclassicism,** that the action and subject matter (idealized), language (heightened), and moral propriety (elevated), should be stylistically integrated and unified.

demonstration Describing the **"alienation effect,"** Bertolt Brecht urged his actors to "demonstrate" the roles they played, rather than identifying with them in the mode of Stanislavskian acting. Acting-as-demonstration keeps the audience aware of both the actor *and* the "character" at the same time.

dengaku-no Form of dance, role-playing, and acrobatics popular in Japan in the eleventh and twelfth centuries; said to be one of the progenitors of **Noh** theater.

desvanes Small open galleries on the third and fourth storeys in a Spanish Golden Age theater, or *corral.*

deus ex machina Literally the "god from the machine," the term refers to the practice of using a crane to lower the character of a god to the stage at the end of a classical Greek tragedy, usually to resolve the action of the play. Modern usage takes the term to refer to any dramatic device that suddenly resolves the action of a play.

dithyramb Choral hymns sung and danced to honor Dionysus as part of the City Dionysia. Choruses of 50 men or 50 boys drawn from each tribe performed dithyrambs prior to the tragedy competition; Aristotle thought tragedy to have originated in these dithyrambic performances.

dokekata Comic roles in **Kabuki** theater.

doll theater Form of Japanese theater originating in the seventeenth century; doll theater uses elaborate dolls, operated by three visible puppeteers, and combines music and narration.

Dottore The "doctor" or old pedant of *commedia dell' arte*; usually a friend of **Pantalone.**

drama A literary composition, usually in dialogue form, and centering on the actions of fictional characters.

emotion memory A term developed by the Russian director Constantin Stanislavski to describe an actor's "work on himself" in acting. After considering a character's circumstances in the play, and his past life leading up to the action of the play, the actor tries to connect the character's situation with important events in his or her own life: this emotional or affectual connection can make the character's display of emotion onstage seem realistic and immediate.

entremeses Short plays performed as interludes between acts of Golden Age dramas.

environmental theater A term coined by Richard Schechner in the late 1960s to describe performances that do not distinguish between the playing area and the audience; the performance takes place throughout the theatrical environment.

epic theater A term associated with the German director Erwin Piscator and theorized by Bertolt Brecht in the late 1920s and 1930s, epic theater uses episodic dramatic action, non-representational staging, and the **"alienation effect,"** to demonstrate the political, social, and economic factors governing the lives of the dramatic characters. In the theater, Brecht advocated the use of placards to announce the action, visible lighting, filmscreens on the stage, and other devices to produce this epic effect.

episode Originally, a dramatic scene in a classical Greek tragedy, as distinct from the choral odes; now, usually refers to any incident or event in a play. Plays that are episodic tend not to subordinate episodes to a causal plot, but simply to arrange them in a series.

exodos The final scene and exit of the characters and chorus in a classical Greek play.

expressionist theater An early twentieth-century movement challenging the **verisimilitude** of realistic theater by staging individual emotional, unconscious states of mind directly. In expressionist plays, the action is usually abrupt and intense; the characters are usually generalized; the plot is typically symbolic or allegorical.

extravaganza Visual spectacle popular in nineteenth-century theater.

Fabian society A late nineteenth-century English socialist political society; Marxist in its orientation to social change, the Fabian society advocated a policy of gradual reform rather than revolution.

farce Usually a short comic play, often relying on a highly coincidental plot.

film noir A genre of black-and-white detective films popular in the 1940s, which frequently used shadowy, nighttime settings to establish an aura of menace and foreboding.

folio A large-format printed volume, in which only four pages (two per side) are printed on each sheet of paper; the paper is folded once to form four pages.

fourth wall Refers to the style of realistic theater since the late nineteenth century, in which the stage is treated as a room with one wall missing. The audience is not acknowledged or addressed by the actors, but overlooks the scene as a silent, invisible observer.

fuebashira Flute-player's pillar in a **Noh** theater, the upstage right pillar where the flute-player is positioned during the performance.

gallery In seventeenth-, eighteenth-, and nineteenth-century theaters, ascending rows of bench seating usually located opposite the stage on the third level of the auditorium; generally the most inexpensive seats in the theater.

genre Literally, "kind" or "type," *genre* in literary and dramatic studies refers to the main types of literary form, principally tragedy and comedy. The term can also refer to forms that are more specific to a given historical era, such as "revenge tragedy" or to more specific sub-genres of **tragedy** and **comedy,** such as "comedy of manners."

given circumstances   Term used by Constantin Stanislavski to describe the situation a character finds himself or herself in at the opening of the play, which the actor must construct as his first step in building the character toward performance.

gracioso   The comic fool of Spanish Golden Age drama, popularized in part by Lope de Vega.

gradas   The steeply raked side seats along the side of the *patio* in a Spanish Golden Age theater, or *corral.*

grave trap   A trap door in the floor of the stage, often in the center.

hamartia   A term used by Aristotle in the *Poetics* to describe the tragic hero's decisive act, the "error" or "mistake" that brings about the tragedy. Sometimes mistranslated as "tragic flaw;" a translation that mistakenly changes the meaning of the term from the description of an action to a feature of the character's moral makeup or personality.

hanamichi   Elevated gangway extending from the rear of **Kabuki** theater to the stage; major characters use this bridge for their entrances and some scenes are played here as well.

Harlequin   The main character of *commedia dell'arte,* and later of English pantomime. Usually a wily schemer, Harlequin was originally played in a patched costume, which became conventionalized as the familiar diamond-covered costume. Harlequin was usually masked and carried a flat bat or paddle.

hashigakari   The long bridge from the **mirror room** to the stage of a **Noh** theater.

heroic tragedy   A seventeenth-century genre, usually on the theme of love vs. honor; associated with Dryden in England, Corneille in France, and Calderón de la Barca in Spain.

hon kyogen   The main play of a **Kabuki** performance, originally lasting from about 7 A.M. until dusk when the theater closed.

hurry door   The small door leading offstage from the *atoza,* or upstage area of a **Noh** theater; used by the chorus, the stage assistants, and by dead characters.

iambic pentameter   English verse meter consisting of ten-syllable lines with alternating stressed and unstressed syllables, the first stress falling on the second syllable.

ideology   A complex term first used in the eighteenth century to categorize political beliefs and attitudes. Used to mean 1) a body of beliefs, a doctrine; 2) a body of illusory beliefs, a false doctrine; 3) a socially-grounded system for producing beliefs and values, a way of producing meanings or doctrines.

Independent Theater Movement   A late nineteenth-century movement in Europe, in which small theaters gambled on the production of new and unconventional plays—by Ibsen, Shaw, Chekhov—to a small audience, usually outside the theatrical mainstream.

Innamorata/o   The attractive young lovers of *commedia dell' arte;* played without masks.

interlude   A short play, usually comic, performed during courtly feasts at the English court in the sixteenth century.

jidaimono   The four- to six-act "history" section of a **Kabuki** performance.

jōruri   Performance of narrative and dialogue to the accompaniment of a *samisen* in Japanese theater; these elements absorbed into **doll theater.**

Kabuki   Form of Japanese popular theater originating in the early seventeenth century. Kabuki tends to encompass both comic and serious elements in elaborate and conventional performances that originally lasted from ten to twelve hours; it includes live acting, narration, music, and singing.

kamyonguk   Dance-drama form practiced in Korea, using colorful costumes, masked actors, and musical accompaniment.

katakiyaku   Villain role in **Kabuki** theater.

komos   A procession and dance in ancient Greece, sometimes thought to be the origin of comic drama.

kyōgen   Brief farcical play performed as interludes between **Noh** plays.

language   One of the six constituent elements of drama defined by Aristotle in the *Poetics*.

line of business   A conventional or stock "character" type that is the specialty of a given actor; his or her "line of business" might be old men, heavy villains, comic heroines, etc.

Little Negro Theater Movement   A movement in U.S. theater in the 1920s to develop theaters owned and operated by African-Americans, playing a dramatic repertory by African-American writers.

Little Theater Movement   A movement in the American theater in the early twentieth century akin to the **Independent Theater Movement** in Europe. Little Theaters offered new, or noncommercial plays to smaller audiences.

liturgical drama   Short dramatized sections of the Catholic Mass performed as part of the service; may have inspired the more elaborate, non-liturgical **cycle plays.**

machina   The Greek term for the crane used in the ancient theater to raise and lower characters, particularly the gods.

machine plays   Term used principally in seventeenth-century French theater to describe spectacular special-effects extravaganzas, in which the dramatic action—usually drawn from mythological subjects—was merely a pretext for the use of stage machinery.

magic if   Term developed by Constantin Stanislavski to describe the actor's attitude toward a role; to play "as if I were in this situation."

mansions   Structures placed at several locations inside medieval churches as settings for liturgical plays.

masque   A brief, usually symbolic, mythological, or allegorical play, with elaborate scenic effects performed at the English court during the sixteenth and seventeenth centuries; performed both by actors and by courtiers.

melodrama   First used in the late eighteenth century, the term originally referred to highly-charged, popular plays using music to reinforce their clear-cut moral action; now refers more generally to plays with a schematic opposition between good and evil, in which good usually prevails.

metatheater   A term used to describe plays that self-consciously comment on the process of theater, or treat the process of theater as a metaphor for off-stage reality. Such plays sometimes use the play-within-the-play device.

Method acting   A technique of acting developed by Constantin Stanislavski at the turn of the twentieth century, which teaches actors to use **emotion memory** to enact the character's feelings persuasively and realistically in performance; method acting became especially popular in the United States in the 1930s, 1940s, and 1950s.

metsukebashira   The "gazing pillar" in a **Noh** theater, where the *shite* looks when delivering his first speech. It is the downstage right pillar.

mie   Exaggerated pose struck for expressive effect by actors in **Kabuki** theater.

mimesis   Greek word for "imitation" used by Aristotle in *Poetics* to describe the function of art.

mirror room   The waiting room of a **Noh** theater, where actors in costume contemplate their characterization.

mise-en-scène   The "putting onstage" of a play, including the setting, scenery, direction, and action.

mitos   Lyrical plays on Mexican-American life devised by Luis Valdez and El Teatro Campesino in the late 1960s and 1970s.

monopoly   The right to exclusive production of the drama.

montage   A technique used in film consisting of a rapid sequence of images.

morality drama   A late-medieval dramatic form using allegorical characters to dramatize moral and ethical problems involved in leading a Christian life.

music   A constituent element of drama as defined by Aristotle in the *Poetics*; Aristotle refers to the flute music that accompanied performance in the ancient Greek theater.

mystery cycles   *See* **cycle plays.**

Naturalism   A late nineteenth-century movement that attempted to achieve an objective **verisimilitude** in art—chiefly in theater and literature—by adopting a "scientific" attitude toward its subject matter. Thematically, naturalism emphasizes the role of society, history, and personality in determining the actions of its characters, usually expressed as a conflict between the characters and their environment.

nautical shows   A type of melodrama popular in England in the eighteenth and nineteenth centuries on seafaring subjects; in aquatic dramas, the stage was actually flooded.

neoclassical drama   Drama written under the influence of **neoclassicism** (see below).

neoclassicism   A movement throughout Europe in the sixteenth to eighteenth centuries to revive the forms and values of art exemplified by ancient literature; associated with the recovery of Aristotle's *Poetics* and its translation into prescriptions for the stage.

new comedy   A form originating in the fourth and third centuries BC, first in Greece and then in Rome. In the plays of Plautus, for instance, new comedy generally concerns a romantic plot involving a conflict between young lovers, an old man, and a tricky servant.

Noh   Japanese classical theater dating from the fourteenth century; the plays are highly poetic dramas given extremely formal production onstage. Noh drama was admired by Yeats and by other modern playwrights.

ode   In Greek drama, a song performed by the chorus while dancing.

old comedy   Satiric social comedy of fifth-century BC Athens; Aristophanes' plays are the only surviving examples.

onnagata   Women's roles in **Kabuki** theater, all of which are played by men.

onna kabuki   Literally, "women's Kabuki," an early name for **Kabuki** companies, which were composed mainly of women.

orchestra   Literally, the "dancing place," the circular area before the **skene** where the chorus performed in ancient Greek theater.

pageant master   The guild officer responsible for gathering funds to finance medieval mystery pageants.

pageant wagons   Wagons carrying the sets for productions of medieval **cycle plays,** on which the plays were performed.

Pantalone   Foolish old man in *commedia dell' arte*; played masked.

pantomime   In general, silent acting using gesture and facial expression. English pantomime is a spoken form, in which spectacular fairy-tale extravaganzas are performed with music and dance during the Christmas holidays.

parabasis   A choral speech in ancient Greek comedy in which the chorus comments on contemporary social issues.

parodos   The entrance song of the chorus in Greek tragedy.

parterre   The standing area in the auditorium of late seventeenth-century Parisian theaters; the **pit.**

pastiche   Term used by Fredric Jameson to describe the toneless quotation of earlier artistic styles in contemporary (or postmodern) works.

patents   Licenses given by the crown permitting a company to give dramatic performances; often, a patent would give a company or a small number of companies a **monopoly** on dramatic performance.

patent theaters   Theaters given **patents** (or licenses) by the crown for dramatic performance, sometimes holding a monopoly on performance. Charles II of England granted two patents and gave their owners a monopoly on dramatic performance.

patio   The flat central courtyard of a Spanish Golden Age theater, or *corral.*

Peking Opera   Elaborate form of Chinese theater involving an onstage orchestra, ornate costumes, music, and dance.

peripeteia   A term used by Aristotle in the *Poetics* to describe the "reversal" in the action of a tragedy.

phallus   A leather phallus worn by male characters in Greek comedy.

pit   Floor area immediately in front of the stage in seventeenth- and eighteenth-century theaters.

plot   The sequence of events in a play or narrative; differs from the "story," which encompasses earlier events. Some works have several plots.

pointing   Common practice in the eighteenth-century theater of delivering a famous speech directly to the audience from a downstage position; to "make a point."

polis   A city-state in ancient Greece.

political theater   In conventional usage, theater that seems to question the inequities and injustices of contemporary society. Bertolt Brecht developed a more searching critique of political theater, however, in which the ideology of theatrical representation itself could be seen as the theater's "politics."

postmodern   A term used to characterize the complex relationship between some contemporary works of art and their modernist forebears. Postmodern works are generally characterized by stylistic "quotation," an invocation and disengagement from history, and the fragmentation of artistic surface.

Prakit   The everyday, prose dialect spoken in **Sanskrit drama,** usually reserved for comic characters, women, and children.

private theaters   In Renaissance England, indoor theaters serving a more privileged audience. Often located on lands within the city limits that were not under city jurisdiction, such as Blackfriars.

prologue   In Greek drama, an introductory scene preceding the entrance of the chorus. In later usage, an introductory scene not directly part of the main action.

proscenium   An arch over the front of the stage. First used in European theaters in the Renaissance; throughout the eighteenth and nineteenth centuries, theater design gradually eliminated the **apron** that extended in front of the proscenium and decorated the proscenium arch itself, emphasizing its frame-like quality.

protagonist   Literally the "first contestant" in the ancient Greek theater, the term referred to the "first" or main actor competing for a prize. In modern usage, refers to the play's main character.

public theaters   In Renaissance England, large outdoor theaters, usually polygonal or round in shape, consisting of three-storey galleries surrounding an open standing pit and a thrust stage.

quarto   A small-size book format, in which eight pages are printed on a single sheet of paper; the paper is folded twice to make eight pages.

raked stage   A stage that is elevated in the back and lower in the front; common in Europe after the seventeenth century. The raked stage gave rise to the terms "upstage" (toward the back, which was higher) and "downstage" (toward the front, which was lower).

rasa An impersonal mood or attitude of contemplation in Hindu philosophy; in **Sanskrit drama,** the play is designed to produce one of eight *rasas* in the audience: erotic, comic, pathetic, furious, heroic, terrible, odious, or marvelous. The basic *rasa* of each play is related to its ***bhava***, or stageable emotion.

Realism A literary and theatrical practice valuing direct imitation or **verisimilitude.** Often associated with **Naturalism,** modern realism is sometimes described as the inheritor of naturalism. In practice, realism is usually more concerned with psychological motives, the "inner reality," and less committed to achieving a superficial verisimilitude alone.

repertory A company that performs several plays in rotation throughout a season is a repertory company; the term also refers to a set of plays.

revenge tragedy A tragic genre popular in English Renaissance, usually involving a complicated intrigue plot in which the hero is force to commit murder in order to avenge himself; madness and supernatural agents (ghosts) are also a common feature. Shakespeare's *Hamlet* is the most well-known example.

role-doubling The practice of using one actor to play more than one part.

romance A modern term used to define idealized narratives and sometimes applied to the idealized comedies written by Shakespeare late in his career, especially *The Winter's Tale* and *The Tempest.*

romantic comedy Comic form centering on the romance between two lovers, or between several sets of lovers. Romantic comedy typically begins with some unreasonable impediment to the lovers' union, and when after a complicated series of events the obstacle is overcome, the play ends in marriage.

ronin *Samurai* warriors who have been disgraced and outcast from society; "men adrift."

ruido A "noise" play or violent comedy in Golden Age theater.

Rupaka The "major drama" of classical **Sanskrit** theater.

samisen Three-stringed instrument that is both plucked and struck as accompaniment to narration in ***jōruri***. In the late sixteenth century, became instrumental in the **doll theater.**

samurai Warrior class of feudal Japan; *samurai* lords both patronized **Noh** playwrights and companies, but provided the code of conduct informing many **Noh, doll theater,** and **Kabuki** plays.

Sanskrit An ancient Indo-European language; once a spoken language, by the modern era it had become mainly a written language reserved for academic and religious purposes. In **Sanskrit drama,** Sanskrit is reserved for elevated scenes and characters, while **Prakit,** the everyday dialect, is spoken by other characters.

Sanskrit drama The drama of ancient India, particularly the plays of the "Golden Age" (second to ninth centuries).

sarugaku-no Form of dance, role-playing, and acrobatics popular in Japan in the eleventh and twelfth centuries; said to be the progenitor of **Noh** theater.

saruwaka Comic roles in **Kabuki** theater, performed by men.

satyr play A brief, rugged comedy performed by actors in satyr costumes (half-man, half-goat) after the performance of a tragic trilogy at the **City Dionysia;** usually on mythological subjects.

scaena Three-storey stage house behind the stage in the Roman theater, facing the audience. Elaborately decorated with columns, panels, and porticos.

scenic unity The practice of harmonizing acting style, costumes, and sets to create the illusion of a single, unified environment on the stage.

sewamono "Domestic plays" of the Japanese **doll theater.**

sharers Actors and playwrights in the English Renaissance theater who, as investors in the company, took a share of the profits; they were responsible for building or leasing a theater and were legally liable for the company's actions.

shite   Principal actor in **Noh** theater.

shitebashira   The upstage right pillar in a **Noh** theater, near the *hashigakari,* where the *shite* delivers his opening speech.

shogun   Hereditary military leader of Japan from the twelfth through the nineteenth centuries; the *shogun* was the most important of the *samurai* (warrior) class, composed of *daimyo* (feudal lords) and lesser *samurai.*

skene   A low building behind the orchestra in the Greek theater facing the audience; possibly used for changing costumes or storage.

social realism   A form of modern realistic drama emphasizing social messages and themes; social realism was the official genre approved by the Communist Party in the Soviet Union after the revolution.

sociétaires   Leading actors and share holders in the Comédie Française; upon serving twenty years, *sociétaires* were entitled to a pension.

soliloquy   A speech delivered by a character alone onstage, speaking to himself or herself, or to the audience.

soubrette   A stock character in drama: a young, pert female character.

spectacle   Aristotle's term for the visual element of theatrical performance in the *Poetics.*

subtext   A term first elaborated by Constantin Stanislavski, "subtext" refers to the unspoken motive for a given line or speech, what the character wants to get or to do by saying the line. It is sometimes now used more generally to suggest a text's underlying sense or meaning.

surrealist theater   A movement originating in Paris in the 1920s attempting to represent subconscious experience directly in art.

symbolist theater   A European movement of the later nineteenth and early twentieth centuries in reaction to **realism** and **naturalism.** Symbolist theater attempted to dramatize more poetic or metaphorical situations, often using unusual stage settings and ethereal dramatic action and language.

Syndicate   A group of investors who developed a massive organization for theatrical production in the United States in the late nineteenth century.

tableau/tableaux (pl.)   A motionless grouping of actors to represent a "picture" of a dramatic scene; sometimes called *tableau vivant,* a "living picture."

tableaux vivants   See **tableau**; *tableaux vivants* is the plural form of *tableau vivant.*

taburetes   The raised and fenced rows of benches near the stage in a Spanish Golden Age theater, or *corral.*

tachiyaku   Leading male role in **Kabuki** theater.

tertulia   An upper gallery occupied by Church officials and intellectuals in a Spanish Golden Age theater, or *corral.*

theater   A structure built for the performance of drama; also refers to the institution of dramatic performance.

theater in the round   The presentation of a play in an arena setting, in which the audience sits on all sides of the stage area, but is separate from the playing space itself.

Theater of Cruelty   Term used by Antonin Artaud to describe his nonrepresentational, mystical, mythological theater.

Theater of the Absurd   A type of late twentieth-century theater and drama, characterized by a relatively abstract setting, and arbitrary and illogical action. It is sometimes said to express the "human condition" in a basic or "existential" way. The term was first coined by Martin Esslin.

theme   A term used to describe a consistent kind of meaning asserted by a work of literature.

tiring house   A structure at the rear of the stage in the Renaissance English **public theater,** where actors would change costumes (attire themselves), and from which they would enter the stage.

tragedy   Originating in the classical Greek theater, tragedy generally refers to serious drama, taking a central character's conflict with himself or herself, with society, or with god as its subject. Aristotle first described tragedy in his *Poetics*, and tragedy has undergone almost continual redefinition.

tragicomedy   In the English Renaissance, a term describing a dramatic form: a play beginning like a tragedy, but ending happily, like a comedy. In modern usage, the term refers most often to a play's tone or attitude: a play that is ironic, both serious and absurd, leaning toward black comedy or tragic farce.

traveling song   Song sung in **Noh** theater by the *waki* during his first entrance; it announces who the *waki* is, and where he is going.

trilogy   Three tragedies produced in sequence as part of the tragic competition in the **City Dionysia** of ancient Greece. Plays were not necessarily on the same subject.

trope   An enlargement on Catholic liturgy, through song or dramatic performance.

tsure   Followers of the *shite* and *waki* in **Noh** theater.

Upa-rupaka   The "minor drama" of classical **Sanskrit** theater.

verisimilitude   Verisimilitude refers to the extent to which the drama or stage setting appears to copy the superficial appearance of life offstage.

wakashugata   Adolescent male roles in **Kabuki** theater.

wakashu kabuki   Literally, "boys' Kabuki," the term refers to **Kabuki** companies composed mainly of adolescent boys, many of whom were prostitutes; banned by the Tokugawa shogunate in 1652.

waki   The secondary actor in **Noh** theater, who responds to the *shite*.

wakibashira   The downstage left pillar in a **Noh** theater, where the *waki* is usually positioned at the opening of the play.

waki-za   A narrow stage area along the stage-left side of a **Noh** theater stage used for seating the chorus.

wayang kulit   Shadow-puppet theater of Java concerning characters and events drawn from the *Ramayana* and *Mahabharata*, the epic poems of classical India. Performances generally begin early in the evening and last until dawn; audiences sit on both sides of a screen, against which puppeteers cast the shadows of elaborate, flat puppets, whose actions are accompanied by dialogue, narration, song, and music.

well-made play   A form of drama popularized in the nineteenth century, especially in France. The plot usually turns on the revelation of a secret and includes a character who explains and moralizes the action of the play to others; the plot is often relentlessly coincidental, often mechanically so.

wings and backdrop   Scenic practice developed in Italy and exported to France and England in the seventeenth century, using staggered painted flats in a receding series, and a painted central backcloth to depict the setting of the play.

yaro kabuki   The "adult male Kabuki" common in Japan today that replaced the boys' and women's **Kabuki** that were popular before such companies were banned in the early seventeenth century.

yugen   The Japanese term for the mysterious beauty, grace, and repose that are the goal of **Noh** performance.

yujo kabuki   Literally, "prostitutes' Kabuki," an early term for **Kabuki** companies, which were composed mainly of women.

Zanni   Wily and clever comic characters, usually clowns or servants, in ***commedia dell' arte***; played masked.

zen   Term in Buddhist thought for a contemplative attitude that is disengaged from worldly desire.

READINGS ON DRAMA AND THEATER

Barish, Jonas. *The Antitheatrical Prejudice.* Berkeley, CA: University of California Press, 1981.

Beckerman, Bernard. *Dynamics of Drama.* New York: Drama Book Specialists, 1979.

Bennett, Susan. *Theatre Audiences: A Theory of Production and Reception.* London: Routledge, 1990.

Bentley, Eric. *The Life of the Drama.* New York: Atheneum, 1964.

Brockett, Oscar G. *History of the Theatre.* Boston: Allyn & Bacon, 1987.

Carlson, Marvin. *Theories of the Theatre: A Historical and Critical Survey, from the Greeks to the Present.* Ithaca, NY: Cornell University Press, 1984.

Case, Sue-Ellen. *Feminism and Theatre.* New York: Methuen, 1988.

———, ed. *Performing Feminisms: Feminist Critical Theory and Theatre.* Baltimore: Johns Hopkins University Press, 1990.

Clark, Barrett H. *European Theories of the Drama.* New York: Crown, 1965.

Dukore, Bernard F. *Dramatic Theory and Criticism: Greeks to Grotowski.* New York: Holt, Rinehart and Winston, 1974.

Elam, Keir. *The Semiotics of Theatre and Drama.* London: Methuen, 1980.

Frye, Northrop. *Anatomy of Criticism.* Princeton, NJ: Princeton University Press, 1957.

Goldman, Michael. *The Actor's Freedom.* New York: Viking, 1975.

Leacroft, Richard, and Helen Leacroft. *Theatre and Playhouse: An Illustrated Survey of Theatre Building from Ancient Greece to the Present Day.* New York: Methuen, 1984.

Nagler, Alois M. *Sources of Theatrical History.* New York: Dover, 1952.

States, Bert O. *Great Reckonings in Little Rooms: On the Phenomenology of Theater.* Berkeley, CA: University of California Press, 1985.

———. *Irony and Drama.* Ithaca, NY: Cornell University Press, 1971.

Turner, Victor. *From Ritual to Theatre: The Human Seriousness of Play.* New York: Performing Arts Journal Publications, 1982.

Worthen, William B. *The Idea of the Actor: Drama and the Ethics of Performance.* Princeton, NJ: Princeton University Press, 1984.

UNIT 1: CLASSICAL ATHENS

Arnott, Peter D. *Greek Scenic Conventions in the Fifth Century, B.C.* Oxford, England: Oxford University Press, 1962.

Beare, William. *The Roman Stage.* London: Methuen, 1969.

Bieber, Margarete. *The History of the Greek and Roman Theatre.* Princeton, NJ: Princeton University Press, 1961.

Else, Gerald F. *The Origin and Early Form of Greek Tragedy.* New York: Norton, 1972.

Hamilton, Edith. *The Greek Way.* New York: Norton, 1983.

Knox, Bernard M. *Word and Action: Essays on the Ancient Theater.* Baltimore: Johns Hopkins University Press, 1979.

Konstan, David. *Roman Comedy.* Ithaca, NY: Cornell University Press, 1983.

Pickard-Cambridge, A. W. *Dithyramb, Tragedy, and Comedy.* Oxford, England: Oxford University Press, 1962.

———. *The Dramatic Festivals of Athens.* Oxford, England: Oxford University Press, 1968.

———. *The Theatre of Dionysus in Athens.* Oxford, England: Oxford University Press, 1945.

Segal, Erich, ed. *Greek Tragedy: Modern Essays in Criticism.* New York: Harper & Row, 1983.

Taplin, Oliver. *Greek Tragedy in Action.* Berkeley, CA: University of California Press, 1978.

Vince, Ronald W. *Ancient and Medieval Theatre: A Historiographical Handbook.* Westport, CT: Greenwood, 1984.

Webster, T. B. L. *Greek Theater Production.* London: Methuen, 1970.

Winkler, John J., and Froma I. Zeitlin, eds. *Nothing to Do with Dionysus? Athenian Drama in Its Social Context.* Princeton, NJ: Princeton University Press, 1990.

Gagarin, Michael. *Aeschylean Drama*. Berkeley, CA: University of California Press, 1976.

Knox, B. M. W., "Aeschylus and the Third Actor." In Bernard M. Knox, ed. *Word and Action: Essays on the Ancient Theater*. Baltimore: Johns Hopkins University Press, 1979.

Lloyd-Jones, Hugh. "The Guilt of Agamemnon." In Erich Segal, ed. *Greek Tragedy: Modern Essays in Criticism*. New York: Harper & Row, 1983.

Rosenmeyer, Thomas G. *The Art of Aeschylus*. Berkeley, CA: University of California Press, 1982.

Taplin, Oliver. *The Stagecraft of Aeschylus*. Oxford, England: Oxford University Press, 1977.

Deardon, C. W. *The Stage of Aristophanes*. London: Athlone, 1976.

Dover, K. J. *Aristophanic Comedy*. Berkeley, CA: University of California Press, 1972.

Harriott, Rosemary. *Aristophanes: Poet and Dramatist*. Baltimore: Johns Hopkins University Press, 1986.

Ussher, Robert Glenn. *Aristophanes*. Oxford, England: Oxford University Press, 1979.

Dodds, E. R. *The Greeks and the Irrational*. Berkeley, CA: University of California Press, 1951.

Foley, Helene P. *Ritual Irony: Poetry and Sacrifice in Euripides*. Ithaca, NY: Cornell University Press, 1985.

Michelini, Ann N. *Euripides and the Tragic Tradition*. Madison, WI: University of Wisconsin Press, 1987.

Dodds, E. R., "On Misunderstanding the *Oedipus Rex*." In Erich Segal, ed. *Greek Tragedy: Modern Essays in Criticism*. New York: Harper & Row, 1983.

Fergusson, Francis. *The Idea of a Theater*. Princeton, NJ: Princeton University Press, 1947.

Knox, B. M. W. *Oedipus at Thebes*. New York: Norton, 1971.

Segal, Charles. *Tragedy and Civilization: An Interpretation of Sophocles*. Cambridge, MA: Harvard University Press, 1981.

Whitman, C. H. *Sophocles: A Study in Heroic Humanism*. Cambridge, England: Cambridge University Press, 1951.

Winnington-Ingram, R. P. *Sophocles: An Interpretation*. New York: Cambridge University Press, 1980.

Arnott, Peter D. *The Theatres of Japan*. New York: St. Martin's Press, 1969.

Bowers, Faubion. *Japanese Theatre*. New York: Hermitage House, 1952.

Brandon, James R. *Theatre in Southeast Asia*. Cambridge, MA: Harvard University Press, 1967.

———, ed. *Traditional Asian Plays*. New York: Hill and Wang, 1972.

Dunn, Charles James, and Bunzo Torigoe, trans. and eds. *The Actors' Analects: Yakusha Rongo*. New York: Columbia University Press, 1969.

Malm, William P. *Japanese Music and Musical Instruments*. Rutland, VT: Tuttle, 1963.

Samson, G. B. *A Short Cultural History of Japan*. London: Cresset Press, 1952.

Brandon, James R., ed. *Chushingura: Studies in Kabuki and the Puppet Theater*. Honolulu: University of Hawaii Press, 1982.

———, trans. *Kabuki: Five Classic Plays*. Cambridge, MA: Harvard University Press, 1975.

Ernst, Earle. *The Kabuki Theatre*. rev. ed. Honolulu: University of Hawaii Press, 1974.

Halford, Aubrey S. and Giovanna M. Halford. *The Kabuki Handbook*. Tokyo: Tuttle, 1952.

Kawatake Toshio. *A History of Japanese Theatre, II: Bunraku and Kabuki*. Tokyo: Kokusai Bunka Shinkokai, 1971

Keene, Donald. *Chushingura: The Treasury of Loyal Retainers*. New York: Columbia University Press, 1971.

———, trans. *Major Plays of Chikamatsu*. New York: Columbia University Press, 1961.

Rimer, J. Thomas, and Yamazaki Masakazu, trans. *On the Art of the No Drama: The Major Treatises of Zeami*. Princeton, NJ: Princeton University Press, 1984.

Scott, Adolphe Clarence. *The Kabuki Theatre of Japan*. London: George Allen and Unwin, 1955.

NOH THEATER

Araki, James T. *The Ballad-Drama of Medieval Japan.* Berkeley, CA: University of California Press, 1964.

Brower, Robert H., and Earl Miner. *Japanese Court Poetry.* Stanford, CA: Stanford University Press, 1961.

Ernst, Earle, *Three Japanese Plays from the Traditional Theatre.* London: Oxford University Press, 1959.

Fenollosa, Ernest, and Ezra Pound. *The Classic Noh Theatre of Japan.* New York: New Directions, 1959.

Keene, Donald. *No, the Classical Theatre of Japan.* Tokyo and Palo Alto, CA: Kodansha International, 1966.

———, ed. *Twenty Plays of the No Theatre.* New York: Columbia University Press, 1970.

Komparo Kunio. *The Noh Theater: Principles and Perspectives.* Jane Corddry and Stephen Comee, trans. Tokyo and New York: Weatherhill, 1983.

Waley, Arthur. *The No Plays of Japan.* London: George Allen and Unwin, 1921.

Yasuda, Kenneth. *Masterworks of the No Theater.* Bloomington, IN: Indiana University Press, 1989.

SANSKRIT THEATER AND DRAMA

Baumer, Rachel V., and James R. Brandon. *Sanskrit Drama in Performance.* Honolulu: University of Hawaii Press, 1981.

Bharata. *Natyasastra.* P. S. R. Appa Rao, trans. Hyderabad, India: Naatyd Maala, 1967.

Keith, A. B. *Sanskrit Drama: Its Origins, Development, Theory and Practice.* Oxford, England: Oxford University Press, 1924.

Tarlekar, G. H. *Studies in the Natyasastra, with Special Reference to the Sanskrit Drama in Performance.* Delhi, 1975.

Wells, Henry W. *Six Sanskrit Plays.* London and Bombay: Asia Publishing House, 1964.

UNIT 3: MEDIEVAL AND RENAISSANCE ENGLAND

Bentley, Gerald Eades. *The Jacobean and Caroline Stage.* 5 vols. Oxford, England: Oxford University Press, 1941–1956.

———. *The Profession of Dramatist in Shakespeare's Time, 1590–1642.* Princeton, NJ: Princeton University Press, 1971.

———. *The Profession of Player in Shakespeare's Time, 1590–1642.* Princeton, NJ: Princeton University Press, 1984.

Bevington, David. *From Mankind to Marlowe: Growth in Structure in the Popular Drama of Tudor England.* Cambridge, MA: Harvard University Press, 1962.

———. *Medieval Drama.* Boston: Houghton, 1975.

Chambers, E. K. *The Elizabethan Stage.* 4 vols. Oxford, England: Oxford University Press, 1923.

———. *The Medieval Stage.* 2 vols. London: Oxford University Press, 1967.

Greenblatt, Stephen, ed. *Representing the English Renaissance.* Berkeley, CA: University of California Press, 1988.

Gurr, Andrew. *The Shakespearean Stage, 1574–1642.* Cambridge, England: Cambridge University Press, 1970.

Hardison, O. B., Jr. *Christian Rite and Christian Drama in the Middle Ages.* Baltimore: Johns Hopkins University Press, 1965.

Kolve, V. A. *The Play Called Corpus Christi.* Stanford, CA: Stanford University Press, 1966.

Orgel, Stephen. *The Illusion of Power: Political Theatre in the English Renaissance.* Berkeley, CA: University of California Press, 1975.

Vince, Ronald W. *Ancient and Medieval Theatre: A Historiographical Handbook.* Westport, CT: Greenwood, 1984.

Wickham, Glynne. *The Medieval Theatre.* New York: Cambridge University Press, 1987.

Woolf, Rosemary. *The English Mystery Plays.* Berkeley, CA: University of California Press, 1972.

EVERYMAN

Bevington, David. *From Mankind to Marlowe: Growth in Structure in the Popular Drama of Tudor England.* Cambridge, MA: Harvard University Press, 1962.

Garner, Stanton B., Jr. "Theatricality in *Mankind* and *Everyman*." *Studies in Philology* 84 (1987): 272–85.

Beadle, Richard, and Pamela M. King, eds. *York Mystery Plays: A Selection in Modern Spelling.* Oxford, England: Clarendon Press, 1984.

Craig, Hardin. *English Religious Drama of the Middle Ages.* Oxford, England: Oxford University Press, 1955.

Davidson, Clifford. "The Realism of the York Realist and the York Passion." *Speculum* 1 (1975): 270–83.

Holding, P. "Stagecraft in the York Cycle." *Theatre Notebook* 34 (1980): 108–25.

Robinson, J. W. "The Art of the York Realist." *Modern Philology* 60 (1962–1963): 241–51.

———. "The Late Medieval Cult of Jesus and the Mystery Plays." *PMLA* 80 (1965): 508–15.

THE YORK CYCLE

Barish, Jonas. *The Antitheatrical Prejudice.* Berkeley, CA: University of California Press, 1981. Chapter 5.

———. *Ben Jonson and the Language of Prose Comedy.* Cambridge, MA: Harvard University Press, 1960.

———, ed. *Volpone: A Casebook.* London: Macmillan, 1972.

Herford, C. H., Percy Simpson and Evelyn Simpson, eds. *The Works of Ben Jonson.* Oxford, England: Clarendon Press, 1925–1952.

Jackson, Gabriele Berhnard. *Vision and Judgment in Ben Jonson's Drama.* New Haven, CT: Yale University Press, 1968.

Kernan, Alvin B. *The Cankered Muse: Satire of the English Renaissance.* New Haven, CT: Yale University Press, 1959.

———. Introduction. *Volpone.* Ed. Alvin B. Kernan. New Haven, CT: Yale University Press, 1962. 1–26.

Leggatt, Alexander. "The Suicide of Volpone." *University of Toronto Quarterly* 39 (1969–1970): 19–32.

BEN JONSON

Bevington, David. *From Mankind to Marlowe: Growth in Structure in the Popular Drama of Tudor England.* Cambridge, MA: Harvard University Press, 1962.

Cole, Douglas. *Suffering and Evil in the Plays of Christopher Marlowe.* Princeton, NJ: Princeton University Press, 1962.

Kernan, Alvin B., ed. *Two Renaissance Mythmakers: Christopher Marlowe and Ben Jonson.* Baltimore: Johns Hopkins University Press, 1977.

Leech, Clifford, ed. *Marlowe: A Collection of Critical Essays.* Englewood Cliffs, NJ: Prentice-Hall, 1964.

Levin, Harry. *The Overreacher: A Study of Christopher Marlowe.* Boston: Beacon Press, 1964.

CHRISTOPHER MARLOWE

Bamber, Linda. *Comic Women, Tragic Men: A Study of Gender and Genre in Shakespeare.* Stanford, CA: Stanford University Press, 1982.

Barber, C. L. *Shakespeare's Festive Comedy.* Princeton, NJ: Princeton University Press, 1968.

Barker, Francis, and Peter Hulme. "Nymphs and Reapers Heavily Vanish: The Discursive Con-texts of *The Tempest.*" In John Drakakis, ed. *Alternative Shakespeares.* New York: Methuen, 1985.

Booth, Stephen. "On the Value of *Hamlet.*" In Norman Rabkin, ed. *Reinterpretations of Elizabethan Drama: Selected Papers from the English Institute.* New York: Columbia University Press, 1969. 137–76.

Brown, Paul. "This thing of darkness I acknowledge mine: *The Tempest* and the Discourse of Colonialism." In Jonathan Dollimore and Alan Sinfield, eds. *Political Shakespeare: New Essays in Cultural Materialism.* Ithaca, NY: Cornell University Press, 1985.

Bullough, Geoffrey, ed. *Narrative and Dramatic Sources of Shakespeare.* 8 vols. New York: Columbia University Press, 1957–1975.

Dollimore, Jonathan, and Alan Sinfield, eds. *Political Shakespeare: New Essays in Cultural Materialism.* Ithaca, NY: Cornell University Press, 1985.

Drakakis, John, ed. *Alternative Shakespeares.* New York: Methuen, 1985.

Forker, Charles R. "Shakespeare's Theatrical Symbolism and its Function in *Hamlet.*" *Shakespeare Quarterly* 14 (1963): 215–29.

WILLIAM SHAKESPEARE

Fergusson, Francis. *The Idea of a Theater.* Princeton, NJ: Princeton University Press, 1947.

Goldman, Michael. *Shakespeare and the Energies of Drama.* Princeton, NJ: Princeton University Press, 1970.

Greenblatt, Stephen. *Shakespearean Negotiations.* Berkeley, CA: University of California Press, 1988.

Hendricks, Margo, and Patricia Parker, eds. *Women, "Race," and Writing in the Early Modern Period.* London: Routledge, 1994.

Howard, Jean E., and Marion F. O'Connor, eds. *Shakespeare Reproduced: The Text in History and Ideology.* London: Methuen, 1987.

Jardine, Lisa. *Still Harping on Daughters: Women and Drama in the Age of Shakespeare.* Totowa, NJ: Barnes & Noble, 1983.

Kernan, Alvin B., ed. *Modern Shakespeare Criticism.* New York: Harcourt, Brace & World, 1970.

———. *The Playwright as Magician.* New Haven, CT: Yale University Press, 1979.

Mack, Maynard. "The World of *Hamlet.*" *Yale Review* 41 (1952): 502–23.

Orgel, Stephen. "Prospero's Wife." In Stephen Greenblatt, ed. *Representing the English Renaissance.* Berkeley, CA: University of California Press, 1988.

Parker, Patricia, and Geoffrey Hartmenn, eds. *Shakespeare and the Question of Theory.* London: Methuen, 1985.

Schoenbaum, S. *Shakespeare: A Documentary Life.* New York: Oxford University Press, 1975.

Schwartz, Murray M., and Coppélia Kahn, eds. *Representing Shakespeare: New Psychoanalytic Essays.* Baltimore: Johns Hopkins University Press, 1981.

Thompson, Marvin, and Ruth Thompson, eds. *Shakespeare and the Sense of Performance.* Newark, DE: University of Delaware Press, 1989.

UNIT 4: EARLY MODERN EUROPE

Allen, John. *The Reconstruction of a Spanish Golden Age Playhouse: El Corral del Principe, 1583–1744.* Gainesville, FL: University of Florida Press, 1983.

Holland, Norman N. *The First Modern Comedies: The Significance of Etheredge, Wycherley, and Congreve.* Cambridge, MA: Harvard University Press, 1959.

Kirsch, Arthur C. *Dryden's Heroic Drama.* Princeton, NJ: Princeton University Press, 1965.

Lancaster, H. C. *A History of French Dramatic Literature in the Seventeenth Century.* 5 vols. Baltimore: Johns Hopkins University Press, 1929–1942.

Loftis, John. *The Politics of Drama in Augustan England.* Oxford, England: Oxford University Press, 1963.

Loftis, John, Richard Southern, Marion Jones, and A. H. Scouten, eds. *The Revels History of Drama in English.* Volume 5: 1660–1750. London: Methuen, 1976.

McKendrick, Melveena. *Theatre in Spain, 1490–1700.* Cambridge, England: Cambridge University Press, 1989.

Staves, Susan. *Players' Scepters: Fictions of Authority in the Restoration.* Lincoln, NE: University of Nebraska Press, 1979.

Styan, J. L. *Restoration Comedy in Performance.* Cambridge, England: Cambridge University Press, 1986.

Waith, Eugene, *The Herculean Hero.* New York: Columbia University Press, 1962.

———. *Ideas of Greatness.* London: Routledge & Kegan Paul, 1971.

Wiley, W. L. *The Early Public Theatre in France.* Cambridge, MA: Harvard University Press, 1920.

Wilson, Margaret. *Spanish Drama of the Golden Age.* New York, 1989.

APHRA BEHN

Diamond, Elin. "Gestus and Signature in Aphra Behn's *The Rover.*" *ELH* 56 (1989): 519–39.

Duffy, Maureen. *The Passionate Shepherdess: Aphra Behn, 1640–89.* London: Methuen, 1977.

Goreau, Angeline. *Reconstructing Aphra: A Social Biography of Aphra Behn.* New York: Dial, 1980.

PEDRO CALDERÓN DE LA BARCA

Armas, F. A., D. M. Gitlitz, J. A. Madrigal, eds. *Critical Perspectives on Calderón de la Barca.* Lincoln, NE: University of Nebraska Press, 1981.

Honig, Edwin. *Calderón and the Seizures of Honor.* Cambridge, MA: Harvard University Press, 1972.

Maraniss, James A. *On Calderón.* Columbia, MO: University of Missouri Press, 1977.

McGaha, Michael D. *Approaches to the Theater of Calderón*. Lanham, MD: Associated University Presses, 1982.

Lillo, George. *The Works of Mr. George Lillo, with Some Account of His Life*. London: T. Davies, 1775.
Steffensen, James L., and Richard Noble, eds. *The Dramatic Works of George Lillo*. Oxford, England: Clarendon Press, 1993.

Gaines, James F. *Molière's Theater*. Columbus, OH: Ohio State University Press, 1984.
Gossman, L. *Men and Masks: A Study of Molière*. Baltimore: Johns Hopkins University Press, 1963.
Gross, Nathan. *From Gesture to Idea: Esthetics and Ethics in Molière's Comedy*. New York: Columbia University Press, 1982.
Guicharnaud, Jacques. *Molière: A Collection of Critical Essays*. Englewood Cliffs, NJ: Prentice-Hall, 1964.

Barthes, Roland. *On Racine*. Richard Howard, trans. New York: Hill and Wang, 1964.
Cook, A. S. *French Tragedy: The Power of Enactment*. Chicago: University of Chicago Press, 1980.
Goldmann, Lucien. *Racine*. Alastair Hamilton, trans. London: Writers and Readers, 1981.

Antoine, André. *Memories of the Théâtre Libre*. Marvin Carlson, trans. Coral Gables, FL: University of Miami Press, 1964.
Bennett, Benjamin. *Modern Drama and German Classicism: Renaissance from Lessing to Brecht*. Ithaca, NY: Cornell University Press, 1979.
————. *Theater as Problem: Modern Drama and Its Place in Literature*. Ithaca, NY: Cornell University Press, 1990.
Bentley, Eric. *The Playwright as Thinker: A Study of Drama in Modern Times*. New York: Harcourt Brace, 1946.
Braun, Edward. *Meyerhold on Theater*. New York: Hill and Wang, 1969.
Brockett, Oscar G., and Robert R. Findlay. *Century of Innovation: A History of European and American Theatre and Drama Since 1870*. Englewood Cliffs, NJ: Prentice-Hall, 1973.
Brustein, Robert. *The Theatre of Revolt*. Boston: Little, Brown, 1964.
Cole, Toby, ed. *Directors on Directing*. Indianapolis: Bobbs-Merrill, 1963.
————, ed. *Playwrights on Playwriting*. New York: Hill and Wang, 1960.
Davis, Tracy C. *Actresses as Working Women: Their Social Identity in Victorian Culture*. London: Routledge, 1991.
Driver, Tom. *Romantic Quest and Modern Query: A History of Modern Theatre*. New York: Delacorte, 1970.
Finney, Gail. *Women in Modern Drama: Freud, Feminism, and European Theater at the Turn of the Century*. Ithaca, NY: Cornell University Press, 1989.
Gilman, Richard. *The Making of Modern Drama*. New York: Farrar, Straus and Giroux, 1974.
Hunt, Hugh, et al., eds. *The Revels History of Drama in English*. Vol. 7: 1880 to the Present Day. London: Methuen, 1979.
Jones, David Richard. *Great Directors at Work*. Berkeley, CA: University of California Press, 1986.
Peter, John. *Vladimir's Carrot: Modern Drama and the Modern Imagination*. Chicago: University of Chicago Press, 1987.
Quigley, Austin. *The Modern Stage and Other Worlds*. London: Methuen, 1985.
Seltzer, Daniel, ed. *The Modern Theatre: Readings and Documents*. Boston: Little, Brown, 1967.
Stanislavski, Constantin. *An Actor Prepares*. Elizabeth Reynolds Hapgood, trans. New York: Theatre Arts, 1936.
————. *Building a Character*. Elizabeth Reynolds Hapgood, trans. New York: Theatre Arts, 1949.
————. *Creating a Role*. Elizabeth Reynolds Hapgood, trans. New York: Theatre Arts, 1961.
————. *My Life in Art*. J. J. Robbins, trans. Boston: Little, Brown, 1924.
Styan, J. L. *The Dark Comedy*. Cambridge, England: Cambridge University Press, 1968.
————. *Modern Drama in Theory and Practice*. 3 vols. Cambridge, England: Cambridge University Press, 1980.

GEORGE LILLO

MOLIÈRE

JEAN RACINE

UNIT 5: MODERN EUROPE

Whitaker, Thomas R. *Fields of Play in Modern Drama.* Princeton, NJ: Princeton University Press, 1977.

Wiles, Timothy J. *The Theater Event: Modern Theories of Performance.* Chicago: University of Chicago Press, 1980.

Williams, Raymond. *Drama from Ibsen to Brecht.* London: Hogarth, 1987.

———. *Modern Tragedy.* Stanford, CA: Stanford University Press, 1966.

Worthen, W. B. *Modern Drama and the Rhetoric of Theater.* Berkeley, CA: University of California Press, 1992.

BERTOLT BRECHT

Benjamin, Walter. *Understanding Brecht.* Anna Bostock, trans. London: NLB, 1973.

Bentley, Eric. *The Brecht Commentaries 1943–1980.* New York: Grove, 1981.

Brecht, Bertolt. *Brecht on Theatre: The Development of an Aesthetic.* John Willett, ed. and trans. New York: Hill and Wang, 1964.

———. *The Messingkauf Dialogues.* John Willett, trans. London: Methuen, 1965.

Dickson, Keith A. *Towards Utopia: A Study of Brecht.* Oxford, England: Oxford University Press, 1978.

Esslin, Martin. *Brecht: The Man and His Work.* Garden City, NJ: Doubleday, 1971.

Ewen, Frederick. *Bertolt Brecht: His Life, His Art and His Times.* New York: Citadel, 1967.

Fuegi, John. *Bertolt Brecht: Chaos According to Plan.* Cambridge, England: Cambridge University Press, 1987.

———. *Brecht and Company.* New York: Grove, 1994.

Lyon, James K. *Bertolt Brecht in America.* Princeton, NJ: Princeton University Press, 1980.

Wright, Elizabeth. *Postmodern Brecht: A Re-Presentation.* London: Routledge, 1989.

GEORG BÜCHNER

Benn, Maurice. *The Drama of Revolt: A Critical Study of Georg Büchner.* Cambridge, England: Cambridge University Press, 1976.

Hilton, Julian. *Georg Büchner.* New York: Grove, 1982.

Reeve, William. *Georg Büchner.* New York: Frederick Ungar, 1979.

Richards, David. *Georg Büchner and the Birth of Modern Drama.* Albany, NY: State University of New York Press, 1977.

ANTON CHEKHOV

Chekhov, Anton. *Letters of Anton Chekhov.* Michael Henry Heim and Simon Karlinsky, trans. New York: Harper & Row, 1973.

Gottlieb, Vera. *Chekhov and the Vaudeville.* Cambridge, England: Cambridge University Press, 1982.

Hingley, Ronald. *Chekhov: A Biographical and Critical Study.* New York: Barnes & Noble, 1966.

Magarshack, David. *Chekhov the Dramatist.* New York: Hill and Wang, 1960.

Peace, Richard. *Chekhov: A Study of the Four Major Plays.* New Haven, CT: Yale University Press, 1983.

Pitcher, Henry. *The Chekhov Play.* London: Chatto and Windus, 1973.

Rayfield, Donald. *Chekhov: The Evolution of His Art.* London: Paul Elek, 1975.

Styan, J. L. *Chekhov in Performance.* Cambridge, England: Cambridge University Press, 1971.

HENRIK IBSEN

Cima, Gay Gibson. "Discovering Signs: The Emergence of the Critical Actor in Ibsen." *Theatre Journal* 35 (1983): 5–22.

Egan, Michael, ed. *Ibsen: The Critical Heritage.* London: Routledge & Kegan Paul, 1972.

Hardwick, Elizabeth. "A Doll's House." In *Seduction and Betrayal.* New York: Random House, 1970.

Lyons, Charles R. *Henrik Ibsen: The Divided Consciousness.* Carbondale, IL: Southern Illinois University Press, 1972.

Marker, Frederick J., and Lise-Lone Marker. *Ibsen's Lively Art: A Performance Study of the Major Plays.* Cambridge, England: Cambridge University Press, 1989.

Meyer, Michael. *Henrik Ibsen: A Biography.* Garden City, NJ: Doubleday, 1971.

Northam, John. *Ibsen: A Critical Study.* Cambridge, England: Cambridge University Press, 1973.

———. *Ibsen's Dramatic Method: A Study of the Prose Dramas.* London: Faber & Faber, 1953.

Shaw, Bernard. *The Quintessence of Ibsenism.* New York: Hill and Wang, 1957.
Sprinchorn, Evert, ed. *Ibsen: Letters and Speeches.* New York: Hill and Wang, 1964.

Bassnet-McGuire, Susan. *Luigi Pirandello.* New York: Grove, 1983.
Bentley, Eric. *The Pirandello Commentaries.* Evanston, IL: Northwestern University Press, 1986.
Guidice, Gaspare. *Pirandello: A Biography.* Alastair Hamilton, trans. Oxford, England: Oxford University Press, 1975.
Kennedy, Andrew K. "*Six Characters:* Pirandello's Last Tape." *Modern Drama* 12 (1969): 1–9.
Oliver, Roger W. *Dreams of Passion: The Theater of Luigi Pirandello.* New York: New York University Press, 1979.
Paolucci, Anne. *Pirandello's Theater.* Carbondale, IL: Southern Illinois University Press, 1974.
Pirandello, Luigi. *On Humor.* Antonio Illiano and Daniel P. Testa, trans. Chapel Hill, NC: University of North Carolina Press, 1974.
Sogluizzo, A. Richard. *Luigi Pirandello, Director: The Playwright in the Theatre.* Metuchen, NJ: Scarecrow, 1982.

Bentley, Eric. *Bernard Shaw.* New York: Norton, 1976.
Berst, Charles A. *Bernard Shaw and the Art of Drama.* Urbana, IL: University of Illinois Press, 1973.
Compton, Louis. *Shaw the Dramatist.* Lincoln, NE: University of Nebraska Press, 1969.
Evans, T. F., ed. *Shaw: The Critical Heritage.* London: Routledge & Kegan Paul, 1976.
Goldman, Michael. "Shaw and the Marriage in Dionysus." In Michael Bertin, ed. *The Play and Its Critic: Essays for Eric Bentley.* New York: University Press of America, 1986.
Holroyd, Michael. *Bernard Shaw.* 3 vols. New York: Random House, 1988–1991.
Meisel, Martin. *Shaw and the Nineteenth-Century Theater.* Princeton, NJ: Princeton University Press, 1963.
Peters, Margot. *Bernard Shaw and the Actresses.* Garden City, NJ: Doubleday, 1980.
Turco, Alfred, Jr. *Shaw's Moral Vision: The Self and Salvation.* Ithaca, NY: Cornell University Press, 1976.
Wisenthal, J. L. *The Marriage of Contraries: Bernard Shaw's Middle Plays.* Cambridge, MA: Harvard University Press, 1974.

Carlson, Harry G. *Strindberg and the Poetry of Myth.* Berkeley, CA: University of California Press, 1982.
Lucas, F. L. *The Drama of Ibsen and Strindberg.* London: Cassell, 1962.
Reinert, Otto, ed. *Strindberg: A Collection of Critical Essays.* Englewood Cliffs, NJ: Prentice-Hall, 1971.
Sprinchorn, Evert. *Strindberg as Dramatist.* New Haven, CT: Yale University Press, 1982.
Strindberg, August. *From an Occult Diary.* Mary Sandbach, trans. New York: Hill and Wang, 1965.
———. *Open Letters to the Intimate Theater.* Walter Johnson, trans. Seattle: University of Washington Press, n.d.
Törnqvist, Egil. *Strindbergian Drama.* Atlantic Highlands, NJ: Humanities Press, 1982.

Berggren, Ruth, ed. *The Definitive Four-Act Version of The Importance of Being Earnest, A Trivial Comedy for Serious People.* New York: Vanguard, 1987.
Cohen, Ed. "Writing Gone Wilde: Homoerotic Desire in the Closet of Representation." *PMLA* 102 (1987): 801–13.
Craft, Christopher. "Alias Bunbury: Desire and Termination in *The Importance of Being Earnest.*" *Representations* 31 (Summer 1990): 19–46.
Ellman, Richard. *Oscar Wilde.* New York: Knopf, 1988.
Gagnier, Regenia. *Idylls of the Marketplace: Oscar Wilde and the Victorian Public.* Stanford, CA: Stanford University Press, 1986.

Bigsby, C. W. E. *A Critical Introduction to Twentieth-Century American Drama.* 3 vols. Cambridge, England: Cambridge University Press, 1982–1985.
Bronner, Edwin, ed. *The Encyclopedia of the American Theatre 1900–1975.* New York: A. S. Barnes, 1980.

LUIGI PIRANDELLO

BERNARD SHAW

AUGUST STRINDBERG

OSCAR WILDE

UNIT 6: THE UNITED STATES

Chinoy, Helen Krich, and Linda Walsh Jenkins, eds. *Women in American Theatre*. New York: Crown, 1981.

Clurman, Harold. *The Fervent Years: The Story of the Group Theatre and the Thirties*. New York: Knopf, 1945.

Cohn, Ruby. *New American Dramatists, 1960–1980*. New York: Grove, 1982.

Coven, Brenda, ed. *American Women Dramatists of the Twentieth Century: A Bibliography*. Metuchen, NJ: Scarecrow, 1982.

Downer, Alan S., ed. *American Drama and Its Critics*. Chicago: University of Chicago Press, 1965.

Flanagan, Hallie. *Arena*. New York: Duell, Sloan and Pearce, 1949.

Garza, Roberto, ed. *Contemporary Chicano Theatre*. Notre Dame, IN: University of Notre Dame Press, 1976.

Harrison, Paul Carter. *The Drama of Nommo*. New York: Grove, 1972.

Hatch, James V., ed. *Black Theatre USA: Forty-Five Plays by Black Americans 1847–1974*. New York: Macmillan, 1974.

Hill, Errol, ed. *The Theatre of Black Americans*. 2 vols. Englewood Cliffs, NJ: Prentice-Hall, 1980.

Huerta, Jorge A. *Chicano Theater: Themes and Forms*. Ypsilanti, MI: Bilingual Press, 1982.

Kanellos, Nicolás. *Hispanic Theatre in the United States*. Houston: Arte Público Press, 1984.

Kernan, Alvin B. *The Modern American Theater: A Collection of Critical Essays*. Englewood Cliffs, NJ: Prentice-Hall, 1967.

Marker, Lise-Lone. *David Belasco: Naturalism in the American Theatre*. Princeton, NJ: Princeton University Press, 1975.

Perkins, Kathy A. *Black Female Playwrights: An Anthology of Plays Before 1950*. Bloomington, IN: Indiana University Press, 1989.

Rabkin, Gerald. *Drama and Commitment: Politics in the American Theatre of the Thirties*. Bloomington, IN: Indiana University Press, 1964.

Shank, Ted. *American Alternative Theatres*. New York: Grove, 1982.

Shewey, Don, ed. *Out Front: Contemporary Gay and Lesbian Plays*. New York: Grove, 1988.

AMIRI BARAKA/ LEROI JONES

Baraka, Imamu Amiri. *The Autobiography of LeRoi Jones/Amiri Baraka*. New York: Freundlich, 1984.

———. "Exaugural Address." *Kulchur* 3.3 (Winter 1964).

———. *Selected Plays and Prose of Amiri Baraka/LeRoi Jones*. New York: William Morrow, 1979.

Bentson, Kimberly W., ed. *Imamu Amiri Baraka (LeRoi Jones): A Collection of Critical Essays*. Englewood Cliffs, NJ: Prentice-Hall, 1978.

Richards, Sandra. "Negative Forces and Positive Non-Entities: Images of Women in the Drama of Amiri Baraka." *Theatre Journal* 32 (1985): 233–40.

Smith, David. "Amiri Baraka and the Politics of Popular Culture." In Adam Sorkin, ed. *Politics and the Muse: Studies in the Politics of Recent American Literature*. Bowling Green, OH: Popular, 1989.

Sollors, Werner. *Amiri Baraka/LeRoi Jones: The Quest for a "Populist Modernism."* New York: Columbia University Press, 1978.

MARIA IRENE FORNES

Cummings, Scott. "Seeing with Clarity: The Visions of Maria Irene Fornes." *Theater* (Yale) 17:1 (Winter 1985): 51–56.

Fornes, Maria Irene. "Interview." *Performing Arts Journal* 2:3 (Winter 1978): 106–11.

Marranca, Bonnie. "The Real Life of Maria Irene Fornes." In *Theatrewritings*. New York: PAJ Publications, 1984.

Worthen, W. B. "*Still playing games*: Ideology and Performance in the Theater of Maria Fornes." In Enoch Brater, ed. *Feminine Focus: The New Women Playwrights*. Oxford, England: Oxford University Press, 1989.

SUSAN GLASPELL

Ben-Zvi, Linda. "Susan Glaspell's Contributions to Contemporary Women Playwrights." In Enoch Brater, ed. *Feminine Focus: The New Women Playwrights*. New York: Oxford University Press, 1989.

Dymkowski, Christine. "On the Edge: The Plays of Susan Glaspell." *Modern Drama* 31 (1988): 91–105.

Kolodny, Annette. "A Map for Rereading: Gender and the Interpretation of Literary Texts." In Elaine Showalter, ed. *The New Feminist Criticism: Essays on Women, Literature, and Theory.* New York: Pantheon, 1985.

Stein, Karen F. "The Women's World of Glaspell's *Trifles.*" In Helen Krich Chinoy and Linda Walsh Jenkins, eds. *Women in American Theatre.* New York: Crown, 1981.

DAVID HENRY HWANG

Garber, Majorie. *Vested Interests: Cross-Dressing and Cultural Anxiety.* London: Routledge, 1992.

Hwang, David Henry. "Afterword." In *M. Butterfly.* New York: New American Library, 1988.

———. *F. O. B.* in *New Plays USA 1.* New York: Theatre Communications Group, 1982.

Moy, James S. "David Henry Hwang's *M. Butterfly* and Philip Kan Gotanda's *Yankee Dawg You Die*: Repositioning Chinese American Marginality on the American Stage." *Theatre Journal* 42 (1990): 48–56.

TONY KUSHNER

Cheever, Susan. Interview with Tony Kushner. *The New York Times* 13 September 1992: II, 7.

Savran, David. "Ambivalence, Utopia, and a Queer Sort of Materialism: How *Angels In America* Reconstructs the Nation." *Theatre Journal* 47(1995): 207–228.

ARTHUR MILLER

Carson, Neil. *Arthur Miller.* New York: Grove, 1982.

Corrigan, Robert W., ed. *Arthur Miller: A Collection of Critical Essays.* Englewood Cliffs, NJ: Prentice-Hall, 1969.

Martin, Robert A., ed. *Arthur Miller: New Perspectives.* Englewood Cliffs, NJ: Prentice-Hall, 1982.

Miller, Arthur. *The Theater Essays of Arthur Miller.* Robert Martin, ed. New York: Viking, 1978.

———. *Timebends: A Life.* New York: Grove, 1987.

EUGENE O'NEILL

Bogard, Travis. *Contour in Time: The Plays of Eugene O'Neill.* Oxford, England: Oxford University Press, 1988.

Cargill, Oscar, N. Bryllion Fagin, and William J. Fisher, eds. *O'Neill and His Plays: Four Decades of Criticism.* New York: New York University Press, 1961.

Chothia, Jean. *Forging a Language: A Study of the Plays of Eugene O'Neil.* Cambridge, England: Cambridge University Press, 1979.

Floyd, Virginia, ed. *Eugene O'Neill at Work: Newly Released Ideas for Plays.* New York: Ungar, 1981.

Gelb, Arthur, and Barbara Gelb. *O'Neill.* New York: Harper & Row, 1973.

Sheaffer, Louis. *O'Neill: Son and Playwright.* Boston: Little, Brown, 1968.

Wainscott, Ronald H. *Staging O'Neill: The Experimental Years, 1920–1934.* New Haven, CT: Yale University Press, 1988.

NTOZAKE SHANGE

Cronacher, Karen. "Unmasking the Minstrel Mask's Black Magic: Ntozake Shange's *spell #7.*" *Theatre Journal* 44 (1992): 177–93.

Shange, Ntozake. *See No Evil: Prefaces, Essays, and Accounts 1976–1983.* San Francisco: Momo's Press, 1984.

Shange, Ntozake. *Three Pieces: spell #7, A Photograph: Lovers in Motion, Boogie Woogie Landscapes.* New York: Penguin, 1982.

SAM SHEPARD

King, Kimball. *Sam Shepard: A Casebook.* New York: Garland, 1988.

Marranca, Bonnie, ed. *American Dreams: The Imagination of Sam Shepard.* New York: Performing Arts Journal Publications, 1981.

Mottram, Ron. *Inner Landscapes: The Theater of Sam Shepard.* Columbia, MO: University of Missouri Press, 1984.

Oumano, Ellen. *Sam Shepard: The Life and Work of an American Dreamer.* New York: St. Martin's, 1986.

LUIS VALDEZ

Broyles-González, Yolanda. *El Teatro Campesino: Theater in the Chicano Movement.* Austin, Texas: University of Texas Press, 1994.

———. "Toward a Re-Vision of Chicano Theatre History: The Women of El Teatro Campesino." In Lynda Hart, ed. *Making a Spectacle: Feminist Essays on Contemporary Women's Theatre.* Ann Arbor, MI: University of Michigan Press, 1989.

Huerta, Jorge A. *Chicano Theater: Themes and Forms.* Ypsilanti, MI: Bilingual Press, 1982.

Kanellos, Nicolás. *Hispanic Theatre in the United States.* Houston: Arte Público, 1984.

Morton, Carlos. "The Teatro Campesino." *Tulane Drama Review* 18:4 (December 1974): 71–6.

Valdez, Luis. *Pensamiento Serpentino.* El Centro Campesino Cultural, CA: Cucaracha, 1973.

Valdez, Luis, and El Teatro Campesino. *Actos.* San Juan Bautista, CA: Menyah Productions, 1971.

von Bardeleben, Renate, ed. *Missions in Conflict: Essays on U.S.–Mexican Relations and Chicano Culture.* Tübingen, Germany: G. Narr, 1986.

TENNESSEE WILLIAMS

Boxill, Roger. *Tennessee Williams.* New York: St. Martin's Press, 1987.

Devlin, Albert J., ed. *Conversations with Tennessee Williams.* Jackson, MS: University of Mississippi Press, 1986.

Leavitt, Richard Freeman, ed. *The World of Tennessee Williams.* New York: Putnam, 1978.

Spoto, Donald. *The Kindness of Strangers: The Life of Tennessee Williams.* Boston: Little, Brown, 1985.

Stanton, Stephen, ed. *Tennessee Williams: A Collection of Critical Essays.* Englewood Cliffs, NJ: Prentice-Hall, 1977.

Williams, Tennessee. *Memoirs.* Garden City, NJ: Doubleday, 1975.

AUGUST WILSON

Ching, Mei-Ling. "Wrestling against History." *Theater/Yale* 19:3 (1988): 70–71.

Henderson, Heather. "Building Fences: An Interview with Mary Alice and James Earl Jones." *Theater/Yale* 16:3 (1985): 67–70.

Shannon, Sandra G. "The Long Wait: August Wilson's *Ma Rainey's Black Bottom.*" *Black American Literature Forum* 25:1 (1991): 135–45.

Wilde, Lisa. "Reclaiming the Past: Narrative and Memory in August Wilson's *Two Trains Running.*" *Theatre/Yale* 22:1 (1991): 73–74.

UNIT 7: THE WORLD STAGE

Artaud, Antonin. *The Theater and Its Double.* Mary Caroline Richards, trans. New York: Grove, 1958.

Bentley, Eric. *Theatre of War.* New York: Viking, 1972.

Betsko, Kathleen, and Rachel Koenig, eds. *Interviews with Contemporary Women Playwrights.* New York: Beech Tree, 1987.

Bigsby, C. W. E. "The Language of Crisis in British Theatre: The Drama of Cultural Pathology." In C. W. E. Bigsby, ed. *Contemporary English Drama.* New York: Holmes and Meier, 1981.

Blau, Herbert. *Eve of the Prey: Subversions of the Postmodern.* Bloomington, IN: Indiana University Press, 1987.

Bradby, David. *Modern French Drama, 1940–1980.* New York: Grove, 1984.

Brater, Enoch, ed. *Feminine Focus: The New Women Playwrights.* New York: Oxford University Press, 1989.

Brook, Peter. *The Empty Space.* New York: Avon, 1968.

Calandra, Denis. *New German Dramatists.* New York: Grove, 1983.

Case, Sue-Ellen. "Toward a Butch-Femme Aesthetic." In Lynda Hart, ed. *Making a Spectacle: Feminist Essays on Contemporary Women's Theatre.* Ann Arbor, MI: University of Michigan Press, 1989.

Chinweizu, Onwuchekwa Jemie, and Ihechukwu Madubuike. *Toward the Decolonization of African Literature.* Vol. 1. Washington, DC: Howard University Press, 1983.

Cohn, Ruby. *From Desire to Godot: Pocket Theater of Postwar Paris.* Berkeley, CA: University of California Press, 1987.

de Lauretis, Teresa. "Sexual Indifferentiation and Lesbian Representation." *Theatre Journal* 40 (1988): 155–77.

Dolan, Jill. *The Feminist Spectator as Critic.* Ann Arbor, MI: UMI Research Press, 1988.

Elsom, John. *Post-War British Theatre.* London: Routledge & Kegan Paul, 1976.

Esslin, Martin. *The Theatre of the Absurd.* New York: Doubleday, 1969.

Grotowski, Jerzy. *Towards a Poor Theatre.* New York: Simon & Schuster, 1968.

Hart, Lynda, ed. *Making a Spectacle: Feminist Essays on Contemporary Women's Theatre.* Ann Arbor, MI: University of Michigan Press, 1989.

Marranca, Bonnie, ed. *The Theatre of Images.* New York: Drama Book Specialists, 1977.

Ndlovu, Duma. *Woza Afrika! An Anthology of South African Plays*. New York: Braziller, 1986.

Ngugi wa Thiong'o. *Decolonising the Mind: The Politics of Language in African Literature*. London: James Currey, 1986.

Rosen, Carol. *Plays of Impasse: Contemporary Drama Set in Confining Institutions*. Princeton, NJ: Princeton University Press, 1983.

Schechner, Richard. *Environmental Theater*. New York: Hawthorn, 1973.

Taylor, John Russell. *Anger and After*. London: Methuen, 1969.

——. *The Second Wave: British Drama of the Sixties*. London: Eyre Methuen, 1978.

Worth, Katharine. *Revolutions in Modern English Drama*. London: G. Bell and Sons, 1972.

SAMUEL BECKETT

Acheson, James, and Kateryna Arthur, eds. *Beckett's Later Fiction and Drama: Texts for Company*. New York: St. Martin's Press, 1987.

Bair, Deirdre. *Samuel Beckett: A Biography*. New York: Harcourt Brace Jovanovich, 1978.

Beckett, Samuel. *Happy Days: The Production Notebook of Samuel Beckett*. James Knowlson, ed. New York: Grove, 1985.

Brater, Enoch, ed. *Beckett at 80/Beckett in Context*. Oxford, England: Oxford University Press, 1986.

——. *Beyond Minimalism: Beckett's Late Style in the Theater*. Oxford, England: Oxford University Press, 1987.

Cohn, Ruby. *Just Play: Beckett's Theater*. Princeton, NJ: Princeton University Press, 1980.

——. *Samuel Beckett: The Comic Gamut*. New Brunswick, NJ: Rutgers University Press, 1962.

Gontarski, S. E. *Beckett's Happy Days: A Manuscript Study*. Columbus, OH: Ohio University Libraries, 1977.

——. *On Beckett: Essays and Criticism*. New York: Grove, 1986.

Graver, Lawrence, and Raymond Federman, eds. *Samuel Beckett: The Critical Heritage*. London: Routledge & Kegan Paul, 1979.

Kalb, Jonathan. *Beckett in Performance*. Cambridge, England: Cambridge University Press, 1989.

Kenner, Hugh. *Samuel Beckett*. Berkeley, CA: University of California Press, 1968.

Worth, Katharine. *The Irish Drama of Europe from Yeats to Beckett*. London: Athlone, 1978.

CARYL CHURCHILL

Churchill, Caryl. "The Common Imagination and the Individual Voice." *New Theatre Quarterly* 4 (February 1988): 3–16.

Diamond, Elin. "Brechtian Theory/Feminist Criticism: Toward a Gestic Feminist Criticism." *Drama Review* 32:1 (Spring 1988): 82–94.

——. "(In)Visible Bodies in Churchill's Theatre." *Theatre Journal* 40 (1988): 188–204.

——. "Refusing the Romanticism of Identity: Narrative Interventions in Churchill, Benmussa, Duras." *Theatre Journal* 37 (1985): 273–86.

Quigley, Austin E. "Stereotype and Prototype: Character in the Plays of Caryl Churchill." In Enoch Brater, ed. *Feminine Focus: The New Women Playwrights*. New York: Oxford University Press, 1989.

Randall, Phyllis R., ed. *Caryl Churchill: A Casebook*. New York: Garland, 1989.

MARGUERITE DURAS

Diamond, Elin. "Refusing the Romanticism of Identity: Narrative Interventions in Churchill, Benmussa, Duras." *Theatre Journal* 37 (1985): 273–86.

Loufti, Martine. "Duras's India." *Literature/Film Quarterly* 14:3 (1986): 151–53.

Papin, Lilian. "Staging Writing or the Ceremony of the Text in Marguerite Duras." *Modern Drama* 34 (1981): 128–37.

Selous, Trista. *The Other Woman: Feminism and Femininity in the Work of Marguerite Duras*. New Haven, CT: Yale University Press, 1988.

Struebig, Patricia. "*India Song / The Vice Consul* of Marguerite Duras: Comparative Techniques in Film and Novel." In JoAnn James and William Cloonan, eds. *Apocalyptic Visions Past and Present*. Tallahassee, FL: Florida State University Press, 1988.

BRIAN FRIEL

Dantanus, Ulf. *Brian Friel: A Study*. London: Faber & Faber, 1988.

Deane, Seamus. *Celtic Revivals: Essays in Modern Irish Literature, 1880–1980*. Winston-Salem, NC: Wake Forest University Press, 1987.

Maxwell, D. E. S. *Brian Friel*. Lewisburg, PA: Bucknell University Press, 1973.
O'Brien, Lance. *Brian Friel*. Boston: Twayne, 1990.
Pine, Richard. *The Diviner: The Art of Brian Friel*. Mullingar, Ireland: Lilliput Press, 1988.

TOMSON HIGHWAY

Baker, Marie Annharte. "An Old Indian Trick Is To Laugh." *Canadian Theatre Review* 68 (Fall 1991): 48–49.
———. "Angry Enough to Spit But with *Dry Lips* It Hurts More Than You Know." *Canadian Theatre Review* 68 (Fall 1991): 88–89.
Dahlquist, Gordon. "I Did It—Highway." *Native Playwrights' Newsletter* (Winter 1994): 22–23.
Filewod, Alan. "Receiving Aboriginality: Tomson Highway and the Crisis of Cultural Authenticity." *Theatre Journal* 46 (1994): 363–73.
Loucks, Bryan. "Another Glimpse: Excerpts from a Conversation with Tomson Highway." *Canadian Theatre Review* 68 (Fall 1991): 9–11.
Rabillard, Sheila. "Absorption, Elimination, and the Hybrid: Some Impure Questions of Gender and Culture in the Trickster Drama of Tomson Highway." *Essays in Theatre/Études Théâtrales* 12:1 (1993): 3–27.
Wilson, Ann. "Tomson Highway." In Linda Hutcheon and Marion Richmond, eds. *Other Solitudes: Canadian Multicultural Fictions*. Toronto: Oxford University Press, 1990.

HAROLD PINTER

Diamond, Elin. *Pinter's Comic Play*. Lewisburg, PA: Bucknell University Press, 1985.
Esslin, Martin. *Pinter*. New York: Norton, 1976.
Ganz, Arthur, ed. *Pinter: A Collection of Critical Essays*. Englewood Cliffs, NJ: Prentice-Hall, 1972.
Postlewait, Thomas. "Pinter's *The Homecoming*: Displacing and Repeating Ibsen." *Comparative Drama* 15 (1981): 195–212.
Quigley, Austin E. *The Pinter Problem*. Princeton, NJ: Princeton University Press, 1975.

WOLE SOYINKA

Gibbs, James. *Wole Soyinka*. London: Macmillan, 1986.
———, ed. *Critical perspectives on Wole Soyinka*. Washington, DC: Three Continents, 1980.
Gibbs, James, Ketu H. Katrak, and Henry Louis Gates, Jr., eds. *Wole Soyinka: A Bibliography of Primary and Secondary Sources*. Westport, CT: Greenwood, 1986.
Gugelberger, Georg M., ed. *Marxism and African Literature*. London: James Currey, 1985.
Jones, Eldred Durosimi. *The Writings of Wole Soyinka*. London: James Currey, 1988.
Nazareth, Peter. *An African View of Literature*. Evanston, IL: Northwestern University Press, 1974.
Ogunba, Oyin. *The Movement of Transition: A Study of the Plays of Wole Soyinka*. Ibadan, Nigeria: Ibadan University Press, 1975.
Soyinka, Wole. "The Fourth Stage." In *The Morality of Art: Essays Presented to G. Wilson Knight by his Colleagues and Friends*. D. W. Jefferson, ed. New York: Barnes & Noble, 1969.
———. *The Man Died*. London: Rex Collings, 1972.

SPLIT BRITCHES

Case, Sue-Ellen. "From Split Subject to Split Britches." In Enoch Brater, ed. *Feminine Focus: The New Women Playwrights*. Ann Arbor, MI: University of Michigan Press, 1989.
———. "Toward a Butch-Femme Aesthetic." In Lynda Hart, ed. *Making a Spectacle: Feminist Essays on Contemporary Women's Theatre*. Ann Arbor, MI: University of Michigan Press, 1989.
Davy, Kate. "Constructing the Spectator: Reception, Context, and Address in Lesbian Performance." *Performing Arts Journal* 10:2 (1986): 43–52.
Dolan, Jill. "The Dynamics of Desire: Sexuality and Gender in Pornography and Performance." *Theatre Journal* 39 (1987): 156–74.
Harris, Hillary. Rev. of *Anniversary Waltz*. *Theatre Journal* 42 (1990): 484–88.
Hart, Lynda. Rev. of *Lesbians Who Kill*. *Theatre Journal* 44 (1992): 515–17.
Leondar, Gail. Rev. of *Belle Reprieve*. *Theatre Journal* 43 (1991): 386–88.

TOM STOPPARD

Bennett, Jonathan. "Philosophy and Mr. Stoppard." *Philosophy* 50 (January 1978): 5–18.
Bigsby, C. W. E. *Tom Stoppard*. Harlow, England: Longman, 1976.
Corballis, Richard. *Stoppard: The Mystery and the Clockwork*. New York: Methuen, 1984.

Jenkins, Anthony. *The Theatre of Tom Stoppard*. Cambridge, England: Cambridge University Press, 1987.

Kelly, Katharine E. *Tom Stoppard and the Craft of Comedy*. Ann Arbor, MI: University of Michigan Press, 1989.

Londré, Felicia Hardison. *Tom Stoppard*. New York: Ungar, 1988.

VIDEO, FILM, AND SOUND RECORDINGS OF PLAYS

UNIT 1   Aeschylus, *Agamemnon*
   VHS. 1983. National Theatre of Great Britain production. Director: Peter Hall. Films for the Humanities.
Aristophanes, *Lysistrata*
   Sound Recording. 1966. Director: Howard Sackler. Cast includes Hermione Gingold and Stanley Holloway. Caedmon Records.
Sophocles, *Oedipus Rex*
   VHS. 1959. Distributed by Encyclopedia Brittanica Educational Corp.
   Film. 1967. Director: Philip Saville. Cast includes Christopher Plummer and Orson Welles.
   VHS. 1975. *The Rise of Greek Tragedy.* Director: Howard Mantell. Cast includes James Mason, Claire Bloom. Set in outdoor amphitheater, using masks. Films for the Humanities, 1982.

UNIT 3   Anonymous, *Everyman*
   Film. 1971. Distributed by Paul Lewison.
   Sound Recording. Cast includes Burgess Meredith. Caedmon Records.
Christopher Marlowe, *Doctor Faustus*
   VHS. 1968. Cast includes Richard Burton, Elizabeth Taylor.
William Shakespeare, *Hamlet*
   Film. 1948. Director: Laurence Olivier. Cast includes Olivier.
   VHS. 1983. The BBC-TV Shakespeare Plays. Cast includes Derek Jacobi.
   VHS. 1990. Cast includes Mel Gibson.
William Shakespeare, *The Tempest*
   VHS. 1983. The BBC-TV Shakespeare Plays. Cast includes Michael Hordern.
   VHS. Director: George Shaefer. Cast includes Maurice Evans, Roddy McDowell, Richard Burton, Lee Remick. Films for the Humanities.

UNIT 4   Molière, *Tartuffe*
   Sound Recording. 1968. Stratford National Theatre of Canada. Director: Jean Gascon. Caedmon Records.

UNIT 5   Anton Chekhov, *The Cherry Orchard*
   Film. 1967. Distributed by Encyclopedia Britannica Educational Corp.
   Sound Recording. Director: Tyrone Guthrie. Cast includes Jessica Tandy. Caedmon Records.
Henrik Ibsen, *A Doll House*
   VHS. 1959. Director: Barry A. Brown. Cast includes Christopher Plummer, Julie Harris, Richard Thomas.
   VHS. 1973. Director: Joseph Losey. Cast includes Jane Fonda, Trevor Howard.
   VHS. 1973. Director: Patrick Garland. Cast includes Claire Bloom, Ralph Richardson, Anthony Hopkins.
Luigi Pirandello, *Six Characters in Search of an Author*
   VHS. 1978. Miami Dade Community College.
George Bernard Shaw, *Major Barbara*
   VHS. 1941. Director: Gabriel Pascal, in consultation with George Bernard Shaw. Cast includes Wendy Hiller, Rex Harrison, Sybil Thorndike.
August Strindberg, *Miss Julie*
   VHS. 1951. Director: Alf Sjöberg. Cast includes Max Von Sydow, Anita Bjork, Ulf Palme.

UNIT 6   Amiri Baraka/LeRoi Jones, *Dutchman*
   Film. 1966. Director: Anthony Harvey. Cast includes Al Freeman, Jr., Shirley Knight.
Sam Shepard, *True West*
   VHS. 1984. Director: Allan Goldstein. Cast includes John Malkovich and Gary Sinise.

Tennessee Williams, *The Glass Menagerie*
  Film. 1950. Director: Irving Rippen. Cast includes Jane Wyman, Kirk Douglas, Arthur Kennedy.
  Film. 1973. Director: Anthony Harvey. Cast includes Kathrine Hepburn, Sam Waterston, Joanna Miles, Michael Moriarty.
  VHS. 1987. Director: Paul Newman. Cast includes John Malkovich, Joanne Woodward, Karen Allen.

Harold Pinter, *The Homecoming*
  Film. 1973. Director: Peter Hall. Cast includes Cyril Cusak, Ian Holm, Vivian Merchant.

UNIT 7

 CREDITS

AESCHYLUS "Agamemnon" from THE ORESTEIA, translated by Robert Fagles. Translation copyright © 1966, 1967, 1975 by Robert Fagles. Used by permission of Viking Penguin, a division of Penguin Books USA Inc.

ARISTOPHANES "Lysistrata" from LYSISTRATA AND OTHER PLAYS by Aristophanes, translated by Alan H. Sommerstein (Penguin Classics, 1973). Copyright © 1973 by Alan H. Sommerstein. Reprinted by permission of Penguin Books, Ltd., London.

ARISTOTLE From "Poetics" in ARISTOTLE POETICS, translated by Gerald F. Else. Copyright © 1967 by The University of Michigan Press. Reprinted by permission of the publisher.

ANTONIN ARTAUD From THE THEATRE AND ITS DOUBLE by Antonin Artaud, translated by Mary Caroline Richard. English translation copyright © 1958 by Grove Press, Inc. Used by permission of Grove Press, Inc.

MIKHAIL BAKHTIN From "The Grotesque Image of the Body" in RABELAIS AND HIS WORLD, translated by Helene Iswolsky. Copyright © 1968 by the MIT Press. Reprinted by permission of the publisher.

AMIRI BARAKA "The Revolutionary Theatre: From Home, Social Essays" and THE DUTCHMAN in SELECTED PLAYS AND PROSE OF AMIRI BARAKA. Copyright © 1979 by Amiri Baraka, published by William Morrow and Co. Reprinted by permission of Sterling Lord Literistic, Inc.

ROLAND BARTHES "The Tasks of Brechtian Criticism" by Roland Barthes, translated by Richard Howard in CRITICAL ESSAYS. Copyright © 1972 by Northwestern University Press. Reprinted by permission of the publisher.

SAMUEL BECKETT ENDGAME by Samuel Beckett. Copyright © 1958 by Grove Press, Inc.; renewed copyright © 1986 by Samuel Beckett. Reprinted by permission of Grove/Atlantic, Inc.

APHRA BEHN THE ROVER edited by Montague Summers. This version published 1915.

LYNDA E. BOOSE From "The Father and the Bride in Shakespeare" in PMLA, Vol. 97, No. 3, May 1982, published by the Modern Language Association of America. Reprinted by permission of the publisher.

KURUWA BANSHO "Love Letter from the Licensed Quarter" by Kuruwa Bansho in KABUKI: FIVE CLASSIC PLAYS, translated by James R. Brandon, Cambridge, MA: Harvard University Press. Copyright © 1975 by the President and Fellows of Harvard College. Reprinted by permission of Harvard University Press.

CALDERÓN DE LA BARCA "Life is a Dream" from LIFE IS A DREAM AND OTHER SPANISH CLASSICS, edited by Eric Bentley and translated by Roy Campbell. Copyright © 1959, 1958 by Eric Bentley. Reprinted by permission of Applause Theatre Book Publishers.

BETTE BOURNE, PEGGY SHAW, PAUL SHAW, AND LOIS WEAVER "Belle Reprieve" from GAY AND LESBIAN PLAYS TODAY, selected and introduced by Terry Helbin, published by Heinemann/Portsmouth, N.H. Copyright © 1991, 1993 by Bette Bourne, Peggy Shaw, Paul Shaw, and Lois Weaver. Reprinted by permission of the authors.
  CAUTION: Lyrics of "I'm a Man" by Ellas McDaniel. Copyright © 1955 (Renewed) Arc Music Corporation. All rights reserved, including the right of public performance for profit. Producers of this play must obtain licensing for this composition from Arc Music Corp. Used by permission of Arc Music Corp.
  Lyrics of "Running Wild" by Joe Grey, Leo Wood, and A. Harrington Gibbs. Copyright © 1922 (renewed) EMI Feist Catalog Inc. All rights reserved. Used by permission of Warner Bros. Publications Inc., Miami, FL, 33014.
  Lyrics of "Pushover" by T. Clarke and B. Davis, Chevis Publishing Corp. Copyright ©. Used by permission.
NOTE: For performance of the songs mentioned in this play, the permission of the copyright owners must be obtained or other songs and recordings in the public domain substituted.

BERTHOLT BRECHT MOTHER COURAGE AND HER CHILDREN. Original work MUTTER COURAGE AND IHRE KINDER by Bertolt Brecht. Copyright 1940 by Arvid Englind Teaterforlag, a.b., renewed June 1967 by Stefan S. Brecht; copyright 1949 by Suhrkamp Verlag, Frankfurt am Main. John Willet's translation of MOTHER COURAGE AND HER CHILDREN and texts by Brecht. Copyright © 1980 by Stefan S. Brecht. Reprinted from MOTHER COURAGE AND HER CHILDREN by Bertolt Brecht, translated by John Willett and edited by John Willett and Ralph Manheim, published by Arcade Publishing, New York, N.Y. Used by permission of Arcade Publishers.

BERTHOLT BRECHT From BRECHT ON THEATRE, translated by John Willett. Translation copyright © 1964 and renewed © 1992 by John Willett. Reprinted by permission of Hill and Wang, a division of Farrar, Straus & Giroux, Inc.

GEORG BUCHNER WOYZECK from GEORG BUCHNER: COMPLETE PLAYS AND PROSE, translated by Carl Richard Mueller. Copyright © 1963 and renewed © 1991 by Carl Richard

AUGUST WILSON From FENCES by August Wilson. Copyright © 1986 by August Wilson. Used by permission of Dutton Signet, a division of Penguin Books USA Inc.

W.B. WORTHEN From "Chekhov's Camera: The Rhetoric of Stage Realism" in "Theater and the Scene of Vision" from MODERN DRAMA AND THE RHETORIC OF THEATER by W.B. Worthen. Copyright © 1992 The Regents of the University of California. Reprinted by permission of the Regents of the University of California and the University of California Press.

ZEAMI MOTOKIYO "Teachings on Style and the Flower" (Fushikaden); "The Aesthetics of Ambiguity: The Artistic Theories of Zeami" (Yamazaki Masakazu); and "A Mirror Held to the Flower" (Kakyo) from ON THE ART OF THE NO DRAMA: THE MAJOR TREATISES OF ZEAMI, translated by J. Thomas Rimer and Yamazaki Masakazu. Copyright © 1986 by Princeton University Press. Reprinted by permission of Princeton University Press.

ÉMILE ZOLA From "Naturalism in the Theatre" by Émile Zola, translated by Albert Bermel in THE THEORY OF THE MODERN STAGE, edited by Eric Bentley, published by Penguin Books USA, 1990. Reprinted by permission of Albert Bermel and his agent Helen Merrill, Ltd.

ILLUSTRATIONS

p. 15   Theatre and Playhouse, by Richard and Helen Leacroft (London, New York: Methuen, 1984, p. 15) © 1984 by Richard and Helen Leacroft. Reprinted by permission of Methuen London.

p. 16   Public domain

pp. 18–19   Public domain

p. 21   Theatre and Playhouse, by Richard and Helen Leacroft (London, New York: Methuen, 1984, p. 29) © 1984 by Richard and Helen Leacroft. Reprinted by permission of Methuen London.

p. 23 top   Photo © T. Charles Erickson

p. 23 bottom   Photo © Joan Marcus

p. 130 top   Photo Nakaza Theatre, Osaka, Japan

p. 130 bottom   Photo Nakaza Theatre, Osaka, Japan

p. 188   Theatre and Playhouse, by Richard and Helen Leacroft (London, New York: Methuen, 1984, p. 39) © 1984 by Richard and Helen Leacroft. Reprinted by permission of Methuen London.

p. 190   Joseph Quincy Adams, Chief Pre-Shakespearean Dramas. Copyright © 1924 by Houghton Mifflin Company. Excerpted with permission.

p. 193   The Shakespearean Stage 1574–1642, 2/e by Andrew Gurr (Cambridge: Cambridge University Press, p. 116) © 1980 by Cambridge University Press.

p. 194   Public domain

p. 195   The Globe Restored, by C. Walter Hodges (London: Ernest Benn, 1953) Ernest C. Benn, A & C Black (Publishers) Limited.

p. 200   Reproduced by permission of the Marquess of Bath, Longleat House, Warminster, Wiltshire, Great Britain.

p. 201 top   Photo © 1994 Martha Swope

p. 201 bottom   Photo by VanDamm

p. 396   Theatre and Playhouse, by Richard and Helen Leacroft (London, New York: Methuen, 1984, p. 73) © 1984 by Richard and Helen Leacroft. Reprinted by permission of Methuen London.

p. 402   Public domain

p. 402   Public domain

p. 404 top   Photo by Richard Feldman

p. 404 bottom   Photo © T. Charles Erickson

p. 557 top   Photo © Richard Feldman

p. 557 bottom left   Photo © Richard Feldman

p. 557 bottom right   Photo Michal Daniel

p. 558 top   Photo © Richard Feldman

p. 558 middle   Photo © Martha Swope

p. 558 bottom   Photo © Carol Rosegg

p. 563   Theatre and Playhouse, by Richard and Helen Leacroft (London, New York: Methuen, 1984, p. 157) © 1984 by Richard and Helen Leacroft. Reprinted by permission of Methuen London.

p. 564   Theatre and Playhouse, by Richard and Helen Leacroft (London, New York: Methuen, 1984, p. 158) © 1984 by Richard and Helen Leacroft. Reprinted by permission of Methuen London.

p. 569   Public domain

p. 572 top   Photo © T. Charles Erickson

p. 572 middle   Photo © Joan Marcus

p. 572 bottom   Photo Billy Rose Theatre Collection, The New York Public Library for the Performing Arts. Astor, Lenox and Tilden Foundations.

p. 801   UPI/Bettmann

p. 803 top left   Photo © 1986 Martha Swope

p. 803 right   Photo © Joan Marcus

p. 803 bottom left   Photo © William B. Carter

p. 1048   Theatre and Playhouse, by Richard and Helen Leacroft (London, New York: Methuen, 1984, p. 187) © 1984 by Richard and Helen Leacroft. Reprinted by permission of Methuen London.

p. 1053   Photo by Jay Thompson

p. 1055 top   Photo © 1985 Martha Swope

p. 1055 middle   Photo © Michael Cooper

p. 1055 bottom   Photo © 1994 Matthew Gilson